INTERNATIONAL HUMAN RIGHTS IN CONTEXT

LAW, POLITICS, MORALS

INTERNATIONAL HUMAN RIGHTS IN CONTEXT

LAW, POLITICS, MORALS

Text and Materials

Third Edition

HENRY J. STEINER

Jeremiah Smith, Jr. Professor Emeritus, and Founder and former Director (1984–2005) of the Human Rights Program at Harvard Law School

PHILIP ALSTON

John Norton Pomeroy Professor of Law and Director of the Center for Human Rights and Global Justice at New York University School of Law

RYAN GOODMAN

Rita E. Hauser Professor of Human Rights and Humanitarian Law and Director of the Human Rights Program at Harvard Law School

OXFORD
UNIVERSITY PRESS

OXFORD
UNIVERSITY PRESS

Great Clarendon Street, Oxford OX2 6DP

Oxford University Press is a department of the University of Oxford.
It furthers the University's objective of excellence in research, scholarship,
and education by publishing worldwide in

Oxford New York

Auckland Cape Town Dar es Salaam Hong Kong Karachi
Kuala Lumpur Madrid Melbourne Mexico City Nairobi
New Delhi Shanghai Taipei Toronto

With offices in

Argentina Austria Brazil Chile Czech Republic France Greece
Guatemala Hungary Italy Japan Poland Portugal Singapore
South Korea Switzerland Thailand Turkey Ukraine Vietnam

Published in the United States
by Oxford University Press Inc., New York

First edition 1996
Second edition 2000
This edition 2007

British Library Cataloguing in Publication Data
Data available

Library of Congress Cataloging in Publication Data
Data available

Typeset by Newgen Imaging Systems (P) Ltd, Chennai, India
Printed in Great Britain
on acid-free paper by
Ashford Colour Press Ltd, Gosport, Hampshire

ISBN 978–0–19–927942–5

5 7 9 10 8 6

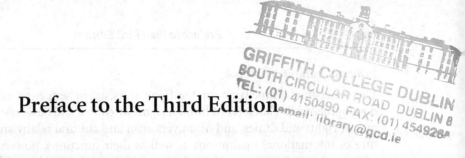

Preface to the Third Edition

Basic purposes

A little more than 60 years after the human rights movement was born out of the disasters of the Second World War, human rights norms and institutions deeply inform the rhetoric, practice and theory of international law and politics, as well as the internal constitutional structures of a large number of states. Although the frailties of human rights as an ideal or ideology or as state practice are evident, that ideal has become a part of modern consciousness, a lens through which to see the world, a universal discourse, a potent aspiration. The coursebook uses the term 'human rights movement' to include post-1945 governmental, intergovernmental and non-governmental developments in both national and international contexts in the recognition and protection of human rights.

However striking and disheartening its major failures and inadequacies, the movement has shown not only staying power and growth, but also a remarkably broad dissemination of its message. Its claims of permanence carry ever greater credibility. Today's university curriculum dwarfs what was available for study in this field as few as 25 years ago. It evidences the significance of international human rights for fields of study as diverse as law, government, international relations, moral theory, public health, world financial institutions, the environment, economic development, ethnic conflict, religion, education, cultural studies and social anthropology.

Although the human rights movement now forms an indelible part of our legal, political and moral landscape, and indeed perhaps precisely because of that status, recent decades have witnessed deeper and more numerous challenges to the foundations upon which the movement has been built, its aspirations to universality, and its claims of growing success in spreading and realizing its message. In response to these many challenges, the book seeks to examine the movement's failures as well as triumphs and dilemmas in seeking to achieve human rights ideals across the world's many histories and cultures.

The book builds on the premise that a basic course in human rights should educate students to see the 'big picture'. Of course it should enable students to master the history, doctrine, and institutional structures of the movement. But it should also persuade students to think critically about the subject as a whole. Thus the text and materials describe, analyse, criticize, and propose, all from a range of political, cultural, moral and geopolitical perspectives. They do not impose any single dogma, direction or method for thinking about the history of or appropriate path for human rights.

These vexing issues are for the student to work out. The book prepares students to work with commitment and critical reflection in a range of roles related to human rights: concerned citizen, advocate, teacher, scholar, activist in a governmental or nongovernmental organization, policy analyst.

Principal features of the book

The conceptual framework for the book consists, in sequence, of the historical development and character of human rights discourse and basic norms; the dilemmas of rights and duties, and of universalism and cultural relativism; the architecture of international institutions as well as their functions, powers and interplay with norms; and the interaction of states with international law and organizations as well as with each other. Certain major themes run through the different parts of the book — for example, changing notions of autonomy and sovereignty, the changing configuration of the public–private divide in human rights ordering, the interplay of duties and rights in the gradual expansion of the human rights movement, the escalating tensions between international human rights and national security, the striking evolution of ideas about the nature and purposes of the movement itself.

Some of our premises about the study of international human rights inform the book as a whole:

1. Human rights are violated within individual states, not in outer space or on the high seas. One might therefore argue that the study of rights should concentrate on different states — say, human rights *in* Nigeria, Peru, China, the United States, Iran, France. Such a book could offer contextual studies of human rights issues — police brutality, press freedom, discrimination, education, freedoms of and from religion, political participation, health care and so on — that would draw on different national histories and political cultures. It would have the character and high value of studies in comparative law, history and culture.

This book follows a different path. The distinctive aspect of the human rights movement of the last six decades has been its invention and development on the international level. Hence the stress is on the *international* human rights system, as well as on the vital relationships between that system and states' internal orders. Although many illustrations throughout the book draw on human rights violations within one or another state, most of the materials address international norms, processes and institutions (governmental and nongovernmental), both in their own terms and in terms of their interaction with states.

2. What are the sensible boundaries of a book that has an important focus on 'law'? Clearly the coursebook could not achieve its goals if it held to a formal or positivist conception that blocked out deeply related fields of inquiry. Thus diverse readings from many fields interact with formal legal materials to form a network of interrelated ideas.

This range of readings is readily accessible to university students with academic backgrounds as varied as law, government, political economy, philosophy, education, theology, cultural studies, business or public health. Human rights courses benefit greatly by including students from such varied backgrounds, as well as from diverse states and cultures. The first two editions served as the principal coursebook in universal human rights courses in numbers of countries, in both graduate schools and colleges that included faculties and departments of law, government, and international relations.

3. A book based on legal norms and institutions characteristically devotes great attention to the work of courts, the paradigmatic legal institutions. Particularly in Western liberal democracies, but also in a growing number of countries in the developing world, courts play a vital role in resolving human rights controversies and developing human rights norms, through constitutional and other bodies of law. However, where governments are authoritarian and repressive, where violations are serious, systemic and brutal, courts are least relevant. Relative to Western democracies, the judiciary's competence to review executive or legislative action, or simply to resolve a controversy without political pressure, may be sharply reduced or eliminated, its jurisdiction limited, its decrees ignored, its judges subjected to threat or worse. The struggle for rights may become fully political, even forceful and violent, before the emergence of an open society with some semblance of the rule of law in which courts can independently function.

For such reasons, in a book giving great attention to both the developed and developing world, to democratic and authoritarian societies, state courts in the large will play a lesser role than in the typical law course in settling major disputes affecting the nature of the polity, and in making and applying law. Nonetheless, even over the 12 years since the publication of the first edition, the importance for human rights of state constitutional courts has markedly increased. A whole field of comparative constitutional law that is worldwide in scope is emerging. During this same period, international tribunals as well as treaty committees with dispute-resolving powers have gained prominence and significance. For such reasons, judicial and quasi-judicial bodies play a larger role in this edition than in the two prior ones.

4. In vital respects, a book that concentrates on international human rights must assume that students have a rudimentary knowledge of international law. How else can a class discuss matters like treaties and custom, intergovernmental institutions and processes, or internalization of treaty or customary norms within a state? Nonetheless, a substantial percentage of students taking basic courses on human rights lacks that knowledge.

How to handle this situation? In its early chapters, the book provides an introduction to basic conceptions, sources, processes and norms of international law. This introduction hardly achieves the depth and sophistication of a course devoted principally to that rich subject. But it suffices to enable students to grapple with the themes of the coursebook.

5. The study of human rights norms without attention to the international organizations that implement, develop, apply and enforce them would create an air of unreality about the entire enterprise. The architecture, powers, functions and processes of international human rights organizations, intergovernmental and nongovernmental, figure importantly in the book. The student is made aware throughout of the pervasive relationships among norms, institutions, and processes at the international as well as national levels.

6. No one substantive human rights problem and no one region dominates the book. The text and readings draw on many problems to illustrate their themes: free speech and the right to education; torture and discrimination against ethnic minorities; laws of war and the right to health care. The chapters illustrate those themes by

drawing on many parts of the world, developed and developing, internationally powerful and weak, and underscore conflicts among regions and cultures in their approaches to and understandings of human rights.

Changes from the second edition

Such changes are pervasive. Of course there has been updating of text and materials throughout, with related changes in emphasis and topics. Several themes absent from or marginal to the prior editions here figure importantly: human rights in relation to terrorism and national security; responsibility of non-state actors for human rights violations; recent substantial changes in sources and processes of international law; achieved and potential reform within United Nations human rights institutions; and theories about international organizations and their influence on state behaviour.

Authors

Ryan Goodman, Rita E. Hauser Professor of Human Rights and Humanitarian Law at Harvard Law School, and Director of its Human Rights Program, has become a third co-author and co-editor of the coursebook.

Practical details and updates on materials

Rather than require students to purchase a separate booklet, we have set forth basic documents like treaties, declarations and constitutions that are necessary companions to the coursebook's materials in a Documents Supplement on a website associated with OUP and the book: www.oxfordtextbooks.co.uk/orc/ihr3e/. Most of these documents have been edited to eliminate sections not relevant to the coursebook's discussions. The website will be periodically revised.

We have sharply edited most of the primary and secondary materials in order to make the readings as compact as possible. Omissions (except for footnotes) are indicated by the conventional use of ellipses. Retained footnotes are renumbered within the consecutive footnote numbering of each chapter.

Acknowledgements

Philip Alston wishes to express his appreciation to Monika Heymann for superb research on Chapter 11, to Katie Young for advice on Chapter 4, to Mara Bustelo for advice on Chapter 9, and to Kelly Ryan for having coordinated the permissions and much else. Ryan Goodman gives his thanks to Naomi Loewith, Brandon Miller, and David Zionts for exceptional research assistance and to Derek Jinks for advice on several chapters.

Henry J. Steiner
Philip Alston
Ryan Goodman
May 2007

Summary of Contents

Contents

PART E: STATES AS PROTECTORS AND ENFORCERS OF HUMAN RIGHTS

Acknowledgements

We gratefully acknowledge the permissions extended by the following publishers and authors to reprint excerpts from the indicated publications:

American Anthropological Association. Excerpts from American Anthropological Association's Statement on Human Rights, 49 American Anthropologist 4, 539 (October–December 1947).

American Society of International Law. Excerpts from Michael J. Dennis and David P. Stewart, Justiciability of Economic, Social and Cultural Rights, 98 Am. J. Int. L. 462 (2004); Felice Gaer, Book Review, 98 Am. J. Int. L. 391 (2004); Sheldon Glueck, The Nuremberg Trial and Aggressive War (1946), 47 Am. J. Int. L. 334 (1947); Ryan Goodman, Human Rights Treaties, Invalid Reservations, and State Consent, 96 Am. J. Int. L. 531 (2002); Frank Hoffmeister, Case Note: Cyprus v. Turkey, 96 Am. J. Intl. L. 445, (2002); Anthea Roberts, Traditional and Modern Approaches to Customary International Law: A Reconciliation, 95 Am. J. Int. L. 757 (2001). Reproduced with permission from *American Journal of International Law*, © 1947, 2001, 2002, 2004 American Society of International Law. Excerpts from José Alvarez, The Internationalization of U.S. Law (28 October 2006); Donna Sullivan, Advancing the Freedom of Religion or Belief Through the UN Declaration on the Elimination of Religious Tolerance and Discrimination, 82 Am. J. Int. L. 487 (1988); Rebecca Cook, Accountability in International Law for Violations of Women's Rights by Non-State Actors, in Dorinda Dallmeyer (ed.) Reconceiving Reality: Women and International Law (1993); Karen Engle, After the Collapse of the Public/Private Distinction: Strategizing Women's Rights, in *ibid.* Copyright © 1988, 1993, 2006 American Society of International Law.

Amnesty International. Excerpts from Facts and Figures on the Death Penalty (27 June 2006); UN Commission on Human Rights Making Human Rights Work: Time to Strengthen the Special Procedures (January 1999) from AI Index: IOR 41/01/99; United Nations Special Procedures: Building on a Cornerstone of Human Rights Protection (2005); Meeting the Challenge: Transforming the Commission on Human Rights into a Human Rights Council (April 2005) from AI Index: IOR 40/008/2005; Rwanda: The Troubled Course of Justice (26 April 2000); Rwanda-GACACA: A Question of Justice (17 December 2002); Irene Khan, Understanding Corporate Complicity: Extending the Notion Beyond Existing Laws (8 December 2005) from AI Index: POL 34/001/2006.

Australian National University, Research School of Pacific Studies. Excerpts from Ben-Huat Chua, Australian and Asian Perceptions of Human Rights, in Ian Russel, Peter van Ness and Beng-Huat Chua (eds.), Australia's Human Rights Diplomacy (1992).

Australian Journal of Human Rights. Excerpts from Domestic Implementation of Human Rights Norms, 5 Aust. J. Human Rights 109 (1999); Elizabeth Evatt, Reflecting on the Role of International Communications in Implementing Human Rights, 5(2) Aust. J. Human Rights 20 (1999). © 1999 University of New South Wales.

Beacon Press. Between Vengeance and Forgiveness by Martha Minow, Copyright © 1998 by Martha Minow, reprinted with permission of Beacon Press, Boston.

Boston Review. Yael Tamir, Hands Off Clitoridectomy, 31 Boston Review 21 (1996). Permission granted by Yael Tamir.

Brill Academic Publishers. Excerpts from: Georges Abi-Saab, The Legal Formulation of a Right to Development in the Right to Development at the International Level, Hague Academy of International Law (1980); Mohammed Bedjaoui, The Right to Development, in M. Bedjaoui and UNESCO (eds.), International Law: Achievements and Prospects (1991); Thomas Buergenthal, The Human Rights Committee, 5 Max Planck Yearbook of United Nations Law 341 (2001); Louis Henkin, International Law: Politics, Values and Functions, 216 Collected Courses of The Hague Academy of International Law 13 (Vol. IV, 1989); Martti Koskenniemi, Between Impunity and Show Trials, 6 Max Planck Yearbook of United Nations Law 1 (2002); Makau Mutua, The Complexity of Universalism in Human Rights in A. Sajo (ed.), Human Rights with Modesty (2004); Virginia Leary, International Labour Conventions and National Law (1982); Oscar Schachter International Law in Theory and Practice (1991); Henry Schermers and Niels M. Blokker, International Institutional Law: Unity within Diversity, 4th rev. edn. (2003); Dinah Shelton, The Promise of Regional Human Rights Systems, in B. Weston and S. Marks (eds.), The Future of International Human Rights (1999); Richard Shweder, Moral Realism without the Ethnocentrism, in A. Sajo (ed.), Human Rights with Modesty (2004); Bruno Simma *et al.*, The Role of German Courts in the Enforcement of International Human Rights in Domestic Courts (1997); M. Weiner, Child Labour in Developing Countries: The Indian Case, 2 International Journal of Children's Rights 121 (1994); Kirsten A. Young, The Law and Process of the UN Human Rights Committee (2002).

University of British Columbia Law Review Society. Karl Klare, Legal Theory and Democratic Reconstruction: Reflections on 1989, 25 U.B.C. L. Rev. 69 (1991). © 1991 University of British Columbia Law Review Society.

The Brookings Institution. Excerpts from Richard Falk, Sovereignty and Human Dignity: The Search for Reconciliation, in F. Deng and T. Lyons (eds.), African Reckoning: A Quest for Good Governance (Brookings Institution 1998).

Brooklyn Journal of International Law. Excerpts from Yuval Shany, How Supreme Is the Supreme Law of the Land? 31 Brook. J. Int'l. L. 341 (2006).

University of California. Excerpts from Stephanie Farrior, Moulding the Matrix: The Historical and Theoretical Foundations of International Law. Berkeley Journal of International Law. Vol. 14, No. 1 (1996), by permission of the Regents of the University of California.

University of California Press. Excerpts from Pnina Lahav, Judgement in Jerusalem (1997). Permission granted by Pnina Lahav.

California Western International Law Journal. Excerpts from Jack Donnelly, In Search of the Unicorn: The Jurisprudence and Politics of the Right to Development, 15 Cal. W. Int'l L. J. 482 (1985).

Cambridge University Press. Excerpts from Carol Anderson, Eyes Off the Prize: The United Nations and the African American Struggle for Human Rights, 1944–1955 (2003); Malcolm Evans, Religious Liberty and International Law in Europe (1997);

Emilie M. Hafner-Burton, Trading Human Rights: How Preferential Trade Agreements Influence Government Repression, 59 (3) International Organization 593 (2005); Barbara Koremenos, Charles Lipson and Duncan Snidal, The Rational Design of International Institutions, 55 International Organization 761 (2001); Andrew Moravcsik, The Origins of Human Rights Regimes: Democratic Delegation in Postwar Europe, 54 International Organization 238 (2000); William Schabas, The Abolition of the Death Penalty in International Law 377, 3rd edn. (2002); Alexander Wendt, Driving with the Rearview Mirror: On the Rational Science of Institutional Design, 55 International Organization 1019 (2001); Stuart White, Social Rights and the Social Contract-Political Theory and the New Welfare Politics, 30 British Journal of Political Science 507 (2000).

Cato Institute. Excerpts from David Kelley, A Life of One's Own: Individual Rights and the Welfare State (1998).

University of Chicago Press. Excerpts from Sally Engle Merry, Human Rights and Gender Violence (2006).

Columbia Human Rights Law Review. Excerpts from: Fionnuala Ni Aolàin, Looking Ahead: Strategic Priorities and Challenges for the United Nations High Commissioner for Human Rights, 35 Colum. Hum. Rts. L. Rec. 469 (2004); Isabelle Gunning, Arrogant Perception, World Traveling and Multicultural Feminism: The Case of Female Genital Surgeries, 23 Colum. Hum. Rts. L. Rec. 238 (1992).

Columbia University Press. Excerpts from Elvin Hatch, Culture and Morality: The Relativity of Values in Anthropology (1983). Permission granted by Elvin Hatch.

Cornell University Press. Excerpts from Activists Beyond Borders: Advocacy Networks in International Politics, by Margaret E. Keck and Kathryn Sikkink. Copyright © 1998 by Cornell University.

DePaul Law Review. Excerpts from Beth Stephens, Individuals Enforcing International Law: The Comparative and Historical Context, 52 DePaul Law Review 433 (2002).

Universidad de Deusto. Excerpts from Christof Heyns and Magnus Killander, The African Regional Human Rights System, in F. Gomez Isa and K. de Feyter (eds.), International Protection of Human Rights: Achievements and Challenges (2006).

Duke Law Journal. Excerpts from: Ryan Goodman and Derek Jinks, How to Influence States: Socialization and International Human Rights Law, 54 Duke Law Journal 621 (2004).

East European Constitutional Review. Cass Sunstein, Against Positive Rights, 2/1 East Eur. Constit'al Rev. (1993).

Emory International Review. Excerpts from Sandra Coliver, Jennie Green and Paul Hoffman, Holding Human Rights Violators Accountable by Using International Law in U.S. Courts, 19 Emory Int'l L. Rev. 169 (2005).

New Encyclopaedia Britannica. Excerpts from Burns Weston, Human Rights. © 1992, by Encyclopaedia Britannica, Inc.

NP Engel Verlag. Excerpts from Manfred Nowak, U.N. Covenant on Civil and Political Rights: ICCPR Commentary (2005); Philip Leach, Access to the European Court of Human Rights: From a Legal Entitlement to a Lottery?, 27 Hum. Rts. L. J. 11 (2006).

European Journal of International Law. Excerpts from Darryl Robinson, Serving the Interests of Justice: Amnesties, Truth Commissions and the International Criminal Court, 14 Eur. J. Int'l L. 481 (2003); Gerald L. Neuman, Counter-Terrorist Operations and the Rule of Law, 15 Eur. J. Int'l L. 1019 (2004); Kenneth Anderson, The Ottawa Convention Banning Landmines, The Role of International Non-Governmental Organization and the Idea of International Civil Society, 11 Eur. J. Int'l L. 92 (2000).

Financial Times. Excerpts from Mure Dickie, Internet Groups Shirk Human Rights Duties in China (20 July 2006); Christopher Caldwell, Historical Truth Speaks for Itself (18 February 2006).

Food and Agriculture Organization. Excerpts from Voluntary Guidelines to Support the Progressive Realization of the Right to Adequate Food in the Context of National Food Security (24 November 2004).

Foreign Affairs. Excerpts from Peter J. Spiro, The New Sovereigntists: American Exceptionalism and its False Prophets, 79 Foreign Affairs, Nov/Dec 2001 © Council on Foreign Relations, Inc. Curtis Bradley and Jack L. Goldsmith, My Prerogative, 80 Foreign Affairs, March/April 2001, © Council on Foreign Relations, Inc. Jonathan D. Tepperman, Truth and Consequences. 81 Foreign Affairs, March/April 2002 © Council on Foreign Relations, Inc.

Foreign Policy. Excerpts from Helena Cobban, Think Again: International Courts, Foreign Policy (March/April 2006); and Letters in Response to Cobban, Foreign Policy (March/April 2006).

Globe and Mail. Excerpts from Colin Freeze and Karen Howlett McGuinty, Government Rule Out Use of Sharia Law (12 September 2005).

The Guardian. Excerpts from Ronald Dworkin, Even Bigots and Holocaust Deniers Must Have Their Say (14 February 2006). Reprinted with permission of Ronald Dworkin.

Harvard Human Rights Journal. Excerpts from Abdullah Ahmed An-Na'im, Human Rights in the Muslim World, 3 Harv. Hum. Rts. J.13 (1990).

Harvard Law Review Association. Excerpts from Henry Steiner, The Youth of Rights, 104 Harv. L. Rev. 917 (1991).

Harvard University Press. Excerpts from A Critique of Adjudication by Duncan Kennedy, pp. 305–306. Copyright © 1997 by the President and Fellows of Harvard College.

Harvard Women's Law Journal. Excerpts from Tracy Higgins, Anti-Essentialism, Relativism and Human Rights, 19 Harv. Women's L. J. 89 (1996); Kay Boulware-Miller, Female Circumcision: Challenges to the Practice as a Human Rights Violation, 8 Harv. Women's L. J. 155 (1985). Copyright © 1985, 1997 by the President and Fellows of Harvard College.

Human Rights Brief. Excerpts from Aryeh Neier, Social and Economic Rights: A Critique, 13 No. 2, Hum. Rts. Brief (2006).

Human Rights Watch. Excerpts from Failing Our Children: Barriers to the Right to Education (2005); Broken People: Caste Violence against India's 'Untouchables' (1991); Backgrounder: Universal Periodic Review 8/18/2006 (2006); Q & A: Crisis in Darfur (December 2006); Race to the Bottom: Corporate Complicity in Chinese Internet Censorship, HRW Index C1808 8/10/2006 (2006); Human Rights Watch and American Civil Liberties Union, Human Rights Violations in the United States: A Report on U.S. Compliance with the International Covenant on Civil and Political Rights (1993). Americas Watch, Criminal Injustice: Violence against Women in Brazil (1992) © 1991, 1992, 1993, 2005, 2006 by Human Rights Watch.

ILSA Journal of International and Comparative Law. Excerpts from Nancy Kaymar, Stafford: A Model War Crimes Court: Sierra Leone, 10 ILSA Journal of Int'l & Comparative Law 117 (2003).

Indiana University Press. Excerpts from J.S. and R.L. Zangrando, ER and Black Civil Rights, in J. Hoff-Wilson and W. Lightman (eds.), Without Precedent: The Life and Career of Eleanor Roosevelt (1984).

The Indian Express. Permission to reprint excerpts from Neeta Lal, Black Spots on Zari Borders (25 July 2005).

International Center for Transitional Justice. Excerpts from The Special Court for Sierra Leone: The First Eighteen Months (March 2004)

International Committee of the Red Cross. Excerpts from International Humanitarian Law and Other Legal Regimes: Interplay in Situations of Violence (2003).

International Review of the Red Cross. Excerpts from Louise Doswald-Beck and Sylvain Vité, International Humanitarian Law and Human Rights Law, 293 Int'l Rev. Red Cross 94 (1993); James Cockayne, The Global Reorganization of Legitimate Violence: Military Entrepreneurs and the Private Face of International Humanitarian Law, 863 Int'l Rev. Red Cross 486 (2006); Andrew Clapham, Human Rights Obligations of Non-State Actors in Conflict Situations, 863 Int'l Rev. Red Cross 503 (2006).

Intersentia Uitgevers N V. Excerpts from Madgalena Sepulveda, The Nature of the Obligations under the International Covenant on Economic, Social and Cultural Rights (2003).

Jewish Publication Society. Excerpts from David Sidorsky, Essays on Human Rights (1979).

The Johns Hopkins University Press. Excerpts from Jan Herman Burgers, The Road to San Francisco: The Revival of the Human Rights Idea in the Twentieth Century, 447 Hum. Rts. Q. 450 (1992); Hilary Charlesworth and Christine Chinkin, The Gender of *Jus Cogens*, 15 Hum. Rts. Q. 63 (1993); James Nickel, How Human Rights Generate Duties to Protect and Provide, 15 Hum. Rts. Q. 77 (1993); Kenneth Roth, Defending Economic, Social and Cultural Rights: Practical Issues Faced by an International Human Rights Organization, 26 Hum. Rts. Q. 63 (2004); Philip Alston, Ships Passing in the Night, 27 Hum. Rts. Q. 802 (2005); Cecilia Medina, The Inter-American Commission on Human Rights and the Inter-American Court of Human Rights: Reflections on a Joint Venture, 12 Hum. Rts. Q. 440 (1990). © Johns Hopkins University Press.

Journal of Law and Religion. Excerpts from Robert Cover, Obligation: A Jewish Jurisprudence of the Social Order 5 J. Law & Rel. 65 (1987). © Hamline University.

Kings College Law Journal. Excerpts from Raymond Plant, Social and Economic Rights Revisited, 14 Kings College L. J. 1 (2003). © Hart Publishing Ltd.

Kluwer Academic Publishers. Excerpts from Nicholas Valticos, Foreword in B.G. Ramcharan (ed.), International Law and Fact-Finding in the Field of Human Rights (1982).

The Law Book Exchange. Excerpts from Hans Kelsen, Principles of International Law (Fletcher School Studies in International Affairs).

Michigan Law Review. Excerpts from Martti Koskenniemi, The Pull of the Mainstream, 88 Michigan L. Rev. 1946 (1990); Mirna E. Adjami, African Courts, International Law and Comparative Case Law: Chimera or Emerging Human Rights Jurisprudence?, 24 Michigan L. Rev. 103 (2002). © Michigan Law Review Association.

MIT Press. Excerpts from Maurice Cranston, Are There Any Human Rights?, 112/4 Daedalus 12 (1983); Jack Goldsmith and Stephen Krasner, The Limits of Idealism, 132 Daedalus 47 (2003). © 1983, 2003 by the American Academy of Arts and Sciences. Excerpts from Jack Snyder and Leslie Vinjamuri, Trials and Errors: Principle and Pragmatism in Strategies of International Justice, 28 Int'l Sec. 43 (2003/04). © 2004 by the President and Fellows of Harvard College and the Massachusetts Institute of Technology. Excerpts from Timothy Savage, Europe and Islam: Crescent Waxing, Cultures Clashing, 27(3) The Wash. Q. 25 (2004). © 2004 by the Center for Strategic and International Studies (CSIS) and the Massachusetts Institute of Technology.

NBR Analysis. Excerpts from Ashley Tellis, Assessing America's War on Terror: Confronting Insurgency, Cementing Primacy, 15(4) NBR Analysis (December 2004). © 2004 by The National Bureau of Asian Research.

Netherlands Yearbook of International Law. Excerpts from E. Vierdag, The Legal Nature of the Rights Granted by the International Convenant on Economic, Social and Cultural Rights, 9 Netherlands Yearbook of Intr'l L. 69 (1978). © T.M.C. Asser Institute.

The New Republic. Excerpts from Amartya Sen, Freedoms and Needs (10 and 17 January 1994).

New York Review of Books. Excerpts from Amartya Sen, More than 100 Million Women are Missing (20 December 1990); Kenneth Roth, The Court the US Doesn't Want (19 November 1998). Reprint permission from The New York Review of Books. Copyright © 1990, 1998 Nyrev. Inc.

New York Times. Excerpts from Sebnem Arsu, Turkish Laureate Criticizes French Legislation (14 October 2006) 5; Lydia Polgreen, As Nigeria Tries to Fight Graft, A New Sordid Tale (29 November 2005) 1; Eduardo Porter Study Finds Wealth Inequality is Widening Worldwide (6 December 2006) 3; Clyde Haberman, Israel is Vary of Long Reach in Rights Cases (28 July 2001) 1; Amy Waldman, States in India Take New Steps to Limit Births (7 November 2003) 1; Joseph Kahn, Exposé of Peasants' Plight is Suppressed by China (9 July 2004); Elaine Sciolino, France Turns to Tough Policy on Students' Religious Garb (2 October 2004) 3; Pankaj Mishra, The Myth of the New India (6 July 2006); Edmund Andrews, German Churches, Ever Givin, Ask to Receive (6 January 1998) A8; Alessandra Stanley, Pope Tells India His Church Has Right to Evangelize (8 November 1999) A3; Barbara Crossette, Testing the Limits of Tolerance as Cultures Mix (6 March 1999) B9; Elaine Sciolino, Ban Religious Attire in School, French Panel Says (12 December 2003) 1; Christopher Marquis, U.S. Chides France on Effort to Bar Religious Garb in Schools (19 December 2003) A8; Elaine Sciolino, French Muslims Protest Rule against Scarves (18 January 2004) sec 1, p. 10; Dan Bilefsky, Denmark is Unlikely Front in

Islam-West Culture War (8 January 2006) sec 1, p. 3; Alen Cowell, More European Papers Print Cartoons of Muhammad, Fueling Dispute with Muslims (12 February 2006) A12; Craig Smith and Ian Fisher, Temperatures Rise over Cartoons Mocking Muhammad (3 February 2006) A3; Outcry over Prophet Cartoons Grows Louder and More Violent (5 February 2006) sec 1, p. 10; Carlotta Gall and Craig Smith, Muslim Protests against Cartoons Spread (7 February 2006) A8; John Vinocur and Dan Bilefsky, Dane Sees Greed and Politics in Crisis (9 February 2006) A9; Robert Wright, The Silent Treatment (17 February 2006) A23; Barbara Crossette, Inquiry Says UN Inertia in '94 Worsened Genocide in Rwanda (17 December 1999) A1; Sarah Lyall, New Course by Royal Navy: A Campaign to Recruit Gays (21 February 2005) A1; John E. Leigh, Bringing it all Back Home (17 April 2006) Op-ed. © 1998/1999/2001/2003/2004/2005/2006 by the New York Times Company.

New York University Law Review. Excerpts from Jed Rubenfeld, Unilateralism and Constitutionalism, 79 NYU L. Rev. 1971 (2004).

Notre Dame Law Review. Excerpts from Cass Sunstein, Rights and Their Critics, 10 Notre Dame L. Rev. 727 (1995). © Notre Dame Law Review, University of Notre Dame.

Oxford University Press. Excerpts from José Alvarez, International Organizations as Law Makers (2005); Henry Steiner and Philip Alston, International Human Rights in Context (1996); Yuji Iwasawa, International Law, Human Rights Law and Japanese Law: The International Law on Japanese Law (1998); Dinah Shelton, Law, Non-Law and the Problem of 'Soft Law' in Dinah Shelton (ed.), Commitment and Compliance: The Role of Non-Binding Norms in the International System (2000); Malcolm Evans, International Law (2006); Cecile Fabre, Social Rights in European Constitutions, in Gráinne de Búrca and Bruno de Witte, Social Rights in Europe (2005); Sandesh Sivakumaran, Binding Armed Opposition Groups in 55 International and Comparative Law Quarterly (2006). Sanford Levinson (ed.), Torture: A Collection (2006); Liam Murphy and Thomas Nagel, Myth of Ownership: Taxes and Justice (2002); Cass Sunstein, Designing Democracy: What Constitutions Do (2003). Reprinted by permission of Oxford University Press, Inc.

Pearson Education. Permission to reprint excerpts Robert Jennings and Arthur Watts (eds.), Oppenheim's International Law (1992).

University of Pennsylvania Press. Excerpts from Joan Fitzpatrick, Human Rights in Crisis: The International System for Protecting Rights During States of Emergency (1994); Makau Mutua, Human Rights, Religion, and Proselytism, in Mutua, Human Rights: A Political and Cultural Critique (2002).

PLAN. Excerpts from Tradition and Rights: Female Genital Cutting in West Africa (2006).

Political Science Quarterly. Excerpts from Professor Herbert Wechsler, The Issues of the Nuremberg Trial, 62 Pol. Sci. Q. 11 (1947). © by The Academy of Political Science.

Princeton University Press. Excerpts from Carol Steiker, Capital Punishment and American Exceptionalism in Michael Ignatieff (ed.), American Exceptionalism and Human Rights 57 (2005); Frederick Schauer, The Exceptional First Amendment in *ibid.*; Henry Shue, Basic Rights, 2nd edn. (1996); Makau Mutua, Human Rights and the African Fingerprint in Mutua, Human Rights: A Political, and Cultural Critique

(2002); Stephen Krasner, Sovereignty: Organized Hypocrisy (1999). © 1996, 1999, 2002, 2005 Princeton University Press.

Random House. Excerpts from Swords into Ploughshares, 4th edn. by Inis L. Claude, Jr., copyright © 1956, 1959, 1964, 1971 by Inis L. Claude, Jr. Used by permission of Random House, Inc. Excerpts from A World Made New by Mary Ann Glendon, copyright © 2001 by Mary Ann Glendon. Used by permission of Random House, Inc. Excerpts from Facing Mount Kenya by Jomo Kenyatta, published by Vintage Books, a division of Random House, Inc. Used by permission of Vintage Books, a division of Random House, Inc. Excerpts from Development as Freedom by Amartya Sen, published by Anchor Books, a division of Random House, Inc. Used by permission of Anchor Books, a division of Random House, Inc.

Shoe String Press. Excerpts from H. Lauterpacht, International Law and Human Rights (1950).

Stanford Law Review. Excerpts from Ryan Goodman and Derek Jinks, Toward an Institutional Theory of Sovereignty, 55 Stanford L. Rev. 1749 (2003).

Taylor and Francis Ltd. Excerpts from K. Hayter, Female Circumcision – Is There a Legal Solution?, Journal of Social Welfare and Family Law (1984). Excerpts from Priscilla Hayner, Unspeakable Truths: Confronting State Terror and Atrocity (2001); Peter Malanczuk, Akehurst's Modern Introduction to International Law, 7th rev. edn. (1997). Reprinted by permission of the publisher (Taylor and Francis Ltd. www.informaworld.com).

Transnational Law and Contemporary Problems. Excerpts from Chidi Anselm Odinkalu, The Individual Complaints Procedures of the African Commission on Human and People's Rights: A Preliminary Assessment, 8 Transnational Law and Contemporary Problems 365 (1998). © University of Iowa College of Law.

UNESCO. Excerpts from Claude Lévi-Strauss, Race and History (1958); Theo van Boven, Distinguishing Criteria of Human Rights, in Karel Vasak and Philip Alston (eds.), The International Dimensions of Human Rights, vol. 1 (1982).

UNICEF. Excerpts from Female Genital Mutilation/Cutting: A Statistical Exploration (2005).

United Nations University. Excerpts from Georges Abi-Saab, The Changing World Order and the International Legal Order: The Structural Evolution of International Law Beyond the State-Centric Model, in Y. Sakamoto (ed.) Global Transformation: Challenges to the State System (1994).

Verso. Excerpts from Richard Rorty, Human Rights, Rationality and Sentimentality, in Obra Savic (ed.), The Politics of Human Rights (1999).

Virginia Journal of International Law. Excerpts from Rebecca Cook, Reservations to the Convention on the Elimination of All Forms of Discrimination against Women, 30 Va. J. of Intr'l L. 643 (1990); M.O. Chibundu, Making Customary International Law Through Municipal Adjudications: A Structural Inquiry, 39 Va. J. of Intr'l L. 1069 (1999).

Washington Post. Excerpts from Jack Goldsmith and Eric A. Posner, A Better Way on Detainees (4 August 2006) Op-Ed, A 17.

Wayne Law Review. Excerpts from Stefan Oeter, International Human Rights and National Sovereignty in Federal Systems: The German Experience, 47 Wayne L. Rev. 871 (2001).

Wiley-Blackwell Publishers. Excerpts from Cécile Fabre, Constitutionalising Social Rights, 6 Journal of Political Philosophy 263 (1998). K.D. Ewing, The Human Rights Act and Parliamentary Democracy, 62 Modern Law Review 79 (1999).

Wm. B. Eerdmans Publishing Company. Excerpts from Cole Durham, Perspectives on Religious Liberty: A Comparative Framework, in Johan van der Vyver and John Witte (eds.), Religious Human Rights in Global Perspective (1996); Dinah Shelton and Alexandre Kiss, A Draft of Model Law on Freedom of Religion, in *ibid.*; Harold Berman, Religious Rights in Russia at a Time of Tumultuous Transition: A Historical Theory in *ibid.* © 1996 Wm. B. Eerdmans Publishing Company, Grand Rapids, Michigan. Reprinted by permission of the publisher; all rights reserved.

World Health Organization. Excerpts from Fact Sheet No. 241 (2000).

Yale Journal of International Law. Excerpts from José Alvarez, Crimes of States/Crimes of Hate: Lessons from Rwanda, 24 Yale J. Int. L. 365 (1999).

Yale Law Journal. Excerpts from Oona Hathaway, Do Human Rights Treaties Make a Difference?, 111 Yale L. Rev. © Yale Law Journal Company and Fred B. Rothman & Company.

Wall Street Journal. Excerpts from Max Boot, Commentary, When 'Justice' and 'Peace' Don't Mix (2 October 2000) A34.

While every care has been taken to establish and acknowledge copyright, and contact the copyright owners, the publishers tender their apologies for any accidental infringement. They would be pleased to come to a suitable agreement with the rightful owners in each case.

PART A

INTRODUCTORY NOTIONS AND BACKGROUND TO INTERNATIONAL HUMAN RIGHTS MOVEMENT

This coursebook examines the world of contemporary human rights, including legal norms, political contexts, moral ideals, humanitarian laws of war, human rights discourse, state interests, international relations and institutions, governmental (state) and nongovernmental (nonstate) actors, and economic development. The boundaries of the subject are steadily expanding. Since the Second World War, the human rights movement that grew out of that war has become an indelible part of our legal, political and moral landscape. The book uses this term 'movement' to include governmental and intergovernmental as well as nongovernmental developments since 1945, unlike some contemporary usage that restricts the term to nongovernmental actors. Given the breadth and complexity of the movement, including its engagement with law, politics, morals and radically different cultures, the coursebook necessarily includes materials from a range of disciplines.

The three principal themes of law, politics and morals are interrelated, indeed inseparable, for an understanding of the movement. The political and moral aspects of international human rights are self-evident; it is the international legal aspect that is novel. The rules and standards of contemporary human rights are expressed not only through states' constitutions, laws and practices, but also through treaties and international custom, as well as the work products (decisions about action, forms of adjudication, studies, investigative reports, resolutions, recommendations) of diverse international institutions and organs.

Throughout, the materials underscore the youth of this movement, and the task of students and others committed to its ideals is to see themselves not as apprentices learning about an established, even static, framework of ideas and institutions, but rather as shapers and architects of the movement's ongoing development. The book's goal is then not only to train students to work effectively within the present structure and boundaries of the human rights movement, but also to impart a broad as well as critical understanding of it, and to provoke ideas about the directions in which it may be or ought to be heading.

The Preface sets forth the book's pedagogical goals, conceptual structure and formal organization. Students may wish to read it now.

1

Human Rights Concepts and Discourse

This introductory chapter assumes no special knowledge about the foundations or content of rights, human rights and international human rights. Rather it is meant to spur thoughts about a range of issues that later chapters examine.

The two parts of the chapter explore these basic questions from complementary perspectives. Part A introduces human rights issues in the large, as they arise and become known. It is not attentive to courts, for in many of the situations it addresses, courts will play only a marginal role, if a role at all. The medium for looking at these issues is newspaper articles.

Part B moves to an examination of the way that courts from different states address and argue about the alleged violations of rights that come before them. The common issue in Part B engaging these courts is the legality of capital punishment under illustrative state laws and under the developing international human rights law. At the same time, these materials examine the growing attention of national courts to foreign law, whether constitutional, or statutory or judicial decisions, to learn how other countries reason and decide about the permissibility of capital punishment (and many other issues). Those inquiries lead us to what many would describe as the 'special case' (or 'situation') of the United States with respect to human rights (and other fields), that involves so-called US exceptionalism or unilateralism.

A. GLOBAL SNAPSHOTS

The following excerpts from newspaper reports draw you into the diverse human rights problems that plague the world. Some but not all of them refer to rights, or human rights, and thereby indicate the current global currency of that term. After reading these reports, consider the following questions:

> What is the source of the rules or standards under which governmental, inter-governmental and nongovernmental organizations evaluate and criticize a state?
>
> What different roles do the types of organizations referred to in these articles seem to play?

How would you identify the alleged human rights violation in each story? Are you clear in each story that (if the reported facts are true) there has been a violation?

Does all conduct that you believe may violate a right address only individuals' rights, or do rights of groups also seem relevant?

Are (international) human rights violations committed only by states, or are nongovernmental forces and individuals also accused of such violations? Do all the stories involve governments as the direct violators of rights?

What steps if any seem to be taken to influence or force a state to end violations?

STORIES FROM THE PRESS: WHAT RELEVANCE TO HUMAN RIGHTS ISSUES?

1. Turkish Laureate Criticizes French Legislation

by Sebnem Arsu, *New York Times*, October 14, 2006, p. 5

Orhan Pamuk, the Turkish novelist who won the Nobel Prize in Literature this week, went on television Friday to criticize the French parliamentary vote that would make it a crime to deny that the Ottoman Turks' mass killing of Armenians constituted genocide. In a telephone interview broadcast live on the private television network NTV, Mr. Pamuk, who faced criminal charges for his statements acknowledging the massacre, said France had acted against its own fundamental principles of freedom of expression.

"The French tradition of critical thinking influenced and taught me a lot," he said. "This decision, however, is a prohibition and didn't suit the libertarian nature of the French tradition." The legislation was approved by the lower house of Parliament, but it is uncertain whether the upper house will concur. [Eds. As of December 2006, the French Senate had not approved the legislation.]

. . .

Some analysts fear that widespread anger against the French legislation may turn more Turks against joining the European Union. A Turkish opinion poll released in July showed a decline in support, to 58 percent from a high of 74 percent in 2003, in part because of the prolonged road to admission.

Mr. Pamuk's statement came after some in the country voiced suspicions that the award was politically motivated. Mr. Pamuk owes part of his celebrity in Europe to his criticism of Turkey's stance on the Armenian genocide. Many in Europe feel that Turkey should acknowledge that the mass killings during and after World War I were genocide, and the country's refusal may complicate its attempts to join the European Union.

. . .

Mr. Pamuk was charged last year with making "anti-Turkish" remarks when he called attention to the Armenian genocide during an interview with a Swiss magazine. Turkish nationalists initiated the criminal case using a law that makes it a crime to insult Turkish identity. Europeans and others who decried Mr. Pamuk's treatment said Turkey was violating his freedom of expression. After much outside pressure, the charges were dropped on a technicality.

...

Sema Munuklu, 38, a restaurant owner, said . . . the French Parliament's action displayed European hesitancy in accepting Turkey into the European Union. Ibrahim Unseli, 55, who runs an electronics shop, said he was as appalled by the French Parliament's attitude as he was by Mr. Pamuk's position on the Armenians and added that he hoped that Turks would boycott French goods.

2. US Human Rights Hypocrisy Attacked

China Daily, May 22, 2004

Human rights experts and religious leaders spoke out on Friday against a recent series of US reports on China's human rights situation, urging Washington to take a closer look at its own army's abuse of Iraqi prisoners. Tian Jin, a member of the China Society for Human Rights Studies, said that the United States wanted to "achieve two goals" by publishing the reports. "It wants to add political pressure on China and demonize China."

The US Government had initially planned to issue its report entitled Supporting Human Rights and Democracy: The US Record 2003–2004, which looks at human rights in over 100 countries, on May 5. But publication was postponed until last Monday amid global fury over the disclosure of atrocities committed by US troops against Iraqi prisoners. "Against the backdrop of the US army's abuse of Iraqi prisoners, the United States should have refrained from issuing such a report," Tian told China Daily. He was echoed by Dong Yunhu, Vice-President of the China Society for Human Rights Studies, who described the US report as "ironic."

The report has allowed the public to see clearly the double standards adopted by the United States concerning human rights and its pursuit for hegemony, said Dong. "The United States should stop interfering in other countries' internal affairs by using human rights, and return to an equal dialogue on human rights," added Dong.

Foreign Ministry spokesman Liu Jianchao said that the United States should take a closer look at the state of human rights in its own country and think about how to improve this. Actions by the US should not violate human rights in other countries.

China can be proud of its human rights achievements over the past decades, although there remains further room for improvement, added the spokesman. This year's session of the National People's Congress in March passed a constitutional amendment which states that China respects and preserves human rights.

The United States and China have had a number of confrontations over human rights this year. The US State Department issued this year's Country Reports on Human Rights Practices in February, which was once again critical of China. That was followed by a US-sponsored anti-China motion at the 60th session of the United Nations Commission on Human Rights which was thrown out by the participating countries on April 16. The recent US actions have prompted China to suspend its human rights dialogue with the United States.

...

3. As Nigeria Tries to Fight Graft, A New Sordid Tale

by Lydia Polgreen, *New York Times*, November 29, 2005, p. 1

Precisely where in the rogue's gallery of corrupt Nigerian leaders Diepreye Alamieyeseigha will fall is a matter for history to judge. Gen. Sani Abacha, the military dictator who helped himself to at least $3 billion and salted it away in foreign bank accounts, doubtless stole far more.

But General Abacha — who ruled the country from 1993 to 1998 — never fled money-laundering charges in a foreign land by donning a dress and a wig to match forged travel documents, as Mr. Alamieyeseigha, the governor of a small oil-producing state in the Niger Delta, did last week, government officials said. For their sheer audacity, his antics are likely to earn him a prominent place among the leaders who in the past four decades are believed to have stolen or misspent $400 billion in government money, most of it the profits from Nigeria's oil reserves.

...

Long associated with rampant corruption and kleptocratic governments, Nigeria has year in and year out gotten one of the worst scores in Transparency International's world corruption perception index, though this year its rating improved slightly.

Corruption touches virtually every aspect of Nigerian life, from the millions of sham e-mail messages sent each year by people claiming to be Nigerian officials seeking help with transferring large sums of money out of the country, to the police officers who routinely set up roadblocks, sometimes every few hundred yards, to extract bribes of 20 naira, about 15 cents, from drivers.

In the past year President Olusegun Obasanjo has ratcheted up the fight against corruption, and several high officials have been ensnared in criminal investigations.

...

"Looting from the people is not a new thing," said Kayode Fayemi of the Center for Democracy and Development, an advocacy group. "We are used to that. But for people who claim to be representatives of their own people to commit this barefaced robbery is shameful. Where is the rule of law?"

...

"There is no real system of checks and balances," said Anyakwee Nsirimovu, executive director of the Institute of Human Rights and Humanitarian Law, based in the Niger Delta. "The legislatures owe all their allegiance to the governors, who control state money."

Here in Mr. Alamieyeseigha's state of Bayelsa, that means serious money. Under a Nigerian law enacted to help develop the oil-rich but long-neglected Niger Delta, 13 percent of the revenue generated in any state is returned there for development. Bayelsa produces 30 percent of the country's oil, and with recent sky-high oil prices, the state budget this year ballooned to $560 million, compared with nearly $300 million in 2003.

...

... Since 2002 the state has spent more than $25 million on the governor's mansion, according to budgets on file in Yenagoa's tiny public library. The fence enclosing the two houses alone cost $5.7 million.

...

Meanwhile, the Poverty Eradication Committee, whose purpose is not explained, has a budget of about $23,000, according to the 2005 spending plan, which is posted on the state's Web site, www.bayelsagov.com. That is a little more than half of what is budgeted for toiletries for state officials.

4. Study Finds Wealth Inequality is Widening Worldwide

by Eduardo Porter, *New York Times*, December 6, 2006, Business Sec. p. 3

Experts have long worried about the skewed distribution of the world's income, with vast rewards massing in the hands of a wealthy elite and precious little left over for the vast majority of the global population.

But even as income inequality has reached near record levels in many countries, the distribution of the world's wealth — things like stocks, bonds or physical assets like land — has become even more narrowly concentrated than income, according to a new report by the World Institute for Development Economics Research of the United Nations University.

In 2000, the top 1 percent of the world's population — some 37 million adults with a net worth of at least $515,000 — accounted for about 40 percent of the world's total net worth, according to the report.

The bottom half of the population owned merely 1.1 percent of the globe's wealth. The net worth of the world's typical person — whose wealth was above that of half the world's population and below that of the other half — was under $2,200.

The widening gap between the global haves and the have-nots in large measure reflects the failure of less-developed countries to develop, while rich countries — particularly the United States — have experienced fast economic growth and a spectacular buildup of assets.

"Developed countries have pulled ahead of the rest of the world," said Edward N. Wolff, a professor of economics at New York University who is a co-author of the new study. "With the notable exception of China and India, the third world has drifted behind."

. . .

Americans have amassed much of the world's treasure. According to the report, in 2000 the United States accounted for 4.7 percent of the world's population but 32.6 percent of the world's wealth. Nearly 4 out of every 10 people in the wealthiest 1 percent of the global population were American.

The average American had a net worth of nearly $144,000, losing only to the average Japanese, who had $180,000, at market exchange rates; the average person in Luxembourg, who had $183,000; and the average Swiss, who had $171,000.

By contrast, in 2000 the average Chinese had a net worth of roughly $2,600, at the official exchange rate. China, home to more than a fifth of the world's population, had only 2.6 percent of the world's wealth. And India, with 16.8 percent of the world's people, accounted for only 0.9 percent of the world's wealth.

Among Americans, wealth is distributed about as unequally as it is around the globe. The new study cited data from the Federal Reserve's Survey of Consumer Finances, which found that the richest 1 percent of Americans held 32 percent of the nation's wealth in 2001. (This excludes the billionaires in the Forbes list, who control roughly another 2 percent of the nation's wealth.)

This tops the inequity in every country but Switzerland, among the 20 nations that measure these wealth disparities and are cited in the report. And it vastly outstrips the inequality in the distribution of income. A recent study by Emmanuel Saez of the University of California, Berkeley, and Thomas Piketty of the Ecole Normale Superieure in Paris, found that in 2004 the top 1 percent of Americans earned a higher share of the nation's income than at any time since the 1920s. Still, that share was only 16 percent.

. . .

Income inequality shows few signs of abating in most countries. Still, there is evidence that the global gap in wealth may close somewhat over coming years. Paradoxically, the reason is the fast growth of China and India. Inequality is growing rapidly in both those countries. As tens of millions of Chinese and Indians climb out of poverty, they are leaving tens of millions of less fortunate Chinese and Indians behind.

. . .

5. Israel Is Wary of Long Reach in Rights Cases
by Clyde Haberman, *New York Times*, July 28, 2001, p. 1

A warning went out this week from Israel's Foreign Ministry to government, army and security officials. Be careful in choosing destinations when travelling abroad, it cautioned, because certain nations might be prepared to charge ranking Israelis with violating Palestinians' human rights.

The advisory was not worded quite that bluntly. It recommended, as a senior ministry official put it today, that high-level officials "do their homework" to avoid stumbling into "a legal embarrassment." But the message was clear:

Some countries, notably in Europe, believe that Israel has been unduly harsh toward the Palestinians — firing on young protesters disproportionately, singling out Islamic extremists for assassination, and restricting the movement of ordinary people to such an extent that Palestinians say their economy is nearing collapse. Israel's insistence that Palestinians have their own leaders to blame for their troubles, and that whatever it does is purely in the name of security, leaves many Europeans cold.

So watch out, the Foreign Ministry told Israeli officials. This is a new age of lawyers without borders when it comes to human rights. Prosecutors are prepared to reach far beyond their own lands to put on trial political figures accused of gross violations. Witness, Israeli officials say, the international cases brought against Augusto Pinochet of Chile and Slobodan Milosevic of Serbia.

While Israelis blanch at the notion that they even remotely qualify for the same league as those two men, they are well aware that Israel often falls short of human-rights standards as interpreted in Western Europe. As a result, the Foreign Ministry has begun compiling a list of nations that claim "universal jurisdiction" in certain cases. Potential worry spots for the Israelis are said to include Belgium, Britain and

Spain. "We're not in a panic," a senior official said, "but I think we must know the facts. And if some system is getting crazy, we should be aware of it."

Concerns here about potential vulnerability have been fueled by two separate cases: an attempt in Belgium to charge Israel's prime minister, Ariel Sharon, with war crimes, and unhappiness in Denmark because Israel has named a former chief of the Shin Bet security service as its new ambassador.

...

[Many Israelis] view the Belgian case as an example of European pro-Arab, anti-Israel and perhaps even anti-Jewish bias. At the least, government officials have said, it is part of an effort to undermine Mr. Sharon politically during this crisis with the Palestinians. And regardless of what human-rights groups may say, they add, Israel's perceived shortcomings pale in comparison with violations in Arab countries that are hardly bastions of democracy and liberty.

...

It was not lost on some Israelis that they themselves have in the past supported the "globalization of the criminal international law," as it was called by Alan Baker, a legal adviser to the Foreign Ministry. Mr. Baker mentioned the Holocaust, seemingly referring to Israel's abduction of the notorious Nazi figure Adolf Eichmann in Argentina in 1960. Eichmann was put on trial in Israel, found guilty and hanged in 1962.

"We always had an interest in true criminals being brought to justice," Mr. Baker told the Israeli radio. The problem now, he said, is "a tendency to exploit this good thing for political achievements such as delegitimizing the State of Israel and its leaders."

6. McGuinty Government Rules Out Use of Sharia Law

by Colin Freeze and Karen Howlett, *Globe and Mail*, September 12, 2005

Seeking to end months of debate, Premier Dalton McGuinty now says 'there will be no sharia law in Ontario' — an announcement that should quell a growing public-relations crisis concerning the use of Islamic law.... Following widespread condemnation of a plan that would formally allow the tenets of sharia to be used in resolving family disputes, the Premier said he'll make the boundaries between church and state clearer by banning faith-based arbitrations.

Ontario explicitly gave the green light to such practices in its 1991 Arbitration Act. But as early as this fall, new Ontario laws may put a stop to religion-based settlements in matters such as child-custody disputes or inheritances. This means that orthodox Jews and some Christian leaders may soon make a common cause with fundamentalist Muslims in seeking to limit the scope of the new proposals.

'Our reaction is we're disappointed, we're very disappointed,' said Joel Richler, chairman of the Ontario wing of the Canadian Jewish Congress. 'It's what we consider to be a knee-jerk reaction against the sharia issue.' He said orthodox Jews have used tribunals to settle family disputes for centuries, but the future of these tribunals is no longer clear in Ontario.

Many moderate Muslims say they are overjoyed by the Premier's announcement. 'I'm so happy today. It's a victory for the women's rights movement,' said Homa Arjomand, an Iranian immigrant who has launched a campaign to stop sharia in

Ontario. 'Women's rights are not protected by any religion,' she said. But fundamentalist Islam, in particular, can be harsh, she said.

'Divorces are happening behind closed doors and the woman is banned from having custody of her children,' Ms. Arjomand said. 'She is being sent back to her home country to live with her relatives.' She went so far as to say that proposed new laws ought to allow for the prosecution of religious leaders involved in faith-based arbitrations.

While it's unlikely that amendments to the Arbitration Act will go that far, Mr. McGuinty told The Canadian Press yesterday that . . ., [t]here will be one law for all Ontarians.' Legislation will be introduced 'as soon as possible,' he said.

The 1991 legislation was originally hailed as a victory for multiculturalism, but since then Canada's Muslim population has grown considerably and now numbers around 650,000.

Already imams are using Islamic law to help settle family disputes — and will likely continue to do so regardless of what Ontario does.

. . .

Last year, former NDP attorney-general Marion Boyd recommended the province handle Islamic arbitrations as it long has other religious arbitrations. She said participants must go into the process voluntarily, and that all decisions could be appealed in court.

Yet the proposal is exceptionally controversial . . . . This past weekend an open letter from prominent Canadian women urged Mr. McGuinty to take a stand against 'the ghettoization of members of religious communities as well as human-rights abuses' that religious tribunals would bring.

. . .

7. States in India Take New Steps to Limit Births

by Amy Waldman, *New York Times*, November 7, 2003, p. 1

A new reckoning is under way in India over how best to stabilize a population that is set to surpass China's as the world's biggest by midcentury. Indian women currently bear an average of just under three children — a steep drop from the six of 50 years ago, but still above the 2.1 that would stabilize a population that already exceeds a billion people.

The burden on development and the growing competition for resources like water and land are prompting a reassessment in which India is struggling to balance its democratic impulses with its demographic pressures. Nearly a decade ago, India embraced the conclusions of a 1994 United Nations conference on population in Cairo, which called for abandoning contraceptive targets, improving education and health for women and children, and offering multiple voluntary contraceptive choices.

India itself had recoiled against coercive policies — like China's — after the ruthless sterilization campaign under Indira Gandhi in the late 1970's. But today, the national mood increasingly favors a tougher approach, and states, free to adopt their own policies, are experimenting.

At least six have laws mandating a two-child norm for members of village councils, and some are extending it to civil servants as well. Some states have considered denying educational benefits to third children. States are also increasingly turning to incentives — pay raises, or access to land or housing — for government servants who choose sterilization after one or two children.

Across some states in North India, local elected officials are increasingly obliged to mount explicit defenses of their decisions to procreate. The reason: laws limiting members of village councils, or panchayats, to two children, on the notion that they should provide models of restraint.

...

But critics of the laws call them gimmicks. They point out that the countries, and even Indian states, that have most successfully limited population growth have done so more by increasing education and work opportunities for women, improving health care and providing a wide range of contraceptive choices.

As seen here, in Chhattisgarh State, the law also provides a case study in the challenges, and perhaps the costs, of even mildly coercive social engineering in a democracy.

...

In July, the Supreme Court seemed to suggest that India needed to do a bit more crushing, when it upheld a two-child limit for village council members in Haryana State. Population control was a matter of such urgency, the court said, that the nation could not place "undue stress on fundamental rights and individual liberty." India is now home to 17 percent of the world's people on only 2.5 percent of its land, the court noted, saying the "torrential increase" in population was hindering socio-economic progress. "Complacency in controlling population in the name of democracy is too heavy a price to pay," the three-judge panel agreed.

...

Now [an interviewed woman] faces dismissal. The couple had six daughters when the law went into effect. They wanted — and subsequently had — a son, a desire that also drove three other panchayat members interviewed to break the law. Some worry that strict enforcement of two-child laws will lead to more abortions of female fetuses, already a problem in North India. "Everyone wants a small family — two children," explained her husband, Rajaram Sonkar, as their girls flitted around his small shop. "But if you have a daughter, you have to keep going."

...

That there is more awareness now is undeniable. Even Mr. Dau's neighbor, Uttra Bai, a 17-year-old with a one-year-old son, said she would prefer only two children. But she also helps explain why so many women have more. Like tens of millions of Indian women, especially across the northern Hindi belt, Ms. Bai was never schooled. She was married off at 15, and had her first child soon after. She said that she did not know how to prevent a pregnancy, and that in any case, the number of children she would bear was for her in-laws to decide.

8. Poll: 44% in U.S. Favor Limits on Muslims' Rights

by William Kates, *South Florida Sun-Sentinel*, December 18, 2004, p. 8A

Nearly half of all Americans believe the U.S. government should restrict the civil liberties of Muslim-Americans, according to a nationwide poll. The survey conducted by Cornell University also found that Republicans and people who described themselves as highly religious were more apt to support curtailing Muslims' civil liberties than Democrats or people who are less religious.

Researchers also found that respondents who paid more attention to television news were more likely to fear terrorist attacks and support limiting the rights of Muslim-Americans.

"It's sad news. It's disturbing news. But it's not unpredictable," said Mahdi Bray, executive director of the Muslim American Society. "The nation is at war, even if it's not a traditional war. We just have to remain vigilant and continue to interface."

The survey found 44 percent favored at least some restrictions on the civil liberties of Muslim Americans. Forty-eight percent said liberties should not be restricted in any way.

The survey showed that 27 percent of respondents supported requiring all Muslim-Americans to register where they lived with the federal government. Twenty-two percent favored racial profiling to identify potential terrorist threats. And 29 percent thought undercover agents should infiltrate Muslim civic and volunteer organizations to keep tabs on their activities and fund-raising.

Cornell student researchers questioned 715 people in the nationwide telephone poll conducted this fall. The margin of error was 3.6 percentage points. James Shanahan, an associate professor of communications who helped organize the survey, said the results indicate "the need for continued dialogue about issues of civil liberties" in a time of war.

While researchers said they were not surprised by the overall level of support for curtailing civil liberties, they were startled by the correlation with religion and exposure to television news.

9. An Endless Wait for Health Care

by Judith Graham, *Chicago Tribune*, December 25, 2005, Metro p. 1

Brenda Yonzon was thrust into Chicago's public health system last year when her husband died suddenly, leaving her without private health insurance. There, she discovered a different world. As a private, insured patient, Yonzon could call her longtime doctors and get an appointment the next day. As an uninsured public patient, she waited eight hours at Stroger Hospital before even seeing a physician who would attend to her kidney stones.

Before, Yonzon could go to a pharmacy and pick up a prescription in 15 minutes. At Stroger, Yonzon stood in line for hours only to have a woman at the counter say the prescription wasn't ready and she would have to come back another day. "That was agony," said Yonzon, 58, who has diabetes and hypertension.

Such stark differences in medical care for the uninsured aren't new. But the rising tide of Americans without health insurance, combined with medical costs that outpace the rate of inflation, is increasingly straining public hospitals and clinics that serve the needy.

...

In the last year, the Bureau of Health Services has closed clinics for diabetes and glaucoma to new patients because it can't accommodate the demand for services.

Colon screenings, recommended for all Americans over age 50, are largely unavailable to poor and uninsured county residents. Non-urgent surgeries are increasingly difficult to schedule. Prescriptions take days, not hours, to fill. The developments mean that more people are putting their names on waiting lists, going without medical care or delaying trying to get services until they are in an acute crisis.

...

Medical advances contribute to the problem.... Today's doctors can do more for sick patients, increasing demand for services.

The trend is national; signs of a similarly overwhelmed system for the uninsured are evident in most major urban centers, from Los Angeles to Atlanta. Uninsured patients in rural America are also hard hit.... In all, some 45.8 million Americans are uninsured, including 1.8 million in Illinois.

...

Two years ago, for instance, the new Stroger Hospital opened with a capacity of nearly 80,000 emergency room visits a year. But in the 12 months ending Nov. 30, visits to the ER totalled 155,000.

...

Specialty clinics are so overburdened that it now takes 14 months to get an appointment with a gastroenterologist and 7 months for an appointment with an orthopedic physician.... Surgical services are so swamped that the county is declining to schedule appointments for non-urgent procedures such as gall bladder surgery or hernia repairs unless patients are in a state of crisis.

...

Also affecting care for uninsured and poor patients are the widening differences between medical institutions in affluent communities and those in disadvantaged communities, according to research published in this month's issue of the policy journal Health Affairs.

In their review of 12 communities–Boston, Miami, Cleveland, Indianapolis, Phoenix, Seattle and others–the authors found that hospitals in wealthy areas invest heavily in the latest medical technology and services, while those in poor neighborhoods cannot do the same.

...

10. Exposé of Peasants' Plight is Suppressed by China

by Joseph Kahn, *New York Times*, July 9, 2004

In their muckraking best seller about abuses against Chinese peasants, the husband-and-wife authors, Chen Guidi and Wu Chuntao, told the stories of farmers who fought the system and lost. The book, "An Investigation of China's Peasantry," describes how one farmer's long struggle against illegal taxes ended only when the police beat him to death with a mulberry club. It profiles a village activist who was jailed on a charge of instigating riots after he accused a local Communist Party boss of corruption.

Now, Mr. Chen and Ms. Wu say, it is their turn to be silenced. Though their tautly written defense of China's 750 million peasants has become a sensation, their names have stopped appearing in the news media. Their publisher was ordered to cease printing at the peak of the book's popularity this spring....

A ranking official sued the authors, accusing them of libel, in his home county court. In a country that does not protect a right to criticize those holding power, it is a case they say they are sure to lose.

Top Beijing leaders acknowledge that China's surging urban economy has done relatively little to benefit the two-thirds of the population living in rural areas. They have put forward new programs to reduce the widening gap between urban and rural living standards. But the effort to quiet Mr. Chen and Ms. Wu makes it clear that officials will not tolerate writers who portray China's vast peasantry as an underclass or who assign blame for peasants' enduring poverty.

"We spoke up for powerless people, but we ourselves are powerless before these officials," Mr. Chen said in an interview near his home in Anhui Province. "The authorities will not allow peasants to have a voice."

Prime Minister Wen Jiabao has ordered the government to address, in the latest slogan, "three peasant problems": farmers, villages and agriculture. But he and other officials rarely emphasize what many rural experts consider the biggest peasant problems: corruption and abuse of power.

"An Investigation of China's Peasantry" deals with little else. It praises the spirit of central government efforts to reduce the rural tax burden and raise farm incomes. But it shows how such policies are sooner or later undone by local party bosses determined to line their own pockets.

It also details how local officials deceive China's top leaders, including Jiang Zemin, the retired party chief who still leads the military, and Zhu Rongji, the retired prime minister. Even Mr. Wen, whom the authors credit with understanding rural problems better than other leaders, is portrayed as being unable to penetrate the local officials' Potemkin displays of fealty.

Mr. Chen and Ms. Wu shocked many urban readers with their tales of rural backwardness. But they appear to have misjudged how much shock the one-party system would accept.

"We had hoped that there would be some support for our work among central government officials," Mr. Chen said. "But it is really sensitive when you write that the general secretary of the Communist Party does not know what's happening in the country."

...

11. France Turns to Tough Policy on Students' Religious Garb

by Elaine Sciolino, *New York Times*, October 22, 2004, p. 3

To enforce its new law banning religious symbols from public schools, the Ministry of National Education has decided to get tough.

...

Nine female Muslim students who have refused to remove their Islamic head coverings have been thrown out of schools across France....

Since school started a month ago, students who have refused to remove what school administrators define as conspicuous religious symbols have been quarantined in study halls or libraries and not allowed to attend class. The banned symbols include anything that can be construed as an Islamic veil (head scarf, bandanna, beret), a Jewish skullcap, a large Christian cross and a Sikh turban.

Officially the law is aimed at enforcing France's republican ideal of secularism. Unofficially it is aimed at stopping female Muslim public school students from swathing themselves in scarves or even long veils.

There have been odd, unintended consequences. Despite the 1905 law separating church and state in France, public schools have been allowed to keep chaplains, most of them Catechism-teaching and Catholic, on their staffs as long as they were not paid by the state....

...

France's Sikh community, meanwhile, challenged the new law in court after the Louise-Michel school in the Parisian suburb of Bobigny barred three male Sikh students from classes because they were wearing turbans.

...

In a letter to President Jacques Chirac nearly a year ago, the Sikh community argued that the turban should be allowed because it is a cultural, not a religious, symbol.

...

In an interview with France Inter radio on Tuesday, Education Minister Francois Fillon said he was pleased with the way things were going. He said that at the start of the school year there were 600 cases of students refusing to remove their religious symbols — most of them Muslim girls in scarves — but that most had agreed to do so after a "dialogue."

A number of opponents of the law criticize the "dialogue" process as nothing more than pressure to break the will of students. "It's a machine that destroys the individual in the name of a fundamentalist secularism," said Dr. Thomas Milcent, a Strasbourg physician and convert to Islam who heads a Muslim lobbying group. "Some girls have been treated with cruelty, kept in isolation for days. This is extremism."

12. Internet Groups 'Shirk Human Rights Duties in China'

by Mure Dickie, *Financial Times* (London), July 20, 2006, Asia-Pacific, p. 10

Amnesty International has accused three of the world's biggest internet companies — Yahoo, Microsoft and Google — of overlooking their human rights obligations in order to tap into China's dynamic online market.

In a report to be issued today the human rights organisation says: "All three companies have in different ways facilitated or participated in the practice of government censorship in China. While companies are under continuous pressure from shareholders to maximise their profits and can be expected to have a presence in lucrative markets, this does not absolve them from their human rights responsibilities." Amnesty also demanded that the three companies lobby Beijing for better human rights protection.

Yahoo, Microsoft and Google have argued that their presence benefits Chinese internet users by giving them greater access to information and promoting the development of the internet. They also say they must abide by Beijing's laws and policies to operate in the country. But Amnesty dismissed their arguments, saying it was significant that "none of the companies has been willing or able to specify precisely which laws and legal processes it has been obliged to follow".

It aimed particular criticism at Yahoo for helping Chinese authorities act against two e-mail users: Shi Tao, a journalist jailed for revealing information about Beijing's media controls, and writer Li Zhi, jailed for writing online essays critical of officials. Yahoo has said it had no choice but to co-operate with authorities and has since transferred control of its China business to a local internet entrepreneur who has made clear he is happy to co-operate with police.

But Amnesty said internet companies in China should "exhaust all judicial remedies and appeal" before co-operating with the state in cases with human rights implications.

The group criticised Microsoft for banning sensitive terms from parts of its Chinese blog service, for shutting down one outspoken blogger's site and for censoring its search service.

Google, the global search market leader, also drew fire for introducing a locally based service that censors sensitive results. Amnesty noted the "welcome first steps" Google had taken by acknowledging that its service did not accord fully with its principles and for telling users when results were censored.

...

13. State Fails to Rescue Child Workers

by Rajiv Shah, *The Times of India*, September 20, 2005

For all its industrialisation, Gujarat has an embarrassingly high number of child labourers and a sorry record of rehabilitation. A latest Sachivalaya document suggests that things have not changed in the past year despite the Comptroller and Auditor General (CAG) indicting the Gujarat government, in its latest report (2003–04), for failing to "eliminate" or at least "minimise" child labour.

The internal report estimates that the state has [about 4,850,000] child workers and Gujarat ranks fifth among states in harbouring child labour. Intriguingly, this report by the state government is based on 1991 Census. Despite the high incidence, the data provided in the internal document shows that as on August 11, 2005, the government was able to rescue only 465 child labourers throughout the state.

...

The document says, in rural areas the incidence of child labour is high among scheduled tribes and other backward classes. In the urban areas, it is high among the scheduled castes.

...

Significantly, the CAG report, basing itself on the data available in 2004, indicted the government for "inadequate compliance" of the Act's provisions to rehabilitate child workers by providing them with education and health care. The state had also ignored Supreme Court directives. It added, there were "defects in the survey of detection of child labour, nonrecovery of compensation from employers and improper functioning of the National Child Labour Project, responsible for implementing the rehabilitation process."

...

QUESTIONS

Many questions concerning human rights are posed about each of these 13 items. Here are a few illustrations:

1. (Item No. 1) Do you believe that either or both states violated a right? What content would such a right have? Whose right?

2. (Item No. 4) How could wealth inequality constitute a violation of a right? What types of rights might be implicated?

3. (Item No. 6) What advantages and problems do you see in authorizing designated ethnic or religious groups to settle certain types of controversies (such as those related to family law) under their own religious law?

4. (Item No. 13) If nonstate actors employ child labourers at their own decision without any state-imposed requirement, how could a state be charged with a rights violation?

B. THE GLOBAL FRAMEWORK FOR CONTEMPORARY HUMAN RIGHTS DISCOURSE: CAPITAL PUNISHMENT, INTERACTIONS AMONG STATES, EXCEPTIONALISM

Part A drew on newspaper accounts to illustrate the large range of issues that have been brought over the last half century into human rights doctrine and discourse. In their descriptions of a number of problems, many of the articles found it necessary to include not only the specific violation that may have been involved, but also the broad political, social, economic or military context. They did not draw on the work of courts.

Section 1 of Part B differs in several respects. It examines one broad issue, capital punishment, either in the large or with respect to a particular category of criminal defendants. And it examines a few illustrative judicial decisions to explore the argument of courts, and the evolving character of human rights discourse in the hands of courts, those most 'legal' of institutions. It is important to bear in mind that much of the invocation of rights and many of the arguments in these decisions are phenomena of the last half-century. The very institutions to which these courts refer simply did not previously exist.

Section 2 considers the degree to which these courts and other national and international organs (like a parliament, or a United Nations body) form part of a global framework of interaction and discourse. For example, do many national courts look to international law, or to the law in foreign states, whether judicial or legislative or constitutional in form, as part of their inquiry and research into a concrete human rights issue? Do they ask (even if not formally bound by a treaty or customary law): what does international law have to say about this, or what do other states have to say about this? In a broader sense, to what extent can we say that some form of world community is developing among the judiciaries or legislatures of many states with respect to human rights issues, at least with respect to interest in what other states are saying about common issues.

Section 3 takes a look at one such country, the United States, and at the critical and sceptical stance that it has taken in recent years toward international law and decisions of other states on controverted human rights issues. This stance goes by many terms that carry different shadings of meaning — unilateralism, or exceptionalism, for example. Sections 1 and 2 provide pertinent background for the readings about and inquiry into these terms. Indeed, section B in its entirety raises questions that reappear and continue to be troubling in later chapters of this book.

1. THE RAPIDLY CHANGING LAW ON CAPITAL PUNISHMENT

AMNESTY INTERNATIONAL, FACTS AND FIGURES ON THE DEATH PENALTY

http://web.amnesty.org/pages/deathpenalty-facts-eng (last updated 27 June, 2006)

Facts and Figures

1. Abolitionist and retentionist countries

Over half the countries in the world have now abolished the death penalty in law or practice.

Amnesty International's latest information shows that:

- 87 countries and territories have abolished the death penalty for all crimes;
- 11 countries have abolished the death penalty for all but exceptional crimes such as wartime crimes;
- 27 countries can be considered abolitionist in practice: they retain the death penalty in law but have not carried out any executions for the past 10 years or more and are believed to have a policy or established practice of not carrying out executions, making a total of 125 countries which have abolished the death penalty in law or practice;
- 71 other countries and territories retain and use the death penalty, but the number of countries which actually execute prisoners in any one year is much smaller.

2. Progress towards worldwide abolition

Over 40 countries have abolished the death penalty for all crimes since 1990. They include countries in Africa (recent examples include Côte d'Ivoire, Senegal), the Americas (Paraguay, Mexico), Asia and the Pacific (Philippines, Bhutan, Samoa, Turkmenistan) and European Asia (Armenia, Bosnia-Herzegovina, Cyprus, Serbia and Montenegro, Turkey).

3. Moves to reintroduce the death penalty

Once abolished, the death penalty is seldom reintroduced. Since 1985, over 50 countries have abolished the death penalty in law or, having previously abolished it for ordinary crimes, have gone on to abolish it for all crimes....

4. Death sentences and executions

During 2005, at least 2,148 people were executed in 22 countries and at least 5,186 people were sentenced to death in 53 countries. These were only minimum figures; the true figures were certainly higher.

In 2005, 94 per cent of all known executions took place in China, Iran, Saudi Arabia, and the USA.

Based on public reports available, Amnesty International estimated that at least 1,170 people were executed in China during the year, although the true figures were believed to be much higher. A Chinese legal expert was recently quoted as stating that the figure for executions is approximately 8,000 based on information from local officials and judges...

Iran executed at least 94 people, and Saudi Arabia at least 86. There were 60 executions in the USA, down from 65 in 2003.

5. Methods of execution

Executions have been carried out by the following methods since 2000:

— Beheading (in Saudi Arabia, Iraq)
— Electrocution (in USA)
— Hanging (in Egypt, Iran, Japan, Jordan, Pakistan, Singapore and other countries)
— Lethal injection (in China, Guatemala, Philippines, Thailand, USA)
— Shooting (in Belarus, China, Somalia, Taiwan, Uzbekistan, Viet Nam and other countries)
— Stoning (in Afghanistan, Iran)

...

7. The deterrence argument

Scientific studies have consistently failed to find convincing evidence that the death penalty deters crime more effectively than other punishments. The most recent survey of research findings on the relation between the death penalty and homicide rates, conducted for the United Nations in 1988 and updated in 2002, concluded: '... *it is not prudent to accept the hypothesis that capital punishment deters murder to a marginally greater extent than does the threat and application of the supposedly lesser punishment of life imprisonment.'*

8. Effect of abolition on crime rates

Reviewing the evidence on the relation between changes in the use of the death penalty and homicide rates, a study conducted for the United Nations in 1988 and updated in 2002 stated: 'The fact that the statistics continue to point in the same direction is persuasive evidence that countries need not fear sudden and serious changes in the curve of crime if they reduce their reliance upon the death penalty'.

Recent crime figures from abolitionist countries fail to show that abolition has harmful effects....

9. International agreements to abolish the death penalty

One of the most important developments in recent years has been the adoption of international treaties whereby states commit themselves to not having the death penalty. Four such treaties now exist:

- The Second Optional Protocol to the International Covenant on Civil and Political Rights, which has been ratified by 57 states. Seven other states have signed the Protocol, indicating their intention to become parties to it at a later date.
- The Protocol to the American Convention on Human Rights to Abolish the Death Penalty, which has been ratified by eight states and signed by one other in the Americas.
- Protocol No. 6 to the European Convention for the Protection of Human Rights and Fundamental Freedoms (European Convention on Human Rights), which has been ratified by 45 European states and signed by one other.
- Protocol No. 13 to the European Convention for the Protection of Human Rights and Fundamental Freedoms (European Convention on Human Rights), which has been ratified by 36 European states and signed by 8 others.

Protocol No. 6 to the European Convention on Human Rights is an agreement to abolish the death penalty in peacetime. The Second Optional Protocol to the International Covenant on Civil and Political Rights and the Protocol to the American Convention on Human Rights provide for the total abolition of the death penalty but allow states wishing to do so to retain the death penalty in wartime as an exception. Protocol No. 13 to the European Convention on Human Rights provides for the total abolition of the death penalty in all circumstances.

10. Execution of the innocent

As long as the death penalty is maintained, the risk of executing the innocent can never be eliminated.

Since 1973, 123 prisoners have been released in the USA after evidence emerged of their innocence of the crimes for which they were sentenced to death.... Recurring features in their cases include prosecutorial or police misconduct; the use of unreliable witness testimony, physical evidence, or confessions; and inadequate defence representation....

...

11. The death penalty in the USA

- 60 prisoners were executed in the USA in 2005, bringing the year-end total to 1004 executed since the use of the death penalty was resumed in 1977.
- Around 3,400 prisoners were under sentence of death as of 1 January 2006.
- 38 of the 50 US states provide for the death penalty in law. The death penalty is also provided under US federal military and civilian law.

Abolitionist and Retentionist States

1. Abolitionist for all crimes

Countries whose laws do not provide for the death penalty for any crime

[List of 87 countries includes among others the European countries, Angola, Cambodia, Colombia, Dominican Republic, Haiti, Namibia, Nepal, South Africa, and Turkey.]

2. Abolitionist for ordinary crimes only

Countries whose laws provide for the death penalty only for exceptional crimes such as crimes under military law or crimes committed in exceptional circumstances

[List of 11 countries includes Albania, Argentina, Brazil, Chile, Israel, and Latvia.]

3. Abolitionist in practice

Countries which retain the death penalty for ordinary crimes such as murder but can be considered abolitionist in practice in that they have not executed anyone during the past 10 years and are believed to have a policy or established practice of not carrying out executions. The list also includes countries which have made an international commitment not to use the death penalty

[List of 27 countries includes Algeria, Bahrain, Congo (Republic), Kenya, Morocco, Myanmar, Russian Federation, Sri Lanka and Tunisia.]

❀ ❀ ❀

Countries which have abolished the death penalty since 1976

[The list includes over 70 countries that have abolished the death penalty in whole or subject to an exception.]

4. Retentionist

Countries and territories which retain the death penalty for ordinary crimes

[The list of 71 countries includes Afghanistan, Bangladesh, Belarus, Chad, China, Cuba, Egypt, Ghana, India, Indonesia, Iran, Iraq, Japan, Kuwait, Malaysia, Nigeria, Pakistan, Palestinian Authority, Saudi Arabia, Singapore, Syria, Taiwan, Uganda, United States, Viet Nam and Zimbabwe.]

NOTE

There follows some further information about the death penalty.

1. The UN Commission on Human Rights (replaced in 2006 by the UN Human Rights Council), the leading intergovernmental organ concerned primarily with human rights issues, issued Resolution 2004/67 on the question of the death penalty in 2004. Such resolutions, while not formally binding on states, can have political and moral significance and influence legal developments. The resolution 'calls upon' states parties to the International Covenant on Civil and Political Rights to join the Second Optional Protocol. It also 'calls upon' states that have retained the death penalty to 'establish a moratorium on executions', with a view to abolishing the death penalty. It urges states retaining capital punishment to ensure that it is not imposed for non-violent acts like 'financial crimes, religious practice or expression of conscience and sexual relations between consenting adults'.

The maximum penalty for persons convicted of war crimes, crimes against humanity, or genocide by the International Criminal Tribunals created by the UN Security Council for the Former Yugoslavia and for Rwanda, or by the International Criminal Court is life imprisonment. (See pp. 1244 and 1291, *infra.*)The Nuremberg and related trials after the Second World War imposed the death sentence on certain defendants.

Religious views

'Preaching consistency in moral values, Pope John Paul II today urged America's Roman Catholics to extend the crusade to protect human life to include murderers on death row. "The new evangelization calls for followers of Christ who are unconditionally pro-life", the Pope preached to 100,000 people [in St Louis]. "Modern society has the means of protecting itself, without definitively denying criminals the chance to reform."' He called the death penalty "cruel and unnecessary", and said it was so "even in the case of someone who has done great evil", *New York Times*, January 28, 1999, p. A14.

'International law arguments may be less convincing in the Islamic world, where an entrenched and immutable religious doctrine insists upon the death penalty in certain cases. Perhaps there is a role for Islamic legal scholars who can demonstrate an alternative and more progressive view of religious law. The intransigence of Islamic States on the subject raises the whole issue of cultural relativism. If there is no universal agreement on the most fundamental of human rights, the right to life, how can anything more be expected in the rest of the catalogue of human rights?' William Schabas, *The Abolition of the Death Penalty in International Law* 377 (3rd edn. 2002).

Arguments about justifications for continuing or abolishing the death penalty

For centuries, law enforcement agencies, defence counsel, criminologists and philosophers, religious figures, and the general public have argued about this issue from many different perspectives. It has become an important factor in political campaigns in democracies. 'Many people still accept the principle of "an eye for an eye, a tooth for a tooth", particularly when atrocious crimes are involved', Schabas, *supra*, at p. x. The debate has intensified as the abolitionist movement has grown over the life of the human rights movement.

The South African judicial decision below at the very start of the post-apartheid regime states many of the leading contemporary arguments. Advocates and courts cast those arguments both in terms of justice and fairness, and in instrumental terms that take into account the effects/consequences of capital punishment on the incidence of crime and other matters. The arguments often fall within the broadly invoked categories of retribution, fairness (including the issue of discrimination), and deterrence.

STATE V. MAKWANYANE

Constitutional Court of the Republic of South Africa, 1995
Case No. CCT/3/94, [1995] 1 LRC 269

[The two appellants were convicted of murder, and sentenced to death by the Witwatersrand Local Division of the Supreme Court. The Appellate Division postponed hearing of the appeals against the death sentence until the new, post-apartheid Constitutional Court decided the question of its constitutionality under the transitional 1993 Constitution. The eleven individual opinions of the Justices of the Constitutional Court were unanimous in holding that the death sentence was unconstitutional. They focused, however, on different constitutional provisions and arguments or elements of the case. There appear below excerpts from the opinion of Justice Chaskalson, President of the Court.]

Relevant provisions of the Constitution

[7] The Constitution

> . . . provides a historic bridge between the past of a deeply divided society characterised by strife, conflict, untold suffering and injustice, and a future founded on the recognition of human rights, democracy and peaceful co-existence and development opportunities for all South Africans, irrespective of colour, race, class, belief or sex.

It is a transitional constitution but one which itself establishes a new order in South Africa; an order in which human rights and democracy are entrenched and in which the Constitution:

> . . . shall be the supreme law of the Republic and any law or act inconsistent with its provisions shall, unless otherwise provided expressly or by necessary implication in this Constitution, be of no force and effect to the extent of the inconsistency.

[8] Chapter Three of the Constitution sets out the fundamental rights to which every person is entitled under the Constitution and also contains provisions dealing

with the way in which the Chapter is to be interpreted by the Courts. It does not deal specifically with the death penalty, but in section 11(2), it prohibits 'cruel, inhuman or degrading treatment or punishment'....

...

[10] ... [S]*ection* 11(2) of the Constitution must not be construed in isolation, but in its context, which includes the history and background to the adoption of the Constitution, other provisions of the Constitution itself and, in particular, the provisions of Chapter Three of which it is part. It must also be construed in a way which secures for 'individuals the full measure' of its protection. Rights with which *section* 11(2) is associated in Chapter Three of the Constitution, and which are of particular importance to a decision on the constitutionality of the death penalty are included in *section* 9, 'every person shall have the right to life', *section* 10, 'every person shall have the right to respect for and protection of his or her dignity', and *section* 8, 'every person shall have the right to equality before the law and to equal protection of the law'. Punishment must meet the requirements of *sections* 8, 9 and 10; and this is so, whether these sections are treated as giving meaning to *Section* 11(2) or as prescribing separate and independent standards with which all punishments must comply.

[11] Mr. Bizos, who represented the South African government at the hearing of this matter, informed us that the government accepts that the death penalty is a cruel, inhuman and degrading punishment and that it should be declared unconstitutional. The Attorney General of the Witwatersrand, whose office is independent of the government, took a different view, and contended that the death penalty is a necessary and acceptable form of punishment and that it is not cruel, inhuman or degrading within the meaning of section 11(2)....

...

[27] The principal arguments advanced by counsel for the accused in support of their contention that the imposition of the death penalty for murder is a 'cruel, inhuman or degrading punishment', were that the death sentence is an affront to human dignity, is inconsistent with the unqualified right to life entrenched in the Constitution, cannot be corrected in case of error or enforced in a manner that is not arbitrary, and that it negates the essential content of the right to life and the other rights that flow from it. The Attorney General argued that the death penalty is recognised as a legitimate form of punishment in many parts of the world, it is a deterrent to violent crime, it meets society's need for adequate retribution for heinous offences, and it is regarded by South African society as an acceptable form of punishment....

International and foreign comparative law

[33] ... The movement away from the death penalty gained momentum during the second half of the present century with the growth of the abolitionist movement. In some countries it is now prohibited in all circumstances, in some it is prohibited save in times of war, and in most countries that have retained it as a penalty for crime, its use has been restricted to extreme cases. According to Amnesty International, 1,831 executions were carried out throughout the world

in 1993 as a result of sentences of death, of which 1,419 were in China, which means that only 412 executions were carried out in the rest of the world in that year. Today, capital punishment has been abolished as a penalty for murder either specifically or in practice by almost half the countries of the world including the democracies of Europe and our neighbouring countries, Namibia, Mozambique and Angola....

[34] ... The international and foreign authorities are of value because they analyze arguments for and against the death sentence and show how courts of other jurisdictions have dealt with this vexed issue. For that reason alone they require our attention. They may also have to be considered because of their relevance to section 35(1) of the Constitution, which states:

> In interpreting the provisions of this Chapter a court of law shall promote the values which underlie an open and democratic society based on freedom and equality and shall, where applicable, have regard to public international law applicable to the protection of the rights entrenched in this Chapter, and may have regard to comparable foreign case law.

[35] ... In the context of *section* 35(1), public international law would include non-binding as well as binding law. They may both be used under the section as tools of interpretation. International agreements and customary international law accordingly provide a framework within which Chapter Three can be evaluated and understood, and for that purpose, decisions of tribunals dealing with comparable instruments, such as the United Nations Committee on Human Rights, the Inter-American Commission on Human Rights, the Inter-American Court of Human Rights, the European Commission on Human Rights, and the European Court of Human Rights, and in appropriate cases, reports of specialized agencies such as the International Labour Organization may provide guidance as to the correct interpretation of particular provisions of Chapter Three.

[36] Capital punishment is not prohibited by public international law, and this is a factor that has to be taken into account in deciding whether it is cruel, inhuman or degrading punishment within the meaning of *section* 11(2). International human rights agreements differ, however, from our Constitution in that where the right to life is expressed in unqualified terms they either deal specifically with the death sentence, or authorize exceptions to be made to the right to life by law....

...

[40] ... From the beginning, the United States Constitution recognized capital punishment as lawful. The Fifth Amendment (adopted in 1791) refers in specific terms to capital punishment and impliedly recognizes its validity. The Fourteenth Amendment (adopted in 1868) obliges the states, not to 'deprive any person of life, liberty, or property, without due process of law' and it too impliedly recognizes the right of the states to make laws for such purposes. The argument that capital punishment is unconstitutional was based on the Eighth Amendment, which prohibits cruel and unusual punishment.... [In a brief discussion of US constitutional law, the Court noted that the federal constitutionality of capital

punishment was affirmed, subject to conditions stated, in *Gregg v. Georgia*, 428 U.S. 153 (1976).]

...

[43] . . . Mr Trengove contended on behalf of the accused that the imprecise language of section 277, and the unbounded discretion vested by it in the Courts, make its provisions unconstitutional.

[44] Section 277 of the Criminal Procedure Act provides:

(1) The sentence of death may be passed by a superior court only and only in the case of a conviction for—
(a) murder;
(b) treason committed when the Republic is in a state of war;
(c) robbery or attempted robbery, if the court finds aggravating circumstances to have been present;
(d) kidnapping;
(e) child-stealing;
(f) rape.

(2) The sentence of death shall be imposed—
(a) after the presiding judge conjointly with the assessors (if any) . . . has made a finding on the presence or absence of any mitigating or aggravating factors;
and
(b) if the presiding judge or court, as the case may be, with due regard to that finding, is satisfied that the sentence of death is the proper sentence.

...

[45] Under our court system questions of guilt and innocence, and the proper sentence to be imposed on those found guilty of crimes, are not decided by juries. In capital cases, where it is likely that the death sentence may be imposed, judges sit with two assessors who have an equal vote with the judge on the issue of guilt and on any mitigating or aggravating factors relevant to sentence; but sentencing is the prerogative of the judge alone. The Criminal Procedure Act allows a full right of appeal to persons sentenced to death, including a right to dispute the sentence without having to establish an irregularity or misdirection on the part of the trial judge. The Appellate Division is empowered to set the sentence aside if it would not have imposed such sentence itself, and it has laid down criteria for the exercise of this power by itself and other courts . . . .

[46] Mitigating and aggravating factors must be identified by the Court, bearing in mind that the onus is on the State to prove beyond reasonable doubt the existence of aggravating factors, and to negative beyond reasonable doubt the presence of any mitigating factors relied on by the accused. Due regard must be paid to the personal circumstances and subjective factors which might have influenced the accused person's conduct, and these factors must then be weighed up with the main objects of punishment, which have been held to be: deterrence, prevention, reformation, and retribution. In this process '[e]very relevant consideration should receive the most scrupulous care and reasoned attention', and the death sentence should only be imposed in the most exceptional cases, where there is no reasonable prospect of reformation and the objects of punishment would not be properly achieved by any other sentence.

[47] There seems to me to be little difference between the guided discretion required for the death sentence in the United States, and the criteria laid down by the Appellate Division for the imposition of the death sentence....

[48] The argument that the imposition of the death sentence under *section* 277 is arbitrary and capricious does not, however, end there. It also focuses on what is alleged to be the arbitrariness inherent in the application of *section* 277 in practice. Of the thousands of persons put on trial for murder, only a very small percentage are sentenced to death by a trial court, and of those, a large number escape the ultimate penalty on appeal. At every stage of the process there is an element of chance. The outcome may be dependent upon factors such as the way the case is investigated by the police, the way the case is presented by the prosecutor, how effectively the accused is defended, the personality and particular attitude to capital punishment of the trial judge and, if the matter goes on appeal, the particular judges who are selected to hear the case. Race and poverty are also alleged to be factors.

[49] Most accused facing a possible death sentence are unable to afford legal assistance, and are defended under the *pro deo* system. The defending counsel is more often than not young and inexperienced, frequently of a different race to his or her client, and if this is the case, usually has to consult through an interpreter. *Pro deo* counsel are paid only a nominal fee for the defence, and generally lack the financial resources and the infrastructural support to undertake the necessary investigations and research, to employ expert witnesses to give advice, including advice on matters relevant to sentence, to assemble witnesses, to bargain with the prosecution, and generally to conduct an effective defence. Accused persons who have the money to do so, are able to retain experienced attorneys and counsel, who are paid to undertake the necessary investigations and research, and as a result they are less likely to be sentenced to death than persons similarly placed who are unable to pay for such services.

...

[54] The differences that exist between rich and poor, between good and bad prosecutions, between good and bad defence, between severe and lenient judges, between judges who favour capital punishment and those who do not, and the subjective attitudes that might be brought into play by factors such as race and class, may in similar ways affect any case that comes before the courts, and is almost certainly present to some degree in all court systems.... Imperfection inherent in criminal trials means that error cannot be excluded; it also means that persons similarly placed may not necessarily receive similar punishment. This needs to be acknowledged....

...

[56] ... The acceptance by a majority of the United States Supreme Court of the proposition that capital punishment is not per se unconstitutional, but that in certain circumstances it may be arbitrary, and thus unconstitutional, has led to endless litigation. Considerable expense and interminable delays result from the exceptionally-high standard of procedural fairness set by the United States courts in attempting to avoid arbitrary decisions. The difficulties that have been experienced in following this path ... persuade me that we should not follow this route.

The right to dignity

[57] Although the United States Constitution does not contain a specific guarantee of human dignity, it has been accepted by the United States Supreme Court that the concept of human dignity is at the core of the prohibition of 'cruel and unusual punishment' by the Eighth and Fourteenth Amendments....

[58] Under our constitutional order the right to human dignity is specifically guaranteed. It can only be limited by legislation which passes the stringent test of being 'necessary'....

[59] In Germany, the Federal Constitutional Court has stressed this aspect of punishment.

> Respect for human dignity especially requires the prohibition of cruel, inhuman, and degrading punishments. [The state] cannot turn the offender into an object of crime prevention to the detriment of his constitutionally protected right to social worth and respect.

[60] That capital punishment constitutes a serious impairment of human dignity has also been recognized by judgments of the Canadian Supreme Court. *Kindler v Canada* [(1992) 6 CRR (2d) SC 4] was concerned with the extradition from Canada to the United States of two fugitives, Kindler, who had been convicted of murder and sentenced to death in the United States, and Ng who was facing a murder charge there and a possible death sentence. Three of the seven judges who heard the cases expressed the opinion that the death penalty was cruel and unusual:

> It is the supreme indignity to the individual, the ultimate corporal punishment, the final and complete lobotomy and the absolute and irrevocable castration. [It is] the ultimate desecration of human dignity.
>
> ...

[61] Three other judges were of the opinion that:

> [t]here is strong ground for believing, having regard to the limited extent to which the death penalty advances any valid penological objectives and the serious invasion of human dignity it engenders, that the death penalty cannot, except in exceptional circumstances, be justified in this country.

...

The International Covenant on Civil and Political Right

[63] *Ng* [another case, *Ng v. Canada*] and *Kindler* took their cases to the Human Rights Committee of the United Nations, contending that Canada had breached its obligations under the International Covenant on Civil and Political Rights. Once again, there was a division of opinion within the tribunal. In Ng's case [*Ng v. Canada*, Communication No. 469/1991, 5 Nov. 1993] it was said:

> The Committee is aware that, by definition, every execution of a sentence of death may be considered to constitute cruel and inhuman treatment within the meaning of article 7 of the covenant.

[64] There was no dissent from that statement. But the International Covenant contains provisions permitting, with some qualifications, the imposition of capital punishment for the most serious crimes. [See Article 6 of the International Covenant.] In view of these provisions, the majority of the Committee were of the opinion that the extradition of fugitives to a country which enforces the death sentence in accordance with the requirements of the International Covenant, should not be regarded as a breach of the obligations of the extraditing country....

...

[The opinion considered the decision by the European Court of Human Rights in *Soering v. United Kingdom* (1989) 11 EHRR 439, involving the question whether the UK would violate the provisions on inhuman and degrading treatment or punishment in Article 3 of the Convention, by extraditing a fugitive to the United States to face murder charges that were subject to capital punishment. In the circumstances, including the experience of 'death row' in the US prisons and possible extradition of the fugitive by the UK for trial in another country that had abolished the death sentence, the European Court concluded that extradition to the United States would violate Article 3.

The opinion next examined a 1980 decision of the Indian Supreme Court holding that capital punishment did not violate the Indian Constitution. It distinguished the Indian decision partly by emphasizing the different wording of relevant provisions in the Constitutions of the two countries].

The right to life

[80] The unqualified right to life vested in every person by *section 9* of our Constitution is another factor crucially relevant to the question whether the death sentence is cruel, inhuman or degrading punishment within the meaning of *section 11(2)* of our Constitution. In this respect our Constitution differs materially from the Constitutions of the United States and India. It also differs materially from the European Convention and the International Covenant. Yet in the cases decided under these constitutions and treaties there were judges who dissented and held that notwithstanding the specific language of the constitution or instrument concerned, capital punishment should not be permitted.

[81] In some instances the dissent focused on the right to life. In *Soering's* case before the European Court of Human Rights, Judge de Meyer, in a concurring opinion, said that capital punishment is 'not consistent with the present state of European civilisation' and for that reason alone, extradition to the United States would violate the fugitive's right to life.

[82] In a dissent in the United Nations Human Rights Committee in *Kindler's* case, Committee member B. Wennergren also stressed the importance of the right to life.

> The value of life is immeasurable for any human being, and the right to life enshrined in article 6 of the Covenant is the supreme human right. It is an obligation of States [P]arties to the Covenant to protect the lives of all human beings on their territory and under their jurisdiction...

[83] An individual's right to life has been described as '[t]he most fundamental of all human rights', and was dealt with in that way in the judgments of the Hungarian Constitutional Court declaring capital punishment to be unconstitutional....

...

Public opinion

[87] ... It was disputed whether public opinion, properly informed of the different considerations, would in fact favour the death penalty. I am, however, prepared to assume that it does and that the majority of South Africans agree that the death sentence should be imposed in extreme cases of murder. The question before us, however, is not what the majority of South Africans believe a proper sentence for murder should be. It is whether the Constitution allows the sentence.

[88] Public opinion may have some relevance to the enquiry, but in itself, it is no substitute for the duty vested in the Courts to interpret the Constitution and to uphold its provisions without fear or favour. If public opinion were to be decisive there would be no need for constitutional adjudication. The protection of rights could then be left to Parliament, which has a mandate from the public, and is answerable to the public for the way its mandate is exercised, but this would be a return to parliamentary sovereignty, and a retreat from the new legal order established by the 1993 Constitution.... The very reason for establishing the new legal order, and for vesting the power of judicial review of all legislation in the courts, was to protect the rights of minorities and others who cannot protect their rights adequately through the democratic process. Those who are entitled to claim this protection include the social outcasts and marginalized people of our society. It is only if there is a willingness to protect the worst and the weakest amongst us, that all of us can be secure that our own rights will be protected.

...

Cruel, inhuman and degrading punishment

...

[94] Proportionality is an ingredient to be taken into account in deciding whether a penalty is cruel, inhuman or degrading. No Court would today uphold the constitutionality of a statute that makes the death sentence a competent sentence for the cutting down of trees or the killing of deer, which were capital offences in England in the 18th Century. But murder is not to be equated with such 'offences'. The wilful taking of an innocent life calls for a severe penalty, and there are many countries which still retain the death penalty as a sentencing option for such cases. Disparity between the crime and the penalty is not the only ingredient of proportionality; factors such as the enormity and irredeemable character of the death sentence in circumstances where neither error nor arbitrariness can be excluded, the expense and difficulty of addressing the disparities which exist in practice between accused persons facing similar charges, and which are due to factors such as race, poverty, and ignorance, and the other subjective factors which have been mentioned, are also factors that can and should be taken into account in dealing with this issue. It may possibly be that none alone would be sufficient under our Constitution

to justify a finding that the death sentence is cruel, inhuman or degrading. But these factors are not to be evaluated in isolation. They must be taken together, and in order to decide whether the threshold set by *section* 11(2) has been crossed they must be evaluated with other relevant factors, including the two fundamental rights on which the accused rely, the right to dignity and the right to life.

[95] The carrying out of the death sentence destroys life, which is protected without reservation under section 9 of our Constitution, it annihilates human dignity which is protected under *section* 10, elements of arbitrariness are present in its enforcement and it is irremediable. Taking these factors into account, as well as the assumption that I have made in regard to public opinion in South Africa, and giving the words of *section* 11(2) the broader meaning to which they are entitled at this stage of the enquiry, rather than a narrow meaning, I am satisfied that in the context of our Constitution the death penalty is indeed a cruel, inhuman and degrading punishment.

...

Section 33 and limitation of rights

[98] *Section* 33(1) of the Constitution provides, in part, that:

> The rights entrenched in this Chapter may be limited by law of general application, provided that such limitation —
> (a) shall be permissible only to the extent that it is —
> (i) reasonable; and
> (ii) justifiable in an open and democratic society based on freedom and equality; and
> (b) shall not negate the essential content of the right in question.

[99] *Section* 33(1)(b) goes on to provide that the limitation of certain rights, including the rights referred to in *section* 10 and *section* 11 'shall, in addition to being reasonable as required in paragraph (a)(I), also be necessary'.

[100] Our Constitution deals with the limitation of rights through a general limitations clause.... [T]his calls for a 'two-stage' approach, in which a broad rather than a narrow interpretation is given to the fundamental rights enshrined in Chapter Three, and limitations have to be justified through the application of section 33. In this it differs from the Constitution of the United States, which does not contain a limitation clause, as a result of which courts in that country have been obliged to find limits to constitutional rights through a narrow interpretation of the rights themselves. Although the 'two-stage' approach may often produce the same result as the 'one-stage' approach, this will not always be the case.

...

[102] Under our Constitution, ... [i]t is not whether the decision of the State has been shown to be clearly wrong; it is whether the decision of the State is justifiable according to the criteria prescribed by section 33. It is not whether the infliction of death as a punishment for murder 'is not without justification', it is whether the infliction of death as a punishment for murder has been shown to be both reasonable and necessary, and to be consistent with the other requirements of *section* 33....

...

[106] Although there is a rational connection between capital punishment and the purpose for which it is prescribed, the elements of arbitrariness, unfairness and irrationality in the imposition of the penalty, are factors that would have to be taken into account in the application of the first component of this test. As far as the second component is concerned, the fact that a severe punishment in the form of life imprisonment is available as an alternative sentence, would be relevant to the question whether the death sentence impairs the right as little as possible.

. . .

[109] The European Convention also has no general limitations clause, but makes certain rights subject to limitation according to specified criteria. The proportionality test of the European Court of Human Rights calls for a balancing of ends and means. The end must be a 'pressing social need' and the means used must be proportionate to the attainment of such an end. The limitation of certain rights is conditioned upon the limitation being 'necessary in a democratic society' for purposes defined in the relevant provisions of the Convention . . . .

. . .

Deterrence

[116] The Attorney General attached considerable weight to the need for a deterrent to violent crime. He argued that the countries which had abolished the death penalty were on the whole developed and peaceful countries in which other penalties might be sufficient deterrents. We had not reached that stage of development, he said. If in years to come we did so, we could do away with the death penalty. Parliament could decide when that time has come . . . .

[117] . . . Without law, individuals in society have no rights. The level of violent crime in our country has reached alarming proportions. It poses a threat to the transition to democracy, and the creation of development opportunities for all, which are primary goals of the Constitution . . . .

. . .

[119] The cause of the high incidence of violent crime cannot simply be attributed to the failure to carry out the death sentences imposed by the courts . . . . It was a progression that started before the moratorium [on executions] was announced. There are many factors that have to be taken into account in looking for the cause of this phenomenon . . . .

[120] Homelessness, unemployment, poverty and the frustration consequent upon such conditions are other causes of the crime wave . . . .

[121] We would be deluding ourselves if we were to believe that the execution of the few persons sentenced to death during this period, and of a comparatively few other people each year from now onwards will provide the solution to the unacceptably high rate of crime . . . .

[122] The greatest deterrent to crime is the likelihood that offenders will be apprehended, convicted and punished. It is that which is presently lacking in our criminal justice system; and it is at this level and through addressing the causes of crime that the State must seek to combat lawlessness.

. . .

[126] ... [B]etween the amendment of the Criminal Procedure Act in 1990, and January 1995 ... 243 death sentences were imposed, of which 143 were confirmed by the Appellate Division. Yet, according to statistics placed before us by the Commissioner of Police and the Attorney General, there were on average approximately 20,000 murders committed, and 9,000 murder cases brought to trial, each year during this period. Would the carrying out of the death sentence on these 143 persons have deterred the other murderers or saved any lives?

...

Retribution

[129] Retribution is one of the objects of punishment, but it carries less weight than deterrence. The righteous anger of family and friends of the murder victim, reinforced by the public abhorrence of vile crimes, is easily translated into a call for vengeance. But capital punishment is not the only way that society has of expressing its moral outrage at the crime that has been committed. We have long outgrown the literal application of the biblical injunction of 'an eye for an eye, and a tooth for a tooth'. Punishment must to some extent be commensurate with the offence, but there is no requirement that it be equivalent or identical to it.... A very long prison sentence is also a way of expressing outrage and visiting retribution upon the criminal.

...

Conclusion

[144] The rights to life and dignity are the most important of all human rights, and the source of all other personal rights in Chapter Three. By committing ourselves to a society founded on the recognition of human rights we are required to value these two rights above all others. And this must be demonstrated by the State in everything that it does, including the way it punishes criminals....

...

[146] ... Taking [all the described] factors into account, as well as the elements of arbitrariness and the possibility of error in enforcing the death penalty, the clear and convincing case that is required to justify the death sentence as a penalty for murder, has not been made out. The requirements of section 33(1) have accordingly not been satisfied, and it follows that the provisions of section 277(1)(a) of the Criminal Procedure Act, 1977 must be held to be inconsistent with section 11(2) of the Constitution. In the circumstances, it is not necessary for me to consider whether the section would also be inconsistent with sections 8, 9 or 10 of the Constitution if they had been dealt with separately and not treated together as giving meaning to section 11(2).

...

[150] The proper sentence to be imposed on the accused is a matter for the Appellate Division and not for us to decide....

...

QUESTIONS

1. Article 6 of the International Covenant on Civil and Political Rights has been much cited and drawn on by both proponents and opponents of capital punishment. In what ways could an abolitionist employ Article 6 to strengthen her position?

2. As an opponent, would you find it advantageous in argument before a court to rely primarily on 'the inherent right to life', as in Article 6(1) of the International Covenant, or on 'cruel, inhuman or degrading treatment or punishment' in Article 7 (compare 'cruel and unusual punishments' in the Eighth Amendment to the US Constitution)? What disadvantages would each have?

3. Would you describe Justice Chaskalson's opinion as ultimately relying on traditional arguments for and against capital punishment that could have been debated by courts anywhere, or relying at least equally on contextual factors that were, if not unique, at least highly specific to South African history and culture? What were the links between these two strands in the opinion?

4. Consider the following comments (reported in Schabas, p. 22, *supra*, at 285) made during a debate in the Parliamentary Assembly of the Council of Europe on the then proposed protocol to the European Convention on Human Rights that would abolish the death penalty. Would you agree or disagree with the speaker, and if the latter, how would you respond to him?

> A Turkish member of the Assembly, Aksoy, said that he supported the report and the recommendation 'in principle', but that it did not take sufficient account of the particular situation of certain member States. He suggested that because of differing economic, social and political structures it was not possible to apply identical sentences in all countries. Were he Swedish, Swiss, Norwegian, Austrian or German, he would most certainly support total abolition of the death penalty, said Aksoy. Yet it would be a grave error to recommend abolition in countries where political assassination and terrorism are organized on a systematic scale.

5. With reference to the preceding opinion, consider (a) the comparative, or horizontal, dimension to the human rights movement — that is, the spread among states of abolition of capital punishment and the cross-referencing by states to each other's legislation or constitutional decisions on this issue. Consider also (b) the vertical dimension — that is, the bearing of treaties and decisions or resolutions of international organs on this issue on how states argue and what they decide to do. In what ways are the horizontal and vertical dimensions of human rights related to each other? Do they appear to constitute equal parts of an international 'human rights movement'?

ADDITIONAL READING

Amnesty International, periodic reports available on its website; R. Hood, *The Death Penalty: A World-Wide Perspective* (3rd edn. 2002); N. Rodley, *The Treatment of Prisoners under International Law* (2nd edn. 1999); W. Schabas, *The Abolition of the Death Penalty in International Law* (3rd edn. 2002); C. Haney, *Death by Design: Capital Punishment as a Social*

Psychological System (2005); H. Bedau and P. Cassell (eds.), *Debating the Death Penalty: Should America Have Capital Punishment?* (2004).

NOTE

Although concluding that the death penalty as applied to the category of defendant involved in the case was unconstitutional, the following opinion of the US Supreme Court makes clear how dramatically the US differs from most states. The opinion is relevant both for its holding and summary of US constitutional jurisprudence of the last few decades with respect to capital punishment, and for the argument among the Justices about the propriety of looking to the law in this field in other states and in international law, a theme to which Section 2 of Part B returns.

ROPER V. SIMMONS

Supreme Court of the United States, 2005

543 U.S. 551, 125 S.Ct. 1183

OPINION OF JUSTICE KENNEDY FOR THE COURT:

This case requires us to address . . . whether it is permissible under the Eighth and Fourteenth Amendments to the Constitution of the United States to execute a juvenile offender who was older than 15 but younger than 18 when he committed a capital crime. In *Stanford* v. *Kentucky*, 492 U.S. 361 (1989), a divided Court rejected the proposition that the Constitution bars capital punishment for juvenile offenders in this age group. We reconsider the question.

[Simmons committed murder at age 17 when a junior (the penultimate year) in secondary school. He was sentenced to death when he was 18. The murder was callous and premeditated. At trial, the judge instructed the jury that it could consider Simmons' age as a mitigating factor in sentencing. The jury recommended the death penalty, which the trial judge imposed. The Missouri Supreme Court affirmed.]

After these proceedings in Simmons' case had run their course, this Court held that the Eighth and Fourteenth Amendments prohibit the execution of a mentally retarded person. *Atkins* v. *Virginia*, 536 U.S. 304 (2002). Simmons filed a new petition for state postconviction relief, arguing that the reasoning of *Atkins* established that the Constitution prohibits the execution of a juvenile who was under 18 when the crime was committed. [The Missouri Supreme Court agreed, and resentenced Simmons to "life imprisonment without eligibility for probation, parole, or release except by act of the Governor."]

The Eighth Amendment provides: "Excessive bail shall not be required, nor excessive fines imposed, nor cruel and unusual punishments inflicted." The provision is applicable to the States through the Fourteenth Amendment. As the Court explained in *Atkins*, the Eighth Amendment guarantees individuals the right not to be subjected to excessive sanctions. The right flows from the basic "'precept of justice that punishment for crime should be graduated and proportioned to [the] offense.'" 536 U.S. at 311. By protecting even those convicted of heinous crimes, the Eighth Amendment reaffirms the duty of the government to respect the dignity of all persons.

The prohibition against "cruel and unusual punishments," like other expansive language in the Constitution, must be interpreted according to its text, by considering history, tradition, and precedent, and with due regard for its purpose and function in the constitutional design. To implement this framework we have established the propriety and affirmed the necessity of referring to "the evolving standards of decency that mark the progress of a maturing society" to determine which punishments are so disproportionate as to be cruel and unusual. *Trop* v. *Dulles*, 356 U.S. 86, 100–101 (1958) (plurality opinion).

In *Thompson* v. *Oklahoma*, 487 U.S. 815 (1988), a plurality of the Court determined that our standards of decency do not permit the execution of any offender under the age of 16 at the time of the crime. The plurality opinion explained that no death penalty State that had given express consideration to a minimum age for the death penalty had set the age lower than 16. The plurality also observed that "[t]he conclusion that it would offend civilized standards of decency to execute a person who was less than 16 years old at the time of his or her offense is consistent with the views that have been expressed by respected professional organizations, by other nations that share our Anglo-American heritage, and by the leading members of the Western European community." The opinion further noted that juries imposed the death penalty on offenders under 16 with exceeding rarity; the last execution of an offender for a crime committed under the age of 16 had been carried out in 1948, 40 years prior.

Bringing its independent judgment to bear on the permissibility of the death penalty for a 15-year-old offender, the *Thompson* plurality stressed that "[t]he reasons why juveniles are not trusted with the privileges and responsibilities of an adult also explain why their irresponsible conduct is not as morally reprehensible as that of an adult." According to the plurality, the lesser culpability of offenders under 16 made the death penalty inappropriate as a form of retribution, while the low likelihood that offenders under 16 engaged in "the kind of cost-benefit analysis that attaches any weight to the possibility of execution" made the death penalty ineffective as a means of deterrence....

The next year, in *Stanford* v. *Kentucky* [*supra*], the Court, over a dissenting opinion joined by four Justices, referred to contemporary standards of decency in this country and concluded the Eighth and Fourteenth Amendments did not proscribe the execution of juvenile offenders over 15 but under 18. The Court noted that 22 of the 37 death penalty States permitted the death penalty for 16-year-old offenders, and, among these 37 States, 25 permitted it for 17-year-old offenders. These numbers, in the Court's view, indicated there was no national consensus "sufficient to label a particular punishment cruel and unusual."...

The same day the Court decided *Stanford*, it held that the Eighth Amendment did not mandate a categorical exemption from the death penalty for the mentally retarded. *Penry* v. *Lynaugh*, 492 U.S. 302 (1989). In reaching this conclusion it stressed that only two States had enacted laws banning the imposition of the death penalty on a mentally retarded person convicted of a capital offense. According to the Court, "the two state statutes prohibiting execution of the mentally retarded, even when added to the 14 States that have rejected capital punishment completely, [did] not provide sufficient evidence at present of a national consensus."

Three Terms ago the subject was reconsidered in *Atkins*. We held that standards of decency have evolved since *Penry* and now demonstrate that the execution of the mentally retarded is cruel and unusual punishment. The Court noted objective indicia of society's standards, as expressed in legislative enactments and state practice with respect to executions of the mentally retarded. When *Atkins* was decided only a minority of States permitted the practice, and even in those States it was rare. On the basis of these indicia the Court determined that executing mentally retarded offenders "has become truly unusual, and it is fair to say that a national consensus has developed against it."

... The *Atkins* Court ... returned to the rule, established in decisions predating *Stanford*, that "'the Constitution contemplates that in the end our own judgment will be brought to bear on the question of the acceptability of the death penalty under the Eighth Amendment.'" Mental retardation, the Court said, diminishes personal culpability even if the offender can distinguish right from wrong. The impairments of mentally retarded offenders make it less defensible to impose the death penalty as retribution for past crimes and less likely that the death penalty will have a real deterrent effect....

...

III

A

The evidence of national consensus against the death penalty for juveniles is similar, and in some respects parallel, to the evidence *Atkins* held sufficient to demonstrate a national consensus against the death penalty for the mentally retarded. When *Atkins* was decided, 30 States prohibited the death penalty for the mentally retarded. This number comprised 12 that had abandoned the death penalty altogether, and 18 that maintained it but excluded the mentally retarded from its reach. By a similar calculation in this case, 30 States prohibit the juvenile death penalty, comprising 12 that have rejected the death penalty altogether and 18 that maintain it but, by express provision or judicial interpretation, exclude juveniles from its reach. *Atkins* emphasized that even in the 20 States without formal prohibition, the practice of executing the mentally retarded was infrequent.... In the present case, too, even in the 20 States without a formal prohibition on executing juveniles, the practice is infrequent....

... Impressive in *Atkins* was the rate of abolition of the death penalty for the mentally retarded. Sixteen States that permitted the execution of the mentally retarded at the time of Penry [*supra*] had prohibited the practice by the time we heard *Atkins*. By contrast, the rate of change in reducing the incidence of the juvenile death penalty, or in taking specific steps to abolish it, has been slower. Five States that allowed the juvenile death penalty at the time of *Stanford* have abandoned it in the intervening 15 years — four through legislative enactments and one through judicial decisions.

Though less dramatic ... we still consider the change from *Stanford* to this case to be significant.... [T]he same consistency of direction of change has been demonstrated....

...

B

A majority of States have rejected the imposition of the death penalty on juvenile offenders under 18, and we now hold this is required by the Eighth Amendment.

Because the death penalty is the most severe punishment, the Eighth Amendment applies to it with special force.... Capital punishment must be limited to those offenders who commit "a narrow category of the most serious crimes" and whose extreme culpability makes them "the most deserving of execution." This principle is implemented throughout the capital sentencing process....

Three general differences between juveniles under 18 and adults demonstrate that juvenile offenders cannot with reliability be classified among the worst offenders. First, as any parent knows and as the scientific and sociological studies respondent and his *amici* cite tend to confirm, "[a] lack of maturity and an underdeveloped sense of responsibility are found in youth more often than in adults and are more understandable among the young. These qualities often result in impetuous and ill-considered actions and decisions." ... It has been noted that "adolescents are overrepresented statistically in virtually every category of reckless behavior." ...

The second area of difference is that juveniles are more vulnerable or susceptible to negative influences and outside pressures, including peer pressure....

The third broad difference is that the character of a juvenile is not as well formed as that of an adult. The personality traits of juveniles are more transitory, less fixed. ... The reality that juveniles still struggle to define their identity means it is less supportable to conclude that even a heinous crime committed by a juvenile is evidence of irretrievably depraved character. From a moral standpoint it would be misguided to equate the failings of a minor with those of an adult, for a greater possibility exists that a minor's character deficiencies will be reformed....

Once the diminished culpability of juveniles is recognized, it is evident that the penological justifications for the death penalty apply to them with lesser force than to adults....

As for deterrence, it is unclear whether the death penalty has a significant or even measurable deterrent effect on juveniles, as counsel for the petitioner acknowledged at oral argument.... [I]t is worth noting that the punishment of life imprisonment without the possibility of parole is itself a severe sanction, in particular for a young person.

Drawing the line at 18 years of age is subject, of course, to the objections always raised against categorical rules.... The age of 18 is the point where society draws the line for many purposes between childhood and adulthood. It is, we conclude, the age at which the line for death eligibility ought to rest.

...

IV

Our determination that the death penalty is disproportionate punishment for offenders under 18 finds confirmation in the stark reality that the United States is the only country in the world that continues to give official sanction to the juvenile death penalty. This reality does not become controlling, for the task of interpreting the Eighth Amendment remains our responsibility. Yet at least from the time of the Court's decision in *Trop* [*supra*], the Court has referred to the laws of other countries and to international authorities as instructive for its interpretation of the Eighth Amendment's prohibition of "cruel and unusual punishments." 356 U.S., at 102–103, 2L. Ed. 2d 630, 78S. Ct. 590 (plurality opinion) ("The civilized nations of the world are in virtual unanimity that statelessness is not to be imposed as punishment for crime"); see also *Atkins, supra*, at 317, n. 21 recognizing that "within the world community, the imposition of the death penalty for crimes committed by mentally retarded offenders is overwhelmingly disapproved"); ...

... Article 37 of the United Nations Convention on the Rights of the Child, which every country in the world has ratified save for the United States and Somalia, contains an express prohibition on capital punishment for crimes committed by juveniles under 18. United Nations Convention on the Rights of the Child, Art. 37, Nov. 20, 1989, 1577 U. N. T. S. 3, 28 I. L. M. 1448, 1468–1470 (entered into force Sept. 2, 1990) .... No ratifying country has entered a reservation to the provision prohibiting the execution of juvenile offenders. Parallel prohibitions are contained in other significant international covenants. See [International Covenant on Civil and Political Rights], Art. 6(5), 999 U. N. T. S., at 175 (prohibiting capital punishment for anyone under 18 at the time of offense) (signed and ratified by the United States subject to a reservation regarding Article 6(5) ....

... [O]nly seven countries other than the United States have executed juvenile offenders since 1990: Iran, Pakistan, Saudi Arabia, Yemen, Nigeria, the Democratic Republic of Congo, and China. Since then each of these countries has either abolished capital punishment for juveniles or made public disavowal of the practice. In sum, it is fair to say that the United States now stands alone in a world that has turned its face against the juvenile death penalty.

Though the international covenants prohibiting the juvenile death penalty are of more recent date, it is instructive to note that the United Kingdom abolished the juvenile death penalty before these covenants came into being. The United Kingdom's experience bears particular relevance here in light of the historic ties between our countries and in light of the Eighth Amendment's own origins. The Amendment was modeled on a parallel provision in the English Declaration of Rights of 1689, which provided: "[E]xcessive Bail ought not to be required nor excessive Fines imposed; nor cruel and unusuall Punishments inflicted." ...

It is proper that we acknowledge the overwhelming weight of international opinion against the juvenile death penalty.... The opinion of the world community, while not controlling our outcome, does provide respected and significant confirmation for our own conclusions.

Over time, from one generation to the next, the Constitution has come to earn the high respect and even, as Madison dared to hope, the veneration of the American people. The document sets forth, and rests upon, innovative principles original to the American experience, such as federalism; a proven balance in political mechanisms through separation of powers; specific guarantees for the accused in criminal cases; and broad provisions to secure individual freedom and preserve human dignity. These doctrines and guarantees are central to the American experience and remain essential to our present-day self-definition and national identity. Not the least of the reasons we honor the Constitution, then, is because we know it to be our own. It does not lessen our fidelity to the Constitution or our pride in its origins to acknowledge that the express affirmation of certain fundamental rights by other nations and peoples simply underscores the centrality of those same rights within our own heritage of freedom.

[Appendix B and Appendix C to the Court's opinion listed state statutes establishing a minimum age to vote (the 26th Amendment to the Constitution provides that the right of citizens who are eighteen or older to vote shall not be denied or abridged on account of age), establishing a minimum age for jury service, and establishing a minimum age for marriage without parental consent. The statutes used overwhelmingly the age of 18.]

JUSTICE O'CONNOR, DISSENTING

...

I turn, finally, to the Court's discussion of foreign and international law.... In short, the evidence of an international consensus does not alter my determination that the Eighth Amendment does not, at this time, forbid capital punishment of 17-year-old murderers in all cases.

Nevertheless, I disagree with Justice Scalia's contention that foreign and international law have no place in our Eighth Amendment jurisprudence. Over the course of nearly half a century, the Court has consistently referred to foreign and international law as relevant to its assessment of evolving standards of decency. This inquiry reflects the special character of the Eighth Amendment, which, as the Court has long held, draws its meaning directly from the maturing values of civilized society.... But this Nation's evolving understanding of human dignity certainly is neither wholly isolated from, nor inherently at odds with, the values prevailing in other countries. On the contrary, we should not be surprised to find congruence between domestic and international values, especially where the international community has reached clear agreement — expressed in international law or in the domestic laws of individual countries — that a particular form of punishment is inconsistent with fundamental human rights. At least, the existence of an international consensus of this nature can serve to confirm the reasonableness of a consonant and genuine American consensus. The instant case presents no such domestic consensus, however....

...

JUSTICE SCALIA, WITH WHOM THE CHIEF JUSTICE AND JUSTICE THOMAS JOIN, DISSENTING

...

Though the views of our own citizens are essentially irrelevant to the Court's decision today, the views of other countries and the so-called international community take center stage.

...

More fundamentally, however, the basic premise of the Court's argument — that American law should conform to the laws of the rest of the world — ought to be rejected out of hand. In fact the Court itself does not believe it. In many significant respects the laws of most other countries differ from our law — including not only such explicit provisions of our Constitution as the right to jury trial and grand jury indictment, but even many interpretations of the Constitution prescribed by this Court itself. The Court-pronounced exclusionary rule, for example, is distinctively American....

...

. . . To begin with, I do not believe that approval by "other nations and peoples" should buttress our commitment to American principles any more than (what should logically follow) disapproval by "other nations and peoples" should weaken that commitment. More importantly, however, the Court's statement flatly misdescribes what is going on here. Foreign sources are cited today, *not* to underscore our "fidelity" to the Constitution, our "pride in its origins," and "our own [American] heritage." To the contrary, they are cited to *set aside* the centuries-old American practice — a practice still engaged in by a large majority of the relevant States — of letting a jury of 12 citizens decide whether, in the particular case, youth should be the basis for withholding the death penalty. What these foreign sources "affirm," " rather than repudiate, is the Justices' own notion of how the world ought to be, and their diktat that it shall be so henceforth in America. . . .

. . .

[Eds.: In the *Atkins* decision relied on in *Roper* by Justice Kennedy, holding that execution of mentally retarded criminals constitutes cruel and unusual punishment, Chief Justice Rehnquist argued in his dissenting opinion that courts should look only to state and federal legislation and to jury determinations about the death sentence to

> ascertain the contemporary American conceptions of decency for purposes of the Eighth Amendment. They are the only objective indicia of contemporary values firmly supported by our precedents. More importantly, however, they can be reconciled with the undeniable precepts that the democratic branches of government and individual sentencing juries are, by design, better suited than courts to evaluating and giving effect to the complex societal and moral considerations that inform the selection of publicly acceptable punishments.

He disapproved of the Court's opinion in *Atkins* for taking account of what other countries had done, for "if it is evidence of a *national* consensus for which we are looking then the viewpoints of other countries simply are not relevant."]

QUESTIONS

1. Consider the fifth paragraph of the opinion discussing approaches to interpreting and applying the Eighth Amendment. What possible approach to interpretation does it not include? Would it include Justice Scalia's view of the appropriate approach to interpretation?

2. How do you react to the idea that finding "consensus" is very helpful or indispensable to concluding that capital punishment is unconstitutional in a given context? Why are the 50 states the appropriate accounting units (as opposed, say, to the total population in states going one or the other way on the issue)? How large a majority (of states, population, etc.) constitutes a consensus? Why is not a trend over a few decades as or more powerful a fact than the "consensus" at a given moment? Why should consensus be decisive for a justice who follows a different approach to the question of constitutionality?

3. How do you assess consensus as an approach by an international tribunal applying international law to concluding that, say, capital punishment as applied in a given context violates the ICCPR? Would the court simply count the number of states going one way or the other? (Consider the questions raised in Question (2) above. Do you reach the same answers in Question (3) that you did in Question (2) addressing the United States federalism? Why, or why not?)

2. SHOULD NATIONAL COURTS LOOK TO FOREIGN DECISIONS AND INTERNATIONAL LAW ABOUT HUMAN RIGHTS ISSUES EVEN WHEN NOT FORMALLY BOUND?

Roper v. *Simmons*, through each of the three excerpted opinions above, exposes the fault line on the U.S. Supreme Court on the topic of this Section 2. In fact, Roper is but one of a number of prominent Supreme Court decisions in recent decades that have debated the appropriateness of looking to and citing foreign and international law, even though neither the judicial decision, statute or treaty referred to may bind the state involved. Apart from its significance for the case at issue, the answer that judges and courts bring to this question sheds light on a country's degree of nationalism or internationalism — matters considered below in Section 3.

THE RELEVANCE OF FOREIGN LEGAL MATERIALS IN US CONSTITUTIONAL CASES: A CONVERSATION BETWEEN JUSTICE ANTONIN SCALIA AND JUSTICE STEPHEN BREYER

3 Int. J. Const. L. 519 (2005)

[There follow excerpts from the transcript of a debate between Associate Justices Stephen Breyer and Antonin Scalia of the US Supreme Court.]

SCALIA

...

But you are talking about using foreign law to determine the content of American constitutional law — to be sure that we're on the right track, that we have the same moral and legal framework as the rest of the world. But we don't have the same moral and legal framework as the rest of the world, and never have. If you told the framers of the Constitution that we're to be just like Europe, they would have been appalled....

...

The Miranda rule, concerning police warnings to suspects of criminal behavior, is a case in point. Well, I don't know the law in Russia. It is said that Russia has adopted the Miranda rule. Has it adopted the exclusionary rule [the rule excluding from trial any evidence gathered in violation of a defendant's constitutional rights, such as a failure to warn a defendant of her right to remain silent] that goes with it?

... The exclusionary rule is distinctively American. I don't think there is any other country in the world that applies the exclusionary rule.

Should we say. "Oh my, we're out of step"? Or, take our abortion jurisprudence: we are one of only six countries in the world that allows abortion on demand at any time prior to viability. Should we change that because other countries feel differently? ... Or do we just use foreign law selectively? When it agrees with what the justices would like the case to say, we use the foreign law, and when it doesn't agree we don't use it.... But we said not a whisper about foreign law in the series of abortion cases.

...

BREYER

...

... I realize full well that the decisions of foreign courts do not bind American courts. Of course they do not. But those cases sometimes involve a human being working as a judge concerned with a legal problem, often similar to problems that arise here, which problem involves the application of a legal text, often similar to the text of our own Constitution, seeking to protect certain basic human rights, often similar to the rights that our own Constitution seeks to protect. To an ever greater extent, foreign nations have become democratic; to an ever greater extent, they have sought to protect basic human rights; to an ever greater extent they have embodied that protection in legal documents enforced through judicial decision making. Judges abroad thus face not only legal questions with obvious answers, e.g., is torture an affront to human dignity, but also difficult questions without obvious answers, where much is to be said on both sides of the issue.

...

Of course. I hope that I, or any other judge, would refer to materials that support positions that the judge disfavors as well as those that he favors. For example, in a case where I took the position that the Establishment Clause prohibited extensive use of school vouchers, I had to face the fact that in countries with somewhat similar traditions of church/state separation, governments subsidized religious school education. And most citizens of those countries, for example Britain and France, believed that doing so caused no relevant harm.... The practice involves opening your eyes to what is going on elsewhere, taking what you learn for what it is worth, and using it as a point of comparison where doing so will prove helpful.

...

SCALIA

I don't know what it means to express confidence that judges will do what they ought to do after having read the foreign law. My problem is I don't know what they ought to do....

Now, my theory of what to do when interpreting the American Constitution is to try to understand what it meant, what it was understood by the society to mean when it was adopted. And I don't think it has changed since then.... It should be easy to understand why, for someone who has my theory of interpretation, why foreign law is irrelevant....

...

... Justice Breyer doesn't have my approach. He applies the principle that the Court adopted about sixty years or so ago — first in the Eighth Amendment area (cruel and unusual punishments) and then elsewhere — the notion that the Constitution is not static. It doesn't mean what the people voted for when it was ratified. Rather, it changes from era to era to comport with — and this is a quote from our cases, "the evolving standards of decency that mark the progress of a maturing society." I detest that phrase, because I'm afraid that societies don't always mature. Sometimes they rot.... It seems to me that the purpose of the Bill of Rights was to prevent change, not to foster change and have it written into a Constitution.

Anyway, let's assume you buy into the evolving Constitution. Still and all, what you're looking for as a judge using that theory is what? The standards of decency of American society — not the standards of decency of the world, not the standards of decency of other countries that don't have our background, that don't have our culture, that don't have our moral views. Of what conceivable value as indicative of American standards of decency would foreign law be?...

...

BREYER

[Referring to opinions in which he described foreign judicial decisions] I did not believe any of these foreign decisions were controlling. But I did think that the issue is not technically legal, but rather a law-related human question, and all concerned, American and foreign judges alike are human beings using similar legal texts, dealing with a somewhat similar human problem. Reaching out to those other nations, reading their decisions, seems useful, even though they cannot determine the outcome of a question that arises under the American Constitution.

...

... But still, with all the uncertainties involved, I would rather have the judge read pertinent foreign cases while understanding that the foreign cases are not controlling. I would rather have the judge treat those cases cautiously, using them with care, than simply to ignore them....

...

It is sometimes difficult for those who live in foreign nations, say Europeans, to understand how Americans can react so negatively to the notion of foreign judges writing opinions that would bind Americans. They may believe that one judge, in a sense, is as good as another. Why does it matter that the judge in question is not American?

... Madison pointed out that the American Constitution is a "Charter of Power granted by Liberty; not a Charter of Liberty granted by Power." In saying this, he was saying that our national government rests upon the theory that all power originates in the people; whatever power government possesses, it possesses by way of delegation from people. But in many foreign countries, governmental power originated in a central authority, perhaps a king, now an elected government; and liberty reflects a delegation of freedom by that central authority. The origins of power and of liberty differ conceptually, even if both nations end up in the same place.

For this reason Americans have a cast of mind that, in respect to anyone's exercise of power, asks, "Who is this person? What opportunity did I have, did the American people have, in authorizing him or her to exercise power over me?" When I hear criticisms of my views based upon this outlook, I do not complain. Even if I disagree with the specific criticism, it reflects a principle that is healthy and important. That principle, in which Americans strongly believe, is that all power has to flow from the people and the people must maintain checks on its exercise. That is a good thing.

...

NOTE

In 'Foreign Law and the Denominator Problem', 119 Harv. L. Rev. 148 (2005), Ernest Young criticizes the Court's opinion in *Roper v. Simmons.* He notes that 'Justices who believe in foreign citation have typically defended it as a form of persuasive authority: American judges look abroad for different or innovative ways of approaching common issues, but the foreign law has no force beyond the persuasiveness of its reasoning.' He contrasts this approach with a court that 'takes account of foreign legal practice as part of a search for "consensus,"' and then 'typically looks to the mere fact of the foreign jurisdiction's position on a particular issue. The process is one of counting noses, with little regard to the reasons that led to the adoption or rejection of a practice in any particular jurisdiction.'

Young analyses *Roper* to fall within this second category. Within the US, with 20 states retaining capital punishment for children committing a crime between ages 16 and 18, it was hardly possible to find a 'consensus.' But by turning to many foreign jurisdictions, it became more plausible for the Court to say that a consensus existed that justified the Court in abolishing capital punishment. The US could be plausibly seen as an 'outlier,' out of step with 'evolving standards of decency.' Foreign jurisdictions are relevant to such a count without consideration of their reasons for their decisions, or the plausibility of those reasons. 'Justice Kennedy's discussion about foreign law is all about noses, not reasons.' Under such a method and approach, the Court is in some sense treating foreign decisions (constitutional, legislative, judicial) as 'authoritative.' 'Foreign practice is not the only reason, of course, and it remains to be seen what the internationalist Justices will do in a case about, say, hate speech or libel law when international authorities point in an opposite direction from their own views about domestic law.' Young is here referring to situations where the great majority of foreign states may, for example, ban 'hate' speech that could be within the protection of the First Amendment in the United States. Young concludes:

> ... A decision like *Roper* [uses decisions of foreign jurisdictions] to proscribe the juvenile death penalty ... in such a way as to foreclose any ability of the political branches to articulate a different view. Incorporation of foreign practice into

constitutional law thus eliminates the political branches' usual prerogative to dissent from the formation of customary norms or to depart from those norms once they have developed. The *Roper* Court thus decided that it — not the President, and not the Congress — would control the way in which the American legal system would respond to developments in international law.

QUESTIONS

1. What differences in context and history might be helpful to explaining the radically different approaches to the question of inquiry into foreign opinions in, say, South Africa (illustrated to some degree by the *Makwanyane* opinion) and by Justice Scalia (and other Supreme Court Justices)?

2. Is Justice Scalia suggesting that federal judges should not consult at all any foreign judicial or legislative decisions on similar issues, or merely that such foreign decisions should not be brought into their opinions' argument (or perhaps even simply cited)? Does his argument apply only to constitutional issues, or also by its logic to statutory questions as well, such as deciding on the extraterritorial reach of a regulatory statute like US antitrust or securities law?

3. EXCEPTIONALISM AND UNILATERALISM: RECENT US APPROACHES TO INTERNATIONAL LAW AND HUMAN RIGHTS

CAROL STEIKER, CAPITAL PUNISHMENT AND AMERICAN EXCEPTIONALISM

In Michael Ignatieff (ed.), American Exceptionalism and Human Rights 57 (2005)

...

What follows is consideration of ten theories of American exceptionalism.... I will close not by declaring a winner among the contending theories, but rather by suggesting that American exceptionalism in the area of capital punishment is better understood as a contingent product of a particular moment in American history than as the ineluctable "fate" that the very abundance of theories of American exceptionalism might seem to suggest.

...

Salience of Crime as a Political Issue

The most persuasive reason to believe that Americans care more intensely about capital punishment is the simple fact that crime and punishment have risen to and remained at the indisputable top of the American political agenda at all levels of government. Since 1968 . . . crime policy has been a hugely salient issue in local, state, and national elections, to a degree not rivaled in any of our peer Western nations. . . .

. . .

In the United States, two things are indisputably true, and "exceptional," at least as a matter of degree, in comparison to the rest of the industrialized West. First, crime has a political salience that is extraordinarily high, almost impossible to overstate. As a result, themes of "law and order" tend to dominate electoral battles at all levels of government. . . . Second, the death penalty has become a potent symbol in the politics of "law and order," despite its relative insignificance as a matter of crime control policy. . . .

Populism

Often proffered more as an alternative than as a complement to the "intensity of preference" theory of American exceptionalism is the theory that populism in American politics, as compared to elitism in European politics, best accounts for differences in death penalty policy. As some Americans like to respond to our European detractors, it is not that Americans have different attitudes about capital punishment, it is that our political institutions are more responsive to the public will. . . . This theory conveniently purports to explain both why the death penalty continues to flourish in the United States and how Western European nations managed to achieve universal abolition despite widespread popular support for capital punishment.

The "American populism" theory has two dimensions to it, one institutional and one that might better be termed cultural. The institutional dimension emphasizes the populist features of the structures of American political organization, especially as compared to European democracies. Obviously, not all American political structures tend toward the populist. . . . The Electoral College and the bicameral structure of Congress have often been noted as antipopulist, at least in the sense of antimajoritarian. . . . The use of the "primary" system to select party candidates in both federal and state elections in the United States is one of the best examples of American political exceptionalism; in other Western democracies, political parties put up candidates for election without throwing the question open to popular intervention — a system much more likely to exclude mavericks and to insulate candidates from hot-button single issues like the death penalty. Similarly, the widespread availability (and somewhat more modest use) of direct democracy tools, such as referenda and initiatives, is another exceptional feature of American politics that, like the "primary" system, tends to increase the power of single-issue voters and to promote populist tendencies in political debates and platforms. . . .

While these differences in democratic organization certainly do exist, differences in political culture between the United States and the rest of the West appear even more striking. In the United States, politicians are conspicuously antielitist in their rhetoric and folksy in their self-presentation. . . .

. . . Unlike the United States, most European countries have a culture of political elitism and careerism, whereby political leaders are produced in large part through education and graduated ascension through professional bureaucracies. The United States simply has no equivalent to France's Ecole Nationale d'Administration (ENA) or Britain's civil service. These institutions both reflect and reinforce a political culture in which political leaders are viewed and view themselves as educated elites who have a duty to make decisions in light of their expertise and thus, more often than in the United States, to lead the public rather than to follow it. In such cultures it is imaginable for a minister of justice to respond to polling revealing substantial popular support for the death penalty with the comment, "They don't really want the death penalty; they are objecting to the increasing violence." . . .

The foregoing is not meant to celebrate the United States as "authentically" democratic in comparison to European bureaucratic elitism; nor, on the other hand, is it meant to exalt European abolition of capital punishment as progressive and "civilized" in comparison to American retention as crude and atavistic. . . .

. . .

Criminal Justice Populism

. . . One of the most clearly "exceptional" aspects of the structure of American government is the much greater degree of both lay participation in the criminal justice system and direct political accountability of institutional actors within the criminal justice system. While many other countries use lay fact finders to a certain extent in criminal trials, no other country authorizes such a large role for criminal trial juries as does the United States. Moreover, the extensive use of lay grand juries in the charging process in the United States is even more truly anomalous. Equally anomalous is the fact that the vast majority of American prosecutors are elected rather than appointed. Judges, too, are directly elected or otherwise politically accountable in a large number of states. This current state of affairs is the result of a uniquely American turn during the nineteenth century toward increasing and entrenching democratic control over state and local governments through state constitutionalism.

These clearly "exceptional" institutional arrangements, like populism in electoral politics, provide a mechanism through which popular support for the use of capital punishment can influence institutional decision making. In this context, however, the influence is not on legislative decision making but rather on prosecutorial charging decisions, judicial conducting of criminal trials, and lay rendering of verdicts and sentences — especially in highly publicized capital, or potentially capital, cases. Elected officials who campaigned on a death penalty platform, or reelected officials who were vigorous advocates for the use of available capital sanctions while in office, no doubt perceive a mandate to use the death penalty in a way that European judges and prosecutors, more isolated products of an elite bureaucracy, could not possibly. There is thus something of a "feedback" loop between voters and elected officials that tends to reinforce and intensify tendencies toward the use of capital punishment. . . .

. . .

Federalism

Another "exceptional" feature of American political organization is American federalism. A number of other Western democracies, such as Germany, Switzerland, and Canada, are structured on a federal model, with discrete governmental units allocated some autonomous spheres of authority within the larger federal nation-state.

However, the United States is the only country that gives full criminal lawmaking power to individual federal units. This grant cannot be superseded by Congress, as the federal constitution is structured to ensure state dominance over criminal law. As a result, criminal lawmaking and law enforcement are understood and experienced in the United States as primarily a state and local concern, with federal lawmaking and enforcement as a limited, specialized adjunct. This arrangement, unique in Western democracies, necessarily permits local or regional enthusiasts to keep the death penalty going within the United States, even when attitudes and trends are moving in the opposite direction in other parts of the country. Nationwide abolition can thus be achieved, as a legislative matter, only through persuasion of the legislatures of fifty different states and the federal legislature as well.

Coordination is the most obvious challenge for a successful nationwide abolitionist movement in such a system. This coordination problem is exacerbated by the radical decentralization of criminal law enforcement authority within states. Local district attorneys control the use of the death penalty on a countywide basis; thus even achieving statewide abolition is difficult without the cooperation and support of local law enforcement officials whose individual political views and agendas must be accommodated....

...

European Exceptionalism

This theory turns the tables and asks whether there is something distinctive about European politics, culture, or history that would lead to wholesale abolition of the death penalty in the space of only a few short decades. A version of this theory has already been explored above as a contrast to American political populism: bureaucratic elitism in European politics has allowed European political leaders to abolish the death penalty despite substantial popular support for capital punishment at the time of abolition. But this theory does not explain what has led European political leaders to conclude that the death penalty must be abandoned at this precise point in time.

The answer to this question may lie in Europe's distinctive historical experiences during the twentieth century. Europeans and others who have recently and vividly experienced terrible abuses of state power may see more reason to remove the death penalty from the state's arsenal of sanctions.... Moreover, Europe has suffered numerous violent ethnic conflicts throughout the last century, and it may fear that the use of the death penalty could play a role in exacerbating such conflicts. Thus it is not surprising that fears that Irishmen might be wrongly convicted and executed for terrorism have changed the minds of some British supporters of capital punishment, or that capital punishment is not on the table as an available sanction for the former Yugoslavia war crimes tribunal....

...

Historical Contingency

...

Moreover, the Court's validation of the continuing use of the death penalty as a matter of constitutional law may have hindered movement toward abolition by creating an impediment to American acceptance of capital punishment as a violation of international human rights law, so prevalent in Europe and elsewhere. Abolition by European countries, especially in the 1980s and 1990s, was almost always couched in the discourse of international human rights. This discourse is much less prominent in, if not absent entirely from, American debates about abolition versus retention, no doubt because it is hard for American political leaders to articulate, or for members of the American public to accept, that there could be a fundamental and universal human right not recognized by our much vaunted Constitution....

...

...The role of the Supreme Court's rejection of constitutional claims against capital punishment in preventing abolition, however, is dwarfed by the other political and institutional impediments to legislative abolition.... No one could seriously entertain the view that nationwide legislative abolition of capital punishment is even remotely likely in the next generation or two. In the context of abolition of capital punishment, however, the Supreme Court has played and will continue to play a much more salient role than the political branches.... Only the Court has the power in this context to effect change throughout the United States; only the Court is sufficiently insulated from political will that it can, on occasion, lead rather than follow public opinion. Moreover there is some suggestion that the Court might be moving in the direction of abolishing or seriously limiting the use of capital punishment in the United States ... The Court's recent declarations in *Roper v. Simmons* [*supra* p. 35, and] *Atkins v. Virginia* [*supra* p. 35] signal a potential shift toward a radically different constitutional stance, one more open to consideration of international practice and norms in developing death penalty jurisprudence....

...

JED RUBENFELD, UNILATERALISM AND CONSTITUTIONALISM

79 N.Y.U.L.Rev. 1971, at 1973 (2004)

Introduction

...

... The United States has been unilateralist since the country was founded — although, historically, U.S. unilateralism was often a device for avoiding war, not making it. Since 1945, however, America has spoken out of both sides of its mouth on international law, championing internationalism in one breath, rejecting it in the next.

...

World War II came to represent, for continental Europe, the horrors of nationalism and populism. As a result, in the war's aftermath, European elites were ready to embrace an antinationalist, antidemocratic international legal system. The United States was not. The war had a very different meaning here, which led to a very different understanding of the internationalist project pursued in its wake.

Basically, the United States promoted the new internationalism as part of an ambition to Americanize as much of the world as it could, which meant both the export of American institutions, including constitutional law, and the strengthening of American global influence.

Whatever its motivations, this ambition created a contradiction at the heart of our post-war internationalist strategy. Because the point of the new international law was to Americanize, the United States, from its own perspective, did not really need international law (being already American). Accordingly, we would lead the world in creating a new international legal order to which we ourselves never fully acceded.... [I]n the ensuing decades, the United States frequently found itself championing international law for other countries, while rejecting or resisting it for itself.

...I suggest that the fundamental issue, whatever the exigencies of current affairs may be, concerns the relationship between international law and the deeper commitments of American constitutionalism.... American constitutionalism differs in certain fundamental respects from contemporary European constitutionalism, and the distinctive features of American constitutionalism have implications not only for ... "jus cogens" or "customary international law," but for supranational legal institutions as a whole.

At the core of any conception of constitutionalism, there has to be an account of the special authority, the higher-law status, claimed by constitutional rules and principles. One such account understands constitutionalism as an inaugurating or foundational act of democratic self-government. On this view, which I will call "democratic constitutionalism," a constitution is, first and foremost, supposed to be the foundational law a particular polity has given itself through a special act of popular lawmaking.

A very different account sees constitutionalism not as an act of democracy, but as a set of checks or restraints on democracy. These restraints are thought to be entitled to special authority because they express universal rights and principles, which in theory transcend national boundaries, applying to all societies alike. From this universalistic perspective, constitutional law is fundamentally antidemocratic; one of its central purposes is to put limits on democratic self-government.

American constitutional history has always displayed a commitment to democratic constitutionalism. The second, universalistic conception has undoubtedly and often prominently figured in American constitutionalism as well, but it has never displaced the commitment to the first. By contrast, European constitutional developments since the Second World War have been increasingly committed to the universalistic view, with a corresponding diminution in the importance attached to democratic constitutionalism. The universalistic picture of constitutional law strongly favors supranational legal and political institutions, because the most important legal and political principles, from this perspective, transcend national boundaries and indeed exist to check national governments. For this reason, I will refer to the second conception as "international constitutionalism."

The great new international charters and international institutions that emerged after the Second World War were built, to a large degree, on the premises of international constitutionalism. For example, these premises underlie the entire contemporary discourse of "international human rights," which is predicated on the idea that there exists an identifiable body of universal law, everywhere binding, requiring no democratic provenance. In this sense, contemporary international law is deeply antidemocratic. That is the true challenge that international law's supporters must meet today.

Part IV [of this article concludes] that the institutions and ideologies surrounding international law, at least in its present form, do in fact pose a significant threat to democracy — not by accident, but structurally and by design. To this extent, America does in fact have a good reason to resist international governance today.

U.S. Unilateralism

. . .

Even after 1945, when America entered the United Nations, American unilateralism continued. Of all the major powers, the United States alone in the late 1940s and 1950s refused to join any of the great new human rights conventions. As of 1993, the United States was a party to only six of twenty principal human rights agreements, and when we did ratify such conventions, we attached "reservations" depriving them of much of their legal force. President Clinton, considered by some a "multilateralist," refused to sign the Landmines Convention and advised against US submission to the International Criminal Court (ICC). But well before we refused to participate in the ICC, we had repeatedly defied or refused to submit to the International Court of Justice (ICJ). And before the 2003 Iraq war, we had used force repeatedly without Security Council approval, as, for example, when the "multilateralist" Clinton administration led the bombing of Kosovo in 1999.

Why, then, does US unilateralism seem to many so new and striking? American unilateralism probably has intensified or accelerated in the last three years. But two other factors are more important.

First, what is genuinely new, as a historical matter, is the extraordinary success of internationalism in Europe and elsewhere since 1945, a development that intensified after 1989. Through their participation in the European Union, many European states today have surrendered prerogatives and trappings of national sovereignty long considered inviolable. This backdrop makes U.S. unilateralism particularly conspicuous today. . . .

Second, and perhaps even more important, the United States has spoken out of both sides of its mouth on the subject of internationalism for the last sixty years. We were the driving engine behind the United Nations. Americans would be among the primary architects of the initial human rights conventions and the strongest champions of international institutions to monitor rights violations and to govern the use of military force. Indeed, America would press on Europe the idea of European union itself — with France, ironically, the primary locus of resistance. At the same time, America would promote a new constitutionalism throughout Europe and the world, a constitutionalism in which fundamental rights as well as protections of minorities would be laid down as part of the world's basic law, ostensibly beyond the reach of ordinary political processes. More than any other single country, the United States is responsible for the existing international legal system, which naturally makes it rather hard for other states to understand how we can act as if that legal system does not apply to us.

. . .

At the same time, however, in one major domain, the United States has been as consistent and devoted a champion of international law as any other country: economics. Although the United States occasionally may act unilaterally in matters of trade, it was and is the world's leading proponent of multilateral economic-governance regimes. The current administration may resist the ICC and the dictates of the U.N. Charter, but it supports North American Free Trade Agreement (NAFTA), which subjects the United States to the jurisdiction of international-trade tribunals, and promotes international free trade and intellectual-property agreements all over the world. A similar tension can be seen in many who otherwise support the familiar, "right-wing" pro-unilateralist position: Many of these seeming unilateralists become die-hard multilateralists when the subject turns to trade and property rights.

. . .

For Europeans, World War II, with its almost sixty million deaths, carried two fundamental lessons. First, it exemplified the horrors of nationalism. In Germany especially, the war left a deep antinationalist scar. . . .

. . .

Second, and more specifically, the war demonstrated the potential horrors of democracy. We may prefer to forget it, but Hitler was elected, and Mussolini rose to power through parliamentary processes. . . . Unpleasant as it is to acknowledge, Nazism and Fascism were populist movements and in fact manifestations of popular sovereignty. From the postwar European perspective, the Allies' victory was a victory not only against nationalism, but against popular sovereignty, against democratic excess.

The American experience of victory could not have differed more starkly. For Americans, the Allies' triumph was a victory for nationalism — for our nation, our kind of nationalism. It was a victory for popular sovereignty (our popular sovereignty) and a victory for democracy (our democracy). . . . If Europe was to develop democratically, it would need American tutelage and assistance. If Europe was to overcome its nationalist pathologies, it might need to become a United States (of Europe). . . .

. . .

. . . The United Nations, the European Union, and international law more generally are expressly understood in Europe as antinationalist; they are constraints on nationalism and national sovereignty, the catastrophic perils of which were made so plain by the Second World War. . . . Just as important, and for the same reasons, international law is also understood, although often more covertly, as a restraint on democracy, at least in the sense of placing increasing power in the hands of international experts — bureaucrats, technocrats, diplomats, and judges — at a considerable remove from popular politics and popular will.

. . .

Two principal motivations lay behind America's leadership in the postwar internationalism, one high-minded, the other geopolitical, both implying a distinctively American mixture of hubris and hypocrisy. The high-minded aspiration involved

America's long-held self-conceit as a beacon to mankind, a "city on the hill," charged with the mission of showing the world the way to freedom, peace, and prosperity.... Thus when drafting international human rights treaties, founding the United Nations and the World Trade Organization (WTO), imposing constitutions on Germany and Japan, and pushing Europe toward integration, Americans were able to see themselves as laboring generously, for the sake of people everywhere, to make the world more American.

In other words, we were bestowing on the world the gift of American law and the American way. Europe might use a different phrase — "human rights" — to describe them....

The second motivation was to increase American wealth and power.... Hence America's internationalist crusade after 1945 was in part intended to establish, throughout as much of the world as possible, a stable legal, political and economic order in which American commerce would flow freely and American military power would reign supreme.

Both these sets of motives could be described as "imperialist." Both shared a common objective: to Americanize the world through a new international order. Naturally, therefore, America would be the great champion of the new international order....

But for just this reason, in the American worldview, all this internationalism, all this multilateralism, was more for the rest of the world than it was for us. This is the root-source of all subsequent American equivocation on international law....

...

...As European integration progressed and as the Soviet fall from world power turned into utter collapse, the "international community" became more discontent with American power. It came to see international law as a vehicle for restraining the "hyperpower," and it became increasingly less tolerant of American "exceptionalism."

...

Unilateralism and Constitutionalism

...

Here is one way constitutionalism can be understood: Constitutional rights are universal. They are rights people have by nature, by virtue of being persons, by reason of morality, or by reason of Reason itself. Constitutional principles — essentially the liberal principles of the Enlightenment — possess an authority superior to that of politics, including, of course, democratic politics. This special authority, residing in a normative domain higher than that of politics, is what allows constitutional law properly to displace the outcomes of political decisionmaking, including democratic decisionmaking.

On this view, constitutional principles and structures ought in principle to be supra-national. Constitutional rights transcend national boundaries. Constitutional principles are superior to claims of national sovereignty or self-determination....

...

In this constitutionalism, a democratic ratification process, if pursued at all, is pursued primarily for reasons of expedience. Ratification of a new constitution may be instrumentally valuable — a means of procuring acquiescence — but, in principle, having a committee of expert jurists draw up a constitution is equally satisfactory. . . .

The alternative conception is democratic constitutionalism. . . . These commitments will include fundamental rights that stand against majority rule at any given moment, but these counter-majoritarian rights are not therefore counter-democratic. . . . The reason . . . is that they represent the nation's self-given law, enacted through a special, democratic, constitutional politics, subject to democratic amendment processes in the future. . . .

From this perspective, a democratic process of constitution-making, particularly when it comes to ratification, is crucial. But the work of drafting and ratification is only the beginning. Just as important, if not more so, is the work of constitutional interpretation, because constitutional law must somehow remain the nation's self-given law even as it is reworked through judicial interpretation and reinterpretation. . . .

. . . The US Constitution differed in one fundamental respect from any democratic constitution that any large state had ever had: It was enacted through a process of popular deliberation and consent.

. . .

Americans at bottom tend to be highly skeptical about the claims of a nonpolitical, neutral constitutional law. They are well aware that judges' values invariably inform constitutional law. Europeans tend to have a different attitude, which is often expressed in the form of a more dogmatic insistence on the separateness of politics from law, including constitutional law. . . .

. . . European constitutionalism today invests courts with full jurisdiction over constitutional rights. . . . [W]hat makes the new European constitutionalism cohere — what gives European constitutional courts their claim to legitimacy — is the ideology of universal or "international human rights," which owe their validity to no particular nation's constitution, and which possess therefore a supranational and almost supraconstitutional character, making them close to unamendable and rendering them peculiarly fit for interpretation by international juridical experts.

. . .

By contrast, in America, where judges still can decry the introduction of international precedents as if they were in the presence of the first spores of a new virus, it would be nothing short of scandalous to suggest that US constitutional questions be decided by an international tribunal, claiming supremacy over our legal system. . . . International law has never quite achieved higher-law status in America; it almost has lower-law status. In the American constitutional perspective, law gains no special authority by virtue of being international law, and courts obtain no special legitimacy by virtue of being international courts. On the contrary, from the American perspective, national constitutional courts, which remain embedded within the nation's democratic processes, are an essential feature of constitutionalism.

. . .

Practical Contrast

. . .

On the European view, human rights transcend national politics. Therefore, at least ideally, human rights ought to be uniform throughout the world. By contrast, on the American view, democratic nations can differ at least on some matters of fundamental rights.

. . .

But turn to the death penalty and to contemporary European attitudes about it. Capital punishment is now viewed as a human rights violation by the European community, and on this ground, Europeans routinely excoriate the United States, where the death penalty remains in force in some jurisdictions . . . .

This position is logical given the European conception of constitutionalism. Human rights are "universal." Therefore, once the death penalty has been deemed a human rights violation, it is a scandal if any nation refuses to recognize it.

For Europeans, one great marker of successful constitutional development is international consensus and uniformity. Internationalists will point to such consensus as if it were supremely validating — as if the fact of agreement on the death penalty throughout the "international community" were itself a source of legal validation and authority . . . .

. . . In American constitutionalism, the US Constitution is supposed to reflect our own fundamental legal and political commitments — not a set of commitments that all civilized nations must share. It is the self-givenness of the Constitution, not its universality, that gives it authority as law. Hence consensus in the "international community" cannot be regarded in the United States as the compelling source of legal or constitutional authority that it is often made out to be in Europe.

. . .

Is International Law Really Antidemocratic?

. . .

. . . [W]hile international law can of course be justiciable in national courts, the natural juridical destination of international law is an international tribunal, if for no reason other than that the interpretation of international law by national courts will always be vulnerable to charges of partisanship.

The shift from national courts to international tribunals has serious implications for democracy. These implications are not apparent to most internationalists, whose thinking runs as follows: Once an issue is taken to be a matter of law, particularly a matter of constitutional law, the issue has been removed from the political domain. And once this has been done — once an issue has been placed in the domain of law, rather than politics — then democratic principles have little to say about whether the court that decides the law is a national or international court. What counts is that the court gets the law right . . . .

. . . Judges [from the American perspective] may, in one sense, be nonpolitical actors, but the judiciary is nevertheless a governmental institution, embedded within a larger political process, and it makes a great difference, democratically speaking, whether adjudication occurs in national or international courts . . . .

. . . When the power of fundamental lawmaking inherent in judicial review is confided to an international tribunal, the aspirations of democratic constitutionalism have been left behind, replaced by those of international constitutionalism.

. . .

QUESTIONS

1. Rubenfeld characterizes the US Constitution as a "democratic constitution." But almost from its origin it contained a Bill of Rights which, with later amendments, and as judicially interpreted, sought to realize a major purpose, to "put limits on democratic self-government," a notion that Rubenfeld associates with universalism and uses to describe the contrasting European-style constitutionalism. But with respect to human rights, is the more important difference between the US and Europe unilateralism vs. universalism, or nationalist vs. internationalist, or internal democracy vs. international constitutionalism?

2. How do you assess Steiker's explanations or Rubenfeld's contrast? To the extent that you agree, do you read the U.S. out of any conception of universalism in human rights, as much for example as one might conclude that some Islamic states are not part of a Western conception of human rights universalism?

2

The Human Rights Movement: Background and Birth

COMMENT ON INTERNATIONAL DIMENSION OF HUMAN RIGHTS MOVEMENT

In its discussion of the legality of the death penalty and related issues, Chapter 1(B) concentrated on the law — often the constitutional law — of different states. The selected opinions of state courts devoted most of their analysis to their own and to foreign legal systems. International law figured through relevant treaty provisions, but in a subsidiary way. It was not at centre stage.

Chapters 2 to 4, on the other hand, concentrate on the international law aspects of the human rights movement. Why has this path been followed? After all, it is possible to study human rights issues not at the international level but in the detailed contexts of different states' histories, socio-economic and political structures, legal systems, religions, cultures and so on. With respect to its legal dimension, a human rights course that was so organized would stress the internal law of states as well as foreign and comparative law. It would engage in a contextual and comparative analysis of bodies of domestic law, perhaps devoting its full attention to states like China, Saudi Arabia, Italy, the United States or Guatemala. It could stress the recent trend in many states toward (at least as a formal matter) liberal constitutionalism. For such a study of human rights, international law could play a peripheral role, relevant only when it exerted some clear influence on the national scene or had a place in the basic logic of a judicial decision.

The attractiveness of such an approach becomes more apparent when one contrasts with international human rights many other international subjects where international law occupies, indeed *must* occupy, a central position. Imagine, for example, that this coursebook's interest was not human rights but the humanitarian law of war as applied to interstate conflicts, or the regulation of fisheries, or immunities of diplomats from arrest, or the regulation of trade barriers like tariffs. Each of those fields is inherently, intrinsically, *international* in character. Each involves relations *between* states or between citizens of one state and other states. We could not profitably examine any one of them without examining international custom and treaties, international institutions and processes.

Violations of human rights are different. Not only are they generally rooted within states rather than in interstate engagements, but they need not on their surface involve any international consequences whatsoever. (Of course, systemic and severe human rights violations that appear to be 'internal' matters — for example, recurrent violence against an ethnic minority — could well have international consequences, perhaps by leading to refugee flows abroad or by angering other states whose populations are related by ethnicity to the oppressed minority.) In typical instances of violations, the police of state X torture defendants to extract confessions; the government of X shuts the opposition press as elections approach; prisoners are raped by their guards; courts decide cases according to executive command; women or a minority group are barred from education or certain work. Each of these events could profitably be studied entirely within a state's (or region's, culture's) internal framework, just as law students in many countries traditionally concentrate on the internal legal–political system, including that system's provision for civil liberties and human rights.

Nonetheless, since the Second World War it would be inadequate or even misleading to develop a framework for the study of human rights in many countries without including as a major ingredient the international legal and political aspects of the field: laws, processes and institutions. In today's world, human rights is characteristically imagined as a movement involving international law and institutions, as well as a movement involving the spread of liberal constitutions among states. Internal developments in many states have been much influenced by international law and institutions, as well as by pressures from other states trying to enforce international law.

Internal or comparative approaches to human rights law and the truly international aspects of human rights are now broadly recognized to be complexly intertwined and reciprocally influential with respect to the growth of human rights norms, the causes and effects of their violations, the reactions and sanctions of intergovernmental bodies or other states, the transformations of internal orders, and so on.

From another perspective as well it would be impossible to grasp the character of the human rights movement without a basic knowledge about international law and its contributions to it. The movement's aspirations to universal validity are necessarily rooted in that body of law. Many of the distinctive organizations intended to help to realize those aspirations are creations of international law.

For such reasons, this coursebook frequently examines but does not concentrate on the internal law and politics of states. It relates throughout this 'horizontal' strand of the human rights movement, as constitutionalism spreads among states, to the 'vertical' strand of the new international law that is meant to bind states and that is implemented by the new international institutions. Both the horizontal and vertical dimensions of the human rights movement are vital to an understanding of the human rights movement. But the truly novel developments of the last half century have involved primarily this second dimension.

Chapter 2 has several functions. It sketches the doctrines and principles in an older international law that served as background to and precedents for the human rights movement that took root and developed immediately after the Second World War. It then examines the early instruments — particularly the Universal Declaration of Human Rights and the International Covenant on Civil and Political Rights — that (together with the later-described International Covenant on Economic, Social and

Cultural Rights) form the substantive core of the movement, an International Bill of Rights. The chapter uses national and international decisions of courts and other tribunals not only to present basic doctrines and principles, but also to convey an understanding of international law: its so-called 'sources', its processes of growth, particularly with respect to customary and treaty law. The two tasks are interrelated. By what means or methods have the international rules and standards of the human rights movement been developed? By what processes are international legal rules made, elaborated, applied and changed?

Several of the opinions and scholarly writings in the chapter draw on Article 38 of the Statute of the International Court of Justice, the judicial organ of the United Nations that was created by the UN Charter of 1945.[1] That article has long served as a traditional point of departure for examining questions about the 'sources' of international law. It repeats (largely in identical language) the similar provisions of the 1921 Statute of its predecessor court, the Permanent Court of International Justice that was linked to the League of Nations and effectively died during the Second World War. It reads:

> 1. The Court, whose function is to decide in accordance with international law such disputes as are submitted to it, shall apply:
>   a. international conventions, whether general or particular, establishing rules expressly recognized by the contesting states;
>   b. international custom, as evidence of a general practice accepted as law;
>   c. the general principles of law recognized by civilized nations;
>   d. subject to the provisions of Article 59 [stating that decisions of the Court have no binding force except between the parties to the case], judicial decisions and the teachings of the most highly qualified publicists of the various nations, as subsidiary means for the determination of rules of law.

Although Article 38 formally instructs this particular Court about the method of applying international law to resolve disputes, its influence has extended to other international tribunals, to national courts, and indeed generally to argument based on international law that is made in settings other than courts.

The Article takes a positivist perspective. It defines the task of the Court in terms of its *application* of an identifiable body of international law that in one or another sense, has been consented to ('expressly recognized', 'accepted as law', 'recognized') directly or indirectly by states. Its skeletal list expresses a formal conception of the judicial function that is radically different from that of, say, a legal realist. Consider the following comments on Article 38 by José Alvarez, *International Organizations as Law Makers*, at 46 (2005):

> Public international lawyers, through at least the greater part of the 20th century, have sought to define their field as relatively autonomous from either politics or

[1] The Court can only hear cases to which states are parties: Article 34 of the Statute. A state's consent is necessary for the Court to exercise jurisdiction over it. That consent generally refers to the Court's adjudicating all 'legal disputes' concerning the 'interpretation of a treaty', a 'question of international law', the existence of a fact which, if established 'would constitute a breach of an international obligation', and the reparation to be made for breach of an international obligation: Article 36. Statute of the International Court of Justice, T.S. No. 993 (at p. 25) (U.S.).

morality. Their endeavor turned many, particularly in Europe and North America, towards legal positivism....

...

Nothing embodies these central positivist tenets in international law as much as the doctrine of sources. For most international lawyers trained in the West, article 38 of the Statute of the International Court of Justice remains the "constitution" of the international community. Its enumerated sources of international law — treaties, custom, and general principles of law — remain, for most, the exclusive means for generating legal obligations on states. Through the doctrine of sources, international lawyers define (and defend) their field as characteristically legal. Thanks to sources doctrine, international lawyers argue that international law, like domestic law, also has a circumscribed set of sources and rules for interpreting them; thanks to article 38, international law is distinguished from morality or politics. Thanks to sources, international rules have a distinctive either/or quality, essential to distinguish mere wishful thinking *(lex ferenda)* from black letter obligation *(lex lata)*: something either is or is not within one of the recognized sources of international law and someone with the requisite skill, like a judge, can do so....

... The doctrine of sources then, has a dual agenda: it tells the lawyer where to find the law in an objective fashion because it is ostensibly based in the concrete practice of states but it also seeks to provide a normatively constraining code for states....

NOTE

The chapter has the following organization: Section A examines customary law, and illustrates its theme through a national court decision in a field now known as 'the humanitarian laws of war'. Section B examines aspects of general principles of law and natural law, in the context of an arbitral decision on the law of state responsibility for injury to aliens. Section C examines treaty law by drawing on a decision of the Permanent Court of International Justice on the minorities regime in Europe between the two World Wars. Section D looks at the judgment at Nuremberg after the Second World War, at the very threshold of the human rights movement. Section E carries the historical narrative into the formation of the movement, stressing the Universal Declaration of Human Rights.

A. LAWS OF WAR AND CUSTOMARY INTERNATIONAL LAW

NOTE

The following decision in *The Paquete Habana* deals with an earlier period in the development of the laws of war, here naval warfare, and with a theme that became central in the later treaty development of this field — the protection of noncombatant civilians and their property (here, civilian fishing vessels) against the ravages of war. Within the framework of the laws of war, this case involves *jus in bello*, the ways in which war ought to be waged, the rules of war itself, rather than the related but distinct *jus ad bellum*, the determination of those conditions (if any) in which a *just* or justified war can be waged, conditions in which (under contemporary international law) going to war is legal.

In its analysis of the question before it, the US Supreme Court here illustrates a classical understanding of customary international law — an understanding that, we shall see, is today open to substantial challenge and reformation. In reading the opinion, keep in mind two questions. What method does the majority opinion employ to conclude that a relevant, indeed decisive, rule of customary international law has developed? Does the dissent differ as to the method itself or as to its application in this case?

THE PAQUETE HABANA

Supreme Court of the United States, 1900

175 U.S. 677, 20 S.Ct. 290

MR. JUSTICE GRAY DELIVERED THE OPINION OF THE COURT

These are two appeals from decrees of the district court of the United States for the southern district of Florida condemning two fishing vessels and their cargoes as prize of war.

Each vessel was a fishing smack, running in and out of Havana, and regularly engaged in fishing on the coast of Cuba; sailed under the Spanish flag; was owned by a Spanish subject of Cuban birth, living in the city of Havana; was commanded by a subject of Spain also residing in Havana; and her master and crew had no interest in the vessel, but were entitled to shares, amounting in all to two thirds, of her catch, the other third belonging to her owner. Her cargo consisted of fresh fish, caught by her crew from the sea, put on board as they were caught, and kept and sold alive. Until stopped by the blockading squadron she had no knowledge of the existence of the war or of any blockade. She had no arms or ammunition on board, and made no attempt to run the blockade after she knew of its existence, nor any resistance at the time of the capture.

. . .

Both the fishing vessels were brought by their captors into Key West. A libel for the condemnation of each vessel and her cargo as prize of war was there filed on April 27, 1898; a claim was interposed by her master on behalf of himself and the other members of the crew, and of her owner; evidence was taken, showing the facts above stated; and on May 30, 1898, a final decree of condemnation and sale was entered, 'the court not being satisfied that as a matter of law, without any ordinance, treaty, or proclamation, fishing vessels of this class are exempt from seizure'.

Each vessel was thereupon sold by auction; the Paquete Habana for the sum of $490; and the Lola for the sum of $800. There was no other evidence in the record of the value of either vessel or of her cargo. . . .

. . .

We are then brought to the consideration of the question whether, upon the facts appearing in these records, the fishing smacks were subject to capture by the armed vessels of the United States during the recent war with Spain.

By an ancient usage among civilized nations, beginning centuries ago, and gradually ripening into a rule of international law, coast fishing vessels, pursuing their vocation of catching and bringing in fresh fish, have been recognized as exempt, with their cargoes and crews, from capture as prize of war.

This doctrine, however, has been earnestly contested at the bar; and no complete collection of the instances illustrating it is to be found, so far as we are aware, in a single published work, although many are referred to and discussed by the writers on international law, notable in 2 Ortolan, *Règles Internationales et Diplomatie de la Mer* (4th ed.) lib. 3, chap. 2, pp. 51–56; in 4 Calvo, *Droit International* (5th ed.) 2367–2373; in De Boeck, *Propriété Privé Ennemie sous Pavillon Ennemie*, 191–196; and in Hall, *International Law* (4th ed.) 148. It is therefore worth the while to trace the history of the rule, from the earliest accessible sources, through the increasing recognition of it with occasional setbacks, to what we may now justly consider as its final establishment in our own country and generally throughout the civilized world.

The earliest acts of any government on the subject, mentioned in the books, either emanated from, or were approved by, a King of England.

In 1403 and 1406 Henry IV issued orders to his admirals and other officers, entitled 'Concerning Safety for Fishermen — *De Securitate pro Piscatoribus*'. By an order of October 26, 1403, reciting that it was made pursuant to a treaty between himself and the King of France; and for the greater safety of the fishermen of either country, and so that they could be, and carry on their industry, the more safely on the sea, and deal with each other in peace; and that the French King had consented that English fishermen should be treated likewise, — it was ordained that French fishermen might, during the then pending season for the herring fishery, safely fish for herrings and all other fish, from the harbor of Gravelines and the island of Thanet to the mouth of the Seine and the harbor of Hautoune....

The same custom would seem to have prevailed in France until towards the end of the seventeenth century. For example, in 1675, Louis XIV and the States General of Holland by mutual agreement granted to Dutch and French fishermen the liberty, undisturbed by their vessels of war, of fishing along the coasts of France, Holland, and England....

The doctrine which exempts coast fishermen, with their vessels and cargoes, from capture as prize of war, has been familiar to the United States from the time of the War of Independence.

...

In the treaty of 1785 between the United States and Prussia, article 23...provided that, if war should arise between the contracting parties, 'all women and children, scholars of every faculty, cultivators of the earth, artisans, manufacturers, and fishermen, unarmed and inhabiting unfortified towns, villages, or places, and in general all others whose occupations are for the common subsistence and benefit of mankind, shall be allowed to continue their respective employments, and shall not be molested in their persons, nor shall their houses or goods be burnt or otherwise destroyed, nor their fields wasted by the armed force of the enemy, into whose power, by the events of war, they may happen to fall; but if anything is necessary to be taken from them for the use of such armed force, the same shall be paid for at a reasonable price'....

Since the United States became a nation, the only serious interruptions, so far as we are informed, of the general recognition of the exemption of coast fishing vessels from hostile capture, arose out of the mutual suspicions and recriminations of England and France during the wars of the French Revolution.

...

On January 24, 1798, the English government by express order instructed the commanders of its ships to seize French and Dutch fishermen with their boats.... After the promulgation of that order, Lord Stowell (then Sir William Scott) in the High Court of Admiralty of England condemned small Dutch fishing vessels as prize of war. In one case the capture was in April, 1798, and the decree was made November 13, 1798. *The Young Jacob and Johanna*, 1 C.Rob. 20....

On March 16, 1801, the Addington Ministry, having come into power in England, revoked the orders of its predecessors against the French fishermen; maintaining, however, that 'the freedom of fishing was nowise founded upon an agreement, but upon a simple concession', that 'this concession would be always subordinate to the convenience of the moment', and that 'it was never extended to the great fishery, or to commerce in oysters or in fish'. And the freedom of the coast fisheries was again allowed on both sides....

Lord Stowell's judgment in *The Young Jacob and Johanna*, 1 C.Rob. 20, above cited, was much relied on by the counsel for the United States, and deserves careful consideration.

The vessel there condemned is described in the report as 'a small Dutch fishing vessel taken April, 1798, on her return from the Dogger bank to Holland'; and Lord Stowell, in delivering judgment, said: 'In former wars it has not been usual to make captures of these small fishing vessels; but this rule was a rule of comity only, and not of legal decision; it has prevailed from views of mutual accommodation between neighbouring countries, and from tenderness to a poor and industrious order of people. In the present war there has, I presume, been sufficient reason for changing this mode of treatment; and as they are brought before me for my judgment they must be referred to the general principles of this court; they fall under the character and description of the last class of cases; that is, of ships constantly and exclusively employed in the enemy's trade'. And he added: 'it is a further satisfaction to me, in giving this judgment, to observe that the facts also bear strong marks of a false and fraudulent transaction'.

Both the capture and the condemnation were within a year after the order of the English government of January 24, 1798, instructing the commanders of its ships to seize French and Dutch fishing vessels, and before any revocation of that order. Lord Stowell's judgment shows that his decision was based upon the order of 1798, as well as upon strong evidence of fraud. Nothing more was adjudged in the case.

But some expressions in his opinion have been given so much weight by English writers that it may be well to examine them particularly. The opinion begins by admitting the known custom in former wars not to capture such vessels; adding, however, 'but this was a rule of comity only, and not of legal decision'. Assuming the phrase 'legal decision' to have been there used, in the sense in which courts are accustomed to use it, as equivalent to 'judicial decision', it is true that so far as appears, there had been no such decision on the point in England. The word 'comity' was apparently used by Lord Stowell as synonymous with courtesy or goodwill. But the period of a hundred years which has since elapsed is amply sufficient to have enabled what originally may have rested in custom or comity, courtesy or concession, to grow, by the general assent of civilized nations, into a settled rule of international law....

The French prize tribunals, both before and after Lord Stowell's decision, took a wholly different view of the general question....

The English government [by orders in council of 1806 and 1810] unqualifiedly prohibited the molestation of fishing vessels employed in catching and bringing to market fresh fish....

Wheaton, in his Digest of the Law of Maritime Captures and Prizes, published in 1815, wrote: 'It has been usual in maritime wars to exempt from capture fishing boats and their cargoes, both from views of mutual accommodation between neighboring countries, and from tenderness to a poor and industrious order of people. This custom, so honorable to the humanity of civilized nations, has fallen into disuse; and it is remarkable that both France and England mutually reproach each other with that breach of good faith which has finally abolished it'. Wheaton, Captures, chap. 2, 18.

This statement clearly exhibits Wheaton's opinion that the custom had been a general one, as well as that it ought to remain so. His assumption that it had been abolished by the differences between France and England at the close of the last century was hardly justified by the state of things when he wrote, and has not since been borne out.

...

In the war with Mexico, in 1846, the United States recognized the exemption of coast fishing boats from capture....

In the treaty of peace between the United States and Mexico, in 1848, were inserted the very words of the earlier treaties with Prussia, already quoted, forbidding the hostile molestation or seizure in time of war of the persons, occupations, houses, or goods of fishermen. 9 Stat. at L. 939, 940.

...

France in the Crimean war in 1854, and in her wars with Italy in 1859 and with Germany in 1870, by general orders, forbade her cruisers to trouble the coast fisheries, or to seize any vessel or boat engaged therein, unless naval or military operations should make it necessary.

...

Since the English orders in council of 1806 and 1810 ... in favor of fishing vessels employed in catching and bringing to market fresh fish, no instance has been found in which the exemption from capture of private coast fishing vessels honestly pursuing their peaceful industry has been denied by England or by any other nation. And the Empire of Japan (the last state admitted into the rank of civilized nations), by an ordinance promulgated at the beginning of its war with China in August, 1894, established prize courts, and ordained that 'the following enemy's vessels are exempt from detention', including in the exemption 'boats engaged in coast fisheries', as well as 'ships engaged exclusively on a voyage of scientific discovery, philanthrophy, or religious mission'. Takahashi, International Law, 11, 178.

International law is part of our law, and must be ascertained and administered by the courts of justice of appropriate jurisdiction as often as questions of right depending upon it are duly presented for their determination. For this purpose, where there is no treaty and no controlling executive or legislative act or judicial decision, resort must be had to the customs and usages of civilized nations, and, as evidence of these, to the works of jurists and commentators who by years of labor, research, and experience have made themselves peculiarly well acquainted with the subjects of which they treat. Such works are resorted to by judicial tribunals, not for the speculations of their authors concerning what the law ought to be, but for trustworthy evidence of what the law really is. Hilton v. Guyot, 159 U.S. 113, 163, 164, 214, 215, 40 L.Ed. 95, 108, 125, 126, 16 Sup.Ct.Rep. 139.

...

Chancellor Kent says: 'In the absence of higher and more authoritative sanctions, the ordinances of foreign states, the opinions of eminent statesmen, and the writings of distinguished jurists, are regarded as of great consideration on questions not settled by conventional law. In cases where the principal jurists agree, the presumption will be very great in favor of the solidity of their maxims; and no civilized nation that does not arrogantly set all ordinary law and justice at defiance will venture to disregard the uniform sense of the established writers on international law'. 1 Kent, Com. 18.

It will be convenient, in the first place, to refer to some leading French treatises on international law, which deal with the question now before us, not as one of the law of France only, but as one determined by the general consent of civilized nations ... [Discussion of French treatises omitted.]

...

No international jurist of the present day has a wider or more deserved reputation than Calvo, who, though writing in French, is a citizen of the Argentine Republic, employed in its diplomatic service abroad. In the fifth edition of his great work on international law, published in 1896, he observes, in 2366, that the international authority of decisions in particular cases by the prize courts of France, of England, and of the United States is lessened by the fact that the principles on which they are based are largely derived from the internal legislation of each country; and yet the peculiar character of maritime wars, with other considerations, gives to prize jurisprudence a force and importance reaching beyond the limits of the country in which it has prevailed. He therefore proposes here to group together a number of particular cases proper to serve as precedents for the solution of grave questions of maritime law in regard to the capture of private property as prize of war. Immediately, in 2367, he goes on to say: 'Notwithstanding the hardships to which maritime wars subject private property, notwithstanding the extent of the recognized rights of belligerents, there are generally exempted, from seizure and capture, fishing vessels'....

The modern German books on international law, cited by the counsel for the appellants, treat the custom by which the vessels and implements of coast fishermen are exempt from seizure and capture as well established by the practice of nations. Heffter, 137; 2 Kalterborn, 237, p. 480; Bluntschli, 667; Perels, 37, p. 217.

. . .

Two recent English text-writers cited at the bar (influenced by what Lord Stowell said a century since) hesitate to recognize that the exemption of coast fishing vessels from capture has now become a settled rule of international law. Yet they both admit that there is little real difference in the views, or in the practice, of England and of other maritime nations; and that no civilized nation at the present day would molest coast fishing vessels so long as they were peaceably pursuing their calling and there was no danger that they or their crews might be of military use to the enemy. . . .

But there are writers of various maritime countries, not yet cited, too important to be passed by without notice. . . .

[The opinion quotes from writing from the Netherlands, Spain, Austria, Portugal and Italy.]

This review of the precedents and authorities on the subject appears to us abundantly to demonstrate that at the present day, by the general consent of the civilized nations of the world, and independently of any express treaty or other public act, it is an established rule of international law, founded on considerations of humanity to a poor and industrious order of men, and of the mutual convenience of belligerent states, that coast fishing vessels, with their implements and supplies, cargoes and crews, unarmed and honestly pursuing their peaceful calling of catching and bringing in fresh fish, are exempt from capture as prize of war. . . .

. . .

This rule of international law is one which prize courts administering the law of nations are bound to take judicial notice of, and to give effect to, in the absence of any treaty or other public act of their own government in relation to the matter.

. . .

To this subject in more than one aspect are singularly applicable the words uttered by Mr. Justice Strong, speaking for this court: 'Undoubtedly no single nation can change the law of the sea. The law is of universal obligation and no statute of one or two nations can create obligations for the world. Like all the laws of nations, it rests upon the common consent of civilized communities. It is of force, not because it was prescribed by any superior power, but because it has been generally accepted as a rule of conduct. Whatever may have been its origin, whether in the usages of navigation, or in the ordinances of maritime states, or in both, it has become the law of the sea only by the concurrent sanction of those nations who may be said to constitute the commercial world . . . [Of these facts] we may take judicial notice. Foreign municipal laws must indeed be proved as facts, but it is not so with the law of nations'. The Scotia, 14 Wall. 170, 187, 188, sub nom. Sears v. The Scotia, 20 L.Ed. 822, 825, 826.

The position taken by the United States during the recent war with Spain was quite in accord with the rule of international law, now generally recognized by civilized nations, in regard to coast fishing vessels.

On April 21, 1898, the Secretary of the Navy gave instructions to Admiral Sampson, commanding the North Atlantic Squadron, to 'immediately institute a blockade of the north coast of Cuba, extending from Cardenas on the east to Bahia Honda on the west'. Bureau of Navigation Report of 1898, appx. 175. The blockade was immediately instituted accordingly. On April 22 the President issued a proclamation declaring that the United States had instituted and would maintain that blockade, 'in pursuance of the laws of the United States, and the law of nations applicable to such cases'. 30 Stat. at L. 1769. And by the act of Congress of April 25, 1898, chap. 189, it was declared that the war between the United States and Spain existed on that day, and had existed since and including April 21. 30 Stat. at L. 364.

On April 26, 1898, the President issued another proclamation which, after reciting the existence of the war as declared by Congress, contained this further recital: 'It being desirable that such war should be conducted upon principles in harmony with the present views of nations and sanctioned by their recent practice'. This recital was followed by specific declarations of certain rules for the conduct of the war by sea, making no mention of fishing vessels. 30 Stat. at L. 1770. But the proclamation clearly manifests the general policy of the government to conduct the war in accordance with the principles of international law sanctioned by the recent practice of nations....

Upon the facts proved in either case, it is the duty of this court, sitting as the highest prize court of the United States, and administering the law of nations, to declare and adjudge that the capture was unlawful and without probable cause; and it is therefore, in each case,—

Ordered, that the decree of the District Court be reversed, and the proceeds of the sale of the vessel, together with the proceeds of any sale of her cargo, be restored to the claimant, with damages and costs.

MR. CHIEF JUSTICE FULLER, WITH WHOM CONCURRED MR. JUSTICE HARLAN AND MR. JUSTICE MEKENNA, DISSENTING

The district court held these vessels and their cargoes liable because not 'satisfied that as a matter of law, without any ordinance, treaty, or proclamation, fishing vessels of this class are exempt from seizure'.

This court holds otherwise, not because such exemption is to be found in any treaty, legislation, proclamation, or instruction granting it, but on the ground that the vessels were exempt by reason of an established rule of international law applicable to them, which it is the duty of the court to enforce.

I am unable to conclude that there is any such established international rule, or that this court can properly revise action which must be treated as having been taken in the ordinary exercise of discretion in the conduct of war.

...

This case involves the capture of enemy's property on the sea, and executive action, and if the position that the alleged rule *proprio vigore* limits the sovereign power in war be rejected, then I understand the contention to be that, by reason of the existence of the rule, the proclamation of April 26 must be read as if it contained the exemption in terms, or the exemption must be allowed because the capture of fishing vessels of this class was not specifically authorized.

The preamble to the proclamation stated, it is true, that it was desirable that the war 'should be conducted upon principles in harmony with the present views of nations and sanctioned by their recent practice', but the reference was to the intention of the government 'not to resort to privateering, but to adhere to the rules of the Declaration of Paris'; and the proclamation spoke for itself. The language of the preamble did not carry the exemption in terms, and the real question is whether it must be allowed because not affirmatively withheld, or, in other words, because such captures were not in terms directed.

. . .

It is impossible to concede that the Admiral ratified these captures in disregard of established international law and the proclamation, or that the President, if he had been of opinion that there was any infraction of law or proclamation, would not have intervened prior to condemnation.

In truth, the exemption of fishing craft is essentially an act of grace, and not a matter of right, and it is extended or denied as the exigency is believed to demand.

It is, said Sir William Scott, 'a rule of comity only, and not of legal decision'.

. . .

It is difficult to conceive of a law of the sea of universal obligation to which Great Britain has not acceded. And I am not aware of adequate foundation for imputing to this country the adoption of any other than the English rule.

. . .

It is needless to review the speculations and repetitions of the writers on international law. Ortolan, De Boeck, and others admit that the custom relied on as consecrating the immunity is not so general as to create an absolute international rule; Heffter, Calvo, and others are to the contrary. Their lucubrations may be persuasive, but not authoritative.

In my judgment, the rule is that exemption from the rigors of war is in the control of the Executive. He is bound by no immutable rule on the subject. It is for him to apply, or to modify, or to deny altogether such immunity as may have been usually extended.

. . .

COMMENT ON THE HUMANITARIAN LAW OF WAR

The opinion in *The Paquete Habana* has the aura of a humane world in which, if war occurs, the fighting should be as compassionate in spirit as possible. It rests the rule of exemption of coastal fishing vessels 'on considerations of humanity to a poor and industrious order of men, and [on] the mutual convenience of fishing vessels'. The opinion seems more than a mere 14 years distant from the savagery of World War I, let alone that war's successors during the last century with their massive civilian casualties, atrocities and wanton destruction in engagements of close to total war by one or both sides.

The intricate body of international humanitarian law considered by the Supreme Court grew out of centuries of primarily customary law, although custom was supplemented, informed and indeed developed centuries ago by selective bilateral treaties. To this day, custom remains essential to argument about the laws of war, indeed to the subject matter jurisdiction of as well as the applicable norms before the international criminal tribunals examined in Chapter 14. Like many other areas of international law, this field is increasingly dominated by multilateral treaties that have both codified customary standards and rules and developed new ones in numerous international conferences. Multilateral declarations and treaties started to achieve prominence in the second half of the nineteenth century. The treaties now include the Hague Conventions concluded around the turn of the century, the four Geneva Conventions of 1949 (as well as two significant protocols of 1977 to those conventions), and several discrete treaties since the Second World War on matters like bans on particular weapons and cultural property.

The basic Geneva Conventions (194 states parties as of January 2007) and the two Protocols (Protocol I, 167 parties; Protocol II, 163 parties) cover a vast range of problems stemming from land, air or naval warfare, including the protection of wounded combatants and prisoners of war, of civilian populations and civilian objects affected by military operations or present in occupied territories, and of medical and religious personnel and buildings. As suggested by this list, the provisions of the four Conventions and the two Protocols constitute the principal contemporary regulation of *jus in bello*, how war ought to be waged.

This entire corpus of custom and treaties has come to be know as the 'international humanitarian law of war', the broad purpose being — in the words of the landmark St. Petersburg Declaration of 1868 — 'alleviating as much as possible the calamities of war'. Here lies the tension, even contradiction, within this body of law. Putting aside the question of a war's legality (an issue central to the Judgment of the International Military Tribunal at Nuremberg, p. 118, *infra*, and today governed by the UN Charter), a war fought in compliance with the standards and rules of the laws of war permits — one might say authorizes or legitimates — massive intentional killing or wounding and massive other destruction that, absent a war, would violate the most fundamental human rights norms.

Hence all these standards and rules stand at some perilous and problematic divide between brutality and destruction (i) that is permitted or privileged and (ii) that is illegal and subject to sanction. Broad standards like 'proportionality' in choosing military means or like the avoidance of 'unnecessary suffering' to the civilian population are employed to help to draw the line. The powerful ideal of reducing human suffering that animates this humanitarian law of war thus is countered by the goal of state parties to a war — indeed, in the eyes of states, the paramount goal — of gaining military objectives and victory while reducing as much as possible the losses to one's own armed forces.

The generous mood of *The Paquete Habana* toward the civilian population and its food-gathering needs was reflected in the various Hague Conventions regulating land and naval warfare that were adopted during the ensuing decade. Note Article 3 of the Hague Convention of 1907 on Certain Restrictions with Regard to the Exercise of the Right to Capture in Naval War, 36 Stat. 2396, T.S. No. 544, which proclaimed in 1910: 'Vessels used exclusively for fishing along the coast . . . are exempt from capture . . . '.

The efforts to protect civilian populations and their property took on renewed vigor after the Second World War through the Geneva Conventions of 1949. Consider Article 48 of Protocol No. 1 to the Geneva Conventions, adopted in 1977.

Article 48 enjoins the parties to a conflict to 'distinguish between the civilian population and combatants and between civilian objects and military objectives'. Their operations are to be directed 'only against military objectives'. Article 52 defines military objectives to be 'objects which, by their nature, location, purposes or use make an effective contribution to military action and whose total or partial destruction, capture or neutralization, in the circumstances ruling at the time, offers a definite military advantage'. Article 54 is entitled, 'Protection of Objects Indispensable to the Survival of the Civilian Population'. It states that '[s]tarvation of civilians as a method of warfare is prohibited'. Specifically, parties are prohibited from attacking or removing 'objects indispensable to the survival of the civilian population, such as foodstuffs . . . , for the specific purpose of denying them for their sustenance value to the civilian population or to the adverse Party . . . '. An exception is made for objects used by an adverse party as sustenance 'solely' for its armed forces or 'in direct support of military action'.

Consider some special characteristics of *The Paquete Habana*:

(1) Note the emphasis on the fact that the Supreme Court here sat as a *prize court* administering the law of nations, and note its references to the international character of the law maritime. Indeed, the Court almost assumed the role of an international tribunal, a consideration stressed in the excerpts from the scholar Calvo. Nonetheless, the Court's statement that 'international law is part of our law' and must be 'ascertained and administered by courts of justice' as often as 'questions of right' depending on it are presented for determination, has been drawn on in many later judicial decisions in the United States involving unrelated international law issues.

(2) An antiquarian aspect of the decision and period is that the naval personnel who captured the fishing vessels participated in the judicial proceedings, for at the time of the war captors were entitled to share in the proceeds of the sale of lawful prizes. That practice has ended and proceeds are now paid into the Treasury. 70A Stat. 475 (1956), 10 U.S.C.A. 7651–81.

(3) The Court looked to a relatively small number of countries for evidence of state practice, dominantly in Western Europe. It referred to Japan as 'the last state admitted into the rank of civilized nations'. Even at the start of the twentieth century, the world community creating international law was a small and relatively cohesive one; today's total of almost 200 states offers a striking contrast. Consider the multinational and multicultural character of an assembly of states today drafting a convention on the laws of war or a human rights convention, and imagine the range of states to which references might be made in a contemporary judicial opinion considering the customary law of international human rights.

COMMENT ON THE ROLE OF CUSTOM

The Supreme Court decision in *The Paquete Habana* raises basic questions about custom, which has been referred to as the oldest and original source of international law. Customary law remains indispensable to an adequate understanding of human rights law. It figures in many fora, from scholarship about the content of human rights law, to the broad debates about human rights within the United Nations, to the arguments of counsel before an international or national tribunal. As this chapter later indicates, the character of such argument today differs in significant respects from the character a century ago at the time of this decision.

Customary law refers to conduct, or the conscious abstention from certain conduct, of states that becomes in some measure a part of international legal order. By virtue of a developing custom, particular conduct may be considered to be permitted or obligatory in legal terms, or abstention from particular conduct may come to be considered a legal duty.

Consider the 1950 statement of a noted scholar describing the character of the state practice that can build a customary rule of international law: (1) 'concordant practice' by a number of states relating to a particular situation; (2) continuation of that practice 'over a considerable period of time'; (3) a conception that the practice is required by or consistent with international law; and (4) general acquiescence in that practice by other states.[2] Other scholars have contested some of these observations, and today many authorities contend that custom has long been a less rigid, more flexible and dynamic force in law-making.

Clause (b) of Article 38(1) states that the ICJ shall apply 'international custom, as evidence of a general practice accepted as law'. The phrase is as confusing as it is terse. Contemporary formulations of custom have overcome some difficulties in understanding it, but three of the terms there used remain contested and vexing: 'general', 'practice', and 'accepted as law'.

Section 102 of the *Restatement (Third), Foreign Relations Law of the United States*, presents a clearer formulation of customary law that draws broadly on scholarly, judicial and diplomatic sources. Many authorities on international law, certainly in the developed world and to varying degrees in the developing states as well, could accept that formulation as an accurate description and guide. After including custom as one of the sources of international law, the *Restatement* provides in clause (2): 'Customary international law results from a general and consistent practice of states followed by them from a sense of legal obligation'.

Each of these terms — 'general', 'consistent', 'practice', 'followed', and 'sense of legal obligation' — is defined in a particular way. For example, the *Restatement*'s comments on Section 102 say:

state practice includes diplomatic acts and instructions, public measures, and official statements, whether unilateral or in combination with other states in international organizations;

inaction may constitute state practice as when a state acquiesces in another state's conduct that affects its legal rights;

the state practice necessary may be of 'comparatively short duration';

a practice can be general even if not universally followed;

[2] M. Hudson, Working Paper on Article 24 of the Statute of the International Law Commission, UN Doc. A/CN.4/16, 3 March 1950, p. 5.

there is no 'precise formula to indicate how widespread a practice must be, but it should reflect wide acceptance among the states particularly involved in the relevant activity'.

The *Restatement* also addresses the question of the sense of legal obligation, or *opinio juris* in the conventional Latin phrase. For example, to form a customary rule, 'it must appear that the states follow the practice from a sense of legal obligation' (*opinio juris sive necessitatis*); hence a practice generally followed 'but which states feel legally free to disregard' cannot form such a rule; *opinio juris* need not be verbal or in some other way explicit, but may be inferred from acts or omissions. The comments also note that a state that is created after a practice has ripened into a rule of international law 'is bound by that rule'.

The *Restatement* (in the Reporter's Notes to Section 102) notes some of the perplexities in the concept of customary law:

> Each element in attempted definitions has raised difficulties. There have been philosophical debates about the very basis of the definition: how can practice build law? Most troublesome conceptually has been the circularity in the suggestion that law is built by practice based on a sense of legal obligation: how, it is asked, can there be a sense of legal obligation before the law from which the legal obligation derives has matured? Such conceptual difficulties, however, have not prevented acceptance of customary law essentially as here defined.

Consider the need to evaluate state practice with respect to (1) *opinio juris* and (2) the reaction of other states to a given state's conduct. Suppose that what is at issue in a case is a state's 'abstention' — for example, state X neither arrests nor asserts judicial jurisdiction over a foreign ambassador, which is one aspect of the law of diplomatic immunities that developed as customary law long before it was subjected to treaty regulation. During the period when this customary law was being developed, it would have been relevant to inquire why states generally did not arrest or prosecute foreign ambassadors. For example, assume that X asserted that it was not legally barred from such conduct but merely exercised its discretion, as a matter of expediency or courtesy, not to arrest or prosecute. Abstention by X coupled with such an explanation would not as readily have contributed to the formation of a customary legal rule. On the other hand, assume that a decision by the executive or courts of X not to arrest or assert judicial jurisdiction over the ambassador rested explicitly on the belief that international law required such abstention. Such practice of X would then constitute classic evidence of *opinio juris*.

Consider a polar illustration, where X acts in a way that immediately and adversely affects the interests of other states rather than abstains from conduct. Suppose that X imprisons without trial the ambassador from state Y, or imprisons many local residents who are citizens of Y. Surely it has not acted out of a sense of an international law *duty*. If it considered international law to be relevant at all, it may have concluded that its conduct was not prohibited by customary law, that customary law was here permissive. Or it may have decided that even if imprisonment was prohibited, it would nonetheless violate international law.

In this type of situation, the conception of *opinio juris* is less relevant, indeed irrelevant to the state's conduct. The state did not act out of duty. What does appear central to a determination of the legality of X's conduct is the *reaction* of other states — in this instance, particularly Y. That reaction of Y might be one of tacit acquiescence, thus tending to support the legality of X's conduct, or, more likely on the facts here given, Y might make a diplomatic protest or criticize X's action in other ways as a violation of international law. Action and reaction, acts by a state perhaps accompanied by claims of the act's legality, followed by reaction-responses by other states adversely affected by those acts, here constitute the critical components of the growth of a customary rule

These simplified illustrations suggest some of the typical dynamics of traditional customary international law. What is common to both illustrations — abstention from arrest, and arrest — is that the interests of at least two states were directly involved: at least the acting state X, and state Y. Of course states other than Y may well have taken an interest in X's action; after all, those states also have ambassadors and citizens in foreign countries. All of these possibilities are relevant to understanding *The Paquete Habana*.

Relationships between Treaties and Custom

Thus far we have considered custom independently of treaties (whose elements are described at p. 106, *infra*). But these two 'sources' or law-making processes of international law are complexly interrelated. For example, the question often arises of the extent to which a treaty should be read in the light of pre-existing custom. A treaty norm of great generality may naturally be interpreted against the background of relevant state practice or policies. In such contexts, the question whether the treaty is intended to be 'declaratory' of pre-existing customary law or to change that law may become relevant.

Moreover, treaties may give birth to rules of customary law. Assume a succession of bilateral treaties among many states, each containing a provision giving indigent aliens who are citizens of the other state party, the right to counsel at the government's expense in a criminal prosecution. The question may arise whether these bilateral treaties create a custom that would bind a state not party to any of them. Polar arguments will likely be developed by parties to such a dispute, for example: (1) The non-party state cannot be bound by those treaties since it has not consented. The series of bilateral treaties simply constitutes special exceptions to the traditional customary law that leaves the state's discretion unimpaired on this matter. Indeed, the necessity that many states saw for treaties underscores that no obligation existed under customary law. (2) A solution worked out among many states should be considered relevant or persuasive for the development of a customary law setting standards for all countries. Similarly, the network of treaties may have become dense enough, and state practice consistent with the treaty may have become general enough, to build a customary norm binding all states. Article 38 of the Vienna Convention signals rather than resolves this issue by stating that nothing in its prior articles providing generally that a treaty does not create obligations for a third state precludes a rule set forth in a treaty from becoming binding on a third state 'as a customary rule of international law, recognized as such'.

In contemporary international law, broadly ratified multilateral treaties are more likely than a series of bilateral treaties to generate the argument that treaty rules have become customary law binding nonparties. Some of the principal human rights treaties, for example, have from 150 to 190 state parties from all parts of the world. Of course, one must distinguish between substantive norms in multilateral treaties that are alleged to constitute customary law that binds non-parties, and institutional arrangements created by the treaties in which parties have agreed, for example, to submit reports or disputes to a treaty organ.

AKEHURST'S MODERN INTRODUCTION TO INTERNATIONAL LAW

Peter Malanczuk (7th revised edn. 1997), at 39

[The following excerpts develop some themes about custom in the preceding Comment.]

...

Where to Look for Evidence of Customary Law

The main evidence of customary law is to be found in the actual practice of states, and a rough idea of a state's practice can be gathered from published material — from newspaper reports of actions taken by states, and from statements made by government spokesmen to Parliament, to the press, at international conferences and at meetings of international organizations; and also from a state's laws and judicial decisions, because the legislature and the judiciary form part of a state just as much as the executive does. At times the Foreign Ministry of a state may publish extracts from its archives; for instance, when a state goes to war or becomes involved in a particular bitter dispute, it may publish documents to justify itself in the eyes of the world. But the vast majority of the material which would tend to throw light on a state's practice concerning questions of international law — correspondence with other states, and the advice which each state receives from its own legal advisers — is normally not published; or, to be more precise, it is only recently that efforts have been made to publish digests of the practice followed by different states....

...

The Problem of Repetition

It has sometimes been suggested that a single precedent is not enough to establish a customary rule, and that there must be a degree of repetition over a period of time....

In the *Nicaragua* case [*Nicaragua v. US (Merits)*, ICJ Rep. 1986, para. 186] the ICJ held:

> It is not to be expected that in the practice of States the application of the rules in question should have been perfect, in the sense that States should have refrained, with complete consistency, from the use of force or from intervention in each

> other's internal affairs. The Court does not consider that, for a rule to be established as customary, the corresponding practice must be in absolutely rigorous conformity with the rule. In order to deduce the existence of customary rules, the Court deems it sufficient that the conduct of States should, in general, be consistent with such rules, and that instances of State conduct inconsistent with a given rule should generally have been treated as breaches of that rule, not as indications of the recognition of a new rule.

In sum, *major* inconsistencies in the practice (that is, a large amount of practice which goes against the 'rule' in question) prevent the creation of a customary rule...

There remains the question of what constitutes 'general' practice. This much depends on the circumstances of the case and on the rule at issue. 'General' practice is a relative concept and cannot be determined in the abstract. It should include the conduct of all states, which can participate in the formulation of the rule or the interests of which are specially affected. 'A practice can be general even if it is not universally accepted; there is no precise formula to indicate how widespread a practice must be, but it should reflect wide acceptance among the states particularly involved in the relevant activity'....

What is certain is that general practice does not require the unanimous practice of all states or other international subjects. This means that a state can be bound by the general practice of other states even against its wishes if it does not protest against the emergence of the rule and continues persistently to do so (persistent objector). Such instances are not frequent and the rule also requires that states are sufficiently aware of the emergence of the new practice and law....

...

The Psychological Element in the Formation of Customary Law (opinio iuris)

...

There is clearly something artificial about trying to analyse the psychology of collective entities such as states. Indeed, the modern tendency is not to look for direct evidence of a state's psychological convictions, but to infer *opinio iuris* indirectly from the actual behaviour of states. Thus, official statements are not required; *opinio iuris* may be gathered from acts or omissions....

...

Customary law has a built-in mechanism of change. If states are agreed that a rule should be changed, a new rule of customary international law based on the new practice of states can emerge very quickly; thus the law on outer space developed very quickly after the first artificial satellite was launched....

...

Universality and the Consensual Theory of International Law

... Can the opposition of a single state prevent the creation of a customary rule? If so, there would be very few rules, because state practice differs from state to state on many topics. On the other hand, to allow the majority to create a rule against the wishes of the minority would lead to insuperable difficulties. How large must the majority be? In counting the majority, must equal weight be given to the practice of

Guatemala and that of the United States? If, on the other hand, some states are to be regarded as more important than others, on what criteria is importance to be based? Population? Area? Wealth? Military power? . . .

. . .

. . . The International Court of Justice has emphasized that a claimant state which seeks to rely on a customary rule must prove that the rule has become binding on the defendant state. The obvious way of doing this is to show that the defendant state has recognized the rule in its own state practice (although recognition for this purpose may amount to no more than failure to protest when other states have applied the rule in cases affecting the defendant's interests). But it may not be possible to find any evidence of the defendant's attitude towards the rule, and so there is a second — and more frequently used — way of proving that the rule is binding on the defendant: by showing that the rule is accepted by other states. In these circumstances the rule in question is binding on the defendant state, unless the defendant state can show that it has expressly and consistently rejected the rule since the earliest days of the rule's existence; dissent expressed after the rule has become well established is too late to prevent the rule binding the dissenting state. . . .

The problem of the 'persistent objector', however, has recently attracted more attention in the literature. Can a disagreeing state ultimately and indefinitely remain outside of new law accepted by the large majority of states? Do emerging rules of *ius cogens* require criteria different to norms of lesser significance? Such questions are far from settled at this point in time. . . .

. . .

Ius cogens

Some of the early writers on international law said that a treaty would be void if it was contrary to morality or to certain (unspecified) basic principles of international law. The logical basis for this rule was that a treaty could not override natural law. With the decline of the theory of natural law, the rule was largely forgotten, although some writers continued to pay lip-service to it.

Recently there has been a tendency to revive the rule, although it is no longer based on natural law . . . The technical name now given to the basic principles of international law, which states are not allowed to contract out of, is 'peremptory norms of general international law', otherwise known as *ius cogens*.

Article 53 of the Convention on the Law of Treaties provides as follows:

> A treaty is void if, at the time of its conclusion, it conflicts with a peremptory norm of general international law. For the purposes of the present Convention, a peremptory norm of general international law is a norm accepted and recognized by the international community of States as a whole as a norm from which no derogation is permitted and which can be modified only by a subsequent norm of general international law having the same character.

What is said about treaties being void would also probably apply equally to local custom. . . .

Although cautiously expressed to apply only 'for the purposes of the present Convention', the definition of a 'peremptory norm' is probably valid for all purposes. The definition is more skilful than appears at first sight. A rule cannot become a peremptory norm unless it is 'accepted and recognized [as such] by the international community of states *as a whole*' . . . It must find acceptance and recognition by the international community at large and cannot be imposed upon a significant minority of states. Thus, an overwhelming majority of states is required, cutting across cultural and ideological differences.

At present very few rules pass this test. Many rules have been suggested as candidates. Some writers suggest that there is considerable agreement on the prohibition of the use of force, of genocide, slavery, of gross violations of the right of people to self-determination, and of racial discrimination. Others would include the prohibition on torture. . . .

. . .

OSCAR SCHACHTER, INTERNATIONAL LAW IN THEORY AND PRACTICE

(1991) at 5

Ch. I. The Nature and Reality of International Law

. . .

The Uses of Law and the Role of Power

In discussing the complexity of international law and its relative autonomy, we have more or less assumed its 'reality'. We did so while recognizing that it is a product of political and social forces, that it is dependent on behaviour and that it is an instrument to meet changing ends and values. All these aspects give rise to questions as to the reality of international law. These questions are epitomized in the not uncommon view that we cannot have genuine and effective law in a society of sovereign States dominated by power and self-interest. . . .

One way of approaching the issues is to consider the views of the sceptics of international law — those who doubt, for one reason or another, that international law can contribute significantly to international order. Four kinds of sceptical positions merit our attention. The first emphasizes the dominance of power over law. The second asserts the dependence of international law on the will of national States. A third position points to the deep divisions of belief, aims and culture in international society and questions whether a common authoritative legal system is realizable. The fourth sceptical position lays stress on the fragility of a legal system that lacks centralized institutions to determine authoritatively what the law is and to enforce it. I will discuss the reasoning behind these positions and comment on their validity.

The thesis that law is subordinate to power is commonly referred to as a 'realist' (or 'realpolitik') point of view. Power, in this context, refers to the ability of a State to impose its will on others or, more broadly, to control outcomes contested by others. The components of power are military, economic, political and psychological; international society exhibits, in striking degree, an unequal distribution of these components of power. The unequal distribution of power is a pervasive and dominating element in the relations of States. States strive to augment their power, perceiving power sometimes as an end in itself and more commonly as a means to attain more freedom of action and other objectives. For the realist, the crucial importance of power and the pursuit of self-interest by States make it virtually inevitable that the law — both in its creation and application — should yield to those determinants. Law may play a subordinate role as an aid to stability, a 'gentle civilizer of events' but it cannot be relied on 'to suppress the chaotic and dangerous aspirations of governments'. Political theorists reach similar conclusions in their analysis of the State system. From a 'structural' standpoint (as they sometimes put it), a system based on the sovereignty of States is a system of 'co-ordinate relations', in which formal authority is decentralized. While this fundamental condition does not rule out the use of a legal system to provide a required degree of order and predictability, the individual States in the last analysis are not subordinated to any superior authority. Hence the effective limits on their action derive from their own perception of national interest and the countervailing power of others. In consequence, as Raymond Aron has put it, international society is 'an anarchical order of power in which might makes right'.

These general theoretical conclusions accord with the widespread popular belief that in international relations power rather than law governs . . . The fact that legal arguments are almost always made by the alleged violators only tends to add to the cynicism about law since such self-serving legal arguments are not submitted to adjudication or other third-party determinations. The absence of compulsory or generally accepted judicial settlement of international disputes is taken as compelling evidence that the law is not taken seriously and hence that 'power politics' prevails.

. . .

We need to consider not only that States break the rules but also that they generally conform to them even against their immediate interest. Nobody denies that States, powerful and not so powerful, observe international law most of the time. There are various reasons why they do so. Much compliance can be attributed to institutionalized habit; officials follow the rules as a matter of practice, and in countless decisions they look to treaty obligations, to precedents that evidence custom and to general principles of law expounded in treatises and manuals. Many of the decisions involve no apparent clash of law and self-interest but numerous cases arise in which a government refrains from action (or non-action) that it would otherwise take if there were no legal grounds limiting its discretion. This is most evident when specific treaties apply — say, of commerce, navigation, reciprocal exchanges — but it is also true of the many cases covered by the unwritten customary rules applicable to many areas of inter-State relations. . . .

It is of course also true that cases arise in which officials do have to consider whether the law should be applied when it appears to be in the immediate interest of the government not to do so. The responses to such situations depend on a variety of considerations. Most obviously, governments will weigh a possible breach by them against their interest in reciprocal observance by the other party. They will also consider the likelihood of retaliation and other self-help measures by that party.

Nor would they ignore the negative consequences of a reputation for repudiating their obligations. In many countries, officials would be sensitive to anticipated criticism by influential domestic leaders or groups who place high value on the country's reputation for legality generally or on observance of the particular obligations involved. The possibility of judicial enforcement in domestic tribunals may in some cases serve as a deterrent to non-compliance. Remedies by the aggrieved State may also be available under some circumstances in international mechanisms, perhaps through arbitral or judicial means or through loss of benefits under treaty régimes.... Violations, in short, are rarely cost-free even to powerful States.

...

The Dependency of International Law on the Will of States

... If States have no superior authority and their relations are 'co-ordinate', rather than hierarchical, does it not follow that a State is bound only by the legal rules to which it agrees to submit?...

These questions are as old as international law itself and have given rise to considerable theoretical writing. The idea that the will of States is the basis of international law and hence that the law is dependent on the consent of States is referred to in international law theory as 'voluntarism' or 'consensualism'. Voluntarism is not only a theory held by academic scholars. It is also an expression of the strongly held conception of State sovereignty dominant in most governments....

The general idea that international law rests on the will of the States has been applied in various ways, with quite different significance. It has been applied to international law as a whole (particularly customary law) and to particular rules of international law. In regard to the latter, the requirement of consent has been directed both to the creation of new rules of law and to their use in particular cases. We will sort out the questions raised in each category by considering the following five propositions:

(1) international law as a general system is accepted by all States and hence is an expression of their will:

...

(3) the creation of a new rule or repeal of an old rule of customary law requires the consent of States;

(4) a State which has not consented to a customary law rule is free at any time to reject its application to the State;

(5) any State is free to exercise its sovereign right to reject the application of a customary law rule on the ground that it is not in accordance with that State's will.

(I should note that the term customary law rule as used above is intended to refer not only to rules in the narrow sense of that term but also to principles, standards, practices, concepts and procedures that are considered as legal grounds for asserting rights and obligations.)

(1) ... [E]ven if it is true that 'membership' in any society presupposes adherence to its basic rules (*ubi societas, ibi ius*), it is not inconsistent with the fact that States

accept the particular system of international law now in force. At least in that sense, the system rests on their consent just as a domestic law system may be said to rest basically on the consent of the people. Without their general consent, there could be no durable operative system of law. Although voluntarism in this form may seem to be a 'weak' version, it is important to recognize that the system of law has in general been accepted by the community of States. Acceptance of the system is in itself a plausible basis for the obligation to abide by the particular rules valid in that system.

...

(3) The third proposition is that the creation of a new rule or repeal of an existing rule requires the consent of States. Inasmuch as customary law arises through uniformities of State conduct accompanied by the belief of States that they are conforming to what amounts to a legal obligation, the States that participated in such conduct and recognize the obligation created by it can reasonably be considered to have consented to the rule thus established....

... For our present purpose, it is enough to note the broad agreement among authorities that general custom does not require universal consent of all States....

(4) The most significant test of voluntarist-consensualist theory is raised by the fourth proposition — namely that a State is not bound by a rule to which it has not consented. The proposition requires critical analysis. Non-consenting States divide into two categories: (1) States that have manifested neither acceptance nor objection: (2) States which have openly objected to the rule in general or to its specific application to the objecting State. If we accept the principle that general custom does not require universal consent it follows that the assent of a particular State is not necessary for a general rule to come into being and to bind all States...

A special problem is presented by the second category of non-consenting States — those that have openly manifested their dissent to a customary rule. One might ask why a dissenting State should be able to avoid a general customary rule if universal consent is not considered necessary and nonassenting States are considered bound.... Even if this is accepted as law, it is subject to some limitations...

... It may be questioned whether the exception for a dissenting State would apply to a new principle of customary law regarded as fundamental or of major importance.... The issue cannot reasonably be decided solely by reference to voluntarist theory. It would be germane to consider a variety of factors including the circumstances of adoption of the new principle, the reasons for its importance to the generality of States, the grounds of dissent, and the relevant position of the dissenting States....

(5) The fifth proposition constitutes the 'strongest' use of voluntarist theory. It would allow a State to reject the application of a customary rule to it simply on the ground that it was contrary to the State's present will.... It would amount to a denial of customary law....

...

Significantly, no State appears to claim a right of this kind although some have interpreted self-defence broadly... or have turned to general notions of sovereignty and independence to justify departing from rules that are deemed against their vital interest.

...

NOTE

Compare with Schachter's views about the relationship between law and force the following observations of Stanley Hoffmann, in 'The Study of International Law and the Theory of International Relations', 1963 Proc. Am. Soc. Int. L. 26:

> It is however essential for the social scientist to understand that law is not merely a policy among others in the hands of statesmen, but that it is a tool with very special characteristics and roles . . . Most important is the fact that law has a distinct solemnity of effects: it is a normative instrument that creates rights and duties. Consequently it has a function that is both symbolic and conservative; it enshrines, elevates, consecrates the interests or ideas it embodies. We understand, thus, why law is an important stake in the contests of nations. What makes international law so special a tool for states is this solemnity of effects, rather than the fact that its norms express common interests; for this is far too simple: some legal instruments such as peace treaties reflect merely the temporary, forced convergence of deeply antagonistic policies. A situation of dependence or of superiority that is just a fact of life can be reversed through political action, but once it is solemnly cast in legal form, the risks of action designed to change the situation are much higher: law is a form of policy that changes the stakes, and often 'escalates' the intensity, of political contests; it is a constraint comparable to force in its effects.

MARTTI KOSKENNIEMI, THE PULL OF THE MAINSTREAM

88 Mich. L. Rev. 1946 (1990)

. . . [I]nternational lawyers have had difficulty accounting for rules of international law that do not emanate from the consent of the states against which they are applied. In fact, most modern lawyers have assumed that international law is not really binding unless it can be traced to an agreement or some other meeting of wills between two or more sovereign states. Once the idea of a natural law is discarded, it seems difficult to justify an obligation that is not voluntarily assumed.

. . .

The matter is particularly important in regard to norms intended to safeguard basic human rights and fundamental freedoms. If the only states bound to respect such rights and freedoms are the states that have formally become parties to the relevant instruments . . . then many important political values would seem to lack adequate protection. It is inherently difficult to accept the notion that states are legally bound not to engage in genocide, for example, only if they have ratified and not formally denounced the 1948 Genocide Convention. Some norms seem so basic, so important, that it is more than slightly artificial to argue that states are legally bound to comply with them simply because there exists an agreement between them to that effect, rather than because, in the words of the International

Court of Justice (ICJ), noncompliance would 'shock[] the conscience of mankind' and be contrary to 'elementary considerations of humanity'.

. . .

. . . Although it seems clear that not all international law can be based upon agreement, it seems much less clear what else, then, it may be founded upon. . . . A Grotian lawyer would not, of course, perceive a great difficulty. He would simply say that some norms exist by force of natural reason or social necessity. Such an argument, however, is not open to a modern lawyer or court, much less an international court, established for the settlement of disputes between varying cultures, varying traditions, and varying conceptions of reason and justice. Such conceptions seem to be historically and contextually conditioned, so that imposing them on a nonconsenting state seems both political and unjustifiable as such.

It is, I believe, for this reason — the difficulty of justifying conceptions of natural justice in modern society — that lawyers have tended to relegate into 'custom' all those important norms that cannot be supported by treaties. In this way, they might avoid arguing from an essentially naturalistic — and thus suspect — position. 'Custom' may seem both less difficult to verify and more justifiable to apply than abstract maxims of international justice.

. . .

Professor Meron [an authority on humanitarian law whose book is here under review by Koskenniemi] follows this strategy. Although he accepts the category of 'general principles' as a valid way to argue about human rights and humanitarian norms, he does not use this argumentative tack. Nor does he examine whether, or to what extent, such norms might be valid as natural law. His reason for so doing is clearly stated: he wishes to 'utilize irreproachable legal methods' to enhance 'the credibility of the norms' for which he argues. The assumption here is that to argue in terms of general principles or natural justice is to engage in a political debate and to fall victim to bias and subjectivism. Following his rationalistic credo, Meron hopes to base human rights and humanitarian norms on something more tangible, something that jurists can look at through a distinct (objective, scientific) method and thus ground their conclusions in a more acceptable way — a way that would also better justify their application against nonconsenting states.

The starting point — hoping to argue nontreaty-based human rights and humanitarian norms as custom — however, does not fare too well in Professor Meron's careful analysis of pertinent case law and juristic opinion. He accepts the orthodox 'two-element theory' of custom (*i.e.*, for custom to exist, there must be both material practice to that effect and the practice must have been motivated by a belief that it is required by law (p. 3)), yet case law contains little to actually support such a theory, although passages paying lip service to it are abundant. . . .

. . .

. . . [The rest of material practice and the *opinio juris*] is useless, first, because the interpretation of 'state behavior' or 'state will' is not an automatic operation but involves the choice and use of conceptual matrices that are controversial and that usually allow one to argue either way. But it is also, and more fundamentally, useless because . . . it is really our certainty that genocide or torture is illegal that allows us to understand state behavior and to accept or reject its legal message, not state behavior itself that allows us to understand that these practices are prohibited by law. It seems to me that if we are uncertain of the latter fact, then there is really little in this world we can feel confident about.

In other words, finding juristic evidence (a precedent, a habitual behaviour, a legal doctrine) to support such a conclusion adds little or nothing to our reasons for adopting it. To the contrary, it contains the harmful implication that it is *only* because this evidence is available that we can justifiably reach our conclusion. It opens the door for disputing the conclusion by disputing the presence of the evidence, or for requiring the same evidence in support of some other equally compelling conclusion, when that evidence might not be so readily available.

It is, of course, true that people are uncertain about right and wrong. The past two hundred years since the Enlightenment and the victory of the principle of arbitrary value have done nothing to teach us about how to know these things or how to cope with our strong moral intuitions. But one should not pretend that this uncertainty will vanish if only one is methodologically 'rigorous'. If the development of the human sciences has taught us anything during its short history, it is that the effort to replace our loss of faith in theories about the right and the good with an absolute faith in our ability to understand human life as a matter of social 'facts' has been a failure. We remain just as unable to derive norms from the facts of state behavior as Hume was. And we are just as compelled to admit that everything we know about norms which are embedded in such behavior is conditioned by an anterior — though at least in some respects largely shared — criterion of what is right and good for human life.

...

QUESTIONS

1. Suppose that an international tribunal rather than US courts had heard the controversy in *The Paquete Habana*, and had sought to decide it within the framework of Article 38 of the Statute of the International Court of Justice. Assuming that this tribunal came to the same conclusion, are any observations in the Supreme Court's opinion likely to have been omitted or changed by such an international tribunal? Which observations? Suppose, for example, that the historical record was identical with that reported by the Supreme Court except for the fact that the United States had consistently objected to this rule of exemption and had often refused to follow it.

2. Does the method of the Court in 'ascertaining' the customary rule appear consistent with some of the observations about the nature of custom and the processes for its development in the preceding readings? Consider, for example, how the Supreme Court deals with:

   (i) the issue of *opinio juris*, and its relation to comity, grace, concession or discretion;

   (ii) the relevance of treaties, as expressing a customary norm or as special rules (*lex specialis*) negating the existence of a custom; and

   (iii) the departure from the rule of exemption during the Napoleonic wars, as a temporary interruption of or as aborting an emerging custom.

About which of these three aspects of the opinion does the dissenting opinion differ? How would you have argued against the Court's resolution of these three aspects?

3. How do you assess Koskenniemi's argument about customary law and natural law? How would you make the argument that the decision in *The Paquete Habana* in fact supports Koskenniemi's view of what underlies argument about customary law and what indeed should be brought to the forefront of argument.

QUESTION

Advocates acting on behalf of prisoners sentenced to death have argued in a number of countries like the United States that the death penalty is now barred by customary international law. Based on the materials in Chapter 1(B), and in light of the preceding discussions of custom, how would you develop the argument that customary international law bars capital punishment? How would you make the opposing argument? In developing your arguments, take account of the evidence of state practice and of *opinio juris*, and of the major difference between (1) ascertaining customary law through interaction between two states or between citizens of one state and the government of another state in a case like *The Paquete Habana*, and (2) ascertaining customary international law in a death penalty case.

ADDITIONAL READING

S. Ratner and A.-M. Slaughter (eds.), 'Symposium on Method in International Law', 93 Am. J. Int. L. 291 (1999); A. Cassese, *International Law* (2nd edn. 2004), M. Shaw, *International Law* (5th edn. 2003); M. Koskenniemi, *Apology and Utopia* (1989, re-issued 2005); C. Reus-Smit (ed.), *The Politics of International Law* (2004); I. Shearer, *Starke's International Law* (11th edn. 1994); B. Simma *et al.* (eds.), *The Charter of the United Nations: A Commentary* (2nd edn. 2002); J. Klabbers, *An Introduction to International Institutional Law* (2002); J.-M. Henckaerts, Jean-Marie and L. Doswold-Beck (eds.), *Customary International Humanitarian Law* (3 vols. 2005).

B. STATE RESPONSIBILITY, GENERAL PRINCIPLES AND NATURAL LAW

COMMENT ON THE LAW OF STATE RESPONSIBILITY

The *Chattin* case described below was decided under a 1923 General Claims Convention between the United States and Mexico, 43 Stat. 1730, T.S. No. 678. That treaty provided that designated claims against Mexico of US citizens (and vice versa) for losses or damages suffered by persons or by their properties that (in the case of the US citizens) had been presented to the US Government for interposition with Mexico and that had remained unsettled 'shall be submitted to a Commission consisting of three members for decision in accordance with the principles of international law, justice and equity'. Each state was to appoint one member, and the presiding third commissioner was to be selected by mutual agreement (and by stipulated procedures failing agreement).

These arbitrations grew out of and further developed the law of state responsibility for injuries to aliens, a branch of international law that was among the important predecessors to contemporary human rights law. That body of law addressed only certain kinds of conflicts — not including, for example, conflicts originating in the first instance in a dispute between a claimant state (X) and a respondent state (Y). Thus it did not cover a dispute, say, based on a claim by X that Y had violated international law by its invasion of X's territory or by its imprisonment of X's ambassador.

Rather, the claims between states that were addressed by the law of state responsibility for injuries to aliens grew out of disputes arising in the first instance between a citizen-national of X and the government of Y. For example, respondent state Y allegedly imprisoned a citizen of claimant state X without hearing or trial, or seized property belonging to citizens of X — allegations which, if true, could show violations of international law. Note that these illustrations involve action leading to injury of X's citizens by governmental officials or organs (executive, legislative, judicial) of Y. The law of state responsibility required that the conduct complained of be that of the state or, in less clear and more complex situations, be ultimately attributable to the state.

In the normal case, the citizen of X would seek a remedy within Y, probably through its judiciary — release from jail, return of the seized property or compensation for it. Indeed, before invoking the aid of his own government, the citizen of X would generally be required under the relevant treaty to pursue such a path, to 'exhaust local remedies'. But that path could prove to be fruitless, because of lack of recourse to Y's judiciary, because that judiciary was corrupt, or because of Y's law adverse to the citizen of X that would certainly be applied by its judiciary. In such circumstances, the injured person may turn to his own government X for diplomatic protection.

The 1924 decision of the Permanent Court of International Justice in the *Mavrommatis Palestine Concessions (Jurisdiction)* case, P.C.I.J., Ser. A, No. 2, gave classic expression to such diplomatic protection. It pointed out that when a state took up the cause of one of its subjects (citizens-nationals) in a dispute originating between that subject and respondent state, the dispute:

> entered upon a new phase; it entered the domain of international law, and became a dispute between two States. . . . It is an elementary principle of international law that a State is entitled to protect its subjects, when injured by acts contrary to international law committed by another State, from whom they have been unable to obtain satisfaction through the ordinary channels. By taking up the case of one of its subjects and by resorting to diplomatic action or international judicial proceedings on his behalf, a State is in reality asserting its own rights — its right to ensure, in the person of its subjects, respect for the rules of international law.

Precisely what action to take, what form of diplomatic protection to extend, lay within the discretion of the claimant state. If it decided to intervene and thereby make the claim its own, it might espouse the claim through informal conversations with the respondent state, or make a formal diplomatic protest, or exert various economic and political pressures to encourage a settlement (extending at times to military intervention), or, if these strategies failed, have recourse to international tribunals. Such recourse was infrequent. International tribunals to whose jurisdiction states had consented for the resolution of disputes between them were rare. Moreover, states were reluctant to raise controversies between their citizens and foreign states to the level of interstate conflict before an international tribunal except where a clear national interest gave reason to do so.

An arbitral tribunal to which the claimant state turned may have been created by agreement between the disputing states to submit to it designated types of disputes. That agreement may have been part of a general arbitration treaty (which after the Second World War found scant use) covering a broad range of potential disputes between the two parties. Or it may have been a so-called 'compromissory clause' (*compromis*) in a treaty dealing with a specific subject that bound the parties to submit to arbitration disputes that might arise under that treaty. Of course, two states could always agree to submit specified disputes to arbitration, as in the 1923 General Claims Convention between the United States and Mexico under which *Chattin* was decided.

In 1921, *ad hoc* arbitral tribunals were first supplemented by an international court, the Permanent Court of International Justice provided for in the Covenant of the League of Nations. Again, problems of states' consent to jurisdiction and states' reluctance to start interstate litigation limited the role of that court (and indeed the role of its successor, the International Court of Justice created under the Charter of the United Nations) in developing the law of state responsibility (or, today, in developing the international law of human rights).

The growth in the nineteenth and twentieth centuries of the law of state responsibility for injury to aliens was the product of and evidenced by a range of state interactions — diplomatic protests and responses, negotiated settlements, arbitral decisions — and the writings of scholars. Before the Second World War, there was little attempt at formal codification or creative development of this body of law through treaties — that is, treaties spelling out the content of what international law required of a state in its treatment of aliens.

As it developed, the international law of state responsibility reflected the more intense identification of the individual with his state (or later, the identification of the corporation with the state of its incorporation, or of most of its shareholders) that accompanied the nationalistic trends of that era. This body of law would not have developed so vigorously but for Western colonialism and economic imperialism that reached their zenith during this period. Transnational business operations centred in Europe, and later in the United States as well, penetrated those regions now known as the Third World or developing countries. The protection afforded aliens under international law had obvious importance for the foreign operations of transnational corporations that were often directed by foreign nationals.

In such circumstances, given the links between the success and wealth of corporations in their foreign ventures and national wealth and power, the security of the person and property of a national or corporation operating in a foreign part of the world became a concern of his or its government. That concern manifested itself in the vigorous assertion of diplomatic protection and in the enhanced activity of arbitral tribunals. In the late nineteenth and early twentieth centuries, some such arbitrations occurred under the pressure of actual or threatened military force by the claimant states, particularly against Latin American governments.

A statement in an arbitral proceeding in 1924 by Max Huber, a Judge of the Permanent Court of International Justice, cogently expressed some basic principles of that era's consensus (among states of the developed world) about the law of state responsibility:[3]

> ... It is true that the large majority of writers have a marked tendency to limit the responsibility of the State. But their theories often have political inspiration and represent a natural reaction against unjustified interventions in the affairs of certain nations....
>
> ... The conflicting interest with respect to the problem of compensation of aliens are, on the one hand, the interest of a State in exercising its public power in its own territory without interference or control of any nature by foreign States and, on the other hand, the interest of the State in seeing the rights of its nationals established in foreign countries respected and well protected.
>
> Three principles are hardly debatable:
>
> ...
>
> (2) In general, a person established in a foreign country is subject to the territorial legislation for the protection of his person and his property, under the same conditions as nationals of that country.
>
> (3) A State whose national established in another State is deprived of his rights has a right to intervene *if the injury constitutes a violation of international law*....
>
> ... The territorial character of sovereignty is so essential a trait of contemporary public law that foreign intervention in relationships between a territorial State and individuals subject to its sovereignty can be allowed only in extraordinary cases....
>
> ... This right of intervention has been claimed by all States; only its limits are under discussion. By denying this right, one would arrive at intolerable results: international law would become helpless in the face of injustices tantamount to the negation of human personality, for that is the subject which every denial of justice touches.
>
> ... No police or other administration of justice is perfect, and it is doubtless necessary to accept, even in the best administered countries, a considerable margin of tolerance. However, the restrictions thus placed on the right of a State to intervene to protect its nationals assume that the general security in the country of residence does not fall below a certain standard....

How was it determined whether, in Huber's words, an 'injury' to an alien 'constitutes a violation of international law', or whether the administration of justice in a

[3] Judge Huber delivered these remarks in his role as a Reporter (in effect, arbitrator) in a dispute between Great Britain and Spain. British Claims in the Spanish Zone of Morocco, 2 U.N.R.I.A.A. 615, 639 (1924).

given country fell below 'a certain standard'? To what materials would, for example, an arbitral tribunal turn for help in defining the content of that standard? What types of argument and justifications would inform the development of this body of international law? Decisions in the many arbitrations, including the *Chattin* case below, shed light on these questions.

COMMENT ON THE *CHATTIN* CASE

The *Chattin* case [4] is among the more interesting of the arbitral decisions. Chattin, a US citizen, was a conductor on a railroad in Mexico from 1908 to 1910, when he was arrested for embezzlement of fares. His trial was consolidated with those of several other Americans and Mexicans who had been arrested on similar charges. In February 1911 he was convicted and sentenced to two years' imprisonment. His appeal was rejected in July 1911. In the meantime the inhabitants of Mazatlán, during a political uprising, threw open the doors of the jail and Chattin escaped to the United States. In asserting Chattin's claims, the United States argued that the arrest was illegal, that Chattin was mistreated while in prison, that his trial was unreasonably delayed, and that there were irregularities in the trial. It claimed that Chattin suffered injuries worth $50,000 in compensation.

Of the three members of the Claims Commission, one came from the United States (Nielsen) and another from Mexico (MacGregor). Each wrote an opinion. Excerpts from the opinion of the third Commissioner follow:

COMMISSIONER VAN VOLLENHOVEN

This opinion examined a range of complaints about the conduct of the trial. The Commissioner gave particular attention to three such complaints.

(1) Chattin claimed that he had not been duly informed of the charges. The opinion concluded that this claim was 'proven by the record, and to a painful extent'. The principal complainant, an American manager of the railroad company, made full statements to the Court 'without ever being confronted with the accused and his colleagues', and indeed was 'allowed to submit to the Court a series of anonymous written accusations . . . It is not shown that the confrontation between Chattin and his accusers amounted to anything like an effort on the Judge's part to find out the truth'. Nonetheless Chattin was generally aware of the details of the investigation.

(2) Van Vollenhoven dismissed Chattin's charge that witnesses were not sworn as irrelevant, 'as Mexican law does not require an "oath" (it is satisfied with a solemn promise, *protesta*, to tell the truth), nor do international standards of civilization'.

(3) Van Vollenhoven found the charge that the hearings in open court lasted only five minutes was proven by the record. That hearing was 'a pure formality', in

[4] *United States of America (B.E. Chattin) v. United Mexican States*, United States-Mexican Claims Commission, 1927. Opinions of Commissioners under the 1923 Convention between the United States and Mexico, 1927, at 422, 4 U.N.R.I.A.A. 282.

which written documents were confirmed and defence counsel said only a word or two. The opinion concludes that 'the whole of the proceedings discloses a most astonishing lack of seriousness on the part of the Court', and cites instances where the judge failed to follow leads or examine certain people. Excerpts follow:

> Neither during the investigations nor during the hearings in open court was any such thing as an oral examination or cross-examination of any importance attempted. It seems highly improbable that the accused have been given a real opportunity during the hearings in open court, freely to speak for themselves. It is not for the Commission to endeavor to reach from the record any conviction as to the innocence or guilt of Chattin and his colleagues; but even in case they were guilty, the Commission would render a bad service to the Government of Mexico if it failed to place the stamp of its disapproval and even indignation on a criminal procedure so far below international standards of civilization as the present one.

Nonetheless, the opinion found the record sufficient to warrant a conviction of Chattin and rejected a charge that the court was biased against American citizens, since four Mexicans were also convicted.

> . . . Since this is a case of alleged responsibility of Mexico for injustice committed by its judiciary, it is necessary to inquire whether the treatment of Chattin amounts even to an outrage, to bad faith, to wilful neglect of duty, or to an insufficiency of governmental action recognizable by every unbiased man . . . and the answer here again can only be in the affirmative.

Taking all these factors into account, the opinion allowed damages in the sum of $5,000.

COMMISSIONER NIELSEN (CONCURRING)

Nielsen observed that counsel for Mexico had stressed that during the period of investigation a Mexican judge was at liberty to receive anything placed before him, including anonymous accusations. Although European procedure allowed 'a similar measure of latitude' for judges, there was one essential difference: after proceedings before a judge of investigation, the case is taken over by another judge who conducts the actual trial. Thus, said Nielsen, under the French law of the period

> the preliminary examination does not serve as a foundation for the verdict of the judge who decided as to the guilt of the accused. The examination allows the examining judge to determine whether there is ground for formal charge, and in case there is, to decide upon the jurisdiction . . . [The trial of the accused] is before a judge whose functions are of a more judicial character than those of a judge of investigation employing inquisitorial methods in the nature of those used by a prosecutor. . . .

Nielsen, 'having further in mind the peculiarly delicate character of an examination of judicial proceedings by an international tribunal, as well as the practical difficulties inherent in such examination', concluded that the Commission should render a small award based on the mistreatment of Chattin during the period of investigation.

COMMISSIONER MACGREGOR (DISSENTING)

In his dissent, Commissioner MacGregor referred to the charge that the trial proper lasted only five minutes, 'implying thereby that there was really no trial and that Chattin was convicted without being heard'. This was an 'erroneous criticism which arises from the difference between Anglo-Saxon procedure and that of other countries'. Mexican criminal procedure consisted of two parts: preliminary proceedings (sumario) and plenary proceedings (plenario). In the sumario, evidence is gathered, investigations occur, the judge or defendant can cross examine. When the judge concludes that there are sufficient facts to establish a case, the sumario ends as the record is given to all parties to be certain that they do not request more testimony and so that they can make final pleas. Then a public hearing (plenario) is held 'in which the parties very often do not have anything further to allege'. That hearing is formal, and serves little new function. Such occurred in the *Chattin* case.

> In view of the foregoing explanation, I believe that it becomes evident that the charge, that there was no trial proper, can not subsist, for, in Mexican procedure, it is not a question of a trial in the sense of Anglo-Saxon law, which requires that the case be always heard in plenary proceedings, before a jury, adducing all the circumstances and evidence of the cause, examining and cross-examining all the witnesses, and allowing the prosecuting attorney and counsel for the defense to make their respective allegations. International law insures that a defendant be judged openly and that he be permitted to defend himself, but in no manner does it oblige these things to be done in any fixed way, as they are matters of internal regulation and belong to the sovereignty of States....
>
> ...
>
> ... It is hardly of any use to proclaim in theory respect for the judiciary of a nation, if, in practice, it is attempted to call the judiciary to account for its minor acts. It is true that sometimes it is difficult to determine when a judicial act is internationally improper and when it is so from a domestic standpoint only. In my opinion the test which consists in ascertaining if the act implies damage, wilful neglect, or palpable deviation from the established customs becomes clearer by having in mind the damage which the claimant could have suffered. There are certain defects in procedure that can never cause damage which may be estimated separately, and that are blotted out or disappear, to put it thus, if the final decision is just. There are other defects which make it impossible for such decision to be just. The former, as a rule, do not engender international liability; the latter do so, since such liability arises from the decision which is iniquitous because of such defects. To prevent an accused from defending himself, either by refusing to inform him as to the facts imputed to him or by denying him a hearing and the use of remedies; to sentence him without evidence, or to impose on him disproportionate or unusual penalties, to treat him with cruelty and discrimination; are all acts which per se cause damage due to their rendering a just decision impossible. But to delay the proceedings somewhat, to lay aside some evidence, there existing other clear proofs, to fail to comply with the adjective law in its secondary provisions

> and other deficiencies of this kind, do not cause damage nor violate international law. Counsel for Mexico justly stated that to submit the decisions of a nation to revision in this respect was tantamount to submitting her to a régime of capitulations. All the criticism which has been made of these proceedings, I regret to say, appears to arise from lack of knowledge of the judicial system and practice of Mexico, and, what is more dangerous, from the application thereto of tests belonging to foreign systems of law. For example, in some of the latter the investigation of a crime is made only by the police magistrates and the trial proper is conducted by the Judge. Hence the reluctance in accepting that one same judge may have the two functions and that, therefore, he may have to receive in the preliminary investigation (instrucción) of the case all kinds of data, with the obligation, of course, of not taking them into account at the time of judgment, if they have no probative weight.... [T]he foreign-law procedure is used to understand what is a trial or open trial imagining at the same time that it must have the sacred forms of common-law and without remembering that the same goal is reached by many roads. And the same can be said when speaking of the manner of taking testimony of witnesses, of cross-examination, of holding confrontations, etc.... In view of the above considerations, I am of the opinion that this claim should be disallowed.

NOTE

The opinions of the Commissioners underscore the methodological problems in developing a minimum international standard of criminal procedure out of such diverse materials — a diversity that was restricted in *Chattin* to Europe and Latin America, hence far less perplexing than today's worldwide diversity of legal cultures and criminal processes. A treaty was relevant to *Chattin*, but as indicated above, it addressed the scope and structure of the arbitration between the United States and Mexico rather than the international norms of criminal procedure to be applied. The only reference of the General Claims Convention to applicable norms was the terse provision in Article 1 that claims should be submitted to the tripartite Commission 'for decision in accordance with the principles of international law, justice and equity'.

Today a dispute like that in *Chattin* could draw on a human rights treaty, the International Covenant on Civil and Political Rights to be discussed in Chapter 3 that (as of January 2007) had 160 state parties. Article 14 of that Covenant dealing with criminal trials provides in relevant part:

> 1. All persons shall be equal before the courts.... [E]veryone shall be entitled to a fair and public hearing by [an] impartial tribunal....
> 2. Everyone... shall have the right to be presumed innocent until proved guilty according to law.
> 3. ... [E]veryone shall be entitled to the following minimum guarantees....
>   (d) To be tried in his presence and to defend himself in person or through legal assistance of his own choosing...;

(e) To examine, or have examined, the witnesses against him and to obtain the attendance and examination of witnesses on his behalf. . . .

QUESTIONS

1. Why is international law relevant to this decision? Were there any international factors in the trial and conviction and, if so, how do they compare with the international factors in *The Paquete Habana*?

2. How would you identify the most serious problem in the judicial process leading to Chattin's conviction — say, on the basis of a comparison with judicial processes in other legal systems?

3. How do the Commissioners approach the task of identifying an 'international standard of civilization' (or, within the terms of the 1923 Convention, the relevant 'international law, justice and equity') against which they are to test the legality of the conviction? Do they resort to customary international law?

4. Would the tribunal's task have been much simpler if there had been a treaty between the United States and Mexico regulating treatment of aliens that included Article 14 of the ICCPR? Would Article 14 have resolved the basic issues on its face?

NOTE

The issues considered in connection with the *Chattin* case illustrate one of the most important building blocks of the twenty-first century law of state responsibility. However, as codified in the International Law Commission's Articles on Responsibility of States for Internationally Wrongful Acts (2001), that law now goes well beyond issues relating to the treatment of aliens, which we have seen was earlier a condition to its applicability. In broad terms, state responsibility today encapsulates the consequences that follow when a state breaches an international obligation, and regulates the permissible range of responses of other states to such breaches. State responsibility exists side by side with treaty law, including those treaties governing human rights. However, when the latter constitute *lex specialis*, or special rules, they take priority if there is any inconsistency. The law of state responsibility prohibits states from taking any countermeasures which would affect 'obligations for the protection of fundamental rights' or 'obligations of a humanitarian character prohibiting reprisals' (Art. 50).[5]

[5] See J. Crawford, *The International Law Commission's Articles on State Responsibility: Introduction, Text and Commentaries* (2002).

OSCAR SCHACHTER, INTERNATIONAL LAW IN THEORY AND PRACTICE

(1991), at 50

Ch. IV. General Principles and Equity

...

The Broad Expanse of General Principles of Law

We can distinguish five categories of general principles that have been invoked and applied in international law discourse and cases. Each has a different basis for its authority and validity as law. They are:

(1) The principles of municipal law 'recognized by civilized nations'.

(2) General principles of law 'derived from the specific nature of the international community'.

(3) Principles 'intrinsic to the idea of law and basic to all legal systems'.

(4) Principles 'valid through all kinds of societies in relationships of hierarchy and co-ordination'.

(5) Principles of justice founded on 'the very nature of man as a rational and social being'.

Although these five categories are analytically distinct, it is not unusual for a particular general principle to fall into more than one of the categories. For example, the principle that no one shall be a judge in his own cause or that a victim of a legal wrong is entitled to reparation are considered part of most if not all, systems of municipal law and as intrinsic to the basic idea of law.

Our first category, general principles of municipal law, has given rise to a considerable body of writing and much controversy. Article 38(1)*(c)* of the Statute of Court does not expressly refer to principles of national law but rather general principles 'recognized by civilized nations'.... Elihu Root, the American member of the drafting committee, prepared the text finally adopted and it seemed clear that his amendment was intended to refer to principles 'actually recognized and applied in national legal systems'. The fact that the subparagraph was distinct from those on treaty and custom indicated an intent to treat general principles as an independent source of law, and not as a subsidiary source. As an independent source, it did not appear to require any separate proof that such principles of national law had been 'received' into international law.

However, a significant minority of jurists holds that national law principles, even if generally found in most legal systems, cannot *ipso facto* be international law. One view is that they must receive the *imprimatur* of State consent through custom or treaty in order to become international law. The strict positivist school adheres to that view. A somewhat modified version is adopted by others to the effect that rules of municipal law cannot be considered as recognized by civilized nations unless there is evidence of the concurrence of States on their status as international law. Such concurrence may occur through treaty, custom or other evidence of recognition. This would allow for some principles, such as *res judicata*, which are not customary law but are generally accepted in international law....

...

... The most important limitation on the use of municipal law principles arises from the requirement that the principle be appropriate for application on the international level. Thus, the universally accepted common crimes — murder, theft, assault, incest — that apply to individuals are not crimes under international law by virtue of their ubiquity....

At the same time, I would suggest a somewhat more positive approach for the emergent international law concerned with the individual, business companies, environmental dangers and shared resources. Inasmuch as these areas have become the concern of international law, national law principles will often be suitable for international application. This does not mean importing municipal rules 'lock, stock and barrel', but it suggests that domestic law rules applicable to such matters as individual rights, contractual remedies, liability for extra-hazardous activities, or restraints on use of common property, have now become pertinent for recruitment into international law. In these areas, we may look to representative legal systems not only for the highly abstract principles of the kind referred to earlier but to more specific rules that are sufficiently widespread as to be considered 'recognized by civilized nations'....

The second category of general principles included in our list comprises principles derived from the specific character of the international community. The most obvious candidates for this category of principles are.... the necessary principles of co-existence. They include the principles of *pacta sunt servanda*, non-intervention, territorial integrity, self-defence and the legal equality of States. Some of these principles are in the United Nations Charter and therefore part of treaty law, but others might appropriately be treated as principles required by the specific character of a society of sovereign independent members.

...

The foregoing comments are also pertinent to the next two categories of general principles. The idea of principles '*jus rationale*' 'valid through all kinds of human societies'... is associated with traditional natural law doctrine. At the present time its theological links are mainly historical as far as international law is concerned, but its principal justification does not depart too far from the classic natural law emphasis on the nature of 'man', that is, on the human person as a rational and social creature.

The universalist implication of this theory — the idea of the unity of the human species — has had a powerful impetus in the present era. This is evidenced in at least three significant political and legal developments. The first is the global movements against discrimination on grounds of race, colour and sex. The second is the move toward general acceptance of human rights. The third is the increased fear of nuclear annihilation. These three developments strongly reinforce the universalistic values inherent in natural law doctrine. They have found expression in numerous international and constitutional law instruments as well as in popular movements throughout the world directed to humanitarian ends. Clearly, they are a 'material source' of much of the new international law manifested in treaties and customary rules.

In so far as they are recognized as general principles of law, many tend to fall within our fifth category — the principles of natural justice. This concept is well known in many municipal law systems (although identified in diverse ways). 'Natural justice' in its international legal manifestation has two aspects. One refers to the minimal standards of decency and respect for the individual human being that are largely spelled out in the human rights instruments. We can say that in this aspect, 'natural justice' has been largely subsumed as a source of general principles by the human rights instruments....

ADDITIONAL READING

J. Crawford, *The International Law Commission's Articles on State Responsibility: Introduction, Text and Commentaries* (2002); D. Bodansky and J. R. Crook, 'Symposium: The ILC's State Responsibility Articles', 96 Am. J. Int. *L.* 773 (2002); 'Symposium: State Responsibility', 10 Eur. J. Int. L. 339 (1999); A. Randelzhofer and C. Tomuschat (eds.), *State Responsibility and the Individual: Reparation in Instances of Grave Violations of Human Rights* (1999); J. Weiler, A. Cassese and M. Spinedi (eds.), *International Crimes of State: A Critical Analysis of the ILC's Draft Article 19 on State Responsibility*; and Malgosia Fitzmaurice and Dan Sarooshi (eds.), *Issues of State Responsibility Before International Judicial Institutions* (2004).

C. INTERWAR MINORITIES REGIME AND THE ROLE OF TREATIES

COMMENT ON THE MINORITIES REGIME AFTER THE FIRST WORLD WAR

The *Minority Schools in Albania* opinion, which follows, illustrates treaties as a source and major expression of international law, and introduces another field of international law that influenced the growth of the human rights movement. This Comment provides some background to the opinion.

Treaties and other special regimes to protect minorities have a long history in international law dating from the emergence in the seventeenth century of the modern form of the political state, sovereign within its territorial boundaries. Within Europe, religious issues became a strong concern since states often included more than one religious denomination, and abuse by a state of a religious minority could lead to intervention by other states where that religion was dominant. Hence peace treaties sometimes included provisions on religious minorities. In the eighteenth and nineteenth centuries, the precarious situation of Christian minorities within the Ottoman Empire and of religious minorities in newly independent East European or Balkan states led to outbreaks of violence and to sporadic treaty regulation.

The First World War ushered in an era of heightened attention to problems of racial, religious or linguistic minorities. The collapse of the great Austro-Hungarian and Ottoman multinational empires, and the chaos as the Russian empire of the Romanoffs was succeeded by the Soviet Union, led to much redrawing of maps and the creation of new states. President Wilson's Fourteen Points, however compromised they became in the Versailles Treaty and later arrangements, nonetheless exerted influence on the postwar settlements. In it and other messages, Wilson stressed the ideals of the freeing of minorities and the related 'self-determination' of peoples or nationalities. That concept of self-determination, so politically powerful and open to such diverse interpretations, continues to this day to be much disputed and to have profound consequences. It not only appears in the UN Charter but is given a position of high prominence in the two principal human rights covenants.

From concepts like 'self-determination' and out of the legacy of nineteenth-century liberal nationalism that saw the development of nation-states like Germany and Italy, the principle of nationalities took on a new force. Here was another ambiguous and disputed concept — the 'nation' or 'nationality' as distinct from the political state, the nation (often identified with a 'people') defined in cultural or historical terms, often defined more concretely in racial, linguistic and religious terms. One goal in displacing the old empires with new or redrawn states was to identify the nation with the state — ideally, to give each 'nation' its own state. Membership in a 'nation' would ideally be equivalent to membership in a 'state' consisting only or principally of that nation.

Within the pure realization of this ideal, all 'Poles', for example, would be situated in Poland; there would be no 'Polish' national minority in other states, and other 'nationalities' would not be resident in Poland. Indeed, the detaching of Poland after the First World War from the empires and states that had absorbed different parts of it represented one of the few instances of relatively strict congruence between the 'nation' and 'state'. There were polar moves; for example, the creation of Yugoslavia as a multiethnic state that after 70 years has had such tragic consequences.

Of course the goal of total identification of state with nation — a goal itself disputed and in contradiction with other conceptions of the political state that did not emphasize cultural homogeneity or ethnic purity — could not be realized. Life and history were and remain too various and complex for such precise correlation. The nineteenth century examples of Germany and Italy, for example, were far from unitary; each had its national, ethnic, linguistic and religious minorities. National or ethnic homogeneity could be achieved in the vast majority of the world's states only by the compulsory and massive migrations of minority groups, migrations far more systematic and coercive than were some of the population movements and exchanges after the First World War. A 'nation' defined, say, in linguistic-religious terms would generally transcend national boundaries and be located in the territories of two or several sovereign states in the new world created by the postwar settlements. A Greek-speaking Christian minority would, for example, be present in the reconfigured Muslim Albania.

Bear in mind another confusing linguistic usage. The term 'national' is generally used in international law to signify the subjects or citizens of a state. Hence members of the 'German' nation (in the sense of a 'people' and 'culture') living in Poland could be Polish 'nationals' in the sense of being citizens of Poland. Or they could possess only German citizenship and be alien residents in Poland. In the *Minority Schools in Albania* case that follows, members of the Greek-speaking Christian minority (part of a 'nation' in the cultural or ethnic sense) in Muslim Albania were 'nationals' (citizens) of Albania. One can imagine the ambiguity attending the frequent usage of the term 'national minorities', which could mean at least (1) a group in a state belonging in the cultural or ethnic sense to a 'nation' that constituted a minority in that state, or (2) all minorities in a state who were 'nationals' (citizens) of that state.

After the First World War, the victorious powers and the new League of Nations sought to address this situation. They confronted the impossibility, even if it were desirable, of creating ethnically homogeneous states. Hence they had to deal with the continuing presence in states of minorities which had frequently been abused in ways ranging from economic discrimination to pogroms and other violence that could implicate other states, spill across international boundaries and lead to war. The immediate trigger for the outbreak of the First World War in the tormented Balkans was fresh in memory.

President Wilson had proposed that the Covenant of the League of Nations include norms governing the protection of minorities that would have embraced all members of the League. The other major powers rejected this approach, preferring discrete international arrangements to handle discrete problems of minorities in particular states of Central-East Europe and the Balkans rather than a universal treaty system. This compromise led to the regime of the so-called 'Minorities Treaties' that were imposed on the new or reconfigured states of Central-East Europe and the Balkans.

For some states like Austria and Hungary, provisions for minority protection were included in the peace treaties. Other states like Poland or Greece signed minority protection treaties with the allied and associated powers. Some states like Albania and Lithuania made minority protection declarations as a condition for their membership in the League of Nations. There were also bilateral treaties protecting minorities such as one between Germany and Poland. Note that one of the features of this new regime was to insulate the victorious powers from international regulation of their treatment of their own citizens belonging to minorities.

Although there were significant variations among these treaties and declarations, many provisions were common. The 1919 Minorities Treaty between the Principal Allied and Associated Powers and Poland served as a model for later treaties and declarations. It provided for protection of life and liberty and religious freedom for all 'inhabitants of Poland'. All Polish nationals (citizens) were guaranteed equality before the law and the right to use their own language in private life and judicial proceedings. Members of racial, religious or linguistic minorities were guaranteed 'the same treatment and security in law and in fact' as other Polish nationals, and the right to establish and control at their expense their own religious, social and educational institutions. In areas of Poland where a 'considerable proportion' of Polish nationals belonged to minorities, an 'equitable share' of public funds would go to such minority groups for educational or religious purposes. In view of the particular history of oppression and violence, there were specific guarantees for Jews.

Jan Herman Burgers[6] has described the special regimes formed by the minority provisions as follows:

> ... [T]he regime consisted of three categories of obligations. Firstly, it guaranteed full and complete protection of life and liberty to all *inhabitants* of the country or region concerned, without distinction of birth , nationality, language, race or religion. Secondly, it guaranteed that all nationals would be equal before the law and

[6] 'The Road to San Francisco: The Revival of the Human Rights Idea in the Twentieth Century', 14 Hum. Rts. Q. 447 (1992), at 450.

> would enjoy the same civil and political rights, without distinction as to race, language or religion. Thirdly, it provided for a series of special guarantees for nationals belonging to minorities, for instance concerning the use of their language and the right to establish social and religious institutions.

Like other minority treaties and declarations, the Polish treaty's provisions were placed under the guarantee of the League of Nations to the extent that 'they affect persons belonging to' minority groups. The League developed procedures to implement its duties, including a right of petition to it by beleaguered minorities claiming that a treaty regime or declaration had been violated, and including a minorities committee given the task of seeking negotiated solutions to such disputes. As shown by the *Minority Schools in Albania* case, the Council of the League could invoke in accordance with its usual procedures the advisory opinion jurisdiction of the Permanent Court of International Justice (PCIJ), the first international court (supplementing *ad hoc* arbitral tribunals as in the *Chattin* case). The Court was created by the League in 1921, became dormant in the Second World War, and was then succeeded by the International Court of Justice created under the UN Charter.

MINORITY SCHOOLS IN ALBANIA

Advisory Opinion, Permanent Court of International Justice, 1935 Series A/B-No. 64

[In 1920, the Assembly of the League of Nations adopted a recommendation requesting that if Albania were admitted into the League, it 'should take the necessary measures to enforce the principles of the Minorities Treaties' and to arrange the 'details required to carry this object into effect' with the Council of the League. Albania was admitted to membership a few days later. In 1921 the Council included on its agenda the question of protection of minorities in Albania.

The Greek government, in view of the presence of a substantial Christian minority of Greek origin in (dominantly Muslim) Albania, communicated to the League proposals for provisions going beyond the Minorities Treaties that were related to Christian worship and to education in the Greek language. The Council commissioned a report, and the reporter submitted to it a draft Declaration to be signed by Albania and formally communicated to the Council. The Declaration was signed by Albania and submitted to the Council in 1921, with basic similarities to but some differences from the typical clauses of the Minorities Treaties. The Council decided that the stipulations in the Declaration about minorities should be placed under the guarantee of the League from the date of the Declaration's ratification by Albania, which took place in 1922.

The first paragraph of Article 5 of the Declaration, at the core of the dispute that later developed, provided as follows:

> Albanian nationals who belong to racial, linguistic or religious minorities, will enjoy the same treatment and security in law and in fact as other Albanian nationals. In particular, they shall have an equal right to maintain, manage and control at their

> own expense or to establish in the future, charitable, religious and social institutions, schools and other educational establishments, with the right to use their own language and to exercise their religion freely therein.

Over the years, numerous changes in the laws and practices of the Albanian government led to questions about compliance with the Declaration. In 1933, the Albanian National Assembly modified Articles 206 and 207 of the Constitution, which had provided that 'Albanian subjects may found private schools' subject to government regulation, to state:

> The instruction and education of Albanian subjects are reserved to the State and will be given in State schools. Primary education is compulsory for all Albanian nationals and will be given free of charge. Private schools of all categories at present in operation will be closed.

The new provisions affecting Greek-language and other private schools led to petitions and complaints to the League from groups including the Greek minority in Albania. Acting within its regular powers, the Council requested the Permanent Court of International Justice in 1935 to give an advisory opinion whether, in light of the 1921 Declaration as a whole, Albania was justified in its position that it had acted in conformity with 'the letter and the spirit' of Article 5 because (as Albania argued) its abolition of private schools was a general measure applicable to the majority as well as minority of Albanian nationals.

There follow excerpts from the opinion for the PCIJ and from a dissenting opinion. For present purposes, the Albanian Declaration can be understood as tantamount to a treaty. The opinions draw no relevant distinction between the two, and refer frequently to the Minorities Treaties to inform their interpretation of the Declaration.]

The contention of the Albanian Government is that the above-mentioned clause imposed no other obligation upon it, in educational matters, than to grant to its nationals belonging to racial, religious, or linguistic minorities a right equal to that possessed by other Albanian nationals. Once the latter have ceased to be entitled to have private schools, the former cannot claim to have them either. This conclusion, which is alleged to follow quite naturally from the wording of paragraph I of Article 5, would, it is contended, be in complete conformity with the meaning and spirit of the treaties for the protection of minorities, an essential characteristic of which is the full and complete equality of all nationals of the State, whether belonging to the majority or to the minority. On the other hand, it is argued, any interpretation which would compel Albania to respect the private minority schools would create a privilege in favour of the minority and run counter to the essential idea of the law governing minorities. Moreover, as the minority régime is an extraordinary régime constituting a derogation from the ordinary law, the text in question should, in case of doubt, be construed in the manner most favourable to the sovereignty of the Albanian State.

According to the explanations furnished to the Court by the Greek Government, the fundamental idea of Article 5 of the Declaration was on the contrary to guarantee freedom of education to the minorities by granting them the right to retain their existing schools and to establish others, if they desired; equality of treatment is, in the Greek Government's opinion, merely an adjunct to that right, and cannot impede the purpose in view, which is to ensure full and effectual liberty in matters of education. Moreover, the application of the same régime to a majority as to a minority, whose needs are quite different, would only create an apparent equality, whereas the Albanian Declaration, consistently with ordinary minority law, was designed to ensure a genuine and effective equality, not merely a formal equality.

. . .

As the Declaration of October 2nd, 1921, was designed to apply to Albania the general principles of the treaties for the protection of minorities, this is the point of view which, in the Court's opinion, must be adopted in construing paragraph 1 of Article 5 of the said Declaration.

The idea underlying the treaties for the protection of minorities is to secure for certain elements incorporated in a State, the population of which differs from them in race, language or religion, the possibility of living peaceably alongside that population and co-operating amicably with it, while at the same time preserving the characteristics which distinguish them from the majority, and satisfying the ensuing special needs.

In order to attain this object, two things were regarded as particularly necessary, and have formed the subject of provisions in these treaties.

The first is to ensure that nationals belonging to racial, religious or linguistic minorities shall be placed in every respect on a footing of perfect equality with the other nationals of the State.

The second is to ensure for the minority elements suitable means for the preservation of their racial peculiarities, their traditions and their national characteristics.

These two requirements are indeed closely interlocked, for there would be no true equality between a majority and a minority if the latter were deprived of its own institutions, and were consequently compelled to renounce that which constitutes the very essence of its being as a minority.

In common with the other treaties for the protection of minorities, and in particular with the Polish Treaty of June 28th, 1919, the text of which it follows, so far as concerns the question before the Court, very closely and almost literally, the Declaration of October 2nd, 1921, begins by laying down that no person shall be placed, in his relations with the Albanian authorities, in a position of inferiority by reason of his language, race or religion. . . .

. . .

In all these cases, the Declaration provides for a régime of legal equality for all persons mentioned in the clause; in fact no standard of comparison was indicated, and none was necessary, for at the same time that it provides for equality of treatment the Declaration specifies the rights which are to be enjoyed equally by all.

. . .

It has already been remarked that paragraph 1 of Article 5 consists of two sentences, the second of which is linked to the first by the words *in particular*: for a right apprehension of the second part, it is therefore first necessary to determine the meaning and the scope of the first sentence. This sentence is worded as follows:

> Albanian nationals who belong to racial, linguistic or religious minorities, will enjoy the same treatment and security in law and in fact as other Albanian nationals.

The question that arises is what is meant by the *same treatment and security in law and in fact.*

It must be noted to begin with that the equality of all Albanian nationals before the law has already been stipulated in the widest terms in Article 4. As it is difficult to admit that Article 5 set out to repeat in different words what had already been said in Article 4, one is led to the conclusion that 'the same treatment and security in law and in fact' which is provided for in Article 5 is not the same notion as the equality before the law which is provided for in Article 4.

. . .

This special conception finds expression in the idea of an equality in fact which in Article 5 supplements equality in law. All Albanian nationals enjoy the equality in law stipulated in Article 4; on the other hand, the equality between members of the majority and of the minority must, according to the terms of Article 5, be an equality in law and in fact.

It is perhaps not easy to define the distinction between the notions of equality in fact and equality in law; nevertheless, it may be said that the former notion excludes the idea of a merely formal equality; that is indeed what the Court laid down in its Advisory Opinion of September 10th, 1923, concerning the case of the German settlers in Poland (Opinion No. 6), in which it said that:

> There must be equality in fact as well as ostensible legal equality in the sense of the absence of discrimination in the words of the law.

Equality in law precludes discrimination of any kind; whereas equality in fact may involve the necessity of different treatment in order to attain a result which establishes an equilibrium between different situations.

It is easy to imagine cases in which equality of treatment of the majority and of the minority, whose situation and requirements are different, would result in inequality in fact; treatment of this description would run counter to the first sentence of paragraph 1 of Article 5. The equality between members of the majority and of the minority must be an effective, genuine equality; that is the meaning of this provision.

The second sentence of this paragraph provides as follows:

> In particular they shall have an equal right to maintain, manage and control at their own expense or to establish in the future, charitable, religious and social institutions, schools and other educational establishments, with the right to use their own language and to exercise their religion freely therein.

This sentence of the paragraph being linked to the first by the words 'in particular', it is natural to conclude that it envisages a particularly important illustration of the application of the principle of identical treatment in law and in fact that is stipulated in the first sentence of the paragraph. For the institutions mentioned in the second sentence are indispensable to enable the minority to enjoy the same treatment as the majority, not only in law but also in fact. The abolition of these institutions, which alone can satisfy the special requirements of the minority groups, and their replacement by government institutions, would destroy this equality of treatment, for its effect would be to deprive the minority of the institutions appropriate to its needs, whereas the majority would continue to have them supplied in the institutions created by the State.

Far from creating a privilege in favour of the minority, as the Albanian Government avers, this stipulation ensures that the majority shall not be given a privileged situation as compared with the minority.

It may further be observed that, even disregarding the link between the two parts of paragraph 1 of Article 5, it seems difficult to maintain that the adjective 'equal', which qualifies the word 'right', has the effect of empowering the State to abolish the right, and thus to render the clause in question illusory; for, if so, the stipulation which confers so important a right on the members of the minority would not only add nothing to what has already been provided in Article 4, but it would become a weapon by which the State could deprive the minority régime of a great part of its practical value. It should be observed that in its Advisory Opinion of September 15th, 1923, concerning the question of the acquisition of Polish nationality (Opinion No. 7), the Court referred to the opinion which it had already expressed in Advisory Opinion No. 6 to the effect that 'an interpretation which would deprive the Minorities Treaty of a great part of its value is inadmissible'.

...

The idea embodied in the expression 'equal right' is that the right thus conferred on the members of the minority cannot in any case be inferior to the corresponding right of other Albanian nationals. In other words, the members of the minority must always enjoy the right stipulated in the Declaration, and, in addition, any more extensive rights which the State may accord to other nationals....

The construction which the Court places on paragraph 1 of Article 5 is confirmed by the history of this provision.

[Analysis of the proposals of the Greek Government and replies of the Albanian Government during the period of drafting of the Declaration omitted.]

The Court, having thus established that paragraph 1 of Article 5 of the Declaration, both according to its letter and its spirit, confers on Albanian nationals of racial, religious or linguistic minorities the right that is stipulated in the second sentence of that paragraph, finds it unnecessary to examine the subsidiary argument adduced by the Albanian Government to the effect that the text in question should in case of doubt be interpreted in the sense that is most favourable to the sovereignty of the State.

...

For these reasons,

The Court is of opinion,

by eight votes to three,

that the plea of the Albanian Government that, as the abolition of private schools in Albania constitutes a general measure applicable to the majority as well as to the minority, it is in conformity with the letter and spirit of the stipulations laid down in Article 5, first paragraph, of the Declaration of October 2nd, 1921, is not well founded.

...

DISSENTING OPINION BY SIR CECIL HURST, COUNT ROSTWOROWSKI, AND MR. NEGULESCO

The undermentioned are unable to concur in the opinion rendered by the Court. They can see no adequate reason for holding that the suppression of the private schools effected in Albania in virtue of Articles 206 and 207 of the Constitution of 1933 is not in conformity with the Albanian Declaration of October 2nd, 1921.

...

The construction of the paragraph is clear and simple. The first sentence stipulates for the treatment and the security being the same for the members of the minority as for the other Albanian nationals. The second provides that as regards certain specified matters the members of the minority shall have an equal right. The two sentences are linked together by the words 'In particular' (*notamment*). These words show that the second sentence is a particular application of the principle enunciated in the first. If the rights of the two categories under the first sentence are to be the same, the equal right provided for in the second sentence must indicate equality between the same two categories, viz. the members of the minority and the other Albanian nationals. The second sentence is added because the general principle laid down in the first sentence mentions only 'treatment and security in law and in fact'— a phrase so indefinite that without further words of precision it would be doubtful whether it covered the right to establish and maintain charitable, religious and social institutions and schools and other educational establishments, but the particular application of the general principle of identity of treatment and security remains governed by the dominating element of equality as between the two categories.

The word 'equal' implies that the right so enjoyed must be equal in measure to the right enjoyed by somebody else. '*They shall have an equal right*' means that the right to be enjoyed by the people in question is to be equal in measure to that enjoyed by some other group. A right which is unconditional and independent of that enjoyed by other people cannot with accuracy be described as an 'equal right'. 'Equality' necessarily implies the existence of some extraneous criterion by reference to which the content is to be determined.

If the text of the first paragraph of Article 5 is considered alone, it does not seem that there could be any doubt as to its interpretation. It is, however, laid down in the Opinion from which the undersigned dissent that if the general purpose of the minority treaties is borne in mind and also the contents of the Albanian Declaration taken as a whole, it will be found that the 'equal right' provided for in the first paragraph of Article 5 cannot mean a right of which the extent is measured by that enjoyed by other Albanian nationals, and that it must imply an unconditional right, a right of which the members of the minority cannot be deprived.

...

As the opinion of the Court is based on the general purpose which the minorities treaties are presumed to have had in view and not on the text of Article 5, paragraph 1, of the Albanian Declaration, it involves to some extent a departure from the principles hitherto adopted by this Court in the interpretation of international instruments, that in presence of a clause which is reasonably clear the Court is bound to apply it as it stands without considering whether other provisions might with advantage have been added to it or substituted for it, and this even if the results following from it may in some particular hypothesis seem unsatisfactory.

. . .

Furthermore, the suppression of the private schools — even if it may prejudice to some appreciable extent the interests of a minority — does not oblige them to abandon an essential part of the characteristic life of a minority. In interpreting Article 5, the question whether the possession of particular institutions may or may not be *important* to the minority cannot constitute the decisive consideration. There is another consideration entitled to equal weight. That is the extent to which the monopoly of education may be of importance to the State. The two considerations cannot be weighed one against the other: Neither of them — in the absence of a clear stipulation to that effect — can provide an objective standard for determining which of them is to prevail.

International justice must proceed upon the footing of applying treaty stipulations impartially to the rights of the State and to the rights of the minority, and the method of doing so is to adhere to the terms of the treaty — as representing the common will of the parties — as closely as possible.

. . .

If the intention of the second sentence: 'In particular they [the minority] shall have an equal right . . . ', had been that the right so given should be universal and unconditional, there is no reason why the draftsman should not have dealt with the right to establish institutions and schools in the earlier articles [of the Declaration that set up fixed and universal standards for all Albanians on matters like protection of life and free exercise of religion]. The draftsman should have dealt with the liberty to maintain schools and other institutions on lines similar to those governing the right to the free exercise of religion, which undoubtedly is conferred as a universal and unconditional right. Instead of doing so the right conferred upon the minority is an 'equal' right. . . .

. . .

COMMENT ON FURTHER ASPECTS OF THE MINORITY TREATIES

The *Minority Schools in Albania* opinions address many current issues that remain vexing. The discussions about the nature of 'equality' and assurances thereof, in particular about equality 'in law' and 'in fact', inform contemporary human rights law as well as constitutional and legislative debates in many states with respect to issues like equal protection and affirmative action. The question whether the Declaration and the Court's opinion recognized only the rights of individual members of a minority, or also the right of the minority itself as a collective or group, remains one that vexes the discussion of minority rights. Protection aiming at the cultural survival of minorities continues to raise the troubling issue of which types of minorities merit such protection, and whether assurance of equal protection (with the majority) is sufficient for the purpose.

But if the issues debated within the minorities regime remain, the regime itself has disappeared. Over the next two decades, its norms were roundly violated. Its international machinery within the League of Nations proved to be ineffectual, partly for the same lack of political will that led to other disastrous events in the interwar period. The failure of the regime was tragic in its consequences. Its noble purposes were distorted or blunted or ignored as Europe of the 1930s moved toward the horrors of the Second World War, the Holocaust and the brutalization and slaughter of so many other minorities. The settlements, norms and institutions after the Second World War designed to prevent further savagery against minorities stressed different principles and created radically different institutions, principally within the universal human rights system built in and around the United Nations.

Nonetheless, it is important to recognize the distinctive dilemmas and advances as well as the shortcomings of this minorities regime. Sovereignty in the sense of a state's (absolute) internal control over its own citizens was to some extent eroded. Treaties-declarations subjected aspects of the state's treatment of its own citizens to international law and international processes — that is, citizens who were members of a racial, religious or linguistic minority. Although the norms were expressed in bilateral treaties or declarations, the regime took on a multilateral aspect through its incorporation into the League as well as through the large number of nearly simultaneous treaties and declarations. The whole scheme was informed by multilateral planning, in contrast with the centuries-old examples of sporadic bilateral treaties protecting (usually religious) minorities. Minorities became a matter of formal international concern, the treaties-declarations fragmented the state into different sections of its citizens, and international law reached beyond the law of state responsibility to protect some of a state's own citizens.

The precise issue of the *Minority Schools in Albania* case is now addressed in the 1960 UNESCO Convention against Discrimination in Education. Article 5(1)(c) recognizes the 'right of members of national minorities to carry on their own educational activities, including the maintenance of schools and, depending on the educational policy of each State, the use or the teaching of their own language . . .'. The article subjects this right to several provisos. For example, its exercise should not prevent minorities from understanding the culture and language of the larger community as well, or prejudice national sovereignty.

COMMENT ON TREATIES

Treaties have inevitably figured in this chapter's prior discussions — for example, the bilateral treaties whose relevance to custom was debated in *The Paquete Habana*, or the convention underlying the *Chattin* litigation. As noted above, the Albanian Declaration can be understood for present purposes as tantamount to a treaty, for the opinions do not distinguish between the two and refer to the Minorities Treaties to advance their interpretation of the Declaration. Hence this Comment, and particularly its sections on issues like interpretation, is here relevant.

In Article 38(1) of the Statute of the International Court of Justice, the Court is instructed in clause (a) to apply 'international conventions, whether general or particular, establishing rules expressly recognized by the contesting states'. Treaties thus head the list. They have become the primary expression of international law and, particularly when multilateral, the most effective if not the only path toward international regulation of many contemporary problems. Multilateral treaties have been the principal means for development of the human rights movement. One striking advantage of treaties over custom should be noted. Only treaties can create, and define the powers or jurisdiction of, international institutions in which state parties participate and to which they may owe duties.

The terminology for this voluminous and diverse body of international law varies. International agreements are referred to as pacts, protocols (generally supplemental to another agreement), covenants, conventions, charters, exchanges of notes and concordats (agreements between a nation and the Holy See), as well as treaties — terms that are more or less interchangeable in legal significance. Within the internal law of some countries such as the United States, the term 'treaty' (as contrasted, say, with international executive agreement) has a particular constitutional significance.

Consider the different purposes which treaties serve. Some reaching critical national interests have a basic political character: alliances, peace settlements, control of atomic weapons. Others, while less politically charged, also involve relationships between governments and affect private parties only indirectly: agreements on foreign aid, cooperation in the provision of governmental services such as the mails. But treaties often have a direct and specific impact upon private parties. For many decades, tariff accords, income tax conventions, and treaties of friendship, commerce and navigation have determined the conditions under which the nationals or residents of one signatory can export to, or engage in business activities within, the other signatory's territory. Most significant for this book's purposes, human rights treaties have sought to extend protection to all persons against governmental abuse.

Domestic analogies to the treaty help to portray its distinctive character: contract and legislation. Some treaties settling particular disputes resemble an accord and satisfaction under contract law: an agreement over boundaries, an agreement to pay a stated sum as compensation for injury to the receiving nation or its nationals. Others are closer in character to private contracts of continuing significance or to domestic legislation for they regulate recurrent problems by defining rights and obligations of the parties and their nationals: agreements over rules of navigation, income taxation or the enforcement of foreign-country judgments. The term 'international legislation' to describe treaties has therefor gained some currency, particularly with respect to multilateral treaties such as those on human rights that impose rules on states intended to regulate their conduct. The Albanian Declaration and the many bilateral treaties that formed part of the minorities regime of the period come within this description.

Nonetheless, domestic legislation differs in several critical respects from the characteristic treaty. A statute is generally enacted by the majority of a legislature and binds all members of the relevant society. Even changes in a constitution, which usually require approval by the legislature and other institutions or groups, can be accomplished over substantial dissent. The ordinary treaty, on the other hand, is a consensual arrangement. With few exceptions, such as Article 2(6) of the UN Charter, it purports to bind or benefit only parties. Alteration of its terms by one state party generally requires the consent of all.

Consider the institution of contract. Like the treaty, a contract can be said to make or create law between the parties — for within the facilitative framework of governing law but subject to that law's mandatory norms and constraints, courts recognize and enforce contract-created duties. The treaty shares a contract's consensual basis, but treaty law lacks the breadth and relative inclusiveness of a national body of contract law. It has preserved a certain Roman law flavour ('*pacta sunt servanda*', '*rebus sic stantibus*') acquired during the long period from the Renaissance to the nineteenth century, when continental European scholars dominated the field. But treaty law often reflects the diversity of approaches to domestic contract law that lawyers bring to the topic, a diversity that is particularly striking on issues of treaty interpretation.

Duties Imposed by Treaty Law

Whatever its purpose or character, the international agreement is generally recognized from the perspective of international law as an authoritative starting point for legal reasoning about any dispute to which it is relevant. The maxim '*pacta sunt servanda*' is at the core of treaty law. It embodies a widespread recognition that commitments publicly, formally and (more or less) voluntarily made by a nation should be honoured. As stated in Article 26 of the Vienna Convention on the Law of Treaties (see below): 'Every treaty in force is binding upon the parties to it and must be performed by them in good faith'.

Whatever the jurisprudential or philosophical bases for this norm, one can readily perceive the practical reasons for and the national interests served by adherence to the principle that *pacta sunt servanda*. The treaty represents one of the most effective means for bringing some order to relationships among states or their nationals, and for the systematic development of new principles responsive to the changing needs of the international community. It is the prime legal form through which that community can realize some degree of stability and predictability, and seek to institutionalize ideals like peaceful settlement of disputes and protection of human rights. Often such goals can be achieved only through international organizations whose powers, structure, membership and purposes will be set forth in the treaties that gave them birth. Treaties then are the basic instruments underlying much contemporary international regulation.

Acceptance of the primary role of the treaty does not, however, mean that a problem between two countries is adequately solved from the perspective of legal ordering simply by execution of a treaty with satisfactory provisions. A body of law has necessarily developed to deal with questions analogous to those addressed by domestic contract law — for example, formation of a treaty, its interpretation and performance, remedies for breach, and amendment or termination. But that body of law is often fragmentary and vague, reflecting the scarcity of decisions of international tribunals and the political tensions which some aspects of treaty law reflect.

There have been recurrent efforts to remedy this situation through more or less creative codification of the law of treaties. The contemporary authoritative text grows out of a United Nations Conference on the Law of Treaties that adopted in 1969 the Convention on the Law of Treaties, UN Doc, A/CONF, 39/27, 63 A.J.I.L. 875 (1969). That Convention became effective in 1980 and (as of January 2007) had been ratified by 90 states from all regions of the world. Excerpts from it appear in the online Documents Supplement. For reasons stemming largely from tensions between the Executive and the Congress over authority over different types of international agreements, the United States has not ratified the Vienna Convention. Nonetheless, in its provisions on international agreements the *Restatement (Third), Foreign Relations Law of the United States* (1987) 'accepts the Vienna Convention as, in general, constituting a codification of the customary international law governing international agreements, and therefore as foreign relations law of the United States. . . . ' Vol. I, p. 145.

Treaty Formation

A treaty is formed by the express consent of its parties. Although there are no precise requirements for execution or form, certain procedures have become standard. By choice of the parties, or in order to comply with the internal rules of a signatory country that are considered at pp. 1087–1122 *infra*, it may be necessary to postpone the effectiveness of the agreement until a national legislative body has approved it and national executive authorities have ratified it. Instruments of ratification for bilateral agreements are then exchanged. In the case of multilateral treaties, such instruments are deposited with the national government or international organization that has been designated as the custodian of the authentic text and of all other instruments relating to the treaty, including subsequent adhesions by nations that were not among the original signatories. Thereafter a treaty will generally be proclaimed or promulgated by the executive in each country.

Consent

Given the established principle that treaties are consensual, what rules prevail as to the character of that consent? Do domestic law contract principles about the effect of duress carry over to the international field?

In a domestic legal system, a party cannot enforce a contract which was signed by a defendant at gunpoint. One could argue that victorious nations cannot assert rights under a peace treaty obtained by a whole army. It is not surprising that the large powers are reluctant to recognize that such forms of duress can invalidate a treaty. If duress were a defence, it would be critical to define its contours, for many treaties result from various forms of military, political or economic pressure. The paucity of and doubts about international institutions with authority to develop answers to such questions underscore the reluctance to open treaties to challenge on these grounds.

The different approaches of the victorious Western powers towards the defeated nations in the First World War and the Second World War reflect the growing awareness that treaties, whatever their 'legal' character, will survive only insofar as they bring satisfactory solutions to developing political, economic and social problems. Even from a legal perspective, the advent of the UN Charter after the Second World War, with its explicit rejection of war as a permitted instrument of national policy, may herald some evolution of legal doctrine in this field. Article 52 of the Vienna Convention states: 'A treaty is void if its conclusion has been procured by the threat or use of force in violation of the principles of international law embodied in the Charter of the United Nations'. Attempts at Vienna to broaden the scope of coercion to include economic duress failed, although they resulted in a declaration condemning the use of such practices.

Reservations

Problems of consent that have no precise parallel in national contract law arise in connection with reservations to treaties, i.e., unilateral statements made by a state accepting a treaty 'whereby it purports to exclude, or vary the legal effect of certain provisions of the treaty in their application to a state' (Article 2(1)(d) of the Vienna Convention). With bilateral treaties, no conceptual difficulties arise: ratification with reservations amounts to a counteroffer; the other state may accept (or reject) explicitly or may be held to have tacitly accepted it by proceeding with its ratification process or with compliance with the treaty. With multilateral treaties the problems may be quite complex. The traditional rule said that acceptance by all parties was required. The expanding number of states has required more flexibility.

Given the increased number of reservations, some of great significance, that many states are attaching to their ratifications of basic human rights treaties, questions about those reservations' validity under general treaty law or under the terms of a specific treaty have become matters of high concern within the human rights movement. See pp. 1124–1155, *infra*.

Violations of and Changes in Treaties

Violation of a treaty may lead to diplomatic protests and a claim before an international tribunal. But primarily because of the limited and qualified consents of nations to the jurisdiction of international tribunals, the offended party will usually resort to other measures. In a national system of contract law, well-developed rules govern such measures. They may distinguish between a minor breach not authorizing the injured party to terminate its own performance, and a material breach providing justification for such a move. Article 60 of the Vienna Convention provides that a material breach (as defined) of a bilateral treaty entitles the other party to terminate the treaty or suspend its performance thereunder. These rules necessarily grow more complex for multilateral treaties. For reasons that Chapters 2 and 3 describe, they may have little relevance for the ways that states respond to violations of human rights treaty norms by other states.

Amendments raise additional problems. The treaty's contractual aspect suggests that the consent of all parties is necessary. Parties may however agree in advance (see Article 108 of the UN Charter) to be bound with respect to certain matters by the vote of a specified number. Such provisions in a multilateral treaty bring it closer in character to national legislation. They may be limited to changes which do not impose new obligations upon a dissenting party, although a state antagonistic to an amendment could generally withdraw. Absent some such provisions, a treaty may aggravate rather than resolve a fundamental problem of international law, how to achieve in a peaceful manner the changes in existing arrangements that are needed to adapt them to developing political, social or economic conditions.

One of the most contentious issues in treaty law is whether the emergence of conditions that were unforeseeable or unforeseen at the time of the treaty's conclusion terminates or modifies a party's obligation to perform. This problem borders the subject of treaty interpretation, considered *infra*, since it is often described as a question whether an implied condition or an escape clause, called the '*clausula rebus sic stantibus*', should be read into a treaty. Mature municipal legal systems have developed rules for handling situations where the performance of one party is rendered impossible or useless by intervening conditions. 'Impossibility', 'frustration', 'force majeure', and 'implied conditions' are the concepts used in Anglo-American law.

At the international level, possibilities of changes in conditions that upset assumptions underlying an agreement are enhanced by the long duration of many treaties, the difficulty in amending them and the rapid political, economic and social vicissitudes in modern times. Thus nations, including the United States, have occasionally used *rebus sic stantibus* as the basis for declaring treaties no longer effective. Article 62 of the Vienna Convention states that a 'fundamental change of circumstances' which was not foreseen by the parties may not be invoked as a ground for terminating a treaty unless '(a) the existence of those circumstances constituted an essential basis of the consent of the parties to transform the extent of obligations still to be performed under the treaty'.

Treaty Interpretation

There is no shortcut to a reliable sense of how a given treaty will be construed. Even immersion in a mass of diplomatic correspondence and cases would not develop such a skill. In view of the variety of treaties and of approaches to their interpretation, such learning would more likely shed light on the possibilities than provide a certain answer to any given question.

One obstacle to helpful generalization about treaty interpretation is the variety of purposes which treaties serve. Different approaches are advisable for treaties that lay down rules for a long or indefinite period, in contrast with those settling past disputes. The long-term treaty must benefit from a certain flexibility and room for development if it is to survive changes in circumstances and relations between the parties. Changes in conditions like those that make *rebus sic stantibus* an attractive doctrine may lead a court or executive official to interpret a treaty flexibly so as to give it a sensible application to new circumstances.

The very style of a treaty will influence the approach of an official charged with interpreting it. Certain categories, such as income tax conventions, lend themselves to a detailed draftsmanship that will often be impractical and undesirable in a constitutional document such as the UN Charter. Conventions such as those relating to human rights necessarily use broad and abstract terms and standards like fairness or *ordre public.*

In a national legal system, lawyers and courts can seek to give specific content to general statutory standards by resort to a common law background or to a constitutional tradition, indeed by reference to the entire legal culture and society within which these standards become operative. Interpretation can reach towards generally understood practices, customs or purposes — even if the lawyer or judge may encounter choice and contradiction in practices and purposes rather than consensus. It may be far more difficult to interpret treaty standards of comparable generality that embrace an international community with diverse national traditions. The problem becomes acute in multilateral treaties among nations from different regions and cultures, for one method of securing agreement to a treaty in the first instance may be to conceal rather than resolve differences through resort to general standards. In addition, the difficulty in achieving agreement over amendments to long-continuing multilateral treaties may encourage their draftsmen to express a 'consensus' through norms of a general character, which have a better chance of surviving and carrying their broad purposes through changed conditions among the signatories.

Maxims similar to those found in domestic fields exist for treaties as well. The Vienna Convention contains several. Article 31 provides that a 'treaty shall be interpreted in good faith in accordance with the ordinary meaning to be given to the terms of the treaty in their context and in the light of its object and purpose'. Article 32 goes on to add that recourse may be had to supplementary means if Article 31 interpretation produces a meaning that is 'ambiguous or obscure' or an outcome 'manifestly absurd or unreasonable'.

One way to build a framework for construing treaties is to consider the continuum which lies between 'strict' interpretation according to the 'plain meaning' of the treaty, and interpretation according to the interpreter's view of the best means of implementing the purposes or realizing the principles expressed by the treaty. Of course, both extremes of the spectrum are untenanted. One cannot wholly ignore the treaty's words, nor can one always find an unambiguous and relevant text that resolves the immediate issue.

Part of the difficulty is that treaties may be drafted in several languages. If domestic courts deem it unwise to 'make a fortress out of the dictionary', it would seem particularly unwise when dictionaries in several languages (and in different legal systems according different meanings to linguistically similar terms) must be resorted to. Sometimes corresponding words in the different versions may shed more light on the intended meaning; at other times, they are plainly inconsistent.

Reliance upon literal construction or 'strict' interpretation may however be an attractive method or technique to an international tribunal that is sensitive to its weak political foundation. It may be tempted to take refuge in the position that its decision is the ineluctable outcome of the drafter's intention expressed in clear text, and not a choice arrived at on the basis of the tribunal's understanding of policy considerations or relevant principles that may resolve a dispute over interpretation. Reliance on legislative history or *travaux préparatoires* can achieve the same result of placing responsibility on the drafters. The charge of 'judicial legislation' evokes strong reactions in the United States; it inevitably influences judges of international tribunals and heightens the temptation to take refuge in the dictionary.

Treaties and International Organizations

In addition to setting forth specific rules which are to govern the conduct of the parties, a treaty may establish machinery for the development of further norms. This applies particularly to multilateral agreements, which may be specialized or general in subject matter, regional or worldwide in scope. At its simplest, such a treaty may provide for periodic meetings at which the signatories' representatives will exchange views. From such discussions the representatives may go on to negotiate new agreements, for the presence of delegates from several countries makes possible the adjustment at one time of interlocking problems that affect each of them. At the next level, the treaty may authorize the parties' delegates to pass advisory or recommendatory resolutions. Such meetings can produce draft conventions which will be submitted to the members for consideration and possible ratification.

In more advanced arrangements the structure created by treaty will include organs or agencies exercising stated powers. Sometimes they are authorized to mediate or put pressure on disputants to arbitrate. Sometimes their authority extends to issuing non-binding declarations on relevant issues and recommendatory resolutions. Such powers can go further and include competence to issue binding interpretations of the treaty as well as regulations, directives or resolutions binding upon the parties (a limited legislative function), or to apply the treaty to specific situations in an authoritative way (a limited judicial function). Finally, the treaty may give a stated majority of the members the power to amend the agreement with respect to some or all provisions so as to bind all parties.

At some point in this progression we find that the treaty has created an international 'organization'. The growth of a permanent staff maintaining a continuous interim activity and the acquisition of a budget and buildings signal the emergence of a distinct entity with some life of its own. The members may endow this entity with a juridical personality and empower it to make contracts or treaties with private parties or governments and be a party to lawsuits. They may also confer upon the organization and its officials various immunities.

Such international organizations' concerns and functions now include diverse fields like peacekeeping, trade and monetary matters, fisheries and other regimes of the high seas, environmental protection, the regulation of basic commodities, and protection of human rights. In all such cases, the issues to be addressed do not lend themselves to adequate resolution through the development of customary rules, through a network of bilateral treaties, or through multilateral treaties that contain only substantive rules without institutional mechanisms for their promotion, implementation or enforcement. Such organizations may be universal or regional.

Issues of human rights, for example, figure pervasively in the work of the United Nations and fully occupy some organs within the UN such as the Commission on Human Rights and its successor, the Human Rights Council (Chapter 9). There are also regional human rights organizations in Europe, the Americas and Africa (Chapter 11).

QUESTIONS

1. The types of protections or assurances given by treaty to a distinctive group within a larger polity can be categorized in various ways, including the following. The assurance can be *absolute* (fixed, unconditional) or *contingent* (dependent on some reference group). For example, treaties of commerce between two states may reciprocally grant to citizens of each state the right to reside (for business purposes) and do business (as aliens) in the other state. Some assurances in such treaties will be absolute — for example, citizens of each state are given the right to buy or lease real property for residential purposes in the other state. Other assurances will be contingent — for example, citizens of each state are given the right to organize a corporation and qualify to do business in the other state on the same terms as citizens of that other state (so called 'national treatment'). Within this framework, how would you characterize the rights given to members of a designated minority by the Albanian Declaration? Do the majority and dissenting opinions differ about how to characterize them?

2. If you were a member of the Greek-speaking Christian minority, would you have been content with a Declaration that contained no more than a general equal protection clause? If not, why not? How would you justify your argument for more protection?

3. Would Albania have been justified in imposing some control on the Greek schools, such as defining subjects to be taught and censoring teaching materials that, say, urged independence from Albania?

4. Why do the opinions refer to this minorities regime as 'extraordinary'? In what respects does it depart from classical conceptions of international law, or differ from the law of state responsibility?

5. Does a treaty necessarily solve the problems of the method to be employed in 'identifying' and 'applying' international law that were present in *The Paquete Habana* and *Chattin*? How would you characterize the methodologies or conceptions of interpretation that the majority and dissenting opinions reveal? How do those approaches to interpretation differ with respect to their basic assumptions about the relation between the minorities regime and general international law?

6. Consider how close to or distant from the minorities regime Article 27 of the International Covenant on Civil and Political Rights appears on its face to be. It provides:

> In those States in which ethnic, religious or linguistic minorities exist, persons belonging to such minorities shall not be denied the right, in community with the other members of their group, to enjoy their own culture, to profess and practise their own religion, or to use their own language.

ADDITIONAL READING

On the minorities regime, see T. Malloy, *National Minority Rights in Europe* (2005); G. Pentassuglia, *Minorities in International Law: An Introductory Study* (2002); M. Weller, *Universal Minority Rights: A Commentary on the Jurisprudence of International Courts and Treaty Bodies* (2007); S. Wheatley, *Democracy, Minorities and International Law* (2005); R. Letschert, *The Impact of Minority Rights Mechanisms* (2005); and P. de Azcarate, *The League of Nations and National Minorities* (1945). On treaty law, see B. Simma, 'Human Rights and General International Law: A Comparative Analysis', in 4 *Collected Courses of the Academy of European Law* 1 (1995); P. Reuter, *Introduction to the Law of Treaties* (3rd edn. 1995); D. Greig, *Invalidity and the Law of Treaties* (2006); S. Davidson, *The Law of Treaties* (2004); S. Scott, *The Political Interpretation of Multilateral Treaties* (2004).

D. JUDGMENT AT NUREMBERG

COMMENT ON THE NUREMBERG TRIAL

The trial at Nuremberg in 1945–1946 of major war criminals among the Axis powers, dominantly Nazi party leaders and military officials, gave the nascent human rights movement a powerful impulse. The UN Charter that became effective in 1945 included a few broad human rights provisions. But they were more programmatic than operational, more a programme to be realized by states over time than a system in place for application to states. Nuremberg, on the other hand, was concrete and applied: prosecutions, convictions, punishment. The prosecution and the Judgment of the International Military Tribunal in this initial, weighty trial for massive crimes committed during the war years were based on concepts and norms, some of which had deep roots in international law and some of which represented a significant development of that law that opened the path toward the later formulation of fundamental human rights norms.

The striking aspect of Nuremberg was that the trial and Judgment applied international law doctrines and concepts to impose criminal punishment on individuals for their commission of any of the three types of crimes under international law that are described below. The notion of crimes against the law of nations for which violators bore an individual criminal responsibility was itself an older one, but it had operated in a restricted field. As customary international law developed from the time of Grotius, certain conduct came to be considered a violation of the law of nations — in effect, a universal crime. Piracy on the high seas was long the classic example of this limited category of crimes. Given the common interest of all nations in protecting navigation against interference on the high seas outside the territory of any state, it was considered appropriate for the state apprehending a pirate to prosecute in its own courts. Since there was no international criminal tribunal, prosecution in a state court was the only means of judicial enforcement. To the extent that the state courts sought to apply the customary international law defining the crime of piracy, either directly or as it had become absorbed into national legislation, the choice of forum became less significant, for state courts everywhere were in theory applying the same law.

One specialized field, the humanitarian laws of war, had long included rules regulating the conduct of war, the so-called '*jus in bello*'. This body of law imposed sanctions against combatants who committed serious violations of the restrictive rules. Such application of the laws of war, and its foundation in customary norms and in treaties, figure in the Judgment, *infra.* But the concept of individual criminal responsibility was not systematically developed. It achieved a new prominence and a clearer definition after the Nuremberg Judgment, primarily through the Geneva Conventions of 1949 and their 1977 Protocols. Gradually other types of conduct have been added to this small list of individual crimes under international law — for example, slave trading long prior to Nuremberg and genocide thereafter. Recent years have seen the creation of the International Criminal Tribunals for the former Yugoslavia and for Rwanda in the 1990s and the initiation of the International Criminal Court in 2002, all discussed in Chapter 14.

As the Second World War came to an end, the Allied powers held several conferences to determine what policies they should follow towards the Germans responsible for the war and for the systematic barbarity and annihilation of the period. The wartime destruction and civilian losses were known. The nature and extent of the Holocaust were first becoming widely known. These conferences culminated in the (United States, USSR, Britain, France) London Agreement of 8 August 1945, 59 Stat. 1544, E.A.S. No. 472, in which the parties determined to constitute 'an International Military Tribunal for the trial of war criminals'. The Charter annexed to the Agreement provided for the composition and basic procedures of the Tribunal and stated the criminal provisions for the trials in its three critical articles:

Article 6.

The Tribunal established by the Agreement referred to in Article 1 hereof for the trial and punishment of the major war criminals of the European Axis countries shall have the power to try and punish persons who, acting in the interests of the European Axis countries, whether as individuals or as members of organizations, committed any of the following crimes.

The following acts, or any of them, are crimes coming within the jurisdiction of the Tribunal for which there shall be individual responsibility:

(a) *Crimes Against Peace*: namely, planning, preparation, initiation or waging of a war of aggression, or a war in violation of international treaties, agreements or assurances, or participation in a common plan or conspiracy for the accomplishment of any of the foregoing;

(b) *War Crimes*: namely, violations of the laws or customs of war. Such violations shall include, but not be limited to, murder, ill-treatment or deportation to slave labor or for any other purpose of civilian population of or in occupied territory, murder or ill-treatment of prisoners of war or persons on the seas, killing of hostages, plunder of public or private property, wanton destruction of cities, towns or villages, or devastation not justified by military necessity;

(c) *Crimes Against Humanity*: namely, murder, extermination, enslavement, deportation, and other inhumane acts committed against any civilian population, before or during the war, or persecutions on political, racial or religious grounds in execution of or in connection with any crime within the jurisdiction of the Tribunal, whether or not in violation of the domestic law of the country where perpetrated.

Leaders, organizers, instigators and accomplices participating in the formulation or execution of a common plan or conspiracy to commit any of the foregoing crimes are responsible for all acts performed by any persons in execution of such plan.

Article 7.
The official position of defendants, whether as Heads of State or responsible officials in Government Departments, shall not be considered as freeing them from responsibility or mitigating punishment.

Article 8.
The fact that the Defendant acted pursuant to order of his Government or of a superior shall not free him from responsibility, but may be considered in mitigation of punishment if the Tribunal determines that justice so requires.

Note the innovative character of these provisions. Although the Tribunal of four judges (one from each of the major Allied Powers) was restricted to the four victorious powers creating it, nonetheless the Tribunal had an international character in its formation and composition, and to that extent was radically different from the national military courts before which the laws of war had to that time generally been enforced. At the core of the Charter lay the concept of international crimes for which there would be 'individual responsibility', a sharp departure from the then-existing customary law or conventions which stressed the duties of (and sometimes sanctions against) states. Moreover, in defining crimes within the Tribunal's jurisdiction, the Charter went beyond the traditional 'war crimes' (paragraph (b) of Article 6) in two ways.

First, the Charter included the war-related 'crimes against peace' — so-called '*jus ad bellum*', in contrast with the category of war crimes or *jus in bello*. International law had for a long time been innocent of such a concept. After a slow departure during the post-Reformation period from earlier distinctions of philosophers, theologians, and writers on international law between 'just' and 'unjust' wars, the European nations moved towards a conception of war as an instrument of national policy, much like any other, to be legally regulated only with respect to *jus in bello*, the manner of its conduct. The Covenant of the League of Nations did not frontally challenge this principle, although it attempted to control aggression through collective decisions of the League. The interwar period witnessed some fortification of the principles later articulated in the Nuremberg Charter, primarily through the Kellogg-Briand pact of 1927 that is referred to in the Judgment. Today the UN Charter requires members (Article 2(4)) to 'refrain in their international relations from the threat or use of force' against other states, while providing (Article 51) that nothing shall impair 'the inherent right of individual or collective self-defence if an armed attack occurs against a Member . . .'. When viewed in conjunction with the Nuremberg Charter, those provisions suggest the contemporary effort to distinguish not between 'just' and 'unjust' wars but between the permitted 'self-defence' and the forbidden 'aggression'—the word used in defining 'crimes against peace' in Article 6(a) of that Charter.

Second, Article 6(c) represented an important innovation. There were few precedents for use of the phrase 'crimes against humanity' as part of a description of international law, and its content was correspondingly indeterminate. On its face, paragraph (c) might have been read to include the entire programme of the Nazi government to exterminate Jews and other civilian groups, in and outside Germany, whether 'before or during the war', and thus to include not only the Holocaust but also the planning for and early persecution of Jews and other groups preceding the Holocaust. Moreover, that paragraph appeared to bring within its scope the persecution or annihilation by Germany of Jews who were German nationals as well as those who were aliens. This would represent a great advance on the international law of state responsibility to aliens as described at pp. 85–93, *supra*. Note, however, how the Judgment of the Tribunal interpreted Article 6(c) with respect to these observations.

In other respects as well, the concept of 'crimes against humanity', even in this early formulation, developed the earlier international law. War crimes could cover discrete as well as systematic action by a combatant — an isolated murder of a civilian by a combatant as well a systematic policy of wanton destruction of towns. Crimes against humanity were directed primarily to planned conduct, to systematic conduct.

In defining the charges against the major Nazi leaders tried at Nuremberg and its successor tribunals, the Allied powers took care to exclude those types of conduct which had not been understood to violate existing custom or conventions and in which they themselves had engaged — for example, the massive bombing of cities with necessarily high tolls of civilians that was indeed aimed at demoralization of the enemy.

JUDGMENT OF NUREMBERG TRIBUNAL

International Military Tribunal, Nuremberg (1946)
41 Am. J. Int. L. 172 (1947)

. . .

[The Law of the Charter]

The jurisdiction of the Tribunal is defined in the [London] Agreement and Charter, and the crimes coming within the jurisdiction of the Tribunal, for which there shall be individual responsibility, are set out in Article 6. The law of the Charter is decisive, and binding upon the Tribunal.

The making of the Charter was the exercise of the sovereign legislative power by the countries to which the German Reich unconditionally surrendered; and the undoubted right of these countries to legislate for the occupied territories has been recognized by the civilized world. The Charter is not an arbitrary exercise of power on the part of the victorious Nations, but in the view of the Tribunal, as will be shown, it is the expression of international law existing at the time of its creation; and to that extent is itself a contribution to international law.

. . . With regard to the constitution of the Court, all that the defendants are entitled to ask is to receive a fair trial on the facts and law.

The Charter makes the planning or waging of a war of aggression or a war in violation of international treaties a crime; and it is therefore not strictly necessary to consider whether and to what extent aggressive war was a crime before the execution of the London Agreement. But in view of the great importance of the questions of law involved, the Tribunal has heard full argument from the Prosecution and the Defence, and will express its view on the matter.

It was urged on behalf of the defendants that a fundamental principle of all law—international and domestic—is that there can be no punishment of crime without a pre-existing law. '*Nullum crimen sine lege, nulla poena sine lege.*' It was submitted that *ex post facto* punishment is abhorrent to the law of all civilized nations, that no sovereign power had made aggressive war a crime at the time that the alleged criminal acts were committed, that no statute had defined aggressive war, that no penalty had been fixed for its commission, and no court had been created to try and punish offenders.

In the first place, it is to be observed that the maxim *nullum crimen sine lege* is not a limitation of sovereignty, but is in general a principle of justice. To assert that it is unjust to punish those who in defiance of treaties and assurances have attacked neighboring states without warning is obviously untrue, for in such circumstances the attacker must know that he is doing wrong, and so far from it being unjust to punish him, it would be unjust if his wrong were allowed to go unpunished . . .

This view is strongly reinforced by a consideration of the state of international law in 1939, so far as aggressive war is concerned. The General Treaty for the Renunciation of War of 27 August 1928, more generally known as the Pact of Paris or the Kellogg-Briand Pact, was binding on 63 nations, including Germany, Italy and Japan at the outbreak of war in 1939. . . .

. . . The nations who signed the Pact or adhered to it unconditionally condemned recourse to war for the future as an instrument of policy, and expressly renounced it. After the signing of the Pact, any nation resorting to war as an instrument of national policy breaks the Pact. In the opinion of the Tribunal, the solemn renunciation of war as an instrument of national policy necessarily involves the proposition that such a war is illegal in international law; and that those who plan and wage such a war, with its inevitable and terrible consequences, are committing a crime in so doing. War for the solution of international controversies undertaken as an instrument of national policy certainly includes a war of aggression, and such a war is therefore outlawed by the Pact. . . .

. . . The Hague Convention of 1907 prohibited resort to certain methods of waging war. These included the inhumane treatment of prisoners, the employment of poisoned weapons, the improper use of flags of truce, and similar matters. Many of these prohibitions had been enforced long before the date of the Convention; but since 1907 they have certainly been crimes, punishable as offenses against the law of war; yet the Hague Convention nowhere designates such practices as criminal, nor is any sentence prescribed, nor any mention made of a court to try and punish offenders. For many years past, however, military tribunals have tried and punished individuals guilty of violating the rules of land warfare laid down by this

Convention. In the opinion of the Tribunal, those who wage aggressive war are doing that which is equally illegal, and of much greater moment than a breach of one of the rules of the Hague Convention.... The law of war is to be found not only in treaties, but in the customs and practices of states which gradually obtained universal recognition, and from the general principles of justice applied by jurists and practised by military courts. This law is not static, but by continual adaptation follows the needs of a changing world. Indeed, in many cases treaties do no more than express and define for more accurate reference the principles of law already existing. ...

All these expressions of opinion, and others that could be cited, so solemnly made, reinforce the construction which the Tribunal placed upon the Pact of Paris, that resort to a war of aggression is not merely illegal, but is criminal. The prohibition of aggressive war demanded by the conscience of the world, finds its expression in the series of pacts and treaties to which the Tribunal has just referred. ...

... That international law imposes duties and liabilities upon individuals as well as upon States has long been recognized. . . . Crimes against international law are committed by men, not by abstract entities, and only by punishing individuals who commit such crimes can the provisions of international law be enforced. ...

The authors of these acts cannot shelter themselves behind their official position in order to be freed from punishment in appropriate proceedings. Article 7 of the Charter expressly declares:

> The official position of Defendants, whether as heads of State, or responsible officials in Government departments, shall not be considered as freeing them from responsibility, or mitigating punishment.

On the other hand the very essence of the Charter is that individuals have international duties which transcend the national obligations of obedience imposed by the individual state. He who violates the laws of war cannot obtain immunity while acting in pursuance of the authority of the state if the state in authorizing action moves outside its competence under international law.

It was also submitted on behalf of most of these defendants that in doing what they did they were acting under the orders of Hitler, and therefore cannot be held responsible for the acts committed by them in carrying out these orders. The Charter specifically provides in Article 8:

> The fact that the Defendant acted pursuant to order of his Government or of a superior shall not free him from responsibility, but may be considered in mitigation of punishment.

The provisions of this article are in conformity with the law of all nations. That a soldier was ordered to kill or torture in violation of the international law of war has never been recognized as a defense to such acts of brutality, though, as the Charter here provides, the order may be urged in mitigation of the punishment. The true test, which is found in varying degrees in the criminal law of most nations, is not the existence of the order, but whether moral choice was in fact possible.

...

War Crimes and Crimes against Humanity

... War Crimes were committed on a vast scale, never before seen in the history of war. They were perpetrated in all the countries occupied by Germany, and on the High Seas, and were attended by every conceivable circumstance of cruelty and horror. There can be no doubt that the majority of them arose from the Nazi conception of 'total war', with which the aggressive wars were waged. For in this conception of 'total war,' the moral ideas underlying the conventions which seek to make war more humane are no longer regarded as having force or validity. Everything is made subordinate to the overmastering dictates of war. Rules, regulations, assurances, and treaties all alike are of no moment; and so, freed from the restraining influence of international law, the aggressive war is conducted by the Nazi leaders in the most barbaric way. Accordingly, War Crimes were committed when and wherever the Führer and his close associates thought them to be advantageous. They were for the most part the result of cold and criminal calculation.

...

... Prisoners of war were ill-treated and tortured and murdered, not only in defiance of the well-established rules of international law, but in complete disregard of the elementary dictates of humanity. Civilian populations in occupied territories suffered the same fate. Whole populations were deported to Germany for the purposes of slave labor upon defense works, armament production, and similar tasks connected with the war effort. Hostages were taken in very large numbers from the civilian populations in all the occupied countries, and were shot as suited the German purposes. Public and private property was systematically plundered and pillaged in order to enlarge the resources of Germany at the expense of the rest of Europe. Cities and towns and villages were wantonly destroyed without military justification or necessity.

...

Murder and Ill-Treatment of Civilian Population

Article 6(b) of the Charter provides that 'ill-treatment ... of civilian population of or in occupied territory ... killing of hostages ... wanton destruction of cities, towns, or villages' shall be a war crime. In the main, these provisions are merely declaratory of the existing laws of war as expressed by the Hague Convention, Article 46....

...

One of the most notorious means of terrorizing the people in occupied territories was the use of concentration camps ... [which] became places of organized and systematic murder, where millions of people were destroyed.

In the administration of the occupied territories the concentration camps were used to destroy all opposition groups....

A certain number of the concentration camps were equipped with gas chambers for the wholesale destruction of the inmates, and with furnaces for the burning of the bodies. Some of them were in fact used for the extermination of Jews as part of the 'final solution' of the Jewish problem. . . .

. . .

Slave Labor Policy

Article 6(b) of the Charter provides that the 'ill-treatment or deportation to slave labor or for any other purpose, of civilian population of or in occupied territory' shall be a War Crime. The laws relating to forced labor by the inhabitants of occupied territories are found in Article 52 of the Hague Convention. . . . The policy of the German occupation authorities was in flagrant violation of the terms of this convention. . . . [T]he German occupation authorities did succeed in forcing many of the inhabitants of the occupied territories to work for the German war effort, and in deporting at least 5,000,000 persons to Germany to serve German industry and agriculture.

. . .

Persecution of the Jews

The persecution of the Jews at the hands of the Nazi Government has been proved in the greatest detail before the Tribunal. It is a record of consistent and systematic inhumanity on the greatest scale. Ohlendorf, Chief of Amt III in the RSHA from 1939 to 1943, and who was in command of one of the Einsatz groups in the campaign against the Soviet Union testified as to the methods employed in the extermination of the Jews. . . .

When the witness Bach Zelewski was asked how Ohlendorf could admit the murder of 90,000 people, he replied: 'I am of the opinion that when, for years, for decades, the doctrine is preached that the Slav race is an inferior race, and Jews not even human, then such an outcome is inevitable'.

. . .

. . . The Nazi Party preached these doctrines throughout its history, *Der Stürmer* and other publications were allowed to disseminate hatred of the Jews, and in the speeches and public declarations of the Nazi leaders, the Jews were held up to public ridicule and contempt.

. . . By the autumn of 1938, the Nazi policy towards the Jews had reached the stage where it was directed towards the complete exclusion of Jews from German life. Pogroms were organized, which included the burning and demolishing of synagogues, the looting of Jewish businesses, and the arrest of prominent Jewish business men. . . .

It was contended for the Prosecution that certain aspects of this anti-Semitic policy were connected with the plans for aggressive war. The violent measures taken against the Jews in November 1938 were nominally in retaliation for the killing of an official of the German Embassy in Paris. But the decision to seize Austria and Czechoslovakia had been made a year before. The imposition of a fine of one billion marks was made, and the confiscation of the financial holdings of the Jews was decreed, at a time when German armament expenditure had put the German treasury in difficulties, and when the reduction of expenditure on armaments was being considered. . . .

It was further said that the connection of the anti-Semitic policy with aggressive war was not limited to economic matters. . . .

The Nazi persecution of Jews in Germany before the war, severe and repressive as it was, cannot compare, however, with the policy pursued during the war in the occupied territories. . . . In the summer of 1941, however, plans were made for the 'final solution' of the Jewish question in Europe. This 'final solution' meant the extermination of the Jews. . . .

The plan for exterminating the Jews was developed shortly after the attack on the Soviet Union. . . .

. . .

. . . Adolf Eichmann, who had been put in charge of this program by Hitler, has estimated that the policy pursued resulted in the killing of 6 million Jews, of which 4 million were killed in the extermination institutions.

The Law Relating to War Crimes and Crimes against Humanity

. . .

The Tribunal is of course bound by the Charter, in the definition which it gives both of War Crimes and Crimes against Humanity. With respect to War Crimes, however, as has already been pointed out, the crimes defined by Article 6, Section (b), of the Charter were already recognized as War Crimes under international law. They were covered by Articles 46, 50, 52, and 56 of the Hague Convention of 1907, and Articles 2, 3, 4, 46, and 51 of the Geneva Convention of 1929. That violation of these provisions constituted crimes for which the guilty individuals were punishable is too well settled to admit of argument.

But it is argued that the Hague Convention does not apply in this case, because of the 'general participation' clause in Article 2 of the Hague Convention of 1907. That clause provided:

> The provisions contained in the regulations (Rules of Land Warfare) referred to in Article 1 as well as in the present Convention do not apply except between contracting powers, and then only if all the belligerents are parties to the Convention.

Several of the belligerents in the recent war were not parties to this Convention.

In the opinion of the Tribunal it is not necessary to decide this question. The rules of land warfare expressed in the Convention undoubtedly represented an advance over existing international law at the time of their adoption. But the convention expressly stated that it was an attempt 'to revise the general laws and customs of war', which it thus recognized to be then existing, but by 1939 these rules laid down in the Convention were recognized by all civilized nations, and were regarded as being declaratory of the laws and customs of war which are referred to in Article 6(b) of the Charter.

. . .

With regard to Crimes against Humanity there is no doubt whatever that political opponents were murdered in Germany before the war, and that many of them were kept in concentration camps in circumstances of great horror and cruelty. The policy of terror was certainly carried out on a vast scale, and in many cases was organized and systematic. The policy of persecution, repression, and murder of civilians in Germany before the war of 1939, who were likely to be hostile to the Government, was most ruthlessly carried out. The persecution of Jews during the same period is established beyond all doubt. To constitute Crimes against Humanity, the acts relied on before the outbreak of war must have been in execution of, or in connection with, any crime within the jurisdiction of the Tribunal. The Tribunal is of the opinion that revolting and horrible as many of these crimes were, it has not been satisfactorily proved that they were done in execution of, or in connection with, any such crime. The Tribunal therefore cannot make a general declaration that the acts before 1939 were Crimes against Humanity within the meaning of the Charter, but from the beginning of the war in 1939 War Crimes were committed on a vast scale, which were also Crimes against Humanity; and insofar as the inhumane acts charged in the Indictment, and committed after the beginning of the war, did not constitute War Crimes, they were all committed in execution of, or in connection with, the aggressive war, and therefore constituted Crimes against Humanity.

[The opinion considered individually each of the 22 defendants at this first trial of alleged war criminals. It found 19 of the defendants guilty of one or more counts of the indictment. It imposed 12 death sentences. Most convictions were for War Crimes and Crimes against Humanity, the majority of those convicted being found guilty of both crimes.]

NOTE

Note the following statement in Ian Brownlie, *Principles of Public International Law* (4th edn. 1990), at 562:

> But whatever the state of the law in 1945, Article 6 of the Nuremberg Charter has since come to represent general international law. The Agreement to which the Charter was annexed was signed by the United States, United Kingdom, France, and USSR, and nineteen other states subsequently adhered to it. In a resolution adopted unanimously on 11 December 1946, the General Assembly affirmed 'the principles of international law recognized by the Charter of the Nuremberg Tribunal and the judgment of the Tribunal'.

There has been considerable expansion in the definitions of two of the crimes defined in Article 6. The field of individual criminal responsibility for war crimes has been both broadened and clarified, through provisions of the Geneva Conventions of 1949 and of the 1998 Rome Statute for the International Criminal Court. Particularly relevant are the provisions for 'grave breaches' in these conventions, later discussed. The concept of crimes against humanity has expanded greatly in coverage and shed some limitations placed on it by the Judgment of the Tribunal. Such developments are described in the materials dealing with the current International Criminal Tribunals for the Former Yugoslavia and for Rwanda and the International Criminal Court in Chapter 14. The notion of 'crimes against peace', however, has fallen into relative disuse.

The problem of *ex post facto* trials has received much commentary, some of which appears below. See in this connection Article 15 of the International Covenant on Civil and Political Rights.

Compare with the Nuremberg Judgment the following provisions of the Convention on the Prevention and Punishment of the Crime of Genocide (140 parties as of January 2007) bearing on personal responsibility. The treaty parties 'confirm' in Article I that genocide 'is a crime under international law which they undertake to prevent and to punish'. Article 2 defines genocide:

> In the present Convention, genocide means any of the following acts committed with intent to destroy, in whole or in part, a national, ethnical, racial or religious group, as such:
>
> (a) Killing members of the group;
> (b) Causing serious bodily or mental harm to members of the group;
> (c) Deliberately inflicting on the group conditions of life calculated to bring about its physical destruction in whole or in part;
> (d) Imposing measures intended to prevent births within the group;
> (e) Forcibly transferring children of the group to another group.

Persons committing acts of genocide 'shall be punished, whether they are constitutionally responsible rulers, public officials or private individuals' (Art. IV). The parties agree (Art. V) to enact the necessary legislation to give effect to the Convention and 'to provide effective penalties for persons guilty of genocide'. Under Article VI, persons charged with genocide are to be tried by a tribunal 'of the State in the territory of which the act was committed, or by such international penal tribunal as may have jurisdiction with respect to those Contracting Parties which shall have accepted its jurisdiction'. No international penal tribunal of general jurisdiction has been created.

VIEWS OF COMMENTATORS

There follow a number of authors' observations about the charges, the Judgment and the principles in the Nuremberg trials.

(1) In a review of a book by Sheldon Glueck entitled *The Nuremberg Trial and Aggressive War* (1946), the reviewer George Finch, 47 Am. J. Int. L. 334 (1947), makes the following arguments:

> As the title indicates, this book deals with the charges at Nuremberg based upon the planning and waging of aggressive war. The author has written it because in his previous volume he expressed the view that he did not think such acts could be regarded as 'international crimes'. He has now changed his mind and believes 'that for the purpose of conceiving aggressive war to be an international crime, the Pact of Paris may, together with other treaties and resolutions, be regarded as evidence of a sufficiently developed *custom* to be accepted as international law' (pp. 4–5)....
>
> The reviewer fully agrees with the author in regard to the place of custom in the development of international law. He regards as untenable, however, the argument

> not only of the author but of the prosecutors and judges at Nuremberg that custom can be judicially established by placing interpretations upon the words of treaties which are refuted by the acts of the signatories in practice, by citing unratified protocols or public and private resolutions of no legal effect, and by ignoring flagrant and repeated violations of non-aggression pacts by one of the prosecuting governments which, if properly weighed in the evidence, would nullify any judicial holding that a custom outlawing aggressive war had been accepted in international law. . . .

(2) In his article, 'The Nurnberg Trial', 33 Va. L. Rev. 679 (1947), at 694, Francis Biddle, the American judge on the Tribunal, commented on the definition of 'crimes against humanity' in Article 6(c) of the Charter:

> . . . The authors of the Charter evidently realized that the crimes enumerated were essentially domestic and hardly subject to the incidence of international law, unless partaking of the nature of war crimes. Their purpose was evidently to reach the terrible persecution of the Jews and liberals within Germany before the war. But the Tribunal held that 'revolting and horrible as many of these crimes were', it had not been established that they were done 'in execution of, or in connection with' any crime within its jurisdiction. After the beginning of the war, however, these inhumane acts were held to have been committed in execution of the war, and were therefore crimes against humanity.
>
> . . .
>
> Crimes against humanity constitute a somewhat nebulous conception, although the expression is not unknown to the language of international law. . . . With one possible exception . . . crimes against humanity were held [in the Judgment of the Tribunal] to have been committed only where the proof also fully established the commission of war crimes. Mr. Stimson suggested [that the Tribunal eliminate from its jurisdiction matters related to pre-war persecution in Germany], which involved 'a reduction of the meaning of crimes against humanity to a point where they became practically synonymous with war crimes'. I agree. And I believe that this inelastic construction is justified by the language of the Charter and by the consideration that such a rigid interpretation is highly desirable in this stage of the development of international law.

(3) Professor Hans Kelsen, in 'Will the Judgment in the Nuremberg Trial Constitute a Precedent in International Law?', 1 Int. L. Q. 153 (1947) at 164, was critical of several aspects of the London Agreement and the Judgment. But with respect to the question of retroactivity of criminal punishment, he wrote:

> The objection most frequently put forward — although not the weightiest one — is that the law applied by the judgment of Nuremberg is an ex post facto law. There can be little doubt that the London Agreement provides individual punishment for acts which, at the time they were performed were not punishable, either under international law or under any national law. . . . However, this rule [against retroactive legislation] is not valid at all within international law, and is valid within national law only with important exceptions. [Kelsen notes several exceptions, including the rule's irrelevance to 'customary law and to law created by a

precedent, for such law is necessarily retroactive in respect to the first case to which it is applied. . . .']

A retroactive law providing individual punishment for acts which were illegal though not criminal at the time they were committed, seems also to be an exception to the rule against ex post facto laws. The London Agreement is such a law. It is retroactive only in so far as it established individual criminal responsibility for acts which at the time they were committed constituted violations of existing international law, but for which this law has provided only collective responsibility. . . . Since the internationally illegal acts for which the London Agreement established individual criminal responsibility were certainly also morally most objectionable, and the persons who committed these acts were certainly aware of their immoral character, the retroactivity of the law applied to them can hardly be considered as absolutely incompatible with justice.

(4) In his biography entitled *Harlan Fiske Stone: Pillar of the Law* (1956), Alpheus Thomas Mason discussed Chief Justice Stone's views about the involvement of Justices of the US Supreme Court in extrajudicial assignments and, in particular, Stone's views about President Truman's appointment of Justice Robert Jackson to be American Prosecutor at the trials. The following excerpts (at 715) are all incorporations by Mason in his book of quotations of Chief Justice Stone's remarks.

So far as the Nuremberg trial is an attempt to justify the application of the power of the victor to the vanquished because the vanquished made aggressive war, . . . I dislike extremely to see it dressed up with a false facade of legality. The best that can be said for it is that it is a political act of the victorious States which may be morally right. . . . It would not disturb me greatly. . . . if that power were openly and frankly used to punish the German leaders for being a bad lot, but it disturbs me some to have it dressed up in the habiliments of the common law and the Constitutional safeguards to those charged with crime.

Jackson is away conducting his high-grade lynching party in Nuremberg. . . . I don't mind what he does to the Nazis, but I hate to see the pretense that he is running a court and proceeding according to common law. This is a little too sanctimonious a fraud to meet my old-fashioned ideas.

(5) Professor Herbert Wechsler, in 'The Issues of the Nuremberg Trial', 62 Pol. Sci. Q. 11 (1947), at 23 observed:

. . . [M]ost of those who mount the attack [on the Judgment on contentions including ex post facto law] hasten to assure us that their plea is not one of immunity for the defendants; they argue only that they should have been disposed of politically, that is, dispatched out of hand. This is a curious position indeed. A punitive enterprise launched on the basis of general rules, administered in an adversary proceeding under a separation of prosecutive and adjudicative powers is, in the name of law and justice, asserted to be less desirable than an ex parte execution list or a drumhead court-martial constituted in the immediate aftermath of the war. . . Those who choose to do so may view the Nuremberg proceeding as 'political' rather than 'legal' — a program calling for the judicial application of principles of liability politically defined. They cannot view it as less civilized an institution than a program of organized violence against prisoners, whether directed from the respective capitals or by military commanders in the field.

(6) Mark Osiel, in *Mass Atrocity, Collective Memory, and the Law* (1997), comments on charges against the defeated states (at 122):

For the Nuremberg and Tokyo courts, it mattered little to the validity of criminal proceedings against Axis leadership that Allied victors had committed vast war crimes of their own. Unlike the law of tort, criminal law has virtually no place for 'comparative fault', no doctrinal device for mitigating the wrongdoing or culpability of the accused in light of the accusers'. . . . For the public, however, . . . it mattered *greatly* in gauging the legitimacy of the trials that they seemed tendentiously selective, aimed at focusing memory in partisan ways. It mattered for such listeners that the defendants . . . had constituted only a single side to a two- or multi-sided conflict, one in which other parties had similarly committed unlawful acts on a large scale. This unsavory feature of the Nuremberg judgment has undermined its authority in the minds of many, weakening its normative weight.

(7) David Luban, in *Legal Modernism* (1994), describes what he sees as a confusion in the Nuremberg charges (at 336):

This idea that Nuremberg was to be the Trial to End All Wars seems fantastic and naïve forty years (and 150 wars) later. It has also done much to vitiate the real achievements of the trial, in particular the condemnation of crimes against humanity. To end all war, the authors of the Nuremberg Charter were led to incorporate an intellectual confusion into it. The Charter criminalized aggression; and by criminalizing aggression, the Charter erected a wall around state sovereignty and committed itself to an old-European model of unbreachable nation-states.

But crimes against humanity are often, even characteristically, carried out by states against their own subjects. The effect, and great moral and legal achievement, of criminalizing such acts and assigning personal liability to those who order them and carry them out is to pierce the veil of sovereignty. As a result, Article 6(a) pulls in the opposite direction from Articles 6(c), 7 and 8, leaving us . . . with a legacy that is at best equivocal and at worst immoral.

(8) Thane Rosenbaum, in 'The Romance of Nuremberg and the Tease of Moral Justice,' 27 Cardozo L. Rev. 1731 (2006), argues about legal and moral justice (at 1736):

When it came to the Nazis, jurisdictional concerns, retroactive punishments, standard causation requirements, and freedom of association principles, were not going to impede moral justice and the development of international law. No one seemed to mind during Nuremberg that these constitutional principles were being upended, and that a strict adherence to constitutional safeguards seemingly did not make the trip to Germany. Given the enormity of the Nazis' crimes and the moral implications of acquitting them on procedural grounds, the Constitution, as a document, apparently was deemed not fit for travel and therefore was left behind. There was little ambivalence among the American prosecutors, including a sitting Supreme Court justice, about applying this new path to justice, one that looked legal but tilted in an entirely moral direction.

QUESTIONS

1. Recall clause (c) of Article 38(1) of the Statute of the ICJ, and the comments thereon of Oscar Schachter, at p. 94, *supra*. Should the Tribunal have relied on that clause to respond to charges of *ex post facto* application of Article 6(c) to individuals who were responsible for the murder of groups of Germans or aliens?

2. Do you agree with the Tribunal's restrictive interpretation of Article 6(c)? Consider the commentary above of Francis Biddle.

3. How do you evaluate the criticism by Finch of the Tribunal's use of treaties in deciding whether customary international law included a given norm? Recall the comments about the growth of customary law by Schachter.

4. How do you evaluate the criticism of the Nuremberg trial by Chief Justice Stone? By Osiel? By Luban? By Rosenbaum?

5. Why do you suppose that Article 6(a) on crimes against peace (wars of aggression) has fallen into disuse with respect to individual criminal liability? It was omitted from the criminal provisions in the Statutes for the International Criminal Tribunals for the Former Yugoslavia and for Rwanda. The Rome Treaty creating the International Criminal Court states that the Court shall have jurisdiction over 'the crime of aggression once a provision is adopted [by the parties to the treaty] defining the crime ...' No such provision has been adopted.

6. How do you assess the significance and consequences of Nuremberg? Even if you agree with some or several of the criticisms above, do you nonetheless conclude that the trial and judgment were justified in their actual historical forms? If so, why?

ADDITIONAL READING

On Nuremberg see three books by Telford Taylor: *Nuremberg Trials: War Crimes and International Law* (1949); *Nuremberg and Vietnam: An American Tragedy* (1978); and *The Anatomy of the Nuremberg Trials: A Personal Memoir* (1992). See also Memorandum Submitted by the Secretary-General, *The Charter and Judgment of the Nürnberg Tribunal: History and Analysis*, UN Doc. A/CN.4/5 (1949); Egon Schwelb, 'Crimes against Humanity', 23 Brit. Ybk. Int. L. 178 (1946); Symposium: The Nuremberg Trials: A Reappraisal and Their Legacy, 27 Cardozo L. Rev. 1549–1738 (2006). More generally, see T. Meron, *War Crimes Law Comes of Age: Essays* (1998).

NOTE

This chapter has offered an illustrative survey of different forms or sources of international law (custom, general principles, treaties) and of several traditional international law topics (laws of war, state responsibility, minority-protection treaties, and international criminal law) as background to the study of the post-Second World War human rights movement. The following excerpts from lectures by Louis Henkin fill in a number of gaps in the history of ways in which pre-1945 international law had been concerned with protection of individuals. Like the earlier materials in this chapter, they too bring contemporary human rights to mind.

LOUIS HENKIN, INTERNATIONAL LAW: POLITICS, VALUES AND FUNCTIONS

216 Collected Courses of The Hague Academy of International Law (Vol. IV, 1989) 13, at 208

Chapter X
State Values and Other Values: Human Rights

. . .

That until recently international law took no note of individual human beings may be surprising. Both international law and domestic legal norms in the Christian world had roots in an accepted morality and in natural law, and had common intellectual progenitors (including Grotius, Locke, Vattel). But for hundreds of years international law and the law governing individual life did not come together. International law, true to its name, was law only between States, governing only relations between States on the State level. What a State did inside its borders in relation to its own nationals remained its own affair, an element of its autonomy, a matter of its 'domestic jurisdiction'.

Antecedents of the International Law of Human Rights

In fact, neither the international political system nor international law ever closed out totally what went on inside a State and what happened to individuals within a State. Early, international law began to attend to internal matters that held special interest for other States, and those sometimes included concern for individual human beings, or at least redounded to the benefit of individual human beings. But what was in fact of interest to other States, and what was accepted as being of legitimate interest to other States (and therefore to the system and to law), were limited *a priori* by the character of the State system and its values. Of course, every State was legitimately concerned with what happened to its diplomats, to its diplomatic mission and to its property in the territory of another State. States were concerned, and the system developed norms to assure, that their nationals (and the property of their nationals) in the territory of another State be treated reasonably, 'fairly', and the system and the law early identified an international standard of justice by which a State must abide in its treatment of foreign nationals. States also entered into agreements, usually on a reciprocal basis, promising protection or privilege — freedom to reside, to conduct business, to worship — to persons with whom the other State party to the treaty identified because of common religion or ethnicity.

Concern for individual human welfare seeped into the international system in the eighteenth and nineteenth centuries in other discrete, specific respects. In the nineteenth century, European (and American) States abolished slavery and slave trade. Later, States began to pursue agreements to make war less inhumane, to outlaw some cruel weapons to safeguard prisoners of war, the wounded, civilian populations. It is noteworthy that, in these instances, even less-than-democratic States began to attend to human values, though humanitarian limitations on the conduct of war may have brought significant cost to the State's military interests.

Following the First World War, concern for individual human beings was reflected in several League of Nations programmes. Building on earlier precedents in the nineteenth century, the dominant States pressed selected other States to adhere to 'minorities treaties' guaranteed by the League, in which States Parties assumed obligations to respect rights of identified ethnic, national or religious minorities among their inhabitants.... The years following the First World War also saw a major development in international concern for individual welfare, a development that is often overlooked and commonly underestimated: the International Labour Office (now the International Labour Organisation (ILO)) was established and it launched a variety of programmes including a series of conventions setting minimum standards for working conditions and related matters.

In general, the principles of customary international law that developed, and the special agreements that were concluded, addressed only what happened to *some* people inside a State, only in respects with which other States were in fact concerned, and only where such concern was considered their proper business in a system of autonomous States. One can only speculate as to why States accepted these norms and agreements, but it may be reasonable to doubt whether those developments authentically reflected sensitivity to human rights generally. States attended to what occurred inside another State when such happenings impinged on their political-economic interests. States were concerned, and were deemed legitimately concerned, for the freedoms, privileges, and immunities of their diplomats because an affront to the diplomat affronted his prince (or his State), and because interference with a diplomat interfered with his functions and disturbed orderly, friendly relations. Injury to a foreign national or to his or her property was also an affront to the State of his or her nationality, and powerful States exporting people, goods, and capital to other countries in the age of growing mercantilism insisted on law that would protect the State interests that these represented.

...

Humanitarian developments in the law of war reflected some concern by States to reduce the horrors of war for their own people and a willingness in exchange to reduce them for others. Powerful States promoted minorities treaties because mistreatment of minorities with which other States identified threatened international peace. Those treaties were imposed selectively, principally on nations defeated in war and on newly created or enlarged States; they did not establish general norms requiring respect for minorities by the big and the powerful as well; they did not require respect for individuals who were not members of identified minorities, or for members of the majority....

Even the ILO conventions, perhaps, served some less-than-altruistic purposes. Improvement in the conditions of labour was capitalism's defence against the spectre of spreading socialism which had just established itself in the largest country in Europe. States, moreover, had a direct interest in the conditions of labour in countries with which they competed in a common international market: a State impelled to improve labour and social conditions at home could not readily do so unless other States did so, lest the increase in its costs of production render its products non-competitive.

I have stressed the possibly political-economic (rather than humanitarian) motivations for early norms and agreements, identifying a State's concern for the welfare of some of its nationals as an extension of its Statehood and perhaps reflecting principally concern for State interests and values. If some norms and agreements in fact were motivated by concern for a State's own people generally, they did not reflect interest in the welfare of those in other countries, or of human beings generally. State interests rather than individual human interests, or at best the interests of a State's own people rather than general human concerns, also inspired voluntary inter-State co-operation to promote reciprocal economic interests. . . .

I would not underestimate the influence of ideas of rights and constitutionalism in the seventeenth and eighteenth centuries, and of a growing and spreading enlightenment generally: Locke, Montesquieu, other Encyclopedists, Rousseau; the example of the Glorious Revolution in England and the establishment of constitutionalism in the United States; the influence of the French Declaration of the Rights of Man and of the Citizen. Such ideas and examples have influenced developments inside countries, but they did not easily enter the international political and legal system. Concern by one country for the welfare of individual human beings inside another country met many obstacles, not least the conception and implications of Statehood in a State system. The human condition in other countries and the treatment of individuals by other Governments were not commonly known abroad since they were not included in the information sources of the time. Information (and concern) were filtered through the State system and through diplomatic sources, and human values as such were not the business of diplomacy. For those reasons, and for other reasons flowing from the State system, other States took little note and expressed little concern for what a Government did to its own citizens. In general, the veil of Statehood was impermeable. If occasionally something particularly horrendous happened — a massacre, pogrom — and was communicated and made known by the available media of communication, it evoked from other States more-or-less polite diplomatic expressions of regret, not on grounds of law but of *noblesse oblige* or of common princely morality wrapped in Christian charity (whose violation gave princes and Christianity a bad name).

Even if the implications of Statehood had not been an obstacle, as regards any but the grossest violations of what we now call human rights, few if any States had moral sensitivity and moral standing to intercede. When a State invoked an international standard of justice on behalf of one of its nationals abroad, it may have been invoking a standard unknown and unheeded at home. Few States had constitutional protections and not many had effective legislative or common-law protections for individual rights. Torture and police brutality, denials of due process, arbitrary detention, perversions of law, were not wildly abnormal. Surely, few States recognized political freedom — freedom of speech, association and assembly, universal suffrage. Many States denied religious freedom to some, and few States granted complete religious toleration; full equality to members of other than the dominant religion was slow in coming anywhere. Women were subject to rampant and deep-rooted inequalities and domination, often to abuse and oppression. Even today such violations are not the stuff of dramatic television programmes and do not arouse international revulsion and reaction; in earlier times, surely, violations of what are today recognized as civil and political rights caused little stir outside the country. A State's failure to provide for the economic and social welfare of its inhabitants was wholly beyond the ken of other States. There were no alert media of information and few civil rights or other non-governmental organizations to sensitize and activate people and Governments.

. . .

E. BIRTH OF THE MOVEMENT: THE UN CHARTER AND THE UDHR

The Nuremberg trial and several provisions of the United Nations Charter of 1945 held centre stage in the incipient human rights movement until 1948, when the UN General Assembly approved the Universal Declaration of Human Rights. For 28 years, the UDHR occupied centre stage. The two fundamental human rights treaties, the International Covenant on Civil and Political Rights and the International Covenant on Economic, Social and Cultural Rights, both became effective in 1976. (Note: only these two human rights treaties bear the solemn title of 'Covenant'.)

Together with the Declaration, the Covenants form the International Bill of Human Rights, which now stands at the core of the *universal* human rights system — universal in the sense that membership is open to states from all parts of the world. Chapter 11 examines three regional human rights systems, each open to members only from the designated part of the world: the European Convention for the Protection of Human Rights and Fundamental Freedoms (known as the 'European Convention on Human Rights'), the American Convention on Human Rights, and the African Charter on Human and Peoples' Rights. Each of these treaties is supported and developed (in different ways) by an intergovernmental body that in most cases is created by the treaty itself. The central institutional participants in the human rights movement also include other intergovernmental bodies such as the International Labour Organization, national governments and human rights agencies, nongovernmental human rights organizations, and a range of nongovernmental (and often international) organizations such as labour unions and churches.

This section focuses on the Charter and Declaration, while the next two chapters examine respectively civil and political rights, and economic and social rights. The Declaration itself includes both categories. These categories are far from airtight. Many treaties declare rights that straddle the two, or that fall clearly within the domains of both of them. Many rights are hard to categorize. Nonetheless, at their core, the conventional distinctions are clear, whatever the relationships and interdependency between the two. Freedom from torture, equal protection, due process and the right to form political associations fall within the first category; the right to health or food or education come within the second.

COMMENT ON THE CHARTER, UDHR AND ORIGINS OF THE HUMAN RIGHTS MOVEMENT

The human rights movement is not simply a systematic ordering, basically through treaties and customary law, of fundamental postulates, ideologies and norms (that is, 'oughts' in the form of rules, standards, principles). To the contrary, these basic elements are imbedded in institutions, some of them state and some international, some governmental or intergovernmental and some nongovernmental and in related international processes. It is impossible to grasp this movement adequately without an appreciation of its close relation to and reliance on international organizations. For example, the basic instruments of the universal system were drafted within the different organs of the United Nations and adopted by its General Assembly, before (in the case of the treaties) being submitted to states for ratification. UN organs play a major role in monitoring, officially commenting on, and applying sanctions to state behaviour.

The United Nations Charter itself first gave formal and authoritative expression to the human rights movement that began at the end of the Second World War. Since its birth in 1945, the UN has served as a vital institutional spur to the development of the movement, as well as serving as a major forum for many-sided debates about it. The purpose of the present comments is to call attention to aspects of the UN and its Charter that bear particularly on the human rights movement.

Readers should now become familiar with the provisions (in the Documents Supplement) of the Charter that are referred to below, and of the UDHR.

Charter Provisions

Consider first the Charter's radical transformation of the branch of the laws of war concerning *jus ad bellum.* Recall that for several centuries that body of law had addressed almost exclusively *jus in bello*, the rules regulating the conduct of warfare rather than the justice or legality of the waging of war. The International Military Tribunal at Nuremberg was empowered to adjudicate 'crimes against peace', part of *jus ad bellum* and the most disputed element of that Tribunal's mandate.

The Charter builds on the precedents to which the Nuremberg Judgment refers and states the UN's basic purpose of securing and maintaining peace. It does so by providing in Article 2(4) that UN members 'shall refrain in their international relations from the threat or use of force against the territorial integrity or political independence of any state', a rule qualified by Article 51's provision that nothing in the Charter 'shall impair the inherent right of individual or collective self-defence if an armed attack occurs' against a member.

The Charter's references to human rights are scattered, terse, even cryptic. The term 'human rights' appears infrequently. Note its occurrence in the following provisions: second paragraph of the Preamble, Article 1(3), Article 13(1)(b), Articles 55 and 56, Article 62(2) and Article 68.

Several striking characteristics of these provisions emerge. Many have a promotional or programmatic character, for they refer principally to the purposes or goals of the UN or to the competences of different UN organs: 'encouraging respect for human rights', 'assisting in the realization of human rights', 'promote . . . universal respect for, and observance of, human rights'. Not even a provision such as Article 56, which refers to action of the Member States rather than of the UN, contains the language of obligation. It notes only that states 'pledge themselves' to action 'for the achievement' of purposes including the promotion of observance of human rights. Note that only one substantive human right, the right to equal protection, receives specific mention in the Charter (Articles 1(3), 13(1)(b) and 55).

The Universal Declaration

Despite proposals to the contrary, the Charter stopped shy of incorporating a bill of rights. Instead, there were proposals for developing one through the work of a special commission that would give separate attention to the issue. That commission was contemplated by Charter Article 68, which provides that one of the UN organs, the Economic and Social Council (ECOSOC), 'shall set up commissions in economic and social fields and for the promotion of human rights'. In 1946, ECOSOC established the Commission on Human Rights (referred to in this book as the UN Commission), which evolved over the decades to become the world's single most important (and perhaps most disputed) human rights organ. At its inception, the new Commission was charged primarily with submitting reports and proposals on an international bill of rights. (The UN Commission was displaced by a newly created Human Rights Council in 2006. Chapter 9 examines the work of both the Commission and Council.)

The UN Commission first met in its present form early in 1947, its individual members (representatives of the states that were members of the Commission) including such distinguished founders of the human rights movement as René Cassin of France, Charles Malik of Lebanon and Eleanor Roosevelt of the United States. Some representatives urged that the draft bill of rights under preparation should take the form of a declaration — that is, a recommendation by the General Assembly to Member States (see Charter Article 13) that would exert a moral and political influence on states rather than constitute a legally binding instrument. Other representatives urged the Commission to prepare a draft convention containing a bill of rights that would, after adoption by the General Assembly, be submitted to states for their ratification.

The first path was followed. In 1948, the UN Commission adopted a draft Declaration, which in turn was adopted by the General Assembly that year as the Universal Declaration of Human Rights (UDHR), with 48 states voting in favour and eight abstaining — Saudi Arabia, South Africa and the Soviet Union together with four East European states and a Soviet republic whose votes it controlled. (It is something of a jolt to realize today, in a decolonized and fragmented world of over 190 states, that UN membership in 1948 stood at 56 states.)

The Universal Declaration was meant to precede more detailed and comprehensive provisions in a single convention that would be approved by the General Assembly and submitted to states for ratification. After all, within the prevailing concepts of human rights at that time, the UDHR seemed to cover most of the field, including economic and social rights (see Art. 22–26) as well as civil and political rights. But during the years of drafting — years in which the Cold War took harsher and more rigid form, and in which the United States strongly qualified the nature of its commitment to the universal human rights movement — these matters became more contentious. The human rights movement was buffeted by ideological conflict and the formal differences of approach in a polarized world. One consequence was the decision in 1952 to build on the UDHR by dividing its provisions between two treaties, one on civil and political rights, the other on economic, social and cultural rights.

The plan to use the Universal Declaration as a springboard to treaties triumphed, but not as quickly as anticipated. The two principal treaties — the International Covenant on Civil and Political Rights (ICCPR) and the International Covenant on Economic, Social and Cultural Rights (ICESCR) — made their ways through the drafting and amendment processes in the Commission, the Third Committee and the General Assembly, where they were approved only in 1966. Another decade passed before the two Covenants achieved in 1976 the number of ratifications necessary to enter into force.

During the 28 years between 1948 and 1976, a number of specialized human rights treaties such as the Genocide Convention entered into force. But not until the two principal Covenants became effective did a treaty achieve as broad coverage of human rights topics as the Universal Declaration. It was partly for this reason that the UDHR became so broadly known and frequently invoked. During these intervening years, it was the only broad-based human rights instrument available. To this day, it:

> has retained its place of honor in the human rights movement. No other document has so caught the historical moment, achieved the same moral and rhetorical force, or exerted as much influence on the movement as a whole.... [T]he Declaration expressed in lean, eloquent language the hopes and idealism of a world released from the grip of World War II. However self-evident it may appear today, the Declaration bore a more radical message than many of its framers perhaps recognized. It proceeded to work its subversive path though many rooted doctrines of international law, forever changing the discourse of international relations on issues vital to human decency and peace.[7]

As a declaration voted in the General Assembly, the UDHR lacked the formal authority of a treaty that binds its parties under international law. Nonetheless, it remains in some sense the constitution of the entire movement, as well as the single most cited human rights instrument.

Other UN Organs Related to Human Rights

Together with the UN Commission, other UN organs have played major roles in developing universal human rights. Their full significance with respect to drafting

[7] Henry Steiner, 'Securing Human Rights: The First Half-Century of the Universal Declaration, and Beyond', Harvard Magazine, September–October 1998, p. 45.

and approving treaties or declarations, monitoring, censuring, and authorizing or ordering state action becomes apparent in later chapters. A brief description follows.

Chapter IV of the Charter sets forth the composition and powers of the General Assembly. Those powers are described in Articles 10–14 in terms such as 'initiate studies', 'recommend', 'promote', 'encourage' and 'discuss'. Particularly relevant are Articles 10 and 13. Article 10 authorizes the General Assembly to 'discuss any questions or any matters within the scope of the present Charter [and] . . . make recommendations to the Members of the United Nations . . . on any such questions or matters'. Article 13 authorizes the GA to 'make recommendations' for the purpose of, *inter alia*, 'assisting in the realization of human rights'. Throughout its history, the GA has been active in voting resolutions related to human rights issues.

Contrast the stronger and more closely defined powers of the Security Council under Chapter VII. Those powers range from making recommendations to states parties about ending a dispute, to the power to authorize and take military action 'to maintain or restore international peace and security' (Article 42) after the Council 'determine[s] the existence of any threat to the peace, breach of the peace, or act of aggression' (Article 39). Under Article 25, member states 'agree to accept and carry out' the Security Council's 'decisions' on these and other matters. No such formal obligation of states attaches to recommendations or resolutions of the General Assembly. As Chapter 9 indicates, the SC has in recent years used its powers to address situations involving major human rights violations.

Two of the seven Main Committees of the General Assembly — committees of the whole, for all UN members are entitled to be represented on them — have also participated in the drafting or other processes affecting human rights. The Social, Humanitarian and Cultural Committee (Third Committee) and the Legal Committee (Sixth Committee) have reviewed drafts of proposed declarations or conventions and often added their comments to the document submitted to the plenary General Assembly for its ultimate approval.

Historical Sequence and Typology of Instruments

That part of the universal human rights movement consisting of intergovernmental instruments — that is, excluding for present purposes both national laws and non-governmental institutions forming part of the movement — can be imagined as a four-tiered normative edifice, the tiers described generally in the order of their chronological appearance.

(1) The UN Charter, at the pinnacle of the human rights system, has relatively little to say about the subject. But what it does say has been accorded great significance. Through interpretation and extrapolation, as well as frequent invocation, the sparse text has constituted a point of departure for inventive development of the entire movement.

(2) The UDHR, viewed by some as a further elaboration of the brief references to human rights in the Charter, occupies in important ways the primary position of constitution of the entire movement. Today many understand the UDHR — or more specifically, numbers of its provisions — to have gained formal legal force by becoming a part of customary international law.

(3) The two principal covenants, which alone among the universal treaties have broad coverage of human rights topics, develop in more detail the basic categories of rights that figure in the Universal Declaration, and include additional rights as well

(4) A host of multilateral human rights treaties (usually termed 'conventions', for there are only the two basic 'covenants'), as well as resolutions or declarations with a more limited or focused subject than the comprehensive International Bill of Rights, have grown out of the United Nations (drafting by UN organs, approval by the General Assembly) and (in the case of treaties) have been ratified by large numbers of states. They develop further the content of rights that are more tersely described in the two covenants or, in some cases, that escape mention in them. This fourth tier consists of a network of treaties, most but not all of which became effective after the two Covenants, including: the Convention on the Prevention and Punishment of the Crime of Genocide (140 states parties as of January 2007), the International Convention on the Elimination of all Forms of Racial Discrimination (173 parties), the Convention on the Elimination of all Forms of Discrimination against Women (185 parties), the Convention against Torture and other Cruel, Inhuman or Degrading Treatment or Punishment (144 parties), and the Convention on the Rights of the Child (193 parties). This book discusses to one or another degree most of these instruments.

QUESTION

Compare the premises to and character and provisions of the UDHR with the prior illustrations in Chapter 2 of certain premises and doctrines in international law that constitute 'background' to the postwar human rights movement. In what respects (putting aside its legal character as a declaration rather than a treaty) does the UDHR stand out as strikingly different, as resting on premises that were not simply alien to but close to heresies within the preceding international law?

NOTE

Consider the following observations in Louis Henkin, *International Law: Politics, Values and Functions*, 216 Collected Courses of The Hague Academy of International Law (Vol. IV, 1989), at 215:

> The United Nations Charter, a vehicle of radical political-legal change in several respects, did not claim authority for the new human rights commitment it projected other than in the present consent of States. Unlike the international standard of justice for foreign nationals, which derived from the age of natural law and clearly reflected common acceptance of some natural rights, the Charter is a 'positivist' instrument. It does not invoke natural rights or any other philosophical basis for human rights. (The principal Powers could not have agreed on any such basis.) The Charter Preamble links human rights with human dignity but treats that value as self-evident, without need for justification. Nor does the Charter

define either term or give other guidance as to the human rights that human dignity requires. In fact, to help justify the radical penetration of the State monolith, the Charter in effect justifies human rights as a State value by linking it to peace and security.

Perhaps because we now wish to, we tend to exaggerate what the Charter did for human rights. The Charter made the promotion of human rights a purpose of the United Nations; perhaps without full appreciation of the extent of the penetration of Statehood that was involved, it thereby recognized and established that relations between a State and its own inhabitants were a matter of international concern. But the Charter did not erode State autonomy and the requirement of State consent to new human rights law....

...

In 1945, the principal Powers were not prepared to derogate from the established character of the international system by establishing law and legal obligation that would penetrate Statehood in that radical way; clearly, they themselves were not ready to submit to such law....

NOTE

From the start, the human rights movement had universal aspirations. It was not to address only the developed countries of the West/North but rather all regions and all states, whatever their form of government, socio-economic situation or religious-cultural traditions. After all, the key document at the very start of the movement was entitled the *Universal* Declaration of Human Rights. Its language, like that of many later human rights treaties, speaks abstractly of 'everyone', or 'no person'. It communicates no sense of differentiation among its subjects based on religion, gender, colour, ethnicity, national origin, wealth, region, education. To the contrary, the human rights texts fasten on equal protection as a cardinal concept.

Over the decades, the question of how 'universal' the postwar human rights are or should seek to become has assumed greater prominence. The 'universal' is often contrasted with the 'particular' or 'culturally specific', or 'cultural relativism.' The different meanings of these concepts and illustrations of their significance for a number of human rights topics figure as a central theme in Chapters 6 and 7. As a preface to those chapters, and as companion to this section's introduction to the UDHR, the excerpts below from Mary Ann Glendon's book on the making of the Declaration comment on the question of its universality and on the political and ethical traditions that inform it.

MARY ANN GLENDON, A WORLD MADE NEW (2001), at 221

Ch. 12. Universality under Siege

The problem of what universality might mean in a multicultural world haunted the United Nations human rights project from the beginning ... Earlier [in 1947] some of the world's best-known philosophers had been asked to ponder the question, "How is an agreement conceivable among men who come from the four corners of the earth and who belong not only to different cultures and civilizations, but to different spiritual families and antagonistic schools of thought?"

No one has yet improved on the answer of the UNESCO philosophers: Where basic human values are concerned, cultural diversity has been exaggerated. The group found, after consulting with Confucian, Hindu, Muslim and European thinkers, that a core of fundamental principles was widely shared in countries that had not yet adopted rights instruments and in cultures that had not embraced the language of rights. Their survey persuaded them that basic human rights rest on "common convictions," even though those convictions "are stated in terms of different philosophic principles and on the background of divergent political and economic systems?"....

...

The hopeful view of the UNESCO philosophers was challenged when a host of new nations appeared on the international stage in the 1950s. With sixteen new members joining the United Nations in 1955 alone and with many Latin American countries retreating from their pro-US positions, the balance of power in the General Assembly had shifted....

Over the years that mood was expressed in characterizations of the Declaration as an instrument of neocolonialism and in attacks on its universality in the name of cultural integrity, self-determination of peoples, or national sovereignty. In some cases the motivations are transparently self-serving. When leaders of authoritarian governments claim that the Declaration is aimed at imposing "foreign" values, their real concern is often domestic: the pressure for freedom building among their own citizens. That might have been the case, for example, when the Iranian representative at a ceremony commemorating the Declaration's fiftieth anniversary in 1998 charged that the document embodies a "Judeo-Christian" understanding of rights, unacceptable to Muslims. Or on the occasions when Singapore's Lee Kuan Yew attempted to justify the suppression of human rights in the name of economic development or national security.

... [M]any challenges to the Declaration's universality are made by individuals who are genuinely concerned about ideological imperialism ... University of Buffalo law professor Makau Mutua described the Declaration as an arrogant attempt to universalize a particular set of ideas and to impose them upon three-quarters of the world's population, most of whom were not represented at its creation. Kenya-born Mutua said, "Muslims, Hindus, Africans, non-Judeo-Christians, feminists, critical theorists, and other scholars of an inquiring bent of mind have exposed the Declaration's bias and exclusivity."

These accusations of cultural relativism and cultural imperialism need to be taken seriously. *Is* the Declaration a "Western" document in some meaningful sense, despite its aspiration to be universal? *Are* all rights relative to time and place? *Is* universality a cover for cultural imperialism? Let us examine the charges on their merits.

Those who label the Declaration "Western" base their claim mainly on two facts: 1) many peoples living in non-Western nations or under colonial rule, especially those in sub-Saharan Africa, were not represented in the United Nations in 1948; and 2) most of the Declaration's rights first appeared in the European and North or South American documents on which John Humphrey based the original draft. Those statements are accurate, but do they destroy the universality of the Declaration?

... It is true that much of the world's population was not represented in the UN in 1948: large parts of Africa and some Asian countries remained under colonial rule; and the defeated Axis powers — Japan, Germany, Italy, and their allies — were excluded as well. But Chang, Malik, Romulo, Mehta, and Santa Cruz were among the most influential, active, and independent members of the Human Rights Commission. And the members of the third committee, who discussed every line of the draft over two months in the fall of 1948, represented a wide variety of cultures.

... Before the whole two-year process from drafting and deliberation to adoption reached its end, literally hundreds of individuals from diverse backgrounds had participated. Thus Malik could fairly say, "The genesis of each article, and each part of each article, was a dynamic process in which many minds, interests, backgrounds, legal systems and ideological persuasions played their respective determining roles."

Proponents of the cultural-imperialism critique sometimes say that the educational backgrounds or professional experiences of men like Chang and Malik "westernized" them, but their performance in the Human Rights Commission suggests something rather different....

...

... On December 10, 1948, Brazil's Belarmino de Athayde summed up sentiments that had been expressed by many other third committee members when he told the General Assembly that the Declaration did not reflect the particular point of view of any one people or group of peoples or any particular political or philosophical system. The fact that it was the product of cooperation among so many nations, he said, gave it great moral authority.

...

The Declaration ... was far more influenced by the modern dignitarian rights tradition of continental Europe and Latin America than by the more individualistic documents of Anglo-American lineage. The fact is that the rights dialect that prevails in the Anglo-American orbit would have found little resonance in Asia or Africa. It implicitly confers its highest priority on individual freedom and typically formulates rights without explicit mention of their limits or their relation to other rights or to responsibilities. The predominant image of the rights bearer, heavily influenced by Hobbes, Locke, and John Stuart Mill, is that of a self-determining, self-sufficient individual.

Dignitarian rights instruments, with their emphasis on the family and their greater attention to duties, are more compatible with Asian and African traditions. In these documents, rights bearers tend to be envisioned within families and communities; rights are formulated so as to make clear their limits and their relation to one another as well as to the responsibilities that belong to citizens and the state....

In the spirit of the latter vision, the Declaration's "Everyone" is an individual who is constituted, in important ways, by and through relationships with others. "Everyone" is envisioned as uniquely valuable in himself (there are three separate references to the free development of one's personality), but "Everyone" is expected to act toward others "in a spirit of brotherhood." "Everyone" is depicted as situated in a variety of specifically named, real-life relationships of mutual dependency: families, communities, religious groups, workplaces, associations, societies, cultures, nations, and an emerging international order. Though its main body is devoted to basic individual freedoms, the Declaration begins with an exhortation to act in "a spirit of brotherhood" and ends with community, order, and society.

Whatever else may be said of him or her, the Declaration's "Everyone" is not a lone bearer of rights.... [The] departure from classical individualism while rejecting collectivism is the hallmark of dignitarian rights instruments such as the Declaration.

In the years since its adoption, the Declaration's aspiration to universality has been reinforced by endorsements from most of the nations that were not present at its creation. Specific references to the Declaration were made in the immediate post-independence constitutions of [the author names 19 African and Asian states]....

...All in all, it has been estimated that the Declaration has inspired or served as a model for the rights provisions of some ninety constitutions.... And in 1993,... representatives of 171 countries at the Vienna Conference on Human Rights affirmed by consensus their "commitment to the purposes and principles contained in the Charter of the United Nations and the Universal Declaration of Human Rights."...

It would be unwise, however, to minimize the danger of human rights imperialism. Today governments and interest groups increasingly deploy the language of human rights in the service of their own political, economic, or military ends. One of the twentieth century's most distinguished diplomats, George F. Kennan, expressed his misgivings about the United States' statements and demands concerning human rights in a 1993 memoir. He sensed in them, he said, "an implied assumption of superior understanding and superior virtue."

...

...Much confusion has been created in current debates by two assumptions that would have been foreign to the framers of the Declaration. Today both critics and supporters of universal rights tend to take for granted that the Declaration mandates a single approved model of human rights for the entire world. Both also tend to assume that the only alternative would be to accept that all rights are relative to the circumstances of time and place.

Nothing could be further from the views of the principal framers. They never envisioned that the document's "common standard of achievement" would or should produce completely uniform practices....

The Declaration's architects expected that its fertile principles could be brought to life in a legitimate variety of ways. Their idea was that each local tradition would be enriched as it put the Declaration's principles into practice and that all countries would benefit from the resulting accumulation of experiences....

There is little doubt about how the principal framers of the Universal Declaration would have responded to the charge of "Western-ness." What was crucial for them — indeed, what made universal human rights possible — was the *similarity* among all human beings. Their starting point was the simple fact of the common humanity shared by every man, woman, and child on earth, a fact that, for them, put linguistic, racial, religious. and other differences into their proper perspective.

NOTE

Makau Mutua, to whose ideas Glendon refers in the preceding excerpts, takes a fundamentally different position about the origin and chacteracter of the UDHR—a position examined in the materials on cultural relativism in Chapters 6 and 7. He states:[8]

> ...Non-Western philosophies and traditions particularly on the nature of man and the purposes of political society were either unrepresented or marginalized during the early formulation of human rights.... There is no doubt that the current human rights corpus is well meaning. But that is beside the point.... International human rights fall within the historical continuum of the European colonial project in which whites pose as the saviors of a benighted and savage non-European world. The white human rights zealot joins the unbroken chain that connects her to the colonial administrator, the Bible-wielding missionary , and the merchant of free enterprise. . . . Thus human rights reject the cross-fertilization of cultures and instead seek the transformation of non-Western cultures by Western cultures.

QUESTIONS

1. As a principle of interpretation, in what direction (if any) would Glendon's understanding of the UDHR'S 'dignitarian' tradition point with respect to, say, (1) a question of freedom of speech as applied to hate speech, (2) a question of individual liberty in relation to the right of others to an adequate standard of living, (3) a question of equal protection in relation to a claim for gay marriage?

2. From a textual examination of the UDHR (that is, independent of locating the UDHR in a larger historical and philosophical context) are you persuaded by Glendon's more community-oriented account of its rights-based prescriptions or by a more individualistic account?

3. Based on Glendon's argument in these excerpts, how do you react to her position that the UDHR was at its origin and is now properly understood as having universal validity?

NOTE

Understandings of the Universal Declaration have inevitably changed over time. Appreciation of earlier ideas at the start of the human rights movement illuminates its general evolution as well as suggests how perceptions of it and, more broadly, international law have developed over the 60 years. There follow some excerpts from an influential book by a preeminent scholar of international law of his generation,

[8] Makau Mutua, 'The Complexity of Universalism in Human Rights,' in András Sajó (ed.), *Human Rights with Modesty* (2004), 51.

Hersch Lauterpacht. At the time of the book's publication, the Declaration was two years old and untested as to its character and significance.

H. LAUTERPACHT, INTERNATIONAL LAW AND HUMAN RIGHTS

(1950), at 61

Chapter 4: The Subjects of the Law of Nations, the Function of International Law, and the Rights of Man

. . .

What have been the reasons which have prompted the changes in the matter of subjects of international law, with regard both to international rights and to international duties? These causes have been numerous and manifold. They have included, with reference to the recognition of the individual as a subject of international rights, the acknowledgment of the worth of human personality as the ultimate unit of all law; the realisation of the dangers besetting international peace as the result of the denial of fundamental human rights; and the increased attention paid to those already substantial developments in international law in which, notwithstanding the traditional dogma, the individual is in fact treated as a subject of international rights. Similarly, in the sphere of international duties there has been an enhanced realisation of the fact that the direct subjection of the individual to the rule of international law is an essential condition of the strengthening of the ethical basis of international law and of its effectiveness in a period of history in which the destructive potentialities of science and the power of the machinery of the State threaten the very existence of civilised life.

Above all, with regard to both international rights and international duties the decisive factor has been the change in the character and the function of modern international law. The international law of the past was to a large extent of a formal character. It was concerned mainly with the delimitation of the jurisdiction of States. . . . In traditional international law the individual played an inconspicuous part because the international interests of the individual and his contacts across the frontier were rudimentary. This is no longer the case. . . .

. . .

. . . [I]t is in relation to State sovereignty that the question of subjects of international law has assumed a special significance. Critics of the traditional theory have treated it as an emanation of the doctrine of sovereignty. In their view it is State sovereignty — absolute, petty, and overbearing — which rejects, as incompatible with the dignity of States, the idea of individuals as units of that international order which they have monopolised and thwarted in its growth. It is the sovereign State, with its claim to exclusive allegiance and its pretensions to exclusive usefulness that interposes itself as an impenetrable barrier between the individual and the greater society of all humanity. . . .

. . .

... [T]he recognition of the individual, by dint of the acknowledgment of his fundamental rights and freedoms, as the ultimate subject of international law, is a challenge to the doctrine which in reserving that quality exclusively to the State tends to a personification of the State as a being distinct from the individuals who compose it, with all that such personification implies. That recognition brings to mind the fact that, in the international as in the municipal sphere, the collective good is conditioned by the good of the individual human beings who comprise the collectivity. It denies, by cogent implication, that the corporate entity of the State is of a higher order than its component parts. ...

... International law, which has excelled in punctilious insistence on the respect owed by one sovereign State to another, henceforth acknowledges the sovereignty of man. For fundamental human rights are rights superior to the law of the sovereign State. ... [T]he recognition of inalienable human rights and the recognition of the individual as a subject of international law are synonymous. To that vital extent they both signify the recognition of a higher, fundamental law not only on the part of States but also, through international law, on the part of the organized international community itself. That fundamental law, as expressed in the acknowledgment of the ultimate reality and the independent status of the individual, constitutes both the moral limit and the justification of the ainternational legal order. ...

Chapter 5: The Idea of Natural Rights in Legal and Political Thought

...

... The law of nature and natural rights can never be a true substitute for the positive enactments of the law of the society of States. When so treated they are inefficacious, deceptive and, in the long run, a brake upon progress. ... The law of nature, even when conceived as an expression of mere ethical postulates, is an inarticulate but powerful element in the interpretation of existing law. Even after human rights and freedoms have become part of the positive fundamental law of mankind, the ideas of natural law and natural rights which underlie them will constitute that higher law which must forever remain the ultimate standard of fitness of all positive law, whether national or international. ...

[Lauterpacht then turns to historical antecedents of 'the notion and the doctrine of natural, inalienable rights of man pre-existent to and higher than the positive law of the State'. He observes that 'ideas of the law of nature date back to antiquity', and briefly describes such ideas and notions of natural right in Greek philosophy and the Greek state, in Roman thought, in the Middle Ages, and in the Reformation and the period of Social Contract. Lauterpacht then addresses 'fundamental rights in modern constitutions'.]

In the nineteenth and twentieth centuries the recognition of the fundamental rights of man in the constitutions of States became, in a paraphrase of Article 38 of the Statute of the Permanent Court of International Justice, a general principle of the constitutional law of civilised States. It became part of the law of nearly all European States. ...

... [T]here is one objection to the notion of natural rights which, far from invalidating the essential idea of natural rights, is nevertheless in a sense unanswerable. It is a criticism which reveals a close and, indeed, inescapable connexion between the idea of fundamental rights on the one hand and the law of nature and the law of nations on the other. That criticism is to the effect that, in the last resort, such rights are subject to the will of the State: that they may — and must — be regulated, modified, and if need be taken away by legislation and, possibly, by judicial interpretation; that, therefore, these rights are in essence a revocable part of the positive law of a sanctity and permanence no higher than the constitution of the State either as enacted or as interpreted by courts and by subsequent legislation. . . .

. . .

Chapter 17: The Universal Declaration of Human Rights

The Universal Declaration of Human Rights . . . has been hailed as an historic event of profound significance and as one of the greatest achievements of the United Nations. . . . Mrs. Roosevelt, Chairman of the Commission on Human Rights and the principal representative of the United States on the Third Committee, said: 'It [the Declaration] might well become the international Magna Carta of all mankind . . . Its proclamation by the General Assembly would be of importance comparable to the 1789 proclamation of the Declaration of the Rights of Man, the proclamation of the rights of man in the Declaration of Independence of the United States of America, and similar declarations made in other countries'. . . .

. . .

The practical unanimity of the Members of the United Nations in stressing the importance of the Declaration was accompanied by an equally general repudiation of the idea that the Declaration imposed upon them a legal obligation to respect the human rights and fundamental freedoms which it proclaimed. The debates in the General Assembly and in the Third Committee did not reveal any sense of uneasiness on account of the incongruity between the proclamation of the universal character of the human rights forming the subject matter of the Declaration and the rejection of the legal duty to give effect to them. The delegates gloried in the profound significance of the achievement whereby the nations of the world agree as to what are the obvious and inalienable rights of man . . . but they declined to acknowledge them as part of the law binding upon their States and Governments. . . .

. . . [T]he representative of the United States, in the same statement before the General Assembly in which she extolled the virtues of the Declaration, said: 'In giving our approval to the declaration today, it is of primary importance that we keep clearly in mind the basic character of the document. It is not a treaty; it is not an international agreement. It is not and does not purport to be a statement of law or of legal obligation. . . .'

. . .

. . . It is now necessary to consider the view, expressed in various forms, that, somehow, the Declaration may have an indirect legal effect.

In the first instance, it may be said — and has been said — that although the Declaration in itself may not be a legal document involving legal obligations, it is of legal value inasmuch as it contains an authoritative interpretation of the 'human rights and fundamental freedoms' which do constitute an obligation, however imperfect, binding upon the Members of the United Nations. It is unlikely that any tribunal or other authority administering international law would accept a suggestion of that kind. To maintain that a document contains an authoritative interpretation of a legally binding instrument is to assert that that former document itself is as legally binding and as important as the instrument which it is supposed to interpret....

... [T]here would seem to be no substance in the view that the provisions of the Declaration may somehow be of importance for the interpretation of the Charter as a formulation, in this field, of the 'general principles of law recognized by civilised nations'. The Declaration does not purport to embody what civilized nations generally recognize as law.... The Declaration gives expression to what, in the fullness of time, ought to become principles of law generally recognized and acted upon by States Members of the United Nations....

...

Undoubtedly the Declaration will occasionally be invoked by private and official bodies, including the organs of the United Nations. But it will not — and cannot — properly be invoked as a source of legal obligation....

Not being a legal instrument, the Declaration would appear to be outside international law. Its provisions cannot form the subject matter of legal interpretation. There is little meaning in attempting to elucidate, by reference to accepted canons of construction and to preparatory work, the extent of an obligation which is binding only in the sphere of conscience....

The fact that the Universal Declaration of Human Rights is not a legal instrument expressive of legally binding obligations is not in itself a measure of its importance. It is possible that, if divested of any pretence to legal authority, it may yet prove, by dint of a clear realisation of that very fact, a significant landmark in the evolution of a vital part of international law....

...

The moral authority and influence of an international pronouncement of this nature must be in direct proportion to the degree of the sacrifice of the sovereignty of States which it involves. Thus conceived, the fundamental issue in relation to the moral authority of the Declaration can be simply stated: That authority is a function of the degree to which States commit themselves to an effective recognition of these rights guaranteed by a will and an agency other than and superior to their own....

Its moral force cannot rest on the fact of its universality — or practical universality — as soon as it is realised that it has proved acceptable to all for the reason that it imposes obligations upon none....

...[C]ompare the Declaration of 1948 with that of [the French Declaration of] 1789 and similar constitutional pronouncements. These may not have been endowed, from the very inception, with all the remedies of judicial review and the formal apparatus of enforcement. But they became, from the outset, part of national law and an instrument of national action. They were not a mere philosophical pronouncement.... One of the governing principles of the Declaration — a principle which was repeatedly affirmed and which is a juridical heresy — is that it should proclaim rights of individuals while scrupulously refraining from laying down the duties of States. To do otherwise, it was asserted, would constitute the Declaration a legal instrument. But there are, in these matters, no rights of the individual except as a counterpart and a product of the duties of the State. There are no rights unless accompanied by remedies. That correlation is not only an inescapable principle of juridical logic. Its absence connotes a fundamental and decisive ethical flaw in the structure and conception of the Declaration.

. . .

QUESTION

Looked at from today's perspective, which of Lauterpacht's ideas or predictions about the UDHR and human rights would require substantial revision?

ADDITIONAL READING

J. Morsink, *The Universal Declaration of Human Rights: Origins, Drafting, and Intent* (1999); G. Alfredsson and A. Eide, *The Universal Declaration of Human Rights: A Common Standard of Achievement* (1999); B. van der Heijden and B. Tahzib-Lie (eds.), *Reflections on the Universal Declaration of Human Rights: A Fiftieth Anniversary Anthology* (1998); Y. Danieli *et al.* (eds.), *Universal Declaration of Human Rights: 50 Years and Beyond* (1999); and M.A. Glendon, *A World Made New* (2001).

PART B

NORMATIVE FOUNDATION OF INTERNATIONAL HUMAN RIGHTS

3

Civil and Political Rights

This chapter introduces basic ideas and instruments of the *universal* human rights movement that concern civil and political rights; the next chapter addresses economic and social rights. It picks up where Chapter 2(E) ended, after the UN Charter entered into force and the General Assembly adopted the Universal Declaration of Human Rights (UDHR). The chapter has four sections:

(A) It begins with an examination of one of the two leading Covenants: the International Covenant on Civil and Political Rights (ICCPR) (160 states parties as of January 2007).

(B) This section reviews some of the methodological and conceptual changes in the character of international law (compared with the descriptions of international law in Chapter 2) that accompanied and influenced the growth of the human rights movement.

(C) The chapter then turns to the Convention on the Elimination of All Forms of Discrimination against Women (CEDAW) (185 states parties) a major treaty that took form several decades after work on drafting the ICCPR began, and that reveals different concerns, goals and strategies of the human rights movement. Comparison of the ICCPR and CEDAW offers insight into the evolution and changing character of civil and political rights and their implementation.

(D) This last section examines a third major treaty, the Convention against Torture, and the resurgence of argument about the permissibility of torture in the context of threats or action by a foreign state or nonstate group involving weapons of mass destruction.

A. THE INTERNATIONAL COVENANT ON CIVIL AND POLITICAL RIGHTS: INTRODUCTION

COMMENT ON RELATIONSHIPS BETWEEN THE UNIVERSAL DECLARATION AND THE ICCPR

You should now become familiar with the substantive part (Articles 1–27) of the International Covenant on Civil and Political Rights. The comparisons below between the UDHR and the ICCPR assume that familiarity. One basic similarity informs all of the following discussion; each instrument aspires to universality. The UDHR was supported by the great majority of states of its time; the ICCPR now includes the great majority of the world's states. The comparison and indeed this section's examination of the ICCPR is brief; Chapter 10 examines the Covenant more intensively through the work of the organ that it creates, the Human Rights Committee.

(1) Under international law, approval by the General Assembly of a declaration like the UDHR has a different consequence from a treaty that has become effective through the required number of ratifications. Of course the declaration will have solemn effects as the formal act of a deliberative body of global importance. Its subject matter, like that of the UDHR, may be of the greatest significance. But when approved or adopted, it is hortatory and aspirational, recommendatory rather than, in a formal sense, binding.

The Covenant, on the other hand, binds the states parties in accordance with its terms and with international law, subject to such formal matters as reservations and the kinds of exceptional circumstances described in the Comment on Treaties, p. 106, *supra*. Of course this statement of international law doctrine and its basic postulate, *pacta sunt servanda*, does not end discussion. The content of important provisions of a treaty may long remain in dispute among the states parties. Differences over interpretation will likely arise; some states will disagree with others as to what even basic provisions of the Covenant (such as, in the case of the ICCPR, the 'right to life') mean and require. What indeed is the 'commitment'? Absent a consensus over meaning, which state party or international institution can provide an interpretation that most parties will view as authoritative and decisive? Even if there is a widespread consensus, one must confront the question of whether states will honour this 'binding' commitment and, if not, whether the UN or some member states will apply pressure against violators sufficient to persuade them to comply. Does or should the probability of enforcement against violators have any bearing on the legally binding character of an international agreement?

In the case of the UDHR, the years have further blurred the threshold contrast between 'binding' and 'hortatory' instruments. The countless references to and invocations of the Declaration as the fountainhead or constitution or grand statement of the human rights movement has its effect on how it is viewed — perhaps as shy of 'binding', but somehow relevant to norm formation and influential with respect to state behaviour as so-called 'soft law' (see p. 160, *infra*). Moreover, broadly supported arguments have developed for viewing all or parts of this Declaration as legally binding, either as a matter of customary international law or as an authoritative interpretation of the UN Charter.

(2) A resolution of the General Assembly (such as that approving the Universal Declaration) with the formal status of a recommendation can hardly create an international institution with defined membership, structure and powers. Neither can customary international law. A treaty can and often does. The Charter creates numerous organs, some organically part of the UN and some distinct from but related to it. The ICCPR creates an ongoing institution, a treaty organ: the Human Rights Committee. That organ gives institutional support to the Covenant's norms, for the Covenant imposes on states parties formal obligations (such as the

submission of periodic reports) to the Committee. This Committee is charged with the performance of the tasks defined both in the Covenant and in its Optional Protocol (109 states parties as of January 2007).

(3) Both the UDHR and ICCPR are terse about their derivations or foundations in moral and political thought. Such statements as are made that have the character of foundational assumptions, justifications or explanations appear in the preambles (with a few exceptions such as Article 21 of the UDHR and Article 25 of the ICCPR). But clearly these instruments differ radically from, say, a tax treaty that expresses a compromise and temporary convergence of interests among its states parties. They speak to matters deep, lasting, purportedly universal. What then are the intuitions that shape them, their sources in intellectual history or moral or religious thought, the important guides to their interpretation and evolution?

(4) Many rights declared in the Covenant closely resemble the provisions of the Universal Declaration, although they are stated in considerably greater detail. Compare, for example, the requirements for criminal trials in Articles 10 and 11 of the Declaration with the analogous provisions in Articles 14 and 15 of the Covenant.

(5) *Individual* rights characterize these instruments. Group or collective rights — that is, rights that pertain to and are exercised by the collectivity as such, perhaps by vote but more likely through representatives — are rare. In a few cases, they are either asserted or hinted at in the Covenant, most directly in Articles 1 (on self-determination of peoples) and 27 (on survival of cultures). The Universal Declaration lacks such provisions. Both the UDHR and the ICCPR refer to the family as the 'natural and fundamental group unit of society'. On the other hand, it should be kept in mind that rights cast in terms of the individual, such as the right to equal protection or the right to practice one's religion or participate in associations, have an inherent group character, either in the sense that the identity at issue in denials of equal protection is a group identity (race, ethnicity, gender, religion) or in the sense that the right is generally practised in community with others (as suggested by ICCPR Art. 27).

(6) In both instruments the idea of *rights* dominates with respect to individuals. Duties characteristically attach to the state. Article 29(1) of the Declaration does provide that everyone 'has duties to the community in which alone the free and full development of his personality is possible'. The Covenant contains no article referring to individuals' *duties*, though its Preamble has such a clause. Recall, however, the argument of Mary Ann Glendon, (p. 139, *supra*).

(7) Article 17 of the Declaration on the 'right to own property' and protection against arbitrary deprivation thereof does not figure among the rights declared in the Covenant. Why do you suppose this is the case?

(8) The UDHR goes little beyond the bare declaration of rights to provide (Art. 8) that everyone has the 'right to an effective remedy by the competent national tribunals' for violations of fundamental rights. The remedial structure of the ICCPR reaches much further. In Article 2, states parties agree to 'ensure' to all persons within their territory the rights recognized by the Covenant, and to adopt such legislative or other measures as may be necessary to achieve that goal. Moreover, the parties undertake to 'ensure' that any person whose rights are violated 'shall have an effective remedy', and that 'the competent authorities shall enforce such remedies when granted'. They undertake in particular 'to develop the possibilities of judicial remedy'.

(9) Two types of provisions in the ICCPR limit states' obligations thereunder:

(a) Under closely stated conditions and limits, Article 4 dealing with a public emergency ('which threatens the life of the nation and the existence of which is officially proclaimed') permits a temporary *derogation* — that is, deviation in the sense of limiting or detracting — from many of the rights declared by the Covenant. Thus states may consciously, purposively depart from such rights as those in Article 9 relating to arrest and detention. Note that under paragraph (2) certain rights are non-derogable. This issue of derogation becomes a major concern in Chapter 5, which deals with national security issues.

(b) A number of articles include *limitation clauses* — that is, provisions indicating that a given right cannot be absolute but must be adapted to meet a state's *interest* in protecting public safety, order, health or morals, or national security. See, for example, Articles 18 and 19. In Articles 21 and 22, the limitation clause is phrased in terms of permitting those restrictions on a right 'which are necessary in a democratic society'. Compare the broad provision of Article 29(2) of the UDHR, which is not linked to a specific right. Note that the limitation clauses may overlap with but are not identical with the common problem of resolving conflicts between *rights* (such as rights to speech and to privacy, as accommodated in the law of defamation) that also may lead to a 'limitation,' in this case of one right to give space to the other.

(10) Article 5 of the UDHR bans 'cruel, inhuman or degrading' punishment, but that instrument does not refer to capital punishment as such. See Article 6, para. 2 of the ICCPR. The Second Optional Protocol to the ICCPR, aiming at abolition of the death penalty, had 60 states parties as of January 2007. Article 1 provides that 'No one within the jurisdiction of a State Party to the present Protocol shall be executed.... Each State Party shall take all necessary measures to abolish the death penalty within its jurisdiction'. Recall the discussion about measures affecting capital punishment at pp. 18–42, *supra*.

❁ ❁ ❁

One can organize or classify the rights declared in the Declaration and Covenant in various ways, depending on the purpose of the typology. Consider the adequacy of the following scheme that embraces most of the Covenant's rights, although it excludes such distinctive provisions as ICCPR Article 1 on the self-determination of peoples and Article 27 on the enjoyment by minorities of their own cultures:

(a) Protection of the individual's physical integrity, as in provisions on torture, arbitrary arrest and arbitrary deprivation of life;
(b) procedural fairness when government deprives an individual of liberty, as in provisions on arrest, trial procedure and conditions of imprisonment;
(c) equal protection norms defined in racial, religious, gender and other terms;
(d) freedoms of belief, speech and association, such as provisions on political advocacy, the practice of religion, press freedom, and the right to hold an assembly and form associations; and
(e) the right to political participation.

These five categories of rights can be imagined as on a spectrum. At one extreme lie killing or torture over which there exists a broad formal-verbal consensus among states (whatever the degree of ongoing violation of the relevant rights by many states). At the other extreme lie rights whose purposes, basic meanings and even validity are formally disputed. For example, few if any states (even those that practise it) formally justify torture (see pp. 224–262, *infra*). A good number of states, however, may justify some form of religious or gender discrimination stemming from religious belief or customary practices, and argue that such practices should be viewed as consistent with the goals of the human rights movement — perhaps because (the argument goes) in such circumstances, equal protection rights should not be viewed as 'universal' so as to bind local cultures or practices or traditions that differ. Or states that reject the core practices of political democracy may justify different forms of political organization ranging from hereditary or elite (say, 'vanguard') leadership to a theocracy.

Among the intergovernmental organs or institutions referred to in this Comment, some such as the UN Commission on Human Rights (replaced in 2006 by the Human Rights Council) are mandated by the UN Charter, others such as the Human Rights Committee by distinct treaties (in this case, the ICCPR). As a matter of convenience, the first set is often referred to as 'Charter-based' organs/institutions, and the second set as 'treaty-based' organs/institutions or 'treaty bodies' (i.e., treaties other than the Charter).

Despite this distinction, bear in mind that almost the entire intergovernmental universal human rights regime is related to the United Nations. Human rights treaties following the Charter are distinct from it only up to a point. Thus the ICCPR and other human rights treaties noted above all grew within the UN, from the time that they were first drafted in an organ like the UN Commission (now the Human Rights Council) to their final approval by the General Assembly and submission to states for ratification. Typically for such treaties, the ICCPR provides for a number of ongoing links to the UN. Article 45 indicates that the Annual Report of the ICCPR Committee should be submitted to the General Assembly. Note also the provisions for amendment of the ICCPR in Article 51. Moreover, each of these separate treaty regimes like the ICCPR depends for funding on the regular biennial budget adopted by the General Assembly.

QUESTIONS

1. Relying only on the preambles and texts of the UDHR and the ICCPR, how would you identify the reasons for those instruments, their justifications in moral and political thought, the moral and political traditions from which they derive? Why do you suppose there was such a sparse statement of reasons or justifications in these instruments?

2. Do you see in either of these instruments any departure from 'universal' premises, rights and related obligations of states? That is, are there concessions in any provisions to different cultures or regions that would allow those cultures or regions to privilege their own practices and traditions rather than follow these instruments' rules — for example, by inflicting certain severe modes of criminal punishment, or governing by theocracy or inherited rule, or imposing restrictions on minority religions or on activities of women?

3. Article 2 of the ICCPR includes states' undertakings 'to respect and to ensure to all individuals' the recognized rights. States parties must 'ensure' that persons whose rights are violated have an 'effective remedy'. Competent authorities 'shall enforce such remedies when granted'.

   a. Is it accurate to say that rights are borne by individuals, and duties are borne only by states since the ICCPR is concerned only with state violations? Who may violate, say, your right to bodily security? Who may violate your right to political participation under Article 25, or your right to procedural due process under Article 14?
   b. Is it accurate to say that the duties of the state are entirely 'negative', in the sense of requiring no more than that the state generally keep its 'hands off' individuals, and refrain from certain conduct such as torture, discrimination, or repression of hostile (to it) political opinion? Is it accurate to say that fulfilment by the state of its duties would then be cost-free?

NOTE

Note the following observations about the progressive or immediate character of the state's obligations under the ICCPR, in Dominic McGoldrick, *The Human Rights Committee* (1991), at 12:

> There were marked differences of opinion during the drafting on the matter of the obligations that would be incurred by a State party to the ICCPR. Some representatives argued that the obligations under the ICCPR were absolute and immediate and that, therefore, a State could only become a party to the ICCPR after, or simultaneously with, its taking the necessary measures to secure those rights. If there were disparities between the Covenant and national law they could best be met by reservations. . . .
>
> Against this view it was argued that the prior adoption of the necessary measures in domestic law was not required by international law. . . .
>
> . . .
>
> Proposals to provide that the necessary measures be taken within a specified time limit or within a reasonable time were rejected as was a suggestion that each State fix its own time limit in its instrument of ratification. The only clear intentions of the [UN Commission on Human Rights] that emerged were those of avoiding excessive delays in the full implementation of the Covenant and of not introducing the general notion of progressiveness that was a feature of the obligations under the then draft [International Covenant on Economic, Social and Cultural Rights].
>
> The objections to the draft article 2(2) were again voiced in the Third Committee but the provision remained unchanged. The Committee's report stated that:
>
> > It represented the minimum compromise formula, the need for which, particularly in new States building up their body of legislation, was manifest. The notion of implementation at the earliest possible moment was implicit in article 2 as a whole. Moreover, the reporting requirement in article 49 (later article 40) would indeed serve as an effective curb on undue delay.

NOTE

It is frequently stated that all rights declared in the ICCPR are 'equal and interdependent'. Within that formulation, the right of an indigent person to be assigned legal assistance in a criminal case in Article 14(3) (c) is of the same rank as and interdependent with the right not to be tortured in Article 7. The following readings explore this issue of equality or hierarchy, and implicitly the notion of interdependence and indivisibility of all rights (terms that have come to describe the entire corpus of international human rights in more recent official documents). Note how the answer may change with the purpose for which the question is asked. These readings are concerned primarily with derogation during emergencies.

THEO VAN BOVEN, DISTINGUISHING CRITERIA OF HUMAN RIGHTS

in Karel Vasak and Alston (eds.), The International Dimensions of Human Rights, Vol. 1 (1982), at 43

There is another argument against making a distinction between fundamental human rights and other human rights. Such a distinction might imply that there is a hierarchy between various human rights according to their fundamental character. However, in modern human rights thinking the indivisibility of human rights and fundamental freedoms is prevalent. This idea of indivisibility presupposes that human rights form, so to speak, a single package and [are not amenable to being ranked] one above the other on a hierarchical scale.

This may all be true, but there still remain weighty arguments which militate in favour of distinguishing fundamental human rights from other human rights. Such fundamental rights can also be called elementary rights or supra-positive rights, i.e. rights whose validity is not dependent on their acceptance by the subjects of law but which are at the foundation of the international community. . . .

. . .

. . . The intensity of the prevailing sentiments against racism and racial discrimination, the awareness of urgency and the political climate have made the principle of racial non-discrimination one of the foundations of the international community as represented in the UN. Members of this community are bound by this principle on the basis of the UN Charter, even if they do not adhere to the various international instruments specifically aimed at the elimination of racial discrimination and apartheid. . . .

There is also a great deal of law in humanitarian conventions and in international human rights instruments supporting the existence of very fundamental human rights. This is that part of human rights law which does not permit any derogation even in time of armed conflict or in other public emergency situations threatening the life of the nation. The common article 3 of the four Geneva Conventions of 1949, setting out a number of minimum humanitarian standards which are to be respected in cases of conflict which are not of an international character, enumerates certain acts which 'are and shall remain prohibited at any time and in any place whatsoever'. The following acts are mentioned:

> (a) violence to life and person, in particular murder of all kinds, mutilation, cruel treatment and torture; (b) taking of hostages; (c) outrages upon personal dignity, in particular, humiliating and degrading treatment; (d) the passing of sentences and the carrying out of executions without previous judgment pronounced by a regularly constituted court, affording all the judicial guarantees which are recognized as indispensable by civilized nations.

The universal validity of these fundamental prescriptions is underlined by the words 'at any time and in any place whatsoever' in this common article 3 of the four 1949 Geneva Conventions.

The International Covenant on Civil and Political Rights enumerates in article 4, para. 2, the rights from which no derogation is allowed in time of public emergency.... Regional human rights conventions contain a similar clause enumerating provisions from which no derogation may be made.

The fact that in a number of comprehensive human rights instruments at the worldwide and the regional level, certain rights are specifically safeguarded and are intended to retain their full strength and validity notably in serious emergency situations, is a strong argument in favour of the contention that there is at least a minimum catalogue of fundamental or elementary human rights.

...

NOTE

Compare with van Boven's observations those in Theodor Meron, *On a Hierarchy of International Human Rights*, 80 Am. J. Int. L. 1 (1986), at 21:

> ... Hierarchical terms constitute a warning sign that the international community will not accept any breach of those rights. Historically, the notions of 'basic rights of the human person' and 'fundamental rights' have helped establish the erga omnes principle, which is so crucial to ensuring respect for human rights. Eventually, they may contribute to the crystallization of some rights, through custom or treaties, into hierarchically superior norms, as in the more developed national legal systems.
>
> Yet the balance of pros and cons does not necessarily weigh clearly on the side of the pros. Resort to hierarchical terms has not been matched by careful consideration of their legal significance. Few criteria for distinguishing between ordinary rights and higher rights have been agreed upon. There is no accepted system by which higher rights can be identified and their content determined. Nor are the consequences of the distinction between higher and ordinary rights clear. Rights not accorded quality labels, i.e., the majority of human rights, are relegated to inferior, second-class, status. Moreover, rather than grapple with the harder questions of rationalizing human rights lawmaking and distinguishing between rights and claims, some commentators are resorting increasingly to superior rights in the

hope that no state will dare — politically, morally and perhaps even legally — to ignore them. In these ways, hierarchical terms contribute to the unnecessary mystification of human rights, rather than to their greater clarity.

Caution should therefore be exercised in resorting to a hierarchical terminology. Too liberal an invocation of superior rights such as 'fundamental rights' and 'basic rights,' as well as *jus cogens*, may adversely affect the credibility of human rights as a legal discipline.

NOTE

The issue arose in the 1990s of a state party's right to withdraw from the ICCPR, which unlike many treaties has no provision about termination of obligations. The Human Rights Committee issued in 1997, at its 61st session, its General Comment 26 on this question. Excerpts follow:

> 1. . . . [T]he possibility of termination, denunciation or withdrawal must be considered in the light of applicable rules of customary international law which are reflected in the Vienna Convention on the Law of Treaties. . . .
>
> . . .
>
> 3. . . . [I]t is clear that the Covenant is not the type of treaty which, by its nature, implies a right of denunciation. Together with the simultaneously prepared and adopted International Covenant on Economic, Social and Cultural Rights, the Covenant codifies in treaty form the universal human rights enshrined in the Universal Declaration of Human Rights, the three instruments together often being referred to as the 'International Bill of Human Rights'. As such, the Covenant does not have a temporary character typical of treaties where a right of denunciation is deemed to be admitted, notwithstanding the absence of a specific provision to that effect.
>
> 4. The rights enshrined in the Covenant belong to the people living in the territory of the State party. The Human Rights Committee has consistently taken the view . . . that once the people are accorded the protection of the rights under the Covenant, such protection devolves with territory and continues to belong to them, notwithstanding change in government of the State party, including dismemberment in more than one State or State succession. . . .
>
> 5. The Committee is therefore firmly of the view that international law does not permit a State which has ratified or acceded or succeeded to the Covenant to denounce it or withdraw from it. . . .

QUESTIONS

1. How does the doctrine of *jus cogens* differ from the effort urged by Van Boven to work out some hierarchy of rights, whether for the purposes indicated by Common Article 3 of the Geneva Conventions or for purposes of stating non-derogable rights in situations of emergency?

2. Does the list of non-derogable rights in Article 4 of the ICCPR necessarily express some abstract, general hierarchy of rights in terms of their 'fundamental' importance or

some similar criterion? How do you compare the rights there listed with others that are derogable? Can you suggest another purpose and criterion for deciding on a list of non-derogable rights in Article 4?

3. Suppose that you are a director of an international nongovernmental human rights organization, like Human Rights Watch or the International Commission of Jurists, that does its work in different regions of the world. You must vote on next year's agenda for that organization indicating what types of violations it should concentrate on in its work, given budget constraints and other limited resources. In general, to what issues would you would give priority with respect to monitoring, reporting and lobbying in the effort to achieve change? From this perspective, how do you react to the views of van Boven and Meron about equality or hierarchy among human rights norms?

ADDITIONAL READING

L. Henkin (ed.), *The International Bill of Rights: The Covenant on Civil and Political Rights* (1981); P. Lauren, *The Evolution of International Human Rights* (1999); M. Nowak, *UN Covenant on Civil and Political Rights: ICCPR Commentary* (2nd edn. 2005); S. Joseph, J. Schultz and M. Castan, *The International Covenant on Civil and Political Rights: Cases, Materials, and Commentary* (2nd edn. 2004); M. Nowak, *Introduction to the International Human Rights Regime* (2003); C. Gearty, *Can Human Rights Survive?* (2006).

B. SIGNIFICANCE FOR HUMAN RIGHTS MOVEMENT OF CHANGING CHARACTER OF CUSTOMARY INTERNATIONAL LAW AND OF 'SOFT LAW'

The UDHR and the ICCPR were part of the soaring growth of postwar multilateral instruments, many of them creating intergovernmental organizations (IGOs). So many fields of international law — human rights, peacekeeping, laws of war, monetary and trade agreements, environmental treaties, criminal law — contributed to this significant trend from bilateral to multilateral agreements and institutions to address some of the problems of the day. Inevitably these treaties and organizations so changed the international law context and the relationships between states and international law as well as each other as to influence some basic concepts and doctrines, such as the vital doctrine of sources that initiated Chapter 2's inquiry into international law.

The preceding materials on the UDHR and ICCPR suggest the importance of this phenomenon for the evolution of the human rights movement. Not only do the basic duties of the state run towards its internal social and political order and population, but other states — independently or as members of one or another of the many international human rights organizations — become involved in the process of attempting to assure the observance by delinquent states of those duties. IGOs become to one or another degree independent actors working toward treaties' goals. Or at least the scheme so suggests, for this book's later materials explore how far shy of that 'assurance' the system has in fact progressed

These and other phenomena, ranging from the development of national and international human rights nongovernmental organizations (NGOs) to globalization embracing multiple cultures, have influenced the very paths of 'making' international law. For example, even outside the world of states and IGOs, there are today so many more voices and places contributing statements, resolutions, declarations, draft codes and other types of instruments about the content of international law — what it 'is', what it 'ought to be'. Our discussion, for example, noted the evolution of the UDHR from its early status as an aspirational statement to a body of norms accepted by many as authoritative — as, for example, part of customary international law, or as an authoritative interpretation of the Charter's human rights provisions. Which individuals, which groups, which institutions, which states served as agents of this process? Do those who understand the UDHR, or important parts of it, as authoritative international law, as much so as a treaty, rely on the traditional criteria of customary law to support their understanding? Do General Assembly resolutions approved with large majorities occupy a special status? Are different criteria for the formation of custom developing, and becoming widely accepted?

And what of the work product of the new international institutions and treaty organs? We have seen that the ICCPR creates its organ (or body), the Human Rights Committee. Six other treaties, now have such treaty bodies, such as CEDAW. The following section of this chapter examines CEDAW together with the different functions and work products of the CEDAW Committee: Concluding Observations, General Recommendations, and 'Views'. What is the formal effect of such output of the Committee on states, or more broadly on the formation of international law? Does this published work of the Committee constitute another 'source' of international law, authoritatively regulating state behaviour? Such questions, addressed not only to treaty bodies or organizations but also to human rights NGOs, to international associations of lawyers or judges, and to a broad range of other nonstate groups issuing proposals about human rights, have led to the concept of 'soft law', which is now another, often perplexing ingredient in the multi-faceted evolution of international law.

For these reasons, we turn to such questions at this point, for they become immediately relevant to an understanding of the elaboration and evolution of civil–political and economic–social rights. The first two articles below develop these themes and questions.

Finally, the development of the international law of human rights has spurred debate over certain doctrinal conceptions that have a direct and forceful bearing on the field. The third reading below comments on two of those conceptions: obligations *erga omnes* and *jus cogens.*

ANTHEA ROBERTS, TRADITIONAL AND MODERN APPROACHES TO CUSTOMARY INTERNATIONAL LAW: A RECONCILIATION

95 Am. J. Int. L. 757 (2001)

[The following excerpts describe a developing mode of thinking about customary international law. They draw on distinctions made by several other scholars to build towards the author's views. These distinctions and the author's analysis thereof can be compared and contrasted with the notions of custom in the *Paquete Habana* decision, p. 62, *supra*, and the readings following that decision. The article bears on the coursebook's discussion of the UDHR, the question of hierarchy of norms, and the interaction within the human rights movement between (1) customary law and (2) human rights treaties and declarations.]

... [C]ustom has become an increasingly significant source of law in important areas such as human rights obligations. Codification conventions, academic commentary, and the case law of the International Court of Justice (the Court) have also contributed to a contemporary resurrection of custom. These developments have resulted in two apparently opposing approaches, which I term "traditional custom" and "modern custom." ...

... Custom is generally considered to have two elements: state practice and *opinio juris*. ... This distinction is problematic because it is difficult to determine what states believe as opposed to what they say. Whether treaties and declarations constitute state practice or *opinio juris* is also controversial. For the sake of clarity, this article adopts Anthony D'Amato's distinction between action (state practice) and statements (*opinio juris*). Thus, actions can form custom only if accompanied by an articulation of the legality of the action. *Opinio juris* concerns statements of belief rather than actual beliefs. Further, treaties and declarations represent *opinio juris* because they are statements about the legality of action, rather than examples of that action....

What I have termed traditional custom results from general and consistent practice followed by states from a sense of legal obligation. It focuses primarily on state practice in the form of interstate interaction and acquiescence. *Opinio juris* is a secondary consideration invoked to distinguish between legal and nonlegal obligations. Traditional custom is evolutionary and is identified through an *inductive* process in which a general custom is derived from specific instances of state practice....

By contrast, modern custom is derived by a *deductive* process that begins with general statements of rules rather than particular instances of practice. This approach emphasizes *opinio juris* rather than state practice because it relies primarily on statements rather than actions. Modern custom can develop quickly because it is deduced from multilateral treaties and declarations by international fora such as the General Assembly, which can declare existing customs, crystallize emerging customs, and generate new customs.... A good example of the deductive approach is the Merits decision in *Military and Paramilitary Activities in and against Nicaragua*

[1986 I.C.J. Rep. 14]. The Court paid lip service to the traditional test for custom but derived customs of non-use of force and nonintervention from statements such as General Assembly resolutions. The Court did not make a serious inquiry into state practice, holding that it was sufficient for conduct to be generally consistent with statements of rules, provided that instances of inconsistent practice had been treated as breaches of the rule concerned rather than as generating a new rule.

. . .

H. L. A. Hart and R. M. Hare distinguish between *descriptive* and *prescriptive* statements and laws. Descriptive laws can be discovered by observation and reasoning because they are statements about what the practice *has been.* By contrast, prescriptive laws are not determined primarily by observations of fact because they state demands about what the practice *should or ought to be.* Legal rules are *always prescriptive* because they make demands about how people and states should behave. However, their prescriptive nature can be justified by what the practice has been and/or what the practice should be. A law is primarily *descriptive* if it conforms to the premise: the *law is* what the practice *has been.* A law is primarily *normative* if it is formulated on the assumption: the *law is* what the practice *ought to be.* What the law *is* (prescription) can be justified by what the practice *has been* (description) or what the practice *ought to be* (normativity). Thus, we should distinguish between what the practice has been, what the law is, and what the practice ought to be: "has/is/ought" (description/prescription/normativity). . . .

. . . Moving from *has* to *is* involves some level of law creation because it requires the formulation of an abstract rule from actual practice, despite the existence of silences, ambiguities, and contradictions in that practice. Determining what the law *is* from what the practice *has been* relies heavily on the choice of characteristics under which precedents are classified and the degree of abstraction employed. . . .

. . .

Traditional custom is closely associated with descriptive accuracy because norms are constructed primarily from state practice — working from practice to theory. Reliance on state practice provides continuity with past actions and reliable predictions of future actions. It results in practical and achievable customs that can actually regulate state conduct. By contrast, modern custom demonstrates a predilection for substantive normativity rather than descriptive accuracy. Modern custom derives norms primarily from abstract statements of *opinio juris* — working from theory to practice. Whereas state practice is clearly descriptive, *opinio juris* is inherently ambiguous in nature because statements can represent *lex lata* (what the law is, a descriptive characteristic) or *lex ferenda* (what the law should be, a normative characteristic). The Court has held that only statements of *lex lata* can contribute to the formation of custom. However, modern custom seems to be based on normative statements of *lex ferenda* cloaked as *lex lata,* for three reasons.

. . .

[Third], treaties and resolutions often use mandatory language to prescribe a model of conduct and provide a catalyst for the development of modern custom. Treaties and declarations do not merely photograph or declare the current state of practice on moral issues. Rather, they often reflect a deliberate ambiguity between actual and desired practice, designed to develop the law and to stretch the consensus on the text as far as possible. For example, some rights set out in the Universal Declaration of Human Rights of 1948 are expressed in mandatory terms and have achieved customary status even though infringements are 'widespread, often gross and generally tolerated by the international community.' As a result, modern custom often represents progressive development of the law masked as codification by phrasing *lex ferenda* as *lex lata.*

...

The moral content of modern custom explains the strong tendency to discount the importance of contrary state practice in the modern approach. Irregularities in description can undermine a descriptive law, but a normative law may be broken and remain a law because it is not premised on descriptive accuracy. For example, *jus cogens* norms prohibit fundamentally immoral conduct and cannot be undermined by treaty arrangement or inconsistent state practice. Since the subject matter of modern customs is not morally neutral, the international community is not willing to accept any norm established by state practice. Modern custom involves an almost teleological approach, whereby some examples of state practice are used to justify a chosen norm, rather than deriving norms from state practice. . . . Thus, the importance of descriptive accuracy varies according to the facilitative or moral content of the rule involved.

...

A critique of modern custom. . . . Deriving customs primarily from treaties and declarations, rather than state practice, is potentially more democratic because it involves practically all states. Most states can participate in the negotiation and ratification of treaties and declarations of international fora, such as the United Nations General Assembly. The notion of sovereign equality (one state, one vote) helps to level the playing field between developed and developing countries. While formal equality cannot remedy all inequalities in power, international fora provide less powerful states with a cost-efficient means of expressing their views. . . . [V]otes in the General Assembly usually receive little media scrutiny and are generally not intended to make law. For example, the General Assembly resolution on torture was adopted unanimously, while a much smaller number of states ratified the Convention Against Torture and others entered significant reservations to it.

...

The greatest criticism of modern custom is that it is descriptively inaccurate because it reflects ideal, rather than actual, standards of conduct. The normative nature of modern custom leads to an enormous gap between asserted customs and state practice. For example, customary international law prohibits torture, yet torture is endemic. A similar criticism is made of the 'emptiness' of *jus cogens* norms, which are often flouted in practice. These laws lack efficacy because states have not internalized them as standards of behavior to guide their actions and judge the behavior of others. The regulatory function of modern custom is doubtful because it appears merely to set up aspirational aims rather than realistic requirements about action. . . . Some theorists characterize modern customs as 'soft laws' or sublegal obligations that do not amount to law. Indeed, norms that are honored in the breach do not yield reliable predictions of future conduct and are likely to bring themselves, and possibly custom as a whole, into disrepute.

. . .

DINAH SHELTON, INTRODUCTION: LAW, NON-LAW AND THE PROBLEM OF 'SOFT LAW'

In Dinah Shelton (ed.), *Commitment and Compliance: The Role of Non-Binding Norms in the International Legal System* (2000), at 1

. . . The subject of compliance with non-binding norms [is] concerned with why states and other international actors choose to conclude non-binding rather than binding normative instruments and whether or to what extent that choice affects their consequent behavior.

. . .

The project to study compliance with international non-binding norms or 'soft law' began with a workshop. . . . In part, the meeting sought to test the hypothesis that countries sometimes comply with non-binding legal instruments as well as they do with binding ones. The term 'soft *law*' itself seems to contain a normative element leading to expectations of compliance.

. . .

. . . [A] decision was made to compare four subject areas: human rights, environment, arms control, and trade and finance. Each of the fields has particularities that result in different uses for non-binding norms and a different ratio of non-binding norms to 'hard' law. Human rights law has developed over the past fifty years into a broad code of behavior for states and state agents, not only in their relations with other states, but primarily as non-reciprocal, unilateral commitments towards all those within the jurisdiction of the state. Environmental law, in contrast, aims more at regulating non-state behavior: most environmental harm is caused by private entities and not by state agents. . . .

. . .

. . . The project participants discussed at length whether or not to include norms adopted by non-state actors. Ultimately it was decided to include them because they are usually intended to impact on state behavior or to circumvent state policies. In addition, with increasing globalization, transnational entities that make their own rules prepare and enter into normative instruments that look much the same as state-adopted norms. . . .

. . .

Throughout the project, participants debated whether binding instruments (law) and non-binding ones (soft law or non-law) are strictly alternative, or whether they are two ends on a continuum from legally binding to complete freedom of action.

Recent inclusion of soft law commitments in hard law instruments suggests that both form and content are relevant to the sense of legal obligation. Some soft law instruments may have a specific normative content that is 'harder' than the soft commitments in treaties. Other non-binding instruments may never be intended to have normative effect, but are promotional, serving as a catalyst to further action. This appears to be the case with some of the concluding acts of international conferences....

...

... A question posed in this study is whether state behavior in adopting and complying with non-binding instruments evidences acceptance of new modes of law-making not reflected in the Statute of the Court. *Ab initio*, however, we take the view that international law is created through treaty and custom, and thus 'soft law' is not legally binding *per se.*

It has become commonplace to note that the international system has undergone tremendous recent changes. From a community of predominately western states, the global arena now contains more than four times the number of states that existed at the beginning of the last century. In addition, other communities have emerged to play important international roles: intergovernmental organizations, non-governmental organizations, professional associations, transnational corporations, and mixed entities comprised of members of different communities. They both contribute to the making of international norms and increasingly are bound by them.

...

The line between law and not-law may appear blurred. Treaty mechanisms are including more 'soft' obligations, such as undertakings to endeavor to strive to cooperate. Non-binding instruments in turn are incorporating supervisory mechanisms traditionally found in hard law texts. Both types of instrument may have compliance procedures that range from soft to hard. The result seems to be a dynamic interplay between soft and hard obligations similar to that which exists between international and national law. In fact, it is rare to find soft law standing in isolation; instead, it is used most frequently either as a precursor to hard law or as a supplement to a hard law instrument. Soft law instruments often serve to allow treaty parties to authoritatively resolve ambiguities in the text or fill in gaps. This is part of an increasingly complex international system with variations in forms of instruments, means, and standards of measurement that interact intensely and frequently, with the common purpose of regulating behavior within a rule of law framework....

... Some scholars have distinguished hard law and soft law by stating that breach of law gives rise to legal consequences while breach of a political norm gives rise to political consequences. Such a distinction is not always easy to make. Testing normativity based on consequences can be confusing, since breaches of law may give rise to consequences that may be politically motivated. A government that recalls its ambassador can either be expressing political disapproval of another state's policy on an issue, or sanctioning noncompliance with a legal norm. Terminating foreign assistance also may be characterized either way. Even binding UN Security Council resolutions based on a threat to the peace do not necessarily depend upon a violation of international law.

... If states expect compliance and in fact comply with rules and principles contained in soft law instruments as well as they do with norms contained in treaties and custom, then perhaps the concept of international law, or the list of sources of international law, requires expansion. Alternatively, it may have to be conceded that legal obligation is not as significant a factor in state behavior as some would think. A further possibility is that law remains important and states choose a soft law form for specific reasons related to the requirements of the problem being addressed and unrelated to the expectation of compliance....

... There are several possible reasons that could explain the choice of soft law over hard law.

...

(5) Legally binding norms may be inappropriate when the issue or the effective response is not yet clearly identified, due to scientific uncertainty or other causes, but there is an urgent requirement to take some action. Similarly, it may be necessary where diverse legal systems preclude legally binding norms. Thus, soft law may be increasingly utilized because it responds to the needs of the new international system. In national legal systems, law-creating methods have always varied, from constitution-writing, to legislation, executive decrees, administrative regulation, and private contract, as well as common law. International law-making itself has changed over time. Where it was once almost entirely customary in origin, treaty-making, first bilateral, then multilateral, has come to be seen as the predominant form of law-making in the modern world.

(6) Soft law allows for more active participation of non-state actors. Where states once created and applied international norms through processes that lacked transparency, participation, and accountability, non-state actors have become a significant source of power alongside, if not outside, state control....

...

ROBERT JENNINGS AND ARTHUR WATTS, (EDS.), OPPENHEIM'S INTERNATIONAL LAW

Vol. 1 (9th edn. 1992), at 4

One can . . . distinguish between those rules of international law which, even though they may be of universal application, do not in any particular situation give rise to rights and obligations *erga omnes*, and those which do. Thus, although all states are under certain obligations as regards the treatment of aliens, those obligations (generally speaking) can only be invoked by the state whose nationality the alien possesses: on the other hand, obligations deriving from the outlawing of acts of aggression, and of genocide, and from the principles and rules concerning the basic rights of the human person, including protection from slavery and racial discrimination, are such that all states have an interest in the protection of the rights involved.[1] Rights and obligations *erga omnes* may even be created by the actions of a limited number of states. There is, however, no agreed enumeration of rights and obligations *erga omnes*, and the law in this area is still developing, as it is in the connected matter of a state's ability, by analogy with the *actio popularis* (or *actio communis*) known to some national legal systems, to institute proceedings to vindicate an interest as a member of the international community as distinct from an interest vested more particularly in itself....

...

States may, by and within the limits of agreement between themselves, vary or even dispense altogether with most rules of international law. There are, however, a few rules from which no derogation is permissible. The latter — rules of *ius cogens*, or peremptory norms of general international law — have been defined in Article 53 of the Vienna Convention on the Law of Treaties 1969 (and for the purpose of that Convention) as norms 'accepted and recognised by the international community of states as a whole as a norm from which no derogation is permitted and which can be modifed only by a subsequent norm of general international law having the same character'; and Article 64 contemplates the emergence of new rules of *ius cogens* in the future.

Such a category of rules of *ius cogens* is a comparatively recent development and there is no general agreement as to which rules have this character. The International Law Commission regarded the law of the Charter concerning the prohibition of the use of force as a conspicuous example of such a rule. Although the Commission refrained from giving in its draft Articles on the Law of Treaties any examples of rules of *ius cogens*, it did record that in this context mention had additionally been made of the prohibition of criminal acts under international law, and of acts such as trade in slaves, piracy or genocide, in the suppression of which every state is called upon to cooperate; the observance of human rights, the equality of states and the principle of self-determination. The full content of the category of *ius cogens* remains to be worked out in the practice of states and in the jurisprudence of international tribunals....

The operation and effect of rules of *ius cogens* in areas other than that of treaties are similarly unclear. Presumably no act done contrary to such a rule can be legitimated by means of consent....

[1] [Eds. The authors here refer in a footnote to the *Case Concerning the Barcelona Traction, Light and Power Company, Limited (New Application 1962) (Belgium v. Spain)* [1970] ICJ Rep. 4. The relevant portion of that opinion of the International Court of Justice reads, at paras 33–34: '[A]n essential distinction should be drawn between the obligations of a State towards the international community as a whole, and those arising vis-à-vis another State in the field of diplomatic protection. By their very nature, the former are the concern of all States. In view of the importance of the rights involved, all States can be held to have a legal interest in their protection; they are obligations *erga omnes*. Such obligations derive, for example, in contemporary international law, from the outlawing of acts of aggression, and of genocide, as also from the principles and rules concerning the basic rights of the human person, including protection from slavery and racial discrimination....']

QUESTIONS

1. How do you assess Roberts' argument? Are you persuaded, for example, that ratifications of human rights treaties should be viewed only as 'statements' or *opinio juris*, not practice? Should a strong consensus (expressed in a declaration or treaty approved by a large majority of states) over an aspiration or ideal be sufficient, or relevant as part of a larger process, to the formation of 'binding' international law — perhaps customary international law or general principles?

2. In any event, are the classical criteria for the formation of custom of the time of *Paquete Habana* and as described in 1950 by Judge Manley Hudson (p. 72, *supra*) workable in modern times? If not, why not? What has changed? If not workable, what criteria for the formation of custom should replace them — those that Roberts describes as now unfolding?

3. Is the upshot of the descriptions and analyses of Roberts and Shelton that the requirement that states 'consent' to the formation of international law, a requirement previously subject to considerable qualification, has become subject to further erosion, by the work, statements and activities of IGOs and other nonstate actors?

NOTE

The discussion of *jus cogens* in *Oppenheim's International Law* (9th edn.) above opens a path toward integrating this Section B with the materials on women's human rights that follow in Section C. Feminist literature about human rights and international law has, as indicated, looked at the subject from many different ideological and methodological perspectives. In several articles, Karen Engle has examined the different approaches — all of which of course give prominence to a gender perspective — and attempted to characterize and classify them. Her latest such effort,[2] covering the last 15 years or so of feminist writings, divides the writings into three periods: (1) liberal inclusion so that women were brought into the basic provisions of international human rights, such as equal protection; (2) criticism of human rights as structurally biased against women; and (3) Third-World feminist approaches. The following article falls within the second category, as the authors contend that the doctrine of *jus cogens* is indeed structurally biased against women.

HILARY CHARLESWORTH AND CHRISTINE CHINKIN, THE GENDER OF *JUS* COGENS

15 Hum. Rts. Q. 63 (1993)

[The authors, drawing on Article 53 of the Vienna Convention on the Law of Treaties and scholarly writing, stress the principal characteristics of the concept of *jus cogens*

[2] Karen Engle, 'International Human Rights and Feminisms: When Discourses Keep Meeting', in Doris Buss and Ambreena Manji (eds.), *International Law: Modern Feminist Approaches* 47 (2005).

as normative superiority and universality, the first inevitably associated with the second. Proponents of the concept emphasize its contribution to the collective international order by playing a role similar to that of constitutionally protected rights in domestic order. The authors contend, however, that the concept of *jus cogens* should not be viewed as universal, for its present content — particularly the category of human rights often designated as norms of *jus cogens* — privileges the experiences of men over women by giving differential protection. The following excerpts advance that claim through the method of structural critique.]

Although human rights law is often regarded as a radical development in international law because of its challenge to that discipline's traditional public/ private dichotomy between states and individuals, it has retained the deeper, gendered, public/private distinction. In the major human rights treaties, rights are defined according to what men fear will happen to them, those harms against which they seek guarantees. The primacy traditionally given to civil and political rights by Western international lawyers and philosophers is directed towards protection for men within their public life — their relationship with government. The same importance has not been generally accorded to economic and social rights which affect life in the private sphere, the world of women, although these rights are addressed to states. This is not to assert that when women are victims of violations of the civil and political rights they are not accorded the same protection, but that these are not the harms from which women most need protection.

All the violations of human rights typically included in catalogues of *jus cogens* norms are of undoubted seriousness; genocide, slavery, murder, disappearances, torture, prolonged arbitrary detention, and systematic racial discrimination. The silences of the list, however, indicate that women's experiences have not directly contributed to it. For example, although race discrimination consistently appears in *jus cogens* inventories, discrimination on the basis of sex does not. And yet sex discrimination is an even more widespread injustice, affecting the lives of more than half the world's population. While a prohibition on sex discrimination, as racial discrimination, is included in every general human rights convention and is the subject of a specialized binding instrument, sexual equality has not been allocated the status of a fundamental and basic tenet of a communal world order.

Of course women as well as men suffer from the violation of the traditional canon of *jus cogens* norms. However the manner in which the norms have been constructed obscures the most pervasive harms done to women. One example of this is the 'most important of all human rights', the right to life set out in Article 6 of the Civil and Political Covenant which forms part of customary international law. The right is concerned with the arbitrary deprivation of life through public action. Important as it is, the protection from arbitrary deprivation of life or liberty through public actions does not address the ways in which being a woman is in itself life-threatening and the special ways in which woman need legal protection to be able to enjoy their right to life. . . .

A number of recent studies show that being a women may be hazardous even from before birth due to the practice in some areas of aborting female fetuses because of the strong social and economic pressure to have sons. Immediately after birth womanhood is also dangerous in some societies because of the higher incidence of female infanticide. During childhood in many communities girls are breast-fed for shorter periods and later fed less so that girls suffer the physical and mental effects of malnutrition at higher rates than boys. Indeed in most of Asia and North Africa, women suffer great discrimination in basic nutrition and health care leading to a disproportionate number of female deaths. The well-documented phenomenon of the 'feminization' of poverty in both the developing and developed world causes women to have a much lower quality of life than men.

Violence against women is endemic in all states; indeed international lawyers could observe that this is one of those rare areas where there is genuinely consistent and uniform state practice. . . .

. . .

The great level of documented violence against women around the world is unaddressed by the international legal notion of the right to life because that legal system is focussed on 'public' actions by the state. A similar myopia can be detected also in the international prohibition on torture. A central feature of the international legal definition of torture is that it takes place in the public realm: it must be 'inflicted by or at the instigation of or with the consent or acquiescence of a public official or other person acting in an official capacity'. Although many women are victims of torture in this 'public' sense, by far the greatest violence against women occurs in the 'private' nongovernmental sphere.

. . .

The problematic structure of traditionally asserted *jus cogens* norms is also shown in the more controversial 'collective' right to self-determination. The right allows 'all peoples' to 'freely determine their political status and freely pursue their economic, social and cultural development'. Yet the oppression of women within groups claiming the right of self-determination has never been considered relevant to the validity of their claim or to the form self-determination should take. An example of this is the firm United States support for the Afghani resistance movement after the 1979 Soviet invasion without any apparent concern for the very low status of women within traditional Afghani society. Another is the immediate and powerful United Nations response after Iraq's 1990 invasion of Kuwait. None of the plans for the liberation or reconstruction of Kuwait were concerned with that state's denial of political rights to women. Although some international pressure was brought to bear on the Kuwaiti government during and after the invasion to institute a more democratic system, the concern did not focus on the political repression of women and was quickly dropped.

. . .

Feminist rethinking of *jus cogens* would also give prominence to a range of other human rights; the right to sexual equality, to food, to reproductive freedom, to be free from fear of violence and oppression, and to peace. . . . In the particular context of the concept of *jus cogens*, which has an explicitly promotional and aspirational character, it should be possible for even traditional international legal theory to accommodate rights that are fundamental to the existence and dignity of half the world's population. . . .

. . .

RESTATEMENT (THIRD), THE FOREIGN RELATIONS LAW OF THE UNITED STATES

American Law Institute (1987), Vol. 2, 161

§702. Customary International Law of Human Rights

A state violates international law if, as a matter of state policy, it practices, encourages, or condones

(a) genocide,
(b) slavery or slave trade,
(c) the murder or causing the disappearance of individuals,
(d) torture or other cruel, inhuman, or degrading treatment or punishment,
(e) prolonged arbitrary detention,
(f) systematic racial discrimination, or
(g) a consistent pattern of gross violations of internationally recognized human rights.

Comment:

a. Scope of customary law of human rights. This section includes as customary law only those human rights whose status as customary law is generally accepted (as of 1987) and whose scope and content are generally agreed. The list is not necessarily complete, and is not closed: human rights not listed in this section may have achieved the status of customary law, and some rights might achieve that status in the future.

b. State policy as violation of customary law. In general, a state is responsible for acts of officials or official bodies, national or local, even if the acts were not authorized by or known to the responsible national authorities, indeed even if expressly forbidden by law, decree or instruction....

...

A government may be presumed to have encouraged or condoned acts prohibited by this section if such acts, especially by its officials, have been repeated or notorious and no steps have been taken to prevent them or to punish the perpetrators.

...

Even when a state is not responsible under this section because a violation is not state policy, the state may be responsible under some international agreement that requires the state to prevent the violation....

...

l. Gender discrimination. The United Nations Charter (Article 1(3)) and the Universal Declaration of Human Rights (Article 2) prohibit discrimination in respect of human rights on various grounds, including sex. Discrimination on the basis of sex in respect of recognized rights is prohibited by a number of international agreements, including the Covenant on Civil and Political Rights, the Covenant on Economic, Social and Cultural Rights, and more generally by the Convention on the

Elimination of All Forms of Discrimination Against Women, which, as of 1987, had been ratified by 91 states and signed by a number of others. The United States had signed the Convention but had not yet ratified it. The domestic laws of a number of states, including those of the United States, mandate equality for, or prohibit discrimination against, women generally or in various respects. Gender-based discrimination is still practiced in many states in varying degrees, but freedom from gender discrimination as state policy, in many matters, may already be a principle of customary international law. . . .

. . .

m. Consistent pattern of gross violations of human rights. The acts enumerated in clauses (a) to (f) are violations of customary law even if the practice is not consistent, or not part of a 'pattern', and those acts are inherently 'gross' violations of human rights. Clause (g) includes other infringements of recognized human rights that are not violations of customary law when committed singly or sporadically (although they may be forbidden to states parties to the International Covenants or other particular agreements); they become violations of customary law if the state is guilty of a 'consistent pattern of gross violations' as state policy. A violation is gross if it is particularly shocking because of the importance of the right or the gravity of the violation. All the rights proclaimed in the Universal Declaration and protected by the principal International Covenants are internationally recognized human rights, but some rights are fundamental and intrinsic to human dignity. Consistent patterns of violation of such rights as state policy may be deemed 'gross' *ipso facto.* These include, for example, systematic harassment, invasions of the privacy of the home, arbitrary arrest and detention (even if not prolonged); denial of fair trial in criminal cases; grossly disproportionate punishment; denial of freedom to leave a country; denial of the right to return to one's country; mass uprooting of a country's population; denial of freedom of conscience and religion; denial of personality before the law; denial of basic privacy such as the right to marry and raise a family; and invidious racial or religious discrimination. A state party to the Covenant on Civil and Political Rights is responsible even for a single, isolated violation of any of these rights; any state is liable under customary law for a consistent pattern of violations of any such right as state policy.

n. Customary law of human rights and jus cogens. Not all human rights norms are peremptory norms (*jus cogens*), but those in clauses (a) to (f) of this section are, and an international agreement that violates them is void.

o. Responsibility to all states (erga omnes)*.* Violations of the rules stated in this section are violations of obligations to all other states and any state may invoke the ordinary remedies available to a state when its rights under customary law are violated.

NOTE

In the United States, the *Restatements of Law* represent an important reference for many legal issues, although they have no official, legal status. These *Restatements* are adopted and promulgated by the American Law Institute, a private organization not affiliated with the United States Government, whose membership consists of judges, legal academicians and lawyers involved in private practice and in government. The drafts presented to the Institute for its approval and adoption are generally prepared by leading academicians, who may consult advisory committees with a broader membership.

Such was the case with the *Restatement (Third) of the Foreign Relations Law of the United States*, other portions of which appear in later chapters. The introduction to that *Restatement* states (at p. ix) that it is 'in no sense an official document of the United States'. It notes that in some particulars its rules 'are at variance' with positions taken by the United States Government. Nonetheless, despite this independence and non-official status, it is inevitable that a *Restatement* dealing with international law will in general reflect the broad positions taken by the United States rather than, say, inconsistent or polar positions taken by other, perhaps hostile states.

NOTE

Professor Louis Henkin was the chief reporter for *Restatement (Third) of the Foreign Relations Law of the United States*. Consider his comments in 'Human Rights and State "Sovereignty"', Ga. J. Int. & Comp. L. 31 (1995/96), at 37:

> ...[T]here is now a significant, and increasing, amount of such nonconventional law of human rights. But though that law is not made by treaty, it ... differs from traditional customary law in fundamental respects. Traditional customary law was not made; it resulted.... Now, in our time, non-conventional law is being *made*, purposefully, knowingly, wilfully, and concern for human rights has provided a principal impetus to its growth....
>
> [Henkin refers to the *Restatement*'s list of violations in Section 702.] Where does this law come from? The Restatement ... supports the non-conventional human rights law it restates by invoking the traditional indicia of traditional customary law — state practice with a sense of legal obligation. But the Reporters of the Restatement admitted that the state practice supporting non-conventional human rights law looks different, is different....
>
> ... I suggest that such law is 'constitutional' in a new sense. The international system, having identified contemporary human values, has adopted and declared them to be fundamental law, international law. But, in a radical derogation from the axiom of 'sovereignty', that law is not based on consent: at least, it does not honor or accept dissent, and it binds particular states regardless of their objection.
>
> How did this happen? Conceptually, it may have sneaked into the law on the back of another idea, *ius cogens* ... *ius cogens* ... does not reflect ancient custom or traditional natural law; it has not been built by state practice. Also, it does not require consent of every state: it reflects 'general' consensus....
>
> And so, international non-conventional human rights law is ... like ius cogens ... [I]t is not the result of practice but the product of common consensus from which few dare dissent....

Compare the earlier articles in this Section by Roberts and Shelton.

C. WOMEN'S RIGHTS AND CEDAW

The study of women's rights illustrates the increasing ambition, breadth and complexity of the human rights movement. We see a proliferation of instruments and institutions, world conferences and NGO initiatives, active proposals in many directions, and growing conflicts about premises and goals within the women's movement itself. The feminist literature relevant to human rights assumptions, goals and strategies has moved adventurously in many directions, sometimes polar directions; its engagement with the human rights movement has enriched and deepened thought about the entire project. The complexity and different currents of advocacy and criticism, idealism and scepticism, views of sexuality and gender, and indeed views of equality are captured in an innovative and ambitious treaty, CEDAW (185 states parties as of January 2007).

Of the several blind spots in the early development of the human rights movement, none is as striking as that movement's failure to give to violations of women's (human) rights the attention, and in some respects the priority, that they require. It is not only that these problems adversely affect half of the world's population. They affect everyone, for a deep change in women's circumstances and possibilities produces change throughout social, economic and political life. Even in a field where the human rights movement acted with vigour in setting standards, passing resolutions and at times imposing sanctions — for example, racial discrimination — it is often the case that progress in many countries has been measured or slight, and that problems of the most serious character not only survive but remain entrenched. Nonetheless, it is instructive to contrast the vigour of the movement in trying to 'eliminate' racial discrimination with its relative apathy until the last 15 years or so in responding to gender discrimination — and to explore why this is so.

The materials in Section C suggest the complexly interwoven socioeconomic, legal, political and cultural strands to the problem of women's subordination and to the content of women's rights. Although a systematic study of economic and social rights must await Chapter 4, Section C demonstrates in many ways the interrelationships and functional interdependence of civil–political and economic-social rights. The title to CEDAW incorporates a classic civil-political issue, discrimination, but the content of this convention's rights and the work of its Committee range more broadly. Moreover, when one focuses specifically on what appear to be women's issues, links between them and other aspects of social order (disorder) appear pervasive. All is interrelated. The problem is truly systemic.

You should bear in mind that Section C is our *first* look at women's rights. Some parts of Chapters 6 and 7 return to this theme, but stress different issues, particularly the tension between universalism and cultural relativism in the understanding of those rights, and the imbedded traditions, practices, attitudes and religiously-based understandings about women that may be broadly accepted (and not only by men) in some parts of the world while abhorred and criticized as violations of rights in other parts.

1. BACKGROUND TO CEDAW: SOCIO-ECONOMIC CONTEXT, DISCRIMINATION AND ABUSE

These introductory materials present reports about women's circumstances in different parts of the world. They suggest the complex relationships among diverse phenomena that bear on women's rights. Several themes recur in the readings.

(1) Legal norms capture and reinforce deep cultural norms and community practices. They entrench ideas and help give them the sense of being natural, part of the inevitable order of things.

(2) Reformers and advocates of deep legal and cultural transformation insist that change is possible, so that what was seen as natural or inevitable comes to be understood as socially constructed and thus contingent, open to change.

(3) Property rights and economic dependence interact with patterns of authority within family and workplace, and with vital issues like education, health, and political participation.

(4) Major economic and political programmes, like a development or privatization scheme or structural adjustment requirements or a stress on deregulated markets and trade, may impose particular and severe costs on women that are not apparent on the face of the programmes.

(5) The statistics created by bureaucracies or scholars structure and confine the imagination. They are often viewed as objective data, without awareness of the disputable methods and categories that determine their formulation. What they record as well as what they do not record influence policies as well as perceptions. New methods and categories in the statistical tables prepared by such institutions as the United Nations Development Program introduce new criteria to judge women's (and other groups') circumstances and progress.

INITIAL REPORT OF GUATEMALA SUBMITTED TO THE CEDAW COMMITTEE

CEDAW/C/Gua/1–2, 2 April 1991

[CEDAW requires in Article 18 that states parties submit periodic reports on 'measures which they have adopted to give effect' to CEDAW's provisions. Those reports 'may indicate factors and difficulties affecting the degree of fulfillment of obligations' under CEDAW. The reports are to be submitted to the Committee created by Article 17 of CEDAW. In its introduction to this report, Guatemala noted the difficulty of assembling it, stressing that 'studies of this type are only a recent innovation'. The task of preparation 'has also been a positive exercise in thought, analysis and self-appraisal with respect to the position of women in Guatemala in 1983, and the changes made to date'. That work stimulated action to design 'strategies and targets . . . to improve the situation encountered in the short and medium term'.

This Guatemalan report offers an unusually graphic and complete picture of the situation of women with family and society. The following excerpts are taken from the report's sections addressing Articles 5 and 16 of the Convention.]

Article 5

46. Guatemala is a multi-ethnic, multi-cultural and multilingual country with traditional, cultural patterns that reinforce the subordination of women on the social, cultural, economic and political planes. Extended Guatemalan families in the country and nuclear families in the city are governed by a patriarchal system in which decisions are taken by men (husband, father or eldest son), who are considered the heads of the household, a role assumed by women only in their absence.

47. In Guatemalan society the man is expected to be the breadwinner, the legal representative, the repository of authority; the one who must 'correct' the children, while the mother is relegated to their care and upbringing, to household tasks, and to 'waiting on' or looking after her husband or partner. These roles often have to be performed in addition to engaging in some profitable activity which generates earnings that are always regarded as 'complementary'.

48. For their childhood, little boys and girls are guided towards work considered 'masculine' or 'feminine'; for example, boys play at working outside the home as carpenters, mechanics, farmers or pilots, and in all those jobs that are considered 'tough' or that require physical strength. Girls, on the other hand, are taught to interest themselves in cooking, weaving, sewing, washing, ironing, or cleaning the house and, especially, caring for the children and helping the mother, as a responsibility and duty more than just a game.

49. Care of the children is strictly considered the responsibility of the mother, grandmother, and/or sister; and in the event of divorce, separation or dissolution of the marriage, custody of the children is generally awarded to the mother.

50. The aforementioned patterns vary slightly with the socio-economic stratum, which generally also determines the social class to which the women belong and which in addition is related to their level of education and knowledge.

51. Notwithstanding what has been said, the woman is the chief social agent in the majority of spheres of action. An empirical profile of a Guatemalan woman may cover the following characteristics.

52. She is responsible for family health and hygiene and for the supervision of the formal and informal upbringing of the children in the home; she organizes and maintains living and sanitary conditions and a supply of water for domestic use. She produces nutritional supplements for the family, including animal proteins (cattle, sheep and goats) and sources of vitamins (fruit and vegetables); she is the one in charge of the purchase, preparation, stocking and distribution of food within the home. In addition, she manages the family income, ensuring that payment in kind and in cash is used in such a way as to maximize the material well-being of the family.

53. She takes responsibility for generating additional income or for producing consumer goods when her partner's income does not cover the minimum family requirements.

54. In the case of an irresponsible father, the entire responsibility for the support of the children devolves upon her, reflected in particular by a considerable increase in her hours of work.

55. Her work is poorly paid or not paid at all and is generally of low productivity owing to lack of access to capital.

56. It is falsely assumed that the man is the one who makes the principal economic contributions to the family, for which reason he is the owner and beneficiary of all payments and services.

57. The educational level of the woman is low, which reflects on the effectiveness of her efforts to maintain and improve the health, feeding, housing and other living conditions of her family.

58. In the paid work that she does, her salary is inferior to a man's and her instability in the sense of a job is greater.

59. The man has traditionally been considered the 'head of the household'.

Article 16

184. Family relations in Guatemala, as regards the guardianship, wardship, trusteeship and adoption of children, the ownership of property, its disposition and enjoyment, etc. are governed by the Guatemalan Civil Code (Decree-Law No. 106).

...

190. The woman's rights and responsibilities in marriage are as follows:

...

(2) The husband owes his wife protection and assistance, and must provide her with all the means necessary to maintain the household, in accordance with his financial resources. The woman has a special right and duty to nurture and care for her children during their minority, and to take charge of domestic affairs.

...

(5) The woman may be employed or ply a trade, occupation, public office or business, where she is able to do so without endangering the interests and the care of her children, or other needs of her household.

...

197. Married women are restricted in representing the marriage and in administration of marital assets, roles which are assigned by law to the husband, and this constitutes a relative incapacity.

198. Parental authority is a right which is virtually forbidden to women, since it is assigned to the father. Women only come to exercise this right when the father is imprisoned or legally barred from such.

...

201. The legal context allows the husband to object to the wife engaging in activities outside the home, thus barring her from the right and freedom to work. The legal context restricts her right to personal fulfillment in areas outside her function as mother and housewife and restricts her personal liberty.

...

203. A judicial declaration of paternity in cases of rape, rape of juveniles and abduction is dependent on the conduct of the mother, based on what the law terms

'notoriously disorderly conduct', an express form of discrimination against women and the product of conception resulting from forced intercourse.

...

209. Adultery defined as an 'offence against honour' protects the legal right of filiation and 'the interests of the family', but makes a clear distinction concerning the gravity of the act, depending on whether it involves the man or the woman, providing a tougher sentence for the woman; the proof and the procedure are different in the two cases, so that in practice it is only applied to women.

210. Offences 'against life' in which women are most affected are defined as abortion, which is defined as criminal conduct by which the death of the foetus is caused deliberately, within the mother's womb or by its premature expulsion. Medical abortion to avoid danger to the health or death of the mother, or due to deformities of the foetus, is not punishable. This is not envisaged when it is the result of rape.

211. With regard to the offence of rape, the punishment is graded according to the age of the victim and the relationship of authority which may exist between the victim and the offender. Reference is made to the 'honourable woman', requiring that the offender has used seduction, promise of marriage or deceit and the woman is a virgin; this emphasizes the value of 'honour', defining it as an offence against honour rather than against personal integrity, as would be correct.

212. Maltreatment of women and children and domestic violence are not defined as offences against the person and in practice are lumped together with injuries, coercion and threats, causing serious difficulties with regard to proof and other procedural problems.

...

COMMENT ON WOMEN'S SOCIAL AND ECONOMIC CONDITIONS

The status of women within the international human rights regime and the task of ensuring human rights for women are incomprehensible without taking into account the social and economic conditions that characterize women's lives around the world. Much information appears in later materials in this section addressing issues such as violence against women. This Comment sets forth some basic comparisons between men and women.

Later readings underscore the degree to which rights abuses are strongly correlated to victims' slight social and economic power, hence political power. Those who are most vulnerable to human rights abuses often lack the favour or protection of the state, as well as the power within their communities to protect and further their basic needs and interests.

According to virtually every indicator of social well-being and status — political participation, legal capacity, access to economic resources and employment, wage differentials, levels of education and health care — women fare significantly and sometimes dramatically worse than men. The gap between vital statistics for women and men tends to grow as inquiry moves from the developed to less developed world. Consider, for example, the following statistics from three states, drawn from the Human Development Report 2005, pp. 299–302, that are respectively characterized as high, medium and low human development. The figures (for 2003) after each state refer, in order, to (1) adult literacy rate for persons 15 and older; and (2) estimated earned income. Within each category, the two figures are, in order, female and male:

> Norway: (1) close to 100% for both female and male; (2) $32,272–$43,148
> Peru: (1) 82.1%–93.5%; (2) $2,231–$8,256
> Nigeria: (1) 59.4%–74.4%; (2) $674–$1,583

A range of special factors influence these state statistics. For example, states of the Arab-Muslim Middle East and North Africa showed considerably larger differences between the genders in these categories. It should be clear that the figures on estimated earned income ignore women's (unvalued and uncompensated) labour in child care and household responsibilities, and that much of their outside labour may remain unvalued and uncompensated where it doesn't form part of the cash economy. The materials of Section C that follow provide information and statistics about several other categories of analysis, such as health care.

Contrary to the expectations that many hold, economic reform and development is not an automatic route to the relative advancement of women within society. Economic globalization and restructuring (such as efforts to convert a Soviet-style economy into a deregulated market economy with accompanying privatization of government enterprises) may in fact worsen their situation, at least during the transition. Like structural adjustment programmes associated with the International Monetary Fund, such market-oriented strategies may involve serious reductions of welfare, social-safety-net programmes that particularly affect women.

Analysis of gender issues has come increasingly to stress cultural context, and has led scholars to surprising statistical reflections of discriminatory practices. Consider an article by Amartya Sen, 'More than 100 Million Women are Missing' (N.Y. Review of Books, December 20, 1990), examining low ratios of women to men (0.94 or lower) in populations in South and West Asia and China, despite the fact that boys worldwide outnumber girls at birth by about 105 to 100. Indeed, in Europe, the U.S. and Japan, despite ongoing forms of gender discrimination, women outnumber men. Why the difference in regions? Sen stresses forms of discrimination that are less common in the West:

> The fate of women is quite different in most of Asia and North Africa. In these places the failure to give women medical care similar to what men get and to provide them with comparable food and social services results in fewer women surviving than would be the case if they had equal care. In India, for example, except in the period immediately following birth, the death rate is higher for women than for men fairly consistently in all age groups until the late thirties. This relates to higher rates of disease from which women suffer, and ultimately to the relative neglect of females, especially in health care and medical attention.

> Similar neglect of women vis-à-vis men can be seen also in many other parts of the world. The result is a lower proportion of women than would be the case if they had equal care — in most of Asia and North Africa, and to a lesser extent Latin America.
>
> This pattern is not uniform in all parts of the third world, however. Sub-Saharan Africa, for example, ravaged as it is by extreme poverty, hunger, and famine, has a substantial excess rather than deficit of women, the ratio of women to men being around 1.02. The 'third world' in this matter is not a useful category, because it is so diverse.
>
> . . .
>
> To get an idea of the numbers of people involved in the different ratios of women to men, we can estimate the number of 'missing women' in a country, say, China or India, by calculating the number of extra women who would have been in China or India if these countries had the same ratio of women to men as obtain in areas of the world in which they receive similar care. If we could expect equal populations of the two sexes, the low ratio of 0.94 women, to men in South Asia, West Asia, and China would indicate a 6 percent deficit of women; but since, in countries where men and women receive similar care, the ratio is about 1.05, the real shortfall is about 11 percent. In China alone this amounts to 50 million 'missing women', taking 1.05 as the benchmark ratio. When that number is added to those in South Asia, West Asia, and North Africa, a great many more than 100 million women are 'missing'. These numbers tell us, quietly, a terrible story of inequality and neglect leading to the excess mortality of women.

Sen discounts two 'simplistic explanations' for this phenomenon: Western civilization is less sexist than Eastern, and unequal nutrition and health care are consequences of underdevelopment. Rather, he suggests we must examine 'the complex ways in which economic, social, and cultural factors can influence the regional differences'. He discusses decision-making within the family as the pursuit of cooperation 'in which solutions for the conflicting aspects of family life are implicitly agreed on'. Analysis of these 'cooperative conflicts' in different regions and cultures can 'provide a useful way of understanding the influences that affect the "deal" that women get in the division of benefits within the family'. Perceptions of who is doing 'productive' work or contributing to the family's welfare can be very influential, and such social perceptions are 'of pervasive importance in gender inequality', particularly 'in sustaining female deprivation in many of the poorer countries'.

Division of a family's joint benefits are apt to be more favourable to women if (1) they earn outside income, (2) their work is recognized as productive, (3) they own some economic resources or hold economic rights, and (4) there is an understanding of ways in which women are deprived. 'Considerable empirical evidence' suggests that gainful employment such as working outside the home for a wage as opposed to unpaid housework 'can substantially enhance the deal that women get'. Not only access to funds but also women's status and standing in the family improve. Moreover, women bring home experience of the outside world, a form of education. Such factors can 'counter the relative neglect of girls as they grow up', as women are seen as economic producers.

Sen discusses the different situation in China, where other explanatory factors may be important, such as the strong measures to control the size of families in the framework of a strong cultural preference for boys:

> To ascribe importance to the influence of gainful employment on women's prospects for survival may superficially look like another attempt at a simple economic explanation, but it would be a mistake to see it this way. The deeper question is why such outside employment is more prevalent in, say, sub-Saharan Africa than in North Africa, or in Southeast and Eastern Asia than in Western and Southern Asia. Here the cultural, including religious, backgrounds of the respective regions are surely important. Economic causes for women's deprivation have to be integrated with other — social and cultural — factors to give depth to the explanation.
>
> Of course, gainful employment is not the only factor affecting women's chances of survival. Women's education and their economic rights — including property rights — may be crucial variables as well. . . .

NOTE

It was the rare report of a human rights NGO before the 1990s that gave specific attention to human rights violations against women, although women often figured with men as victims in reports dealing with themes like arbitrary detention, disappearances, or torture. Numbers of NGOs have been organized during the past 15 years that are devoted to women's human rights issues, and leading NGOs now frequently address women's problems, particularly violence against women perpetrated directly by the state and violence in the home followed by state inaction. Examples of contemporary reports and analytic frameworks appear later in the materials.

Consider two earlier reports, starting with Amnesty International, Rape and Sexual Abuse: Torture and Ill Treatment of Women in Detention (1992). It stressed that 'many governments persistently refuse to recognize that rape and sexual abuse by government agents are serious human rights violations'. Effective investigations do not take place, perpetrators are not brought to justice. 'In 1986 a Peruvian prosecutor told an AI delegation in Ayacucho that rape was to be expected when troops were conducting counter-insurgency operations, and that prosecutions for such assaults were unlikely.' Government forces in such circumstances use the threat of sexual abuse to extract military information. 'The official failure to condemn or punish rape gives it an overt political sanction, which allows rape and other forms of torture and ill-treatment to become tools of military strategy.' The report cited victim's reports of serious abuse in a broad range of countries: Greece, Northern Ireland, Israel-occupied territories, Turkey, Syria and Pakistan. Often perpetrators go free 'because their victims are too terrified or shamed to file a complaint'.

Americas Watch (a unit of Human Rights Watch), Criminal Injustice: Violence against Women in Brazil (1992), attempted more cultural analysis of domestic violence, focusing on wife-murder, domestic battery and rape. It constituted the first report of a newly formed Women's Rights Project of HRW. The report noted that 'domestic violence is a common and serious problem in developed and developing countries alike'. Like the AI report, it gave graphic examples of and statistics about domestic violence:

> A police chief in Rio de Janeiro told Americas Watch that to her knowledge, of more than 2,000 battery and sexual assault cases registered at her station in 1990, not a single one had ended in punishment of the accused. The São Luis women's police station in the northeastern state of Maranhão reported that of over 4,000 cases of physical and sexual assault registered with the station, only 300 were ever forwarded for processing and only two yielded punishment for the accused.
>
> Brazil's criminal law is part of the problem. In the Brazilian Penal Code, rape is defined as a crime against custom rather than a crime against an individual person — society rather than the female victim is the offended party. Most other sex crimes are deemed crimes only if the victim is a 'virgin' or 'honest' woman. If a woman does not fit this 'customary' stereotype, she is likely to be accused of having consented to the crime and it is unlikely to be investigated.

The report included information from a 1989 study of violence in a Brazilian state, which included such practices as:

> beating, tying up and spanking, burning the genitals and breasts with cigarettes, strangulation, inserting objects in the victim's vagina (such as bottles and pieces of wood) and throwing alcohol and fire on the victim. The study also noted repeated physical abuse of pregnant women in which the aggressors 'aimed for the womb, breasts and vagina'.

The report also described the growing and effective women's movement that pressed for changes in the state's response. Their pressures led to numbers of improvements, such as establishment of a woman's police station staffed entirely by women and dedicated to crimes of violence against women. These stations were designed to investigate and to provide psychological and legal counselling. They 'represented an integrated approach to the problem of domestic violence'. Pressures from the women's movement also contributed to Brazil's becoming a party to CEDAW.

2. CEDAW: PROVISIONS AND COMMITTEE

COMMENT ON CEDAW'S SUBSTANTIVE PROVISIONS

The Convention is among the many that elaborate in one particular field the norms and ideals that are generally and tersely stated in the Universal Declaration, and stated somewhat more amply in the ICCPR. Its preamble suggests how deeply the issues run and that the norms of this Convention must be placed in a broader transformative context. It recognizes 'that a change in the traditional role of men as well as the role of women in society and in the family is needed to achieve full equality between men and women'.

The reader should be familiar with the provisions of the Convention, a few of which are addressed by the following comments.

Article 1: Note three vital characteristics of the definition of 'discrimination against women'. (a) The article refers to *effect* as well as *purpose*, thus directing attention to the consequences of governmental measures as well as the intentions underlying them. (b) The definition is not limited to discrimination through 'state action' or action by persons acting under colour of law, as are the definitions of many rights such as the definition of torture under the Convention against Torture. (c) The definition's range is further expanded by the concluding phrase, 'or any other field'.

Article 2: The goals stated in this article are to be pursued 'without delay'. Consider the possible meanings of the terms 'equality' in clause (a) and 'any act of discrimination' in clause (c). Note the breadth of clauses (e) and (f) with respect to the private, non-governmental sectors of society, particularly in relation to the definition in Article 1. Note throughout the Convention the blurred lines between the private and public spheres of life, and the range of obligations on states to intervene in the private sector, to go beyond 'respect' in order to 'protect', 'ensure', and 'promote'.

Article 3: Note the grand goal set forth for states, to 'ensure the full development and advancement of women', and consider whether the other human rights instruments examined contain a similar conception for any group, or for people in general.

Article 4: This 'affirmative action' clause, duly qualified, appears as well in the Convention on the Elimination of all Forms of Racial Discrimination, but not in the ICCPR. Consider this article in relation to Article 2(e) and (f), and Article 11.

Article 5: The breadth and aspiration of this article can be described only as striking. Provisions such as Article 10(c) impose a similar obligation on states in defined contexts. Other human rights treaties lack a similar provision, although Article 2 of the Racial Discrimination Convention comes close. Consider how a state in good faith might decide on 'appropriate measures' under this article, bearing in mind the injunction in Article 2 to proceed 'without delay' as well as the claims of the Convention's other provisions.

Articles 6–16: These articles evidence how a treaty devoted to one set of problems — here, ending discrimination against women and achieving equality — makes possible discrete, disaggregated treatment of the different issues relevant to these problems. Clearly the variety and detail in these articles would have been out of place, indeed impossible, in a treaty of general scope like the ICCPR. Note the great range of verbs that are used throughout these articles to define states parties' duties, including: eliminate, provide, encourage, protect, introduce, accord, ensure.

> *Article 6* is typical of many provisions in requiring a state party to regulate specific non-governmental activity.
>
> *Articles 7–9*, to the contrary, deal with the traditional notion of state action, here barring discrimination by the state.
>
> *Article 10* concerns a particular field, education, and lists specific goals which, in their totality, take on a programmatic character. Note paragraph (h) on family planning and its relationship to three other provisions: Articles 12(1), 14(2)(b) and 16(e). The Convention does not address as such the question of abortion.

Article 12 together with a number of other provisions indicate the degree to which CEDAW involves and interrelates the classical categories of civil-political rights and economic-social rights. It imposes a limited duty to provide free health care.

Article 14 disaggregates women's problems in regional and functional terms. It underscores strategies for realizing goals that permeate the entire Convention, such as mobilization through functional grass roots groups and participation in local decision making. CEDAW is not a convention in which solutions are to be provided only by the central authority of the state.

Article 16 orders the states to sweep away a large number of fundamental, traditional discriminations against and forms of subordination of women. Like several other articles, it could be understood as a complement to, as one specification of, the broad goals stated in Article 5. Compare its provisions with the Report of Guatemala, p. 176, *supra*.

NOTE

More states have entered reservations to their ratification of CEDAW than to any other human rights treaty. Some reservations seriously qualify a state's commitment, particularly those that base the reservation on conflicting principles or rules in a religion or culture. The Comment at p. 1125, *infra*, gives examples of reservations and examines them in the context of a discussion about universalism and cultural relativism.

COMMENT ON TYPES OF STATE DUTIES IMPOSED BY HUMAN RIGHTS TREATIES

To understand the significance and implications of the rights stated in the ICCPR, CEDAW and other human rights treaties, it is helpful to examine the related duties/obligations of states — even though human rights conventions rarely talk of duties. Attention to such duties clarifies the significance and even content of the related rights. It also points to strategies to realize a right, as by persuading the state to change its behaviour in one or another respect. The effort, then, is to deconstruct a right into its related state duties, perhaps duties that an advocate seeks to have imposed on the state.

Some of these duties can fairly be called correlative (corresponding) to the right — for example, implying from your right not to be tortured the state's correlative duty not to torture you. These may be the duties that come most promptly and naturally to the mind of the rights-holder. As a practical matter and from a functional perspective, other duties may be necessary implications from the nature of a given right even if they are not spelled out in treaty text — for example, a state's duty to create and operate electoral institutions and processes if the citizen's right to vote is to be realized.

Different rights may point to different types of state duties. All depends on the nature of the right, on the problems that it was meant to overcome or to prevent. Some types of state duties described below are more prominent in the ICCPR, some in CEDAW, some in the International Covenant on Economic, Social and Cultural Rights discussed in Chapter 4, or in other human rights treaties. Identifying the multiple duties that may be relevant to any one right sharpens an understanding of what is distinctive to and necessary to realize that right.

Two points should be kept in mind as we examine different kinds of rights from the perspective of related variable state duties.

(1) At the start of the human rights movement, much weight was given to a distinction between so-called 'negative' and 'positive' rights. The negative rights basically imposed a duty of 'hands-off', a duty of a state not to interfere with, say, an individual's physical security. The illustration of torture noted above fits well here. Thus, the right not to be tortured was imagined to impose only such a negative duty — the state's correlative duty not to torture. Positive rights, on the other hand, imposed affirmative (positive) duties on the state — in the classic case, a duty to provide food (food stamps/subsidies and so on) if such provision was essential to satisfy the right to food. Thus economic and social rights such as the right to food were considered positive rights, which frequently required financial expenditures by the state, unlike the classic negative rights that were thought to require merely abstention from unjustified interference with another person. It will be important to consider how much of this negative-positive distinction remains valid in the light of the illustrations and analysis below, and whether it clarifies or confuses the issues before us.

Consider the following classic presentation of this distinction in Maurice Cranston, 'Are There Any Human Rights?', in 112/4 Daedalus 12 (1983):

> The traditional political and civil rights are not difficult to institute. For the most part, they require governments, and other people generally, to leave a man alone.... Do not injure, arrest, or imprison him. To respect a man's right to life, liberty, and property is not a very costly exercise. As Locke and others have explained, it requires a system of law that recognizes those rights to protect those rights. But rulers are not called upon to do anything that it is unreasonable to expect of them.... Political... rights can be secured by fairly simple legislation. Since those rights are largely rights against government interference, the greatest effort will be directed toward restraining the government's own executive arm. But this is no longer the case where economic and social rights are concerned....

(2) Rights are not static. They evolve. They broaden or contract over time. One way of understanding an expansion of the content of a given right (to speech, to food) is to examine the duties related to that right, and to inquire whether and how they have expanded. The argument for a broader construction of a given right often amounts to the claim that further duties ought to be imposed on the state in order to satisfy the right. Consider some examples. The right to speech implies at a minimum the government's correlative duty not to interfere with it. It should not enjoin or penalize the rights-holder who indeed speaks. A modest expansion of this 'hands-off' right imposes the further duty on government to protect a speaker against

deliberate interference by nonstate actors. Your right to speak loses meaning if others are permitted to block you in various ways from publishing or orally communicating your ideas. An argument for further expansion can be based on the claim that government must facilitate speech by assuring access of political groups to the media (that is, to newspapers or electronic media whether or not owned or controlled by the state). Such arguments for expansion of the kinds of state duties can constitute a strategy of change. So attention to duties, how they differ among rights within a treaty and among treaties, and how they change over time is one vital way of examining and fostering change in the human rights movement as a whole.

The following scheme of five types of state duties derives from but modifies earlier writings, particularly Henry Shue, *Basic Rights* (2nd edn. 1996), and G. J. H. van Hoof, 'The Legal Nature of Economic, Social and Cultural Rights', in Philip Alston and K. Tomasevski (eds.), *The Right to Food* (1984), at 97.

(1) Respect Rights of Others

This duty requires the state to treat persons equally, to respect their individual dignity and worth, and hence not to interfere with or impair their declared rights, whether they be physical security rights or rights to due process, equal protection, speech or political participation. This duty of respect has often been described as 'negative' in the sense of being a 'hands-off' duty. The broad idea is not to worsen an individual's situation by depriving that person of the enjoyment of a declared right.

Of course the observance by states of this duty of respect would itself, without the possibility of any further state duties, lead to a vast improvement in the human condition. In this sense, the duty of respect can be seen to lie at the core of the human rights movement. Compliance with it would avoid most of the worst calamities: genocides, massacres, torture. The duty of respect is in this sense allied to the 'antidisaster' element of the human rights movement — the notion that the human rights movement arose and developed to prevent recurrence of the massive abominations of the twentieth century that preceded it. But observance would achieve far more, such as realizing the basic conditions for a democratic society.

For many but not all rights declared in the treaties, the duty of respect reaches beyond states to obligate individuals and nonstate entities. A person's right to bodily security or to vote imposes a correlative duty on all other persons to refrain from interfering with it. My right to bodily security mean little unless my neighbors are prohibited by the state from violating it. On the other hand, the other duties identified in categories (2) — (5) below are in most cases associated only with the state. Under the human rights treaties, individuals or nonstate entities do not, for example, bear direct duties to protect other individuals against physical attack or to provide housing for them. Such issues about the character and range of individual duties are considered elsewhere at pp. 496 and 501, *infra*. This Comment covers only state duties.

(2) Create Institutional Machinery Essential to Realization of Rights

Some rights may be impaired or effectively annulled not only by government's direct interference with them (torture, preventing a citizen from expressing ideas or voting), but also by its failure to put in place the institutional machinery essential for the realization or practice of the right. Political participation offers a simple illustration. A citizen's right to vote means little unless a government maintains fair electoral machinery that makes possible the act of voting, counting of ballots and so on. Voting rights are, then, hardly cost-free for government. It is not simply a matter of 'hands off'. Public funds must be expended to create the infrastructure on which the practical realization of the right depends. Public care must be taken to be certain the voting mechanisms function fairly and honestly. The negative–positive distinction, while having some utility, is inadequate to describe this duty, as well as the state's duty to institutionalize rights that is described in category (3) below.

(3) Protect Rights/Prevent Violations

Several human rights treaties make explicit the state's duty to protect against and to prevent violations of rights — for example, Article 2 of the ICCPR that gives victims of violations the right to a remedy. Again institutional machinery is required, in this instance to comply with a specific command of the treaties. In the case of the ICCPR, that command is expressed through the state's duty in Article 2 to 'ensure to all individuals' the recognized rights. States must then do the necessary to ensure. Surely they must provide a police force to protect people against violations of their rights (to physical security, or free speech, or property) either by state or nonstate ('private') actors. They must create normative systems like tort or criminal law, as well as institutions like courts or jails, processes like civil suits or criminal prosecutions, in order to maintain a system of justice that provides remedies for violations and imposes sanctions on violators. This duty to protect has been vital to the development of CEDAW and women's rights.

As in category (2) above, the state's duty to protect/prevent involves state expenditures.

Again, the negative-positive rights distinction is not helpful. The classic 'negative' rights here demand the classic 'positive' protection. It is difficult to imagine a right for which this is not true. As Henry Shue, in *Basic Rights* (2nd edn. 1996) puts it:

> All these activities and institutions [of government, like police, courts, jails] are attempts at providing social guarantees for individuals' security so that they are not left to face alone forces that they cannot handle on their own. How much more than these expenditures one thinks would be necessary in order for people actually to be reasonably secure . . . depends on one's theory of violent crime, but it is not unreasonable to believe that it would involve extremely expensive, 'positive' programs. . . . A demand for physical security is not normally a demand simply to be left alone, but demand to be protected against harm. It is a demand for positive action. . . .

Note that the concepts of protect and prevent, though linked in this category (3), can take on quite different meanings, depending on context. For example, promotion of cultural change (category (5) below) about, say, violence against women may help to prevent such violence. Prevention may then be realized in the long run through strategies well outside such everyday forces for protection as police.

(4) Provide Goods and Services to Satisfy Rights

The state's duty here is primarily to provide material resources to the rights-bearer, like housing or food or health care, matters associated with the International Covenant on Economic, Social and Cultural Rights. (Resources provided by the state may go directly from it to the individual rights-bearer, as by providing food stamps or subsidized public housing, *or* it may go indirectly to the ultimate beneficiary through, say, subsidies to construction firms that will then offer low-rent housing.) Unlike the duty of respect (do not worsen the situation of the rights-bearer), this duty to provide generally is meant to improve the situation of the rights-bearer.

It is most evident and explicit in this category (4) that the state must expend public funds to meet its duties. It is for this reason that state duties related to welfare rights have most frequently been described as affirmative (positive). Unlike categories (2) and (3) above, both of which also involve state expenditures, these expenditures are at the core of, are the very essence of, the individual right. They are not merely incidental to it, essential means to realize some other right, as for example state expenditures for police are essential to fulfil a duty to protect.

On the other hand, the realization of economic and social rights need not depend on 'direct' or 'indirect' provision by the state in the sense described above. Other, radically different policies may achieve the goal of satisfying a right to, say, food. For example, one way of overcoming poverty and malnutrition in rural areas might be to undertake a programme of expropriation and land reform that would increase employment and yield and thereby make more people self-sufficient with respect to food. Again, monetary or fiscal policy designed to lower unemployment and hence malnutrition and homelessness could reduce the need for direct provision of funds or goods. Such characteristic policies of the modern welfare state may then make the direct or indirect provision of funds or goods measures of last rather than first resort.

(5) Promote Rights

This state duty refers to bringing about changes in public consciousness or perception or understanding about a given problem or issue, with the purpose of alleviating the problem. In certain contexts, such promotion of rights may be a useful or indeed essential path towards their better recognition by nonstate actors. Like the duty of protection, it generally requires the state to expend funds and create the institutions that are necessary to promoting acceptance of the right. Thus a state's duty to promote often involves public education — for example, school education or public campaigns meant to change attitudes about violence towards women or children. Promotion to achieve such types of cultural change plays a vital role in CEDAW.

Promotion underscores the point that these categories of duties are not discrete. They are often complexly interrelated, and indeed overlap. For example, fulfilment of a duty to promote may bear on the duty not only to provide but also to protect, as when the state promotes and disseminates knowledge about the evil consequences of discrimination that may reduce, say, racism or homophobic violence.

JAMES NICKEL, HOW HUMAN RIGHTS GENERATE DUTIES TO PROTECT AND PROVIDE

15 Hum. Rts. Q. 77 (1993), at 80

[The following excerpts, which use different terms from those appearing in the preceding Comment, bear out and expand some ideas in that Comment.]

The feasibility of a general right is typically concerned with the duties or burdens of several parties. For example, an adequate response to the claim-to freedom from torture will involve a high-priority duty to refrain from torturing. This duty not to torture can feasibly be borne and fulfilled by all, so this duty can be addressed to everyone. But an adequate response to the claim-to freedom from torture also requires finding individuals or institutions that can protect people against torture. As noted earlier, this positive duty, although connected with a universal right, need not be addressed to everyone, or even to some worldwide agency. The claim-to freedom from torture may be universal without all of the corresponding duties being universal in the sense of being against everyone, or against some worldwide agency. All that is required is that for every rightholder, there is at least one agent or agency with duties to protect that person from torture.

To illustrate how this might work, consider the addressees of the right to freedom from torture. First, all persons and all institutions have duties to refrain from torturing, from using torture to achieve their ends. This part of the claim-against *is* universal in the sense of being against everyone. Second, each government has the duty or responsibility to protect people within its territory from torture, to take steps to prevent, deter, and stop torture. Negative duties to refrain fall on everyone; positive duties to protect fall on governments. In addition to these primary addressees of the right against torture, one can also identify secondary addressees who bear secondary or back-up responsibilities connected with the right against torture. The people of a country are secondary addressees with respect to fundamental rights. They bear the responsibility of creating and maintaining a political system that respects and protects the right to freedom from torture. International institutions such as the United Nations and the World Bank are also secondary addressees. They bear the responsibility of assisting, encouraging, and — if necessary — pressuring governments to refrain from torture and to provide protections against torture. . . .

. . .

One advantage of the emphasis on duties connected with rights is that it moves the debate in the direction of implementation, towards the question of who has to do what if these rights are to be realized. In the case of the right to education in Brazil, an emphasis on the duties connected with this right would lead one to ask, who bears primary responsibility for educating the millions of youngsters in Brazil whose parents are too poor to pay for their education. Many of these children are not in school, and many others are in schools of extremely low quality. Under this analysis, the Brazilian government bears this primary responsibility, and accordingly it ought to be sternly criticized for its historic failure to invest much in educational opportunities to the children of the poor. The citizens of Brazil are the secondary addressees of this right, and they bear the responsibility to act politically to bring about changes in government agencies to effectively implement the right to education. . . .

. . .

QUESTIONS

1. Consider CEDAW's stress on eliminating discrimination to achieve equality between men and women, as well as its means for realizing that equality. The phrase 'on the basis of equality of men and women' recurs in many of its articles. Compare the notion of equality in the ICCPR — say, in ICCPR Article 3 ('to ensure the equal rights of men and women to the enjoyment of all civil and political rights' in that covenant), or ICCPR Article 26 ('All persons are equal before the law and are entitled without any discrimination to the equal protection of the law'). Are the two treaties' conceptions of equality identical, similar, very different?

2. Note that CEDAW has no provision specifically addressing bodily security in the manner that other human rights instruments do by, for example, prohibiting arbitrary deprivation of life, torture or arbitrary detention. What provisions of CEDAW would you rely on to assert a woman's right to bodily security?

3. Do the provisions of CEDAW on their face make any concession to cultural relativism, to cultural diversity in regional, ethnic, religious or other terms? Or do they insist throughout on universal application of its norms without variation, no matter what the cultural context, history or circumstances of the state involved?

4. Under Article 2, states parties agree to pursue the required policies, 'by all appropriate means and without delay'. Contrast the description of state obligations in Article 2 of the Covenant on Economic, Social and Cultural Rights: 'achieving progressively the full realization' of the recognized rights. Is this textual contrast accurate with respect to CEDAW? How do you understand the question of CEDAW's 'time frame' in comparison, say, with the ICCPR?

5. Which provisions of CEDAW fall into which of the categories of state duties that are described in the preceding Comment and article? Does any one category appear to dominate? Which category represents the most significant change from the ICCPR?

6. Anti-discrimination measures followed a certain chronology both in the United States and in the international human rights movement: prohibition first of racial discrimination and then of types of sex discrimination, while today the debate rages about what measures to take, indeed whether to take measures, against discrimination on the basis of sexual orientation

As far as the international movement is concerned, racism was considered an evil from the start. Because of its connections with the issues of apartheid and colonialism it fuelled the entire movement. Sex discrimination was also barred in the Universal Declaration of Human Rights, but had to wait several decades before becoming a focus of attention and being incorporated into the mainstream discussion of human rights. The normative consensus regarding certain elements of gender discrimination (such as non-discrimination in employment) started to develop about that time. Today that consensus obtains on certain core issues, while on many others dispute continues at the practical, doctrinal and ideological level in political fora and within the women's movement. As yet we see no consensus at the universal level regarding the rights of sexual minorities or the right to sexual orientation.

How can you explain this sequence of race, gender and sexual orientation both at the international level and in many states' internal reform and human rights movements? Is it significant, or merely an accident of history? Do the feared consequences of ending discrimination differ radically among these three fields? Is there an implicit hierarchy, some forms of discrimination being considered worse than others?

NOTE

Two institutions within the universal human rights system are concerned exclusively with women's rights. The older of the two, the UN Commission on the Status of Women, is formally the body with primary responsibility for monitoring and encouraging implementation of international law on women's rights.[3] It was established by the General Assembly at the same time as the Human Rights Commission, but it has been a less effective and influential body.

The more significant and influential organ has been the Committee formed under CEDAW. Hence the following materials examine principally the work of the CEDAW Committee, a 'treaty organ' rather than a 'Charter organ' within the distinction made at p. 155, *supra*. Chapter 10 will examine the ICCPR Committee. You should now read Articles 17–21 of the Convention.

COMMENT ON THE COMMITTEE ON THE ELIMINATION OF DISCRIMINATION AGAINST WOMEN

[Some information in this Comment is taken from Andrew Byrnes, The Committee on the Elimination of Discrimination against Women, published in the second edition of Steiner and Alston, *International Human Rights in Context* (2000), at p. 188. All quotations below are from Byrnes.]

The UN General Assembly, in deciding on the appropriate type of supervisory body for CEDAW, drew on the model of the ICCPR Committee. Thus the CEDAW Committee was constituted as a body of independent experts — that is, not state officials or other persons representing the state or subject to its instructions — given the task of monitoring states' efforts to meet their obligations through review of periodic reports submitted by the states parties. Moreover, the Committee was authorized to issue General Recommendations to all states. Finally, pursuant to a later Optional Protocol to the Convention, the Committee gained authority to hear contentious cases before it based on alleged violations of CEDAW and to issue recommendatory 'views'. The Committee also provides input into conferences on

[3] See Sandra Coliver, 'United Nations Commission on the Status of Women: Suggestions for Enhancing its Effectiveness', 9 Whittier L. Rev. 435 (1987).

women's issues. The Committee's importance has steadily increased over its life, partly as a consequence of the greater attention given women's rights on the world scene, from world conferences to new international instruments.

Committee members have had diverse backgrounds, from fields like sociology, medicine, international relations, education, political science, law and government. With very few exceptions, all Committee members have been women.

> This is perhaps no surprise, since the membership of treaty bodies reflects one national selection process multiplied many times, and in most countries there is likely to be a higher percentage of women than men working on issues relating to women's equality, thus making it more likely that a woman will be nominated. Nevertheless, perhaps the time has come for the Committee and States Parties to consider once again whether some members of CEDAW should be men. Given that they should be experts in the field covered by the Convention, one beneficial effect of a better gender balance would be to avoid the impression that all-female membership may create, namely that discrimination against women is a concern only of women, and not something that men should be concerned with.
>
> At the same time, the all-female membership of CEDAW must be seen in the context of the overall gender imbalance in the treaty bodies. The overwhelming majority of treaty body members are still male, though the number of women has increased slightly in recent years.

The large question posed by the illustrations that follow of Concluding Comments, General Recommendations, and Views concerns the effectiveness of the Committee's work in moving states towards the goal of equality of dignity and equal protection for women. It will immediately become apparent that the Committee itself lacks means of 'enforcing' its policies and understanding of CEDAW on states. How then can it influence state behaviour? How can it influence the course of law-making about women's rights, both national and international law, since it has no explicit power to legislate?

We start inquiry into the Committee by looking at its function of monitoring states parties with respect to their compliance with the Convention. It does so via the examination of the periodic reports on compliance that states parties are required to submit to the Committee. The Committee, like other treaty organs, has developed the practice of holding a meeting between Committee members and representatives of the state party to discuss the submitted report and then preparing its own concluding observations, which are given to the state.

CONCLUDING COMMENTS OF CEDAW COMMITTEE

www.un.org/womenwatch/daw/cedaw

China, 36th Sess., 25 August 2006 (5th and 6th periodic reports)

CEDAW/C/C/CHN/CO/6

. . .

Positive aspects

5. The Committee commends the State party on the range of recent legal reforms and policies and programmes aimed at eliminating discrimination against

women. . . . [The Committee refers to the] 2005 amendment to the Law on the Protection of Rights and Interests of Women, the 2001 amendment to the Marriage Law adding provisions in a number of areas, including on domestic violence, property of couples and relations among family members, the promulgation in 2002 of the Law on Contracting of Rural Land, and the 2006 amendment to the Law on Compulsory Education. It also welcomes the Programme for the Development of Chinese Women (2001–2010), which makes gender equality a basic State policy for the enhancement of national social progress.

. . .

Principal areas of concern and recommendations

. . .

11. . . . The Committee also notes that the Convention does not appear to have ever been invoked in a court of law.

12. The Committee encourages the State party to ensure that the Convention, the Committee's general recommendations and related domestic legislation are made an integral part of the legal education and training of judicial officers, including judges, lawyers and prosecutors. . . . It also calls upon the State party to enhance availability of effective legal remedies and implement further awareness-raising and sensitization measures about such legal remedies against discrimination so that women can avail themselves of them. It encourages the State party . . . to include in its next periodic report detailed statistics on the use by women of the legal system to obtain redress for discrimination in all fields covered by the Convention, and trends over time.

. . .

13. The Committee is concerned that the report did not include sufficient data disaggregated by sex, regions and ethnic groups, and information comparing the situation of women to that of men, to enable it to obtain a comprehensive understanding of the current situation of women. . . .

. . .

15. While commending the State party for the significant economic growth and related reduction in poverty rates achieved in recent years, the Committee is concerned that those benefits continue to be unevenly distributed between urban and rural areas and that women may not benefit to the same extent as men from overall economic growth and development. . . .

16. The Committee calls upon the State party to enhance its monitoring of the impact of economic development and changes on women and to take proactive and corrective measures, including increasing social spending, so that women can fully and equally benefit from growth and poverty reduction. To that end, it recommends that a gender impact analysis of all social and economic policies and poverty reduction measures be conducted regularly, including of the budget. . . .

17. The Committee expresses concern at the persistence of deep-rooted stereotypes regarding the roles and responsibilities of women and men in the family and society, reflected in concerns such as son-preference, which lead to high adverse sex-ratio and illegal sex-selective abortion. The Committee is concerned that these prevailing attitudes continue to devalue women and violate their human rights.

18. The Committee calls upon the State party to put in place a comprehensive approach to overcoming traditional stereotypes regarding the role of women and men in society, in accordance with articles 2 (f) and 5 (a) of the Convention. Such an approach should include legal, policy and awareness-raising measures, involve public officials and civil society and target the entire population, in particular men and boys. It should include the use of different media, including radio, television and print, and encompass both specialized and general programmes. The Committee calls upon the State party to evaluate the gender sensitivity of the curriculum and textbook reform it has undertaken since 2000 and to further ensure that it explicitly addresses the principle of equality between women and men.

. . .

20. . . . The Committee also urges the State party to take measures aimed at the rehabilitation and reintegration of women in prostitution into society, to enhance other livelihood opportunities for women to leave prostitution, provide support for them to do so and to prevent any detention of women without due legal process. . . .

. . .

24. The Committee recommends the utilization of temporary special measures in accordance with article 4, paragraph 1, of the Convention and the Committee's general recommendation 25 [see p. 206, *infra*] to accelerate the practical realization of the goal of de facto or substantive equality of women with men in all areas of the Convention.

. . .

26. The Committee encourages the State party to take sustained measures, including temporary special measures, such as the establishment of adequate numerical goals and targets, and timetables, in order to progress more expeditiously towards women's full and equal representation in elected and appointed bodies in all areas of public life, from the local to the national levels, and in all branches of Government, including in the country's foreign service. The Committee recommends that the State party conduct training programmes on leadership and negotiation skills for current and future women leaders. It further urges the State party to undertake awareness-raising about the importance of women's participation in decision-making processes at all levels of society.

. . .

28. The Committee recommends that the State party take all necessary measures to strengthen the active participation of rural women in the design, development, implementation and monitoring of rural development policies and programmes so as to enhance implementation of article 14 of the Convention. The measures should include efforts to ensure that all rural girls complete the nine years of compulsory education, free of all miscellaneous fees and tuition. Urgent attention should also be given to improving rural women's free access to health care and services in all rural areas. The Committee urges the State party to further assess the reasons for the disproportionate representation of women among the rural landless and to take appropriate remedial action, including measures and steps to change customs that result in discrimination against women. The Committee recommends enhancing

the availability of affordable and quality mental health and counselling services in rural areas to further reduce the female suicide rate....

...

31. While noting that legal measures prohibiting sex-selective abortions and female infanticide and other measures are in place, such as the nationwide campaign, 'Operation Caring for Girls', launched in 2006 and a system of incentives, the Committee remains concerned at the persistence of illegal practices of sex-selective abortion, female infanticide and the non-registration and abandonment of female children, and about forced abortions. The Committee is concerned about the impact of the adverse sex ratio, which may contribute to the increase in trafficking in women and girls.

32. The Committee urges the State party to strengthen its monitoring of the implementation of existing laws against selective abortion and female infanticide and to enforce them through fair legal procedures that sanction officials acting in excess of their authority. It also urges the State party to investigate and prosecute the reports of abuse and violence against ethnic minority women by local family planning officials, including forced sterilization and forced abortion.... It further recommends that the State party vigorously address the causes of son-preference, which remain strong in rural areas, and of the negative consequences of the one-child policy as regards the adverse sex ratio by expanding insurance systems and old-age pensions to the population at large, in particular in rural areas.

...

Guatemala, 35th Sess., 2 June 2006 (6th periodic report)
CEDAW/C/GUA/CO/6

...

12. ... [The Committee] urges the State party to carry out awareness-raising campaigns on the Convention and its Optional Protocol, including on the meaning and scope of substantive equality between women and men, aimed, inter alia, at the general public, legislators, the judiciary and the legal profession. Such efforts should focus on the systematic use of the Convention to respect, promote and fulfil women's human rights, and of the use of the Optional Protocol.

13. [T]he Committee is concerned that, in spite of the recommendations it addressed to the State party on the occasion of the consideration of Guatemala's initial and second periodic reports in 1994 and its combined, third and fourth, and fifth periodic reports in 2002, the domestic legislation is still not in conformity with the Convention....

14. The Committee urges the State party to put in place an effective strategy with clear priorities and timetables to achieve the required amendments to discriminatory provisions in the Civil, Criminal and Labour Codes .... [The Government should] ensure that the national machinery for the advancement of women has the necessary authority and human and financial resources to undertake awareness-raising initiatives for a full understanding of women's human rights in light of the provisions of the Constitution among the legislative and judicial branches.

15. While noting the adoption of the various laws and decrees ... the Committee is concerned about the lack of enforcement, coordination, effective implementation and monitoring of those laws and decrees.

...

23. The Committee is deeply concerned about the continuing and increasing cases of disappearances, rape, torture and murders of women, the engrained culture of impunity for such crimes, and the gender-based nature of the crimes committed, which constitute grave and systematic violations of women's human rights. It is concerned about the insufficient efforts to conduct thorough investigations, the absence of protection measures for witnesses, victims and victims' families and the lack of information and data regarding the cases, the causes of violence and the profiles of the victims.

24. . . . [The Committee] encourages the State party to institutionalize the Commission on Femicide as a permanent body, with its own human and financial resources. It requests the State party to provide in its next periodic report detailed information on the causes, scope and extent of the disappearances, rape and murder of women and of the impact of measures taken to prevent such cases, to investigate occurrences and prosecute and punish perpetrators and to provide protection, relief and remedies, including appropriate compensation to victims and their families.

25. . . . The Committee is concerned about . . . the lack of social awareness about and condemnation of violence against women and girls in the country.

26. The Committee . . . recommends gender sensitivity training on violence against women for public officials, particularly law enforcement personnel, the judiciary, teaching personnel and health service providers, so as to ensure that they are sensitized to all forms of violence against women and can adequately respond to it.

27. While noting the efforts to amend the Act on Elections and Political Parties to impose a quota of 44 per cent for women's participation, the Committee remains concerned about the underrepresentation of women, in particular indigenous women, in political and public positions at all levels. The Committee is also concerned about the persistence and pervasiveness of patriarchal attitudes and deep-rooted stereotypes regarding the roles and responsibilities of women and men in the family and society, which constitute a significant impediment to the participation of women in decision-making at all levels and a root cause of women's disadvantaged position in all spheres of life.

28. The Committee calls upon the State party to accelerate amending of the Act on Elections and Political Parties and strengthen the use of temporary special measures, including quotas, in accordance with article 4, paragraph 1, of the Convention and the Committee's general recommendation 25, to increase the number of women, in particular indigenous women, in political and public life and in decision-making positions. It suggests that the State party implement leadership training programmes aimed at women. . . .

. . .

31. The Committee observes with concern the possible adverse impact that the free trade agreements may have on the living and working conditions of Guatemalan women.

32. The Committee suggests that the State party undertake a study to determine the impact of the free trade agreements on the socio-economic conditions of women and to consider the adoption of compensatory measures that take into consideration women's human rights.

. . .

34. The Committee urges the State party to ensure that all poverty eradication policies and programmes integrate a gender perspective and explicitly address the structural nature and various dimensions of poverty faced by women, in particular women living in rural areas. . . .

41. The Committee requests the State party to respond to the concerns expressed in the present concluding comments in its next periodic report under article 18 of the Convention, which is due in September 2007.

QUESTIONS

1. Do these excerpts from the concluding comments suggest that the Committee is urging compliance with the full range of duties described in the typology of duties at p. 185, *supra*, or that it is giving priority to one strategy and related duty? What strategy would you employ if you were a member of the Committee?

2. What relationships do the concluding comments suggest between civil-political and economic-social rights?

3. In what ways and to what extent do the concluding observations bear on the conduct of nonstate/private actors?

4. Compare the Report of Guatemala to the CEDAW Committee in 1991 (p. 176, *supra*) with these Concluding Comments. Bear in mind the tone of the Committee's Concluding Comments. What comments would you make about the course of events in Guatemala during this period? What can the Committee do about it?

5. In what ways, if any, could these concluding comments serve to put pressure on the Chinese government to act in accordance with the recommendations? How do you assess the utility or significance for realizing the goals of CEDAW of these periodic reports and reactions by the Committee?

6. In his book, *Human Rights Law-Making in the United Nations* (1986), at p. 66, Theodor Meron signals the danger that CEDAW's mandate, as through its Article 5, to regulate social and cultural patterns of conduct, whether private or public, in order to reach the treaty's goals may lead to curtailment 'to an undefined extent [of] privacy and associational interests and the freedom of opinion and expression'. He goes on to state that,

> since social and cultural behaviour may be patterned according to factors such as ethnicity or religion, state action authorized by para. (a) [of Article 5] which is directed towards modifying the way in which a particular ethnic or religious group treats women may conflict with the principles forbidding discrimination on the basis of race or religion. The danger of intrusive state action and possible violation of the rights of ethnic or religious groups might have been mitigated by limiting state action to educational measures.

Consider in this respect para. 18 of the Concluding Comments for China. Do you see any such danger in its advice for a 'comprehensive' programme of eliminating gender stereotypes, which should 'include the use of different media, including radio, television and print, and encompass both specialized and general programmes'.

NOTE

A detailed process has developed over the years for the examination of states' reports. The concerns and recommendations set forth above for China and Guatemala come near the end of that process. Prior to the broad and general Concluding Comments, a meeting has taken place in which representatives of the state appear before the Committee to respond to questions. Prior to this meeting, the Committee has formulated and given to the state involved detailed questions based on the report, and has received (or at least should have received) the state's answers, to be sure their quality depending on the state, ranging from the complete and responsive to the selective and evasive.

Review paragraphs 17 and 18 of the Concluding Comments for China's report. There appear below excerpts from the Committee's questions to China, during the meeting of China's representatives and Committee members, about part of the subject matter of those paragraphs, and from the answers provided by China.[4]

1. Excerpts from the Committee's question and China's response on the question of sex-selective abortion follow:

> 19. **In spite of China's recent efforts to combat sex-selective abortions and infanticide of baby girls, the 2000 census in China showed 117 boys born for every 100 girls. . . . Please describe the concrete measures in place to ensure full adherence to the Law on Population and Family Planning of 2001, as well as cases brought under the law since 2001 and sanctions imposed on offenders.**
>
> (Response): . . .[T]he Law on Population and Family Planning of 2001 again clearly stipulates that the identification of foetal gender for non-medical purposes or to bring about sex-selective pregnancy termination for non-medical purposes constitutes an unlawful act. In 2002, eleven Government ministries and committees . . . collaborated in drawing up an official document clearly delineating each agency's operational responsibilities and duties in dealing comprehensively with problematic gender ratios in newborns. . . .
>
> Beginning in 2003, the Government began testing a campaign to promote caring for girl children in some areas around the country, with the purpose of fostering a social environment favourable to the lives and development of girls and eliminating the prejudice favouring male offspring in child-bearing through promoting the equality of men and women, providing economic assistance to households having only girl children, rigorously investigating and dealing with unlawful foetal sex selection, and gradually establishing a system of social guarantees for rural villages. In 2006, "Operation Caring for Girls" was launched nationwide. In 2004, the Government formulated and began to implement a system of incentives and assistance for family planning in some rural villages, focusing on rural couples with only one child or with two daughters; for those age 60 and over, the Government provides lifetime incentives and financial assistance. A variety of local policies and measures benefiting girls' lives have also been drawn up in different localities; for

[4] The questions and responses can be found at the same website as the Concluding Comments: www.un.org/womenwatch/daw/cedaw. Responses to the list of issues and questions for consideration of the combined fifth and sixth periodic report of China, CEDAW/C/CHN/Q/6/Add. 1.

example, families with daughters only are given priority in the deployment of development items and assistance, in the provision of educational, medical and subsistence aid, and (for rural parents of daughters only) in being included in the basic social and old-age insurance system. With regard to cases of unlawful identification of foetal gender and the artificial termination of pregnancies for purposes of sex selection, [two Laws] both provide for penalizing those involved, confiscating the equipment used and suspending the operation of the business involved. Currently, some problems remain with regard to uncovering and verifying such unlawful activity, and concrete laws and regulations to combat it are lacking. China is currently studying the legislative experiences of such countries as the Republic of Korea and India, and researching the issue of amending the relevant regulations of the Criminal Law. The Chinese Government has set a goal of effectively halting the trend of higher ratios of male births and normalizing the gender ratios of newborns overall by the year 2010.

2. Excerpts from the Committee's question and China's response on the question of gender stereotypes and education follow:

12. **The Committee, in its previous concluding comments, recommended that school textbooks and curricula be revised to eliminate gender stereotypes. Please provide an update on the implementation of this recommendation and, in particular, indicate how the principle of equality between women and men has been incorporated in the new curriculum referred to [in] the report.**

(Response): . . .[T]he Government has been carrying out a reform of the basic curriculum and teaching materials, and putting forward the need to fully incorporate the principle of equality between men and women.

. . .

(b) Close attention is paid to ensure that equality in education is an important component of curriculum content. For example, the standards for ideological and moral character education at the junior-secondary level call for students to understand that people are equal in dignity and in their status before the law; to be able to treat people equally and refrain from mistreating the weak and bullying or cheating strangers; and not to allow differences of family background, physical appearance, or intellectual ability to give rise to feelings of excessive pride or inferiority.

(c) With regard to the compilation and evaluation of teaching materials, care is taken to increase content fostering equality awareness and action; to avoid exposing students to the imperceptible influences of mechanistic gender stereotypes in the illustrations for teaching materials; to preserve a numerical balance of males and females; and to choose literary compositions featuring female main characters in language-teaching materials and to introduce outstanding female historical figures in materials for history courses.

(d) Learning activities featuring education on the legal system and the protection of human rights have been developed; human-rights content is included in elementary and middle-school textbooks, with text and illustrations being equally high in quality; and laws are explained on the basis of actual cases. Excellent results have already been obtained in propagating knowledge of the law and human rights and forming a concept of equality between men and women among elementary and middle-school students.

32. Please ... [i]ndicate in particular any strategies in place to eradicate stereotypes through the education system.

...

The education system is based on the principle that everyone has the right to education, and is orientated to favour the global development of the personality, along with social progress and the democratization of society. Article 122 (1) of the Basic Law guarantees that all educational institutions in the MSAR shall enjoy their autonomy and teaching and academic freedom in accordance with law. Therefore, the Government must respect the autonomy of private schools and does not interfere with their programmes of education but, by law, the principle of equality of opportunity in access to and achievement in education must be obeyed. To eliminate roles stereotypes, the Education and Youth Affairs Bureau often organizes workshops and seminars to which parents and teachers are invited and giving them greater familiarity with the issue. Many schools also promote elimination of gender stereotyping by means of seminars, projects, programmes, workshops, conferences, surveys, etc. on the subjects of sexual education and personal and social development.

QUESTIONS

1. Suppose that you are a member of the Committee. (a) How do you assess the answers to the Committee's questions? (b) If the Committee had the opportunity to press China further in these proceedings (other than through its Concluding Comments), what further questions might you ask or what further information or clarifications would you seek? (c) Suppose that you doubt the accuracy of some of the information provided. Do you believe it appropriate to seek outside information to challenge the responses? To what sources would you turn?

2. How do you assess, from the perspective of international human rights, the prohibition of sex-selective abortion (after learning the sex of the foetus through routine tests that are now neither expensive nor dangerous)? Why is not freedom for the parent(s) to act as they choose protected within the human rights corpus? What rights would be relevant?

NOTE

Note that the very title to CEDAW refers only to discrimination as the target of the Convention. Contrast the ICCPR, which specifies no single forbidden practice and embraces a vast range of violations. How then does CEDAW embrace perhaps the most fundamental concern to the world's women: physical violence, sexual and other, often domestic violence of the 'private' world, but often the violence of abusive employment, of armed conflicts, of street crime, and other 'public' events outside the family?

Consider General Recommendation No. 19 of CEDAW, entitled 'Violence against Women'.[5] Excerpts follow:

> 6. . . . The definition of discrimination includes gender-based violence, that is, violence that is directed against a woman because she is a woman or that affects women disproportionately. It includes acts that inflict physical, mental or sexual harm or suffering, threats of such acts, coercion and other deprivations of liberty. Gender-based violence may breach specific provisions of the Convention, regardless of whether those provisions expressly mention violence.
>
> 7. Gender-based violence, which impairs or nullifies the enjoyment by women of human rights and fundamental freedoms under general international law or under human rights conventions, is discrimination within the meaning of article 1 of the Convention. [The rights violated by gender-based violence amounting to discrimination include the right to life, to liberty and security of the person, to equality in the family, to the highest standard attainable of physical and mental health, and to just and favourable conditions of work.]
>
> . . .
>
> 9. It is emphasized, however, that discrimination under the Convention is not restricted to action by or on behalf of Governments (see articles 2(e), 2(f) and 5).... Under general international law and specific human rights covenants, States may also be responsible for private acts if they fail to act with due diligence to prevent violations of rights or to investigate and punish acts of violence, and for providing compensation.
>
> . . .
>
> 11. Traditional attitudes by which women are regarded as subordinate to men or as having stereotyped roles perpetuate widespread practices involving violence or coercion, such as family violence and abuse, forced marriage, dowry deaths, acid attacks and female circumcision. Such prejudices and practices may justify gender-based violence as a form of protection or control of women. The effect of such violence on the physical and mental integrity of women is to deprive them of the equal enjoyment, exercise and knowledge of human rights and fundamental freedoms. While this comment addresses mainly actual or threatened violence, the underlying consequences of these forms of gender-based violence help to maintain women in subordinate roles and contribute to their low level of political participation and to their lower level of education, skills and work opportunities.
>
> . . .
>
> 20. In some States there are traditional practices perpetuated by culture and tradition that are harmful to the health of women and children. These practices include dietary restrictions for pregnant women, preference for male children and female circumcision or genital mutilation.
>
> . . .
>
> 23. Family violence is one of the most insidious forms of violence against women. It is prevalent in all societies. . . .

The Committee recommends that states parties should (among other measures) take a range of steps to 'overcome all forms of gender-based violence, whether by public or private act', provide adequate protective and support services for victims of family

[5] 11th Sess., 1992, UN Doc. A/47/38, www.un.org/womenwatch/daw/cedaw/recomm.htm.

violence and provide gender-sensitive training to police and judges, take measures 'to ensure that the media respect and promote respect for women', take measures to eliminate prejudices and attitudes that lead to violence, and ensure that women needn't resort to illegal abortion 'because of lack of appropriate services in regard to fertility control'.

NOTE

The UN Economic and Social Council endorsed in 1994 (Decision 1994/254) a resolution of the UN Commission on Human Rights (Resolution 1994/45) to appoint a special rapporteur 'on violence against women, its causes and consequences'. These instruments authorized the special rapporteur to engage (among other activities) in field missions, seek information from governments and other sources, and submit reports on such missions to the Commission. Yakin Ertürk from Turkey succeeded to the position of special rapporteur in 2003. (The functions of Special Rapporteurs and other appointees of the Commission (replaced in 2006 by the Human Rights Council) are examined in Chapter 9, pp. 765–790, *infra.*)

YAKIN ERTÜRK, REPORT ON MISSION TO THE RUSSIAN FEDERATION

UN Commission on Human Rights, E/CN.4/2006/61/Add.2, 26 January 2006

[The Report is based on the visit of the Special Rapporteur on Violence against Women to the Russian Federation from 17 to 24 December, 2004. Excerpts follow:]

1. Emergence of the Russian Federation

...

7. The process of political and economic transition in Russia, which entailed the transformation from a command economy to a market economy as well as restructuring of the State apparatus has had contradictory effects on women. Under communism, minimum levels of social welfare and the enjoyment of certain economic, social and cultural rights were guaranteed to the population at large, much of which disappeared under market liberalization. Despite recent improvements, high unemployment rates, wage cuts and wage arrears, and limited access to health care and education continue to be persisting problems. Violations of women's human rights in particular are largely related to this process of transition as women carry a disproportionate share of the burden of the transition, including as concerns poverty, domestic violence, sexual assault and trafficking.

8. ... Today, women still have many formal rights; however, real opportuniti for women have considerably decreased with the transition to a market econor which is accompanied by the reassertion of patriarchal values....

9. Women's political participation has also decreased, resulting in underrepr tation in decision-making positions. While in 1993, women held 14 per cent

seats in the State Duma, the lower house of Parliament, two years later this dropped to 11 per cent. In the parliamentary elections in 2000 women won only 7.7 per cent of the seats in the Duma and 0.6 per cent of seats in the upper house, the Federation Council. Women are also grossly underrepresented in public sector decision-making positions. Although 55 per cent of civil servants are women, they hold only 1.3 per cent of decision-making posts. Their position is considerably better in the private sector, where mainly in small enterprises, women occupy 35 per cent of managerial positions.

10. . . . Although they tend to be more educated, women also generally earn less than men – with reports indicating that women's average salaries can be as much as 70 per cent below men's average salaries for work of equal value. . . .

11. The three years of parental leave, taken nearly exclusively by women, is another factor constraining the employment of women. Since an employer must retain the workplace of the absent employee and continue to pay social benefits, they reportedly prefer hiring men. . . .

12. All these factors disempower women and make them increasingly dependent on fathers or husbands. . . . Apart from the obvious discriminatory implications, these practices also have an adverse impact on women's overall status in the society, thus increasing the risk of human rights violations, including violence in the private and public spheres.

. . .

19. The 1993 Constitution of the Russian Federation provides for primacy of international law over domestic law. The Constitution guarantees many rights, including the right to life, the right to be free from torture, freedom of thought and expression, the right to health, the right to education and the right to housing. In particular, article 19 states that "all people shall be equal before the law and in the court of law" and that "man and woman shall have equal rights and liberties and equal opportunities for their pursuit". . . .

. . .

21. With respect to regional human rights instruments, Russia has ratified the European Convention on Human Rights and its Protocols Nos. 1, 4 and 7, and the right of citizens to take their case to the European Court of Human Rights is constitutionally guaranteed. . . .

22. At the international level, Russia has ratified [CEDAW, the two Covenants, and a number of other human rights treaties].

II. Domestic Violence in Russia

. . .

26. . . . [E]xisting data reveals a worrisome increase in domestic violence since the collapse of the Soviet Union. Reportedly, 80 per cent of violent crimes against women are cases of domestic violence. Between 1994 and 2000, the number of reported cases increased by 217 per cent to 169,000. Over a 10-month period in 2004, the Ministry of Interior reported 101,000 crimes related to the family — a 16 per cent increase over the previous year. The State . . . acknowledged that 14,000 women were killed annually by their husbands or other family members. . . .

27. . . . In many meetings held by the Special Rapporteur, authorities referred to an ancient Russian proverb, "a beating man is a loving man!" Due to strong patriarchal

values, husbands in Russia are generally considered superior to their wives with the right to assert control over them, legitimizing the general opinion that domestic violence is a private issue....

28. ... [S]ocial stigma is connected to sexual and domestic violence, pressuring victims to keep silent and "solve it" within the family. This stigma results in weak public pressure for State action, which may explain why the problem is low on the State agenda.

...

31. Women attempting to escape violent situations are frequently unable to access independent housing. In many cases, women are compelled to share the same residence with a violent partner, even after an official divorce. In the past decade, access to housing has worsened with the privatization of the housing market.

...

36. The lack of a specific law on domestic violence in Russia is a major obstacle to combating this violence. While the State Duma has considered as many as 50 draft versions of a law on domestic violence, none has been adopted....

...

38. The lack of specific legislation contributes to impunity for crimes committed in the private sphere. It deters women from seeking recourse and reinforces police unwillingness, or even refusal, to deal seriously with the problem, as they do not consider it a crime....

39. Where women are assertive in trying to file a complaint, the officers allegedly delay the filing process or make it difficult. Police also reportedly blame victims and treat them in a discriminatory and degrading manner....

40. ... With no system of restraining or civil protection orders, local officials lack a legal mechanism to protect the victim from further violence once the perpetrator has been released.

...

6. ... Female Duma representatives, the Chairperson of the Presidential Human Rights Council and women's groups are concerned that there is now an institutional vacuum within the State structure. The fact that there is no specialized body, with clout, authority and resources, to address women's rights and equality issues will seriously jeopardize the coordination and monitoring of the implementation of the Convention....

...

48. ... The Chairperson of the Presidential Human Rights Council particularly emphasized the importance of shelters in combating violence against women. Currently there are only 5 shelters throughout the Federation and 120 crisis centres. In recent years, there has been an increase in the number of crisis centres and telephone hotlines funded by local authorities and managed by non-governmental organizations, offering psychological, legal, medical and other services for women and girls who have experienced violence....

...

[The Report concluded with a number of recommendations to the Government.]

QUESTIONS

1. Note that a report on violence against women, with a stress on domestic violence, embarks on multiple paths involving multiple disciplines and perspectives: historical, political, ideological, economic, sociological—and, yes, legal also. Do you understand all these dimensions of the report to bear on the basic topic? To be interdependent and indispensable, to form a whole that best explains the situation of women?

2. What should be the special rapporteur's most important recommendations?

3. What do you imagine to be the future course of the report and recommendations? Who will be likely to read and discuss it? What effect is it likely to have on the Russian State's conduct and decisions about this topic?

GENERAL RECOMMENDATION NO. 25 OF CEDAW COMMITTEE, 30TH SESS., 2004

www.un.org/womenwatch/daw/cedaw/recomm.htm

[This General Recommendation is entitled Temporary Special Measures, and is based on Article 4(1) of CEDAW.]

...

3. The Convention is a dynamic instrument. [The Committee has]contributed through progressive thinking to the clarification and understanding of the substantive content of the Convention....

...

8. ... [T]he Convention requires that women be given an equal start and that they be empowered by an enabling environment to achieve equality of results. It is not enough to guarantee women treatment that is identical to that of men. Rather, biological as well as socially and culturally constructed differences between women and men must be taken into account. Under certain circumstances, non-identical treatment of women and men will be required in order to address such differences....

...

10. ... [M]easures [must be] adopted towards a real transformation of opportunities, institutions and systems so that they are no longer grounded in historically determined male paradigms of power and life patterns.

...

14. ... [T]he application of temporary special measures in accordance with the Convention is one of the means to realize de facto or substantive equality for women, rather than an exception to the norms of nondiscrimination and equality.

18. ... While the application of temporary special measures often remedies the effects of past discrimination against women, the obligation of States parties under the Convention to improve the position of women to one of de facto or substantive

equality with men exists irrespective of any proof of past discrimination. The Committee considers that States parties that adopt and implement such measures under the Convention do not discriminate against men.

. . .

20. Article 4, paragraph 1, explicitly states the "temporary" nature of such special measures. Such measures should therefore not be deemed necessary forever, even though the meaning of "temporary" may, in fact, result in the application of such measures for a long period of time. The duration of a temporary special measure should be determined by its functional result in response to a concrete problem and not by a predetermined passage of time. . . .

. . .

22. The term 'measures' encompasses a wide variety of legislative, executive, administrative and other regulatory instruments, policies and practices, such as outreach or support programmes; allocation and/or reallocation of resources; preferential treatment; targeted recruitment, hiring and promotion; numerical goals connected with time frames; and quota systems. . . .

23. . . . As temporary special measures aim at accelerating achievement of de facto or substantive equality, questions of qualification and merit, in particular in the area of employment in the public and private sectors, need to be reviewed carefully for gender bias as they are normatively and culturally determined. For appointment, selection or election to public and political office, factors other than qualification and merit, including the application of the principles of democratic fairness and electoral choice, may also have to play a role.

24. Article 4, paragraph 1, read in conjunction with articles 1, 2, 3, 5 and 24, needs to be applied in relation to articles 6 to 16 which stipulate that States parties "shall take all appropriate measures". Consequently, the Committee considers that States parties are obliged to adopt and implement temporary special measures in relation to any of these articles if such measures can be shown to be necessary and appropriate in order to accelerate the achievement of the overall, or a specific goal of, women's de facto or substantive equality.

. . .

37. The Committee reiterates its general recommendations Nos. 5, 8 and 23, wherein it recommended the application of temporary special measures in the fields of education, the economy, politics and employment, in the area of women representing their Governments at the international level and participating in the work of international organizations, and in the area of political and public life. . . .

. . .

GENERAL RECOMMENDATION NO. 23 OF CEDAW COMMITTEE, 16TH SESS., 1997

www.un.org/womenwatch/daw/cedaw/recomm.htm

[This GR is entitled Political and Public Life and is based on Article 7 of CEDAW.]

...

5. Article 7 obliges States parties to take all appropriate measures to eliminate discrimination against women in political and public life and to ensure that they enjoy equality with men in political and public life.... The political and public life of a country is a broad concept. It refers to the exercise of political power, in particular the exercise of legislative, judicial, executive and administrative powers. The term covers all aspects of public administration and the formulation and implementation of policy at the international, national, regional and local levels. The concept also includes many aspects of civil society, including public boards and local councils and the activities of organizations such as political parties, trade unions, professional or industry associations, women's organizations, community-based organizations and other organizations concerned with public and political life.

...

14. No political system has conferred on women both the right to and the benefit of full and equal participation. While democratic systems have improved women's opportunities for involvement in political life, the many economic, social and cultural barriers they continue to face have seriously limited their participation. Even historically stable democracies have failed to integrate fully and equally the opinions and interests of the female half of the population. Societies in which women are excluded from public life and decision-making cannot be described as democratic.... The examination of States parties' reports shows that where there is full and equal participation of women in public life and decision-making, the implementation of their rights and compliance with the Convention improves.

15. ... Under article 4, the Convention encourages the use of temporary special measures in order to give full effect to articles 7 and 8. Where countries have developed effective temporary strategies in an attempt to achieve equality of participation, a wide range of measures has been implemented, including recruiting, financially assisting and training women candidates, amending electoral procedures, developing campaigns directed at equal participation, setting numerical goals and quotas and targeting women for appointment to public positions such as the judiciary or other professional groups that play an essential part in the everyday life of all societies....

16. ... Research demonstrates that if women's participation reaches 30 to 35 per cent (generally termed a 'critical mass'), there is a real impact on political style and the content of decisions, and political life is revitalized.

...

22. The system of balloting, the distribution of seats in Parliament, the choice of district, all have a significant impact on the proportion of women elected to Parliament. Political parties must embrace the principles of equal opportunity and democracy and endeavour to balance the number of male and female candidates.

...

29. Measures that have been adopted by a number of States parties in order to ensure equal participation by women in senior cabinet and administrative positions and as members of government advisory bodies include: adoption of a rule whereby, when potential appointees are equally qualified, preference will be given to a woman nominee; the adoption of a rule that neither sex should constitute less than 40 per cent

of the members of a public body; a quota for women members of cabinet and for appointment to public office; and consultation with women's organizations to ensure that qualified women are nominated for membership in public bodies and offices and the development and maintenance of registers of such women in order to facilitate the nomination of women for appointment to public bodies and posts. . . .

. . .

31. Examination of the reports of States parties also demonstrates that in certain cases the law excludes women from exercising royal powers, from serving as judges in religious or traditional tribunals vested with jurisdiction on behalf of the State or from full participation in the military. These provisions discriminate against women, deny to society the advantages of their involvement and skills in these areas of the life of their communities and contravene the principles of the Convention.

32. . . . Political parties should be encouraged to adopt effective measures to . . . ensure that women have an equal opportunity in practice to serve as party officials and to be nominated as candidates for election.

33. Measures that have been adopted by some political parties include setting aside for women a certain minimum number or percentage of positions on their executive bodies, ensuring that there is a balance between the number of male and female candidates nominated for election, and ensuring that women are not consistently assigned to less favourable constituencies or to the least advantageous positions on a party list. . . .

34. Other organizations such as trade unions and political parties have an obligation to demonstrate their commitment to the principle of gender equality in their . . . memberships with gender-balanced representation on their executive boards so that these bodies may benefit from the full and equal participation of all sectors of society and from contributions made by both sexes. . . .

. . .

39. The globalization of the contemporary world makes the inclusion of women and their participation in international organizations, on equal terms with men, increasingly important. The integration of a gender perspective and women's human rights into the agenda of all international bodies is a government imperative. . . .

. . .

[The Committee's recommendations identify concrete measures to be implemented and specifies the details and statistical data on these issues to be provided in the periodic state reports.]

QUESTIONS

1. With reference to the typology of state duties at p. 187, *supra*, categorize the different duties which states are to bear under the two preceding general recommendations. Does any one category appear to represent a priority for the Committee?

2. In what ways do these general recommendations reach beyond state conduct to regulate the conduct of nonstate/private parties? Is any of this regulation direct, in the

sense that the Committee interprets CEDAW to impose duties directly on such nonstate parties? Do the recommendations point toward criminal sanctions imposed by the state against private parties not complying with the stated policies?

3. How do you react to the provisions in both General Recommendations on affirmative action, either by the state or by political parties? As a member of the Committee, which if any of these provisions would you oppose? How do you react to para. 31 of GR No. 23?

4. GR No. 23 is intended to apply to, among other types of states, democratic states. It recommends policies including minimum quotas for women for candidates for election, gender-specific percentages of seats in a legislature or in a judiciary, and so on. How are such policies or laws consistent with Article 25 of the ICCPR, guaranteeing the right to vote? Are voters freely deciding on their legislative representatives if their choices are structured as GR No. 23 intends? Are executive officials necessarily selecting the people they consider best qualified for high positions in the executive branch or judiciary if their choices are constrained by such gender requirements?

5. What influence do you believe that these general recommendations will have on the conduct of states? What measures are at the Committee's disposal to put pressure on states to comply?

COMMENT ON EFFORTS TOWARDS US RATIFICATION OF CEDAW

Ratification has been considered by the United States on several occasions and, in October 1994, almost occurred. President Clinton had submitted the Convention to the Senate, and the Senate Committee on Foreign Relations, after hearings, had recommended to the Senate, by a vote of 13–5, that it consent to ratification.[6] It observed among other things that failure to ratify had limited US leadership in the promotion of equality for women.

The Committee recommended ratification subject to a number of reservations, understandings and declarations, including the following:

> [T]he Constitution and laws of the United States establish extensive protections against discrimination, reaching all forms of governmental activity as well as significant areas of non-governmental activity. However, individual privacy and freedom from governmental interference in private conduct are also recognized as among the fundamental values of our free and democratic society. The United States understands that by its terms the Convention requires broad regulation of private conduct, in particular under Articles 2, 3 and 5. The United States does not accept any obligation under the Convention to enact legislation or to take any other action with respect to private conduct except as mandated by the Constitution and laws of the United States.

[6] See S384–10, Exec. Rep. Sen. Comm. on For. Rel., 3 October 1994. Various related documents and the text of all reservations are set forth in 89 Am. J. Int. L. 102 (1995).

The Committee also proposed reservations to the right to equal pay understood as comparable worth, the right to paid maternity leave, and any obligation under Articles 5, 7, 8 and 13 of the Convention that might restrict constitutional rights to speech, expression and association.

Five senators (a Republican minority) on the Committee objected to ratification. Their statement of Minority Views recognized the 'unfortunate prevalence of violence and human rights abuses against women around the world' and shared the 'majority's strong support for eliminating discrimination against women'. Nonetheless, they were not 'persuaded' that CEDAW was 'a proper or effective means of pursuing that objective'. The Minority Views made the following points:

> (1) CEDAW may enable ratifying states to generate 'political capital', but is 'unlikely to convince governments to make policy changes they would otherwise avoid'.
>
> (2) Countries like the United States 'must guard against treaties that overreach', and must not promise 'more than we can deliver or we risk diluting the moral suasion that undergirds existing covenants'. Indeed, the fear exists that 'creating another set of unenforceable international standards will further dilute respect for international human rights'.
>
> (3) More than 30 states ratifying CEDAW had made significant reservations, sometimes 'so broad as to appear to be at variance with the object and purpose of the treaty itself'. The Minority Views drew illustrations from Islamic states. The statement questioned 'whether such behavior does not, in fact, "cheapen the coin" of human rights treaties generally'. These reservations suggest that CEDAW 'may reach beyond the necessarily restrictive scope of an effective human rights treaty'.
>
> (4) 'Improvement in the status of women in countries such as India, China, and Sudan will ultimately be made in those countries, not in the United States Senate'.
>
> (5) Evolution of 'internationally accepted norms' on human rights 'is important and must be carefully encouraged. It must, however, take place within an international system of sovereign nations with differing cultural, religious and political systems. Pushing a normative agenda beyond that system's ability to incorporate it leads, we believe, to what is represented by this convention. . . .'

In the end, as the session of Congress came to an end, the Convention was never brought to a full vote in the Senate. There has been little subsequent action. President Clinton sent a letter to Congressional leaders on 11 March 1998, seeking their support for gaining Senate consent to ratification.[7] In 2002, the Senate Foreign Relations Committee held a brief hearing on CEDAW involving testimony by those favouring and opposing ratification. By a vote of 12–7, the Committee approved a resolution of advice and consent to ratification of the Convention, subject to most of the earlier proposed reservations, understandings and declarations, plus two additional ones. Senator Biden, chairman of the Committee, sponsored an understanding to the effect that 'the CEDAW Committee has no authority to compel parties to follow its recommendations'.[8] However, the treaty did not come up for a vote before the full Senate before adjournment of the 107th Congress. There the matter rests.

[7] Weekly Compilation of Presidential Documents, 16 March 1998.

[8] Congressional Research Service Report for Congress, The Convention to Eliminate All Forms of Discrimination against Women: Congressional Issues (updated 14 December 2006).

QUESTIONS

1. Which objections to ratification of CEDAW that were set forth in the Minority Views seem particular to CEDAW, and which could refer generally to many human rights treaties?

2. The Minority Views state that CEDAW 'may reach beyond the necessarily restrictive scope of an effective human rights treaty'. The Views refer to the differing cultural, religious and political systems among states, and assert that '[p]ushing a normative agenda beyond [the international system's] ability to incorporate it leads . . . to what is represented by this convention. . . . ' Though the US is a party to the ICCPR, it is unclear whether the senators supporting the Minority Views would have approved the ICCPR at that time. Would such approval have been consistent with the Minority Views? Does CEDAW raise special and more difficult problems than the ICCPR for the US (or for other countries, despite the fact that it now has 185 states parties)? If so, why?

NOTE

Another mechanism within the international system has been increasingly used to advance human rights as well as other objectives: large inter-governmental conferences organized around specific themes. These conferences provide an occasion for governments to discuss and perhaps ultimately agree on common strategies of action to resolve issues of global concern. Recent conferences have included the 1990 World Summit for Children, the 1992 Rio de Janeiro Conference on Environment and Development, the 1993 Second World Conference on Human Rights at Vienna (leading to the Vienna Declaration and Programme of Action with its strong statements of gender equality), the 1994 Cairo Conference on Population and Development, the 1995 Copenhagen World Summit for Social Development, the Fourth World Conference on Women in Beijing in 1995, the Beijing + 5 Process and Program for Action in 2000, and the World Conference against Racism in 2001.

Recent conferences have tended to follow a similar format. Apart from publicizing the Member States' recognition of the importance of the subject under consideration, the main object of the Conference is often to obtain agreement on a draft document, such as a declaration or charter, and on a related programme of action.

Much of the difficult work in identifying the nature of the issue and proposing solutions to particular problems, is accomplished prior to the opening of the conference. An initial draft may be drawn up by a branch of the UN Secretariat. Expert group meetings are often convened around specific issues or areas of concern. Through a series of regional and global preparatory meetings attended by delegations of the Member States, the draft document may be refined or significantly altered. By the time the conference opens, normally a significant portion of the text or programme has been agreed upon. At this point, it becomes a 'battle of the brackets'—the term arises from the practice of bracketing clauses in the text that are not yet agreed on — that is to say, an exercise in resolving the parts of the programme that have remained contentious.

Throughout this process, sometimes at parallel meetings designed to facilitate it, NGOs engage in an attempt to influence the substance of the document, by providing relevant information to the Secretariat, lobbying Member States or publicizing issues of concern in the press. Reflecting NGOs' increasing influence and activity, it is becoming more common for Member States to consult with them — at least ones from their own countries — prior to establishing their positions, and even to include NGO representation in their official delegations to the preparatory and world conferences.

3. THE PUBLIC/PRIVATE DIVIDE: DISCRIMINATION AND VIOLENCE BY NONSTATE ACTORS

Earlier materials in this chapter — indeed the very terms of CEDAW — sometimes refer to abuse of women not by the state ('public') but by nonstate/nongovernmental ('private') actors and action. This theme — the relevance of the public-private divide — inevitably surfaces with respect to women's rights as much as, if not more than, with respect to other human rights fields.

One can state the distinction between these two terms or concepts in different ways. Indeed much confusion has resulted from failure to identify which meaning is intended in a particular context. Moreover, the notion of 'privacy' must be kept distinct from the notions of a 'public/private' divide.

Consider this basic distinction between meanings of public and private: (1) In the opening paragraph above, the distinction had to do with the nature or character of the actor (state or nonstate). Both a man and woman, for example, working in a law firm would be classified within the private sector. (2) The distinction concerns different spheres of life and action. The 'private' is frequently associated within relations and conduct within the home, family, domestic life. The 'public' is identified with the relations and conduct of a working life, outside the home or family: employment, business, professions, the give and take of the market, being 'out in the world'. Thus a woman who acts as homemaker and home manager but who works in a business office would have both private and public dimensions to her life though she holds no employment from the state.

The section examines some of the issues presented by the opposition of public and private for both of these broad meanings:

- the practical, political and ideological significance of the divide;
- the shifting boundary line between the two as conceptions of their significance and content change;
- the degree to which human rights treaties should require states parties to regulate the relevant conduct of private (in the sense of nonstate) actors; and
- the degree to which human rights treaties should directly regulate the relevant conduct of such private actors and impose sanctions on such actors for violations of their duties within the regulatory scheme.

The readings start with what has become a classic judicial opinion in international human rights because of its clarification of a state's duty with respect to violence committed by nonstate actors.

VELÁSQUEZ RODRIGUEZ CASE

Inter-American Court of Human Rights, 1988
Ser. C, No. 4, 9 Hum. Rts L. J. 212 (1988)

[A petition against Honduras was received by the Inter-American Commission of Human Rights, alleging that Velásquez Rodriguez was arrested without warranty by national security units of Honduras. Knowledge of his whereabouts was consistently denied by police and security forces. Velásquez had disappeared. Petitioners argued that through this conduct, Honduras had violated several articles of the American Convention on Human Rights. After hearings and conclusions, the Commission referred the matter to the Inter-American Court of Human Rights, whose contentious jurisdiction had been recognized by Honduras. The Court concluded that Honduras had violated the Convention.

In the excerpts below, the Court addresses the issue of just what the obligations of Honduras were under the Convention? Was Honduras obligated only to 'respect' individual rights and not directly violate them, as by torture or illegal arrest? Or was Honduras obligated to take steps, within reasonable limits, to protect people like Velásquez from seizure even by nonstate, private persons? In an earlier portion of the opinion, the Court had found that the Honduran state was implicated in the arrest and disappearance, and that the acts of those arresting Velásquez could be imputed to the state. In the present excerpts, the Court reviews that information, and considers what might be the responsibility of Honduras even if the seizure and disappearance of Velásquez were caused by private persons unconnected with the government.]

161. Article 1(1) of the Convention provides:

> 1. The States Parties to this Convention undertake to respect the rights and freedoms recognized herein and to ensure to all persons subject to their jurisdiction the free and full exercise of those rights and freedoms....

...

164. Article 1(1) is essential in determining whether a violation of the human rights recognized by the Convention can be imputed to a State Party. In effect, that article charges the States Parties with the fundamental duty to respect and guarantee the rights recognized in the Convention. Any impairment of those rights which can be attributed under the rules of international law to the action or omission of any public authority constitutes an act imputable to the State, which assumes responsibility in the terms provided by the Convention itself.

165. The first obligation assumed by the States Parties under Article 1(1) is 'to respect the rights and freedoms' recognized by the Convention....

166. The second obligation of the States Parties is to ['ensure'] the free and full exercise of the rights recognized by the Convention to every person subject to its

jurisdiction. This obligation implies the duty of the States Parties to organize the governmental apparatus and, in general, all the structures through which public power is exercised, so that they are capable of juridically ensuring the free and full enjoyment of human rights. As a consequence of this obligation, the States must prevent, investigate and punish any violation of the rights recognized by the Convention and, moreover, if possible attempt to restore the rights violated and provide compensation as warranted for damages resulting from the violation.

. . .

169. According to Article 1(1), any exercise of public power that violates the rights recognized by the Convention is illegal. . . .

170. This conclusion is independent of whether the organ or official has contravened provisions of internal law or overstepped the limits of his authority. Under international law a State is responsible for the acts of its agents undertaken in their official capacity and for their omissions, even when those agents act outside the sphere of their authority or violate internal law.

. . .

172. Thus, in principle, any violation of rights recognized by the Convention carried out by an act of public authority or by persons who use their position of authority is imputable to the State. However, this does not define all the circumstances in which a State is obligated to prevent, investigate and punish human rights violations, nor all the cases in which the State might be found responsible for an infringement of those rights. An illegal act which violates human rights and which is initially not directly imputable to a State (for example, because it is the act of a private person or because the person responsible has not been identified) can lead to international responsibility of the State, not because of the act itself, but because of the lack of due diligence to prevent the violation or to respond to it as required by the Convention.

. . .

174. The State has a legal duty to take reasonable steps to prevent human rights violations and to use the means at its disposal to carry out a serious investigation of violations committed within its jurisdiction, to identify those responsible, impose the appropriate punishment and ensure the victim adequate compensation.

175. This duty to prevent includes all those means of a legal, political, administrative and cultural nature that promote the safeguard of human rights and ensure that any violations are considered and treated as illegal acts, which, as such, may lead to the punishment of those responsible and the obligation to indemnify the victims for damages. It is not possible to make a detailed list of all such measures, as they vary with the law and the conditions of each State Party. Of course, while the State is obligated to prevent human rights abuses, the existence of a particular violation does not, in itself, prove the failure to take preventive measures. . . .

. . .

177. In certain circumstances, it may be difficult to investigate acts that violate an individual's rights. The duty to investigate, like the duty to prevent, is not breached merely because the investigation does not produce a satisfactory result. Nevertheless, it must be undertaken in a serious manner. . . . Where the acts of

private parties that violate the Convention are not seriously investigated, those parties are aided in a sense by the government, thereby making the State responsible on the international plane.

178. In the instant case, the evidence shows a complete inability of the procedures of the State of Honduras, which were theoretically adequate, to ensure the investigation of the disappearance of Manfredo Velásquez and the fulfillment of its duties to pay compensation and punish those responsible, as set out in Article 1(1) of the Convention.

179. As the Court has verified above, the failure of the judicial system to act upon the writs brought before various tribunals in the instant case has been proven. Not one writ of habeas corpus was processed. No judge had access to the places where Manfredo Velásquez might have been detained. The criminal complaint was dismissed.

180. Nor did the organs of the Executive Branch carry out a serious investigation to establish the fate of Manfredo Velásquez. There was no investigation of public allegations of a practice of disappearances nor a determination of whether Manfredo Velásquez had been a victim of that practice. The Commission's requests for information were ignored to the point that the Commission had to presume, under Article 42 of its Regulations, that the allegations were true. . . .

. . .

182. The Court is convinced, and has so found, that the disappearance of Manfredo Velásquez was carried out by agents who acted under cover of public authority. However, even had that fact not been proven, the failure of the State apparatus to act, which is clearly proven, is a failure on the part of Honduras to fulfill the duties it assumed under Article 1(1) of the Convention, which obligated it to guarantee Manfredo Velásquez the free and full exercise of his human rights.

. . .

NOTE

Earlier materials in this chapter examined two work products of the CEDAW Committee: concluding comments responding to periodic reports of states parties, and general recommendations. We now encounter a third competence and activity of the Committee. Indeed these three functions are characteristic of a number of so-called 'treaty bodies', organs formed pursuant to a treaty and authorized to consider only issues arising under that same treaty. The competence of the CEDAW committee for this third function extends only to states parties to the so-called 'Optional Protocol to CEDAW' (the OP) which creates this competence. The OP is open to ratification only by parties to CEDAW itself. This OP became effective in 2000. As of January 2007, it had 83 states parties, compared with 185 parties to CEDAW itself. (Chapter 10 on the Human Rights Committee created by the ICCPR examines in more detail the workings of that Committee under a similar OP to the ICCPR.)

This brief sketch of several of the OP's provisions provides sufficient background for the 'views' of the Committee that follow this note. States parties to the

OP agree to recognize the competence of the Committee 'to receive and consider communications'. Individuals or 'groups of individuals' under the 'jurisdiction' of a State party may submit communications to the Committee, 'claiming to be victims of a violation [by the state] of any of the rights set forth in the Convention'. Communications must meet certain conditions and criteria to be judged admissible—for example, submission following exhaustion of domestic remedies. The Committee brings the communication confidentially to the attention of the State party involved. After finding the communication admissible and examining it, the Committee transmits its 'views' on the communication, 'together with its recommendations', to the concerned parties. The State party 'shall give due consideration to the views of the Committee, together with its recommendations'.

Ms. A. T. v. HUNGARY

Communication No. 2/2003, CEDAW Committee
Views of CEDAW Committee, Jan. 26, 2005, UN Doc. CEDAW/C/32/D/2/2003 (2005)

[The author stated that she had been subjected for four years "to regular severe domestic violence and serious threats by her common law husband, L.F., father of her two children," one of whom was brain-damaged. L.F. threatened to kill the author and rape the children, but the author didn't go to a shelter "because no shelter in the country is equipped to take on a fully disabled child together with his mother and sister." Moreover, no protection orders or restraining orders are available under Hungarian law. Civil proceedings brought no relief. Ten medical certificates have been issued in connection with separate incidents of "severe physical violence," even after L.F. left the family residence to live with another woman. At one stage, L.F. broke into the apartment when he no longer had a key. One beating required hospitalization and caused serious kidney injury. The author lives "at serious risk" and"in constant fear." Criminal proceedings against L.F. were initiated but have come to no conclusion; "no action has been taken by the Hungarian authiorities to protect the author from [L.F.]."]

3.1 The author alleges that she is a victim of violations by Hungary of articles 2 (a), (b) and (e), 5 (a) and 16 of the Convention on the Elimination of All Forms of Discrimination against Women for its failure to provide effective protection from her former common law husband. She claims that the State party passively neglected its "positive" obligations under the Convention and supported the continuation of a situation of domestic violence against her.

3.2 She claims that the irrationally lengthy criminal procedures against L. F., the lack of protection orders or restraining orders under current Hungarian law and the fact that L. F. has not spent any time in custody constitute violations of her rights under the Convention as well as violations of general recommendation 19 of the Committee. She maintains that these criminal procedures can hardly be considered effective and/or immediate protection.

. . .

3.4 The author is also seeking the Committee's intervention into the intolerable situation, which affects many women from all segments of Hungarian society. In particular, she calls for the (a) introduction of effective and immediate protection for victims of domestic violence into the legal system, (b) provision of training programmes on gender-sensitivity, the Convention on the Elimination of All Forms of Discrimination against Women and the Optional Protocol, including for judges, prosecutors, police and practising lawyers, and (c) provision of free legal aid to victims of gender-based violence, including domestic violence.

...

[The State's account of some of these events and descriptions differed, at times substantially, from the author's, generally presenting the civil and criminal proceedings in a more favorable light. Nonetheless, 'the State party admits that [such remedies as were provided] were not capable of providing immediate protection to the author from ill-treatment by her former partner. Having realized that the system of remedies against domestic violence is incomplete in Hungarian law and that the effectiveness of the existing procedures is not sufficient, the State party states that it has instituted a comprehensive action programme against domestic violence in 2003.'

The State emphasized Hungarian Parliament resolutions presenting a national strategy 'for the prevention and effective treatment of violence within the family.' The proposals included introduction of restraining orders, training of and protocols governing the police, childcare organs, better shelters for victims of violence and establishing victim protection crisis centres, providing free legal aid to victims, introducing a rehabilitation program, giving priority to court cases based on alleged family violence, educating and raising awareness of home violence among judges, and spurring a media campaign to bring these problems before the public. Some of these proposals were underway. The author's response to these comments by the state concluded:]

6.9 The author requests that the Committee . . . decide on the merits that the rights under the Convention have been violated by the State party. She requests that the Committee recommend to the State party to urgently introduce effective laws and measures towards the prevention of and effective response to domestic violence, both in her specific case and in general. . . . The author believes that the most effective way would be to provide her with a safe home, where she could live in safety and peace with her children, without constant fear of her batterer's "lawful" return and/or substantial financial compensation.

...

Consideration of the merits

...

9.2 The Committee recalls its general recommendation No. 19 on violence against Women [p. 202, supra]. . . . "[U]nder general international law and specific human rights covenants, States may also be responsible for private acts if they fail to act with due diligence to prevent violations of rights or to investigate and punish acts of violence, and for providing compensation". [The issue] is whether the author of the communication is the victim of a violation of articles 2 (a), (b) and (e), 5 (a) and 16 of the Convention because, as she alleges, for the past four years the State party has failed in its duty to provide her with effective protection. . . .

9.3 With regard to article 2 (a), (b), and (e), the Committee notes that the State party has admitted that the remedies pursued by the author were not capable of providing immediate protection to her against ill -treatment by her former partner and, furthermore, that legal and institutional arrangements in the State party are not yet ready to ensure the internationally expected, coordinated, comprehensive and effective protection and support for the victims of domestic violence. While appreciating the State party's efforts at instituting a comprehensive action programme against domestic violence and the legal and other measures envisioned, the Committee believes that these have yet to benefit the author and address her persistent situation of insecurity. The Committee further notes the State party's general assessment that domestic violence cases as such do not enjoy high priority in court proceedings. The Committee is of the opinion that the description provided of the proceedings resorted to in the present case, both the civil and criminal proceedings, coincides with this general assessment. Women's human rights to life and to physical and mental integrity cannot be superseded by other rights, including the right to property and the right to privacy. The Committee also takes note that the State party does not offer information as to the existence of alternative avenues that the author might have pursued that would have provided sufficient protection or security from the danger of continued violence. In this connection, the Committee recalls its concluding comments from August 2002 on the State party's combined fourth and fifth periodic report. . . . Bearing this in mind, the Committee concludes that the obligations of the State party set out in [CEDAW] remain unfulfilled and constitute a violation of the author's human rights and fundamental freedoms, particularly her right to security of person.

9.4 The Committee . . . has stated on many occasions that traditional attitudes by which women are regarded as subordinate to men contribute to violence against them. [The Committee restates the author's failed attempts to get relief from beatings and threats, and the absence of legal remedies.] None of these facts have been disputed by the State party and, considered together, they indicate that the rights of the author under articles 5 (a) and 16 of the Convention have been violated.

. . .

9.6 Acting under article 7, paragraph 3, of the Optional Protocol . . .[the Committee] makes the following recommendations to the State party:

I. Concerning the author of the communication

(a) Take immediate and effective measures to guarantee the physical and mental integrity of A. T. and her family;

(b) Ensure that A. T. is given a safe home in which to live with her children, receives appropriate child support and legal assistance as well as reparation proportionate to the physical and mental harm undergone and to the gravity of the violations of her rights;

II. General

[The general recommendations to the State included: respecting and promoting women's human 'right to be free from all forms of domestic violence'; taking measures for 'prevention and effective treatment of violence . . . promptly implemented and evaluated'; providing regular training of judges and law enforcement officials about CEDAW's requirements; seeking enactment of laws providing for 'protection and exclusion orders as well as support services, including shelters'; and providing offenders with rehabilitation programs. The State was requested to publish and widely distribute the Committee's views 'in order to reach all relevant sectors of society.']

NOTE

In *Szijjarto v. Hungary*, Communication No. 4/2004, Views of the CEDAW Committee, August 29, 2006, U.N. Doc. CEDAW/C/36/D/4/2004, the author, a Hungarian Roma woman, with three children, encountered serious problems in another pregnancy and was brought into a Hungarian hospital when in an emergency situation and in considerable pain and confusion and in a state of shock.

> While on the operating table, the author was asked to sign a form consenting to the caesarean section. She signed this as well as a barely legible note that had been hand-written by the doctor and added to the bottom of the form, which read: "Having knowledge of the death of the embryo inside my womb I firmly request my sterilization [a Latin term unknown to the author was used]. I do not intend to give birth again; neither do I wish to become pregnant."

Within 17 minutes of the ambulance's arrival at the hospital, the caesarean section was performed and the author's fallopian tubes were tied. The author's narrative, accepted in large part by the Committee, made clear that she had no idea of what she had signed and in fact desired more children. The sterilization violated her Catholic beliefs and led to a depression and feeling of having violated the Roma culture in which she lived. Her civil action against the hospital for pecuniary and non-pecuniary damages failed at the trial and appellate level. In this case initiated before the CEDAW Committee under the Optional Protocol, the author claimed that she had been 'subjected to coerced sterilization by medical staff at a Hungarian hospital', and that Hungary thereby violated her rights under articles 10(h), 12, and 16 (parag. 1(e)) of CEDAW.

The Committee agreed. The 'recommendations' that it made to the State first referred to 'appropriate compensation' for the author 'commensurate with the gravity of the violations of her rights'. Its 'general' recommendations to the state included taking measures 'to ensure' that CEDAW's relevant provisions and some earlier general recommendations of the Committee 'are known and adhered to by all relevant personnel in public and private health centres'; reviewing legislation on informed consent 'to ensure its conformity with international human rights and medical standards'; and monitoring public and private health centres performing sterilization procedures 'so as to ensure that fully informed consent is being given . . . with appropriate sanctions in place in the event of a breach'. The State party was requested to publish the Committee's view and distribute them widely 'in order to reach all relevant sectors of society'.

QUESTIONS

1. Identify the important similarities and differences between the judgment in *Velasaquez Rodriguez* and the views in *Ms. A.T. v. Hungary*, with respect to nature and functions of the forum, specificity and breadth of the conclusions, and character and effect of remedies. Is it accurate to say that the views are a direct and unproblematic application to women's rights of the ideas in the judgment?

2. 'Given the nature of the recommendations to the state in the Committee's views in both *Ms. A.T. v. Hungary* and *Szijjarto v. Hungary*, the Committee appears to have interpreted its powers under the Optional Protocol to resemble those relating to General Recommendations under Article 21 of CEDAW.' Do you agree? If so, do you approve or disapprove the reach of the Committee's views? What advantages relative to General Recommendations (and indeed relative to Concluding Comments responding to periodic reports) does the OP bring to women who have been victims of violations?

NOTE

In her article 'Accountability in International Law for Violations of Women's Rights by Non-State Actors', appearing in Dorinda Dallmeyer (ed.), *Reconceiving Reality: Women and International Law* (1993), at 93, Rebecca Cook asks why it is necessary or useful to inquire into a state's accountability in international law for violations of women's rights by nonstate actors including private persons. She suggests:

> Women's experiences confirm the endemic character of denials of rights committed by public agencies, for instance regarding access to government, to political power, and to legal status based on nationality. Women's initial experiences of discrimination arise more intimately, however, through their inferior status as daughters and impaired access to education, employment, wage equity, and equitable distribution of family assets. Vulnerability to domestic violence may be encountered as daughters, sisters, brides, and wives. Accordingly, women's exposure to discrimination and other denials of human rights will originate through acts of private persons and institutions, and will continue at this level as women mature to recognize parallel denials of rights directly attributable to state action that they encounter in the political, economic and other spheres of national life. The denials of rights that states permit women to suffer in their private relationships are an important part of the total subjugation of women.

> Women's human rights warrant defense when their violation originates in state action and also in private action. It is not a reason to disregard privately originating violations because violations also occur in the public sector of national life, or because they remain unremedied when they are directly attributable to organs of the state, or because they are more difficult to tackle when they arise through non-state actors.... The identification of violations of women's rights both by organs of state and by conduct of non-state actors for which the state can be shown accountable are complementary goals, and not alternatives to or in competition with each other.

...

KAREN ENGLE, AFTER THE COLLAPSE OF THE PUBLIC/PRIVATE DISTINCTION: STRATEGIZING WOMEN'S RIGHTS

in Dorinda Dollmeyer (ed.), Reconceiving Reality: Women and International Law (1993), at 143

...

Central to the critiques of international law have been analyses of the public/private distinction. They generally take one of two forms. Either women's rights advocates argue that public international law, and particularly human rights theory, is fiawed because it is not really universal. That is, because international law excludes from its scope the private, or domestic sphere — presumably the space in which women operate — it cannot include them. Or advocates argue that international law does not really exclude the private, but rather uses the public/private divide as a convenient screen to avoid addressing women's issues.

Those who take the first approach, then, take for granted that public international law in its present form cannot enter what they see as the private sphere. For women to be included, they maintain, international law must be reconceptualized to include the private.

Those who take the second approach, on the other hand, assume that doctrinal tools are present in international law — particularly in human rights law — to accommodate women. The public/private dichotomy, they assert, is both irrational and inconsistently applied. According to this second approach, the human rights regime and states are disingenuous in their claim that they do not enter the private sphere. The private sphere is entered all the time, for example, through regulation of the family, or the ability to impute to states the acts of non-state actors in disappearance cases. Moreover, these critics argue, a state's failure to protect rights in the private sphere is not distinguishable from direct state action. Finally, they point out that the human rights regime applies a double standard when talking about women. The international legal regime would never argue, for example, that it could not intervene to ensure that states end certain forms of 'private' violence, such as cannibalism or slavery.

...

Concentrating too much on the public/private distinction excludes important parts of women's experiences. Not only does such a focus often omit those parts of women's lives that figure into the 'public', however that gets defined, it also assumes that 'private' is bad for women. It fails to recognize that the 'private' is a place where many have tried to be (such as those involved in the market), and that it might ultimately afford protection to (at least some) women.

...

[... The critiques of the private-public distinction] make us think of the unregulated private as something that is necessarily bad for women. We rarely look at the ways in which privacy (even if only because it seems the best available paradigm) is seen by at least some women to offer them protection. A number of examples immediately come to mind, each of which centers on women's bodies and, not surprisingly, on women's sexuality. The language of privacy, and sketching out zones of privacy, many would argue, is our best shot at legally theorizing women's sexuality. In United States legal jurisprudence, the First Amendment has been used to a similar end as often seen in the debates about pornography.

Examples of where 'the private' is sometimes seen to have liberating potential for women are abortion (which is most obvious to us in the United States); battering; the protection of 'alternative' sexual lifestyles; prostitution; right to wear the veil as protection from sexual harassment; right to participate in *or be free of* clitoridectomies, sati, breast implants, the wearing of spike-heeled shoes. Failure to focus on these issues affecting women's relationships to our bodies obscures the ways that many women see their lives.

... [T]he critiques often prevent us from taking seriously women who claim not to want the regulation or protection of international law. Arguments about 'culture', particularly those that attempt to use claims of cultural integrity or community to maintain practices that some women might find abhorrent, get transformed into arguments about the private. That is, women's rights advocates often treat these arguments as though they are yet another manifestation of the mainstream legal regime's exclusion of the private or women (or both) at all costs. As a result, advocates either ignore those women who defend practices they see as an important part of their culture, or assume that such women are replete with false consciousness.

...

... [T]he critiques often lead us to conspiracy theories. Our exclusion indicates that they're all out to get us. We point out that *they* don't include *us* in the mainstream, that *they* give *us* our own marginal institutions and then ensure that the institutions lack enforcement mechanisms, that *they* don't really care about *us* or take us seriously. We rarely ask, though, who *they* are, who *we* are, and why they're out to get us. We also fail to notice that others are singing a similar tune to our own. Those who argue for economic and social rights, for example, seem to feel just as isolated and outside as women's advocates do. In fact, sometimes it seems that international law, particularly human rights law, has been built by its own criticism. That is every time some group or cause feels outside the law, it pushes for inclusion, generally through a new official document. The vast proliferation of human rights documents, then, is as much a testament to exclusion as it is to inclusion.

ADDITIONAL READING

On women's rights generally see: K. Askin and D. Koenig (eds.), *Women and International Human Rights Law* (3 vols. 1999–2000); F. Banda, *Women, Law and Human Rights: An African Perspective* (2005); S. Mullally, *Gender, Culture and Human Rights: Reclaiming Universalism* (2006); D. Buss and A. Manji (eds.), *International Law: Modern Feminist Approaches* (2005); L. Welchman and S. Hossain (eds.), *'Honour': Crimes, Paradigms, and Violence against Women* (2005); H. Charlesworth and C. Chinkin, *The Boundaries of International Law: A Feminist Analysis* (2000); R. Cook (ed.), *Human Rights of Women* (1994). On CEDAW, see S. Engle Merry, *Human Rights and Gender Violence: Translating International Law into Local Justice* (2006); M. Bustelo, 'CEDAW at the Crossroads', in P. Alston and J. Crawford (eds.), *The Future of UN Human Rights Treaty Monitoring* 79 (2000); Annotated CEDAW Bibliography, at http://www.iwrp.org/pdf/biblio.pdf .

On issues of public and private, see: A. Clapham, *Human Rights Obligations of Non-State Actors* (2006); A. Clapham, *Human Rights in the Private Sphere* (1993); Law Commission of Canada, *New Perspectives on the Public-Private Divide* (2003); Dawn Oliver, *Common Values and the Public-Private Divide* (1999); C. Chinkin, 'A Critique of the Public/Private Dimension', 10 *Eur. J. Int. L.* 387 (1999); Barbara Arneil, 'Women as Wives, Servants and Slaves: Rethinking the Public/Private Divide'. 34 *Canadian J. Pol. Sci.* 29 (2001); C. MacKinnon, 'On Torture: A Feminist Perspective on Human Rights', in K. Mahoney and P. Mahoney (eds.), *Human Rights in the Twenty-First Century* 21 (1993); F. Olsen, 'Feminist Critiques of the Public/Private Distinction', in D. Dallmeyer (ed.), *Reconceiving Reality: Women and International Law* (1993), at 157; C. Pateman, *Part A. Contemporary Human Rights: Background and Context* 224 'Feminist Critiques of the Public/ Private Distinction', in S. J. Benn and Gaus (eds.), *Public and Private in Social Life* (1983), at 281.

D. TORTURE REVISITED

If one were to ask a representative number of people committed to human rights values which if any right among, say, those declared in the UDHR had priority in importance, torture would surely rank high on the list. It occupies a vital place in the human rights lexicon, a 'no' strongly and universally felt and expressed. 'If anything is a human right, then it's the right not to be tortured.' Consider its prominence in human rights texts. Article 5 of the UDHR states that no one shall be subjected 'to torture or to cruel, inhuman or degrading treatment or punishment'. Article 7 of the ICCPR restates this language. An entire treaty — the Convention against Torture and other Cruel, Inhuman or Degrading Treatment or Punishment — addresses the problem of state-inflicted torture. As of January 2007, that treaty had 144 states parties. The regional conventions reveal the same emphasis on the prohibition, in both general and torture-specific treaties.

Nonetheless, despite this broad normative consensus over prohibition of torture by states, its systematic incidence remains significant and widespread, more in authoritarian than liberal regimes, more in the developing than developed worlds, but in developed and democratic countries as well. Recall the discussions about customary international law where commentators questioned whether the prohibition of torture by states could be viewed as part of customary law (indeed, of *jus cogens*) because, despite the consistent *opinio juris* about its illegality, so much state practice remained to the contrary.

A certain amount of torture by the state will stem from truly aberrational conduct by a state official violating state policy (savage beatings and rapes by prison guards, for example) and possibly later subjected to sanctions. But torture by the state dominantly takes place because of explicit policies allowing or requiring it or because of quiet toleration of violations of formal policy. Some of those policies have been constants over the centuries, while others have disappeared or been newly invoked over historical periods. Undoubtedly sheer venality — the satisfaction of sexual and sadistic desires or the desire to humiliate and exercise total physical dominion over another's body — has always played its role. It appears that periods of mass violence of horrific proportions, such as the Cambodian and Rwandan genocides, weaken inherent or acquired inhibitions against vile behavior so as to make commonplace the torture of helpless civilian populations and prisoners. Such abominations, themselves often fostered by state propaganda to enlist the participation of nonstate actors in the savaging of the target population, may constitute both a response to and heightening of the process of dehumanization that underlies mass violence, to the extreme of genocide.

Torture by state officials is then rarely gratuitous or attributable simply to aberrational conduct stemming from the dark side of our human nature. It generally serves an instrumental purpose as a means to some further goal, as in a broad sense dehumanization serves a genocidal program. A state, for example, may systematically employ torture as a method for terrorizing a population and discouraging dissent or other behavior condemned by the government. As Amnesty International has long said, torture can be understood as the 'price of dissent', a familiar instrument of terror of the repressive and ruthless authoritarian state to maintain a given structure or ideology and to assure those holding power of their position. Stalin's Soviet Union, Nazi Germany and Maoist China offer the most striking and tragic examples during a century rich in illustrations.

Torture as broadly understood today has figured in many cultures as a part of punishment itself after the criminal process has ended in a conviction. The historical punishments of being drawn and quartered, or placed on the rack, or burned at the stake, provide classic illustrations. Today few such formal institutions of punishment remain, though dispute continues over methods of capital punishment used in many countries, and over methods of punishment that may be religiously based such as amputation of limbs. Historically in the West, torture served for hundreds of years another related function that was largely abolished by the eighteenth century. It had long been routinely and deeply a formal, judicially sanctioned part of criminal procedure, used in many European states to investigate a suspect once some threshold of facts leading to suspicion had been uncovered, and used (subject to certain safeguards designed to heighten the credibility of what was revealed or confessed) both to extract incriminating information and to achieve a confession that, despite the coercion, was used by courts to establish guilt.

If then progress has been made, principally in normative terms but also in the diminishing incidence of torture as part of a broad system of investigation or punishment, the current resurgence of interest and concern of state use of torture suggests today that the human rights movement is not uni-directional, that prohibitions of state conduct once thought settled as a matter of normative consensus are again in contention. Not surprisingly, perhaps, the movement finds itself in new circumstances in which assumed foundational beliefs have been challenged and again figure in high-level and popular discussion. The question is with us not simply in terms of actual use but also in terms of normative justification for such use. Moreover, the question is centred in the West where such important progress seemed to have been achieved — in the United States and other Western democracies as they confront the perils of a post-9/11 world: weapons of mass destruction, non-state actors, terrorism, threats of massive killing. And it is centred on interrogation, on the effort to extract information from suspected terrorists that may destroy networks, bring mass killers to justice, and prevent attacks from occurring that could cost thousands if not millions of lives. Such is the limited focus of this section: the question of state torture to obtain information in this new, threatening context.

INTERNATIONAL INSTRUMENTS PROHIBITING TORTURE

The following illustrations of prohibitions and (where the instrument provides) definitions of torture are drawn from a few major declarations and treaties on human rights as well as on the humanitarian laws of war.

Universal Declaration of Human Rights

Article 5. No one shall be subjected to torture or to cruel, inhuman or degrading treatment or punishment.

International Covenant on Civil and Political Rights

Article 7. [Same text as Universal Declaration]

Article 4. [This article concerns the conditions to derogations by parties from their obligations under the Covenant. Paragraph 2 provides that no derogation may be made from certain articles, including Art. 7.]

Convention against Torture and Other Cruel, Inhuman or Degrading Treatment or Punishment

Article 1(1). For the purposes of this Convention, the term 'torture' means any act by which severe pain or suffering, whether physical or mental, is intentionally inflicted on a person for such purposes as obtaining from him or a third person information or a confession, punishing him for an act he or a third person has committed or is suspected of having committed, or intimidating or coercing him or a third person, or for any reason based on discrimination of any kind, when such pain or suffering is inflicted by or at the instigation of or with the consent or acquiescence of a public official or other person acting in an official capacity. It does not include pain or suffering arising only from, inherent in or incidental to lawful sanctions.

Article 2(2). No exceptional circumstances whatsoever, whether a state of war or a threat of war, internal political instability or any other public emergency, may be invoked as a justification of torture.

Article 4(1). Each State Party shall ensure that all acts of torture are offences under its criminal law. . . .

Article 16. Each State Party shall undertake to prevent in any territory under its jurisdiction other acts of cruel, inhuman or degrading treatment or punishment which do not amount to torture as defined in article 1. . . .

European Convention for the Protection of Human Rights and Fundamental Freedoms

Article 3. No one shall be subjected to torture or to inhuman or degrading treatment or punishment.

Geneva Conventions

[All four Geneva Conventions of 1949 prohibit torture. The term appears in a number of articles, including]

Common Article 3. In the case of armed conflict not of an international character occurring in the territory of one of the High Contracting Parties, each Party to the conflict shall be bound to apply, as a minimum, the following provisions:

(1) Persons taking no active part in the hostilities, including members of armed forces who have laid down their arms and those placed hors de combat by sickness, wounds, detention, or any other cause, shall in all circumstances be treated humanely. . . .

To this end the following acts are and shall remain prohibited at any time and in any place whatsoever with respect to the above-mentioned persons:

(a) violence to life and person, in particular murder of all kinds, mutilation, cruel treatment and torture;. . .

[The term 'torture' also appears in the similarly worded provision of each convention on the definition and consequences of 'grave breaches'. The following illustration is drawn from the Third Geneva Convention Relative to the Treatment of Prisoners of War.]

Article 129. The High Contracting Parties undertake to enact any legislation necessary to provide effective penal sanctions for persons committing, or ordering to be committed, any of the grave breaches of the present Convention defined in the following Article.

. . .

Article 130. Grave breaches to which the preceding Article relates shall be those involving any of the following acts, if committed against persons or property protected by the Convention: wilful killing, torture or inhuman treatment, including biological experiments, wilfully causing great suffering or serious injury to body or health, compelling a prisoner of war to serve in the forces of the hostile Power, or wilfully depriving a prisoner of war of the rights of fair and regular trial prescribed in this Convention.

...

BENTHAM ON TORTURE

W.L. Twining and P.E. Twining (eds. and commentary),
24 N. Ireland Leg. Q. 305 (1973)

[These previously unpublished manuscripts of Jeremy Bentham, a principal and influential expounder of utilitarianism for modern Western thought, were written mid-1770s to 1780, almost two centuries before the birth of the international human rights movement. The excerpts below are taken from Bentham Manuscripts, University College, London, 46/56–70.]

...

Torture, as I understand it, is where a person is made to suffer any violent pain of body in order to compel him to do something or to desist from doing something which done or desisted from the penal application is immediately made to cease.

...

The very circumstance by which alone what is called Torture stands distinguished from what is commonly called punishment is a circumstance that operates in its favour. This circumstance is, that as soon as the purpose for which it is applied is answered, it can at any time be made to cease. With punishment it is necessarily otherwise. Of punishment, in order to make sure of applying as much as is necessary you must commonly run a risque of applying considerably more: of Torture there need never be a grain more applied than what is necessary. . . . Two men are caught setting a house on fire; one of them escapes: set the prisoner on the rack, ask him who his Accomplice is, the instant he has answered you may untie him. Torture then when not abused, Torture considered in itself is in this point of view less liable to exception than punishment is.

The great objection against Torture is, that it is so liable to abuse. . . . [O]f Torture a very great quantity may be employed and the purpose not answered. . . .

...

There seem to be two Cases in which Torture may with propriety be applied.

1. The first is where the thing which a Man is required to do being a thing which the public has an interest in his doing, is a thing which for a certainty is in his power to do; and which therefore so long as he continues to suffer for not doing he is sure not to be innocent.

2. The second is where a man is required what probably though not certainly it is in his power to do; and for the not doing of which it is possible that he may suffer, although he be innocent; but which the public has so great an interest in his doing

that the danger of what may ensue from his not doing it is a greater danger than even that of an innocent person's suffering the greatest degree of pain. . . . Are there in practice any cases that can be ranked under this head? If there be any, it is plain there can be but very few.

. . . It may now be time to . . . state in a more concise manner the Rules that seem requisite to be observed in order to prevent its being employed to an improper degree, or in improper Cases. With regard to the first of the two Cases in which it may be admitted, the following Rules may be proper to be observed.

Rule 1st

I. First then it ought not to be employed without good proof of its being in the power of the prisoner to do what is required of him.

Rule 2d

2. This proof ought to be as strong as that which is required to subject him to a punishment equal to the greatest degree of suffering to which he can in this way be exposed.

Rule 3d

3. It ought not to be employed but in cases which admit of no delay; in cases in which if the thing done were not done immediately there is a certainty, at least a great probability, that the doing it would not answer the purpose.

Rule 4

4. In cases which admit of delay a method of compulsion apparently less severe and therefore less unpopular ought to be employed in preference.

Rule 5

5. Even on occasions which admit not of delay, it ought not to be employed but in Cases where the benefit produced by the doing of the thing required is such as can warrant the employing of so extreme a remedy.

. . .

Rule 7

7. In order that as little misery may be incurred in waste as possible the torture employed should be of such a kind as appears to be the most acute for the time the dolorific application lasts, and of which the pain goes off the soonest after the application is at an end.

. . .

Next with regard to the remaining case of the two in which it may be admitted the following additional Rules seem proper to be observed.

Rule 1

Torture ought not to be employed but in Cases where the exigency will not wait for a less penal method of compulsion.

Rule 2

2. It ought not to be employed but where the safety of the whole state may be endangered for want of that intelligence which it is the object of it to procure.

Rule 3

3. The power of employing it ought not to be vested in any hands but such as from the business of their office are best qualified to judge of that necessity: and from the dignity of it perfectly responsible in case of their making an ill use of so terrible a power.

Rule 4

4. In whatever hands the power is reposed, as many and as efficacious checks ought to be applied to the exercise of it as can be made consistent with the purpose for which it is conferred.

...

Upon the whole therefore it appears, that provided the utmost of suffering that can be inflicted in this way be limited, there is no more danger in trusting a Judge to decide upon this question, whether it is in the power of the prisoner to give such or such a piece of information, than in trusting him to decide upon any other question, by the event of which a man may be subjected to punishment equally severe.

What reconciles me the better to it in the cases in which I have proposed it should be established, is that it may very well be established and answer all the purposes it is designed to answer, without ever being actually applied. In general Cases a man's knowing that it may be applied will be sufficient. In countries where Torture is absolutely forbidden a malefactor scarce ever betrays his accomplice; for why should he?... Establish Torture, and you give him the compleatest of all Excuses, irresistable Necessity.

...

Torture, by many of those who have sitten in judgement over it, seems to have been regarded in one single point of view, as if it were one single individual thing, applied constantly to one and the same purpose. Those who viewed it in this light which ever part they take, whether they approve it, or whether they condemn it, can not fail of being mistaken. On this subject as much as on most others it behoves us to be on our guard not to be led astray by words. There is no approving it in the lump, without militating against reason and humanity: nor condemning it without falling into absurdities and contradictions.

...

QUESTIONS

1. A number of discussions below employ the 'ticking bomb' hypothetical case. As you read ahead, ask: how would Bentham approach and resolve that issue?

2. With respect to interrogation, what if any safeguards for the detainee does Bentham propose?

3. Consider the final sentence in the preceding excerpts, arguing against approving or condemning torture 'in the lump'. What is its relevance to Bentham's larger scheme?

IRELAND V. UNITED KINGDOM

European Court of Human Rights, 1978
2 EHRR 25

[The Republic of Ireland brought this case against the U.K. under the European Convention for the Protection of Human Rights and Fundamental Freedoms. It sought 'to ensure the observance in Northern Ireland of the engagements undertaken by the respondent Government as a High Contracting Party to the Convention'.

The European Court of Human Rights reviewed the course of violence, including the escalating numbers of deaths and injuries, over several decades of this 'tragic and lasting crisis in Northern Ireland', a part of the U.K. contiguous with the Republic of Ireland. Extensive legislation and regulations from 1922 on by local Northern Ireland authorities and the U.K. Government were intended to combat what the U.K. termed a 'violent terrorist campaign' executed by the Irish Republican Army (IRA, a nonstate Northern Ireland group) in the effort to gain independence of Northern Ireland from Britain.

From 1971 to 1975 a series of extrajudicial powers of arrest, detention and internment were put in place and weakened or strengthened over the following years. The U.K. gave as one reason for resort to such measures 'the view that the normal procedures of investigation and criminal prosecution had become inadequate to deal with IRA terrorists; it was considered that the ordinary criminal courts could no longer be relied on as the sole process of law for restoring peace and order. . . . The authorities therefore came to the conclusion that it was necessary to introduce a policy of detention and internment of persons suspected of serious terrorist activities but against whom sufficient evidence could not be laid in court.' Police and other centres, some identified and some not, were established to hold and interrogate persons detained or interned under these special regulations.

The Court's opinion examined the measures taken by the Northern Ireland authorities and the U.K. Government in the light of several articles of the European Convention. The excerpts below concern only the Court's inquiry into the legality of various methods of interrogation of detained suspects under Article 3: 'No one shall be subjected to torture or inhuman or degrading treatment or punishment.']

93. Allegations of ill-treatment have been made by the applicant Government in relation both to the initial arrests and to the subsequent interrogations. . . . The Commission [Eds.: then an organ of the European Convention which initially heard a case prior to its possible later reference to the European Court of Human Rights] examined in detail with medical reports and oral evidence 16 "illustrative" cases selected at its request by the applicant Government.

. . .

The following account of events is based on the information set out in the Commission's report and in the other documents before the Court.

96. Twelve persons arrested on 9 August 1971 and two persons arrested in October 1971 were singled out and taken to one or more unidentified centres. There . . . they were submitted to a form of "interrogation in depth" which involved the combined

application of five particular techniques. These methods, sometimes termed "disorientation" or "sensory deprivation" techniques, were not used in any cases other than the fourteen so indicated above. It emerges from the Commission's establishment of the facts that the techniques consisted of:

(a) wall-standing: forcing the detainees to remain for periods of some hours in a "stress position", described by those who underwent it as being "spreadeagled against the wall, with their fingers put high above the head against the wall, the legs spread apart and the feet back, causing them to stand on their toes with the weight of the body mainly on the fingers";

(b) hooding: putting a black or navy coloured bag over the detainees' heads and, at least initially, keeping it there all the time except during interrogation;

(c) subjection to noise: pending their interrogations, holding the detainees in a room where there was a continuous loud and hissing noise;

(d) deprivation of sleep: pending their interrogations, depriving the detainees of sleep;

(e) deprivation of food and drink: subjecting the detainees to a reduced diet during their stay at the centre and pending interrogations....

97. From the start, it has been conceded by the respondent Government that the use of the five techniques was authorised at "high level". Although never committed to writing or authorised in any official document, the techniques had been orally taught to members of the RUC [Royal Ulster Constabulary, the police force in Northern Ireland] by the English Intelligence Centre at a seminar held in April 1971.

98. The two operations of interrogation in depth by means of the five techniques led to the obtaining of a considerable quantity of intelligence information, including the identification of 700 members of both IRA factions and the discovery of individual responsibility for about 85 previously unexplained criminal incidents....

[The following excerpts refer to one or another group of persons suspected of terrorism and held in one or another of several detention centres.]

167. The five techniques were applied in combination, with premeditation and for hours at a stretch; they caused, if not actual bodily injury, at least intense physical and mental suffering to the persons subjected thereto and also led to acute psychiatric disturbances during interrogation. They accordingly fell into the category of inhuman treatment within the meaning of Article 3 [of the Convention]. The techniques were also degrading since they were such as to arouse in their victims feelings of fear, anguish and inferiority capable of humiliating and debasing them and possibly breaking their physical or moral resistance.

On these two points, the Court is of the same view as the Commission. In order to determine whether the five techniques should also be qualified as torture, the Court must have regard to the distinction, embodied in Article 3, between this notion and that of inhuman or degrading treatment. In the Court's view, this distinction derives principally from a difference in the intensity of the suffering inflicted. The Court considers in fact that, whilst there exists on the one hand violence which is to be condemned both on moral grounds and also in most cases under the domestic law of the Contracting States but which does not fall within Article 3 of the Convention, it appears on the other hand that it was the intention that the Convention, with its distinction between "torture" and "inhuman or degrading treatment", should by the first of these terms attach a special stigma to deliberate inhuman treatment causing very serious and cruel suffering.

. . .

Although the five techniques, as applied in combination, undoubtedly amounted to inhuman and degrading treatment, although their object was the extraction of confessions, the naming of others and/or information and although they were used systematically, they did not occasion suffering of the particular intensity and cruelty implied by the word torture as so understood.

. . .

174. . . . The evidence before the Court reveals that, at the time in question, quite a large number of those held in custody at Palace Barracks were subjected to violence by members of the RUC. This violence, which was repeated violence occurring in the same place and taking similar forms, did not amount merely to isolated incidents; it definitely constituted a practice. It also led to intense suffering and to physical injury which on occasion was substantial; it thus fell into the category of inhuman treatment. According to the applicant Government, the violence in question should also be classified, in some cases, as torture.

On the basis of the data before it, the Court does not share this view. Admittedly, the acts complained of often occurred during interrogation and, to this extent, were aimed at extracting confessions, the naming of others and/or information, but the severity of the suffering that they were capable of causing did not attain the particular level inherent in the notion of torture as understood by the Court.

. . .

180. The RUC, with the assistance of the army, used Ballykinler as a holding and interrogation centre for a few days early in August 1971. Some dozens of people arrested in the course of Operation Demetrius were held there in extreme discomfort and were made to perform irksome and painful exercises. . . .

181. The Court has to determine whether this practice violated Article 3. Clearly, it would not be possible to speak of torture or inhuman treatment, but the question does arise whether there was not degrading treatment. . . . [T]he matters of which Mr. Moore complained were, if nothing else, contrary to the domestic law then in force in the United Kingdom. Furthermore, the way in which prisoners at Ballykinler were treated was characterised in the judgment of 18 February 1972 as not only illegal but also harsh.

However, the judgment does not describe the treatment in detail; it concentrates mainly on reciting the evidence tendered by the witnesses and indicates that the judge rejected that given on behalf of the defence. The Compton Committee for its part considered that, although the exercises which detainees had been made to do involved some degree of compulsion and must have caused hardship, they were the result of lack of judgment rather than an intention to hurt or degrade.

To sum up, the RUC and the army followed at Ballykinler a practice which was discreditable and reprehensible but the Court does not consider that they infringed Article 3.

. . .

[The Court held by sixteen votes to one that the use of the five techniques constituted inhuman and degrading treatment but, by thirteen votes to four, that it did not constitute torture.]

NOTE

In her analysis of the European Convention's prohibition of torture, Fionnuala Ni Aoláin notes the Court's observations in the preceding opinion, particularly its stress on the degree of suffering experienced by detainees that distinguishes torture from inhuman treatment. 'The Court's standards have shifted over the intervening twenty-five years; were this case to appear on the Court's docket today, the outcome might well be a very different one.'[9] She speculates that this 1978 decision was influenced by its context and that the case was seen as very politically sensitive, arising relatively early in the Court's history and involving a leading Western democracy. Ni Aoláin also emphasizes the significance for the Court's judgments in this field of intentionality and deliberateness with respect to the perpetrators' conduct.

QUESTIONS

1. Torture and cruel, inhuman and degrading treatment are both illegal. What difference might it make, both in this case and in the broader context of other human rights treaties, if state conduct is determined to fall within one or the other category? Do the excerpts above from CAT suggest one difference?

2. How objective or subjective do the standards for one or the other category appear to be?

3. Would you favour a convention that provided concrete illustrations for each category so as to give greater guidance to the state? What illustrations would you use to suggest what kinds of conduct crossed the line into torture?

PUBLIC COMMITTEE AGAINST TORTURE IN ISRAEL V. GOVERNMENT OF ISRAEL

Supreme Court of Israel, 1999
H.C. 5100/94

[English translation: http://www.jewishvirtuallibrary.org/jsource/Politics/GSStext.html]

[The applications for relief brought before the Court concerned interrogation methods used by the General Security Service (GSS) to investigate individuals

[9] Fionnuala Nì Aoláin, The European Convention on Human Rights and its Prohibition on Torture, in Sanford Levinson (ed.), *Torture: A Collection*, 213 (2004) at 216.

suspected of committing crimes against Israel's security. The Court noted the 'unceasing struggle' of Israel for its existence and security, in particular the combat against terrorist organizations committed to Israel's annihilation. Terrorist attacks that included suicide bombings against civilian and military targets led to 121 deaths and 707 injured people from 1996 to May 1998. For an in-depth description, the Court referred to the 1987 Report of the Commission of Inquiry Regarding the GSS' Interrogation Practices with Respect to Hostile Terrorist Activities, headed by (ret.) Supreme Court Justice M. Landau (the 'Commission of Inquiry Report'). The GSS is the main body charged with fighting terrorism. Its investigation and interrogation of suspects seek information 'for the purpose of thwarting and preventing [terrorists] from carrying out these attacks'. It used 'physical means' in the interrogations.

GSS investigators informed the Court of the physical means employed. Internal regulations of the GSS, approved by a special Ministerial Committee on GSS interrogations, provided when physical means were to be used in particular instances, and required permission from officials within the GSS hierarchy. The Court's opinion written by its President A. Barak explored the physical means at issue.]

Shaking

9. A number of applicants claimed that the shaking method was used against them. Among the investigation methods outlined in the GSS' interrogation regulations, shaking is considered the harshest. The method is defined as the forceful shaking of the suspect's upper torso, back and forth, repeatedly, in a manner which causes the neck and head to dangle and vacillate rapidly. According to an expert opinion submitted in one of the applications, the shaking method is likely to cause serious brain damage, harm the spinal cord, cause the suspect to lose consciousness, vomit and urinate uncontrollably and suffer serious headaches.

... To [the State's] contention, there is no danger to the life of the suspect inherent to shaking;.... In any event, they argue, doctors are present....

All agree that in one particular case the suspect in question expired after being shaken.... [T]he State argues in its response that the shaking method is only resorted to in very particular cases, and only as a last resort. The interrogation directives define the appropriate circumstances for its application and the rank responsible for authorizing its use. The investigators ... must probe the severity of the danger that the interrogation is intending to prevent; consider the urgency of uncovering the information presumably possessed by the suspect in question; and seek an alternative means of preventing the danger. ... According to the respondent, shaking is indispensable to fighting and winning the war on terrorism.... Its use in the past has lead to the thwarting of murderous attacks.

Waiting in the "Shabach" Position

10. ... [A] suspect investigated under the "Shabach" position has his hands tied behind his back. He is seated on a small and low chair, whose seat is tilted forward, towards the ground. One hand is tied behind the suspect, and placed inside the gap between the chair's seat and back support. His second hand is tied behind the chair, against its back support. The suspect's head is covered by an opaque sack, falling

down to his shoulders. Powerfully loud music is played in the room. . . . [S]uspects are detained in this position for a prolonged period of time, awaiting interrogation at consecutive intervals.

The aforementioned affidavits claim that prolonged sitting in this position causes serious muscle pain in the arms, the neck and headaches. The State [submitted] that both crucial security considerations and the investigators' safety require tying up the suspect's hands as he is being interrogated. The head covering is intended to prevent contact between the suspect in question and other suspects. The powerfully loud music is played for the same reason.

[The opinion described three additional 'physical means' included in the applications: (1) the 'frog crouch', consecutive, periodical crouches on tip toes each crouch lasting five minutes, (2) excessive tightening of hand or leg cuffs, allegedly leading to serious injuries, and (3) sleep deprivation while being tied in the 'Shabach' position, involving long interrogations without breaks.]

Applicants' Arguments

14. . . . *Second*, [applicants] argue that the physical means employed by GSS investigators not only infringe upon the human dignity of the suspect undergoing interrogation, but in fact constitute criminal offences. These methods, argue the applicants, are in violation of International Law as they constitute "Torture," which is expressly prohibited under International Law. Thus, the GSS investigators are not authorized to conduct these interrogations. . . .

We asked the applicants' attorneys whether the "ticking time bomb" rationale was not sufficiently persuasive to justify the use of physical means, for instance, when a bomb is known to have been placed in a public area and will undoubtedly explode causing immeasurable human tragedy if its location is not revealed at once. This question elicited a variety of responses from the various applicants before the Court. There are those convinced that physical means are not to be used under any circumstances; the prohibition on such methods to their mind is absolute, whatever the consequences may be. On the other hand, there are others who argue that even if it is perhaps acceptable to employ physical means in most exceptional "ticking time bomb" circumstances, these methods are in practice used even in absence of the "ticking time bomb" conditions. The very fact that, in most cases, the use of such means is illegal provides sufficient justification for banning their use altogether, even if doing so would inevitably absorb those rare cases in which physical coercion may have been justified. . . .

The State's Arguments

15. . . . With respect to the physical means employed by the GSS, the State argues that these do not violate International Law. Indeed, it is submitted that these methods cannot be qualified as "torture," "cruel and inhuman treatment" or "degrading treatment," that are strictly prohibited under International Law. Instead, the practices of the GSS do not cause pain and suffering, according to the State's position.

Moreover, the State argues that these means are equally legal under Israel's internal (domestic) law. This is due to the "necessity" defence outlined in article 34(11) of the Penal Law (1977). Hence, in the specific cases bearing the relevant conditions inherent to the "necessity" defence, GSS investigators are entitled to use "moderate physical pressure" as a last resort in order to prevent real injury to human life and well being. Such "moderate physical pressure" may include shaking, as the "necessity" defence provides in specific instances. Resorting to such means is legal, and does not constitute a criminal offence. . . . [E]ven in these rare cases [where physical means are allowed], the application of such methods is subject to the strictest of scrutiny and supervision, as per the conditions and restrictions set forth in the Commission of Inquiry's Report. . . .

The Commission of Inquiry's Report

16. . . . [T]he Commission concluded that in cases where the saving of human lives necessarily requires obtaining certain information, the investigator is entitled to apply both psychological pressure and "a moderate degree of physical pressure." Thus, an investigator who, in the face of such danger, applies that specific degree of physical pressure, which does not constitute abuse or torture of the suspect, but is instead proportional to the danger to human life, can avail himself of the "necessity" defence, in the face of potential criminal liability. The Commission was convinced that its conclusions to this effect were not in conflict with International Law, but instead reflect an approach consistent with both the Rule of Law and the need to effectively safeguard the security of Israel and its citizens.

The Commission approved the use of "a moderate degree of physical pressure" with various stringent conditions including directives that were set out in the second (and secret) part of the Report, and for the supervision of various elements both internal and external to the GSS. The Commission's recommendations were duly approved by the government.

[The Court explored bases for the authority of the GSS to conduct interrogations and concluded that it was so authorized.]

The Means Employed for Interrogation Purposes

21. [The State] argued before this Court that some of the physical means employed by the GSS investigators are permitted by the "law of interrogation" itself. . . .

22. . . . Quite accurately, it was noted that:

> Any interrogation, be it the fairest and most reasonable of all, inevitably places the suspect in embarrassing situations, burdens him, intrudes his conscience, penetrates the deepest crevices of his soul, while creating serious emotional pressure. (Y. Kedmi, *On Evidence*, Part A, 1991 at 25).

. . . In crystallizing the interrogation rules, two values or interests clash. *On the one hand*, lies the desire to uncover the truth, thereby fulfilling the public interest in exposing crime and preventing it. *On the other hand*, is the wish to protect the dignity and liberty of the individual being interrogated. This having been said, these interests and values are not absolute. A democratic, freedom-loving society does not accept that investigators use any means for the purpose of uncovering the truth. . . . At times, the price of truth is so high that a democratic society is not prepared to pay it. To the same extent however, a democratic society, desirous of liberty seeks to fight crime and to that end is prepared to accept that an interrogation may infringe upon the human dignity and liberty of a suspect provided it is done for a proper purpose and that the harm does not exceed that which is necessary. . . .

Our concern, therefore, lies in the clash of values and the balancing of conflicting values. The balancing process results in the rules for a 'reasonable interrogation'. These rules are based, *on the one hand*, on preserving the "human image" of the suspect, and on preserving the "purity of arms" used during the interrogation. *On the other hand*, these rules take into consideration the need to fight the phenomenon of criminality in an effective manner generally, and terrorist attacks specifically. These rules reflect "a degree of reasonableness, straight thinking (right mindedness) and fairness". The rules pertaining to investigations are important to a democratic state. They reflect its character. An illegal investigation harms the suspect's human dignity. It equally harms society's fabric.

23. . . . The "law of interrogation" by its very nature, is intrinsically linked to the circumstances of each case. This having been said, a number of general principles are nonetheless worth noting:

First, a reasonable investigation is necessarily one free of torture, free of cruel, inhuman treatment of the subject and free of any degrading handling whatsoever. There is a prohibition on the use of "brutal or inhuman means" in the course of an investigation. This conclusion is in perfect accord with (various) International Law treaties — to which Israel is a signatory — which prohibit the use of torture, "cruel, inhuman treatment" and "degrading treatment". These prohibitions are "absolute". There are no exceptions to them and there is no room for balancing. Indeed, violence directed at a suspect's body or spirit does not constitute a reasonable investigation practice. The use of violence during investigations can potentially lead to the investigator being held criminally liable. *Second*, a reasonable investigation is likely to cause discomfort; It may result in insufficient sleep; The conditions under which it is conducted risk being unpleasant. . . . In the end result, the legality of an investigation is deduced from the propriety of its purpose and from its methods. Thus, for instance, sleep deprivation for a prolonged period, or sleep deprivation at night when this is not necessary to the investigation time wise may be deemed a use of an investigation method which surpasses the least restrictive means.

From the General to the Particular

24. . . . Plainly put, shaking is a prohibited investigation method. It harms the suspect's body. It violates his dignity. It is a violent method which does not form part of a legal investigation. It surpasses that which is necessary. . . . In any event, there is no doubt that shaking is not to be resorted to in cases outside the bounds of "necessity" or as part of an "ordinary" investigation.

25. . . . [O]ne of the investigation methods employed consists of the suspect crouching on the tips of his toes for five minute intervals. . . . This is a prohibited investigation method. It does not serve any purpose inherent to an investigation. It is degrading and infringes upon an individual's human dignity.

26. The "Shabach" method is composed of a number of cumulative components: the cuffing of the suspect, seating him on a low chair, covering his head with

an opaque sack (head covering) and playing powerfully loud music in the area. Are any of the above acts encompassed by the general power to investigate? Our point of departure is that there are actions which are inherent to the investigation power. Therefore, we accept that the suspect's cuffing, for the purpose of preserving the investigators' safety, is an action included in the general power to investigate. . . . Notwithstanding, the cuffing associated with the "Shabach" position is unlike routine cuffing. . . . This is a distorted and unnatural position. The investigators' safety does not require it. . . . The use of these methods is prohibited. . . .

[The opinion explored further possible justifications for the "Shabach" position and found them wanting. "All these methods do not fall within the sphere of a 'fair' interrogation. They are not reasonable. They impinge upon the suspect's dignity, his bodily integrity, and his basic rights in an excessive manner (or beyond what is necessary)." It examined the State's justifications for covering a suspect's head with an opaque sack. ". . . [L]ess harmful means must be employed [for example, to prevent communication with other suspects being interrogated] It degrades [the suspect]. . . . It suffocates him."]

30. . . . A similar — though not identical — combination of interrogation methods were discussed in the case of *Ireland v. United Kingdom* (1978) 2 EHRR 25. . . .

31. The interrogation of a person is likely to be lengthy. . . . Indeed, a person undergoing interrogation cannot sleep as does one who is not being interrogated. . . . This is part of the "discomfort" inherent to an interrogation. This being the case, depriving the suspect of sleep is, in our opinion, included in the general authority of the investigator. . . .

The above described situation is different from those in which sleep deprivation shifts from being a "side effect" inherent to the interrogation, to an end in itself. If the suspect is intentionally deprived of sleep for a prolonged period of time, for the purpose of tiring him out or "breaking" him — it shall not fall within the scope of a fair and reasonable investigation. Such means harm the rights and dignity of the suspect in a manner surpassing that which is required.

32. All that was stated regarding the exceptions pertinent to an interrogation, flowing from the requirement that an interrogation be fair and reasonable, is the accepted law with respect to a regular police interrogation. The power to interrogate given to the GSS investigator by law is the same interrogation powers the law bestows upon the ordinary police force investigator. . . .

Physical Means and the "Necessity" Defence

33. . . . [A]n explicit authorization permitting GSS to employ physical means is not to be found in our law. An authorization of this nature can, in the State's opinion, be obtained in specific cases by virtue of the criminal law defense of "necessity", prescribed in [Article 34 (1) of] the Penal Law. . . .

> A person will not bear criminal liability for committing any act immediately necessary for the purpose of saving the life, liberty, body or property, of either himself or his fellow person, from substantial danger of serious harm, imminent from the particular state of things [circumstances], at the requisite timing, and absent alternative means for avoiding the harm.

The State's position is that by virtue of this "defence" to criminal liability, GSS investigators are also authorized to apply physical means, such as shaking, in the appropriate circumstances, in order to prevent serious harm to human life or body, in the absence of other alternatives. . . . It is choosing the lesser evil. Not only is it legitimately permitted to engage in the fighting of terrorism, it is our moral duty to employ the necessary means for this purpose. . . . [T]here is no obstacle preventing the investigators' superiors from instructing and guiding them with regard to when the conditions of the "necessity" defence are fulfilled and the proper boundaries in those circumstances. From this flows the legality of the directives with respect to the use of physical means in GSS interrogations. In the course of their argument, the State's attorneys submitted the "ticking time bomb" argument. . . . Is a GSS investigator authorized to employ physical means in order to elicit information regarding the location of the bomb in such instances? The State's attorneys answer in the affirmative.

34. We are prepared to assume that — although this matter is open to debate — the "necessity" defence is open to all, particularly an investigator, acting in an organizational capacity of the State in interrogations of that nature. Likewise, we are prepared to accept — although this matter is equally contentious — that the "necessity" exception is likely to arise in instances of "ticking time bombs", and that the immediate need ("necessary in an immediate manner" for the preservation of human life) refers to the imminent nature of the act rather than that of the danger. . . .

. . .

35. . . . This however, is not the issue before this Court. We are not dealing with the potential criminal liability of a GSS investigator. . . . Moreover, we are not addressing the issue of admissibility or probative value of evidence obtained as a result of a GSS investigator's application of physical means against a suspect. . . . The question before us is whether it is possible to infer the authority to, in advance, establish permanent directives setting out the physical interrogation means that may be used under conditions of "necessity". . . . According to the State, it is possible to imply from the "necessity" defence, available (*post factum*) to an investigator indicted of a criminal offence, an advance legal authorization. . . .

36. In the Court's opinion, . . . [t]he "necessity" defence does not constitute a source of authority, allowing GSS investigators to make use of physical means during the course of interrogations. [That defence] . . .deals with deciding those cases involving an individual reacting to a given set of facts; It is an ad hoc endeavour, in reaction to an event. . . . [T]he very nature of the defence does not allow it to serve as the source of a general administrative power. The administrative power is based on establishing general, forward looking criteria. . . .

. . .

. . . The very fact that a particular act does not constitute a criminal act (due to the "necessity" defence) does not in itself authorize the administration to carry out this deed, and in doing so infringe upon human rights. The Rule of Law (both as a formal and substantive principle) requires that an infringement on a human right be prescribed by statute, authorizing the administration to this effect. . .

37. . . . If the State wishes to enable GSS investigators to utilize physical means in interrogations, they must seek the enactment of legislation for this purpose. This authorization would also free the investigator applying the physical means from

criminal liability. This release would flow not from the "necessity" defence but from the "justification" defense which states [Article 34(13) of the Penal Law]:

> A person shall not bear criminal liability for an act committed in one of the following cases:
> (1) He was obliged or authorized by law to commit it.

The defence to criminal liability by virtue of the "justification" is rooted in an area outside of the criminal law. This "external" law serves as a defence to criminal liability. . . . These questions and the corresponding answers must be determined by the Legislative branch. This is required by the principle of the Separation of Powers and the Rule of Law, under our very understanding of democracy.

38. Our conclusion is therefore the following: According to the existing state of the law, neither the government nor the heads of security services possess the authority to establish directives and bestow authorization regarding the use of liberty infringing physical means during the interrogation of suspects suspected of hostile terrorist activities, beyond the general directives which can be inferred from the very concept of an interrogation. Similarly, the individual GSS investigator — like any police officer — does not possess the authority to employ physical means which infringe upon a suspect's liberty during the interrogation, unless these means are inherently accessory to the very essence of an interrogation and are both fair and reasonable.

An investigator who insists on employing these methods, or does so routinely, is exceeding his authority. His responsibility shall be fixed according to law. His potential criminal liability shall be examined in the context of the "necessity" defence, and according to our assumptions, the investigator may find refuge under the "necessity" defence's wings (so to speak), provided this defence's conditions are met by the circumstances of the case. . . .

A Final Word

39. This decision opens with a description of the difficult reality in which Israel finds herself security wise. We shall conclude this judgment by re-addressing that harsh reality. We are aware that this decision does not ease dealing with that reality. This is the destiny of democracy, as not all means are acceptable to it, and not all practices employed by its enemies are open before it. . . . Preserving the Rule of Law and recognition of an individual's liberty constitutes an important component in its understanding of security. At the end of the day, they strengthen its spirit and its strength and allow it to overcome its difficulties. . . . If it will nonetheless be decided that it is appropriate for Israel, in light of its security difficulties to sanction physical means in interrogations . . ., this is an issue that must be decided by the legislative branch which represents the people. We do not take any stand on this matter at this time. . . . It is there that the required legislation may be passed, provided, of course, that a law infringing upon a suspect's liberty "befitting the values of the State of Israel," is enacted for a proper purpose, and to an extent no greater than is required. (Article 8 to the Basic Law: Human Dignity and Liberty).

40. Deciding these applications weighed heavy on this Court. True, from the legal perspective, the road before us is smooth. We are, however, part of Israeli society. Its

problems are known to us and we live its history. We are not isolated in an ivory tower. We live the life of this country. We are aware of the harsh reality of terrorism in which we are, at times, immersed. Our apprehension . . . that this decision will hamper the ability to properly deal with terrorists and terrorism, disturbs us. We are, however, judges. Our brethern require us to act according to the law. . . .

. . .

Consequently . . . we declare that the GSS does not have the authority to "shake" a man, hold him in the "Shabach" position . . . force him into a "frog crouch" position and deprive him of sleep in a manner other than that which is inherently required by the interrogation. . . .

[Seven Justices agreed with the opinion. Justice J'Kedmi accepted the opinion's conclusion but would have suspended the judgment's effectiveness for one year.]

QUESTIONS

1. Is allowing the defence of 'necessity' consistent with an 'absolute' view of protection against torture, such that exceptions and balancing are both forbidden (see para. 23)? How would you state the criteria for and the conditions to a 'necessity' defence?

2. What is the relationship between, on the one hand, a required standard of reasonableness and fairness in the policies and practices of the state during interrogations, and on the other hand, an absolute protection against torture? Would you expect a consensus among states about what kind of conduct in what circumstances would clearly violate an absolute ban, but might be viewed as permissible within the reasonableness standard?

3. Consider para. 31 and its terms like 'general authority', 'inherent', and an 'end in itself'. What if any actions can the state take that are intended to apply pressures on the detainee that may lead to useful information? Compare what was approved by the Court in *Ireland v. U.K.*

4. What is the effect of this opinion? Does it 'ban' torture (as defined or understood) in Israel? If not, what does it achieve? Is 'torture' indeed a category of analysis and definition in the opinion?

5. Both the ECHR and Israeli decisions are directed to national security and terrorism. Do these contexts for the decisions adequately distinguish such cases from certain common types of criminal cases, such as those involving drug dealers or networks of those who sexually abuse children whose activity may seriously injure (or kill) thousands of people? Can an exception realistically be drawn for the context of security and terrorism without substantial risk of its slipping into interrogations inquiring into other forms of criminal activity?

NOTE

Compare *A (FC) v. Secretary of State for the Home Department*, [2005] UKHL 71. Under British legislation, the Secretary of State has authority to issue a certificate to the effect that he reasonably believes a named non-UK national to pose a national security risk and to be a terrorist. A person so certified can challenge the certification before the Special Immigration Appeals Commission (SIAC). Appellants brought their appeals to the House of Lords after losing a challenge before SIAC as well as their appeal to the Court of Appeals, which held that evidence that was (as claimed by appellants), or might have been, 'procured by torture inflicted by foreign officials without the complicity of the British authorities' was admissible before SIAC. Appellants argued before the House of Lords that the common law, as well as the European Convention on Human Rights, barred admission of such evidence.

The House of Lords unanimously held that evidence obtained by torture by officials of a foreign state without the participation of British authorities was not admissible before SIAC. Lord Bingham delivered the main judgment, stating that he was 'startled . . . at the suggestion . . . that this deeply-rooted tradition [abhorrence of torture] and an international obligation solemnly and explicitly undertaken [the Convention against Torture] can be overridden by a statute and a procedural rule which makes no mention of torture at all. . . . The issue is one of constitutional principle . . . irrespective of where, or by whom, or on whose authority the torture was inflicted'. The common law, as well as the European Convention, required exclusion of such evidence. Lord Bingham did observe that ' . . . it would of course be within the power of a sovereign Parliament (in breach of international law) to confer power on SIAC to receive third party torture evidence.'

QUESTION

Should the distinct question relevant to this decision — the admissibility of evidence in a legal proceeding, rather than the criminality or permissibility of certain methods of interrogation — affect a legislature's or court's view of the nature or consequences of torture? Should it, for example, be relevant (a) whether the alleged conduct constituted 'torture' or some other form of coercive interrogation such as 'cruel, inhuman or degrading' treatment, or (b) whether the torture leading to the evidence involved might be viewed as justified within a 'ticking bomb' scenario?

SANFORD LEVINSON (ED.), TORTURE: A COLLECTION
(2004)

Sanford Levinson, Contemplating Torture: An Introduction, at 23

. . .

It turns out to be surprisingly hard to avoid granting some element of "legitimacy" to torture, unless one resolutely believes, in the face of all the evidence, that any and all known events of torture will be prosecuted with significant severity under a doctrine of what lawyers call "strict liability," that is, limiting the legal issue to whether the alleged activity occurred at all, accepting no possible arguments by the defendant that it was justifiable or even excusable . . . [F]ew theorists, and no legal systems, have endorsed such strict liability. Most telling, in a way, is that even Professor Shue, who insists that all acts of "torture ought to remain illegal," nonetheless added immediately that "anyone who sincerely believes such an act to be the least available evil" should be

> placed in the position of needing to justify his or her act morally in order to defend himself or herself legally.... Anyone who thinks an act of torture is justified should have no alternative but to convince a group of peers in a public trial that all necessary conditions for a morally permissible act were indeed satisfied.... If the situation approximates those in the imaginary examples in which torture seems possible to justify, *a judge can surely be expected to suspend the sentence.* (Emphasis added)

...

Few governments, including the United States, Great Britain, and Israel, among others that could no doubt be cited, appear eager, or even particularly willing, to prosecute as criminals agents of the state who engaged in violations of the relevant prohibitions. As John Conroy writes, "throughout the world torturers are rarely punished, and when they are, the punishment rarely corresponds to the severity of the crime." Miscreants, for example, sometimes lose their jobs, but they rarely go to jail.

Conroy's explanation for the infrequency of punishment is derived from the very title of his excellent book *Unspeakable Acts, Ordinary People.* Torturers cannot be reduced to the obvious "sadists" one would, for moral clarity's sake, like them to be. They view themselves as servants of a state — fighting a just war; indeed, as Osiel points out, they are often encouraged in their views by the clergy — in the case of Argentina, Catholic priests....

Jean Bethke Elshtain, Reflection on the Problem of 'Dirty Hands', at 77

...

A certain asceticism is required of those who may be required, in a dangerous and extreme situation, to temporarily override a general prohibition. They should not seek to legalize it. They should not aim to normalize it. And they should not write elaborate justifications of it, as if there were a tick-list one can do down and, if a sufficient number of ticks appears, one is given leave to torture. The tabooed and forbidden, the extreme, nature of this mode of physical coercion must be preserved so that it never becomes routinized as just the way we do things around here.

...

... The position I have developed pushes in the following direction: there is no absolute prohibition to what some call torture. Once again, torture is not sufficiently disaggregated. Recall the possibilities: pulling out fingernails; grinding the teeth down or pulling teeth ...; raping men or women; burning breasts, genitalia; hanging for hours from the arms; crucifying; torturing the spouse or children. There should be — and are — prohibitions against such practices. In an exceptional and truly extreme circumstance, would it be defendable to do any of these things? Everything in me says no and tells me that when we think of torture it is these sorts of extreme forms of physical torment we are thinking of. If torture is the inflicting of severe and devastating pain, as the dictionary defines it, the horrors I have listed are certainly torture.

But there are other options that also come under condemnation as torture. In a striking piece, "The Dark Art of Interrogation," Mark Bowden details some of these. They are called "torture lite:" and, Bowden tells us, some argue that such methods are not properly torture at all. This list includes

> sleep deprivation, exposure to heat or cold, the use of drugs to cause confusion, rough treatment (slapping, shoving or shaking), forcing a prisoner to stand for days at a time or sit in uncomfortable positions, and playing on his fears for himself and his family. Although excruciating for the victim, these tactics generally leave no permanent marks and do no lasting physical harm.

The Geneva Convention, however, makes no distinctions of any kind between these tactics and the horrific possibilities I noted earlier. Torture is torture, it says in effect.

. . . It seems to be the case, as Bowden documents it, that techniques like solitary confinement and sensory deprivation often suffice to induce a prisoner to give up sensitive information about terrorist operations. The skilled interrogator often finds that the fear that something may happen is "more effective than any drug, tactic, or torture device. . . . The threat of coercion usually weakens or destroys resistance more effectively than coercion itself." Forms of psychological pressure and the arts of deception and trickery — for example, telling a captive that others have capitulated so he might as well talk — are standard tools of the interrogator's trade, though some absolutists would forbid them, too. . . .

Bowden concludes that few "moral imperatives make such sense on a large scale" — referring to the prohibition against torture — "but break down so dramatically in the particular." . . . It follows that when human rights groups label "unpleasant or disadvantageous treatment of any kind" torture, they . . . embrace a moralistic "code fetishism" that flies in the face of the harsh and dangerous realities of the world in which we find ourselves . . . ;

. . . The ban on torture must remain. But "moderate physical pressure" to save innocent lives, "coercion" by contrast to "torture," is not only demanded in certain extreme circumstances, it is arguably the "least bad" thing to do. . . .

. . .

Let's sum up this unhappy subject. Far greater moral guilt falls on a person in authority who permits the deaths of hundreds of innocents rather than choosing to "torture" one guilty or complicit person. One hopes and prays such occasions emerge only rarely. Were I the parent or grandparent of a child whose life might be spared, I confess, with regret, that I would want officials to rank their moral purity as far less important in the overall scheme of things than eliciting information that might spare my child or grandchild and all those other children and grandchildren. But I do not want a law to "cover" such cases, for, truly, hard cases do make bad laws. Instead, we work with a rough rule of thumb in circumstances in which we believe an informant might have information that would probably spare the lives of innocents. In a world of such probabilities, we should demur from Torture 1 — the extreme forms of physical torment. But Torture 2, for which we surely need a different name, like coercive interrogation, may, with regret, be used. . . . This is a distinction with a difference.

. . .

John Parry, Escalation and Necessity, at 145

...

International tribunals have given additional content to these definitions and to the distinctions between them. Thus, severe beatings that do not break bones or cause lesions but cause intense pain and swelling are "classic" forms of torture. Torture also includes the combination of being made to stand all day for days at a time, beatings, and withholding food; beatings and being buried alive; electric shocks, beatings, being hung with one's arms behind one's back, having one's head forced under water until nearly asphyxiated, and being made to stand for hours. Rape or threats of physical mutilation are torture as well.

Another series of cases has found that certain combinations of conduct are torture *and* cruel or inhuman treatment.... In a third group of cases, the European Commission of Human Rights found that beatings and one or more instances of electric shock, mock execution, or refusal of food and water were either torture *or* inhuman treatment.

...

The most significant case to examine the difference between torture and cruel or inhuman treatment is *Ireland v. United Kingdom* [*supra*]....

...

The Israeli situation presents the potential importance under the Convention for determining the difference between torture and the lesser — but still illegal — category of cruel, inhuman, or degrading treatment. The Convention [against Torture] bars torture absolutely. . . . By contrast, states that ratify the Convention must "undertake to prevent" cruel, inhuman, or degrading treatment, but the "no exceptional circumstances" provision does not apply. Thus, if conduct similar to Israel's former practices would not be torture under the Convention, an exceptional circumstances justification could be available....

...

... [T]he Senate's statement that the definition of cruel, inhuman, or degrading treatment or punishment must be tied to the Fifth, Eighth, and Fourteenth Amendments gives federal courts the ultimate power to define our international obligations. A series of cases assessing the voluntariness of confessions under the due process clause suggests that these obligations could be broad. But if the Court limits the applicability of these cases or changes course and determines that a particular practice is constitutional, then that practice is permitted under international law as well, at least as the United States understands it.

...

Oren Gross, The Prohibition on Torture and the Limits of Law, at 229

...

Absolutists — those who believe that an unconditional ban on torture ought to apply without exception regardless of circumstances — frequently base their position on deontological grounds, that is, they assess the intrinsic moral value of things independent of their consequences. For them, torture is inherently wrong. It is an evil that can never be justified or excused. It violates the physical and mental integrity of the person subjected to it, negates her autonomy and humanity, and deprives her of human dignity. It reduces her to a mere object, a body, from which information is to be exacted, while coercing her to act in a manner that may be contrary to her most fundamental beliefs, values, and interests. Torture is also wrong because of its depraving and corrupting effects on individual torturers as well as on society at large. . . .

Others support an absolutist view of the ban on torture by arguing that social costs of permitting the use of torture, even in narrowly defined exceptional circumstances . . ., would always outweigh the social benefits that could be derived from applying torture. . . .

It is easy to see why this uncompromising point of view is castigated by its opponents as utopian, naive, or even outright hypocritical. The case of the ticking bomb is used by those who advocate the position that use of coercive interrogation methods may be justified in certain — albeit exceptional and extraordinary — circumstances. . . .

The most prevalent arguments in support of the conditionality of the prohibition on torture are consequentialist claims comparing costs and benefits on a case-by-case basis. . . .

One attempt to escape both sets of criticisms calls for the use of what Charles Black coined "orders of magnitude" assessment. Thus, even if a straightforward cost-benefit analysis leads to the conclusion that, in a given case, the benefits from use of torture outweigh the costs involved, torture is not to be used unless the magnitude of the threat to society (which may be prevented or minimized as a result of resorting to torture) is of a particularly large scale (e.g., the "nuclear weapon in a suitcase in the middle of a major metropolis" scenario). Under this approach, the prohibition on torture sets out a strong presumption against the use of torture. That presumption is, however, rebuttable. Yet to refute it in any given case a showing must be made of the exceptional magnitude of the risk involved. . . .

A third set of arguments put forward by the conditionalists suggests that the prohibition on torture cannot be defensible as a moral absolute. . . . Thus, for example, when the choice is between the physical integrity and dignity of a suspected terrorist, on the one hand, and the lives of a great many innocent persons (e.g., those who are highly likely to be killed or be seriously injured should the ticking bomb actually go off), on the other hand, an absolute ban on torture cannot be morally defensible. . . .

In this article I defend an absolute prohibition on torture while at the same time arguing that the ticking-bomb case should not be brushed aside as merely hypothetical or as either morally or legally irrelevant. . . . [T]he proposal made herein focuses on the possibility that truly exceptional cases may give rise to official disobedience: public officials may step outside the legal framework, that is, act extralegally, and be ready to accept the legal ramifications of their actions. However, there is also the possibility that the extralegal actions undertaken by those officials will be legally (if not morally) excused ex post. . . .

My focus is on what I call *preventive interrogational torture*.... By adding "preventive" I seek to limit the discussion to that use of torture whose aim is to gain information that would assist the authorities in foiling exceptionally grave future terrorist attacks. Hence, the aim is entirely forward-looking....

A second clarification concerns the scope of the term "torture".... [T]he argument I develop hereafter seeks to address instances where interrogation methods that clearly fall within the ambit of "torture" are used....

...

... To deny the use of preventive interrogational torture in [catastrophic] cases ... is also hypocritical: as experience tells us, when faced with serious threats to the life of the nation, government will take whatever measures it deems necessary to abate the crisis....

... As a result, particular norms, and perhaps the legal system in general, may break down, as the ethos of obedience to law may be seriously shaken and challenges emerge with respect to the reasonableness of following these norms. Thus, legal rigidity in the face of severe crises is not merely hypocritical but is, in fact, detrimental to long-term notions of the rule of law.... It may also lead to more, rather than less, radical interference with individual rights and liberties....

...

... We want our leaders and our public officials to possess the highest moral character. But I do not believe we want them to be brazen Kantians.... [F]ew would want a leader who follows Kant's absolutist view to its extreme rather than act to save the lives of innocent civilians. As Judge Posner aptly put it, "if the stakes are high enough, torture is permissible. No one who doubts that this is the case should be in a position of responsibility."...

...

I peg my belief on the twin notions of *pragmatic absolutism* and *official disobedience*. ... [T]he way to reconcile that absolute ban on torture with the necessities of the catastrophic case is not through any means of legal accommodation (such as recognizing an explicit legal exception to the ban on torture that applies to catastrophic cases) but rather through a mechanism of extralegal action that I would term *official disobedience:* in circumstances amounting to a catastrophic case, the appropriate method of tackling extremely grave national dangers and threats *may* entail going outside the legal order, at times even violating otherwise accepted constitutional principles.

Going completely outside the law in appropriate cases preserves, rather than undermines, the rule of law in a way that bending the law to accommodate for catastrophes does not.... [T]o say that governments are going to use preventive interrogational torture in the catastrophic case is not the same as saying that they should be authorized to do so through a priori, ex ante legal rules. It is extremely dangerous to provide for such eventualities and such awesome powers within the framework of the existing legal system because of the large risks of contamination and manipulation of that system and the deleterious message involved in legalizing such actions (e.g., constitutional protections are really designed only for ordinary times and are easily suspended precisely when they are needed the most).

Instead, my proposal calls on public officials having to deal with the catastrophic case to consider the possibility of acting outside the legal order while openly acknowledging their actions and the extralegal nature of such actions. Those officials must assume the risks involved in acting extralegally. State agents may regard strict obedience to legal authority (such as the absolute legal ban on torture) as irrational or immoral under circumstances of a true catastrophic case. . . . Society retains the role of making the final determination whether the actor ought to be punished and rebuked or rewarded and commended for her actions . . .

. . . [T]he acting official may . . . for example, need to resign her position, face criminal charges or civil suits, or be subjected to impeachment proceedings. Alternatively, the people may approve the actions and ratify them. . . . [L]egal modes of ratification may include exercising prosecutorial discretion not to bring criminal charges against persons accused of using torture, jury nullification where criminal charges are brought, executive pardoning or clemency where criminal proceedings result in conviction, or governmental indemnification of state agents who are found liable for damages to persons who were tortured.

. . .

Alan Dershowitz, Tortured Reasoning, at 257

. . .

The Supreme Court of Israel [see p. 234, *supra*] left the security services a tiny window of opportunity in extreme cases. Borrowing from the Landau Commission, it cited the traditional common-law defense of necessity. . . . This leaves each individual member of the security services in the position of having to guess how a court would ultimately resolve his case. That is unfair to such investigators. It would have been far better, in my view, had the court required any investigator who believed that torture was necessary in order to save lives to apply to a judge, when feasible. The judge would then be in a position either to authorize or refuse to authorize a "torture warrant." Such a procedure would require judges to dirty their hands by authorizing torture warrants or bear the responsibility for failing to do so. . . .

In response to the decision of the Supreme Court of Israel, it was suggested that the Knesset — Israel's parliament — could create a procedure for advance judicial scrutiny, akin to the warrant requirement in the Fourth Amendment to the United States Constitution. It is a traditional role for judges to play, since it is the job of the judiciary to balance the needs for security against the imperatives of liberty. Interrogators from the security service are not trained to strike such a delicate balance. Their mission is single-minded: to prevent terrorism. . . . The essence of a democracy is placing responsibility for difficult choices in a visible and neutral institution like the judiciary.

. . .

. . . I sought a debate [after September 11]: . . . if torture would, *in fact* be employed by a democratic nation under the circumstances, would the rule of law and principles of accountability require that any use of torture be subject to some kind of judicial (or perhaps executive) oversight (or control)? . . . My answer, unlike that of the Supreme Court of Israel, is yes. To elaborate, I have argued that unless a democratic nation is prepared to have a proposed action governed by the rule of law, it should not undertake, or authorize, that action. As a corollary, if it needs to take the proposed action, then it must subject it to the rule of law. Suggesting that an after-the-fact "necessity defense" might be available in extreme cases is not an adequate substitute for explicit advance approval.

... In explaining my preference for a warrant, I [earlier] wrote the following.

...

> There is, of course, a downside: legitimating a horrible practice that we all want to see ended or minimized. Thus we have a triangular conflict unique to democratic societies: If these horrible practices continue to operate below the radar screen of accountability, there is no legitimation, but there is continuing and ever expanding *sub rosa* employment of the practice. If we try to control the practice by demanding some kind of accountability, then we add a degree of legitimation to it while perhaps reducing its frequency and severity. If we do nothing, and a preventable act of nuclear terrorism occurs, then the public will demand that we constrain liberty even more. There is no easy answer.

...

The strongest argument against my preference for candor and accountability is the claim that it is better for torture — or any other evil practice deemed necessary during emergencies — to be left to the low-visibility discretion of low-level functionaries than to be legitimated by high-level, accountable decision-makers. Posner makes this argument:

> Dershowitz believes that the occasions for the use of torture should be regularized — by requiring a judicial warrant for the needle treatment, for example. But he overlooks an argument for leaving such things to executive discretion. If rules are promulgated permitting torture in defined circumstances, some officials are bound to want to explore the outer bounds of the rules. Having been regularized, the practice will become regular. Better to leave in place the formal and customary prohibitions, but with the understanding that they will not be enforced in extreme circumstances.

...

QUESTIONS

1. Which approach do you believe preferable: (1) the decision of the Israeli Supreme Court, or the argument of Dershowitz? (2) the proposals of Gross or Dershowitz? What considerations point you in one or the other direction in each case?

2. Is any one of these varied proposals more likely than others to avoid the danger signalled by Posner in the closing paragraph above?

3. Do any proposals in these materials respond to the risk that the probability of a given detainee's possessing information relevant to stopping a terrorist attack will be overstated, or in many cases be simply indeterminate? How would you respond to it?

4. Make a list of considerations that you believe relevant to a legislative debate about what limits if any to place on methods of interrogation by military or police personnel in cases posing national security concerns.

NOTE

In contrast to the conventions of the last three decades, the eighteenth-century US Constitution and its amendments do not refer to torture as such. The first ten amendments to the Constitution, effective two years after the Constitution itself, constitute the Bill of Rights. Two striking differences emerge between the Eighth Amendment and the postwar conventions. It provides: 'Excessive bail shall not be required, nor excessive fines imposed, nor cruel and unusual punishments inflicted.' The phrase 'cruel and unusual', rather than torture, describes the limit imposed on state action. Moreover, the phrase refers only to 'punishments,' whereas the ICCPR characteristically bars 'torture' and 'cruel, inhuman or degrading *treatment or punishment*.' (emphasis added).[10]

Outside the context of punishment, then, the courts have had to resort to other constitutional provisions to determine whether, for example, incriminating evidence obtained coercively from a defendant could be admitted in evidence at the criminal trial. The principally invoked provisions have been the 'due process' clauses of the Fifth and Fourteenth Amendments.

A decision of the U.S. Supreme Court growing out of a California criminal case — Rochin v. California, 342 U.S. 165 (1952) — illustrates such due process jurisprudence. Police officers had information that defendant Rochin was selling narcotics. They illegally entered his home, and Rochin promptly swallowed two capsules seen by the police. The police took him to a hospital, where a doctor was ordered to insert into his stomach an emetic solution through a tube. Defendant therefore vomited and brought up the two capsules, which contained morphine. Primarily on that evidence, he was convicted of illegal possession of morphine. The US Supreme Court upset the conviction, concluding that the evidence obtained by coercion could not be admitted. The opinion stated (at p. 172):

> . . .[W]e are compelled to conclude that the proceedings by which this conviction was obtained do more than offend some fastidious squeamishness or private sentimentalism about combating crime too energetically. This is conduct that shocks the conscience. Illegally breaking into the privacy of the petitioner, the struggle to open his mouth and remove what was there, the forcible extraction of his stomach's contents — this . . . is bound to offend even hardened sensibilities. They are methods too close to the rack and the screw to permit of constitutional differentiation. . . . [C]onvictions cannot be brought about by methods that offend 'a sense of justice.' Coerced confessions offend the community's sense of fair play and decency. . . .

Note that no federal statute bars 'torture' as such. The State Department has argued that the constitutional protections noted above as well as several common crimes defined in federal and state statutes (such as the long-standing crimes of assault and battery) adequately cover the issue. Note also that 18 U.S.C. 2340A, p. 253, *infra*, criminalizes 'torture' only *outside* the United States.

[10] *Roper v. Simmons, supra* p. 35, illustrates the contemporary application by the Supreme Court of the Eighth (and Fourteenth) Amendments to decide if capital punishment of criminals who committed the crime when juveniles would be constitutional.

COMMENT ON US GOVERNMENT POLICY AND RECENT LEGISLATION BEARING ON THE QUESTION OF TORTURE

The events of 11 September led the Bush Administration to develop and institutionalize a broad policy of counter-terrorism. It proposed, and Congress enacted, broad legislation like the Patriot Act. In important part, it also proceeded through the Executive Branch, independently of Congress — for example, by interpretations of both domestic legislation and treaties that bore on vital matters including the question of prohibited methods of interrogation of persons detained on suspicion of participation in terrorism.

The issue of torture, and its regulation under US legislation as well as by the Convention against Torture and the Geneva Conventions to which the US was a party, thereby became prominent within the Administration, in Congressional debate, and among the broad public. The decisions reached, particularly those within the Executive Branch, provoked foreign criticism of US policy. The question of torture, once thought settled and closed as a normative matter (despite its ongoing practice in the world), became newly relevant in a domestic and international context. The US had entered the following reservation to its ratification of the Convention against Torture:

> That the United States considers itself bound by the obligation under Article 16 to prevent "cruel, inhuman or degrading treatment or punishment," only insofar as the term "cruel, inhuman or degrading treatment or punishment" means the cruel, unusual and inhumane treatment or punishment prohibited by the Fifth, Eighth, and/or Fourteenth Amendments to the Constitution of the United States.

A similarly worded reservation to US ratification of the International Covenant on Civil and Political Rights was entered with respect to Article 7 of the Covenant.

The ratification of the Convention against Torture was also made subject to the following 'understanding' of the US:

> That with reference to Article 1, the United States understands that, in order to constitute torture, an act must be specifically intended to inflict severe physical or mental pain or suffering and that mental pain or suffering refers to prolonged mental harm caused by or resulting from: (1) the intentional infliction or threatened infliction of severe physical pain or suffering; (2) the administration or application, or threatened administration or application, of mind altering substances or other procedures calculated to disrupt profoundly the senses or the personality; (3) the threat of imminent death; or (4) the threat that another person will imminently be subjected to death, severe physical pain or suffering, or the administration or application of mind altering substances or other procedures calculated to disrupt profoundly the senses or personality.

There follow excerpts from a few memoranda issuing from officials holding important positions in the Department of Justice. They concern both the definition of torture and the broad issue of the heightened role and powers of the Executive Branch *vis-a-vis* Congress and the Judiciary on national security matters in the age of terrorism.

U. S. Department of Justice, Memorandum from Jay Bybee, Assistant Attorney General, to Alberto Gonzales, Counsel to the President, August 1, 2002

This memorandum concerned standards of conduct for interrogation of detainees outside the United States under the Torture Act, 18 U.S.C. §§2340–2340A implementing the Convention against Torture (CAT) and the provisions for grave breaches in the Geneva Conventions. It separately analysed the statute and treaty. Section 2340 reads in part:

As used in this chapter —

(1) 'torture' means an act committed by a person acting under the color of law specifically intended to inflict severe physical or mental pain or suffering (other than pain or suffering incidental to lawful sanctions) upon another person within his custody or physical control;

(2) 'severe mental pain or suffering' means the prolonged mental harm caused by or resulting from —

(A) the intentional infliction or threatened infliction of severe physical pain or suffering;

(B) the administration or application, or threatened administration or application, of mind-altering substances or other procedures calculated to disrupt profoundly the senses or the personality;

(C) the threat of imminent death; or

(D) the threat that another person will imminently be subjected to death, severe physical pain or suffering, or the administration or application of mind-altering substances or other procedures calculated to disrupt profoundly the senses or personality. . . .

. . .

Section 2340A states in part:

> Whoever outside the United States commits or attempts to commit torture shall be fined under this title or imprisoned not more than 20 years, or both, and if death results to any person from conduct prohibited by this subsection, shall be punished by death or imprisoned for any term of years or for life.

The statute does not define the critical word 'severe'. Turning to dictionary definitions to identify the 'ordinary or natural meaning' of that term, the memo concludes that 'the pain or suffering must be of such a high level of intensity that the pain is difficult for the subject to endure'. Turning to other statutes using the term 'severe' such as those defining an emergency medical condition for the purpose of providing health care, Bybee understood them to suggest that 'severe' pain in Section 2340:

> must rise to a similarly high level — the level that would ordinarily be associated with a sufficiently serious physical condition or injury such as death, organ failure, or serious impairment of body functions — in order to constitute torture.

The memo then refers to the statute's four-part definition of severe 'mental' pain or suffering, and summarizes its views:

> Each component of the definition emphasizes that torture is not the mere infliction of pain or suffering on another, but is instead a step well removed. The victim must experience intense pain or suffering of the kind that is equivalent to the pain that would be associated with serious physical injury so severe that death, organ failure, or permanent damage resulting in a loss of significant body function will likely result. If that pain or suffering is psychological, that suffering must result from one of the acts set forth in the statute. In addition, these acts must cause long-term mental harm.

The memo understands the statutory requirement of 'prolonged mental harm' to mean that 'the acts giving rise to the harm must cause some lasting, though not necessarily permanent, damage . . . [T]he development of a mental disorder such as post-traumatic stress disorder, which can last months or even years, or even chronic depression, which also can last for a considerable period of time if untreated, might satisfy the prolonged harm requirement.' The memo states that it is not enough for the victim to suffer prolonged mental suffering. The perpetrator must also specifically intend, in other words purposefully aim to achieve, that result.

The memo then addressed treaties. It recalled that CAT distinguishes between 'torture' and 'cruel, inhuman or degrading treatment or punishment which does not amount to torture as defined in Article 1.' Recall the 'understanding' informing the U.S. ratification of CAT, p. 252, *supra*, that later found its way into the definition of mental pain or suffering in Section 2340.

The Bybee memo referred to testimony at the time of the memo of an official from the Department of Justice stating that 'torture is understood to be that barbaric cruelty which lies at the top of the pyramid of human rights misconduct'. That testimony gave as examples 'the needle under the fingernail, the application of electrical shock to the genital area, the piercing of eyeballs, etc'. In conclusion, the memo argued that CAT's text, ratification history and negotiating history confirmed that torture 'is a step far-removed from other cruel, inhuman or degrading treatment or punishment'. CAT reaches only 'the most heinous acts'. Such an interpretation gave the Administration and U.S. military more leeway in deciding on methods of interrogation seeking information from suspected terrorists that were shy of the ultimate prohibition of torture.

The memo further considered the President's power as Commander-in-Chief. It noted his clear constitutional power to respond with force to the attack on September 11, and power to deploy the armed forces domestically to protect against foreign terrorist attack. Interrogation of individuals connected to Al Qaeda 'is clearly imperative to our national security and defense [and] may prove invaluable in preventing further direct attacks . . .' The President 'enjoys complete discretion in the exercise of his Commander-in-Chief authority and in conducting operations against hostile forces'. Therefore, 'without a clear statement otherwise, we will not read a criminal statute as infringing on the President's ultimate authority in these areas'. Hence, 'Section 2340A must be construed as not applying to interrogations undertaken pursuant to his Commander-in-Chief authority.' More broadly,

> Congress lacks authority under Article I to set the terms and conditions under which the President may exercise his authority as Commander-in-Chief to control the conduct of operations during a war. A construction of Section 2340A that applied the provision to regulate the President's authority as Commander-in-Chief to determine the interrogation and treatment of enemy combatants would raise serious constitutional issues. Congress may no more regulate the President's ability to detain and interrogate enemy combatants than it may regulate his ability to direct troop movements on the battlefield. . . . Just as statutes that order the President to conduct warfare in a certain manner or for specific goals would be unconstitutional, so too are laws that work to prevent the President from gaining the intelligence he believes necessary to prevent attacks upon the United States.

The memorandum concludes that the 'application of Section 2340A to interrogations undertaken pursuant to the President's Commander-in-Chief power may be unconstitutional'.

The memorandum also considers 'defenses', including that of 'necessity'. Such a defense could eliminate criminal liability even if the statutory definition of torture was found to have been violated and the statute was found constitutional in its criminal application. The memo stresses two factors: (1) The greater the certainty of government officials that the person under interrogation has information needed to prevent a serious attack, the more necessary the interrogation. (2)The greater the likelihood that a terrorist attack will occur, and the greater the damage expected from such an attack, the more the interrogation would be necessary. Much then depends on the knowledge of the government official conducting the interrogation. 'While every interrogation that might violate Section 2340A does not trigger a necessity defense, we can say that certain circumstances would support such a defense.'

❀ ❀ ❀

U.S. Department of Justice, Memorandum from Daniel Levin, Acting Assistant Attorney General, to James B. Comey, Deputy Attorney General, December 30, 2004

[The Bybee memorandum above provoked extensive debate and much criticism, some of which was directed to its very restrictive definition of torture. The memorandum below examined the legal standards applicable under 18 U.S.C. §§ 2340–2340A. Excerpts follow:]

> Torture is abhorrent both to American law and values and to international norms. This universal repudiation of torture is reflected in our criminal law . . . ; international agreements . . .; customary international law, centuries of Anglo-American law and the longstanding policy of the United States, repeatedly and recently reaffirmed by the President.
>
> This Office interpreted the federal criminal prohibition against torture — codified at 18 U.S.C. §§ 2340–2340A — in [the August 2002 Memorandum appearing above, which] also addressed a number of issues beyond interpretation of those statutory provisions, including the President's Commander-in-Chief power. . . . Questions have since been raised, both by this Office and by others, about the appropriateness and relevance of the non-statutory discussion in the August 2002 Memorandum, and also about various aspects of the statutory analysis. . .
>
> We decided to withdraw the August 2002 Memorandum. . . . This memorandum supersedes the August 2002 Memorandum in its entirety. Because the discussion in that memorandum concerning the President's Commander-in-Chief power . . . was — and remains — unnecessary, it has been eliminated from the analysis that follows. Consideration of the bounds of any such authority would be inconsistent with the President's unequivocal directive that United States personnel not engage in torture.
>
> We have also modified in some important respects our analysis of the legal standards applicable under 18 U.S.C. §§ 2340–2340A. For example, we disagree with statements in the August 2002 Memorandum limiting "severe" pain under the statute to "excruciating and agonizing" pain, *id.* at 19, or to pain "equivalent in intensity to the pain accompanying serious physical injury, such as organ failure, impairment of bodily function, or even death." . . .
>
> . . .
>
> Congress enacted sections 2340–2340A to carry out the United States' obligations under the CAT. The CAT, among other things, obligates state parties to take effective measures to prevent acts of torture in any territory under their jurisdiction, and requires the United States, as a state party, to ensure that acts of torture, along with attempts and complicity to commit such acts, are crimes under U.S. law. Sections 2340–2340A satisfy that requirement with respect to acts committed outside the United States. Conduct constituting "torture" occurring within the United States was — and remains — prohibited by various other federal and state criminal statutes that we do not discuss here.
>
> . . .
>
> [The memo notes that the Senate attached an understanding to its advice and consent to ratification of the CAT that differs from the constituent elements of an act of torture set forth in the CAT. That understanding is generally tracked in Sections 2340–2340A.]
>
> Although Congress defined "torture" under sections 2340–2340A to require conduct specifically intended to cause "severe" pain or suffering, we do not believe Congress intended to reach only conduct involving "excruciating and agonizing" pain or suffering. . . . We are not aware of any evidence suggesting that the standard was raised in the statute and we do not believe that it was.
>
> . . .

(2) The meaning of 'severe physical pain or suffering.'

> . . .Although we think the meaning of "severe physical pain" is relatively straightforward, the question remains whether Congress intended to prohibit a category of "severe physical suffering" distinct from "severe physical pain." We conclude that under some circumstances "severe physical suffering" may constitute torture even if it does not involve "severe physical pain." Accordingly, to the extent that the August 2002 Memorandum suggested that "severe physical suffering" under the statute could in no circumstances be distinct from "severe physical pain," we do not agree.

. . .

The memorandum's discussion about the meaning of 'severe mental pain or suffering' and 'specific intent' is omitted. In that discussion, it drew further distinctions between its understanding and that of the earlier, withdrawn August 2002 memorandum.

❁ ❁ ❁

Following the public debate over dissemination of pictures from the Abu Ghraib prison facility in Iraq, President Bush issued a statement in 2004 that said in part:

> Today, on United Nations International Day in Support of Victims of Torture, the United States reaffirms its commitment to the worldwide elimination of torture. . . . Freedom from torture is an inalienable human right, and we are committed to building a world where human rights are respected and protected by the rule of law. . . . We will investigate and prosecute all acts of torture and undertake to prevent other cruel and unusual punishment in all territory under our jurisdiction. . . . The United States also remains steadfastly committed to upholding the Geneva Conventions, which have been the bedrock of protection in armed conflict for more than 50 years. . . . We expect other nations to treat our service members and civilians in accordance with the Geneva Conventions.

During 2005 and 2006, intense debate continued about the treatment of prisoners with respect to a range of issues, including interrogation methods. Senator McCain introduced an amendment to legislation on the defence budget which bore his name. As enacted as part of the Detainee Treatment Act of 2005, it provided that (1) no one in the custody of the Department of Defense 'shall be subject to any treatment or technique of interrogation not authorized by and listed in the United States Army Field Manual on Intelligence Interrogation', and that (2) no one in the custody of the U.S. Government, 'regardless of nationality or physical location, shall be subject to cruel, inhuman, or degrading treatment or punishment'. It did not refer to 'torture' as such, but stated that the term 'cruel, inhuman, or degrading treatment of punishment' means (as provided in the Reservations, Declarations and Understandings to the US ratifications of the ICCPR and CAT) such treatment or punishment prohibited by the Fifth, Eighth, and Fourteenth Amendments to the Constitution. The McCain Amendment leaves open a number of key questions bearing on its consistency with the international standard for state-inflicted torture — for example, whether the due-process test employed (through the Fourteenth Amendment) in the *Rochin* case, p. 251, *supra*, to bar evidence would now permit national security considerations to be employed in a balancing test. Such a test might ask whether the harm inflicted in interrogation is worth the information gained.

The Graham-Levin Amendment, a further modification incorporated into the Detainee Treatment Act of 2005, qualified the significance of the McCain Amendment. For example, it permitted the Department of Defense to consider evidence 'obtained as a result of coercion' in determining whether to detain an individual at Guantanamo, it withdrew habeas corpus for Guantamo detainees, and it created some forms of independent court review for a narrow set of claims raised after initial designation as an enemy combatant by a Combatant Status Review Tribunal and after canviction by a military commission. We discuss the procedural provisions in chapter 5, see p. 415 *infra*.

In approving the bill including these amendments, President Bush issued a signing statement to the effect that the executive branch would construe such measures affecting detainees 'in a manner consistent with the constitutional authority of the President to supervise the unitary executive branch and as Commander in Chief and consistent with the constitutional limitations of the judicial power' to protect America from further terrorist attacks.

In late 2006, the US Government passed the Military Comissions Act of 2006 (MCA). The Act followed the Supreme Court's decision in *Hamdan v. Rumsfeld*, which held that Common Article 3 of the Geneva Conventions applies to the conflict with A1 Qaeda, see p. 445 *infra*. Among other things, the MCA amended the War Crimes Act of 1996 by specifically defining those violations of Common Article 3 that incur criminal liability. Several of the MCA provisions involve the definition of torture under US law.

Prior to the MCA, the War Crimes Act criminalized 'violation[s] of common article 3'. Common article 3 prohibits 'violence to life and person, in particular murder of all kinds, mutilation, cruel treatment and torture' as well as 'outrages upon personal dignity, in particular, humiliation and degrading treatment'. The MCA designates only certain violations of Common Article 3 as a criminal offence under the War Crimes Act. Included in that category is torture, which the MCA defines as follows:

> TORTURE. — The act of a person who commits, or conspires or attempts to commit, an act specifically intended to inflict severe physical or mental pain or suffering (other than pain or suffering incidental to lawful sanctions) upon another person within his custody or physical control for the purpose of obtaining information or a confession, punishment, intimidation, coercion, or any reason based on discrimination of any kind.

The MCA also defines cruel or inhuman treatment as a criminal offence:

> CRUEL OR INHUMAN TREATMENT. — The act of a person who commits, or conspires or attempts to commit, an act intended to inflict severe or serious physical or mental pain or suffering (other than pain or suffering incidental to lawful sanctions), including serious physical abuse, upon another within his custody or control.

Under the MCA, the meaning of 'serious physical pain or suffering' is further defined as bodily injury that involves:

(i) a substantial risk of death;
(ii) extreme physical pain;
(iii) a burn or physical disfigurement of a serious nature (other than cuts, abrasions, or bruises); or
(iv) significant loss or impairment of the function of a bodily member, organ, or mental faculty

Compare with this definition that used by the Department of Justice in the August 2002 memo to define 'severe pain' as requiring 'the level that would ordinarily be associated with a sufficiently serious physical condition or injury such as death, organ failure, or serious impairment of body functions'.

The definition of severe mental pain or suffering in 18 USC 2340A(2), discussed above, applies to the MCA's definition of serious mental pain or suffering, with one exception. For conduct occurring after the enactment of the MCA, the term 'prolonged mental harm' is replaced by the term 'serious and non-transitory mental harm (which need not be prolonged)'.

The MCA's definitions of torture and cruel or inhuman treatment apply only to the War Crimes Act's criminalization of Common Article 3 violations. It does not apply to other proscriptions on torture and coercive interrogation, including the McCain Amendment. Nor does it preclude other crimnal offences, such as assault, which may exist in other statutes. The Detainee Treatment Act and MCA, however, may make it more difficult for detainees to challenge their treatment. The legislation strips courts of jurisdiction over habeas corpus petitions by aliens who are determined to have been properly detained as enemy combatants (while still providing limited independent review of detention and military commission proceedings under the Graham-Levin Amendment). These procedural restrictions, discussed in Chapter 5, have been subject to constitutional challenge.

The MCA also expressly permits the use of statements obtained by coercive interrogation as evidence before a military commission. The Act authorizes military commissions (as opposed to courts martial or normal criminal courts) for trial of foreign national enemy combatants, including members of Al Qaeda and the Taliban. The MCA excludes statements obtained by torture. The Act, however, permits the admission of statements obtained by coercive measures short of torture. For statements made before the enactment of the Detainee Treatment Act of 2005 if 'the degree of coercion is disputed', a military judge must determine whether :

(1) the totality of the circumstances renders the statement reliable and possessing sufficient probative value;
(2) the interests of justice would best be served by admission of the statement into evidence; and
(3) the interrogation methods used to obtain the statement do not amount to cruel, inhuman, or degrading treatment prohibited by . . .the Detainee Treatment Act of 2005.

For statements made before the enactment of the Detainee Treatment Act, the first two criteria above are repeated, but the third criterion is conspicuously omitted.

Note that the MCA also bars all persons from invoking the Geneva Conventions as a source of rights in any civil action (including habeas corpus) to which the United States or a US official is a party.

CONCLUSIONS AND RECOMMENDATIONS OF COMMITTEE AGAINST TORTURE RELATING TO REPORT SUBMITTED BY THE UNITED STATES

CAT/C/USA/CO/2, 25 July 2006

[The Committee against Torture created by the CAT serves several functions comparable to those of the CEDAW Committee discussed in Section C of this chapter. Those functions include receiving and reacting to reports about compliance with CAT that states parties are required to submit periodically to the Committee. In 2006, the Committee issued its conclusions and recommendations concerning a report submitted by the United States that year. The excerpts below include both expressions of 'concern' and formal recommendations.]

13. . . . The Committee also regrets that, despite the occurrence of cases of extraterritorial torture of detainees, no prosecutions have been initiated under the extraterritorial criminal torture statute (arts. 1, 2, 4 and 5).

The Committee reiterates its previous recommendation that the State party should enact a federal crime of torture consistent with article 1 of the Convention.... The State party should ensure that acts of psychological torture, prohibited by the Convention, are not limited to "prolonged mental harm" as set out in the State party's understandings lodged at the time of ratification of the Convention, but constitute a wider category of acts, which cause severe mental suffering, irrespective of their prolongation or its duration. . . .

14. The Committee regrets the State party's opinion that the Convention is not applicable in times and in the context of armed conflict, on the basis of the argument that the "law of armed conflict" is the exclusive *lex specialis* applicable, and that the Convention's application "would result in an overlap of the different treaties which would undermine the objective of eradicating torture".

The State party should recognize and ensure that the Convention applies at all times, whether in peace, war or armed conflict, in any territory under its jurisdiction and that the application of the Convention's provisions are without prejudice to the provisions of any other international instrument, pursuant to paragraph 2 of its articles 1 and 16.

15. . . . The State party should recognize and ensure that the provisions of the Convention expressed as applicable to "territory under the State party's jurisdiction" apply to, and are fully enjoyed, by all persons under the effective control of its authorities, of whichever type, wherever located in the world.

16. The Committee notes with concern that the State party does not always register persons detained in territories under its jurisdiction outside the United

States, depriving them of an effective safeguard against acts of torture (art. 2). The State party should register all persons it detains in any territory under its jurisdiction, as one measure to prevent acts of torture....

17. The Committee is concerned by allegations that the State party has established secret detention facilities, which are not accessible to the International Committee of the Red Cross. Detainees are allegedly deprived of fundamental legal safeguards, including an oversight mechanism in regard to their treatment and review procedures with respect to their detention.

The Committee is also concerned by allegations that those detained in such facilities could be held for prolonged periods and face torture or cruel, inhuman or degrading treatment....

...

22. The Committee, noting that detaining persons indefinitely without charge constitutes per se a violation of the Convention, is concerned that detainees are held for protracted periods at Guantánamo Bay, without sufficient legal safeguards and without judicial assessment of the justification for their detention (arts. 2, 3 and 16).

The State party should cease to detain any person at Guantánamo Bay and close this detention facility, permit access by the detainees to judicial process or release them as soon as possible, ensuring that they are not returned to any State where they could face a real risk of being tortured, in order to comply with its obligations under the Convention.

...

24. ... The State party should rescind any interrogation technique, including methods involving sexual humiliation, "waterboarding", "short shackling" and using dogs to induce fear, that constitutes torture or cruel, inhuman or degrading treatment or punishment, in all places of detention under its de facto effective control, in order to comply with its obligations under the Convention.

...

27. The Committee is concerned that the Detainee Treatment Act of 2005 aims to withdraw the jurisdiction of the State party's federal courts with respect to habeas corpus petitions, or other claims by or on behalf of Guantánamo Bay detainees, except under limited circumstances....

The State party should ensure that independent, prompt and thorough procedures to review the circumstances of detention and the status of detainees are available to all detainees, as required by article 13 of the Convention.

...

NOTE

President Bush and other high officials of the Executive Branch, as well as a number of legislators, disputed the Committee's conclusions and recommendations and characterized them as seriously inaccurate in major respects.

QUESTION

How do you assess US policy and legislation on torture since 11 September with respect to its consistency with international human rights?

ADDITIONAL READING

Amnesty International, *Torture Worldwide: An Affront to Human Dignity* (2000); Karen Greenberg (ed.), *The Torture Debate in America* (2005); Karen Greenberg and Joshua Dratel (eds.), *The Torture Papers: The Road to Abu Ghraib* (2005); John Langbein, *Torture and the Law of Proof: Europe and England in the Ancien Regime* (2006, republication of 1977 book of same title); Sanford Levinson (ed.), *Torture: A Collection* (2004); Manfred Nowak, 'What Practices Constitute Torture?: US and UN Standards', 28 Hum. Rts Q. 809 (2006); Kenneth Roth, Minky Worden and Amy Bernstein, *Torture: Does It Make Us Safer? Is It Ever OK?: A Human Rights Perspective* (2005); 'Symposium: Torture and the War on Terror', 37 Case Western Reserve J. of Int. L. Nos. 2 and 3 (2006).

4

Economic and Social Rights

A. SOCIO-ECONOMIC CONTEXT AND HISTORICAL BACKGROUND

The Universal Declaration of Human Rights recognizes two sets of human rights: the 'traditional' civil and political rights, as well as economic, social and cultural rights. In transforming the Declaration's provisions into legally binding obligations, the United Nations adopted two separate International Covenants which, taken together, constitute the bedrock of the international normative regime for human rights. The issues raised in earlier Chapters concentrated on civil and political rights. This chapter explores the International Covenant on Economic, Social and Cultural Rights (ICESCR).

The 'official' position, dating back to the Universal Declaration and reaffirmed in innumerable resolutions since that time, is that the two covenants and sets of rights are, in the words adopted by the 1993 second World Conference on Human Rights in Vienna, 'universal, indivisible and interdependent and interrelated. The international community must treat human rights globally in a fair and equal manner, on the same footing, and with the same emphasis.' (Vienna Declaration, para. 5). But this formal consensus, although restated by the UN General Assembly in its 2005 resolution creating the Human Rights Council, masks a deep and enduring disagreement over the proper status of economic, social and cultural rights. At one extreme lies the view that these rights are superior to civil and political rights in terms of an appropriate value hierarchy and in chronological terms. Of what use is the right to free speech to those who are starving and illiterate? The homeless cannot register to vote, the illiterate cannot fully exercise their political rights. At the other extreme we find the view that economic and social rights ('ESR') do not constitute rights (as properly understood) at all. Treating them as rights undermines the enjoyment of individual freedom, distorts the functioning of free markets by justifying large-scale state intervention in the economy, and provides an excuse to downgrade the importance of civil and political rights.

Although variations on these extremes have dominated both diplomatic and academic discourse, the great majority of governments has taken some sort of intermediate position. For the most part that position has involved (a) support for the equal status and importance of ESR (as of January 2007, 155 states were parties to the ICESCR, compared with 160 parties to the ICCPR), together with (b) failure to take steps to entrench those rights constitutionally, to adopt legislative or administrative provisions based explicitly on the recognition of specific ESR as international human rights, or to provide effective means of redress to individuals or groups alleging violations of those rights. Indeed, one of the puzzles in the field lies in the rare invocation of the ICESCR in the play of internal politics or in the judiciaries in most states, compared with the frequent invocation of civil and political rights treaties.

Even before the final adoption of the UDHR, the debate over the relationship between the two sets of rights had become a casualty of the Cold War: the Communist countries abstained from voting on its adoption by the General Assembly on the grounds that the ESR provisions were inadequate, and the Western countries were insistent that there should be two Covenants rather than a single integrated one. Since the 1970s, the debate has also taken on important North-South dimensions. These include claims that developing countries should not be held to the same standards in some respects and that respect for rights by poorer states must be linked to international aid, and trade and other concessions. As a result, the debate carries a lot of ideological baggage. With the rejection of communism and the widespread embrace of free-market economic solutions within the ongoing processes of globalization, ESR are certain to remain among the most controversial issues in the years ahead. Those issues will have important implications for other aspects of human rights law.

In a statement to the Vienna World Conference in 1993, the UN Committee on Economic, Social and Cultural Rights (hereafter the ESCR Committee) drew attention to:

> [t]he shocking reality . . . that States and the international community as a whole continue to tolerate all too often breaches of economic, social and cultural rights which, if they occurred in relation to civil and political rights, would provoke expressions of horror and outrage and would lead to concerted calls for immediate remedial action. In effect, despite the rhetoric, violations of civil and political rights continue to be treated as though they were far more serious, and more patently intolerable, than massive and direct denials of economic, social and cultural rights. . . .
>
> . . . Statistical indicators of the extent of deprivation, or breaches, of economic, social and cultural rights have been cited so often that they have tended to lose their impact. The magnitude, severity and constancy of that deprivation have provoked attitudes of resignation, feelings of helplessness and compassion fatigue. Such muted responses are facilitated by a reluctance to characterize the problems that exist as gross and massive denials of economic, social and cultural rights. Yet it is difficult to understand how the situation can realistically be portrayed in any other way.[1]

SOCIAL AND ECONOMIC STATISTICS

Despite the ESCR Committee's sense that statistical indicators of deprivation have lost much of their impact it is essential to have at least a general sense of the major

[1] UN Doc. E/1993/22, Annex III, paras 5 and 7.

dimensions of poverty, against the backdrop of which the debate about ESR takes place. Consider the following snapshots.

International Cooperation at a Crossroads: Aid, Trade and Security in an Unequal World

UNDP, Human Development Report 2005 (New York, 2005) p. 1

The year 2004 ended with an event that demonstrated the destructive power of nature and the regenerative power of human compassion. The tsunami that swept across the Indian Ocean left some 300,000 people dead. Millions more were left homeless. Within days of the tsunami, one of the worst natural disasters in recent history had given rise to the world's greatest international relief effort, showing what can be achieved through global solidarity when the international community commits itself to a great endeavour.

The tsunami was a highly visible, unpredictable and largely unpreventable tragedy. Other tragedies are less visible, monotonously predictable and readily preventable. Every hour more than 1,200 children die away from the glare of media attention. This is equivalent to three tsunamis a month, every month, hitting the world's most vulnerable citizens — its children. The causes of death will vary, but the overwhelming majority can be traced to a single pathology: poverty. Unlike the tsunami, that pathology is preventable. With today's technology, financial resources and accumulated knowledge, the world has the capacity to overcome extreme deprivation. Yet as an international community we allow poverty to destroy lives on a scale that dwarfs the impact of the tsunami.

The state of human development

...

Much has been achieved since [1990]. On average, people in developing countries are healthier, better educated and less impoverished — and they are more likely to live in a multiparty democracy. Since 1990 life expectancy in developing countries has increased by 2 years. There are 3 million fewer child deaths annually and 30 million fewer children out of school. More than 130 million people have escaped extreme poverty. These human development gains should not be underestimated.

Nor should they be exaggerated. In 2003, 18 countries with a combined population of 460 million people registered lower scores on the human development index (HDI) than in 1990 — an unprecedented reversal. In the midst of an increasingly prosperous global economy, 10.7 million children every year do not live to see their fifth birthday, and more than 1 billion people survive in abject poverty on less than $1 a day. The HIV/AIDS pandemic has inflicted the single greatest reversal in human development. In 2003 the pandemic claimed 3 million lives and left another 5 million people infected. Millions of children have been orphaned.... In human development terms the space between countries is marked by deep and, in some cases, widening inequalities in income and life chances. One-fifth of humanity live in countries where many people think nothing of spending $2 a day on a cappuccino. Another fifth of humanity survive on less than $1 a day and live in countries where children die for want of a simple anti-mosquito bednet.

At the start of the twenty-first century we live in a divided world. The size of the divide poses a fundamental challenge to the global human community. Part of that challenge is ethical and moral....

...

Debates about trends in global income distribution continue to rage. Less open to debate is the sheer scale of inequality. The world's richest 500 individuals have a combined income greater than that of the poorest 416 million. Beyond these extremes, the 2.5 billion people living on less than $2 a day — 40% of the world's population — account for 5% of global income. The richest 10%, almost all of whom live in high-income countries, account for 54%. An obvious corollary of extreme global inequality is that even modest shifts in distribution from top to bottom could have dramatic effects on poverty. Using a global income distribution database, we estimate a cost of $300 billion for lifting 1 billion people living on less than $1 a day above the extreme poverty line threshold. That amount represents 1.6% of the income of the richest 10% of the world's population. Of course, this figure describes a static transfer. Achieving sustainable poverty reduction requires dynamic processes through which poor countries and poor people can produce their way out of extreme deprivation. But in our highly unequal world greater equity would provide a powerful catalyst for poverty reduction....

Beyond Scarcity: Power, Poverty and the Global Water Crisis, UNDP, Human Development Report 2006

(New York, 2006) Foreword, p. v

...

Access to water for life is a basic human need and a fundamental human right. Yet in our increasingly prosperous world, more than 1 billion people are denied the right to clean water and 2.6 billion people lack access to adequate sanitation. These headline numbers capture only one dimension of the problem. Every year some 1.8 million children die as a result of diarrhoea and other diseases caused by unclean water and poor sanitation. At the start of the 21st century unclean water is the world's second biggest killer of children. Every day millions of women and young girls collect water for their families — a ritual that reinforces gender inequalities in employment and education. Meanwhile, the ill health associated with deficits in water and sanitation undermines productivity and economic growth, reinforcing the deep inequalities that characterize current patterns of globalization and trapping vulnerable households in cycles of poverty.

As this Report shows, the sources of the problem vary by country, but several themes emerge. First, few countries treat water and sanitation as a political priority, as witnessed by limited budget allocations. Second, some of the world's poorest people are paying some of the world's highest prices for water, reflecting the limited coverage of water utilities in the slums and informal settlements where poor people live. Third, the international community has failed to prioritize water and sanitation in the partnerships for development that have coalesced around the Millennium Development Goals. Underlying each of these problems is the fact that the people suffering the most from the water and sanitation crisis — poor people in general and poor women in particular — often lack the political voice needed to assert their claims to water.

. . . At the start of the 21st century we have the finance, technology and capacity to consign the water and sanitation crisis to history just as surely as today's rich countries did a century ago. What has been lacking is a concerted drive to extend access to water and sanitation for all through well designed and properly financed national plans, backed by a global plan of action to galvanize political will and mobilize resources.

. . .

U.S. Census Bureau, 'Income Climbs, Poverty Stabilizes, Uninsured Rate Increases'

29 August 2006[2]

[The following are excerpts from this press statement.]

Poverty

[In the U.S. there] were 37 million people in poverty (12.6 percent) in 2005.

[T]he average poverty threshold for a family of four in 2005 was $19,971; for a family of three, $15,577; for a family of two, $12,755; and for unrelated individuals, $9,973.

Poverty rates remained statistically unchanged for blacks (24.9 percent) and Hispanics (21.8 percent).

The poverty rate in 2005 for children under 18 (17.6 percent) remained higher than that of 18-to-64-year olds (11.1 percent) and that of people 65 and older (10.1 percent).

Health Insurance Coverage

The number of people with health insurance coverage increased by 1.4 million to 247.3 million between 2004 and 2005, and the number without such coverage rose by 1.3 million to 46.6 million (from 15.6 percent in 2004 to 15.9 percent in 2005).

The proportion and number of uninsured children increased between 2004 and 2005, from 10.8 percent to 11.2 percent and from 7.9 million to 8.3 million, respectively.

Pankaj Mishra, 'The Myth of the New India'

New York Times, July 6, 2006

"India is a roaring capitalist success story." So says the latest issue of *Foreign Affairs* [magazine] . . . .

. . .

[2] At http://www.census.gov/Press-Release/www/releases/archives/income_wealth/007419.html.

It was not so long ago that India appeared in the American press as a poor, backward and often violent nation, saddled with an inefficient bureaucracy....

...

Since the early 1990's, when the Indian economy was liberalized, India has emerged as the world leader in information technology and business outsourcing, with an average growth of about 6 percent a year. Growing foreign investment and easy credit have fueled a consumer revolution in urban areas....

But the increasingly common, business-centric view of India suppresses more facts than it reveals .... [T]he country's $728 per capita gross domestic product is just slightly higher than that of sub-Saharan Africa and that ... even if it sustains its current high growth rates, India will not catch up with high-income countries until 2106.

Nor is India rising very fast on [UNDP's] Human Development Index, where it ranks 127, just two rungs above Myanmar and more than 70 below Cuba and Mexico. Despite a recent reduction in poverty levels, nearly 380 million Indians still live on less than a dollar a day.

Malnutrition affects half of all children in India, and there is little sign that they are being helped by the country's market reforms, which have focused on creating private wealth rather than expanding access to health care and education. Despite the country's growing economy, 2.5 million Indian children die annually, accounting for one out of every five child deaths worldwide; and facilities for primary education have collapsed in large parts of the country (the official literacy rate of 61 percent includes many who can barely write their names). In the countryside, where 70 percent of India's population lives, the government has reported that about 100,000 farmers committed suicide between 1993 and 2003.

Feeding on the resentment of those left behind by the urban-oriented economic growth, communist insurgencies (unrelated to India's parliamentary communist parties) have erupted in some of the most populous and poorest parts of north and central India. The Indian government no longer effectively controls many of the districts where communists battle landlords and police, imposing a harsh form of justice on a largely hapless rural population.

The potential for conflict — among castes as well as classes — also grows in urban areas, where India's cruel social and economic disparities are as evident as its new prosperity. The main reason for this is that India's economic growth has been largely jobless. Only 1.3 million out of a working population of 400 million are employed in the information technology and business processing industries that make up the so-called new economy.

No labor-intensive manufacturing boom of the kind that powered the economic growth of almost every developed and developing country in the world has yet occurred in India....

... [R]egular elections may not be enough to contain the frustration and rage of millions of have-nots, or to shield them from the temptations of religious and ideological extremism.

Many serious problems confront India. They are unlikely to be solved as long as the wealthy, both inside and outside the country, choose to believe their own complacent myths.

QUESTION

Do the preceding analyses describe violations of ESR or simply regrettable, but perhaps inevitable, inequalities? Is the ESCR Committee fudging important terminological issues when it claims that we tolerate 'breaches of economic, social and cultural rights which, if they occurred in relation to civil and political rights, would provoke expressions of horror and outrage'?

COMMENT ON HISTORICAL ORIGINS OF ECONOMIC AND SOCIAL RIGHTS

The historical origins of the recognition of ESR are diffuse. Those rights have drawn strength from the injunctions expressed in different religious traditions to care for those in need and those who cannot look after themselves. In Catholicism, papal encyclicals have long promoted the importance of the right to subsistence with dignity, while 'liberation theology' has sought to build upon this 'preferential option for the poor'. Virtually all of the major religions manifest comparable concern for the poor and oppressed (see pp. 293–4 *infra*). Other sources include philosophical analyses and political theory from authors as diverse as Thomas Paine, Karl Marx, Immanuel Kant and John Rawls; the political programmes of the nineteenth century Fabian socialists in Britain, Chancellor Bismarck in Germany (who introduced social insurance schemes in the 1880s), and the New Dealers in the United States; and constitutional precedents such as the Mexican Constitution of 1917, the first and subsequent Soviet Constitutions, and the 1919 Constitution of the Weimar Republic (embodying the *Wohlfahrtsstaat* concept).

This comment concentrates on the evolution of these ideas in international human rights law. The most appropriate starting point is the International Labour Organization (ILO). Established by the Treaty of Versailles in 1919 to abolish the 'injustice, hardship and privation' which workers suffered and to guarantee 'fair and humane conditions of labour', it was conceived as the response of Western countries to the ideologies of Bolshevism and Socialism arising out of the Russian Revolution.[3]

In the interwar years, the ILO adopted international minimum standards in relation to a wide range of matters which now fall under the rubric of ESR. They included, *inter alia*, conventions dealing with freedom of association and the right to organize trade unions, forced labour, minimum working age, hours of work, weekly rest, sickness protection, accident insurance, invalidity and old-age insurance, and freedom from discrimination in employment. The Great Depression of the early 1930s underscored the need for social protection of those who were unemployed and gave a strong impetus to full employment policies such as those advocated by Keynes in his *General Theory of Employment, Interest and Money* (1936).

[3] J.T. Shotwell, 'The International Labor Organization as an Alternative to Violent Revolution', 166, The Annals of the American Academy of Political and Social Science (1933) 18.

Partly as a result of these developments, various proposals were made during the drafting of the UN Charter for the inclusion of provisions enshrining the maintenance of 'full employment' as a commitment to be undertaken by Member States. The strongest version, known after its principal proponents as the 'Australian Pledge', committed UN members to take action to secure 'improved labour standards, economic advancement, social security, and employment for all who seek it'.[4]

Despite significant support, the United States opposed the proposal on the grounds that any such undertaking would involve interference in the domestic, economic and political affairs of states. Ultimately agreement was reached on Article 55(a) of the Charter, which simply states that the United Nations shall promote 'higher standards of living, full employment, and conditions of economic and social progress and development' but does not call for specific follow-up at the international level.

US opposition in this context did not signify the rejection of ESR *per se*. Indeed, in 1941 President Roosevelt had nominated 'freedom from want' as one of the four freedoms that should characterize the future world order. He spelled out this vision in his 1944 State of the Union address.[5]

> We have come to a clear realization of the fact that true individual freedom cannot exist without economic security and independence. 'Necessitous men are not free men.' People who are out of a job are the stuff of which dictatorships are made.
>
> In our day these economic truths have become accepted as self-evident. We have accepted, so to speak, a second bill of rights, under which a new basis of security and prosperity can be established for all — regardless of station, race, or creed.
>
> Among these are:
>
> The right to a useful and remunerative job in the industries, or shops, or farms, or mines of the Nation;
> The right to earn enough to provide adequate food and clothing and recreation;
> The right of every farmer to raise and sell his products at a return which will give him and his family a decent living;
> The right of every businessman, large and small, to trade in an atmosphere of freedom from unfair competition and domination by monopolies at home or abroad;
> The right of every family to a decent home;
> The right to adequate medical care and the opportunity to achieve and enjoy good health;
> The right to adequate protection from the economic fears of old age, sickness, accident, and unemployment;
> The right to a good education.
>
> All of these rights spell security. And after this war is won we must be prepared to move forward, in the implementation of these rights, to new goals of human happiness and well-being.

[4] See generally Ruth Russell and Jean Muther, *A History of the United Nations Charter: The Role of the United States* 1940–1945 (1958), at 786.

[5] Eleventh Annual Message to Congress (11 January 1944), in J. Israel (ed.), *The State of the Union Messages of the Presidents* (1966), Vol. 3, at 2881. See generally Cass Sunstein, *The Second Bill of Rights: FDR's Unfinished Revolution and Why We Need It More than Ever* (2004).

This approach was subsequently reflected in a draft international Bill of Rights, completed in 1944, by a Committee appointed by the American Law Institute. In addition to listing the rights contained in the US Bill of Rights (the first ten amendments to the Constitution), the Institute's proposal advocated international recognition of a range of rights and acceptance of the correlative duties in relation to education, work, reasonable conditions of work, adequate food and housing, and social security.[6] In relation to each of the proposed rights, a Comment by the Committee drew attention to the fact that it had already been recognized in the 'current or recent constitutions' of many countries; e.g., 40 countries in the case of the right to education; 9 for the right to work; 11 for the right to adequate housing; 27 for the right to social security.

Although these proposals of the Committee were never formally endorsed by the American Law Institute, they were submitted to the United Nations and were to prove highly influential in the preparation of the first draft of the Universal Declaration in 1947. In the drafting of Articles 22–28 of the UDHR, strong support for the inclusion of ESR came from the United States (a delegation led by Eleanor Roosevelt), Egypt, several Latin American countries (particularly Chile) and from the (Communist) countries of Eastern Europe. Australia and the United Kingdom opposed their inclusion,[7] as did South Africa which objected first that 'a condition of existence does not constitute a fundamental human right merely because it is eminently desirable for the fullest realization of all human potentialities' and secondly that if the proposed economic rights were to be taken seriously it would be 'necessary to resort to more or less totalitarian control of the economic life of the country'.[8]

After the adoption of the Universal Declaration in 1948, the next step was to translate the rights it recognized in Articles 22–28 into binding treaty obligations. This process took from 1949 to 1966. The delay was due to reasons including the Cold War, developing US opposition to the principle of international human rights treaties, and the scope and complexity of the proposed obligations. By 1955, the main lines of what was to become the ICESCR were agreed.

The following analysis of the drafting process, prepared by the United Nations, captures the main dilemmas and controversies relating to the inclusion of economic, social and cultural rights.[9]

> ... [Between 1949 and 1951 the Commission on Human Rights worked on a single draft covenant dealing with both of the categories of rights. But in 1951 the General Assembly, under pressure from the Western-dominated Commission, agreed to draft two separate covenants] ... to contain 'as many similar provisions as possible' and to be approved and opened for signature simultaneously, in order to emphasize the unity of purpose.
>
> ...

[6] See Statement of Essential Human Rights, UN Doc. A/148 (1947), Arts 11–15.

[7] See B. Andreassen, 'Article 22', A. and W. B. Eide, 'Article 25', in G. Alfredsson and A. Eide (eds.), *The Universal Declaration of Human Rights* (1999); and J. Morsink, *The Universal Declaration of Human Rights: Origins, Drafting and Intent* (1999) Chs 5–6.

[8] UN Doc. E/CN.4/82/Add.4 (1948) 11, 13.

[9] Annotations on the Text of the Draft International Covenants on Human Rights, UN Doc. A/2929 (1955), at 7.

8. Those who were in favour of drafting a single covenant maintained that human rights could not be clearly divided into different categories, nor could they be so classified as to represent a hierarchy of values. All rights should be promoted and protected at the same time. Without economic, social and cultural rights, civil and political rights might be purely nominal in character; without civil and political rights, economic, social and cultural rights could not be long ensured . . .

9. Those in favour of drafting two separate covenants argued that civil and political rights were enforceable, or justiciable, or of an 'absolute' character, while economic, social and cultural rights were not or might not be; that the former were immediately applicable, while the latter were to be progressively implemented; and that, generally speaking, the former were rights of the individual 'against' the State, that is, against unlawful and unjust action of the State, while the latter were rights which the State would have to take positive action to promote. Since the nature of civil and political rights and that of economic, social and cultural rights, and the obligations of the State in respect thereof, were different, it was desirable that two separate instruments should be prepared.

10. The question of drafting one or two covenants was intimately related to the question of implementation. If no measures of implementation were to be formulated, it would make little difference whether one or two covenants were to be drafted. Generally speaking, civil and political rights were thought to be 'legal' rights and could best be implemented by the creation of a good offices committee, while economic, social and cultural rights were thought to be 'programme' rights and could best be implemented by the establishment of a system of periodic reports. Since the rights could be divided into two broad categories, which should be subject to different procedures of implementation, it would be both logical and convenient to formulate two separate covenants.

11. However, it was argued that not in all countries and territories were all civil and political rights 'legal' rights, nor all economic, social and cultural rights 'programme' rights. A civil or political right might well be a 'programme' right under one régime, an economic, social or cultural right a 'legal' right under another. A covenant could be drafted in such a manner as would enable States, upon ratification or accession, to announce, each in so far as it was concerned, which civil, political, economic, social and cultural rights were 'legal' rights, and which 'programme' rights, and by which procedures the rights would be implemented.

. . .

NOTE

This Covenant was adopted by the General Assembly in Res. 2200A (XXI) of 16 December 1966 and entered into force on 3 January 1976. It is divided into five 'Parts'. Part I (like Part I of the ICCPR) recognizes the right of peoples to self-determination; Part II defines the general nature of states parties obligations; Part III enumerates the specific substantive rights; Part IV deals with international implementation; and Part V contains typical final provisions of a human rights treaty. In terms of substantive rights the right to property, although recognized in the Universal Declaration, was not included, primarily because of the inability of governments to agree on a formulation governing public takings and the compensation therefor.

Economic and social rights are not in any sense restricted to the ICESCR. To the contrary, they figure in most of the other major treaties.

While it is essential to read the full text of the Covenant, the following excerpts from Parts II and III provide a flavour of some of the key issues. Later materials explore the meaning of Article 2.

EXCERPTS FROM THE ICESCR

...

PART II
Article 2

1. Each State Party to the present Covenant undertakes to take steps, individually and through international assistance and co-operation, especially economic and technical, to the maximum of its available resources, with a view to achieving progressively the full realization of the rights recognized in the present Covenant by all appropriate means, including particularly the adoption of legislative measures.

...

PART III
Article 6

1. The States Parties to the present Covenant recognize the right to work, which includes the right of everyone to the opportunity to gain his living by work which he freely chooses or accepts, and will take appropriate steps to safeguard this right.

2. The steps to be taken by a State Party to the present Covenant to achieve the full realization of this right shall include technical and vocational guidance and training programmes, policies and techniques to achieve steady economic, social and cultural development and full and productive employment under conditions safeguarding fundamental political and economic freedoms to the individual.

Article 7

The States Parties to the present Covenant recognize the right of everyone to the enjoyment of just and favourable conditions of work which ensure, in particular:

(a) Remuneration which provides all workers, as a minimum, with:

(i) Fair wages and equal remuneration for work of equal value . . . ;
(ii) A decent living for themselves and their families . . . ;

(b) Safe and healthy working conditions;

...

(d) Rest, leisure and reasonable limitation of working hours and periodic holidays with pay, as well as remuneration for public holidays

. . .

Article 9

The States Parties to the present Covenant recognize the right of everyone to social security, including social insurance.

. . .

Article 11

1. The States Parties to the present Covenant recognize the right of everyone to an adequate standard of living for himself and his family, including adequate food, clothing and housing, and to the continuous improvement of living conditions . . . .

2. The States Parties to the present Covenant, recognizing the fundamental right of everyone to be free from hunger, shall take, individually and through international co-operation, the measures, including specific programmes, which are needed:

(a) To improve methods of production, conservation and distribution of food . . .

. . .

Article 12

1. The States Parties to the present Covenant recognize the right of everyone to the enjoyment of the highest attainable standard of physical and mental health.

2. The steps to be taken by the States Parties to the present Covenant to achieve the full realization of this right shall include those necessary for:

(a) The provision for the reduction of the stillbirth-rate and of infant mortality and for the healthy development of the child;
(b) The improvement of all aspects of environmental and industrial hygiene;
(c) The prevention, treatment and control of epidemic, endemic, occupational and other diseases;
(d) The creation of conditions which would assure to all medical service and medical attention in the event of sickness.

Article 13

1. The States Parties to the present Covenant recognize the right of everyone to education . . . .

2. The States Parties to the present Covenant recognize that, with a view to achieving the full realization of this right:

(a) Primary education shall be compulsory and available free to all;
(b) Secondary education . . . shall be made generally available and accessible to all by every appropriate means, and in particular by the progressive introduction of free education;

(c) Higher education shall be made equally accessible to all, on the basis of capacity, by every appropriate means, and in particular by the progressive introduction of free education;

...

COMMENT ON ASPECTS OF ICESCR

Differences between the ICESCR and the ICCPR

There are many differences between the two major Covenants, including terminology. For example, the ICCPR contains terms such as 'everyone has the right to ...', or 'no one shall be ...', whereas the ICESCR usually employs the formula 'States Parties recognize the right of everyone to ...'. Two major differences should be noted, both appearing in the key provision of Article 2(1). First, the obligation of states parties stated in that provision is recognized to be subject to the availability of resources ('to the maximum of its available resources'). And second, the obligation is one of progressive realization ('with a view to achieving progressively').

This language has been subject to conflicting critiques. On the one hand, it is often suggested that the nature of the obligation under the ICESCR is so onerous that virtually no government will be able to comply. Developing countries, in particular, are seen to be confronting an impossible challenge. On the other hand, it is argued that the relative open-endedness of the concept of progressive realization, particularly in light of the qualification about availability of resources, renders the obligation devoid of meaningful content. Governments can present themselves as defenders of ESR without international imposition of any precise constraints on their policies and behaviour. A related criticism is that the Covenant imposes only 'programmatic' obligations upon governments — that is, obligations to be fulfilled incrementally through the ongoing execution of a programme. It therefore becomes difficult if not impossible to determine when those obligations ought to be met or indeed have been met.

Interdependence of the two Covenants

The interdependence of the two categories of rights has always been part of UN doctrine. The UDHR of 1948 included both categories without any sense of separateness or priority. The Preamble to the ICESCR, in terms mirroring those used in the ICCPR, states that 'in accordance with the Universal Declaration ..., the ideal of free human beings enjoying freedom from fear and want can only be achieved if conditions are created whereby everyone may enjoy his economic, social and cultural rights, as well as his civil and political rights'.

The interdependence principle, apart from its use as a political compromise between advocates of one or two covenants, reflects the fact that the two sets of rights can neither logically nor practically be separated in watertight compartments. Civil and political rights may constitute the condition for and thus be implicit in ESR.

Or a given right might fit equally well within either covenant, depending on the purpose for which it is declared. Some illustrations follow:

(1) The right to form trade unions is contained in the ICESCR, while the right to freedom of association is recognized in the ICCPR.
(2) The ICESCR recognizes various 'liberties' and 'freedoms' in relation to scientific research and creative activity.
(3) While the right to education and the parental liberty to choose a child's school are dealt with in the ICESCR (Art. 13), the liberty of parents to choose their child's religious and moral education is recognized in the ICCPR (Art. 18).
(4) The prohibition of discrimination in relation to the provision of, and access to, educational facilities and opportunities can be derived from both Art. 2 of the ICESCR and Art. 26 of the ICCPR.
(5) Even the European Convention on Human Rights, which is generally considered to cover only civil and political rights issues, states (in Art. 2 of Protocol 1) that 'no person shall be denied the right to education'.

Economic rights, social rights, cultural rights

The ICESCR does not make explicit any distinction between economic, social or cultural rights. Commentators differ as to their characterization of one or the other of the declared rights,[10] or ignore the distinction. The original drafting rationale was an essentially bureaucratic one: the rights of concern to the ILO (Arts. 6–9) were assumed to be 'economic', those relevant to UN agencies such as the Food and Agriculture Organization and the World Health Organization (Arts. 10–12) were treated as 'social', and those that fell within the sphere of interest of UNESCO (Arts 13–15) were designated as 'cultural'. In practice, however, most such distinctions are difficult to maintain. Education, for example, can arguably be classified as belonging to all of the relevant categories — economic, social, and cultural, not to mention civil and political.

Although the title of the ICESCR expressly refers to 'cultural rights' and Article 15(1) recognizes 'the right of everyone . . . to take part in cultural life', such rights have attracted relatively little attention in this context. Rather, they have tended to be dealt with in relation to the ICCPR, whether under its non-discrimination clause (Art. 2(1)), the minorities provision (Art. 27), or specific rights such as freedoms of expression, religion, and association and the right to 'take part in the conduct of public affairs'. The consequence has been a clear neglect of the specifically economic and social rights dimensions of cultural rights.

Implementation — the ESCR Committee

The greatest challenge is to identify effective approaches to implementation — i.e., to the means by which ESCR can be given effect and governments can be held

[10] E.g. Henry Steiner, 'Social Rights and Economic Development: Converging Discourses?', 4 Buffalo Hum. Rts. L. Rev. 25 (1998), at 27.

accountable to fulfil their obligations. The Covenant says only that governments must use 'all appropriate means' to work towards the stated ends. Such means may be universally valid or relevant or may be quite specific to a particular culture or legal system. The Covenant gives no further pointers, beyond noting that 'appropriate means' includes 'particularly the adoption of legislative measures'. It is clear, however, that neither legislation nor effective remedies of a judicial nature, which are both central to the domestic implementation framework contained in the ICCPR (Art. 2), will play the same roles or *per se* be sufficient in relation to the ICESCR.

The principal UN body concerned with ESCR is the Committee on Economic, Social and Cultural Rights (the ESCR Committee). The creation of the Committee was not foreseen in the text of the Covenant. It first met in 1987, having been established by a 1985 resolution of the Economic and Social Council after earlier monitoring arrangements had failed. The Committee has 18 independent expert member, elected for four-year terms on the basis of equitable geographic representation. In most respects it functions along the same lines as the ICCPR Committee, the work of which is analyzed in detail in Chapter 10, *infra*, and the CEDAW Committee discussed in Chapter 3, *supra*. For that reason, little detail as to procedures etc is provided in the present context. Its task is to supervise compliance by states parties with their obligations under the ICESCR. It does this on the basis of regular reports submitted by states parties in accordance with its 'reporting guidelines'. An initial report by each state party is due within two years, and subsequent reports are required at five-yearly intervals. It has also been active in producing General Comments.[11] The Committee seeks to: (1) develop the normative content of the rights recognized in the Covenant; (2) act as a catalyst to state action in developing national mechanisms for establishing accountability, and providing means of vindication to aggrieved individuals and groups; and (3) hold states accountable at the international level through the examination of reports. The ICESCR does not yet have a complaints procedure, although a draft protocol for this purpose is being prepared (see p. 362 *infra*). The Committee also holds a 'day of general discussion' at most of its sessions to enable experts from civil society, academia, international agencies and elsewhere to discuss key issues relating to ESCR. The examination of a state's report by the Committee culminates in the adoption of the Committee's concluding observations.

An example, dealing with Albania, follows. Note by way of background that Albania is one of the poorest countries in Europe and has been undergoing major economic restructuring after the end of Communist rule in 1990. Since 1990, one-fifth of the population has moved abroad. The tax revenue-to-GDP ratio is about

[11] Between 1989 and January 2007 the ESCR Committee adopted 18 General Comments. The subjects and dates of adoption are as follows: No. 1: Reporting by States parties (1989); No. 2: International technical assistance (1990); No. 3: The nature of States parties' obligations (1990); No. 4: Right to adequate housing (1991); No. 5: Persons with disabilities (1994); No. 6: ESCR of older persons (1995); No. 7: Forced evictions (1997); No. 8: Economic sanctions and ESCR (1997); No. 9: Domestic application of the Covenant (1998); No. 10: National human rights institutions and ESCR (1998); No. 11: Plans of action for primary education (1999); No. 12: Right to adequate food (1999); No. 13: Right to education (1999); No. 14: Right to health (2000); No. 15: Right to water (2002); No. 16: Equal right of men and women to ESCR (2005); No. 17: Authorial rights under Art. 15(1)(c); and No. 18: Right to work (2005). In 2007 work was continuing on the drafting of General Comments on Article 2 (2) (non-discrimination) and on Article 9 (the right to social security). The Committee's are published annually. See UN Doc. HRI/GEN/1/Rev.8 (2006). Or see http://www.ohchr.org/english/bodies/cescr/comments.htm.

23% compared to 40% in comparable countries, and the black market is huge. Poverty is pervasive and one Albanian in four lives below the poverty line.[12]

CONCLUDING OBSERVATIONS OF THE ESCR COMMITTEE: ALBANIA

UN Doc. E/C.12/ALB/CO/1 (2006)

. . .

E. Suggestions and recommendations

. . .

44. The Committee urges the State party to ensure the justiciability of the Covenant rights in domestic courts and draws its attention to General Comment No. 9 . . . .

45. . . . The Committee strongly urges the State party to take all necessary measures to ensure the independence, integrity, security and training of the judiciary.

46. The Committee strongly urges the State party to take effective measures to combat corruption and preferential treatment based on family ties within all areas of government and public administration and, in particular, to increase transparency and consultations at all levels of decision-making.

47. The Committee . . . urges the national statistical agency and relevant ministries to review the ways in which data relating to all rights are collected in accordance to the provisions of the Covenant.

48. The Committee urges the State party to ensure that the lack of registration and other personal identity documents do not become an obstacle to the enjoyment of [ESCR] . . . . In this regard, the Committee also recommends the State party to undertake public awareness campaigns on the importance of birth and other forms of civil registration, and consider lowering the registration fees.

49. . . . The Committee also urges the State party to provide specific training to law enforcement officers to ensure that, in the performance of their duties, they respect and protect human rights of all persons without distinction as to race, colour, national or ethnic origin. Incidents of police violence should be thoroughly investigated and perpetrators promptly brought to justice.

. . .

51. The Committee recommends that the State party step up the necessary measures, legislative or otherwise, to promote equality between men and women . . . .

52. The Committee urges the State party to increase its efforts to combat unemployment through special targeted programmes, including programmes aimed at reducing unemployment among disadvantaged and marginalized groups. The Committee, also noting the high levels of rural to urban migration, recommends that the State party take measures to stimulate rural development, inter alia, through local employment initiatives . . . .

[12] Albania: Sustaining Growth Beyond the Transition, A World Bank Country Economic Memorandum, 27 December 2004.

...

56. The Committee calls upon the State party to ensure that targeted social assistance depending on family income is guaranteed to all disadvantaged and marginalized individuals and families, and that such assistance does not fall below the subsistence level. . . .

...

58. The Committee . . . strongly recommends that the State party strengthen its efforts to eliminate the practice of "vendetta" killings and other forms of violence . . . .

...

60. The Committee urges the State party to ensure the full integration of economic, social and cultural rights in its social development and poverty reduction strategies, and allocate sufficient funds for the implementation of these strategies . . . . The Committee encourages the State party to develop indicators and benchmarks on an annual basis, disaggregated by gender, age, urban-rural population and ethnic background for the purpose of specifically assessing the needs of disadvantaged and marginalised individuals and groups . . . .

61. The Committee urges the State party to take effective measures to provide evicted persons with adequate compensation or with alternative accommodation . . . .

62. The Committee urges the State party to undertake the necessary measures to improve its health services, by, *inter alia*, increasing the budgetary allocations to the health sector and extending basic health services to rural areas . . . .

63. The Committee urges the State party to allocate sufficient resources to ensure that reproductive health services and education, as well as adequate perinatal and postnatal healthcare services are available and fully accessible to women and girls, including those in rural areas.

...

66. The Committee urges the State party to take all necessary measures to allocate the required resources to improve the quality of education offered in schools at all levels . . . .

69. The Committee encourages the State party to consider increasing the proportion of budget allocated to cultural development and participation in cultural life.

QUESTIONS

1. Consider the following issues in relation to the excerpts from the ICESCR: does the right to work amount to a guarantee of employment? Is Article 7 on working conditions utopian or relevant only to an advanced industrial economy? Is the much-derided 'right to holidays with pay' defensible? How could the right to social security be meaningful in a poor developing country? Why is the right to health not formulated in terms of a right of access to health care? Is the vision of the right to education in Article 13 outdated?

2. Based on the example of Albania how would you assess the approach of the Committee in its Concluding Observations?

ADDITIONAL READING

P. Alston, 'The Committee on Economic, Social and Cultural Rights', in P. Alston and F. Mégret (eds.), *The UN and Human Rights* (2nd edn. 2007); P. Alston and G. Quinn, 'The Nature and Scope of States Parties' Obligations Under the International Covenant on Economic, Social and Cultural Rights', 9 Hum. Rts Q. 156 (1987).

B. COMPETING PERSPECTIVES ON ESR

In the following materials we examine some of the philosophical, religious, economic and legal challenges that are frequently posed by the critics of ESR, both at the national and international levels. The materials tend to emphasize the United States debate, partly because the US has been the key dissenter on these issues in international fora and partly because US-style economic liberalism is increasingly being followed elsewhere.

Before reviewing the various critiques, however, it is important to note that there are many situations in which the concept and practice of ESR are widely accepted. The right to education, at least at primary school level, is almost universally recognized and has achieved extensive constitutional recognition. When people are forcibly evicted from their homes and have nowhere else to live, most legal systems recognize some dimensions of their right to shelter or housing. The deliberate denial of access to food — whether in relation to detainees, displaced persons, disfavoured ethnic or racial groups, or in the context of an embargo — is widely acknowledged to violate basic human rights norms. When states fail to establish and enforce basic minimal health and safety protections for workers the international community considers a violation of labour rights to have occurred. But despite such examples there remain many objections to these rights, as the following readings indicate.

1. COMMENT ON GOVERNMENTAL AMBIVALENCE

ESR have been challenged on many grounds. Governments have been especially ambivalent in relation to them, both at the national level and in international fora. Consider the following examples:

- Applicants for membership of the Council of Europe must undertake to ratify the European Convention on Human Rights, but are not required to give assurances of any type as to the European Social Charter (which is the European Convention's counterpart in the field of ESR). As of 1 January 2007, 8 of the Council's 46 members had not ratified either the 1961 Charter or the 1996 revision; and
- The Additional Protocol to the American Convention on Human Rights in the Area of Economic, Social and Cultural Rights, of 1988 (the 'Protocol of

San Salvador'), has only been ratified by 14 countries, compared with the 24 parties to the Convention itself.

The only open hostility to this group of rights has come from the United States, whose attitude has varied considerably from one administration to another. Eleanor Roosevelt, who represented the Truman administration, was a strong proponent of ESR. The US, under President Johnson, voted in the General Assembly in 1966 to adopt the Covenant. Although neither the Nixon nor Ford Administrations were opposed to these rights, neither actively promoted them. The Carter Administration adopted a different approach epitomized by Secretary of State Vance's 'Law Day Speech' at the University of Georgia, in which he defined human rights as including:

> First, . . . the right to be free from governmental violation of the integrity of the person . . . . Second, . . . the right to the fulfilment of such vital needs as food, shelter, health care and education . . . . Third, . . . the right to enjoy civil and political liberties . . . .[13]

In 1978, President Carter signed the Covenant and sent it to the Senate for its advice and consent to ratification. At the time, however, no action was taken on the Covenant by the Senate, even in Committee. The Reagan and Bush Administrations reversed official policy and opposed the concept of ESR on the grounds that while:

> the urgency and moral seriousness of the need to eliminate starvation and poverty from the world are unquestionable . . . the idea of economic and social rights is easily abused by repressive governments which claim that they promote human rights even though they deny their citizens the basic . . . civil and political rights.[14]

Subsequently, in international fora, the US opposed measures designed to promote ESR. In 1993, Secretary of State Christopher indicated that the Clinton Administration would press for ratification of the Covenant, although nothing was subsequently done. To the contrary, during these years the US strongly opposed the inclusion of all references to rights such as the right to adequate housing and the right to adequate food in international diplomatic settings. The administration of George W. Bush has maintained this approach while being less focused on objecting to use of the terminology of ESR. For example, the US argued that the right to food must be seen as 'a goal or aspiration to be realized progressively' and that it translates into 'the opportunity to secure food; it is not a guaranteed entitlement'.[15] Similarly, ESR 'are aspirational' whereas civil and political rights are 'inalienable and immediately enforceable'.[16]

In 2004 the US proposed the inclusion of the following paragraph in all ESR-related resolution adopted by the UN Commission on Human Rights:

> Bearing in mind that sovereign States must determine from time to time through open, participatory debate and democratic processes the combination of policies

[13] 76 Dept. of State Bulletin 505 (1977).

[14] Introduction, U.S. Dept of State, Country Reports on Human Rights Practices for 1992, 5.

[15] See http://www.humanrights-usa.net/statements/0421Food.htm.

[16] See http://www.us-mission.ch/humanrights/statements/0407Item10.htm.

> and programs they consider will be most effective in progressively realizing the achievement of economic, social and cultural rights and objectives; that each State must determine in accord with its own system the role of various institutions in its society in carrying out such policies and programs; and that each State must define in a manner consistent with its own legal system the administrative and legal recourse available to those seeking review of the implementation of those policies and programs.[17]

It is noteworthy, however, that while the State Department's annual *Country Report on Human Rights Practices* does not address ESR, it does include a range of labour rights (which are classified as ESR by UN instruments).

But the United States is not alone in its ambivalence. Although formal support for economic, social and cultural rights has been near universal, in practice no group of states has consistently followed up its rhetorical support at the international level with practical and sustained programmes of implementation. Western European social democracies would seem best placed to promote the importance of these rights. But while being consistently supportive of initiatives they have been generally cautious, in part because the rights are often not accorded constitutional or other recognition as rights *per se*, and in part because of the consistent calls within some states for a reduction in the scope of the European welfare state. Developing countries continue to be the most vocal proponents of these rights but they have made few concrete proposals beyond calling for more attention to be accorded to them. Cuba, for example, was so reluctant to treat these rights as individually enforceable that it initially resisted the appointment of a special rapporteur to investigate situations with respect to economic, social and cultural rights:

> The Government of Cuba is of the opinion that ... such a step would be contrary to United Nations efforts to simplify the Organization's structures and make them more efficient and effective ... [Such a rapporteur] could only give an inventory of rights that are not being realized and of daily calamities in all parts of the world, with which we are all familiar. What is needed ... [is] to take more decisive steps towards the inalienable right to development, understood not only as economic growth but also as eradication of poverty ....

Cuba's view was that the focus should be on the rich countries, for whom the provision of assistance to developing countries is 'a moral and historical obligation'.[18] Another reason for reticence on the part of developing countries is illustrated by developments in China. Since the 1980s economic reforms have created great wealth. But it has come at the expense of 'the collapse of socialized medicine and staggering cost increases' in Chinese health care. In 2006 it was estimated that 79% of the rural population, which used to enjoy universal basic health insurance, is uninsured.[19]

17 See http://geneva.usmission.gov/humanrights/2004/statements/0329Leland.htm.
18 UN Doc. E/CN.4/1998/25, para. 16.
19 H. French, 'Wealth Grows, but Health Care Withers in China', New York Times, 14 January 2006, p. A1.

QUESTION

Given the reticence of many states, how would you explain the fact that ESR continue to occupy an important place within the international regime? What factors might lead any given government to be strongly supportive of the concept and practice of such rights?

2. PHILOSOPHICAL PERSPECTIVES

Much of the literature on ESR focuses on the feasibility of recognizing them as legal, or even constitutional, rights, and of making them justiciable. The deeper philosophical dimensions of the issue are too often overlooked in such contexts, but they are nonetheless very important. In the readings that follow, Neier and Kelley provide a general overview of the principal arguments used for not treating ESR as 'rights'. The excerpts from Plant and White place these critiques within a broader philosophical perspective.

ARYEH NEIER,SOCIAL AND ECONOMIC RIGHTS: A CRITIQUE[20]

13/2 Hum. Rts. Brief (2006)

... [L]et me first make clear that I favor a fairer distribution of the world's resources; [but] through the political process. For the most part, ... it cannot take place through the assertion of rights. ... Rights only have meaning if it is possible to enforce them. But there has to be some mechanism for that enforcement, and adjudication seems to be the mechanism that we have chosen. Therefore, from my standpoint, if one is to talk meaningfully of rights, one has to discuss what can be enforced through the judicial process.

... [A]lthough there certainly will be economic ramifications of efforts to enforce [civil and political rights such as access to counsel for accused persons, and decent prisons], they do not involve a broad redistribution of society's resources or its economic burdens. Therefore, I would distinguish the incidental costs of protecting civil and political rights from the much more substantial costs of economic redistribution.

Furthermore, there will always be, in unfair economic distribution, elements of invidious discrimination, discrimination on grounds of race or gender, or denials of due process. In these circumstances, I believe it is appropriate to invoke rights. For example, if a town provides roads and sewage collection, or water and electricity, to people of one race and not to those of another .... But I think of these matters in terms of race discrimination, which involves a denial of civil and political rights, and

[20] Neier is President of the Open Society Institute and former Executive Director of Human Rights Watch.

not economic redistribution. Finally, I want to make it clear that certain constitutions incorporate some things that could be called economic and social rights with a certain degree of legislative specificity. For example, a constitution may provide that every child shall be entitled to a free primary school or a free secondary school education. When a constitution provides that level of legislative specificity, I think it is certainly appropriate to use the judicial mechanism to enforce one's rights accordingly.

Social/economic rights and the democratic process

The concern I have with economic and social rights is when there are broad assertions . . . of a right to shelter or housing, a right to education, a right to social security, a right to a job, and a right to health care. There, I think, we get into territory that is unmanageable through the judicial process and that intrudes fundamentally into an area where the democratic process ought to prevail.

In my view, the purpose of the democratic process is essentially to deal with two questions: public safety and the development and allocation of a society's resources. . . . Economic and security matters ought to be questions of public debate. To withdraw either of them from the democratic process is to carve the heart out of that process.

Everybody has an opinion on what should be done to protect the public's safety, and . . . as to what is appropriate in the allocation of a society's resources and its economic burdens. . . . These issues ought to be debated by everyone in the democratic process, with the legislature representing the public and with the public influencing the legislature in turn. To suggest otherwise undermines the very concept of democracy by stripping from it an essential part of its role.

Indeed, whenever you get to these broad assertions of shelter or housing or other economic resources, the question becomes: What shelter, employment, security, or level of education and health care is the person entitled to? It is only possible to deal with this question through the process of negotiation and compromise. . . . [A] court is not the place where it is possible to engage in [the necessary] sort of negotiation and compromise. . . . That is the heart of the political process . . . .

Consider the question of health care. . . . If you are allocating the resources of a society, how do you deal with the person who says they need [a] kidney transplant or [a] bypass or . . . anti-retroviral drugs to save their life when the cost of these procedures may be equivalent to providing primary health care for a thousand children? Do you say the greater good for the greater number, a utilitarian principle, and exclude the person whose life is at stake if they do not get the health care that they require? I do not believe that is the kind of thing a court should do. . . .

Consider next the question of education. What if a constitution talks about a right to an education but is silent as to the type of education people should be entitled to? A society may say that it needs a certain elite — scientists, engineers, and brain surgeons — as well as people who are going to able to work effectively in factories and service jobs. Does someone have a right to say they are entitled to an elite education . . . ? Can you deal with these questions through the adjudicatory process? Again, I do not believe it is possible.

Finally, consider the question of jobs. Suppose that a decision is made through the legislative process that we have to spend a certain amount on building roads because we want peasants to be able to take their goods to market for sale. Suppose further that we have to build a port to export those goods. . . . Can the judicial process deal with the question of the short-term need for jobs and social security as opposed to that of long-term socio-economic growth? . . .

Civil and political rights

. . . I am a believer in very strong civil and political rights: the right to free speech, the right to assemble, the right not to be tortured, etc. Those rights have to mean exactly the same thing every place in the world. With social and economic "rights," however, it is inevitable that they are going to be applied differently in different places. That is, if you are talking about one country with extensive resources and one that is very poor, there is not going to be the same right to shelter or to health care. . . .

But suppose that one takes that same idea — that different stages of development mean different things for each country — and applies it to the concept of civil and political rights. Suppose China or Zimbabwe says it is not a developed country and therefore cannot provide the same civil and political rights as a developed country. . . .

Another way in which the idea of social and economic rights is dangerous is that you can only address economic and social distribution through compromise, but compromise should not enter into the adjudication of civil and political rights. I do not want a society to say that it cannot afford to give individuals the right to speak or publish freely, or the right not to be tortured. . . .

. . .

DAVID KELLEY, A LIFE OF ONE'S OWN: INDIVIDUAL RIGHTS AND THE WELFARE STATE

(1998), at 1

In our personal lives, most of us realize that the world doesn't owe us a living . . . .

Yet in our public lives we have accepted an obligation to provide food, shelter, jobs, education, pensions, medical care, child support, and other goods to every member of society. The premise of the welfare state — the sprawling network of programs for transferring wealth from taxpayers to recipients — is that the world *does* owe us a living. If someone is unable or unwilling to support himself, the government will provide food stamps, housing subsidies, and possibly cash assistance as well . . . .

. . .

. . . [T]he welfare state is a specific historical phenomenon. In its modern form it is just over 100 years old. During the 1880s, Germany under Otto von Bismarck created social insurance programs for old age, job-related accidents, and other medical costs. Great Britain began building its welfare state, partly on Bismarck's model, in the early years of this century. In the United States, . . . the major welfare programs were created during the 1930s and 1960s . . . .

. . . The welfare state . . . rests on an idea. The thinkers and activists who built it insisted that the social provision of goods be treated as a right possessed by all people as citizens, rather than as an act of charity or noblesse oblige, a gift from some to others....

...

[Ch.] 2. What is a Welfare Right?

...America remains unique in the role that rights play in the national culture. [The Declaration of Independence reflects the principles of Enlightenment individualism, including] the idea that the individual's primary need is for liberty: the freedom to act without interference, to be secure against assault on his person or property, to think and speak his mind freely, to keep the fruits of his labor. And while government is necessary to secure that freedom, it is also the greatest danger to it. Thus, the concept of rights served two functions in the political theory of the Enlightenment: to legitimate government and to control it....

It is against that background that we must understand the concept of welfare rights, a concept that reflects a more expansive view of the role of government than anything envisioned by the classical liberals of the Enlightenment. 'For Jefferson,... the poor had no right to be free from want', observes legal scholar Louis Henkin. 'The framers saw the purposes of government as being to police and safeguard, not to feed and clothe and house'....

...

Welfare rights differ from the classical rights to life, liberty, and property in the nature of the claim that they embody....

The primary difference is one of content, a difference in what it is that people are said to have a right *to*. The classical rights are rights to freedom of action, whereas welfare rights are rights to goods. That distinction has often been described as the difference between 'freedom from' and 'freedom to'. The classical rights guarantee freedom from interference by others — and may thus be referred to as liberty rights — whereas welfare rights guarantee freedom to have various things that are regarded as necessities. What that means, in essence, is that the classical liberty rights are concerned with processes, whereas welfare rights are concerned with outcomes.

Liberty rights set conditions on the way in which individuals interact. Those rights say that we cannot harm, coerce, or steal from each other as we go about our business in life, but they do not guarantee that we will succeed in our business....

Welfare rights, by contrast, are intended to guarantee success, at least at a minimum level. They are conceived as entitlements to have certain goods, not merely to pursue them. They are rights to have the goods provided by others if one cannot (or will not) earn them oneself....

...

On whom does the obligation fall [to provide what welfare rights require]? Here is another point of difference between liberty and welfare rights. One person's liberty rights impose on every other human being the obligation to respect them. I am obliged not to murder or steal from other individuals, even those I have never encountered and with whom I have no relationship. But am I obliged to respect their welfare rights? No advocate of welfare rights would say that a poor person has a right to appear at my door and demand food, or a place to sleep, or any of the other goods to which he is said to have a right. The obligation to supply those goods does not fall upon me as a particular individual; it falls upon all of us indifferently, as members of society .... Insofar as welfare rights are implemented through government programs, for example, the obligation is distributed among all taxpayers.

...

To implement the liberty rights of individuals, government must protect them against incursions by other individuals .... The laws involved are relatively simple; they essentially prohibit specific types of actions. The government apparatus required is relatively small, the 'night-watchman state' of classical liberalism. The only significant expense involved is that of the military, to protect against foreign aggression.

The implementation of welfare rights requires a much more activist form of government. The welfare state typically involves large-scale transfer programs ... through which wealth is transferred from taxpayers to those on whom the state confers entitlements to various goods.

...

... [T]he administration of the transfer programs is enormously complex by contrast with the relatively simple prohibitions involved in protecting the rights to life, liberty, and property. The welfare state involves government in running large-scale business enterprises: pension plans, health insurance, and so on. A complex set of regulations is required to define the entitlements of people, depending on the diverse circumstances of their lives, and a large bureaucracy is required to enforce those regulations. [Kelley also refers to the high amount of total spending on social welfare by government at all levels in the United States.]

Liberty and welfare rights differ, finally, in the level at which it is possible to implement them. The economic and technological development of a society affects the degree to which it can provide welfare rights to its members. A preindustrial society obviously cannot guarantee access to modern medical equipment and procedures. Even in a wealthy society, the potential demand for goods like health care or insurance against economic risks is open-ended. If individuals have rights to at least minimum levels of such goods, then the political process must decide what constitutes the minimum, the level that represents need rather than luxury. There is no universal and nonarbitrary standard for distinguishing need from luxury and thus for defining the content of welfare rights. It depends on the level of wealth in a given society.

The implementation of liberty rights, however, is not historically relative in the same way. The protection of an individual's liberty rights requires that other individuals, and the government itself, refrain from forcibly harming or constraining him or appropriating his property. The ability to forbear such actions is not a function of wealth....

...

In short, liberty rights reflect an individualist political philosophy that prizes freedom, welfare rights a communitarian or collectivist one that is willing to sacrifice freedom....

QUESTION

Based on the preceding readings, how would you identify the salient distinctions between civil and political and ESR? How useful is it to think in terms of rights versus needs, negative versus positive, individual versus collective, determinate versus open textured, law versus policy?

RAYMOND PLANT, SOCIAL AND ECONOMIC RIGHTS REVISITED

14 King's College L. J. (2003) 1, at 13

...

Rights and social justice

...

Some critics of social justice and social and economic rights make [the] point about intention a central plank in their case against both. This is for example a major theme of Hayek. The argument goes as follows. An injustice can only be caused by an intentional act in the same way as for Fried a wrong in relation to a right can only result from an intentional act. So, Hayek argues, this is the underlying reason why we do not regard the consequences of the weather or of the genetic lottery as injustices even though they may cause great suffering. They are not injustices and nor do they infringe the rights of anyone because they are not intended. This argument is then transposed to the operation of free economic markets. In a market, individuals buy and sell on an intentional basis and in this, wrong and injustice can arise between individual parties to transactions. These are dealt with by contract law and other forms of law covering the buying and selling of goods. However, the overall outcomes of markets and, in particular, the so called "distribution" of income and wealth are not intended. They are the aggregate effects of individual acts of intentional buying and selling. The distribution of resources which a market produces at any moment is an unintended consequence of this activity. Because market outcomes are unintended they are not wrongful nor do they cause injustice to those whose share of resources falls below say, the level at which they can meet their needs. Hence market outcomes do not produce wrong and injustice and for this reason there is no case for assuming collective responsibility for these outcomes and conferring on individuals social and economic rights to protect against such outcomes.

...

This argument may, however, be doubted because while it is no doubt true that the outcomes of markets are unintended they can, at least in aggregate, be foreseen and it is this degree of foreseeability that grounds the idea of collective responsibility. It would be a very odd thing if it was claimed that market outcomes were not foreseeable because part of the justification for extending markets in areas currently covered by the state or by voluntary action is that, if a market mechanism is adopted, efficiencies will be achieved and supply will be increased. . . . At the level of individual responsibility both in morality and the law we can be held morally and legally responsible for the reasonably foreseeable, albeit unintended, outcomes of our actions. Given this, there is a case for arguing that, if there are unintended but reasonably foreseeable outcomes of markets, and if, for individuals disadvantaged by such outcomes, it is possible to compensate them for their position without causing similar hardship to those involved in funding the compensation, then we have a collective responsibility to do that. In this way it would be possible to argue in favour of tax funded social and economic rights as a way of expressing collective responsibility for market outcomes.

. . .

[A related issue concerns] . . . the question about the relationship between the wrongfulness of the infringement of a right and the identification of the individual who is under the duty to respect the right and has committed the wrong. . . . In the case of social and economic rights however, [a negative rights theorist would argue that] it is not clear who is the duty bearer. Is it an individual so that another individual without the means to meet his social and economic rights has a direct right in respect of the resources of the first individual, and this first individual has a duty in respect of the [second] individual's rights? This point is made very fairly by Jan Narveson in the course of a critique of social and economic rights:

> But a duty has to be someone's duty. It can't just be no one's in particular. Consequently the thing to do is to make it everyone's duty to do something, even if that something is a matter of seeing that someone else does it.

This would seem to be correct and would follow from the earlier argument about collective responsibility. The strict duty for individuals in the case of social and economic rights would not be that of personal provision of resources for deprived individuals . . . but rather a duty to support the tax system, and other aspects of provision for social and economic rights which the entity, usually a state, through which collectively accepted responsibility for market outcomes takes place . . . .

STUART WHITE, SOCIAL RIGHTS AND THE SOCIAL CONTRACT — POLITICAL THEORY AND THE NEW WELFARE POLITICS

30 Brit. J. Pol. S. (2000) 507, at 509

Welfare contractualism makes the payment of a publicly-financed minimum income (welfare) to the individual conditional on his/her satisfying behavioural requirements, such as active job search, retraining or work itself. . . . [This is said to be] incompatible with the idea of social rights: for rights necessarily have a quality of unconditionality, and making the payment of welfare benefits which are notionally covered by a social right conditional on doing *X* or *Y*, as contractualism entails, apparently violates this necessary quality of unconditionality. . . .

. . . The distinction to which we must pay attention here is the distinction between: (1) a right to be *given* some resource, *X*, unconditionally; and, (2) an unconditional right of *reasonable access* to a given resource, *X*, where reasonable access means, in part, that the resource in question can be acquired and enjoyed by the individual concerned without unreasonable effort. . . . The notion of a social right can quite intelligibly be understood in the second way as well as in the first: as an unconditional right of reasonable access to a given resource, rather than as a right to be given this same resource unconditionally. This distinction is important for our purposes because while welfare contractualism does seem incompatible with a social right of the first kind it is by no means necessarily incompatible with a social right of the second. If, for example, Smith is perfectly capable of working, then it is not clear that making Smith's eligibility for welfare benefits conditional on, say, active job search, necessarily violates Smith's unconditional right of reasonable access to a decent minimum of income.

It might be objected that I am revising the traditional conception of social rights here. . . . But this is not the case. When we look at the work of political theorists who are typically credited with being intellectual pioneers of the British welfare state, we see exactly this distinction being made and, in some cases, a clear preference for social rights of the second kind . . . . [The] early social democrats recognized that in a market economy many citizens will lack reasonable access, in the sense defined above, to certain vital resources. The state, on their view, has a responsibility to ensure that all citizens do have reasonable access to these resources. In some cases it may be appropriate for the state simply to give citizens the relevant resources. But this need not, and probably ought not, always to be the case. In particular, a right of reasonable access to a decent minimum of income does not necessarily have to take the form of a universal right to be given a minimum income unconditionally. . . .

IV. The fair reciprocity approach to welfare contractualism

The citizen's putative obligation to make a productive contribution to the community—the obligation that he/she putatively has under the reciprocity principle—will be enforced against some background distribution of assets and opportunities. . . .

. . . I think it is possible to discern certain conditions of fair reciprocity which would follow from any broadly egalitarian conception of distributive justice. I shall now sketch out four of these *intuitive conditions of fair reciprocity*, as one might call them.

(1) *Guarantee of a decent share of the social product for those meeting a minimum standard of productive participation.* This . . . is frequently violated by workfare initiatives in practice, certainly in the United States.

(2) *Decent opportunities for (and in) productive participation.* It is essential that citizens have adequate opportunity to work to meet their reciprocity-based obligations in a meaningful way, so that they do not suffer the loss of self-respect that comes from failure to reciprocate. . . .

(3) *Equitable treatment of different forms of productive participation.* What kind of activities count as forms of contribution in satisfaction of the reciprocity

principle? . . . There is surely something to the idea that care workers (for example, those caring for infirm relatives or for very young children), whose work is not remunerated in the market, may nevertheless be providing productive services of sufficiently significant benefit to the wider community as to justify public recognition and subsidy. . . .

(4) *Universal enforcement of the minimum standard of productive participation.* If we are going to insist that any one citizen satisfies reciprocity-based obligations in return for assurance of a minimum standard of living, then fairness requires that we apply the same logic to all citizens (or all productively capable citizens). . . .

. . .

IMMANUEL KANT, THE DOCTRINE OF VIRTUE

in The Metaphysics of Morals (1797, M. J. Gregor, trans. 1964), at 116

[24.] When we are speaking of laws of duty (not laws of nature) and, among these, of laws governing men's external relations with one another, we are considering a moral (intelligible) world where, by analogy with the physical world, attraction and repulsion bind together rational beings (on earth). The principle of mutual love admonishes men constantly to come nearer to each other; that of the respect which they owe each other, to keep themselves at a distance from one another. And should one of these great moral forces fail, 'then nothingness (immorality), with gaping throat, would drink the whole kingdom of (moral) beings like a drop of water'. . . .

[25.] In this context, however, love is not to be taken as a feeling (aesthetic love), i.e. a pleasure in the perfection of other men; it does not mean emotional love (for others cannot oblige us to have feelings). It must rather be taken as a maxim of benevolence (practical love), which has beneficence as its consequence.

The same holds true of the respect to be shown to others: it is not to be taken merely as the feeling that comes from comparing one's own worth with another's (such as mere habit causes a child to feel toward his parents, a pupil toward his teacher, a subordinate in general toward his superior). Respect is rather to be taken in a practical sense (*observantia aliis praestanda*), as a maxim of limiting our self-esteem by the dignity of humanity in another person.

Moreover, the duty of free respect to others is really only a negative one (of not exalting oneself above others) and is thus analogous to the juridical duty of not encroaching on another's possessions. Hence, although respect is a mere duty of virtue, it is considered narrow in comparison with a duty of love, and it is the duty of love that is considered wide.

The duty of love for one's neighbour can also be expressed as the duty of making others' ends my own (in so far as these ends are only not immoral), The duty of respect for my neighbour is contained in the maxim of not abasing any other man to a mere means to my end (not demanding that the other degrade himself in order to slave for my end).

By the fact that I fulfill a duty of love to someone I obligate the other as well: I make him indebted to me. But in fulfilling a duty of respect I obligate only myself, contain myself within certain limits in order to detract nothing from the worth that the other, as a man, is entitled to posit in himself.

. . .

[30.] It is every man's duty to be beneficent — that is, to promote, according to his means, the happiness of others who are in need, and this without hope of gaining anything by it.

For every man who finds himself in need wishes to be helped by other men. But if he lets his maxim of not willing to help others in turn when they are in need become public, i.e. makes this a universal permissive law, then everyone would likewise deny him assistance when he needs it, or at least would be entitled to. Hence the maxim of self-interest contradicts itself when it is made universal law — that is, it is contrary to duty. Consequently the maxim of common interest — of beneficence toward the needy — is a universal duty of men, and indeed for this reason: that men are to be considered fellow-men — that is, rational beings with needs, united by nature in one dwelling place for the purpose of helping one another.

. . .

[*Casuistical Questions*]

. . .

The ability to practice beneficence, which depends on property, follows largely from the injustice of the government, which favours certain men and so introduces an inequality of wealth that makes others need help. This being the case, does the rich man's help to the needy, on which he so readily prides himself as something meritorious, really deserve to be called beneficence at all?

. . .

[38.] Every man has a rightful claim to respect from his fellow-men and is reciprocally obligated to show respect for every other man.

Humanity itself is a dignity; for man cannot be used merely as a means by any man (either by others or even by himself) but must always be treated at the same time as an end . . . .

QUESTIONS

1. Kelley stresses the redistributive character of social welfare programmes and their high expense. Need such programmes necessarily rest on, say, progressive taxation at higher rates for the rich to finance distributions in cash or kind to the needy? Consider in this regard the five levels of duties identified in Chapter 3, *supra* (p. 185)

2. Rights and duties go together. But "collective responsibility" of the type proposed by Plant makes a mockery of that idea because the resultant duty-holder remains vague and amorphous.' Discuss.

3. Is welfare contractualism compatible with the notion of a human right?

4. 'If we were to make a rough analogy, Kant's duty of respect recalls the ICCPR, while the duty of beneficence recalls the ICESCR.' Do you agree or disagree, and why?

3. RELIGIOUS PERSPECTIVES

Isaiah, Ch. 58 (Holy Scriptures, Masoretic Text, 1917)

[The reference is to a fast of repentance.]

Behold, in the day of your fast ye pursue your business, and exact all your labours.
Behold, ye fast for strife and contention, and to smite with the fist of wickedness;
Ye fast not this day so as to make your voice to be heard on high.
Is such the fast that I have chosen? The day for a man to afflict his soul?
Is it to bow down his head as a bulrush, and to spread sackcloth and ashes under him?
Wilt thou call this a fast, and an acceptable day to the Lord?
Is not this the fast that I have chosen? To loose the fetters of wickedness, to undo the bands of the yoke,
And to let the oppressed go free, and that ye break every yoke?
Is it not to deal thy bread to the hungry, and that thou bring the poor that are cast out to thy house?
When thou seest the naked, that thou cover him, and that thou hide not thyself from thine own flesh?

...

And if thou draw out thy soul to the hungry, and satisfy the afflicted soul;
Then shall thy light rise in darkness, and thy gloom be as the noonday;
And the Lord will guide thee continually, and satisfy thy soul in drought, and make strong thy bones;
And thou shalt be like a watered garden, and like a spring of water, whose waters fail not.

Matthew, Ch. 26 (Holy Bible, King James Version)

When the Son of man shall come in his glory, and all the holy angels with him, then shall he sit upon the throne of his glory;

...

Then shall the King say unto them on his right hand. Come, ye blessed of my Father, inherit the kingdom prepared for you from the foundation of the world.

For I was an hungered, and ye gave me meat; I was thirsty, and ye gave me drink; I was a stranger, and ye took me in;

Naked, and ye clothed me. I was sick, and ye visited me; I was in prison, and ye came unto me.

Then shall the righteous answer him, saying, Lord, when saw we thee an hungred, and fed thee, or thirsty, and gave thee drink?

...

And the King shall answer and say unto them. Verily I say unto you, Inasmuch as you have done it unto any of the least of these my brethren, ye have done it unto me.

Surah 63: Al Munafiqun, 9 and 10 (Holy Qur'an, Abdullah Yusuf 'Ali trans. 1989)

O ye who believe!
Let not your riches
Or your children divert you
From the remembrance of Allah.
If any act thus,
The loss is their own.
And spend something (in charity)
Out of the substance
Which We have bestowed
On you

QUESTIONS

1. Compare as a group the verses from the Hebrew Bible, the Christian Bible, and the Qur'an *with* Article 11 of the ICESCR. Based on these religious texts and on the prior readings in this chapter, what similarities and what differences do you find with respect to the invocation of rights and duties, and with respect to who bears what rights or duties?

2. A critic of economic-social rights might respond to these readings by saying that they well illustrate the distinction which must be drawn between ethical or moral duties on the one hand, and legal obligations which are correlative to human rights on the other. Would you agree?

ADDITIONAL READING

H. Shue, *Basic Rights: Subsistence, Affluence, and U.S. Foreign Policy* (2nd edn. 1996); A. Gewirth, *The Community of Rights* (1997); E. Frankel Paul *et al.* (eds.), *Economic Rights* (1992); R. Plant, *Modern Political Thought* (1991); Friedrich von Hayek, Law, The Mirage of Social Justice, vol. 2 of *Legislation and Liberty* (1976); S. Holmes and C. Sunstein, *The Cost of Rights: Why Liberty Depends on Taxes* (1999); D. Beetham, 'What Future For Economic And Social Rights?', 43 *Political Studies* 41 (1995); J. Waldron, 'A Rights-Based Critique of Constitutional Rights', 13 Oxford J. Legal Studies (1993) 18.

C. THE PROBLEM OF RESOURCES

The competing perspectives on ESR considered earlier (p. 283 *supra*) make it clear that perhaps the two most contested questions are (1) the issue of 'available resources', which in turn holds the key to the possibilities for 'progressive development', and

(2) how to give content to vague norms such as the right to housing or the right to food. In this part of the chapter we examine the relationship between resources and the realization of ESR, and then consider the relevance of fiscal, or tax, policy in determining available resources. A central political and philosophical issue which derives from the progressive realization qualification to the ICESCR is whether poverty is, *per se*, a violation of human rights. Some perspectives on that question are presented in section 3 *infra*.

Sections D and E *infra* are devoted to the various sources from which content is derived in the interpretation and application of ESR.

1. 'AVAILABLE RESOURCES'

One of the major distinctions between ESR and civil and political rights is that obligations in relation to the former are limited to steps that can be taken within 'available resources'. No equivalent limitation is mentioned in relation to the latter, leading many experts to suggest that they are therefore not resource contingent. As a result, it is often argued that while wealthy industrialized countries may be able to afford policies designed to protect ESR, most developing countries do not enjoy the luxury of being able to pursue such policies. For example, Maurice Cranston has written that: '[f]or a government to provide social security ... it has to have access to great capital wealth . . . . The government of India, for example, simply cannot command the resources that would guarantee' each Indian an adequate standard of living.[21] Another issue concerns trade-offs. It is argued that more money on health inevitably means less for education, or water, or food etc. For many critics it follows that, in the absence of large-scale international aid or of rapid domestic economic growth (or both), the government's hands are tied and little can be expected of it in response to its obligations under the Covenant. (Note that the issue of international aid is considered in Chapter 16, *infra*.) Pressures to reduce the size of the public sector, to privatize various functions previously performed by governments, and to stimulate growth by reducing taxes, all render governments less able to accept responsibility for ESR. Recall the provisions of Article 2(1) of the ICESCR:

> Each State Party to the present Covenant undertakes to take steps, individually and through international assistance and co-operation, especially economic and technical, to the maximum of its available resources, with a view to achieving progressively the full realization of the rights recognized in the present Covenant by all appropriate means, including particularly the adoption of legislative measures.

The following readings survey a range of responses to this dilemma, with particular emphasis on the right to education. The section concludes with the 'solution' identified by the ESCR Committee in its General Comment No. 3 (1990). We start with different perspectives on the empirical dimension.

21 'Human Rights: Real and Supposed', in D.D. Raphael (ed.), *Political Theory and the Rights of Man* 43 (1967), at 51.

WEINER, CHILD LABOUR IN DEVELOPING COUNTRIES: THE INDIAN CASE

2 Int. J. Children's Rts. 121 (1994)

Governments do not advocate child labour or oppose compulsory education. . . . Why, then, is child labour so widespread in developing countries? Why are so many children not in school?

The answers are well known and widely accepted. Governments in developing countries, it is said, lack the financial resources for universal compulsory primary school education; governments lack the administrative resources to enforce child labour laws; poor families need the labour and the income of their children; and children and their parents often find the schools in developing countries irrelevant to meet their needs.

By drawing upon examples from India, I will argue that these explanations are unsatisfactory. India is the world's largest producer of non-school going child workers; a review of the Indian experience will therefore help in understanding the reasons for the persistence of child labour not only in India but perhaps also in other developing states. I propose to develop three alternative explanations, firstly, that child labour is not simply an unfortunate feature of low income developing countries that cannot be eliminated until national incomes grow but is in fact sustained by government policies on primary education; secondly, that in India the establishment of compulsory primary education has not been in the interests of the middle classes who are concerned with the expansion of government expenditures on higher education; and finally, that child labour has become part of the government's industrial strategy to promote the small scale sector and to expand exports.

. . .

. . . [One] conclusion is that the establishment of compulsory education is a necessary condition for the reduction and abolition of child labour. Without compulsory education governments are unable to enforce child labour laws. In one country after another the phased extension of the age of compulsory education went hand in hand with a phased extension of restrictions on the employment of children. If the school-leaving age is lower than the age of admission to employment, children are likely to illegally seek employment, and the enforcement of child labour laws is rendered more difficult. It is administratively easier to monitor school attendance than to monitor children in the work place, and easier to force parents to send their children to school than to force employers not to hire children. No country has successfully ended child labour without first making education compulsory. So long as children are free not to attend school, they will enter the labour force.

India need not wait until incomes rise to make primary education universal and compulsory. The sooner India acts, the quicker will be the fall in the illiteracy rate, the more likely it is that child labour will be reduced, and the greater are the prospects for a reduction in fertility rates as children are no longer seen as financial assets to the family. But Indian policy makers continue to be mired in a set of views that preclude their taking the necessary steps to get children into school and out of the labour force and a set of industrial policies that promote the employment of children in the small scale sector. Moreover, these views are so widely shared in India that no political parties of the left or right, none of the trade unions, no religious organizations, and not even the educational establishment is pressing for policy changes. There is little indication of fundamental rethinking within the state or central governments. Even officials who recognize that regular school attendance is a solution to the problem of child labour continue to believe that the responsibility of sending children to school should be with parents, not with the state. Policy makers continue to believe that parents should be permitted to send their children into the labour force, and that child labour cannot be eliminated while there is poverty. Government policy is to work around the fringes of the problem: promote adult literacy campaigns, provide non-formal education to working children, and provide free school lunches to encourage children to remain in school. But neither the central nor the state governments have been willing to do what has been done historically by every developed and now by many developing countries: declare that all children ages six to twelve or fourteen *must* attend school, that parents, no matter how needy, will *not be* permitted to remove their children from school, that school attendance *will* be enforced by local authorities, and that the government *will* be obligated to locate a primary school within reasonable distance of all school age children. Only through such a policy will it be possible to end child labour in India, and within a generation raise India's literacy rate to that of other large developing countries.

DIVERSE VIEWS

Human Rights Watch, Failing our Children: Barriers to the Right to Education

(2005), at 6

...

II. School Fees

In many countries around the world, school fees and related education costs create formidable barriers to children's right to education. A 2000–2001 World Bank survey found fees levied in seventy-seven of seventy-nine low-income countries; most had several different types of fees. Although formal tuition fees have been abolished in many countries, particularly in Africa since 2000, the associated costs of education — books, uniforms, supplies, transportation — are still extremely common and prohibitively expensive for many families. In many countries where formal fees have been lifted without an effective reallocation of resources, local schools have imposed additional 'informal' fees to make up for the lost income. In such cases, the financial burden still falls upon children and their families.

...

Recommendations

Governments should ensure that all children enjoy their right to free primary education. No child should ever be denied their right to education because of school fees or related costs of education. Strategies to eliminate or reduce the costs of attending school could include lifting fees, providing stipends conditional on school attendance, provision of free uniforms or lifting of uniform requirements, provision of free textbooks, provision of transportation (for example, bicycles or bus service) or free school meals to attract poor children to school.

...

Donor governments should provide long-term technical and financial support to governments that lift school fees in order to off-set lost revenue and ensure that education systems are prepared to meet increased demand.

BBC News, 'Burundians Flock To Free Schools'

19 September 2005[22]

Burundi's primary schools are struggling to cope with a huge increase in numbers of pupils on the first day of term after fees were scrapped. Some children have been sent home because there are not enough desks. Other are being taught in tents.

In one province, three times as many children were registered as were expected before fees were abolished by new President Pierre Nkurunziza. In some areas of the war-torn country, there are 150 pupils in a single class. . . .

Single mother of three Nzeyimana Marie Goreth, who sells second-hand clothes, told the BBC that the government had taken the right decision. 'It is not easy to feed them, clothe them and pay school fees, especially when you are alone,' she said.

But some parents have criticised the government for not doing more to prepare for the expected influx. They are also unhappy with the new huge class sizes.

BBC News, China Ends School Fees for 150m

13 December 2006[23]

China is to abolish tuition and other fees for 150 million rural students, in a bid to narrow the gap between wealthy coastal provinces and poorer regions. The students will be exempt from tuition fees over the course of their compulsory nine-year education.

The move would cost 15bn yuan ($1.9bn) a year, the China Daily said, or about 140 yuan ($18) a child. But children of rural families who have migrated to China's booming cities will not be included.

The new policy is "part of a major move to relieve the financial burden of farmers and to develop a new countryside," the state-owned newspaper said. . . .

In theory, Chinese children are offered education that is free or almost free from age six to 15. But in practice, cash strapped local authorities and schools charge extra fees and education taxes. Poorer families . . . can find these prohibitive.

[22] At http://news.bbc.co.uk/1/hi/world/africa/4260092.stm.
[23] At http://news.bbc.co.uk/2/hi/asia-pacific/6174847.stm.

United Nations Development Programme, Human Development Report (1990), at 4

...

7. Developing countries are not too poor to pay for human development and take care of economic growth.

The view that human development can be promoted only at the expense of economic growth poses a false tradeoff. It misstates the purpose of development and underestimates the returns on investment in health and eduction. These returns can be high, indeed. Private returns to primary education are as high as 43% in Africa, 31% in Asia and 32% in Latin America. Social returns from female literacy are even higher — in terms of reduced fertility, reduced infant mortality, lower school dropout rates, improved family nutrition and lower population growth.

Most budgets can, moreover, accommodate additional spending on human development by reorienting national priorities. In many instances, more than half the spending is swallowed by the military, debt repayments, inefficient parastatals, unnecessary government controls and mistargetted social subsidies. Since other resource possibilities remain limited, restructuring budget priorities to balance economic and social spending should move to the top of the policy agenda for development in the 1990s.

Special attention should go to reducing military spending in the Third World—it has risen three times as fast as that in the industrial nations in the last 30 years.... Developing countries as a group spend more on the military (5.5% of their combined GNP) than on education and health (5.3%).... There are eight times more soldiers than physicians in the Third World.

Governments can also do much to improve the efficiency of social spending by creating a policy and budgetary framework that would achieve a more desirable mix between various social expenditures, particularly by reallocating resources:

- from curative medical facilities to primary health care programmes,
- from highly trained doctors to paramedical personnel,
- from urban to rural services,
- from general to vocational education,
- from subsidising tertiary education to subsidising primary and secondary education,
- from expensive housing for the privileged groups to sites and services projects for the poor,
- from subsidies for vocal and powerful groups to subsidies for inarticulate and weaker groups and
- from the formal sector to the informal sector and the programmes for the unemployed and the underemployed.

Such a restructuring of budget priorities will require tremendous political courage. But the alternatives are limited, and the payoffs can be enormous.

...

VARUN GAURI, SOCIAL RIGHTS AND ECONOMICS: CLAIMS TO HEALTH CARE AND EDUCATION IN DEVELOPING COUNTRIES

in Philip Alston and Mary Robinson (eds.), Human Rights and Development: Towards Mutual Reinforcement (2005), at 65

[The author compares the approaches of economists and human rights advocates in relation to ESR. He argues that they have a great deal in common but also identifies] three important, though not irreconcilable, differences in policy. First, the mechanisms and processes for the delivery of health and education services are, in the rights approach, themselves morally compelling. . . . That means that consent to treatment, norms for due process in delivery and allocation, participation and consultation, and transparency regarding professional and bureaucratic decision making not only facilitate good service delivery but are constitutive of it. On the other hand, the economic approach views those processes instrumentally: they could in principle be reconciled with authoritarian styles in medicine and school governance if those lowered mortality and raised literacy. But the entire thrust of normative micro-economic theory is to expand choices available to consumers, both because choices raise utility directly and because competition among providers increases social welfare. In addition, benchmark theories of competitive equilibrium require full information on prices, quantities, quality, and preferences; and contemporary accounts of service delivery endorse reducing information asymmetries among principals and agents. In other words, the processes of service delivery are critical in the economic approach, even if they do not have intrinsic value.

Second, in the rights approach, evaluations of health and education programs emphasize distributions in outcomes, not only averages. The entire distribution is of concern because rights theories take seriously the idea that every human being is worthy of respect. If systematic discrepancies appear among large populations, rights advocates take this as evidence that services are unavailable or inadequate for some groups. Typically, the rights approach views these discrepancies as direct evidence of inequity, whereas the economic approach would first examine whether they are the result of household choices. Rights advocates pay particular attention to disaggregated data among ethnic and religious minorities, women, and the poor because they are particularly liable to practices and prejudices that weaken their agency and the social basis of their self-esteem. Economists, of course, are also concerned with the distribution of outcomes. But usually, economists disaggregate data by income level because standard assumptions regarding the poor and the rich, such as the degree of risk aversion and the marginal utility of consumption, are available to build positive accounts of individual and household behavior. But there is nothing inherent in economic theory that conflicts with a normative concern for excluded groups, or with the development of new behavioral assumptions regarding women or ethnic groups.

Third, rights approaches accommodate adaptive preferences. Some constraints to the fulfillment of rights are external. For example, many cannot afford the direct or opportunity costs of schooling, do not receive information about how to receive medical care, or live in communities where collective action is costly or impossible.

Economic analyses highlight the important role of these factors — resources, information, and coordination — in the quality of service delivery. Especially in the guise of the capabilities framework, rights approaches emphasize, in addition to these, constraints internal to individuals, such as adaptive preferences — the habit of individuals subject to deprivation to lower their standards regarding what they need, want, and deserve. Rights advocates call for consciousness raising, political education, and other measures to expand the imagination and demands of excluded groups. The discipline of economics does not easily accommodate individuals who do not maximize their welfare. But many of the mechanisms through which economists propose second best solutions involve changes in available information, participation, and incentives that, in practice, also change people's awareness of what they have and what they deserve. . . .

There are two additional and less easily reconciled challenges that economic analysis poses for rights approaches. First, rights based approaches have no distributional metric. The question arises: in the rights framework, just how high is the high priority status of educational and health care goods and services, and how should governments and other actors make allocative decisions, both within and across sectors? Economics offers alternative approaches. Allocations can be based on consumer preferences and existing endowments, or on an objective social welfare function, such as cost per life saved or real social returns to human capital investments. Both of these approaches are problematic. The former simply assumes that market allocations are just and offers no ground for moral criticism, and the latter places no value on deliberative procedures and on actual preferences, which might or might not prioritize welfare and material well-being. Still, the approaches have the virtue of being clear and calculable.

Rights-based approaches do not offer an explicit metric for making tradeoffs, and are in fact premised on the incommensurabilty of human dignity. It is true that some aspects of health care and education, such as skilled attendance at birth and literacy, can be identified as more fundamental to agency, social inclusion, and life chances than others, say contact lenses and earth science. But there are also countless close calls, both within and across sectors. As a result, from a rights perspective, there are always ambiguous tradeoffs, and recommended allocations are not robust to small changes in circumstances. Sorting out the various claims and counterclaims in a large population is, from the rights perspective, inevitably an activity without a formula, and one that relies on judgment guided by principle. . . . As a result of complexities like these, when making policy proposals, some rights advocates tend for the sake of simplicity to fall back on modest versions of social rights, such as the right to subsistence, basic education, and minimal health, note that even these are not available in developing countries, and argue that, globally, resources are available to fulfill at least some basic rights without having to confront the most vexing tradeoffs.

The second tough problem that economic analysis poses for rights involves the behavioral distortions associated with subsidies. If a rights approach leads to subsidies or otherwise more accessible services for at least some individuals or groups, those who receive the (implicit or explicit) subsidies will spend less of their own money on the services, or will engage in more costly activities (moral hazard), with the result that the government or the entity supporting the services will buy them at a higher social cost than anticipated. . . .

COMMITTEE ON ECONOMIC, SOCIAL AND CULTURAL RIGHTS, GENERAL COMMENT NO. 3 (1990)

UN Doc. E/1991/23, Annex III

The nature of States parties obligations (article 2, paragraph 1)

1. Article 2 . . . describes the nature of the general legal obligations undertaken by States parties to the Covenant. Those obligations include both what may be termed (following the work of the International Law Commission) obligations of conduct and obligations of result . . . [W]hile the Covenant provides for progressive realization and acknowledges the constraints due to the limits of available resources, it also imposes various obligations which are of immediate effect. Of these, two are of particular importance in understanding the precise nature of States parties obligations. One of these, . . . is the 'undertaking to guarantee' that relevant rights 'will be exercised without discrimination . . . '.

2. The other is the undertaking in article 2(1) 'to take steps', which in itself, is not qualified or limited by other considerations . . . . [W]hile the full realization of the relevant rights may be achieved progressively, steps towards that goal must be taken within a reasonably short time after the Covenant's entry into force for the States concerned. Such steps should be deliberate, concrete and targeted as clearly as possible towards meeting the obligations recognized in the Covenant.

3. The means which should be used in order to satisfy the obligation to take steps are stated in article 2(1) to be 'all appropriate means, including particularly the adoption of legislative measures'. The Committee recognizes that in many instances legislation is highly desirable and in some cases may even be indispensable. For example, it may be difficult to combat discrimination effectively in the absence of a sound legislative foundation for the necessary measures. In fields such as health, the protection of children and mothers, and education, as well as in respect of the matters dealt with in articles 6 to 9, legislation may also be an indispensable element for many purposes.

4. . . . [H]owever, the adoption of legislative measures, as specifically foreseen by the Covenant, is by no means exhaustive of the obligations of States parties. Rather, the phrase 'by all appropriate means' must be given its full and natural meaning . . . . [T]he ultimate determination as to whether all appropriate measures have been taken remains for the Committee to make.

. . .

7. Other measures which may also be considered 'appropriate' for the purposes of article 2(1) include, but are not limited to, administrative, financial, educational and social measures.

. . .

9. . . . The concept of progressive realization constitutes a recognition of the fact that full realization of all economic, social and cultural rights will generally not be able to be achieved in a short period of time. In this sense the obligation differs significantly from that contained in article 2 of the Covenant on Civil and Political Rights which embodies an immediate obligation to respect and ensure all of the relevant rights. Nevertheless, the fact that realization over time, or in other words

progressively, is foreseen under the Covenant should not be misinterpreted as depriving the obligation of all meaningful content. It is on the one hand a necessary flexibility device, reflecting the realities of the real world and the difficulties involved for any country in ensuring full realization of economic, social and cultural rights. On the other hand, the phrase must be read in the light of the overall objective, indeed the *raison d'être* of the Covenant which is to establish clear obligations for States parties in respect of the full realization of the rights in question. It thus imposes an obligation to move as expeditiously and effectively as possible towards that goal. Moreover, any deliberately retrogressive measures in that regard would require the most careful consideration and would need to be fully justified....

10. ... [T]he Committee is of the view that a minimum core obligation to ensure the satisfaction of, at the very least, minimum essential levels of each of the rights is incumbent upon every State party. Thus, for example, a State party in which any significant number of individuals is deprived of essential foodstuffs, of essential primary health care, of basic shelter and housing, or of the most basic forms of education is, prima facie, failing to discharge its obligations under the Covenant. If the Covenant were to be read in such a way as not to establish such a minimum core obligation, it would be largely deprived of its *raison d'être.* By the same token, it must be noted that any assessment as to whether a State has discharged its minimum core obligation must also take account of resource constraints applying within the country concerned. Article 2(1) obligates each State party to take the necessary steps 'to the maximum of its available resources'. In order for a State party to be able to attribute its failure to meet at least its minimum core obligations to a lack of available resources it must demonstrate that every effort has been made to use all resources that are at its disposition in an effort to satisfy, as a matter of priority, those minimum obligations.

11. ... [T]he obligations to monitor the extent of the realization, or more especially of the non-realization, of economic, social and cultural rights, and to devise strategies and programmes for their promotion, are not in any way eliminated as a result of resource constraints....

12. Similarly, the Committee underlines the fact that even in times of severe resource constraints whether caused by a process of adjustment, of economic recession, or by other factors, the vulnerable members of society can and indeed must be protected by the adoption of relatively low-cost targeted programmes.

...

COMMITTEE ON ECONOMIC, SOCIAL AND CULTURAL RIGHTS, GENERAL COMMENT NO. 11 (1999)

UN Doc. E/C.12/1999/4

Plans of action for primary education

1. Article 14 of the [ICESCR] requires each State party which has not been able to secure compulsory primary education, free of charge, to undertake within

two years, to work out and adopt a detailed plan of action for the progressive implementation, within a reasonable number of years, to be fixed in the plan, of the principle of compulsory primary education free of charge for all....

...

6. *Compulsory*. The element of compulsion serves to highlight the fact that neither parents, nor guardians, nor the State is entitled to treat as optional the decision as to whether the child should have access to primary education....

7. *Free of charge*. The nature of this requirement is unequivocal. The right is expressly formulated so as to ensure the availability of primary education without charge to the child, parents or guardians. Fees imposed by the Government, local authorities or the school, and other direct costs, constitute disincentives to the enjoyment of the right and may jeopardize its realization. They are also often highly regressive in effect. Their elimination is a matter which must be addressed by the required plan of action. Indirect costs, such as compulsory levies on parents (sometimes portrayed as being voluntary, when in fact they are not), or the obligation to wear a relatively expensive school uniform, can also fall into the same category. Other indirect costs may be permissible, subject to the Committee's examination on a case-by-base basis....

8. *Adoption of a detailed plan*. The State party is required to adopt a plan of action within two years....

9. *Obligations*. A State party cannot escape the unequivocal obligation to adopt a plan of action on the grounds that the necessary resources are not available. If the obligation could be avoided in this way, there would be no justification for the unique requirement contained in article 14 which applies, almost by definition, to situations characterized by inadequate financial resources. By the same token, and for the same reason, the references to 'international assistance and cooperation' in articles 2.1 and 23 of the Covenant are of particular relevance in this situation. Where a State party is clearly lacking in the financial resources and/or expertise required to 'work out and adopt' a detailed plan, the international community has a clear obligation to assist.

10. *Progressive implementation*.... Unlike the provision in article 2.1, however, article 14 specifies that the target date must be 'within a reasonable number of years' and moreover, that the time-frame must 'be fixed in the plan'. In other words, the plan must specifically set out a series of targeted implementation dates for each stage of the progressive implementation of the plan....

QUESTIONS

1. Is there an argument to be made, on the basis of these materials, that almost every country can in fact afford to provide universal primary education if it wishes?

2. Does Gauri make a convincing case that the concept of ESR, as understood in international human rights law, could be accepted by most economists? Or are there still essential incompatibilities in the assumptions made by economists and human rights advocates?

3. Do the ESCR Committee's General Comments reflect a workable balance that resolves the objections of ESR critics to the effect that such rights are unaffordable if taken seriously and almost meaningless if the emphasis is placed on resources which will never be sufficiently 'available'?

2. THE FISCAL DIMENSION OF DETERMINING 'AVAILABLE RESOURCES'

Human rights advocates have largely neglected what is arguably the single most important element in determining the resources 'available' to a government to promote the realizations of ESR. Consider the number of issues which fall under the rubric of fiscal policy in the following list of factors determining the resources available to a government:

- size and structure of the economy and its rate of growth
- structure of tax rates
- effectiveness of tax administration
- structure of user fees
- effectiveness of administration of user fees
- availability of other sources of revenue
- inflow of foreign aid
- government borrowing
- interest payments for domestic and foreign creditors
- underlying distribution of resources in the society.[24]

Schumpeter observed that 'nothing shows so clearly the character of a society and of a civilization as does the fiscal policy that its political sector adopts'.[25] And Murphy and Nagel have noted that while '[n]othing could be more mundane than taxes, . . . they provide a perfect setting for constant moral argument and possible moral progress.'[26]

For them, taxation has two primary functions.

> (1) It determines how much of a society's resources will come under the control of government, for expenditure in accordance with some collective decision procedure, and how much will be left to the discretionary control of private individuals, as their personal property. . . . (2) It plays a central role in determining how the social product is shared out among different individuals, both in the form of private property and in the form of publicly provided benefits.[27]

When we talk about fiscal policy we are talking about far more than transfers to the poor. Tax policy can reward the rich (for certain types of investments such as

[24] D. Elson, *Budgeting for Women's Rights* (2006) 15.
[25] J. Schumpeter, *History of Economic Analysis* (1954) 769.
[26] Liam Murphy and Thomas Nagel, *The Myth of Ownership: Taxes and Justice* (2002) 188.
[27] Ibid., at 76.

housing or capital stock), can exempt certain groups, and determines the overall pool of available resources. In the readings that follow, Elson outlines the impact of budget policies, and thus of fiscal measures, and a report on Guatemala illustrates, albeit in relation to a civil and political rights issue, the crucial role of tax policy.

VIEWS ON RESOURCES

Diane Elson, Budgeting for Women's Rights: Monitoring Government Budgets for Compliance with CEDAW

(UNIFEM, 2006), at 10

Budgets . . . entail moral claims and obligations, resting on social and political norms about willingness to pay taxes, and expectations of what kinds of social protection governments should provide (for instance, universal schemes which involve everyone or targeted schemes that reach only particular social groups). Thus Government budgets rest upon what has been described as a 'fiscal covenant': 'the basic socio-political agreement that legitimizes the role of the State and establishes the areas and scope of government responsibility in the economic and social spheres' . . . .

Government budgets affect people in multiple ways: their primary impact is through distributing resources to people via expenditure and claiming resources from them via tax and other measures. They also have secondary impacts via their impacts on job creation, economic growth and inflation. Drawing up a budget entails consideration of how to balance the different claims and obligations; how to balance total expenditure, total revenue and government borrowing, so as to avoid high rates of inflation on the one hand and economic stagnation or recession on the other. This means setting priorities and considering costs; and trying to make the most effective use of resources. It is not possible to meet all the demands that citizens make about revenue and expenditures. Choices have to be made about which ones will be met in any given year. Budgets are always constrained by legal claims and obligations and by the moral claims and obligations inherent in the fiscal covenant.

Report of the Special Rapporteur on Extrajudicial, Summary or Arbitrary Executions, Philip Alston, Mission to Guatemala

UN Doc. A/HRC/4/20/Add.2 (2007)

. . . The killing of women, the execution of selected individuals by elements within the police and military, gang and crime-related killings, social cleansing, and other acts of violence have created a widespread sense of insecurity among the population. There are 5,000 or more killings per year, and the responsibility for this must rest with the State. [T]he death toll is only the beginning of the cost, for a society that lives in fear of killing is unable to get on with its life and business in the ways that it wants. The rich can protect themselves, up to a point, but the rest of the society lives with the fear that a random killing could affect them or their loved ones at any moment.

...

It is important to emphasize that while limited resources may provide some excuse for particular Government agencies, it provides no excuse at all for the State as a whole. Guatemala is not an exceptionally poor country, and it could readily afford a criminal justice system on par with that provided in other Central American countries....

The reason the executive branch of the Guatemalan State has so little money to spend on the criminal justice system is that the legislative branch, the Congress, imposes exceptionally low taxes.... [T]ax revenue amounted to 9.6 percent of GDP in 2005. In regional comparison, its tax revenue is a lower percentage of GDP than that of [its neighbours] ... and radically lower than that of the countries of South America [the average for the latter is around 23%; in the US it is 26% and in Canada 34%]. Neither would higher taxation need to impose any greater burden on the poorer segments of the population given that Guatemala has higher income inequality than every other country in the region....

... Guatemala could so readily afford a far better criminal justice system.... The lack of resources is due to a lack of political will: Rather than funding a high-quality criminal justice system, Congress has decided to impose very low levels of taxation and, thus, to starve the criminal justice system and other parts of Government. Insofar as impunity is due to a lack of resources, it is also due to a lack of political will.

QUESTIONS

1. What does the ICESCR have to say about fiscal policies? If it is silent, does this not mean that a government retains complete discretion as to such matters?

2. If a government decides to reduce tax rates dramatically, with the result that funding is no longer available for basic ESR programs, how could it be argued that this is a violation of ESR obligations? What if the government responds that lower tax rates will mean higher growth which will greatly benefit all members of society, including the poorest?

3. A US Government report on Guatemala notes that 'The wealthiest 10% of the population receives almost one-half of all income; the top 20% receives two-thirds of all income. As a result, about 80% of the population lives in poverty, and two-thirds of that number — or 7.6 million people — live in extreme poverty. Guatemala's social development indicators, such as infant mortality and illiteracy, are among the worst in the hemisphere.'[28] A report by a Canadian Government agency concluded that 'Guatemala's chronic problem with social development has been its elite's unwillingness to pay taxes or to participate in any initiative to redistribute resources'.[29] Could you rely upon the ICESCR, ratified by Guatemala in 1988, to make an argument that the government is obligated to raise taxes?

28 Department of State, Background Note: Guatemala (October 2006) at http://www.state.gov/r/pa/ei/bgn/2045.htm.

29 Canadian International Development Agency at http://www.acdi-cida.gc.ca/CIDAWEB/acdicida.nsf/En/NIC-22312396-NQ3#2.

3. IS POVERTY A VIOLATION OF HUMAN RIGHTS?

According to Nelson Mandela '[m]assive poverty and obscene inequality are such terrible scourges of our times — times in which the world boasts breathtaking advances in science, technology, industry and wealth accumulation — that they have to rank alongside slavery and apartheid as social evils.'[30] The question is whether that makes poverty a violation of human rights? UNESCO has launched a programme 'emphasizing that freedom from poverty is a human right, a global ethical imperative, and a top priority for governments and the international community'. But these three characterizations have radically different consequences. What is meant by characterizing poverty as a violation of rights and what content could such a right have? What legal analysis, grounded in international law, could sustain the proposition that freedom from poverty is, *per se*, a human right? Consider the following perspectives.

PERSPECTIVES ON POVERTY

International Cooperation at a Crossroads: Aid, Trade and Security in an Unequal World

UNDP, Human Development Report 2005 (New York, 2005), at 5

Why inequality matters

Human development gaps within countries are as stark as the gaps between countries. These gaps reflect unequal opportunity — people held back because of their gender, group identity, wealth or location. Such inequalities are unjust. They are also economically wasteful and socially destabilizing. Overcoming the structural forces that create and perpetuate extreme inequality is one of the most efficient routes for overcoming extreme poverty [and] enhancing the welfare of society....

...

Multiple and interlocking layers of inequality create disadvantages for people throughout their lives. Income inequality is increasing in countries that account for more than 80% of the world's population. Inequality in this dimension matters partly because of the link between distribution patterns and poverty levels.... High levels of income inequality are bad for growth, and they weaken the rate at which growth is converted into poverty reduction: they reduce the size of the economic pie and the size of the slice captured by the poor. Income inequalities interact with other life chance inequalities. Being born into a poor household diminishes life chances, in some cases in a literal sense.... Poor women are less likely to be educated and less likely to receive antenatal care when they are pregnant. Their children are less likely

[30] Quoted in UNDP, *International Cooperation at a Crossroads* (2005) p. 4.

to survive and less likely to complete school, perpetuating a cycle of deprivation that is transmitted across generations. Basic life chance inequalities are not restricted to poor countries. Health outcomes in the United States, the world's richest country, reflect deep inequalities based on wealth and race....

...

None of this implies that achieving greater equity in human development is easy. Extreme inequalities are rooted in power structures that deprive poor people of market opportunities, limit their access to services and — crucially — deny them a political voice. These pathologies of power are bad for market-based development and political stability....

Philip Alston, 'Ships Passing in the Night: The Current State of the Human Rights and Development Debate Seen Through the Lens of the Millennium Development Goals'

27 Hum. Rts Q. (2005) 755, at 786

[Former UN HCHR, Mary Robinson, once stated:] "I am often asked what is the most serious form of human rights violations in the world today, and my reply is consistent: extreme poverty."

In legal terms this [proposition] is only true to the extent that a government or other relevant actor has failed to take measures that would have been feasible ("to the maximum of its available resources," as the language of the ICESCR puts it) and that could have had the effect of avoiding or mitigating the plight in which an individual living in poverty finds him or herself. In a country with adequate resources, the proposition will almost always be valid. The only qualification in that context, and it is highly unlikely to be a problem, is that the definition of poverty is not more expansive than the definition of the economic and social rights involved. In a country with very limited resources, it will often also be valid, in the sense that the government has failed to take possible steps to improve the situation and instead has opted to devote scarce resources to other objectives that do not address directly the realization of basic rights.

Consistent with this legal analysis (but also with the reluctance of governments to accept a legal responsibility in relation to poverty) the Vienna Declaration of the 1993 World Conference on Human Rights observed that the "existence of widespread extreme poverty inhibits the full and effective enjoyment of human rights," and that "extreme poverty and social exclusion constitute a violation of human dignity." Indeed this formulation points to a principal justification of Mary Robinson's proposition — poverty is incompatible with human dignity, human dignity is the foundation stone of human rights, and in cases where a national government does not have the resources to remedy (extreme) poverty, a human rights based responsibility falls upon the international community. International lawyers might argue on this basis that a violation of human dignity is tantamount to a violation of human rights; however, this is not the message that the carefully negotiated Vienna Declaration language was designed to convey. The [Human Development Report] 2000 similarly avoided characterizing poverty as a violation of human rights, instead noting that "Poverty eradication is not only a development goal — it is a central challenge for human rights in the 21st century." Finally, the Millennium Declaration also does not characterize poverty as a human rights violation per se. It does, however, resolve to "spare no efforts to free [people] from the abject and dehumanizing conditions of extreme poverty." . . .

Tom Campbell, Poverty as a Violation of Human Rights: Inhumanity or Injustice? (2003)[31]

. . . If poverty is a violation of human rights precisely what does the violation consist of? . . .

. . . [T]here often seems to be a confusion of poverty with either its causes or its effects or both. In asserting that poverty is a violation of human rights we may be taken to mean that when other (non-poverty) rights are violated then this causes poverty, as when in violation of a person's civil rights they are held in confinement without justification and their family is reduced to poverty.

Or we may take the violation to occur when as a result of being poor people are then despised and disrespected and discriminated against, so that poverty leads to a violation of their human rights in general. This assumption is frequently associated with the view that the poor are systematically excluded from society.

. . .

There is another possible interpretation . . . , namely that all or very many human rights violations can be classified as poverty violations, since almost all human rights violations can be read as reducing the capacities of the right holders to lead a truly human right so making them impoverished. This is an approach which may be encouraged by conceiving all human rights as deriving from the existence of certain human needs or . . . the capabilities whose absence indicates the existence of a need. . . .

However, I assume that the proposal is directed primarily at least at the idea that the condition of poverty is to be viewed as a distinct violation of specific human rights, such as the right to subsistence or the right to a tolerable standard of living. . . .

But what is the violation when . . . extreme material poverty . . . occurs? Two possibilities suggest themselves. The first is that the violation occurs when the poverty is caused. More particularly, the analysis might be that poverty is a condition that is brought about by the conduct of other people, and that conduct is the violation.

Alternatively we may identify the violation not in the causation of harm but in the failure to act so as to enable those who are in extreme poverty to escape from that condition. The violation lies in the inactivity of those who are in a position to do something effective about it.

. . .

[31] At http://www.cappe.edu.au/PDF%20Files/Campbell4.pdf.

THOMAS POGGE, RECOGNIZED AND VIOLATED BY INTERNATIONAL LAW: THE HUMAN RIGHTS OF THE GLOBAL POOR

at http://www.ucl.ac.uk/spp/download/seminars/0506/ Paper-Thomas-Pogge.doc

...

... I contend that most of the vast human rights deficits persisting in today's world can be traced back to institutional factors — to the national institutional arrangements in many so-called developing countries, for which their political and economic elites bear primary responsibility, as well as to present global institutional arrangements, for which the governments and citizens of the affluent countries bear primary responsibility. Focusing on the latter subject, I argue that current global institutional arrangements as codified in international law constitute a collective human rights violation of enormous proportions to which most of the world's affluent are making uncompensated contributions.

The *moral* plank of my argument was concisely stated 57 years ago:

> Everyone is entitled to a social and international order in which the rights and freedoms set forth in this Declaration can be fully realized. [Art. 28 UDHR]

I read this Article in light of four straightforward interpretive conjectures:

(1) Alternative institutional designs that do not satisfy the requirement of Article 28 can be ranked by how close they come to enabling the full realization of human rights: Any social system ought to be structured so that human rights can be realized in it as fully as is reasonably possible.
(2) How fully human rights *can* be realized under some institutional design is measured by how fully these human rights generally are, or (in the case of a hypothetical design) generally would be, realized in it.
(3) An institutional design *realizes* a human right insofar as (and fully if and only if) this human right is *fulfilled* for the persons upon whom this order is imposed.
(4) A human right is fulfilled for some person if and only if this person enjoys *secure access to the object of this human right.*

Taking these four conjectures together, Article 28 should be read as holding that the moral quality, or justice, of any institutional order depends primarily on the extent to which it affords all its participants secure access to the objects of their human rights: Any institutional order is to be assessed and reformed principally by reference to its relative impact on the realization of the human rights of those on whom it is imposed. An institutional order and its imposition are human-rights-violating if and insofar as this order foreseeably gives rise to a substantial and avoidable human rights deficit.

2. How Features of the Present Global Order Cause Massive Severe Poverty

Each day, some 50,000 human beings — mostly children, mostly female and mostly people of color — die from starvation, diarrhea, pneumonia, tuberculosis, malaria, measles, perinatal conditions and other poverty-related causes. . . .

I believe that most of this annual death toll and of the much larger poverty problem it epitomizes are avoidable through minor modifications in the global order that would entail at most slight reductions in the incomes of the affluent. Such reforms have been blocked by the governments of the affluent countries, which are ruthlessly advancing their own interests and those of their corporations and citizens, designing and imposing a global institutional order that, continually and foreseeably, produces vast excesses of severe poverty and premature poverty deaths.

There are three main strategies for denying this charge. One can deny that variations in the design of the global order have any significant impact on the evolution of severe poverty worldwide. Failing this, one can claim that the present global order is optimal or close to optimal in terms of poverty avoidance. And, should this strategy fail as well, one can still contend that the present global order, insofar as it is suboptimal in terms of poverty avoidance, is not *causing* severe poverty but merely failing to alleviate such poverty (caused by other factors) as much as it might. . . .

2.4 Conclusion

This catastrophe [of vast poverty] was and is happening, foreseeably, under a global institutional order designed for the benefit of the affluent countries' governments, corporations and citizens and of the poor countries' political and military elites. There are feasible alternative designs of the global institutional order, feasible alternative paths of globalization, under which this catastrophe would have been largely avoided. Even now severe poverty could be rapidly reduced through feasible reforms that would modify the more harmful features of this global order or mitigate their impact.

QUESTIONS

1. Is poverty *per se* a violation of human rights? What arguments would you use to defend such a proposition?

2. Are the analyses of Campbell and Pogge really grounded in international human rights law, or are they essentially philosophical or policy-based?

ADDITIONAL READING

Entries on 'Food', 'Health', 'Housing' and 'Work' in S. Marks and A. Clapham, *International Human Rights Lexicon* (2005); A. Chapman and S. Russell (eds.), *Core Obligations: Building a Framework for Economic, Social and Cultural Rights* (2002); M. Dowell-Jones, *Contextualising the International Covenant on Economic, Social and Cultural Rights: Assessing the Economic Deficit* (2004); On some specific rights see: Brigit Toebes, *The Right to Health as a Human Right in International Law* (1999); S. Narula, 'The Right to Food: Holding Global Actors Accountable under International Law', 44 Colombia J. Transnat'l L. (2006) 691; P. Alston and K. Tomaševski (eds.), *The Right To Food* (1984); S. Leckie (ed.), *National Perspectives on Housing Rights* (2003); Centre on Housing Rights and Evictions, *Forced Evictions and Human Rights: A Manual for Action* (1999); K. D. Beiter, *The Protection of the Right to Education by International Law* (2006); *Public Report on Education in India (Probe)* (1999); W.R. Böhning, *Labour Rights in Crisis: Measuring the Achievement of Human Rights in the World of Work* (2005); R. Cook, B. Dickens and M. Fathalla, *Reproductive Rights and Human Health* (2003)

D. GIVING CONTENT TO ESR: JUSTICIABILITY

The accountability of governments and other entities, as well as the availability of a remedy in cases of a violation, are indispensable elements of international human rights law. Article 8 of the UDHR states that 'Everyone has the right to an effective remedy by the competent national tribunals for acts violating the fundamental rights granted him by the constitution or by law.' The Declaration recognizes ESR and there is nothing to indicate that this provision was intended to apply only to civil and political rights. The ICCPR (Art. 2(3)(b)) requires states parties to 'develop the possibilities of judicial remedy', but there is no equivalent provision in the ICESCR. This seems to have encouraged many governments and commentators to assume that traditional legal remedies such as court actions are either inappropriate or at best impracticable for the vindication of ESR.

The response of many participants in the debate is that the need for remedies and accountability need not be automatically equated with judicial remedies. There are many other ways in which ESR might be effectively vindicated. They include administrative remedies, and legislative responsiveness to reports by human rights commissions and the like. Greater flexibility and responsiveness of some of those techniques can be better suited than litigation for achieving the goals of ESR.

Nevertheless, many observers continue to insist upon the benchmark of justiciability (i.e., the ability of courts to provide a remedy for aggrieved individuals claiming a violation of those rights) as the true test of a 'real' human right. In addition, there are clearly some aspects of ESR the promotion of which is best achieved through judicial remedies. For these reasons considerable importance has been attached to whether ESR are in fact justiciable and the past few years have seen very important developments in this regard. In the next section of this chapter consideration is given to the drafting of an Optional Protocol to the ICESCR under which complaints would be examined by the ESCR Committee in a quasi-judicial procedure similar to that used under the Optional Protocol to the ICCPR (see p. 891 *infra*). In many respects this is a reflection of the developments at the national level which are reviewed in the present section.

The materials that follow begin with an important general defence of judicial remedies for ESR by the ESCR Committee in a General Comment. Then, after considering some of the arguments for and against justiciability of ESR, we look at the recent experience in this regard in four jurisdictions: India, South Africa, the USA and Europe.

COMMITTEE ON ECONOMIC, SOCIAL AND CULTURAL RIGHTS, GENERAL COMMENT NO. 9 (1998)

UN Doc. E/1999/22, Annex IV

Domestic Application of the Covenant

A. The duty to give effect to the Covenant in the domestic legal order

1. . . . The central obligation in relation to the Covenant is for States parties to give effect to the rights recognized therein. By requiring governments to do so 'by all appropriate means', the Covenant adopts a broad and flexible approach which enables the particularities of the legal and administrative systems of each State, as well as other relevant considerations, to be taken into account.

2. But this flexibility co-exists with the obligation upon each State Party to use *all* the means at its disposal to give effect to the rights recognised in the Covenant. In this respect, the fundamental requirements of international human rights law must be borne in mind. Thus the norms themselves must be recognised in appropriate ways within the domestic legal order, appropriate means of redress, or remedies, must be available to any aggrieved individual or group, and appropriate means of ensuring governmental accountability must be put in place.

. . .

C. The role of legal remedies

Legal or judicial remedies?

9. The right to an effective remedy need not be interpreted as always requiring a judicial remedy. Administrative remedies will, in many cases, be adequate . . . . Any such administrative remedies should be accessible, affordable, timely, and effective. . . . [But] whenever a Covenant right cannot be made fully effective without some role for the judiciary, judicial remedies are necessary.

Justiciability

10. In relation to civil and political rights, it is generally taken for granted that judicial remedies for violations are essential. Regrettably, the contrary presumption is too often made in relation to economic, social and cultural rights. This discrepancy is not warranted either by the nature of the rights or by the relevant Covenant provisions. The Committee has already made clear that it considers many of the provisions in the Covenant to be capable of immediate implementation. Thus in General Comment No. 3 it cited, by way of example: articles 3, 7(a)(i), 8, 10(3), 13(2)(a), 13(3), 13(4) and 15(3). It is important in this regard to distinguish between justiciability (which refers to those matters which are appropriately resolved by the courts) and norms which are self-executing (capable of being applied by courts without further elaboration). While the general approach of each legal system needs to be taken into account, there is no Covenant right which could not, in the great majority of systems, be considered to possess at least some significant justiciable dimensions. It is sometimes suggested that matters involving the

allocation of resources should be left to the political authorities rather than the courts. While the respective competences of the different branches of government must be respected, it is appropriate to acknowledge that courts are generally already involved in a considerable range of matters which have important resource implications. The adoption of a rigid classification of economic, social and cultural rights which puts them, by definition, beyond the reach of the courts would thus be arbitrary and incompatible with the principle that the two sets of human rights are indivisible and interdependent. It would also drastically curtail the capacity of the courts to protect the rights of the most vulnerable and disadvantaged groups in society.

NOTE

The rights referred to by the Committee in the preceding General Comment No. 9 are equal rights of men and women (Art. 3), equal pay for equal work (Art. 7(a)(i)), the right to form and join trade unions and the right to strike (Art. 8), the right of children to special protection (Art. 10(3)), the right to free, compulsory, primary education (Art. 13(2)(a)), the liberty to choose a non-public school (Art. 13(3)), the liberty to establish schools (Art. 13(4)), and the freedom for scientific research and creative activity (Art. 15(3)). The extent to which these rights are actually justiciable varies considerably from one country to another.

In relation to the remaining rights in the ICESCR, such as the rights to work (Art. 6), health (Art. 12), food, clothing, housing (Art. 11) and education (Art. 13), Vierdag concludes a lengthy critique of the Covenant in the following terms:[32]

> What are laid down in provisions such as Articles 6, 11 and 13 of the ICESCR are consequently not rights of individuals, but broadly formulated programmes for governmental policies in the economic, social and cultural fields.
>
> It is suggested that it is misleading to adopt an instrument that by its very title and by the wording of its relevant provisions purports to grant 'rights' to individuals but in fact appears not to do so, or to do so only marginally. It is also regrettable that, in this way, a notion of 'right' is introduced into international law that is utterly different from the concept of 'right of an individual' as it is traditionally understood in international law and employed in practice....

CÉCILE FABRE, CONSTITUTIONALIZING SOCIAL RIGHTS
6 J. Polit. Phil. 263 (1998), at 280–283

... Now, the institutional logic of social rights is said to preclude their constitutionalisation because judges lack the *legitimacy* and/or the *competence* to deal with such issues. That is, it is claimed that they ought not to be allowed to adjudicate constitutional social rights because it is the democratic majority's moral right to

[32] E. Vierdag, 'The Legal Nature of the Rights Granted by the International Covenant on Economic, Social and Cultural Rights', 9 Neths. Ybk. Int. L. 69 (1978), at 103.

allocate resources as they see fit, and/or they should not be allowed to adjudicate these rights because they are not equipped to do so. I shall examine these two claims in turn.

There are two reasons why one might think that the judiciary does not have the legitimacy to adjudicate constitutional social rights. First, were it to do so, it would have to interfere with the drawing of the budget, thereby encroaching upon one of the main prerogatives of the legislature.

. . . It may be that there are no welfare policies which give effect to constitutional social rights; or it may be that there are such policies but that they do not, or so it is claimed, give people what the constitution entitles them to get. The judiciary has two courses of action. It can either ask the government to implement welfare policies or to allocate resources in such a way as to respect people's social rights, or it can draft policies itself and decide in great detail how resources should be allocated. I believe it should do the first; that is, it should remind the government that it is under a duty to do x: it should not tell the government *how* to fulfil this duty, precisely so as to allow for greater scope in democratic decision-making.

The second reason why it is thought that the judiciary does not have the legitimacy to adjudicate constitutional social rights is that . . . resources are scarce and the interests protected by social rights are therefore likely to conflict. As a result, adjudicating between them requires that very difficult choices be made (who will get resources? homeless people or the sick?) which will shape what society looks like. Only the elected representatives of the people, it is argued, ought to be allowed to make those difficult choices. Now, admittedly, these may be difficult matters to deal with; however, adjudicating conflicts between interests protected by negative rights may be as difficult (how, for instance, is one to decide that someone's interest in privacy has been violated by someone else's exercise of their freedom of speech?), and if one thinks that the judiciary can adjudicate the latter conflicts on the grounds that the value of autonomy must be protected from attacks by the democratic majority then one must argue that the judiciary has legitimacy to adjudicate conflicts between the interests protected by social rights, precisely because these interests must be safeguarded for people to be autonomous.

Whether judges are competent to deal with constitutional social rights raises different issues. Judges, it is said, are not competent to ask the government to allocate resources in certain ways: they do not have the training and the information-gathering tools that are required to decide whether funds have been spent the way they should have and whether a particular individual got the resources the constitution entitles him to have. In fact, or so it is argued, faced with such difficulties, judges would be unwilling to adjudicate social rights, which would give their constitutionalisation no more than symbolic value . . . . [Judges] now increasingly assess whether resources have been allocated according to the law, most notably, in the UK, with respect to education, housing and health care, which suggests that they would not be reluctant to adjudicate constitutional social rights. These judgements are usually taken into account by governments, and have led some governments to adjust their welfare policies. This tells us two things. First, courts have not always been reluctant to adjudicate allocations of resources. Second, when they have done so, they have done so with some degree of success.

Now, it is likely that they are not always as successful as they should be. However, to bemoan this fact and reject constitutional social rights on that ground is misguided. Clearly, poring over budget reports and assessing welfare policies require some specific skills; but there is no reason why specialised judges could not be trained to acquire those skills, or could not seek advice from independent experts, as they actually already do.

[The author then asks whether judges are well placed to adjudicate individual cases and tentatively concludes that it might sometimes] be virtually impossible for them to assess whether a social right of a given *individual* has been violated. However, that is no reason to reject the constitutionalisation of social rights altogether. The government could be put under weaker constitutional constraints, which could be formulated as follows: 'the government of the day must take all steps to ensure that it satisfies social rights to minimum income, housing, education and health care, as far as it can, within the constraints of resources reasonably available to pursue them'. The judiciary would be able, I think, to make sure that the government does indeed take those steps. Furthermore, there are other ways of protecting constitutional social rights than constitutional judicial review of individual cases, which admittedly would not offer as good a protection, but would offer some protection nonetheless. For example, one might provide for group action, whereby associations of, say, homeless people, would be able to challenge government housing policies on grounds of unconstitutionality. Or one might provide for constitutional judicial *preview* of the law, as is the case in France and in the Republic of Ireland....

CASS R. SUNSTEIN, AGAINST POSITIVE RIGHTS

2/1 East Eur. Constit'al Rev. 35 (1993)

...

If we look at the actual and proposed constitutions for Eastern Europe, we will find a truly dazzling array of social and economic rights....

I think that this is a large mistake, possibly a disaster. It seems clear that Eastern European countries should use their constitutions to produce two things: (a) firm liberal rights — free speech, voting rights, protection against abuse of the criminal justice system, religious liberty, barriers to invidious discrimination, property and contract rights; and (b) the preconditions for some kind of market economy. The endless catalogue of what I will be calling 'positive rights', many of them absurd, threatens to undermine both of these important tasks.

Three qualifications are necessary at the outset. First, the argument against these rights applies with distinctive force to countries in the unique position of transition from Communism to a market economy. Other countries, especially in the West, are in a much different situation, and here it is by no means clear that social and economic rights would be harmful....

Second, there is a big difference between what a decent society should provide and what a good constitution should guarantee. A decent society ensures that its citizens have food and shelter; it tries to guarantee medical care; it is concerned to offer good education, good jobs, and a clean environment. . . . If the Constitution tries to specify everything to which a decent society commits itself, it threatens to become a mere piece of paper, worth nothing in the real world. . . . Opposition to social and economic rights in the Constitution does not entail a belief that nations in Eastern Europe should eliminate social and economic programs that provide crucial protection against the vicissitudes of the free market.

Third, not all positive rights are the same. The right to education, for example, is more readily subject to judicial enforcement than the right to a clean environment. Some of the relevant rights pose especially severe risks; others are relatively harmless. But I believe that few of them belong in Eastern European constitutions. Here's why:

Governments should not be compelled to interfere with free markets. Some positive rights establish government interference with free markets as a constitutional obligation. For countries that are trying to create market economies, this is perverse. A constitution that prevents the operation of free labor markets may defeat current aspirations in Eastern Europe. Recall that the Hungarian Constitution protects not merely the right to equal pay for equal work, but also the right to an income conforming with the quantity and quality of work performed. This provision will have one of two consequences. (a) If the provision is to mean something, courts will have to oversee labor markets very closely, [in which case] it will be impossible to have a labor market. (b) The relevant provisions will be ignored — treated as goals or aspirations not subject to legal enforcement. . . .

The Hungarian provision is an extreme example, but similar problems are raised by provisions calling for specified maximum hours, for paid parental leave, for paid holidays, and much else. Many of these provisions may make sense if they are placed in ordinary legislation. But this is where they belong — not in the constitution. The constitution should not undertake close control of the private sphere, of civil society and economic markets . . . . Perhaps some small companies in the East should be allowed to get ahead by paying their workers a great deal in return for long hours, or for less in the way of leave; perhaps not. Perhaps medical care should not be free — especially for people who have the money to pay for it. These issues should be subject to democratic debate, not constitutional foreclosure.

Many positive rights are unenforceable by courts. Courts lack the tools of a bureaucracy. They cannot create government programs. They do not have a systematic overview of government policy. In these circumstances, it is unrealistic to expect courts to enforce many positive rights. . . . One of the enduring legacies of Communism is a large degree of cynicism about constitutions — a belief that constitutions may be pretty, but that they do not have meaning in the real world. If the right to 'the highest possible level of physical health' is not subject to judicial enforcement, perhaps the same will become true of the right to free speech and to due process of law.

The inclusion of many positive rights could work against general current effort to diminish sense of entitlement to state protection and to encourage individual initiative. . . . [I]f positive dispensations from the state are seen as a matter of individual entitlement, there can be corrosive effects on individual enterprise and initiative. This effect can be seen in both the West and the East. The risk of corrosion is no reason to eliminate programs that provide for subsistence. But in today's Eastern Europe, it is important to undertake a cultural shift through which people will look less to the state for their support, and more to their own efforts and enterprise.... A constitution that indiscriminately merges guarantees of 'just pay' and 'recreation' with traditional liberal rights is likely to send just the wrong signals.

...

In these circumstances, what ought to be done? I suggest three routes for the future. First, people now drafting constitutions for Eastern Europe should delete or minimize provisions that call for positive rights....

Second, [they] might put the positive rights in a separate section,... making clear that such rights are not for judicial enforcement, that they occupy a separate status, and that they are intended to set out general aspirations for public officials and for the citizenry at large.

Third, judges and lawyers in Eastern Europe... might adopt the notion that rights are 'nonjusticiable' — not subject to judicial enforcement — when they call for large-scale interference with the operation of free markets, or when they call for managerial tasks not within judicial competence. Any such notion must, however, make it clear that courts will vigorously enforce the basic political and civil rights whose violation was a daily affair under Communist rule — rights such as free speech, religious liberty, freedom from police abuse, due process, and nondiscrimination on grounds of ethnicity, race, religion, and sex.

CASS R. SUNSTEIN, DESIGNING DEMOCRACY: WHAT CONSTITUTIONS DO

(2001), at 222.

... [T]he American Constitution, and most constitutions before the twentieth-century, protected such rights as free speech, religious liberty, and sanctity of the home, without creating rights to minimally decent conditions of life. But in the late twentieth century, the trend is otherwise, with international documents, and most constitutions, creating rights to food, shelter, and more.

Some skeptics have doubted whether such rights make sense from the standpoint of constitutional design. On one view, a constitution should protect 'negative' rights, not 'positive' rights. Constitutional rights should be seen as individual protections *against* the aggressive state, not as private entitlements to protection by the state. A constitution that protects socioeconomic rights might, on this view, jeopardize constitutional rights altogether, by weakening the central function against preventing the abusive or oppressive exercise of government power.

But there are many problems with this view. Even conventional individual rights, like the right to free speech and private property, require governmental action. Private property cannot exist without a governmental apparatus, ready and able to secure people's holdings as such. So-called negative rights are emphatically positive rights. In fact all rights, even the most conventional, have costs. Rights of property and contract, as well as rights of free speech and religious liberty, need significant taxpayer support. In any case we might well think that the abusive or oppressive exercise of government power consists, not only in locking people up against their will, or in stopping them from speaking, but also in producing a situation in which people's minimal needs are not met.

If the central concerns are citizenship and democracy, the line between negative rights and positive rights is hard to maintain. The right to constitutional protection of private property has a strong democratic justification: If people's holdings are subject to ongoing governmental adjustment, people cannot have the security, and independence, that the status of citizenship requires. The right to private property should not be seen as an effort to protect wealthy people; it helps ensure deliberative democracy itself. But the same things can be said for minimal protections against starvation, homelessness, and other extreme deprivation. For people to be able to act as citizens, and to be able to count themselves as such, they must have the kind of independence that such minimal protections ensure.

On the other hand, a democratic constitution does not protect every right and interest that should be protected in a decent or just society. Perhaps ordinary politics can be trusted; if so, there is no need for constitutional protection. The basic reason for constitutional guarantees is to respond to problems faced in ordinary political life. If minimal socio-economic rights will be protected democratically, why involve the Constitution? The best answer is that to doubt the assumption and to insist such rights are indeed at systematic risk in political life, especially because those who would benefit from them lack political power. It is not clear if this is true in every nation. But certainly it is true in many places.

. . .

QUESTIONS

1. What desirable goals might human rights proponents expect the constitutional recognition of ESR to achieve? Do the views of Sunstein appear to have changed between 1993 and 2001? In what ways?

2. Fabre's proposed formulation looks rather like the obligation expressed in Article 2(1) of the ICESCR. Take some current examples of welfare policy in your country and reflect on whether they could be impugned on the basis of such a formulation.

3. Starting in 1992 the Israeli Knesset (parliament) considered various proposals for a Basic Law dealing with social rights. In 1997, the Ministry of Justice proposed the inclusion of the following formulation in such a law:

> The State of Israel will pursue the promotion and development of the conditions required for the guarantee of an existence worthy of human dignity to all residents, including, in this respect, matters of employment, education, health, housing, social welfare and environment, as determined by law or in accordance [with] the law or governmental decisions.

How would you evaluate this proposal, taking account of the fact that Israel is a party to the ICESCR?

NOTE

Although there is no formal requirement in the Covenant that ESR be constitutionally enshrined by states, there are many examples of such provisions. While the façade constitutions of the Soviet Union and other Communist states of the pre-1989 period are often cited in order to discredit such an approach, the practice is far more widespread than this reference point might suggest.

The following materials seek to give a reasonable cross-section of examples by drawing on cases in India, South Africa, the United States, and Europe. When reading these materials, bear in mind several aspects of the question of justiciability that underlie some of the courts' discussion.

(1) Are the rights as recognized in the ICESCR formulated in a manner that is sufficiently precise to enable judges to apply them in concrete cases?
(2) To the extent that such cases will involve decisions about public spending priorities, should such decisions remain the exclusive domain of the executive and legislature?
(3) Are judges well suited in terms of their expertise, social and political background and the facilities available to them to make such decisions?
(4) Does the justiciability test need to be applied to issues of ESR in a narrow, traditional manner, or are there more creative approaches, still involving the courts in some way, which would satisfy those demanding formal, institutionalized measures of implementation for ESR?

Bear in mind also the suggestion that quite similar questions might well be posed, in theory at least, in relation to key civil and political rights norms such as the prohibition on cruel, inhuman, or degrading treatment or punishment or the right to due process.

1. INDIA: 'DIRECTIVE PRINCIPLES'

In India the concept of 'directive principles of state policy' was originally developed in contra-distinction to that of 'fundamental rights'. Such principles are considered to be distinct from, and usually inferior in status to, rights that appear in the constitution without the qualification 'directive'. They appear in different forms in diverse constitutions including those of Ireland, Papua New Guinea and Nigeria. The Indian experience holds the greatest interest for our purposes. The Indian Constitution of 1950 contains one chapter dealing with 'fundamental rights' which consists largely of civil and political rights which figure in litigation as do a great range of legal claims, and another chapter dealing with 'directive principles of state policy'. Some illustrations from the Constitution follow.

Part III. Fundamental Rights

...

Article 21. No person shall be deprived of his life or personal liberty except according to procedure established by law.

...

Part IV. Directive Principles of State Policy

...

Article 37. The provisions contained in this Part shall not be enforced by any court, but the principles therein laid down are nevertheless fundamental in the governance of the country and it shall be the duty of the State to apply these principles in making laws.

Article 39. The State shall, in particular, direct its policy towards securing—

(a) that the citizens, men and women equally, have the right to an adequate means of livelihood;
(b) that the ownership and control of the material resources of the community are so distributed as best to subserve the common good;
(c) that the operation of the economic system does not result in the concentration of wealth and means of production to the common detriment;
(d) that there is equal pay for equal work for both men and women;
(e) that the health and strength of workers, men and women, and the tender age of children are not abused and that citizens are not forced by economic necessity to enter avocations unsuited to their age or strength;
(f) that children are given opportunities and facilities to develop in a healthy manner and in conditions of freedom and dignity and that childhood and youth are protected against exploitation and against moral and material abandonment.

...

Article 41. The State shall, within the limits of its economic capacity and development, make effective provision for securing the right to work, to education and to public assistance in cases of unemployment, old age, sickness and disablement, and in other cases of undeserved want.

...

Article 47. The State shall regard the raising of the level of nutrition and the standard of living of its people and the improvement of public health as among its primary duties...

Over the years the Indian courts as well as the legislature have redefined the relationship between fundamental rights and directive principles. The Court has approached the two categories in an integral manner, one result of which is to give some directive principles the status of fundamental rights. In the following materials the Olga Tellis case provides a classic illustration of the Court's activism, while Jean Ziegler describes one of the most important (and, as of 2007, ongoing) cases which deals with the right to food. Rajagopal then offers a critique of the experience of such 'public interest litigation'.

OLGA TELLIS V. BOMBAY MUNICIPAL CORPORATION

Supreme Court of India, 1985

AIR 1986 Supreme Court 18

CHANDRACHUD, C.

1. These Writ Petitions portray the plight of lakhs [hundreds of thousands] of persons who live on pavements and in slums in the city of Bombay. They constitute nearly half the population of the city. . . . Those who have made pavements their homes exist in the midst of filth and squalor, which has to be seen to be believed. Rabid dogs in search of stinking meat and cats in search of hungry rats keep them company. . . .

It is these men and women who have come to this Court to ask for a judgment that they cannot be evicted from their squalid shelters without being offered alternative accommodation. They rely for their rights on Art. 21 of the Constitution which guarantees that no person shall be deprived of his life except according to procedure established by law. They do not contend that they have a right to live on the pavements. Their contention is that they have a right to live, a right which cannot be exercised without the means of livelihood. . . .

. . .

32. . . . For purposes of argument, we will assume the factual correctness of the premise that if the petitioners are evicted from their dwellings, they will be deprived of their livelihood. Upon that assumption, the question which we have to consider is whether the right to life includes the right to livelihood. We see only one answer to that question, namely, that it does. The sweep of the right to life conferred by Art. 21 is wide and far-reaching. . . . That, which alone makes it possible to live, leave aside what makes life livable, must be deemed to be an integral component of the right to life. Deprive a person of his right to livelihood and you shall have deprived him of his life. Indeed, that explains the massive migration of the rural population to big cities. . . .

33. Article 39(a) of the Constitution, which is a Directive Principle of State Policy, provides that the State shall, in particular, direct its policy towards securing that the citizens, men and women equally, have the right to an adequate means of livelihood. [Reference is made to Arts. 41 and 37, see p. 322 *supra*] . . . The Principles contained in Arts. 39(a) and 41 must be regarded as equally fundamental in the understanding and interpretation of the meaning and content of fundamental rights. If there is an obligation upon the State to secure to the citizens an adequate means of livelihood and the right to work, it would be sheer pedantry to exclude the right to livelihood from the content of the right to life. . . .

. . .

35 . . . . It would be unrealistic on our part to reject the petitions on the ground that the petitioners have not adduced evidence to show that they will be rendered jobless if they are evicted from the slums and pavements. Commonsense, which is

a cluster of life's experiences, is often more dependable than the rival facts presented by warring litigants.

. . .

37. Two conclusions emerge from this discussion: one, that the right to life which is conferred by Art. 21 includes the right to livelihood and two, that it is established that if the petitioners are evicted from their dwellings, they will be deprived of their livelihood. But the Constitution does not put an absolute embargo on the deprivation of life or personal liberty. By Art. 21, such deprivation has to be according to procedure established by law. . . .

. . .

57. To summarise, . . . pavement dwellers who were censused or who happened to be censused in 1976 should be given, though not as a condition precedent to their removal, alternate [sites] at Malavani or at such other convenient place as the Government considers reasonable but not farther away in terms of distance; slum dwellers who were given identity cards and whose dwellings were numbered in the 1976 census must be given alternate sites for the resettlement: slums which have been in existence for a long time, say for twenty years or more, and which have been improved and developed will not be removed unless the land on which they stand or the appurtenant land, is required for a public purpose, in which case, alternate sites or accommodation will be provided to them . . . . In order to minimise the hardship involved in any eviction, we direct that the slums, wherever situated, will not be removed until one month after the end of the current monsoon season . . . .

REPORT OF THE SPECIAL RAPPORTEUR ON THE RIGHT TO FOOD, JEAN ZIEGLER, MISSION TO INDIA

UN Doc. E/CN.4/2006/44/Add.2 (2006)

[Note: In 2006 Jean Ziegler was reporting to the UN Human Rights Council in his capacity as Special Rapporteur. See Chapter 9 below.]

C. Access to justice and human rights institutions

24. . . . India provides one of the best examples in the world in terms of the justiciability of economic, social and cultural rights, with the right to life interpreted extensively by the Supreme Court to include the right to food. Under the Constitution, public-interest litigation is permitted to protect the basic human rights of the most vulnerable, which explains why so many social movements have sought appropriate remedies before the Supreme Court. In 2001, the PUCL approached the Supreme Court on behalf of starving people. Their original petition addressed the situation in six states, but the Supreme Court broadened its scope to cover the entire country. For the Supreme Court, the Government has a direct responsibility to prevent starvation:

> The anxiety of the Court is to see that the poor and the destitute and the weaker sections of the society do not suffer from hunger and starvation. The prevention of

> the same is one of the prime responsibilities of the Government — whether Central or the State. Mere schemes without any implementation are of no use. What is important is that the food must reach the hungry. [*People's Union for Civil Liberties v. Union of India & Ors*, 2001]

25. To ensure the fulfilment of the right to food, the Supreme Court directed that all destitute people be identified and included in existing food-based schemes and directed state governments to implement fully all these schemes, including the Targeted Public Distribution Scheme (TPDS), the Antyodaya Anna Yojana (AAY), the Integrated Child Development Scheme (ICDS), the Mid-Day Meals Scheme (MDMS). The Supreme Court also directed the most vulnerable, including the primitive tribes, to be placed in the AAY lists to ensure their access to food at a highly subsidized price. To increase access to information, it directed that all its orders and the lists of beneficiaries be made publicly available. The Supreme Court also directed that Chief Secretaries/Administrations of the states/Union territories should be held responsible in case of starvation or malnutrition deaths or persistent default in compliance with the orders. These directions have significantly improved the implementation of many food security schemes in many states, particularly since the Court has also appointed two Commissioners to monitor the implementation of its orders.

26. The PUCL case represents a great advance in the justiciability of the right to food as a human right, as the orders of the Supreme Court in this case have transformed the policy choices of the Government into enforceable, justiciable rights of the people. Although this relates primarily to the obligation to fulfil the right to food, the Court has also made judgements that are related to the obligations to respect and to protect the right to food. It has, for example, protected the right to water of Dalits against discrimination by the upper castes, [*State of Karnataka v. Appa Balu Ingale*, 1993] the right to livelihood of traditional fisherpeople against the shrimp industry [the *Aquaculture case: S. Jagannath v. Union of India*, 1996], and the right to livelihood of scheduled tribes against the acquisition of land by a private company [*Samatha v. State of Andhra Pradesh*, 1997]. For the Supreme Court, "any person who is deprived of his right to livelihood except according to just and fair procedure established by law, can challenge the deprivation as offending the right to life conferred by article 21" [*Olga Tellis v. Bombay Municipal Corporation*, 1985] It is now essential that small farmers who are arbitrarily evicted from their land, or women or members of the Scheduled Castes or Scheduled Tribes who are deprived of their access to productive resources, should have the same access to justice before the Supreme Court.

27. Despite these advances in the justiciability of the right to food, there remain difficulties in enforcing existing legislation, in ensuring the implementation of court decisions and in ensuring access to justice for the poor. The decisions of the Supreme Court in the *Aquaculture case* and *Samatha case* have, for example, never been fully implemented.... Lack of implementation, high costs, long delays in court proceedings and the lack of full independence of the judiciary at the local level have made the judicial system virtually inaccessible.

BALAKRISHNAN RAJAGOPAL, SOCIO-ECONOMIC RIGHTS AND THE INDIAN SUPREME COURT: REFLECTIONS FROM A SOCIAL MOVEMENT PERSPECTIVE

(Draft, August 2004)

. . . [M]ost social movements in India since 1970s have actively used the courts — especially the Supreme Court — as part of their struggles, whether it be the women's movement, the labor movement, the human rights movement or the environmental movement. Despite this activism, it is now increasingly recognized that the impact of the Court on ground reality has not been consistent. In the area of human rights for instance, studies show that the Court's seminal rulings are often not translated into reality for a range of reasons. In addition, the Court's activism, especially under the umbrella of social action litigation (SAL), has itself come under criticism for its undemocratic nature, lack of effectiveness and judicial grandstanding as well as its alleged violation of separation of powers. As one distinguished observer of judicial activism [Upendra Baxi] puts it, "judicial activism is at once a peril and a promise, an assurance of solidarity for the depressed classes of Indian society as well as a site of betrayal".

In this essay, I join this critique and call attention to the limitations of judicial activism, as it has been practiced more recently, for a progressive social movement politics. Rather than criticizing judicial activism for its counter-majoritarian character or its lack of effectiveness on the ground, I focus attention on the ideological character of the Court's particular approach to human rights. In particular, I suggest that the Court's activism increasingly manifests several biases — in favor of the state and development, in favor of the rich and against workers, in favor of the urban middle class and against rural farmers, and in favor of a globalitarian class and against the distributive ethos of the Indian Constitution — that, when taken together, result in an ideological interpretation of human rights . . . .

. . .

II. Explaining the mixed judicial record: Judicial Governance and the ideology of judging

. . .

As a result of the Court's assumption of governance functions, its approach to human rights is determined by its congruence, at any given time, with the overarching ideologies of *statism* and *developmentalism* which remain dominant ideologies of governance. Put differently, the Court is generally loath to find for a petitioner who is asserting rights that openly contradict with either the dominance of the state or with the vision of socio-economic and cultural change that is implied in the grand vision of development. . . .

A second reason why the Court may be biased in favor of some rights over others has to do with the particular history of the Court's long tussle with the legislature over the question of property rights. . . . [T]he Court has come to see itself, for historical reasons, principally as the defender of Chapter III [fundamental] rights. This has resulted in creating a structural bias in favor of civil and political rights. This could be evidenced, for instance, in the way in which almost all implied rights — livelihood, environment, education — have been read into Article 21 and therefore translated as a civil and political right. . . .

A third reason for the bias of the Court in favor of some rights over others has to do with social movement politics itself. Social movements in India, as elsewhere, tend to be highly suspicious of courts and law because of their perception as elite defenders of the status quo. . . . As such, social movements tend to approach courts relatively rarely unless they stand to gain immediately either through publicity, or to stave off disasters. . . .

A fourth reason for the bias of the Court can be found in the individual class and political alignments of judges, as well as their individual training and outlook towards socio-economic issues. . . .

A final reason for the bias of the Court in favor of some rights has to do with the role of the Bar itself. The Indian Bar, while tremendously talented, has not aggressively pushed for adjudication of socio-economic rights and does not seem to draw on the most current trends in international and comparative law. . . .

QUESTIONS

1. 'Courts overstep their proper roles by making radical interpretations of constitutional terms that expand both state duties and courts' power. The *Olga Tellis* decision reads a right to livelihood or work at a living wage (an economic-social right) into the right to life (a classic civil-political right), and moreover ties housing to the right to a livelihood. It thereby converts a "directive principle" into a "fundamental right". In light of this decision, every economic-social right that contributes importantly to an adequate life becomes part of the right to life. What economic and social planning now stands outside a court's jurisdiction? The court has become the legislature of the welfare state.' Comment, as applied to the *Olga Tellis* decision.

2. Compare Articles 39(a) and 41 of the Indian Constitution with Articles 2, 6 and 7 of the ICESCR. Are they equivalent with respect to the obligations put on the state, or are there significant differences between them?

3. Ziegler begins by praising the Indian model as one of the best in the world, but ends by lamenting the difficulties in enforcing legislation, implementing decisions, and ensuring access to justice. Rajagopal is also critical. What picture of the Indian experience emerges? Is it an example to follow elsewhere?

2. SOUTH AFRICA: A MODEL SOCIAL RIGHTS CONSTITUTION?

When South Africa's post-apartheid constitution was being debated, consideration was given to following the directive principles approach in relation to social rights. This was rejected, however, and full constitutional recognition was accorded to them. In the decade since, the South African jurisprudence has had a major impact on discussions of ESR globally, with many commentators arguing that the *Grootboom* and *TAC*cases in particular show the way forward for an effective and manageable approach to making these rights justiciable.[33] Some of the relevant provisions of the Constitution (1996) are provided below, followed by excerpts from the three major cases.

Section 1

The Republic of South Africa is one sovereign democratic state founded on the following values:

(a) Human dignity, the achievement of equality and the advancement of human rights and freedoms.

...

Section 7

(1) This Bill of Rights is a cornerstone of democracy in South Africa. It enshrines the rights of all people in our country and affirms the democratic values of human dignity, equality and freedom.
(2) The state must respect, protect, promote and fulfil the rights in the Bill of Rights.
(3) The rights in the Bill of Rights are subject to the limitations contained or referred to in section 36, or elsewhere in the Bill.

...

Section 10

Everyone has inherent dignity and the right to have their dignity respected and protected.

Section 11

Everyone has the right to life.

...

Section 26

(1) Everyone has the right to have access to adequate housing.
(2) The state must take reasonable legislative and other measures, within its available resources, to achieve the progressive realisation of this right.
(3) No one may be evicted from their home, or have their home demolished, without an order of court made after considering all the relevant circumstances. No legislation may permit arbitrary evictions.

[33] Two other notable ESR cases are *Khosa v. Minister for Social Development* 2004 (6) BCLR 569 (social security for non-citizens) and *Port Elizabeth Municipality v. Various Occupiers* 2004 (12) BCLR 1268 (housing rights).

Section 27

(1) Everyone has the right to have access to —
(a) health care services, including reproductive health care;
(b) sufficient food and water; and
(c) social security, including, if they are unable to support themselves and their dependants, appropriate social assistance.

(2) The state must take reasonable legislative and other measures, within its available resources, to achieve the progressive realisation of each of these rights.

(3) No one may be refused emergency medical treatment.

Section 28

(1) Every child has the right:

. . .

(b) to family care or parental care, or to appropriate alternative care when removed from the family environment;
(c) to basic nutrition, shelter, basic health care services and social services;

. . .

Section 39

(1) When interpreting the Bill of Rights, a court, tribunal or forum:
(a) must promote the values that underlie an open and democratic society based on human dignity, equality and freedom;
(b) must consider international law; and
(c) may consider foreign law.

(2) When interpreting any legislation, and when developing the common law or customary law, every court, tribunal or forum must promote the spirit, purport, and objects of the Bill of Rights.

SOOBRAMONEY V. MINISTER OF HEALTH (KWAZULU-NATAL)

Constitutional Court of South Africa, Case CCT 32/97, 27 November 1997

www.law.wits.ac.za/judgements/soobram.html

CHASKALSON P.

[1] The appellant, a 41 year old unemployed man, is a diabetic who suffers from ischaemic heart disease and cerebro-vascular disease which caused him to have a stroke during 1996. In 1996 his kidneys also failed. Sadly his condition is irreversible and he is now in the final stages of chronic renal failure. His life could be prolonged by means of regular renal dialysis. He has sought such treatment from the renal unit of the Addington state hospital in Durban. The hospital can, however, only provide

dialysis treatment to a limited number of patients. The renal unit has 20 dialysis machines available to it, and some of these machines are in poor condition. . . . Because of the limited facilities that are available for kidney dialysis the hospital has been unable to provide the appellant with the treatment he has requested.

[2] . . . Additional dialysis machines and more trained nursing staff are required to enable it to do this, but the hospital budget does not make provision for such expenditure. The hospital would like to have its budget increased but it has been told by the provincial health department that funds are not available for this purpose.

[3] Because of the shortage of resources the hospital follows a set policy in regard to the use of the dialysis resources. Only patients who suffer from acute renal failure, which can be treated and remedied by renal dialysis are given automatic access to renal dialysis at the hospital. Those patients who, like the appellant, suffer from chronic renal failure which is irreversible are not admitted automatically to the renal programme. A set of guidelines has been drawn up and adopted to determine which applicants who have chronic renal failure will be given dialysis treatment. . . .

[The opinion noted that the appellant did not qualify under the guidelines. He alleged that he could not afford treatment at private hospitals, and he sought a judicial order directing Addington Hospital to provide the necessary treatment. His application was dismissed, and he then applied for leave to appeal to the Constitutional Court. His claim was based on sections 27(3) and 11 of the 1996 Constitution, *supra.*

The Court stressed the great disparities in wealth in South Africa, and the deplorable conditions and poverty in which millions of people lived, including lack of access to adequate health facilities. It referred to the commitment in the preamble of the Constitution to address these issues 'and to transform our society into one in which there will be human dignity, freedom and equality . . . ', and to sections 26 and 27, *supra.*]

. . .

[11] What is apparent from these provisions is that the obligations imposed on the state by sections 26 and 27 in regard to access to housing, health care, food, water and social security are dependent upon the resources available for such purposes, and that the corresponding rights themselves are limited by reason of the lack of resources. Given this lack of resources and the significant demands on them that have already been referred to, an unqualified obligation to meet these needs would not presently be capable of being fulfilled. This is the context within which section 27(3) must be construed.

[14] Counsel for the appellant argued that section 27(3) should be construed consistently with the right to life entrenched in section 11 of the Constitution and that everyone requiring life-saving treatment who is unable to pay for such treatment herself or himself is entitled to have the treatment provided at a state hospital without charge.

[15] This Court has dealt with the right to life in the context of capital punishment but it has not yet been called upon to decide upon the parameters of the right to life or its relevance to the positive obligations imposed on the state under various provisions of the bill of rights. In India the Supreme Court has developed a jurisprudence around

the right to life so as to impose positive obligations on the state in respect of the basic needs of its inhabitants. . . . Unlike the Indian Constitution ours deals specifically in the bill of rights with certain positive obligations imposed on the state, and where it does so, it is our duty to apply the obligations as formulated in the Constitution and not to draw inferences that would be inconsistent therewith.

. . .

[17] The purposive approach [to constitutional interpretation] will often be one which calls for a generous interpretation to be given to a right to ensure that individuals secure the full protection of the bill of rights, but this is not always the case, and the context may indicate that in order to give effect to the purpose of a particular provision 'a narrower or specific meaning' should be given to it.

[18] In developing his argument on the right to life counsel for the appellant relied upon a decision of a two-judge bench of the Supreme Court of India in *Paschim Banga Khet Mazdoor Samity and others v. State of West Bengal and another*, where it was said:

> The Constitution envisages the establishment of a welfare State at the federal level as well as at the State level. In a welfare State the primary duty of the Government is to secure the welfare of the people. Providing adequate medical facilities for the people is an essential part of the obligations undertaken by the Government in a welfare State. The Government discharges this obligation by running hospitals and health centres which provide medical care to the person seeking to avail those facilities. Article 21 imposes an obligation on the State to safeguard the right to life of every person. Preservation of human life is thus of paramount importance. The Government hospitals run by the State and the medical officers employed therein are duty bound to extend medical assistance for preserving human life. Failure on the part of a Government hospital to provide timely medical treatment to a person in need of such treatment results in violation of his right to life guaranteed under Article 21.

These comments must be seen in the context of the facts of that case which are materially different to those of the present case. It was a case in which constitutional damages were claimed. The claimant had suffered serious head injuries and brain haemorrhage as a result of having fallen off a train. He was taken to various hospitals and turned away, either because the hospital did not have the necessary facilities for treatment, or on the grounds that it did not have room to accommodate him. As a result he had been obliged to secure the necessary treatment at a private hospital. It appeared from the judgment that the claimant could in fact have been accommodated in more than one of the hospitals which turned him away and that the persons responsible for that decision had been guilty of misconduct. This is precisely the sort of case which would fall within section 27(3). It is one in which emergency treatment was clearly necessary. The occurrence was sudden, the patient had no opportunity of making arrangements in advance for the treatment that was required, and there was urgency in securing the treatment in order to stabilize his condition. The treatment was available but denied.

[19] In our Constitution the right to medical treatment does not have to be inferred from the nature of the state established by the Constitution or from the

right to life which it guarantees. It is dealt with directly in section 27. If section 27(3) were to be construed in accordance with the appellant's contention it would make it substantially more difficult for the state to fulfill its primary obligations under sections 27(1) and (2) to provide health care services to 'everyone' within its available resources. It would also have the consequence of prioritising the treatment of terminal illnesses over other forms of medical care and would reduce the resources available to the state for [non-life threatening medical needs]. In my view much clearer language than that used in section 27(3) would be required to justify such a conclusion.

[20] Section 27(3) itself is couched in negative terms — it is a right not to be refused emergency treatment. The purpose of the right seems to be to ensure that treatment be given in an emergency, and is not frustrated by reason of bureaucratic requirements or other formalities. . . . What the section requires is that remedial treatment that is necessary and available be given immediately to avert that harm.

[21] The applicant suffers from chronic renal failure. To be kept alive by dialysis he would require such treatment two to three times a week. This is not an emergency which calls for immediate remedial treatment. It is an ongoing state of affairs resulting from a deterioration of the applicant's renal function which is incurable. In my view section 27(3) does not apply to these facts.

[22] The appellant's demand to receive dialysis treatment at a state hospital must be determined in accordance with the provisions of sections 27(1) and (2) and not section 27(3). These sections entitle everyone to have access to health care services provided by the state 'within its available resources'.

. . .

[24] At present the Department of Health in KwaZulu-Natal does not have sufficient funds to cover the cost of the services which are being provided to the public. [For two years it has already greatly overspent its budget.] . . . The renal unit at the Addington Hospital has to serve the whole of KwaZulu-Natal and also takes patients from parts of the Eastern Cape. There are many more patients suffering from chronic renal failure than there are dialysis machines to treat such patients. This is a nation-wide problem and resources are stretched in all renal clinics throughout the land. Guidelines have therefore been established [and] . . . were applied in the present case.

[25] By using the available dialysis machines in accordance with the guidelines more patients are benefited than would be the case if they were used to keep alive persons with chronic renal failure, and the outcome of the treatment is also likely to be more beneficial because it is directed to curing patients, and not simply to maintaining them in a chronically ill condition. It has not been suggested that these guidelines are unreasonable or that they were not applied fairly and rationally . . . .

. . .

[28] . . . It is estimated that the cost to the state of treating one chronically ill patient by means of renal dialysis provided twice a week at a state hospital is approximately R60,000 per annum. If all the persons in South Africa who suffer from chronic renal failure were to be provided with dialysis treatment . . . the cost of doing so would make substantial inroads into the health budget. And if this principle were to be applied to all patients claiming access to expensive medical treatment or

expensive drugs, the health budget would have to be dramatically increased to the prejudice of other needs which the state has to meet.

[29] The provincial administration which is responsible for health services in KwaZulu-Natal has to make decisions about [health care] funding.... These choices involve difficult decisions to be taken at the political level in fixing the health budget, and at the functional level in deciding upon the priorities to be met. A court will be slow to interfere with rational decisions taken in good faith by the political organs and medical authorities whose responsibility it is to deal with such matters.

[30] . . . The dilemma confronting health authorities faced with such cases was described by Sir Thomas Bingham MR in in *R v. Cambridge Health Authority, ex parte B*:[34]

> ... health authorities of all kinds are constantly pressed to make ends meet.... Difficult and agonising judgments have to be made as to how a limited budget is best allocated to the maximum advantage of the maximum number of patients. That is not a judgment which the court can make.

[31] One cannot but have sympathy for the appellant and his family... [b]ut the state's resources are limited and the appellant does not meet the criteria for admission to the renal dialysis programme. Unfortunately, this is true not only of the appellant but of many others who need access to renal dialysis units or to other health services. There are also those who need access to housing, food and water, employment opportunities, and social security....

The state has to manage its limited resources in order to address all these claims. There will be times when this requires it to adopt a holistic approach to the larger needs of society rather than to focus on the specific needs of particular individuals within society.

[37]... The appeal... is dismissed.

GOVERNMENT OF SOUTH AFRICA V. GROOTBOOM

Constitutional Court of South Africa, Case CCT 11/00, 4 October 2000

[Irene Grootboom and most other respondents (390 adults and 510 children) lived in a squatter settlement called Wallacedene. Their living conditions were 'lamentable': very low income population, overcrowded shacks (95% of which lacked electricity), no water or sewage or refuse removal services, the area partly waterlogged and dangerously close to a main thoroughfare. Many inhabitants who had applied for subsidized low-cost housing from the municipality had been on the waiting list up to seven years.

Facing the prospect of indefinitely long intolerable conditions, respondents began to move out of Wallacedene in September 1998, putting up shacks on vacant privately owned land (named 'New Rust') that was earmarked for eventual low-cost

[34] [1995] 2 All ER 129 (CA) at 137d–f.

housing. Court proceedings brought by the owner resulted in an order of May 1999 instructing the sheriff to evict respondents and dismantle their shacks. The magistrate also ordered the parties and municipality to identify alternative land for permanent or temporary occupation by the New Rust residents. No mediation occurred, and respondents were evicted, their houses bulldozed and possessions destroyed. They then took shelter on the Wallacedene sports fields under such temporary structures as were feasible, at the time when winter rains began.

Respondents' court-appointed attorney then applied to the Cape of Good Hope High Court for an order requiring the government to provide them with adequate basic housing until they obtained permanent accommodation. The High Court ordered the appellants to provide the respondents who were children and their parents with shelter. Its judgment stated that 'tents, portable latrines and a regular supply of water (albeit transported) would constitute the bare minimum.' The appellants, representing all spheres of government responsible for housing (central government, province of the Western Cape, and municipality), brought the present appeal to challenge that order].

JUSTICE YACOOB WROTE THE OPINION FOR THE UNANIMOUS CONSTITUTIONAL COURT.

[6] The cause of the acute housing shortage lies in apartheid.

[The High Court concluded that the respondents' challenge under section 26 failed, because the appellant had taken 'reasonable legislative measures and other measures within its available resources to achieve the progressive realisation of the right to have access to adequate housing.' The Constitutional Court interpreted section 26 to impose certain obligations in this case.

Respondents' second claim was under section 28(1)(c), which provides that children have (among other rights) the right to shelter. The High Court had ordered that temporary accommodation be provided for those of the respondents who were children and for one parent of each child who required supervision. This part of the High Court's order was reversed by the Constitutional Court.]

The following excerpts from Justice Yacoob's opinion concern only section 26....

...

[20] ... Section 7(2) of the Constitution requires the state "to respect, protect, promote and fulfil the rights in the Bill of Rights" and the courts are constitutionally bound to ensure that they are protected and fulfilled. The question is therefore not whether socio-economic rights are justiciable under our Constitution, but how to enforce them in a given case....

...

ii) *The relevant international law and its impact*

[26] During argument, considerable weight was attached to the value of international law in interpreting section 26....

[The Court turned to a discussion of the ICESCR and the work of the UN Committee on ESCR. The opinion emphasized Art. 11 (the right of everyone to an adequate standard of living..., including adequate food, clothing and housing) and

Art. 2 (States parties will take appropriate steps to ensure the realization of this right . . . to the maximum of available resources etc.). The opinion drew particular attention to para. 10 of General Comment No. 3 (at p. 303 *supra*) in relation to a minimum core obligation.]

[31] . . . Each right has a "minimum essential level" that must be satisfied by the states parties. . . . Minimum core obligation is determined generally by having regard to the needs of the most vulnerable group that is entitled to the protection of the right in question. It is in this context that the concept of minimum core obligation must be understood in international law.

[32] It is not possible to determine the minimum threshold for the progressive realisation of the right of access to adequate housing without first identifying the needs and opportunities for the enjoyment of such a right. These will vary according to factors such as income, unemployment, availability of land and poverty. The differences between city and rural communities will also determine the needs and opportunities for the enjoyment of this right. Variations ultimately depend on the economic and social history and circumstances of a country. All this illustrates the complexity of the task of determining a minimum core obligation for the progressive realisation of the right. . . .

[33] . . . [T]he real question in terms of our Constitution is whether the measures taken by the state to realise the right afforded by section 26 are reasonable. There may be cases where it may be possible and appropriate to have regard to the content of a minimum core obligation to determine whether the measures taken by the state are reasonable . . . .

iii) *Analysis of section 26*

. . .

[34] . . . Subsections (1) and (2) are related and must be read together . . . . Although the subsection does not expressly say so, there is, at the very least, a negative obligation placed upon the state and all other entities and persons to desist from preventing or impairing the right of access to adequate housing. The negative right is further spelt out in subsection (3) which prohibits arbitrary evictions. Access to housing could also be promoted if steps are taken to make the rural areas of our country more viable so as to limit the inexorable migration of people from rural to urban areas in search of jobs.

[35] . . . A right of access to adequate housing also suggests that it is not only the state who is responsible for the provision of houses, but that other agents within our society, including individuals themselves, must be enabled by legislative and other measures to provide housing. The state must create the conditions for access to adequate housing for people at all economic levels of our society . . . .

[36] . . . For those who can afford to pay for adequate housing, the state's primary obligation lies in unlocking the system, providing access to housing stock and a legislative framework to facilitate self-built houses through planning laws and access to finance. Issues of development and social welfare are raised in respect of those who cannot afford to provide themselves with housing. State policy needs to address both these groups. The poor are particularly vulnerable and their needs require special attention. It is in this context that the relationship between sections 26 and

27 and the other socio-economic rights is most apparent. If under section 27 the state has in place programmes to provide adequate social assistance to those who are otherwise unable to support themselves and their dependants, that would be relevant to the state's obligations in respect of other socio-economic rights.

[37] The state's obligation to provide access to adequate housing depends on context, and may differ from province to province, from city to city, from rural to urban areas and from person to person. Some may need access to land and no more; some may need access to land and building materials; some may need access to finance; some may need access to services such as water, sewage, electricity and roads....

...

Reasonable legislative and other measures

[39] What constitutes reasonable legislative and other measures must be determined in the light of the fact that the Constitution creates different spheres of government: national government, provincial government and local government.... The Constitution allocates powers and functions amongst these different spheres emphasising their obligation to co-operate with one another in carrying out their constitutional tasks. In the case of housing, it is a function shared by both national and provincial government. A reasonable programme therefore must clearly allocate responsibilities and tasks to the different spheres of government and ensure that the appropriate financial and human resources are available.

...

[41] The measures must establish a coherent public housing programme directed towards the progressive realisation of the right of access to adequate housing within the state's available means.... The precise contours and content of the measures to be adopted are primarily a matter for the legislature and the executive. They must, however, ensure that the measures they adopt are reasonable.... A court considering reasonableness will not enquire whether other more desirable or favourable measures could have been adopted, or whether public money could have been better spent. The question would be whether the measures that have been adopted are reasonable. It is necessary to recognise that a wide range of possible measures could be adopted by the state to meet its obligations. Many of these would meet the requirement of reasonableness....

[42] ... Mere legislation is not enough....

...

[43] Those whose needs are the most urgent and whose ability to enjoy all rights therefore is most in peril, must not be ignored .... It may not be sufficient to meet the test of reasonableness to show that the measures are capable of achieving a statistical advance in the realisation of the right....

...

[46] ... Section 26 does not expect more of the state than is achievable within its available resources .... The measures must be calculated to attain the goal

expeditiously and effectively but the availability of resources is an important factor in determining what is reasonable.

. . .

[51] It emerges from the general principles [of the national Housing Act] read together with the functions of national, provincial and local government that the concept of housing development as defined is central to the Act. Housing development, as defined, seeks to provide citizens and permanent residents with access to permanent residential structures with secure tenure ensuring internal and external privacy and to provide adequate protection against the elements. What is more, it endeavours to ensure convenient access to economic opportunities and to health, educational and social amenities. . . .

[52] . . . [T]here is no express provision to facilitate access to temporary relief for people who have no access to land, no roof over their heads, for people who are living in intolerable conditions and for people who are in crisis because of natural disasters such as floods and fires, or because their homes are under threat of demolition. These are people in desperate need. Their immediate need can be met by relief short of housing which fulfils the requisite standards of durability, habitability and stability encompassed by the definition of housing development in the Act.

. . .

[66] . . . The nationwide housing programme falls short of obligations imposed upon national government to the extent that it fails to recognise that the state must provide for relief for those in desperate need. They are not to be ignored in the interests of an overall programme focussed on medium and long-term objectives. It is essential that a reasonable part of the national housing budget be devoted to this, but the precise allocation is for national government to decide in the first instance.

. . .

[68] Effective implementation requires at least adequate budgetary support by national government. This, in turn, requires recognition of the obligation to meet immediate needs in the nationwide housing programme. Recognition of such needs in the nationwide housing programme requires it to plan, budget and monitor the fulfilment of immediate needs and the management of crises. This must ensure that a significant number of desperate people in need are afforded relief, though not all of them need receive it immediately . . . .

[69] In conclusion . . . the programmes adopted by the state fell short of the requirements of section 26(2) in that no provision was made for relief to the categories of people in desperate need identified earlier . . . .

. . .

H. *Evaluation of the conduct of the appellants towards the respondents*

. . .

[81] . . . It cannot be said, on the evidence before us, that the respondents moved out of the Wallacedene settlement and occupied the land earmarked for low-cost housing development as a deliberate strategy to gain preference in the allocation of housing resources over thousands of other people who remained in intolerable conditions and who were also in urgent need of housing relief. It must be borne in mind however, that

the effect of any order that constitutes a special dispensation for the respondents on account of their extraordinary circumstances is to accord that preference.

...

[83] ... Section 26, read in the context of the Bill of Rights as a whole, must mean that the respondents have a right to reasonable action by the state in all circumstances and with particular regard to human dignity....

...

[88] ... The state had an obligation to ensure, at the very least, that the eviction was humanely executed. However, the eviction was reminiscent of the past and inconsistent with the values of the Constitution. The respondents were evicted a day early and to make matters worse, their possessions and building materials were not merely removed, but destroyed and burnt...

...

[92] This judgment must not be understood as approving any practice of land invasion for the purpose of coercing a state structure into providing housing on a preferential basis to those who participate in any exercise of this kind. Land invasion is inimical to the systematic provision of adequate housing on a planned basis. It may well be that the decision of a state structure, faced with the difficulty of repeated land invasions, not to provide housing in response to those invasions, would be reasonable. Reasonableness must be determined on the facts of each case.

I. *Summary and conclusion*

...

[94] I am conscious that it is an extremely difficult task for the state to meet these obligations in the conditions that prevail in our country. This is recognised by the Constitution .... I stress however, that despite all these qualifications, these are rights, and the Constitution obliges the state to give effect to them. This is an obligation that courts can, and in appropriate circumstances, must enforce.

[95] ... [S]ection 26 does oblige the state to devise and implement a coherent, co-ordinated programme designed to meet its section 26 obligations. The programme that has been adopted ... fell short of the obligations imposed....

...

J. *The Order*

[99] ... It is declared that:

2....

(a) Section 26(2) of the Constitution requires the state to devise and implement within its available resources a comprehensive and coordinated programme progressively to realise the right of access to adequate housing.

(b) The programme must include reasonable measures ... to provide relief for people who have no access to land, no roof over their heads, and who are living in intolerable conditions or crisis situations.

(c) As at the date of the launch of this application, the state housing programme in the area of the Cape Metropolitan Council fell short of compliance with the requirements in paragraph (b), in that it failed to make reasonable provision within its available resources for people in the Cape Metropolitan area with no access to land, no roof over their heads, and who were living in intolerable conditions or crisis situations.

TREATMENT ACTION CAMPAIGN V. MINISTER OF HEALTH

Constitutional Court of South Africa, Case CCT 8/02, 5 July 2002

[The Treatment Action Campaign (TAC) was the lead applicant among various other civil society groups working on HIV/AIDS. The respondents were the national Minister of Health and the various Provincial authorities.]

...

[2] This appeal is directed at reversing orders made in a high court against government because of perceived shortcomings in its response to an aspect of the HIV/AIDS challenge. The court found that government had not reasonably addressed the need to reduce the risk of HIV-positive mothers transmitting the disease to their babies at birth. More specifically the finding was that government had acted unreasonably in (a) refusing to make an antiretroviral drug called nevirapine available in the public health sector where the attending doctor considered it medically indicated and (b) not setting out a timeframe for a national programme to prevent mother-to-child transmission of HIV.

[3] ... The drug is currently available free to government and its administration is simple: a single tablet taken by the mother at the onset of labour and a few drops fed to the baby within 72 hours after birth....

[4] [A] Government ... programme imposes restrictions on the availability of nevirapine in the public health sector. This is where the first of two main issues in the case arose. The applicants contended that these restrictions are unreasonable when measured against the Constitution .... At issue here is the right given to everyone to have access to public health care services and the right of children to be afforded special protection.... [see sections 27–28, p. 329 *supra*].

[5] The second main issue ... is whether government is constitutionally obliged and had to be ordered forthwith to plan and implement an effective, comprehensive and progressive programme for the prevention of mother-to-child transmission of HIV throughout the country....

[6] The affidavits lodged by the applicants addressed these two central issues from a variety of specialised perspectives, ranging from paediatrics, pharmacology and epidemiology to public health administration, economics and statistics....

...

The Issues

[19] ... [As noted in the TAC affidavit] the Applicants' case is as follows: 22.1 The HIV/AIDS epidemic is a major public health problem in our country, and has reached catastrophic proportions. 22.2 One of the most common methods of

transmission of HIV in children is from mother to child at and around birth. Government estimates are that since 1998, 70,000 children are infected in this manner every year. 22.3 The Medicines Control Council has the statutory duty to investigate whether medicines are suitable for the purpose for which they are intended, and the safety, quality and therapeutic efficacy of medicines. 22.4 The Medicines Control Council has registered Nevirapine for use to reduce the risk of mother-to-child transmission of HIV. This means that Nevirapine has been found to be suitable for this purpose, and that it is safe, of acceptable quality, and therapeutically efficacious. 22.5 The result is that doctors in the private profession can and do prescribe Nevirapine for their patients when, in their professional judgment, it is appropriate to do so. 22.6 In July 2000 the manufacturers of Nevirapine offered to make it available to the South African government free of charge for a period of five years, for the purposes of reducing the risk of mother-to-child transmission of HIV. 22.7 The government has formally decided to make Nevirapine available only at a limited number of pilot sites, which number two per province. 22.8 The result is that doctors in the public sector, who do not work at one of those pilot sites, are unable to prescribe this drug for their patients, even though it has been offered to the government for free. 22.9 The Applicants are aware of the desirability of a multiple-strategy approach to the prevention of mother-to-child transmission. However, they cannot and do not accept that this provides a rational or lawful basis for depriving patients at other sites of the undoubted benefits of Nevirapine, even if at this stage the provision can not be done as part of a broader integrated strategy — a point that is not conceded. 22.10 To the extent that there may be situations in which the use of Nevirapine is not indicated, this is the situation in both the private and the public sector. Whether or not to prescribe Nevirapine is a matter of professional medical judgment.... 22.11 There is no rational or lawful basis for allowing doctors in the private sector to exercise their professional judgment in deciding when to prescribe Nevirapine, but effectively prohibiting doctors in the public sector from doing so. 22.12 ... [T]he government has failed over an extended period to implement a comprehensive programme for the prevention of mother-to-child transmission of HIV. 22.13 The result of this refusal and this failure is the mother-to-child transmission of HIV in situations where this was both predictable and avoidable. 22.14 This conduct of the government is irrational, in breach of the Bill of Rights, and contrary to the values and principles prescribed for public administration in section 195 of the Constitution. Furthermore, government conduct is in breach of its international obligations...."

...

[22] In their argument counsel for the government raised issues pertaining to the separation of powers. This may be relevant in two respects — (i) in the deference that courts should show to decisions taken by the executive concerning the formulation of its policies; and (ii) in the order to be made where a court finds that the executive has failed to comply with its constitutional obligations...

Enforcement of socio-economic rights

...

[25] ... The question is whether the applicants have shown that the measures adopted by the government to provide access to health care services for HIV-positive

mothers and their newborn babies fall short of its obligations under the CESCR General Comment 3 "The nature of States parties obligations....

Minimum core

[26] [T]he first and second amici . . . contended that section 27(1) of the Constitution establishes an individual right vested in everyone. This right, so the contention went, has a minimum core to which every person in need is entitled. The concept of "minimum core" was developed by the United Nations Committee on [ESCR]....

...

[28] ... In the case of sections 26 and 27 . . . rights and obligations are stated separately. There is accordingly a distinction between the self-standing rights in sections 26(1) and 27(1), to which everyone is entitled, and which in terms of section 7(2) of the Constitution "[t]he state must respect, protect, promote and fulfil", and the independent obligations imposed on the state by sections 26(2) and 27(2). This minimum core might not be easy to define, but includes at least the minimum decencies of life consistent with human dignity. No one should be condemned to a life below the basic level of dignified human existence. The very notion of individual rights presupposes that anyone in that position should be able to obtain relief from a court.

[29] In effect what the argument comes down to is that sections 26 and 27 must be construed as imposing two positive obligations on the state: one an obligation to give effect to the 26(1) and 27(1) rights; the other a limited obligation to do so progressively through "reasonable legislative and other measures, within its available resources". Implicit in that contention is that the content of the right in subsection (1) differs from the content of the obligation in subsection (2). This argument fails to have regard to the way subsections (1) and (2) of both sections 26 and 27 are linked in the text of the Constitution itself, and to the way they have been interpreted by this Court in *Soobramoney* and *Grootboom.*

...

[34] Although Yacoob J [in *Grootboom*] indicated that evidence in a particular case may show that there is a minimum core of a particular service that should be taken into account in determining whether measures adopted by the state are reasonable, the socio-economic rights of the Constitution should not be construed as entitling everyone to demand that the minimum core be provided to them. Minimum core was thus treated as possibly being relevant to reasonableness under section 26(2), and not as a self-standing right conferred on everyone under section 26(1).

[35] A purposive reading of sections 26 and 27 does not lead to any other conclusion. It is impossible to give everyone access even to a "core" service immediately. All that is possible, and all that can be expected of the state, is that it act reasonably to provide access to the socio-economic rights identified in sections 26 and 27 on a progressive basis....

[36] The state is obliged to take reasonable measures progressively to eliminate or reduce the large areas of severe deprivation that afflict our society. The courts will

guarantee that the democratic processes are protected so as to ensure accountability, responsiveness and openness, as the Constitution requires in section 1. As the Bill of Rights indicates, their function in respect of socio-economic rights is directed towards ensuring that legislative and other measures taken by the state are reasonable. As this Court said in *Grootboom*, "[i]t is necessary to recognise that a wide range of possible measures could be adopted by the State to meet its obligations".

[37] It should be borne in mind that in dealing with such matters the courts are not institutionally equipped to make the wide-ranging factual and political enquiries necessary for determining what the minimum-core standards called for by the first and second amici should be, nor for deciding how public revenues should most effectively be spent. There are many pressing demands on the public purse. . . .

[38] Courts are ill-suited to adjudicate upon issues where court orders could have multiple social and economic consequences for the community. The Constitution contemplates rather a restrained and focused role for the courts, namely, to require the state to take measures to meet its constitutional obligations and to subject the reasonableness of these measures to evaluation. Such determinations of reasonableness may in fact have budgetary implications, but are not in themselves directed at rearranging budgets. In this way the judicial, legislative and executive functions achieve appropriate constitutional balance.

[39] We therefore conclude that section 27(1) of the Constitution does not give rise to a self-standing and independent positive right enforceable irrespective of the considerations mentioned in section 27(2). Sections 27(1) and 27(2) must be read together as defining the scope of the positive rights that everyone has and the corresponding obligations on the state to "respect, protect, promote and fulfil" such rights. The rights conferred by sections 26(1) and 27(1) are to have "access" to the services that the state is obliged to provide in terms of sections 26(2) and 27(2).

. . .

The applicants' contentions

[44] It is the applicants' case that the measures adopted by government . . . were deficient in two material respects: first, because they prohibited the administration of nevirapine at public hospitals and clinics outside the research and training sites; and second, because they failed to implement a comprehensive programme for the prevention of mother-to-child transmission of HIV.

. . .

[46] In *Grootboom* . . . this Court held that "[a]lthough [section 26(1)] does not expressly say so, there is, at the very least, a negative obligation placed upon the State and all other entities and persons to desist from preventing or impairing the right of access to adequate housing." . . . . This is relevant to the challenges to the measures adopted by government . . . .

[47] The applicants' contentions raise two questions, namely, is the policy of confining the supply of nevirapine reasonable in the circumstances; and does government have a comprehensive policy for the prevention of mother-to-child transmission of HIV.

The policy confining nevirapine to the research and training sites

...

[51–55] In substance four reasons were advanced in the affidavits for confining the administration of nevirapine to the research and training sites. [(1) Where the comprehensive package was unavailable the benefits of nevirapine would be counteracted by the transmission of HIV from mother to infant through breast-feeding. But delivery of that package is costly and problematic in some contexts. (2) The administration of nevirapine to the mother and her child might lead to the development of resistance to the efficacy of nevirapine and related antiretrovirals in later years. (3) In safety terms the hazards of using neviripine are unknown. (4) It is unclear if the public health system has the capacity to provide the package.]

...

[56] We deal with each of these issues in turn.

Efficacy

[57] ... It is clear from the evidence that the provision of nevirapine will save the lives of a significant number of infants even if it is administered without the full package ....

[58] ... [T]he wealth of scientific material produced by both sides makes plain that sero-conversion of HIV takes place in some, but not all, cases and that nevirapine thus remains to some extent efficacious in combating mother-to-child transmission even if the mother breastfeeds her baby.

Resistance

[59] ... The prospects of the child surviving if infected are so slim and the nature of the suffering so grave that the risk of some resistance manifesting at some time in the future is well worth running.

Safety

[60] The evidence shows that safety is no more than a hypothetical issue. ... That is why [nevirapine's] use is recommended without qualification for this purpose by the World Health Organization.

...

Considerations relevant to reasonableness

[67] The policy of confining nevirapine to research and training sites ... fails to distinguish between the evaluation of programmes for reducing mother-to-child transmission and the need to provide access to health care services required by those who do not have access to the sites.

[68] ... A programme for the realisation of socio-economic rights must "be balanced and flexible and make appropriate provision for attention to ... crises and to short, medium and long term needs. A programme that excludes a significant segment of society cannot be said to be reasonable." [*Grootboom*]

...

Children's rights

[74] There is another consideration that is material. This case is concerned with newborn children. [see Sections 28(1)(b) and (c) of the Constitution, p. 329 *supra*] . . .

. . .

[76] Counsel for the government, relying on . . . the *Grootboom* judgment, submitted that section 28(1)(c) imposes an obligation on the parents of the newborn child, and not the state, to provide the child with the required basic health care services.

[77] While the primary obligation to provide basic health care services no doubt rests on those parents who can afford to pay for such services, it was made clear in *Grootboom* that "[t]his does not mean . . . that the State incurs no obligation in relation to children who are being cared for by their parents or families."

[78] The provision of a single dose of nevirapine to mother and child for the purpose of protecting the child against the transmission of HIV is, as far as the children are concerned, essential. . . . Their rights are "most in peril" as a result of the policy that has been adopted and are most affected by a rigid and inflexible policy that excludes them from having access to nevirapine.

[79] The state is obliged to ensure that children are accorded the protection contemplated by section 28 that arises when the implementation of the right to parental or family care is lacking. Here we are concerned with children born in public hospitals and clinics to mothers who are for the most part indigent and unable to gain access to private medical treatment which is beyond their means. They and their children are in the main dependent upon the state to make health care services available to them.

. . .

The powers of the courts

[96] Counsel for the government contended that even if this Court should find that government policies fall short of what the Constitution requires, the only competent order . . . that a court can make is to issue a declaration of rights to that effect. That leaves government free to pay heed to the declaration made and to adapt its policies in so far as this may be necessary to bring them into conformity with the court's judgment. This, so the argument went, is what the doctrine of separation of powers demands.

[97] In developing this argument counsel contended that under the separation of powers the making of policy is the prerogative of the executive and not the courts, and that courts cannot make orders that have the effect of requiring the executive to pursue a particular policy.

[98] This Court has made it clear on more than one occasion that although there are no bright lines that separate the roles of the legislature, the executive and the courts from one another, there are certain matters that are pre-eminently within the domain of one or other of the arms of government and not the others. All arms of government should be sensitive to and respect this separation. This does not mean, however, that courts cannot or should not make orders that have an impact on policy. . . .

[99] The primary duty of courts is to the Constitution and the law . . . . The Constitution requires the state to "respect, protect, promote, and fulfil the rights in the Bill of Rights". Where state policy is challenged as inconsistent with the Constitution, courts have to consider whether in formulating and implementing such policy the state has given effect to its constitutional obligations. If it should hold in any given case that the state has failed to do so, it is obliged by the Constitution to say so. In so far as that constitutes an intrusion into the domain of the executive, that is an intrusion mandated by the Constitution itself. There is also no merit in the argument advanced on behalf of government that a distinction should be drawn between declaratory and mandatory orders against government. Even simple declaratory orders against government or organs of state can affect their policy and may well have budgetary implications. Government is constitutionally bound to give effect to such orders whether or not they affect its policy and has to find the resources to do so. . . .

. . .

[102] . . . Particularly in a country where so few have the means to enforce their rights through the courts, it is essential that on those occasions when the legal process does establish that an infringement of an entrenched right has occurred, it be effectively vindicated. The courts have a particular responsibility in this regard and are obliged to 'forge new tools' and shape innovative remedies, if needs be, to achieve this goal." . . .

. . .

[106] We thus reject the argument that the only power that this Court has in the present case is to issue a declaratory order. Where a breach of any right has taken place, including a socio-economic right, a court is under a duty to ensure that effective relief is granted. The nature of the right infringed and the nature of the infringement will provide guidance as to the appropriate relief in a particular case. . . .

[107] . . . In the United States, for example, frequent use has been made of the structural injunction — a form of supervisory jurisdiction exercised by the courts over a government agency or institution. Most famously, the structural injunction was used in the case of *Brown v Board of Education* . . . .

[108] Even a cursory perusal of the relevant Indian case law demonstrates a willingness on the part of the Indian courts to grant far-reaching remedial orders. . . .

[109] Although decisions of the German Federal Constitutional Court are mostly in the form of declaratory orders, the Court also has the power to prescribe for a temporary period which steps have to be taken in order to create a situation in conformity with the Basic Law. . . .

. . .

[112] What this brief survey [also covering Canada and the UK] makes clear is that in none of the jurisdictions surveyed is there any suggestion that the granting of injunctive relief breaches the separation of powers. The various courts adopt different attitudes to when such remedies should be granted, but all accept that within the separation of powers they have the power to make use of such remedies — particularly when the state's obligations are not performed diligently and without delay.

[114] A factor that needs to be kept in mind is that policy is and should be flexible. It may be changed at any time and the executive is always free to change policies where

it considers it appropriate to do so. The only constraint is that policies must be consistent with the Constitution and the law. Court orders concerning policy choices made by the executive should therefore not be formulated in ways that preclude the executive from making such legitimate choices. . . .

. . .

Orders

[135] . . .

. . .

3. Government is ordered without delay to:
   a) Remove the restrictions that prevent nevirapine from being made available for the purpose of reducing the risk of mother-to-child transmission of HIV at public hospitals and clinics that are not research and training sites.
   b) Permit and facilitate the use of nevirapine for the purpose of reducing the risk of mother-to-child transmission of HIV and to make it available for this purpose at hospitals and clinics when in the judgment of the attending medical practitioner acting in consultation with the medical superintendent of the facility concerned this is medically indicated, which shall if necessary include that the mother concerned has been appropriately tested and counselled.
   c) Make provision if necessary for counsellors based at public hospitals and clinics other than the research and training sites to be trained for the counselling necessary for the use of nevirapine to reduce the risk of mother-to-child transmission of HIV.
   d) Take reasonable measures to extend the testing and counselling facilities at hospitals and clinics throughout the public health sector to facilitate and expedite the use of nevirapine for the purpose of reducing the risk of mother-to-child transmission of HIV.
4. The orders made in paragraph 3 do not preclude government from adapting its policy in a manner consistent with the Constitution if equally appropriate or better methods become available to it for the prevention of mother-to-child transmission of HIV.
5. The government must pay the applicants' costs, including the costs of two counsel.

. . .

QUESTIONS

1. Compare the approaches taken by the Court in *Soobramoney*, *Grootboom* and TAC. Is the approach consistent or does the Court shift the goalposts significantly from one case to the next?

2. As a government housing official how would you respond to the *Grootboom* decision? What choices are before you? Would new legislation or administrative regulations be necessary, and what kinds of provisions should they include? Does the Court's opinion give any clue about the degree of revision of the housing schemes or extent of new tax measures that should flow from the decision?

3. 'In the TAC case the Court rolls out all the classic statements of deference to the legislature before it engages in an aggressive demolition of the government's policy choices and replaces them with its own.' Comment.

4. The concept of minimum core obligations is a key element in the approach adopted by the UN ESCR Committee in General Comment No. 3. It is accorded a pivotal role in *Grootboom* but seemingly rejected in TAC. How would you respond to the following critique? Is the concept likely to be useful in the future?

> [I]n a case such as TAC, there are likely to be very different notions of what counts as the absolute core of the right to access health-care services, according to whether one prioritizes the need to respond to urgent and concrete threats to life (life), urgent demands for palliative care and treatment for debilitating and painful disease, demands which count as inherently reasonable from a cost-benefit point of view, and thus, refusal of which might tend to demean citizens' sense of self-worth, or the need to respond to claims made on behalf of the poorest and most neglected South Africans, from a health-care point of view (equality).[35]

3. THE UNITED STATES: EDUCATION RIGHTS

Since 1982 the United States has been a strong opponent of ESR at the international level. The situation in terms of domestic jurisprudence is, however, rather more complex. The right to education provides an interesting case study. It has been addressed, in different ways, in the constitutions of many of the 50 component states.[36] In 1954 in the landmark case of *Brown v. Board of Education*[37] a unanimous Court recognized 'education [as] perhaps the most important function of state and local governments' and declared it to be 'a right which must be made available to all on equal terms.' But, almost two decades later, in *San Antonio Independent School District* v. *Rodriguez*[38] the Court took a very different approach. While much of the 5–4 majority decision was concerned with the finer points of US equal protection law, the court also considered whether education was a Constitutionally protected fundamental right. It insisted that such a right could not be derived from arguments about the 'relative societal significance of education' but only from the text of the Constitution. And it found that, despite dramatic differences in the funding provided for education from

[35] Rosalind Dixon, Creating Dialogue about Socio-Economic Rights: Strong V. Weak-Form Judicial Review Revisited, NYU Center for Human Rights and Global Justice Working Paper No. 3, 2006, p. 15

[36] Allen Hubsch, 'Note: The Emerging Right to Education under State Constitutional Law', 65 Temple L. Rev. 1325 (1992); and Woods and Lewis, *Human Rights and the Global Marketplace: Economic, Social and Cultural Dimensions* (2005) 901–11.

[37] 347 U.S. 483 (1954).

[38] 411 U.S. 1 (1973).

one district to another, there was no 'absolute denial of educational opportunities to any' children, and thus no right to education issue. In doing so it expressed concerns that a finding of a right to education might logically lead to findings relating to issues such as denials of 'decent food and shelter'. The majority decision indicated that it was enough for education reforms to 'take one step at a time', and was concerned about the federalism implications of intervening in state decisions. It also claimed the Court lacked the 'expertise and the familiarity with local problems' necessary to decide issues of local taxation. Finally, the Court attached importance to the view that better financing would not necessarily bring better education.

In reaction to *Rodriguez*, most subsequent action has been at the state level.[39] In 1989, the Kentucky Supreme Court declared the state's 'entire system of common schools . . . unconstitutional' and ordered the provision of funding 'sufficient to provide each child in Kentucky an adequate education'.[40] This prompted extensive litigation in other states, and especially in New York.

Article XI (1) of the New York Constitution states: 'The legislature shall provide for the maintenance and support of a system of free common schools, wherein all the children of this state may be educated.' In *Levittown v. Nyquist* (1982) the NY Court of Appeals had ruled that despite substantial inequities in funding, equal funding across different school districts was not required. It did, however, assert that the state constitution entitled students to a 'sound basic education'. This provided the basis for a suit brought in 1995 by the Campaign for Fiscal Equity claiming that New York City students were being denied such an education. The litigation ended only in 2006 with the following judgment of the Court of Appeal.

CAMPAIGN FOR FISCAL EQUITY V. STATE OF NEW YORK

New York Court of Appeal, 2006 NYSlipOp 02284

BUCKLEY, P.J. . . .

History of the Case

At the conclusion of the first appellate round, the Court of Appeals declared that the Education Article "requires the State to offer all children the opportunity of a sound basic education," consisting of "the basic literacy, calculating, and verbal skills necessary to enable children to eventually function productively as civic participants capable of voting and serving on a jury," as well as "minimally adequate physical facilities and classrooms which provide enough light, space, heat, and air to permit children to learn," "minimally adequate instrumentalities of learning such as desks, chairs, pencils, and reasonably current textbooks," and "minimally adequate teaching of reasonably up-to-date basic curricula such as reading, writing, mathematics,

[39] For a review and critique, see Goodwin Liu, 'Education, Equality, and National Citizenship', 116 Yale L.J. (2006) 330.
[40] *Rose v. Council for Better Education*, 790 S.W.2d 186.

science, and social studies, by sufficient personnel adequately trained to teach those subject areas."

On the second appeal, the Court of Appeals held that "the opportunity of a sound basic education" means "the opportunity for a meaningful high school education," though not pegged to any particular grade level, Board of Regents standard, or high school diploma eligibility requirement.

The Court of Appeals upheld the trial court's findings that various "inputs" (teaching, school facilities, classrooms, and instrumentalities of learning) and "outputs" (school graduation rates and test results) demonstrated that New York City schoolchildren were not receiving the opportunity for the constitutional sound basic education, and that there was a causal link between the State's current funding system and such failure.

With respect to the remedy, the Court of Appeals acknowledged that the judiciary should "defer to the Legislature in matters of policymaking" and directed the State to "ascertain the actual cost of providing a sound basic education in New York City," to reform the current system of school funding and management to furnish every school in the City with the resources necessary for providing the opportunity for a sound basic education, and to "ensure a system of accountability to measure whether the reforms actually provide the opportunity for a sound basic education". The Court of Appeals set a deadline of July 30, 2004, a little more than one year after the date of the decision, for defendants "to implement the necessary measures".

... [T]he deadline passed without an agreement....

In August 2004, Supreme Court appointed three Referees "to hear and report with recommendations on what measures defendants [had] taken" to follow the directives of the Court of Appeals.

The Defendants' Proposals

At the Referees' hearing defendants submitted a State Education Reform Plan, which proposed $4.7 billion in additional annual funds for the city schools, phased in over five years, plus various accountability reforms. That plan largely drew upon the report of the New York State Commission on Education Reform, the "Zarb Commission," appointed by the Governor in 2003.

The Zarb Commission had identified three methods of determining the actual cost of providing city schoolchildren with the opportunity for a sound basic education: (1) the "econometric method," which uses a statistical model to estimate the costs associated with different levels of school district performance; (2) the "professional judgment method," which uses panels of education professionals to determine the scholastic elements needed to attain certain goals and then assigns costs to those elements; and (3) the "successful schools method," which examines the expenditures of school districts that meet or exceed performance standards. The Zarb Commission rejected both the econometric method, since it had not been used by any other state, and the professional judgment method, which is based only on hypothetical constructs. The Commission selected the successful schools method as the most reliable, because it is based on actual data from school districts with a proven record of success, and is used by the State Board of Regents.

[Using this method, an annual spending gap for the city schools ranging from $1.93 billion to $4.69 billion was calculated.] . . .

. . .

In July 2004, the Governor proposed legislation that would . . . increase funding of the city school districts by $4.7 billion annually, phased in over five years. However, that legislation was not enacted. . . .

The Proposals of Plaintiffs, the City, and the Board of Regents

Plaintiffs submitted to the Referees a report by the American Institutes for Research (AIR) and Management Analysis and Planning, Inc. (MAP), which recommended additional annual expenditures of $5.63 billion. The AIR/MAP study used the professional judgment method . . .

The City submitted a plan calling for $5.3 billion in additional annual funds and $13.1 billion in capital improvements. . . .

The Referees' Recommendations

In November 2004, the Referees issued their report, recommending additional annual funds of $5.63 billion, phased in over four years, and capital improvements of $9.179 billion over a five-year period. . . . [The judgment then recounts the differences of opinion over the appropriate bases for calculation, etc.]

The Standard of Review and Constitutional Requirements

. . .

. . . Just as the other branches of government may not compel the judiciary to perform nonjudicial functions of government, the courts must refrain from arrogating such powers to themselves. . . . As pointed out by the Court of Appeals in CFE II, "in a budgetary matter the Legislature must consider that any action it takes will directly or indirectly affect its other commitments". Thus, without the ability or the authority to review the entire state budget, "it is untenable that the judicial process . . . should intervene and reorder priorities, allocate the limited resources available, and in effect direct how the vast [city and state] enterprise[s] should conduct [their] affairs" (*Jones v Beame* 45 NY2d 402, 407 [1978]). "While it is within the power of the judiciary to declare the vested rights of a specifically protected class of individuals, . . . the manner by which the State addresses complex societal and governmental issues is a subject left to the discretion of the political branches of government".

The principle is well stated in *Klostermann v Cuomo* (61 NY2d 525 [1984]), relied on by plaintiffs. In *Klostermann*, the plaintiffs, patients and former patients of state psychiatric hospitals, claimed that their constitutional and statutory rights had been violated when they were released into the community without residential placement, supervision, and care, under the least restrictive conditions suitable to their condition. The Court of Appeals held that it had the authority to compel the State to exercise its mandatory duties, even if those duties are to be executed through discretionary means, but lacked the power to direct the State to act in a particular manner.

The Court could compel the State to perform a legal duty, but not direct how it should perform that duty, since

> [t]he activity that the courts must be careful to avoid is the fashioning of orders or judgments that go beyond any mandatory directives of existing statutes and regulations [and constitutional provisions] and intrude upon the policy-making and discretionary decisions that are reserved to the legislative and executive branches.

...

It is undisputed that the State has failed to appropriate an adequate amount of funding to meet its educational mandate as outlined in CFE II. However, that neglect does not give the Court the authority to participate in budget negotiations or, absent a constitutional failing, to exercise a veto power over the State's calculations of the cost of a sound basic education. The fact that the other two branches of government have not remedied constitutional failings in the past does not authorize the courts to commit their own constitutional violations now.

...

Order

[I]n enacting a budget for the fiscal year commencing April 1, 2006, the Governor and the Legislature [are directed to] consider, as within the range of constitutionally required funding for the New York City School District, the proposed funding plan of at least $4.7 billion in additional annual operating funds, and the Referees' recommended annual expenditure of $5.63 billion, or an amount in between, phased in over four years, and that they appropriate such amount, in order to remedy constitutional deprivations, and that, in enacting such budget, the Governor and the Legislature implement a capital improvement plan that expends $9.179 billion over the next five years or otherwise satisfies the city schools' constitutionally recognized capital needs....

...

SAXE, J. (DISSENTING)....

...

The majority asserts that "in the final analysis it is for the Governor and the Legislature to make the determination as to the constitutionally mandated amount of funding." However, the majority ignores the fact that the deadline for making that determination has already passed without the Legislature successfully enacting such legislation. Indeed, the Legislature has proven itself unable to either agree upon the necessary level of constitutionally mandated funding or to make provision for its allocation.......

The majority's "direction," at this juncture, leaves the students of the New York City public schools without any more of a remedy for this substantial constitutional violation than they had on July 31, 2004, the day noncompliance with the Court of Appeals' prior directive was clear. I am unable to read the majority's decretal paragraph as containing the type of clear and exact directive that, if ignored, may be the subject of enforcement proceedings. Without that type of clarity, it merely amounts to a suggestion to consider taking action, an illusory and possibly unenforceable remedy.

... By framing the discussion, and the purported remedy, as it does, the majority is consigning the schoolchildren of New York to further constitutional violations and neglect. Under these circumstances, where the legislative and executive branches of government have repeatedly failed to confront and solve a problem of state constitutional dimension, it is the obligation of the judiciary to assert its historic role.

QUESTIONS

1. Would the analysis and outcome in *Rodriguez* have been significantly different if the US had been a party to the ICESCR? How and why?

2. Can a right to adequate education be derived from any constitutional obligation upon a state to provide a school system?

3. How would you characterize the outcome of the very extended *CFE* litigation? A success story for the justiciability of ESR, or vindication for those who argue that such policy and budgetary decisions must be left to the legislature?

4. EUROPE: CONSTITUTIONAL SOCIAL JUSTICE

In the following analysis Fabre indicates that 26 out of 29 European Constitutions (the 27 members of the European Union and two applicants for membership) enshrine ESR. The materials then present two very similar cases from Europe and the US which resulted in diametrically opposed outcomes.

CÉCILE FABRE, SOCIAL RIGHTS IN EUROPEAN CONSTITUTIONS

in G. de Búrca and B. de Witte (eds.), Social Rights in Europe (2005), at 15

...

Reviewing each European constitution one by one would be both cumbersome and not particularly interesting. Instead, let me make six general observations.... [First, these constitutions do not generally address violations of ESR by] private actors such as firms and corporations, and by foreign actors such as foreign states and international institutions....

Secondly, many European constitutions specify that such rights should be respected to an adequate standard. But what does constitute an adequate standard of provision? Consider, for example, the right to a minimum income. . . . An *adequate* income . . . will vary from country to country and, within a country, over time. Accordingly, when entrenching social rights, constitution-makers must be careful not to be too specific, since levels of provision may have to vary depending on the country's level of economic and social development. However, they must also be careful not to be too vague, so as to give courts a sense of how best to respect the constitution when adjudicating those rights.

When assessing how European constitutions deal with social rights, and in particular which rights they enshrine and in which terms, we shall need to bear those considerations in mind. However, there is no need to do so as far as Austria, Germany, and the United Kingdom are concerned, since they (alone out of twenty-nine constitutions) do not enshrine social rights as such.... [A]t the other end of the scale, the Portuguese Constitution is very detailed, without falling into the trap of being too specific. It lists all social rights . . . , distinguishes between various categories of people who might need, and deserve, material assistance: the young, the elderly, the disabled, workers, the unemployed.... Article 64 states that all individuals have a right to health care, and goes on to specify that such a right can be respected through preventive, curative, and rehabilitative care, and that the state ought to supervise private medicine....

All other twenty-five countries fall somewhere in between: some enshrine all social rights, others focus on one or two. Some use rather terse language; others take greater care to elucidate the content of those rights. For example, the Constitution of Cyprus merely stipulates at Article 9 that individuals have a right to 'decent existence and social security', without specifying further what that could mean.... Sweden's Instrument of Government also rather succinctly states ... 'that it shall be incumbent upon the public administration to secure the right to work, housing and education, and to promote social care and social security'....

So far, I have mentioned only those social rights the promotion of which is incumbent on governments. It is worth noting, though, and thirdly, that many European constitutions enshrine a number of rights in the workplace — in other words, rights which ought to be protected by law, but which it is incumbent upon employers to respect....

...

Finally, many European constitutions (for example, the Danish and Finnish constitutions) tend to rely, sometimes explicitly, sometimes implicitly, on the distinction between those who are needy through no fault of their own, and those who are responsible for their predicament. The phrases 'those who cannot work', or 'those who cannot secure the means for their own subsistence' are often used in connection with the right to a minimum income. In so doing, European constitutions strongly distinguish between the deserving and the undeserving poor....

...

III. Justiciability

...

Not all European constitutions allow the courts to adjudicate conflicts between public authorities and individuals regarding constitutional social rights. The Constitution of Denmark is entirely silent on the issue. Others, such as the Dutch

Constitution, explicitly disallow judicial interference with legislative action; still others explicitly disallow judicial interference with social policy specifically....

However, the majority of countries provide for justiciability....

...

V. Conclusion

... European constitutions ... converge to enough of a degree that it is appropriate to speak of a European constitutional order with respect to social justice....

Z AND OTHERS V. THE UNITED KINGDOM

29392/95 [2001] ECHR 333 (10 May 2001)

[This case involved the extended and chronic abuse of four children (Z, A, B, and C) over a period of more than four years in which the responsible local authorities recorded much of the abuse but failed to take any decisive action. The case went to the UK House of Lords which declined for reasons of public policy to find a common law duty of care applicable to the relevant authorities. The case eventually went to the European Court of Human Rights, sitting as a Grand Chamber. On the Court and the European Convention, see Chapter 11, *infra*.]

48. ... It was claimed on behalf of Z that she had suffered severe neglect and chronic deprivation which rendered it likely that specialist care would be necessary during her adolescence, a time where emotional repercussions of the abuse might become apparent; on behalf of A that he had suffered physical deprivation, emotional abuse, physical abuse and possible sexual abuse — he had suffered permanent physical scarring and was still receiving treatment from a child psychiatrist; on behalf of B that he had suffered extreme physical and emotional deprivation and shown signs of sexual abuse — he also had suffered permanent physical scarring and was receiving therapy; and on behalf of C that she had suffered extreme physical and emotional deprivation, and in addition that her need for eye treatment was not being met by her parents.

...

69. The applicants alleged that the local authority had failed to protect them from inhuman and degrading treatment contrary to Article 3 of the Convention, which provides:

> No one shall be subjected to torture or to inhuman or degrading treatment or punishment.

...

74. There is no dispute in the present case that the neglect and abuse suffered by the four applicant children reached the threshold of inhuman and degrading treatment .... This treatment was brought to the local authority's attention, at the earliest in October 1987. It was under a statutory duty to protect the children and had a range of powers available to them, including the removal of the children from their home. These were, however, only taken into emergency care, at the insistence of the mother, on 30 April 1992. Over the intervening period of four and a half years,

they had been subjected in their home to what the consultant child psychiatrist who examined them referred as horrific experiences . . . . The Criminal Injuries Compensation Board had also found that the children had been subject to appalling neglect over an extended period and suffered physical and psychological injury directly attributable to a crime of violence . . . The Court acknowledges the difficult and sensitive decisions facing social services and the important countervailing principle of respecting and preserving family life. The present case, however, leaves no doubt as to the failure of the system to protect these applicant children from serious, long-term neglect and abuse.

75. Accordingly, there has been a violation of Article 3 of the Convention.

. . .

105. The applicants submitted that they had not been afforded any remedy for the damage which they had suffered as a result of the failure of the local authority to protect them, relying on Article 13 of the Convention, which provides:

> Everyone whose rights and freedoms as set forth in [the] Convention are violated shall have an effective remedy before a national authority notwithstanding that the violation has been committed by persons acting in an official capacity.

. . .

110. The applicants have argued that in their case an effective remedy could only be provided by adversarial court proceedings against the public body responsible for the breach. The Court notes that the Government have conceded that the range of remedies at the disposal of the applicants was insufficiently effective. . . . The Court does not consider it appropriate in this case to make any findings as to whether only court proceedings could have furnished effective redress, though judicial remedies indeed furnish strong guarantees of independence, access for the victim and family, and enforceability of awards in compliance with the requirements of Article 13 . . . .

111. The Court finds that in this case the applicants did not have available to them an appropriate means of obtaining a determination of their allegations that the local authority failed to protect them from inhuman and degrading treatment and the possibility of obtaining an enforceable award of compensation for the damage suffered thereby. Consequently, they were not afforded an effective remedy in respect of the breach of Article 3 and there has, accordingly, been a violation of Article 13 of the Convention.

COMMENT ON DESHANEY V. WINNEBAGO COUNTY DEPARTMENT OF SOCIAL SERVICES

489 U.S. 189 (1989)

Joshua DeShaney, the petitioner in this decision of the U.S. Supreme Court, 489 U.S. 189 (1989), was a very young boy who was repeatedly and seriously beaten by his father. He and his mother sued for damages from the respondent, the Department of Social Services (DSS) of the state of Wisconsin, under a federal statute, 42 U.S.C. 1983 bearing on the denial of constitutional rights. He claimed that, by failing to protect him, the DSS had denied him the liberty guaranteed by the Due Process Clause of the Fourteenth Amendment to the Constitution ('No State shall . . . deprive any person of life, liberty, or property, without due process of law').

Joshua lived with his twice-divorced father, to whom an earlier court decision had awarded custody. From 1982 to 1984, DSS was advised on several occasions that Joshua might be a victim of child abuse. On several occasions, local hospitals to which Joshua had been admitted with multiple bruises and abrasions had informed DSS of its suspicions. A former wife of the father had termed the father 'a prime case for child abuse.' An ad hoc 'team' of experts formed by Winnebago County had concluded there was insufficient evidence of child abuse to remove Joshua from his home, but recommended measures to which the father had agreed. A DSS caseworker then made monthly visits to the DeShaney home, observed suspicious injuries, noted that the father had broken his agreement, and 'dutifully recorded' such information in her files, together with her 'continuing suspicion' that Joshua was being physically abused, 'but she did nothing more.' In 1984, the father beat four-year-old Joshua into a life-threatening coma. Joshua suffered severe brain damage and was expected to spend his life confined to an institution for the profoundly retarded.

This action in a federal district court claimed that DSS violated Joshua's rights under the Due Process Clause by failing to intervene to protect him against a risk of violence which it knew of or ought to have known. Joshua was thereby deprived of his liberty interest in freedom from unjustified intrusions on his personal security. In a 6–3 decision, the US Supreme Court affirmed the decision of the Court of Appeal denying the claim. Chief Justice Rehnquist's opinion for the Court said in part:

> But nothing in the language of the Due Process Clause itself requires the State to protect the life, liberty, and property of its citizens against invasion by private actors. The Clause is phrased as a limitation of the State's power to act, not as a guarantee of certain minimal levels of safety and security . . . [I]ts language cannot fairly be extended to impose an affirmative obligation on the State to ensure that those interests do not come to harm through other means. Nor does history support such an expansive reading of the constitutional text. Like its counterpart in the Fifth Amendment, the Due Process Clause of the Fourteenth Amendment was intended to prevent government [quoting from a prior decision] 'from abusing [its] power, or employing it as an instrument of oppression.' . . . Its purpose was to protect the people from the State, not to ensure that the State protected them from each other. The Framers [of the Constitution] were content to leave the extent of governmental obligation in the latter area to the democratic political processes.
>
> Consistent with these principles, our cases have recognized that the Due Process Clauses generally confer no affirmative right to governmental aid, even where such aid may be necessary to secure life, liberty, or property interests of which the government itself may not deprive the individual . . . . As a general matter, then, we conclude that a State's failure to protect an individual against private violence simply does not constitute a violation of the Due Process Clause.

The opinion further rejected petitioners' contention that, 'even if the Due Process Clause imposes no affirmative obligation on the State to provide the general public with adequate protective services, such a duty may arise out of certain "protective relationships" created or assumed by the State with respect to particular individuals.' It distinguished prior cases imposing such a duty when the state took individuals into its custody, as in prisons or mental health institutions.

A dissenting opinion of Justice Brennan stated in part:

> It may well be, as the Court decides, that the Due Process Clause as construed by our prior cases creates no general right to basic governmental services. That, however, is not the question presented here.... No one, in short, has asked the Court to proclaim that, as a general matter, the Constitution safeguards positive as well as negative liberties.

Criticizing the majority opinion's emphasis on state *inaction* as the asserted basis for the state's liability, Justice Brennan stressed the degree to which the state in this case had indeed *acted* (1) by encouraging citizens and other state agencies to rely on the DSS to handle instances of child abuse, and (2) by actively intervening through DSS in several ways in this case. He drew an analogy between the facts in *DeShaney* and the custody cases that Justice Rehnquist had concluded were not in point. 'My disagreement with the Court arises from its failure to see that inaction can be every bit as abusive of power as action, that oppression can result when a State undertakes a vital duty and then ignores it.'

In his dissenting opinion, Justice Blackmun termed the facts and decision 'a sad commentary upon American life.'

QUESTIONS

1. From Fabre's description of the different approaches in Europe would you agree that there is a single European constitutional order with regard to social justice? Is this the same as saying that ESR, as human rights, are part of the prevailing order?

2. The facts in *Z v. UK* and *DeShaney* are remarkably similar, but the outcomes are radically different. In seeking to explain the divergence Michelman considers, but does not find compelling, the following factors: the US notion of federalism, the different texts being interpreted (the ECHR versus the 14th Amendment), the history of the relevant provisions and the original understandings of their drafters, contemporary constitutional culture and the prevailing political 'philosophy' in each place.[41] How would you explain the different outcomes?

[41] Frank Michelman, 'The protective function of the state in the United States and Europe: the constitutional question', in G. Nolte (ed.), *European and US Constitutionalism* (2005) 156, at 160.

ADDITIONAL READING

S. Liebenberg 'Socio-economic Rights', in M. Chaskalson *et al.* (eds.) *Constitutional Law of South Africa* (2nd edn. 2004), Ch. 33; D. Brand and C. Heyns (eds.), *Socio-Economic Rights in South Africa* (2005); J. Dugard and T. Roux, 'The Record of the South African Constitutional Court in Providing an Institutional Voice for the Poor: 1995–2004', in R. Gargarella, P. Domingo and T. Roux (eds.), *Courts and Social Transformation in New Democracies: An Institutional Voice for the Poor?* (2006); J. Klaaren, 'A Second Look at the South African Human Rights Commission, Access to Information, and the Promotion of Socioeconomic Rights', 27 Hum. Rts Q. (2005) 539; S. Muralidhar, 'Economic, Social and Cultural Rights: An Indian Response to the Justiciability Debate,' in Y. Ghai and J. Cottrell (eds.), *Economic, Social and Cultural Rights in Practice* (2004) 23; S.P. Sathe, *Judicial Activism in India: Transgressing Borders and Enforcing Limits* (2002); R. Howard-Hassmann and C. Welch, *Economic Rights in Canada and the United States* (2006).

E. GIVING CONTENT TO ESR: INTERNATIONAL MONITORING

The preceding section emphasized the role of national judicial decisions in giving content to ESR norms. But another important element is the contribution made in that regard by various domestic and international monitoring arrangements. Mention should also be made of litigation under regional human rights treaties. For example, a considerable number of cases dealing with ESCR have been raised under the Inter-American system (see Chapter 11, p. 1037, *infra*). In addition, the collective complaints procedure under the European Social Charter has made an important contribution in terms of normative clarification (see Chapter 11, p. 1018, *infra*). The following materials focus on the international dimension, including the role played by General Comments adopted by the ESCR Committee, the possibility of a complaints procedure for the ICESCR, the role played by international organizations such as the Food and Agriculture Organization, and by non-governmental organizations.

1. GENERAL COMMENT: A CASE STUDY OF THE RIGHT TO WATER

VIEWPOINTS

In 2002 the ESCR Committee adopted a General Comment (GC) on the right to water, a right not recognized *per se* in either the UDHR or the ICESCR. Paul Hunt, a former Committee Rapporteur describes the challenge inherent in drafting GCs.

Paul Hunt, 'Ten Years After The Vienna World Conference On Human Rights',[42] (2003)

. . . [W]hat these General Comments are trying to do is complex and controversial. They are trying to outline the normative content of complicated ESCR, as well as the obligations deriving from these norms. They are also trying to identify ways by which these norms and obligations can be monitored by states, civil society and others. Moreover, they are trying to do all this in a way that is meaningful to rich and poor states alike; in other words, they have to speak to the realities of Canada and Chad. Further, as is well-known, the national legal tradition of ESCR is not as rich as the national legal tradition regarding civil and political rights, and thus it provides fewer precedents to help international work on ESCR. In summary, the challenge is to identify the contours and content of specific international ESCR, and also to establish the conceptual tools by which this can be done. By any standards, this is a difficult and ambitious undertaking.

ESCR Committee, The Right to Water, General Comment No. 15[43] (2002)

1. . . . The human right to water is indispensable for leading a life in human dignity. It is a prerequisite for the realization of other human rights. . . .

2. The human right to water entitles everyone to sufficient, safe, acceptable, physically accessible and affordable water for personal and domestic uses. An adequate amount of safe water is necessary to prevent death from dehydration, to reduce the risk of water-related disease and to provide for consumption, cooking, personal and domestic hygienic requirements.

3. Article 11, paragraph 1, of the Covenant specifies a number of rights emanating from, and indispensable for, the realization of the right to an adequate standard of living 'including adequate food, clothing and housing'. The use of the word 'including' indicates that this catalogue of rights was not intended to be exhaustive. The right to water clearly falls within the category of guarantees essential for securing an adequate standard of living, particularly since it is one of the most fundamental conditions for survival. . . .

. . .

10. The right to water contains both freedoms and entitlements. The freedoms include the right to maintain access to existing water supplies necessary for the right to water, and the right to be free from interference, such as the right to be free from arbitrary disconnections or contamination of water supplies. By contrast, the entitlements include the right to a system of water supply and management that provides equality of opportunity for people to enjoy the right to water.

11. The elements of the right to water must be *adequate* for human dignity, life and health . . . . The adequacy of water should not be interpreted narrowly, by mere

[42] At http://www2.essex.ac.uk/human_rights_centre/rth/docs/FIAN.docp. 3.

[43] UN doc. E/C.12/2002/11.

reference to volumetric quantities and technologies. Water should be treated as a social and cultural good, and not primarily as an economic good. . . .

12. While the adequacy of water required for the right to water may vary according to different conditions, the following factors apply in all circumstances:

Availability. The water supply for each person must be sufficient and continuous for personal and domestic uses. . . . ;

Quality. The water required for each personal or domestic use must be safe, therefore free from micro-organisms, chemical substances and radiological *hazards* that constitute a threat to a person's health. Furthermore, water should be of an acceptable colour, odour and taste for each personal or domestic use.

Accessibility. Water and water facilities and services have to be accessible to *everyone* without discrimination, within the jurisdiction of the State party. . . .

. . .

International obligations

30. [ICESCR Articles 2(1), 11(1) and 23] require that States parties recognize the essential role of international cooperation and assistance and take joint and separate action to achieve the full realization of the right to water.

31. To comply with their international obligations in relation to the right to water, States parties have to respect the enjoyment of the right in other countries. International cooperation requires States parties to refrain from actions that interfere, directly or indirectly, with the enjoyment of the right to water in other countries. Any activities undertaken within the State party's jurisdiction should not deprive another country of the ability to realize the right to water for persons in its jurisdiction.

32. States parties should refrain at all times from imposing embargoes or similar measures, ...

33. Steps should be taken by States parties to prevent their own citizens and companies from violating the right to water of individuals and communities in other countries . . . .

34. Depending on the availability of resources, States should facilitate realization of the right to water in other countries, for example through provision of water resources, financial and technical assistance, and provide the necessary aid when required . . . .

35. . . . States parties should take steps to ensure that [any international agreements to which they are parties] do not adversely impact upon the right to water. Agreements concerning trade liberalization should not curtail or inhibit a country's capacity to ensure the full realization of the right to water.

. . .

While the GC on the right to water was enthusiastically received in some quarters, others had reservations. The following excerpt notes some of the opposition and explains it primarily in terms of interpretive techniques.

Matthew Craven, 'Some Thoughts on the Emergent Right to Water' in E. Riedel & P. Rothen (eds.), *The Human Right to Water* (2006) 37, at 39.

... [The Committee's] creative affirmation [of a right to water] did not go entirely unnoticed. In a subsequent debate within the UN Commission on Human Rights in 2003, the Canadian representative [said]:

> While accepting that governments owed a responsibility to their own people to provide access to a clean drinking water supply and sanitation, it did not agree that there was a 'right' to drinking water and sanitation owed between states. The internationalization of a right to water between states was not grounded on any plausible reading of the [ICESCR] and was therefore opposed by his government.

...

On the surface, the Canadian opposition to the position adopted by the UN Committee may be understood as turning upon a rival interpretive strategy. Whereas the UN Committee had ... pursued what might be called a 'teleological' or 'purposive' approach to interpretation, Canada by contrast, insisted upon a narrow 'literalist' construction ....

...

[But] ... different modes of interpretation do not neatly align themselves by reference to 'conservative' or 'progressive' traditions .... A desire to conserve the status quo may involve occasionally reading an instrument such as the Covenant in a 'teleological' or 'evolutive' manner, just as a desire to transform or change social relations may involve reading it 'literally'. Governments are as unlikely to insist upon one particular mode of interpretation being the only or definitive means by which the Covenant is to be construed, as the Committee is to insist upon another. No mode of interpretation is, as such, 'innately' better than another from whichever perspective one may [be looking].

...

[The Committee's] main role ... is to concern itself with outcomes and questions of due process, rather than the substantive process of policy formulation.... [T]he Committee resists the temptation, for example, to decide in advance, that certain polices were inappropriate or inadequate in the circumstances, or further than that, simply contrary to the terms of the Covenant.

...

QUESTIONS

1. How strong is the Committee's case in favour of 'deriving' a right to water from the ICESCR? What is the significance of the Canadian objection to the process?

2. When might the Committee be likely to insist upon a literal approach to Covenant interpretation and when might a government opt for a teleological one?

3. The Committee member principally responsible for drafting the GC noted that, instead of seeking to draft a treaty on the right to water, it would be preferable to use 'the traditional cascade model of norm-creation culminating in treaties, starting from resolutions, via declarations, recommendations, voluntary guidelines or codes of conduct . . . '.[44] What steps might then be expected to be taken by the Committee or other actors by way of follow-up to the GC?

2. A COMPLAINTS PROCEDURE UNDER THE ICESCR?

Only two of the seven major UN human rights treaties lack a complaints procedure — the CRC and the ICESCR. In 1990 the ESCR Committee began discussing such a procedure, in 1993 the Vienna World Human Rights Conference authorized further work on the question, and in 1997 the Committee submitted a complete draft Optional Protocol (UN Doc. E/CN.4/1997/105, annex). For the past decade the matter has been under consideration, reflecting a distinct lack of enthusiasm on the part of governments.

VIEWPOINTS

Dennis and Stewart are strongly critical of the proposal. Although they were both US State Department legal advisers, they were writing in their personal capacities.

Michael J. Dennis and David P. Stewart, 'Justiciability of Economic, Social, and Cultural Rights'

98 Am. J. Int. L. (2004) 462, at 514

VII. Conclusion

The effective realization of [ESCR] remains a global challenge of gigantic proportions. . . .

Establishment of a new international adjudicative mechanism will not remediate this situation. In the vast majority of circumstances, the origins of individual privations are not legal, and their ultimate resolution will not be found in legal edicts or directives. . . .

But because the underlying causes for states' failure to achieve the goals of the Covenant are most often grounded in the absence or misuse of resources, there is scant reason to believe that the Committee's legally binding "decision" in a specific case would prove any more persuasive or authoritative to a receptive government than a perceptive Concluding Observation on a periodic report or a carefully crafted General Comment. There is little basis for concluding that external dictates (in the form of binding decisions from an independent adjudicative body) would prove more effective than external development assistance in ameliorating internal privation.

[44] Eibe Riedel, 'The Human Right to Water and General Comment No. 15 of the CESCR', in E. Riedel and P. Rothen (eds.), *The Human Right to Water* (2006) 19 at 35.

...

... We strongly support inclusion of human rights considerations in development activities and do not reject out of hand the notion that some [ESR] may be domestically justiciable. The question is whether a new international complaints mechanism would help to bridge the still growing gap between human rights commitments and concrete action. We think not.

The challenges to a new complaints mechanism along the lines of the proposed optional protocol are substantial. Beyond the issues of criteria, capacity, costs, and conflicts with other existing adjudicative procedures as discussed above, the success of a complaints mechanism would depend in substantial part on the overall competence of the adjudicators.... [T]here is still no reason to believe that they would, in fact, have better access to, or understanding of, the relevant economic, demographic, and statistical data than the government concerned, much less the time and ability to make more informed or effective choices about the allocation of limited resources in a malfunctioning economic system. Even if the [adjudicators were to prove enlightened, it must be asked] would it be the most desirable political choice to vest international adjudicators with the authority to proclaim what must be done domestically? Again, we think not.

The proposal for a new individual-complaints mechanism remains an ill-considered effort to mimic the structures of the ICCPR — and largely for mimicry's sake. The principal justifications put forward in its favor are, at base, attacks on decisions made by the negotiators and participating states fifty years ago, and the proponents have failed to make a convincing case for reversing those decisions or for establishing a new mechanism. Even if justified within a narrow perspective, the proposal ignores practical issues, overlooks the important role of specialized agencies and other existing mechanisms, and fails to describe the criteria by which compliance with the ICESCR would be measured in the context of individual complaints. The proposal proceeds from questionable premises — namely, that a punitive approach will be effective, especially as to the worst violators, and that binding adjudication will be more effective than encouragement, assistance, and leadership by persuasive example. It offers formalistic structures and procedures in place of concrete, cooperative, "on the ground" efforts to improve peoples' lives. It promises paper judgments and learned opinions in lieu of practical achievements.

The rights and obligations contained in the ICESCR were never intended to be susceptible to judicial or quasi-judicial determination. The negotiators and drafters of the UDHR] and the two Covenants well understood the differences between [the two sets of rights]. Those differences have not disappeared.

Philip Alston, 'Establishing a Right to Petition under the Covenant on Economic, Social and Cultural Rights'

4/2 Collected Courses of the Academy of European Law (1995), at 107

... [T]he principal criteria are whether the adoption of a complaints procedure ... will (1) contribute to the understanding of economic and social rights in general and (2) enhance the standing and practical relevance of the Covenant in particular. There are at least six ways in which the proposed protocol could contribute to both of those objectives.

First, a complaints procedure brings concrete and tangible issues into relief. The real problems confronting individuals and groups come alive in a way that can never be the case in the context of the abstract discussions that arise in the setting of the reporting procedure....

Second, the focus on a particular case provides a framework for inquiry which is otherwise absent. It should ideally involve the submission of precise and detailed information by a petitioner which, in turn, should ensure the provision of equally clearly focused information by the Government concerned. Even where the dialogue is in writing the capacity to get to the nub of issues is vastly greater than it is under the reporting procedure....

Third, the mere possibility that complaints might be brought in an international forum should encourage Governments to ensure that more effective local remedies are available in respect of [ESR]....

Fourth, the existence of a potential 'remedy' at the international level provides an incentive to individuals and groups to formulate some of their economic and social claims in more precise terms and in relation to the specific provisions of the Covenant....

Fifth, the possibility of an adverse finding by an international committee would give ESR a salience in terms of the political concerns of Governments that those rights very largely lack at present....

Finally, a complaints procedure produces a tangible result which, in terms of 'human interest' potential, is far more likely to generate interest in, and an understanding of, the Covenant in general and of the specific issues concerned....

Elements for an Optional Protocol to the ICESCR, Analytical Paper by the Chairperson-Rapporteur, Catarina de Albuquerque

UN Doc. E/CN.4/2006/WG.23/2 (2005)

[This analysis was prepared for the Commission on Human Rights' open-ended working group on an optional protocol to the ICESCR, February 2006. Probably the most controversial question under consideration concerned the range of rights to which any complaints procedure would be applicable. Note that similar debates took place when the Optional Protocol to CEDAW was being drafted and the final decision reflected a comprehensive approach.]

3. There are five main approaches for identifying which rights contained in the Covenant would be subject to a communications procedure. These are as follows:
   (a) The comprehensive approach can take two forms. The first allows an author to bring a communication alleging a violation of any of the provisions of the Covenant. The second allows an author to bring a communication alleging a violation of any of the Part III provisions, read in conjunction with Parts I and II. All existing communications procedures under the international system have adopted the comprehensive approach;

(b) The "à la carte" approach allows States to limit the application of the communications procedure to certain provisions of the Covenant. The Revised European Social Charter allows each State party to consider itself bound by [selected rights, and the Additional Protocol builds upon that system.] . . . ;

(c) The reservation approach or the "opt-out à la carte" approach allows a State party to exclude the application of the communications procedure from one or several provisions of the Covenant. . . .

(d) The time-limited approach allows States to limit the application of the communications procedure to certain provisions of the Covenant while at the same time obliging States parties to increase the number of provisions subject to the procedure within set time limits with a view to achieving comprehensive coverage;

(e) The limited approach allows an author to bring communications in relation to only some Parts of the Covenant or some provisions of the Covenant. . . .

4. [In determining the best option the following factors are relevant]:

(a) The implications for each approach on the principles of indivisibility, interdependence and interrelatedness of all human rights;

(b) The views of the [ESCR Committee reflected in its 1997 draft];

(c) The approach that could promote rapid ratification of an optional protocol . . . ;

(d) The potential effects of excluding provisions from the application of a communications procedure . . . ;

(e) The relative importance of allowing States flexibility . . . ;

(f) The effects of the different approaches on affirming justiciability and promoting the realization of [ESCR] at the national level;

(g) Whether the objectives pursued through "opting-in" or "opting-out" could be achieved by the entry of reservations to the optional protocol.

. . .

QUESTIONS

1. Which of Dennis and Stewart's objections apply exclusively to ESCR and could not reasonably be directed to a complaints procedure dealing with civil and political rights?

2. Would Dennis and Stewart's analysis lead to the conclusion that development, rather than accountability, is the answer to the promotion of ESR? Would such a position be the mirror image of that put forward by China and many developing countries in relation to civil and political rights? Are there grounds for suggesting that the two arguments are fundamentally different?

3. Which, if any, of the options for coverage of the Protocol would you support, and why?

3. INSTRUMENTS ADOPTED BY INTERNATIONAL ORGANIZATIONS OUTSIDE OF THE HUMAN RIGHTS FRAMEWORK

International organizations outside the human rights field narrowly defined have made important contributions towards elaborating the normative content of ESCR rights. In addition to the example of FAO given below, mention can also be made of instruments adopted by agencies such as the ILO, WHO and UNESCO.

FOOD AND AGRICULTURE ORGANIZATION, VOLUNTARY GUIDELINES TO SUPPORT THE PROGRESSIVE REALIZATION OF THE RIGHT TO ADEQUATE FOOD IN THE CONTEXT OF NATIONAL FOOD SECURITY

24 November 2004

www.fao.org/righttofood/en/

[The Guidelines are 37 pages long.]

Section I: Preface and Introduction

. . .

2. In the Rome Declaration on World Food Security, Heads of State and Government "reaffirm[ed] the right of everyone to have access to safe and nutritious food, consistent with the right to adequate food and the fundamental right of everyone to be free from hunger." Objective 7.4 of the World Food Summit Plan of Action established the task: "to clarify the content of the right to adequate food and the fundamental right of everyone to be free from hunger, as stated in the [ICESR] and other relevant international and regional instruments . . . ."

. . .

9. These Voluntary Guidelines are a human rights-based practical tool addressed to all States. They do not establish legally binding obligations for States or international organizations, nor is any provision in them to be interpreted as amending, modifying or otherwise impairing rights and obligations under national and international law. States are encouraged to apply these Voluntary Guidelines in developing their strategies, policies, programmes and activities, and should do so without discrimination of any kind . . . .

. . .

17. States have obligations under relevant international instruments relevant to the progressive realization of the right to adequate food. Notably, States Parties to the [ICESCR] have the obligation to respect, promote and protect and to take appropriate steps to achieve progressively the full realization of the right to adequate

food. [The remaining part of this paragraph builds upon the following statement by the ESCR Committee in its GC No. 12 on the right to food]:

> The right to adequate food, like any other human right, imposes three types or levels of obligations on States parties: the obligations to *respect*, to *protect* and to *fulfil*. In turn, the obligation to *fulfil* incorporates both an obligation to *facilitate* and an obligation to *provide*. The obligation to *respect* existing access to adequate food requires States parties not to take any measures that result in preventing such access. The obligation to *protect* requires measures by the State to ensure that enterprises or individuals do not deprive individuals of their access to adequate food. The obligation to *fulfil* (*facilitate*) means the State must pro-actively engage in activities intended to strengthen people's access to and utilization of resources and means to ensure their livelihood, including food security. Finally, whenever an individual or group is unable, for reasons beyond their control, to enjoy the right to adequate food by the means at their disposal, States have the obligation to *fulfil* (*provide*) that right directly. This obligation also applies for persons who are victims of natural or other disasters.[45]

[There follow 19 separate guidelines dealing '*inter alia*' with democracy, good governance, human rights and the rule of law, economic development policies, strategies (states should consider adopting a national human rights based strategy for the progressive realization of the right to adequate food), market systems (states should improve the functioning of their markets), institutions (states should assess performance of relevant public institutions and, where necessary, reform them), stakeholders, legal framework (consider including provisions in domestic law and constitutions), access to resources and assets, food safety and consumer protection, nutrition ('if necessary, states should take measures to maintain, adapt or strengthen dietary diversity and healthy eating habits and food preparation, as well as feeding patterns'), education and awareness raising, support for vulnerable groups, safety nets, international food aid, natural and human-made disasters (food should never be used as a means of political and economic pressure), monitoring, indicators and benchmarks ('states may wish to establish mechanisms to monitor and evaluate' implementation of the guidelines, and to conduct domestic 'right to food impact assessments'), and national human rights institutions.]

Annex 2, Statement by the United States, September 23, 2004

The United States is pleased to join consensus in the adoption of the Voluntary Guidelines . . . .

. . . In joining in the adoption of these Voluntary Guidelines, the United States does not recognize any change in the current state of conventional or customary international law regarding rights related to food. The United States believes that the attainment of any "right to adequate food" or "fundamental freedom to be free from hunger" is a goal or aspiration to be realized progressively that does not give rise to any international obligations nor diminish the responsibilities of national governments toward their citizens.

[45] Committee on Economic, Social and Cultural Rights, General Comment No. 12 (1999), para 15, UN Doc. E/C.12/1999/5.

QUESTIONS

1. What is the potential value of instruments such as the Voluntary Guidelines?

2. Does the US statement conform to existing international human rights law in all respects?

4. ADVOCACY BY NON-GOVERNMENTAL ORGANIZATIONS

Until 1993 Human Rights Watch (HRW) eschewed ESCR. Amnesty International effectively did the same until 2001. Since then both organizations have sought to develop a coherent strategy in relation to these rights, with varying degrees of success. In the readings that follow Kenneth Roth, the Executive Director of HRW, seeks to identify the circumstances under which international NGOs might take on issues concerning ESR. It should be emphasized that while the largest of the NGOs have struggled with these challenges, a number of more specialized groups such as Physicians for Human Rights, the Centre on Housing Rights and Evictions, the FoodFirst Information and Action Network, and the Center for Economic and Social Rights, along with the International Commission of Jurists, have made important contributions to enhanced understanding of these rights.[46]

KENNETH ROTH, DEFENDING ECONOMIC, SOCIAL AND CULTURAL RIGHTS: PRACTICAL ISSUES FACED BY AN INTERNATIONAL HUMAN RIGHTS ORGANIZATION

26 Hum. Rts Q. (2004), at 63

. . .

In my view, the most productive way for international human rights organizations, like Human Rights Watch, to address ESC rights is by building on the power of our methodology. The essence of that methodology . . . is not the ability to mobilize people in the streets, to engage in litigation, to press for broad national plans, or to provide technical assistance. Rather, the core of our methodology is our ability to investigate, expose, and shame. We are at our most effective when we can hold governmental (or, in some cases, nongovernmental) conduct up to a disapproving public. . . .

[46] See especially various interpretive guides adopted by civil society groups. such as (i) the Limburg Principles on the Implementation of the International Covenant on Economic, Social and Cultural Rights (1986), 9 Hum. Rts. Q. (1987) 122; (ii) the Maastricht Guidelines on Violations of Economic, Social and Cultural Rights (1997), 20 Hum. Rts Q. (1998) 691; and (iii) the Montréal Principles on Women's Economic, Social and Cultural Rights (2002), 26 Hum. Rts. Q. (2004) 760.

. . . [T]o shame a government effectively — to maximize the power of international human rights organizations like Human Rights Watch — clarity is needed around three issues: violation, violator, and remedy. We must be able to show persuasively that a particular state of affairs amounts to a violation of human rights standards, that a particular violator is principally or significantly responsible, and that a widely accepted remedy for the violation exists. If any of these three elements is missing, our capacity to shame is greatly diminished. . . .

. . .

Broadly speaking, [these elements are] clearest when it is possible to identify arbitrary or discriminatory governmental conduct that causes or substantially contributes to an ESC rights violation. These three dimensions are less clear when the ESC shortcoming is largely a problem of distributive justice. If all an international human rights organization can do is argue that more money be spent to uphold an ESC right — that a fixed economic pie be divided differently — our voice is relatively weak. We can argue that money should be diverted from less acute needs to the fulfillment of more pressing ESC rights, but little reason exists for a government to give our voice greater weight than domestic voices. On the other hand, if we can show that the government (or other relevant actor) is contributing to the ESC shortfall through arbitrary or discriminatory conduct, we are in a relatively powerful position to shame: we can show a violation (the rights shortfall), the violator (the government or other actor through its arbitrary or discriminatory conduct), and the remedy (reversing that conduct).

. . .

To conclude, let me offer a hypothesis about the conduct of international human rights organizations working on ESC rights. It has been clear for many years that the movement would like to do more in the ESC realm. Yet despite repeated professions of interest, its work in this area remains limited. Part of the reason, of course, is expertise; the movement must staff itself somewhat differently to document shortfalls in such matters as health or housing than to record instances of torture or political imprisonment. But much of the reason, I suspect, is a sense of futility. International human rights activists see how little impact they have in taking on matters of pure distributive justice so they have a hard time justifying devoting scarce institutional resources for such limited ends. . . .

QUESTIONS

1. Are ESR matters of 'pure distributive justice', and if so, does this make them any less human rights than civil and political rights?

2. Does Roth's strategy risk focusing only on ESR when there is a civil and political rights dimension to a violation?

F. THE RELATIONSHIP BETWEEN THE TWO SETS OF RIGHTS

The phrase first coined in 1950 and then adapted at the 1993 Vienna World Conference — that all rights are 'indivisible and interdependent and interrelated' — expresses the international community's attempt to resolve in the context of its discussions of human rights the longstanding debate over the relationship between freedom and equality. But the constant reaffirmation of the slogan of indivisibility has not prevented regular claims that one set of rights or the other must in fact be accorded priority. Throughout the 1980s the United States claimed that because 'the idea of economic and social rights is easily abused by repressive governments', it would omit all discussion of those rights from its focus. China has constantly sought to downgrade civil and political rights on the grounds that 'when poverty and lack of adequate food are commonplace and people's basic needs are not guaranteed, priority should be given to economic development'.[47] The Right to Development has also often been used as a surrogate for this claim (see p. 1420, *infra*).

International human rights NGOs have tended to be preoccupied with civil and political rights despite occasional affirmations of intent to adopt a broader focus.

In the materials that follow we consider different perspectives on the relationship between the two sets of rights. The case study of the Dalits suggests that, in the absence of civil and political rights, their ESR will continue to be systematically violated. Sen goes beyond this and argues that civil and political rights are even constitutive of ESR. Gauri challenges assumptions that ESR will automatically be addressed in a democratic polity.

HUMAN RIGHTS WATCH, BROKEN PEOPLE: CASTE VIOLENCE AGAINST INDIA'S 'UNTOUCHABLES'

(1999), at 1

More than one-sixth of India's population, some 160 million people, live a precarious existence, shunned by much of society because of their rank as 'untouchables' or Dalits — literally meaning 'broken' people — at the bottom of India's caste system. Dalits are discriminated against, denied access to land, forced to work in degrading conditions, and routinely abused at the hands of the police and of higher-caste groups that enjoy the state's protection. In what has been called India's 'hidden apartheid', entire villages in many Indian states remain completely segregated by caste. National legislation and constitutional protections serve only to mask the social realities of discrimination and violence faced by those living below the 'pollution line'.

[47] Henkin, 'International Human Rights and Rights in the United States', in Theodor Meron (ed.), *Human Rights in International Law* (1984), at 43.

Despite the fact that 'untouchability' was abolished under India's constitution in 1950, the practice of 'untouchability' — the imposition of social disabilities on persons by reason of their birth in certain castes — remains very much a part of rural India. 'Untouchables' may not cross the line dividing their part of the village from that occupied by higher castes. They may not use the same wells, visit the same temples, drink from the same cups in tea stalls, or lay claim to land that is legally theirs. Dalit children are frequently made to sit in the back of classrooms, and communities as a whole are made to perform degrading rituals in the name of caste.

Most Dalits continue to live in extreme poverty, without land or opportunities for better employment or education. With the exception of a minority who have benefited from India's policy of quotas in education and government jobs, Dalits are relegated to the most menial of tasks, as manual scavengers, removers of human waste and dead animals, leather workers, street sweepers, and cobblers. Dalit children make up the majority of those sold into bondage to pay off debts to upper-caste creditors....

Dalit women face the triple burden of caste, class, and gender. Dalit girls have been forced to become prostitutes for upper-caste patrons and village priests. Sexual abuse and other forms of violence against women are used by landlords and the police to inflict political 'lessons' and crush dissent within the community....

...

Lacking access to mainstream political organizations and increasingly frustrated with the pace of reforms, Dalits have begun to resist subjugation and discrimination in two ways: peaceful protest and armed struggle. Particularly since the early 1990s, Dalit organizations have sought to mobilize Dalits to protest peacefully against the human rights violations suffered by their community. These movements have quickly grown in membership and visibility and have provoked a backlash from the higher-caste groups most threatened — both economically and politically — by Dalit assertiveness.

...

This report is about caste, but it is also about class, gender, poverty, labor, and land. For those at the bottom of its hierarchy, caste is a determinative factor for the attainment of social, political, civil, and economic rights.

...

AMARTYA SEN, FREEDOMS AND NEEDS

The New Republic (January 10 and 17, 1994) 31, at 32

...

... Do needs and rights represent a basic contradiction? Do the former really undermine the latter? I would argue that this is altogether the wrong way to understand, first, the force of economic needs and, second, the salience of political rights. The real issues that have to be addressed lie elsewhere, and they involve taking note of extensive interconnections between the enjoyment of political rights and the appreciation of economic needs. Political rights can have a major role in providing incentives and information toward the solution of economic privation. But the connections between rights and needs are not merely instrumental, they are also constitutive. For our conceptualization of economic needs depends on open public debates and discussions, and the guaranteeing of those debates and those discussions requires an insistence on political rights.

...

Consider the matter of famine. I have tried to argue elsewhere that the avoidance of such economic disasters as famines is made much easier by the existence, and the exercise, of various liberties and political rights, including the liberty of free expression .... But famines have never afflicted any country that is independent, that goes to elections regularly, that has opposition parties to voice criticisms, that permits newspapers to report freely and to question the wisdom of government policies without extensive censorship.

...

Why might we expect a general connection between democracy and the non-occurrence of famines? The answer is not hard to seek. Famines kill millions of people in different countries in the world, but they do not kill the rulers. The kings and the presidents, the bureaucrats and the bosses, the military leaders and the commanders never starve. And if there are no elections, no opposition parties, no forums for uncensored public criticism, then those in authority do not have to suffer the political consequences of their failure to prevent famine. Democracy, by contrast, would spread the penalty of famine to the ruling groups and the political leadership.

There is, moreover, the issue of information. A free press, and more generally the practice of democracy, contributes greatly to bringing out the information that can have an enormous impact on policies for famine prevention, such as facts about the early effects of droughts and floods, and about the nature and the results of unemployment .... Indeed, I would argue that a free press and an active political opposition constitute the best 'early warning system' that a country threatened by famine can possess.

...

In making such arguments, of course, there is the danger of exaggerating the effectiveness of democracy. Political rights and liberties are permissive advantages, and their effectiveness depends on how they are exercised. Democracies have been particularly successful in preventing disasters that are easy to understand, in which sympathy can take an especially immediate form. Many other problems are not quite so accessible. Thus India's success in eradicating famine is not matched by a similar success in eliminating non-extreme hunger, or in curing persistent illiteracy or in relieving inequalities in gender relations. While the plight of famine victims is easy to politicize, these other deprivations call for deeper analysis, and for greater and more effective use of mass communication and political participation — in sum, for a fuller practice of democracy.

...

NOTE

Varun Gauri[48] offers the following observation related to electoral democracy:

> [E]mpowerment, participation, and information become critical because regular elections do not as a matter of routine lead to universal access to minimally decent health care and education.
>
> From the human rights perspective, the reason for this is that explicit legal discrimination, prolonged social exclusion, patterns of prejudice, and/or the internalization of low expectations lead to inadequate service utilization for some groups and individuals. Problems such as these are acute in developing countries, where former colonial powers bequeathed varying group-based civil law for different ethnicities and religions, and where liberal constitutions are contemporaneous with feudal, clientelist, and patriarchal practices. The remedy requires correcting legal defects, as well as empowering citizens and the civil society organizations that act on their behalf to campaign against the informal cultural, social, and economic practices that sustain unfairness in access and utilization.
>
> The economic approach is skeptical that electoral democracy by itself creates accountability in the health and education sectors for two reasons. Drawing on public choice theory, some economic analysts argue that interest groups, such as teachers unions, "capture" the institutions of service delivery for their own purposes. Using the principal findings of social choice theory, others contend that the preferences of service recipients are so heterogeneous that efforts to aggregate them, whether through democratic procedures or through market provision of jointly provided services like health care and education, are invariably bedeviled by impossibility, arbitrariness, and instability. Economic solutions to interest group capture entail strengthening the market and political position of recipients by giving consumers choices, exposing providers to competitive pressures, and, where services remain publicly provided, allowing service recipients more direct participation in decision making and monitoring. One solution to the aggregation problem involves group deliberation and the development of trust.

QUESTIONS

1. Is Sen's analysis consistent with the indivisibility thesis or does it give a clear priority to civil and political rights?

2. In 1992 the ESCR Committee asserted that 'there is no basis whatsoever to assume that the realization of economic, social and cultural rights will necessarily result from the achievement of civil and political rights', or that democracy can be a sufficient condition for their realization unless it is accompanied by targeted policies. Is this consistent with Sen's analysis? Does it seem to you to be empirically verifiable?

[48] 'Social Rights and Economics: Claims to Health Care and Education in Developing Countries', in P. Alston and M. Robinson (eds.), *Human Rights and Development: Towards Mutual Reinforcement* (2005), at 65.

3. Lee Kuan Yew, the former Prime Minister of Singapore, adopted an ESR policy which has been described in the following terms:

> [It is government policy] not to provide direct funds to individuals in its 'welfare' programs. Instead, much is spent on education, public housing, health care and infrastructure build-up as human capital investments to enable the individual and the nation as a whole to become economically competitive in a capitalist world.... For those who fall through the economic net ... public assistance is marginal and difficult to obtain.... The government's position is that 'helping the needy' is a moral responsibility of the community itself and not just of the state. So construed, the recipients of the moral largesse of the community are to consider themselves privileged and bear the appropriate sense of gratitude.[49]

Does such an approach give priority to ESR or does it instead put economic growth ahead of both sets of rights? If Singapore were to decide to become a party to the ICESCR, would it need to change such policies?

4. As the adviser to a local human rights NGO, what general governmental strategy would you suggest to respond to the problems of Dalits? Would government programmes to provide ESR figure at the outset of that strategy, or at a later stage in your recommendations, or at all? Would it make sense to focus solely on civil and political rights, on the theory that such rights, when genuinely assured and exercised, will themselves open the paths toward economic and social progress?

ADDITIONAL READING

R. Hirschl, *Toward Juristocracy: The Origins and Consequences of the New Constitutionalism* (2004); S. Leckie and A. Gallagher (eds.), *Economic, Social and Cultural Rights: A Legal Resource Guide* (2006); J.M. Woods and H. Lewis, *Human Rights and the Global Marketplace: Economic, Social and Cultural Dimensions* (2005); P. Alston and J. Heenan, *Economic and Social Rights: A Bibliography* (2007); M. Craven, *The International Covenant on Economic, Social and Cultural Rights: A Perspective on its Development* (1995); A Eide, C. Krause and A. Rosas (eds.), *Economic, Social and Cultural Rights: A Textbook* (2nd edn. 2001); M. Sepúlveda, *The Nature of the Obligations under the International Covenant on Economic, Social and Cultural Rights* (2003); Grainne Mckeever and Fionnuala ni Aoláin, 'Thinking Globally, Acting Locally: Enforcing Socio Economic Rights in Northern Ireland', Eur. Hum. Rts L. Rev. (2004) 158; C. Scott and P. Macklem, 'Constitutional Ropes of Sand or Justiciable Guarantees: Social Rights in a New South African Constitution?', 141 U. Penn. L. Rev. 1 (1992); L. Arbour, 'Economic and Social Justice for Societies in Transition', NYU Center For Human Rights And Global Justice, Working Paper 10/2006.

[49] Beng-Huat Chua, 'Australian and Asian Perceptions of Human Rights', in I. Russell, P. van Ness and Beng-Huat Chua (eds.), *Australia's Human Rights Diplomacy* (1992), at 95.

5

National Security, Terrorism and Limitations on Human Rights

The intersection of national security and human rights has long troubled international law. This chapter explores the subject through the prism of counter-terrorism law and practice. In this specific domain, international legal institutions have gained considerable experience over several decades in dealing with situations involving terrorism and states of emergency. A rich body of legal rules and principles has developed in response to the interests and aspirations of various actors over time. As a result, significant insights can be drawn from past experiences, while appreciating that new threats — both to security and to rights and freedoms — may require different responses than those previously adopted.

This chapter explores recent historical cases such as the response of Latin American governments to insurgencies in the late twentieth century and contemporary cases including Turkey's battle with Kurdish separatist movements, British and US confrontation with Al Qaeda, and the Israeli-Palestinian conflict. Each of these cases involved the resort to international tribunals, national courts, or regional bodies. They accordingly raise important considerations about the distribution of interpretative and regulatory authority in times of public emergency. The selected cases also demonstrate the prospect of sweeping changes in response to modern terrorism. We have previously discussed some of these issues with respect to the law and practice of torture, see Chapter 3. The potential implications span not only civil and political rights, but also social and economic rights. This chapter explores this wider range of implications. In the world being remade after 11 September 2001, recurring questions include whether the proper balance is being struck between security and rights, and which rules and which institutions are best equipped to achieve that balance. A threshold issue for such discussions, however, is the definition of terrorism itself.

A. TERRORISM AND HUMAN RIGHTS: DEFINITIONS AND RELATIONSHIPS

At the international level, states have long struggled to find a generally, if not universally, acceptable definition of terrorism. The adage that 'one person's terrorist is another person's freedom fighter' might reflect more of a political challenge than a legal or semantic challenge to achieving this goal. Competent lawyers are presumably capable of classifying specific acts as illicit under any circumstance and without regard to the motivation of fighting forces. Instead, at different points in history various states and other international actors have employed the legal craft to create exceptions for their favoured political groups or ideological struggles.

Without a strong political consensus, states interested in outlawing terrorism through international treaties had to resign themselves for decades to codifying the definition and prohibition of specific acts — such as hostage taking and seizure of civilian aircraft. The UN began this piecemeal approach with the adoption of the 1963 Tokyo Convention on Offences and Certain Other Acts Committed on Board Aircraft. Eight conventions of a similar character were adopted in the 1970s and 1980s, and two more before 1999. A general definition of terrorism and a categorical outlawing of the practice remained politically elusive.

Over the latter half of the twentieth century, success on those fronts was stymied by divergent political interests. Some argued that any definition and accompanying regulatory regime ought to recognize the legitimacy of armed struggle by national liberation groups, such as the Palestine Liberation Organization and the African National Congress, and groups resisting colonial domination. In contrast, others argued that no definition of terrorism would be acceptable if it implied that attacks on civilians could be excused in the case of armed resistance or insurgencies waged for particular purposes. Another political impasse involved the regulation of 'state terrorism'. That is, some proposed definitions of terrorism faced stiff opposition because they focused on actions by nonstate actors and failed to address violence that governments employed against civilians. Finally, a nagging legal question was whether crimes against humanity — a widespread or systematic attack against a civilian population — already covered significant acts of terrorism. That set of crimes, however, lacked codification and, in the view of many, it also lacked specificity.

More recently, states have taken significant steps towards a comprehensive definition of terrorism. Developments include the International Convention for the Suppression of the Financing of Terrorism, agreed to by the UN General Assembly near the close of the twentieth century. The Terrorism Financing Convention, adopted in December 1999, includes the first general definition of terrorism in an international treaty:

> Any other act intended to cause death or serious bodily injury to a civilian, or to any other person not taking an active part in the hostilities in a situation of armed conflict, when the purpose of such act, by its nature or context, is to intimidate a population, or to compel a Government or an international organization to do or to abstain from doing any act.

By mid 2001, only four states had ratified the Convention — far short of the 22 required for the treaty to enter into force. In the days following the attacks on 11 September, the Security Council called on states to become party to the Convention 'as soon as possible'. Within five years, 155 states had done so.

Another significant step towards achieving a universal definition was spurred by the Security Council. In August 2004, the government of Russia introduced resolution

1566 on terrorism. The previous month, Russia had experienced one of the worst hostage crises in its history. A Chechnyan armed group seized a Russian school in the town of Beslan, and the standoff ended in the deaths of over 300 civilians, most of them children. The resolution was intended, in part, to expand the work of a Security Council committee beyond its existing focus on Al Qaeda and the Taliban. The Council broke new ground with language that effectively provided a general definition of terrorism:

> The Security Council . . . acting under Chapter VII . . . [r]ecalls that criminal acts, including against civilians, committed with the intent to cause death or serious bodily injury, or taking of hostages, with the purpose to provoke a state of terror in the general public or in a group of persons or particular persons, intimidate a population or compel a government or an international organization to do or to abstain from doing any act, and all other acts which constitute offences within the scope of and as defined in the international conventions and protocols relating to terrorism, are under no circumstances justifiable by considerations of a political, philosophical, ideological, racial, ethnic, religious or other similar nature . . .

The Security Council members adopted the resolution unanimously (Res. 1566).

These various developments, however, have not completely resolved the legal ambiguities and political controversy surrounding a definition. Upon ratifying the Terrorism Financing Convention, three states (Egypt, Jordan and Syria) submitted a reservation to the definition of terrorism. Jordan's reservation, for example, stated that its government 'does not consider acts of national armed struggle and fighting foreign occupation in the exercise of people's right to self-determination as terrorist acts within the context of paragraph 1(b) of Article 2 of the Convention'. Two dozen states formally objected to the reservation. Most of them contended that the reservation was incompatible with the object and purpose of the treaty.[1] None of the objections was made by an Islamic or African country.

Similar cleavages emerged with respect to Security Council resolution 1566. In statements immediately before and after the Council vote, the governments of Turkey (on behalf of the fifty-seven member Organization of the Islamic Conference), Algeria and Pakistan (both Security Council members at the time) claimed diplomatic victories. They reportedly obtained compromises during the negotiations that assured them the text would not undermine their position on liberation struggles. The resolution's definition, for example, arguably refers only to existing international conventions that outlaw specific terrorist acts. Additionally, a Security Council committee specifically targets and sanctions a list of individuals and groups associated with Al Qaeda and the Taliban. An early draft of resolution 1566 would have added to the list individuals and groups involved in terrorist activities without an association with Al Qaeda or the Taliban. That language was dropped. 'It doesn't open any new doors', Pakistan's UN ambassador stated after passage of the resolution. 'We ought not, in our desire to confront terrorism, erode

[1] Argentina, Austria, Belgium, Canada, Czech Republic, Denmark, Estonia, Finland, France, Germany, Hungary, Ireland, Italy, Japan, Latvia, the Netherlands, Norway, Poland, Portugal, Russia, Spain, Sweden, United Kingdom, United States of America.

the principle of the legitimacy of national resistance that we have upheld for 50 years'.

Given the persistent international disagreement, it may be helpful to try to understand how acts of terrorism become, expressly or tacitly, accepted by perpetrators and third parties. The discussion in Chapter 3 explored how absolute ethical proscriptions — against torture — erode under the pressure from extraordinary threats to national security. Analogously, proscriptions on attacking civilians may erode in the pursuit of certain ideological struggles, such as struggles to achieve national liberation. In *Through Our Enemies' Eyes: Osama Bin Laden, Radical Islam and the Future of America*, Michael Scheuer draws provocative comparisons between the 'idealistic' visions of Osama Bin Laden, leaders of the American revolution, and the militant John Brown who helped inspire the abolitionist movement against American slavery. The goal for Scheuer, who served for 22 years in the CIA and headed the agency's Osama Bin Laden Unit, is not to justify Al Qaeda's actions, but to explain (and defeat) them. Social scientists and other experts on terrorism also discuss political and ideological objectives as a motivating force behind the resort to terrorist violence. Political scientist Martha Crenshaw, for example, has written that '[t]he first condition that can be considered a direct cause of terrorism is the existence of concrete grievances among an identifiable subgroup of a larger population, such as an ethnic minority discriminated against by the majority'.

A particular form of terrorism — suicidal terrorism — may provide special insights into sociopolitical or other conditions that give rise to extreme acts of violence. Suicidal terrorism, indeed, requires the suspension of profound moral and psychological constraints. It often depends upon a broader social system to encourage individuals to end their own lives and disregard or dehumanize the lives of civilians. In his book, *Dying to Win: The Strategic Logic of Suicidal Terrorism*, political scientist Robert Pape concludes that historical and contemporary cases demonstrate that the perceived foreign occupation of a group's homeland is a strong motivating factor for such extreme cases of terrorism. Pape considers not only the logic of individual terrorists and terrorist organizations; he also explores the support of the broader social community that is needed to sustain such campaigns. For terrorism more generally, the international political environment may also be shaped by such 'root causes' including the perceived legitimacy of the purpose of the struggle. That sense of legitimacy may involve not only quests for self-determination, which Pape emphasizes, but also quests for the primacy of a particular vision of society and the extermination of others. Indeed, other experts such as professor of political psychology and international affairs Jerrold Post argue that the primary determinants of terrorism are psychological and are reflected in the polarizing, intolerant, and absolutist visions of terrorist group members.

These various explanations naturally do not exhaust theories of terrorism. Nevertheless, they help one to begin to appreciate the background against which human rights institutions must operate in addressing the scourge of terrorism, often adopted in the name of self-determination, and extreme governmental actions and reactions, often adopted in the name of self-defence. Exploring the possible explanations for terrorism may also help to understand why international political cleavages have impeded a universal definition and the transnational regulation of terrorism.

While (and perhaps because) the international rules remain unsettled, national legal conceptions of terrorism vary significantly. Not only do diverse definitions of terrorism exist across nations, but even within a single state the domestic legal order may include multiple formulations. The definition of terrorism in the criminal code might be one among many. Different definitions of terrorism may be found in provisions for civil law suits, grounds for immigration exclusion and deportation, and standards for regulating nonprofit and charitable organizations. There may be logistical or administrative reasons to employ definitions of different scope in each of these domains. Maintaining vague or excessively broad definitions to control individuals' behavior, however, raises rights-related concerns. The Inter-American Commission on Human Rights recently examined problems with vague statutes in the context of fair trial rights:

> 261. . . . [M]ost fundamental fair trial requirements cannot justifiably be suspended under either international human rights law or international humanitarian law. These protections therefore apply to the investigation, prosecution and punishment of crimes, including those relating to terrorism, regardless of whether such initiatives may be taken in time of peace or times of national emergency, including armed conflict, and include the following:
>
> (a) The right to respect for fundamental principles of criminal law, including the *non-bis-in-idem* principle, the *nullum crimen sine lege* and *nulla poena sine lege* principles, the presumption of innocence, and the right not to be convicted of an offense except on the basis of individual penal responsibility. Of particular pertinence in the context of terrorism, these principles demand that any laws that purport to proscribe conduct relating to terrorism be classified and described in precise and unambiguous language that narrowly defines the punishable offense, and accordingly require a clear definition of the criminalized conduct establishing its elements and the factors that distinguish it from behaviors that are not punishable or involve distinct forms of punishment. Ambiguities in laws proscribing terrorism not only undermine the propriety of criminal processes that enforce those laws, but may also have serious implications beyond criminal liability and punishment, such as the denial of refugee status.
>
> As indicated above, the Commission and the Court have previously found certain domestic anti-terrorism laws to violate the principle of legality because, for example, they have attempted to prescribe a comprehensive definition of terrorism that is inexorably overbroad and imprecise . . . .[2]

Concerns about vagueness relate not only to the definition of terrorism but also to the scope of direct and indirect responsibility ascribed to individuals and organizations. Resolution 1566, for example, also includes language calling on states to 'find, deny safe haven and bring to justice . . . any person who supports, facilitates, participates or attempts to participate in the financing, planning, preparation or

[2] Report on Terrorism and Human Rights, Inter-American Commission on Human Rights, 22 October 2002, available at http://www.cidh.org/Terrorism/Eng/toc.htm.

commission of terrorist acts or provides safe havens'. Amnesty International criticized this construction on the grounds that the

> language casts the net so wide that people, including human rights advocates or peaceful political activists can easily and unintentionally fall victim to the measures advocated in the resolution. The resolution does not even require that acts contributing to 'terrorists acts' [sic], such as unknowingly providing lodging, have to be intentional or done with the knowledge that they will assist the crime. In resorting to such exceptionally broad language, the resolution would call for measures which do not even permit individuals to foresee whether their acts will be lawful or not, a basic requirement in criminal law....

B. 11 SEPTEMBER 2001: A TURNING POINT

The attacks on 11 September 2001 constituted a turning point in the relationships between international law, global institutions, and terrorism. Why (and how much) did 11 September change the international legal and political landscape?

It was one of the deadliest days in American history, totaling more deaths — nearly 3,000 — than the attack on Pearl Harbor and rivalling, if not exceeding, the number of Americans killed on D-Day. Nineteen members of Al Qaeda hijacked four commercial jets, two of which crashed into the 110-story twin towers of the World Trade Center, one into the Pentagon, and one in a field in Pennsylvania. Almost two hours passed between the first collision and the collapse of the second WTC tower, with the loss of life and panic televised around the world as the events unfolded. The near simultaneous attacks exposed major vulnerabilities in the security system of the world's superpower. Al Qaeda cells had resided within US territory. They had converted public transportation into catastrophic weapons. Their members' willingness to embrace (if not glory in) suicide represented a unique strategic threat, one less susceptible to traditional modes of deterrence. Now, given the demonstrated commitment of Al Qaeda to murder thousands of people, intelligence agencies began considering with special intensity the prospect of a terrorist organization acquiring and employing weapons of mass destruction.

International institutions responded in a swift and extraordinary manner. In a resolution passed on 12 September, the UN Security Council determined that the attacks constituted a 'threat to international peace and security' and also recognized the 'inherent right of individual or collective self-defence in accordance with the Charter' (Res. 1368). Accordingly, the resolution implicitly recognized that the acts of 11 September constituted an 'armed attack' under Article 51 of the UN Charter. Although the US and other countries had experienced and responded to terrorist attacks with force in the past, the Council had never before issued such a finding. Also unprecedented, both the North Atlantic Treaty Organization and the Organization of American States formally considered 11 September an 'armed attack' and invoked the collective self-defence provisions of their respective treaties.

In late September, the Security Council, acting under its binding Chapter VII powers, required all states to take financial, penal, and other regulatory measures against individuals and organizations involved in terrorist activities (Res. 1373). The Council also established the Counter-Terrorism Committee (CTC) to monitor implementation of the resolution. Professor José Alvarez describes the special significance of the CTC:

> To date [the CTC] has received hundreds of reports from the UN's members purporting to explain how each has implemented the Council's edicts within their domestic law and practice. . . . In . . . prior instances, it could readily be assumed that the Council's enforcement action would cease when such specific situations were resolved. Resolution 1373, by contrast, has no express or implied time or geographic limitations. It is the closest thing we have in international institutional law to real 'law-making' as some define it. This is action that is binding, backed by the possibility of real coercive sanction, affecting all relevant actors, and capable of repeated application across time in comparable instances.[3]

The CTC has been criticized for not considering whether governmental actions reported to it or adopted pursuant to the Council's dictates comply with universal human rights obligations. The first Chair of the CTC expressed the Committee's policy in a briefing to the Security Council:

> Monitoring performance against other international conventions, including human rights law, is outside the scope of the Counter-Terrorism Committee's mandate. But we will remain aware of the interaction with human rights concerns, and we will keep ourselves briefed as appropriate. It is, of course, open to other organizations to study States' reports and take up their content in other forums.

In 2004, however, the Council adopted resolutions '[r]eminding States that they must ensure that any measures taken to combat terrorism comply with all their obligations under international law, and should adopt such measures in accordance with international law, in particular international human rights, refugee, and humanitarian law' (Res. 1535 and 1566). And, in a 'policy guidance' adopted in mid 2006, the CTC instructed its Executive Directorate to liaise with the Office of the High Commissioner for Human Rights and to 'advise the CTC on how to ensure that any measures States take to implement the provisions of [Security Council anti-terrorism mandates] comply with their obligations under international law, in particular international human rights law, refugee law, and humanitarian law'.

The Security Council's actions, and those of influential countries, may have helped set in motion two streams of legal and policy changes across the world. First, some commentators argue that these developments have encouraged repressive states to exploit anti-terrorism discourse. As one commentator explains:

> Some States have deployed the international legitimacy conferred by Council authorization to define terrorism to repress or de-legitimize political opponents, and to conflate them with Al-Qaeda. Thus, China bluntly characterizes Uighur

[3] José E. Alvarez, *International Organizations as Law-Makers*, 196–197 (2005).

> separatists in Xinjiang as terrorists; Russia asserts that Chechen rebels are terrorists, even though many are fighting in an internal conflict; and India seldom distinguishes militants from terrorists in Kashmir. In Indonesia, insurgencies in Aceh and West Papua have been described and combated as terrorism, as have a Maoist insurgency in Nepal and an Islamist movement in Morocco. Predictably, Israel has identified Palestinians with Al-Qaeda, with Ariel Sharon calling Arafat 'our Bin Laden'.[4]

After 11 September, the organization Human Rights Watch stated that 'many countries around the globe cynically attempted to take advantage of this struggle to intensify their own crackdowns on political opponents, separatists and religious groups, or to suggest they should be immune from criticism of their human rights practices'. A catalogue of such practices can be found on the organization's website.[5]

Second, the Security Council's actions, along with legislation adopted by especially influential countries, have propelled a cascade of national terrorism laws. These laws often have similar structural features despite varying conditions within countries. Professor Kent Roach argues that, as a result, counter-terrorism legislation in a given country may not be tailored to combat security threats efficiently or to do so with human rights safeguards suited to the particular political context:

> In the five years since the terrorist attacks on the United States, a staggering array of new anti-terrorism laws have been enacted throughout the world. . . . [I]nternational and domestic organizations often draft anti-terrorism initiatives on the fly, engaging in bricolage with what is at hand, but with limited information about the effects of various measures on security or human rights. The sources and process used to make anti-terrorism laws can reveal much about their substance. In particular, it can expose the contingent, questionable but not easily reversed choices that have been made with respect to both security and human rights.
>
> . . . [T]hree influential sources for the anti-terrorism laws [are] found in a number of jurisdictions including Australia, Canada, South Africa, the United Kingdom and the United States. It is possible to focus on only a few sources in part because there has been a faddish aspect to post 9/11 anti-terrorism laws with a number of countries following trends established by a small number of influential international and domestic instruments.
>
> . . .
>
> . . . Many countries have followed the lead of the Security Council and used immigration law as anti-terrorism law. This has had adverse effects on various human rights because immigration proceedings typically offer less procedural protections for detainees than criminal proceedings and because a number of countries are re-evaluating the right not to be deported to torture. The focus on immigration law also has had adverse effects on security as it has encouraged some western states to focus anti-terrorism efforts on non-citizens even though, as the London bombings tragically confirm, citizens can also commit acts of terrorism.

[4] Ben Saul, 'Definition of "Terrorism" in the UN Security Council: 1985–2004', 4 Chinese Journal of International Law 141 (2005).

[5] Human Rights Watch, Opportunism in the Face of Tragedy: Repression in the name of anti-terrorism, at http://www.hrw.org/campaigns/september11/opportunismwatch.htm.

> . . . There is a need for continued critical evaluation of broad definitions of terrorism on both human rights and security. There is a danger that broad definitions of terrorism could facilitate the targeting of extremists in domestic protest movements as opposed to those who identify with al Qaeda. Broad definitions of terrorism could have adverse effects on security, as well as human rights, if they result in a misallocation of limited law enforcement and security intelligence resources.[6]

In assessing these accounts of post-11 September legislation, one should also consider the baseline against which these changes occurred. For example, do you think the *actions* of opportunistic states changed after 11 September or just their rhetoric? Does the international discourse surrounding terrorism mean that states will engage in a level of rights violations that they would otherwise refrain from committing? Separately, Professor Roach identifies inefficiencies in anti-terrorism legislation adopted around the world. Without the international impetus to enact counter-terrorism legislation, however, there might have been an 'undersupply' of laws focusing on this transnational security threat. Is it not better for more countries to adopt counterterrorism laws with some inefficiency than for them to adopt none at all? Finally, what motivates countries to adopt, in Professor Roach's words, 'faddish' counter-terrorism legislation? If all these accounts of the pitfalls and problems with the global spread of counter-terrorism law are accurate, what measures should be taken to counteract the negative effects while preserving the positive aspects?

Finally, 11 September also represented a turning point in the strategic approach of the United States to terrorism and Al Qaeda in particular. The Bush administration has proclaimed a 'Global War on Terrorism' and, in more technical legal terms, contends that the United States is in an 'armed conflict' with Al Qaeda and its affiliates. This strategic posture has entailed the adoption of a 'war model' in dealing with terrorism in contrast with an exclusively 'criminal law model'. A war model employs the instruments of warfare such as armed interventions, armed forces and military violence. A criminal law model employs the instruments of law enforcement, policing and prosecutions.

Choosing to adopt a war model may have a greater effect on political discourse and psychological frames than on rights and obligations under international human rights law. As will be discussed shortly, international human rights law adjusts state obligations regardless of whether a public emergency is designated a war or another type of threat to public order and national security. The nature of the threat — its gravity and probability — is the critical variable. That said, domestic legal questions, such as constitutional presidential powers, may turn on the classification of a situation as a war or something else. Furthermore, as discussed at length below, the existence of an armed conflict triggers the application of international humanitarian law (IHL). Whether IHL supplements, displaces, or discounts human rights law raises a host of interesting and important questions.

[6] Kent Roach, 'Sources and Trends in Post 9/11 Anti-Terrorism Laws', in Benjamin Goold and Liora Lazarus (eds.), *Security and Human Rights* (forthcoming).

QUESTIONS

1. Consider for the purpose of discussion the following statement:

[W]hether the global war on terrorism is truly a war is difficult to answer. On balance, the answer is affirmative. At the most abstract level, it is best understood as a politico-moral campaign against the abhorrent practice of targeting innocents for certain strategic ends. In this sense, the fight against terrorism is a war akin to the great campaigns against piracy and slavery earlier. All these struggles . . . involved military, diplomatic, economic, and ideological instruments of warfare. The current battle against terrorism, therefore, has a long and distinguished lineage. Viewed in this perspective, it is indeed appropriate. . . . to conceive of the current struggle as a war against terrorism itself — terrorism now understood not as some abstract Platonic form that cannot be defeated at a world-historical level, but as an inhumane political practice that can be targeted and, more importantly, delegitimized, even if it cannot be totally eradicated. Given this objective, President Bush has been right all along: terrorism is, and ought to be, an unacceptable instrumentality because it sacrifices innocent life in the service of some political vision that, no matter how attractive or justifiable, subordinates means to ends and, accordingly, paves the way for a tyranny that obliterates the respect for persons that lies at the center of every good political order.[7]

2. Consider broader ramifications of the relationship between terrorism and human rights law beyond national security. The issue whether existing international law — including crimes against humanity — prohibits terrorism and the insistence that states bring terrorists to justice lends insights into the content of human rights law more generally. A fundamental issue is whether terrorism constitutes a human rights violation, and, if so, what legal consequences follow for state and nonstate actors. As we explore in other chapters, some international human rights obligations may apply directly to nonstate actors. Some obligations may also apply indirectly to nonstate actors such that states have international duties to prevent private actors from interfering with individuals' rights. Terrorism obviously implicates the right to be free from the arbitrary deprivation of life. Several of the readings in this chapter accordingly refer to a state's obligation to combat terrorism. Does a deep understanding of such obligations in the context of terrorism inform prevailing notions of state responsibility for human rights protection more broadly? If one accepts the premise that states have a duty to combat terrorist threats to their citizenry, does it follow that states have similar obligations to prevent and redress violence against women, malnutrition, natural disasters, infectious disease? Has the law developed to confront terrorism but not these other cases, and, if so, why the imbalance?

ADDITIONAL READING

Kent Roach, 'The Post 9/11 Migration of Britain's Terrorism Act, 2000', in S. Choudhry (ed.), *The Migration of Constitutional Ideas* (forthcoming); Catharine A. MacKinnon, 'Women's

[7] Ashley J. Tellis, Assessing America's War on Terror: Confronting Insurgency, Cementing Primacy, 15 NBR Analysis [National Bureau of Asian Research], no. 4, Dec. 2004, available at http://www.carnegieendowment.org/files/ NBRAnalysis-Tellis_December2004.pdf.

September 11th: Rethinking the International Law of Conflict', 47 Harv. Int. L J. 1 (2006); Christian Terrorism as a Challenge for National and International Law: Security versus Liberty? (2004); Derek Jinks, Walter, Frank Schorkopf, Silja Vöneky, Volker Röben, and Christian Walter (eds.), 'September 11 and the Laws of War', 28 Yale J. Int. L. 1 (2003); Derek Jinks, 'State Responsibility for the Acts of Private Armed Groups', 4 Chicago J. of Int. L. 83 (2003); Dinah Pokempner, 'Terrorism and Human Rights: The Legal Framework', in Michael Schmitt and Gian Luca Beruto (eds.), *Terrorism and International Law* (2003); Alex P. Schmid and Albert J. Jongman, *Political Terrorism: A New Guide to Actors, Authors, Concepts, Data Bases, Theories, and Literature* (1988).

C. THE LEGAL FRAMEWORK: PUBLIC EMERGENCIES, DEROGATIONS AND THE LAWS OF WAR

International law permits states to limit or suspend part of their legal obligations, and thus restrict some rights, under certain circumstances. To that end, the legal recourse available to states includes limitation clauses (discussed in the context of civil and political rights in Chapter 3 and economic, social and cultural rights in Chapter 4) and derogations systems codified in various treaties or available through norms of customary international law.

Limitation and derogation clauses in treaties have a similar function in the sense that both provide legal avenues for states to break free of obligations that would ordinarily constrain their actions. They are also similar in that neither permits states to ignore their human rights obligations altogether. However, one significant difference between the two is that derogations were designed to be applicable only in the exceptional case of a grave threat to the survival and security of a nation. The implication is that derogations were intended to be invoked as temporary measures. In contrast, limitation clauses apply across the spectrum, from everyday public order maintenance and policing strategies to national security and large-scale military actions.

In human rights instruments, limitation clauses are commonplace. The UDHR, as discussed in Chapter 3, contains a general limitation clause in Article 29. The ICESCR contains a general limitation clause in Article 4. It permits state parties to subject the rights contained in the Covenant 'only to such limitations as are determined by law only in so far as this may be compatible with the nature of these rights and solely for the purpose of promoting the general welfare'. The ICCPR, by contrast, does not contain a general limitation clause. Instead, limitation clauses are included in various rights provisions such as those pertaining to freedom of association (Article 22), freedom of movement (Article 12), expulsion of foreign nationals (Article 13), and access of the press and public to criminal trials (Article 14). Several provisions in the ICCPR, such as those prohibiting torture (Article 7) and slavery (Article 8), are subject to no limitation.

Article 4 of the ICCPR codifies the rules for states to derogate from obligations during a state of emergency. Specific conditions are attached to a state's exercise of this option. For example, governmental measures must generally be prescribed and determined by law, shown to be necessary, and designed to protect particular public interests. These conditions and associated rules perform multiple functions. Most obviously, they are designed to strike a balance between security and human rights. In important respects, they are also designed to avoid balancing or, rather, do more than just balance. Some of the rules, for example, preclude any relaxation of obligations with respect to core rights. The prohibition on genocide is a prime example. The categorical prohibition on genocidal acts is subject to no qualification. In addition to balancing competing interests, the rules are also designed to ensure that governments do not restrict rights that have no rational or reasoned connection to meeting national concerns during a time of emergency.

The following readings examine the derogation system in contrast with the protections (and limitations) that ordinarily apply.

JOAN FITZPATRICK, HUMAN RIGHTS IN CRISIS: THE INTERNATIONAL SYSTEM FOR PROTECTING RIGHTS DURING STATES OF EMERGENCY (1994)

Approaching [the law on derogations] chronologically, the first legally significant standard is Article 3 common to the four Geneva Conventions of 1949, also known as "Common Article 3." Applicable during periods of internal armed conflict, a frequent setting for the invocation of emergency powers in the past several decades, Common Article 3 prescribes a set of minimal protections that must be afforded even under these dire circumstances. The guarantees of Common Article 3 are further elaborated in Articles 4 to 6 of Protocol II [to the Geneva Conventions, adopted in 1977], particularly with respect to non-derogable fair trial standards. Indeed, the entire body of international humanitarian law, both customary and codified, is highly relevant to protection of human rights during states of emergency, especially in defining non-derogable rights. International humanitarian law by nature is designed to apply in full force during the subset of emergencies involving armed conflict, so in a sense it is all emergency law. And because situations of armed conflict tend to be among the direst of emergencies, protections available then should logically be available in any other emergency context.

Two crucial sets of treaty standards were also drafted at approximately the same time as Common Article 3. Article 15 of the European Convention was drafted primarily during early 1950 with the benefit of almost three years of discussion by drafters of the Covenant on Civil and Political Rights within the United Nations. The derogation article of the European Convention served as a focal point for the debate between two alternate approaches to treaty drafting, which might be called "general enumeration" and "precise definition." The proponents of general enumeration favored drafting a document with positive definitions of rights and no exceptions or restrictions other than a single general limitations clause, similar to Article 29 of the Universal Declaration. The proponents of precise definition, on the other hand, wanted not only specific limitations clauses in many provisions defining particular rights but also a derogation article for emergencies, arguing that these clauses would actually prevent abusive suspension or denial of rights. During the final stages of the drafting process, the attraction of entrenching a list of non-derogable rights swayed a majority to favor inclusion of the derogation article.

Whereas the drafting of the Covenant on Civil and Political Rights dragged on until 1966, debate on the advisability and specific terms of a derogation article occurred during the relatively compressed period between 1947 and 1952. Article 4 became the focus of the division of opinion between the general-enumeration and precise-definition camps, as had Article 15 in the case of the European Convention. Another key division, leading to an awkward compromise, developed on the question whether the clause on non-derogable rights should include only those rights most important and central to human dignity and most at risk during typical emergencies, or should be expanded to include all rights that no reasonable government would need to limit substantially in any conceivable emergency.

The drafters of the American Convention on Human Rights, who began work in earnest in the 1960s, had the benefit of earlier-drafted human rights treaties as a model and began with an apparent consensus on the precise-definition approach.... The special interest developed within the OAS on protecting human rights during states of emergency may help explain the rather different form the derogation article takes in the American Convention, as compared to those in the European Convention and the Covenant.

A brief comparison of the three derogation articles in the human rights treaties to the relevant portions of the major humanitarian law instruments reveals some interesting similarities and differences, as well as "lacunae," that have attracted ongoing efforts to formulate additional, more complete standards. Discussion will be limited to the substantive aspects of these emergency provisions....

...

Along with the threshold of severity, the principle of proportionality is the most important and yet most elusive of the substantive limits imposed on the privilege of derogation.... The principle of proportionality embodied in the derogation clauses has its roots in the principle of necessity, which also forms one of the key pillars of international humanitarian law. The existence of competent active, and informed organs of supervision, both at the national as well as at the international level, is vital if the proportionality principle is to have meaning in practice. As the ensuing chapters will demonstrate both logistical (access to information and ability to act promptly) and attitudinal (deference to national authorities, e.g., by extension of a "margin of appreciation") factors affect the functioning of the various treaty implementation organs.

The Covenant and the American Convention include clauses specifying that derogation measures may not be imposed in a manner that discriminates on the grounds of race, color, sex, language, religion, or social origin...

Article 15 of the European Convention is silent on the issue of discrimination in the application of emergency measures.... The issue of discriminatory treatment of minorities in the application of emergency measures was touched on during the drafting of the European Convention, but it never achieved prominence in the discussions, and no concrete proposals for a nondiscrimination clause were made. Nevertheless, arbitrary discrimination against disfavored groups of various types would be difficult to justify as being "strictly required." Thus, there may be no substantive difference between the silence of the European Convention and the explicit non-discrimination clauses of the other two treaties, if only arbitrary distinctions are outlawed by the latter.

Draft non-discrimination provisos to the Covenant's derogation article were proposed by the United States (in 1948) and by France (in 1949), but adding the element of non-discrimination was not easily accomplished. The Commission on Human Rights voted in May 1950 on the basis of an oral amendment during debate to add Article 20, the non-discrimination article to the list of non-derogable rights in Article 4. Objections were immediately raised that disparate treatment of enemy aliens would be necessary during wartime, and the decision was reversed the following day. A way around this impasse was found in 1952 when a non-discrimination clause not including the classification of national origin was added to the draft derogation article.

The idea that only arbitrary discrimination is outlawed by Article 4(1) is underlined by the deliberate inclusion of the word "solely" in its text.[8] Even without this term, however, the reference to discrimination in Article 4 conveys the implication that only arbitrary and unjustifiable distinctions in the application of emergency measures would be outlawed. Thus, where an identifiable racial or religious group poses a distinct security threat not posed by other members of the community, presumably, emergency measures could be deliberately targeted against the group, despite the non-discrimination clause.

The absence of the word "solely" from the non-discrimination clause in Article 27(1) of the American Convention on Human Rights apparently has no intended significance. The word was included in the draft prepared by the IACHR but "disappeared from the final text, and the records of the conference provide no clue as to the reason." Thus, the three treaties would seem to impose a virtually identical nondiscrimination obligation, despite disparate phraseology.

The three treaties diverge dramatically with respect to defining absolute rights never subject to suspension. The process of defining non-derogable rights has been a markedly progressive one, with each later drafted instrument expanding the core of non-derogable rights. The European Convention begins with just four, sparely defined: the right to life, excepting deaths resulting from lawful acts of war (Article 2); the ban on torture or inhuman or degrading treatment or punishment (Article 3); the prohibition on slavery or servitude (Article 4(1)); and the prohibition on retroactive criminal penalties (Article 7).

[8] A separate vote was taken on the UK proposal to frame the clause in terms of discrimination 'solely' on one of the forbidden grounds. Support of the inclusion of 'solely' was premised on the notion that wartime measures aimed at a particular nationality, for example, might predominantly affect persons of a particular race without being race-based.

HUMAN RIGHTS COMMITTEE, STATES OF EMERGENCY, GENERAL COMMENT 29 (ON ARTICLE 4)

24 July 2001

1. . . . The restoration of a state of normalcy where full respect for the Covenant can again be secured must be the predominant objective of a State party derogating from the Covenant. . . .

2. . . . Before a state moves to invoke Article 4, two fundamental conditions must be met: the situation must amount to a public emergency that threatens the life of the nation, and the state party must have officially proclaimed a state of emergency. The latter requirement is essential for the maintenance of the principles of legality and rule of law at times when they are most needed. When proclaiming a state of emergency with consequences that could entail derogation from any provision of the Covenant, States must act within their constitutional and other provisions of law that govern such proclamation and the exercise of emergency powers; it is the task of the Committee to monitor the laws in question with respect to whether they enable and secure compliance with Article 4. In order that the Committee can perform its task, States parties to the Covenant should include in their reports submitted under Article 40 sufficient and precise information about their law and practice in the field of emergency powers.

3. Not every disturbance or catastrophe qualifies as a public emergency which threatens the life of the nation . . . . If States parties consider invoking Article 4 in other situations than an armed conflict, they should carefully consider the justification and why such a measure is necessary and legitimate in the circumstances. On a number of occasions the Committee has expressed its concern over States parties that appear to have derogated from rights protected by the Covenant, or whose domestic law appears to allow such derogation in situations not covered by Article 4. [The Committee cites to situations in Tanzania; the Dominican Republic; the United Kingdom; Peru; Bolivia; Colombia; Lebanon; Uruguay; and Israel.]

4. . . . [The requirement that derogation measures are limited to the extent strictly required by the exigencies of the situation] relates to the duration, geographical coverage and material scope of the state of emergency and any measures of derogation resorted to because of the emergency. Derogation from some Covenant obligations in emergency situations is clearly distinct from restrictions or limitations allowed even in normal times under several provisions of the Covenant. Nevertheless, the obligation to limit any derogations to those strictly required by the exigencies of the situation reflects the principle of proportionality which is common to derogation and limitation powers. Moreover, the mere fact that a permissible derogation from a specific provision may, of itself, be justified by the exigencies of the situation does not obviate the requirement that specific measures taken pursuant to the derogation must also be shown to be required by the exigencies of the situation. In practice, this will ensure that no provision of the Covenant, however validly derogated from will be entirely inapplicable to the behaviour of a State party. . . .

5. The issues of when rights can be derogated from, and to what extent, cannot be separated from the provision in Article 4, paragraph 1, of the Covenant according to which any measures derogating from a State party's obligations under the

Covenant must be limited 'to the extent strictly required by the exigencies of the situation'. This condition requires that States parties provide careful justification not only for their decision to proclaim a state of emergency but also for any specific measures based on such a proclamation. If States purport to invoke the right to derogate from the Covenant during, for instance, a natural catastrophe, a mass demonstration including instances of violence, or a major industrial accident, they must be able to justify not only that such a situation constitutes a threat to the life of the nation, but also that all their measures derogating from the Covenant are strictly required by the exigencies of the situation. In the opinion of the Committee, the possibility of restricting certain Covenant rights under the terms of, for instance, freedom of movement (Article 12) or freedom of assembly (Article 21) is generally sufficient during such situations and no derogation from the provisions in question would be justified by the exigencies of the situation.

...

7. ... Conceptually, the qualification of a Covenant provision as a non-derogable one does not mean that no limitations or restrictions would ever be justified. The reference in Article 4, paragraph 2, to Article 18, a provision that includes a specific clause on restrictions in its paragraph 3, demonstrates that the permissibility of restrictions is independent of the issue of derogability. Even in times of most serious public emergencies, States that interfere with the freedom to manifest one's religion or belief must justify their actions by referring to the requirements specified in Article 18, paragraph 3. ...

8. According to Article 4, paragraph 1, one of the conditions for the justifiability of any derogation from the Covenant is that the measures taken do not involve discrimination solely on the ground of race, colour, sex, language, religion or social origin. Even though Article 26 or the other Covenant provisions related to non-discrimination (Articles 2, 3, 14, paragraph 1, 23, paragraph 4, 24, paragraph 1, and 25) have not been listed among the non-derogable provisions in Article 4, paragraph 2, there are elements or dimensions of the right to non-discrimination that cannot be derogated from in any circumstances.

...

10. Although it is not the function of the Human Rights Committee to review the conduct of a State party under other treaties, in exercising its functions under the Covenant the Committee has the competence to take a State party's other international obligations into account when it considers whether the Covenant allows the State party to derogate from specific provisions of the Covenant. Therefore, when invoking Article 4, paragraph 1, or when reporting under Article 40 on the legal framework related to emergencies, States parties should present information on their other international obligations relevant for the protection of the rights in question, in particular those obligations that are applicable in times of emergency. In this respect, States parties should duly take into account the developments within international law as to human rights standards applicable in emergency situations.[9]

[9] [Eds. In a footnote, the Committee refers to UN and other international initiatives involving the identification of fundamental standards of humanity applicable in all circumstances, and the report of the International Committee of the Red Cross on customary international humanitarian law.]

...

12. In assessing the scope of legitimate derogation from the Covenant, one criterion can be found in the definition of certain human rights violations as crimes against humanity. If action conducted under the authority of a State constitutes a basis for individual criminal responsibility for a crime against humanity by the persons involved in that action, Article 4 of the Covenant cannot be used as justification that a state of emergency exempted the State in question from its responsibility in relation to the same conduct. Therefore, the recent codification of crimes against humanity, for jurisdictional purposes, in the Rome Statute of the International Criminal Court is of relevance in the interpretation of Article 4 of the Covenant.[10]

13. In those provisions of the Covenant that are not listed in Article 4, paragraph 2, there are elements that in the Committee's opinion cannot be made subject to lawful derogation under Article 4. Some illustrative examples are presented below.

(a) All persons deprived of their liberty shall be treated with humanity and with respect for the inherent dignity of the human person . . . a norm of general international law not subject to derogation. . . .
(b) The prohibitions against taking of hostages, abductions or unacknowledged detention . . . justified by their status as norms of general international law.
(c) . . . [T]he rights of persons belonging to minorities includes elements that must be respected in all circumstances. . . .
(d) . . . [D]eportation or forcible transfer of population without grounds permitted under international law . . .
(e) No declaration . . . may be invoked as justification for a State party to engage itself, contrary to Article 20, in propaganda for war, or in advocacy of national, racial or religious hatred that would constitute incitement to discrimination, hostility or violence.

14. Article 2, paragraph 3, of the Covenant requires a State party to the Covenant to provide remedies for any violation of the provisions of the Covenant. This clause is not mentioned in the list of non-derogable provisions in Article 4, paragraph 2, but it constitutes a treaty obligation inherent in the Covenant as a whole. Even if a State party, during a state of emergency, and to the extent that such measures are strictly required by the exigencies of the situation, may introduce adjustments to the practical functioning of its procedures governing judicial or other remedies, the State party must comply with the fundamental obligation, under Article 2, paragraph 3, of the Covenant to provide a remedy that is effective.

15. It is inherent in the protection of rights explicitly recognized as non-derogable in Article 4, paragraph 2, that they must be secured by procedural guarantees, including, often, judicial guarantees. The provisions of the Covenant

[10] . . . [T]he category of crimes against humanity as defined in [the Rome Statute] covers . . . violations of some provisions of the Covenant that have not been mentioned in the said provision of the Covenant. For example, certain grave violations of Article 27 may at the same time constitute genocide under Article 6 [genocide] of the Rome Statute, and Article 7 [crimes against humanity], in turn, covers practices that are related to, besides Articles 6, 7 and 8 of the [ICCPR], also Articles 9, 12, 26 and 27.

relating to procedural safeguards may never be made subject to measures that would circumvent the protection of non-derogable rights. Article 4 may not be resorted to in a way that would result in derogation from non-derogable rights. Thus, for example, as Article 6 of the Covenant is non-derogable in its entirety, any trial leading to the imposition of the death penalty during a state of emergency must conform to the provisions of the Covenant, including all the requirements of Articles 14 and 15.

16. Safeguards related to derogation, as embodied in Article 4 of the Covenant, are based on the principles of legality and the rule of law inherent in the Covenant as a whole. As certain elements of the right to a fair trial are explicitly guaranteed under international humanitarian law during armed conflict, the Committee finds no justification for derogation from these guarantees during other emergency situations. The Committee is of the opinion that the principles of legality and the rule of law require that fundamental requirements of fair trial must be respected during a state of emergency. Only a court of law may try and convict a person for a criminal offence. The presumption of innocence must be respected. In order to protect non-derogable rights, the right to take proceedings before a court to enable the court to decide without delay on the lawfulness of detention, must not be diminished by a State party's decision to derogate from the Covenant.[11]

17. In paragraph 3 of Article 4 ... [s]uch notification is essential not only for the discharge of the Committee's functions, in particular in assessing whether the measures taken by the State party were strictly required by the exigencies of the situation, but also to permit other States parties to monitor compliance with the provisions of the Covenant.... Sometimes, the existence of a state of emergency and the question of whether a State party has derogated from provisions of the Covenant have come to the attention of the Committee only incidentally, in the course of the consideration of a State party's report. The Committee emphasizes the obligation of immediate international notification whenever a State party takes measures derogating from its obligations under the Covenant. The duty of the Committee to monitor the law and practice of a State party for compliance with Article 4 does not depend on whether that State party has submitted a notification.

[11] See the Committee's concluding observations on Israel: '... The Committee considers the present application of administrative detention to be incompatible with Articles 7 and 16 of the Covenant, neither of which allows for derogation in times of public emergency .... The Committee stresses, however, that a State party may not depart from the requirement of effective judicial review of detention.' See also the recommendation by the Committee to the Sub-Commission on Prevention of Discrimination and Protection of Minorities concerning a draft third optional protocol to the Covenant: 'The Committee is satisfied that States parties generally understand that the right to habeas corpus and amparo should not be limited in situations of emergency. Furthermore, the Committee is of the view that the remedies provided in Article 9, paragraphs 3 and 4, read in conjunction with Article 2 are inherent to the Covenant as a whole.' [Eds. The Human Rights Committee provided the latter comments in response to a proposal for a draft optional protocol to the ICCPR which would have added Article 9 paras. 3 and 4 (arrest and detention) and Article 14 (criminal procedure) to the list of non-derogable provisions under Article 4(2). The Committee also commented that there was a 'considerable risk' that such an optional protocol 'might implicitly invite States parties to feel free to derogate from the provisions of article 9 of the Covenant during states of emergency if they do not ratify the proposed optional protocol'. UN Doc. A/49/40, paras. 22–25.]

NOTE

If the ICCPR contained no derogation clause, could state parties lawfully suspend particular treaty obligations in the event of a public emergency? Two areas of international law are relevant to answering this question: rules governing the suspension of treaties and rules governing circumstances precluding wrongfulness. As to the former, the Vienna Convention on the Law of Treaties sets forth default rules for treaty interpretation. Article 62 provides that a state can suspend its treaty obligations due to a 'fundamental change in circumstances'. The suspension may apply to the treaty as a whole or to a single clause or provision. *See* Vienna Convention, Article 44. In the drafting process, states can elect to modify the default rules with respect to a specific treaty. For example, treaty drafters could narrow (or expand) the scope of conditions that permit a state to suspend its obligations. Likewise, treaty drafters could condition the ability to suspend a treaty obligation on the satisfaction of procedural criteria.

Second, the Articles on Responsibility of States for International Wrongful Acts drafted by the International Law Commission[12] describe rules for 'circumstances precluding wrongfulness'. The draft articles of state responsibility define conditions under which a state may justify its failure to perform an international legal obligation. In the preceding analysis of derogation clauses, Joan Fitzpatrick alludes to one such justification: necessity. According to the articles of state responsibility, '[n]ecessity may not be invoked by a State as a ground for precluding the wrongfulness of an act unless the act [i]s the only way for the State to safeguard an essential interest against a grave and imminent peril'.

Another justification that may be relevant is *force majeure*. This principle excuses a state from legal responsibility if 'the occurrence of an irresistible force or of an unforeseen event, beyond the control of the State, mak[es] it materially impossible in the circumstances to perform the obligation', according to the draft articles. The practice of the International Labour Organization, for example, suggests that states can derogate from ILO conventions in the event of an armed conflict by invoking *force majeure* — whether or not the convention contains an explicit suspension clause. These issues have begun to receive attention as part of a general study by the International Law Commission under the heading 'effects of armed conflicts on treaties'. The Law Commission's special rapporteur, Professor Ian Brownlie, has issued a handful of insightful reports that serve as a useful resource on the topic.

In addition to the substantive scope of the right to derogate, consider the specific procedures a state is supposed to follow in derogating from its treaty obligations. Article 4 contains two procedural elements: official proclamation of a public emergency and notification to other state parties. In a landmark decision, *Silva v. Uruguay*, Communication No. 34/1978 (1981), the Human Rights Committee

[12] The International Law Commission is a body of 34 independent experts created by the UN General Assembly with the purpose of helping to promote and codify international law.

elaborated its views on the notification requirement:

> Although the sovereign right of a State party to declare a state of emergency is not questioned, yet, in the specific context of the present communication, the Human Rights Committee is of the opinion that a State, by merely invoking the existence of exceptional circumstances, cannot evade the obligations which it has undertaken by ratifying the Covenant. Although the substantive right to take derogation measures may not depend on a formal notification being made pursuant to Article 4(3) of the Covenant, the State party concerned is duty-bound to give a sufficiently detailed account of the relevant facts when it invokes Article 4(1) of the Covenant in proceedings under the Protocol. It is the function of the Human Rights Committee, acting under the Optional Protocol, to see to it that States parties live up to their commitments under the Covenant. In order to assess whether a situation of the kind described in Article 4(1) of the Covenant exists in the country concerned, it needs full and comprehensive information. If the respondent Government does not furnish the required justification itself, as it is required to do under Article 4(2) of the Optional Protocol and Article 4(3) of the Covenant, the Human Rights Committee cannot conclude that valid reasons exist to legitimize a departure from the normal legal regime prescribed by the Covenant.

QUESTIONS

1. Should a state's failure to satisfy the notification requirement forfeit its right to derogate from the ICCPR? In *Silva v. Uruguay*, the Committee clearly concludes no. Consider the other procedural element of Article 4 as well. General Comment 29 suggests that the proclamation of a public emergency constitutes one of two 'fundamental conditions' before a state can avail itself of Article 4. What purposes does such a condition serve? Should a government lose its right to adopt a derogation measure to address a serious security threat simply because it failed to proclaim an emergency?

2. All *jus cogens* norms are nonderogable under Article 4, but not all nonderogable rights under Article 4 are *jus cogens* norms. In other words, there is a residual category in Article 4: ICCPR provisions that do not reflect *jus cogens* norms but nevertheless may not be suspended due to a public emergency. What are the general features of such provisions? What is the logic behind their receiving this extraordinary protection if they do not implicate peremptory norms?

3. In General Comment 24, the Committee provides an expanded list of nonderogable rights beyond those explicitly enumerated in Article 4(2). Did the Committee go too far or not far enough? What would you exclude or include?

4. Do you agree with the Committee's reasoning that other international legal norms, such as those contained in the Rome Statute for the International Criminal Court, should be applied in interpreting the Covenant? These appear to be international instruments that directly relate to human rights, but what defines 'human rights' for this purpose and how direct does the relationship have to be? Are environmental treaties, peace agreements, or other instruments also relevant to assessing states' human rights obligations?

Note that according to a general rule of treaty interpretation, sources to be consulted in interpreting a treaty include 'any relevant rules of international law applicable in the relations between the parties'. Vienna Convention, art. 31.

ADDITIONAL SOURCES

Dominic McGoldrick, 'The Interface Between Public Emergency Powers and International Law', 2 Int. J. Const. L. 380 (2004); Anna-Lena Svensson-McCarthy, *The International Law of Human Rights and States of Exception* (1998); Oren Gross and Fionnuala Ní Aoláin, *Law in Times of Crisis: Emergency Powers in Theory and Practice* (2006).

COMMENT ON RELATIONSHIPS BETWEEN INTERNATIONAL HUMAN RIGHTS AND HUMANITARIAN LAW

International law protects the rights of individuals during wartime. A potential difficulty in securing such protection, however, is determining how two areas of international law — international humanitarian law (IHL) and human rights law — interrelate. Also which institutions should have the power to interpret and apply the law? For example, should human rights bodies have the authority and competence to interpret IHL? For the moment we focus on the first set of concerns, namely, the relationship between IHL and human rights. Once we better understand those issues, we can consider questions about the appropriate role of various institutions in interpreting the law.

A principle familiar to many legal systems, public international law included, is *lex specialis derogat generali*. That is, a specific or special rule should take precedence over a general rule. This principle raises an important challenge for the legal regulation of warfare: should IHL supplant human rights law in defining the rights and obligations of individuals and states during an armed conflict?

IHL is certainly a specialized body of law. It applies only in situations of armed conflict and military occupation. It regulates, often in exacting detail, the methods of conducting hostilities and the treatment of victims of warfare, that is, individuals who are not, or no longer, taking part in hostilities. The principal instruments of humanitarian law are the four Geneva Conventions of 1949. In late 2006, they became the first treaties in modern history to achieve ratification by every state in the world. The conventions were drafted in the aftermath of the Second World War, during the same period in which war crimes trials were taking place on the European continent and in East Asia. Collectively, the 1949 Conventions provide rules for the wounded, sick, and shipwrecked (the First and Second Geneva Conventions), prisoners of war (the Third Geneva Convention), and civilians (the Fourth Geneva Convention). Most of these rules apply to international armed conflicts — war between two or more states — and foreign military occupation.

However, Article 3 common to all four Conventions, which has been called a 'convention in miniature', contains rules that apply to non-international conflicts such as civil wars. Common Article 3 governs armed conflicts between state and nonstate actors as well as conflicts between two or more nonstate actors. It imposes direct legal obligations on all parties to a conflict. These obligations include the most basic rights of individuals such as freedom from torture, murder, mutilation, and cruel treatment; the right to a fair trial, and the general right 'in all circumstances [to] be treated humanely'. The International Court of Justice famously referred to the rules in Common Article 3 as 'a minimum yardstick' for all armed conflicts because they reflect 'elementary considerations of humanity'.

In the midst of the Cold War, states reconvened in Geneva to negotiate two additional protocols to the 1949 Conventions. Additional Protocol I of 1977 elaborates the rules that apply in international armed conflicts. It also defines as an 'international armed conflict' national liberation and other armed struggles in exercise of the right of self-determination. One hundred and sixty-seven states (recently including France and the United Kingdom and for a longer time including China and Russia) are now party to the Protocol, and many of its provisions are considered customary international law applicable in all armed conflicts. The United States is one of the few states not to ratify the Protocol (along with India, Iran, Iraq, Pakistan and Sri Lanka), but the US Government considers much of the Protocol binding customary international law. The United Kingdom ratified the Protocol in 1998 but notably attached a reservation stating that 'the term "armed conflict" of itself and in its context denotes a situation of a kind which is not constituted by the commission of ordinary crimes including acts of terrorism whether concerted or in isolation'. Additional Protocol II (with 163 state parties and also not ratified by the US) contains more modest rules for internal armed conflicts.

The most recent international instrument including a wide range of IHL prohibitions is the Rome Statute for the International Criminal Court. The drafters of the Rome Statute considered it their task to draft treaty text reflecting existing international law, not developing new law. As a consequence, Article 8 is widely understood to codify customary IHL and thus serves as a useful reference point.

In contrast with IHL, international human rights law applies during peacetime and wartime. The first formal recognition of the application of human rights law to armed conflicts is often dated back to the 1968 International Conference on Human Rights at Teheran. The world conference also spurred a series of annual UN General Assembly Resolutions entitled 'Respect for Human Rights in Armed Conflicts', and those resolutions were a prelude to the 1977 Geneva Protocols.

The recognition of the interconnections between human rights law and armed conflicts, however, was a growing trend that began before the Teheran conference. Human rights instruments, some finalized before 1968 and some after, clearly contemplate situations of warfare and military matters. The European Human Rights Convention (adopted in 1950) and its Inter-American counterpart (adopted in 1969) both contain derogation clauses referring to 'time of war'. The European Convention also lists the right to life as nonderogable 'except in respect of deaths resulting from lawful acts of war'. The derogation clause in the ICCPR (adopted in 1966) uses the phrase 'public emergency which threatens the life of the nation' and is well understood to encompass armed conflicts. Article 2 of the Torture Convention (adopted in 1984) states: 'No exceptional circumstances whatsoever, whether a state of war or a threat or war . . . may be invoked as a justification of torture'. The Convention on the Rights of the Child (adopted in 1989) commits states to promoting the recovery and reintegration of 'child victim[s] of . . . armed conflicts'. Article 30 of the Declaration on the Rights of Indigenous Peoples, adopted by the UN Human Rights Council in 2006, places restrictions on 'military activities' in the lands and territories of indigenous peoples.[13]

In corresponding fashion, conventions related to IHL indicate the applicability of human rights norms to situations of armed conflict. The 1949 Geneva Conventions might have referred to universal human rights in preambular language, but disputes over unrelated language culminated in dropping the idea of having a preamble. As the historian Geoffrey Best explains, 'What seems beyond doubt is that the human rights affiliation expressly claimed by the original, minimal preambles was in itself accepted by all parties to the 1949 diplomatic conference to the point even of being taken for granted'.[14] The most apparent influence of human rights norms is Common Article 3, which regulates practices within states' sovereign borders. According to the ICRC Commentaries, the article reflects 'the few essential rules of humanity which all civilized nations consider as valid everywhere and under all circumstances and as being above and outside war itself'.

The 1977 Additional Protocols to the Geneva Conventions continued this trend. Protocol II contains a preamble, which notes that 'international instruments relating to human rights offer a basic protection to the human person'. Article 72 of Additional Protocol I, which delineates the convention's field of application, acknowledges the relevance of human rights law: 'The provisions of this Section are additional to the rules concerning humanitarian protection of civilians and civilian objects in the power of a Party to the conflict contained in the Fourth Convention . . . as well as to other applicable rules of international law relating to the protection of fundamental human rights during international armed conflict'.

Notably, the 1977 Protocols represented a significant shift towards the convergence of human rights and humanitarian law norms. One of the most influential commentators on the subject, Professor Colonel G.I.A.D. Draper, issued a series of cautions at the time. He argued that actors engaged in promoting such a fusion should consider the divergent interests and distinct structural concerns that animate the two domains of law. In a controversial essay that retains some influence, Draper explained his position:

> The law of armed conflicts purports to govern the hostile relations of states engaged in armed confrontation. It was, and is, part of the law of nations. Human-rights law purports to govern part of the relations between government and

[13] Specific provisions of two of the most recent human rights treaties also deserve mention, though their relationship to armed conflict and IHL is ambiguous. Consider Article 38 (concerning protections for children in armed conflicts including restrictions on the use of child soldiers) of the Convention of the Rights of the Child and Article 43 (stating that the 'Convention is without prejudice to the provisions of international humanitarian law') of the newly minted Convention for the Protection of All Persons from Enforced Disappearance (2006).

[14] Geoffrey Best, *War and Law Since 1945* (1994), 72.

governed by setting limits to the intrusions by governments upon those areas of human freedom thought to be essential for the proper functioning of the human being in society and for his development therein. A war or 'emergency' situation impinges, within specified limits, upon those guaranteed rights and freedoms, in relation to the governed i.e. 'everyone within their jurisdiction', and not in relation to an enemy. These freedoms, when internationalized in human-rights instruments, are neither intended nor adequate to govern an armed conflict between two states in a condition of enmity. The relevance of war to a human-rights regime is that the regime determines what happens to those human rights in that event. The regime in no way purports to regulate the conduct of the war between two states even assuming that both were subject to that human-rights regime. Hostilities and government-governed relationships are different in kind, origin, purpose, and consequences. Accordingly, the law that relates to them, respectively, has the like differences. Human-rights regimes and the humanitarian law of war deal with different and distinct relationships. [T]he process whereby human-rights law ha[s] now been 'internationalized' has not changed the quality of the relationships to which that law applies. What has happened is that certain states, sharing a common civilization and ideas about the limits of government and the freedom of the individual in society, have entered into a system of binding mutual guarantees of specific human rights and freedoms, listed and defined, in their respective states, enforceable by international organs established by the convention concerned. It is not possible to have a regional law of war. It is possible to have a regional regime of human rights....

...

The attempt to confuse the two regimes of law is insupportable in theory and inadequate in practice. The two regimes are not only distinct but are diametrically opposed....

If there be a common base for the two regimes, it might be found in the shared base of the idea of humanity, but the conception is too vague to justify the confusion attempted by the UN in the application of the two regimes of law here considered. At the end of the day, the law of human rights seeks to reflect the cohesion and harmony in human society and must, from the nature of things, be a different and opposed law to that which seeks to regulate the conduct of hostile relationships between states or other organized armed groups, and in internal rebellions. The humanitarian nature of the modern law of war neither justifies the confusion with, nor dispels the opposition to, human rights.[15]

More recently a different version, if not revision, of Draper's points has emerged: some commentators and a few states (the United States included) have argued that IHL should displace or supplant the application of human rights law in armed conflicts.[16]

[15] G.I.A.D. Draper, 'Humanitarian Law and Human Rights', Act Juridica 193 (1979).

[16] Notably, a contrary position may be reflected in a remarkable provision of the Rome Statute for the International Criminal Court. The Rome Statute covers crimes involving violations of both IHL and human rights law. Article 21 sets forth the 'applicable law' for the Court to employ such as the Statute itself and 'established principles of the international law of armed conflict'. Article 21(3) contains a notable rider: 'The application and interpretation of law pursuant to this Article must be consistent with internationally recognized human rights'. It appears that human rights law may obtain primacy under this framework. Alain Pellet, 'Applicable Law', in John R.W.D. Jones, Paola Gaeta and Antonio Cassese (eds.), *The Rome Statute of the International Criminal Court: A Commentary* 1051 (2002).

The International Court of Justice provided one of the most influential statements on this matter in an Advisory Opinion, *Legality of the Threat or Use of Nuclear Weapons*. The Court was faced with various opposing arguments. One argument maintained that the possession, threat or use of nuclear weapons violated the right to life under the ICCPR, a position supported by a General Comment of the Human Rights Committee in 1984. Another position held that the ICCPR protects human rights only in peacetime. And, some states (including the Netherlands, the United Kingdom, and the United States) took the position that IHL provides a safe harbor for parties to an armed conflict: if deaths result from actions that comply with IHL, those actions cannot be considered 'arbitrary' deprivations of the right to life. The British government, for example, stated, 'The only sensible construction which can be placed on the term "arbitrary" in this context is that it refers to whether or not the deliberate taking of life is unlawful under that part of the international law which was specifically designed to regulate the conduct of hostilities, that is the laws of armed conflict'.[17] In an oft-quoted passage, the ICJ stated:

> [T]he protection of the International Covenant of Civil and Political Rights does not cease in times of war, except by operation of Article 4 of the Covenant whereby certain provisions may be derogated from in a time of national emergency. Respect for the right to life is not, however, such a provision. In principle, the right not arbitrarily to be deprived of one's life applies also in hostilities. The test of what is an arbitrary deprivation of life, however, then falls to be determined by the applicable *lex specialis*, namely, the law applicable in armed conflict which is designed to regulate the conduct of hostilities.

As with many judicial opinions, the meaning of this statement has been subject to different, and sometimes conflicting, interpretations. Consider the following articulation of the Court's analysis and the rationale behind a broad application of the *lex specialis* doctrine:

> Confronted with two legal regimes — human rights law and humanitarian law — containing rules on the taking of lives, the ICJ resorted to the principle that *lex specialis derogat lex generali* to reconcile them, holding that the ICCPR provision on the right to life must be construed by making a *renvoi* to humanitarian law. *Lex specialis derogat lex generali*, or, the specific provision overcomes the general provision, is a canon of construction that is widely considered to be a general principle of law, as applicable in the international legal system as it is in national legal systems. Koskenniemi [in a 2003 paper] provides the principle's rationale: a 'special rule is more to the point ("approaches more nearly the subject in hand") than a general one and it regulates the matter more effectively ("are ordinarily more effective") than general rules do'. The thinking goes that because many of the same states have negotiated and acceded to the human rights law and humanitarian law

[17] The Netherlands, like other states, also referred to the negotiating history of the ICCPR:

> [T]he *travaux preparatoires* of Article 6 of the International Covenant make clear that, instead of listing the circumstances in which the deprivation of life would not be considered contrary to the right to life, the drafters decided to agree on the formulation that 'No one shall be *arbitrarily* deprived of his life.' One of the instances mentioned in this connection by the drafters as an example of a deprivation of life which is not arbitrary was 'the performance of lawful acts of war'.

treaties, we should presume that these treaties are consistent with one another. We should not think, for example, that it violates the right to liberty under the ICCPR or ECHR to hold a combatant as a prisoner of war until the end of active hostilities when, after all, the same states that negotiated the ICCPR and ECHR also negotiated an entire treaty on prisoners of war that allows exactly that. Because general rules ('No one shall be subjected to arbitrary arrest or detention.') may be interpreted in more than one way, we should interpret them in light of specific rules ('Prisoners of war shall be released and repatriated without delay after the cessation of hostilities.') rather than vice versa.[18]

The ICJ recently issued two opinions involving the application of human rights in armed conflict and military occupation. The first, in 2004, concerned Israel's construction of a physical barrier in occupied Palestinian territory, see *infra* p. 461 The second, in 2006, involved an armed conflict between the Democratic Republic of the Congo and Uganda. On both occasions, the Court provided the following formulation:

> The protection offered by human rights conventions does not cease in case of armed conflict, save through the effect of provisions for derogation of the kind to be found in Article 4 of the International Covenant on Civil and Political Rights. As regards the relationship between international humanitarian law and human rights law, there are thus three possible situations: some rights may be exclusively matters of international humanitarian law; others may be exclusively matters of human rights law; yet others may be matters of both these branches of international law.

Some of the following commentaries predate this most recent statement by the ICJ. Consider, among other issues, how the ICJ's general formulation might affect the analysis in the following commentaries. Australian Navy Commander Dale Stephens, for example, argues that the *Nuclear Weapons* opinion suggests placing greater weight upon human rights commitments in interpreting and applying the law of armed conflict:

> While human rights proponents welcomed [the] ICJ's application of Article 6 of the ICCPR during times of armed conflict, the interpretation of its Opinion remains ambiguous. The Court did not determine that the law of armed conflict had been modified in any structural manner by the parallel application of non-derogable provisions of the ICCPR. Rather, the Opinion suggests that 'humanitarian law is to be used to actually interpret a human rights rule.' Such an interpretation suggests that the possible legal content of Article 6 completely assimilates into the applicable rules of the law of armed conflict. Indeed, according to one authoritative view, it suggests that 'in the context of the conduct of hostilities, human rights law cannot be interpreted differently from humanitarian law.'[19]
>
> While this interpretation may be formalistically correct, it nonetheless is quite narrow. It is based upon an orthodox interpretation by acknowledging that the

[18] William Abresch, 'A Human Rights Law of Internal Armed Conflict: The European Court of Human Rights in Chechnya', 16 Eur. J. Int. L. 741 (2005).

[19] Louise Doswald-Beck, 'International Humanitarian Law and the Advisory Opinion of the International Court of Justice on the Legality of the Threat or Use of Nuclear Weapons', 1997 Int. Rev. Red Cross 35, at 51.

language of Article 6 is very general. In contrast, the plethora of rules governing the protection (and destruction) of life as contained within the law of armed conflict are quite detailed and therefore should, under common cannons [sic] of interpretation, continue to be the exclusive governing regime. Those seeking to ensure specific separation of the two streams of international law have applauded this manner of interpretation. These commentators contend that the rules of the law of armed conflict were largely the product of strenuous and specific negotiation. Accordingly, the import of applying operative peacetime human rights concepts, such as the right to life, would undermine the integrity of the existing rules and only promote numerous reservations and declarations to current and future law of armed conflict regimes. While possibly representative of realpolitik, such views represent a narrow assessment of the import of the Court's approach to the issue.

Though the Court formally maintained the priority of the law of armed conflict, it interpreted that law in terms of the underlying principles of humanity. This emphasis elevated the humanitarian aspects and priorities of the law of armed conflict and ensured that these 'weighted' humanitarian aspects must be considered when determining the legitimacy of military actions. . . . Hence, the Court develops its reasoning by re-interpreting the law of armed conflict with a new-found emphasis on promoting humanitarian considerations.[20]

INTERNATIONAL COMMITTEE OF THE RED CROSS, INTERNATIONAL HUMANITARIAN LAW AND OTHER LEGAL REGIMES: INTERPLAY IN SITUATIONS OF VIOLENCE

(2003)

http://www.icrc.org/Web/Eng/siteeng0.nsf/iwpList575/ ACF03C9E9B96AB23C1256DFF00332E15

[In 2003, the International Committee of the Red Cross co-sponsored a gathering in which 200 governmental and nongovernmental experts participated. Following is the ICRC summary of the participants' views on the relationship between IHL and human rights law, including on the ICJ's Nuclear Weapons opinion.]

. . . [A] consensus emerged that, even in this hypothesis of conflict, at least the non-derogable rules of human rights law continue to apply and to complement IHL.

. . .

. . . [T]he great majority of the participants simply recalled that IHL represented a special law in as much as it has been specifically framed to apply in a period of armed conflict. They noted that, in offering ground rules adapted to this particular context of violence, this body of law makes it possible — in many cases — to specify

[20] Dale Stephens, 'Human Rights and Armed Conflict — The Advisory Opinion of the International Court of Justice in the Nuclear Weapons Case', 4 Yale H. R. and Development L. J. 1, 14–15 (2001), available at http://islandia.law.yale.edu/ yhrdlj/pdf/Vol%204/Stephens.pdf.

the precise content of the non-derogable human rights. In this regard, many references were made to the reasoning followed by the International Court of Justice in its advisory opinion rendered on 8 July 1996 in the matter of the *Legality of the Threat or Use of Nuclear Weapons.* In this case, the Court, having confirmed the non-derogable nature of the right to life, held in effect that it was appropriate to refer to IHL — framed as *lex specialis* — to determine what could be considered as an arbitrary deprivation of life.

However, several participants pointed out that this reasoning — though perfectly consistent for interpreting the precise content of the right to life — could not necessarily be generalised to all relations between IHL and human rights law. On the contrary, as human rights law is more precise than IHL in certain domains, the relation of interpretation must also be able to operate in the other direction. For example, Article 3(1)(d) common to the Geneva Conventions explicitly refers to the "judicial guarantees recognised as indispensable by civilised peoples" but without further specifying the meaning of this expression. It was suggested that . . . reference [can] be made to human rights law in order to deduce the substantive guarantees resulting from this general formula. The lively debate that ensued between the participants as to the extent to which IHL could be "supplemented" by human rights law did not come to any final conclusion. . . . [S]ome of the experts maintained that only the non-derogable human rights could be appropriate in this regard and that any other approach would lead to an extension of the scope of application of human rights law without any legal basis.

INTERNATIONAL LAW COMMISSION, REPORT OF THE STUDY GROUP FINALIZED BY MARTTI KOSKENNIEMI, FRAGMENTATON OF INTERNATIONAL LAW

Fifty-eighth session, 1 May-9 June and 3 July-11 August 2006
http://daccessdds.un.org/doc/UNDOC/LTD/G06/610/77/PDF/G0661077.pdf

[In 2002, the International Law Commission included the topic of 'Fragmentation of international law' in its programme of work and established a Study Group. Professor Martti Koskenniemi is the current Chair. Following is an extract of his 2006 report to the Commission.]

88. There are two ways in which law may take account of the relationship of a particular rule to general one. A particular rule may be considered an application of a general standard in a given circumstance. The special relates to the general as does administrative regulation to law in domestic legal order. Or it may be considered as a modification, overruling or a setting aside of the latter. The first case is sometimes seen as not a situation of normative conflict at all but is taken to involve the simultaneous application of the special and the general standard. Thus, only the latter is thought to involve the application of a genuine *lex specialis.*

. . .

91. . . . [T]he European Court of Human Rights has thought the *lex specialis* applicable even in the absence of direct conflict between two provisions and where it might be said that both apply concurrently. This is the proper approach. There are two reasons for why it is useful to consider the case of "application" in connection with the case where the *lex specialis* sets up an exception or involves a "setting aside". First, it follows from the definition of the *lex specialis* adopted above that this case is also included: the norm of application is more specific because it contains the general rule itself as one element in the definition of its scope of application. Second, and more important, though the distinction is analytically sound, it is in practice seldom clear-cut. It may often be difficult to say whether a rule "applies" a standard, "modifies" it or "derogates from" it. An "application" or "modification" involves also a degree of "derogation" and "setting aside"....

96. Or what to say of the place of *lex specialis* in the Legality of the Threat or Use of Nuclear Weapons case (1996)? Here the ICJ observed that both human rights law (namely the International Covenant on Civil and Political Rights) and the laws of armed conflict both applied "in times of war". Nevertheless, when it came to determine what was an "arbitrary deprivation of life" under Article 6 (1) of the Covenant, this fell "to be determined by the applicable *lex specialis*, namely the law applicable to armed conflict". In this respect, the two fields of law applied concurrently, or within each other. From another perspective, however, the law of armed conflict — and in particular its more relaxed standard of killing — set aside whatever standard might have been provided under the practice of the Covenant.

...

104. The example of the laws of war focuses on a case where the rule itself identifies the conditions in which it is to apply, namely the presence of an "armed conflict". Owing to that condition, the rule appears more "special" than if no such condition had been identified. To regard this as a situation of *lex specialis* draws attention to an important aspect of the operation of the principle. Even as it works so as to justify recourse to an exception, what is being set aside does not vanish altogether. The [ICJ] was careful to point out that human rights law continued to apply within armed conflict. The exception — humanitarian law — only affected one (albeit important) aspect of it, namely the relative assessment of "arbitrariness". Humanitarian law as *lex specialis* did not suggest that human rights were abolished in war. It did not function in a formal or absolute way but as an aspect of the pragmatics of the Court's reasoning.... Legality of Nuclear Weapons was a "hard case" to the extent that a choice had to be made by the Court between different sets of rules none of which could fully extinguish the others. *Lex specialis* did hardly more than indicate that though it might have been desirable to apply only human rights, such a solution would have been too idealistic, bearing in mind the speciality and persistence of armed conflict....

119. *Lex specialis derogat lege generali* refers to a standard technique of legal reasoning, operative in international law as in other fields of law understood as systems. Its power is entirely dependent on the normative considerations for which it provides articulation: sensitivity to context, capacity to reflect State will, concreteness, clarity, definiteness. Its functioning cannot be assessed independently of the

role of considerations of the latter type in specific context of legal reasoning. How does a particular agreement relate to the general law around it? Does it implement or support the latter, or does it perhaps deviate from it? Is the deviation tolerable or not? No general, context-independent answers can be given to such questions. In this sense, the *lex specialis* maxim cannot be meaningfully codified.

120. The role of *lex specialis* cannot be dissociated from assessments about the nature and purposes of the general law that it proposes to modify, replace, update or deviate from. This highlights the systemic nature of the reasoning of which arguments from "special law" are an inextricable part. No rule, treaty, or custom, however special its subject-matter or limited the number of the States concerned by it, applies in a vacuum. Its normative environment includes . . . not only whatever general law there may be on that very topic, but also principles that determine the relevant legal subjects, their basic rights and duties, and the forms through which those rights and duties may be supplemented, modified or extinguished.

D. REGULATING DETENTION

1. CASE STUDY: GUANTÁNAMO DETAINEES — PROCESS FOR DETERMINING STATUS AND GROUNDS FOR DETENTION

Following the 11 September attacks and the Security Council recognition of the US right to self-defence, US and British forces invaded Afghanistan on 7 October 2001. By January 2002, the United States began transporting alleged Taliban and Al Qaeda members to its military base at Guantánamo Bay, Cuba. Individuals linked to Al Qaeda were apprehended not only in Afghanistan, but in other countries as well including Bosnia-Herzegovina, Egypt, Gambia, Mauritania, Pakistan and Thailand, before being transferred to Guantánamo.

The US government contended that all Taliban and Al Qaeda members were 'unlawful combatants' who, therefore, failed to qualify as prisoners of war (POW) under the Third Geneva Convention. What was at stake? According detainees POW status would require the Government to guarantee specific trial rights not provided by the US military commissions. POW status would also provide combatant immunity for membership in an enemy armed force (though no immunity applies to the commission of acts of terrorism, perfidy, or other war crimes). POW status would also oblige the United States to provide for certain conditions of detention, though these conditions are not clearly far superior to conditions of detention required under the Civilians (Fourth Geneva) Convention.[21]

Article 4 of the Third Convention sets forth the requirements for POW status. Under Article 4(a), POWs include individuals who belong to any of the

[21] Derek Jinks, 'The Declining Significance of POW Status', 45 Harv. Int. L. J. 367 (2004).

following categories:

(1) Members of the armed forces of a Party to the conflict, as well as members of militias or volunteer corps forming part of such armed forces.
(2) Members of other militias and members of other volunteer corps, including those of organized resistance movements, belonging to a Party to the conflict and operating in or outside their own territory, even if this territory is occupied, provided that such militias or volunteer corps, including such organized resistance movements, fulfil the following conditions:
   (a) that of being commanded by a person responsible for his subordinates;
   (b) that of having a fixed distinctive sign recognizable at a distance;
   (c) that of carrying arms openly;
   (d) that of conducting their operations in accordance with the laws and customs of war.

...

(4) Persons who accompany the armed forces without actually being members thereof, such as ... supply contractors, members of labour units or of services responsible for the welfare of the armed forces ...

Article 5 of the POW Convention states that '[s]hould any doubt arise as to whether persons, having committed a belligerent act and having fallen into the hands of the enemy, belong to any of the categories enumerated in Article 4, such persons shall enjoy the protection of the present Convention until such time as their status has been determined by a competent tribunal'.

The US Government declared that the Geneva Conventions applied to the international armed conflict with Afghanistan. The United States, however, contended that the Taliban and Al Qaeda failed to satisfy the criteria of Article 4(a)2; that the criteria of Article 4(a)2 apply to 4(a)1 groups that Al Qaeda as a nonstate actor (and especially as a terrorist group) could not receive the protections of the Geneva Conventions in any case; and that no doubt about status existed and hence there was not need for a tribunal under Article 5 of the POW Convention.

Several international intergovernmental and nongovernmental organizations opposed the US position including the European Parliament, the International Committee for the Red Cross, the UN High Commissioner for Human Rights, UN human rights special mechanisms such as the UN Working Group on Arbitrary Detention, and a number of foreign governments.

In early 2002, a group of organizations (the Center for Constitutional Rights, the Human Rights Clinic at Columbia Law School, and the Center for Justice and International Law) petitioned the Inter-American Commission on Human Rights. They argued, *inter alia*, that the United States violated the American Declaration on the Rights and Duties of Man in failing to comply with the procedures established under the Third Geneva Convention and in holding the individuals in prolonged detention without access to a court.

In March 2002, the Commission issued a communication requesting the United States to adopt precautionary measures — to 'take the urgent measures necessary to have the legal status of the detainees at Guantánamo Bay determined by a competent tribunal'. In 2002–2005, the US Government and petitioners submitted numerous briefs and participated in oral hearings before the Commission. During this period, the Commission issued multiple decisions reiterating and amplifying its March 2002 communication. The Commission also recognized that intervening developments, including US Supreme Court decisions and Department of Defense policy changes, partially satisfied US obligations identified in the Commission's initial decision. Some commentators credit the pressure from the Commission and other international authorities as helping bring about those developments.

Throughout its exchanges with the Commission, the US government contended that IHL has the status of *lex specialis* and displaces the application of human rights law. The United States also contended that the Commission lacked the jurisdictional competence to interpret and apply IHL. These and other arguments are explored in the following materials.

INTER-AMERICAN COMMISSION ON HUMAN RIGHTS ORGANIZATION OF AMERICAN STATES DETAINEES IN GUANTÁNAMO BAY, CUBA REQUEST FOR PRECAUTIONARY MEASURES

13 March 2002

[The Organization of American States] charge[s] the Commission with supervising member states' observance of human rights in the Hemisphere. These rights include those prescribed under the American Declaration of the Rights and Duties of Man, which constitutes a source of legal obligation for all OAS member states in respect of persons subject to their authority and control. . . .

. . . [W]hile its specific mandate is to secure the observance of international human rights protections in the Hemisphere, this Commission has in the past looked to and applied definitional standards and relevant rules of international humanitarian law in interpreting the American Declaration and other Inter-American human rights instruments in situations of armed conflict.

In taking this approach, the Commission has drawn upon certain basic principles that inform the interrelationship between international human rights and humanitarian law. It is well-recognized that international human rights law applies at all times, in peacetime and in situations of armed conflict. In contrast, international humanitarian law generally does not apply in peacetime and its principal purpose is to place restraints on the conduct of warfare in order to limit or contain the damaging effects of hostilities and to protect the victims of armed conflict, including civilians and combatants who have laid down their arms or have been placed hors de combat. Further, in situations of armed conflict, the protections under international human rights and humanitarian law may complement and reinforce one another, sharing as they do a common nucleus of non-derogable rights and a common purpose of promoting human life and dignity. In certain circumstances, however, the test for evaluating the observance of a particular right, such as the right to liberty, in a situation of armed conflict may be distinct from that applicable in time of peace. In such situations, international law, including the jurisprudence of this Commission, dictates that it may be necessary to deduce the applicable standard by reference to international humanitarian law as the applicable *lex specialis*.

Accordingly, where persons find themselves within the authority and control of a state and where a circumstance of armed conflict may be involved, their fundamental rights may be determined in part by reference to international humanitarian law as well as international human rights law. Where it may be considered that the protections of international humanitarian law do not apply, however, such persons remain the beneficiaries at least of the non-derogable protections under international human rights law. In short, no person under the authority and control of a state, regardless of his or her circumstances, is devoid of legal protection for his or her fundamental and non-derogable human rights.

This basic precept is reflected in the Martens clause common to numerous long-standing humanitarian law treaties, including the Hague Conventions of 1899 and 1907 respecting the laws and customs of war on land, according to which human persons who do not fall within the protection of those treaties or other international agreements remain under the protection of the principles of the law of nations, as they result from the usages established among civilized peoples, from the laws of humanity, and the dictates of the public conscience. And according to international norms applicable in peacetime and wartime, such as those reflected in Article 5 of the Third Geneva Convention and Article XVIII of the American Declaration of the Rights and Duties of Man, a competent court or tribunal, as opposed to a political authority, must be charged with ensuring respect for the legal status and rights of persons falling under the authority and control of a state.

Specifically with regard to the request for precautionary measures presently before it, the Commission observes that certain pertinent facts concerning the detainees at Guantánamo Bay are well-known and do not appear to be the subject of controversy. These include the fact that the government of the United States considers itself to be at war with an international network of terrorists, that the United States undertook a military operation in Afghanistan beginning in October 2001 in defending this war, and that most of the detainees in Guantánamo Bay were apprehended in connection with this military operation and remain wholly within the authority and control of the United States government.

It is also well-known that doubts exists [*sic*] as to the legal status of the detainees. This includes the question of whether and to what extent the Third Geneva Convention and/or other provisions of international humanitarian law apply to some or all of the detainees and what implications this may have for their international human rights protections. According to official statements from the United States government, its Executive Branch has most recently declined to extend prisoner of war status under the Third Geneva Convention to the detainees, without submitting the issue for determination by a competent tribunal or otherwise ascertaining the rights and protections to which the detainees are entitled under US domestic or international law. To the contrary, the information available suggests that the detainees remain entirely at the unfettered discretion of the United States government. Absent clarification of the legal status of the detainees, the Commission considers that the rights and protections to which they may be entitled under international or domestic law cannot be said to be the subject of effective legal protection by the State.

In light of the foregoing considerations, and without prejudging the possible application of international humanitarian law to the detainees at Guantánamo Bay, the Commission considers that precautionary measures are both appropriate and necessary in the present circumstances, in order to ensure that the legal status of each of the detainees is clarified and that they are afforded the legal protections commensurate with the status that they are found to possess, which may in no case fall below the minimum standards of non-derogable rights. On this basis, the Commission hereby requests that the United States take the urgent measures necessary to have the legal status of the detainees at Guantánamo Bay determined by a competent tribunal.

...

The Commission wishes to note in accordance with ... the Commission's Rules of Procedure that the granting of these measures and their adoption by the State shall not constitute a prejudgment on the merits of a case.

RESPONSE OF THE UNITED STATES TO REQUEST FOR PRECAUTIONARY MEASURES, DETAINEES IN GUANTÁNAMO BAY, CUBA, 15 APRIL 2002

41 I.L.M. 1015 (2002)

... [T]he Commission's request for precautionary measures and the precautionary measures themselves are not premised on any rights set forth in the American Declaration. This case is not about the American Declaration. Rather, this case is about the detention of captured enemy combatants who took part in hostilities during an armed conflict .... It involves solely the interpretation and application of specific articles of the Geneva Convention and related customary international humanitarian law, neither of which lies within the scope of the Commission's competence. In order to request provisional measures in this case, the Commission necessarily has had to interpret and apply humanitarian law, specifically Article 5 and other provisions of the Geneva Convention — a body of law separate and distinct from the American Declaration and the body of human rights law.

...

Petitioners' ... citation to international human rights law is misguided, in part because it rests on the assumption that human rights law is equally applicable during armed conflict and indeed takes precedence over international humanitarian law. In fact, international human rights law is not applicable to the conduct of hostilities or the capture and detention of enemy combatants, which are governed by the more specific laws of armed conflict.

...

. . . Furthermore, the detainees in this case . . . are not subject to the Fourth Geneva Convention on civilians. Rather they are unlawful enemy combatants who were captured while taking part in hostilities against the United States and its allies. . . .

. . .

Nor can Petitioners save the jurisdictional competence of the Commission by framing the issues in terms of human rights law, evidently ignoring the separate and distinct humanitarian law rules at issue. For example, the Petitioners assert that the United States has violated the detainees' human rights to be free from, inter alia, arbitrary and prolonged detention without, however, any reference to the separate and distinct rules of detention in international humanitarian law. Under international humanitarian law, states engaged in armed conflict have the right to capture and detain enemy combatants, whether or not the combatants are POWs.[22] In this case, active hostilities are ongoing. The United States is therefore fully entitled to hold the detainees.

. . .

Under the ICJ's methodology, the Commission would have to interpret the American Declaration in light of the *lex specialis,* i.e., international humanitarian law and the Geneva Convention. The ICJ explained in its Advisory Opinion on the Legality of the Threat or Use of Nuclear Weapons that, to the extent human rights law is applicable during armed conflict, it must be interpreted in light of relevant *lex specialis* as set forth in the body of humanitarian law.

Accordingly, the ICJ's analysis would require the Commission to take the following analytical steps in this case:

- First, the Commission would determine the generally applicable human rights norm. The generally applicable norm under the American Declaration, Article XVIII, provides that individuals may resort to the courts to protect their legal rights. American Declaration, Art. XVIII. Absent applicable *lex specialis,* therefore, detainees generally would have recourse to the courts to challenge their detentions.
- Second, the Commission would determine whether there is any applicable *lex specialis.* In this case, the *lex specialis* would be international humanitarian law because the detainees were captured in the context of an ongoing armed conflict.
- Third, the Commission would determine whether the *lex specialis* forms a separate and distinct rule altogether, or rather, merely refines the otherwise applicable concepts embodied in the American Declaration.
- Fourth, if the *lex specialis* forms a separate and distinct rule altogether, the Commission would determine whether it had competence to interpret the

[22] The underlying principle that a State has the authority to detain combatants for the duration of hostilities certainly is not diminished by the mere fact that a combatant is acting unlawfully, as opposed to lawfully. Geneva Convention Article 118, which sets forth release and repatriation obligations and conditions with respect to lawful combatants, i.e., POWs reflects the international humanitarian law principle that combatants may be detained for at least the duration of hostilities. The authority to detain unlawful combatants is at a minimum equal to that with respect to lawful combatants. To afford rights to unlawful combatants greater than those afforded to lawful combatants would be entirely inconsistent with the letter and spirit of the Geneva Convention, as well as customary international humanitarian law. . . .

> separate and distinct *lex specialis*. In this case, the Commission would recognize that the international humanitarian laws on detention are quite explicit, as well as separate and distinct from the human rights norms in the American Declaration. The Commission would recognize that it, unlike the ICJ, has a very limited jurisdictional competence which does not include international humanitarian law, for reason previously discussed. The Commission would then acknowledge that where it lacks the competence to interpret and apply the relevant law, it must decline to grant the Petitioners' request.

...

... [T]he *lex specialis* in this case is the body of international humanitarian law relating to detentions, which affords the detainees, as captured unlawful enemy combatants, no right of access to the detaining power's courts.

...

The Commission Letter states that "precautionary measures are both appropriate and necessary . . . in order to ensure that the legal status of each of the detainees is clarified. . . ." This statement assumes that the legal status of the detainees needs clarification. In fact, however, their legal status has been stated clearly and is widely known.

The United States has stated publicly that the detainees are not entitled to POW status because they are unlawful combatants. For example, the United States has said:

> Under Article 4 of the Geneva Convention, . . . Taliban detainees are not entitled to POW status. . . . The Taliban have not effectively distinguished themselves from the civilian population of Afghanistan. Moreover, they have not conducted their operations in accordance with the laws and customs of war . . . . Al Qaeda is an international terrorist group and cannot be considered a state party to the Geneva Convention. Its members, therefore, are not covered by the Geneva Convention, and are not entitled to POW status under the treaty.

...

Thus, contrary to the Commission's assertion, the detainees' legal status is clear. The United States has made it a matter of public record that the detainees are not POWs because they do not meet the criteria applicable to lawful combatants. . . .

In light of the fact that the status already has been clarified, precautionary measures are unnecessary.

INTER-AMERICAN COMMISSION ON HUMAN RIGHTS, REITERATION OF PRECAUTIONARY MEASURES REGARDING DETAINEES IN GUANTÁNAMO, 23 JULY 2002

45 I.L.M. 667 (2006)

...

The additional information provided by the Petitioners in their observations May 13, 2002, to which the United States chose not to respond in substance, have augmented the Commission's concerns. In particular, as indicated by the Petitioners and as reported in the media, the manner in which certain detainees at Guantánamo Bay were captured raises reasonable doubts concerning whether they belong to the enemy's armed forces or related groups. These detainees are alleged to include, for example, six Algerian citizens arrested by US authorities in Bosnia and ten Kuwaiti nationals arrested in Pakistan. Without more, this information raises further serious concerns regarding the legal status of each of the detainees at Guantánamo Bay and the international rights and protections to which they may be entitled.

INTER-AMERICAN COMMISSION ON HUMAN RIGHTS, DETAINEES IN GUANTÁNAMO BAY, CUBA, REITERATION AND FURTHER AMPLIFICATION OF PRECAUTIONARY MEASURES, 28 OCTOBER 2005

45 I.L.M. 673 (2006)

[In 2004, the U.S. Supreme Court decided two cases relevant to the proceedings before the Inter-American Commission. One case, *Rasul v. Bush*, is directly discussed in the following excerpt from the Commission. The other case, *Hamdi v. Rumsfeld*, is dealt with indirectly. *Hamdi* involved a U.S. citizen alleged to have been a Taliban member and held in the United States without trial. The Supreme Court ruled that Hamdi was entitled, under the U.S. Constitution, to a hearing to determine whether he was indeed a combatant who could consequently be detained until the cessation of hostilities. After *Hamdi*, the United States created Combatant Status Review Tribunals (CSRTs) for all foreign nationals held by the Defense Department at Guantánamo. CSRTs, composed of three military officers, are mandated to determine whether an individual is an 'enemy combatant'. The Order establishing CSRTs defines 'enemy combatant' as 'an individual who was part of or supporting Taliban or Al Qaeda forces, or associated forces that are engaged in hostilities against the United States or its coalition partners. This includes any person who has committed a belligerent act or has directly supported hostilities in aid of enemy armed forces'. The United States also established Administrative Review Boards to review periodically whether an enemy combatant should continue to be detained.]

... [T]he Commission observes that when it first adopted these precautionary measures in March 2002, the urgency of the matter arose from the fact that according to available information, the detainees at Guantanamo Bay remained entirely at the unfettered discretion of the United States government. As no person under the authority and control of a state, regardless of his or her circumstances, is devoid of legal protection for his or her fundamental and non-derogable human rights, the Commission considered that the rights and protections to which the detainees may be entitled under international or domestic law could not be said to be the subject of effective legal protection by the State absent clarification of the legal status of the detainees. Over two years later, the U.S. Supreme Court reached essentially the same conclusion in its judgment in the case of *Rasul v. Bush* [in 2004], in which a majority of the Court held that United States courts have jurisdiction to consider challenges to the legality of detention of foreign nationals captured abroad in connection with hostilities and incarcerated at Guantanamo Bay. The Court's finding in this respect was based upon, inter alia, the longstanding and fundamental role that the writ of habeas corpus plays as a means of reviewing Executive detention. In this respect, Mr. Justice Stevens, writing for the majority, quoted Justice Jackson's statement from his dissenting opinion in the case of *Shaughnessey v. United States ex rel. Mezei*, that

> Executive imprisonment has long been considered oppressive and lawless since John, at Runnymede, pledged that no free man should be imprisoned, dispossessed, outlawed, or exiled save by the judgment of his peers or by the law of the land. The judges of England developed the writ of habeas corpus largely to preserve these immunities from executive restraint.

Notwithstanding the Supreme Court's pronouncement, the information before the Commission indicates that over one year since the decision, nearly half of the detainees at Guantanamo Bay have not been given effective access to counsel or otherwise provided with a fair opportunity to pursue a habeas corpus proceeding in accordance with the Supreme Court's ruling, despite the fact that the purpose of habeas is intended to be a timely remedy aimed at guaranteeing personal liberty and humane treatment.[23] Moreover, in those habeas petitions that have been filed, no final determinations have yet been reached as to the legal status of the detainees or the rights to which they are entitled under domestic or international law. While the State argues that the procedures before the Combatant Status Review Board and the Administrative Review Boards likewise satisfy the Commission's request, it remains entirely unclear from the outcome of those proceedings what the legal status of the detainees is or what rights they are entitled to under international or domestic law. The information available only indicates that 558 of the 596 detainees have been found by the Combatant Status Review Tribunal to be "enemy combatants not entitled to prisoner of war protections." Accordingly, the Commission does not consider that these procedures have adequately responded to the concerns at the base of the Commission's request for precautionary measures.

In these circumstances, the Commission considers that the urgent situation at Guantanamo Bay continues to exist and, moreover, has been exacerbated by the fact that some detainees have been subjected to additional processes and proceedings, including removal to third countries and trial by military commission, while their legal status remains unclear. Based upon these considerations, the Commission finds that the State has not complied with this aspect of the Commission's request for precautionary measures, that a serious and urgent situation of irreparable harm to persons remains at Guantanamo Bay, and therefore reiterates its request that the State take the immediate measures necessary to have the legal status of the detainees at Guantanamo Bay effectively determined by a competent tribunal.

[23] See I/A Court H.R., Castillo Paéz Case, Judgment of 3 November 1997, Ser. C No. 34, para. 83 (holding that '[t]he purpose of habeas corpus is not only to guarantee personal liberty and humane treatment, but also to prevent disappearance or failure to determine the place of detention, and, ultimately, to ensure the right to life').

DETAINEE TREATMENT ACT OF 2005

[On 30 December 2005, President Bush signed into law the Detainee Treatment Act of 2005. The Act eliminates *habeas corpus* for claims concerning conditions of confinement, including conditions of interrogation, for individuals held at Guantanamo Bay. It does, however, provide for judicial review of CSRTs and military commissions. It also includes the 'McCain Amendment', discussed in Chapter 3, which prohibits torture and cruel, inhuman, or degrading treatment or punishment applicable to all persons held in U.S. custody.]

SEC. 1005. PROCEDURES FOR STATUS REVIEW OF DETAINEES OUTSIDE THE UNITED STATES.

...

(e) Judicial Review of Detention of Enemy Combatants —

... Except as provided in section 1005 of the Detainee Treatment Act of 2005, no court, justice, or judge shall have jurisdiction to hear or consider —

(1) an application for a writ of habeas corpus filed by or on behalf of an alien detained by the Department of Defense at Guantanamo Bay, Cuba; or

(2) any other action against the United States or its agents relating to any aspect of the detention by the Department of Defense of an alien at Guantanamo Bay, Cuba, who —

(A) is currently in military custody; or

(B) has been determined by the United States Court of Appeals for the District of Columbia Circuit in accordance with the procedures set forth in section 1005(e) of the Detainee Treatment Act of 2005 to have been properly detained as an enemy combatant.

(2) REVIEW OF DECISIONS OF COMBATANT STATUS REVIEW TRIBUNALS OF PROPRIETY OF DETENTION —

(A) IN GENERAL — . . . the United States Court of Appeals for the District of Columbia Circuit shall have exclusive jurisdiction to determine the validity of any final decision of a Combatant Status Review Tribunal that an alien is properly detained as an enemy combatant.

(B) LIMITATION ON CLAIMS — The jurisdiction of the United States Court of Appeals for the District of Columbia Circuit under this paragraph shall be limited to claims brought by or on behalf of an alien —

(i) who is, at the time a request for review by such court is filed, detained by the Department of Defense at Guantanamo Bay, Cuba; and

(ii) for whom a Combatant Status Review Tribunal has been conducted, pursuant to applicable procedures specified by the Secretary of Defense.

(C) SCOPE OF REVIEW — The jurisdiction of the United States Court of Appeals for the District of Columbia Circuit on any claims with respect to an alien under this paragraph shall be limited to the consideration of —

(i) whether the status determination of the Combatant Status Review Tribunal with regard to such alien was consistent with the standards and procedures specified by the Secretary of Defense for Combatant Status Review Tribunals (including the requirement that the conclusion of the Tribunal be supported by a preponderance of the evidence and allowing a rebuttable presumption in favor of the Government's evidence); and

(ii) to the extent the Constitution and laws of the United States are applicable, whether the use of such standards and procedures to make the determination is consistent with the Constitution and laws of the United States.

(D) TERMINATION ON RELEASE FROM CUSTODY — The jurisdiction of the United States Court of Appeals for the District of Columbia Circuit with respect to the claims of an alien under this paragraph shall cease upon the release of such alien from the custody of the Department of Defense.

(3) REVIEW OF FINAL DECISIONS OF MILITARY COMMISSIONS —

(A) IN GENERAL — . . . the United States Court of Appeals for the District of Columbia Circuit shall have exclusive jurisdiction to determine the validity of any final decision rendered pursuant to Military Commission Order No. 1, dated August 31, 2005 (or any successor military order).

(B) GRANT OF REVIEW— Review under this paragraph —

(i) with respect to a capital case or a case in which the alien was sentenced to a term of imprisonment of 10 years or more, shall be as of right; or

(ii) with respect to any other case, shall be at the discretion of the United States Court of Appeals for the District of Columbia Circuit.

(C) LIMITATION ON APPEALS — The jurisdiction of the United States Court of Appeals for the District of Columbia Circuit under this paragraph shall be limited to an appeal brought by or on behalf of an alien —

(i) who was, at the time of the proceedings pursuant to the military order referred to in subparagraph (A), detained by the Department of Defense at Guantanamo Bay, Cuba; and

(ii) for whom a final decision has been rendered pursuant to such military order.

(D) SCOPE OF REVIEW — The jurisdiction of the United States Court of Appeals for the District of Columbia Circuit on an appeal of a final decision with respect to an alien under this paragraph shall be limited to the consideration of—

(i) whether the final decision was consistent with the standards and procedures specified in the military order referred to in subparagraph (A); and

(ii) to the extent the Constitution and laws of the United States are applicable, whether the use of such standards and procedures to reach the final decision is consistent with the Constitution and laws of the United States.

...

QUESTIONS

1. Is the US Government's position on the relationship between the two bodies of law — IHL and human rights law — persuasive? Do human rights bodies, such as the Inter-American Commission, have the proper expertise and competence to interpret and apply IHL? What factors should determine the appropriate role for such an institution?

2. Should the administrative detention of suspected terrorists, or unlawful combatants in an armed conflict, be subject to review by a court? Human rights law says one thing, and IHL arguably says another. Articles XVIII and XXV of the Declaration on the Rights and Duties of Man contemplate 'resort to the courts' and 'legality of ... detention ascertained ... by a court'. So does a corresponding provision in the ICCPR: Article 9(4). Article 5 of the POW Convention, however, refers only to a 'competent tribunal', which most authorities conclude could be satisfied by an administrative body composed of military personnel. The ICRC Commentaries on a similar article in Protocol I state:

> This rule is more or less based on Article 5 of the Third Convention and the question which arises is obviously that of knowing what is meant by a 'competent tribunal'. This problem had already arisen for the drafters of Article 5 of the Third Convention. ... The drafters finally agreed upon the expression 'competent tribunal', and the Rapporteur indicated in his report that 'as in the case of Article 5, such a tribunal may be administrative in nature', which includes, in particular, military commissions.

Can the principle of *lex specialis derogat generali* resolve this conflict? Or, should the *lex specialis* principle operate only in the case of a 'true conflict' of law — when one rule prohibits an action that another rule requires? Should Article 5 be interpreted differently in light of the evolution of human rights norms since 1949?

3. Does the nature of the conflict with Al Qaeda amplify or reduce the need for judicial review of detention decisions? Does the special threat posed by terrorism suggest that older, more protective rules are less applicable in this new context? Or is the nature of the conflict so vague and open-ended such that greater judicial safeguards are needed?

4. Evaluate the following statement.

> The Inter-American Human Rights Commission was correct. The US Combatant Status Review Tribunals could never dispose of the question whether an individual is a

POW, nor the broader question concerning his rights and status under international law. First, the CSRTs are mandated only to determine whether an individual is 'an enemy combatant'. Being an enemy combatant is not inconsistent with being a POW. On the contrary, an adverse finding in a CSRT would support a finding of POW status in an Article 5 tribunal: being a 'combatant' satisfies an element of Article 4(a)1 and 2 of the POW Convention. Accordingly, the CSRT process does not assign detainees any rights-bearing status. The outcome of the process is fundamentally inconclusive for achieving that purpose. Second, determining that an individual is an 'unlawful combatant' does not resolve his rights or status under international law despite the U.S. government's assertions before the Commission. The US Government had also taken the position that unlawful combatants are not legally entitled to protections under the POW or Civilians Convention and that human rights law does not apply to the situation. Under this scheme, 'unlawful combatants' are held in legal limbo if not a legal abyss.

Also, consider the above statement in light of the Detainee Treatment Act of 2005. Does the legislation resolve concerns raised in the comment? In a 2006 decision, which is discussed shortly, the Supreme Court held that Al Qaeda members are covered by Common Article 3. Does that ruling help resolve the concerns raised in the comment?

2. CASE STUDY: INDEFINITE DETENTION IN EUROPE

Prior to 11 September, the UK Parliament passed the Terrorism Act 2000. The law provides a general definition of terrorism, which serves as the backbone of British anti-terrorism laws and practices. Section 1 of the legislation reads:

1 Terrorism: interpretation

(1) In this Act 'terrorism' means the use or threat of action where—

- (a) the action falls within subsection (2),
- (b) the use or threat is designed to influence the government or to intimidate the public or a section of the public, and
- (c) the use or threat is made for the purpose of advancing a political, religious or ideological cause.

(2) Action falls within this subsection if it—

- (a) involves serious violence against a person,
- (b) involves serious damage to property,
- (c) endangers a person's life, other than that of the person committing the action,
- (d) creates a serious risk to the health or safety of the public or a section of the public, or
- (e) is designed seriously to interfere with or seriously to disrupt an electronic system.

(3) The use or threat of action falling within subsection (2) which involves the use of firearms or explosives is terrorism whether or not subsection (1)(b) is satisfied.

(4) In this section—

(a) 'action' includes action outside the United Kingdom,

(b) a reference to any person or to property is a reference to any person, or to property, wherever situated,

(c) a reference to the public includes a reference to the public of a country other than the United Kingdom, ...

...

(5) In this Act a reference to action taken for the purposes of terrorism includes a reference to action taken for the benefit of a proscribed organisation.

In the aftermath of 11 September, the United Kingdom took two significant steps. First, Parliament passed the Anti-terrorism, Crime and Security Act 2001 (ATCSA). The Act provides broad powers to detain foreign nationals who cannot be deported, for example, due to the threat of torture on their return or the lack of agreement with their home country. Section 23(1) states:

(1) A suspected international terrorist may be detained ... despite the fact that his removal or departure from the United Kingdom is prevented (whether temporarily or indefinitely) by—

(a) a point of law which wholly or partly relates to an international agreement, or

(b) a practical consideration.

Second, the government submitted a detailed Derogation Order under the European Convention on Human Rights and the ICCPR in contemplation of the new detention rules.

Under the ATCSA, the UK Home Secretary certified a total of 17 foreign nationals as 'suspected international terrorists'. These individuals were detained without the prospect of a criminal trial. They were alleged by the Home Secretary to have engaged in various activities including maintaining 'extensive contacts to senior terrorists worldwide', being 'at the centre in the UK of terrorist activities associated with al-Qaeda', being an 'active supporter of various international terrorist groups, including those with links to Osama Bin Laden's terrorist network ... [and engaging in] activities on their behalf include[ing] fund raising', and being 'an active supporter of the Tunisian Fighting Group, a terrorist organisation with close links to al-Qaeda ... [and having] provided direct assistance to a number of active terrorists'.

The petitioners in the case brought before Britain's highest court, the House of Lords, were certified as suspected international terrorists between December 2001 and early 2002. They could not be deported to their home countries because they faced a risk of torture or inhuman or degrading treatment. The Home Secretary accordingly detained the petitioners pursuant to section 23(1) of the ATCSA. Two of the detainees exercised their right to leave the United Kingdom: one went to Morocco and the other went to France. One detainee was released on bail on strict conditions in April 2004. The Home Secretary revoked the certification of another detainee in September 2004. Due to the significance of the case, the House of Lords convened a panel of nine rather than the ordinary five Law Lords, an action that had occurred only once since World War II. Lord Bingham delivered the lead opinion. Only one Law Lord dissented in the case.[24]

A AND OTHERS V. SECRETARY OF STATE FOR THE HOME DEPARTMENT

United Kingdom House of Lords, 16 December 2004
[2004] UKHL 56

LORD BINGHAM

9. . . . [R]eference must be made to the important decision of the European Court of Human Rights in *Chahal v United Kingdom* (1996). Mr Chahal was an Indian citizen who had been granted indefinite leave to remain in this country but whose activities as a Sikh separatist brought him to the notice of the authorities both in India and here. The Home Secretary of the day decided that he should be deported from this country because his continued presence here was not conducive to the public good for reasons of a political nature, namely the international fight against terrorism. He resisted deportation on the ground (among others) that, if returned to India, he faced a real risk of death, or of torture in custody . . . [The Court] said, in paras 79–80 of its judgment:

> "79. Article 3 [of the European Convention] enshrines one of the most fundamental values of democratic society. The Court is well aware of the immense difficulties faced by States in modern times in protecting their communities from terrorist violence. However, even in these circumstances, the Convention prohibits in absolute terms torture or inhuman or degrading treatment or punishment, irrespective of the victim's conduct. . . .

The Court went on to consider whether Mr Chahal's detention, which had lasted for a number of years, had exceeded the period permissible under Article 5(1)(f) [of the European Convention]. On this question the Court, differing from the unanimous decision of the Commission, held that it had not. But it reasserted that "any deprivation of liberty under Article 5(1)(f) will be justified only for as long as deportation proceedings are in progress". . . . But a non-national who faces the prospect of torture or inhuman treatment if returned to his own country, and who cannot be deported to any third country and is not charged with any crime, may not under Article 5(1)(f) of the Convention and Schedule 3 to the Immigration Act 1971 be detained here even if judged to be a threat to national security.

. . .

The Derogation Order

11. The derogation related to Article 5(1), in reality Article 5(1)(f), of the Convention. The proposed notification by the United Kingdom was set out in a

[24] Sangeeta Shah, 'The UK's Anti-Terror Legislation and the House of Lords: The First Skirmish', 6 Hum.R.L.R. 416 (2006).

schedule to the Order. The first section . . . referred to the attacks of 11 September and to United Nations Security Council resolutions recognising those attacks as a threat to international peace and security and requiring all states to take measures to prevent the commission of terrorist attacks, "including by denying safe haven to those who finance, plan, support or commit terrorist attacks". . . .

. . . In a section entitled "Article 5(1)(f) of the Convention" the effect of the Court's decision in *Chahal* was summarised. In the next section it was recognised that the extended power in the new legislation to detain a person against whom no action was being taken with a view to deportation might be inconsistent with Article 5(1)(f). Hence the need for derogation. Formal notice of derogation was given to the Secretary General on 18 December 2001. . . .

The 2001 Act

12. . . . Section 21 provides for certification of a person by the Secretary of State [for the Home Department]:

'*21 Suspected international terrorist: certification*

(1) The Secretary of State may issue a certificate under this section in respect of a person if the Secretary of State reasonably—

(a) believes that the person's presence in the United Kingdom is a risk to national security, and
(b) suspects that the person is a terrorist.

(2) In subsection (1)(b) 'terrorist' means a person who—

(a) is or has been concerned in the commission, preparation or instigation of acts of international terrorism,
(b) is a member of or belongs to an international terrorist group, or
(c) has links with an international terrorist group.

(3) A group is an international terrorist group for the purposes of subjection (2)(b) and (c) if—

(a) it is subject to the control or influence of persons outside the United Kingdom, and
(b) the Secretary of State suspects that it is concerned in the commission, preparation or instigation of acts of international terrorism.

(4) For the purposes of subsection (2)(c) a person has links with an international terrorist group only if he supports or assists it.
(5) In this Part—'terrorism' has the meaning given by section 1 of the Terrorism Act 2000 [see para. 5 above], and 'suspected international terrorist' means a person certified under subsection (1).

. . .

15. The Act makes provision in section 24 for the grant of bail by the Special Immigration Appeals Commission ("SIAC"), in section 25 for appeal to SIAC against certification by a certified suspected international terrorist, in section 26 for periodic reviews of certification by SIAC. . . .

Public emergency

16. The appellants repeated . . . that there neither was nor is a "public emergency threatening the life of the nation" within the meaning of Article 15(1). . . .

17. The European Court considered the meaning of this provision in *Lawless v Ireland (No 3)* (1961) 1 EHRR 15, a case concerned with very low-level IRA terrorist activity in Ireland and Northern Ireland between 1954 and 1957. . . . [T]he Court held that it was for it to determine whether the conditions laid down in Article 15 for the exercise of the exceptional right of derogation had been made out. In paras 28–29 it ruled:

> "28. . . . The Court, after an examination, finds this to be the case; the existence at the time of a 'public emergency threatening the life of the nation' was reasonably deduced by the Irish Government from a combination of several factors, namely: in the first place, the existence in the territory of the Republic of Ireland of a secret army engaged in unconstitutional activities and using violence to attain its purposes; secondly, the fact that this army was also operating outside the territory of the State, thus seriously jeopardising the relations of the Republic of Ireland with its neighbour; thirdly, the steady and alarming increase in terrorist activities from the autumn of 1956 and throughout the first half of 1957.
>
> 29. Despite the gravity of the situation, the Government had succeeded, by using means available under ordinary legislation, in keeping public institutions functioning more or less normally, but the homicidal ambush on the night of 3 to 4 July 1957 in the territory of Northern Ireland near the border had brought to light, just before 12 July — a date, which, for historical reasons, is particularly critical for the preservation of public peace and order — the imminent danger to the nation caused by the continuance of unlawful activities in Northern Ireland by the IRA and various associated groups, operating from the territory of the Republic of Ireland."

18. In the *Greek Case* (1969) 12 YB 1 the Government of Greece failed to persuade the Commission that there had been a public emergency threatening the life of the nation such as would justify derogation. In para 153 of its opinion the Commission described the features of such an emergency:

> "153. Such a public emergency may then be seen to have, in particular, the following characteristics:
>
> (1) It must be actual or imminent.
> (2) Its effects must involve the whole nation.
> (3) The continuance of the organised life of the community must be threatened.
> (4) The crisis or danger must be exceptional, in that the normal measures or restrictions, permitted by the Convention for the maintenance of public safety, health and order, are plainly inadequate."

In *Ireland v United Kingdom* (1978) . . . the Court made valuable observations about its role where the application of the article is challenged:

"(a) *The role of the Court*

> 207. The limits on the Court's powers of review are particularly apparent where Article 15 is concerned.

> It falls in the first place to each Contracting State, with its responsibility for 'the life of [its] nation', to determine whether that life is threatened by a 'public emergency' and, if so, how far it is necessary to go in attempting to overcome the emergency. By reason of their direct and continuous contact with the pressing needs of the moment, the national authorities are in principle in a better position than the international judge to decide both on the presence of such an emergency and on the nature and scope of derogations necessary to avert it. In this matter, Article 15(1) leaves those authorities a wide margin of appreciation.
>
> Nevertheless, the States do not enjoy an unlimited power in this respect. The Court, which, with the Commission, is responsible for ensuring the observance of the States' engagements (Art. 19), is empowered to rule on whether the States have gone beyond the 'extent strictly required by the exigencies' of the crisis. The domestic margin of appreciation is thus accompanied by a European supervision."

...

20. The appellants did not seek to play down the catastrophic nature of what had taken place on 11 September 2001 nor the threat posed to western democracies by international terrorism. But they argued that there had been no public emergency threatening the life of the British nation, for three main reasons: if the emergency was not (as in all the decided cases) actual, it must be shown to be imminent, which could not be shown here; the emergency must be of a temporary nature, which again could not be shown here; and the practice of other states, none of which had derogated from the European Convention, strongly suggested that there was no public emergency calling for derogation. All these points call for some explanation.

21. The requirement of imminence is not expressed in Article 15 of the European Convention or Article 4 of the ICCPR but it has, as already noted, been treated by the European Court as a necessary condition of a valid derogation. It is a view shared by the distinguished academic authors of the Siracusa Principles, who in 1985 formulated the rule (applying to the ICCPR):

> "54. The principle of strict necessity shall be applied in an objective manner. Each measure shall be directed to an actual, clear, present, or imminent danger and may not be imposed merely because of an apprehension of potential danger."

In submitting that the test of imminence was not met, the appellants pointed to ministerial statements in October 2001 and March 2002: "There is no immediate intelligence pointing to a specific threat to the United Kingdom, but we remain alert, domestically as well as internationally;" and "[I]t would be wrong to say that we have evidence of a particular threat."

...

23. No state other than the United Kingdom has derogated from Article 5. In Resolution 1271 adopted on 24 January 2002, the Parliamentary Assembly of the Council of Europe resolved (para 9) that:

> "In their fight against terrorism, Council of Europe members should not provide for any derogations to the European Convention on Human Rights."

...

In Opinion 1/2002 of the Council of Europe Commissioner for Human Rights, Mr Alvaro Gil-Robles observed, in para 33:

> "Whilst acknowledging the obligation of governments to protect their citizens against the threat of terrorism, the Commissioner is of the opinion that general appeals to an increased risk of terrorist activity post September 11th 2001 cannot, on their own, be sufficient to justify derogating from the Convention. Several European states long faced with recurring terrorist activity have not considered it necessary to derogate from Convention rights. Nor have any found it necessary to do so under the present circumstances. Detailed information pointing to a real and imminent danger to public safety in the United Kingdom will, therefore, have to be shown."

. . .

24. The appellants . . . were able to rely on a series of reports by the Joint Committee on Human Rights. In its Second Report of the Session 2001–2002, made on 14 November 2001 when the 2001 Act was a Bill before Parliament, the Joint Committee stated:

> "Having considered the Home Secretary's evidence carefully, we recognise that there may be evidence of the existence of a public emergency threatening the life of the nation, although none was shown by him to this Committee."

. . . In its report of 23 February 2004, the Joint Committee stated, in para 34:

> "Insufficient evidence has been presented to Parliament to make it possible for us to accept that derogation under ECHR Article 15 is strictly required by the exigencies of the situation to deal with a public emergency threatening the life of the nation."

. . .

25. The Attorney General, representing the Home Secretary, answered these points. He submitted that an emergency could properly be regarded as imminent if an atrocity was credibly threatened by a body such as Al-Qaeda which had demonstrated its capacity and will to carry out such a threat, where the atrocity might be committed without warning at any time. The Government, responsible as it was and is for the safety of the British people, need not wait for disaster to strike before taking necessary steps to prevent it striking. As to the requirement that the emergency be temporary, the Attorney General did not suggest that an emergency could ever become the normal state of affairs, but he did resist the imposition of any artificial temporal limit to an emergency of the present kind, and pointed out that the emergency which had been held to justify derogation in Northern Ireland in 1988 had been accepted as continuing for a considerable number of years (see *Marshall v United Kingdom* (10 July 2001, Appn No 41571/98) para 18 above). . . .

. . .

26. . . . In the result, however, not without misgiving . . . I would resolve this issue against the appellants . . .

28. . . . The European Court decisions in *Ireland v United Kingdom* (1978) 2 EHRR 25; *Brannigan and McBride v United Kingdom* (1993) 17 EHRR 539; *Aksoy v Turkey* (1996) 23 EHRR 553 and *Marshall v United Kingdom* (10 July 2001, Appn. No. 41571/98) seem to me to be, with respect, clearly right. In each case the member state had actually experienced widespread loss of life caused by an armed body dedicated to destroying the territorial integrity of the state. To hold that the Article 15 test was not satisfied in such circumstances, if a response beyond that provided by the ordinary course of law was required, would have been perverse. But these features were not, on the facts found, very clearly present in *Lawless v Ireland*. That was a relatively early decision of the European Court, but it has never to my knowledge been disavowed. . . .

29. . . . I would accept that great weight should be given to the judgment of the Home Secretary, his colleagues and Parliament on this question, because they were called on to exercise a pre-eminently political judgment. It involved making a factual prediction of what various people around the world might or might not do, and when (if at all) they might do it, and what the consequences might be if they did. . . . It would have been irresponsible not to err, if at all, on the side of safety. As will become apparent, I do not accept the full breadth of the Attorney General's argument on what is generally called the deference owed by the courts to the political authorities. It is perhaps preferable to approach this question as one of demarcation of functions or what Liberty in its written case called "relative institutional competence". The more purely political (in a broad or narrow sense) a question is, the more appropriate it will be for political resolution and the less likely it is to be an appropriate matter for judicial decision. The smaller, therefore, will be the potential role of the court. It is the function of political and not judicial bodies to resolve political questions. Conversely, the greater the legal content of any issue, the greater the potential role of the court, because under our constitution and subject to the sovereign power of Parliament it is the function of the courts and not of political bodies to resolve legal questions. The present question seems to me to be very much at the political end of the spectrum . . . I conclude that the appellants have shown no ground strong enough to warrant displacing the Secretary of State's decision on this important threshold question.

Proportionality

30. Article 15 requires that any measures taken by a member state in derogation of its obligations under the Convention should not go beyond what is "strictly required by the exigencies of the situation." . . . In determining whether a limitation is arbitrary or excessive, the court must ask itself:

> "whether: (i) the legislative objective is sufficiently important to justify limiting a fundamental right; (ii) the measures designed to meet the legislative objective are rationally connected to it; and (iii) the means used to impair the right or freedom are no more than is necessary to accomplish the objective."

. . .

31. The appellants' argument under this head can, I hope fairly, be summarised as involving [the following claims:] …

…

(4) Sections 21 and 23 [of the Anti-terrorism, Crime and Security Act] did not rationally address the threat to the security of the United Kingdom presented by Al-Qaeda terrorists and their supporters because (a) it did not address the threat presented by UK nationals, (b) it permitted foreign nationals suspected of being Al-Qaeda terrorists or their supporters to pursue their activities abroad if there was any country to which they were able to go, and (c) the sections permitted the certification and detention of persons who were not suspected of presenting any threat to the security of the United Kingdom as Al-Qaeda terrorists or supporters.

(5) If the threat presented to the security of the United Kingdom by UK nationals suspected of being Al-Qaeda terrorists or their supporters could be addressed without infringing their right to personal liberty, it is not shown why similar measures could not adequately address the threat presented by foreign nationals.

…

32. … The evidence before SIAC [Special Immigration Appeals Commission] was that the Home Secretary considered "that the serious threats to the nation emanated predominantly (albeit not exclusively) and more immediately from the category of foreign nationals." In para 95 of its judgment SIAC held:

> "But the evidence before us demonstrates beyond argument that the threat is not so confined. [i.e. is not confined to the alien section of the population]. There are many British nationals already identified — mostly in detention abroad — who fall within the definition of 'suspected international terrorists,' and it was clear from the submissions made to us that in the opinion of the [Home Secretary] there are others at liberty in the United Kingdom who could be similarly defined."

… The Newton Committee recorded the Home Office argument that the threat from Al-Qaeda terrorism was predominantly from foreigners but drew attention (para 193) to

> "accumulating evidence that this is not now the case. The British suicide bombers who attacked Tel Aviv in May 2003, Richard Reid ('the Shoe Bomber'), and recent arrests suggest that the threat from UK citizens is real. Almost 30% of Terrorism Act 2000 suspects in the past year have been British. We have been told that, of the people of interest to the authorities because of their suspected involvement in international terrorism, nearly half are British nationals."

…

33. … [S]ections 21 and 23 do permit a person certified and detained to leave the United Kingdom and go to any other country willing to receive him, as two of the appellants did when they left for Morocco and France respectively. Such freedom to leave is wholly explicable in terms of immigration control: if the British authorities wish to deport a foreign national but cannot deport him to country "A" because of *Chahal* their purpose is as well served by his voluntary departure for country "B". But allowing a suspected international terrorist to leave our shores and depart to

another country, perhaps a country as close as France, there to pursue his criminal designs, is hard to reconcile with a belief in his capacity to inflict serious injury to the people and interests of this country. It seems clear from the language of section 21 of the 2001 Act, read with the definition of terrorism in section 1 of the 2000 Act, that section 21 is capable of covering those who have no link at all with Al-Qaeda (they might, for example, be members of the Basque separatist organisation ETA), or who, although supporting the general aims of Al-Qaeda, reject its cult of violence....

34. Some of these features of the 2001 Act were the subject of comment by the European Commissioner for Human Rights in his Opinion 1/2002 (28 August 2002):

> "The proportionality of the derogating measures is further brought into question by the definition of international terrorist organisations provided by section 21(3) of the Act. The section would appear to permit the indefinite detention of an individual suspected of having links with an international terrorist organisation irrespective of its presenting a direct threat to public security in the United Kingdom and perhaps, therefore, of no relation to the emergency originally requiring the legislation under which his Convention rights may be prejudiced.
>
> ...
>
> It would appear, therefore, that the derogating measures of the Anti-Terrorism, Crime and Security Act allow both for the detention of those presenting no direct threat to the United Kingdom and for the release of those of whom it is alleged that they do. Such a paradoxical conclusion is hard to reconcile with the strict exigencies of the situation."

35. The fifth step in the appellants' argument permits of little elaboration. But it seems reasonable to assume that those suspected international terrorists who are UK nationals are not simply ignored by the authorities. When G, one of the appellants, was released from prison by SIAC on bail, it was on condition (among other things) that he wear an electronic monitoring tag at all times; that he remain at his premises at all times; that he telephone a named security company five times each day at specified times; that he permit the company to install monitoring equipment at his premises; that he limit entry to his premises to his family, his solicitor, his medical attendants and other approved persons; that he make no contact with any other person; that he have on his premises no computer equipment, mobile telephone or other electronic communications device; that he cancel the existing telephone link to his premises; and that he install a dedicated telephone link permitting contact only with the security company. The appellants suggested that conditions of this kind, strictly enforced, would effectively inhibit terrorist activity. It is hard to see why this would not be so.

...

37. ... [The Attorney General] submitted that as it was for Parliament and the executive to assess the threat facing the nation, so it was for those bodies and not the courts to judge the response necessary to protect the security of the public. These were matters of a political character calling for an exercise of political and not judicial judgment. Just as the European Court allowed a generous margin of

appreciation to member states, recognising that they were better placed to understand and address local problems, so should national courts recognise, for the same reason, that matters of the kind in issue here fall within the discretionary area of judgment properly belonging to the democratic organs of the state. It was not for the courts to usurp authority properly belonging elsewhere....

38. ... In *R v Director of Public Prosecutions, Ex p Kebilene* [2000] 2 AC 326, 381, Lord Hope of Craighead said:

> "It will be easier for such [a discretionary] area of judgment to be recognised where the Convention itself requires a balance to be struck, much less so where the right is stated in terms which are unqualified. It will be easier for it to be recognised where the issues involve questions of social or economic policy, much less so where the rights are of high constitutional importance or are of a kind where the courts are especially well placed to assess the need for protection."

Another area in which the court was held to be qualified to make its own judgment is the requirement of a fair trial: *R v A (No 2)* [2002]. The Supreme Court of Canada took a similar view in *Libman v Attorney General of Quebec* (1997). In his dissenting judgment (cited with approval in *Libman*) in *RJR- MacDonald Inc v Attorney General of Canada* [1995], La Forest J, sitting in the same court, said:

> "Courts are specialists in the protection of liberty and the interpretation of legislation and are, accordingly, well placed to subject criminal justice legislation to careful scrutiny. However, courts are not specialists in the realm of policymaking, nor should they be."

Jackson J, sitting in the Supreme Court of the United States in *West Virginia State Board of Education v Barnette* 319 US 624 (1943), para 3, stated, speaking of course with reference to an entrenched constitution:

> "The very purpose of a Bill of Rights was to withdraw certain subjects from the vicissitudes of political controversy, to place them beyond the reach of majorities and officials and to establish them as legal principles to be applied by the courts.... We cannot, because of modest estimates of our competence in such specialties as public education, withhold the judgment that history authenticates as the function of this Court when liberty is infringed."

40. The Convention regime for the international protection of human rights requires national authorities, including national courts, to exercise their authority to afford effective protection....

... [T]he European Commissioner for Human Rights had authority for saying (Opinion 1/2002, para 9):

> "It is furthermore, precisely because the Convention presupposes domestic controls in the form of a preventive parliamentary scrutiny and posterior judicial review that national authorities enjoy a large margin of appreciation in respect of derogations. This is, indeed, the essence of the principle of the subsidiarity of the protection of Convention rights."

. . .

41. Even in a terrorist situation the Convention organs have not been willing to relax their residual supervisory role: *Brogan v United Kingdom* above, para 80; *Fox, Campbell & Hartley v United Kingdom*, above, paras 32–34. In *Aksoy v Turkey* (1996) 23 EHRR 553, para 76, the Court, clearly referring to national courts as well as the Convention organs, held:

> "The Court would stress the importance of Article 5 in the Convention system: it enshrines a fundamental human right, namely the protection of the individual against arbitrary interference by the State with his or her right to liberty. Judicial control of interferences by the executive with the individual's right to liberty is an essential feature of the guarantee embodied in Article 5(3), which is intended to minimise the risk of arbitrariness and to ensure the rule of law."

. . .

. . . [T]he function of independent judges charged to interpret and apply the law is universally recognised as a cardinal feature of the modern democratic state, a cornerstone of the rule of law itself. The Attorney General is fully entitled to insist on the proper limits of judicial authority, but he is wrong to stigmatise judicial decision-making as in some way undemocratic. It is particularly inappropriate in a case such as the present in which Parliament has expressly legislated in section 6 of the 1998 Act to render unlawful any act of a public authority, including a court, incompatible with a Convention right, has required courts (in section 2) to take account of relevant Strasbourg jurisprudence, has (in section 3) required courts, so far as possible, to give effect to Convention rights and has conferred a right of appeal on derogation issues. The effect is not, of course, to override the sovereign legislative authority of the Queen in Parliament, since if primary legislation is declared to be incompatible the validity of the legislation is unaffected (section 4(6)) and the remedy lies with the appropriate minister (section 10), who is answerable to Parliament. The 1998 Act gives the courts a very specific, wholly democratic, mandate. As Professor Jowell has put it

> "The courts are charged by Parliament with delineating the boundaries of a rights-based democracy."

. . .

43. The appellants' proportionality challenge to the Order and section 23 is, in my opinion, sound, for all the reasons they gave and also for those given by the European Commissioner for Human Rights and the Newton Committee. The Attorney General could give no persuasive answer. In a discussion paper Counter-Terrorism Powers: Reconciling Security and Liberty in an Open Society (Cm 6147, February 2004) the Secretary of State replied to one of the Newton Committee's criticisms in this way:

> "32. It can be argued that as suspected international terrorists their departure for another country could amount to exporting terrorism. . . . But that is a natural consequence of the fact that Part 4 powers are immigration powers: detention is

> permissible only pending deportation and there is no other power available to detain (other than for the purpose of police enquiries) if a foreign national chooses voluntarily to leave the UK. (Detention in those circumstances is limited to 14 days after which the person must be either charged or released.) Deportation has the advantage moreover of disrupting the activities of the suspected terrorist."

This answer, however, reflects the central complaint made by the appellants: that the choice of an immigration measure to address a security problem had the inevitable result of failing adequately to address that problem (by allowing non-UK suspected terrorists to leave the country with impunity and leaving British suspected terrorists at large) while imposing the severe penalty of indefinite detention on persons who, even if reasonably suspected of having links with Al-Qaeda, may harbour no hostile intentions towards the United Kingdom. The conclusion that the Order and section 23 are, in Convention terms, disproportionate is in my opinion irresistible.

...

Discrimination

45. As part of their proportionality argument, the appellants attacked section 23 as discriminatory. They contended that, being discriminatory, the section could not be "strictly required" within the meaning of Article 15 and so was disproportionate....

46. The appellants complained that in providing for the detention of suspected international terrorists who were not UK nationals but not for the detention of suspected international terrorists who were UK nationals, section 23 unlawfully discriminated against them as non-UK nationals in breach of Article 14 of the European Convention....

Jackson J reflected this belief in his well-known judgment in *Railway Express Agency Inc v New York* 336 US 106, 112–113 (1949), when he said:

> "I regard it as a salutary doctrine that cities, states and the Federal Government must exercise their powers so as not to discriminate between their inhabitants except upon some reasonable differentiation fairly related to the object of regulation. This equality is not merely abstract justice. The framers of the Constitution knew, and we should not forget today, that there is no more effective practical guaranty against arbitrary and unreasonable government than to require that the principles of law which officials would impose upon a minority must be imposed generally. Conversely, nothing opens the door to arbitrary action so effectively as to allow those officials to pick and choose only a few to whom they will apply legislation and thus to escape the political retribution that might be visited upon them if larger numbers were affected. Courts can take no better measure to assure that laws will be just than to require that laws be equal in operation."

...

47. The United Kingdom did not derogate from Article 14 of the European Convention (or from Article 26 of the ICCPR, which corresponds to it). The Attorney General did not submit that there had been an implied derogation, an argument advanced to SIAC but not to the Court of Appeal or the House.

...

52. . . . [T]he appellants' chosen comparators were suspected international terrorists who were UK nationals. The appellants pointed out that they shared with this group the important characteristics (a) of being suspected international terrorists and (b) of being irremovable from the United Kingdom. Since these were the relevant characteristics for purposes of the comparison, it was unlawfully discriminatory to detain non-UK nationals while leaving UK nationals at large.

53. Were suspected international terrorists who were UK nationals, the appellants' chosen comparators, in a relevantly analogous situation to the appellants? . . . The Court of Appeal thought not because (per Lord Woolf, para 56) "the nationals have a right of abode in this jurisdiction but the aliens only have a right not to be removed". This is, however, to accept the correctness of the Secretary of State's choice of immigration control as a means to address the Al-Qaeda security problem, when the correctness of that choice is the issue to be resolved. In my opinion, the question demands an affirmative answer. Suspected international terrorists who are UK nationals are in a situation analogous with the appellants because, in the present context, they share the most relevant characteristics of the appellants.

54. . . . The undoubted aim of the relevant measure, section 23 of the 2001 Act, was to protect the UK against the risk of Al-Qaeda terrorism. As noted above that risk was thought to be presented mainly by non-UK nationals but also and to a significant extent by UK nationals also. The effect of the measure was to permit the former to be deprived of their liberty but not the latter. The appellants were treated differently because of their nationality or immigration status. . . .

64. . . .

In his discussion paper published in response to the Newton Report ("Counter-Terrorism Powers"—see para 43 above) the Secretary of State said:

> "36. Secondly Lord Newton proposed that new legislation should apply equally to all nationalities including British citizens. The Government believes it is defensible to distinguish between foreign nationals and our own citizens and reflects their different rights and responsibilities. Immigration powers and the possibility of deportation could not apply to British citizens. While it would be possible to seek other powers to detain British citizens who may be involved in international terrorism it would be a very grave step. The Government believes that such draconian powers would be difficult to justify. Experience has demonstrated the dangers of such an approach and the damage it can do to community cohesion and thus to the support from all parts of the public that is so essential to countering the terrorist threat."

. . .

67. The Court of Appeal differed from SIAC on the discrimination issue: [2004] QB 335. Lord Woolf CJ referred (para 45) to a tension between Article 15 and Article 14 of the European Convention. He held (para 49) that it would be "surprising indeed" if Article 14 prevented the Secretary of State from restricting his power to detain to a smaller rather than a larger group. . . .

68. I must respectfully differ from this analysis. . . . Any discriminatory measure inevitably affects a smaller rather than a larger group, but cannot be justified on the ground that more people would be adversely affected if the measure were applied

generally. What has to be justified is not the measure in issue but the difference in treatment between one person or group and another. What cannot be justified here is the decision to detain one group of suspected international terrorists, defined by nationality or immigration status, and not another. . . .

NOTE

Subsequent to the House of Lords decision, Parliament passed the Prevention of Terrorism Act of 2005 (PTA). The Act was passed before Britain experienced devastating bomb attacks on 7 July 2005. The PTA provides for 'control orders' to be imposed on individuals of any origin who are suspected of being 'involved in terrorism-related activity'. Control orders are intended to apply when there is insufficient evidence to pursue criminal prosecution. The measures taken with respect to Defendant G in the House of Lords case (para. 35 of the opinion) served as a template for this new approach. The PTA makes provision for two types of control orders: derogating control orders, which impose obligations on an individual that are incompatible with the right to liberty under Article 5 of the European Convention and which require a specific order of derogation; and non-derogating control orders. Control orders potentially include various measures such as confinement to specific premises, electronic monitoring, restrictions on use of certain services or facilities, restrictions in respect of work or other occupation, prohibitions and restrictions on associations and communications, and prohibitions on being at specified places or within specified areas at specified times. Notably, Australia has also adopted a system of control orders modelled on the PTA.

In August 2006, the UK Court of Appeal considered a set of non-derogating control orders. The petitioners were five Iraqi nationals and one Iraqi/Iranian national. They were detained under immigration powers pending deportation on national security grounds. All deportation proceedings were discontinued on the issuance of the control orders. The six petitioners were each subject to similar restrictions:

> The obligations imposed by the control orders are . . . essentially identical. Each respondent is required to remain within his 'residence' at all times, save for a period of 6 hours between 10 am and 4 pm. In the case of GG the specified residence is a one bedroom flat provided by the local authority in which he lived before his detention. In the case of the other five applicants the specified residences are one bedroom flats provided by NASS. During the curfew period the respondents are confined in their small flats and are not even allowed into the common parts of the buildings in which these flats are situated. Visitors must be authorised by the Home Office, to which name, address, date of birth and photographic identity must be supplied. The residences are subject to spot searches by the police. During the six hours when they are permitted to leave their residences, the respondents are confined to restricted urban areas, the largest of which is 72 square kilometres. These deliberately do not extend, save in the case of GG, to any area in which they lived before. Each area contains a mosque, a hospital, primary health care facilities, shops and entertainment and sporting facilities. The respondents

> are prohibited from meeting anyone by pre-arrangement who has not been given the same Home Office clearance as a visitor to the residence.

The Court of Appeal ruled that the control orders constituted an unlawful deprivation of liberty under Article 5 of the Convention.

QUESTIONS

1. Is the definition of terrorism in the Terrorism Act 2000 excessively vague? Which provisions are most vulnerable to criticism along those lines? What purposes might be served by the use of ambiguity? Is this vagueness more (or less) acceptable in the context of immigration and nationality law than other legal domains such as criminal law? For example, should the state retain greater power and discretion in the regulation of its borders?

2. Consider the analysis of the discrimination claim by the House of Lords. Can you think of any reasons that could justify treating the class of individuals subject to detention differently than British nationals? The court suggests that the level of threat posed by the two groups is indistinguishable. Do you agree? Could British nationals generally pose a greater threat than foreign nationals? Are there other factors the court should have used to compare the two classes of individuals? Is this decision compatible with the war model for combating terrorism discussed previously?

3. On 13 November 2001, President Bush issued a Military Order providing for the detention (and trial by military commission) of Al Qaeda members and others suspected of involvement in acts of 'international terrorism'. The order expressly applies to noncitizens only. Similarly, the US Congress passed the Military Commission Act of 2006, *see infra* p. 258, which provides for trial by military commission of 'alien unlawful enemy combatants'. Do such acts run afoul of anti-discrimination principles articulated in the House of Lords opinion?

4. In its examination of the nature of the public emergency, does the House of Lords defer excessively to the Home Secretary and other governmental authorities? Would it be better for the court to adopt a general presumption of deference, which could be overcome when authorities within the government express differences of opinion on a factual issue—such as whether the United Kingdom faced a direct threat to the life of the nation?

In determining the level of deference given to the Government, did Lord Bingham err in relying on European Court of Human Rights jurisprudence that pertains to the relationship between a supranational body and national authorities? In a concurring opinion, Lord Hoffman remarked: 'Nor do I find the European cases particularly helpful. All that can be taken from them is that the Strasbourg court allows a wide "margin of appreciation" to the national authorities in deciding "both on the presence of such an emergency and on the nature and scope of derogations necessary to avert it". What this means is that we, as a United Kingdom court, have to decide the matter for ourselves'.

5. The House of Lords asserts an active role for the judiciary in determining the proportionality of a derogation measure. In doing so, the opinion relies on cases involving

fair trial rights and freedom from arbitrary detention under Article 5(3) of the European Convention. Does the court's explanation extend beyond these rights (for example to freedom of association) or do these rights have characteristics that especially favour the judiciary serving as a referee of governmental actions? Additionally, a distinction might be drawn between (i) rights to a fair *process* (e.g., Article 5(3)) and (ii) *substantive* rights that concern the fairness of defining which particular individuals or actions are subject to detention and punishment (e.g., Article 5(1)(c)). Do the reasons that support an active role for the judiciary in the former apply equally to determining the appropriate role of the judiciary in the latter?

6. Evaluate the following assessment of the court's opinion.

The House of Lords demonstrated how antiquated the derogation system is when it comes to transnational terrorism in the twenty-first century. In the proceedings before the Law Lords, the British government invoked Security Council resolutions calling on states to fight transnational terrorism, and the British Terrorism Act of 2000 accordingly applies to terrorist acts outside UK territory. Not only do the derogation rules fail to take such concerns into account; acting on such concerns may discredit a state's position. In paragraphs 33–34 of his opinion, Lord Bingham treated the government's actions to combat terrorist threats to other countries as further evidence of a lack of proportionality. This reasoning is unfair and absurd. It also undercuts global efforts to orchestrate an effective transnational response to terrorism. Human rights doctrine needs to be drastically updated, and that task can be performed without the risk of introducing unwarranted loopholes into the law of derogations.

E. GUARANTEEING FAIR TRIALS

The right to a fair trial ranks among the most basic protections in humanitarian and human rights law. Three provisions of the 1949 Geneva Conventions and their Protocols deserve special mention. First, Common Article 3 outlaws 'the passing of sentences and the carrying out of executions without previous judgment pronounced by a regularly constituted court, affording all the judicial guarantees which are recognized as indispensable by civilized peoples'. The ICRC Commentaries explain that this provision calls for extension of the general law concerning fair trials to the arena of warfare: 'All civilized nations surround the administration of justice with safeguards aimed at eliminating the possibility of judicial errors. The Convention has rightly proclaimed that it is essential to do this even in time of war'. Second, the Civilians Convention contains a 'security proviso' permitting states to suspend treaty obligations when dealing with unlawful combatants such as spies and saboteurs; yet it too requires that 'such persons shall nevertheless be treated with humanity and, in case of trial, shall not be deprived of the rights of fair and regular trial prescribed by the present Convention'. Third, Article 75 (entitled 'Fundamental Guarantees') of Additional Protocol I is generally recognized, including by the United States, as binding customary law. It specifies elements of the right to a fair trial that are guaranteed to all individuals who do not benefit from more favourable treatment under the 1949 Conventions or the Additional Protocol. These three IHL provisions establish a floor of fair trial rights below which no state may pass. Recall that General Comment 29 relies on such fundamental protections in reasoning that if certain elements of a fair trial cannot be lawfully transgressed in war, they can never be subject to derogation under the ICCPR. A difficulty is defining the content of those core fair trial rights.

One of the most vexing issues in defining the right to a fair trial in the national security context involves military tribunals. Can a military tribunal provide a fair trial and, if so, under what conditions? The following readings address this set of concerns. A recent report by the Inter-American Commission on Human Rights sets the stage by discussing the broader legal and normative framework. The Inter-American Commission took up the general subject of human rights law and terrorism, and issued a lengthy report in 2002. The report provides, *inter alia*, one of the most comprehensive formal pronouncements on the content of derogable and nonderogable fair trial rights. The Commission developed these legal principles partly in response to the use of military courts by Latin American governments in the 1980s and early to mid 1990s. Governmental practices that sparked international criticism included Colombia's use of 'faceless' prosecutors, judges, witnesses and attorneys in cases of terrorism and subversion; Peru's trials of civilians accused of treason and terrorism in closed proceedings before a military court and with defense counsel prohibited from accessing the government's evidence or questioning military and police witnesses; Guatemala's Special Courts for subversive activities which operated in secret locations, relied on confessions from the accused taken without counsel present, and provided little time for the accused to prepare a defence; and Uruguay's secret hearings, materially ineffective appeals process for objecting to an indictment, and inadequate access of defence counsel to evidentiary files.

With respect to a specific issue — prosecution of civilians before military tribunals — the Inter-American Commission is among the international bodies that most strongly oppose such practices. A December 2001 Resolution by the Commission states: 'According to the doctrine of the IACHR, military courts may not try civilians, except when no civilian courts exist or where trial by such courts is materially impossible'. The content of the 2002 Report, however, is arguably more qualified. Pay particular attention to the Commission's understanding of 'civilians' charged with involvement in terrorism and of 'unlawful combatants' in an armed conflict. Also, look closely at the Commission's concerns that might provide the basis for a categorical prohibition on prosecuting civilians before military tribunals. Is it, for example, the troubled history of military courts in the Americas that explains the Commission's position? If that is the case, the particular experience of summary proceedings might inspire a prophylactic rule against military trials. Such a rule might be advisable even if, theoretically, a government could establish a military court system that secures the rights of defendants. Otherwise, why not disallow particular procedures rather than deem military trials of civilians *per se* illegal? Alternatively, consider whether the concerns regarding military trials may have more to do with the institutional relationship of the military and the executive rather than specific trial procedures. The related readings that follow, from the

Human Rights Committee and the European Court of Human Rights, provide other examples of approaches to regulating such courts.

INTER-AMERICAN COMMISSION ON HUMAN RIGHTS, REPORT ON TERRORISM AND HUMAN RIGHTS, 22 OCTOBER 2002

http://www.cidh.org/Terrorism/Eng/toc.htm

Right to a Hearing by a Competent, Independent and Impartial Tribunal previously established by Law

229. Underlying this aspect of the right to a fair hearing are the fundamental concepts of judicial independence and impartiality . . . . The requirement of independence in turn necessitates that courts be autonomous from the other branches of government, free from influence, threats or interference from any source and for any reason, and benefit from other characteristics necessary for ensuring the correct and independent performance of judicial functions, including tenure and appropriate professional training. . . . These requirements in turn require that a judge or tribunal not harbor any actual bias in a particular case, and that the judge or tribunal not reasonably be perceived as being tainted with any bias.

230. In the context of these fundamental requirements, the jurisprudence of the inter-American system has long denounced the creation of special courts or tribunals that displace the jurisdiction belonging to the ordinary courts or judicial tribunals and that do not use the duly established procedures of the legal process. This has included in particular the use of ad hoc or special courts or military tribunals to prosecute civilians for security offenses in times of emergency, which practice has been condemned by this Commission, the Inter-American Court and other international authorities. The basis of this criticism has related in large part to the lack of independence of such tribunals from the Executive and the absence of minimal due process and fair trial guarantees in their processes.

231. It has been widely concluded in this regard that military tribunals by their very nature do not satisfy the requirements of independent and impartial courts applicable to the trial of civilians, because they are not a part of the independent civilian judiciary but rather are a part of the Executive branch, and because their fundamental purpose is to maintain order and discipline by punishing military offenses committed by members of the military establishment. In such instances, military officers assume the role of judges while at the same time remaining subordinate to their superiors in keeping with the established military hierarchy.

232. . . . Military tribunals are also precluded from prosecuting civilians, although certain human rights supervisory bodies have found that in exceptional circumstances military tribunals or special courts might be used to try civilians but only where the minimum requirements of due process are guaranteed. During armed conflicts, a state's military courts may also try privileged and unprivileged combatants, provided that the minimum protections of due process are guaranteed. Article

84 of the Third Geneva Convention, for example, expressly provides that

> [a] prisoner of war shall be tried only by a military court, unless the existing laws of the Detaining Power expressly permit the civil courts to try a member of the armed forces of the Detaining Power in respect of the particular offense alleged to have been committed by the prisoner of war. In no circumstances whatever shall a prisoner of war be tried by a court of any kind which does not offer the essential guarantees of independence and impartiality as generally recognized, and, in particular, the procedure of which does not afford the accused the rights and means of defence provided for in Article 105....

Although the provisions of international humanitarian law applicable to unprivileged combatants, including Article 75 of Additional Protocol I, do not specifically address the susceptibility of such combatants to trial by military courts, there appears to be no reason to consider that a different standard would apply as between privileged and unprivileged combatants. In any event, the standards of due process to which unprivileged combatants are entitled may in no case fall below those under Article 75 of Additional Protocol I.

...

Fair Trial, Due Process of Law and Derogation

...

246. ... [N]o human rights supervisory body has yet found the exigencies of a genuine emergency situation sufficient to justify suspending even temporarily basic fair trial safeguards....

249. Without detracting from the above standards, prevailing norms suggest that there may be some limited aspects of the right to due process and to a fair trial from which derogation might in the most exceptional circumstances be permissible. Any such suspensions must, however, comply strictly with the principles of necessity, proportionality and non-discrimination, and must remain subject to oversight by supervisory organs under international law.

250. Due process and fair trial protections that might conceivably be subject to suspension include the right to a public trial where limitations on public access to proceedings are demonstrated to be strictly necessary in the interests of justice. Considerations in this regard might include matters of security, public order, the interests of juveniles, or where publicity might prejudice the interests of justice. Any such restrictions must, however, be strictly justified by the state concerned on a case by case basis and be subject to on-going judicial supervision.

251. The right of a defendant to examine or have examined witnesses presented against him or her could also be, in principle, the subject of restrictions in some limited instances. It must be recognized in this respect that efforts to investigate and prosecute crimes, including those relating to terrorism, may in certain instances render witnesses vulnerable to threats to their lives or integrity and thereby raise difficult issues concerning the extent to which those witnesses can be safely identified during the criminal process. Such considerations can never serve to compromise a defendant's non-derogable due process protections and each situation must be carefully evaluated on its own merits within the context of a particular justice system....

252. Similarly, the investigation and prosecution of terrorist crimes may render judges and other officials involved in the administration of justice vulnerable to threats. As noted above, states are obliged to take all necessary measures to prevent violence against such persons. Accordingly, states may be compelled by the exigencies of a particular situation to develop mechanisms to protect a judge's life, physical integrity and independence . . . subject to such measures as are necessary to ensure a defendant's right to challenge the competence, independence or impartiality of his or her prosecuting tribunal. . . .

. . .

International Humanitarian Law

. . .

256. As noted above, while international human rights law prohibits the trial of civilians by military tribunals, the use of military tribunals in the trial of prisoners of war is not prohibited . . .

261. . . . [M]ost fundamental fair trial requirements cannot justifiably be suspended under either international human rights law or international humanitarian law . . . includ[ing] the following:

. . . The right to be tried by a competent, independent and impartial tribunal in conformity with applicable international standards. In respect of the prosecution of civilians, this requires trial by regularly constituted courts that are demonstrably independent from the other branches of government and comprised of judges with appropriate tenure and training, and generally prohibits the use of ad hoc, special, or military tribunals or commissions to try civilians. A state's military courts may prosecute members of its own military for crimes relating [to] the functions that the law assigns to military forces and, during international armed conflicts, may try privileged and unprivileged combatants, provided that the minimum requirements of due process are guaranteed.

. . .

HUMAN RIGHTS COMMITTEE, ADMINISTRATION OF JUSTICE, GENERAL COMMENT NO. 13

(U.N. Doc. HRI/GEN/1/Rev. 1 (1984))

. . . The Committee notes the existence, in many countries, of military or special courts which try civilians. This could present serious problems as far as the equitable, impartial and independent administration of justice is concerned. Quite often the reason for the establishment of such courts is to enable exceptional procedures to be applied which do not comply with normal standards of justice. While the Covenant does not prohibit such categories of courts, nevertheless the conditions which it lays down clearly indicate that the trying of civilians by such courts should be very exceptional and take place under conditions which genuinely afford the full guarantees stipulated in Article 14. The Committee has noted a serious lack of information in this regard in the reports of some States parties whose judicial institutions include such courts for the trying of civilians. In some countries such military and special courts do not afford the strict guarantees of the proper administration of justice in accordance with the requirements of Article 14 which are essential for the effective protection of human rights. If States parties decide in circumstances of a public emergency as contemplated by Article 4 to derogate from normal procedures required under Article 14, they should ensure that such derogations do not exceed those strictly required by the exigencies of the actual situation, and respect the other conditions in paragraph 1 of Article 14.

INCAL v. TURKEY

European Court of Human Rights Grand Chamber
Case No. 41/1997/825/1031, 9 June 1998

[In Turkey's third largest city, İzmir, Mr İbrahim Incal served on the local executive committee of a pro-Kurdish political party (the People's Labour Party). The executive committee decided to distribute a leaflet criticising the local government's restrictions on small-scale illegal trading and squatter camps. The leaflet stated that these restrictions were part of a larger campaign to drive Kurds back to their own regions; that 'passivity as a form of defence against this devastation has encouraged the State'; and that the Kurdish population should organize themselves into 'neighbourhood communities . . . to assume their responsibilities and oppose this special war being waged'.

The public prosecutor instituted criminal proceedings in the İzmir National Security Court against Incal and other members of the People's Labour Party. The prosecutor accused them of attempting to incite hatred and hostility through racist words and asked the court to apply the Criminal Code, the Prevention of Terrorism Act and the Press Act. The National Security Court, composed of three judges, one of whom was a member of the military, refused to apply the Prevention of Terrorism Act but otherwise found the applicant guilty of the offences charged and sentenced him to nearly seven months' imprisonment and a fine of 55,555 Turkish liras. Following is the decision of the Grand Chamber of the European Court of Human Rights.]

. . .

B. The National Security Courts

26. The National Security Courts were created by Law no. 1773 of 11 July 1973, in accordance with Article 136 of the 1961 Constitution. That Law was annulled by the Constitutional Court on 15 June 1976. The courts in question were later reintroduced into the Turkish judicial system by the 1982 Constitution. The relevant part of the statement of reasons contains the following passage:

> "There may be acts affecting the existence and stability of a State such that when they are committed special jurisdiction is required in order to give judgment expeditiously and appropriately. For such cases it is necessary to set up National Security Courts. According to a principle inherent in our Constitution, it is forbidden to create a special court to [give judgment on] a specific act after it has been

> committed. For that reason the National Security Courts have been provided for in our Constitution to try cases involving the above-mentioned offences. Given that the special provisions laying down their powers have [thus] been enacted in advance and that the courts have been created before the commission of any offence . . . , they may not be described as courts set up to deal with this or that offence after the commission of such an offence."

The composition and functioning of the National Security Courts are subject to the following rules.

1. The Constitution

27. The constitutional provisions governing judicial organisation are worded as follows:

Article 138 §§ 1 and 2

"In the performance of their duties, judges shall be independent; they shall give judgment, according to their personal conviction, in accordance with the Constitution, statute and the law.

No organ, authority, officer or other person may give orders or instructions to courts or judges in the exercise of their judicial powers, or send them circulars or make recommendations or suggestions to them."

Article 139 § 1

"Judges . . . shall not be removed from office or compelled to retire without their consent before the age prescribed by the Constitution . . ."

Article 143 § 4

"Presidents, regular members and substitute judges of the National Security Courts shall be appointed for a renewable period of four years."

Article 145 § 4

"The personal rights and obligations of military judges . . . shall be regulated by law in accordance with the principles of the independence of the courts, the safeguards enjoyed by the judiciary and the requirements of military service. Relations between military judges and the commanders under whom they serve as regards their non-judicial duties shall also be regulated by law . . ."

2. Law no. 2845 on the creation and rules of procedure of the National Security Courts

28. Based on Article 143 of the Constitution, the relevant provisions of Law no. 2845 on the National Security Courts, provide as follows:

Section 1

"In the capitals of the provinces of . . . National Security Courts shall be established to try persons accused of offences against the Republic—whose constituent qualities are enunciated in the Constitution — against the indivisible unity of the State — meaning both the national territory and its people — or against the free, democratic system of government and offences directly affecting the State's internal or external security."

Section 3

"The National Security Courts shall be composed of a president and two other regular members. In addition, there shall sit at each National Security Court two substitute members."

Section 5

"The president of a National Security Court, one of the other regular members and one of the substitutes shall be civilian ... judges, the other members, whether full or substitute, military judges of the first rank ..."

...

3. *The Military Legal Service Act (Law no. 357)*

29. The relevant provisions of the Military Legal Service Act are worded as follows:

Additional section 7

"The aptitude of military judges ... shall be determined on the basis of assessment reports drawn up according to the procedure laid down below, subject to the provisions of the present Act and the Turkish Armed Forces Personnel Act (Law no. 926). ..."

Additional section 8

"Members ... of the National Security Courts belonging to the Military Legal Service ... shall be appointed by a committee composed of the personnel director and legal advisor of the General Staff, the personnel director and legal adviser attached to the staff of the arm in which the person concerned is serving and the Director of Military Judicial Affairs at the Ministry of Defence ..."

Section 16(1) and (3)

...

The procedure for appointment as a military judge shall take into account the opinion of the Court of Cassation, the reports by Ministry of Justice assessors and the assessment reports drawn up by the immediate superiors ...

...

Section 38

"When military judges ... sit in court they shall wear the special dress of their civilian counterparts ..."

4. *Article 112 of the Military Criminal Code*

30. Article 112 of the Military Criminal Code of 22 May 1930 provides:

"It shall be an offence, punishable by up to five years' imprisonment, to abuse one's authority as a [public] official in order to influence the military courts."

. . .

C. Case-law

1. *The Supreme Military Administrative Court*

32. The Government produced several judgments of the First Division of the Supreme Military Administrative Court setting aside decisions concerning the appointment and promotion of military judges or disciplinary sanctions applied to them. . . .

It appears from these judgments that in setting aside the transfer decisions concerned, the First Division gave as its grounds either lack of consent on the part of the person concerned or abuse of the military authorities' discretionary power. In connection with assessment reports, failure to state reasons or a lack of objectivity on the part of the immediate superior was taken into account. Lastly, in connection with a disciplinary sanction, against which in principle no appeal lies, the First Division held that the acts of which the person concerned stood accused had been incorrectly established and that the sanction was accordingly null and void.

2. *The National Security Courts*

33. The Government also submitted a number of judgments rendered by National Security Courts relevant to the impartiality of military judges sitting as members of such courts. . . . Most of these decisions declared the accused guilty but also contained separate opinions by military judges adopting a dissenting opinion with regard to the establishment and classification of the facts, the way sentence was determined or the finding of guilt itself.

[The European Court of Human Rights Grand Chamber first analyzed and decided that Incal's criminal conviction infringed his right to freedom of expression under the Convention.]

II. ALLEGED VIOLATION OF ARTICLE 6 § 1 OF THE CONVENTION

. . .

A. The proceedings in the National Security Court

1. *Arguments of the participants*

62. Mr Incal submitted that the İzmir National Security Court could not be regarded as an "independent and impartial tribunal" within the meaning of Article 6 § 1 [of the European Convention]. The military judge who sat in it was dependent on the executive and, more specifically, on the military authorities, because while performing his judicial duties he remained an officer and maintained his links with the armed forces and his hierarchical superiors. The latter retained the power to influence his career by means of the assessment reports they drew up on him.

Mr Incal maintained that the National Security Courts were special courts set up to protect the State's interests rather than to do justice as such; in that respect their function was similar to that of the executive. The presence of a military judge in the court's composition only served to confirm the army's authority and its intimidating influence over both the defendant and public opinion in general. The fact that a military judge was able to pass judgment on a civilian, and a politician at that, in connection with an offence that had nothing to do with military justice, evidenced the armed forces' influence over the handling of Turkey's political problems.

63. The Government submitted that the . . . arguments concerning these judges' responsibility towards their commanding officers and the rules governing their professional assessment were overstated; their duties as officers were limited to obeying military regulations and observing military courtesies. They were safe from any pressure from their hierarchical superiors, as such an attempt was punishable under the Military Criminal Code. The assessment system applied only to military judges' non-judicial duties. In addition, they had access to their assessment reports and could even challenge their content in the Supreme Military Administrative Court.

In the present case, neither the colleagues or hierarchical or disciplinary superiors of the military judge in question nor the public authorities who had appointed him had any connection with the parties to Mr Incal's trial or any interest whatsoever in the judgment to be delivered.

. . .

2. The Court's assessment

65. The Court reiterates that in order to establish whether a tribunal can be considered "independent" for the purposes of Article 6 § 1, regard must be had, *inter alia*, to the manner of appointment of its members and their term of office, the existence of safeguards against outside pressures and the question whether it presents an appearance of independence.

As to the condition of "impartiality" within the meaning of that provision, there are two tests to be applied: the first consists in trying to determine the personal conviction of a particular judge in a given case and the second in ascertaining whether the judge offered guarantees sufficient to exclude any legitimate doubt in this respect. It was not contested before the Court that only the second of these tests was relevant in the instant case.

In the instant case, however, the Court will consider both issues — independence and impartiality — together.

66. . . . National Security Courts . . . are composed of three judges, one of whom is a regular officer and member of the Military Legal Service.

As the independence and impartiality of the two civilian judges is not disputed, the Court must determine what the position was with regard to the military judge.

67. The Court notes that the status of military judges sitting as members of National Security Courts provides certain guarantees of independence and impartiality. For example, military judges undergo the same professional training as their civilian counterparts, which gives them the status of career members of the Military Legal Service. When sitting as members of National Security Courts, military judges enjoy constitutional safeguards identical to those of civilian judges; in addition,

with certain exceptions, they may not be removed from office or made to retire early without their consent; as regular members of a National Security Court they sit as individuals; according to the Constitution, they must be independent and no public authority may give them instructions concerning their judicial activities or influence them in the performance of their duties.

68. On the other hand, other aspects of these judges' status make it questionable. Firstly, they are servicemen who still belong to the army, which in turn takes its orders from the executive. Secondly, they remain subject to military discipline and assessment reports are compiled on them by the army for that purpose. Decisions pertaining to their appointment are to a great extent taken by the administrative authorities and the army. Lastly, their term of office as National Security Court judges is only four years and can be renewed.

...

70. At the hearing before the Court the Government submitted that the only justification for the presence of military judges in the National Security Courts was their undoubted competence and experience in the battle against organised crime, including that committed by illegal armed groups. For years the armed forces and the military judges — in whom, moreover, the people placed great trust — had acted, partly under martial law, as the guarantors of the democratic and secular Republic of Turkey, while assuming their social, cultural and moral responsibilities. For as long as the terrorist threat persisted, military judges would have to continue to lend their full support to these special courts, whose task was extremely difficult.

It is not for the Court — which is aware of the problems caused by terrorism — to pass judgment on these assertions. Its task is not to determine *in abstracto* whether it was necessary to set up such courts in a Contracting State or to review the relevant practice, but to ascertain whether the manner in which one of them functioned infringed the applicant's right to a fair trial.

71. In this respect even appearances may be of a certain importance. What is at stake is the confidence which the courts in a democratic society must inspire in the public and above all, as far as criminal proceedings are concerned, in the accused. In deciding whether there is a legitimate reason to fear that a particular court lacks independence or impartiality, the standpoint of the accused is important without being decisive. What is decisive is whether his doubts can be held to be objectively justified.

72. Mr Incal was convicted of disseminating separatist propaganda capable of inciting the people to resist the government and commit criminal offences, for participating in the decision to distribute the leaflet in issue .... As the acts which gave rise to the case were considered likely to endanger the founding principles of the Republic of Turkey, or to affect its security, they came *ipso jure* under the jurisdiction of the National Security Courts.

The Court notes, however, that in considering the question of compliance with Article 10 it did not discern anything in the leaflet which might be regarded as incitement of part of the population to violence, hostility or hatred between citizens [The Court refers to the earlier section of the opinion holding that the government violated Incal's right to freedom of expression.]. Moreover, the National Security Court refused to apply the Prevention of Terrorism Act (Law no. 3713). In addition, the Court attaches great importance to the fact that a civilian had to appear before a court composed, even if only in part, of members of the armed forces.

It follows that the applicant could legitimately fear that because one of the judges of the İzmir National Security Court was a military judge it might allow itself to be unduly influenced by considerations which had nothing to do with the nature of the case. The Court of Cassation was not able to dispel these concerns, as it did not have full jurisdiction.

73. In conclusion, the applicant had legitimate cause to doubt the independence and impartiality of the İzmir National Security Court.

There has accordingly been a breach of Article 6 § 1.

JOINT PARTLY DISSENTING OPINION OF JUDGES THÓR VILHJÁLMSSON, GÖLCÜKLÜ, MATSCHER, FOIGHEL, SIR JOHN FREELAND, LOPES ROCHA, WILDHABER AND GOTCHEV

Given the security situation in Turkey and the involvement of the armed forces in the process of countering terrorism, the Turkish authorities have considered it necessary to reinforce the National Security Courts, as specialised courts of criminal justice, by the inclusion of a military judge.

...

In a number of cases the Court has acknowledged that a special court whose members include "experts" may be a "tribunal" within the meaning of Article 6 § 1. The domestic legislation of the Council of Europe member States provides many examples of courts in which professional judges sit alongside specialists in a particular sphere whose knowledge is desirable and even necessary in deciding certain cases, provided that all the members of the court can offer the required guarantees of independence and impartiality.

As to military judges who are members of the National Security Courts, paragraph 67 of the judgment describes the constitutional safeguards they enjoy, and paragraph 68 goes on to say that certain aspects of their status make it questionable. We consider the conclusions the Court drew from these aspects . . . unconvincing.

In that connection we would observe that it is possible for ordinary judges too to be subject to assessment and to disciplinary rules and for decisions pertaining to their appointment to be taken by the administrative authorities, and that the Court has held even a three-year term of office to be sufficient. In addition, at the end of their term of office as National Security Court judges, where that term is not renewed, the judges in question remain military judges for the whole duration of their careers.

As to the argument that the composition of the court may have caused the applicant to harbour doubts about its impartiality and independence, from the point of view of "appearances", we consider that, in view of the constitutional safeguards enjoyed by military judges, doubts about their independence and impartiality cannot be regarded as objectively justified.

The logical consequence of asserting the contrary would be to cease to consider that even specialised courts can be "tribunals" for the purposes of Article 6 § 1, thus departing from the Court's well-established case-law.

COMMENT ON MILITARY JUDGES AND MILITARY COURTS AFTER INCAL AND 11 SEPTEMBER

European Court of Human Rights: Öcalan v. Turkey Grand Chamber, App. No. 46221/99 (2005)

In a high profile case and one of the first international court decisions following 11 September, the Grand Chamber reaffirmed its ruling in *Incal v. Turkey*. The case involved the capture and trial of Abdullah Öcalan, the leader of the militant separatist group, Kurdistan Workers Party. In early 1999, Turkish forces captured Öcalan in Kenya and transferred him to Turkey where he was subject to prosecution before a State Security Court. A 139-page indictment accused him of founding an armed group to secede from Turkey's national territory and of instigating numerous terrorist acts.

Öcalan's trial before the Ankara State Security Court, composed of two civilian and one military judge, began in late March 1999. Following the *Incal* judgment, Turkey started to amend its Constitution and national legislation to permit only civilian judges to sit on state security courts. The legislative amendments passed on 22 June 1999 and went into immediate effect. The next day a civilian judge replaced the military judge in Öcalan's trial court. The replacement judge had been present throughout the proceedings and attended all the hearings of the State Security Court from the beginning of the trial. On 29 June, the security court found Öcalan guilty.

A majority of the Grand Chamber of the ECHR held that the presence of the military judge violated Öcalan's right to be tried by an independent and impartial tribunal:[25]

> 113. It is understandable that the applicant — prosecuted in a State Security Court for serious offences relating to national security — should have been apprehensive about being tried by a bench which included a regular army officer belonging to the military legal service. On that account he could legitimately fear that the State Security Court might allow itself to be unduly influenced by considerations which had nothing to do with the nature of the case.
>
> 114. As to whether the military judge's replacement by a civilian judge in the course of the proceedings before the verdict was delivered remedied the situation, the Court considers, firstly, that the question whether a court is seen to be independent does not depend solely on its composition when it delivers its verdict. In order to comply with the requirements of Article 6 regarding independence, the court concerned must be seen to be independent of the executive and the legislature at each of the three stages of the proceedings, namely the investigation, the trial and the verdict (those being the three stages in Turkish criminal proceedings according to the Government).

[25] The Court also held, *inter alia*, that the government violated the right of Öcalan to be brought promptly before a judge following his arrest, the right to initiate proceedings to determine the lawfulness of his detention, and the right to legal assistance.

116. In its previous judgments, the Court attached importance to the fact that a civilian had to appear before a court composed, even if only in part, of members of the armed forces (see, among other authorities, *Incal*). Such a situation seriously affects the confidence which the courts must inspire in a democratic society.

President of the ECHR, Judge Luzius Wildhaber together with five other judges issued a dissenting opinion disagreeing strongly with the majority's view on the independence and impartiality of the trial court. The dissenting opinion stated:

6. . . . To say that the presence of a military judge, who was replaced under new rules (that were introduced to comply with the case-law of the European Court of Human Rights) made the State Security Court appear not to be independent and impartial is to take the "theory" of appearances very far. That, in our opinion at least, is neither realistic, nor even fair.

. . .

8. In addition, in Mr Oçalan's case [*sic*], and without departing from the principles established in the *Incal* judgment itself, it is hard to agree with what is said in paragraph 116 of the judgment. The applicant is there described as a civilian (or equated to a civilian). However, he was accused of instigating serious terrorist crimes leading to thousands of deaths, charges which he admitted at least in part. He could equally well be described as a warlord, which goes a long way to putting into perspective the fact that at the start of his trial one of the three members of the court before which he appeared was himself from the military.

United States: Hamdan v. Rumsfeld, 126 S. Ct. 2749 (2006) and Military Commission Act of 2006

In June 2006, the US Supreme Court decided a case involving an alleged member of Al Qaeda who was held at Guantánamo Bay and designated for trial by military commission. The Court invalidated the President's military commissions on the ground that they were not properly authorized by Congress. The Court held that the commissions violated a congressional statute requiring the President to adhere to IHL. The Court thus left open the possibility that Congress could subsequently authorize such commissions, a path the President pursued in late 2006.

A majority of the Court ruled that Common Article 3 applies to the conflict between the United States and Al Qaeda and that the military commissions violated the fair trial provisions of the article. The majority held that the US commissions did not constitute a 'regularly constituted court', because the Government failed to justify setting up special ad hoc tribunals outside the existing courts martial system. The majority thus implicitly accepted that a courts martial — a standing US military tribunal — would constitute a regularly constituted court. A plurality of the Supreme Court went on to conclude that particular procedures of the military commission — precluding the defendant from seeing classified evidence — failed to 'afford[] all the judicial guarantees which are recognized as indispensable by civilized peoples'. Following are excerpts from *Hamdan*:

> [T]here is at least one provision of the Geneva Conventions that applies here even if the relevant conflict is not one between signatories.[26] . . .
>
> . . .
>
> . . . While the term "regularly constituted court" is not specifically defined in either Common Article 3 or its accompanying commentary, other sources disclose its core meaning. The commentary accompanying a provision of the Fourth Geneva Convention, for example, defines " 'regularly constituted' " tribunals to include "ordinary military courts" and "definitely exclud[e] all special tribunals." GCIV Commentary 340 (defining the term "properly constituted" in Article 66, which the commentary treats as identical to "regularly constituted"); see also *Yamashita*, 327 U.S., at 44, 66 S.Ct. 340 (Rutledge, J., dissenting) (describing military commission as a court "specially constituted for a particular trial"). And one of the Red Cross' own treatises defines "regularly constituted court" as used in Common Article 3 to mean "established and organized in accordance with the laws and procedures already in force in a country." Int'l Comm. of Red Cross, 1 Customary International Humanitarian Law 355 (2005); see also GCIV Commentary 340 (observing that "ordinary military courts" will "be set up in accordance with the recognized principles governing the administration of justice").
>
> . . . At a minimum, a military commission "can be 'regularly constituted' by the standards of our military justice system only if some practical need explains deviations from court-martial practice."[27] . . .
>
> [A plurality of the Court continued.]
>
> Inextricably intertwined with the question of regular constitution is the evaluation of the procedures governing the tribunal and whether they afford "all the judicial guarantees which are recognized as indispensable by civilized peoples." Like the phrase "regularly constituted court," this phrase is not defined in the text of the Geneva Conventions. But it must be understood to incorporate at least the barest of those trial protections that have been recognized by customary international law. Many of these are described in Article 75 of [Protocol I]. Although the United States declined to ratify Protocol I, its objections were not to Article 75 thereof. Indeed, it appears that the Government "regard[s] the provisions of Article 75 as an articulation of safeguards to which all persons in the hands of an enemy are entitled." Taft, The Law of Armed Conflict After 9/11: Some Salient

[26] Hamdan observes that Article 5 of the Third Geneva Convention requires that if there be 'any doubt' whether he is entitled to prisoner-of-war protections, he must be afforded those protections until his status is determined by a 'competent tribunal'. Because we hold that Hamdan may not, in any event, be tried by the military commission the President has convened . . . the question whether his potential status as a prisoner of war independently renders illegal his trial by military commission may be reserved.

[27] Further evidence of this tribunal's irregular constitution is the fact that its rules and procedures are subject to change midtrial, at the whim of the Executive. See Commission Order No. 1, ß 11 (providing that the Secretary of Defense may change the governing rules 'from time to time').

> Features, 28 Yale J. Int'l L. 319, 322 (2003). Among the rights set forth in Article 75 is the "right to be tried in [one's] presence." Protocol I, Art. 75(4)(e).[28]
>
> . . . [V]arious provisions of Commission Order No. 1 dispense with the principles, articulated in Article 75 and indisputably part of the customary international law, that an accused must, absent disruptive conduct or consent, be present for his trial and must be privy to the evidence against him. That the Government has a compelling interest in denying Hamdan access to certain sensitive information is not doubted. But, at least absent express statutory provision to the contrary, information used to convict a person of a crime must be disclosed to him.

Subsequent to the Supreme Court decision, Congress passed the Military Commission Act (MCA) of 2006. Notably the Act embraced the application of Common Article 3 to the conflict between the United States and Al Qaeda. The Act is a complex piece of legislation encompassing a wide range of measures including rules on interrogation, detention and habeas corpus.[29] Provisions concerning military commissions include those excerpted below. Consider whether these provisions satisfy the IHL standards discussed in *Hamdan*. How about the standards set forth by the Inter-American Commission and the European Court of Human Rights?

UNITED STATES MILITARY COMMISSION ACT (MCA) OF 2006

http://frwebgate.access.gpo.gov/cgi-bin/getdoc.cgi?dbname = 109_cong_bills&docid = f:s3930enr.txt.pdf

§ 948a. Definitions

> . . . Unlawful enemy combatant.— (A) The term "unlawful enemy combatant" means—
>
> (i) a person who has engaged in hostilities or who has purposefully and materially supported hostilities against the United States or its co-belligerents who is not a lawful enemy combatant (including a person who is part of the Taliban, al Qaeda, or associated forces); or
>
> (ii) a person who, before, on, or after the date of the enactment of the Military Commissions Act of 2006, has been determined to be an unlawful enemy combatant by a Combatant Status Review Tribunal or another

[28] Other international instruments to which the United States is a signatory include the same basic protections set forth in Article 75. See, e.g., International Covenant on Civil and Political Rights, Art. 14, ¶3(*d*), Mar. 23, 1976, 999 U.N.T.S. 171 (setting forth the right of an accused "[t]o be tried in his presence, and to defend himself in person or through legal assistance of his own choosing"). Following World War II, several defendants were tried and convicted by military commission for violations of the law of war in their failure to afford captives fair trials before imposition and execution of sentence. In two such trials, the prosecutors argued that the defendants' failure to apprise accused individuals of all evidence against them constituted violations of the law of war. *See* 5 UN War Crimes Commission 30 (trial of Sergeant-Major Shigeru Ohashi), 75 (trial of General Tanaka Hisakasu)

[29] For a useful synopsis of the Act, see John Cerone, The Military Commissions Act of 2006: Examining the Relationship between the International Law of Armed Conflict and US Law, 10 ASIL Insight No. 30, 13 Nov. 2006 at http://www.asil.org/insights/2006/11/insights061114.html.

competent tribunal established under the authority of the President or the Secretary of Defense.

... Co-belligerent. — In this paragraph, the term "co-belligerent", with respect to the United States, means any State or armed force joining and directly engaged with the United States in hostilities or directly supporting hostilities against a common enemy.

§ 948b. Military commissions generally

...

(b) Authority for military commissions under this chapter. — The President is authorized to establish military commissions under this chapter for offenses triable by military commission as provided in this chapter.

(c) Construction of provisions. — The procedures for military commissions set forth in this chapter are based upon the procedures for trial by general courts-martial under chapter 47 of this title (the Uniform Code of Military Justice)....

(d) Inapplicability of certain provisions. — (1) The following provisions of this title shall not apply to trial by military commission under this chapter:

[The Act lists provisions related to 'speedy trial, including any rule of courts-martial relating to speedy trial', compulsory self-incrimination, and pretrial investigation.]

(2) Other provisions of chapter 47 of this title shall apply to trial by military commission under this chapter only to the extent provided by this chapter.

...

(f) Status of commissions under common Article 3. — A military commission established under this chapter is a regularly constituted court, affording all the necessary "judicial guarantees which are recognized as indispensable by civilized peoples" for purposes of common Article 3 of the Geneva Conventions.

(g) Geneva Conventions not establishing source of rights. — No alien unlawful enemy combatant subject to trial by military commission under this chapter may invoke the Geneva Conventions as a source of rights.

...

§ 948d. Jurisdiction of military commissions

(a) Jurisdiction. — A military commission under this chapter shall have jurisdiction to try any offense made punishable by this chapter or the law of war when committed by an alien unlawful enemy combatant before, on, or after September 11, 2001.

...

(c) Determination of unlawful enemy combatant status dispositive. — A finding, whether before, on, or after the date of the enactment of the Military Commissions Act of 2006, by a Combatant Status Review Tribunal or another competent tribunal established under the authority of the President or the Secretary of Defense that a person is an unlawful enemy combatant is dispositive for purposes of jurisdiction for trial by military commission under this chapter.

(d) Punishments. — A military commission under this chapter may, under such limitations as the Secretary of Defense may prescribe, adjudge any punishment not forbidden by this chapter, including the penalty of death when authorized under this chapter or the law of war.

...

§ 948h. Who may convene military commissions

Military commissions under this chapter may be convened by the Secretary of Defense or by any officer or official of the United States designated by the Secretary for that purpose.

§ 948i. Who may serve on military commissions

(a) In general. — Any commissioned officer of the armed forces on active duty is eligible to serve on a military commission under this chapter.

...

§ 948j. Military judge of a military commission

(a) Detail of military judge. — A military judge shall be detailed to each military commission under this chapter. The Secretary of Defense shall prescribe regulations providing for the manner in which military judges are so detailed to military commissions. The military judge shall preside over each military commission to which he has been detailed.

...

(d) Consultation with members; ineligibility to vote. — A military judge detailed to a military commission under this chapter may not consult with the members of the commission except in the presence of the accused (except as otherwise provided in section 949d of this title), trial counsel, and defense counsel, nor may he vote with the members of the commission.

...

§ 949a. Rules

(a) Procedures and rules of evidence. — Pretrial, trial, and post-trial procedures, including elements and modes of proof, for cases triable by military commission under this chapter may be prescribed by the Secretary of Defense, in consultation with the Attorney General. Such procedures shall, so far as the Secretary considers practicable or consistent with military or intelligence activities, apply the principles of law and the rules of evidence in trial by general courts-martial. Such procedures and rules of evidence may not be contrary to or inconsistent with this chapter.

(b) Rules for military commission. — (1) Notwithstanding any departures from the law and the rules of evidence in trial by general courts-martial authorized by subsection (a), the procedures and rules of evidence in trials by military commission under this chapter shall include the following:

(A) The accused shall be permitted to present evidence in his defense, to cross-examine the witnesses who testify against him, and to examine and respond to evidence admitted against him on the issue of guilt or innocence and for sentencing, as provided for by this chapter.

(B) The accused shall be present at all sessions of the military commission (other than those for deliberations or voting), except when excluded under section 949d of this title.

. . .

§ 949d. Sessions

. . .

(d) Closure of proceedings. — (1) The military judge may close to the public all or part of the proceedings of a military commission under this chapter, but only in accordance with this subsection.

(2) The military judge may close to the public all or a portion of the proceedings under paragraph (1) only upon making a specific finding that such closure is necessary to —

(A) protect information the disclosure of which could reasonably be expected to cause damage to the national security, including intelligence or law enforcement sources, methods, or activities; or

(B) ensure the physical safety of individuals.

(3) A finding under paragraph (2) may be based upon a presentation, including a presentation ex parte or in camera, by either trial counsel or defense counsel.

. . .

(f) Protection of classified information. —

(1) National security privilege. — (A) Classified information shall be protected and is privileged from disclosure if disclosure would be detrimental to the national security. . . .

(2) Introduction of classified information. —

(A) Alternatives to disclosure. — To protect classified information from disclosure, the military judge, upon motion of trial counsel, shall authorize, to the extent practicable —

(i) the deletion of specified items of classified information from documents to be introduced as evidence before the military commission;

(ii) the substitution of a portion or summary of the information for such classified documents; or

(iii) the substitution of a statement of relevant facts that the classified information would tend to prove.

(B) Protection of sources, methods, or activities. — The military judge, upon motion of trial counsel, shall permit trial counsel to introduce otherwise admissible evidence before the military commission, while protecting from disclosure the sources, methods, or activities by which the United States acquired the evidence if the military judge finds that (i) the sources, methods, or activities by which the United States acquired the evidence are classified, and (ii) the evidence is reliable. The military judge may require trial counsel to present to the military commission and the defense, to the extent practicable and consistent with national security, an unclassified summary of the sources, methods, or activities by which the United States acquired the evidence.

...

(3) Consideration of privilege and related materials. — A claim of privilege under this subsection, and any materials submitted in support thereof, shall, upon request of the Government, be considered by the military judge in camera and shall not be disclosed to the accused.

(4) Additional regulations. — The Secretary of Defense may prescribe additional regulations, consistent with this subsection, for the use and protection of classified information during proceedings of military commissions under this chapter. A report on any regulations so prescribed, or modified, shall be submitted to the Committees on Armed Services of the Senate and the House of Representatives not later than 60 days before the date on which such regulations or modifications, as the case may be, go into effect.

...

§ 950b. Review by the convening authority

...

(c) Action by convening authority. — (1) The authority under this subsection to modify the findings and sentence of a military commission under this chapter is a matter of the sole discretion and prerogative of the convening authority.

...

(2)(C) In taking action under this paragraph, the convening authority may, in his sole discretion, approve, disapprove, commute, or suspend the sentence in whole or in part. The convening authority may not increase a sentence beyond that which is found by the military commission.

(3) The convening authority is not required to take action on the findings of a military commission under this chapter. If the convening authority

takes action on the findings, the convening authority may, in his sole discretion, may . . . dismiss any charge or specification by setting aside a finding of guilty thereto . . .

. . .

§ 950c. Appellate referral; waiver or withdrawal of appeal

(a) Automatic referral for appellate review. — Except as provided under subsection (b) [providing for waiver of right to review], in each case in which the final decision of a military commission (as approved by the convening authority) includes a finding of guilty, the convening authority shall refer the case to the Court of Military Commission Review. . . .

. . .

§ 950f. Review by Court of Military Commission Review

. . . The Secretary of Defense shall establish a Court of Military Commission Review which shall be composed of one or more panels, and each such panel shall be composed of not less than three appellate military judges. For the purpose of reviewing military commission decisions under this chapter, the court may sit in panels or as a whole in accordance with rules prescribed by the Secretary.

. . .

. . . In a case reviewed by the Court of Military Commission Review under this section, the Court may act only with respect to matters of law.

§ 950g. Review by the United States Court of Appeals for the District of Columbia Circuit and the Supreme Court

(a) Exclusive appellate jurisdiction. — (1)(A) Except as provided in subparagraph (B), the United States Court of Appeals for the District of Columbia Circuit shall have exclusive jurisdiction to determine the validity of a final judgment rendered by a military commission (as approved by the convening authority) under this chapter.

(B) The Court of Appeals may not review the final judgment until all other appeals under this chapter have been waived or exhausted.

. . .

(b) Standard for review. — In a case reviewed by it under this section, the Court of Appeals may act only with respect to matters of law.

(c) Scope of review. — The jurisdiction of the Court of Appeals on an appeal under subsection (a) shall be limited to the consideration of —

(1) whether the final decision was consistent with the standards and procedures specified in this chapter; and

(2) to the extent applicable, the Constitution and the laws of the United States.

(d) Supreme court. —The Supreme Court may review by writ of certiorari the final judgment of the Court of Appeals . . .

GERALD L. NEUMAN, COUNTER-TERRORIST OPERATIONS AND THE RULE OF LAW

15 E.J.Int.L. 1019 (2004)

... European states have responded to the new terrorism threats since 2001 primarily by means of traditional law enforcement methods. It is to be hoped that conditions will remain favourable enough that they can continue to do so....

1. The Military Model

Since 2001, the United States Government has felt impelled to supplement the criminal justice model of counter-terrorist action with military action. There is no war on terrorism as such, but there does exist an armed conflict between the United States and Al Qaeda.....

This conflict differs from the kinds of struggles involved in most decisions of the European Court of Human Rights about terrorism. Most such decisions have concerned either separatist violence or revolutionary violence within a state. Local insurgents seeking to gain control of all or part of a state's territory face different incentives that limit the degree of their destructiveness against people and places. Separatists who appeal to world opinion to validate their claims confront different constraints than groups that reject the legitimacy of international law.

When the military model frames counter-terrorist operations, rule of law aspirations have lesser relevance than in the criminal justice model. They continue to play an important role, but in a more limited manner. Armed conflict should not be wholly unrestrained, and rule of law conceptions inform both the restrictions that international humanitarian law imposes and the means of enforcing them....

...

2. Military Trials

... Among the debated issues ... is the choice between military and civilian tribunals for prosecution of unprivileged combatants and war crimes. European human rights case law has broadly disapproved of the participation of even a single military judge in security trials of civilians...

The disapproval of military tribunals seems understandable in the context of alleged internal subversion, where judicial independence provides an important protection for domestic political opponents. The Court appears to strike a balance, creating a prophylactic, institutionally justified rule that avoids the need for case-by-case inquiry and reduces the risk of unfair trial. As dissenting judges have sometimes warned, however, the limits of its reasoning are unclear, and it would potentially call into question all forms of military justice....

The Court's prophylactic rule is not necessarily appropriate for international armed conflict, or conflict with a foreign terrorist organization. In international armed conflicts, military jurisdiction over regular forces of the enemy is not only traditional, but is specifically sanctioned by the Third Geneva

Convention.[30] Arguably, in war, civilians may be as biased, or more biased, against the enemy than military professionals. Moreover, military judges may interpret the laws of war with the knowledge that their own forces will be bound by their interpretations, and may be less inclined to use adjudication as a vehicle for the progressive development of international humanitarian law than civilian judges. These considerations may have lesser force in the asymmetrical context of conflict between a state and a non-state actor. But military trials, with compensating procedural guarantees that both international humanitarian law and human rights law require, can be a legitimate consequence of the shift to the military model.

QUESTIONS

1. What aspect, if any, of the European Court of Human Rights' analysis in *Incal* turns on the status of the defendant (civilian versus military) or on the nature of the offence? Do those distinctions explain the source of disagreement between the majority and dissenting opinions? Why should the test for an independent and impartial tribunal turn on such considerations? Should it matter whether a conflict is between a government and an internal separatist movement, a state and a transnational terrorist organization, or two states?

2. 'The United States is at war with Al Qaeda. The sooner we all agree on that fact the more the conflict will be regulated by a more rights-protective regime. The Supreme Court's decision in *Hamdan* is exhibit A. The Court held that the situation constitutes an armed conflict under Common Article 3, and, by extension, its fair trial rights govern military commissions and its prohibition on torture, cruel, humiliating, and degrading treatment regulates interrogations. Were the situation not an armed conflict, rights protections would not be so obvious, courts may not be bound to apply international treaties, derogation clauses would risk overprotecting state interests, and the moral force of the Geneva Conventions would be missing' Comment.

3. In *Incal*, the Court found that the participation of a military judge violates the guarantee of an independent and impartial tribunal partly because military judges 'are servicemen who still belong to the army, which in turn takes its orders from the executive'. Does the logical extension of the Court's analysis invalidate courts-martial and military tribunals in which the entire judicial panel or jury are comprised of service members answerable ultimately to the executive? Does the Court's analysis turn on the specific structural position of the military judges in Turkey's system or on the mere fact that they are members of a military? How does the US Military Commission Act of 2006 fare under this analysis?

[30] Professor Neuman references Articles 84 and 102 of the POW Convention. Article 84 is quoted in full in the Inter-American Commission Report, *supra.* p. 435 Article 102 states: 'A prisoner of war can be validly sentenced only if the sentence has been pronounced by the same courts according to the same procedure as in the case of members of the armed forces of the Detaining Power'.

4. Should the presence of a single military judge on a three-judge panel be a sufficient reason to invalidate the proceedings? Does the presence of civilian judges help counteract potential bias? How might military judges be different from other 'expert' judges that the dissenters in *Incal* suggest are permitted under the Court's case law? Would modifying other aspects of the proceedings — a different number and ratio of civilian and military judges, weighted voting rules, or appellate review — make the presence of military judges acceptable in your view? Chapter 14 returns to a similar set of questions about the composition and biases of judges in the case of hybrid tribunals such as the Special Court for Sierra Leone. In that context, panels are composed of international and national judges, and the latter are often criticized for being too closely connected to the conflict.

5. Could problems associated with holding war crimes and terrorism trials be averted by suspending prosecutions at least until the conclusion of the conflict? Wouldn't the political atmosphere, for example, generally be more conducive to ensuring the fairness of proceedings after a state of emergency? Consider the following text from ICRC Commentaries to the Geneva Conventions:

> Proceedings in respect of war crimes may not be brought against prisoners of war in conditions and at a time when any normal defence of the prisoners' interests is impossible. As long as hostilities continue, a prisoner of war accused of such offences will usually be unable to adduce the proof or evidence which might absolve him of responsibility or reduce that responsibility. It seems necessary that, except in special cases, prisoners of war accused of war crimes should not be tried until after the end of hostilities, that is to say when communications have been re-established between the belligerent countries and the prisoner is in a position to procure the necessary documents for his defence and to call witnesses.
>
> If prisoners of war were nevertheless tried while hostilities were still in progress, in conditions which would not afford them a proper defence, they would in fact be deprived of the regular trial to which they are entitled under Article 99. A trial conducted in such circumstances could then constitute a grave breach of the Convention, as covered by Article 130.

Consider also the following argument by Professors Jack Goldsmith and Eric Posner:

> . . . The United States holds more than 400 terrorism suspects at Guantanamo Bay, and 500 or so more at Bagram air base in Afghanistan. Five years after the Sept. 11 attacks, it has announced plans for military trials for only 10 of these detainees. . . .
>
> Why only 10? Because it is difficult to try terrorists in this war. For most detainees, the government lacks evidence of overt crimes such as murder. It can prosecute these detainees only for the vague and problematic crime of conspiracy to commit a terrorist act based on membership in and training with al-Qaeda or the Taliban. Beyond this problem, witnesses are scattered around the globe, and much of the evidence is in a foreign language, or classified, or hearsay — in many cases all of these things.
>
> Even if these obstacles are overcome, . . . trials of political enemies are more difficult, more time-consuming and, in the end, more circuslike than an ordinary criminal trial. The defendant or his lawyers will use a trial not to contest guilt but rather to rally followers and demoralize foes.
>
> . . .

> There is a better and easier way to deal with captured terrorists. The Supreme Court has made clear that the conflicts with al-Qaeda and the Taliban are governed by the laws of war, and the laws of war permit detention of enemy soldiers without charge or trial until hostilities end....
>
> The main concern with military detentions is that the war will last a long time, perhaps indefinitely. If so, detention could mean a life sentence. We don't yet know whether this concern is warranted. But there are several ways to assure Americans and the world that the system is as fair and humane as circumstances permit.
>
> ...
>
> When hostilities in the war against al-Qaeda and its affiliates cease, of course, the detention rationale will dissipate and detainees must be released or (if they have committed law-of-war violations) tried. For such people, if there are any, regular criminal trial procedures should be adequate. If hostilities are really over, the risk that a former terrorist might walk free as a result of insufficient evidence is no more troublesome than it is for trials of ordinary criminals...[31]

F. NATIONAL SECURITY AND ECONOMIC AND SOCIAL RIGHTS

Discussions about potential relationships between national security and human rights law commonly focus on civil and political rights. In this section, we turn our attention to relationships between national security and economic and social rights.

One set of questions concerns whether the political and strategic landscape post 11 September will (and should) affect rights protections within this domain. Does the mantra that the full range of human rights are 'indivisible, interdependent and interrelated' suggest that accommodations for national security concerns in the civil and political rights realm will (and should) translate into accommodations across the human rights system? More generally, what economic and social rights protections might national security interests directly or indirectly affect? Should these rights protections, just like civil and political rights guarantees, regulate the acts of belligerents in times of war, or does the programmatic nature of economic and social rights necessitate alternative ways of thinking about the rights-security relationship?

On the face of it, the Covenant on Economic, Social and Cultural Rights suggests little direct connection between its subject of concern and national security. The Covenant specifically references 'national security' only in an article dealing with trade union rights (a corollary to rights of association). In contrast, the International Covenant on Civil and Political Rights references 'national security' in limitations clauses of six separate articles. Also, Article 4 of the ICCPR contains

[31] Jack Goldsmith and Eric A. Posner, 'Op-Ed, A Better Way on Detainees', Washington Post, 4 August 2006, A17.

a derogation mechanism for public emergencies. The CESCR has no such device.[32]

Nevertheless, situations involving armed conflict, militarization and terrorism can directly implicate economic and social rights. And various international human rights mechanisms have begun to address such matters. The UN supervisory committee that monitors and evaluates implementation of the CESCR, for example, denounced the housing, health and nutritional conditions of civilians displaced in the Sri Lankan civil war and criticized the Government's failure to implement a peace plan to devolve power to regional authorities. That committee has also reviewed the record of Israel on multiple occasions. In its most recent evaluation, in 2003, the committee stated that it was

> gravely concerned about the deplorable living conditions of the Palestinians in the occupied territories, who — as a result of the continuing occupation and subsequent measures of closures, extended curfews, roadblocks and security checkpoints — suffer from impingement of their enjoyment of economic, social and cultural rights enshrined in the Covenant, in particular access to work, land, water, health care, education and food.

Other examples include the committee's review of Russia in 2003, concerning conditions in Chechnya, and Colombia in 2001, concerning displacement of Afro-Colombian communities and street children affected by the armed conflict.

The European Committee on Social Rights, a similar body responsible for monitoring and evaluating implementation of a regional treaty, has also issued opinions addressing national security. The European Committee is aided by the fact that its governing treaty, the revised European Social Charter, explicitly contemplates such questions. The Charter includes a general limitation clause permitting governments to restrict economic and social rights when such measures are 'prescribed by law and are necessary in a democratic society for the protection of . . . national security'. The Charter also includes a general derogation provision modelled on provisions in civil and political rights treaties. It permits a state to suspend treaty obligations 'in time of war or other public emergency threatening the life of the nation'. Notably, no economic and social rights are listed as nonderogable.

Under this framework, the European Committee has rendered decisions delineating which economic and public sectors are sufficiently related to national security. Those determinations affect whether particular areas of the workforce are subject to exceptional government powers such as prohibiting strikes, prohibiting collective action or excluding foreign nationals from employment. The European Committee has also decided whether specific governmental measures are proportionate to meeting national security objectives. Measures subject to such an inquiry have included blanket prohibitions on the right to strike, an exceptionally lengthy

[32] The Additional Protocol to the American Convention on Human Rights in the Area of Economic, Social and Cultural Rights ('Protocol of San Salvador') contains no derogation clause. The African Charter on Human and Peoples' Rights recognizes both civil and political rights and economic and social rights, but it does not contain a derogation clause for either.

period of compulsory service for military officers, and disparate periods of governmental service for conscientious objectors.

UN officials whose mandate covers economic and social rights have increasingly addressed violations occurring in situations of armed conflict.[33] In 2001 and 2002, the UN Special Rapporteur on the Right to Food reported on the use of food as 'a method of warfare against insurgents and civilian populations' by the government of Myanmar including 'the deliberate destruction by government armed forces of staple crops and confiscation of food from civilians'. The Special Rapporteur also reported on situations in Afghanistan and occupied Palestinian territories. The Special Rapporteur on the Right to Adequate Housing criticized house demolitions in occupied Palestinian territory in 2003, forced evictions in Afghanistan in 2004, and displacement of civilian populations in Sudan in 2005. The Special Rapporteur on the Right to Health, on one occasion, urged the Coalition Provisional Authority in Iraq to inquire into the health of the civilian population in the city of Falluja following massive military operations by US-led forces and, on another occasion, sent an urgent appeal following the bombing of a field clinic by Iraqi and multinational forces.

State obligations might seem relatively straightforward in these contexts. The cases generally do not involve positive obligations requiring a state to *protect* individuals from the depredations of private actors, nor do they involve obligations to take affirmative steps to promote and *fulfil* economic and social wellbeing. Rather, the cases involve the obligation to *respect* economic and social rights. They refer to acts of commission not omission, and they concern direct governmental intrusions that interfere with and undermine human welfare. Governmental actions in many of these instances also clearly contravene the principle of non-regression. Along all these dimensions, the analysis of state obligations appears to rest on politically and philosophically less controversial ground than other situations involving economic and social rights.

These cases are, at the same time, deceptively simple. Indeed, national security cases reveal the significant difficulties that can arise in determining whether the obligation of a state to respect economic and social rights is lawfully discharged. When economic and social rights conflict with national security and military imperatives, which interests should prevail? What constitutes a proportional loss of health, housing, or livelihood, for example, in the face of a proffered national security or military justification? What role should courts — international or domestic — play in addressing such questions? How should judicial and other authorities frame an analysis that decides when such economic and social interests trump national security objectives proffered by state officials? The establishment of a physical barrier by Israel in occupied territory, a case we turn to shortly, foregrounds many of these issues.

Another important dimension of the relationship between national security and economic and social rights is the significance of international humanitarian law. Recall our discussion of debates about *lex specialis* earlier in this chapter. Are there special reasons for having international humanitarian law displace (or supplement) human rights law in the area of economic and social rights? When reading the following commentary by Louise Doswald-Beck and Sylvain Vité consider the

[33] We introduce the general responsibilities and practices of these offices in Chapter 9.

advantages and disadvantages of an international humanitarian law framework in regulating practices that implicate economic and social welfare of civilians during armed conflict. Also consider whether international human rights standards would unduly complicate or reduce obligations of parties to a conflict by introducing imprecision to international humanitarian law or by providing broad justifications for restricting rights that would not otherwise exist under international humanitarian law. In an issue of the International Review of the Red Cross, Doswald-Beck and Vité analyze distinctions between the IHL and human rights regimes:

> [T]here is a phenomenon in human rights law which is quite alien to humanitarian law, namely . . . the fact that most of these treaties make a distinction between so-called "civil and political rights" and "economic, social and cultural" rights. The legal difference between these treaties is that the "civil and political" ones require instant respect for the rights enumerated therein, whereas the "economic, social and cultural" ones require the State to take appropriate measures in order to achieve a progressive realization of these rights. . . .
>
> . . .
>
> . . . [I]t is a fact that the implementation of most of the economic rights does necessitate some resources and thought as to the best economic arrangement in order to achieve the best standard of living possible. The genuine difficulty thus created in giving a proper interpretation to the ESC Covenant in the particular circumstances of each State has a direct effect on the nature of the individual's economic rights. . . .
>
> [T]he major difficulty of applying human rights law as enunciated in the treaties is the very general nature of the treaty language. Even outside armed conflict situations, we see that the documents attempt to deal with the relationship between the individual and society by the use of limitation clauses. Thus the manner in which the rights may be applied in practice must be interpreted by the organs instituted to implement the treaty in question. Although the United Nations Human Rights Committee, created by the [ICCPR], has made some general statements on the meaning of certain articles, the normal method of interpretation by both the United Nations and regional systems has been through a decision or an opinion on whether a particular set of facts constitutes a violation of the article in question. . . . The major legal difference is that humanitarian law is not formulated as a series of rights, but rather as a series of duties that combatants have to obey. This does have one very definite advantage from the legal theory point of view, in that humanitarian law is not subject to the kind of arguments that continue to plague the implementation of economic and social rights.
>
> . . .
>
> . . . [T]he Protocol protects life in a way that goes beyond the traditional civil right to life. First, it prohibits the starvation of civilians as a method of warfare and consequently the destruction of their means of survival (which is an improvement on earlier customary law).[34] Secondly, it offers means for improving their chance

[34] Article 54 of Additional Protocol I provides in part:

1. Starvation of civilians as a method of warfare is prohibited.

2. It is prohibited to attack, destroy, remove or render useless objects indispensable to the survival of the civilian population, such as food-stuffs, agricultural areas for the

of survival by, for example, providing for the declaration of special zones that contain no military objectives and consequently may not be attacked. Thirdly, there are various stipulations in the Geneva Conventions and their Additional Protocols that the wounded must be collected and given the medical care that they need. In human rights treaties this would fall into the category of "economic and social rights". Fourthly, the Geneva Conventions and their Protocols specify in considerable detail the physical conditions that are needed in order to sustain life in as reasonable a condition as possible in an armed conflict. Thus, for example, the living conditions required for prisoners of war are described in the Third Geneva Convention and similar requirements are also laid down for civilian persons interned in an occupied territory. With regard to the general population, an occupying power is required to ensure that the people as a whole have the necessary means of survival and to accept outside relief shipments if necessary to achieve this purpose.[35] There are also provisions for relief for the Parties' own populations, but they are not as absolute as those that apply in occupied territory. Once again, these kinds of provisions would be categorized by a human rights lawyer as "economic and social".[36]

QUESTIONS

1. Does international humanitarian law offer a framework superior to human rights law for regulating violations of economic and social rights in times of war? Do you agree with Doswald-Beck and Vité's comparisons?

2. Are the international humanitarian law rules precise but too narrow? Does Article 54 of Additional Protocol I, for example, outlaw actions taken only with a specific intent — e.g., purposefully depriving civilians of sustenance rather than knowingly or negligently engaging in such acts? Does this feature demonstrate that international humanitarian law cannot adequately address the full range of human rights concerns in armed conflicts?

production of food-stuffs, crops, livestock, drinking water installations and supplies and irrigation works, for the specific purpose of denying them for their sustenance value to the civilian population or to the adverse Party, whatever the motive, whether in order to starve out civilians, to cause them to move away, or for any other motive.

[35] Article 55 of the Civilians Convention provides: 'To the fullest extent of the means available to it, the Occupying Power has the duty of ensuring the food and medical supplies of the population; it should, in particular, bring in the necessary foodstuffs, medical stores and other articles if the resources of the occupied territory are inadequate.'

Article 56 of the Convention provides: 'To the fullest extent of the means available to it, the Occupying Power has the duty of ensuring and maintaining, with the cooperation of national and local authorities, the medical and hospital establishments and services, public health and hygiene in the occupied territory, with particular reference to the adoption and application of the prophylactic and preventive measures necessary to combat the spread of contagious diseases and epidemics. Medical personnel of all categories shall be allowed to carry out their duties.'

Article 69 of Additional Protocol I states: 'In addition to the duties specified in Article 55 of the [Civilians] Convention concerning food and medical supplies, the Occupying Power shall, to the fullest extent of the means available to it and without any adverse distinction, also ensure the provision of clothing, bedding, means of shelter, other supplies essential to the survival of the civilian population of the occupied territory . . . .'

[36] Louise Doswald-Beck and Sylvain Vité, 'International Humanitarian Law and Human Rights Law', 293 International Review of the Red Cross 94–119 (1993), available at http://www.icrc.org/web/eng/siteeng0.nsf/html/57JMRT.

3. In 2002, the CESCR Committee issued General Comment No. 15 on the right to water. Consider the following excerpt from that Comment:

> The Committee notes that during armed conflicts, emergency situations and natural disasters, the right to water embraces those obligations by which States parties are bound under international humanitarian law.[37] This includes protection of objects indispensable for survival of the civilian population, including drinking water installations and supplies and irrigation works, protection of the natural environment against widespread, long-term and severe damage and ensuring that civilians, internees and prisoners have access to adequate water.

In a detailed analysis of the subject, the Special Rapporteur on the Right to Food adopted a similar position: 'The right to food must be protected in times of peace, but also in times of war. This section looks at the right to food in situations of armed conflict in which international humanitarian law comes into effect and is the more appropriate way to protect people suffering from hunger and malnutrition.'

Should international humanitarian law standards completely substitute for human rights law during armed conflict as the Committee's and Rapporteur's analysis might suggest? The Committee references the Nuclear Weapons Advisory Opinion of the International Court of Justice which we discuss earlier in the chapter. The ICJ stated: 'The test of what is an arbitrary deprivation of life, however, then falls to be determined by the applicable *lex specialis*, namely, the law applicable in armed conflict which is designed to regulate the conduct of hostilities'. If IHL serves as the test for arbitrary deprivations of life, does it necessarily follow that this body of law should serve as the test for unlawful deprivations of economic and social rights in armed conflict as well?

LEGAL CONSEQUENCES OF THE CONSTRUCTION OF A WALL IN THE OCCUPIED PALESTINIAN TERRITORY INTERNATIONAL COURT OF JUSTICE

International Court of Justice, 9 July 2004
Advisory Opinion, ICJ Reports 2004, at 136

[The second Intifada began in Israel and occupied Palestinian territory in September 2000. In 2002, the Government of Israel decided to construct a physical barrier consisting of a network of fences located partly within the West Bank and partly along the border between the West Bank and Israel. The Government's stated purpose was to decrease infiltrations by terrorists intent on attacking Israeli citizens.

[37] For the interrelationship of human rights law and humanitarian law, the Committee notes the conclusions of the International Court of Justice in *Legality of the Threat or Use of Nuclear Weapons (Request by the General Assembly), ICJ Reports* (1996) p. 226, para 25.

In December 2003, the UN General Assembly adopted a resolution (by a vote of 90 in favour to 8 against, with 74 abstentions) to request the International Court of Justice to issue an Advisory Opinion concerning 'the legal consequences arising from the construction of the wall being built by Israel, the occupying Power, in the Occupied Palestinian Territory, including in and around East Jerusalem'. Israel argued that an Advisory Opinion would constitute an improper exercise of jurisdiction, and the government declined to participate in the oral hearings.

On 30 June 2004, the Supreme Court of Israel issued a decision ordering the Government to modify a segment of the barrier that was the object of the petitioners' complaint. The Court held that military commanders have the authority to erect a barrier in occupied territory. The specific route chosen, however, failed the Court's proportionality analysis. The security advantage of the route compared with potential alternative routes 'd[id] not stand in reasonable proportion' to the injury suffered by the Palestinian population. The Court stated: 'The injury caused by the separation fence is not restricted to the lands of the inhabitants and to their access to these lands. The injury is of far wider a scope. It strikes across the fabric of life of the entire population'. Notably, the Supreme Court expressed its view of the appropriate role of the judiciary in adjudicating such issues: 'The military commander is the expert regarding the military quality of the separation fence route. We are experts regarding the humanitarian aspects. The military commander determines where, on hill and plain, the separation fence will be erected. That is his expertise. We examine whether this route's harm to the local residents is proportional. That is our expertise'.

A few days later, the ICJ issued its Advisory Opinion. The Court held, by 14 votes to 1, that the barrier violated various international obligations including international humanitarian law and human rights law. The Court's analysis of economic and social rights obligations follows.]

103. On 3 October 1991 Israel ratified both the International Covenant on Economic, Social and Cultural Rights . . . and the International Covenant on Civil and Political Rights . . . .

105. In [the Court's] Advisory Opinion of 8 July 1996 on the *Legality of the Threat or Use of Nuclear Weapons* . . . certain States had argued that "the Covenant was directed to the protection of human rights in peacetime, but that questions relating to unlawful loss of life in hostilities were governed by the law applicable in armed conflict". The Court rejected this argument, stating that:

> "the protection of the International Covenant of Civil and Political Rights does not cease in times of war, except by operation of Article 4 of the Covenant whereby certain provisions may be derogated from in a time of national emergency. Respect for the right to life is not, however, such a provision. In principle, the right not arbitrarily to be deprived of one's life applies also in hostilities. The test of what is an arbitrary deprivation of life, however, then falls to be determined by the applicable *lex specialis*, namely, the law applicable in armed conflict which is designed to regulate the conduct of hostilities."

106. More generally, the Court considers that the protection offered by human rights conventions does not cease in case of armed conflict, save through the effect

of provisions for derogation of the kind to be found in Article 4 of the International Covenant on Civil and Political Rights. As regards the relationship between international humanitarian law and human rights law, there are thus three possible situations: some rights may be exclusively matters of international humanitarian law; others may be exclusively matters of human rights law; yet others may be matters of both these branches of international law. In order to answer the question put to it, the Court will have to take into consideration both these branches of international law, namely human rights law and, as *lex specialis*, international humanitarian law.

[The Court concludes that the ICESCR and ICCPR apply outside national territory and cover individuals subject to a state's exercise of jurisdiction in occupied territory.]

112. . . . [T]he territories occupied by Israel have for over 37 years been subject to its territorial jurisdiction as the occupying Power. In the exercise of the powers available to it on this basis, Israel is bound by the provisions of the International Covenant on Economic, Social and Cultural Rights. Furthermore, it is under an obligation not to raise any obstacle to the exercise of such rights in those fields where competence has been transferred to Palestinian authorities.

. . .

127. The International Covenant on Civil and Political Rights . . . contains several relevant provisions. Before further examining these, the Court will observe that Article 4 of the Covenant allows for derogation to be made, under various conditions, to certain provisions of that instrument. Israel made use of its right of derogation under this Article by addressing [a] communication to the Secretary-General of the United Nations on 3 October 1991 . . . .

The Court notes that the derogation so notified concerns only Article 9 of the International Covenant on Civil and Political Rights, which deals with the right to liberty and security of person and lays down the rules applicable in cases of arrest or detention. The other Articles of the Covenant therefore remain applicable not only on Israeli territory, but also on the Occupied Palestinian Territory.

. . .

130. As regards the International Covenant on Economic, Social and Cultural Rights, that instrument includes a number of relevant provisions, namely: the right to work (Articles 6 and 7); protection and assistance accorded to the family and to children and young persons (Article 10); the right to an adequate standard of living, including adequate food, clothing and housing, and the right "to be free from hunger" (Art. 11); the right to health (Art. 12); the right to education (Arts. 13 and 14).

. . .

133. Th[e] construction [of the wall], the establishment of a closed area between the Green Line and the wall itself and the creation of enclaves have moreover imposed substantial restrictions on the freedom of movement of the inhabitants of the Occupied Palestinian Territory (with the exception of Israeli citizens and those assimilated thereto). Such restrictions are most marked in urban areas, such as the Qalqiliya enclave or the City of Jerusalem and its suburbs. They are aggravated by the fact that the access gates are few in number in certain sectors and opening hours appear to be restricted and unpredictably applied. For example, according to the

Special Rapporteur of the Commission on Human Rights on the situation of human rights in the Palestinian territories occupied by Israel since 1967, "Qalqiliya, a city with a population of 40,000, is completely surrounded by the Wall and residents can only enter and leave through a single military checkpoint open from 7 a.m. to 7 p.m." (Report of the Special Rapporteur of the Commission on Human Rights, John Dugard, on the situation of human rights in the Palestinian territories occupied by Israel since 1967, submitted in accordance with Commission resolution 1993/2 A and entitled "Question of the Violation of Human Rights in the Occupied Arab Territories, including Palestine", E/CN.4/2004/6, 8 September 2003, para. 9.)

There have also been serious repercussions for agricultural production, as is attested by a number of sources. According to the Special Committee to Investigate Israeli Practices Affecting the Human Rights of the Palestinian People and Other Arabs of the Occupied Territories

> "an estimated 100,000 dunums [approximately 10,000 hectares] of the West Bank's most fertile agricultural land, confiscated by the Israeli Occupation Forces, have been destroyed during the first phase of the wall construction, which involves the disappearance of vast amounts of property, notably private agricultural land and olive trees, wells, citrus grows and hothouses upon which tens of thousands of Palestinians rely for their survival" (Report of the Special Committee to Investigate Israeli Practices Affecting the Human Rights of the Palestinian People and Other Arabs of the Occupied Territories, A/58/311, 22 August 2003, para. 26).

Further, the Special Rapporteur on the situation of human rights in the Palestinian territories occupied by Israel since 1967 states that "Much of the Palestinian land on the Israeli side of the Wall consists of fertile agricultural land and some of the most important water wells in the region" and adds that "Many fruit and olive trees had been destroyed in the course of building the barrier." (E/CN.4/2004/6, 8 September 2003, para. 9.) The Special Rapporteur on the Right to Food of the United Nations Commission on Human Rights states that construction of the wall "cuts off Palestinians from their agricultural lands, wells and means of subsistence" (Report by the Special Rapporteur of the United Nations Commission on Human Rights, Jean Ziegler, "The Right to Food", Addendum, Mission to the Occupied Palestinian Territories, E/CN.4/2004/10/Add.2, 31 October 2003, para. 49). In a recent survey conducted by the World Food Programme, it is stated that the situation has aggravated food insecurity in the region, which reportedly numbers 25,000 new beneficiaries of food aid (report of the Secretary-General, para. 25).

It has further led to increasing difficulties for the population concerned regarding access to health services, educational establishments and primary sources of water. This is also attested by a number of different information sources. Thus the report of the Secretary-General states generally that "According to the Palestinian Central Bureau of Statistics, so far the Barrier has separated 30 localities from health services, 22 from schools, 8 from primary water sources and 3 from electricity networks." (Report of the Secretary-General, para. 23.) The Special Rapporteur of the United Nations Commission on Human Rights on the situation of human rights in the Palestinian territories occupied by Israel since 1967 states that "Palestinians between the Wall and Green Line will effectively be cut off from their land and workplaces, schools, health clinics and other social services." (E/CN.4/2004/6, 8 September 2003, para. 9.) In relation specifically to water resources, the Special Rapporteur on the Right to Food of the United Nations Commission on Human Rights observes that "By constructing the fence Israel will also effectively annex most of the western aquifer system (which provides 51 per cent of the West Bank's water resources)." (E/CN.4/2004/10/Add.2, 31 October 2003, para. 51.) Similarly, in regard to access to health services, it has been stated that, as a result of the enclosure of Qalqiliya, a United Nations hospital in that town has recorded a 40 per cent decrease in its caseload (report of the Secretary-General, para. 24).

At Qalqiliya, according to reports furnished to the United Nations, some 600 shops or businesses have shut down, and 6,000 to 8,000 people have already left the region (E/CN.4/2004/6, 8 September 2003, para. 10; E/CN.4/2004/10/Add.2, 31 October 2003, para. 51). The Special Rapporteur on the Right to Food of the United Nations Commission on Human Rights has also observed that "With the fence/wall cutting communities off from their land and water without other means of subsistence, many of the Palestinians living in these areas will be forced to leave." (E/CN.4/2004/10/Add.2, 31 October 2003, para. 51.) In this respect also the construction of the wall would effectively deprive a significant number of Palestinians of the "freedom to choose [their] residence". In addition, however, in the view of the Court, since a significant number of Palestinians have already been compelled by the construction of the wall and its associated régime to depart from certain areas, a process that will continue as more of the wall is built, that construction, coupled with the establishment of the Israeli settlements mentioned in paragraph 120 above, is tending to alter the demographic composition of the Occupied Palestinian Territory.

134. To sum up, the Court is of the opinion that the construction of the wall and its associated régime impede the liberty of movement of the inhabitants of the Occupied Palestinian Territory (with the exception of Israeli citizens and those assimilated thereto) as guaranteed under Article 12, paragraph 1, of the International Covenant on Civil and Political Rights. They also impede the exercise by the persons concerned of the right to work, to health, to education and to an adequate standard of living as proclaimed in the International Covenant on Economic, Social and Cultural Rights. . . .

136. The Court would further observe that some human rights conventions, and in particular the International Covenant on Civil and Political Rights, contain provisions which States parties may invoke in order to derogate, under various conditions, from certain of their conventional obligations. In this respect, the Court would however recall that the communication notified by Israel to the Secretary-General of the United Nations under Article 4 of the International Covenant on Civil and Political Rights concerns only Article 9 of the Covenant, relating to the right to freedom and security of person (see paragraph 127 above); Israel is accordingly bound to respect all the other provisions of that instrument.

The Court would note, moreover, that certain provisions of human rights conventions contain clauses qualifying the rights covered by those provisions. There is no clause of this kind in Article 17 of the International Covenant on Civil and Political Rights. On the other hand, Article 12, paragraph 3, of that instrument provides that restrictions on liberty of movement as guaranteed under that Article "shall not be subject to any restrictions except those which are provided by law, are necessary to protect national security, public order (*ordre public*), public health or morals or the rights and freedoms of others, and are consistent with the other rights recognized in the present Covenant". As for the International Covenant on Economic, Social and Cultural Rights, Article 4 thereof contains a general provision as follows:

> "The States Parties to the present Covenant recognize that, in the enjoyment of those rights provided by the State in conformity with the present Covenant, the State may subject such rights only to such limitations as are determined by law only in so far as this may be compatible with the nature of these rights and solely for the purpose of promoting the general welfare in a democratic society."

The Court would observe that the restrictions provided for under Article 12, paragraph 3, of the International Covenant on Civil and Political Rights are, by the very terms of that provision, exceptions to the right of freedom of movement contained in paragraph 1. In addition, it is not sufficient that such restrictions be directed to the ends authorized; they must also be necessary for the attainment of those ends. As the Human Rights Committee put it, they "must conform to the principle of proportionality" and "must be the least intrusive instrument amongst those which might achieve the desired result" (CCPR/C/21/Rev.1/Add.9, General Comment No. 27, para. 14). On the basis of the information available to it, the Court finds that these conditions are not met in the present instance.

The Court would further observe that the restrictions on the enjoyment by the Palestinians living in the territory occupied by Israel of their economic, social and cultural rights, resulting from Israel's construction of the wall, fail to meet a condition laid down by Article 4 of the International Covenant on Economic, Social and Cultural Rights, that is to say that their implementation must be "solely for the purpose of promoting the general welfare in a democratic society".

137. To sum up, the Court, from the material available to it, is not convinced that the specific course Israel has chosen for the wall was necessary to attain its security objectives. The wall, along the route chosen, and its associated régime gravely infringe a number of rights of Palestinians residing in the territory occupied by Israel, and the infringements resulting from that route cannot be justified by military exigencies or by the requirements of national security or public order. The construction of such a wall accordingly constitutes breaches by Israel of various of its obligations under the applicable international humanitarian law and human rights instruments.

...

140. The Court has, however, considered whether Israel could rely on a state of necessity which would preclude the wrongfulness of the construction of the wall. In this regard the Court is bound to note that some of the conventions at issue in the present instance include qualifying clauses of the rights guaranteed or provisions for derogation (see paragraphs 135 and 136 above). Since those treaties already address considerations of this kind within their own provisions, it might be asked whether a state of necessity as recognized in customary international law could be invoked with regard to those treaties as a ground for precluding the wrongfulness of the measures or decisions being challenged. However, the Court will not need to

consider that question. As the Court observed in the case concerning the *Gabčíkovo-Nagymaros Project (Hungary/Slovakia)*, "the state of necessity is a ground recognized by customary international law" that "can only be accepted on an exceptional basis"; it "can only be invoked under certain strictly defined conditions which must be cumulatively satisfied; and the State concerned is not the sole judge of whether those conditions have been met" (*I.C.J. Reports 1997*, p. 40, para. 51). One of those conditions was stated by the Court in terms used by the International Law Commission, in a text which in its present form requires that the act being challenged be "the only way for the State to safeguard an essential interest against a grave and imminent peril" (Article 25 of the International Law Commission's Articles on Responsibility of States for Internationally Wrongful Acts; see also former Article 33 of the Draft Articles on the International Responsibility of States, with slightly different wording in the English text). In the light of the material before it, the Court is not convinced that the construction of the wall along the route chosen was the only means to safeguard the interests of Israel against the peril which it has invoked as justification for that construction.

141. The fact remains that Israel has to face numerous indiscriminate and deadly acts of violence against its civilian population. It has the right, and indeed the duty, to respond in order to protect the life of its citizens. The measures taken are bound nonetheless to remain in conformity with applicable international law.

Separate opinion of Judge Kooijmans

13. Although the Court certainly has taken into account the arguments put forward by Israel and has dealt with them in a considerate manner, I am of the view that the present Opinion could have reflected in a more satisfactory way the interests at stake for all those living in the region. The rather oblique references to terrorist acts which can be found at several places in the Opinion, are in my view not sufficient for this purpose. . . .

. . .

34. Proportionality — The Court finds that the conditions set out in the qualifying clauses in the applicable humanitarian law and human rights conventions have not been met and that the measures taken by Israel cannot be justified by military exigencies or by requirements of national security or public order (paras. 135–137). I agree with that finding but in my opinion the construction of the wall should also have been put to the proportionality test, in particular since the concepts of military necessity and proportionality have always been intimately linked in international humanitarian law. And in my view it is of decisive importance that, even if the construction of the wall and its associated régime could be justified as measures necessary to protect the legitimate rights of Israeli citizens, these measures would not pass the proportionality test. The route chosen for the construction of the wall and the ensuing disturbing consequences for the inhabitants of the Occupied Palestinian Territory are manifestly disproportionate to interests which Israel seeks to protect, as seems to be recognized also in recent decisions of the Israeli Supreme Court.

Declaration of Judge Buergenthal

1. Since I believe that the Court should have exercised its discretion and declined to render the requested advisory opinion, I dissent from its decision to hear the case. . . . I am compelled to vote against the Court's findings on the merits because the Court did not have before it the requisite factual bases for its sweeping findings; it should therefore have declined to hear the case. . . .

2. I share the Court's conclusion that international humanitarian law, including the Fourth Geneva Convention, and international human rights law are applicable to the Occupied Palestinian Territory and must there[fore] be faithfully complied with by Israel. I accept that the wall is causing deplorable suffering to many Palestinians living in that territory. In this connection, I agree that the means used to defend against terrorism must conform to all applicable rules of international law and that a State which is the victim of terrorism may not defend itself against this scourge by resorting to measures international law prohibits.

3. . . . The nature of these cross-Green Line attacks and their impact on Israel and its population are never really seriously examined by the Court, and the dossier provided the Court by the United Nations on which the Court to a large extent bases its findings barely touches on that subject. I am not suggesting that such an examination would relieve Israel of the charge that the wall it is building violates international law, either in whole or in part, only that without this examination the findings made are not legally well founded. In my view, the humanitarian needs of the Palestinian people would have been better served had the Court taken these considerations into account, for that would have given the Opinion the credibility I believe it lacks.

. . .

7. In summarizing its finding that the wall violates international humanitarian law and international human rights law, the Court has the following to say: [Judge Buergenthal repeats paragraph 137 of the majority opinion.]

The Court supports this conclusion with extensive quotations of the relevant legal provisions and with evidence that relates to the suffering the wall has caused along some parts of its route. But in reaching this conclusion, the Court fails to address any facts or evidence specifically rebutting Israel's claim of military exigencies or requirements of national security. It is true that in dealing with this subject the Court asserts that it draws on the factual summaries provided by the United Nations Secretary-General as well as some other United Nations reports. It is equally true, however, that the Court barely addresses the summaries of Israel's position on this subject that are attached to the Secretary-General's report and which contradict or cast doubt on the material the Court claims to rely on. Instead, all we have from the Court is a description of the harm the wall is causing and a discussion of various provisions of international humanitarian law and human rights instruments followed by the conclusion that this law has been violated. Lacking is an examination of the facts that might show why the alleged defences of military exigencies, national security or public order are not applicable to the wall as a whole or to the individual segments of its route. The Court says that it "is not convinced" but it fails to demonstrate why it is not convinced, and that is why these conclusions are not convincing.

. . .

9. . . . [G]iven the demonstrable great hardship to which the affected Palestinian population is being subjected in and around the enclaves created by those segments of the wall, I seriously doubt that the wall would here satisfy the proportionality requirement to qualify as a legitimate measure of self-defence.

NOTE

In July 2004, the General Assembly voted (150–6 with 10 abstentions) to endorse the ICJ Opinion and 'demand[] that Israel, the occupying Power, comply with its legal obligations as mentioned in the advisory opinion'. A/RES/ES-10/15.

In 2005, the Supreme Court of Israel issued a second decision involving a different segment of the barrier. The Court nullified this segment as well. In its earlier decision, *Beit Sourik v. Israel*, the Court held that the incremental security benefit of a particular route did not outweigh the injury to the Palestinian population. In the 2005 case, the Court held that the chosen route failed a different part of its proportionality analysis. The Government failed to establish that a route less harmful to the Palestinians would have provided less security than the existing route. In other words, a less restrictive means (without compromising security) was potentially available. The Court avoided what it considered the most difficult question of all:

> And what will be the case if examination of the alternative route leads to the conclusion that the only route which provides the minimum required security is the existing route? Without it, there is no security for the Israelis. With it, there [is] a severe injury to the fabric of life of the residents of the villages. What will the case be in such a situation ('absolute' implementation of narrow proportionality: *see The Beit Sourik Case*)? That is the most difficult of the questions. We were not confronted with it in *The Beit Sourik Case*, since we found that there was an alternative which provides security to Israelis. How shall we solve this difficulty in the case before us? It seems to us that the time has not yet come to confront this difficulty, and the time may never come.[38]

QUESTIONS

1. In a separate opinion in the ICJ case, Judge (now ICJ President) Rosalyn Higgins admitted, 'So far as the International Covenant on Economic, Social and Cultural Rights is concerned, the situation is even stranger, given the programmatic requirements for the fulfilment of this category of rights'. Did the ICJ correctly employ the framework for analyzing economic and social rights, including limitation clauses, under the Covenant? Does the Covenant contemplate that its rights provisions can impose such stiff obligations on a state especially in the context of a military occupation?

[38] *Mara'abe v. The Prime Minister of Israel*, Israeli High Court of Justice 7957/04 (2005).

Relatedly, does the nature of these rights (or the structure of the Covenant) suggest that they are not applicable to situations of armed conflict and military occupation? Recall the commentary from G.I.A.D. Draper above. Another commentator writes specifically with respect to the ICJ opinion: 'The fact that [derogation] provisions are absent [in the CESCR] is itself indicative of the fact that they were not intended to apply to occupation situations or in times of armed conflict'. He also contends that for specific economic and social rights, such as education,

> greater interference with the education system of the sort described in some parts of the human rights instruments would be assuming the longer term rights of a sovereign, thereby overstepping occupation authority and thereby appearing 'annexationist'.... [T]here is no aspect of the human rights instruments' provisions cited by the Court that has not been excluded by the *lex specialis* provisions of the IHL instruments. The Court's recourse to these provisions was therefore wrong in law and it should have confined itself to an analysis of the adherence by Israel to the relevant IHL.[39]

2. Did the ICJ adequately consider Israel's security concerns? What reasons might justify not delving into a deeper inquiry of the countervailing security interests? Is there a category of governmental actions, or impact on civilian lives, for which no plausible security rationale could be provided? If so, do the actions in this case rise to that level?

In a separate opinion, Judge Owada criticized the majority opinion: 'an in-depth effort could have been made by the Court, *proprio motu*, to ascertain the validity of this [security] argument on the basis of facts and law, and to present an objective picture surrounding the construction of the wall in its entirety, on the basis of which to assess the merits of the contention of Israel'. Yet Judge Owada also remarked that 'the political, social, economic and humanitarian impacts of the construction of the wall... are so overwhelming that I am ready to accept that no justification based on the "military exigencies", even if fortified by substantiated facts, could conceivably constitute a valid basis for precluding the wrongfulness of the act on the basis of the stringent conditions of proportionality'.

In balancing security objectives with human rights concerns, consider the following data presented in the Israeli Supreme Court's more recent decision:

> [A]ccording to the figures of the General Security Service, in the (approximately) 34 months between the outbreak of the armed conflict and until the completion of the first part of the separation fence, the terrorist infrastructure committed 73 mass murder attacks in the Samaria area, in which 293 Israelis were killed, and 1950 injured. Since the completion of the separation fence — that is, the year between August 2003 and August 2004 — the terrorist infrastructure succeeded in committing five mass murder attacks, in which 28 Israelis were killed and 81 injured. Comparison between the year prior to commencement of work on the separation fence (September 2001–July 2002) and the year after construction of the fence (August 2003–2004) indicates an 84% drop in the number of killed and a 92% drop in the number of wounded.

[39] Michael J. Kelly, 'Critical Analysis of the International Court of Justice Ruling on Israel's Security Barrier', 29 Fordham Int. L. J. 181 (2005).

3. Would the CESCR have been better designed with a derogation system similar to Article 4 of the ICCPR? How would you craft derogation rules for economic and social rights? Consider the following:

> [T]he lack of a derogation provision is an appropriate omission in the Covenant because the very nature of economic, social and cultural rights does not allow for the kind of derogation contemplated in civil and political rights instruments. It is important to bear in mind that the rationale for derogation provisions is to strike a balance between the sovereign right of a government to maintain peace and order during public emergencies, and the protection of the rights of the individual from abuse by the State.... [I]t seems difficult to imagine a circumstance in which derogation from the rights contained in the ICESCR would be necessary to maintain peace and order from the perspective of human rights law. For example, it is difficult to see how derogation from the right to food . . . would assist in resolving a conflict situation rather than worsening it.[40]

Professor Walter Kälin, who served as UN Special Rapporteur on the situation of human rights in Kuwait under Iraqi occupation, writes,

> There are good reasons for [the lack of a derogation provision]: Guarantees like the rights to food, housing or health constitute, in their core, subsistence-rights and therefore help to secure survival in times of armed conflict. The Committee on Economic, Social and Cultural Rights has recognized the existence of 'a minimum core obligation to ensure the satisfaction of . . . minimum essential levels of each rights'.

Does the absence of a derogation clause indicate that a state's obligations under the Covenant are nonderogable? On the contrary, should obligations be presumed derogable unless an express treaty provision stipulates otherwise? In other words, what is the correct presumption if the treaty text is silent on the matter? Consider our earlier discussion of the Vienna Convention on the Law of Treaties, which provides that a state can suspend its treaty obligations due to a 'fundamental change in circumstances'. Also recall our discussion of international legal doctrine involving 'circumstances precluding wrongfulness'. Would those rules apply to the CESCR?

ADDITIONAL READING

Michael J. Dennis, 'Application of Human Rights Treaties Extraterritorially in Times of Armed Conflict and Military Occupation', 99 Am. J. Int. L. 119 (2005); Jelena Pejic, 'The Right to Food in Situations of Armed Conflict: The Legal Framework', 844 International Review of the Red Cross 1097 (2001); Phillip Alston and Gerard Quinn, 'The Nature and Scope of States Parties' Obligations under the International Covenant on Economic, Social, and Cultural Rights', 9 Hum. R. Q. 156 (1987).

[40] M. Magdalena Sepulveda, *The Nature of the Obligations under the International Covenant on Economic, Social and Cultural Rights* (2003), Ch. VI, ß 3.4

PART C

RIGHTS, DUTIES AND DILEMMAS OF UNIVERSALISM

The preceding chapters surely conveyed no sense of a uniform, coherent, uncontested human rights movement. From the controversies over capital punishment in Chapter 1, the dispute over permitted methods for interrogating prisoners in Chapter 3, the implementation of economic and social rights in Chapter 4, and the issues of national security in Chapter 5, we have seen major differences in understandings of human rights both among legal orders of different states and within states. Such contests and struggles within and about the human rights movement can be contrasted with conduct (police brutality, summary executions, racial discrimination, sham trials, coerced religious practice) that the vast majority of states throughout the world view as violations of universally accepted human rights norms.

Part C concentrates on notions of rights and of contests and disputes about them, exploring the very idea of rights more systematically than did the prior materials. Chapter 6 examines the nature of rights and rights discourse, and the character and consequences of duty-oriented rather than rights-oriented social systems. Chapter 7 begins with exploration of the opposition between universalism and cultural relativism in one's understanding of the character of the human rights movement. Theoretical writings introduce these notions, followed by illustrative case studies.

6

Rights or Duties as Organizing Concepts

Thus far the materials have described but barely commented on the fundamental characteristic of the UDHR and ICCPR, their foundation in the rhetoric and concept of *rights*. Many view that rhetoric as unproblematic, as the central and inevitable component of a universal discourse about human dignity and humane treatment of individuals by governments. Others, to the contrary, view a discourse about rights as alien and harmful to their states or cultures, disruptive of traditional social structures, subversive of authority. Consider the following queries:

(1) Why does the language of rights dominate the texts of the declarations and treaties as well as, in many states, the new constitutions and even the slogans and polemics of political debate?

(2) Is that language intrinsically superior to other possible ones — for example, the language of duties that might lead to a Universal Declaration of Human Duties, or the language and methods of utility? Is rights language essential to the values and goals of the human rights movement? Or is the currency of that language a matter of historical contingency, in that the postwar movement to protect human dignity found its roots in liberal political cultures in which rights had long ago taken root.

(3) Does a particular substantive content necessarily attach to the language of rights? For example, do 'rights' necessarily express the principles of the liberal political tradition, as with respect to nondiscrimination, or fair procedures, or freedom of religion or speech? Are the same questions as relevant to the language of duties? Are either rights or duties empty receptacles that are open to many different types of values and ideas, some of which might be antagonistic to the liberal tradition?

(4) Universality informs the discourse and content of rights in the UDHR and the basic treaties. But why should we accept that the stated norms are universal? Are arguments about their universal character accepted worldwide? Or do some parts of the world view many important provisions in the basic human rights instruments as particular to the Western liberal tradition, hence inapplicable to radically different states and cultures? Would the same criticism be as applicable to a duty-based Universal Declaration?

A. IDEAS ABOUT RIGHTS AND THE EFFECTS OF RIGHTS RHETORIC

We here consider different understandings, historical and contemporary, of the notion of 'rights' and inquire whether rights have inherent implications for a society's moral, political and socio-economic order. For example, does rights rhetoric in a constitution and statutes, or in a dominant moral and political theory, point to an individualistic, communitarian, or other type of society? Does it necessarily assume certain institutional arrangements for government, such as a constitutional separation of powers and an independent judiciary?

The readings begin with a brief description of the evolution from earlier concepts of natural law and natural rights to contemporary notions of rights in domestic and international contexts.

BURNS WESTON, HUMAN RIGHTS

20 New Encyclopedia Britannica (15th edn. 1992)

. . .

The expression 'human rights' is relatively new, having come into everyday parlance only since World War II and the founding of the United Nations in 1945. It replaces the phrase 'natural rights', which fell into disfavour in part because the concept of natural law (to which it was intimately linked) had become a matter of great controversy, and the later phrase 'the rights of Man' . . .

. . .

It was primarily for the 17th and 18th centuries, however, to elaborate upon this modernist conception of natural law as meaning or implying natural rights. The scientific and intellectual achievements of the 17th century . . . encouraged a belief in natural law and universal order; and during the 18th century, the so-called Age of Enlightenment, a growing confidence in human reason and in the perfectability of human affairs led to its more comprehensive expression. Particularly to be noted are the writings of the 17th-century English philosopher John Locke — arguably the most important natural law theorist of modern times — and the works of the 18th-century Philosophes centred mainly in Paris, including Montesquieu, Voltaire, and Jean-Jacques Rousseau. Locke argued in detail, mainly in writings associated with the Revolution of 1688 (the Glorious Revolution), that certain rights self-evidently pertain to individuals as human beings (because they existed in 'the state of nature' before humankind entered civil society); that chief among them are the rights to life, liberty (freedom from arbitrary rule), and property; that, upon entering civil society (pursuant to a 'social contract'), humankind surrendered to the state only the right to enforce these natural rights, not the rights themselves; and that the state's failure to secure these reserved natural rights (the state itself being under contract to safeguard the interests of its members) gives rise to a right to responsible, popular revolution. The Philosophes, building on Locke and others and embracing many and varied currents of thought with a common supreme faith in reason, vigorously attacked religious and scientific dogmatism, intolerance, censorship, and social-economic restraints. They sought to discover and act upon universally valid principles harmoniously governing nature, humanity, and society, including the theory of the inalienable 'rights of Man' that became their fundamental ethical and social gospel.

All this liberal intellectual ferment had, not surprisingly, great influence on the Western world of the late 18th and early 19th centuries. Together with the practical example of England's Revolution of 1688 and the resulting Bill of Rights, it provided the rationale for the wave of revolutionary agitation that then swept the West, most notably in North America and France. Thomas Jefferson, who had studied Locke and Montesquieu and who asserted that his countrymen were a 'free people claiming their rights as derived from the laws of nature and not as the gift of their Chief Magistrate', gave poetic eloquence to the plain prose of the 17th century in the Declaration of Independence proclaimed by the 13 American Colonies on July 4, 1776: 'We hold these truths to be self-evident, that all men are created equal, that they are endowed by their Creator with certain unalienable Rights, that among these are Life, Liberty and the Pursuit of Happiness'. Similarly, the Marquis de Lafayette . . . imitated the pronouncements of the English and American revolutions in the [French] Declaration of the Rights of Man and of the Citizen of August 26, 1789. Insisting that 'men are born and remain free and equal in rights', the declaration proclaims that 'the aim of every political association is the preservation of the natural and imprescriptible rights of man', identifies these rights as 'Liberty, Property, Safety and Resistance to Oppression', and defines 'liberty' so as to include the right to free speech, freedom of association, religious freedom, and freedom from arbitrary arrest and confinement (as if anticipating the Bill of Rights added in 1791 to the Constitution of the United States of 1787).

In sum, the idea of human rights, called by another name, played a key role in the late 18th- and early 19th-century struggles against political absolutism. It was, indeed, the failure of rulers to respect the principles of freedom and equality, which had been central to natural law philosophy almost from the beginning, that was responsible for this development . . .

. . . [B]ecause they were conceived in essentially absolutist — 'inalienable', 'unalterable', 'eternal' — terms, natural rights were found increasingly to come into conflict with one another. Most importantly, the doctrine of natural rights came under powerful philosophical and political attack from both the right and the left.

In England, for example, conservatives Edmund Burke and David Hume united with liberal Jeremy Bentham in condemning the doctrine, the former out of fear that public affirmation of natural rights would lead to social upheaval, the latter out of concern lest declarations and proclamations of natural rights substitute for effective legislation. In his *Reflections on the Revolution in France* (1790), Burke, a believer in natural law who nonetheless denied that the 'rights of Man' could be derived from it, criticized the drafters of the Declaration of the Rights of Man and of the Citizen for proclaiming the 'monstrous fiction' of human equality, which, he argued, serves but to inspire 'false ideas and vain expectations in men destined to travel in the obscure walk of laborious life'. Bentham, one of the founders of Utilitarianism and a nonbeliever, was no less scornful. 'Rights', he wrote, 'is the child of law; from real law come real rights; but from imaginary laws, from "law of nature", come imaginary rights.... Natural rights is simple nonsense; natural and imprescriptible rights (an American phrase), rhetorical nonsense, nonsense upon stilts'. Hume agreed with Bentham: natural law and natural rights, he insisted, are unreal metaphysical phenomena.

This assault upon natural law and natural rights, thus begun during the late 18th century, both intensified and broadened during the 19th and early 20th centuries. John Stuart Mill, despite his vigorous defense of liberty, proclaimed that rights ultimately are founded on utility. The German jurist Friedrich Karl von Savigny, England's Sir Henry Maine, and other historicalists emphasized that rights are a function of cultural and environmental variables unique to particular communities. And the jurist John Austin and the philosopher Ludwig Wittgenstein insisted, respectively, that the only law is 'the command of the sovereign' (a phrase of Thomas Hobbes) and that the only truth is that which can be established by verifiable experience. By World War I, there were scarcely any theorists who would or could defend the 'rights of Man' along the lines of natural law....

Yet, though the heyday of natural rights proved short, the idea of human rights nonetheless endured in one form or another. The abolition of slavery, factory legislation, popular education, trade unionism, the universal suffrage movement — these and other examples of 19th-century reformist impulse afford ample evidence that the idea was not to be extinguished even if its transempirical derivation had become a matter of general skepticism. But it was not until the rise and fall of Nazi Germany that the idea of rights — human rights — came truly into its own....

...

To say that there is widespread acceptance of the principle of human rights on the domestic and international planes is not to say that there is complete agreement about the nature of such rights or their substantive scope — which is to say, their definition. Some of the most basic questions have yet to receive conclusive answers. Whether human rights are to be viewed as divine, moral, or legal entitlements; whether they are to be validated by intuition, custom, social contract theory, principles of distributive justice, or as prerequisites for happiness; whether they are to be understood as irrevocable or partially revocable; whether they are to be broad or limited in number and content — these and kindred issues are matters of ongoing debate and likely will remain so as long as there exist contending approaches to public order and scarcities among resources.

...

NOTE

In 'Contemporary Reinterpretations of the Concept of Human Rights', (in David Sidorsky (ed.), *Essays on Human Rights* (1979)), Sidorsky observes:

> ... [A] major characterization of natural rights derived from [the] belief that rights are the properties of persons capable of exercising rational choice. For, when men

> asserted their natural rights they were expressing their autonomy as individuals. Hence, the model or pattern for the exercise of natural rights became the protection of the sphere of the autonomous individual from arbitrary incursion by the state or other coercive association. The listing of the right to life, for example, did not involve a commitment to the extension or universalization of health care or to actions for shaping a safer environment but to a rule of law that would restrain arbitrary acts of violence, especially those of governmental authorities, against individuals. Similarly, the natural right to liberty did not refer to support of policies that would enhance self-realization through the universalization of education, but it did require the legal protection of individuals against arbitrary imprisonment.

Sidorsky illustrates his remarks by referring to health care and education, and seems to be broadly contrasting civil-political and economic-social rights. Recall that from the start, the canonical texts of the international human rights movement gave these two bodies of rights a formal equal significance.

❁ ❁ ❁

The following readings describe their authors' understandings of basic characteristics of rights in contemporary legal and political discourse and argument. The brief excerpt from Eugene Kamenka distinguishes claims of rights from other types of claims, taking a positivist position about rights. Duncan Kennedy analyzes rights discourse as it has evolved in a liberal political culture such as the United States. He is thus more attentive to the role of rights in adjudication than are most of the materials in this coursebook, which examine rights discourse in the framework not only of judicial opinions but also of broader political processes — advocacy and speeches, UN resolutions, committee reports, investigative missions, scholarly writings and so on. Nonetheless, the analysis and critique of rights in Kennedy's book inform rights discourse throughout the international human rights movement as well. In two readings that follow, Cass Sunstein and Karl Klare respond in different ways to aspects of the broad 'critique of rights' that schools of thought and groups throughout the world have developed over recent decades. David Kennedy raises underlying questions about contradictions within the human rights movement, the socio-economic and political consequences of rights-based advocacy, and arguments for and against a rights-based strategy for achieving reform.

Ideas in these readings are central to grasping the special characteristics, strengths and weaknesses of a movement based on rights, whether rights language figures in broad political debates or in the opinions of courts. They bear importantly on the discussion of cultural relativism in Chapter 7.

EUGENE KAMENKA, HUMAN RIGHTS, PEOPLES' RIGHTS

in James Crawford (ed.), The Rights of Peoples (1988), at 127

Rights are claims that have achieved a special kind of endorsement or success: legal rights by a legal system; human rights by widespread sentiment or an international order. All rights arise in specific historical circumstances. They are claims made, conceded or granted by people who are themselves historically and socially shaped. They are asserted by people on their own behalf or as perceived and endorsed implications of specific historical traditions, institutions and arrangements or of a historically conditioned theory of human needs and human aspirations, or of a human conception of a Divine plan and purpose. In objective fact as opposed to (some) subjective feeling, they are neither eternal nor inalienable, neither prior to society or societies nor independent of them. Some such rights can be singled out, and they often are singled out, as social ideals, as goals to strive toward. But even as such, they cannot be divorced from social content and context.

Claims presented as rights are claims that are often, perhaps usually, presented as having a special kind of importance, urgency, universality, or endorsement that makes them more than disparate or simply subjective demands. Their success is dependent on such endorsement — by a government or a legal system that has power to grant and protect such rights, by a tradition or institution whose authority is accepted in those circles that recognize these claims as rights, by widespread social sentiment, regionally, nationally, or internationally.

Claims, whether presented as rights or not, conflict. So do the traditions, institutions and authorities that endorse the claim as a right. They conflict both with each other and, often, in their internal structure, implications and working out....

The concept of human rights is no longer tied to belief in God or natural law in its classical sense. But it still seeks or claims a form of endorsement that transcends or pretends to transcend specific historical institutions and traditions, legal systems, governments, or national and even regional communities. Like moral claims more generally, it asserts in its own behalf moral and sometimes even logical priority — connection with the very concept (treated as morally loaded) of what it means to be a human being or a person, or of what it means to behave morally. These are questions on which moral philosophers do have a certain expertise, at least in seeing where the difficulties lie, and on which they, like ordinary people throughout the world, have long disagreed and continue to disagree.

NOTE

Compare the following remarks of Norberto Bobbio, in *The Age of Rights* (trans. Allan Cameron) (1996), at p. 18:

> My theoretical approach has always been . . . that human rights however fundamental are historical rights and therefore arise from specific conditions characterized by the embattled defence of new freedoms against old powers. . . . Religious freedom resulted from the religious wars, civil liberties from the parliamentarian struggles against absolutism, and political and social freedoms from the birth, growth and experience of movements representing workers, landless peasants and smallholders....
>
> . . .

... The expression rights of man is certain emphatic, and even if that emphasis is expedient, it can be misleading because it implies that there are rights belonging to an abstract man and thus removed from the historical context, and that by contemplating this essential and eternal man we can arrive at the certain knowledge of his rights and duties. Today we know that the so-called human rights are the product of human civilization and not nature, because historical rights are changeable and therefore susceptible to transformation and growth. It is sufficient to look at the writings of the early advocates of natural law to realize how the list of rights has been getting longer and longer. Indeed Hobbes only recognized one right, the right to life.... If someone had told Locke, the champion of the rights to liberty, that all citizens should have the right to participate in politics, or even worse that they had the right to paid employment, he would have called it madness....

The rights listed in the [Universal] Declaration ... are the rights of a historical man as perceived by those who drew up the Declaration following the tragedy of the Second World War, in an époque which commenced with the French Revolution and included the Soviet Revolution....

DUNCAN KENNEDY, A CRITIQUE OF ADJUDICATION
(1997), at 305

[Kennedy, a leading scholar in the critical legal studies movement that started in the United States and spread to other countries, devotes part of his book to the examination and critique of rights. He is not directly concerned with the substance of rights — for example, whether a right to free speech should have broader or narrower boundaries — but rather with the discourse of rights itself, with the way in which advocates and courts argue and reason about rights. Thus Kennedy examines matters such as the assumptions made by courts and advocates about rights, the distinctive characteristics of rights rhetoric, and the types of reasoning (legal and other) that are explicitly or implicitly involved in the interpretation, elaboration and application of rights to given cases or contexts.

These ideas, although rooted in this book in the American experience, bear directly on rights discourse in the international human rights movement. The ideas below figure in the responses by Karl Klare and Cass Sunstein to criticism of rights and rights rhetoric that appear in the next following materials.

Kennedy notes that rights 'play a central role in the American mode of political discourse'. He describes rights as 'mediators' between two elements or domains in that discourse: *value judgments*, which he describes as matters of preference, related to subjectivity of views and to 'philosophical' premises; and *factual judgments* (also referred to as *factoid*) that represent the domain of the scientific, the empirical, objective judgments.

Excerpts from the chapters on rights follow.]

... [I]t seems to me that in American political discourse [the ways of understanding the nature of rights] all presuppose a basic distinction between rights argument and other kinds of normative argument. The point of an appeal to a right, the reason for making it, is that it *can't be reduced* to a mere 'value judgment' that one outcome is better than another. Yet it is possible to make rights arguments about matters that fall outside the domain commonly understood as factual, that is, about political or policy questions of how the government ought to act. In other words, rights are mediators between the domain of pure value judgments and the domain of factual judgments.

The word 'mediation' here means that reasoning from the right is understood to have properties from both sides of the divide: 'value' as in value judgment, but 'reasoning' as in 'logic', with the possibility of correctness. Rights reasoning, in short, allows you to be right about your value judgments, rather than just stating 'preferences', as in 'I prefer chocolate to vanilla ice cream'. The mediation is possible because rights are understood to have two crucial properties.

First, they are 'universal' in the sense that they derive from needs or values or preferences that every person shares or ought to share. For this reason, everyone does or ought to agree that they are desirable. This is the first aspect of rights as mediators: they follow from values but are neither arbitrary nor subjective because they are universal.

Second, they are 'factoid', in the sense that 'once you acknowledge the existence of the right, then you have to agree that its observance *requires x, y*, and *z*'. For example, everyone recognizes that the statement 'be good' is too vague to help resolve concrete conflicts, even though it is universal. But once we have derived a *right* from universal needs or values, it is understood to be possible to have a relatively objective, rational, determinate discussion of how it ought to be instantiated in social or legal rules.

...

I pointed out [earlier] that rights occupy an ambiguous status with respect to the distinction between rules and reasons for rules. 'Congress shall make no law abridging the freedom of speech' is an enacted rule of the legal system, but 'protecting freedom of speech' is a reason for adopting a rule, or for choosing one interpretation of a rule over another. In this second usage, the right is understood to be something that is outside and preexists legal reasoning.

The outside right is something that a person has even if the legal order doesn't recognize it and even if 'exercising' it is illegal. 'I have the right to engage in homosexual intercourse, even if it is forbidden by the sodomy statutes of every government in the universe'. Or 'slavery denies the right to personal freedom, which exists in spite of and above the law of slave states'.

The Constitution, and state and federal statutes, legalize some highly abstract outside rights, such as the right of free speech in the First Amendment or of property in the Fourteenth. Positive law also legalizes less abstract rights that are understood to derive from more abstract, but not enacted, outside rights....

...

[Kennedy observes that these 'outside' rights, which preexist any incorporation of them into law (for example, the right not to be tortured by state officials exists whether or not the formal legal system incorporates it and thus makes it a 'legal' right), can be analogized to 'natural rights' in classical liberal political theory.

When a party to litigation makes a legal claim of right, other factors come into play, such as the 'duty of interpretive fidelity' of judges who are bound by the legal formulation of the right and have a duty to be faithful to it in their interpretation and application. The adjudication of constitutional rights brings all these problems together. When incorporated in a constitution, such as the First Amendment to the United States Constitution, constitutional rights 'are both legal rights embedded in and formed by legal argumentative practice (legal rules) and entities that "exist" prior to and outside the constitution'. Thus argument based on constitutional rights involves both 'legal argument (under a duty of interpretive fidelity) and legislative argument (appealing to the political values of the community)'. By 'legislative argument', Kennedy refers to the broad range of arguments based on preferences, values, and policies that are characteristically advanced by opposing parties and interests within the legislative political process.

Kennedy then discusses legal rights in legal reasoning. He notes that rights arguments 'are open to the same analysis of open texture of indeterminacy as legal argument in general'. He describes one of the ways in which the critique of legal rights collapses the distinction between rights-based argument and policy argument in general. For example, suppose that a claimant appeals to the right to free speech to urge a court to interpret some rule in a way that protects free speech. The court will frequently 'balance' the conflicting claims, perhaps the right to free speech and (with respect to sexually abusive speech in the workplace) the other party's right to a nonabusive workplace. What determines the balance struck by the court is not any logical chain of reasoning from the asserted right, or from two asserted conflicting rights, but the court's 'considering obviously open-textured arguments from morality, social welfare, expectations, and institutional competence and administrability'.]

The upshot, when both sides are well represented, is that the advocates confront the judge with two plausible but contradictory chains of rights reasoning, one proceeding from the plaintiff's rights and the other from the defendant's. Yes, the employer has property rights, but the picketers have free-speech rights. Yes, the harasser has free-speech rights, but the harassed has a right to be free of sex discrimination in the workplace. Yes, the landowner has the right to do whatever he wants on his land, but his neighbor has a right to be free from unreasonable interference. And each chain is open to an internal critique.

Sometimes the judge more or less arbitrarily endorses one side over the other; sometimes she throws in the towel and balances. The lesson of practice for the doubter is that the question involved cannot be resolved without resort to policy, which in turn makes the resolution open to ideological influence. The critique of legal rights reasoning becomes just a special case of the general critique of policy argument: once it is shown that the case requires a balancing of conflicting rights claims, it is implausible that it is the rights themselves, rather than the 'subjective' or 'political' commitments of the judges, that are deciding the outcome.

. . .

People sometimes say, 'A critique of rights? But if you got rid of rights, then the state could do anything it wanted to you! What about the right of privacy? We wouldn't have any way to object to state intrusion!' They are just missing the point!

In the Western democracies, rights 'exist' in the sense that there are legal rules limiting what people can do to one another and limiting the executive and the legislature. The critique of rights recognizes the reality of rule-making, rule-following, and rule-enforcing behavior. It is about faith in the rational procedures through which legislators, adjudicators, or enforcers elaborate gaps, conflicts, and ambiguities in the 'text' of inside or outside rights.

There is nothing in the critique that might suggest a reduction in the rights of citizens vis-à-vis their governments. Having lost one's faith in rights discourse is perfectly consistent with, indeed often associated with, a passionate belief in radical expansion of citizen rights against the state. Moreover, loss of faith is consistent with advocacy of greatly increased tenant rights in dealings with landlords, as well as with the reverse, just as it is consistent with favoring more or less government control over abortion decisions. It is not about the question of how we ought to define rights but rather about how we should *feel about the discourse in which we claim them.*

...

CASS R. SUNSTEIN, RIGHTS AND THEIR CRITICS

70 Notre Dame L. Rev. 727 (1995), at 730

[This article, though written with respect to ongoing debate about rights in the United States, bears also on the international discourse of rights. The author develops six different categories of charges against rights drawn from judicial opinions and from critics. Excerpts follow.]

B. The Rigidity of Rights

Other critics charge that rights have a strident and absolutist character, and that for this reason they impoverish political discourse. Rights do not admit of compromise. They do not allow room for competing considerations. For this reason, they impair and even foreclose deliberation over complex issues not realistically soluble by simple formulas.

Rooted in nineteenth-century ideas of absolute sovereignty over property, rights are said to be ill-adapted to what we usually need, that is, a careful discussion of trade-offs and competing concerns. If rights are (in Ronald Dworkin's suggestive and influential phrase, criticized below) 'trumps', they are for that very reason harmful to the difficult process of accommodating different goals and considerations in resolving such thorny problems as abortion, the environment, and plant closings.

C. Indeterminacy

In one of his greatest aphorisms, Justice Holmes wrote that '[g]eneral propositions do not decide concrete cases'. Rights, of course, take the form of general propositions. For this reason they are said to be indeterminate and thus unhelpful.

If we know that there is a right to private property, we do not know whether an occupational safety and health law or a law requiring beach access is permissible.

In fact, we know relatively little. Standing by itself, the constitutional protection against government 'takings' tells us very little about how to handle particular problems. This is true of rights generally. To say that there is a right to equal protection of the law is not to say, for example, that affirmative action programs are acceptable, mandatory, or prohibited. In fact, the right to equal protection of the law requires a great deal of supplemental work to decide cases. The right must be specified in order to have concrete meaning. The specification will depend on premises not contained within the announcement of the right itself. Rights purport to solve problems, but when stated abstractly—it is claimed—they are at most the beginning of a discussion.

Perhaps the area of free speech is the most vivid illustration. Everyone agrees that such a right exists; but without supplemental work, we cannot know how to handle the hard questions raised by commercial speech, libel, obscenity, or campaign finance restrictions. A serious problem with modern free speech discussions is that the term 'free speech' tends to be used as if it handled the hard questions by itself.

D. *Excessive Individualism*

A different objection is that rights are unduly individualistic and associated with highly undesirable characteristics, including selfishness and indifference to others. Rights miss the 'dimension of sociality'; they posit selfish, isolated individuals who assert what is theirs, rather than participating in communal life. Rights, it is said, neglect the moral and social dimensions of important problems.

The important and contested right of privacy, for example, is said to have emerged as an unduly individual right, rooted in the 'property paradigm' and loosened from connections to others. Critics urge that this conception of the issues involved in the so-called privacy cases misses crucial aspects of the relevant problems — abortion, family living arrangements, and the asserted right to die. Such issues do not involve simple privacy; they call up a range of issues about networks of relationships, between individuals and the state, between individuals and families, between individuals and localities. . . .

. . .

F. *Rights Versus Responsibilities*

A final and especially prominent objection is that the emphasis on rights tends to crowd out the issue of responsibility. In American law and in American public discourse, some critics complain, it is too rare to find the idea that people owe duties to each other, or that civic virtue is to be cultivated, prized, and lived. Rights, and especially new protections of rights since the 1960s, are said to be a major problem here.

In a simple formulation: People who insist on their rights too infrequently explore what it is right to do. Or they become dependent on the official institutions charged with safeguarding rights, rather than doing things for themselves. The controversy over whether rights turn women or blacks into a 'dependent class' is in part about this issue. People who insist that their status as victims entitles them to enforce their legal rights may not conceive of themselves in ways that engender equality and equal citizenship.

. . .

[The author then turns to clarification of some conceptual issues raised by the criticism, and concludes that the critique, while embodying some limited and important truths, 'does not by any means support a general challenge to rights.' He starts by noting the position advanced by many rights advocates — Ronald Dworkin comes immediately to mind — that rights refer to important human interests 'that operate as "trumps", in the sense that they cannot be compromised by reference to collective policies or goals.' He doubts that this conception is helpful.]

. . . The first problem is that almost every right is defeasible at some point, and defeasible just because the collective interest is very strong. In American law, no right is absolute. If, for example, the rest of the human race will be eliminated because of the protection of a right, the right will certainly be redefined or legitimately infringed, probably under some version of the 'compelling interest' test. The real question then becomes when rights are defeasible because of collective justifications — under what conditions and for what reasons. The formula of 'trumps' is misleading for this reason. We need to know what sorts of reasons are admissible and how weighty they must be; these are the key questions in the exploration of rights.

Rights characteristically limit the kinds of arguments that can be used by way of justification, and they characteristically require justification of special weight. Above all, rights exclude certain otherwise admissible reasons for action. But ideas of this kind do not support the 'trumps' metaphor and indeed lead in quite different directions.

The second problem is that many conceptual puzzles are raised by the understanding of right as interests operating 'against' the collectivity. Often rights are something that the collectivity recognizes and protects in order to protect its interests. If this is so, there is no easy opposition between rights and the collectivity. . . . Rights are collectively conferred and designed to promote collective interests. They are protected by social institutions for social reasons. . . .

[Sunstein turns his attention to what he describes as 'truths and partial truths' in the 'highly eclectic' views of the critics of rights. He observes:]

It is also important to point out that references to rights can make for unduly rigid understandings of complex problems and can sometimes stop discussion in its tracks before analysis has even started. Claims of right often have the vices of rules. Even worse, rights can be conclusions masquerading as reasons. In thinking about claims of right, it is often necessary to be detailed and concrete about the social consequences of competing courses of action. The invocation of 'rights' can be a serious obstacle to this process. Consider, for example, the current debates over regulation of the electronic media, violent pornography, hate speech at universities, or advertising for cigarettes. To say that any restriction on these forms of expression violates the 'right to free speech' may in the end be correct; but this requires a long and complex argument, not a shorthand phrase. The claim of a 'right to free speech' is far too general and abstract to support the argument. Here it does seem important and true to say that rights, stated abstractedly, do not solve concrete cases. They are indeterminate until they are specified.

As they operate in law, rights generally *are* specified. Hence the rights protected by the Constitution and the common law are far from indeterminate, however hard it is to know what they are when stated abstractly. The claim of indeterminacy is for this reason far too broad. The problem, to which the critics have correctly drawn attention, lies in the use of general claims of right to resolve cases in which the specification has not yet occurred.

It is also true that efforts to think about many social and economic problems in terms or rights can obscure those problems. A claimed right to clean air and water or to safe products and workplaces makes little sense in light of the need for close assessment, in particular cases, of the advantages of greater environmental protection or more safety, as compared with the possible accompanying disadvantages— higher prices, lower wages, less employment, and more poverty. Perhaps the legal system will create rights of a kind after it has undertaken this assessment. But to the extent that the regulatory programs of the 1970s were billed as simple vindications of 'rights', they severely impaired political deliberation about their content and about the necessity for trade-offs.

...

D. Confusions and Misconceptions

Despite the various partial truths in the attack on rights, there is a pervasive problem in that attack: Rights need not have the functions or consequences that they are alleged to have. The challenge to rights is properly directed against certain kinds of rights, not against rights in general. At most, the challenge to rights creates a contingent, partial warning about the appropriate content of rights and about the possibly harmful role of certain social institutions safeguarding rights....

...

... Often critics write as if rights and responsibilities are opposed, or as if those who favor the former are completely different from these who favor the latter. As they see it, rights are individual, atomistic, selfish, crude, licentious, antisocial, and associated with the Warren Court. Responsibilities, on the other hand, are seen as collective, social, altruistic, nuanced, and associated with appropriate or traditional values. But this understanding is quite inadequate, for some rights lack the characteristics claimed for them, and other rights have the features associated with responsibilities.

For example, the right to freedom of speech may be owned by individuals, but it is a precondition for a highly social process, that of democratic deliberation. That right keeps open the channels of communication; it is emphatically communal in character. It ensures a sine qua non of sociality, an opportunity for people to speak with one other. Indeed, everyone who owns a speech right does so partly so as to contribute to the collectivity; it is this fact that explains the government's inability to 'buy' speech rights even when a speaker would like to sell. So too, the right to associational freedom is hardly individualistic. It is meant precisely to protect collective action and sociality.

...

. . . Moreover, a principal characteristic of totalitarian states is the endless cataloguing of responsibilities owed by citizens to the state. The Soviet Constitution was an ignoble example. For example, that Constitution created a duty 'to make thrifty use of the people's wealth', 'to preserve and protect socialist property', to 'work conscientiously', and 'to concern themselves with the upbringing of children'. The Soviet Constitution offers a cautionary note against enthusiasm for responsibilities…

…

KARL KLARE, LEGAL THEORY AND DEMOCRATIC RECONSTRUCTION

25 U. of Brit. Colum. L. Rev. 69 (1991), at 97

[The author discusses the appropriate place of 'rights' in the formal legal structures and guarantees and in the legal-political discourse of the postcommunist states of Central-East Europe. He concludes that 'it seems obvious that post-communist law should be founded upon an explicit charter of human rights guarantees. How could there be any doubt of the central place of rights in democratic legal reconstruction?' Nonetheless, Klare notes, recent debates among Western legal scholars have developed a serious 'critique of rights', and he undertakes to summarize 'some of the major lines of criticism advanced by the rights skeptics'. The following excerpts deal with two aspects of this critique and Klare's responses thereto.]

A second branch of rights skepticism concerns the efficacy and limitations of the rights tradition in relationship to social change. [T]he skeptics call attention to certain self-imposed limitations internal to rights discourse stemming from its embrace of the public/private distinction. Rights thinking has predominantly concerned the relationship between the individual and the state. As traditionally understood, the human rights project is to erect barriers between the individual and the state, so as to protect human autonomy and self-determination from being violated or crushed by governmental power.

Unquestionably, a just society requires such protections, but human freedom can also be invaded or denied by nongovernmental forms of power, by domination in the so-called 'private sphere'. Human dignity is denied by *de jure* racial segregation, but it is also denied by employers who discriminate on the basis of race.… Rights charters almost invariably concern restrictions on state power and therefore leave intact many forms of 'private' domination, including hierarchies of class, race, gender and sexual preference.…

Given the injustices committed by the Stalinist regimes, it is understandable that the first priority of postcommunist lawyers is to guard against the abuse of state power.… Granting this, the argument goes, to realize freedom in all aspects of life, to establish arrangements in all social contexts that will be committed to human dignity, self-realization and equality, requires a deep transformation, in both East and West, not only of governmental but also of non-state institutions and practices that are left untouched by conventional human rights doctrine. A strong version of rights skepticism suggests that the fixation on the individual/state relationship in the rights tradition actually diverts intellectual and political resources from other, needed approaches to social justice.

. . .

This brings us to a third aspect of contemporary rights skepticism, the so-called 'indeterminacy critique'. . . .

. . . Because human rights concepts tend to be very elastic and open-ended, they are capable of being given a wide range of meanings, including inconsistent meanings. Take freedom of speech, for example. One meaning is the right to dissent and to criticize the powers that be. Yet the right to free speech can also be given quite a different meaning, as, e.g., in the American cases barring government from trying to prevent the distortion of the electoral process by corporate campaign contributions. In the former interpretation, free speech permits individuals to unfreeze hierarchy and open up political debate, whereas in the latter case, the right to free speech is mobilized to reinforce domination by entrenched power. . . .

Thus, rights concepts are sufficiently elastic so that they can mean different things to different people. People who seek to reinforce hierarchy and perpetuate domination can speak the language of rights, often with sincerity. But there is an even deeper problem. Even those who would consistently invoke rights in the service of self-determination, autonomy and equality find that rights concepts are internally contradictory. That is because, like all of legal discourse, rights theory is an arena of conflicting conceptions of justice and human freedom. . . . Proponents of democracy have advanced conceptions of rights to freedom of association and also conceptions of rights of excluded minorities to insist on membership in important groups. . . .

. . .

The problem is that rights discourse itself does not provide neutral decision procedures with which to make such choices.

. . .

. . . My point here is that, by itself, rights discourse does not and probably cannot provide us with the criteria for deciding between conflicting claims of right. In order to resolve rights conflicts, it is necessary to step outside the discourse. One must appeal to more concrete and therefore more controversial analyses of the relevant social and institutional contexts than rights discourse offers; and one must develop and elaborate conceptions of and intuitions about human freedom and self-determination by reference to which one seeks to assess rights claims and resolve rights conflicts.

If the processes of concretizing rights concepts and of resolving rights conflicts extend beyond the traditional discourse of rights onto the terrain of social theory and political philosophy, it follows that rights rhetoric must be politicized in order to serve as a foundation for legal reconstruction. . . . Surely it is insufficient to think of human rights practice in terms of obtaining the correct list of rights and then enacting them into a code. Rather, postcommunist lawyers must think of rights discourse and rights charters as relatively open media in which to advance visions of socially desirable institutions and practices. That is, the rights foundation of legal reconstruction is an invitation to make political philosophy, not only in promulgating the initial charters, but at every step along the way of articulating and interpreting rights concepts and filling them with concrete legal and institutional meaning. But this revised, 'politicized' conception of human rights discourse and practice in postcommunist legal reconstruction sits uneasily with the idea of an autonomous rule of law that is ostensibly the basis of the whole enterprise.

...

NOTE

A number of different understandings about rights — their derivation, nature, content and consequences — appear in the readings in Chapters 3–5 and the immediately preceding readings. Consider the following lists, (1) setting forth in the left column assertions or understandings about rights that derive from natural rights or related deep premises about the nature of human beings or divine law, and typify much (surely not all) rights discourse within liberal societies, in opposition to a list (2) setting forth in the right column very different understandings that, for example, (a) inform arguments in favour of cultural relativism that Chapter 7(A) discusses, and (b) inform utilitarian or policy-oriented argument as opposed to argument derived from natural rights or related deep premises about the nature of human beings or divine law.

inalienable	as opposed to	socially constructed, given and taken
absolute		qualified, contingent, content dependent on context
universal		particular, culturally specific
eternal, ahistorical		historicist, evolving, open to change
based on equal human dignity		based on utility, power

Note that — as Duncan Kennedy and Cass Sunstein's articles make clear — the same 'content' of a right may be argued toward and justified starting with the assumptions in lists in the left or right columns. Indeed, the same result may be reached whether argument to justify a given rule or its interpretation is rights-based at all or rather uses the different language and methodology associated with utilitarian-consequentialist-cost/benefit thought. Often both modes of justification may be at issue, and may be seen as complementary and mutually supportive. For example: (1) Free speech may be justified as a right inhering in human personality, a mode of self-realization, a recognition of equal human dignity. Or it may be justified as contributing to the 'marketplace of ideas', offering many competitive ideas from which rational conclusions and the 'best' regulation of speech may be more readily devised. (2) A rule excluding from court proceedings any evidence that the police illegally seize may be understood as resting on notions of right and fairness and basic relations between individual and state, or as a method of disciplining the police not to act illegally for their evidence cannot be used in trial. (3) Torture may be viewed as a violation of human dignity and personality, a violation of a basic and eternal human right, or it may be viewed as illegal because it is often an unreliable path toward procuring accurate and reliable evidence. Recall the arguments of Bentham and other authors in Chapter 3(D).

DAVID KENNEDY, THE DARK SIDE OF VIRTUE (2004), at 3

Chapter One: The International Human Rights Movement: Part of the Problem?

. . . Among well-meaning legal professionals in the United States and Europe — humanitarian, internationalist, liberal, compassionate in all the best senses of these terms — the human rights movement has become a central object of devotion.

But are there also dark sides? This chapter develops a short list of hypotheses about the possible risks, costs, and unanticipated consequences of human rights activism. . . . [I]n the end, one cannot think pragmatically about human rights work without some such list of possible costs in mind.

. . .

A checklist of possible downsides is not a general critique of human rights. Benefits and harms must be analyzed in particular cases, under specific conditions, at particular times. The cases and conditions may be extremely specific (pursuing this petition will make this magistrate less likely to grant this other petition) or quite general (articulating social welfare needs as individual "rights" makes people everywhere more passive and isolated). . . .

. . . Ultimately, we must also compare whatever assessment we make of the human rights vocabulary against the costs and benefits of *other* emancipatory vocabularies which might be used to the same ends.

In the end, of course, different observers will weigh the costs and benefits of human rights activism in different ways. . . .

. . .

. . . [F]or me, nothing goes in the "costs" column until the human rights movement has a bad *effect*. A bad effect means influencing someone to act (or fail to act) or to think in a way which counts as a cost (again, ethically, politically, philosophically, aesthetically) for the person making the argument. . . .

. . .

Here is my short list of pragmatic worries.

Human Rights Occupies the Field of Emancipatory Possibility

[The author here discusses the 'hegemony' of human rights as resource allocation, criticism and distortion.]

The claim here is that this institutional and political hegemony makes other valuable, often more valuable, emancipatory strategies less available. This argument is stronger, of course, when one can say something about what those alternatives are — or might be. But there may be something to the claim that human rights has so dominated the imaginative space of emancipation that alternatives can now be thought only, perhaps unhelpfully, as negations of what human rights asserts — passion to its reason, local to its global. . . . This is easiest to see when human rights attracts institutional energy and resources which would otherwise flow elsewhere. But this is not only a matter of scarce resources.

Human rights also occupies the field by implicit or explicit delegitimation of other emancipatory strategies. . . . Where this is so, pursuing a human rights initiative or promoting the use of human rights vocabulary may have fully unintended negative consequences for other existing emancipatory projects, including those relying on more religious, national, or local energies. . . .

To the extent emancipatory projects must be expressed in the vocabulary of "rights" to be heard, good policies which are not framed that way go unattended. This also distorts the way projects are imagined and framed for international consideration. For example, it is often asserted that the international human rights movement makes an end run around local institutions and strategies which would often be better — ethically, politically, philosophically, aesthetically. . . . A "universal" idea of what counts as a problem and what works as a solution snuffs out all sorts of promising local political and social initiatives to contest local conditions in other terms. But there are other lost vocabularies which are equally global — vocabularies of duty, of responsibility, of collective commitment. Encouraging people concerned about environmental harm to rethink their concerns as a human rights violation will have bad consequences if it would have turned out to be more animating, for example, to say there is a duty to work for the environment, rather than a right to a clean environment.

The "right to development" is a classic — and well-known — example. Once concerns about global poverty are raised in these terms, energy and resources are drawn to developing a literature and an institutional practice of a particular sort at the international level. Efforts which cannot be articulated in these terms seem less legitimate, less practical, less worth the effort. Increasingly, people of goodwill concerned about poverty are drawn into debate about a series of ultimately impossible legal quandaries — rights of whom, against whom, remediable how — and into institutional projects of codification and reporting familiar from other human rights efforts, without evaluating how these might compare with other deployments of talent and resources. . . .

. . .

Human Rights Views the Problem and the Solution too Narrowly

People have made many different claims about the narrowness of human rights. Here are some: the human rights movement foregrounds harms done explicitly by *governments* to individuals or groups — leaving potentially more severe harms brought about by private groups or indirect governmental action largely unaddressed and more legitimate by contrast. Even when addressing private harms, human rights focuses attention on *public* remedies — explicit rights formalized and implemented by the state. One criticizes the *state* and seeks *public* law remedies, but leaves unattended or enhanced the powers and felt entitlements of private actors . . . .

When combined, these ideas about human rights often define problems and solutions in ways unlikely to change the economy. Human rights foregrounds problems of *participation* and *procedure*, at the expense of distribution. As a result, existing distributions of wealth, status, and power can seem more legitimate after rights have been legislated, formal participation in government achieved, and institutional remedies for violations provided. However useful saying "that's my right" is in extracting things from the state, it is not good for extracting things from the economy, unless you are a property holder. Indeed, a practice of rights claims against the state may actively weaken the capacity of people to challenge economic arrangements.

. . . [T]he imbalance between civil/political and social/economic rights is neither an accident of politics nor a matter which could be remedied by more intensive commitment. It runs deep in the philosophy of human rights, and seems central to the conditions of political possibility that make human rights an emancipatory strategy in the first place, and to the institutional character of the movement.

The strong attachment of the human rights movement to the legal formalization of rights and the establishment of legal machinery for their implementation makes the achievement of these forms an end in itself. . . . These are the traditional problems of form: form can hamper peaceful adjustment and necessary change, can be overinclusive or underinclusive. Is the right to vote a floor — or can it become a ceiling?

The emphasis on human rights can leave unattended the wide array of laws that do not explicitly condone violations, but that certainly affect their frequency and may in fact be doing more harm than the absence of rights. These background laws, left with clean hands, can seem more legitimate. . . .

Even very broad social movements of emancipation — for women, for minorities, for the poor — have their vision bunkered by the promise of recognition in the vocabulary and institutional apparatus of human rights. They will be led away from the economy and toward the state, away from political and social conditions and toward forms of legal recognition. . . .

. . .

Human Rights is Limited by its Relationship to Western Liberalism

. . .

Human rights encourages people to seek emancipation in the vocabularies of reason rather than faith, in public rather than private life, in law rather than politics, in politics rather than economics. The human rights vocabulary helps draw the lines between these spheres. In each case, it underestimates what it takes as the natural base and overestimates our ability to instrumentalize what it takes as the artificial domain of emancipation. Moreover, human rights is too quick to conclude that emancipation *means* progress forward from the natural passions of politics into the civilized reason of law. The urgent need to develop a more vigorous human politics is sidelined by the effort to throw thin but plausible nets of legal articulation across the globe. Work to develop law comes to be seen as an emancipatory end in itself, leaving the human rights movement too ready to articulate problems in political terms and solutions in legal terms.

The posture of human rights as an emancipatory political project which extends and operates within a domain above or outside politics — a political project repackaged as a form of knowledge — delegitimates other political voices and makes less visible the local, cultural, and political dimensions of the human rights movement itself. . .

. . .

[T]he human rights movement contributes to the framing of political choices in the third world as oppositions between "local/traditional" and "international/modern" forms of government and modes of life. This effect is strengthened by the presentation of human rights as part of belonging to the modern world, but coming from some place outside political choice, from the universal, the rational, the civilized. By strengthening the articulation of third world politics as a choice between tradition and modernity, the human rights movement impoverishes local political discourse, often strengthening the hand of self-styled "traditionalists" who are offered a commonsense and powerful alternative to modernization for whatever politics they may espouse.

. . .

Human Rights Promotion Can Be Bad Politics in Particular Contexts

It may be that this is all one can say — promoting human rights can sometimes have bad consequences. All of the first nine types of criticism suggested that human rights suffered from one or another design defect — as if these defects would emerge, these costs would be incurred, regardless of context. Perhaps this is so. But so long as none of these criticisms has been proven in such a general way (and it is hard to see just how they could be), it may be that all we have is a list of possible downsides, open risks, bad results which have sometimes occurred, which might well occur. In some context, for example, it might turn out that pursuing emancipation as entitlement could reduce the capacity and propensity for collective action. Something like this seems to have happened in the United States in the last twenty years — the transformation of political questions into legal questions, and then into questions of legal "rights," has made other forms of collective emancipatory politics less available. But it is hard to see that this is always and everywhere the destiny of human rights initiatives. . . .

. . .

QUESTIONS

1. How damaging to a rights-oriented international movement are the criticisms about rights discourse and argument that are developed (and in some cases, responded to) in the preceding articles? To which of them are the UDHR, treaties and other materials examined in Chapters 3–5 most vulnerable?

2. Duncan Kennedy and Klare both stress that, at a given point, rights-based assertions give out, and a claimant or judge or other decision-maker must resort to (Kennedy) 'open-textured arguments from morality, social welfare, expectations, and institutional competence and administrability'. Klare stresses that 'choices must be made in elaborating any structure of human rights guarantees . . . and the choices bear socially and politically

significant consequences. The problem is that rights discourse itself does not provide neutral decision procedures with which to make such choices.... In order to resolve rights conflicts, it is necessary to step outside the discourse'.

Apply these observations to a conception as basic as the 'right to life'. What 'choices' about the meaning of this conception are before treaty-makers, legislatures, courts or advocates elaborating this right, and through what methods or processes can those choices be resolved? What different issues are posed by, say, a 'right to health care'?

3. Duncan Kennedy, Klare and Sunstein all stress the significance of the indeterminacy of rights-based argument, including the problem of conflicting rights. Kennedy notes that these features of 'open texture or indeterminacy' are open to the same analysis 'as legal argument in general'. That is, they are not particular to rights. Give some examples, other than those stated in the preceding writings, of pressing and difficult issues raised by the ICCPR, CEDAW or the ICESCR that stem from the indeterminacy of the texts or contradictions among rights? How would you go about resolving a concrete issue about the content and reach of a right that involves indeterminacy or contradiction (say, the right to speech or privacy)? Bear in mind that for many international human rights issues and in many states, it will be impractical or impossible to invoke the jurisdiction of a court that could issue a 'binding' precedent.

4. Do you understand David Kennedy's "dark side" of human rights to advance significantly different criticism of rights, rights rhetoric, and rights-based advocacy and strategy than do the three articles preceding it? In what respects? To the extent that these three earlier (in time) articles address in different ways some of Kennedy's concerns, how do you assess their arguments?

5. With respect to David Kennedy's arguments, consider: (a) What illustrations could you offer of situations where reliance on rights rhetoric to advance popular claims crowded out other "emancipatory vocabularies" and strategies — for example, mass political action — that could possibly or even likely have achieved more? Consider, for example, earlier materials examining the struggles for "women's rights", the arguments against torture, and arguments in favour of economic/social rights like health care or housing. Is mass political action — electoral campaigns, marches by protestors to a capital city, boycotts — necessarily independent of rights rhetoric embedded in such action? (b) Suppose that a human rights advocate argued to a minister of education in a developing country that giving schoolgirls equal educational opportunities would improve talent, energy, productivity and the level of economic well-being within the family and the country — that is, benefits will far exceed costs. Is the "hegemony" of rights rhetoric apt to block such argument? Could both modes of argument be used together? What of using simultaneously several different modes of argument — utilitarian, fairness-based, rights-based — with respect to environmental degradation? (c) Do this book's earlier materials support the author's argument that human rights directs so much attention to the public sector (that is, the state as the only identified violator of human rights in the conventions and in human rights discourse) that many violations occurring in the nonstate sector (employment discrimination, family violence) are apt to remain hidden and untouched? (d) The author several times characterizes human rights as claims and arguments based on reason, whereas other emancipatory languages and strategies rely on faith and passion. Do you agree with this distinction, which tends to characterize "rights" as cerebral and abstract, while other languages/strategies are more basic, emotional, appealing, stimulating to people?

B. DUTY-BASED SOCIAL ORDERS

COMMENT ON DUTIES

The following readings describe and analyse duty-oriented rather than rights-oriented social ordering through law and cultural tradition. Robert Cover comments on the legal culture of Judaism with its stress on obligations imposed by God rather than on rights. He suggests historical reasons why Western states and Judaism developed in these different ways. Jomo Kenyatta describes aspects of the education of the young in the Gikuyu people in Kenya, particularly the inculcation of elements of social obligations and duty. Although the cultural and religious contexts and the content of the duties referred to are radically different in these readings, they both suggest important consequences of an orientation towards duty/obligation and the gap between such an orientation and the liberal political culture that influenced the human rights movement.

Note that the duties/obligations referred to in these readings are *not* the same as duties within a *scheme of rights* that are correlative to the described rights. For example, the individual's basic right to be free from torture imposes a correlative (corresponding) duty on the state not to torture. The following readings talk of duties imposed on *individuals* rather than on the state or some other collective entity. That is, they are not correlative duties to others' rights, but initially imposed on the individual. Article 29(1) of the UDHR offers an analogy to such use of duties, as does the preamble to the ICCPR. But explicit language of individual duty to other individuals (other than the implied, traditional correlative duties), to society, or to the state in the universal human rights system is rare. A closer analogy to the present readings, particularly the excerpts from Kenyatta, is provided by the African Charter on Human and Peoples' Rights, examined at p. 504, *infra*.

ROBERT COVER, OBLIGATION: A JEWISH JURISPRUDENCE OF THE SOCIAL ORDER

5 J. of L. and Relig. 65 (1987)

I. Fundamental Words

Every legal culture has its fundamental words. When we define our subject this weekend as human rights, we also locate ourselves in a normative universe at a particular place. The word 'rights' is a highly evocative one for those of us who have grown up in the post-enlightenment secular society of the West. . . .

Judaism is, itself, a legal culture of great antiquity. It has hardly led a wholly autonomous existence these past three millennia. Yet, I suppose it can lay as much claim as any of the other great legal cultures to have an integrity to its basic categories. When I am asked to reflect upon Judaism and human rights, therefore, the first thought that comes to mind is that the categories are wrong. I do not mean, of course, that basic ideas of human dignity and worth are not powerfully expressed in the Jewish legal and literary traditions. Rather, I mean that because it is a legal tradition Judaism has its own categories for expressing through law the worth and dignity of each human being. And the categories are not closely analogous to 'human rights'. The principal word in Jewish law, which occupies a place equivalent in evocative force to the American legal system's 'rights', is the word 'mitzvah' which literally means commandment but has a general meaning closer to 'incumbent obligation'.

Before I begin an analysis of the differing implications of these two rather different key words, I should like to put the two words in a context — the contexts of their respective myths. For both of us these words are connected to fundamental stories and receive their force from those stories as much as from the denotative meaning of the words themselves. The story behind the term 'rights' is the story of social contract. The myth postulates free and independent if highly vulnerable beings who voluntarily trade a portion of their autonomy for a measure of collective security. The myth makes the collective arrangement the product of individual choice and thus secondary to the individual. 'Rights' are the fundamental category because it is the normative category which most nearly approximates that which is the source of the legitimacy of everything else. Rights are traded for collective security. But some rights are retained and, in some theories, some rights are inalienable. In any event the first and fundamental unit is the individual and 'rights' locate him as an individual separate and apart from every other individual.

I must stress that I do not mean to suggest that all or even most theories that are founded upon rights are 'individualistic' or 'atomistic'. Nor would I suggest for a moment that with a starting point of 'rights' and social contract one must get to a certain end. Hobbes as well as Locke is part of this tradition. And, of course, so is Rousseau. Collective solutions as well as individualistic ones are possible but, it is the case that even the collective solutions are solutions which arrive at their destination by way of a theory which derives the authority of the collective from the individual....

The basic word of Judaism is obligation or mitzvah. It, too, is intrinsically bound up in a myth — the myth of Sinai. Just as the myth of social contract is essentially a myth of autonomy, so the myth of Sinai is essentially a myth of heteronomy. Sinai is a collective — indeed, a corporate — experience. The experience at Sinai is not chosen. The event gives forth the words which are commandments. In all Rabbinic and post Rabbinic embellishment upon the Biblical account of Sinai this event is the Code for all Law. All law was given at Sinai and therefore all law is related back to the ultimate heteronomous event in which we were chosen-passive voice.

...

What have these stories to do with the ways in which the law languages of these respective legal cultures are spoken? Social movements in the United States organize around rights. When there is some urgently felt need to change the law or keep it in one way or another a 'Rights' movement is started. Civil rights, the right to life, welfare rights, etc. The premium that is to be put upon an entitlement is so coded. When we 'take rights seriously' we understand them to be trumps in the legal game. In Jewish law, an entitlement without an obligation is a sad, almost pathetic thing....

Indeed, to be one who acts out of obligation is the closest thing there is to a Jewish definition of completion as a person within the community. A child does not become emancipated or 'free' when he or she reaches maturity. Nor does she/he become *sui juris*. No, the child becomes bar or bat mitzvah, literally one who is of the obligations. Traditionally, the parent at that time says a blessing. Blessed is He that has exonerated me from the punishment of this child. The primary legal distinction between Jew and non-Jew is that the non-Jew is only obligated to the 7 Noachide commandments....

The Uses of Rights and Obligations

The Jewish legal system has evolved for the past 1900 years without a state and largely without much in the way of coercive powers to be exercised upon the adherents of the faith. I do not mean to idealize the situation. The Jewish communities over the millennia have wielded power. Communal sanctions of banning and shunning have been regularly and occasionally cruelly imposed on individuals or groups. Less frequently, but frequently enough, Jewish communities granted quasi-autonomy by gentile rulers, have used the power of the gentile state to discipline dissidents and deviants. Nonetheless, there remains a difference between wielding a power which draws on but also depends on pre-existing social solidarity, and, wielding one which depends on violence....

In a situation in which there is no centralized power and little in the way of coercive violence, it is critical that the mythic center of the Law reinforce the bonds of solidarity. Common, mutual, reciprocal obligation is necessary. The myth of divine commandment creates that web.... It was a myth that created legitimacy for a radically diffuse and coordinate system of authority. But while it created room for the diffusion of authority it did not have a place for individualism. One might have independent and divergent understandings of the obligations imposed by God through his chosen people, but one could not have a world view which denied the obligations.

The jurisprudence of rights, on the other hand, has gained ascendance in the Western world together with the rise of the national state with its almost unique mastery of violence over extensive territories. Certainly, it may be argued, it has been essential to counterbalance the development of the state with a myth which a) establishes the State as legitimate only in so far as it can be derived from the autonomous creatures who trade in their rights for security—i.e., one must tell a story about the State's utility or service to us, and b) potentially justifies individual and communal resistance to the Behemoth. It may be true as Bentham so aptly pointed out that natural rights may be used either apologetically or in revolutionary fashion, and there is nothing in the concept powerful enough analytically to constrain which use it shall be put to. Nevertheless, it is the case that natural right apologies are of a sort that in their articulation they limit the most far-reaching claims of the State, and the revolutionary ideology that can be generated is also of a sort which is particularly effective in countering organic statist claims.

Thus, there is a sense in which the ideology of rights has been a useful counter to the centrifugal forces of the western nation state while the ideology of mitzvoth or obligation has been equally useful as a counter to the centripetal forces that have beset Judaism over the centuries.

. . .

. . . [T]he Maimonides system contrasts the normative world of mitzvoth with the world of vanity — hebel. It seems that Maimonides, in this respect, as in so many others has hit the mark. A world centered upon obligation is not, really cannot be, an empty or vain world. Rights, as an organizing principle, are indifferent to the vanity of varying ends. But mitzvoths because they so strongly bind and locate the individual must make a strong claim for the substantive content of that which they dictate. The system, if its content be vain, can hardly claim to be a system. The rights system is indifferent to ends and in its indifference can claim systemic coherence without making any strong claims about the fullness or vanity of the ends it permits.

. . .

JOMO KENYATTA, FACING MOUNT KENYA: THE TRIBAL LIFE OF THE GIKUYU

(1965), at 109

[These excerpts are taken from a description by Kenyatta, who later became the first post-colonial president of Kenya, of the Gikuyu people (often rendered in English as 'Kikuyu') in that country. The excerpts stress elements of duty inculcated in Gikuyu children, and appear in Chapter 5, 'System of Education.']

[The children] are also taught definitely at circumcision the theory, as it were, of respect to their parents and kinsfolk. Under all circumstances they must stay with them and share in their joys and sorrows. It will never do to leave them and go off to see the world whenever they take the notion, especially when their parents are in their old age. They must give them clothes, look after their garden, herd their cattle, sheep and goats, build their grain stores and houses. It thus becomes a part of their outlook on life that their parents shall not suffer want nor continue to labour strenuously in their old age while their children can lend a hand and do things to give them comfort.

This respect and duty to parents is further emphasised by the fact that the youth or girl cannot advance from one stage to another without the parent's will and active assistance. The satisfaction of all a boy's longings and ambitions depends on the father's and family's consent . . . .

. . .

The teaching of social obligations is again emphasised by the classification of age-groups to which we have already referred. This binds together those of the same status in ties of closest loyalty and devotion. Men circumcised at the same time stand in the very closest relationship to each other. When a man of the same age-group injures another it is a serious magico-religious offence. They are like blood brothers; they must not do any wrong to each other. It ranks with an injury done to a member of one's own family. The age-group (*riika*) is thus a powerful instrument for securing conformity with tribal usage. The selfish or reckless youth is taught by the opinion of his gang that it does not pay to incur displeasure. He will not be called to eat with the others when food is going. He may be put out of their dances, fined, or even ostracised for a time. If he does not change his ways he will find his old companions have deserted him.

. . . The age-groups do more than bind men of equal standing together. They further emphasise the social grades of junior and senior, inferior and superior. We see the same principle in evidence all through the various grades . . .

Owing to the strength and numbers of the social ties existing between members of the same family, clan and age-group, and between different families and clans through which the tribe is unified and solidified as one organic whole, the community can be mobilised very easily for corporate activity. House-building, cultivation, harvesting, digging trap-pits, putting up fences around cultivated fields, and building bridges, are usually done by the group; hence the Gikuyu saying: '*Kamoinge koyaga ndere*', which means collective activities make heavy tasks easier. In the old days sacrifices were offered and wars were waged by the tribe as a whole or by the clan. Marriage contracts and ceremonies are the affairs of families and not of individuals. Sometimes even cattle are bought by joint effort. Thus the individual boy or girl soon learns to work with and for other people. An old man who has no children of his own is helped by his neighbour's children in almost everything. His hut is built, his garden dug, firewood is cut and water is fetched for him. If his cattle, sheep or goats are lost or in difficulties the children of his neighbour will help to bring them back, at great pains and often at considerable risk. The old man reciprocates by treating the children as though they were his own. Children learn this habit of communal work like others, not by verbal exhortations so much as by joining with older people in such social services . . . All help given in this way is voluntary, and kinsfolk are proud to help one another. There is no payment or expectation of payment. They are well feasted, of course. This is not regarded as payment, but as hospitality. The whole thing rests on the principle of reciprocal obligations. It is taken for granted that the neighbour whom you assist in difficulty or whose house you help to build will do the same for you when in similar need. Those who do not reciprocate these sentiments of neighbourliness are not in favour . . . .

. . .

The selfish or self-regarding man has no name or reputation in the Gikuyu community. An individualist is looked upon with suspicion and is given a nickname of *mwebongia*, one who works only for himself and is likely to end up as a wizard. He may lack assistance when he needs it . . .

In the Gikuyu community there is no really individual affair, for every thing has a moral and social reference. The habit of corporate effort is but the other side of corporate ownership; and corporate responsibility is illustrated in corporate work no less than in corporate sacrifice and prayer.

In spite of the foreign elements which work against many of the Gikuyu institutions and the desire to implant the system of wholesale Westernisation, this system of mutual help and the tribal solidarity in social services, political and economic activities are still maintained by the large majority of the Gikuyu people. It is less practised among those Gikuyu who have been Europeanised or detribalised. The rest of the community look upon these people as mischief-makers and breakers of the tribal traditions, and the general disgusted cry is heard: '*Mothongo ne athogonjire borori*', i.e. the white man had spoiled and disgraced our country.

...

The striking thing in the Gikuyu system of education, and the feature which most sharply distinguishes it from the European system of education, is the primary place given to personal relations. Each official statement of educational policy repeats this well-worn declaration that the aim of education must be the building of character and not the mere acquisition of knowledge....

...

QUESTIONS

1. 'A duty-based social order seems inherently less subject to universalization (with respect to the duties imposed on individuals) than a rights-based social order (with respect to the rights attributed to individuals). That is, the content of duties (obligations toward elders, toward the community, toward God) seems to be very particular and bound to a given context, a product of a given religion or political or social culture or history, whereas individuals' rights seem to be more divorced from a particular context and can therefore be stated more abstractly.' Do you agree? Any examples?

2. "Individual rights" necessarily imply equality among all rights holders, which is to say among all members of society. This in fact is what the contemporary human rights instruments declare. To the contrary, duties can be (and frequently are) defined so as to impose hierarchy, status, and discrimination in a given social order.' Do you agree? Any examples?

3. 'Different from a regime of rights, a regime of duties intrinsically exerts an inward, centripetal force. It draws individual duty-bearers into the society, connects them intricately with other individuals and the community in a variety of ways, blurs the separate identity of the individual from society, and leads to a more communal and collective structure of life.' Do you agree?

4. Note that Article 2(3) of the ICCPR requires states to provide all persons whose rights have been violated with 'an effective remedy', and to develop particularly the possibilities of 'judicial remedy'. Do rights imply a preference for or even require individual (judicial or other) remedies against the state, whereas a regime of individual duties is less likely to provide such remedies?

COMMENT ON DUTY PROVISIONS OF NATIONAL CONSTITUTIONS

In modern constitutions, as in human rights treaties, provisions conferring rights on individuals far outnumber those imposing duties. There appear below English translations of articles in a number of state constitutions that, as of recent dates, expressed such duties. Presented here in isolation from the context of the constitutions and political societies in which they take meaning, these articles serve merely to illustrate the range of such duties. Within their national contexts, they may be understood or interpreted to impose slight or significant duties, which moreover may be viewed merely as hortatory or may be subject to enforcement by civil or criminal actions brought by the state or by nonstate parties.

Belarus

Article 53: Everyone shall respect the dignity, rights, liberties, and legitimate interests of others.

Article 55: It shall be the duty of everyone to protect the environment.

Cambodia

Article 47: Parents shall have the duty to take care of and educate their children to become good citizens. Children shall have the duty to take good care of their elderly mother and father according to Khmer traditions.

China

Article 42: (3) Work is the glorious duty of every able-bodied citizen. All working people in state enterprises and in urban and rural economic collectives should perform their tasks with an attitude consonant with their status as masters of the country. . . .

Article 49: (2) Both husband and wife have the duty to practice family planning. (3) Parents have the duty to rear and educate their minor children, and children who have come of age have the duty to support and assist their parents.

Article 54: It is the duty of citizens of the People's Republic of China to safeguard the security, honour, and interests of the motherland; they must not commit acts detrimental to the security, honour and interests of the motherland.

India

Article 51A: It shall be the duty of every citizen of India . . . (b) to cherish and follow the noble ideals which inspired our national struggle for freedom; . . . (e) to promote harmony and the spirit of common brotherhood amongst all the people of India transcending religious, linguistic and regional or sectional diversities; to renounce practices derogatory to the dignity of women; . . . (g) to protect and improve the natural environment . . . and to have compassion for living creatures. . . .

Italy

Article 4: The Republic recognizes the right of all citizens to work and promotes such conditions as will make this right effective. (2) Every citizen shall undertake, according to his possibilities and his own choice, an activity or a function contributing to the material and moral progress of society.

Poland

Article 86: Everyone shall care for the quality of the environment and shall be held responsible for causing its degradation. The principles of such responsibility shall be specified by statute.

Saudi Arabia

Article 12: The consolidation of national unity is a duty, and the state will prevent anything that may lead to disunity, sedition and separation.

Spain

Article 45: (1) Everyone has the right to enjoy an environment suitable for the development of the person as well as the duty to preserve it.

Thailand

Article 68: Every person shall have a duty to exercise his or her right to vote at an election. The person who fails to attend an election for voting without notifying the appropriate cause of such failure shall lose his or her right to vote as provided by law.

Uganda

Article 39: The exercise and enjoyment of rights and freedoms is inseparable from the performance of duties and obligations, and accordingly, it shall be the duty of every citizen . . . (c) to foster national unity and live in harmony with others; (d) to engage in gainful employment for the good of himself, the family, the common good and to contribute to the national development; . . . (f) to contribute to the well-being of the community where the citizen lives; (g) to protect and safeguard the environment; and (h) to promote democracy and the rule of law.

QUESTIONS

1. Which if any of the preceding provisions are inconsistent with, or indeed threaten, the human rights declared by the leading international instruments? Which if any do you view as implicitly incorporated in those instruments?

2. How do you understand, and would you support for inclusion in your own country's constitution, the provisions relating to work, to environment, and to voting?

COMMENT ON COMPARISONS BETWEEN RIGHTS AND DUTIES IN THE AFRICAN CHARTER AND IN OTHER HUMAN RIGHTS INSTRUMENTS

The newest, the least developed or effective (in relation to the European and Inter-American regimes), the most distinctive and the most controversial of the three established regional human rights regimes involves African states. In 1981 the Assembly of Heads of States and Government of the Organization of African Unity adopted the African Charter on Human and Peoples' Rights (appearing in the Documents Supplement). It entered into force in 1986. The OAU was succeeded in 2002 by the African Union, which as of January 2007 had 53 member states. All such states are parties to the African Charter.

The present discussion of the Charter emphasizes the distinctive attention that the African system gives to duties as well as rights. This distinctive emphasis is obvious on the face of the African Charter, even before one considers any elaboration or application of the provisions on duties by the African Commission. You should now become familiar with the provisions of the Charter. Other aspects of the Charter, and of the role of the Commission created by it, are discussed at pp. 1062–1083 *infra.*

The Charter's Preamble itself suggests some of the striking differences from other human rights instruments, universal and regional. Its key theme is regional cultural distinctiveness, as when it refers to '[t]aking into consideration the virtues of [African states'] historical tradition and the values of African civilization'.

Rights

Consider first Chapter 1 of Part I, dealing with 'human and peoples' rights'.

1. Compare the important opening provisions (Articles 1 and 2) of the Charter on the obligations of states with the analogous provisions in Article 2 of the ICCPR.

2. Several of the rights are expressed in ways that differ in wording from equivalent provisions in other instruments but that amount in the large to a similar conception. See, for example, Article 4.

3. Many rights are expressed in significantly different ways from the equivalent provisions in, say, the ICCPR. Compare, for example, Article 7 of the Charter on criminal procedure with Articles 14 and 15 of the ICCPR; and Article 13 of the Charter on political participation with Article 25 of the ICCPR. Note the respects in which Article 25 is more specific.

4. The protection of the property right in Article 14 recalls Article 17 of the UDHR but finds no equivalent in the ICCPR. The European Convention as first drafted included no such provision, but its First Protocol extends protection to the property right.

5. Some provisions state familiar norms, but illustrate them or make them specific in ways that recall Africa's experience with the Western slave trade and with colonization. They bear out the phrase in the Preamble quoted above. See, for

example, Articles 5, 19 and 20. Other provisions refer to abuses in Africa's own post-colonial history, such as Article 12(5) that recalls Uganda's expulsion of its citizens of Asian descent.

6. A number of provisions draw attention to the attempts of the states to reconcile humane treatment of individuals with their interests in territorial integrity and security. See for example, Article 23(2).

7. Compare the characteristic limitations on rights in the Charter with those in the ICCPR. See, for example, Articles 18(3) and 22(2) of the ICCPR. Compare with them Article 6 of the Charter, assuring the right to liberty 'except for reasons and conditions previously laid down by law'; Article 8 providing that freedom of conscience and religion are 'subject to law and order'; and Article 10 declaring the right to free association 'provided that [the individual] abides by the law'. See also Articles 11 and 12(2).

8. Note that the Charter has no provision for derogation of rights in situations of national emergency, equivalent to Article 4 of the ICCPR.

9. The Charter includes economic-social rights as in Articles 15 and 16, but does not qualify these rights with respect to their progressive realization and with respect to resource constraints to which the rights are subject, as does Article 1 of the International Covenant on Economic, Social and Cultural Rights.

10. The Charter includes several collective or peoples' rights, sometimes referred to as 'third-generation' human rights, in provisions like those in Articles 23 and 24 dealing with peoples' rights 'to national and international peace and security' and 'to a generally satisfactory environment favourable to their development.' The Charter's title itself signals the importance of this feature.

Duties

Consider now the distinctive Chapter 2 of Part I, on 'duties'. As prior materials in this chapter stress, references to 'duties' are not alien to human rights instruments: Article 29 of the UDHR, the preamble to the ICCPR, indeed the preamble to the UN Charter itself.

Nonetheless, the Charter is the first human rights treaty to include an enumeration of, to give forceful attention to, individuals' duties. In this respect, it goes well beyond the conventional notion that duties may be correlative to rights, such as the obvious duties of states that are correlative (corresponding) to individual rights — for example, states' duties not to torture or to provide a structure for voting in political elections. The Charter also goes beyond correlative duties of individuals that many human rights instruments explicitly or implicitly impose — for example, an individual's right to bodily security imposes a duty an other individuals not to invade that right. The Charter differs by defining duties that are not simply the 'other side' of individual rights, and that run from individuals to the state as well as to other groups and individuals. Hence the Charter directly raises the issues of universalism and cultural relativism that are addressed in Chapter 7.

Depending on their interpretation and their possible application within the African human rights regime, the duties declared in the Charter could constitute part of the deep structure of the society contemplated by that instrument. For example, they could determine in basic ways the relationships between the individual on the one hand, and society and state on the other. They could resolve in specific ways the tension between the individual and the collective. They could contradict some provisions in the Charter's preceding elaboration of rights.

Note some of the vital phrases in Articles 27–29. Article 27 refers to duties towards one's 'family and society, the State and other legally recognized communities and the international community'. Rights are to be exercised with 'due regard to the rights of others, collective security, morality and common interest'.

The language of Article 29 is striking. Note such phrases as the 'harmonious development of the family', 'cohesion and respect', 'serve the national community', 'not to compromise the security of the state', 'strengthen social and national solidarity', 'strengthen positive African cultural values in [one's] relations with other members of the society', and 'contribute to the best of [one's] abilities . . . to the promotion and achievement of African unity'.

This theme of solidarity appears also in the African Charter's definitions of rights. Article 10(2) protects individuals against being compelled 'to join an association', but '[s]ubject to the obligation of solidarity provided for in Article 29'. Article 25 provides that states must 'promote and ensure through teaching, education and publication' respect for the rights declared and to assure that such rights 'as well as corresponding obligations and duties are understood'.

That is, depending on their interpretation and application, duties and ideals of solidarity may impinge in clear and serious ways on the Charter's definitions of rights themselves. Moreover, the Charter imposes individual duties not only on the state but also on different groups or communities within (or perhaps transcending) that state.

Consider some of the problems raised by these provisions about individual duties:

1. Sometimes what appear to be conventional terms of reference may bear plural meanings that affect the nature of the duty. For example, what definition applies to the word 'family' in Article 27 — the nuclear or extended family? In the African context, one might think of the extended family. Nonetheless, the only specific reference to family relationships in the three articles on duties deals with parents and children (Article 29(1)).

Or how are we to understand 'society' in Article 27 — as referring to the nation state, or to prevailing social and cultural structures within the state? It is striking that the article does not mention or seem to include ethnic groups, for they are frequently not 'legally' recognized.

2. As in the other two articles on duties, the requirements put on the individual by Article 28 raise the question of whether, and by whom, these duties are to be enforced. Who or what institution is to give meaning and application to them, or even provide general guidance for their performance? To the present, the African Commission has taken no steps toward interpretation or general elaboration of the provisions on duties. The question remains open whether the three articles are to constitute in some sense 'binding' and enforceable obligations.

3. The duties are of such breadth and so ambiguous in their connotations that a regime of serious enforcement without some degree of prior elaboration is difficult

to imagine. Consider, for example, Article 28's provision that non-discrimination is not simply a duty of the state, but individuals also must not discriminate against other individuals. The article does not list any forbidden grounds for discrimination. Nor does it on its face distinguish between discrimination in the so-called private and public spheres — that is, discrimination in personal social relationships, and in employment or housing.

4. Article 29 raises a host of such issues, none more salient than the question whether it imposes on individuals a duty to uphold extant, traditional structures ranging from the family to the government. The critical terms seem to be 'harmonious', 'cohesion', 'community', 'security', 'social and national solidarity', 'territorial integrity', 'positive African cultural values', 'moral well-being of society', and last but not least, 'African unity'. How are these injunctions to be reconciled with the rights earlier declared?

Consider the following analysis of duties and their relationships both to rights and to African tradition and culture.

MAKAU MUTUA, HUMAN RIGHTS AND THE AFRICAN FINGERPRINT

in *Mutua, Human Rights: A Political and Cultural Critique* (2002), at 71

...

... [M]uch of the criticism of the Charter has been directed at its inclusion of duties on individuals .... This criticism ... should [lead us to] examine the concept of duty in precolonial African societies and demonstrate its validity in conceptualizing a unitary, integrated conception of human rights in which the extreme individualism of current human rights norms is tempered by the individual's obligation to the society.

Capturing the view of many Africans, B. Obinna Okere has written that the 'African conception of man is not that of an isolated and abstract individual, but an integral member of a group animated by a spirit of solidarity.' ...

...

In practical terms, this philosophy of the group-centered individual evolves through a series of carefully taught rights and responsibilities. At the root were structures of social and political organization, informed by gender and age, which served to enhance solidarity and ensure the existence of the community into perpetuity. ... Relationships, rights, and obligations flowed from these organizational structures, giving the community cohesion and viability. Certain obligations, such as the duty to defend the community and *its* territory, attached by virtue of birth and group membership. ...

...

Defense of the community, a state-type right exacted on those who came under its protection, was probably the most serious positive public obligation borne by young men. ... [M]ost individual duties attached at the family and kinship levels ...

...

This conception, that of the individual as a moral being endowed with rights but also bounded by duties, proactively uniting his needs with the needs of others, was the quintessence of the formulation of rights in precolonial societies. It radically differs from the liberal conception of the individual as the state's primary antagonist. . . . Moreover, it provides those concerned with the universal conception of human rights with a basis for imagining another dialectic: the harmonization of duties and rights. . . . This African worldview, [Cobbah] writes, "is for all intents and purposes as valid as the European theories of individualism and the social contract." Any concept of human rights with pretensions of universality cannot avoid mediating between these two seemingly contradictory notions.

The Duty/Rights Conception

. . . [T]he African Charter is the first human rights document to articulate the concept [of duty] in any meaningful way. . . .

. . . Perhaps at no other time in the history of the continent have Africans needed each other more than they do today. Although there is halting progress toward democratization in some African countries, the continent is generally on a steady track to political and economic collapse. Now in the fifth decade of postcolonialism, African states have largely failed to forge viable, free, and prosperous countries. . . . The new African states have failed to inspire loyalty in the citizenry; to produce a political class with integrity and a national interest; to inculcate in the military, the police, and the security forces their proper roles in society; to build a nation from different linguistic and cultural groups; and to fashion economically viable policies. . . .

. . .

Ironically, colonialism, though a divisive factor, created a sense of brotherhood or unity among different African nations within the same colonial state, because they saw themselves as common victims of an alien, racist. and oppressive structure. Nevertheless, as the fissures of the modern African state amply demonstrate, the unity born out of anticolonialism has not sufficed to create an enduring identity of nationhood in the context of the postcolonial state. . . .

This difficult social and political transformation from self-governing ethnocultural units to the multilingual, multicultural modern state — the disconnection between the two Africas: one precolonial, the other post-colonial — lies at the root of the current crisis. . . .

. . .

. . . While acknowledging that it is impossible to recapture and reinstitute precolonial forms of social and political organization, this chapter nonetheless asserts that Africa must partially look inward, to its precolonial past, for possible solutions. Certain ideals in precolonial African philosophy, particularly the conception of humanity, and the interface of rights and duties in a communal context as provided for in the African Charter, should form part of that process of reconstruction. . . .

. . .

The series of explicit duties spelled out in articles 27 through 29 of the African Charter could be read as intended to recreate the bonds of the precolonial era among individuals and between individuals and the state. They represent a rejection of the individual "who is utterly free and utterly irresponsible and opposed to society." In a proper reflection of the nuanced nature of societal obligations in the precolonial era, the African Charter explicitly provides for two types of duties: direct and indirect. A direct duty is contained, for example, in article 29(4) of the Charter which requires the individual to "preserve and strengthen social and national solidarity, particularly when the latter is threatened." There is nothing inherently sinister about this provision; it merely repeats a duty formerly imposed on members of precolonial communities. If anything, there exists a heightened need today, more than at any other time in recent history, to fortify communal relations and defend national solidarity....

The African Charter provides an example of an indirect duty in article 27(2), which states that "The rights and freedoms of each individual shall be exercised with due regard to the rights of others, collective security, morality and common interest." This duty is in fact a limitation on the enjoyment of certain individual rights. It merely recognizes the practical reality that in African societies, as elsewhere in the world, individual rights are not absolute. Individuals are asked to reflect on how the exercise of their rights in certain circumstances might adversely affect other individuals or the community....

Duties are also grouped according to whether they are owed to individuals or to larger units such as the family, society, or the state. Parents, for example, are owed a duty of respect and maintenance by their children. Crippling economic problems do not allow African states to contemplate some of the programs of the welfare state. The care of the aged and needy falls squarely on family and community members. This requirement — a necessity today — has its roots in the past: it was unthinkable to abandon a parent or relative in need....

Some duties are owed by the individual to the state. These are not distinctive to African states; many of them are standard obligations that any modern state places on its citizens.... Such duties are rights that the community or the state, defined as all persons within it, holds against the individual....

The duties that require the individual to strengthen and defend national independence, security, and the territorial integrity of the state are inspired by the continent's history of domination and occupation by outside powers over the centuries. The duties represent an extension of the principle of self-determination, used in the external sense, as a shield against foreign occupation.... Likewise, the duty to place one's intellectual abilities at the service of the state is a legitimate state interest, for the "brain drain" has robbed Africa of massive intellect. In recognition of the need for the strength of diversity, rather than its power to divide, the Charter asks individuals to promote African unity, an especially critical role given arbitrary balkanization by the colonial powers and the ethnic animosities fostered within and between the imposed states.

... [T]he Charter also requires the state to protect the family, which it terms "the natural unit and basis of society," and the "custodian of morals and traditional values." There is an enormous potential for advocates of equality rights to be concerned that these provisions could be used to support the patriarchy and other repressive practices of precolonial social ordering. It is now generally accepted that one of the strikes against the precolonial regime was its strict separation of gender roles and, in many cases, the limitation on, or exclusion of, women from political participation. . . .

However, these are not the practices that the Charter condones when it requires states to assist families as the "custodians of morals and traditional values." Such an interpretation would be a cynical misreading of the Charter. The reference is to those traditional values which enhanced the dignity of the individual and emphasized the dignity of motherhood and the importance of the female as the central link in the reproductive chain; women were highly valued as equals in the process of the regeneration of life. The Charter guarantees, unambiguously and without equivocation, the equal rights of women in its gender equality provision by requiring states to "eliminate every discrimination against women" and to protect women's rights in international human rights instruments." . . .

. . .

The most damaging criticism of the language of duties in Africa sees them as "little more than the formulation, entrenchment, and legitimation of state rights and privileges against individuals and peoples." However, critics who question the value of including duties in the Charter point only to the theoretical danger that states might capitalize on the duty concept to violate other guaranteed rights. The fear is frequently expressed that emphasis on duties may lead to the "tramping" of individual rights if the two are in opposition. . . .

. . .

. . . It should be the duty of the African Commission in its jurisprudence to clarify which, if any, of these duties are moral or legal obligations, and what the scope of their application ought to be. The Commission could lead the way in suggesting how some of the duties — on the individual as well as the state — might be implemented. The concept of national service, for example, could utilize traditional notions in addressing famine, public works, and community self-help projects. The care of parents and the needy could be formalized in family/state burden-sharing. The Commission should also indicate how, and in what forum, the state would respond to the breach of individual duties. It might suggest the establishment of community arbitration centers to work out certain types of disputes. . . .

. . .

This chapter was not intended to dismiss concerns about the potential *for* the misuse of the duty/rights conception by political elites to achieve narrow, personal ends. However, any notions are subject to abuse by power-hungry elites. There is no basis for concluding that the duty/rights conception is unique in this respect . . . Is it possible to introduce in the modern African state grassroots democracy, deepening it in neighborhood communities and villages in the tradition of the precolonial council of elders? Can the family reclaim its status as the basic organizational political unit in this redemocratization process? Is it possible to create a state of laws — where elected officials are bound by checks and balances — as in the days of old, where rulers were held accountable, at times through destooling?

. . .

QUESTIONS

1. Does Mutua's article (a) explain and seek to justify in terms of African history and culture the relevant provisions of the Charter, or (b) seek to reconcile those provisions with the human rights movement, or (c) both? Do you believe that he succeeds in the second task? Does he suggest that the West and Africa should in some respects go their separate ways, or that Africa has indeed much to teach the West about the directions of its own rights-oriented thought?

2. Does the Charter protect an advocate of radical reform who seeks significant changes in her state with respect to gender relationships or the character of the family? How, for example, would you reconcile the provisions of Article 29 with Article 18, to the effect that the state should 'ensure the elimination of every discrimination against women'? How would you state your argument for the supremacy of Article 18? Are you persuaded by Mutua's argument?

3. What effect might Articles 27–29 have on the Charter's provisions for speech and association, which are the very conditions of effective political participation? Are Mutua's views here helpful?

4. 'Whatever the African Charter says, African states like all states are subject to the universal human rights system of the UDHR and the two basic Covenants. If there is a conflict, if this regional regime requires or permits state conduct that universal norms prohibit, those norms must prevail. Else the "universal" human rights movement collapses into regional anarchy'. Comment.

NOTE

As prior readings underscore, rights as a fundamental language of law, politics and morals grew within and are associated with the Western liberal tradition. This is not, however, to say that the claims, interests, values and ideals expressed through rights language in the basic human rights instruments are exclusive to the Western lieral tradition. Many of them, as we have seen, may be expressed through other languages as well — for example, the language of duty and responsibility of the state, government, and individuals.

To place the basic instruments in historical context, and as background for the discussion of cultural relativism in Chapter 7, it will be helpful to have in mind some notions about liberal political thought and the liberal state. The following Comment sketches basic characteristics.

COMMENT ON SOME CHARACTERISTICS OF THE LIBERAL POLITICAL TRADITION

Observers from different regions and cultures can agree that the human rights movement, with respect to its language of rights and the civil and political rights that it declares, stems principally from the liberal tradition of Western political and legal thought. That observation lies at the core of argument by states from non-Western parts of the world that some basic provisions in instruments like the UDHR or ICCPR are inappropriate and inapplicable to their circumstances. Those instruments, the argument goes, purport to give a genuinely universal expression to certain tenets of liberal political culture, and advocates basing their criticism of counties in the developing world on the human rights movement are effectively advancing a contemporary form of imperialism. Thus liberal thought and practices inform much contemporary debate examined in Chapter 7 about the meaning and relevance of cultural relativism.

For the purpose of facilitating some comparisons between liberalism and the human rights movement, this Comment sketches characteristics that observers would associate with the different expressions of the liberal tradition during the twentieth century. The Comment has a limited historical scope. It does not reach back to the origins of liberal thought in the seventeenth century and Age of Enlightenment, or to changes in that body of thought in the nineteenth century.

The liberal political tradition has never been and surely is not today a monolithic body of thought requiring one and only one form of government. The very term 'liberal' has assumed different meanings, from the liberal economics associated with the *laissez faire* school of the nineteenth century to contemporary associations of liberalism in a country like the United States with a more active and engaged state concerned with the general welfare of the population and with regulation of the market and nongovernmental actors — the modern regulatory and welfare state so familiar to Western states.

The contemporary expressions of liberal thought by theorists like Dworkin or Rawls depart significantly from the writings of the classical theorists influencing its development, like Bentham, Kant, Locke, Mill, Rousseau and Tocqueville. The differences among such classical writers are reflected in the distinct versions of liberal ideology and the varied structures and practices of self-styled liberal democracies. This variety and ongoing transformation suggest caution in making inclusive and dogmatic comparisons between, say, liberalism and the human rights movement, which has during the last six decades generated its own internal conflicts and has itself undergone significant change.

No characteristic of the liberal tradition is more striking than its emphasis on the individual. Liberal political theory and the constitutive instruments of many liberal states frequently employ basic concepts or premises like the dignity and autonomy of the individual, and the respect that is due to all individuals. The vital concept of equality informs these terms: the equal dignity of all human beings, the equal respect to which individuals are entitled, the equal right for self-realization. It is not then surprising that equal protection and equal opportunities without repressive discrimination constitute so cardinal a value of contemporary liberalism. In general, the protection of members of minorities against invidious discrimination continues to be a central concern for the liberal state.

Such stress on the individual informs basic justifications for the state. The liberal state rests on, its very legitimacy stems from, the consent of the people within it. Within liberal theory, that consent is both hypothetical, as in the notion of a social contract among the inhabitants of a state of nature to create the political state, and institutionalized through typical practices such as periodic elections. Such ideas are explicit in the basic human rights instruments. Note Article 21 of the UDHR ('The will of the people shall be the basis of the authority of government') and Article 25 of the ICCPR (the importance of elections 'guaranteeing the free expression of the will of the electors').

From the start, liberal theory has been attentive to the risk of abuse of the individual by the state. The rights language that is found in constitutional bills of rights, statutory provisions for basic rights, political traditions not expressed in positive law, and writings of theorists and advocates respond to this need for protection against the state. The rights with which the individual is endowed limit governmental power — the right not to be tortured, not to be discriminated against on stated grounds. Until the early twentieth century, liberal theory and the liberal state were far less attentive to violations of rights by non-state actors, corporations or individuals, but heightened regulation of the non-state (private) sector and the growth of international human rights have brought significant change, particularly since World War II.

Historically the protection of the property right against interference by the state and others played a major role in liberal theory. Indeed, questions of the relationships between liberalism and free enterprise or capitalism have long been debated. They take on a particular pungency in the post Cold-War world of spreading markets, spreading democracy, and globalization.

Sometimes the types of rights just referred to are described as 'negative': the hands-off or non-interference rights (don't touch), or the right to be interfered with (as by arrest, imprisonment) only pursuant to stated processes. It is partly the prominence of the rights related to notions of individual liberty, autonomy and choice and the right related to property protection that produces the sharp division in much liberal thought between the state and individual, between government and nongovernmental sectors, between what are often referred to as the public and private realms or spheres of action.

This conception of negative rights, and of negative freedom as the absence of external constraints, together with the historical alliance of political liberalism with conceptions of a free market and *laissez faire*, led to liberalism's early emphasis on sharply limited government. The tension between that early ideology and background, and the growing emphasis over more than a century on the welfare and regulatory functions of the modern liberal state, remain central to much political and moral debate today.

That debate is related to an opposition that has developed in liberal thought between *negative* rights or negative liberty (freedom), and *positive* or *affirmative* rights or liberty (freedom). Those terms have acquired different meanings, to be explored in this and later chapters. For example, 'positive rights' have been described as entitlements of individuals to the effect that the state should not simply respect the 'private' sphere of inviolability of the individual (the negative rights), but should also 'act' in particular ways to benefit the individual, perhaps by providing education or health care. In this sense, the 'positive rights' of individuals such as the right to education or health care impose duties on the state to provide the necessary institutions or resources. Compare the Comment on state duties at p. 185, *supra*.

In a different and more ample sense, *positive liberty* has been described as 'liberty to' as opposed to 'liberty from'—for example, the liberty to realize oneself, to satisfy one's real interests, to achieve individual self-determination. One form of such positive liberty facilitated by the state would be governmental policies and institutions fostering the active political participation of citizens in electoral and other processes that help to determine the exercise of public power. Through such positive liberty, the individual can participate in the creation and recreation of self and state. The state readily and naturally becomes involved in this search of individuals for positive liberty, characteristically by creating the conditions that make the individual quest more likely to succeed, but at the dangerous authoritarian extreme by attempting to define the content of genuine self-realization and by coercing individuals to achieve it.

What an individual should seek in life, what idea of the good in life that individual holds, how the individual seeks self-realization, remain in the liberal state matters of individual choice to which both negative and positive conceptions of rights and freedom are relevant. That state must be open to a variety of ends, a variety of conceptions of the good, that individuals will express. The liberal state must then be a pluralist state. Its structure of rights, going beyond the rights to personal security and equal protection to include rights of conscience and speech and association, facilitates and protects the many types of diversity within pluralism, as well as ongoing argument in the public arena about the forms and goals of social and political life.

Precisely what governmental structures best realize such liberal principles is among the disputed features of the liberal tradition. The liberal state is closely associated with the ideal of the rule of law, hence with some minimum of separation of government powers such as an independent judiciary that can protect individual rights against executive abuse. The fear of tyranny of the majority lies at the foundation of the argument for restrictions on governmental power through a constitutional bill of rights limiting or putting conditions on what government can do. How to enforce that bill of rights against the executive and legislature has never achieved a consensus among liberal states. They vary in the degree to which they subject legislative action to judicial review, hence in the degree to which governmental power, even if supported by a freely voting majority of the population, can abridge or transform or abolish rights. The trend among liberal democracies over the last few decades has been toward judicial review of legislative as well as executive action.

The liberal tradition continues to be subjected to deep challenges from within and without, and thus continues its process of evolutionary change. During and particularly after the Cold War, its interaction with states of the developing world posed complex issues in relation to efforts of some of those states to develop new forms of government and economy. For example, the relationships in the former Communist states of Central and East Europe between liberalism, privatization and property rights, markets and regulation thereof, and the provision of welfare remain ambiguous and in flux. More generally, questions of the relationship between liberalism and a market economy, or liberalism and ethnic nationalism, have assumed heightened prominence. In a Western country such as the United States, liberalism responds to challenges from diverse perspectives such as communitarian ideas, civic republicanism, and multiculturalism (cultural particularism).

Some of these contemporary challenges underscore a continuing debate within liberalism, the two sides to which can lead to significantly different political and social orders: *individual* or *group* identity as primary. The group may be — to use the conventional porous and overlapping terms — national, linguistic, religious, cultural, ethnic. At the extreme, it is not compatible with a liberal creed for a governing order to subordinate individuals fully to the demands of such kinds of groups. With respect to the core values of liberalism, individual rights remain lexically prior to the demands of a culture or group, to the claims of any collective identity or group solidarity.

Nonetheless, the liberal state is hardly hostile to groups as such. It is not blind to the influence of groups (religious, cultural, ethnic) or of group and cultural identity in shaping the individual. Indeed, the political life of modern liberal democracies is largely constituted by the interaction, lobbying and other political participation of groups, some of which are natural in their defining characteristic (race, sex, elderly citizens), and some formed out of shared interests (labour unions, business associations, environmental groups). The liberal state, by definition committed to pluralism, must accommodate different types of groups, and maintain the framework of rights in which they can struggle for recognition, power and survival.

Such issues indicate how much is open and debated within liberalism about the significance of the priority of the individual in the contemporary liberal state — or different types of liberal states. Should we, for example, understand the 'individual' *abstractly*, as similar in vital respects everywhere, both within the same state and universally? Or do we understand the individual *contextually*, as influenced or even determined by ethnic, cultural, national, religious and other traditions and communities? Should we even phrase the question in such dramatic contrasts, or should we rather assume that the answers are too complex for any clear choice between them?

Since the birth of the human rights movement, and particularly since the collapse of the Soviet Union, such issues about the individual and the collective have taken on great pungency in the contradictions bred, on the one hand, by the spread of both liberal ideology with its emphasis on the individual and of market ideology with its stress on private initiative, and on the other hand, by the often savage bursts of ethnic nationalism in many parts of the world with their stress on collective rather than individual identity.

The emphasis in both liberalism and the human rights movement on individual 'rights' leads to one final observation related to several of this chapter's readings. Rights are no more determinate in meaning, no less susceptible to varying interpretations and disputes among states, than any other moral, political or legal conception — for example, 'property', or 'sovereignty', or 'consent', or 'national security'. Within liberal states, different institutional solutions have been brought to the question of who should determine and develop the content of rights, and who should resolve the many and puzzling conflicts among rights. In the international arena, this problem becomes all the more complex. What mechanisms, what institutional framework, what allocation or separation of powers, what blend of overtly political and judicial resolution of these issues, will we find in the international human rights movement? Such issues are examined in Part D of this coursebook.

ADDITIONAL READING

On theories of rights see the following collections: M. Ishay (ed.), *The Human Rights Reader: Major Political Essays, Speeches, and Documents from the Bible to the Present* (1997); J. Waldron (ed.), *Theories of Rights* (1984); C. Nino (ed.), *Rights* (1992); D. Boaz (ed.), *The Libertarian Reader* (1997). In relation to duties see: D. Selbourne, *The Principle of Duty* (1994); and F. Van Hoof, 'A Universal Declaration of Human Responsibilities: Far-Sighted or Flawed?', in M. Bulterman, A. Hendriks, and J. Smith (eds.), *To Baehr in Our Minds* (1998), at 55. On liberalism see: H. Laski, *The Rise of Liberalism* (1936); G. De Ruggiero, *The History of European Liberalism* (1927); N. Rosenblum (ed.), *Liberalism and the Moral Life* (1989); M. Sandel (ed.), *Liberalism and its Critics* (1984); C. Taylor, 'What's Wrong with Negative Liberty?', in A. Ryan (ed.), *The Idea of Freedom* (1979), at 175. More generally, see R. Rorty, *Contingency, Irony, and Solidarity* (1989); R. Unger, *Democracy Realized* (1998); A. Gewirth, *The Community of Rights* (1998); and C. Nino, *The Ethics of Human Rights* (1991).

7

Conflict in Culture, Tradition and Practices: Challenges to Universalism

A. UNIVERSALISM AND CULTURAL RELATIVISM

COMMENT ON THE UNIVERSALIST-RELATIVIST DEBATE

The question of the 'universal' or 'relative' character of the rights declared in the major instruments of the human rights movement has been a source of debate and contention from the movement's start. These understandings of the character of human rights have sometimes been cast as alternatives, as polar visions with no neutral ground between them, and sometimes as allowing for a more complex view that understands some norms as universal, some as relative to context and culture. The generally antagonistic positions have borne a number of descriptions — for example, 'absolute' rights (compare 'universal') as opposed to 'contingent' rights (compare 'relative'), or imperialism in imposing rights (compare 'universal') as opposed to self-determination of peoples (compare 'relative'). The contest between these positions took on renewed vigour as the human rights movement slowly developed, and in important respects weakened, earlier more robust understandings of the scope of national sovereignty and of domestic jurisdiction. Indeed, significant links have developed over the decades between some of the claims associated with cultural relativism and claims of sovereign autonomy for a state to follow its own path.

Put simply, the partisans of universality claim that international human rights like rights to equal protection, physical security, fair trials, free speech, freedom of religion and free association, are and must be the same everywhere. This claim applies at least to the rights' general content, for advocates of the position that rights are universal of course recognize that many basic rights (such as the right to a fair criminal trial) allow for historically and culturally influenced forms of implementation or realization (i.e., states are not required to use the Anglo-American jury to assure a fair trial; states need not follow any one particular voting system to meet the requirement of a government that represents the will of the people).

Advocates of cultural relativism claim that (most, some) rights and rules about morality are encoded in and thus depend on cultural context, the term 'culture' often being used in a broad and diffuse way that reaches beyond indigenous traditions and customary practices to include political and religious ideologies and institutional structures. Hence notions of right (and wrong) and moral rules based on them necessarily differ throughout the world because the cultures in which they take root and inhere themselves differ. This relativist position can then be understood simply to assert as an empirical matter that the world contains an impressive diversity in views about right and wrong that is linked to the diverse underlying cultures.

But the strong relativist position goes beyond arguing that there is — as a matter of fact, empirically — an impressive diversity. It attaches an important consequence to this diversity: that no transcendent or transcultural ideas of right can be found or agreed on, and hence that no culture or state (whether or not in the guise of enforcing international human rights) is justified in attempting to impose on other cultures or states what must be understood to be ideas associated particularly with it. In this strong form, cultural relativism necessarily contradicts a basic premise of the human rights movement. Its strong values are respect for diversity and the related local autonomy.

On their face, human rights instruments (which in their treaty form mean to impose legal obligations, to convert moral rules into legal rules) are surely on the 'universalist' side of this debate. The landmark instrument is the *Universal* Declaration of Human Rights, parts of which have clearly become customary international law. The two Covenants, with states parties from all the world's regions, also speak in universal terms: 'everyone' has the right to liberty, 'all persons' are entitled to equal protection, 'no one' shall be subjected to torture, 'everyone' has the right to an adequate standard of living. Neither in the definitions of rights nor in the limitation clauses (such as limitations of rights because of public order or policy or public health) does the text of these basic instruments make any explicit concession to cultural variation. (The regional instruments examined in Chapter 11, and particularly the aspects of the African Charter on Human and Peoples' Rights examined at p. 504, *supra*, do express an important degree of cultural variation.)

To the relativist, these instruments and their pretension to universality may suggest primarily the arrogance or 'cultural imperialism' of the West, given the West's traditional urge — expressed for example in political ideology (liberalism) and in religious faith (Christianity) — to view its own forms and beliefs as universal, and to attempt to universalize them. Moreover, the push to universalization of norms is said by some relativists to destroy diversity of cultures and hence to amount to another path toward cultural homogenization in the modern world — itself a contradiction of the value of cultural survival stressed in Article 27, for example, of the ICCPR. But the debate between these two positions follows no simple route. It is open to a range of views and strategies that the materials in this Section A explore at a general and theoretical level — and that the case studies in Section B further probe.

During the Cold War, such debates (sometimes no more than highly politicized accusations, routine polemics) were dominantly between the Communist world (and its sympathizers) and the Western democracies. The Western democracies charged the Communist world with violating many basic rights, particularly those of a civil and political character. That world replied both by charging the West with violations of the more important economic and social rights, and by asserting that the political and ideological structures of Communist states pointed toward a different understanding of rights.

That debate died more-or-less together with the Soviet Union, though some of its themes survive in different form. Today the universal-relative debate takes place primarily in a North-South (or West-East) framework between developed and less developed countries, or in a religious (West-Islam) framework. It also includes non-state actors such as indigenous peoples.

NOTE

The principle of universalism of human rights norms that permeates the universal instruments starting with the UDHR rests on a few basic postulates, beliefs, assumptions. Perhaps the fundamental postulate, one that embraces all human beings, is equal human dignity. Denial of that principle, at least with respect to the regulation of action and behaviour, itself shatters universalism in the sense of the human rights corpus, without even reaching the divisive issues posed by cultural relativism. That denial has been a commonplace in world history, strikingly evident in the history of the twentieth century. Consider the following observations of a philosopher, Richard Rorty, in 'Human Rights, Rationality and Sentimentality', in Obrad Saviá (ed), *The Politics of Human Rights* 67 (1999), at 74:

> ... [E]verything turns on who counts as a fellow human being, as a rational agent in the only relevant sense — the sense in which rational agency is synonymous with membership in *our* moral community.
>
> For most white people, until very recently, most Black people did not so count. For most Christians, up until the seventeenth century or so, most heathens did not so count. For the Nazis, Jews did not so count. For most males in countries in which the average annual income is under four thousand dollars, most females still do not so count. Whenever tribal and national rivalries become important, members of rival tribes and nations will not so count. Kant's account of the respect due to rational agents tells you that you should extend the respect you feel for people like yourself to all featherless bipeds. This is an excellent suggestion, a good formula for secularizing the Christian doctrine of the brotherhood of man. But it has never been backed up by an argument based on neutral premises, and it never will be. Outside the circle of post-Enlightenment European culture ... most people are simply unable to understand why membership in a biological species is supposed to suffice for membership in a moral community. This is not because they are insufficiently rational. It is, typically, because they live in a world in which it would be just too risky — indeed, would often be insanely dangerous — to let one's sense of moral community stretch beyond one's family, clan, or tribe.
>
> To get whites to be nicer to Blacks, males to females, Serbs to Muslims, or straights to gays, to help our species link up into what Rabossi calls a 'planetary community' dominated by a culture of human rights, it is of no use whatever to say, with Kant: notice that what you have in common, your humanity, is more important than these trivial differences. For the people we are trying to convince

> will rejoin that they notice nothing of the sort. Such people are *morally* offended by the suggestion that they should treat someone who is not kin as if he were a brother ... They are offended by the suggestion that they treat people whom they do not think of as human as if they were human....
>
> This rejoinder is not just a rhetorical device, nor is it in any way irrational. It is heartfelt. The identity of these people, the people whom we should like to convince to join our Eurocentric human rights culture, is bound up with their sense of who they are *not*. Most people — especially people relatively untouched by the European Enlightenment — simply do not think of themselves as, first and foremost, human beings. Instead, they think of themselves as being a certain *good* sort of human being — a sort defined by explicit opposition to a particularly bad sort. It is crucial for their sense of who they are that they are *not* an infidel, not a queer, not a woman, *not* an untouchable. Just in so far as they are impoverished, and as their lives are perpetually at risk, they have little else than pride in not being what they are not to sustain their self-respect....

NOTE

The three introductory readings below come out of the rich anthropological literature on culture and cultural relativism. Anthropologists have long had to wrestle with these issues, in the context of their ethnographic writings about diverse cultures whose practices and values depart radically from the West. Often those practices would be subject to serious moral criticism from the perspectives of Western thought. The anthropological writings have sought primarily to describe, explain and understand the alien culture, within the framework of one or another theoretical perspective or methodology. They have not historically sought to pass judgement on the practices involved, to condemn or praise even as they describe.

Thus the role of the anthropologist has traditionally been very different from that of the human rights investigator who monitors and reports and the human rights advocate who works to arrest the described violations. To be sure, investigators and advocates may also seek to understand and to describe the cultural contexts in which they are working. But those working with the large international human rights organizations characteristically combine their description with moral and legal assessment of a given state's conduct against international human rights standards. They will in appropriate cases condemn the state's conduct and urge the state or others to take corrective or coercive measures. Their work is inherently judgmental, normatively based. They seek to vindicate and advance the human rights movement.

As noted in the readings, the traditional anthropologists' approach to these questions has come under recurrent challenge. Questions have been raised about the appropriate stance of the anthropologist toward practices and values that are offensive from a Western viewpoint. Ought she be critical of them, or on the contrary be tolerant and accepting, or simply be distant and neutral while in the role of observer and explainer. If critical, under what standards would she criticize?

Most of the anthropological debate on such issues developed before the international human rights movement became prominent in the 1970s, and makes no reference to that movement. The Statement on Human Rights, p. 528, *infra*, is an exception to this observation. Moreover, bear in mind in the following readings that the human rights movement addresses primarily states — and primarily individuals' rights against the state — whereas ethnographic writings involve primarily peoples or tribes or societies, which may be nonstate (often sub-state) entities or which in any event are objects of study distinct from the political organization and political acts of the state itself.

ELVIN HATCH, CULTURE AND MORALITY: THE RELATIVITY OF VALUES IN ANTHROPOLOGY

(1983), at 8

... Herskovits wrote that cultural relativism developed because of

> the problem of finding valid cross-cultural norms. In every case where criteria to evaluate the ways of different peoples have been proposed, in no matter what aspect of culture, the question has at once posed itself: 'Whose standards?' ... [T]he need for a cultural relativistic point of view has become apparent because of the realization that there is no way to play this game of making judgments across cultures except with loaded dice.

Ethical relativism is generally conceived as standing at the opposite pole from absolutism, which is the position that there is a set of moral principles that are universally valid as standards of judgment. One absolutist ethical theory is the traditional Christian view that right and wrong are God-given, and that all people may be judged according to Christian values. A wide range of purely secular ethical theories have also developed....

It is the *content* of moral principles, not their existence, that is variable among human beings. It seems that all societies have some form of moral system, for people everywhere evaluate the actions of kinsmen, neighbors, and acquaintances as virtuous, estimable, praiseworthy, and honorable, or as unworthy, shameful, and despicable. These evaluations take objective form as sanctions, such as open praise or rebuke; and in extreme cases, violence and execution. The ubiquity of the moral evaluation of behavior apparently is a feature which sets humanity apart from other organisms....

...

Chapter 4. The Call for Tolerance

... By and large ethical relativists have been anthropologists and not philosophers, and it is chiefly in the anthropological literature that we find arguments in its favor. Two people in particular have stood out as its proponents in the United States, Melville Herskovits and Ruth Benedict, both of whom were students of Boas. Almost without exception, the philosophers are disapproving, for usually they mention ethical relativism only to criticize it while in the course of arguing some other ethical theory.

At least two very different versions of ethical relativism have been advanced by anthropologists, and these need to be distinguished since they have their own faults and virtues. The first is sometimes classified (erroneously, as we shall see) as a form of skepticism, and I will call it the Boasian version of ethical relativism.... Skepticism in ethics is the view that nothing is really either right or wrong, or that there are no moral principles with a reasonable claim to legitimacy. It has been suggested that the Boasian position differs from this on one main point: Boasian relativism implies that principles of right and wrong do have some validity, but a very limited one, for they are legitimate only for the members of the society in which they are found. The values of the American middle class are valid for middle-class Americans, but not for the Trobriand Islanders, and vice versa.

Philosophers have presented a wide range of arguments against Boasian ethical relativism ... According to this argument, Boasian relativism is in essence a moral theory that gives a central place to one particular value.... It contains a more or less implicit value judgment in its call for tolerance: it asserts that we *ought* to respect other ways of life....

...The call for tolerance was an appeal to the liberal philosophy regarding human rights and self-determinism. It expressed the principle that others ought to be able to conduct their affairs as they see fit, which includes living their lives according to the cultural values and beliefs of their society. Put simply, what was at issue was human freedom.

The call for tolerance (or for the freedom of foreign peoples to live as they choose) was a matter of immediate, practical importance in light of the pattern of Western expansion. As Western Europeans established colonies and assumed power over more and more of the globe, they typically wanted both to Christianize and civilize the indigenous peoples. Christian rituals were fostered or imposed, and 'pagan' practices were prohibited, sometimes with force. The practice of plural marriage was condemned as a barbaric custom, and Western standards of modesty were enforced in an attempt to improve morals by covering the body. In the Southwest of North America, Indians who traditionally had lived in scattered encampments were made to settle in proper villages like 'civilized' people. The treatment of non-Western societies by the expanding nations of the West is a very large blot on our history, and had the Boasian call for tolerance — and for the freedom of others to define 'civilization' for themselves — been heard two or three centuries earlier, this blot might not loom so large today.

...

To develop a moral theory around the principle of tolerance raises the need to justify that principle: what reasons or grounds can be given to make the case that cultural differences ought to be respected? ... The relativists make the error of deriving an 'ought' statement from an 'is' statement. To say that values vary from culture to culture is to describe (accurately or not) an empirical state of affairs in the real world, whereas the call for tolerance is a value judgment of what ought to be, and it is logically impossible to derive the one from the other. The fact of moral diversity no more compels our approval of other ways of life than the existence of cancer compels us to value ill-health.

...

Chapter 5. The Limits of Tolerance

The Boasian version of ethical relativism is subject to even harsher criticism . . . in its commitment to the status quo. The approval it enjoins seems to be absolute, leaving no room for judgment . . .

. . .

The moral principle of tolerance that is proposed by Boasian relativism carries the obligation that one cannot be indifferent toward other ways of life — it obligates us to approve what others do. So if missionaries or government officials were to interfere in Yanomamo affairs for the purpose of reducing violence, the relativist would be obligated to oppose these moves in word if not action. Similarly, by the strict logic of relativism, Chagnon was wrong to insist that the mother feed her emaciated child. The Boasian relativist is placed in the morally awkward position of endorsing the infant's starvation, the rape of abducted women, the massacre of whole villages . . .

Chapter 6. A Growing Disaffection

. . .

We can now understand why ethical relativism has fallen on such hard times in spite of the resurgence of pessimism during the 1960s and later. First, it has been the experience of most anthropologists that non-Western peoples (and especially Third World nations) want change, at least to some extent: second, it is clear that they are often disadvantaged if it does not come; third, anthropologists by and large have altered their thinking about the relativity of material interests and improvement: most today consider these to be general values that can be applied throughout the world.

Not only has relativism fallen on hard times, it has become the subject of angry criticism, much of it from the Third World, which tends to conceive anthropologists as conservative in their attitudes toward change and therefore as promoting the subservience of the underdeveloped nations. . . .

. . .

Whatever the cause, according to the radical critique, relativism has played directly into the hands of the oppressors throughout the world by its tacit support of the status quo. The relativists have not recognized that the exotic cultures to which they grant equal validity are poverty-stricken, powerless, and oppressed. William Willis comments that the relativist 'avoids the distress and misery' of foreign peoples who are 'cringing and cursing at the aggressive cruelty' of the Western nations. This avoidance of the matter of oppression 'helps explain the lack of outrage that has prevailed in anthropology until recent years'. Willis writes: 'Since relativism is applied only to 'aboriginal' customs, it advises colored peoples to preserve those customs that contributed to initial defeat and subsequent exploitation. . . . Hence, relativism defines the good life for colored peoples differently than for white people, and the good colored man is the man of the bush'. Instead of leaving cultures as they are, as museum pieces, we should help to bring about change — or, better, we should help the oppressed to bring about change.

. . .

SALLY ENGLE MERRY, HUMAN RIGHTS AND GENDER VIOLENCE

(2006), at 2

Ch. 1. Culture and Transnationalism

...

... Human rights ideas, embedded in cultural assumptions about the nature of the person, the community, and the state, do not translate easily from one setting to another. If human rights ideas are to have an impact, they need to become part of the consciousness of ordinary people around the world. Considerable research on law and everyday social life shows that law's power to shape society depends not on punishment alone but on becoming embedded in everyday social practices, shaping the rules people carry in their heads. Yet, there is a great distance between the global sites where these ideas are formulated and the specific situations in which they are deployed. We know relatively little about how individuals in various social and cultural contexts come to see themselves in terms of human rights.

Nor do ideas and approaches move readily the other way from local to global settings. Global sites are a bricolage of issues and ideas brought to the table by national actors. But transnational actors, and even some national elites, are often uninterested in local social practices or too busy to understand them in their complicated contexts.... Transnational reformers must adhere to a set of standards that apply to all societies if they are to gain legitimacy....

The division between transnational elites and local actors is based less on culture or tradition than on tensions between a transnational community that envisions a unified modernity and national and local actors for whom particular histories and contexts are important. Intermediaries such as NGO and social movement activists play a critical role in interpreting the cultural world of transnational modernity for local claimants... [T]hey take local stories and frame them in ... human rights language....

This book ... explains how human rights create a political space for reform using a language legitimated by a global consensus on standards. But this political space comes with a price. Human rights promote ideas of individual autonomy, equality, choice, and secularism even when these ideas differ from prevailing cultural norms and practices. Human rights ideas displace alternative visions of social justice that are less individualistic and more focused on communities and responsibilities, possibly contributing to the cultural homogenization of local communities....

...

There are several conundrums in applying human rights to local places. First, human rights law is committed to setting universal standards using legal rationality, yet this stance impedes adapting those standards to the particulars of local context. This perspective explains why local conditions often seem irrelevant to global debates. Second, human rights ideas are more readily adopted if they are packaged in familiar terms, but they are more transformative if they challenge existing assumptions about power and relationships. Activists who use human rights for local social movements face a paradox. Rights need to be presented in local cultural terms in order to be persuasive, but they must challenge existing relations of power in order to be effective. Third, to have local impact, human rights ideas need to be framed in terms of local values and images, but in order to receive funding, a wider audience, and international legitimacy, they have to be framed in terms of transnational rights principles....

...

Theorizing the Global-Local Interface

The global-local divide is often conceptualized as the opposition between rights and culture, or even civilization and culture. Those who resist human rights often claim to be defending culture. For example, male lineage heads in the rural New Territories of Hong Kong claimed that giving women rights to inherit land would destroy the social fabric.... [T]hese arguments depend on a very narrow understanding of culture and the political misuse of this concept....

Even as anthropologists and others have repudiated the idea of culture as a consensual, interconnected system of beliefs and values, the idea has taken on new life in the public sphere, particularly with reference to the global South....

...

Seeing culture as contested and as a mode of legitimating claims to power and authority dramatically shifts the way we understand the universalism-relativism debate. It undermines those who resist changes that would benefit weaker groups in the name of preserving "culture," and it encourages human rights activists to pay attention to local cultural practices. This view of culture emphasizes that culture is hybrid and porous and that the pervasive struggles over cultural values within local communities are competitions over power. More recent anthropological scholarship explores processes by which human rights ideas are mobilized locally, adapted, and transformed and, in turn, how they shape local political struggles. As Cowan, Dembour, and Wilson point out, "Rather than seeing universalism and cultural relativism as alternatives which one must choose, once and for all, one should see the tension between the positions as part of the continuous process of negotiating ever-changing and interrelated global and local norms". Culture in this sense does not serve as a barrier to human rights mobilization but as a context that defines relationships and meanings and constructs the possibilities of action.

...

Deconstructing Culture

Although culture is a term on everyone's lips, people rarely talk about what they mean by it. The term has many meanings in the contemporary world. It is often seen as the basis of national, ethnic, or religious identities. Culture is sometimes romanticized as the opposite of globalization, resolutely local and distinct.... In international human rights meetings, culture often refers to traditions and customs: ways of doing things that are justified by their roots in the past. There is a whiff of the notion of the primitive about this usage of the term culture. It is not what modern urbanites do but what governs life in the countryside.... Culture was often juxtaposed to civilization during the civilizing mission of imperialism, and this history has left a legacy in contemporary thinking.

...

There is a critical need for conceptual clarification of culture in human rights practice. Insofar as human rights relies on an essentialized model of culture, it does not take advantage of the potential of local cultural practices for change. . . .

. . . Cultures consist of repertoires of ideas and practices that are not homogeneous but continually changing because of contradictions among them or because new ideas and institutions are adopted by members. They typically incorporate contested values and practices. Cultures are not contained within stable borders but are open to new ideas and permeable to influences from other cultural systems, although not all borders are equally porous. Cultural discourses legitimate or challenge authority and justify relations of power.

Of the myriad ways culture is imagined in transnational human rights discussions, two of the most common ones reflect an essentialized concept of culture. . . .

[1] *Culture as Tradition*

Within the discourse of human rights activism, culture is often used as a synonym for tradition. Labeling a culture as traditional evokes an evolutionary vision of change from a primitive form to something like civilization. . . . So-called traditional societies are at an earlier evolutionary stage than modern ones, which are more evolved and more civilized. Culture in this sense is not used to describe the affluent countries of the global North but the poor countries of the global South, particularly isolated and rural areas. . . .

Although some human rights activists refer to "good" cultural practices and "harmful" cultural practices and a few feminist scholars examine cultural practices that protect women from violence, many who write about women's right to protection from violence identify culture and tradition as the source of the problem. . . . [T]he human rights process seeks to replace cultural practices that are discriminatory with other cultural practices rooted in modern ideas of gender equality. Thus, like the colonial state, they seek to move ethnically defined subjects into the realm of rights-bearing modernity. This effort sometimes demonizes culture as it seeks to save individuals from its oppressive effects.

Female genital cutting (also called female genital mutilation) is the poster child for this understanding of culture. . . .

. . .

[2] *Culture as National Essence*

A second common understanding of culture is as national essence or identity This concept of culture grows out of the German romantic tradition of the nineteenth century. Confronted with the claims to universal civilization of England and France, Germans began to draw a distinction between the external trappings of civilization and the inward, spiritual reality of culture. German romantics asserted the importance of a distinct culture, or *Kultur*, which formed the spiritual essence of their society. Each people, or *Volk*, has its own history and culture that expresses its genius. This includes its language, its laws, and its religion. The cosmopolitan elite corrupts it, while foreign technological and material values undermine it. . . .

Culture as national essence is fundamental to claims to indigenous sovereignty and ethnonationalism, often in resistance to human rights. In 1993, when Lee Kuan Yew of Singapore claimed that human rights failed to incorporate Asian values, he drew on this understanding of culture. With support from several other Asian leaders, he argued that Asian values differed from Western conceptions of human rights. In some ways, the Asian values argument replays the German romantic resistance to French and English claims to civilization. Indeed, one critic of the Asian values argument notes that it falls into Orientalist notions of a communitarian East, with communal values, and an individualistic West.

Although the Asian values argument is less often articulated now, it represents one of many ways that leaders assert that human rights violate the fundamental cultural principles of a nation or a religion and therefore cannot be adopted. Women's rights are often opposed by those who claim to defend culture. . . .

Culture as Contentious

. . . Over the last two decades, anthropology has elaborated a conception of culture as unbounded, contested, and connected to relations of power, as the product of historical influences rather than evolutionary change. Cultural practices must be understood in context, so that their meaning and impact change as their context shifts. . . . [Cultures] include institutional arrangements, political structures, and legal regulations. As institutions such as laws and policing change, so do beliefs, values, and practices. Cultures are not homogeneous and "pure" but produced through hybridization or creolization.

. . . These different perspectives on culture affect policies concerning women. For example, in Uruguay's country report to the committee monitoring the Women's Convention, the government expressed regret that more women were not involved in politics but blamed cultural traditions, women's involvement in domestic tasks, and the differences in wages by gender. In contrast, facing the same absence of women politicians, Denmark offered funds to offset babysitting expenses when women attended meetings. In the first case, the barrier to change is theorized as cultural tradition; in the second case, as institutional arrangements of child care. The first model sees culture as fixed; the second assumes that the meanings of gender will change as institutional and legal arrangements change.

. . .

. . . [C]ulture is as important in shaping human rights conferences as it is in structuring village mortuary rituals. Thinking of those peoples formerly labeled "backward" as the only bearers of culture neglects the centrality of culture to the practice of human rights. UN meetings are deeply shaped by a culture of transnational modernity, one that specifies procedures for collaborative decision-making, conceptions of global social justice, and definitions of gender roles. Human rights law is itself primarily a cultural system. Its limited enforcement mechanisms mean that the impact of human rights law is a matter of persuasion rather than force, of cultural transformation rather than coercive change. Its documents create new cultural frameworks for conceptualizing social justice. It is ironic that the human rights system tends to promote its new cultural vision through a critique of culture.

. . .

AMERICAN ANTHROPOLOGICAL ASSOCIATION, STATEMENT ON HUMAN RIGHTS

49 Amer. Anthropologist No. 4, 539 (1947)

[In 1947, the Commission on Human Rights created under the UN Charter was considering proposals for a declaration on basic human rights. Ultimately the instrument took the form of the Universal Declaration of Human Rights voted by the UN General Assembly in 1948. The Statement from which the following excerpts are taken was submitted to the Commission in 1947 by the Executive Board of the American Anthropological Association. It uses several terms to refer to the pending document that became the UDHR.]

The problem faced by the Commission on Human Rights of the United Nations in preparing its Declaration on the Rights of Man must be approached from two points of view. The first, in terms of which the Declaration is ordinarily conceived, concerns the respect for the personality of the individual as such and his right to its fullest development as a member of his society. In a world order, however, respect for the cultures of differing human groups is equally important.

These are two facets of the same problem, since it is a truism that groups are composed of individuals, and human beings do not function outside the societies of which they form a part. The problem is thus to formulate a statement of human rights that will do more than just phrase respect for the individual as an individual. It must also take into full account the individual as a member of the social group of which he is a part, whose sanctioned modes of life shape his behavior, and with whose fate his own is thus inextricably bound.

... How can the proposed Declaration be applicable to all human beings and not be a statement of rights conceived only in terms of the values prevalent in the countries of Western Europe and America?

...

If we begin, as we must, with the individual, we find that from the moment of his birth not only his behavior, but his very thought, his hopes, aspirations, the moral values which direct his action and justify and give meaning to his life in his own eyes and those of his fellows, are shaped by the body of custom of the group of which he becomes a member. ... [I]f the essence of the Declaration is to be, as it must, a statement in which the right of the individual to develop his personality to the fullest is to be stressed, then this must be based on a recognition of the fact that the personality of the individual can develop only in terms of the culture of his society.

...

... Doctrines of the 'white man's burden' have been employed to implement economic exploitation and to deny the right to control their own affairs to millions of peoples over the world, where the expansion of Europe and America has not meant the literal extermination of whole populations. Rationalized in terms of ascribing cultural inferiority to these peoples, or in conceptions of their backwardness in development of their 'primitive mentality', that justified their being held in the tutelage of their superiors, the history of the expansion of the western world has been marked by demoralization of human personality and the disintegration of human rights among the peoples over whom hegemony has been established.

The values of the ways of life of these peoples have been consistently misunderstood and decried. Religious beliefs that for untold ages have carried conviction and permitted adjustment to the Universe have been attacked as superstitious, immoral, untrue. And, since power carries its own conviction, this has furthered the process of demoralization begun by economic exploitation and the loss of political autonomy....

We thus come to the first proposition that the study of human psychology and culture dictates as essential in drawing up a Bill of Human Rights in terms of existing knowledge:

1. The individual realizes his personality through his culture, hence respect for individual differences entails a respect for cultural differences.

There can be no individual freedom, that is, when the group with which the individual identifies himself is not free. There can be no full development of the individual personality as long as the individual is told, by men who have the power to enforce their commands, that the way of life of his group is inferior to that of those who wield the power.

...

2. Respect for differences between cultures is validated by the scientific fact that no technique of qualitatively evaluating cultures has been discovered.

This principle leads us to a further one, namely that the aims that guide the life of every people are self-evident in their significance to that people....

3. Standards and values are relative to the culture from which they derive so that any attempt to formulate postulates that grow out of the beliefs or moral codes of one culture must to that extent detract from the applicability of any Declaration of Human Rights to mankind as a whole.

Ideas of right and wrong, good and evil, are found in all societies, though they differ in their expression among different peoples. What is held to be a human right in one society may be regarded as anti-social by another people, or by the same people in a different period of their history. The saint of one epoch would at a later time be confined as a man not fitted to cope with reality. Even the nature of the physical world, the colors we see, the sounds we hear, are conditioned by the language we speak, which is part of the culture into which we are born.

The problem of drawing up a Declaration of Human Rights was relatively simple in the eighteenth century, because it was not a matter of *human* rights, but of the rights of men within the framework of the sanctions laid by a single society....

Today the problem is complicated by the fact that the Declaration must be of worldwide applicability. It must embrace and recognize the validity of many different ways of life. It will not be convincing to the Indonesian, the African, the Indian, the Chinese, if it lies on the same plane as like documents of an earlier period...

...

NOTE

In 1999, the American Anthropological Association adopted a Declaration on Anthropology and Human Rights, www.aaanet.org/stmts/humanrts.htm. Excerpts follow:

> As a professional organization of anthropologists, the AAA has long been, and should continue to be, concerned whenever human difference is made the basis for a denial of basic human rights, where "human" is understood in its full range of cultural, social, linguistic, psychological, and biological senses.
>
> [The AAA in its working definition of principles of respect for difference "builds on" the UDHR and the basic human rights covenants and conventions.] The AAA definition thus reflects a commitment to human rights consistent with international principles but not limited by them. Human rights is not a static concept. Our understanding of human rights is constantly evolving as we come to know more about the human condition. It is therefore incumbent on anthropologists to be involved in the debate on enlarging our understanding of human rights on the basis of anthropological knowledge and research.

NOTE

The excerpts from Merry's book engage briefly in the deconstruction of culture. The human rights discourse of the last half century often raises the question of what the different proponents in the ongoing debate mean by culture, or cultural tradition or identity. What is being asserted by the claim that a given state or region must be free to follow its own 'cultural tradition', even if thereby violating norms in universal treaties? Many meanings of the term appear and disappear in this debate; often 'culture' as a justification for difference is not referred to as such but is implicit in a state's argument. Or that broad term is disaggregated into some of its complex components, such as language, religion, traditions, rituals and other practices.

Meanings of culture may also differ across the divides of different languages. Consider some definitions for 'culture' in the American Heritage Dictionary of the English Language (1969).

> … 4. Intellectual and social formation. 5. The totality of socially transmitted behavior patterns, arts, beliefs, characteristic of a community or population. 6. A style of social and artistic expression peculiar to a society or class. 7. Intellectual and artistic activity.

❀ ❀ ❀

Consider:

BRITANNUS (*shocked*):

Caesar, this is not proper.

THEODOTUS (*outraged*):
How?
CAESAR (*recovering his self-possession*):
Pardon him Theodotus: he is a barbarian, and thinks that the customs of his tribe and island are the laws of nature.

George Bernard Shaw, *Caesar and Cleopatra*, Act II

The following article explores cultural relativism from the perspective of Islam. An-Na'im looks at the 'Muslim world'. Committed to international human rights and of the Islamic faith, he argues that 'human rights advocates in the Muslim world must work within the framework of Islam to be effective . . . [and] should struggle to have their interpretations of the relevant [Islamic] texts adopted as the new Islamic scriptural imperatives for the contemporary world'. Those interpretations would be broadly consistent with the norms of international human rights. An-Na'im is then attentive to the relation between the international system and a given religious tradition, and to the possibility of reconciliation through reinterpretation of the tradition, rather than through identification of cross-cultural values among different systems that in some sense transcend or trump aspects of the religious tradition that defy or are otherwise inconsistent with them.

. . .

ABDULLAHI AHMED AN-NA'IM, HUMAN RIGHTS IN THE MUSLIM WORLD

3 Harv. Hum. Rts. J. 13 (1990)

Introduction

Historical formulations of Islamic religious law, commonly known as Shari'a, include a universal system of law and ethics and purport to regulate every aspect of public and private life. The power of Shari'a to regulate the behavior of Muslims derives from its moral and religious authority as well as the formal enforcement of its legal norms. As such, Shari'a influences individual and collective behavior in Muslim countries through its role in the socialization processes of such nations regardless of its status in their formal legal systems. For example, the status and rights of women in the Muslim world have always been significantly influenced by Shari'a, regardless of the degree of Islamization in public life. Of course, Shari'a is not the sole determinant of human behavior nor the only formative force behind social and political institutions in Muslim countries.

. . .

I conclude that human rights advocates in the Muslim world must work within the framework of Islam to be effective. They need not be confined, however, to the particular historical interpretations of Islam known as Shari'a. Muslims are obliged, as a matter of faith, to conduct their private and public affairs in accordance with the dictates of Islam, but there is room for legitimate disagreement over the precise nature of these dictates in the modern context. Religious texts, like all other texts, are open to a variety of interpretations. Human rights advocates in the Muslim world should struggle to have their interpretations of the relevant texts adopted as the new Islamic scriptural imperatives for the contemporary world.

A. Cultural Legitimacy for Human Rights

The basic premise of my approach is that human rights violations reflect the lack or weakness of cultural legitimacy of international standards in a society. Insofar as these standards are perceived to be alien to or at variance with the values and institutions of a people, they are unlikely to elicit commitment or compliance. While cultural legitimacy may not be the sole or even primary determinant of compliance with human rights standards, it is, in my view, an extremely significant one. Thus, the underlying causes of any lack or weakness of legitimacy of human rights standards must be addressed in order to enhance the promotion and protection of human rights in that society.

. . . This cultural illegitimacy, it is argued, derives from the historical conditions surrounding the creation of the particular human rights instruments. Most African and Asian countries did not participate in the formulation of the Universal Declaration of Human Rights because, as victims of colonization, they were not members of the United Nations. When they did participate in the formulation of subsequent instruments, they did so on the basis of an established framework and philosophical assumptions adopted in their absence. For example, the pre-existing framework and assumptions favored individual civil and political rights over collective solidarity rights, such as a right to development, an outcome which remains problematic today. Some authors have gone so far as to argue that inherent differences exist between the Western notion of human rights as reflected in the international instruments and non-Western notions of human dignity. In the Muslim world, for instance, there are obvious conflicts between Shari'a and certain human rights, especially of women and non-Muslims.

. . . In this discussion, I focus on the principles of legal equality and nondiscrimination contained in many human rights instruments. These principles relating to gender and religion are particularly problematic in the Muslim world.

. . .

II. Islam, Shari'a and Human Rights

. . .

A. The Development and Current Application of Shari'a

To the over nine hundred million Muslims of the world, the Qur'an is the literal and final word of God and Muhammad is the final Prophet. During his mission, from 610 A.D. to his death in 632 A.D., the Prophet elaborated on the meaning of the Qur'an and supplemented its rulings through his statements and actions. This body of information came to be known as Sunna. He also established the first Islamic state in Medina around 622 A.D. which emerged later as the ideal model of an Islamic state....

While the Qur'an was collected and recorded soon after the Prophet Muhammad's death, it took almost two centuries to collect, verify, and record the Sunna. Because it remained an oral tradition for a long time during a period of exceptional turmoil in Muslim history, some Sunna reports are still controversial in terms of both their authenticity and relationship to the Qur'an.

Because Shari'a is derived from Sunna as well as the Qur'an, its development as a comprehensive legal and ethical system had to await the collection and authentication of Sunna. Shari'a was not developed until the second and third centuries of Islam....

...

Shari'a is not a formally enacted legal code. It consists of a vast body of jurisprudence in which individual jurists express their views on the meaning of the Qur'an and Sunna and the legal implications of those views. Although most Muslims believe Shari'a to be a single logical whole, there is significant diversity of opinion not only among the various schools of thought, but also among the different jurists of a particular school....

Furthermore, Muslim jurists were primarily concerned with the formulation of principles of Shari'a in terms of moral duties sanctioned by religious consequences rather than with legal obligations and rights and specific temporal remedies. They categorized all fields of human activity as permissible or impermissible and recommended or reprehensible. In other words, Shari'a addresses the conscience of the individual Muslim, whether in a private, or public and official, capacity, and not the institutions and corporate entities of society and the state.

...

Whatever may have been the historical status of Shari'a as the legal system of Muslim countries, the scope of its application in the public domain has diminished significantly since the middle of the nineteenth century. Due to both internal factors and external influence, Shari'a principles had been replaced by European law governing commercial, criminal, and constitutional matters in almost all Muslim countries. Only family law and inheritance continued to be governed by Shari'a....

Recently, many Muslims have challenged the gradual weakening of Shari'a as the basis for their formal legal systems. Most Muslim countries have experienced mounting demands for the immediate application of Shari'a as the sole, or at least primary, legal system of the land. These movements have either succeeded in gaining complete control, as in Iran, or achieved significant success in having aspects of Shari'a introduced into the legal system, as in Pakistan and the Sudan. Governments of Muslim countries generally find it difficult to resist these demands out of fear of being condemned by their own populations as anti-Islamic. Therefore, it is likely that this so-called Islamic fundamentalism will achieve further successes in other Muslim countries.

The possibility of further Islamization may convince more people of the urgency of understanding and discussing the relationship between Shari'a and human rights, because Shari'a would have a direct impact on a wider range of human rights issues if it became the formal legal system of any country....

I believe that a modern version of Islamic law can and should be developed. Such a modern 'Shari'a' could be, in my view, entirely consistent with current standards of human rights. These views, however, are appreciated by only a tiny minority of contemporary Muslims. To the overwhelming majority of Muslims today, Shari'a is the sole valid interpretation of Islam, and as such *ought* to prevail over any human law or policy.

B. *Shari'a and Human Rights*

In this part, I illustrate with specific examples how Shari'a conflicts with international human rights standards....

...

The second example is the Shari'a law of apostasy. According to Shari'a, a Muslim who repudiates his faith in Islam, whether directly or indirectly, is guilty of a capital offense punishable by death. This aspect of Shari'a is in complete conflict with the fundamental human right of freedom of religion and conscience. The apostasy of a Muslim may be inferred by the court from the person's views or actions deemed by the court to contravene the basic tenets of Islam and therefore be tantamount to apostasy, regardless of the accused's personal belief that he or she is a Muslim.

The Shari'a law of apostasy can be used to restrict other human rights such as freedom of expression. A person may be liable to the death penalty for expressing views held by the authorities to contravene the official view of the tenets of Islam. Far from being an historical practice or a purely theoretical danger, this interpretation of the law of apostasy was applied in the Sudan as recently as 1985, when a Sudanese Muslim reformer was executed because the authorities deemed his views to be contrary to Islam.[1]

A third and final example of conflict between Shari'a and human rights relates to the status and rights of non-Muslims. Shari'a classifies the subjects of an Islamic state in terms of their religious beliefs: Muslims, *ahl al-Kitab* or believers in a divinely revealed scripture (mainly Christian and Jews), and unbelievers. In modern terms, Muslims are the only full citizens of an Islamic state, enjoying all the rights and freedoms granted by Shari'a and subject only to the limitations and restrictions imposed on women. *Ahl al-Kitab* are entitled to the status of *dhimma*, a special compact with the Muslim state which guarantees them security of persons and property and a degree of communal autonomy to practice their own religion and conduct their private affairs in accordance with their customs and laws. In exchange for these limited rights, *dhimmis* undertake to pay *jizya* or poll tax and submit to Muslim sovereignty and authority in all public affairs....

According to this scheme, non-Muslim subjects of an Islamic state can aspire only to the status of *dhimma*, under which they would suffer serious violations of their

[1] ... The Salman Rushdie affair illustrates the serious negative implications of the law of apostasy to literary and artistic expression. Mr Rushdie, a British national of Muslim background, published a novel entitled *The Satanic Verses*, in which irreverent reference is made to the Prophet of Islam, his wives, and leading companions. Many Muslim governments banned the book because their populations found the author's style and connotations extremely offensive. The late Imam Khomeini of Iran sentenced Rushdie to death *in absentia* without charge or trial....

human rights. *Dhimmis* are not entitled to equality with Muslims. [Economic and family law illustrations omitted.]

...

IV. A Case Study: The Islamic Dimension of the Status of Women

...

The present focus on Muslim violations of the human rights of women does not mean that these are peculiar to the Muslim world.[2] As a Muslim, however, I am particularly concerned with the situation in the Muslim world and wish to contribute to its improvement.

The following discussion is organized in terms of the status and rights of Muslim women in the private sphere, particularly within the family, and in public fora, in relation to access to work and participation in public affairs. This classification is recommended for the Muslim context because the personal law aspects of Shari'a, family law and inheritance, have been applied much more consistently than the public law doctrines.[3] The status and rights of women in private life have always been significantly influenced by Shari'a regardless of the extent of Islamization of the public debate.

A. Shari'a and the Human Rights of Women

... The most important general principle of Shari'a influencing the status and rights of women is the notion of *qawama*. *Qawama* has its origin in verse 4:34 of the Qur'an: 'Men have *qawama* [guardianship and authority] over women because of the advantage they [men] have over them [women] and because they [men] spend their property in supporting them [women]'. According to Shari'a interpretations of this verse, men as a group are the guardians of and superior to women as a group, and the men of a particular family are the guardians of and superior to the women of that family.

... For example, Shari'a provides that women are disqualified from holding general public office, which involves the exercise of authority over men, because, in keeping with the verse 4:34 of the Qur'an, men are entitled to exercise authority over women and not the reverse.

Another general principle of Shari'a that has broad implications for the status and rights of Muslim women is the notion of *al-hijab*, the veil. This means more than requiring women to cover their bodies and faces in public. According to Shari'a

[2] It is difficult to distinguish between Islamic, or rather Shari'a, factors and extra-Shari'a actors affecting the status and rights of women. The fact that women's human rights are violated in all parts of the world suggests that there are universal social, economic, and political factors contributing to the persistence of this state of affairs. Nevertheless, the articulation and operation of these factors varies from one culture or context to the next. In particular, the rationalization of discrimination against the denial of equality for women is based on the values and customs of the particular society. In the Muslim world, these values and customs are supposed to be Islamic or at least consistent with the dictates of Islam. It is therefore useful to discuss the Islamic dimension of the status and rights of women.

[3] The private/public dichotomy, however, is an artificial distinction. The two spheres of life overlap and interact. The socialization and treatment of both men and women at home affect their role in public life and vice versa. While this classification can be used for analysis in the Muslim context, its limitations should be noted. It is advisable to look for both the private and public dimensions of a given Shari'a principle or rule rather than assume that it has only private or public implications.

interpretations of verses 24:31, 33:33,[4] 33:53, and 33:59[5] of the Qur'an, women are supposed to stay at home and not leave it except when required to by urgent necessity. When they are permitted to venture beyond the home, they must do so with their bodies and faces covered. *Al-hijab* tends to reinforce women's inability to hold public office and restricts their access to public life. They are not supposed to participate in public life, because they must not mix with men even in public places.

... In family law for example, men have the right to marry up to four wives and the power to exercise complete control over them during marriage, to the extent of punishing them for disobedience if the men deem that to be necessary.[6] In contrast, the co-wives are supposed to submit to their husband's will and endure his punishments. While a husband is entitled to divorce any of his wives at will, a wife is not entitled to a divorce, except by judicial order on very specific and limited grounds. Another private law feature of discrimination is found in the law of inheritance, where the general rule is that women are entitled to half the share of men.

In addition to their general inferiority under the principle of *qawama* and lack of access to public life as a consequence of the notion of *al-hijab*, women are subjected to further specific limitations in the public domain. For instance, in the administration of justice, Shari'a holds women to be incompetent witnesses in serious criminal cases, regardless of their individual character and knowledge of the facts. In civil cases where a woman's testimony is accepted, it takes two women to make a single witness. *Diya*, monetary compensation to be paid to victims of violent crimes or to their surviving kin, is less for female victims than it is for male victims.

... These overlapping and interacting principles and rules play an extremely significant role in the socialization of both women and men. Notions of women's inferiority are deeply embedded in the character and attitudes of both women and men from early childhood.

...

C. Muslim Women in Public Life

A similar and perhaps more drastic conflict exists between reformist and conservative trends in relation to the status and rights of women in the public domain. Unlike personal law matters, where Shari'a was never displaced by secular law, in most Muslim countries, constitutional, criminal, and other public law matters have come to be based on secular, mainly Western, legal concepts and institutions. Consequently, the struggle over Islamization of public law has been concerned with the re-establishment of Shari'a where it has been absent for decades, or at least since the creation of the modern Muslim nation states in the first half of the twentieth century. In terms of women's rights, the struggle shall determine whether women

[4] [O Consorts of the Prophet ...] And stay quietly in your houses, and make not a dazzling display, like that of the former Times of Ignorance; and establish regular prayer, and give regular charity; and obey God and His Apostle. And God only wishes to remove all abomination from you, ye Members of the Family, and to make you pure and spotless.

[5] O Prophet! Tell thy wives and daughters, and the believing women, that they should cast their outer garments over their persons (when abroad): that is most convenient, that they should be known (as such) and not molested. And God is Oft-Forgiving, Most Merciful.

[6] Polygamy is based on verse 4:3 of the Qur'an. The husband's power to chastise his wife to the extent of beating her is based on verse 4:34 of the Qur'an.

can keep the degree of equality and rights in public life they have achieved under secular constitutions and laws.

. . .

. . . Educated women and other modernist segments of society may not be able to articulate their vision of an Islamic state in terms of Shari'a, because aspects of Shari'a are incompatible with certain concepts and institutions which these groups take for granted, including the protection of all human rights. To the extent that efforts for the protection and promotion of human rights in the Muslim world must take into account the Islamic dimension of the political and sociological situation in Muslim countries, a modernist conception of Islam is needed.

V. *Islamic Reform and Human Rights*

. . .

Islamic reform needs must be based on the Qur'an and Sunna, the primary sources of Islam. Although Muslims believe that the Qur'an is the literal and final word of God, and Sunna are the traditions of his final Prophet, they also appreciate that these sources have to be understood and applied through human interpretation and action. . . .

A. *An Adequate Reform Methodology*

. . . The basic premise of my position, based on the work of the late Sudanese Muslim reformer *Ustadh* Mahmoud Mohamed Taha, is that the Shari'a reflects a historically-conditioned interpretation of Islamic scriptures in the sense that the founding jurists had to understand those sources in accordance with their own social, economic, and political circumstances. In relation to the status and rights of women, for example, equality between men and women in the eighth and ninth centuries in the Middle East, or anywhere else at the time, would have been inconceivable and impracticable. It was therefore natural and indeed inevitable that Muslim jurists would understand the relevant texts of the Qur'an and Sunna as confirming rather than repudiating the realities of the day.

In interpreting the primary sources of Islam in their historical context, the founding jurists of Shari'a tended not only to understand the Qur'an and Sunna as confirming existing social attitudes and institutions, but also to emphasize certain texts and 'enact' them into Shari'a while de-emphasizing other texts or interpreting them in ways consistent with what they believed to be the intent and purpose of the sources. Working with the same primary sources, modern Muslim jurists might shift emphasis from one class of texts to the other, and interpret the previously enacted texts in ways consistent with a new understanding of what is believed to be the intent and purpose of the sources. This new understanding would be informed by contemporary social, economic, and political circumstances in the same way that the 'old' understanding on which Shari'a jurists acted was informed by the then prevailing circumstances. The new understanding would qualify for Islamic legitimacy, in my view, if it is based on specific texts in opposing the application of other texts, and can be shown to be in accordance with the Qur'an and Sunna as a whole.

For example, the general principle of *qawama*, the guardianship and authority of men over women under Shari'a, is based on verse 4:34 of the Qur'an.

... This verse presents *qawama* as a consequence of two conditions: men's advantage over and financial support of women. The fact that men are generally physically stronger than most women is not relevant in modern times where the rule of law prevails over physical might. Moreover, modern circumstances are making the economic independence of women from men more readily realized and appreciated. In other words, neither of the conditions — advantages of physical might or earning power — set by verse 4:34 as the justification for the *qawama* of men over women is tenable today.

The fundamental position of the modern human rights movement is that all human beings are equal in worth and dignity, regardless of gender, religion, or race. This position can be substantiated by the Qur'an and other Islamic sources as understood under the radically transformed circumstances of today. For example, in numerous verses the Qur'an speaks of honor and dignity for 'humankind' and 'children of Adam', without distinction as to race, color, gender, or religion. By drawing on those sources and being willing to set aside archaic and dated interpretations of other sources, such as the one previously given to verse 4:34 of the Qur'an, we can provide Islamic legitimacy for the full range of human rights for women.

Similarly, numerous verses of the Qur'an provide for freedom of choice and non-compulsion in religious belief and conscience.[7] These verses have been either de-emphasized as having been 'overruled' by other verses which were understood to legitimize coercion, or 'interpreted' in ways which permitted such coercion. For example, verse 9:29 of the Qur'an was taken as the foundation of the whole system of *dhimma*, and its consequent discrimination against non-Muslims. Relying on those verses which extoll freedom of religion rather than those that legitimize religious coercion, one can argue now that the *dhimma* system should no longer be part of Islamic law and that complete equality should be assured regardless of religion or belief. The same argument can be used to abolish all negative legal consequences of apostasy as inconsistent with the Islamic principle of freedom of religion. [Discussion omitted of mechanisms and methods within Islam for development and reform.]

... The ultimate test of legitimacy and efficacy is, of course, acceptance and implementation by Muslims throughout the world.

B. *Prospects for Acceptance and Likely Impact of the Proposed Reform*

...

... Governments of Muslim countries, like many other governments, formally subscribe to international human rights instruments because, in my view, they find the human rights idea an important legitimizing force both at home and abroad...

Nevertheless, the proposed reform will probably be resisted because it challenges the vested interests of powerful forces in the Muslim world and may upset male-dominated traditional political and social institutions. These forces probably

[7] See, for example, verse 2:256 of the Qur'an which provides: 'Let there be no compulsion in religion: Truth stands out clear from error ...' In verse 18:29 God instructs the Prophet: 'Say, the Truth is from your Lord. Let him who will, believe, and let him who will, reject [it]'.

will try to restrict opportunities for a genuine consideration of this reform methodology....

Consequently, the acceptance and implementation of this reform methodology will involve a political struggle within Muslim nations as part of a larger general struggle for human rights. I would recommend this proposal to participants in that struggle who champion the cause of justice and equality for women and non-Muslims, and freedom of belief and expression in the Muslim world. Given the extreme importance of Islamic legitimacy in Muslim societies, I urge human rights advocates to claim the Islamic platform and not concede it to the traditionalist and fundamentalist forces in their societies. I would also invite outside supporters of Muslim human rights advocates to express their support with due sensitivity and genuine concern for Islamic legitimacy in the Muslim world.

...

QUESTION

An-Na'im suggests an approach to the questions of how to understand divergences among cultures with respect to human rights issues and how to go about finding common ground. How would you describe that approach? Exogenous, endogenous, some mix? Does it appear helpful in resolving contemporary disputes over, say, gender discrimination or capital punishment? Do Merry's observations about culture and modes of cultural change support or call into question An-Na'im's project?

NOTE

Consider the following observation in Rosalyn Higgins, *Problems and Process: International Law and How We Use It* (1994), at 96:

> It is sometimes suggested that there can be no fully universal concept of human rights, for it is necessary to take into account the diverse cultures and political systems of the world. In my view this is a point advanced mostly by states, and by liberal scholars anxious not to impose the Western view of things on others. It is rarely advanced by the oppressed, who are only too anxious to benefit from perceived universal standards. The non-universal, relativist view of human rights is in fact a very state-centred view and loses sight of the fact that human rights are human rights and not dependent on the fact that states, or groupings of states, may behave differently from each other so far as their politics, economic policy, and culture are concerned. I believe, profoundly, in the universality of the human spirit. Individuals everywhere want the same essential things: to have sufficient food and shelter; to be able to speak freely; to practise their own religion or to abstain from religious belief; to feel that their person is not threatened by the state; to know that they will not be tortured, or detained without charge, and that, if charged, they will have a fair trial. I believe there is nothing in these aspirations that is dependent upon culture, or religion, or stage of development. They are as keenly felt by the African tribesman as by

> the European city-dweller, by the inhabitant of a Latin American shanty-town as by the resident of a Manhattan apartment.

Consider also these excerpts from remarks by Louise Arbour, UN High Commissioner for Human Rights, on the opening of the 61st session of the Commission on Human Rights, Geneva, 14 March 2005:

> Yet the normative framework of rights is by and large in place: its shape and outlines are clear. Our core treaties, historical declarations from Teheran, Vienna and Durban, together with decades of jurisprudence from treaty bodies and international tribunals provide the architectural drawings.
>
> But it is equally a truism that there is no right without a remedy and that such a paper framework should not be mistaken for a bricks and mortar dwelling.... The unfulfilled promises of equality, justice and dignity betray the rights on which these promises were said to rest.
>
> ...
>
> I am further concerned that we have unduly embroiled our normative discourse in unnecessary clashes of vision, creating competing images, each incomplete and ineffective without the addition of the other. Are human rights universal or culturally specific? Are they collectively or individually held? Should we promote them, or protect them? Which is the more effective: technical cooperation or naming and shaming; country analysis or thematic debates? Which comes first: peace or justice; economic, social and cultural rights, or civil and political rights; development or democracy?
>
> Such questions serve, in practice, as little more than a series of diversions to the real task in hand. They become the theoretical playground within which we demonstrate our irrelevance and justify our inaction, whether than inaction is borne of indifference, shrewd calculation, or despair.

ADDITIONAL READING

K. Dalacoura, *Islam, Liberalism and Human Rights* (1998); E. Cotran and A. Sherif (eds.), *Democracy, The Rule of Law and Islam* (1999); A. Pollis and P. Schwab (eds.), *Human Rights: Cultural and Ideological Perspectives* (1979); T. Dunne and N. Wheeler (eds.), *Human Rights in Global Politics* (1999); R. Schweder, M. Minow and Markus (eds.), *Engaging Cultural Differences: The Multicultural Challenges in Liberal Democracies* (2002); and A. Sajó (ed.), *Human Rights with Modesty: The Problem of Universalism* (2004).

B. DISSONANCE AND CONFLICT: ILLUSTRATIONS

Against the background of Chapters 6 and 7(A), with their examination of rights discourse and presentation of different perspectives on universalism and cultural relativism, this chapter explores four topics that are among the human rights issues now in contention and active debate among and within countries.

In the illustrations below, two different phenomena become central to the debate. (1) The asserted universal norm itself may be challenged, perhaps on the ground that it lacks universal validity, or that it conflicts with ultimate religious commands, or that it violates long-standing tradition that assures cultural integrity and survival. That is, the legitimacy or validity of the human rights norm is itself challenged. In such respects, this chapter's illustrations further develop the theme of cultural relativism. (2) Sometimes related to cultural relativism and sometimes distinct, the second phenomenon involves a conflict among rights that are all recognized to some extent in the leading human rights instruments. The dispute is formally internal to the human rights corpus. What, for example, are the respective boundaries of rights that in given contexts squarely conflict with each other? Freedom of religious belief and practice may conflict with nondiscrimination norms; freedom of speech may conflict with the protection of minority groups. As materials in Chapter 6(A) made clear, such types of conflict are endemic to rights discourse, as they are to law in general.

In several of the following studies, the issues have to do with family, gender, and religion — interrelated topics that have characterized much discussion of the last decade about cultural relativism and that often involve conflicting rights. Thus the studies examine gender and family in relation to a state's or ethnic group's internal custom, or in relation to religion.

The problems discussed in this chapter have become acute within many developing countries. In recent decades, such countries experienced strong external and internal pressures to rethink and revise, sometimes radically, their traditional beliefs and practices. The relentless assault of the developed world on other cultures, the penetration of those cultures by trade, investment, high-tech media, and tourism, as well as the universalization of ideas and values like human rights, have launched transformative processes that are often referred to under the broad rubric of globalization. The challenge to a state or region's traditional ways and to other state practices that depart from the universal human rights instruments increasingly comes from internal groups as well as from international advocates and organizations. The battle is joined.

1. GENDER

The potential for conflict in a large number of states between the objectives of several human rights treaties, on the one hand, and customary laws and practices as well as religious beliefs, on the other, has become a salient contemporary concern. Gender-related issues are here prominent, for many traditional norms and much local custom that retain power and influence today impose different roles and duties on men and women. To some extent, such problems stem from the increasing power and prominence in recent years of fundamentalist religious groups, many of which actively oppose the transformative impetus of the human rights movement with respect to traditional gender roles.

Customary laws and practices may conflict with prohibitions in the text of the ICCPR and CEDAW or in the action taken by the bodies created by these treaties. Recall Articles 2(f) and 5(a) of CEDAW that require states to take all appropriate measures to modify or abolish customs, practices, and social and cultural patterns of conduct that constitute discrimination or that are based on the idea of inferiority or on stereotyped roles for women.

This section begins with a reading that explores some problems in developing a feminist perspective on human rights related to gender, problems that bear on the following case studies. It then explores a practice that is variously referred to, with strikingly different political and moral innuendo and sometimes agendas, as female circumcision *or* female genital mutilation.

TRACY HIGGINS, ANTI-ESSENTIALISM, RELATIVISM, AND HUMAN RIGHTS

19 Harvard Women's L. J. 89 (1996)

During the Fourth United Nations World Conference on Women [in 1995], cultural differences among women presented a series of practical and theoretical problems. The practical problems arose out of the enormous task of negotiating among a large group of people a single, albeit complex, document that would set an agenda for addressing the problems of women globally. Differences in culture, language, religion, and education presented complications at every stage of the process. As a theoretical matter, such differences presented a less immediate but in some ways more difficult and persistent problem: In the face of profound cultural differences among women, how can feminists maintain a global political movement yet avoid charges of cultural imperialism?

This theoretical dilemma has become a serious political hurdle for global feminism as the challenge of cultural relativism permeates the politics of any discussion of women's rights on the international stage. For example, at the 1994 United Nations Population Conference in Cairo, the Vatican joined with several Muslim governments to condemn what they viewed as the imposition of Western norms of sexual license and individual autonomy on the rest of the world....

Feminist responses to this charge are complicated and sometimes conflicting. On the one hand, feminists note that culture and religion are often cited as justifications for denying women a range of basic rights, including the right to travel, rights in marriage and divorce, the right to own property, even the right to be protected by the criminal law on an equal basis with men. Women have much to lose, therefore, in any movement away from a universal standard of human rights in favor of deference to culture. On the other hand, feminists acknowledge that feminism itself is grounded in the importance of participation, of listening to and accounting for the particular experiences of women, especially those on the margins of power. Indeed, much feminist criticism of traditional human rights approaches has focused on the tendency of international policymakers to exclude women's experiences and women's voices. Thus, the claim that Western concepts of women's equality are exclusionary or imperialist strikes at the heart of one of feminism's central commitments — respect for difference.

In short, both the move to expand universal human rights to include those rights central to women's condition and the move toward a relativist view of human rights are consistent with and informed by feminist theory. Indeed, the tension between them reflects a tension within feminism itself, between describing women's experience collectively as a basis for political action and respecting differences among women. Addressing this tension, this Article endeavors to sort out the degree to which feminism, by virtue of its own commitments, must take cultural defenses seriously, particularly when articulated by women themselves.

. . .

Despite the general consensus [over the universality of human rights that was reflected in the Universal Declaration], differences have persisted over the scope and priorities of the international human rights agenda, differences that are translated with surprising frequency into the rhetoric of universality versus cultural relativism, imperialism versus self-determination. Notwithstanding the language of universality, the question remains: To what extent may a state depart from international norms in the name of culture? . . .

. . .

The influence of the universalist/relativist divide on the politics of human rights is perhaps nowhere more evident than in debates over women's rights as human rights. Cultural relativists have targeted feminism itself as a product of Western ideology and global feminism as a form of Western imperialism. Ironically, cultural relativists have accused feminist human rights activists of imposing Western standards on non-Western cultures in much the same way that feminists have criticized states for imposing male-defined norms on women. The complexity of this debate has sown confusion among feminist human rights activists, undermining the effectiveness of the global feminist movement . . .

[Higgins considers the criticism of some feminists that the movement in general has been characterized by 'essentialism' — that is, the belief that many categories (like gender) or groups (like women) have a real, true essence, and thus fixed properties that define what they are. Essentialism in this sense is likely to be linked to a universalist position.]

Much incisive and insightful criticism, particularly by feminists of color, has revealed that treating gender difference as the primary concern of feminism has had the effect of reinforcing gendered categories and collapsing differences among women. These critics have argued convincingly that early feminist descriptions of women's experience focused on white, middle-class, educated, heterosexual women. Consequently, the political priorities of the women's movement in the West (e.g., equal access to education and employment, abortion rights) have reflected the most urgent concerns of a relatively more powerful group of women . . . Accused of essentialism, feminists who theorized a commonality among women were criticized for committing the dual sin of reinforcing patriarchal assumptions about women as a group and marginalizing some women along the lines of race, class, and sexual orientation.

Despite its theoretical and political vulnerabilities, the practical appeal of essentialism, like the appeal of universalism, persists. Essentialist assumptions offer the promise of uniting women in a way that transcends or precedes politics . . .

Much feminist activism on the international level has been premised on two assumptions, both of which may be characterized as essentialist: first, that women share types of experiences and are oppressed in particular ways as women; and second, that these experiences are often different than those of men . . . [F]eminist progress in reshaping the scope of the international human rights agenda stands as an important example of the power of organizing around assumptions of commonality.

. . .

[Higgins explores two views about culture and coercion that are relevant to a response by feminists who are committed to universalism to the criticisms and challenge of cultural relativists and anti-essentialists. The first view has to do with the tendency in some strands of cultural relativism to 'essentialize' the local culture itself and in the process to obscure coercion.]

Feminists have questioned arguments based on a simple assertion of cultural integrity for several reasons. First, cultural relativists may inadequately attend to the degree to which power relationships within the culture itself constrain the ability of individuals to renegotiate cultural norms. Yet, this inattention is inconsistent with a concern about coercion. The relativist cannot criticize Western imperialism and at the same time ignore non-Western states' selective use of the defense of culture in the service of state power. The risk of such intra-cultural coercion seems especially great when that selective invocation of culture has differential effects on groups within the state such as minority ethnic or racial groups or women.

Second, cultural relativist arguments may oversimplify the complexity and fluidity of culture by treating culture as monolithic and moral norms within a particular culture as readily ascertainable. Yet, a single, inward glance at Western culture reveals the absurdity of this assumption. The multiplicity of beliefs in the United States (or even within a single community or family) about the legitimacy of abortion or the role of women in the family illustrates the complexity of translating imperfectly shared assumptions into evaluative standards. Such oversimplification seems inconsistent with the very premises of cultural relativism. Indeed, cultural relativists' tendency to describe differences in terms of simple opposition — Western versus non-Western — without exploring how specific cultural practices are constituted and justified 'essentializes' culture itself.

Treating culture as monolithic fails to respect relevant intra-cultural differences just as the assumption of the universality of human rights standards fails to respect cross-cultural differences. Cultural differences that may be relevant to assessing human rights claims are neither uniform nor static. Rather, they are constantly created, challenged, and renegotiated by individuals living within inevitably overlapping cultural communities.

This oversimplification of culture may lead relativists to accept too readily a cultural defense articulated by state actors or other elites on the international level, actors that tend not to be women. Yet, it seems unlikely that a cultural defense offered by the state will adequately reflect the dynamic, evolving, and possibly conflicting cultural concerns of its citizens.

Given the complexity and multiplicity of culture, the ability or inclination of heads of state to identify and translate cultural practices into specific defenses against the imposition of Western human rights norms is questionable. Feminists in particular have cited example after example in which culture has been selectively and perhaps cynically invoked to justify oppressive practices.

...

[The second view about culture and coercion raises the question of the role of private ordering in coercion.]

In contrast to cultural relativists and liberal pluralists, feminist anti-essentialists are centrally concerned with the interplay between culture and self, exploring ways in which culture constructs gendered individuals. ... [F]eminism emphasizes the role of private power. The most important premise of this feminist view is that the sex/gender system is substantially a product of culture rather than divine will, human biology or natural selection. Implicit in this assumption is the claim that cultural norms — language, law, myth, custom — are not merely products of human will and action but also define and limit the possibilities for human identity.

Connected with this view of cultural limitations on human subjectivity is the notion that cultural norms function as a source of power and control within modern society. Consistent with this recognition, many feminists have rejected a theory of power that posits monolithic control held by a coherent or unified sovereign. Yet, it is precisely this model of power that traditional human rights standards are designed to regulate and to which cultural relativists often defer when exercised within cultural boundaries. In contrast, feminists ... have emphasized the degree to which power is exercised both from above, by sovereigns, and within concrete social interactions and relationships — in short, through culture. For feminists, culture itself becomes a source of control and a site of resistance, a form of power that feminist human rights activists must engage directly along with more traditional public and private forms.

...

Conclusion

Confronted with the challenge of cultural relativism, feminism faces divergent paths, neither of which seems to lead out of the woods of patriarchy. The first path, leading to simple tolerance of cultural difference, is too broad. To follow it would require feminists to ignore pervasive limits on women's freedom in the name of an autonomy that exists for women in theory only.

The other path, leading to objective condemnation of cultural practices, is too narrow. To follow it would require feminists to dismiss the culturally distinct experiences of women as false consciousness. Yet to forge an alternative path is difficult, requiring feminists to confront the risks inherent in global strategies for change.

Building upon women's shared experiences inevitably entails a risk of misdescription, or worse, cooptation but contains the promise of transforming and radicalizing women's understanding of their own condition. Emphasizing difference threatens to splinter women politically, undermining hard-won progress, but may simultaneously uncover new possibilities for re-creating gender relations. Forging a combined strategy that respects both commonality and difference requires feminists to acknowledge that we cannot eliminate the risk of coercion altogether, but the risk of inaction is also ever present.

VIEWS OF COMMENTATORS ABOUT FEMALE GENITAL MUTILATION

World Health Organization, Fact Sheet No. 241 (2000)

www.who.int/mediacentre/factsheets/fs241/en/

What is female genital mutilation

Female genital mutilation (FGM), often referred to as 'female circumcision', comprises all procedures involving partial or total removal of the external female genitalia or other injury to the female genital organs whether for cultural, religious or other non-therapeutic reasons. There are different types of female genital mutilation known to be practised today. They include:

- Type I — excision of the prepuce, with or without excision of part or all of the clitoris;
- Type II — excision of the clitoris with partial or total excision of the labia minora;
- Type III — excision of part or all of the external genitalia and stitching/narrowing of the vaginal opening (infibulation);
- Type IV — pricking, piercing or incising of the clitoris and/or labia; stretching of the clitoris and/or labia; cauterization by burning of the clitoris and surrounding tissue;
- scraping of tissue surrounding the vaginal orifice (angurya cuts) or cutting of the vagina (gishiri cuts);
- introduction of corrosive substances or herbs into the vagina to cause bleeding or for the purpose of tightening or narrowing it; and any other procedure that falls under the definition given above.

The most common type of female genital mutilation is excision of the clitoris and the labia minora, accounting for up to 80% of all cases; the most extreme form is infibulation, which constitutes about 15% of all procedures.

Health Consequences of FGM

The immediate and long-term health consequences of female genital mutilation vary according to the type and severity of the procedure performed.

Immediate complications include severe pain, shock, haemorrhage, urine retention, ulceration of the genital region and injury to adjacent tissue. Haemorrhage and infection can cause death.

More recently, concern has arisen about possible transmission of the human immunodeficiency virus (HIV) due to the use of one instrument in multiple operations, but this has not been the subject of detailed research.

Long-term consequences include cysts and abscesses, keloid scar formation, damage to the urethra resulting in urinary incontinence, dyspareunia (painful sexual intercourse) and sexual dysfunction and difficulties with childbirth.

Psychosexual and psychological health: Genital mutilation may leave a lasting mark on the life and mind of the woman who has undergone it. In the longer term, women may suffer feelings of incompleteness, anxiety and depression.

Who Performs FGM, at What Age, and for What Reasons?

In cultures where it is an accepted norm, female genital mutilation is practiced by followers of all religious beliefs as well as animists and non believers. FGM is usually performed by a traditional practitioner with crude instruments and without anaesthetic. Among the more affluent in society it may be performed in a health care facility by qualified health personnel. WHO is opposed to medicalization of all the types of female genital mutilation.

The age at which female genital mutilation is performed varies from area to area. It is performed on infants a few days old, female children and adolescents and, occasionally, on mature women.

...

Prevalence and Distribution of FGM

Most of the girls and women who have undergone genital mutilation live in 28 African countries, although some live in Asia and the Middle East. They are also increasingly found in Europe, Australia, Canada and the USA, primarily among immigrants from these countries.

Today, the number of girls and women who have been undergone female genital mutilation is estimated at between 100 and 140 million. It is estimated that each year, a further 2 million girls are at risk of undergoing FGM.

World Health Organization, Female Genital Mutilation and Obstetric Outcome

(2006) www.who.int/reproductive-health/fgm/

A new study published by the World Health Organization (WHO) has shown that women who have had Female Genital Mutilation (FGM) are significantly more likely to experience difficulties during childbirth and that their babies are more likely to die as a result of the practice. Serious complications during childbirth include the need to have a caesarean section, dangerously heavy bleeding after the birth of the baby and prolonged hospitalization following the birth. The study showed that the degree of complications increased according to the extent and severity of the FGM.

In the case of caesarean section, women who have been subjected to the most serious form of FGM ("FGM III") will have on average 30 per cent more caesarean sections compared with those who have not had any FGM. Similarly there is a 70 per cent increase in numbers of women who suffer from postpartum haemorrhage in those with FGM III compared to those women without FGM.

... The death rate among babies during and immediately after birth is also much higher for those born to mothers with FGM: 15 per cent higher in those with FGM I, 32 per cent higher in those with FGM II, and 55 per cent higher in those with FGM III....

...

PLAN, Tradition and Rights: Female Genital Cutting in West Africa (2006) http://www.crin.org/resources/infodetail.asp?id = 11060

Each year, an estimated two million girls undergo excision. Most of these girls live in Sub-Saharan and North-eastern Africa. To a lesser extent, female genital cutting is also practiced in some countries in the Middle East and parts of Asia and the Pacific. The practice of excision among immigrant communities in Europe, North America, and Australia has recently drawn much public attention.Female genital cutting is practiced throughout West Africa....

...

The practitioners of excision

... The act of excision is usually performed by female traditional practitioners who have inherited their role from a relative. ... Recent campaigns to create awareness about the dangers of excision have lead to an increasing medicalisation of the practice, especially in cities and larger towns. ... Parents who can afford it may call a nurse to assist the procedure. An ever increasing number of excisions throughout West Africa are performed by health care workers.

Most practitioners have an interest in the continuation of female genital cutting. In some areas, the practice is a lucrative business. Most practitioners have no other stable source of income. Some of them work as traditional midwives, others are herbalists or spiritual healers. But financial rewards are not always the main motivation. In some regions of Mali, for instance, the payment is small and symbolic. Performing excisions is a social duty of designated women, something they have to do to contribute to the well-being of society....

...

Motives for Practicing Female Genital Cutting

By excising their daughters, parents show respect for their culture and to their ancestors. The practice of excision is perceived as a means whereby one can become aware of cultural and traditional values that are precious to society. Although many parents do not see any benefit in the practice, it would be inconceivable to them to disrespect ancestral customs by not excising their daughters.

...

In communities where female genital cutting is widely practiced, it is the social norm. The pressure to undergo excision is immense. Those who disrespect the norm are likely to be stigmatised, treated as non-adults, or even ostracized from society. Non-excised girls fear being mocked and ridiculed by their peers. Their parents worry that they may not find a husband. It is therefore quite common that young girls demand to be excised in order to be accepted by their peers and their community.

...

In a number of African societies, the practice of excision is an important part of an initiation ritual that marks the transition into adulthood. The initiation is necessary in order to become a "complete" or a "full-grown" woman. Non initiated women (and men) are treated like children, even if they have reached an advanced age. ... Excision is only one part of initiation. Other aspects include training in skills such as cooking, dancing, traditional healing, and taking care of household, husband, and children. Initiation is intended to prepare girls for their future role as household managers, wives, and mothers. The pain endured during excision is seen as part of the girl's education. It is believed to change her into a respectful, calm, and less demanding person who accepts her role as a servant to her husband. This belief reveals the patriarchal social structures that maintain the practice of female genital cutting.

...

Some African Muslims believe that excision is recommended, or even required, by Islam. They hold on to the practice of female genital cutting to fulfil a religious obligation. Sometimes this belief is reinforced by local Islamic leaders. ... In fact, no form of female genital cutting is mentioned in the Koran.

Excision in West Africa is practiced by Muslims, Christians, and Animists. It is cultural and not a religious practice that predates both Christianity and Islam. (29,30)

...

Some communities consider excision as a tool to control female sexuality and to safeguard the honour of the family. The ablation of the clitoris is supposed to help protect the virginity of the young girl and to ensure the fidelity of the married woman. Another reason cited is to prevent girls from masturbating or experimenting with their body. ... Hence, excision is understood as a means of exercising control over a woman's sexuality.

However, this perception cannot be generalised. In some societies female genital cutting is believed to promote sexual intercourse and fertility. ...

...

Among women interviewed in the field studies, excision was rarely perceived as a subordination of their sexual life. On the contrary, in some communities it is cherished as a symbol of women's power and freedom from men. It creates a "women's space", a realm over which they have power that cannot be taken away or challenged by men ...

...

... [I]nitiation rites during which the excisions are performed present the only opportunity to get away from daily work and to unite female power against the authority of men. During initiation women step out of the reach of male authority and celebrate the legitimacy of female authority, the authority of their mothers and grandmothers....

...

During the PLAN field studies, the researchers encountered many communities who defended the practice of female genital cutting because of beliefs that were clearly false. These included:

- The belief that excision facilitates sexual intercourse and child birth, or that it enhances fertility.

...

- The belief that the clitoris is a dangerous organ that can kill or harm men during intercourse or the infant during delivery.
- The belief that the clitoris represents the male part of the body. In order to become a "true" woman, it has to be cut off.

TRADITION AND RIGHTS:

...

Most people are aware that the practise of excision is not without danger. Deaths of girls during initiation ceremonies are quite common....

...

Laws against Female Genital Cutting in West Africa

In November 2005, the Republic of Togo became the 15th Member State of the African Union to ratify the 2003 Protocol to the African Charter on Human and Peoples' Rights on the Rights of Women in Africa, commonly known as the Maputo Protocol. This means that the Protocol is now in force, and all African countries are obliged to pass legislation prohibiting excision. Legislation prohibiting female genital cutting already exists in most West African countries. ... However, with the exception of Burkina Faso, prosecutions under the laws are rare. In Guinea, for example, almost all girls are excised, yet there has never been a court case.

...

The practice of excision is severely sanctioned in Burkina Faso since 1996.... The law against female genital cutting is applied rigorously. Between 1996 and 2005 more than 400 convictions have been recorded. However, the application of the law is not the only strategy pursued by the State. The Government, has conducted public information campaigns about excision. Members of the police and the army have been trained to intervene in support of the law. The topic of excision is integrated in school curricula. Women suffering from complications of female genital cutting are treated free of charge in public health care facilities. A telephone hotline has been set up to help the denunciation of planned excisions. It receives approximately 150 calls a year. The Government and civil society actions against excision appear to be effective. The number of girls being excised is falling rapidly....

The Complex Dynamics of Female Genital Cutting

...The underlying dynamics of excision in West Africa are complex. They are linked to social, cultural, political and developmental issues in the region.

...[A] large proportion of the population practicing excision is illiterate and lives below the line of poverty. National public education campaigns rarely reach these people, and when they do they are not understood....

Talking about genital organs is a sensitive and uncomfortable subject in all cultures. In addition, the subject of female genital cutting is considered taboo in many West African societies. It is only discussed under specific circumstances by selected members of the community....[I]n communities where the practice of excision is strongly supported by local opinion leaders, campaigners against female genital cutting may be afraid to speak out, fearing for their reputation or even their lives.

The most commonly heard argument in favour of continuing the practice of female genital cutting is: "It is a tradition that we have found with our ancestors". What is hiding behind this statement? ... Excision is often associated with ethnic identity in West Africa. The practice is a heritage of the ancestors and a source of pride. It is understandable that communities react with hostility when outsiders criticise practices linked to their ethnic identity. Traditions are maintained to preserve values. These values allow the individual to be socially accepted. They stand for dignity, security, and a source of identity within the community....

Campaigners against female genital cutting cannot ignore the conflict between human rights and societal norms. Clearly, girls have the right to be protected from harm and the right to have an intact body. But they also have a need to get married and to be accepted members of their community. This conflict needs to be resolved before there can be progress towards the abandonment of female genital cutting.

...

PLAN'S Work on Female Genital Cutting in West Africa

For the communities who practice excision, the Government and the international organisations are external actors. Engagement of foreign anti-excision activists has often done more harm than good. In some communities it has created the prejudice that the abandonment of excision is a "project of white people", an attempt to destroy African culture....

...

An acceptable and frequently used door opener is to start a discussion about the health risks and long-term reproductive health complications of excision. This information is usually of interest to all community members. It is, however, important not to become stuck in the discussion at this point. Information about the risks does not prevent people from excising their daughters. It may lead to an increasing medicalisation of the practice. But tradition and social conformism are much stronger behavioural motivators than information about adverse health outcomes....

...

The abandonment of female genital cutting is not a priority for communities; it is a priority for development agencies. Community members become easily annoyed when a development organisation appears to have no concern for their daily problems and insists to speak only about excision. . . . In order to be effective, efforts to promote the abandonment of excision have to be integrated into a development program that is consistent with the needs and demands articulated by the community. This can be an education program, a micro-finance program, a health program or any other program that is seen as a priority. . . .

. . .

Men are intimately involved in the issue of female genital cutting. In many communities they play a major role in preserving the practice.(29) But the PLAN field studies also found that sometimes men are most interested in abandoning excision because of the burden of having to pay for the ceremony. This points to a common error of anti-excision activists to "feminise" the issue. Female genital cutting is not a "women's problem", it is a gender and a child protection issue that affects the whole community.

. . .

UNICEF, Female Genital Mutilation/Cutting: A Statistical Exploration (2005)

. . .

VIII. Conclusions and Recommendations

In its many and complex cultural meanings, FGM/C is a long-standing tradition that has become inseparable from ethnic and social identity among many groups. As stated by the International Conference on Population and Development, "For women it is not only a painful ordeal but a means of social bargaining and negotiation; for societies it is a collective identity marker — a status symbol in the fullest sense — as well as a creator of cohesion."

The following summarizes five essential points resulting from this statistical analysis.

FGM/C prevalence rates are slowly declining in some countries. Evidence of change can be obtained by comparing the experiences of different age cohorts within a given country. The most recent survey data indicate consistently, for all countries, that women aged 15–19 are less likely to have been circumcised than women in the older age groups. In countries with high prevalence rates (particularly in Egypt, Guinea, Mali and Sudan), the difference between the 15–19 and 20–24 age cohorts is less than 1 per cent. Nevertheless, it is believed to indicate the beginning of change.

Attitudes towards FGM/C are slowly changing as more and more women oppose its continuation. In almost all countries that have conducted more than one survey during the past decade, data indicate that opposition to the practice is increasing. These results are reinforced by the fact that support for the discontinuation of the practice is particularly high among younger women. As FGM/C is deeply ingrained in the social fabric, and in most countries has been practised for a very long time, any increase in opposition, even a small one, represents a significant indication of change. . . .

Strategies to end FGM/C must be accompanied by holistic, community-based education and awareness-raising. As a social behaviour, the practice of FGM/C derives its roots from a complex set of belief systems. ... In many ways, bringing an end to FGM/C requires changing community norms and societal attitudes that discriminate against women and subjugate their rights to those of men. ... [T]his study shows the close link between women's ability to exercise control over their lives and their belief that FGM/C should be ended. Programmatic interventions must aim to promote the empowerment of women and girls through awareness-raising campaigns and increasing their access to education, as well as their access to and control of economic resources....

Programmes must be country specific and adapted to reflect regional, ethnic and socio-economic variances. ... [T]he practice of FGM/C differs significantly between and within countries. Any strategy to end FGM/C must address the specific situation for each country and reflect regional and ethnic differences.... Furthermore, as the section on attitudes illustrates, FGM/C is practised for a wide variety of cultural reasons. For some communities, it is related to rites of passage. In others, it is considered aesthetically pleasing. Some practise it for reasons related to morality and sexuality. Research into why and how FGM/C is practised among a given group or region is essential for the design of culturally appropriate, effective programmatic interventions.

Detailed segregation of data by socio- economic variables can significantly enhance and strengthen advocacy efforts at the country level. Advocacy efforts are instrumental in influencing behaviour change and awareness. In many situations, however, advocacy can be severely hampered by the lack of systematic and accurate data. In the field of FGM/C, the link between advocacy efforts and accurate data is particularly strong due to the availability of such instruments. ... Programmatic interventions to end FGM/C should continue to draw upon the available measurement tools and use data to better tailor their advocacy messages. By examining the different factors and variables that surround the practice, this study attempts to identify girls most at risk and thus take the first step towards ensuring their protection. FGM/C is no longer a cultural practice alone, removed from the scrutiny of international attention and human rights concerns. Rather, it has become a phenomenon that cannot be independently evaluated without looking at the social and economic injustices surrounding women and girls. Any approach that aims to end FGM/C must incorporate a holistic strategy that addresses the multitude of factors that perpetuate it.

Kay Boulware-Miller, Female Circumcision: Challenges to the Practice as a Human Rights Violation

8 Harv. Women's L. J. 155 (1985), at 165

...

A. The Rights of the Child

The Declaration of the Rights of the Child, adopted by the UN General Assembly in 1959, asserts that children must be guaranteed the opportunity to develop physically in a healthy and normal way.

...

First, to challenge female circumcision as a violation of the rights of the child suggests that women who permit the operation are incompetent and abusive mothers who, in some ways, do not love their children. The success of this approach therefore depends in part on how it is implemented; if African women are offended by the implication that they are poor mothers, they will likely reject the children's rights argument altogether.

The second problem with the rights of the child approach is that it conflicts with parents' desires to rear children independently and their notions of what is in their children's best interests. While women may not wish to see their daughters harmed, they may also feel strongly that they should be able to rear their children according to their own cultural norms and traditions. Besides, if mothers value the economic, social, and cultural benefits of the operation, they are unlikely to be persuaded that it should not be performed on their daughters. Moreover, the strong social and cultural pressures to continue the practice work against parents who would prefer not to submit their daughters to the operation....

The third problem with this approach is that it almost exclusively focuses on the physical harm done to a child when she is circumcised and does not address the positive feelings she may have as a circumcised woman. In African communities with strong cultural and traditional ties, the perceived need to be circumcised mitigates the hellish remembrances of the event. Little girls who are initially hurt, betrayed, and degraded by the operation later come to feel socially and morally acceptable because they have been circumcised. As the girls grow into women they may forget the pain and argue that the practice need not be banned. Furthermore, it is difficult to attack a practice as harmful to children when it later gives them both social and economic benefits.

A final problem with approaching this issue from the rights of the child perspective is that many young girls believe that they want to be circumcised. The stigma associated with not being circumcised attaches early, virtually compelling a choice to undergo the operation....

...

Isabelle Gunning, Arrogant Perception, World Travelling and Multicultural Feminism: The Case of Female Genital Surgeries

23 Colum. Hum. Rts. L. Rev. 189 (1991–1992), at 238

...

Arguably, most of the activity reviewed and criticized by the human rights system is not culturally based. In cases of torture or forced disappearances, accused governments generally deny the fact or any knowledge thereof. With a cultural practice, the condemned act is acknowledged and defended: the practice is viewed 'as conduct which has evolved for a specific purpose within a culture and is endorsed as a legitimate expression of that purpose'. However governments may not be actually involved in the practice, because private citizens willingly nurture their cultural norms.

One problem therefore is whether human rights which, like the rest of international law, is aimed at public or government actions can be used to alter the behavior of private parties. Feminists have argued persuasively that the public-private distinction is a false one and that the real question is not whether law, in this case human rights law, should apply to the private as well as the public, but rather 'what types of private acts are and are not protected'. If one can decide that a particular act is a violation, even if performed by private citizens, one can hold governments responsible. For example, when one reviews the international definition of torture one sees that it is not only active or direct government participation which is prohibited, but also government 'consent or acquiescence'.

It may be argued that that language is designed to hold accountable governments that are believed to be responsible for torturous acts but who have created sufficient 'plausible deniability' to make it difficult to prove complicity. Still, it reflects a willingness to pressure governments to do something about 'private' acts. The practical problem is that if governments really do not have control over private actions, then the primary tool of human rights enforcement, governmental embarrassment, will not be nearly as effective. This is particularly true with a practice like female genital surgeries, where the governments involved may either refuse to be embarrassed or become angry at the attack on the culture; thus they reject the interference. Moreover, even if a government is embarrassed, the cost of implementing an eradication law, as has been explained, could be enormously socially disruptive and ineffective.

...

... One is not stuck between choosing 'universal standards' and 'everything is relative'. It is not that there are 'universals' out there waiting to be discovered. But through dialogue, shared values can become universal and be safeguarded. The process by which these universal standards are created is important. A dialogue, with a tone that respects cultural diversity, is essential. From that dialogue a consensus may be reached, understanding that as people and cultures interact they do change and learn from each other.

CEDAW, Female Circumcision

General Recommendation. No. 14, 9th Sess., 1990

Un Doc. A/45/38/1 Int. Hum. Rts. Re. 21 (No. 1, 1994)

[The Committee on the Elimination of Discrimination against Women (see p. 192, *supra*), created by the Convention on the Elimination of all Forms of Discrimination against Women, is authorized to make general recommendations based on reports that it receives from the states parties.]

Recommends that States parties:

(a) Take appropriate and effective measures with a view to eradicating the practice of female circumcision. Such measures could include:

(i) The collection and dissemination by universities, medical or nursing associations, national women's organizations or other bodies of basic data about such traditional practices;

(ii) The support of women's organizations at the national and local levels working for the elimination of female circumcision and other practices harmful to women;

(iii) The encouragement of politicians, professionals, religious and community leaders at all levels, including the media and the arts, to co-operate in influencing attitudes towards the eradication of female circumcision;

(iv) The introduction of appropriate educational and training programmes and seminars based on research findings about the problems arising from female circumcision;

(b) Include in their national health policies appropriate strategies aimed at eradicating female circumcision in public health care. Such strategies could include the special responsibility of health personnel, including traditional birth attendants, to explain the harmful effects of female circumcision;

(c) Invite assistance, information and advice from the appropriate organizations of the United Nations system to support and assist efforts being deployed to eliminate harmful traditional practices;

(d) Include in their reports to the Committee under articles 10 and 12 of the Convention on the Elimination of All Forms of Discrimination against Women information about measures taken to eliminate female circumcision.

Female Genital Mutilation, 18 U.S.C.A. §116

Section 116 of this federal criminal statute was enacted in 1996. It reads:

(a) Except as provided in subsection (b), whoever knowingly circumcises, excises, or infibulates the whole or any part of the labia majora or labia minora or clitoris of another person who has not attained the age of 18 years shall be fined under this title or imprisoned not more than 5 years, or both.

(b) A surgical operation is not a violation of this section if the operation is — [Clauses (1) and (2) refer to the operation's being necessary for health/medical purposes and being performed by a licensed medical practitioner.]

(c) In applying subsection (b)(1) , no account shall be taken of the effect on the person on whom the operation is to be performed of any belief on the part of that person, or any other person, that the operation is required as a matter of custom or ritual.

K. Hayter, Female Circumcision — Is There a Legal Solution?

J. of Soc. Welf. L. (U.K.) 323 (November 1984), at 355

[These remarks concerned a pending bill in Parliament to prohibit female circumcision in the UK]

Clearly the effects of female circumcision and the enforced suppression of female sexuality is to be abhorred. The overall response of members of the House of Lords reflects this view, as summarised in the speech of Baroness Gaitskell's where she states, 'The primitive attitude to female circumcision rests not only on tradition, but on the male desire for the female to be pure for him ... That is not only the most cruel, but also ... the most primitive, and the most important aspect of the matter which we should reject'. But is this moral indignation sufficient to justify legal intervention to prohibit consensual acts performed on women over 16 in accordance with the cultural requirements of a minority group? ... It is interesting to note here that clitoradectomies were openly performed on children and women in England and the United States as late as 1945 as a 'cure' for masturbation and 'promiscuity'. The demise of this practice in recent years may indicate a general change in attitudes towards female sexuality. If this is correct then, it is suggested, the legality of certain western practices will also require review. Purely elective cosmetic surgery is an obvious case where the right of the individual to consent to treatment is not seriously questioned. Breast reduction, for example, is an unnecessary and mutilating operation involving considerable pain and scarring to the patient. If justification for its performance were called for, medical evidence of anxiety and depression brought on by the woman's dissatisfaction with her body would undoubtedly be sufficient to outweigh the injury inherent in the treatment. Indeed, the Government's proposed amendment to the Bill which would safeguard the right of western women to undergo surgery on mental health grounds reinforces this view. Precisely the same justification would be pleaded in support of the legality of female circumcision and should, by analogy, in the absence of further justification for its prohibition, be sufficient. In both cases the women's perception of themselves reflects the demands of the social group to which they belong. This justification is the greater in the case of female circumcision where its necessity extends beyond mere aesthetic appeal, being crucial to the women's status within the group.

Additionally, the imposition of the moral values of the majority onto minority groups would seem inappropriate in a multiracial society in which the current trend is towards tolerance of others' cultural practices. An analogy can be drawn here between female circumcision and the circumcision of Jewish males, which does receive social and legal tolerance. Clearly nice distinctions can be drawn between a mere custom in the case of female circumcision and a strict religious requirement in the latter case. But is this really the criteria to be used to limit the bounds of toleration? The essential element in both appears to be the unquestioned and entrenched nature of the practices which are part of the social fabric of the groups concerned. Arguably both should, prima facie, be tolerated on this basis alone. A valid distinction between the two practices, however, is the degree of injury involved in female circumcision which is not associated with male circumcision.

... Legal intervention is, however, justified to protect persons from what is offensive or injurious, particularly where the individual is young, weak in body or mind or in a state of particular physical or economic dependence. Arguably the practice of female circumcision bears characteristics which bring it within these exceptions thus justifying legal intervention, which are not present in other forms of elective surgery. Clearly it is applicable to the circumcision of female children and this approach has been taken to prohibit indigenous practices, notably the tattooing of minors. To subject women over 16 to the same degree of legal paternalism appears, prima facie, to be a denial of their right to self-determination and a slight on the intellectual capacity of the women members of these groups. This issue underlies objections to legal limitations on a woman's right to elect for abortion. It is possible, however, that the cloistered lifestyle and acute state of economic dependence in which the women practising female circumcision find themselves may provide some justification for a paternalistic approach here. Access to research findings and wider views which refute the necessity for female circumcision are denied to them and the traditional view of the practice is enforced within the closed environment. They are not, therefore, in a position to form a balanced judgment in their own best interests. By criminalising female circumcision the law may assist in freeing women who are powerless to help themselves by reducing the social pressure to conform.

...

AAWORD, A Statement on Genital Mutilation

Miranda Davies (ed.), *Third World-Second Sex: Women's Struggles and National Liberation* (1983), at 217

[The Association of African Women for Research and Development (AAWORD) is a group of African women researchers dedicated to doing women's research from an African perspective. They are based in Dakar, Senegal, where their first official meeting was held in December 1977.]

...

This new crusade of the West has been led out of the moral and cultural prejudices of Judaeo-Christian Western society: aggressiveness, ignorance or even contempt, paternalism and activism are the elements which have infuriated and then shocked many people of good will. In trying to reach their own public, the new crusaders have fallen back on sensationalism, and have become insensitive to the dignity of the very women they want to 'save'. They are totally unconscious of the latent racism which such a campaign evokes in countries where ethnocentric prejudice is so deep-rooted. And in their conviction that this is a 'just cause', they have forgotten that these women from a different race and a different culture are also *human beings*, and that solidarity can only exist alongside self-affirmation and mutual respect.

...

AAWORD, whose aim is to carry out research which leads to the liberation of African people and women in particular, *firmly condemns* genital mutilation and all other practices — traditional or modern — which oppress women and justify exploiting them economically or socially, as a serious violation of the fundamental rights of women.

...

However, as far as AAWORD is concerned, the fight against genital mutilation, although necessary, should not take on such proportions that the wood cannot be seen for the trees....

... [T]o fight against genital mutiliation without placing it in the context of ignorance, obscurantism, exploitation, poverty, etc., without questioning the structures and social relations which perpetuate this situation, is like 'refusing to see the sun in the middle of the day'. This, however, is precisely the approach taken by many Westerners, and is highly suspect, especially since Westerners necessarily profit from the exploitation of the peoples and women of Africa, whether directly or indirectly.

Feminists from developed countries — at least those who are sincerely concerned about this situation rather than those who use it only for their personal prestige — should understand this other aspect of the problem. They must accept that it is a problem for *African women*, and that no change is possible without the conscious participation of African women....

...

Merwine, Letter to Editor

***New York Times*, November 24, 1993, at A24**

To the Editor:

A. M. Rosenthal condemns female circumcision, a traditional practice common to many African and Arabic peoples, as 'female mutilation'... From the Western liberal tradition, and certainly from a feminist perspective, Mr. Rosenthal is correct.

However, from the African viewpoint the practice can serve as an affirmation of the value of woman in traditional society.

This tradition has long been a source of conflict between Western and African values.

...

The operation completed, a fee was provided by the young women, usually in the form of a cooked meal, to their moruithia. At this point, they became full members of the Kikuyu and were no longer considered girls.

The importance of the ceremony among traditional Kikuyu cannot be understated, for each girl showed by her act of courage that she was ready to be married. Of equal importance, she now became a member of an age-set. An age-set is a group of people of similar age who tend to act together in their society for the rest of their lives. To the Kikuyu, female circumcision is much more than a mere physical act.

...

The sentiments expressed long ago in Kenya are almost certainly shared by the peoples who practice the custom today. To demand, as Mr. Rosenthal does, that economic aid be used to force a change in a tradition central to many Africans and Arabs is the height of ethnocentrism.

A better approach would be for Western peoples to try to understand the importance of these traditions to those who practice them. The West could encourage Africans to have the surgical part of the ceremony performed by competent medical practitioners. That would eliminate potential infection and restrict the extent of excision. This is being done in many African states. Such a policy would allow the West to uphold its values while avoiding the appearance of arrogance.

Richard Shweder, Moral Realism without the Ethnocentrism

in A. Sajó (ed.), *Human Rights with Modesty: The Problem of Universalism* (2004) 65, at 100

... [T]he following points need to be addressed and debated, if there is to be a serious evenhanded non-ethnocentric discussion of the topic:

1. Despite claims to the contrary, the practice of genital alteration is a rather poor example of gender inequality or of society picking on women. If one surveys the cultures of the world, one finds very few cultures where genital surgeries are done to girls but not to boys, although there are many cultures where they are done only to boys or to both sexes. ... [S]ocial recognition for both boys and girls of their ritual transformation into a more mature status as empowered men and women is not infrequently a major point of the ceremony. ... [F]emale circumcision, when and where it occurs in Africa, is much more a case of a society treating boys and girls equally. ...

2. The practice is also a rather poor example of patriarchal domination. Many patriarchal cultures in Europe and Asia do not engage in genital alterations at all or ... exclude girls from participation. ... Moreover, the African ethnic groups that circumcise both females and males are very different from each other. ...

3. ... [T]he practice is almost always controlled, performed, and most strongly upheld by women, although male kin often do provide material and moral support. Typically, however, men have rather little to do with these female operations, may not know very much about them, and may feel it is not really their business to butt in. ... It is the women of the society who are the cultural experts in this intimate feminine domain ...

4. Imagine an African mother living in the United States who [believes for several reasons in the importance of circumcision for her daughter by a modest surgical procedure that is] no more substantial from a medical point of view than the customary male circumcision operation. Why should we not extend that option to (e.g.) the Kono parents of daughters as well as to (e.g.) the Jewish parents of sons? Principles of gender equity, due process before the law, religious and cultural freedom, and family privacy would seem to support the option.

...

Yael Tamir, Hands off Clitoridectomy

31 Boston Review 21 (Summer 1996)

...

Clitoridectomy is obviously a deplorable practice. It is, among other things, an extremely painful, traumatizing mutilation of young girls that leaves them permanently disfigured and deprived of sexual enjoyment. We should express no sympathy toward those who practice it, and support those who struggle to end it.

But we also should be suspicious about the role of clitoridectomy in current political debate. Despite their liberal appearance, references to clitoridectomy commonly reveal a patronizing attitude toward women, suggesting that they are primarily sexual beings. Moreover, those references involve a certain degree of dishonesty. They intentionally widen the gap between our culture and those in which clitoridectomy is practiced, thus presenting those other cultures as incommensurable with ours. The effect of this distancing is to disconnect criticism of their practices from criticism of our own, and turn reflection on other cultures into yet another occasion for celebrating our special virtues. We should resist such self-congratulation. And if we do, the debate about clitoridectomy takes on an entirely different cast.

...

Moreover, we are all aware of painful practices of body piercing, tattooing, and abnormal elongation of lips, ear lobes, and necks. National Geographic runs cover photos of women and men who have undergone such severe malformations, not in protest but as a neutral representation of other ways of life with their different conceptions of beauty. So hostility to clitoridectomy is not driven principally by concerns about physical suffering. Those who object to it would be no less hostile if it were performed in hygienic conditions under anesthesia.

It might be said that these examples are all irrelevant as they do not include the mutilation of the body. But when is the body improved and when is it mutilated? Are parents who force their children to wear braces mutilating their children's teeth or improving them? In most cases, the answer depends on one's conception of beauty.... To be sure, parents say (sincerely) that these treatments will improve their children's life chances, self-image, and social standing. But parents who perform clitoridectomy on their daughters invoke precisely the same arguments.

Furthermore, it seems clear that Western conceptions of female beauty encourage women to undergo a wide range of painful, medically unnecessary, and potentially damaging processes — extreme diets, depilation, face lifts, fat pumping, silicone implants. Of course, adult women do these things to their own bodies, and, it is said, their decisions are freely made. But would our gut reaction to female circumcision be very different if it were performed on consenting adults? It is not unlikely that girls at the age of 13 or 14, who are considered in traditional societies as adults mature enough to wed and bear children, would 'consent' to the mutilation of their bodies if they were convinced that marriage and children were contingent on so doing. Many women who followed the tradition of Sati seemed to do it as a matter of choice. Did their 'consent' make this tradition defensible? Women 'consent' to such practices because the alternative is even more painful — a life of solitude, humiliation, and deprivation.

...

Perhaps, then, we object to clitoridectomy because it is performed on minors. But think of the parents in our culture who foster in their daughters bad eating habits that might destroy their teeth or their vital organs, or, in more tragic cases, lead to life-threatening eating disorders. Are we ready to judge these parents as harshly as we judge parents who require clitoridectomies?

In both cases, parents sincerely believe that they are serving the interests of their children and allowing them to live what is, according to their conception of the good, a meaningful life. Both cases may thus be taken to demonstrate that parents are not the most trustworthy guardians of their children, but why should one case be more harshly judged than the other?

…

The common answer is that clitoridectomy damages women's sexual organs, thus depriving them of sexual enjoyment — a basic need, perhaps even a right. One may wonder, however, when precisely our society became so deeply committed to women's sexual enjoyment.

…

Sexual enjoyment has acquired a mythical status in our society, advocated both as the most sublime and most corruptive pleasure. Advocates of clitoridectomy see the corruption: Performing clitoridectomy will restrict the sexual desires of women, thereby turning them into more chaste and righteous wives and mothers. They believe that the pursuit of sexual pleasures may lead a person astray, and that women are more likely to be influenced by such desires and act unscrupulously.

Both assumptions are also well grounded in the Western tradition. The failure to control the pursuit of sexual pleasures was seen by religious thinkers, as well as by many secular liberals, as undermining virtue, fostering bad habits and pernicious behavior, and hindering the possibility of true love (either of God or of other human beings). In the Christian tradition celibacy was affirmed as the highest ideal, and 'sex within marriage was regarded as an evil necessary for the continuation of the species'.

…

… Societies discriminate, dominate, and abuse their members in various ways, but there is something common to all expressions of oppression. We should place this core aspect, repeated in all traditions in different forms, at the center of our criticism. In the cases discussed here, it is not a particular practice but a set of ill-motivated efforts to control the sexuality of women and to restrict their ability to compete for social and political resources that we should find reprehensible.

Does the overwhelming disgust at clitoridectomy signal an emerging social commitment to structural change — to ensuring equal social, economic, and political status for women? I'm afraid not. Of course, the absence of such commitment is no justification for clitoridectomy. My purpose, however, is not to justify clitoridectomy, but to expose the roots of the deep hostility to it — to reveal the smug, unjustified self-satisfaction lurking behind the current condemnation of clitoridectomy. Referring to clitoridectomy, and emphasizing the distance of the practice from our own conventions, allows us to condemn them for what they do to their women, support the struggle of their women against their primitive, inhuman culture, and remain silent on the status of women in our society.

…

Multicultural exchanges raise acute concerns not because they point to the incommensurability of cultures, or the impossibility of cross-cultural conversation, but because they confront us with our own deficiencies....

[This article of Yael Tamir was followed by several commentators on the article. One such commentator, Martha Nussbaum, wrote:]

> I am prepared to agree with Tamir to this extent. The attention given FGM seems to me somewhat disproportionate, among the many gross abuses the world practices against women — lack of equality under the law, lack of equal access to education, sex-selective infanticide and feticide, domestic violence, marital rape, rape in police custody, and many more.... [T]he reason for this focus is not a fascination with sex but the relative tractability of FGM as a practical problem, given the fact that it is already widely resisted and indeed illegal; how much harder to grapple with women's legal inequality before Islamic courts, their pervasive danger, their illiteracy.... Surely Tamir is right that we should not focus on this one abuse while relaxing our determination to make structural changes that would bring women closer to full equality worldwide.

NOTE

As comments in the preceding readings make clear, the practice of female genital mutilation raises the distinctive question of who (if anyone), which party or actor, is violating international human rights. Apparently no state enforces the practice, or instructs or advocates through its affiliated religious or educational institutions that the practice be continued.

The practice then raises the question addressed in the discussions of the ICCPR and CEDAW in Chapter 3: the degree to which the human rights movement regulates directly or indirectly the conduct of nonstate — and in this sense, private — actors. Again we consider the reach of the human rights movement to 'private' actors and to actions that cannot readily be attributed directly to the 'public' state, another instance of the public-private question that recurs throughout the coursebook.

Note that this question also points towards the serious obstacles to practical implementation of human rights norms, even by states that are hostile to and seek to curb the challenged practice. A government may find it difficult to disregard the sentiments of politically powerful groups or segments of society that wish to maintain religious or customary law. Moreover, a state's motivation to bring about change will depend on that change's relation to other state objectives and on the depth of the socio-cultural roots of the practices. Indeed, the state might not possess the necessary influence or power to proceed. Authority may be divided among the central government and regional or ethnic leaders. The supervision and enforcement of some customary laws may rest not with the state but with another body, such as a religious court or officials. And as the preceding materials have indicated, secular remedies, even if available, may have limited utility or not even be the best route to follow for critics of the practice.

QUESTIONS

1. African state X is a party to the ICCPR and CEDAW. Its government takes no formal, legal position on female genital mutilation, which is undergone by a substantial number of girls in X in the different ways described in the readings. No law, no subsidy, no official policy, requires or facilitates or prohibits the practice. Suppose that you are a member of a nongovernmental human rights organization in X criticizing this widespread practice before an international human rights body such as the committees created by the ICCPR (see Chapter 10) and CEDAW, on the ground that it violates those treaties.

   a. Precisely what is the violation, and whom would you charge with committing it? The state? Why? If not the state, are any nonstate actors subject to duties under these instruments?

   b. On what provisions of these treaties would you rely for your claim of a human rights violation? What arguments would you make based on them?

2. 'It's no wonder that challenges to female circumcision have generated so much controversy in states where it is practiced. Could the line-up be worse from the perspective of getting things done? It's West vs. the rest, the uneducated and backward rest. It's whites vs. non-whites. It's science vs. culture.' Comment. If you agree, how would you attempt to change this line-up?

3. In view of the preceding commentaries about fgm, what kind of information would you (as a member of an NGO that believes fgm is a violation of human rights and that is planning a visit to a country where it is widely practiced) seek to obtain about that country?

4. Are the articles by Merry and An-Na'im in Section A of this chapter helpful in devising a strategy to reduce the incidence of fgm in countries or regions where it now prevails?

NOTE

Consider the remarks of Yakin Ertürk, Special Rapporteur of the UN Commission on Human Rights on Violence against Women, in her Report on Integration of the Human Rights of Women and the Gender Perspective, E/CN.4/2004/66, at 13:

> ... [CEDAW] draws attention to the contradictions that may arise in the intersectionality of collective rights and the human rights of women. This paradox begs the question, "Does the right to cultural difference and specificity, as embedded in the freedom of religion and belief, contradict the universality of human rights of women?" Alternatively, the question can be turned around as follows; "Is control

over the regulation of women the only means by which cultural specificity and tradition can be sustained?" "Is is culture, or authoritarian patriarchal coercion and the interests of hegemonic masculinity that violates the human rights of women everywhere?" "When a man beats his wife, is he exercising his right in the name of culture? If so, are culture, tradition and religion the property of men alone?"

Universal human rights norms are clear on these questions. The Declaration [on the Elimination of Violence against Women, UN Doc. A/48/629, Art. 4] stresses that States "should not invoke any custom, tradition or religious consideration to avoid their obligations with respect to [the elimination of violence against women]."

RADHIKA COOMARASWAMY, REPORT ON CULTURAL PRACTICES IN THE FAMILY THAT ARE VIOLENT TOWARDS WOMEN

Commission on Human Rights, E/CN.4/2002/83, 2002

[Radhika Coomaraswamy submitted this Report to the Commission on Human Rights, in her capacity as Special Rapporteur on Violence against Women.]

I. Introduction

1. Throughout the world, there are practices in the family that are violent towards women and harmful to their health ... but have avoided national and international scrutiny because they are seen as cultural practices that deserve tolerance and respect. ... Cultural relativism is therefore often an excuse to allow for inhumane and discriminatory practices against women in the community. ...

...

5. Despite these international norms and standards, the tension between universal human rights and cultural relativism is played out in the everyday lives of millions of women throughout the globe. The situation is made more complex by the fact that women also identify with their culture and are offended by the arrogant gaze of outsiders who criticize their way of doing things. Since their sense of identity is integrally linked to the general attitude towards their community, their sense of dignity and self-respect often comes from being members of the larger community. In minority communities and third world communities that already suffer from discrimination, this sense of identity poses major problems for women. Some women have told the Special Rapporteur that they do not mind wearing the veil because they see the veil as subversive against imperialism. Cultural markers and cultural identity that allow a group to stand united against the oppression and discrimination of a more powerful ethnic or political majority often entail restrictions on the rights of women. ... For this reason, the issue of cultural relativism requires a measure of sensitivity. Women's rights must be vindicated but women should win those rights in a manner that allows them to be full participants in a community of their choosing. ...

6. Nevertheless, many of the practices enumerated in the next section are unconscionable and challenge the very concept of universal human rights. Many of

them involve "severe pain and suffering" and may be considered "torture like" in their manifestation. ... [T]hose cultural practices that involve "severe pain and suffering" for the woman or the girl child, those that do not respect the physical integrity of the female body, must receive maximum international scrutiny and agitation....

...

II. Cultural Practices in the Family that Violate Women's Rights

11. There are many cultural practices throughout the world that are violent toward women. In this section some of the more disturbing violations are described, in order to highlight the nature of the problem.

[The Report describes a number of practices omitted from these excerpts, including female genital mutilation, witch hunting, caste, honour killings, parentally determined marriage, practices violating reproductive rights, required dress in public, and incest.]

H. Son Preference

70. Son preference, the preference of parents for male children, often manifests itself in neglect, deprivation or discriminatory treatment of girls to the detriment of their physical and mental health. It is generally recognized to exist in most African and Asian countries, but varies in intensity and expression from one country to another.

71. In many regions of the world, entrenched patriarchal systems perpetuate bias and discrimination against females from the time they are conceived and even before they are born. But economic considerations such as the traditional role of men with regard to agriculture and as property owners underlie this type of discrimination against women. This is seen in practices such as prenatal sex selection, female infanticide and gender differences in nutrition, health and education....

72. ... [W]ith modern technology such as amniocentesis or sonograms, it is easier to determine the sex of the unborn child. This advancement of science and technology is exploited to select the sex of the child through aborting the unwanted child instead of merely monitoring the health of the foetus. Most often, it is the female foetus that is considered unwanted. UNICEF has provided the following statistics:

> A study of 10,000 abortions following gender tests by amniocentesis in Bombay, India revealed that 9,999 of the foetuses were female; A recent official survey in China revealed that 12 per cent of all female foetuses were aborted or otherwise unaccounted for, mainly the result of ultrasound screening throughout the country to determine the sex of unborn children; In one survey in Bangladesh, 96 per cent of women said that they wanted their next child to be a boy. Only 3 per cent wanted a girl.

73. In India, where there is a strong societal preference for sons, many sex identification clinics have started up. Sex identification before birth was made unlawful many years ago but is commonly practised throughout India. It is argued that a girl will be a financial burden that will only increase as she grows. A modern saying in

India, "Better 500 rupees now than 5,000 rupees later", compares the cost of sex selective technology and the future dowry.

74. In many cultures, the revulsion towards the birth of a daughter is so strong that female infanticide is accepted as a necessary evil. A baby girl may be deprived of food and water in the hope that she will die or she may even be killed. ... In China, many families prefer that the one child they are allowed under the Sate one-child policy should be a son, for various reasons. Many baby girls are put in dying rooms and left to die without food or water. This wilful neglect of girls is common throughout their lives. Given the number of men in India and China at present, there should today be 30 million more women in India and 38 million more women in China than there are.

75. ... In Taiwan, daughters are commonly referred to by epithets such as "goods on which one loses" and "water spilled on the ground". In Arabic, the term *Abu-banat*, meaning the father of daughters, is an insult. ... Such terms are never used with reference to a boy even as a joke. These are some of the countless ways women learn how little they are valued.

76. ... UNICEF estimates that more than 1 million female babies die each year from malnutrition and abuse who would have lived if they were boys. Many mothers stop breastfeeding a girl child early in order to try and get pregnant with a male. ... If there are shortages of money and food, sons have priority treatment over the daughters. Daughters are trained to wait patiently while their father and brothers finish their meal, and eat what is remaining. ...

77. Traditionally, females are not taken to hospital or to other medical providers until their illness reaches a critical stage. They are more often treated at home or taken to a traditional healer. More boys are immunized and treated by hospitals than girls. ... A boy is more carefully taken care of to ensure that he will grow into a strong man to provide for the family.

78. ... It is thought that boys need a better education to look after their families when they grow up. In societies where girls are married off at a young age, they are withdrawn from school even primary school. ...

...

80. There are various cultural, religious and economic reasons for the above-mentioned practices. In many societies, male children carry on the family lineage. ... Among many communities in Asia and Africa, men perform most religious ceremonies and sons perform burial rites for parents. ... In agricultural societies, the need for a strong labour force is a factor which perpetuates son preference. ... The deprived economic status of women and the low esteem attached to women's economic contribution result in the preference for sons.

81. This is illustrated in a saying common in societies where son preference is prevalent: "To have a son is good economics and good politics, whereas bringing up a girl is like watering the neighbour's garden".

III. Ideologies that Perpetuate Cultural Practices that are Violent towards Women

98. Violence against women in the family in the name of culture is often sanctioned by dominant ideologies and structures within societies. These ideologies and

structures emerged in a different era but continue to dominate public opinion and individual lifestyles, thus preventing the eradication of practices that are harmful to women.

A. The regulation of female sexuality

99. Many of the cultural practices discussed above are often based on a society's belief that the freedom of a woman, especially with regard to her sexual identity should be curtailed and regulated....

100. In many cases, female sexuality is regulated by physical violence and force. Honour killings ... are the most obvious examples. Women who fall in love, commit adultery, request divorce, or choose their own husbands are seen as transgressors of the boundaries of appropriate sexual behaviour. As a result, they are subject to direct violence of the most horrific kind. The killing of women with impunity for these transgressions is perhaps the most overt example of the brutal control of female sexuality.

...

B. Masculinity and violence

105. In recent times, anthropologists and scholars have pointed out that, in certain contexts and in certain societies, being "masculine" in an ideal sense involves a tolerance of violence. In many societies, the ideal of heroic masculinity requires acceptance of the notion of honour and the violent regulation of female sexuality.... Heroic men in these societies use violence as a means of furthering justice and the social good, but they also use violence to ensure that women behave and are subordinate to their will.

...

QUESTION

In light of the Report of the Special Rapporteur, what strategies might you urge as a member of the CEDAW Committee or of an international human rights NGO to reduce or eliminate prevalent practices in a given country or region such as honour killings, denial of equal health care to girls, or abortion of female feotuses after determination of sex? In planning a strategy, what specific information would you think useful to you about the country or region involved?

ADDITIONAL READING

K. Askin and D. Koenig (eds.), *Women and International Human Rights Law* (1999); R. Schweder, M. Minow and Markus (eds.), *Engaging Cultural Differences* (2002); M. Sunder, 'Piercing the Veil', 112 Yale L. J. 1399 (2003); K. Knop (ed.), *Gender and Human Rights* (2004); C. MacKinnon, *Are Women Human?: And Other International Dialogues* (2007).

2. RELIGION

No topic generates more controversy — or indeed more complex ideas — than relationships between (1) institutionalization of religion in the state or religious belief or practice and (2) human rights norms. From one perspective, religious beliefs and human rights are complementary expressions of similar ideas, even though religious texts invoke the language of duties rather than rights. Important aspects of the major religious traditions — canonical text, scholarly exegesis, ministries — provide the foundation or justification for, or reinforce, many basic human rights. Evident examples include rights to bodily security, or to economic and social provision for the needy. From another perspective, religious traditions may impinge on human rights, and religious leaders may assert the primacy of those traditions over rights. Recall the illustrations in *Human Rights in the Muslim World*, p. 531, *supra*. The banner of cultural relativism may here be held high. If notions of state sovereignty represent one powerful concept and a force that challenges and seeks to limit the reach of the international human rights movement, religion can then represent another.

The topics in this section explore selected issues within this large theme. They involve the distinction sketched by some scholars between freedom *of* religion, and freedom *from* religion. The first freedom is threatened primarily by state conduct that prohibits public expression of religious belief and sharply restricts religious practice or ritual. Such conduct may stem from an ideologically secular state (such as the Peoples' Republic of China) that seeks to limit the role of organized religions, or at the other extreme from fundamentalist states that will not tolerate other forms of religious expression. The second freedom *from* again is threatened primarily by the state, which may impose the beliefs or practices of an official or dominant religion on all citizens, whatever their religious community (if any, for some citizens will be secular or atheist). In such circumstances, human rights additional to the right to freedom of religion may also be implicated. Forms of gender discrimination enforced by the state may find roots in sacred religious text. The state may repress certain speech that is widely viewed as offensive to the dominant religion. And so on.

These issues do not involve a simple dichotomy of the 'state' and 'citizens'. As the materials in Chapters 6 and 7 have illustrated, religion-based restraints or obligations may be rooted in a broad religious culture that is both closely related to and distinct from the state, and that may be insisted on or enforced by a range of non-state actors. Religion and society will often be as apt a framework for discussion as religion and state. The state itself may adopt many attitudes and pursue many policies, ranging from support of the religious culture, to a pose of neutrality, to active opposition to a religion's teachings and demands.

The following materials start with a comparative survey of questions of religion and state and freedom of religion. These comparisons among states highlight a vital issue that permeates this section: what are the links between religious communities, or one religious community, and the state? The spectrum is large, from notions of separation that are strong in the United States (the 'establishment' clause of the First Amendment to the Constitution, the metaphor much used by courts of the 'wall of separation' between church and state), to the pervasive interrelationships in several countries between Islam and the state.

This section continues with analyses of ways in which the international human rights instruments address the broad array of issues sketched in the preceding paragraphs.

a. COMPARATIVE PERSPECTIVES AMONG STATES

COLE DURHAM, PERSPECTIVES ON RELIGIOUS LIBERTY: A COMPARATIVE FRAMEWORK

in Johan van der Vyver and Witte (eds.), Religious Human Rights in Global Perspective (1996), at 12

...

Up to this point, we have identified various cultural tensions that make religion potentially divisive and the countervailing considerations that have helped moderns since Locke to understand how respect for religion and its potential divisiveness can result in stabilization rather than disintegration of a society and its political institutions. We turn now to an effort to provide a comparative framework for possible configurations of religious and state institutions and resulting patterns of religious freedom.

...

The Relationship between Religious Freedom Rights and Church-State Separation

... The degree of religious liberty in a particular society can be assessed along two dimensions — one involving the degree to which state action burdens religious belief and conduct and another involving the degree of identification between government and religious institutions. In the United States, because of the wording of the religion clause of the First Amendment of the U.S. Constitution, these two dimensions are thought of respectively as the 'free exercise' and 'establishment' aspects of religious liberty. But for comparative purposes, it is useful to think more broadly in terms of varying degrees of religious freedom and church-state identification.

At least in lay thought, there is a tendency to assume that there is a straightforward linear correlation between these two values that could be represented as shown in Figure 1.

This picture considerably oversimplifies matters. The primary difficulties arise in connection with the church-state identification gradient and its correlation to the

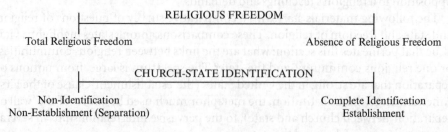

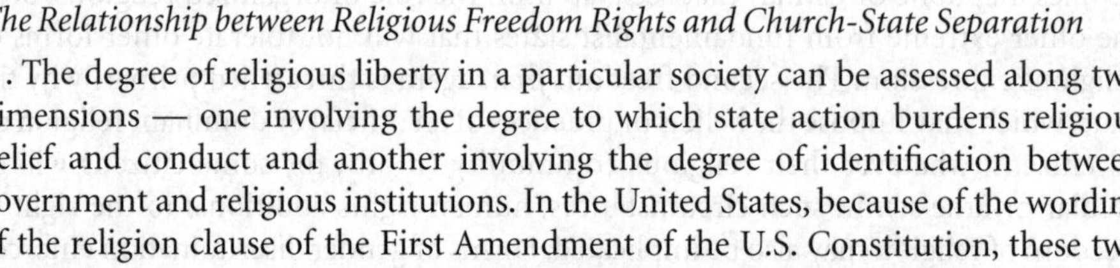

Figure 1

religious freedom continuum. Few religious establishments have ever been so totalistic as to achieve complete identification of church and state. To the extent that extreme situation is reached or approached, there is clearly an absence of religious freedom. This is obviously true for adherents of minority religions, and even the majority religion is likely to suffer because of extensive state involvement in or regulation of its affairs or due to the enervation that results from excessive dependence of religious institutions on the state.

At the other end of the church-state identification continuum, things seem more confused. The mere fact that a state does not have a formally established church does not necessarily mean that it has a separationist regime characterized by rigorous non-identification with religion. Moreover, there is considerable disagreement about the exact configuration of relationships between church and state that maximizes religious liberty, and it may well be that the optimal configuration for one culture may be different than that for another. Further, it is not clear whether 'non-identification' accurately marks the end of this particular continuum. Non-establishment and separation may mark intermediate points along a longer continuum that actually ends with 'negative' identification: i.e., overt hostility or persecution. But if persecution lies at both ends of the church-state identification continuum, it is not at all clear how this continuum correlates with the religious liberty continuum.

[The author draws on an article by George Ryskamp, 'The Spanish Experience in Church-State Relations: A Comparative Study of the Interrelationship between Church-State Identification and Religious Liberty', 1980 Brigham Young Univ. L. Rev. 616, including that article's diagram using the same two continua as in Figure 1 above. But countries in Ryskamp's diagram appear at different points of the two continua; there is no precise correlation. The author challenges Ryskamp's location of several countries on these continua, but asks generally 'why states located at opposite ends of the identification gradient should be located so close to each other on the religious freedom gradient'.]

The answer to this seeming puzzle lies in reconceptualizing the church-state identification continuum as a loop that correlates with the religious freedom continuum as shown in Figure 3.

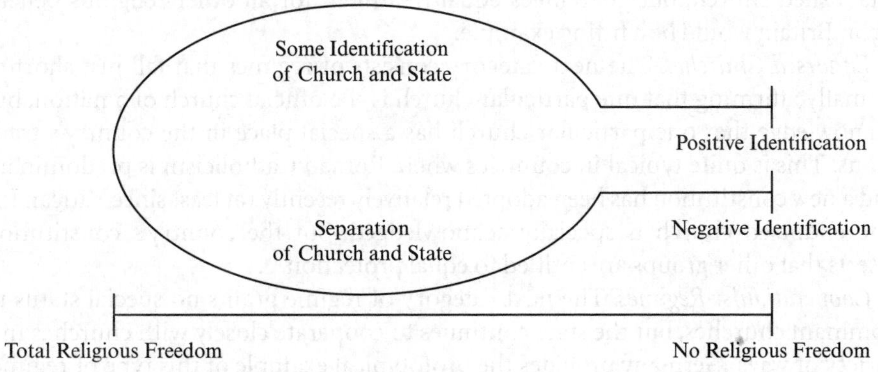

Figure 3

This model accurately reflects the fact that both strong positive and strong negative identification of church and state correlate with low levels of religious freedom. In both situations, the state adopts a sharply defined attitude toward one or more religions, leaving little room for dissenting views.

...

Another significant aspect of religious liberty clarified by the model is that one cannot simply assume that the more rigidly one separates church and state, the more religious liberty will be enhanced. At some point, aggressive separationism becomes hostility toward religion. Mechanical insistence on separation at all costs may accordingly push a system toward inadvertent insensitivity and ultimately intentional persecution. Stalinist constitutions generally had very strong church-state separation provisions, but these can hardly be said to have maximized religious liberty. Rather, they were construed as a demand that religion should be excluded from any domain where the state was present. But in a totalitarian state, this became a demand in practice that religion be marginalized to the vanishing point....

...

Turning first to the identification continuum, one can conceive it as a representation of a series of types of church-state regimes. Beginning at the positive identification end of the continuum, one first encounters *absolute theocracies* of the type one associates with stereotypical views of Islamic fundamentalism. In fact, a range of regimes is possible in Muslim theory, depending on the scope given to internal Muslim beliefs about toleration and also depending on the extent to which flexible interpretation of Shari'a law creates normative space for modernization.

Established Churches. The notion of an 'established church' is vague, and can in fact cover a range of possible church-state configurations with very different implications for the religious freedom of minority groups. At one extreme, a regime with an established church that is granted a strictly enforced monopoly in religious affairs is closely related to one with theocratic rule. Spain or Italy at some periods are classical exemplars. The next position is held by countries that have an established religion that tolerates a restricted set of divergent beliefs. An Islamic country that tolerates 'people of the Book' (but not others) would be one example; a country with an established Christian church that tolerates a number of major faiths, but disparages others would be another. The next position is a country that maintains an established church, but guarantees equal treatment for all other religious beliefs. Great Britain would be a fitting example.

Endorsed Churches. The next category consists of regimes that fall just short of formally affirming that one particular church is the official church of a nation, but acknowledge that one particular church has a special place in the country's traditions. This is quite typical in countries where Roman Catholicism is predominant and a new constitution has been adopted relatively recently (at least since Vatican II). The endorsed church is specially acknowledged, but the country's constitution asserts that other groups are entitled to equal protection....

Cooperationist Regimes. The next category of regime grants no special status to dominant churches, but the state continues to cooperate closely with churches in a variety of ways. Germany provides the prototypical example of this type of regime, though it is certainly not alone in this regard. Most notably, the cooperationist state may provide significant funding to various church-related activities, such as religious education or maintenance of churches, payment of clergy, and so forth. Very often in such regimes, relations with churches are managed through special agreements, concordats, and the like. Spain, Italy and Poland as well as several Latin American countries follow this pattern. The state may also cooperate in helping with the gathering of contributions (e.g., the withholding of 'church tax' in Germany). Cooperationist countries frequently have patterns of aid or assistance that benefit larger denominations in particular. However, they do not specifically endorse any religion, and they are committed to affording equal treatment to all religious organizations. . . .

. . .

Accommodationist Regimes. A regime may insist on separation of church and state, yet retain a posture of benevolent neutrality toward religion. Accommodationism might be thought of as cooperationism without the provision of any direct financial subsidies to religion or religious education. An accommodationist regime would have no qualms about recognizing the importance of religion as part of national or local culture, accommodating religious symbols in public settings, allowing tax, dietary, holiday, Sabbath, and other kinds of exemptions, and so forth. Many scholars in the United States argue that the United States religion clause should be construed to allow a more accommodationist approach to religious liberty. Note that the growth of the state intensifies the need for accommodation. As state influence becomes more pervasive and regulatory burdens expand, refusal to exempt or accommodate shades into hostility.

Separationist Regimes. As suggested by the earlier comments on Stalinist church-state separation, the slogan 'separation of church and state' can be used to cover a fairly broad and diverse range of regimes. At the benign end, separationism differs relatively little from accommodationism. The major difference is that separationism, as its name suggests, insists on more rigid separation of church and state. Any suggestion of public support for religion is deemed inappropriate. Religious symbols in public displays such as Christmas creches are not allowed. Even indirect subsidies to religion through tax deductions or tax exemptions are either suspect or proscribed. Granting religiously-based exemptions from general public laws is viewed as impermissible favoritism for religion. No religious teaching or indoctrination of any kind is permitted in public schools (although some teaching about religions from an objective standpoint may be permitted). The mere reliance on religious premises in public argument is deemed to run afoul of the church-state separation principle. Members of the clergy are not permitted to hold public office.

More extreme forms of separationism make stronger attempts to cordon off religion from public life. One form this can take is through tightening the state monopoly on certain forms of educational or social services. In the educational realm, the state can ban home schooling altogether, can proscribe private schools, or can submit either of the foregoing to such extensive accreditation requirements that it is virtually impossible for independent religious education to function. Different regimes make differing judgments about the extent to which religious marriages will be recognized. A range of social or charitable services (including health care) may be regulated in ways that make it difficult for religious organizations to carry out their perceived ministries in this area. 'Separation' in its most objectionable guise demands that religion retreat from any domain that the state desires to occupy, but is untroubled by intrusive state regulation and intervention in religious affairs. . . .

Hostility and Overt Persecution. The test in this area is how smaller religious groups are treated. Government officials seldom persecute larger religious groups (though this was certainly not unheard of in communist lands). Persecution can take the form of imprisonment of those who insist on acting in accordance with divergent religious beliefs. In its most egregious forms, it involves 'ethnic cleansing' or most extreme, genocide. More typical problems involve less dramatic forms of bureaucratic roadblocks which cumulatively have the effect of significantly impairing religious liberty. These can take the form of denying or delaying registration (granting entity status) and obstructing land use approvals.

With the foregoing categories in mind, the relationship between the more refined identification gradient and the religious freedom gradient can be modeled as shown in Figure 4.

There is some room for argument about which type of regime should be displayed as the type most likely to maximize religious liberty. My contention is that accommodationist regimes have the best claim to this position. Historical experience suggests that maximal religious liberty tends to be achieved when church-state identification is in the accommodation or non-hostile separation mode. Of course, substantial religious liberty can also exist in cooperationist or endorsed church regimes, at least where genuine religious equality is present. However, there is always a sense in such regimes that smaller religious communities have a kind of second-class status, and to the extent that public funds are directly supporting programs of major churches, there is a sense that members of religious minorities are being coerced to support religious programs with which they do not agree. As between

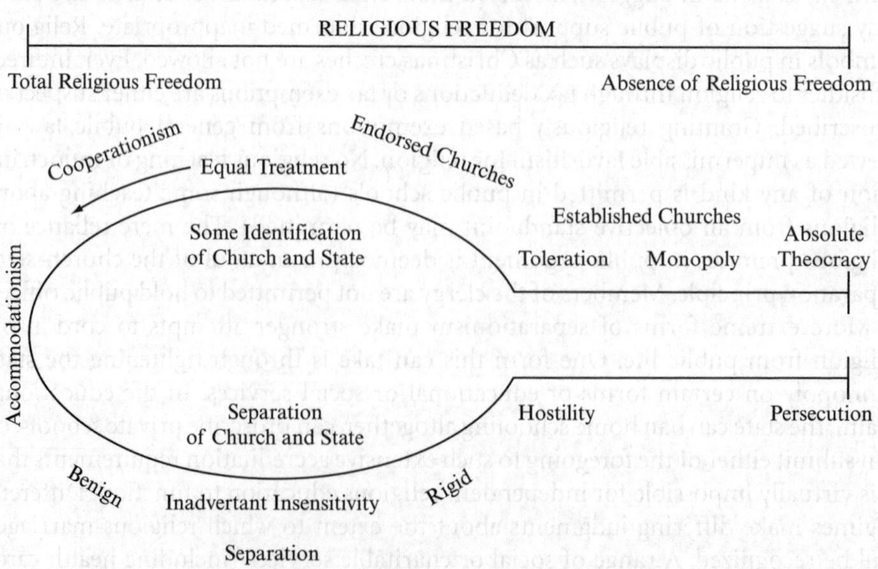

Figure 4

separationist and accommodationist regimes, accommodationism has the edge in contemporary settings where the modern secular 'performance state' has emerged with its welfare and regulatory dimensions. As state action or influence pervades more and more of social life, wooden insistence on separation too easily slips into marginalization of religion. Moreover, as regulations proliferate, there is increased demand for exceptions that can sensitively accommodate religious needs. In the last analysis, if accommodation can be achieved without undue difficulty, a regime which fails to accommodate manifests a lesser degree of religious liberty.

. . .

The church-state identification loop is useful not only in comparing types of institutional configurations, but also in keeping institutional issues in perspective. It is useful to note, for example, that the often highly polarized constitutional debates in the United States are in fact debates about which of a fairly narrow range of institutional options is optimal. . . .

. . .

DINAH SHELTON AND ALEXANDRE KISS, A DRAFT MODEL LAW ON FREEDOM OF RELIGION

in Johan van der Vyver and J. Witte, Jr. (eds.), Religious Human Rights in Global Perspective (1996), at 572

. . .

The freedom to have a religion means that the government does not prescribe orthodoxy or prohibit particular religions or beliefs. In practice, this is not always the case. Among the examples that may be cited, Indonesia bans the Jehovah's Witness religion because of 'its aggressive manner in propagating its teachings, trying to convert other adherents to this faith'. According to the government, 'misleading cults' are banned in order to maintain peace and harmony between and among adherents of the various religions. 'Without the Government's handling in the matter, the activities of "cults" (including Jehovah's Witnesses and Baha'is) may create disturbances and disrupt the existing religious tolerance'. Similar justifications are put forward by other states that ban specific religions. In some countries, coercion is employed to force renunciation of banned religions.

Short of banning, laws may severely interfere with minority religions. In Pakistan, the Ahmadis are prevented by law from calling themselves Muslims and using Muslim practices in worship or in the public manifestations of their faith.

. . .

The constitutions of some states establish the primacy of a religion over the state, granting privileges that are incompatible with religious liberty and non-discrimination. Even in states with excellent human rights records, links between religion and state pose problems. In Norway, the king and a majority of the cabinet are required to be members of the state church. Christianity is still a mandatory subject in the Norwegian public schools. Nonconformists have been permitted to teach it since 1969 as long as they do so in accordance with evangelical Lutheran doctrine.

Only in 1964 was the constitution amended to guarantee all inhabitants the free exercise of religion. A 1969 Law Concerning Religious Denominations extends the right to form denominations and stipulates that groups registered with the Department of Justice may receive financial aid from both the national and municipal governments on the same basis as parishes of the state church in proportion to their membership statistics. The majority remains opposed to disestablishment of the state church. It is seen as 'a public institution in which membership does not require a commitment of faith and which presently has approximately equal numbers of atheists and "personal Christians" on its rolls'.

In England, the Anglican Church remains at the center of public policy and has substantial support from the state. Prime ministers appoint bishops and the House of Lords contains 26 Anglican bishops who are the lords spiritual. The Parliament can rule on doctrinal and liturgical matters — most recently on the issue of ordination of women. Although there may be little real intervention in the internal affairs of the church, its strongly privileged position can be seen to discriminate against minority religions.

State budgets provide for some religious denominations in Spain, Italy, Greece, Belgium, and Luxembourg. Religious taxes exist in Austria, Switzerland, Denmark, Germany, Norway, and Finland. Indirect support is provided in France, Great Britain, the Netherlands, and Sweden.

Established religions exist in all parts of the world. In Africa, the constitutions of the Comores, Mauritania, Libya, and Somalia proclaim Islam as the religion of the state. Libya also declares that 'the Holy Koran is the constitution of the Socialist People's Libyan Arab Jamahiriya'. In the Sudan, all legislation must conform to Islamic prescriptions. The head of state must be a Muslim, and non-Muslims are incompetent to testify against Muslims. Propagation of heretical beliefs is a crime. In contrast, the constitution of Botswana specifically recognizes the individual's right to propagate his religion. Proselytizing or converting others is permissible.

...

Mexico's constitution contains some of the more restrictive provisions. Its articles provide that no minister of any faith may be a candidate for elected office. Article 130 provides that ministers cannot form associations for political purposes or rally in favor of or against any candidate, political party or association. ... It is also forbidden to hold political meetings in the churches. ...

...

NOTE

The two preceding articles provide rich illustrations of different types of relationships between religion and state throughout the world. The First Amendment to the United States Constitution, prohibiting Congress from making laws 'respecting an establishment of religion, or prohibiting the free exercise thereof', would appear to stand at the end of a spectrum with respect to establishment, although as Durham demonstrates, it is problematic to place the United States at the extreme, for all depends on how the spectrum is defined. For example, the United States and Iran (excerpts from the Iranian Constitution appear below) do represent extremes with respect to involvement of religion in the state, and the state in religion. But the United States would be located on a different point in a spectrum if states like Iran were at one end, and states hostile to and suppressing all religious belief and practice (which of course would be non-establishment states) were at the other.

Although there continues to be extensive constitutional litigation in the United States with respect to both the 'establishment' and 'free exercise' clauses, it is important to bear in mind that, relative to most of the countries discussed below, 'the often highly polarized constitutional debates in the United States are in fact debates about which of a fairly narrow range of institutional options is optimal'. Durham, *supra*. We here introduce some illustrations of these observations, starting with a well-known US Supreme Court decision that explores aspects of the establishment clause, and continuing with illustrations from societies and states that depart substantially or radically from the underlying assumptions, constitutional doctrine, and practice in the United States.

LYNCH V. DONNELLY

Supreme Court of the United States, 1984

465 U.S. 669, 104 S.Ct. 1355

[For at least 40 years during the Christmas season, the city of Pawtucket, R.I. had erected a display within a park owned by a nonprofit organization that was located in the heart of the shopping district. The display consisted of several objects owned by the city, including a Christmas tree, a banner reading 'Seasons Greetings', and a creche or scene of the Nativity that included the traditional figures of the Infant Jesus, Mary and Joseph, and angels. The city's expenses in installing and repairing objects in the creche were negligible.

Respondents in this case had brought an action in the Federal District Court challenging the city's inclusion of the creche in the display by contending that it violated the Establishment Clause as made applicable to states by the Fourteenth Amendment. The District Court upheld the challenge, enjoining the city from including the creche in the display, and the Court of Appeals affirmed. There follow excerpts from the opinion for the Court by Chief Justice Burger that reversed the Court of Appeals by a 5–4 decision.]

... The concept of a "wall" of separation [between church and state] is a useful figure of speech [serving] as a reminder that the Establishment Clause forbids an established church or anything approaching it. But the metaphor itself is not a wholly accurate description of the practical aspects of the relationship that in fact exists between church and state.

...

Executive Orders and other official announcements of Presidents and of the Congress have proclaimed both Christmas and Thanksgiving National Holidays in religious terms. And, by Acts of Congress, it has long been the practice that federal employees are released from duties on these National Holidays, while being paid from the same public revenues that provide the compensation of the Chaplains of the Senate and the House and the military services. . . .

Other examples of reference to our religious heritage are found in the statutorily prescribed national motto "In God We Trust," which Congress and the President mandated for our currency, and in the language "One nation under God," as part of the Pledge of Allegiance to the American flag.

. . .

Rather than mechanically invalidating all governmental conduct or statutes that confer benefits or give special recognition to religion in general or to one faith — as an absolutist approach would dictate — the Court has scrutinized challenged legislation or official conduct to determine whether, in reality, it establishes a religion or religious faith, or tends to do so. . . .

. . . The line between permissible relationships and those barred by the Clause can no more be straight and unwavering than due process can be defined in a single stroke or phrase or test. The Clause erects a "blurred, indistinct, and variable barrier depending on all the circumstances of a particular relationship."

In the line-drawing process we have often found it useful to inquire whether the challenged law or conduct has a secular purpose, whether its principal or primary effect is to advance or inhibit religion, and whether it creates an excessive entanglement of government with religion. . . .

. . .

. . . The District Court inferred from the religious nature of the creche that the city has no secular purpose for the display. . . . When viewed in the proper context of the Christmas Holiday season, it is apparent that, on this record, there is insufficient evidence to establish that the inclusion of the creche is a purposeful or surreptitious effort to express some kind of subtle governmental advocacy of a particular religious message. In a pluralistic society a variety of motives and purposes are implicated. The city, like the Congresses and Presidents, however, has principally taken note of a significant historical religious event long celebrated in the Western World. The creche in the display depicts the historical origins of this traditional event long recognized as a National Holiday.

The narrow question is whether there is a secular purpose for Pawtucket's display of the creche. The display is sponsored by the city to celebrate the Holiday and to depict the origins of that Holiday. These are legitimate secular purposes. The District Court's inference, drawn from the religious nature of the creche, that the city has no secular purpose was, on this record, clearly erroneous.

. . .

The dissent asserts some observers may perceive that the city has aligned itself with the Christian faith by including a Christian symbol in its display and that this serves to advance religion. We can assume, *arguendo*, that the display advances religion in a sense; but our precedents plainly contemplate that on occasion some advancement of religion will result from governmental action. The Court has made it abundantly clear, however, that "not every law that confers an 'indirect,' 'remote,' or 'incidental' benefit upon [religion] is, for that reason alone, constitutionally invalid." Here . . . display of the creche is no more an advancement or endorsement of religion than the Congressional and Executive recognition of the origins of the Holiday itself as "Christ's Mass," or the exhibition of literally hundreds of religious paintings in governmentally supported museums.

...

... This case does not involve a direct subsidy to church-sponsored schools or colleges, or other religious institutions, and hence no inquiry into potential political divisiveness is even called for. In any event, apart from this litigation there is no evidence of political friction or divisiveness over the creche in the 40-year history of Pawtucket's Christmas celebration....

...

Of course the creche is identified with one religious faith but no more so than the examples we have set out from prior cases in which we found no conflict with the Establishment Clause.... To forbid the use of this one passive symbol — the creche — at the very time people are taking note of the season with Christmas hymns and carols in public schools and other public places, and while the Congress and legislatures open sessions with prayers by paid chaplains, would be a stilted overreaction contrary to our history and to our holdings. If the presence of the creche in this display violates the Establishment Clause, a host of other forms of taking official note of Christmas, and of our religious heritage, are equally offensive to the Constitution.

The Court has acknowledged that the "fears and political problems" that gave rise to the Religion Clauses in the 18th century are of far less concern today. We are unable to perceive the Archbishop of Canterbury, the Bishop of Rome, or other powerful religious leaders behind every public acknowledgment of the religious heritage long officially recognized by the three constitutional branches of government. Any notion that these symbols pose a real danger of establishment of a state church is farfetched indeed.

...

JUSTICE O'CONNOR, CONCURRING

...

The Establishment Clause prohibits government from making adherence to a religion relevant in any way to a person's standing in the political community. Government can run afoul of that prohibition in two principal ways. One is excessive entanglement with religious institutions, which may interfere with the independence of the institutions, give the institutions access to government or governmental powers not fully shared by nonadherents of the religion, and foster the creation of political constituencies defined along religious lines. The second and more direct infringement is government endorsement or disapproval of religion. Endorsement sends a message to nonadherents that they are outsiders, not full members of the political community, and an accompanying message to adherents that they are insiders, favored members of the political community. Disapproval sends the opposite message.

...

... I would find that Pawtucket did not intend to convey any message of endorsement of Christianity or disapproval of non-Christian religions. The evident purpose of including the creche in the larger display was not promotion of the religious content of the creche but celebration of the public holiday through its traditional symbols. Celebration of public holidays, which have cultural significance even if they also have religious aspects, is a legitimate secular purpose.

...

... The display celebrates a public holiday, and no one contends that declaration of that holiday is understood to be an endorsement of religion. The holiday itself has very strong secular components and traditions. Government celebration of the holiday, which is extremely common, generally is not understood to endorse the religious content of the holiday, just as government celebration of Thanksgiving is not so understood....

...

These features combine to make the government's display of the creche in this particular physical setting no more an endorsement of religion than such governmental "acknowledgments" of religion as legislative prayers ... government declaration of Thanksgiving as a public holiday, printing of "In God We Trust" on coins, and opening court sessions with "God save the United States and this honorable court." Those government acknowledgments of religion serve, in the only ways reasonably possible in our culture, the legitimate secular purposes of solemnizing public occasions, expressing confidence in the future, and encouraging the recognition of what is worthy of appreciation in society. For that reason, and because of their history and ubiquity, those practices are not understood as conveying government approval of particular religious beliefs....

...

JUSTICE BRENNAN, WITH WHOM JUSTICE MARSHALL, JUSTICE BLACKMUN, AND JUSTICE STEVENS JOIN, DISSENTING

...

... [O]ur precedents in my view compel the holding that Pawtucket's inclusion of a life-sized display depicting the biblical description of the birth of Christ as part of its annual Christmas celebration is unconstitutional. Nothing in the history of such practices or the setting in which the city's creche is presented obscures or diminishes the plain fact that Pawtucket's action amounts to an impermissible governmental endorsement of a particular faith.

...

... [A]ll of Pawtucket's "valid secular objectives can be readily accomplished by other means." Plainly, the city's interest in celebrating the holiday and in promoting both retail sales and goodwill are fully served by the elaborate display of Santa Claus, reindeer, and wishing wells that are already a part of Pawtucket's annual Christmas display. More importantly, the nativity scene, unlike every other element of the Hodgson Park display, reflects a sectarian exclusivity that the avowed purposes of celebrating the holiday season and promoting retail commerce simply do not encompass. ... The inclusion of a distinctively religious element like the creche, however, demonstrates that a narrower sectarian purpose lay behind the decision to include a nativity scene....

... The effect on minority religious groups, as well as on those who may reject all religion, is to convey the message that their views are not similarly worthy of public recognition nor entitled to public support. It was precisely this sort of religious chauvinism that the Establishment Clause was intended forever to prohibit....

Finally, it is evident that Pawtucket's inclusion of a creche as part of its annual Christmas display does pose a significant threat of fostering "excessive entanglement." ... Jews and other non-Christian groups, prompted perhaps by the Mayor's remark that he will include a Menorah in future displays, can be expected to press government for inclusion of their symbols, and faced with such requests, government will have to become involved in accommodating the various demands....

...

Finally, and most importantly, even in the context of Pawtucket's seasonal celebration, the creche retains a specifically Christian religious meaning. I refuse to accept the notion implicit in today's decision that non-Christians would find that the religious content of the creche is eliminated by the fact that it appears as part of the city's otherwise secular celebration of the Christmas holiday. The nativity scene is clearly distinct in its purpose and effect from the rest of the Hodgson Park display for the simple reason that it is the only one rooted in a biblical account of Christ's birth. It is the chief symbol of the characteristically Christian belief that a divine Savior was brought into the world and that the purpose of this miraculous birth was to illuminate a path toward salvation and redemption. For Christians, that path is exclusive, precious, and holy. But for those who do not share these beliefs, the symbolic reenactment of the birth of a divine being who has been miraculously incarnated as a man stands as a dramatic reminder of their differences with Christian faith ...

...

... While I remain uncertain about these questions, I would suggest that such practices as the designation of "In God We Trust" as our national motto, or the references to God contained in the Pledge of Allegiance to the flag can best be understood, in Dean Rostow's apt phrase, as a form a "ceremonial deism," protected from Establishment Clause scrutiny chiefly because they have lost through rote repetition any significant religious content. ... The practices by which the government has long acknowledged religion are therefore probably necessary to serve certain secular functions, and that necessity, coupled with their long history, gives those practices an essentially secular meaning.

...

Under our constitutional scheme, the role of safeguarding our "religious heritage" and of promoting religious beliefs is reserved as the exclusive prerogative of our Nation's churches, religious institutions, and spiritual leaders. ... [T]he city's action should be recognized for what it is: a coercive, though perhaps small, step toward establishing the sectarian preferences of the majority at the expense of the minority, accomplished by placing public facilities and funds in support of the religious symbolism and theological tidings that the creche conveys....

...

QUESTIONS

1. Based on the preceding excerpts from *Lynch v. Donnelly*, how would you describe the major purposes in the United States of the establishment clause? Does one or do several of those purposes appear essential to the character of the US as a liberal democratic country protecting freedoms of conscience, speech, assembly, association and religion?

2. What do you understand to be the relationship, if any, between the establishment clause and the free exercise clause? For example, is the first relevant to the second? Essential to the second?

3. 'I don't understand why the question posed in *Lynch v. Donnelly* is thought to raise a constitutional issue. Most Americans are Christian — simply a fact. Non-Christian Americans — whether Jews or Muslims or Hindus or any other of the many religions observed in the United States — are therefore minorities. Many aspects of a state's practices stem from the majority culture and beliefs — the Christmas holiday, for example. Minorities rarely feel completely at home in a country in which the large majority of the population is different — whether the factor making them minorities is race, ethnicity, cultural practices, or religion. They may feel excluded, left out, uncomfortably different. There's nothing "wrong" with that from a legal or moral point of view. It's inevitable.' Comment.

EDMUND ANDREWS, GERMAN CHURCHES, EVER GIVING, ASK TO RECEIVE

New York Times, January, 6, 1998, p. A8

...

Under an unusual century-old system, religious institutions in Germany get almost all their revenue from a 9 percent church surtax imposed on the income tax of every registered Catholic, Protestant and Jew. Taxpayers are asked to declare their religion on their income tax returns, and churchgoers are pressed to register their religion with the Government. Those who are not members of the religions covered by the tax do not pay it, nor do those who have taken the bureaucratic step of revoking their registration.

Church taxes totaled about $11 billion in 1996, almost as much as the sin tax on cigarettes. In striking contrast to the United States, with its separation of church and state, Germany uses its religion taxes for the salaries of priests and rabbis, the construction of churches and a sprawling array of church-run social programs, from Christian day-care centers and kindergartens to drug-counseling clinics and hospitals.

But now the church-state partnership is cracking. With 4.3 million Germans, or more than 11 percent of the work force, unemployed, and thus paying no taxes, church revenue fell about 4 percent in 1996. It could have plunged as much as 10 percent in 1997. That would represent a combined drop in revenues for all religions of more than $1 billion.

...

Germany's church tax supports three main religious groups: the Evangelical Churches, an umbrella organization of Protestants that oversees the Lutheran, Reform and United Protestant branches; Roman Catholicism, and Judaism. Protestants, most of them Lutherans, account for 45 percent of the German population, with Roman Catholics at 37 percent. Jews represent only a small percentage. Muslims and others are not part of the tax structure.

Much like German industry, German religion is now preaching the need to cut costs, become more efficient and refocus priorities. In Munich, Protestant leaders even got a free strategic analysis from the management consultants McKinsey & Company. And they are talking about trying to wean themselves, at least partly, from the tax system.

In early November, Protestant leaders in Hesse announced plans to cut 25 percent of spending on 19 programs, like psychological counseling and adult education. Pastors will also be sent into retirement as soon as they turn 60, while new seminarians will be kept out. In addition, the church will sharply reduce its extensive support for kindergartens and cut the number of religion teachers it sends to public schools.

. . .

The financial crunch is causing religious people at all levels to rethink their partnership with the Government. It began when the state took it upon itself to tax people who went to church and to funnel that money back to the denominations. In exchange, the churches assumed a range of nonreligious responsibilities in areas like adult education and social work as well as providing religious instruction in public schools.

. . .

Meanwhile, churches have begun to pull away from responsibilities not directly related to church life. In the case of kindergartens, Protestant officials want to force either the state or parents to pay more. Under the budget plan here in Hesse, the church's contribution to kindergarten costs would drop to 15 percent, from 40 percent in some schools. And children who do not belong to the church will have to pay extra.

. . .

CONSTITUTION OF IRAN

1979 (as amended)

[Events of the last few years underscore the severe tensions and at times outright conflict between the forces for religious or secular rule in Iran, which became an Islamic republic in 1979 when the ruling monarchy was overthrown. In the process, the implications and very meaning of the 1979 revolution against the Shah led by Ayatollah Khomeini (Khumayni), and the Constitution that it spawned, are brought into public debate. The paradoxes and indeed contradictions of Iran's complex governmental structure (religious leader, institutionalization of Islamic principles, elected president and assembly) are reflected in the excerpts below from the Constitution.[8]]

[8] Original text is based on a translation provided by the Iranian Embassy in London. It has been extensively changed in 1994 and 1995 to adapt it to ICL standards.

Chapter I: General Principles

Article 1 [Form of Government]

The form of government of Iran is that of an Islamic Republic, endorsed by the people of Iran on the basis of their longstanding belief in the sovereignty of truth and Koranic justice, in the referendum of 29 and 30 March 1979, through the affirmative vote of a majority of 98.2% of eligible voters, held after the victorious Islamic Revolution led by Imam Khumayni.

Article 2 [Foundational Principles]

The Islamic Republic is a system based on belief in:

(1) the One God (as stated in the phrase 'There is no god except Allah'), His exclusive sovereignty and right to legislate, and the necessity of submission to his commands;

(2) Divine revelation and its fundamental role in setting forth the laws;

...

(6) the exalted dignity and value of man, and his freedom coupled with responsibility before God; in which equity, justice, political, economic, social, and cultural independence, and national solidarity are secured by recourse to: (a) continuous leadership of the holy persons, possessing necessary qualifications, exercised on the basis of the Koran and the Sunnah, upon all of whom be peace; ...

Article 3 [State Goals]

In order to attain the objectives specified in Article 2, the government of the Islamic Republic of Iran has the duty of directing all its resources to the following goals:

(1) the creation of a favorable environment for the growth of moral virtues based on faith and piety and the struggle against all forms of vice and corruption;

(2) raising the level of public awareness in all areas, through the proper use of the press, mass media, and other means;

...

(6) the elimination of all forms of despotism and autocracy and all attempts to monopolize power;

(7) ensuring political and social freedoms within the framework of the law;

(8) the participation of the entire people in determining their political, economic, social, and cultural destiny;

...

(16) framing the foreign policy of the country on the basis of Islamic criteria, fraternal commitment to all Muslims, and unsparing support to the freedom fighters of the world

Article 4 [Islamic Principle]

All civil, penal financial, economic, administrative, cultural, military, political, and other laws and regulations must be based on Islamic criteria. This principle applies absolutely and generally to all articles of the Constitution as well as to all other laws and regulations, and the wise persons of the Guardian Council are judges in this matter.

...

Article 6 [Administration of Affairs]

In the Islamic Republic of Iran, the affairs of the country must be administered on the basis of public opinion expressed by the means of elections, including the election of the President, the representatives of the Islamic Consultative Assembly, and the members of councils, or by means of referenda in matters specified in other articles of this Constitution.

. . .

Article 8 [Community Principle]

In the Islamic Republic of Iran, 'al-'amr bilma'ruf wa al-nahy 'an al-munkar' is a universal and reciprocal duty that must be fulfilled by the people with respect to one another, by the government with respect to the people, and by the people with respect to the government. The conditions, limits, and nature of this duty will be specified by law. (This is in accordance with the Koranic verse 'The believers, men and women, are guardians of one another; they enjoin the good and forbid the evil'. [9:71])

. . .

Article 12 [Official Religion]

The official religion of Iran is Islam and the Twelver Ja'fari school, and this principle will remain eternally immutable. Other Islamic schools are to be accorded full respect, and their followers are free to act in accordance with their own jurisprudence in performing their religious rites. These schools enjoy official status in matters pertaining to religious education, affairs of personal status (marriage, divorce, inheritance, and wills) and related litigation in courts of law. In regions of the country where Muslims following any one of these schools constitute the majority, local regulations, within the bounds of the jurisdiction of local councils, are to be in accordance with the respective school, without infringing upon the rights of the followers of other schools.

Article 13 [Recognized Religious Minorities]

Zoroastrian, Jewish, and Christian Iranians are the only recognized religious minorities, who, within the limits of the law, are free to perform their religious rites and ceremonies, and to act according to their own canon in matters of personal affairs and religious education.

Article 14 [Non-Muslims' Rights]

In accordance with the sacred verse 'God does not forbid you to deal kindly and justly with those who have not fought against you because of your religion and who have not expelled you from your homes' [60:8], the government of the Islamic Republic of Iran and all Muslims are duty-bound to treat non-Muslims in conformity with ethical norms and the principles of Islamic justice and equity, and to respect their human rights. This principle applies to all who refrain from engaging in conspiracy or activity against Islam and the Islamic Republic of Iran.

. . .

Chapter III: The Rights of the People

Article 19 [No Discrimination, No Privileges]

All people of Iran, whatever the ethnic group or tribe to which they belong, enjoy equal rights; color, race, language, and the like, do not bestow any privilege.

Article 20 [Equality Before Law]

All citizens of the country, both men and women, equally enjoy the protection of the law and enjoy all human, political, economic, social, and cultural rights, in conformity with Islamic criteria.

Article 21 [Women's Rights]

The government must ensure the rights of women in all respects, in conformity with Islamic criteria, and accomplish the following goals:

(1) create a favorable environment for the growth of woman's personality and the restoration of her rights, both the material and intellectual;

...

Article 22 [Human Dignity and Rights]

The dignity, life, property, rights, residence, and occupation of the individual are inviolate, except in cases sanctioned by law.

Article 23 [Freedom of Belief]

The investigation of individuals' beliefs is forbidden, and no one may be molested or taken to task simply for holding a certain belief.

Article 24 [Freedom of the Press]

Publications and the press have freedom of expression except when it is detrimental to the fundamental principles of Islam or the rights of the public. The details of this exception will be specified by law.

...

Article 26 [Freedom of Association]

The formation of parties, societies, political or professional associations, as well as religious societies, whether Islamic or pertaining to one of the recognized religious minorities, is permitted provided they do not violate the principles of independence, freedom, national unity, the criteria of Islam, or the basis of the Islamic Republic....

[Sections of economic and social rights are omitted.]

Chapter V: The Rights of National Sovereignty

Article 57 [Separation of Powers]

The powers of government in the Islamic Republic are vested in the legislature, the judiciary, and the executive powers, functioning under the supervision of the absolute religious Leader and the Leadership of the Ummah, in accordance with the forthcoming articles of this Constitution. These powers are independent of each other.

Article 58 [Legislature]

The functions of the legislature are to be exercised through the Islamic Consultative Assembly, consisting of the elected representatives of the people. Legislation approved by this body, after going through the stages specified in the articles below, is communicated to the executive and the judiciary for implementation.

...

Article 60 [Executive]

The functions of the executive, except in the matters that are directly placed under the jurisdiction of the Leadership by the Constitution, are to be exercised by the President and the Ministers.

Article 61 [Judiciary]

The functions of the judiciary are to be performed by courts of justice, which are to be formed in accordance with the criteria of Islam, and are vested with the authority to examine and settle lawsuits, protect the rights of the public, dispense and enact justice, and implement the Divine limits.

Chapter VI: The Legislative Power

Article 62 [Election]

(1) The Islamic Consultative Assembly is constituted by the representatives of the people elected directly and by secret ballot.

(2) The qualifications of voters and candidates, as well as the nature of election, will be specified by law.

...

Article 64 [270 Members, Religious Representatives]

(1) There are to be two hundred seventy members of the Islamic Consultative Assembly....

(2) The Zoroastrians and Jews will each elect one representative; Assyrian and Chaldean Christians will jointly elect one representative; and Armenian Christians in the north and those in the south of the country will each elect one representative.

(3) The delimitation of the election constituencies and the number of representatives will be determined by law.

...

Article 72 [Limits]

The Islamic Consultative Assembly cannot enact laws contrary to the official religion of the country or to the Constitution. It is the duty of the Guardian Council to determine whether a violation has occurred, in accordance with Article 96.

Article 89 [Interpellation]

...

(2) In the event at least one-third of the members of the Islamic Consultative Assembly interpellate the President [formally question about government policy] concerning his executive responsibilities in relation with the Executive Power and the executive affairs of the country the President must be present in the Assembly within one month after the tabling of the interpellation in order to give adequate explanations in regard to the matters raised. In the event, after hearing the statements of the opposing and favoring members and the reply of the President, two-thirds of the members of the Assembly declare a vote of no confidence, the same will be communicated to the Leadership for information and implementation of Article 110(10).

...

Article 91 [Guardian Council]

With a view to safeguard the Islamic ordinances and the Constitution, in order to examine the compatibility of the legislation passed by the Islamic Consultative Assembly with Islam, a council to be known as the Guardian Council is to be constituted with the following composition:

1. six religious men, conscious of the present needs and the issues of the day, to be selected by the Leader, and
2. six jurists, specializing in different areas of law, to be elected by the Islamic Consultative Assembly from among the Muslim jurists nominated by the Head of the Judicial Power.

...

Article 94 [Review of Legislation]

All legislation passed by the Islamic Consultative Assembly must be sent to the Guardian Council. The Guardian Council must review it within a maximum of ten days from its receipt with a view to ensuring its compatibility with the criteria of Islam and the Constitution. If it finds the legislation incompatible, it will return it to the Assembly for review. Otherwise the legislation will be deemed enforceable.

...

Article 98 [Authoritative Interpretation]

The authority of the interpretation of the Constitution is vested with the Guardian Council, which is to be done with the consent of three-fourths of its members.

...

Chapter VIII: The Leader or Leadership Council

Article 107 [Religious Leader]

(1) After the demise of Imam Khumayni, the task of appointing the Leader shall be vested with the experts elected by the people. The experts will review and consult among themselves concerning all the religious men possessing the qualifications specified in Articles 5 and 109. ... The Leader thus elected by the Assembly of Experts shall assume all the powers of the religious leader and all the responsibilities arising therefrom.

...

Article 109 [Leadership Qualifications]

(1) Following are the essential qualifications and conditions for the Leader:

a. Scholarship, as required for performing the functions of religious leader in different fields.

b. Justice and piety, as required for the leadership of the Islamic Ummah.

c. Right political and social perspicacity, prudence, courage, administrative facilities, and adequate capability for leadership.

...

Article 110 [Leadership Duties and Powers]

(1) Following are the duties and powers of the Leadership:

1. Delineation of the general policies of the Islamic Republic of Iran after consultation with the Nation's Exigency Council.
2. Supervision over the proper execution of the general policies of the system.
3. Issuing decrees for national referenda.
4. Assuming supreme command of the Armed Forces.
5. Declaration of war and peace and the mobilization of the Armed Forces.
6. Appointment, dismissal, and resignation of:

   a. the religious men on the Guardian Council,
   b. the supreme judicial authority of the country,
   c. the head of the radio and television network of the Islamic Republic of Iran,
   d. the chief of the joint staff,
   e. the chief commander of the Islamic Revolution Guards Corps, and
   f. the supreme commanders of the Armed Forces.

7. Resolving differences between the three wings of the Armed Forces and regulation of their relations.
8. Resolving the problems which cannot be solved by conventional methods, through the Nation's Exigency Council.
9. Signing the decree formalizing the election of the President of the Republic by the people. The suitability of candidates for the Presidency of the Republic, with respect to the qualifications specified in the Constitution, must be confirmed before elections take place by the Guardian Council, and, in the case of the first term of a President, by the Leadership.
10. Dismissal of the President of the Republic, with due regard for the interests of the country, after the Supreme Court holds him guilty of the violation of his constitutional duties, or after a vote of the Islamic Consultative Assembly testifying to his incompetence on the basis of Article 89.

...

[Selected Provisions]

Article 144 [Islamic Army]

The Army of the Islamic Republic of Iran must be an Islamic Army, i.e., committed to Islamic ideology and the people, and must recruit into its service individuals who have faith in the objectives of the Islamic Revolution and are devoted to the cause of realizing its goals.

...

Article 167 [Rule of Law for Judiciary]

The judge is bound to endeavor to judge each case on the basis of the codified law. In case of the absence of any such law, he has to deliver his judgment on the basis of authoritative Islamic sources and authentic fatawa....

QUESTIONS

1. What similarities with and differences from Iran would you stress in comparing the Western states noted above with respect to relationships between religion and state?

2. What do you believe to be the likely implications of a close (or closer than the United States) relationship between religion and state for nondiscrimination among religions or their adherents?

3. Does the state's 'entanglement' with churches in Germany appear to violate the US establishment clause? Does it seem to impair freedom of religion? How would you answer the same questions with respect to Iran?

b. INTERNATIONAL LAW PERSPECTIVES

Here we turn to the universal human rights instruments. Note the limited degree to which those instruments have developed ideas about religion and state or religion and human rights, at least in relation to their far greater development of human rights ideas in fields like race, gender or democratic participation. A purpose of this section is to explore why this should be the case.

GENERAL COMMENT NO. 22 (ON ICCPR ARTICLE 18) OF THE HUMAN RIGHTS COMMITTEE

Adopted 1993, UN Doc. HRI/GEN/1/Rev.1 (1994), at 35

[The Human Rights Committee created by the International Covenant on Civil and Political Rights has authority to issue 'general comments,' effectively used by the Committee to issue interpretive comments on the Covenant's provisions. This General Comment addresses Article 18 (*infra*) of the ICCPR. See pp. 873–890, *infra*, for a discussion of the Committee's General Comments and their effects.]

Article 18, ICCPR

1. Everyone shall have the right to freedom of thought, conscience and religion. This right shall include freedom to have or to adopt a religion or belief of his choice, and freedom, either individually or in community with others and in public or private, to manifest his religion or belief in worship, observance, practice and teaching.
2. No one shall be subject to coercion which would impair his freedom to have or to adopt a religion or belief of his choice.
3. Freedom to manifest one's religion or beliefs may be subject only to such limitations as are prescribed by law and are necessary to protect public safety, order, health, or morals or the fundamental rights and freedoms of others.
4. The States Parties to the present Covenant undertake to have respect for the liberty of parents and, when applicable, legal guardians to ensure the religious and moral education of their children in conformity with their own convictions.

General Comment No. 22

...

2. Article 18 protects theistic, non-theistic and atheistic beliefs, as well as the right not to profess any religion or belief. The terms 'belief' and 'religion' are to be broadly construed. Article 18 is not limited in its application to traditional religions or to religions and beliefs with institutional characteristics or practices analogous to those of traditional religions....

3. Article 18 distinguishes the freedom of thought, conscience, religion or belief from the freedom to manifest religion or belief. It does not permit any limitations whatsoever on the freedom of thought and conscience or on the freedom to have or adopt a religion or belief of one's choice. These freedoms are protected unconditionally....

4. The freedom to manifest religion or belief may be exercised 'either individually or in community with others and in public or private'. The freedom to manifest religion or belief in worship, observance, practice and teaching encompasses a broad range of acts. The concept of worship extends to ritual and ceremonial acts giving direct expression to belief, as well as various practices integral to such acts, including the building of places of worship, the use of ritual formulae and objects, the display of symbols, and the observance of holidays and days of rest. The observance and practice of religion or belief may include not only ceremonial acts but also such customs as the observance of dietary regulations, the wearing of distinctive clothing or headcoverings, participation in rituals associated with certain stages of life, and the use of a particular language customarily spoken by a group. In addition, the practice and teaching of religion or belief includes acts integral to the conduct by religious groups of their basic affairs, such as the freedom

to choose their religious leaders, priests and teachers, the freedom to establish seminaries or religious schools and the freedom to prepare and distribute religious texts or publications.

5. The Committee observes that the freedom to 'have or to adopt' a religion or belief necessarily entails the freedom to choose a religion or belief, including the right to replace one's current religion or belief with another or to adopt atheistic views, as well as the right to retain one's religion or belief. Article 18.2 bars coercion that would impair the right to have or adopt a religion or belief, including the use of threat of physical force or penal sanctions to compel believers or non-believers to adhere to their religious beliefs and congregations, to recant their religion or belief or to convert....

6. The Committee is of the view that article 18.4 permits public school instruction in subjects such as the general history of religions and ethics if it is given in a neutral and objective way. ... The Committee notes that public education that includes instruction in a particular religion or belief is inconsistent with article 18.4 unless provision is made for non-discriminatory exemptions or alternatives that would accommodate the wishes of parents and guardians.

7. In accordance with article 20, no manifestation of religion or belief may amount to propaganda for war or advocacy of national, racial or religious hatred that constitutes incitement to discrimination, hostility or violence....

8. Article 18.3 permits restrictions on the freedom to manifest religion or belief only if limitations are prescribed by law and are necessary to protect public safety, order, health or morals, or the fundamental rights and freedoms of others. The freedom from coercion to have or to adopt a religion or belief and the liberty of parents and guardians to ensure religious and moral education cannot be restricted. In interpreting the scope of permissible limitation clauses ... limitations may be applied only for those purposes for which they were prescribed and must be directly related and proportionate to the specific need on which they are predicated....

9. The fact that a religion is recognized as a state religion or that it is established as official or traditional or that its followers comprise the majority of the population, shall not result in any impairment of the enjoyment of any of the rights under the Covenant, including articles 18 and 27, nor in any discrimination against adherents to other religions or non-believers. In particular, certain measures discriminating against the latter, such as measures restricting eligibility for government service to members of the predominant religion or giving economic privileges to them or imposing special restrictions on the practice of other faiths, are not in accordance with the prohibition of discrimination based on religion or belief and the guarantee of equal protection under article 26....

10. If a set of beliefs is treated as official ideology in constitutions, statutes, proclamations of ruling parties, etc., or in actual practice, this shall not result in any impairment of the freedoms under article 18 or any other rights recognized under the Covenant nor in any discrimination against persons who do not accept the official ideology or who oppose it.

...

DECLARATION ON THE ELIMINATION OF ALL FORMS OF INTOLERANCE AND OF DISCRIMINATION BASED ON RELIGION OR BELIEF

G.A. Res. 36/55, 1981

The General Assembly

. . .

Considering that the disregard and infringement of human rights and fundamental freedoms, in particular of the right to freedom of thought, conscience, religion or whatever belief, have brought, directly or indirectly, wars and great suffering to mankind, especially where they serve as a means of foreign interference in the internal affairs of other States and amount to kindling hatred between peoples and nations,

Considering that religion or belief, for anyone who professes either, is one of the fundamental elements in his conception of life and that freedom of religion or belief should be fully respected and guaranteed,

Considering that it is essential to promote understanding, tolerance and respect in matters relating to freedom of religion and belief . . . ,

. . .

Proclaims this Declaration on the Elimination of All Forms of Intolerance and of Discrimination Based on Religion or Belief:

Article 1

1. Everyone shall have the right to freedom of thought, conscience and religion. This right shall include freedom to have a religion or whatever belief of his choice, and freedom, either individually or in community with others and in public or private, to manifest his religion or belief in worship, observance, practice and teaching.
2. No one shall be subject to coercion which would impair his freedom to have a religion or belief of his choice.
3. Freedom to manifest one's religion or belief may be subject only to such limitations as are prescribed by law and are necessary to protect public safety, order, health or morals or the fundamental rights and freedoms of others.

Article 2

1. No one shall be subject to discrimination by any State, institution, group of persons, or person on the grounds of religion or other belief.
2. For the purposes of the present Declaration, the expression 'intolerance and discrimination based on religion or belief' means any distinction, exclusion, restriction or preference based on religion or belief and having as its purpose or as its effect nullification or impairment of the recognition, enjoyment or exercise of human rights and fundamental freedoms on an equal basis.

Article 3

Discrimination between human being on the grounds of religion or belief constitutes an affront to human dignity and a disavowal of the principles of the Charter of the United Nations, and shall be condemned as a violation of the human rights and fundamental freedoms proclaimed in the Universal Declaration of Human Rights and enunciated in detail in the International Covenants on Human Rights, and as an obstacle to friendly and peaceful relations between nations.

Article 4

1. All States shall take effective measures to prevent and eliminate discrimination on the grounds of religion or belief in the recognition, exercise and enjoyment of human rights and fundamental freedoms in all fields of civil, economic, political, social and cultural life.

2. All States shall make all efforts to enact or rescind legislation where necessary to prohibit any such discrimination, and to take all appropriate measures to combat intolerance on the grounds of religion or other beliefs in this matter.

Article 5

1. The parents or, as the case may be, the legal guardians of the child have the right to organize the life within the family in accordance with their religion or belief and bearing in mind the moral education in which they believe the child should be brought up.

2. Every child shall enjoy the right to have access to education in the matter of religion or belief in accordance with the wishes of his parents or, as the case may be, legal guardians, and shall not be compelled to receive teaching on religion or belief against the wishes of his parents or legal guardians, the best interests of the child being the guiding principle.

. . .

Article 6

In accordance with article 1 of the present Declaration, and subject to the provisions of article 1, paragraph 3, the right to freedom of thought, conscience, religion or belief shall include, inter alia, the following freedoms:

. . .

(d) To write, issue and disseminate relevant publications in these areas;

(e) To teach a religion or belief in places suitable for these purposes;

(f) To solicit and receive voluntary financial and other contributions from individuals and institutions;

(g) To train, appoint, elect or designate by succession appropriate leaders called for by the requirements and standards of any religion or belief;

(h) To observe days of rest and to celebrate holidays and ceremonies in accordance with the precepts of one's religion or belief;

(i) To establish and maintain communications with individuals and communities in matters of religion and belief at the national and international levels.

Article 7

The rights and freedoms set forth in the present Declaration shall be accorded in national legislation in such a manner that everyone shall be able to avail himself of such rights and freedoms in practice.

...

Article 8

Nothing in the present Declaration shall be construed as restricting or derogating from any right defined in the Universal Declaration of Human Rights and the International Covenants on Human Rights.

DONNA SULLIVAN, ADVANCING THE FREEDOM OF RELIGION OR BELIEF THROUGH THE UN DECLARATION ON THE ELIMINATION OF RELIGIOUS TOLERANCE AND DISCRIMINATION

82 Am. J. Int. L. 487 (1988)

[The General Assembly adopted this Declaration in 1981 by consensus, 19 years after efforts began in the UN system to develop protections for religious freedom that went beyond the provisions of what became Article 18 of the ICCPR. As the author notes, this long delay in producing a Declaration — not a Convention — may be attributed partly 'to the potential for controversy inherent in the subject matter itself'. The excerpts below discuss a few of the Declaration's provisions.]

Although it lacks, of course, the nature of an international agreement, the Declaration is 'regarded throughout the world as articulating the fundamental rights of freedom of religion and belief'. The Declaration gives specific content to the general statements of the rights to freedom of religion or belief and freedom from discrimination based on religion or belief contained in the major human rights instruments.... That the United Nations General Assembly intended that it be normative and not merely hortatory is apparent from its Articles 4 and 7.... There is no consensus on whether the prohibition of discrimination on grounds of religion or belief already constitutes a norm of customary law. As the Declaration acquires concrete material content through its implementation, it will contribute to the acceptance of the customary law status of this important principle.

...

I. *Preliminary Observations*

The norms stated in the Declaration hold a striking potential for conflict with other rights.... Two general features of the Declaration are likely to affect the resolution of such conflicts. First, it is directed primarily toward actions taken by governments, or by individuals who do not subscribe to a given religion or belief, against individuals who do hold and practice that belief. Interactions among members of the same religious groups are therefore not easily analyzed under the Declaration. Second, application of the Declaration is most straightforward when the belief or practice under consideration corresponds to a typically Western model of religion, in which religious institutions and authority are structurally separable from political and other social institutions. ... [T]he protections offered in the Declaration are not premised upon the separation of church and state and are clearly distinguished in this regard from First Amendment rights under the United States Constitution.

...

II. The Scope of Article 1

...

[Coercion]

Coercive forms of persuasion, which attack the intellectual and psychological aspects of belief, should be encompassed by the prohibited forms of coercion. In two common situations, such 'moral' coercion generates conflict between principles stated in the Declaration itself. Proselytizing activities, the first of these, by their very nature attempt moral compulsion to some degree. [Such activities are examined at pp. 600–616, *infra.*]

A desire to avoid the implicit approval of proselytizing was one of the considerations underlying the omission from the Declaration of an explicit reference to the freedom to change one's religion or belief....

The right of individuals to maintain their own beliefs is central to the concerns that motivated the drafting of the Declaration itself. This principle necessarily entails not only the right to retain a belief, but also the freedom to choose a belief without coercion, including the right to reject one's current belief and accept another. Although explicit reference to the right to change beliefs was dropped from the Declaration, that right remains implicit in the right to have a religion or belief. Moreover, Article 8, the savings clause of the Declaration, preserves the standards set forth in the Universal Declaration of Human Rights and the International Covenants on Human Rights.... The Universal Declaration affirms the freedom to change beliefs and the Political Covenant refers to the freedom to adopt a religion or belief.

Nonetheless, the parameters of the right to change one's religion or belief remain uncertain, as illustrated by the difficulty of evaluating the treatment to be accorded apostates and heretics under the Declaration, a second area implicated by the prohibition of coercion.... History is replete with examples of religious persecution perpetrated in the guise of punishment for heresy....

...

[Boundary Between Religion and Politics]

...

Governments do have a legitimate interest in controlling violence against the state or disruptions of public order, and may do so by using methods consistent with other human rights obligations. Nonetheless, governmental violations of religious freedoms and persecution of religious leaders and groups under the pretense of restraining impermissible political activity are far more prevalent than is the use of a religious identity to camouflage actions motivated by purely partisan political concerns. . . .

. . . [T]the distinction between religious and political activities may be artificial. For example, pacifist religious convictions may prompt an individual to participate in public protest, to refuse to pay taxes used for military expenses and to attempt to influence decisions made by political leaders. Religious beliefs inevitably assume political significance in such circumstances.

. . . Moreover, the structural separation of secular and religious authority is obviously not a universal feature of societies, as demonstrated by Iran. Finally, political beliefs are presumably subsumed within the general category of 'beliefs' to which the Declaration extends and are protected under that rubric. . . .

. . .

III. The Scope of the Prohibition of Discrimination and Intolerance

. . .

[Intolerance]

. . . Two general views have been taken of the meaning of 'intolerance' and its significance in the Declaration. . . .

. . . The view that intolerance describes the emotional, psychological, philosophical and religious attitudes that may prompt acts of discrimination or violations of religious freedoms is persuasive. Where intolerance fuels such conduct as killing or the destruction of property, these acts constitute violations of substantive international human rights, such as the right to life, and, in most cases, violations of national law. If intolerance motivates deprivations of the freedom to manifest religion or belief, these acts again constitute violations of substantive rights protected by the Declaration itself.

. . .

. . . [E]ducational measures to eradicate intolerance are of vital significance. Educational activities obviously lie within the scope of the 'appropriate' measures contemplated by Article 4(2), although no express reference to such activities appears in the Declaration. Efforts to promote and implement the Declaration should compensate for the omission of a provision explicitly calling for educational measures by emphasizing the importance of such activities.

A second approach to combating intolerance, which was proposed during drafting but rejected, is to prohibit the expression of ideas based on religious hatred and the incitement of hatred and discrimination based on religion or belief. [See Article 20 of the ICCPR.] . . .

[Religious Law and Human Rights Law]

Although the rights to establish religious courts and administer religious law are not stated in the Declaration, religious tribunals and the implementation of religious law are manifestations of religious belief to which the protections of Article 1 should apply. Nevertheless, the extent to which religious law may be administered without restrictions by the state or without limitations derived from other human rights obligations may vary with the substantive content of the law itself, and with the scope of the subject matter and personal jurisdiction vested in the religious courts. . . .

QUESTIONS

1. In what respects does the General Comment of the Human Rights Committee appear to go beyond Article 18 itself with respect to notions of religious freedom, and beyond the 1981 Declaration? What implications have Article 18 and the 1981 Declaration for the issue of 'establishment'?

2. Does the Declaration reach beyond action by the state to cover conduct (that is, to require or prohibit certain conduct) by private (nonstate) actors? If so, under what provisions and with respect to what kinds of conduct?

3. How would you resolve apparent conflicts between the Declaration and other human rights instruments — for example, requirements of nondiscrimination in employment under CEDAW and a religiously based belief that women should not be given certain kinds of employment? Do the savings clauses — Article 8 of the Declaration and Article 23 of CEDAW — provide an answer?

4. Under the Declaration, what are the state's duties with respect to religious intolerance that expresses itself in interactions among individuals and nonstate entities but that state organs or officials do not themselves urge or actively reinforce? The same as a state's duties under CEDAW?

5. Assess the consistency of the provisions of the Iranian Constitution with (a) Article 18 of the ICCPR, and (b) the 1981 Declaration, assuming (contrary in some instances to fact) that all religious faiths including Sunni Moslems, Christians of all sects, Jews, Baha'is, and others are allowed freely to hold and observe their religious beliefs and to practice their religious commandments in groups and in houses of worship. How likely is it that a state committed to a constitution similar to Iran's will afford freedom of religion to all faiths?

NOTE

Consider the following comments in Malcolm Evans, *Religious Liberty and International Law in Europe* (1997), at 257. The author speculates about prospects for a convention on religious freedom and discrimination, and notes that the complexity and variety of views on religious issues suggests how arduous the legal and political paths would be toward agreement on its provisions. He notes that there have been suggestions for such a treaty in the UN Commission on Human Rights and the Sub-Commission, and that reports examining this possibility have been prepared. Evans states that these reports highlight one factor among the many that need to be addressed in preparing such a treaty—namely, 'the intolerant attitude of believers themselves. This is seen as a handicap which can be overcome with copious doses of education concerning human rights'. He quotes from one such report, which observed that:

> the reservations concerning religious freedom that have been expressed... should be dealt with patiently and deliberately, through further dialogue. Such dialogue should take into account the factors, be based on internationally established principles... and set a long-term course without any concessions.... The only way to make progress in promoting religious freedom is to avoid categorical, inflexible attitudes....

Reacting to these observations and to similar ones in other reports, Evans states:

> If this means anything, it means that the freedom of religion does not include the right to adhere to a religion which is intolerant of the beliefs of others. On this view, 'Human Rights' has itself become a 'religion or belief' which is itself as intolerant of other forms of value systems which may stand in opposition to its own central tenets as any of those it seeks to address.

Evans also refers to a recommendation of the Parliamentary Assembly of the Council of Europe that described the current 'crisis of values' in society, and the inadequacy of a market society to meet needs for (quoting from the recommendation) 'individual well-being and social responsibility. The recourse to religion as an alternative has, however, to be reconciled with the principles of democracy and human rights'. Evans expresses his opinion about these assertions:

> In seeking to assert itself in this fashion, the international community risks becoming the oppressor of the believer, rather than the protector of the persecuted. Clearly the time is not yet ripe for a convention: not because of the unwillingness of States to adopt such an instrument, but because of the reluctance of the international community to accept that in the religious beliefs of others the dogmas of human rights are met with an equally powerful force which must be respected, not overcome.

QUESTIONS

1. Do you agree with the views of Evans about resolution of the tension between 'religious beliefs of others and the dogmas of human rights'? In what directions would his views point, for example, with respect to dealing with gender discrimination based on religion?

2. Do you agree that the time is not ripe for a convention? Given all the problems, what kind of changes from the terms of the 1981 Declaration would you advocate in such a convention, and what strategies would you follow in working toward agreement among diverse states and religions on the proposed terms?

c. PROSELYTISM

KOKKINAKIS V. GREECE

European Court of Human Rights, 1993
Ser. A, No. 260-A

[Minos Kokkinakis, a Greek national, was born in 1919 into an Orthodox Christian family. In 1936, he became a Jehovah's Witnesses, a Christian sect originating in the nineteenth century, and known for intense door-to-door canvassing by its members. He was arrested more than 60 times for proselytism, and on several occasions imprisoned for a period of months. In 1986, he and his wife called at the home of a Mrs. Kyriakaki to engage her in discussion about religion. Her husband, cantor at a local Orthodox church, informed the police who arrested him. Kokkinakis was convicted under Law No. 1363/1938 of the crime of engaging in proselytism and was sentenced to four months' imprisonment. The Court of Appeal upheld the conviction. The Court of Cassation dismissed an appeal, rejecting the plea that the Law violated Article 13 of the Greek Constitution and hence could not be applied.

Kokkinakis then brought a case against Greece before the European Commission of Human Rights, claiming that his conviction violated provisions of the European Convention on Human Rights. Greece, a party to that Convention, had accepted the jurisdiction of the Commission to hear individual complaints. The Commission found that Greece had violated Article 9 of the Convention. It then referred the case to the European Court of Human Rights, whose jurisdiction Greece had also accepted. (The jurisdiction and work of this Court are examined at pp. 938–1000, *infra*.)

Section 4 of Law No. 1363/1938, as later amended, made 'engaging in proselytism' a crime, and further provided:

> 2. By 'proselytism' is meant, in particular, any direct or indirect attempt to intrude on the religious beliefs of a person of a different religious persuasion, with the aim of undermining those beliefs, either by any kind of inducement or promise of an inducement or moral support or material assistance, or by fraudulent means or by taking advantage of his inexperience, trust, need, low intellect or naïvety.

The Greek Constitution of 1975 stated in Article 3 that the 'dominant religion in Greece is that of the Christian Eastern Orthodox Church'. The opinion of the European Court of Human Rights noted:

> Greece's successive Constitutions have referred to the Church as being 'dominant'. The overwhelming majority of the population are members of it, and, according to Greek conceptions, it represents de jure and de facto the religion of the State itself, a good number of whose administrative and educational functions (marriage and family law, compulsory religious instruction, oaths sworn by members of the Government, etc.) it moreover carries out. Its role in public life is reflected by, among other things, the presence of the Minister of Education and Religious Affairs at the sessions of the Church hierarchy at which the Archbishop of Athens

is elected and by the participation of the Church authorities in all official State events; the President of the Republic takes his oath of office according to Orthodox ritual (Article 33 para. 2 of the Constitution); and the official calendar follows that of the Christian Eastern Orthodox Church.

Article 13 of the Constitution provided:

1. Freedom of conscience in religious matters is inviolable. The enjoyment of personal and political rights shall not depend on an individual's religious beliefs.
2. There shall be freedom to practise any known religion; individuals shall be free to perform their rites of worship without hindrance and under the protection of the law. The performance of rites of worship must not prejudice public order or public morals. Proselytism is prohibited.

Several accounts appeared in the opinions of the Greek courts of the interaction between Kokkinakis and Kryiakaki. The trial court stated that the defendant:

> attempted to proselytise and, directly or indirectly, to intrude on the religious beliefs of Orthodox Christians, with the intention of undermining those beliefs, by taking advantage of their inexperience, their low intellect and their naïvety. In particular, they went to the home of [Mrs Kyriakaki] ... and told her that they brought good news; by insisting in a pressing manner, they gained admittance to the house and began to read from a book on the Scriptures which they interpreted with reference to a king of heaven, to events which had not yet occurred but would occur, etc., encouraging her by means of their judicious, skilful explanations ... to change her Orthodox Christian beliefs.

The Court of Appeal repeated this account, and added that Kokkinakis began to read out passages from Holy Scripture, which he:

> skillfully analysed in a manner that the Christian woman, for want of adequate grounding in doctrine, could not challenge, and at the same time offered her various similar books and importunately tried, directly and indirectly, to undermine her religious beliefs. He must consequently be declared guilty of the above-mentioned offence.

One appeal judge dissented, asserting that no evidence showed that Kyriakaki was particularly inexperienced in Orthodox Christian belief or was of particularly low intellect or naïve.

There follow excerpts from the opinion of the European Court:]

[A 1953 judgment of the Greek Supreme Administrative Court had stated with respect to the meaning of the prohibition of proselytism that the Constitutional ban]

> means that purely spiritual teaching does not amount to proselytism, even if it demonstrates the errors of other religions and entices possible disciples away from them, who abandon their original religions of their own free will; this is because spiritual teaching is in the nature of a rite of worship performed freely and without

> hindrance. Outside such spiritual teaching, which may be freely given, any determined, importunate attempt to entice disciples away from the dominant religion by means that are unlawful or morally reprehensible constitutes proselytism as prohibited by the aforementioned provision of the Constitution.

18. The Greek courts have held that persons were guilty of proselytism who ... offered a scholarship for study abroad; ... distributed 'so-called religious' books and booklets free to 'illiterate peasants' or to 'young schoolchildren'; or promised a young seamstress an improvement in her position if she left the Orthodox Church, whose priests were alleged to be 'exploiters of society'.

[The opinion noted that the Jehovah's Witnesses movement had been present in Greece for about a century, and that its membership in Greece was estimated to be between 25,000 and 70,000. Between 1975 and 1992, 4,400 members had been arrested, 1,233 committed to trial, and 208 convicted, some for other offences than proselytism. It then turned to Kokinnakis's claim that Article 9 of the European Convention had been violated.]

28. The applicant's complaints mainly concerned a restriction on the exercise of his freedom of religion. The Court will accordingly begin by looking at the issues relating to Article 9 (art. 9), which provides:

> 1. Everyone has the right to freedom of thought, conscience and religion; this right includes freedom to change his religion or belief and freedom, either alone or in community with others and in public or private, to manifest his religion or belief, in worship, teaching, practice and observance.
>
> 2. Freedom to manifest one's religion or beliefs shall be subject only to such limitations as are prescribed by law and are necessary in a democratic society in the interests of public safety, for the protection of public order, health or morals, or for the protection of the rights and freedoms of others.

29. The applicant did not only challenge what he claimed to be the wrongful application to him of section 4 of Law no. 1363/1938. His submission concentrated on the broader problem of whether that enactment was compatible with the right enshrined in Article 9 (art. 9) of the Convention ... He pointed to the logical and legal difficulty of drawing any even remotely clear dividing-line between proselytism and freedom to change one's religion or belief and, either alone or in community with others, in public and in private, to manifest it, which encompassed all forms of teaching, publication and preaching between people.

The ban on proselytism, which was made a criminal offence during the Metaxas dictatorship, was not only unconstitutional, Mr Kokkinakis submitted, but it also formed, together with the other clauses of Law no. 1363/1938, 'an arsenal of prohibitions and threats of punishment' hanging over the adherents of all beliefs and all creeds.

Mr Kokkinakis complained, lastly, of the selective application of this Law by the administrative and judicial authorities; it would surpass 'even the wildest academic hypothesis' to imagine, for example, the possibility ... that an Orthodox Christian would be prosecuted for proselytising on behalf of the 'dominant religion'.

...

31. ...According to Article 9, freedom to manifest one's religion is not only exercisable in community with others, 'in public' and within the circle of those whose faith one shares, but can also be asserted 'alone' and 'in private'; furthermore, it includes in principle the right to try to convince one's neighbour, for example through 'teaching', failing which, moreover, 'freedom to change [one's] religion or belief', enshrined in Article 9, would be likely to remain a dead letter.

...

33. ...[The limitations clause in Article 9(2)] refers only to 'freedom to manifest one's religion or belief'. In so doing, it recognises that in democratic societies, in which several religions coexist within one and the same population, it may be necessary to place restrictions on this freedom in order to reconcile the interests of the various groups and ensure that everyone's beliefs are respected.

...

36. The sentence passed by the Lasithi Criminal Court and subsequently reduced by the Crete Court of Appeal (see paragraphs 9–10 above) amounts to an interference with the exercise of Mr Kokkinakis's right to 'freedom to manifest [his] religion or belief'. Such an interference is contrary to Article 9 unless it is 'prescribed by law', directed at one or more of the legitimate aims in paragraph 2 and 'necessary in a democratic society' for achieving them.

...

[Kokkinakis claimed that the requirement that a prohibition be 'prescribed by law' had not been met by Section 4 of the Greek Law. The definition of proselytism had no 'objective' base, perhaps a deliberate decision 'to make it possible for any kind of religious conversation or communication to be caught by the provision'. The Law was vague throughout, using phrases like an 'indirect attempt' to intrude on religious beliefs.

> Punishing a non-Orthodox Christian even when he was offering 'moral support or material assistance' was tantamount to punishing an act that any religion would prescribe and that the Criminal Code required in certain emergencies.... Consequently, no citizen could regulate his conduct on the basis of this enactment....

The Court noted that it was indeed essential to avoid 'excessive rigidity' in legislation in order to keep pace with changing circumstances. Many criminal statutes 'to a greater or lesser extent are vague'. Practice under the proselytism statute and a "body of settled national case-law interpreting the Law were such as to 'enable Mr. Kokkinakis to regulate his conduct in the matter'. Hence the Law was 'prescribed by law' within the meaning of Article 9(2).

The Court next inquired into whether there had been a 'legitimate aim' for the Law within the meaning of Article 9(2).]

43. In the applicant's submission, religion was part of the 'constantly renewable flow of human thought' and it was impossible to conceive of its being excluded from public debate. A fair balance of personal rights made it necessary to accept that others' thought should be subject to a minimum of influence, otherwise the result would be a 'strange society of silent animals that [would] think but ... not express

themselves, that [would] talk but ... not communicate, and that [would] exist but... not coexist'.

44. Having regard to the circumstances of the case and the actual terms of the relevant courts' decisions, the Court considers that the impugned measure was in pursuit of a legitimate aim under Article 9 para. 2, namely the protection of the rights and freedoms of others, relied on by the Government.

[The Court turned to the requirement that a restrictive measure be 'necessary in a democratic society.']

45. Mr Kokkinakis did not consider it necessary in a democratic society to prohibit a fellow citizen's right to speak when he came to discuss religion with his neighbour. He was curious to know how a discourse delivered with conviction and based on holy books common to all Christians could infringe the rights of others. Mrs Kyriakaki was an experienced adult woman with intellectual abilities; it was not possible, without flouting fundamental human rights, to make it a criminal offence for a Jehovah's Witness to have a conversation with a cantor's wife. Moreover, the Crete Court of Appeal, although the facts before it were precise and absolutely clear, had not managed to determine the direct or indirect nature of the applicant's attempt to intrude on the complainant's religious beliefs; its reasoning showed that it had convicted the applicant 'not for something he had done but for what he was'.

...

46. The Government ... pointed out that if the State remained indifferent to attacks on freedom of religious belief, major unrest would be caused that would probably disturb the social peace.

47. The Court has consistently held that a certain margin of appreciation is to be left to the Contracting States in assessing the existence and extent of the necessity of an interference, but this margin is subject to European supervision, embracing both the legislation and the decisions applying it, even those given by an independent court. The Court's task is to determine whether the measures taken at national level were justified in principle and proportionate.

...

48. First of all, a distinction has to be made between bearing Christian witness and improper proselytism. The former corresponds to true evangelism, which a report drawn up in 1956 under the auspices of the World Council of Churches describes as an essential mission and a responsibility of every Christian and every Church. The latter represents a corruption or deformation of it. It may, according to the same report, take the form of activities offering material or social advantages with a view to gaining new members for a Church or exerting improper pressure on people in distress or in need; it may even entail the use of violence or brainwashing; more generally, it is not compatible with respect for the freedom of thought, conscience and religion of others.

Scrutiny of section 4 of Law no. 1363/1938 shows that the relevant criteria adopted by the Greek legislature are reconcilable with the foregoing if and in so far as they are designed only to punish improper proselytism, which the Court does not have to define in the abstract in the present case.

49. The Court notes, however, that in their reasoning the Greek courts established the applicant's liability by merely reproducing the wording of section 4 and

did not sufficiently specify in what way the accused had attempted to convince his neighbour by improper means. None of the facts they set out warrants that finding.

That being so, it has not been shown that the applicant's conviction was justified in the circumstances of the case by a pressing social need. The contested measure therefore does not appear to have been proportionate to the legitimate aim pursued or, consequently, 'necessary in a democratic society ... for the protection of the rights and freedoms of others'.

50. In conclusion, there has been a breach of Article 9 (art. 9) of the Convention.

...

[Since a breach of the Convention had been found, the Court found it unnecessary to consider an additional charge of Kokkinakis, namely that his conviction also violated Article 10, protecting freedom of expression. It held that Greece was to pay Kokkinakis 400,000 drachmas for non-pecuniary damage and 2,789,500 drachmas for costs and expenses. There follow some excerpts from the separate concurring and dissenting opinions.]

PARTLY CONCURRING OPINION OF JUDGE PETTITI:

I was in the majority which voted that there had been a breach of Article 9 but I considered that the reasoning given in the judgment could usefully have been expanded.

Furthermore, I parted company with the majority in that I also took the view that the current criminal legislation in Greece on proselytism was in itself contrary to Article 9.

...

In the first place, I take the view that what contravenes Article 9 (art. 9) is the Law. ... [T]he definition is such as to make it possible at any moment to punish the slightest attempt by anyone to convince a person he is addressing.

... [T]he mere threat of applying a provision, even one that has fallen into disuse, is sufficient to constitute a breach.

The expression "proselytism that is not respectable", which is a criterion used by the Greek courts when applying the Law, is sufficient for the enactment and the case-law applying it to be regarded as contrary to Article 9.

...

... [T]he haziness of the definition leaves too wide a margin of interpretation for determining criminal penalties.

...

Proselytism is linked to freedom of religion; a believer must be able to communicate his faith and his beliefs in the religious sphere as in the philosophical sphere. Freedom of religion and conscience is a fundamental right and this freedom must be able to be exercised for the benefit of all religions and not for the benefit of a single Church, even if this has traditionally been the established Church or 'dominant religion'.

Freedom of religion and conscience certainly entails accepting proselytism, even where it is 'not respectable'. Believers and agnostic philosophers have a right to expound their beliefs, to try to get other people to share them and even to try to convert those whom they are addressing.

The only limits on the exercise of this right are those dictated by respect for the rights of others where there is an attempt to coerce the person into consenting or to use manipulative techniques.

The other types of unacceptable behaviour — such as brainwashing, breaches of labour law, endangering of public health and incitement to immorality, which are found in the practices of certain pseudo-religious groups — must be punished in positive law as ordinary criminal offences. Proselytism cannot be forbidden under cover of punishing such activities.

...

... Non-criminal proselytism remains the main expression of freedom of religion. Attempting to make converts is not in itself an attack on the freedom and beliefs of others or an infringement of their rights.

...

Spiritual, religious and philosophical convictions belong to the private sphere of beliefs and call into play the right to express and manifest them. Setting up a system of criminal prosecution and punishment without safeguards is a perilous undertaking, and the authoritarian regimes which, while proclaiming freedom of religion in their Constitutions, have restricted it by means of criminal offences of parasitism, subversion or proselytism have given rise to abuses....

The wording adopted by the majority of the Court in finding a breach, namely that the applicant's conviction was not justified in the circumstances of the case, leaves too much room for a repressive interpretation by the Greek courts in the future, whereas public prosecution must likewise be monitored. In my view, it would have been possible to define impropriety, coercion and duress more clearly and to describe more satisfactorily, in the abstract, the full scope of religious freedom and bearing witness.

...

DISSENTING OPINION OF JUDGE VALTICOS:

...

Let us look now at the facts of the case. On the one hand, we have a militant Jehovah's Witness, a hardbitten adept of proselytism, a specialist in conversion, a martyr of the criminal courts whose earlier convictions have served only to harden him in his militancy, and, on the other hand, the ideal victim, a naïve woman, the wife of a cantor in the Orthodox Church (if he manages to convert her, what a triumph!). He swoops on her, trumpets that he has good news for her (the play on words is obvious, but no doubt not to her), manages to get himself let in and, as an experienced commercial traveller and cunning purveyor of a faith he wants to spread, expounds to her his intellectual wares cunningly wrapped up in a mantle of universal peace and radiant happiness. Who, indeed, would not like peace and happiness? But is this the mere exposition of Mr Kokkinakis's beliefs or is it not rather an attempt to beguile the simple soul of the cantor's wife? Does the Convention afford its protection to such undertakings? Certainly not.

...

I should certainly be inclined to recommend the Government to give instructions that prosecutions should be avoided where harmless conversations are involved, but not in the case of systematic, persistent campaigns entailing actions bordering on unlawful entry.

That having been said, I do not consider in any way that there has been a breach of the Convention.

...

MAKAU MUTUA, HUMAN RIGHTS, RELIGION, AND PROSELYTISM

***in Mutua, Human Rights: A Political and Cultural Critique* (2002), at 94**

... This chapter is an exploration of the historical experience of religious penetration and advocacy in a very specific context and a quest to demonstrate the possibilities of conflict between certain forms of evangelistic advocacy and certain human rights norms. With the African theater as the basic laboratory, I intend to unpack the meaning of religious freedom at the point of contact between the messianic faiths and African religions and illustrate how that meeting resulted in a phenomenon akin to cultural genocide. The main purpose here is not merely to defend forms of religion or belief but rather to problematize the concept of the right to the free exercise of messianic faiths, which includes the right to proselytize in the marketplace of religions. In societies such as those in Africa where religion is woven into virtually every aspect of life, its delegitimiation can eventually lead to the collapse of social norms and cultural identities. The result, as has been the case in most of sub-Saharan Africa, is a culturally disconnected people, neither themselves nor the outsiders in Europe, North America, and the Arab world that they seek to imitate. In other words, I argue that imperial religions have necessarily violated the individual conscience and the communal expressions of Africans and their communities by subverting African religions. In so doing, they have robbed Africans of essential elements of their humanity....

Since the right to religious freedom includes the right to be left alone — to choose freely whether to believe and what to believe in — the rights regime by requiring that African religions compete in the marketplace of ideas incorrectly assumes a level playing field. The rights corpus not only forcibly imposes on African religions the obligation to compete — a task for which as nonproselytizing, noncompetitive creeds they are not historically fashioned — but also protects evangelizing religions in their march toward universalization. In the context of religious freedom, the privileging by the rights regime of the competition of ideas over the right against cultural invasion, in a skewed contest, amounts to condoning the dismantling of African religions.

I also argue that the playing field, the one crucial and necessary ingredient in a fair fight, is heavily weighted against Africans. Messianic religions have been forcibly imposed or their introduction was accomplished as part of the cultural package borne by colonialism. Missionaries did not simply offer Jesus Christ as the savior of benighted souls, his salvation was frequently a precondition for services in education and health, which were quite often the exclusive domain of the Church and the colonial state. It makes little sense to argue that Africans could avoid acculturation by opting out of the colonial order; in most cases, the embrace of indigenous societies by the European imperial powers was so violent and total that conformity was the only immediate option. In making this argument, I also rely on notions of human rights law which, as I seek to show, suggest that indigenous beliefs have a right to be respected and left alone by more dominant external traditions.

...

A discussion about limitations on religious rights at first blush appears to frustrate some of the major ideals of the human rights movement. It raises the question about the tension between the restriction of the right to evangelize or advocate a point of view and one of the central ideals of the human rights movement, the promotion of diversity and the right to advocate ideas or creeds. An exploration of the manner in which the human rights corpus ought to view religious rights — whether to further limit or to expand the protections they currently enjoy — raises a fundamental tension: how does a body of principles that promotes diversity and difference protect the establishment and manifestation of religious orders that seek to destroy difference and forcibly impose an orthodoxy in Africa — as both Christianity and Islam, the two major proselytizing religions, attempted, and in many cases successfully did? Precisely because of the ethos of universalization common to both, the messianic faiths sought to eradicate, with the help of the state, all other forms of religious expression and belief and close off any avenues through which other competing faiths could be introduced or sustained....

...While I explore the nature, context, and purposes of proselytization in Africa from a rights perspective, I also seek to see whether proselytization in that context constituted a human rights violation and, if so, what the response of the human rights regime should be.

...

The challenge for the human rights movement is to move beyond the singular obsession with wrongs committed directly by the state — although it remains the most important obligee of the discourse — and confront nonstate actors in order to contain and control human rights violations in the private sphere. To do so, the movement has to take on powerful private institutions in the private realm, including established religion. It is my argument that although religious human rights must be defined, secured, and protected, there is a correlative duty on the part of religions to respect the human rights of nonbelievers and adherents of other religions or faiths and not to seek their coerced conversion either directly or through the manipulation and destruction of other cultures.

...

Demonizing the "Other"

The two most geographically diverse religions — Christianity and Islam — are also the most imperial; they are proselytizing and universalist in their attempts to convert into their faith the entire human race. Although these religions are not spread through physical violence today, they have historically been forcibly introduced.

They have also been negatively competitive against each other as well as other creeds as they have fought over the souls of both different religious groups and individuals. But central to them is the belief in the racial superiority of the proselytizers . . . It does not require a profound knowledge of history to prove that both Arab and European perceptions of Africa have been decidedly racist over the centuries. . . .

. . .

The Legal Invisibility of Indigenous Religions

. . . I shall focus my attention on "indigenous religions" which I define as nonmessianic faiths but excluding dominant and politically established religions such as Judaism, Buddhism, and Hinduism. The key to the inclusion of a religion as indigenous is its history of attack and domination by the imperial faiths and colonialism and its status as the cultural inheritance and spiritual expression of the original, nonwhite, non-Arabic peoples of Africa. But I also examine United Nations documents regarding the cultural rights of indigenous peoples to indicate how the human rights regime might consider thinking about the protection of indigenous religions.

The UDHR and the ICCPR do not specially recognize indigenous religions in relation to dominant faiths or cultures; they do not even refer to them. Article 18 [of the ICCPR] simply provides the right of everyone "to freedom of thought, conscience and religion" and prohibits the use of coercion to "impair" the freedom of others to have or to adopt a religion or a belief of their choice. The freedom to "manifest one's religion or beliefs may be subject to such limitations as are prescribed by law" or limited to protect public "morals or the fundamental rights and freedoms of others." This provision prohibits the use of force to make converts as was the case in early European crusades in Africa and the conquest of parts of the continent by Arab Muslims. It would also appear to disallow using state resources — such as educational, health, and other services — to disadvantage particular faiths. Missionaries who worked against other religions with the help of colonial regimes would seem to be in violation of this provision.

While no authoritative human rights body has issued a definitive interpretation of such construction, the Human Rights Committee has adopted a General Comment on article 27 of the ICCPR, providing that states are under an obligation to protect the cultural, linguistic, and religious rights of minorities. It said, in part:

> Although the rights protected under Article 27 are individual rights, they depend in turn on the ability of the minority group to maintain its culture, language or religion. Accordingly, positive measures by States may also be necessary to protect the identity of a minority and the rights of its members to enjoy and develop their culture and language and to practice their religion, in community with other members of the group.

. . .

Ideals Versus Realities

. . . The emphasis placed on the importance of creating and maintaining a diverse society is one of the most striking characteristics of human rights law. Diversity is encouraged, though not required, by the rights corpus in cultural, religious, political, and other endeavors and pursuits. Through this emphasis, human rights law "evidences throughout its hostility to imposed uniformity."

...

Although human rights law amply protects the right to proselytize through the principles of free speech, assembly, and association, the pecking order of rights problematizes the right to evangelize where the result is the destruction of other cultures or the closure of avenues for other religions. It is my argument that the most fundamental of all human rights is that of self-determination and that no other right overrides it. Without this fundamental group or individual right, no other human right could be secured, since the group would be unable to determine for its individual members under what political, social, cultural, economic, and legal order they would live. Any right which directly conflicts with this right ought to be void to the extent of that conflict.

Traditionally, the self-determination principle has been employed to advance the cause of decolonization or to overcome other forms of external occupation. The principle was indispensable to the decolonization process. This usage of the principle — as a tool for advancing demands for external self-determination — could be expanded to disallow cultural and religious imperialism or imposition by external agencies through acculturation, especially where the express intent of the invading culture or religion, as was the case in Africa, is to destroy its indigenous counterparts and seal off the entry or growth of other traditions. Furthermore, the principle could also be read to empower internal self-determination, that is, the right of a people to "cultural survival." ...

...

The Moral Equivalency of Cultures

... Although many of the rights enumerated in human rights law attach to individuals, they only make sense in a collective, social perspective. This is the case because the creation or development of a culture or a religion are societal, not individual, endeavors. I make this point to underline the importance of culture or religion to individuals and groups. An individual's morals, attitudes toward life and death, and identity come from this collective construction of reality through history.

No one culture or religion is sovereign in relationship to any other culture or religion. Proper human rights ought to assume that all cultures are equal. This view rejects the notion that there is a hierarchy of cultures or religions; that some cultures are superior to others even though they may more technologically advanced. Belief in the contrary has led to military invasions to "civilize," colonize, and enslave, as was the case with Christianity in Africa. Cultures, however, have always interacted throughout history; there are no pure cultures, as such, although many traditions retain their distinctive personality. In many cases, the voluntary, unforced commingling of cultures has led to a more vital and creative existence. Several lessons can be drawn from this premise. The human rights movement should encourage the crossbreeding of cultures and tolerance for diversity. But it should frown upon homogenization and the imposition of uniformity.

...

Perhaps there is nothing that can be done today to reverse the negative effects of forced or coerced religious proselytization during the era of colonialism in Africa. Nor is it possible to reclaim wholly the African past as though history has stood still. This does not mean, however, that we should simply forget the past and go on as if nothing happened. The anguish and deprivation caused by that historical experience is with me and millions of other Africans today. We bear the marks of that terrible period. For those Africans who choose not to be Christians or Muslims, the past is not really an option: it was so effectively destroyed and delegitimized that it is practically impossible to retrieve as a coherent scheme of values. It is this loss that I mourn and for which I blame Christianity and Islam. The human rights corpus should outlaw those forms of proselytization used in Africa, because their purpose and effect have been the dehumanization of an entire race of people. It could do so by elaborating a treaty that addresses religious human rights but provides for the protection and mechanisms of redress for forms of proselytization that seek to unfairly assimilate or impose dominant cultures on indigenous religions.

HAROLD BERMAN, RELIGIOUS RIGHTS IN RUSSIA AT A TIME OF TUMULTUOUS TRANSITION: A HISTORICAL THEORY

in Johan van der Vyver and J. Witte (eds.), Religious Human Rights in Global Perspective (1996), at 301

...

'Are you a believer?' I once asked a Muscovite. He replied, 'I'm Russian, I'm Orthodox'.

During a visit to Moscow in September, 1994, I had the opportunity to ask questions about this ethnic dimension of Russian Christianity in a two-hour interview with a representative of the Moscow Patriarchate. In defending the aborted 1993 legislation, he said that the Lutherans should be free to give religious leadership to the German population of Russia, the Roman Catholics to the Polish population of Russia, the Jews to the Jews, the Muslims to the Turks in Russia, and so forth — but the Russians ..., the ethnic Russians, the *russkie*, he said, belong chiefly to Russian Orthodoxy.

It is difficult for Western Christians to accept, or even to understand, the belief in ethnic Christian churches. In the Western Christian tradition, now embodied in secular constitutional law in most countries and adopted by the human rights covenants, religious freedom is conceived primarily in terms of the religious faith of the individual believer, including his right to manifest that faith in collective bodies which are conceived to be voluntary associations. ...

It is, above all, this conception of the common Christian faith of the people, the *narod*, of Russian nationality that is the principal source of opposition to the influx of foreign evangelical missionaries. It is not the purpose of the vast majority of these missionaries to draw Russians away from Russian Orthodoxy, and for the most part they have attracted Russians who formerly were atheist or agnostic. When I made this point to the representative of the Moscow Patriarchate with whom I spoke in 1994, he replied: 'It is true that after more than 75 years of Marxist-Leninist education and Communist Party pressure, a great many Russians are ignorant of Russian Orthodoxy or indifferent to it. But their roots are Orthodox. It is our task to return them to Orthodoxy'.

...

But the objection to foreign missionaries goes deeper. The historical argument of the Patriarchate is directed not only to the past but also to the present and future. Russia is now experiencing a severe spiritual crisis, which, in the view not only of the Moscow Patriarchate but of many Russian people, whether or not they are believers, is being aggravated by the foreign evangelical missionaries. My informant in the Moscow Patriarchate expressed this point in the following way:

'The changes now taking place in Russia', he said, 'including especially the economic reforms, require a new post-Soviet psychology among the people. For three generations the people has been brought up on a simple monolithic ideology that is now repudiated. The belief in Soviet superiority is gone. The belief in progress toward a bright future is gone. The people feels lost'.

'The foreign evangelical missionaries,' he continued, 'know that there is a spiritual crisis but they do not understand it. In fact, they are offering to the people another simple solution. Like the Communists, they offer salvation in return for a commitment which requires little effort. "Just believe, and you will be saved." This reinforces the old psychology, in which simple slogans were offered in return for immediate minimum rewards but great rewards in the future. Russian Orthodoxy is more complex and more difficult. It teaches not rewards but sacrifice. It teaches the positive value of suffering. Its spiritual demands are great'.

My interlocutor went on to a different aspect of the same theme of spiritual crisis. 'In the past,' he said, 'whenever there has been a spiritual crisis of this intensity, the people has turned to the Russian Church. That was true at the time of the Napoleonic Wars. It was true in the First World War. It was true even under Stalin in the Second World War. Now we are in a comparable crisis. Moreover, both the extreme nationalist on the right and the radical democrats on the left can be reconciled on this point, namely, that to meet our spiritual crisis it is important that a strong role be played not only by the Russian Orthodox Church but also by other traditional Russian confessions, confessions that have been tested by repression for seventy-five years and that have forged a fraternal relationship with each other'.

I responded that many think the Russian Orthodox Church is simply afraid of competition. 'Not at all,' he replied, 'But Russia needs time to recover her health before they descend on us. The Russian Orthodox Church is like a very sick person that is only beginning to recover her health'.

'Moreover,' he added, 'we lack both the material and the human resources needed to compete on an equal basis. The foreign missionaries are pouring huge sums of money into evangelization, paying for billboard advertisements and for television programs featuring American preachers and hiring huge stadiums for spreading their message'. Also in human resources, the Russian Church, he said, is lacking in people who are trained to attract outsiders. 'For 75 years we were permitted to talk only to the faithful in our congregations. We are only beginning now to educate clergy in how to speak to non-believers'.

. . .

'The August law,' my informant said, 'was a reaction against the premature invasion of Western missionaries. Of course we do not want to violate international law or our own constitution or principles of human rights. But we hope that those legal and moral norms can be adapted to enable us to meet the acute spiritual crisis that now confronts us'.

. . .

ALESSANDRA STANLEY, POPE TELLS INDIA HIS CHURCH HAS RIGHT TO EVANGELIZE

New York Times, November 8, 1999, p. A3

Summoning all his moral authority, Pope John Paul II tried today to persuade leaders of other religions here that interfaith understanding should lead them to recognize the Roman Catholic Church's right to evangelize. 'Religious freedom constitutes the very heart of human rights', the pope, on a three-day visit to India, said at a interreligious gathering that included Hindus, Muslims, Sikhs, Jews and representatives of several other faiths. 'Its inviolability is such that individuals must be recognized as having the right even to change their religion, if their conscience so demands.'

But that is an argument that many religious leaders in India accept only with difficulty. Christian conversions are at the heart of a political and religious dispute that has made the 79-year-old pope's visit a tense one. Christian proselytizing is fuel for Muslim fundamentalists, but it is also a source of uneasiness between the pope and some of his more moderate and like-minded religious peers.

'Conversions are a fundamental right,' Samdhong Rinpoche, a Buddhist monk who is the speaker of the Tibetan Parliament in exile, said after leaving the podium he shared with the pope. 'But what we fear is that between indoctrination and anybody's inner-consciousness to choose his religion, there is a clean line.' 'Any kind of action to encourage, or to persuade or to motivate in favor of any particular religion, that is a form of conversion that we as Buddhists cannot recommend,' the monk said.

. . .

. . . Shankaracharya Madhavananda Saraswati, a moderate Hindu leader who has criticized fundamentalist protests against the visit . . . also expressed private misgivings about Christian evangelization. He said later that Hindus could not really ever be diverted from their original faith: 'Religion comes from the heart. Something may change outwardly, but what is inside remains with the human being forever. That does not change'.

The pope, who came to India to close a synod of Asian bishops, has declared the evangelization of Asia, where Catholics remain a tiny minority, to be one of the church's top priorities for the next millennium. He said it was a 'mystery' why Christ is largely unknown on the continent and added, 'The peoples of Asia need Jesus Christ and his Gospel'.

In India, however, Hindu fundamentalists accuse Christian missionaries, who are most active in poor rural and tribal areas, of preying on the most susceptible in society—buying their souls with education, medical aid and economic assistance.

Anti-Christian attacks by Hindu fundamentalists, often encouraged by political extremists, have increased dramatically in the last two years, with more than 150 recorded incidents of church lootings, beatings, rapes and killings. In Orissa, the state that was recently devastated by a cyclone, a missionary and his two young children were killed in January.

The pope came to India with two agendas: He preached ardently for religious tolerance for all faiths, but also instructed his own to convert new followers. To even the mildest leaders of other religions, the two messages do not easily blend.

'Religious people are more busy with increasing the number of their followers rather than paying attention to the challenges that beset religion,' Acharya Mahapragya, head of the Jain faith, said at the podium. Speaking through a lavender-colored surgical mask — Jains are Hindus who revere all forms of life and veil their speech to prevent their breath from destroying living micro-organisms — he was the only leader, besides the pope, to address the issue of conversions publicly.

In the current climate, some Indian Catholics say, their simplest acts of charity are misunderstood. 'We help people with scholarships and medical aid,' said Bartholomew Abraham, 40, a businessman who traveled almost 1,500 miles by train to see the pope. 'If we were really bribing converts, after 2,000 years we wouldn't still only be 2 percent of the population'.

The pope wants church leaders to adapt their pastoral style to suit the culture and customs of their native lands, and he showed the way today by presiding over a colorful sitar Mass for 40,000 worshipers in Nehru Stadium. The Mass coincided with the most important Hindu celebration of the year, Diwali, the festival of light, which was noisily celebrated all over New Delhi with fireworks. At the Mass, under a huge abstract poster of Mother Teresa of Calcutta, women in brown and gold saris danced before the altar while a choir of sitar-players performed Indian-style hymns.

...

NOTE

Consider the following observations of Claude Lévi-Strauss in *Race and History* (1958), at 12. Rather than view the diversity of cultures as a 'natural phenomenon', people 'have tended rather to regard diversity as something abnormal or outrageous', to the point of rejecting 'out of hand the cultural institutions ... which are furthest removed from those with which we identify ourselves'. One sees 'crude reactions', 'instinctive antipathy', 'repugnance' toward ways of life or beliefs to which we are unaccustomed and which we term 'barbarous'.

Nonetheless, collaboration between cultures has been the key to achievement. The greater achievements stem not from 'isolated' cultures but from those which have 'combined their play' through such means as migration, borrowing, trade or warfare. 'For, if a culture were left to its own resources, it could never hope to be "superior"'. Indeed, the greater the diversity between the cultures concerned, the 'more fruitful' such a 'coalition of cultures' will be.

Lévi-Strauss turns to a problem stemming from his preceding observations, that of cultural uniformity. He proposes some solutions to it, but emphasizes that he is describing a process that is inherently 'contradictory'. That is, progress requires collaboration among cultures, but 'in the course of their collaboration, the differences in their contributions will gradually be evened out, although collaboration was originally necessary and advantageous simply because of these differences.' To this contradiction he finds no clear solution. He stresses that

> man must, no doubt, guard against the blind particularism which would restrict the dignity of humankind to a single race, culture or society; but he must never forget, on the other hand, that no section of humanity has succeeded in finding universally applicable formulas; and that it is impossible to imagine mankind pursuing a single way of life for, in such a case, mankind would be ossified.

The currents toward both unification and diversity are essential. One must preserve diversity as such, diversity itself, the idea and substance of it, rather than any one historically realized form. One must look for 'stirrings of new life, foster latent potentialities', and see each form of diversity as 'contributions to the fullness of all the others'.

QUESTIONS

1. How do you assess the *Kokkinakis* opinion? Do you find justification for any restriction on proselytizing other than those related to coercion, undue imposition on the listener, and similar matters?

2. How do you assess Mutua's views? Can they be limited to matters or religion, or would his arguments carry with the same effect to other attributes of a culture, such as discrimination, or extreme forms of punishment, or authoritarian rule by priests or by elders of a community? How would you seek to resolve the tensions that Mutua underscores, such as through arguments in favour of cultural variety and survival as opposed to arguments for universal norms?

3. How do you compare the arguments advanced in the article by Berman by a representative of the Moscow Patriarchate with respect to proselytizing in Russia with Mutua's arguments about Africa? What similarities and differences? How do both compare with the apparent position of the Greek Government in Kokkinakis? Should these different arguments carry different weight with respect to assessing the legality of restrictions on proselytizing under the ICCPR or the European Convention?

4. 'The human rights instruments are very attentive to the rights of parents to persuade their children to particular beliefs, including religious beliefs and related practices. For example, Article 18(4) of the ICCPR commits the states parties "to have respect for

the liberty of parents . . . to ensure the religious and moral education of their children in conformity with their own convictions". Religious belief is of fundamental importance to a human being. Why should parents be given this authority, and states then be permitted to prohibit efforts of others to persuade adults to a different belief?' Respond.

5. 'If cultural survival and maintenance of old traditions, religious and other, is to prevail, it must do so by the inner strength of these traditions, by their ability to resist, not through the state's protection in the form of banning foreign ideas and influence of a religious or other character. Here as elsewhere, consumer choice in the larger marketplace of ideas should prevail. Cultures grow through interaction, not through artificial isolation.' Comment.

3. DRESS AND SYMBOLS, IMMIGRATION AND MULTICULTURALISM

The larger flows of immigrants in recent decades from developing countries to Europe and the United States have led to more complex and sometimes abrasive cultural mixes. Immigrants carry cultural and religious beliefs and practices with them; many immigrants continue to adhere to those beliefs and seek to continue the practices accompanying them as well as the beliefs' manifestations in routine daily behaviour. Sometimes, as in the case of female genital mutilation, the practices grow out of deeply rooted culture and traditions. Sometimes, as in the issue of headscarves that is discussed below, they have at least in part a religious foundation. In either case, in the increasingly multicultural states of the developed world, the newcomers' practices and routine behaviour — one or another form of dress is frequently at issue — stir discomfort, concern and even intense hostility in the host state. That concern and hostility will often continue after the immigrants or their children have become citizens. The issue is starkly posed whether the immigrants or new citizens should be allowed to continue their practices, or whether they should be required to follow laws and practices of the developed country that effectively require their abolition. Severe sanctions, including expulsion from schools and criminal proceedings, may await the newcomers who refuse to surrender their beliefs and ways.

Of course, such conflicts raise serious human rights issues. Such is the concern of this Section 3. The opening materials concern immigrant communities, while the later materials examine similar issues that arise in national settings among long-present groups of citizens.

BARBARA CROSSETTE, TESTING THE LIMITS OF TOLERANCE AS CULTURES MIX

New York Times, March 6, 1999, p. B9

In Maine, a refugee from Afghanistan was seen kissing the penis of his baby boy, a traditional expression of love by this father. To his neighbors and the police, it was child abuse, and his son was taken away. In Seattle, a hospital tried to invent a harmless female circumcision procedure to satisfy conservative Somali parents wanting to keep an African practice alive in their community. The idea got buried in criticism from an outraged public.

How do democratic, pluralistic societies like the United States, based on religious and cultural tolerance, respond to customs and rituals that may be repellent to the majority? As new groups of immigrants from Asia and Africa are added to the demographic mix in the United States, Canada and Europe, balancing cultural variety with mainstream values is becoming more and more tricky.

Many Americans confront the issue of whether any branch of government should have the power to intervene in the most intimate details of family life.

'I think we are torn,' said Richard A. Shweder, an anthropologist at the University of Chicago and a leading advocate of the broadest tolerance for cultural differences. 'It's a great dilemma right now that's coming up again about how we're going to deal with diversity in the United States and what it means to be an American.'

Anthropologists have waded deeply into this debate, which is increasingly engaging scholars across academia, as well as social workers, lawyers and judges who deal with new cultural dimensions in immigration and asylum. Some, like Mr. Shweder, argue for fundamental changes in American laws, if necessary, to accommodate almost any practice accepted as valid in a radically different society if it can be demonstrated to have some social or cultural good.

For example, although Mr. Shweder and others would strongly oppose importing such practices as India's immolation of widows, they defend other controversial practices, including the common African ritual that opponents call female genital mutilation, which usually involves removing the clitoris at a minimum. They say that it is no more harmful than male circumcision and should be accommodated, not deemed criminal, as it now is in the United States and several European countries. At the Harvard Law School, Martha Minow, a professor who specializes in family and school issues, said that intolerance often arises when the behavior of immigrants seems to be 'nonmodern, nonscientific and nonrational'. She cites as an example the practice of 'coining' among Cambodians, where hot objects may be pressed on a child's forehead or back as cures for various maladies, leaving alarming welts that for teachers and social workers set off warnings of child abuse.

Americans are more than happy to accept new immigrants when their traditions seem to reinforce mainstream ideals. There are few cultural critics of the family values, work ethic or dedication to education found among many East Asians, for example.

But going more than halfway to tolerate what look like disturbing cultural practices unsettles some historians, aid experts, economists and others with experience in developing societies. Such relativism, they say, undermines the very notion of progress. What's more, it raises the question of how far acceptance can go before there is no core American culture, no shared values, left.

Many years of living in a variety of cultures, said Urban Jonsson, a Swede who directs the United Nations Children's Fund, Unicef, in sub-Saharan Africa, has led him to conclude that there is 'a global moral minimum', which he has heard articulated by Asian Buddhists and African thinkers as well as by Western human rights advocates.

'There is a nonethnocentric global morality,' he said, and scholars would be better occupied looking for it rather than denying it. 'I am upset by the anthropological interest in mystifying what we have already demystified. All cultures have their bad and good things.'

...

Scholars like Mr. Shweder are wary of attempts to catalogue 'good' and 'bad' societies or practices ... [H]e helped form a group of about 15 legal and cultural experts to investigate how American law affects ethnic customs among African, Asian, Caribbean and Latin American immigrants.

...

'Despite our pluralistic ideals, something very much like a cultural un-American activities list seems to have begun circulating among powerful representatives and enforcers of mainstream culture', the group says in its statement. 'Among the ethnic minority activities at risk of being dubbed "un-American" are the use of disciplinary techniques such as shaming and physical punishment, parent/child co-sleeping arrangements, rituals of group identity and ceremonies of initiation involving scarification, piercing and genital alterations, arranged marriage, polygamy, the segregation of gender roles, bilingualism and foreign language use and many more'.

Some sociologists and anthropologists on this behavioral frontier argue that American laws and welfare services have often left immigrants terrified of the intrusive power of government. The Afghan father in Maine who lost his son to the social services, backed by a lower court, did not prevail until the matter reached the state Supreme Court, which researched the family's cultural heritage and decided in its favor — while making clear that this was an exceptional case, not a precedent.

Spanking, puberty rites, animal sacrifices, enforced dress codes, leaving children unattended at home and sometimes the use of narcotics have all been portrayed as acceptable cultural practices. But who can claim to be culturally beyond the prevailing laws and why?

...

Paradoxically, while some Americans want judgment-free considerations of immigrants' practices and traditional rituals in the countries they come from, asylum seekers from those same countries are turning up at American airports begging to escape from tribal rites in the name of human rights. Immigration lawyers and judges are thus drawn into a debate that is less and less theoretical.

Mr. Jonsson of Unicef ... labels those who would condemn many in the third world to practices they may desperately want to avoid as 'immoral and unscientific.' In their academic towers, Mr. Jonsson said, cultural relativists become 'partners of the tormentors'.

Jessica Neuwirth, an international lawyer who is director of Equality Now, a New York-based organization aiding women's groups in the developing world and immigrant women in this country, asks why the practices that cultural relativists want to condone so often involve women: how they dress, what they own, where they go, how their bodies can be used.

'Culture is male-patrolled in the way that it is created and transmitted,' she said. 'People who control culture tend to be the people in power, and who constitutes that group is important. Until we can break through that, we can't take the measure of what is really representative'.

...

TIMOTHY SAVAGE, EUROPE AND ISLAM: CRESCENT WAXING, CULTURES CLASHING

27 The Washington Quarterly No. 3, p. 25 (2004)

... Internally, Europe must integrate a ghettoized but rapidly growing Muslim minority that many Europeans view as encroaching upon the collective identity and public values of European society....

...

More than 23 million Muslims reside in Europe, comprising nearly 5 percent of the population....

...

Currently, the waves of immigrants and asylum seekers from the Middle East and North Africa (MENA) — the region with the world's second-highest fertility rate — have had more to do with the worsening conditions in the MENA countries than with labor shortages in Europe, the region with the world's lowest fertility rate. As the MENA population doubles in the next three decades and Europe's shrinks, increased migratory flows from south to north appear unavoidable — a trend augmented by Europe's graying population, as opposed to the youthful MENA average. In 2000 the UN projected that, to counterbalance their increasingly graying populations, EU states annually would need 949,000 migrants to maintain their 1995 populations; 1,588,000 migrants to maintain their 1995 working-age populations; or 13,480,000 migrants to maintain their population support ratios (the ratio of people aged 15–64 to those aged 65 and older). Furthermore, rather than help alleviate the problem, the demographics of the 10 new EU member states increase these gaps. Whichever goal is pursued, most of these individuals will be Muslims.

...

The growing Muslim presence in Europe has tended to cluster geographically within individual states, particularly in industrialized, urban areas within clearly defined, if not self-encapsulated, poorer neighborhoods such as Berlin's Kreuzberg district, London's Tower Hamlets, and the *banlieues* (suburbs) of major French cities, further augmenting its visibility and impact yet circumscribing day-to-day contact with the general population....

...

The nature of the Muslim presence in Europe is also changing. No longer "temporary guest workers," Muslims are now a permanent part of western European national landscapes, as they have been for centuries in southeastern Europe. The institutionalization of Islam in Europe has begun, as has a "re-Islamization" of Muslims in Europe.

... Like European Christians and Jews, European Muslims are not a monolithic group. Nonetheless, Muslims increasingly identify first with Islam rather than with either their family's country of origin or the European country in which they now reside. Moreover, this phenomenon is significantly more pronounced among younger Muslims.

... The current generation is also modernizing and acculturating to aspects of contemporary European society at a faster rate than the first waves of Muslim immigrants did. Younger Muslims are adopting attributes of the European societies in which they were born and raised, such as language; socialization through schooling; and, in many cases, some of the secular perspectives of the country in which they reside. Yet, generally they do not feel part of the larger society nor that they have a stake in it. Conversely, even though they may be third-generation citizens, they often are not viewed as fellow citizens by the general public but are still identified as foreigners and immigrants instead.

...

Despite these trends in citizenship, younger Muslims are resisting assimilation into secular European societies even more steadfastly than the older generation did. Europe's Muslims, including the younger generation, are willing to integrate and respect national norms and institutions as long as they can, at the same time, maintain their distinct Islamic identity and practices. They fear that assimilation, that is, total immersion into European society, will strip them of this identity. Yet, this is the price many Muslims increasingly see European governments and publics demanding: to have Europe become a melting pot without accommodation by or modifications of the existing culture. Studies in France and Germany find that second- and particularly third-generation Muslims are less integrated into European societies than their parents or grandparents were. The recent headscarf affairs in France and Germany underscore and further exacerbate this basic clash.

Perceived discrimination in European societies affecting employment, education, housing, and religious practices is compelling many second- and third-generation Muslims to embrace Islam as their badge of identity. Indeed, the unemployment rate among Muslims is generally double that of non-Muslims, and it is worse than that of non-Muslim immigrants. Educational achievement and skill levels are relatively low, participation by Muslim women in the workforce is minimal, opportunities for advancement are limited, and biases against Muslims are strong. Such factors contribute to the isolation — and self-encapsulation — of Muslim communities in Europe....

...

The rapidly growing Muslim populations seem to be overwhelming the ability of European governments to draw the lines of tolerance rationally, consistently, and convincingly. Europeans see Muslims as a direct challenge to the collective identity, traditional values, and public policies of their societies, as demonstrated by the heated controversies over the hijab [scarf], Muslim food (*halal*), the construction of mosques, the teaching of Islam in schools, and Muslim burial rites. This attitude is also reflected in intense debates over women's rights, church-state relations, and Islam's compatibility with democracy. Politicians, pundits, and ordinary citizens are all seized with the "Islamic challenge."

... The threat is framed in terms of security (terrorism) and economics (jobs); yet, the core issue is identity and the perceived cultural threat Islam poses to the

European way of life. Europeans have even coined a name for it: Islamophobia. Conversely, this tendency to see Muslims as a monolith has its reverse image in Muslim allegiance to the umma, which transcends other loyalties; tends to reinforce the "we/them" perspective; and is part of the reason why Muslims resist assimilation — the total loss of identity-related indicators of existing differences from European societies — and insist on integration — a reconstituted identity that stresses remaining differences — or, in some cases, recommunalization — a physical presence in Europe but no accommodation with European society. . . .

. . . [T]he challenge for Europe seems more daunting [than that of the United States with respect to racial hostility and tolerance] because it involves not only integration and tolerance but also redefining both parties' identities. Each side will have to change and move toward the other. Europe's Muslims will need to accept the norms, customs, and cultures of the states in which they live and reject efforts to establish a parallel society, while the general European population will need to broaden its horizons to embrace and accommodate diversity, accepting integration and not just complete assimilation as a valid relationship to society.

. . .

For their part, Muslims in Europe, who must confront poverty, bigotry, de facto segregation, and limited social mobility, are likely to find it difficult to embrace Europe's liberal democratic views on gender equality; sexual liberalization; and the principles of compromise, egalitarianism, and identification with the state. These are all issues that challenge the traditional views not only of Muslims but also of individuals with an Arab, Turkish, or South Asian heritage, as the vast majority of Europe's Muslims are. These cultural backgrounds have not included the Enlightenment as a central pillar, and the idea of a secular society is for the most part alien. Moreover, as Mustafa Malik notes, in these societies, "[Resistance] to liberalism was heightened by hatred for European colonialists, who represented liberal values." Lack of organization and political standing, diversity of views and interests, economic weakness, and the absence of clear leadership pose major complicating hurdles, all of which Europe's Muslims will need to address if they are to contribute their part to Europe's transformation.

. . .

Although the situation in Europe is not quite there, the tipping point may be closer than is generally realized. As intolerance toward Muslim communities grows in Europe, European Muslims are growing more self-confident but also more dissatisfied, particularly as Europe's economy continues to sputter. The percentage of Muslims in France is rapidly approaching that of African-Americans in the United States in 1950 (10 percent), and the percentage of Muslims in Europe as a whole will pass that benchmark within the next decade. . . .

. . .

Conversely, however, a success in dealing with the building clash of cultures and identities, which results in a shift of both Muslim and non-Muslim European mind-sets, and crafts a societal framework that encourages integration and respects individual as well as national identities would negate Huntington's thesis of the inevitable incompatibility of Islam and the West. It would require change in European society, to be sure. As with all change, there would be winners and losers. Yet, success holds out the hope of reinvigorating and redefining Europe, proffering a possible corrective to its projected political, economic, and demographic decline as well as moving European integration to a new level and giving it new meaning.

…

NOTE

In 2004, a French law became effective that effectively banned from public schools the headscarf worn by many Muslim girls as well as designated clothing or symbols of several other religions that indicated a student's religious affiliation, including large crosses for Christians and skullcaps for Jewish boys. The law was stimulated by concern about and hostility of the French people toward the increasingly common practice of girls within the growing immigrant Muslim community of wearing the headscarf in public, including at public schools. The preceding and following readings suggest some of the reasons for that concern and hostility.

ELAINE SCIOLINO, BAN RELIGIOUS ATTIRE IN SCHOOL, FRENCH PANEL SAYS

New York Times, December 12, 2003, Sec. A, p. 1

A report delivered to President Jacques Chirac on Thursday called for a new law banning the wearing of "conspicuous" religious symbols in French public schools — large crosses for Christians, head scarves for Muslim girls, or skullcaps for Jewish boys. The recommendation was the most striking in an official reassessment of how to preserve the principle of the separation of religion and state in France in light of such developments as the rise of a large Muslim population and a new wave of anti-Semitism. That principle, the report said, would be guaranteed by impartiality and the banning of all conspicuous religious symbols in official institutions, but individuals using those institutions would not be barred from wearing "discreet symbols like, for example, medallions, small crosses, Stars of David, hands of Fatima, or small Korans."

In today's France, no social issue provokes more emotion and debate and cuts across political lines more sharply than the Islamic veil. This week's Elle magazine, for example, printed an open letter to Mr. Chirac signed by leading French women — Muslim and non-Muslim — calling for an outright ban.

The report, prepared by an independent commission appointed by the government, also recommended that public schools add Jewish and Muslim holidays to the Christian holidays now observed, a move so far untested in Europe, and to provide special meals for Jews and Muslims in school cafeterias. In addition, employers were urged to allow employees to choose the religious holidays they take off — for example, Yom Kippur for Jews, Id al-Kebir for Muslims or the Orthodox Christmas for Orthodox Christians.

The 67-page report is the work of a 20-member commission of religious leaders, teachers, politicians and sociologists that was created in July by Mr. Chirac. It is certain to intensify rather than quiet the increasingly shrill debate in France over the intrusion of religion into public institutions as the country struggles to retain the ideal of strict separation between religion and state it codified into law a century ago.

...

The commission said that a 1905 law codifying the separation of church and state was no longer adequate given the cultural and religious composition of present-day France. It said that organized groups were testing the secular state by demands on public services in the name of religion and pressuring Muslims to identify first with their faith and then with their French citizenship. "In one century, because of immigration, French society has become diverse in terms of its spiritual and religious aspect," the report said. "The challenge today is to give space to new religions while at the same time to succeed in integration and struggle against political-religious manipulation."

Bernard Stasi, a former education minister who headed the commission, said at a news conference announcing its conclusions that the commission had been "astonished to see that the situation was more serious than what we previously thought." "There are without any doubt forces in France that try to destabilize the republic, and it's time for the republic to react," he said.

Currently, there is no uniform regulation on wearing veils in public schools. A ruling in 1989 by France's Council of State declared that religious symbols could not be worn in public schools if they "constitute an act of intimidation, provocation, proselytizing or propaganda," threaten health, security or the freedom of others or "disturb order."

...

Supporters of a ban say that it is the only way to stop what they see as increasing demands by France's large Muslim community for special privileges, like the separation of men and women in public swimming pools and treatment of female patients exclusively by female doctors. The open letter in Elle said, "The Islamic veil sends us all — Muslims and non-Muslims — back to a discrimination against women that is intolerable."

...

Even within the French government, there are deep divisions. Mr. Chirac has made no secret of his opposition to head scarves in schools, telling students at the French high school in Tunis last week that he saw "something aggressive" in the wearing of Muslim veils and pledging that the French state would forbid students to wear what he called "ostentatious signs of religious proselytism." By contrast, France's interior minister, Nicolas Sarkozy, opposes such a law, arguing that an outright ban would represent "secular fundamentalism."

NOTE

In an article entitled 'U.S. Chides France on Effort to Bar Religious Garb in Schools', *New York Times*, December 19, 2003, Sec. A, p. 8, Christopher Marquis reported:

> The Bush administration on Thursday gently criticized a French proposal to ban head scarves and other conspicuous religious items from the public schools, saying that such displays constitute "a basic right that should be protected." In the first public comment by a United States official about the controversy, John V. Hanford, the administration's top-ranking official on issues of religious freedom, took issue with President Jacques Chirac's call for legislation to prevent the wearing of head scarves for Muslim girls, large crosses for Christians and skullcaps for Jewish boys.
>
> "A fundamental principle of religious freedom that we work for in many countries of the world, including on this very issue of head scarves, is that all persons should be able to practice their religion and their beliefs peacefully, without government interference, as long as they are doing so without provocation and intimidation of others in society," Mr. Hanford said. Mr. Hanford said that as long as people were wearing such items "as a heartfelt manifestation of their beliefs" — rather than as a provocative act — "this is, we believe, a basic right that should be protected."

In an article entitled 'French Muslims Protest Rule against Scarves, *New York Times*, January 18, 2004, Sec. 1, p. 10, Elaine Sciolino reported:

> In a speech in December announcing his recommendation for passage of a law banning religious symbols from schools, President Jacques Chirac said that if France succumbed to the demands of its religious communities, "it would lose its soul."
>
> . . .
>
> The demonstrators in Paris sought to portray the struggle as one of loyal French citizens demanding their rights. Many waved French flags; some women among the protesters wore the red, white and blue French flag as a head covering or as a shawl. "The Marseillaise" was played. One banner displayed in the demonstration read, "France, you are my country; Veil, you are my life." Another said, "Down with the racist laws of the Catholics and Mr. Chirac against the Arabs and the head scarf." A third read, "Secular fundamentalism is a danger for the Republic."

NOTE

The two following cases, *Dahlab* and *Sahin*, do not involve immigrants but rather Muslim citizens of the country banning the wearing of a headscarf by the citizen involved in designated educational institutions. (These two decisions of the European Court of Human Rights, like the *Kokkinakis* decision at p. 600, *supra*, anticipate the systematic examination of that Court in Chapter 11.)

Four years earlier than the *Sahin v. Turkey* decision following this Note, the European Court of Human Rights decided *Dahlab v. Switzerland*, Application

No. 42393/98 (2001). Applicant, a Catholic, was appointed a primary school teacher in the secular school system in Geneva to work with young children. She converted to Islam and soon began to 'observe a precept laid down in the Koran whereby woman were enjoined to draw their veils over themselves in the presence of men.' She refused the request of the Director General of Primary Education to stop wearing a headscarf to class, and was soon dismissed. Applicant was not given relief by the Swiss authorities, and therefore brought an action before the European Court to have this decision reversed, on the ground that the prohibition of the headscarf infringed her freedom to manifest her religion pursuant to Article 9 of the Convention. The Court agreed with the conclusions of the Swiss administrative and judicial authorities and declared the application inadmissible. It stated in part:

> The Court accepts that it is very difficult to assess the impact that a powerful external symbol such as the wearing of a headscarf may have on the freedom of conscience and religion of very young children [between four and eight]. . . . [T]he wearing of a headscarf might have some kind of proselytizing effect, seeing that it appears to be imposed on women by a precept which is laid down in the Koran and which . . . is hard to square with the principle of gender equality. It therefore appears difficult to reconcile the wearing of an Islamic headscarf with the message of tolerance, respect for others and, above all, equality and non-discrimination that all teachers in a democratic society must convey to their pupils. . . . [H]aving regard, above all, to the tender age of the children for whom the applicant was responsible as a representative of the State, the Geneva authorities did not exceed their margin of appreciation and . . . the measure they took was therefore not unreasonable.

SAHIN V. TURKEY

European Court of Human Rights, 2005
Judgment of Grand Chamber, Application No. 44774/98

[Applicant came from a traditional family of practicing Muslims, and considered it her religious duty to wear the Islamic headscarf. She did so during her four years studying medicine in a Turkish university. Applicant then transferred to Istanbul University to continue her studies. In a series of episodes beginning in 1998 she was censured by university authorities for refusing to comply with university circulars based on legislation banning students wearing headscarves from lectures and courses. After being denied enrolment and admission to lectures, she sought unsuccessfully relief from Turkish courts. Relevant provisions of the Turkish Constitution provide:

> Article 2: The Republic of Turkey is a democratic, secular (*laik*) and social State based on the rule of law that is respectful of human rights in a spirit of social peace. . . .
>
> Article 10: All individuals shall be equal before the law without any distinction based on language, race, colour, sex, political opinion, philosophical belief, religion, membership of a religious sect or other similar grounds. . . .

> Article 13: Fundamental rights and freedoms may be restricted only by law and on the grounds set out in special provisions of the Constitution.... Any such restriction shall not conflict with the letter or spirit of the Constitution or the requirements of a democratic, secular social order and shall comply with the principle of proportionality.
>
> Article 14: The rights and freedoms set out in the Constitution may not be exercised with a view to undermining the territorial integrity of the State, the unity of the Nation or the democratic and secular Republic founded on human rights....
>
> Article 24: Everyone shall have the right to freedom of conscience, belief and religious conviction. Prayers, worship and religious services shall be conducted freely, provided that they do not violate the provisions of Article 14. No one shall be compelled to participate in prayers, worship or religious services or to reveal his or her religious beliefs and convictions; no one shall be censured or prosecuted for his religious beliefs or convictions....

Ultimately, applicant abandoned her studies in Turkey and pursued her medical education at Vienna University. After failing to secure judicial relief in Turkey, she initiated proceedings against Turkey under the European Convention on Human Rights. In a 2004 judgment, a Chamber of the European Court of Human Rights held unanimously that there had been no violation of the Convention. Applicant's request that the case be referred to the Court's Grand Chamber was accepted. In its 2005 judgment, the Grand Chamber also ruled against applicant. Excerpts from that opinion and a dissenting opinion follow.]

B. History and background

30. The Turkish Republic was founded on the principle that the State should be secular (*laik*). Before and after the proclamation of the Republic on 29 October 1923, the public and religious spheres were separated through a series of revolutionary reforms....

31. The principle of secularism was inspired by developments in Ottoman society in the period between the nineteenth century and the proclamation of the Republic.... Significant advances in women's rights were made during this period (equality of treatment in education, the introduction of a ban on polygamy in 1914, the transfer of jurisdiction in matrimonial cases to the secular courts that had been established in the nineteenth century).

32. The defining feature of the Republican ideal was the presence of women in public life and their active participation in society. Consequently, the ideas that women should be freed from religious constraints and that society should be modernised had a common origin.... [W]omen obtained equal political rights with men. ...

35. In Turkey wearing the Islamic headscarf to school and university is a recent phenomenon which only really began to emerge in the 1980s.... Those in favour of the headscarf see wearing it as a duty and/or a form of expression linked to religious identity. However, the supporters of secularism ... see the Islamic headscarf as a symbol of a political Islam ...

[In the Turkish Constitutional Court's opinion that upheld the university's position, the judges stated that secularism had achieved so important a position among constitutional values because of the country's historical experience and the particularities of Islam compared to other religions; secularism was an essential condition for democracy and acted as a guarantor of freedom of religion and of equality before the law. Students must be allowed to work in a tolerant atmosphere without being deflected from their goals by signs of religious affiliation such as the headscarf.

The ECHR opinion included a comparative survey about laws about headscarves in a number of European countries. The survey indicated that state legislation varied on many details — for example, how if at all the headscarf was regulated, and the level of school/university that was covered by any regulation.]

I. ALLEGED VIOLATION OF ARTICLE 9 OF THE CONVENTION

70. The applicant submitted that the ban on wearing the Islamic headscarf in institutions of higher education constituted an unjustified interference with her right to freedom of religion, in particular, her right to manifest her religion. She relied on Article 9 of the Convention, which provides:

> 1. Everyone has the right to freedom of thought, conscience and religion; this right includes freedom to change his religion or belief and freedom, either alone or in community with others and in public or private, to manifest his religion or belief, in worship, teaching, practice and observance.
>
> 2. Freedom to manifest one's religion or beliefs shall be subject only to such limitations as are prescribed by law and are necessary in a democratic society in the interests of public safety, for the protection of public order, health or morals, or for the protection of the rights and freedoms of others.

...

104. The Court reiterates that as enshrined in Article 9, freedom of thought, conscience and religion is one of the foundations of a "democratic society" within the meaning of the Convention. This freedom is, in its religious dimension, one of the most vital elements that go to make up the identity of believers and their conception of life, but it is also a precious asset for atheists, agnostics, sceptics and the unconcerned. The pluralism indissociable from a democratic society, which has been dearly won over the centuries, depends on it. That freedom entails, *inter alia*, freedom to hold or not to hold religious beliefs and to practise or not to practise a religion.

105. While religious freedom is primarily a matter of individual conscience, it also implies, *inter alia*, freedom to manifest one's religion, alone and in private, or in community with others, in public and within the circle of those whose faith one shares. Article 9 lists the various forms which manifestation of one's religion or belief may take, namely worship, teaching, practice and observance....

106. In democratic societies, in which several religions coexist within one and the same population, it may be necessary to place restrictions on freedom to manifest one's religion or belief in order to reconcile the interests of the various groups and ensure that everyone's beliefs are respected....

107. The Court ... also considers that the State's duty of neutrality and impartiality is incompatible with any power on the State's part to assess the legitimacy of religious beliefs or the ways in which those beliefs are expressed ...

...

29. Where questions concerning the relationship between State and religions are at stake, on which opinion in a democratic society may reasonably differ widely, the role of the national decision-making body must be given special importance. This will notably be the case when it comes to regulating the wearing of religious symbols in educational institutions, especially in view of the diversity of the approaches taken by national authorities on the issue. It is not possible to discern throughout Europe a uniform conception of the significance of religion in society and the meaning or impact of the public expression of a religious belief will differ according to time and context. Rules in this sphere will consequently vary from one country to another according to national traditions and the requirements imposed by the need to protect the rights and freedoms of others and to maintain public order. ...

30. This margin of appreciation goes hand in hand with a European supervision embracing both the law and the decisions applying it. The Court's task is to determine whether the measures taken at national level were justified in principle and proportionate. In delimiting the extent of the margin of appreciation in the present case the Court must have regard to what is at stake, namely the need to protect the rights and freedoms of others, to preserve public order and to secure civil peace and true religious pluralism, which is vital to the survival of a democratic society. ...

111. [The Court briefly discusses and quotes from the *Dahlab* case, p. 624, *supra.*]

...

115. After examining the parties' arguments, the Grand Chamber sees no good reason to depart from the approach taken by the Chamber as follows [Ed. Indented paragraphs are quotations from the 2004 judgment of the Chamber]:

> ... The Court ... notes the emphasis placed in the Turkish constitutional system on the protection of the rights of women ... Gender equality — recognised by the European Court as one of the key principles underlying the Convention and a goal to be achieved by member States of the Council of Europe — was also found by the Turkish Constitutional Court to be a principle implicit in the values underlying the Constitution ...
>
> ... In addition, like the Constitutional Court ..., the Court considers that, when examining the question of the Islamic headscarf in the Turkish context, there must be borne in mind the impact which wearing such a symbol, which is presented or perceived as a compulsory religious duty, may have on those who choose not to wear it. As has already been noted, the issues at stake include the protection of the "rights and freedoms of others" and the "maintenance of public order" in a country in which the majority of the population, while professing a strong attachment to the rights of women and a secular way of life, adhere to the Islamic faith. Imposing limitations on freedom in this sphere may, therefore, be regarded as meeting a pressing social need by seeking to achieve those two legitimate aims, especially since, as the Turkish courts stated ..., this religious symbol has taken on political significance in Turkey in recent years.

> ... The Court does not lose sight of the fact that there are extremist political movements in Turkey which seek to impose on society as a whole their religious symbols and conception of a society founded on religious precepts... It has previously said that each Contracting State may, in accordance with the Convention provisions, take a stance against such political movements, based on its historical experience. The regulations concerned have to be viewed in that context and constitute a measure intended to achieve the legitimate aims referred to above and thereby to preserve pluralism in the university.

....

117. The Court must now determine whether in the instant case there was a reasonable relationship of proportionality between the means employed and the legitimate objectives pursued by the interference.

118. Like the Chamber ..., the Grand Chamber notes at the outset that it is common ground that practising Muslim students in Turkish universities are free, within the limits imposed by educational organisational constraints, to manifest their religion in accordance with habitual forms of Muslim observance. In addition, the resolution adopted by Istanbul University on 9 July 1998 shows that various other forms of religious attire are also forbidden on the university premises.

...

121. ... By reason of their direct and continuous contact with the education community, the university authorities are in principle better placed than an international court to evaluate local needs and conditions or the requirements of a particular course....

122. In the light of the foregoing and having regard to the Contracting States' margin of appreciation in this sphere, the Court finds that the interference in issue was justified in principle and proportionate to the aim pursued.

123. Consequently, there has been no breach of Article 9 of the Convention.

II. ALLEGED VIOLATION OF ARTICLE 2 OF PROTOCOL NO. 1

[Applicant also argued that Article 2 of Protocol No. 1 of the European Convention should be interpreted to uphold her right to wear a headscarf while attending the university. That article provides:

> No person shall be denied the right to education. In the exercise of any functions which it assumes in relation to education and to teaching, the State shall respect the right of parents to ensure such education and teaching in conformity with their own religious and philosophical convictions.

The Grand Chamber relied heavily on its reasoning with respect to freedom of religion in concluding that there had been no violation of Article 2 of Protocol No. 1. It said in part:]

157. ... [T]he Court is able to accept that the regulations on the basis of which the applicant was refused access to various lectures and examinations for wearing the Islamic headscarf constituted a restriction on her right to education, notwithstanding the fact that she had had access to the University and been able to read the

subject of her choice in accordance with the results she had achieved in the university entrance examination. However, an analysis of the case by reference to the right to education cannot in this instance be divorced from the conclusion reached by the Court with respect to Article 9....

158. ... The obvious purpose of the restriction was to preserve the secular character of educational institutions.

159. As regards the principle of proportionality, the Court found in paragraphs 118 to 121 above that there was a reasonable relationship of proportionality between the means used and the aim pursued. In so finding, it relied in particular on the following factors which are clearly relevant here. Firstly, the measures in question manifestly did not hinder the students in performing the duties imposed by the habitual forms of religious observance. Secondly, the decision-making process for applying the internal regulations satisfied, so far as was possible, the requirement to weigh up the various interests at stake. The university authorities judiciously sought a means whereby they could avoid having to turn away students wearing the headscarf and at the same time honour their obligation to protect the rights of others and the interests of the education system. Lastly, the process also appears to have been accompanied by safeguards — the rule requiring conformity with statute and judicial review — that were apt to protect the students' interests.

...

161. Consequently, the restriction in question did not impair the very essence of the applicant's right to education....

III. ALLEGED VIOLATION OF ARTICLES 8, 10 AND 14 OF THE CONVENTION

[Based on its arguments with respect to Article 9, the Court summarily and unanimously concluded that there had been no violations of Articles 8, 10 and 14.]

❀ ❀ ❀

[By sixteen votes to one, the Court concluded that there had been no violation of Article 9 or of the first sentence of Article 2 of Protocol No. 2.]

DISSENTING OPINION OF JUDGE TULKENS

...

2. ... Underlying the majority's approach is the *margin of appreciation* which the national authorities are recognised as possessing and which reflects, *inter alia*, the notion that they are "better placed" to decide how best to discharge their Convention obligations in what is a sensitive area. The Court's jurisdiction is, of course, subsidiary and its role is not to impose uniform solutions, especially "with regard to establishment of the delicate relations between the Churches and the State"....

3. I would perhaps have been able to follow the margin-of-appreciation approach had not two factors drastically reduced its relevance in the instant case.

The first concerns the argument the majority use to justify the width of the margin, namely the diversity of practice between the States on the issue of regulating the wearing of religious symbols in educational institutions and, thus, the lack of a European consensus in this sphere. The comparative-law materials do not allow of such a conclusion, as in none of the member States has the ban on wearing religious symbols extended to university education, which is intended for young adults, who are less amenable to pressure. The second factor concerns the European supervision that must accompany the margin of appreciation. ... [O]ther than in connection with Turkey's specific historical background, European supervision seems quite simply to be absent from the judgment. However, the issue raised in the application, whose significance to the right to freedom of religion guaranteed by the Convention is evident, is not merely a "local" issue, but one of importance to all the member States. European supervision cannot, therefore, be escaped simply by invoking the margin of appreciation.

4. On what grounds was the interference with the applicant's right to freedom of religion through the ban on wearing the headscarf based? In the present case, relying exclusively on the reasons cited by the national authorities and courts, the majority put forward, in general and abstract terms, two main arguments: secularism and equality. ... In a democratic society, I believe that it is necessary to seek to harmonise the principles of secularism, equality and liberty, not to weigh one against the other.

5. As regards, firstly, *secularism* ...: Religious freedom is, however, also a founding principle of democratic societies. Accordingly, the fact that the Grand Chamber recognised the force of the principle of secularism did not release it from its obligation to establish that the ban ... met a "pressing social need". ... [W]here there has been interference with a fundamental right, the Court's case-law clearly establishes that mere affirmations do not suffice: they must be supported by concrete examples. ...

6. Under Article 9 of the Convention, the freedom with which this case is concerned is not freedom to have a religion (the internal conviction) but to manifest one's religion (the expression of that conviction). If the Court has been very protective (perhaps over-protective) of religious sentiment ... it has shown itself less willing to intervene in cases concerning religious practices. ... which only appear to receive a subsidiary form of protection.

...

7. ... The majority thus consider that wearing the headscarf contravenes the principle of secularism. In so doing, they take up position on an issue that has been the subject of much debate. ...

In the present case, a generalised assessment of that type gives rise to at least three difficulties. Firstly, the judgment does not address the applicant's argument — which the Government did not dispute — that she had no intention of calling the principle of secularism, a principle with which she agreed, into doubt. Secondly, there is no evidence to show that the applicant, through her attitude, conduct or acts, contravened that principle. ... Lastly, the judgment makes no distinction between teachers and students, whereas in the *Dahlab v. Switzerland* decision of

15 February 2001, which concerned a teacher, the Court expressly noted the role-model aspect which the teacher's wearing the headscarf had ... [T]he position of pupils and students seems to me to be different.

8. Freedom to manifest a religion entails everyone being allowed to exercise that right, whether individually or collectively, in public or in private, subject to the dual condition that they do not infringe the rights and freedoms of others and do not prejudice public order.

As regards the first condition, this could have been satisfied if the headscarf the applicant wore as a religious symbol had been ostentatious or aggressive or was used to exert pressure, to provoke a reaction, to proselytise or to spread propaganda and undermined — or was liable to undermine — the convictions of others. However, the Government did not argue that this was the case and there was no evidence before the Court to suggest that Ms Sahin had any such intention. As to the second condition, it has been neither suggested nor demonstrated that there was any disruption in teaching or in everyday life at the University. ...

9. ...[T]he possible effect which wearing the headscarf, which is presented as a symbol, may have on those who do not wear it does not appear to me, in the light of the Court's case-law, to satisfy the requirement of a pressing social need. ...

10. In fact, it is the threat posed by "extremist political movements" seeking to "impose on society as a whole their religious symbols and conception of a society founded on religious precepts" which, in the Court's view, serves to justify the regulations in issue, which constitute "a measure intended ... to preserve pluralism in the university". ...

While everyone agrees on the need to prevent radical Islamism, a serious objection may nevertheless be made to such reasoning. Merely wearing the headscarf cannot be associated with fundamentalism and it is vital to distinguish between those who wear the headscarf and "extremists" who seek to impose the headscarf as they do other religious symbols. Not all women who wear the headscarf are fundamentalists and there is nothing to suggest that the applicant held fundamentalist views. ... [T]he judgment fails to provide any concrete example of the type of pressure concerned. ...

11. Turning to *equality*, the majority focus on the protection of women's rights and the principle of sexual equality. ... By converse implication, wearing the headscarf is considered synonymous with the alienation of women. The ban on wearing the headscarf is therefore seen as promoting equality between men and women. However, what, in fact, is the connection between the ban and sexual equality? The judgment does not say. ... [W]earing the headscarf has no single meaning; it is a practise that is engaged in for a variety of reasons. It does not necessarily symbolise the submission of women to men and there are those who maintain that, in certain cases, it can even be a means of emancipating women. What is lacking in this debate is the opinion of women, both those who wear the headscarf and those who choose not to.

12. On this issue, the Grand Chamber refers in its judgment to the *Dahlab v. Switzerland* decision of 15 February 2001, citing what to my mind is the most questionable part of the reasoning in that decision, namely that wearing the headscarf

represents a "powerful external symbol", which "appeared to be imposed on women by a religious precept that was hard to reconcile with the principle of gender equality" and that the practice could not easily be "reconciled with the message of tolerance, respect for others and, above all, equality and non-discrimination that all teachers in a democratic society should convey to their pupils".

... The applicant, a young adult university student, said — and there is nothing to suggest that she was not telling the truth — that she wore the headscarf of her own free will. In this connection, I fail to see how the principle of sexual equality can justify prohibiting a woman from following a practice which, in the absence of proof to the contrary, she must be taken to have freely adopted. ...

13. ... In these circumstances, there has been a violation of the applicant's right to freedom of religion, as guaranteed by the Convention.

...

[The dissenting opinion also disagreed on several grounds with the majority's disposition of applicant's claim based on Article 2 of Protocol No. 1.]

20. I end by noting that all these issues must also be considered in the light of the observations set out in the annual activity report published in June 2005 of the European Commission against Racism and Intolerance (ECRI), which expresses concern about the climate of hostility existing against persons who are or are believed to be Muslim and considers that the situation requires attention and action in the future. Above all, the message that needs to be repeated over and over again is that the best means of preventing and combating fanaticism and extremism is to uphold human rights.

NOTE

In an article entitled, 'Blair Criticizes Full Islamic Veils as "Mark of Separation"', *New York Times*, October 18, 2006, p. A3. Alan Cowell reported:

> Prime Minister Tony Blair joined a passionate and increasingly contentious debate on Tuesday over the full-face veils worn by some British Muslim women, calling it a "mark of separation." It was the first time Mr. Blair had so explicitly backed Jack Straw, the leader of the House of Commons, who raised Muslim ire this month by saying he did not believe that women should wear the full-face veil, a headdress with only a narrow slit for the eyes. Mr. Straw had asked Muslim women meeting with him to remove their veils, arguing that it prevented communication and set the wearer apart. "It is a mark of separation, and that is why it makes other people from outside the community feel uncomfortable," Mr. Blair said at a regular news conference, echoing some of Mr. Straw's sentiments.
>
> His remarks reflected a sense that British society is heading toward ever deeper fissures between Muslims and non-Muslims, evoking questions about the nation's readiness to embrace Muslims, and Muslims' willingness to adapt. The discussion mirrors earlier public disputes in France, Turkey and elsewhere about head scarves, though in Britain it is largely limited to the use of the full-face veil, the niqab.

QUESTIONS

1. What arguments would you make under the ICCPR (France is a State Party) to challenge the legality of the French ban on headscarves for girls in public schools? Would exactly the same arguments apply if you were challenging the law's ban on 'large' crosses for Christian children or skullcaps for Jewish boys?

2. Putting challenges to the law's legality to the side, what is your view of the appropriateness or likely effectiveness (with respect to what French goals?) of the law, given the context that it addresses? Should the Government have pursued other policies? Which?

3. Turkey's situation showed some similarities to the French concerns and some dramatic differences. How do you evaluate the *Sahin* decision with respect to its consistency with the European Convention on Human Rights? Is the *Dahlab* decision an easier or more difficult decision to justify under that Convention?

4. Does Article 9 of the European Convention lead you to a different decision with respect to the legality of the French law from that reached in Question (1) when examining that law in relation to the ICCPR ? Do you believe that as a matter of policy the ban of headscarves in public educational institutions was equally justified or unjustified in France and Turkey or more justified in one country than the other ?

NOTE

The two following decisions of the supreme courts of Canada and the United States pose similar issues to the headscarf cases though involving different objects of clothing or symbols. Both cases are decided exclusively under national constitutional law without reference to international law.

MULTANI V. COMMISSION SCOLAIRE MARGUERITE-BOURGEOYS

Supreme Court of Canada, 2006
2006 SCC 6 (CanLII)

[G and his father B are orthodox Sikhs, who believe that their religion requires them to wear a kirpan — a religious object resembling a dagger that must be made of metal — at all times. G accidentally dropped the kirpan he wore under his clothing when in the school yard. The school's governing board concluded that wearing a kirpan at school violated the school's code of conduct, which prohibited the carrying of weapons. The board's council of commissioners agreed and notified G and B that G could carry a symbolic kirpan made of a material that made it harmless. B sought judicial relief. The Court of Appeal agreed with the council of commissioners, concluding that the council's decision did infringe G's freedom of religion under the *Canadian Charter of Rights and Freedoms* and the *Quebec Charter of Human Rights and Freedoms*, but that the infringement was justified for the purposes of relevant sections in both instruments. In this decision, the Canadian Supreme Court held that the appeal should be allowed, and the decision of the council of commissioners should be declared to be null. Excerpts follow.]

PER MCLACHLIN C.J. AND BASTARACHE, BINNIE, FISH AND CHARRON JJ.:

...

... [O]nly freedom of religion is in issue here. However, that freedom is not absolute and can conflict with other constitutional rights.... [T]he Court has never called into question the principle that rights are reconciled through the constitutional justification required by s. 1 of the *Canadian Charter*.... [Section 1 provides: 'The *Canadian Charter of Rights and Freedoms* guarantees the rights and freedoms set out in it subject only to such reasonable limits prescribed by law as can be demonstrably justified in a free and democratic society.']

The council of commissioners' decision prohibiting G from wearing his kirpan to school infringes his freedom of religion. G genuinely believes that he would not be complying with the requirements of his religion were he to wear a plastic or wooden kirpan, and none of the parties have contested the sincerity of his belief. The interference with G's freedom of religion is neither trivial nor insignificant, as it has deprived him of his right to attend a public school. The infringement of G's freedom of religion cannot be justified under s. 1 of the *Canadian Charter*. Although the council's decision to prohibit the wearing of a kirpan was motivated by a pressing and substantial objective, namely to ensure a reasonable level of safety at the school, and although the decision had a rational connection with the objective, it has not been shown that such a prohibition minimally impairs G's rights.

... In the circumstances of the instant case, the decision to establish an absolute prohibition against wearing a kirpan does not fall within a range of reasonable alternatives. The arguments in support of such a prohibition must fail. The risk of G using his kirpan for violent purposes or of another student taking it away from him is very low, especially if the kirpan is worn under conditions such as were imposed by the Superior Court. It should be added that G has never claimed a right to wear his kirpan to school without restrictions. Furthermore, there are many objects in schools that could be used to commit violent acts and that are much more easily obtained by students, such as scissors, pencils and baseball bats. The evidence also reveals that not a single violent incident related to the presence of kirpans in schools has been reported. Although it is not necessary to wait for harm to be done before acting, the existence of concerns relating to safety must be unequivocally established for the infringement of a constitutional right to be justified. Nor does the evidence support the argument that allowing G to wear his kirpan to school could have a ripple effect. Lastly, the argument that the wearing of kirpans should be prohibited because the kirpan is a symbol of violence and because it sends the message that using force is necessary to assert rights and resolve conflict is not only contradicted by the evidence regarding the symbolic nature of the kirpan, but is also disrespectful to believers in the Sikh religion and does not take into account Canadian values based on multiculturalism. Religious tolerance is a very important value of Canadian society. If some students consider it unfair that G may wear his kirpan to school while they are not allowed to have knives in their possession, it is incumbent on the schools to discharge their obligation to instil in their students this value that is at the very foundation of our democracy. A total prohibition against wearing a kirpan to school undermines the value of this religious symbol and sends students the message that some religious practices do not merit the same protection as others. Accommodating G and allowing him to wear his kirpan under certain conditions demonstrates the importance that our society attaches to protecting freedom of religion and to showing respect for its minorities. The deleterious effects of a total prohibition thus outweigh its salutary effects.

Given that G no longer attends his school, the appropriate and just remedy is to declare the decision prohibiting him from wearing his kirpan to be null.

GOLDMAN V. WEINBERGER

Supreme Court of the United States, 1986

475 U.S. 503, 106 S. Ct. 1310

[Goldman, an Orthodox Jew and ordained rabbi, was accepted into the Armed Forces Health Professions Scholarship Program while studying clinical psychology, and therefore received for three years of study a scholarship and monthly stipend. Participants in the scholarship programme are required to serve one year of active duty for each year of subsidized education. After gaining his Ph.D., he entered active service in the United States Air Force as a commissioned officer. He served as a clinical psychologist at the mental health clinic of a base in the US, where he was free to wear a yarmulke (a skullcap), and wore his service cap over the yarmulke when out of doors.

After he testified as a defence witness at a court-martial wearing his yarmulke but not his service cap, opposing counsel lodged a complaint with the Hospital Commander, arguing that wearing a yarmulke was a violation of Air Force Regulation (AFR) 35–10, stating that '[headgear] will not be worn … [while] indoors except by armed security police in the performance of their duties.' Petitioner was ordered not to wear a yarmulke while on duty. He received a letter of reprimand and was given a negative recommendation with respect to his application to extend his term of service. Petitioner than resorted to litigation based upon his right under the Free Exercise Clause of the First Amendment to exercise his religious beliefs. The Federal Court of Appeals ruled against him on the ground that the Air Force's strong interest in discipline justified the strict enforcement of its uniform dress requirements. The following excerpts are from the opinion by Justice Rehnquist for the US Supreme Court that affirmed the judgment of the Court of Appeals.]

Our review of military regulations challenged on First Amendment grounds is far more deferential than constitutional review of similar laws or regulations designed for civilian society. The military need not encourage debate or tolerate protest to the extent that such tolerance is required of the civilian state by the First Amendment; to accomplish its mission the military must foster instinctive obedience, unity, commitment, and esprit de corps. The essence of military service "is the subordination of the desires and interests of the individual to the needs of the service."

... In the context of the present case, when evaluating whether military needs justify a particular restriction on religiously motivated conduct, courts must give great deference to the professional judgment of military authorities concerning the relative importance of a particular military interest...

The considered professional judgment of the Air Force is that the traditional outfitting of personnel in standardized uniforms encourages the subordination of personal preferences and identities in favor of the overall group mission. Uniforms encourage a sense of hierarchical unity by tending to eliminate outward individual distinctions except for those of rank....

To this end, the Air Force promulgated AFR 35–10, a 190-page document, which states that "Air Force members will wear the Air Force uniform while performing their military duties, except when authorized to wear civilian clothes on duty." The rest of the document describes in minute detail all of the various items of apparel that must be worn as part of the Air Force uniform. It authorizes a few individualized options with respect to certain pieces of jewelry and hairstyle, but even these are subject to severe limitations. In general, authorized headgear may be worn only out of doors. Indoors, "[headgear] [may] not be worn ... except by armed security police in the performance of their duties." A narrow exception to this rule exists for headgear worn during indoor religious ceremonies....

...

... The Air Force has drawn the line essentially between religious apparel that is visible and that which is not, and we hold that those portions of the regulations challenged here reasonably and evenhandedly regulate dress in the interest of the military's perceived need for uniformity. The First Amendment therefore does not prohibit them from being applied to petitioner even though their effect is to restrict the wearing of the headgear required by his religious beliefs.

...

JUSTICE BRENNAN, WITH WHOM JUSTICE MARSHALL JOINS, DISSENTING

...

... The fact that "the regulations do not permit the wearing of ... a yarmulke," does not simply render military life for observant Orthodox Jews "objectionable." It sets up an almost absolute bar to the fulfillment of a religious duty....

...

... When a military service burdens the free exercise rights of its members in the name of necessity, it must provide, as an initial matter and at a minimum, a *credible* explanation of how the contested practice is likely to interfere with the proferred military interest...

...

The contention that the discipline of the Armed Forces will be subverted if Orthodox Jews are allowed to wear yarmulkes with their uniforms surpasses belief.

...

...

...In its brief, the Government characterizes the yarmulke as an assertion of individuality and as a badge of religious and ethnic identity, strongly suggesting that, as such, it could drive a wedge of divisiveness between members of the services.

...

...[T]he services allow, and rightly so, other manifestations of religious diversity. It is clear to all service personnel that some members attend Jewish services, some Christian, some Islamic, and some yet other religious services. Barracks mates see Mormons wearing temple garments, Orthodox Jews wearing tzitzit, and Catholics wearing crosses and scapulars. That they come from different faiths and ethnic backgrounds is not a secret that can or should be kept from them.

... [A] yarmulke worn with a United States military uniform is an eloquent reminder that the shared and proud identity of United States serviceman embraces and unites religious and ethnic pluralism.

...

...Although turbans, saffron robes, and dreadlocks are not before us in this case and must each be evaluated against the reasons a service branch offers for prohibiting personnel from wearing them while in uniform, a reviewing court could legitimately give deference to dress and grooming rules that have a *reasoned* basis in, for example, functional utility, health and safety considerations, and the goal of a polished, professional appearance....

...

Implicit ... in the Government's arguments, is what might be characterized as a fairness concern. It would be unfair to allow Orthodox Jews to wear yarmulkes, while prohibiting members of other minority faiths with visible dress and grooming requirements from wearing their saffron robes, dreadlocks, turbans, and so forth.... What puzzles me is the implication that a neutral standard that could result in the disparate treatment of Orthodox Jews and, for example, Sikhs is *more* troublesome or unfair than the existing neutral standard that does result in the different treatment of Christians, on the one hand, and Orthodox Jews and Sikhs on the other. *Both* standards are constitutionally suspect; before either can be sustained, it must be shown to be a narrowly tailored means of promoting important military interests.

...

....A critical function of the Religion Clauses of the First Amendment is to protect the rights of members of minority religions against quiet erosion by majoritarian social institutions that dismiss minority beliefs and practices as unimportant, because unfamiliar. It is the constitutional role of this Court to ensure that this purpose of the First Amendment be realized.

QUESTION

How do you evaluate the judgments of these two courts? In what relevant respects are the situations presented to the Canadian and American courts similar to or different from the facts and contexts in the *Dahlab* and *Sahin* cases? Given the reasoning of those two decisions and Article 9 of the European Convention, how do you think the European Court would have decided the *Goldman* case?

4. FREEDOM OF SPEECH

Freedom of speech forms one of the obvious boundary lines between relatively open and closed societies, between liberal democracies and different types of authoritarian states like China, Iran, North Korea or Zimbabwe. Whatever the form of authoritarian regime, a liberal value like speech and its related rights such as assembly and association will bow to one or another degree to censorship and other repressive controls. In some instances, the explanations for different understandings of this human right would stress factors like an authoritarian regime's guiding ideology and its rulers' concern about resistance or subversion. Relatively free speech may pose too great a danger for the survival of the existing political system. In other cases, different conceptions of free speech and its relation to other rights and state interests may reflect religious beliefs, cultural patterns, or long-standing traditions and practices.

Section 4 examines such different conceptions of free speech and its limitations. Some of these differences exist among states within the world of liberal democracies, whereas others involve liberal democracies and authoritarian states in such diverse regions as Europe and the Middle East. The topics selected to explore these issues concern 'hate speech' and blasphemy (ranging from offensive texts to cartoons).

COMMENT ON HATE SPEECH

The view of the ICCPR Committee under that Convention's Optional Protocol that appears below, the *Faurisson* case, involves a so-called 'Holocaust-denial law' that has a close affinity with laws making 'hate speech' a criminal offence (that may also be subject to civil sanctions). This Comment provides background on the general issue of hate speech, several definitions of which appear in the official texts below. The fundamental idea covers abusive, denigrating, harassing speech based on a group or individual's national, religious, racial or ethnic identity. In some but not all definitions, such speech must incite to violence or discrimination.

The laws imposing criminal and other sanctions on hate speech clearly impinge on freedom of speech, a core value of the human rights movement that is protected under the major universal and regional human rights instruments. Consider the universal instruments, which at once proclaim and limit this freedom:

> *Article 19, UDHR*: Everyone has the right to freedom of opinion and expression; this right includes freedom to . . . impart information and ideas through any media and regardless of frontiers.
>
> *Article 19, ICCPR*: . . .
>
> (2) Everyone shall have the right to freedom of expression; this right shall include freedom to . . . impart information and ideas of all kinds, regardless of frontiers. . . .
>
> (3) The exercise of the right provided for in paragraph 2 of this article carries with it special duties and responsibilities. It may therefore be subject to certain restrictions, but these shall only be such as are provided by law and are necessary: (a) For respect of the rights or reputations of others; (b) For the protection of national security or of public order (*ordre public*), or of public health or morals.

Note also the following ICCPR articles, each of which has a comparable UDHR article: (1) the equal protection clause in Article 26; (2) the provision in ICCPR Article 5 that nothing in the Covenant should be interpreted as implying 'for any group or person any right to engage in any activity . . . aimed at the destruction of any of the rights and freedom recognized herein. . . .'; and (3) the provision in Article 17 that no one shall be subject to 'arbitrary or unlawful interference with his privacy . . . nor to unlawful attacks on his honour and reputation'.

The arguments in favour of free speech are broadly familiar, for example: the full realization of the individual human personality, the challenge to existing beliefs (the 'marketplace of ideas') and the related stimulus to inquiry and debate and development of knowledge, the relation to principles of democratic government and pluralism, and its close functional association with other human rights like freedoms of belief, religion and association. But are these arguments sufficient to justify the protection of hate speech directed to particular racial, ethnic, religious, gender or other groups or their members? Such speech itself attacks basic premises of the human rights system, premises as deep as equal human dignity, respect for others and equal protection. It may deny that the targeted group is entitled to benefit together with the rest of the population from human rights protections. It may advocate, indeed passionately urge, discriminatory or even violent action against members of the targeted group. It may pose threats of a greater or lesser immediacy of such violence.

The quoted provisions above of the ICCPR include qualifications to free speech that bear generally on these types of restrictive laws. Several human rights instruments are more explicit on these issues — for example, Article 20(2) of the ICCPR: 'Any advocacy of national, racial or religious hatred that constitutes incitement to discrimination, hostility or violence shall be prohibited by law.' Manfred Nowak, in his *U.N. Covenant on Civil and Political Rights: CCPR Commentary* (1993), observes (p. 365) that the 'legal formulation of this provision is not entirely clear'. The wording of paragraph (2):

> literally means that incitement to discrimination without violence must also be prohibited. . . . Particularly inexplicable is the insertion of the word 'discrimination'.

> ... It is most difficult to conceive of an advocacy of national, racial or religious hatred that does not simultaneously incite discrimination.... Art. 20(2)... may be sensibly interpreted only in light of its object and purpose, i.e., taking into consideration its *responsive character* with regard to the Nazi racial hatred campaigns.... Thus, despite its unclear formulation, States Parties are not obligated by Art. 20(2) to prohibit advocacy of hatred in private circles that instigates non-violent actions of racial or religious discrimination. What the delegates ... had in mind was to ... prevent the public incitement of racial hatred and violence within a State or against other States and peoples.

Some states have forbidden political groups or parties that are based on racism, and hence that employ hate speech, from participating in elections. In Israel, for example, a system of proportional representation works by having a candidates' list from different parties or political formations presented to the electorate, which votes for a list as a whole. Amendment No. 9 to the Basic Law on the Knesset (Parliament) provides: 'A candidate's list shall not participate in elections to the Knesset if its objects or actions, expressly or by implication, include one of the following: ... (3) incitement to racism'.

The *Jersild* Decision

Consider the approach of the European Court of Human Rights in *Jersild v. Denmark*, Ser. A, No. 298-A (1994). The question posed was whether Jersild, a Danish journalist, was criminally liable for aiding and abetting three youths who made racist remarks on interviews conducted by Jersild on a television programme on matters of public interest. The three young men were members of a group, the Greenjackets, that engaged in hate speech against particular groups — in this case people, particularly Danish residents, of African descent. In the course of the interview conducted by Jersild after he had located the men, and which had been sharply edited by Jersild from an initial length of hours to a few minutes, the men made numerous ugly and denigrating remarks about blacks. There was no allegation in the criminal charge that Jersild or the broadcasting station shared those views. On the other hand, since the point of the programme was to convey information to the Danish public about atypical, small racist groups, there was no effort by Jersild or the broadcasting station to challenge or oppose the racist views expressed.

A Danish penal statute, responsive to obligations of Denmark under the Convention on the Elimination of All Forms of Racial Discrimination, imposed a fine or imprisonment on '[a]ny person who, publicly or with the intention of disseminating it to a wide circle of people, makes a statement, or other communication, threatening insulting or degrading a group of persons on account of their race, colour, national or ethnic origin or belief ...'. The three youths were found guilty of violating the statute, and did not appeal. Jersild was found guilty of aiding and abetting the three youths. His conviction was affirmed by the Danish appellate courts, and he then instituted proceedings before the European Commission on Human Rights, which ultimately referred the case to the European Court of Human Rights.

The Court decided that the conviction — that is, not the hate-speech statute abstractly, but the statute as here applied to Jersild for aiding and abetting — violated the free expression provisions (including freedom of media) of Article 10 of the European Convention on Human Rights. Its opinion stressed the need to protect freedom of the press, and that news reporting through interviews was an important means of informing the public. Conviction of a journalist in these circumstances could hamper discussion of matters of public interest. It concluded that the limitation on Jersild's freedom of expression was not 'necessary in a democratic society', a requirement of Article 10. The prosecution and conviction were disproportionate to the state's interest, also expressed in Article 10, of protecting the reputation or rights of others.

One of the dissenting opinions observed:

> ... The applicant has cut the entire interview down to a few minutes, probably with the consequence or even the intention of retaining the most crude remarks. That being so, it was absolutely necessary to add at least a clear statement of disapproval. The majority of the Court sees such disapproval in the context of the interview, but this is an interpretation of cryptic remarks. Nobody can exclude that certain parts of the public found in the television spot support for their racist prejudices.
>
> And what must be the feelings of those whose human dignity has been attacked, or even denied, by the Greenjackets? Can they get the impression that seen in context the television broadcast contributes to their protection? A journalist's good intentions are not enough in such a situation, especially in a case in which he has himself provoked the racist statements.

Another dissenting opinion noted:

> While appreciating that some judges attach particular importance to freedom of expression, the more so as their countries have largely been deprived of it in quite recent times, we cannot accept that this freedom should extend to encouraging racial hatred, contempt for races other than the one to which we belong, and defending violence against those who belong to the races in question. It has been sought to defend the broadcast on the ground that it would provoke a healthy reaction of rejection among the viewers. That is to display an optimism, which to say the least, is belied by experience. Large numbers of young people today, and even of the population at large, finding themselves overwhelmed by the difficulties of life, unemployment and poverty, are only too willing to seek scapegoats who are held up to them without any real word of caution; for — and this is an important point — the journalist responsible for the broadcast in question made no real attempt to challenge the points of view he was presenting, which was necessary if their impact was to be counterbalanced, at least for the viewers.

Hate Speech in Former Yugoslavia and Rwanda

The effect of years of intense Serbian-nationalist rhetoric under the rule of Milosevich on the internal and international wars in the Former Yugoslavia is well known. A news article reported in 1999 that the United States and its Western allies in the Bosnia peacekeeping operation were creating a tribunal with power to close radio and television stations and punish newspapers that issued propaganda undermining peace efforts. Western officials described the broadcasts that they wished to arrest as 'poisonous propaganda'. Groups of journalists and civil liberties groups expressed their concern about these efforts by democratic states to place restraints on the media. The Western officials avoided use of the term censorship, and explained that they' had no other option, given the venomous propaganda that they said often masquerades as news coverage in Bosnia and that can threaten the safety of the American-led NATO peacekeeping force there'. One spokesman said, 'Basically, there's a tradition here of propaganda in the class of Goebbels'. A State Department official said: 'There are obvious free-speech concerns, but we need to put in place something to deal with the abuses of the media — the hate, the racial epithets and ethnic slurs': *New York Times*, April 24, 1998, p. A8.

NOTE

Recall the 1946 Judgment of the International Military Tribunal at Nuremberg, which makes sparse reference to the Holocaust but includes the following observation, p. 122, *supra*:

> The persecution of the Jews at the hands of the Nazi Government has been proved in the greatest detail before the Tribunal. It is a record of consistent and systematic inhumanity on the greatest scale. Ohlendorf, Chief of Amt III in the RSHA from 1939 to 1943, and who was in command of one of the Einsatz groups in the campaign against the Soviet Union testified as to the methods employed in the extermination of the Jews. ... When the witness Bach Zelewski was asked how Ohlendorf could admit the murder of 90,000 people, he replied: 'I am of the opinion that when, for years, for decades, the doctrine is preached that the Slav race is an inferior race, and Jews not even human, then such an outcome is inevitable'.... The Nazi Party preached these doctrines throughout its history, *Der Stürmer* and other publications were allowed to disseminate hatred of the Jews, and in the speeches and public declarations of the Nazi leaders, the Jews were held up to public ridicule and contempt....
>
> ... In the summer of 1941, however, plans were made for the 'final solution' of the Jewish question in Europe. This 'final solution' meant the extermination of the Jews.... Adolf Eichmann, who had been put in charge of this program by Hitler, has estimated that the policy pursued resulted in the killing of 6 million Jews, of which 4 million were killed in the extermination institutions.

Consider the following observations about Rwanda by Bill Berkeley, 'Radio in Rwanda: The Sounds of Silence', *San Diego Union-Tribune*, August 18, 1994:

> ...
>
> ... Human rights groups, the United Nations and even, reluctantly, the U.S. State Department have described this systematic slaughter [In Rwanda] as 'genocide', yet no one has explained how thousands of peasants who say they had never killed before could have been lured, incited or coerced into participating in mass

murder on par with this century's worst massacres. One answer, according to captive killers like Kiruhura and other moderate Hutus who were targeted by death squads but managed to escape, lies in the sinister propaganda broadcast by radio stations affiliated with the now-deposed Rwandan government. This was the match that started the fire, they say.

...

.... The Tutsis were demonized ... Radio Rwanda and a station owned by members of [the former Hutu President] Habyarimana's inner circle, Radio Milles Collines, had been terrorizing the Hutus with warnings about the evil Tutsi-led RPF and Hutu oppositionists, who were labeled 'enemies' or 'traitors' and who 'deserved to die'. Endless speeches, songs and slogans demonized the Tutsis....

Throughout the terror, Radio Rwanda and Radio Milles Collines have systematically blurred the distinction between rebel soldiers and Tutsi civilians. On May 23, for example, Radio Rwanda warned its listeners of what it called the 'means and clues that the Inyenzi [cockroaches] use to infiltrate in a given zone'. It said RPF soldiers 'change their clothing appearance most of the time, trying to be confused with ordinary people who till the soil and go to the market'.

Hutus were urged to 'guard seriously the roadblock', a reference to the checkpoints where Tutsis were selected for slaughter. On June 1 Radio Milles Collines described the rebels as 'criminals' responsible for a series of harrowing massacres, a fact it claimed had been 'confirmed by international sources'.... [T]he broadcast concluded: 'This is the real face of the RPF. These people are not Rwandans, they are revengeful Ugandans. We hate them; we are disgusted with them, and nobody will accept that they take power....'

...

'All the Westerners who come here ask us this question', says Sixbert Musangamfura, a Hutu journalist. 'They forget the evil of Hitler's propaganda. The propaganda heard here resembles the propaganda made by Joseph Goebbels. People received this propaganda all day long. It is the propaganda that is at the base of this tragedy.'...

❁ ❁ ❁

The *Faurisson* opinion that follows deals with 'Holocaust denial laws' that have been enacted by several states including Austria, Belgium, France, Germany, Israel, Lithuania, Spain and Switzerland. As noted in McGoldrick and O'Donnell, 'Hate-Speech Laws: Consistency with National and International Human Rights Law,' 18 Leg. Studies 453 (1997), at 457, these laws vary a great deal:

> The essential feature of the laws which attracts the label of holocaust denial is that they make it a criminal offence to deny certain things in a certain way.... [F]or the French law it is 'crimes against humanity as defined by the Nuremberg International Military Tribunal'. The German law is wider, as it refers to 'persecution under National Socialism or any other form of despotism or tyranny'. The Israeli law is even wider again: 'acts committed in the period of the Nazi regime, which are crimes against the Jewish people or crimes against humanity'. The Austrian law extends to denial of the 'nationalist socialist genocide or other national socialist crimes against humanity'. The Austrian law extends to cover the gross trivialisation, approval or justification of the same. The German law is similar.

The following excerpts from Frederick Schauer, 'The Exceptional First Amendment', in Michael Ignatieff, *American Exceptionalism and Human Rights* (2005), at 32, underscore the breadth of the concept.

> ... Although the label "hate speech" tends to be applied capaciously, the phrase can be understood as encompassing four distinct but interrelated freedom of speech issues. First, there is the question of the legitimacy of prohibiting various racial, ethnic, and religious epithets — *nigger, wog, kike, paki, kaffir*, and the like — words whose use, except as ironic self-reference by members of those groups, is invariably intended to harm, to offend, and to marginalize. Second, the question of hate speech sometimes involves the issue of restrictions on circulating certain demonstrably false factual propositions about various racial or religious groups, with prohibitions on Holocaust denial being the most common example. A third hate speech issue arises with respect to laws prohibiting the advocacy of or incitement to racial or religious intolerance, hatred, or violence, as with explicit calls to race-based violence, explicit appeals for racial exclusion, and explicit calls for repatriation of members of racial or religious minorities to the countries of their ancestry. Finally, hate speech questions are presented, especially in the context of gender when it is argued that epithets, and occasionally pictures, create a hostile, and therefore marginalizing or excluding, workplace or educational or cultural environment.
>
> ... The precise form of attempting to control hate speech by law varies considerably among the nations of the world. Germany and Israel, among other countries, ban the Nazi Party and its descendants, as well as prohibiting other political parties whose programs include racial hatred, racial separation, and racial superiority.' ... Germany, Israel, and France are among the nations that prohibit the sale and distribution of various Nazi items, including swastikas, Nazi flags, and, on occasion, images of Adolph Hitler and copies of *Mein Kampf*.' ... Canada, Germany, and France, along with others, permit sanctions against those who would deny the existence of the Holocaust.' ... France imposes fines with some frequency on public utterances espousing the racial or religious inferiority of various groups, or advocating the exclusion of people from France on the basis of their race, their religion, their ethnicity, or their national origin. The Netherlands outlaws public insults based on race, religion, or sexual preference." ... And South Africa, New Zealand, Australia, Canada, the United Kingdom, and all of the Scandinavian countries, among many others, follow the mandates of Article 20(2) of the International Covenant on Civil and Political Rights, and Articles 4(a) and 4(b) of the Convention on the Elimination of all Forms of Racial Discrimination, by making it a crime to engage in the incitement to racial, religious, or ethnic hatred or hostility.

FAURISSON V. FRANCE

Communication No. 550/1993, Human Rights Committee
Views of Committee, November 8, 1996, UN Doc. A/52/40 (1999), Vol. II, at 84

[Robert Faurisson, author of the communication and a former professor of literature, was removed from his university chair in 1991. He had expressed doubt about or denial of the accuracy of conventional accounts of the Holocaust, including

(i) his conviction that there were no homicidal gas chambers for the extermination of Jews in Nazi concentration camps, (ii) his doubts over the number of people killed, and (iii) his disbelief in the records and evidence of the Nuremberg trial that were used to convict Nazis.

In 1990, the French legislature passed the so-called 'Gayssot Act'. It amended the 1881 law on Freedom of the Press by adding Article 24 *bis*, which made it an offence to contest (*contestation*) the existence of the category of crimes against humanity as defined in the London Charter of 1945, on the basis of which Nazi leaders were convicted by the International Military Tribunal at Nuremberg in 1945–1946. For the relevant provision of the Charter and excerpts from the Nuremberg judgment, see pp. 115–124, *supra*.

Faurisson attacked the 1990 law as a threat to academic freedom, including freedom of research and expression. He claimed that the Gayssot Act raised to the rank of infallible dogma the proceedings and verdict at Nuremberg, and endorsed forever the orthodox Jewish version of the Second World War. Arguing that the Nuremberg records could not be treated as infallible, he cited examples of historical revision such as the Katyn massacre in Poland of Polish army officers that was initially attributed to Germans but that was later shown to be of Soviet responsibility. Faurisson described as 'exorbitant' the 'privilege of censorship' from which the representatives of the Jewish community in France benefited.

The State Party noted that anti-racism legislation adopted by France in the 1980s was considered insufficient to bring legal action against the trivialization of Nazi crimes. There was governmental concern over 'revisionism' by individuals justifying their writing through their status as historians. The French Government viewed these revisionist theses as a 'subtle form of contemporary anti-semitism'. The Gayssot Act was meant to fill a legal vacuum while defining the new criminal conduct as precisely as possible.

Associations of French resistance fighters and of deportees to German concentration camps filed a private criminal action against Faurisson, who was convicted in 1991 of violating the Gayssot Act. The Court of Appeal of Paris upheld the conviction and imposed a fine. Faurisson took the position that further appeal to the Court of Cassation would be futile and filed the present communication. He argued that the Act violated the ICCPR, although his communication did not invoke specific provisions.

The ICCPR Committee concluded in an earlier proceeding that the communication was admissible and that it raised issues under Article 19 of the Covenant. This proceeding led to the views of the Committee under Article 5(4) of the Optional Protocol, as well as five individual opinions signed by seven Committee members. Excerpts from the views of the Committee and several individual opinions follow.]

9.3 Although it does not contest that the application of the terms of the Gayssot Act... may lead, under different conditions than the facts of the instant case, to decisions or measures incompatible with the Covenant, the Committee is not called upon to criticize in the abstract laws enacted by States parties. The task of the Committee under the Optional Protocol is to ascertain whether the conditions of the restrictions imposed on the right to freedom of expression are met in the communications which are brought before it.

9.4 Any restriction on the right to freedom of expression must cumulatively meet the following conditions: it must be provided by law, it must address one of the aims set out in paragraph 3 (a) and (b) of article 19, and must be necessary to achieve a legitimate purpose.

9.5 ... [T]he Committee concludes ... that the finding of the author's guilt [in the French proceedings] was based on his following two statements: '... I have excellent reasons not to believe in the policy of extermination of Jews or in the magic gas chambers ... I wish to see that 100 per cent of the French citizens realize that the myth of the gas chambers is a dishonest fabrication'. His conviction therefore did not encroach upon his right to hold and express an opinion in general. Rather the court convicted Mr. Faurisson for having violated the rights and reputation of others. For these reasons the Committee is satisfied that the Gayssot Act, as read, interpreted and applied to the author's case by the French courts, is in compliance with the provisions of the Covenant.

9.6 To assess whether the restrictions placed on the author's freedom of expression by his criminal conviction were applied for the purposes provided for by the Covenant, the Committee begins by noting ... that the rights for the protection of which restrictions on the freedom of expression are permitted by article 19, paragraph 3, may relate to the interests of other persons or to those of the community as a whole. Since the statements made by the author, read in their full context, were of a nature as to raise or strengthen anti-semitic feelings, the restriction served [sic] the respect of the Jewish community to live free from fear of an atmosphere of anti-semitism. The Committee therefore concludes that the restriction of the author's freedom of expression was permissible under article 19, paragraph 3 (a), of the Covenant.

9.7 Lastly the Committee needs to consider whether the restriction of the author's freedom of expression was necessary. The Committee noted the State party's argument contending that the introduction of the Gayssot Act was intended to serve the struggle against racism and anti-semitism. It also noted the statement of a member of the French Government, the then Minister of Justice, which characterized the denial of the existence of the Holocaust as the principal vehicle for anti-semitism. ... [T]he Committee is satisfied that the restriction of Mr. Faurisson's freedom of expression was necessary within the meaning of article 19, paragraph 3, of the Covenant.

10. The Human Rights Committee, acting under article 5, paragraph 4, of the Optional Protocol to the International Covenant on Civil and Political Rights, is of the view that the facts as found by the Committee do not reveal a violation by France of article 19, paragraph 3, of the Covenant.

Statement of Thomas Buergenthal

As a survivor of the concentration camps of Auschwitz and Sachsenhausen whose father, maternal grandparents and many other family members were killed in the Nazi Holocaust, I have no choice but to recuse myself from participating in the decision of this case.

INDIVIDUAL OPINION BY NISUKE ANDO (CONCURRING)

... In my view the term 'negation' ('contestation'), if loosely interpreted, could comprise various forms of expression of opinions and thus has a possibility of threatening or encroaching the right to freedom of expression, which constitutes an indispensable prerequisite for the proper functioning of a democratic society. In order to eliminate this possibility it would probably be better to replace the Act with a specific legislation prohibiting well-defined acts of anti-semitism or with a provision of the criminal code protecting the rights or reputations of others in general.

INDIVIDUAL OPINION BY ELIZABETH EVATT AND DAVID KRETZMER, CO-SIGNED BY ECKART KLEIN (CONCURRING)

...

2. ... The main issue is whether the restriction has been shown by the State party to be necessary, in terms of article 19, paragraph 3 (a), for respect of the rights or reputations of others.

3. ... While we entertain no doubt whatsoever that the author's statements are highly offensive both to Holocaust survivors and to descendants of Holocaust victims (as well as to many others), the question under the Covenant is whether a restriction on freedom of expression in order to achieve this purpose may be regarded as a restriction necessary for the respect of the rights of others.

4. Every individual has the right to be free not only from discrimination on grounds of race, religion and national origins, but also from incitement to such discrimination. This is stated expressly in article 7 of the Universal Declaration of Human Rights. It is implicit in the obligation placed on States parties under article 20, paragraph 2, of the Covenant to prohibit by law any advocacy of national, racial or religious hatred that constitutes incitement to discrimination, hostility or violence. The crime for which the author was convicted under the Gayssot Act does not expressly include the element of incitement, nor do the statements which served as the basis for the conviction fall clearly within the boundaries of incitement, which the State party was bound to prohibit, in accordance with article 20, paragraph 2. However, there may be circumstances in which the right of a person to be free from incitement to discrimination on grounds of race, religion or national origins cannot be fully protected by a narrow, explicit law on incitement that falls precisely within the boundaries of article 20, paragraph 2. This is the case where, in a particular social and historical context, statements that do not meet the strict legal criteria of incitement can be shown to constitute part of a pattern of incitement against a given racial, religious or national group, or where those interested in spreading hostility and hatred adopt sophisticated forms of speech that are not punishable under the law against racial incitement, even though their effect may be as pernicious as explicit incitement, if not more so.

...

6. The notion that in the conditions of present-day France, Holocaust denial may constitute a form of incitement to anti-semitism cannot be dismissed....

7. The Committee correctly points out, as it did in its General Comment 10, that the right for the protection of which restrictions on freedom of expression are permitted by article 19, paragraph 3, may relate to the interests of a community as a whole. This is especially the case in which the right protected is the right to be free from racial, national or religious incitement.... It appears ... that the restriction on the author's freedom of expression served to protect the right of the Jewish community in France to live free from fear of incitement to anti-semitism....

8. The power given to States parties under article 19, paragraph 3, to place restrictions on freedom of expression, must not be interpreted as license to prohibit unpopular speech, or speech which some sections of the population find offensive. Much offensive speech may be regarded as speech that impinges on one of the values mentioned in article 19, paragraph 3(a) or (b) (the rights or reputations of others, national security, ordre public, public health or morals). The Covenant therefore stipulates that the purpose of protecting one of those values is not, of itself, sufficient reason to restrict expression. The restriction must be necessary to protect the given value. This requirement of necessity implies an element of proportionality. The scope of the restriction imposed on freedom of expression must be proportional to the value which the restriction serves to protect....

9. The Gayssot Act is phrased in the widest language and would seem to prohibit publication of bona fide research connected with matters decided by the Nuremburg Tribunal. Even if the purpose of this prohibition is to protect the right to be free from incitement to anti-semitism, the restrictions imposed do not meet the proportionality test. They do not link liability to the intent of the author, nor to the tendency of the publication to incite to anti-semitism. Furthermore, the legitimate object of the law could certainly have been achieved by a less drastic provision that would not imply that the State party had attempted to turn historical truths and experiences into legislative dogma that may not be challenged, no matter what the object behind that challenge, nor its likely consequences. In the present case we are not concerned, however, with the Gayssot Act, in abstracto, but only with the restriction placed on the freedom of expression of the author by his conviction for his statements in the interview in Le Choc du Mois. Does this restriction meet the proportionality test?

10. The French courts examined the author's statements in great detail. Their decisions, and the interview itself, refute the author's argument that he is only driven by his interest in historical research. In the interview the author demanded that historians 'particularly Jewish historians' who agree that some of the findings of the Nuremburg Tribunal were mistaken be prosecuted. The author referred to the 'magic gas chamber' ('la magique chambre à gaz') and to 'the myth of the gas chambers' ('le mythe des chambres à gaz'), that was a 'dirty trick' ('une gredinerie') endorsed by the victors in Nuremburg. The author has, in these statements, singled out Jewish historians over others, and has clearly implied that the Jews, the victims of the Nazis, concocted the story of gas chambers for their own purposes. While there is every reason to maintain protection of bona fide historical research against restriction, even when it challenges accepted historical truths and by so doing offends people, anti-semitic allegations of the sort made by the author, which violate the rights of others in the way described, do not have the same claim to protection against restriction. The restrictions placed on the author did not curb the core of his right to freedom of expression, nor did they in any way affect his freedom of research.... It is for these reasons that we joined the Committee....

INDIVIDUAL OPINION BY RAJSOOMER LALLAH (CONCURRING)

...

11. I conclude, therefore, that the creation of the offence provided for in the Gayssot Act, as it has been applied by the Courts to the author's case, falls more

appropriately, in my view, within the powers of France under article 20, paragraph 2, of the Covenant. The result is that there has, for this reason, been no violation by France under the Covenant.

. . .

13. Recourse to restrictions that are, in principle, permissible under article 19, paragraph 3, bristles with difficulties, tending to destroy the very existence of the right sought to be restricted. The right to freedom of opinion and expression is a most valuable right and may turn out to be too fragile for survival in the face of the too frequently professed necessity for its restriction in the wide range of areas envisaged under paragraphs (a) and (b) of article 19, paragraph 3.

. . .

NOTE

Consider the following views of Christopher Caldwell, in 'Historical Truth Speaks for Itself', *Financial Times*, February 18, 2006:

> Madeleine Reberioux, the late leftist historian, warned of the biggest danger of the Gayssot law as soon as it was passed. "One day", she wrote, "it's going to lead into other areas besides the genocide against the Jews — other genocides and other assaults on what will be called 'historical truth.'" She was right. A law declaring the Turkish killings of Armenians early last century to be a "genocide" was passed in 2001; later that year, another law defined the slave trade as a "crime against humanity"; a year ago, legislation mandated that teachers stress the "positive role" of the French presence in North Africa. Each new officialisation of remembrance calls into being more "moral lobbies", which press their claims with ever more insistence in ever more obscure corners of political life and with ever more legal clout.
>
> . . .
>
> Mr Dworkin's case [*infra*] for abolishing laws against Holocaust denial on grounds of political legitimacy is the right one. Of course, no one should be under the illusion that being able to go out and deny the Holocaust will add much to any "debate". The official truth of western governments about the Holocaust happens to be the truth. Allowing delusions or anti-Semitic propaganda to masquerade as "opinions" will not change that. So those western countries with laws against Holocaust denial are now in a tricky position. They must undo laws that have proved unworkable and counterproductive — and at a moment when some of those laws' most vocal detractors are violent people of ill will.

QUESTIONS

1. As a legislator, would you have voted for the Gayssot Act? How would you have reacted to the following argument in general, or as applied to the passage of that Act?

> Freedom of expression is indeed a fundamental right. While its protection may sometimes be an end in itself, its exercise may not disturb the fundamental goals

underlying human rights law. One of the most fundamental of those goals is achieving equality and non-discrimination. In fact, if there is any right which enjoys primacy among rights, it is arguably the principle of equality and non-discrimination. ... The goal of hate mongers is to convince others that the members of the target group are not entitled to equal protection of the law; the hate mongers seek a society of discrimination. ... They should not be entitled to claim protection under the right to freedom of expression for their abuse of speech rights to achieve that goal.[9]

2. Suppose that an author's statements leading to a prosecution under the Gayssot Act appeared in a periodical article that was the only writing by the author on the subject. The author concludes that the Nuremberg judgment, later judicial decisions describing the Holocaust, and 'official' accounts of the Holocaust were part of a conscious conspiracy among the victorious Allies to spur feelings of guilt by Germans and hatred of others toward them.

Would a conviction by French courts be likely to be upheld under the opinion above for the Committee? Under the concurring opinion by Elizabeth Evatt and David Kretzmer? How do these opinions differ, and which do you view as the better one?

3. Should the opinions have referred to arguments in favour of freedom of speech, or to the criteria in Section 19 for limiting speech, such as 'public order' or 'public morals'? What could have been the bases or events in France and French history for relying on such criteria to uphold the statute and affirm the conviction? Would comparable bases have been available in the United States to justify legislation similar to the Gayssot Act?

4. Do you think that the opinions as a whole succeed in illuminating the relevant aspects of the ICCPR, or indeed of human rights in general? Do they advance understanding of the value and limitations of free speech, and of the dilemmas of resolving conflicts among rights within the human rights instruments?

NOTE

The United States ratified the ICCPR in 1992. In giving its consent to ratification, and acting consistently with proposals made to it by the Bush administration (see p. 1139, *infra*), the Senate entered a reservation to Article 20 that then qualified the US ratification. It reads: 'Article 20 does not authorize or require legislation or other action by the United States that would restrict the right to free speech and association protected by the Constitution and laws of the United States'.

Compare with Article 20 an equivalent provision, Article 4 of the Convention on Elimination of All Forms of Racial Discrimination. In that article, the states parties 'condemn all propaganda ... based on ideas or theories of superiority of one race or group of persons or one colour or ethnic origin'. They undertake to declare a punishable offence 'all dissemination of ideas based on racial superiority or hatred,

[9] Stephanie Farrior, 'Moulding the Matrix: The Historical and Theoretical Foundations of International Law Concerning Hate Speech', 14 Berkeley J. of Int. L. 1 (1996), at 6, 98.

incitement of racial discrimination, as well as all acts of violence' against such a race or group. Article 1 defines 'racial discrimination' to mean any distinction based on 'race, colour, descent, or national or ethnic origin' that has the purpose or effect of impairing equal enjoyment of rights 'in the political, economic, social, cultural or any other field of public life'. When the United States ratified the Racial Convention, it reserved as to Article 4.

The primary constitutional provision referred to in these two reservations by the United States is the First Amendment: 'Congress shall make no law ... abridging the freedom of speech....'

FREDRICK SCHAUER, THE EXCEPTIONAL FIRST AMENDMENT

in Michael Ignatieff (ed.), American Exceptionalism and Human Rights (2005), at 29

... [A]lthough a constitutional or quasi-constitutional right to freedom of expression is the international norm, the contours of that right vary widely even among the liberal democracies that understand the value of the right and the importance of enforcing it seriously. And among the most interesting manifestations of that variety among liberal democracies is the way in which the American First Amendment, as authoritatively interpreted, remains a recalcitrant outlier to a growing international understanding of what the freedom of expression entails. In numerous dimensions, the American approach is *exceptional*. ... [P]rotection of freedom of expression is generally stronger than that represented by an emerging multinational consensus — but stronger in ways that may also reflect an exceptional though not necessarily correct understanding of the relationship between freedom of expression and other goals, other interests, and other rights.

...

... [The effects of the U.S. reservations in several treaties like the ICCPR on hate-speech issues] are important in their own right but also reflect a deeper division between the United States and the rest of the world on freedom of expression issues; for as a matter of formal legal doctrine and significantly as a matter of public opinion as well, the American understanding is that principles of freedom of speech do not permit government to distinguish protected from unprotected speech on the basis of the point of view espoused. Specifically, this prohibition on what is technically called "viewpoint discrimination" extends to the point of view that certain races or religions are inferior, to the point of view that hatred of members of minority races and religions is desirable, and to the point of view that violent or otherwise illegal action is justified against people because of their race, their ethnicity, or their religious beliefs. If government may not under the First Amendment distinguish between Republicans and Communists, or prohibit the speeches of the flat-earthers because of the patent falsity of their beliefs, then the government may not, so American First Amendment doctrine insists, distinguish between espousals of racial equality and espousals of racial hatred, nor may the government prohibit public denials of the factuality of the Holocaust just because of the demonstrable falsity of that proposition and the harm that would ensue from its public articulation.

Some of the American aversion to discriminating against speech because of its point of view, including racist points of view, was spawned when the Supreme Court in 1969 established the still-prevailing test distinguishing permitted advocacy from regulable incitement. Advocacy even of illegal conduct, the Court held, was protected by the First Amendment, and only if that advocacy was explicitly directed to urging "imminent" lawless acts in a context in which such imminent lawless acts were "likely" — essentially standing in front of an angry mob and verbally leading them to immediate violence — could the constraints of the First Amendment be overridden. This doctrine applies to the full range of public political or ideological utterances, but for our purposes what is most important is that the doctrine was created in the context of a case [*Brandenburg v. Ohio*, 395 U.S. 444 (1969)] in which Clarence Brandenburg, a local leader of the Ku Klux Klan in southern Ohio, had called for acts of "revengance" against African Americans and Jews. But because Brandenburg's advocacy fell short of explicitly urging "imminent" unlawful acts in a context in which those unlawful acts were "likely," his speech was held to be constitutionally immune from criminal (and, almost certainly, civil as well) punishment. In the context of hate speech, therefore, *Brandenburg* stands for the proposition that in the United States restrictions on the incitement of racial hatred can be countenanced under the First Amendment only when they are incitements to *violent* racial hatred, and even then only under the rare circumstances in which the incitements unmistakably call for immediate violent action, and even then only under the more rare still circumstances in which members of the listening audience are in fact likely immediately to act upon the speaker's suggestion.... Jean Le Pen could not be sanctioned in the United States, as he was in France, for accusing Jews of exaggerating the Holocaust, nor could Brigitte Bardot be fined in the United States, as she was in France, for crusading against Islam and urging the deportation of those of Arab-ethnicity. Ernst Zundel and James Keegstra can be charged with crimes in Canada for denying the Holocaust, but not in the United States.

The distinction between American practice and that in other liberal democracies, exists not only with respect to incitement, but also with respect to racial epithets and insults intended not to rally or motivate the speaker's allies but rather to cause psychic harm and mental distress to those to whom the words are directed. When Frank Cohn, then the leader of the American Nazi Party, proposed in 1977 to march with his followers, in full Nazi regalia, in Skokie, Illinois, a community disproportionately populated by survivors of the Holocaust, both the state and federal courts made clear that under the First Amendment there was no plausible cause for prohibiting the march. More recent cases involving racial intimidation, membership in racist groups, and restrictions on racist speech on university campuses have all emphasized that this form of "hate speech" will not be treated differently under the First Amendment... from any other viewpoint or any other form of public offensiveness.... In much of the developed world one uses racial epithets at one's legal peril, one displays Nazi regalia and the other trappings of ethnic hatred at significant legal risk, and one urges discrimination against religious minorities under threat of fine or imprisonment, but in the United States all such speech remains constitutionally protected.

The divergence between American and international approaches to freedom of expression is hardly unique to the issue of hate speech. A similar divergence, for example, exists between American and non-American free speech and free press understandings with respect to defamation law — the law of libel (written) and slander (spoken). Traditionally, the United States shared with the rest of the common law world an English law heritage in which defamation was treated as a strict liability tort. In order to win a lawsuit and recover money damages, a person suing for libel or slander needed only to prove by a bare preponderance of the evidence (the normal burden of proof in civil, as opposed to criminal, cases) that the defendant had uttered (or, more commonly, published) words tending to injure the alleged victim's reputation. The plaintiff/victim was not required to prove that the defendant/publisher was negligent or in any other way at fault, and indeed the plaintiff did not even have to prove that the imputation was false. The defendant could, to be sure, prevent recovery by asserting an affirmative defense and showing that the words were true ... but the fact that the burden of proof was on the publisher to demonstrate truth rather than on the target to demonstrate falsity underscores the way in which the common law of defamation traditionally embodied the view that one published at one's peril....

The United States departed dramatically from this tradition in 1964. In *New York Times* Co. *v. Sullivan* [376 U.S. 264 (1964)], the Supreme Court, in the name of the First Amendment, constitutionalized what had previously been the constitutionally untouched common law of defamation, concluding that actions for libel and slander brought by public officials could succeed only upon proof by clear and convincing evidence (and not merely by a preponderance of the evidence, as would be the case in other civil actions) of *intentional* falsity, a burden of proof almost impossible to meet. To the Supreme Court, the traditional common law approach imposed all of the risk of falsity upon the publisher, making publishers wary of publishing even those charges that turned out to be true. This phenomenon, now widely labeled "the chilling effect," was to the Court inconsistent with a First Amendment part of whose goal was to encourage exposing and thus checking the abuses of those in power. Although requiring intentional falsity to sustain liability would undoubtedly increase the amount of published falsehood, this error, the Court implicitly concluded, was far less grave than the opposite error of inhibiting the publication of political truth. And even if some of what would be published under the new rule turned out to be vituperative and uncivil, this was only to be expected, for the common law approach was inconsistent with a First Amendment centered on the importance of "uninhibited," "robust," and "wide-open" public debate.

In the ensuing years, the Supreme Court has refused to back away from the *Sullivan* approach and has indeed substantially extended it. A few years after *Sullivan* it applied its basic holding to candidates for public office as well as to office holders, and, more surprisingly and more significantly, to public figures as well as to public officials, even to those public figures — pop stars, television chefs, and professional athletes, for example — who have little to no involvement in or effect on public policy or political debates. The Court then required that even private individuals prove negligence in order to prevail, and thus by 1975 the constitutionalization of American defamation law was complete.... For all practical purposes the availability in the United States of defamation remedies for public officials and public figures, even in cases of provable falsity, has come to an end.

Largely through the efforts of journalists, newspapers, and their lawyers, there has been an active effort to persuade other countries to adopt the American approach, and to conclude that the harm of unpublished truth about public officials and public figures is far greater than the harm of unsanctioned falsity. Yet although these efforts have been successful in moving most common law countries slightly away from the strictest version of the common law model, and in securing some modifications of analogous remedies even in civil law countries, the overwhelming reaction of the rest of the world to the American approach has been negative. In Australia, New Zealand, Canada, the United Kingdom, and a number of other countries, the unalloyed American approach has been rejected....

... In disputes over the persistent and inevitable conflict between freedom of the press to report on criminal prosecutions and the right of the accused to a fair trial uninfluenced by potentially inflammatory pretrial and midtrial publicity, the United States favors the former over the latter to a degree unmatched in the world. In much of the rest of the world, press restrictions, often under the label of sanctions for "contempt," are acceptable as means to preserve the sanctity of the trial process, but in the United States considerable interference with that sanctity is tolerated so that trials, no less than other governmental processes, are open for all that is best and worst about press coverage and public scrutiny. In the same vein, disputes between the interest in privacy of victims of crimes and the interest of the press in reporting on criminal proceedings are typically resolved in favor of the press and against the victim's privacy.

...

... Where in the rest of the world freedom of expression appears to be understood as an important value to be considered along with other important values of fairness, equality, dignity, health, privacy, safety and respect, among others, in the United States the freedom of expression occupies pride of place, prevailing with remarkable consistency in its conflicts with even the most profound of other values and the most important of other interests.

QUESTION

What historical and other factors come to mind that could help to explain the significant differences between European (and other) countries and the US with respect to defining the boundaries of free speech in relation to competing interests and concerns?

COMMENT ON BLASPHEMY CASES

In *Otto-Preminger-Institut v. Austria*, Ser. A, 295-A, 1994, the European Court of Human Rights decided by 6 votes to 3 that the seizure and forfeiture of a blasphemous film did not violate the freedom of expression guaranteed by Article 10 of the

European Convention. The applicant association had advertised the screening of the film, *Das Liebeskonzil*, based on an 1894 play, which:

> . . . portrays the God of the Jewish religion, the Christian religion and the Islamic religion as an apparently senile old man prostrating himself before the devil with whom he exchanges a deep kiss and calling the devil his friend. . . . Other scenes show the Virgin Mary permitting an obscene story to be read to her and the manifestation of a degree of erotic tension between the Virgin Mary and the devil. The adult Jesus Christ is portrayed as a low grade mental defective and in one scene is shown lasciviously attempting to fondle and kiss his mother's breasts, which she is shown as permitting.

The film was presented by the association as a 'satirical tragedy'. 'Trivial imagery and absurdities of the Christian creed are targeted in a caricatural mode and the relationship between religious beliefs and worldly mechanisms of oppression is investigated.' The Innsbruck Regional Court in Austria ordered seizure and forfeiture of the film under Section 188 of the Austrian Penal Code for the criminal offence of 'disparaging religious precepts'. The criminal proceedings against the association were eventually dropped.

Since there was no dispute that the seizure constituted an interference with the association's freedom of expression, the European Court considered whether the seizure was permissible under the conditions set by of Article 10, paragraph 2. The Court concluded that the interference had the 'legitimate aim' of protecting the rights of others to freedom of religion. Interpreting Article 9 of the Convention to include the right to respect for one's religious feelings, the Court found that such considerations outweighed the film's contribution to public debate. The Court reasoned:

> The respect for the religious feelings of believers as guaranteed in Article 9 can legitimately thought to have been violated by provocative portrayals of objects of religious veneration; and such portrayals can be regarded as malicious violation of the spirit of tolerance, which must also be a feature of democratic society. The Convention is to be read as a whole and therefore the interpretation and application of Article 10 in the present case must be in harmony with the logic of the Convention. . . . [T]he Court accepts that the impugned measures pursued a legitimate aim under Article 10 para. 2, namely 'the protection of the rights of others'.

The Court stressed that freedom of expression applies not only to ideas that are favourably received, but also to those 'that shock, offend or disturb the State or any sector of the population. Such are the demands of that pluralism, tolerance and broadmindedness without which there is no "democratic society."' Nonetheless, people exercising their rights under Article 10 were subject to duties, among which could legitimately be included 'an obligation to avoid as far as possible expressions that are gratuitously offensive to others and thus an infringement of their rights, and which therefore do not contribute to any form of public debate capable of further progress in human affairs'.

The Court determined that the seizure could be considered 'necessary in a democratic society'. There was no 'uniform conception of the significance of religion in society' throughout Europe, 'even within a single country'. A 'certain margin of appreciation is therefore to be left to the national authorities in assessing the existence and extent of the necessity of such interference'. It is 'for the national authorities, who are better placed than the international judge, to assess the need for such a measure in the light of the situation obtaining locally'. Given that the Tyrolean population was 87 per cent Roman Catholic, the Court found that the Austrian authorities had acted within their margin of appreciation 'to ensure religious peace in that region and to prevent that some people should feel the object of attacks on their religious beliefs in an unwarranted and offensive manner'.

Three judges dissented. Given the precautions against offence to viewers taken by the association through a warning announcement, the showing of the film to a paid audience only, and the restriction of viewing to those over 17 years of age, the dissent found the seizure and forfeiture to be disproportionate to the aim pursued, and thus not necessary in a democratic society.

❁ ❁ ❁

In *Wingrove v. United Kingdom*, European Court of Human Rights, 1996, Rep. 1996-V, fasc. 23, a film director who was a British national brought a complaint before the European Commission alleging that the United Kingdom had violated Article 10 by interfering with the director's freedom of expression through refusing to grant a distribution certificate for the director's 18-minute video work, *Visions of Ecstasy*. The video work involved visions of St. Teresa about the crucified Christ, and in the view of the British Board of Film Classification, drew Christ graphically into the erotic desire of St. Teresa. The refusal to grant the certificate was based on the Board's conclusion that the video constituted blasphemy, defined in a recent case as 'any contemptuous, reviling, scurrilous or ludicrous matter related to God, Jesus Christ or the Bible'. The decision was upheld by the Video Appeals Committee.

The European Commission expressed the opinion in a 14–2 vote that there had been a violation of Article 10. The Commission and the United Kingdom brought the case before the European Court, which concluded by a 7–2 vote that there had been no violation of Article 10. Some of its observations about the requirement in Article 10 that a restriction be 'necessary in a democratic society' follow:

> 57. The Court observes that the refusal to grant Visions of Ecstasy a distribution certificate was intended to protect 'the rights of others', and more specifically to provide protection against seriously offensive attacks on matters regarded as sacred by Christians. . . .
>
> . . . [B]lasphemy legislation is still in force in various European countries. It is true that the application of these laws has become increasingly rare and that several States have recently repealed them altogether. . . . Strong arguments have been advanced in favour of the abolition of blasphemy laws, for example, that such laws may discriminate against different faiths or denominations. . . . However, the fact remains that there is as yet not sufficient common ground in the legal and social orders of the member States of the Council of Europe to conclude that a system whereby a State can impose restrictions on the propagation of material on the

> basis that it is blasphemous is, in itself, unnecessary in a democratic society and thus incompatible with the Convention....
>
> 58. Whereas there is little scope under Article 10 para. 2 of the Convention for restrictions on political speech or on debate of questions of public interest, ... a wider margin of appreciation is generally available to the Contracting States when regulating freedom of expression in relation to matters liable to offend intimate personal convictions within the sphere of morals or, especially, religion. Moreover, as in the field of morals, and perhaps to an even greater degree, there is no uniform European conception of the requirements of 'the protection of the rights of others' in relation to attacks on their religious convictions. What is likely to cause substantial offence to persons of a particular religious persuasion will vary significantly from time to time and from place to place, especially in an era characterised by an ever growing array of faiths and denominations. By reason of their direct and continuous contact with the vital forces of their countries, State authorities are in principle in a better position than the international judge to give an opinion on the exact content of these requirements with regard to the rights of others as well as on the 'necessity' of a 'restriction' intended to protect from such material those whose deepest feelings and convictions would be seriously offended....
>
> This does not of course exclude final European supervision. Such supervision is all the more necessary given the breadth and open-endedness of the notion of blasphemy and the risks of arbitrary or excessive interferences with freedom of expression under the guise of action taken against allegedly blasphemous material. ... Moreover the fact that the present case involves prior restraint calls for special scrutiny by the Court....

The Court (para. 50) also considered the fact that the English law of blasphemy 'only extends to the Christian faith'. It was not, however, for the European Court 'to rule *in abstracto*' about the compatibility of British law with the Convention. 'The extent to which English law protects other beliefs is not in issue before the Court which must confine its attention to the case before it.... The uncontested fact that the law of blasphemy does not treat on an equal footing the different religions practised in the United Kingdom does not detract from the legitimacy of the aim pursued in the present context'. A concurring opinion of Judge Pettiti observed that the Convention left 'scope for review under Article 14. In the present case no complaint had been made to the European Court under that article'.

A dissenting opinion of Judge Lohmus noted that the law of blasphemy 'only protects the Christian religion and, more specifically, the established Church of England.... This in itself raises the question whether the interference was (in the language of Article 10) "necessary in a democratic society".'

QUESTIONS

1. How do these opinions resolve the question of who in the liberal state must show tolerance to whom? Must the majority put up with the minority's views and modes of expression (at least where those views and expressions are not 'forced' on the majority

through unavoidable public acts)? Or is it the minority that must take account of the majority's sensibility and refrain from offending it?

2. During the colonial period, the British colonial government in India enacted several laws as part of the Indian Penal Code that defined offences including 'defiling a place of worship', 'acts insulting religion or religious beliefs', 'disturbing a religious assembly', 'trespassing on burial grounds', and 'utterances wounding religious feelings'. Punishments were a maximum of two years imprisonment, a fine, or both.

These laws were amended or supplemented by the Government of Pakistan. Section 295-B of the Pakistan Penal Code, added in 1982, provided:

> Whoever willfully defiles, damages or desecrates a copy of the Holy Quran or an extract therefrom or uses it in any derogatory manner or for any unlawful purpose shall be punishable with imprisonment for life.

Section 295-C was enacted in 1986. It stated:

> Whoever by words, either spoken or written, or by any visible representation, or by any imputation, innuendo, or insinuation, directly or indirectly, defiles the sacred name of the Holy Prophet Mohammed (peace be upon him) shall be punished with death, or imprisonment for life and shall also be liable to fine.

Compare the Pakistani statutes with the laws and action described in the *Otto-Preminger-Institut* and *Wingrove* cases. What are the salient differences? How would the Pakistani statutes be judged under the European Convention?

NOTE

The final materials in this section 4 concern the publication in a Danish newspaper in September 2005 of cartoons that proved to be offensive to a number of Muslim countries and that led in January 2006 to popular demonstrations and violent protests in those countries. The cartoons consisted of unflattering and mocking notions about Muslims and caricatures of the Prophet Mohammed, including a cartoon portraying Mohammed wearing a turban in the shape of a bomb ready to explode — an obvious reference to Muslim terrorist and other bellicose and dangerous groups. The protests were the stronger because many Muslims understand that Islam bans any image, let alone caricatures, of the Prophet; such images are often viewed as blasphemous. The controversy led in some instances to a break in diplomatic relations between an Arab state and Denmark, and to death threats made to those responsible for the publications. The cartoons were republished by newspapers in several European countries, including France and Germany, and were rapidly available on the Internet.

The entire episode drew substantial comment from diverse sources in the Arab and Western worlds, examples of which appear in the readings below. In a comment entitled 'No Laughing Matter', in Findlaw, Feb. 15, 2006 (http://writ.news.findlaw.com/commentary/20060215_teitel.html), Ruti Teitel observes:

> Many people saw the cartoons as ... exhibiting intolerance toward those whose religion is Islam. ... To understand why so many Muslims were so gravely

offended, it is important to see that the cartoons don't stand alone, but rather were published against a backdrop of political and legislative action that, to many Muslims, reflects a repeated pattern of disparagement of Islam in the public sphere. At present, Europe is struggling with issues of identity.... The crisis arises because of new demographics, at the same time as new regionalism. Many Muslims feel they are being relegated to second-class citizenship in Europe. And they relate the publication of the cartoons — by a newspaper they feel would not consider publishing anti-Christian or anti-Jewish cartoons — to this wrongful sense that they are not full citizens.

NEWSPAPER REPORTS ON MUSLIM REACTION TO CARTOONS ABOUT MOHAMMED

There follow excerpts from several articles.

Dan Bilefsky, Denmark is Unlikely Front in Islam-West Culture War

New York Times, **January 8, 2006, Sec. 1, p. 3**

The cartoons were published amid the growth of an anti-immigrant sentiment in Denmark, reflected in the rise of the far-right Danish People's Party....

Soren Krarup, a retired priest and leading voice in the party, said the Muslim response to the cartoons showed that Islam was not compatible with Danish customs. He said Jesus had been satirized in Danish literature and popular culture for centuries — including a recent much-publicized Danish painting of Jesus with an erection — so why not Muhammad? He also argues that Muslims must learn to integrate. "Muslims who come here reject our culture," he said. "Muslim immigration is a way for Muslims to conquer us, just as they have done for the past 1,400 years."

Muslim leaders say that such talk helped create the atmosphere that allowed the cartoons to be published. And they contend that it is alienating the people the Danish People's Party says it wants to assimilate.

...

Mr. Rose, the editor [of the paper publishing the cartoons], said free speech, no matter how radical, should be allowed to flourish, from all varieties of perspectives. "Muslims should be allowed to burn the Danish flag in a public square if that's within the boundaries of the law," he said.

Alan Cowell, More European Papers Print Cartoons of Muhammad, Fueling Dipuste with Muslims

New York Times, **February 2, 2006, p. A12**

...

Indeed, the culture editor, Flemming Rose, said in an interview: 'This is a far bigger story than just the question of 12 cartoons in a small Danish newspaper. This is about the question of integration and how compatible is the religion of Islam with a modern secular society — how much does an immigrant have to give up and how much does the receiving culture have to compromise.'

In recent days, Denmark has become the object of a widespread boycott of its goods in Muslim countries, its diplomats have been summoned to be dressed down in Tehran and Baghdad, and protesters have taken to the streets of Gaza.

The Danish prime minister, Anders Fogh Rasmussen, has rejected demands by Arab governments for an official apology, saying: "I can't call a newspaper and tell them what to put in it. That's not how our society works."

...

In support of the Danish position, newspapers in France, Germany, Italy, the Netherlands, Spain and Switzerland reprinted some of the cartoons on Wednesday....

...

Robert Menard, the secretary general of Reporters Without Borders, a Paris-based body that monitors media developments, said in a telephone interview: "All countries in Europe should be behind the Danes and Danish authorities to defend the principle that a newspaper can write what it wishes to, even if it offends people. I understand that it may shock Muslims, but being shocked is part of the price of being informed."

...

In Germany, the conservative Die Welt printed one image on its front page and declared in an editorial: "The protests from Muslims would be taken more seriously if they were less hypocritical. When Syrian television showed drama documentaries in prime time depicting rabbis as cannibals, the imams were quiet."

...

Craig Smith and Ian Fisher, Temperatures Rise over Cartoons Mocking Muhammad

***New York Times*, February 3, 2006, p. A3**

A newly elected legislator from Hamas, the radical Islamic group that swept the Palestinian elections last week, said large rallies were planned in Gaza in the next few days ... "We are angry — very, very, very angry," said the legislator, Jamila al-Shanty. "No one can say a bad word about our prophet."

... Islam is Europe's fastest growing religion and is now the second largest religion in most European countries. Racial and religious discrimination against Muslims in Europe's weakest economies adds to the strains.

...

Most European commentators concede that the cartoons were in poor taste but argue that conservative Muslims must learn to accept Western standards of free speech and the pluralism that those standards protect.

Several accused Muslims of a double standard, noting that media in several Arab countries continue to broadcast or publish references to "The Protocols of the Elders of Zion," a notorious early 20th-century anti-Semitic hoax that presented itself as the Jews' master plan to rule the world.

...

Afghanistan's president, Hamid Karzai, issued a statement condemning "in the strongest terms" France Soir's publication of the cartoons. "Any insult to the holy prophet (peace be upon him) is an insult to more than one billion Muslims," his statement read.

...

AP, Outcry over Prophet Cartoons Grows Louder and More Violent

New York Times, February 5, 2006, Sec. 1, p. 10

Thousands of Syrians enraged by caricatures of Islam's revered prophet torched the Danish and Norwegian embassies in Damascus on Saturday — the most violent in days of furious protests by Muslims in Asia, Europe and the Middle East. In Gaza, Palestinians marched through the streets, storming European buildings and burning German and Danish flags. Protesters smashed the windows of the German cultural center and threw stones at the European Commission building, the police said.

...

The Vatican deplored the violence but said certain provocative forms of criticism were unacceptable. "The right to freedom of thought and expression cannot entail the right to offend the religious sentiment of believers," the Vatican said in its first statement on the controversy.

...

Carlotta Gall and Craig Smith, Muslim Protests against Cartoons Spread

New York Times, February 7, 2006, p. A8

...

Arab governments have met the growing wave of protests with tacit acceptance, if not support, while seeking to prevent violence.

Qatar's Chamber of Commerce said it had halted dealings with Danish and Norwegian delegations, urging other Muslim states to follow suit. In cities where protests are unheard of, like Dubai, demonstrations against Denmark have been held openly. In some, demonstrators were bused in, paid for by the government. An official at a religious affairs ministry in the United Arab Emirates, speaking on condition of anonymity, said: "You have no choice but to join the chorus. Anyone who doesn't speak up will look as if they tacitly accept the prophet to be insulted."

...

John Vinocur and Dan Bilefsky, Dane Sees Greed and Politics in Crisis

New York Times, February 9, 2006, p. A9

Prime Minister Anders Fogh Rasmussen said Thursday that attempts by European companies in the Middle East to disassociate themselves from Denmark or Danish products were "disgraceful."

...

... Mr. Rasmussen reiterated that there would be no Danish apology for the cartoons. He brushed aside any suggestion that Denmark's policies requiring immigrants to accommodate themselves to Danish tradition were at fault, and asserted, "We are on the right track." More broadly, he said, "I see a very clear tendency that other European countries will go in our direction."

...

Mr. Rasmussen said he believed that Islam was compatible with democracy but argued that it was incumbent on Muslim immigrants in Denmark and Europe in general to embrace the liberal values of their adopted countries.

"Denmark is a liberal country," he said. "We do believe in individual liberty and freedom. People can live according to their own customs. However, I think we have to insist on respecting our core values, including freedom of expression, gender equality for women and men, and a clear distinction between politics and religion."

...

Robert Wright, The Silent Treatment

***New York Times*, February 17, 2006, p. A23**

...

... The Muslim uproar over those Danish cartoons isn't as alien to American culture as we like to think. Once you see this, a benign and quintessentially American response comes into view. Even many Americans who condemn the cartoon's publication accept the premise that the now-famous Danish newspaper editor set out to demonstrate: in the West we don't generally let interest groups intimidate us into what he called "self-censorship." What nonsense.

...

... [S]o many of the grievances coalesce in a sense that Muslims aren't respected by the affluent, powerful West (just as rioting American blacks felt they weren't respected by affluent, powerful whites.) A cartoon that disrespects Islam by ridiculing Muhammad is both trigger and extremely high octane fuel.

None of this is to say that there aren't big differences between American culture and culture in many Muslim parts of the world.... What isn't a big difference is the Muslim demand for self-censorship by major media outlets. That kind of self-censorship is not just an American tradition, but a tradition that has helped make American one of the most harmonious multiethnic and multireligious societies in the history of the world.

RONALD DWORKIN, EVEN BIGOTS AND HOLOCAUST DENIERS MUST HAVE THEIR SAY

***The Guardian*, 14 February 2006**

The British media were right, on balance, not to republish the Danish cartoons that millions of furious Muslims protested against in violent and terrible destruction around the world. Reprinting would very likely have meant more people killed and more property destroyed. It would have caused many British Muslims great pain. . . . [T]he public does not have a right to read or see whatever it wants no matter what the cost, and the cartoons are in any case widely available on the internet.

There is a real danger, however, that the decision of British media not to publish, though wise, will be wrongly taken as an endorsement of the widely held opinion that freedom of speech has limits, that it must be balanced against the virtues of multiculturalism, and that the government was right after all to propose that it be made a crime to publish anything "abusive or insulting" to a religious group. Freedom of speech is not just a special and distinctive emblem of western culture that might be generously abridged or qualified as a measure of respect for other cultures that reject it, the way a crescent or menorah might be added to a Christian religious display. Free speech is a condition of legitimate government. Laws and policies are not legitimate unless they have been adopted through a democratic process, and a process is not democratic if government has prevented anyone from expressing his convictions about what those laws and policies should be. Ridicule is a distinct kind of expression; its substance cannot be repackaged in a less offensive rhetorical form without expressing something very different from what was intended. That is why cartoons and other forms of ridicule have for centuries, even when illegal, been among the most important weapons of both noble and wicked political movements.

So in a democracy no one, however powerful or impotent, can have a right not to be insulted or offended. That principle is of particular importance in a nation that strives for racial and ethnic fairness. If weak or unpopular minorities wish to be protected from economic or legal discrimination by law — if they wish laws enacted that prohibit discrimination against them in employment, for instance — then they must be willing to tolerate whatever insults or ridicule people who oppose such legislation wish to offer to their fellow voters, because only a community that permits such insult may legitimately adopt such laws. If we expect bigots to accept the verdict of the majority once the majority has spoken, then we must permit them to express their bigotry in the process whose verdict we ask them to respect. Whatever multiculturalism means — whatever it means to call for increased "respect" for all citizens and groups — these virtues would be self-defeating if they were thought to justify official censorship.

Muslims who are outraged by the Danish cartoons point out that in several European countries it is a crime publicly to deny, as the president of Iran has denied, that the Holocaust ever took place. They say that western concern for free speech is therefore only self-serving hypocrisy, and they have a point. But of course the remedy is not to make the compromise of democratic legitimacy even greater than it already is but to work toward a new understanding of the European convention on human rights that would strike down the Holocaust-denial law and similar laws across Europe for what they are: violations of the freedom of speech that that convention demands.

It is often said that religion is special, because people's religious convictions are so central to their personalities that they should not be asked to tolerate ridicule in that dimension, and because they might feel a religious duty to strike back at what they take to be sacrilege. Britain has apparently embraced that view because it retains the crime of blasphemy, though only for insults to Christianity. But we cannot make an exception for religious insult if we want to use law to protect the free exercise of religion in other ways. If we want to forbid the police from profiling people who look or dress like Muslims for special searches, for example, we cannot also forbid people from opposing that policy by claiming, in cartoons or otherwise, that Islam is committed to terrorism, however silly we think that opinion is. Religion must be tailored to democracy, not the other way around. No religion can be permitted to legislate for everyone about what can or cannot be drawn any more than it can legislate about what may or may not be eaten. No one's religious convictions can be thought to trump the freedom that makes democracy possible.

NOTE

An article in the *Boston Sunday Globe*, 'A Test of Principles, not Presidents', January 22, 2006, p. A1, reported that the Office of Citizenship in the State Department was designing a new test for immigrants seeking citizenship through naturalization. Current requirements include proof of their ability to read, write and speak English, and to answer correctly six of ten questions on the present test. The questions required such information as knowing the colors of the stars in the U.S. flag, or who becomes president if the president and vice-president both die while in office. The Government now finds such testing 'trivial,' largely because the examination 'tests only their ability to memorize answers.' The new test to be designed will be first used in 2008. 'It will ask aspiring citizens about what it means to be American, rather than quiz them on picayune facts. Officials say that it is more important to ask immigrants about such principles as freedom of speech and religion. . . .' Alfonso Aguilar, chief of the Office of Citizenship, described the goal of the new text to be producing citizens who are more involved, more aware of their rights and responsibilities, and more American. He said: 'We want to celebrate diversity and encourage the common values that link every American. . . .Immigrants who embrace those values become fully American.'

QUESTIONS

1. What provisions of the ICCPR could you have relied on to seek relief for the publication in a European country of the cartoons? Would it be relevant if you were a resident Muslim in such a country or were a national and resident of a Middle Eastern country?

2. Do you agree with the views expressed by Dworkin?

ADDITIONAL READING

John Bowen, *Why the French Don't Like Headscarves* (2006); Sandra Coliver (ed.), *Striking a Balance: Hate Speech, Freedom of Expression and Non-Discrimination* (1992); Kent Greenawalt, *Fighting Words: Individuals, Communities, and Liberties of Speech* (1995); S. Douglas-Scott, 'The Hatefulness of Protected Speech: A Comparison of the American and European Approaches', 7 Wm. & Mary Bill of Rts. J. 305 (1999); Kent Greenawalt, *Fighting Words: Individuals, Communities, and Liberties of Speech* (1995); Michael Rosenfeld, 'Hate Speech in Comparative Perspective', 24 Cardozo L. Rev. 1523 (2003).

PART D

INTERNATIONAL HUMAN RIGHTS ORGANIZATIONS

Part D turns to an examination of the international organizations embodying, developing, monitoring and enforcing the rules and standards of the human rights movement whose character and evolution were explored in the preceding chapters. The creation of organizations by the movement has been among its most striking and important features. None of the institutions discussed in Part D existed before the end of the Second World War. Some have become operational only in the last few decades. The youth of the movement becomes more apparent as we move our attention from norms to institutions.

Neither Parts B nor D can fully exclude the other and become an airtight compartment. Norms and institutions are too intricately and fundamentally connected. Several UN organs necessarily figured in the discussion in Chapters 2 and 3 of the development of the UDHR, ICCPR and CEDAW, as well as in the discussion in Chapter 4 of the ICESCR. They did so because standard-setting, the grandest achievement of the human rights movement's first half century, began within the new institutions — drafting by the UN Commission on Human Rights, for example. Similarly, the materials in Part D, though stressing institutions' role in the implementation of treaties, necessarily involve their law-making powers as well through their interpretive comments on treaty texts and the dispute-resolving decisions by international committees or courts that stem from such texts.

Nonetheless our concerns here sharply change. These new chapters look at institutions as such: constitutional structures, processes, functions, powers. Above all, the chapters are concerned with institutions' role in elaboration, implementation, application and enforcement rather than standard-setting.

Part D examines intergovernmental organizations, both universal and regional in scope, whose work involves primarily international human rights. Inevitably its materials pose broader issues about international organizations or institutions in general, whatever their fields of specialization. An analogy to Part A is pertinent. There we gave some attention to characteristics of international law as such, as essential background to the study of international human rights norms. Here too, particularly in Chapter 8, we give brief attention to characteristics of international organizations as such. Chapters 9 to 11 start with the UN Charter human rights organs (or bodies), continue with treaty bodies, and move to regional human rights organizations in Europe, the Americas and Africa.

8

Design and Functions of International Institutions, and Issues of Sovereignty

The international institutions and organs examined in Part D were created by multilateral treaties or derive their authority and legitimacy from decisions taken within the framework of those treaties. Customary international law cannot create institutions. These materials explore the more developed and complex institutional arrangements, going well beyond the kind of rudimentary organization created by a multilateral treaty that, say, provides only for periodic meetings of states parties to exchange views on certain matters or to draft conventions to be submitted to states for ratification.

The principal treaties relevant to Part D — the UN Charter, the ICCPR and its Optional Protocol, and the treaties creating the three regional human rights systems — each creates a distinctive human rights regime involving both norms and one or more treaty organs intended to perform stated functions by exercising stated powers. To one or another extent, that regime (or organization) takes on a life of its own. It will have one or many of such attributes as its own officials, staff and budget. Despite its pervasive links with the states parties creating it (parties that are directly represented in the membership of many Charter organs such as the UN General Assembly), the regime or organization can be meaningfully considered separately from those parties (unlike, say, the 'rudimentary' form of organization described above). If in some major respects it depends entirely on the states parties' 'will' as expressed in voting or other forms of decision-making, in other major respects the regime/organization possesses autonomy. Thus a regime organ like the Human Rights Council or the European Court of Human Rights becomes a significant participant in international relations, expanding on the traditional international system of sovereign states and qualitatively changing the nature of international law and life.

Bear in mind that Chapter 8 examines almost exclusively international *governmental* organizations (IGOs), though the text refers occasionally to activities of *nongovernmental* organizations (NGOs) as well. Starting with Chapter 1, the book has frequently examined aspects of the work of NGOs, perhaps an NGO working exclusively in one country (the American Civil Liberties Union in the US, thousands of such human rights organizations throughout the world engaged only in their country of organization) or in several countries (Amnesty International and Human

Rights Watch, for example, sometimes referred to as international non-governmental organizations, or INGOs). Preceding chapters have looked at such typical NGO activities as investigating, monitoring and reporting on violations; advocating before international human rights organs (such as the Human Rights Council) or national organs (such as Congressional committees or an executive department in the US) in favour of a given human rights policy or sanction; and publishing systematic analyses of particular problems often accompanied by proposals for policies responding to them. The book examines aspects of the structure and decision-making processes of NGOs in general at p. 1420, *infra*.

A. CHARACTERISTICS OF IGOs WITHIN THE HUMAN RIGHTS MOVEMENT

Form and function obviously bear some relationship in the creation of IGOs. An organization created to monitor, implement and develop rules governing trade among treaty parties, and perhaps to resolve disputes under the treaty as well, may have little in common with a peacekeeping organization, an environmental or public health organization, or a human rights organization. On the other hand, the kind of regime that an international organization may in some sense 'govern' hardly *determines* its structure, functions, and powers, or indeed the powers exercised by the membership of states parties to the treaty. Nor does it determine the duties, if any, owed by member states to certain decisions of the organization — similar perhaps to the duties of states to comply with decisions taken by the UN Security Council under Chapter VII of the Charter.

Of course much depends on states' diverging interests in constructing one or another kind of organization, with respect to such fundamental matters as the power exercised over member states by the IGO or the functions that it is charged with. Inevitably the final agreement over the organization will reflect the distribution of power among states, and among blocs of states, whose interests differ. Negotiations are apt to be tough and exacting, sometimes as much or more so over institutional arrangements and powers as over a treaty's substantive provisions. To be sure, questions about the IGO's functions or powers are not definitively resolved by the text of the agreement, for ambiguities (which may have been left in the text intentionally because of the difficulty in then resolving them) and the inevitable uncertainty of language and meaning in changing contexts will require later interpretation as issues arise. Indeed, the question of who if anyone — perhaps an organ within the IGO, perhaps a specified number of member states through further agreement — has the authority to interpret the treaty authoritatively so as to 'bind' all member states will characteristically be one of the major issues in the initial negotiation.

Section A introduces Part D with two readings. The first identifies distinctive characteristics of international human rights in relation to other fields of international law and suggests ways in which those characteristics will inevitably influence how an IGO is constructed. The second analyses characteristics of IGOs themselves, in human rights and other fields, to underscore how deeply their large number and many uses and modes of operation have changed fundamental aspects of international law and relations.

HENRY STEINER, INTERNATIONAL PROTECTION OF HUMAN RIGHTS

in Malcolm Evans (ed.), International Law (2nd edn. 2006), 753

...

II. The Kinds of Protection Provided by International Organizations

A. Why Create International Organizations

Is it necessary or even useful to create intergovernmental human rights organizations (IGOs) to debate, interpret, develop and apply customary and treaty law? Are not matters like implementation and protection better left in the hands of governments and civil society in the different States, particularly since human rights issues are imbedded in national (and sub-national, local) governments, traditions, and cultures? In such respects, the field of human rights differs from situations presented, for example, by international trade or environmental law, where a State's violation of a treaty adversely affects other treaty parties' interests as or (usually) more severely than it does its own population. In such treaty regimes based on reciprocity, the relevant issues about trade or environment may be very significant for a State but are not rooted in its political structures, traditional practices, and cultural underpinnings. Unlike many human rights issues, they only rarely implicate constitutional principles and text. Hence enforcement of treaty commitments and dispute settlement may more readily be entrusted to IGOs.

These doubts become the more plausible when we take into account that standard-setting by itself — the declarations and treaties that dominated the early decades of the human rights movement, and the related spread to interest groups, media and the general population of this new discourse of international human rights — will advance the cause of human rights. The internalization and constitutionalization of treaty norms by many States has made those norms a key ingredient of the domestic legal system. They become institutionalized, and infiltrate political and popular debate. In the longer run, they will influence how some or many people think about issues.

As a consequence, human rights advocates and politically mobilized groups may come to base their demands for political and social change primarily on the State's international commitment and internal law responsive to treaty commitments. Disaffected citizens can invoke the State's own words against it rather than invoke only 'foreign' or 'international' texts or the more amorphous customary international law, all of which the State may have ignored or explicitly rejected. The gap between the treaty commitment and government policy, between assurance of human rights norms and peoples' precarious lives, becomes strikingly and publicly apparent. The resulting cognitive dissonance as official state norms clash with state conduct may itself generate unrest and demands for change. In such ways, the treaty text itself can serve to empower a population, spur demands for reform, and heighten the pressure on a State....

One can question the need for IGOs from another perspective. We can imagine a world where all States are committed in good faith to observe human rights, and hence where international organizations would be unnecessary. But even in this ideal world, disputes will inevitably arise over questions of interpretation stemming from conflicts between rights, diverse political and cultural understandings about the meaning of a term in the treaties, and the effect of such changed circumstances as the end of the Cold War on the human rights corpus. IGOs appear at least useful, perhaps essential, to contribute to resolving such disputes. The possibilities range from merely a forum for States to explore such disputes, to an international court whose opinions could have an advisory character or stand as judgments binding on respondent States.

More to the point, the assumption of a good-faith commitment of all States to a human rights regime defies our knowledge of the world and of the human rights movement's history. Massive violations of basic physical security norms including genocide have captured the world's attention. Cambodia and Rwanda offer extreme examples. As most of these episodes demonstrate, we have no basis for relying on other States to apply economic or military force against such systemic violations, whether unilaterally or through coordinated action — let alone against delinquent States committing less dramatic violations of rights, perhaps related to a free press or imprisonment of dissenters.

If then the human rights treaties were left free floating rather than anchored in intergovernmental organizations endowed with some powers to monitor, report and protect, the movement would have achieved some but a very modest advance. But the conclusion that IGOs are indispensable for an effective movement raises a host of questions: How should membership in such organizations be organized, what relationships should they bear to national systems, what powers and functions should they exercise vis-à-vis States? Moreover, what duties should States bear toward IGOs or their decisions?

Such issues were never systematically examined for IGOs as a group during the evolution of the universal human rights system. The UN Charter and UN organs created or authorized the creation of the major bodies and official posts that are now concerned with human rights issues: the Security Council and General Assembly, the UN Commission on Human Rights (replaced in 2006 by a newly created Human Rights Council), the Sub-Commission on the Promotion and Protection of Human Rights, related working groups and rapporteurs, and the Office of the High Commissioner of Human Rights. In addition, each of seven human rights treaties [which were drafted and approved within the UN before being submitted to States for ratification] is serviced by its own committee, the so-called treaty bodies or organs. These committees bear a close family resemblance, and as a whole differ markedly from the former UN Commission and new Council.

This range of universal organizations and organs was created at different times and in different contexts over a half century; indeed, many of them have played significant

roles only over the last two decades. Moreover, each of them has experienced independent and ongoing internal development with respect to its powers and functions, such that the original understandings about such matters now appear more modest. In the last decade, institutions and centres like the World Bank and the UN Development Programme, as well as the International Criminal Tribunals and the new International Criminal Court, have become important actors in the field of human rights, further expanding the types of pressure against and forms of dialogue with delinquent States.
. . .

Substantive provisions of the human rights treaties drew on several centuries of an evolving tradition of rights. But neither the architecture nor powers and functions of most of the intergovernmental institutions seemed obvious at the time of the drafting of their constitutive instruments. We can contrast a State in a period of transition from a repressive authoritarian regime to political democracy. Planners of the structure of its new governmental regime might well adopt broadly understood principles for democratic government like the rule of law and the related separation of powers. But no common stock of principles was available to suggest the design of IGOs intended to protect human rights. In the universal system, close analogies to national legal-political institutions such as a world court of human rights lay beyond political possibility or even imagination.

The inevitably novel architecture and powers of these new institutions raised deep concerns among their planners — and potential members. After all, the IGO under negotiation might have power to implement a treaty through authoritative interpretation or even to apply telling pressure against a member State. Such powers would pose a far greater threat to a State's sovereign control over its own territory and population than would its bare agreement to observe treaty norms. Indeed, many States viewed even that bare agreement as a significant qualification of the sovereign control over one's citizens that was thought to inhere in statehood. If IGOs gained in stature and increased their armoury of pressures against violator States, they could cut to the very bone of sovereignty. . . .

Negotiations during the drafting of the treaties over powers and functions of IGOs were notoriously contentious. The inevitable compromises sometimes led to terse and vague provisions that left much for future decision. Neither basic principles nor a master plan, but rather contingent compromises over time responsive to the positions of the great powers and of regional or ideological blocs of countries, all as supplemented by a gradual increase in powers of international organizations through their internal development, explain our present institutional arrangements. However limited and inadequate those arrangements now appear, we should keep in mind how radical and politically implausible they would have seemed when the human rights movement was born.
. . .

III. Characteristics of International Human Rights Relevant to the Nature of Protection

. . . This section develops five inter-related and distinctive characteristics of international human rights. Together they suggest why international protection is weak in comparison with the ordinary sanctions of national legal-political systems or with some other types of international regulatory regimes, and frequently has so hortatory, dialogic, and recommendatory a nature.

These characteristics demonstrate the need for a different and expanded conception of what the protection of human rights amounts to through the universal human rights system. Such a conception would emphasize pressures against a State to arrest violations, but at the same time, would urge assistance to that State to find plausible paths toward reform and compliance. It would look beyond current violations to ways of forestalling their recurrence in later years, most importantly by fostering change in the background circumstances and cultural understandings that often underlie violations. The task of protection . . . could not be analogized to conventional modes of protection in developed countries like arrest and criminal trial or tort remedies. It requires a grasp of context, persistence, and time.

The following analysis . . . simply attempts to describe the human rights movement as it is. . . . Far from defeatist, a realistic portrayal of the complexity and duration of the task [of implementation and protection] should point towards the more fruitful paths for international protection to follow in order to achieve greater realization of human rights ideals.

A. *Human Rights Violations Generally Occur within and Affect Only People within a Single State*

. . .

. . . In the treaty and customary law [of human rights] of the last half century, no trace of a foreign element is essential to the conclusion that a State has violated its international obligations regarding individual rights. . . . For many kinds of violations — police brutality, press censorship, bribed or coerced judges — only the population of the delinquent State is likely to feel the effects. Other States individually are unlikely to protest, let alone take weightier measures to end the violations, even though the violator may have broken its obligations *erga omnes*, vis-à-vis all other States or at least those within a given treaty regime. These other States lack any narrowly conceived interest to act — that is, material interest related characteristically to power or resources. [They] are not likely to . . . impose significant sanctions against the delinquent State — selective trade barriers, general embargoes or boycotts including financial transactions like bank loans. Reducing or cancelling military support or financial aid has occurred somewhat more frequently. . . .

At the same time, the classical self-help remedies or countermeasures allowed by treaty or customary law for injuries to a State caused by the delinquent State's breach of a reciprocal obligation — for example, suspending obligations to the delinquent State that are proportionate to the broken promises made by that State in a tax or trade treaty — lose meaning. . . .

. . .

The reluctance of other States to become directly involved in responding to violations elsewhere as serious as gender discrimination, press censorship, or corrupt political trials underscores the need for a system of international organizations. . . .

B. Human Rights Violations Often Have a Systemic Character and Reflect Deep Aspects of a State's Political Structure

... [T]he violation and injury are rarely idiosyncratic, disconnected from a larger political system or prevailing cultural practices. They tend to fall within a practice or pattern — perhaps widespread torture or abuse of prisoners, electoral fraud, repression of religious worship, gender discrimination, or disappearance of political dissenters.

Human rights norms may then threaten a State's political structure and ideology, for often systemic violations will appear essential to maintaining authoritarian rule ... [—] far more so than would international responses to a State's violation of trade, commercial, or environmental treaties, or rules of the law of the sea.

... Commonplace illustrations of systemic violations whose termination would shake the viability of authoritarian regimes and increase the chances for fundamental change include denial of the right to associate and suppression of an independent press ... violations [that moreover] often pose issues of constitutional breadth and significance....

...

... [A] decision by an IGO to react to serious and systemic violations by an authoritarian State may raise complex questions of strategy and of the relevant time frame. The task is to solve the problem not only for today but for later days as well. ... Such a notion of the ongoing involvement of human rights institutions amounts to an enlarged conception of protection. Surely it puts extra burdens on any international mechanism....

C. The Extensive Reach of Human Rights Duties to Non-State (Private) Actors

International law, classically defined as the law among States, breaks dramatically with this tradition in its human rights instruments....

Like many liberal constitutions, the treaties rest on the assumption that the State constitutes the primary threat to individual rights (as well indeed as the prime agency for their protection). Hence they stress the duty to respect individual rights by not interfering or acting inconsistently with them. But of course non-State actors ... themselves fail to respect others' rights. The rapist or the abusing spouse violates the right to physical security; the discriminatory employer violates equal protection norms....

... [I]nternational law does directly subject non-State as well as State-related violators to criminal liability — with respect, for example, to war crimes, crimes against humanity, and genocide....

[Moreover,] the conduct of non-State actors is frequently *indirectly* regulated by international human rights law. States' obligations under most treaties ... include duties of 'protecting' or 'ensuring' rights-holders from interference by non-State actors, fulfilled in most instances by regulating those actors' conduct. Much of the significance of the State/non-State (public-private) distinction with respect to the reach of international law in general thereby collapses with respect to human rights....

In order to fulfill [the duty under CEDAW to eliminate discrimination] the State must develop a complex web of government policy and legislation, including proactive measures, that will be extremely context-sensitive. Considerable discretion must be allowed the State in deciding on strategies and working out the 'appropriate measures'. Consider, for example, the requirement in CEDAW that parties eliminate discrimination in employment. Should the State criminalize discrimination by corporate officials in hiring or advancement? Would it be preferable to provide only for civil suits for injunctions and damages? Or mandate a policy of affirmative action? Or appoint members of the discriminated-against group to high public office to set an example? Or establish a supervisory agency to which corporations submit periodic reports . . . ?

Ongoing dialogue [of the IGO] with the delinquent State naturally forms an integral part of this enlarged process of protection.

D. The Progressive Realization of Civil and Political Rights

Most treaties express at their creation a convergence of interests of States parties, or a compromise shaped by the distribution of power and influence among the parties. The rules stated in a multilateral treaty are not exactly those that any one party would have initially proposed. The treaty regimes intend those rules to regulate State behaviour from the moment of ratification — diplomatic immunities, treaties on intellectual property, commercial or environmental treaties, the law of the sea. . . .

Human rights treaties differ. Far from representing compromises of points of view between, say, liberal democratic and authoritarian polities, far from accepting the interests or practices of most or all major States as decisive, these treaties declare ideals of State conduct that no State can fully match, and that tower above many States' conduct. . . . The size of the gap between treaty norms and State behaviour varies dramatically among States. . . .

. . . If China were to ratify the ICCPR tomorrow without reservations, a long internal struggle would doubtless precede implementation of rights to speech and association, not to mention the right to vote. . . . Nonetheless other States, IGOs, and NGOs would not protest and condemn China for entering a treaty as a violator. Rather the human rights community would applaud the move as a vital first step that might over time lead to China's deeper sensitivity to and engagement with the movement and heightened degree of compliance.

Consider the famous provision in Article 2 of the ICESCR requiring States to take steps 'with a view to achieving progressively the full realization' of the rights stated in that Covenant. . . . [T]he Committee on Economic, Social and Cultural Rights has made clear that [the] notion of progressive realization or achievement in no sense invalidates or compromises the idea of State obligation. . . . [S]teps forming part of progressive achievement 'must be taken within a reasonably short time' after ratification. They must be 'deliberate, concrete and targeted' toward meeting the State's obligations.

. . .

. . . [M]ost of the civil-political rights treaties make no allowance on their face for gradual implementation over period of time. The command is unambiguous: comply now with your duty to respect, and to protect or ensure. . . .

But common sense as well as the practice of IGOs and NGOs suggest the inevitability of that kind of process for many basic rights. The direction in which State X is moving noticeably influences IGOs and NGOs in the tone and content of their reports and resolutions on X.... Evaluation and criticism will depend greatly on the pace and significance of the steps that X must continue to take....

...

E. The State's Duty to Promote and Transform: Cultural Obstacles

...

What may have been less evident [than conflicting systems of government or ideologies] at the time of the human rights movement's birth were cultural obstacles of a deeper, more diffuse and tenacious character — those aspects of culture that draw on religious belief, political ideology, cosmology, traditional practice and ritual, myth, and symbolic representation. Consider, for example, the structure of the ICCPR.... Article 2 sets forth the obligations of States to 'respect and ensure' to all individuals within their territory the recognized rights, and to take 'necessary steps' to adopt legislative or other measures to give effect to those rights. States also undertake to 'ensure... an effective remedy' to persons whose rights are violated....

The image is one of the rule of law within a liberal democracy; the assumption is that legal processes and institutions are in place or will become available to vindicate claims of right. The Covenant has nothing to say about how to get 'from here to there', how to achieve in government and civil society the observance of deep human rights norms that stand in sharp contradiction to existing practices. Surely there is no recognition in the treaty of cultural relativism or diversity....

Some later conventions evidence a heightened awareness of the need to transform certain assumptions and practices. Within this evolving framework of thought about human rights, police and courts and other familiar State institutions within a conventional understanding of the rule of law can best be understood as essential but insufficient instruments for achieving compliance with the treaties.

CEDAW is most striking. States undertake to ensure the 'full development and advancement of women' (Article 3).... To achieve such goals, States must encourage appropriate education, revise textbooks and school programmes, and introduce new teaching methods (Article 10(c))....

These and similar provisions in other human rights instruments have created what may now be described as a necessary function, if not quite a general duty, of States. That function is to *promote* new understandings with respect to both State-citizen relationships and to interactions among non-State actors in contexts ranging from the family or market to institutions of civil society. These understandings may reach into the most significant and intimate aspects of public action and personal lives. Now that promotion has come to include, as it must, efforts to change aspects of a culture that embraces the rulers and the ruled, the human rights movement has further eroded the traditional distinction between State and non-State actors. If the State's duty to *respect* rights were at the forefront in the early years of the movement, the related tasks of *protection* and *promotion* have become ever more prominent, both tasks pointing toward the necessity of a proactive State attentive to cultural obstacles [and thereby further complicating the construction of international institutions capable of performing these tasks] [italics within this sentence added].

...

Let us turn to two illustrations of the kind of instrumental approach to culture stressed in this [article]:

[The article illustrates what is meant by an 'instrumental' approach to culture by drawing on the right to political participation included in the UDHR and the ICCPR, a right that includes the periodic vote. How can that idea, one 'of increasing salience in a world caught up in the rhetoric of democratization', be realized in authoritarian regimes that may see in the vote their own destruction? This question has become vital in the wars in Afghanistan and Iraq. 'Inevitably the process will be gradual. . . . Complementary institutions and processes must ultimately be put in place, and for the while, a healthy experimentalism including grassroots innovations may heighten chances for success far more than would an imposed blueprint from a stable democracy.']

...

One upshot of this discussion of the characteristics of human rights bearing on protection [and the architecture of human rights IGOs] concerns the question of how to assess States' observance of these mandatory norms. . . .

. . . [D]o the answers hold the same salience as if they addressed tax, trade, commercial, or transportation treaties? In those circumstances, treaty parties appropriately expect immediate and ongoing compliance. . . . As this chapter has argued, a longer-run perspective and time frame often become essential for human rights.

To return to an earlier example, the vital questions if China were to ratify the ICCPR would address the process of change and commitment to it — continuity, depth, apparent strength, the alignment of internal forces, speed of reforms in relation to observers' assessments of what was realistically possible. Answers to those question would appear to be more relevant than the fact of continuing violations — in China's case, for example, denial of genuine elections contested by independent political parties — to the decisions of IGOs, other States, and NGOs about strategies and pressures for encouraging change. Such assessment of progress — in a sense, of 'compliance' — would lack the certainty and finality of measurement that a simpler 'yes, no' approach might yield with respect to current practice. It will complicate the question of what external pressures are appropriate. Despite such drawbacks, a longer time frame will permit the key questions to be examined. The findings about current violations become the start rather than end of inquiry into treaties' effectiveness.

...

QUESTIONS

1. Do you agree with Steiner's list of distinctive attributes of international human rights that distinguish it from most other fields of international law, indeed with his argument that the field is distinctive? Would you have stressed other attributes?

2. In view of the characteristics noted about international human rights and their protection, in what directions might they point with respect to the membership, structure, functions and powers of a human rights IGO? Would your answer be affected by whether the IGO was universal or regional (Europe, the Inter-American system, Africa) in scope, or whether you responded from the perspective of a leading power like the US, another established democracy, or a country under authoritarian rule accused of serious and systemic violations of civil and political rights?

JOSÉ ALVAREZ, INTERNATIONAL INSTITUTIONS AS LAW MAKERS (2005)

Preface

...

... A large portion of the rules that we have to govern nations, both those that are formally legally binding and those that are not, are now initiated, formulated, negotiated, interpreted, and often implemented through the efforts of IOs [International Organizations]....

... [T]he lawyers most familiar with such rules remain in the grip of a positivistic preoccupation with an ostensibly sacrosanct doctrine of sources, now codified in article *38* of the Statute of the International Court of Justice, which originated before most modern IOs were established and which, not surprisingly, does not mention them.... [W]e continue to pour an increasingly rich normative output into old bottles labeled "treaty;" "custom," or (much more rarely) "general principles."

... The notion that these doctrines as applied to IOs are mere parasitical variations on familiar rules applied to states reflects a prevailing assumption that such organizations are merely the agents of states and not in any real sense autonomous entities....

...

... [T]his book contends that we need to reconsider the state-centric ways in which public international law-making processes are described. This conclusion may appear odd for a book that focuses on entities that are composed largely if not entirely of states. Inter-governmental organizations lend themselves to state-centric description. We continue to assume ... that these organizations are merely "new settings for old techniques of diplomacy." ... [Alvarez later states: 'The thesis here is that the IOs that are the primary focus of this book — namely those that aspire to universal participation — have transformed the processes by which international norms are produced, the nature of the actors that produce these rules, as well as the content of much of general public international law itself.']

...

... An international charter like the UN Charter or a series of interwoven obligations subject to binding institutionalized dispute settlement like the WTO covered agreements, or a modern environmental framework convention continuously revised through periodic meetings of the parties, is each subject to a significantly different interpretative process than is the bilateral treaty-contract between two states.... A treaty produced through modern collective processes is likely to be different not merely in its origins, but also in its final text and in its subsequent evolution. Process affects substance.

...

The study of organizations permits us to see as well their many failings and especially their shortcomings from the perspective of democratic theory.... As the missions of these organizations intrude more deeply into the fabric of domestic law, as more national judges, parliamentarians, and executive agencies are required to deal with rules produced at the international level, and as more individuals are affected by them, it makes sense to many to ask whether domestic legal doctrines — such as principles relating to "separation of powers" or "improper delegation" — should pose limits on the incorporation or enforcement of international law within national law.

...

1
Introduction
1.1 Why Focus on "International Organizations"?

...

The premise is not that organizations like the UN are more important, or more likely to be active in more than one state, or are more powerful or even legally relevant than are TNCs [Transnational Corporations] or NGOs. A variety of non-state actors, from IOs to TNCs and NGOs, and even individuals, are helping to make and enforce modern international law, even if they are not formally recognized as "international legal persons" alongside of states. NGOs like Amnesty International may be the single greatest promulgators and de facto enforcers of international human rights, for example. TNCs like Exxon, many of which have a presence in more countries than most IOs, have exerted considerable power, particularly over the domestic law of small states whose gross national products they dwarf; and they have also influenced international law — as with respect to standards of compensation upon expropriation. Both IOs and TNCs have at times been seen as competitors to sovereign states. TNCs have also been the subject of considerable efforts at international regulation, no less than IOs. The potential clout and legal impact of other non-state entities such as the Roman Catholic Church is also not in doubt....

...

1.3 An Intellectual History

There is no single over-arching scholarly framework that comprehensively explains IO law-making or indeed suggests uniform agreement about what IOs are for. As we shall examine below, for some, IOs have been and remain primarily beholden to those with power, mere vassals for the hegemon. Others agree that IOs are the agents of states but argue that states have diverse tradable interests and that IOs serve the needs of states to cooperate on the international level, with consequent beneficial effects, notably in law. Some contend that IOs are not merely vessels for the individual and collective interests of states, but vehicles by which national and transnational groups take action at the international level. And some would even turn the causal arrows the other way, to suggest that IOs shape what states (and possibly others) want. . . .

1.3.1 Functionalist Theories

The most common perspective on IOs remains functionalism, a school with many rooms but which, at its core, credits changing state needs for both the rise in, and the subsequent development of, IOs. . . .

. . .

Functionalist accounts of international organizations assume that states are the dominant actors in international relations; that states, in the absence of institutions, engage in the anarchic pursuit of power but do have some common interests; that, over time, they respond rationally to (primarily technologically driven) developments; and that, given time, they "learn" from prior experience. As adherents to institutionalism (a version of functionalism that emerged in the 1980s within political science) argued, IOs create the "conditions for orderly multilateral relations" by, for example, reducing the costs of making transactions, legitimating different forms of (inter-)state action, facilitating linkages among issues and between regimes, and increasing the symmetry and the quality of information states receive. On this view, IOs are not only capable of modifying the conditions of anarchy in which states find themselves by permitting cooperation: they are as fundamental to the determination of international outcomes as the distribution of capabilities among states.

To a functionalist, IOs are simply agencies called into being by states, sustained by states, and actually or potentially directed by states on the supposition that the organization's existence and operation are useful to themselves. . . . They are seen as natural a product of international society as states, and as inevitable. They are no more and no less the subject of praise or of criticism than the state-centric international system of which they are a product.

. . .

"Learning" plays an important role in this version of history . . . . States learned from the defects of ad hoc conferences, which had proven unsatisfactory for the resolution of many issues because: they were dependent on the initiative of a state willing to convene the event, limited to the specific agenda the organizer had in mind and could not serve as a forum for more general debate, restricted to those states invited by the host, and rigorously adhered to a rule of unanimity on the basis of one state/one vote. Such conferences gave way to the periodic conference system whose regularized meetings and other attributes would eventually culminate in a permanent body: the League of Nations. International law-making was also expedited (if not transformed) by the creation of multilateral treaties (as opposed to a series of bilateral arrangements). . . . International unions gave states the further insight that institutional permanence was a virtue, and that votes (and budgetary contributions) could be weighed on the basis of differing criteria, as appropriate to the object of the organization or the organ within an organization. States also learned that . . . not all state participants needed to be treated for purposes of voting or participation rights as equal within institutional organs.

…

… Functionalists such as David Mitrany have seen IOs as a kind of rear guard action against state sovereignty, as an interim step towards political integration at the international level. Mitrany and others have argued that by learning to cooperate in technical areas through supranational institution-building, states eventually learn to cooperate with respect to more political issues, including the prevention of war. They theorize that states will gradually learn a larger lesson: that international cooperation through institutions does not involve the surrendering of sovereignty but merely "pooling as much of it as may be needed for the joint performance of a particular task." They hope that world order, if not necessarily "world government" involving a politically difficult decision to renounce sovereignty in favor of centralized political authority, will gradually evolve as governments learn that functions can be integrated internationally as much as they are internally. For such functionalists, IOs hold out the prospect of "federalism by installments" or "peace by pieces."

… They contend that IOs gradually extend their powers through new interpretations of their charters, an expansion of the role of organs or secretariat, the growth of their bureaucracy (committees, staff), or an expansion of their budgets. They explain that while states often resist such changes and the consequential interference with their sovereignty, the pressure to accede arises from the substantive advantages provided by institutional integration itself, with often startling results. Thus Luard, although critical of much of Mitrany's views, concludes his 1977 book as follows:

> Only thirty years ago the right to impose exchange restrictions and quotas, or to raise tariffs, the right to determine what human rights were to be accorded minority populations, the right to determine exchange rate policies, all these were almost universally regarded as matters solely within domestic jurisdiction, for each government to decide for itself; today it is equally taken for granted that they are all subject to international influence, to the norms established by the international community. It is above all through this gradual erosion of the barriers between subjects regarded as national and as international that international authority is slowly extended, and the power of the nation-state gradually challenged.

…

1.3.2 Realism

… While there are as many schools or varieties of realists as there are within functionalism, realists share certain assumptions with functionalists: namely, that the only important international actor is the state, that states rationally pursue power within a system that is largely anarchic, and that the clash of competing state interests defines the significant issues of foreign affairs. Realists also agree that states respond rationally to stimuli and would even accept the possibility that states can learn. They would therefore not dispute much of the functionalist account of the rise and fall of IOs, subject to three significant caveats.

First, realists deny any suggestion that IOs (or their products such as international law or regimes) have fundamentally altered the conditions in which states find themselves. Where functionalists of various stripes look out into the world and see islands of cooperation, realists see a much larger ocean of continued disorder and anarchy. To them, IOs' regulatory schemes are epiphenomenal and less significant than they appear to be since the law they propound is generally ineffective or merely constitutes "agreements to disagree." Whether because they see human nature as impossible to control in the absence of a hierarchically superior, centralized, and powerful authority or because they believe that the anarchic structure of the international system of horizontal states makes this inevitable, realists disparage the power of IOs (or international law, for that matter) to change the fundamental behavior of states....

...

... [T]here is a third distinction between realists and functionalists: to realists, the only IOs that might conceivably matter are those concerned with 'high" politics, which they define to be those involving national security issues. This provides yet another reason for disparaging the ultimate value of IOs; realists argue that none of the universal IOs in existence and only one with a unique regional mandate, the European Union, aspires to serious governance over states and even the European Union has wavered on intruding on matters of high politics. To them the UN system is neither an incipient world government nor even an effective collective security system since its restrictive purposes and powers preclude the former and the veto (accorded to the five permanent members of the Security Council) makes its security capabilities derisible in the most significant cases: where a great power either becomes an aggressor or is allied with one....

...

1.3.5 Constructivism

The critique from culture, gender, ideology; and race/ethinicity is suggestive of another failing shared by realists, functionalists, and liberals: none of these concern themselves with how the primary actors of each of these approaches — states, hegemons, state-centric entities like IOs or individuals — form their own preferences. All of these frameworks for analysis presume instrumental calculation by different actors each seeking to advance predetermined sets of interests. Constructivists are concerned precisely with those interests and whether these interests are in fact preformed. For constructivists, as with respect to some crits, ideology and gender matters, along with much else in the construction of what people, including states, want.

Keohane suggests that these theories of regime formation share a "sociological approach to the study of institutions, which stresses the role of impersonal social forces as well as the impact of cultural practices, norms, and values that are not derived from calculations of interests." As Keohane indicates, constructivists (whom he categorizes as reflectionists) argue that:

> individuals, local organizations, and even states develop within the context of more encompassing institutions. Institutions do not merely reflect the preferences and power of the units constituting them; the institutions themselves shape those preferences and that power. Institutions are therefore constitutive of actors as well as vice versa. It is therefore not sufficient in this view to treat the preferences of individuals as given exogenously: they are affected by institutional arrangements,

by prevailing norms, and by historically contingent discourse among people seeking to pursue their purposes and solve their self-defined problems.

For this group of theorists, neither states' nor individuals' interests are fixed. On the contrary; interests flow from a constructed identity and the identities of all actors in international relations fluctuate either through different associations with others (as through participation in an IO) or through changing self-perceptions (which can also be influenced through the normative activity of IOs). On this "normative" as opposed to "instrumentalist" optic, states are socialized, including through their participation in IOs, to see themselves as, for example, defenders of trans-Atlantic political/economic values through their membership in NATO, the European Union, the Inter-American and European human rights regimes, or the Helsinki process. They come to believe that they have an interest in protecting the human rights of their own nationals (and understand what this means) at least in part because of the "norm cascades" produced by a gamut of IOs of which they are an active part....

...

10

Conclusion: the promise and perils of international organizations

...

10.1 IOs and the Traditional Sources of Law

...

IOs have also transformed the second source of law in article 38, customary international law. [See discussions of changing custom and 'soft law' at pp. 160–174, *supra.*]

... [N]o one would deny that relevant actors today increasingly rely on IO-generated legislative treaties to suggest custom binding even on non-parties to such agreements, resolutions adopted by organizational plenary bodies (most notably the UN General Assembly but including, for example, WTO members as in their Doha Declaration), the practice of IO organs or their secretariats (especially with respect to "international institutional law"), and even the occasional principle proclaimed at a gathering not authorized to generate law at all.... Public international lawyers are also finding custom and general principles of law (as well as new, sometimes unexpected, interpretations of treaty law) in another product of institutions: in the judgments issued by the proliferating number of international dispute settlers ... even though none of these judicialized or non-judicialized fora are authorized to make law. Yet ... institutionalized adjudicators are as much promulgators of law, both treaty-based and customary; as they are settlers of disputes.

... From the annual sessions of the GA to the commentaries provided by the [International Law Commission (ILC)] that accompany its efforts (such as the commentaries to its Articles of State Responsibility), IO venues ... make possible what would otherwise be increasingly difficult in a world of nearly 200 nation states: finding concrete, preferably written, evidence that virtually all states accept a rule as one of custom. In addition . . . the sustained interaction between institutional organs (GA/SC/Secretariat) and other actors (states/NGOs), has produced dramatic changes in customary rules on such significant topics as the rights and duties of states and other international legal persons, human rights and their application, and the (ever-diminishing) concept of "domestic jurisdiction." . . .

. . .

. . . Apart from the more egalitarian and transparent nature of this form of evidence (at least as compared to reliance on those privileged states that can and do produce digests of their practice), reliance on IOs tends to make the resulting rules the product of a *consciously* deliberative process that approximates the intentional processes involved in treaty-making. Rules of custom discussed by the GA, in proposed commentaries of the ILC, or in the legal memoranda circulated by the UN Legal Counsel, for example, are circulated in written form — as would draft texts of a treaty — and all states (and NGOs involved) are on notice if they wish to respond. Unlike rules of law that have to be gleaned from the practices or reactions of states in specific factual contexts, such IO texts, cast in "sufficient expression in legal form," are ready made to form viable rules of custom. . . . What constitutes "repetition of state practice across time" has been changed as well; it is more likely to include rhetorical repetition (as through repeated GA resolutions) or the repeated practices of IO organs. . . .

. . .

. . . [T]he making of "internal" international institutional law, even if implicitly authorized by these organizations' constitutive instruments, proves hard to disentangle from external law-making — with direct consequences on states' ever shrinking *domaine réservé*. . . . The categories of treaty, custom, and general principle do not provide satisfactory rubrics for describing such phenomena as . . . the World Bank's Guidelines, or IMF-imposed conditions. Such norms, as much as those UN General Assembly resolutions deemed to be expressions of the "general will," are "global law" unique to the age of international organization.

. . .

. . . [M]any of the new rules involve the participation of, or purport to affect, the conduct of non-state actors, fail to evince traditional expressions of state consent to be bound, or lack the precision often associated with rules of law. . . .

. . .

. . . The distinction between hard treaty and soft law obligations is no longer as clear cut as it was, and it is no longer as easy to tell whether states are complying because of a treaty or customary law obligation, or merely because they are dutifully following organizational expectations. This means as well that it is sometimes difficult to tell whether certain institutional legal products — whether "core" ILO Conventions or opinions issued by the ILO Labor Office — impose obligations only for those who have ratified particular treaties and are therefore a species of contractual obligation, or are general obligations on all and therefore a new phenomenon, namely, a species of international legislation.

. . .

. . . IOs have also blurred the distinctions between making law, interpreting it, and adjudicating it. This is most evidently true to the extent many IOs rely on adjudicative fora (as in the WTO) to clarify and amplify the treaty obligations of members, and not merely settle discrete disputes....

To the extent general rules of law are produced through such methods — by actions of bureaucrats, dispute settlers, or political organs — this necessarily implies a shift of power to those making these decisions and a shift away from positivist state consent as the basis for all international obligations. The rise of such organizational forms of law-making explains why, to commentators, "[t]he image of a sovereign state exercising freedom of choice in its participation in international community no longer seems valid, or even desirable, except perhaps for the most powerful of nation-states."....

...

10.2 IOs and the Changing Content of International Law

...

Thanks to IO organs, we know that "sovereign equality" means at least the equal right to participate in international negotiations and, in the context of particular IOs, may entitle states to many more procedural rights. At the same time, the unequal standing of states formally accepted in terms of the governance structures of the IMF and the World Bank, not to mention the authorized privileges of the Permanent Members of the Security Council, are an apt reminder that this sovereign right may not have much greater substantive content....

...

10.3 IOs and the Changing Law-Makers

...

....[I]n the modern world, thanks at least in part to the actions of IOs, states can no longer be said to hold "absolute" power over their own peoples or territory even with respect to matters that were once seen as "domestic" having nothing to do with inter-state relations. International law now embraces the full spectrum of matters that national law covers, from family relations to the labeling of food products....

...

... [S]cholars and policy-makers increasingly take the view that sovereign power is not a "zero-sum game" in which delegations of power to IOs necessarily lessen a state's own power. Participation within IOs is increasingly portrayed by diplomats and scholars as "sovereignty-strengthening" since it enhances a state's ability to engage in the standard-setting activities, and secure other benefits, needed to fulfill the regulatory needs generated by a globalizing world. The exercise as traditionally understood today required ... participation in IOs....

...

10.5 New Challenges to the Legitimacy of International Law

...

The uncertainties attendant to "soft" law ... though they cannot all be laid at the feet of IOs, can be partly attributed to IO processes that encourage treaties with vague provisions or that reflect a false "consensus" among states, rhetorical statements of the law disguised as existing law (such as GA resolutions), reliance on the practice of organs instead of the actual practices of states, and attempts at law-making by persons (IO bureaucrats, experts, international dispute settlers) having no readily demonstrable authority to legislate on behalf of states. Even those who criticize the state-centricity of the current list of international sources of law recognize that states need some list, or at least a reliable checklist of factors, that distinguish law from non-law, political aspiration from firm obligation. When everything — from "guidelines" to commitments made in loan agreements — can be regarded as legally significant, even if not equally legally binding, there is understandable fear that law and lawyers will lose their value to the policymaker, that if everything is "law," nothing, in the end, will be.

...

10.6 Conclusion

...

... IOs are seen as primary vehicles for transforming international law from rudimentary frameworks for bilateral barter to systems of governance premised on multilateral cooperation. IOs provide greater opportunities for all states, regardless of wealth or power, to participate in the formation of law. The making of international law in the age of IOs is now open to non-European states that would have been dismissed as "uncivilized" in the 19th century and to ever increasing number of non-state actors, from NGOs to multinational corporations. . . . IOs have produced *more* law, more democratically and transparently, and, given the diversity of adjudication and compliance efforts now in use, presumably, to more effect.

...

... While it is difficult to say whether IOs have improved public international law and the jury is still out on whether they have made states more likely to behave in conformity with international rules, there is little doubt that the institutionalization of public international law has radically altered how state power, hard and soft, is exercised and has created competing sites for its exercise.

...

... The legal standards established — whether through treaties or forms of national regulation — are less like black/white prohibitions than managerial structures for dynamic interactions intended to encourage adaptability and iterative learning, including re-defining problems in the course of implementation and continued re-examination of rules over time.

... From the start IOs have lowered the barriers of entry to non-state actors seeking to influence the law, thereby helping to turn individuals, NGOs, and even multinational corporations, into norm-generating subjects. . . . Nonetheless, the numerous innovations in international law's norms, content, actors, and forms of compliance brought about in the age of IOs may themselves provide the best hope for eventually generating efficient, politically legitimate, and democratic forms of standards — both within the administrative state and outside of it. That is the continued promise offered by the move to international institutions.

NOTE

The preceding readings raise a plethora of questions and problems stimulated by the growing prominence of international organizations. We have inevitably omitted some topics relevant to recent developments and current issues, including a theme that has become important over the last decade: the question whether IGOs are consistent with the principles of democratic government, or more broadly democracy, that characterize the internal orders of a large number of their member states. Ever more frequently, critics of the participation of democratic countries like the US in IGOs underscore the nondemocratic character of IGOs. Those organizations may often make important decisions affecting the external relations and internal life of member states. Human rights IGOs provide an obvious illustration. Critics argue, for example, that 'delegation' of such decision-making to IGOs, despite the charge of a 'democracy deficit' in such organizations, deprives democratic countries' populations of their right to participate politically.

The topic is rich in basic and puzzling questions, such as: What structural characteristics and processes would we include within the notion of a democratically based IGO? Would they be identical with reigning conceptions of democracy within states (note the many significant variations in these 'conceptions' and political structures among democratic states)? If fundamental characteristics of democracies such as popular election by the adult population are radically implausible for a universal IGO like the WTO, CEDAW Committee, or indeed UN, what surrogates or alternatives might be available? Should all types of IGOs be equally subject to this demand and criticism, from the European Union to the Law of the Sea to the UN? One finds no scholarly or political consensus on these questions, but the contentious scholarly literature well illuminates the issues. See, e.g., Andrew Moravcsik, 'Is there a "*Democratic Deficit*" *in World Politics? A Framework for Analysis*', 39(2) Government and Opposition 336 (online issue 17 March 2004).

QUESTION

Recall earlier discussions about changes over recent decades in the structure and basic elements of international law and relations — the discussions at pp. 160–174, *supra*, for example, about the 'new' customary international law and 'soft law.' Are these developments closely related to the trend described by Alvarez with respect to IOs? Are they all part of a systematically interrelated larger picture displacing reigning notions a half century ago? How would you describe that picture?

B. SOVEREIGNTY AND DOMESTIC JURISDICTION

At its very threshold and to this day, the human rights movement has inevitably confronted antagonistic claims based on conceptions of sovereignty. How could its premises coexist with the then-reigning conceptions of state sovereignty? Or have the nature of the state, and the content of that protean concept as well as of allied concepts like domestic jurisdiction and autonomy, themselves undergone substantial change over the six decades of this movement?

The basic ideas in this section will be familiar from earlier chapters examining the normative content of the human rights movement. Indeed, those chapters could not have avoided them. In one or another of its meanings or incarnations, the notion of sovereignty inserts itself into many of the diverse topics in this coursebook. The introduction in Chapter 2 to international law inevitably considered the clash between international regulation and national governments' internal control of their polity — cases like *Chattin* or *Minority Schools in Albania*, for example. States' arguments based on sovereignty provided a counterpoint in Chapter 3 to the description of the growth of the human rights movement. States' claims based on notions of cultural relativism in Chapters 6 and 7 often spoke the language of autonomy and sovereign independence. The broad theme of sovereignty in its modern dress(es) continues to inform discussion in the following chapters: topics including actions of the UN Security Council under Chapter VII of the Charter (Chapter 9); supranational regional organizations as in Europe that appropriate former economic, political and human rights prerogatives of the state (Chapter 11); and changing notions of internal sovereignty and independence or interdependence in an era of globalization, free trade and deregulated markets (Chapter 15).

Consider at the outset brief comments of several scholars about the meaning of this notion in contemporary international law and argument.

Malanczuk[1] notes that the origin of the modern theory lies in internal analyses of state structure, analyses that reach to writings of theorists like Machiavelli, Bodin and Hobbes. Originally used to describe the commands of a sovereign within a state (internal sovereignty), sovereignty later came to be used to describe as well the relationship of the ruler towards other rulers or states (external sovereignty, a continuing deep concern of international law). He suggests that the word 'sovereignty' should be replaced by 'independence'. 'In so far as "sovereignty" means anything in addition to "independence", it is not a legal term with any fixed meaning but a wholly emotive term. Everyone knows that states are powerful, but the emphasis on sovereignty exaggerates their power and encourages them to abuse it . . . '.

Brownlie[2] states that:

> sovereignty and equality of states represent the basic constitutional doctrine of the law of nations, which governs a community consisting primarily of states having a

[1] Peter Malanczuk, *Akehurst's Modern Introduction to International Law* (7th edn. 1997), 17–18.

[2] Ian Brownlie, *Principles of Public International Law* (4th edn. 1990), Ch. XIII, 287.

> uniform legal personality. If international law exists, then the dynamics of state sovereignty can be expressed in terms of law, and, as states are equal and have legal personality, sovereignty is in a major aspect a relation to other states (and to organizations of states) defined by law.

He describes the principal corollaries of states' sovereignty and equality as:

> (1) a jurisdiction, prima facie exclusive, over a territory and the permanent population living there; (2) a duty of non-intervention in the area of exclusive jurisdiction of other states; and (3) the dependence of obligations arising from customary law and treaties on the consent of the obligor.

Koskenniemi[3] observes that it is 'notoriously difficult to pin down the meaning of sovereignty', but that nonetheless the literature characteristically starts with a definition. Usually the concept is connected with ideas of independence (external sovereignty) and self-determination (internal sovereignty). He quotes a classic definition in an arbitral decision to the effect that sovereignty 'in the relations between States signifies independence: independence in regard to a portion of the globe is the right to exercise therein, to the exclusion of any other States, the functions of a State'. Sovereignty thus implies freedom of action by a state.

If, argues Koskenniemi, this or any agreed-on definition of sovereignty had a clear, ascertainable meaning, then 'whether an act falls within the State's legitimate sphere of action could always be solved by simply applying [that definition] to the case'. But '[t]here simply is no fixed meaning, no natural extent to sovereignty at all'. Thus in disputes between two states, each may base its argument on its own sovereignty. Assuming that 'sovereignty had a fixed content would entail accepting that there is an antecedent material rule which determines the boundaries of State liberty regardless of the subjective will or interest of any particular State'. Such material boundaries not stemming from the free choice of the state 'will appear as unjustified coercion'. It is indeed 'impossible to define "sovereignty" in such a manner as to contain our present perception of the State's full subjective freedom and that of its objective submission to restraints to such freedom'.

STEPHEN KRASNER, SOVEREIGNTY: ORGANIZED HYPOCRISY

(1999), at 9

[Krasner identifies four different ways in which the term sovereignty is commonly used: domestic, interdependence, international legal and Westphalian sovereignty.]

[3] Martti Koskenniemi, *From Apology to Utopia: The Structure of International Legal Argument* (1989), Ch. 4.

Domestic sovereignty

The intellectual history of the term sovereignty is most closely associated with domestic sovereignty.

. . . Domestic sovereignty, the organization and effectiveness of political authority, is the single most important question for political analysis, but the organization of authority within a state and the level of control enjoyed by the state are not necessarily related to international legal or Westphalian sovereignty.

. . .

Interdependence sovereignty

In contemporary discourse it has become commonplace for observers to note that state sovereignty is being eroded by globalization. Such analysts are concerned fundamentally with questions of control, not authority. The inability to regulate the flow of goods, persons, pollutants, diseases, and ideas across territorial boundaries has been described as a loss of sovereignty.

. . .

Interdependence sovereignty, or the lack thereof, is not practically or logically related to international legal or Westphalian sovereignty. A state can be recognized as a juridical equal by other states and still be unable to control movements across its own borders. Unregulated transborder movements do not imply that a state is subject to external structures of authority, which would be a violation of Westphalian sovereignty. Rulers can lose control of transborder flows and still be recognized and be able to exclude external actors.

. . .

International legal sovereignty

The third meaning of sovereignty, international legal sovereignty, has been concerned with establishing the status of a political entity in the international system. Is a state recognized by other states? Is it accepted as a juridical equal? Are its representatives entitled to diplomatic immunity? Can it be a member of international organizations? Can its representatives enter into agreements with other entities?

. . .

The classic model of international law is a replication of the liberal theory of the state. The state is treated at the international level as analogous to the individual at the national level. Sovereignty, independence, and consent are comparable with the position that the individual has in the liberal theory of the state.

International legal sovereignty . . . does not guarantee that legitimate domestic authorities will be able to monitor and regulate developments within the territory of their state or flows across their borders; that is, it does not guarantee either domestic sovereignty or interdependence sovereignty.

. . .

Westphalian sovereignty

Finally, sovereignty has been understood as the Westphalian model, an institutional arrangement for organizing political life that is based on two principles: territoriality and the exclusion of external actors from domestic authority structures. Rulers may be constrained, sometimes severely, by the external environment, but they are still free to choose the institutions and policies they regard as optimal. Westphalian sovereignty is violated when external actors influence or determine domestic authority structures.

Domestic authority structures can be infiltrated through both coercive and voluntary actions, through intervention and invitation. Foreign actors, usually the rulers of other states, can use their material capabilities to dictate or coerce changes in the authority structures of a target; they can violate the rule of nonintervention in the internal affairs of other states.

. . .

While Westphalian sovereignty can be compromised through invitation as well as intervention, invitation has received less notice in the literature because observers have confounded international legal and Westphalian sovereignty. Intervention violates both. Invitation violates only Westphalian sovereignty. Invitation occurs when a ruler voluntarily compromises the domestic autonomy of his or her own polity. Free choices are never inconsistent with international legal sovereignty.

Invitations can, however, infringe domestic autonomy. Rulers may issue invitations for a variety of reasons, including tying the hands of their successors, securing external financial resources, and strengthening domestic support for values that they, themselves, embrace. Invitations may sometimes be inadvertent; rulers might not realize that entering into an agreement may alter their own domestic institutional arrangements. Regardless of the motivation or the perspicacity of rulers, invitations violate Westphalian sovereignty by subjecting internal authority structures to external constraints. The rulings of the European Court of Justice, for instance, have legitimacy in the judicial systems of the member states of the European Union. IMF conditionality agreements, which may include stipulations requiring changes in domestic structures, carry weight not only because they are attached to the provision of funding but also because the IMF has legitimacy for some actors in borrowing countries derived from its claims to technical expertise. Human rights conventions can provide focal points that alter conceptions of legitimacy among groups in civil society and precipitate possibly unanticipated changes in the institutional arrangements of signatory states.

. . . [T]he most important empirical conclusion of the present study is that the principles associated with both Westphalian and international legal sovereignty have always been violated. Neither Westphalian nor international legal sovereignty has ever been a stable equilibrium from which rulers had no incentives to deviate. . . .

. . .

GEORGES ABI-SAAB, THE CHANGING WORLD ORDER AND THE INTERNATIONAL LEGAL ORDER: THE STRUCTURAL EVOLUTION OF INTERNATIONAL LAW BEYOND THE STATE-CENTRIC MODEL

in Y. Sakamoto (ed.), Global Transformation: Challenges to the State System (1994), at 439

The origins of the present international legal order go back to the disintegration of what Vinogradoff has called 'the World State of Medieval Christendom', as a result of the Reformation and the Wars of Religion in Europe. Its traits were fixed in the Peace of Westphalia, which definitively broke away from the formally theocratic character and hierarchic structure of the existing system, invalidating once and for all the assumption — already negated in practice — of the double allegiance of princes to Pope and Emperor, and replacing it by a new egalitarian set-up epitomized in the dictum '*cujus regio, ejus religio*' (each region follows its prince's religion).

This formula provided the basis for the coexistence of princes adhering to different versions of 'truth' (i.e. with different ideologies), the Wars of Religion having shown that neither camp was in a position to impose its truth on the other. It thus recognized, in terms of the ideological conflict of the moment (to which it was supposed to provide a final and stable solution), the paramountcy of every prince in his territory and over his subjects; whence the twin legal principles, governing the new international distribution of power, of sovereignty and equality (or of the 'sovereign equality' of Article 2(1) of the UN Charter).

In other words, as the legal system was meant to govern relations between antagonistic units, it had to gloss over the sources of their antagonism. It thus postulated a horizontal international structure where no hierarchy prevailed; where princes were 'sovereign', both in the sense of exercising exclusive power over their territory and their subjects (internal sovereignty), and in the sense of depending on no higher authority in the international sphere (external sovereignty or independence). But in order to maintain this situation, princes had to recognize each other (i.e. to be considered) as legally equal on the international level, regardless of size, wealth, strength, form of government, religion, or ideology.

Given the main purpose of the system of making it possible for antagonistic units to coexist, it aimed — to borrow the words of David Mitrany — at keeping them 'peacefully apart' rather than at bringing them 'actively together'. In the logic of this system, there was only one general obligation, the obligation to respect the sovereignty of others. It was an essentially passive obligation of abstention, of not trespassing on the spatial and functional confines of their sovereignty.

But if the sovereigns decided to establish or entertain relations, the system provided them with the 'legal recipes' or the 'how to do' formulae. In other words, to the extent that relations did take place, international law provided them with a convenient frame of reference. Indeed, the most developed chapters of classical international law fall in this category, such as the law of diplomatic and consular relations, and the law of treaties and of state responsibility.

Two important consequences flowed from this scheme of things, one relating to the representation of the new system of its rising subjects, the states, the other to the consistency and structure of the system itself. And both reflected its patently 'state-centric', indeed its 'state-deist', character.

...

As far as the consistency (or density) and structure of the system are concerned, states did not want to give with the left hand what they had just acquired with the right, namely their affranchisement from any and all dependence on, or submission to, a higher authority. They particularly did not want to see (re)established above them any new superior instance, whatever it might be. The new structure of international law thus had a precise and well-delimited (as well as limited) task: formally to sanction the new distribution of power in international society, i.e. to legitimize and sanction sovereignty in its newly acquired sense, without encroaching or trespassing on it.

...

In conclusion, two remarks are in order concerning the real social hold of this initial design, and the place of the ensuing system in the world then and now.

First, what is described above is the inner logic of the system or the manner in which it was initially articulated, in the light and as a function of the new constellation of power in the civil society it purported to regulate. But its 'fit' to external social reality comprised a good part of artifice and reification. For when we speak of the centrality and all-inclusiveness or all-mightiness of the state, we are speaking of the abstract model, on the basis of abstract equality. In reality, this model eliminates from its field of vision sources of inequality and conflict of interests, and the attendant vulnerability of weak states to diktats and interventions by stronger powers, usually on the pretext of alleged violations of international law by the former, put forward and unilaterally acted upon by the latter, in the absence of autonomous organs capable of objectively verifying their veracity at the request of either party.

In the second place, it should be recalled that, at its inception, this system was not the only one contending for the status of international legal order. It had to coexist, even in Europe, with the system of Islam as well as with other existing regional systems with similar universalist pretentions. However, with time, it progressively managed to dispose of these contending systems, either by direct control, via its subjects, of large parts of the non-Western world through colonialism; or, for those communities that managed to remain formally independent (e.g. because they served as a buffer between two European empires or to avoid upsetting the European balance of power), through forced assimilation, in order to qualify as 'civilized nations'.

Thus, what started objectively as a regional system in the seventeenth century, ended up becoming the universal system by the end of the nineteenth century.

...

NOTE

The following readings underscore the significance of international human rights for the internal distribution of power within a state, suggest new understandings of sovereignty that might impose internal human rights observance upon the legitimacy of a state's defensive invocation of the concept, and challenge and defend the notion of the sovereign state itself.

HENRY STEINER, THE YOUTH OF RIGHTS

104 Harv. L. Rev. 917 (1991), at 929

. . . Unlike many components of classical international law, the human rights movement was not meant to work out matters of reciprocal convenience among states — for example, sovereign or diplomatic immunities — or to aim only at regulating areas of historical conflict among states — for example, uses of the sea or airspace, or treatment by a state of its alien population. Rather it reached broad areas of everyday life within states that are vital to the internal rather than international distribution of political power. As international law's aspirations grew, as that law became more critical of and hence more distanced from states' behavior, the potential for conflict between human rights advocates within a state and that state's controlling elites escalated.

Even the most consensual of rights, the right not to be tortured, has a subversive potential. If, as [an] Amnesty International report suggests, torture amounts to the price of dissent because it is 'most often used as an integral part of a government's security strategy', abolishing torture lowers that price. Oppressive regimes prefer to keep the price high.

Other rights included in the *Universal Declaration* and the *Civil–Political Rights Covenant* influence the structure of government more directly. Abolishing discrimination on grounds of race, ethnicity, religion, or gender can radically alter economic and social arrangements and redirect political power. Protecting rights of speech, expression, and association will give citizens not only security against arbitrary state action, but also the chance to develop a diverse and vibrant civil society that can influence the directions of the state as effectively as governmental policies influence it. Entrenched structures of domination — landholding patterns, power over rural labor, virtual enslavement of children or women or given minorities — may become open to effective challenge.

The stakes for power rise as we move further along the spectrum of human rights. The major human rights instruments empower citizens to 'take part' in government and to vote in secrecy in genuine, periodic, and nondiscriminatory elections. In given circumstances, an authoritarian government can stop torturing and arresting without surrendering its monopoly of power. As events in Eastern Europe illustrate, however, such a government cannot grant the right to political participation without signing its death warrant. 'Throw out the rascals' speaks the more dramatically after decades of unchosen and oppressive regimes.

. . .

Particular clusters of civil-political rights thus challenge many of the world's governments in unavoidable, implacable ways. To some extent the range of human rights that I have mentioned respond to a 'disaster' dimension of the human rights movement. . . .

But the aspirations of the human rights movement reach beyond the goal of preventing disasters. The movement also has a 'utopian' dimension that envisions a vibrant and broadly based political community. Such a vision underscores the potential of the human rights movement for conflict with regimes all over the world. A society honoring the full range of contemporary human rights would be hospitable to many types of pluralism [and unwilling to embrace or impose] one final truth, at least to the point of allowing and protecting difference....

QUESTION

Richard Falk (*On Human Governance: Towards a New Global Politics* (1995), at 251), observes that 'sovereignty and democracy are profoundly affected by the realization of human rights.... In particular, the citizenry is morally and legally empowered to the extent it appreciates that its leaders can be challenged when they transgress the restraints on power as contained in the international law of human rights. In these regards, the protection of human rights represents a radical tendency in our historical period...'.

Given the observations of Steiner and Falk with respect to the human rights movement's radical effects on internal power and external sovereignty, why would any state sign up to a human rights treaty other than in bad faith?

RICHARD FALK, SOVEREIGNTY AND HUMAN DIGNITY: THE SEARCH FOR RECONCILIATION

in Francis Deng and Terrence Lyons (eds.), African Reckoning: A Quest for Good Governance (1998), at 12

If the doctrine of sovereignty could be erased from the minds of political leaders, would it reduce those forms of human suffering associated with extreme governmental failure? Would such an erasure strengthen sentiments of human solidarity on which an ethos of collective responsibility and individual accountability depends?

This still dominant image of sovereignty is essentially negative, a prerogative to resist claims and encroachments coming from outside national boundaries — the right to say no. Such a view of sovereignty is especially prevalent among sub-Saharan countries, which look back on their pre-independence past in sorrow and anger because of the harms generally perceived to have resulted from the predatory interventions that lay at the core of the colonial experience. With this image still uppermost in political consciousness, the acquisition of independence and with it sovereign rights was most often and influentially understood as an inversion of colonialism. Instead of complete domination from *outside* the country, there was now to be unencumbered freedom to act *inside* borders.

But the predicaments of postcolonial Africa are very different from those of colonial Africa. If one follows the lines of reasoning that flow from the American and French Revolutions, sovereignty inheres ultimately not in the state but in the citizenry and is associated with the rights of people, although it may be exercised by the people's representatives. Such international moral, legal, and political ideas as the right of self-determination and the right of development are direct expressions of this understanding of sovereignty, but such an understanding has not yet formally conditioned the interplay between state, society, and the organized international community.

Under present circumstances sovereignty calls for a more balanced, complex view of this foundational idea of the contemporary state that continues to provide the ideological underpinning of world order. The spread of support for human rights and the emergence of a norm of democratic entitlement [lend] credence to the view that the state is itself the subject of obligations as well as entitled to rights, and that these obligations may be implemented both by a politics of resistance on the part of citizens and by a process of humanitarian intervention by the international community. This conditioning of sovereignty is further evolved in relation to the capacity of a state to carry out governmental functions. When the state fails to provide governance, other political actors are needed to protect a vulnerable citizenry from the perils of chaos and civil strife as well as from unleashed forces of ethnic and religious extremism. This is particularly true in much of Africa where the intermediate structures of civil society are very weak, offering little protection in the event that government institutions at the center collapse or even seriously erode.

. . .

Aside from doctrinal confusion, manipulation, and uncertainty, there is a clear trend away from the idea of unconditional sovereignty and toward a concept of responsible sovereignty. Governmental legitimacy that validates the exercise of sovereignty involves adherence to minimum humanitarian norms and a capacity to act effectively to protect citizens from acute threats to their security and well-being that derive from adverse conditions within a country. As with other fundamental norms and principles, sovereignty evolves in relation to practice and to changes in community expectations. . . .

NOTE

Compare the following comment of Margaret Keck and Kathryn Sikkink:[4]

> . . . Northerners within networks usually see third world leaders' claims about sovereignty as the self-serving positions of authoritarian or, in any case, elite actors. They consider that a weaker sovereignty might actually improve the political clout of the most marginalized people in developing countries.
>
> In the south, however, many activists take quite a different view. Rather than seeing sovereignty as a stone wall blocking the spread of desired principles and norms, they recognize its fragility and worry about weakening it further. The doctrines of sovereignty and nonintervention remain the main line of defense against foreign efforts to limit domestic and international choices that third world states (and their citizens) can make. Self-determination, because it has so rarely been

[4] *Activists beyond Borders: Advocacy Networks in International Politics* (1998), at 215.

practiced in a satisfactory manner, remains a desired, if fading, utopia. Sovereignty over resources, a fundamental part of the discussions about a new international economic order, appears particularly to be threatened by international action on the environment. Even where third world activists may oppose the policies of their own governments, they have no reason to believe that international actors would do better, and considerable reason to suspect the contrary. In developing countries it is as much the idea of the state, as it is the state itself, that warrants loyalty.

...

... The issue of sovereignty, for third world activists, is deeply embedded in the issue of structural inequality.

AMBASSADOR RICHARD N. HAASS, SOVEREIGNTY: EXISTING RIGHTS, EVOLVING RESPONSIBILITIES

Remarks presented at Georgetown University, School of Foreign Service, 14 January 2003

...

... For the past two years, as Director of Policy Planning [at the U.S. Department of State], I have been privileged to be able to look at the entire mosaic of U.S. foreign policy. George C. Marshall created the Policy Planning Staff 55 years ago, to provide a broad strategic perspective that could guide and inform daily diplomacy. ...

...

... Sovereignty is so fundamental, so embedded in our conceptions about the way our world works, that we often take its existence for granted. We should not. ...

...

The final challenge to sovereignty I want to highlight arises not when states cede it voluntarily but when it is taken away. This is the result of one of the most significant developments of the past decades: the emerging global consensus that sovereignty is not a blank check. Rather, sovereign status is contingent on the fulfillment by each state of certain fundamental obligations, both to its own citizens and to the international community. When a regime fails to live up to these responsibilities or abuses its prerogatives, it risks forfeiting its sovereign privileges including, in extreme cases, its immunity from armed intervention.

I believe that exceptions to the norm of non-intervention are warranted in at least three circumstances.

The first qualification of sovereignty comes when a state commits or fails to prevent genocide or crimes against humanity on its territory. The international community then has the right and, indeed, in some cases, the obligation to act to safeguard the lives of innocents.

As Czech President Vaclav Havel said at the NATO summit in Prague in November, "human life, human freedom and human dignity represent higher values than state sovereignty." A growing body of humanitarian and human rights law, enshrined in the Genocide Convention and the Covenant on Civil and Political Rights, recognizes that individuals, as well as states, possess fundamental rights.

. . . Non-intervention is no longer sacrosanct, even at the United Nations, a body formed by and committed to sovereign states. As U.N. Secretary-General Kofi Annan declared in September 1999, "States bent on criminal behavior [should] know that frontiers are not an absolute defense that massive and systematic violations of human rights wherever they may take place should not be allowed to stand."

Within the developing world, too, there is a budding recognition that sovereignty must have limits. We see this in the founding act of the African Union, which recently replaced the Organization of African Unity (OAU). In contrast to the OAU, which regarded non-interference as a bedrock principle, the new African Union commits all members to respect human rights and good governance, establishing a peer review mechanism to monitor compliance with these commitments. We witness a similar evolution in the Western Hemisphere, where all the members of the Organization of American States except Cuba have committed to a Democratic Charter, pledging to oppose any interruption of democratic processes.

We see a comparable change in international views of state responsibilities to fight terrorism. This is the second point of growing global consensus: Quite simply, countries have the right to take action to protect their citizens against those states that abet, support, or harbor international terrorists, or are incapable of controlling terrorists operating from their territory.

. . .

Finally, states risk forfeiting their sovereignty when they take steps that represent a clear threat to global security. When certain regimes with a history of aggression and support for terrorism pursue weapons of mass destruction, thereby endangering the international community, they jeopardize their sovereign immunity from intervention including anticipatory action to destroy this developing capability.

The right to self-defense including the right to take "pre-emptive" action against a clear and imminent threat has long been recognized in international law and practice. The challenge today is to adapt the principle of self-defense to the unique dangers posed by the proliferation of weapons of mass destruction. Traditionally, international lawyers have distinguished between pre-emption against an imminent threat, which they consider legitimate, and "preventive action" taken against a developing capability, which they regard as problematic. . . . The deception practiced by rogue regimes has made it harder to discern either the capability or imminence of attack. It is also often difficult to interpret the intentions of certain states, forcing us to judge them against a backdrop of past aggressive behavior. Most fundamentally, the rise of catastrophic weapons means that the cost of underestimating these dangers is potentially enormous. . . .

In all three of the situations I have just outlined stopping genocide, fighting terrorism, and preventing the spread of weapons of mass destruction, the principle remains the same: With rights come obligations. Sovereignty is not absolute. It is conditional. . . .

The world is still groping towards consensus on the obligations of sovereignty and on the steps that are warranted when states refuse to live up to them. In all cases, the bar to armed intervention must be set high. . . .

The reason for prudence is clear-cut. Although sovereignty is less absolute and more contingent than in the past, it remains, as it has been for the past three-and-a-half centuries, a central pillar — and arguably the central pillar — of world order. We do not want to return to a world in which governments routinely intervene in one another's affairs. In an age of advanced conventional weapons and new instruments of mass destruction, this would be a recipe for catastrophe. Accordingly, there should be a general presumption in favor of respecting sovereignty. But as my remarks this evening suggest, we need to strike a new balance between the rights and responsibilities of states....

QUESTIONS

1. If you were to flesh out Falk's notion of 'responsible sovereignty', what ingredients might it contain? The entire human rights corpus? What consequences might flow from a failure to exercise such 'responsible sovereignty' because of, say, gross and massive human rights violations like massacres of political opponents? What entities — states, IGOs, NGOS, others — might impose those consequences?

2. How do you assess the comment of Keck and Sikkink? Do you understand it to be consistent with Falk's proposal?

3. Do you agree with Richard Haass's view on 'conditional sovereignty'? Should the systematic violations of economic and social rights trigger the suspension or qualification of sovereignty with the same implications that Haass describes for other rights violations?

4. Has the human rights movement contributed to an erosion of state sovereignty and thus ineluctably lent support to proposals like Haass's? Consider the following comment.

> What distinguishes the use of force to prevent genocide from the use of force for pre-emptive self-defense? If it is known that a despot is arming himself to eradicate a minority population within his country, sovereignty should be no defense against states willing to employ force to prevent the atrocity. A fortiori, democratic states should not be expected to remain idle when they know that a despotic nation is arming itself with the intent to attack their countries. Indeed, a state has a greater obligation to use force to prevent an attack against its own citizens in the latter situation than it does to use force to prevent an attack against foreign citizens by their government in the former situation.

COMMENT ON DOMESTIC JURISDICTION

In the human rights context, especially within the United Nations, many perspectives on sovereignty have been brought into debate primarily in the context of two issues: (1) the interplay between Article 2(7), on the one hand, and Articles 55–56 of the Charter and provisions of human rights treaties, on the other; and (2) proposed action by the Security Council in response to a threat to international peace and security or in cases of humanitarian intervention, such as in Kosovo in 1999. Article 2(7) reads:

> Nothing contained in the present Charter shall authorize the United Nations to intervene in matters which are essentially within the domestic jurisdiction of any

State . . ., but this principle shall not prejudice the application of enforcement measures under Chapter VII.

Although this provision does not sit easily with the undertakings in Articles 55–56 to cooperate with the UN in promoting respect for human rights, nor with the explicit duties of states set forth in the human rights treaties, the tensions were left to be dealt with over time through the developing practice of UN organs. Apart from mandating the creation of a Commission/Council on Human Rights, the Charter did not spell out the measures that it envisaged might be taken to give effect to one of the UN's principal purposes, listed in Article 1(3), of promoting and encouraging respect for human rights. The General Assembly was empowered to 'discuss any questions or any matters within the scope of the . . . Charter' (Article 10) and to 'initiate studies and make recommendations for the purpose of . . . [*inter alia*] assisting in the realization of human rights' (Article 13). Neither the type of studies nor the ways in which they might be prepared were spelled out. Nor was it clear what, if any, limits applied to the type of recommendations that might be made. So the task remained of working out the relationship between the traditional themes of state sovereignty in paragraphs (1) and (7) of Article 2 with the internationalist spirit of Article 1 and the later human rights provisions.

Some critics have stressed that the Charter did not give the Assembly or other UN organs the power to make authoritative interpretations of these or any other provisions. In Watson's view, 'as a result, the power of autointerpretation still remains with individual states'.[5] Each state, when addressed by a UN organ (other than the Security Council acting under explicit powers), would then decide for itself whether or not the matter raised was part of its *domaine reservé* (domestic jurisdiction) and thus off limits to the UN under Article 2(7). The overwhelming majority of commentators have rejected this analysis, and have instead argued that (1) the General Assembly must have the power to interpret its own mandate, including the implications of Article 2(7); (2) a teleological approach should be applied in interpreting Article 2(7) in the light of the (developing) purposes of the Organization (Article 1); (3) the resolutions of the UN and other bodies have made clear that a narrow interpretation is to be given to Article 2(7); and (4) as legitimate matters of international concern, human rights cannot reasonably be characterized as being exclusively an internal matter.

Over the course of more than half a century, UN organs have systematically reduced the scope claimed for the domestic jurisdiction 'defence'. The early case of South Africa was critical. Although Article 2(7) was invoked in many diplomatic exchanges and public statements by a variety of states in the late 1940s and early 1950s, apartheid led to a major breakthrough. A special Commission on the Racial Situation in the Union of South Africa appointed by the General Assembly in 1952 concluded that Article 2(7) prohibited only 'dictatorial interference', a phrase interpreted as implying 'a peremptory demand for positive conduct or abstention — a demand which, if not complied with, involves a threat of or recourse to compulsion . . .'. Article 2(7) referred 'only to direct intervention in the domestic economy,

[5] James Shand Watson, *Theory and Reality in the International Protection of Human Rights* (1999), at 205.

social structure, or cultural arrangements of the State concerned but does not in any way preclude recommendations, or even inquiries conducted outside the territory of such State'.[6] The Commission's report gave rise to extensive debate, in which South Africa took the position that the General Assembly could not even discuss the subject of race relations in that country. Only rarely today does one hear even distant echoes of that extreme position. (Later developments with respect to South Africa are described at p. 836, *infra*.)

Although regularly invoked, the domestic jurisdiction defence proved equally unsuccessful in relation to debate and recommendations about other cases such as those of Vietnam in the early 1960s, Israel since the late 1960s, Chile in the 1970s and countries such as Iran and Afghanistan in the 1980s.[7] It has been difficult to assemble a wide range of governments to advance a strong defensive interpretation (that is, a broad interpretation) of Article 2(7) that is consistent, because states arguing for such an interpretation in their own defence have nonetheless occasionally or frequently insisted that measures be taken against other violator states.

The only significant exception in this regard has been the People's Republic of China, which has abstained in the UN from condemning human rights violations in other states of which it clearly did not approve. But even China supported resolutions condemning human rights violations in Afghanistan, southern Africa and the Israeli Occupied Territories, and has expressed its concern about human rights violations in countries such as Indonesia in the late 1990s.

The end of the Cold War brought a dramatic change of policy by many states and within the UN with respect to domestic jurisdiction. For example, Poland had insisted in 1983, when its own declaration of martial law was under scrutiny, that UN organs could consider human rights questions in a particular state only 'if the following criteria were met: firstly, that a particular situation represented a gross, massive and flagrant violation of human rights and fundamental freedoms; secondly, that the situation represented a consistent pattern of such violations; thirdly, that the situation endangered international peace and security; and lastly, that consideration of the situation was without prejudice to the functions and powers of organs already in existence'.[8] But by October 1991 Poland endorsed the following conclusion of the Moscow Meeting of the Conference on the Human Dimension of the Conference on Security and Co-operation in Europe (the CSCE, or Helsinki process, described at p. 1016, *infra*):

> The participating States emphasize that issues relating to human rights, fundamental freedoms, democracy and the rule of law are of international concern, as respect for these rights and freedoms constitutes one of the foundations of the international order. They categorically and irrevocably declare that the commitments undertaken in the field of the human dimension of the CSCE are matters of direct and legitimate concern to all participating States and do not belong exclusively to the internal affairs of the State concerned.[9]

[6] UN Doc. A/2505 (1953), 16–22.

[7] Menno Kamminga, *Inter-State Accountability for Violations of Human Rights* (1992).

[8] UN Doc. E/CN.4/1983/SR.40/Add.1.

[9] 30 Int. Leg. Mat. 1670, 1672 (1991).

Today the issue of domestic jurisdiction is rarely raised in other than a perfunctory manner in UN fora. Even when raised by a state like China whose human rights record is under criticism, a substantive debate about a resolution or other aspects of the criticism usually takes place and the outcome (a resolution, say, passed or defeated) reflects a variety of legal and political considerations among which Article 2(7) as such is not a substantial factor.

PETER J. SPIRO, THE NEW SOVEREIGNTISTS: AMERICAN EXCEPTIONALISM AND ITS FALSE PROPHETS

79 Foreign Affairs (2000), 9–15

[A]nti-internationalism claims a growing intellectual following. This group of academics — many of whom are highly credentialed and attached to prestigious institutions or conservative Washington think tanks — has developed a coherent blueprint for defending American institutions against the alleged encroachment of international ones. This school does not oppose international engagement per se and thus cannot be classified simply as isolationist. Rather, it holds that the United States can pick and choose the international conventions and laws that serve its purpose and reject those that do not. Call it international law à la carte.

...

This "New Sovereigntist" vision explains the continuing U.S. refusal to participate in a broad array of international regimes, some of them now nearly universally accepted by other nations. It drove the Senate's recent rejection of the Comprehensive Test Ban Treaty, the Clinton administration's refusal to sign on to the Land Mines Convention and the Rome Treaty establishing an international criminal court, and the U.S. failure to submit the Kyoto Protocol on global warming for Senate approval. It also explains Washington's persistent refusal to conform U.S. practices to international human rights regimes. The United States stands alone with Somalia in not acceding to the Convention on the Rights of the Child. Washington heavily qualified its acceptance of the International Covenant on Civil and Political Rights (ICCPR).... Only the free-trade agreements — provided they are limited to trade and do not include the environment, labor issues, or human rights — pass muster under New Sovereigntism because they are thought to serve American interests.

...

New Sovereigntists relentlessly characterize most international law standards as too amorphous to justify American agreement. A favorite whipping post is the broader provisions of human rights treaties. Jack Goldsmith, a law professor at the University of Chicago [now Harvard], asks "would the ICCPR's 'protection against discrimination on any ground,' including 'status,' extend to discrimination on the basis of homosexuality? Age? Weight? Beauty? Intelligence?" This reasoning warns, in effect, of the bait-and-switch possibilities in some international treaties: Washington should not sign on to innocuous generalities today that may become dangerously specific tomorrow.

...

On the process side, New Sovereigntists assert the deficiency of international lawmaking by raising the specter of international bureaucrats who lack accountability within the American constitutional scheme. John Yoo, a law professor at the University of California at Berkeley, warns that "novel forms of international cooperation increasingly call for the transfer of rulemaking authority to international organizations that lack American openness and accountability." New Sovereigntists highlight the lack of direct elections at the international level to strike an unfavorable contrast with the selection of U.S. lawmakers. In the tradition of Cold War critiques of international law, they also question the enforceability and vitality of international law by underscoring the acceptance of human rights regimes by such brazen violators as Iraq, Serbia, and North Korea. This argument echoes historical campaigns against U.S. participation in international regimes: We live up to our word when no one else does, so if we agree to international obligations we are effectively tying one hand behind our back against an enemy who keeps both hands free. At bottom, the New Sovereigntists question whether international law is about anything more than international power.

Here again the arguments fall short. Accountability deficits in increasingly powerful international institutions do exist (the central point of the Seattle and Washington demonstrations), but international organizations are not free-floating entities with unconfined powers. In fact, they are kept on the usually tight leash of their nation-state members. But where mainstream environmentalists, human rights advocates, and labor interests could accept global governance (if it heard their voices), New Sovereigntists reject even the possibility that international institutions can be made accountable. Indeed, in a strange twist betraying their neoconservative tendencies, the New Sovereigntists paint the institutional influence of nongovernmental organizations (NGOs) as part of the accountability problem rather than part of its solution.

...

The linchpin of New Sovereigntism is its premise that America has the power to opt out of international norms, even those universally accepted by other nations. "As the strongest and richest country in the world, the United States can afford to safeguard its sovereignty," argues Rabkin....

This approach echoes the realist conception of international relations as a matter of might, not right — a sticks-and-stones view of international law. At the same time, New Sovereigntists contend that, within the American domestic framework, the federal government lacks the constitutional power to participate in some international regimes. Curtis Bradley, a professor at the University of Virginia Law School [now Duke Law School], has argued that the unconditional adoption of international human rights conventions would violate federalism constraints.... In a 1997 Harvard Law Review article (the opening salvo in the New Sovereigntist crusade), Bradley and Goldsmith argued that federal courts have no place enforcing norms of international law, including established human rights. The bottom line: Not only does the United States have the power to reject international regimes, but in many instances the federal government has a constitutional duty to reject them. America does not have to play by the rules that everybody else plays by because nobody can make it play by them — and besides, it has its own set of more important ones.

These arguments are grounded in highly formalistic readings of the Constitution and selective interpretations of its history. Some revive arguments already made and defeated at other times of critical change in America's relationship to the rest of the world. Most important, the New Sovereigntists forget that the Constitution — hardly blind to the national interest — has always adapted itself successfully to new exigencies of the international system. Such values as federalism, the separation of powers, and individual rights are not so brittle that they will shatter at the intersection with globalization.

Indeed, the Constitution will have to adapt to global requirements sooner or later, for the New Sovereigntist premise of American impermeability is flawed. . . . True, Washington will continue to maintain the fiction of an opt-out capability, and the international community cannot yet force formal participation in international regimes. But economic globalization will inevitably bring the United States in line.

Meanwhile, the international community can advance the rule of international law by working against key U.S. actors — most notably corporations but also states — in trade and investment decisions. That way, it can directly discipline U.S. entities, circumventing and constraining anti-internationalist federal policymakers in the process. Take the test-ban case. . . . When France undertook nuclear tests in 1995, NGOs launched a campaign against French wine that helped force President Jacques Chirac to back down from future testing. Something similar would happen if America announced an intention to test. Boycotts might threaten certain powerful U.S. industries (e.g., fast-food chains) with lost sales, which would in turn press the federal government to respect the test ban.

A similar story is likely to unfold in the human rights context. The United States stands increasingly isolated, at least among Western nations, in its continued use of the death penalty. . . . On the one hand, no one expects Washington to sign on to international accords limiting capital punishment. On the other, international actors are now moving against the U.S. states that continue the practice. Executions in the United States consistently make headlines in Europe, where state-level responsibility for the death penalty is widely understood. As a result, European and other foreign leaders are bypassing Washington to make direct protests to states with frequent or controversial executions, such as Texas, Virginia, and Georgia. Where economic pressure and shaming campaigns might not work against the United States, they can prove effective on the state level. . . . In the medium term, states will almost certainly eliminate the more internationally offensive uses of the death penalty, and over the long run they will likely end it altogether. Again, the United States will end up complying with an international norm even if it does not take formal steps to accept it. The New Sovereigntists may win high-profile battles on Capitol Hill, but they will lose the war on the more important fronts.

For now, however, the New Sovereigntist grip over Washington imposes significant costs by retarding the advance of international law. The United States may be increasingly vulnerable to international pressure, but it is still the biggest kid on the block. Persistent American rejection will hurt the progress of even well-established international regimes by giving cover to other nonparticipants, and incipient norms will lose the boost that would otherwise come with American acceptance. And U.S. noncompliance with international accords saps its authority to press other nations to respect the rule of international law.

Above all, the United States compromises its own interests by formally refusing to adopt widely accepted international regimes. Treaty committees and other international institutions usually extend participation rights only to member states. America thereby forfeits any right to help shape those regimes that it rejects. It has no voice in shaping international norms at a critical stage of their development, even as its ability to resist their imposition diminishes. It plays the part of the complaining, unregistered voter on the international stage, refusing to participate in processes that nevertheless bind him. . . .

CURTIS A. BRADLEY AND JACK L. GOLDSMITH, MY PREROGATIVE

80 Foreign Affairs 188 (2001)

Peter Spiro cites us as examples of his article's title villains . . . He defines this awkward term ["New Sovereigntists"] (which is his, not ours) as those who believe "the United States can pick and choose the international conventions and laws that serve its purpose and reject those that do not."

But the idea that a nation can decide which international laws to embrace is not new and should not be controversial. In a world of diverse cultures, political systems, and power relationships, international law derives its legitimacy and efficacy from national consent. And the power to give consent naturally implies the power to withhold it.

Spiro describes our position as "anti-internationalist." It is not a rejection of international law, however, to examine whether treaties or customary international rules are consistent with U.S. interests and constitutional standards, or to consider how these international norms should best be implemented within the U.S. system. The United States has long supported the development of an international rule of law. It has also insisted, however, that its international commitments have the support of its people through elected representatives, and that these commitments respect basic constitutional principles such as the separation of powers, federalism, and individual liberties.

Spiro dismisses these domestic democratic and constitutional concerns. For him, more international law, regardless of its content, is always better and should always trump domestic standards. Thus, he claims that the "New Sovereigntism" is "retarding the advance of international law." As for the possibility that some of this "advancing" international law might actually contravene U.S. constitutional values, Spiro simply asserts that "the Constitution will have to adapt." Fortunately, our elected officials have been more sensitive to the domestic costs of international regimes than Spiro has.

Ironically, it is Spiro's unalloyed internationalism, not the New Sovereigntism, that is likely to foster U.S. rejection of international law. Washington often pulls back from international commitments and institutions when such obligations no longer respond to American needs and values. The more advocates such as Spiro justify international law as an end in itself without regard to national consent, the more likely it is that they will fuel the very anti-internationalism they decry.

RYAN GOODMAN AND DEREK JINKS, TOWARD AN INSTITUTIONAL THEORY OF SOVEREIGNTY

55 Stanford L. Rev. 1749 (2003)

... [T]his Article offers a sociological model of state sovereignty. We suggest that the state should be understood as a highly institutionalized organizational form that is embedded in a global cultural order. In many important respects, states are enactors and enactments of models that are substantially organized and legitimated through global culture....

Our model calls into question several basic assumptions of current debates about international law and state sovereignty. According to conventional wisdom, there is a structural tension between state sovereignty and a range of practices including compliance with international obligations, participation in multilateral regimes, and acceptance of international legal principles. Major concerns include preserving national control over domestic legal and policy choices, and, in international affairs, avoiding exogenous constraints on sovereign prerogatives.... We contend, however, that these concerns are, at best, misspecified and, at worst, misleading (and, as a consequence, amenable to ideological manipulation). Quite plainly, a new vocabulary is needed to resolve these paradoxes and to explain the interests that are actually at stake.

First, the putative tension between international law and state sovereignty must be reexamined. According to the sociological model we advance, the constitutive features of states derive from world-level cultural models, and the nature of sovereignty itself is a global cultural product. State commitments to, and specific designs for, "domestic" policies (e.g., programs for education, science, welfare, suffrage) reflect globally legitimated agendas.... [S]everal fundamental features of "national security" — including the practices in pursuit of it, interests that motivate it, and cognitive systems that frame it — are also derived, in significant part, from worldwide institutional environments. Indeed, the very principles of state autonomy and sovereign independence (as well as the domestic and international practices employing these principles) follow global scripts.

These insights reveal a number of paradoxes in the conventional understanding of sovereignty. Consider a few stylized examples. In country X, military elites resist application of an international humanitarian rule on the ground that it intrudes on "sovereignty" and their military authority; yet their conception of sovereignty, their zone of authority, and perhaps the nature of the resistance itself are derived, in significant part, from global cultural and associational processes. . . . The important point is that several constitutive features of the modern state (including the very notion of being an autonomous actor) are socially constructed at a global level. This perspective directly challenges the normative appeal and conceptual coherence of state resistance to other potentially conflicting global norms on the basis that these norms undermine its "autonomy," "individuality," and "self-determination." . . .

. . .

Second, world models of sovereignty differ sharply from the idealized notions of "autonomous states." Indeed, globally legitimated notions of sovereignty not only empower, but also constrain the "legitimate actorhood" of states. For example, appeals to sovereignty inhibit humanitarian-oriented states from intervening in other countries to stop mass slaughter; limit the capacity of states to constrain dangerous arms races and the proliferation of weapons of mass destruction; and arguably generate inefficiencies in achieving free trade and flexible movement of labor. Following the global script of sovereignty can also hamper the ability to achieve pragmatic concessions over contested territory, and instead can push states toward armed conflict and displays of brinkmanship. Similarly, sovereignty and the integrity of the state can also promote protracted internal armed conflicts. Not only are states less willing to concede for symbolic reasons, national liberation groups are less willing to ask or settle for anything less than their own state as a means to international legitimacy and self-determination.

Appeals to sovereignty can also threaten constitutional norms and protections. Consider U.S. foreign-affairs scholars who advocate suspending regular forms of judicial review when cases involve questions of sovereignty. Similarly, in U.S. immigration law, the Supreme Court's plenary power doctrine is grounded in strong notions of sovereignty. On this basis, courts have held that the judiciary may not exercise its regular authority in protecting individual rights.

At bottom, our point is that "sovereignty," as a highly institutionalized global norm, complicates and constrains state action. Although the concept of sovereignty assigns to the state supreme political authority within a delimited territory, the scope and content of this "authority" are defined and legitimated by global cultural processes.

Conversely, our model also illuminates surprising ways in which institutional constraints empower states. A basic insight in sociology is that social structure not only constrains, but also empowers actors. . . . [W]orld society is no different. As discussed in greater detail . . . global culture legitimates purposive states with the formal responsibility for promoting certain globally legitimated goals. In this sense, the institutional constraints of global culture define the organizational field within which states are highly legitimated actors. By following that global script, states are empowered to act. They are also tasked with objectives — both internationally and domestically — for action.

. . .

QUESTIONS

1. Is Professors Bradley and Goldsmith's rejoinder an effective response to Professor Spiro's central claim? Are Bradley and Goldsmith correct that arguments like Spiro's 'fuel

the very anti-internationalism they decry'? Based on the article by Professor Jed Rubenfeld in Chapter 1, p. 50 *supra*, how might he respond to Spiro's analysis?

2. Do international human rights institutions always threaten state sovereignty or create, sustain, and, in some cases, bolster it as Professors Goodman and Jinks suggest? Does their analysis help counter concerns that 'new sovereigntists' have about international human rights law?

C. INSTITUTIONAL DESIGN: BUILDING GLOBAL STRUCTURES TO INFLUENCE STATES

Part D examines numerous international human rights institutions. The features of these institutions vary across several dimensions. For example, they may extend globally or regionally, provide for open or restricted membership, forge formal or informal agreements, cover multiple or single issues, codify precise rules or abstract guidelines, emphasize coercive authority or voluntarism, and afford meaningful or nominal opportunities for NGO participation. Each of these design choices can potentially affect the distributional consequences and overall effectiveness of an international institution. Accordingly, the following discussion considers how to fashion international institutions with competing design choices in mind.

Various interdisciplinary perspectives can inform the study and practice of institutional design. The approaches that scholars and practitioners have brought to bear on this subject include empirical social science research, economic-analytic modelling, historical inquiry, and more. Interdisciplinary approaches may lend insight into such matters as the logic of action that drives state behaviour, the influence of military and economic power versus ethical norms in shaping global politics, and the capacity of multilateral organizations to resolve collective action problems. A better understanding of those issues can assist in fashioning institutions to define and safeguard human rights in the most effective and normatively desirable manner.

The following readings include diverse approaches to and perspectives on institutional design. These readings can help frame your examination of human rights institutions in subsequent chapters. First there follow excerpts from the Table of Contents of a leading treatise on international organizations that suggest a formal typology for thinking about the constitution and operations of international institutions. It indicates how much choice states have, and how many possibilities are before them, when they negotiate about the form and reform of multilateral institutions.

HENRY G. SCHERMERS AND NIELS M. BLOKKER, INTERNATIONAL INSTITUTIONAL LAW: UNITY WITHIN DIVERSITY

(4th rev. edn. 2003), at ix–xxvi

Table of Contents

a. Need for regional representation
b. Composition of regions
F. Election of non-plenary organs
1. Election by the entire organization
2. Election by the region or group concerned
3. Election or rotation?
III. Functioning
...
2. Frequency and duration
3. Specialized sessions
...
5. Place
6. Public and private meetings, publicity and transparency
...
9. Procedure
B. Officers
1. Chairman
...
2. Vice-presidents and bureau
3. Rapporteurs
...
III. Secretariat
...
CHAPTER 5 Advisory and Supervisory Organs
I. Parliamentary organs
...
II. Judicial organs
...
CHAPTER 6 Decision-making process
...
III. Initiative
A. Necessity for initiatives
B. Initiatives by governments
C. Initiatives by organs of the organization
...
E. Initiatives by interest groups
F. Initiatives by individuals
...
V. Decision-making by consensus
...
VI. Voting
A. Unanimity
B. Voting power
1. Equality of voting power

2. Inequality of voting power
   a. Permanent seats and weighted representation

...

   c. Veto

C. Required majority
1. Kinds of majorities
2. Calculation of majorities
   a. Majority of membership
   b. Majority of the votes
   c. Abstention

...

   f. Invalid vote
3. Unqualified majority
   a. Voting between two alternatives
   b. Voting between several alternatives
   c. Multiple elections

...

D. Methods of voting
1. Simultaneous open voting
2. Roll-call or recorded vote
3. Secret vote
4. Vote by correspondence
5. Alteration of votes cast

...

VIII. Termination of decisions

...

CHAPTER 7 Financing

...

CHAPTER 8 Legal order

...

II. Constitution

...

C. Amendment of the constitution

...

III. Decisions of the organization
A. Internal rules
1. Rules concerning the functioning of the organization

...

B. External rules
1. Recommendations

...

2. Declarations

...

3. Conventions

...

4. Binding rules

...

CHAPTER 10 Supervision and sanctions

...

II. Supervision of the implementation of rules
   A. Supervision by other members acting on their own account
   B. Supervision by or on behalf of the organization

...

III. Official recognition of violations

...

V. Sanctions

BARBARA KOREMENOS, CHARLES LIPSON AND DUNCAN SNIDAL, THE RATIONAL DESIGN OF INTERNATIONAL INSTITUTIONS

55 International Organization (2001), 761–799

...

We begin with a simple observation: major institutions are organized in radically different ways. . . .

Why do these differences exist? Do they really matter, both for members and for international politics more generally? Do they affect what the institutions themselves can do? We focus on these large questions of institutional design. Our basic presumption, grounded in the broad tradition of rational-choice analysis, is that states use international institutions to further their own goals, and they design institutions accordingly. This might seem obvious, but it is surprisingly controversial.

One critique comes from constructivists, who argue that international institutions play a vital, independent role in spreading global norms. We agree that normative discourse is an important aspect of institutional life (though surely not the whole of it) and that norms are contested within, and sometimes propagated by, international institutions. But it is misleading to think of international institutions solely as outside forces or exogenous actors. They are the self-conscious creation of states (and, to a lesser extent, of interest groups and corporations).

The realist critique is exactly the opposite. For them, international institutions are little more than ciphers for state power. This exaggerates an important point. States rarely allow international institutions to become significant autonomous actors. Nonetheless, institutions are considerably more than empty vessels. States spend significant amounts of time and effort constructing institutions precisely because they can advance or impede state goals. . . . States fight over institutional design because it affects outcomes. . . .

. . . We explore — theoretically and empirically — the implications of our basic presumption that states construct and shape institutions to advance their goals. The most direct implication is that design differences . . . are the result of rational, purposive interactions among states and other international actors to solve specific problems.

We define international institutions as explicit arrangements, negotiated among international actors, that prescribe, proscribe, and/or authorize behavior. . . .

Although in most arrangements negotiators are typically states, this is not part of our definition; it is an empirical observation that may vary across issues and over time. In fact, nonstate actors participate with increasing frequency in institutional design. Multinational firms, nongovernmental organizations (NGOs), and intergovernmental organizations have all shaped international institutions, solely especially those dealing with the world economy, the environment, and human rights.

Thus our definition of international institutions is relatively broad. It includes formal organizations like the World Health Organization and International Labor Organization, as well as well-defined (and explicit) arrangements like "diplomatic immunity" that have no formal bureaucracy or enforcement mechanisms but are fundamental to the conduct of international affairs.

. . .

. . . [I]nstitutional rules must be "incentive compatible" so that actors create, change, and adhere to institutions because doing so is in their interests. Consider an institution that can be sustained only through sanctions and whose members must apply these sanctions themselves. This is an equilibrium institution only if the members who are supposed to apply sanctions actually have incentives to do so. Incentive compatibility does not mean that members always adhere to rules or that every state always benefits from the institutions to which it belongs. It does mean that over the long haul states gain by participating in specific institutions — or else they will abandon them.

. . .

Membership

Who belongs to the institution? Is membership exclusive and restrictive, like the G-7's limitation to rich countries? Or is it inclusive by design, like the UN? Is it regional, like ASEAN, or is it universal? Is it restricted to states, or can NGOs join?

. . .

Scope

What issues are covered? . . .

Sometimes two seemingly unrelated issues are linked. A trade issue, for example, may be linked to a security issue to facilitate agreement and compliance. . . .

. . .

Sometimes scope is not open to design choice because of technical considerations or shared perceptions. In the Law of the Sea negotiations, for example, jurisdiction over ocean territories could not be separated from coastal environment and fishing rights issues. Technological interactions required that these issues be dealt with together in a comprehensive settlement. But other Law of the Sea issues seemed to have little in common. Here linkage was more cognitive — a result of how issues were framed, especially under the rubric of the "common heritage of mankind."

...

Centralization

Are some important institutional tasks performed by a single focal entity or not? Scholars often misleadingly equate centralization with centralized enforcement. We use the term more broadly to cover a wide range of centralized activities. In particular we focus on centralization to disseminate information, to reduce bargaining and transaction costs, and to enhance enforcement. These categories are not exhaustive....

...

Control

How will collective decisions be made? Control is determined by a range of factors, including the rules for electing key officials and the way an institution is financed. We focus on voting arrangements as one important and observable aspect of control.

...

Flexibility

How will institutional rules and procedures accommodate new circumstances? Institutions may confront unanticipated circumstances or shocks, or face new demands from domestic coalitions or clusters of states wanting to change important rules or procedures. What kind of flexibility does an institution allow to meet such challenges?

It is important to distinguish between two kinds of institutional flexibility: adaptive and transformative. "Escape clauses" are a good example of adaptive flexibility. They allow members to respond to unanticipated shocks or special domestic circumstances while preserving existing institutional arrangements. . . . This limited flexibility is designed to deal chiefly with outlying cases, to wall them off from run-of-the-mill issues.

Some institutions have built-in arrangements to transform themselves in ways that are more profound. This deeper kind of flexibility usually involves clauses that permit renegotiation or sunset provisions that require new negotiations and ratification for the institution to survive. . . .

...

Conjectures about Rational Design

In this section we develop a series of conjectures . . .. We call these "conjectures" to indicate that they represent generalizations based on a common rational-choice theoretical framework. . . .

1. Rational design: States and other international actors, acting for self-interested reasons, design institutions purposefully to advance their joint interests.

We thus make standard assumptions: actors have (well-behaved) preferences over various goals; and the pursuit of those goals is guided by their beliefs about each others' preferences and the relative costs and benefits of different outcomes; and actors are constrained by their capabilities. . . .

. . .

2. Shadow of the future: The value of future gains is strong enough to support a cooperative arrangement.

. . .

3. Transaction costs: Establishing and participating in international institutions is costly.

When creating institutions, states need, for example, to acquire information about the issue, about each other, and about the likely effects of alternative institutional forms. One way they do this is through negotiations. There are other types of transaction costs as well, such as safeguards to ensure compliance and sustain cooperation. . . .

. . .

4. Risk aversion: States are risk-averse and worry about possible adverse effects when creating or modifying international institutions.

Risk-averse actors prefer a certain outcome to a chancy one when each has the same expected value. This assumption is the bedrock of modern realism, where states' fears of destruction and keen interest in preserving their sovereignty dominate their strategic calculations. However, even realist states may trade off some sovereignty if they reap large enough gains in return. Institutionalists have a broader view of what states value, but they, too, typically assume states are risk-averse.

With these four assumptions in mind, we now turn to specific conjectures about international institutional design. . . .

. . .

Conjecture M1: Restrictive Membership Increases With The Severity Of The Enforcement Problem

The more severe the enforcement problem, the more restricted the membership. When actors face an enforcement problem (that is, when individuals do not have an incentive to voluntarily contribute to group goals), collective action is problematic. Moreover, the severity of the enforcement problem increases with the number of actors . . . .

. . . Furthermore, when uncertainty about a state's capacity to comply is at issue, inclusive membership may be suboptimal because, as George Downs and David Rocke argue, "every time the third state violates the treaty, the other two states are forced to suspend the cooperation between them to punish it."

. . .

Conjecture M2: Restrictive Membership Increases With Uncertainty About Preferences

Membership enables states to learn about each others' preferences if the membership mechanism can distinguish cooperators from noncooperators. Ideally, a state that values the goals of an organization will want to join, whereas one that wants a free ride will find it too costly to join a regime they intend to violate. In formal terms, membership is a costly signal. Effective membership rules create a separating equilibrium where only those who share certain characteristics will bear the costs necessary to be included in an equilibrium. . . .

The WTO, for example, requires prospective members to bring key domestic economic rules in line with WTO rules — perhaps with phase-in allowances or special considerations for certain categories of states. Similarly, NATO will not accept a new member until it meets certain domestic political requirements and brings its military up to certain agreed-upon levels. By requiring concessions, these organizations ensure that prospective members are willing to bear the necessary adjustment costs and are likely to be cooperating members down the road. When the price of membership is too low, membership is not informative.

. . .

Conjecture S1: Issue Scope Increases With Greater Heterogeneity Among Larger Numbers Of Actors

. . .

When actors have heterogeneous interests, issue linkage may generate new opportunities for resolving conflicts and reaching mutually beneficial arrangements. James K. Sebenius demonstrates how adding issues "can yield joint gains that enhance or create a zone of possible agreement." . . . When one actor values issue X more than issue Y, and the other ranks them the opposite way, both can be made better off by exchange, that is, by agreeing to defer to each other on these issues. Environmental issues that are important to postindustrial states, for example, are often linked to issues of development and technology when less-developed states with less intrinsic interest in environmental quality are essential to the arrangement.

Conjecture S2: Issue Scope Increases With The Severity Of The Distribution Problem

Linkage not only allows states to increase efficiency but may also allow them to overcome distributional obstacles. When the benefits of an issue accrue primarily to a few, and the costs fall disproportionately on others, linkage to another issue with different distributional consequences allows cost-bearing states to be compensated by those who reap the gains. When each state cares relatively more about one of two issues, linking the negotiations may be the mutually preferred option. . . .

Conjecture S3: Issue Scope Increases With The Severity Of The Enforcement Problem

When the incentives on an issue are insufficient for decentralized enforcement, linkage to other issues can provide enforcement. . . .

Since all three conjectures point to advantages of greater scope, the question naturally arises, Why isn't everything linked to everything else? The answer is that increased scope also has costs. These include the extra bargaining costs associated with additional issues and the greater probability that some actor will "hold up" the agreement to gain additional benefits. The risk of unraveling, whereby failure in one issue may lead to failure in all linked issues, is also greater. . . .

Conjecture C1: Centralization Increases With Uncertainty About Behavior

The Folk theorem holds that when states interact over extended periods they can achieve cooperative outcomes on a decentralized basis through strategies of reciprocity. But when states are uncertain about others' behavior, they cannot achieve the same mutually beneficial outcomes. Greater noise lowers the joint gains they can achieve.... However, centralized information may offer a more effective alternative if it can reduce uncertainty about behavior to make (otherwise) decentralized cooperation more effective.

...

Centralized information not only lets states know how others have behaved but also can provide valuable interpretations of that behavior. States will know better whether others' noncooperation is intentional and deserves retaliation or is excusable because of extenuating circumstances. When states retaliate, their targets and third parties will better understand the action as retaliation rather than unilateral noncooperation or error....

[The authors go on to describe the following series of conjectures that illustrate their rational design approach.

Conjecture C2: Centralization Increases with Uncertainty about the State of the World.

Conjecture C3: Centralization Increases with Number.

Conjecture C4: Centralization Increases with the severity of the Enforcement Problem.

Conjecture V1: Individual Control Decreases as Number Increases.

Conjecture V2: Asymmetry of Control Increases with Asymmetry among Contributors (Number).

Conjecture V3: Individual Control (To Block Undesirable Outcomes) Increases with Uncertainty about the State of the World.

Conjecture F1: Flexibility Increases with Uncertainty about the State of the World.

Conjecture F2: Flexibility Increases with the Severity of the Distribution Problem.

Conjecture F3: Flexibility Decreases with Number.]

ALEXANDER WENDT, DRIVING WITH THE REARVIEW MIRROR: ON THE RATIONAL SCIENCE OF INSTITUTIONAL DESIGN

55 International Organization (2001), 1019–1049

... At base, the theory of rational design is that states and other actors choose international institutions to further their own interests. This amounts to a functionalist claim: actors choose institutions because they expect them to have a positive function....

... At first glance it might seem hard to identify plausible rivals. One is tempted to say, Of course actors design institutions to further their interests — what else would they do? But in fact there are some interesting rivals, both to the proposition that institutions are rationally chosen and to the proposition that they are designed....

...

Alternatives to "Rational"

What makes the choice of an institutional design "rational"? Rationality can be defined in various ways. In rational-choice theory it refers to instrumental or "logic of consequences" thinking: Actors are rational when they choose strategies that they believe will have the optimal consequences given their interests. The expected costs and benefits of different choices are compared, and the one with the highest net value is chosen. . . .

If for a single actor rational action is what subjectively maximizes its interests, then when there are multiple actors, as in international politics, a rationally chosen institution will be one that solves their collective-action problem, not one that necessarily solves a problem in the external world. . . . Collective-action problems, in short, are subjective at the group level, in that they are constituted by a shared perception of some facts in the world as (1) being a "problem" (versus not), (2) requiring "collective action" (versus not), and (3) having certain features that constitute what kind of collective-action problem it is (coordination, cooperation, security, economic, and so on). These understandings are only partly determined by objective facts in the world. . . . They are also constructed by a communicative process of interpreting what that world means and how and why designers should care about it. As such, there is ample room for institutional designers to ignore issues that others might see as problems (global justice?), or to define problems in mistaken ways ("fighting the last war").

This process of problem construction takes place prior to the questions in which [Koremenos et al. are] interested and structures how institutional design proceeds. Given a definition of the design problem, the rational action is to maximize the expected value of institutional choices. This subjectivism gives the Rational Design framework a curiously "post-modern" feel, since the rationality of institutional choices is always internal to the discourses by which collective-action problems are constituted. That the Bermuda aviation regime studied by John Richards was a rational choice, for example, presupposes that states were committed to preserving national carriers. While that desire makes sense from the standpoint of the symbolic concerns emphasized by sociological institutionalists, it is less clear how it comports with the material economic interests rationalists tend to emphasize. . . .

What are the alternatives to the hypothesis that states choose subjectively rational institutions? . . .

One alternative is that states choose institutional designs according to the "logic of appropriateness": Instead of weighing costs and benefits, they choose on the basis of what is normatively appropriate. This explanation is usually treated as a rival to the logic of consequences. . . . In international politics there are many examples of decision making on appropriateness grounds. . . . [An] interesting example is provided by Nina Tannenwald's study of the "nuclear taboo," which suggests that even when instrumental factors weighed in favor of using nuclear weapons, as in the Vietnam War, U.S. decision makers refrained on normative grounds. The way such a logic ultimately works is through the internalization of norms. As actors become socialized to norms, they make them part of their identity, and that identity in turn creates a collective interest in norms as ends in themselves.

The result is internalized self-restraint: actors follow norms not because it is in their self-interest, but because it is the right thing to do in their society. Society would not be as stable as it is if people always applied a logic of consequences to their actions, and so internalized norms may explain much of the rule-following we see in international life.

. . .

Nevertheless, there are at least three ways in which normative logics might be rivals to rational explanations of institutional design. One is by supplying desiderata for institutions that make little sense on consequentialist grounds. A norm of universal membership, for example, operates in many international regimes. Why do land-locked states have a say in the Law of the Sea, or Luxembourg a vote in the EU? It is not obvious that the answers lie in the enforcement and distributional considerations emphasized by the Rational Design framework. Or consider the norm that Great Powers have special prerogatives. Without reference to this idea, it is hard to explain the inclusion of Russia in the Group of Eight, or to make sense of debates about the future of the UN Security Council. The norm that the control of international institutions should be democratic is also gaining strength. The Rational Design framework proposes that designs for institutional control reflect degrees of uncertainty and asymmetries of contribution, yet in debates about how to fix the "democratic deficit" in the EU and other international organizations such cost-benefit considerations seem less salient than questions of legitimacy and principle. Arguably, this is because decision makers themselves see democratic accountability as an intrinsic good. Then there are solidarity norms stemming from collective identities, which to their credit Mitchell and Keilbach suggest may be necessary to explain German and Swiss contributions to the Rhine River regime. One wonders about the possible future role of norms of justice in international politics. And so on. . . .

A second, converse, way in which logics of appropriateness may constitute rival hypotheses is by taking design options that might be instrumentally attractive off the table as "normative prohibitions." Peter Rosendorff and Helen Milner point to plausible rational reasons why trade regimes will include "escape clauses." Yet in other regimes such clauses are absent — there is no exemption for murder in the human rights regime, for example — which seems hard to explain on such grounds, since the norms are equally difficult to enforce. This example also suggests that the relative tolerance of the POW regime for violations may be due to more than just enforcement problems, but reflects a "boys will be boys" belief that a certain level of murder on the battlefield is legitimate. Similarly, Mitchell and Keilbach note that in negotiations over the whaling regime the United States relied on coercion in part because of a reluctance to pay bribes to stop what was seen as an immoral activity. Moving beyond the cases in this volume, in turn, one might expect a purely rational regime for dealing with "failed states" to include a trusteeship option, but because of its association with colonialism, this is unacceptable to the international community. Finally, norms about what kinds of coercion may be used in different contexts may also factor into regime design. Military intervention to collect sovereign debts was legitimate in the nineteenth century, but it is hard to imagine this being done today. . . . A true test of rational-design theory would include all instrumentally relevant options, not just those that are normatively acceptable.

Finally, logics of appropriateness can affect the modalities used to design institutions, which as a result may be historically specific. For example, the ongoing conferences in the aviation regime discussed by Richards and the "clustered negotiations" on trade studied by Robert Pahre presuppose a belief that issue-specific conferences could be kept insulated from military competition, but this belief is a relatively recent notion, dating to the Concert of Europe.... Finally, there is the most general question of how states came to see "institutions" as solutions to collective-action problems in the first place. States have always had such problems, yet for most of the past five thousand years they never thought to create institutions to address them. Why not? Was it irrational, or was it that the very idea of using institutions to solve international problems was unknown or considered inappropriate? Following Hedley Bull, we might point to the norms of international society as a prerequisite, such that it is only with the attainment of a certain level of collective identity that the rational design of institutions becomes possible.

In at least three ways, then, logics of appropriateness may help structure international institutions. These possibilities do not mean that consequentialism is wholly absent, as the case studies in this volume make clear. But insofar as our objective is to assess variance explained, the logic of appropriateness suggests that rival factors may be important as well.

...

Alternatives to "Design"

...

[I]nstitutional designs today may play a causal feedback role in constructing the actors who make designs tomorrow.... As Koremenos, Lipson, and Snidal briefly note, one level would be institutional designs that expand the set of members who make up the subsequent designing actor.... A second kind of feedback on actors occurs when institutions affect designers' identities and interests. NATO is a good example: Even if its original design reflected the self-interests of its members, over time they arguably have come to identify with the institution and thus see themselves as a collective identity, valuing NATO as an end in itself rather than just as a means to an end. One wonders whether Morrow's POW regime has had a similar effect, helping to create a "we" of "civilized" states who even in war feel bound by norms.... Over time, designs cause designers as much as designers cause designs.

... To the extent that they are not separable, actors cannot be said to cause institutional designs, but are instead constituted by them. In international politics the institution of sovereignty provides perhaps the most fundamental example. By acting as the members of sovereign states are expected to act — defending their autonomy, privileging their citizens over foreigners, recognizing the rights of other states to do likewise, and, now, engaging in practices of international institutional design — certain groups of individuals constitute themselves as the corporate actors known as "sovereign states," which have particular powers and rights in international politics.... This suggests that the identity of a state lies not in the state itself, as if it were an object, but in the process by which people who would be a state project themselves into that which they are not. Since this process is continuous, state identity is always an ongoing accomplishment, not ontologically given.

...

JACK GOLDSMITH AND STEPHEN KRASNER, THE LIMITS OF IDEALISM

132 Daedalus (2003), 47–63

. . .

Three developments in particular — the rise of universal jurisdiction, the creation of a new International Criminal Court [ICC], and recurring demands for humanitarian intervention — reflect a renewed commitment to international idealism. Supporters of these institutions and policies tend to believe that justice is best served when it is isolated from politics and power. Only by insulating international institutions and practice from the bargaining and compromise that characterize political decision-making, and from the domestic political pressure to which politicians must always be alert, can justice be fully realized. On this view, institutions and principles that minimize the influence of power better achieve justice than those in which power plays an important role; and decisions made by unaccountable actors, especially judges, are more likely to be just than decisions made by political leaders responsible to their electorates.

. . .

Our claim is not that idealism in international politics is irrelevant or inherently harmful. . . . [I]deals can be pursued effectively only if decisionmakers are alert to the distribution of power, national interests, and the consequences of their policies. . . .

1.

Universal jurisdiction is the power of a domestic court to try foreign citizens, including government officials, for certain egregious international crimes committed anywhere in the world. This authority is premised on the idea that human rights violations are an affront to all humanity and thus may be punished anywhere, regardless of the defendants' nationality or the place of the crime. Universal jurisdiction aims to strengthen international human rights law by marshaling politically independent domestic courts to enforce that law. . . .

. . .

The inability of universal jurisdiction prosecutors to weigh judiciously the consequences of their actions distinguishes them from purely domestic prosecutors, and attests to the importance of democratic accountability in the enforcement of criminal law. . . In many instances the adverse community consequences of holding an individual accountable for a past crime can lead prosecutors to forgo prosecution, or to strike a plea deal favorable to the accused. (And of course political accountability also dampens the likelihood that this discretionary process will be abused.) Because universal jurisdiction prosecutions take place outside affected communities, universal jurisdiction courts and prosecutors lack the incentive, or the institutional capacity, to consider such tradeoffs.

. . .

2.

. . .

[T]he ICC has most of the other characteristics — and flaws — of universal jurisdiction. Its norms are still much too open-ended and contested to permit a consensus on proscribed behavior; it suppresses considerations of power; it lacks democratic accountability; and it cannot reliably balance legal benefits against possible political costs.

. . .

. . . Its structure is remarkably similar to the much-maligned U.S. Independent Counsel statute. By guaranteeing independence at the price of political control, it invites questionable and even politically motivated prosecutions. Legal restrictions and definitional limitations are not likely to provide real checks on the ICC's behavior, for the ICC itself is the ultimate interpreter of these norms. . . .

. . .

There are at least two problems with this attempt to eliminate power politics from the enforcement of international criminal law and to subvert the recognition of national power incorporated in the UN Security Council. The first parallels a problem with universal jurisdiction: the ICC could initiate prosecutions that aggravate bloody political conflicts and prolong political instability in the affected regions. Relatedly, the possibilities for compromise that exist in a political environment guided by prudential calculation are constricted when political deliberation must compete with an independent judicial process. . . . The best strategy for stability often depends on context and contingent political factors that are not reducible to a rule of law. . . .

. . .

Even if no U.S. defendant is brought before the ICC, it can still cause mischief for the United States by being a public forum for official criticism and judgment of U.S. military actions. For all these reasons, the ICC will more likely affect the activities of the generally human-rights-protecting but militarily active United States than rogue state actors who hide behind walls of sovereignty (or in ungoverned areas) and care little about world public opinion and international legitimacy.

. . .

U.S. opposition to the ICC is important because U.S. military and financial backing have been crucial to the operation of ad hoc international criminal tribunals. Consider how Milosevic wound up in The Hague. It was not the gravitational pull of international norms that brought him there. Rather, the United States wielded enormous diplomatic and military power to oust him from office, and then threatened to withhold some $50 million in aid to the successor regime in Yugoslavia. . . .

The Milosevic episode teaches a general lesson. The ICC simply cannot, without U.S. support, fulfill its dream of prosecuting big-time human rights abusers who hide behind national borders. This is why the ICC's alienation of the United States may actually hinder rather than enhance human rights enforcement. . . . [T]he ICC will most likely chill U.S. military action not when central U.S. strategic interests are at stake (as in Afghanistan), but rather in humanitarian situations (like Rwanda and perhaps Kosovo) where the strategic benefits of military action are low, and thus even a low probability of prosecution weighs more heavily. . . .

. . . The international idealists who rejected U.S. demands for Security Council control over ICC prosecutions aimed to decouple the enforcement of international criminal law from international politics. They wanted "equal justice under law"—the equal application of international human rights law to weak and powerful nations alike.... In demanding a full loaf of neutral justice rather than a half loaf of justice that accords with the interests of nations that can enforce it, and in creating an institution that relies on legal norms wholly removed from considerations of power, international idealists may diminish rather than enhance the protection of human rights.

3.

...

This absence of democratic support is a fundamental problem for those who insist that nations should intervene to arrest human suffering in other nations.... [P]olitical leaders cannot engage in acts of altruism abroad much beyond what constituents and/or interest groups will support. This conclusion is fatal to the interventionist project. The most we can expect is that when a nation's strategic interests dovetail with an inclination toward genuine humanitarian intervention, it will intervene — as the United States did in Bosnia, Haiti, and Kosovo.

Once again, this means that international justice will depend on the power and interest of nations, and will often result in uneven patterns of enforcement that critics deride as hypocritical. Opportunistic interventions are also what give rise to the (not unjustified) concern that many so-called humanitarian interventions are ruses for invasions motivated in large part by strategic ends. A clear-eyed analysis of interventions would realize that such mixed-motive cases are probably the best we can hope for. The presence of mixed motives does not detract from the fact that some such interventions might help local populations, as the Kosovo intervention arguably did.

... Political prudence demands that foreign policy actions be judged in terms of their consequences, not their intentions.

...

4.

We have offered reasons to be pessimistic about the efficacy of three regimes ... that aim to enforce international human rights norms. Our point is not to criticize the norms themselves, but to focus attention on pathologies that may result from the inadequate institutions in which they are embedded. International institutions can damage rather than promote international ideals if they are incompatible with the interests of those states whose support is needed for their success.

...

When self-enforcement fails, the alternative is a system of selective justice enforced by the powerful, one consequence of which is effective immunity for the powerful. What has not proved possible in international affairs is universal international justice based on legal norms that operate in the absence of either self-enforcement or hegemonic dominance.

...

... The ICC and universal jurisdiction sever the link between norm enforcement and political accountability. One consequence of this separation is that the institutions are practically, and in some circumstances legally, discouraged from engaging in assessments of costs and benefits that are often so important for the prevention of human suffering. As a result, such institutions may worsen rather than alleviate human rights catastrophes.

RYAN GOODMAN AND DEREK JINKS, HOW TO INFLUENCE STATES: SOCIALIZATION AND INTERNATIONAL HUMAN RIGHTS LAW

54 Duke L. J. 621 (2004)

. . . Prevailing approaches [in human rights scholarship] suggest that law changes human rights practices by either (1) coercing states (and individuals) to comply with regime rules, or (2) persuading states (and individuals) of the validity and legitimacy of human rights law. In our view, the former approach fails to grasp the complexity of the social environment within which states act, and the latter fails to account for many ways in which the diffusion of social and legal norms occurs. Indeed, a robust cluster of empirical studies in interdisciplinary scholarship documents particular processes that socialize states in the absence of coercion or persuasion. These studies conclude that the power of social influence can be harnessed even if (1) collective action problems and political constraints that inhibit effective coercion are not overcome and (2) the complete internalization sought through persuasion is not achieved. . . .

. . . [W]e provide a more complete conceptual framework by identifying a third mechanism by which international law might change state behavior — acculturation. By acculturation, we mean the general process by which actors adopt the beliefs and behavioral patterns of the surrounding culture. . . . We do not suggest that international legal scholarship has completely failed to identify aspects of this process. Rather, we maintain that the mechanism is underemphasized and poorly understood, and that it is often conflated (or even confused) with other constructivist mechanisms such as persuasion. . . .

. . . We link each of the three mechanisms of social influence to specific regime characteristics — identifying several ways in which identifying acculturation as distinct from the better-understood mechanisms of coercion and persuasion may occasion a rethinking of fundamental design problems in human rights law. In short, we reverse-engineer structural regime design principles from the salient characteristics of underlying social processes. . . .

Careful readers may argue that the best approach to regime design should incorporate elements of all three mechanisms. . . . [T]he kind of analysis contemplated by this line of criticism (i.e., the development of an integrated theory of regime design accounting for each mechanism) first requires, in our view, identification and clear differentiation of these mechanisms. This conceptual clarification is a first step, which enables subsequent work aimed at identifying the conditions under which each of the mechanisms would predominate, potentially reinforcing or frustrating the operation of the others. . . .

. . .

I. Three Mechanisms of Social Influence

... [T]he microprocesses of social influence are often underspecified, underanalyzed, or, at best, underexplained. Several important questions merit more sustained reflection. For example, how exactly do norms change behavior or attitudes? Do social sanctions impose costs that states weigh against other interests, or do social sanctions function more as cognitive cues? If one mechanism through which norms influence actors is "persuasion," what exactly are the microprocesses by which persuasion works? ...

...

A. Coercion

The first, and most obvious, social mechanism is coercion — whereby states and institutions influence the behavior of other states by escalating the benefits of conformity or the costs of nonconformity through material rewards and punishments....

...

B. Persuasion

The second mechanism of social influence is persuasion — the active, often strategic, inculcation of norms. Persuasion theory suggests that international law influences state behavior through processes of social "learning" and other forms of information conveyance. Persuasion ... "requires argument and deliberation in an effort to change the minds of others." Persuaded actors "internalize" new norms and rules of appropriate behavior and redefine their interests and identities accordingly. The touchstone of this approach is that actors are consciously convinced of the truth, validity, or appropriateness of a norm, belief, or practice....

Next, consider how persuasion works — a matter explored in depth in a vast, interdisciplinary literature. At the risk of oversimplifying this rich and varied body of work, we highlight two factors that determine, in substantial part, the persuasiveness of counterattitudinal messages. The first and most important technique of persuasion is "framing." The basic idea is that the persuasive appeal of a counterattitudinal message increases if the issue is strategically framed to resonate with already accepted norms....

...

C. Acculturation

A burgeoning, interdisciplinary literature suggests another important mechanism of social influence — acculturation. ... This mechanism induces behavioral changes through pressures to assimilate — some imposed by other actors and some imposed by the self. Acculturation encompasses a number of microprocesses, including orthodoxy, mimicry, identification, and status maximization. Our claim is that individual behavior (and community-level behavioral regularities) is in part a function of social structure — the relations between individual actors and some reference group(s). Acculturation induces behavioral changes not only by changing the target actor's incentive structure or mind but also by changing the actor's social environment....

. . .

First, acculturation is propelled by cognitive pressures. . . . These internal pressures include (1) social-psychological costs of nonconformity (such as dissonance associated with conduct that is inconsistent with an actor's identity or social roles), and (2) social-psychological benefits of conforming to group norms and expectations (such as the "cognitive comfort" associated with both high social status and membership in a perceived "in-group"). . . . Therefore, there are internal pressures driving actors to act and think in ways consistent with the social roles and expectations internalized by such actors. An implication of this pressure is that, once actors internalize some role (or any other identity formation), they are impelled to act and think in ways consistent with the highly legitimated purposes and attributes of that role. As a consequence, orthodoxy and social legitimacy are internalized as authoritative guides for human action.

Second, acculturation is also propelled by social pressures — real or imagined pressures applied by a group. These pressures — which are no doubt more familiar to many readers — include (1) the imposition of social-psychological costs through shaming or shunning and (2) the conferral of social-psychological benefits through "back-patting" and other displays of public approval. . . . Consider, for example, social-psychological studies of conformity. Substantial empirical evidence demonstrates that, in the face of real or perceived social pressure from a reference group, actors often change their behavior to conform to the behavioral patterns of the group. Moreover, actors systematically conform (under the right conditions) even if the group is clearly wrong and even if there are strong incentives to be accurate. . . .

. . .

Despite the obvious similarities, acculturation differs from persuasion in important respects. First, persuasion requires acceptance of the validity or legitimacy of a belief, practice, or norm — acculturation requires only that an actor perceive that an important reference group harbors the belief, engages in the practice, subscribes to the norm. Second, persuasion requires active assessment of the merits of a belief. Acculturation processes, in contrast, frequently operate tacitly; it is often the very act of conforming that garners social approval and alleviates cognitive discomfort. Persuasion involves assessment of the content of the message (even if only indirectly); acculturation involves assessment of the social relation (the degree of identification) between the target audience and some group. Acculturation occurs not as a result of the content of the relevant rule or norm but rather as a function of social structure — the relations between individual actors and some reference group. Acculturation depends less on the properties of the rule than on the properties of the relationship of the actor to the community. Because the acculturation process does not involve actually agreeing with the merits of a group's position, it may result in outward conformity with a social convention without private acceptance or corresponding changes in private practices.

. . .

. . . [T]here is good reason to question whether states as such are amenable to acculturation. . . .

Numerous empirical studies now suggest that states are significantly shaped and legitimated through their broader organizational environment. States are highly legitimated actors in world society, and their formal structures (e.g., administrative bodies, policy commitments) substantially derive from institutionalized models promulgated at the global level. These studies generally proceed by collecting quantitative data for all available states over several decades and employing analytic techniques . . . to test predictions of acculturation. The studies demonstrate that states emulate standardized models of structural organization in areas such as environmental policy, educational curricula, militarization, the laws of war, and human rights. As many commentators point out, the extent of isomorphism across states is remarkable, and it is seemingly inexplicable without reference to acculturation processes. Importantly, the studies do not suggest that this structural convergence reflects actual practices or effects on the ground. On the contrary, the convergence (across states) is accompanied by substantial and persistent "decoupling" (within states): official purposes and formal structure are disconnected from functional demands. Rather than correlating with local task demands, structural attributes and official goals of the state correlate in important ways with attributes and goals of other states in the world.

With respect to human rights, extensive research identifies these patterns of norm diffusion in fundamental areas of governance including welfare and labor policy, civil rights guarantees, and public order maintenance. For example, the number of constitutions that include provisions committed to the state management of childhood and the right to education has increased dramatically. A study of every national constitution in effect during the 1870–1970 period shows that the adoption of such constitutional provisions over time does not correlate with local forms of social organization (such as urbanization and national wealth) or with technical capacities of the relevant states. Moreover, each group of newly established states shows a significantly higher probability of adopting such constitutional provisions than the preceding group of entrants. The overall findings suggest that "[n]ational constitutions do not simply reflect processes of internal development," but rather "reflect legitimating ideas dominant in the world system at the time of their creation."

Consider, also, state convergence with respect to women's rights. A leading study uses sophisticated analytic techniques to examine state definitions of political citizenship over a hundred-year period. According to the study, once universal suffrage became a legitimating principle associated with the modern nation-state, state enactment of women's suffrage followed a pattern anticipated by theories of acculturation. After an initial stage of early adopters, the number of states providing women the right to vote increased steeply and included most states before the rate of adoption tapered off; the likelihood that a state would adopt women's suffrage correlated with world trend lines; and adoption correlated far less with domestic political conditions once isomorphism took hold. Additionally, an important finding indicates a "contagion" effect: once the norm was institutionalized, a strong predictor for whether an individual state would enact women's suffrage was whether other states in its region had done so in the past five years. The overall findings suggest that, compared with local conditions such as the strength of domestic women's rights groups, "[c]ountries apparently are affected much less strongly by internal factors and much more strongly by shifts in the international logic of political citizenship."

. . .

II. Conditional Membership

An important choice in designing human rights regimes involves deciding between an inclusive or restrictive membership rule in multilateral organizations. . . . An inclusive approach would allow all comers to join the organization. . . . In contrast, a restrictive approach would reject candidate states or expel member states that do not meet particular human rights standards. . . .

. . .

Unlike the other two approaches, the acculturation mechanism suggests that membership rules are of high importance in regime design. According to this view, broad membership would amplify social pressure and help substantiate the claim that the principled commitments of the regime are, indeed, universal. Moreover, one of the principal empirical insights of acculturation studies is that the degree to which states are embedded in international organizations is strongly associated with the state's conformity to global models of appropriate behavior. Participation in international institutions thus plays a significant role in promoting standardized, socially legitimated models of appropriate state behavior. Importantly, institutions with broad membership advance the social processes by which states adopt norms identified with being a "modern state." Accordingly, the mechanism of acculturation — unlike coercion and persuasion — operates much more effectively, and sometimes necessarily, through international organizations.

. . .

. . . [T]he logic of acculturation, in contrast to the logic of the other mechanisms, highlights the importance of discouraging certain relationships that can arise between organizational insiders and outsiders. As a model of culture, acculturation predicts the institutionalization of deviance within subcultures that can form among outsiders who have been denied access to the dominant group. . . .

. . .

The mechanics of acculturation also suggest potential advantages to a restrictive rule. First, membership itself can serve as a device for affirmation or censure. That is, inclusion can provide a form of back-patting, whereas exclusion can shame and shun. In a related context, Dean Anne-Marie Slaughter advocates calibrating the application of doctrines of judicial deference to different forms of government. She proposes that national courts exercise jurisdiction over the acts of liberal foreign states but abstain from reviewing the acts of illiberal ones. Dean Slaughter contends that shielding illiberal states from judicial scrutiny entails "salving their sovereign sensitivities, but at the price of . . . moral ostracism from the liberal community." Indeed, her proposal is designed to confer a "badge of alienage" on illiberal states and a "badge of legitimacy" on liberal states. Although substantial empirical evidence now suggests that these categories are socially meaningful, Dean Slaughter does not consider countervailing effects within the terms of the same social logic. That is, the same body of empirical work provides strong reasons for bringing recalcitrant states into the fold. Specifically, as discussed above, processes of assimilation suggest that illiberal states will begin to imitate the group in which they are included. This "identification" with a group — not banishment from the group — is perhaps more likely to propel the legal and political systems of illiberal states toward conformity with prevailing norms.

. . .

III. Precision of Obligations

...

The acculturation model departs significantly from canonical approaches to the "level of precision" problem. ... Under the coercion and persuasion approaches, obtaining precision is generally considered essential to the long-term effectiveness of the regime....

...

[I]t is necessary to distinguish the two types of acculturation discussed earlier: conformity resulting from cognitive cues and conformity resulting from social sanctions. ... Conformity depends less on the properties of the rule than on the properties of the actor's relationship to the community. Because the convention or norm is associated in general terms with the identity of the group, rules best foster conformity by "establish[ing] broad hortatory goals with few specific proscribed or prescribed activities." This effect suggests that imprecision mobilizes "cognitive pressures" to adopt social norms (the first type of acculturation). Precision, on the other hand, is more likely to emphasize disagreements — triggering cognitive cues that the would-be reference group is importantly dissimilar from the target actor. There are, nevertheless, good reasons to suspect that precision might facilitate social rewards and sanctions — one of the two types of acculturation that we identify....

Professor Thomas Franck's discussion of "determinacy" helps explain both the distinction between the two types of acculturation and the potential benefits to precision. Franck discusses how precise rules promote compliance — emphasizing the social value of precision. His analysis of precision, however, generally suggests only one type of acculturation — the distribution of social sanctions.... Franck suggests that the determinacy of a rule will narrow the range of permissible interpretations and thus facilitate the regulatory effects of social sanctions. He contends that states, in trying to avoid the wrath of the community, will attempt to evade the application of a rule "by interpreting the rule permissively" and "using clever sophistry." Precision limits that possibility.

We agree that precision may strengthen social pressure by enhancing the legitimacy of a sanction. In that respect, an acculturation approach would value precision....

... Professor Franck's concern with self-serving and evasive interpretations does not easily fit the conceptual apparatus of acculturation through cognitive processes. Indeed, cognitive pressures suggest that states may be more inclined to conform their behavior to community expectations — and that they are unlikely to sustain, over the long term, an idiosyncratic interpretation of any norm that the international community considers central. The motivation to mimic the reference group is also self-directed. Indeed, states will even adopt legitimated practices under conditions of little or no surveillance by the international community. On this view, it is inaccurate to suggest that states embedded in international organizations will invariably engage in "unilateral, self-serving exculpatory interpretations of . . . rules." Furthermore, Professor Franck's analysis of this issue emphasizes the penalties side of social pressures, rather than social rewards or cognitive impulses to conform. In that respect, Professor Franck's analysis indicates that precision may be a less valuable tool under conditions in which social sanctions are underutilized, infeasible, or expensive.

IV. Implementation: Monitoring and Enforcement

... [Several reform] proposals reflect the view that compliance is best induced by the exercise of coercive authority — such as military intervention or binding decisions of third-party monitoring institutions. This view, we maintain, is called into question by the acculturation approach. Indeed, we posit that, under certain conditions, "soft law" mechanisms will be more effective in establishing durable norms.

...

A. Coercion

...

The coercion approach does not value highly soft strategies such as publishing best practices or monitoring and reporting human rights abuses — except insofar as these strategies are integrated into some coercive apparatus....

The coercion approach also considers official criticism to be largely unimportant. As a direct coercive technique, criticism constitutes a nominal sanction. It is, indeed, difficult to conceive of the net benefit of criticism alone once transaction costs are taken into account....

B. Persuasion

Under the persuasion approach, "managerialism" is the central medium for promoting regime objectives. Managerialism suggests that human rights regimes can encourage desirable behavior in two ways: (1) by systematically engaging governments in discussion about controversial practices and (2) by fostering structural opportunities for transnational networks to engage governments (or other relevant audiences). On this view, states can be convinced to embrace regime norms (1) through organizational arrangements that facilitate meaningful communicative exchanges among stakeholders (e.g., the International Labor Organization) and (2) through the exercise of "good offices" by high-level officials (e.g., the High Commissioner on National Minorities of the Organization for Security and Cooperation in Europe).

Furthermore, according to the persuasion approach, monitoring and reporting can induce change if conducted in a sensitive manner. Some persuasion scholars recommend these strategies as means of generating useful information and cooperative solutions.... Monitoring and reporting can also serve an important function in cuing states to think harder about human rights violations — another valuable ingredient in the persuasion process....

Less clear in the persuasion model is the effectiveness of criticism and sanctions. The literature is ambivalent on this issue. One school of thought maintains that criticism and more severe penalties can complement efforts at persuasion. Indeed, the (implicit or explicit) threat of sanctions may bring states to the table in the first place. Moreover, some scholarship stresses the importance of persuasion but finds its greatest impact in encouraging transnational political movements and foreign states to leverage concessions from recalcitrant states. In sharp contrast, other scholarship argues that criticism and more severe penalties have a deleterious effect on the communicative atmosphere required for collective deliberation to thrive. Criticism may, therefore, also discourage states from systematically reviewing new types and patterns of human rights violations.

C. Acculturation

Under the acculturation approach, power is understood as productive, cultural, and diffuse — not merely prohibitory, material, and centralized. Treaty regimes can induce desirable behavior through processes that institutionalize models of legitimate state practice and that link states and their citizenry to forums that elaborate and apply such standards. . . .

Acculturation values the publication of best practices more highly than does either of the other mechanisms. Admittedly, the general approach would not suggest relying heavily on this method. Nevertheless, publishing best practices can contribute to the process of standardization. States may be more willing to adopt such models, at faster rates and more durably, than the other approaches suggest. The emulation of best practices will not require persuading relevant actors. State policies that "mimic" best practices should also be more durable than policy shifts caused by coercion — the policies should generally persist even when material pressure is no longer applied or available.

. . . With respect to conformity through social rewards and sanctions, it is vital to expose wrongdoing (and to tie exposure to external praise and criticism). Accordingly, external surveillance and reporting — especially by third-party states and organizations — should be significant parts of the monitoring and reporting apparatus.

With respect to acculturation through cognitive pressure, monitoring and reporting serve different functions. States will formally adopt particular conventions even under conditions of nonsurveillance. That is, they will accede to particular norms in the process of identity formation and mimicry of globally promulgated models. External monitoring and reporting are thus not necessarily required. . . . Nevertheless, visibility might perform a regulatory function. Indeed, the leading social theorist on discursive practices, Michel Foucault, emphasizes the power of visibility in regulating social behavior. A regime attempting to exploit these attributes might stress reporting by a state's own organs, not simply reporting by third parties. Indeed, the very process of identifying, describing, and controlling human rights practices helps the diffusion of the human rights discourse through global and local levels. This general approach, however, would require care not to institutionalize noncompliance. As suggested by recent studies of domestic order maintenance, international regimes should be concerned that emphasizing the prevalence of violations might promote disorder and further violations.

QUESTIONS

1. Do these readings cause you to reconsider the prudence or effectiveness of human rights norm promotion strategies discussed in earlier chapters?

2. An important, controversial law review article by Professor Oona Hathaway presents statistical research indicating that under certain conditions, ratification of human rights treaties is associated with a subsequent increase in human rights violations.[10] As an explanation of these findings, Hathaway posits that ratification is virtually costless due to the lack of monitoring and enforcement. International actors nevertheless reward ratifying states by relaxing political pressure on these states to promote human rights, and the relaxation of external pressure results in an increase of human rights violations. As a solution, Hathaway suggests the following institutional reforms:

> [T]o the extent that noncompliance with many human rights treaties is commonplace, the current treaty system may create opportunities for countries to use treaty ratification to displace pressure for real change in practices.... Revisions of the existing treaty system aimed at exposing and publicizing noncompliance are needed if the reputational costs of noncompliance are truly to be enhanced.
>
> ...
>
> ... [B]odies charged with implementing the treaties should be empowered to compel countries to participate in the reporting and monitoring systems to which they have subscribed.... The bodies should provide NGOs with more regular opportunities to participate in the process of evaluating and assessing state practices. ... [F]uture human rights treaties should be written with a closer eye to effective monitoring. Declarations of rights that are not easily defined and measured, or that are not accompanied by an effective plan for securing true remedies for violations of those rights, may actually be counterproductive.
>
> The findings of this study may also give reason to reassess the current policy of the United Nations of promoting universal ratification of the major human rights treaties. Although universal ratification of a treaty can make a strong statement to the international community that the activity covered by the treaty is unacceptable, pressure to ratify, if not followed by strong enforcement and monitoring of treaty commitments, may be counterproductive. Indeed, it may be worthwhile to develop, consider, and debate more radical approaches to improving human rights through the use of new types of treaty membership policies. If countries gain some expressive benefit from ratifying human rights treaties, perhaps this benefit ought to be less easily obtained. Countries might, for example, be required to demonstrate compliance with certain human rights standards before being allowed to join a human rights treaty. This would ensure that only those countries that deserved an expressive benefit from treaty membership would obtain it. Or membership in a treaty regime could be tiered, with a probationary period during the early years of membership followed by a comprehensive assessment of country practices for promotion to full membership. Or treaties could include provisions for removing countries that are

[10] Oona A. Hathaway, 'Do Human Rights Treaties Make a Difference?', 111 Yale L. J. 1935 (2002). For a debate about this study, see Ryan Goodman and Derek Jinks, 'Measuring the Effects of Human Rights Treaties', 13 Euro. J. of Int. L. 171 (2003); Oona A. Hathaway, 'Testing Conventional Wisdom', 13 Euro. J. of Int. L. 185 (2003).

habitually found in violation of the terms of the treaty from membership in the treaty regime.

Do the rational design and other approaches articulated in this chapter help you to evaluate Hathaway's proposed reforms? Are the reforms well-designed and politically feasible? What are their potential costs and benefits?

3. The rational design project focuses on states motivated by instrumental calculations and material interests. Yet the authors acknowledge, at least as an aside, the role of NGOs in shaping international institutions. If NGOs are motivated predominantly by a logic of appropriateness, does this affect the rational design project? In Goldsmith and Krasner's view, should NGOs be restricted, if not excluded, from the design stage of institutional institutions for this very reason — the idealism of NGOs does not function well in creating politically durable and effective organizations that states will support over the long term?

9

The United Nations Human Rights System

This chapter takes a systematic look at the United Nations human rights system created by, and in response to, the United Nations Charter, and traces the evolution of that system over more than sixty years. While it consists of a complex and often confusing set of institutional arrangements, it is crucial to an understanding of the universal regime which now exists. The materials focus particularly on the Human Rights Council, created in 2006, to replace the Commission on Human Rights which had functioned since 1946. Consideration is given to the vital role played in the setting of new human rights standards by these intergovernmental bodies and to the techniques they have developed for responding to violations. Consideration is also given to two of the other 'principal organs' of the UN, the Security Council and the International Court of Justice. The role of each in relation to human rights has developed very significantly in recent years.

COMMENT ON CONCEPTIONS OF ENFORCEMENT

For individuals whose human rights are being violated, and for the groups that seek to defend them, the effectiveness of the UN's human rights system depends to an important degree upon its ability to 'enforce' respect for the legal norms that originated within it. But the very concept of such international 'enforcement' is controversial and resisted by a significant number of governments (a few of which do so overtly, while many others use more subtle methods). As suggested by Chapter 8, it is therefore not surprising that the UN's often hotly contested efforts to establish institutions and procedures capable of securing enforcement have been less successful than its work in setting human rights standards, often consensually.

An evaluation of the UN's performance will be strongly influenced by the observer's starting point or perspective on world order. For example:

1. Do we assume that the 'globalization' of issues such as human rights is desirable, even unavoidable, so that a nation's treatment of its own nationals is a legitimate concern of all others (an *erga omnes* approach, p. 167, *supra*)? Or do we hold to a more traditional image of the sovereign state that emphasizes the inviolability of national boundaries for at least most human rights issues as well as other purposes?

2. Even if the former, do we envisage a world in which an effective multilateral organization (which might or might not be the UN) should be able to act against the

will of the government(s) concerned to enforce universal norms? Or do we believe that although we live in a globalizing context, the actual implementation by individual governments of human rights standards, each in its own way, remains the most effective, desirable or realistic approach?

3. Are we prepared to accept that the measures that we would happily support against another country might, in a different context, be applied against our own? Do we assume that international enforcement actions must be applied equally to powerful nations and to smaller states, so that we should only adopt policies that can be applied across the board, consistently? Or are there legitimate differences in the ways in which the international community should respond to human rights violations in different types of states (democratic — non-democratic, large — small, developed — developing, etc.)?

The answers to such questions depend partly on the definition of enforcement. Do we refer only to the relatively rare peacekeeping and so-called 'police' actions that involve the presence in a state of UN or other foreign forces? The only use of the term 'enforcement' in the UN Charter occurs in relation to the enforcement under Chapter VII of decisions of the Security Council (Article 45). This has led some international lawyers to equate enforcement with the use of, or threat to use, economic or other sanctions or armed force. Although most dictionary definitions of enforcement include an element of compulsion, it is nonetheless true that compulsion may be moral as well as physical. It is also true that the use of force for human rights purposes has won increasing support in recent years, especially in light of developments in relation to Kosovo and East Timor, but this is surely not what is meant by calls for the UN to 'enforce', routinely, universal human rights norms.

At the other extreme from the use of sanctions or armed force, enforcement has been defined as 'comprising all measures intended and proper to induce respect for human rights'.[1] That definition could extend to the other extreme of UN action, the frequent debates or recommendatory resolutions of the Human Rights Council or the General Assembly. But such a definition is so open-ended that it provides no criteria against which to evaluate the UN's performance. It puts the emphasis on intentions rather than on results achieved, and suggests that 'enforcement' measures might be confined to the adoption of resolutions and other such hortatory activities of the UN.

QUESTION

Is the term 'enforcement' the right term to use to describe what you would like the UN to be able to do in response to its findings that gross violations of human rights are taking place or are likely to take place? Are there other powers, stopping short of this sense of 'enforcement', that you would wish to vest in the UN or any other international organization to respond to gross violations?

[1] Rudolf Bernhardt, 'General Report', in Bernhardt and Jolowicz (eds.), *International Enforcement of Human Rights* (1985), at 5.

A. THE UN SYSTEM: CHARTER-BASED INSTITUTIONS

The UN's human rights monitoring arrangements consists of a 'two-track' approach:

(1) *Charter-based organs* including those (a) whose creation is directly mandated by the UN Charter, such as the General Assembly and the Human Rights Council (as the successor to the Commission on Human Rights and the role previously played by the Economic and Social Council), or (b) which have been authorized by one of those bodies, such as the Sub-Commission on the Promotion and Protection of Human Rights, and the Commission on the Status of Women; and

(2) *Treaty-based organs* such as the Human Rights Committee formed under the ICCPR, referred to in this book as the 'ICCPR Committee' in order to reduce confusion with the UN Human Rights Council that is identified as the 'UN Council', that have been created by a range of other human rights treaties originating in UN processes. These organs are intended to monitor compliance by states with their obligations under those treaties.

The focus of this chapter is on Charter-based organs. Treaty-based organs are dealt with especially in Chapters 3 (CEDAW Committee), 4 (ESCR Committee) and 10 (ICCPR Committee). While the work of the UN Council is of particular importance, other UN organs are also significant.

COMMENT ON CHARTER ORGANS

The 'principal organs' created by the UN Charter of 1945 are the Security Council, General Assembly, Economic and Social Council, Trusteeship Council, the Secretariat and the International Court of Justice. One of these organs is now virtually defunct — the highly successful post-War decolonization processes overseen by the UN rendered the *Trusteeship Council* superfluous and it suspended its work in 1994. Although the *Economic and Social Council* (ECOSOC) once played a major role as an intermediary between the Assembly and the Commission on Human Rights, and still has a theoretically important role of coordination within an increasingly disparate UN system, its substantive contributions to the human rights debate since the 1970s have been extremely limited and its coordination efforts have had little practical impact. One of the aims of creating the Human Rights Council in 2006 was to bypass the role of the ECOSOC and enable the new Council to report directly to the General Assembly. As a result the main human rights-relevant role played today by ECOSOC concerns the granting of 'consultative status' with the UN to nongovernmental organizations.

We turn now to the organs whose work is examined in this chapter. Until the mid 1990s, the *Security Council* was extremely reluctant to become involved in human rights matters. Since that time, its role in the field has become significant in a variety of ways. Similarly, the *International Court of Justice* (ICJ) exerted a relatively marginal influence over the understanding and interpretation of international human rights law until the mid 1990s, despite its consideration of a handful of important cases focusing on issues such as self-determination and genocide. Over the past decade, however, the ICJ has adopted a series of judgments of major importance in terms of their contribution to an understanding of aspects of the international human rights regime.

The *Secretariat* is led by the *Secretary-General*, who is appointed for five years by the General Assembly on the recommendation of the Security Council. A nominee may thus be vetoed by any of the five permanent members of the Council (China, France, Russia, the United Kingdom and the USA). The Secretary-General is the chief administrative officer of the UN and also exerts important moral authority within the wider international system. For decades successive Secretaries-General were very reluctant to embrace human rights concerns actively for fear of offending governments and jeopardizing their wider role in the promotion of international peace and security. Two examples illustrate this reluctance. In the 1950s Dag Hammarskjöld of Sweden was said to have kept the UN human rights programme cruising at no more than 'minimum flying speed'. In 1993 the proposal that led to the creation of the post of High Commissioner for Human Rights in December 1993 was strongly opposed by then Secretary-General Boutros Boutros-Ghali (of Egypt). In contrast, Kofi Annan, of Ghana, the Secretary-General for a decade from 1997, took a much more active human rights stance than any of his predecessors and appointed a series of strong High Commissioners. He also oversaw a process of 'mainstreaming' human rights throughout the organization which meant that bodies dealing with issues such as development, peacekeeping and environment were encouraged to address systematically the human rights dimensions of their work. It remains to be seen what approach will be adopted by his successor Ban Ki-moon, of South Korea, whose term of office began on 1 January 2007.

Under the Secretary-General, the *High Commissioner for Human Rights* (HCHR) is the UN official with principal responsibility for human rights. In formal terms she is subject to the direction and authority of the Secretary-General and acts within the mandate given her by the policy organs. In practice she and her Office (the OHCHR) are increasingly viewed as central players in their own right. The High Commissioner is appointed by the Secretary-General with the approval of the General Assembly, due regard being paid to geographical rotation, for a four-year term with the possibility of one renewal. The fourth High Commissioner, Louise Arbour, of Canada, took office in July 2004 (see p. 824, *infra*). Her Office has close to 670 staff members and its operational role has expanded rapidly in recent years. As of January 2007 it was running seven regional offices and 15 country offices.

Much of this chapter concentrates on the work of the UN Human Rights Council and its predecessor, the Commission on Human Rights. Since the debates, declarations, resolutions and recommendations of the General Assembly, the vital plenary organ, play an important role, various readings draw also on its work. A brief description of each of these organs follows.

The *General Assembly*. The Charter empowers the Assembly to 'discuss any questions or any matters within the scope of the . . . Charter' (Article 10) and to 'initiate studies and make recommendations for the purpose of . . . [*inter alia*] assisting in the realization of human rights' (Article 13). The Assembly's principal significance derives from the fact that it is composed of all UN Member States, each of which has one vote regardless of population, wealth or other factors. While most issues are decided by a simple majority vote, decisions on important questions, such as those on peace and security, admission of new Members, and budgetary matters, require a two-thirds majority. Nevertheless, much of its work is carried out on a consensus basis, thus avoiding the need for a vote. The Assembly meets intensively from September to December each year and at other times as required. Its resolutions are not *per se* legally binding but they are an important reflection of the will of the world community. Much of the debate and drafting occurs in six Main Committees, three of which are of particular relevance to human rights: the Third (Social, Humanitarian and Cultural issues); the Fifth (Administrative and Budgetary issues); and the Sixth (Legal issues).

In 2006 the *Human Rights Council* replaced the *Commission on Human Rights* which had functioned since 1946. The Commission was widely said to have become discredited, although as we shall see (p. 791, *infra*) the reasons cited to justify that assessment vary dramatically from one government or commentator to the next. The Council consists of 47 member governments, one-third of which are elected every year by an absolute majority of the UN General Assembly. States are limited to two consecutive three-year terms. The Council must meet in at least three sessions each year for a total minimum of ten weeks. It can also meet in Special Sessions provided one-third of its members agree.

The tendency of the UN generally to promote geographical and political balance through a system of regional groupings influences much of the work of the Council. The five groups are Asia, Africa, Eastern Europe, Latin America, and Western Europe and Others — the last category including Canada, Australia and New Zealand, and, in practice, the United States. As the European Union has expanded, the traditional historical division of Europe into East and West for these purposes has become increasingly problematic. The position of President of the Council rotates annually among the groups and the regional groups caucus regularly during the Council's sessions. Working groups of five member governments are commonly established to ensure that one member from each group can be included.[2] Although the old Commission was hierarchically inferior to the Assembly and the ECOSOC, in the human rights area it was in practice often more significant than those other bodies. The Council has been established as a subsidiary body of the General Assembly and its work and functioning are scheduled for review in 2011.

Three other bodies warrant a mention at this stage. The first is the *Commission on the Status of Women*. It was established in 1946 and reports to the ECOSOC in relation to policies to promote women's rights in the political, economic, civil, social

[2] Israel is the only country in an anomalous position in relation to the geographical groups. Geographically, it is part of the Asian region but that group has refused to admit Israel. In 2000 it was given 'temporary' membership, with restricted nominating and other rights, by the Western Europe group.

and educational fields. It consists of 45 governmental representatives, who normally meet for only ten days each year. It drafted many of the key treaties dealing with women's rights ranging from the 1952 Convention on the Political Rights of Women to the 1979 Convention on the Elimination of All Forms of Discrimination against Women. Its mandate includes follow-up to the four UN Women's Conferences held since 1975, and especially that held in Beijing in 1995.

The second is the *Permanent Forum of Indigenous Peoples* which discusses all aspects of indigenous issues — economic, social, cultural, environmental — as well as human rights, and advises the ECOSOC and other UN bodies and agencies. Since 2002 it has met annually in New York for two weeks.

The third body is the *Sub-Commission on the Promotion and Protection of Human Rights* (known from 1947 to 1999 as the Sub-Commission on Prevention of Discrimination and Protection of Minorities). Its future, in the context of the transition from the Commission to the Council, remained unclear as of January 2007. In contrast to the Council (and the Commission), which is composed entirely of governmental representatives, the Sub-Commission consists of 26 independent experts, elected upon the nomination of governments. It meets annually in Geneva in August, and much of its preparatory work is undertaken in various Working Groups such as those dealing with communications (complaints under the 1503 procedure, see p. 754, *infra*), the rights of indigenous populations, contemporary forms of slavery, minorities, transnational corporations, the administration of justice, terrorism, and a Social Forum.

The degree of independence of Sub-Commission members varies radically. For many years it stood out because of its relative independence, its flexible agenda and working methods, its preparedness to act as a pressure group *vis-à-vis* its parent body (the Commission), and its ambiguous and often antagonistic relationship with that parent. It came under increasing attack in the late 1990s and since 1999 has been instructed not to adopt resolutions on country situations under consideration by the Commission. It previously played an important role by adopting resolutions which put pressure on the Commission to act in relation to specific situations. Although the Sub-Commission continued to generate a large number of detailed studies on specific subjects (a total of 73 between 1956 and 2006, its reputation suffered significantly in the final years prior to the creation of the Council and there were many calls for its abolition. It fought back and proposed that instead it should be renamed, reinvigorated and given a more comprehensive advisory and coordinating role under the new Council.[3] As of January 2007 it seemed likely that it would be succeeded by an Expert Advice Body which would carry out most of the Sub-Commission's functions.

In contrast with the treaty-based bodies discussed earlier, the Charter-based bodies are political organs which have a much broader mandate to promote awareness, to foster respect, and to respond to violations of human rights standards. They derive their legitimacy and their mandate, in the broadest sense, from the human rights provisions of the Charter. Consider the following contrasts between the two types of organs.

[3] See UN Doc. A/HRC/Sub.1/58 (2006).

Treaty-based organs are distinguished by: a limited clientele consisting only of states parties to the treaty in question; a limited mandate reflecting the terms of the treaty; a limited range of procedural options for responding to violations; consensus-based decision-making as far as possible; a preference for a non-adversarial relationship with states parties (particularly with respect to state reports) based on the concept of a 'constructive dialogue'; and a particular concern with addressing issues in ways that contribute to developing the normative understanding of the relevant rights.

By contrast, the political organs generally: focus on a diverse range of issues; insist that every state is an actual or potential client (or respondent), regardless of its specific treaty obligations; work on the basis of a flexible and expanding mandate designed to crises as they emerge; engage, as a last resort, in adversarial actions *vis-à-vis* states; rely more heavily upon NGO inputs and public opinion generally to ensure the effectiveness of their work; take decisions by often strongly contested majority voting; pay less attention to normative issues *per se*; and are very wary about establishing specific procedural frameworks within which to work, preferring a more *ad hoc* approach in most situations.

The materials illustrate some of the key themes and approaches that have emerged from the work of these institutions, with particular reference to standard-setting and responding to violations. Before examining the record in those areas a general observation on the current political context is in order. Up until around 1990 the Cold War exerted a major influence over what the UN could and could not do in the human rights area. Some initiatives were simply off-limits because of the strong hostility of either East or West. Others proved feasible either because of a general consensus or because of coalition building by one side or the other with countries of the South in relation to specific issues. During the 1990s the human rights mood within the UN was a relatively open and expansive one and much was achieved. In very recent years, however, strong tensions have again emerged. They are primarily of a North-South character, and have manifested themselves mainly in relation to significantly different assumptions as to: (1) the emphasis that should be placed on specific country situations as opposed to more generic phenomena; (2) the balance between the two sets of rights, and the importance to be attributed to the right to development; and (3) the division of labour between experts and political representatives in making assessments and recommending action.

The result of these tensions, partly manifested by the replacement of the Commission by the Human Rights Council and the ensuing debate over potentially far-reaching structural reforms, is that the UN system is in a state of considerable flux.

One symptom of these tensions is the fact that the principal criterion used by the majority of governments and commentators in assessing the UN's performance is the extent to which it reacts effectively to gross violations. But the priority accorded to this criterion should not be accepted uncritically. A significant amount of the UN's important work concentrates on longer term, structural dimensions of human rights issues: standard-setting, the promotion of greater awareness of those standards both within (e.g., in peacekeeping, or in the work of the World Bank and UN Development Programme) and outside the UN system, and the provision of advice and assistance (formerly known in the UN human rights context as 'advisory services' but now referred to as 'technical co-operation'). The organization of world conferences and 'summit meetings' has also been important, particularly for present purposes those relating to human rights (Teheran 1968 and Vienna 1993), children (New York 1990), population and reproductive rights (Cairo 1994), women (Beijing 1995), food (Rome 1996 and 2002), and racism (Durban 2001).

NOTE

In historical terms it might well be considered that the single most important contribution made by the Charter-based bodies, and especially by the Commission and now the Council which have frequently played the lead role, has been through the elaboration of an ever growing body of standards designed to flesh out the meaning and implications of the relatively bare norms enunciated in the Universal Declaration. Although the Commission's 1946 terms of reference included a general mandate to address any human rights matter, it spent most of its first 20 years engaged almost exclusively in standard-setting. This included the preparation of the first draft of the UDHR and the two Covenants, as well as a range of other instruments. Even today this standard-setting function continues to be important.[4]

The following materials are designed to provide some historical and political context to the drafting of the UDHR, the majority of which was done in the context of the Commission. The aim is to give some sense of the complex array of factors at work when delegates have the dual challenge of garnering support at home for a particular set of positions and then engaging in multilateral diplomacy to advance those positions in the face of sometimes radically different bargaining postures by the representatives of other states. The focus is on Eleanor Roosevelt, the US delegate, who chaired the UN Commission on Human Rights between 1946 and 1950 and also chaired the Commission's working group which drafted the UDHR. She was a universally admired figure and, by all accounts, played a key role both in bringing the Declaration to fruition and in ensuring official US support for the outcome.[5] The following materials go beyond the usual approach of paying homage to the unquestionably vital role she played. Instead they illustrate the ways in which even someone of Eleanor Roosevelt's standing can be obliged to make tradeoffs and compromises in the context of domestic and international negotiations over the drafting of a human rights instrument.

[4] In 2006 alone the General Assembly adopted both the Convention on the Rights of Persons with Disabilities (and its Optional Protocol) and the International Convention for the Protection of All Persons from Enforced Disappearances. The Declaration on the Rights of Indigenous Peoples, under consideration by the Commission since 1995 when it received a complete draft from the Sub-Commission, was also adopted by the Human Rights Council in June 2006. It was, however, subsequently rejected by the General Assembly, which called for further work on the draft. And there were ongoing drafting exercises being undertaken by the Council Working Group on an Optional Protocol to the ICESCR, and the Ad Hoc Committee on the Elaboration of Complementary Standards relating to racism, racial discrimination, xenophobia and related intolerance.

[5] See Mary Ann Glendon, *A World Made New: Eleanor Roosevelt and the Universal Declaration of Human Rights* (2001).

J.S. AND R.L. ZANGRANDO, ER AND BLACK CIVIL RIGHTS

in J. Hoff-Wilson and M. Lightman (eds.), Without Precedent: The Life and Career of Eleanor Roosevelt (1984) 88, at 91

[Eleanor Roosevelt was] an advocate of equal opportunities rather than a social critic or an architect of structural change. . . .

There were reasons for these limitations. Eleanor Roosevelt and her cohorts . . . had been reared in the late-nineteenth and early twentieth-century presumptions of racism, in which theories of racial hierarchies abounded. . . .

As they questioned and challenged social injustices, Roosevelt and her contemporaries came to value "tolerance", "reform", and "brotherhood" in pursuit of the American dream. Accordingly, they looked with suspicion upon the programs of [black nationalist] Marcus Garvey and of the American Communist party. . . . Relying upon the moderate, procedural instruments of a progressive liberalism, Eleanor Roosevelt embraced the New Deal-type solutions that became synonymous with her public behavior.

. . .

She was the first President's wife thus to be fully engaged in public affairs, and the first to openly espouse a concern for civil rights. In this, she was far ahead of her husband. He argued that he could not promote civil rights because he needed the cooperation of southern Democrats, first for economic recovery measures and later for defense expenditures. . . .

. . .

The postwar decolonization movement among Third World peoples put the question of race in an entirely new light, one that many traditional white Americans found unsettling. Decolonization efforts provided Afro-Americans with models of initiative that challenged existing racial assumptions and jeopardized long-standing racial arrangements that whites had taken for granted. . . .

. . . [Roosevelt's position was that] 'We have . . . to make sure that we have civil rights in this country . . . [because] it isn't any longer a domestic question — its an international question. It is perhaps the question which may decide whether democracy or communism wins out in the world.'

Ironically, the issue of communism cut in both directions simultaneously: the Cold War and McCarthyism imposed a certain conformist mentality on all Americans, even while their eagerness to improve America's international image intensified a concern for racial reform. This contradiction also appeared in the postwar career of Eleanor Roosevelt. . . . [A]s a member of the American delegation to the UN, she had steadfastly refused to introduce the NAACP's[6] 1947 *Appeal to the World*. . . . [T]his was a stinging indictment of American race relations and a request for UN monitoring of racial injustices. Roosevelt worried that the document would damage America's international reputation , and resented the fact that its introduction

[6] The National Association for the Advancement of Colored People was the leading African-American lobbying group of the day and a group with which Eleanor Roosevelt had worked closely.

would throw the spotlight on American domestic behavior while leaving the Soviets untouched.

. . .

[One of the leaders of the NAACP wrote in 1955 that Eleanor Roosevelt's] enemies and critics used every device of criticism and slander to stop her, but undaunted, she continued to speak out and act as her conscience dictated. She gave to many Americans, particularly Negroes, hope and faith which enabled them to continue the struggle for full citizenship'.

CAROL ANDERSON, EYES OFF THE PRIZE: THE UNITED NATIONS AND THE AFRICAN AMERICAN STRUGGLE FOR HUMAN RIGHTS, 1944–1955

(2003), 2

[T]oward the end of the Second World War, the African American leadership, led by the [NAACP], had already decided that only human rights could repair the damage that more than three centuries of slavery, Jim Crow, and racism had done to the African American community. Civil rights, no matter how noble, could only maintain the gap. The NAACP, therefore, marshaled its resources — including a war chest of more than one million dollars, nearly 500,000 members, and access to power brokers throughout the world — to make human rights *the* standard for equality. . . . Yet, even with all its clout and prestige, the Association recognized that it could not singlehandedly alter the trajectory of America's sordid racial history.

The NAACP, therefore, forged important, but ultimately flawed, alliances with Eleanor Roosevelt and Harry S. Truman to aid in the struggle for African Americans' human rights. Yet, whereas Roosevelt and Truman were clearly committed to some measure of civil rights, they were both unable and unprepared to fight for a world that embraced full equality for African Americans. Truman was emphatic. "'I wish to make clear'," he told a group of black Democrats, "that I am not appealing for social equality for the Negro. The Negro himself knows better than that, and the highest type of Negro leaders say quite frankly that they prefer the society of their own people. Negroes want justice, not social equality." . . .

Similarly, although scholars and admirers speak glowingly about Eleanor Roosevelt's unstinting support for African American equality, she, too, was one of the masters of symbolic equality. The stories of her battles to allow Marian Anderson to sing at the Lincoln Memorial, coupled with her act of racial defiance in a Southern Jim Crow theater, cemented Roosevelt's reputation as "a friend of the Negro." A closer examination of her actions in the UN and the repercussions of those actions for the black community, however, reveal a very different story. Thus, in her role as chair of the UN Commission on Human Rights, although she sympathized with the plight of the African Americans, she was even more responsive to the public relations exigencies of the Cold War, which called for sanitizing and camouflaging the reality of America's Jim Crow democracy. She, therefore, joined with Texas Senator Tom Connally and others in an attempt to thwart a complaint to the

UN charging South Africa with racial discrimination and systematic human rights violations. Roosevelt, Connally, and the other members of the U.S. delegation voiced strong concerns that, if the complaint succeeded, it would set a dangerous precedent that could ultimately lead to the United Nations investigating the condition of "negroes in Alabama."

Roosevelt also used her chairmanship and influence to manipulate the human rights treaties in ways that would shield the United States from UN scrutiny and assuage the powerful Southern Democrats, who "were afraid" that the UN's treaties just "might affect the Colored question." After all, the senators from Georgia and Texas railed, those treaties were nothing more than a "back-door method of enacting federal anti-lynching legislation." Mrs. Roosevelt, therefore, fought for the insertion of a clause in the Covenant on Human Rights that would allow states that were in a federal system, such as Georgia, to disregard the treaty completely. Mrs. Roosevelt explained the benefits of this federal-state clause to a skeptical Southern audience as she promised that, even with a Covenant on Human Rights, the federal government would never interfere in "murder cases," investigate concerns over "fair trials," or insist on "the right to education." In essence, Eleanor Roosevelt had just assured the Dixiecrats that the sacred troika of lynching, Southern Justice, and Jim Crow schools would remain untouched, even with an international treaty to safeguard human rights. Obviously, then, although the United States was willing to use the rhetoric of human rights to bludgeon the Soviet Union and play the politics of moral outrage that the Holocaust engendered, the federal government, even the liberals, steadfastly refused to make human rights a viable force in the United States or in international practice.

QUESTIONS

1. The materials relating to the drafting of the UDHR emphasize the importance of the political context, and of individual personalities, and also highlight the complex domestic political considerations which might influence the approach adopted by delegates. Do any of these dimensions give you cause for concern? If so, why?

2. In 1986 the General Assembly (Res. 41/120) adopted 'guidelines' for future human rights standard-setting. It suggested that proposed instruments should, *inter alia*:

(a) be consistent with the existing body of international human rights law;
(b) be of fundamental character and derive from the inherent dignity and worth of the human person;
(c) be sufficiently precise to give rise to identifiable and practicable rights and obligations;
(d) provide, where appropriate, realistic and effective implementation machinery, including reporting systems;
(e) attract broad international support.

Are these guidelines likely to exclude very many proposals? What factors do you consider might be the most crucial in deciding whether or not to embark upon a new standard-setting exercise?

B. TECHNIQUES FOR RESPONDING TO VIOLATIONS

While the Human Rights Council was designed to remedy the perceived shortcomings of the Commission, an understanding of the latter's approach is essential in order to appreciate the challenges confronting the Council. The following materials focus primarily on the Commission's endeavours to respond to violations. Those efforts began only in 1967 when it effectively overturned a much-criticized statement it adopted in 1947 to the effect that it had 'no power to take any action in regard to any complaints concerning human rights'.

The early efforts to address serious violations were directed only to problems associated with racism and colonialism. In 1979, however, the Commission's work entered a third phase in which it began to apply the procedures it had developed in an increasingly creative fashion to an ever-widening range of countries and violations. For purposes of evaluating the Commission's work, one should bear in mind that it is less than 30 years since it first began to respond to violations in general.

By the time of the Commission's demise in 2006 it was using several different procedures to deal with alleged violations. They were: (1) confidential consideration of a situation under the 1503 procedure; (2) public debate under the 1235 procedure, which might have led to the appointment of a Special Rapporteur, a Special Representative of the Secretary-General, or some other designated individual or group to investigate a situation; (3) the designation of one or more experts to consider all aspects, including violations, of a specific theme; and (4) the appointment of an expert to report on the situation in a given country under the rubric of providing technical advice. Use of the latter approach was more palatable to governments than the appointment of a rapporteur to examine violations per se. While the reports produced under (4) often differed little from those under (2), it was assumed that the government concerned could save face as a result.

In principle, each of these procedures is relatively distinct from the others in terms of its origins, the nature of its mandate, the steps to be followed and the types of outcome available. In practice, there is considerable overlap. For our purposes it is sufficient to distinguish between the 1503 procedure and the 'special procedures' which encompass (2) and (3) above. Under the Commission's rules 'special procedures' might be concerned either with themes such as torture or the right to education, or with specific countries ('country rapporteurs'). While Resolution 1235 provided the formal mandate for both (2) and (3), by 2006 its significance had become purely formal and historical.

Before turning to look at the functioning of 1503 and the special procedures, we consider the role of fact-finding which is a central element in all of the procedures and raises very complex issues that go to the heart of the aspirations and potential achievements of the international human rights regime.

1. FACT-FINDING

Fact-finding is a term which has long been used to describe the function of international human rights monitors whose task is to ascertain what is going on in a given situation and to report thereon in relation to international human rights standards. The notion that the international community would seek to 'find facts' that may not accord with, or even flatly contradict, those provided officially by a sovereign government would have been virtually unthinkable not many years ago. For example, when the 1907 Hague Convention relating to international commissions of inquiry was adopted, its scope was carefully limited so as to cover only 'disputes involving neither honour nor essential interests'. Today, international fact-finding is an accepted and relatively common activity. It is carried out not only by a large number of international organizations but also by individual states and above all NGOs.

Fact-finding depends for its credibility and potential impact upon the extent to which it is perceived to have been thorough, politically objective and procedurally fair. For that reason attempts have been made to draw up rules or guidelines for fact-finders. The procedures and guidelines set forth in the following materials bear directly on investigations and reporting within the UN system. But they are also relevant to fact-finding by NGOs and by regional organs such as the Inter-American Commission on Human Rights (p. 1039, *infra*).

In the following materials, Nicholas Valticos introduces some general issues. An excerpt from the State Department's annual Country Report on Human Rights Practices emphasizes the difficulty of getting to the truth of the matter. We then examine the standards that are used by Special Rapporteurs appointed by the Human Rights Council.

NICHOLAS VALTICOS, FOREWORD

in B.G. Ramcharan (ed.), International Law and Fact-Finding in the Field of Human Rights (1982), at vii

[Fact-finding] is no longer a matter of ascertaining the facts in cases which merely involve the interests of two States.... [I]ssues of major importance to both the international community and the State concerned are often at stake. What type of action can be taken in such cases to meet the requirements of the international community while taking account of the susceptibilities of the State involved?

...

... [F]act-finding in the field of human rights has a special importance, and also encounters special difficulties, both because of the subject-matter and because of the importance attached to it by public opinion, which regards it as the acid test of the effectiveness of international organisations. [It] is however all the more difficult, because it frequently concerns the action and essential interests, if not indeed the very structure, of the States involved, who are therefore less inclined to accept international intervention in such matters. The issues often have political aspects and are the subject of discussion in political bodies, a factor which necessarily complicates their examination. Lastly, . . . fact-finding on questions concerning human rights has been undertaken by various organisations and bodies in differing contexts, and the methods used have not always been similar.

. . .

Having myself taken part in such procedures, I should like to set out some general reflections on the problem.

In the first place, as we are on the frequently unstable terrain of international law, it is necessary, as has previously been recognized, not to confine oneself within unduly rigid categories or rules. In international law, functions intertwine — at times, indeed, too much — and judicial aspects cannot always be distinguished clearly from non-judicial ones. It is therefore not always possible, in international fact-finding, to transpose internal judicial procedures in full. Nor is it always possible — or even desirable — to establish unduly detailed rules which may turn out not to be applicable in practice. If procedures are too formal and judicial and rules too detailed, they may prove not to be adapted to the great variety of situations, to the susceptibilities and objections of the States concerned, or to practical needs.

One conclusion to be drawn from this is that it is necessary to have available a variety of procedures suited to different situations, ranging from quasi-judicial inquiries to methods involving a minimum of formality such as 'direct contacts'. . . .

. . .

The principles must be such that, having regard to the procedure followed and the persons entrusted with it, the fact-finding process enjoys the confidence of the international community as well as of the State concerned. It thus becomes possible more readily to obtain the co-operation of the latter, while not leaving the international community in any doubt about the integrity and reliability of the findings.

These principles must naturally be based on the principal concepts of *due process of law* in domestic procedures (such as the age-old rule 'auditur et altera pars'), but they must also make allowance for the special features of this kind of international action. Thus, in the event of on-the-spot visits, it will not normally be possible for a representative of the complainant to be present, nor will it be appropriate for a representative of the party complained against to take part in interviews with private individuals. The latter party should, however, be given an opportunity to comment on allegations received in the course of such visits. Similarly, precautions have sometimes to be taken to ensure the safety of witnesses and to protect them against intimidation or reprisals (or the mere fear of reprisals). . . .

A process as difficult as human rights fact-finding calls not only for procedural safeguards. In a divided and distrustful world, and on questions where there exist profound differences of views, fact-finding itself and the conclusions and recommendations emanating from it are more likely to find acceptance if it is entrusted to independent and impartial persons. Not only logic, but also several decades of experience lead to that conclusion.

COMMENT ON FRAMEWORKS FOR FACT-FINDING

Issues of fact-finding, including the quest for accuracy in the face of limited access to information and the incentive for governments and others to provide misinformation, arise in the context of almost all human right reporting, whether undertaken by the UN, NGOs or governments. Note the following comments in US Department of State, *Country Reports on Human Rights Practices — 2005* (2006):[7]

> [The State Department's Bureau of Democracy, Human Rights, and Labor (DRL)] strives to learn the truth and state the facts in all of its human rights investigations . . . . Each year, DRL develops, edits, and submits to Congress a 5,000-page report on human rights conditions in over 190 countries that is respected globally for its objectivity and accuracy.
>
> Appendix A: Notes on Preparation of the Country Reports and Explanatory Notes
>
> We have attempted to make the reports as comprehensive, objective and uniform as possible in both scope and quality of coverage. We have paid particular attention to attaining a high standard of consistency in the reports despite the multiplicity of sources and the obvious problems associated with varying degrees of access to information, structural differences in political, legal, and social systems, and differing trends in world opinion regarding human rights practices in specific countries.
>
> Evaluating the credibility of reports of human rights abuses is often difficult. With the exception of some terrorist organizations, most opposition groups and certainly most governments deny that they commit human rights abuses and sometimes go to great lengths to conceal any evidence of such acts. There are often few eyewitnesses to specific abuses, and they frequently are intimidated or otherwise prevented from reporting what they know. On the other hand, individuals and groups opposed to a government sometimes have powerful incentives to exaggerate or fabricate abuses, and some governments similarly distort or exaggerate abuses attributed to opposition groups. We have made every effort to identify those groups (for example, government forces or terrorists) or individuals that are believed, based on all the evidence available, to have committed human rights or other abuses. Where credible evidence is lacking, we have tried to indicate why it is not available. Many governments that profess to oppose human rights abuses in fact secretly order or tacitly condone them or simply lack the will or the ability to control those responsible for them. Consequently, in judging a government's policy, the reports look beyond statements of policy or intent and examine what a government has done to prevent human rights abuses, including the extent to which it investigates, brings to trial, and appropriately punishes those who commit such abuses.

There have been various efforts by the international community to 'codify' some of the responsibilities of governments and the rights and obligations of fact-finders in the human rights context. The most important precedent in the UN context was a

[7] http://www.state.gov/g/drl/rls/hrrpt/2005/61746.htm.

'Memorandum of Understanding with the Government of Chile',[8] which was negotiated in advance of a visit by an Ad Hoc Working Group established by the UN Commission on Human Rights. It subsequently became a template for other fact-finding missions, and much of its content was reflected in 'The Belgrade Minimum Rules of Procedure for International Human Rights Fact-Finding Missions', adopted in 1981 by the International Law Association.[9]

In 1997 the Special Rapporteurs and other independent experts of the Commission on Human Rights adopted their own terms of reference which have since been used extensively:[10]

> During fact-finding missions, special rapporteurs or representatives of the Commission on Human Rights, as well as United Nations staff accompanying them, should be given the following guarantees and facilities by the Government that invited them to visit its country:
>
> (a) Freedom of movement in the whole country, including facilitation of transport, in particular to restricted areas;
> (b) Freedom of inquiry, in particular as regards:
>   (i) Access to all prisons, detention centres and places of interrogation;
>   (ii) Contacts with central and local authorities of all branches of government;
>   (iii) Contacts with representatives of non-governmental organizations, other private institutions and the media;
>   (iv) Confidential and unsupervised contact with witnesses and other private persons, including persons deprived of their liberty, considered necessary to fulfil the mandate of the special rapporteur; and
>   (v) Full access to all documentary material relevant to the mandate;
> (c) Assurance by the Government that no persons, official or private individuals who have been in contact with the special rapporteur/representative in relation to the mandate will for this reason suffer threats, harassment or punishment or be subjected to judicial proceedings;
> (d) Appropriate security arrangements without, however, restricting the freedom of movement and inquiry referred to above;
> (e) Extension of the same guarantees and facilities mentioned above to the appropriate United Nations staff who will assist the special rapporteur/representative before, during and after the visit.

REPORTS BY THE SPECIAL RAPPORTEUR ON TORTURE, MANFRED NOWAK

Consider the following excerpts from reports by the Special Rapporteur on Torture, Manfred Nowak in relation to the terms of reference for missions.

[8] UN Doc. A/33/331 (1978), Annex VII.

[9] 75 Am. J. Int. L. 163 (1981).

[10] Terms of Reference for Fact-Finding Missions by Special Rapporteurs/Representatives of the Commission on Human Rights, UN Doc. E/CN.4/1998/45, appendix V.

Annual Report, 2006, UN Doc E/CN.4/2006/6

...

21. . . . The aim of carrying out country visits is to see first-hand what the true practice and situation of torture and ill-treatment is: to identify gaps as well as acknowledge positive measures, to recommend ways to improve the situation, and to initiate a process of sustained constructive cooperation with the Government together with the international community and civil society in order to eradicate torture and ill-treatment. Such visits necessarily entail meetings with authorities most directly concerned with the issues, alleged victims or their families, as well as NGOs and relevant international actors.

22. To ensure that any assessment of the situation of torture and ill-treatment will be honest, credible and objective, a number of basic preconditions must be guaranteed by the Government. . . . [The 1997 terms of reference, reproduced above,] are integral to his methods of work. The Special Rapporteur notes that similar standards for conducting visits to detention facilities have been recognized in international instruments, such as in the European Convention for the Prevention of Torture . . . .

23. [I]t is axiomatic that freedom of inquiry in places of detention implies: unimpeded access, with or without prior notice, to any place where persons may be deprived of their liberty (e.g. police lock-up, pretrial, prison, juvenile, administrative, psychiatric or other facilities, as well as detention facilities within military installations); not being subject to arbitrary time limits for carrying out his work (e.g. visiting hours, working hours of daytime prison staff, etc.); free movement within the facility and access to any room in order to gather information, including by use of electronic means, such as photography; having access to any detainee or staff, and the possibility of conducting confidential and private interviews, unsupervised by government officials, in places either chosen by the Special Rapporteur or in cooperation with the detainee; being assisted by independent medical specialists who are qualified to document and assess injuries, in accordance with the Istanbul Protocol, as well as being assisted by independent interpreters; and being provided with copies of relevant information and documentation as requested.

24. The Special Rapporteur observes that in recent years much concern has been raised by Governments with respect to the above-mentioned terms of reference, particularly with regard to unannounced visits to places of detention. . . . Were he to announce in advance, in every instance, which facilities he wished to see and whom he wished to meet, there might be a risk that existing circumstances could be concealed or changed, or persons might be moved, threatened or prevented from meeting with him. This is an unfortunate reality that the Special Rapporteur faces. In fact, such incidents have even occurred where he has been delayed in entering a facility by as little as 30 minutes.

25. On occasion, in order to deny the Special Rapporteur the unimpeded access described above, it has been argued that national legislation restricts access to facilities except for a select number of enumerated individuals. However, it must be pointed out that an official visit of the United Nations Special Rapporteur, undertaken at the express invitation of a Government, is clearly an exceptional event.

Therefore, one would expect that the Government would demonstrate its good faith and cooperation by facilitating the work of the Special Rapporteur to the fullest extent possible. In practical terms, this has been achieved by providing the Special Rapporteur with letters of authorization signed by the relevant ministries, as was done recently in Georgia, Mongolia and Nepal. . .

26. In the view of the Special Rapporteur, these terms of reference are fundamental, necessary and common sense considerations. Moreover, by their nature, "common sense" methods for fact-finding cannot be subject to negotiation or selective approval by States. This was one of the reasons for the cancellation of the visit to Guantánamo Bay. Any suggestion to the contrary can only be considered as an attempt to compromise later findings. Likewise, subsequent violations of these conditions would seriously call into question the intentions behind inviting the Special Rapporteur.

. . .

Report on Mission to China, UN Doc. E/CN.4/2006/6/Add.6

[Eds.: The Special Rapporteur first requested a mission to China in 1995. Four years later the government suggested a 'friendly visit', which would not have followed the standard methodology for country visits by rapporteurs. The invitation was declined. In 2004 an unconditional invitation was extended. Behind the scenes, the issue of the Special Rapporteur's visit was the subject of extensive bilateral discussions by the USA and the European Union in their diplomatic exchanges with China.]

. . .

I. Particular circumstances of fact-finding

9. The Special Rapporteur . . . credits the Ministry [of Foreign Affairs] for its great efforts in ensuring that the mission proceeded as smoothly as possible and that his terms of reference (TOR) were in principle respected. All meetings with detainees were carried out in privacy and in locations designated by the Special Rapporteur. No request for a meeting or interviewing of a particular individual nor for a visit to any particular detention centre was refused. Prison staff were generally cooperative and helped the Special Rapporteur meet with prisoners on his list, even those who had been transferred to different facilities.

10. The Special Rapporteur feels, however, compelled to point out that security and intelligence officials attempted to obstruct or restrict his attempts at fact-finding, particularly at the outset of the visit when his team was followed in their Beijing hotel and its vicinity. Furthermore, during the visit a number of alleged victims and family members, lawyers and human rights defenders were intimidated by security personnel, placed under police surveillance, instructed not to meet the Special Rapporteur, or were physically prevented from meeting with him.

11. Prison officials restricted interviews to their own working hours, which limited the number of facilities visited and detainees interviewed. The Special Rapporteur and his team were also prevented from bringing photographic or electronic equipment

into prisons. Furthermore, as the Special Rapporteur was unable to obtain a letter of authorization from the relevant authorities to visit detention centres alone (in contrast to his previous country visits), officials from the Ministry of Foreign Affairs accompanied him to detention centres to ensure unrestricted access. As the authorities were generally informed approximately an hour in advance, the visits could not be considered to have been strictly "unannounced". Nonetheless, this practice significantly improves upon the modalities employed in previous visits to China of the special procedures of the Commission on Human Rights.

Press Release on 'Postponement of Visit to Russian Federation'
4 October 2006

As the Special Rapporteur announced on 6 July 2006 . . ., he was invited by the Government of the Russian Federation to carry out a fact-finding visit from 9 to 20 October 2006, with a particular focus on the North Caucasus Republics of Chechnya, Ingushetia, North Ossetia and Kabardino-Balkaria.

However, at a very late stage in the preparations, he was informed by the Government that certain elements of his Terms of Reference for carrying out visits to detention facilities would contravene Russian Federation law, particularly with respect to carrying out unannounced visits, and holding private interviews with detainees. Since these issues could not be resolved prior to the visit, he regrets to announce that he is not in a position to proceed as planned.

. . .

QUESTIONS

1. Is the account by Valticos convincing in terms of the feasibility of combining respect for due process with the sort of flexibility and adaptability that he says is essential?

2. Given the State Department's emphasis upon the incentives that various actors have to present misinformation, are the standards reflected in the 1997 UN 'terms of reference' sufficient to enable UN investigators to find the 'truth'?

3. The 'Terms of reference for fact-finding missions' used by UN Special Rapporteurs have never been formally endorsed by the Commission or the Council. Is this problematic in any way? Should such rules be 'negotiated' by an intergovernmental body such as the Council, or adopted by the relevant experts?

4. Is it reasonable to expect governments to provide a UN rapporteur with the sort of guaranteed privileged access insisted upon by Nowak?

5. Suppose the killing of 20 residents of a small village by hooded men takes place one night. The government denies responsibility, which it places on a guerrilla group seeking to prevent villagers from cooperating with the government. What options are open to a UN rapporteur to pursue an inquiry, and are they adequate?

2. THE 1503 PROCEDURE: PROS AND CONS OF CONFIDENTIALITY

The 1503 procedure is named after Economic and Social Council Resolution 1503 (XLVIII) (1970). The resolution authorized the Commission to establish a procedure for the examination of communications (complaints) pertaining to 'situations which appear to reveal a consistent pattern of gross and reliably attested violations of human rights requiring consideration by the Commission'. Its origins lay in a dramatic change in the composition of the major UN organs by the mid 1960s as a result of the influx of new members, mainly newly independent African and Asian states. Membership of the Commission went from 18 in 1960 to 32 in 1967 (20 of which were from the Third World), en route to 53 members in 2006.

In 1965 a complaints procedure had been included in the Convention on the Elimination of All Forms of Racial Discrimination (CERD). The willingness of the Third World majority to develop new procedures for treaty bodies applied even though there was a significant 'risk' that the scope or reach of these procedures might eventually be extended to address a broader range of problems for which Third World governments might be responsible. And indeed this development cleared the way for an Optional Protocol to the Covenant on Civil and Political Rights to be adopted the following year.

At the same time, Third World countries, strongly supported by the Eastern Europeans, were pressing for a general, non-treaty-based, communications-type procedure as an additional means by which to pursue the struggle against racist and colonialist policies, particularly in southern Africa. These efforts resulted in the adoption of what eventually turned out to be two separate procedures, the scope of each of which was extended to include violations anywhere in the world. The first, established under ECOSOC Resolution 1235 (XLII), laid down the principle that violations could be examined by the Commission and responded to. It provided the necessary authorization for the Commission to engage in public debate on the issue each year. The second was the 1503 procedure. Although it was adopted after, and built upon, the 1235 procedure, it developed more rapidly than the latter, and has often been used as a precursor to action under it. Thus we consider the 1503 procedure first.

The UN Commission had previously (under Resolutions 75 (V) (1947) and 728 F (XXVIII) (1959)) used communications only as a means of identifying general trends, thus providing no response whatsoever to the particular violations at issue. The adoption of the 1503 procedure involved a typical horse-trading exercise in which governments with competing objectives sought to reconcile their goals through the use of open-ended and flexible language. Both the resolution itself and the subsequent Sub-Commission resolution that laid down the admissibility criteria for communications are perfect case studies in ambiguity.

Under the terms of the 1503 resolution the Sub-Commission was authorized to establish a Working Group which would review all communications and government replies to those communications and bring to the attention of the Sub-Commission any of them which appeared 'to reveal a consistent pattern of gross and reliably attested violations of human rights and fundamental freedoms within the terms of reference of the Sub-Commission'. The Sub-Commission would then decide which, if any, of those situations should be brought to the attention of the Commission.

For its part the Commission could determine that the situation warranted either 'a thorough study' followed by a public report to the Commission and ECOSOC, or the appointment of an '*ad hoc* committee' of investigation. The latter would require 'the express consent of the State concerned and shall be conducted in constant co-operation with that State and under conditions determined by agreement with it'. Even the membership of the committee was subject to the consent of the government concerned. Its work was to be entirely confidential and it should 'strive for friendly solutions' at all times. This committee procedure has never been used. The 1503 resolution provided that all activities pursuant to it would 'remain confidential until such time as the Commission may decide to make recommendations to the' ECOSOC.

In 1971, the Sub-Commission (Res. 1 (XXIV)) adopted procedures on admissibility under 1503. They permitted communications to come from any person or group who is a victim or has direct and reliable knowledge of violations, including NGOs. Communications would not be accepted if they were anonymous, prejudiced arrangements of other UN agencies, contained insulting references, were manifestly politically motivated or contrary to the UN Charter, if viable domestic remedies have not been exhausted, or if not submitted within a reasonable time.

CASE STUDY OF SAUDI ARABIA UNDER THE 1503 PROCEDURE

Until the mid 1980s the United Nations received around 25,000 complaints per year. In 1993 the number ballooned to around 300,000, but many of these complaints were identical as a result of letter-writing campaigns by groups with large and active memberships. It seems that, on average, about 50,000 complaints are still received each year. The processes involved are tedious and time-consuming. This is because the procedure was carefully designed to ensure that governments would not lightly be accused of violations and because it is concerned not with individual cases, but with 'situations'.

In statistical terms, the 1503 procedure has 'touched' an impressive number of countries. Between 1972 and 2005, 86 states have been subject to scrutiny. Of these, 27 were in Africa, 27 in Asia (including the Middle East), 16 in Latin America, 10 in Eastern Europe, and 6 in Western Europe.[11] While no final decision had been taken as of January 2007, it seems highly likely that the 1503 procedure will be maintained, with minor amendments, by the new Human Rights Council. At its second session, in 2006, the Council considered only three countries under the 1503 procedure — the Islamic Republic of Iran, Kyrgyzstan, and Uzbekistan. Its only action was to

[11] Source: http://www.ishr.ch/handbook/Annexes/CommProcs/1503outcms.pdf.

remove Kyrgyzstan from the procedure on the grounds that the situation had changed and the government had committed itself to taking positive steps.

The entire 1503 procedure is shrouded in secrecy, with each of its stages being accomplished in confidential sessions by the bodies concerned. The only public statement is an indication provided by the Chairperson of the Commission each year of the names of the countries which are currently under consideration and those cases which have been discontinued. Nevertheless, the details have invariably been leaked to the media for one reason or another and the complete documentation on several country situations has been made available as a result of Commission decisions to release all relevant documentation in cases concerning Equatorial Guinea, Uruguay, Argentina and the Philippines. Since those cases are now too old to provide a reliable guide to current practice, this case study on Saudi Arabia was compiled on the basis of 'confidential' but leaked UN documents as well as information gleaned from interviews with participants.

In April 1996 Amnesty International submitted a communication entitled 'Continuing Human Rights Violations in Saudi Arabia' to the UN, and sent a copy to the Saudi Government for information. It followed two previous communications submitted in April 1994 and April 1995. While the precise form of the ten-page report differed from Amnesty's published reports, the content reflected long-standing concerns published in various contexts by Amnesty and, according to the communication, repeatedly raised by Amnesty with the government without any response. The content was accurately reflected in Amnesty's public report issued in advance of the 1999 Commission session. A US State Department assessment issued prior to the Commission's 1998 session spoke in similar terms. Excerpts from the two reports follow:

Amnesty International, 1999 UN Commission on Human Rights — Making Human Rights Work: Time to Strengthen the Special Procedures[12]

. . .

Gross and systematic human rights violations continue in Saudi Arabia. Hundreds of people are detained indefinitely on political grounds. Although Saudi Arabia is a party to the Convention against Torture, torture and ill-treatment are widespread. Amputations, a form of torture, and floggings, amounting to torture or cruel, inhuman and degrading treatment, continue to be imposed and carried out as judicial punishments. Saudi Arabia has one of the highest execution rates per capita in the world. People continue to be executed, often in public, after summary and secret trials in blatant disregard of the most basic standards for fair trial.

Contrary to international standards, defendants are denied access to lawyers. They are denied the basic right to bring witnesses in their defence or to cross examine those appearing for the prosecution. Appeals are conducted in total secrecy and the defendant is denied access to the proceedings and even knowledge of their progress.

[12] Report IOR 41/01/99, January 1999.

Prisoners are often held for indefinite periods without charge, in incommunicado detention, and there is no independent, impartial judicial supervision of arrest and detention. Such conditions foster torture and a climate of impunity for the perpetrators of torture and other gross human rights violations.

US Department of State, Saudi Arabia Country Report on Human Rights Practices for 1997

January 30, 1998[13]

. . .

The Government commits and tolerates serious human rights abuses. Citizens have neither the right nor the legal means to change their government. Security forces continued to abuse detainees and prisoners, arbitrarily arrest and detain persons, and facilitate incommunicado detention. Prolonged detention is a problem. Security forces committed such abuses, in contradiction of law, but with the acquiescence of the Government. . . . The Government disagrees with internationally accepted definitions of human rights and views its interpretation of Islamic law as its sole source of guidance on human rights.

In August 1996, the Sub-Commission agreed to forward the communication from Amnesty to the Commission under the 1503 procedure. The Saudi Government was then invited by the Commission to respond, which it did in a reply dated March 1998, just as the Commission session was getting under way. The 17-page reply alleged that the Amnesty figures relating to matters like execution, amputations and public floggings were inaccurate, but supplied no alternative figures on any of these issues. The Amnesty report was variously described as exaggerated, extreme, groundless, inaccurate, selective, ambiguous and distorted. At one point the Government questioned how Amnesty could characterize any Saudi trials as being unfair since its complaint lacked precise case details.

The two reports — one by Amnesty and the Government's reply — were the principal documents before the UN Commission when it met in private session on 8 April 1998 under the 1503 procedure. In the course of about one hour the Commission disposed of the case. It first heard the Saudi representative affirm the Government's faith in human rights and its confidence in the UN's human rights mechanisms. He also indicated that the Government was considering contributing more money to a UN Trust Fund for the Victims of Torture, that it had respected international standards and had sought to improve the functioning of its judicial system. A succession of speakers — from Pakistan, Sri Lanka, Sudan, Morocco, Bangladesh, Malaysia, South Korea, the Philippines, China, Uganda, Indonesia and Tunisia — then welcomed the Government's cooperative attitude and proposed that the Commission's 1503 examination of the situation in Saudi Arabia be discontinued. The US representative remained silent throughout, while speakers from Denmark and Germany posed some questions based on the Government's report.

[13] http://www.state.gov/www/global/human_rights/1997_hrp_reports/saudiara.html.

After the Saudi representative indicated that note had been taken of the questions put, the Commission decided to discontinue the case. The Chairperson of the Commission provided neither reasons for the outcome nor details of the debate. The documentation remained confidential. NGOs were highly critical of the decision and at a subsequent press conference, the US Permanent Representative to the UN in Geneva was asked to comment on the issue. Ambassador Moose replied as follows:

> I would say that indeed the issues of human rights in Saudi Arabia received intensive discussion and consideration in this Commission this year. In fact, one of the things we did see this year was a much greater readiness on the part of the Saudi government to respond to the concerns that have been raised in the Commission. Frankly it was on the basis of that responsiveness that the Commission determined to drop Saudi Arabia from the 1503 Procedures. On this issue, as on every other issue, I would simply say that we continue to look to the future, we will continue to monitor and to dialogue with the Saudis and with others to ensure that the responsiveness that we have seen is in fact the beginning of a process of ongoing dialogue and response.[14]

NOTE

In the mid-1970s, Amnesty International characterized the confidentiality of 1503 as 'an undisguised stratagem for using the United Nations, not as an instrument for promoting and protecting and exposing large-scale violations of human rights, but rather for concealing their occurrence'. In a similar vein, the then Director of the UN's human rights Secretariat, Theo van Boven, made this thinly veiled allusion to the procedure in his opening statement to the Commission in 1980:

> Is it satisfactory to place so much emphasis on the consideration of situations in confidential procedures thereby shutting out the international community and oppressed peoples? Are certain procedures in danger of becoming, in effect, screens of confidentiality to prevent cases discussed thereunder from being aired in public? While there is probably no alternative to trying to co-operate with the Governments concerned, should we allow this to result in the passage of several years while the victims continue to suffer and nothing meaningful is really done?[15]

Some commentators have strongly defended the procedure on the grounds that: (1) 1503 review facilitates subsequent consideration of a country under the public procedures; and (2) it enables attention to be paid to situations that would otherwise be ignored. Others have commented that: 'While the 1503 process is painfully slow, complex, secret, and vulnerable to political influence at many junctures, it does afford an incremental technique for placing gradually increasing pressure on

[14] Transcript of a press conference of 24 April 1998 at: http://www3.itu.ch/MISSIONS/US/hrcom/0424bri.htm.

[15] T. van Boven, *People Matter: Views on International Human Rights Policy* (1982), at 65.

offending governments'.[16] In 2007 it was under review and various proposals for reform have been made.[17]

QUESTIONS

1. One way to grasp loopholes for governments in the 1503 procedure is to imagine a case and formulate arguments based on the procedure to the effect that the matter does not fit within the relevant guidelines and therefore should not be considered. Suppose that the government you represent is responding to a communication alleging that a hundred members of a group have been arbitrarily detained for six months. The communication was submitted by a small NGO based in your country. The group's secretary is also the leader of a political party opposed to the government. The complaint, based upon newspaper reports and accounts provided by relatives of eleven detained persons, mentions that the government is widely considered to be both oppressive and exploitative. The communication notes that the state's courts have always done the government's bidding and that it would be a waste of time and resources to ask the courts to order the release of the detainees. What arguments would you make against admissibility?

2. What criteria for effectiveness would you use in evaluating the 1503 procedure? Under what circumstances do you consider the use of confidentiality in such procedures to be justified? What reforms would you suggest to improve this procedure?

3. THE 1235 PROCEDURE

ECOSOC Resolution 1235 (XLII) (1967) established the procedure on the basis of which the Commission held an annual public debate focusing on gross violations in a number of states. The pertinent parts of the resolution are as follows.

ECOSOC RESOLUTION 1235 (XLII) (1967)

The Economic and Social Council

. . .

1. *Welcomes* the decision of the Commission on Human Rights to give annual consideration to the item entitled 'Question of the violation of human rights and fundamental freedoms, including policies of racial discrimination and segregation and of *apartheid*, in all countries, with particular reference to colonial and other dependent countries and territories. . . .'.

2. *Authorizes* the Commission on Human Rights and the Sub-Commission on Prevention of Discrimination and Protection of Minorities, . . . to examine

[16] F. Newman and D. Weissbrodt, *International Human Rights* (1990), at 122–3.

[17] International Service for Human Rights, A New Chapter for Human Rights (2006) at http://www.ishr.ch/handbook/Handbook.pdf.

information relevant to gross violations of human rights and fundamental freedoms, as exemplified by the policy of *apartheid* as practised in the Republic of South Africa and in the Territory of South West Africa . . . and to racial discrimination as practised notably in Southern Rhodesia. . . .

3. *Decides* that the Commission on Human Rights may, in appropriate cases, and after careful consideration of the information thus made available to it, in conformity with the provisions of paragraph 1 above, make a thorough study of situations which reveal a consistent pattern of violations of human rights, as exemplified by the policy of *apartheid* as practised in the Republic of South Africa and in the Territory of South West Africa . . . and racial discrimination as practised notably in Southern Rhodesia, and report, with recommendations thereon, to the Economic and Social Council;

. . .

COMMENT ON THE 1235 PROCEDURE AND ITS POTENTIAL OUTCOMES

The provisions of Resolution 1235 provide a vivid illustration of the extent to which the Commission's mandate has evolved. The ways in which violations are now dealt with by the Commission under the rubric of the 1235 procedure bear only a passing resemblance to the Resolution. It was not until the late 1970s that the procedure began to fulfil its potential. In 1976 to 1977 the Commission had notably failed to act publicly with regard to horrendous violations in Pol Pot's Democratic Kampuchea (Cambodia), Amin's Uganda, Bokassa's Central African Empire, Macias' Equatorial Guinea, the military's Argentina and Uruguay, and several other situations. Developing public opinion about these failures (almost by definition among the elites in the West and a limited number of Third World countries) combined with the higher profile given to human rights issues by the Carter Administration in the United States, and several of its allies, contributed to a political climate in which expansion of the Commission's work was almost an imperative. Starting with Equatorial Guinea and Cambodia in the late 1970s the UN Commission gradually widened the range of countries whose records were publicly scrutinized under the 1235 procedure.

That procedure eventually operated to provide the foundation for two types of activity. The first, in accordance with the mandate, involved the holding of a public debate during the Commission's annual session in which governments and NGOs were given an opportunity to identify publicly those country-specific situations that they considered to merit the Commission's attention. The second involved studying and investigating particular situations (or individual cases) through the use of whatever techniques the Commission deemed appropriate. Such investigative activity was only authorized in relation to a small proportion of the situations identified during the annual debate. This did not mean that the remaining situations were entirely neglected, for the Commission could contribute in other ways to pressures on a government accused of violations. A broad range of outcomes might follow the identification of a serious country situation by a government or an NGO within the framework of the 1235 debate. They included:

- the mere mention of a situation in the debate might embarrass a country (sometimes referred to as the sanction of 'shaming'), generate media coverage, or influence another country's foreign policy;
- an NGO might use the occasion to pressure other governments to take up the issue on a bilateral or multilateral basis;
- a draft resolution might be circulated, and then withdrawn, perhaps after a strong lobbying effort by the government concerned or in response to concessions offered by that government; or
- the Chairperson of the Commission might issue a statement of exhortation, with the (either formal or *de facto*) approval of the Commission.

If the Commission did take up the matter it might:

- decide that the country concerned should be provided with 'advisory services', thus avoiding condemnation but making clear its concern;
- adopt a resolution calling for all available information to be submitted to it with a view to considering the matter at a later session;
- call upon the government to respond to the allegations in detail and in writing before its next session;
- adopt a resolution criticizing the government (for which purpose, language ranging from the diplomatic to the highly critical might be used) and calling upon the government to take specific measures;
- appoint an independent expert to provide the country with 'technical assistance', which is essentially a face-saving way of appointing someone who acts very much like a Special Rapporteur;
- appoint a Special Rapporteur or other individual or group to examine the situation and submit a report to the Commission on the basis of a visit (if possible) to the country;
- call upon the Secretary-General to appoint a Special Representative to perform a similar function; or
- call upon the Security Council to take up the issue, with a view to considering the adoption of sanctions or some other punitive measure.

The impact of any of these measures varied greatly depending on factors such as the nature of the violations and especially the extent to which their continuation was central to the government's strategy for retaining power, the relative influence of domestic pressure groups, the degree of support for the measure in the Commission, the openness of the country concerned to external influences, the vulnerability of the country to trade, aid or other pressures; and the attitude taken by the country's allies and its regional neighbours.

As of January 2007 the following 13 country situations, all inherited from the Commission, were being examined under separate 'country mandates' by the Human Rights Council: Belarus, Burundi, Cambodia, Cuba, Democratic People's

Republic of Korea, Democratic Republic of the Congo, Haiti, Liberia, Myanmar, Palestinian Territories Occupied since 1967, Somalia, Sudan and Uzbekistan.

The following excerpts illustrate the approach to reporting taken by country rapporteurs, in this case in relation to the Democratic People's Republic of Korea (North Korea).

REPORT OF THE SPECIAL RAPPORTEUR ON THE SITUATION OF HUMAN RIGHTS IN THE DEMOCRATIC PEOPLE'S REPUBLIC OF KOREA, VITIT MUNTARBHORN

UN Doc. E/CN.4/2006/35

...

2. ... It is regrettable that, to date, the Democratic People's Republic of Korea [DPRK] has declined to invite him to the country. His approach remains constructive, thus inviting the [DPRK] to view this mandate as a window of opportunity to engage with the United Nations system.

3. The Special Rapporteur welcomes the fact that the [DPRK] is a party to four key human rights treaties — [the ICCPR, the ICESCR, the CEDAW and the CRC] — which offer a platform for the country to promote and protect human rights. ...

A. General concerns

...

10. To guarantee food security, there is also a need to move towards more sustainable agricultural techniques which are environment-friendly, given that the country suffers from limited arable land and overexploitation of such land. In addition, it cannot be overstated that the excessive expenditure by the authorities on its defence sector, based upon the country's "military-first" policy causes serious distortions in the national budget and its use of national resources. This is a key impediment to the country's development process as well as the right to food and life and other rights.

11. Second, with regard to the right to security of the person, humane treatment, non-discrimination and access to justice, given the non-democratic and repressive nature of the regime in power, there continue to be many reports of transgressions by the authorities ... The incarceration system has been described as follows:

> The criminals sentenced to correctional punishment are typically economic or violent criminals, rather than political criminals, and would be detained in the correctional centres managed by the correctional bureau of the People's Security Agency. In addition to official correctional facilities, North Korea has been criticized for operating political concentration camps, collection points and labour training camps. Political criminals are incarcerated in *kwanliso* operated by the "farm guidance bureau" of the State Security Agency . . . [Fn: *White Paper on Human Rights in North Korea 2005*, Korean Institute for National Unification, Seoul, 2005, pp. 69–70.]

. . .

13. Third, there is the question of freedom of movement, asylum and refugee protection. Throughout 2005, there were reports of potential or actual forced return ("refoulement") of [DPRK] nationals who had sought asylum in neighbouring countries — without adequate guarantees of safety. . . .

. . .

18. The opaque and non-democratic nature of the State militates against the right to self-determination and the need for democracy in the country. Although the advent of technology and globalization has meant that some [DPRK] nationals have more access to foreign information, there is still no genuine free access to information, since media and related information are State-controlled and it is illegal to listen to foreign radio, watch foreign TV or to own computers without official permission. Political dissent is repressed, with a pervasive security network and detention camps for political prisoners. Interestingly, at the end of 2005, with various media speculation on the issue of succession in regard to the leadership of the country, it was reported that the authorities had issued an instruction forbidding discussion of the subject, with the threat of life imprisonment for those who failed to follow the instruction.

19. While there are official claims that freedom of religion is allowed, the reality suggests otherwise, as seen in a recent report on the issue, based upon many interviews, which highlights a myriad of threats not only to religious freedom but also to the right to life and humane treatment:

> Ownership of a Bible or other religious materials is illegal, with sentences ranging from imprisonment to execution. One other interviewee, while imprisoned following repatriation to North Korea, met a fellow prisoner who was imprisoned because a Bible had been found in his home. Another interviewee reported that while detained following repatriation . . . , six other detainees were sent to prison camp for political prisoners after confessing that they were followers of Jesus . . . In 2002, the North Korean Government formally notified the United Nations that State and religion are separated from each other and the State neither interferes in nor discriminates against any religion. This statement is disingenuous at best. All legally sanctioned religious activity in North Korea takes place under the auspices of Government-controlled federations . . . . [FN: *Thank You, Father Kim Il Sung: Eyewitness Accounts of Severe Violations of Freedom of Thought, Conscience, and Religion in North Korea*, United States Commission on International Religious Freedom, Washington (pp. 14–16).]

. . .

IX. RECOMMENDATIONS

81. The [DPRK] should take the following measures/actions:

(a) Abide effectively by human rights, particularly by implementing the four human rights treaties to which it is a party, in addition to acceding to and implementing the totality of human rights instruments, and accord adequate resources to ensure their implementation, especially to reallocate military budgets for this purpose;

(b) Allow humanitarian agencies to stay in the country to ensure food distribution to target groups with effective monitoring, and promote sustainable agricultural development to ensure food security;

(c) Reform the national law in order to not require travel permits and prohibit punishment of those who leave the country without permission;

(d) Initiate reform of its prison system under the concept of the rule of law, with improvement of the criminal justice system, due safeguards for the accused, independent judiciary and access to justice, and abolish sanctions for political dissent;

(e) Liberalize its laws, policies and practices to ensure respect for the totality of civil, political, economic, social and cultural rights;

(f) Address the specific concerns of women, children, older persons, those with disabilities and the ethnic dimension by substantively promoting non-discrimination;

. . .

82. The rest of the international community should:

(a) Support the various recommendations of the Special Rapporteur . . .;

(b) Continue to provide food aid . . .;

(c) Respect the principle of asylum . . .;

(d) Assist the [DPRK] to reform its prison system and to abide by the rule of law;

(e) Respond in a balanced manner to the [DPRK's] concerns about "security" by packaging human rights initiatives with security guarantees and incentives for economic and other development, reflective of a comprehensive approach to human rights with practical implementation measures.

NOTE

In response to the resolution appointing the Special Rapporteur the Government replied to the Commission as follows:

> The DPRK has already repeatedly stated its resolute rejection of the resolution and still remains invariable in its position. The resolution, as initiated by the European Union, is based on political motivations, taking sides with the United States policy of hostility against the DPRK and, therefore, has nothing to do with genuine promotion and protection of human rights.
>
> The resolution is also in pursuit of confrontation and double standards in flagrant violation of internationally recognized principles including universal, non-selective and objective handling of human rights issues through dialogue and cooperation. Consequently, the resolution in its entirety represents one of the major factors contributing to the serious undermining of the credibility of the Commission on Human Rights in whose activities the principle of non-politicization, objectivity

> and impartiality should be thoroughly observed. The DPRK rejects and does not even recognize the resolution itself since it runs counter to the genuine promotion and protection of human rights in actual fact.[18]

The following summarizes a 2006 Government reply to a communication from several thematic special procedures alleging the trafficking of women from the DPRK to China:

> the forces hostile to the DPRK were becoming ever more reckless in their attempts to defame, disintegrate and overthrow the state and social system of the country. As part of these attempts they were resorting to every possible means in the international human rights field including by continuing to circulate fabricated information on and forcing the allies and various individuals of the world to join their plot against the DPRK. In the light of its political motives, provocative nature and fabricated contents, the joint letter, was construed as a product of a conspiracy undertaken in line with hostile forces' attempts.[19]

QUESTIONS

1. When, if ever, might a state view a country-specific mandate 'as a window of opportunity to engage with the United Nations system'?

2. What, if any, limits are there to the type of issue that a country rapporteur can reasonably address? Consider, for example, the reference to the need for environment-friendly agricultural policies, the assertion that the national defence budget should be reduced, and the decision to address apparent human rights violations (refoulement) by neighbouring countries.

3. What sources should a rapporteur make use of? Is it appropriate to cite lengthy quotations from South Korean and US sources?

4. How compelling are Muntarbhorn's recommendations? How would you suggest they might be improved?

C. THE THEMATIC 'SPECIAL PROCEDURES' OF THE COMMISSION AND COUNCIL

COMMENT ON SPECIAL PROCEDURES

In 2006 former UN Secretary-General Kofi Annan described the special procedures as 'the crown jewel of the [UN human rights] system'. Those procedures consist of

[18] UN Doc. E/CN.4/2005/G/13.

[19] UN Doc. E/CN.4/2006/62/Add.1, para. 68.

the country mandates described in the preceding section and a range of 'thematic procedures'. The latter are devoted to a theme rather than a state or region and hence their concerns are likely to have global reach. The first such mechanism was the Working Group on Disappearances, established by the Commission in 1980. Its origins lay in efforts to respond to the massive 'disappearances' that took place during the 1970s in Argentina's 'dirty war' against leftist and other forces opposed to the military government. The government's strategy was effective in avoiding condemnation by international human rights forua until 1978 when the Inter-American Commission on Human Rights issued a damning indictment. Despite this precedent, within the UN context many governments were reluctant to 'name' Argentina, for a variety of reasons ranging from trade interests to fear that they themselves might be next on the list.

To get around this opposition the UN Commission opted to avoid a country-specific inquiry and instead established the first 'thematic' mechanism. Argentina hoped that the thematic approach would not single out any one country, would demonstrate that Argentina was only one of many countries that had problems, and would give a significant number of governments a strong incentive to ensure that the new mechanism would be kept under careful political control and thus remain ineffectual. But in the first few years of its existence, the Disappearances Working Group played an important role in developing techniques which were subsequently to serve as a model for a growing range of mechanisms dealing with other themes.

Number and scope

The thematic mechanisms have grown almost exponentially. In 1985 there were three, in 1990 six, in 1995 fourteen, in 2000 twenty-one, and in January 2007 there were twenty-eight. Of these, there were eight each dealing with civil and political rights, economic, social and cultural rights, and specific groups. In addition, there were four working groups — on disappearances, arbitrary detention, mercenaries, and people of African descent. In 2004, by way of example, these mechanisms submitted over 100 reports to the Commission, including reports on the human rights situation in some 40 countries. The same year, more than 1,300 communications were sent to 142 governments concerning 4,448 individual cases.

The 28 mandates deal with (1) disappearances, (2) extrajudicial executions, (3) torture, (4) freedom of religion or belief, (5) the sale of children, child prostitution and child pornography, (6) arbitrary detention, (7) freedom of opinion and expression, (8) contemporary forms of racism, racial discrimination, xenophobia and related intolerance, (9) independence of judges and lawyers, (10) violence against women, (11) toxic and dangerous products and waste, (12) extreme poverty, (13) migrants; (14) foreign debt, (15) the right to education, (16) the right to food, (17) the right to housing, (18) human rights defenders, (19) indigenous peoples, (20) people of African descent, (21) the right to health, (22) internally displaced persons, (23) trafficking in persons, (24) mercenaries, (25) terrorism, (26) international solidarity, (27) transnational corporations, and (28) minority issues. Thus, in the 26 years since the creation of the first mechanism the Commission created an average of slightly more than one new mechanism every year.

The terminology used for the different mechanisms is confusing — 'Working Group', 'Special Rapporteur', 'Independent Expert', 'Representative' or 'Special Representative' of the Secretary-General — but relatively little significance attaches to it in practice. A few are appointed by the Secretary-General or the HCHR but most are appointed by the Chairperson of the Council who is expected to 'consult' with the regional groups before making an appointment. Those selected are generally prominent personalities from human rights-related backgrounds, including academics, lawyers, economists and NGO leaders. The first female expert was not appointed until 1994 and the current proportion of women is only about one-third. The experts receive no financial reward for their work, although their expenses are covered. They rely upon the Office of the UN High Commissioner for Human Rights for secretariat services, but they have long complained of the gross inadequacy of the assistance available to them as a result of chronic financial and staff shortages within the OHCHR.

Functions

The functions undertaken by the Special Procedures include the following:

- Act urgently on information that suggests that a human rights violation is about to happen, or is already occurring. Urgent action usually takes the form of direct contact with the foreign ministry of the country concerned, or through the release of a public statement.
- Respond to allegations that a violation has already taken place, through direct contact with the permanent mission of the country concerned in Geneva (or New York if necessary), or through a public statement.
- Undertake fact-finding missions to examine, at first-hand, allegations of violations and provide detailed recommendations and advice to the government concerned.
- Examine the global phenomenon of a type of violation through studies in order to provide an understanding of the problem and its solutions.
- Clarify the applicable international legal framework to address a particular violation.
- Present annual reports to the Commission (and in some cases interim reports to the General Assembly) documenting their activities, which can include a summary of communications with governments, mission reports and mission follow-up, studies and recommendations.[20]

Evaluation and reform

Comment by Amnesty International: 'The Special Procedures are at the core of the UN human rights machinery. As independent and objective experts who are able to monitor and rapidly respond to situations and allegations of violations against

[20] Amnesty International, United Nations Special Procedures: Building on a Cornerstone of Human Rights Protection (2005), p. 5.

individuals or groups occurring anywhere in the world, they play a critical and often unique role in promoting and protecting human rights. This poses a dilemma when it comes to reviewing their effectiveness and identifying ways to strengthen them. The Special Procedures have evolved haphazardly and without any overall institutional framework. Over a period of nearly forty years, they have been undermined by chronic under-funding, a lack of cooperation from states, marginalization by the Commission in its political decision-making processes, and the variable quality of work of the mandate-holders. At the same time, there is the suspicion that some governments would like to use efforts to enhance the Special Procedures in order to emasculate them by imposing unnecessary restrictions on their working methods. As the Special Procedures were never conceived as a 'system', there are recurring difficulties associated with co-ordination, consistency and overlap, which were identified by the World Conference on Human Rights and have continued to resonate through subsequent resolutions adopted by the Commission.'[21]

Comment by the High Commissioner for Human Rights: 'The strength of the special procedures lies in their independence and the concerted focus with which they address a single issue or situation. The special procedures constitute a unique link between governments, national institutions, and non-governmental and civil society organizations. They address human rights concerns and make recommendations directly to governments and at the highest levels of the United Nations' intergovernmental machinery. They interact daily with actual and potential victims of human rights violations around the world and advocate vocally for the respect of their rights. Through the expertise they have developed over the years, the special procedures have advanced the discourse on human rights.

All major stakeholders have, however, emphasized that the special procedures, both as individual mandates and as a system, lack the tailored support and resources they need. As a result, they argue, the special procedures cannot adequately fulfil their mandate to affect positively the human rights situation around the world. Observers have noted a number of weaknesses in the system, particularly a lack of coordination among the various mandates, inadequate public awareness about the special procedures in general, and only limited follow-up to recommendations and individual complaints.'[22]

The future

General Assembly Res. 60/251 requires the Council to 'assume, review and, where necessary, improve and rationalize all mandates, mechanisms, functions and responsibilities of the Commission on Human Rights in order to maintain a system of special procedures . . .; the Council shall complete this review within one year after the holding of its first session' (i.e. by June 2007).

Of the functions performed by the Special Procedures, three stand out in importance: (1) the presentation of an annual report and associated efforts to develop

[21] Ibid, p. 3.

[22] High Commissioner's Strategic Management Plan 2006–2007, p. 26, at http://www.ohchr.org/english/about/docs/strategic.pdf.

jurisprudence; (2) country fact-finding missions; and (3) the sending of complaints ('communications'). The following materials consider examples of the ways in which each of these functions is carried out.

1. ANNUAL REPORTS AND THE DEVELOPMENT OF JURISPRUDENCE

While it is risky to generalize too much when seeking to capture the practice of 28 different thematic procedures, most mandate-holders use their 'annual report' to provide an overview of current and pressing issues, to systematize in some way the approach adopted to the mandate and the lessons learned, and to develop particular interpretations of the norms in question. In the excerpts below the Special Rapporteur on adequate housing uses his final report to reflect on the key issues confronting his mandate and to launch a new set of soft law principles. In the following example, the report of the Representative of the Secretary-General on the human rights of internally displaced persons illustrates the extensive use made under that mandate of techniques designed to generate soft law and to influence the way in which states and others interpret the relevant norms.

REPORT OF THE SPECIAL RAPPORTEUR ON ADEQUATE HOUSING . . ., MILOON KOTHARI

UN Doc. E/CN.4/2006/41

. . .

II. Main obstacles and contemporary trends

29. [Based on the six years of his mandate, the Special Rapporteur uses the occasion of what was expected to be his final report (in the transitional arrangements from the Commission to the Council his mandate was extended for one year) to] highlight a number of main obstacles and contemporary trends that require urgent attention:

Adequate housing and land and property concerns. Testimonies, country missions to Afghanistan, Brazil, Cambodia or Kenya, and other sources of information have clearly demonstrated that the realization of the right to adequate housing cannot be examined in isolation from land and property considerations. Relevant concerns include: land and property speculation and the unwillingness of States to intervene in the market to ensure that low-income persons can access rental and owner-occupied housing; land occupation/grabbing; land confiscation and expropriation; destruction and deterioration of land; inequality in land ownership; agrarian reform; housing and property restitution in the context of the return of refugees, evicted persons, and internally displaced persons; and the inability of States to control the growth and power of land mafias and cartels;

Natural disasters and humanitarian emergencies. Tragic events in recent years, such as the earthquake in Bam, Islamic Republic of Iran, in December 2003; the Indian Ocean tsunami in December 2004; the South Asia earthquake in October 2005 that affected areas of Pakistan and India; Hurricane Katrina, which caused flooding along the Gulf Coast of the United States; and Hurricane Mitch, which devastated parts of Nicaragua, have shown that there is a need to integrate human rights standards into relief and rehabilitation efforts. Concerns raised in recent evaluation studies include discrimination and corruption in distribution of aid, compensation and reconstruction work; and overcrowding, lack of water and sanitation, and violations of the human rights to adequate housing, and privacy and security of the person in temporary and intermediate shelters. Attention should be paid to the elaboration of means by which the international community, including international financial institutions and non-government organizations, can incorporate human rights standards in their policies and practices including the speedy transition from temporary shelter to permanent housing. …

Urban and rural. Urban areas across the world today are scenes of violations of the right to adequate housing, due to the inability and unwillingness of Governments at local, national and international levels to adequately control land and house speculation, to reverse concentration of land and hoarding of property, to promote affordable rental housing and to invest in social housing. This has led to an increase in the number of people who live in slums; and a rise in "urban apartheid", "segregation", and "ghettoization" with physical borders of separation between wealthy and poor urban residents. While recognizing the enormous challenges stemming from rapid urbanization and the need to respond thereto, the Special Rapporteur has, on numerous occasions, emphasized the need to also urgently address the housing rights of rural populations and the distressed reality of inadequate housing and homelessness in rural areas. This includes paying attention to large-scale projects like dams and mining and other extractive industries that promote urban development while resulting in the displacement and loss of homes and livelihoods of large sections of the rural population. Given the grim status of housing rights, it is imperative that States and other involved actors urgently develop policies for both urban and rural areas. Agrarian reform must be given priority in rural development, and planning must address complex trends such as inequality in land ownership, rapid urbanization, growing homelessness, forced evictions, forced migration, land-grabbing, and segregation;

Housing finance for the very poor. The Special Rapporteur has continuously pointed out the worldwide failure to finance and ensure adequate housing for the poor who comprise the bottom 20 per cent of national populations. … [I]t should be possible to restructure the national housing finance system to meet the needs of this group;

Groups in focus. The Special Rapporteur has undertaken considerable work on women and adequate housing. Having identified the persistent "culture of silence" as one of the main obstacles confronting women in their struggle for their right to adequate housing and land, it is critical that the situation of women be attentively addressed in the future. The same is true with respect to the situation of the world's growing homeless population. In addition, an in-depth analysis will be needed on homelessness and discrimination faced by other groups, such as children, youth, the elderly, persons with disabilities, indigenous peoples, refugees, migrants, minorities, and the poorest of the poor.

III. Practical tools of implementation: Basic principles and guidelines on development-based evictions and displacement

30. Throughout his mandate, the Special Rapporteur has favoured a constructive approach with a view to suggesting concrete recommendations and developing practical implementing tools to this end.... In this last report to the Commission, the Special Rapporteur wishes to present practical guidelines for States on development-based evictions and displacement....

34. The basic principles and guidelines on development-based evictions and displacement represent a further development of the United Nations Comprehensive Human Rights Guidelines on Development-based Displacement (E/CN.4/Sub.2/1997/7, annex). They offer several new prescriptions, based on experiences gathered worldwide since 1997, which render more clear the obligations of States within this context. These include: the need for States to conduct comprehensive impact assessments in advance of evictions that take into account their differential impact on women, children and other vulnerable groups; calling for States to take intervening measures to ensure that market forces do not increase the vulnerability of low-income and marginalized groups to forced eviction; affirming the obligation of States to recognize the fundamental human rights of evicted persons to return, resettlement and fair and just compensation; and the requirement that all affected persons be notified in writing and sufficiently in advance with a view towards minimizing the adverse impacts of evictions; the enumeration of detailed steps to be taken by States to protect human rights prior to, during and after evictions; and the establishment of stringent criteria for initiating and carrying out evictions in exceptional circumstances.

REPORT OF THE REPRESENTATIVE OF THE SECRETARY-GENERAL ON THE HUMAN RIGHTS OF INTERNALLY DISPLACED PERSONS, WALTER KÄLIN

UN Doc. E/CN.4/2006/71

...

I. Protection of internally displaced persons:

A. Conceptual framework

4. Protection of IDPs is the foundation of the Representative's mandate, and the essential point of departure for all operational and practical recommendations. A comprehensive understanding of protection in the various phases and contexts of displacement accordingly is at the heart of the Representative's methodology. In all activities pursuant to his mandate, the Representative uses as a framework the

Guiding Principles, and the underlying norms of international human rights, humanitarian and refugee law which they reflect and with which they are consistent.

. . .

6. The primary duty and responsibility to protect and assist IDPs within their jurisdiction lies with national authorities from whom IDPs have the right to request and receive such protection and assistance (Guiding Principle 3). . . .

7. From a practical perspective, and in line with best practices from all parts of the world, national Governments are encouraged to take 12 key steps in order to fulfil their responsibility. They should:

(a) Take effective measures to prevent displacement and minimize its adverse effects;
(b) Acknowledge the existence of internal displacement where it happens and raise national awareness of the problem;
(c) Collect data on the number and conditions of IDPs;
(d) Support training of government officials at all levels on the rights of IDPs;
(e) Create a legal framework for upholding the rights of IDPs;
(f) Develop, on the basis of such legislation, a national policy or plan of action on internal displacement;
(g) Designate an institutional focal point on IDPs;
(h) Encourage national human rights institutions, where they exist, to integrate internal displacement into their work;
(i) Ensure the participation of IDPs in decision-making affecting them;
(j) Support durable solutions based on the free choice of the IDPs concerned, including return to their homes, integration at the place of displacement or resettlement to another part of the country;
(k) Allocate adequate resources to the problem;
(l) Cooperate with the international community to the extent that national capacity is insufficient.

. . .

Protection in the context of internal displacement resulting from natural disasters

9. The human rights implications of internal displacement arising from natural disasters have not heretofore thoroughly been examined and have only begun to gather wider attention in the wake of the catastrophic natural disasters suffered in late 2004 and 2005. Following the Representative's working visit to South Asia, he spelled out the human rights aspects of natural disasters in his report on the visit. Further, the Representative proposed the development of operational guidelines for United Nations human rights and humanitarian organizations on the human rights of IDPs in situations of natural disaster. The IASC Working Group welcomed that proposal and the guidelines will be presented to that body in 2006 . . .

The protection role of national human rights institutions

10. National human rights institutions (NHRIs), with their specific knowledge of local conditions and institutional capacities, have a particularly important role to play in promoting and protecting the human rights of IDPs. Over the last year, the important role to be played by NHRIs has been particularly apparent in the response to the tsunamis of December 2004. In particular, after meeting with South Asian NHRIs, the Asia Pacific Forum of National Human Rights Institutions (APF) decided to develop Guidelines on the human rights of internally displaced persons in the context of natural disasters: a common methodology for NHRIs. Based on the Guiding Principles, these Guidelines, set forth recommendations, in pre- and post-disaster phases, for strengthening NHRI capacity and working with Governments, the United Nations, civil society and other non-State actors in raising awareness, handling complaints and engaging in regional cooperation . . .

. . .

Protection role of international human rights mechanisms

12. International human rights mechanisms have an important protection role to play at the monitoring and supervisory levels. United Nations treaty bodies are increasingly addressing issues of displacement, through their examination of State reports and in their resolution of individual complaints. . . . [I]n order to increase awareness of the international human rights protection mechanisms, the Brookings-Bern Project, which the Representative co-directs, is preparing a comprehensive manual, setting out the major human rights protection mechanisms which exist at regional and international levels. The manual provides practical information on mandates, procedures, outcomes and comparative advantages of the different mechanisms, in order to assist IDPs and their advocates determine the most appropriate mechanism to use in any particular context.

QUESTIONS

1. How useful is the review of obstacles and trends undertaken by the Special Rapporteur on housing? Are these issues about which the Human Rights Council could do something?

2. The Guiding Principles on Internal Displacement were submitted by the Representative to the Commission on Human Rights in 1998 but were never formally adopted by a UN body. One commentator has argued that states and other actors 'are not legally bound to respect them and cannot be held liable for violating them. The obvious danger is that they could become a dead letter, as there is no mechanism to ensure their proper implementation.'[23] Comment in light of the report.

[23] Catherine Phuong, *The International Protection of Internally Displaced Persons* (2004), 66. Cf. on the limited effectiveness of treaty-making in such areas Simon Bagshaw, *Developing a Normative Framework for the Protection of Internally Displaced Persons* (2005).

2. COUNTRY FACT-FINDING MISSIONS

The system of on-site country visits by mandate-holders is an indispensable component of the special procedures. Such visits give the Council the opportunity to respond effectively, systematically, and even-handedly to alleged violations of human rights. As of January 2007, 56 countries had provided 'standing invitations' to all of the special procedures. Perhaps inevitably, most of the countries which are most likely to be 'of interest' to mandate-holders dealing with the more controversial issues have not issued such invitations and are loath to respond to requests for invitations to visit. Thus the Special Rapporteur on torture listed 31 countries to which requests had been sent and remained pending. The Special Rapporteur on extrajudicial executions reported in 2006 that he had requested visits to 22 countries, only three of which had accepted. He noted that '[t]he responses of the remaining 19 countries have ranged from complete silence, through formal acknowledgement, to acceptance in principle but without meaningful follow-up.' He also observed that 8 of the 19 were members of the Human Rights Council who, in seeking election to that body, had pledged to cooperate with it.[24]

The first excerpt below indicates the understanding shared by the mandate-holders as to the rules by which such visits should be governed. Three examples, drawn from three different special procedures, are then given of reports and of the subsequent reactions by the governments concerned.

DRAFT MANUAL OF THE UNITED NATIONS HUMAN RIGHTS SPECIAL PROCEDURES

January 2007, at http://www.ohchr.org/english/bodies/chr/special/docs/Manual_English.pdf

[This Manual was adopted by the annual Meeting of Special Procedure mandate-holders in 1999. In 2006 it was revised, and made public in draft form with a request to all stakeholders to submit comments, with a view to finalization of the Manual in 2007.]

53. Country visits are an essential means to obtain direct and first-hand information. They allow for direct observation of the human rights situation and facilitate an intensive dialogue with all relevant state authorities, including those in the executive, legislative and judicial branches. They also allow for contact with and information gathering from victims, witnesses, international and local NGOs and other members of civil society, the academic community, and officials of international agencies present in the country concerned.

54. Country visits generally vary in duration between one and two weeks but can be either shorter or longer if the circumstances so require. The visit occurs at the invitation of a State....

[24] UN Doc. A/61/311 (2006), paras. 4–5.

55. Country visits by mandate-holders provide an opportunity to enhance awareness at the country, regional and international levels of the specific problems under consideration. This is done, *inter alia*, through meetings, briefings, press coverage of the visit and dissemination of the report.

. . .

56. A Government may invite a mandate-holder on its own initiative. Alternatively a mandate-holder may solicit an invitation by communicating with the Government concerned . . . . The General Assembly, the Human Rights Council, or the High Commissioner for Human Rights might also suggest or request that a visit be undertaken.

57. In instances in which an invitation is not forthcoming it is appropriate for a mandate-holder to remind the Government concerned, to draw the attention of the Council to the outstanding request, and to take other appropriate measures designed to promote respect for human rights. . . .

58. Considerations which might lead a mandate-holder to request to visit a country include, *inter alia*, human rights developments at the national level (whether positive or negative), the availability of substantive information giving rise to concern, or a wish to pursue a particular thematic interest. Other factors which might be taken into account in determining which visits to undertake at any particular time might include considerations of geographical balance, the expected impact of the visit and the willingness of national actors to cooperate with the mandate-holder, the likelihood of follow-up on any recommendations made, the recent adoption by one or more treaty bodies of relevant concluding observations, the upcoming examination of the situation by one or more treaty bodies, recent or proposed visits by other Special Procedure mandate-holders, the list of countries scheduled for consideration under the Council's Universal Periodic Review (UPR) mechanism, and the priorities reflected in OHCHR's country engagement strategy.

59. The Commission on Human Rights strongly encouraged all States to extend a 'standing invitation' to all thematic Special Procedures. By extending such an invitation States announce that they will automatically accept a request to visit by any of the Special Procedures. . . .

REPORT OF THE SPECIAL RAPPORTEUR ON THE QUESTION OF TORTURE, THEO VAN BOVEN: VISIT TO SPAIN, 5–10 OCTOBER 2003

UN Doc. E/CN.4/2004/56/Add.2

4. The issues examined by the Special Rapporteur can be summarized as follows:

(a) Legal framework and safeguards for the protection of detainees from torture or ill-treatment, in particular with regard to detainees held in connection with counter-terrorism measures;

(b) Review of the occurrence and extent of the practice of torture or ill-treatment;

(c) Investigation and punishment of acts of torture, and the right to fair and adequate compensation and rehabilitation for victims of torture.

5. During his mission the Special Rapporteur visited the cities of Madrid, Vitoria and Bilbao. In Madrid, he held meetings with, among others . . .: [the Secretary of State for Foreign Affairs, the Minister of the Interior, the Attorney-General, the Secretary of State for Justice, the Director-General for the Modernization of Justice, the Director-General of Legislative Policy, the Secretary of State for Security, the Director-General of the Civil Guard, the Deputy Director-General for Operations of the Civil Guard, the President of the Criminal Law Chamber of the Supreme Court, the President of the Audiencia Nacional . . . [etc]

. . .

II. Scope and Context: Actors and Factors

A. Terrorism and its effects

23. . . . [T]he Special Rapporteur focused his inquiry on the treatment of individuals held in police detention, and in particular on the treatment and regime applicable to suspected members or collaborators of terrorist groups.

24. In this respect, the Special Rapporteur wishes to underline that he is fully aware of the acts of violence and terrorism confronting Spain. The crimes committed by *Euskadi Ta Askatasuna* (ETA) flout the principles of international and national human rights law and the dictates of public conscience. ETA has been criminally involved in shootings, bombings and campaigns of intimidation, which has had an enormous impact on the daily lives of people. Many in Spain live in constant fear: politicians, judges, lawyers, members of law enforcement forces, academics and journalists have received death threats against themselves and their families. According to the information received, since 1984 ETA has killed 831 individuals, injured 2,392 and abducted 77.

25. The Ministry of the Interior emphasized that terrorism was a grave security threat. The Government told the Special Rapporteur that it was fighting terrorism on three main fronts: the rule of law, international cooperation, and the stability pact for liberty and against terrorism (*Acuerdo por las libertades y contra el terrorismo*), an agreement concluded on 8 December 2000 between the People's Party and the Spanish Socialist Workers' Party.

26. The Special Rapporteur recognizes that Spain has a right, and indeed an obligation, to protect its citizens and the security of the State against such acts and threats thereof. However, he wishes to reiterate, as he has done most recently in his report to the General Assembly (A/57/173), that the legal and moral basis for the prohibition of torture and other cruel, inhuman or degrading treatment or punishment is absolute and imperative and must under no circumstances yield or be subordinate to other interests, policies or practices, including the legitimate need to prevent terrorist acts and bring those responsible for having financed, planned, supported or committed these acts, to justice. It follows that legislation must provide sufficient legal safeguards to prevent, prohibit and combat torture and other forms of ill-treatment and ensure that impunity will not prevail in cases of torture under

any circumstances, and that such normative safeguards must be duly implemented and applied.

27. Before and during his visit to the country, the Special Rapporteur received a great deal of information from non-governmental sources, including personal testimonies from former detainees, to the effect that torture and cruel, inhuman and degrading treatment continues to occur in Spain. The majority of the information received, in line with the focus of the visit, was concerned with detainees arrested and held incommunicado as suspected members or supporters of ETA. According to testimonies provided to the Special Rapporteur during the mission, a certain pattern had emerged. Suspects were arrested and transferred to Madrid. During transfer they were allegedly handcuffed, hooded, forced to keep their head between their knees and beaten. They were reportedly held incommunicado by the police or the Civil Guard for three to five days, when they were reportedly subjected to torture or cruel, inhuman or degrading treatment. Former detainees described the following methods of treatment during incommunicado detention: hooding, forced nudity, physical exercise, being forced to stand for prolonged periods facing the wall, sleep deprivation, disorientation, the "*bolsa*" (asphyxiation with a plastic bag), sexual humiliation, threatened rape, and threats of execution.

28. During the visit the Special Rapporteur provided the Government with a selection of alleged recent cases that reportedly occurred between March 2002 and February 2003. The Government responded by letter dated 17 November 2003 . . . .

29. The Special Rapporteur has observed a reluctance to discuss the occurrence and extent of the practice of torture in Spain as torture has become a highly politically charged issue. The prevailing opinion among authorities interviewed by the Special Rapporteur was that reports of torture by persons detained in connection with counter-terrorism measures were false and made systematically as part of the ETA strategy to undermine the Spanish criminal justice system. The Government provided the Special Rapporteur with a document reportedly found in the residence of members of the "ARABA/98" terrorist squad arrested on 19 March 1998. The document is said to provide instructions on how to claim that one was tortured when in detention. The decree of silence that surrounds the subject and the denial by authorities without investigating the allegations of torture has made it particularly difficult to provide the necessary monitoring of protection and guarantees.

. . .

V. Recommendations

64. The highest authorities, in particular those responsible for national security and law enforcement, should officially and publicly reaffirm and declare that torture and cruel, inhuman or degrading treatment or punishment are prohibited under all circumstances and that information on and allegations of the practice of torture in all its forms will be promptly and thoroughly investigated.

65. Taking into account the recommendations of international monitoring mechanisms, the Government should draw up a comprehensive plan to prevent and suppress torture and other forms of cruel, inhuman or degrading treatment or punishment.

66. Since incommunicado detention creates conditions that facilitate the perpetration of torture and can in itself constitute a form of cruel, inhuman or degrading treatment or even torture, the incommunicado regime should be abrogated.

67. All persons held in detention by law enforcement agencies should promptly and effectively be ensured (a) the right of access to a lawyer, including the right to consult the lawyer in private; (b) the right to be examined by a doctor of their own choice, it being understood that such examination may take place in the presence of a State-appointed forensic doctor; and (c) the right to have relatives informed of their arrest and place of detention.

68. Each interrogation should begin with the identification of all persons present. All interrogation sessions should be recorded, preferably video-recorded, and the identity of all persons present should be included in the record. In this regard, the practice of blindfolding and hooding should be explicitly forbidden.

69. Complaints and reports of torture or ill-treatment should be investigated promptly and effectively. Legal action should be taken against the public officials involved, and they should be suspended from their duties pending the outcome of the investigation and any subsequent legal or disciplinary proceedings. The investigation should be independent of suspected perpetrators and the agency they serve....

NOTE

This is how the Spanish Government responded to the report of the Special Rapporteur:

> ... [T]he report of the Special Rapporteur ... contains so many major factual errors that the conclusions drawn by the Special Rapporteur are seriously undermined, with the result that the report is virtually unacceptable in its entirety, being unfounded and lacking in rigour, substance and method.... [T]he "legal aspects" are inadequately presented ... and contain numerous factual errors.... As regards the "factual aspects", much of [the] information ... has not been verified, or has been obtained at second hand or from unidentified sources, information that, moreover, is lacking in even the most basic details that would allow its credibility to be established. Yet the Special Rapporteur gives these reports credence, and consequently uses them to include in his report serious allegations concerning the situation of human rights in Spain that are false. Particularly serious factual errors ... are to be found in paragraphs 26, 27, 28 and 57 .... [T]he Special Rapporteur levels the serious accusation that a "wall of silence" is being maintained by the authorities and society in Spain as they deny the existence of torture or ill-treatment. On the other hand, the Special Rapporteur has collected alleged statements from sources identified only as "former detainees", whose anonymity the Government believes is completely unjustified. The Special Rapporteur considers these sources to be credible precisely because "a certain pattern had emerged" from their statements. From this Mr. Van Boven goes on to conclude that these statements cannot be considered to be "fabrications". It is outrageous that the Special Rapporteur should have failed to consider that the versions of these

"former detainees" might agree precisely because they were acting on the basis of instructions from the organization to which they belonged.[25]

REPORT OF THE SPECIAL RAPPORTEUR ON EXTRAJUDICIAL, SUMMARY OR ARBITRARY EXECUTIONS, PHILIP ALSTON, ON HIS MISSION TO NIGERIA (27 JUNE–8 JULY 2005)

UN Doc. E/CN.4/2006/53/Add.4

…

Case study 4: the sharia courts and stoning to death for homosexuality

21. In 2000 the jurisdiction of the sharia courts, which exist in twelve states, was extended from civil and personal matters to criminal cases. Concerns have long been expressed that the sharia judges lacked the training necessary to deal with criminal matters, that a confession alone was sufficient to convict, that defendants were unrepresented or poorly represented, and that some penalties violated human rights standards. After considerable publicity and lengthy legal proceedings, the widely-publicized convictions of several women sentenced to death by stoning for adultery were overturned. In a lengthy discussion of these issues, several judges of the Appeals Court of the Grand Khadi of Kano sought to allay the concerns of the Special Rapporteur by recalling the injunction attributed to the Prophet to "[p]ut off the hudud (prescribed) penalties in cases of uncertainty".

22. The day after meeting the judges the Special Rapporteur asked to meet with all death row prisoners in Kano prison. One of them was a 50 year old man awaiting death by stoning after being convicted of sodomy. A neighbour had reported him to the local Hisbah Committee [Islamic volunteers monitoring respect for Sharia law] which carried out a citizen arrest and handed him to the police. He claimed to have been comprehensively beaten by both groups. The official court records show that he admitted to the offence, but sought the court's forgiveness. He had no legal representation and failed to appeal within the time provided. The Special Rapporteur subsequently took steps so that a late appeal could be lodged and the case is now under review.

23. In December 2005 the Katsina Sharia Court acquitted two other men charged with the capital offence of sodomy, because there were no witnesses. They had nevertheless spent six months in prison on remand which the judge reportedly said should remind them "to be of firm character and desist from any form of immorality".

24. Regardless of the circumstances of the individual case, however, the incident serves to highlight several major problems. They are the use of stoning to death as a punishment, and the prescription of the death penalty for private sexual conduct.

…

[25] UN Doc. E/CN.4/2004/G/19.

(c) Sharia law in Nigeria

32. Under the Sharia Penal Codes in force in twelve northern states, capital offences include sodomy, "adultery (zina), apostasy (ridda), rebellion (bag'yi), and Hiraba, translated as highway robbery . . . ". The issue of punishment for zina (adultery) has attracted extensive media attention because of cases in which the sharia courts prescribed death by stoning for women found guilty of zina. In the Special Rapporteur's discussions with them, judges of the Appeals Court of the Grand Khadi of Kano emphasized the extent to which the version of the sharia which they applied (following the Maliki School) contains provisions which ensure that only very few cases will ever satisfy the requirements for the imposition of the death penalty.

33. In March 2002 a Sharia Court in Katsina State sentenced Ms. Amina Lawal to death by stoning for *zina*. A higher court upheld the judgment in August 2002. On appeal in September 2003 the Katsina State Sharia Court of Appeal (by a 4–1 majority) overturned the conviction. Several grounds were cited: (i) the evidence against her should have been presented not just by the police but by four witnesses as required by the Koran; (ii) her initial conviction should have been rendered by a three judge panel, rather than only a single judge; (iii) under Islamic law she should have been permitted to withdraw her confession at any point prior to execution; and (iv) the child of a divorced woman is presumed to have been fathered by her ex-husband, a presumption which only he could refute. The alleged father of the baby denied paternity and had been discharged at an early stage on the grounds that the required four witnesses could not be found to testify against him.

34. In late 2004 two women, Hajara Ibrahim and Daso Adamu, were sentenced to death for *zina* by Sharia Courts in Bauchi State. Both convictions were later overturned by Upper Sharia Courts. Ms. Ibrahim was acquitted on the basis that her marriage had never been consummated so she could not be guilty of adultery and Ms. Adamu was acquitted on the basis of the principle that a pregnancy can reasonably be attributed to the ex-husband up to five years after a divorce.

35. Fortunately, the accused in all of these cases were ultimately acquitted. But reason for continuing concern remains. Firstly, characterizing adultery and sodomy as capital offences leading to death by stoning is contrary to applicable Nigerian and international law. Neither can be considered to be one of the most serious crimes for which the death penalty may be prescribed. Secondly, even if the sentence is never carried out, the mere possibility that it can threaten the accused for years until overturned or commuted constitutes a form of cruel, inhuman or degrading treatment or punishment. Assurances that an offence which continues to be recognized by the law will never be applied in practice are neither justified nor convincing. The very existence of such laws invites abuse by individuals. This is all the more so in a context in which sharia vigilante groups have been formed with strong Government support. The maintenance of such laws on the books is an invitation to arbitrariness and in the case of *zina* to a campaign of persecution of women.

. . .

37. In relation to sodomy, the imposition of the death sentence for a private sexual practice is clearly incompatible with Nigeria's international obligations. Moral sanction is a matter for the consciences of individuals and the beliefs of religious

groups. Criminal sanctions are an entirely different matter and when the threat of execution is involved the State cannot stand idly by and permit the two types of sanctions to be conflated in a way that violates international law.

38. The constitutionality of sharia criminal law has been widely challenged for violating the principle of non-discrimination, the federal-state division of powers, freedom of religion and the prohibitions against a state religion. Indeed the Federal Government has itself asserted that the northern states are acting unconstitutionally. Yet it has so far failed to take legal action to uphold the Constitution.

NOTE

Alston's report led to the following exchange:

H.E. Mr. Joseph U. Ayalogu, Ambassador/Permanent Representative of Nigeria, Geneva, 19th September 2006

[Address to the Human Rights Council]

Mr. President,

. . .

Where we wish to differ slightly with the Rapporteur is on the case of the death penalty by stoning under Shari'a law for unnatural sexual acts. It is our belief that these should not be equated with extrajudicial killings, and indeed should not have featured in the report. Our position is informed by the following considerations.

1. There has been a long standing moratorium on executions in the country. Indeed, the question of death penalty is being reviewed in its entirety in the country.
2. Shari'a law is [sic] judicial system that has existed in Nigeria for long and recognized by the Constitution as one of the methods of dispensing of justice.
3. No executions have taken place even after death sentences have been passed on the offenders by the Shari'a courts. Also, death penalties are reviewed by higher appellate courts which are wholly secular. There is also recourse to review of such judgements and the prerogative of mercy exercised by the Chief Executives of States and the President.
4. Also, the notion that executions for offences such as homosexuality and lesbianism are excessive is judgemental rather than objective. What may be seen by some as disproportional penalty in such serious offences and odious conduct such may be seen by others as appropriate and just punishment.
5. The practice of death by stoning is not pervasive and has not been mainstreamed into Nigeria's juridical procedures.

Response by Philip Alston, Human Rights Council, 20 September 2006

In relation to the comments by the government of Nigeria, I thank them for their very cooperative approach. I would only want to take issue with the question that arose in relation to the crimes of sodomy and adultery. The explanation offered by the representative is not in my view a compelling one . . . . [T]he suggestion that there are some who would consider the death penalty to be an appropriate and just punishment is, of course, entirely inconsistent with the federal law in Nigeria. The Federal Government has never taken this position and my request to the Government is simply that it reaffirms its legal obligations and acts in such a way as to ensure conformity on the part of the states.

QUESTIONS

1. What in your view should the Human Rights Council do in response to governments which consistently refuse to 'invite' a Special Procedure mandate-holder who has sought a visit?

2. Is the report of Theo van Boven fatally flawed in the ways suggested by the Spanish Government?

3. How would you respond to the arguments made by the Nigerian Ambassador in response to the report on Nigeria's stoning laws?

3. SENDING COMMUNICATIONS

The third main technique used by special procedures mandate-holders is the sending of communications, either in the form of 'allegation letters', requesting governments to respond to allegations, or 'urgent actions', requesting governments to take immediate action to prevent or mitigate a violation. In the materials below consideration is given to the general practice followed in this area. Concrete examples are then taken from communications sent by the Special Representative of the Secretary-General on human rights defenders and by the Working Group on Arbitrary Detention.

DRAFT MANUAL OF THE UNITED NATIONS HUMAN RIGHTS SPECIAL PROCEDURES

January 2007, at http://www.ohchr.org/english/bodies/chr/special/docs/Manual_English.pdf

28. Most Special Procedures provide for the relevant mandate-holders to receive information from different sources and to act on credible information by sending a communication to the relevant Government(s) in relation to any actual or anticipated human rights violations which fall within the scope of their mandate.

29. Communications may deal with cases concerning individuals, groups or communities, with general trends and patterns of human rights violations in a

particular country or more generally, or with the content of existing or draft legislation considered to be a matter of concern.

30. Communications do not imply any kind of value judgment on the part of the Special Procedure concerned and are thus not per se accusatory. They are not intended as a substitute for judicial or other proceedings at the national level. Their purpose is to obtain clarification in response to allegations of violations and to promote measures designed to protect human rights.

...

35. In communications sent to Governments, the source is normally kept confidential in order to protect against reprisals or retaliation. An information source may, however, request that its identity be revealed.

36. In light of information received in response from the Government concerned, or of further information from other sources, the mandate-holder will determine how best to proceed. This might include the initiation of further inquiries, the elaboration of recommendations or observations to be published in the relevant report, or other appropriate steps designed to achieve the objectives of the mandate.

37. All communications sent and responses received thereon are confidential until such time as they are published in the relevant report of the mandate-holder or the mandate-holder determines that the specific circumstances require action to be taken before that time. Periodic reports issued by the Special Procedures should reflect the communications sent by the mandate-holder and the governments' responses thereto. They may also contain observations of the mandate-holders in relation to the outcome of the exchange of views. The names of alleged victims are reflected in the reports, although exceptions may be made in relation to children and other victims of violence in relation to whom publication would be problematic.

...

40. Allegations should ideally contain: the name of individual victim(s) or other identifying information, such as date of birth, sex, passport no. and place of residence; the name of any community or organization subject to alleged violations, information as to the circumstances, including available information as to the date and place of any incident(s), alleged perpetrators, suspected motives, contextual information; and any steps already taken at the national, regional or international level in relation to the case.

...

42. In determining whether to act the mandate-holder will generally take account of the reliability of the source, the internal consistency of the information received, the precision of the factual details, and the relevance of the issues raised in terms of the mandate. It is open to mandate-holders to seek additional information from the original source or from other appropriate sources in order to clarify the issues or verify the credibility of the information.

43. Unlike the requirements of communication procedures established under human rights treaties, the exhaustion of domestic remedies is not a pre-requisite for the consideration of an allegation by the Special Procedures. The Special Procedures are not quasi-judicial mechanisms. Rather, they are premised upon the need for

rapid action, designed to protect victims and potential victims, and do not preclude in any way the taking of appropriate judicial measures at the national level.

REPORT OF THE SPECIAL REPRESENTATIVE OF THE SECRETARY-GENERAL [ON HUMAN RIGHTS DEFENDERS], HINA JILANI

Summary of cases transmitted to Governments and replies received
UN Doc. E/CN.4/2006/95/Add.1

Australia

20. On 10 March 2005, the Special Representative, together with the Special Rapporteur on the situation of human rights and fundamental freedoms of indigenous people, sent an urgent appeal concerning reports they have received of efforts, including with the support of the Government, to close down the Aboriginal and Torres Strait Islander Commission (ATSIC), an organization established to defend human rights. The Special Representative and the Special Rapporteur noted that while ATSIC was established by Statute and receives its funding through the State, the organization was nevertheless intended to retain independence from Government and benefits from Special Consultative Status at the United Nations in a manner similar to non- Governmental organizations. The Special Representative and the Special Rapporteur were informed of actions taken by the State to transfer the substantive responsibilities of ATSIC to other State funded bodies which do not have the same independent status, to withdraw funding, and reportedly to close ATSIC down entirely. They have also received reports of legal prosecution pursued against an ATSIC member. . . . Information was requested from the Government that would reassure the Special Representative and the Special Rapporteur in the context of Government actions with regard to ATSIC, that the provisions of the Declaration on human rights defenders and other relevant provisions of international human rights law are being fully respected.

Observations

21. The Special Representative regrets that no response was received to her communication.

. . .

Indonesia

252. On 23 November 2005, the Special Representative, together with the Special Rapporteur on the independence of judges and lawyers, sent a letter of allegation concerning the investigation into the death of Mr. Munir, a human rights lawyer and co-founder of human rights group Imparsial and the National Commission for Disappeared Persons and Victims of Violence (Kontras). . . . Mr. Munir died on 7 September 2004 aboard a Garuda flight from Jakarta to Amsterdam . . . . The presidential fact-finding team (TPF) established in December 2004 . . . produced a

lengthy report with detailed findings and recommendations. The TPF suggested the involvement of high-ranking intelligence officials and senior employees of Garuda Airlines with Mr. Munir's death. According to the new information received, since the police took over the investigation, no progress had been made into investigating the involvement of high-ranking intelligence officials and senior employees of Garuda Airlines, apart from the prosecution of Mr. Pollycarpus, a low ranking Garuda pilot. The four month delay raised questions as to the Prosecution and the police investigation team's commitment to properly investigate the case and to ensure that there is no impunity for Mr. Munir's murder and that those responsible for his death are brought before a fair trial.

Communications received

253. [The Government replied on 27 December 2005 stating] that much progress had been achieved in bringing the facts of the case to light and in arresting viable suspects. The Indonesian police team coordinated their efforts with the Dutch Forensic Institute and questioned over 30 people, including intelligence officials. The Government stated that the TPF began their investigations at the end of 2004 and upon completion of their mandate, they handed their concluding report and investigations to the police. As well as Mr. Pollycarpus Priyanto, [there were] other suspects . . . . However, the Government stated, Mr. Pollycarpus Priyanto remained the chief suspect and after five days of interrogation was charged with violating Article 240 of the Criminal Code. His trial began in September 2005.

Observations

254. . . . [The Special Representative] remains concerned that the detailed findings of the TPF investigation team, including those suggesting the involvement of high-ranking intelligence officials and senior employees of Garuda airlines, were not fully taken into account when the authorities proceeded with the case against the sole suspect Mr. Pollycarpus Priyanto who has since been convicted of the murder. [Eds: Mr Pollycarpus was convicted, but the conviction was overturned on appeal in 2006 on the grounds of insufficient evidence.]

Kazakhstan

293. On 7 September 2005, the Special Representative sent an urgent appeal concerning the Kazakhstan International Bureau for Human Rights and the Rule of Law (KIBHR), an independent non-governmental human rights organization. According to the information received, between 13 and 14 August 2005, the offices of the KIBHR in Almaty were allegedly broken into and robbed by unknown individuals. Members of the organization reported noticing that six LCD monitors and thirteen processors had been removed from the offices. It is reported that the perpetrators did not steal any of the other valuable objects present in the office such as a fax machine, telephones or printers. A report was filed and the Almaty Criminal Police and representatives of the Department of Internal Affairs have begun an investigation into the robbery. Concern was expressed that this robbery may have aimed at seizing some of the information and material linked to the

human rights work of the organization. According to the information received, previously, on 9 March 2005, following a request from a member of parliament concerning about 30 NGOs, including the KIBHR, an investigation was launched into the finances of the organization by the Almaty City Prosecutor's Office. Yet it was reported that no conclusion of this investigation had been communicated. . . . In addition, in 1999, the KIBHR offices were reportedly set on fire. The fire-police allegedly found the incident to be a result of arson yet nobody has been brought to justice in this case.

Observations

294. The Special Representative regrets that at the time this report was being finalized, no response had been received from the Government of Kazakhstan.

Myanmar

350. On 17 January 2005, the Special Representative, together with the Special Rapporteur on the promotion and protection of the right to freedom of opinion and expression, sent an urgent appeal concerning Mr. Saw Pan Koo, a 30-year old member of National League for Democracy, who was arrested on 6 December 2004 with 13 other NLD members. Initially, they were charged with attempting to celebrate Burmese National Day; subsequently Saw Pan Koo was singled out by the authorities and charged with distributing leaflets containing the Universal Declaration of Human Rights. Reportedly, Saw Pan Koo and the other MLD members have been detained at Pyapon Prison where their trial should soon be completed.

. . .

Communications received

356. On 7 March 2005 the Government replied to the communication of 17 January 2005 concerning Mr. Saw Pan Koo, Aung Zaw Ok, Kyaw Zeya and Thein Tun. The Government stated that they were charged by the Pyapon District Police under section 17 of the Printing and Registration Act. The Pyapon District Court opened the case on 16 December 2004. Aung Zaw Ok, Kyaw Zeya and Thein Tun did not appear in court as a result of which action was taken against them as absconders. Saw Pan Koo only appeared at the time of the proceedings. After hearing the witnesses, the Judge found that Saw Pan Koo and the other three were not guilty . . . .

Observations

357. The Special Representative thanks the Government of Myanmar for its response to her communication of 17 January 2005, but deeply regrets not having received responses to [various] other communications of 2005.

358. She welcomes the release and the dropping of the charges against Saw Pan Koo.

WORKING GROUP ON ARBITRARY DETENTION, OPINION NO. 31/2006 (IRAQ AND UNITED STATES OF AMERICA), 1 SEPTEMBER 2006

UN Doc. A/HRC/4/40/Add. 1 (2007), p. 103

[Eds.: The five-member Working Group on Arbitrary Detention was established in 1991 and developed a format for dealing with communications which is significantly more sophisticated than those used by other special procedures. The Group receives cases from any relevant source, transmits the allegations to governments with a request for a reply within 90 days, and then adopts an 'opinion' on the case. It was previously termed a 'decision', but this characterization was resisted by governments.]

Communication addressed to the Governments on 3 May 2005
Concerning: Mr. Saddam Hussein Al-Tikriti

. . .

3. On 30 November 2005, the Working Group adopted [an earlier] opinion no. 46/2005 concerning the communication on behalf of Mr. Saddam Hussein Al-Tikriti against the Governments of Iraq and the United States of America. . . . [The Working Group decided not to deal with the lawfulness of Saddam's detention during the period when an international armed conflict was ongoing; that the international responsibility of the US might be implicated in any decision because Saddam was in the physical custody of US authorities; and that rather than making a determination on alleged violations of fair trial rights, the Group would keep the case pending.]

. . .

[Early in 2006 the Group received new allegations from the source. They were transmitted to the US and Iraq for comments and the US replied on 30 August 2006.]

9. A first set of allegations and arguments presented by the source regard the composition of the SICT [Supreme Iraqi Criminal Tribunal]. In January 2006 the presiding judge of the Dujail trial, Rizar Amin, resigned. His resignation followed public criticism of his handling of the trial by senior Iraqi government officials and was, according to the source, due to pressure by a high level member of a Shi'a party in the Interim Legislature. His successor as presiding judge of the Dujail trial chamber, Saeed al-Hameesh, was transferred to a different chamber of the SICT after being accused of being a former member of the Baath party. On 24 January 2006, a new judge, Raouf Rasheed Abdel-Rahman, was nominated to preside the Dujail trial. The source expresses serious doubts regarding his impartiality, since he was born in Halabja, the Kurdish town which was attacked with poison gas by the Iraqi armed forces in 1988, and reportedly lost several family members in the attack. Moreover, judge Abdel-Rahman made statements indicating that the guilt of

Saddam Hussein is a foregone conclusion. In particular, before assuming his position as presiding judge, he is reported to have stated on Iraqi national television that Saddam Hussein should be executed without trial....

10. The source further reports that the identity of the judges sitting on Saddam Hussein's trial in the Dujail case is not disclosed, with the exception of the presiding judge. It argues that as a consequence of the judges' "facelessness", the defense cannot verify whether they meet the requirements for judicial office and are impartial and independent.

11. A second set of allegations and arguments presented by the source concern restrictions of Saddam Hussein's rights to be represented by lawyers of his own choosing and to communicate with his lawyers. Most fundamentally, the source states that the lawyers were not allowed to meet the defendant in private, all meetings taking place in the presence of United States officials. Moreover, the source reports numerous instances of obstruction of the lawyers' work....

12. The source states that the setting and cancellation of hearing dates at very short notice often made it impossible for Saddam Hussein's lawyers to attend hearings in the case....

13. According to the source, the failure of the authorities to take steps to protect the life and physical integrity of defense lawyers further contributed to undermining the fairness of proceedings. As publicly reported, defense lawyers have been the object of several attacks which resulted in the death of three of them....

14. The third set of allegations and arguments presented by the source relates to the right to present the defense case in conditions of equality with the prosecution. In this respect, the source states that evidence was reportedly read into the record on the basis of affidavits of which the defense counsel had no adequate prior notice, and which they therefore could not meaningfully question. Moreover, the defense was not provided with copies of the statements of prosecution witnesses.

...

16. In its submission of 30 August 2006, the [US argued] ... that Mr. Hussein had domestic remedies available which had not been exhausted. The United States Government also reiterates its position that, although it has physical custody of the detainee, Mr. Hussein is being held under the legal authority of an Iraqi court, and that, therefore the appropriate Iraqi authorities are best placed to respond to the questions about his continued detention. The United States Government accordingly chose not to comment on the new allegations of the source.

17. While noting with appreciation the cooperation of the United States Government, the Working Group regrets that neither the Government of Iraq nor the Government of the United States have submitted information in respect of the new allegations of the source or their position on its merits. Nonetheless, the Working Group believes that it is in a position to consider the case again and render an opinion on the facts and circumstances in the context of the new substantiated allegations made.

18. With regard to the doctrine of exhaustion of domestic remedies . . ., the Working Group recalls [its position] that ... "the Commission [...] never intended the doctrine of exhaustion of domestic remedies to apply to the activity of the Working Group as a criterion for the admissibility of communications". This does

not, however, preclude the Working Group from keeping in mind the rationale underlying the doctrine, i.e. that the State where a human rights violation has allegedly occurred should have the opportunity to redress the alleged violation by its own means within the domestic framework.

19. . . . Since [the submission of the original communication], nine months have passed, the Governments concerned have not cooperated with the Working Group, and the source alleges that the violations of international law in the trial of Saddam Hussein have grown worse. Most importantly, Article 27(2) of the Iraqi Special Court's Statute provides that sentences shall be enforced within 30 days of becoming final, which in the case of imposition of the death penalty could result in a precipitous and irremediable end to the proceedings. Therefore, the Working Group considers that it can no longer delay giving its opinion on the communication submitted to it two years ago.

20. In the light of the allegations summarized above, which have not been refuted by the governments despite an invitation to do so, and also in the light of all the information publicly available about the trial of Mr. Saddam Hussein before the SICT, the Working Group notes that no action has been taken to correct the deficiencies identified in its opinion rendered on 30 November 2005. In addition, new procedural flaws have been reported to the Working Group.

21. In opinion no. 46/2005, the Working Group had clearly stated that the proper way to ensure that the detention of Mr. Saddam Hussein does not amount to arbitrary deprivation of liberty would be to ensure that his trial is conducted by an independent and impartial tribunal in strict conformity with international human rights standards.

22. More specifically, the Working Group finds that Saddam Hussein did not enjoy the right to be tried by an independent and impartial tribunal as required by Article 14(1) ICCPR. As reported by the source, the presiding judge of the chamber trying Saddam Hussein changed twice, both times as a result of political pressure exercised on the SICT. The current presiding judge is reported to have made statements incompatible with the requirement of impartiality and the presumption of innocence enshrined in Article 14(2) ICCPR. The known circumstances surrounding the changes of the presiding judge of the trial chamber render the fact that the identities of the other judges composing the chamber are not known all the more preoccupying. As pointed out by the source, neither the defendants nor the public are in a position to verify whether these judges meet the requirements for judicial office, whether they are affiliated with political forces, whether their independence and impartiality is otherwise undermined.

23. Saddam Hussein did not "have adequate time and facilities for the preparation of his defence", as required by Article 14(3)(b) ICCPR. . . .

24. Finally, Saddam Hussein did not enjoy the possibility "to obtain the attendance and examination of witnesses on his behalf under the same conditions as witnesses against him", as required by Article 14(3)(e) ICCPR. . . .

25. It is because the Working Group is deeply committed to the principle that serious violations of human rights, whether committed by political leaders or others, must be inquired into and redressed by putting the perpetrators to justice, that it considers that procedures to hold the perpetrators of gross human rights violations

accountable must scrupulously respect the rules and standards elaborated and accepted by the international community to guarantee a fair trial to any person charged with a criminal offence. This is all the more necessary when the death penalty could be imposed.

26. The Working Group believes that also from the perspective of the victims, who under international law enjoy the right to reparation, truth and justice, it is particularly important that the investigation of the gross violation of human rights and the trial of their alleged perpetrators are conducted in a legitimate and transparent legal process. For them as well, it is essential that justice is not only fair but also be seen to be fair.

27. In the light of the foregoing, the Working Group renders the following opinion:

> The deprivation of liberty of Mr. Saddam Hussein is arbitrary, being in contravention of article 14 of the International Covenant on Civil and Political rights to which Iraq and the United States are parties....

28. As a consequence of the opinion rendered, the Working Group requests the Governments of Iraq and the United States to take the necessary steps to remedy the situation of Mr. Saddam Hussein.... In this context, the Working Group invites the Government of Iraq to give serious consideration to the question whether a trial of the former Head of State in conformity with international law is at all possible before an Iraqi tribunal in the current situation in the country, or whether the case should not be referred to an international tribunal.

QUESTIONS

1. What purposes are potentially served by the communications procedures? Based on the examples provided, how well do you think the procedure measures up in practice?

2. Asian and other governments have called for an exhaustion of domestic remedies rule in relation to communications sent by the special procedures. Amnesty International has explained its opposition in the following terms: 'For the Special Procedures system, which is neither quasi-judicial, nor treaty-based, or accusatory, the introduction of a threshold requiring exhaustion of domestic remedies before mandate-holders can act would stifle the responsiveness of the Special Procedures that has been so important in saving lives and preventing violations. As former rapporteur Prof Peter Kooijmans commented: "... humanitarian intervention asks for speed and effectiveness rather than for proper procedures connected with the concept of State responsibility." '[26] What do you consider to be the arguments for and against such a rule in this context?

3. The communication to Australia concerns domestic policy-making in relation to government institutions. What specific human rights violations are identified by the Special Representative?

[26] Amnesty International, UN Special Procedures, note 20, *supra*, p. 12.

4. In the Saddam case the Working Group bases itself entirely on the allegations received and on unspecified press reports. It is now clear that a number of the allegations were incorrect. Is this a problem? How convincing is the Group's 'opinion' and does it effectively justify its conclusion as to some US responsibility in the situation?

D. THE UN HUMAN RIGHTS COUNCIL

1. BACKGROUND

COMMENT ON EVENTS LEADING TO COUNCIL

The Human Rights Council replaced the old Commission on Human Rights in 2006. Its inaugural two-week session, in June 2006, attracted several thousand participants, including representatives of the 47 Member States, 108 other states, 25 UN and other international organizations, and 154 international NGOs. Before examining the terms of General Assembly Res. 60/151 (2006) which established the Council it is important to gain some sense of the political events which led to the demise of the Commission and shaped the Council. Some of the key ingredients are reflected in the following snapshots on the road to the demise of the Commission.

(1) China responds to criticism, 1997

Following the suppression of the Chinese 'democracy movement' in Tiananmen Square in 1989, Western states began to use the UN Human Rights Commission to criticize China's human rights record. A series of proposed resolutions which would have censured China were, however, defeated in the mid 1990s. As a result, China launched a counter-attack on the international system itself, an attack which as we shall see below (p. 799) bore important fruit in the language used to replace the Commission and establish the Human Rights Council in 2006. For present purposes the Chinese critique serves to raise important questions as to the political and other assumptions on which a system of human rights enforcement could operate.

Statement by H.E. Ambassador Wu Jianmin, Head of the Chinese Delegation to the UN Commission, April 8, 1997

...

After the end of the Cold War, the East–West confrontation at the Commission was replaced by the North–South confrontation which has lasted five years. It is provoked by the North and imposed on the South.

... Since 1992, the Commission has adopted altogether seventy-two country resolutions. Almost all of them are directed at the developing countries. This is no coincidence. As the representative from a developing country, I cannot help asking, are they qualified to pass judgment on the developing countries? The answer is NO. Because:

First, the majority of these developed countries do not have a decent human rights record in history.... The Western countries had been engaging in the trade of black slaves for about four centuries....

Since the fifteenth century, the Western countries had waged colonial wars for several centuries. They massacred the people of the colonies and plundered their wealth on a large scale....

Secondly, the developed Western countries have the unshirkable responsibility for the human rights problems the world faces today .... How come 1.3 billion people are living in poverty? Does it have nothing to do with the aggression, exploitation and plundering by the colonialists in the past? Isn't it the consequence of the irrational international economic order established by the developed countries?...

Thirdly, the human rights records of the developed countries are far from perfect. Let's take that largest developed country for an instance .... [w]e see racism that plagued the country for hundreds of years still running amok.

...

A large number of developing countries are fed up with the atmosphere of confrontation and politicization at this Commission. They have appealed time and again for an end to it. Yet, some developed countries stubbornly cling to confrontation. Their statements under this item sound like indictments in a tribunal, and are presented with intolerable arrogance. Why do they cling to confrontation? There are at least three reasons.

First, to revive the old dream of colonialists....

Secondly, to divert public attention. . . . In this way, the massive violation of human rights in their own countries, such as racism, discrimination against women, xenophobia and maltreatment of migrant workers could be cast to the winds.

Thirdly, to shift the blame onto others....

... [T]he Commission has squandered a great deal of time, resources and energy on the North–South confrontation. It is high time we put an end to this situation. For that purpose, the Chinese delegation would like to propose the following:

I. The Commission should encourage cooperation and reject confrontation. Confrontation intensifies mutual hostility and leads the Commission astray....

II. The Commission should encourage democracy and oppose the practice of imposing on others by a few developed countries ....

III. The Commission should abide by the principle of equality and mutual respect and oppose the practice of the big oppressing the small, the strong bullying the weak.... This is a gross violation of the principle of equality which is not only the basic principle of human rights, but also the foundation for fruitful cooperation. Only when the principle of sovereign equality and mutual respect is sincerely adhered to and dialogue and cooperation encouraged, can the Commission make great achievements in promoting the human rights cause.

(2) The USA fails in bid for election to the UN Human Rights Commission, 2001

In May 2001 the USA failed, for the first time ever, to be elected to the UN Commission on Human Rights. Various explanations were given. Commentators suggested that the vote reflected resentment of the general attitude of the new Bush Administration to international organizations, its reluctance to ratify human rights treaties, and its opposition to the International Criminal Court. While it was clear that various other Western countries had not backed the US, China's role was highlighted by some observers: 'China had quietly lobbied to get the United States removed, striking back for the annual [Commission] resolution that Washington sponsors condemning Beijing's treatment of dissidents and, this year, the Falun Gong movement.'[27] A threat by Congressmen to withhold $244 million in dues owed to the UN did not eventuate, but the US was elected the following year. The fact that countries like Sudan, Libya, and Pakistan were elected when the US was not also gave rise to a concerted US-led effort to focus on which countries were elected to the Commission and particularly to seek to exclude those governments perceived to be major violators.

(3) Civil society disillusionment, 2003

Reporters Without Borders, UN Commission On Human Rights loses all credibility

http://www.rsf.org/IMG/pdf/Report_ONU_gb.pdf, July 2003

[E]xpectations were low for the [2003] annual session of the [CHR]. But it exceeded the worst fears .... [T]he UN high commissioner for human rights, Sergio Vieira de Mello of Brazil, ... voiced disappointment and incomprehension at the impossibility of overcoming the divisions within the commission and the readiness of members to block resolutions rather than compromise.

In his closing statement, the high commissioner echoed the widespread malaise: "There really is nothing more serious than the protection of human rights. Yet at times I have felt that, in the course of competitive debate, delegates were losing sight of the noble goal of protecting human rights, in the very body whose duty it is to promote them." UN Secretary-General Kofi Annan was even more explicit when he openly chided the commission in a speech the day before: "Divisions and disputes in recent months have made your voice not stronger, but weaker; your voice in the great debates about human rights more muffled, not clearer. This must change ...."

The war in Iraq clearly overshadowed the start of the session in mid-March, ...

Judges and defendants at the same time, the commission's 53 member states have always indulged in their little diplomatic games for big political stakes. Blithely bending democratic procedures, authoritarian and totalitarian regimes have pulled off dazzling feats of sleight of hand. Draft resolutions calling Russia to order because of Chechnya or Zimbabwe and Sudan because of abuses against their own populations were dropped thanks to fleeting alliances. Iran also managed to slip through

[27] David Sanger, 'House Threatens to Hold U.N. Dues in Loss of a Seat', *New York Times*, 8 May 2001, p. A1.

the net after the European Union decided not to propose a resolution on the grounds that a dialogue was now under way with Tehran.

A few days after going so far as to sentence 79 dissidents to heavy prison sentences and execute three ferry hijackers while the commission was in mid-session, Cuba got off with a painless resolution that simply asked it to receive a UN envoy. Cuba's crackdown elicited frowns and the high commissioner's condemnation, but President Castro's friends were never seriously discomfited. Returning favours, Algeria, China, Pakistan, Russia, Syria, Vietnam, Zimbabwe and Sudan rushed to regime's rescue.

On the other hand, a few countries without support in the commission such as Burma and Burundi received condemnations that were clearly deserved while the commission found easier targets by singling out Belarus, North Korea and Turkmenistan for the first time. One cannot of course forget Israel, which is invariably condemned and enjoys the dubious privilege of being the subject of a half-dozen resolutions each year for it alone.

The United States was back after a year of penitence, distinguishing itself by its cynicism and hypocrisy. Clearly treating its "adversarial partners" with care, the United States chose not to sponsor any resolution on China or Russia. China got away without any reproach at all, while Russia was pleased that the commission took note of "improvements" in Chechnya....

... Trapped by their own fears and a failure to stick to their principles, the democracies for their part offered the sad spectacle of impotence and a lack of political will.

And human rights in all of this? The "collateral damage" column includes Kurds, Tibetans, Uighurs, Moluccan Christians, Pakistani Ahmadis, Pygmies, Buddhist Chakmas in Bangladesh, the Papuans of Irian Jaya and indigenous everywhere. Look, they are nowhere to be seen. The UN commission that is supposed to defend and protect fundamental freedoms is sinking in a maelstrom of culpable insignificance where George Orwell's newspeak reigns supreme. It remains to be seen whether there is any will to extricate the commission from this dead end, in a UN in crisis, and whether it will still be possible to rise to the challenge of the future of human dignity.

...

... The main human rights NGOs have issued repeated warnings over the years. Disarray, farce, fiasco, slim pickings — they could not find harsh enough words to describe the [2002] session's "disastrous outcome," which Amnesty International thought was the worst ever. One assumed it had hit rock bottom and could sink no lower, but 2003 was beyond belief. [It] proved "even more disappointing than last year," said a disillusioned Human Rights Watch. "An abusers club of governments hostile to human rights has further consolidated its position" within the commission, the US-based NGO said....

(4) The big powers avoid scrutiny, 2004

Five states make up the Permanent (veto-holding) members of the Security Council: China, France, Russia, the United Kingdom and the United States. The following excerpts from the 2004 report of Commission[28] illustrate the difficulty of holding them to account.

Situation of human rights in the Republic of Chechnya of the Russian Federation

184. . . . Ireland (on behalf of the European Union) introduced [the following] draft resolution . . .:

"*The Commission on Human Rights,*

. . .

"2. *Strongly condemns*:
"(*a*) All terrorist attacks in Chechnya and elsewhere in the Russian Federation . . .;
"(*b*) The ongoing serious violations of international human rights law and international humanitarian law in Chechnya, including forced disappearances, extrajudicial, summary or arbitrary executions, torture, ill-treatment, arbitrary detentions and abductions;

"3. *Expresses its concern* at reports of difficulties experienced by the local population in obtaining proper investigations by local law enforcement structures and the public or military prosecutor, and prosecutions, where warranted, of human rights abuses by the security forces, and that the return of internally displaced persons is not taking place on a strictly voluntary basis;

"4. *Urges* the Government of the Russian Federation:
"(*a*) To cooperate with human rights mechanisms . . .;
"(*b*) To facilitate the delivery of humanitarian aid . . .;
"(*c*) To cooperate fully with the Organization for Security and Cooperation in Europe and the Council of Europe . . .;
"(*d*) To take urgently all necessary measures to stop and prevent violations of human rights and international humanitarian law, including the full and prompt prosecution of all perpetrators;

. . .

186. [T]he draft resolution . . . was rejected by 23 votes to 12, with 18 abstentions . . . .

Situation of human rights in China

191. . . . [T]he representative of the United States of America introduced [the following draft resolution]:

"*The Commission on Human Rights,*

. . .

[28] UN doc. E/2004/23.

"1. *Expresses concern* at continuing reports of severe restrictions on freedom of assembly, association, expression, conscience and religion, legal processes that continue to fall short of international norms of due process and transparency, and arrests and other severe sentences for those seeking to exercise their fundamental rights, including those in Tibet and Xinjiang;

"2. *Encourages* China to permit visits by United Nations mechanisms . . .;

. . .

193. Under . . . the rules of procedure . . . China moved that the Commission take no decision on the draft resolution.

195. [T]he motion . . . was carried by 28 votes to 16, with 9 abstentions.

Question of arbitrary detentions in the area of the United States naval base in Guantánamo

633. . . . Cuba introduced [the following] draft resolution:

"*The Commission on Human Rights,*

. . .

"1. *Requests* the State exercising effective jurisdiction over the detention camps located in the areas of the United States naval base in Guantánamo to provide to the Office of the High Commissioner and to the other States the necessary information to clarify the living conditions and legal status of the persons being held at present in these camps, as well as the steps taken to secure respect for their human rights and fundamental freedoms and their protection under international humanitarian law;

"2. *Also requests* the State concerned to investigate the alleged violations mentioned above and to take the necessary steps to prevent those that may take place while such persons are still under its effective jurisdiction;

"3. *Requests* [several Special Procedures mechanisms to investigate] and to report on their findings to the United Nations High Commissioner for Human Rights;

. . .

The draft resolution was subsequently withdrawn before a vote could be taken, presumably because the sponsor had concluded that it would not garner the votes needed to pass. As a result, no action was taken by the Commission itself, although several Special Procedures subsequently decided to act on their own initiative.[29]

(5) Developing country attacks on the Commission, 2005

Commission on Human Rights Opens Sixty-first Session

UN Press Release HR/CN/1107, 15 March 2005

[The following excerpts are reports of speeches made at the Commission's opening session in 2005.]

[29] That report was published in UN Doc. E/CN.4/2006/120.

MASOOD KHAN (Pakistan), speaking on behalf of the Organization of the Islamic Conference (OIC), said . . . Islamic countries were perturbed at the increasing trend in the last few years of defamatory statements against Islam and Muslims at human rights forums . . . .

The OIC rejected that practice of targeting developing countries, including Islamic countries, through country-specific resolutions. Those resolutions were often politically motivated and did not help in the promotion and protection of human rights. . . . The OIC believed that the problems confronting the human rights system were not rooted in the membership of the Commission, or the need of an advisory body or lack of reports by the High Commissioner.

MAHY ABDEL LATIF (Egypt) said the work of the Commission should take place in an enabling environment which was conducive to effectiveness and seriousness, and which was conducted through constructive dialogue among the Commission's members and its groups. That work should be free from defamatory and negative references . . . .The contributions of non-governmental organizations to the Commission's work should be provided in three languages at least one week before the relevant debate . . . .

JUAN ANTONIO FERNANDEZ-PALACIOS (Cuba) said the Commission was a sinking boat, wrecked because of its growing lack of credibility and prestige; sinking as a result of political manipulation and its double standards. Its sinking was marked by its inconsistencies and the impunity enjoyed by a privileged few, who benefited from the irrational world order in which everyone had to live. It was not the poor and marginalized developing countries that were responsible for this state of affairs. They had always been the defendants in the forum, turned into an inquisition tribunal for the rich.

The Commission on Human Rights could not be half-reformed; it had to be re-founded from its own foundations. The problems were not organizational or technical. Its legitimacy was undermined by the membership of a superpower which trampled upon human rights and curtailed liberties. The problems of the Commission were fundamentally marked by political manipulation, and the organizational deficiencies were an expression of that manipulation. A true reform should begin by eliminating the pernicious practice of imposing unjust resolutions against countries, putting an end to double standards and to the impunity of the most powerful, reorienting the work through dialogue and cooperation, and devoting more time and allocating more resources to the effective realisation of economic, social and cultural rights and particularly the always postponed right to development.

(6) Amnesty seeks to keep the Commission's shortcomings in perspective, 2005

Amnesty International, Meeting the Challenge: Transforming the Commission on Human Rights into a Human Rights Council

April 2005, AI Index: IOR 40/008/2005

. . .

Achievements of the Commission on Human Rights

Despite persistent criticisms of the Commission . . ., some aspects of its work are extremely valuable and must be preserved, and strengthened, in a new human rights body:

Creating the space for dialogue

Since its establishment, the Commission has provided a unique international forum for human rights discourse. . . .

Prompting governments to act

Amnesty International has been told by victims and national NGOs that the resolutions adopted by the Commission and the reports published by its Special Procedures are extremely important as statements of both concern and intent by the international community. Although it can be difficult to measure the impact of the Commission's actions, especially at the national level, the lengths to which states go to evade Commission scrutiny are a clear indication of their sensitivity to criticism by that body. Sometimes the risk of scrutiny can be a powerful incentive for states to act to improve the human rights situation. . . .

Building a framework for human rights protection

The elaboration of treaties and other standards has been an on-going task and constitutes a major accomplishment . . .

Dealing with all human rights

Over the last decade, the Commission has broadened its agenda to include the full spectrum of civil, cultural, economic, political and social rights, including the right to development. . . .

Developing a system of independent human rights experts

Another major legacy of the Commission is its system of "Special Procedures". . . .

Yet the Special Procedures' system is undermined by the failure of many states to co-operate with mandate-holders and implement their recommendations, as well as a chronic lack of adequate resources . . .

Shortcomings of the Commission on Human Rights

[The Amnesty report emphasizes the Commisions's political selectivity in responding to situations of massive violations, including especially its failure to respond to 'violations perpetrated by powerful states and, increasingly, their allies'; and its flawed working methods ('highly compressed and politicized')].

Another procedural factor which inhibits constructive discussion of human rights at the Commission is that the analysis of the human rights situation and the corresponding policy response are combined in one process, as the Commission works largely on the basis of draft resolutions presented by governments without first, routinely, reviewing the situation in a particular country in an objective manner. . . .

QUESTIONS

1. What could be meant in practice by the need to 'reorient' the Commission's work 'through dialogue and cooperation'? Is an international human rights system which seeks to bring pressure on individual countries to change their policies and practices simply incompatible with the approach advocated by China and the group of developing countries?

2. Should the big powers, such as the USA, China and Russia enjoy any sort of special treatment, either more or less demanding, than other states? How could equal treatment be ensured given power realities in a political body such as the Commission?

3. 'The major international NGOs are caught in a dilemma. They perceive the Commission to be dysfunctional and often ineffectual, but they have no choice but to faithfully support it.' Comment.

2. ESTABLISHING THE HUMAN RIGHTS COUNCIL

The terms on which the Human Rights Council was established were negotiated over a period of almost a year. The most contentious issues concerned the principles and approach which would guide its deliberations, its composition, the statement of its functions, including new procedures to be developed, and its relationship to the procedures and mechanisms it 'inherited' from the Commission. In broad-brush terms most of these matters were resolved in the heavily negotiated text which became the General Assembly resolution establishing the Council, which we now consider. In practice, a great deal remains to be determined in the course of the next few years.

GENERAL ASSEMBLY RESOLUTION 60/251 (2006): HUMAN RIGHTS COUNCIL

The General Assembly,

...

Reaffirming further that all human rights are universal, indivisible, interrelated, interdependent and mutually reinforcing, and that all human rights must be treated in a fair and equal manner, on the same footing and with the same emphasis,

Reaffirming that, while the significance of national and regional particularities and various historical, cultural and religious backgrounds must be borne in mind, all States, regardless of their political, economic and cultural systems, have the duty to promote and protect all human rights and fundamental freedoms,

...

Affirming the need for all States to continue international efforts to enhance dialogue and broaden understanding among civilizations, cultures and religions, and emphasizing that States, regional organizations, non-governmental organizations, religious bodies and the media have an important role to play in promoting tolerance, respect for and freedom of religion and belief,

Recognizing the work undertaken by the Commission on Human Rights and the need to preserve and build on its achievements and to redress its shortcomings,

Recognizing also the importance of ensuring universality, objectivity and non-selectivity in the consideration of human rights issues, and the elimination of double standards and politicization,

...

1. *Decides* to establish the Human Rights Council, based in Geneva, in replacement of the Commission on Human Rights, as a subsidiary organ of the General Assembly; the Assembly shall review the status of the Council within five years;

2. *Decides* that the Council shall be responsible for promoting universal respect for the protection of all human rights and fundamental freedoms for all, without distinction of any kind and in a fair and equal manner;

3. *Decides also* that the Council should address situations of violations of human rights, including gross and systematic violations, and make recommendations thereon. It should also promote the effective coordination and the mainstreaming of human rights within the United Nations system;

4. *Decides further* that the work of the Council shall be guided by the principles of universality, impartiality, objectivity and non-selectivity, constructive international dialogue and cooperation, with a view to enhancing the promotion and protection of all human rights, civil, political, economic, social and cultural rights, including the right to development;

5. *Decides* that the Council shall, inter alia:

(*a*) Promote human rights education and learning as well as advisory services, technical assistance and capacity-building, to be provided in consultation with and with the consent of Member States concerned;

(*b*) Serve as a forum for dialogue on thematic issues on all human rights;

(*c*) Make recommendations to the General Assembly for the further development of international law in the field of human rights;

(*d*) Promote the full implementation of human rights obligations undertaken by States and follow-up to the goals and commitments related to the promotion and protection of human rights emanating from United Nations conferences and summits;

(*e*) Undertake a universal periodic review, based on objective and reliable information, of the fulfilment by each State of its human rights obligations and commitments in a manner which ensures universality of coverage and equal treatment with respect to all States; the review shall be a cooperative mechanism, based on an interactive dialogue, with the full involvement of the country concerned and with consideration given to its capacity-building needs; such a mechanism shall complement and not duplicate the work of treaty bodies; the Council shall develop the modalities and necessary time allocation for the universal periodic review mechanism within one year after the holding of its first session;

(*f*) Contribute, through dialogue and cooperation, towards the prevention of human rights violations and respond promptly to human rights emergencies;

(*g*) Assume the role and responsibilities of the Commission on Human Rights relating to the work of the Office of the United Nations High Commissioner for Human Rights, as decided by the General Assembly in its resolution 48/141 of 20 December 1993;

(*h*) Work in close cooperation in the field of human rights with Governments, regional organizations, national human rights institutions and civil society;

(*i*) Make recommendations with regard to the promotion and protection of human rights;

(*j*) Submit an annual report to the General Assembly;

6. *Decides also* that the Council shall assume, review and, where necessary, improve and rationalize all mandates, mechanisms, functions and responsibilities of the Commission on Human Rights in order to maintain a system of special procedures, expert advice and a complaint procedure; the Council shall complete this review within one year after the holding of its first session;

7. *Decides further* that the Council shall consist of forty-seven Member States, which shall be elected directly and individually by secret ballot by the majority of the members of the General Assembly; the membership shall be based on equitable geographical distribution, and seats shall be distributed as follows among regional groups: Group of African States, thirteen; Group of Asian States, thirteen; Group of Eastern European States, six; Group of Latin American and Caribbean States, eight; and Group of Western European and other States, seven; the members of the Council shall serve for a period of three years and shall not be eligible for immediate re-election after two consecutive terms;

8. *Decides* that the membership in the Council shall be open to all States Members of the United Nations; when electing members of the Council, Member States shall take into account the contribution of candidates to the promotion and protection of human rights and their voluntary pledges and commitments made thereto; the General Assembly, by a two-thirds majority of the members present and voting, may suspend the rights of membership in the Council of a member of the Council that commits gross and systematic violations of human rights;

9. *Decides also* that members elected to the Council shall uphold the highest standards in the promotion and protection of human rights, shall fully cooperate with the Council and be reviewed under the universal periodic review mechanism during their term of membership;

10. *Decides further* that the Council shall meet regularly throughout the year and schedule no fewer than three sessions per year, including a main session, for a total duration of no less than ten weeks, and shall be able to hold special sessions, when needed, at the request of a member of the Council with the support of one third of the membership of the Council;

...

12. *Decides also* that the methods of work of the Council shall be transparent, fair and impartial and shall enable genuine dialogue, be results oriented, allow for

subsequent follow-up discussions to recommendations and their implementation and also allow for substantive interaction with special procedures and mechanisms; ...

QUESTIONS

1. Does the text support the approach of those governments who would opt to abolish all country-specific responses to violations on the part of the Council? What language would you point to in arguing for and against such a proposition? What implications flow from the emphasis on 'dialogue and cooperation'?

2. What do you think is the significance of the references to religion in the text?

3. A major debate in establishing the Council concerned its optimum size. The Commission had 53 members and the US proposed that the Council should have only 20, or a maximum of 30. After an examination of the issue a High-Level Panel reporting to the UN Secretary-General in December 2004 concluded that efforts to identify membership criteria would have little chance of changing the negative dynamics in the Commission and only risked 'further politicizing the issue'. The Panel thus advocated universal membership of a revamped Council, thus opening the way for the full participation of all 193 UN Member States.[30] The compromise chosen was 47. What are the arguments for and against a universal or a very selective membership for the Council?

NOTE

One of the major issues that led to the disbanding of the Commission was the criticism that its members included Governments which were themselves major violators of human rights. As the US Ambassador put it:

> ... [T]hose countries that respect the rights of their own citizens [are] the ones best entitled to serve on this Commission. It is enigmatic at best that abusers sit on this Commission, band together to weaken or forestall resolutions against themselves and sit in judgment of others. The membership of the UN Commission on Human Rights must be the firefighters of the world, not the arsonists.[31]

But the subsequent debate over criteria for membership suggested that it was not so easy to identify the good guys from the bad guys.

[30] High-Level Panel on Threats, Challenges and Change, *A More Secure World — Our Shared Responsibility*, UN Doc A/59/565 (2004) 282–291.

[31] Senator Rudy Boschwitz, US Ambassador to the Commission on Human Rights, 31 March 2005, at http://geneva.usmission.gov/humanrights/2005/0331FreedomHouse.htm.

PHILIP ALSTON, PROMOTING THE ACCOUNTABILITY OF MEMBERS OF THE NEW UN HUMAN RIGHTS COUNCIL

15 J. Transnat'l L. & Pol'y 49, 57 (2005)

During the long decades of the Cold War one side's human rights violators were the other side's champions of resistance. . . . There was thus an unstated but widely shared tolerance for the presence of human rights violators in many of the decision-making fora of the United Nations.

The end of the Cold War made possible a reconsideration of this policy and, as the principles of economic liberalism and political democracy spread, it became feasible to contemplate the option of establishing some sort of criteria for membership. After all, the Council of Europe had long required applicant states to sign on to a statement of democratic principles and more specifically to adhere to the European Convention on Human Rights. . . .

Various scholars have suggested that international human rights bodies might be composed exclusively of states whose records are such that they can be considered democratic or committed to the rule of law. . . . [Others] argued that it was not only infeasible but potentially counter-productive to create an exclusionist system which would put many countries completely beyond the purview of the regime and would definitively undermine the formal universalist claims of human rights law. . . .

[But the issue of criteria for Commission membership came to a head when the United States failed] in May 2001 to win re-election, for the first time since the Commission had been established in 1946. The response of then National Security Adviser Condoleezza Rice was fairly typical. She condemned the vote and lamented the sad fact 'that the country that has been the beacon for those fleeing tyranny for 200 years is not on this commission, and Sudan is. . . . It's very bad for those people who are suffering under tyranny around the world and it is an outrage.' A rather different approach was taken by China's official Xinhua News Agency which said the US lost because it had 'undermined the atmosphere for dialogue' and had used 'human rights . . . as a tool to pursue its power politics and hegemony in the world'.

[By 2004 the US position was that the Commission] 'should not be allowed to become a protected sanctuary for human rights violators who aim to pervert and distort its work.' Its proposed solution was to ensure that only 'real democracies' should enjoy the privilege of membership.

This approach was driven by the fact that a number of states which the United States Government considered to be major violators of human rights were regularly elected to membership of the Commission . . . such as China, Cuba, Nepal, Russia, Sudan, Zimbabwe and Saudi Arabia . . .

. . . The only criteria which had ever previously been acknowledged in determining the composition of the Commission were representation of different cultures and a more precisely formulated geographical balance reflecting the five regional groupings . . . Criteria such as relative economic strength, the ability to contribute to the effective implementation of relevant resolutions, compliance with particular standards, or membership of specific treaty regimes were never seriously contemplated. It should be added, however, that there was a presumption during the years of the Cold War that each of the five permanent members of the Security Council should always be members.

... Human Rights Watch ... proposed in 2003 that 'as a prerequisite for membership of the Commission, governments should have ratified core human rights treaties, complied with their reporting obligations, issued open invitations to U.N. human rights experts and not have been condemned recently by the Commission for human rights violations.'

[The analysis then suggests that each of these criteria would either be infeasible or yield highly problematic results. For example, requiring only ratification of both International Covenants would exclude the USA, China and South Africa, among others. Timely submission of reports would eliminate the great majority of countries on the basis of current practices, although a more flexible definition of undue delay could be developed for this purpose. While the requirement that countries should have issued 'open invitations' to UN experts would be valuable, it would at the time have excluded the great majority of African and Asian countries (including China) as well as the United States and Russia. Exclusion of countries recently condemned by the Commission would have affected only 13 countries, by no means including all of those usually singled out as the major violators. An additional criterion, that a country not be the subject of Security Council sanctions, would also have affected only 12 countries.]

The approach finally adopted rejected substantive criteria in favour of procedural solutions. As reflected in the resolution these include: (i) election of states on an individual basis, thus avoiding regional 'slates' which in effect assured of election every state nominated by its regional group; (ii) election by a majority of states represented in the General Assembly, thus requiring at least 96 votes; (iii) the elimination of de facto permanent membership by requiring rotation after two consecutive terms; (iv) requiring candidate states to pledge to take human rights initiatives if elected (see paras. 8 and 9 of GA res. 60/251); (v) the possibility of suspending Council members for human rights violations; and (vi) the imposition of particular obligations upon members, including a review of their human rights record ward for election to the Council.[32]

NOTE

Paragraph 8 of Res. 60/251 called upon UN member states to take account of a state's 'pledges and commitments' in the election process for membership of the

[32] For an analysis of these provisions see Alston, 'Reconceiving the UN Human Rights Regime: Challenges Confronting the New UN Human Rights Council', 7 Melb. J. Int. L. (2006) 185. In the 2006 Council elections many of the countries targeted by human rights groups as being unsuitable candidates were nevertheless elected. The larger states such as China, India, Russia, Nigeria, South Africa, Brazil, Germany, France and the UK all succeeded. Four of the five permanent members of the Security Council were elected, with the fifth — the US — opting not to run.

Council. Since no criteria were provided for such pledges the Office of the High Commissioner for Human Rights sought to fill the vacuum by identifying the elements that should be addressed in such pledges.

OHCHR, SUGGESTED ELEMENTS FOR VOLUNTARY PLEDGES AND COMMITMENTS BY CANDIDATES FOR ELECTION TO THE HUMAN RIGHTS COUNCIL

April 2006, at http://www.ohchr.org/english/13042006.pdf

... [T]he guidance offered herein provides a framework within which Member States can provide relevant information when presenting candidatures.... These suggestions are not intended to be exhaustive .... To the extent possible, States are encouraged to include specific, measurable and verifiable commitments in their submissions.

1. International contribution, pledges and commitments

- List of international human rights instruments to which the State is already party and indications of intent to ratify further instruments and to withdraw reservations
- Cooperation with special procedures, accepting requests for visits, extending standing invitations, and responding positively to communications and follow-up on recommendations
- Cooperation with treaty monitoring bodies, timely submission of reports and implementation of concluding observations and contribution to the global reform of the treaty body system
- Contribution to international initiatives for the promotion and protection of human rights through the provision of human, technical and financial resources
- Cooperation with OHCHR and support for its activities
- Contribution to the deliberation of international human rights fora
- Commitment to fully support and engage constructively in the deliberations of the Human Rights Council, its subsidiary bodies and mechanisms including the special procedures
- Commitment to open and constructive engagement in a robust universal review procedure including reporting on measures taken to follow-up on its recommendations
- Commitment to the meaningful engagement of NGOs with the Council.

2. National contribution, pledges and commitments

- Description of national human rights policy, including information on national human rights planning, the existence of independent national human rights institutions, guarantees of effective remedies to redress human rights abuses, etc.

- Identification of principal human rights challenges as well as indication of steps to be taken to meet those challenges
- Indication of approach to the contribution of civil society, including in the formulation and implementation of domestic human rights policy and programmes
- Commitment to protect against and prevent discrimination in all its forms, in both law and in practice
- Pledge to uphold the highest standards in the promotion and protection of human rights.

In the final outcome, however, many of the pledges made were vague and limited in scope. Some states confined themselves to general expressions of good intentions, while others failed to submit any pledge at all.[33]

3. UNIVERSAL PERIODIC REVIEW

The General Assembly's decision that the Council would 'undertake a universal periodic review based on objective and reliable information of the fulfilment by each State of its human rights obligations and commitments' represented a major departure from the practice of the Commission and a significant victory for the so-called 'Like-Minded Group' of developing countries which had opposed the Commission's emphasis upon gross violations committed by a handful of countries. Cuba, a leading critic of the Commission, accused it of placing the countries of the South as 'the defendants in the forum', and providing an 'inquisition tribunal for the rich'. Reforms were needed to eliminate 'the pernicious practice of imposing unjust resolutions against countries' and 'putting an end to double standards and to the impunity of the most powerful'.[34] But Western governments and most NGOs also warmly welcomed the proposal, on the assumption that it would facilitate a regular in-depth review of the human rights performance of all states.

In June 2007, after extensive negotiations[35] the following procedure for the implementation of the UPR was agreed upon by the Human Rights Council.

UNITED NATIONS HUMAN RIGHTS COUNCIL, RESOLUTION 5/1 ON INSTITUTION BUILDING

June 18, 2007

Universal Periodic Review Mechanism

[The review will be based upon the UN Charter, the UDHR, human rights instruments to which the State is party, voluntary pledges and commitments made by States, including

[33] For the content of the pledges made see http://www.un.org/ga/60/elect/hrc/.

[34] UN Doc HR/CN/1107 (14 March 2005).

[35] In relation to the different options put forward, see *International Service For Human Rights, A New Chapter For Human Rights* (2006), Chap. 6; and *Human Rights Watch, Backgrounder: Universal Periodic Review*, August 18, 2006, at http://hrw.org/backgrounder/un/un0806/index.htm

those made by candidates in elections to the Human Rights Council, and 'international humanitarian law, as and where applicable'.]

B. Principles and Objectives

1. Principles

The Universal Periodic Review (UPR) should:

- Promote the universality, interdependence, indivisibility and interrelatedness of all human rights;
- Be a cooperative mechanism based on objective and reliable information and on interactive dialogue;
- Ensure universal coverage and equal treatment of all States;
- Be an intergovernmental process, United Nations Member-driven and action-oriented;
- Fully involve the country under review;
- Complement and not duplicate other human rights mechanisms, thus representing an added value;
- Be conducted in an objective, transparent, non-selective, constructive, non-confrontational and non-politicized manner;
- Not be overly burdensome to the concerned State or to the agenda of the Council;
- Not be overly long. It should be realistic and not absorb a disproportionate amount of time, human and financial resources;
- Not diminish the Council's capacity to respond to urgent human rights situations;
- Ensure that a gender perspective is fully integrated in the UPR;
- UPR should, without prejudice to the obligations contained in the elements provided for in the basis of review, take into account the level of development and specificities of countries;
- Ensure participation of all relevant stakeholders, including non-governmental organizations (NGOs) and national human rights institutions (NHRIs) . . . .

2. Objectives

- Improvement of the human rights situation on the ground;
- Fulfilment of the State's human rights obligations and commitments and assessment of positive developments and challenges faced by the State;
- Enhancement of the State's capacity and technical assistance . . . ;
- Sharing of best practices among States and other stakeholders in consultation with and with the consent of the State concerned;
- Support for cooperation in the promotion and protection of human rights;
- Encouragement of full cooperation and engagement with the Council, other human rights bodies and the [OHCHR].

C. Periodicity and Order of the Review

. . .

- The periodicity of the review for the first cycle will be of four years. This will imply the consideration of 48 States per year during three sessions of the working group of two weeks each.

D. Process and Modalities of Review

1. Documentation

a. The documents on which the review would be based are:

- Information prepared by the State concerned, which can take the form of a national report, on the basis of General Guidelines to be adopted by the Council ..., and any other information considered relevant by the State concerned, which could be presented either orally or in writing; provided that the written presentation summarizing the information will not exceed 20 pages, to guarantee equal treatment to all States and not to overburden the mechanism. States are encouraged to prepare this presentation through a broad consultation process at the national level with all relevant stakeholders;
- Additionally OHCHR will prepare a compilation of the information contained in the reports of treaty bodies, special procedures, including observations and comments by the State concerned, and other relevant official United Nations documents, which shall not exceed 10 pages;
- In the review, the Council should also take into consideration additional credible and reliable information provided by other relevant stakeholders to UPR. OHCHR will prepare a summary of such information that shall not exceed 10 pages;
- The documents prepared by OHCHR should be elaborated following the structure of the General Guidelines adopted by the Council regarding the information prepared by the State concerned;
- Both the State's written presentation and the summaries prepared by OHCHR shall be ready six weeks prior to the review by the Working Group . . . .

2. Modalities

The modalities of the review shall be as follows:

- The review will be conducted in one Working Group, chaired by the President of the Council and composed of the 47 Member States of the Council. Each Member State will decide on the composition of its delegation;
- Observer States can participate in the review, including in the interactive dialogue;
- Other relevant stakeholders can attend the conduct of the review in the Working Group;

- A group of three rapporteurs, selected by drawing of lots among the members of the Council and from different Regional Groups (troika) will be formed to facilitate each review, including the preparation of the report of the Working Group. The OHCHR will provide the necessary assistance and expertise to the rapporteurs;
- The concerned country may request that one of the rapporteurs be from its own Regional Group and may also request the inclusion of an alternate rapporteur in [sic] only one occasion;
- A rapporteur may request to be excused from its participation in a specific review process;
- Interactive dialogue between the country under review and the Council will take place in the Working Group. The rapporteurs could collate issues or questions to be transmitted to the State under review to facilitate its preparation and focus the interactive dialogue, while guaranteeing fairness and transparency;
- The duration of the review will be three hours for each country in the Working Group. Additional time of up to one hour will be allocated for the consideration of the outcome by the Council plenary;
- Half an hour will be allocated for the adoption of the report of each country under review in the Working Group;
- A reasonable time frame should be allocated in between the review and the adoption of the report of each State in the Working Group;
- The final outcome will be adopted by the plenary of the Council.

E. Outcome of the review

1. Format of the outcome

A report consisting of a summary of the proceedings of the review process; recommendations and/or conclusions; and voluntary commitments.

2. Content of the outcome

UPR is a cooperative mechanism. Its outcome could include, inter alia:

- Assessment in an objective and transparent manner of the human rights situation in the reviewed country, including positive developments and challenges faced by the country;
- Sharing of best practices;
- Emphasis on enhancing cooperation for the promotion and protection of human rights;
- Provision of technical assistance and capacity-building in consultation with and with the consent of the country concerned;
- Voluntary commitments and pledges made by the country reviewed.

3. Adoption of the outcome

- The reviewed country should be fully involved in the outcome;
- Before the adoption of the outcome by the plenary of the Council, the State concerned should be offered the possibility to present replies to

questions or issues that were not sufficiently addressed during the interactive dialogue;

- The State concerned and the Member States of the Council, as well as observer States, will be given the opportunity to express their views on the outcome of the review before the plenary takes action on it;
- Other relevant stakeholders will have the opportunity to make general comments before the adoption of the outcome by the plenary;
- Recommendations that enjoy the support of the State concerned will be identified as such. Other recommendations, together with the comments of the State concerned thereon, will be noted. Both will be included in the outcome report to be adopted by the Council.

F. Follow-up to the review

- The outcome of UPR, as a cooperative mechanism, should be implemented primarily by the State concerned and, as appropriate, by other relevant stakeholders;
- The subsequent review should focus, inter alia, on the implementation of the preceding outcome;
- The Council should have a standing item on its agenda devoted to UPR;
- The international community will assist in implementing the recommendations and conclusions regarding capacity-building and technical assistance, in consultation with and with the consent of the country concerned;
- In considering the UPR outcome, the Council will decide if and when any specific follow-up would be necessary.
- After exhausting all efforts to encourage a State to cooperate with the UPR mechanism, the Council will address, as appropriate, cases of persistent non-cooperation with the mechanism.

QUESTIONS

1. 'If membership of the UN Human Rights Council is open to serious violators of human rights it can never be expected to become an effective, let alone a credible, champion of rights'. Comment.

2. How could the 'pledge' system be adjusted so as to provide a real incentive for states to comply?

3. 'The UPR is predestined to fail. There are too many states to review in too short a time, no significant resources to support what should be a very complex task, little expert input into the process and, worst of all, no incentive for governments to police themselves in other than a cosmetic or symbolic way.' Comment.

4. THE COUNCIL'S RESPONSE TO VIOLATIONS

In terms of the legal basis for procedures for responding to violations of human rights, ECOSOC Res. 1235 has effectively been superseded by para. 3 of GA Res. 60/251 (see above). After a year of consultations the Human Rights Council decided in June 2007 to maintain the system of special procedures described above. Mandate-holders are to be appointed upon the recommendation of a Consultative Group, consisting of five government representatives assisted by the Office of the High Commissioner for Human Rights, and after extensive consultations with all stakeholders. It was decided that 'individuals holding decision-making positions in governments or in any other organization or entity which could represent a conflict of interest with the responsibilities arising from the mandate shall be excluded'. Tenure would be for a maximum of six years. The Council also decided to undertake a review of the thematic mandates which left open the possibility to 'streamline, merge or eventually dismantle' mandates, as long as such decisions are 'guided by the need for improvement of the enjoyment and protection of human rights for all.' As of June 2007 it remained unclear whether the Council would retain country-specific, or 'geographic' mandates.

The Council decided to replace the old Sub-Commission with a new Human Rights Council Advisory Committee (HRCAC), composed of 18 independent experts who would 'function as a think-tank to the Council and work at its direction'. In electing the experts 'due consideration should be given to gender balance and to an appropriate representation of different civilizations and legal systems' and seats were allocated as follows: 5 to Africa, 5 to Asia, 2 to Eastern Europe, 3 to Latin American and the Caribbean, and 3 to Western European and Other States. Experts may serve a maximum of two three-year terms. The Committee's stated function is 'to provide expertise to the Council in the manner and form requested by the Council, focusing mainly on studies and research-based advice. Further, such expertise shall be rendered only upon the latter's request, in compliance with its resolutions and under its guidance.' The Committee is specifically precluded from adopting resolutions or decisions and will meet for up to two sessions for a maximum of ten working days per year, with the possibility of ad hoc sessions approved by the Council. A further indication of the determination of governments to keep full control over the activities of the Advisory Committee is that it is prohibited from establishing any working group on its own volition.

The Council agreed to retain the essence of the 1503 procedure, 'improved where necessary, so as to ensure that [it] would be impartial, objective, efficient, victims-oriented and conducted in a confidential and timely manner'. For this purpose, it established two working groups. The Working Group on Communications would consist of five of the independent expert members of the new HRCAC and will operate in a comparable manner to the old Sub-Commission Working Group. The other group will be a Working Group on Situations, composed of five government representatives. On the basis of information and recommendations presented to it by the Communications Working Group it shall report to the Council on situations involving 'consistent patterns of gross and reliably attested violations of human rights and fundamental freedoms'. The work of both groups shall be confidential unless the Council decides otherwise in specific instances.

The most controversial aspect of the new Council's work to date has concerned its approach to country-specific situations. During its first year, through June 2007, the Special Procedures established by the Commission continued to report, and various highly troubling situations were raised in debate. However, the Council generally eschewed country-specific resolutions. The main exception was Israel which was a distinct pre-occupation of the Council. Of four special sessions convened in six months, the first three concerned Israel and the fourth focused on Darfur. The materials that follow review these two situations.

COMMENT ON ISRAEL

At its first session, in June 2006, the only country-specific resolution was on the Human Rights Situation in Palestine and Other Occupied Arab territories. The Council requested several Special Rapporteurs to report to it on Israeli violations in occupied Palestine. In July it convened its first special session and called upon the UN High Commissioner 'to undertake an urgent visit to the Occupied Palestinian Territory and to report on the Israeli human rights violations there' (Res. S-1/1). Following the conflict in Lebanon starting in July 2006 the Council called a second special session in August 2006. Even though a group of four rapporteurs (those dealing with executions, internally displaced persons, health, and housing) had indicated that they would visit Lebanon and Israel in early September, the Council (in Res. S-2/1) appointed a Commission of Inquiry: (a) to investigate the systematic targeting and killings of civilians by Israel in Lebanon; (b) to examine the types of weapons used by Israel and their conformity with international law; and (c) to assess the extent and deadly impact of Israeli attacks on human life, property, critical infrastructure and the environment.[36] On 15 November 2006 a third special session was held in response to an Israeli attack one week earlier on Beit Hannoun, in Gaza which killed 18, including 8 children. The result was the appointment of a High-Level Fact-Finding Commission to visit Beit Hannoun. Although led by Archbishop Desmond Tutu, it failed to gain the cooperation of Israel and was unable to visit.

At that special session, Pakistan, speaking on behalf of the Organization of the Islamic Conference explained the OIC's position thus:

> Some say that too frequent special sessions will devalue the currency of the Human Rights Council. We say too frequent human rights violations targeting one particular region make a mockery of the human rights machinery if it cannot respond or take action in real time.
>
> ...
>
> The Council has failed to implement its resolutions on the appalling human rights situation in Gaza for the last six months. It should not now be under a gag

[36] For the Commission's report, see http://www.ohchr.org/english/bodies/hrcouncil/docs/CoI-Lebanon.pdf.

order so that it cannot even speak up when egregious rights violations take place .... People speak in the Council because they still believe that it is the world's conscience on human rights. If the Council ceases to speak on such horrendous acts, it would give a green light for human rights violations.[37]

While Amnesty International and many other major NGOs called for action by the Council, the European Union took no position on the outcome of the special session but deplored 'Israeli military action in Gaza' and 'deeply regretted' the growing number of civilian casualties. In contrast, the US argued that the 'Council should not address particular military actions taken during a period of armed conflict that are clearly governed by the law of war. It is indeed unfortunate that the Council is using its limited resources to discuss subjects not squarely within its mandate . . .'

At its third regular session, which concluded in December 2006, the Council adopted six resolutions, one of which dealt with the human rights situation in the Occupied Palestinian Territory, calling for the urgent dispatch of a fact-finding mission which the Council had called for in its first special session (S-1/Res.1), and another of which focused on follow-up to the report of the Commission of Inquiry into Israel's actions in Lebanon. None of the other resolutions addressed a country-specific situation. This accumulated imbalance led to a highly unusual rebuke from the outgoing Secretary-General who said in a video-taped message to the session:

> You have focused especially on the Arab-Israeli conflict, which indeed has escalated during these months in ways that cause deep concern to us all....
>
> I hope, however, that the Council will take care to handle this issue in an impartial way, and not allow it to monopolize attention at the expense of others where there are equally grave or even graver violations. There are surely other situations, besides the one in the Middle East, which would merit scrutiny by a special session of this Council. I would suggest that Darfur is a glaring case in point.[38]

In a later speech the Secretary-General said:

> I am worried by [the Council's] disproportionate focus on violations by Israel. Not that Israel should be given a free pass. Absolutely not. But the Council should give the same attention to grave violations committed by other states as well.
>
> And I am also worried by the efforts of some Council members to weaken or abolish the system of Special Procedures — the independent mechanisms for reporting on violations of particular kinds, or in specific countries.
>
> The Special Procedures are the crown jewel of the system. They, together with the High Commissioner and her staff, provide the independent expertise and judgement which is essential to effective human rights protection. They must not be politicized, or subjected to governmental control.[39]

[37] Statement by Ambassador Mashood Khan, Pakistan's Permanent Representative, Geneva, 15 November 2006.

[38] Available at http://www.un.org/apps/sg/sgstats.asp?nid=2333.

[39] Address to mark International Human Rights Day, New York City, 8 December 2006, at http://www.un.org/News/ossg/sg/stories/statments_full.asp?statID=39.

Another important element in the overall equation is that the Security Council has been effectively unable to take action in relation to most proposed resolutions concerning Israel. Over 40 resolutions have been vetoed since 1972 and since 2001 the United States has cast its veto, usually the sole negative vote, in response to the following proposed resolutions: (1) appointment of UN observer force in OPT (2001, 9 votes in favour, 1 — the US — against), (2) condemning acts of terror and proposing observers (2001, 12–1), (3) killing of UN employees and destruction of World Food Programme warehouse (2002, 12–1), (4) calling on Israel not to expel Palestinian leader (2003, 11–1), (5) calling on Israel not to extend the wall (2003, 10–1), (6) condemning Israel for targeted assassination of Sheik Yassin and 6 others (2004, 11–1), (7) calling for an end to military activities in Gaza (2004, 11–1), (8) calling on Israel to release Palestinian cabinet ministers and cease shelling of Gaza (2006, 10–1), (9) calling for Gaza force withdrawal and inquiry into attack on Beit Hanoun (2006, 10–1).[40]

In terms of the Council and the old Commission it should be noted that the very heavy focus on Israel has not, however, involved an examination of the human rights situation within Israel itself. Rather it has been concerned with the consequences of occupation, and the inevitably fraught situation arising in such a context (the Occupied Palestinian Territories — OPT), and with the invasion of another country (Lebanon).

In terms of Israel's domestic human rights situation, the relationship with the relevant UN bodies has been relatively routine. Israel is a party to all six of the core treaties and has reported on a reasonably regular basis, most recently to the CEDAW and CERD Committees in 2005. Concluding observations on reports by Israel have been adopted by the ICCPR and ICESCR Committees (2003), the Committee on the Rights of the Child (2002) and the Committee against Torture (2002). The great majority of the concerns expressed by those committees relate also to Israel's conduct in the OPT, but issues of discrimination, against Arabs in particular, as well as other problems have also been identified. The ICESCR Committee, for example, expressed concern about:

> 16. . . . the continuing difference in treatment between Jews and non-Jews, in particular Arab and Bedouin communities, with regard to their enjoyment of economic, social and cultural rights in the State party's territory. The Committee reiterates its concern that the "excessive emphasis upon the State as a 'Jewish State' encourages discrimination and accords a second-class status to its non-Jewish citizens" (ibid., para. 10). This discriminatory attitude is apparent in the continuing lower standard of living of Israeli Arabs as a result, inter alia, of higher unemployment rates, restricted access to and participation in trade unions, lack of access to housing, water, electricity and health care and a lower level of education, despite the State party's efforts to close the gap. In this regard, the Committee expresses its concern that the State party's domestic legal order does not enshrine the general principles of equality and non-discrimination.
>
> 18. . . . the status of "Jewish nationality", which is a ground for exclusive preferential treatment for persons of Jewish nationality under the Israeli Law of Return,

[40] The text of the resolutions is available at http://www.jewishvirtuallibrary.org/jsource/UN/usvetoes.html.

granting them automatic citizenship and financial government benefits, thus resulting in practice in discriminatory treatment against non-Jews, in particular Palestinian refugees ...

...

21. ... the persisting inequality in wages of Jews and Arabs in Israel, as well as the severe under-representation of the Arab sector in the civil service and universities.[41]

...

VIEWS ABOUT DARFUR

[The situation in Darfur has been deeply problematic since 2003. The Commission on Human Rights had addressed it, the Security Council has been very active, and a special Commission of Inquiry appointed by the Commission on Human Rights had led the Security Council to refer the matter to the International Criminal Court. The materials that follow give a sense of the background and then illustrate the response by various governments in the context of the only sustained debate within the Human Rights Council to focus on any situation other than Israel and the Middle East.]

Human Rights Watch, Q & A: Crisis in Darfur, December 2006

http://www.hrw.org/english/docs/2004/05/05/darfur8536.htm

What has happened in Darfur?

Since early 2003, Sudanese government forces and ethnic militia called "Janjaweed" have engaged in an armed conflict with rebel groups called the Sudanese Liberation Army/Movement (SLA/SLM) and the Justice and Equality Movement (JEM). As part of its operations against the rebels, government forces have waged a systematic campaign of "ethnic cleansing" against the civilian population who are members of the same ethnic groups as the rebels.

Sudanese government forces and the Janjaweed militias burned and destroyed hundreds of villages, killed and caused the deaths of possibly 200,000 people, and raped and assaulted thousands of women and girls. As of November 2006, approximately two million displaced people live in camps in Darfur and at least 218,000 people have fled to neighboring Chad, where they live in refugee camps. In addition to the people displaced by the conflict, at least 1.7 million other people need some form of food assistance because the conflict has destroyed the local economy, markets, and trade in Darfur.

Rebel allegiances have shifted and split since the conflict began, most notably in November 2005, when the SLA split into two factions. As of late 2006, there are more than a dozen splinter factions of the SLA and JEM. The rebel movements are broadly divided into those groups supporting the May 2006 Darfur Peace Agreement and others who have refused to sign the agreement, some of whom operate under an umbrella organization known as the National Redemption Front (NRF).

[41] UN Doc. E/C.12/1/Add.90 (2003).

What is happening in Darfur now?

. . . [T]he situation has dramatically worsened, particularly after the May 2006 Darfur Peace Agreement.

Since August 2006 fighting has increased between the government and rebel forces and among the rebel factions. There has been indiscriminate bombing by the Sudanese government in North Darfur and government-backed militias have also intensified their attacks on the civilian population in South Darfur, including on camps for internally displaced persons. . . .

. . .

Has the Darfur Peace Agreement brought peace?

No. On May 5, 2006, the Sudanese government signed the Darfur Peace Agreement (DPA) in Abuja, Nigeria with a faction of SLA . . . . However, two other rebel movements, JEM and [another] SLA faction . . . , refused to sign, putting the DPA on uncertain footing from the start. Rebel leaders say they rejected the DPA because it failed to sufficiently address key issues including a victim's compensation fund, power-sharing, rebel representation in government and disarmament of the Janjaweed militias.

Many internally displaced persons also oppose the DPA also because they claim that it does not provide them adequate protection from militia groups . . .

. . .

Why has the situation in Darfur deteriorated?

One of the key problems is that over the past three years the Sudanese government has continued to follow a policy of supporting ethnic militias, organizing attacks on civilians and permitting serious violations of international law to go unpunished — including attacks on African Union forces and humanitarian aid workers and their convoys. The continuing conflict and fragmentation of the rebel groups has also contributed to increasing lawlessness in parts of Darfur. This in turn has allowed bandits to flourish and rebels to attack aid convoys and kill civilians. . . .

. . .

How does the Sudanese government explain the situation in Darfur?

In the first few years of the conflict, the Sudanese government regularly described the situation in Darfur as "tribal clashes" and consistently refused to acknowledge its responsibility for systematic attacks on civilians. Khartoum has accused international journalists and human rights groups of "fabricating" the Darfur situation, despite the overwhelming evidence of the Sudanese government's responsibility for the crimes, and has tried to limit media access to Darfur. The government has consistently harassed journalists and restricted press freedom in an effort to stop the information flow from Darfur.

. . .

What is the UN Security Council doing about Darfur?

Despite passing a dozen resolutions demanding that the Sudanese government take certain steps, including disarming its militias and ceasing attacks on civilians, there has been little united effort by the UN Security Council to ensure these demands are implemented. The main reason is that the UN Security Council is divided on Sudan because different member states have divergent interests. Russia and China have often supported the Sudanese government because of ideological commitments (non-interference in internal affairs of member states) and both have economic interests in Sudan. China, for instance, imports between 4–7 percent of its oil from Sudan and the Sudan oil project is its most successful international oil development endeavor.

The Security Council took two important steps in 2005, however. One was the referral of the situation in Darfur to the International Criminal Court . . . . The second step was establishing a sanctions committee and a panel of experts to investigate individuals who violate the arms embargo, commit abuses of human rights, or impede the peace process. A crucial third step was taken in 2006 with the adoption of UN Security Council Resolution 1706 deploying UN peacekeepers to Darfur. However, to date none of these actions has succeeded in ensuring that civilians in Darfur are protected from further abuses.

. . .

UN Body 'Must Investigate' Darfur

BBC News, 12 December 2006, at http://news.bbc.co.uk/2/hi/africa/6170651.stm

The UN Human Rights Council has been urged by UN Secretary-General Kofi Annan to send a team to investigate abuses in Sudan's Darfur region. . . . The world's top human rights body has remained silent on Darfur, and is now under huge pressure to take a stand. . . .

The Sudanese government has rejected a UN Security Council resolution authorising the deployment of UN troops and police to Darfur. Khartoum denies accusations that it is backing the militias to put down the uprising and says the scale of the crisis has been exaggerated. Sudanese President Omar al-Bashir said recently that only 9,000 had been killed during the Darfur conflict.

A small force of 7,000 African Union (AU) peacekeepers has struggled to protect civilians in the absence of a UN contingent. Sudan has agreed to let the UN provide logistical support to a larger AU force, but refuses to allow UN forces into Darfur.

. . .

. . . Despite Mr Annan's calls for action, African countries have consistently resisted any action which appears critical of the Sudanese government. Human rights groups hope that the emergency session will bring an end to the silence . . .

Secretary-General strongly urges Human Rights Council to send experts to investigate latest escalation of abuses in Darfur

Statement by Kofi Annan, UN Press Release SG/SM/10794, 12 December 2006

. . .

For more than three years now, the people of Darfur have endured a nightmare. In recent weeks, the fighting has escalated and conditions for the civilian population have got even worse. Armed militias continue to attack defenceless civilians with impunity, destroying dozens of villages and displacing thousands more in the last few weeks alone. Large numbers of women are still being subjected to rape and other forms of violence. Some 4 million people need humanitarian assistance, including 2 million internally displaced, and conditions are such that many of the most vulnerable can no longer be reached by humanitarian relief workers. And the violence has now spread to two neighbouring countries.

...

I urge you to lose no time in sending a team of independent and universally respected experts to investigate the latest escalation of abuses. It is urgent that we take action to prevent further violations, including by bringing to account those responsible for the numerous crimes that have already been committed.

That is the very least you can do to show the people of Darfur that their cries for help are being heard.

Address by Ms. Louise Arbour (UN HCHR) to the 4th special session of the Human Rights Council

12 December 2006

... The unrelenting tragedy in Darfur demands the commensurate engagement and vigilance of the Human Rights Council.

... A lack of accountability allows and even emboldens perpetrators to hold sway over the population in Darfur....

... To provide a more comprehensive picture of the deteriorating conditions in Darfur, my Office has gathered an extensive compilation of documents, which includes reports from our field work since 2004, as well as material from other UN sources..... What emerges from these documents is a compelling, factual account of the systematic failure to prevent violence in Darfur, to protect the civilian population, and to bring the perpetrators to justice. [See www.ohchr.org/english/countries/sd/index.htm.]

The failure to prevent, to protect and to provide justice must prompt this Council, the whole international community and, above all, the Government of Sudan to enforce all the measures pledged or agreed upon thus far, which taken together and implemented, would help to deliver relief, justice and remedy to the people of Darfur.

...

... [T]he UN Panel of Experts of the sanction committee on Sudan ... concluded that not only has the Government of Sudan failed to disarm militia as required by the Darfur Peace Agreement, but that there is credible evidence pointing to the responsibility of the Government in upgrading the militia's arsenals and mobility.

The gravity of the situation is compounded by the rebels' abusive conduct. They, too, are responsible for killing, raping, maiming, torturing and destroying the livelihoods of civilians who have the misfortune of standing in their destructive path. And they, too, must be held accountable for such violations of international human rights and humanitarian law as it applies to non-State actors.

Yet impunity is rampant. The vast majority of crimes are not prosecuted and go unpunished at all levels, from foot-soldiers up to high-level Government officials and rebel leaders with command responsibility. In response to national and international criticism, the Government did put in place mechanisms to hold parties to the conflict accountable. But these mechanisms have yet to prove effective. Only one high-ranking official was ever charged. He was later acquitted. Ten State officials were convicted by special courts, but they were all low-level officers.

. . .

STATEMENTS MADE AT THE SPECIAL SESSION ON DARFUR

12 December 2006

Sudan

. . .

1. Once more, we reiterate our firm belief in, and commitment to the promotion of human rights, and to ridding it of politicization and selectivity.

. . .

3. . . . [T]he motives behind the call [for this special session] differ. For some, it is not the protection and promotion of human rights. Rather, it is tarnishing in turns the dignity, independence and sovereignty of the countries deemed weak, whereas our goal is to faithfully represent the truth . . .

. . .

8. . . . [T]he reports of the international media and the High Commissioner not only overlook these violations of the armed groups, but blame the government and its armed forces for such violations . . .

. . .

10. The High Commissioner adopted a political and unprofessional position partial to the positions of certain countries . . .

. . .

13. Facing this situation, the African Union was objective and true to itself when it decided . . . that:

- The Darfur conflict can only be resolved through a political process,
- The DPA is the only basis for this process and should not be re-negotiated,
- No party outside the DPA should be allowed to undermine its implementation,
- The African Union remains the lead actor in the process of implementing the DPA.

. . .

17. The statistics made available by Sudan to the international institutions and civil society organizations indicate clearly that incidents of violence against women have been exaggerated. . . . We assure you that the moral and cultural tradition of the

Sudanese people and the laws based on these tenets do not tolerate this very sensitive matter.

18. The Sudan will continue to be open to dialogue and cooperation to promote human rights in the Sudan generally and in Darfur particularly. However, we are aware of the difference between genuine concerns for human rights and ideological and political drives that push some countries and organizations which control the power, wealth and media in crucial centers of the world. Wars begin first in the minds of men.

...

21. We are confident that the contribution of the international community and donors in the peaceful settlement will be decisive if the financial pledges made are fulfilled.

...

24. [We ask] . . . whether the end to be achieved by such mobilization and continuing campaigns is genuinely to protect human rights in Darfur or just an ignominious targeting of Sudan, its people, resources and territorial integrity.

Algeria, in the name of the African Group

...

3. As is the case in all civil conflicts and wars, the conflict in Darfur is accompanied by far-reaching propaganda campaigns where information is manipulated and the human rights situation is politicised.

Thus, an analysis by a major NGO headquartered in an advanced country, disseminated at this session, presents the case in term of an ethnic conflict of apocalyptic proportion between an Arab oppressor Government with its militia targeting non Arab-tribes. There is not a single mention of the true nature of the conflict between herders and pastoralists or of rebel group action using civilian human shields and attacking humanitarian assistance convoys.

4. . . . In this exercise, we must be driven by facts obtained first-hand on the ground and not simply by media driven interpretations as a wrong-footed or heavy-handed response aimed simply at naming and shaming an African Government would be self-defeating. For sovereignty is not an abstract notion and can only be ignored at the peril, not only of national unity, but of regional peace, as recent experience has shown.

Cuba

...

. . . [T]here is a persistent campaign of discredit [sic] and exaggeration orchestrated against the Government of Sudan with the clear aim of encouraging the hegemonic pretensions of the West. . . . [We have been informed by the Deputy Governor of the State of South Darfur] that severe measures have been adopted against those guilty of human rights violations . . . .The complex situation in Darfur can never be solved with external impositions from New York or Geneva. The measures adopted by this Council, will only be effective if they fully involve and are accepted by the Government of Sudan. . . .

... The solution to the situation in Darfur requires a long-term strategy for development and cooperation, doing away with inflammatory language and pretensions of imposing sanctions and unnecessary condemnation.

Finland, on behalf of the European Union

...

... Darfur is experiencing a severe and large-scale human rights and humanitarian crisis as we speak.

It is against the background of this grave suffering by civilians that we are calling on this Council to ... scrutinize the situation in Darfur and to decide on immediate measures. This new Human Rights Council simply must act.

...

... [A]n urgent Assessment Mission to Darfur, with the essential levels of expertise, objectivity and independence, including the Special Rapporteur in Sudan, has been called for.

Extensive and detailed information based on independent monitoring notably by OHCHR and other Agencies on the human rights situation in Darfur already exists. ... The suggested mission should therefore build on these existing efforts, and seek to identify ways in which the Government of Sudan should implement recommendations for the better protection of the human rights of its citizens, and in which all parties can alleviate the dire human rights situation.

...

Pakistan, on behalf of the Organization of the Islamic Conference

...

Without a doubt, the people of Darfur have suffered. Relief has been provided to them. More relief needs to be sent to the region. Human rights abuses by all parties must come to an end.

...

[T]he session's resolution/decision should not be one-sided. It must fully reflect and respect the views of the Sudanese Government which is cooperating with the human rights machinery.

[T]here is conflicting information about almost everything: from killings to IDPs to the measures being taken. These gaps must be ascertained through objective means, not by muzzling opposite view.

...

The Human Rights Council is a new body. It should build bridges not create new fissures. The Council, while dealing with issues in its current phase, should look at the broader, strategic and long term picture so that human rights norms, standards and laws are strengthened; and implemented effectively. Moreover, they should create a global environment for the respect of fundamental human rights. The Council should not become a battleground for pushing narrow, parochial or neo-provincial agendas. It must pursue the vision of all human rights and human rights for all.

The United Kingdom

...

Despite this plethora of eyewitness information we have nevertheless agreed that this Council should receive its own report on the human rights situation. The UK has agreed, but clearly those who write such a report must be objective, independent and universally respected experts .... [T]he team that visits Darfur must have free and unrestricted access to all the key players: the UN, AMIS, and civil society as well as to the Government of Sudan and other parties.

...

The United Kingdom wants to see a consensus approach to tackling violations in Darfur. We seek cooperation; we encourage dialogue. Yet cooperation and dialogue and the search for consensus cannot be ends in themselves. They, and by extension we, must surely serve the founding purpose of this Council: the promotion and protection of human rights. Today, we must seek effective action for the people of Darfur. Without this, we are guilty of reverting to just so many of those political phrases we play with here in Geneva to duck the difficult issues: and perhaps make our diplomatic lives a little more comfortable. I would submit that our comfort must not come at the price of more deaths uncommented upon; of more suffering ignored, of more violence against women and children.

...

India

...

... [T]he cooperation extended by the Government of Sudan to the Special Rapporteur on the situation of human rights in Sudan is noteworthy. It is only through such cooperative efforts with the UN and the African Union that the condition of the affected people on the ground can be ameliorated.

We look forward to the report of the Assessment Mission to Sudan so that measures can be quickly put in place in consultation with the Government of Sudan to bring relief and succor to those most in need....

Canada

...

The primary reason we are here today is to signal first and foremost to the people of Darfur that we have not forgotten them; secondly to remind the Government of Sudan that it has the primary responsibility to protect its population; and thirdly, that the international community is ready to work in cooperation, openness and transparency with the Sudanese government to improve the human rights and humanitarian situation in Darfur. However, in the absence of the Government of Sudan's willingness or ability to protect its population, the international community, in accordance with the Responsibility to Protect [see pp. 838, *infra*] which it accepted in 2005, must do all that it can to provide protection to the people of Darfur. We are greatly concerned that the international community is failing to do just that.

...

... It is critical that perpetrators of violations of human rights and international humanitarian law be brought to justice in accordance with international standards and through a transparent and legitimate process. Combating impunity is a deterrent to further abuse and an essential part of building long-term peace and stability in Darfur.

...

NOTE

The following decision of the Human Rights Council, (Decision S-4/101) 13 December 2006, was adopted by consensus:

The Human Rights Council

1. *Expresses* its concern regarding the seriousness of the human rights and humanitarian situation in Darfur;

2. *Welcomes* the signing of the Darfur Peace Agreement, urges its full implementation, and calls upon parties who have not signed it to do so, and all parties to observe the cease fire;

3. *Welcomes* the cooperation established by the Government of Sudan with the Special Rapporteur on the situation of human rights in Sudan and calls upon the Government to continue and intensify its cooperation with the Human Rights Council, its mechanisms, and the Office of the High Commissioner for Human Rights;

4. *Decides* to dispatch a High-Level Mission to assess the human rights situation in Darfur and the needs of Sudan in this regard, comprising five highly qualified persons, to be appointed by the President of the Human Rights Council following consultation with the members of the Council; as well as the Special Rapporteur on the situation of human rights in Sudan;

5. *Requests* the Secretary-General and the United Nations High Commissioner for Human Rights to provide all administrative, technical and logistical assistance required to enable the High-Level Mission to fulfil its mandate promptly and efficiently, in coordination with the President of the Human Rights Council and also requests the latter to consult as appropriate with the concerned country; ...

QUESTIONS

1. 'The Council's pre-occupation with Israel reflects the state of international relations in general rather than the shortcomings of the Council. In any event, the optimal course is not for a reduced focus on violations such as those of which Israel is accused, but a more systematic targeting of this type focusing on a wide range of countries involved in systematic violations.' Comment.

2. What conclusions might be drawn from the Council's debate over Darfur? What appear to be the key fault lines and what expectations for future actions in country-specific situations emerge?

E. THE ROLE OF THE HIGH COMMISSIONER FOR HUMAN RIGHTS

For over 40 years, starting in 1947, various proposals have been put forward involving the creation of the post of UN High Commissioner for Human Rights. The Soviet Union and its allies were strongly opposed, most developing countries were very wary, and the West was most enthusiastic when it was clear that the proposal was unlikely to be taken up. The breakthrough came at the Vienna World Conference on Human Rights in 1993. A combination of factors were at play: the demise of the Socialist bloc and associated post-Cold War optimism, the election of the Clinton Administration in the US which was keen to find new ideas in the human rights area, and, curiously, the opposition of the then UN Secretary-General, Boutros Boutros-Ghali which reassured nervous governments that any appointee would be kept under a tight reign. The Office has been filled by José Ayala-Lasso (Ecuador) 1994–1997, Mary Robinson (Ireland) 1997–2002, Sergio Vieira de Mello (Brazil) 2002–2003, B.G. Ramcharan, acting-HC (Guyana) 2003–2004, and Louise Arbour (Canada) 2004–present. By 2006 the Office had approximately 272 posts funded from the regular budget and another 395 from extra-budgetary funds (voluntary donations), making a total of 667 staff. The dynamic leadership, especially of Mary Robinson and Louise Arbour, has turned the HC into one of the key actors in the international human rights regime.

The materials begin with the resolution creating the Office. It reveals the tradeoffs made between those keen to establish the new office and those seeking to ensure that it would be limited in reach and impact.

HIGH COMMISSIONER FOR THE PROMOTION AND PROTECTION OF ALL HUMAN RIGHTS

GA Res. 48/141 (1993)

The General Assembly,

. . .

1. Decides to create the post of the High Commissioner for Human Rights;
2. Decides that the High Commissioner for Human Rights shall:

   (a) Be a person of high moral standing and personal integrity and shall possess expertise, including in the field of human rights, and the general knowledge and understanding of diverse cultures necessary for impartial, objective, non-selective and effective performance of the duties of the High Commissioner;

   (b) Be appointed by the Secretary-General of the United Nations and approved by the General Assembly, with due regard to geographical rotation, and have a fixed term of four years with a possibility of one renewal for another fixed term of four years;

   . . .

3. Decides that the High Commissioner for Human Rights shall:

(a) Function within the framework of the Charter of the United Nations, the Universal Declaration of Human Rights, other international instruments of human rights and international law, including the obligations, within this framework, to respect the sovereignty, territorial integrity and domestic jurisdiction of States and to promote the universal respect for and observance of all human rights, in the recognition that, in the framework of the purposes and principles of the Charter, the promotion and protection of all human rights is a legitimate concern of the international community;
(b) Be guided by the recognition that all human rights — civil, cultural, economic, political and social — are universal, indivisible, interdependent and interrelated and that, while the significance of national and regional particularities and various historical, cultural and religious backgrounds must be borne in mind, it is the duty of States, regardless of their political, economic and cultural systems, to promote and protect all human rights and fundamental freedoms;
(c) Recognize the importance of promoting a balanced and sustainable development for all people and of ensuring realization of the right to development, as established in the Declaration on the Right to Development;

4. Decides that the High Commissioner for Human Rights shall be the United Nations official with principal responsibility for United Nations human rights activities under the direction and authority of the Secretary-General; within the framework of the overall competence, authority and decisions of the General Assembly, the Economic and Social Council and the Commission on Human Rights, the High Commissioner's responsibilities shall be:

(a) To promote and protect the effective enjoyment by all of all civil, cultural, economic, political and social rights;
(b) To carry out the tasks assigned to him/her by the competent bodies of the United Nations system in the field of human rights and to make recommendations to them with a view to improving the promotion and protection of all human rights;
(c) To promote and protect the realization of the right to development and to enhance support from relevant bodies of the United Nations system for this purpose;
(d) To provide, through the Centre for Human Rights of the Secretariat and other appropriate institutions, advisory services and technical and financial assistance, at the request of the State concerned and, where appropriate, the regional human rights organizations, with a view to supporting actions and programmes in the field of human rights;
(e) To coordinate relevant United Nations education and public information programmes in the field of human rights;

(f) To play an active role in removing the current obstacles and in meeting the challenges to the full realization of all human rights and in preventing the continuation of human rights violations throughout the world, as reflected in the Vienna Declaration and Programme of Action;

(g) To engage in a dialogue with all Governments in the implementation of his/her mandate with a view to securing respect for all human rights;

(h) To enhance international cooperation for the promotion and protection of all human rights;

(i) To coordinate the human rights promotion and protection activities throughout the United Nations system;

(j) To rationalize, adapt, strengthen and streamline the United Nations machinery in the field of human rights with a view to improving its efficiency and effectiveness;

(k) To carry out overall supervision of the Centre for Human Rights;

5. Requests the High Commissioner for Human Rights to report annually on his/her activities, in accordance with his/her mandate, to the Commission on Human Rights and, through the Economic and Social Council, to the General Assembly;

...

FELICE GAER, 'BOOK REVIEW'

98 Am. J. Int. L. 391 (2004)

...

Although some calls for a high commissioner for human rights had emerged in the United Nations' earliest years, it was not until 1963 that the idea ... gained serious political backing — notably from the Kennedy administration .... Introduced at the United Nations by Costa Rica in 1967 and bounced from one UN body to another until it barely resembled the initial conception, the proposal to create a high commissioner was all but abandoned by the late 1980s.

...

Among the obvious deficiencies in the early 1990s — despite all the mechanisms created to inquire about, and report on, human rights abuses — was the continuing marginalization and isolation of the United Nations' human rights program: it was based in Geneva, invisible in New York, and absent from the field. Denounced by diplomats and bureaucrats as "political," the human rights program was considered by some countries as a threat to development assistance, and by others, to the resolution of long-standing armed conflicts.

Human rights advocates wanted a high commissioner who would focus on human rights violations and develop strategies for immediate and effective responses. The officeholder had to live up to the post's title: many NGOs argued that a high commissioner should be high level, independent, and able not only to heighten attention to human rights in the United Nations and throughout the world, but to galvanize concern, act rapidly in emerging crises, and produce actions and results that would help individual victims. As suggested by the title, the occupant of the post should be able to commission projects, supervise them, and take charge of the issues. Many spoke of the high commissioner as a "champion" of human rights for all, and as a "conscience" or moral voice able to speak out honestly when political forces kept others silent or fearful. For these purposes, the high commissioner would have to be a critic, a communicator, and a colleague and confidant of human rights defenders the world over. The high commissioner was thus expected to enhance the global visibility of human rights, to integrate human rights concerns throughout the UN system, to develop new strategies for action and effectiveness, and, at the same time, to be a manager or coordinator of the UN human rights programs, rationalizing and streamlining them.

UN General Assembly Resolution 48/141, which created the post of high commissioner, formally assigned the officeholder a range of impossibly broad tasks but little or no resources with which to achieve them.... Since then, relevant UN bodies have assigned numerous other specific tasks to the high commissioner.

What individual could meet all the expectations? And did the individual matter more than the bureaucratic section established and its particular mandate within the UN system?

Observers were generally critical of the first UN high commissioner for human rights, Ambassador Jose Ayala Lasso of Ecuador. In his initial speeches as high commissioner, Ayala commonly emphasized the sensitivity of the post and called for international cooperation in order to achieve results. He had chaired the UN negotiations creating the post and never forgot how many governments, especially the Asian ones that supported his candidacy, had opposed creation of an activist, independent high commissioner.

Former president of Ireland Mary Robinson became the second high commissioner in 1997. Her appointment received considerable praise from human rights NGOs. After being named to the post, she promised to "stand up to bullies" and to be a "moral voice" favoring human rights and aiming to "narrow the gap" between civil and political rights, on the one hand, and economic and social rights, on the other. Later, her troubled leadership of the Durban World Conference Against Racism marked a period of oft-bumpy relations with the secretary-general, the United States, and other governments.

The third high commissioner, Sergio Vieira de Mello — a prominent, longtime UN employee — stressed in his initial speeches that human rights was now "fully at the centre of intergovernmental debate" and that strengthening the "rule of law" was the key goal of his term of office, as it would entrench the universality of human rights.

These initial remarks by the occupants of the high commissioner's post indicate the very different perspectives brought by each of the individuals occupying the position, and how each high commissioner has tried to shape the post. Because such hopes were placed in the independence and moral voice of the high commissioner, however, it is not surprising that the first two high commissioners had difficulties with the UN secretary-general. Large institutions rarely value officials who are "out of sync" with prevailing organizational culture. Secretary-General Boutros

Boutros-Ghali did not want an independent high commissioner and kept the post weak and ineffective. Ambassador Ayala was a quiet consensus builder, who spent much of his time in office fighting with another official who served as head of the United Nations' Centre for Human Rights. Ayala emphasized "quiet diplomacy" in his country visits, arguing that this approach would bring permission for visits of special rapporteurs who would otherwise be refused entry. President Robinson came into office as the selection of Kofi Annan, a secretary-general who, in this post-Rwanda, post-Bosnia period, explicitly encouraged more attention to human rights across the UN system — but who sometimes found it difficult to work with a high commissioner so unschooled in the ways of bureaucracy and so often out in front of him. On many country visits, she was outspoken on behalf of victims, offering her views and exhortations in public. Annan's appointment of de Mello was seen as reflecting his preference for a high commissioner who would, as Resolution 48/141 states, function "under the authority and direction of the Secretary-General."

Personality and individual preferences have thus played an important role in the performance of each of the high commissioners for human rights — which poses a challenge to anyone interested in evaluating the impact of the post.

...

... Has the high commissioner brought a new voice, an independent voice of conscience, into the human rights field? If so, analysts, advocates, and diplomats may well ask whether such independence makes a difference in terms of protecting those who are suffering human rights violations. And even on the assumption that, by speaking out, the high commissioner gives individuals the courage to speak up against those who abuse their rights, will that sort of opposition lead to better enforcement of existing human rights standards? That is, does the high commissioner's independent voice ultimately serve to deter the state from perpetrating or permitting abuses? This question still needs to be examined.

The second high commissioner, Robinson, spoke out and added a new perspective and new issues to the rights debate. She pressed to see that trafficking in persons would be addressed as a human rights issue. Early in her tenure she condemned the governments of Algeria and Democratic Republic of the Congo for human rights abuses. She urged that issues related to reparations for slavery (and also to the Palestinian conflict) be part of the Durban World Conference document. Noteworthy, too — among her many acts of publicly giving voice to human rights concerns — was that she called for a bombing halt within a week after the United States started to bomb Afghanistan. Praised by the media as independent and as a moral voice, she left office encouraging those who support human rights to "keep their nerve." Many from the NGO community view her as the prime example of independence (of both governmental and UN authorities), but there are others in government and the United Nations who saw her as unsuited to that organization's international bureaucratic environment. Given such views, it is apparent that there is a continuing tension between the expectations of NGOs and those of governmental and intergovernmental insiders — who continue to see the post as being "under the authority and direction of the Secretary General," as defined by the General Assembly resolution that created it.

The advantage of independence in human rights is the ability to point to wrongs as they occur — to "tell the truth" and thus to stigmatize unforgivable action and to demand its correction. That is what NGOs continually demand of public officials who work on "human rights." But in intergovernmental (and governmental) bodies, the key to effectiveness is, in general, to be able to change behavior and reach negotiated agreements, rather than to speak out and to pass judgment according to unbending standards.

One must therefore ask: although speaking out is usually prioritized as an ideal in the field of human rights, is it always, or even usually, the most effective course of action? We would benefit from a study of violations that the high commissioner or the secretary-general, using his good offices, has identified — either publicly or privately — to see what approach has, in fact, been most effective in improving human rights. . . .

FIONNUALA NI AOLÁIN, LOOKING AHEAD: STRATEGIC PRIORITIES AND CHALLENGES FOR THE UNITED NATIONS HIGH COMMISSIONER FOR HUMAN RIGHTS

35 Colum. Hum. Rts. L. Rev. 469 (2004)

[The author suggests that there are three different models according to which the HCHR could operate: '(1) the co-ordinator model; (2) the managerial model; and (3) the moral standard-bearer model.' In her view '[t]he magnitude of the High Commissioner's role requires a flexible amalgamation of all three although, at certain points, one mode of operation may be in ascendancy over others. The main thrust of her analysis, however, is that the HCHR should identify priorities.]

. . .

. . . I advocate for a consistently applied set of criteria that can be used to make hard choices between pressing human rights issues. Formalized criteria provide a basis for making difficult decisions about what inputs the High Commissioner's Office can make, and may help to marry the Office's external and internal personas. This will sometimes mean that the High Commissioner's Office will be unable to respond to genuine and real human rights situations, issues, and violations. Nonetheless, the message of deliverable priorities is important and strategic to convey, and can serve to bolster, rather than undermine, the Office.

. . .

The starting point for this process is the minimalist position that a human rights issue must initially pass a threshold test for the High Commissioner's Office to be seized of it . . . .

A. Threshold Criteria

The first threshold criterion is that the human rights intervention must fall within the scope of the High Commissioner's mandate [GA Res. 48/141]. 15 The issue also must be consistent with . . . the protection of human rights . . . [and] must concern a human rights matter that is not being protected adequately by any other U.N. body or state party within whose territory the human rights issue arises.

B. Imperative Criteria

. . .

The first criterion requires the matter to be urgent. Urgency would generally mean that the High Commissioner is satisfied that there is a pressing need to address the human rights concern, that there are time-bounded implications for the protection of the rights in question if the High Commissioner fails to intervene, or that there is a threat to the well-being of persons or groups because of action or inaction by the state or third parties.

. . .

Under the second imperative criterion, the matter must implicate systemic experiences of a human rights violation. This means that the High Commissioner should be satisfied that the scale of the issue and/or the number of people affected ensures that the work undertaken will have the potential for a wide effect. Third, the matter must involve a fundamental principle of human rights protection, and it must be evident that no measures have been taken to resolve the human rights violations experienced by individuals or groups. Lastly, the issue must provide an opportunity for the High Commissioner's Office to use its particular powers and expertise to make a distinct and positive contribution to the enhancement of human rights protections.

C. Important Additionality

[Four other questions should also be considered.] First, would addressing the issue allow the High Commissioner to contribute to the augmentation of a human rights culture within the United Nations or its member states? Second, is the human rights issue of symbolic significance? . . . The third question asks whether addressing the human rights issue can advance strategic reform. . . . Finally, the Office should identify whether the human rights issue has been an ongoing source of frustration and/or exclusion for particular individuals or groups.

HIGH COMMISSIONER'S STRATEGIC MANAGEMENT PLAN, 2006–2007

http://www.ohchr.org/english/about/docs/strategic.pdf, at 9

OHCHR's mission is to work for the protection of all human rights for all people; to help empower people to realize their rights; and to assist those responsible for upholding such rights in ensuring that they are implemented.

In carrying out its mission OHCHR will:

- Give priority to addressing the most pressing human rights violations, both acute and chronic, particularly those that put life in imminent peril;

- Focus attention on those who are at risk and vulnerable on multiple fronts;
- Pay equal attention to the realization of civil, cultural, economic, political, and social rights, including the right to development; and
- Measure the impact of its work through the substantive benefit that is accrued, through it, to individuals around the world.

...

Operationally, OHCHR works with governments, legislatures, courts, national institutions, civil society, regional and international organizations, and the United Nations system to develop and strengthen capacity, particularly at the national level, for the protection of human rights in accordance with international norms.

Thus, the present plan envisages attention to a range of "implementation gaps" on the ground, including those related to knowledge, capacity, commitment, and security. Helping to close those gaps and thereby protecting people and helping to empower them to realize their rights must be seen as the essential mission of the United Nations human rights office.

To these ends, the plan sets forth action points in five areas:

(a) Greater country engagement through an expansion of geographic desks, increased deployment of human rights staff to countries and regions, the establishment of standing capacities for rapid deployment, investigations, field support, human rights capacity-building, advice and assistance, and work on transitional justice and the rule of law;

(b) An enhanced human rights leadership role for the High Commissioner, including through greater interaction with relevant United Nations bodies and actors and regular system-wide human rights consultations, a reinforced New York presence, an annual thematic World Human Rights Report, a global campaign for human rights, and more involvement in efforts to advance poverty reduction and the Millennium Development Goals;

(c) Closer partnerships with civil society and United Nations agencies through the establishment of a civil society support function, support for human rights defenders, stepped up commitment to Action 2 [i.e. national level] activities for rights-based approaches and national protection systems, and human rights guidance to the resident coordinator system;

(d) More synergy in the relationship between OHCHR and the various United Nations human rights bodies, an intergovernmental meeting to consider options for a unified standing human rights treaty body, . . . and a review of the special procedures; and

(e) Strengthened management and planning for OHCHR . . . .

...

Technical Cooperation, and Field Activities

. . . Field offices will manage technical cooperation projects, integrate OHCHR's thematic expertise into their work, and assist countries in working with the special fact-finding procedures of the Commission on Human Rights, or its successor, and with the bodies that monitor the implementation of human rights treaties. Field presences take the form of regional offices, country offices, support for peace missions, or the assignment of human rights officers to the United Nations Country Teams. OHCHR has regional offices in Central Asia (Almaty); East Africa (Addis Ababa); Latin America (Santiago de Chile); the Middle East and the Gulf countries (Beirut); the Pacific (Suva); Southeast Asia (Bangkok) and Southern Africa (Pretoria); as well as a Regional Human Rights Centre for Central Africa in Yaoundé. In the next biennium OHCHR intends to open new regional offices in North Africa, Central America and West Africa and a regional human rights centre in Qatar for the Arab Region and Southwest Asia....

OHCHR has country offices in Angola, Bosnia and Herzegovina, Burundi, Cambodia, Colombia, Democratic Republic of the Congo, Guatemala, Mexico, Nepal, Palestine, the Russian Federation, Serbia and Montenegro (including Kosovo) and Uganda. In the next biennium OHCHR intends to open new country offices in Bolivia and Togo. . . . Human rights officers are deployed in the United Nations Country Teams in Ecuador, Guyana, Mongolia, Southern Caucasus (Georgia) and Sri Lanka. In the next biennium, support to the human rights components of peace missions will be strengthened....

REPORT OF THE UNHCHR ON THE SITUATION OF HUMAN RIGHTS AND THE ACTIVITIES OF HER OFFICE, INCLUDING TECHNICAL COOPERATION, IN NEPAL

UN Doc. E/CN.4/2006/107

[Eds.: By 2005 the situation in Nepal had deteriorated greatly and there was international pressure on the Commission on Human Rights to take strong action. The Nepalese Government wished to avoid the international censure implied by the appointment of a country rapporteur and instead acquiesced in a proposal to deal with the issue under the rubric of technical cooperation, rather than violations, and to set up a country office of the HCHR (CHR Res. 2005/78). 95. By January 2006, OHCHR-Nepal was made up of 39 international staff, 20 UN Volunteers and 2 Junior Professional Officers, together with 22 National Professional Officers and 58 local support staff. In April 2006, after this report was submitted, a popular mass movement brought an end to King Gyanendra's direct rule. On 21 November 2006 a comprehensive peace agreement was signed between the government and the Maoist rebels.]

1. [The 10 April 2005 agreement between the Government of the Kingdom of Nepal and the OHCHR] mandated the OHCHR-Nepal office, inter alia, to assist the authorities in promoting and protecting human rights, to monitor the situation of human rights and observance of international humanitarian law, and to report to the Commission on Human Rights and the General Assembly....

...

I. Context

A. Political context

4. In February 1996 the Communist Party of Nepal (CPN) (Maoist) declared a so-called "people's war" against the State. The ensuing armed conflict escalated in succeeding years. . . .

5. In May 2002 Parliament was dissolved . . . . Since October 2002 four Prime Ministers either resigned or were dismissed by His Majesty King Gyanendra Bir Bikram Shah Dev. The last Prime Minister was removed on 1 February 2005 when the King dismissed the Government, citing its failure to hold elections or to effectively combat the armed insurgency, and declared a three-month state of emergency. Many fundamental rights were suspended and hundreds of political leaders and activists, human rights defenders, journalists and others were imprisoned. The state of emergency was revoked on 29 April 2005 and those imprisoned were released by July, although some restrictions on civil liberties remained in effect or were reintroduced under other legislation.

6. From 1 February 2005 King Gyanendra assumed direct executive authority . . .

. . .

8. In early October 2005, the Government announced that municipal elections would be held on 8 February 2006 and parliamentary elections by April 2007. An alliance of seven political parties, which have opposed the royal takeover and refused to accept the King's executive role, decided to boycott elections . . . . CPN (Maoist) declared that it would disrupt the elections. On 22 November 2005, the seven-party alliance and CPN (Maoist) announced their common adoption of a 12-point "Letter of Understanding", including a call for an "end to autocratic monarchy" and the election of a constituent assembly. The "Understanding" committed CPN (Maoist) to multiparty democracy, human rights and the rule of law, and stated that the armed Maoist force and RNA [the Royal Nepalese Army] would be kept "under the supervision of the United Nations or any other reliable international supervision" during constituent assembly elections. The Secretary-General welcomed the Understanding, but it was strongly criticized by government ministers. . . .

. . .

C. Government human rights commitments and cooperation

13. The Government has provided regular opportunities to meet with the Representative and officers of OHCHR-Nepal, and members of security forces have made themselves available at short notice in Kathmandu and in the regions. The authorities continue to show good cooperation in assuring access for OHCHR-Nepal monitors visiting places of detention without prior notice.

14. OHCHR-Nepal maintains regular communication with the human rights cells in RNA and Nepal Police. Frequent communications were sent to security forces requesting urgent information on the whereabouts of persons reported to have been arrested. In most of those instances, security forces replied confirming the arrests and giving assurances in regard to concerns over risk of torture or disappearance. In the majority of cases concerning deaths in custody or alleged summary executions, the response fell far short of the information requested.

15. A new human rights coordination structure, comprising a national coordination committee chaired by the Minister for Foreign Affairs and two sub-committees chaired by the Chief Secretary and the Attorney-General, was set up by the Government in August. OHCHR-Nepal met with the Chief Secretary and the Secretary responsible for human rights coordination in the Office of the Prime Minister and Council of Ministers in the context of their coordinating responsibility.

D. Communist Party of Nepal (Maoist) human rights commitments and cooperation

16. The establishment of OHCHR's office in Nepal was welcomed publicly and in communications to the Representative by the leadership of CPN (Maoist), which committed itself to allow OHCHR-Nepal staff to travel freely, to investigate incidents and to meet with party members and others. In accordance with article V (1) (b) of the Agreement, OHCHR-Nepal met and raised concerns with CPN (Maoist) leaders and cadres. CPN (Maoist) has responded and taken action with respect to a number of individual cases, but a majority have not received any response.

...

HUMAN RIGHTS WATCH, RESPONSE TO CRITICISM OF THE UN HIGH COMMISSIONER FOR HUMAN RIGHTS

13 December 2005, at http://hrw.org/english/docs/2005/12/15/usint12295.htm

. . . In a statement for Human Rights Day [the HCHR, Louise] Arbour expressed serious and legitimate concerns that the right to be free from torture and cruel, inhuman, and degrading treatment had become a casualty of the "war on terror." She highlighted the United States' use of secret prisons and reliance on diplomatic assurances of proper treatment of suspects from governments that routinely torture detainees as two practices that violate international human rights law and the Convention against Torture. [The US Permanent Representative to the UN] Ambassador Bolton is reported to have said that it was "inappropriate and illegitimate for an international civil servant to second-guess the conduct that we're engaged in [within] the war on terror, with nothing more as evidence than what she reads in the newspapers."

The United States government has every right to disagree with the substance of Ms. Arbour's comments. But Ambassador Bolton's decision to move from substance to a personal attack on Ms. Arbour and her ability to speak publicly about human rights abuses is both misguided and ill timed.

The High Commissioner for Human Rights is no mere international civil servant; she is the leading voice of the U.N. system on human rights issues. To do her job effectively, she must operate entirely independently of governments and have the ability to raise concerns about the human rights conduct of any government. Victims of oppression worldwide have reason to be grateful for her independence and her ability and courage to raise human rights concerns wherever and whenever they occur.

...

QUESTIONS

1. The role of the HCHR has evolved considerably since 1993. Much depends on the office-holder and on her relationship with governments and the Secretary-General. The question of her accountability is a vexed one. If she is seen to be accountable to the Secretary-General for every decision then her role as an independent voice is at risk, since he is likely to come under regular pressure from powerful states to 'rein her in'. If she is subject to the direction of the Human Rights Council then her office becomes a mere secretariat. How then is she to be held to account?

2. Should the HCHR only take up issues and cases which fit strict criteria of gravity etc. or is more discretion needed?

F. THE SECURITY COUNCIL AND THE RESPONSIBILITY TO PROTECT

COMMENT ON EARLIER WORK OF SECURITY COUNCIL

Until fairly recently the role of the Security Council in human rights matters had been remarkably limited. With the end of the Cold War the Council's role has expanded significantly and many of the issues coming before it have had human rights dimensions. The Council has, for example, played an important role in matters such as ensuring the inclusion of human rights provisions in peace agreements, efforts to eliminate the use of children in armed conflicts, and considering the role of human rights protections in the work of its own Counter-Terrorism Committee established in the wake of the 9/11 attacks on the US. Its biggest conceptual challenge, however, has been to move from the notion of humanitarian intervention to that of the 'responsibility to protect'.

The Security Council consists of 15 members, five of which are permanent — China, France, Russia, the UK and the USA. Ten others are elected by the General Assembly for two-year terms. Each member has one vote. Substantive decisions require nine votes out of the 15, and must include the concurring votes (defined by the Council to include abstentions) of all five permanent members. This is the so-called 'veto' power. The Council is able to be convened at any time and non-members may be invited to participate, but without a vote, when their interests are affected.

The Council is given 'primary responsibility' for the maintenance of international peace and security under the collective security system provided for in the UN Charter (Article 24), and member states are obligated to carry out its decisions

(Article 25). It can act under *Chapter VI* of the Charter (Articles 33–38) to achieve the pacific settlement of 'any dispute, the continuance of which is likely to endanger the maintenance of international peace and security'. It is empowered to investigate any such dispute and to recommend 'appropriate procedures or methods of adjustment'. It can act under *Chapter VII* (Articles 39–51) whenever it determines 'the existence of any threat to the peace, breach of the peace, or act of aggression'. In such situations, the Council can call on states to apply sanctions of various kinds (Article 41) or to take such military action 'as may be necessary to restore international peace and security' (Article 42). Since all states are obligated by Article 2(4) of the Charter to 'refrain in their international relations from the threat or use of force against the territorial integrity or political independence of any state', except in the exercise of the right of self-defence against an armed attack (Article 51), the Council enjoys a legal monopoly over the use of force in all other circumstances. This monopoly extends to Article 53(1) which authorizes the Council to make use of 'regional arrangements or agencies for enforcement action under its authority'. But the latter are not permitted to act without the Council's authorization.

Precedents set in the struggle against apartheid

Many procedures and techniques which were eventually developed by the General Assembly and the Security Council to deal with human rights were hammered out on the anvil of the South African apartheid system. The issue was first brought to the Assembly in 1946 by India which complained of the discriminatory treatment of persons of Indian origin. Very early on, India suggested that such conduct could be seen as a threat to international peace and thus as requiring the attention of the Council. South Africa replied that most of those concerned were its nationals and that, in any event, the issue was exclusively a domestic affair.

The battle lines were thus set for a struggle continuing until today to clarify two key issues: (1) the relationship between the human rights provisions of the UN Charter and the domestic jurisdiction clause in Article 2(7) of the Charter (considered at pp. 689, *supra*); and (2) the circumstances under which gross human rights violations (and especially those with no significant international element such as the involvement of foreign nationals or the prompting of refugee flows) can be considered to threaten international peace and security and thus warrant Security Council measures under Chapter VII. While South Africa was the main focus of these debates, the situations in Southern Rhodesia (Zimbabwe) and the Portugese colonies in southern Africa (Angola and Mozambique) also figured in them.

With the influx of newly independent states into the United Nations from the late 1950s onwards, the South African case pitted a Security Council dominated by Western governments that were reluctant to act, against a General Assembly which was increasingly frustrated at the intransigence of the racist governments in southern Africa and the failure of the Assembly's barrage of resolutions to make any difference. In 1962 the Assembly tested the limits of its division of labour with the Security Council by itself calling upon member states to break off diplomatic relations with South Africa, to refuse entry to its ships and aircraft, to boycott its goods, and to impose an arms embargo. It also established what became the Special

Committee against Apartheid to monitor developments and report, as appropriate, to either the Assembly or the Council. The resolution also called upon the Council to impose binding sanctions. In 1963 the Council characterized the South African situation as 'seriously disturbing international peace and security' and called for, but did not mandatorily impose, an arms embargo. The Assembly raised the stakes again in 1966 by condemning apartheid as 'a crime against humanity', an approach which was taken further by its adoption in 1973 of the Convention on the Suppression and Punishment of the Crime of Apartheid (GA Res. 3068 (XXVIII)). Three years later, the Assembly concluded that 'the continued brutal repression, including indiscriminate mass killings' by the apartheid regime left 'no alternative to the oppressed people of South Africa but to resort to armed struggle to achieve their legitimate rights', thus giving its imprimatur to the national liberation struggle.

It was not until 1977 that the Council (Res. 418) imposed a mandatory arms embargo under Chapter VII. In 1984, the Council rejected a new constitution that had been adopted by an exclusively white electorate as contrary to UN principles and thus 'null and void'. With the end of apartheid and the transition to democracy the Council terminated the arms embargo and all other restrictions in May 1994.

From humanitarian intervention to the 'responsibility to protect'

It has long been claimed that, despite the prohibition on the use of force contained in Article 2(4) of the UN Charter, there is a humanitarian exception of some sort which would justify the use of force by a state to protect individuals in another state from egregious violations of human rights. With the end of the Cold War, the 1990s brought a distinctly greater willingness on the part of some states, including the US, to intervene for such reasons. Somalia, Haiti and the former Yugoslavia were key examples. But the failure to intervene in the face of genocide in Rwanda traumatized the UN and other actors and led to extensive soul-searching as to the nature of any principle of intervention for humanitarian reasons. In part, this ambiguity reflects the traumas of recent years when the Council was accused of not having acted forcefully enough in response to massive violations in Bosnia and Rwanda. The UN commissioned inquiries into both failings. The report on Rwanda characterized the 1994 genocide in which 800,000 people were killed in about 100 days as 'one of the most abhorrent events of the twentieth century'. It condemned the failure to 'prevent, and subsequently, to stop the genocide in Rwanda' as a failure by the UN system as a whole. 'The fundamental failure was the lack of resources and political commitment devoted to developments in Rwanda and to the United Nations presence there. There was a persistent lack of political will by Member States to act, or to act with enough assertiveness . . . '. It called upon the 'Security Council and troop contributing countries . . . to act to prevent acts of genocide or gross violations of human rights wherever they may take place.'[42]

In the same year as the UN published the strongly self-critical reviews of action and inaction in Bosnia and Rwanda a crisis erupted in Kosovo, then a province of

[42] Report of the Independent Inquiry into the Actions of the United Nations During the 1994 Genocide in Rwanda, UN Doc. S/1999. For a detailed inquiry into failings in Bosnia, see: 'The Fall of Srebrenica', UN Doc. A/54/549 (1999).

Serbia. Since 1993 reports to the UN Commission on Human Rights had documented serious human rights abuses by Serbia against the Kosovo Albanians who made up 90 per cent of the province's population. In 1998 the Security Council, acting under Chapter VII, imposed an arms embargo (Res. 1160) and subsequently determined that there was 'a threat to peace and security in the region' (Res. 1199). Russia, however, made clear that it would veto any Council resolution authorizing the use of force. After a grave deterioration of the situation, and the failure of talks among the relevant parties held in Rambouillet, the North Atlantic Treaty Organization (NATO) launched military action against Serbia for non-compliance with the Council resolutions and in the name of 'humanitarian intervention'. It was estimated that 90 per cent of the Kosovo Albanian population — some 1.45 million people — had been displaced by the conflict by the time it ended.[43]

Although the Security Council had never authorized the intensive bombing campaign, it endorsed the political settlement that was reached and agreed to deploy an extensive 'international security presence' along with a parallel 'international civil presence' (Res. 1244).

VIEWS ON THE RESPONSIBILITY TO PROTECT

Kofi Annan, Implications of International Response to Events in Rwanda, Kosovo Examined by Secretary-General

UN Press Release GA/9595, 20 September 1999

[This is a report of a speech to the General Assembly by the UN Secretary-General, Kofi Annan.]

'While the genocide in Rwanda will define for our generation the consequences of inaction in the face of mass murder, the more recent conflict in Kosovo had prompted important questions about the consequences of action in the absence of unity on the part of the international community', he said. In the case of Kosovo, the inability of that community to reconcile the question of the legitimacy of an action taken by a regional organization without a United Nations mandate, on one side, and the universally accepted imperative of effectively halting gross and systematic violations of human rights, on the other, could only be viewed as a tragedy. It had revealed the core challenge to the Security Council and the United Nations in the next century: To forge unity behind the principle that massive, systematic violations of human rights — wherever they might take place — should not be allowed to stand.

He said that, to those for whom the greatest threat to the future of international order was the use of force in the absence of a Council mandate, one might ask — not in the context of Kosovo, but in the context of Rwanda — if a coalition of States had been prepared to act in defence of the Tutsi population, but had not received

[43] OSCE, Kosovo/Kosova: As Seen, As Told, December 1999, at www.osce.org/kosovo/reports/hr.

prompt Council authorization, should such a coalition have stood aside and allowed the horror to unfold? To those for whom the Kosovo action heralded a new era when States and groups of States could take military action outside the established mechanisms for enforcing international law, one might ask: Was there not a danger of such intervention undermining the imperfect, yet resilient, security system created after the Second World War, and of setting dangerous precedents for future interventions?

. . .

. . . [I]n the Charter's own words, 'armed force shall not be used, save in the common interest'. What was the common interest, who should define it, who would defend it, and under whose authority and with what means of intervention? he asked. . . .

. . .

. . . In [Rwanda and Kosovo] Member States of the United Nations should have been able to find common ground in upholding the principles of the Charter, and acting in defence of 'our common heritage'. The Charter required the Council to be the defender of the 'common interest'. Unless it was seen to be so, there was a danger that others could seek to take its place.

The Responsibility to Protect Report, 2001

In order to address systematically the policy issues emerging from situations such as Rwanda and Kosovo the Canadian Government established an International Commission on Intervention and State Sovereignty which reported in 2001. Its Report, entitled *The Responsibility to Protect* put forward a series of 'core principles' premised on the argument that while the notion of state sovereignty could not be brushed aside in the name of intervention, it should be interpreted as implying that 'the primary responsibility for the protection of its people lies with the state itself'. But where a state is 'unwilling or unable' to halt or avert serious harm to its own population, 'the principle of non-intervention yields to the international responsibility to protect.'[44] A similar approach was subsequently endorsed by a 'High-level Panel' appointed by the UN Secretary-General.

A More Secure World: Our Shared Responsibility, Report of the High-Level Panel on Threats, Challenges and Change (2004)

http://www.un.org/secureworld/report3.pdf

. . .

201. The successive humanitarian disasters in Somalia, Bosnia and Herzegovina, Rwanda, Kosovo and now Darfur, Sudan, have concentrated attention not on the immunities of sovereign Governments but their responsibilities, both to their own people and to the wider international community. There is a growing recognition that the issue is not the "right to intervene" of any State, but the "responsibility to protect" of *every* State when it comes to people suffering from avoidable catastrophe — mass

[44] http://www.iciss.ca/pdf/Commission-Report.pdf.

murder and rape, ethnic cleansing by forcible expulsion and terror, and deliberate starvation and exposure to disease. And there is a growing acceptance that while sovereign Governments have the primary responsibility to protect their own citizens from such catastrophes, when they are unable or unwilling to do so that responsibility should be taken up by the wider international community — with it spanning a continuum involving prevention, response to violence, if necessary, and rebuilding shattered societies. The primary focus should be on assisting the cessation of violence through mediation and other tools and the protection of people through such measures as the dispatch of humanitarian, human rights and police missions. Force, if it needs to be used, should be deployed as a last resort.

202. The Security Council so far has been neither very consistent nor very effective in dealing with these cases, very often acting too late, too hesitantly or not at all. But step by step, the Council and the wider international community have come to accept that, under Chapter VII and in pursuit of the emerging norm of a collective international responsibility to protect, it can always authorize military action to redress catastrophic internal wrongs if it is prepared to declare that the situation is a "threat to international peace and security", not especially difficult when breaches of international law are involved.

203. We endorse the emerging norm that there is a collective international responsibility to protect, exercisable by the Security Council authorizing military intervention as a last resort, in the event of genocide and other large-scale killing, ethnic cleansing or serious violations of international humanitarian law which sovereign Governments have proved powerless or unwilling to prevent.

B. The question of legitimacy

...

207. In considering whether to authorize or endorse the use of military force, the Security Council should always address — whatever other considerations it may take into account — at least the following five basic criteria of legitimacy:

(a) *Seriousness of threat.* Is the threatened harm to State or human security of a kind, and sufficiently clear and serious, to justify *prima facie* the use of military force? In the case of internal threats, does it involve genocide and other large-scale killing, ethnic cleansing or serious violations of international humanitarian law, actual or imminently apprehended?
(b) *Proper purpose.* Is it clear that the primary purpose of the proposed military action is to halt or avert the threat in question, whatever other purposes or motives may be involved?
(c) *Last resort.* Has every non-military option for meeting the threat in question been explored, with reasonable grounds for believing that other measures will not succeed?
(d) *Proportional means.* Are the scale, duration and intensity of the proposed military action the minimum necessary to meet the threat in question?
(e) *Balance of consequences.* Is there a reasonable chance of the military action being successful in meeting the threat in question, with the consequences of action not likely to be worse than the consequences of inaction?

2005 World Summit Outcome, General Assembly Res. 60/1

. . .

138. Each individual State has the responsibility to protect its populations from genocide, war crimes, ethnic cleansing and crimes against humanity. This responsibility entails the prevention of such crimes, including their incitement, through appropriate and necessary means. We accept that responsibility and will act in accordance with it. The international community should, as appropriate, encourage and help States to exercise this responsibility and support the United Nations in establishing an early warning capability.

139. The international community, through the United Nations, also has the responsibility to use appropriate diplomatic, humanitarian and other peaceful means, in accordance with Chapters VI and VIII of the Charter, to help to protect populations from genocide, war crimes, ethnic cleansing and crimes against humanity. In this context, we are prepared to take collective action, in a timely and decisive manner, through the Security Council, in accordance with the Charter, including Chapter VII, on a case-by-case basis and in cooperation with relevant regional organizations as appropriate, should peaceful means be inadequate and national authorities are manifestly failing to protect their populations from genocide, war crimes, ethnic cleansing and crimes against humanity. We stress the need for the General Assembly to continue consideration of the responsibility to protect populations from genocide, war crimes, ethnic cleansing and crimes against humanity and its implications, bearing in mind the principles of the Charter and international law. We also intend to commit ourselves, as necessary and appropriate, to helping States build capacity to protect their populations from genocide, war crimes, ethnic cleansing and crimes against humanity and to assisting those which are under stress before crises and conflicts break out.

Russia harshly criticizes United States for raising Belarus at U.N. Security Council

The Associated Press, 13 December 2006

Russia's Foreign Ministry on Wednesday criticized the United States for raising the plight of an opposition leader in Belarus in the United Nations Security Council, saying the move violated U.N. procedures.

. . .

It added that the discussion of human rights issues was a prerogative of other U.N. structures and condemned what it called "the violation of the existing Security Council procedures" by the United States.

. . .

"We all need to make efforts to ensure that the U.N. Security Council focuses on issues crucial to world peace and international security and is not distracted by issues that have nothing to do with its mandate," Foreign Minister Sergey Lavrov said.

China and Russia veto US/UK-backed Security Council draft resolution on Myanmar[45]

12 January 2007

China and Russia today vetoed a draft resolution in the Security Council — the first use of multiple vetoes at the Council since 1989 — that had called on Myanmar to release all political prisoners, begin widespread dialogue and end its military attacks and human rights abuses against ethnic minorities.

Sponsored by the United States and the United Kingdom, the text received nine votes in favour, the necessary number for a majority. Those in favour were Belgium, France, Ghana, Italy, Panama, Peru, Slovakia, the UK and the US. But the permanent members China and Russia issued vetoes, and South Africa also voted against the resolution. There were three abstentions: Indonesia, Qatar and the Republic of the Congo.

Opponents of the text said that while Myanmar was experiencing clear social and economic problems, the country was not a serious threat to international peace and security and therefore the issue should not be dealt with by the Security Council.

Speaking before the vote, Chinese Ambassador Wang Guangya said the problems in Myanmar were largely the internal affairs of a sovereign State and the Government and other groups should be allowed to continue their efforts towards reconciliation.

Russian Ambassador Vitaly Churkin said the issue would be better handled by other UN organs, particularly the Human Rights Council, the General Assembly and humanitarian agencies such as the World Health Organization (WHO).

QUESTIONS

1. Are the criteria identified by the High-level Panel likely to be very helpful in resolving a concrete situation that comes before the Security Council? If not, why not?

2. How far does the General Assembly's 2005 resolution go towards resolving the problems that arise when the Security Council is unable to act in a given crisis situation because of the threat of a veto by one of the Permanent Members?

3. What is the significance of the positions taken, especially by Russia and China, in response to human rights issues recently raised in the Security Counci?

ADDITIONAL READING

H. Morsink, *The Universal Declaration of Human Rights: Origins, Drafting and Intent* (1999); International Service for Human Rights, *Human Rights Monitor* (1989–present); M. Lempinen, *The United Nations Commission on Human Rights and the Different Treatment*

[45] http://www.un.org/apps/news/story.asp?NewsID=21228&Cr=myanmar&Cr1=.

of Governments (2005); K. Tomaševski, *Responding to Human Rights Violations 1946–1999* (2000); M. O'Flaherty, 'The Concluding Observations of United Nations Human Rights Treaty Bodies', 6 Hum. Rts. L. Rev. 27 (2006); O. Hoehne, 'Special Procedures and the New Human Rights Council — A Need for Strategic Positioning', 4/1 Essex Hum. Rts. Rev. (Feb. 2007), at http://projects.essex.ac.uk/ehrr/; J. Gutter, *Thematic Procedures of the United Nations Commission on Human Rights and International Law: in Search of a Sense of Community* (2006); and P. Alston and F. Mégret, *The UN and Human Rights* (2nd edn. 2008).

10

Treaty Bodies: The ICCPR Human Rights Committee

This chapter continues the inquiry into the structure, roles, functions and processes of international human rights bodies. We continue to emphasize the relationships among human rights norms, institutions and processes, as well as the reasons and techniques for 'institutionalization' of norms.

The Human Rights Council, created under the UN Charter (thus a 'Charter organ') as a successor to the Commission on Human Rights, which was examined in Chapter 9, remains the most complex and politically charged of the specifically human rights organs with universal reach. It differs markedly in organization, functions and powers, as well as notoriety, from the seven 'treaty bodies' established to monitor implementation of the eight universal human rights treaties (dealing respectively with civil and political rights, economic and social rights, racial discrimination, gender discrimination, torture, children's rights, migrant workers' rights, and persons with disabilities. Each of the treaty bodies is distinctive in some respects; each has functions only with respect to the treaty creating it; each such treaty regime is now to some extent 'monitored' or 'implemented' or 'developed' by that body.

Chapter 10 provides a systematic study of one such treaty body, the Human Rights Committee created by and functioning within one of the UN's two principal human rights treaties, the International Covenant on Civil and Political Rights. As of January 2007, 160 states are parties to the ICCPR. We continue to use the abbreviation 'ICCPR Committee' to distinguish it from the 'Human Rights Council'.

Previous chapters have introduced the work of other treaty bodies, including the CEDAW Committee and the CAT Committee (Chapter 3) as well as the ICESCR Committee (Chapter 4). The emphasis of the present chapter is on institutional structure, functions, powers and efficacy. Why has the ICCPR Committee assumed the character, structure and functions that it has? After thirty years in existence, is it now time for a significant overhaul? But this chapter also addresses important substantive issues, albeit through the lens of the work of the Committee.

Two thoughts should be kept in mind: (1) The ICCPR Committee forms part of a complex system of universal bodies concentrating on human rights issues, both Charter and treaty bodies. Should it then be understood and evaluated not only as an isolated organ functioning under and within the ICCPR, but also as part of this larger complex? If so, it becomes relevant to assess the Committee's work in relation to that of the Human Rights Council, and of other actors such as NGOs. (2) Even when we examine the Committee's work only within the ICCPR, can we understand each of its basic functions in isolation from the others, or should each discrete function be seen as part of an overall ICCPR system?

A. POWERS, FUNCTIONS AND PERFORMANCE OF THE ICCPR COMMITTEE

1. INTRODUCTION

COMMENT ON THE FORMAL ORGANIZATION OF THE ICCPR COMMITTEE

Based on Articles 40 and 41 of the Covenant, and on the first Optional Protocol to the ICCPR, the Committee has four main functions: (1) the consideration of states' reports; (2) the adoption of 'general comments'; (3) the examination of 'communications' (i.e. complaints) from individuals claiming to be victims of violations by states parties of the Covenant; and (4) an interstate complaints procedure (Article 21). While the latter was considered to be potentially important when the Covenant was drafted, it has never been used by states. Governments apparently prefer to resolve such matters on a bilateral basis, or through the political organs of international or regional organizations.

Before considering the first three of these functions we consider the organizational arrangements reflected in the ICCPR.

Article 28

1. There shall be established a Human Rights Committee .... It shall consist of eighteen members and shall carry out the functions hereinafter provided.
2. The Committee shall be composed of nationals of the States Parties to the present Covenant who shall be persons of high moral character and recognized competence in the field of human rights, consideration being given to the usefulness of the participation of some persons having legal experience.
3. The members of the Committee shall be elected and shall serve in their personal capacity.

...

Article 31

1. The Committee may not include more than one national of the same State.
2. In the election of the Committee, consideration shall be given to equitable geographical distribution of membership and to the representation of the different forms of civilization and of the principal legal systems.

...

Article 38

> Every member of the Committee shall, before taking up his duties, make a solemn declaration in open committee that he will perform his functions impartially and conscientiously.
>
> . . .

Article 39

> . . .
>
> (2)(b) Decisions of the Committee shall be made by a majority vote of the members present.

The professional background of Committee members has varied considerably and includes judges, university teachers, public interest lawyers, former diplomats, and former government officials. In general, members have demonstrated a high level of competence. Because Article 31(2) does not actually set regional quotas the group of experts elected to the Committee has not always reflected the 'equitable geographical' balance called for. As of January 2007, the 18 Committee members came from Australia, Benin, Colombia, Egypt, France, India, Ireland, Japan, Mauritius, Panama, Peru, Romania, South Africa, Sweden, Switzerland, Tunisia, United Kingdom and the United States.

Under Article 28(3), all members are to be 'elected and shall serve in their personal capacity'. The UN term for such members is 'experts', as opposed to the 'representatives' of states who sit on the UN Human Rights Council. The inference is that Committee members are to act independently of the governments of their states.

Generally this aspiration appears to have been realized, but in many contexts, 'independence' in the sense identified has been a relative rather than absolute concept. Consider members who are nationals of (and originally nominated for election by) states of an authoritarian character directed, say, by a single party, a military clique, or a personal dictator. Moreover, since membership on the Committee is a part-time business, a minority of members have continued to hold government (diplomatic and other) posts, again qualifying the degree of possible independence from their governments' positions on given issues. Consider the following 'Guidelines' adopted by the Committee:

> 1. The independence of members of the Committee is essential. The principle of independence requires that the members are not removable during their term of office and are not subject to direction or influence of any kind, or to pressure from the State or its agencies in regard to the performance of their duties....
>
> 2. In their work . . . members . . . should not only be impartial, but should also appear to be so.
>
> 3. . . . [I]t is important that the election of one of its nationals to the Committee should not result in, or be thought to result in, either more favourable or less favourable treatment for the nominating State.
>
> . . .

4. It is the practice of the Committee that a member does not participate in the examination of the reports presented by his or her country....

...

6. ... [A] member [should] take no part whatsoever, formally or informally, in the discussion of communications from his or her own country....

...

8. It is desirable for a member of the Committee to abstain from being on the Board of Directors or the Executive Committee of an international non-governmental organization which regularly submits reports and information to the Committee, so as to avoid the appearance of any conflict in their respective capacities.

...

9. ... Members should abstain from participation in any political body of the United Nations or of any other intergovernmental organization concerned with human rights. They should also abstain from acting as experts, consultants or counsels for any Government in a matter that might come up for consideration before the Committee.[1]

The Committee meets for three sessions annually, each three weeks long, at the UN Office in Geneva (twice) and at UN headquarters in New York. There is some intersessional work by individual members in the context of working groups, which meet for one week prior to the start of each session. Living and travel expenses are paid by the UN but since 2002 an annual honorarium of $3,000 previously paid to members has been reduced to a token $1, in order to save money. The work is part-time, members hold 'regular', often full-time, jobs, and must fit the Committee's work into already busy schedules. Most meetings (other than those considering 'communications' under the Optional Protocol) are public. Public attendance is usually rather limited, although reports from certain countries can attract a 'full house' in a small conference room. Press coverage is generally very limited, but again there are major exceptions. In general, however, the ICCPR Committee has neither enjoyed nor sought the publicity and notoriety of the UN Council

Decisions of the Committee should formally be by majority vote pursuant to Article 39(2). In fact, all decisions to date have been taken by consensus, although as a formal matter any member could demand a vote on any issue. This unbroken practice of reaching decisions by consensus (e.g., on decisions about the Committee's concluding observations on a state's report, p. 850, *infra*, or about the text of a General Comment, p. 873, *infra*) meets with varying reactions from Committee members. Its advantages in avoiding the factional battles that have dominated much of the life of the UN political organs and in permitting the Committee to move ahead as a unit are obvious. Its undoubted if indeterminate historical effects on the action taken by the Committee are as obvious: compromise, the blunting of positions, the failure to take the bolder step.

[1] Report of the Human Rights Committee, 1998, UN doc. A/53/40, p. 89, Annex III.

Committee members have said that the practice has had the general effect of not permitting an individual member to hold out for a different position from the large majority, but also has generated a lot of give-and-take while encouraging members holding minority views to go along with a clear trend or dominant opinion. In one activity, the writing of 'Views' about communications discussed at p. 891, *infra*, Committee practice has allowed individual members to write concurring or dissenting opinions.

Like the UN Council (and the Commission before it), the ICCPR Committee has witnessed vast changes in global politics since it first met in 1977. The disputes and compromises over the Committee's basic structure and functions that marked the drafting of the Covenant and the Optional Protocol have left a strong imprint on the Committee today. History's traces are indeed everywhere in the Committee's activities, as part of the section below on General Comments seeks to illustrate.

NOTE

Consider the following brief summaries by two authors of the nature of the earlier disputes and their continuing influence. The first is taken from Dominic McGoldrick, *The Human Rights Committee* (1991) at 13–14:

> 1.18 There was general agreement during the drafting that the primary obligation under the ICCPR would be implementation at the national level by States. There was continuing disagreement, however, on the question whether there should also be international measures of implementation. A minority of States, principally the Soviet bloc, insisted that there should be provisions to ensure implementation but that there should be no international measures of implementation. It was argued that such measures were a system of international pressure intended to force States to take particular steps connected with the execution of obligations under the Covenant. They were, therefore, contrary to the principle of domestic jurisdiction in article 2(7) of the United Nations Charter, would undermine the sovereignty and independence of States and would upset the balance of powers established by the UN Charter. Moreover, the establishment of petitions systems would transform complaints into international disputes with consequent effects upon peaceful international relations.
>
> 1.19 Against these views it was argued that the undertaking of international measures of implementation was an exercise of domestic jurisdiction and not an interference with it. International measures were essential to the effective observance of human rights, which were matters of international concern. However, even within those States that agreed that international measures were essential, there were significant differences of opinion as to the appropriate types of measures. The proposals included an International Court of Human Rights empowered to settle disputes concerning the Covenant; settlement by diplomatic negotiation and, in default, by *ad hoc* fact-finding Committees; the establishment of an Office of High Commissioner (or Attorney-General) for Human Rights; the establishment of reporting procedures covering some or all of the provisions in the Covenant; empowering the proposed Human Rights Committee to collect

information on all matters relevant to the observance and enforcement of human rights and to initiate an inquiry if it thought one necessary.

...

1.21 The lengthy drafting process of the ICCPR largely coincided with the depths of cold war confrontation, the explosive development of notions of self-determination and independence, the accompanying political tensions of large scale decolonization, and the consequential effects of a rapidly altering balance of diplomatic power within the United Nations. In retrospect then it must be acknowledged that it was much more difficult to agree on the text of a Covenant containing binding legal obligations and limited measures of international implementation than it had been to agree upon the statement of political principles in the Universal Declaration in 1948....

The second summary is by Torkel Opsahl, 'The Human Rights Committee', in Philip Alston (ed.), *The United Nations and Human Rights* (1992), at 371:

... The draft Covenant prepared in 1954 by the Commission envisioned a quasi-judicial Human Rights Committee quite different in its powers and functions from that which actually came into existence. It was another twelve years before the General Assembly's Third Committee debated the proposed implementation provisions, at which time they were drastically altered. The majority was opposed to making obligatory the procedure for interstate communications....

All of the various positions, except that of dispensing with the Committee altogether, were taken into account by a formula worked out by the Afro-Asian group. According to this version, the Committee's only compulsory role would be to study and comment generally upon the reports of States Parties, a function originally intended for the Commission on Human Rights. Many of the details of this proposal were amended, which later caused doubts and disagreements about the proper role of the Committee in the reporting system. The functions relating to communications were made entirely optional, and arrangements providing for the consideration of individual complaints of violations were separated from the Covenant and put in the Optional Protocol. In other words, the result was a compromise between those States which favoured strong international measures and those which emphasized the primacy of national sovereignty and responsibility. As is inevitably the case with such compromises, many specific issues were left unresolved, perhaps intentionally. As a result the subsequent evolution of the arrangements has had to be shaped by a continuing give-and-take within the Committee over many years.

QUESTION

Some commentators would like to characterize the ICCPR Committee as a 'quasi-judicial' body. How is this affected by the part-time, unpaid basis of the work, the very limited conflict of interest provisions contained in the Guidelines, and the fact that the Committee generally works by consensus? What changes would be desirable if the Committee were to seek to resemble more closely a quasi-judicial model?

2. STATE REPORTING

COMMENT ON REPORTS OF STATES

Submission by states of reports to a human rights treaty body about their implementation of that treaty has become a familiar requirement. But consider how revolutionary a practice this must have appeared at the time of the first proposals about 60 years ago. To many, it would have seemed nearly inconceivable that most of the world's states would periodically submit a report to an international body about their internal matters involving many politically significant aspects of relations between government and citizens, and then participate in a discussion about that report with members of that body drawn from all over the world.

The critical provision is Article 40:

> 1. The States Parties to the present Covenant undertake to submit reports on the measures they have adopted which give effect to the rights recognized herein and on the progress made in the enjoyment of those rights:
>
> (*a*) Within one year of the entry into force of the present Covenant for the States Parties concerned;
>
> (*b*) Thereafter whenever the Committee so requests.
>
> 2. . . . Reports shall indicate the factors and difficulties, if any, affecting the implementation of the present Covenant.
>
> . . .
>
> 4. The Committee shall study the reports . . . [and shall submit them], and such general comments as it may consider appropriate, to the States Parties. . . .
>
> 5. The States Parties to the present Covenant may submit to the Committee observations on any comments that may be made in accordance with paragraph 4 of this article.

Discussions of reports are public proceedings, with attendance varying considerably depending on the country concerned, and the vibrancy of the domestic NGO community and of the national media. The proceedings amount less to a systematic 'study' (to use the term of Article 40) than to an examination of the report with members speaking individually, making comments and posing questions. The representative of the state responds to comments and questions. Reports are generally presented by a state party every five years or at other intervals determined by the Committee in its Concluding Observations. A practice of requesting 'emergency reports', pioneered by the Committee in 1992 in relation to Iraq, Rwanda and the former Yugoslavia, has not since been reactivated in this form.

The Committee has encountered various problems in the reports submitted to it: incomplete coverage, abstraction and formality that leads states to stress their formal constitutional or statutory provisions rather than to offer a realistic description of practices; and great delays in filing reports.

The Covenant makes no provision about the way in which a state should prepare a report, but the Committee has issued general guidelines UN Doc. CCPR/C/

66/GUI/Rev.2 (2001). In addition, each state is generally expected to frame its reports around the issues of concern identified by the Committee at the conclusion of its consideration of the state's previous report.

The ICCPR Committee's sister treaty body, the Committee on Economic, Social and Cultural Rights, has stated that much of the value of the reporting process lies at the domestic level rather than in the formal hearing and its outcome in Geneva or New York:

> The process of reporting provides an opportunity for an individual State party to conduct a comprehensive review of the measures it has taken to bring its national law and policy into line with the provisions of the treaties to which it is a party. The preparation of reports provides a platform for national dialogue on human rights amongst the various stakeholders in a State party. The report itself provides the Government and others, including civil society, with a baseline for the elaboration of clearly stated and targeted policies, which include priorities consistent with the provisions of the treaties. The process of reporting also encourages and facilitates public scrutiny at the national level of Government approaches to implementation and stimulates constructive discussion with civil society of ways to advance the enjoyment by all of the rights laid down in the various conventions. Consideration of the reports by the Committtees, through constructive dialogue with States parties, allows individual States and States as a whole to exchange experience on the problems faced in implementation of the instruments, and good practices that facilitate enhanced implementation. It also allows for international scrutiny, which underlines States' responsibility and accountability for human rights protection.[2]

In most cases, however, the reporting process, from a report's preparation by a state through Committee proceedings, gets little publicity. Only a few states include groups of their citizens — interest groups, particular lobbies, ethnic or gender groups or indigenous peoples, human rights NGOs and so on — in the process of the report's preparation or in the process of considering the Committee's reaction to the report. The most participatory dimension of the process in many cases is an informal one which involves the preparation of a shadow report by civil society groups. It is then submitted to the Committee in the form of an NGO document and serves both to critique the governmental report and to provide information on issues which the Committee might wish to take up in its dialogue with the state.

It has been suggested that the effectiveness of reporting will depend on:

> the willingness and capacity of States to report regularly, use the process as an opportunity for a frank and comprehensive assessment of implementation of international obligations, and engage in a dialogue with national stakeholders before and after the consideration of reports by the Committee. It also depends on the awareness and knowledge of national constituencies and their interest in participating in the process and using it to assess progress in implementation and

[2] 'Concept Paper on the High Commissioner's proposal for a unified standing treaty body', UN doc. HRI/MC/2006/2 (2006) summarizing the approach of Committee on Economic, Social and Cultural Rights, General Comment 1 (1989): Reporting by States Parties, UN Doc. HRI/GEN/1/Rev.8, p. 9, para. 8.

raise issues, including obstacles to implementation, at the national and international levels. In addition, it depends on the lapse of time between submission and consideration of a report, the quality and fairness of the dialogue, concluding observations and recommendations and any follow-up action that may occur.[3]

THOMAS BUERGENTHAL, THE HUMAN RIGHTS COMMITTEE

5 Max Planck Yearbook of United Nations Law (2001) 341, at 347

[Thomas Buergenthal was a Committee member until 1999, when he was elected to the International Court of Justice.]

...

... [W]hile states have tended to believe that inter-state and individual petition systems would threaten their freedom of action, reporting systems have on the whole not been seen by them as involving much of a risk in that regard. This explains why most of the human rights treaties adopted within the United Nations framework provide for a mandatory reporting system. Dispute resolution mechanisms are less common and usually optional, particularly those that give individuals a right of action, which states see as particularly threatening.

These same considerations entered into the drafting of the measures of implementation of the Covenant and explain why only the reporting requirement is mandatory. It should be emphasized, however, that the assumption that the reporting requirement is 'harmless' is not necessarily valid. Whether or not it is, will frequently depend upon the composition of the supervisory body, its commitment to the cause of human rights, its creativity and the larger political climate within which it exercises its functions. In fact, experience suggests that there is nothing inherently weaker about a reporting system when compared with other measures of implementation than the preconceived notion that quasi-judicial mechanisms of settlement or investigation are by their very nature better suited to achieve results in the human rights field. Whether one or the other implementation measure will produce the desired result in terms of improving a given country's human rights situation which, after all, is the object of the exercise, depends on a variety of factors....

A. The Committee's role

...

The language of Article 40 indicates that those who drafted this provision did not wish to spell out very clearly what powers the Committee had in dealing with State reports....

...

In 1984 it was agreed that individual members could voice their own assessment or observations with regard to a State report at the conclusion of its review by the

[3] *Ibid.*, para. 10.

Committee. These individual observations were then summarized and reproduced in the Committee's annual report to the UN General Assembly. Finally, in 1992, after again reviewing its functions under Article 40(4), the Committee decided that 'observations or comments reflecting the views of the Committee as a whole at the end of the considerations of any State party report should be embodied in a written text, which would be dispatched to the State party concerned as soon as practicable'.

This is the current practice of the Committee. It consists of the adoption by the Committee of so-called 'Concluding Observations'. These observations consist of an assessment of the state's human rights situation in light of the information provided in the State report, the answers the Committee received to the questions posed by its members during the examination of the report, and information available to the members from other sources, all analyzed in terms of the country's obligations under the Covenant. The Committee transmits its concluding observations to the State Party concerned shortly after the hearing; they are also reproduced in the Committee's annual report to the General Assembly....

Concluding observations are adopted by the Committee as a whole in closed meetings after a thorough paragraph-by-paragraph discussion of a draft text prepared by a country rapporteur.... [T]he findings set out in concluding observations must be viewed as authoritative pronouncements on whether a particular state has or has not complied with its obligations under the Covenant. What we have here is a type of Committee 'jurisprudence', which provides some insights about the manner in which the Committee interprets the Covenant.

COMMENT ON PROCEDURES IN EXAMINING REPORTS

Diverse and accurate sources of information are essential to the work of the Committee in scrutinizing the reports of states. But the question of the 'acceptable' sources of information upon which Committee members could draw proved to be a very vexed one during the Committee's early years. Even reference to information contained in other official UN documents was objected to when the reporting procedure began. During the Cold War period there were concerted efforts by experts from the Socialist states to prevent the submission of information by UN agencies, such as the ILO or the Office of the High Commissioner for Refugees. Information from NGOs was resisted and, for a significant period, more or less forced underground, and information from the media was deemed unacceptable. All but the last of these limitations have long since disappeared. Following the procedures pioneered by the Committee on Economic, Social and Cultural Rights, the Committee now receives regular briefings from UN agencies, and holds meetings (usually the first one at each session, and additional informal lunchtime gatherings) at which it is briefed by NGOs on the situation in the countries whose reports it is about to consider.

The formal procedure for examining reports consists of several steps. The first is the appointment of a 'country report task force' of 4–6 members. They have the main responsibility for the conduct of the debate on the report. One of these members will also be designated as the 'country rapporteur'. He or she takes the lead in preparing a list of issues to be sent to the state party. The list, which takes account of information from NGOs and other sources, is adopted by the Committee at the session preceding the official examination, and sent to the reporting state. The latter is requested to provide written replies of not more than 30 pages in length.

An important development over the past decade has been the submission of increasingly high quality 'alternative reports', prepared by civil society groups, and designed to cover largely the same ground as the government report but to provide a much more critical perspective. When such reports are accurate, detailed, and concise they can have a major impact on the process.

During the 'constructive dialogue' with the representatives of the state party the country rapporteur and other task force members take the lead in posing questions, with other members free to join in thereafter. The task force then drafts the concluding observations, based on the dialogue, and taking account of inputs from individual Committee members. The observations are debated in private, adopted, and usually released at the end of the relevant session. The Committee normally deals with no more than 5–6 reports at each of its three-week sessions. Governments are encouraged to inform it of the measures taken in response to the observations, and it has appointed a Special Rapporteur on follow-up to concluding observations. Many states have, however, failed to provide the requested follow-up information and the issue remains a major challenge to the Committee.[4]

One final problem concerns the failure of states to report at all, or to delay greatly the submission of reports. This is a problem which the ICCPR Committee shares with most of the other treaty bodies. In relation to the ICCPR, some states are as much as 20 years behind in their submission of reports. For example, in its 2006 Annual Report the Committee listed Gambia (21 years overdue), Equatorial Guinea (17), Somalia (15), Nicaragua (15), along with others such as Bulgaria (11), Iran (11), Jordan (9), and Spain (7). The reports overdue by 5 years or more also included 20 initial reports, meaning that states had ratified the Covenant but not bothered to submit even an initial report. The Committee observed that this conduct frustrates 'a major objective of the Covenant'.[5] In 2002 the Committee adopted a procedure by which it proceeded to consider the situation in non-reporting states, if necessary in the absence of a report and even a delegation from the country concerned. The results were generally very positive, in terms of encouraging some states to report at long last, and enabling the Committee to adopt concluding observations in relation to some that continued to ignore the procedure.[6]

In the next part of the chapter we consider three case studies of reporting, all from 2006. The most detailed is that of the USA, and the others concern the Democratic Republic of the Congo and the UN Interim Administration Mission in Kosovo.

[4] UN Doc. CCPR/C/SR.2412 (2006), paras. 41–44.

[5] Annual Report 2006, UN Doc. A/61/40 (2005), paras. 70–72.

[6] *Ibid.* The procedure is described in General Comment No. 30 (2002).

CASE STUDY: REPORT OF THE USA TO THE ICCPR COMMITTEE, JULY 2006

The US ratified the ICCPR on 8 June 1992 and the treaty entered into force for the US on 8 September 1992. Its initial report was submitted on time in September 1993 and examined by the Committee in July 1994. It submitted its second and third periodic reports in November 2005, some seven years late in the case of the first of these. In March 2006 a six-page list of issues was drawn up and submitted to the US Government, and a 102 page reply sent to the Committee. The Committee received almost 50 detailed NGO submissions.[7] Excerpts from two of these follow.

A coordinated U.S. NGO response to the U.S. Second and Third Periodic Reports and to CCPR/C/USA/Q/3

http://www.ohchr.org/english/bodies/hrc/docs/ngos/Summary%20final.pdf

This document is a collaborative effort put together by a coalition of NGOs to provide an overview of the various 'shadow reports' each of them had submitted to the Committee.

Constitutional and legal framework...

12. When the U.S. signed the treaty, it simultaneously issued broad RUDs [reservations, understandings and declarations] limiting the scope of its obligations and rendering the treaty unenforceable. In essence, the RUDs strip the ICCPR of all its authority and relevance to the U.S....

...

14. The U.S. ratified the ICCPR in a way that precludes the treaty from having any real effect domestically. Under the "federalism understanding," the U.S. government pledges that it will implement the ICCPR to the extent that it has legislative and judicial jurisdiction, and allow state and local governments to implement the treaty where they have respective jurisdiction. However, the federal government has yet to name the types of matters where state and local governments have unique jurisdiction and therefore specific obligations under the ICCPR treaty. Nor has the federal government taken steps to pass implementing legislation to ensure that all branches of government understand their human rights obligations. Finally, should states and local governments fail to uphold their obligations under the ICCPR, the federal government has not clarified its authority to ensure the treaty is upheld and enforced.

...

17. As a matter of domestic law, millions of individuals in the United States do not have the right to remedy violations of federal civil rights laws as a result of Supreme Court opinions that restrict the private right of action of individuals. The inability to redress these civil rights violations is contrary to Article 2(3).

[7] All these documents are available at http://www.ohchr.org/english/bodies/hrc/hrcs87.htm.

. . .

19. U.S. Supreme Court decisions that have restricted the ability of individuals to obtain compensatory damages against state actors violate Article 2(3) and the failure to compensate an individual for harms caused by civil rights violations means that the remedy is insufficient and thus inappropriate.

Memorandum to Members of the U.N. Human Rights Committee from Human Rights Watch, January 10, 2006

http://www.ohchr.org/english/bodies/hrc/docs/ngos/hrw.doc

(1) The Cloak of Federalism: . . . [T]he United States' system of federalism is used to justify the failures to abide by its treaty obligations.

The United States has consistently failed to develop, monitor, or enforce any national standards for law enforcement personnel and treatment of prisoners and detained persons within the United States. The national government has consistently left such practices up to the individual states and localities, with little to no guidance or monitoring.

This failure is reflected in the report itself. Whereas the report cites a long list of court cases and statutes, it fails to provide any description of the reality on the ground; i.e. how these statutes are being implemented and any how violations of the Convention are monitored. The report does not contain such a description because the federal government does not know — it has not established mechanisms to acquire the necessary information. Moreover, the report heavily emphasizes federal statutes and federal standards, while stating little about the state statutes, standards and enforcement mechanisms — even though law enforcement personnel are almost all state or local, and most prisoners are in state or local facilities.

HRW urges the committee to ask the United States questions about law enforcement and corrections policies and practices within the states, in particular the policies and practices with regard to the treatment of juveniles in the criminal justice system, use of force (including restraint devices and electronic stun devices) by law, sexual abuse of prisoners, the operation of supermaximum prisons, and the treatment of the mentally ill in prison.

(2) Article 2 — Effective Remedies: Courts provide the primary vehicle by which individuals in the United States can seek redress of violations of their rights. Over the last ten years the U.S. government has increasingly restricted access to courts for persons who believe public officials have violated their rights to liberty, due process or to be free from torture or other cruel, inhuman or degrading treatment. Of particular concern are the limitations on prisoners, immigrants, and "enemy combatant" detainees' access to the courts, as highlighted in the coalition's submission under Article 2.

HRW urges the committee to question the United States about the availability of judicial and other effective remedies available to certain groups of persons, including prisoners, immigrants, and detainees in the so-called "war on terror."

DIALOGUE BETWEEN THE HUMAN RIGHTS COMMITTEE AND THE DELEGATION OF THE USA

Second and third periodic reports of the United States of America, 18 July 2006

UN doc. CCPR/C/SR.2380, 27 July 2006

2. *Mr. WAXMAN* (United States of America) said that his Government did not consider questions concerning the war on terrorism, and detention and interrogation outside United States territory to fall within the scope of the Covenant. However, his delegation would use the opportunity to exchange views and share information with the Committee and NGOs. He agreed that measures taken to combat terrorism should not compromise human rights principles. The Al-Qaida attacks on the United States constituted a global threat that did not correspond to existing legal categories....

3. The Government drew a clear distinction between the global threat posed by transnational terrorism and the legal status of his country's armed conflict with Al-Qaida, and its affiliates and supporters. While the Covenant continued to apply to the treatment of prisoners in domestic United States prisons, the law of armed conflict governed United States detention operations in Guantánamo Bay, Afghanistan and Iraq....

4. In accordance with the traditional rule of warfare, enemy fighters could be held until the end of the conflict in order to prevent them from returning to the battlefield. Given the unique nature of the current war, however, his Government had made significant efforts to develop individualized administrative procedures to review each case in Guantánamo and elsewhere. Once the Government was convinced that detainees would have adequate security and humane treatment on returning to their home countries, they were released or returned to those countries.

5. *Mr. HARRIS* (United States of America) said that his Government regretted the delay in submitting its second and third periodic reports.... The Covenant was well known in his country and had been cited in many legal cases. All reports were published on the State Department and other websites. The legislative branch of government was familiar with the Covenant thanks to the ratification process, which had included extensive public discussion. Several training programmes on international treaty obligations for federal judges covered the Covenant.

6. The Government had taken measures to engage individual states in the preparation of the report. Given that United States civil rights protections were enforced through federal and state legal processes, and that the Constitution was applicable to both, the absence of detailed reporting did not, however, indicate a failure to implement the Covenant at state level. Should the Committee have concerns regarding a particular state, it would be helpful if it could inform the Government prior to preparation of the fourth periodic report.

7. His Government had not entered a derogation under article 4 of the Covenant because no actions in his country had derogated from the obligations under the Covenant....

8. [In relation to the scope of article 2 (1) of the Covenant], his delegation found it difficult to accept that the conjunction in the phrase "within its territory and subject to its jurisdiction" could be interpreted as meaning "and/or". That was particularly implausible given that the Covenant negotiators had rejected the proposal to substitute the word "or" for "and". In general, only the parties to a treaty were empowered to give a binding interpretation of its provisions unless the treaty provided otherwise. That was not the case in the Covenant, nor did it authorize the International Court of Justice to issue legally binding interpretations of its provisions.

...

10. His Government respectfully disagreed with the Committee's conclusion that article 7 of the Covenant contained a non-refoulement obligation[8] with respect to torture and cruel, inhuman or degrading treatment or punishment. That conclusion went well beyond the language of article 7 and the scope of the non-refoulement provision contained in article 3 of the Convention against Torture and Other Cruel, Inhuman or Degrading Treatment or Punishment. His Government did not accept that the obligations of a State party under a treaty were affected by non-binding general comments or individual complaints procedures that the State had not accepted....

11. *Ms. HODGKINSON* (United States of America) said that detainees were being held in Guantánamo in order to remove them to a location safe from the continuing battle, while keeping dangerous terrorists from the proximity of the American public. Guantánamo had been the best option as a military base with existing facilities.

...

19. His [sic] country did not transfer detainees to States where it was "more likely than not" that they would be tortured, and did not transport any individual to a third country to be tortured. In accordance with domestic legislation and policy, his delegation would not discuss specific intelligence activities. Nevertheless, many countries, including the United States, had used renditions for decades to transport individuals between countries for law enforcement purposes. Where appropriate, the United States negotiated diplomatic assurances to ensure that individuals transferred from Guantánamo would not be tortured on return to their countries, and that they did not pose a significant threat to the United States or its allies. Diplomatic assurances were not, however, deemed a substitute for a thorough review of whether it was "more likely than not" that a person would be tortured. Rather, they were one of many components considered when analysing each situation.

...

21. *Mr. KIM* (United States of America) said that several laws safeguarded the constitutional rights of all prisoners, including women. The Civil Rights Division of the Department of Justice investigated and prosecuted prison officials found guilty of violating inmates' and detainees' constitutional rights. Between 2001 and 2005, 334 police and prison officials had been charged with misconduct. The Department of Justice also monitored conditions in state local prisons and juvenile detention facilities. Since 2001, it had concluded formal investigations of 42 jails, prisons and

[8] This is an obligation not to return a person to a country in which there is a possibility he will be tortured.

juvenile facilities to ensure that constitutional rights were protected. It was currently monitoring agreements involving 97 such institutions and would remain vigilant in protecting the rights of women in custody.

. . .

27. On the question of surveillance, in some instances it was necessary to gather evidence of an ongoing crime, and alerting the criminal to the fact that the evidence being gathered was not practicable. Nevertheless, numerous safeguards ensured that delayed-notice search warrants were used appropriately. . . .

28. Protection against racial profiling was provided by the Fourteenth Amendment, which prohibited law enforcement actions motivated solely by race or national origin. The current Government had further prohibited the use of racial profiling in federal law enforcement. . . .

. . .

37. *Mr. TIMOFEYEV* (United States of America) said that his country strongly supported the United Nations Guiding Principles on Internal Displacement. His Government's response to the internal displacement caused by Hurricane Katrina had included providing relief assistance to all victims as quickly as possible without discrimination. . . . Despite the extensive displacement caused by the hurricane, the situation did not come within the challenges that the Guiding Principles were designed to address.

. . .

46. [*Mr. KIM* (United States of America)] . . . said that the federal maximum security facility . . . was used only for offenders who were hardened and dangerous criminals. Inmates in the facility had access to a broad range of classes, programmes and services, regular access to the prison chaplain, and five hours of out-of-cell recreation per week. On prison rape, he said that the rape of an inmate was a serious crime, which was vigorously prosecuted. . . . It was not general policy or practice to shackle women giving birth in detention. Inmates were only restrained during labour and delivery in the unlikely event that they posed a threat to themselves, their babies or others around them. Although the use of shackles was not prohibited, allegations of their misuse in federal or state prisons were investigated by the Department of Justice.

47. The Prison Litigation Reform Act contained provisions to curtail frivolous lawsuits by prison inmates (question 22). Civil action for damages could not be brought by a prisoner for mental or emotional injury suffered in custody, without a prior showing of physical injury. A civil action could, however, be brought by a prisoner to redress torture or cruel, inhuman or degrading treatment or punishment. A wide range of alternative avenues was open, through which prisoners could file complaints and express grievances.

. . .

49. Persons under the age of 18 in the United States could be sentenced to life in prison without the possibility of parole (question 24). Lengthy sentences had been imposed on persons who, despite their youth, were hardened criminals who had been convicted of extremely serious crimes and constituted an extreme danger to society. Each state handled the prosecution, rehabilitation, treatment and imprisonment of young offenders pursuant to its own statutes . . . .

...

52. *Mr. O'FLAHERTY* [Committee member] reminded the delegation that some of the Committee's questions had remained unanswered. In some instances, the delegation had failed to acknowledge situations of fact and to analyse the effectiveness of government responses to those situations. A mere statement of how much money had been allocated to addressing a certain situation did not constitute an explanation or justification of government activities....

53. ... Any programme that increased the risk of infection or death raised issues under the Covenant. Research had shown that abstinence programmes increased the risk of contracting HIV, falling pregnant, undergoing unsafe abortions and death. He wished to know what measures were being taken to reduce those risks. The Committee had been informed that 49 per cent of pregnancies in the United States were unplanned. He wished to know if that figure was correct.

...

55. *Mr. LALLAH* [Committee member] ... Although legislative guarantees were in place to protect all prisoners from cruel, inhuman or degrading treatment or punishment, the Committee had been informed that the provisions of that legislation were not always implemented effectively. He wondered what the results had been of the adoption of the Prison Rape Elimination Act, and whether there was any monitoring of the implementation of that legislation.... He asked what efforts were being made to improve conditions for women in prison, and in particular to review the procedure of shackling women detainees during childbirth.

56. *Mr. KÄLIN* [Committee member] said that although the delegation's responses had been clear and enlightening, he regretted its minimalist approach to some issues and its tendency merely to insist that the United States had not violated the Covenant. The examination of a State party's report was not a quasi-judicial procedure. States were required under article 2 not only to respect the Covenant but also to ensure that all individuals enjoyed Covenant rights. The purpose of the Committee's review of periodic reports was to explore with each State how it could move beyond the current stage of implementation of the Covenant, on the understanding that there was always room for improvement when it came to protecting human rights.

57. With regard to continuing differences between the State party and the Committee on how to interpret important parts of the Covenant, he agreed that there was no binding procedure for determining the correct interpretation. However, that did not bar the International Court of Justice (ICJ) from ruling on any questions of law that arose.... Moreover, the Committee was mandated by article 40 to make general comments on the Covenant, so that its findings, though not legally binding, had considerable authoritative status.

58. Several States parties had informed the Committee that they accepted the principle of extraterritorial applicability of the Covenant. Some were even training their armed forces in Covenant rights since they might be stationed abroad not only in combat situations but also as part of a peacekeeping mission to which international humanitarian law no longer applied. It would be very odd if no human rights protection was available under such circumstances and troops were free to behave as they wished.

59. He had taken note of the delegation's statement that there was no rendition to a place where it was "more likely than not" that a person would be tortured. It must therefore unfortunately be inferred that persons could be rendered to a place where the risk of torture was as great as 49 per cent. [O]ther common law jurisdictions . . . had concluded that it could not be considered an appropriate standard under international law or even under common law.

. . .

62. He agreed that the Covenant did not rule out the possibility of excluding criminals from the right to vote. However, it was a matter of concern that such exclusions had led in the United States to the disenfranchisement of millions of voters. In Florida alone an estimated 600,000 people of voting age had been prevented from casting their vote in the last two presidential elections . . . . The right to vote had a collective dimension — the right to have at least some chance of securing a majority.

. . .

64. *Sir Nigel RODLEY* [Committee member] said that some of the delegation's responses had been dogged reaffirmations of positions already stated in the report . . . .

. . .

69. The Committee had been assured that persons in prolonged incommunicado detention were humanely treated in accordance with the prohibition of torture and cruel, inhuman or degrading treatment or punishment. . . . [According to resolutions of the Commission on Human Rights] prolonged incommunicado detention could violate that prohibition. As the United States had invariably joined in the consensus on that resolution, it was unclear how consistent its current interpretation of the scope of article 7 was with its earlier position.

. . .

77. The United States had incarcerated some 2,270,000 people out of a population of approximately 280 million, which was equivalent to 757 per 100,000 members of the population, a ratio that was between 500 and 1,000 per cent higher than for any other developed country. He wondered why such high levels of incarceration were necessary.

. . .

79. *Mr. WIERUSZEWSKI* [Committee member] . . . asked whether the State party had taken any steps to ratify the Convention on the Rights of the Child. The fact that the United States was one of only two States that had failed to ratify the Convention was an unfortunate example of exceptionalism and an impediment to universality.

. . .

83. *Mr. SHEARER* [Committee member] noted with dismay the increasingly strident rejection of the relevance of international law and standard-setting by significant public figures in the United States such as judges and government officials.

. . .

105. *Mr. HARRIS* (United States of America) said that his delegation's views on the scope of certain provisions of the Covenant differed from the views held by the Committee. Each Government had the sovereign right to decide which obligations

to assume under international treaty law. When acceding to a treaty, his Government reviewed all of its provisions carefully to determine which of the resulting obligations could be implemented at both the State and federal levels. Reservations were entered in respect of those provisions whose implementation was considered unfeasible. As a result, the country became bound by a set of obligations set forth in the treaty. It was not for the Committee to change his country's obligations flowing from the Covenant or to issue authoritative guidance in that respect. His Government did not agree with all opinions adopted and jurisprudence developed by the Committee over time.

106. The way in which questions were raised during his delegation's dialogue with the Committee at times appeared to suggest that the United States acted in violation of its obligations, which, in turn, sparked a perhaps overly defensive reaction on the part of the delegation. He hoped that the clarification concerning his Government's approach to its treaty obligations might dispel certain misconceptions and tensions pervading his delegation's dialogue with the Committee and facilitate a more constructive dialogue in the future.

...

CONCLUDING OBSERVATIONS OF THE HUMAN RIGHTS COMMITTEE, UNITED STATES OF AMERICA

UN doc. A/61/40 (Vol. 1) (2006), p. 60[9]

[Eds.: The Committee's document alternates between diagnosis, in regular font, and prescriptions, in bold font.]

Introduction

...

3. The Committee regrets that the State party has not integrated into its report information on the implementation of the Covenant with respect to individuals under its jurisdiction and outside its territory. The Committee notes however that the State party has provided additional material "out of courtesy". The Committee further regrets that the State party, invoking grounds of non-applicability of the Covenant or intelligence operations, refused to address certain serious allegations of violations of the rights protected under the Covenant.

4. The Committee regrets that only limited information was provided on the implementation of the Covenant at the State level.

B. Positive aspects

5–9. The Committee welcomes [various Supreme Court decisions including *Hamdan v. Rumsfeld* (2006) establishing the applicability of common article 3 of the Geneva Conventions; *Roper v. Simmons* (2005), prohibiting the juvenile death

[9] As amended by UN Doc. A/61/40 (Vol.1)/Corr.1 (2006).

penalty; *Atkins v. Virginia* (2002), prohibiting the execution of mentally retarded criminals; and *Lawrence et al. v. Texas* (2003), declaring unconstitutional legislation criminalizing homosexual relations between consenting adults. It also welcomes the National Detention Standards (2000), establishing minimum standards for detention facilities holding Department of Homeland Security detainees.]

C. Principal subjects of concern and recommendations

10. The Committee notes with concern the restrictive interpretation made by the State party of its obligations under the Covenant, as a result in particular of (a) its position that the Covenant does not apply with respect to individuals under its jurisdiction but outside its territory, nor in time of war, despite the contrary opinions and established jurisprudence of the Committee and the International Court of Justice; (b) its failure to take fully into consideration its obligation under the Covenant not only to respect, but also to ensure the rights prescribed by the Covenant; and (c) its restrictive approach to some substantive provisions of the Covenant, which is not in conformity with the interpretation made by the Committee before and after the State party's ratification of the Covenant.

The State party should review its approach and interpret the Covenant in good faith, in accordance with the ordinary meaning to be given to its terms in their context, including subsequent practice, and in the light of its object and purpose. . . .

11. The Committee expresses its concern about the potentially overbroad reach of the definitions of terrorism under domestic law . . .

The State party should ensure that its counter-terrorism measures are in full conformity with the Covenant . . . .

12. . . . **The State party should immediately cease its practice of secret detention and close all secret detention facilities. It should also grant the International Committee of the Red Cross prompt access to any person detained in connection with an armed conflict. The State party should also ensure that detainees, regardless of their place of detention, always benefit from the full protection of the law.**

13. The Committee is concerned with the fact that the State party has authorized for some time the use of enhanced interrogation techniques, such as prolonged stress positions and isolation, sensory deprivation, hooding, exposure to cold or heat, sleep and dietary adjustments, 20-hour interrogations, removal of clothing and deprivation of all comfort and religious items, forced grooming, and exploitation of detainees' individual phobias. Although the Committee welcomes the assurance that, according to the Detainee Treatment Act of 2005, such interrogation techniques are prohibited by the present Army Field Manual on Intelligence Interrogation, the Committee remains concerned that (a) the State party refuses to acknowledge that such techniques, . . . violate . . . article 7 of the Covenant; (b) no sentence has been pronounced against an officer, employee, member of the Armed Forces, or other agent of the United States Government for using harsh interrogation techniques that had been approved; (c) these interrogation techniques may still be authorized or used by other agencies, including intelligence agencies and "private contractors"; and (d) the State party has provided no information to the fact that oversight systems of such agencies have been established to ensure compliance with article 7. . . .

14. ... **The State party should conduct prompt and independent investigations into all allegations concerning suspicious deaths, torture or cruel, inhuman or degrading treatment or punishment inflicted by its personnel (including commanders) as well as contract employees, in detention facilities in Guantanamo Bay, Afghanistan, Iraq and other overseas locations. The State party should ensure that those responsible are prosecuted and punished in accordance with the gravity of the crime. The State party should adopt all necessary measures to prevent the recurrence of such behaviors,....**

...

16. The Committee notes with concern the State party's restrictive interpretation of article 7 of the Covenant according to which it understands (a) that the obligation not to subject anyone to treatment prohibited by article 7 of the Covenant does not include an obligation not to expose them to such treatment by means of transfer, rendition, extradition, expulsion or refoulement; (b) that in any case, it is not under any other obligation not to deport an individual who may undergo cruel, inhuman or degrading treatment or punishment other than torture, as the State party understands the term; and (c) that it is not under any international obligation to respect a non-refoulement rule in relation to persons it detains outside its territory. ... Its concern is deepened by the so far successful invocation of State secrecy in cases where the victims of [renditions] have sought a remedy before the State party's courts (e.g. the cases of *Maher Arar v. Ashcroft* (2006) and *Khaled Al-Masri v. Tenet* (2006)).

The State party should review its position, in accordance with the Committee's general comments No. 20 [and No. 31]. ... The State party should exercise the utmost care in the use of diplomatic assurances and adopt clear and transparent procedures with adequate judicial mechanisms for review before individuals are deported, as well as effective mechanisms to monitor scrupulously and vigorously the fate of the affected individuals. The State party should further recognize that the more systematic the practice of torture or cruel, inhuman or degrading treatment or punishment, the less likely it will be that a real risk of such treatment can be avoided by such assurances, however stringent any agreed follow-up procedures may be.

17. The Committee is concerned that the Patriot Act and the 2005 REAL ID Act of 2005 may bar from asylum and withholding of removal any person who has provided "material support" to a "terrorist organization", whether voluntarily or under duress. It regrets having received no response on this matter from the State party.

...

18. ... **The State party should ensure, in accordance with article 9 (4) of the Covenant, that persons detained in Guantanamo Bay are entitled to proceedings before a court to decide, without delay, on the lawfulness of their detention or order their release. Due process, independence of the reviewing courts from the executive branch and the army, access of detainees to counsel of their choice and to all proceedings and evidence, should be guaranteed in this regard.**

19. The Committee ... is concerned by reports that, following the September 11 attacks, many non-U.S. citizens, suspected to have committed terrorism-related offences have been detained for long periods pursuant to immigration laws with

fewer guarantees than in the context of criminal procedures, or on the basis of the Material Witness Statute only. The Committee is also concerned with the compatibility of the Statute with the Covenant since it may be applied for up-coming trials but also to investigations or proposed investigations.

...

21. The Committee ... notes that section 213 of the Patriot Act, expanding the possibility of delayed notification of home and office searches; section 215 regarding access to individuals' personal records and belongings; and section 505, relating to the issuance of national security letters, still raise issues of concern in relation to article 17 of the Covenant. In particular, the Committee is concerned about the restricted possibilities for the concerned persons to be informed about such measures and to effectively challenge them. Furthermore, the Committee is concerned that the State Party, including through the National Security Agency (NSA), has monitored and still monitors phone, email, and fax communications of individuals both within and outside the U.S., without any judicial or other independent oversight.

... The State party should ensure that any infringement on individual's rights to privacy is strictly necessary and duly authorized by law, and that the rights of individuals to follow suit in this regard are respected.

22. The Committee is concerned with reports that some 50 % of homeless people are African American although they constitute only 12 % of the United States population.

The State party should take measures, including adequate and adequately implemented policies, to bring an end to such de facto and historically generated racial discrimination.

23. The Committee notes with concern reports of de facto racial segregation in public schools, reportedly caused by discrepancies between the racial and ethnic composition of large urban districts and their surrounding suburbs, and the manner in which schools districts are created, funded and regulated. The Committee is concerned that the State party, despite measures adopted, has not succeeded in eliminating racial discrimination such as regarding the wide disparities in the quality of education across school districts in metropolitan areas, to the detriment of minority students. It also notes with concern the State party's position that federal government authorities cannot take legal action if there is no indication of discriminatory intent by state or local authorities.

... The State party should conduct in-depth investigations into the de facto segregation described above and take remedial steps, in consultation with the affected communities.

24. ... **The State party should continue and intensify its efforts to put an end to racial profiling used by federal as well as state law enforcement officials. The Committee wishes to receive more detailed information about the extent to which such practices still persist, as well as statistical data on complaints, prosecutions and sentences in such matters.**

25. The Committee notes with concern allegations of widespread incidence of violent crime perpetrated against persons of minority sexual orientation, including by law enforcement officials. It notes with concern the failure to address such crime

in the legislation on hate crime adopted at the federal level and in many states. It notes with concern the failure to outlaw employment discrimination on the basis of sexual orientation in many states. . . .

26. . . . **In the aftermath of Hurricane Katrina, the State party should increase its efforts to ensure that the rights of the poor, and in particular African-Americans, are fully taken into consideration in the reconstruction plans with regard to access to housing, education and healthcare. . . .**

27. The Committee regrets that it has not received sufficient information on the measures the State party considers adopting in relation to the reportedly nine million undocumented migrants now in the United States. . . . [T]he Committee remains concerned about the increased level of militarization on the southwest border with Mexico.

. . .

28. The Committee regrets that many federal laws which address sex-discrimination are limited in scope and restricted in implementation. The Committee is especially concerned about the reported persistence of employment discrimination against women. (articles 3 and 26)

The State party should take all steps necessary, including at state level, to ensure the equality of women before the law and equal protection of the law, as well as effective protection against discrimination on the ground of sex, in particular in the area of employment.

29. . . . **The State party should review federal and state legislation with a view to restricting the number of offences carrying the death penalty. The State party should also assess the extent to which death penalty is disproportionately imposed on ethnic minorities and on low-income population groups . . . . In the meantime, the State party should place a moratorium on capital sentences, bearing in mind the desirability of abolishing death penalty.**

30. The Committee reiterates its concern about reports of police brutality and excessive use of force by law enforcement officials. . . .

. . .

32. The Committee reiterates its concern that conditions in some maximum security prisons are incompatible with the obligation contained in article 10 (1) of the Covenant to treat detainees with humanity and respect for the inherent dignity of the human person. It is particularly concerned by the practice in some such institutions to hold detainees in prolonged cellular confinement, and to allow them out-of-cell recreation for only five hours per week, in general conditions of strict regimentation in a depersonalized environment. . .

. . .

33. . . . **The Committee reiterates its recommendation that male officers should not be granted access to women's quarters, or at least be accompanied by women officers. The Committee also recommends the State party to prohibit the shackling of detained women during childbirth.**

34. The Committee notes with concern reports that forty-two states and the Federal government have laws allowing persons under the age of eighteen at the time the offence was committed, to receive life sentences, without parole, and that about 2,225 youth offenders are currently serving life sentences in United States

prisons. . . . The Committee is of the view that sentencing children to life sentence without parole is of itself not in compliance with article 24 (1) of the Covenant.

. . .

35. The Committee is concerned that about five million citizens cannot vote due to a felony conviction, and that this practice has significant racial implications. The Committee also notes with concern that the recommendation made in 2001 by the National Commission on Federal Election Reform that all states restore voting rights to citizens who have fully served their sentences has not been endorsed by all states. The Committee is of the view that general deprivation of the right to vote for persons who have received a felony conviction, and in particular those who are no longer deprived of liberty, do not meet the requirements of articles 25 or 26 of the Covenant, nor serves the rehabilitation goals of article 10 (3).

. . .

38. The Committee sets 1st August 2010 as the date for the submission of the fourth periodic report of the United States of America. It requests that the State party's second and third periodic reports and the present concluding observations be published and widely disseminated in the State party, to the general public as well as to the judicial, legislative and administrative authorities, and that the fourth periodic report be circulated for the attention of the non-governmental organizations operating in the country.

39. [T]he State party should submit within one year information on the follow-up given to the Committee's recommendations in paragraphs 12, 13, 14, 16, 20 and 26 above. The Committee requests the State party to include in its next periodic report information on its remaining recommendations and on the implementation of the Covenant as a whole, as well as about the practical implementation of the Covenant, the difficulties encountered in this regard, and the implementation of the Covenant at state level. . . .

. . .

CONCLUDING OBSERVATIONS OF THE HUMAN RIGHTS COMMITTEE, THE DEMOCRATIC REPUBLIC OF CONGO

UN doc. A/61/40 (2006), Vol. 1, p. 40

A. Introduction

[The DRC reported to the Committee in 1987 and 1989. Its next report was not submitted until 2006, a delay which the Committee characterized as a breach of Covenant obligations.]

3. The Committee . . . [regrets that the report] contains only partial information on the implementation of the Covenant in daily life and on the factors and difficulties encountered, focusing rather on the listing of relevant existing legislation or pending draft laws. The Committee also regrets that the delegation was unable to respond in detail to some of the questions and concerns expressed in the list of issues and during the consideration of the report.

4. The Committee has taken note of . . . the fact that the eastern regions of the country — against which the Security Council, in its resolution 1493 (2003), has imposed an arms embargo — are not under the effective control of the Government. It reminds the Government, nonetheless, that the provisions of the Covenant and all the obligations thereunder apply to the territory in its entirety.

B. Positive aspects

5. The Committee is pleased at the democratic transition . . . . [The 2006 elections were the first since 1960.]

. . .

C. Principal subjects of concern and recommendations

8. The Committee notes that, under article 215 of the Constitution, the authority of treaties supersedes that of laws and that . . . the Covenant may be and sometimes is directly invoked before national courts. It regrets, however, that the delegation did not draw its attention to specific cases in which the direct applicability of the Covenant was invoked, or in which the national courts were asked to judge the compatibility of national laws with the Covenant. It also regrets the absence of precise information on the compatibility between customary law, which continues to be practised in some parts of the country, and the provisions of the Covenant.

. . .

9. . . .

The State party should follow up on the Committee's recommendations in [various sets of views issued under the Optional Protocol] and submit a report thereon to the Committee as soon as possible. The State party should also accept a mission by the Committee's special rapporteur to follow up the Views and discuss possible ways and means of implementing the Committee's recommendations, with a view to ensuring more effective cooperation with the Committee.

10. Despite the information from the delegation on several criminal proceedings against human rights violators, the Committee notes with concern the impunity with which many serious human rights violations have been and continue to be committed in the territory of the Democratic Republic of the Congo, even though the identity of the perpetrators of these violations is often known.

. . .

11. The Committee notes with concern the persistent practice of discrimination against women with regard to education, equal rights of both spouses within marriage and the management of family assets. . . . The Committee expresses its concern at the State party's admission that women do not enjoy equal rights with men in the areas of political participation and access to education and employment and at the legislation on forced marriage, which is incompatible with the Covenant.

(a) The State party should speed up the process of adapting the Family Code to international legal instruments . . . .

(b) The State party should increase its efforts to promote women's participation in political affairs and their access to education and employment. In its next report, the State party should inform the Committee of any relevant actions taken and their outcomes.

12. The Committee is concerned at the reports of domestic violence in the Democratic Republic of the Congo and of failures by the authorities to ensure the prosecution of the perpetrators and care of the victims. It reminds the State party that the distinctive nature of such violence calls for the enactment of special legislation.

. . .

13. In view of article 15 of the Constitution, which stipulates that the authorities should ensure the elimination of sexual violence, the Committee is concerned at the number of acts of aggravated assault, including sexual abuse and many cases of rape, committed against women and children in the war zones. It also notes the reports alleging that members of the United Nations Organization Mission in the Democratic Republic of the Congo (MONUC) committed sexual abuse.

The State party should take all necessary steps to strengthen its capacity to protect civilians in the zones of armed conflict, especially women and children. Relevant guidelines should be made available to all members of the armed forces and human rights training should be made compulsory for all members of the State party's armed forces. The State party should prevail upon the States of origin of MONUC troops suspected of having committed acts of sexual abuse to open inquiries into the matter and take the appropriate measures.

14. The Committee remains concerned by the very high maternal and infant mortality rates in the Democratic Republic of the Congo, owing in particular to the difficulty of access to health and family planning services and the low level of education.

The State party should strengthen, in particular, its efforts to increase access to health services. The State party should ensure that health-care personnel receive better training.

. . .

20. The Committee notes that the report (para. 112) and the delegation frankly acknowledge the poor conditions of detention in the country's prisons, including the unacceptable state of sanitation and nutrition and the widespread overcrowding in these institutions.

The State party should ensure that conditions of detention in the country's prisons are compatible with the United Nations Standard Minimum Rules for the Treatment of Prisoners, and that prisoners are adequately fed. The country's prisons should also be modernized.

21. The Committee is concerned at the continued existence of military courts and at the absence of guarantees of a fair trial in proceedings before these courts. It is also concerned at the clearly insufficient number of active judges in the Democratic Republic of the Congo, and at the low pay they receive, which frequently results in their corruption, according to information provided to the Committee. The shortage of judges contributes to the increase in crime and to the failure to prosecute criminal offences.

The State party should abolish military courts for ordinary offences. It should fight the corruption of judges, recruit and train enough judges to ensure the proper administration of justice throughout the territory of the Republic, fight crime and impunity, and allocate sufficient budgetary resources for the administration of justice.

CONCLUDING OBSERVATIONS OF THE HUMAN RIGHTS COMMITTEE ON THE REPORT ON KOSOVO (REPUBLIC OF SERBIA) SUBMITTED BY THE UNITED NATIONS INTERIM ADMINISTRATION MISSION IN KOSOVO (UNMIK)

UN DOC. A/61/40 (2006), Vol. 1, p. 68

A. Introduction

2. The Committee welcomes the submission by [UNMIK] of a report on the human rights situation in Kosovo since 1999, pursuant to a request formulated by the Committee in its concluding observations on the initial report of Serbia and Montenegro in 2004. The Committee notes with appreciation that UNMIK, on the basis of its obligations under Security Council resolution 1244 to protect and promote human rights in Kosovo, prepared its report in general conformity with the harmonized guidelines . . . .

3. The Committee regrets the lack of statistical data and of information on the practical implementation of the Covenant in Kosovo since 1999. It appreciates the dialogue with the UNMIK delegation. The Committee acknowledges with appreciation the efforts undertaken by the Republic of Serbia to facilitate this dialogue and takes note of its introductory statement.

. . .

B. Positive aspects

5. The Committee notes that the Covenant was made part of the applicable law in Kosovo, . . . binding on all persons undertaking public duties or holding public office in Kosovo, and that it was subsequently included in the Constitutional Framework for the Provisional Institutions of Self-Government, promulgated by UNMIK Regulation 2001/9.

. . .

C. Principal subjects of concern and recommendations

9. The Committee expresses its concern that, despite the establishment of various advisory bodies on human rights, as well as of human rights units within the Ministries, human rights concerns are often not sufficiently attended to in the programmes of UNMIK and the PISG [Provisional Institutions of Self-Government].

UNMIK, in cooperation with the PISG, should ensure that institutional structures and capacities are in place and actually utilized to fully integrate human rights in their programmes.

. . .

11. The Committee is concerned about the persistence of male-dominated attitudes within Kosovar society, low representation of women in the Ministries and central institutions of Kosovo, under-reporting of incidents of domestic violence, low numbers of convictions related to domestic violence, limited capacity of victim assistance programmes, and the absence of a comprehensive evaluation of the effectiveness of measures to combat domestic violence.

UNMIK, in cooperation with the PISG, should take prompt and effective measures with the goal of achieving equal representation of women in public offices and intensify training for judges, prosecutors and law enforcement officers on the application of existing laws and other instruments to combat gender discrimination and domestic violence. It should further facilitate the reporting of gender-related crimes, the obtaining of protection orders against perpetrators, enhance victim assistance programmes, and ensure effective remedies.

...

22. The Committee is concerned about the selective use of certain official languages in official dealings and the lack of opportunities for minority children, in particular Roma children, to receive instruction in, and of, their languages.

UNMIK should ensure that the PISG respect the right of minority communities to use any official language of Kosovo in correspondence with public authorities, that all official documents are translated into these languages, that minority children have adequate opportunities to receive instruction in, and of, their language, and that sufficient funds are allocated and teachers trained for that purpose.

23. The Committee requests that the text of the present report and these concluding observations be made public and broadly disseminated throughout Kosovo, and that the next periodic report be made available by relevant authorities to civil society and to non-governmental organizations operating in Kosovo.

QUESTIONS

1. What does the Committee's use of soft terminology such as 'regrets' or 'is concerned' say about the underlying assumptions of the process of 'constructive dialogue' and of the system's aspirations in terms of 'compelling' change at the domestic level?

2. The Committee's concluding observations on the US run to 12 single-spaced pages, with no indication of priorities among the many concerns identified. Should the Committee indicate priority concerns? This would facilitate follow-up and make it easier for others, including domestic actors, to generate pressure for change in relation to the State concerned. Would it, however, undermine the principle of indivisibility of all rights? Would it be likely to lead to the downgrading of certain concerns — such as those relating to women, children and minorities — which might be less likely than anti-terrorism policies and torture to feature among the top concerns identified in relation to most countries?

3. What options are available to the various actors where the Committee and a government clearly disagree on legal interpretation as illustrated by the US position disputing the Committee's view that Article 7 obliges non-refoulement or prohibits renditions, or that Article 2 means the Covenant can apply to US activities 'outside its territory'. Consider the following statement by Prof. José Alvarez, President of the American Society of International Law, in 2006:

> A panoply of UN experts and assorted others — from human rights treaty bodies to the special rapporteur on torture — now routinely make ever more specific legal pronouncements — about such things as the propriety or consequences of

"invalid" treaty reservations, specific interrogation techniques, or states' reliance on diplomatic assurances when engaging in the foreign rendition of suspects. While our Executive contests many of these pronouncements, even the 100 plus lawyers of the U.S. State Department are no match for the sheer quantity and variety of this institutionalized output, which, as amplified by the voice of organizations like Human Rights Watch, may achieve a legitimacy greater than the views of any single nation, including our own.

... [E]ven our relatively nativist judges ... sometimes find themselves citing, as never before, 'soft' law such as General Assembly resolutions, reports of human rights rapporteurs, judgments issued by international criminal courts, or guidelines for multinational corporations — at least by way of interpreting U.S. law and even in some rare cases, the U.S. Constitution.[10]

4. How could the Committee seek to resolve factual disagreements, such as those that result when the US Government simply denies problems described in detail in reports submitted by Human Rights Watch and other groups to the Committee on issues such as prison rape, or the shackling of female prisoners when giving birth?

5. In 2001, Jack Goldsmith warned against the incorporation of the ICCPR in US domestic law: '[A] domesticated ICCPR would generate enormous litigation and uncertainty, potentially changing domestic civil rights law in manifold ways. Human rights protections in the United States are not remotely so deficient as to warrant these costs. Although there is much debate around the edges of domestic civil and political rights law, there is a broad consensus about the appropriate content and scope of this law. This consensus has built up slowly over the past century. It is the product of years of judicial interpretation of domestic statutory and constitutional law, various democratic processes, lengthy and varied experimentation, and a great deal of practical local experience. Domestic incorporation of the ICCPR would threaten to upset this balance. It would constitute a massive, largely standardless delegation of power to federal courts to rethink the content and scope of nearly every aspect of domestic human rights law.'[11] Comment in light of the Committee's 2006 examination of the US report.

6. How important should 'context' be in determining the Committee's approach to a particular country situation? Consider the following assessment of the situation in the DRC:

[There were] 16,850 UN peacekeeping troops in the country, [and] government control of certain areas of the country remained weak, particularly in the rural areas ... where armed groups continued to operate outside of government control. Although the government made progress integrating key institutions such as the army, police, and local administrations, different components of the government sometimes acted independently of, or contrary to, the interests of other components. Civilian authorities generally did not maintain effective control of the security forces, which were poorly trained, poorly paid, undisciplined, and committed

[10] José E. Alvarez, The Internationalization of U.S. Law, 28 October 2006, at http://www.asil.org/aboutasil/documents/ILAweekend061102.pdf.

[11] Jack Goldsmith, 'Should International Human Rights Law Trump US Domestic Law?', 1 Chi. J. Int. L. (2000) 327, at 332.

numerous serious human rights abuses with impunity, particularly in eastern parts of the country. In all areas of the country, the human rights record remained poor, and numerous serious abuses were committed ....[12]

7. What is the significance of the fact that the UN Mission (UNMIK) is presenting a report to the Committee, which, in turn, addresses its concerns and recommendations to the Mission?

3. GENERAL COMMENTS

The text of the ICCPR is characteristically terse and ambiguous about what is intended by 'general comments'. Article 40, after setting forth the undertaking of states to submit periodic reports to the Committee, provides in paragraph 4 that the Committee 'shall study the reports' submitted by states and 'shall transmit its reports, and such *general comments* as it may consider appropriate' to the states (emphasis added). Under paragraph 5, states 'may submit to the Committee observations on any [such] comments'.

Many options existed for the interpretation of this opaque text, depending on how the Committee answered questions like: Should the general comments be directed only to states' reports? Should they vary with the report, addressing concretely this or that problem of this or that state? Alternatively, should they remain truly 'general' in the sense that they do not pertain exclusively to one state but rather address issues of general relevance to all or many states? Should they deal only with the processes of reporting or also with substantive provisions of the Covenant? Should they elaborate upon those substantive provisions?

The following materials focus on such questions of institutional and systemic policy, as well as on a selection of the substantive issues addressed by the Committee in its GCs.

PHILIP ALSTON, THE HISTORICAL ORIGINS OF THE CONCEPT OF 'GENERAL COMMENTS' IN HUMAN RIGHTS LAW

in L. Boisson de Chazournes and V. Gowland Debbas (eds.), The International Legal System in Quest of Equity and Universality: Liber Amicorum Georges Abi-Saab (2001), at 763.

It would be difficult to imagine a more oddly and even misleadingly named instrument than a 'General Comment'. What, after all, could be the jurisprudential value of a mere 'comment', and an explicitly 'general' one at that? Yet the adoption of such

[12] US Department of State, *Country Reports on Human Rights Practices 2005* (2006).

a statement is today one of the potentially most significant and influential tools available to each of the [then] six United Nations human rights treaty bodies . . .

Commentators' assessments cover a broad spectrum. They range from those which seek to portray them as authoritative interpretations of the relevant treaty norms, through others that see them as a de facto equivalent of advisory opinions which are to be treated with seriousness but not more, to highly critical approaches which classify them as broad, unsystematic, statements which are not always well founded, and are not deserving of being accorded any particular weight in legal settings.

Their reception in the world of practice has been equally mixed. Some governments have launched highly critical attacks on them as representing an unwarranted and unacceptable attempt to attribute to treaty provisions a meaning which they do not have. But this is a double-edged sword in the sense that while it reflects governmental dissent both from the specifics of the Comment in question, and challenges the proposition that the committees have a powerful and legitimate interpretative weapon at their disposal, it also draws attention to the relevant interpretation and helps to establish it as a benchmark against which alternative interpretations will be forced to compete at something of a disadvantage. A similarly uneven reception can be discerned in relation to the treatment accorded to General Comments in national courts. While the great majority of courts continue to take little or no notice of them, others are beginning to accord an important role to selected General Comments in the context of judgments which deal with the domestic significance of international standards or with the relevance of international jurisprudence in interpreting domestic constitutional or other legislative provisions. . . .

The task is further complicated by the existence of incentives which lead different actors to present radically differing characterizations of the significance of General Comments, depending upon the context and the broader objectives which each actor has in mind. . . .

The potential significance of General Comments derives from the fact that a great many international human rights norms are notoriously, but unavoidably, vague or open-ended. As Beccaria reminded us, terms such as 'rights' and 'obligations' are, in some respects at least, "abbreviated symbols of a rational argument" rather than ideas in themselves. It is thus hardly surprising that the governments, courts and administrators who are supposed to be applying them can invoke that vagueness, sometimes with conviction, sometimes not, sometimes creatively and other times brazenly, in ways which effectively avoid the 'risk' that the norms might have any significant practical impact. Consistent with this experience, it is often assumed that the challenge of combating the marginalisation of applicable international human rights treaties within the domestic legal order of most states is one that belongs essentially to municipal rather than international lawyers. In other words, overstating the role and importance of the internationalists should be avoided and instead it should be left to the constitutional, administrative, public interest, civil rights, and other lawyers at the national level to consider how best they can enhance use of the international norms within their own domestic systems. But, even apart from the fact that there have been too few sustained efforts of this type, such an abdication of responsibility on the part of international lawyers would be too simple. It is they, along with their diplomatic interlocutors and other participants in the international regime itself, who bear a large responsibility for the extent to which international norms are 'usable' within national legal systems.

. . .

The Improbable Origins of the Concept of 'General Comments'

. . .

By the time the General Assembly got around to debating the Covenants' implementation provisions in 1966, it was envisaged that the Human Rights Committee would submit to the states parties 'its report, and such comments as it may consider appropriate' . . . . At the last moment, however, the sponsors proposed the inclusion of the word 'general' before comments and this was adopted by a vote of 44 in favour, 29 against, and 12 abstentions. Thus there was a strong division of opinion as to whether the examination of states reports under the Covenant should give rise to 'comments' of a general or a specific nature. Nevertheless, neither side ever spelled out precisely what might have been envisaged by their respective formulae. . . . [One precedent, provided by a system of periodic reporting under the UDHR, set up by the Commission on Human Rights in 1956 and terminated in 1981 resulted in 'general' comments which were] largely descriptive, more or less positive in orientation, and determinedly general.

The Human Rights Committee Re-Shapes the Concept

[In its first four years in existence the Committee devoted much time to debating what meaning should be given to the term 'general comments'.] A fundamental East-West difference of opinion emerged, with the Western European experts . . . suggesting that general comments could be country-specific, and violations focused. . . . This was all too much for the East Europeans . . . who rejected both specificity and appraisal and insisted that since the Covenant was not a 'control mechanism' General Comments should be directed to all States parties rather than one.

[In 1980, a Western European member] opened the debate by combining a conciliatory approach to the East European position with an insistence upon the possibility that General Comments might be issue-specific and perhaps even country-specific. He sought to distinguish between violations and the failure to implement. . . . The distinction was, however, patently artificial . . . . He also insisted that General Comments could be used to 'assist States' and to do so 'without expressing condemnations'. But the dual agenda became clear when he suggested in closing that while 'particular States [should not be] singled out' and that '[i]n no case should the Committee report on violations . . . under article 40', nevertheless 'general comments on that subject might be made in exceptional circumstances — for instance, when a State party had admitted violations.'

[The compromise that emerged in October 1980] . . . consisted of two key elements: (1) the principles which would guide the Committee in formulating its General Comments; and (2) the subjects to be addressed. The list of principles provided that:

> They should be addressed to the States parties . . .;
> They should promote co-operation between States parties . . .:
> They should summarize the experience the Committee has gained in considering States reports;
> They should draw the attention of States parties to matters relating to the improvement of the reporting procedure and the implementation of the Covenant;
> They should stimulate activities of States parties . . . .

This non-specific approach, determinedly rooted in the reporting process itself and emphasising its constructive and helpful intent, remains the formal framework invoked even today by the various committees. As to the topics to be addressed, 'general comments could be related, inter alia, to the following subjects':

> The implementation of the obligation to submit reports . . .;
> The implementation of the obligation to guarantee the rights set forth in the Covenant;
> Questions related to the application and the content of individual articles of the Covenant;
> Suggestions concerning co-operation between States parties . . . .

. . .

Drawing Some Conclusions

In many ways the evolution of General Comments from a concept of unclear and contested meaning to a tool of fundamental importance in the armoury of those seeking to promote international human rights law provides a classic case study of the techniques and processes which are so familiar to international lawyers, yet so puzzling and even dubious to many outsiders. The process has several steps. The first is the articulation of a series of clearly incompatible positions or perspectives in the context of diplomatic negotiations over the relevant treaty provisions. These provisions are then 'accommodated' within a draft text on which a compromise is able to be reached based on the incorporation of language which has already been used elsewhere and partly on the inherent open-endedness of the formulation adopted. While the proponents of each of the different starting positions insist that the outcome reflects, or at least fully compatible with, their preferred approach, all recognise implicitly that the key points of contention remain unresolved and that they will need to be addressed again in due course. A different group is then entrusted with the task of determining which interpretation will be adopted. That group (the Human Rights Committee, in this case) undertakes its own debate against a very different background and has a very different make-up. While arguments made in the original debate are cited in defence of the different positions put forward, the outcome actually reflects a significantly changed set of considerations. . . .

COMMENT ON EVOLUTION OF GENERAL COMMENTS

Between 1981 and 2007 the ICCPR Committee adopted 32 General Comments. While most are devoted to specific rights or articles, there are also a number of wide-ranging General Comments which deal with broader issues such as reservations, emergencies, gender equality and State's obligations in general.[13]

A close reading of these Comments and of the evolution in style and substance reflected therein reveals that the Committee's record might usefully be understood by distinguishing four somewhat, but not entirely, separate phases in its approach to General Comments. They are: (i) consolidation of procedures — 1981–1983; (ii) tentative first substantive steps — 1984–1988; (iii) the post-Cold War period in which agreement could be reached on expansive interpretations of key substantive rights; and (iv) since 2000 when the Committee has adopted an important set of umbrella comments designed to consolidate its understanding of the system as a whole.

The output in the first of these phases has been described as 'laconic', 'hesitant', 'bland and uninspiring'.[14] Judged by today's standards this is fair, but in fact the General Comments adopted during this phase played a very important role in consolidating various procedural and organizational innovations in the Committee's working methods which, up until that point, might have been reversible. These included, for example, the 'requirement' that states' representatives make an oral presentation and respond to questions, and the need for states' reports to follow the Committee's reporting guidelines. Neither practice is specifically authorized by the terms of the Covenant. The caution of this phase was also justified by the need to ensure that states would acquiesce in the development of the notion of General Comments.

The second phase saw the adoption of only three Comments but they were considerably longer, more detailed, and reflected more sophisticated legal analysis. The constraints imposed by political factors were nevertheless evident, both in the Comments that were adopted and those that were not (for example, a long-term effort to adopt a draft on the rights of minorities had to be abandoned)[15] and the jurisprudential innovations were rather limited.

[13] The subjects and dates of adoption are as follows: No. 1. Reporting obligations (1981); No. 2. Reporting guidelines (1981); No. 3. Implementation at the national level (1981); No. 4. Equal right of men and women (1981); No. 5. Derogations; No. 6. Right to life (1982); No. 7. Prohibition of torture or cruel, inhuman or degrading treatment or punishment (1982); No. 8. Right to liberty and security of persons (1982); No. 9. Article 10 (Humane treatment of persons deprived of their liberty (1982); No. 10. Freedom of opinion (1983); No. 11. Article 20 (propaganda for war and advocacy of hatred)(1983); No. 12. Right to self-determination (1984); No. 13. Administration of justice (1984); No. 14. Right to life (1984); No. 15. The position of aliens under the Covenant (1986); No. 16. Right to privacy (1998); No. 17. Rights of the child (1989); No. 18. Non-discrimination (1989); No. 19. The family (1990); No. 20. Prohibition of torture, or other cruel, inhuman or degrading treatment or punishment (1992); No. 21. Humane treatment of persons deprived of their liberty (1992); No. 22. Freedom of thought, conscience religion (1993); No. 23. Rights of minorities (1994); No. 24. Reservations (1994); No. 25. Participation in public affairs and the right to vote (1996); No. 26. Continuity of obligations (1997); No. 27. Freedom of movement (1999); No. 28. The equality of rights between men and women (2000); No. 29. Derogations during a state of emergency (2001); No. 30. Reporting obligations (2002); No. 31. The Nature of the General Legal Obligation Imposed on States Parties to the Covenant (2004); No. 32. Right to a Fair Trial (2007). The text of all GCs are published annually. See UN Doc. HRI/GEN/1/Rev.8 (2006).

[14] T. Buergenthal, 'The Human Rights Committee', 5 *Max Planck Yearbook of United Nations Law* (2001) 341, 387.

[15] For the record of debates over an aborted draft, see UN Docs. CCPR/C/SR 590, 607, 618, 633 (1985).

The third phase, after 1989, showed a Committee which had freed itself from most of the limitations that flowed from competing socialist and liberal perceptions both of the nature of human rights and of the appropriate role of treaty bodies and from the constraints that flowed from the early understandings of the limited functions of General Comments. It adopted expansive Comments on the rights of the child, non-discrimination, and the family and it marked a definitive break with the past by adopting revised Comments on Articles 7 and 10 of the Covenant which replaced the very tentative efforts it had made during the first phase with much longer and more assertive texts. The end of the influence of the Cold War was also strongly underlined by the range of topics on which detailed and progressive Comments were adopted after 1992. In particular, the Comments on freedom of expression (1993), minorities (1994), the right to vote and take part in government (1996), and freedom of movement (1999) could never have been agreed during the earlier phases and each contains very important jurisprudential elements.

The fourth phase, since 2000, has seen the Committee consolidate its views on the system as a whole with detailed and expansive statements on gender equality, rights in emergency contexts, reporting obligations and the legal nature of state's obligations under the Covenant.

ILLUSTRATIONS OF GENERAL COMMENTS

In reading the sampling of GCs that follows you should re-read the relevant articles of the Covenant.[16] Consider: the functions played by GCs, what their evolution reflects in terms of the changing roles of the Covenant and of the Committee, what they reveal about the Committee's understanding of the Covenant, the significance of GCs in expanding the interpretive reach of the Covenant and its norms, and the relevance of GCs in relation to the human rights movement in general.

1. Phase 1 (1981–1983)

> The purpose of [the Committee's] general comments is to make this experience available for the benefit of all States parties in order to promote their further implementation of the Covenant; to draw their attention to insufficiencies disclosed by a large number of reports; to suggest improvements in the reporting procedure and to stimulate the activities of these States and international organizations in the promotion and protection of human rights. . . .[17]

GC No. 2, 'Reporting Guidelines' (1981):

> 3. The Committee considers that the reporting obligation embraces not only the relevant laws and other norms relating to the obligations under the Covenant

[16] In addition to those excerpted below, other GCs feature elsewhere in the book. See e.g.: (1) GC No. 26 at p. 888, *infra*, on a states withdrawal from the Covenant; (2) GC No. 22 at p. 590, *supra*, on freedom of religion; (3) GC No. 24 at p. 1144, *infra*, on reservations to the ICCPR; (4) GC No. 29 at p. 389, *supra*, on states of emergency; and (5) GC No. 13 at p. 436, *supra*, on the administration of justice.

[17] UN Doc. HRI/GEN/1/Rev.8 (2006).

but also the practices and decisions of courts and other organs of the State party as well as further relevant facts which are likely to show the degree of the actual implementation and enjoyment of the rights recognized in the Covenant, the progress achieved and factors and difficulties in implementing the obligations under the Covenant.

GC No. 3, 'Implementation at the National Level' (1981):

1. The Committee notes that article 2 of the Covenant generally leaves it to the States parties concerned to choose their method of implementation in their territories within the framework set out in that article. It recognizes, in particular, that the implementation does not depend solely on constitutional or legislative enactments, which in themselves are often not per se sufficient. The Committee considers it necessary to draw the attention of States parties to the fact that the obligation under the Covenant is not confined to the respect of human rights, but that States parties have also undertaken to ensure the enjoyment of these rights to all individuals under their jurisdiction. This aspect calls for specific activities by the States parties to enable individuals to enjoy their rights. This is obvious in a number of articles, but in principle this undertaking relates to all rights set forth in the Covenant.

2. In this connection, it is very important that individuals should know what their rights under the Covenant (and the Optional Protocol, as the case may be) are and also that all administrative and judicial authorities should be aware of the obligations which the State party has assumed under the Covenant. To this end, the Covenant should be publicized in all official languages of the State and steps should be taken to familiarize the authorities concerned with its contents as part of their training. It is desirable also to give publicity to the State party's cooperation with the Committee.

2. Phase 2 (1984–1988)

GC No. 14, 'Article 6' (1984) builds on *GC No. 6, 'Article 6'* (1982). Both address the right to life, and their orientation reflects the revived influence of Cold War concerns, as well efforts to explore how the ICCPR Covenant might relate to economic and social rights type concerns. The Committee did not take up either of these issues systematically in its later work. Consider the following excerpt from *GC No. 6*:

1. The right to life enunciated in article 6 of the Covenant has been dealt with in all State reports. It is the supreme right from which no derogation is permitted even in time of public emergency which threatens the life of the nation (art. 4). However, the Committee has noted that quite often the information given concerning article 6 was limited to only one or other aspect of this right. It is a right which should not be interpreted narrowly.

...

5. Moreover, the Committee has noted that the right to life has been too often narrowly interpreted. The expression 'inherent right to life' cannot properly be understood in a restrictive manner, and the protection of this right requires that States adopt positive measures. In this connection, the Committee considers that it

would be desirable for States parties to take all possible measures to reduce infant mortality and to increase life expectancy, especially in adopting measures to eliminate malnutrition and epidemics.

Compare these provisions from the earlier GC with *GC No. 14*, two years later:

3. While remaining deeply concerned by the toll of human life taken by conventional weapons in armed conflicts, the Committee has noted that, during successive sessions of the General Assembly, representatives from all geographical regions have expressed their growing concern at the development and proliferation of increasingly awesome weapons of mass destruction, which not only threaten human life but also absorb resources that could otherwise be used for vital economic and social purposes, particularly for the benefit of developing countries, and thereby for promoting and securing the enjoyment of human rights for all.

4. The Committee associates itself with this concern. It is evident that the designing, testing, manufacture, possession and deployment of nuclear weapons are among the greatest threats to the right to life which confront mankind today. This threat is compounded by the danger that the actual use of such weapons may be brought about, not only in the event of war, but even through human or mechanical error or failure.

...

6. The production, testing, possession, deployment and use of nuclear weapons should be prohibited and recognized as crimes against humanity.

7. The Committee accordingly, in the interest of mankind, calls upon all States, whether Parties to the Covenant or not, to take urgent steps, unilaterally and by agreement, to rid the world of this menace.

❁ ❁ ❁

GC No. 16, 'Article 17' (1988) (p. 21) elaborates the article's reference to interference with privacy. The following excerpt illustrates the Committee's preparedness to go into substantive issues in more depth and to read more into the terms of the Covenant than it had been prepared to do at the outset:

10. The gathering and holding of personal information on computers, databanks and other devices, whether by public authorities or private individuals or bodies, must be regulated by law. Effective measures have to be taken by States to ensure that information concerning a person's private life does not reach the hands of persons who are not authorized by law to receive, process and use it, and is never used for purposes incompatible with the Covenant. In order to have the most effective protection of his private life, every individual should have the right to ascertain in an intelligible form, whether, and if so, what personal data is stored in automatic data files, and for what purposes. Every individual should also be able to ascertain which public authorities or private individuals or bodies control or may control their files. If such files contain incorrect personal data or have been collected or processed contrary to the provisions of the law, every individual should have the right to request rectification or elimination.

3. Phase 3 (1989–1999)

GC No. 18, 'Non-discrimination' (1989) deals with several provisions of the Covenant — Articles 2, 3 and 26 among others — that state the principle of non-discrimination. Compare it with GC No. 28 on equality, adopted during the fourth phase.

> 7. ... [T]he Committee believes that the term 'discrimination' as used in the Covenant should be understood to imply any distinction, exclusion, restriction or preference which is based on any ground such as race, colour, sex, language, religion, political or other opinion, national or social origin, property, birth or other status, and which has the purpose or effect of nullifying or impairing the recognition, enjoyment or exercise by all persons, on an equal footing, of all rights and freedoms.
>
> ...
>
> 10. The Committee also wishes to point out that the principle of equality sometimes requires States parties to take affirmative action in order to diminish or eliminate conditions which cause or help to perpetuate discrimination prohibited by the Covenant. For example, in a State where the general conditions of a certain part of the population prevent or impair their enjoyment of human rights, the State should take specific action to correct those conditions. Such action may involve granting for a time to the part of the population concerned certain preferential treatment in specific matters as compared with the rest of the population. However, as long as such action is needed to correct discrimination in fact, it is a case of legitimate differentiation under the Covenant.
>
> ...
>
> 12. ... In the view of the Committee, article 26 does not merely duplicate the guarantee already provided for in article 2 but provides in itself an autonomous right. ... [T]he application of the principle of non-discrimination contained in article 26 is not limited to those rights which are provided for in the Covenant.
>
> 13. Finally, the Committee observes that not every differentiation of treatment will constitute discrimination, if the criteria for such differentiation are reasonable and objective and if the aim is to achieve a purpose which is legitimate under the Covenant.

❁ ❁ ❁

GC No. 20, 'Article 7' (1992) concerns torture and cruel or degrading treatment or punishment. Note the detail in the following provisions that bear on implementation.

> 11. ... To guarantee the effective protection of detained persons, provisions should be made for detainees to be held in places officially recognized as places of detention and for their names and places of detention, as well as for the names of persons responsible for their detention, to be kept in registers readily available and accessible to those concerned, including relatives and friends. To the same effect, the time and place of all interrogations should be recorded, together with the names of all those present and this information should also be available for

purposes of judicial or administrative proceedings. Provisions should also be made against incommunicado detention. In that connection, States parties should ensure that any places of detention be free from any equipment liable to be used for inflicting torture or ill-treatment. The protection of the detainee also requires that prompt and regular access be given to doctors and lawyers and, under appropriate supervision when the investigation so requires, to family members.

12. It is important for the discouragement of violations under article 7 that the law must prohibit the use of admissibility in judicial proceedings of statements or confessions obtained through torture or other prohibited treatment.

...

15. The Committee has noted that some States have granted amnesty in respect of acts of torture. Amnesties are generally incompatible with the duty of States to investigate such acts; to guarantee freedom from such acts within their jurisdiction; and to ensure that they do not occur in the future. States may not deprive individuals of the right to an effective remedy, including compensation and such full rehabilitation as may be possible.

4. Phase 4 (2000–present)

GC No. 28, 'Equality of rights between men and women' (2000):

3. The obligation to ensure to all individuals the rights recognized in the Covenant, established in articles 2 and 3 of the Covenant, requires that States parties take all necessary steps to enable every person to enjoy those rights. These steps include the removal of obstacles to the equal enjoyment of such rights, the education of the population and of State officials in human rights, and the adjustment of domestic legislation so as to give effect to the undertakings set forth in the Covenant. The State party must not only adopt measures of protection, but also positive measures in all areas so as to achieve the effective and equal empowerment of women. States parties must provide information regarding the actual role of women in society so that the Committee may ascertain what measures, in addition to legislative provisions, have been or should be taken to give effect to these obligations, what progress has been made, what difficulties are encountered and what steps are being taken to overcome them.

4. States parties are responsible for ensuring the equal enjoyment of rights without any discrimination. Articles 2 and 3 mandate States parties to take all steps necessary, including the prohibition of discrimination on the ground of sex, to put an end to discriminatory actions, both in the public and the private sector, which impair the equal enjoyment of rights.

5. Inequality in the enjoyment of rights by women throughout the world is deeply embedded in tradition, history and culture, including religious attitudes. The subordinate role of women in some countries is illustrated by the high incidence of prenatal sex selection and abortion of female foetuses. States parties should ensure that traditional, historical, religious or cultural attitudes are not used to justify violations of women's right to equality before the law and to equal enjoyment of all Covenant rights. States parties should furnish appropriate information on those aspects of tradition, history, cultural practices and religious attitudes which jeopardize, or may jeopardize, compliance with article 3, and indicate what measures they have taken or intend to take to overcome such factors.

GC No. 31, 'Nature of the General Legal Obligation' (2004):

2. While article 2 is couched in terms of the obligations of State parties towards individuals as the right-holders under the Covenant, every State party has a legal interest in the performance by every other State party of its obligations. This follows from the fact that the "rules concerning the basic rights of the human person" are *erga omnes* obligations.... *[The Committee then urges States parties to make use of the so far moribund inter-state complaints procedure provided for in Article 41.]* To draw attention to possible breaches of Covenant obligations by other States parties and to call on them to comply with their Covenant obligations should, far from being regarded as an unfriendly act, be considered as a reflection of legitimate community interest.

...

4. The obligations of the Covenant in general and article 2 in particular are binding on every State party as a whole. All branches of government (executive, legislative and judicial), and other public or governmental authorities, at whatever level (national, regional or local) are in a position to engage the responsibility of the State party. The executive branch that usually represents the State party internationally, including before the Committee, may not point to the fact that an action incompatible with the provisions of the Covenant was carried out by another branch of government as a means of seeking to relieve the State party from responsibility for the action and consequent incompatibility....

...

13. Article 2, paragraph 2, requires that States parties take the necessary steps to give effect to the Covenant rights in the domestic order. It follows that, unless the Covenant's rights are already protected by their domestic laws or practices, States parties are required on ratification to make such changes to domestic laws and practices as are necessary to ensure their conformity with the Covenant. Where there are inconsistencies between domestic law and the Covenant, article 2 requires that the domestic law or practice be changed to meet the standards imposed by the Covenant's substantive guarantees. Article 2 allows a State party to pursue this in accordance with its own domestic constitutional structure and accordingly does not require that the Covenant be directly applicable in the courts, by incorporation of the Covenant into national law. The Committee takes the view, however, that Covenant guarantees may receive enhanced protection in those States where the Covenant is automatically or through specific incorporation part of the domestic legal order. The Committee invites those States parties in which the Covenant does not form part of the domestic legal order to consider incorporation of the Covenant to render it part of domestic law to facilitate full realization of Covenant rights as required by article 2.

14. The requirement under article 2, paragraph 2, to take steps to give effect to the Covenant rights is unqualified and of immediate effect. A failure to comply with this obligation cannot be justified by reference to political, social, cultural or economic considerations within the State.

15. Article 2, paragraph 3, requires that in addition to effective protection of Covenant rights States parties must ensure that individuals also have accessible and effective remedies to vindicate those rights. Such remedies should be appropriately adapted so as to take account of the special vulnerability of certain categories of person, including in particular children. The Committee attaches importance to States parties' establishing appropriate judicial and administrative

mechanisms for addressing claims of rights violations under domestic law. The Committee notes that the enjoyment of the rights recognized under the Covenant can be effectively assured by the judiciary in many different ways, including direct applicability of the Covenant, application of comparable constitutional or other provisions of law, or the interpretive effect of the Covenant in the application of national law. Administrative mechanisms are particularly required to give effect to the general obligation to investigate allegations of violations promptly, thoroughly and effectively through independent and impartial bodies. National human rights institutions, endowed with appropriate powers, can contribute to this end. A failure by a State party to investigate allegations of violations could in and of itself give rise to a separate breach of the Covenant. Cessation of an ongoing violation is an essential element of the right to an effective remedy.

16. Article 2, paragraph 3, requires that States parties make reparation to individuals whose Covenant rights have been violated. Without reparation to individuals whose Covenant rights have been violated, the obligation to provide an effective remedy, which is central to the efficacy of article 2, paragraph 3, is not discharged. In addition to the explicit reparation required by articles 9, paragraph 5, and 14, paragraph 6, the Committee considers that the Covenant generally entails appropriate compensation. The Committee notes that, where appropriate, reparation can involve restitution, rehabilitation and measures of satisfaction, such as public apologies, public memorials, guarantees of non-repetition and changes in relevant laws and practices, as well as bringing to justice the perpetrators of human rights violations.

17. In general, the purposes of the Covenant would be defeated without an obligation integral to article 2 to take measures to prevent a recurrence of a violation of the Covenant. . . .

18. . . . [W]here public officials or State agents have committed violations of the Covenant rights referred to in [Articles 6, 7 or 9], the States parties concerned may not relieve perpetrators from personal responsibility, as has occurred with certain amnesties (see general comment No. 20 (44)) and prior legal immunities and indemnities. Furthermore, no official status justifies persons who may be accused of responsibility for such violations being held immune from legal responsibility. Other impediments to the establishment of legal responsibility should also be removed, such as the defence of obedience to superior orders or unreasonably short periods of statutory limitation in cases where such limitations are applicable. States parties should also assist each other to bring to justice persons suspected of having committed acts in violation of the Covenant that are punishable under domestic or international law.

19. The Committee further takes the view that the right to an effective remedy may in certain circumstances require States parties to provide for and implement provisional or interim measures to avoid continuing violations and to endeavour to repair at the earliest possible opportunity any harm that may have been caused by such violations.

QUESTIONS

1. Today's General Comments go well beyond the literal text of the ICCPR. Using examples taken from above, how would you describe the Committee's approach? Making

the text operational by drawing reasonable inferences from it? Interpretation in light of the interaction among different provisions or of the broad object and purpose of the ICCPR as a whole? Creative development in the light of changing world conditions and ideologies? Or working out a common understanding that emerges from the approach adopted in interpreting particular provisions by a representative cross-section of states parties to the ICCPR?

2. The drafting of General Comments now takes place in public meetings of the Committee and, in practice, suggestions are put forward by NGOs and UN agencies. In 2006 Canada called for standardization of the drafting procedures, and for steps to formalize the participation of NGOs and states parties in the process. What role do you think states should play? Should they, for example, have a right to put forward a draft, to make specific suggestions on key issues, or to comment on the Committee's own draft?

3. General Comments are regularly invoked by: UN bodies such as the Human Rights Council and the General Assembly, the International Court of Justice, national courts and, on occasion, the regional human rights courts. What authority should they be accorded and from whence does that authority derive? Is it desirable for the Committee to have a power of authoritative interpretation of the ICCPR?

4. In paragrapgh 14 of GC No. 31, the Committee says the requirement in Article 2(2) to 'take the necessary steps ... to adopt such legislative or other measures as may be necessary to give effect to the rights' is 'unqualified and of immediate effect'. It goes on to state that 'failure to comply with this obligation cannot be justified by reference to ... economic considerations within the State'.

Consider the following account of the Committee's practice in this regard:

> [T]he HRC has not generally accepted economic, relativist arguments. For example in *Mukong v Cameroon* (458/91), it refused to accept that economic hardship and budgetary considerations could excuse the State from liability for the atrocious prison conditions suffered by the author. In *Lubuto v. Zambia* (390/90), economic hardship could not justify the delay in the author's appeal of his conviction. Finally, in its General Comment 21 on Article 10, the HRC noted that the obligation to treat detainees with respect for their dignity 'cannot be dependent on the material resources available in the State party.' Underdevelopment cannot therefore justify overcrowding in prisons, or the failure to provide adequate resources to detainees. On the other hand, in *Aumeeruddy-Cziffra et al v Mauritus* (35/78), the HRC did state that the level of protection required for families under article 23 may vary according to 'different social, economic, political and cultural conditions and traditions.' This may indicate that economic relativism does apply, perhaps uniquely within the ICCPR, to the level of entitlement entailed in article 23 rights. However, economic relativism does not generally apply to ICCPR rights unlike the rights in the ICESCR.[18]

[18] Joseph, Schultz, and Castan, *The International Covenant on Civil and Political Rights: Cases, Materials, and Commentary* (2nd edn. 2004), at 44.

Compare this formal approach with the following observation by Ken Roth, Executive Director of Human Rights Watch:

> ... tradeoffs of scarce resources can arise in the realm of civil and political rights. Building prisons or creating a judicial system can be expensive. However, my experience has been that international human rights organizations implicitly recognize these tradeoffs by avoiding recommendations that are costly. For example, Human Rights Watch in its work on prison conditions routinely avoids recommending large infrastructure investments. Instead, we focus on improvements in the treatment of prisoners that would involve relatively inexpensive policy changes. Similarly, our advocacy of due process in places such as Rwanda with weak and impoverished judicial systems implicitly takes account of the practical limitations facing the country leading us to be more tolerant of prosecutorial compromises such as *gacaca* courts than we would be in a richer country.[19]

How realistic is the Committee's approach? Is an absolutist approach which precludes consideration of economic resources likely to succeed? Is Roth's approach compatible with that espoused by the Committee?

COMMENT ON SOME CONTROVERSIES ADDRESSED IN GCs

In some important instances GCs have been the Committee's chosen vehicle for propounding far-reaching and often controversial, interpretations of the Covenant. Consider the following examples relating to reservations, succession and jurisdiction. The GC on reservations was adopted after the United States had made its ratification of the Covenant subject to a significant number of reservations, and before a US expert had been elected to the Committee. Ironically, the first such member was Louis Henkin, who had previously argued that it would have been preferable for the US not to become a party at all rather than to have ratified subject to reservations, understandings and declarations which he found highly problematic.

(i) Reservations: GC No. 24 (1994)[20]

> 8. ... [P]rovisions in the Covenant that represent customary international law (and a fortiori when they have the character of peremptory norms) may not be the subject of reservations. Accordingly, a State may not reserve the right to engage in slavery, to torture, to subject persons to cruel, inhuman or degrading treatment or punishment, to arbitrarily deprive persons of their lives, to arbitrarily arrest and detain persons, to deny freedom of thought, conscience and religion, to presume a person guilty unless he proves his innocence, to execute pregnant women or children, to permit the advocacy of national, racial or religious hatred, to deny to persons of marriageable age the right to marry, or to deny to minorities the right to

[19] Kenneth Roth, 'Defending Economic, Social and Cultural Rights: Practical Issues Faced by an International Human Rights Organization', 26 Hum. Rts. Q. 63 (2004).

[20] Note that more detailed excerpts from this GC appear *infra* at p. 1144.

enjoy their own culture, profess their own religion, or use their own language. And while reservations to particular clauses of article 14 may be acceptable, a general reservation to the right to a fair trial would not be.

...

18. It necessarily falls to the Committee to determine whether a specific reservation is compatible with the object and purpose of the Covenant. This is in part because, as indicated above, it is an inappropriate task for States parties in relation to human rights treaties, and in part because it is a task that the Committee cannot avoid in the performance of its functions. In order to know the scope of its duty to examine a State's compliance under article 40 or a communication under the first Optional Protocol, the Committee has necessarily to take a view on the compatibility of a reservation with the object and purpose of the Covenant and with general international law. Because of the special character of a human rights treaty, the compatibility of a reservation with the object and purpose of the Covenant must be established objectively, by reference to legal principles, and the Committee is particularly well placed to perform this task....

Nowak notes that, prior to the adoption of GC No. 24, several members of the Committee had expressed the view that it was not authorized to review the validity of reservations. He notes that several governments — in particular France, the US, and the UK — expressly objected to some of the conclusions reached in the GC, and that some academic commentators have also been critical.[21] Nowak characterizes GC No. 24 as 'one of the most important legal documents ever adopted on the controversial question of reservations to human rights treaties'. While supportive of the Committee's conclusions as to its own competence, he questions the broad range of reasons given to justify the incompatibility. 'First of all, the Committee made no clear distinction between customary international law and peremptory norms (ius cogens).... Secondly, the list of provisions regarded as representing customary law seems far too broad.... [Since rights relating to self-determination, marriage, minorities and incitement to hatred] have in fact been the subject of reservations by a considerable number of States, it is not surprising that Governments objected to this comprehensive list which, according to the Committee, may not be the subject of reservations'.[22] In written comments, submitted in 1995, France rejected the 'entire analysis' contained in paragraph 18 and stated that:

As for the opinion that the Committee is particularly well placed to take decisions on the compatibility of a reservation with the object and purpose of the Covenant, France points out that the Committee, like any other treaty body or similar body established by agreement, owes its existence exclusively to the treaty and has no powers other than those conferred on it by the States parties; it is therefore for the latter, and for them alone, unless the treaty states otherwise, to decide whether a reservation is incompatible with the object and purpose of the treaty.[23]

[21] See p. 1143, *infra.*

[22] Nowak, *UN Covenant on Civil and Political Rights: ICCPR Commentary* (2nd edn. 2005) pp. XXXI–XXXIII.

[23] UN Doc. CCPR A/51/40 (1995), Annex VI, para. 14.

(ii) Succession and denunciation: GC No. 26 (1997)

Two very important issues in relation to treaty law concern whether (i) a successor state is automatically bound by the international human rights treaty obligations of its predecessor; and (ii) whether a state which is a party to the ICCPR can denounce it, and thus be no longer bound by its provisions. The text of the Covenant is silent on both issues, although Article 12 of the first Optional Protocol to the ICCPR explicitly provides for a state to denounce the Protocol.

GC No. 26, Continuity of obligations (1997)

> 1. [The Committee observes that the issue is governed by customary law as reflected in the Vienna Convention on the Law of Treaties]. On this basis, the Covenant is not subject to denunciation or withdrawal unless it is established that the parties intended to admit the possibility of denunciation or withdrawal or a right to do so is implied from the nature of the treaty.
>
> 2. [The Committee notes that denunciation is specifically provided for in relation to (i) the inter-state procedure under Article 41(2); (ii) the first Optional Protocol to the ICCPR; and (iii) the International Convention on the Elimination of All Forms of Racial Discrimination, adopted before the ICCPR.] It can therefore be concluded that the drafters of the Covenant deliberately intended to exclude the possibility of denunciation. The same conclusion applies to the Second Optional Protocol in the drafting of which a denunciation clause was deliberately omitted.
>
> 3. Furthermore, it is clear that the Covenant is not the type of treaty which, by its nature, implies a right of denunciation. Together with the simultaneously prepared and adopted [ICESCR], the Covenant codifies in treaty form the universal human rights enshrined in the [UDHR], the three instruments together often being referred to as the "International Bill of Human Rights". As such, the Covenant does not have a temporary character typical of treaties where a right of denunciation is deemed to be admitted, notwithstanding the absence of a specific provision to that effect.
>
> 4. The rights enshrined in the Covenant belong to the people living in the territory of the State party. The Human Rights Committee has consistently taken the view, as evidenced by its long-standing practice, that once the people are accorded the protection of the rights under the Covenant, such protection devolves with territory and continues to belong to them, notwithstanding change in government of the State party, including dismemberment in more than one State or State succession or any subsequent action of the State party designed to divest them of the rights guaranteed by the Covenant.
>
> 5. The Committee is therefore firmly of the view that international law does not permit a State which has ratified or acceded or succeeded to the Covenant to denounce it or withdraw from it.

The succession issue arose in relation to some of the successor states to the former Soviet Union and Hong Kong and Macau. While most of the former group accepted the continuing applicability of the ICCPR obligations, they nonetheless deposited instruments of succession, rather than assuming the automaticity of the process.[24] Kazakhstan was the exception, but the Committee continued to treat it as a state party and request reports. Eventually, in 2006, Kazakhstan ratified the Covenant. When China resumed its control of Hong Kong and Macau in 1997 it also agreed to succeed to the pertinent ICCPR obligations of the United Kingdom (in relation to Hong Kong) and Portugal (Macau), and has since presented a report to the ICCPR Committee on compliance with the Covenant in those two territories.

Denunciation was more complex. The GC was adopted in October 1997 in direct response to North Korea's purported denunciation of the ICCPR, lodged with the UN in August 1997. North Korea did not pursue it plans, and subsequently presented a report to the Committee. But other states had also previously contemplated denunciation. Thus, for example, the Netherlands considered withdrawal after decisions of the ICCPR Committee on non-discrimination in relation to social security law which had major financial implications.[25]

(iii) Jurisdiction

Consider the following extracts from GC No. 31 on the 'Nature of the General Legal Obligation' (2004) in light of the objections raised by the US in its reporting to the Committee, excerpted above.[26]

> 10. States parties are required by article 2, paragraph 1, to respect and to ensure the Covenant rights to all persons who may be within their territory and to all persons subject to their jurisdiction. This means that a State party must respect and ensure the rights laid down in the Covenant to anyone within the power or effective control of that State party, even if not situated within the territory of the State party.... This principle also applies to those within the power or effective control of the forces of a State party acting outside its territory, regardless of the circumstances in which such power or effective control was obtained, such as forces constituting a national contingent of a State party assigned to an international peacekeeping or peace-enforcement operation.
>
> 11. As implied in general comment No. 29, the Covenant applies also in situations of armed conflict to which the rules of international humanitarian law are applicable. While, in respect of certain Covenant rights, more specific rules of international humanitarian law may be especially relevant for the purposes of the interpretation of Covenant rights, both spheres of law are complementary, not mutually exclusive.
>
> 12. Moreover, the article 2 obligation requiring that States parties respect and ensure the Covenant rights for all persons in their territory and all persons under their control entails an obligation not to extradite, deport, expel or otherwise remove a person from their territory, where there are substantial grounds for believing that there is a real risk of irreparable harm, such as that contemplated by articles 6 and 7 of the Covenant, either in the country to which removal is to be effected or in any country to which the person may subsequently be removed.

[24] One Committee member subsequently indicated in remarks under an Optional Protocol case that he agreed with para. 4 of GC No. 26 'as a matter of policy, but I cannot agree with it as a statement of a rule of customary international law' (Mr Ando in *Kuok Koi v Portugal*, No. 925/00).

[25] See *Broeks v The Netherlands*, No. 172/1984; and generally Nowak, note 22 *supra*, XXXVI.

[26] See p. 862, *supra*.

Consider the following defence of the Committee's position by Nowak:

> States are basically responsible only for the legal security of persons who are located on their territory and subject to their sovereign authority. This means, on the one hand, that States parties are not responsible for violations of the Covenant by persons who are on their territory but not subject to their jurisdiction (e.g., for actions by international organizations against their officials or for actions by occupation troops). On the other hand, this means that States are not responsible for violations against persons over whom they have personal jurisdiction (in particular, nationals), when such violations take place on foreign territory and are attributable to some other sovereign. The motive behind the formulation of Art. 2(1) was to preclude this responsibility of States parties.
>
> When States parties, however, take *actions on foreign territory* that violate the rights of persons subject to their sovereign authority, it would be contrary to the purpose of the Covenant if they could not be held responsible. It is irrelevant whether these actions are permissible under general international law (e.g., sovereign act by diplomatic or consular representatives, or in border traffic or by border officials in customs-free zones; actions by occupation forces in accordance with the rules of the law of war) or constitute illegal interference, such as the kidnapping of persons by secret service agents.
>
> Departing from earlier views in the literature, which had adhered to a literal reading of Art. 2(1), the Committee has sought to correct the wording of this provision by developing case law oriented along the object and purpose of the Covenant and affording increased legal protection. In the first place, it has made it clear that persons who have fled abroad are not prevented by Art. 2(1) from submitting individual communications. Second, in the so-called *Passport cases* concerning Uruguay, it held that States parties are also responsible for violations of the Covenant (at least of Art. 12) by foreign diplomatic representatives. Third, it has considered communications by persons who had been kidnapped by Uruguayan agents in neighbouring States to be admissible, reasoning that States parties are responsible for the actions of their agents on foreign territory.[27]

QUESTIONS

1. How does the Committee's list of customary international law rights in GC No. 24 compare with that drawn up, albeit some seven years earlier, by the American Law Institute (p. 172 *supra*), and how would you explain the differences.

2. What are the characteristics of the ICCPR which make it the type of treaty which is not susceptible to denunciation? How potentially far-reaching are the implications of the Committee's reasoning, especially in paragraph 3 of GC No. 26?

3. Is the Committee's reasoning persuasive in defence of its interpretation of Article 2 (1) as covering persons who are subject to a state's jurisdiction, even when they are not within its territory?

[27] Nowak, n. 22 *supra*, 43–44.

4. INDIVIDUAL COMMUNICATIONS[28]

COMMENT ON COMMUNICATIONS

As of January 2007, 108 of the 160 states parties to the ICCPR were also parties to the first Optional Protocol, which allows for individuals to submit 'communications' (complaints). Note some of its critical provisions. The communications must be 'from individuals . . . who claim to be victims of a violation' by a state party to the Protocol 'of any of the rights set forth in the Covenant'. After being notified of the communication, the state party shall 'submit to the Committee written explanations or statements clarifying the matter . . .'. The Committee considers communications 'in the light of all written information made available to it by the individual and by the State Party concerned'. It will not consider a communication before ascertaining that the matter is 'not being examined under another procedure of international investigation or settlement'. Examination of the communications takes place at 'closed meetings'. The Committee is to forward 'its views' to the individual and state concerned. The goals of the procedure are said to be to: (i) enable the Committee 'to identify steps that States should take to comply with their international legal obligations in the context of concrete individual situations'; (ii) to 'offer individual relief to victims of human rights violations'; and (iii) to 'stimulate general legal, policy and programme change.'[29]

The historical background to the adoption of the Optional Protocol highlights two aspects: (1) the deep disagreement over whether such a procedure was appropriate; and (2) the extremely vague understanding of how such a procedure should work which emerged from the hurried drafting process. Consider the following description:[30]

> [A complaints procedure] was intensely discussed in the early stages of the [Human Rights Commission's] deliberations [in drafting the Covenant]. In 1950, the [General Assembly] called upon the [Human Rights Commission] 'to proceed with the consideration of provisions, to be inserted in the draft covenant or in separate protocols, for the receipt and examination of petitions from individuals and organizations with respect to alleged violations of the covenant.' However, all the [relevant drafts] were either withdrawn or defeated, usually by narrow majorities. Since the [Human Rights Commission] was dominated by proponents of State sovereignty, the draft adopted in 1954 contained no provision for an individual communication.
>
> Twelve years passed before the [General Assembly] once again took up this issue. In 1966 the Netherlands [proposed] an optional right of communication on the part of individuals and groups; in a supplementary motion, Jamaica even sought to make this procedure obligatory. . . . But opposition persisted from a

[28] Most of the main UN human right treaties provide for communications procedures. The ICCPR Committee, however, is the oldest of them all and has received and examined far more complaints than the others put together. See table at p. 920 *infra*.

[29] UN Doc. HRI/MC/2006/2 (2006) para. 9.

[30] Nowak, 'Historical Background to the OP', in *UN Covenant on Civil and Political Rights: ICCPR Commentary* (2nd edn. 2005), at 821.

> variety of States, particularly Socialist countries, all of whom viewed the individual communication as a violation of State sovereignty, a threat to international relations and a departure from the principle that individuals are not subjects of international law. On account of this, France introduced a compromise that sought to limit the function of the Committee to the mere acknowledgement of and confidential reply to communications by individuals and groups. The three drafts were ultimately withdrawn in favour of a proposal introduced by 10 States from all geopolitical regions with the exception of Eastern Europe. [In response to warnings by the Socialist States] that the adoption of this proposal in the text of the Covenant would threaten its chances for ratification, [it was proposed to make the protocol separate and optional]....
>
> Time began to run out for the concrete drafting of the OP. The text finally adopted is based on a Nigerian proposal, which was clearly oriented along the "10-State Draft" ... This motion was then discussed quite superficially, which means that the *travaux preparatoires* are of only limited assistance for the interpretation of the various provisions of the OP. The time pressure under which these provisions were drafted led to a rather rudimentary description of the procedure, to systematic absurdities and to lack of clarity at points. It is thus not incorrect to assume that the Committee had been provided with quite wide discretion ... to work out the details of the procedure....

The terse and ambiguous provisions described by Nowak set the scene for the development of a rather barebones procedure. Note the following characteristics:

1. The proceedings are in no sense a continuation of, or appeal from, judicial proceedings (if there were any) in the state in which the dispute originated. They are fresh, distinct proceedings that may involve the same two parties to prior proceedings, or different parties.
2. Unlike some complaints procedures, communications to the ICCPR Committee need not allege that the violation complained of is systemic — that is, involves a consistent pattern of violations reaching a certain level of gravity. Thus, an isolated, atypical violation can suffice to found a communication.
3. There are no provisions for oral hearings, let alone direct confrontation between the parties, or for independent fact-finding (such as examination of the parties or witnesses or independent experts, or on-site visits) by the Committee. The Optional Protocol refers only to written proceedings.
4. There are no public hearings or debates by the Committee about how to deal with a particular communication.
5. There is no provision setting forth the precise legal effect of Views, and certainly no provision in the text to indicate that the Views are binding. Nor does the text set forth what follow-up should take place if the Committee's Views indicating that a state should take particular action (such as payment of compensation or release of a prisoner) are ignored by that state.

But the procedures described in these provisions have evolved significantly through the practice of the Committee, much of which is then reflected in its Rules of Procedure. This evolving practice sets the scene for the main challenge in evaluating the work of the Committee under the Optional Protocol: how to reconcile the paucity of powers and resources given to the Committee for this purpose as a reflection of the determinedly modest original vision of the drafters, with the substantial subsequent evolution of the Committee's, and more generally the human rights movement's, aspirations in relation to such procedures. The questions to focus upon in reading the following materials are (i) the extent to which the ICCPR Committee is using rather primitive tools to achieve increasingly sophisticated goals, and (ii) whether such an approach is sustainable without major procedural innovations designed to create a better equilibrium between the tools used and the goals sought.

The Committee's caseload

Between 1977 and 2006 the Committee registered 1,490 communications concerning 81 States Parties. Of those, 547 led to the adoption of Views, including 429 in which violations of the Covenant were found. 449 were declared inadmissible, 218 were discontinued or withdrawn, and 276 were pending. Several hundred other petitioners were told that more information would be needed if the Committee was to proceed and well over 4,000 communications were rejected on the grounds that they fell clearly outside the scope of the application of the Covenant or the Optional Protocol.[31] The most frequent respondent states are (1) Jamaica 177 cases registered amounting to 12.18% of the total; (2) Canada 118 cases, 8.12%; (3) Australia 98 cases, 6.74%; (4) Spain 93 cases, 6.40%; (5) Netherlands 82 cases, 5.64%; (6) Uruguay 79 cases, 5.44%; (7) Uzbekistan 71 cases, 4.89%; and (8) France 66 cases, 4.54%.[32]

The Committee's working methods

Complaints which are submitted to the UN Secretary-General and which allege a violation of the ICCPR by a State Party to the Optional Protocol are sent on to the Committee's Special Rapporteur on New Communications, who may decide to register them and send them on to states for a response. In appropriate circumstances he or she might also request interim measures (see p. 895, *infra*). The Working Group on Communications meets for one week prior to each of the Committee's sessions, and can declare some communications to be inadmissible without needing to refer them to the government concerned. While the Protocol envisages two separate stages in the examination of a communication — the first considering its admissibility and the second examining the merits of a complaint once it has been declared admissible — the Committee's practice now generally involves consideration of both issues at the same time. The bulk of the Committee's work on any particular communication is carried out by the Special Rapporteur and the Working Group, and the Committee as a whole will generally only examine a communication once in light of the recommendations of the Working Group.

[31] Annual Report, 2006, UN Doc. A/61/40, Vol. I, paras. 89–96.
[32] UN Doc. HRI/MC/2006/2, Annex 4.

This description of the formalities does little to capture the key challenges confronting members of the Committee in their work on communications. Consider the following comment by a former Committee member:

> ... When dealing with communications, members ... listen to each other, learn from each other, adjust their own prejudices and assumptions and try to reach an agreed position. But it is not always possible to agree. In the past few years, there has been a tendency ... to adopt individual opinions. ... Some decisions of the Committee appear rather obscure or brief because of amendments and deletions carried out in order to arrive at consensus. While consensus is desirable and maintains the collegial approach and the anonymity of decisions, in some cases the price of consensus is too high. ... In those cases it is better for different shades of opinion to be separately presented rather than to undermine or truncate the reasoning of the majority.[33]

Finding of facts

One of the biggest challenges for the Committee is its inability to undertake independent fact-finding when confronted with contradictory evidence offered by a complainant and a state party. Consider for example the following response by the Committee to a claim that an individual on death row in Guyana had been tortured.

> 5.1. ...In the current case, the Committee notes that the testimony of 3 doctors at the trial, that Mr. Deolall displayed injuries, ... as well as Mr. Deolall's own statement, would prima facie support the allegation that such ill-treatment indeed occurred during the police interrogations, prior to his signing of the confession statement. ...
>
> 5.2 The Committee maintains its position that it is generally not in the position to evaluate facts and evidence presented before a domestic court. In the current case, however, the Committee takes the view that the instructions to the jury raise an issue under article 14 of the Covenant, as the defendant had managed to present prima facie evidence of being mistreated, and the Court did not alert the jury that the prosecution must prove that the confession was made without duress. This error constituted a violation of Mr. Deolall's right to a fair trial as required by the Covenant, as well as his right not to be compelled to testify against himself or confess guilt ...[34]

In dealing with cases in which clearly conflicting evidence is presented, it has been observed that:

> The HRC's Views often give little information regarding what evidence it considered and why it accorded the evidence the value it did...
>
> ...
>
> The HRC appears to rely frequently on circumstantial evidence, including evidence of a consistent pattern of conduct. ... The use of inference can be highly

[33] Elizabeth Evatt, 'Reflecting on the Role of International Communications in Implementing Human Rights', 5(2) Australian J. of Hum. Rts. 20 (1999).

[34] *Deolall v. Guyana*, Communication No. 912/2000, UN Doc. CCPR/C/82/D/912/2000 (28 January 2005).

> prejudicial to a state party as it is a very small shift in logic to conclude from the existence of a general pattern that this person, the author, suffered from the alleged violation. It therefore becomes particularly important that the HRC identify the circumstantial evidence, such as patterns of conduct, that it is using to raise an inference or a rebuttable presumption.[35]

The same author suggests that there are ways in which the Committee could transform the process if it wished to do so. In particular she advocates the use of oral proceedings and, based on the Committee's willingness to adopt innovative procedures in so many other respects, rejects the argument that it does not have competence to initiate such an approach. In her view:

> The Committee's refusal ... is probably more motivated by logistics: oral proceedings would increase the HRC's workload when it already lacks adequate means to deal with its current burden....
>
> The HRC's fact-finding could also be enhanced if it were enabled to go beyond the materials provided by the parties.... This would not necessarily entail embarking on on-site missions or extensive research in every case. In some cases, the HRC could simply charge its Secretariat with using material obtained through other treaty or U.N. bodies that would confirm the author's allegations. In addition, there are many NGOs that could be invited to provide evidence in support of allegations, such as corroborative testimony or relevant statistics.
>
> The HRC is in no way barred from sending missions to a state party where that state party has consented....[36]

QUESTION

How feasible do you consider these various proposals to be? Would they transform the role of the Committee in problematic ways, such as moving it from a relatively light and non-costly procedure into a judicial model which would require fundamental reforms and challenge many of the assumptions on the basis of which the procedure was established and has been operating? Or is the Committee moving inexorably in this direction? Recall its request (p. 868, *supra*) to the Democratic Republic of the Congo that it accept a mission by the Committee's special rapporteur to follow up on Views already adopted but not implemented.

COMMENT ON REMEDIES AND INTERIM MEASURES

In some contexts the Committee does little more than identify violations and leave it to the state party to work out how best to remedy the problem, or, in the words now used at the end of every set of Views, to adopt 'measures ... to give effect to the Committee's Views'. Overall, however, the Committee is increasingly specific as to

[35] Kirsten A. Young, *The Law and Process of the U.N. Human Rights Committee* (2002), at 299–300.
[36] *Ibid.*

the specific measures it believes states should take. They include: (a) undertaking a public investigation to establish the facts; (b) bringing the perpetrators to justice; (c) providing compensation (d) ensuring that the violation will not be repeated; (e) amending the law; (f) providing restitution of liberty, employment, or property; (g) providing medical care and treatment; (h) permitting the victim to leave the country; or (i) enjoining an imminent violation.[37]

One of the most controversial aspects of the remedies that might be sought by the Committee concerns 'interim measures' which call upon the state to suspend any action while the communication is being considered. Thus Rule 92 of the Committee's Rules of Procedures states:

> The Committee may, prior to forwarding its Views on the communication to the State party concerned, inform that State of its Views as to whether interim measures may be desirable to avoid irreparable damage to the victim of the alleged violation. In doing so, the Committee shall inform the State party concerned that such expression of its Views on interim measures does not imply a determination on the merits of the communication.

In its 2005 Annual Report the Committee noted that it 'continues to apply this rule on suitable occasions, mostly in cases submitted by or on behalf of persons who have been sentenced to death and are awaiting execution and who claim that they were denied a fair trial.' Interim measures have also been sought 'in other circumstances, for instance in cases of imminent deportation or extradition which may involve or expose the author to a real risk of violation of rights protected under the Covenant.' In a one-year period, 2004–2005, 17 of 112 new communications transmitted to states involved requests for interim measures to be taken.[38] Consider the following examples.

Piandiong et al. v. The Philippines, Communication No. 869/1999, Views adopted 19 October 2000

UN Doc. CCPR/C/70/D/869/1999

1.1 The authors of the communication . . . claim [to be] victims of violations of articles 6, 7 and 14 of the [ICCPR] . . . .

1.2 On 7 November 1994, [they] were convicted of robbery with homicide and sentenced to death by the Regional Trial Court of Caloocan City. The Supreme Court denied the appeal, and confirmed both conviction and sentence . . . . [A subsequent request for clemency by the President was denied. The Committee invoked its Rule on interim measures and requested the Philippines not to execute the petitioners while their case was under consideration by the Committee. Shortly thereafter the men were executed.]

. . .

3.5 In respect to counsel's request to the Committee for interim measures of protection as a matter of urgency, the State party notes that counsel found no need to

[37] Dinah Shelton, *Remedies in International Human Rights Law* (2nd edn. 2005) 184–185.

[38] Annual Report, 2005, UN Doc. A/60/40, paras. 146 and 107.

address the Committee during the year that his clients were on death row after all domestic remedies had been exhausted. Even after the President granted a 90 day reprieve, counsel waited until the end of that period to present a communication to the Committee. The State party argues that in doing so counsel makes a mockery of the Philippine justice system and of the constitutional process.

3.6 The State party assures the Committee of its commitment to the Covenant and states that its action was not intended to frustrate the Committee. . . .

. . .

5.1 By adhering to the Optional Protocol, a State party to the Covenant recognizes the competence of the Human Rights Committee to receive and consider communications . . . . Implicit in a State's adherence to the Protocol is an undertaking to cooperate with the Committee in good faith . . . . It is incompatible with these obligations for a State party to take any action that would prevent or frustrate the Committee in its consideration and examination of the communication, and in the expression of its Views.

5.2 . . . [A] State party commits grave breaches of its obligations under the Optional Protocol if it acts to prevent or frustrate consideration by the Committee of a communication alleging a violation of the Covenant, or to render examination by the Committee moot and the expression of its Views nugatory and futile. [In this case] . . . the State party breaches its obligations under the Protocol, if it proceeds to execute the alleged victims before the Committee concludes its [work]. It is particularly inexcusable for the State to do so after the Committee has [requested] that the State party refrain from doing so.

5.3 . . . There is nothing in the Optional Protocol that restricts the right of an alleged victim of a violation of his or her rights under the Covenant from submitting a communication after a request for clemency or pardon has been rejected, and the State party may not unilaterally impose such a condition that limits both the competence of the Committee and the right of alleged victims to submit communications. Furthermore, the State party has not shown that by acceding to the Committee's request for interim measures the course of justice would have been obstructed.

5.4 Interim measures . . . are essential to the Committee's role under the Protocol. Flouting of the Rule, especially by irreversible measures such as the execution of the alleged victim or his/her deportation from the country, undermines the protection of Covenant rights through the Optional Protocol.

. . .

Mansour Ahani v. Canada, Communication No. 1051/2002, Views adopted 29 March 2004

UN Doc. CCPR/C/80/D/1051/2002

1.1 [The author of the communication, dated 10 January 2002, is Mansour Ahani, an Iranian citizen, detained in Canada] pending conclusion of legal proceedings in the Supreme Court of Canada concerning his deportation. He claims to be a victim of violations by Canada of articles 2, 6, 7, 9, 13 and 14 of the [ICCPR]. . . .

1.2 On 11 January 2002, the Committee . . . requested the State party, in the event that the Supreme Court's decision expected the same day would permit the author's deportation, "to refrain from deportation until the Committee has had an opportunity to consider the allegations, in particular those that relate to torture, other inhuman treatment or even death as a consequence of the deportation". . . . On 10 June 2002, the State party deported the author to Iran.

. . .

2.1 . . . On 1 April 1992, the Immigration and Refugee Board determined that the author was a Convention refugee based on his political opinion and membership in a particular social group.

2.2 On 17 June 1993, the Solicitor-General of Canada and the Minister of Employment & Immigration, having considered security intelligence reports stating that the author was trained to be an assassin by the Iranian Ministry of Intelligence and Security ("MIS"), both certified . . . [under the relevant Act that] there were reasonable grounds to believe that he would engage in terrorism, that he was a member of an organization that would engage in terrorism and that he had engaged in terrorism. On the same date, . . . he was taken into mandatory detention, where he remained until his deportation nine years later.

. . .

2.10 . . . On 15 January 2002, the Ontario Superior Court (Dambrot J) rejected the author's argument that the principles of fundamental justice, protected by the Charter, prevented his removal prior to the [Human Rights] Committee's consideration of the case. On 8 May 2002, the Court of Appeal for Ontario upheld the decision, holding that the request for interim measures was not binding upon the State party. On 16 May 2002, the Supreme Court, by a majority, dismissed the author's application for leave to appeal (without giving reasons). On 10 June 2002, the author was deported to Iran.

. . .

5.2 By submissions dated 5 December 2002, the State party, in response to the Committee's request for explanation, argued that it fully supported the important role mandated to the Committee and would always do its utmost to co-operate with the Committee. It contended that it took its obligations under the Covenant and the Optional Protocol very seriously and that it was in full compliance with them. The State party points out that alongside its human rights obligations it also has a duty to protect the safety of the Canadian public and to ensure that it does not become a safe haven for terrorists.

5.3 The State party noted that neither the Covenant nor the Optional Protocol provide for interim measures requests and argues that such requests are recommendatory, rather than binding. Nonetheless, the State party usually responded favourably to such requests. As in other cases, the State party considered the instant request seriously, before concluding in the circumstances of the case, including the finding (upheld by the courts) that he faced a minimum risk of harm in the event of return, that it was unable to delay the deportation. The State party pointed out that usually it responds favourably to requests[;] its decision to do so was determined to be legal and consistent with the Charter up to the highest judicial level. The State party argues that interim measures in the immigration context raise "some particular difficulties" where, on occasion, other considerations may take precedence over a request for interim measures. The particular circumstances of the case should thus not be construed as a diminution of the State party's commitment to human rights or the Committee.

...

8.1 The Committee finds, in the circumstances of the case, that the State party breached its obligations under the Optional Protocol, by deporting the author before the Committee could address the author's allegation of irreparable harm to his Covenant rights. The Committee observes that torture is, alongside the imposition of the death penalty, the most grave and irreparable of possible consequences to an individual of measures taken by the State party. Accordingly, action by the State party giving rise to a risk of such harm, as indicated a priori by the Committee's request for interim measures, must be scrutinized in the strictest light.

8.2 Interim measures... are essential to the Committee's role under the Protocol. Flouting of the Rule, especially by irreversible measures such as the execution of the alleged victim or his/her deportation from a State party to face torture or death in another country, undermines the protection of Covenant rights through the Optional Protocol....

QUESTIONS

1. One commentator, reflecting on the Committee's Views in Piandiong, suggests that the 'Committee's reasoned justification for its conclusion, [consistent] with the "dynamic and evolutive" approach to human rights treaties, must be considered correct, if only on the utilitarian ground of seeking to ensure maximum protection for people at risk.'[39] What other factors might reasonably be taken into account in evaluating whether the Committee's approach to interim measures is justified?

2. What do you make of the fact that the Governments of both the Philippines and Canada insist on their respect for the interim measures procedure in principle but reject it in the case at hand? What would be the consequences from the Committee's perspective of accepting the Canadian view that interim measures 'requests are recommendatory, rather than binding'?

3. Do you agree that '[a] State that has accepted the right of individual petition... has bound itself to support that process by complying with any interim measures ordered. It would be incompatible with the obligations voluntarily undertaken by the State for the State to act or refrain from acting in a way that frustrates the consideration of an individual petition.'[40]

❀ ❀ ❀

[39] Gino Naldi, 'Interim Measures in the UN Human Rights Committee', 53 Int. & Comp. L. Q. (2004) 445, at 454.

[40] Jo M. Pasqualucci, 'Interim Measures in International Human Rights: Evolution and Harmonization', 38 Vand. J. Transnat'l L. 1, 48 (2005).

There follows a selection of views adopted by the ICCPR Committee in relation to communications.

BABAN V. AUSTRALIA

Communication No. 1014/2001, Views adopted August 6, 2003
UN Doc. CCPR/C/78/D/1014/2001

[Omar Sharif Baban, an Iraqi national of Kurdish ethnicity, and his 20-month old son, arrived in Australia without travel documents in June 1999, and applied for refugee status. They were immediately detained in Villawood Detention Centre, near Sydney. Baban's application for asylum was denied by the immigration authorities, a subsequent appeal to the Refugee Review Tribunal was dismissed, and the Federal Court denied review of that decision. In July 2000, he participated in a hunger strike, in response to which the strikers were allegedly cut off from the outside world and mistreated by the guards. He and his son were subsequently removed to another detention centre in which they were held for eight days in an isolation cell without a window or toilet and allegedly denied access to legal counsel. These claims were dismissed by the Committee on the grounds that available domestic remedies in relation to them had not been exhausted. Baban also alleged that his detention for almost two years was unjustified and violated Art. 9 of the ICCPR.]

...

Consideration of the merits

...

7.2 As to the claims under article 9, the Committee recalls its jurisprudence that, in order to avoid a characterization of arbitrariness, detention should not continue beyond the period for which the State party can provide appropriate justification. In the present case, the author's detention as a non-citizen without an entry permit continued, in mandatory terms, until he was removed or granted a permit. While the State party advances particular reasons to justify the individual detention, the Committee observes that the State party has failed to demonstrate that those reasons justified the author's continued detention in the light of the passage of time and intervening circumstances such as the hardship of prolonged detention for his son or the fact that during the period under review the State Party apparently did not remove Iraqis from Australia. In particular, the State party has not demonstrated that, in the light of the author's particular circumstances, there were not less invasive means of achieving the same ends, that is to say, compliance with the State party's immigration policies, by, for example, the imposition of reporting obligations, sureties or other conditions. The Committee also notes that in the present case the author was unable to challenge his continued detention in court. Judicial review of detention would have been restricted to an assessment of whether the author was a non-citizen without valid entry documentation, and, by direct operation of the relevant legislation, the relevant courts would not have been able to consider arguments that the individual detention was unlawful in terms of the Covenant. Judicial review of the lawfulness of detention under article 9, paragraph 4, is not limited to mere compliance of the detention with domestic law but must include the possibility to order release if the detention is incompatible with the requirements of the Covenant, in particular those of article 9, paragraph 1. In the present case, the author and his son were held in immigration detention for almost two years without individual justification and without any chance of substantive judicial review of the continued compatibility of their detention with the Covenant. Accordingly, the rights of both the author and his son under article 9, paragraphs 1 and 4, of the Covenant were violated.

...

9. In accordance with article 2, paragraph 3 (a), of the Covenant, the State party is under an obligation to provide the authors with an effective remedy, including compensation.

...

INDIVIDUAL OPINION OF COMMITTEE MEMBER
MS. RUTH WEDGWOOD (DISSENTING)

I am unable to agree with the Committee's supposition that any legislative standards requiring the detention of any class of unlawful entrants and limiting a court's discretion during the pendency of immigration proceedings must *per se* violate article 9 of the Covenant. The guarantee of article 9 against arbitrary detention, in the Committee's view, requires not simply that a person must have access to court review, but that the standards for the court's evaluation must be unfettered. The legislature's own factual conclusions about the success or failure of policies of supervised release or problems of non-reporting by particular classes of unlawful entrants do not, apparently, merit weight.

This same logic could be deployed to challenge any mandatory penal sentences in criminal cases, since there too a court is limited to evaluating facts without discretion to alter the consequences that flow from those facts.

While article 9, paragraphs 1 and 4, of the Covenant may well require reference to substantive standards beyond domestic law — i.e., an action could be arbitrary under the Covenant even though it complies with domestic law — nonetheless there is no grounding in the Covenant to dictate that courts must be the repository of all policy judgments and standard-setting in difficult areas such as unlawful immigration....

The author ... argues that his detention as an asylum applicant was arbitrary and unreasonable because in his individual case, conditions of supervised release might have sufficed to prevent his flight, and a court should have had a chance to assess the matter. ... [T]he parliament of Australia could reasonably have concluded that illegal entrants who have received a[n] administrative or lower court denials of their asylum claims are not thereafter likely to report for possible deportation after appeals are exhausted. This competence of the parliament does not preclude some limit, under the Covenant, on the ultimate length of time that unsuccessful asylum-seekers can be detained, where there is no possibility of their return to another country. Nor does it preclude some reasonable time limit on the decision of appeals, where the applicant is detained. But the author of this communication does not present such facts.

We may wish that the world had no borders, and that the conditions which give rise to legitimate asylum claims no longer existed. But especially in the present time we must recognize as well that states have a right to control entry into their own countries, and may use reasonable legislative judgments to that end.

SINGARASA V. SRI LANKA

Communication No. 1033/2001

UN Doc. CCPR/C/81/D/1033/2001 (23 August 2004)

...

Facts as submitted by the author

2.1 On 16 July 1993, at about 5am, the author was arrested, by Sri Lankan security forces while sleeping at his home. 150 Tamil men were also arrested in a "round up" of his village. None of them were informed of the reasons for their arrest. They were all taken to the Komathurai Army Camp and accused of supporting the Liberation Tigers of Tamil Eelam (known as "the LTTE"). During his detention at the camp, the author's hands were tied together, he was kept hanging from a mango tree, and was allegedly assaulted by members of the security forces.

2.2 ... He was detained pursuant to ... the Prevention of Terrorism Act No. 48 of 1979....

2.3 [Between July and September 1993 he was interrogated, held incommunicado, and denied legal representation and medical assistance. For two days he claims to have been tortured] which included being pushed into a water tank and held under water, and then blindfolded and laid face down and assaulted....

...

2.5 [During his interrogation, since] the author could not speak Sinhalese, the PC [Police Constable] interpreted between Tamil and Sinhalese. The author was then requested to sign a statement, which had been translated and typed in Sinhalese by the PC. The author refused to sign as he could not understand it. He alleges that the ASP [Assistant Superintendent of Police] then forcibly put his thumbprint on the typed statement. The prosecution later produced this statement as evidence of the author's alleged confession....

...

2.9 On 12 January 1995, in an application to the High Court, defence counsel submitted that there were visible marks of assault on the author's body, and moved for a medical report to be obtained. On the Court's order, a Judicial Medical Officer then examined him. According to the author, the medical report stated that the author displayed scars on his back and ... a corneal scar on his left eye ... [and] that 'injuries to the lower part of the left back of the chest and eye were caused by a blunt weapon while that to the mid back of the chest was probably due to application of sharp force'.

2.10 On 2 June 1995, the author's alleged confession was the subject of a voir dire hearing by the High Court, at which the ASP, PC and author gave evidence, and the medical report was considered. The High Court concluded that the confession was admissible, pursuant to section 16(1) of the PTA, which renders admissible any statement made before a police officer not below the rank of an ASP, provided that it is not found to be irrelevant under section 24 of the Evidence Ordinance. Section 16(2) of the PTA put the burden of proof that any such statement is irrelevant on the accused. (4) The Court did not find the confession irrelevant, despite defence counsel's motion to exclude it on the grounds that it was extracted from the author under threat.

2.11 According to the author, the High Court gave no reasons for rejecting the medical report. . . . In holding that the confession was voluntary, the High Court relied upon the author's failure to complain to anyone at any time about the beatings . . . .

2.12 On 29 September 1995, the High Court convicted the author on all five counts, and on 4 October 1995, sentenced him to 50 years imprisonment. The conviction was based solely on the alleged confession. . . .

. . .

The State party's submissions on admissibility and merits

. . .

4.8 On the claim of torture, the State party submits that the trial court and the Court of Appeal made clear and unequivocal findings that these allegations were inconsistent with the medical report adduced in evidence, and that the author had failed to make such allegations to the Magistrate or to the police, prior to the trial.

4.9 . . . On the issue of a violation of article 14, paragraph 5, it notes that the author was afforded every opportunity to have his conviction and sentence reviewed by a tribunal according to law, and that he merely seeks to question the findings of fact made by the domestic courts before the Committee. . . .

. . .

Issues and proceedings before the Committee

Consideration of the Merits

. . .

7.2 . . . [A]s clearly appears from the court proceedings, the confession took place in the sole presence of the two investigating officers . . . . The Committee concludes that the author was denied a fair trial in accordance with article 14, paragraph 1, of the Covenant by solely relying on a confession obtained in such circumstances.

. . .

7.4 On the claim of a violation of the author's rights under article 14, paragraph 3 (g), in that he was forced to sign a confession and subsequently had to assume the burden of proof that it was extracted under duress and was not voluntary, the Committee must consider the principles underlying the right protected in this provision. . . . The Committee considers that it is implicit in this principle that the prosecution prove that the confession was made without duress. . . . [T]he Committee also notes that the burden of proving whether the confession was voluntary was on the accused.... Even if, as argued by the State party, the threshold of proof is "placed very low" and "a mere possibility of involuntariness" would suffice to sway the court in favour of the accused, it remains that the burden was on the author. The Committee notes in this respect that the willingness of the courts at all stages to dismiss the complaints of torture and ill-treatment on the basis of the inconclusiveness of the medical certificate (especially one obtained over a year after the interrogation and ensuing confession) suggests that this threshold was not complied with. Further, insofar as the courts were prepared to infer that the author's allegations lacked credibility by virtue of his failing to complain of ill-treatment before its Magistrate, the Committee finds that inference to be manifestly unsustainable in the light of his expected return to police detention. Nor did this treatment of the complaint by its courts satisfactorily discharge the State party's obligation to investigate effectively complaints of violations of article 7....

...

7.6 In accordance with article 2, paragraph 3 (a), of the Covenant, the State party is under an obligation to provide the author with an effective and appropriate remedy, including release or retrial and compensation. The State party is under an obligation to avoid similar violations in the future and should ensure that the impugned sections of the PTA are made compatible with the provisions of the Covenant.

...

Subsequent to this set of Views adopted by the Committee, Singarasa requested the Sri Lankan Supreme Court to revise its earlier decision taking into consideration the views of the Committee. *Singarasa* was the sixth case against Sri Lanka in which the Committee had found violations. The Chief Justice was involved in several of those, including the *Singarasa* case.

NOTE

Following the Committee's View in Singarasa, the Sri Lankan Supreme Court returned to the issues raised:

Nallaratnam Singarasa v. Attorney-General, Supreme Court of the Democratic Socialist Republic of Sri Lanka

15 September 2006, S.C. Spl(LA) No. 182/99

SARATH N SILVA, C.J.

...

(i) [T]he alternative remedies specified by the Committee [see paragraph 7.6, *supra*] cannot be comprehended in the context of our court procedure. A release and compensation (to be sought in a separate civil action) predicate a baseless mala fide prosecution. Whereas a retrial is ordered when there is sufficient evidence but the conviction is flawed by a serious procedural illegality. The High Court convicted the Petitioner on the basis of his confession after a full *voir dire* inquiry as to its voluntariness. If the confession is adequate to base a conviction, a retrial (as contemplated by the Committee) would be a superfluous re-enactment of the same process.

(ii) The Petitioner has been convicted with [sic] having conspired with others to overthrow the lawfully elected Government of Sri Lanka and for that purpose attacked several Army camps. The offences are directly linked to the Sovereignty of the People of Sri Lanka, and the Committee at Geneva, not linked with the Sovereignty of the People, has purported to set aside the orders made at all three levels of Courts that exercise the judicial power of the People of Sri Lanka.

...

The resulting position is that the Petitioner cannot seek to "vindicate and enforce' his rights through the Human Rights Committee at Geneva, which is not reposed with judicial power under our Constitution. A fortiori it is submitted that this Court being "the highest and final Superior Court of record in the Republic" in terms of Article 118 of the Constitution cannot set aside or vary its order as pleaded by the Petitioner on the basis of the findings of the Human Rights Committee in Geneva which is not reposed with any judicial power under or in terms of the Constitution.

...

... [W]here the President enters into a treaty or accedes to a Covenant the content of which is "inconsistent with the provisions of the Constitution or written law" it would be a transgression of the limitation in Article 33(f) [of the Constitution] and ultra vires. Such act of the President would not bind the Republic qua state....

...

[Recognition of the role of the ICCPR Committee to receive and consider communications] is a purported conferment of a judicial power on the Human Rights Committee at Geneva....

Therefore the accession to the Optional Protocol in 1997 by the then President and Declaration made under Article 1 is inconsistent with the provisions of the Constitution specified above and is in excess of the power of the President as contained in Article 33(f) of the Constitution. The accession and declaration does not bind the Republic qua state and has no legal effect within the Republic.

...

In these circumstances the Petitioner cannot plead a legitimate expectation to have the findings of the Human Rights Committee enforced or given effect to by an order of this Court.

Consider the following comment on this judgment.

Interights, Sri Lankan Ruling Undermines UN Complaints Mechanism

http://www.interights.org/iain%20Singarasa%20redft3.pdf

... The Court's conclusion is all the more remarkable given the fact that the validity of the accession to the Optional Protocol was not raised in this case. In so holding, the judgment completely ignores the basic customary international law principle of *pacta sunt servanda*... that every treaty is binding on states parties and must be performed by them in good faith. It also disregards those rules of international law governing how binding treaties are entered into, reflected in Article 7 of the Vienna Convention. It is therefore clear that, despite the Supreme Court's judgment, the Sri Lankan state remains fully bound by its obligations under the Optional Protocol.

The Supreme Court's decision is as surprising as it is disappointing given that Article 27(15) of Sri Lanka's own Constitution requires the state to 'endeavour to foster respect for international law and treaty obligations in dealings among nations'. This obligation was expressly recognised by the Court in a previous ruling when it was held to imply that 'the State must likewise respect international law and treaty obligations in its dealings with its own citizens, particularly when their liberty is involved. The State must afford to them the benefit of the safeguards which international law recognizes.'

QUESTIONS

1. Is it reasonable for the Committee in *Baban* to put the burden of proof on the state party to demonstrate that imprisonment was the only reasonable way to ensure compliance with its policies? Or is it, as Wedgwood suggests, up to states to make their own 'reasonable legislative judgments'?

2. Are the Committee's procedures adequate to enable it to deal with a case such as *Singarasa*? How could its procedures in such cases be improved?

3. Does the ICCPR Committee exercise judicial power, as indicated by the Court? Would the situation be different if the Committee's Views were considered binding upon states parties?

K.N.L.H. V. PERU

Communication No. 1153/2003
UN Doc. CCPR/C/85/D/1153/2003/Rev.1 (14 August 2006)

...

Factual background

2.1 The author became pregnant in March 2001, when she was aged 17. On 27 June 2001 she was given a scan at the Archbishop Loayza National Hospital in Lima, part of the Ministry of Health. The scan showed that she was carrying an anencephalic foetus.

2.2 On 3 July 2001, [a specialist at the hospital] ... advised termination by means of uterine curettage. The author decided to terminate the pregnancy ....

2.3 On 19 July 2001, when the author [sought hospital admission, the specialist] informed her that she needed to obtain written authorization from the hospital director. Since she was under age, her mother, Ms. E.H.L., requested the authorization. On 24 July 2001, Dr. Maximiliano Cárdenas Díaz, the hospital director, replied in writing that the termination could not be carried out as to do so would be unlawful, since under article 120 of the Criminal Code, abortion was punishable by a prison term of no more than three months when it was likely that at birth the child would suffer serious physical or mental defects, while under article 119, therapeutic abortion was permitted only when termination of the pregnancy was the only way of saving the life of the pregnant woman or avoiding serious and permanent damage to her health.

2.4–2.5 [Reports were submitted by both a social worker and a psychiatrist attesting to the highly adverse consequences of not permitting the applicant to terminate her pregnancy.]

. . .

2.6 On 13 January 2002, three weeks late with respect to the anticipated date of birth, the author gave birth to an anencephalic baby girl, who survived for four days, during which the mother had to breastfeed her. Following her daughter's death, the author fell into a state of deep depression. . . .

2.7 The author has submitted to the Committee a statement made by [experts who] . . . stated that anencephaly is a condition which is fatal to the foetus in all cases. Death immediately follows birth in most cases. It also endangers the mother's life. . . .

. . .

The complaint

3.1 The author claims a violation of article 2 of the Covenant, since the State party failed to comply with its obligation to guarantee the exercise of a right. The State should have taken steps to respond to the systematic reluctance of the medical community to comply with the legal provision authorizing therapeutic abortion, and its restrictive interpretation thereof. . . .

3.2 The author claims to have suffered discrimination in breach of article 3 of the Covenant, in the following forms:

(a) In access to the health services, since her different and special needs were ignored because of her sex. . . .

(b) Discrimination in the exercise of her rights, since although the author was entitled to a therapeutic abortion, none was carried out because of social attitudes and prejudices . . . .

(c) Discrimination in access to the courts, bearing in mind the prejudices of officials in the health system and the judicial system where women are concerned and the lack of appropriate legal means of enforcing respect for the right to obtain a legal abortion when the temporal and other conditions laid down in the law are met.

3.3 The author claims a violation of article 6 of the Covenant. . . . [T]he violation of the right to life lay in the fact that Peru did not take steps to ensure that the author secured a safe termination of pregnancy on the grounds that the foetus was not viable. She states that the refusal to provide a legal abortion service left her with two options which posed an equal risk to her health and safety: to seek clandestine (and hence highly risky) abortion services, or to continue a dangerous and traumatic pregnancy which put her life at risk.

...

3.5 [In claiming a violation of Article 7 the author] ... points out that, after considering Peru's report in 1996, the Committee expressed the view that restrictive provisions on abortion subjected women to inhumane treatment, in violation of article 7 of the Covenant, and that in 2000, the Committee reminded the State party that the criminalization of abortion was incompatible with articles 3, 6 and 7 of the Covenant.

3.6 The author claims a violation of article 17, arguing that this article protects women from interference in decisions which affect their bodies and their lives, and offers them the opportunity to exercise their right to make independent decisions on their reproductive lives....

3.7 The author claims a violation of article 24, since she did not receive the special care she needed from the health authorities, as an adolescent girl.

...

State party's failure to cooperate under article 4 of the Optional Protocol

4. On 23 July 2003, 15 March 2004 and 25 October 2004, reminders were sent to the State party inviting it to submit information to the Committee concerning the admissibility and the merits of the complaint. The Committee notes that no such information has been received....

Issues and proceedings before the Committee

Consideration of admissibility

...

5.3 The Committee considers that the author's claims of alleged violations of articles 3 and 26 of the Covenant have not been properly substantiated, since the author has not placed before the Committee any evidence relating to the events which might confirm any type of discrimination under the article in question. Consequently, the part of the complaint referring to articles 3 and 26 is declared inadmissible under article 2 of the Optional Protocol.

...

Consideration of the merits

...

6.3 ... The omission on the part of the State in not enabling the author to benefit from a therapeutic abortion was, in the Committee's view, the cause of the suffering she experienced. The Committee has pointed out in its General Comment No. 20 that the right set out in article 7 of the Covenant relates not only to physical pain but also to mental suffering, and that the protection is particularly important in the case of minors. In the absence of any information from the State party in this regard, due weight must be given to the author's complaints. Consequently, the Committee considers that the facts before it reveal a violation of article 7 of the Covenant. In the light of this finding the Committee does not consider it necessary in the circumstances to make a finding on article 6 of the Covenant.

6.4 The . . . refusal to act in accordance with the author's decision to terminate her pregnancy was not justified and amounted to a violation of article 17 of the Covenant.

6.5 The author claims a violation of article 24 of the Covenant, since she did not receive from the State party the special care she needed as a minor. . . . [I]n the absence of any information from the State party, due weight must be given to the author's claim that she did not receive, during and after her pregnancy, the medical and psychological support necessary in the specific circumstances of her case. Consequently, the Committee considers that the facts before it reveal a violation of article 24 of the Covenant.

6.6 . . . [The Committee] concludes that the facts before it also reveal a violation of article 2 in conjunction with articles 7, 17 and 24.

. . .

8. In accordance with article 2, paragraph 3 (a), of the Covenant, the State party is required to furnish the author with an effective remedy, including compensation. The State party has an obligation to take steps to ensure that similar violations do not occur in the future.

APPENDIX, DISSENTING OPINION BY COMMITTEE MEMBER HIPÓLITO SOLARI-YRIGOYEN

. . .

It is not only taking a person's life that violates article 6 of the Covenant but also placing a person's life in grave danger, as in this case. Consequently, I consider that the facts in the present case reveal a violation of article 6 of the Covenant.

QUESTIONS

1. What are the consequences of the Government's failure to submit any information in this case? Does it undermine the precedential value of the decision?

2. Does this decision amount to recognition that there is a right to abortion under the ICCPR? What do you make of the Committee's refusal to entertain the various claims of discrimination? What sort of evidence might have been submitted to substantiate such claims?

3. Do you agree with the following critique of the majority's position on Article 6:

> The separate opinion is to be preferred to the majority's decision. The majority chose not to address Article 6 because it had found a violation of Article 7. The complaints regarding Article 7 concerned the complainant's mental trauma, whereas the complaint concerning Article 6 concerned the endangerment to her life

caused by the pregnancy, and the possibility that she might seek a dangerous clandestine abortion. The Article 6 complaint was not specifically related to the author's mental state (for example, the possibility of suicide), apart from the possibility that she might seek an illegal abortion out of desperation. Hence, the [Committee's] evasion of the Article 6 issue . . . is regrettable and unjustifiable. The importance of the issue is highlighted by a World Health Organisation (WHO) report from 1998, indicating that 13% of maternal deaths are caused by unsafe abortions.[41]

TOONEN V. AUSTRALIA

Communication No. 488/1992, Views adopted 31 March 1994
UN Doc. CCPR/C/50/D/488/1992

[The author of this communication was an Australian citizen resident in the Australian state of Tasmania, and a leading member of the Tasmanian Gay Law Reform Group. He claimed that he was a victim of violations by Australia of Articles 2(1), 17 and 26 of the ICCPR. Article 2(1) provides that each state party will ensure to all individuals the 'rights recognized in the present Covenant, without distinction of any kind, such as . . . sex . . . political or other opinion . . . or other status'. Article 17 provides that no one shall be subjected 'to arbitrary or unlawful interference with his privacy . . . '. Article 26 provides that all persons 'are equal before the law and are entitled without any discrimination to the equal protection of the law'. Forbidden discriminations are similar to those in Article 2(1).

Toonen challenged in particular two provisions of the Tasmanian Criminal Code (Australia being internationally responsible for acts of a component state within its federal structure) which made criminal 'various forms of sexual conduct between men, including all forms of sexual contacts between consenting adult homosexual men in private'. The Tasmanian police had not charged anyone with violations of these statutes, such as 'intercourse against nature', but there remained a threat of enforcement. Moreover, the author alleged that the criminalization of homosexuality had nourished prejudice and 'created the conditions for discrimination in employment, constant stigmatization, vilification, threats of physical violence and the violation of basic democratic rights'. Tasmania alone among Australian jurisdictions continued to have such laws in effect, and the Federal Government's position before the Human Rights Committee was critical of those laws.

Excerpts from the Committee's view follow, starting with some of Australia's observations.]

6.5 The state party does not accept the argument of the Tasmanian authorities that the retention of the challenged provisions is partly motivated by a concern to protect Tasmania from the spread of HIV/AIDS, and that the laws are justified on public health and moral grounds. This assessment in fact goes against the Australian Government's National HIV/AIDS Strategy, which emphasizes that laws criminalizing homosexual activity obstruct public health programmes promoting safer sex.

[41] Sarah Joseph, 'Landmark Decision regarding Abortion Rights', 6 Hum. Rts. L. Rev. (2006) 361, at 364.

The State party further disagrees with the Tasmanian authorities's contention that the laws are justified on moral grounds, noting that moral issues were not at issue when article 17 of the Covenant was drafted.

6.6 None the less, the State party cautions that the formulation of article 17 allows for *some* infringement of the right to privacy if there are reasonable grounds, and that domestic social mores may be relevant to the reasonableness of an interference with privacy. The State party observes that while laws penalizing homosexual activity existed in the past in other Australian states, they have since been repealed with the exception of Tasmania. Furthermore, discrimination on the basis of homosexuality or sexuality is unlawful in three of six Australian states and the two self-governing internal Australian territories. The Federal Government has declared sexual preference to be a ground of discrimination that may be invoked under ILO Convention No. 111 (Discrimination in Employment or Occupation Convention), and created a mechanism through which complaints about discrimination in employment on the basis of sexual preference may be considered by the Australian Human Rights and Equal Opportunity Commission.

6.7 On the basis of the above, the State party contends that there is now a general Australian acceptance that no individual should be disadvantaged on the basis of his or her sexual orientation. Given the legal and social situation in all of Australia except Tasmania, the State party acknowledges that a complete prohibition on sexual activity between men is unnecessary to sustain the moral fabric of Australian society. On balance, the State party 'does not seek to claim that the challenged laws are based on reasonable and objective criteria'.

...

Examination of the merits:

...

8.2 Inasmuch as article 17 is concerned, it is undisputed that adult consensual sexual activity in private is covered by the concept of 'privacy', and that Mr. Toonen is actually and currently affected by the continued existence of the Tasmanian laws.

...

8.3 The prohibition against private homosexual behaviour is provided for by law, namely, Sections 122 and 123 of the Tasmanian Criminal Code. As to whether it may be deemed arbitrary, the Committee recalls that pursuant to its General Comment 16 on article 17, the 'introduction of the concept of arbitrariness is intended to guarantee that even interference provided for by the law should be in accordance with the provisions, aims and objectives of the Covenant and should be, in any event, reasonable in the circumstances'. The Committee interprets the requirement of reasonableness to imply that any interference with privacy must be proportional to the end sought and be necessary in the circumstances of any given case.

...

8.5 As far as the public health argument of the Tasmanian authorities is concerned, the Committee notes that the criminalization of homosexual practices cannot be considered a reasonable means or proportionate measure to achieve the aim of preventing the spread of AIDS/HIV....

8.6 The Committee cannot accept either that for the purposes of article 17 of the Covenant, moral issues are exclusively a matter of domestic concern, as this would open the door to withdrawing from the Committee's scrutiny a potentially large number of statutes interfering with privacy. It further notes that with the exception of Tasmania, all laws criminalizing homosexuality have been repealed throughout Australia and that, even in Tasmania, it is apparent that there is no consensus as to whether Sections 122 and 123 should not also be repealed. Considering further that these provisions are not currently enforced, which implies that they are not deemed essential to the protection of morals in Tasmania, the Committee concludes that the provisions do not meet the 'reasonableness' test in the circumstances of the case, and that they arbitrarily interfere with Mr. Toonen's right under article 17, paragraph 1.

8.7 The State party has sought the Committee's guidance as to whether sexual orientation may be considered an 'other status' for the purposes of article 26. The same issue could arise under article 2, paragraph 1, of the Covenant. The Committee confines itself to noting, however, that in its view the reference to 'sex' in articles 2, paragraph 1, and 26 is to be taken as including sexual orientation.

9. The Human Rights Committee, acting under article 5, paragraph 4, of the Optional Protocol to the International Covenant on Civil and Political Rights, is of the view that the facts before it reveal a violation of articles 17, paragraph 1, *juncto* 2, paragraph 1, of the Covenant.

10. Under article 2(3)(a) of the Covenant, the author, victim of a violation of articles 17, paragraph 1, *juncto* 2, paragraph 1, of the Covenant, is entitled to a remedy. In the opinion of the Committee, an effective remedy would be the repeal of Sections 122 (a), (c) and 123 of the Tasmanian Criminal Code.

11. Since the Committee has found a violation of Mr. Toonen's rights under articles 17(1) and 2(1) of the Covenant requiring the repeal of the offending law, the Committee does not consider it necessary to consider whether there has also been a violation of article 26 of the Covenant.

12. The Committee would wish to receive, within 90 days of the date of the transmittal of its views, information from the State party on the measures taken to give effect to the views.

NOTE

A former member of the Committee from Australia offered the following comment on Australia's position in the *Toonen* case:

> Australians are only too well aware of the lack of domestic remedies to enforce ICCPR rights. For example, in *Toonen*, the Author's claim that Tasmania's anti-gay law violated his right to privacy could not be taken to the Australian courts. The only remedy available to Mr. Toonen was to take his case to the Committee under the Optional Protocol. . . . Australia had not fulfilled its obligations under Article 2(3) [of the ICCPR]. The Australian Government's response to the finding of violation . . . was to do what should have been done already, that is to introduce

> legislation to provide a remedy enforceable in the courts for any arbitrary interference with the privacy of sexual conduct between consenting adults [The Human Rights (Sexual Conduct) Act 1994 (Cth.)]. Had that remedy been available in the first place — as one might reasonably expect if Article 2(3) were taken seriously — the Committee might not have needed to consider Mr. Toonen's case. . . .[42]

Discussion of homosexual acts and of other implications for gay and lesbian people of rights to privacy and equal protection continues at pp. 965–79, *infra*, in the framework of the European Convention on Human Rights.

QUESTIONS

1. Suppose that a communication comes from a state making sodomy between consenting adult males a criminal offence. The communication's author has been charged with this offence and faces trial. The state's defence before the Committee rests on biblical condemnation of such conduct and related moral views to the same effect held by a large majority of the state's population. What issues should be raised by the parties and discussed by the Committee? What relevance has the *Toonen* view to such a case?

2. How do you understand and assess paragraph 8.7? As a Committee member, would you have supported or opposed inclusion of this paragraph in its present form, or in any form? Was it necessary? What distinct issues are raised by inclusion of sexual orientation in the term 'sex' in Articles 2(1) and 26?

3. How do you assess the Committee's argument related to Article 17? Would you have taken a different approach?

4. What differences do you see between the Committee's expressing its understanding of Articles 17 and 2(1) in relation to homosexual acts through a View such as *Toonen*, or through a General Comment expressing the same ideas? Which route would you favour?

COMMENT ON OUTCOME OF THE COMMUNICATIONS PROCEDURES

One of the key issues in evaluating the impact of the elaborate communications procedure provided for in the Optional Protocol is the extent to which states have complied with the Views adopted in relevant cases. Closely linked to this empirical question is the more doctrinal issue of whether or not the Views are binding upon states.

In terms of the empirical issue, Australia provides a useful case study. It is the state with the third highest number of registered cases. Between December 1991 and January 2007 the Committee adopted decisions in response to 48 cases concerning

[42] Evatt, 'Reflecting on the Role of International Communications in Implementing Human Rights', 5(2) Australian J. of Hum. Rts. (1999) 20, at 24.

Australia. It found violations in 14 of the 19 cases in which it adopted Views. Thus around one in every 30 of the Committee's total number of registered communications, and findings of violations, have concerned Australia. Part of the explanation is that Australia does not have a constitutional bill of rights. In the context of the reporting procedure the Committee has expressed concern over this fact. In response the Australian Government has informed the Committee that it does not support a bill of rights because Australia 'already has a robust constitutional structure, an extensive framework of legislation protecting human rights and prohibiting discrimination, and an independent human rights institution, the [Human Rights and Equal Opportunity] Commission. The latter mechanism holds the legislative branch and Australian Government accountable against human rights standards and thereby substantively achieves the same outcome in this respect as would legislation that directly implements the Covenant. Australia adds that human rights are also protected and promoted by Australia's strong democratic institutions.'[43]

Australia has, however, consistently challenged the Views of the Committee. In one case the Government bluntly rejected the Committee's Views that the complainant's detention was arbitrary and its conclusion that the Government had not provided sufficient justification. It also rejected the recommendation to pay compensation and disagreed with most elements in the Committee's interpretation of Article 9(4).[44]

There are two ways in which the Committee has sought to respond to the challenge presented by states such as Australia which comply with the formal requirements of the procedure but reject the Views adopted by the Committee. The first is to develop a 'follow-up procedure' and the second is to argue that states are *obligated* to respect the Views.

Follow-up

In an effort to expand the number of states which take appropriate action in response to the Views adopted under the Optional Protocol, the Committee has adopted a follow-up procedure:

> 1. The Committee shall designate a Special Rapporteur for follow-up . . . for the purpose of ascertaining the measures taken by States parties to give effect to the Committee's Views.
> 2. The Special Rapporteur may make such contacts and take such action as appropriate for the due performance of the follow-up mandate. The Special Rapporteur shall make such recommendations for further action by the Committee as may be necessary. . . .[45]

In implementing its follow-up policies, letters are sent requesting information, the Special Rapporteur meets with state's representatives, the matter is discussed in

[43] Response to Views in Faure, 1036/2001, Human Rights Committee Annual Report 2006, UN Doc. A/61/40, Vol. II. For a critique of Australia's position see Hilary Charlesworth *et al.*, *No Country is an Island: Australia and International Law* (2006) 82–91.

[44] *A v. Australia*, Communication No. 560/1993, *Human Rights Committee Annual Report 1998*, UN Doc. A/53/40, Vol 1, para. 491.

[45] Rules of Procedure of the Human Rights Committee, UN Doc. CCPR/C/3/Rev.8 (2005), Rule 101.

a public meeting,[46] all replies and non-replies are recorded in detail in the Annual Report,[47] and in some cases the Special Rapporteur has requested a country visit. In addition to proposing more frequent use of follow-up missions, a member of the Committee (Prof. Wedgwood) has called on the Committee to make use of the internet to publicize 'case opinions and [indicate] the compliance or non-compliance' of states, to 'find ways to speak to States and to parliaments directly, without, of course, evading diplomatic channels' and to seek 'to increase the influence and didactic effectiveness of its jurisprudence'.[48]

The Legal Status of Views

The status of the Committee's Views is linked to the perceived nature of the Committee itself. Nowak suggests that it is a 'quasi-judicial' body:

> Because it is a body of experts largely independent of the United Nations and States parties, and considering its decision-making powers in individual and inter-State communications and the manner in which these procedures have thus far been conducted in practice, the Committee may be considered a '*quasi-judicial organ*'. The fact that . . . it cannot be termed a court in the strict sense of the word follows not only from the relatively brief term of office of its members and the lack of internationally binding effect of its decisions but also from its designation as a 'Committee'.[49]

But the Committee itself, and many commentators have nonetheless suggested that its Views are, in effect, binding. Scheinin, for example, argues that:

> it would be wrong to categorize the Committee's views as mere 'recommendations'. They are the end result of a quasi-judicial adversarial international body established and elected by the States Parties for the purpose of interpreting the provisions of the Covenant and monitoring compliance with them. It would be incompatible with these preconditions of the procedure if a state that voluntarily has subjected itself to such a procedure, would, after first being one of the two parties in a case, then after receiving the Committee's views, simply replaces the Committee's position with its own interpretation as to whether there has been a violation of the Covenant or not. If a state wishes to question the correctness of a legal interpretation by the Committee, it should as least resort to some other procedure before an international court or independent expert body. As this is not likely to happen in practice, the presumption should be that the Committee's views in Optional Protocol cases are treated as the authoritative interpretation of the Covenant under international law.[50]

Joseph has noted that the Committee 'is the pre-eminent interpreter of the ICCPR which is itself legally binding. The [Committee's] decisions are therefore

[46] See, e.g., UN doc. CCPR/C/SR.2392 (2006).

[47] A comprehensive account of the Committee's follow-up in response to all pending Views is contained in its Annual Report. See, e.g., Annual Report 2006, Vol. II, Annex VII.

[48] UN Doc. CCPR/C/SR.2412 (2006), para. 52.

[49] Nowak, n. 22, *supra*, pp. 668–669.

[50] R. Hanski and M. Scheinin (eds.), *Leading Cases of the Human Rights Committee* (2003), p. 22.

strong indicators of legal obligations, so rejection of these decisions is good evidence of a State's bad faith attitude towards its ICCPR obligations.'[51]

While the attitude of individual Committee members seem to vary, they have reached a consensus on the following formulation which is used to conclude every set of Views adopted by the Committee:

> Bearing in mind that, by becoming a State party to the Optional Protocol, the State party has recognized the competence of the Committee to determine whether there has been a violation of the Covenant or not and that, pursuant to article 2 of the Covenant, the State party has undertaken to ensure to all individuals within its territory and subject to its jurisdiction the rights recognized in the Covenant and to provide an effective and enforceable remedy in case a violation has been established, the Committee wishes to receive from the State party, within ninety days, information about the measures taken to give effect to the Committee's Views.

Redefining the Committee's role under the Optional Protocol

Steiner has argued that the Committee cannot realistically serve the basic dispute-resolution function that informs adjudication by courts in many national legal systems. Nor can it effectively do justice in the individual case within the limits of its jurisdiction and to that extent vindicate the rule of law. Nor can it effectively protect rights under the ICCPR through deterrence. What remains is the function of 'expounding (elucidating, interpreting and explaining) the Covenant so as to engage the Committee in an ongoing, fruitful dialogue' with all relevant actors.

HENRY STEINER, INDIVIDUAL CLAIMS IN A WORLD OF MASSIVE VIOLATIONS: WHAT ROLE FOR THE HUMAN RIGHTS COMMITTEE?

in Philip Alston and James Crawford (eds.), The Future of UN Human Rights Treaty Monitoring 15 (2000), at 38

Despite its stark differences from courts, the Committee could contribute to the international adjudicatory processes that elaborate human rights law in the same manner as do opinions of the European and Inter-American Courts of Human Rights....

Two significant changes in the Committee's mode of functioning under the Protocol would be necessary for realising these proposals: breaking with the historical pattern and style of writing views, and moving from a mandatory to a discretionary jurisdiction.

[In developing his first point, Steiner criticizes the 'formulaic presentations' of the great majority of the Committee's views, particularly because of their lack of readability and the frequent terse, unelaborated statement of the Committee's conclusions following an exhaustive presentation of the parties' arguments. He notes that

[51] Joseph, n. 18, *supra*, p. 24.

'the very effort to reach consensus has sapped the views of strength .... The upshot is that views ... hardly summon the human rights community to debate and dialogue. They fail to educate their readership ....']

The writing of views that possess the suggested characteristics requires that the Committee husband its energies under the Protocol, to allow more time to research and reflect on an issue, and to write. The Committee would have to allocate time to cases meriting exploration for the development of the Covenant, rather than depend on the flow of registered communications. These requirements would be difficult to satisfy in light of the overload of cases before the Committee and the prospects for its increase.

What then can be done to enable the Committee to establish some control over its caseload and the allocation of its time? ...

Achieving [the necessary reduction in caseload] could then require amending the Protocol to make the jurisdiction of the Committee (in whole or in substantial part) discretionary rather than mandatory....

Operating under a discretionary jurisdiction, the Committee might be able to issue 20 to 30 views a year, an ample number for making significant contributions to the understanding and development of the Covenant, and for stimulating thought and dialogue with diverse actors. In so different a system, the Committee would necessarily develop criteria for selection of communications. Such criteria might, for example, lead to rejection of cases where the case turned on controverted matters of fact that the Committee was not in a good position to resolve. They could disfavour cases raising issues that had been settled in prior views or that were not of general significance. The criteria might give priority to emergent issues affecting many states. The Committee might decide to handle a group of related problems, such as issues of criminal procedure or free speech, over several sessions.

... The Judicial Code of the United States gives the United States Supreme Court (with minor exceptions) discretion whether to review any case decided below by a federal or state court—even cases of the highest significance, involving the constitutionality of federal or state statutes, that had previously been subject to mandatory jurisdiction. The Court's criteria for exercising discretion in favour of review include a decision by a state or federal court on 'an important question of federal law that has not been, but should be, settled by this Court'.

...

QUESTIONS

1. What techniques do you think the Committee should use to promote compliance with its Views? What are the implications of these techniques in terms of the nature of states' obligations?

2. Do you consider states to be 'bound' by the Views? If so, on the basis of what theory of obligation? Is it desirable for the communications procedure to have a binding outcome?

3. Why do you suppose Steiner rejects certain functions as impractical or unrealistic for the Committee, such as (a) general dispute resolution for the states parties, (b) vindication of the rule of law by achieving justice in the individual case, and (c) acting as a deterrent to violations of the ICCPR? Do you agree?

4. How do you assess Steiner's proposal? What guidelines would you suggest for determining whether to hear on the merits a given communication?

5. 'Each of the Committee's three functions can be found inadequate from different perspectives. But if we look at the Committee as a totality, and examine these functions not discretely but as complementary approaches, we reach a far more favourable judgment about the significance of the Committee's contribution to the human rights regime'. Do you agree?

B. COMMENT ON THE OVERALL UN HUMAN RIGHTS TREATY BODY SYSTEM

While this chapter has focused on the ICCPR, many of the techniques used are followed by the other treaty bodies operating within the UN human rights regime. Until 2003 there were six 'core' treaties in force, each with its own monitoring body. In recent years, however, the situation has begun to change very significantly. The result, as of early 2007, is that in addition to the ICCPR Committee, there are the following UN treaty bodies, either in existence, or soon to be:

- *ESCR Committee*: Committee on Economic, Social and Cultural Rights (ICESCR — see Chapter 4);
- *CERD Committee*: Committee on the Elimination of Racial Discrimination (International Convention on the Elimination of All Forms of Racial Discrimination);
- *CEDAW Committee*: Committee on the Elimination of Discrimination against Women (CEDAW Convention — see Chapter 3);
- *CAT*: Committee: Committee against Torture (Convention against Torture and Other Cruel, Inhuman or Degrading Treatment or Punishment);
- *CRC*: Committee on the Rights of the Child (Convention on the Rights of the Child);
- *CMW*: Committee on the Protection of All Migrant Workers and Members of Their Families (Convention on the Protection of All Migrant Workers and Members of Their Families);
- *CRPD*: Committee on the Rights of Persons with Disabilities (Convention on the Rights of Persons with Disabilities)
- *CED*: Committee on Enforced Disappearances (International Convention for the Protection of All Persons from Enforced Disappearance)

The precise details as to dates, composition, functions, number of cases, etc., are too complex to warrant detailed analysis here. Instead the Table below provides the salient facts.[52] This final section contains a brief note on some of the new approaches to monitoring that have emerged over the past few years and that go well beyond the standard techniques reflected in the ICCPR, and an overview of proposals to streamline or reform the treaty body system as a whole.

New Approaches to Monitoring

Both the Convention against Torture (Art. 20) and the Optional Protocol to the CEDAW Convention (Art. 8) provide for an on-site visit, or inquiry, on an initially confidential basis, to be undertaken by one or more committee members where violations have been reliably attested and the state concerned agrees to the visit. The confidentiality may be, and consistently has been, waived once the visit has been made. Mexico, for example, has been the subject of visits under both procedures, one dealing with consistent reports of police torture, and the other concerning the killing of hundreds of young women in Ciudad Juarez between 1993 and 2003, and both reports have been published.[53]

More recent treaties have been even more creative in terms of monitoring arrangements. At one end of the spectrum is the Optional Protocol to the Torture Convention of 2002, which entered into force in 2006. Its emphasis is on prevention and it establishes a Subcommittee for Prevention which can make on-site visits at any time. It also obligates states to establish their own national preventive mechanisms (NPMs) to monitor regularly all places of detention. At the other end of the spectrum is the proposed Committee on Enforced Disappearances. In addition to the traditional functions of state reporting, individual complaints, and interstate complaints, the proposed committee has an urgent, humanitarian procedure, is empowered to undertake on-site inquiries and may call the attention of the UN General Assembly to situations of widespread and systematic disappearances.

Proposals to streamline the treaty body system

Even when there were only six treaty bodies, and many fewer states parties to the key treaties than is now the case, concerns had been raised about the sustainability of a system which is fragmented, complex, and under-resourced. Critics identified shortcomings in all aspects of the reporting process. They noted widespread non-reporting and significant tardiness in reporting by states, and that reports are often superficial. Governments are reluctant to facilitate domestic debate around the reports. In relation to the committees themselves, the level of expertise and independence of members has been questioned, the Concluding Observations on states reports are often excessively general, the approach adopted to reports by different states by a single treaty body is not always consistent, and there is inadequate follow-up to recommendations made to governments.

[52] The best general sources are: 'Report on the working methods of the human rights treaty bodies relating to the state party reporting process', UN Doc. HRI/MC/2006/4; and the information provided at www.bayefsky.com.

[53] See UN Doc. CAT/C/75 (2003) and CEDAW/C/2005/OP.8/MEXICO (2005).

International human rights treaties overseen by monitoring bodies

Treaty	ICCPR	ICESCR	ICERD	CEDAW	CAT	CRC	CMW	CRPD	ICED
Adopted in	1966	1966	1965	1979	1984	1989	1990	2006	2006
Entry into force	1976	1976	1969	1981	1987	1990	2003		
States parties, 01/2007	160	155	173	185	144	193	34		
OPs adopted/in force	1:1966/1976 2:1989/1991			1999/2000	2002/2006	1:2000/2002* 2:2000/2002		2006	
States parties to OPs, 1/2007	1: 109 2: 60			83	28	1: 113 2. 110			
Treaty Body	HR C'ee	ESCR C'ee	CERD C'ee	CEDAW C'ee	C'ee agst Torture	C'eeRC	C'ee MW	C'ee RPD	C'eeED
C'ee Members	18	18	18	23	10+10–25**	18	10–14	12–18	10
Reporting periodicity: first/periodic	1/4 yrs	2/5 yrs	1/2 yrs	1/4 yrs	1/4 yrs	2/5 yrs	1/5 yrs	2/4 yrs	2/- yrs
Weeks of mtgs per year	9	6	6	9	6	9	2		
No of reports examined per year	12	10	16–22	31	12	48	1		
Inter-state complaint procedure?	Yes	No	Yes	No	Yes	No	No	Yes-in OP	Yes
Individual complaints procedure?	Yes	No	Yes	Yes	Yes	No	Yes	Yes	Yes
Cases registered to 2006	1,453		35	6	288				
Cases decided 2005 + 2006	151		6	4	38				
On-site inquiry visits	No	No	No	Yes-OP	Yes-in CAT & OP	No	No	No	Yes
No. of GC's etc up to 1/2007	31	18	31	25	1	8			
Day of General discussion?	No	Yes	Yes	No	No	Yes	Yes		

* 1: OP on Sale of children; 2: OP on Armed conflict.

** The OP to CAT establishes a Subcommittee on Prevention, which will begin with 10 members, rising to 25.

Another pressing issue concerns the duplication of reporting obligations under the different treaty regimes. As originally conceived, the system was designed to enable a state to become a party to one treaty, even if it had no interest in any of the others. Now that the majority of states has ratified the majority of the six treaties, the overlapping reporting burden and the uncoordinated responses by the different committees are increasingly being challenged by governments. And identical reports might elicit different responses from different committees. NGOs with sparse resources must deal with the difficulties of monitoring states' compliance with each of these treaties and seeking to give adequate publicity to the work of each.

In statistical terms the following figures provide part of the overall picture as of 2006. All States are party to at least one of the seven treaties and 75% are party to four or more; for the first six of the treaties, 77% of all possible ratifications have been undertaken. The seven treaties bodies combined consist of 115 members and meet for 57 weeks of sessions per year. The average time from submission to consideration of State party reports by the treaty bodies in 2005 was 17.4 months. The ICCPR Committee had 316 cases pending in 2006. For ICESCR and CAT only 72% of initial reports have been submitted, and for CAT 62% of states parties had overdue reports. The total annual cost of running the existing seven treaty bodies, including UN staff, interpretation and translation, travel and subsistence of members is close to $25 million.[54]

Reports by an 'independent expert' appointed by the UN Secretary-General suggested three long-term options for reducing reporting burdens: (i) reducing the number of treaty bodies and hence the number of reports required; (ii) encouraging states to produce a single 'global' report to be submitted to all relevant treaty bodies; and (iii) replacing the requirement of comprehensive periodic reports with specifically-tailored reports.[55] Governments responded in mixed terms to these reports[56] but a new impetus to reform came from a report by the UN Secretary-General in 2005:

> 95. The United Nations human rights treaty system is one of the Organization's great achievements....
>
> 96. The problems with the current system are well documented and there is a large degree of consensus on the basic defects....
>
> ...
>
> 99. ... In the long term ... it seems clear that some means must be found to consolidate the work of the seven treaty bodies and to create a unified standing treaty body....[57]

[54] Source: UN Doc. HRI/MC/2006/2, Annexes.

[55] P. Alston, Final Report on Enhancing the Long-Term Effectiveness of the United Nations Human Rights Treaty System, UN Doc. E/CN.4/1997/74.

[56] See UN Docs. E/CN.4/1998/85 and E/CN.4/2000/98.

[57] In larger freedom: towards development, security and human rights for all: Report of the Secretary-General, UN Doc. A/59/2005/Add.3.

CONCEPT PAPER ON THE HIGH COMMISSIONER'S PROPOSAL FOR A UNIFIED STANDING TREATY BODY

UN Doc. HRI/MC/2006/2

[In this analysis the HCHR spells out the arguments in favour of replacing the existing seven treaty bodies with a single treaty body, composed of full-time experts.]

7. The High Commissioner's proposal is underpinned by several principles. These are that the human rights treaty system has a key role to play in the promotion and protection of human rights at national and international levels. The achievements of the current system should be built on, in order to provide a stronger framework for implementation and monitoring of existing treaty obligations, and those which may be elaborated by future international human rights treaties, such as with respect to disappearances and disability. The specificities of each treaty must be preserved and their focus on specific rights, such as freedom from torture or racial discrimination, and the rights of particular rights-holders, such as children, women, and migrant workers, should not be diminished. At the same time, the interdependent and indivisible nature of the obligations set out in the treaties must be highlighted. Implementation of existing obligations of States parties, must be strengthened, but substantive obligations of States parties should not be affected or renegotiated.

...

[Challenges facing the system]

16. The system . . . faces challenges because many States accept the human rights treaty system on a formal level, but do not engage with it, or do so in a superficial way, either as a result of lack of capacity or lack of political will. . . .

...

17. The growth in the number of treaties and treaty bodies has been ad hoc and their provisions and competencies overlap. . . .

18. The growth in the number of treaties and ratifications has resulted in a steep increase in the workload of the treaty bodies and the Secretariat, backlogs in the consideration of reports and individual complaints, and increasing resource requirements. At the same time, the treaty bodies have been under-resourced, and their meeting time has been insufficient to handle their workload. Individual complaints procedures are underutilized, but the time between submission of a complaint and pronouncement of a final decision currently averages 30 to 33 months . . . .

...

[Advantages of a unified approach]

27. The proposal of a unified standing treaty body is based on the premise that, unless the international human rights treaty system functions and is perceived as a unified, single entity responsible for monitoring the implementation of all international human rights obligations, with a single, accessible entry point for rights-holders, the

lack of visibility, authority and access which affects the current system will persist. The proposal is also based on the recognition that, as currently constituted, the system is approaching the limits of its performance, and that, while steps can be taken to improve its functioning in the short and medium term, more fundamental, structural change will be required in order to guarantee its effectiveness in the long term. Unlike the current system of seven part-time Committees, a unified standing treaty body comprised of permanent, full-time professionals is more likely to produce consistent and authoritative jurisprudence. A unified standing treaty body would be available to victims on a permanent basis and could respond rapidly to grave violations. As a permanent body, it would have the flexibility to develop innovative working methods and approaches to human rights protection and be able to develop clear modalities for the participation of United Nations partners and civil society, which build on the good practices of the current system....

NOTE

The following are among the advantages of a unified body suggested by the paper: it could adopt a holistic approach; its procedures could be more flexible and creative; its relative simplicity would facilitate the work of NGOs, national human rights institutions and other stakeholders; the interpretation of comparable provisions of different treaties would be consistent; General Comments would be consistent and clear; pending individual complaints would be adjudicated expeditiously, which would make the system more effective and attractive; follow-up capacity would be enhanced; it could be flexible in terms of the timing and venue of its sessions; it could take on the supervision of new treaty standards if necessary; and it could work more closely with other human rights bodies, such as the special procedures or regional human rights bodies. Perhaps, most importantly, it 'would inevitably be more visible than the existing treaty bodies, and would be able to make its procedures, recommendations and decisions better known at the national level.'

The report acknowledges that a unified body could adopt various modes of operation including (1) a single body with no chambers, (2) chambers operating in parallel, (3) chambers along functional lines, (4) chambers along treaty lines, (5) chambers along thematic lines, and (6) chambers along regional lines. In terms of the legal challenge of introducing such a system the report notes: 'At a minimum, a simplified ratification procedure, or the provisional application of the new monitoring regime pending the entry into force of the amendments ... could be envisaged.'

QUESTION

What do you see as the principal disadvantages of a unified treaty body? Could these be overcome through creative arrangements in establishing the new body, or would too much of the appeal of the existing system be lost?

ADDITIONAL READING

M. Nowak, *UN Covenant on Civil and Political Rights: ICCPR Commentary* (2nd edn. 2005); P. Alston and J. Crawford (eds.), *The Future of UN Human Rights Treaty Monitoring* (2000); C. Heyns and F. Viljoen, *The Impact of the United Nations Human Rights Treaties on the Domestic Law* (2002); I. Boerefijn, *The Reporting Procedure under the Covenant on Civil and Political Rights: Practice and Procedures of the Human Rights Committee* (1999); G. Alfredsson *et al.* (eds.), *International Human Rights Monitoring Mechanisms* (2001); A. Bayefsky, *The UN Human Rights Treaty System: Universality at the Crossroads* (2001); K. Young, *The Law and Process of the U.N. Human Rights Committee* (2002); S. Joseph, J. Schultz and M. Castan, *The International Covenant on Civil and Political Rights: Cases, Materials, and Commentary* (2nd edn. 2004); M. Banton, *International Action Against Racial Discrimination* (1996). The best website for primary documents relating to the UN treaty bodies is www.bayefsky.com, and see 'How to Complain About Human Rights Treaty Violations' at www.bayefsky.com/tree.php/area/complain. Another excellent site is International Service for Human Rights, *Treaty Body Monitor*, at www.ishr.ch/hrm/TMBs/index.htm.

11

Regional Arrangements

Part D's materials on intergovernmental institutions concludes with a look at the world's major regional human rights systems. After an introductory section comparing the advantages and disadvantages of regional systems versus a universal one, this chapter turns to the regional arrangements in Europe, the Americas and Africa.

The materials describe the norms, institutional structure and processes of the regional systems, and invite comparisons among them as well as with the UN system. The European and Inter-American systems have innovative institutions and processes; the African system has distinctive norms. Thus the regional arrangements add in important ways to knowledge derived from the United Nations and UN-related treaties like the two International Covenants about possible methods for protecting and promoting human rights. They illustrate the full range of the human rights movement's institutional architecture.

Chapter 11 concentrates on one distinctive aspect of each system. The remarkable feature of the European system is its productive and effective Court; the materials illustrate its work and the dilemmas of supranational adjudication through its decisions on issues of homosexuality and political democracy, and its response to the admission of new members with complex and often problematic human rights records such as Russia. In the Inter-American system, the materials look briefly at its Court but concentrate on its Commission on Human Rights, a powerful organ with tasks and functions not found in the European system. The African system is the least developed institutionally. Part of Chapter 6 on cultural relativism looked at its distinctive stress on duties as well as rights; the present materials look primarily at the communications procedure of the African Commission on Human and Peoples' Rights.

A. COMPARISON OF UNIVERSAL AND REGIONAL SYSTEMS

The relationship between 'universal' (meaning, in this context, United Nations-sponsored) and regional human rights arrangements is a complex one. In addition to the three major systems, there is a largely dormant Arab system and a proposal for the creation of Asian regional or sub-regional systems. Although Chapter VIII of the United Nations Charter makes provision for regional arrangements in relation to peace and security, it is silent as to human rights cooperation at that level. Nevertheless, the Council of Europe moved as early as 1950 to adopt the European Convention on Human Rights. It was not until 1969 that the analogous American Convention was adopted. In the meantime, at least until the mid 1960s, the UN remained at best ambivalent about such developments. Vasak has noted some of the reasons for its reluctance:

> For a long time, regionalism in the matter of human rights was not popular at the United Nations: there was often a tendency to regard it as the expression of a breakaway movement, calling the universality of human rights into question. However, the continual postponements of work on the International Human Rights Covenants led the UN to rehabilitate, and to be less suspicious (less jealous, some would say) towards, regionalism in human rights, especially after the adoption of the Covenants in 1966.[1]

It was not then coincidental that the UN General Assembly began to contemplate the active encouragement of regional mechanisms only in 1966, when the two basic Covenants were finally adopted by the General Assembly. In 1977, it formally endorsed a new approach by appealing 'to States in areas where regional arrangements in the field of human rights do not yet exist to consider agreements with a view to the establishment within their respective regions of suitable regional machinery for the promotion and protection of human rights' (GA Res. 32/127 (1977)). Four years later, the African Charter of Human and Peoples' Rights was adopted. Throughout this period the Communist states of Eastern Europe were strongly opposed to regional arrangements, and the Asian and Pacific countries generally argued that their region was much too heterogeneous to permit the creation of a regional mechanism.

Despite the UN General Assembly's annual adoption of a resolution calling upon the relevant regions to act, no significant regional or sub-regional systems has been created since 1981. Although states from the former Soviet Union adopted a Commonwealth of Independent States Convention on Human Rights in Minsk in 1995, the Convention has been much criticized and appears to have amounted to little in practice.[2] The current climate is somewhat more hospitable, in view of the desire of Eastern and Central European governments to become full partners in a united Europe, and even to join the European Union, which has prompted many of them to join the European human rights system. Moreover, the transformation of the Organization for Security and Co-operation in Europe (OSCE) from an East-West debating forum (or shouting match) into an organization designed to promote respect for a broadly defined range of human rights, has added another important dimension to regional human rights cooperation.

The successful example of the OSCE in promoting political cooperation, combined with the dramatically increased importance of the role of regional trading blocs — exemplified by the European Union Treaty in Europe, as well as the North American Free Trade Agreement between the United States, Canada and Mexico — and efforts

[1] In K. Vasak and P. Alston (eds.), *The International Dimensions of Human Rights* (Vol. 2, 1982), at 451.

[2] See text in 17 Hum. Rts L. J. 159 (1996) and critiques in *ibid.*, 164 and 181.

to develop the Association of South-East Asian Nations (ASEAN) and the Asian-Pacific Economic Cooperation (APEC) initiative, have given renewed impetus to regional cooperation arrangements. Over time, this development may have important consequences for human rights.

❁ ❁ ❁

The following readings develop some comparisons between universal and regional systems, both in general and with respect to human rights. Several themes suggested by these materials recur throughout the chapter: what are the relations between these systems — for example, are there hierarchical 'controls' between them; in what ways is it preferable from the perspective of observance of human rights to have a regional system complement a universal one; how do we explain the different institutional structures and differences in norms among these systems; what can we learn from these differences about effective architecture for intergovernmental human rights organizations?

INIS CLAUDE, SWORDS INTO PLOWSHARES

(4th edn. 1984), at 102

Regionalism is sometimes put forward as an alternative to globalism, a superior substitute for the principle of universality. Emphasis is placed upon the bigness and heterogeneity of the wide world, and the conclusion is drawn that only within limited segments of the globe can we find the cultural foundations of common loyalties, the objective similarity of national problems, and the potential awareness of common interests which are necessary for the effective functioning of multilateral institutions. The world is too diverse and unwieldy; the distances — physical, economic, cultural, administrative, and psychological — between peoples at opposite ends of the earth are too formidable to permit development of a working sense of common involvement and joint responsibility. Within a region, on the other hand, adaptation of international solutions to real problems can be intelligently carried out, and commitments by states to each other can be confined to manageable proportions and sanctioned by clearly evident bonds of mutuality.

...

The advocacy of regionalism can be, and often is, as doctrinaire and as heedless of concrete realities as the passion for all-encompassing organization. It should be stressed that the suitability of regionalism depends in the first place upon the nature of the problem to be dealt with. Some problems of the modern world are international in the largest sense, and can be effectively treated only by global agencies. Others are characteristically regional, and lend themselves to solution by correspondingly delimited bodies. Still others are regional in nature, but require for their solution the mobilization of extra-regional resources.

...

The nature of a problem is significant not only for the determination of the most appropriate means of solution, but also for the measurement of the range of its impact. A problem may be regional in location, and susceptible of regional management, and yet have such important implications for the whole world that it becomes a fit subject for the concern of a general organization. The world-at-large cannot be disinterested in such 'regional' matters as the demographic problem in Asia or racialism in Southern Africa. Thus, the question of the ramifications of a problem as well as that of its intrinsic quality affects the choice between regional and universal approaches.

...

However, . . . [t]he world does not in fact break easily along neatly perforated lines. Rational regional divisions are difficult to establish, boundaries determined for one purpose are not necessarily appropriate for other purposes, and the most carefully chosen dividing lines have a perverse way of changing or coming to require change, and of overlapping. It is true that brave universalist experiments tend to give way to sober regionalist afterthoughts, but it is equally true that carefully cut regional patterns tend to lose their shape through persistent stretching in the direction of universalism. In a sense, the adoption of the universal approach is the line of least resistance, since it obviates the difficulties of defining regions and keeping them defined.

. . . Intraregional affinities may be offset by historically rooted intraregional animosities, and geographical proximity may pose dangers which states wish to diminish by escaping into universalism, rather than collaborative possibilities which they wish to exploit in regional privacy. While global organization may be too large, in that it may ask states to be concerned with matters beyond the limited horizons of their interests, regional organization may be too small, in that it may represent a dangerous form of confinement for local rivalries. Global stretching, in short, may be no worse than regional cramping.

...

In a very general sense, it may be contended that regional organizations are particularly suitable for the cultivation of intensive cooperation among states, while global organizations have special advantages for dealing with conflict among states. If the goal is the development of linkages that bind states together in increasingly intimate collaboration and perhaps culminate in their integration, it would appear to be essential to restrict the enterprise to a few carefully selected states.

. . . On the other hand, the capacity of an organization to promote the control and resolution of conflicts may be enhanced by its inclusiveness. A global agency is inherently better equipped than a regional one to provide the mediatorial services of governments and individuals whose disinterested attitude toward any given pair of disputants is likely to be regarded as credible, and its potency as a mobilizer of pressure upon states engaged in conflict is a function of the broad scope of its membership and jurisdiction. The European Community may be treated as the model for international organization as a workshop for collaboration, and the United Nations as the model for international organization as an arena for conflict.

...

WALDEMAR HUMMER AND MICHAEL SCWEITZER, ARTICLE 52

in B. Simma *et al.* (eds.), The Charter of the United Nations: A Commentary (2nd edn. 2002), at 807, 812

. . .

Regionalism versus Universalism

. . .

The 'universalist' approach, on the one hand, assumed that systems not conceived on a world-wide basis would necessarily create rivalries, thus containing within themselves the seeds of future conflicts; these conflicts could only be avoided by a universal organization invested with far-reaching powers. On the other hand, the 'regionalist' approach expressed the opinion that in the light of the size and heterogeneity of the world, regional sub-systems represent indispensable intermediary structures of co-operation over which a universal superstructure — although merely supervisory in nature — could possibly span.

. . .

At the Dumbarton Oaks Conference [of the four major powers, in1944] the universalist approach prevailed, in that a world Organization under the primary responsibility of the permanent members of the SC was conceived, leaving almost no room for regional groupings. By way of contrast, at the San Francisco Conference from April to June 1945, 36 of the 50 State representatives advocated a 'regionalist' approach. However, due to their entirely divergent particular interest, these representatives were initially only able to push through negligible changes to the text of the Charter as formulated at Dumbarton Oaks in 1944.

. . .

The decisive and ultimately successful push for modification of the universalist principle came from the Latin American States. The continental/regional element has existed on the American continent since the beginning of Pan-Americanism in 1889–90, and, since 1933, had grown progressively stronger. . . .

. . .

The UN Charter contains no further provisions regarding any other regional organizations of a political, economic, technical, cultural, or any other nature. Since organizations are in any case so inconsistent with the universal approach of the UN that they could not even achieve the status of specialized agency. . . . Accordingly, regionalism plays only a subordinate role within the UN as a principle of that organization.

REGIONAL PROMOTION AND PROTECTION OF HUMAN RIGHTS

Twenty-Eighth Report of the Commission to Study the Organization of Peace (1980), at 15

[The report notes four arguments favouring regional human rights commissions]: (1) the existence of geographic, historical, and cultural bonds among States of a particular region; (2) the fact that recommendations of a regional organization may meet with less resistance than those of a global body; (3) the likelihood that publicity about human rights will be wider and more effective; and (4) the fact that there is less possibility of 'general, compromise formulae', which in global bodies are more likely to be based on 'considerations of a political nature'.

...

Opposition to the establishment of regional human rights commissions has been expressed on numerous occasions by the Eastern European States and other Members of the United Nations, on several grounds. First, they argue that human rights, being global in nature and belonging to everyone, should be defined in global instruments and implemented by global bodies. 'The African and the Asian should have the same human rights as the European or the American'. Second, regional bodies in the human rights field would, at best, duplicate the work of United Nations bodies and, at worst, develop contradictory policies and procedures. . . . Third, the Eastern European States in particular object that any cooperation between regional commissions and the United Nations would add to the financial burdens of the latter. Fourth, several Western European States contend that preoccupation with regional arrangements might deflect official and public attention from the two International Covenants and delay their ratification.

It may be argued that the global approach and the regional approach to promotion and protection of human rights are not necessarily incompatible; on the contrary, they are both useful and complementary. The two approaches can be reconciled on a functional basis: the normative content of all international instruments, both global and regional, should be similar in principle, reflecting the Universal Declaration of Human Rights, which was proclaimed 'as a common standard of achievement for all peoples and all nations'. The global instrument would contain the minimum normative standard, whereas the regional instrument might go further, add further rights, refine some rights, and take into account special differences within the region and between one region and another.

Thus what at first glance might seem to be a serious dichotomy — the global approach and the regional approach to human rights — has been resolved satisfactorily on a functional basis. . . .

Implementation procedures may well vary even more from region to region, as the Governments therein desire. Indeed, they may vary within a region.

...

It may also be argued that the regional approach involves certain possible risks. First, a regional or sub-regional commission might serve to insulate the area from outside influences and encourage it to ignore the global standards and institutions of the United Nations system. Second, institutions of one region or sub-region might become involved in competition or conflict with those of another area. Given a modicum of good will and statesmanship on the part of any newly-established regional institutions, however, these risks should be minimal.

The further question arises whether if human rights commissions were established in certain regions, they might interpret international standards too narrowly and thus adversely affect the work of global bodies in this field. It might be necessary in such a case to establish the right of global institutions to consider a particular matter *de novo*.

. . .

NOTE

Consider the following cautions of Vasak about conditions for the success of a regional human rights organization:

> The experience of the European Convention of Human Rights . . . tends to show that the regional protection of human rights can achieve full success only if it constitutes an element in a policy of integration on the part of the States of a given region. Only at this price is it possible to permit the blow struck by regionalism in the matter of human rights against that necessary universalism which springs from the intrinsically identical nature of all human beings. The recent entry into force of the [UN Covenants], which should be preserved as a legal expression of the universal character of the human being, should even lead us to be more exacting in the future in respect of regionalism than we were in the past when no universal system for the effective protection of human rights seemed feasible. In the last analysis, regional protection must come within the framework of regional organization in accordance with the Charter of the United Nations and become one aspect of the policy of integration. If, however, regional protection were but a *form of intergovernmental co-operation*, the parochial and perhaps even selfish attitudes of which it would also be the expression, would by no means justify the danger of such a serious blow to universalism.[3]

Shelton, on the other hand, is very optimistic in describing the results of the interaction of the various regional systems with one another and with the UN:

> As the systems have evolved, the universal framework within which they began, together with their own interactions, have had surprisingly strong influence, leading to converging norms and procedures in an overarching interdependent and dynamic system. In many respects they are thinking globally and acting regionally. Each uses the jurisprudence of the other systems and amends and strengthens its procedures with reference to the experience of the others. In general, their mutual influence in highly progressive, both in normative development and institutional reform.[4]

[3] Note 1 above, at p. 455.

[4] Dinah Shelton, 'The Promise of Regional Human Rights Systems', in B. Weston and S. Marks (eds.), *The Future of International Human Rights* (1999) 351, at 356.

Note the flexibility of conceptions of the term 'region'. For a range of purposes, such as caucuses among state representatives in the UN Commission on Human Rights, the UN divides the world into five geo-political regions: Asia, Africa, Eastern Europe, Latin America and Western Europe and Others (including the United States). That classification need bear no relation whatsoever to appropriate definition of regions for purposes of a human rights regime. For example, the Pacific region (with or excluding Australia and New Zealand), South Asia, West Asia, Southeast Asia and possibly other groupings of states might all be considered appropriate units for the creation of a given type of joint human rights mechanism.

QUESTIONS

1. Consider the observation that '[r]egional and sub-regional blocs and groupings, whatever their purpose, are by their very nature inward-looking and designed to serve specific ends. Like the states of which they are composed, these blocs and groupings are more concerned with the exploitation of immediate advantages than with long-range world plans . . .'.[5] Is this view as appropriate for a human rights regime as for, say, a regional trading bloc?

2. To date, there have been no major conflicts (as opposed to minor differences) of interpretation, or formal decisions between the existing regional bodies and their UN counterparts, although the texts of the different regional treaties suggest on their face that serious conflicts with UN-related treaties could arise. In theory, such conflicts are to be avoided through the application of some basic guidelines or rules. How do you assess the following guidelines, and what alternatives might you propose to them?

   a. The standards in the Universal Declaration and in any other UN-related treaties accepted by the state or states concerned must be respected.
   b. Human rights standards forming part of general principles of international law must also be respected.
   c. Where standards conflict, the one most favourable to the individual concerned should prevail.

3. Should regional organizations provide an opening for cultural relativism — that is, for regionally specific norms that should be respected rather than superseded by the universal systems? How do the guidelines in the preceding question bear on that possibility?

ADDITIONAL READING

H. Hashimoto, *The Prospects for a Regional Human Rights Mechanism in East Asia* (2003); D. Shelton, 'The Promise of Regional Human Rights Systems', in B. Weston and S. Marks (eds.), *The Future of International Human Rights* (1999) 351; 'Chapter

[5] M. Moscowitz, *The Politics and Dynamics of Human Rights* (1968), at 48.

VIII: Regional Arrangements', in B. Simma *et al.* (eds.), *The Charter of the United Nations: A Commentary* 807 (2nd edn. 2002).

B. THE EUROPEAN CONVENTION SYSTEM

1. INTRODUCTION AND OVERVIEW

The European Convention for the Protection of Human Rights and Fundamental Freedoms (ECHR) was signed in 1950 and entered into force in 1953. The ECHR is of particular importance within the context of international human rights for several reasons: it was the first comprehensive treaty in the world in this field; it established the first international complaints procedure and the first international court for the determination of human rights matters; it remains the most judicially developed of all the human rights systems; it has generated a more extensive jurisprudence than any other part of the international system; and it now applies to some 30% of the nations in the world. Our principal concern in this selective examination of the European Convention is with its evolving institutional architecture, particularly with the European Court of Human Rights and the manner in which it has performed the judicial function.

The impetus for the adoption of a European Convention came from three factors. It was first a regional response to the atrocities committed in Europe during the Second World War and an affirmation of the belief that governments respecting human rights are less likely to wage war on their neighbours. Secondly, both the Council of Europe, which was set up in 1949 (and under whose auspices the Convention was adopted), and the European Union (previously the European Community or Communities, the first of which was established in 1952) were partly based on the assumption that the best way to ensure that Germany would be a force for peace, in partnership with France, the United Kingdom and other Western European states, was through regional integration and the institutionalizion of common values. This strategy contrasted strongly with the punitive, reparations-based, approach embodied in the 1919 Versailles Treaty after the First World War.

Thus, the Preamble to the European Convention refers (perhaps somewhat optimistically at the time) to the 'European countries which are likeminded and have a common heritage of political traditions, ideals, freedom and the rule of law . . . '. But this statement also points to the third major impetus towards a Convention — the desire to bring the non-Communist countries of Europe together within a common ideological framework and to consolidate their unity in the face of the Communist threat. 'Genuine democracy' (to which the Statute of the Council of Europe commits its members) or the 'effective political democracy' to which the Preamble of the Convention refers, had to be clearly distinguished from the 'people's democracy' which was promoted by the Soviet Union and its allies.

The European Convention's transformation of abstract human rights ideals into a concrete legal framework followed a path which has characterized virtually all subsequent attempts. The initial enthusiasm was soon tempered by concerns over sovereignty and a reluctance to take the concept of a state's accountability too far. Thus a call by the Congress of Europe in 1948 for the adoption of a Charter of Human Rights to be enforced by a Court of Justice 'with adequate sanctions for the implementation of this Charter' went further than Western European governments were prepared to go. Instead, the final version of the Convention acknowledges in the Preamble that it constitutes only 'the first steps for the collective enforcement of certain of the Rights stated in the Universal Declaration'.

Both during the drafting of the Convention and in the years after its adoption there was considerable reluctance on the part of key states in relation to many of its key provisions. In this regard the most detailed historical analyses have been undertaken in relation to the United Kingdom and it is an instructive example.[6] During the Second World War, Prime Minister Churchill often returned to the theme that the war was being fought 'to establish, on impregnable rocks, the rights of the individual', and commentators such as Hersch Lauterpacht insisted that the war was, in large part, about 'the enthronement of the rights of man' and the correlative limitation of state sovereignty.[7] But when victory brought the opportunity to draft a human rights treaty, British diplomats and politicians raised a host of objections, as the following excerpt shows.

ANDREW MORAVCSIK, THE ORIGINS OF HUMAN RIGHTS REGIMES: DEMOCRATIC DELEGATION IN POSTWAR EUROPE

54 Int. Org. 217 (2000), at 238

The British . . . supported international declaratory norms but firmly opposed any attempt to establish binding legal obligations, centralized institutions, individual petition, or compulsory jurisdiction. As W. E. Beckett, legal advisor to the Foreign Office and the initiator of the British government's participation [in the drafting of the ECHR], put it, "We attach the greatest importance to a well-drafted Convention of Human Rights but we are dead against anything like an international court to which individuals who think they are aggrieved in this way could go." . . .

What issues were raised in confidential British deliberations? The secondary literature on British human rights policy makes much of two British concerns: the fear that residents of British colonies and dependencies might invoke the ECHR, and aversion to European federalism. To judge from confidential discussions, however, neither appears to have been a dominant concern. . . .

. . .

Instead British officials and politicians — most notably in Cabinet discussions — dwelled primarily on the fear that the convention would threaten idiosyncratic (but

[6] See A.W. B. Simpson, *Human Rights and the End of Empire: Britain and the Genesis of the European Convention* (2004); and G. Marston, 'The United Kingdom's Part in the Preparation of the European Convention on Human Rights, 1950', Int. & Comp. L. Q. 796 (1993).

[7] See M. Mazower, *Dark Continent: Europe's Twentieth Century* (1998) 193–194.

not unambiguously undemocratic) political practices and institutions in the United Kingdom....

The defense of British institutional idiosyncrasy elicited the most violent rhetoric from British politicians and officials. Lord Chancellor Jowitt's official paper criticized the draft convention... as:

> so vague and woolly that it may mean almost anything. Our unhappy legal experts ... have had to take their share in drawing up a code compared to which ... the Ten Commandments ... are comparatively insignificant.... It completely passes the wit of man to guess what results would be arrived at by a tribunal composed of elected persons who need not even be lawyers, drawn from various European states possessing completely different systems of law, and whose deliberations take place behind closed doors.... Any student of our legal institutions must recoil from this document with a feeling of horror.

A common complaint was that judicial review would undermine parliamentary sovereignty. Beckett wrote: "It seems inconceivable that any Government, when faced with the realities of this proposal, would take the risk of entrusting these unprecedented powers to an international court, legislative powers which Parliament would never agree to entrust to the courts of this country which are known and which command the confidence and admiration of the world." "Our whole constitution," a government document intoned, "is based on the principle that it is for the Parliament to enact the laws and for the judges to interpret the laws."...

The specific issue cited most often by the government's legal authorities was the British policy toward political extremists. A ministerial brief referred to a "blank cheque" that would "allow the Governments to become the object of such potentially vague charges by individuals as to invite Communists, crooks, and cranks of every type to bring actions." ... Lord Chancellor Jowitt's complaint was that "the Convention would prevent a future British government from detaining people without trial during a period of emergency ... or judges sending litigants to prison for throwing eggs at them; or the Home Secretary from banning Communist or Fascist demonstrations."

...

What blunted British opposition to any postwar European human rights regime was, above all, the fear of resurgent totalitarianism abroad that might pose an eventual military threat to the United Kingdom — precisely as republican liberal theory predicts. This fear reflected not just a concern with a resurgence of Fascism, but also a turnaround in British foreign policy in 1948 in response to the perceived rise of the Communist threat in Western Europe. The West, the government argued, needed not only to maintain the military balance but also to strengthen continental democracies....

In the minds of British officials, however, the primacy of domestic sovereignty over collective defense of the democratic peace remained unchallenged. The cabinet mandated efforts to water down the force of any agreement in Britain. British representatives sought to limit the potential risk of open-ended jurisprudence by calling for the careful enumeration and definition of human rights before agreeing on any enforcement mechanism. The expectation was that governments would not be able to agree on a list both extensive and precise. Acting on Prime Minister Clement Attlee's direct instruction, the British delegation successfully pressed to place the right of individual petition and the jurisdiction of the court into optional clauses. Foreign Minister Ernest Bevin himself instructed British negotiators to veto any mandatory right of individual petition "even if it [means] being in a minority of one." . . .

Having secured these concessions, which essentially rendered the convention unenforceable in Britain, the cabinet unanimously accepted the desirability of signing it. . . .

COMMENT ON ADMISSION TO MEMBERSHIP AND CONTENT OF RIGHTS

This historical review seems a long way from the world of the twenty-first century in which the UK Human Rights Act 1998, however distinctly formulated, made all of the rights recognized in the Convention an integral part of domestic law. More generally, major reforms of institutional provisions of the Convention have helped to move the system closer to that envisaged by the maximalists of the early 1950s. As with most systems for the protection of human rights, progress has required the gradual growth of popular expectations and an accumulation of experience in the functioning of the procedures that has served to assuage the worst fears of governments.

An Overview of the ECHR System

The Council of Europe was established in 1949 by a group of ten states, primarily to promote democracy, the rule of law, and greater unity among the nations of Western Europe. It represented both a principled commitment of its members to these values and an ideological stance against Communism. Over the years its activities have included the promotion of cooperation in relation to social, cultural, sporting and a range of other matters. Until 1990, the Council had 23 members, all from Western Europe. Post-Cold War developments, however, made a major impact upon the Council and by 2007 it had double that number.[8]

The conditions for the admission of a state to the Council of Europe are laid down in Article 3 of its Statute. The state must be a genuine democracy that respects the rule of law and human rights and must 'collaborate sincerely and effectively' with the Council in these domains. In practice, such collaboration involves becoming

[8] Albania, Andorra, Armenia, Austria, Azerbaijan, Belgium, Bosnia and Herzegovina, Bulgaria, Croatia, Cyprus, Czech Republic, Denmark, Estonia, Finland, France, Georgia, Germany, Greece, Hungary, Iceland, Ireland, Italy, Latvia, Liechtenstein, Lithuania, Luxembourg, Malta, Moldova, Monaco, Netherlands, Norway, Poland, Portugal, Romania, Russian Federation, San Marino, Serbia, Slovakia, Slovenia, Spain, Sweden, Switzerland, The Former Yugoslav Republic of Macedonia, Turkey, Ukraine and the United Kingdom.

a party to the European Convention on Human Rights. An applicant state must satisfy the Council's Committee of Ministers that its legal order conforms with the requirements of Article 3. The opinion of the Parliamentary Assembly is sought and the Assembly in turn will appoint an expert group to advise it.

The opinion of the experts is based upon an on-site visit.[9] For example, a 1994 expert report on the situation in Russia concluded that the requirements were not met. The report noted 'important shortcomings with regard to the rights to liberty and security of person and to fair trial' as well as the absence of the rule of law in view of the fact that the 'activities of public authorities are mainly decided upon according to general policy choices, personal allegiance and the effective power structure'.[10] Russia was admitted, nevertheless, in 1996. This decision by the Council's Parliamentary Assembly, and another to admit Croatia, were strongly criticized at the time by some human rights advocates.

Since that time the Parliamentary Assembly of the Council of Europe has adopted its own procedure, and established a specialist committee, to monitor 'the honouring of obligations and commitments' by all member states. The committee continues to report regularly on progress in all states, including for example its visit to Russia in 2006.[11]

The importance attached by the states of Central and Eastern Europe to membership of the Council reflected not only a commitment to human rights but a determination to gain respectability within Europe and, perhaps most importantly, to qualify for certain membership benefits as well as for admission to the European Union. Although the process of becoming a party to the Convention is not required to be completed prior to obtaining membership in the Council, it is generally assumed that the domestic legislative and other measures required to enable the state to ratify or accede will be completed within a period of two years.

The rights recognized in the ECHR

Although the initial moves to create a European Convention pre-dated the UN's adoption of the Universal Declaration, the text of the latter was available to those responsible for the final drafting of the Convention. Eventually the drafters defined rights in terms similar to the early version of the draft Covenant on Civil and Political Rights. (You should now read Articles 2–12 and 14 of the Convention.) Since the Covenant went through numerous changes before adoption, the formulations used in the two treaties sometimes differ significantly. Several weighty provisions appear in only one or the other. For example, the European Convention contains no provision relating to self-determination or to the rights of members of minority groups (Articles 1 and 27 of the ICCPR). Each treaty limits freedoms of expression, association and religion in similar ways (criteria of public safety or

[9] For a recent example, see 'Accession of the Republic of Montenegro to the Council of Europe: Opinion', Council of Europe Parliamentary Assembly, Doc. 11205 (12 March 2007).

[10] R. Bernhardt *et al.*, 'Report on the Conformity of the Legal Order of the Russian Federation with Council of Europe Standards', 15 Hum. Rts. L. J. 249 (1994), at 287.

[11] http://assembly.coe.int/ASP/APFeaturesManager/defaultArtView.asp?ArtId=430.

national security, for example), but the European Convention consistently requires that a limitation be 'necessary in a democratic society' (Articles 8–11). The derogation clauses (Article 4 of the ICCPR, Article 15 of the Convention) differ with respect to the list of non-derogable provisions.

Article 1 requires the Parties to 'secure [these rights] to everyone within their jurisdiction', while Article 13 requires the state to provide 'an effective remedy before a national authority' for everyone whose rights are violated. Compare the more demanding Article 2 of the ICCPR, which refers to states' duty to adopt legislative and other measures to give effect to the recognized rights and to 'develop the possibilities of judicial remedy'.

When the Convention was adopted in 1950, there were several outstanding proposals on which final agreement could not be reached. It was therefore agreed to adopt Protocols containing additional provisions. Since 1952, eleven protocols have been adopted. While the majority are devoted to procedural matters, others have recognized the following additional rights: the right to property ('the peaceful enjoyment of [one's] possessions'), the right to education, and the obligation to hold free elections (Protocol 1 of 1952); freedom from imprisonment for civil debts, freedom of movement and residence, freedom to leave any country, freedom from exile, the right to enter the country of which one is a national, and no collective expulsion of aliens (Protocol 4 of 1963); abolition of the death penalty (Protocol 6 of 1983); the right of an alien not to be expelled without due process, the right to appeal in criminal cases, the right to compensation for a miscarriage of justice, immunity of double prosecution for the same offence, and equality of rights and responsibility of spouses (Protocol 7 of 1984); the general prohibition of discrimination (Protocol 12 of 2000); and abolition of the death penalty, in all circumstances (Protocol 13 of 2002). Acceptance of each of the Protocols is optional.

By March 2007, all 46 member states of the Council of Europe were parties to the European Convention, and to Protocol Nos. 2, 3, 5, 8 and 11. Ratifications for the other Protocols were: No. 1–43; No. 4–40; No. 6–45; No. 7–39; No. 9–24; No. 10–25; No. 12–14; No. 13–38; and No. 14–45.

2. THE EUROPEAN COURT AND ITS PROCEDURES

The ECHR provides for both individual petitions (Art. 34) and interstate complaints (Art. 33). The latter are rare, but the opportunity continues to be significant. In contrast, the former, which may be brought by individuals, legal persons (such as corporations), groups of individuals, or non-governmental organisations, have grown exponentially in numerical terms.

The Convention makes clear that the primary responsibility for implementation rests with the member states themselves. The implementation machinery of the Convention comes into play only after domestic remedies are considered to have been exhausted. The great majority of complaints submitted are deemed inadmissible, frequently on the grounds that domestic law provides an effective remedy for any violation that may have taken place. Recall the obligations of member states under Articles 1 and 13 of the Convention to 'secure to everyone' the Convention's rights and to provide 'an effective remedy before a national authority' for violations of those rights. This preference for domestic resolution is also reinforced by the requirement to seek a 'friendly settlement' wherever possible and by the procedures for full government consultation in the examination of complaints.

The remedy given by a domestic court may be pursuant to provisions of domestic law that stand relatively independently of the Convention, although perhaps influenced by it, such as a human rights act, a code of criminal procedure or a constitutional provision that are consistent with the Convention. Or a remedy may be given as a result of the incorporation of the Convention into domestic law, which may be achieved as an automatic consequence of ratification or through the adoption of special legislation. See generally pp. 1087–1099, *infra*.

COMMENT ON THE DRAMATIC EVOLUTION OF THE ECHR SYSTEM

The system of considering individual complaints is the hallmark of the ECHR regime. Its evolution from a tentative and optional procedure which was used relatively sparingly to one which is now compulsory and extremely widely used has compelled the Contracting States (or states parties, to use UN terminology) to undertake a series of fundamental reforms. Driven by a flood of applications and the ever-present risk that the system will collapse from overload, the Court has been forced to consider very far-reaching and controversial changes and, in the process, to reflect carefully on what exactly it aspires to achieve. Much of the latter debate has taken place under the rubric of whether the ECHR is, or should be, a 'constitutional court'.

When originally devised in the 1950s, and for several decades thereafter, the petition procedure was optional. Only three of the original ten members accepted it from the outset, while many of the rest made clear that they wanted no part of it. For example, It was not until 1981 that France accepted the right of individual complaint for its citizens. And during the 1970s the British Government regularly raised the prospect that it might withdraw its acceptance of the procedure. Until the late 1990s the procedures used were much less 'judicial' than they are today, and were surrounded by safeguards aimed at providing reassurances to governments that they need not fear too much encroachment on their national sovereignty.

In terms of institutions, all complaints were first considered by the European Commission on Human Rights ('the Commission'). It initially considered whether a complaint was admissible. If it was, an effort was made to broker a 'friendly settlement', as provided for in the Convention. In the absence of such a settlement the Commission reported on the facts and expressed its opinion on the merits of the case. That report went to the Committee of Ministers, a political body, which could endorse or reject it. In instances where the state concerned had opted to accept the compulsory jurisdiction of the Court, either the Commission or that state could refer the case to the Court for a final, binding adjudication including, where appropriate, an award of compensation. The Court was thus dependent on the Commission or the state concerned in order to be able to consider a case. When cases did not go to the

Court but to the Committee of Ministers, which found there had been a violation of the Convention, it might award 'just satisfaction' to the victim.

Over time, more and more states accepted the compulsory jurisdiction of the Court and acceptance of the complaints procedure itself had become uninamous by 1990. A major reform introduced in 1994 (when Protocol No. 9 entered into force) allowed applicants to submit their case to a screening panel composed of three judges, which decided whether the Court should take it up. As the Court's workload grew, and an increasing number of states from eastern and central Europe joined the ECHR, the need for even more major reforms became irresistible.

There have since been three waves of reform, resulting in Protocol No. 11 of 1994 which took effect in 1998, Protocol No. 14, adopted in 2004 but not yet in force as of May 2007, and a series of subsequent reform proposals that remain the subject of debate. The debate over Protocol No. 14 and subsequent proposals are considered below at p. 1007.

The entire system was streamlined by Protocol No. 11. The right of individual petition became compulsory, the Commission ceased to exist (as of October 1999), the Court became full-time and assumed all of the relevant functions of the Commission, individuals gained direct access to the Court, and the political (and too often problematic) role played by the Committee of Ministers is now limited to matters of enforcement.

The System

Proceedings under the individual petitions procedure of Article 34 begin with a complaint by an individual, group or NGO against a state party. To be declared admissible a petition must not be anonymous, manifestly ill-founded, or constitute an abuse of the right of petition. Domestic remedies must have been exhausted, it must be presented within six months of the final decision in the domestic forum and it must not concern a matter which is substantially the same as one which has already been examined under the ECHR or submitted to another procedure of international investigation or settlement.

As a result of the Protocol No. 11 reforms, the organization of the Court is rather complicated. It has been described as follows:

> . . . The Court is composed of a number of judges equal to that of the Contracting States (currently forty-six). Judges are elected by the Parliamentary Assembly of the Council of Europe, which votes on a shortlist of three candidates put forward by Governments. The term of office is six years, and judges may be re-elected. Their terms of office expire when they reach the age of seventy, although they continue to deal with cases already under their consideration.
>
> Judges sit on the Court in their individual capacity and do not represent any State. They cannot engage in any activity which is incompatible with their independence or impartiality or with the demands of full-time office.
>
> The Plenary Court has a number of functions that are stipulated in the Convention. It elects the office holders of the Court, i.e. the President, the two Vice-Presidents (who also preside over a Section) and the three other Section Presidents. In each case, the term of office is three years. The Plenary Court also

elects the Registrar and Deputy Registrar. The Rules of Court are adopted and amended by the Plenary Court. It also determines the composition of the Sections.

Under the Rules of Court, every judge is assigned to one of the five Sections, whose composition is geographically and gender balanced and takes account of the different legal systems of the Contracting States. The composition of the Sections is varied every three years.

The great majority of the judgments of the Court are given by Chambers. These comprise seven judges and are constituted within each Section. The Section President and the judge elected in respect of the State concerned sit in each case. Where the latter is not a member of the Section, he or she sits as an *ex officio* member of the Chamber. If the respondent State in a case is that of the Section President, the Vice-President of the Section will preside. In every case that is decided by a Chamber, the remaining members of the Section who are not full members of that Chamber sit as substitute members.

Committees of three judges are set up within each Section for twelve-month periods. Their function is to dispose of applications that are clearly inadmissible.

The Grand Chamber of the Court is composed of seventeen judges, who include, as *ex officio* members, the President, Vice-Presidents and Section Presidents. The Grand Chamber deals with cases that raise a serious question of interpretation or application of the Convention, or a serious issue of general importance. A Chamber may relinquish jurisdiction in a case to the Grand Chamber at any stage in the procedure before judgment, as long as both parties consent. Where judgment has been delivered in a case, either party may, within a period of three months, request referral of the case to the Grand Chamber. Where a request is granted, the whole case is reheard.[12]

The election of judges

A major challenge facing all international human rights bodies is how to come up with a process which ensures that the highest quality judges or committee members are chosen as members of bodies such as the European Court of Human Rights ('ECtHR'). The Council of Europe has gone further than most other international bodies in an effort to ensure the objectivity of the process and the likelihood that highly qualified candidates will be chosen. The main safeguards are to require each state to nominate three candidates for each vacancy, and to provide the Human Rights Directorate of the Council, as well as the Committee of Ministers, with an opportunity to evaluate candidates. In addition, candidates are interviewed by a sub-committee of the Parliamentary Assembly, which then makes recommendations to the Assembly before it votes. However, this relatively elaborate procedure appears, in practice, to be rather flawed. After carefully examining its functioning a leading European non-governmental group, Interights, identified the following list of key problems:

1. States have absolute discretion with respect to the nomination system they adopt. Governments are not given guidelines on procedures, nor are they required to report on or account for their national nomination processes. In practice, even in the most established democracies, nomination often involves a 'tap on the shoulder'

[12] European Court of Human Rights, Survey of Activities 2006 (2007), at 4.

from the Minister of Justice or Foreign Affairs, and frequently rewards political loyalty more than merit. Nominees often lack the necessary experience and even fail to meet the very general criteria set out in the Convention.

2. The Committee of Ministers, while on paper the body that should be empowered to engage with governments on their nomination procedures and reject acceptable lists, is concerned more with safeguarding State sovereignty than with ensuring the quality of nominated candidates. Accordingly it fails to engage in meaningful dialogue with States on their internal nomination procedures and to evaluate the quality of candidates submitted

3. The only safeguard in the procedure lies at the Sub-Committee level. Regrettably, this mechanism is at best limited and at worst is fundamentally flawed. The Sub-Committee consists of parliamentarians, most of whom lack human rights or international law expertise. The Sub-Committee ranks candidates after a cursory 15-minute interview. Its deliberations are secret and it does not give reasons for its ranking of candidates. There have been cases where its ranking of candidates has appeared to be based on or influenced by party politics rather than the merits of the prospective judges.

4. At the final stage, the Parliamentary Assembly is provided with limited information on candidates and the five political groups appear to dictate voting patterns. Lobbying by States, and occasionally by judicial candidates, jeopardizes the future independence (actual and apparent) of judges.

5. The current possibility of re-appointing sitting judges renders them particularly susceptible to unacceptable interference from their governments and risks obedience to their governments.

6. The result is a Court less qualified and less able to discharge its crucial mandate than it might otherwise be. The Court also suffers from gender imbalance, at least in part due to the opaque and politicized nature of the nomination and election procedure.[13]

In 2006, a Group of Wise Persons appointed by the Council made the following policy recommendations:

> The professional qualifications and knowledge of languages of candidates for the post of judge should be carefully examined during the election procedure. For this purpose, before the Parliamentary Assembly considers the candidatures, an opinion on the suitability of the candidates could be given by a committee of prominent personalities possibly chosen from among former members of the Court, current and former members of national supreme or constitutional courts and lawyers with acknowledged competence. As regards the members of the proposed Judicial Committee, the prior opinion should be given by the Court.
>
> The Group also looked at the particularly sensitive issue of the number of judges. In the Group's opinion, the logic underlying the new role proposed for the Court [See p. 1013 *infra*] and the setting up of the Judicial Committee should lead in due course to a reduction in the number of judges.[14]

[13] Jutta Limbach *et al., Judicial Independence: Law and Practice of Appointments to the European Court of Human Rights* (Interights, 2003) 9.

[14] Report of the Group of Wise Persons to the Committee of Ministers, Council of Europe doc. CM(2006) 203, 15 November 2006, paras. 144–145.

NOTE

The procedures followed by the ECtHR are, especially since the entry into force of Protocol No. 11 and in response to its very heavy workload, complex and not easy to follow. The rather dry description that follows illustrates both the key rules and the resulting complexity. The flowchart then seeks to capture the key points from filing an application all the way through the execution of judgment phase.

EUROPEAN COURT OF HUMAN RIGHTS, SURVEY OF ACTIVITIES 2006

(2007), at 5

1. General

Any Contracting State (State application) or individual claiming to be a victim of a violation of the Convention (individual application) may lodge directly with the Court in Strasbourg an application alleging a breach by a Contracting State of one of the Convention rights. A notice for the guidance of applicants and the official application form are available on the Court's internet site. They may also be obtained directly from the Registry.

The procedure before the European Court of Human Rights is adversarial and public. It is largely a written procedure. Hearings, which are held only in a very small minority of cases, are public, unless the Chamber/Grand Chamber decides otherwise on account of exceptional circumstances. Memorials and other documents filed with the Court's Registry by the parties are, in principle, accessible to the public.

Individual applicants may present their own cases, but they should be legally represented once the application has been communicated to the respondent Government [see flowchart at p. 945, *infra*]. The Council of Europe has set up a legal aid scheme for applicants who do not have sufficient means.

The official languages of the Court are English and French, but applications may be submitted in one of the official languages of the Contracting States. Once the application has been declared admissible, one of the Court's official languages must be used, unless the President of the Chamber/Grand Chamber authorises the continued use of the language of the application.

2. The handling of applications

Each application is assigned to a Section, where it will be dealt with by a Committee or a Chamber.

An individual application that clearly fails to meet one of the admissibility criteria will be referred to a Committee, which will declare it inadmissible or strike it off. A unanimous vote is required, and the Committee's decision is final. All other individual applications, as well as inter-State applications are referred to a Chamber. One member of the Chamber will be designated to act as rapporteur for the case.

The identity of the rapporteur is not divulged to the parties. The application will be communicated to the respondent State, which will be asked to address the issues of admissibility and merits that arise, as well as the applicant's claims for just satisfaction. The parties will also be invited to consider whether a friendly settlement is possible. The Registrar facilitates friendly settlement negotiations, which are confidential and without prejudice to the parties' positions.

The Chamber will determine both admissibility and merits. As a rule, both aspects are taken together in a single judgment, although the Chamber may take a separate decision on admissibility, where appropriate. Such decisions, which are taken by majority vote, must contain reasons and be made public.

The President of the Chamber may, in the interests of the proper administration of justice, invite or grant leave to any Contracting State which is not party to the proceedings, or any person concerned who is not the applicant, to submit written comments, and, in exceptional circumstances, to make representations at the hearing. A Contracting State whose national is an applicant in the case is entitled to intervene as of right.

Chambers decide by a majority vote. Any judge who has taken part in the consideration of the case is entitled to append to the judgment a separate opinion, either concurring or dissenting, or a bare statement of dissent.

A Chamber judgment becomes final three months after its delivery. Within that time, any party may request that the case be referred to the Grand Chamber if it raises a serious question of interpretation or application or a serious issue of general importance. If the parties declare that they will not make such a request, the judgment will become final immediately. Where a request for referral is made, it is examined by a panel of five judges composed of the President of the Court, two Section Presidents designated by rotation, and two more judges also designated by rotation. No judge who has considered the admissibility and/or merits of the case may be part of the panel that considers the request. If the panel rejects the request, the Chamber judgment becomes final immediately. A case that is accepted will be re-heard by the Grand Chamber. Its judgment is final.

All final judgments of the Court are binding on the respondent States concerned.

Responsibility for supervising the execution of judgments lies with the Committee of Ministers of the Council of Europe. The Committee of Ministers verifies whether the State in respect of which a violation of the Convention is found has taken adequate remedial measures, which may be specific and/or general, to comply with the Court's judgment.

Note that footnotes and most internal citations and cross-references have been removed in the excerpts from judgments in this Chapter.

The following flowchart, produced by the Court's Registry, provides a visual representation of the main features of the system described above. As the authors note, it 'indicates the progress of a case through the different judicial formations. In the interests of readability, it does not include certain stages in the procedure — such as communication of an application to the respondent State, consideration of a re-hearing request by the Panel of the Grand Chamber and friendly settlement negotiations.'

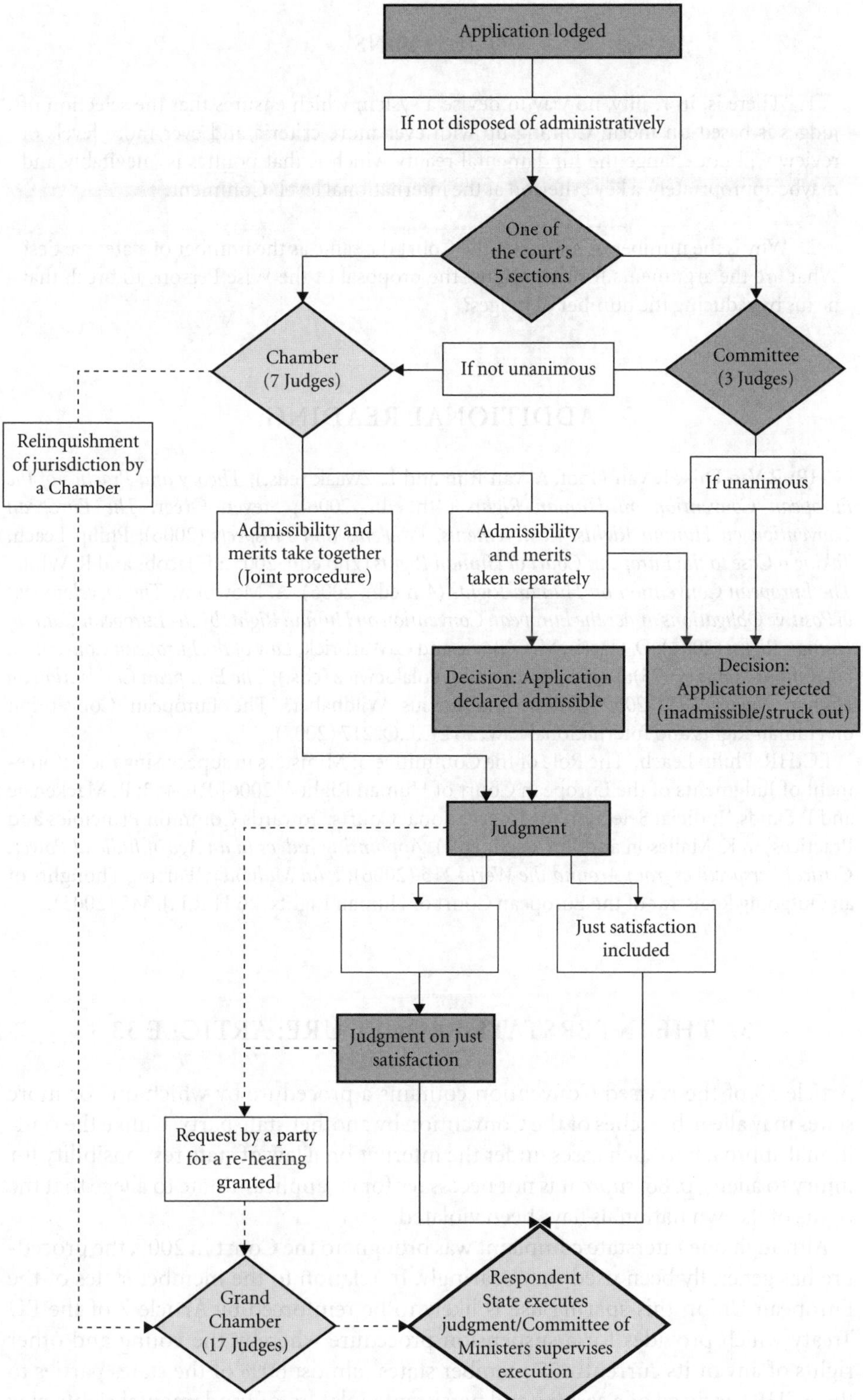
Application lodged
If not disposed of administratively
One of the court's 5 sections
Chamber (7 Judges)
If not unanimous
Committee (3 Judges)
Relinquishment of jurisdiction by a Chamber
If unanimous
Admissibility and merits take together (Joint procedure)
Admissibility and merits taken separately
Decision: Application declared admissible
Decision: Application rejected (inadmissible/struck out)
Judgment
Just satisfaction included
Judgment on just satisfaction
Request by a party for a re-hearing granted
Grand Chamber (17 Judges)
Respondent State executes judgment/Committee of Ministers supervises execution

QUESTIONS

1. 'There is, in reality, no way to devise a system which ensures that the selection of judges is based on merit. Coming up with ever more criteria and ever more levels of review will not change the fundamental reality which is that politics is, inevitably and maybe appropriately, a key criterion at the international level.' Comment.

2. Why is the number of judges on the Court the same as the number of states parties? What are the arguments for and against the proposal of the Wise Persons to break that nexus by reducing the number of judges?

ADDITIONAL READING

ECHR: P. Van Dijk, F. Van Hoof, A. van Rijn and L. Zwaak (eds.), *Theory and Practice of the European Convention on Human Rights* (4th edn. 2006); Steven Greer, *The European Convention on Human Rights: Achievements, Problems and Prospects* (2006); Philip Leach, *Taking a Case to the European Court of Human Rights* (2nd edn. 2005); F. Jacobs and R. White, *The European Convention on Human Rights* (4th edn. 2006); A. Mowbray, *The Development of Positive Obligations under the European Convention on Human Rights by the European Court of Human Rights* (2004); D. Harris, M. O'Boyle and C. Warbrick, *Law of the European Convention on Human Rights* (1995); R. Blackburn and J. Polakiewicz (eds.), *The European Convention on Human Rights 1950–2000* (2000); and Luzius Wildhaber, 'The European Convention on Human Rights and International Law', 56 I.C.L.Q. 217 (2007).

ECtHR: Philip Leach, 'The Role of the Committee of Ministers in supervising the enforcement of Judgments of the European Court of Human Rights' [2006] P.L. 443; R. Mackenzie and P. Sands, 'Judicial Selection for International Courts: Towards Common Principles and Practices', in K. Malleson and P. Russell (eds.), *Appointing Judges in an Age of Judicial Power: Critical Perspectives from Around the World* 213 (2006); *Paul Mahoney*, 'Parting Thoughts of an Outgoing Registrar of the European Court of Human Rights', 26 H.R.L.J. 345 (2005).

3. THE INTERSTATE PROCEDURE: ARTICLE 33

Article 33 of the revised Convention contains a procedure by which one or more states may allege breaches of the Convention by another state party. Unlike the traditional approach to such cases under the international law of state responsibility for injury to aliens, p. 86, *supra* it is not necessary for an applicant state to allege that the rights of its own nationals have been violated.

Although one interstate complaint was brought to the Court in 2007, the procedure has generally been used very sparingly. In relation to the member states of the European Union this sparing use is likely to be reinforced by Article 7 of the EU Treaty which provides for a suspension procedure whereby the voting and other rights of any of its currently 27 member states (almost 60% of the states parties to the ECHR) accused of a serious and persistent violation of fundamental rights may be suspended. The EU procedure is both a more immediate one and one with more serious consequences. But the ECHR interstate procedure will continue to be the only option in relation to disputes between non-EU member states.

In general states are reluctant to set in motion a formal condemnation procedure when they do not have a direct stake in the matter or when they perceive a serious risk of antagonizing the target state through what will be seen as a hostile act. One predictable result of such litigation would be the filing of a counter-suit. The reluctance to use the ECHR's interstate procedure is consistent with the fact that a comparable procedure involving the Human Rights Committee under Articles 41–43 of the ICCPR has also never been invoked.

Between 1956 and 1999, the former Commission considered 17 interstate applications, the most significant of which addressed only seven different situations: (i) *Greece v. United Kingdom* (1956 and 1957) relating to the declaration of a state of exception in Cyprus (then a British colony); (ii) *Austria v. Italy* (1960) concerning the murder trial of six members of the German-speaking minority in the South Tyrol; (iii) *Denmark, Netherlands, Norway and Sweden v. Greece* (1967, 1970) relating to the coup d'état carried out by the Greek colonels in 1967. The Commission's response in that case has been described as a model 'for demonstrating both the possibilities and the political limitations of the international protection of human rights'.[15] The case also provided an early illustration of a model of international fact-finding, undertaken by a sub-commission of the former Commission, which was path-breaking at the time, although it has since become commonplace;[16] (iv) *Ireland v. the United Kingdom* (1971 and 1972) relating to the state of emergency in Northern Ireland; (v) *Cyprus v. Turkey* (1974, 1975, 1977 and 1996) cases arising out of the Turkish armed intervention in Cyprus; (vi) *Denmark, France, the Netherlands, Norway and Sweden v. Turkey* (1982), alleging violations, including torture, by the military government. Under the settlement approved by the Commission, the Turkish Government gave a number of vague undertakings such as a commitment to instruct 'the State Supervisory Council . . . to have special regard to the observance by all public authorities' of the Convention's prohibition against torture. The settlement was widely criticized on the ground that it was not based on the respect for human rights required by the Convention; and (vii) *Denmark v. Turkey* in 1997, alleging torture of a Danish citizen during detention by Turkish authorities, and resulting in a friendly settlement.

Since 1959, the Court has delivered judgment in only three interstate cases — *Ireland v. the United Kingdom* (1978); *Denmark v. Turkey* (2000) and *Cyprus v. Turkey* (2001) — but a fourth application was lodged in March 2007 by Georgia against Russia. The first of these cases was examined in Chapter 3 (p. 231, *supra*) in relation to the characterization of certain interrogation techniques as amounting to 'inhuman and degrading treatment', but not torture. It was also noteworthy for the fact that the Court rejected a British submission that the case should effectively be considered moot on the grounds that the UK had not contested the finding by the Commission of a violation of Article 3, that the practices in question had been renounced and a solemn undertaking not to reintroduce them had been given, and

[15] Francis Jacobs, *The European Convention on Human Rights* (1975), at 27.

[16] For a description, see A. Robertson and J. Merrills, *Human Rights in Europe: A Study of the European Convention on Human Rights* (3rd edn. 1993), at 277–279.

that individuals had been punished for the acts in question. The Court held, however, that:

> [T]he responsibilities assigned to it within the framework of the system under the Convention extend to pronouncing on the non-contested allegations of violation of Article 3. The Court's judgments in fact serve not only to decide those cases brought before the Court but, more generally, to elucidate, safeguard and develop the rules instituted by the Convention, thereby contributing to the observance by the States of the engagements undertaken by them as Contracting Parties.[17]

In the case that was lodged on 26 March 2007, Georgia accused the Russian Federation of a wide range of ECHR violations in the context of its response to an incident in September 2006 in which four Russian officers were arrested in Tbilisi, Georgia, on spying charges. Subsequently Russia deported hundreds of Georgians, cut off mail and transport links with Tbilisi, and cracked down on Georgian businesses alleged to have been operating illegally in Russia. Georgia alleges that the resulting harassment of the Georgian immigrant population in the Russian Federation led to 'interferences with the respect for private and family life, home and correspondence, the peaceful enjoyment of possessions and the right to education together with widespread arrests and detention generating a generalized threat to security of the person and multiple interferences with the right to liberty on arbitrary grounds'. The Georgian Government also complained of the conditions in which 'at least 2,380 Georgians' had been detained. According to the Georgians:

> [T]he collective expulsion of Georgians from the Russian Federation involved systematic and arbitrary interference with documents evidencing a legitimate right to remain, due process requirements and the statutory appeal process. In addition closing the land, air and maritime border between the Russian Federation and Georgia, thereby interrupting all postal communication, frustrated access to remedies for the persons affected.[18]

The case will be heard by a Chamber of seven judges, including both the Georgian and Russian judges.

Finally, we turn to the case of *Cyprus v. Turkey* which illustrates the potentially very complex nature of interstate cases.

FRANK HOFFMEISTER, CASE NOTE: CYPRUS V. TURKEY[19]

96 Am. J. Int. L. 445 (2002)

In the first interstate case after the reform of 1998, the European Court of Human Rights, sitting as a grand chamber of seventeen judges, rendered the longest judgment

[17] *Ireland v. United Kingdom*, Application no. 5310/71, 18 January 1978, para. 154.

[18] European Court of Human Rights, Press Release, 27 March 2007.

[19] Application No. 25781/94, 10 May 2001.

in its history. It ruled . . . that Turkey was responsible for various breaches of the [ECHR] in the "Turkish Republic of Northern Cyprus" (TRNC)....

... Cyprus alleged that, with respect to the situation that has existed in Cyprus since the start of Turkey's military operations in northern Cyprus in July 1974, Turkey was in breach of the entire set of human rights guaranteed by the Convention (Articles 1–11, 13, 14, and 17), with the exception of the right to marry (Article 12)....

... [T]he Court rejected Turkey's contention that only the TRNC had jurisdiction in northern Cyprus. The Court concluded that "having effective overall control over northern Cyprus, [Turkey's] responsibility cannot be confined to the acts of its own soldiers or officials in northern Cyprus but must also be engaged by virtue of the acts of the local administration which survives by virtue of Turkish military and other support." It would frustrate the purpose of the Convention as an instrument of European public order if Cyprus's continuing inability to exercise its Convention obligations in northern Cyprus was allowed to result in a vacuum in human rights protection in that territory, now under the effective control of Turkey.

With respect to the requirement of exhaustion of local remedies . . . , Cyprus argued that local judicial authorities of the TRNC could not be expected to "issue effective decisions against persons exercising authority with the backing of the [Turkish] army in order to remedy violations of human rights committed in furtherance of the general policies of the regime." Turkey maintained, however, that the local judiciary was fully developed and independent. . . . Referring to the need to avoid a vacuum in the protection of human rights in northern Cyprus, the European Court thus found that the absence of TRNC courts would work to the detriment of the people living there. Therefore, the judicial organs of the TRNC could not be simply disregarded. The Court concluded that the inhabitants of the territory were required to exhaust local remedies unless the absence or ineffectiveness of such remedies can be proved — a question that needs to be settled on a case-by-case basis.

Turning to the merits, the Court first examined the matter of Greek Cypriot missing persons. It noted that there was no proof that any of the missing persons had been unlawfully killed by Turkish troops in 1974. In any case, the six-month period for bringing a claim under the Convention was long past, and the relevant events did not come within the scope *ratione temporis* of the application. Nevertheless, the Court also determined that it could examine the matter of the missing persons from the perspective of a contracting state's procedural obligation under Article 2 to protect the right to life — an obligation that arises upon "proof of an arguable claim" that a person, last seen in the custody of state agents, subsequently disappeared in a context that could be considered life-threatening.

In addressing this question, the Court observed that many persons now missing were detained either by Turkish or Turkish Cypriot forces at a time when the conduct of military operations was accompanied by arrests and killings on a large scale. The Court rejected Turkey's claim that its cooperation with the UN Committee on Missing Persons (CMP) satisfied the need to inquire into the whereabouts of the missing persons. As the Court noted, the CMP's task was to determine only whether any of the missing persons on the list were dead or alive; it was not empowered to make findings either on the cause of death or on the issue of responsibility for any deaths. The Court therefore concluded that the CMP's investigations could not be regarded as effective. It found, moreover, a continuing violation of the right to life because no effective investigation has ever been undertaken into the whereabouts and fate of Greek Cypriot missing persons who disappeared in 1974 under life-threatening circumstances. The Court added that it was incumbent on the authorities to account for the whereabouts of given individuals after they had assumed control over them. By virtue of the failure of Turkish authorities to do so, there was also, according to the Court, a continuing violation of the right to liberty under Article 5 of the Convention. The Court held, moreover, that the silence of the Turkish authorities in the face of the legitimate concerns of the missing persons' relatives was inhuman treatment within the meaning of Article 3 of the Convention.

The second substantive matter addressed by the Court related to the rights of displaced persons with respect to their homes and property....

...As regards property rights, the Court repeated its finding in the *Loizidou* judgment that Article 159 of the 1985 TRNC Constitution, which provides that abandoned property devolves to the TRNC, is deemed to be invalid for the purposes of the Convention. Hence, the Greek Cypriots remained the owners of their property lying in the north....

The third substantive matter addressed by the Court concerned the living conditions of the remaining 429 Greek Cypriots in the Karpas region of northern Cyprus. It found that their freedom of religion was infringed since TRNC authorities prevented them from traveling outside their villages to attend religious ceremonies. Furthermore, the censorship regime imposed upon Greek-language schoolbooks violated the freedom of expression (Article 10 of the Convention), and the absence of appropriate secondary-school facilities for Greek Cypriots violated the right to education (Article 2 of Protocol No. 1)....

...

Finally, the Court decided that the question of the possible application of Article 41 of the Convention — under which it can grant just satisfaction if the internal law of the respondent state allows only partial reparation to be made for the consequences of the violations found — was "not ready for decision"; the Court therefore "adjourn[ed] consideration" of the Article 41 request.

QUESTIONS

1. Some of the largest European countries, including the United Kingdom, Germany and Spain, have never lodged an interstate complaint against another European government. Does this mean that this procedure is only likely to be invoked by small countries with limited political clout? If so, would that indicate a fundamental weakness of the procedure?

2. Under what circumstances might the lodging of an interstate complaint be most productive and when might it be considered counter-productive?

3. In the Cyprus case, six dissenting judges criticized the proposition that the TRNC courts should be considered to provide appropriate 'domestic remedies' that needed to be exhausted before appealing to the ECHR. They cited an 'obvious and justifiable lack of confidence' in those courts. What do you see as the reasons for, and the implications of, the Court's finding in this regard?

4. THE COURT'S JURISDICTION

The ECtHR cannot consider an application unless it ascertains that it has jurisdiction over the case. If an event occurred prior to the state becoming a party to the ECHR and has no continuing dimension, if the state whose conduct is complained about is not a party to the Convention, and so on, the Court will have no jurisdiction. One of the most controversial and complex issues currently giving cause for concern is the extent to which the Court has jurisdiction over events which occur beyond the territory of a Contracting Party. The issue of extraterritorial jurisdiction arises in connection with situations which have become increasingly common. They include, to take the examples dealt with below, situations in which a military strike is launched from within the legal space (*l'éspace juridique*) of the Council of Europe but results in damage outside that area, actions taken by armed forces of one state operating in the territory of another which may or may not be a member of the Council of Europe, and the responsibility of a state contributing troops to a United Nations or other multilateral peace-keeping force under the auspices of the UN Security Council.

These issues highlight the challenge of evolving approaches in response to challenges that were not foreseen at the time of the drafting of the ECHR. The Court has often affirmed the importance of a dynamic, evolutive or teleological approach to interpretation, but in relation to territorial jurisdiction it seems surprisingly reticent to adopt such an approach. The challenges discussed below also underscore the impact of globalization and the extent to which it remains possible to defend the notion that the Convention is essentially designed to uphold the human rights of those within the *éspace juridique.* As boundaries become ever more porous and European states deepen their involvement in complex ways in neighbouring countries and beyond, such a restrictive notion will be increasingly challenged.

The most contentious of the cases below is *Banković,* in which forces operating under the control of the North Atlantic Treaty Organization (NATO) fired a missile which killed and injured civilians in the course of an air strike on a television station. The Court's rejection of jurisdiction in that case seems to have been qualified in the *Issa* case which follows, which concerns the acts of Turkish Government troops in neighbouring Iraq which resulted in the killing of a number of individuals. Finally, the British Court of Appeals in *Al-Skeini* explored what it would mean, in terms of the applicability of the ECHR, to say that British troops had been in 'effective control' of an area near Basrah in Iraq in which civilians had been shot and killed.

BANKOVIĆ AND OTHERS V. BELGIUM AND OTHERS

European Court of Human Rights
Application no. 52207/99, Grand Chamber, 12 December 2001

[On 23 April a missile launched from a NATO forces' aircraft hit the building in Belgrade which housed the master control room of RTS which operated three television channels and four radio stations. In total 24 targets were hit in the Federal Republic of Yugoslavia (FRY) on the same night, including three in Belgrade. The applicants in the case included one person injured and five relatives of some of the sixteen persons killed in the RTS attack. The respondent Governments were all NATO members who were party to the ECHR: Belgium, the Czech Republic, Denmark, France, Germany, Greece, Hungary, Iceland, Italy, Luxembourg, the Netherlands, Norway, Poland, Portugal, Spain, Turkey and the United Kingdom.

After considering a range of issues the Court concluded that 'the essential question to be examined therefore is whether the applicants and their deceased relatives were, as a result of that extra-territorial act [of firing a missile], capable of falling within the jurisdiction of the respondent States'. Before addressing the jurisdiction issue the Court noted the applicable rules of interpretation. The framework is that reflected in the rules set out in the Vienna Convention on the Law of Treaties and involves ascertaining the 'ordinary meaning to be given to the phrase "within their jurisdiction" in its context and in the light of the object and purpose of the Convention', and taking account of any additional applicable rules of international law. The Court also noted that 'it must remain mindful of the Convention's special character as a human rights treaty', as well as interpreting it 'as far as possible in harmony with other principles of international law of which it forms part'. In addition, the *travaux préparatoires* can be consulted with a view to confirming the ordinary meaning of a provision or when such an approach to interpretation 'leaves the meaning "ambiguous or obscure" or leads to a result which is "manifestly absurd or unreasonable"' (Arts. 31–32 of the VCLT).]

(b) The meaning of the words "within their jurisdiction"

59. As to the "ordinary meaning" of the relevant term in Article 1 of the Convention, the Court is satisfied that, from the standpoint of public international law, the jurisdictional competence of a State is primarily territorial. While international law does not exclude a State's exercise of jurisdiction extra-territorially, the suggested bases of such jurisdiction (including nationality, flag, diplomatic and consular relations, effect, protection, passive personality and universality) are, as a general rule, defined and limited by the sovereign territorial rights of the other relevant States.

60. Accordingly, for example, a State's competence to exercise jurisdiction over its own nationals abroad is subordinate to that State's and other States' territorial competence. In addition, a State may not actually exercise jurisdiction on the territory of another without the latter's consent, invitation or acquiescence, unless the former is an occupying State in which case it can be found to exercise jurisdiction in that territory, at least in certain respects.

61. The Court is of the view, therefore, that Article 1 of the Convention must be considered to reflect this ordinary and essentially territorial notion of jurisdiction, other bases of jurisdiction being exceptional and requiring special justification in the particular circumstances of each case.

62. . . . [In terms of state practice] no State has indicated a belief that its extra-territorial actions involved an exercise of jurisdiction within the meaning of Article 1 of the Convention by making a derogation pursuant to Article 15 of the Convention. . . .

63. Finally, the Court finds clear confirmation of this essentially territorial notion of jurisdiction in the *travaux préparatoires* which demonstrate that the Expert Intergovernmental Committee replaced the words "all persons residing within their territories" with a reference to persons "within their jurisdiction" with a view to expanding the Convention's application to others who may not reside, in a legal sense, but who are, nevertheless, on the territory of the Contracting States.

64. It is true that the notion of the Convention being a living instrument to be interpreted in light of present-day conditions is firmly rooted in the Court's case-law. The Court has applied that approach not only to the Convention's substantive provisions . . . but more relevantly to its interpretation of former Articles 25 and 46 concerning the recognition by a Contracting State of the competence of the Convention organs. . . .

65. However, the scope of Article 1, at issue in the present case, is determinative of the very scope of the Contracting Parties' positive obligations and, as such, of the scope and reach of the entire Convention system of human rights' protection as opposed to the question, under discussion in the Loizidou case (*preliminary objections*), of the competence of the Convention organs to examine a case. In any event, the extracts from the *travaux préparatoires* detailed above constitute a clear indication of the intended meaning of Article 1 of the Convention which cannot be ignored. The Court would emphasise that it is not interpreting Article 1 "solely" in accordance with the *travaux préparatoires* or finding those *travaux* "decisive"; rather this preparatory material constitutes clear confirmatory evidence of the ordinary meaning of Article 1 of the Convention as already identified by the Court (Article 32 of the Vienna Convention 1969).

66. Accordingly, and as the Court stated in the Soering case:

> "Article 1 sets a limit, notably territorial, on the reach of the Convention. In particular, the engagement undertaken by a Contracting State is confined to 'securing' ('*reconnaître*' in the French text) the listed rights and freedoms to persons within its own 'jurisdiction'. Further, the Convention does not govern the actions of States not Parties to it, nor does it purport to be a means of requiring the Contracting States to impose Convention standards on other States."

(c) Extra-territorial acts recognised as constituting an exercise of jurisdiction

67. In keeping with the essentially territorial notion of jurisdiction, the Court has accepted only in exceptional cases that acts of the Contracting States performed, or producing effects, outside their territories can constitute an exercise of jurisdiction by them within the meaning of Article 1 of the Convention.

68. Reference has been made in the Court's case-law, as an example of jurisdiction "not restricted to the national territory" of the respondent State (the Loizidou judgment (*preliminary objections*), at § 62), to situations where the extradition or expulsion of a person by a Contracting State may give rise to an issue under Articles 2 and/or 3 (or, exceptionally, under Articles 5 and or 6) and hence engage the responsibility of that State under the Convention.

However, the Court notes that liability is incurred in such cases by an action of the respondent State concerning a person while he or she is on its territory, clearly within its jurisdiction, and that such cases do not concern the actual exercise of a State's competence or jurisdiction abroad.

. . .

70. Moreover, in that first Loizidou judgment (*preliminary objections*), the Court found that, bearing in mind the object and purpose of the Convention, the responsibility of a Contracting Party was capable of being engaged when as a consequence of military action (lawful or unlawful) it exercised effective control of an area outside its national territory. The obligation to secure, in such an area, the Convention rights and freedoms was found to derive from the fact of such control whether it was exercised directly, through the respondent State's armed forces, or through a subordinate local administration. The Court concluded that the acts of which the applicant complained were capable of falling within Turkish jurisdiction within the meaning of Article 1 of the Convention.

. . .

In its subsequent *Cyprus v. Turkey* judgment, the Court added that since Turkey had such "effective control", its responsibility could not be confined to the acts of its own agents therein but was engaged by the acts of the local administration which survived by virtue of Turkish support. Turkey's "jurisdiction" under Article 1 was therefore considered to extend to securing the entire range of substantive Convention rights in northern Cyprus.

71. In sum, the case-law of the Court demonstrates that its recognition of the exercise of extra-territorial jurisdiction by a Contracting State is exceptional: it has done so when the respondent State, through the effective control of the relevant territory and its inhabitants abroad as a consequence of military occupation or through the consent, invitation or acquiescence of the Government of that territory, exercises all or some of the public powers normally to be exercised by that Government.

. . .

73. Additionally, the Court notes that other recognised instances of the extra-territorial exercise of jurisdiction by a State include cases involving the activities of its diplomatic or consular agents abroad and on board craft and vessels registered in, or flying the flag of, that State. In these specific situations, customary international law and treaty provisions have recognised the extra-territorial exercise of jurisdiction by the relevant State.

(d) Were the present applicants therefore capable of coming within the "jurisdiction" of the respondent States?

74. The applicants maintain that the bombing of RTS by the respondent States constitutes yet a further example of an extra-territorial act which can be

accommodated by the notion of "jurisdiction" in Article 1 of the Convention, and are thereby proposing a further specification of the ordinary meaning of the term "jurisdiction" in Article 1 of the Convention. The Court must be satisfied that equally exceptional circumstances exist in the present case which could amount to the extra-territorial exercise of jurisdiction by a Contracting State.

75. In the first place, the applicants suggest a specific application of the "effective control" criteria developed in the northern Cyprus cases. . . . The Court considers that the applicants' submission is tantamount to arguing that anyone adversely affected by an act imputable to a Contracting State, wherever in the world that act may have been committed or its consequences felt, is thereby brought within the jurisdiction of that State for the purpose of Article 1 of the Convention.

The Court is inclined to agree with the Governments' submission that the text of Article 1 does not accommodate such an approach to "jurisdiction". Admittedly, the applicants accept that jurisdiction, and any consequent State Convention responsibility, would be limited in the circumstances to the commission and consequences of that particular act. However, the Court is of the view that the wording of Article 1 does not provide any support for the applicants' suggestion that the positive obligation in Article 1 to secure "the rights and freedoms defined in Section I of this Convention" can be divided and tailored in accordance with the particular circumstances of the extra-territorial act in question and, it considers its view in this respect supported by the text of Article 19 of the Convention. Indeed the applicants' approach does not explain the application of the words "within their jurisdiction" in Article 1 and it even goes so far as to render those words superfluous and devoid of any purpose. Had the drafters of the Convention wished to ensure jurisdiction as extensive as that advocated by the applicants, they could have adopted a text the same as or similar to the contemporaneous Articles 1 of the four Geneva Conventions of 1949.

Furthermore, the applicants' notion of jurisdiction equates the determination of whether an individual falls within the jurisdiction of a Contracting State with the question of whether that person can be considered to be a victim of a violation of rights guaranteed by the Convention. These are separate and distinct admissibility conditions, each of which has to be satisfied in the afore-mentioned order, before an individual can invoke the Convention provisions against a Contracting State.

76. Secondly, the applicants' alternative suggestion is that the limited scope of the airspace control only circumscribed the scope of the respondent States' positive obligation to protect the applicants and did not exclude it. The Court finds this to be essentially the same argument as their principal proposition and rejects it for the same reasons.

. . .

78. Fourthly, the Court does not find it necessary to pronounce on the specific meaning to be attributed in various contexts to the allegedly similar jurisdiction provisions in the international instruments to which the applicants refer because it is not convinced by the applicants' specific submissions in these respects. . . . [A]s to Article 2 § 1 the CCPR 1966, as early as 1950 the drafters had definitively and specifically confined its territorial scope and it is difficult to suggest that exceptional recognition by the Human Rights Committee of certain instances of extra-territorial

jurisdiction (and the applicants give one example only) displaces in any way the territorial jurisdiction expressly conferred by that Article of the CCPR 1966 or explains the precise meaning of "jurisdiction" in Article 1 of its Optional Protocol 1966. . . .

79. Fifthly and more generally, the applicants maintain that any failure to accept that they fell within the jurisdiction of the respondent States would defeat the *ordre public* mission of the Convention and leave a regrettable vacuum in the Convention system of human rights' protection.

80. The Court's obligation, in this respect, is to have regard to the special character of the Convention as a constitutional instrument of *European* public order for the protection of individual human beings and its role, as set out in Article 19 of the Convention, is to ensure the observance of *the engagements undertaken* by the Contracting Parties (the above-cited Loizidou judgment (*preliminary objections*), at § 93). It is therefore difficult to contend that a failure to accept the extra-territorial jurisdiction of the respondent States would fall foul of the Convention's *ordre public* objective, which itself underlines the essentially regional vocation of the Convention system, or of Article 19 of the Convention which does not shed any particular light on the territorial ambit of that system.

It is true that, in its above-cited *Cyprus v. Turkey* judgment (at § 78), the Court was conscious of the need to avoid "a regrettable vacuum in the system of human-rights protection" in northern Cyprus. However, and as noted by the Governments, that comment related to an entirely different situation to the present: the inhabitants of northern Cyprus would have found themselves excluded from the benefits of the Convention safeguards and system which they had previously enjoyed, by Turkey's "effective control" of the territory and by the accompanying inability of the Cypriot Government, as a Contracting State, to fulfil the obligations it had undertaken under the Convention.

In short, the Convention is a multi-lateral treaty operating, subject to Article 56 of the Convention, in an essentially regional context and notably in the legal space (*espace juridique*) of the Contracting States. The FRY clearly does not fall within this legal space. The Convention was not designed to be applied throughout the world, even in respect of the conduct of Contracting States. Accordingly, the desirability of avoiding a gap or vacuum in human rights' protection has so far been relied on by the Court in favour of establishing jurisdiction only when the territory in question was one that, but for the specific circumstances, would normally be covered by the Convention.

. . .

4. The Court's conclusion

82. The Court is not therefore persuaded that there was any jurisdictional link between the persons who were victims of the act complained of and the respondent States. Accordingly, it is not satisfied that the applicants and their deceased relatives were capable of coming within the jurisdiction of the respondent States on account of the extra-territorial act in question.

. . .

ISSA AND OTHERS V. TURKEY

European Court of Human Rights
Application no. 31821/96, 16 November 2004

[The case was brought by six Iraqi nationals, shepherdesses who earn their living by shepherding sheep, who complained of the alleged unlawful arrest, detention, ill-treatment and subsequent killing of their relatives in the course of a military operation conducted by the Turkish army in northern Iraq in April 1995. The Turkish Government responded that while a military operation had taken place in this region at the relevant time, its forces had not been within ten kilometres of the area where the alleged violations occurred.]

II. Whether the applicants' relatives came within the jurisdiction of Turkey

. . .

B. The Court's assessment

. . .

67. The established case-law in this area indicates that the concept of "jurisdiction" for the purposes of Article 1 of the Convention must be considered to reflect the term's meaning in public international law.

From the standpoint of public international law, the words "within their jurisdiction" in Article 1 of the Convention must be understood to mean that a State's jurisdictional competence is primarily territorial (see *Bankovic and Others*, § 59), but also that jurisdiction is presumed to be exercised normally throughout the State's territory.

68. However, the concept of "jurisdiction" within the meaning of Article 1 of the Convention is not necessarily restricted to the national territory of the High Contracting Parties (see *Loizidou v. Turkey*, pp. 2235–2236 § 52). In exceptional circumstances the acts of Contracting States performed outside their territory or which produce effects there ("extra-territorial act") may amount to exercise by them of their jurisdiction within the meaning of Article 1 of the Convention.

69. According to the relevant principles of international law, a State's responsibility may be engaged where, as a consequence of military action — whether lawful or unlawful — that State in practice exercises effective control of an area situated outside its national territory. The obligation to secure, in such an area, the rights and freedoms set out in the Convention derives from the fact of such control, whether it be exercised directly, through its armed forces, or through a subordinate local administration (*ibid.* § 52).

70. It is not necessary to determine whether a Contracting Party actually exercises detailed control over the policies and actions of the authorities in the area situated outside its national territory, since even overall control of the area may engage the responsibility of the Contracting Party concerned (*ibid.*, pp. 2235–2236, § 56).

71. Moreover, a State may also be held accountable for violation of the Convention rights and freedoms of persons who are in the territory of another State but who are found to be under the former State's authority and control through its agents operating — whether lawfully or unlawfully — in the latter State. . . . Accountability in such situations stems from the fact that Article 1 of the Convention cannot be interpreted so as to allow a State party to perpetrate violations of the Convention on the territory of another State, which it could not perpetrate on its own territory (*ibid.*).

2. Application of the above principles

72. In the light of the above principles the Court must ascertain whether the applicants' relatives were under the authority and/or effective control, and therefore within the jurisdiction, of the respondent State as a result of the latter's extra-territorial acts.

73. In this connection, the Court notes that it is undisputed between the parties that the Turkish armed forces carried out military operations in [the relevant area at the time]. . . .

74. The Court does not exclude the possibility that, as a consequence of this military action, the respondent State could be considered to have exercised, temporarily, effective overall control of a particular portion of the territory of northern Iraq. Accordingly, if there is a sufficient factual basis for holding that, at the relevant time, the victims were within that specific area, it would follow logically that they were within the jurisdiction of Turkey (and not that of Iraq, which is not a Contracting State and clearly does not fall within the legal space (*espace juridique*) of the Contracting States (see the above-cited *Bankovic* decision, § 80).

75. However, notwithstanding the large number of troops involved in the aforementioned military operations, it does not appear that Turkey exercised effective overall control of the entire area of northern Iraq. . . .

76. The essential question to be examined in the instant case is whether at the relevant time Turkish troops conducted operations in the area where the killings took place. The fate of the applicants' complaints in respect of the killing of their relatives depends on the prior establishment of that premise. The Government have vigorously denied that their troops were active in or around Azadi village in the Spna area (see paragraphs 25 and 58 above). The reasonableness of that assertion must be tested in the light of the documentary and other evidence which the parties have submitted to the Court, having regard to the standard of proof which it habitually employs when ascertaining whether there is a basis in fact for an allegation of unlawful killing, namely proof "beyond reasonable doubt", it being understood that such proof may follow from the coexistence of sufficiently strong, clear and concordant inferences or of similar unrebutted presumptions of fact.

. . .

81. On the basis of all the material in its possession, the Court considers that it has not been established to the required standard of proof that the Turkish armed forces conducted operations in the area in question, and, more precisely, in the hills above the village of Azadi where, according to the applicants' statements, the victims were at that time.

3. The Court's conclusion

82. In the light of the above, the Court is not satisfied that the applicants' relatives were within the "jurisdiction" of the respondent State for the purposes of Article 1 of the Convention.

...

R (AL-SKEINI) V. SECRETARY OF STATE FOR DEFENCE

Court of Appeals [2005] EWCA Civ 1609

LORD JUSTICE BROOKE

1. This is an appeal by the first five claimants and a cross-appeal by the defendant from an order made by the Divisional Court (Rix LJ and Forbes J) on 14th December 2004. The first five claimants appeal against the declaration by that court to the effect that the [ECHR] and the Human Rights Act 1998 ("HRA") do not apply to the circumstances of their cases. The defendant appeals against the court's declaration to the effect that the HRA applies to the circumstances of the case of the sixth claimant....

12. ... [The] sixth claimant, Daoud Mousa, ... sues in relation to the death and inhuman treatment of his son Baha Mousa while he was in the custody of British troops in a military detention centre in Basrah City....

...

108. ... In my judgment, Mr Mousa came within the control and authority of the UK from the time he was arrested at the hotel and thereby lost his freedom at the hands of British troops.

109. [The judgment then recalls the circumstances surrounding the deaths of the first five claimants.] Hazam Al-Skeini was at liberty in a city street when a patrol of British soldiers shot him dead. Muhammed Salim was at liberty in his brother-in-law's home when British soldiers entered the house and shot him dead. Hannan Shmailawi was at liberty in her own home when a chance bullet entered the house and killed her. Waleed Sayay Mezban was driving his mini-bus, and even on the soldiers' story he had accelerated away and then seemed to be reaching for a weapon when he was shot dead. Raid Al-Musawi was also at liberty in a city street when he was shot dead.

110. None of them were under the control and authority of British troops at the time when they were killed....

...

112. It is therefore necessary to turn to the facts to see if British troops could be said to have been in effective control of Basrah City for the purposes of Strasbourg jurisprudence at the relevant time....

...

124. In my judgment it is quite impossible to hold that the UK, although an occupying power for the purposes of the Hague Regulations and Geneva IV, was in effective control of Basrah City for the purposes of ECHR jurisprudence at the material time. If it had been, it would have been obliged, pursuant to the *Bankovic*

judgment, to secure to everyone in Basrah City the rights and freedoms guaranteed by the ECHR. One only has to state that proposition to see how utterly unreal it is. The UK possessed no executive, legislative or judicial authority in Basrah City, other than the limited authority given to its military forces, and as an occupying power it was bound to respect the laws in force in Iraq unless absolutely prevented (see Article 43 of the Hague Regulations). It could not be equated with a civil power: it was simply there to maintain security, and to support the civil administration in Iraq in a number of different ways.

125. It would indeed have been contrary to the Coalition's policy to maintain a much more substantial military force in Basrah City when its over-arching policy was to encourage the Iraqis to govern themselves. . . .

LORD JUSTICE SEDLEY

. . .

184. . . . [T]hat the Convention governs the UK's acts in relation to the military prison in Basra . . . is now conceded because the Crown accepts that such an establishment is analogous to a diplomatic legation: not an extension of British territory but a United Kingdom enclave within another state, and so within the *espace juridique* of the Convention.

. . .

188. . . . [T]he next question is whether the Convention . . . extends either to areas controlled, however imperfectly, by British troops . . . , or to any operations undertaken by them. . . .

4. The applicability of the ECHR . . .

189. It is here that the claimants' case encounters an increasingly steep terrain of practical reality. It starts with [counsel for the claimants] Mr Singh's straightforward proposition, which I have mentioned, that there is no distinction of principle between prisoners held within and prisoners held outside a British military prison. . . .

190. [Counsel for the Government] Mr Greenwood's argument against any such reach has two limbs: first, that the legal test is effective control, not state agency, and that there was no effective control in these cases; second, that the Convention is applicable either in full, as it manifestly was not in the prevailing situation of civil disorder, or not at all. . . .

5. What is effective control?

191. . . . [S]uch control as was being exercised in the Basra area at the material time was being exercised by the Crown, and not by either the United States or a coalition force lacking international legal personality or responsibility. The evidence . . . shows that such control was intermittent and incomplete. In no practical way did it replicate that of a functioning civil authority.

192. The decisions of the European Court of Human Rights do not speak with a single voice on the question whether such a level of presence and activity engages the responsibility of a member state on foreign soil. *Issa v Turkey* contains a clear indication that even a brief incursion into a non-member state by a member state's

troops will bring with it liability for any violation of local people's human rights which they can be proved to have committed. Effective control here is equated with immediate presence and power. *Bankovic v Belgium*, by contrast, rejects state liability where Convention rights are violated by aerial bombardment of a non-member state. Effective control here is distinguished from immediate presence and power.

193. I do not accept Mr Greenwood's submission that *Bankovic* is a watershed in the Court's jurisprudence. *Bankovic* is more accurately characterised, in my view, as a break in a substantial line of decisions, nearly all of them relating to the Turkish occupation of northern Cyprus, which hold a member state answerable for what it does in alien territory following a de facto assumption of authority....

194. ... [The key question is] how much control is, for this purpose, effective control. International human rights law in its present phase does not answer this question. On the one hand, it sits ill in the mouth of a state which has helped to displace and dismantle by force another nation's civil authority to plead that, as an occupying power, it has so little control that it cannot be responsible for securing the population's basic rights. On the other, the fact is that it cannot: the invasion brought in its wake a vacuum of civil authority which British forces were and still are unable to fill. On the evidence before the Court they were, at least between mid-2003 and mid-2004, holding a fragile line against anarchy.

195. In respectful disagreement with what Brooke LJ says in paragraph 124, I do not see why the presence or absence of adequate civil power for effective control in international law should be tested by asking whether there is sufficient control to enforce the full range of Convention rights. Nor does the ECtHR seem to have thought so in *Bankovic*. What seems to me more material is the fact that, as Brooke LJ explains in his preceding paragraphs, the United Kingdom was an occupying power within the meaning of Article 42 of the Hague Regulations because the Basra region was under the authority of its armed forces. Article 43 then made it incumbent upon the UK "to take all the measures in [its] power to restore, and ensure, *as far as possible*, public order and safety, while respecting, *unless absolutely prevented*, the laws in force in the country". (I will return to the words I have italicised.) These obligations are predicated not on effective control but on "the authority of the legitimate power having in fact passed into the hands of the occupant". Geneva IV, Article 27, adds to them an obligation to respect "in all circumstances" the persons of civilians and to protect them from acts of violence.

196. No doubt it is absurd to expect occupying forces in the near-chaos of Iraq to enforce the right to marry vouchsafed by Art. 12 or the equality guarantees vouchsafed by Art. 14. But I do not think effective control involves this. If effective control in the jurisprudence of the ECtHR marches with international humanitarian law and the law of armed conflict, as it clearly seeks to do, it involves two key things: the de facto assumption of civil power by an occupying state and a concomitant obligation to do all that is possible to keep order and protect essential civil rights. It does not make the occupying power the guarantor of rights; nor therefore does it demand sufficient control for all such purposes. What it does is place an obligation on the occupier to do all it can.

197. If this is right, it is not an answer to say that the UK, because it is unable to guarantee everything, is required to guarantee nothing. The question is whether our

armed forces' effectiveness on the streets in 2003–4 was so exiguous that despite their assumption of power as an occupying force they lacked any real control of what happened from hour to hour in the Basra region. My own answer would be that the one thing British troops did have control over, even in the labile situation described in the evidence, was their own use of lethal force....

...

[The judgment concludes, however, that Bankovic constitutes a 'road-block' to the type of solution which would follow from his analysis.]

9. Conclusions

205. I ... see good grounds of principle and of substantive law for holding that, at least where the right to life is involved, these parts extend beyond the walls of the British military prison and include the streets patrolled by British troops.

206. The reason why, nevertheless, I express doubt rather than dissent is that such a conclusion would probably not be compatible with the central reasoning of *Bankovic*. Given, however, that there are passages in the Grand Chamber's judgment itself which point the other way and reasoning in critical parts of it which may be thought less than compelling, I would be content if on consideration at a higher level my doubts were to prove misplaced.

...

LORD JUSTICE RICHARDS

209. I agree ... for the reasons given by Brooke LJ....

NOTE

In June 2007 the House of Lords (Al-Skeini v. Secretary of State for Defence [2007] UKHL 26) affirmed the applicability of the Banković case and upheld the decision of the majority in the Court of Appeals.

Another important issue, which has not yet reached the ECtHR concerns whether actions taken by national forces in furtherance of a binding UN Security Council resolution could be evaluated for compliance with the ECHR. The matter was evaluated by the Court of Appeals in *R (Al-Jedda) v. Secretary of State for Defence* ([2006] EWCA Civ 327). Mr Al-Jedda was a dual British and Iraqi national, imprisoned without trial as a suspected terrorist in Iraq since October 2004. In response to his claim under ECHR, Article 5, the UK Government asserted that his detention was authorized by UN Security Council Resolution 1546 which authorized internment for imperative reasons of security, irrespective of nationality. Lord Justice Richards has described the outcome in the following terms:

> The court ... had to rule on the question whether in international law, through the operation of the UN Charter, UNSCR 1546 qualified the rights contained in the ECHR. Article 103 of the UN Charter provides that in the event of a conflict

between the obligations of the members of the United Nations under the Charter and their obligations under any other international agreement, their obligations under the Charter shall prevail. The court held that . . . the United Kingdom was subject to the obligations in the resolution rather than under any human rights conventions in so far as the resolution was in conflict with the latter. In so far as the resolution sanctioned the continued use of internment as a means of restoring peace in Iraq, it was inconsistent with, and therefore qualified, the requirements of article 5 of the ECHR.

It followed from all this that Mr Al-Jedda could not succeed in a claim under article 5 against the United Kingdom in Strasbourg.[20]

QUESTIONS

1. Is the international law definition of jurisdiction used by the Court in *Banković* adequate to take account of the notion of accountability for the exercise of state authority in situations in which the state enjoys a degree of effective control?

2. In *Issa* the Court observes that Article 1 'cannot be interpreted so as to allow a State party to perpetrate violations of the Convention on the territory of another State, which it could not perpetrate on its own territory'. Is this not essentially what occurred in *Banković*?

3. It has been argued that acceptance of the *Al-Skeini* approach of extending the jurisdiction of the ECHR beyond the Council of Europe's *éspace juridique* would mean that 'the Court's decisions are likely to backfire in that they create a disincentive for member states to participate in peacekeeping missions worldwide'. What, in your view, might be the policy arguments in favour of a restrictive approach to jurisdiction, such as that adopted in *Banković*?

4. The disagreements between Lord Justices Brooke and Sedley in the *Al-Skeini* case turn largely on the feasibility of a nuanced effective control test. Do you see a problem in adopting Sedley's approach of holding British troops accountable to ECHR standards in relation to any particular actions over which they did clearly seem to have control, such as the use of lethal force in a particular situation?

ADDITIONAL READING

Olivier de Schutter, 'Globalization and Jurisdiction: Lessons from the European Convention on Human Rights', 6 Baltic Yearbook of Int. L. 185 (2006); Fons Coomans & Menno Kamminga (eds.), *Extraterritorial Application of Human Rights Treaties* (2004); Stefka Kavaldjieva, 'Jurisdiction of the European Court of Human Rights: Exorbitance in Reverse?', 37 *Geo. J. Int. L.* 507 (2006); Tariq Abdel-Monem, 'How Far do the Lawless Areas of Europe Extend? Extraterritorial Application of the European Convention on Human Rights', 14 J. Transnat'l L. & Pol'y 159 (2005).

[20] Lord Justice Richards, 'The International Dimension of Judicial Review', The 2006 Gray's Inn Reading, 7 June 2006, at http://www.judiciary.gov.uk/publications_media/speeches/2006/sp070606.htm

5. THE EUROPEAN COURT IN ACTION: SOME ILLUSTRATIVE CASES

The role of the European Court is of particular importance for several reasons. First, in quantitative terms, is the fact that it now has the final say in relation to the interpretation of the human rights standards applicable in relation to 46 different nations and covering over 800 million people. Second, its caseload has expanded exponentially over the past decade alone and this has important consequences in terms of the quantity and range of case law or jurisprudence being generated. Thus in 1996 the ECtHR handed down 72 judgments (a number far exceeding that of any other international human rights tribunal). By 2006 that number had increased by over 2,000% to 1,560. By the end of 2006 there were almost 90,000 applications pending before the Court. The challenges posed by this potentially overwhelming caseload are considered at pp. 1007–13, *infra*. Another consequence of this judicial output is the extent to which the ECtHR's jurisprudence is likely to influence, or be taken into account, in the work of the other leading human rights adjudicatory organs such as the Inter-American Court and the ICCPR Committee.

Third, in qualitative terms, the jurisdiction of the Court now spans a diverse array of cultural contexts, political systems, social perspectives and levels of economic development. As a result, where once it might have been portrayed as a Court whose docket covered only a rather limited range of issues, and often not necessarily those which were seen to be the most pressing, today it is confronted on a daily basis with virtually the full range of human rights challenges of the utmost importance within the societies concerned. A fourth reason for its importance is the crucial role it now plays both as a constitutional court in its own right, and in relation to national constitutional courts, across the whole of Europe. While it does not enjoy formal hierarchical superiority *vis-à-vis* the highest court in the EU, the European Court of Justice, that court is now showing a growing degree of deference to the normative pronouncements of the ECtHR.

The decisions below explore some of the characteristic problems that arise when international tribunals decide human rights issues that may deeply affect the internal order of states. They involve some examples of cases that have arisen in relation to the newer members of the ECHR system, and Russia in particular. Other cases focus on two of the more controversial areas in which the European Court has been active — the rights of homosexuals and electoral democracy — among the vast range of matters that have come before the Court. That range indeed approximates to the breadth of issues that come before national constitutional courts or the US Supreme Court with respect to its constitutional decisions. Indeed, the United States offers a useful comparison: relationships between the European Court and the (judiciaries of the) member states of the European Convention, on the one hand; relationships between the US Supreme Court and the (judiciaries of the) component states of American federalism, on the other.

The differences between the handling of complaints within the UN system by a body such as the ICCPR Human Rights Committee and the European Court are striking. Of course, deep and often disputed moral and political premises inform the work of both types of body and sometimes enter into explicit debate. But the Court's opinions take the traditional forms of the law — the facts of the dispute, argument about the interpretation of the text and related argument about the policies or principles involved, reflection on the institutional role of the Court in relation to national political orders, the ultimate decision applying the Convention in a decision binding the states parties, and possible recourse to a political body if a state does not comply with the Court's decision. From this point of view, a study of the European Court's decisions best illustrates the promise of an international (regional) *legal* order brought to bear on national human rights issues.

The question inevitably arises of how transferable this experience of the European human rights system may be — whether, for example, an equally effective judicial system aspiring to such a high record of compliance by states could function under a universal human rights treaty such as the ICCPR, or in a different kind of regional regime such as the Americas or Africa.

An important jurisprudential and political theme that is unique in the ECHR system is the doctrine of margin of appreciation, critical to an understanding of the dilemmas before this international court and the ways in which it tries to come to terms with them. It is especially important in relation to issues of morality, as illustrated by the cases dealing with homosexuality.

a. ISSUES OF SEXUALITY

The following materials deal with the rights of homosexuals with respect to sexual relations and military service, principally within the context of the right to privacy. The *Handyside* decision introduces those materials since it provides background for the European Court's decision in *Norris v. Ireland*, below. The following excerpts consider only issues bearing directly on *Norris*.

HANDYSIDE CASE

European Court of Human Rights, 1976
Ser. A, No. 24

[In 1971, Handyside, a UK publisher was about to publish an English translation of 'The Little Red Schoolbook', a Danish book published in a number of continental countries which was meant to serve as a reference work for schoolchildren. It treated education and teaching in general, advancing in many instances unorthodox, counter-cultural perspectives. About 10% of the book dealt with sexual matters, including 'reference' sections on masturbation, intercourse, contraceptives, homosexuality, pornography and venereal disease. Here too the advice offered was unorthodox: experiment, learn for yourself, don't fear disapproval. The publicity given the book drew adverse reactions from quarters such as schools, churches and parents' groups.

Before publication, government authorities acted under the Obscene Publications Acts 1959 and 1964, seizing all found copies of the book. Handyside was convicted, fined, and all the books were ordered to be destroyed. The appellate court affirmed, concluding that the book, seen as a whole, would tend to corrupt and deprave a significant portion of children who would read it, and that despite its virtues as an educational document, the book could not benefit from a statutory defence to the effect that on balance publication could be justified as being in the public good. A revised edition of the book was published later in 1971 and its distribution was permitted.

In 1972 Handyside filed an application before the European Commission of Human Rights, alleging several violations of the Convention but stressing Article 10. The Commission in effect concluded that there had been no breach of the Convention, and it referred the case to the ECtHR in 1976. The Court decided that no breach of Article 10 (or any other article) had been established. Article 10 provides:

> 1. Everyone has the right to freedom of expression. This right shall include freedom to hold opinions and to receive and impart information and ideas without interference by public authority and regardless of frontiers. . . .
>
> 2. The exercise of these freedoms, since it carries with it duties and responsibilities, may be subject to such formalities, conditions, restrictions or penalties as are prescribed by law and are necessary in a democratic society, in the interests of national security, territorial integrity or public safety, for the prevention of disorder or crime, for the protection of health or morals, for the protection of the reputation or rights of others, for preventing the disclosure of information received in confidence, or for maintaining the authority and impartiality of the judiciary.

After review of the book and the evidence before the English courts, the Court concluded that the English judges had a basis, in the exercise of the discretion left them by the Convention, for finding that the book would have a pernicious effect on the morals of the likely readers between ages 12 and 18. The excerpts below from the opinion treat matters relevant to a determination whether the UK restrictions on publication were 'necessary in a democratic society' within the meaning of Article 10(2).]

48. . . . These observations apply, notably, to Article 10(2). In particular, it is not possible to find in the domestic law of the various Contracting States a uniform European conception of morals. The view taken by their respective laws of the requirements of morals varies from time to time and from place to place, especially in our era which is characterised by a rapid and far-reaching evolution of opinions on the subject. By reason of their direct and continuous contact with the vital forces of their countries, State authorities are in principle in a better position than the international judge to give an opinion on the exact content of these requirements as well as on the 'necessity' of a 'restriction' or 'penalty' intended to meet them. . . . [I]t is for the national authorities to make the initial assessment of the reality of the pressing social need implied by the notion of 'necessity' in this context.

Consequently, Article 10(2) leaves to the Contracting States a margin of appreciation. This margin is given both to the domestic legislator ('prescribed by law') and to the bodies, judicial amongst others, that are called upon to interpret and apply the laws in force. . . .

49. Nevertheless, Article 10(2) does not give the Contracting States an unlimited power of appreciation. The Court, which, with the Commission, is responsible for ensuring the observance of those States' engagements (Article 19), is empowered to give the final ruling on whether a 'restriction' or 'penalty' is reconcilable with freedom of expression as protected by Article 10. The domestic margin of appreciation thus goes hand in hand with a European supervision. Such supervision concerns both the aim of the measure challenged and its 'necessity'....

The Court's supervisory functions oblige it to pay the utmost attention to the principles characterising a 'democratic society'. Freedom of expression constitutes one of the essential foundations of such a society, one of the basic conditions for its progress and for the development of every man. Subject to paragraph 2 of Article 10, it is applicable not only to 'information' or 'ideas' that are favourably received or regarded as inoffensive or as a matter of indifference, but also to those that offend, shock or disturb the State or any sector of the population. Such are the demands of that pluralism, tolerance and broadmindedness without which there is no 'democratic society'. This means, amongst other things, that every 'formality', 'condition', 'restriction' or 'penalty' imposed in this sphere must be proportionate to the legitimate aim pursued.

From another standpoint, whoever exercises his freedom of expression undertakes 'duties and responsibilities' the scope of which depends on his situation and the technical means he uses. The Court cannot overlook such a person's 'duties' and 'responsibilities' when it enquires, as in this case, whether 'restrictions' or 'penalties' were conducive to the 'protection of morals' which made them 'necessary' in a 'democratic society'.

50. It follows from this that it is in no way the Court's task to take the place of the competent national courts but rather to review under Article 10 the decisions they delivered in the exercise of their power of appreciation.

...

NOTE

The judgment below of the European Court of Human Rights in *Norris v. Ireland* refers both to the *Handyside* case and to the *Dudgeon Case*, Ser. A, No. 45 (1981). Dudgeon, a homosexual resident of Northern Ireland, brought proceedings against the United Kingdom based on his complaint against laws of Northern Ireland that made certain sexual acts between consenting adult males criminal offences. The Court concluded that Dudgeon had suffered an unjustified interference with his right to respect for his private life and accordingly found a breach by the UK of ECHR Article 8:

1. Everyone has the right to respect for his private and family life, his home and his correspondence.

2. There shall be no interference by a public authority with the exercise of this right except such as is in accordance with the law and is necessary in a democratic society in the interests of national security, public safety or the economic well-being

of the country, for the prevention of disorder or crime, for the protection of health or morals, or for the protection of the rights and freedoms of others.

We turn to two judicial decisions interpreting and applying the ECHR in relation to this issue.

NORRIS V. IRELAND

European Court of Human Rights, 1989
Ser. A, No. 142

[The applicant, an Irish national and member of the Irish Parliament, was a homosexual and chairman of the Irish Gay Rights Movement. In 1977, he instituted proceedings in the High Court of Ireland, seeking a declaration that certain laws prohibiting homosexual relations were invalid under the Irish Constitution. Those laws included (i) section 62 of the Person Act 1861 to the effect that '[w]hosoever shall attempt to commit the said abominable crime [of buggery], or shall be guilty of any... indecent assault upon a male person', is guilty of a misdemeanor and subject to a prison sentence not exceeding ten years, and (ii) section 11 of the Criminal Law Amendment Act 1885 to the effect that any 'male person who, in public or in private, commits... any act of gross indecency with another male person', is guilty of a misdemeanor and subject to imprisonment not exceeding two years. The term 'gross indecency' was not statutorily defined and was to be given meaning by courts on the particular facts of each case. Later acts gave courts discretion to impose more lenient sentences.

At no time was the applicant charged with any offence in relation to his admitted homosexual activities, although he was continuously at risk of being so prosecuted on the basis of an indictment laid by the Director of Public Prosecutions. The Director made a statement in connection with this litigation to the effect that '[t]he Director has no *stated* prosecution policy on any branch of the criminal law. He has no unstated policy *not* to enforce any offence. Each case is treated on its merits'. Since the Office of the Director was created in 1984, no prosecution had been brought in respect of homosexual activities except where minors were involved or the acts were committed in public or without consent.

Mr Norris offered evidence of the ways in which this legislation had interfered with his right to respect for his private life, including evidence (i) of deep depression on realizing that 'any overt expression of his sexuality would expose him to criminal prosecution', and (ii) of fear of prosecution of him or of another man with whom he had a physical relationship.

The judge in the High Court found that '[o]ne of the effects of criminal sanctions against homosexual acts is to reinforce the misapprehension and general prejudice of the public and increase the anxiety and guilt feelings of homosexuals leading, on occasions, to depression... '. However, he dismissed the action on legal grounds, and his decision was upheld in 1983 by the Supreme Court of Ireland. That court concluded that the applicant had standing (*locus standi*) to bring an action for a declaration even though he had not been prosecuted, for the threat continued.

The Supreme Court rejected the applicant's argument that the Irish Constitution should be interpreted in the light of the European Convention on Human Rights, for the Convention was 'an international agreement [which] does not and cannot form part of [Ireland's] domestic law, nor affect in any way questions which arise thereunder'. Article 29(6) of the Irish Constitution declared: 'No international agreement shall be part of the domestic law of the State save as may be determined by the Oireachtas', and the Oireachtas (legislature) had not taken action to enact the Convention as domestic legislation.

The Supreme Court found the laws complained of to be consistent with the Constitution, since no right of privacy encompassing consensual homosexual activity could be derived from the 'Christian and democratic nature of the Irish State'. It observed (i) that homosexuality 'has always been condemned in Christian teaching as being morally wrong' and has been regarded for centuries 'as an offence against nature and a very serious crime', (ii) that '[e]xclusive homosexuality, whether the condition be congenital or acquired, can result in great distress and unhappiness for the individual and can lead to depression, despair and suicide', and (iii) that male homosexual conduct resulted in many states in 'all forms of venereal disease', which had become a 'significant public health problem'.

When the European Commission on Human Rights considered Norris' case it found, by six votes to five, that there had been a violation of Article 8. The case was then referred to the European Court, which agreed with the conclusion in *Dudgeon* that the applicant could claim to be a victim of a violation of the Convention because of the risk of criminal prosecution that constituted a continuing interference with the applicant's right to respect for his private life. Excerpts from the judgment follow:]

39. The interference found by the Court does not satisfy the conditions of paragraph (2) of Article 8 unless it is 'in accordance with the law', has an aim which is legitimate under this paragraph and is 'necessary in a democratic society' for the aforesaid aim.

40. It is common ground that the first two conditions are satisfied. As the Commission pointed out in paragraph 58 of its report, the interference is plainly 'in accordance with the law' since it arises from the very existence of the impugned legislation. Neither was it contested that the interference has a legitimate aim, namely the protection of morals.

41. It remains to be determined whether the maintenance in force of the impugned legislation is 'necessary in a democratic society' for the aforesaid aim. According to the Court's case law, this will not be so unless, *inter alia*, the interference in question answers a pressing social need and in particular is proportionate to the legitimate aim pursued.

...

42. ... It was not contended before the Commission that there is a large body of opinion in Ireland which is hostile or intolerant towards homosexual acts committed in private between consenting adults. Nor was it argued that Irish society had a special need to be protected from such activity. In these circumstances, the Commission concluded that the restriction imposed on the applicant under Irish

law, by reason of its breadth and absolute character, is disproportionate to the aims sought to be achieved and therefore is not necessary for one of the reasons laid down in Article 8(2) of the Convention.

...

44. . . . As early as 1976, the Court declared in its *Handyside* judgment of 7 December 1976 that, in investigating whether the protection of morals necessitated the various measures taken, it had to make an 'assessment of the reality of the pressing social need implied by the notion of 'necessity' in this context' and stated that 'every 'restriction' imposed in this sphere must be proportionate to the legitimate aim pursued'. It confirmed this approach in its *Dudgeon* judgment.

. . . [A]lthough of the three aforementioned judgments two related to Article 10 of the Convention, it sees no cause to apply different criteria in the context of Article 8.

...

46. As in the *Dudgeon* case, . . . not only the nature of the aim of the restriction but also the nature of the activities involved will affect the scope of the margin of appreciation. The present case concerns a most intimate aspect of private life. Accordingly, there must exist particularly serious reasons before interferences on the part of public authorities can be legitimate for the purposes of paragraph (2) of Article 8.

Yet the Government has adduced no evidence which would point to the existence of factors justifying the retention of the impugned laws which are additional to or are of greater weight than those present in the aforementioned *Dudgeon* case. [The Court then recalled that most European States no longer criminalize homosexual conduct.]

It was clear that 'the authorities [had] refrained in recent years from enforcing the law in respect of private homosexual acts between consenting [adult] males . . . capable of valid consent'. There was no evidence to show that this '[had] been injurious to moral standards in Northern Ireland or that there [had] been any public demand for stricter enforcement of the law'.

Applying the same tests to the present case, the Court considers that, as regards Ireland, it cannot be maintained that there is a 'pressing social need' to make such acts criminal offences. On the specific issue of proportionality, the Court is of the opinion that 'such justifications as there are for retaining the law in force unamended are outweighed by the detrimental effects which the very existence of the legislative provisions in question can have on the life of a person of homosexual orientation like the applicant. Although members of the public who regard homosexuality as immoral may be shocked, offended or disturbed by the commission by others of private homosexual acts, this cannot on its own warrant the application of penal sanctions when it is consenting adults alone who are involved'.

47. The Court therefore finds that the reasons put forward as justifying the interference found are not sufficient to satisfy the requirements of paragraph (2) of Article 8. There is accordingly a breach of that Article.

...

49. [The Court then rejected the applicant's request for compensation on the grounds that] its finding of a breach of Article 8 constitutes adequate just satisfaction. . . .

QUESTIONS

1. Do you think *Handyside* would be decided in the same way today? Is the deference to national preferences a characteristic of a lower degree of European integration?

2. Do you believe that it was significant that *Norris* was decided on the basis of the right to 'respect' for 'private life' rather than of some other provisions of the ECHR? If there were no Article 8 in the European Convention, how would you as counsel for the applicants have argued the case? How might the Court have resolved it?

3. What method do you think the Court should explicitly follow in deciding a case like *Norris*, or the birching case from the Isle of Man, with respect to trends in European states? Should it survey the legislation and the practice under that legislation (whether or not to prosecute, nature of punishment, and so on) in all member states? What should it make of the survey? Would all states have equal 'weight' in the decision? What relevance would a 'trend' have — for example, 30 years ago 90% of the states barred the practice at issue, but now only 60% bar it (or the reverse, earlier permitted and now often barred)?

NOTE

The South African Constitution of 1996 includes the right to privacy and the right to dignity. The equal protection provision of Section 9 states:

(1) Everyone is equal before the law and has the right to equal protection and benefit of the law.
(2) Equality includes the full and equal enjoyment of all rights and freedoms. To promote the achievement of equality, legislative and other measures designed to protect or advance persons, or categories of persons, disadvantaged by unfair discrimination may be taken.
(3) The state may not unfairly discriminate directly or indirectly against anyone on one or more grounds, including race, gender, sex, pregnancy, marital status, ethnic or social origin, colour, sexual orientation, age, disability, religion, conscience, belief, culture, language and birth.
(4) No person may unfairly discriminate directly or indirectly against anyone on one or more grounds in terms of subsection (3). National legislation must be enacted to prevent or prohibit unfair discrimination.
(5) Discrimination on one or more of the grounds listed in subsection (3) is unfair unless it is established that the discrimination is fair.

Article 36 of the Constitution provides: 'The rights in the Bill of Rights may be limited only in terms of law of general application to the extent that the limitation is reasonable and justifiable in an open and democratic society based on human dignity, equality and freedom . . .'.

A number of decisions have involved challenges — based on the equal protection, privacy and dignity provisions of the Constitution — to laws concerning homosexuals. In *National Coalition for Gay and Lesbian Equality v. Minister of Justice*, CCT 11/98, 1999(1) SA6 (CC), 1998 (1) BCLR 1517 (CC), the Constitutional Court of

South Africa declared the common law offences of sodomy between males and related statutory offences to be inconsistent with the Constitution because — as applied to consensual sexual relations in privacy between adult males — they breach the rights of equality, dignity and privacy.

QUESTION

In what ways does Article 9 of the South African Constitution differ from the analogous provisions in the ECHR? Does it suggest that the advocate of gay and lesbian rights should rely on it alone, or is there reason to rely also on the right to privacy?

LUSTIG-PREAN AND BECKETT V. UNITED KINGDOM

European Court of Human Rights, 1999
www.echr.coe.int/eng/Judgments.htm

[The two applicants, British nationals, complained that 'investigations into their homosexuality and their discharge from the Royal Navy on the sole ground that they are homosexual' violated Article 8 of the European Convention taken alone and in conjunction with Article 14. By 1999 the European Commission had ceased to function and so the applications went directly to the ECtHR.

Lustig-Prean began his career in the Royal Navy in 1982, and his performance evaluations were consistently very positive. In 1992, he began a steady relationship with a civilian partner. In early 1994, he was interviewed, on the basis of an anonymous tip, by the Royal Navy Special Investigations Branch (the 'service police'). He was asked personal questions about his homosexual relationships, and whether he was HIV-positive. His final evaluation in June 1994 rated him as outstanding. Six months later, the Admiralty Board notified him that he would be administratively discharged on grounds of his sexual orientation. His term of service would otherwise have ended in 2009, with possibility of renewal.

Beckett too had a successful career in the Royal Navy, with positive evaluations. He too admitted his homosexuality to the service police. The questions put to him were highly personal and detailed about his sexual life with his partner. His administrative discharge on grounds of homosexuality took place in 1993.

The applicants sought judicial review of the decisions to discharge them. The High Court dismissed their application, and the Court of Appeal later dismissed their appeal. The main opinion, written by the Master of the Rolls, concluded that:

> the court may not interfere with the exercise of an administrative discretion on substantive grounds save where the court is satisfied that the decision is unreasonable in the sense that it is beyond the range of responses open to a reasonable decision-maker. But in judging whether the decision-maker has exceeded this margin of appreciation the human rights context is important. The more substantial the interference with human rights, the more the court will require by way of justification before it is satisfied that the decision is reasonable in the sense outlined above.

The opinion noted that the greater the policy content of the decision and the more remote the subject matter of a decision from ordinary judicial experience, the more hesitant the court had to be in holding a decision to be irrational.

Leave to appeal to the House of Lords was denied.

Britain had decriminalized homosexual acts in private between consenting adults in the Sexual Offences Act 1967. The Criminal Justice and Public Order Act 1994 provided that nothing prevented a homosexual act from constituting a ground for discharging a member of the armed forces. In 1994, Armed Forces' Policy and Guidelines on Homosexuality were updated to state in part:

> Homosexuality, whether male or female, is considered incompatible with service in the armed forces. This is not only because of the close physical conditions in which personnel often have to live and work, but also because homosexual behaviour can cause offence, polarize relationships, induce ill-discipline and, as a consequence, damage morale and unit effectiveness. If individuals admit to being homosexual whilst serving and their Commanding Officer judges that this admission is well-founded they will be required to leave the services. . . .

A Homosexuality Policy Assesment Team (HPAT) was then established by the Ministry of Defence to make an internal assessment of the armed forces' policy.

> The starting-point of the assessment was an assumption that homosexual men and women were in themselves no less physically capable, brave, dependable and skilled than heterosexuals. It was considered that any problems to be identified would lie in the difficulties which integration of declared homosexuals would pose to the military system which was largely staffed by heterosexuals.

The following excerpts from the opinion of the European Court of Human Rights start with a discussion of the HPAT.]

47. The focus throughout the assessment was upon the anticipated effects on fighting power and this was found to be the 'key problem' in integrating homosexuals into the armed forces. It was considered well established that the presence of known or strongly suspected homosexuals in the armed forces would produce certain behavioural and emotional responses and problems which would affect morale and, in turn, significantly and negatively affect the fighting power of the armed forces.

These anticipated problems included controlling homosexual behaviour and heterosexual animosity, assaults on homosexuals, bullying and harassment of homosexuals, ostracism and avoidance, 'cliquishness' and pairing, leadership and decision-making problems including allegations of favouritism, discrimination and ineffectiveness . . . , privacy/decency issues, increased dislike and suspicions (polarized relationships), and resentment over imposed change especially if controls on heterosexual expression also had to be tightened.

. . .

55. The HPAT found that 'the key problem remains and its intractability has indeed been re-confirmed. The evidence for an anticipated loss in fighting power has been set out . . . and forms the centrepiece of this assessment . . . '.

Current service attitudes were considered unlikely to change in the near future. . . . [The HPAT] considered that it was not possible to draw any meaningful comparison between the integration of homosexuals and of women and ethnic minorities into the armed forces since homosexuality raised problems of a type and intensity that gender and race did not. . . .

. . .

60. [A 1996 Parliamentary Select Committee report noted that] since its last report, a total of 30 officers and 331 persons of other rank had been discharged or dismissed on grounds of homosexuality. The committee was satisfied that no reliable lessons could as yet be drawn from the experience of other countries. . . . The matter was then debated in the House of Commons and members, by 188 votes to 120, rejected any change to the existing policy.

61. . . . [O]n 1 September 1995 the armed forces introduced a Service Statement to be read and signed [by potential recruits] before enlistment. Paragraph 8 of that statement is headed 'Homosexuality' and states that homosexuality is not considered compatible with service life and 'can lead to administrative discharge'.

AS TO THE LAW

I. Alleged Violation of Article 8 of the Convention

. . .

64. . . . [T]he Court is of the view that the investigations by the military police . . . constituted a direct interference with the applicants' right to respect for their private lives. Their consequent administrative discharge on the sole ground of their sexual orientation also constituted an interference with that right.

65. Such interferences can only be considered justified if the conditions of the second paragraph of Article 8 are satisfied. Accordingly, the interferences must be 'in accordance with the law', have an aim which is legitimate under this paragraph and must be 'necessary in a democratic society' for the aforesaid aim (see the *Norris v. Ireland* judgment of 26 October 1988, Series A no. 142, p. 18, 39).

. . .

2. Legitimate aim

67. . . . The Court finds no reason to doubt that the policy was designed with a view to ensuring the operational effectiveness of the armed forces or that investigations were, in principle, intended to establish whether the person concerned was a homosexual to whom the policy was applicable. To this extent, therefore, the Court considers that the resulting interferences can be said to pursue the legitimate aims of 'the interests of national security' and 'the prevention of disorder'.

3. 'Necessary in a democratic society'

. . .

(C) The Court's assessment

(i) Applicable general principles

. . .

81. The Court recognizes that . . . [a] margin of appreciation is left open to Contracting States in the context of this assessment, which varies according to the nature of the activities restricted and of the aims pursued by the restrictions. . . .

82. Accordingly, when the relevant restrictions concern 'a most intimate part of an individual's private life', there must exist 'particularly serious reasons' before such interferences can satisfy the requirements of Article 8(2) of the Convention.

When the core of the national security aim pursued is the operational effectiveness of the armed forces, it is accepted that each State is competent to organise its own system of military discipline and enjoys a certain margin of appreciation in this respect. The Court also considers that it is open to the State to impose restrictions on an individual's right to respect for his private life where there is a real threat to the armed forces' operational effectiveness, as the proper functioning of an army is hardly imaginable without legal rules designed to prevent service personnel from undermining it. However, the national authorities cannot rely on such rules to frustrate the exercise by individual members of the armed forces of their right to respect for their private lives, which right applies to service personnel as it does to others within the jurisdiction of the State. Moreover, assertions as to a risk to operational effectiveness must be 'substantiated by specific examples'.

(ii) Application to the facts of the case

83. . . . In the case of the present applicants, the Court finds the interferences to have been especially grave for the following reasons.

84. In the first place, the investigation process was of an exceptionally intrusive character. . . .

85. Secondly, the administrative discharge of the applicants had . . . a profound effect on their careers and prospects. . . . The Court notes, in this respect, the unique nature of the armed forces . . . and, consequently, the difficulty in directly transferring essentially military qualifications and experience to civilian life. . . .

86. Thirdly, the absolute and general character of the policy which led to the interferences in question is striking. . . .

. . .

89. Even accepting that the views on the matter which were expressed to the HPAT may be considered representative, the Court finds that the perceived problems which were identified in the HPAT report as a threat to the fighting power and operational effectiveness of the armed forces were founded solely upon the negative attitudes of heterosexual personnel towards those of homosexual orientation. The Court observes, in this respect, that no moral judgment is made on homosexuality by the policy. . . .

90. . . . The Court observes from the HPAT report that these attitudes, even if sincerely felt by those who expressed them, ranged from stereotypical expressions of hostility to those of homosexual orientation, to vague expressions of unease about the presence of homosexual colleagues. To the extent that they represent a predisposed bias on the part of a heterosexual majority against a homosexual minority, these negative attitudes cannot, of themselves, be considered by the Court to amount to sufficient justification for the interferences with the applicants' rights outlined above, any more than similar negative attitudes towards those of a different race, origin or colour.

...

92. The Court notes the lack of concrete evidence to substantiate the alleged damage to morale and fighting power that any change in the policy would entail....

93. However, in the light of the strength of feeling expressed in certain submissions to the HPAT and the special, interdependent and closely knit nature of the armed forces' environment, the Court considers it reasonable to assume that some difficulties could be anticipated as a result of any change in what is now a long-standing policy. Indeed, it would appear that the presence of women and racial minorities in the armed forces led to relational difficulties of the kind which the Government suggest admission of homosexuals would entail...

...

95. The Court considers it important to note, in the first place, the approach already adopted by the armed forces to deal with racial discrimination and with racial and sexual harassment and bullying. The January 1996 Directive, for example, imposed both a strict code of conduct on every soldier together with disciplinary rules to deal with any inappropriate behaviour and conduct. This dual approach was supplemented with information leaflets and training programmes, the army emphasising the need for high standards of personal conduct and for respect for others.

The Government, nevertheless, underlined that it is 'the knowledge or suspicion of homosexuality' which would cause the morale problems and not conduct, so that a conduct code would not solve the anticipated difficulties. However, in so far as negative attitudes to homosexuality are insufficient, of themselves, to justify the policy, they are equally insufficient to justify the rejection of a proposed alternative....

...[E]ven if it can be assumed that the integration of homosexuals would give rise to problems not encountered with the integration of women or racial minorities, the Court is not satisfied that the codes and rules which have been found to be effective in the latter case would not equally prove effective in the former....

...

97. The Government, referring to the relevant analysis in the HPAT report, further argued that no worthwhile lessons could be gleaned from the relatively recent legal changes in those foreign armed forces which now admitted homosexuals. The Court disagrees. It notes the evidence before the domestic courts to the effect that the European countries operating a blanket legal ban on homosexuals in their armed forces are now in a small minority. It considers that, even if relatively recent, the Court cannot overlook the widespread and consistently developing views and associated legal changes to the domestic laws of Contracting States on this issue....

98. Accordingly, the Court concludes that convincing and weighty reasons have not been offered by the Government to justify the policy....

...

104. In sum, the Court finds that neither the investigation conducted into the applicants' sexual orientation, nor their discharge on the grounds of their homosexuality ... were justified under Article 8.2 of the Convention.

[The Court then considered the charge of violation of Article 14, the anti-discrimination clause of the ECHR. It concluded that because Article 14 would raise the very same issues, 'albeit seen from a different angle,' that had been considered under Article 8 that no separate issues arise which would warrant examination.]

JUDGE LOUCAIDES (PARTLY CONCURRING, PARTLY DISSENTING)

I agree with the majority on all points except as regards the finding that there has been a violation of Article 8 of the Convention by reason of the applicants' discharge from the armed forces on account of their homosexuality.

In this respect I have been convinced by the argument of the Government that particular problems might be posed by the communal accommodation arrangements in the armed forces. The applicants would have to share single-sex accommodation and associated facilities (showers, toilets, etc.) with their heterosexual colleagues. To my mind, the problems in question are in substance analogous to those which would result from the communal accommodation of male members of the armed forces with female members. What makes it necessary for males not to share accommodation and other associated facilities with females is the difference in their sexual orientation. It is precisely this difference between homosexuals and heterosexuals which makes the position of the Government convincing.

... '[C]onduct codes and disciplinary rules' cannot change the sexual orientation of people and the relevant problems which ... in the analogous case of women makes it incumbent to accommodate them separately from male soldiers....

...

... I agree with the Government that the narrow margin of appreciation which is applied to cases involving intimate private-life matters is widened in cases like the present, in which the legitimate aim of the relevant restriction relates to the operational effectiveness of the armed forces and, therefore, to the interests of national security....

Regard must also be had to the principle that limitations incapable of being imposed on civilians may be placed on certain of the rights and freedoms of members of the armed forces...

I believe that the Court should not interfere simply because there is a disagreement with the necessity of the measures taken by a State. Otherwise the concept of the margin of appreciation would be meaningless. The Court may substitute its own view for that of the national authorities only when the measure is patently disproportionate to the aim pursued....

NOTE

Note the contrasting approaches described in the following two stories

Sarah Lyall, 'New Course by Royal Navy: A Campaign to Recruit Gays'

New York Times, 21 February 2005, p. A1

Five years after Britain lifted its ban on gays in the military, the Royal Navy has begun actively encouraging them to enlist and has pledged to make life easier when they do.

The navy announced Monday that it had asked Stonewall, a group that lobbies for gay rights, to help it develop better strategies for recruiting and retaining gay men and lesbians. It said, too, that one strategy may be to advertise for recruits in gay magazines and newspapers....

The partnership with Stonewall, Commodore Docherty [Director of Naval Life Management] said, will help "make more steps toward improving the culture and attitude within the service as a whole, so gays who are still in the closet feel that much more comfortable about coming out."

Gays in Britain have benefited from a number of new laws, including one that makes it illegal for employers to discriminate on the basis of workers' sexuality.

Last year, Parliament passed the Civil Partnership Act, which gives marriage-style rights to British gays who have registered as couples. The entire military is subject to the legislation, and starting in the fall, gay couples in the military who have registered under the act will be allowed to apply for housing in quarters previously reserved for married couples.

The new effort continues a pattern of changing official attitudes in the navy — once derided as running on rum, sodomy and the lash, in a phrase usually attributed to Winston Churchill....

...

'Gays In Military Debate Resurfaces'

CBS News, 7 October 2006, at
http://www.cbsnews.com/stories/2006/10/08/eveningnews/main2072456.shtml

Former Naval Petty Officer Rhonda Davis says she now serves her country on the front lines for homosexual rights. As Randall Pinkston reports, the Navy dismissed her because she violated the "don't ask, don't tell" policy on homosexuality.

Earlier this summer, she publicly acknowledged her sexual orientation at a rally supporting gay marriage.

"I said I would like to get married. I am dating a woman, we're very much in love and this is where I broke the policy," Davis says. Since 1994 when the don't ask, don't tell policy went into effect, an estimated 10,000 military personnel have been discharged — 2,000 since the war in Iraq began. The General Accounting Office reports the coast of training and replacing them totals nearly $200 million.

The war in Iraq is taking a toll on overall recruitment, and meeting the minimum enlistment goals remains a challenge. The Pentagon says it has met this year's quotas, but that was because the Army changed its enlistment requirements and increased financial incentives just to get people to sign up.

You can now get a waiver [sic] for lack of a high school diploma — even past drug use or minor incarcerations. But no branch of service will give a waiver for open homosexuality.

For that to happen, Congress has to change the law, and a House bill to do just that is encountering tough opposition.

The Pentagon contends it is following the policy set by the Commander-In-Chief. But some conservative groups say they want don't ask, don't tell eliminated because it allows gays to serve discreetly.

"Homosexuality is incompatible with military service. It's that simple," Elaine Donnelly, Director of the Center for Military Readiness says....

QUESTIONS

1. 'At least with respect to dismissal from the armed forces, the *Lustig-Prean* decision could better have been decided under Article 14 alone, rather than (effectively) under Article 8 alone. The problem of discrimination is pervasive in many states with respect to activities in the public or private sectors — employment and housing, for example. Gender and race discrimination were stopped by anti-discrimination laws. This is the clearer and stronger path to follow with respect to sexual orientation also'. Do you agree? Would it be essential under Article 14 to involve Article 8 as well? Compare the *Toonen* decision, p. 910, *supra*, under Article 17 of the ICCPR.

2. The 'Yogyakarta Principles on the Application of International Human Rights Law in Relation to Sexual Orientation and Gender Identity', adopted by a group of non-governmental experts in 2007, states that 'Every citizen has the right to take part in the conduct of public affairs, ... and to have equal access to all levels of public service and employment in public functions, including serving in the police and military, without discrimination on the basis of sexual orientation or gender identity.'[21] In your view, would this formulation provide a sounder basis than the principles relating to privacy or non-discrimination, for validating the rights of homosexuals to participate in the military?

3. What conclusions about the European human rights regime would you draw from the contrast between the policy prescribed by the ECtHR and the approach still followed in the United States in relation to the service of homosexuals in the military?

4. In 1996, the British Government proposed that the Council of Europe should seeks means:

> ... for encouraging wider and more consistent application of the margin of appreciation. One possible approach might be a resolution in the Committee of Ministers, drawing *inter alia* on the following points:
>
> (a) account should be taken of the fact that democratic institutions and tribunals in Member States are best placed to determine moral and social issues in accordance with regional and national perspectives;
> (b) full regard should be paid to decisions by democratic legislatures and to differing legal traditions;
> (c) long-standing laws and practices should be respected, except where these are manifestly contrary to the Convention.[22]

What do you see as the implications of this position? Should the democratic character of the state and its institutions have independent weight, so that (at the extreme) a law from an authoritarian state might be struck down whereas a similar law from a democratic state might be sustained?

[21] Available at http://yogyakartaprinciples.org/.

[22] European Court and Commission on Human Rights: Note on the Position of the British Government', 4 IHRR 260 (1997).

ADDITIONAL READING

A. Clapham and K. Waaldijk (eds.), *Homosexuality: A European Community Issue* (1993); Eric Heinze, *Sexual Orientation: A Human Right* (1995); R. Wintemute, *Sexual Orientation and Human Rights* (1997); Janet Halley, '*Don't: A Reader's Guide to the Military's Anti-Gay Policy*' (1999); *id.*, 'Reasoning about Sodomy: Act and Identity in and after *Bowers v. Hardwick*', 79 Va. L. Rev. 1721 (1993); *id.*, 'The Politics of the Closet: Towards Equal Protection for Gay, Lesbian, and Bisexual Identity', 36 U.C.L.A. L. Rev. 915 (1989).

b. DEMOCRACY AND POLITICAL PARTICIPATION

The following materials address the links between political participation, elections and democratic government. They start with two of the six cases decided by the European Court since 1998 involving the banning or dissolution of political parties in Turkey, and continue with a case dealing with questions of political participation and elections in Latvia, and one dealing with the regulation of political participation in Greece.

The literature in this area often distinguishes between 'procedural' and 'militant' democracy. The former are comparatively permissive and do not seek to limit the political rights even of those seeking to undermine or overthrow the constitutional order. They will, of course, use the criminal law in individual cases of transgression but will not ban political parties. Militant democracy on the other hand refers to an approach which seeks to place certain core foundational values beyond the reach of the democratic process. Those who seek to trespass upon those values will face the risk of being excluded from the political process. The German Constitution adopted after the Second World War is a classic example of the latter approach. The dilemma is simple:

> Must a democratic system stand idly by and watch antidemocratic forces gather strength? Must liberal constitutions, because they support tolerance and openness, function as suicide pacts, preventing effective self-defense? …
>
> The correct answer is "no." Constitutional democracies can and do act preemptively; for instance, by banning extremist parties while they are still relatively weak. Endangered democracies can curtail freedom of speech, freedom of association, and associated political rights to vote and compete for office and still remain recognizably liberal and democratic. To be sure, honest debate remains possible about the most effective and least restrictive ways of defending democracy against its most virulent enemies. And there is another important question that remains unanswered: What constitutional obstacles can be put in place to prevent political incumbents from opportunistically invoking the defense of democracy against antidemocratic forces as a justification for cracking down on perfectly legitimate political rivals?[23]

It might be thought that the issues arising in the cases that follow concerning Turkey and Latvia would be unlikely to arise in the context of the established democracies

[23] Stephen Holmes, Book Review, 4 Int'l J Con Law, 586 (2006).

that make up the core of the 'old' Council of Europe. But this would be a mistake. Consider for example the 2004 banning by the Belgian High Court of the Vlaams Blok, a Flemish independence party focusing strongly on 'nationalist' issues such as immigration and crime. The Court found its programme to be racist and soon after it was dissolved. Its leadership, however, started another party with an appropriately toned down platform.

In the United Kingdom, then Prime Minister Tony Blair responded to the July 2005 bombings of the London Underground railway by, *inter alia*, proposing to ban an Islamic political party, Hizb-ut-Tahrir, which had campaigned for the introduction of Sharia law in all countries. After extensive domestic controversy, and on the basis of legal and police advice, the proposal was eventually dropped in December 2006. And in Spain, Batasuna, a political party which supported the formation of a separate Basque state was proscribed by the Supreme Court in 2003 on the grounds that it was the political wing of a banned armed group, the ETA. That ban was again renewed in February 2006. The cases that follow demonstrate the complexity of dealing with extremist political parties whose goals or activities are characterized as being incompatible with the human rights and democratic principles on which they rely in order to convey their message, but which would be at great risk if they were to be elected.

UNITED COMMUNIST PARTY OF TURKEY V. TURKEY

European Court of Human Rights
Application No. 133/1996/752/951,
Grand Chamber judgment of 30 January 1998

. . .

7. The United Communist Party of Turkey ('the TBKP'), the first applicant, was a political party that was dissolved by the Constitutional Court. Mr Nihat Sargin and Mr Nabi Yagci, the second and third applicants, were respectively Chairman and General Secretary of the TBKP. They live in Istanbul.

8. The TBKP was formed on 4 June 1990. On the same day, its constitution and programme were submitted to the office of Principal State Counsel at the Court of Cassation for assessment of their compatibility with the Constitution and Law no. 2820 on the regulation of political parties.

9. On 14 June 1990, when the TBKP was preparing to participate in a general election, Principal State Counsel at the Court of Cassation ('Principal State Counsel') applied to the Constitutional Court for an order dissolving the TBKP. He accused the party of having sought to establish the domination of one social class over the others . . . , of having incorporated the word 'communist' into its name . . . , of having carried on activities likely to undermine the territorial integrity of the State and the unity of the nation . . . and of having declared itself to be the successor to a previously dissolved political party, the Turkish Workers' Party. . . .

[The following excerpts from the opinion concern almost exclusively the principal charge of undermining the unity of the nation. In omitted portions, the opinion found the other three grounds inadequate to justify interference with the right of association under Article 11.]

In support of his application Principal State Counsel relied in particular on passages from the TBKP's programme, mainly taken from a chapter entitled 'Towards a peaceful, democratic and fair solution for the Kurdish problem'; that chapter read as follows:

...

> The TBKP will strive for a peaceful, democratic and fair solution of the Kurdish problem, so that the Kurdish and Turkish peoples may live together of their free will within the borders of the Turkish Republic, on the basis of equal rights and with a view to democratic restructuring founded on their common interests.
>
> ...

10. On 16 July 1991 the Constitutional Court made an order dissolving the TBKP, [resulting in the liquidation of the party, the transfer of its assets to the Treasury, and the banning of its founders and managers from holding similar office in any other political body].

...

As to the allegation that the TBKP's constitution and programme contained statements likely to undermine the territorial integrity of the State and the unity of the nation, the Constitutional Court noted, inter alia, that those documents referred to two nations: the Kurdish nation and the Turkish nation. But it could not be accepted that there were two nations within the Republic of Turkey, whose citizens, whatever their ethnic origin, had Turkish nationality. In reality the proposals in the party constitution covering support for non-Turkish languages and cultures were intended to create minorities, to the detriment of the unity of the Turkish nation.

Reiterating that self-determination and regional autonomy were prohibited by the Constitution, the Constitutional Court said that the State was unitary, the country indivisible and that there was only one nation....

...

AS TO THE LAW

I. Alleged Violation of Article 11 of the Convention[24]

...

25. ... [P]olitical parties are a form of association essential to the proper functioning of democracy. In view of the importance of democracy in the Convention system, there can be no doubt that political parties come within the scope of Article 11.

...

[24] [Eds. Article 11 provides:

1. Everyone has the right to freedom of . . . association with others, including the right to form and to join trade unions. . . .

2. No restrictions shall be placed on the exercise of these rights other than such as are prescribed by law and are necessary in a democratic society in the interests of national security . . . or for the protection of the rights and freedoms of others.]

27. . . . [A]n association, including a political party, is not excluded from the protection afforded by the Convention simply because its activities are regarded by the national authorities as undermining the constitutional structures of the State. . . .

[W]hile it is in principle open to the national authorities to take such action as they consider necessary to respect the rule of law or to give effect to constitutional rights, they must do so in a manner which is compatible with their obligations under the Convention and subject to review by the Convention institutions.

28. The Preamble to the Convention refers to the 'common heritage of political traditions, ideals, freedom and the rule of law', of which national constitutions are in fact often the first embodiment. . . .

. . .

30. The political and institutional organization of the member States must accordingly respect the rights and principles enshrined in the Convention. It matters little in this context whether the provisions in issue are constitutional or merely legislative. . . .

. . .

32. It does not, however, follow that the authorities of a State in which an association, through its activities, jeopardizes that State's institutions are deprived of the right to protect those institutions. In this connection, the Court points out that it has previously held that some compromise between the requirements of defending democratic society and individual rights is inherent in the system of the Convention. For there to be a compromise of that sort any intervention by the authorities must be in accordance with paragraph 2 of Article 11, which the Court considers below. . . .

. . .

37. Such an interference [by Turkey with Article 11] will constitute a breach of Article 11 unless it was 'prescribed by law', pursued one or more legitimate aims under paragraph 2 and was 'necessary in a democratic society' for the achievement of those aims.

. . .

(b) Legitimate aim

. . .

41. [T]he Court considers that the dissolution of the TBKP pursued at least one of the 'legitimate aims' set out in Article 11: the protection of 'national security'.

(c) 'Necessary in a democratic society'

42. The Court reiterates that notwithstanding its autonomous role and particular sphere of application, Article 11 must also be considered in the light of Article 10. The protection of opinions and the freedom to express them is one of the objectives of the freedoms of assembly and association as enshrined in Article 11.

43. That applies all the more in relation to political parties in view of their essential role in ensuring pluralism and the proper functioning of democracy.

As the Court has said many times, there can be no democracy without pluralism. . . .

. . .

45. Democracy is without doubt a fundamental feature of the European public order. . . . The Court has . . . pointed out several times that the Convention was designed to maintain and promote the ideals and values of a democratic society.

. . . The only type of necessity capable of justifying an interference with any of those rights is, therefore, one which may claim to spring from 'democratic society'. Democracy thus appears to be the only political model contemplated by the Convention and, accordingly, the only one compatible with it. . . .

46. Consequently, . . . only convincing and compelling reasons can justify restrictions on such parties' freedom of association. In determining whether a necessity within the meaning of Article 11(2) exists, the Contracting States have only a limited margin of appreciation, which goes hand in hand with rigorous European supervision embracing both the law and the decisions applying it, including those given by independent courts. . . .

47. When the Court carries out its scrutiny, [it does not have] to confine itself to ascertaining whether the respondent State exercised its discretion reasonably, carefully and in good faith; it must look at the interference complained of in the light of the case as a whole and determine whether it was 'proportionate to the legitimate aim pursued' and whether the reasons adduced by the national authorities to justify it are 'relevant and sufficient'. . . .

2. Application of the principles to the present case

. . .

49. The Government pointed out that . . . faced with a challenge to the fundamental interests of the national community, such as national security and territorial integrity, the Turkish authorities had not in any way exceeded the margin of appreciation conferred on them by the Convention.

. . .

51. The Court notes at the outset that the TBKP was dissolved even before it had been able to start its activities and that the dissolution was therefore ordered solely on the basis of the TBKP's constitution and programme, which . . . contain nothing to suggest that they did not reflect the party's true objectives and its leaders' true intentions. Like the national authorities, the Court will therefore take those documents as a basis for assessing whether the interference in question was necessary.

. . .

55. The second submission accepted by the Constitutional Court was that the TBKP sought to promote separatism and the division of the Turkish nation. . . .

56. The Court notes that although the TBKP refers in its programme to the Kurdish 'people' and 'nation' and Kurdish 'citizens', it neither describes them as a 'minority' nor makes any claim — other than for recognition of their existence — for them to enjoy special treatment or rights, still less a right to secede from the rest of the Turkish population. On the contrary, the programme states: 'The TBKP will strive for a peaceful, democratic and fair solution of the Kurdish problem, so that the Kurdish and Turkish peoples may live together of their free will within the borders of the Turkish Republic, on the basis of equal rights and with a view to democratic restructuring founded on their common interests'. With regard to the right to

self-determination, the TBKP does no more in its programme than deplore the fact that because of the use of violence, it was not 'exercised jointly, but separately and unilaterally', adding that 'the remedy for this problem is political' and that '[i]f the oppression of the Kurdish people and discrimination against them are to end, Turks and Kurds must unite'.

...

57. The Court considers one of the principal characteristics of democracy to be the possibility it offers of resolving a country's problems through dialogue, without recourse to violence, even when they are irksome. Democracy thrives on freedom of expression. From that point of view, there can be no justification for hindering a political group solely because it seeks to debate in public the situation of part of the State's population and to take part in the nation's political life in order to find, according to democratic rules, solutions capable of satisfying everyone concerned....

...

59. The Court is also prepared to take into account the background of cases before it, in particular the difficulties associated with the fight against terrorism....

60. Nor is there any need to bring Article 17 into play as nothing in the constitution and programme of the TBKP warrants the conclusion that it relied on the Convention to engage in activity or perform acts aimed at the destruction of any of the rights and freedoms set forth in it.

61. Regard being had to all the above, a measure as drastic as the immediate and permanent dissolution of the TBKP, ordered before its activities had even started and coupled with a ban barring its leaders from discharging any other political responsibility, is disproportionate to the aim pursued and consequently unnecessary in a democratic society. It follows that the measure infringed Article 11 of the Convention.

...

REFAH PARTİSİ (THE WELFARE PARTY) AND OTHERS V. TURKEY

European Court of Human Rights
Applications nos. 41340/98, 41342/98, 41343/98 and 41344/98
Grand Chamber, 13 February 2003

[Four applications were submitted by the Turkish Welfare Party (Refah) and three of its members in May 1998. They alleged that the dissolution of Refah by the Turkish Constitutional Court and the suspension of certain political rights of the party leaders breached Articles 9, 10, 11, 14, 17 and 18 of the ECHR and Articles 1 and 3 of Protocol No. 1. The case was first heard by a Chamber. In July 2001 it held by a vote of four to three that there had been no violation of Article 11 and that it was unnecessary to examine the other alleged breaches. In December 2001, after a request by the applicants, the case was referred to the Grand Chamber.]

THE FACTS

...

11. Refah took part in a number of general and local elections. In the local elections in March 1989 Refah obtained about 10% of the votes...

Ultimately, Refah obtained approximately 22% of the votes in the general election of 24 December 1995 and about 35% of the votes in the local elections of 3 November 1996.

The results of the 1995 general election made Refah the largest political party in Turkey.... On 28 June 1996 Refah came to power by forming a coalition government with the centre-right.... According to an opinion poll carried out in January 1997,... Refah might obtain 67% of the votes in the general election to be held roughly four years later.

B. Proceedings in the Constitutional Court

...

12. On 21 May 1997 Principal State Counsel at the Court of Cassation applied to the Turkish Constitutional Court to have Refah dissolved on the grounds that it was a "centre" (*mihrak*) of activities contrary to the principles of secularism. In support of his application, he referred to the following acts and remarks by certain leaders and members of Refah.

— Whenever they spoke in public Refah's chairman and other leaders advocated the wearing of Islamic headscarves in State schools and buildings occupied by public administrative authorities, whereas the Constitutional Court had already ruled that this infringed the principle of secularism enshrined in the Constitution.

— At a meeting on constitutional reform Refah's chairman, Mr Necmettin Erbakan, had made proposals tending towards the abolition of secularism in Turkey. He had suggested that the adherents of each religious movement should obey their own rules rather than the rules of Turkish law.

— On 13 April 1994 Mr Necmettin Erbakan had asked Refah's representatives in the Grand National Assembly to consider whether the change in the social order which the party sought would be "peaceful or violent" and would be achieved "harmoniously or by bloodshed".

— At a seminar held in January 1991 in Sivas, Mr Necmettin Erbakan had called on Muslims to join Refah, saying that only his party could establish the supremacy of the Koran through a holy war (jihad) and that Muslims should therefore make donations to Refah rather than distributing alms to third parties.

...

— Several members of Refah, including some in high office, had made speeches calling for the secular political system to be replaced by a theocratic system. These persons had also advocated the elimination of the opponents of this policy, if necessary by force. Refah, by refusing to open disciplinary proceedings against the members concerned and even, in certain cases, facilitating the dissemination of their speeches, had tacitly approved the views expressed.

— On 8 May 1997 a Refah MP, Mr İbrahim Halil Çelik, had said in front of journalists in the corridors of the parliament building that blood would flow if an attempt was made to close the "*İmam-Hatip*" theological colleges. . . .

. . .

THE LAW

I. Alleged Violation of Article 11 of the Convention

[The Court considered whether the interference had been 'prescribed by law' and had been in pursuance of a 'legitimate aim'. It responded affirmatively on both issues.]

. . .

3. "Necessary in a democratic society"

. . .

98. [T]he Court considers that a political party may promote a change in the law or the legal and constitutional structures of the State on two conditions: firstly, the means used to that end must be legal and democratic; secondly, the change proposed must itself be compatible with fundamental democratic principles. It necessarily follows that a political party whose leaders incite to violence or put forward a policy which fails to respect democracy or which is aimed at the destruction of democracy and the flouting of the rights and freedoms recognised in a democracy cannot lay claim to the Convention's protection against penalties imposed on those grounds. . . .

99. The possibility cannot be excluded that a political party, in pleading the rights enshrined in Article 11 and also in Articles 9 and 10 of the Convention, might attempt to derive therefrom the right to conduct what amounts in practice to activities intended to destroy the rights or freedoms set forth in the Convention and thus bring about the destruction of democracy (see *Communist Party (KPD) v. Germany*, no. 250/57, Commission decision of 20 July 1957, Yearbook 1, p. 222). In view of the very clear link between the Convention and democracy, no one must be authorised to rely on the Convention's provisions in order to weaken or destroy the ideals and values of a democratic society. Pluralism and democracy are based on a compromise that requires various concessions by individuals or groups of individuals, who must sometimes agree to limit some of the freedoms they enjoy in order to guarantee greater stability of the country as a whole.

In that context, the Court considers that it is not at all improbable that totalitarian movements, organised in the form of political parties, might do away with democracy, after prospering under the democratic regime, there being examples of this in modern European history.

100. The Court reiterates, however, that the exceptions set out in Article 11 are, where political parties are concerned, to be construed strictly; only convincing and compelling reasons can justify restrictions on such parties' freedom of association.

In determining whether a necessity within the meaning of Article 11 § 2 exists, the Contracting States have only a limited margin of appreciation. Although it is not for the Court to take the place of the national authorities, which are better placed than an international court to decide, for example, the appropriate timing for interference, it must exercise rigorous supervision embracing both the law and the decisions applying it, including those given by independent courts. Drastic measures, such as the dissolution of an entire political party and a disability barring its leaders from carrying on any similar activity for a specified period, may be taken only in the most serious cases. . . . Provided that it satisfies the conditions set out in paragraph 98 above, a political party animated by the moral values imposed by a religion cannot be regarded as intrinsically inimical to the fundamental principles of democracy, as set forth in the Convention.

. . .

(ε) *The appropriate timing for dissolution*

102. In addition, the Court considers that a State cannot be required to wait, before intervening, until a political party has seized power and begun to take concrete steps to implement a policy incompatible with the standards of the Convention and democracy, even though the danger of that policy for democracy is sufficiently established and imminent. The Court accepts that where the presence of such a danger has been established by the national courts, after detailed scrutiny subjected to rigorous European supervision, a State may "reasonably forestall the execution of such a policy, which is incompatible with the Convention's provisions, before an attempt is made to implement it through concrete steps that might prejudice civil peace and the country's democratic regime" (see the Chamber's judgment, § 81).

103. . . . A Contracting State may be justified under its positive obligations in imposing on political parties, which are bodies whose *raison d'être* is to accede to power and direct the work of a considerable portion of the State apparatus, the duty to respect and safeguard the rights and freedoms guaranteed by the Convention and the obligation not to put forward a political programme in contradiction with the fundamental principles of democracy.

(ζ) *Overall examination*

104. In the light of the above considerations, the Court's overall examination . . . must concentrate on the following points: (i) whether there was plausible evidence that the risk to democracy, supposing it had been proved to exist, was sufficiently imminent; (ii) whether the acts and speeches of the leaders and members of the political party concerned were imputable to the party as a whole; and (iii) whether the acts and speeches imputable to the political party formed a whole which gave a clear picture of a model of society conceived and advocated by the party which was incompatible with the concept of a "democratic society".

105. . . . [T]he Court must [also] take account of the historical context in which the dissolution of the party concerned took place and the general interest in preserving the principle of secularism in that context in the country concerned to ensure the proper functioning of "democratic society".

(ii) Application of the above principles to the present case

...

(α) Pressing social need

The appropriate timing for dissolution

...

108. The Court ... considers that at the time of its dissolution Refah had the real potential to seize political power without being restricted by the compromises inherent in a coalition. If Refah had proposed a programme contrary to democratic principles, its monopoly of political power would have enabled it to establish the model of society envisaged in that programme.

...

110. While it can be considered, in the present case, that Refah's policies were dangerous for the rights and freedoms guaranteed by the Convention, the real chances that Refah would implement its programme after gaining power made that danger more tangible and more immediate....

In short, the Court considers that in electing to intervene at the time when they did in the present case the national authorities did not go beyond the margin of appreciation left to them under the Convention.

...

The main grounds for dissolution cited by the Constitutional Court

116. The Court considers on this point that among the arguments for dissolution pleaded by Principal State Counsel at the Court of Cassation those cited by the Constitutional Court as grounds for its finding that Refah had become a centre of anti-constitutional activities can be classified into three main groups: (i) the arguments that Refah intended to set up a plurality of legal systems, leading to discrimination based on religious beliefs; (ii) the arguments that Refah intended to apply sharia to the internal or external relations of the Muslim community within the context of this plurality of legal systems; and (iii) the arguments based on the references made by Refah members to the possibility of recourse to force as a political method. The Court must therefore limit its examination to those three groups of arguments cited by the Constitutional Court.

(a) The plan to set up a plurality of legal systems

...

119. The Court sees no reason to depart from the Chamber's conclusion that a plurality of legal systems, as proposed by Refah, cannot be considered to be compatible with the Convention system. In its judgment, the Chamber gave the following reasoning:

> "70. ... the Court considers that Refah's proposal that there should be a plurality of legal systems would introduce into all legal relationships a distinction between individuals grounded on religion, would categorise everyone according to his religious beliefs and would allow him rights and freedoms not as an individual but according to his allegiance to a religious movement.

The Court takes the view that such a societal model cannot be considered compatible with the Convention system, for two reasons.

Firstly, it would do away with the State's role as the guarantor of individual rights and freedoms. . . .

Secondly, such a system would undeniably infringe the principle of non-discrimination between individuals as regards their enjoyment of public freedoms. . . .

(b) Sharia

122. . . . [After examining the various comments attributed to Refah leaders the Court accepted] the Constitutional Court's conclusion that these remarks and stances of Refah's leaders formed a whole and gave a clear picture of a model conceived and proposed by the party of a State and society organised according to religious rules.

123. The Court concurs in the Chamber's view that sharia is incompatible with the fundamental principles of democracy, as set forth in the Convention:

"72. Like the Constitutional Court, the Court considers that sharia, which faithfully reflects the dogmas and divine rules laid down by religion, is stable and invariable. Principles such as pluralism in the political sphere or the constant evolution of public freedoms have no place in it. The Court notes that, when read together, the offending statements, which contain explicit references to the introduction of sharia, are difficult to reconcile with the fundamental principles of democracy, as conceived in the Convention taken as a whole. It is difficult to declare one's respect for democracy and human rights while at the same time supporting a regime based on sharia, which clearly diverges from Convention values, particularly with regard to its criminal law and criminal procedure, its rules on the legal status of women and the way it intervenes in all spheres of private and public life in accordance with religious precepts. . . . In the Court's view, a political party whose actions seem to be aimed at introducing sharia in a State party to the Convention can hardly be regarded as an association complying with the democratic ideal that underlies the whole of the Convention."

124. The Court must not lose sight of the fact that in the past political movements based on religious fundamentalism have been able to seize political power in certain States and have had the opportunity to set up the model of society which they had in mind. It considers that, in accordance with the Convention's provisions, each Contracting State may oppose such political movements in the light of its historical experience.

125. The Court further observes that there was already an Islamic theocratic regime under Ottoman law. When the former theocratic regime was dismantled and the republican regime was being set up, Turkey opted for a form of secularism which confined Islam and other religions to the sphere of private religious practice. Mindful of the importance for survival of the democratic regime of ensuring respect for the principle of secularism in Turkey, the Court considers that the Constitutional Court was justified in holding that Refah's policy of establishing sharia was incompatible with democracy.

. . .

(d) The possibility of recourse to force

...

130. The Court considers that, whatever meaning is ascribed to the term "jihad" used in most of the speeches mentioned above (whose primary meaning is holy war and the struggle to be waged until the total domination of Islam in society is achieved), there was ambiguity in the terminology used to refer to the method to be employed to gain political power. In all of these speeches the possibility was mentioned of resorting "legitimately" to force in order to overcome various obstacles Refah expected to meet in the political route by which it intended to gain and retain power.

131. Furthermore, the Court endorses the following finding of the Chamber:

> "74. ... While it is true that [Refah's] leaders did not, in government documents, call for the use of force and violence as a political weapon, they did not take prompt practical steps to distance themselves from those members of [Refah] who had publicly referred with approval to the possibility of using force against politicians who opposed them. Consequently, Refah's leaders did not dispel the ambiguity of these statements about the possibility of having recourse to violent methods in order to gain power and retain it."

Overall examination of "pressing social need"

132. . . . [Taking account of the factors above the Court concluded that the dissolution order] may reasonably be considered to have met a "pressing social need".

Proportionality of the measure complained of

133. After considering the parties' arguments, the Court sees no good reason to depart from the following considerations in the Chamber's judgment:

> "82. ... [A]fter [Refah's] dissolution only five of its MPs (including the applicants) temporarily forfeited their parliamentary office and their role as leaders of a political party. The 152 remaining MPs continued to sit in Parliament and pursued their political careers normally.... The Court considers in that connection that the nature and severity of the interference are also factors to be taken into account when assessing its proportionality...."

4. The Court's conclusion regarding Article 11 of the Convention

135. Consequently, following a rigorous review to verify that there were convincing and compelling reasons justifying Refah's dissolution and the temporary forfeiture of certain political rights imposed on the other applicants, the Court considers that those interferences met a "pressing social need" and were "proportionate to the aims pursued". It follows that Refah's dissolution may be regarded as "necessary in a democratic society" within the meaning of Article 11 § 2.

136. Accordingly, there has been no violation of Article 11 of the Convention. [The Court therefore concluded that there was no need to examine the same issues in relation to the other provisions of the Convention cited by the applicants.]

NOTE

The consequences of the Refah case proved to be far less dire for Islamist political parties in Turkey than was predicted at the time of the dissolution. Issacharof notes that after its dissolution:

> . . . the Welfare Party fractured. A more moderate wing, led by former Istanbul mayor Recep Tayyip Erdoğan, himself a former protégé of Erbakan, broke off to form the Justice and Development Party, a far more moderate Islamic Party. In 2002, Erdoğan became Prime Minister when Justice and Development emerged as the largest bloc in Parliament. Under his tutelage, Turkey has pursued its efforts at EU integration and remains a bastion of moderation in the Middle East. Far from creating an insuperable barrier to an Islamic voice in Turkish politics, the effect of the dissolution of the Welfare Party appears to have sparked a realignment in which committed democratic voices from the self-proclaimed Islamic communities found a means of integration into mainstream Turkish political life.[25]

QUESTIONS

1. Commenting upon the *Refah* case Issacharof stated that 'On first impression, the opinion jars many democratic sensibilities, particularly those formed in the free speech environment of the United States.... [T]he use of a deferential "reasonableness" standard for the political exclusion of a party with broad popular support gives a great deal of latitude to national determinations that are necessarily problematic.' Do you think the Court went too far in this case? What other options might have been available to the Government or the Court to deal with such perceived threats to democracy without going so far as to dissolve an entire political party?

2. Comment on the following evaluation: 'The difference between the Communist Party and Refah cases is that the first involved the sort of balancing long familiar to human rights courts while the second hinged on a challenge by a religious party. The Court's statement that "sharia is incompatible with the fundamental principles of democracy" went much further and was far less nuanced than any equivalent assessment of a Christian party with otherwise comparable aims would have gone.'

3. After reviewing the European Court's political party dissolution cases, Mersel argues that the Court should also pay attention to the internal structures of political parties to ensure that they too meet appropriate criteria of democracy.[26] Where they are not democratically structured they might reasonably be banned. In your view, would this be an appropriate extension of the Court's existing jurisprudence?

[25] Samuel Issacharoff, 'Fragile Democracies', 120 Harv. L. Rev 1405, at 1446 (2007).

[26] Yigal Mersel, 'The Dissolution of Political Parties: The Problem of Internal Democracy', 4 Int. J. Con. L. 84 (2006).

ŽDANOKA V. LATVIA

European Court of Human Rights
Grand Chambers Application no. 58278/00, 16 March 2006

[The applicant was a Latvian national, Ms Tatjana Ždanoka, who alleged that her disqualification from standing for election to the Latvian Parliament and to municipal elections infringed her rights under Article 3 of Protocol No. 1, and Articles 10 and 11 of the Convention. The case was first heard by a Chamber of the Court which, in March 2003, by five votes to two, found a violation of Article 3 of Protocol No. 1 and of Article 11. It was considered unnecessary to examine separately the claim under Article 10. In November 2004, after an application by the Government, the case was referred to the Grand Chamber. The historical background to the case is complex and the actual facts were strongly contested by the two sides. In essence, the case arose out of the illegal 1940 Soviet occupation and annexation of a previously independent Latvia.

Ždanoka was born in Latvia into a Russian-speaking family. In 1971 she joined the Communist Party of Latvia (CPL), which was directly affiliated with the Communist Party of the Soviet Union. In March 1990, when the Soviets had agreed under strong political pressure to hold independent elections, she was elected as a CPL candidate to the parliament (the Supreme Council). At that time the CPL continued to support Soviet rule in Latvia. In May 1990, the Supreme Council declared transitional measures to ensure Latvia's independence, but the CPL parliamentary group ('Equal Rights') did not participate in the vote. Instead the CPL's Central Committee strongly criticised the Declaration and called for Soviet intervention. In January 1991 the Soviet army launched military operations against the neighbouring country of Lithuania, whose Government had been formed in the same way as the Latvian Government. Thirteen Lithuanian civilians were killed and hundreds injured. At precisely the same time a coup was launched in Latvia with CPL support. It failed. In August 1991 there was an attempted coup in Moscow, for which the CPL declared its full support. That coup also failed, and the Latvian authorities responded by proclaiming the country's immediate and absolute independence. The Supreme Council also declared the CPL unconstitutional, and some of its representatives were subsequently expelled from parliament, but Ms 6Zdanoka was not among them.

In February 1993 she became chairperson of a political party. The authorities, however, refused to include her on the residents' register as a Latvian citizen which prevented her participation in various elections between 1993 and 1995. After an appeal the courts vindicated her right to register in 1996. In March 1997 Ždanoka was elected to the Riga City Council. To be eligible she had signed a written statement confirming that she had not 'actively participated' in the Soviet Communist Party or the CPL after 13 January 1991. But she acknowledged in a separate letter that she had been a CPL member until 10 September 1991, the date of the CPL's official dissolution. The electoral authorities accepted her eligibility. In 1998 she was presented as a candidate for the parliamentary elections and made the same statements. On that basis the Central Electoral Commission rejected her candidacy and subsequently asked the Prosecutor General to examine the legitimacy of her election to the Riga City Council. The latter concluded that she had not committed any offence under the Criminal Code.

But in 1999 the Prosecutor General submitted documentation to the Riga Regional Court alleging her continued participated in the CPL after 13 January 1991.The court endorsed this view of the facts and dismissed the applicant's arguments that she was only formally a member of the CPL, did not participate in the meetings of its Central Committee and that, accordingly, she could not be held to have 'actively participated' in the party's activities. The Court's findings were upheld on appeal and Ždanoka's efforts to stand in the 2002 parliamentary elections failed accordingly. In 2004, however, she was elected to the European Parliament, on the basis of the European Parliament Elections Act, which did not contain the same restrictions on the eligibility of candidates.]

103. The rights guaranteed under Article 3 of Protocol No. 1 are crucial to establishing and maintaining the foundations of an effective and meaningful democracy governed by the rule of law. Nonetheless, these rights are not absolute. There is room for "implied limitations", and Contracting States must be given a margin of appreciation in this sphere. The Court re-affirms that the margin in this area is wide . . . . There are numerous ways of organising and running electoral systems and a wealth of differences, *inter alia*, in historical development, cultural diversity and political thought within Europe, which it is for each Contracting State to mould into its own democratic vision.

104. It is however for the Court to determine in the last resort whether the requirements of Article 3 of Protocol No. 1 have been complied with; it has to satisfy itself that the conditions imposed on the rights to vote or to stand for election do not curtail the exercise of those rights to such an extent as to impair their very essence and deprive them of their effectiveness; that they are imposed in pursuit of a legitimate aim; and that the means employed are not disproportionate. In particular, any such conditions must not thwart the free expression of the people in the choice of the legislature — in other words, they must reflect, or not run counter to, the concern to maintain the integrity and effectiveness of an electoral procedure aimed at identifying the will of the people through universal suffrage.

105. . . . [T]he Court has found that domestic legislation imposing a minimum age or residence requirements for the exercise of the right to vote is, in principle, compatible with Article 3 of Protocol No. 1. The Convention institutions have also held that it was open to the legislature to remove political rights from persons convicted of serious or financial crimes. In the . . . *Hirst* case, however, the Grand Chamber underlined that the Contracting States did not have *carte blanche* to disqualify all detained convicts from the right to vote without having due regard to relevant matters such as the length of the prisoner's sentence or the nature and gravity of the offence. A general, automatic and indiscriminate restriction on all detained convicts' right to vote was considered by the Court as falling outside the acceptable margin of appreciation.

106. The Convention institutions have had fewer occasions to deal with an alleged violation of an individual's right to stand as a candidate for election . . . . In this regard the Court has emphasised that the Contracting States enjoy considerable latitude in establishing constitutional rules on the status of members of parliament, including criteria governing eligibility to stand for election. . . .

[The Court then reviewed a series of relevant precedents. In *Podkolzina v. Latvia*, in 2002 the Court accepted that a person could be barred as a parliamentary candidate on account of an insufficient knowledge of the official language of the State. In that case, however, a violation was found because the language-testing procedure did not meet the requirements of procedural fairness and legal certainty. In *Melnychenko v. Ukraine*, in 2004, it was accepted that domestic residence requirements could be required for a parliamentary candidate, although in that case the domestic law governing proof of a candidate's residence lacked the necessary certainty and precision to prevent arbitrary treatment. In earlier cases (*X. v. the Netherlands*, 1974 and *X. v. Belgium*, 1979, *Van Wambeke v. Belgium*, 1991) the former Commission upheld laws depriving persons convicted of treason of the right to vote. Laws proscribing political activities by specific categories of persons, such as police officers or members of the armed forces, have also been upheld (*Rekvényi v. Hungary*, 1999).]

(c) The Court's conclusion as to the principles to be applied under Article 3 of Protocol No. 1

115. Against the background of the aforementioned cases, the Court reaches the following conclusions . . . :

(a) Article 3 of Protocol No. 1 is akin to other Convention provisions protecting various forms of civic and political rights . . . . However, where an interference with Article 3 of Protocol No. 1 is at issue the Court should not automatically adhere to the same criteria . . . . Because of the relevance of Article 3 of Protocol No. 1 to the institutional order of the State, this provision is cast in very different terms from Articles 8–11. Article 3 of Protocol No. 1 is phrased in collective and general terms, although it has been interpreted by the Court as also implying specific individual rights. The standards to be applied for establishing compliance with Article 3 of Protocol No. 1 must therefore be considered to be less stringent than those applied under Articles 8–11 of the Convention.

(b) . . . Given that Article 3 is not limited by a specific list of "legitimate aims" such as those enumerated in Articles 8–11, the Contracting States are therefore free to rely on an aim not contained in that list to justify a restriction, provided [it is compatible with the rule of law and the general objectives of the Convention].

(c) The "implied limitations" concept under Article 3 of Protocol No. 1 also means that the Court does not apply the traditional tests of "necessity" or "pressing social need". . . . [Instead] the Court has focused mainly on two criteria: whether there has been arbitrariness or a lack of proportionality, and whether the restriction has interfered with the free expression of the opinion of the people. In this connection, the wide margin of appreciation enjoyed by the Contracting States has always been underlined. In addition, the Court has stressed the need to assess any electoral legislation in the light of the political evolution of the country concerned, with the result that features unacceptable in the context of one system may be justified in the context of another.

(d) The need for individualisation of a legislative measure alleged by an individual to be in breach of the Convention, and the degree of that individualisation where it is required by the Convention, depend on the circumstances of each particular case, namely the nature, type, duration and consequences of the impugned statutory restriction. For a restrictive measure to comply with Article 3 of Protocol No. 1, a lesser degree of individualisation may be sufficient. . . .

(e) As regards the right to stand as a candidate for election, . . . the Court has been even more cautious in its assessment of restrictions in that context than when it has been called upon to examine restrictions on the right to vote . . . .

3. Application of these principles in the present case

. . .

117. The Court points out in the first place that the criterion of political loyalty which may be applied to public servants is of little, if any, relevance to the circumstances of the instant case, which deals with the very different matter of the eligibility of individuals to stand for Parliament. The criterion of "political neutrality" cannot be applied to members of Parliament in the same way as it pertains to other State officials, given that the former cannot be "politically neutral" by definition.

118. The Court further finds that the impugned restriction pursued aims compatible with the principle of the rule of law and the general objectives of the Convention, namely the protection of the State's independence, democratic order and national security.

119. It remains to be established whether the restriction was proportionate. [The Court then recounted the historical record and the consistent support of the CPL for the role played by the Soviet Union.]

. . .

121. The impugned restriction . . . precluding persons from standing for Parliament where they had "actively participated" in the activities of the CPL between 13 January 1991 and the date of that party's dissolution in September 1991, must be assessed with due regard to this very special historico-political context and the resultant wide margin of appreciation enjoyed by the State in this respect.

122. The parties disagree as to whether the impugned restriction constituted a preventive or punitive measure. In the Court's opinion, what was at the heart of the impugned legislation was not an intention to punish those who had been active in the CPL. Rather, it was to protect the integrity of the democratic process by excluding from participation in the work of a democratic legislature those individuals who had taken an active and leading role in a party which was directly linked to the attempted violent overthrow of the newly-established democratic regime. . . .

123. . . . In view of the critical events surrounding the survival of democracy in Latvia which occurred after 13 January 1991, it was reasonable for the Latvian legislature to presume that the leading figures of the CPL held an anti-democratic stance, unless by their actions they had rebutted this presumption . . . .

. . .

125. It should also be recalled that the Convention does not exclude a situation where the scope and conditions of a restrictive measure may be determined in detail by the legislature, leaving the courts of ordinary jurisdiction only with the task of verifying whether a particular individual belongs to the category or group covered by the statutory measure at issue. This is particularly so in matters relating to Article 3 of Protocol No. 1. The Court's task is essentially to evaluate whether the measure

defined by Parliament is proportionate from the standpoint of this provision, and not to find fault with the measure simply on the ground that the domestic courts were not empowered to "fully individualise" the application of the measure in the light of an individual's specific situation and circumstances.

...

4. The Court's observations in conclusion

132. The Latvian authorities' view that even today the applicant's former position in the CPL, coupled with her stance during the events of 1991, still warrant her exclusion from standing as a candidate to the national Parliament, can be considered to be in line with the requirements of Article 3 of Protocol No. 1. The impugned statutory restriction as applied to the applicant has not been found to be arbitrary or disproportionate. The applicant's current or recent conduct is not a material consideration, given that the statutory restriction in question relates only to her political stance during the crucial period of Latvia's struggle for "democracy through independence" in 1991.

133. While such a measure may scarcely be considered acceptable in the context of one political system, for example in a country which has an established framework of democratic institutions going back many decades or centuries, it may nonetheless be considered acceptable in Latvia in view of the historico-political context....

134. The Court therefore accepts in the present case that the national authorities of Latvia, both legislative and judicial, are better placed to assess the difficulties faced in establishing and safeguarding the democratic order. Those authorities should therefore be left sufficient latitude to assess the needs of their society in building confidence in the new democratic institutions, including the national Parliament....

...

136. The Court concludes that there has been no violation of Article 3 of Protocol No. 1 to the Convention.

III. Alleged Violation of Articles 10 and 11 of the Convention

137. The applicant complained that her disqualification ... [violated] Articles 10 and 11 of the Convention....

...

141. The Court considers in the circumstances of the case that Article 3 of Protocol No. 1 is *lex specialis*, and no separate examination of the applicant's complaints is warranted under Article 11. Nor can the Court find any argument that would require a separate examination of the applicant's complaints about her inability to stand for election from the point of view of Article 10.

...

DISSENTING OPINION OF JUDGE ZUPANČIČ

...

... [T]he travesty of former oppressors subsequently appealing to and profiting from democracy and the rule of law is not specific to Latvia....

...

[P]eople cannot be prevented from actively participating in the democratic process simply because they are likely to be elected. The alleged political subversiveness of Mrs Ždanoka does not derive from any illegal activity on her part established by a Latvian criminal court. Moreover, she would be politically irrelevant were it not for the *real odds*, past, present or future, that she *would* be elected. By whom? By members of the Russian-speaking minority? When she *was* permitted to stand (successfully) for election to the European Parliament this *was* tolerated because her political impact in the European Parliament is diluted and does not threaten the autonomist rule in Latvia. The fact, incidentally, that she was elected proves the real odds mentioned above.

In other words, I do not believe for a moment that the Latvian authorities would have prevented Mrs Ždanoka from standing in national elections in Latvia were it only for her Communist *past*. Neither is the true reason her *present* unwillingness to recant and repudiate her Communist views. The domestic Latvian point of view concerns no more (and no less) than Mrs Ždanoka's *future* political dangerousness. This has to do with the demographic *fact* that thirty per cent of the existing Latvian population speaks Russian. Presumably, this puts in jeopardy the pro-autonomy rule of the autochthonous majority in whose name the separation of Latvia (and the other two Baltic states) from the Soviet Union was carried out in the first place.

Now that we have reached the stage where we can, without legalistic smoke-screens, call a spade a spade, we can finally address the real question. The large Russian-speaking minority in Latvia is a demographic by-product of the long-term illegal occupation by the Soviet Union. Does the historical fact that the occupation *was* illegal ... imply that the residence of the Russian-speaking population in Latvia is itself illegal?

In different terms the same issue arose in *Slivenko*. The critical distinction when an individual's human right is at stake is precisely between an individual's *personal* situation on the one hand — and the larger historical and *collective* situation of the group to which he or she happens to belong. In principle, human rights are strictly individual rights. Historical and collective aspects of the situation are beyond the scope of our jurisdiction.

Yet the majority opinion ... rightly treats her situation as representative not merely of her private predicament. Obviously, the right to stand for election — for this reason considered in a separate Protocol — affects the individual (Mrs Ždanoka) *and* the collectivity (the Russian-speaking minority) he or she has the ambition to represent politically. The majority opinion, however, *implicitly* amalgamates the two aspects. The consequence of this mingling of issues is *explicit* endorsement of the denial of the right to stand for election. The reason for this denial was that Mrs Ždanoka had a real chance of being elected. So much for democracy.

Admittedly, this result is a consequence of the narrow scope of our jurisdiction. Yet, are we here to correct the historical wrongs? Are we to say that thirty per cent of the Latvian population is there illegally? Even if these people were regarded as aliens, their collective expulsion would be explicitly forbidden by Article 4 of Protocol No. 4. The prohibition of the collective expulsion of aliens indicates a clear *legal* answer to this question, if indeed there is a need for one. This answer is tolerance in the passage of time.

. . .

. . . [I]ntolerance is the European scourge. Because European history is replete with instances of aggression deriving from regressive nationalism, the European Court of Human Rights must take an unambiguous and unshakable *moral* stand on this predicament. Inter-ethnic tolerance is a categorical imperative of modernity. From intolerance derive too many violations of human dignity and human rights.

QUESTIONS

1. Compare the approach of the Court in *Ždanoka* with the judgment in *Refah*. What are the similarities and differences and to what extent do you consider the principles enunciated in *Refah* to be transposable to *Ždanoka*?

2. The Court characterizes Article 3 of Protocol No. 1 as *lex specialis*, and concludes that consideration should therefore not be given to any alleged violations of Ms Ždanoka's rights under Articles 10 or 11 of the ECHR. How does this comport with the Court's earlier insistence that the standards to be applied in relation to the different rights are fundamentally different?

3. In your view, what significance should be attributed to the fact that no criminal prosecution was ever undertaken against Ms Ždanoka?

4. How would the Court's majority respond to the criticism directed at them in the dissenting opinion of Judge Zupančič

5. In 2000 the European Commission for Democracy through Law (Venice Commission) recommended that every effort be made to use alternative measures designed to avoid having to ban political parties. They included fines, administrative measures, withdrawal of state subsidies, boycotts by other political factions, and bringing members of the political party involved to justice. In your view how far could effective use of these techniques go in eliminating the need to ban political parties?

NOTE

If there is one concept that appears in almost all of the preceding cases, and is an essential element in the ECtHR's overall approach, it is the 'margin of appreciation' doctrine. Former President Wildhaber notes that it cannot apply to ECHR Articles 2 and 3 and is particularly important in relation to procedural obligations:

> . . . This area of discretion is a necessary element inherent in the nature of international jurisdiction when applied to democratic States that respect the rule of law. It reflects on the one hand the practical matter of the proximity to events of national authorities and the sheer physical impossibility for an international court, whose jurisdiction covers 43 States with a population of some 800 million inhabitants, to operate as a tribunal of fact. Thus the Court has observed that it must be cautious in

taking on the role of first instance tribunal of fact. Nor is it the Court's task to substitute its own assessment of the facts for that of the domestic courts, it requires cogent finding of fact to depart from findings of fact reached by those courts.

But the margin of appreciation also embraces an element of deference to decisions taken by democratic institutions, a deference deriving from the primordial place of democracy within the Convention system. It is not the role of the European Court systematically to second guess democratic legislatures. What it has to do is to exercise an international supervision in specific cases to ensure that the solutions found do not impose an excessive or unacceptable burden on one sector of society or individuals. The democratically elected legislature must be free to take measures in the general interest even where they interfere with a given category of individual interests. The balancing exercise between such competing interests is most appropriately carried out by the national authorities. There must however be a balancing exercise, and this implies the existence of procedures which make such an exercise possible. Moreover the result must be that the measure taken in the general interest bears a reasonable relationship of proportionality both to the aim pursued and the effect of the individual interest concerned. In that sense the area of discretion accorded to the States, the margin of appreciation, will never be unlimited and the rights of individuals will ultimately be protected against the excesses of majority rule. The margin of appreciation recognizes that where appropriate procedures are in place a range of solutions compatible with human rights may be available to the national authorities. The Convention does not purport to impose uniform approaches to the myriad different interests which arise in the broad field of fundamental rights protection; it seeks to establish common minimum standards to provide an Europe-wide framework for domestic human rights protection.[27]

QUESTIONS

1. Based on the cases reviewed in this chapter, what meaning(s) or methods or premises do you attach to invocation by a judge of the margin of appreciation? Does that doctrine or principle appear to have the same meaning in all the decisions, or does its meaning change with the context?

2. Do you agree that the 'margin of appreciation, with its principled recognition of moral relativism, is at odds with the concept of the universality of human rights. If applied liberally, this doctrine can undermine seriously the promise of international enforcement of human rights that overcomes national policies.'[28]

ADDITIONAL READING

Henry Steiner, 'Political Participation as a Human Right', 1 Harv. Y'bk Int. L. 77 (1988); András Sajó (ed.), *Militant Democracy* (2004); Patrick Macklem, 'Militant Democracy,

[27] Luzius Wildhaber, 'A Constitutional Future for the European Court of Human Rights?', 23 Hum. Rts. L. J. 161, 162 (2002).

[28] Eyal Benvenisti, 'Margin of Appreciation, Consensus, and Universal Standards', 31 N.Y.U. J. Int. L. & Pol'y 843, at 844 (1999).

Legal Pluralism, and the Paradox of Self-Determination', 4. J. Int. Con. L. 488 (2006); Paul Mahoney, 'Marvellous Richness of Diversity or Invidious Cultural Relativism', 19 Hum. Rts L. J. 1 (1998); Franz Matscher, 'Methods of Interpretation of the Convention', in R. St. J. Macdonald, F. Matscher and H. Petzold (eds.), *The European System for the Protection of Human Rights* (1993), at 75; R. Macdonald, 'The Margin of Appreciation', in *ibid.* at 122; J. Sweeney, 'Margins of Appreciation: Cultural Relativity and the European Court of Human Rights in the Post-Cold War Era', 54 I.C.L.Q. 459 (2005).

6. THE CONVENTION AND THE COURT AT THE NATIONAL LEVEL

For all the importance of streamlining the Court's procedures and trying to make the system as a whole more efficient and more readily able to cope with the ever increasing caseload, there are two closely related challenges which hold the key to almost everything else. Both concern what happens or does not happen at the national level. The first is to ensure that the Convention, or at least its normative provisions, are as fully integrated as possible into the domestic legal system. Given the diversity of systems among the 46 Contracting Parties there can be no simple formula for achieving such an outcome. But, unless a state's domestic judicial system is promoting ECHR compliance, the number of cases being taken to Strasbourg will inevitably be great. In part the problem must be resolved by the national authorities, both judicial and executive. In the readings below Hoffmeister gives a sense of the different approaches to the status of the ECHR in domestic law. (On that issue, see also Chapter 12 *infra*).

The second challenge is to ensure that states provide effective domestic remedies in response to the judgments of the Court, and excerpts below from reports by the Parliamentary Assembly illustrate some of the political efforts to pressure states to comply with judgments, and to desist from interfering with those who seek to petition Strasbourg. A key part of this broader effort has also been to devise a means by which to deal effectively with a large number of cases taken to the Court from the same state and which address essentially the same problem. A dramatic breakthrough in that respect occurred in 2004 and 2005 with the emergence of the concept of 'pilot-judgments', which was first developed in the *Broniowski* case.

FRANK HOFFMEISTER, GERMANY: STATUS OF EUROPEAN CONVENTION ON HUMAN RIGHTS IN DOMESTIC LAW

4 Int. J. Con. L. 722 (2006)

Under Article 46 of the [ECHR] the high contracting parties undertake to abide by the final judgment of the [ECtHR] in any case to which they are parties. Does this obligation bind only the government — or the courts, as well — of a state party? If the courts are similarly obligated, what are the repercussions of a finding of the ECtHR on the domestic proceedings? Do the judgments of the Strasbourg court have binding force? Can an applicant bring a constitutional complaint against a decision of a German court, if the latter ignores a relevant finding of the ECtHR? These were the central issues raised in the [decision of the Bundesverfassungsgericht (the German Federal Constitutional Court or 'FCC') in the *Görgülü* decision of October 14, 2004, 2 BvR 1481/04].

[Christopher was born in August 1999. His parents were unmarried and separated and the mother gave him up for adoption immediately after birth. He went to live with prospective adoptive parents. The applicant, the father, married another woman, and in 2000 initiated custody-and-access proceedings in relation to Christopher. Access was granted initially but subsequently suspended by the German courts. His application to the ECtHR was decided in February 2004. The Court found a violation of ECHR Article 8, and pursuant to Article 46 held that Germany was under an obligation to facilitate access. The case was taken up again in the German judicial system at the same time and in October 2004 the FCC rendered its judgment.]

First, it held that the ... Convention had to be applied by German courts, like ... federal statutes, "in the framework of accepted methods of interpretation." According to the Court, the Convention influences the interpretation of fundamental rights and the rule of law, as enshrined in the Basic Law. Hence, the text of the Convention and the jurisprudence of the ECtHR serve as interpretative tools of German norms of a constitutional nature.

...

Second, the FCC held that judgments of the ECtHR reflect the actual status of Convention law.... If the ECtHR finds that the state has violated Convention provisions, the party must strive for *restitutio in integrum*. If the violation is ongoing, the state party will be obliged to ensure that the wrongdoing has ceased. Failing to act to prevent repetition of the illegal conduct would represent a further violation of the Convention....

Third, German administrative and judicial organs may not disregard such judgments. ... Administrative practice with regard to the interpretation of German statutes may have to be changed; administrative acts that violate the Convention may have to be revoked. Court decisions may have to be reviewed; if that were impossible due to the principle of *res judicata*, the Strasbourg findings could play, nevertheless, an important role in similar cases where new procedures are allowed due to changing circumstances....

Fourth, it ... must be possible to allege before the FCC that state organs did not properly take into consideration the judgments of the ECtHR....

...

As for the domestic position of the ECHR in Germany, the Court has confirmed its well-known dualist approach to international treaty law. ... [C]ertain international treaties must be submitted to the federal legislature prior to ratification.... Only when the federal legislature [adopts] an international convention as a federal statute, does that Convention become part of German domestic law, enjoying in principle the same weight as other federal statutes. By according this rank to the Convention, Germany may be grouped with Belgium, Finland, Italy, Liechtenstein, Lithuania, San Marino, Hungary, Denmark, Sweden, Iceland, and the United Kingdom. Evidently, equality with other federal statutes may lead to conflicts if a statute — adopted later — is itself not in conformity with the Convention (*lex posterior derogat legi priori*). To avoid such a situation, other Council of Europe states, such as Bulgaria, Estonia, France, Greece, the Netherlands, Luxembourg, Poland, Portugal, Russia, Slovenia, Spain, Cyprus, Latvia, Malta, Norway, Romania, the Czech Republic, Slovakia, and most recently Turkey, opted to accord the Convention a rank higher than that of federal statutes but lower than that of their respective constitutions. In Austria, the Convention enjoys the rank of formal constitutional law, while in Switzerland it is part of substantive constitutional law.

. . .

[T]he Constitutional Court has now clarified the scope and significance of the Convention for German law. . . . It rightly rejects the traditional theory that judgments of [the ECtHR] were not binding on domestic courts, broadly interpreting the duty to abide by judgments under article 46(1) of the Convention as covering all state organs. Furthermore, it does away with the narrow view that the judgments emanating from Strasbourg would only address past violations, with no practical significance for ongoing cases. With no ambiguity, the FCC follows the more recent tendency of the ECtHR in prescribing concrete action as to how a state party should implement a judgment. . . .

IMPLEMENTATION OF JUDGMENTS OF THE EUROPEAN COURT OF HUMAN RIGHTS

Council of Europe, Parliamentary Assembly, Doc. 11020, 18 September 2006, Report of the Committee on Legal Affairs and Human Rights

1. Past experience convincingly shows that the Assembly has contributed, in various ways, to a quicker resolution of often difficult issues of non-compliance with the judgments of the [ECtHR]. . . .

2. This contribution has taken a variety of forms such as the raising of the political visibility of outstanding issues, exerting pressure on responsible decision-makers, putting forward constructive proposals for solutions and ensuring adequate parliamentary action at the national level. In so doing the Assembly has adopted a number of reports and issued a series of resolutions notably for the attention of domestic authorities and recommendations to the Committee of Ministers. It has also organized debates and engaged a constructive dialogue with the Committee of Ministers through oral and written questions. The Assembly has also sought to ensure that its national parliamentary delegations involve themselves more actively in the pursuit of solutions. . .

. . .

iv. Greece

...

26. These judgments reveal a systemic problem of poor conditions of detention due to, notably, the overcrowding of Greek prisons or detention centres....

...

28. . . . [T]he recent report of the Council of Europe's Human Rights Commissioner to Greece... states that "in December 2005, none of the 17 new prisons had been completed"....

...

v. Italy

...

31. [T]he problem of Italy's compliance with the Court's judgments remains a serious concern, both as regards the number of cases pending for a long time before the Committee of Ministers (more than a half of all cases are Italian cases) and the number and the extent of structural problems that remain to be solved to comply with the judgments (some 12% of the structural problems concern Italy).

32. The Committee of Ministers has adopted a number of Interim Resolutions, repeatedly calling for Italy's compliance and suggesting specific measures. However, in spite of these efforts, real, effective progress by Italy has remained insufficient.

33. ... [T]he ... following problems remain of major concern:

- Structural deficiencies of the judicial system resulting in excessively lengthy proceedings, especially in civil cases, ... which also leads to ineffective protection of a wide range of other substantial rights; this causes large numbers of repetitive violations of the ECHR and represents a serious danger to the Rule of Law and efficient government in Italy;
- Italian law still does not allow reopening of domestic criminal proceedings impugned by the Court....

...

ix. Russian Federation

...

56. The Russian Federation is presently confronted with an increasing number of complex issues raised in recent judgments of the Court, including with some important systemic problems. These problems have already been described [elsewhere] ... and will only be briefly recalled below:

- the deficient judicial review over pretrial detention, which results in its excessive length and overcrowding of detention facilities;
- chronic non-enforcement of domestic judicial decisions delivered against the State;
- violations of the requirement of legal certainty by extensive quashing of binding judicial decisions through the nadzor procedure [such decisions may be quashed for any material or procedural violations];

- violations found by the Court on account of abuses by the security forces in the Chechen Republic or elsewhere disclose other problems requiring comprehensive measures, including those relating to disappearances....

NOTE

Another major problem, especially but not only in relation to Russia, concerns violations of States parties obligations under Article 34 of the ECHR not to hinder in any way the effective exercise of the right of individual application. The issue has been taken up by the Committee on Legal Affairs and Human Rights, of the Parliamentary Assembly of the Council of Europe. Its draft report on 'Member states' duty to co-operate with the European Court of Human Rights' (Doc. 11183, 9 February 2007) provides an indication of the problems:

> [T]he Committee is deeply worried about the fact that a number of cases involving the alleged killing, disappearance, beating or threatening of applicants initiating cases before the Court have still have not been fully and effectively investigated by the competent authorities. On the contrary, in a significant number of cases there are clear signs of lack of willingness to effectively investigate the allegations and in some cases the intention of whitewashing is clearly apparent.
>
> Illicit pressure has also been brought to bear on lawyers who defend applicants before the Court, and who assist victims of human rights violations in exhausting national remedies before applying to the Court. Such pressure has included trumped-up criminal charges, discriminatory tax inspections and threats of prosecution for "abuse of office". Similar pressure has been brought to bear on NGOs who assist applicants in preparing their cases.
>
> ... [M]ember states ... should take robust action to prosecute and punish the perpetrators and instigators of such acts, in such a way as to send out a clear message that such action will not be tolerated by the authorities.
>
> It also encourages the Court to continue taking an assertive stand in counteracting pressure on applicants and their lawyers, as well as on lawyers working on the exhaustion of internal remedies, including by an increased use of interim measures, and the granting of priority to relevant cases. As regards the lack of co-operation of member states in the establishment of facts, concrete measures proposed by the Committee include increased recourse, in appropriate cases, to factual inferences and the reversal of the burden of proof.

COMMENT ON THE PILOT-JUDGMENT PROCEDURE

The ECtHR has long faced the challenge of how best to deal with situations in which a particular defect in a state's legal system has resulted in a large number of applications to the European Court. In 2004, as part of a reform package, the Committee of Ministers invited the Court to identify in those of its judgments in which found it a violation 'what it considers to be an underlying systemic problem and the source of that problem, in particular when it is likely to give rise to numerous applications, so as to assist States in finding the appropriate solution and the Committee of Ministers in supervising the execution of judgments'.

But it remained very unclear how such an approach might work in practice until the Court experimented with the so-called 'pilot-judgment' scheme in the 2003 case of *Broniowski v. Poland*.[29] That case involved a claim by the heir of an individual whose home was forfeited when formerly Polish territory was given to the Soviet Union following the Second World War. Under international agreements, as well as domestic law, the 1.2 million people who were displaced from their homes were entitled to compensation in kind. Subsequent changes in the law, and the adoption of new laws and institutions as a result of the demise of Communism, had interminably delayed, and in the end effectively extinguished, Broniowski's claim. He brought a case before the ECtHR alleging a breach of Article 1 of Protocol No. 1 concerning the right to peaceful enjoyment of his possessions.

The property in question was in the so-called 'territories beyond the Bug River' in what is now Lviv, in Ukraine. The Court examined whether the Polish authorities had respected the principle of lawfulness, pursued a 'legitimate aim' in terms of the Convention, and had struck a fair balance between legitimate state interests and the rights of the individual. It found a violation, based on the interminable delays suffered by the applicant and by the extremely low compensation offered. In brief, the applicant had borne 'a disproportionate and excessive burden' which could not be justified 'in terms of the legitimate general community interest' (para. 186). But the Court then went on to note that Broniowski's problem, far from being isolated, 'originated in a widespread problem which resulted from a malfunctioning of Polish legislation and administrative practice and which has affected and remains capable of affecting a large number of persons' (para. 189).

The Court grounded the new procedure in Article 46 of the Convention which commits states which are parties to a case to abide by the Court's final judgments, and provides for execution of the judgment to be supervised by the Committee of Ministers. It held that in addition to providing compensation to those concerned, the state must also 'select, subject to supervision by the Committee of Ministers, the general and/or, if appropriate, individual measures to be adopted in their domestic legal order to put an end to the violation found by the Court and to redress so far as possible the effects' (para. 192). While the choice of approach was for the state itself, and not for the Court, to determine 'the measures adopted must be such as to remedy the systemic defect underlying the Court's finding of a violation so as not to overburden the Convention system with large numbers of applications deriving from the same cause' (para. 193). The Court thus reserved a decision on the possible award of damages pending submission within six months by both the Government and the applicant of their written observations, and hinted strongly that a friendly settlement would be the ideal outcome.

In September 2005 the Court, having reviewed a friendly settlement submitted by the parties to ensure its consistency with the ECHR, proceeded to strike the application out of its list.[30] It observed that its 'objective in designating the principal

[29] Application no. 31443/96, 22 June 2004.

[30] *Broniowski v. Poland*, Application no. 31443/96, Friendly settlement, 28 September 2005.

judgment as a "pilot judgment" was to facilitate the most speedy and effective resolution of a dysfunction' at the national level, thus securing respect for human rights, providing more rapid redress, and easing the Court's own backlog (para. 35).

As of May 2007 the Court has applied this procedure in only a handful of cases, all of which dealt with property rights. There remains much work to be done to determine how the pilot-judgment process will be developed and how well the Committee of Ministers might monitor agreements of this type which have been approved by the Court.

QUESTIONS

1. 'Getting 46 States, with such a vast array of legal systems and ongoing human rights challenges to adopt the measures necessary to ensure effective domestic implementation and avoid acts of intimidation against those who would submit claims to Strasbourg is surely wishful thinking'. Discuss.

2. Can you think of any objections to the pilot-judgment scheme in light of the aims of the Convention? And how easy will it be to apply it to rights other than the right to property?

3. Are there analogues to the ECHR's friendly settlement procedure in the domestic law of most states, or does this represent an unusual conciliation procedure for a court to be overseeing?

7. THE CONTINUING NEED FOR REFORM

While the ECHR system has already undergone dramatic changes since 1990, many of the most difficult challenges lie ahead. In the materials that follow, former Judge Caflisch underscores the extent of the problem and provides the basis for concluding that, despite the reforms expected to be introduced as a result of Protocol No. 14, much more remains to be done. Former ECtHR President Wildhaber then makes the argument in favour of moving beyond the concern of providing individual relief, while Philip Leach reviews the arguments raised against greater selectivity.

LUCIUS CAFLISCH, THE REFORM OF THE EUROPEAN COURT OF HUMAN RIGHTS: PROTOCOL NO. 14 AND BEYOND

6 Hum. Rts. L. Rev. 403, 404 (2006)

. . . With its [now 46] judges and about 250 Registry lawyers, the Court is presently confronted with an accumulated case-load of 82,600 applications, out of which 45,550 were made in 2005, the yearly capacity of absorption of the Court now being at around 28,000 cases. This means that: (i) the yearly input exceeds the output by about 17,000 cases and (ii) if applications were stopped altogether from coming in at this very moment — an absurd supposition — it would take the Court a minimum of three years to dispose of its accumulated case-load.

Before examining the more realistic means to gain control over an alarming situation, it may be interesting to look at the origins and the content of the applications brought before the Court. Regarding their origin, the situation is the following as of 1 April 2006:

[Russia, 19.5%; Romania, 11.6%; Turkey, 10.4%; Poland, 8.6%; Ukraine, 6.3%; France, 5.3%; Germany, 4.5%; Italy, 4.2%; Czech Republic, 3.7%; United Kingdom, 3.0%; and Bulgaria, 2.7%.]

This means that 11 States, i.e. roughly a quarter of the States Parties, are the source of more than three quarters of the total number of cases, or that 34 States (three quarters) of the total number of States Parties are accountable for only 20.2% of all applications. The number of applications from a country is not necessarily indicative of the human rights situation there; however, it can be, as is witnessed in the high-count States: Russia, Turkey and Romania. . . . A reason for the high number of applications from Eastern Europe is the distrust of individuals vis-à-vis their national judicial systems. . . .

. . . While no reliable statistics are available, one can say intuitively that more than half of the applications addressed to the Court concern Article 6 (fair trial), and at least half of these — i.e. one quarter of the total number of applications — concern the excessive length of proceedings. A great number of complaints relate to Article 5 (right to liberty), more particularly to the length of detention on remand. Both problems point to defects in the organisation of justice at the domestic level. . . . [The entry into force in 2004 of Protocol No. 12] which, contrary to Article 14 of the ECHR, forbids discrimination across the board and not only when it pertains to substantive rights protected by the Convention and its Additional Protocols . . . is likely to increase [the number of applications] by about one-third. . . .

All this goes to show that the Strasbourg Court is in a serious predicament. First, it is true that the Court has been able, in the past year, to increase its output by about one quarter; but did it do so at the expense of quality? It is also true that over 90% of the applications are inadmissible; but in order to reach that conclusion, applications must be summarily examined, and that, too, takes time. It follows that the Court, which has fallen victim to its own success, faces a difficult situation.

NOTE

In response to these various pressures the Council of Europe adopted Protocol No. 14 in 2004. As of May 2007 it had been ratified by 45 of the 46 Contracting Parties. The Russian Federation, which also happened to be the country against which almost one of every five applications to the Court have been lodged, was the sole holdout. While its Government had indicated it was supportive, the Duma (Parliament) has not taken the action required, despite innumerable pleas from the Court and all other Contracting Parties. This experience raises the question as to whether reforms of the system, especially those of a procedural nature, can be permitted to be held hostage in this way by one or even a small handful of states.

The main changes to be instituted when Protocol No. 14 enters into force have been described in the following terms:

> Protocol 14 will change the current organisation and procedure of the Court in a number of respects. When it takes effect, judges will be elected for a single term of nine years. The present judicial formations will be modified. The function discharged by a Committee will be taken on by a single judge, who cannot be the judge sitting in respect of the State concerned. The judge will be assisted by a new category of Court officers, to be known as rapporteurs. Committees will have the power to give judgment in cases to which well-established case law is applicable. The competence of Chambers will not change, although the Plenary Court may request the Committee of Ministers to reduce their size from seven members to five for a fixed period of time. The procedures before the Chambers and the Grand Chamber will remain as described above, although the Council of Europe Commissioner for Human Rights will be entitled to submit written comments and take part in the hearing in any case.
>
> Protocol No. 14 will institute two new procedures regarding the execution phase. The Committee of Ministers will be able to request interpretation of a judgment of the Court. It will also be able to take proceedings in cases where, in its view, the respondent State refuses to comply with a judgment of the Court. In such proceedings, the Court will be asked to determine whether the State has respected its obligation under Article 46 to abide by a final judgment against it.[31]

But it is universally agreed that Protocol No. 14 will not, of itself, be sufficient to deal with the huge mounting pressures resulting from the Court's ever-growing caseload. Some of the reforms which were considered during the drafting of Protocol No. 14 but were not adopted continue to be debated. And much of the debate focuses on the question of the appropriate role to be played by the Court. These developments are considered in the following readings. The first two, by Luzius Wildhaber, who was President of the Court from 1998 until 2006, address the latter question. The next article, by Philip Leach, considers some of the objections that have been raised by a wide range of commentators to the new criterion for admissibility of applications which was added by Protocol No. 14. And the final note refers to the report presented in November 2006 by a Group of Wise Persons, appointed by the Committee of Ministers to consider the 'long-term effectiveness of the ECHR control mechanism' and to make recommendations for further reforms.

[31] European Court of Human Rights, Survey of Activities 2006, p. 6.

LUZIUS WILDHABER, A CONSTITUTIONAL FUTURE FOR THE EUROPEAN COURT OF HUMAN RIGHTS?

23 Hum. Rts. L. J. 161 (2002)

1. A European Constitutional Court

Whether the European Court of Human Rights is itself a "Constitutional Court" is largely a question of semantics. We can always call it a quasi-Constitutional Court, sui generis. . . .

2. The procedural obligation implicit in Convention guarantees

. . .

It is where grievances have not been, or have not been effectively, tested in national proceedings that the Court finds itself in something of a dilemma. Should it examine the substantive complaint at the root of the application, or confine itself to establishing a procedural violation? In a number of cases involving alleged breaches of the right to life guaranteed by Article 2 of the Convention where it has been unable to establish to the required standard of proof the substantive violation, the Court has found a "procedural" violation on account of the lack of an effective investigation or effective judicial proceedings at national level capable of establishing the true facts at the origin of the allegation. In any event the Convention has a strong procedural bias. . . . It is fundamental to the machinery of protection established by the Convention that the national systems themselves provide redress for breaches of its provisions, the Court exerting its supervisory role subject to the principle of subsidiarity. . . .

. . .

4. Individual relief or constitutional mission

[T]here is a fundamental dichotomy running throughout the Convention. This is as to whether the primary purpose of the Convention system is to provide individual relief or whether its mission is more a "constitutional" one of determining issues on public policy grounds in the general interest. If the latter is the case then the mechanism of individual applications is to be seen as the means by which defects in national protection of human rights are detected with a view to correcting them and thus raising the general standard of protection of human rights. . . . [Thus the Court has]consistently confirmed that it is not empowered to order consequential measures. It establishes the existence of a violation, and the process of giving effect to that finding is left to the Committee of Ministers of the Council of Europe, "peer pressure" being the most likely way to ensure proper execution of the judgment of what is, after all, an international court. The function of this execution process is to secure the elimination of the causes of the violation. In this sense the role of the Convention and the Court is prospective as much as it is retrospective.

On this view the place of individual relief, while important and particularly so in respect of the most serious violations, is secondary to the primary aim of raising the general standard of human rights protection and extending human rights jurisprudence throughout the community of Convention States. In terms of the effectiveness of the system the emphasis will thus be on the need to avoid repetition of the circumstances giving rise to the violation. Now I would be the first to admit that the analysis of the Convention system is not universally accepted, but . . . the future of the system cannot be exclusively individual-relief based.

PHILIP LEACH, ACCESS TO THE EUROPEAN COURT OF HUMAN RIGHTS: FROM A LEGAL ENTITLEMENT TO A LOTTERY?

27 Hum. Rts. L. J. 11, 21 (2006)

[Article 12 of Protocol No. 14 provides that the Court may declare an application inadmissible if it considers that 'the applicant has not suffered a significant disadvantage, unless respect for human rights as defined by the Convention and the Protocols thereto requires an examination of the application on the merits and provided that no case may be rejected on this ground which has not been duly considered by a domestic tribunal.']

. . . [T]he European Coordinating Group for National Institutions for the Promotion and Protection of Human Rights argued [in 2003] that:

> "... the right of individual petition enshrined in the European Convention should remain sacrosanct. Any alteration of this right per se would bring the whole of the European Convention system into disrepute and would send a signal to Member States that they can dilute their obligations in the field of human rights".

Are such principled objections justified, however? Steven Greer has suggested that arguments in favour of the provision of systematic individual justice. . . have tended to "take the form of blunt and unsupported assertions . . .". . . .

As a body, the Strasbourg judges have clearly been split on this fundamental question, as was acknowledged by the Court's *Position Paper* adopted in September 2003:

> " . . . some judges are of the opinion that any further restriction on the right of individual petition is wrong in principle, whereas others consider that the only solution to the caseload problem is to give the Court some discretion as to which cases it examines in full."

Sir Stephen Sedley, the Court of Appeal Judge, who has sat as an ad hoc UK judge on the European Court, has [argued that]: . . .

> "The proposal to introduce a discretion to refuse to entertain, or to refer back, cases which are legally admissible, as final appeal courts such as the House of Lords and the Unites States Supreme Court can do, is a counsel of despair. Instead of addressing the reason for the excessive number of admissible applications, it seeks to reduce the load by transforming admission from a legal entitlement into a lottery.

> To do this would be to abandon the Court's crucial role, which is not that of a supreme court, but that of a tribunal of last resort for citizens of non-compliant states. It would be to forget that the second, the third, the hundredth or the thousandth identical violation of the Convention by a state is even more serious than the first. A power to say that such an issue, though admissible, is no longer interesting may be attractive to judges. It is less attractive for the citizens of states which persistently or systematically fail to observe the Convention."

...

[The United Kingdom judge on the Court] Sir Nicolas Bratza, has expressed "the gravest reservations" about the proposal to exclude cases of "minor or secondary" importance from detailed treatment. He has argued that any attempt to define what is 'substantial' will be "fraught with difficulty". He has questioned:

> "What is to be regarded as a case of 'minor' or 'secondary' importance? Or, contrarily, what case is to be seen as a 'substantial' one? Who decides whether a case is worthy of detailed treatment and how is such a decision practically to be arrived at? And perhaps most importantly, what is to happen to those well-founded complaints which are not ajudged worthy of the Court's detailed attention?"

Does this proposal risk creating a hierarchy of human rights which implicitly tolerates more minor breaches? That is another view which has been expressed within the Court itself.

[T]he Parliamentary Assembly of the Council of Europe [also argued] that it would discriminate (unintentionally) against female applicants to the Court, by having the effect of stressing the need to establish financial disadvantage. . . .

> "How will such a significant disadvantage be measured? In monetary terms? It is rarely women who suffer great financial losses and 'disadvantages'; they are more likely to suffer discrimination and gender-based violence. How much is rape or genital mutilation 'worth'? Will they constitute a 'significant disadvantage' in the eyes of the Court?"

...

[A group of expert advisers] seemed to be equally opposed to a *certiorari* system, when it argued:

> " . . . that accepting this suggestion would be tantamount to calling into question the entire philosophy on which the European Convention on Human Rights was based. If the idea of transforming the Court into a constitutional court were to be adopted, the *certiorari* system could be envisaged, but this would be tantamount to giving general jurisdiction to the Court to decide not to hear a case that it did not consider sufficiently important (the practice of the Unites States Supreme Court). If this were accepted, it would imply a radical change in the current system as anyone was entitled, in principle, to have his or her case examined by the Court, and that was the cornerstone of the Convention mechanism. The principle whereby anyone had the right to apply to the Court should be upheld and reaffirmed".

...

NOTE

As noted in the preceding reading, although Protocol No. 14 will allow the Court to deal more rapidly with certain types of case, this is only the tip of the reform iceberg. It is widely acknowledged that additional steps are essential. To this end the Committee of Ministers adopted five Recommendations in 2004 urging States to take appropriate measures to improve domestic implementation. An English judge, Lord Woolf, reported on the ECtHR's Working Methods in December 2005, and a Group of Wise Persons drew up 'a comprehensive strategy to secure the long-term effectiveness of the [ECHR] and its control mechanism'.

The Wise Persons Report (Doc. CM(2006)203, 15 November 2006) recommended against the creation of 'regional courts of first instance', which they feared would risk divergent case law, significant cost and procedural complexity. They also rejected a *certiorari*-type procedure giving the Court a discretion as to which cases to examine. It would undermine the 'philosophy' of the ECHR and the need to be selective would risk 'politicising the system', and might lead to inconsistencies and arbitrariness. Instead, it recommended: more flexible arrangements for authorizing procedural reforms of the judicial machinery; the establishment of an entirely new Judicial Committee to filter cases before they get to the Court ('to hear all applications raising admissibility issues and all cases which could be decided on the basis of well-established case-law of the Court allowing an application to be declared either manifestly well-founded or manifestly ill-founded'); reforms at the national level to ensure greater recognition and dissemination of the Court's jurisprudence; a procedure enabling national constitutional courts to request advisory opinions; imposing an obligation on States Parties to introduce domestic legal mechanisms to redress the damage resulting from any ECHR violation; compensation awards should be determined by national courts and only overseen by the ECtHR; full use should be made of the 'pilot-judgment' procedure; and greater recourse to friendly settlements or national-level mediation should be encouraged.

The Wise Persons also recommended that the role of the Council of Europe's Commissioner for Human Rights should be developed. That office was established in 1999 and was held by Alvaro Gil-Robles until 2006, who was succeeded by Thomas Hammarberg. The Commissioner's principal activities have been: a system of country visits in order to undertake a comprehensive evaluation of the human rights situation (following a report on Russia by Mr. Gil-Robles, President Vladimir Putin said in June 2005: 'We'll pay careful attention to the conclusions . . . and will work strenuously during the next two years not merely to react, but to change the situation in some areas.'); provision of advice on specific issues and organization of public awareness-raising events; and cooperating closely with national human rights bodies, such as ombudsmen, and national human rights institutions.

QUESTIONS

1. What do you see as the strongest arguments for and against the transformation of the ECtHR into a truly European Constitutional Court, with a discretion to select a limited number of cases to be heard? If the time is not yet ripe for such a move, when will it be?

2. By comparison with most other human rights institutions which run on a shoe-string, the ECHR is not cheap. Its budget for 2006 was 44,189,000 euros (US$58,740,000), which covers Judges' remuneration, staff salaries and operational expenditure, but not building and infrastructure. This was almost exactly the same as the budget of the US Supreme Court. But, given that the ECHR has more than five times as many judges, huge language translations costs, and a clientele almost three times as large as that of the US Supreme Court (in terms of national populations), is there an argument that European states are seeking to get justice at bargain basement rates rather than investing the amount of money which would be justified in such a vital enterprise?

ADDITIONAL READING

Christina Hioureas, 'Behind the Scenes of Protocol No. 14: Politics in Reforming the European Court of Human Rights', 24 Berkeley J. Int. L. 717 (2006); *Steven Greer*, Protocol 14 and the Future of the European Court of Human Rights [2005] Public Law 63; Martin Eaton and Jeroen Schokkenbroek, 'Reforming the Human Rights System Established by the European Convention on Human Rights', 26 H.R.L.J. 1 (2005).

8. THE BROADER EUROPEAN INSTITUTIONAL CONTEXT: THE EU AND THE OSCE

The European Union

The origins of the European Union (EU) lie in the Treaty of Paris of 1952 establishing the European Coal and Steel Community (ECSC) and subsequently in the two Treaties of Rome of 1957 creating the European Economic Community (EEC) and the European Atomic Energy Community. Upon the entry into force in 1993 of the Treaty on Economic Union these communities became the European Union, and the Treaty of Paris expired in 2002. From six founding members in 1957 the EU has grown to 27 in 2007.

The impetus for the first step of creating the ECSC came essentially from a desire to ensure that the heavy industries of the Ruhr, which had underpinned Germany's military might in two World Wars, would be 'contained' within an intergovernmental structure bringing together West Germany and its former antagonists. The expansion into an EEC in 1957 was an attempt to promote closer economic integration within Europe for both federalist and economic reasons. While the adoption of a bill of rights based on the ECHR had been proposed in the early 1950s, none of the subsequent treaties contained such a bill or a list of enumerated rights. The 1957 treaties were more concerned with the freedom of the marketplace than the rights of individuals. The latter were seen to be appropriately protected at the national level.

Despite the absence of a bill of rights, the European Court of Justice (the judicial organ of the EU) began in 1969 to evolve a specific doctrine of human rights, the original motivation for which probably owed more to a desire to protect the primacy of EC law over national law than to any concern to provide extended protection to individuals. Over the years during which the human rights doctrine has evolved, the Court has identified several different normative underpinnings for 'the general principles of EC law' of which human rights (referred to by the European Court of Justice as 'fundamental rights') were one category. These normative underpinnings include certain provisions of the Treaty of Rome, the constitutional traditions of the member states, and international treaties accepted by member states. The European Court of Justice has applied this concept of human rights to the actions of the Community itself, and, with certain qualifications, to the actions of the member states.[32] The Court's jurisprudence was subsequently reflected in the Maastricht and Amsterdam Treaties, the latter of which came into force in 1999. Article 6 of the Treaty on European Union provides that:

> 1. The Union is founded on the principles of liberty, democracy, respect for human rights and fundamental freedoms, and the rule of law, principles which are common to the Member States.
>
> 2. The Union shall respect fundamental rights, as guaranteed by the [ECHR] … and as they result from the constitutional traditions common to the Member States, as general principles of Community law.

…

The Amsterdam Treaty also established a procedure (Article 7) whereby certain membership rights in the EU can be suspended if 'a serious and persistent breach' of human rights is deemed to exist within a member state. This was reformed again by the Nice Treaty — following the Haider debacle in Austria[33] — to improve the procedures and to allow for action to be taken before a serious breach occurs. Despite these changes, high-level expert groups called for other major reforms in EU human rights policies in order to make them 'coherent, balanced, substantive and professional'.[34] A number of the reforms proposed by these groups were in fact subsequently introduced, including the creation of a new post of Personal Representative on Human Rights to the existing Council Secretary General and High Representative for the EU's Common Foreign and Security Policy in 2004, and the establishment of a (primarily advisory) Fundamental Rights Agency in 2007.

[32] See P. Alston, M. Bustelo and J. Heenan (eds.), *The EU and Human Rights* (1999); and P. Craig and G. de Búrca, *EU Law: Text, Cases, and Materials* (4th edn. 2007), Ch. 11.

[33] The Haider affair involved a series of controversial diplomatic sanctions adopted by fourteen of the then fifteen member states against Austria, in protest against the entry of the far-right Freedom Party into a coalition government in Austria in 2000.

[34] 'Leading by Example: A Human Rights Agenda for the European Union for the Year 2000', in Alston, above n. 32 at 919; and European Commission, *Affirming Fundamental Rights in the European Union: Report of the Expert Group on Fundamental Rights* (1999).

Further a network of independent experts was established in 2002 to carry out monitoring and advisory functions.

While the ECHR (a Council of Europe treaty) has been accorded a privileged position within the Community legal order, proposals that the European Community or the European Union should adhere to the treaty have not yet borne fruit. In 1996 the European Court of Justice held in its Opinion 2/94 on 'Accession by the Community to the ECHR' that such a step could not be taken in the absence of a specific treaty amendment to that effect.[35] A provision requiring the EU to accede to the ECHR was included in the EU's Constitutional Treaty in 2004, but the Treaty remains unratified after being rejected by popular referendum in France and the Netherlands in 2005. However, that provision clearly indicated a change of political will within the EU and it seems likely to be proposed again before long. Further, ECHR Protocol No. 14 specifically allows for accession by the European Union. Equally importantly, the EU in 2000 adopted its own 'Charter of Fundamental Rights'.[36] Although the decision to give this Charter full legal effect by incorporating it into the EU Constitutional Treaty has been subverted by the non-ratification of that Treaty, the Charter at present has a kind of soft-law status within the EU. It is treated by the EU legislative institutions as binding upon them and is cited in the preamble to many pieces of the legislation, as well as being cited by the European Court of Justice and European Court of First Instance.

Although arrangements exist to facilitate consultation and coordination between the EU and the Council of Europe,[37] they remain separate entities operating in very different settings despite the fact that the activities of each organization are very relevant to those of the other.

The Organization for Security and Co-operation in Europe (OSCE)

The Conference on Security and Co-operation in Europe (CSCE) opened in 1973 and concluded in August 1975 with the signing of the Final Act of Helsinki (known as the Helsinki Accord) by the 35 participating states (including all European States except Albania, plus Canada and the United States). The Soviet Union was motivated mainly by a desire to obtain formal recognition of its European frontiers, while the West took advantage of a period of East–West *détente* to obtain concessions primarily in relation to security matters. Human rights were of only secondary concern.

The CSCE process continued in the form of conferences designed to follow up and elaborate on the obligations contained in the Helsinki Accord. These agreements are reflected in various 'Concluding Documents', the most important of which in the human rights field ('the human dimension of the CSCE') are those adopted in Vienna and Paris in 1989, Copenhagen in 1990, Moscow in 1991 and Geneva in 1992.

[35] [1996] ECR I-1759.

[36] See [2000] Official Journal of the European Communities C364/1.

[37] See 'Council of Europe — European Union: A Sole Ambition for the European Continent', Report of Luxembourg Prime Minister Jean Claude Juncker of 11 April 2006, available at http://assembly.coe.int/Documents/WorkingDocs/doc06/EDOC10897.pdf.

Several characteristics distinguish the work of the CSCE from that of other entities in the human rights field. Its standards are all formally non-binding (in the sense that they are solemn undertakings, but are not in treaty form and thus not ratified or acceded to by states). Secondly, its membership is far broader than that of the European Union or even the Council of Europe. By 2007, it had grown to 56 states. Thirdly, until 1991 it had no more than a token institutional structure designed only to arrange its periodic meetings. It performed no operational tasks.

The non-binding diplomatic nature of the Helsinki Process led many observers to question its utility. Whatever contribution the process ultimately made to the demise of Communism, it clearly played an important role, especially in the second half of the 1980s and early 1990s, in legitimating human rights discourse within Eastern Europe, providing a focus for nongovernmental activities at both the domestic and international levels, and developing standards in relation to democracy, the rule of law, 'human contacts', national minorities and freedom of expression which went beyond those already in existence in other contexts such as the Council of Europe and the UN. To a large extent, its formally non-binding nature enabled the CSCE standard-setting process to yield more detailed and innovative standards than those adopted by its counterparts.

In 1995 the CSCE was officially transformed into the Organisation for Security and Co-operation in Europe (OSCE). Its official organs include the Parliamentary Assembly of the OSCE, the Ministerial Council (Foreign Ministers), the Permanent Council (which meets weekly), the 'Chairman-in-Office' which is a rotating post held by each member state Foreign Minister in turn, and Summit Meetings of Heads of State or Government. In 2005, the OSCE had over 3,500 staff, 18 field operations, and an annual budget of €159.4 million.

The OSCE's basic priorities today are: the consolidation of democratic institutions, civil society and the rule of law, conflict prevention and resolution, and the promotion of a cooperative security system. Its principal institutions are its Secretariat in Vienna, the Office for Democratic Institutions and Human Rights (ODIHR) in Warsaw, a Representative on Freedom of the Media, in Vienna, and a High Commissioner on National Minorities, based in The Hague. His role is to identify and resolve ethnic tensions that threaten peace and stability. OSCE organs or the country concerned may request a mission, but the decision whether to make an on-site visit is his own. His recommendations address both short-term policy towards minorities and longer-term measures to encourage a continuing dialogue between the government and minority members.

The OSCE has played an important role in the field in a wide range of situations, and has been especially active in electoral observation.

QUESTION

How would you characterize the division of labour in relation to human rights among the Council of Europe, the EU and the OSCE? Is there too much overlap, or does each organization make a very distinctive contribution?

9. OTHER HUMAN RIGHTS CONVENTIONS ADOPTED BY THE COUNCIL OF EUROPE

COMMENT ON THREE CONVENTIONS

The European Social Charter

Although economic and social rights were reflected in the post-Second World War constitutions of France, Germany and Italy, they were not included in the European Convention. One of the key drafters, Pierre-Henri Teitgen, explained this decision in 1949 on the grounds that it was first necessary 'to guarantee political democracy in the European Union and then to co-ordinate our economies, before undertaking the generalisation of social democracy'. These rights were subsequently recognized in the European Social Charter of 1961.

The ESC system consists of: (1) the original Charter of 1961 (ratified by 27 states, as of January 2007), (2) an Additional Protocol of 1988 extending some of the rights (13 states), (3) an amending Protocol of 1991 which revises some of the original monitoring arrangements (22 states), (4) a revised (consolidated) Charter of 1996 which brings the earlier documents up to date and adds some new rights (22 states), and (5) a further Additional Protocol of 1995 which provides for a system of collective complaints (12 states). All but the 1991 Protocol have entered into force. The resulting picture is heavily fragmented since different states are governed by different regimes depending on which parts of the system they have ratified. It is noteworthy that, while every Council of Europe state has ratified the ECHR, 17 out of 41 have ratified none of the Social Charter instruments.

The Charter and its Additional Protocol of 1988 guarantee a series of 'rights and principles' with respect to employment conditions and 'social cohesion'. The former relate to: non-discrimination, prohibition of forced labour, trade union rights, decent working conditions, equal pay for equal work, prohibition of child labour and maternity protection. Among the latter are: health protection, social security, and certain rights for children, families, migrant workers and the elderly. These rights are not legally binding *per se*. The legal obligations designed to ensure their effective exercise are contained in Part II, which details the specific measures to be taken in relation to each of the rights. Part III reflects the principle of progressive implementation tailored to suit the circumstances of individual states. Each contracting party must agree to be bound by at least five of seven rights which are considered to be of central importance. It must also accept at least five of the other rights as listed in Part II.

Part IV provides for a monitoring system based on the submission of regular reports by contracting parties. The reports are examined by the European Committee of Social Rights whose assessments of compliance and non-compliance are then considered by the Parliamentary Assembly and a Governmental Committee. Finally, on the basis of all these views, the Committee of Ministers may make specific recommendations to the state concerned. The Additional Protocol providing for collective complaints entered into force in July 1998, although by March 2007 only 42 complaints had been registered. Decisions had been adopted in relation to issues such as: the right to strike in Bulgaria, housing rights for the Roma in Italy and in Bulgaria, the right to collective bargaining in Belgium, corporal punishment in several states, and discrimination against autism sufferers in France.

The European Convention for the Prevention of Torture

In 1987 the Council of Europe adopted the European Convention for the Prevention of Torture and Inhuman or Degrading Treatment or Punishment (ECPT) which places a particular emphasis on prevention. As of April 2007 the ECPT had been ratified by 46 states and is also open to non-Council of Europe states by invitation.

The Convention establishes a Committee for the Prevention of Torture (CPT) which is composed of independent experts. Its function is 'to examine the treatment of persons deprived of their liberty with a view to strengthening, if necessary, the protection of such persons' from torture, inhuman or degrading treatment (Article 1). The Convention is not concerned solely with prisoners but with any 'persons deprived of their liberty by a public authority'. Each state party is required to permit the Committee to visit any such place within the state's jurisdiction (Article 2), unless there are exceptional circumstances (which will rarely be the case). Most visits are routine and scheduled well in advance, but there is also provision for *ad hoc* visits with little advance notice (Article 7).

As of April 2007 the CPT had made 142 periodic, and 88 *ad hoc* visits. It meets *in camera* and its visits and discussions are confidential as, in principle, are its reports. The latter, however, may be released, either at the request of the state concerned or if a state refuses to cooperate and the Committee decides by a two-thirds majority to make a public statement. This occurred in 1992 when the Committee concluded after three visits to Turkey that the Government had failed to respond to its recommendations. Since then, virtually all states have voluntarily agreed to the release of the Committee's report and (as of April 2007) 177 have been published.

Framework Convention for the Protection of National Minorities

Despite the importance of national minorities within Europe and discussions about appropriate measures since 1949, the issue had proven too controversial and complex for the Council of Europe to adopt specific standards until 1994, when the Framework Convention was adopted. In part, the impetus was the adoption of the 1992 UN Declaration on Rights of Persons Belonging to Minorities, and the development of non-binding standards and promotional activities in this field by the CSCE. The Council sought to avoid longstanding controversies by, among other things, confining the Convention to programmatic obligations that are not directly applicable and that leave considerable discretion about implementation to the state concerned. International supervision is undertaken by the Committee of Ministers of the Council based upon periodic reports to be submitted by states parties. The Convention entered into force in February 1998 and as of April 2007 had been ratified by 39 states.

ADDITIONAL READING

The EU: P. Alston, M. Bustelo and J. Heenan (eds.), *The EU and Human Rights* (1999); Marc Weller (ed.), *The Rights of Minorities in Europe: A Commentary on the European Framework Convention for the Protection of National Minorities* (2006); G. de Búrca and B. de Witte (eds.), Social Rights (2005); L. Betten and D. MacDevitt (eds.), *The Protection of Fundamental Social Rights in the European Union* (1996); P. Alston and O. de Schutter (eds), *Monitoring Fundamental Rights in the EU: The Contribution of the Fundamental Rights Agency* (2005); ODIHR, *Common Responsibility: Commitment and Implementation* (2006); Tove Malloy, *National Minority Rights in Europe* (2005); W. Zellner, *On the Effectiveness of the OSCE Minority Regime* (1999); Steven Wheatley, *Democracy, Minorities and International Law* (2005); W. Korey, *The Promises We Keep: Human Rights, the Helsinki Process, and American Foreign Policy* (1993).

C. THE INTER-AMERICAN SYSTEM

Section C illustrates the work of the Inter-American system, both the Inter-American Commission on Human Rights (IACHR) and the Inter-American Court of Human Rights (IACtHR). The applicable standards in the Inter-American system consist of the originally non-binding American Declaration on the Rights and Duties of Man (1948) and the American Convention on Human Rights (1969). The relationship between the two is comparable in some ways to that between the UDHR and the two International Covenants. Similarly, many of the techniques that are used by the Commission and Court will be familiar from our study of the UN and ECHR systems.

By the same token, the Inter-American system is distinctive in many ways. The issues it has been forced to address are often quite different from those that have preoccupied the ECHR, for example. Disappearances, killings, the death penalty, amnesty laws and related issues have been on the agenda of the Commission since the 1970s and of the Court since the 1980s. The Commission has undergone a significant evolution over time and now engages, albeit on a very limited budget, in a diverse range of activities. We focus below on the system of country reporting that it has developed. In relation to the Court, particular attention is given to judgments dealing with one of its early landmark cases dealing with responsibility for disappearances, and to two recent cases dealing with the rights of indigenous peoples and the response to prison riots.

1. BACKGROUND AND INSTITUTIONS

COMMENT ON DEVELOPMENT OF THE INTER-AMERICAN SYSTEM

In May 1948 the ninth Inter-American Conference, held in Bogotá, established the Organization of American States (OAS). Its predecessor organizations date back to the

International Union of American Republics of 1890. The 1948 Charter entered into force in December 1951 and has since been amended by the Protocol of Buenos Aires of 1967, the Protocol of Cartagena de Indias of 1985, the Protocol of Washington of 1992 and the Protocol of Managua of 1993. The purposes of the OAS are:

> to strengthen the peace and security of the continent; to promote and consolidate representative democracy, with due respect for the principle of nonintervention; to prevent possible causes of difficulties and to ensure the pacific settlement of disputes that may arise among the member states; to provide for common action on the part of those States in the event of aggression; to seek the solution of political, juridical and economic problems that may arise among them; to promote by cooperative action, their economic, social and cultural development, and to achieve an effective limitation of conventional weapons that will make it possible to devote the largest amount of resources to the economic and social development of the member states. (*Annual Report of the Inter-American Commission on Human Rights 1994* (1995), at 347.)

Its principal organs are the General Assembly that meets annually and in additional special sessions if required, the Meeting of Consultation of Ministers of Foreign Affairs that considers urgent matters, the Permanent Council and the General Secretariat. The latter two organs are based in Washington DC.

The Bogotá Conference of 1948 also adopted the American Declaration of the Rights and Duties of Man. The Inter-American system thus had a human rights declaration seven months before the United Nations had adopted the Universal Declaration and two and a half years before the European Convention was adopted. Nevertheless, the development of a regional treaty monitored by an effective supervisory machinery was to take considerably longer. The Inter-American Commission on Human Rights was created in 1959 and the American Convention on Human Rights was adopted in 1969. It entered into force in 1978.

The development of the Inter-American system followed a different path from that of its European counterpart. Although the institutional structure is superficially very similar and the normative provisions are in most respects very similar, the conditions under which the two systems developed were radically different. Within the Council of Europe, military and other authoritarian governments have been rare and short-lived, while in Latin America they were close to being the norm until the changes that started in the 1980s.

In contrast to the type of cases and issues that have preoccupied the ECHR regime, states of emergency have been common in Latin America, the domestic judiciary has often been extremely weak or corrupt, and large-scale practices involving torture, disappearances and executions have not been uncommon. Many of the governments with which the Inter-American Commission and Court have had to work have been ambivalent towards those institutions at best and hostile at worst.

In May 2007 there were 35 member states of the OAS, of which 25 had ratified the American Convention on Human Rights and 22 had recognized the jurisdiction of the Court. Although the United States signed the Convention in 1978, it has yet to ratify. Cuba remains, technically, a member of the OAS, but the Communist Government has been excluded from participation in its work since 1962. As we shall see below these facts have not prevented the Inter-American Commission from scrutinizing the human rights records of the two states.

COMMENT ON RIGHTS RECOGNIZED IN THE AMERICAN DECLARATION AND CONVENTION

You should now become familiar with these two instruments, excerpts from which appear in the online Documents Supplement.

In terms of rights, the American Declaration on the Rights and Duties of Man is similar in content to the Universal Declaration, including the economic and social rights therein. What distinguishes it are ten articles setting out the duties of the citizen: the duty 'so to conduct himself in relation to others that each and every one may fully form and develop his personality'; to 'aid support, educate and protect his minor children', to 'acquire at least an elementary education', to vote in popular elections, to 'obey the law and other legitimate commands of the authorities', to 'render whatever civil and military service his country may require for its defence and preservation', to cooperate with the state with respect to social security and welfare; to pay taxes; and to work.

The process of drafting an Inter-American treaty began in 1959. The result was the American Convention on Human Rights of 1969 (also known as the Pact of San José, Costa Rica) which contains 26 rights and freedoms, 21 of which are formulated in similar terms to the provisions of the ICCPR. Consider some comparisons:

1. Article 27 of the ICCPR, which recognizes the rights of members of minority groups, has no counterpart in the American Convention.
2. The five provisions which are in that Convention but not in the ICCPR are the right of reply (Article 14), the right to property (Article 21), freedom from exile (Article 22(5)), the right to asylum (Article 22(7)), and prohibition of 'the collective expulsion of aliens' (Article 21(9)).
3. Some provisions in the American Convention express the same general idea as in other human rights treaties but give it a distinctive specification — for example, Article 4 on the right to life that provides in paragraph 1 that the right 'shall be protected by law and, in general, from the moment of conception'.
4. Article 23 on participation in government, which figures in the later materials, contains the same rights and requirements as the analogous Article 21 of the UDHR and Article 25 of the ICCPR.

When the Convention was adopted in 1969 it was decided not to have a separate treaty relating to economic, social and cultural rights but rather to include a general provision (Article 26) in the following terms:

> The States Parties undertake to adopt measures, both internally and through international cooperation, especially those of an economic and technical nature,

> with a view to achieving progressively by legislation or other means, the full realization of the rights implicit in the economic, social, educational, scientific and cultural standards set forth in the Charter of the Organization of American States as amended by the Protocol of Buenos Aires.

The OAS Charter, as amended, sets up an Inter-American Council for Education, Science and Culture, as well as an Economic and Social Council, both of which are supposed to set standards, consider reports made by States, and make recommendations. That machinery has, however, achieved very little indeed in relation to economic, social and cultural rights. In 1988 the OAS adopted an Additional Protocol to the American Convention on Human Rights in the Area of Economic, Social and Cultural Rights (known as the Protocol of San Salvador). It obliges parties to adopt measures, 'to the extent allowed by their available resources, and taking into account their degree of development', for the progressive achievement of the rights listed. The Protocol became effective in 1999 and had, as of May 2007, 13 states parties.

The rights recognized in the Protocol are similar to those in the International Covenant on Economic, Social and Cultural Rights, although the formulations differ significantly. The Protocol does not recognize the rights to adequate clothing and housing or to an adequate standard of living (Art. 11 of the ICESCR), but it does include the right to a healthy environment, the right to special protection in old age, and the rights of persons with disabilities, none of which are explicitly recognized in the ICESCR.

NOTE

Compare the individual duties expressed in the American Declaration with the ICCPR, in which duties are only referred to in the preamble that paraphrases Article 29(1) of the Universal Declaration ('Everyone has duties to the community in which alone the free and full development of his personality is possible'). The conception and nature of the duties expressed in the African Charter on Human and Peoples' Rights, p. 504, *supra*, is radically different.

CECILIA MEDINA, THE INTER-AMERICAN COMMISSION ON HUMAN RIGHTS AND THE INTER-AMERICAN COURT OF HUMAN RIGHTS: REFLECTIONS ON A JOINT VENTURE

12 Hum. Rts. Q. 439 (1990), at 440

[When the Inter-American Commission was established in 1959, the assumption was that it would confine itself to 'abstract investigations'. When complaints immediately flowed in, the Commission was compelled to respond in some way.]

. . .

A significant part of the Commission's work was addressing the problem of countries with gross, systematic violations of human rights, characterized by an absence or a lack of effective national mechanisms for the protection of human rights and a lack of cooperation on the part of the governments concerned. The main objective of the Commission was not to investigate isolated violations but to document the existence of these gross, systematic violations and to exercise pressure to improve the general condition of human rights in the country concerned. For this purpose, and by means of its regulatory powers, the Commission created a procedure to 'take cognizance' of individual complaints and use them as a source of information about gross, systematic violations of human rights in the territories of the OAS member states.

The Commission's competence to handle individual communications was formalized in 1965, after the OAS reviewed and was satisfied with the Commission's work. The OAS passed Resolution XXII, which allowed the Commission to 'examine' isolated human rights violations, with a particular focus on certain rights. This procedure, however, provided many obstacles for the Commission. Complaints could be handled only if domestic remedies had been exhausted, a requirement that prevented swift reactions to violations. Also, the procedure made the Commission more dependent on the governments for information. This resulted in the governments' either not answering the Commission's requests for information or answering with a blanket denial that did not contribute to a satisfactory solution of the problem.

Furthermore, once the Commission had given its opinion on the case, there was nothing else to be done; the Commission would declare that a government had violated the American Declaration of the Rights and Duties of Man and recommend the government take certain measures, knowing that this was unlikely to resolve the situation.... [I]n order not to lose the flexibility it had, the Commission interpreted Resolution XXII as granting the Commission power to 'examine' communications concerning individual violations of certain rights specified in the resolution without diminishing its power to 'take cognizance' of communications concerning the rest of the human rights protected by the American Declaration. The Commission preserved this broader power for the purposes of identifying gross, systematic human rights violations.

The procedure to 'take cognizance' of communications evolved and became the general case procedure and was later used in examining the general human rights situation in a country.... [T]he Commission could publicize its findings in order to put pressure upon the governments. Finally, the report resulting from the investigation could be sent to the political bodies of the OAS, thereby allowing for a political discussion of the problem which, at least theoretically, could be followed by political measures against the governments involved.

Since financial and human resources were limited, the Commission concentrated all its efforts on the examination of the general situation of human rights in each country. The examination of individual cases clearly took a secondary place....

In short, the Commission was the sole guarantor of human rights in a continent plagued with gross, systematic violations, and the Commission was part of an international organization for which human rights were definitely not the first priority, and these facts made an imprint on the way the Commission looked upon its task.... Apparently, the Commission viewed itself more as an international organ with a highly political task to perform than as a technical body whose main task was to participate in the first phase of a quasi-judicial supervision of the observance of human rights. The Commission's past made it ill-prepared to efficiently utilize the additional powers the [American] Convention subsequently granted it.

A. The system under the American Convention on Human Rights

The Convention vested the authority to supervise its observance in two organs: the Inter-American Commission, which pre-existed the Convention, and Inter-American Court of Human Rights, which was created by the Convention.

The Inter-American Commission is composed of seven members elected in a non-governmental capacity by the OAS General Assembly and represents all the OAS member states. The entry into force of the Convention in 1978 invested the Commission with a dual role. It has retained its status as an organ of the OAS, thereby maintaining its powers to promote and protect human rights in the territories of all OAS member states. In addition, it is now an organ of the Convention, and in that capacity it supervises human rights in the territories of the states parties to the Convention.

The Commission's functions include: (1) promoting human rights in all OAS member states; (2) assisting in the drafting of human rights documents; (3) advising member states of the OAS; (4) preparing country reports, which usually include visits to the territories of these states; (5) mediating disputes over serious human rights problems; (6) handling individual complaints and initiating individual cases on its own motion, both with regard to states parties and states not parties to the Convention; and (7) participating in the handling of cases and advisory opinions before the Court.

The Inter-American Court consists of seven judges irrespective of the number of states that have recognized the jurisdiction of the Court. Although the Court is formally an organ of the Convention and not of the OAS, its judges may be nationals of any member state of the OAS whether or not they are parties to the Convention.

The Court has contentious and advisory jurisdiction. In exercising its contentious jurisdiction, the Court settles controversies about the interpretation and application of the provisions of the American Convention through a special procedure designed to handle individual or state complaints against states parties to the Convention. Under its advisory jurisdiction, the Court may interpret not only the Convention but also any other treaty concerning the protection of human rights in the American states.

... The advisory jurisdiction of the Court may be set in motion by any OAS member state, whether or not it is a party to the Convention, or by any OAS organ listed in Chapter X of the OAS Charter, which includes the Commission.

The procedure for handling individual or state complaints [under the Convention] begins before the Commission. The procedure resembles those set forth in the European Convention and in the Additional Protocol to the International Covenant on Civil and Political Rights. It is a quasi-judicial mechanism which may be started by any person, group of persons, or nongovernmental entity legally recognized in one or more of the OAS member states, regardless of whether the complainant is the victim of a human rights violation. This right of individual petition is a mandatory provision in the Convention, binding on all states parties. Inter-state communications, however, are dependent upon an explicit recognition of the competence of the Commission to receive and examine them. In addition, the Commission may begin processing a case on its own motion.

...

The Commission has powers to request information from the government concerned and, with the consent of the government, to investigate the facts in the complaint at the location of the alleged violation. If the government does not cooperate in the proceedings by providing the requested information within the time limit set by the Commission, Article 42 of the Commission's Regulations allows the Commission to presume that the facts in the petition are true, 'as long as other evidence does not lead to a different conclusion'. Following this, the Commission need investigate the case no further.

...

The Court may consider a case that is brought either by the Commission or by a state party to the Convention. For the Commission to refer a case to the Court, the case must have been admitted for investigation and the Commission's draft report sent to the state party. In addition, the state must recognize the Court's general contentious jurisdiction or a limited jurisdiction specified by a time period or case. For a state party to be able to place a case before the Court, the only requirement is that both states must have recognized the Court's contentious jurisdiction.

...

If a state does not comply with the decision of the Court, the Court may inform and make recommendations to the OAS General Assembly. There is no reference in the Convention to any action that the General Assembly might take; the assembly, being a political body, may take any political action it deems necessary to persuade the state to comply with its international obligations.

...

In addition to the problems posed by the Commission's status as part of a political organization and by the lack of cooperation among the states, financial limitations are also potentially troublesome. The OAS does not provide the Commission with the necessary means to carry out all its various activities.

. . . Under these circumstances, the Commission inevitably makes a choice as to what it can accomplish and places a priority on tasks it perceives as most likely to increase the general respect for human rights. In this ordering, the handling of individual complaints does not rank very high.

...

DAVID HARRIS, REGIONAL PROTECTION OF HUMAN RIGHTS: THE INTER-AMERICAN ACHIEVEMENT

in David Harris and S. Livingstone (eds.), The Inter-American System of Human Rights (1998), at 1

...

The inter-American system differs in many ways from the other well established regional system for the protection of human rights, namely that under the European Convention on Human Rights. . . . The inter-American system is more complex than that of the European Convention in that it is based upon two overlapping instruments, namely the American Declaration on the Rights and Duties of Man and the American Convention. . . . It also has more than one dimension in that the Inter-American Commission not only hears petitions but also conducts *in loco* visits, leading to the adoption of country reports on the human rights situation in OAS member states. This second, very important dimension to the Inter-American Commission's work has no counterpart in the European system.

Another crucial difference is the political context within which the two systems operate. Whereas the European system has during its forty year history generally regulated democracies with independent judiciaries and governments that observe the rule of law, the history of much of the Americas since 1960 has been radically different, with military dictatorships, the violent repression of political opposition and of terrorism and intimidated judiciaries for a while being the order of the day in a number of countries. The result is that human rights issues in the Americas have often concerned gross, as opposed to ordinary, violations of human rights. They have been much more to do with the forced disappearance, killing, torture and arbitrary detention of political opponents and terrorists than with particular issues concerning, for example, the right to a fair trial or freedom of expression that are the stock in trade of the European Commission and Court. This difference is apparent both in the country reports of the Inter-American Commission and in its decisions on individual petitions. A remarkable feature of the Commission's annual reports has been the long sequences of cases of forced disappearances on the street and extra-judicial killings by state agents in which the Commission, in the absence of any government response, finds a breach of the right to life on the basis of the petitioner's credible allegations.

. . .

A final difference exists at the stage of enforcing final decisions and judgments. The inter-American system provides no counterpart to the supervisory role of the Committee of Ministers of the Council of Europe. Related to this is the fact that the outcome of proceedings in the inter-American system is not necessarily a legally binding decision. The judgments of the Inter-American Court are legally binding upon the parties. . . .

One further introductory comment that may be made about the inter-American system is that it applies to the whole of a region that has a certain dislocation within it, between the United States and Canada and the rest. As one reads the annual reports of the Commission and the judgments of the Court, one has the sense that the system is essentially a Latin American one, with the United States and, more recently, Canada making an occasional appearance.[38]

. . .

There have been few signs that the Commission or the Court are overtly following national law standards common to the Americas. To the contrary, it is noticeable

[38] A small number of individual petitions have been brought under the Declaration against the US and, in a few cases, Canada (neither are bound by the Convention) and the Commission has made *in loco* visits to the US. But otherwise, outside of the political organs, and despite the active participation of US nationals on the Commission and the Court, the impression is very much one of Latin American concerns and priorities. . . .

that the Court has stated that a 'certain tendency to integrate the regional and universal system for the protection of human rights can be perceived in the Convention'. In accordance with such an approach, both the Court and the Commission have referred to, and generally followed, the jurisprudence of the European Court and Commission of Human Rights where appropriate.

...

This contrasts with the approach of the European Commission and Court which tend to set their standards quite openly by reference to the law in the great majority of European states. Moreover, on matters touching upon public morality (for example, obscenity, blasphemy), where values vary from one European state or group of European states to another, the tendency of the European Court has been to permit particular states a measure of discretion through the use of the 'margin of appreciation' doctrine. The European system has also had to accommodate the differences between common and civil law judicial systems, generally allowing each to operate in their own ways provided that justice can be seen to be done overall.

Given that most of the cases that reach the Inter-American Commission and Court involve gross violations of basic human rights upon which all legal systems and societies would agree, there has yet been little occasion for the application of specifically American standards or for cultural relativism otherwise to become an issue. Nor has the question whether a change in social values has been sufficiently generally acknowledged throughout the region for the Commission or the Court, applying a dynamic approach to interpretation, to recognise a new social standard arisen in practice. It may be anticipated that, as the American system evolves, with the number and percentage of ordinary, as opposed to gross, human rights violations increasing, these kinds of issues will arise for the Inter-American Commission and Court. Certainly, there are varying conceptions of morality and honour and kinds of legal systems in different parts of South and North America.

...

In the first fifteen or so years of its history, the Commission made *in loco* visits and country reports the central part of its work, not the examination of individual petitions. Faced with gross violations of human rights by military regimes that would be unlikely to respond to rulings against them of the European kind, the Commission prioritised the need to establish and publicise what was happening and to seek change by negotiation, and possibly by pressure through the General Assembly of the OAS, rather than through adverse ruling in petition cases. Consequently, the Commission focused on visiting states and talking with governments and on the publication of country reports and their presentation to the General Assembly for debate. The Commission's work in this regard parallels that of the UN Commission on Human Rights. On occasions, the Inter-American Commission's reports have acted as a catalyst or had some other beneficial effect. A vivid example was the 1980 report that brought home to people in Argentina the record of their military government on disappeared persons in the late 1970s. Such effect as the Commission's reports have achieved has not been with the backing of the General Assembly of the OAS. Apart from a short period in the late 1970s when pressure from the Carter Government in Washington led the Assembly to discuss the Commission's reports and generally support its work, the non-interventionalist tradition within the OAS has led other states largely to ignore the evidence presented to them, with such criticism as has been mounted in the Assembly being addressed against the Commission by the state that it has dared to attack, rather than by other states against the delinquent state.

While *in loco* visits and country reports remain an important and necessary part of the Commission's work, the consideration of individual petitions has come to play an increasing role in its activities in recent years. This has been prompted by the entry into force of the American Convention in 1979, which introduced the possibility of cases being referred to the Inter-American Court for a final, legally binding decision, and the return to democracy and law and order in South and Central American states since then, which has reduced the number of instances of gross violations of human rights for which *in loco* visits are particularly appropriate.

. . .

2. THE STANDARDS TO BE APPLIED TO DIFFERENT STATES

The American Convention applies to each of the 25 states that have ratified it. But the Commission and the Court have had to confront complex issues in relation to some of the remaining ten states, especially Cuba and the United States, which have not ratified the Convention. In relation to Cuba, the Commission has adopted a series of reports ever since the Communist Government came to power in 1959. In relation to the United States, the debate turns around the status of the American Declaration. The US has signed the American Convention but not ratified it. Its official position is that the American Declaration is clearly non-binding. It is a 'noble statement of human rights aspirations' which 'lacks the precision necessary to resolve complex legal questions'. 'It would seriously undermine the process of international lawmaking . . . to impose legal obligations on states through a process of "reinterpretation" or "inference" from a non-binding statement of principles.' It is hardly surprising then, given (i) the willingness of the US to apply to other nations the Universal Declaration of Human Rights, the status of which is very similar, and (ii) the enthusiasm of the US for holding its Latin American neighbours to their human rights obligations, that other states within the Inter-American system were keen to clarify the status of the American Declaration. The Advisory Opinion below does not mention the USA in any way but its target is fairly clear.

In its 2006 Annual Report the IACHR re-states the rationale for its endeavours to hold Cuba to account and indicates the outlines of its analysis:

> 54. Cuba is a member state of the Organization of American States since July 16, 1952. . . . The Commission has maintained that the Cuban State "is juridically answerable to the Inter-American Commission in matters that concern human rights" inasmuch as it "is party to the first international instruments established in the American hemisphere to protect human rights" and because "Resolution VI of the Eighth Meeting of Consultation excluded the Government of Cuba, not the State, from participating in the intra-American system." In this connection the IACHR stated:

> (...) it was not the intention of the Organization of American States to leave the Cuban people without protection. That Government's exclusion from the regional system in no way means that it is no longer bound by its international human rights obligations.

56. ... [The following analysis refers] specifically to the need for ending economic and commercial sanctions against the Government of Cuba, inasmuch as they tend to aggravate restrictions on the actual exercise of economic, social and cultural rights by the Cuban people.

57. Restrictions on political rights, freedom of expression and dissemination of ideas have amounted for decades to a permanent and systematic violation of the fundamental rights of Cuban citizens, a situation that is made worse, in particular, by the lack of independence of the judiciary.

58. The Commission finds it necessary to reiterate that the absence of free and fair elections based on universal secret suffrage as the sovereign expression of the people violates the right to political participation...

INTER-AMERICAN COURT OF HUMAN RIGHTS, ADVISORY OPINION OC-10/89, JULY 14, 1989

Interpretation of the American Declaration of the Rights and Duties of Man within the Framework of Article 64 of the American Convention on Human Rights: Requested by the Government of the Republic of Colombia

...

2. [In February 1988, the Government of Colombia sought an advisory opinion on] the following question:

> Does Article 64 authorize the Inter-American Court of Human Rights to render advisory opinions at the request of a member state or one of the organs of the OAS, regarding the interpretation of the American Declaration of the Rights and Duties of Man, adopted by the Ninth International Conference of American States in Bogotá in 1948?

...

17. [At the public hearing the] representatives of the United States of America said that:

> It is the position of the United States that the American Declaration is not a treaty, and that therefore the Court does not have jurisdiction under Article 64 to interpret it or determine its normative status within the inter-American human rights system.
>
> ...
>
> Because the Declaration is not and never has been a treaty, the United States believes that the Court has no jurisdiction to consider the present request, and should therefore dismiss it.

...

> In the event that the Court does reach the issues of the normative status of the Declaration, the United States' view is that the Declaration remains for all member states of the O.A.S. what it was when it was adopted: an agreed statement of non-binding general human rights principles.
>
> ...
>
> The United States must state, with all due respect, that it would seriously undermine the established international law of treaties to say that the Declaration is legally binding.
>
> ...

IV

29. The Court will now address the merits of the question before it.

30. Article 64(1) of the Convention authorizes the Court to render advisory opinions "regarding the interpretation of this Convention or of other treaties concerning the protection of human rights in the American states." ...

...

33. In attempting to define the word "treaty" as the term is employed in Article 64(1), it is sufficient for now to say that a "treaty" is, at the very least, an international instrument of the type that is governed by the two Vienna Conventions [on the law of treaties]. ... [It is clear] that the Declaration is not a treaty as defined by the Vienna Conventions because it was not approved as such, and that, consequently, it is also not a treaty within the meaning of Article 64(1).

34. Here it must be recalled that the American Declaration was adopted by the Ninth International Conference of American States (Bogotá, 1948) through a resolution adopted by the Conference itself. It was neither conceived nor drafted as a treaty....

...

[As noted] on September 26, 1949, by the Inter-American Committee of Jurisconsults ...:

> It is evident that the Declaration of Bogotá does not create a contractual juridical obligation, but it is also clear that it demonstrates a well-defined orientation toward the international protection of the fundamental rights of the human person....

35. The mere fact that the Declaration is not a treaty does not necessarily compel the conclusion that the Court lacks the power to render an advisory opinion containing an interpretation of the American Declaration.

36. In fact, the American Convention refers to the Declaration in paragraph three of its Preamble which reads as follows:

> *Considering* that these principles have been set forth in the Charter of the Organization of the American States, in the American Declaration of the Rights and Duties of Man, and in the Universal Declaration of Human Rights, and that they have been reaffirmed and refined in other international instruments, worldwide as well as regional in scope.

And in Article 29(d) which indicates:

. . .

> No provision of this convention shall be interpreted as:
>
> . . .
>
> d. excluding or limiting the effect that the American Declaration of the Rights and Duties of Man and other international acts of the same nature may have.

From the foregoing, it follows that, in interpreting the Convention in the exercise of its advisory jurisdiction, the Court may have to interpret the Declaration.

37. . . . [T]o determine the legal status of the American Declaration it is appropriate to look to the inter-American system of today in the light of the evolution it has undergone since the adoption of the Declaration, rather than to examine the normative value and significance which that instrument was believed to have had in 1948.

38. The evolution of the here relevant "inter-American law" mirrors on the regional level the developments in contemporary international law and specially in human rights law, which distinguished that law from classical international law to a significant extent. That is the case, for example, with the duty to respect certain essential human rights, which is today considered to be an *erga omnes* obligation. . . .

39. The Charter of the Organization refers to the fundamental rights of man in [various provisions] . . . but it does not list or define them. The member states of the Organization have, through its diverse organs, given specificity to the human rights mentioned in the Charter and to which the Declaration refers.

40. This is the case of Article 112 of the Charter . . . :

> There shall be an Inter-American Commission on Human Rights, whose principal function shall be to promote the observance and protection of human rights and to serve as a consultative organ of the Organization in these matters.
>
> An inter-American convention on human rights shall determine the structure, competence, and procedure of this Commission, as well as those of other organs responsible for these matters.

Article 150 of the Charter provides as follows:

> Until the inter-American convention on human rights, referred to in Chapter XVIII (Chapter XVI of the Charter as amended by the Protocol of Cartagena de Indias), enters into force, the present Inter-American Commission on Human Rights shall keep vigilance over the observance of human rights.

41. These norms authorize the Inter-American Commission to protect human rights. These rights are none other than those enunciated and defined in the American Declaration. That conclusion results from Article 1 of the Commission's Statute . . . [adopted in 1979]:

> 1. The Inter-American Commission on Human Rights is an organ of the Organization of the American States, created to promote the observance and

defense of human rights and to serve as consultative organ of the Organization in this matter.

2. For the purposes of the present Statute, human rights are understood to be:
   a. The rights set forth in the American Convention on Human Rights, in relation to the States Parties thereto;
   b. The rights set forth in the American Declaration of the Rights and Duties of Man, in relation to the other member states.

Articles 18, 19 and 20 of the Statute enumerate these functions.

42. The General Assembly of the Organization has also repeatedly recognized that the American Declaration is a source of international obligations for the member states of the OAS. . . .

43. Hence it may be said that by means of an authoritative interpretation, the member states of the Organization have signaled their agreement that the Declaration contains and defines the fundamental human rights referred to in the Charter. Thus the Charter of the Organization cannot be interpreted and applied as far as human rights are concerned without relating its norms, consistent with the practice of the organs of the OAS, to the corresponding provisions of the Declaration.

44. In view of the fact that the Charter of the Organization and the American Convention are treaties with respect to which the Court has advisory jurisdiction by virtue of Article 64(1), it follows that the Court is authorized, within the framework and limits of its competence, to interpret the American Declaration and to render an advisory opinion relating to it whenever it is necessary to do so in interpreting those instruments.

QUESTIONS

1. Is the Commission's rationale for continuing to examine the human rights situation in Cuba convincing?

2. On the basis of the Court's Advisory Opinion, what is the legal status of the American Declaration, and how would you compare it in that respect with the Universal Declaration, discussed at pp. 151, *supra*?

3. THE COMMISSION AT WORK: COMPLAINTS AND STATE REPORTS

The Inter-American Commission has evolved significantly in terms of its techniques. In the materials that follow a former Commission President, Tom Farer, provides some essential historical context. Thereafter there is a note on the individual and interstate complaints mechanism and on the system of reporting on state compliance with human rights obligations.

TOM FARER, THE RISE OF THE INTER-AMERICAN HUMAN RIGHTS REGIME: NO LONGER A UNICORN, NOT YET AN OX

in David Harris and S. Livingstone (eds.), The Inter-American System of Human Rights (1998), at 32

[The author was a member of the Inter-American Commission on Human Rights from 1976–1983 and served as its President from 1980–1982.]

Introduction: the birth of a big surprise

...

Some six years after creating the Commission and providing it with a vaguely-worded mandate to assist in the defense of human rights, the OAS had given the Commission explicit authority to investigate individual instances of alleged human rights violations. . . . Armed with its new mandate, the Commission could have concentrated on individual cases, futilely but respectably pursuing an endless paper trail of victims' complaints and official denials. . . . Instead, focusing upon the investigation of the facts and the preparation of country reports on the actual conditions that it found, the Commission converted itself into an accusatory agency, a kind of Hemispheric Grand Jury, storming around Latin America to vacuum up evidence of high crimes and misdemeanors and marshaling it into bills of indictment in the form of country reports for delivery to the political organs of the OAS and the court of public opinion.

Western Europe's human rights institutions, the Commission and the Court, also charged governments with violations of human rights. But the violations almost invariably involved actions undertaken openly on the thinly marked border between the legitimate exercise of public authority on behalf of the community and the irreducible claims of individual liberty. The various European governments employing challenged acts no doubt regarded them as useful but hardly as means essential to the preservation of order or the execution of any other important public function. Moreover, both competitive elections and, in most if not all the countries then subject to the regime, constitutional restraints enforced by independent courts broadly limited their ends and means to those generally consistent in fact with internationally recognized human rights. Thus the European human rights regime largely reinforced national restraints on the exercise of executive and legislative power rather than adding on strong additional ones.

Latin American constitutions also contained long lists of protected rights and corresponding checks on government action. But few, if any, countries had effectively independent judiciaries available and committed to enforcing them. Furthermore, on close inspection constitutional restraints were often riddled with specific exceptions and were for the most part subject to derogation in times of emergency. And the region's constitutional courts had shown little zeal for auditing executive branch claims that the required emergency existed and that the particular suspension of guarantees was reasonably necessary to protect public order. Their determined passivity may not have been entirely unconnected to the fact that judges, certainly judges of the courts with powers of constitutional review, came from the same middle and upper classes suffused with anxiety about Leftist threats to the established order of things. Serving in the midst of what luminaries of that order (in the United States no less than in Latin America) declared to be a global Cold War and in ideologically polarized societies, judges would be naturally inclined to concede to governments a very large margin of appreciation about the requirements of domestic security. In actual fact, however, governments rarely tested the full measure of that inclination, since they committed the most flagrant human rights delinquencies secretly or at least behind the often thin veil of official denial.

So although the norms invoked by the inter-American human rights institutions often mirrored those of national constitutions, the conjunction of multiple exceptions with an auto-restrained judiciary and a secretive state made constitutional norms ineffective. In actual fact, therefore, the Commission, unlike its European counterpart, was attempting to impose on governments restraints without domestic parallel. It was trying to do this, moreover, in the face of the conviction held by many regimes and their class supporters that grave violations of human rights were a regrettable but absolutely necessary means, if not for survival altogether, then at least for the restoration of their domestic tranquillity.

...

Whither the Commission in a democratic era?

At the end of the 1980s even Central America began to step back from remorseless civil war. Throughout Latin America, then, the grosser human rights violations subsided from the old torrent to a trickle, and elected — if not always liberal — democratic regimes began to seem normal. The end of the Hemispheric state of emergency and the proliferation of credible investigating agencies, some with greater competence and drive than the Commission, provided two reasons for it to consider shifting a *modest* proportion of its human and financial resources to individual cases, which continued to arrive. For as an official institution, it had a role denied to the NGOs, namely building a body of doctrine interpreting the American Declaration and Convention.

As long as governments were simply torturing and maiming, interpretation was hardly necessary. But with governments striving with varying degrees of effort to establish the rule of law, the Commission naturally began to receive more cases from the gray borderland where the state's authority to promote the general interest collides with individual rights. From such governments, moreover, one might expect at least a measure of cooperation with the Commission, substituting for brazen denial open legal defense of their position on questions of fact and law.

Unlike the Buenos Aires Protocol with its broad grant of authority to the Commission, the Convention deals in some detail with individual petition cases and, being modeled on the European Convention, arguably envisions a modestly formal presentation of evidence by petitioner and the accused state....

... But with an exiguous staff, numerous cases and a continuing commitment to general reports, the Commission continued to handle cases casually. In doing so, it came under increasing criticism not only from some governments, but from human rights lawyers as well. Like any good lawyers, they wanted to feel that technical competence in the accumulation and presentation of evidence mattered. And they wanted deadlines, so that decisions came predictably and with reasonable dispatch. In addition, they wanted formal precedents that could then be deployed in arguments with governments. And finally, they wanted more than a Commission conclusion in favor of their clients. They wanted injunctions and reparations which they could secure only from the Inter-American Court. And they could not get to that Court until the Commission had finished processing the case and, even then, only if the Commission or the target state decided to invoke the Court's jurisdiction. . . .

The Commission's seeming indifference to the Court, even reluctance to send it business, had two sources . . . [U]ntil the mid-1980s the main inhibitor was continuing emphasis on reports; and thereafter it was in part limited time and resources. Preparation for and the conduct of formal hearings for many cases made huge demands on a staff very poorly equipped to respond, not to mention the demands on Commissioners who functioned as it were in their spare time. Nevertheless, pressured by commentators, lawyers and governments, the Commission has gradually begun to move toward a more case-oriented existence and correspondingly to generate much more business for the Court.

Yet there remains a great need for country reports. Despite the spread of elected governments and great improvement in the condition of human rights, indisputable and grave violations continued to occur in many countries, albeit with less international hue and cry, since once again almost all of the victims are drawn from the only episodically visible and relatively mute lower classes. And given an enduring culture of impunity for public security agencies, weak judicial systems, a tradition of broad executive discretion in the exercise of power and a continuing tendency of elites to dismiss non-governmental human rights activists as 'Leftists,' grave violations of basic rights are likely to continue as a feature of life in many countries. Reports, in part because they bring together many cases of abuse and reveal a pattern of delinquency by public officials, attract far more attention than conclusions in individual cases. In addition, they provide members of the target country and the international community with a far more accurate appreciation of the extent and endemic character of human rights violations. *Therefore they must continue to be the central preoccupation of the Commission and its most important contribution to the mitigation of officially inflicted pain and humiliation in the Western Hemisphere.*

Reports must continue. However, the altered and enhanced but not transformed conditions of life in the Western Hemisphere call for additional dimensions to the Commission's reporting efforts. Beyond its traditional single-country focus, peculiarly appropriate where gross violations are epidemic or a country has undergone what appear to be dramatic changes, the Commission should attempt occasional thematic reports. For instance, it might look cross-nationally at the access of the poor to the civil courts or at the output of justice systems in a number of countries. Equally challenging and important would be reports on economic and social rights. The Commission has construed the single reference to them in the Declaration and

Convention as creating two obligations for states. One is to develop a serious plan for mitigating extreme poverty. The other is to begin implementing such a plan giving priority to health and nutrition. Compliance with those minimal obligations is measurable.

Human rights lawyers were not the Commission's only critics. As a kind of peace settled over Latin American societies, democratic governments began lashing out at the one organ of the OAS which had battled with their authoritarian predecessors, battled to create the space in which democracy could grow. This was ironic but not really anomalous. For where in a democratic era is one likely to find greater self righteousness than in the offices of elected leaders? To be elected is to enjoy the Peoples' mandate which, in an age also secular, is as close to heaven's mandate as one can get.

When you accuse an authoritarian government of human rights violations, you arguably accuse only the people who run it. Accuse a democratic one, and you slander the Nation; for what is a nation but the people who comprise it and democratic leaders are their chosen voice. That at least is how some of the newly elected regimes appeared to feel when confronted with adverse Commission rulings.

Two kinds of issues have excited the greatest irritation. One concerns the legality of various sorts of legal immunity coerced from their elected successors by military establishments as they withdrew. In the case of Uruguay, where an electorate threatened with the restoration of military rule had endorsed immunity, the Commission inevitably found that popular majorities could not for any reason deny remedies to the victims of human rights delinquencies, any more than popular majorities could legitimate the denial of due process to or the torture of some despised individual or group. The other issue concerned elections, more particularly the Commission's claim of right to hear and resolve claims that elections had not been conducted fairly. Despite the proliferation of official monitoring missions all over the globe, regimes formed by the winners in contested cases claimed that Commission review constituted an unauthorized interference in their internal affairs, claimed that despite the clear language of the Convention giving to every person a right to 'vote and to be elected in genuine periodic elections, which shall be by universal and equal suffrage and by secret ballot that guarantees the free expression of the will of the voters...'.

...

The Individual Complaints System

For an instructive example of the Inter-American Commission's complaints procedure at work you should review the materials in Chapter 5, *supra* (see pp. 404–16) relating to the treatment of detainees in Guantanamo.

The number of complaints being received each year by the Commission has grown steadily in recent ten years. In 1997 there were 435, in 2001, 885, and by 2006, 1,325. Over the same period the number of friendly settlements reached under the auspices of the Commission has also grown and in 2006 it hailed the progress made in this regard. It cited, in particular, the signing of an agreement by Argentina to eliminate the special military jurisdiction and thus bring fair trial protections for the military into line with those for civilians.

In its 2006 report the Commission attempted to provide a picture of compliance, or otherwise, with its recommendations. Of 86 reports adopted by the Commission, its own analysis indicated that total compliance had been achieved in only one case, partial compliance in 59 cases, and compliance was still awaited in 26 cases.

It is clear from this mixed track record that the Commission cannot rely exclusively on its complaints mechanism. This is especially true in light of its very limited staffing. Indeed, both the Commission and the Court are significantly under-resourced. In 2007 the Commission had 28 professional officers and 14 administrators, in addition to the Executive Secretary and his assistant. The problems of the Court are even more significant, especially since 2001 when the Commission began to refer almost all cases on to the Court. Neither the members of the Commission nor the Court are paid a salary. In recent years only around 3.5% of the total OAS budget has gone to the Commission, and about two-thirds of that amount goes to staff salaries and benefits.

Two different techniques to promote domestic compliance without the time-consuming processes involved in complaints are to enhance domestic implementation and to devise other means by which the Commission is able to encourage compliance through its own work. Domestic implementation of the Convention remains highly unsatisfactory in the Americas. For the most part, states have failed to take effective measures to promote domestic implementation of the standards contained in the American Convention, even when these nominally enjoy superior status within the domestic legal order. The result is that while many states indicate that international standards are applicable within their domestic legal systems, those standards are rarely invoked and even more rarely given effect by the courts.

The other technique the Commission has used in order to enhance the effectiveness of its own work in key areas involves the appointment of special rapporteurs. In 2006 it amended its Rules of Procedure to provide that Special Rapporteurs, who are not Commission members, will be appointed following a competitive public process. Vacancy announcements will be made, member states and civil society will be able to comment on candidates, the finalists will be interviewed by the Commission, and a vote will then take place. As of 2007 there are Special Rapporteurs for the rights of the child, women, indigenous peoples, detainees, those of African descent, migrant workers and freedom of expression. There is also a secretariat unit concerned with the rights of human rights defenders. Most of those mechanisms are supported by voluntary financial contributions, especially from the European Union and the Inter-American Development Bank.

Interstate Complaints

The American Convention establishes an interstate complaints procedure (Art. 45–51). As in the United Nations setting, such procedures have proved unpopular with governments. In March 2007, however, the Inter-American Commission presented its first report on such a complaint.[39] It concerned allegations of systematic

[39] Report No. 11/07, Interstate Case 01/06, *Nicaragua v. Costa Rica*, 8 March 2007.

discrimination against Nicaraguan citizens resident in Costa Rica. The procedures under the Convention provide that a State Party may recognize the Commission's competence to receive such complaints either when it ratifies or at any later date (Art. 45). Domestic remedies must have been exhausted, unless they are unavailable, inaccessible or unduly delayed, and the petition must be lodged within six months of a final judgment (Art. 46). If the complaint is deemed admissible the Commission may request the states concerned to furnish any pertinent information, and is to seek to reach a friendly settlement (Art. 48). If a settlement is not reached, the Commission shall report and may 'make such proposals and recommendations as it sees fit' (Art. 50).

In the case brought by Nicaragua, the Commission concluded that the complaint was not admissible by virtue of the complainant's failure to submit the complaint within six months of its having been notified of a final decision being handed down in Costa Rica. Nonetheless, the Commission took the opportunity, in a 69-page judgment, to explore the applicable procedures, develop its jurisprudence on admissibility in such cases, exculpate Costa Rica in relation to some of the most serious charges, acknowledge Costa Rica's admission of the existence of discrimination and xenophobia in its territory, and conclude by condemning 'all acts of discrimination or xenophobia against migrant persons of any origin' and recall the 'obligation of states to protect individuals against discrimination, whether this occurs within the public sphere or among private parties'.

Country Visits

As noted in some of the readings above, the Commission's early success with *in loco* visits to countries experiencing significant human rights problems contributed greatly to enhancing its stature. Its reports on Argentina at the height of the problem of disappearances, in 1978, remains a classic in terms of effective fact-finding and follow-up. Such visits continue to be important but today there are relatively few visits undertaken by the Commission as a whole. Instead a single Commissioner undertakes a 'working visit' and issues a detailed press release at the end of the visit which outlines the major problems he or she has identified. Similarly, there are now fewer reports focusing on every aspect of a country's human rights situation, and a greater likelihood of focusing on a specific set of issues or sectors of the population.

In addition, the Commission includes a Chapter on 'Human Rights Developments in the Region' in each of its Annual Reports. The stated aim is to provide the OAS with updated information on the human rights situation in countries that have 'been the subject of the Commission's special attention' or where an emerging problem is seen. Inclusion in the Chapter is an unwelcome 'honour' for any state. Since 1997, the Commission has sought to apply five criteria in selecting countries for this purpose: (i) states ruled by governments that have not come to power through secret, genuine, periodic and free elections; (ii) states in which human rights 'have been, in effect, suspended totally or in part, by virtue of the imposition of exceptional measures'; (iii) states which commit 'massive and grave violations'; (iv) 'states that are in a process of transition from any of the above three situations'; and (v) where 'temporary or structural situations', such as major institutional crises, 'seriously affect the enjoyment of fundamental rights'. Based on these criteria the Commission's 2006 report (issued in March 2007) focused on four states: Colombia, Cuba, Haiti and Venezuela. An excerpt from the section on Cuba is at p. 1029, *supra*. The section on Venezuela, which follows, provides an example of the approach used in a situation in which the Commission has been unable to gain access to the country concerned.

ANNUAL REPORT OF THE INTER-AMERICAN COMMISSION ON HUMAN RIGHTS 2006

OEA/Ser.L/V/II.127, Doc. 4 rev. 1, 3 March 2007, Chap. IV

Venezuela

[The Government provided comments on a draft of the following report]

140. The Commission has monitored the human rights situation in Venezuela closely. The Commission here addresses issues that, in its opinion, hinder the completion of the mandate assigned by the States to the IACHR, as well as such matters as the administration of justice, the problem of sicariato [paid killings] in Venezuela, the impunity that surrounds reports of extrajudicial executions at the hands of agents of the State, the substandard prison conditions, and the climate of political pressure to reportedly imposed on various sectors of civil society, in particular those that do not express open alignment with the discourse and objectives of the present government.

II. Preliminary considerations

141. In its observations to this Chapter, the State questions the sources of information on the grounds that they are partial or incomplete in verifying some of the subjects analyzed by the Commission.

142. [T]he information utilized in the preparation of the present Chapter consists of diverse sources of information such as press releases, information sent to the Commission by diverse Venezuelan civil society organizations and international organizations, as well as information presented by the State during hearings or in responses to requests of information, or from case decisions and urgent measures already published by the bodies of the System....

...

III. The impossibility of arranging a visit to Venezuela

...

145. Since its last on-site visit to Venezuela in May 2002, the Commission has fruitlessly sought the consent of the State, both verbally and in writing, to visit the country again....

. . .

147. It has been 20 years since the IACHR began its practice of on-site visits to the different countries of the hemisphere to verify the situation of human rights in them. The possibility of firsthand knowledge on the ground of different issues and programs connected with human rights in the countries has helped to strengthen a close dialogue with government authorities and society as a whole. . . .

. . .

152. Based on the foregoing, the IACHR considers that the impossibility for the IACHR to visit a member state due to lack of consent or political will on the part of the government runs contrary to the very spirit that led the States to create the agencies of the system for protection of human rights and, therefore, obstructs fulfillment of the specific mandates adopted by the States in Charter of the Organization, the American Convention on Human Rights, the Statutes of the IACHR, and, more recently, the Inter-American Democratic Charter.

. . .

IV. Administration of justice and impunity for violations of the rights to life and humane treatment

. . .

167. . . . The Commission reiterates that it finds [the situation regarding public prosecutors] particularly troubling since, in addition to possible irregularities in terms of independence and impartiality as well as the lack of transparency that may underlie the constant dismissals and new appointments, the provisional status and correlative lack of job stability of the officials responsible for conducting criminal investigations and moving them forward inevitably also impairs the pursuit and conclusion of specific lines of investigation as well as compliance with deadlines in the investigation stage. . . . Accordingly, this situation may have negative consequences for victims' rights in the context of criminal proceedings related to human rights violations.

. . .

169. According to official data provided by the Office of the Attorney General between 2000 and 2005, the number of victims of homicides committed by agents of the state security forces came to 6,377, in which a total of 6,110 police officials were involved. . . . [T]he Commission finds that serious levels of impunity similar to those of the last five years would appear to persist since it transpires from the report presented by the Prosecutor General to the National Assembly in April 2006 that in the more than 5,684 cases investigated by the Office of the Attorney General in which government servants are thought to be involved, only 1,560 officials have been accused, 760 formally charged, 315 deprived of their liberty, and 113 policemen convicted.

170. . . . According to publicly available information, in 2006, of the 891 cases of persons thought to been killed in presumed confrontations with the police of [the state of Bolivar], only four have gone to trial. . . .

. . .

QUESTIONS

1. How would you explain the fact that the Inter-American Commission receives less than 1,500 cases per year, in contrast to the tens of thousands received by the ECtHR?

2. How satisfactory is a procedure of reporting on a state's human rights performance in the absence of a visit to the country?

4. THE COURT IN ACTION

In the Inter-American system, the Court plays a more restricted and modest role than does its equivalent in the European system. Its governing provisions bear a close relationship to those for the European Court of Human Rights. Hence the following materials illustrate its work through a single decision, to be understood within the framework for the Court's work that was described in the preceding articles by Medina, Harris and Farer.

In the mid 1980s, a cooperative relationship began to evolve between the Commission and Court, commencing with the referral by the Commission of three contentious cases to the Court, each involving instances of disappearances in Honduras. The principal case, *Velásquez Rodríguez*, appears below. It was the first contentious case initiated by an individual that involved systemic state violence, and was one of three cases leading to decisions by the Court on the question of disappearances in Honduras. Outside as well as inside the Inter-American system, it has also proved to be one of the most influential and cited decisions of an international human rights tribunal.

The three cases placed in a judicial setting the same issues that occupied the UN Commission on Human Rights and its Working Group on Disappearances, p. 766, *supra*, and the Inter-American Commission in its function of investigating and reporting on systemic violations. Indeed, one of the striking aspects of the *Velásquez Rodríguez* decision is how effectively it links the individual and systemic aspects of a violation.

After this decision, the Commission started to generate a small but steady flow of cases for the Court.

VELÁSQUEZ RODRÍGUEZ CASE

Inter-American Court of Human Rights, 1988
Ser. C No. 4

[This case arose out of a period of political turbulence, violence and repression in Honduras. It originated in a petition against Honduras received by the Inter-American Commission on Human Rights in 1981. The thrust of the petition was that Angel Manfredo Velásquez Rodríguez was arrested without warrant in 1981 by members of the National Office of Investigations (DNI) and the G-2 of the Armed Forces. The 'arrest' was a seizure by seven armed men dressed in civilian clothes who abducted him in an unlicensed car. The petition referred to eyewitnesses reporting his later detention, 'harsh interrogation and cruel torture'. Police and security forces continued to deny the arrest and detention. Velásquez had disappeared. The petition alleged that through this conduct, Honduras violated several articles of the American Convention on Human Rights.

In 1986, Velásquez was still missing, and the Commission concluded that the Government of Honduras 'had not offered convincing proof that would allow the Commission to determine that the allegations are not true'. Honduras had recognized the contentious jurisdiction of the Inter-American Court of Human Rights, to which the Commission referred the matter. The Court held closed and open hearings, called witnesses and requested the production of evidence and documents. The statement of facts below is taken from the Court's opinion and consists both of its independent findings and its affirmation of some findings of the Commission.

The Commission presented witnesses to testify whether 'between the years 1981 and 1984 (the period in which Manfredo Velásquez disappeared) there were numerous cases of persons who were kidnapped and who then disappeared, these actions being imputable to the Armed Forces of Honduras and enjoying the acquiescence of the Government of Honduras', and whether in those years there were effective domestic remedies to protect such kidnapped persons. Several witnesses testified that they were kidnapped, imprisoned in clandestine jails and tortured by members of the Armed Forces. Explicit testimony described the severity of the torture — including beatings, electric shocks, hanging, burning, drugs and sexual abuse — to which witnesses had been subjected. Several witnesses indicated how they knew that their captors and torturers were connected with the military. The Court received testimony indicating that 'somewhere between 112 and 130 individuals were disappeared from 1981 to 1984'.

According to testimony, the kidnapping followed a pattern, such as use of cars with tinted glass, with false licence plates and with disguised kidnappers. A witness who was President of the Committee for the Defense of Human Rights in Honduras testified about the existence of a unit in the Armed Forces that carried out the disappearance, giving details about its organization and commanding personnel. A former member of the Armed Forces testified that he had belonged to the battalion carrying out the kidnapping. He confirmed parts of the testimony of witnesses, claiming that he had been told of the kidnapping and later torture and killing of Velásquez, whose body was dismembered and buried in different places. All such testimony was denied by military officers and the Director of Honduran Intelligence.

The Commission also presented evidence showing that from 1981–1984 domestic judicial remedies in Honduras were inadequate to protect human rights. Courts were slow and judges were often ignored by police. Authorities denied detentions. Judges charged with executing the writs of habeas corpus were threatened and on several occasions imprisoned. Law professors and lawyers defending political prisoners were pressured not to act; one of the two lawyers to bring a writ of habeas corpus was arrested. In no case was the writ effective in relation to a disappeared person.

In view of threats against witnesses it had called, the Commission asked the Court to take provisional measures contemplated by the Convention. Soon thereafter, the Commission reported the death of a Honduran summoned by the Court to appear as a witness, killed 'on a public thoroughfare [in the capital city] by a group of armed men who . . . fled in a vehicle'. Four days later the Court was informed of two more assassinations, one victim being a man who had testified before the Court as a witness hostile to the Government. After a public hearing, the Court decided on 'additional provisional measures' requiring Honduras to report within two weeks (1) on measures that it adopted to protect persons connected with the case, (2) on its judicial investigations of threats against such persons, and (3) on its investigations of the assassinations.

The Court's opinion refers to several articles of the American Convention. *Article 4* gives every person 'the right to have his life respected. . . . No one shall be arbitrarily deprived of his life'. *Article 5* provides that no one 'shall be subjected to torture or to cruel, inhuman, or degrading punishment or treatment'. *Article 7* gives every person 'the right to personal liberty and security', prohibits 'arbitrary arrest or imprisonment', and provides for such procedural rights as notification of charges, recourse of the detained person to a competent court, and trial within a reasonable time or release pending trial. There follow excerpts from the opinion. (Other excerpts at p. 214, *supra*, discuss the liability of Honduras for the disappearance, whether the actual abductors were state or nonstate actors.)

[VII]

. . .

123. Because the Commission is accusing the Government of the disappearance of Manfredo *Velásquez*, it, in principle, should bear the burden of proving the facts underlying its petition.

124. The Commission's argument relies upon the proposition that the policy of disappearances, supported or tolerated by the Government, is designed to conceal and destroy evidence of disappearances. When the existence of such a policy or practice has been shown, the disappearance of a particular individual may be proved through circumstantial or indirect evidence or by logical inference. Otherwise, it would be impossible to prove that an individual has been disappeared.

. . .

126. . . . If it can be shown that there was an official practice of disappearances in Honduras, carried out by the Government or at least tolerated by it, and if the disappearance of Manfredo *Velásquez* can be linked to that practice, the Commission's allegations will have been proven to the Court's satisfaction, so long as the evidence presented on both points meets the standard of proof required in cases such as this.

127. The Court must determine what the standards of proof should be in the instant case. Neither the Convention, the Statute of the Court nor its Rules of Procedure speak to this matter. Nevertheless, international jurisprudence has recognized the power of the courts to weigh the evidence freely, although it has always avoided a rigid rule regarding the amount of proof necessary to support the judgment.

. . .

130. The practice of international and domestic courts shows that direct evidence, whether testimonial or documentary, is not the only type of evidence that may be legitimately considered in reaching a decision. Circumstantial evidence, indicia, and presumptions may be considered, so long as they lead to conclusions consistent with the facts.

131. Circumstantial or presumptive evidence is especially important in allegations of disappearances, because this type of repression is characterized by an attempt to suppress any information about the kidnapping or the whereabouts and fate of the victim.

...

134. The international protection of human rights should not be confused with criminal justice. States do not appear before the Court as defendants in a criminal action. The objective of international human rights law is not to punish those individuals who are guilty of violations, but rather to protect the victims and to provide for the reparation of damages resulting from the acts of the States responsible.

135. In contrast to domestic criminal law, in proceedings to determine human rights violations the State cannot rely on the defense that the complainant has failed to present evidence when it cannot be obtained without the State's cooperation.

136. The State controls the means to verify acts occurring within its territory. Although the Commission has investigatory powers, it cannot exercise them within a State's jurisdiction unless it has the cooperation of that State.

...

138. The manner in which the Government conducted its defense would have sufficed to prove many of the Commission's allegations by virtue of the principle that the silence of the accused or elusive or ambiguous answers on its part may be interpreted as an acknowledgment of the truth of the allegations, so long as the contrary is not indicated by the record or is not compelled as a matter of law. This result would not hold under criminal law, which does not apply in the instant case...

...

[IX]

147. The Court now turns to the relevant facts that it finds to have been proven. They are as follows:

a. During the period 1981 to 1984, 100 to 150 persons disappeared in the Republic of Honduras, and many were never heard from again....
b. Those disappearances followed a similar pattern....
c. It was public and notorious knowledge in Honduras that the kidnappings were carried out by military personnel, police or persons acting under their orders....
d. The disappearances were carried out in a systematic manner, regarding which the Court considers the following circumstances particularly relevant:
i. The victims were usually persons whom Honduran officials considered dangerous to State security.... [Omitted paragraphs deal with arms used, details of the kidnappings and interrogations, denials by officials of any

knowledge about the disappeared person, and the failure of any investigative committees to produce results.]

e. On September 12, 1981, between 4:30 and 5:00 p.m., several heavily armed men in civilian clothes driving a white Ford without license plates kidnapped Manfredo *Velásquez* from a parking lot in downtown Tegucigalpa. Today, nearly seven years later, he remains disappeared, which creates a reasonable presumption that he is dead....

f. Persons connected with the Armed Forces or under its direction carried out that kidnapping....

g. The kidnapping and disappearance of Manfredo *Velásquez* falls within the systematic practice of disappearances referred to by the facts deemed proved in paragraphs a–d.

...

[X]

149. Disappearances are not new in the history of human rights violations. However, their systematic and repeated nature and their use, not only for causing certain individuals to disappear, either briefly or permanently, but also as a means of creating a general state of anguish, insecurity and fear, is a recent phenomenon. Although this practice exists virtually worldwide, it has occurred with exceptional intensity in Latin America in the last few years.

150. The phenomenon of disappearances is a complex form of human rights violation that must be understood and confronted in an integral fashion.

151. The establishment of a Working Group on Enforced or Involuntary Disappearances of the United Nations Commission on Human Rights by Resolution 20(XXXVI) of February 29, 1980, is a clear demonstration of general censure and repudiation of the practice of disappearances.... The reports of the rapporteurs or special envoys of the Commission on Human Rights show concern that the practice of disappearances be stopped, the victims reappear and that those responsible be punished.

152. Within the inter-American system, the General Assembly of the Organization of American States (OAS) and the Commission have repeatedly referred to the practice of disappearances and have urged that disappearances be investigated and that the practice be stopped....

153. International practice and doctrine have often categorized disappearances as a crime against humanity, although there is no treaty in force which is applicable to the States Parties to the Convention and which uses this terminology....

...

155. The forced disappearance of human beings is a multiple and continuous violation of many rights under the Convention that the States Parties are obligated to respect and guarantee. The kidnapping of a person is an arbitrary deprivation of liberty, an infringement of a detainee's right to be taken without delay before a judge and to invoke the appropriate procedures to review the legality of the arrest, all in violation of Article 7 of the Convention....

156. Moreover, prolonged isolation and deprivation of communication are in themselves cruel and inhuman treatment, harmful to the psychological and moral integrity of the person and a violation of the right of any detainee to respect for his inherent dignity as a human being. Such treatment, therefore, violates Article 5 of the Convention....

157. The practice of disappearances often involves secret execution without trial, followed by concealment of the body to eliminate any material evidence of the crime and to ensure the impunity of those responsible. This is a flagrant violation of the right to life, recognized in Article 4 of the Convention....

158. The practice of disappearances, in addition to directly violating many provisions of the Convention, such as those noted above, constitutes a radical breach of that treaty in that it implies a crass abandonment of the values which emanate from the concept of human dignity and of the most basic principles of the inter-American system and the Convention....

...

[The part of the Court's opinion examining the obligation of a state not only to respect individual rights (such as by not 'disappearing' the government's opponents), but also to ensure free exercise of rights (such as by protecting those expressing political opinions against violence by private, nongovernmental actors), appears at p. 215, *supra.*]

[XII]

189. Article 63(1) of the Convention provides:

> If the Court finds that there has been a violation of a right or freedom protected by this Convention, the Court shall rule that the injured party be ensured the enjoyment of his right or freedom that was violated. It shall also rule, if appropriate, that the consequences of the measure or situation that constituted the breach of such rights or freedom be remedied and that fair compensation be paid to the injured party.

Clearly, in the instant case the Court cannot order that the victim be guaranteed the enjoyment of the right or liberty violated. The Court, however, can rule that the consequences of the breach of the rights be remedied and rule that just compensation be paid.

190. During this proceeding, the Commission requested the payment of compensation, but did not offer evidence regarding the amount of damages or the manner of payment. Nor did the parties discuss these matters.

191. The Court believes that the parties can agree on the damages. If an agreement cannot be reached, the Court shall award an amount. The case shall, therefore, remain open for that purpose. The Court reserves the right to approve the agreement and, in the event no agreement is reached, to set the amount and order the manner of payment.

[In the concluding paragraphs, the Court unanimously declared that Honduras violated Articles 4, 5 and 7 of the Convention, all three read in conjunction with Article

1(1); and unanimously decided that Honduras was required to pay fair compensation to the victim's next-of-kin.]

QUESTIONS

1. The facts are contested. What method does the Court employ to resolve them? Does it employ such traditional notions of the law of evidence in systems of national law as burdens of proof (burdens of persuasion) or presumptions? For example:

   a. What is the relevance to the Court's finding of Honduran responsibility of the Court's use of terms like (the Honduran) 'practice' or 'policy', or the characterization of disappearances as 'systemic'?

   b. What is the significance of the Court's observation that the state 'controls the means to verify acts occurring within its territory'? Is the Court threatening the state with an adverse finding if it fails to make that effort?

2. 'It is wrong to argue that contentious cases before the Court can effectively address only individual situations and violations, while the Commission must expose structural and systemic violations of human rights through its state reports. The *Velásquez Rodríguez* case shows that the two tasks can be accomplished effectively at the same time. The Court is an adequate alternative to the Commission'. Comment.

NOTE

Among the significant contributions made by the Inter-American Court to human rights jurisprudence in general have been its defence of the rights of indigenous peoples and its emphasis upon the provision of extensive and carefully tailored reparations by states found to have violated their human rights obligations. Cassel has suggested that there are six factors which have contributed to the expansive approach taken by the Court in relation to reparations: (i) it has been pushed to do so by the Commission and by victims; (ii) substantial compliance by states with its reparations orders has encouraged a continued emphasis in this regard; (iii) the increasing acceptance of the Court within Latin America; (iv) its experience with political violence and impunity has encouraged more sweeping remedies; (v) doctrinal evolution on the issue; and (vi) the influence of the approach of some 'particularly creative jurists on the Court'.[40]

[40] Douglas Cassel, 'The Expanding Scope and Impact of Reparations Awarded by the Inter-American Court of Human Rights', in K. de Feyter *et al.* (eds.), *Out of the Ashes: Reparation for Victims of Gross and Systematic Human Rights Violations* (2005) 191, at 211.

SAWHOYAMAXA INDIGENOUS COMMUNITY V. PARAGUAY

Inter-American Court of Human Rights
Judgment of March 29, 2006

...

73. Having assessed [all the evidence] ..., the Court finds the following facts to be proven:

a) The Sawhoyamaxa Indigenous Community and the traditional occupation of the lands claimed

73(1) Towards the end of the 19th century vast stretches of land in the Paraguayan Chaco were acquired by British businessmen through the London Stock Exchange as a consequence of the debt owed by Paraguay after the so-called War of the Triple Alliance. The division and sale of such territories were made while their inhabitants, who, at the time, were exclusively Indians, were kept in full ignorance of the facts.

...

73(2) The economy of the indigenous peoples in the Chaco was mainly based on hunting, fishing, and gathering, and therefore, they had to roam their lands to make use of nature....

73(3) Over the years, and particularly after the Chaco War between Bolivia and Paraguay (1933–1936), the non-indigenous occupation of the Northern Chaco which had started by the end of the 19th century was extended. The estates that started settling in the area used the Indians who had traditionally lived there as workers, who thus became farmhands and employees of new owners. Although the indigenous peoples continued occupying their traditional lands, the effect of the market economy activities into which they were incorporated turned out to be the restriction of their mobility, whereby they ended by becoming sedentary.

73(4) Since then, the lands of the Paraguayan Chaco have been transferred to private owners and gradually divided. This increased the restrictions for the indigenous population to access their traditional lands, thus bringing about significant changes in its subsistence activities....

73(5) The Sawhoyamaxa ("from the place where coconuts have run out") Community is an indigenous community, typical of those traditionally living in the Paraguayan Chaco that has become sedentary....

...

73(7) At present most members of the Sawhoyamaxa Indigenous Community live in the settlements known as "Santa Elisa" and "KM 16." "Santa Elisa" [both lying alongside roads....]

73(8) [In 2006], the Community has 407 members, grouped in approximately eighty-three dwelling places.

73(9) The lands claimed ... are within the lands which they have traditionally occupied and which are part of their traditional habitat.

73(10) The lands claimed are suitable for the Indigenous Community members to continue with their current subsistence activities and to ensure their short and mid-term survival, as well as the beginning of a long-term process of development of alternative activities which will allow their subsistence to become sustainable

[The court considered several issues including whether the plea of non-exhaustion of domestic remedies could be invoked at this late stage, whether the existing indigenous land claim administrative procedure was effective and whether the time taken to consider claims had been reasonable. It reached negative conclusions on each issue.]

[Right to property — Article 21]

. . .

116. Article 21 of the American Convention declares that:

1. Everyone has the right to the use and enjoyment of his property. The law may subordinate such use and enjoyment to the interest of society.
2. No one shall be deprived of his property except upon payment of just compensation, for reasons of public utility or social interest, and in the cases and according to the forms established by law.
3. Usury and any other form of exploitation of man by man shall be prohibited by law.

117. In analyzing [Article 21] in relation to the communal property of the members of indigenous communities, the Court has taken into account Convention No. 169 of the ILO in the light of the general interpretation rules established under Article 29 of the Convention, in order to construe . . . Article 21 in accordance with the evolution of the Inter-American system. . . . The State ratified Convention No. 169 and incorporated its provisions to domestic legistlation by Law No. 234/93.

118. . . . [T]he close ties the members of indigenous communities have with their traditional lands and the natural resources associated with their culture . . ., must be secured under Article 21 of the American Convention. The culture of the members of indigenous communities reflects a particular way of life, of being, seeing and acting in the world, the starting point of which is their close relation with their traditional lands and natural resources, not only because they are their main means of survival, but also because they form part of their worldview, of their religiousness, and consequently, of their cultural identity.

119. [Article 13 of Convention No. 169 requires States to] respect "the special importance for the cultures and spiritual values of the peoples concerned of their relationship with the lands or territories, or both as applicable, which they occupy or otherwise use, and in particular the collective aspects of this relationship."

120. Likewise, this Court considers that indigenous communities might have a collective understanding of the concepts of property and possession, in the sense that ownership of the land "is not centered on an individual but rather on the group and its community." This notion of ownership and possession of land does not necessarily conform to the classic concept of property, but deserves equal protection under Article 21. . . . Disregard for specific versions of use and enjoyment of property, springing from the culture, uses, customs, and beliefs of each people, would be

tantamount to holding that there is only one way of using and disposing of property, which, in turn, would render protection under Article 21 . . . illusory for millions of persons.

121. Consequently, the close ties of indigenous peoples with their traditional lands and the native natural resources thereof, associated with their culture, as well as any incorporeal element deriving therefrom, must be secured under Article 21. . . . [In the Court's jurisprudence] "property" as used in Article 21, includes "material things which can be possessed, as well as any right which may be part of a person's patrimony; that concept includes all movable and immovable, corporeal and incorporeal elements and any other intangible object capable of having value".

122. The Paraguayan Constitution recognizes the existence of indigenous peoples as groups which have preceded the formation of the State, as well as their cultural identity, the relation with their respective habitat and their communal characteristics of their land-tenure system, and further grants them a series of specific rights which serve as basis for the Court to define the scope of Article 21 of the Convention.

123. On the other hand, Article 3 of Law No. 43/89 points out that settlements of indigenous communities are "constituted by a physical area made up of a core of houses, natural resources, crops, plantations, and their environs, linked insofar as possible to their cultural tradition [. . .]"

. . .

125. The State has pointed out that it "does not deny its obligation to restore rights to these peoples," but the members of the Sawhoyamaxa Community "claim title to a piece of real estate based exclusively on an anthropologic report that, worthy as it is, collides with a property title which has been registered and has been conveyed from one owner to another for a long time." Likewise, the State fears that, would [the] claim by the Community be granted, "it would be convicted for the 'sins' committed during the [C]onquest" (inner quotation marks as used in the original text), and that this could lead to the "absurd situation in which the whole country could be claimed by indigenous peoples, for they are the primitive inhabitants of the stretch of territory that is nowadays called Paraguay."

126. Consequently, in order to address the issues in the instant case, the Court will proceed to examine, in the first place, whether possession of the lands by the indigenous people is a requisite for official recognition of property title thereto. In the event that possession not be a requisite for restitution rights, the Court will analyze, in the second place, whether enforcement of said rights is time-restricted. Finally, the Court will address the actions that the State must take to enforce indigenous communal property rights.

i) The possession of the lands

127. Acting within the scope of its adjudicatory jurisdiction, the Court has had the opportunity to decide on indigenous land possession in three different situations. On the one hand, in the *Case of the Mayagna (Sumo) Awas Tingni Community*, the Court pointed out [in 2001] that possession of the land should suffice for indigenous communities lacking real title to property of the land to obtain official recognition of that

property, and for consequent registration. On the other hand, in the *Case of the Moiwana Community*, the Court considered [in 2005] that the members of the N'djuka people were the "legitimate owners of their traditional lands" although they did not have possession thereof, because they left them as a result of the acts of violence perpetrated against them. In this case, the traditional lands have not been occupied by third parties. Finally, in the *Case of the Indigenous Community Yakye Axa*, the court [in 2005] considered that the members of the Community were empowered, even under domestic law, to file claims for traditional lands and ordered the State, as measure of reparation, to individualize those lands and transfer them on a for no consideration basis.

128. The following conclusions are drawn from the foregoing: 1) traditional possession of their lands by indigenous people has equivalent effects to those of a state-granted full property title; 2) traditional possession entitles indigenous people to demand official recognition and registration of property title; 3) the members of indigenous peoples who have unwillingly left their traditional lands, or lost possession therof, maintain property rights thereto, even though they lack legal title, unless the lands have been lawfully transferred to third parties in good faith; and 4) the members of indigenous peoples who have unwillingly lost possession of their lands, when those lands have been lawfully transferred to innocent third parties, are entitled to restitution thereof or to obtain other lands of equal extension and quality. Consequently, possession is not a requisite conditioning the existence of indigenous land restitution rights. The instant case is categorized under this last conclusion.

129. Paraguay acknowledges the right of indigenous peoples to claim restitution of their lost traditional lands....

...

iii) Actions to enforce the rights of the community members over their traditional lands

135. Once it has been proved that land restitution rights are still current, the State must take the necessary actions to return them to the members of the indigenous people claiming them. However, as the Court has pointed out, when a State is unable, on objective and reasoned grounds, to adopt measures aimed at returning traditional lands and communal resources to indigenous populations, it must surrender alternative lands of equal extension and quality, which will be chosen by agreement with the members of the indigenous peoples, according to their own consultation and decision procedures.

136. Nevertheless, the Court can not ... decide that Sawhoyamaxa Community's property rights to traditional lands prevail over the right to property of private owners or *vice versa*, since the Court is not a domestic judicial authority with jurisdiction to decide disputes among private parties. This power is vested exclusively in the Paraguayan State. Nevertheless, the Court has competence to analyze whether the State ensured the human rights of the members of the Sawhoyamaxa Community.

137. [The Court rejects three] arguments put forth by the State to justify non-enforcement of the indigenous people's property rights have not sufficed to release it from international responsibility....

138. [First] ... the fact that the claimed lands are privately held by third parties is not in itself an "objective and reasoned" ground for dismissing *prima facie* the

claims by the indigenous people. Otherwise, restitution rights become meaningless and would not entail an actual possibility of recovering traditional lands, as it would be exclusively limited to an expectation on the will of the current holders, forcing indigenous communities to accept alternative lands or economic compensations. In this respect, the Court has pointed out that, when there be conflicting interests in indigenous claims, it must assess in each case the legality, necessity, proportionality and fulfillment of a lawful purpose in a democratic society (public purposes and public benefit), to impose restrictions on the right to property, on the one hand, or the right to traditional lands, on the other. . . .

139. [The same rationale applies to the second argument which suggests] that indigenous communities are not entitled, under any circumstances, to claim traditional lands the when they are exploited and fully productive, viewing the indigenous issue exclusively from the standpoint of land productivity and agrarian law, something which is insufficient for it fails to address the distinctive characteristics of such peoples.

140. [The third argument is that the owner's right is protected under a bilateral agreement between Paraguay and Germany which, because of its treaty status, has become part of the law of the land.] . . . [T]he Court has not been furnished with the aforementioned treaty [but it is said to allow] . . . for capital investments made by a contracting party to be condemned or nationalized for a "public purpose or interest", which could justifiy land restitution to indigenous people. . . . [The] enforcement [of such bilateral treaties] should always be compatible with the American Convention, which is a multilateral treaty on human rights that stands in a class of its own and that generates rights for individual human beings and does not depend entirely on reciprocity among States.

141. Based on the foregoing, the Court dismisses the three arguments of the State described above and finds them insufficient to justify non-enforcement of the right to property of the Sawhoyamaxa Community.

142. Finally, it is worth recalling that, under Article 1(1) of the Convention, the State is under the obligation to respect the rights recognized therein and to organize public authority in such a way as to ensure to all persons under its jurisdiction the free and full exercise of human rights.

143. Even though the right to communal property of the lands and of the natural resources of indigenous people is recognized in Paraguayan laws, such merely abstract or legal recognition becomes meaningless in practice if the lands have not been physically delimited and surrendered because the adequate domestic measures necessary to secure effective use and enjoyment of said right by the members of the Sawhoyamaxa Community are lacking. The free development and transmission of their culture and traditional rites have thus been threatened.

144. For the aforementioned reasons, the Court concludes that the State violated Article 21 of the American Convention, to the detriment of the members of the Sawhoyamaxa Community, in relation to Articles 1(1) and 2 therein.

[Right to life — Article 4]

. . .

155. It is clear for the Court that a State cannot be responsible for all situations in which the right to life is at risk. Taking into account the difficulties involved in the

planning and adoption of public policies and the operative choices that have to be made in view of the priorities and the resources available, the positive obligations of the State must be interpreted so that an impossible or disproportionate burden is not imposed upon the authorities. In order for this positive obligation to arise, it must be determined that at the moment of the occurrence of the events, the authorities knew or should have known about the existence of a situation posing an immediate and certain risk to the life of an individual or of a group of individuals, and that the necessary measures were not adopted within the scope of their authority which could be reasonably expected to prevent or avoid such risk.

...

163. The Court acknowledges the criterion of the State in the sense that it has not induced or encouraged the members of the Community to move and settle by the side of the road. However, the Court considers that there were powerful reasons for the members of the Community to abandon the estates where they lived and worked, due to the extremely hard physical and labor conditions they had to endure. Likewise, this argument is not enough for the State to disregard its duty to protect and guarantee the right to life of the alleged victims. It is necessary that the State proves that it carried out all necessary actions [to] take the indigenous peoples from the roadside, and in the meantime, to adopt all necessary measures to reduce the risk that they were facing.

164. In that respect, the Court notes that the principal means available for the State to get the members of the Community out of the side of the road was to give them their traditional lands....

...

166. Consequently, this Court considers that the State has not adopted the necessary measures for the members of the Community to leave the roadside, and thus, abandon the inadequate conditions that endangered, and continue endangering, their right to life.

...

170. . . . Presidential Order N° 3789 [of 1999 declared] the Sawhoyamaxa Community in a state of emergency. However, the measures adopted by the State in compliance with such order cannot be considered sufficient and adequate. Indeed, for six years after the effective date of the order, the State only delivered food to the alleged victims on ten opportunities, and medicine and educational material on two opportunities, with long intervals between each delivery.... [A]fter the emergency Presidential Order became effective, at least 19 persons died.

171. ... [M]ost of the Community members that died were boys and girls under 3 years of age, and the causes of their deaths range from *enterocolitis*, dehydration, cachexia, tetanus, measles, and respiratory illnesses, such as pneumonia and bronchitis; all of them are reasonably foreseeable diseases that can be prevented and treated at a low cost.

...

173. The Court does not accept the State argument regarding the joint responsibility of the ill persons to go to the medical centers to receive treatment, and of the Community leaders to take them to such centers or to communicate the situation to the health authorities. From the issuance of the emergency Order, [the Government authorities] had the duty to take "the actions that might be necessary to immediately

provide food and medical care to the families that form part of [the Sawhoyamaxa Community] . . .). Therefore, the provision of goods and health services did no longer specifically depend on the individual financial capacity of the alleged victims, and therefore, the State should have taken action contributing to the provision of such goods and services. . . .

. . .

178. Considering the aforesaid, the Court finds that the State violated Article 4(1) . . . since it has not adopted the necessary positive measures within its powers, which could reasonably be expected to prevent or avoid risking the right to life of the members of the Sawhoyamaxa Community. . . .

[Right to juridical personality—Article 3]

. . .

187. In the instant case, neither the Commission nor the representatives have alleged the violation of Article 3 of the American Convention. However, from the facts of the case, it . . . appears that there has been no registration or official documentation of the existence of several members of the indigenous Sawhoyamaxa Community. The Court considers that the parties have had the opportunity of addressing such situation[sic], thus, it is pertinent to examine the obligations stemming from Article 3 of the American Convention which provides as follows:

> "Every person has the right to recognition as a person before the law."

. . .

192. The above mentioned members of the Community have remained in a legal limbo in which, though they have been born and have died in Paraguay, their existence and identity were never legally recognized, that is to say, they did not have personality before the law. Indeed, the State, in the instant proceeding before the Court, has intended to use this situation for its own benefit. In fact, at the time of referring to the right to life, the State alleged:

> If neither the existence of these persons nor even their death has even been proved, it is not possible to claim liability from anyone, lest [sic] the State, where are their birth and death certificates?

. . .

194. On the basis of the above considerations, and notwithstanding the fact that other members of the Community may be in the same situation, the Court finds that the State violated the right to personality before the law enshrined in Article 3. . . .

[Reparations]

. . . Article 63(1) of the American Convention states the following:

> If the Court finds that there has been a violation of a right or freedom protected by this Convention, the Court shall rule that the injured party be ensured the enjoyment of his right or freedom that was violated. It shall also rule, if appropriate, that the

> consequences of the measure or situation that constituted the breach of such right or freedom be remedied and that fair compensation be paid to the injured party.

...

198. The reparations, as the term itself indicates, consist of measures tending to eliminate the effects of the breaches perpetrated. Their nature and amount depend on both the pecuniary and non-pecuniary damages caused. The reparations cannot imply enrichment or detriment for the victims or their successors.

...

210. ... [T]he Court orders that the State shall adopt all legislative, administrative or other type of measures necessary to guarantee the members of the Community ownership rights over their traditional lands, and consequently the right to use and enjoy those lands.

211. ... [R]estitution of such lands to the Community is barred, since these lands are currently privately owned.

212. ... [T]he State must consider the possibility of purchasing these lands or the lawfulness, need and proportionality of condemning these lands in order to achieve a lawful purpose in a democratic society.... If restitution of ancestral lands ... is not possible on objective and sufficient grounds, the State shall make over alternative lands, selected upon agreement with the aforementioned Indigenous Community, in accordance with the community's own decision-making and consultation procedures, values, practices and customs. In either case, the extension and quality of the lands must be sufficient to guarantee the preservation and development of the Community's own way of life.

...

215. The State shall, within three years ... formally and physically grant tenure [of] the lands to the victims, irrespective of whether they be acquired by purchase or by condemnation, or whether alternative lands are selected. The State shall guarantee all the necessary funds for the purpose.

...

219. Non-pecuniary damage may include distress and suffering caused directly to the victims or their relatives, tampering with individual core values, and changes of a non pecuniary nature in the living conditions of the victims or their families.... [S]aid damage may only be compensated in one of two ways. Firstly, ... by paying an amount of money or delivering property or services. ... And secondly, ... through public actions or works, such as the publication of an official message repudiating the human rights violations at stake and committing to prevent further similar violations ...

...

221. This Court finds that the non enforcement of the right to hold title ... and the detrimental living conditions imposed upon them ... must be taken into account....

222. Similarly, the Court finds that the special meaning that these lands have for indigenous peoples, in general, and for the members of the Sawhoyamaxa Community, in particular, implies that the denial of those rights over land involves a detriment to values that are highly significant to the members of those communities, who are at risk of losing or suffering irreparable damage to their lives and identities, and to the cultural heritage of future generations.

224. . . . The State shall allocate the amount of US$ 1,000,000.00 (one million United States Dollars) to [a community development] fund, which will be used to implement educational, housing, agricultural and health projects, as well as to provide drinking water and to build sanitation infrastructure, for the benefit of the members of the Community. These projects must be established by an implementation committee, as described below, and must be completed within two years as from delivery of the lands to the members of the Indigenous Community.

. . .

226. . . . [T]he Court . . . orders the State to pay compensation in the amount of US$ 20,000.00 . . . to each of the 17 members of the Community who died as a result of the events in the instant case. That amount must be distributed among the next of kin of the victims pursuant to the cultural practices of the Sawhoyamaxa Community. . . .

. . .

230. . . . [T]he Court orders that, while the members of the Community remain landless, the State shall immediately, regularly and permanently adopt measures to: a) supply sufficient drinking water . . . ; b) provide medical check-ups, tests and care . . . ; c) deliver sufficient quantity and quality of food; d) set up latrines . . . , and e) provide the school of the "Santa Elisa" settlement with all necessary material and human resources . . .

. . .

235. . . . [T]he State shall, within a reasonable time, enact into its domestic legislation, as per Article 2 of the American Convention, the legislative, administrative and other measures necessary to provide an efficient mechanism to claim the ancestral lands of indigenous peoples enforcing their property rights and taking into consideration their customary law, values, practices and customs.

. . .

236. As ordered in prior cases, the Court finds that, as a measure of satisfaction, the State shall publish . . . in the Official Gazette and in another national daily newspaper, [parts of the judgment, and shall finance the radio broadcasting of key paragraphs] in the language indicated by the members of the Community, in a radio station accessible to them. Said radio broadcasting shall be made at least four times in two-week intervals. . . .

. . .

248 [14] The Court shall monitor full compliance with this Judgment and shall consider the instant case closed upon full compliance by the State with the provisions therein. Within a year . . . the State shall submit to the Court a report on the measures adopted to comply herewith . . . .

THE MIGUEL CASTRO CASTRO PRISON V. PERU

Inter-American Court of Human Rights
Judgment of November 25, 2006

. . .

197(1) During the period that goes from the beginning of the eighties until the end of the year 2000, Peru lived a conflict between armed groups and agents of the police force and the military. This conflict got worse in the midst of a systematic practice of violations to human rights, among them extrajudicial killings and forced disappearances of people suspected of belonging to armed groups that existed on the fringe of the law, such as Sendero Luminoso (hereinafter SL) and the Revolutionary Movement Tupac Amarú (hereinafter MRTA), all practices carried out by state agents following orders given by military and police leaders.

. . .

197(8) In the final report issued [in 2003] by the CVR [the Commission for Truth and Reconciliation] it established that "during the years of political violence, [the prisons] were not only areas for the imprisonment of those accused or convicted for crimes of terrorism, but scenarios in which the Communist Party of Peru [PCP-Sendero Luminoso] and, in less measure, the Revolutionary Movement Túpac Amaru, extended the armed conflict."

197(9) [From April 1992,] in order to fight subversive and terrorist groups, the State implemented in the prisons practices not compatible with the effective protection of the right to life and other rights, such as extrajudicial killings and cruel and inhuman treatments, as well as the disproportionate use of force in critical circumstances.

. . .

197(11) The national press [warned] that Sendero Luminoso was exercising territorial control within the Miguel Castro Castro Prison, that from within said center it was planning several attacks and that they had turned their pavilions "into teaching centers."

Miguel Castro Castro Prison

. . .

197(13) In the time in which the events occurred, pavilion 1A of the Miguel Castro Castro Prison was occupied by around 135 female inmates and 50 male, and pavilion 4B was occupied by approximately 400 male inmates. The inmates of pavilions 1A and 4B were accused or convicted for the crimes of terrorism or treason, and they were allegedly members of the Sendero Luminoso. Many of them had been accused and were awaiting conviction, and in some cases they were acquitted.

. . .

197(15) Law Decree No. 25421 of April 6, 1992 ordered the reorganization of the National Penitentiary Institute (INPE) and put the National Police of Peru in charge of the control of security at the penitentiaries. It was within the framework of this stipulation that "Operative Transfer 1" was planned and executed. The official version was that said "operative" consisted in the transfer of the women that were imprisoned in pavilion 1A of the Miguel Castro Castro Prison, to the maximum security prison for women in Chorrillos. The state authorities did not inform the Director of the criminal center, the prisoners, their next of kin or attorneys of the mentioned transfer.

197(16) The real objective of the "operative" was . . . a premeditated attack . . . designed to attack the life and integrity of the prisoners located in pavilions 1A and 4B of the Miguel Castro Castro Prison. . . .

...

197(20) At [4am on May 6 the security forces] knocked down part of the external wall of the yard of pavilion 1A using explosives....

197(21) The state, police, and military agents used war weapons, explosives, tear gas, vomiting, and paralyzing bombs against the inmates, from the start of the operation. The bullets and grenades used would fragment upon impact with the walls, injuring many inmates with splinters. Snipers were located on the roofs and windows of the other pavilions. ...

197(22) [O]n May 6th the National Police introduced grenades, white phosphorous gas bombs, and tear gas bombs in pavilion 1A, which produced asphyxia, and a burning feeling in the respiratory system, eyes, and skin of the inmates....

...

197(30) [On May 7 the President and the authorities took action] ... [T]he presence of human rights organizations in the surrounding areas of the criminal center was forbidden, the supply of electricity, water, and food to inmates was cut off, and the attacks with fire weapons and explosives was increased.

197(31) In the afternoon, police officers and members of the Armed Forces intensified the attacks against pavilion 4B, using grenades, machine guns, and tear gas bombs.

197(32) On May 8, 1992, the third day of the "operative", the police and military officials continued the attack with rockets fired from helicopters, mortar fire, and grenades.

...

197(37) [On May 9] the inmates announced to the state agents that they were coming out and they asked them to stop shooting. Groups of unarmed inmates, made up mainly by people labeled as members of the head of Sendero Luminoso, exited the pavilion, when they were reached by bursts of bullets fired by state agents. The majority of those inmates died. Later, a large number of inmates exited pavilion 4B, at a fast pace. The security agents of the State shot at them indiscriminately and in different parts of their bodies, even when they were injured on the floor....

197(38) When the inmates were under the control of state agents, some were separated from the group and killed by state agents. One of the bodies presented mutilations and signs of torture.

197(39) The majority of the inmates that were killed presented between 3 and 12 bullet wounds to the head and thorax.

197(40) During the events of May 6 to 9, 1992 a police officer died, as a consequence of having received bullet wounds in the head and thorax; and approximately 9 police officers were injured.

[In total, it was estimated by the Inter-American Commission that at least 42 inmates died, 175 were injured, and 322 were subjected to cruel, inhuman and degrading treatment. The Court determined that there was no justification for the legitimate use of force by the authorities under the circumstances. Based in part on acknowledgements of responsibility by the state the Court concluded that the state was responsible for violations of Articles 4, 5, 8(1) and 25 of the American Convention, and of violations of the provisions of the Inter-American Convention to Prevent, Punish, and Eradicate Violence Against Women, and of the Inter-American Convention to Prevent and Punish Torture.]

413. . . . The Court has established, on several occasions, that all violation of an international obligation that has produced damage involves the duty to adequately repair it. To these effects, Article 63(1) of the American Convention states that:

> [i]f the Court finds that there has been a violation of a right or freedom protected by [this] Convention, the Court shall rule that the injured party be ensured the enjoyment of his right or freedom that was violated. It shall also rule, if appropriate, that the consequences of the measure or situation that constituted the breach of such right or freedom be remedied and that fair compensation be paid to the injured party.

414. As previously stated by the Court, Article 63(1) of the American Convention constitutes a rule of customary law that enshrines one of the fundamental principles in contemporary international law on state responsibility. Thus, when an illicit act is imputed to the State, its international responsibility arises for the violation of the corresponding international norm, together with the subsequent duty of reparation and to put an end to the consequences of said violation. Said international responsibility is different to the responsibility in domestic legislation.

415. The reparation of the damage caused by a violation of an international obligation requires, whenever possible, full restitution. . . . When this is not possible, the international court will determine a series of measures to guarantee the rights violated, repair the consequences caused by the infractions, and establish payment of an indemnity as compensation for the harm caused or other means of satisfaction. The obligation to repair, regulated in all its aspects (scope, nature, modalities, and determination of the beneficiaries) by International Law, may not be modified or ignored by the State obliged, by invoking stipulations of its domestic law.

416. Reparations, as indicated by the term itself, consist in those measures necessary to make the effects of the committed violations disappear. Their nature and amount depend on the harm caused at both material and moral levels. Reparations cannot entail either enrichment or impoverishment of the victim or his successors.

[The Court then considered and awarded various forms of pecuniary and non-pecuniary damages.]

D) Other forms of reparation

(Measures of Satisfaction and Non-Repetition Guarantees)

. . .

435. In this section the Tribunal will determine those measures of satisfaction that seek to repair non-pecuniary damages, that do not have a pecuniary scope, and it will establish measures of a public scope or repercussion. In cases such as the present that are characterized by extreme seriousness these measures acquire a special relevance.

. . .

441. [T]he State must, within a reasonable period of time, effectively carry out the ongoing criminal proceedings and the ones that may be opened, and it must adopt all measures necessary to elucidate all the facts of the present case and not only those that resulted in the death of the victims, in order to determine the intellectual and material responsibility of those who participated in the violations. The results of these proceedings must be publicly diffused by the State, so that the Peruvian society may know the truth regarding the facts of the present case.

442. Likewise, as a guarantee of non-repetition, the Court rules that the State must, within a reasonable period of time, establish the necessary means in order to ensure that the information and documentation related to police investigations regarding facts as serious as those of the present case be conserved in a manner such that they do not obstruct the corresponding investigations.

. . .

445. [I]t is necessary, in order to repair the damage caused to the victims and their next of kin, and to avoid that facts like those of the present case repeat themselves, that the State carry out a public act of acknowledgment of its international responsibility in relation to the violations declared in this Judgments in amends to the victims and for the satisfaction of their next of kin. This act must be carried out in a public ceremony, with the presence of high State authorities and of the victims and their next of kin. The State must transmit said act through the media, including the transmission on radio and television. For this, the State has one year, as of the notification of the present Judgment.

. . .

451. The violations attributable to the State in the present case were perpetrated by police, and army personnel, as well as special security forces. . . .

452. Therefore, the State must design and implement, within a reasonable period of time, human rights education programs, addressed to agents of the Peruvian police force, on the international standards applicable to matters regarding treatment of inmates in situations of alterations of public order in penitentiary centers.

453. Regarding the measures requested by the Commission and the intervener, on the construction of monuments and the creation of a park in "the area of Canto Grande", the State argued that "a monument (called the Eye that Cries) has already been erected in a public place of the capital of the Republic in favor of all the victims of the conflict, and that it is the subject of continuous memorial and commemoration acts."

454. In this sense, the Court values the existence of the monument and public area called "The Eye that Cries", created upon the request of civil society and with the collaboration of state authorities, which constitutes an important public acknowledgment to the victims of violence in Peru. However, the Tribunal considers that, within a one-year period, the State must ensure that all the people declared as deceased victims in the present Judgment be represented in said monument. For this, it must coordinate with the next of kin of the deceased victims an act, in which they may include an inscription with the name of the victim as corresponds according to the monument's characteristics.

. . .

NOTE

Reporting on this judgment, the *New York Times* noted that the 'verdict set off a wave of anger in Peru over what many see as honoring terrorists and killers'. It added that the judgment had 'reopened scars of a rebellion that raged from 1980 to 1998' and reported that the Congressional leader of the governing party 'said after meeting with President Alan García . . . that the authorities were mulling Peru's withdrawal from the Inter-American Court of Human Rights . . . '.[41]

QUESTIONS

1. How compelling is the Court's justification for providing privileged treatment for the indigenous peoples in the Sawhoyamaxa Community?

2. 'The Court has gone too far in developing innovative remedies. It has turned itself into a dispenser of transitional justice and the righter of all wrongs. It would be better off confining itself to individual remedies and avoiding sweeping structural remedies.' Discuss.

ADDITIONAL READING

J. Pasqualucci, *The Practice and Procedure of the Inter-American Court of Human Rights* (2003); D. Rodríguez-Pinzón and C. Martin, *The Prohibition of Torture and Ill-Treatment in the Inter-American Human Rights System* (2006); J. Cavallaro and E. Schaffer, 'Less as More: Rethinking Supranational Litigation of Economic and Social Rights in the Americas', 56 Hastings L. J. 217; (2004) T. Melish, 'Rethinking the "Less as More" Thesis: Supranational Litigation of Economic Social, and Cultural Rights in the Americas', 39 N.Y.U. J. Int. L. & Pol. 171 (2007); B. Tittemore, 'Guantanamo Bay and the Precautionary Measures of the Inter-American Commission on Human Rights', 6 Hum. Rts. L. Rev. 378 (2006); J. Pasqualucci, 'The Evolution of International Indigenous Rights in the Inter-American Human Rights System', 6 Hum. Rts. L. Rev. 281 (2006); D. Harris and S. Livingstone (eds.), *The Inter-American System of Human Rights* 395 (1998); S. Davidson, *The Inter-American Human Rights System* (1996); *ibid.*, *The Inter-American Court of Human Rights* (1992); C. Cerna, 'The Structure and Functioning of the Inter-American Court of Human Rights (1979–1992)', 63 Brit. Y.B. Int. L. 135 (1992); T. Buergenthal, 'The Inter-American System for the Protection of Human Rights', in T. Meron (ed.), *Human Rights in International Law: Legal and Policy Issues* 439 (1984).

D. THE AFRICAN SYSTEM

The newest, the least developed or effective (in relation to the European and Inter-American regimes), the most distinctive and the most controversial of the three

[41] 'Ruling on Shining Path Rebels Angers Peru', *New York Times*, 11 January 2007, p. 1.

established regional human rights regimes involves African states. In 1981 the Assembly of Heads of States and Government of the Organization of African Unity adopted the African Charter on Human and Peoples' Rights. It entered into force in 1986. As of May 2007, 53 African states were parties.

In Chapter 6's discussion of rights and duties, at pp. 504–7, *supra*, the Charter itself served as an important illustration of a human rights regime that was more duty-oriented than the universal human rights system or the two other regional systems. This present section focuses primarily on the institutional aspects of the African system, and especially on the work of the African Commission on Human and Peoples' Rights. The examination is relatively brief, because although the overall system has become increasingly elaborate, the lack of resources and the limited political will of governments have served to limit its achievements. The Commission has been in existence for only two decades, its workload has expanded only gradually and it has been cautious in exercising its limited powers or creatively interpreting and developing them. The judges of the African Court of Human and Peoples' Rights were elected only in 2006, and the Court has yet to begin functioning. Moreover, the basic structure and tasks of the Commission and the Court do not introduce novel themes to Part D's examination of the architecture of intergovernmental human rights institutions.

It follows that the African system has not yet yielded anywhere near the same amount of information and 'output' of recommendations or decisions — state reports and reactions thereto, communications (complaints) from individuals about state conduct, studies of 'situations' or investigations of particular violations — as have the other systems. In comparison with those systems, the states parties and Commission have taken only a few forceful or persuasive actions within the structure of the Charter to attempt to curb serious human rights violations, although recent years have shown promise of a more insistent and active stance.

This examination of institutional aspects of the African system begins with a brief description of the African Union. You should be familiar with the provisions of the African Charter.

COMMENT ON THE AFRICAN UNION

In 1963 the Organization of African Unity was established as the official regional body of African states. It was inspired by the anti-colonial struggles of the late 1950s, and was primarily dedicated to the eradication of colonialism. The emergent African states created through it a political bloc to facilitate intra-African relations and to forge a regional approach to Africa's relationships with external powers. In 2001 the OAU was replaced by the African Union ('AU'). Today, 53 of 54 African states are members of the AU. The exception is Morocco which withdrew from the OAU in 1984 after the organization recognized Western Sahara.

For a variety of reasons, especially its experience of colonialism, the OAU Charter attached major importance to 'unity and solidarity' among African states, and defence of 'their sovereignty, their territorial integrity and independence'. Thus the inviolability of territorial borders, expressed through the principle of non-interference in the internal affairs of member states, was one of the OAU's central creeds. But concern at the Organization's failure to react to various gross violations of human rights committed by dictators like Idi Amin in Uganda, Jean-Bédel Bokassa in the then Central African Empire, and Francisco Macias Nguema in Equatorial Guinea, combined with a growing recognition of the importance of human rights led the OAU to adopt, in 1981, the African Charter on Human and Peoples' Rights.

This development, in addition to the rapid expansion in national constitutions within Africa which contained detailed provisions relating to human rights, facilitated the inclusion of a wide range of human rights objectives and principles in the AU Charter. By comparison, the OAU Charter had said very little. Thus among the objectives of the AU, listed in Article 3, are to '(e) encourage international cooperation, taking due account of the Charter of the United Nations and the Universal Declaration of Human Rights' and to '(h) promote and protect human and peoples' rights in accordance with the African Charter on Human and Peoples' Rights and other relevant human rights instruments'. Similarly, Article 4 lists the following principles in accordance with which the Union is to function:

> (g) non-interference by any Member State in the internal affairs of another;
> (h) the right of the Union to intervene in a Member State pursuant to a decision of the Assembly in respect of grave circumstances, namely: war crimes, genocide and crimes against humanity;
> ...
> (j) the right of Member States to request intervention from the Union in order to restore peace and security;
> ...
> (l) promotion of gender equality;
> (m) respect for democratic principles, human rights, the rule of law and good governance;
> (n) promotion of social justice to ensure balanced economic development;
> (o) respect for the sanctity of human life, condemnation and rejection of impunity and political assassination, acts of terrorism and subversive activities;
> (p) condemnation and rejection of unconstitutional changes of governments.

While the AU Charter does not contain any human rights requirements relating to admission to the Union, it does provide for the possible suspension of certain rights or the imposition of sanctions upon states that fail to comply with AU decisions and policies (Art. 23(2)). In addition, governments that 'come to power through unconstitutional means shall not be allowed to participate' in AU activities (Art. 30).

In addition to the African Charter, the OAU adopted two other important instruments addressing specifically the rights of women and of children. The African Charter on the Rights and Welfare of the Child was adopted in 1990 and entered into force in 1999. As of May 2007 it had 39 ratifications.

The Protocol to the African Charter on Human and Peoples' Rights on the Rights of Women in Africa was adopted in 2003 and entered into force in November 2005.

As of May 2007 it had 20 ratifications. Activists welcomed the Protocol as an antidote to what is seen as the African Charter's relative neglect of women's issues. The Protocol is far-reaching, especially in certain areas. It defines 'discrimination against women' to include 'any distinction, exclusion or restriction or any differential treatment based on sex and whose objectives or effects compromise or destroy the recognition, enjoyment or the exercise by women, regardless of their marital status, of human rights and fundamental freedoms in all spheres of life'. It has detailed provisions dealing, *inter alia*, with 'harmful practices' ('all behaviour, attitudes and/or practices which negatively affect the fundamental rights of women and girls, such as their right to life, health, dignity, education and physical integrity', Art. 5), violence against women (Art. 4), equality in and after marriage (Art. 6–7), the right to political participation (Art. 9), protection of women in armed conflicts (Art. 11), health and reproductive rights (Art. 14), and widow's rights (Art. 20). Its implementation is to be overseen in the same way as the African Charter.

The African Union has also been active in the provision of peacekeepers to support various regional initiatives. The most recent are the African Union Mission in the Sudan (AMIS) which was created in 2004. As of May 2007 it consisted of over 7,000 persons. In January 2007 the African Union Mission in Somalia (AMISOM) was established with a planned 8,000 peace-keepers. These forces perform some human rights-related functions and cooperate with UN missions etc. focusing on issues of human rights.

COMMENT ON INSTITUTIONAL IMPLEMENTATION: THE AFRICAN COMMISSION

The 11 members of the Commission, elected by secret ballot by the Assembly of Heads of State and Government from a list of persons nominated by parties to the Charter, are to serve (Art. 31) 'in their personal capacity'. Article 45 defines the mandate or functions of the Commission to be (1) to 'promote Human and Peoples' Rights', (2) to 'ensure the protection of human and peoples' rights' under conditions set by the Charter, (3) to 'interpret all the provisions of the Charter' when so requested by states or OAU institutions; and (4) to perform other tasks that may be committed to it by the Assembly. So the three dominant functions appear to be promotion, ensuring protection, and interpretation.

The Commission's task of 'promotion' includes (Article 45) undertaking 'studies and researches on African problems in the field of human and peoples' rights', as well as organizing seminars and conferences, disseminating information, encouraging 'local institutions concerned with human and peoples' rights', giving its views or making recommendations to governments, and formulating principles and rules 'aimed at solving legal problems related to human and peoples' rights . . . upon which African Governments may base their legislation'. Article 46 states tersely that the Commission 'may resort to any appropriate method of investigation'. In general, the 'Charter gives pre-eminence to the promotion of human rights and vests a wide range of responsibility on the Commission. In this regard, it has functions that are not directly vested in the ... American Commission'.[42] Several steps have been taken to implement the task of promotion — for example, resolutions by the Commission to the effect that states should include the teaching of human rights at all levels of the educational curricula, should integrate the Charter's provisions into national laws, and should establish committees on human rights.

Communications (complaints) and state reports are the most significant functions or processes involving the Commission that are identified in the Charter. Thus far, the procedures in the Charter involving communications by a state party concerning another state party have not been used. Individuals and national and international institutions can also send communications to the Commission, as provided in Articles 55–59. These provisions recall, but differ significantly from, the First Optional Protocol of the ICCPR examined at pp. 891–917, *supra.*

The Charter refers tersely to reports. Under Article 62, each party 'shall undertake to submit every two years ... a report on the legislative or other measures taken with a view to giving effect to the rights' under the Charter. Compare the more elaborate provisions in Article 40 of the ICCPR about the role of the ICCPR Committee in reviewing states' reports under that Covenant.

Although there is some irony in the observation that the Commission, addressing a continent rife with state-imposed abuses, should have promotion as its primary function, that concentration of energy makes some sense in view of Africa's large uneducated population that is ignorant of its rights or lacks organization and capacity for mobilization to vindicate them. Creating a 'rights awareness' could understandably be considered to be a primary function.

But in the long run, promotion alone will not be sufficient. This human rights regime governs states that have committed rampant violations, and that lack experience in and institutions for curbing the abuse of governmental power. Such a regime must depend on the effectiveness of intervention and protection of individuals, in order to effect long-term change. The African system — in part through the work of the Commission — must raise the costs to states of violations through one or another of the sanctions with which other human rights regimes are familiar.

CHRISTOF HEYNS AND MAGNUS KILLANDER, THE AFRICAN REGIONAL HUMAN RIGHTS SYSTEM

in F. Gomez Isa and K. de Feyter (eds.), International Protection of Human Rights: Achievements and Challenges 2006, at 524

5.2. The African Commission on Human and Peoples' Rights

... The Commission is not formally an organ of the AU, as it was created by a separate treaty.

[42] U.O. Umozurike, 'The African Commission on Human and Peoples' Rights', 1 Rev. Afr. Comm. Hum. & Peoples' Rts. 5 (1991), at 8.

5.2.1. The Commissioners

The African Commission consists of 11 commissioners, who serve in their individual capacities. The Commission meets twice a year in regular sessions for a period of up to two weeks. They are nominated by state parties to the Charter and elected by the Assembly. The Secretariat of the Commission is based in Banjul, The Gambia. The Commission alternates its meetings between Banjul and other African capitals. The Commission has a protective as well as a promotional mandate.

Although the Charter provides that the Commissioners should be independent there have been many instances where the independence of individual Commissioners has been questioned. The fact that many Commissioners have been serving civil servants or ambassadors has received criticism. . . . [But, starting in April 2005,] the AU Commission provided guidelines that excluded senior civil servants and diplomatic representatives. . . .

5.2.2. The Complaints Procedure

Both states and individuals may bring complaints to the African Commission alleging violations of the African Charter by state parties.

The procedure by which one state brings a complaint about an alleged human rights violation by another state is not often used. Currently one such case is pending before the Commission, between the Democratic Republic of Congo and three neighbouring countries.

The so-called individual communication or complaints procedure is not [c]learly provided for in the African Charter. One reading of the Charter is that communications could be considered only where "serious or massive violations" are at stake, which then triggers the rather futile Article 58 procedure, described below. However, the African Commission has accepted from the start that it has the power to deal with complaints about any human rights violations under the Charter even if "serious or massive" violations are not at stake, provided the admissibility criteria are met.

The Charter is silent on the question who can bring such complaints, but the Commission practice is that complaints from individuals as well as NGOs are accepted. From the case law of the Commission it is clear that the complainant does not need to be a victim or a family member of a victim. . . .

The individual complaints procedure is [not used] . . . as frequently as one would have expected on a continent with the kind of human rights problems that Africa has. This could to some extent be attributed to a lack of awareness about the system, but even where there is awareness, there is often not much faith that the system can make a difference. [The authors then cite the study excerpted below by Viljoen and Louw.]

As with other complaints systems, the African Charter poses certain admissibility criteria before the Commission may entertain complaints. The criteria include the requirement of exhausting local remedies. The Commission may be approached only once the matter has been pursued in the highest court in the country in question, without success, or a reasonable prospect of success.

The Commission has stated that for a case not to be admissible local remedies must be available, effective, sufficient and not unduly prolonged. In *Purohit and*

Moore v the Gambia, a case dealing with detention in a mental health institution, the Commission gave a potentially far-reaching decision on the exhaustion of local remedies when it held that:

> the category of people being represented in the present communication are likely to be people picked up from the streets or people from poor backgrounds and as such it cannot be said that the remedies available in terms of the Constitution are realistic remedies for them in the absence of legal aid services.

The Charter also has a requirement that the communications are "not written in disparaging or insulting language directed against the state concerned and in institutions or to the Organization of African Unity".

When a complaint is lodged, the state in question is asked to respond to the allegations against it. If the state does not respond, the Commission proceeds on the basis of the facts as provided by the complainant. If the decision of the Commission is that there has indeed been a violation or violations of the Charter, the Commission sometimes also makes recommendations that continuing violations should stop (e.g. prisoners be released); or specific laws be changed, but often the recommendations are rather vague, and the state party is merely urged to "take all necessary steps to comply with its obligations under the Charter." Sometimes there is no provision at all as to remedies, while in other cases the remedies provided are elaborate. Recently the Commission required some states to report on measures taken to comply with the recommendations in their state reports to the Commission.

Article 58 provides that "special cases which reveal the existence of serious or massive violations of human and peoples' rights" must be referred by the Commission to the Assembly, which "may then request the Commission to undertake an in-depth study of these cases". Where the Commission has followed this route, the Assembly has failed to respond, but the Commission has nevertheless made findings that such massive violations have occurred. Today, the Commission does not seem to refer cases anymore to the Assembly in terms of Article 58.

The Charter does not contain a provision in terms of which the Commission has the power to take provisional or interim measures requesting state parties to abstain from causing irreparable harm. However, the Rules of Procedure of the Commission grants the Commission the power to do so. The Commission has used these provisional or interim measures in a number of cases. . . .

5.2.3. Consideration of State Reports

Each state party is required to submit a report every two years on its efforts to comply with the African Charter. Although it is not provided for in the African Charter [these reports are now, with the approval of the Assembly, reviewed by the Commission.]. NGOs are allowed to submit shadow or alternative reports, but the impact of this avenue is diminished by the lack of access of NGOs to the state reports to which they are supposed to respond. The reports are considered by the Commission in public sessions. . . .

Reporting under the Charter, as in other systems, is aimed at facilitating both introspection and inspection. "Introspection" refers to the process when the state, in writing its report, measures itself against the norms of the Charter. "Inspection" refers to the process when the Commission measures the performance of the state in question against the Charter. The objective is to facilitate a "constructive dialogue" between the Commission and the states.

Reporting has been very tardy, and 18 of the 53 state parties to the African Charter have never submitted any report. In 2001 the Commission started to issue concluding observations in respect of reports considered. Their usefulness is diminished by the fact that neither the state reports nor the concluding observations are published by the Commission.

5.2.4. Special Rapporteurs and Working Groups

The Commission has appointed a number of special rapporteurs, with varying degrees of success. There is no obvious legal basis for the appointment of the special rapporteurs in the Charter. . . .

There has been widespread criticism of the lack of effective action on the part of the Special Rapporteur on Summary, Arbitrary and Extrajudicial Executions, while the same is true of at least the first incumbent of the position of Special Rapporteur on the Conditions of Women in Africa. In contrast, the Special Rapporteur on Prisons and Conditions of Detention in Africa has set the standards for years to come.

The Commission has recently appointed special rapporteurs on freedom of expression; refugees and internally displaced persons; and human rights defenders [as well as a committee to monitor guidelines on torture and Working Groups on Indigenous People or Communities and on Economic, Social and Cultural Rights]. Some of the members of these working groups are not members of the Commission.

5.2.5. On-Site Visits

The Commission has since 1995 conducted a number of on-site visits. These involve a range of activities, from fact finding to good offices and general promotional visits. Many mission reports have never been published.

5.2.6. Resolutions

The Commission has adopted resolutions on a number of human rights issues in Africa. . . .

5.2.7. Relationship with NGOs

NGOs have a special relationship with the Commission. Large numbers have registered for observer status. NGOs are often instrumental in bringing cases to the Commission; they sometimes submit shadow reports; propose agenda items at the outset of Commission sessions; and provide logistical and other support to the Commission, for example by placing interns at the Commission and providing support to the special rapporteurs and missions of the Commission. NGOs often organize special NGO workshops just prior to Commission sessions, and participate actively in the public sessions of the Commission. NGOs also collaborate with the Commission in developing normative resolutions and new protocols to the African Charter.

5.2.8. Interaction with AU Political Bodies

The Annual Activity Reports of the Commission ... are submitted each year for permission to publish to the meetings of the Assembly.... [The task has since been delegated to the Executive Council.] ...

In practice the Assembly has served as a rubber stamp for the publication of the report by the Commission containing its decisions, but the principle that the very people in charge of the institutions whose human rights practices are at stake — the Heads of State- should take the final decision on publicity undermines the legitimacy of the system....

5.2.9. Information on the Commission

... Information on the work of the Commission is available on a number of websites. It is unclear why the Commission makes little use of its own web site.... [Eds: As of May 2007 the most recently available report of the Commission is that of the Eighteenth Session, covering the period up to June 2005].

CHIDI ANSELM ODINKALU, THE INDIVIDUAL COMPLAINTS PROCEDURES OF THE AFRICAN COMMISSION ON HUMAN AND PEOPLES' RIGHTS: A PRELIMINARY ASSESSMENT

8 Transnat'l L. & Contemp. Probs 359 (1998), at 365

...

IV. Objective of the individual complaints procedure

The African Charter does not expressly define an objective for the individual complaints procedure. In the Free Legal Assistance Group Case [a 1996 decision involving Zaire], the Commission established that the objective of the communications procedure is 'to initiate a positive dialogue, resulting in an amicable resolution between the complainant and the state concerned, which remedies the prejudice complained of'. The attainment of this objective, the Commission continued, was dependent on 'the good faith of the parties concerned, including their willingness to participate in a dialogue'. The Commission thus recognizes that the bottom line of the communications procedure is the redress of violations complained of. To enable it to reach this objective, it is prepared to seek an amicable settlement between the parties, which must fulfill a two-pronged, subjective and objective criteria. Subjectively, the parties must be satisfied with the result, a difficult standard to meet given that the interests and aims of the victims and perpetrators of violations are often at odds. Objectively, both parties are called upon to act in good faith so as to bring about a resolution which 'remedies the prejudice complained of'.

. . .

In a series of communications, the Commission was presented with serious and massive allegations of violations of human rights against the state of Malawi. The Commission sent several requests and reminders to the state party which were neither answered nor acknowledged. The Commission designated a member of the Commission, the Late Chief Justice Moleleki Mokama of Botswana, to undertake a mission to Malawi and report back to it, but the Malawi authorities refused to admit him into their territory or to co-operate with him. [In December] 1993, the Commission took the then-unprecedented step of adopting and publishing a strongly worded resolution deploring the attitude of the Malawi government in apparently ignoring the Commission's inquiries and finding Malawi 'guilty of massive and serious violations of human rights'. Following this experience, the Commission decided in 1994 that 'where allegations of human rights abuse go uncontested by the government concerned, even after repeated notifications, the Commission must decide on the facts provided by the complainant and treat those facts as given'. . . .

. . .

IX. Problems encountered by the African Commission

Foremost among the problems that the Commission has encountered is the very text of the African Charter itself, which, like the Rules of Procedure, is opaque and difficult to interpret.

. . .

Another set of problems is found in what a former member of the Commission has bluntly described as 'a lack of money, lack of funds, lack of ability to act'. The resource and personnel problems of the Commission are endemic. . . .

X. Conclusion: What prospects for the Commission?

. . .

The [slow] development of the individual petition procedure [reflects] possibly, a low level of awareness about the mechanism or cynicism about the utility of adjudication mechanisms generally in addressing the kinds of violations of human rights that are witnessed in many parts of Africa. Jurisprudentially, the Commission has tilted the balance of its conciliation efforts in favour of the states parties by appearing too ready to affirm the existence of amicable settlements without clarifying their terms or setting accompanying compliance and verification guidelines. . . . Given the gravity of the complaints that it receives, the enthusiasm of the African Commission for amicable settlements that are not capable of either compliance or verification can only damage its credibility. To avoid this result, the Commission must evolve better principles and practice for negotiating settlements and inducing states parties to respect them.

On its interpretation of the Charter, the Commission has been mostly positive and sometimes even innovative. . . . In cases where it has proceeded to the merits, it has interpreted the rights in the Charter effectively, although its application of the principles thus established has not always been consistent. . . .

One question that I am often asked is whether the decisions of the Commission are effective.... [A]ny temptation to dismiss [the Commission] as a worthless institution today must be regarded as premature, ill-informed, or both. The individual petition procedure of the Commission offers a point of pressure which, if used creatively, can make a difference, as exemplified by a case involving capital punishment [in which the Commission's and NGOs' interventions ultimately led the Nigerian government to free prisoners whose convictions rested on procedures violating due process.] ...

...

[The statistics on the number of communications received and considered annually] indicate that the Commission is very much under-capacitated and under-utilized. The responsibility for changing this situation must be shared between the Commission and its interlocutors, including the states parties, victims and their representatives, and the NGO community. In the context of its individual petition procedures in particular, the most effective avenue for positively transforming the Commission's procedure is to confront it with actual cases and problems. With the imminent creation of an African Court of Human Rights, the likelihood is that the number of individual petitions brought to the attention of the Commission will continue to increase as will the burden on the institution. The proposed Court will not replace the Commission but will complement and reinforce its mandate....

...

NOTE

In a recent study designed to evaluate compliance with the Commission's decisions Viljoen and Louw[43] note that:

> [T]he attempt to chart compliance empirically and analytically is fraught with methodological difficulties. The most important of these is the Commission's failure to enunciate clear and specific remedies, leaving an unreliable yardstick for measuring compliance. Even when the yardstick is clearer, linking the steps toward compliance to the required remedial action often remains a matter of causal conjecture.
>
> Our analysis of cases of full and clear noncompliance suggests that the most important factors predictive of compliance are political, rather than legal. The only factor relating to the treaty body itself that shows a significant link to improved compliance is its follow-up activities. This finding lends support to arguments for a fully developed and effectively functional follow-up mechanism in the secretariat of the Commission, the consistent integration of follow-up activities into the Commission's mandate, and the appointment of a Special Rapporteur on follow-up....

[43] Frans Viljoen and Lirrette Louw, 'State Compliance with the Recommendations of the African Commission on Human and Peoples' Rights, 1994–2004', 101 Am. J. Int. L. 1 (2007), at 32.

> [T]he Commission in November 2006 [called upon states parties to the Charter] . . . to report on compliance within ninety days of being notified of decisions against them [and] decided to include a report on "the compliance with its recommendations" in future activity reports.
>
> . . . [O]ur study suggests that the mere fact that the [African] Court will provide legally binding and specific remedies and better formulated judgments will not in itself guarantee improved state compliance. The advent of the Court may coincide with a gradual hardening of human rights commitments and lead to improved human rights adherence, but it would then be on the strength of a stronger domestic and regional political commitment, increased publicity, and greater involvement of civil society.
>
> Inadequate political commitment at the regional level is an important factor underlying the lack of state compliance. . . .
>
> . . . [During the OAU period, the] absence of debate or the imposition of sanctions on states found in violation of the Charter translated into a lack of political pressure within the regional system to comply with the Commission's recommendations.
>
> . . .

The authors conclude that while the AU Charter has brought significant improvements in institutional arrangements, it still remains to be seen whether the AU will take effective action based on the opportunities available to it.

The materials that follow look first at an example of fact-finding undertaken by the Commission and then consider three recent examples of communications decided by the Commission.

REPORT OF THE FACT-FINDING MISSION TO ZIMBABWE, 24–28 JUNE 2002

Executive Summary, in Seventeenth Annual Activity Report of the African Commission on Human and Peoples' Rights 2003–2004, Annex II, at 13

Following widespread reports of human rights violations in Zimbabwe, the African Commission [decided in May 2001] . . . to undertake a fact-finding mission to the Republic of Zimbabwe from 24th to 28th June 2002.

. . .

FINDINGS

1. The Mission observed that Zimbabwean society is highly polarised. It is a divided society with deeply entrenched positions. The land question is not in itself the cause of division. It appears that at heart is a society in search of the means for change and divided about how best to achieve change after two decades of dominance by a political party that carried the hopes and aspirations of the people of Zimbabwe through the liberation struggle into independence.

2. There is no doubt that from the perspective of the fact-finding team, the land question is critical . . . [but recent legal and other developments mean] that land reform and land distribution can now take place in a lawful and orderly fashion.

3. There was enough evidence placed before the Mission to suggest that, at the very least during the period under review, human rights violations occurred in Zimbabwe. The Mission was presented with testimony from witnesses who were victims of political violence and others victims of torture while in police custody. There was evidence that the system of arbitrary arrests took place....

4. There were allegations that the human rights violations that occurred were in many instances at the hands of ZANU PF [the ruling Zimbabwe African National Union — Patriotic Front] party activists. The Mission is however not able to find definitively that this was part of an orchestrated policy of the government of the Republic of Zimbabwe....

5. The Mission is prepared and able to rule, that the Government cannot wash its hands from responsibility for all these happenings. It is evident that a highly charged atmosphere has been prevailing, many land activists undertook their illegal actions in the expectation that government was understanding and that police would not act against them — many of them, the War Veterans, purported to act as party veterans and activists. Some of the political leaders denounced the opposition activists and expressed understanding for some of the actions of ZANU (PF) loyalists. Government did not act soon enough and firmly enough against those guilty of gross criminal acts. By its statements and political rhetoric, and by its failure at critical moments to uphold the rule of law, the government failed to chart a path that signalled a commitment to the rule of law.

LAWYERS FOR HUMAN RIGHTS V. SWAZILAND

African Commission on Human and Peoples' Rights
Application 251/2002 (May 2005)

[A Swaziland NGO, Lawyers for Human Rights, lodged a complaint on 3 June 2002 alleging that King Sobhuza I vested all legislative, executive and judicial power in himself through a Proclamation of 12 April 1973. It also repealed the 1968 democratic Constitution of Swaziland which enshrined democratic principles such as the supremacy of the Constitution, separation of powers, amendment procedures, and a Bill of Rights.]

...

Law

...

Decision on the merits

...

40. The complainant prays the African Commission to:

- find the King's Proclamation of 12 April, 1973 to be in violation of the African Charter on Human and Peoples' Rights; and
- recommend and mandate strongly the Kingdom of Swaziland to take constitutional measures forthwith to give effect to all the provisions of the African Charter, specifically Articles 1, 7, 10, 11, 13 and 26 thereof.

Commission's decision on the merits

41. . . . The decision on the merits was taken without any response from the State. . . . Under such circumstances, the Commission is left with no other option than to take a decision based on the information at its disposal.

42. It must be stated however that, by relying on the information provided by the complainant, the Commission did not rush into making a decision. The Commission analyzed each allegation made and established the veracity thereof.

. . .

51. In the opinion of the Commission, by ratifying the Charter without at the same time taking appropriate measures to bring domestic laws in conformity with it, the Respondent State's action defeated the very object and spirit of the Charter and thus violating [sic] Article 1 thereof.

52. The complainant also alleges violation of Article 7 of the Charter stating that the Proclamation vests all powers of State to the King, including judicial powers and the authority to appoint and remove judges and Decree No.3/2001 which ousts the Courts' jurisdiction to grant bail on matters listed in the Schedule. According to the complainant this illustrates that Courts are not independent.

53. Article 7 of the African Charter provides for fair trial guarantees — safeguards to ensure that any person accused of an offence is given a fair hearing. . . .

54. [T]he Proclamation of 1973 and the Decree of 2001 vested judicial power in the King and ousted the jurisdiction of the court on certain matters. . . . [These acts] not only constitute a violation of the right to fair trial . . . , but also tend to undermine the independence of the judiciary.

55. Article 26 of the Charter provides that States Parties shall have the duty to guarantee the independence of the courts. [The Commission then invokes provisions of the UN Basic Principles on the Independence of the Judiciary and of the International Bar Association (IBA)'s Minimum Standards of Judicial Independence].

56. By entrusting all judicial powers to the Head of State with powers to remove judges, the Proclamation of 1973 seriously undermines the independence of the judiciary in Swaziland. . . .

57. In its Resolution on the Respect and the Strengthening on the Independence of the Judiciary adopted [in 1996] . . . the African Commission "recognised the need for African countries to have a strong and independent judiciary enjoying the confidence of the people for sustainable democracy and development". . .

58. Clearly, retaining a law which vest all judicial powers in the Head of State with possibility of hiring and firing judges directly threatens the independence and security of judges and the judiciary as a whole. The Proclamation of 1973, to the extent that it allows the Head of State to dismiss judges and exercise judicial power is in violation of Article 26 of the African Charter.

59. With regards allegation of violation of Articles 10 and 11, the complainant submits that the Proclamation of 1973 abolishes and prohibits the existence and the formation of political parties or organisations of a similar nature and that the Proclamation also violates Article 11 — right to assemble peacefully as the right to associate cannot be divorced from the right to assembly freely and peacefully.

...

61. ... By ratifying the Charter without taking appropriate steps to bring its laws in line with the same, the African Commission is of the opinion that the State has not complied with its obligations under Article 1 .... The Commission therefore finds the State to have violated these two articles by virtue of the 1973 proclamation.

62. The complainant also alleges violation of Article 13 of the African Charter claiming that the King's Proclamation of 1973 restricted participation of citizens... in issues of governance only within [local government] structures....

63. ... By prohibiting the formation of political parties, the King's Proclamation seriously undermined the ability of the Swaziland people to participate in the government of their country and thus violated Article 13 of the Charter.

From the above reasoning, the African Commission is of the view that the Kingdom of Swaziland by its Proclamation of 1973 and the subsequent Decree No.3 of 2001 violated Articles 1, 7, 10, 11, 13 and 26 of the African Charter.

The Commission hereby recommends as follows:

- that the Proclamation and the Decree be brought in conformity with the provisions of the African Charter;
- that the State engages with other stakeholders, including members of civil society in the conception and drafting of the New Constitution; and
- that the Kingdom of Swaziland should inform the African Commission in writing within six months on the measures it has taken to implement the above recommendations.

CURTIS FRANCIS DOEBBLER V. SUDAN

African Commission on Human and Peoples' Rights
Application 236/2000 (May 2003)

Summary of Facts:

1. The Complainant alleges that on 13th June 1999, the students of the Nubia Association at Ahlia University held a picnic in Buri, Khartoum along the banks of the river....

2. After ... some hours, security agents and policemen accosted the students, beating some of them and arresting others. They were alleged to have violated 'public order' contrary to Article 152 of the Criminal Law of 1991 because they were not properly dressed or acting in a manner considered being immoral.

3. The Complainant avers that the acts constituting these offences comprised of girls kissing, wearing trousers, dancing with men, crossing legs with men, sitting with boys and sitting and talking with boys.

...

5. On 14th June 1999, the eight [female] students ... were convicted and sentenced to fines and or lashes. The said punishment was executed through the supervision of the court. This type of punishment is widespread in Sudan.

...

7. No written record of the proceedings is publicly available.

8. The Complainant submits on the issue of exhaustion of local remedies that since the sentences have already been executed, domestic remedies would no longer be effective.

...

LAW

Admissibility

...

23. ... The Complainant submits that a remedy that has no prospect of success does not constitute an effective remedy and states that the Criminal Code of Sudan had been steadfastly applied in numerous cases and hence there was no reasonable prospect of success of having it declared invalid.

24. He adds that a visa was denied to the legal representative of the victims....

...

27. In order to exhaust the local remedies within the spirit of Article 56(5) of the Charter, one needs to have access to those remedies but if victims have no legal representation it would be difficult to access domestic remedies.

28. For the above reasons, the African Commission declares the communication admissible.

Merits

29. Article 5 of the African Charter reads: *"Every individual shall have the right to the respect of the dignity inherent in a human being and to the recognition of his legal status. All forms of exploitation and degradation of man, particularly slavery, slave trade, torture, cruel, inhuman or degrading punishment and treatment shall be prohibited".*

30. Complainant alleges that [all eight students were] sentenced to fines and between 25 and 40 lashes, the lashes were carried out in public on the bare backs of the women using a wire and plastic whip that leaves permanent scares [sic] on the women.

31. He points out that the instrument used to inflict the lashes was not clean and no doctor was present to supervise the execution of punishment and that the punishment therefore, could have resulted in severe infections to the victims.

32. Complainant alleges that the punishment of lashings are disproportionate and humiliating because they require a girl to submit to baring her back in public and to the infliction of physical harm which is contrary to the high degree of respect accorded to females in Sudanese society.

...

35. There is little or no dispute between the Complainant and the Government of Sudan concerning the facts recounted above. The only dispute that arises is to whether or not the lashings for the acts committed in this instance violate the prohibition of article 5 as being cruel, inhumane, or degrading punishment.

36. Article 5 of the Charter prohibits not only cruel but also inhuman and degrading treatment. This includes not only actions which cause serious physical or

psychological suffering, but which humiliate or force the individual against his will or conscience.

37. While ultimately whether an act constitutes inhuman degrading treatment or punishment depends on the circumstances of the case. The African Commission has stated that the prohibition of torture, cruel, inhuman, or degrading treatment or punishment is to be interpreted as widely as possible. . . .

38. The European Court of Human Rights in *Tyler v. United Kingdom* . . . has similarly held that even lashings that were carried out in private, with appropriate medical supervision, under strictly hygienic conditions . . . violated the rights of the victim. The Court stated that: "the very nature of judicial corporal punishment is that it involves one human being inflicting physical violence on another human being. Furthermore, it is institutionalised violence that is in the present case violence permitted by law, ordered by the judicial authorities of the State and carried out by the police authorities of the State. Thus, although the applicant did not suffer any severe or long lasting physical effects, his punishment whereby he was treated as an object in the power of authorities — constituted an assault on precisely that which it is one of the main purposes of Article 3 to protect, namely a person dignity and physical integrity. Neither can it be excluded that the punishment may have had adverse psychological effects".

39. The Complainant alleges that the punishment meted out was grossly disproportionate, as the acts for which the students were punished were minor offences, which ordinarily would not have attracted such punishments.

40. The Complainant submits that according to Islamic law the penalty of lashings may be meted out for some serious crimes. For example, *hadd* offenses may be punished with lashes under *Shari'a* because they are considered grave offences and strict requirements of proof apply. Minor offenses, however, cannot be punished as *hadd* because the *Qur'an* does not expressly prohibit them with a prescribed penalty. The acts committed by the students were minor acts of friendship between boys and girls at a party.

41. The African Commission, however, wishes to assert that it was not invited to interpret Islamic *Shari'a* Law as obtains in the Criminal Code of the Respondent State. No argument was presented before it nor did the African Commission consider arguments based on the *Shari'a* Law. The African Commission hereby states that the inquiry before it was confined to the application of the African Charter in the legal system of a State Party to the Charter.

42. There is no right for individuals, and particularly the government of a country to apply physical violence to individuals for offences. Such a right would be tantamount to sanctioning State sponsored torture under the Charter and contrary to the very nature of this human rights treaty.

. . .

44. The law under which the victims in this communication were punished has been applied to other individuals. This continues despite the government being aware of its clear incompatibility with international human rights law.

For these reasons, the African Commission,

Finds the Republic of Sudan violation of Article 5 of the African Charter on Human and Peoples' Rights and,

Requests the Government of Sudan to —:

- **Immediately amend** the Criminal Law of 1991, in conformity with its obligations under the African Charter and other relevant international human rights instruments;
- **Abolish** the penalty of lashes; and
- **Take appropriate measures** to ensure compensation of the victims.

INTERIGHTS ON BEHALF OF SAFIA YAKUBU HUSAINI ET AL. V. NIGERIA

African Commission on Human and Peoples' Rights Application 269/2003

1. The complaint is filed by Interights [a London-based NGO] on behalf of Safiya Yakubu Husaini and others who have been allegedly subjected to gross and systematic violations of fair trial and due process rights in the Sharia Courts in Nigeria.

2. The Complainant alleges that Ms Safiya Hussaini, a Nigerian woman and nursing mother was sentenced to death by stoning by a Sharia Court in Gwadabawa, Sokoto State Nigeria, for an alleged crime of adultery. . . .

3. The Complainant alleges that Safiya's case is only one of the many cases to be decided under the recently introduced pieces of Sharia penal legislation in northern Nigerian States. All laws in Nigeria, at both Federal and State levels, ought to be compatible with both the constitution of 1999 and international (including regional) treaties ratified by Nigeria, and are required to particularly comply with the African Charter on Human and Peoples' Rights which is domestic law in the country.

4. [T]he complainant also enumerates other similar instances of alleged violations of fair trial, personal dignity and the right to life. It alleged that in December 2002, a Ms Hafsatu Abubakar from Sokoto State was charged with "Zina," which is either voluntary premarital sexual intercourse or, if the person is married, to adultery.

5. On 19 January 2001, an unmarried woman called Bariya Magazu received 100 lashes in Zamfara State for having committed the offence of Zina. Ms. Magazu was also initially convicted of false accusation for failing to prove her declaration that three particular men had coerced her into having sexual intercourse, which men were not prosecuted. By an order of an Islamic Court in the same State, a Mr. Umaru Bubeh received 80 strokes of the cane on 9 March 2001 for drinking alcohol. On 4 May 2001, a Mr. Lawal Incitara's hand was amputated after a Sharia Court in same State found him guilty of stealing bicycles.

6. In Sokoto State, Sani Shehu and Garga Dandare were sentenced to have their right hands and left feet amputated after being convicted by a Sharia Court in Sokoto State on 20 December 2001. On 27 December 2001, the Upper Sharia Court in the same State convicted a Mr. Aminu Bello of theft and sentenced him to have his right hand amputated.

7. The Complainant alleges that in none of these case did the victims/accused persons receive nor were they offered competent or any legal representation. The

rights of legal representation in the Sharia Courts are very limited and, even where they allow legal representation, only lawyers who are muslims can practice in them.

8. It is further alleged that the new Sharia penal legislations that are adopted in the various Nigeria States contain specifications that limit their application to people of Muslim faith but they dispense with all the fair trial safeguards recognised in the African Charter. . . . In effect, the Sharia penal legislation subject persons of Muslim faith to lower standards of fair trial merely by reason of their faith. In all the cases regarding the application of Sharia law for criminal cases, there is discrimination on grounds of the faith of the accused.

9. The Complaint also alleges that the rights of those tried under Sharia law are protected to a lesser extent than in the Penal Code for Northern Nigeria, valid for non-Muslim people, particularly concerning the right of representation, the right of appeal and the lack of knowledge of criminal procedure by the court. Under Sharia law, the death penalty is applied for offences that are not punishable with the death penalty under the Penal Code for Northern Nigeria. The criteria for appointing judges to the same court also falls short of international standards of training judicial personnel, and there is no requirement for judges to be legally qualified in law.

10. [T]he Complainant submitted a request for provisional measures . . . .

Complaint

11. The Complainant alleges serious and massive violations of Articles 2, 3, 4, 5, 6, 7, and 26 of the African Charter on Human and Peoples' Rights.

Procedure

. . .

13. [In February 2002, the Secretariat of the African Commission requested Interights to provide] evidentiary materials on the developments surrounding the application of the Penal Provisions of Sharia religious law before Nigerian Sharia Courts, and to forward to it complete and specific cases of alleged irregularities supported by relevant documentations. The Complainant was also asked to indicate to the Commission which of the specific decisions of the Sharia Courts had been executed, and which were pending.

14. On 6th February 2002, the Chairman of the African Commission addressed an Urgent Appeal to . . . [President Obasanjo] of Nigeria, respectfully urging Him to suspend further implementation of the Sharia Penal Statutes and decisions as well as convictions thereof, including the case of Ms. Safiya Yakubu, pending the outcome of the consideration of the complaints before the African Commission.

. . .

19. . . . On 21 March 2002, the Chief of Staff to the President of [Nigeria wrote on behalf of the President to assure the Chairman of the African Commission] that the administration and many Nigerians equally shared his concern. The letter further expressed his optimism that, in the long run, justice would be done and Safiya's life would be spared. While noting that the Federal Government could not unilaterally suspend the Sharia Penal Statutes and decisions which were within the prerogative of the State government in accordance with the Nigerian Constitution, the letter

assured the Chairman that the Administration would leave no stone unturned in ensuring that the right to life and human dignity of Safiya, and that of all other Nigerians that may be affected in future were adequately protected.

…

21. On 2 April 2002, the Secretariat of the African Commission wrote to the Complainant reminding it of the need for further information on Ms. Amina Lawal who was alleged to have been sentenced to a similar punishment by a Sharia Court in Katsina State. . . . On 19 April 2002, the [Nigerian Government informed the Commission] of the decision by the Federal Court of Appeal in Nigeria overturning the death sentence imposed on Safiya by a lower Court in Sokoto State thereby making the need to make further Presidential intervention unnecessary.

…

26. [I]n October 2002, the complainant orally informed the Secretariat that it was unable to compile the requested information in time. . . .

…

38. [In December 2004], the complainant orally informed the Rapporteur of the Communication of his wish to withdraw the case.

39. [T]he African Commission decided to defer its decision . . . pending a written confirmation of the same by the complainant.

…

42. [T]he African Commission received a written request for withdrawal, dated 2nd May 2005, from the complainant.

For the abovementioned reason the African Commission on Human and Peoples' Rights,

Takes note of the withdrawal of the communication by the Complainant and decides to close the file.

COMMENT ON PROTOCOL FOR AN AFRICAN COURT ON HUMAN AND PEOPLES' RIGHTS

When the African Charter was adopted in 1981 a clear decision was taken to opt for a Commission rather than a Court as the principal institutional arrangement. Negotiations to establish a Court continued, however, and in 1998 the OAU Assembly adopted a Protocol to the African Charter on Human and Peoples' Rights to establish an African Court on Human and Peoples' Rights. The Protocol entered into force in 2004, after 15 states parties to the Charter had ratified it. As of May 2007 there were 23 parties. And in 2006 the newly elected judges of the Court were sworn in. The Preamble recites that the states parties to the Charter are 'firmly convinced that the attainment of the objectives' of the Charter 'requires the establishment of an African court' to 'complement and reinforce the functions' of the Commission.

The Court consists of 11 judges 'elected in an individual capacity'; no two judges may be nationals of the same state. (Article 11). Its membership is to include 'representation of the main regions of Africa and of their principal legal traditions', and in the election of judges the Assembly 'shall ensure that there is adequate gender representation'. (Article 14) Judicial independence is to be fully ensured. (Article 17). All judges must be from Africa and a judge must not sit in a case concerning his or her own state of nationality.

The Court's jurisdiction extends to cases and disputes 'concerning the interpretation and application' of the Charter, Protocol, 'and any other relevant human rights instrument ratified by the States concerned' (Article 3). At the request of a member state of the OAU or the OAU, the Court may give its advisory opinion 'on any legal matter related to the Charter or any other relevant human rights instruments', provided that the matter is not then being examined by the Commission (Article 4).

To invoke the Court's contentious jurisdiction, the Commission, a state party that has brought a complaint before the Commission or against whom a complaint has been brought, a state party whose citizen is a victim of a violation, and African intergovernmental organizations can submit a case to the Court (Article 5). On the other hand, the capacity of individuals and NGOs to bring a complaint against a state depends both on a special declaration by the state and on the discretion of the Court (Articles 5 and 34). This double barrier represents a sharp contrast with the access of individuals to the other two regional courts.

The Commission continues to play an important role under the Protocol. The provisions on admissibility provide that the Court 'may consider cases or transfer them to the Commission' (Article 6). The Court's Rules of Procedure are to state the conditions under which the Court shall consider cases, 'bearing in mind the complementarity between the Commission and the Court' (Article 8). The communications procedure itself of the Commission is not reconciled with the new Court; it remains unclear when one or the other path should be followed by an institution or individual intending to submit a complaint against a state. Thus the two organs appear to be in competition with each other, without any clear hierarchy, posing a large risk of duplication of effort.

If the Court finds a violation, 'it shall make appropriate orders to remedy the violation' (Article 27). States parties to the Protocol 'undertake to comply with the judgment in any case to which they are parties . . . and to guarantee its execution' (Article 30). The OAU Council of Ministers is to 'monitor' a judgment's execution (Article 29).

The Court is to be based in Arusha, Tanzania, using the facilities developed for the International Criminal Tribunal for Rwanda. Negotiations are also currently underway to merge the new Court with the proposed African Court of Justice. The agreement creating the latter has never entered into force. The consequences of such a merger are unclear.

QUESTIONS

1. Rachel Murray, one of the most prolific authors writing about the AU human rights system, has criticized many scholars, including the authors of the present book, for having too readily dismissed the importance of African human rights institutions. This is said to be 'due to neglect by international human rights discourse of views outside of the ruling,

or dominant, Western and European States. . . . The result is that international literature on human rights and international institutions often do not cite African institutions' case law or activities as examples or suggestions of best practice or indicators of the development of international human rights law'.[44] Comment.

2. How well did the Commission deal with the Islamic law issues addressed in the *Doebbler* and *Interights* cases?

3. Should the Commission in the Swaziland case have undertaken an analysis more along the lines of the ECtHR to assess whether the King might have been justified in taking some of the measures contained in the Procalamation complained of?

4. Given the provisions of the Protocol and the present circumstances of the Commission and of the African human rights regime in general, would you as an African human rights advocate have urged the present creation of a court? What plausible arguments could be made for or against such a move at this time?

ADDITIONAL READING

H. Onoria, 'The African Commission on Human and Peoples' Rights and the Exhaustion of Local Remedies under the African Charter', 3 Af. Hum. Rts. J. 1 (2003); G.W. Mugwanya, *Human Rights in Africa* (2003); R. Murray, *Human Rights in Africa: From the OAU to the African Union* (2004); P.T. Zeleza and P. McConnaughay (eds.), *Human Rights, The Rule of Law, and Development in Africa* (2004); M. Evans and R. Murray (eds.), *The African Charter on Human and Peoples' Rights: The System in Practice, 1986–2000* (2002); *Compendium of Key Human Rights Documents of the African Union* (2005); C. Heyns, 'The African Regional Human Rights System: The African Charter', 108 Penn St. L. Rev. 679 (2004); and M. Mutua, 'The African Human Rights Court: A Two-Legged Stool?', 21 Hum. Rts. Q. 342 (1999).

[44] R. Murray, 'International Human Rights: Neglect of Perspectives from African Institutions' 55 I.C.L.Q. 193 (2006), at 195–196.

PART E

STATES AS PROTECTORS AND ENFORCERS OF HUMAN RIGHTS

Part E completes the basic structure of this coursebook. We first examined in Parts A–C the processes for the creation of international human rights norms and the basic categories of civil, political, economic, and social rights. Our attention then turned in Part D to the relations between norms and institutions, particularly to the significance of international institutions and processes for the development and enforcement of norms.

Those parts gave primary attention to the international dimensions of the human rights movement. Of course, states — the creators of the norms, the designers and members of the institutions, the participants in the processes, as well as the primary duty-bearers under international human rights law — figured prominently in these earlier materials. They appeared frequently as the violators, the defendants, the entities being monitored, investigated and reported on by intergovernmental and nongovernmental organizations.

Part E shifts focus. Here we observe primarily the internal processes of the states themselves, particularly the decisions and acts of governments bearing on human rights issues. Our perspective is that of the state rather than the international community. For the most part, we examine executive, legislative and judicial action looking towards the observance and protection of human rights, rather than state action violating rights. In short, we here imagine states as the first-line enforcers of the international human rights system that they have created. Such is indeed the primary focus of the entire human rights movement. In a state-organized world, the highest human rights aspiration would imagine states as fully adequate protectors of human rights, to the point where international enforcement machinery would become redundant.

Part E has two chapters, both of which involve the interpenetration of national legal-political orders and the international system. Chapter 12 examines ways in which states observe and protect human rights. Chapter 13 inquires into the ways in which a state acts abroad as an enforcer of human rights norms against violator states.

In both chapters, as in the entire coursebook, the materials view the state primarily *in its relationships* to the international system. That is, these chapters do not examine state politics, history or culture *independently* of that system. Within this framework, states are meant to draw from and work to increase the efficacy of the international standards. The chapters discuss variations of state practice across several countries and types of legal systems.

12

Vertical Interpenetration: International Human Rights Law Within States' Legal and Political Orders

Human rights violations occur *within* a state, rather than on the high seas or in outer space outside the jurisdiction of any one state. Ultimately, effective protection must come from within the state. The international human rights system does not typically place delinquent states in political bankruptcy and through some form of receivership take over the administration of a country in order to assure the enjoyment of human rights — although the measures implemented by the international community in Bosnia-Herzegovina after the 1995 Dayton Peace Agreement and in Kosovo (see p. 837, *supra*) represent steps in that direction. Rather the international system seeks to compel states to fulfil their obligations through one or another method — either observing national law (constitutional or statutory) that is consistent with the international norms, or making the international norms themselves part of the national legal and political order.

Such is the focus of Chapter 12, which falls into two sections. *Section A* studies how states generally 'internalize' *treaty* norms — that is, how they absorb the provisions of human rights treaties within the state's legal and political order so that they can be implemented and enforced by state authorities. *Section B* discusses the particular issue of reservations to treaties, including the rules for determining the scope and consequence of illegal reservations.

A. DOMESTIC INTERNALIZATION OF HUMAN RIGHTS TREATIES

Section A focuses attention on the domestic incorporation of international instruments, specifically human rights treaties, in domestic legal and political systems. It examines the interpenetration of the international and national systems, the significance of treaties within states. The broad questions explored are: how do these treaties influence the national legal and political systems of states parties? Are they automatically absorbed into a state legal system, or reproduced in state legislation, and with what effects on the different branches of government such as the executive and judiciary? Or do they remain distinct from the state system, 'above' it as part of international law? The readings draw on the techniques and experiences of a range of countries in this excursion into comparative constitutional and foreign affairs law.

CHRISTOF HEYNS AND FRANS VILJOEN, THE IMPACT OF THE UNITED NATIONS HUMAN RIGHTS TREATIES ON THE DOMESTIC LEVEL

(2002)

[The following presents the findings of a study initiated in collaboration with the Office of the High Commissioner for Human Rights. The study examines the effectiveness of the UN human rights treaty system across a variety of states.]

. . .

[T]he position in the following countries was investigated:

African region: Egypt, Senegal, South Africa, Zambia
Asian region: India, Iran, Japan, the Philippines
Eastern European region: the Czech Republic, Estonia, Romania, the Russian Federation (Russia)
Latin American and Caribbean region: Brazil, Colombia, Jamaica, Mexico
Western Europe and Other (WEOG) region: Australia, Canada, Finland, Spain

. . .

Compatibility studies comparing the treaties with domestic legislation prior to ratification or accession were done in respect of all six treaties in Brazil, Canada, Egypt, Japan and South Africa. Compatibility studies were done only in respect of some of the treaties, or were done to a limited extent only, in Australia, Finland, India, Iran, Jamaica, Romania, Senegal, Spain and Zambia. (In Senegal a study comparing the treaties and the Senegalese Constitution, but not ordinary legislation, was undertaken.) . . .

Compatibility studies have sometimes resulted in legislative amendments as part of the process of ratification or accession. Finland amended its Penal Code before ratifying CERD.

Compatibility studies have also culminated in the entering of reservations upon ratification (eg Australia (CERD), Finland, India, Japan). As mentioned above, a compatibility study in respect of CEDAW resulted in Iran not ratifying that Convention. In respect of CRC it led to a controversial reservation.

. . .

C IMPACT OF THE TREATIES

...

i Level of awareness of the treaties

The younger generation of urbanised lawyers, government officials (mostly from departments of foreign affairs) and academics who deal with the treaties, and NGOs with a specific focus on an area covered by the treaties are the groups most likely to be familiar with the treaties throughout the world.

CERD is well known in some countries where race (ethnicity or religion) is an issue (eg Australia (especially in respect of indigenous peoples' issues), the Czech Republic, but not in Egypt, Finland (this is changing), Jamaica, Japan, the Philippines, Zambia). If one has to generalise, there seems to be a higher level of awareness in a number of countries of CEDAW and CRC than of other treaties (eg Canada, Japan, Mexico (especially CRC), South Africa, Spain, Zambia). NGOs are mobilised around these special treaties (eg Senegal). CESCR seems not to be well known in a number of countries (eg India, Japan, Mexico, Philippines), although in other countries (eg Romania, South Africa) NGOs are mobilised around this Covenant. CCPR has attracted special attention in a number of societies (eg Finland). In Iran CRC, in respect of which the controversial reservation cited above was made, ironically seems to be the only treaty of which there is some awareness. Knowledge of CAT is largely confined to those responsible for its implementation (eg Japan, Mexico).

...

Through a systematic newspaper search, less than 10 articles directly referring to the treaties were found in Brazil, Colombia, the Philippines and South Africa. Only Australia, Canada and Finland revealed a significant number of articles. (Over 800 are reported from Australia; over 100 from Canada; and from Finland the number of articles about two controversial cases before the HRC is estimated to exceed "several dozens".)

ii Constitutional recognition of treaty norms

The treaty norms form the basis of, or at least coincide with, most of the constitutional human rights provisions, such as the bills and charters of rights, of the 20 countries reviewed. This method of internalising treaty norms into the domestic legal system, especially where the constitutional human rights provisions are justiciable, constitutes one of the most powerful ways in which treaty norms could be enforced on the local level.

... In some instances ... the treaties have impacted on the bills of rights even when they had not been ratified at the time (eg CRC in Brazil, CESCR in South Africa)....

The impact of the treaties on the constitutional human rights provisions in respect of which they have played a role may be categorised as follows:

- The treaties played an identifiable and significant role in the drafting process of constitutional human rights provisions

  To this category belong South Africa's 1993 and 1996 Constitutions (the greatest impact on the bill of rights recorded in the study); Brazil (most of the treaties, especially CESCR; also CRC even before it was ratified); Canada (especially CCPR was used as the basis of the 1982 Charter); Finland (when the bill of rights was changed in 1995, the treaties were clearly influential in the drafting, to the extent that the specific wording was followed).

- Many of the treaty norms are mirrored in bills of rights, and there is some (but not a very clear) causal link between the treaties and the constitutional human rights provisions

  This applies to Colombia (CESCR, CCPR were relied on by delegates in the Constitutional Convention who redrafted the constitution in 1991); the Czech Republic (CECSR is linked to the inclusion of socio-economic rights; CCPR also mirrored); Estonia (although the European Convention was more influential in the 1992 redraft); the Philippines (the 1987 Bill of Rights reflects the rights in CESCR and CCPR); Romania (the 1991 Constitution includes most of the rights in CESCR and CCPR, and some of those in the other treaties); Russia (a government report indicates that only one provision in the two Covenants is not affirmed in the Russian Constitution); and Spain (the 1978 Bill of Rights was drafted one year after the ratification of CCPR and CESCR, but there was little influence).

- Only some norms are reflected in constitutional human rights provisions, and there is no clear link between them.

  Egypt, Iran

iii Legislative reform

Numerous instances of legislative reform that were prompted by the treaties have been identified. Some of this reform took place as a result of compatibility studies, other in response to concluding observations, and some in the course of ordinary legislative review. A sample of only that legislation in which explicit reference was made to the treaties is given below:

Australia: Human Rights and Equal Opportunities Commission Act 1986 (CERD, CCPR and CRC); Native Titles Act of 1993 (CERD and CESCR); Aboriginal and Torres Strait Islander Commission Act of 1989 (CERD and CESCR); Workplace Relations Act 1996 (CESCR and CEDAW); Industrial Relations Reform Act 1993 (CESCR and CEDAW); Commonwealth and NSW Evidence Act of 1995 (CCPR); Sex Discrimination Act of 1984 (CEDAW); Various extradition legislation refers to CAT; the Australian Law Reform Commission often refers to CCPR in its law reform activities.

Brazil: Children's and Adolescents' Statute (CRC).

Canada: Canadian Multiculturalism Act (CERD and CCPR); Emergencies Act (CCPR).

Finland: Amendment of the Penal Code (CERD); enactment of the Equality Act and amendments to other laws (CEDAW); amendments to the Aliens Act, Act on Military Discipline and Act on Public Meetings (CCPR).

India: The Protection of Human Rights Act 1993, which created the National Human Rights Commission, defines "human rights" with reference to the Covenants.

Japan: The explanatory note of the Alien Registration Act cites the Covenants. (Especially CEDAW prompted dramatic changes in the laws of Japan.)
Mexico: The government of the Federal District (Mexico City) has incorporated the definition of discrimination as contained in CERD in its legislation; the Law for Minor lnfractors (CRC).
Philippines: Inter Country Adoption Act 1995, Family Courts Act 1997, Domestic Adoption Act 1998 (CRC).
Senegal: Amendment of the Criminal Code (CRC and CEDAW).
South Africa: Equality Bill (CERD and CEDAW); Domestic Violence Act (CEDAW and CRC); Maintenance Act (CRC and CEDAW).
Spain: The Penal Code was amended in accordance with CAT.
Zambia: Affiliation and Maintenance of Children Act (CRC).

There is ample evidence of the impact of the treaties on legislation in Finland (where they have been incorporated into national law) and Russia. They have played a very limited role in Colombia.

iv Judicial decisions

In some isolated instances, treaties have been used as an independent basis on which the substantive outcome of cases in domestic courts has hinged. Much more frequently, however, courts have used the treaties as interpretative guides to clarify legislative provisions, such as those of the national bills of rights.

Treaties have been used as the basis for substantive outcomes in Estonia (CRC) and Japan (CCPR was held to be self-executing). The Colombian Constitutional Court has an exceptional record of reference to the treaties, and has in 129 cases between 1992 and 1998 based their decisions on CCPR. CCPR has also played a significant role in the high courts in India.

Based purely on the number of references to the treaties as a tool of interpretation in decided cases traced in the course of this study, the following categories may be identified:

- Frequent use of treaties as an interpretative tool
  Australia (844 instances in which reference was made to at least one of the six treaties on the basis of a Lexis database case search); Canada (169 references); Finland (more than 36 references); South Africa (at least 28 references); Spain (at least 28 references)
- Infrequent use of treaties as an interpretative tool
  The Philippines (at least 8 references); the Czech Republic (at least 6 references)
- Very limited reference to treaties
  India (about 14 references), Romania (at least 7 references), Russia (a "very limited number of cases"), Egypt (at least 1 case), Zambia (one reference). In respect of Jamaica the only reference was in a decision of the Privy Council.
- No reference whatsoever to treaties found
  Iran, Mexico, Senegal

v Development of policy, etc.

In a number of countries national action plans on human rights in general, or plans that focus on particular interest groups that were largely inspired by the treaties have been developed....

National human rights institutions (or similar institutions) often make use of the treaties (eg in Colombia, Finland, India). The South African Human Rights Commission has a special mandate to monitor socio-economic rights, in respect of which CESCR (and to some extent the concomitant jurisprudence such as the General Comments of the CESCR Committee) plays a significant role. The Parliamentary Ombudsman in Finland and the Colombian Human Rights Ombudsman often make use of the treaties.

...

vi Use by NGOs

NGOs use specific treaties as focal points for lobbying activities (eg in Australia, Canada, India, the Philippines, Romania, Russia, Senegal). In Iran and Zambia this has happened in respect of children's and women's rights. Women's NGOs in Japan rally around CEDAW....

vii Academic publications

References to the treaties in academic publications (largely legal journals or books) are found in most of the countries reviewed. However, as systematic searches were not performed in each case, conclusive figures are not available.

The Australian, Canadian and South African reports cited the most references to the treaties, while Brazil, Colombia, Mexico, the Philippines and Senegal cited the least.

...

G LIMITING AND ENHANCING FACTORS

...

i Factors limiting the impact of the treaties

- There is ample evidence in the study that because governments guard their sovereignty jealously, they resist international supervision and are reluctant to implement recommendations and views.
- In many instances, however, conscious resistance is not necessary. The widespread ignorance of the treaty system in government circles, among lawyers and in civil societies around the world, effectively blocks any impact which the treaties may otherwise have had....
- The absence of a domestic human rights culture is another obvious factor that limits the impact of the UN treaties in many societies. A low level of domestic implementation of human rights norms in a particular country makes international supervision more important, but in practice the system is less likely to have an effect under such circumstances (Egypt, Iran, Zambia). In order for international human rights treaties to have an impact,

an enabling domestic environment is required. The Japanese report mentions that the treaties need "domestic constituencies". An inactive civil society is also reflected in the absence of a strong domestic NGO sector....

- In some countries there is a shortage of journalists with human rights training (eg Czech Republic, Senegal)....
- Socio-economic factors often have a negative influence on the potential impact of the treaties. Illiteracy of the population is an important factor in this regard (eg Egypt, Senegal, Zambia)....

...

- In some instances treaties are associated with unpopular political causes (such as the abolition of the death penalty and restraints on the police in Jamaica; the fate of migrants and gypsies in Spain, secessionist movements in Senegal and India) and as such they are more readily discounted by governments and civil society, and human rights groups become reluctant to rely on these treaties. (At the same time the relevance of human rights to these causes inevitably enhances their legitimacy in the eyes of those who support them.)

...

- In some instances the progressive and effective protection of human rights on the domestic level could render the international system redundant. The South African Bill of Rights, for example, has incorporated most of the international norms, and in some cases provides a higher level of protection than the treaties (also Finland (CEDAW)).
- There is a lack of co-ordination within governments (between departments on the national level, and between national and local levels), between NGOs and between governments and NGOs. Making a treaty the exclusive responsibility of a certain government department limits its reach (eg CEDAW in Spain), although it is seen as necessary for one department to co-ordinate the others (eg CRC in Spain).
- The treaties cover six separate areas of human rights, but government departments are not organised in that way. The international and national systems are not synchronised. For example, normally a single government body is not responsible for children's rights. This makes it difficult in practice to pinpoint responsibility on the domestic level (Canada).
- Reporting is widely seen as an ad hoc activity, a once-off burden which the state has to deal with every few years, and not a continuous effort which involves an ongoing cycle of reporting...

  ... From the Russian perspective the reporting cycles are regarded as too long. Successive administrations are given the chance effectively to deny responsibility for what happened before the previous elections.
- Federal states find it more difficult to report (Canada) and at times also to take decisions to ratify treaties (Australia). In any event, awareness and impact is least at the lower levels of government, such as in the local government sphere (eg in South Africa).

...

- Correspondents report a widespread preference for regional systems above the UN system. . . . According to the report on Estonia, the Council of Europe supports its human rights system better than the UN, by means of seminars, financial assistance and help with compatibility studies. . . .

. . .

iii Best practices

The following practices that were encountered are among those that seem to have the potential to enhance the impact of the system:

- Interdepartmental institutions have been created to co-ordinate reporting on a continuous scale in a number of countries.
- In Finland public hearings are held on the basis of draft reports prior to their submission to the UN.

. . .

- In Estonia the state translated the concluding observations into Estonian and distributed them. It then took the initiative to have these published in privately owned newspapers. The concluding observations also were tabled in cabinet.
- A "tripartite follow-up" of politicians, government officials and NGOs was convened in respect of the concluding observations of the HRC in respect of the CCPR report in Japan, although it did not reach its full potential.
- In Colombia and Finland there are special procedures for the enforcement of the views of the treaty bodies.

. . .

- The Australian Law Reform Commission is required by statute to take international human rights treaties (and particularly CCPR) into account.

. . .

- In Japan the Prime Minister has been questioned in parliament on the implementation of concluding observations of the HRC. . . .
- In South Africa the new constitution was tested by the Constitutional Court to establish whether it gave recognition to all internationally recognised human rights before it became law. The constitution states that courts must consider international law in interpreting the bill of rights.
- The Indian Supreme Court has overruled a reservation that India has entered in respect of CCPR, to the effect that victims of unlawful detention would not have a right to claim compensation.
- In Finland the Bill of Rights Drafting Commission that drafted the 1995 constitutional changes started their work by drawing up a comparative chart of those human rights contained in treaties ratified by Finland.
- In Australia country reports are tabled in parliament.

. . .

IV PROPOSALS

. . .

(6) National human rights institutions (or similar institutions) are found in an increasing number of countries around the world today. It is proposed that they

should be involved more prominently in mediating the interface between the UN and the relevant role players in the various states (civil servants as well as members of civil society). In particular, they should be encouraged to do their own follow-up of UN procedures, both as regards concluding observations and individual complaints, and to keep track of what has been done by governments in this respect. This information should be included in the yearly reports of national human rights institutions....

...

V AFTERWORD

When one compares the world as it is with what it would have been without the treaties, treaties have made a huge difference. But when one considers their potential impact, much still remains to be done.

VIRGINIA LEARY, INTERNATIONAL LABOUR CONVENTIONS AND NATIONAL LAW

(1982), at 1

[The efficacy of human rights treaties] depends essentially on the incorporation of their provisions in national law...

...

International law determines the validity of treaties in the international legal system, i.e., when and how a treaty becomes binding upon a state as regards other State Parties. It also determines the remedies available on the international plane for its breach. But it is the national legal system which determines the status or force of law which will be given to a treaty within that legal system, i.e., whether national judges and administrators will apply the norms of a treaty in a specific case.... When the treaty norms become domestic law, national judges and administrators apply them, and individuals in the ratifying states may receive rights as a result of the treaty provisions. Thus, developed municipal legal systems supplement the more limited enforcement system of international law.

While the international legal system does not reach *directly* into the national systems to enforce its norms it attempts to do so *indirectly*. States are required under international law to bring their domestic laws into conformity with their validly contracted international commitments. Failure to do so, however, results in an international delinquency but does not change the situation within the national legal systems where judges and administrators may continue to apply national law rather than international law in such cases....

The status of treaties in national law is determined by two different constitutional techniques referred to in this study as 'legislative incorporation' and 'automatic incorporation'. In some states the provisions of ratified treaties do not become national law unless they have been enacted as legislation by the normal method. The legislative act creating the norms as domestic law is an act entirely distinct from the act of ratification of the treaty. The legislative bodies may refuse to enact legislation implementing the treaty. In this case the provisions of the treaty do not become national law. This method, referred to as 'legislative incorporation', is used, inter alia, in the United Kingdom, Commonwealth countries and Scandinavian countries. In other states, which have a different system, ratified treaties become domestic law by virtue of ratification. This method is referred to as 'automatic incorporation' and is the method adopted, inter alia, by France, Switzerland, the Netherlands . . . and many Latin American countries and some African and Asian countries. . . . Even in such states, however, some treaty provisions require implementing legislation before they will be applied by the courts. Such provisions are categorized as 'non-self-executing'.

. . .

International law does not dictate that one or the other of the methods of legislative or automatic incorporation must be used. Either is satisfactory assuming that the norms of treaties effectively become part of national law. Conversely, neither method is *ipso facto* satisfactory under international law, if, in practice, the norms of ratified treaties are not applied by national judges and administrators. The method by which treaties become national law is a matter in principle to be determined by the constitutional law of the ratifying state and not a matter ordained by international law. The international community, lacking more effective means of enforcement, is often dependent on the constitutional system of particular states for the effective application of treaties intended for internal application.

Some national constitutions provide for automatic incorporation of treaty provisions. In other states, judicial decisions have determined that treaties are to be automatically incorporated. A correlation appears to exist between legislative consent to ratification and automatic incorporation. In states with the system of automatic incorporation, legislative consent by at least one house of the legislature is generally required before the executive may ratify treaties. In states with the system of legislative incorporation, ratification of treaties is frequently a purely executive act not requiring prior approbation of the legislature. In the United Kingdom, and other common law countries which have followed UK precedent in this regard, parliamentary consent to ratification is normally not required and express legislative enactment of treaty provisions is necessary before they become domestic law.

. . .

An individual may invoke the provisions of a treaty before national courts in automatic incorporation states in the absence of implementing legislation only when its provisions are considered to be self-executing and when he has standing to do so. . . . [I]n general, treaty provisions are considered by national courts and administrators as self-executing when they lend themselves to judicial or administrative application without further legislative implementation. . . .

. . .

COMMENT ON MONISM AND DUALISM

Comparative analyses of different constitutional approaches to incorporating international law often refer to 'monist' and 'dualist' theories concerning the relationship between international and national law. Monist theories imagine a unitary world legal system in which national and international law have 'comparable, equivalent, or identical subjects, sources, and substantive contents'.[1] Monists argue for the supremacy of international law in relation to national law. In its classical formulation, monism asserts that all activity of states is regulated by the superior international law. Thus the so-called 'domestic affairs' of a state are not affairs unregulated by international law, but rather affairs which a state has exclusive competence to regulate pursuant to and under international law.

Dualist theories distinguish between the system or public order of international law and of national law. Each has 'its own distinguishable subjects, distinguishable structures and processes of authority, and distinguishable substantive content'. Thus the subjects of international law are only states, its sources lie only in treaties and custom made by states, and its content involves only relations between states. Neither international law nor national law can *per se* create or invalidate the other. Of course a state may by its own custom or national law adopt rules of international law as the law of the land, through practices and theories of incorporation, transformation, adoption and so on.

Hans Kelsen has stressed the different perspectives on institutions, world values and order that these two theories express:

> . . . It may be that our choice . . . is guided by ethical or political preferences. A person whose political attitude is that of nationalism and imperialism may be inclined to accept as a hypothesis the basic norm of his own national law. A person whose sympathy is for internationalism and pacifism may be inclined to accept as a hypothesis the basic norm of international law and thus proceed from the primacy of international law. From the point of view of the science of law, it is irrelevant which hypothesis one chooses. But from the point of view of politics, the choice [between dualism and monism] may be important since it is tied up with the ideology of sovereignty.[2]

The monist theory is illustrated by the Dutch Constitution of 1983, discussed in the following excerpts:[3]

> . . . Art. 93 of the Constitution provides that provisions of treaties and decisions of international organisations, the contents of which may be binding on everyone, shall have this binding effect as from the time of publication. The words 'the contents of which may be binding on everyone' are generally understood to refer to the self-executing character which is required for their application by Dutch Courts. The rights contained in the ECHR are considered self-executing by the courts and are therefore directly applicable.
>
> . . .
>
> . . . [Pursuant to Art. 94 of the Dutch Constitution, Dutch courts must] give precedence to self-executing treaty provisions over domestic law that is not in

[1] All quotations in this Note are taken from Myres McDougal, 'The Impact of International Law upon National Law: A Policy-Oriented Perspective', 4 S. Dak. L. Rev. 25 (1959), at 27–31.

[2] *Principles of International Law* (1952), at 446, quoted in McDougal, *supra* n. 1.

[3] Jörg Polakiewicz and V. Jacob-Foltzer, 'The European Human Rights Convention in Domestic Law', 12 Hum. Rts. L. J. 65 (1991), at 125.

> conformity therewith, be it antecedent or posterior, statutory or constitutional law.... But the courts have no competence to nullify, repeal or amend the legislation in question. The provision remains in force, but will not be applied.
>
> ...
>
> *3. Case-law*
>
> ...
>
> [The earlier] reticent attitude of Dutch courts towards the ECHR has changed quite dramatically during the 1980s. The statistical survey recently given by Van Dijk shows a considerable increase of references to the ECHR. The percentage of cases, however, in which the Supreme Court has found a violation of the Convention remains small (an average of 9%). When confronted with a conflict between a provision of the ECHR and a provision of Dutch law, the Supreme Court tends to circumvent it by giving to the latter an interpretation or scope different from its original meaning and from the anterior legal practice, or by inserting a new principle into Dutch law derived from the treaty provision....

Dualist theories are illustrated in the practice and constitutional norms of several of the states described below.

NOTE

Several constitutional courts employ a canon of construction that favours interpreting domestic law to be consistent with international law. This interpretive approach reappears in various readings in this chapter. Should this canon of construction apply to interpreting the text of a national constitution as well as a parliamentary statute? The following discusses existing practice:[4]

> ... [One] factor for assessing the ability of interpretative canons to harmonize [constitutional law] and IHR treaties is the existence of judicial discretion, i.e., whether courts may or should harmonize [constitutional law] and IHR treaties. One common model for incorporating international law in domestic law is the 'presumption of conformity' doctrine. Many domestic legal systems ... apply a rule of interpretation prescribing that ordinary legislation be construed, as far as possible, in harmony with the international obligations of the state. This presumption is often presented as reflective of a hypothetical parliamentary intent — that, barring contrary evidence, judges must assume that legislators had not intended to compromise their state's international obligations via legislation.
>
> However, courts in most of the surveyed legal systems do not apply this canon of interpretation to their [constitutional law], even when they are prepared to seek guidance from international law sources. Instead, references to IHR treaties often seem to be based on a weaker, comparative law framework of analysis, based upon

[4] Yuval Shany, 'How Supreme is the Supreme Law of the Land? Comparative Analysis of the Influence of International Human Rights Treaties upon the Interpretation of Constitutional Texts by Domestic Courts', 31 Brook. J. Int. L. 341 (2006).

> the inherent persuasiveness of IHR law (whether binding or not upon the relevant jurisdiction), and not on a recognized duty to incorporate it into [constitutional law]. Under this interpretive model, courts retain considerable discretion on whether or not to harmonize [constitutional law] and IHR treaties. For example, in the rare cases where IHR instruments and their treaty bodies' case law were invoked by U.S. Supreme Court justices, they were addressed within a weak interpretive framework alluding to the informative value of comparative law or non-binding international law, and not within the stronger Charming Betsy canon. [The author elsewhere explains, 'The doctrine has also been referred to as the "presumption of compatibility," "presumption of compliance," or, in the United States, as the Charming Betsy canon of interpretation. See Murray v. Schooner Charming Betsy, 6 U.S. 64, 118 (1804) ("[A]n act of [C]ongress ought never to be construed to violate the law of nations if any other possible construction remains . . . ").']

Some of the readings that follow raise the question whether courts should also apply the Charming Betsy analysis in interpreting federal laws as well as provincial and local laws and in interpreting parliamentary legislation as well as executive and administrative acts.

BRUNO SIMMA ET AL., THE ROLE OF GERMAN COURTS IN THE ENFORCEMENT OF INTERNATIONAL HUMAN RIGHTS

in B. Conforti and F. Francioni (eds.), Enforcing International Human Rights in Domestic Courts (1997), at 107

Our review of the jurisprudence of German courts on international human rights will probably leave the observer with mixed feelings. On the one hand, the implementation of human rights treaties and customary human rights law in the German legal order, combined with the extensive jurisdiction and broad powers of review available to the judiciary, would offer a good starting-point for German courts to take an active part in the formation of an extensive body of case law on international human rights. The demand of the Bundesverfassungsgericht [Federal Constitutional Court] to pursue an interpretation in favour of public international law . . . grants German courts further possibilities to apply international human rights indirectly in their jurisprudence. Unfortunately, however, the number of cases in which German courts deal with international human rights is rather meagre except in some areas like expulsion and extradition, where domestic statutes explicitly require the consideration of international human rights standards.

Why do German courts apply international human rights norms so rarely? In part at least, practical reasons can explain this reluctance of German courts:

1. International human rights norms are not part of the core curricula in the legal education and practical training of lawyers and judges.
2. Some courts may have difficulties in obtaining German translations. . . .
3. Access to the texts of international norms sometimes proves to be difficult. . . .

The most plausible explanation for the reluctance of German courts to consider international human rights norms in their case law, however, seems to be the far-reaching *prime facie* parallelism of some international rights and domestic constitutional and statutory rights. Whenever courts can enforce an individual right simply on the basis of a constitutional or statutory provision they will do so, simply because they can rely on an elaborate case law, commentaries and other secondary literature.... In addition, German courts, and German jurists in general, seem convinced that the German legal system establishes such a high standard of protection for individual rights guaranteed in the Basic law that international human rights law could hardly offer any improvement. Thus, it is not surprising that courts often refer to international human rights only in the way of stating briefly that the application of these rights would not lead to a different result in the specific case. Judgments of the European Court of Human Rights which found a violation of the Convention by German authorities have proved that this general assumption is erroneous. In the long run, these decisions had quite considerable impact insofar as they changed the general attitude of German courts towards the European Convention....
...

STEFAN OETER, INTERNATIONAL HUMAN RIGHTS AND NATIONAL SOVEREIGNTY IN FEDERAL SYSTEMS: THE GERMAN EXPERIENCE

47 Wayne L. Rev. 871 (2001)

... German public authorities and judicial courts are so accustomed to the idea that the standard of internal fundamental rights protection is above the standard of international human rights that they automatically tend to imply that a public act compatible with the fundamental rights of the Constitution will create no problems under international human rights. If state authorities, the legislator or judicial organs violate international human rights, they usually do not do so with the conscience of disregarding international human rights. They are simply not accustomed to keeping international human rights foremost in mind. In this regard there is probably no great difference between Germany and the United States.

... In most arenas, the elaborate system of constitutional protection of fundamental rights that has transformed large parts of the German legal order de facto ensures that the corresponding requirements of international human rights are observed. But there are certain specific fields, like freedom of assembly and association of foreigners, that largely fall outside the scope of protection of fundamental rights of the federal constitution....

The intrinsic inwardness of the intellectual perspective of ordinary lawyers often blurs the problem, however, and leads to neglecting the standards of international human rights. The current discourse on severely limiting the political activities of foreign citizens living in Germany, in particular refugees and asylum seekers, delivers an example of such neglect of international human rights standards in the legal and political arena. This is probably no particularity of the German legal and political system, since conservative populists campaigning with slogans of law and order and tight immigration control everywhere in the world will tend to repress the limits which international human rights place to their proposed policy changes. Perhaps such a systematic neglect of international human rights standards is part of the political game, proposing radical measures that mobilize voters, knowing that they can never be implemented due to legal impediments of a constitutional as well as international legal character. Even the most elaborate system of inclusion of international legal obligations in the internal legal order cannot prevent such political games. What it should prevent, however, is the spill-over of such radical discourses into administrative and judicial practice. To be efficient, there should exist a rapid and effective procedural mechanism that forces administrative authorities and judicial courts to observe international human rights.

Here the German record is far from perfect. Usually the mechanism works well, but if the judiciary becomes blind itself, forgets about requirements of international human rights protection, or even consciously disregards these requirements, the system breaks down. . . .

YUJI IWASAWA, INTERNATIONAL LAW, HUMAN RIGHTS LAW AND JAPANESE LAW: THE IMPACT OF INTERNATIONAL LAW ON JAPANESE LAW

(1998), at 288–306

A. The Relationship between International Law and Japanese Law

. . .

International law is accorded high formal authority in Japan; both treaties and customary international law have the force of law and override statutes, even if the statutes were enacted later in time.

. . .

B. Impact of International Law on Japanese Law

. . .

(a) *Tendency of the courts to ignore arguments based on international human rights law*

. . .

[T]he courts are generally reluctant to adjudicate on the basis of international human rights law. Japanese courts often restrict their interpretation to the Japanese Constitution, ignoring arguments based on international human rights law.

. . .

(b) *Tendency of the courts to summarily dismiss arguments based on international human rights law*

Japanese courts tend to dismiss arguments based on international human rights law without detailed analysis of their substance. The courts often interpret the Japanese Constitution and then apply the same reasoning to a comparable provision in a human rights treaty. Japanese courts assume that the meaning, scope, and effect of human rights provisions under international human rights law are the same as those under the Japanese Constitution. Accordingly, if a governmental action is found to be lawful under the Japanese Constitution, it is automatically regarded as lawful under international human rights law as well.

. . .

. . . To justify restrictions of human rights, the courts have preferred to rely on the familiar Japanese concept of 'public welfare' rather than the international concepts of 'national security, public order (*ordre public*), public health or morals'. . . .

. . .

(c) *Reluctance of the courts to find violations of international human rights law*

. . . In recent years, more and more individuals and attorneys have come to invoke international human rights law, particularly the International Covenants on Human Rights, before the courts. Yet, the courts have so far applied the ICCPR directly in only a few instances. Occasionally, the courts have used international human rights law as an aid in the interpretation of domestic law to hold in favour of the individual who had invoked it.

. . .

(d) *Japanese courts and the practice of judicial restraint*

. . .

. . . Japanese courts are highly restrained in judicial review and generally reluctant to invalidate legislation on constitutional grounds. Even when Japanese courts sympathize with the plaintiff, they hesitate to find a government action to be unconstitutional, preferring instead to dispose of the case by statutory interpretation. . . .

. . . In the five decades since the enactment of the Constitution, statutes have been found to be unconstitutional on only five occasions.

. . .

2. Revision of Domestic Law in Accordance with International Law

(a) *Revision of domestic law upon ratification of treaties*

Since treaties have the force of law and override domestic laws in Japan, when the Japanese Government decides to enter into a treaty, it makes scrupulous efforts to bring Japanese law into conformity with the treaty. . . . Thus, upon ratification of treaties, Japanese law significantly improves through revision of laws. The most conspicuous such changes have occurred in the area of human rights — in the treatment of aliens and women.

. . .

K.D. EWING, THE HUMAN RIGHTS ACT AND PARLIAMENTARY DEMOCRACY

62 Modern L. Rev. 79 (1999)

The UK Human Rights Act 1998 . . . represents an unprecedented transfer of political power from the executive and legislature to the judiciary, and a fundamental re-structuring of our 'political constitution'. As such it is unquestionably the most significant formal redistribution of political power in this country since 1911, and perhaps since 1688. . . .

. . .

The nature and extent of incorporation

The Human Rights Act 1998 does not incorporate the ECHR into domestic law in the way that the European Communities Act 1972 incorporates the EC Treaty. Rather what it does is to give effect to certain provisions of the Convention and some of its protocols by providing that these so-called 'Convention rights' are to have a defined status in English law. There is no question of the Convention rights in themselves 'becoming part of our substantive domestic law': rather, certain defined provisions of the Convention enjoy a defined legal status. The terms of the Convention which are given effect to in this way by section 1 of the Act are articles 2 to 12 and 14, as well as articles 1 to 3 of the First Protocol and . . . articles 1 and 2 of the Sixth Protocol. The major omissions here are articles 1 and 13 of the Convention, the former providing that 'The High Contracting Parties shall secure to everyone within their jurisdiction the rights and freedoms defined in Section 1 of [the] Convention'; and the latter providing that 'Everyone whose rights and freedoms as set forth in this Convention are violated shall have an effective remedy before a national authority'. There was little objection to the omission of article 1, which was properly excluded on the ground that it was an inter-state obligation.

. . .

In giving effect to Convention rights in this way, by section 2 the Act also directs the courts to have regard to the jurisprudence of the different enforcement and supervisory bodies in Strasbourg. For this purpose the Act refers expressly to the European Court of Human Rights, the European Commission of Human Rights, and the Committee of Ministers. As we have seen, the Commission and the Committee of Ministers will have been abolished or removed from questions of adjudication by the time the Act comes into force, though the jurisprudence of these bodies will continue to be relevant. It is to be noted, however, that the courts are required simply to take into account the jurisprudence of the Strasbourg bodies, but are not bound by it, and that the government rejected an amendment in the Lords which would have imposed the stronger obligation. . . .

. . .

The fact remains that the Convention is meaningful only because of the principles of interpretation developed in the case law, and the decisions on points of substance, issues which are of universal application. As a text the Convention is meaningless without the jurisprudence, as is true of any other legal text: to sever the jurisprudence from the treaty is like severing the limbs from a torso. But whatever the reasons for refusing to be bound by Strasbourg jurisprudence, it should be clear that the nature and extent of judicial power under the Act are greater than may be realised. Convention rights are now free standing and autonomous (even if not 'substantive') rights of British law which the judges are empowered to develop as they wish, guided but unconstrained by the Convention jurisprudence.

...

Statutory interpretation

The first way by which the Convention will impact upon domestic law is through the obligations in respect of statutory interpretation in section 3. This provides that 'so far as possible to do so', both primary legislation and delegated [subordinate, secondary] legislation are to be read and given effect to in a way which is compatible with Convention rights....

... Parliament has also been careful to point out in section 3, however, that the duty of construction which it embraces does not 'affect the validity, continuing operation or enforcement of any incompatible primary legislation'. Nor does it affect the continuing operation or enforcement of any incompatible subordinate legislation 'if primary legislation prevents removal of the incompatibility'.

But what happens if legislation — primary or subordinate — is incompatible with Convention rights, and it is not possible to construe the former to meet the demands of the latter? The answer lies in section 4 which empowers the courts to make a declaration of incompatibility ... [Discussion of secondary legislation omitted.]

The power to grant a declaration of incompatibility is limited to the higher courts.... The duty to construe legislation to comply with Convention rights is one which in contrast is imposed on all courts. The granting of a declaration of incompatibility is discretionary even where a 'mismatch' has been found, and the government resisted an amendment that it should be mandatory. If granted, a declaration of incompatibility has 'no operative or coercive effect', and 'does not prevent either party relying on, or the courts enforcing, the law in question': it does not affect the validity, continuing operation or enforcement of the legislation in question; nor is it binding on the parties in the proceedings in which it is made....

...

Liability of public authorities

The second way by which the Act gives effect to the Convention is by imposing an obligation on public authorities to comply with Convention rights, an obligation which is directly enforceable in the courts. Section 6 provides that it is unlawful for a public authority to act in a way which is incompatible with one or more of the Convention rights, with a 'public authority' being widely defined to include a court; a tribunal which exercises functions in relation to legal proceedings; and any person certain of whose functions are functions of a public nature. The definition is fluid and open ended.... But the intention clearly is that they should apply to central government (including executive agencies), local government, the police, immigration officers, and the prison service, as well as to others. One of the most difficult questions under the Act relates to the inclusion of courts and tribunals within the definition of a public authority. The precise meaning and implications of this are unclear. . . .

According to the Lord Chancellor, the government 'believe that it is right as a matter of principle for the courts to have the duty of acting compatibly with the Convention not only in cases involving other public authorities but also in developing the common law in deciding cases between citizens'. But what does this mean, given the government's belief that 'full horizontal effect' would be 'a step too far in a Bill which . . . is designed to allow the Convention rights to be invoked in this country by people who would have already a case in Strasbourg', and given also the rejection by the Lord Chancellor of the view that the courts will be required to legislate by way of judicial decision 'whenever a law cannot be found either in the statute book or as a rule of common law to protect a convention right'? The answer it seems is that Convention rights may be relied upon in litigation between private parties, but cannot themselves be the basis of a cause of action. So although a worker dismissed for a reason incompatible with the Convention may not sue his or her employer for breach of a Convention right, the worker in question may be able to sue for wrongful dismissal, claiming that a dismissal for a reason incompatible with a Convention right is wrongful.

. . .

Remedial action

As we have seen, section 4 of the Act permits the courts to declare an Act of Parliament to be incompatible with Convention rights, though they are required still to enforce and apply it until such time as the legislation has been amended. The government considered but rejected the option of giving the courts the power to set aside an Act of Parliament believed to be incompatible with Convention rights, 'because of the importance the Government attaches to Parliamentary sovereignty'. The White Paper continues in powerful and convincing terms, as follows:

> In this context, Parliamentary sovereignty means that Parliament is competent to make any law on any matter of its choosing and no court may question the validity of any Act that it passes. In enacting legislation, Parliament is making decisions about important matters of public policy. The authority to make those decisions derives from a democratic mandate because they are elected, accountable and representative.

Concern was expressed that to permit the courts to set aside Acts of Parliament 'would confer on the judiciary a general power over the decisions of Parliament', and 'would be likely on occasions to draw the judiciary into serious conflict with Parliament'. Crucially there 'is no evidence to suggest that they desire this power, nor that the public wish them to have it'.

So why give the courts the power to rule on the compatibility of an Act of Parliament with Convention rights? How can this be reconciled with the authority of the mandate? The answer is that it is open to the government to decide how to deal with the decision of the courts, and to refuse to take steps to remedy the incompatibility if it deems it appropriate to do so. This after all is the position currently with decisions of the European Court of Human Rights which do not change domestic law but require amending legislation, which the government cannot be compelled to introduce and Parliament cannot be compelled to pass. But although these are weighty and logical considerations, we should be careful about distinguishing form from substance, principle from practice. As a matter of constitutional legality, Parliament may well be sovereign, but as a matter of constitutional practice it has transferred significant power to the judiciary.

…

MIRNA E. ADJAMI, AFRICAN COURTS, INTERNATIONAL LAW, AND COMPARATIVE CASE LAW: CHIMERA OR EMERGING HUMAN RIGHTS JURISPRUDENCE?

24 Mich. J. Int. L. 103 (2002)

…

African States inherited the international law frameworks of their colonial powers. Most Francophone African countries that were under French or Belgian colonial rule have adopted a monist view of international law, while Anglophone States of British colonial heritage have embraced the dualist position. Of the national judiciaries examined [here], Nigeria, Tanzania, and Zambia are Anglophone, common law countries that operate under the dualist theory. Botswana and Zimbabwe are also former British colonies with common law legal systems that follow the dualist tradition. Given their particular colonial experience, South Africa and Namibia follow the Roman-Dutch law model, while also adopting an English common law approach to adjudication, including its dualism.

…

… [M]any African courts have overcome the technical obstacle that nonincorporation would normally impose through their use of international human rights instruments as persuasive authority in national court decisions. Indeed, many of the decisions examined in [this Article] include explicit statements to this end. As the Chief Justice declared in one Ghanaian case:

> Ghana is a signatory to this African Charter and Member States of the [OAU] and parties to the Charter are expected to recognize the rights, duties and freedoms enshrined in the Charter and to undertake to adopt legislative and other measures to give effect to the rights and duties. I do not think the fact that Ghana has not passed specific legislation to give effect to the Charter means that the Charter cannot be relied upon.
>
> …

Furthermore, the lack of autochthonous principles in African constitutions presents an obstacle for their societal legitimacy. . . . Although the legal structures of these countries are a legacy of their colonial experience, enforcing human rights through national judiciaries is a move toward more entrenched human rights constitutionalism.

. . . Properly functioning judiciaries that enforce the bills of rights that codify international human rights norms articulate these norms through a national voice that may be accepted as more legitimate. Given the heavy influence of international human rights instruments on the drafting of bills of rights in African countries, when a litigant brings a claim under these provisions and a court enforces them, they are in effect nationalizing international human rights norms.

. . .

The experience of the national courts . . . indicates that thus far, litigants and national courts in Africa have embraced the universalist and internationalist discourse on human rights with fewer cultural hesitations than the staunch proponents of African particularism would predict. This is a striking phenomenon with implications for the future enforcement of human rights in Africa.

. . .

Although only one Justice from an African court attended th[e] first colloquium in Bangalore [see p. 1111, *infra*], subsequent colloquia have involved greater participation from and a greater focus on Africa. In particular, the judicial colloquia in Harare, Zimbabwe in 1989, in Banjul, The Gambia in 1990, in Abuja, Nigeria in 1991, at Balliol College at Oxford in the United Kingdom in 1992, and in Bloemfontein, South Africa in 1993 were attended by numerous justices from common law African countries . . . . [N]ational African courts have cited the Bangalore Principles and other statements from these judicial colloquia as justification for their liberal use of international human rights instruments and comparative jurisprudence in their domestic adjudication.

. . .

Not only do judges have an activist role in advancing human rights in Africa, so too do the lawyers in national legal systems. Lawyers determine when to raise claims under constitutional guarantees of fundamental rights and have the ability to draw international and comparative law parallels in their briefs and arguments before the courts. This encourages judges in the national court systems to take these sources into account in their adjudication.

. . .

. . . The cases studied here come from the Courts of Appeal, High Courts, and Supreme Courts of Botswana, Namibia, Nigeria, South Africa, Tanzania, Zambia, and Zimbabwe.

. . . The parallels between fundamental rights guaranteed in national bills of rights and those enshrined in international instruments have led national judges to look to international human rights instruments and foreign jurisprudence to support their analyses of the scope of fundamental rights in their national context.

. . . First, they used international and comparative sources to support their court's adoption of a particular approach to constitutional and statutory interpretation. Some judges reflected on their role in defining the scope of rights embedded in a national constitution, given the novelty of constitutional interpretation as an exercise for them. For the most part, these judges adopted the purposive approach to constitutional and statutory interpretation, playing an activist role in broadening the scope of the indeterminate language that is used to define fundamental rights. The judges did so consciously as part of an effort to follow the emerging consensus or trends in guaranteeing fundamental rights and join the ranks of judges of "civilized nations."

Second, these courts used international and comparative sources as an interpretive tool to establish the substantive definition of particular rights....

The national judges do not always embrace the universalist discourse on human rights without reservations.... [P]assages from various cases ... display an awareness of the tension between the universalist and particularist views of human rights in Africa ... [including] cases involving women's rights, an area in which rights to equality often come into direct conflict with traditional rules of customary law....

...

African courts' use of international and comparative case law as persuasive authority in their jurisprudence challenges the framework in which traditional scholars of international law and human rights in Africa have foreseen the role of such international norms in the national context.... [T]he traditional model of the status of international law in domestic courts does not account for the actual ways in which international sources and comparative case law have been used in African fundamental rights jurisprudence. Classic dualism of common law systems should serve as a barrier to the invocation of international human rights norms in national courts in Africa. But the courts studied here defy these constraints. Even though litigants before these courts plead their claims in terms of violations of fundamental rights found in their national constitutions, the courts draw parallels to international human rights norms, as expressed in treaties or statements of principles, and the pronouncements of foreign courts regarding these rights in order to determine the scope of their national constitutional guarantees. Most striking is that the courts do so seamlessly, without noting or explaining the binding nature or level of persuasive authority of these international and comparative sources.

...

QUESTIONS

1. It has often been observed that respect for human rights begins and ends at home and that international organizations have little more than a catalytic or intermediary role. On the basis of the preceding descriptions of states' relationships to international human rights norms, how satisfactory have the efforts of each of the states been to ensure that its legal order respects the relevant norms?

2. Is the *de facto* preference for applying domestic constitutional rather than international human rights norms desirable, neutral or dangerous from the perspective of realizing international human rights?

3. Some commentators have suggested that Articles 1 and 13 of the European Convention, taken together, create a legal obligation upon state parties to make the provisions of the

Convention applicable in domestic law. What are arguments for and against such an approach, which stands in clear contradiction to the approach of the UK?

4. Should future international human rights treaties require ratifying states to guarantee the full incorporation in and enforcement by domestic law of their provisions?

5. Compare the approach reflected in the UK Human Rights Act with the statement of the UK Government at p. 979. Are they two versions of the same theme? What do they say about the status in the UK of the debate over state sovereignty and the supremacy of international human rights norms?

NOTE

The preceding readings have focused primarily on the extent to which courts in different states are required to apply international human rights norms in domestic cases. But regardless of any such legal requirements, there are important ways referred to in those readings in which both the judiciary and the executive have a role in giving domestic effect to applicable human rights standards. Beyond the African courts that Mirna Adjami analyzes, Murray Hunt has observed more generally that the international human rights regime has tended, in a variety of ways, to blur the old distinctions between incorporated and unincorporated norms:

> The language of 'incorporation' presupposes a dualist position derived from an uncompromising premise of the sovereignty of Parliament. The question of the domestic status of international law in that binary framework is an 'in/out' question: has the international norm been made 'part of' domestic law or not? The concepts and the language lack the sophistication to capture the more nuanced reality that there are many different ways in which international law may be of relevance to an issue before a domestic court. A norm of international treaty law may not be 'part of' domestic law in the sense that it gives rise to a right or obligation which is directly enforceable in domestic courts and on which individuals may therefore found their case, but, insofar as judicial recourse to it is permitted by the treaty presumption, to assist in the interpretation of domestic statute law, or its customary or near-customary status provides guidance in the development of domestic common law, it is clearly of legal relevance.[5]

This argument could also be extended (although Hunt explicitly does not do so) to ground a presumption that the executive branch of government will not act inconsistently with treaty norms even if domestic law does not formally obligate the executive to apply those standards. This issue is of particular relevance in countries such as the United Kingdom, Australia and New Zealand, which follow a system of legislative incorporation that leaves unclear the status or significance of treaties which have been ratified but have not been given effect in domestic law by legislation.

[5] M. Hunt, *Using Human Rights Law in English Courts* (1998), at 41–42.

The following materials examine some of the difficulties in reaching a general understanding among states of the nature of their obligation to give domestic effect to their treaty commitments.

COMMITTEE ON ECONOMIC, SOCIAL AND CULTURAL RIGHTS, GENERAL COMMENT NO. 9

Domestic Application of the Covenant, UN Doc. E/1999/22, Annex IV, 1998

A. The duty to give effect to the Covenant in the domestic legal order

...

2. [The Covenant requires] each State Party to use *all* the means at its disposal to give effect to the rights recognized in the Covenant .... Thus the norms themselves must be recognised in appropriate ways within the domestic legal order, appropriate means of redress, or remedies, must be available to any aggrieved individual or group, and appropriate means of ensuring governmental accountability must be put in place.

...

B. The status of the Covenant in the domestic legal order

4. In general, legally binding international human rights standards should operate directly and immediately within the domestic legal system of each State party, thereby enabling individuals concerned to seek enforcement of their rights before national courts and tribunals. The rule requiring the exhaustion of domestic remedies reinforces the primacy of national remedies in this respect ....

5. The Covenant itself does not stipulate the specific means by which its terms are to be implemented in the national legal order. And there is no provision obligating its comprehensive incorporation or requiring it to be accorded any specific type of status in national law. Although the precise method by which Covenant rights are given effect in national law is a matter for each State Party to decide, the means used should be appropriate in the sense of producing results which are consistent with the full discharge of its obligations by the State Party. The means chosen are also subject to review as part of the Committee's examination of the State Party's compliance with its Covenant obligations.

...

C. The role of legal remedies

...

11. The Covenant itself does not negate the possibility that the rights may be considered self-executing in systems where that option is provided for. Indeed, when it was being drafted, attempts to include a specific provision in the Covenant providing that it be considered 'non-self-executing' were strongly rejected. In most

States the determination of whether or not a treaty provision is self-executing will be a matter for the courts, not the executive or the legislature. In order to perform that function effectively the relevant courts and tribunals must be made aware of the nature and implications of the Covenant and of the important role of judicial remedies in its implementation.... [W]hen Governments are involved in court proceedings, they should promote interpretations of domestic laws which give effect to their Covenant obligations....

...

D. The treatment of the Covenant in domestic courts

...

13. ... [S]ome courts have applied the provisions of the Covenant either directly or as interpretive standards. Other courts are willing to acknowledge, in principle, the relevance of the Covenant for interpreting domestic law, but in practice, the impact of the Covenant on the reasoning or outcome of cases is very limited. Still other courts have refused to give any degree of legal effect to the Covenant in cases in which individuals have sought to rely on it....

14. Within the limits of the appropriate exercise of their functions of judicial review, courts should take account of Covenant rights where this is necessary to ensure that the State's conduct is consistent with its obligations under the Covenant. Neglect by the courts of this responsibility is incompatible with the principle of the Rule of Law which must always be taken to include respect for international human rights obligations.

...

MICHAEL KIRBY, THE ROLE OF INTERNATIONAL STANDARDS IN AUSTRALIAN COURTS

in P. Alston and M. Chiam (eds.), Treaty-Making and Australia: Globalization versus Sovereignty (1995), at 82

The Bangalore Principles

The traditional view of most common law countries has been that international law is not part of domestic law. Blackstone in his Commentaries, suggested that:

> The law of nations (whenever any question arises which is properly the object of its jurisdiction) is here [in England] adopted in its full extent by the common law, and is held to be part of the law of the land.

Save for the United States, where Blackstone had a profound influence, this view came to be regarded, virtually universally, as being 'without foundation'...

More recently, however, a new recognition has come about of the use that may be made by judges of international human rights principles and their exposition by the courts, tribunals and other bodies established to give them content and effect.

This reflects both the growing body of international human rights law and the instruments, both regional and international, which give effect to that law. It furthermore recognizes the importance of the content of those laws. An expression that seems to encapsulate the modern approach was given [at a meeting among jurists from many states] in February 1988 in Bangalore, India in the so-called *Bangalore Principles.*

The Bangalore Principles state, in effect, that:

(1) International law, whether human rights norms or otherwise, is not, as such, part of domestic law in most common law countries;
(2) Such law does not become part of domestic law until Parliament so enacts or the judges, as another source of law-making, declare the norms thereby established to be part of domestic law;
(3) The judges will not do so automatically, simply because the norm is part of international law or is mentioned in a treaty, even one ratified by their own country;
(4) But if an issue of uncertainty arises, as by a lacuna in the common law, obscurity in its meaning or ambiguity in a relevant statute, a judge may seek guidance in the general principles of international law, as accepted by the community of nations; and
(5) From this source material, the judge may ascertain and declare what the relevant rule of domestic law is. It is the action of the judge, incorporating the rule into domestic law, which makes it part of domestic law.

...

High judicial pronouncements

In the seven years since Bangalore, . . . something of a sea change has come over the approach of courts in Australia, as well as in New Zealand and England.

The clearest indication of the change in Australia can be found in the remarks of Brennan J (with the concurrence of Mason CJ and McHugh J) in *Mabo v Queensland (No 2).* In the course of explaining why a discriminatory doctrine, such as that of *terra nullius* (which refused to recognize the rights and interests in land of the indigenous inhabitants of a settled colony such as Australia) could no longer be accepted as part of the law of Australia, Brennan J said:

> The expectations of the international community accord in this respect with the contemporary values of the Australian people. The opening up of the international remedies to individuals pursuant to Australia's accession to the *Optional Protocol* to the *International Covenant on Civil and Political Rights* brings to bear on the common law the powerful influence of the *Covenant* and the international standards it imports. The common law does not necessarily conform with international law, but international law is a legitimate and important influence on the development of the common law, especially when international law declares the existence of universal human rights.

...

NOTE

Justice Kirby has commented further on the developments noted in his preceding article:[6]

...

> Critics of [these] developments ... list a number of considerations which need to be kept in mind by judges as they venture upon this new source of principle for judicial law-making. The expressed concerns include:
>
> 1. Treaties are typically negotiated by the executive government. They may, or may not, reflect the will of the people as expressed in parliament. . . .
> 2. The processes of ratification are often defective. . . .
> 3. In federal countries, such as Australia, Canada, Malaysia, and others, special concern may be expressed that the ratification of international treaties could be used as a means to undermine the constitutional distribution of powers. . . .
> 4. Judicial introduction of human rights norms may sometimes divert the community from the more open, principled and democratic adoption of such norms in constitutional or statutory amendments which have the legitimacy of popular endorsement.
> 5. Some commentators have also expressed scepticism about the international courts, tribunals and committees which pronounce upon human rights. They argue that often they are composed of persons from legal regimes very different from our own.
> 6. To similar effect, critics have pointed to the broad generality of the expression of the provisions contained in international human rights instruments. Of necessity, these are expressed in language that lacks precision. This means that those who use them may be tempted to read into their broad language what they hope, expect or want to see. Whilst the judge of the common law tradition has a creative role, such creativity must be in the minor key. The judge must proceed in a judicial way. He or she must not undermine the primacy of democratic law-making by the organs of government directly or indirectly accountable to the people.
> 7. Finally, some critics warn against undue, premature undermining of the sovereignty of a State by judicial *fiat* without the authority of the State's democratically accountable law-makers. The latter is, generally, the proper institution to develop human rights in the State's own way.
>
> ...

MINISTER OF STATE FOR IMMIGRATION AND ETHNIC AFFAIRS V. AH HIN TEOH

High Court of Australia, 1995 183 CLR 273

[Mr Teoh, a Malaysian citizen, entered Australia in May 1988 on a temporary entry permit. In July he married an Australian citizen who had been the *de facto* spouse of

[6] 'Domestic Implementation of Human Rights Norms', 5 Aust. J. Hum. Rts. 109 (1999), at 119.

his deceased brother. In November 1990 he was convicted on charges of heroin importation and possession and sentenced to six years' imprisonment. The offences were clearly related to Mrs Teoh's heroin addiction. In 1991 Teoh was ordered to be deported on the ground that he had committed a serious crime. At that time Mrs Teoh had six of her children living with her, all under ten years old, and three of them had been fathered by Teoh. The deportation order was appealed to the Federal Court, which upheld the appeal partly on the grounds that the requirement in the Convention on the Rights of the Child, that the child's best interests be considered in such matters, had not been taken into account. The Minister appealed that decision to the High Court.]

MASON CJ AND DEANE J:

...

25. It is well established that the provisions of an international treaty to which Australia is a party do not form part of Australian law unless those provisions have been validly incorporated into our municipal law by statute....

26. But the fact that the Convention [on the Rights of the Child] has not been incorporated into Australian law does not mean that its ratification holds no significance for Australian law. Where a statute or subordinate legislation is ambiguous, the courts should favour that construction which accords with Australia's obligations under a treaty or international convention to which Australia is a party, at least in those cases in which the legislation is enacted after, or in contemplation of, entry into, or ratification of, the relevant international instrument. That is because Parliament, *prima facie*, intends to give effect to Australia's obligations under international law.

27. ...If the language of the legislation is susceptible of a construction which is consistent with the terms of the international instrument and the obligations which it imposes on Australia, then that construction should prevail. So expressed, the principle is no more than a canon of construction and does not import the terms of the treaty or convention into our municipal law as a source of individual rights and obligations.

28. Apart from influencing the construction of a statute or subordinate legislation, an international convention may play a part in the development by the courts of the common law. The provisions of an international convention to which Australia is a party, especially one which declares universal fundamental rights, may be used by the courts as a legitimate guide in developing the common law. But the courts should act in this fashion with due circumspection when the Parliament itself has not seen fit to incorporate the provisions of a convention into our domestic law. Judicial development of the common law must not be seen as a backdoor means of importing an unincorporated convention into Australian law. A cautious approach ... would be consistent with the approach which the courts have hitherto adopted....

...

34. ...[R]atification by Australia of an international convention ... is a positive statement by the executive government of this country to the world and to the Australian people that the executive government and its agencies will act in accordance

with the Convention. That positive statement is an adequate foundation for a legitimate expectation, absent statutory or executive indications to the contrary, that administrative decision-makers will act in conformity with the Convention and treat the best interests of the children as 'a primary consideration'....

...

36. ... To regard a legitimate expectation as requiring the decision-maker to act in a particular way is tantamount to treating it as a rule of law. It incorporates the provisions of the unincorporated convention into our municipal law by the back door....

37. But, if a decision-maker proposes to make a decision inconsistent with a legitimate expectation, procedural fairness requires that the persons affected should be given notice and an adequate opportunity of presenting a case against the taking of such a course.

...

TOOHEY J:

...

27. In *Reg. v. Home Secretary; Ex parte Brind* the House of Lords rejected the broad proposition that the Secretary of State should exercise a statutory discretion in accordance with the terms of the [ECHR], which was not part of English domestic law. That decision was considered by the New Zealand Court of Appeal in *Tavita v. Minister of Immigration* where a deportee argued that those concerned with ordering his deportation were bound to take into account the Convention and the [ICCPR], both of which had been ratified by New Zealand. In the end the Court did not have to determine the point. But it said of the contrary proposition: 'That is an unattractive argument, apparently implying that New Zealand's adherence to the international instruments has been at least partly window-dressing ... there must at least be hesitation about accepting it'.

...

MCHUGH J:

...

37. ... The people of Australia may note the commitments of Australia in international law, but, by ratifying the Convention, the Executive government does not give undertakings to its citizens or residents. The undertakings in the Convention are given to the other parties to the Convention. How, when or where those undertakings will be given force in Australia is a matter for the federal Parliament....

38. If the result of ratifying an international convention was to give rise to a legitimate expectation that that convention would be applied in Australia, the Executive ... would have effectively amended the law of this country. ... The consequences for administrative decision-making in this country would be enormous.... Australia is a party to about 900 treaties. Only a small percentage of them has been enacted into law. Administrative decision-makers would have to ensure that their decision-making complied with every relevant convention or inform a person affected that they would not be complying with those conventions.

39. I do not think that it is reasonable to expect that public officials will comply with the terms of conventions which they have no obligation to apply or consider merely because the federal government has ratified them. . . . Total compliance with the terms of a convention may require many years of effort, education and expenditure of resources. For these and similar reasons, the parties to a convention will often regard its provisions as goals to be implemented over a period of time rather than mandates calling for immediate compliance. . . .

NOTE

In a more recent decision, *Re Minister for Immigration and Multicultural Affairs: Ex parte Lam* (2003) 214 C.L.R. 1, various Justices on the Australian High Court indicated that they were inclined to overrule *Teoh*. Justices McHugh and Gummow stated, 'An aspect of the rule of law under the Constitution is that the role or function of [Chapter] III courts does not extend to the performance of the legislative function of translating policy into statutory form or the executive function of administration. . . . If *Teoh* is to have continued significance at a general level for the principles which inform the relationship between international obligations and the domestic constitutional structure, then further attention will be required to the basis upon which *Teoh* rests'. Justice Callinan stated, '[T]he view is open that for the Court to give the effect to the Convention that it did, was to elevate the Executive above the parliament. This in my opinion is the important question rather than whether the Executive act of ratification is, or is not to be described as platitudinous or ineffectual. Whatever may be the current utility or status of the doctrine of "legitimate expectation", I agree with McHugh and Gummow JJ, for the reasons that their Honours give, that on no view can it give rise to substantive rights rather than to procedural rights'. Justice Hayne helped explain the context of *Teoh*:

> Legitimate expectation is a phrase which, although used in administrative law for more than 30 years . . .
>
> [L]ater, however, the phrase legitimate expectation has come to be used in very different ways. Instead of being used to describe why procedural fairness should be afforded to a person it has sometimes been used to refer to what matters the decision-maker should take into account in making a decision or, in England, to what decision the decision-maker should reach. This last development, said to engage concepts of abuse of power, directs attention to whether a person has a legitimate expectation of a benefit which is substantive rather than merely procedural and to whether to frustrate that expectation is unfair.
>
> I was not suggested that principles of this last-mentioned kind had any application in this case. . . . I mention this use of the phrase legitimate expectation in connection with substantive rather than procedural benefits only to emphasise the dangers of using the phrase without careful articulation of the content of the principle which is said to be engaged in the particular case.
>
> . . . [In *Teoh*, the] legitimate expectation identified was an expectation about what would be taken into account in reaching a decision.

ILLUSTRATIONS OF NATIONAL EXECUTIVE VIEWS ABOUT METHODS OF COMPLIANCE

(1) In direct response to the *Teoh* judgment the Australian Government issued a statement. While opposition in the Senate to the statement prevented its enactment into law, it is nonetheless of obvious importance for administrative law. It reads:[7]

> (3) . . . The High Court in the *Teoh* case . . . gave treaties an effect in Australian law . . . which they did not previously have. The Government is of the view that this development is not consistent with the proper role of Parliament in implementing treaties in Australian law. . . . It is for Australian parliaments . . . to change Australian law to implement treaty obligations.
>
> (4) The purpose of this statement is to ensure that the executive act of entering into a treaty does not give rise to legitimate expectations in administrative law.
>
> (5) . . . The prospect was left open by the *Teoh* case of decisions being challenged on the basis of a failure sufficiently to advert to relevant international obligations including where the decision-maker and person affected had no knowledge of the relevant obligation at the time of the decision. This is not conducive to good administration.
>
> (6) Therefore, we indicate on behalf of the Government that the act of entering into a treaty does not give rise to legitimate expectations in administrative law which could form the basis for challenging any administrative decision made from today. This is a clear expression by the Executive Government of the Commonwealth of a contrary indication referred to by the majority of the High Court in the *Teoh* case.
>
> . . .

(2) Consider the following problem about international human rights and federalism. In February 2000, a 15-year-old Aboriginal boy in the Northern Territory of Australia committed suicide in his prison cell. He had been jailed for 28 days for stealing pencils and stationery and breaking a window, under Territory legislation which mandates imprisonment for property offences. In 1997 the UN Committee on the Rights of the Child expressed concern at the legislation and suggested that it was inconsistent with Article 37(b) of the Convention, which requires that detention of a child should only be 'used as a measure of last resort'. The issue was complicated by the reluctance of Australia's Federal Government to use its powers to overrule criminal laws adopted by the Territory legislature. When asked about Australia's compliance with its treaty obligations, Prime Minister John Howard replied:[8]

> Australia decides what happens in this country through the laws and the parliaments of Australia. I mean in the end we are not told what to do by anybody. We make our own moral judgments. . . . Australia's human rights reputation compared with the rest of the world is quite magnificent. We've had our blemishes

[7] Joint Statement, The Minister for Foreign Affairs and the Attorney-General and Minister for Justice: http://law.gov.au/aghome/agnews/1997news/attachjs.htm, 25 February 1997.

[8] See www.pm.gov.au/media/pressrel/2000/AM1802.htm, 18 February 2000.

and we've made our errors and I'm not saying we're perfect. But I'm not going to cop this country's human rights name being tarnished in the context of a domestic political argument. Now this is a difficult issue. Traditionally these matters are the prerogative of States. And if you have Federal governments seeking to overturn laws of this kind you really are remaking the rule book.

(3) Compare the following 1998 Presidential Executive Order in the United States:[9]

By the authority vested in me as President . . . it is hereby ordered as follows:

Sec. 1. Implementation of Human Rights Obligations.

(a) It shall be the policy and practice of the Government of the United States, . . . fully to respect and implement its obligations under the international human rights treaties to which it is a party, including the ICCPR, the CAT, and the CERD. . . .

Sec. 2. Responsibility of Executive Departments and Agencies.

(a) All executive departments and agencies . . . shall maintain a current awareness of United States international human rights obligations that are relevant to their functions and shall perform such functions so as to respect and implement those obligations fully. . . .

Sec. 3. Human Rights Inquiries and Complaints.

Each agency shall take lead responsibility, in coordination with other appropriate agencies, for responding to inquiries, requests for information, and complaints about violations of human rights obligations that fall within its areas of responsibility. . . .

. . .

Sec. 6. Judicial Review, Scope, and Administration.

(a) Nothing in this order shall create any right or benefit, substantive or procedural, enforceable by any party against the United States, its agencies or instrumentalities, its officers or employees, or any other person.
(b) This order does not supersede Federal statutes and does not impose any justiciable obligations on the executive branch.
(c) The term "treaty obligations" shall mean treaty obligations as approved by the Senate pursuant to Article II, section 2, clause 2 of the United States Constitution.
(d) To the maximum extent practicable and subject to the availability of appropriations, agencies shall carry out the provisions of this order.

[9] US Executive Order 13107 on Implementation of Human Rights Treaties, Federal Register, 15 December 1998, Vol. 63, No. 240, pp. 68991–93.

QUESTIONS

1. To what extent does the Economic, Social and Cultural Rights Committee's General Comment go beyond the position about international law's requirements for state incorporation described by Leary at p. 1095, *supra*? How would you justify its position?

2. How would you respond to the concerns enumerated by Justice Kirby about the approach reflected in the Bangalore Principles?

3. Do the political and administrative consequences of the *Teoh* decision go beyond what can reasonably be expected of a state party to a human rights treaty? What are the implications of the Government's subsequent 'Joint Statement'?

4. Should the approach reflected in the US Executive Order be the norm for all states? Does it matter that, in ratifying various international human rights treaties, the US Government has declared that it considers the substantive provisions to be non-self-executing and thus unable to be invoked by US courts to decide cases?

5. As a member of the Committee on the Rights of the Child, how would you respond to the statement by the Australian Prime Minister, bearing in mind the sensitivity of federal-state issues in countries such as Canada, the United States and Australia?

ADDITIONAL READING

H. Knop, 'Here and There: International Law in Domestic Courts,' 32 N.Y.U. J. Int. L. & Pol. 501 (2000); J. Doyle and B. Wells, 'How Far Can the Common Law Go in Protecting Human Rights?', in P. Alston (ed.), *Promoting Human Rights Through Bills of Rights* (1999), at 17; T. Schweisfurth and R. Alleweldt, 'The Position of International Law in the Domestic Legal Orders of Central and Eastern European Countries', in 40 German Yearbook of International Law 164 (1997); E. Stein, 'International Law in Internal Law: Toward Internationalisation of Central-Eastern European Constitutions', 88 Am. J. Int. L. 427 (1994); E. Benvenisti, 'The Influence of International Human Rights Law on the Israeli Legal System: Present and Future', 28 Israel L. Rev. 136 (1994); K. Port, 'The Japanese International Law "Revolution": International Human Rights Law and its Impact in Japan', 28 Stanford J. of Int. L. 139 (1991).

COMMENT ON TREATIES IN THE UNITED STATES

Read the references to 'treaties' in the following provisions of the US Constitution: Article I, Section 10; Article II, Section 2; Article III, Section 2; and Article VI. The term 'treaty' has a special constitutional significance in the United States. The following materials speak of *treaties* in this constitutional sense, as opposed to another form of international agreement (so-called 'executive agreements') into which the

United States enters. The information below complements the Comment on Treaties at p. 106, *supra*, which describes treaties from an international law rather than national perspective.

The conclusion of a treaty binding on the United States normally involves three stages. (1) Negotiation of the treaty is usually conducted by an agent of the Executive, although members of the Senate have occasionally been brought into the process at an early stage as observers and advisers. (2) The President submits the treaty to the Senate for the advice and consent required by Article II, Section 2. If the treaty fails to receive the required two-thirds vote of those present, no further action may be taken on it. If it receives that vote, the President may ratify it. (3) Ratification takes place by an exchange of instruments or, in the case of multilateral agreements, by deposit with a designated depositary. The President then proclaims the treaty, making it a matter of public notice and often effective as of that time.

Of course, the United States has had to resolve the same issues as other countries about the internal status and effect of treaties. Constitutional decisions have brought reasonably clear answers to some basic questions. For example, treaties that have become part of the internal legal order have the same domestic effect as federal statutes. A treaty thus supersedes earlier inconsistent legislation. Just as a statute can be superseded by a later inconsistent statute, so can a treaty be superseded, although maxims of interpretation encourage a judicial effort to construe the later-in-time statute so as not to violate the treaty. If that effort fails, the legislative rule prevails internally, although as a matter of international law the United States has broken its obligations to the other treaty party.

Perhaps one of the most important questions about a treaty effective as domestic law is its status *vis-à-vis* the Constitution. Will a treaty provision — perhaps one requiring a government to ban certain types of 'hate' speech — be given effect internally even if legislation to the same effect that was independent of any treaty commitment would be judged to be unconstitutional? In *Reid v. Covert*, the U.S. Supreme Court rejected such a proposition. The Court held that civilian dependents of members of the armed forces overseas could not constitutionally be tried by a court-martial in time of peace for capital offences. The Fifth and Sixth Amendment, according to the Court, prohibited these military trials. At the time, an agreement between the United States and the United Kingdom permitted the trials. Justice Black stated emphatically, 'It would be manifestly contrary to the objectives of those who created the Constitution, as well as those who were responsible for the Bill of Rights — let alone alien to our entire constitutional history and tradition — to construe Article VI as permitting the United States to exercise power under an international agreement without observing constitutional prohibitions. . . . This Court has regularly and uniformly recognized the supremacy of the Constitution over a treaty'.

Self-executing treaties

A question that frequently arises in the United States, as in the European states earlier examined, is whether a treaty is 'self-executing', in the sense that it creates rights and obligations for individuals that are enforceable in the courts without legislative implementation of the treaty. The concept of 'self-executing' is close to the concept of 'automatic incorporation' in the excerpts from Virginia Leary, p. 1095, *supra*.

Each country here faces distinct problems. In the United States, the answer to the question posed is bound up in constitutional text and in the allocation of powers over treaties among the Executive Branch, the Senate and the Congress as a whole. For example, note the status of 'supreme law' that is accorded the treaty under Article VI of the Constitution (the Supremacy Clause), and the relationship of that clause to the self-executing character of treaties.

Consider the following excerpts from Section 111 of the *Restatement (Third), Foreign Relations Law of the United States* (1987):

> (3) Courts in the United States are bound to give effect to international law and to international agreements of the United States, except that a 'non-self-executing' agreement will not be given effect as law in the absence of necessary implementation.
> (4) An international agreement of the United States is 'non-self-executing' (a) if the agreement manifests an intention that it shall not become effective as domestic law without the enactment of implementing legislation, (b) if the Senate in giving consent to a treaty, or Congress by resolution, requires implementing legislation, or (c) if implementing legislation is constitutionally required.

Comment (h) to Section 111 provides:

> In the absence of special agreement, it is ordinarily for the United States to provide how it will carry out its international obligations. Accordingly, the intention of the United States determines whether an agreement is to be self-executing in the United States or should await implementation by legislation or by appropriate executive or administrative action. If the international agreement is silent as to its self-executing character and the intention of the United States is unclear, account must be taken of… any expression by the Senate or by Congress in dealing with the agreement.
> … Whether an agreement is to be given effect without further legislation is an issue that a court must decide when a party seeks to invoke the agreement as law…. Some provisions of an international agreement may be self-executing and others non-self-executing. If an international agreement or one of its provisions is non-self-executing, the United States is under an international obligation to adjust its laws and institutions as may be necessary to give effect to the agreement.

Certain types of treaties have traditionally been understood to be self-executing and have been applied by courts without any implementing legislation. Consider bilateral treaties giving (reciprocally) rights to nationals of each party to establish residence for certain purposes in the territory of the other party, establish corporations, conduct business there, and so on, frequently on national-treatment terms. Courts have long entertained actions by nationals of a treaty party seeking to enforce one or another of the rights provided for in the treaty.

Under US law (as developed through constitutional decisions of the courts), certain types of treaties cannot be self-executing but require implementing legislation to have domestic effects. Note Section 111(4)(c) above of the *Restatement*. For example, a treaty obligating the United States to make certain conduct criminal, even if it closely defined that conduct and stated its penalty, would nonetheless require such legislation. A treaty obligating the United States to pay funds to another state may require an appropriation of funds by the Congress.

Generally it is not relevant from an international law perspective whether a treaty is self-executing, since a state is obligated under international law to do whatever may be required under its internal law (such as legislative enactment) to fulfil its treaty commitments. The state can follow either path.

The question of the attributes of a self-executing treaty has assumed a new prominence in recent years through a number of human rights treaties ratified by the United States — the ICCPR, for example — that were approved by the Senate and ratified subject to a declaration that the treaties were not self-executing. The terms of the declaration have varied among treaties. The precise effect of some of these declarations on courts remains a matter of dispute — for example, whether the treaty could be invoked defensively by a defendant in a prosecution, even if it could not be used by a plaintiff as the foundation for an action. See p. 1142, *infra*.

QUESTIONS

1. What advantages do you see in the UK system (legislation) and in the US system (self-executing treaties) for giving treaty provisions internal effect? If you were drafting the US Constitution anew, which of the constitutional arrangements in the prior readings for giving treaties internal effect would you select?

2. What relation do you see between the conception of self-executing treaties in the United States and the provision of Article VI of the Constitution that treaties consistent with the Constitution form part of the 'supreme law' of the land?

3. 'The path of self-executing treaty can frustrate fundamental democratic principles. It would be satisfactory if the House of Representatives, the more popular and representative House in Congress, participated in giving consent to ratification, but only the Senate does. If two-thirds of that body will go along with treaty provisions that might bring about deep internal change in U.S. law, the treaty has the force of "supreme law". But there has been no full legislative process and debate, and that's not how laws should be made in the U.S.' Comment. Can you give realistic illustrations for the argument made? Are they apt to be common in treaty making?

ADDITIONAL READING

L. Henkin, *Foreign Affairs and the United States Constitution* (2nd edn. 1996); H. Koh, 'Why Do Nations Obey International Law?', 106 Yale L. J. 2599 (1997); D. Sloss, 'The Domestication of International Human Rights', 24 Yale J. Int. L. 129 (1999); K. Starmer, *European Human Rights Law: The Human Rights Act 1998 and the European Convention on Human Rights* (1999); D. Kinley (ed.), *Human Rights in Australian Law* (1968).

COMMENT ON NATIONAL HUMAN RIGHTS INSTITUTIONS

An important development over the last two decades is the emergence of national human rights institutions (NHRIs). NHRIs include governmental bodies such as national human rights commissions and human rights ombudsmen. These institutions are generally tasked with addressing a range of human rights issues — including civil and political as well as economic and social rights. In 1991, the UN convened an international workshop in Paris to review existing NHRIs, with an eye towards establishing normative standards on the role, composition, status and function of these bodies. The resulting standards, the so-called 'Paris Principles', were adopted by the General Assembly in 1993 (A/RES/48/134). The Office of the High Commissioner for Human Rights played an instrumental role in helping establish NHRIs over the course of the next several years.

Since the early 1990s, upwards of a hundred NHRIs have been established in such diverse countries as Argentina, Australia, India, Indonesia, Ireland, Kenya, Mexico, Morocco, Nepal, Nigeria, the Philippines and South Africa. One commentator notes the recognition and spread of NHRIs:[10]

> In addition to the general recommendations, the UN treaty bodies have underlined the role of national institutions when dealing with the reports of individual governments. This tendency has clearly gained momentum since the late 1990s and can, of course, be partly explained by the growth of the number of national institutions worldwide. However, there is no doubt that a role has also been played by the independent experts who have become more familiar with the concept of national institutions and have understood the great potential of such institutions in the national implementation of UN human rights treaties. For instance, the CRC and the CESCR have systematically started to refer to the Paris Principles in their concluding observations and encouraged States Parties to create national institutions that comply with these standards....
>
> Since the end of the 1990s, UN special rapporteurs and representatives have also attached growing importance to national institutions and to the Paris Principles. Although it seems that the endorsement of national institutions has not yet become as central part to the work of extraconventional mechanisms as it has become within treaty monitoring bodies, it is evident that the idea is gaining ground....
>
> The fact that the Paris Principles have become widely known in the past ten years and are now accepted as a benchmark for governmental human rights bodies implies that the concept of national human rights institutions has become something of a "norm". To use theoretical terms, the critical threshold of acceptance, which was reached already ... in 1993, has gradually led to such a broad acceptance of the concept of national institutions that, by the late 1990s, such institutions are almost taken for granted. As one observer concludes, "[t]he creation of National Human Rights Institutions is viewed as an important governmental step in becoming a legitimate member of the international community". It could be argued that the influence of the concept of national institution has

[10] Anna-Elina Pohjolainen, *The Evolution of National Human Rights Institution* (The Danish Institute for Human Rights 2006), at 12–13, http://www.nhri.net/pdf/Evolution_of_NHRIs.pdf.

> been particularly strong on post-authoritarian and emerging democracies, which have modified their national structures in accordance with international values and principles in the 1990s and have therefore often resorted to external sources for appropriate institutional models.

The formal power and practices of NHRIs can include a range of activities such as receiving and adjudicating complaints, auditing proposed legislation, training public officials, undertaking education campaigns, and encouraging ratification of treaties. These institutions are often uniquely situated. They work at the boundary of international and domestic legal orders and operate in the space between governments and civil society. In other words, these institutions can often contribute to the reception of global human rights norms into domestic legal and cultural systems. NHRIs, however, require sufficient political and financial support as well as confidence of the public to be effective.

The study by Christof Heyns and Frans Viljoen, which began this section, suggests NHRIs should assume greater responsibility in interfacing with the work of treaty bodies, see p. 1094, *supra*. Importantly two of the most recent human rights instruments envisage a role for national institutions: the Optional Protocol to the Convention Against Torture (Art. 18(4)) and the Convention on the Rights of Persons with Disabilities (Art. 33).

B. CONDITIONING CONSENT: RATIFICATION WITH RESERVATIONS

Article 2(1)(d) of the Vienna Convention on the Law of Treaties defines a reservation as 'a unilateral statement' made by a state when ratifying a treaty 'whereby it purports to exclude or to modify the legal effect of certain provisions of the treaty in their application to that State'. Article 19 provides that a state ratifying a treaty may make a reservation unless it is 'prohibited by the treaty' or 'is incompatible with the object and purpose of the treaty'. Section 313 of the *Restatement (Third), Foreign Relations Law of the United States* (1987), is to the same effect. Comment (g) to Section 313 refers to the terms *declaration* and *understanding*.

> When signing or adhering to an international agreement, a state may make a unilateral declaration that does not purport to be a reservation. Whatever it is called, it constitutes a reservation in fact if it purports to exclude, limit, or modify the state's legal obligation. Sometimes, however, a declaration purports to be an 'understanding', an interpretation of the agreement in a particular respect. Such an interpretive declaration is not a reservation if it reflects the accepted view of the agreement. But another contracting party may challenge the expressed understanding, treating it as a reservation which it is not prepared to accept.

The International Court of Justice addressed the question of the effect of reservations to a multilateral human rights treaty in its 1951 advisory opinion on *Reservations to the Genocide Convention*,[11] which influenced the Vienna Convention's provisions above. The principal questions put to the I.C.J. by the UN General Assembly were whether a reserving state could be regarded as a party to the Genocide Convention if its reservation was objected to by one or more existing parties but not by others, and, if so, what effect the reservation then had between the reserving state and the accepting or rejecting parties.

In responding to those questions,[12] the Court addressed the 'traditional concept . . . that no reservation was valid unless it was accepted by all the contracting parties without exception. . . .' In the context of the Genocide Convention, the Court found it 'proper' to take into account circumstances leading to 'a more flexible application of this principle'. It emphasized the universal character and aspiration of multilateral human rights treaties. Widespread ratifications had 'already given rise to greater flexibility in the international practice' concerning them.

After concluding that the Genocide Convention (whose provisions were silent on the issue of reservations) permitted a state to enter a reservation, the Court considered 'what kind of reservations may be made and what kind of objections may be taken to them'. It underscored the special character of the Convention, which was 'manifestly adopted for a purely humanitarian and civilizing purpose.' In such a convention the contracting states have a common interest in the 'accomplishment of those high purposes which are the *raison d'être* of the convention'. In such circumstances, one cannot 'speak of individual advantages or disadvantages to States, or of the maintenance of a perfect contractual balance between rights and duties'. Permitting any one state that objected to another state's reservation to block adherence to the convention by the reserving state would frustrate the Convention's goal of universal membership.

On the other hand, the Court could not accept the argument that 'any State entitled to become a party to the Genocide Convention may do so while making any reservation it chooses by virtue of its sovereignty'. It followed that 'it is the compatibility of a reservation with the object and purpose of the Convention that must furnish the criterion for the attitude of a State in making the reservation on accession as well as for the appraisal by a State in objecting to the reservation'.

COMMENT ON RESERVATIONS TO CEDAW

The high number of reservations that have accompanied ratification of CEDAW have become a regrettably notorious feature of the Convention, which is in this respect first among the human rights treaties. By way of contrast, few states have entered reservations to the Convention on Racial Discrimination. Moreover, many of the CEDAW reservations are directed to fundamental provisions.

[11] Advisory Opinion, 1951 I.C.J. 15.

[12] The Court concluded (1) that a state whose reservation has been objected to by one or more parties but not by others can be regarded as a party to the Convention 'if the reservation is compatible with the object and purposes of the Convention', and (2) that a state party objecting to a reservation that it views as incompatible with the Convention can consider the reserving state not to be a party.

Unlike the ICCPR, which is silent on the issue, CEDAW addresses reservations in Article 28(2), which prohibits those incompatible with the 'object and purpose' of the Convention. Tolerance of reservations has been urged on various grounds—for example, the desirability of securing widespread participation in treaties serving a 'purely humanitarian and civilizing purpose' (in the words of the *Genocide Convention* advisory opinion), and hence the reluctance to view a ratification as invalid because of its reservations. A commentator suggests another ground:[13]

> Most states are apprehensive about the possible consequences of accepting a human rights treaty, not least because such treaties may have a dynamic force and interpretation of their scope and impact is less certain that that of commercial treaties.... Reservations are seen to offer an assurance that the state can protect its interest to the fullest extent possible.

Other commentators have considered reservations to Article 2 of CEDAW to be 'manifestly incompatible' with the object and purpose of the Convention.[14] As noted below, several state parties have objected to these reservations on the ground that they threaten the integrity of the Convention and the human rights regime in general. Reservations that purport to be consistent with Article 28(2) of CEDAW raise issues of religious intolerance and of cultural relativism. The net result, claims one commentator, has been the diffuse and widespread view that international obligations assumed through the ratification of CEDAW are somehow 'separate and distinct' from and less binding than those of other human rights treaties.[15]

Consider the following suggestions of Rebecca Cook about criteria for distinguishing between reservations that are compatible and incompatible with the Convention:[16]

> The thesis of this article is that the object and purpose of the Women's Convention are that states parties shall move progressively towards elimination of all forms of discrimination against women and ensure equality between men and women. Further, states parties have an obligation to provide the means to move progressively toward[s] this result. Although the Women's Convention envisions that states parties shall move progressively towards elimination of all forms of discrimination against women and ensure equality between men and women, reservations to the Convention's substantive provisions pose a threat to the achievement of this goal... Accordingly, reservations that contemplate the provision of means towards the pursuit of this goal will be regarded as compatible with 'the object and purpose of the treaty' as provided by article 28(2) of the Women's Convention and article 19(c) of the Vienna Convention. Similarly, any reservation that contemplates enduring inconsistency between state law or practice and the

[13] Rebecca Cook, 'Reservations to the Convention on the Elimination of All Forms of Discrimination against Women', 30 Va. J. Int. L. 643, 650 (1990).

[14] Belinda Clark, 'The Vienna Convention Reservations Regime and the Convention on Discrimination against Women', 85 Am J. Int. L. 281 (1991).

[15] Ibid.

[16] Rebecca Cook, n. 13, *supra*, at 648.

obligations of the Women's Convention is incompatible with the treaty's object and purpose.

Recall the reservations recommended by the US Senate Foreign Relations Committee with respect to the potential US ratification of CEDAW, p. 210, *supra*. As of January 2007, 61 states parties had entered reservations or declarations to the Convention (though some of these reservations were simply to Article 29 providing for arbitration and adjudication by the ICJ). Twenty-one states had registered one or more objections to other states' reservations. Selected illustrations of reservations from several states, as well as a characteristic objection by another state party, appear below.[17]

Austria

Austria reserves its right to apply the provision of article 7(b) as far as service in the armed forces is concerned, and the provision of article 11 as far as night work of women and special protection of working women is concerned, within the limits established by national legislation.

Bangladesh (subsequently withdrawn with respect to Articles 13(a); 16(1)(c) and (f))

The Government of the People's Republic of Bangladesh does not consider as binding upon itself the provisions of articles 2, 13(a) and 16(1)(c) and (f) as they conflict with Shariah law based on Holy Koran and Sunna.

Belgium (subsequently withdrawn)

The application of article 7 shall not affect the validity of the provisions of the Constitution ... which reserves for men the exercise of royal powers ...

Brazil (subsequently withdrawn)

The Government of the Federative Republic of Brazil hereby expresses its reservations to article 15, paragraph 4, and to article 16, paragraph 1(a),(c),(g) and (f)....

Egypt

Reservation to the text of article 9, paragraph 2, concerning the granting to women of equal rights with men with respect to the nationality of their children, without prejudice to the acquisition by a child born of a marriage of the nationality of his father. ... It is clear that the child's acquisition of his father's nationality is the procedure most

[17] The full text of all reservations etc. is available on the UN website at http://www. un.org/womenwatch/daw/cedaw/reservations.htm. Note that the reservations listed above made by Bangladesh in relation to Arts. 13(a) and 16(1)(c) and (f), and those made by Belgium and Brazil, have all subsequently been withdrawn.

suitable for the child and that this does not infringe upon the principle of equality between men and women, since it is customary for a woman to agree, upon marrying an alien, that her children shall be of the father's nationality.

Reservation to the text of article 16 concerning the equality of men and women in all matters relating to marriage and family relations during the marriage and upon its dissolution, without prejudice to the Islamic Shariah provisions whereby women are accorded rights equivalent to those of their spouses so as to ensure a just balance between them. This is out of respect for the sacrosanct nature of the firm religious beliefs which govern marital relations in Egypt and which may not be called in question and in view of the fact that one of the most important bases of these relations is an equivalency of rights and duties so as to ensure complementarity which guarantees true equality between the spouses, not a quasi-equality that renders the marriage a burden on the wife. . . . The provisions of the Shariah lay down that the husband shall pay bridal money to the wife and maintain her fully and shall also make a payment to her upon divorce, whereas the wife retains full rights over her property and is not obliged to spend anything on her keep. The Shariah therefore restricts the wife's rights to divorce by making it contingent on a judge's ruling, whereas no such restriction is laid down in the case of the husband.

The Arab Republic of Egypt is willing to comply with the content of [Art. 2], provided that such compliance does not run counter to the Islamic Shariah.

France

The Government of the French Republic declares that no provision of the Convention must be interpreted as prevailing over provisions of French legislation which are more favourable to women than to men.

Ireland

[Re Art. 16(1)(d) and (f)] Ireland is of the view that the attainment in Ireland of the objectives of the Convention does not necessitate the extension to men of rights identical to those accorded to women in respect of the guardianship, adoption and custody of children born out of wedlock and reserves the right to implement the Convention subject to that understanding.

Malta

The Government of Malta does not consider itself bound by subparagraph (e) of Article 16, insofar as the same may be interpreted as imposing an obligation on Malta to legalize abortion.

Oman

Reservations:

1. All provisions of the Convention not in accordance with the provisions of the Islamic sharia and legislation in force in the Sultanate of Oman;

2. Article 9, paragraph 2, which provides that States Parties shall grant women equal rights with men with respect to the nationality of their children;

3. Article 15, paragraph 4, which provides that States Parties shall accord to men and women the same rights with regard to the law relating to the movement of persons and the freedom to choose their residence and domicile;

4. Article 16, regarding the equality of men and women, and in particular subparagraphs (a), (c), and (f) (regarding adoption).

...

Singapore

In the context of Singapore's multi-racial and multi-religious society and the need to respect the freedom of minorities to practise their religious and personal laws, the Republic of Singapore reserves the right not to apply the provisions of articles 2 and 16 where compliance with these provisions would be contrary to their religious or personal laws.

Singapore interprets article 11, paragraph 1, in the light of the provisions of article 4, paragraph 2 as not precluding prohibitions, restrictions or conditions on the employment of women in certain areas, or on work done by them where this is considered necessary or desirable to protect the health and safety of women or the human foetus....

Turkey

The Government of the Republic of Turkey [makes reservations] with regard to the articles of the Convention dealing with family relations which are not completely compatible with the provisions of the Turkish Civil Code....

Objections

Germany

The Federal Republic of Germany considers that the reservations made by Egypt regarding article 2, article 9, paragraph 2, and article 16, by Bangladesh regarding article 2, article 13 (*a*) and article 16, paragraph 1 (*c*) and (*f*), by Brazil regarding article 15, paragraph 4, and article 16, paragraph 1 (*a*), (*c*), (*g*) and (*h*), by Jamaica regarding article 9, paragraph 2, by the Republic of Korea regarding article 9 and article 16, paragraph 1 (*c*), (*d*), (*f*) and (*g*), and by Mauritius regarding article 11, paragraph 1 (*b*) and (*d*), and article 16, paragraph 1 (*g*), are incompatible with the object and purpose of the Convention (article 28, paragraph 2) and therefore objects to them. In relation to the Federal Republic of Germany, they may not be invoked in support of a legal practice which does not pay due regard to the legal status afforded to women and children in the Federal Republic of Germany in conformity with the above-mentioned articles of the Convention.

This objection shall not preclude the entry into force of the Convention as between Egypt, Bangladesh, Brazil, Jamaica, the Republic of Korea, Mauritius and the Federal Republic of Germany.

QUESTIONS

1. Which of the preceding reservations do you view as objectionable within the criteria of the Vienna Convention? Consider the reservations of Egypt. What arguments would you make for the validity of its reservations under the criteria stated in the Vienna Convention and CEDAW?

2. Which of the reservations raise issues of cultural relativism? Only those based on a state's local custom or religion?

3. How do you assess the criteria suggested by Cook? Would you judge any of the reservations above differently under her criteria?

4. Why do you suppose that CEDAW has attracted more reservations by states than other human rights treaties?

NOTE

In comparison with other democratic states, and even with many one-party and authoritarian states that are persistent and cruel violators of basic human rights, the United States has a modest record of ratification of human rights treaties. That comparison cuts both ways. One might say that the United States has a lesser commitment to and concern with developing international human rights than do many (say, European and Commonwealth) states of a roughly similar political and economic character. As the world's leading power, its lesser commitment necessarily weakens the human rights movement. *Or*, one might say that the United States does not engage in the hypocrisy of many states in ratifying and then ignoring treaties. If it ratifies, it means to comply, and hence will take a careful look to be certain that full compliance is possible.

One can be certain that neither of these 'pure' explanations captures the complexity of the arguments within the Executive Branch and the Senate about ratification of these treaties. This section examines aspects of the ratification process of the ICCPR to illustrate that complexity.

As background to the materials on the ICCPR, the introductory readings below describe earlier attitudes within the United States about involvement in the international human rights system, and indicate the reasons why the United States effectively withdrew from participation in human rights treaties in the early 1950s. Recall the significant role played by the United States just a few years earlier in helping to launch the International Bill of Rights through the drafting of the Universal Declaration.

LOUIS SOHN AND THOMAS BUERGENTHAL, INTERNATIONAL PROTECTION OF HUMAN RIGHTS (1973), at 961

1. In 1945, during the Senate Foreign Relations Committee's hearings on the U.N. Charter, a principal Department of State expert on the Charter, Dr. Leo Pasvolsky, was questioned extensively on the relationship between Article 2(7) and the human rights provisions of the Charter. The following is an excerpt from his testimony:

> Senator Millikin. I notice several reiterations of the thought of the Charter that the Organization shall not interfere with domestic affairs of any country. How can you get into these social questions and economic questions without conducting investigations and making inquiries in the various countries?
>
> Mr. Pasvolsky. Senator, the Charter provides that the Assembly shall have the right to initiate or make studies in all of these economic or social fields. . . .
>
> Senator Millikin. Might the activities of the Organization concern themselves with, for example, wage rates and working conditions in different countries?
>
> Mr. Pasvolsky. The question of what matters the Organization would be concerned with would depend upon whether or not they had international repercussions. This Organization is concerned with international problems. International problems may arise out of all sorts of circumstances. . . .
>
> Senator Millikin. Could such an Organization concern itself with various forms of discrimination which countries maintain for themselves, bloc currency, subsidies to merchant marine, and things of that kind?
>
> Mr Pasvolsky. I should think that the Organization would wish to discuss and consider them. It might even make recommendations on any matters which affect international economic or social relations. The League of Nations did. The International Labor Office has done that. This new Organization being created will be doing a great deal of that. . . .
>
> Senator Millikin. Would the investigation of racial discriminations be within the jurisdiction of this body?
>
> Mr. Pasvolsky. Insofar, I imagine, as the Organization takes over the function of making studies and recommendations on human rights, it may wish to make studies in those fields and make pronouncements.
>
> Senator Vandenberg. At that point I wish you would reemphasize what you read from the Commission Report specifically applying the exemption of domestic matters to the Social and Economic Council.
>
> Mr. Pasvolsky. I will read that paragraph again.
>
> Senator Vandenberg. Yes, please.
>
> Mr. Pasvolsky. (reading): The members of Committee 3 of Commission II are in full agreement that nothing contained in chapter IX can be construed as giving authority to the Organization to intervene in the domestic affairs of Member states . . .
>
> Senator Millikin. Is there any other international aspect to a labor problem or a racial problem or a religious problem that does not originate domestically? . . .
>
> Mr. Pasvolsky. Well, Senator, I suppose we can say that there is no such thing as an international problem that is not related to national problems, because the word 'international' itself means that there are nations involved. What domestic jurisdiction relates to here, I should say, as it does in all of these matters, is that

there are certain matters which are handled internally by nations which do not affect other nations or may not affect other nations. On the other hand, there are certainly many matters handled internally which do affect other nations and which by international law are considered to be of concern to other nations.

Senator Millikin. For example, let me ask you if this would be true. It is conceivable that there are racial questions on the southern shores of the Mediterranean that might have very explosive effects under some circumstances; but they originate locally, do they not, Doctor?

Mr Pasvolsky. Yes.

Senator Millikin. And because they might have explosive effects, this Organization might concern itself with them; is that correct?

Mr. Pasvolsky. It might, if somebody brings them to the attention of the Organization.

Senator Millikin. And by the same token, am I correct in this, that in any racial matter, any of these matters we are talking about, that originates in one country domestically and that has the possibility of making international trouble, might be subject to the investigation and recommendations of the Organization?

Mr. Pasvolsky. I should think so, because the Organization is created for that.

2. A number of different versions of a proposal to amend the treatymaking power under the U.S. Constitution were considered by the Congress in the course of the so-called 'Bricker Amendment' debate, which lasted roughly from 1952 to 1957.[18]

...

4. It is generally acknowledged that the defeat of the proposed constitutional amendment was due in large measure to the vigorous lobbying by the Eisenhower Administration and its concomitant undertaking, articulated in the above-quoted testimony by Secretary of State John Foster Dulles, not to adhere to human rights treaties. This undertaking was also embodied in a policy statement issued by Mr. Dulles in the form of a letter addressed to Mrs. Oswald B. Lord, the United States Representative on the United Nations Commission on Human Rights. 28 DSB 579–80 (1953); 13 M. M. Whiteman, Digest of International Law 667–68 (Washington, D.C., 1970). This letter read in part:

> In the light of our national, and recently, international experience in the matter of human rights, the opening of a new session of the Commission on Human Rights appears an appropriate occasion for a fresh appraisal of the methods through which we may realize the human rights goals of the United Nations. These goals have a high place in the Charter as drafted at San Francisco and were articulated in greater detail in the Universal Declaration of Human Rights....
>
> Since the establishment of these goals, much time and effort has been expended on the drafting of treaties, that is, Covenants on Human Rights, in which it was sought to frame, in mutually acceptable legal form, the obligations to be assumed by national states in regard to human rights. We have found that such drafts of

[18] [Eds. The Bricker Amendment, a series a proposals for constitutional amendments, would have significantly limited executive power over treaties and correspondingly increased the power of the Senate or the Congress as a whole. Different versions of the amendments would have curtailed the use of self-executing treaties rather than treaties followed by legislation, and redrawn the boundary line between treaties and executive agreements so as to require larger Senate participation.]

Covenants as had a reasonable chance of acceptance in some respects established standards lower than those now observed in a number of countries.

While the adoption of the Covenants would not compromise higher standards already in force, it seems wiser to press ahead in the United Nations for the achievement of the standards set forth in the Universal Declaration of Human Rights through ways other than the proposed Covenants on Human Rights. This is particularly important in view of the likelihood that the Covenants will not be as widely accepted by United Nations members as initially anticipated. Nor can we overlook the fact that the areas where human rights are being persistently and flagrantly violated are those where the Covenants would most likely be ignored.

In these circumstances, there is a grave question whether the completion, signing and ratification of the Covenants at this time is the most desirable method of contributing to human betterment particularly in areas of greatest need. Furthermore, experience to date strongly suggests that even if it be assumed that this is a proper area for treaty action, a wider general acceptance of human rights goals must be attained before it seems useful to codify standards of human rights as binding international legal obligations in the Covenants.

With all these considerations in mind, the United States Government asks you to present to the Commission on Human Rights at its forthcoming session a statement of American goals and policies in this field; to point out the need for reexamining the approach of the Human Rights Covenants as the method for furthering at this time the objectives of the Universal Declaration of Human Rights; and to put forward other suggestions of method, based on American experience, for developing throughout the world a human rights conscience which will bring nearer the goals stated in the Charter....

... By reason of the considerations referred to above, the United States Government has reached the conclusion that we should not at this time become a party to any multilateral treaty such as those contemplated in the draft Covenants on Human Rights, and that we should now work toward the objectives of the Declaration by other means. While the Commission continues, under the General Assembly's instructions, with the drafting of the Covenants, you are, of course, expected to participate. This would be incumbent on the United States as a loyal Member of the United Nations.

NOTE

A 1953 memorandum prepared within the State Department[19] listed the pros and cons of US support for the then draft international covenants. The arguments noted in the memorandum for changing the present policy of support included: (1) It was doubtful that a covenant on civil and political rights could gain the necessary Senate consent. (2) It was 'by no means clear' that many countries ratifying the covenants would 'actually give effect to their provisions'. (3) The Covenants:

could work to the disadvantage of United States interests, whether this country becomes a party or not. The Covenants would be a source of propaganda attack on

[19] United States Policy Regarding Draft International Covenants on Human Rights, Foreign Relations of the United States 1952–1954, Vol. III (1979), p. 1550.

positions taken by the United States and on conditions within this country. The Covenants might contain provisions on economic self-determination and the right of nationalization which would be detrimental to United States interests in certain areas abroad.

(4) US support appeared to some critics as 'inconsistent with the Administration's policy on civil rights in the United States, where the emphasis is now on persuasion as against any new federal civil rights legislation'.

COMMENT ON BACKGROUND TO SUBMISSION OF ICCPR TO SENATE

In the years following the decision to withdraw from participation in the two major Covenants, the United States did ratify a few human rights treaties, including the Slavery Convention, the Protocol Relating to the Status of Refugees, the Convention on the Political Rights of Women, and the four Geneva Conventions on the laws of war. But it was not until the Carter administration in the late 1970s that a President sought the Senate's consent for ratification of a number of major treaties (including the two Covenants).

In recent years, the record of the United States has substantially improved, for it has become a party not only to the ICCPR but also to the Convention on the Prevention and Punishment of the Crime of Genocide; the Convention against Torture and other Cruel, Inhuman or Degrading Treatment or Punishment; and the International Convention on the Elimination of All Forms of Racial Discrimination. But there has never been sustained debate in the Senate or broader political debate in the country about participation in four major and widely ratified treaties: the Convention on the Elimination of All Forms of Discrimination against Women, the American Convention on Human Rights, the International Covenant on Economic, Social and Cultural Rights, or the Convention of the Rights of the Child.

The following materials deal with aspects of the ratification process of the International Covenant on Civil and Political Rights. Given the similarities between the provisions of that Covenant and the US tradition of liberal constitutionalism and a Bill of Rights, no opponents of ratification then expressed doubt about the broad consistency between the principles of the Covenant and the US Constitution. There were statements from civil liberties groups stressing significant if more limited ways in which the United States, were it to become a party without making numerous legislative and policy changes, would be in violation of several ICCPR provisions.[20]

One of the recurrent issues before the Executive Branch and the Senate in deciding whether the United States should become a party to the ICCPR was whether the Covenant, or salient parts of it, should be understood to be self-executing. Note

[20] See, e.g., Human Rights Watch and American Civil Liberties Union, *Human Rights Violations in the United States: A Report on U.S. Compliance with the International Covenant on Civil and Political Rights* (1993).

that the ICCPR itself makes no reference to its self-executing or non-self-executing character but provides in Article 2(2):

> Where not already provided for by existing legislation or other measures, each State Party to the present Covenant undertakes to take the necessary steps, in accordance with its constitutional processes and with the provisions of the present Covenant, to adopt such legislative or other measures as may be necessary to give effect to the rights recognized in the present Covenant.

Article 2(3) bears out this obligation by stating the further undertaking to 'ensure that any persons whose rights . . . are violated shall have an effective remedy', and to 'ensure that any person claiming such a remedy shall have his right thereto determined by competent judicial, administrative or legislative authorities . . . and to develop the possibilities of judicial remedy'. How the states fulfil these obligations lies within their discretion; they are not obligated to incorporate the treaty *as such* within their domestic legal order, whether through automatic incorporation (self-executing treaty) or legislative incorporation. Consider the following comments on the ICCPR:

> In its examination of individual communications and State reports, the [ICCPR Human Rights Committee] has originally confirmed that the States Parties may implement the Covenant domestically as they see fit. On the other hand, however, from the beginning there was a certain tendency of the Committee to promote the *direct applicability* of the Covenant. . . . In practice, a growing number of States parties are in fact enhancing the status of the Covenant in domestic law. . . . Of those countries in which the Covenant forms part of domestic law, only the United States has declared the operative articles (1 to 27) to be non-self-executing.[21]

SENATE HEARINGS ON INTERNATIONAL HUMAN RIGHTS TREATIES

S. Comm. For. Rel., 96th Cong., 1st Sess. (1979)

[In 1977, President Carter signed four human rights treaties on behalf of the United States and soon thereafter submitted them to the Senate for its consent to ratification. The Carter Administration proposed that the Senate adopt a number of reservations, understandings and declarations as part of its consent. The following excerpts from the 1979 Senate hearings on the treaties concern only one of them, the International Covenant on Civil and Political Rights. The treaties were never brought to vote in the Senate, and the matter effectively died until the Bush Administration revived in 1991 the question of US participation in this Covenant. It submitted the Covenant afresh to the Senate, together with modestly amended proposals for reservations, understandings and declarations that are set forth at p. 1139, *infra*.

[21] Manfred Nowak, *UN Covenant on Civil and Political Rights: CCPR Commentary* (2nd edn. 2005), at 58.

There follow some brief excerpts from the lengthy Senate hearings.]

Statement of Charles Yost, Former Ambassador to United Nations

...

There are, in my judgment, few failures or omissions on our part which have done more to undermine American credibility internationally than this one. Whenever an American delegate at an international conference, or an American Ambassador making representations on behalf of our Government, raises a question of human rights, as we have in these times many occasions to do, the response public or private, is very likely to be this: If you attach so much importance to human rights, why have you not even ratified the United Nations' conventions and covenants on this subject? . . .

Our refusal to join in the international implementation of the principles we so loudly and frequently proclaim cannot help but give the impression that we do not practice what we preach, that we have something to hide, that we are afraid to allow outsiders even to inquire whether we practice racial discrimination or violate other basic human rights. Yet we constantly take it upon ourselves to denounce the Soviet Union, Cuba, Vietnam, Argentina, Chile, and many other states for violating these rights. . . .

Many are therefore inclined to believe that our whole human rights policy is merely a cold war exercise or a display of self-righteousness directed against governments we dislike. . . .

...

Prepared Statement of Robert Owen, Legal Adviser, Department of State

...

. . . [Objections to the human rights treaties] tend to fall into three categories. First, it is said that the human rights treaties could serve to change our laws as they are, allowing individuals in courts of law to invoke the treaty terms where inconsistent with domestic law or even with the Constitution. The second type of objection is that the treaties could be used to alter the jurisdictional balance between our federal and state institutions. . . . The third type of objection is that the relationship between a government and its citizens is not a proper subject for the treaty-making powers at all, but ought to be left entirely to domestic legislative processes. . . .

. . . [T]he treaties do diverge from our domestic law in a relatively few instances. Critics fear that this divergence will cause changes in that domestic law outside the normal legislative process, or at least will subject the relations between the government and the individual to conflicting legal standards.

This fear is not well-founded, in our judgment, for two reasons. First, the President has recommended that to each of the four treaties there is appended a declaration that the treaties' substantive provisions are not self-executing.

...

. . . This does not mean that vast new implementing legislation is required, as the great majority of the treaty provisions are already implemented in our domestic law. It does mean that further changes in our laws will be brought about only through the normal legislative process. This understanding as to the non-self-executing nature of the substantive provisions of the treaties would not derogate from or diminish in any way our international obligations under the treaties; it touches only upon the role the treaty provisions will play in our domestic law.

A second reason why we need not fear a confusion of standards due to possible conflicts between the treaty provisions and domestic law rests in this Administration's recommended reservations and understandings. In the few instances where it was felt that a provision of the treaties could reasonably be interpreted to diverge from the requirements of our constitution or from federal or state law presently in force, the Administration has suggested that a reservation or understanding be made to that provision. In our view, these reservations do not detract from the object and the purpose of the treaties — that is, to see to it that minimum standards of human rights are observed throughout the world — and they permit us to accept the treaties in a form consonant with our domestic legal requirements.

. . .

. . . The primary objective is the fostering of international commitments to erect and observe a minimum standard of rights for the individual as set forth by the treaties. This standard is met by our domestic system in practice, although not always in precisely the same way that the treaties envision. By ratification, we would commit ourselves to maintain the level of respect we already pay to the human rights of our people; we would commit ourselves not to backslide, and we would be subjecting this commitment and our human rights performance as a whole to international scrutiny.

. . .

Another reason why the Administration has proposed a number of reservations, understandings and declarations is pragmatic. We believe these treaties to be important and necessary, and we are anxious to secure the advice and consent of the Senate to their ratification. It is our judgment that the prospects for securing that ratification would be significantly and perhaps decisively advanced if it were to be clear that, by adopting these treaties, the United States would not automatically be bringing about changes in its internal law without the legislative concurrence of the federal or state governments.

❀ ❀ ❀

Senator Pell. Do you think by affixing reservations we may be making an error in that we would be permitting other nations also to affix reservations and reinterpret the covenants according to their own ideologies?

Mr. Owen. The reservations that we have recommended in some cases are absolutely essential in order to avoid conflicts with our own Constitution.

As to the other reservations, if the Senate should decide that they are not necessary, I think the administration would be willing to dispense with them. Then we would be, in effect, bringing about a more rigorous civil rights regime and there would be no possible criticism that we were not fulfilling the treaties as a whole.

. . .

Senator Pell. Where do you think the opposition has been to the passage of these treaties? Why is it we have had to delay for 20 years or more?

...

Mr. Farer. . . . I think that race relations have been one factor, if we will be perfectly frank. A lot of opposition came from representatives of States where law or practice were crudely discriminatory.

But I also think that like most other countries, particularly large countries, we tend to react instinctively with some belligerence to the idea that other countries and peoples can assess for themselves what we are doing, and the idea that they may fault the level of achievement that we have managed to reach.

...

Senator Pell. What would you think, Professor Sohn?

Mr. Sohn. I agree with the two other speakers that the fears have been exaggerated and that it is simply part of the general feeling that the United States knows better about various things and therefore should not be subject to other peoples' judgments. It reminds me of what happened in the United Kingdom when they finally ratified the European Convention on Human Rights. The Foreign Minister made a statement in the House of Commons saying of course we are willing to ratify it because nobody can find anything wrong with the British laws on human rights. Well, of course, two weeks later all of the cases relating to immigration from Kenya to the United Kingdom by people nominally British citizens and the restrictions on them by immigration authorities immediately were taken to the European Commission. The United Kingdom had to admit that its administrative procedures were not in accordance with the standards of the Convention.

I think on the one hand we always say to everybody else that our standards are higher than those of anyone else; but we will discover, if we are subject to international supervision, that there are some skeletons in our closet and they will be paraded in public, and we do not like that idea.

...

Statement of Phyllis Schlafiy, Alton, III

...

I oppose Senate ratification of these international human rights treaties for the following reasons.

First, the treaties do not give Americans any rights whatsoever. They do not add a minuscule of benefit to the marvelous human rights proclaimed by the Declaration of Independence, guaranteed by the U.S. Constitution, and extended by our Federal and State laws.

Second, the treaties imperil or restrict existing rights of Americans by using treaty law to restrict or reduce U.S. constitutional rights, to change U.S. domestic Federal or State laws, and to upset the balance of power within our unique system of federalism.

Third, the treaties provide no tangible benefit to peoples in other lands and, even if they did, that would not justify sacrificing American rights.

...

This covenant sets up a Human Rights [Committee] of 18 members on which the United States would have at most one or perhaps no representative at all. It would have the competence to hear complaints against us, and who knows what they would do.

. . .

QUESTION

Based on the prior readings, how would you identify the principal concerns that a President who believed it important to ratify a given human rights treaty should be aware of when seeking the Senate's consent? Can you think of ways in which the President might seek to alleviate or dispose of those concerns before submitting the treaty to the Senate?

NOTE

President George H. W. Bush sent a letter to the Senate Foreign Relations Committee in 1991,[22] urging the Senate to give its advice and consent to ratification of the ICCPR. It stated in part:

> The end of the Cold War offers great opportunities for the forces of democracy and the rule of law throughout the world. I believe the United States has a special responsibility to assist those in other countries who are now working to make the transition to pluralist democracies. . . .
>
> United States ratification of the Covenant on Civil and Political Rights at this moment in history would underscore our natural commitment to fostering democratic values through international law. . . . Subject to a few essential reservations and understandings, it is entirely consonant with the fundamental principles incorporated in our own Bill of Rights. U.S. ratification would also strengthen our ability to influence the development of appropriate human rights principles in the international community. . . .
>
> . . .

PROPOSALS BY BUSH ADMINISTRATION OF RESERVATIONS TO INTERNATIONAL COVENANT ON CIVIL AND POLITICAL RIGHTS

Rep. of S. Comm. For. Rel. to Accompany Exec. E, 95–2 (1992), at 10

[In 1978, the Carter Administration had proposed a list of reservations, understandings and declarations when it put four human rights treaties, including the ICCPR, to the Senate for its consent to ratification. In 1991, when the Bush Administration

[22] Rep. of S. Comm. for For. Rel. to Accompany Exec. E, 95–2 (1992), at 25.

revived the ICCPR alone among the four treaties, it submitted a revised list to the Senate Foreign Relations Committee. The following excerpts from this 1991 submission set forth the Bush Administration's reasons for proposing several of the reservations, understandings and declarations.]

General Comments

...

In a few instances, however, it is necessary to subject U.S. ratification to reservations, understandings or declarations in order to ensure that the United States can fulfill its obligations under the Covenant in a manner consistent with the United States Constitution, including instances where the Constitution affords greater rights and liberties to individuals than does the Covenant. Additionally, a few provisions of the Covenant articulate legal rules which differ from U.S. law and which, upon careful consideration, the Administration declines to accept in preference to existing law....

Formal Reservations

1. *Free Speech (Article 20)*

Although Article 19 of the Covenant specifically protects freedom of expression and opinion, Article 20 directly conflicts with the First Amendment by requiring the prohibition of certain forms of speech and expression which are protected under the First Amendment to the U.S. Constitution (i.e., propaganda for war and advocacy of national, racial or religious hatred that constitutes incitement to discrimination, hostility or violence). The United States cannot accept such an obligation.

Accordingly, the following reservation is recommended:

> Article 20 does not authorize or require legislation or other action by the United States that would restrict the right of free speech and association protected by the Constitution and laws of the United States.

...

2. *Article 6 (capital punishment)*

Article 6, paragraph 5 of the Covenant prohibits imposition of the death sentence for crimes committed by persons below 18 years of age and on pregnant women. In 1978, a broad reservation to this article was proposed in order to retain the right to impose capital punishment on any person duly convicted under existing or future laws permitting the imposition of capital punishment. The Administration is now prepared to accept the prohibition against execution of pregnant women. However, in light of the recent reaffirmation of U.S. policy towards capital punishment generally, and in particular the Supreme Court's decisions upholding state laws permitting the death penalty for crimes committed by juveniles aged 16 and 17, the prohibition against imposition of capital punishment for crimes committed by minors is not acceptable. Given the sharply differing view taken by many of our future treaty partners on the issue of the death penalty (including what constitutes 'serious crimes' under Article 6(2)), it is advisable to state our position clearly.

Accordingly, we recommend the following reservation to Article 6:

> The United States reserves the right, subject to its Constitutional constraints, to impose capital punishment on any person (other than a pregnant woman) duly convicted under existing or future laws permitting the imposition capital punishment, including such punishment for crime committed by persons below eighteen years of age.

3. *Article 7 (torture/punishment)*

. . .

[We discuss the US reservation to Article 7 at p. 252, *supra.*]

4. *Article 15(1) (post-offense reductions in penalty)*

Article 15, paragraph 1, precludes the imposition of a heavier penalty for a criminal offense than was applicable at the time the offense was committed, and requires States Party to comply with any post-offense reductions in penalties: '[i]f, subsequent to the commission of the offense, provision is made by law for the imposition of the lighter penalty, the offender shall benefit thereby.' Current federal law, as well as the law of most states, does not require such relief and in fact contains a contrary presumption that the penalty in force at the time the offense is committed will be imposed, although post-sentence reductions are permitted (see 18 U.S.C. 3582 (c)(2) and the Federal Sentencing Guidelines) and are often granted in practice when there have been subsequent statutory changes. Upon consideration, there is no disposition to require a change in U.S. law to conform to the Covenant. [A reservation was proposed.]

Understandings

1. *Article 2(1), 4(1) and 26 (non-discrimination)*

The very broad anti-discrimination provisions contained in the above articles do not precisely comport with long-standing Supreme Court doctrine in the equal protection field. In particular, Articles 2(1) and 26 prohibit discrimination not only on the bases of 'race, colour, sex, language, religion, political or other opinion, national or social origin, property, birth' but also on any 'other status.' Current U.S. civil rights law is not so open-ended: discrimination is only prohibited for specific statuses, and there are exceptions which allow for discrimination. For example, under the Age Discrimination Act of 1975, age may be taken into account in certain circumstances. In addition, U.S. law permits additional distinctions, for example between citizens and non-citizens and between different categories of non-citizens, especially in the context of the immigration laws.

. . .

Notwithstanding the very extensive protections already provided under U.S. law and the Committee's interpretive approach to the issue, we recommend [an understanding that expresses the preceding concerns.] [Eds. The text of that understanding is here omitted.]

4. *Article 14 (right to counsel, compelled witness, and double jeopardy)*

In a few particular aspects, this Article could be read as going beyond existing U.S. domestic law. . . . Under the Constitution, double jeopardy attaches only to multiple prosecutions by the same sovereign and does not prohibit trial of the same defendant for the same crime in, for example, state and federal courts or in the courts of two states. See *Burton v. Maryland*, 395 U.S. 784 (1969).

To clarify our reading of the Covenant with respect to these issues, we recommend the following understanding, similar to the one proposed in 1978:

> . . . The United States understands the prohibition upon double jeopardy in paragraph 7 to apply only when the judgment of acquittal has been rendered by a court of the same governmental unit, whether the Federal Government or a constituent unit, as is seeking a new trial for the same cause.

Declarations

1. Non-self-executing Treaty

For reasons of prudence, we recommend including a declaration that the substantive provisions of the Covenant are not self-executing. The intent is to clarify that the Covenant will not create a private cause of action in U.S. courts. As was the case with the Torture Convention, existing U.S. law generally complies with the Covenant; hence, implementing legislation is not contemplated.

We recommend the following declaration . . .

> The United States declares that the provisions of Articles 1 through 27 of the Covenant are not self-executing.

. . .

3. Article 41 (state-to-state complaints)

Under Article 41, States Party to the Covenant may accept the competence of the Human Rights Committee to consider state-to-state complaints by means of a formal declaration to that effect . . . .

Accordingly, we recommend informing the Senate of our intent, subject to its approval, to make an appropriate declaration under Article 41 at the time of ratification, as follows:

> The United States declares that it accepts the competence of the Human Rights Committee to receive and consider communications under Article 41 in which a State Party claims another State Party is not fulfilling its obligations under the Covenant.

. . .

QUESTIONS

1. Several NGOs participating in the Senate hearings on ratification of the ICCPR opposed the proposed (and later adopted) declaration to the effect that the substantive provisions of the Covenant would not be self-executing. Note the following comments in

a report by the largest domestic civil liberties organization and the largest US-based international human rights organization in the United States:[23]

> ... Americans would have been able to enforce the treaty in U.S. courts either if it had been declared to be self-executing or if implementing legislation had been enacted to create causes of action under the treaty. The Bush administration rejected both routes. The result was that ratification became an empty act for Americans: the endorsement of the most important treaty for the protection of civil rights yielded not a single additional enforceable right to citizens and residents of the United States.
>
> We issue this report to demonstrate the inaccuracy of the view that Americans do not need the protection of the ICCPR. As we show, the Bush administration was wrong in its assessment that the United States is already complying with all the treaty's obligations, even after the administration nullified some of the rights through its reservations, declarations and understandings. In the areas of racial and gender discrimination, prison conditions, immigrants' rights, language discrimination, the death penalty, police brutality, freedom of expression and religious freedom, we show that the United States is now violating the treaty in important respects. As a result, the Clinton administration is under an immediate legal obligation to remedy these human rights violations at home, through specific steps that we outline.
>
> Moreover, to ensure that these remedies are sufficient, we believe the U.S. government is obligated to grant Americans the right to invoke the protections of the treaty in U.S. courts, at least through specific legislation enabling them to do so, but preferably through a formal declaration that the treaty is self-executing, and thus invocable in U.S. courts without further legislation. ...

Do you agree with these observations about the need for a self-executing Covenant? What arguments would you make against this position?

2. What remedial path has a US citizen who plausibly claims that the government has violated his rights under the ICCPR, but who lacks any plausible claim under US law? What steps could he realistically take to pressure the US government to accept his position?

3. Ratification by the United States of the ICCPR Optional Protocol does not seem to have been discussed. No such proposal was put to the Senate. (a) Why do you suppose this to have been the case? (b) As a member of the State Department, would you have argued for or against joining the Optional Protocol? (c) 'Ratification of the Optional Protocol would have been the correct solution, preferable to making the ICCPR self-executing.' Comment.

COMMENT ON EFFECTS OF RESERVATIONS WITH RESPECT TO OTHER STATE PARTIES

The Senate consented to ratification subject to the described (and other) reservations, understandings and declarations. In the Senate debate preceding the approving vote, Senator Moynihan noted that '[o]thers have raised the legitimate concern that the number of reservations in the administration's package might imply to some that the

[23] Human Rights Watch and American Civil Liberties Union, *Human Rights Violations in the United States: A Report on U.S. Compliance with the International Covenant on Civil and Political Rights* (1993), at 2.

United States does not take the obligations of the covenant seriously'. He stressed how few and selective the package was, in the context of the entire covenant, and argued that 'a wholly different interpretation' could be placed on it — namely, as an indication of the seriousness with which the United States approached its new obligations, unlike 'nations of the totalitarian block [that] ratified obligations without reservation — obligations that they had no intention of carrying out'. He observed that 'a Senator might well conclude that it is in the interests of the United States to ratify the covenant with this package of reservations even if that Senator disagrees strongly with a particular domestic practice which has prompted a reservation'. Efforts to change that domestic practice through legislation could continue (138 Cong. Rec. S4781, April 2, 1992).

The United States then ratified the Covenant. A number of states parties to the ICCPR objected to one or more of the reservations. Several states — including Belgium, Denmark, Finland, France, Germany, Italy, Netherlands, Norway, Portugal, Spain and Sweden — objected to the reservation regarding Article 6, paragraph 5, prohibiting the imposition of the death sentence for crimes committed by persons below 18 years of age, and found that reservation incompatible with the ICCPR's provisions and with its object and purpose. Most of these states also objected to other reservations (or to understandings), particularly the one relating to Article 7. The objections, however, stressed that (to take one illustration) the state's position on the relevant reservations 'does not constitute an obstacle to the entry into force of the Covenant between the Kingdom of Spain and the United States of America'. Compare in this respect Articles 20–21 of the Vienna Convention on the Law of Treaties.

In objecting to three reservations and three understandings, Sweden observed that under international treaty law, the name 'assigned to a statement' that excluded or modified the effect of certain treaty provisions:

> does not determine its status as a reservation to the treaty. Thus, the Government considers that some of the understandings made by the United States in substance constitute reservations to the Covenant.
>
> A reservation by which a State modifies or excludes the application of the most fundamental provisions of the Covenant, or limits its responsibilities under that treaty by invoking general principles of national law, may cast doubts upon the commitment of the reserving State to the object and purpose of the Covenant. The reservations made by the United States of America include both reservations to essential and non-derogable provisions, and general references to national legislation. Reservations of this nature contribute to undermining the basis of international treaty law. All States parties share a common interest in the respect for the object and purpose of the treaty to which they have chosen to become parties.

HUMAN RIGHTS COMMITTEE, GENERAL COMMENT NO. 24

CCPR/C/21/Rev.1/Add.6, 2 November 1994.

[At its 52nd session in 1994, the ICCPR Committee adopted General Comment No. 24 entitled: 'General comment on issues relating to reservations made upon ratification of accession to the Covenant or the Optional Protocols thereto, or in relation to declarations under article 41 of the Covenant'. (Earlier General Comments (GCs) of the Committee appear at p. 878, *supra*). This GC was adopted after the ratification of the ICCPR by the United States described above, and preceded the Committee's consideration of the first periodic report submitted by the United States in 1995. It refers to the judicial decision and to the provisions of the Vienna Convention on the Law of Treaties described at p. 1124, *supra.*

The GC notes that as of its date, 46 of the 127 states parties to the ICCPR had entered a total of 150 reservations, ranging from exclusion of the duty to provide particular rights, to insistence on the 'paramountcy of certain domestic legal provisions' and to limitation of the competence of the Committee. Those reservations 'tend to weaken respect' for obligations and 'may undermine the effective implementation of the Covenant'. The Committee felt compelled to act, partly under the necessity of clarifying for states parties just what obligations had been undertaken, a clarification that would require the Committee to determine 'the acceptability and effects' of a reservation or unlilateral declaration.

The GC observed that the ICCPR itself makes no reference to reservations (as is true also for the First Optional Protocol; the Second Optional Protocol limits reservations), and that the matter of reservations is governed by international law. It found in Article 19(3) of the Vienna Convention on the Law of Treaties 'relevant guidance'. Therefore, that article's 'object and purpose test ... governs the matter of interpretation and acceptability of reservations'. The GC continues:]

8. Reservations that offend peremptory norms would not be compatible with the object and purpose of the Covenant. Although treaties that are mere exchanges of obligations between States allow them to reserve *inter se* application of rules of general international law, it is otherwise in human rights treaties, which are for the benefit of persons within their jurisdiction. Accordingly, provisions in the Covenant that represent customary international law (and *a fortiori* when they have the character of peremptory norms) may not be the subject of reservations. Accordingly, a State may not reserve the right to engage in slavery, to torture, to subject persons to cruel, inhuman or degrading treatment or punishment, to arbitrarily deprive persons of their lives, to arbitrarily arrest and detain persons, to deny freedom of thought, conscience and religion, to presume a person guilty unless he proves his innocence, to execute pregnant women or children, to permit the advocacy of national, racial or religious hatred, to deny to persons of marriageable age the right to marry, or to deny to minorities the right to enjoy their own culture, profess their own religion, or use their own language. And while reservations to particular clauses of Article 14 may be acceptable, a general reservation to the right to a fair trial would not be.

9. Applying more generally the object and purpose test to the Covenant, the Committee notes that, for example, ... a State [may not] reserve an entitlement not to take the necessary steps at the domestic level to give effect to the rights of the Covenant (Article 2(2)).

10. ... [I]t falls for consideration as to whether reservations to the non-derogable provisions of the Covenant are compatible with its object and purpose. While there is no hierarchy of importance of rights under the Covenant, the operation of certain rights may not be suspended, even in times of national emergency. This underlines

the great importance of non-derogable rights. But not all rights of profound importance, such as articles 9 and 27 of the Covenant, have in fact been made non-derogable. One reason for certain rights being made non-derogable is because their suspension is irrelevant to the legitimate control of the state of national emergency (for example, no imprisonment for debt, in article 11). Another reason is that derogation may indeed be impossible (as, for example, freedom of conscience). At the same time, some provisions are non-derogable exactly because without them there would be no rule of law. . . .

11. . . . The Committee's role under the Covenant, whether under article 40 or under the Optional Protocols, necessarily entails interpreting the provisions of the Covenant and the development of a jurisprudence. Accordingly, a reservation that rejects the Committee's competence to interpret the requirements of any provisions of the Covenant would also be contrary to the object and purpose of that treaty.

12. . . . Domestic laws may need to be altered properly to reflect the requirements of the Covenant; and mechanisms at the domestic level will be needed to allow the Covenant rights to be enforceable at the local level. Reservations often reveal a tendency of States not to want to change a particular law. And sometimes that tendency is elevated to a general policy. Of particular concern are widely formulated reservations which essentially render ineffective all Covenant rights which would require any change in national law to ensure compliance with Covenant obligations. No real international rights or obligations have thus been accepted. And when there is an absence of provisions to ensure that Covenant rights may be sued on in domestic courts, and, further, a failure to allow individual complaints to be brought to the Committee under the first Optional Protocol, all the essential elements of the Covenant guarantees have been removed.

. . .

17. . . . [Human rights] treaties, and the Covenant specifically, are not a web of inter-State exchanges of mutual obligations. . . . Because the operation of the classic rules on reservations is so inadequate for the Covenant, States have often not seen any legal interest in or need to object to reservations. The absence of protest by States cannot imply that a reservation is either compatible or incompatible with the object and purpose of the Covenant. . . .

18. It necessarily falls to the Committee to determine whether a specific reservation is compatible with the object and purpose of the Covenant. . . . Because of the special character of a human rights treaty, the compatibility of a reservation with the object and purpose of the Covenant must be established objectively, by reference to legal principles, and the Committee is particularly well placed to perform this task. The normal consequence of an unacceptable reservation is not that the Covenant will not be in effect at all for a reserving party. Rather, such a reservation will generally be severable, in the sense that the Covenant will be operative for the reserving party without benefit of the reservation.

19. Reservations must be specific. . . . States should not enter so many reservations that they are in effect accepting a limited number of human rights obligations, and not the Covenant as such. So that reservations do not lead to a perpetual non-attainment of international human rights standards, reservations should not systematically reduce the obligations undertaken only to the presently existing in

less demanding standards of domestic law. Nor should interpretative declarations or reservations seek to remove an autonomous meaning to Covenant obligations, by pronouncing them to be identical, or to be accepted only insofar as they are identical, with existing provisions of domestic law.

. . .

COMMENT ON SEVERABILITY

France, the United Kingdom and the United States submitted observations to the ICCPR Committee on General Comment No. 24. The US Government stated that the GC 'appears to go much too far' and that the ICCPR does not 'impose on States Parties an obligation to give effect to the Committee's interpretations or confer on the Committee the power to render definitive interpretations of the Covenant'. The observations stated that paragraphs 16–20 of the GC 'appear to reject the established rules of interpretation of treaties' in the Vienna Convention and in customary international law. It criticized the GC's condemnation of the types of reservations that the United States had entered.

The observations were particularly critical of paragraph 18, which stated that in the indicated circumstances, 'the Covenant will be operative for the reserving party without benefit of the reservations'. This conclusion is 'completely at odds with established legal practice and principles. . . .' If it were determined that any one or more of the US reservations were ineffective, the consequence would be that the ratification as a whole could thereby be nullified, and the United States would not be party to the Covenant. France and the United Kingdom submitted similar observations. On the severability question, France 'reject[ed] this entire analysis. . . . [I]f these reservations are deemed incompatible with the purpose and object of the treaty, the only course open is to declare that this consent is not valid and decide that these States cannot be considered parties to the instrument in question'. On this point of law, the UK Government stated similar concerns and added a pragmatic one: 'questions of principle aside, an approach as outlined in . . . the General Comment would risk discouraging States from ratifying human rights conventions (since they would not be in a position to reassure their national Parliaments as to the status of treaty provisions on which it was felt necessary to reserve)'.

Despite these responses, other treaty bodies subsequently endorsed General Comment 24, and the Human Rights Committee employed its severability approach. In a communication submitted to the International Law Commission, the chairpersons of the treaty bodies stated: 'The Chairpersons express[] their firm support for the approach reflected in General Comment No. 24 of the Human Rights Committee and they urge[] that the conclusions proposed by the International Law Commission should be adjusted accordingly to reflect that approach'. Shortly thereafter, the Human Rights Committee applied its severability approach in a First Optional Protocol proceeding involving a death row inmate from Trinidad and Tobago.

KENNEDY V. TRINIDAD AND TOBAGO

Communication No 845/1999, Human Rights Committee, 31 December 1999, UN Doc. CCPR/C/67/D/845/1999 (2 November, 1999)

1. The author of the communication is Mr. Rawle Kennedy, a citizen of Trinidad and Tobago, awaiting execution in the State prison in Port of Spain. . . .

3.3 The author claims to be a victim of violations of [various articles of the ICCPR on grounds of the mandatory nature of the death penalty for murder in Trinidad and Tobago, the imposition of the death penalty without consideration of mitigating circumstances in his particular situation as a secondary party to the killing, the lack of a fair hearing for the prerogative of mercy, torture prior to trial, inhumane conditions of detention on death row, and] that carrying out his death sentence in such circumstances would constitute a violation of his rights under articles 6 and 7. Reference is made to the Judicial Committee of the Privy Council's judgment in *Pratt and Morgan v. The Attorney General of Jamaica* (1994) 2 AC1, in which it held that prolonged detention under sentence of death would violate, in that case, Jamaica's constitutional prohibition on inhuman and degrading treatment. . . .

4.1 . . . [T]he State party makes reference to its instrument of accession to the Optional Protocol of 26 May 1998, which included the following reservation:

> ". . . Trinidad and Tobago re-accedes to the Optional Protocol to the International Covenant on Civil and Political Rights with a Reservation to article 1 thereof to the effect that the Human Rights Committee shall not be competent to receive and consider communications relating to any prisoner who is under sentence of death in respect of any matter relating to his prosecution, his detention, his trial, his conviction, his sentence or the carrying out of the death sentence on him and any matter connected therewith."

6.2 On 26 May 1998, the Government of Trinidad and Tobago denounced the first Optional Protocol to the International Covenant on Civil and Political Rights. On the same day, it reacceded, including in its instrument of reaccession the reservation set out in paragraph 4.1 above.

6.3 To explain why such measures were taken, the State party makes reference to the decision of the Judicial Committee of the Privy Council in Pratt and Morgan v. the Attorney General for Jamaica, in which it was held that "in any case in which execution is to take place more than five years after sentence there will be strong grounds for believing that the delay is such as to constitute 'inhuman or degrading punishment or other treatment'" in violation of section 17 of the Jamaican Constitution. The effect of the decision for Trinidad and Tobago is that inordinate delays in carrying out the death penalty would contravene . . . the Constitution of Trinidad and Tobago, which contains a provision similar to that in section 17 of the Jamaican Constitution. The State party explains that as the decision of the Judicial Committee of the Privy Council represents the constitutional standard for Trinidad and Tobago, the Government is mandated to ensure that the appellate process is expedited by the elimination of delays within the system in order that capital sentences imposed pursuant to the laws of Trinidad and Tobago can be enforced. Thus, the State party chose to denounce the Optional Protocol:

> "In the circumstances, and wishing to uphold its domestic law to subject no one to inhuman and degrading punishment or treatment and thereby observe its obligations under article 7 of the International Covenant on Civil and Political Rights, the Government of Trinidad and Tobago felt compelled to denounce the Optional Protocol. Before doing so, however, it held consultations on 31 March 1998, with the Chairperson and the Bureau of the Human Rights Committee with a view to seeking assurances that the death penalty cases would be dealt with expeditiously and completed within 8 months of registration. For reasons which the Government of Trinidad and Tobago respects, no assurance could be given that these cases would be completed within the timeframe sought."

6.6 In its General Comment No. 24, the Committee expressed the view that a reservation aimed at excluding the competence of the Committee under the Optional Protocol with regard to certain provisions of the Covenant could not be considered to meet th[e] test [whether or not the reservation by the State party can be considered to be compatible with the object and purpose of the Optional Protocol.]

6.7 The present reservation, which was entered after the publication of General Comment No. 24, does not purport to exclude the competence of the Committee under the Optional Protocol with regard to any specific provision of the Covenant, but rather to the entire Covenant for one particular group of complainants, namely prisoners under sentence of death. This does not, however, make it compatible with the object and purpose of the Optional Protocol. On the contrary, the Committee cannot accept a reservation which singles out a certain group of individuals for lesser procedural protection than that which is enjoyed by the rest of the population. In the view of the Committee, this constitutes a discrimination which runs counter to some of the basic principles embodied in the Covenant and its Protocols, and for this reason the reservation cannot be deemed compatible with the object and purpose of the Optional Protocol. The consequence is that the Committee is not precluded from considering the present communication under the Optional Protocol.

6.8 The Committee, noting that the State party has not challenged the admissibility of any of the author's claims on any other ground than its reservation, considers that the author's claims are sufficiently substantiated to be considered on the merits.

7. The Human Rights Committee therefore decides . . . the State party shall be requested to submit to the Committee, within six months of the date of transmittal to it of this decision, written explanations or statements clarifying the matter and the measures, if any, that may have been taken . . . .[24]

INDIVIDUAL, DISSENTING, OPINION OF COMMITTEE MEMBERS NISUKE ANDO, PRAFULACHANDRA N. BHAGWATI, ECKART KLEIN AND DAVID KRETZMER

6. . . . If a State party is free either to accept or not accept an international monitoring mechanism, it is difficult to see why it should not be free to accept this mechanism

[24] [Eds. In response to the Committee's conclusion, Trinidad and Tobago denounced and withdrew from the Optional Protocol in 2000.]

only with regard to some rights or situations, provided the treaty itself does not exclude this possibility. All or nothing is not a reasonable maxim in human rights law.

8. It goes without saying that a State party could not submit a reservation that offends peremptory rules of international law. Thus, for example, a reservation to the Optional Protocol that discriminated between persons on grounds of race, religion or sex, would be invalid. However, this certainly does not mean that every distinction between categories of potential victims of violations by the State party is unacceptable. All depends on the distinction itself and the objective reasons for that distinction.

9. . . . As we are talking about a reservation to the Optional Protocol, and not to the Covenant itself, this requires us to examine not whether there should be any difference in the substantive rights of persons under sentence of death and those of other persons, but whether there is any difference between communications submitted by people under sentence of death and communications submitted by all other persons. . . .

10. The grounds for the denunciation of the Optional Protocol by the State party are set out in paragraph 6.3 of the Committee's views and there is no need to rehearse them here. What is clear is that the difference between communications submitted by persons under sentence of death and others is that they have different results. . . .

16. It is not our intention within the framework of the present case to reopen the whole issue dealt with in General Comment no. 24. Suffice it to say that even in dealing with reservations to the Covenant itself the Committee did not take the view that in every case an unacceptable reservation will fall aside, leaving the reserving state to become a party to the Covenant without benefit of the reservation. As can be seen from the section of General Comment no. 24 quoted above, the Committee merely stated that this would normally be the case. The normal assumption will be that the ratification or accession is not dependent on the acceptability of the reservation and that the unacceptability of the reservation will not vitiate the reserving state's agreement to be a party to the Covenant. However, this assumption cannot apply when it is abundantly clear that the reserving state's agreement to becoming a party to the Covenant is dependent on the acceptability of the reservation. The same applies with reservations to the Optional Protocol.

17. . . . [I]f we had accepted the Committee's view that the reservation is invalid we would have had to hold that Trinidad and Tobago is not a party to the Optional Protocol. . . .

18. . . . [W]e wish to stress that we share the Committee's view that the reservation submitted by the State party is unfortunate. . . . [T]he reservation is wider than required in order to cater to the constitutional constraints of the State party, as it disallows communications by persons under sentence of death even if the time limit set by the Privy Council has already been exceeded (as would seem to be the case in the present communication). We understand that since the State party's denunciation and reaccession there have been developments in the jurisprudence of the Privy Council that may make the reservation unnecessary. These factors do not affect the question of the compatibility of the reservation with the object and purpose of the

Optional Protocol. However, we do see fit to express the hope that the State party will reconsider the need for the reservation and withdraw it. . . .

RYAN GOODMAN, HUMAN RIGHTS TREATIES, INVALID RESERVATIONS, AND STATE CONSENT

96 Am. J. Int. L. 531 (2002)

[The theory that] an invalid reservation can be severed . . . has recently encountered strong opposition. According to . . . the anti-severability (AS) position, international law [does not permit the option of severing an invalid reservation]. . . . Proponents of the AS position ground their argument on a foundational precept of international law: the principle of state consent. . . .

. . . I argue that reservations to human rights treaties should be presumed to be severable unless for a specific treaty there is evidence of a ratifying state's intent to the contrary. This argument has two parts: the first part contends that severability should be an option for a third-party institution (e.g., a domestic court, a national human rights commission, a regional court, the International Court of Justice (ICJ), a treaty body) to invoke after having found a reservation invalid; the second part contends that severance should be presumed to be the optimal remedy. . . .

This approach better reflects and protects state consent than the AS position. . . .

. . .

. . . [A] state may include more reservations than required to obtain its consent. Whether counting on other states not to object to its reservations or discounting the cost of such objections, a state may include supererogatory conditions in its package of reservations. Although some reservations are essential — integral to the state's consent to the treaty — others may be described as what Judge Armand-Ugon, in a related context, called "an accessory stipulation."

In various multilateral agreements, especially those without a juridical supervisory organ, states may incur little cost for submitting accessory reservations. . . .

. . .

Newly established democracies. The greatest potential cost of an AS regime would be to newly established democracies. Andrew Moravcsik . . . argues that . . . the accession by newly democratic states to binding human rights agreements: " . . . is a tactic used by governments to 'lock in' and consolidate democratic institutions, thereby enhancing their credibility and stability vis-à-vis nondemocratic political threats." That is, these regimes attempt to entrench certain political choices in fear, or anticipation, that a future illiberal regime will roll back liberal gains. . . .

. . . Under an AS regime, newly established democracies could not rely on the treaties for the purposes they desire. Without severance as a remedial option, they might more easily lose their membership in human rights treaties at some point in the future. This level of prospective uncertainty is not what these states want, nor is it the ground on which their consent to the treaty was built.

. . .

Established democracies.... Moravcsik explains that established democracies perceive little domestic gain in agreeing to such international commitments and a significant sovereignty cost in doing so.... In terms of the lack of domestic benefits, these states operate with a high baseline of strong democratic traditions and civil rights protections.... Moravcsik concludes that the factor that ultimately encouraged the United Kingdom to ratify the Convention was the perception that a regional human rights regime would help stave off the threat of totalitarianism in Western Europe, a concern well within the security interests of the British government....

...

The breadth of U.S. objectives in joining human rights treaties should suggest that in some circumstances those interests would outweigh the interests served by a particular reservation. If the government were faced with the choice of (1) the complete loss of membership in a treaty or (2) the loss of the application or effect of a particular reservation, in some circumstances the government would prefer the latter. Certain features of the American political system suggest that the number of times when that choice would prevail is not trivial. In her extended analysis of the subject, Natalie Kaufman discusses institutional relationships between executive agencies, the president, and the Senate that lead to "attachments [that] are unnecessary." According to Kaufman, wounds left by the debates on the Bricker Amendment in the 1950s often lead the executive branch to overcompensate in submitting its package of reservations to the Senate as a means of securing approval. Kaufman explains that this attitude frequently results in reservations that sweep much more broadly than required for passage ...

...

Although the above discussion relies partly on Moravcsik's empirical work, his findings do not suffice for our purposes.... [S]everal established democracies, such as the Netherlands and Belgium, follow a consistent standard with regard to international human rights law. They evince a deep commitment to incorporating human rights treaties in their domestic law and to promoting international human rights abroad: hence, they can be characterized as consistent, rather than double, standard states.

...

... Because their domestic systems are closely tied to international regimes, they also potentially incur significant costs and benefits from developments in the law of treaties. All of these states have submitted reservations to the ICCPR. If a reservation were found invalid — by a domestic court or by another third-party institution — the determination whether the government was still bound to the treaty would have considerable ramifications.

...

A strict AS rule would release the government from this self-constraint, and suspend a panoply of civil and political rights protections in a manner the system would have a difficult time withstanding....

The double- and consistent-standard states analyzed above constitute opposite ends of a spectrum. Between the two lies an intermediate category of established democracies (such as Australia, Canada, Switzerland, and arguably India). In contrast to the double-standard democracies, these states evince genuine interest in incorporating human rights treaties in domestic law and in maintaining membership in them by dint of domestic political interests, not simply external foreign policy goals. However, their domestic systems of governance are not reliant on, or committed to, these treaties for the same ideational and pragmatic purposes as the consistent-standard states. The intermediate states, like all states, have an incentive to enter both essential and accessory reservations when ratifying multilateral agreements....

...

Nondemocratic states.... International relations scholars have recently begun to use sociological tools to understand the processes by which states pass from illiberal to liberal regimes....

Most significant for our purposes is the critical step in the socialization process from a phase of "tactical concessions" to one of "prescriptive status." These are the moments when we can expect states to ratify human rights treaties, and thus the political context in which the value the government attaches to a reservation would be indicated. In the "tactical concession" phase, such governments make cosmetic changes to placate domestic and international pressure groups. For example, a government may release some political prisoners, exercise greater permissiveness toward political demonstrations, or pass relatively superficial legislation. These concessions can propel certain causal mechanisms, resulting in further dynamic changes that potentially lead to the phase of "prescriptive status."...

...At first glance, the minimal use of reservations by nondemocratic states might suggest that the concern about where to place such states in a severability model is marginal. While the small number of reservations does diminish the concern, this phenomenon should also prompt heightened attention when nondemocratic states actually use reservations.

... [A] nondemocratic state that ratifies a treaty with reservations has begun to accept the prescriptive legitimacy of international rules. In these contexts, a state may be genuinely balancing competing goals so that a particular reservation may not be an essential condition of its accession to the treaty.

...

... [I]n some cases, honoring a state's initial act of ratification and the expression of political pressures reflected in that decision may require treating a reservation as dispensable. This result would reflect the nondemocratic state's consent.

A treaty regime that respects the choice of nondemocratic states' consent in the same manner that it respects the consent of other states may raise some normative concerns.... [I]t is worth emphasizing two aspects of the impact of a severability regime on the human rights practices of nondemocratic states. First, a severability regime provides a meaningful opportunity to keep a state bound to a human rights treaty despite an invalid reservation. In sharp contrast, an AS regime would consistently nullify a state's ratification without ever inquiring into the severability question....

...

[Second, a regime that permits severability] facilitates progressive movement through the phases [of socialization]...

...

. . . [Thomas] Risse argues that inducing nondemocratic governments to engage openly in the discourse of international legal norms, including juridical justifications to defend their actions, helps to facilitate progressive change. A severability regime — especially one that applies the default rule proposed [below] — includes an information-forcing mechanism that stimulates discourse by the nondemocratic state in international legal terms. . . .

The above analysis of state treaty practice not only demonstrates the need for severing invalid reservations in particular circumstances, but also points toward the way to structure a regime that distinguishes between those circumstances and ones in which severance is inappropriate. A central problem in designing or administering such a regime concerns what an adjudicator should do in the face of silence or ambiguity. . . . When the text is silent or ambiguous, however, a default rule or interpretive presumption is required to determine the outcome. Such a rule will also be required for cases in which states have already acceded to a treaty without knowing to specify their intent at the time; for existing human rights treaties, that retrospective tail will be exceptionally long.

. . . [A]djudicators should assume an invalid reservation is not an essential condition of a state's decision to ratify a treaty unless evidence to the contrary is provided. A significant factor in setting the appropriate presumption involves reducing error costs. For example, if the adjudicator misjudges the state's intent, is it better for the error to fall in the domain of underinclusiveness or overinclusiveness?

The record of state treaty practice strongly suggests that error costs derived from a nonseverance presumption exceed those from a presumption favoring severance. . . . An adjudicator's erroneous expulsion of a state from a treaty risks significant costs along two dimensions: international (e.g., a sovereignty impact from the state's expulsion against its will, reputational costs to the state's international standing, loss of a leadership or participatory role in the regime) and domestic (e.g., the unhinging of a wide array of judicially enforceable civil and political rights protections, facilitation of illiberal rollbacks). The result would probably involve significant transaction costs in the process of reratifying the agreement.

. . .

A presumption favoring nonseverance risks more harmful outcomes than the severance presumption. Perhaps most important is the corrective action that states can adopt: reratification (in response to an erroneous decision not to sever) and withdrawal (in response to an erroneous decision to sever). The corrective action is far more difficult in the former case than in the latter.

QUESTIONS

1. Why was there near unanimity among the states parties to the ICCPR that objected to the reservations by the United States about the particular reservation concerning Article 6, paragraph 5 (death sentence)? Did that reservation raise a special problem under the Covenant? On the other hand, was there special reason for the United States to reserve as to that provision?

2. In the light of General Comment No. 24, if you were a Senator committed to US ratification of the major human rights instruments, would you have voted for *any* reservation? Did any one of the reservations have a special justification?

3. Is General Comment No. 24 consistent with the spirit of the *Genocide Convention* advisory opinion described above, p. 1124, *supra*? Using that opinion, how would you argue that the reservations of the United States should be accepted in their entirety as valid under international law?

4. In *Kennedy v. Trinidad and Tobago*, the dissenting members of the Committee noted that application of the reservation in the present case 'is wider than required in order to cater to the constitutional constraints of the State party'. In such circumstances, should the Committee take a minimalist approach: sever, or refuse to apply, a particular aspect of a reservation and not sever the reservation as whole? Is that approach better suited to institutions such as national courts?

5. The UK Government raised a significant pragmatic concern about General Comment 24 — that the Committee's severability approach 'would risk discouraging States from ratifying human rights conventions (since they would not be in a position to reassure their national Parliaments as to the status of treaty provisions on which it was felt necessary to reserve)', see p. 1147, *supra*. How do you evaluate these concerns in light of the article by Goodman? Would different types of states respond the same way to a severability rule? Does it depend on a state's purposes in joining a human rights treaty regime? Would you anticipate the same effects for CEDAW, ICESCR or CERD?

13

Horizontal Interpenetration: Transnational Influence and Enforcement of Human Rights

Chapter 12 offered the promise or ideal. States will take the necessary measures to assure internal compliance with international human rights. In many states, their own constitutions, whether predating or instituted during the human rights movement, will achieve broad compliance. In other contexts, states will internalize the international norms so that their courts apply those norms directly.

Our concern of course is with states that fall short of this ideal, sometimes far short. We have seen principally in Chapters 9 and 10, but also in the regional systems of Chapter 11, the efforts of intergovernmental institutions and their organs to secure compliance by violator states. Such modes of enforcement can be understood as *vertical*, in the sense that pressures are exerted and perhaps sanctions applied by international organs 'above' the state. Such organs apply international law. From the perspective of that law, those international bodies exercise authority over all member states in accordance with the terms of the treaties creating them.

Of course, international organizations' decision-making about what action, if any, to take is not divorced from the decisions of their member states. To the contrary, the international bodies attempting to ensure, or at least to heighten the probability of, compliance are often 'intergovernmental' in two senses. First, the treaties creating them were ratified by their member states. Second, within the UN Charter system (apart from the International Court of Justice), the decision-making bodies for compliance and enforcement measures are composed of representatives of such states. Their decisions are not then 'divorced' from these states' separate decisions, for each member of a given body must decide how to vote — say, within the Human Rights Council or General Assembly or Security Council. Nonetheless, the organ's vote (say, to pass a resolution, make an investigation, authorize or order sanctions or intervention, or to refuse to take any of these actions) is a collective vote, an organizational decision, which may in the end impose obligations on many states individually. The organization, however influenced in its decision it may be by a few member states, is in a formal and vital sense the acting party.

Here, in Chapter 13, we consider entirely *horizontal* modes of implementing and enforcing human rights. Nations are increasingly providing formal mechanisms for victims seeking to redress human rights violations committed in foreign countries. This chapter focuses principally on judicial means of norm enunciation and enforcement. Indeed, both criminal prosecutors and civil courts are increasingly engaged with cases seeking to establish the wrongdoing of individuals for violations committed abroad. Such cases constitute a bridge between Chapters 12 and 13. Although they are decided by domestic institutions and domestic law plays a vital role, they may impose liability for activities occurring in other countries that involved citizens of those countries and did not involve citizens of the forum, and their decrees may impose remedies which affect officials or other citizens of those countries. Of course these vehicles for redress may complement or interfere with other governmental approaches to influencing the human rights practices in other states. Those interactions are considered along with the cases studied in this chapter.

As a matter of international law, a threshold question is whether a national body has legal authority to exercise jurisdiction. Should courts, for example, be presumed to have such power unless international law expressly prohibits it? Or should courts be presumed not to have such power unless international law affirmatively authorizes it? Also consider different classes of defendants. That is, in addition to those thorny jurisdictional issues, should high state officials be immune from criminal and civil proceedings in foreign courts? In particular, should standard forms of diplomatic and sovereign immunity protect individuals who have allegedly engaged in crimes against humanity and other gross human rights violations? What is the proper balance between the need to protect sovereign prerogatives and the need to redress human rights abuses in these contexts? What principles should be developed to strike the correct balance and who should decide? These are some of the issues we explore in the sections that follow.

These issues variously concern the lawful authority and desirability of different forms of influence over foreign human rights practices. They demand answers to questions about the proper allocation of power between private individuals and public authorities. They also invite an exploration of the vices and virtues of criminal prosecution and civil litigation and the impact on foreign policy relationships in taking such cases to court.

The focus of Chapter 13 falls into three sections. *Section A* examines jurisdictional principles. It attends foremost to human rights enforcement by national bodies in cases having no direct nexus to the forum state. *Section B* turns to state judiciaries providing remedies to victims of human rights violations that occurred in other countries. It stresses the role of legislation in the United States, the Alien Tort Statute, and judicial doctrines regulating the power provided by that law. Finally, *Section C* considers sovereign and official immunity. It discusses the prospect of achieving justice in light of these defences and examines the competing interests at stake.

COMMENT ON INTERSTATE SANCTIONS

In this chapter, we consider horizontal modes of implementing and enforcing human rights between countries. Acting singly or as part of a consortium, states may apply a range of pressures to punish a violator state or to prevent violations from occurring. One of the softer forms of coercive power includes immigration and travel restrictions. In contrast, one of the most severe forms is the use of armed force. In Chapter 9, we discussed NATO's intervention in Kosovo in 1999 as a defining moment for 'humanitarian intervention' conducted without the authority of the Security Council, p. 837, *supra*. Historical examples of unilateral humanitarian intervention post 1945 might include India's invasion of East Pakistan; Tanzania's invasion of Uganda (to oust Idi Amin's regime) and Vietnam's invasion of Cambodia (to oust Pol Pot's regime). After the Cold War, examples of humanitarian intervention without prior Security Council approval include the Economic Community of West African States' intervention in Liberia; safe havens and no fly zones in northern and southern Iraq established by British, French and US forces following the 1991 Iraq War; and the Economic Community of West African States' intervention in Sierra Leone. After the 1999 NATO campaign, the Independent International Commission on Kosovo was established on the initiative of Sweden's Prime Minister and co-chaired by Justice Richard Goldstone and Mr. Carl Tham. The Commission issued a report which concluded that NATO's intervention was 'illegal but legitimate'. The Commission explained: 'It was illegal because it did not receive prior approval from the United Nations Security Council. However, . . . the intervention was justified because all diplomatic avenues had been exhausted and because the intervention had the effect of liberating the majority population of Kosovo from a long period of oppression under Serbian rule'. The Responsibility to Protect, discussed in Chapter 9, drew in part from the Kosovo experience. Although unilateral military force is seldom employed to promote human rights, it is worth contemplating as a reference point on the spectrum of interstate sanctions.

One of the primary and more common tools of interstate sanctions involves the use of economic incentives. The range of such measures includes both carrots and sticks. These measures may rely on damaging the reputation of the state involved — 'shaming', to use a term commonly invoked as one of a range of strategies. Such efforts may impose boycotts or embargoes, suspend trade or encourage disinvestment. They may impose conditions on security assistance, development aid or trade advantages — conditions that require the targeted state to comply with fundamental human rights norms. Within such a 'horizontal' (state-to-state) application of inducements and pressures, the state imposing human rights conditions — so-called 'conditionality' — as part of its foreign policy becomes part of a multi-layered system of enforcement of international human rights.

A specific category of human rights inducements involves preferential trade agreements (PTAs). The following excerpt from an article on the topic describes some illustrative agreements as well as the empirical assumptions that underpin such mechanisms for influencing state behaviour:[1]

> PTAs [Preferential trade agreements] are a rapidly growing class of international institutions that govern market access between member states of an economic region. Semi-autonomous from the global structure of the World Trade Organization (WTO), PTAs frequently regulate spheres of social governance that increasingly include human rights standards. Some, such as the Euro-Mediterranean Association Agreements, supply "hard" standards that tie agreement benefits to member compliance with specific human rights principles. Others, such as the West African

[1] Emilie M. Hafner-Burton, Trading Human Rights: How Preferential Trade Agreements Influence Government Repression, International Organization, Vol. 59, Issue 3, 593–629 (2005).

> Economic and Monetary Union, supply "soft" standards that are only vaguely tied to market access and unconditional on member states' actions.
>
> . . .
>
> [Some] PTAs provide member governments with "harder" institutional channels to manage and enforce their policy commitments (that is, benefits that are in some way conditional on member states' actions). These PTAs do so by placing the language of human rights in an enforceable incentive structure designed to provide members with the economic and political benefits of various forms of market access. These benefits are supplied under conditions of compliance with the protection of human rights principles or laws identified in the agreement. Behavioral change is a side payment for market gains, enforced through threat (direct or tacit) to disrupt integration or exchange unless a trade partner complies with their human rights commitments specified in the contract. . . .
>
> The Lomé and Cotonou Agreements are strong examples of these types of PTAs. Cotonou provides the new institutional structure for the European Community's largest financial and political framework for cooperation, offering nonreciprocal trade benefits for certain African, Caribbean, and Pacific states, including nearly unlimited entry to the EC market for a wide range of goods. The agreement, which replaced successive Lomé Agreements, commits "Parties [to] undertake to promote and protect all fundamental freedoms and human rights, be they civil and political, or economic, social and cultural." These principles are supported through a political dialogue designed to share information, to cultivate mutual understanding, and to facilitate the formation of shared priorities, including those concerning the respect for human rights. Obligations are binding on recipients. They are supported by a review mechanism established in the consultation procedures of Article 96, which require habitual assessments of national developments concerning human rights. Alongside the agreement are conditional financial protocols allocating resources available to eligible countries through the European Development Fund. When members are perceived to violate agreement terms, a variety of different actions can be taken to influence behavior. These include the threat or act of withdrawal of membership or financial protocols, as well as the enforcement of economic or political sanctions. Cotonou thus supplies strong elements of both coercion and persuasion.
>
> . . . PTAs with hard standards can, under certain conditions, influence through coercion by changing repressive actors' costs and benefits of actualizing their preferences for repression. Consider again the abusive elite with strong preferences for repression. Where persuasion alone is likely to fail, hard standards can influence the problem of compliance without changing actors' preferences. They provide an economic motivation to promote human rights policy reforms that would not otherwise be implemented, and they do so in a relatively short time horizon. When institutionalized PTAs create new and valuable gains, hard agreements can also commit future elites with preferences for liberalization to human rights reforms they would not otherwise select. While influence through persuasion requires leveling a campaign to change a new leader's preferences for repression, influence through coercion requires only that the leader value the gains of integration more than the gains of repression.

The debate within the United States about the relevance of human rights to foreign economic policy has been active and contentious for decades. A centerpiece in this regard is the US Foreign Assistance Act, which is designed to restrict foreign aid to states 'engag[ing] in a consistent pattern of gross violations of internationally recognized human rights'. US foreign policy measures have also ranged from security assistance and development aid to trade and foreign investment. The contexts in which political controversies have arisen include US involvement with global 'hot spots' since the early 1970s — for example, US security or economic aid to, investment in, or trade with regimes in Chile, China, Cuba, Nicaragua, South Africa and others. The economic importance of aid and trade has concerned major sectors of the US economy — defence industries anxious to export their products, manufacturing and service-oriented firms fearful of losing foreign markets in retaliation for elimination by the United States of other states' advantages in trade, consumer groups fearful of losing cheaper imported products, and so on. Such strong consequences raise the stakes for a politics of conditionality.

Of course, overall US foreign policy also has a 'carrot' side, or range of positive inducements. That is, the US Government offers help to states that are willing to attempt certain changes, such as a move toward democratic government or the rule of law. Launched in 2004, the Millennium Challenge Account (MCA) is one of the latest manifestations in this regard. The MCA is stylized as a 'reward' programme. It increases US development assistance to countries that demonstrate a willingness to meet certain performance indicators such as civil and political rights protections and investments in health care and education. More broadly, for decades various US or US-funded agencies have provided foreign states with a range of assistance — such as expert consultants and training government branches (particularly the judiciary) to observe basic principles of the rule of law. Such aid programmes, stressing relationships between democracy and the rule of law on the one hand, and market economies and free trade on the other, form part of the current globalization debate, discussed in Chapter 16.

The US is not alone in these efforts. The European Union employs 'restrictive measures' to promote human rights. According to the EU, the range of measures includes:[2]

> diplomatic sanctions (expulsion of diplomats, severing of diplomatic ties, suspension of official visits);
> suspension of cooperation with a third country;
> boycotts of sport or cultural events;
> trade sanctions (general or specific trade sanctions, arms embargoes);
> financial sanctions (freezing of funds or economic resources, prohibition on financial transactions, restrictions on export credits or investment);
> flight bans; and
> restrictions on admission.

In early 2007, the list of countries subject to various EU measures included Belarus, Burma, Serbia and Montenegro, and Zimbabwe. Additionally, the European Community and Council of Development Ministers, in particular, promote human rights through project aid under such titles as 'governance and civil society' and 'social infrastructure projects in education and training'. Other countries have also

[2] See http://ec.europa.eu/comm/external_relations/cfsp/sanctions/index.htm.

followed suit, at least in their formal commitments. For instance, at the end of the Cold War, Japan adopted the Official Development Assistance Charter, which includes a commitment to condition foreign aid to promote human rights. In 2003, the Government revised the Charter and maintained the commitment to consider human rights, among other factors, in its foreign aid programmes. Whether the Government has implemented this principle in practice is subject to debate.

Some of the 'case studies' in the balance of this chapter explore the potential interactions between economic sanctions, foreign policy more generally, and judicial cognizance of foreign human rights violations. Regardless of those relationships, economic sanctions should be recognized, in their own right, as alternative measures for state-to-state influence on human rights norms.

ADDITIONAL READING

Fumitaka Furuoka, 'Human Rights Conditionality and Aid Allocation: Case Study of Japanese Foreign Aid Policy', *Perspectives on Global Development and Technology*, Vol. 4, No. 2, 125–146 (2005); Sarah H. Cleveland, 'Norm Internalization and U.S. Economic Sanctions', 1 Yale Journal of International Law 1 (2001); Adeno Addis, 'Economic Sanctions and the Problem of Evil', Human Rights Quarterly, Vol. 25, No. 3, pp. 573–623 (2003); Diego Nogueras and Luis Hinojosa, 'Human Rights Conditionality in the External Trade of the European Union', 7 Colum. J. Eur. L. 307 (2001); K. Tomaševski, *Between Sanctions and Elections: Aid Donors and their Human Rights Performance* (1997); D. Price and J. Hannah, 'The Constitutionality of United States State and Local Sanctions', 39 Harv. Int. L. J. 443 (1998);. Poe *et al.*, 'Human Rights and US Foreign Aid Revisited: The Latin American Region', 16 Hum. Rts. Q. 539 (1994); K. Arts, *Integrating Human Rights into Development Cooperation: The Case of the Lomé Convention* (2000); P. Alston (ed.), The EU and Human Rights (1999); P. J. Kuyper, 'Trade Sanctions, Security and Human Rights and Commercial Policy', in M. Maresceau (ed.), The *European Community's Commercial Policy after 1992: The Legal Dimension* 387 (1993).

A. UNIVERSAL JURISDICTION

The principle of universal jurisdiction emerged primarily in the context of criminal prosecutions and subsequently extended to areas of civil litigation. It is accordingly helpful to review basic jurisdictional principles on which states prescribe (make law), particularly laws imposing individual criminal responsibility, and the basic jurisdictional principles on which a state's courts hear civil and criminal cases.

Criminal litigation, unlike civil litigation, ordinarily requires that the state whose courts are trying a case have custody of the defendant. Holding criminal trials *in absentia* is rare. Choice of law, so vital an element of many civil cases, generally does not figure in criminal litigation; the court applies only the law of the state from which it derives its authority, almost always the one in which it sits, even if the conduct occurred or the effects were felt in other states. The principle of universal jurisdiction examined below, constitutes a major exception to this generalization.

The bases on which states enact the criminal laws to which their courts look therefore becomes a critical issue. There are certain conventional categories, some of which are more broadly accepted internationally than others. Several of these categories appear in the following description, based on the American Law Institute, *Restatement (Third), The Foreign Relations Law of the United States* (1987), section 402.

> (1) *Territorial principle*, or prescribing with respect to conduct taking place within a state's territory. This principle is surely the most common and the most readily accepted throughout the world. (2) *Effects principle*, prescribing with respect to conduct outside the territory that has effects within it. (3) *Nationality principle*, prescribing with respect to acts, interests or relations of a state's nationals within and outside its territory. (4) *Protective principle*, prescribing with respect to certain conduct of non-nationals outside a state's territory that is directed against the security of the state or against a limited class of state interests that threaten the integrity of governmental functions (such as counterfeiting). (5) *Passive personality principle*, or prescribing with respect to acts committed outside a state by a non-national where the victim was a national. This principle is surely the least recognized among states as a valid basis for criminal legislation.

These principles are bounded by a number of qualifications and competing considerations, some of which are sketched in section 403 of the *Restatement*. Consider the following discussion in the *Restatement on universal jurisdiction.*

> 404. Universal jurisdiction to Define and Punish Certain Offenses
>
> A state has jurisdiction to define and prescribe punishment for certain offenses recognized by the community of nations as of universal concern, such as piracy, slave trade, attacks on or hijacking of aircraft, genocide, war crimes, and perhaps certain acts of terrorism....
>
> COMMENT:
>
> *a. Expanding class of universal offenses*... [I]nternational law permits any state to apply its laws to punish certain offenses although the state has no links of territory with the offense, or of nationality with the offender (or even the victim). Universal jurisdiction over the specified offenses is a result of universal condemnation of those activities and general interest in cooperating to suppress them, as reflected in widely-accepted international agreements and resolutions of international organizations. These offenses are subject to universal jurisdiction as a matter of customary law. Universal jurisdiction for additional offenses is provided by international agreements, but it remains to be determined whether universal jurisdiction over a particular offense has become customary law for states not party to such an agreement....
>
> ...
>
> REPORTERS' NOTES
>
> 1. *Offenses subject to universal jurisdiction.* Piracy has sometimes been described as 'an offense against the law of nations' — an international crime. Since there is no international penal tribunal, the punishment of piracy is left to any state that seizes the offender.... Whether piracy is an international crime, or is rather a matter of international concern as to which international law accepts the jurisdiction of all states, may not make an important difference.
>
> ...

> That genocide and war crimes are subject to universal jurisdiction was accepted after the Second World War...
>
> The [Genocide] Convention provides for trial by the territorial state or by an international penal tribunal to be established, but no international penal tribunal with jurisdiction over the crime of genocide has been established. Universal jurisdiction to punish genocide is widely accepted as a principle of customary law...
>
> International agreements have provided for general jurisdiction for additional offenses, e.g., the Hague Convention for the Suppression of Unlawful Seizure of Aircraft... and the International Convention against the Taking of Hostages... These agreements include an obligation on the parties to punish or extradite offenders, even when the offense was not committed within their territory or by a national.... An international crime is presumably subject to universal jurisdiction.

COMMENT ON THE *EICHMANN* TRIAL

The *Eichmann* trial and conviction in 1961 illustrate issues concerning the application of universal jurisdiction at an early stage of the post-Nuremberg evolution of human rights law.

Adolf Eichmann, operationally in charge of the mass murder of Jews in Germany and German-occupied countries, fled Germany after the war. He was abducted from Argentina by Israelis, and brought to trial in Israel under the Nazi and Nazi Collaborators (Punishment) Law, enacted after Israel became a state. Section 1(a) of the Law provided:

> A person who has committed one of the following offences — (1) did, during the period of the Nazi regime, in a hostile country, an act constituting a crime against the Jewish people; (2) did, during the period of the Nazi regime, in a hostile country, an act constituting a crime against humanity; (3) did, during the period of the Second World War, in a hostile country, an act constituting a war crime; is liable to the death penalty.

The Law defined 'crimes against the Jewish people' to consist principally of acts intended to bring about physical destruction. The other two crimes were defined similarly to the like charges at Nuremberg. The 15 counts against Eichmann involved all three crimes. The charges stressed Eichmann's active and significant participation in the 'final solution to the Jewish problem' developed and administered by Nazi officials. Eichmann was convicted in 1961 and later executed. There appear below summaries of portions of the opinions of the trial and appellate courts.

The Attorney-General of the Government of Israel v. Eichmann[3]

Eichmann argued that the prosecution violated international law by inflicting punishment (1) upon persons who were not Israeli citizens (2) for acts done by them

[3] District Court of Jerusalem, Judgment of 11 December 1961. This summary and the selective quotations are drawn from 56 Am. J. Int. L. 805 (1962) (unofficial translation).

outside Israel and before its establishment, (3) in the course of duty, and (4) on behalf of a foreign country. In reply, the Court noted that, in the event of a conflict between an Israeli statute and principles of international law, it would be bound to apply the statute. However, it then concluded that 'the law in question conforms to the best traditions of the law of nations. The power of the State of Israel to enact the law in question or Israel's 'right to punish' is based... from the point of view of international law, on a dual foundation: The universal character of the crimes in question and their specific character as being designed to exterminate the Jewish people'.

Thus the Court relied primarily on the universality and protective principles to justify its assertion of jurisdiction to try the crimes defined in the Law. It held such crimes to be offences against the law of nations, much as was the traditional crime of piracy. It compared the conduct made criminal under the Israeli statute (particularly the 'crime against the Jewish people') and the crime of genocide, as defined in Article 1 of the Convention for the Prevention and Punishment of Genocide.

> The Contracting Parties confirm that genocide, whether committed in time of peace or in time of war, is a crime under international law which they undertake to prevent and to punish.[4]

The Court also stressed the relationship between the Law's definition of 'war crime' and the pattern of crimes defined in the Nuremberg Charter. It rejected arguments of Eichmann based upon the retroactive application of the legislation, and stated that 'all the reasons justifying the Nuremberg judgments justify *eo ipse* the retroactive legislation of the Israeli legislator'.

The Court then discussed another 'foundation' for the prosecution — the offence specifically aimed at the Jewish people.

> [This foundation] of penal jurisdiction conforms, according to [the] acknowledged terminology, to the protective principle... The 'crime against the Jewish people,' as defined in the Law, constitutes in effect an attempt to exterminate the Jewish people.... If there is an effective link (and not necessarily an identity) between the State of Israel and the Jewish people, then a crime intended to exterminate the Jewish people has a very striking connection with the State of Israel.... The connection between the State of Israel and the Jewish people needs no explanation.

Eichmann v. The Attorney-General of the Government of Israel[5]

After stating that it fully concurred in the holding and reasoning of the district court, the Supreme Court proceeded to develop arguments in different directions. It

[4] Article 6 of the Convention, the meaning and implications of which were viewed differently by the parties, states: 'Persons charged with genocide or any of the other acts enumerated in Article III shall be tried by a competent tribunal of the State in the territory of which the act was committed, or by such international penal tribunal as may have jurisdiction with respect to those Contracting Parties which shall have accepted its jurisdiction'.

[5] Supreme Court sitting as Court of Criminal Appeals, 29 May 1962. This summary is based upon an English translation of the decision appearing in 36 Int. L. Rep. 14–17, 277 (1968).

stressed that Eichmann could not claim to have been unaware at the time of his conduct that he was violating deeply rooted and universal moral principles. Particularly in its relatively underdeveloped criminal side, international law could be analogized to the early common law, which would be similarly open to charges of retroactive law making. Because the international legal system lacked adjudicatory or executive institutions, it authorized, for the time being, national officials to punish individuals for violations of its principles, either directly under international law or by virtue of municipal legislation adopting those principles.

Moreover, in this case Israel was the most appropriate jurisdiction for trial, a *forum conveniens* where witnesses were readily available. It was relevant that there had been no requests for extradition of Eichmann to other states for trial, or indeed protests by other states against a trial in Israel.

The Court affirmed the holding of the district court that each charge could be sustained. It noted, however, much overlap among the charges, and that all could be grouped within the inclusive category of 'crimes against humanity'.

PNINA LAHAV, JUDGMENT IN JERUSALEM

(1997), at 150

[In this portion of her biography of Simon Agranat, Justice and later Chief Justice of the Israeli Supreme Court, Lahav analyses his role in the Supreme Court's affirmance of Eichmann's conviction and death sentence. The Court delivered its judgment in a *per curiam* opinion. Justice Agranat had prepared the section of that opinion dealing with jurisdictional challenges to the trial.]

Agranat also understood that more than appearance was at stake: the soul of the Zionist project was reshaped by the brutal confrontation with the Holocaust. The old tension within Zionism between universalism and particularism now tilted in favor of particularism. Israelis were perceiving themselves as special: a special target for genocide and special in their right to ignore international norms in pursuit of justice. Popular hubris was growing, nurturing a victim mentality, a sense of self-righteousness and excessive nationalism, threatening to weaken the already shaky foundations of universalism in Israeli political culture.

...

Agranat understood that the legal reasoning he chose would affect the resolution of the tension between particularism and universalism. The Supreme Court could either let the conviction stand on the basis of crimes against the Jewish people, thereby lending force to the contention that Israel operated by its own rules, impervious to the laws developed by the community of nations, or it could try to show that Eichmann's trial was compatible with international norms of justice and fairness.

Most of the legal arguments advanced by Eichmann were designed to prove that Israel lacked jurisdiction to try him. Two of these arguments received extensive attention from the international community. The first was that the 1950 Israeli Law against the Nazis and Nazi Collaborators, which vested jurisdiction in the Israeli courts, was an ex post facto criminal law and as such could not apply to foreign nationals; the second was that, because the crimes were 'extra-territorial offenses' committed by a foreign national, Israel could not prosecute Eichmann according to the territoriality principle of international law.

In rejecting these arguments, the district court stressed the superiority of Israeli law in the sovereign state of Israel. The Law against the Nazis and Nazi Collaborators, the district court held, was a part of Israeli positive law and, as such, was binding on the courts of the land. It did hold that the law agreed with international norms, but emphasized the impact of the Holocaust on the evolution of the law of nations. This holding contained a symbolic message: Jewish national pride and self-assertion ruled the day. There was poetic justice in this interpretation. If the Final Solution was about the lawless murder of Jews, the *Eichmann* case was about the subjection of the perpetrators to Jewish justice, conceived and applied by the very heirs of those murdered.

There was ambivalence in Agranat's handling of this theme. On one hand, he endorsed the district court's analysis; on the other, his own reasoning went in a different direction. He sought to prove that the validity of the Law against the Nazis and Nazi Collaborators stemmed not from its superiority to the law of nations but from its compatibility with international law. Jewish justice was thereby not different from or superior to the law of nations; rather, it was a part of it.

...

...Citing scholarly works and judicial opinions, he asserted that international law did not prohibit ex post facto laws and was not dogmatic about the territoriality principle. Thus Israel's decision to prosecute, far from being a violation of international law, was simply a perfectly legitimate reluctance to recognize principles not fully endorsed by the community of nations.... He wanted to show that Israel's law was not an aberration but an affirmation of the law of nations.

The Law against the Nazis and Nazi Collaborators created a new category of crimes: crimes against the Jewish people. As such, it was a unique ex post facto law. The crime was specific to Jews and created a category hitherto unknown in any legal system. It was precisely for this reason that the crime formed a coherent part of Zionism.... Zionism portrayed the Holocaust less as the vile fruit of totalitarianism and more as the culmination of two millennia of anti-Semitism. The Jews had been defenseless because they did not possess political power. Even in Nuremberg the Allies refused to recognize that the Jews as a nation were especially targeted by the Nazis. The offense, 'crimes against the Jewish people', was designed to correct that myopia and to assert, ex post facto and forever, the Jewish point of view....

Speaking for the Supreme Court, Agranat raised a different voice. He reviewed the four categories of the indictment, and he concluded that they had a common denominator, a 'special universal characteristic'. About 'crimes against the Jewish people' he had this to say: 'Thus, the category of "crimes against the Jewish people" is nothing but ... "the gravest crime against humanity". It is true that there are certain differences between them ... but these are not differences material to our case'. Therefore, he concluded, in order to determine whether international law recognized Israeli jurisdiction stemming from this ex post facto statute, the Court could simply collapse the entire indictment into 'the inclusive category of "crimes against humanity"'. This 'simple' technique enabled Agranat to devote the bulk of his opinion to the universal aspects of the *Eichmann* case.

QUESTIONS

1. Consider the alternatives to trial of Eichmann by the Israeli court. Would any international tribunal have been competent? What would have been involved in an effort to establish another *ad hoc* international criminal tribunal like Nuremberg, and would that effort have been likely to succeed? Would trial before the courts of another state have been preferable? Which state?

2. What problems, if any, do you see in reliance on 'crimes against the Jewish people'? How would you distinguish it from, for example, legislation by an African state defining 'crimes against the black people' that could reach persons in Western or other states who are accused of violence against black people? Are both types of statutes good ideas?

COMMENT ON *EX PARTE* PINOCHET AND UNIVERSAL JURISDICTION

General Augusto Pinochet resigned as head of state of Chile in 1990 and became a 'Senator for life'. In 1998, he traveled to the United Kingdom for medical treatment. Judicial authorities in Spain sought to extradite him to stand criminal trial in Spain on several charges, including torture, related to the right-wing military overthrow of President Allende on 11 September 1973 and the subsequent political repression during Pinochet's term as head of state. An international warrant for his arrest was issued in Spain, and a British magistrate issued a provisional warrant under the UK Extradition Act of 1989. None of the conduct alleged by the Spanish authorities was committed against UK citizens or in the United Kingdom. Seeking to return to Chile, Pinochet initiated proceedings for habeas corpus and for judicial review of the warrant.

On appeal, the House of Lords decided the case, but this judgment was set aside due to a conflict of interest involving one of the Lords. A differently constituted seven-member panel reheard the appeal in 1999. Six of the seven Lords upheld the extradition process, but (in the majority of their opinions) only with respect to a small number of the charges. Extradition was appropriate only for charges satisfying the 'double criminality' principle, which requires the conduct in question to have been criminal in both Spain and the United Kingdom at the time it was committed. A majority of the Lords concluded that because a section of the Criminal Justice Act 1988, incorporating the United Kingdom's obligations under the Convention Against Torture, had created a new domestic crime for torture committed outside of the country, only the charges of torture committed after the Act's entry into force could proceed.[6]

[6] We discuss below analogous US domestic legislation implementing the Torture Convention, see p. 1203, *infra*.

Lord Browne-Wilkinson discussed the foundation for universal jurisdiction over torture:

> I have no doubt that long before the Torture Convention of 1984 state torture was an international crime in the highest sense.
>
> But there was no tribunal or court to punish international crimes of torture. Local courts could take jurisdiction: see... *Attorney-General of Israel v. Eichmann.* But the objective was to ensure a general jurisdiction so that the torturer was not safe wherever he went.... The Torture Convention was agreed not in order to create an international crime which had not previously existed but to provide an international system under which the international criminal — the torturer — could find no safe haven....
>
> ...
>
> Under Article 5(2) a state party has to take jurisdiction over any alleged offender who is found within its territory.
>
> ...
>
> [I]n my judgment the Torture Convention did provide what was missing: a worldwide universal jurisdiction.

Other Lords expressed a range of opinions concerning universal jurisdiction. Consider, for example, Lord Millett's opinion:

> ...[C]rimes prohibited by international law attract universal jurisdiction under customary international law if two criteria are satisfied. First, they must be contrary to a peremptory norm of international law so as to infringe a jus cogens. Secondly, they must be so serious and on such a scale that they can justly be regarded as an attack on the international legal order. Isolated offences, even if committed by public officials, would not satisfy these criteria....
>
> ...
>
> ...Customary international law is part of the common law, and accordingly I consider that the English courts have and always have had extra-territorial criminal jurisdiction in respect of crimes of universal jurisdiction under customary international law.
>
> In my opinion, the systematic use of torture on a large scale and as an instrument of state policy had joined piracy, war crimes and crimes against peace as an international crime of universal jurisdiction well before 1984. I consider that it had done so by 1973. For my own part, therefore, I would hold that the courts of this country already possessed extra-territorial jurisdiction in respect of torture and conspiracy to torture on the scale of the charges in the present case and did not require the authority of statute to exercise it....
>
> ...
>
> Whereas the international community had condemned the widespread and systematic use of torture as an instrument of state policy, the Convention extended the offence to cover isolated and individual instances of torture provided that they were committed by a public official. I do not consider that offences of this kind were previously regarded as international crimes attracting universal jurisdiction.... Whereas previously states were entitled to take jurisdiction in respect of the offence wherever it was committed, they were now placed under an obligation to do so.

In contrast, Lord Phillips remarked:

> I believe that it is still an open question whether international law recognises universal jurisdiction in respect of international crimes — that is the right, under international law, of the courts of any state to prosecute for such crimes wherever they occur. In relation to war crimes, such a jurisdiction has been asserted by the State of Israel, notably in the prosecution of Adolf Eichmann, but this assertion of jurisdiction does not reflect any general state practice in relation to international crimes. Rather, states have tended to agree, or to attempt to agree, on the creation of international tribunals to try international crimes. They have however, on occasion, agreed by conventions, that their national courts should enjoy jurisdiction to prosecute for a particular category of international crime wherever occurring.

After the decision, the extradition case continued while Pinochet remained under house arrest. France, Belgium and Switzerland also made extradition requests. In 2000, the British Home Secretary stated that medical examinations of Pinochet led him to conclude that the 84-year-old general was incapable of standing trial and should be released to return to Chile. Later that year, Pinochet was permitted to fly home, to a radically different political context in which he was an isolated, far less influential and potent figure. Judicial steps were underway toward intense investigation into Pinochet's connection with the killings and torture. The Chilean Supreme Court stripped Pinochet of immunity, and several charges were brought against him. However, on 10 December 2006, Pinochet died before any prosecution was brought.

CASE CONCERNING THE ARREST WARRANT OF 11 APRIL 2000 (DEMOCRATIC REPUBLIC OF THE CONGO V. BELGIUM)

International Court of Justice, 2002

[A leading treatment of the scope and viability of universal jurisdiction arose in recent proceedings before the International Court of Justice (ICJ). The case involved Belgium's 'universal jurisdiction' law, which has since been modified. At the time, the law permitted Belgian judicial authorities to prosecute violations of international humanitarian law regardless of where the acts were committed and regardless of the nationality of the perpetrators and victims. In late 1998, twelve individuals lodged a complaint with a Belgian investigating judge at the Brussels Court of First Instance. Of the twelve complainants, five were of Belgian nationality, seven were of Congolese nationality, and all were resident in Belgium. The complaint concerned events that had taken place in the Democratic Republic of the Congo (DRC).

In mid-2000, the Belgian judge issued an arrest warrant in absentia against Mr Abdulaye Yerodia Ndombasi, who was the DRC's Minister for Foreign Affairs at the time. The warrant accused Mr Yerodia of committing war crimes and crimes against humanity before serving in his ministerial post. The complaint alleged that he made public speeches that incited the massacre of several hundred people, mainly of Tutsi origin, in the DRC. The Government of the DRC initiated proceedings against the Government of Belgium before the ICJ claiming that the issuance and international distribution of the arrest warrant unlawfully infringed the foreign minister's immunity and violated international rules on jurisdiction. A majority of the ICJ did not reach the issue of universal jurisdiction, holding instead that the promulgation and circulation of the arrest warrant violated Mr Yerodia's official immunity as Foreign Minister. A separate opinion joined by Judges Rosalyn Higgins, Peter Kooijmans and Thomas Buergenthal squarely addressed the issue of universal jurisdiction in one of the most extensive treatments of the subject to date. We return to the majority's assessment of the official immunity claim later in this chapter, p. 1233, *infra*. Excerpts of the separate joint opinion follow.]

JOINT SEPARATE OPINION OF JUDGES HIGGINS, KOOIJMANS AND BUERGENTHAL

19. We . . . turn to the question whether States are entitled to exercise jurisdiction over persons having no connection with the forum State when the accused is not present in the State's territory. . . .

20. Our analysis may begin with national legislation, to see if it evidences a State practice. . . . [N]ational legislation, whether in fulfilment of international treaty obligations to make certain international crimes offences also in national law, or otherwise, does not suggest a universal jurisdiction over these offences. Various examples typify the more qualified practice. The Australian War Crimes Act of 1945, as amended in 1988, provides for the prosecution in Australia of crimes committed between 1 September 1939 and 8 May 1945 by persons who were Australian citizens or residents at the times of being charged with the offences. The United Kingdom War Crimes Act of 1991 enables proceedings to be brought for murder, manslaughter or culpable homicide, committed between 1 September 1935 and 5 June 1945, in a place that was part of Germany or under German occupation, and in circumstances where the accused was at the time, or has become, a British citizen or resident of the United Kingdom. . . .

The Criminal Code of Canada 1985 allows the execution of jurisdiction when at the time of the act or omission the accused was a Canadian citizen or "employed by Canada in a civilian or military capacity;" or the "victim is a Canadian citizen or a citizen of a State that is allied with Canada in an armed conflict," or when "at the time of the act or omission Canada could, in conformity with international law, exercise jurisdiction over the person on the basis of the person's presence in Canada".

21. All of these illustrate the trend to provide for the trial and punishment under international law of certain crimes that have been committed extraterritorially. But none of them, nor the many others that have been studied by the Court, represent a classical assertion of a universal jurisdiction over particular offences committed elsewhere by persons having no relationship or connection with the forum State.

22. The case law under these provisions has largely been cautious so far as reliance on universal jurisdiction is concerned. In the Pinochet case in the English courts, the jurisdictional basis was clearly treaty based, with the double criminality rule required for extradition being met by English legislation in September 1988, after which date torture committed abroad was a crime in the United Kingdom as it already was in Spain. . . .

. . .

26. In some of the literature on the subject it is asserted that the great international treaties on crimes and offences evidence universality as a ground for the exercise of jurisdiction recognized in international law. This is doubtful.

27. Article VI of the Convention on the Prevention and Punishment of the Crime of Genocide, 9 December 1948, provides:

> "Persons charged with genocide or any of the other acts enumerated in Article III shall be tried by a competent tribunal of the State in the territory of which the act was committed, or by such international penal tribunal as may have jurisdiction with respect to those Contracting Parties which shall have accepted its jurisdiction."

This is an obligation to assert territorial jurisdiction, though the travaux preparatoires do reveal an understanding that this obligation was not intended to affect the right of a State to exercise criminal jurisdiction on its own nationals for acts committed outside the State (A/C 6/SR, 134; p. 5). Article VI also provides a potential grant of non-territorial competence to a possible future international tribunal — even this not being automatic under the Genocide Convention but being restricted to those Contracting Parties which would accept its jurisdiction. In recent years it has been suggested in the literature that Article VI does not prevent a State from exercising universal jurisdiction in a genocide case. (And see, more generally, Restatement (Third) of the Foreign Relations Law of the United States (1987), § 404.)

28. Article 49 of the First Geneva Convention, Article 50 of the Second Geneva Convention, Article 129 of the Third Geneva Convention and Article 146 of the Fourth Geneva Convention, all of 12 August 1949, provide:

> "Each High Contracting Party shall be under the obligation to search for persons alleged to have committed, or to have ordered to be committed, . . . grave breaches, and shall bring such persons, regardless of their nationality, before its own courts. It may also, if it prefers, and in accordance with the provisions of its own legislation, hand such persons over for trial to another High Contracting Party concerned, provided such High Contracting Party has made out a prima facie case."

29. Article 85, paragraph 1, of the First Additional Protocol to the 1949 Geneva Convention incorporates this provision by reference.

30. The stated purpose of the provision was that the offences would not be left unpunished (the extradition provisions playing their role in this objective). It may immediately be noted that this is an early form of the aut dedere aut prosequi to be seen in later conventions. But the obligation to prosecute is primary, making it even stronger.

31. No territorial or nationality linkage is envisaged, suggesting a true universality principle. But a different interpretation is given in the authoritative Pictet Commentary: Geneva Convention for the Amelioration of the Condition of the Wounded and Sick in Armed Forces in the Field (1952), which contends that this obligation was understood as being an obligation upon States parties to search for offenders who may be on their territory. Is it a true example of universality, if the obligation to search is restricted to the own territory? Does the obligation to search imply a permission to prosecute in absentia, if the search had no result?

. . .

35. The Hague Convention for the Suppression of Unlawful Seizure of Aircraft, 16 December 1970, making preambular reference to the "urgent need" to make such acts "punishable as an offence and to provide for appropriate measures with respect to prosecution and extradition of offenders," provided in Article 4(1) for an obligation to take such measures as may be necessary to establish jurisdiction over these offences and other acts of violence against passengers or crew:

> "(a) when the offence is committed on board an aircraft registered in that State;
>
> (b) when the aircraft on board which the offence is committed lands in its territory with the alleged offender still on board;
>
> (c) when the offence is committed on board an aircraft leased without crew to a lessee who has his principal place of business or, if the lessee has no such place of business, his permanent residence, in that State."

Article 4(2) provided for a comparable obligation to establish jurisdiction where the alleged offender was present in the territory and if he was not extradited pursuant to Article 8 by the territory. Thus here too was a treaty provision for aut dedere aut prosequi, of which the limb was in turn based on the principle of "primary universal repression." The jurisdictional bases provided for in Articles 4(1)(b) and 4(2), requiring no territorial connection beyond the landing of the aircraft or the presence of the accused, were adopted only after prolonged discussion. The travaux preparatoires show States for whom mere presence was an insufficient ground for jurisdiction beginning reluctantly to support this particular type of formula because of the gravity of the offence. Thus the representative of the United Kingdom stated that his country "would see great difficulty in assuming jurisdiction merely on the ground that an aircraft carrying a hijacker had landed in United Kingdom territory." Further, "normally his country did not accept the principle that the mere presence of an alleged offender within the jurisdiction of a State entitled that State to try him. In view, however, of the gravity of the offence. . . he was prepared to support. . . [the proposal on mandatory jurisdiction on the part of the State where a hijacker is found]." (Hague Conference, p. 75, para. 18.)

36. It is also to be noted that Article 4, paragraphs 1 and 2, provides for the mandatory exercise of jurisdiction in the absence of extradition; but does not preclude criminal jurisdiction exercised on alternative grounds of jurisdiction in accordance with national law (though those possibilities are not made compulsory under the Convention).

37. Comparable jurisdictional provisions are to be found in Articles 5 and 8 of the International Convention against the Taking of Hostages of 17 December 1979. The obligation enunciated in Article 8 whereby a State party shall "without exception whatsoever and whether or not the offence was committed in its territory," submit the case for prosecution if it does not extradite the alleged offender, was again regarded as necessary by the majority, given the nature of the crimes (Summary Record, Ad Hoc Committee on the Drafting of an International Convention Against the Taking of Hostages (A/AC.188/SR.5, 7, 8, 11, 14, 15, 16, 17, 23, 24 and 35)). The United Kingdom cautioned against moving to universal criminal jurisdiction

(ibid., A/AC.188/SR.24, para. 27) while others (Poland, para. 18; Mexico, para. 11) felt the introduction of the principle of universal jurisdiction to be essential. The USSR observed that no State could exercise jurisdiction over crimes committed in another State by nationals of that State without contravening Article 2, paragraph 7, of the Charter. The Convention provisions were in its view to apply only to hostage taking that was a manifestation of international terrorism — another example of initial and understandable positions on jurisdiction being modified in the face of the exceptional gravity of the offence.

38. The Convention against Torture, of 10 December 1984, establishes in Article 5 an obligation to establish jurisdiction

> "(a) When the offences are committed in any territory under its jurisdiction or on board a ship or aircraft registered in that State;
> (b) When the alleged offender is a national of that State;
> (c) When the victim is a national of that State if that State considers it appropriate."

If the person alleged to have committed the offence is found in the territory of a State party and is not extradited, submission of the case to the prosecuting authorities shall follow (Art. 7). Other grounds of criminal jurisdiction exercised in accordance with the relevant national law are not excluded (Art. 5, para. 3), making clear that Article 5, paragraphs 1 and 2, must not be interpreted a contrario. (See J. H. Burgers and H. Danelius, The United Nations Convention against Torture, 1988, p. 133.)

39. The passage of time changes perceptions. The jurisdictional ground that in 1961 had been referred to as the principle of "primary universal repression" came now to be widely referred to by delegates as "universal jurisdiction" — moreover, a universal jurisdiction thought appropriate, since torture, like piracy, could be considered an "offence against the law of nations." (United States: E/CN.4/1367, 1980). Australia, France, the Netherlands and the United Kingdom eventually dropped their objection that "universal jurisdiction" over torture would create problems under their domestic legal systems. (See E/CN.4/1984/72.)

40. This short historical survey may be summarized as follows:

41. The parties to these treaties agreed both to grounds of jurisdiction and as to the obligation to take the measures necessary to establish such jurisdiction. The specified grounds relied on links of nationality of the offender, or the ship or aircraft concerned, or of the victim. See, for example, Article 4(1) Hague Convention; Article 3(1) Tokyo Convention; Article 5, Hostages Convention; Article 5, Torture Convention. These may properly be described as treaty-based broad extraterritorial jurisdiction. But in addition to these were the parallel provisions whereby a State party in whose jurisdiction the alleged perpetrator of such offences is found, shall prosecute him or extradite him. By the loose use of language the latter has come to be referred to as "universal jurisdiction," though this is really an obligatory territorial jurisdiction over persons, albeit in relation to acts committed elsewhere.

42. Whether this obligation (whether described as the duty to establish universal jurisdiction, or, more accurately, the jurisdiction to establish a territorial jurisdiction over persons for extraterritorial events) is an obligation only of treaty law, inter partes or, whether it is now, at least as regards the offences articulated in the treaties,

an obligation of customary international law was pleaded by the Parties in this case but not addressed in any great detail.

. . .

44. However, we note that the inaccurately termed "universal jurisdiction principle" in these treaties is a principle of obligation, while the question in this case is whether Belgium had the right to issue and circulate the arrest warrant if it so chose.

. . .

45. That there is no established practice in which States exercise universal jurisdiction, properly so called, is undeniable. As we have seen, virtually all national legislation envisages links of some sort to the forum State; and no case law exists in which pure universal jurisdiction has formed the basis of jurisdiction. This does not necessarily indicate, however, that such an exercise would be unlawful. In the first place, national legislation reflects the circumstances in which a State provides in its own law the ability to exercise jurisdiction. But a State is not required to legislate up to the full scope of the jurisdiction allowed by international law. The war crimes legislation of Australia and the United Kingdom afford examples of countries making more confined choices for the exercise of jurisdiction. . . . Moreover, while none of the national case law to which we have referred happens to be based on the exercise of a universal jurisdiction properly so called, there is equally nothing in this case law which evidences an opinio juris on the illegality of such a jurisdiction. In short, national legislation and case law, — that is, State practice — is neutral as to exercise of universal jurisdiction.

46. There are, moreover, certain indications that a universal criminal jurisdiction for certain international crimes is clearly not regarded as unlawful. The duty to prosecute under those treaties which contain the aut dedere aut prosequi provisions opens the door to a jurisdiction based on the heinous nature of the crime rather than on links of territoriality or nationality (whether as perpetrator or victim). The 1949 Geneva Conventions lend support to this possibility, and are widely regarded as today reflecting customary international law.

47. The contemporary trends, reflecting international relations as they stand at the beginning of the new century, are striking. The movement is towards bases of jurisdiction other than territoriality. "Effects" or "impact" jurisdiction is embraced both by the United States and, with certain qualifications, by the European Union. Passive personality jurisdiction, for so long regarded as controversial, is now reflected not only in the legislation of various countries (the United States, Ch. 113A, 1986 Omnibus Diplomatic and Antiterrorism Act; France, Art. 689, Code of Criminal Procedure, 1975), and today meets with relatively little opposition, at least so far as a particular category of offences is concerned.

48. In civil matters we already see the beginnings of a very broad form of extraterritorial jurisdiction. Under the Alien Torts Claim Act, the United States, basing itself on a law of 1789, has asserted a jurisdiction both over human rights violations and over major violations of international law, perpetrated by non-nationals overseas. Such jurisdiction, with the possibility of ordering payment of damages, has been exercised with respect to torture committed in a variety of countries (Paraguay, Chile, Argentina, Guatemala), and with respect to other major human

rights violations in yet other countries. While this unilateral exercise of the function of guardian of international values has been much commented on, it has not attracted the approbation of States generally.

...

53. This brings us once more to the particular point that divides the Parties in this case: is it a precondition of the assertion of universal jurisdiction that the accused be within the territory?

54. Considerable confusion surrounds this topic, not helped by the fact that legislators, courts and writers alike frequently fail to specify the precise temporal moment at which any such requirement is said to be in play. Is the presence of the accused within the jurisdiction said to be required at the time the offence was committed? At the time the arrest warrant is issued? Or at the time of the trial itself? ... The only prohibitive rule ... is that criminal jurisdiction should not be exercised, without permission, within the territory of another State. The Belgian arrest warrant envisaged the arrest of Mr. Yerodia in Belgium, or the possibility of his arrest in third States at the discretion of the States concerned. This would in principle seem to violate no existing prohibiting rule of international law.

...

58. If the underlying purpose of designating certain acts as international crimes is to authorize a wide jurisdiction to be asserted over persons committing them, there is no rule of international law (and certainly not the aut dedere principle) which makes illegal co-operative overt acts designed to secure their presence within a State wishing to exercise jurisdiction.

59. If, as we believe to be the case, a State may choose to exercise a universal criminal jurisdiction in absentia, it must also ensure that certain safeguards are in place. They are absolutely essential to prevent abuse and to ensure that the rejection of impunity does not jeopardize stable relations between States.

No exercise of criminal jurisdiction may occur which fails to respect the inviolability or infringes the immunities of the person concerned. We return below to certain aspects of this facet, but will say at this juncture that commencing an investigation on the basis of which an arrest warrant may later be issued does not of itself violate those principles. The function served by the international law of immunities does not require that States fail to keep themselves informed.

A State contemplating bringing criminal charges based on universal jurisdiction must first offer to the national State of the prospective accused person the opportunity itself to act upon the charges concerned. The Court makes reference to these elements in the context of this case at paragraph 16 of its Judgment.

Further, such charges may only be laid by a prosecutor or juge d'instruction who acts in full independence, without links to or control by the government of that State. Moreover, the desired equilibrium between the battle against impunity and the promotion of good inter-State relations will only be maintained if there are some special circumstances that do require the exercise of an international criminal jurisdiction and if this has been brought to the attention of the prosecutor or juge d'instruction. For example, persons related to the victims of the case will have requested the commencement of legal proceedings.

60. It is equally necessary that universal criminal jurisdiction be exercised only over those crimes regarded as the most heinous by the international community.

. . .

64. The arrest warrant issued against Mr. Yerodia accuses him both of war crimes and of crimes against humanity. As regards the latter, charges of incitement to racial hatred, which are said to have led to murders and lynchings, were specified. Fitting of this charge within the generally understood substantive context of crimes against humanity is not without its problems. "Racial hatred" would need to be assimilated to "persecution on racial grounds," or, on the particular facts, to mass murder and extermination. [The opinion analyzes whether incitement is an acceptable form of liability under international criminal law, and concludes that it is.]

65. It would seem (without in any way pronouncing upon whether Mr. Yerodia did or did not perform the acts with which he is charged in the warrant) that the acts alleged do fall within the concept of "crimes against humanity" and would be within that small category in respect of which an exercise of universal jurisdiction is not precluded under international law.

QUESTIONS

1. What does the Joint Separate Opinion mean by 'pure universal jurisdiction'? Are the distinctions between universal jurisdiction and forms of extraterritorial jurisdiction analytically coherent?

2. States can consent through a treaty to forms of jurisdiction that otherwise would not be permitted under international law. Should the existence of a treaty provision allowing broad-based jurisdiction such as a 'prosecute or extradite' provision support — or undermine — the proposition that substantive offences contained in that treaty are subject to universal jurisdiction as a matter of customary international law?

3. Assuming the Joint Separate Opinion correctly states prevailing international law, could Belgium pass a law authorizing the prosecution of individuals who become Belgian citizens or residents for acts committed before they become naturalized citizens or lawful residents? How about for acts committed by a foreign national visiting Belgium if the acts took place before her date of entry? Must these acts in question constitute universal crimes? Should international law be fashioned such that a line is drawn between citizens and foreign national residents? Between long-term residents and temporary visitors?

4. Does the exercise of universal jurisdiction interfere unjustifiably with the domestic affairs of another country? What about situations in which the relevant acts could not be prosecuted due to an amnesty passed in the foreign state (such as in South Africa)? In such situations, a strong argument could be made that criminal prosecutions would trample on the prerogatives of a democratic country deciding how best to deal with its past. Should the balance tip in favour of exercising jurisdiction when victims-complainants are nationals of the prosecuting state? Should the presence of a single Belgian victim (or a single Belgian perpetrator) change the calculus of whether to override a foreign state's approach to dealing with the past?

5. Does the Joint Separate Opinion strike the correct balance between the interests of the international community in punishing the commission of universal crimes and the interests of states in conducting diplomatic affairs?

6. The Joint Separate Opinion suggests that Belgium's exercise of jurisdiction is lawful unless an international rule clearly prohibits it. As a law clerk to one of the judges in the case would you have advised supporting such a presumption? Why or why not?

7. In the United Kingdom, complainants in civil suits have claimed that national courts have jurisdiction over torture committed in a foreign country on the ground that psychological harm caused by the torture was sustained in the United Kingdom. Those types of arguments are generally framed to meet domestic legal requirements for jurisdiction, but how do they comport with the distribution of jurisdictional authority on the global level? Is it appropriate for the United Kingdom to vindicate such interests through judicial proceedings and civil remedies?

ADDITIONAL READING

Donald Francis Donovan and Anthea Roberts, 'The Emerging Recognition of Universal Civil Jurisdiction,' 100 Am. J. Int. L. 142 (2006); Naomi Roht-Arriaza, *The Pinochet Effect: Transnational Justice in the Age of Human Rights* (2005); Stephen Macedo (ed.), *Universal Jurisdiction: National Courts and the Prosecution of Serious Crimes under International Law* (2004); Henry J. Steiner, 'Three Cheers for Universal Jurisdiction — Or is it Only Two?' 5 Theoretical Inquiries L. 199 (2004); Beth Van Schaack, 'In Defense of Civil Redress: The Domestic Enforcement of Human Rights Norms in the Context of the Proposed Hague Judgments Convention,' 42 Harv. Int. L J. 141 (2001).

B. US CIVIL LITIGATION AND GLOBAL COMPARISONS

Within the realm of judicial enforcement of human rights violations committed in foreign countries, one of the most important lines of cases involves the US Alien Tort Statute (ATS). The ATS is a statutory provision enacted by the US Congress in 1789, but given new life by a decision of the Court of Appeals for the Second Circuit in 1980. Codified at 28 U.S.C. 1350, the ATS states in full: 'The district courts shall have original jurisdiction of any civil action by an alien for a tort only, committed in violation of the law of nations or a treaty of the United States'. In *Filartiga v. Pena-Irala*, the Court of Appeals for the Second Circuit permitted two Paraguayan citizens, Dr. Joel Filartiga and his daughter, to file an ATS suit against a Paraguayan official for allegedly torturing to death Dr. Filartiga's teenage son. That decision has since been cited, for various propositions, in well over a hundred US federal court cases. Other federal courts subsequently permitted suits to be brought under the ATS for international law violations including genocide, slavery, disappearances and war crimes.

Congressional passage of the US Torture Victim Protection Act of 1991, which we discuss below (p. 1199 *infra*), added another dimension to the opportunities afforded by the ATS for human rights litigation in US courts. In addition, courts in other countries have expanded opportunities to entertain private law causes of action as well as criminal prosecution as a means for seeking redress for human rights violations. One result is that the central concerns of private international law (jurisdiction, including *forum non conveniens*[7] and state immunity; choice of law, including 'act of state' determinations; and enforcement of judgments) are now increasingly relevant to litigation based on human rights law. Another result may be the increased willingness of institutions within the countries in which violations were committed to undertake efforts to address injustices.

ELLEN LUTZ AND KATHRYN SIKKINK, THE JUSTICE CASCADE: THE EVOLUTION AND IMPACT OF FOREIGN HUMAN RIGHTS TRIALS IN LATIN AMERICA

2 Chi. J. Int. L. 1 (2001)

[T]he British government arrested Chilean General and former President Augusto Pinochet on a Spanish extradition warrant for torture and other human rights crimes.... British courts assiduously considered the jurisdictional issues posed by the Spanish request and determined that the Spanish courts had jurisdiction to try Pinochet for crimes committed in Chile over a decade before. Although British authorities ultimately allowed Pinochet to return to Chile, finding that he was too incapacitated to stand trial, the events in Europe had important political repercussions in Chile that are now rippling across Latin America and the rest of the world....

...This Article examines what changed... that made Pinochet's arrest in Britain possible. We address two main questions: (1) why, in the last two decades of the 20th century, was there a major international norms shift towards using foreign or international judicial processes to hold individuals accountable for human rights crimes; and (2) what difference have foreign judicial processes made for human rights practices in the countries whose governments were responsible for those crimes.

...

...Because most of the work on norms cascades has been done by legal theorists interested in domestic norms, there have not been efforts to model what an international norms cascade would look like....

...

The justice norms cascade is being operationalized through a series of norm-affirming events including the decisions of foreign courts to try cases involving violations of international human rights, the active participation of non-governmental organizations ("NGOs") and governments in the process of establishing the ICC,

[7] A common law doctrine which allows, or may even require, courts to decide not to take jurisdiction over a case because another country's court system is better suited to hear the case.

and the willingness of states to ratify the ICC treaty. Even cases like Pinochet, in which a foreign court recognized the legitimacy of a third country's jurisdiction but ultimately did not take steps to ensure the trial of the perpetrator, can be seen as norm-affirming events.

The transnational justice network operates by enabling individuals whose access to justice is blocked in their home country to go outside their state and seek justice abroad. This dynamic is similar to the primary mechanism of other transnational advocacy networks. Foreign court rulings against rights-abusing defendants have the effect of putting pressure "from above" on the state where the rights abuses occurred. Increasingly, this pressure serves to open previously blocked domestic avenues for pursuing justice. Looking at other advocacy networks, Keck and Sikkink have called this dynamic a "boomerang pattern" — domestic activists bypass their states and directly search out international allies to bring outside pressure on their states. . . .

. . .

A. The US Cases

The practice of "borrowing" foreign judicial systems to seek justice for past human rights abuses began in the United States in 1979 with the path- breaking *Filartiga v Peña-Irala*, and the family of cases that followed. The US cases differed from the later Spanish cases in that they were civil instead of criminal, and they required as a basis for jurisdiction that the defendant be physically present in the United States. . . .

. . .

The success of *Filartiga* provided US human rights lawyers with a new avenue for striking back at perpetrators of human rights abuses and the means to offer some satisfaction to individuals who had suffered. A network of US lawyers mobilized to take on these cases and before long the nuances of the legal theories first raised in *Filartiga* were being tested in the courts. Many of the lawsuits involved victims and perpetrators of human rights abuses from Latin America. . . .

. . .

B. The European Cases

Latin American human rights advocates also collaborated with their counterparts in Europe to apply outside pressure on their governments to bring rights violators to justice. . . . This was possible for two reasons. First, many European countries, unlike the United States, recognize the passive personality basis for criminal jurisdiction in which a state may exercise criminal jurisdiction over anyone who injures one of their nationals, no matter where the crime occurred. Second, the Southern Cone countries were populated by Spaniards, Italians, and others of European descent, and many of these European countries recognize as nationals their children and even subsequent generations. As a result, transnational justice network lawyers were able to convince European judges that they had jurisdiction to criminally try Latin American perpetrators of rights abuses for the torture, disappearance, or murder of their nationals.

…

The impact of the European cases turned out to be more significant. The turning point was *Pinochet.* Although most of those indicted or charged with human rights crimes have, until now, evaded punishment, momentum for such trials has built and more and more cases are moving forward. The Argentine and Chilean cases before Judge Garzón, though initially brought on behalf of only a handful of victims, have swelled to include hundreds, and international arrest warrants have been issued for dozens of former junta members and military officers from those two countries.

…

In Chile, the arrest of Pinochet appears to have lifted psychological, political, and juridical barriers to justice by weakening the powerful forces blocking such trials in Chile since the return to democracy. …

Since Pinochet's arrest, twenty-five Chilean officers have been arrested on charges of murder, torture, and kidnapping. In an interview, Defense Minister Edmundo Perez Yoma discussed a "new attitude" emerging among the military high command: "You deal with it or it will never go away. You have to confront it — that's the changed attitude." In July 1999, Chile's Supreme Court upheld a lower court decision that the amnesty law was no longer applicable to cases in which people had disappeared. …

…

The European cases against the Argentine military officers had the unanticipated effect of spurring change in Argentina's willingness to try human rights cases. The decision by the Argentine government to imprison Admiral Massera and General Videla pending trial apparently was a preemptive measure in response to the Spanish judge's international arrest warrants. …

…

Meanwhile, Pinochet and the efforts of Menchu to bring former Guatemalan dictators to account in Spain have contributed to an aura of contrition among Guatemala's senior policymakers. In August 2000, Guatemalan President Alfonso Portillo admitted government responsibility for atrocities committed during the country's thirty-six-year civil war and pledged to investigate massacres, prosecute those responsible, and compensate the victims. Moreover, in a show of good faith, President Portillo signed an agreement with the Inter-American Human Rights Commission ("IACHR") that affirms Guatemala's institutional responsibility for war crimes and empowers the IACHR to monitor the actions of the Guatemalan government in light of its new promises to redress those past wrongs. In December 2000, the Inter-American Court found that the Guatemalan government had killed Efrain Bamaca Velasquez, a rebel leader, and the husband of human rights activist Jennifer Harbury. …

…

Latin American countries also have enthusiastically supported efforts to establish the ICC. …

…

Conclusion

We have argued that a justice cascade is underway in Latin America today. This norms cascade was the result of the concerted efforts of a transnational justice advocacy network, made up of connected groups of activist lawyers with expertise in international and domestic human rights law....

...

...With respect to the perpetrators, even if they never face punishment, or even trial, they are finding themselves "landlocked." Even where their own government is willing to protect them from the reach of foreign courts, they dare not travel abroad for fear that the country they travel to will extradite them to a country seeking to try them....

The much bigger casualty seems to be the amnesty decrees that past Latin American dictators gave themselves before leaving office, or post-dictatorship democratic regimes gave their predecessors in exchange for their allowing democracy to flourish by not seizing power again. Old amnesties are not bearing up well against current national sovereignty concerns....No Latin American country, particularly those with rapidly consolidating democracies, wants to foster the perception that its courts lack the competence, capacity, or independence necessary to effectively try its own nationals....

Still, there is plenty of evidence that in Latin America the justice cascade is far from complete. In countries that have not yet faced the possibility that foreign judiciaries will try their nationals, policy-makers have had far less enthusiasm for trials even though they find the Pinochet precedent worrisome. Thus Uruguay has taken steps to restrict the foreign travel of its nationals who were implicated in past abuses of human rights, while at the same time stepping up other initiatives, such as the establishment of a national commission to investigate the disappearances of Uruguayan nationals.... Even in countries where internalization of the justice cascade is more advanced, it is far from fully realized. Thus in Argentina, where there has been substantial progress with respect to conducting trials, there is far less movement when it comes to executing judgments for civil damages in human rights trials that occurred abroad....

We conclude that in Latin America, while the justice cascade is in progress, the extent of its realization in each country depends on numerous factors including: (1) the degree of consolidation of that country's democracy and legal system, (2) whether that country has directly faced the possibility that one of its former senior political figures would be tried abroad, (3) the amount of publicity and support foreign judicial processes have received, (4) the intensity of the determination of domestic human rights advocates and victims, amply supported by their international counterparts, to pressure their government to realize justice for past wrongs, (5) the degree to which each country feels it will bear some embarrassment or other international consequence for not conducting trials that is not outweighed by domestic political pressures exerted by the supporters of those it would try, and (6) the extent to which those now in power have internalized the justice norm and believe that trying past perpetrators is the right thing to do.

...

BETH STEPHENS, INDIVIDUALS ENFORCING INTERNATIONAL LAW: THE COMPARATIVE AND HISTORICAL CONTEXT

52 DePaul L. Rev. 433 (2002)[8]

Analysis of U.S. human rights litigation often assumes that in permitting such claims the United States is out on a limb, unsupported by the practices of any other nation. In fact, the U.S. line of cases bears important similarities to legal approaches that are underway in several nations and developing just as rapidly as the U.S. precedents.

First, civil lawsuits have been filed in several common law legal systems challenging corporate abuses committed by domestic corporations in their operations abroad. One case filed in England, for example, charged that a British asbestos corporation had permitted its foreign subsidiary in South Africa to operate in a way that endangered the health of black workers and their families. The plaintiffs alleged that the company forced black workers into the most dangerous jobs, without health care, while white workers were protected from the asbestos dust and received proper health care. A similar case filed against a British chemical company, Thor Chemical Holdings, resulted in a series of settlements that compensated South African workers poisoned by mercury. . . .

Although properly styled as violations of domestic law, these lawsuits share the goals of much human rights litigation: holding accountable those who violate the fundamental rights of individuals around the world. Claims in the United States that might be styled as international law violations have been filed as negligence claims in England, Canada, and Australia. This litigation strategy may be necessitated by the absence of domestic statutory authorization such as that provided by the Alien Tort Claims Act.

Second, civil lawsuits in the United States have much in common with privately initiated criminal prosecutions in civil law legal systems. These similarities are often overlooked because of a tendency among domestic lawyers to assume that the lines dividing the categories of criminal and civil are fixed and definable and are constant across different legal systems. In fact, such lines are difficult to pin down even within a single legal system and do not transfer automatically from one system to another.

It is not surprising that these distinctions would vary across national lines. Even within legal systems, they are hard to define. In the United States, the civil/criminal divide has important constitutional consequences: defendants in criminal proceedings have the right to a panoply of constitutional protections that are not afforded to civil litigants. Despite repeated efforts, however, the U.S. Supreme Court has not been able to draw a clear line. The European regional system has confronted similar difficulties in applying criminal law protections to procedures that originate in diverse domestic legal systems. Rather than rely upon the domestic label, the European Court of Human Rights conducts an independent inquiry to determine the

[8] See also Beth Stephens, 'Translating Filártiga: A Comparative and International Law Analysis of Domestic Remedies for International Human Rights Violations', 27 Yale J. Int. L. 1 (2002).

proper classification of legal actions. In deciding whether a proceeding is properly classified as criminal rather than civil, the court considers whether the purpose of the proceedings is "deterrent and punitive" and whether the sanction imposed is "in its nature and degree" appropriate "to the 'criminal' sphere."

...

One commonly identified distinction between civil actions and criminal prosecutions is a difference in the purpose of a judgment: civil actions are said to be designed to compensate the injured party, without any attendant moral condemnation of the offender, while criminal actions aim to punish the guilty party for morally blameworthy conduct. United States tort actions, however, particularly those that include punitive damages, are designed to deter and punish as well as to compensate, and entail moral condemnation. . . .

On the other hand, criminal prosecutions in many countries include the possibility of monetary compensation to those injured by the criminal acts. In some systems, compensation is an automatic feature of a criminal prosecution. In others, compensation is obtained by means of a coordinated civil suit, attached to the criminal prosecution and relying on the facts developed at the criminal trial. In such systems, if acts are subject to criminal prosecution, it may not be necessary for a private person to undertake an independent civil action for compensation.

Another traditional distinction between criminal and civil actions focuses on the party in charge of the proceeding: public prosecutors handle criminal prosecutions while private parties litigate torts. . . . But comparative analysis also blurs the public/private distinction. In many civil law legal systems, private parties can file and even prosecute criminal proceedings. Moreover, criminal prosecutions in many systems rely upon an inquiry conducted by an investigating magistrate; those magistrates may operate with a great deal of independence from the executive branch of their governments. The Spanish prosecution of Augusto Pinochet, which led to the attempt to extradite him from England, illustrates both of these strands of independence: the prosecution was initiated by private parties over the objection of the public prosecutors, and the investigation was conducted by a magistrate despite the opposition of the country's executive branch.

Examples of such privately initiated, magistrate-driven prosecutions for human rights violations are common across Europe; in addition, one is underway in Paraguay, while another was filed but later dismissed in Senegal. As with the Pinochet case, the potential for embarrassment of the political branches of the government is high. A criminal case filed against Ariel Sharon in Belgium, for example, charges him with responsibility for the massacre of hundreds of Palestinians in refuge camps in Lebanon. Approximately thirty similar private criminal complaints have been filed in Belgium, under a broad criminal jurisdiction statute that permitted criminal prosecutions for universal crimes committed anywhere in the world, even where the defendant was not present in Belgium at the time the complaint was filed.

Private criminal prosecutions may also be filed against corporations. A new, non-profit organization in France was formed for the sole purpose of pursuing criminal human rights prosecutions against corporations. Its first prosecution was filed in March 2002 against a French corporation, alleging illegal plundering of resources in

Cameroon. Criminal investigations have also been initiated in Belgium against an oil company for activities in Burma.

...

Civil human rights litigation in the United States bears a strong resemblance to actions termed criminal in other nations. These examples indicate that private parties are engaged in the enforcement of international human rights norms in the domestic courts of many nations. In the United States, such efforts are limited to civil lawsuits. In many countries, they are more likely to entail privately initiated criminal prosecutions, requests to magistrates to open investigations, or civil claims attached to criminal prosecutions.

These varied approaches reflect the diversity and strength of national legal systems as a means to enforce international law. All of these actions are part of the expanding international movement toward accountability for violations of international law. In each, the individual plays a key role as an enforcer of international norms. Each domestic legal system implements the international norms in a manner consistent with its local procedures.... Despite our unique line of civil litigation, the United States has significant company in this growing trend towards private enforcement of international law in domestic courts.

SOSA V. ALVAREZ-MACHAIN

Supreme Court of the United States, 2004
542 U.S. 692

[Beginning with *Filartiga* in 1980, the first wave of human rights litigation in US courts confronted the question whether the Alien Tort Statute provided a cause of action for violations of contemporary international human rights law. In 2004, the US Supreme Court finally addressed the issue and, at the same time, provided guidance for judicial management of future ATS litigation. Excerpts of the opinion follow.]

In 1985, an agent of the Drug Enforcement Administration (DEA), Enrique Camarena-Salazar, was captured on assignment in Mexico and taken to a house in Guadalajara, where he was tortured over the course of a 2-day interrogation, then murdered. Based in part on eyewitness testimony, DEA officials in the United States came to believe that respondent Humberto Alvarez-Machain (Alvarez), a Mexican physician, was present at the house and acted to prolong the agent's life in order to extend the interrogation and torture.

In 1990, a federal grand jury indicted Alvarez for the torture and murder of Camarena-Salazar, and the United States District Court for the Central District of California issued a warrant for his arrest. The DEA asked the Mexican Government for help in getting Alvarez into the United States, but when the requests and negotiations proved fruitless, the DEA approved a plan to hire Mexican nationals to seize Alvarez and bring him to the United States for trial. As so planned, a group of

Mexicans, including petitioner Jose Francisco Sosa, abducted Alvarez from his house, held him overnight in a motel, and brought him by private plane to El Paso, Texas, where he was arrested by federal officers.

...

The case was tried in 1992, and ended at the close of the Government's case, when the District Court granted Alvarez's motion for a judgment of acquittal.

...

So far as it matters here, Alvarez sought damages ... from Sosa under the ATS [Alien Tort Statute], for a violation of the law of nations.

...

A divided en banc court ... relied upon what it called the "clear and universally recognized norm prohibiting arbitrary arrest and detention," to support the conclusion that Alvarez's arrest amounted to a tort in violation of international law....

We granted certiorari ... to clarify the scope of ... the ATS.

...

... Sosa ... argues (as does the United States supporting him) that there is no relief under the ATS because the statute does no more than vest federal courts with jurisdiction, neither creating nor authorizing the courts to recognize any particular right of action without further congressional action. Although we agree the statute is in terms only jurisdictional, we think that at the time of enactment the jurisdiction enabled federal courts to hear claims in a very limited category defined by the law of nations and recognized at common law. We do not believe, however, that the limited, implicit sanction to entertain the handful of international law cum common law claims understood in 1789 should be taken as authority to recognize the right of action asserted by Alvarez here.

Judge Friendly called the ATS a "legal Lohengrin," *IIT v. Vencap, Ltd.*, 519 F.2d 1001 (C.A.2 1975); "no one seems to know whence it came," and for over 170 years after its enactment it provided jurisdiction in only one case. The first Congress passed it as part of the Judiciary Act of 1789....

The parties and amici here advance radically different historical interpretations of this terse provision. Alvarez says that the ATS was intended not simply as a jurisdictional grant, but as authority for the creation of a new cause of action for torts in violation of international law. We think that reading is implausible.... [W]e think the statute was intended as jurisdictional in the sense of addressing the power of the courts to entertain cases concerned with a certain subject.

But holding the ATS jurisdictional raises a new question, this one about the interaction between the ATS at the time of its enactment and the ambient law of the era. Sosa would have it that the ATS was stillborn because there could be no claim for relief without a further statute expressly authorizing adoption of causes of action. Amici professors of federal jurisdiction and legal history take a different tack, that federal courts could entertain claims once the jurisdictional grant was on the books, because torts in violation of the law of nations would have been recognized within the common law of the time. We think history and practice give the edge to this latter position.

"When the United States declared their independence, they were bound to receive the law of nations, in its modern state of purity and refinement." *Ware v. Hylton*, 3

Dall. 199 (1796) (Wilson, J.). In the years of the early Republic, this law of nations comprised two principal elements, the first covering the general norms governing the behavior of national states with each other....

The law of nations included a second, more pedestrian element, however, that did fall within the judicial sphere, as a body of judge-made law regulating the conduct of individuals situated outside domestic boundaries and consequently carrying an international savor. To Blackstone, the law of nations in this sense was implicated "in mercantile questions, such as bills of exchange and the like; in all marine causes, relating to freight, average, demurrage, insurances, bottomry...; [and] in all disputes relating to prizes, to shipwrecks, to hostages, and ransom bills." The law merchant emerged from the customary practices of international traders and admiralty required its own transnational regulation. And it was the law of nations in this sense that our precursors spoke about when the Court explained the status of coast fishing vessels in wartime grew from "ancient usage among civilized nations, beginning centuries ago, and gradually ripening into a rule of international law...." *The Paquete Habana*, 175 U.S. 677 (1900).

There was, finally, a sphere in which these rules binding individuals for the benefit of other individuals overlapped with the norms of state relationships. Blackstone referred to it when he mentioned three specific offenses against the law of nations addressed by the criminal law of England: violation of safe conducts, infringement of the rights of ambassadors, and piracy. An assault against an ambassador, for example, impinged upon the sovereignty of the foreign nation and if not adequately redressed could rise to an issue of war....

Before there was any ATS, a distinctly American preoccupation with these hybrid international norms had taken shape owing to the distribution of political power from independence through the period of confederation. The Continental Congress was hamstrung by its inability to "cause infractions of treaties, or of the law of nations to be punished," J. Madison, Journal of the Constitutional Convention 60 (E. Scott ed. 1893), and in 1781 the Congress implored the States to vindicate rights under the law of nations....

Appreciation of the Continental Congress's incapacity to deal with this class of cases was intensified by the so-called Marbois incident of May 1784, in which a French adventurer, Longchamps, verbally and physically assaulted the Secretary of the French Legion in Philadelphia. See *Respublica v. De Longchamps*, 1 Dall. 111, 1 L.Ed. 59 (O.T. Phila.1784). Congress called again for state legislation addressing such matters, and concern over the inadequate vindication of the law of nations persisted through the time of the constitutional convention....

...

...There is no record of congressional discussion about private actions that might be subject to the jurisdictional provision, or about any need for further legislation to create private remedies; there is no record even of debate on the section.... Still, the history does tend to support... [the proposition] that Congress intended the ATS to furnish jurisdiction for a relatively modest set of actions alleging violations of the law of nations. Uppermost in the legislative mind appears to have been offenses against ambassadors; violations of safe conduct were probably understood to be actionable, and individual actions arising out of prize captures and piracy may well have also been contemplated. But the common law appears to have understood only those three of the hybrid variety as definite and actionable, or at any rate, to have assumed only a very limited set of claims.

...

In sum, although the ATS is a jurisdictional statute creating no new causes of action, the reasonable inference from the historical materials is that the statute was intended to have practical effect the moment it became law. The jurisdictional grant is best read as having been enacted on the understanding that the common law would provide a cause of action for the modest number of international law violations with a potential for personal liability at the time.

We think it is correct, then, to assume that the First Congress understood that the district courts would recognize private causes of action for certain torts in violation of the law of nations... We assume, too, that no development in the two centuries from the enactment of § 1350 to the birth of the modern line of cases beginning with *Filartiga v. Pena-Irala*, has categorically precluded federal courts from recognizing a claim under the law of nations as an element of common law; Congress has not in any relevant way amended § 1350 or limited civil common law power by another statute. Still, there are good reasons for a restrained conception of the discretion a federal court should exercise in considering a new cause of action of this kind. Accordingly, we think courts should require any claim based on the present-day law of nations to rest on a norm of international character accepted by the civilized world and defined with a specificity comparable to the features of the 18th-century paradigms we have recognized. This requirement is fatal to Alvarez's claim.

A series of reasons argue for judicial caution when considering the kinds of individual claims that might implement the jurisdiction conferred by the early statute. First, the prevailing conception of the common law has changed since 1789 in a way that counsels restraint in judicially applying internationally generated norms. When § 1350 was enacted, the accepted conception was of the common law as "a transcendental body of law outside of any particular State but obligatory within it unless and until changed by statute." *Black and White Taxicab & Transfer Co. v. Brown and Yellow Taxicab & Transfer Co.*, 276 U.S. 518 (1928) (Holmes, J., dissenting). Now, however, in most cases where a court is asked to state or formulate a common law principle in a new context, there is a general understanding that the law is not so much found or discovered as it is either made or created....

Second, along with, and in part driven by, that conceptual development in understanding common law has come an equally significant rethinking of the role of the federal courts in making it. *Erie R. Co. v. Tompkins*, 304 U.S. 64 (1938), was the watershed in which we denied the existence of any federal "general" common law, which largely withdrew to havens of specialty, some of them defined by express congressional authorization to devise a body of law directly, e.g., *Textile Workers v. Lincoln Mills of Ala.*, 353 U.S. 448 (1957) (interpretation of collective-bargaining agreements); Fed. Rule Evid. 501 (evidentiary privileges in federal-question cases). Elsewhere, this Court has thought it was in order to create federal common law rules in interstitial areas of particular federal interest.... the general practice has been to look for legislative guidance before exercising innovative authority over substantive law. It would be remarkable to take a more aggressive role in exercising a jurisdiction that remained largely in shadow for much of the prior two centuries.

Third, this Court has recently and repeatedly said that a decision to create a private right of action is one better left to legislative judgment in the great majority of cases. The creation of a private right of action raises issues beyond the mere consideration whether underlying primary conduct should be allowed or not, entailing, for example, a decision to permit enforcement without the check imposed by prosecutorial discretion. Accordingly, even when Congress has made it clear by statute that a rule applies to purely domestic conduct, we are reluctant to infer intent to provide a private cause of action where the statute does not supply one expressly. While the absence of congressional action addressing private rights of action under an international norm is more equivocal than its failure to provide such a right when it creates a statute, the possible collateral consequences of making international rules privately actionable argue for judicial caution.

Fourth, the subject of those collateral consequences is itself a reason for a high bar to new private causes of action for violating international law, for the potential implications for the foreign relations of the United States of recognizing such causes should make courts particularly wary of impinging on the discretion of the Legislative and Executive Branches in managing foreign affairs. It is one thing for American courts to enforce constitutional limits on our own State and Federal Governments' power, but quite another to consider suits under rules that would go so far as to claim a limit on the power of foreign governments over their own citizens, and to hold that a foreign government or its agent has transgressed those limits. Cf. *Banco Nacional de Cuba v. Sabbatino*, 376 U.S. 398, 431–432 (1964).... Since many attempts by federal courts to craft remedies for the violation of new norms of international law would raise risks of adverse foreign policy consequences, they should be undertaken, if at all, with great caution....

The fifth reason is particularly important in light of the first four. We have no congressional mandate to seek out and define new and debatable violations of the law of nations, and modern indications of congressional understanding of the judicial role in the field have not affirmatively encouraged greater judicial creativity. It is true that a clear mandate appears in the Torture Victim Protection Act of 1991, providing authority that "establish[es] an unambiguous and modern basis for" federal claims of torture and extrajudicial killing, H.R.Rep. No. 102–367, pt.1, p.3 (1991). But that affirmative authority is confined to specific subject matter, and although the legislative history includes the remark that § 1350 should "remain intact to permit suits based on other norms that already exist or may ripen in the future into rules of customary international law," id., at 4, Congress as a body has done nothing to promote such suits. Several times, indeed, the Senate has expressly declined to give the federal courts the task of interpreting and applying international human rights law, as when its ratification of the International Covenant on Civil and Political Rights declared that the substantive provisions of the document were not self-executing. 138 Cong. Rec. 8071 (1992).

...

Whereas Justice Scalia sees these developments as sufficient to close the door to further independent judicial recognition of actionable international norms, other considerations persuade us that the judicial power should be exercised on the understanding that the door is still ajar subject to vigilant doorkeeping, and thus open to a narrow class of international norms today. *Erie* did not in terms bar any judicial recognition of new substantive rules, no matter what the circumstances, and post-Erie understanding has identified limited enclaves in which federal courts may derive some substantive law in a common law way. For two centuries we have affirmed that the domestic law of the United States recognizes the law of nations. See, e.g., *Sabbatino*, 376 U.S., at 423 ("[I]t is, of course, true that United States courts apply international law as a part of our own in appropriate circumstances"); The *Paquete Habana*, 175 US., at 700 ("International law is part of our law, and must be ascertained and administered by the courts of justice of appropriate jurisdiction, as often as questions of right depending upon it are duly presented for their determination"); *The Nereide*, 9 Cranch 388, 423 (1815) (Marshall, C.J.) ("[T]he Court is bound by the law of nations which is a part of the law of the land"). It would take some explaining to say now that federal courts must avert their gaze entirely from any international norm intended to protect individuals.

... The First Congress, which reflected the understanding of the framing generation and included some of the Framers, assumed that federal courts could properly identify some international norms as enforceable in the exercise of § 1350 jurisdiction. We think it would be unreasonable to assume that the First Congress would have expected federal courts to lose all capacity to recognize enforceable international norms simply because the common law might lose some metaphysical cachet on the road to modern realism. Later Congresses seem to have shared our view. The position we take today has been assumed by some federal courts for 24 years, ever since the Second Circuit decided *Filartiga v. Pena-Irala*... Congress, however, has not only expressed no disagreement with our view of the proper exercise of the judicial power, but has responded to its most notable instance by enacting legislation supplementing the judicial determination in some detail. See supra (discussing the Torture Victim Protection Act).

...

... Whatever the ultimate criteria for accepting a cause of action subject to jurisdiction under § 1350, we are persuaded that federal courts should not recognize private claims under federal common law for violations of any international law norm with less definite content and acceptance among civilized nations than the historical paradigms familiar when § 1350 was enacted.... This limit upon judicial recognition is generally consistent with the reasoning of many of the courts and judges who faced the issue before it reached this Court. See *Filartiga, supra*, at 890 ("[F]or purposes of civil liability, the torturer has become — like the pirate and slave trader before him — hostis humani generis, an enemy of all mankind"); *Tel-Oren v. Libyan Arab Republic*, 726 F.2d 774, 781 (C.A.D.C.1984) (Edwards, J., concurring) (suggesting that the "limits of section 1350's reach" be defined by "a handful of heinous actions — each of which violates definable, universal and obligatory norms"); see also *In re Estate of Marcos Human Rights Litigation*, 25 F.3d 1467, 1475 (C.A.9 1994) ("Actionable violations of international law must be of a norm that is specific, universal, and obligatory"). And the determination whether a norm is sufficiently definite to support a cause of action[9] should (and, indeed, inevitably must) involve an element of judgment about the practical consequences of making that cause available to litigants in the federal courts.[10]

. . .

To begin with, Alvarez cites two well-known international agreements that, despite their moral authority, have little utility under the standard set out in this opinion. He says that his abduction by Sosa was an "arbitrary arrest" within the meaning of the Universal Declaration of Human Rights. And he traces the rule against arbitrary arrest not only to the Declaration, but also to article nine of the International Covenant on Civil and Political Rights to which the United States is a party, and to various other conventions to which it is not. But the Declaration does not of its own force impose obligations as a matter of international law. And, although the Covenant does bind the United States as a matter of international law, the United States ratified the Covenant on the express understanding that it was not self-executing and so did not itself create obligations enforceable in the federal courts. Accordingly, Alvarez cannot say that the Declaration and Covenant themselves establish the relevant and applicable rule of international law. He instead attempts to show that prohibition of arbitrary arrest has attained the status of binding customary international law.

Here, it is useful to examine Alvarez's complaint in greater detail. As he presently argues it, the claim does not rest on the cross-border feature of his abduction. . . . [I]t relied on the conclusion that the law of the United States did not authorize Alvarez's arrest, because the DEA lacked extraterritorial authority under 21 U.S.C. § 878, and because Federal Rule of Criminal Procedure 4(d)(2) limited the warrant for Alvarez's

[9] A related consideration is whether international law extends the scope of liability for a violation of a given norm to the perpetrator being sued, if the defendant is a private actor such as a corporation or individual. Compare *Tel-Oren v. Libyan Arab Republic*, 726 F.2d 774, 791–795 (C.A.D.C.1984) (Edwards, J., concurring) (insufficient consensus in 1984 that torture by private actors violates international law), with *Kadic v. Karadzic*, 70 F.3d 232, 239–241 (C.A.2 1995) (sufficient consensus in 1995 that genocide by private actors violates international law).

[10] This requirement of clear definition is not meant to be the only principle limiting the availability of relief in the federal courts for violations of customary international law, though it disposes of this case. For example, the European Commission argues as amicus curiae that basic principles of international law require that before asserting a claim in a foreign forum, the claimant must have exhausted any remedies available in the domestic legal system, and perhaps in other fora such as international claims tribunals. See Brief for European Commission as Amicus Curiae 24, n. 54 (citing I. Brownlie, Principles of Public International Law 472–481 (6th ed.2003)); cf. Torture Victim Protection Act of 1991, ß 2(b), 106 Stat. 73 (exhaustion requirement). We would certainly consider this requirement in an appropriate case.

Another possible limitation that we need not apply here is a policy of case-specific deference to the political branches. For example, there are now pending in federal district court several class actions seeking damages from various corporations alleged to have participated in, or abetted, the regime of apartheid that formerly controlled South Africa. See *In re South African Apartheid Litigation*, 238 F.Supp.2d 1379 (JPML 2002) (granting a motion to transfer the cases to the Southern District of New York). The Government of South Africa has said that these cases interfere with the policy embodied by its Truth and Reconciliation Commission, which "deliberately avoided a 'victors' justice' approach to the crimes of apartheid and chose instead one based on confession and absolution, informed by the principles of reconciliation, reconstruction, reparation and goodwill." Declaration of Penuell Mpapa Maduna, Minister of Justice and Constitutional Development, Republic of South Africa, reprinted in App. to Brief for Government of Commonwealth of Australia *et al.* as Amici Curiae (emphasis deleted). The United States has agreed. See Letter of William H. Taft IV, Legal Adviser, Dept. of State, to Shannen W. Coffin, Deputy Asst. Atty. Gen., Oct. 27, 2003, reprinted in id., at 2a. In such cases, there is a strong argument that federal courts should give serious weight to the Executive Branch's view of the case's impact on foreign policy. Cf. *Republic of Austria v. Altmann*, 541 U.S. — (2004) (discussing the State Department's use of statements of interest in cases involving the Foreign Sovereign Immunities Act of 1976).

arrest to "the jurisdiction of the United States." It is this position that Alvarez takes now: that his arrest was arbitrary and as such forbidden by international law not because it infringed the prerogatives of Mexico, but because no applicable law authorized it.

Alvarez thus invokes a general prohibition of "arbitrary" detention defined as officially sanctioned action exceeding positive authorization to detain under the domestic law of some government, regardless of the circumstances. Whether or not this is an accurate reading of the Covenant, Alvarez cites little authority that a rule so broad has the status of a binding customary norm today.[11] He certainly cites nothing to justify the federal courts in taking his broad rule as the predicate for a federal lawsuit, for its implications would be breathtaking. His rule would support a cause of action in federal court for any arrest, anywhere in the world, unauthorized by the law of the jurisdiction in which it took place, and would create a cause of action for any seizure of an alien in violation of the Fourth Amendment, supplanting the actions under Rev. Stat. § 1979, 42 U.S.C. § 1983 and Bivens v. Six Unknown Fed. Narcotics Agents, 403 U.S. 388 (1971), that now provide damages remedies for such violations. It would create an action in federal court for arrests by state officers who simply exceed their authority; and for the violation of any limit that the law of any country might place on the authority of its own officers to arrest. And all of this assumes that Alvarez could establish that Sosa was acting on behalf of a government when he made the arrest, for otherwise he would need a rule broader still.

Alvarez's failure to marshal support for his proposed rule is underscored by the Restatement (Third) of Foreign Relations Law of the United States (1987), which says in its discussion of customary international human rights law that a "state violates international law if, as a matter of state policy, it practices, encourages, or condones... prolonged arbitrary detention." Although the Restatement does not explain its requirements of a "state policy" and of "prolonged" detention, the implication is clear. Any credible invocation of a principle against arbitrary detention that the civilized world accepts as binding customary international law requires a factual basis beyond relatively brief detention in excess of positive authority. Even the Restatement's limits are only the beginning of the enquiry, because although it is easy to say that some policies of prolonged arbitrary detentions are so bad that those who enforce them become enemies of the human race, it may be harder to say which policies cross that line with the certainty afforded by Blackstone's three common law offenses. In any event, the label would never fit the reckless policeman who botches his warrant, even though that same officer might pay damages under municipal law.

Whatever may be said for the broad principle Alvarez advances, in the present, imperfect world, it expresses an aspiration that exceeds any binding customary rule having the specificity we require.[12] Creating a private cause of action to further that aspiration would go beyond any residual common law discretion we think it

[11] Specifically, he relies on a survey of national constitutions, Bassiouni, Human Rights in the Context of Criminal Justice: Identifying International Procedural Protections and Equivalent Protections in National Constitutions, 3 Duke J. Comp. & Int'l L. 235, 260–261 (1993); a case from the International Court of Justice, *United States v. Iran*, 1980 I.C.J. 3, 42; and some authority drawn from the federal courts, see Brief for Respondent Alvarez-Machain 49, n. 50. None of these suffice. The Bassiouni survey does show that many nations recognize a norm against arbitrary detention, but that consensus is at a high level of generality. . . .

[12] It is not that violations of a rule logically foreclose the existence of that rule as international law. Cf. *Filartiga v.*

appropriate to exercise.[13] It is enough to hold that a single illegal detention of less than a day, followed by the transfer of custody to lawful authorities and a prompt arraignment, violates no norm of customary international law so well defined as to support the creation of a federal remedy.

...

JUSTICE BREYER, CONCURRING IN PART AND CONCURRING IN THE JUDGMENT

...

I would add one further consideration. Since enforcement of an international norm by one nation's courts implies that other nations' courts may do the same, I would ask whether the exercise of jurisdiction under the ATS is consistent with those notions of comity that lead each nation to respect the sovereign rights of other nations by limiting the reach of its laws and their enforcement. In applying those principles, courts help ensure that "the potentially conflicting laws of different nations" will "work together in harmony," a matter of increasing importance in an ever more interdependent world....

...

Since different courts in different nations will not necessarily apply even similar substantive laws similarly, workable harmony, in practice, depends upon more than substantive uniformity among the laws of those nations. That is to say, substantive uniformity does not automatically mean that universal jurisdiction is appropriate. Thus, in the 18th century, nations reached consensus not only on the substantive principle that acts of piracy were universally wrong but also on the jurisdictional principle that any nation that found a pirate could prosecute him....

Today international law will sometimes similarly reflect not only substantive agreement as to certain universally condemned behavior but also procedural agreement that universal jurisdiction exists to prosecute a subset of that behavior. That subset includes torture, genocide, crimes against humanity, and war crimes.

The fact that this procedural consensus exists suggests that recognition of universal jurisdiction in respect to a limited set of norms is consistent with principles of international comity.... That consensus concerns criminal jurisdiction, but consensus as to universal criminal jurisdiction itself suggests that universal tort jurisdiction would be no more threatening. That is because the criminal courts of many nations combine civil and criminal proceedings, allowing those injured by criminal conduct to be represented, and to recover damages, in the criminal proceeding itself.... Thus, universal criminal jurisdiction necessarily contemplates a significant degree of civil tort recovery as well.

Pena-Irala, 630 F.2d 876, 884, n. 15 (C.A.2 1980) ("The fact that the prohibition of torture is often honored in the breach does not diminish its binding effect as a norm of international law"). Nevertheless, that a rule as stated is as far from full realization as the one Alvarez urges is evidence against its status as binding law; and an even clearer point against the creation by judges of a private cause of action to enforce the aspiration behind the rule claimed.

[13] Alvarez also cites, Brief for Respondent Alvarez-Machain 49–50, a finding by a United Nations working group that his detention was arbitrary under the Declaration, the Covenant, and customary international law. See Report of the United Nations Working Group on Arbitrary Detention, U.N. Doc. E/CN.4/1994/27, pp. 139–140 (Dec. 17, 1993). That finding is not addressed, however, to our demanding standard of definition, which must be met to raise even the possibility of a private cause of action. If Alvarez wishes to seek compensation on the basis of the working group's finding, he must address his request to Congress.

JUSTICE SCALIA, WITH WHOM CHIEF JUSTICE REHNQUIST AND JUSTICE THOMAS JOIN, CONCURRING IN PART AND CONCURRING IN THE JUDGMENT

...

The analysis in the Court's opinion departs from my own in this respect: After concluding in Part III that "the ATS is a jurisdictional statute creating no new causes of action," the Court addresses at length in Part IV the "good reasons for a restrained conception of the *discretion* a federal court should exercise in considering a new cause of action" under the ATS. (emphasis added). By framing the issue as one of "discretion," the Court skips over the antecedent question of authority. This neglects the "lesson of *Erie*," that "grants of jurisdiction alone" (which the Court has acknowledged the ATS to be) "are not themselves grants of law-making authority." Meltzer, supra, at 541. On this point, the Court observes only that no development between the enactment of the ATS (in 1789) and the birth of modern international human rights litigation under that statute (in 1980) "has categorically *precluded* federal courts from recognizing a claim under the law of nations as an element of common law." (emphasis added). This turns our jurisprudence regarding federal common law on its head. The question is not what case or congressional action prevents federal courts from applying the law of nations as part of the general common law; it is what authorizes that peculiar exception from *Erie*'s fundamental holding that a general common law does not exist.

...

The Court recognizes that *Erie* was a "watershed" decision heralding an avulsive change, wrought by "conceptual development in understanding common law... [and accompanied by an] equally significant rethinking of the role of the federal courts in making it." The Court's analysis, however, does not follow through on this insight, interchangeably using the unadorned phrase "common law" in Parts III and IV to refer to pre-*Erie* general common law and post-*Erie* federal common law. This lapse is crucial, because the creation of post-*Erie* federal common law is rooted in a positivist mindset utterly foreign to the American common-law tradition of the late 18th century. Post-*Erie* federal common lawmaking (all that is left to the federal courts) is so far removed from that general-common-law adjudication which applied the "law of nations" that it would be anachronistic to find authorization to do the former in a statutory grant of jurisdiction that was thought to enable the latter. Yet that is precisely what the discretion-only analysis in Part IV suggests.

...

... In holding open the possibility that judges may create rights where Congress has not authorized them to do so, the Court countenances judicial occupation of a domain that belongs to the people's representatives. One does not need a crystal ball to predict that this occupation will not be long in coming, since the Court endorses the reasoning of "many of the courts and judges who faced the issue before it reached this Court," including the Second and Ninth Circuits.

The Ninth Circuit brought us the judgment that the Court reverses today. Perhaps its decision in this particular case, like the decisions of other lower federal courts that receive passing attention in the Court's opinion, "reflects a more assertive view of federal judicial discretion over claims based on customary international law than the position we take today." But the verbal formula it applied is the same verbal formula that the Court explicitly endorses. Compare ante (quoting *In re Estate of Marcos Human Rights Litigation*, 25 F.3d 1467, 1475 (C.A.9 1994), for the proposition that actionable norms must be " 'specific, universal, and obligatory' "), with 331 F.3d 604, 621 (C.A.9 2003) (en banc) (finding the norm against arbitrary arrest and detention in this case to be "universal, obligatory, and specific"); id., at 619 ("[A]n actionable claim under the [ATS] requires the showing of a violation of the law of nations that is specific, universal, and obligatory" (internal quotation marks omitted)). Endorsing the very formula that led the Ninth Circuit to its result in this case hardly seems to be a recipe for restraint in the future.

. . .

Though it is not necessary to resolution of the present case, one further consideration deserves mention: Despite the avulsive change of *Erie*, the Framers who included reference to "the Law of Nations" in Article I, § 8, cl. 10, of the Constitution would be entirely content with the post-Erie system I have described, and quite terrified by the "discretion" endorsed by the Court. That portion of the general common law known as the law of nations was understood to refer to the accepted practices of nations in their dealings with one another (treatment of ambassadors, immunity of foreign sovereigns from suit, etc.) and with actors on the high seas hostile to all nations and beyond all their territorial jurisdictions (pirates). Those accepted practices have for the most part, if not in their entirety, been enacted into United States statutory law, so that insofar as they are concerned the demise of the general common law is inconsequential. The notion that a law of nations, redefined to mean the consensus of states on any subject, can be used by a private citizen to control a sovereign's treatment of its own citizens within its own territory is a 20th-century invention of internationalist law professors and human-rights advocates. See generally Bradley and Goldsmith, Critique of the Modern Position, 110 Harv. L.Rev., at 831–837. The Framers would, I am confident, be appalled by the proposition that, for example, the American peoples' democratic adoption of the death penalty, see, e.g., Tex. Penal Code Ann. § 12.31 (2003), could be judicially nullified because of the disapproving views of foreigners.

We Americans have a method for making the laws that are over us. We elect representatives to two Houses of Congress, each of which must enact the new law and present it for the approval of a President, whom we also elect. For over two decades now, unelected federal judges have been usurping this lawmaking power by converting what they regard as norms of international law into American law. Today's opinion approves that process in principle, though urging the lower courts to be more restrained.

This Court seems incapable of admitting that some matters — any matters — are none of its business. See, e.g., *Rasul v. Bush*, 124 S.Ct. 2686 (2004); *INS v. St. Cyr*, 533 U.S. 289 (2001). In today's latest victory for its Never Say Never Jurisprudence, the Court ignores its own conclusion that the ATS provides only jurisdiction, wags a finger at the lower courts for going too far, and then — repeating the same formula the ambitious lower courts themselves have used — invites them to try again.

It would be bad enough if there were some assurance that future conversions of perceived international norms into American law would be approved by this Court itself. (Though we know ourselves to be eminently reasonable, self-awareness of eminent reasonableness is not really a substitute for democratic election.) But in this illegitimate lawmaking endeavor, the lower federal courts will be the principal actors; we review but a tiny fraction of their decisions. And no one thinks that all of them are eminently reasonable.

. . .

NOTE

Which human rights norms satisfy the test set forth in *Sosa*? Indeed, what are the elements of that test? Under the test, can only *jus cogens* norms, in effect, satisfy the criteria? The following discusses recent cases that have grappled with defining these boundaries.

Economic and social rights. Would economic and social rights ever satisfy the *Sosa* test? Consider the following statement by the Court of the Appeals for the Second Circuit involving a case, in which Peruvians sued a mining company alleging that 'egregious' pollution caused severe lung disease and deaths among the local population[14]:

> [W]e hold that the asserted "right to life" and "right to health" are insufficiently definite to constitute rules of customary international law. . . . [I]n order to state a claim under the ATCA, we have required that a plaintiff allege a violation of a "clear and unambiguous" rule of customary international law. . . .
>
> Far from being "clear and unambiguous," the statements relied on by plaintiffs to define the rights to life and health are vague and amorphous. For example, the statements that plaintiffs rely on to define the rights to life and health include the following:
>
> > Everyone has the right to a standard of living adequate for the health and well-being of himself and of his family . . . .
>
> Universal Declaration of Human Rights, Art. 25.
>
> > The States Parties to the present Covenant recognize the right of everyone to the enjoyment of the highest attainable standard of physical and mental health.
>
> International Covenant on Economic, Social, and Cultural Rights, Art. 12.
>
> > Human beings are . . . entitled to a healthy and productive life in harmony with nature.
>
> Rio Declaration on Environment and Development ("Rio Declaration"), United Nations Conference on Environment and Development, Rio de Janeiro, Brazil, June 13, 1992, Principle 1.
>
> These principles are boundless and indeterminate. They express virtuous goals understandably expressed at a level of abstraction needed to secure the adherence of States that disagree on many of the particulars regarding how actually to achieve them. But in the words of a sister circuit, they "state abstract rights and liberties devoid of articulable or discernable standards and regulations." *Beanal v. Freeport-McMoran, Inc.*, 197 F.3d 161 (5th Cir.1999). The precept that "[h]uman

[14] *Flores v. Southern Peru Copper Corp.*, 414 F.3d 233 (2d Cir. 2003); see also *Abdullahi v. Pfizer, Inc.*, 2005 WL 1870811 (S.D.N.Y. 2005) (holding that claim alleging pharmaceutical company's dangerous medical experiments on Nigerian children without informed consent does not satisfy *Sosa* test).

beings are... entitled to a healthy and productive life in harmony with nature," for example, utterly fails to specify what conduct would fall within or outside of the law. Similarly, the exhortation that all people are entitled to the "highest attainable standard of physical and mental health" proclaims only nebulous notions that are infinitely malleable.

In support of plaintiffs' argument that the statements and instruments discussed above are part of customary international law, plaintiffs attempt to underscore the universality of the principles asserted by pointing out that they "contain *no limitations as to how or by whom these rights may be violated.*" Pls.' Br. at 10 (emphasis added). However, this assertion proves too much; because of the conceded absence of any "limitations" on these "rights," they do not meet the requirement of our law that rules of customary international law be clear, definite, and unambiguous.

Cruel, inhuman, or degrading treatment. Is the prohibition on cruel, inhuman or degrading treatment (CIDT) sufficiently precise to be cognizable under the ATS? Federal courts have disagreed on this issue. Prior to *Sosa*, the Federal District Court for the Northern District of California concluded that a plaintiff 'failed to establish that there is any international consensus as to what conduct falls within the category of "cruel, inhuman or degrading treatment." Absent such consensus as to the content of this alleged tort, it is not cognizable under the Alien Tort Statute.' *Forti v. Suarez-Mason*, 694 F.Supp. 707, 712 (N.D.Cal.1988). Subsequent to *Sosa*, the Court of Appeals for the Eleventh Circuit overturned previous lower court decisions that had found CIDT actionable. The court stated: 'those courts relied on the International Covenant on Civil and Political Rights... [and] *Sosa* explains that the International Covenant did not "create obligations enforceable in the federal courts."' *Aldana v. Del Monte Fresh Produce*, 416 F.3d 1242, 1247 (11th Cir. 2005).[15]

Subsequent to *Sosa*, the Federal District Court for the Northern District of California took a different approach. Falun Gong practitioners sued local government officials of the People's Republic of China under the ATS and TVPA. The court's analysis of the CIDT claim follows[16]:

> [T]he court in *Xuncax v. Gramajo*, 886 F.Supp. 162 (D.Mass.1995), while acknowledging the complex definitional problem of this tort, reasoned that "[i]t is not necessary for every aspect of what might comprise a standard... be fully defined and universally agreed before a given action meriting the label is clearly proscribed under international law..." The focus, under *Xuncax*, is on the specific conduct at issue, and the question under the ATCA is whether that conduct is universally condemned as cruel, inhuman, or degrading....
>
> This Court is persuaded that the *Xuncax* approach is correct.... Moreover, subsequent to *Forti*, the United States ratified the International Covenant of Civil and Political Rights which prohibits, inter alia, "cruel, inhuman or degrading treatment or punishment." The fact that there may be doubt at the margins — a fact that inheres in any definition — does not negate the essence and application of that definition in clear cases.

[15] Judge Barkett issued a dissent from the decision not to rehear the case en banc because she concluded the CIDT ruling constituted a 'precedent-setting error of exceptional importance.' *Aldana v. Del Monte Fresh Produce, N.A., Inc.*, 452 F.3d 1284 (11th Cir.(Fla.) Jun 23, 2006) (NO. 04–10234).

[16] *Doe v. Qi*, 349 F. Supp. 2d 1258, 1321 (N.D. Cal. 2004).

> This approach is entirely consistent with *Sosa*. The Court in *Sosa* acknowledged that the prohibition under international law of prolonged and arbitrary detention entailed a gray area at which it may be "hard [ ] to say which policies cross that line with the certainty" sufficient to state a common law claim under the ATCA; yet there are "some policies of prolonged arbitrary detentions [which] are so bad that those who enforce them become enemies of the human race." The inquiry turns on the specific facts of each case and is not precluded simply because there are questions at the margins.
>
> ... As previously noted, Plaintiffs Larsson, Lemish, and Odar allege that they were subjected to one day of incarceration and interrogation during which they were pushed, shoved, hit, and placed in a chokehold. Plaintiff Petit alleges that a police office[r] attempted to force his hand into her vagina while several other officers pinned her down.
>
> The allegations of specific conduct must be compared with existing authorities on international law to determine whether the specific conduct alleged violated universally established norms. [The court examines several decisions by the Human Rights Committee, Committee Against Torture, the Inter-American Commission on Human Rights, the European Court of Human Rights and Fundamental Freedoms, and the African Commission on Human and Peoples' Rights.] Without diminishing the mistreatment allegedly suffered by Plaintiffs Larsson, Lemish, and Odar, their treatment pales in comparison to the acts which have been found by various courts and international authorities to constituted cruel, inhuman or degrading treatment. Simply put, a review of the authorities discussed above does not establish that the specific conduct alleged by these plaintiffs is universally prohibited by the international community as a whole. On the other hand, the sexual abuse suffered by Plaintiff Petit is different. The United Nations Committee Against Torture's Initial Report specifically lists sexual abuse as a cruel act.... Plaintiff Petit has stated a claim for cruel, inhuman or degrading treatment in violation of the ATCA. Plaintiffs Larsson, Lemish, and Odar have not.

In *Mujica v. Occidental Petroleum Corp.*, 381 F.Supp.2d 1164 (C.D.Cal. 2005), another federal district court cited the Falun Gong case in distinguishing between different types of CIDT claims:

> Plaintiffs' claims of cruel, inhuman, and degrading treatment allege that Defendant's acts resulted in gross humiliation, fear, and anguish. These actions caused Plaintiffs to fear for their lives and forced them to flee their homes. It would be impractical to recognize these allegations as constituting an ATS claim because it would allow foreign plaintiffs to litigate claims in U.S. courts that bear a strong resemblance to intentional infliction of emotional distress. While the Court [holds] that there is an international norm against cruel, inhuman, and degrading treatment, the broad swaths of conduct that could result in extreme fear and anguish counsel against recognizing such a claim. However, this should be taken to indicate that claims of cruel, inhuman, and degrading treatment should not be recognized when they arise out of more severe situations such as those involving sexual abuse.

The *Mujica* court explained that it was heeding *Sosa*'s admonition to consider the 'practical consequences' of expanding the causes of action under the ATS. *Mujica* noted that *Sosa* 'observed that the implications of recognizing a cause of action for arbitrary detention ' "would be breathtaking." '

Is it desirable for courts, including the Supreme Court, to consider such 'practical consequences'? Should the political branches, instead of the judiciary, reign in the scope of such claims? Why is the consequence of exercising jurisdiction over acts of arbitrary detention 'breathtaking,' but doing so for a single act of torture or a single act of sexual abuse is not? Have the courts drawn a sensible boundary?

QUESTIONS

1. Consider how the Court analysed various sources of international law. Did the Court's analysis depart from conventional approaches in determining the content of customary international law? Consider the following commentary:[17]

> [M]any pre-*Sosa* lower court decisions downplayed the traditional state practice requirement for CIL [customary international law] and emphasized instead state acceptance as reflected in instruments like General Assembly resolutions, multilateral treaties, national constitutions, and official pronouncements of international bodies. *Sosa* appears to render some of these sources irrelevant, minimize the significance of others, and reemphasize the importance of looking to state practice in ATS cases.
>
> . . .
>
> . . . [T]he Court in *Sosa* gave little weight to both the Universal Declaration of Human Rights and the ICCPR, narrowed the relevance of national constitutions and the Restatement, and reduced the allowable gap between a CIL norm's aspiration and the actual practice of states. It is no surprise, in this light, that the Court in *Sosa* envisioned that, under its approach, only a modest number of claims would be recognized under the ATS.
>
> It remains unclear, however, precisely how far *Sosa* went in this regard. The lack of clarity results from the Court's favorable citation to prior lower court opinions that had embraced the very methods and sources of CIL identification that the Court in *Sosa* appeared to discount. . . .
>
> . . .
>
> In recent years, the Supreme Court has cited and relied on international and foreign materials in the course of interpreting provisions of the US Constitution. . . .
>
> . . .
>
> . . . The Court has been much less rigorous with respect to foreign and international materials in its constitutional interpretation cases than it was with respect to these sources in the context of the ATS in *Sosa*. In *Roper v. Simmons*, for example, in which the Court held that the execution of juvenile offenders violates the Eighth Amendment, the Court cited, among other things, the Convention on the Rights of the Child, a treaty that had not been ratified by the United States, and the ICCPR, which the U.S. had ratified with a reservation declining to agree to the ban in that treaty on the juvenile death penalty. By contrast, in *Sosa*, as we discussed earlier, the

[17] Curtis A. Bradley, Jack L. Goldsmith and David H. Moore, 'Sosa, Customary International Law, and the Continuing Relevance of Erie', 120 Harv. L. Rev. 869 (2007).

Court described the ICCPR as having "little utility" in its analysis, even though, unlike in *Roper*, there was no relevant reservation with respect to the issue before the Court.

It is difficult to know what to make of the Supreme Court's differing treatment of foreign and international sources in the constitutional and ATS contexts....

2. The ATS provides jurisdiction for injuries 'committed in violation of the law of nations or a treaty of the United States'. After *Sosa*, is there any hope of successfully bringing a claim solely under the ICCPR? What if the self-executing declaration accompanying the US ratification of the ICCPR is incompatible with the object and the purpose of the treaty?

3. Do you agree with Justice Breyer that 'consensus as to universal criminal jurisdiction itself suggests that universal tort jurisdiction would be no more threatening'? Could civil jurisdiction be more threatening to a foreign state than a system of criminal jurisdiction?

4. How should US reservations, understandings or declarations to a treaty affect the interpretation of custom under the 'law of nations' prong of the ATS? Consider the following discussion in a recent lower federal court opinion[18]:

> The Plaintiffs urge that finding cruel, inhuman or degrading treatment could be consistent with the Senate's ratifications of both the CAT and the ICCPR which reflects its intent to incorporate the constitutional test for cruel and unusual treatment or punishment prohibited by the Firth, Eighth, or Fourteenth Amendment....
>
> ...
>
> ... [I]rrespective of the Senate's interpretation, the constitutional standards of one nation is not necessarily determinative of standards to be followed by the international community as a whole. While one nation's practices may inform the question as to the existence of an internationally accepted standard, only those domestic standards rising to the level of customary usage and practice of the international community can constitute "the law of nations" under the ATCA....

5. Should the 'law of nations' prong of the ATS apply only to customary international law norms? Would it be appropriate for a court to consider an international norm derived from general principles of law? Does *Sosa* foreclose that legal avenue?

TORTURE VICTIM PROTECTION ACT

106 Stat. 73 (1992), 28 U.S.C.A. 1350 Notes

...

Section 2. Establishment of Civil Action

(a) LIABILITY. — An individual who, under actual or apparent authority, or color of law, of any foreign nation —

(1) subjects an individual to torture shall, in a civil action, be liable for damages to that individual; or

[18] *Doe v. Qi*, 349 F. Supp. 2d 1258, 1324 n. 44 (N.D. Cal. 2004).

(2) subjects an individual to extrajudicial killing shall, in a civil action, be liable for damages to the individual's legal representative, or to any person who may be a claimant in an action for wrongful death.

(b) EXHAUSTION OF REMEDIES. — A court shall decline to hear a claim under this section if the claimant has not exhausted adequate and available remedies in the place in which the conduct giving rise to the claim occurred.

(c) STATUTE OF LIMITATIONS. — No action shall be maintained under this section unless it is commenced within 10 years after the cause of action arose.

Section 3. Definitions

(a) EXTRAJUDICIAL KILLING. — For the purposes of this Act, the term 'extrajudicial killing' means a deliberated killing not authorized by a previous judgment pronounced by a regularly constituted court affording all the judicial guarantees which are recognized as indispensable by civilized peoples. Such term, however, does not include any such killing that, under international law, is lawfully carried out under the authority of a foreign nation.

(b) TORTURE. — For the purposes of this Act —

(1) the term 'torture' means any act, directed against an individual in the offender's custody or physical control, by which severe pain or suffering (other than pain or suffering arising only from or inherent in; or incidental to; lawful sanctions), whether physical, or mental, is intentionally inflicted on that individual for such purposes as obtaining from that individual or a third person information or a confession, punishing that individual for an act that individual or a third person has committed or is suspected of having committed, intimidating or coercing that individual or a third person, or for any reason based on discrimination of any kind; and

(2) mental pain or suffering refers to prolonged mental harm caused by or resulting from —

(A) the intentional infliction or threatened infliction of severe physical pain or suffering;

(B) the administration or application, or threatened administration or application, of mind altering substances or other procedures calculated to disrupt profoundly the senses or the personality;

(C) the threat of imminent death; or

(D) the threat that another individual will imminently be subjected to death, severe physical pain or suffering, or the administration or application of mind altering substances or other procedures calculated to disrupt profoundly the senses or personality.

SENATE REPORT ON THE TORTURE VICTIM PROTECTION ACT

S. Rep. 102–249, Committee on the Judiciary, 102nd Cong., 1st Sess., 1991

... This legislation will carry out the intent of the Convention against Torture and Other Cruel, Inhuman or Degrading Treatment or Punishment, which was ratified by the U.S. Senate on October 27, 1990. The convention obligates state parties to adopt measures to ensure that torturers within their territories are held legally accountable for their acts. This legislation will do precisely that — by making sure that torturers and death squads will no longer have a safe haven in the United States.

...

The TVPA would establish an unambiguous basis for a cause of action that has been successfully maintained under an existing law, section 1350 of title 28 of the U.S. Code....

...

The TVPA would... enhance the remedy already available under section 1350 in an important respect: while the Alien Tort Claims Act provides a remedy to aliens only, the TVPA would extend a civil remedy also to U.S. citizens who may have been tortured abroad.

...

IV. Analysis of Legislation

...

D. Who can be sued

First and foremost, only defendants over which a court in the United States has personal jurisdiction may be sued. In order for a Federal court to obtain personal jurisdiction over a defendant, the individual must have "minimum contacts" with the forum state, for example through residency here or current travel. Thus, this legislation will not turn the U.S. courts into tribunals for torts having no connection to the United States whatsoever.

The legislation uses the term "individual" to make crystal clear that foreign states or their entities cannot be sued under this bill under any circumstances: only individuals may be sued. Consequently, the TVPA is not meant to override the Foreign Sovereign Immunities Act (FSIA) of 1976, which renders foreign governments immune from suits in U.S. courts, except in certain instances.

The TVPA is not intended to override traditional diplomatic immunities which prevent the exercise of jurisdiction by U.S. courts over foreign diplomats. The United States is a party to the Vienna Convention on Diplomatic Relations, under which diplomats are immune from civil lawsuits except with regard to certain commercial activities.

Nor should visiting heads of state be subject to suit under the TVPA. Article 2(1) of the United Nations Convention on Special Missions provides that, when one state sends an official mission to another, the visiting head of state "shall enjoy in the receiving State or in a third State the facilities, privileges and immunities accorded by international law to Heads of State on an official visit."

However, the committee does not intend these immunities to provide former officials with a defense to a lawsuit brought under this legislation. To avoid liability by invoking the FSIA, a former official would have to prove an agency relationship to a state, which would require that the state "admit some knowledge or authorization of relevant acts." 28 U.S.C. 1603(b). Because all states are officially opposed to torture and extrajudicial killing, however, the FSIA should normally provide no defense to an action taken under the TVPA against a former official.

Similarly, the committee does not intend the "act of state" doctrine to provide a shield from lawsuit for former officials. In *Banco Nacional de Cuba v. Sabbatino*, 376 U.S. 398 (1964), the Supreme Court held that the "act of state" doctrine is meant to prevent U.S. courts from sitting in judgment of the official public acts of a sovereign foreign government. Since this doctrine applies only to "public" acts, and no state commits torture as a matter of public policy, this doctrine cannot shield former officials from liability under this legislation.

E. Scope of liability

In order for a defendant to be liable, the torture or extrajudicial killing must have been taken "under actual or apparent authority or under color of law of a foreign nation." Consequently, this legislation does not cover purely private criminal acts by individuals or nongovernmental organizations. However, because no state officially condones torture or extrajudicial killings, few such acts, if any, would fall under the rubric of "official actions" taken in the course of an official's duties. Consequently, the phrase "actual or apparent authority or under color of law" is used to denote torture and extrajudicial killings committed by officials both within and outside the scope of their authority. Courts should look to principles of liability under U.S. civil rights laws, in particular section 1983 of title 42 of the United States Code, in construing "under color of law" as well as interpretations of "actual or apparent authority" derived from agency theory in order to give the fullest coverage possible.

The legislation is limited to lawsuits against persons who ordered, abetted, or assisted in the torture. It will not permit a lawsuit against a former leader of a country merely because an isolated act of torture occurred somewhere in that country. However, a higher official need not have personally performed or ordered the abuses in order to be held liable. Under international law, responsibility for torture, summary execution, or disappearances extends beyond the person or persons who actually committed those acts — anyone with higher authority who authorized, tolerated or knowingly ignored those acts is liable for them....

...

F. Exhaustion of remedies

...Cases involving torture abroad which have been filed under the Alien Tort Claims Act show that torture victims bring suits in the United States against their alleged torturers only as a last resort. Usually, the alleged torturer has more substantial assets outside the United States and the jurisdictional nexus is easier to prove outside the United States. Therefore, as a general matter, the committee recognizes that in most instances the initiation of litigation under this legislation will be virtually prima facie evidence that the claimant has exhausted his or her remedies in the jurisdiction in which the torture occurred. The committee believes that courts should approach cases brought under the proposed legislation with this assumption.

More specifically, as this legislation involves international matters and judgments regarding the adequacy of procedures in foreign courts, the interpretation of section 2(b), like the other provisions of this act, should be informed by general principles of international law. The procedural practice of international human rights tribunals generally holds that the respondent has the burden of raising the nonexhaustion of remedies as an affirmative defense and must show that domestic remedies exist that the claimant did not use....

VII. Minority Views of Messrs. Simpson and Grassley

...

The executive branch, through the Department of Justice, has expressed a most serious concern with S. 313, which we share. Senate bill 313 could create difficulties in the management of foreign policy. For example, under this bill, individual aliens could determine the timing and manner of the making of allegations in a U.S. court about a foreign country's alleged abuses of human rights.

There is no more complex and sensitive issue between countries than human rights. The risk that would be run if an alien could have a foreign country judged by a U.S. court is too great. Judges of U.S. courts would, in a sense, conduct some of our Nation's foreign policy. The executive branch is and should remain, we believe, left with substantial foreign policy control.

In addition the Justice Department properly notes that our passage of this bill could encourage hostile foreign countries to retaliate by trying to assert jurisdiction for acts committed in the United States by the U.S. Government against U.S. citizens. For example, if this bill's principles were adopted abroad, Saddam Hussein could try a United States citizen police officer who happened to be present in Iraq, in an Iraqi court, for alleged human rights abuses against any United States citizen that the policeman happened to arrest while performing his duties in the United States.

...

COMMENT ON CRIMINAL PROSECUTION UNDER CONVENTION AGAINST TORTURE

Although the preceding Senate Report states that the TVPA 'will carry out the intent' of the Torture Convention, it does so only with respect to *civil liability*. Article 14 of that Convention provides that each State Party 'shall ensure in its legal system that the victim of an act of torture obtains redress and has an enforceable right to fair and adequate compensation ...'.

Compare the provisions for *criminal prosecution* under Article 1 of the Convention, which applies (with respect to torture, as there defined) to pain and suffering that is 'inflicted by or at the instigation of or with the consent or acquiescence of a public official or other person acting in an official capacity'. Article 2 provides that States Parties 'shall take effective... measures to prevent acts of torture' in their territory. But the Convention reaches beyond this traditional territorial base for a state's criminal jurisdiction. Under Article 4, each State Party 'shall ensure that all acts of torture are offences under its criminal law', and 'shall make these offences punishable by appropriate penalties'. Under Section (1) of Article 5, each Party 'shall take such measures as may be necessary to establish its jurisdiction over the offences referred to in article 4':

(a) when offences are committed in the state's territory;
(b) when 'the alleged offender is a national of that State'; and
(c) when 'the victim is a national of that State if that State considers it appropriate'.

In addition, jurisdiction is to be established under Section (2) of Article 5, where the alleged offender is present in the state's territory and the state does not extradite him pursuant to the Convention to other indicated and involved states for criminal prosecution there.

In 1990, the Senate Committee on Foreign Relations reported favourably on the Convention and recommended that the Senate give its consent to ratification. With respect to Section (1) of Article 5, the Committee report states:[19]

> A major concern in drafting Article 5... was whether the Convention should provide for possible prosecution by any State in which the alleged offender is found — so-called universal jurisdiction.[20] The United States strongly supported the provision for universal jurisdiction, on the grounds that torture, like hijacking, sabotage, hostage-taking, and attacks on internationally protected persons, is an offense of special international concern, and should have similarly broad, universal recognition as a crime against humanity, with appropriate jurisdictional consequences. Provision for 'universal jurisdiction' was also deemed important in view of the fact that the government of the country where official torture actually occurs may seldom be relied on to take action.... [E]xisting federal and state law appears sufficient to establish jurisdiction when the offense has allegedly been committed in any territory under U.S. jurisdiction.... Implementing legislation is therefore needed only to establish Article 5(1)(b) jurisdiction over offenses committed by U.S. nationals outside the United States, and to establish Article 5(2) jurisdiction over foreign offenders committing torture abroad who are later found in territory under U.S. jurisdiction.... Similar legislation has already been enacted to implement comparable provisions of the Conventions on Hijacking, Sabotage, Hostages, and Protection of Diplomats.

In 1990, the Senate consented to ratification of the Convention, provided that the criminal legislation required by the Convention first be enacted by Congress. The

[19] Sen. Comm. For. Relations, Report on Convention against Torture, 100th Cong., 2d Sess. (1990).

[20] [Eds. A discussion and illustrations of general bases for jurisdiction including universal jurisdiction appear at p. 1161, *supra*.]

Torture Convention Implementing Legislation was enacted in 1994, 18 U.S.C.A. 2340–2340B. Section 2340A gives courts jurisdiction for torture (as defined) committed 'outside the United States' where the alleged offender is a US national or 'is present in the United States, irrespective of the nationality of the victim or alleged offender'. The United States then ratified the Convention.

In December 2006, the Government launched the first US prosecution for the crime of torture. US attorneys charged Roy Belfast, aka Charles 'Chuckie' Taylor Jr, son of former Liberian President Charles Taylor, for various crimes related to an alleged torture of a person in Liberia. At the time of the incident, the defendant commanded the Liberian Antiterrorist Unit. He allegedly participated in repeatedly burning the victim's flesh with a hot iron, burning various parts of his body with scalding water, repeatedly electrically shocking the victim's genitalia and other body parts, and rubbing salt into the victim's wounds.

SANDRA COLIVER, JENNIE GREEN AND PAUL HOFFMAN, HOLDING HUMAN RIGHTS VIOLATORS ACCOUNTABLE BY USING INTERNATIONAL LAW IN US COURTS: ADVOCACY EFFORTS AND COMPLEMENTARY STRATEGIES

19 Emory Int. L. Rev. 169 (2005)

[The authors are among the leading litigators who have helped bring many of the ATS and TVPA cases. They are respectively Executive Director, the Center for Justice & Accountability; Senior Attorney, Center for Constitutional Rights; Partner, Schonbrun, DeSimone, Seplow, Harris & Hoffman, LLP.]

Since 1980, at least sixteen human rights perpetrators (including Pena-Irala, the defendant in the landmark *Filartiga* case) have been sued successfully.[21] One of those was a current high-ranking government official: the Bosnian Serb leader Radovan Karadzic. Seven were former high-ranking civilian or military officials who continued to exercise considerable influence in their countries. All were found to have had substantial responsibility for egregious human rights violations, to be subject to the personal jurisdiction of the court, and not to be entitled to immunity from suit (sovereign, diplomatic, or otherwise). In all cases, the plaintiffs satisfied the requirements of standing and the statute of limitations, and demonstrated that they had exhausted any available and effective remedies in their home countries. In several cases the courts expressly found that the cases did not pose a significant interference to U.S. foreign policy or that the act of state doctrine applied.

...

[21] [Eds. The authors list numerous federal court decisions and defendants including a Paraguayan police chief, Argentinian general, Bosnian Serb leader, Guatemalan former defence minister, Bolivian corporation and civilian, Ghanaian security officer, former President of the Philippines, Rwandan radio station owner and political party leader, Indonesian general, former Haitian military ruler, Bosnian Serb paramilitary member, Ethiopian former municipal official, Chilean former member of military death squad, Salvadoran key organizer of Archbishop Romero assassination, Beijing Mayor, and former Salvadoran generals and ministers of defence.]

1. Ensuring that the U.S. Does Not Remain a Safe Haven for Human Rights Abusers

The Center for Justice and Accountability ("CJA") estimates that several hundred human rights abusers now live in the United States with substantial responsibility for heinous atrocities, and that several dozen high-level perpetrators visit every year. These figures are supported by estimates from the U.S. Bureau of Immigration and Customs Enforcement (ICE). They have come from more than seventy countries, including Bosnia, Cambodia, Chile, El Salvador, Ethiopia, Guatemala, Haiti, Honduras, India, Liberia, Pakistan, Peru, Rwanda, Sierra Leone, Somalia, Sri Lanka, and Vietnam. Only a few dozen human rights abusers have been deported, in addition to the approximately ninety who were denaturalized, deported, or extradited for Naziera crimes. Most of the non-Nazis have been deported since 2000. Most of them are low-level abusers and nearly half are Haitian. The majority of them are identified in the asylum process when they declare that their fear of persecution is based on the fact that they were part of a unit that participated in human rights atrocities....

...Of the sixteen individuals who have been successfully sued using the ATS, one was deported based on information uncovered by the plaintiffs, one was extradited, one died, and ten left the country never to return (as far as we know), including five who had moved to the United States to settle. Only three of the sixteen remain in the United States and, of those, one has been denaturalized and is in detention while he awaits deportation; the other two are subject to deportation investigations based in large part on evidence uncovered during the course of the ATS cases.

These sixteen cases appear to have deterred numerous human rights perpetrators from coming to the United States. Following the ATS case against Paraguayan police chief Pena-Irala, the U.S. consulate in Paraguay reported a decrease in visas to visit the United States requested by Paraguayan officials and military officers. The Shah of Iran was the last major human rights abuser to seek medical treatment openly in the United States.... Salvadorans who have been watching for the entry of Salvadoran military officers who used to travel regularly to Miami and southern California report that they are no longer coming here. Immigration agents have confirmed that certain named human rights abusers from Central America stopped coming to the States after mid-2002, after two Salvadoran former defense ministers were found liable by a Florida jury and ordered to pay $54 million to the plaintiffs.

2. Holding Perpetrators Accountable

...Although the punishment does not fit the severity of the crimes, these civil cases are generally the only remedies available to survivors. The cases expose what the perpetrators have done and cause embarrassment to the perpetrators. In some cases, being sued under the ATS or TVPA may limit the careers of foreign officials if their advancement depends on their ability to travel to the United States without controversy. The lawsuits prevent foreign human rights violators from visiting or resettling in the United States with impunity.... In addition, lawyers continue to pursue the collection of assets in past judgments and increasingly are pursuing defendants with assets that may be reachable by U.S. courts.

Hector Gramajo, a Guatemalan ex-general, was one of those who fled the United States after being served with an ATS complaint in 1991. He had been grooming himself to run for the presidency of his country and had come to the United States to obtain a degree from the Kennedy School at Harvard. On his graduation day, he was served with the lawsuit. He immediately returned to Guatemala, his U.S. visa was revoked, and his party decided not to choose him as its presidential candidate. His inability to travel to the United States without embarrassment was a liability. Gramajo's political ambitions were harmed by the lawsuit and the public exposure surrounding it.

. . .

Kelbessa Negewo, held responsible by a federal court in Atlanta for acts of torture during the "Red Terror" in Ethiopia, lost several jobs as a result of the civil judgment and was denaturalized largely based on evidence produced at the civil trial. . . .

The collection of ATS monetary judgments, however, has been difficult. It is believed that there has been money collected in only three of the individual defendant cases: a little more than $1 million from the estate of Philippine President Ferdinand Marcos,[22] and approximately $1,000 each from General Suarez-Mason and Kelbessa Negewo. In 2003, $270,000 was collected from one of the defendants in the Romagoza case.[23]

. . .

3. Official Acknowledgment and Reparation for the Human Rights Victims and Survivors

These cases often help survivors experience a sense of justice, a sense of meaning in their survival, and tremendous satisfaction in knowing that they have brought dignity to the memories of those who were killed or tortured. . . . [T]he cases can serve as a kind of mini-truth commission. . . .

For instance, Juan Romagoza, a Salvadoran torture survivor, stated:

> When I testified, a strength came over me. I felt like I was in the prow of a boat and that there were many, many people rowing behind. I felt that if I looked back, I'd weep because I'd see them again: wounded, tortured, raped, naked, torn, bleeding. So, I didn't look back, but I felt their support, their strength, their energy. Being involved in this case, confronting the generals with these terrible facts — that's the best possible therapy a torture survivor could have.

7. Contributing to Transitional Justice

ATS cases can serve as a catalyst for the process of transitional justice in the home country. . . . By demonstrating that impunity can be challenged, ATS cases can

[22] A $150 million settlement was approved in the Marcos case but the Philippine courts blocked the transfer of Marcos's assets after the Philippine government intervened to claim the assets for itself. . . . Of course, all of the Holocaust Assets cases included ATS claims and billions of dollars in settlements have been achieved in those cases. Lawyers involved in these suits . . . have credited the foundation of ATS jurisprudence as being crucial in their efforts to obtain justice for victims of the Holocaust. See, e.g., Burt Neuborne, Preliminary Reflections on Aspects of Holocaust-Era Litigation in American Courts, 80 Wash.U. L.Q. 795 nn. 29–30 (2002).

[23] However, unless the reversal of this judgment is overturned, the funds collected will have to be returned. CJA has put special focus on collecting the assets of the individual defendants it sues and on taking cases where such collection is possible. . . .

stimulate discussion about the crimes of the past and build support for bringing perpetrators to justice in their own domestic courts. For instance, the Abebe-Jira case had an effect on public opinion in Ethiopia and on the commitment of the Ethiopian government to move forward with trials of former officials of the Dergue.[24]

...

The Romagoza case also stimulated witnesses to come forward with evidence against two more Salvadoran perpetrators who have lived in the United States for more than fifteen years: one of the organizers of the 1980 assassination of Archbishop Oscar Romero and Colonel Carranza, Head of the Hacienda (Treasury) Police, who was forced out of the military in 1985 as a result of his responsibility for atrocities which endangered the continuation of U.S. military aid to El Salvador. Following the issuance of the verdict in the Romero case in September 2004, key representatives of the Catholic Church in El Salvador for the first time called for revisions to the amnesty law and a reopening of the criminal investigation into the assassination. The Archbishop of San Salvador stated that the verdict should help to establish Archbishop Romero's martyrdom, by having proved who was involved in the assassination plot.

M. O. CHIBUNDU, MAKING CUSTOMARY INTERNATIONAL LAW THROUGH MUNICIPAL ADJUDICATION: A STRUCTURAL INQUIRY

39 Va. J. Int. L. 1069 (1999)

...

Even when one accepts the underlying norms of individual rights ..., the proposition that these rights should be enforced in the domestic courts of any country without regard to the traditional concerns over sovereignty is flawed for numerous reasons, not the least of which are the paradoxes that are embedded in the claim.

The most obvious but telling paradox is that these "individual rights" claims invariably seem to arise from the most contested political conflicts in the Third World. Indeed, a recent survey of the litigation of "international human rights claims" in U.S. courts might easily have substituted as a current affairs topics primer of the trouble-spots of the non-Western world.... [T]he persistent and unilaterally-arrived-at decision by the courts of one nation to sit in judgment over political cases that consistently touch on the raw nerves of the internal conflicts of other societies surely push right up against (if it does not cross) well-tested norms in international law such as those of self-determination.

And here is to be found another paradox. One significant effect of "individual rights" litigation in courts purporting to apply "universal" law may be to deprive the local courts in strife-ridden countries the opportunity to develop and internalize those very same norms.... The losing elites in the political turbulences of the Third World, aided and abetted by the contingent interest groups that invariably emerge

[24] Plaintiffs' counsel was invited to give a nationally televised address during a visit to Ethiopia after the trial in March 1994. The case received substantial publicity within Ethiopia and within Ethiopian communities outside the country.

in the West — sometimes in response to the pull of social affinities like race, religion, ethnicity and national origin, and other times to the push of ideology or visual journalism — will invoke the well-developed, efficient and potentially remunerative Western judiciary to continue "by other means" the wars lost at home. Meanwhile, their local judiciaries atrophy. Individual rights are ignored in the home country, and the success of the local victors will continue to depend less on the judicial fashioning and enforcement of "individual rights" than on the extrajudicial mauling of opponents. Thus, even if one accepts that "human rights" are "universal" and "individual," the process by which the norm is actualized makes a good deal of difference.... To deprive turbulent societies of this necessary process under the guise of international humanism is no less imperial — and with about the same likely consequences — as were the European colonial "civilizing missions" of the nineteenth and early twentieth centuries.... [W]hatever its benefits may be to specific individuals in the short run, its effect is to contribute mightily to deprive the "backward societies" of the opportunity for nurture from within and the internalization of the necessary experiences without which those very cherished Western seeds of "democratic pluralism" and "individual rights" will not flourish.

...

...Interest groups in the United States, for example, purporting to act on behalf of individuals and groups living under such acknowledged repressive regimes as that of Ferdinand Marcos in the Philippines, Sani Abacha in Nigeria, and Suharto in Indonesia, have not limited their claims to core human rights claims such as torture, arbitrary arrests, unexplained disappearances or even "extrajudicial" killings — as substantial as such claims may be — but have asserted as remediable in U.S. courts alleged economic wrongs such as the uncompensated taking of the property of a local national by that local government, or the unregulated pollution of the local environment as a result of ill-advised policies by those governments. Nor have such actions been limited to miscreant government officials whose future conduct is sought to be deterred. Rather, these *Filartiga*-type actions have been read to embrace conduct by commercial concerns integrally involved in structuring the national economy, as well as by rebel movements in conflicts that are essentially about the internal self-determination and alignment of political power within these countries. In short, such proponents of the "universal jurisdiction" of U.S. courts in human rights cases assert, under the aegis of the ATCA and U.S. law, the imperial right to judicially impose wholesale structural reforms — political, social and economic — on societies whose human rights practices are deemed to be backward. Perhaps the societies would benefit from such changes, but it is surely questionable whether it is within the province of a judicial proceeding to undertake such systemic reconfiguration of a foreign society.

...

When one factors in such other considerations as the non-contemporaneity of the interests that are weighed (that is, power, interests, burdens and benefit are all dynamic and will have different weights over time), it becomes all too clear why civil judicial relief by the courts of a political system far removed from the events that it seeks to regulate is not only a blunt tool, but is entirely inadequate for the task...

...

... Although fashionable, it is a mistake to equate "justice" with "punishment." What is important is that the experience of trying to come to grips with the interplay of criminality and politics within the particular society is one that shapes the structures and institutions of that society, not the least of which are the judiciary and related institutions. Whether South Africa's Truth and Reconciliation Commission works or fails, the one certainty is that South Africans will learn from it, and cannot shift the responsibility for its failure (or for that matter allot the credit for its success) to others. Similarly, but of no small consequence, Westerners will not always saddle themselves with the guilt of failure, or, as is more likely the case, invariably take credit for the "new South Africa," effectively minimizing the role of the local population in its self-actualization.

...

As appealing as it may thus appear at first blush, the arrogation by a municipal court of the unbridled power to punish wrongdoing under the guise of enforcing international law should be resisted not only on account of its effectiveness, but more fundamentally because of what it says about the social distribution of power within the international community.... Just as colonial outposts were incidental objects of metropolitan politics in late nineteenth and early twentieth centuries' European politics, so also is the fixation today on the undoubted atrocities taking place in some developing societies. Consider, for example, how much knowledge of these developing societies is possessed by those who, at the drop of a hat, are only too willing to brandish summons and complaints of human rights violations in those societies? Is the television camera any less superficial as a recorder of history than the yellow rags of the late nineteenth century?

... If the international community of jurists is to create an enduring jurisprudence of international human rights law, it will be because those norms converge from adjudications in multiple jurisdictions each reflecting the socio-political structures of its constitution, while seeking to conform local practices to evolving international standards.

QUESTIONS

1. Are you persuaded by Professor Chibundu's critique of ATS litigation? How much, if any, of his argument hinges on the notion that ATS cases will be used to vindicate norms far in excess of *jus cogens* violations (e.g., property violations)? If courts do not actually accept such attempts to stretch the doctrine, is his general argument substantially weakened?

2. Professor Chibundu's admonitions might apply not only to courts, but also directly to the organizations litigating these cases. What recommendations, if any, would you suggest to such an organization in light of his critiques?

3. Does ATS and TVPA litigation 'deprive the local courts in strife-ridden countries the opportunity to develop and internalize those very same norms'? Can US federal courts develop and apply legal doctrines to address such concerns while still fully vindicating human rights? Consider, for example, the requirement that plaintiffs exhaust

domestic remedies, which is referenced in *Sosa* and codified in the TVPA, p. 1200, *supra.* How might Lutz and Sikkink's article relate to this set of questions? Consider the following application of Lutz and Sikkink's work by the Court of Appeals for the Ninth Circuit in a recent ATS decision[25]:

> [T]he argument that requiring exhaustion will improve compliance with international human rights law in other countries because it provides an incentive for those countries to improve their legal systems appears plausible on its face. (See Dissent at 1116–17.) Although advanced with some frequency, however, this argument remains fairly speculative and most often lacks any empirical data showing improvements in the quality or accessibility of local remedies as a result of the application of the local remedies rule at the international level. An alternative and perhaps equally plausible hypothesis is that "[f]oreign court rulings against rights-abusing defendants have the effect of putting pressure 'from above' on the state where the rights abuses occurred." Ellen Lutz & Kathryn Sikkink, The Justice Cascade: The Evolution and Impact of Human Rights Trials in Latin America, 2 Chi. J. Int. L. 1, 4 (2001); see also id. at 24–25, 30 (discussing the possibility that the arrest and near trial of General Pinochet in Europe and European court cases against Argentine military officers were catalysts in Chile and Argentina, respectively, for more aggressive pursuit of human rights suits in those countries). If this alternative hypothesis were true, the absence of the exhaustion rule, not its presence, would contribute to the development of effective remedies for human rights abuses.
>
> [The majority analysis responds, in part, to the following passages from Judge Jay Bybee in dissent.]
>
> By accepting jurisdiction over foreign suits that can be appropriately handled locally, the federal courts embroil the nation in a kind of judicial "imperialism" . . .
>
> . . . The principle in international practice is "not to submit [the claimant] to a mere judicial exercise," but is "intended to afford the territorial government an opportunity actually to repair the injury sustained." The exhaustion rule is part of a concerted international effort to encourage countries to provide effective local remedies.
>
> This consideration provides perhaps the most important practical consideration for the adoption of an exhaustion requirement in ATCA. If litigants are allowed to seek refuge in U.S. courts before pursuing available remedies at home, we will have facilitated parties-including politically-minded parties-who wish to circumvent the creation and refinement of local remedies.
>
> . . .
>
> Moreover, litigation is not always the best vehicle for resolving difficult internal matters. Exhaustion may thus encourage creative political solutions beyond our ken. The exhaustion requirement 'acknowledges that a sovereign is not only in the best position to succeed, particularly when acting within its own territory, but that a sovereign is also most familiar with the situation and best able to fashion a remedy appropriate to local circumstances.' Richard D. Glick, Environmental Justice in the United States: Implications of the International Covenant on Civil and Political Rights, 19 Harv. Envt'l. L. Rev. 69, 99 (1995).

[25] *Sarei v. Rio Tinto, PLC.*, 456 F.3d 1069 (9th Cir. 2006).

COMMENT ON FOREIGN POLICY IMPACT

In *Sosa*, the Court stated that 'another possible limitation that we need not apply here is a policy of case-specific deference to the political branches'. When is such deference, if ever, appropriate? The Court, in a remarkable step, referred to ongoing ATS litigation (against corporations that allegedly supported South Africa's apartheid regime). The Court added, '[i]n such cases, there is a strong argument that federal courts should give serious weight to the Executive Branch's view of the case's impact on foreign policy'.

Subsequent to *Sosa*, several federal courts have grappled with these issues. A starting point in their analyses is often the political question doctrine. Under that doctrine, courts may decline to exercise jurisdiction over a case if the controversy is determined to involve a political question. According to the leading Supreme Court decision, *Baker v. Carr*, 369 U.S. 186 (1962), such a determination involves six factors:

> Prominent on the surface of any case held to involve a political question is found [1] a textually demonstrable constitutional commitment of the issue to a coordinate political department; or [2] a lack of judicially discoverable and manageable standards for resolving it; or [3] the impossibility of deciding without an initial policy determination of a kind clearly for nonjudicial discretion; or [4] the impossibility of a court's undertaking independent resolution without expressing lack of the respect due coordinate branches of government; or [5] an unusual need for unquestioning adherence to a political decision already made; or [6] the potentiality of embarrassment from multifarious pronouncements by various departments on one question.

The US Government submitted Statements of Interest (SOI) in multiple cases decided subsequent to *Sosa*. Courts generally responded by closely parsing the text of the Statement to determine the nature and strength of the Government's concern and by analysing whether the exercise of jurisdiction would interfere with existing US policy. In short, they engaged in case-by-case analyses. Consider the following examples.

DOE v. EXXON MOBIL

473 F.3d 345 (Court of Appeals for the District of Columbia 2007)

[Eleven Indonesian villagers alleged that Exxon's security forces, comprised exclusively of members of the Indonesian military and serving under the 'direction and control' of Exxon, committed murder, torture, sexual assault, battery, false imprisonment and other torts. The defendants asked the Court of Appeals to halt the lower court proceedings by issuing a writ of mandamus. Such an interlocutory motion would, according to the court, need to satisfy an especially high standard, that is, the appellate court would 'have to hold that the district court "clearly and indisputabl[y]" exceeded its jurisdiction by refusing to dismiss this case under the political question doctrine.' On that basis, the Court of Appeals proceeded to analyze Exxon's petition.]

At the outset, we note that the district court has taken several steps to limit the scope of this litigation. For example, the court dismissed the plaintiffs' claims against a natural gas company that was partially owned by the Indonesian government because including this entity as a party would "create a significant risk of interfering in Indonesian affairs and thus U.S. foreign policy concerns." Likewise, the district court has greatly curtailed discovery in this case; for example, Exxon will not be required to produce documents from its Indonesian operations unless it receives all "necessary authorizations" from the Indonesian government. The district court imposed this limitation to ensure that there would be no discovery of documents that the Indonesian government deems classified or confidential.

We disagree with Exxon's contention that there is a conflict between the views of the State Department and those of the district court. In a letter . . . the Legal Adviser of the State Department noted that adjudication of the plaintiffs' claims would "risk a potentially serious adverse impact on significant interests of the United States." However, the letter also contained several important qualifications. It noted that the effects of this suit on U.S. foreign policy interests "cannot be determined with certainty." Moreover, the letter stated that its assessment of the litigation was "necessarily predictive and contingent on how the case might unfold in the course of litigation." Most importantly, the State Department emphasized that whether this case would adversely affect U.S. foreign policy depends upon "the nature, extent, and intrusiveness of discovery." We interpret the State Department's letter not as an unqualified opinion that this suit must be dismissed, but rather as a word of caution to the district court alerting it to the State Department's concerns. Indeed, the fact that the letter refers to "how the case might unfold in the course of the litigation" shows that the State Department did not necessarily expect the district court to immediately dismiss the case in its entirety. Thus, we need not decide what level of deference would be owed to a letter from the State Department that unambiguously requests that the district court dismiss a case as a non-justiciable political question. See *Sosa v. Alvarez-Machain*, 542 U.S. 692, 733 n. 21 (2004). Of course, if we have misinterpreted this letter, or if the State Department has additional concerns about this litigation, it is free to file further letters or briefs with the district court expressing its views. . . .

But given the letter before us in the record, we cannot say it is "indisputable" that the district court erroneously failed to dismiss the plaintiffs' claims under the political question doctrine, no matter what level of deference is owed to the State Department's letter.

JOO v. JAPAN

413 F.3d 45 (Court of Appeals for the District of Columbia 2005)

[Fifteen former 'comfort women', from China, the Philippines, South Korea and Taiwan, brought an ATS action against Japan. The plaintiffs alleged that they were abducted, forced into sexual slavery, and routinely subject to rape, torture and mutilation by the Japanese Army during the Second World War. The defendant argued that their claims were foreclosed by a series of peace agreements between

Japan and the plaintiffs' governments. Relying on *Sosa* and *Baker*, the Court of Appeals held that the court was an inappropriate forum to resolve such issues.]

As we explained in our previous opinion, Article 14 of the 1951 Treaty of Peace between Japan and the Allied Powers "expressly waives... 'all claims of the Allied Powers and their nationals arising out of any actions taken by Japan and its nationals in the course of the prosecution of the war.'"

The appellants from China, Taiwan, and South Korea argue that because their governments were not parties to the 1951 Treaty, the waiver of claims provision in Article 14 did not extinguish their claims.... Although the appellants acknowledge that "it may seem anomalous that aliens may sue where similar claims of U.S. nationals are waived," they argue "that is precisely the result contemplated by... the [Alien Tort Statute].

"Anomalous" is an understatement. See Statement of Interest of the United States ("it manifestly was not the intent of the President and Congress to preclude Americans from bringing their war-related claims against Japan... while allowing federal or state courts to serve as a venue for the litigation of similar claims by non-U.S. nationals"). Even if we assume, however, as the appellants contend, that the 1951 Treaty does not of its own force deprive the courts of the United States of jurisdiction over their claims, it is pellucidly clear the Allied Powers intended that all war-related claims against Japan be resolved through government-to-government negotiations rather than through private tort suits. Indeed, Article 26 of the Treaty obligated Japan to enter "bilateral" peace treaties with non-Allied states "on the same or substantially the same terms as are provided for in the present treaty"....

...

As evidenced by the 1951 Treaty itself, when negotiating peace treaties,

> governments have dealt with... private claims as their own, treating them as national assets, and as counters, 'chips', in international bargaining. Settlement agreements have lumped, or linked, claims deriving from private debts with others that were intergovernmental in origin, and concessions in regard to one category of claims might be set off against concessions in the other, or against larger political considerations unrelated to debts.

Louis Henkin, Foreign Affairs and the Constitution 300 (2d edition 1996).

... Indeed, Professor Henkin reports that "except as an agreement might provide otherwise, international claim settlements generally wipe out the underlying private debt, terminating any recourse under domestic law as well."...

...

... In order to adjudicate the plaintiffs' claims, the court would have to resolve their dispute with Japan over the meaning of the treaties between Japan and Taiwan, South Korea, and China, which, as the State Department notes... would require the court to determine "the effects of those agreements on the rights of their citizens with respect to events occurring outside the United States."

The question whether the war-related claims of foreign nationals were extinguished when the governments of their countries entered into peace treaties with Japan is one that concerns the United States only with respect to her foreign relations, the authority for which is demonstrably committed by our Constitution not to the courts but to the political branches, with "the President [having] the 'lead role.'" *Garamendi*, 539 U.S. at 423 n. 12. And with respect to that question, the history of management by the political branches, *Baker*, 369 U.S. at 211, is clear and consistent: Since the conclusion of World War II, it has been the foreign policy of the United States "to effect as complete and lasting a peace with Japan as possible by closing the door on the litigation of war-related claims, and instead effecting the resolution of those claims through political means." ...

...

... [T]he United States is not a party to the treaties the meaning of which is in dispute, and the Executive does not urge us to adopt a particular interpretation of those treaties. Rather, the Executive has persuasively demonstrated that adjudication by a domestic court not only "would undo" a settled foreign policy of state-to-state negotiation with Japan, but also could disrupt Japan's "delicate" relations with China and Korea, thereby creating "serious implications for stability in the region." ... Is it the province of a court in the United States to decide whether Korea's or Japan's reading of the treaty between them is correct, when the Executive has determined that choosing between the interests of two foreign states in order to adjudicate a private claim against one of them would adversely affect the foreign relations of the United States? Decidedly not. The Executive's judgment that adjudication by a domestic court would be inimical to the foreign policy interests of the United States is compelling and renders this case nonjusticiable under the political question doctrine.

... [W]e defer to "the considered judgment of the Executive on [this] particular question of foreign policy." *Republic of Austria v. Altmann*, 541 U.S. at 702. For the court to disregard that judgment, to which the Executive has consistently adhered, and which it persuasively articulated in this case, would be imprudent to a degree beyond our power.

SAREI v. RIO TINTO

456 F.3d 1069 (Court of Appeals for the Ninth Circuit 2006)

[Current and former residents of Bougainville, an island province of Papua New Guinea (PNG), sued Rio Tinto, an international mining company headquartered in London. Rio Tinto, with the assistance of the PNG Government, allegedly engaged in war crimes involving aerial bombardment of civilian targets, burning of villages and rape. In November 2001, the US Department of State filed an SOI in response to a request by the US federal district court. The opinion of the Court of Appeals follows.]

After noting that the district court had not asked the United States to comment on the act of state and political question doctrines, the State Department reported that "in our judgment, continued adjudication of the claims ... would risk a potentially serious adverse impact on the peace process, and hence on the conduct of our foreign relations," and that PNG, a "friendly foreign state," had "perceive[d] the potential impact of this litigation on U.S.-PNG relations, and wider regional interests, to be 'very grave.'" Attached to the SOI was the PNG government's communique stating that the case "has potentially very serious social, economic, legal, political and security implications for" PNG, including adverse effects on PNG's international relations, "especially its relations with the United States."

. . .

We first observe that without the SOI, there would be little reason to dismiss this case on political question grounds, and therefore that the SOI must carry the primary burden of establishing a political question. There is no independent reason why the claims presented to us raise any warning flags as infringing on the prerogatives of our Executive Branch. As such, these claims can be distinguished from cases in which the claims by their very nature present political questions requiring dismissal. See, e.g., *Alperin v. Vatican Bank*, 410 F.3d 532, 562 (9th Cir.2005) (identifying nonjusticiable political question presented by claims regarding alleged war crimes of an enemy of the United States committed during World War II). The Supreme Court has been clear that "it is error to suppose that every case or controversy which touches foreign relations lies beyond judicial cognizance," and that the doctrine "is one of 'political questions,' not of 'political cases'." *Baker*, 369 U.S. at 211, 217. Without the SOI, this case presents claims that relate to a foreign conflict in which the United States had little involvement (so far as the record demonstrates), and therefore that merely "touch[ ] foreign relations." Id. at 211.

When we take the SOI into consideration and give it "serious weight," we still conclude that a political question is not presented. Even if the continued adjudication of this case does present some risk to the Bougainville peace process, that is not sufficient to implicate the final three *Baker* factors.... The State Department explicitly did not request that we dismiss this suit on political question grounds, and we are confident that proceeding does not express any disrespect for the executive, even if it would prefer that the suit disappear. Nor do we see any "unusual need for unquestioning adherence" to the SOI's nonspecific invocations of risks to the peace process. And finally, given the guarded nature of the SOI, we see no "embarrassment" that would follow from fulfilling our independent duty to determine whether the case should proceed. We are mindful of *Sosa*'s instruction to give "serious weight" to the views of the executive, but we cannot uphold the dismissal of this lawsuit solely on the basis of the SOI.[26]

Our holding today is consistent with our recent dismissal of ATCA war crimes claims in *Vatican Bank*... There, a proposed class of Holocaust survivors sued the

[26] The plaintiffs have submitted recent letters from members of PNG's government urging that the suit will not harm or affect the ongoing Bouagainville peace process. The Chief Secretary to the Government of PNG, Joseph Kalinoe, wrote to the United States Ambassador to PNG on 30 March 2005 that "the [PNG Government] does not see the case presently before the U.S. courts in the U.S. affecting diplomatic and bilateral relations between our two countries nor does it see it affecting the peace process on the island of Bougainville." And on January 8, 2005, John Momis, the Interim Bougainville Provincial Governor, wrote to the State Department's legal advisor under whose name the SOI was written, "urg[ing] the Government of the United States to support the Prime Minister's position to permit the case to proceed in the courts of America, and to explain that the people of Bougainville strongly desire the case to proceed in America...." Momis' letter includes detail about the current state of the Bougainville peace process, and about how "the litigation has not hindered or in any way adversely affected the peace negotiations." Indeed, the letter adds that "the *Sarei* litigation has helped facilitate the process as it is viewed as another source of rectifying the historic injustices perpetrated against the people of Bougainville." Finally, the letter asserts that "the only way that the litigation will impact [U.S./PNG] foreign relations is if the litigation is discontinued."

Whether these letters are properly authenticated is in dispute. But if they are authentic and their authors accurately describe the current state of affairs in PNG,

Vatican Bank (a financial institution connected to the Vatican) for its complicity in various war crimes of the Nazi-sympathizing Ustasha puppet regime in Croatia, including Vatican Bank's profiting from the Ustasha regime's theft of the class's property. We concluded that... "the broad allegations tied to the Vatican Bank's alleged assistance to the war objectives of the Ustasha, including the slave labor claims, which essentially call on us to make a retroactive political judgment as to the conduct of the war... are, by nature, political questions."...

We do not understand *Vatican Bank* as foreclosing the plaintiffs' claims that relate to the PNG regime's alleged war crimes, but instead read its holding to apply only to the narrower category of war crimes committed by enemies of the United States. Considering such claims would necessarily require us to review the acts of an enemy of the United States, which would risk creating a conflict with the steps the United States actually chose to take in prosecuting that war. See id. at 560 (expressing unwillingness to "intrude unduly on certain policy choices and value judgments that are constitutionally committed to the political branches... for we do not and cannot know why the Allies made the policy choice not to prosecute the Ustasha and the Vatican Bank.").

Reading *Vatican Bank* to preclude any ATCA war crimes claims would work a major, and inadvisable, shift in our ATCA jurisprudence.... [I]t would contradict *Sosa*,... when it stated that "[f]or two centuries we have affirmed that the domestic law of the United States recognizes the law of nations. It would take some explaining to say now that federal courts must avert their gaze entirely from any international norm intended to protect individuals."

PRESBYTERIAN CHURCH OF SUDAN V. TALISMAN
No. 01 Civ. 9882, 2005 WL 2082846
S.D.N.Y. 2005

[Some of the competing human rights and foreign policy concerns were presented to the court in an acute form in a suit involving the Sudan. The plaintiffs, residents of southern Sudan, brought an ATS suit for claims of genocide and crimes against humanity against the Sudanese Government and a Canadian energy company, Talisman Energy, Inc. The US Government submitted a Statement of Interest, containing a letter from the Department of State (State Letter) and a diplomatic note from the Embassy of Canada (Canada Letter). The court explained the content of these documents:

> ... [In its letter,] Canada emphasizes its concerns... Canada has spent millions of dollars in humanitarian aid and to support peace efforts in the Sudan. Canada

that would seriously undercut the State Department's concerns expressed in its November 5, 2001 SOI-which itself depended on assessments by local government officials, including Joseph Kalinoe's predecessor as Chief Secretary to the Government of PNG. For whatever reason, the State Department has declined to update the SOI. Under these circumstances, we do not rely on the letters' substantive representations. But the letters, by suggesting there exists today a different reality in PNG from that portrayed in the SOI, illustrate why it is inappropriate to give the SOI final and conclusive weight as establishing a political question under Baker.

states that it uses trade support services as "both a stick and carrot in support of peace," and that while the "inducement for Sudan if they achieve peaceful resolution of their internal disputes will be the reinstatement of trade support services[,] ... the impending U.S. court action removes that inducement." According to Canada, in the event that Sudan's peaceful resolution of its internal disputes justifies the resumption of Canadian trade support services, "Canadian firms will likely absent themselves from Sudan and therefore not contribute to its economic revitalization out of fear of U.S. courts." ...

...

The State Letter explains that "[t]he Department of State takes no position on the merits of the pending litigation but shares the government of Canada's concern about the difficulties that can arise from an expansive exercise of jurisdiction by the federal courts under the ATS."

...

According to the State Letter, "... This Administration has been working actively and directly with the government of Sudan and with the international community for several years to bring an end to the decades-old conflict in southern Sudan and to bring relief to the many thousands of victims of that conflict. Most recently, the United States led the humanitarian relief effort for the displaced in Darfur and refugees in Chad, as well as provided support to the African Union ceasefire-monitoring mission. In both of these efforts, Canada has also played a prominent role".[27]

The State Letter argues that "when the government in question protests that the U.S. proceeding interferes with the conduct of its foreign policy in pursuit of goals that the United States shares, we believe that considerations of international comity and judicial abstention may properly come into play." It also contends that concerns about the proper scope of the ATS should be strong where, among other things, "a foreign government has interposed a specific and strong objection ... [and] claims regulatory and jurisdictional competence over its nationals and the conduct in question," and the lawsuit has little or no nexus to the United States.

On the basis of the Statement of Interest, Talisman argued that the action should be dismissed under principles of international comity, to avoid undue interference with the discretion of the executive and legislative branches in managing foreign affairs, or in the alternative, as a nonjusticiable political question pursuant to the Supreme Court's reasoning in *Sosa*. The court's opinion follows.]

Courts have assigned varying weight to statements of interest by the United States Government according to the circumstances.... Where the State Department had submitted a statement of interest, the Second Circuit has held that "an assertion of the political question doctrine by the Executive Branch [would be] entitled to respectful consideration, [but] would not necessarily preclude adjudication." *Kadic v. Karadzic*, 70 F.3d 232, 250 (2d Cir.1995)....

There is comparatively little guidance regarding the appropriate weight to assign to statements of interest made by foreign governments transmitted directly to a court, or as in this case, that accompany a United States Government statement of interest...

[27] Darfur is in western Sudan; this lawsuit is brought on behalf of residents in southern Sudan.

Because the amount of weight to assign to the Statement, including the State Letter and the Canada Letter, does not affect the disposition of Talisman's motion, it will be assumed, without deciding, that "serious weight" should be assigned to each part of the Statement. See *Alvarez-Machain*, 124 S.Ct. at 2766 n. 21. . . .

1. International Comity

Declining to exercise jurisdiction for reasons of international comity is a discretionary act that "generally means deference to a foreign nation's legislative, executive, or judicial enactment." ...

. . . Talisman likens this action to *In re South African Apartheid Litig.*, 346 F. Supp.2d 538 (S.D.N.Y.2004), which considered, among other things, the plaintiffs' theory that the defendant corporations "violated the law of nations by doing business in apartheid South Africa." In *South African Apartheid*, the United States, the United Kingdom, Germany, and Switzerland had all adopted a "policy of constructive engagement" by supporting and encouraging business investment in apartheid South Africa, and the United States and South Africa had submitted statements of interest expressing their concern for the effect of the lawsuit on business investment in South Africa. Noting that it "must be extremely cautious in permitting suits here based upon a corporation's doing business in countries with less than stellar human rights records, especially since the consequences of such an approach could have significant, if not disastrous, effects on international commerce," the court dismissed the plaintiffs' ATS claims. *Id.* at 554.

Talisman argues that Canada adopted a similar policy of constructive engagement towards Sudan in 1999, and that permitting this lawsuit to continue will cause this Court to render judgment on a Canadian executive policy in a manner that the *South African Apartheid* court refused to permit. *South African Apartheid*, however, does not apply to the facts of this case, because the plaintiffs allege that Talisman knowingly assisted Sudan in perpetrating a campaign of genocide and crimes against humanity, not that Talisman merely transacted business in and with Sudan. Unlike *South African Apartheid*, where business transactions — the result of States' executive policies of encouraging investment — were the basis for the plaintiffs' ATS claims, the claims here involve knowing assistance in the commission of grave human rights abuses, including jointly planning attacks on civilians and supporting and facilitating those attacks. Therefore, this action does not require a judgment that Canada's executive policy of constructive engagement was or caused a violation of the law of nations; it merely requires a judgment as to whether Talisman acted outside the bounds of customary international law while doing business in Sudan.

In any event, the Canada Letter does not argue that Talisman's presence in the Sudan was pursuant to Canadian government policy or that this lawsuit requires a judgment to be rendered about any past Canadian policy. The State Letter explicitly denies any view as to the merits of this lawsuit. For each of these reasons, Talisman's first argument is rejected.

. . .

It is assumed that Canada's judgment that this lawsuit will interfere with its foreign policy and handicap its efforts to promote peace in the Sudan is entitled to great weight and must be carefully considered. As a nation with a long and distinguished record of working to promote peace in many troubled areas of the world and a nation that has made a sustained commitment to international humanitarian efforts, its judgment brings particular credibility.

. . .

The Canada Letter explains that Canada has promised to restore trade support services in the event that the peace process is sufficiently successful in the Sudan, and that this is part of a "stick and carrot" approach to encouraging peace. That promise implies that, should Canada make a judgment that the Sudan is not experiencing genocide or crimes against humanity on the scale alleged in this lawsuit, it will reinstate trade support services. The trade support services, as described in the Canada Letter, appear to be for the benefit of Canadian companies exporting to the Sudan and doing business with Sudanese companies.

While this Court may not question either the accuracy of the description of Canada's foreign policy in its Letter, or the wisdom and effectiveness of that foreign policy, it remains appropriate to consider the degree to which that articulated foreign policy applies to this litigation. As the Supreme Court has explained, deference is appropriate to the extent that a sovereign's opinion has been stated with particularity, that is, regarding "*particular* petitioners in connection with *their* alleged conduct." *Republic of Austria v. Altmann*, 541 U.S. at 702 (emphasis in original). This lawsuit does not concern a Canadian company exporting to and engaged in trade with the Sudan, but a Canadian company operating in the Sudan as an oil exploration and extraction business. Moreover, the allegations in this lawsuit concern participation in genocide and crimes against humanity, not trading activity. While there is no requirement that a government's letter must support its position with detailed argument, where the contents of the letter suggest a lack of understanding about the nature of the claims in the ATS litigation, a court may take that into account in assessing the concerns expressed in the letter.

Given the commitment by the United States to the Sudan peace process, it is telling that the United States has not advised this Court that the continuation of this lawsuit will adversely affect the Government's relations with Canada or threaten the goal of achieving peace in Sudan. In other cases, the United States Department of State has not hesitated to warn courts where it believes continuation of a lawsuit will affect a foreign government's policy to the extent that it would disturb U.S. relations with that foreign government or would adversely affect U.S. efforts to promote peace.

. . .

Finally, the United States and the international community retain a compelling interest in the application of the international law proscribing atrocities such as genocide and crimes against humanity. To the extent that the Canada Letter and Talisman's arguments request this Court in its discretion to decline to exercise its jurisdiction over past events in order to avoid conflict with future Canadian foreign policy, the seriousness of the alleged past events counsel in favor of exercising jurisdiction.

2. *Political Question Doctrine and Executive and Legislative Discretion*

. . .

Talisman also contends that recent Supreme Court precedent requires dismissing this action to avoid undue interference with executive and legislative discretion in managing foreign policy towards Sudan and Canada. The Supreme Court recently discussed in *dicta* the "policy of case-specific deference to the political branches" in the context of pending ATS cases addressing the South African apartheid regime....

Talisman does not contend that the United States has participated in, supported, or approved of, a political decision to address serious human rights violations in Sudan with an approach mirroring the South African Truth and Reconciliation Commission, or any other form of comprehensive amnesty or absolution. Talisman is therefore at pains to identify United States foreign policies towards Sudan with which this action interferes, other than to speculate more generally about its effects on efforts to promote peace in Sudan. This action, however, evidently did not hinder the conclusion of the Peace Agreement. Moreover, as noted above, neither the Statement nor the State Letter contend that this case will impact on United States foreign policy towards Sudan or Canada.

QUESTIONS

1. Consider the following statement. '*Talisman* demonstrates the problem with ATS litigation. The judge essentially engaged in foreign policy determinations that are not fit for a court to decide. Courts should operate with a presumption of abstaining from adjudication in such matters unless the US Government expressly gives a green light for the court to do otherwise'. Likewise, should the court in *Exxon* have erred in favour of the Government's foreign policy concerns?

2. In *Talisman*, the court states that it is 'appropriate to consider the degree to which [Canada's] articulated foreign policy applies to this litigation'. Does the court demand too close a nexus between the foreign policy agenda of Canada and the particular situation of the defendant company?

3. Should a court be more or less reluctant to exercise jurisdiction if the case involves actions that have no direct connection to the United States?

4. Could *Sosa*'s directing courts to give 'serious weight to the Executive Branch's view of the case's impact on foreign policy' place the Executive in a difficult position? Are there situations in which the Executive Branch would prefer not to be asked its views concerning a case's potential impact on foreign policy? Consider the following commentary concerning a related context:

> [P]roblems...occurred under the pre-FSIA [Foreign Sovereign Immunity Act] regime of executive suggestion. Under that regime, the State Department established an informal administrative process to 'pre-adjudicate' immunity claims, the results of which were binding on courts. This process became heavily politicized, and had the effect of offending foreign nations more than when determinations were made by courts alone applying legal standards. There are ways to avoid this conundrum, including making the administrative determination of susceptibility to suit subject to strict legal standards. This latter approach may capture both rule of law benefits and expertise benefits in a manner akin to modern administrative agencies.[28]

[28] Jack Goldsmith and Ryan Goodman, 'U.S. Civil Litigation and International Terrorism', in *Civil Litigation and International Terrorism* 109, 154 (John Norton Moore ed., 2004).

Could a similar solution work with respect to evaluating a case's impact on foreign policy? Is such an inquiry amenable to strict legal standards? To any legal standards? Is a better solution to discard universal civil jurisdiction in favour of a system of universal criminal jurisdiction? In the criminal law context, public officials would be able to control assessments of foreign policy ramifications and perhaps do so without publicly exposing the nature of those internal decisions. Is lack of transparency a desirable institutional feature given the foreign relations implications of such cases?

C. SOVEREIGN AND OFFICIAL IMMUNITY

Civil suits, especially those pursued under the ATS and TVPA, often end in default judgments and generally do not result in actual payment of damages. Several obstacles thwart the attainment of financial compensation. Individual defendants often do not have deep pockets. In contrast with criminal cases, defendants may also freely leave the country. Also, foreign enforcement of judgments is usually difficult if not practically impossible. Suits against two types of defendants — corporations and governments — do not pose such obstacles. This section considers obstacles that uniquely affect suits against governments and governmental agencies, the type of cases in which plaintiffs might have a real prospect of achieving compensation but principles of sovereign immunity can close off such avenues. Indeed, questions of sovereign immunity have frequently arisen in cases under the ATS. These cases concern the ability of plaintiffs to sue a foreign state directly. They also concern the ability of plaintiffs to sue particular individuals in their personal capacity when those individuals claim to be protected by sovereign immunity.

The Foreign Sovereign Immunities Act of 1976 (FSIA), codified principally at 22 U.S.C.A. 1602–11, provides a comprehensive legislative framework for claims of immunity by foreign state defendants. Foreign states, including 'an agency or instrumentality' thereof, are immune from judicial jurisdiction, subject to enumerated exceptions. Those exceptions include court actions growing out of a state's commercial activities occurring in the United States, actions involving property expropriated by the foreign government in violation of international law, and actions in which the foreign state has 'waived its immunity either explicitly or by implication'.

Argentine Republic v. Amerada Hess Shipping Corp., 488 U.S. 428 (1989), involved an ATS action growing out of the Falklands (Malvinas) war between the UK and Argentina. It was based on the damage to plaintiff's ship by an attack of Argentinean aircraft. The Supreme Court refused to find an exception to the rule of immunity for suits under the ATS because of Argentina's alleged violation of international law. The Court held that the FSIA is 'the sole basis for obtaining jurisdiction over a foreign state in our courts'. It drew from the FSIA 'the plain implication that immunity is granted in those cases involving alleged violations of international law that do not come within one of the FSIA's exceptions'. Plaintiffs were accordingly required as a threshold matter to satisfy one of the conditions under the FSIA for suspending sovereign immunity.

Saudi Arabia v. Nelson, 507 U.S. 349 (1993), involved tort claims based on alleged human rights violations. The Supreme Court held that alleged conduct of the defendant state did not fall within the FSIA exception for 'commercial activity'. The plaintiff, a US citizen employee at a Saudi state hospital, claimed that Saudi government agents subjected him to unlawful detention and torture as retaliation for his persistence in reporting hospital safety violations. The Supreme Court concluded that '[t]he conduct [complained of by plaintiff] boils down to abuse of the power of its police by the Saudi Government, and however monstrous such abuse undoubtedly may be, a foreign state's exercise of the power of its police has long been understood... as peculiarly sovereign in nature'. Sovereign immunity was granted to Saudi Arabia.

In *Siderman de Blake v. Republic of Argentina*, 965 F.2d 699 (9th Cir. 1992), the Court of Appeals agreed with the plaintiff's argument that official acts of torture attributed to Argentina constituted a violation of a *jus cogens* norm of the 'highest status within international law'. Nonetheless, taking its lesson from the *Amareda Hess* decision in which the Supreme Court was so specific, the court concluded that it was Congress that would have to make any further exceptions to sovereign immunity. 'The fact that there has been a violation of *jus cogens* does not confer jurisdiction under the FSIA.' *See also Sampson v. Federal Republic of Germany*, 250 F.3d 1145 (7th Cir.2001); *Smith v. Socialist People's Libyan Arab Jamahiriya*, 101 F.3d 239 (2d Cir.1996); *Princz v. Federal Republic of Germany*, 26 F.3d 1166 (D.C.Cir.1994).

In view of the FSIA and the case law described above, US plaintiffs in 1350 actions have also sought to avoid the issue of sovereign immunity by suing not the state itself but individual perpetrators — as indeed occurred in *Filartiga*. Courts required to sort out the relevance of sovereign immunity when individual defendants are before it have taken different approaches in characterizing the relationship between the individual and the state.

Consider *In re Estate of Ferdinand Marcos*, 25 F.3d 1467 (9th Cir. 1994). The court held that the FSIA did not bar jurisdiction under 1350 over the estate of former President Ferdinand Marcos for alleged acts of torture and wrongful death, since those were not official acts perpetrated within the scope of his official authority in the Philippines but rather acts outside the scope of his authority as President. Quoting from a prior related case, the court stated that '[o]ur courts have had no difficulty in distinguishing the legal acts of a deposed ruler from his acts for personal profit that lack a basis in law'. At the same time, the requirement of state action under the definition of official torture could still be met by an official acting under colour of authority, though not within an official mandate. That is, such an official could violate international law for purposes of the ATS.

In *Jones v. Saudi Arabia* (2006), the British House of Lords adopted a very different approach. Plaintiffs brought claims of torture against various defendants including the head of the Ministry of the Interior, a captain and a lieutenant in the Saudi Arabian police force, and a colonel in the Ministry of Interior and deputy governor of a prison facility. The Court held that government officials should be equated with the state for the purpose of sovereign immunity. In an unusual line of reasoning, the Court explained, in part, that because states are liable for actions of governmental officials (including actions in excess of authority or contravention of instructions) under international principles of state responsibility, it follows that civil suits against governmental officials activate sovereign immunity. Lord Bingham stated:

> It is certainly true that in *Pinochet* (No 1) and *Pinochet* (No 3) certain members of the House held that acts of torture could not be functions of a head of state or governmental or official acts. But the case was categorically different from the present, since it concerned criminal proceedings falling squarely within the universal criminal jurisdiction mandated by the Torture Convention...The essential ratio of the decision, as I understand it, was that international law could not without absurdity require criminal jurisdiction to be assumed and exercised where the Torture Convention conditions were satisfied and, at the same time, require immunity to be granted to those properly charged.[29] The Torture Convention was the mainspring of the decision, and certain members of the House expressly accepted that the grant of immunity in civil proceedings was unaffected. It is, I think, difficult to accept that torture cannot be a governmental or official act, since under article 1 of the Torture Convention torture must, to qualify as such, be inflicted by or with the connivance of a public official or other person acting in an official capacity. The claimants' argument encounters the difficulty that it is founded on the Torture Convention; but to bring themselves within the Torture Convention they must show that the torture was (to paraphrase the definition) official; yet they argue that the conduct was not official in order to defeat the claim to immunity.
>
> ...
>
> ...A state is not criminally responsible in international or English law, and therefore cannot be directly impleaded in criminal proceedings. The prosecution of a servant or agent for an act of torture within article 1 of the Torture Convention is founded on an express exception from the general rule of immunity. It is, however, clear that a civil action against individual torturers based on acts of official torture does indirectly implead the state since their acts are attributable to it. Were these claims against the individual defendants to proceed and be upheld, the interests of the Kingdom would be obviously affected, even though it is not a named party.

Compare the logic of *Jones v. Saudi Arabia* with the Senate Report on the Torture Victim Protection Act, p. 1201, *supra*.

COMMENT ON *EX PARTE* PINOCHET AND IMMUNITY

We previously discussed the case involving General Augusto Pinochet before the British House of Lords, see p. 1167, *supra*. In addition to holding that the United Kingdom had jurisdiction over acts of torture allegedly committed by Pinochet after the Torture Convention had been incorporated into UK law, six of the seven Lords concluded that Pinochet did not enjoy state immunity from prosecution for these acts.

[29] [Eds. In a concurring opinion, Lord Hoffman added: 'To produce a conflict with state immunity, it is therefore necessary to show that the prohibition on torture has generated an ancillary procedural rule which, by way of exception to state immunity, entitles or perhaps requires states to assume civil jurisdiction over other states in cases in which torture is alleged'.]

Lord Saville reasoned that the Torture Convention necessarily eliminated Pinochet's official immunity for the crime of torture:

> A former head of state who it is alleged resorted to torture for state purposes falls in my view fairly and squarely within those terms [of the Torture Convention] and on the face of it should be dealt with in accordance with them.
>
> ...
>
> To my mind these terms demonstrate that the states who have become parties have clearly and unambiguously agreed that official torture should now be dealt with in a way which would otherwise amount to an interference in their sovereignty.

Lord Browne-Wilkinson wrote:

> Can it be said that the commission of a crime which is an international crime against humanity and jus cogens is an act done in an official capacity on behalf of the state? I believe there to be strong ground for saying that the implementation of torture as defined by the Torture Convention cannot be a state function.
>
> ...
>
> I have doubts whether, before the coming into force of the Torture Convention, the existence of the international crime of torture as jus cogens was enough to justify the conclusion that the organisation of state torture could not rank for immunity purposes as performance of an official function. At that stage there was no international tribunal to punish torture and no general jurisdiction to permit or require its punishment in domestic courts. Not until there was some form of universal jurisdiction for the punishment of the crime of torture could it really be talked about as a fully constituted international crime.

Lord Hope of Craighead added:

> ... [T]here remains the question whether the immunity can survive Chile's agreement to the Torture Convention if the torture which is alleged was of such a kind or on such a scale as to amount to an international crime....
>
> ...
>
> Despite the difficulties which I have mentioned, I think that there are sufficient signs that the necessary developments in international law were in place by [29 September 1998, the date of entry into force of the Criminal Justice Act].
>
> ...
>
> I would not regard this as a case of waiver. Nor would I accept that it was an implied term of the Torture Convention that former heads of state were to be deprived of their immunity ratione materiae with respect to all acts of official torture as defined in article 1. It is just that the obligations which were recognised by customary international law in the case of such serious international crimes by the date when Chile ratified the Convention are so strong as to override any objection by it on the ground of immunity ratione materiae to the exercise of the jurisdiction over crimes committed after that date which the United Kingdom had made available.

❁ ❁ ❁

Two recent decisions by international courts have directly addressed the question of sovereign and official immunity.

AL-ADSANI V. UNITED KINGDOM

European Court of Human Rights (Grand Chamber), 21 November 2001
Application no. 35763/97

[Mr Sulaiman Al-Adsani, a dual British-Kuwaiti national, initiated civil proceedings in the United Kingdom against the Government of Kuwait and individual Kuwaitis for his alleged torture in Kuwait. Mr Al-Adsani's specific allegations involved being beaten over several days, having his head held underwater in a swimming pool containing corpses, and being severely burnt. The UK appellate court permitted Mr Al-Adsani to proceed against the individual Kuwaitis but held that UK law on state immunity barred suit against the Government of Kuwait.

Mr Al-Adsani appealed to the European Court of Human Rights, claiming in significant part that the application of state immunity denied him access to a court in violation of Article 6 of the European Convention for the Protection of Human Rights and Fundamental Freedoms. The Grand Chamber heard the appeal and, by a slim majority (nine votes to eight), rejected his claim. Parts of the majority and dissenting opinions follow.]

Relevant Legal Materials

[The State Immunity Act 1978]

21. The relevant parts of the State Immunity Act 1978 provide:

> "1. (1) A State is immune from the jurisdiction of the courts of the United Kingdom except as provided in the following provisions of this Part of this Act.
>
> ...
>
> 5. A State is not immune as regards proceedings in respect of—
> (a) death or personal injury;
>
> ...
>
> caused by an act or omission in the United Kingdom ..."

[The Basle Convention]

22. The above provision (section 5 of the 1978 Act) was enacted to implement the 1972 European Convention on State Immunity ("the Basle Convention"), a Council of Europe instrument, which entered into force on 11 June 1976.... Article 11 of the Convention provides:

> "A Contracting State cannot claim immunity from the jurisdiction of a court of another Contracting State in proceedings which relate to redress for injury to the person or damage to tangible property, if the facts which occasioned the injury or damage occurred in the territory of the State of forum, and if the author of the injury or damage was present in that territory at the time when those facts occurred."

Article 15 of the Basle Convention provides that a Contracting State shall be entitled to immunity if the proceedings do not fall within the stated exceptions.

[State immunity in respect of civil proceedings for torture]

23. In its Report on Jurisdictional Immunities of States and their Property (1999), the working group of the International Law Commission (ILC) found that over the preceding decade a number of civil claims had been brought in municipal courts, particularly in the United States and United Kingdom, against foreign governments, arising out of acts of torture committed not in the territory of the forum State but in the territory of the defendant and other States. The working group of the ILC found that national courts had in some cases shown sympathy for the argument that States are not entitled to plead immunity where there has been a violation of human rights norms with the character of jus cogens, although in most cases the plea of sovereign immunity had succeeded....

24. The working group of the ILC did, however, note two recent developments which it considered gave support to the argument that a State could not plead immunity in respect of gross human rights violations. One of these was the House of Lords' judgment in *ex parte Pinochet* (No. 3) (see paragraph 34 below). The other was the amendment by the United States of its Foreign Sovereign Immunities Act (FSIA) to include a new exception to immunity. This exception,... applies in respect of a claim for damages for personal injury or death caused by an act of torture, extra-judicial killing, aircraft sabotage or hostage-taking, against a State designated by the Secretary of State as a sponsor of terrorism, where the claimant or victim was a national of the United States at the time the act occurred.

...

30. In its judgment in *Prosecutor v. Furundzija*, the International Criminal Tribunal for the Former Yugoslavia observed as follows:

> 144. ... the prohibition on torture is a peremptory norm or jus cogens.... This prohibition is so extensive that States are even barred by international law from expelling, returning or extraditing a person to another State where there are substantial grounds for believing that the person would be in danger of being subjected to torture.
>
> 145. ... all States parties to the relevant treaties have been granted, and are obliged to exercise, jurisdiction to investigate, prosecute and punish offenders....
>
> 146. The existence of this corpus of general and treaty rules proscribing torture shows that the international community, aware of the importance of outlawing this heinous phenomenon, has decided to suppress any manifestation of torture by operating both at the interstate level and at the level of individuals. No legal loopholes have been left.
>
> ...
>
> 153. ... Because of the importance of the values it protects, this principle has evolved into a peremptory norm or jus cogens,... The most conspicuous consequence of this higher rank is that the principle at issue cannot be derogated from by States through international treaties or local or special or even general customary rules not endowed with the same normative force.
>
> ...

31. Similar statements were made in *Prosecutor v. Delacic and Others* and in *Prosecutor v. Kunarac.*

[Criminal jurisdiction of the United Kingdom over acts of torture]

32. The United Kingdom ratified the UN Convention with effect from 8 December 1988.

...

34. In its *Regina v. Bow Street Metropolitan Stipendiary Magistrate and Others, ex parte Pinochet Ugarte* (No. 3), judgment of 24 March 1999 [2000] Appeal Cases 147, the House of Lords held that the former President of Chile, Senator Pinochet, could be extradited to Spain in respect of charges which concerned conduct that was criminal in the United Kingdom at the time when it was allegedly committed. The majority of the Law Lords considered that extraterritorial torture did not become a crime in the United Kingdom until section 134 of the Criminal Justice Act 1988 came into effect. The majority considered that although under Part II of the State Immunity Act 1978 a former head of State enjoyed immunity from the criminal jurisdiction of the United Kingdom for acts done in his official capacity, torture was an international crime and prohibited by jus cogens (peremptory norms of international law). The coming into force of the UN Convention had created a universal criminal jurisdiction in all the Contracting States in respect of acts of torture by public officials, and the States Parties could not have intended that an immunity for ex-heads of State for official acts of torture would survive their ratification of the UN Convention. The House of Lords (and, in particular, Lord Millett, at p. 278) made clear that their findings as to immunity ratione materiae from criminal jurisdiction did not affect the immunity ratione personae of foreign sovereign States from civil jurisdiction in respect of acts of torture.

The Law

I. Alleged Violation of Article 3 of the Convention

[The Court rejected a separate claim, raised by Al-Adsani, that the United Kingdom violated an obligation to secure to everyone within its jurisdiction the freedom from torture and the right to an effective remedy. The Court unanimously concluded, 'The applicant does not contend that the alleged torture took place within the jurisdiction of the United Kingdom or that the United Kingdom authorities had any causal connection with its occurrence. In these circumstances, it cannot be said that the High Contracting Party was under a duty to provide a civil remedy to the applicant in respect of torture allegedly carried out by the Kuwaiti authorities.']

II. Alleged Violation of Article 6 § 1 of the Convention

42. The applicant alleged that he was denied access to a court in the determination of his claim against the State of Kuwait and that this constituted a violation of Article 6 § 1 of the Convention, which provides in its first sentence:

> "In the determination of his civil rights and obligations or of any criminal charge against him, everyone is entitled to a fair and public hearing within a reasonable time by an independent and impartial tribunal established by law."

...

47. Whether a person has an actionable domestic claim may depend not only on the substantive content, properly speaking, of the relevant civil right as defined under national law but also on the existence of procedural bars preventing or limiting the possibilities of bringing potential claims to court. In the latter kind of case Article 6 § 1 may be applicable. Certainly the Convention enforcement bodies may not create by way of interpretation of Article 6 § 1 a substantive civil right which has no legal basis in the State concerned. However, it would not be consistent with the rule of law in a democratic society or with the basic principle underlying Article 6 § 1 — namely that civil claims must be capable of being submitted to a judge for adjudication — if, for example, a State could, without restraint or control by the Convention enforcement bodies, remove from the jurisdiction of the courts a whole range of civil claims or confer immunities from civil liability on large groups or categories of persons (see *Fayed v. the United Kingdom*, judgment of 21 September 1994, Series A no. 294-B, pp. 49–50, § 65).

48. The proceedings which the applicant intended to pursue were for damages for personal injury, a cause of action well known to English law. The Court does not accept the Government's submission that the applicant's claim had no legal basis in domestic law since any substantive right which might have existed was extinguished by operation of the doctrine of State immunity. It notes that an action against a State is not barred in limine: if the defendant State waives immunity, the action will proceed to a hearing and judgment. The grant of immunity is to be seen not as qualifying a substantive right but as a procedural bar on the national courts' power to determine the right.

49. The Court is accordingly satisfied that there existed a serious and genuine dispute over civil rights. It follows that Article 6 § 1 was applicable to the proceedings in question.

Compliance with Article 6 § 1

1. Submissions of the parties

50. The Government contended that the restriction imposed on the applicant's right of access to a court pursued a legitimate aim and was proportionate. The 1978 Act reflected the provisions of the Basle Convention (see paragraph 22 above), which in turn gave expression to universally applicable principles of public international law... Article 6 § 1 of the Convention could not be interpreted so as to compel a Contracting State to deny immunity to and assert jurisdiction over a non-Contracting State. Such a conclusion would be contrary to international law and would impose irreconcilable obligations on the States that had ratified both the Convention and the Basle Convention.

There were other, traditional means of redress for wrongs of this kind available to the applicant, namely diplomatic representations or an inter-State claim.

51. The applicant submitted that the restriction on his right of access to a court did not serve a legitimate aim and was disproportionate. The House of Lords in *ex parte Pinochet* (No. 3) (see paragraph 34 above) had accepted that the prohibition of torture had acquired the status of a jus cogens norm in international law and that torture had become an international crime. In these circumstances there could be

no rational basis for allowing sovereign immunity in a civil action when immunity would not be a defence in criminal proceedings arising from the same facts.

Other than civil proceedings against the State of Kuwait, he complained that there was no effective means of redress available to him. He had attempted to make use of diplomatic channels but the Government refused to assist him....

2. The Court's assessment

53. The right of access to a court is not... absolute, but may be subject to limitations; these are permitted by implication since the right of access by its very nature calls for regulation by the State. In this respect, the Contracting States enjoy a certain margin of appreciation, although the final decision as to the observance of the Convention's requirements rests with the Court. It must be satisfied that the limitations applied do not restrict or reduce the access left to the individual in such a way or to such an extent that the very essence of the right is impaired. Furthermore, a limitation will not be compatible with Article 6 § 1 if it does not pursue a legitimate aim and if there is no reasonable relationship of proportionality between the means employed and the aim sought to be achieved (see *Waite and Kennedy v. Germany* [GC], no. 26083/94, § 59, ECHR 1999-I).

54. The Court must first examine whether the limitation pursued a legitimate aim. It notes in this connection that sovereign immunity is a concept of international law, developed out of the principle par in parem non habet imperium, by virtue of which one State shall not be subject to the jurisdiction of another State. The Court considers that the grant of sovereign immunity to a State in civil proceedings pursues the legitimate aim of complying with international law to promote comity and good relations between States through the respect of another State's sovereignty.

55. The Court must next assess whether the restriction was proportionate to the aim pursued....

56. It follows that measures taken by a High Contracting Party which reflect generally recognised rules of public international law on State immunity cannot in principle be regarded as imposing a disproportionate restriction on the right of access to a court as embodied in Article 6 § 1. Just as the right of access to a court is an inherent part of the fair trial guarantee in that Article, so some restrictions on access must likewise be regarded as inherent, an example being those limitations generally accepted by the community of nations as part of the doctrine of State immunity.

57. The Court notes that the 1978 Act, applied by the English courts so as to afford immunity to Kuwait, complies with the relevant provisions of the 1972 Basle Convention, which, while placing a number of limitations on the scope of State immunity as it was traditionally understood, preserves it in respect of civil proceedings for damages for personal injury unless the injury was caused in the territory of the forum State. Except insofar as it affects claims for damages for torture, the applicant does not deny that the above provision reflects a generally accepted rule of international law. He asserts, however, that his claim related to torture, and contends that the prohibition of torture has acquired the status of a jus cogens norm in international law, taking precedence over treaty law and other rules of international law.

...

61. While the Court accepts, on the basis of these authorities, that the prohibition of torture has achieved the status of a peremptory norm in international law, it observes that the present case concerns not, as in *Furundzija* and *Pinochet*, the criminal liability of an individual for alleged acts of torture, but the immunity of a State in a civil suit for damages in respect of acts of torture within the territory of that State. Notwithstanding the special character of the prohibition of torture in international law, the Court is unable to discern in the international instruments, judicial authorities or other materials before it any firm basis for concluding that, as a matter of international law, a State no longer enjoys immunity from civil suit in the courts of another State where acts of torture are alleged. In particular, the Court observes that none of the primary international instruments referred to (Article 5 of the Universal Declaration of Human Rights, Article 7 of the International Covenant on Civil and Political Rights and Articles 2 and 4 of the UN Convention) relates to civil proceedings or to State immunity.

...

65. As to the *ex parte Pinochet* (No. 3) judgment, the Court notes that the majority of the House of Lords held that, after the UN Convention and even before, the international prohibition against official torture had the character of jus cogens or a peremptory norm and that no immunity was enjoyed by a torturer from one Torture Convention State from the criminal jurisdiction of another. But, as the working group of the ILC itself acknowledged, that case concerned the immunity ratione materiae from criminal jurisdiction of a former head of State, who was at the material time physically within the United Kingdom. As the judgments in the case made clear, the conclusion of the House of Lords did not in any way affect the immunity ratione personae of foreign sovereign States from the civil jurisdiction in respect of such acts (see in particular, the judgment of Lord Millett, mentioned in paragraph 34 above). In so holding, the House of Lords cited with approval the judgments of the Court of Appeal in *Al-Adsani* itself.

66. The Court, while noting the growing recognition of the overriding importance of the prohibition of torture, does not accordingly find it established that there is yet acceptance in international law of the proposition that States are not entitled to immunity in respect of civil claims for damages for alleged torture committed outside the forum State. The 1978 Act, which grants immunity to States in respect of personal injury claims unless the damage was caused within the United Kingdom, is not inconsistent with those limitations generally accepted by the community of nations as part of the doctrine of State immunity.

67. In these circumstances, the application by the English courts of the provisions of the 1978 Act to uphold Kuwait's claim to immunity cannot be said to have amounted to an unjustified restriction on the applicant's access to a court.

It follows that there has been no violation of Article 6 § 1 of the Convention in this case.

For these reasons, the Court

1. Holds unanimously that there has been no violation of Article 3 of the Convention;
2. Holds by nine votes to eight that there has been no violation of Article 6 § 1 of the Convention.

CONCURRING OPINION OF JUDGE PELLONPÄÄ JOINED BY JUDGE SIR NICOLAS BRATZA

...

The acceptance of the applicant's argument concerning access to a court would thus have required a possibility of having judgments — probably often default judgments — delivered in torture cases executed against respondent States. This in turn would raise the question whether the traditionally strong immunity of public property from execution would also have had to be regarded as incompatible with Article 6. It would seem that this indeed would have been the inevitable consequence of the acceptance of the minority's line. If immunity from jurisdiction were to be regarded as incompatible with Article 6 because of the jus cogens nature of the prohibition of torture, which prevails over all other international obligations not having that same hierarchical status, it presumably would also have to prevail over rules concerning immunity from execution. Consequently, the Contracting States would have had to allow attachment and execution against public property of respondent States if the effectiveness of access to a court could not otherwise be guaranteed.

The acceptance of the applicant's argument indeed would have opened the door to much more far-reaching consequences than did the amendment to the United States Foreign Sovereign Immunities Act.... As appears from the plaintiff's futile efforts of execution in *Flatow v. the Islamic Republic of Iran* [*Flatow v. Islamic Republic of Iran* (999 F. Supp. 1 (D.D.C. 1998)); *Flatow v. the Islamic Republic of Iran and Others* (76 F. Supp. 2d 16, 18 (D.D.C. 1999))], this narrowly limited statutory amendment did not affect the immunity of a foreign State's public property from attachment and execution, causing the District Court Judge Royce C. Lamberth to characterise the plaintiff's original judgment against Iran as an epitome of the phrase "Pyrrhic victory."

...

... [I]n order not to contradict itself the Court would have been forced to hold that the prohibition of torture must also prevail over immunity of a foreign State's public property, such as bank accounts intended for public purposes, real estate used for a foreign State's cultural institutes and other establishments abroad (including even, it would appear, embassy buildings), etc., since it has not been suggested that immunity of such public property from execution belongs to the corps of jus cogens. Although giving absolute priority to the prohibition of torture may at first sight seem very "progressive", a more careful consideration tends to confirm that such a step would also run the risk of proving a sort of "Pyrrhic victory". International cooperation, including cooperation with a view to eradicating the vice of torture, presupposes the continuing existence of certain elements of a basic framework for the conduct of international relations. Principles concerning State immunity belong to that regulatory framework, and I believe it is more conducive to orderly international cooperation to leave this framework intact than to follow another course.

...

JOINT DISSENTING OPINION OF JUDGES ROZAKIS AND CAFLISCH JOINED BY JUDGES WILDHABER, COSTA, CABRAL BARRETO AND VAJIĆ

...

In our opinion, the distinction made by the majority and their conclusions are defective on two grounds.

Firstly, the English courts, when dealing with the applicant's claim, never resorted to the distinction made by the majority. They never invoked any difference between criminal charges or civil claims, between criminal and civil proceedings, in so far as the legal force of the rules on State immunity or the applicability of the 1978 Act was concerned. The basic position of the Court of Appeal — the last court which dealt with the matter in its essence — is expressed by the observations of Lord Justice Stuart-Smith who simply denied that the prohibition of torture was a jus cogens rule. In reading the Lord Justice's observations, one even forms the impression that if the Court of Appeal had been convinced that the rule of prohibition of torture was a norm of jus cogens, they could grudgingly have admitted that the procedural bar of State immunity did not apply in the circumstances of the case.

Secondly, the distinction made by the majority between civil and criminal proceedings, concerning the effect of the rule of the prohibition of torture, is not consonant with the very essence of the operation of the jus cogens rules. It is not the nature of the proceedings which determines the effects that a jus cogens rule has upon another rule of international law, but the character of the rule as a peremptory norm and its interaction with a hierarchically lower rule. The prohibition of torture, being a rule of jus cogens, acts in the international sphere and deprives the rule of sovereign immunity of all its legal effects in that sphere. The criminal or civil nature of the domestic proceedings is immaterial. The jurisdictional bar is lifted by the very interaction of the international rules involved, and the national judge cannot admit a plea of immunity raised by the defendant State as an element preventing him from entering into the merits of the case and from dealing with the claim of the applicant for the alleged damages inflicted upon him.

...

CASE CONCERNING THE ARREST WARRANT OF 11 APRIL 2000 (DEMOCRATIC REPUBLIC OF THE CONGO V. BELGIUM)

International Court of Justice, 2002

[The background to these proceedings are discussed earlier in the chapter, p. 1169, *supra*. The following excerpts of the majority's opinion concern the issue of immunity raised by the Congolese Government.]

47. The Congo maintains that... no criminal prosecution may be brought against a Minister for Foreign Affairs in a foreign court as long as he or she remains in office, and that any finding of criminal responsibility a domestic court in a

foreign country, or any act of investigation undertaken with a view to bringing him or her to court, would contravene the principle of immunity from jurisdiction....

...

49. Belgium maintains for its part that, while Ministers for Foreign Affairs in office generally enjoy an immunity from jurisdiction before the courts of a foreign State, such immunity applies only to acts carried out in the course of their official functions, and cannot protect such persons in respect of private acts or when they are acting otherwise than in the performance of their official functions.

50. Belgium further states that, in the circumstances of the present case, Mr. Yerodia enjoyed no immunity at the time when he is alleged to have committed the acts of which he is accused, and that there is no evidence that he was then acting in any official capacity. It observes that the arrest warrant was issued against Mr. Yerodia personally.

51. The Court would observe at the outset that in international law it is firmly established that, as also diplomatic and consular agents, certain holders of high-ranking office in a State, such as the Head of State, Head of Government and Minister for Foreign Affairs, enjoy immunities from jurisdiction in other States, both civil and criminal. For the purposes of the present case, it is only the immunity from criminal jurisdiction and the inviolability of an incumbent Minister for Foreign Affairs that fall for the Court to consider.

52. A certain number of treaty instruments were cited by the Parties in this regard...

...

These conventions provide useful guidance on certain aspects of the question of immunities. They do not, however, contain any provision specifically defining the immunities enjoyed by Ministers for Foreign Affairs. It is consequently on the basis of customary international law that the Court must decide the questions relating to the immunities of such Ministers raised in the present case.

53. In customary international law, the immunities accorded to Ministers for Foreign Affairs are not granted for their personal benefit, but to ensure the effective performance of their functions on behalf of their respective States. In order to determine the extent of these immunities, the Court therefore first consider the nature of the functions exercised by a Minister for Foreign Affairs. He or she is in charge of his or her Government's diplomatic activities and generally acts as its representative in international negotiations and intergovernmental meetings.... In the performance of these functions, he or she frequently required to travel internationally, and thus must be in a position freely to do so whenever the need should arise. He or she must also be in constant communication with the Government, and with its diplomatic missions around the world, and be capable at any time of communicating with representatives of other States. The Court further observes that a Minister for Foreign Affairs, responsible for the conduct of his or her State's relations with all other States, occupies a position such that, like the Head of State or the Head of Government, he or she is recognized under international law as representative of the State solely by virtue of his or her office....

54. The Court accordingly concludes that the functions of a Minister for Foreign Affairs are such that, throughout the duration of his or her office, he or she when

abroad enjoys full immunity from criminal jurisdiction and inviolability. That immunity and that inviolability protect the individual concerned against any act of authority of another State which would hinder him or her in the performance of his or her duties.

55. In this respect, no distinction can be drawn between acts performed by a Minister for Foreign Affairs in an "official" capacity, and those claimed to have been performed in a "private capacity", or, for that matter, between acts performed before the person concerned assumed office as Minister for Foreign Affairs and acts committed during the period of office, Thus, if a Minister for Foreign Affairs is arrested in another State on a criminal charge, he or she is clearly thereby prevented from exercising the functions of his or her office.... Furthermore, even the mere risk that, by travelling to or transiting another State a Minister for Foreign Affairs might be exposing himself or herself to legal proceedings could deter the Minister from travelling internationally when required to do so for the purposes of the performance of his or her official functions.

❁ ❁

56. The Court will now address Belgium's argument that immunities accorded to incumbent Ministers for Foreign Affairs can in no case protect them where they are suspected of having committed war crimes or crimes against humanity....

Belgium begins by pointing out that certain provisions of the instruments creating international criminal tribunals state expressly that the official capacity of a person shall not be a bar to the exercise by such tribunals of their jurisdiction.

Belgium also places emphasis on certain decisions of national courts, and in particular on the judgments rendered on 24 March 1999 by the House of Lords in the United Kingdom and on 13 March 2001 by the Court of Cassation in France in the *Pinochet* and *Qaddafi* cases respectively, in which it contends that an exception to the immunity rule was accepted in the case of serious crimes under international law. Thus, according to Belgium, the *Pinochet* decision recognizes an exception to the immunity rule when Lord Millett stated that "[i]nternational law cannot be supposed to have established a crime having the character of a jus cogens and at the same time to have provided an immunity which is co-extensive with the obligation it seeks to impose", or when Lord Phillips of Worth Matravers said that "no established rule of international law requires state immunity rationae materiae to be accorded in respect of prosecution for an international crime"....

57. The Congo, for its part, states that, under international law as it currently stands, there is no basis for asserting that there is any exception to the principle of absolute immunity from criminal process of an incumbent Minister for Foreign Affairs where he or she is accused of having committed crimes under international law.

In support of this contention, the Congo refers to State practice, giving particular consideration in this regard to the *Pinochet* and *Qaddafi* cases, and concluding that such practice does not correspond to that which Belgium claims but, on the contrary, confirms the absolute nature of the immunity from criminal process of Heads of State and Ministers for Foreign Affairs. Thus, in the *Pinochet* case, the Congo cites

Lord Browne-Wilkinson's statement that "[t]his immunity enjoyed by a head of state in power and an ambassador in post is a complete immunity attached to the person of the head of state or ambassador and rendering him immune from all actions or prosecutions..." ....

As regards the instruments creating international criminal tribunals and the latter's jurisprudence, these, in the Congo's view, concern only those tribunals, and no inference can be drawn from them in regard to criminal proceedings before national courts against persons enjoying immunity under international law.

58. The Court has carefully examined State practice, including national legislation and those few decisions of national higher courts, such as the House of Lords or the French Court of Cassation. It has been unable to deduce from this practice that there exists under customary international law any form of exception to the rule according immunity from criminal jurisdiction and inviolability to incumbent Ministers for Foreign Affairs, where they are suspected of having committed war crimes or crimes against humanity.

The Court has also examined the rules concerning the immunity or criminal responsibility of persons having an official capacity contained in the legal instruments creating international criminal tribunals, and which are specifically applicable to the latter (see Charter of the International Military Tribunal of Nuremberg, Art. 7; Charter of the International Military Tribunal of Tokyo, Art. 6; Statute of the International Criminal Tribunal for the former Yugoslavia, Art.7, para.2; Statute of the International Criminal Tribunal for Rwanda, Art.6, para. 2; Statute of the International Criminal Court, Art. 27). It finds that these rules likewise do not enable it to conclude that any such an exception exists in customary international law in regard to national courts.

Finally, none of the decisions of the Nuremberg and Tokyo international military tribunals, or of the International Criminal Tribunal for the former Yugoslavia, cited by Belgium deal with the question of the immunities of incumbent Ministers for Foreign Affairs before national courts where they are accused of having committed war crimes or crimes against humanity. The Court accordingly notes that those decisions are in no way at variance with the findings it has reached above.

In view of the foregoing, the Court accordingly cannot accept Belgium's argument in this regard.

...

60. The Court emphasizes, however, that the immunity from jurisdiction enjoyed by incumbent Ministers for Foreign Affairs does not mean that they enjoy impunity in respect of any crimes they might have committed, irrespective of their gravity. Immunity from criminal jurisdiction and individual criminal responsibility are quite separate concepts. While jurisdictional immunity is procedural in nature, criminal responsibility is a question of substantive law. Jurisdictional immunity may well bar prosecution for a certain period or for certain offences; it cannot exonerate the person to whom it applies from all criminal responsibility.

61. Accordingly, the immunities enjoyed under international law by an incumbent or former Minister for Foreign Affairs do not represent a bar to criminal prosecution in certain circumstances.

First, such persons enjoy no criminal immunity under international law in their own countries, and may thus be tried by those countries' courts in accordance with the relevant rules of domestic law.

Secondly, they will cease to enjoy immunity from foreign jurisdiction if the State which they represent or have represented decides to waive that immunity.

Thirdly, after a person ceases to hold the office of Minister for Foreign Affairs, he or she will no longer enjoy all of the immunities accorded by international law in other States. Provided that it has jurisdiction under international law, a court of one State may try a former Minister for Foreign Affairs of another State in respect of acts committed prior or subsequent to his or her period of office, as well as in respect of acts committed during that period of office in a private capacity.

Fourthly, an incumbent or former Minister for Foreign Affairs may be subject to criminal proceedings before certain international criminal courts, where they have jurisdiction. Examples include the International Criminal Tribunal for the former Yugoslavia, and the International Criminal Tribunal for Rwanda, established pursuant to Security Council resolutions under Chapter VII of the United Nations Charter, and the future International Criminal Court created by the 1998 Rome Convention. The latter's Statute expressly provides, in Article 27, paragraph 2, that "[i]mmunities or special procedural rules which may attach to the official capacity of a person, whether under national or international law, shall not bar the Court from exercising its jurisdiction over such a person".

...

PROSECUTOR V. CHARLES TAYLOR, SPECIAL COURT FOR SIERRA LEONE (DECISION ON IMMUNITY FROM JURISDICTION)

31 May 2004

[What institutions qualify as an 'international criminal court' according to the ICJ in *Congo v. Belgium*? Does the International Military Tribunal of Nuremberg qualify even though it was established by four states (France, the Soviet Union, the United Kingdom and the United States)? How about the International Military Tribunal of Tokyo, which was established by a military order of General MacArthur and included the participation of eleven states?[30] Why should international criminal courts, in contrast with national courts, be permitted to suspend sovereign immunities?

These issues arose in a case decided by the Special Court for Sierra Leone involving Charles Taylor, the former President of Liberia. In the 1990s, Sierra Leone was ravaged by a civil war that claimed over 75,000 lives and displaced a third of the population. In June 2000, the President of Sierra Leone formally requested the UN Secretary-General to assist in prosecuting perpetrators of atrocities committed during

[30] The states taking part in the prosecution and judgment were Australia, Canada, China, France, India, the Netherlands, New Zealand, the Philippines, the Soviet Union, the United Kingdom and the United States.

the civil war. In response, the Security Council authorized the Secretary-General to negotiate an agreement between the UN and the Government of Sierra Leone to establish a criminal tribunal. The subsequent agreement, which was signed in January 2002, created the legal framework for the Special Court for Sierra Leone. The Special Court is seated in the capital Freetown. The Court is composed of international and domestic judges, prosecutors and administrative staff. The jurisdiction of the Court includes international and domestic crimes.]

1. This is an application by Mr. Charles Taylor, the former President of the Republic of Liberia, to quash his Indictment and to set aside the warrant for his arrest on the grounds that he is immune from any exercise of the jurisdiction of this court. The Indictment and arrest warrant were approved ... on 7 March 2003, when Mr. Taylor was Head of State of Liberia.

...

5. The Indictment against Mr. Taylor contains seventeen counts. It accuses him of the commission of crimes against humanity and grave breaches of the Geneva Conventions, with intent "to obtain access to the mineral wealth of the Republic of Sierra Leone, in particular the diamond wealth of Sierra Leone, and to destabilize the state". It is alleged that he "provided financial support, military training, personnel, arms, ammunition and other support and encouragement" to rebel factions throughout the armed conflict in Sierra Leone. The counts variously accuse him of responsibility for "terrorizing the civilian population and ordering collective punishment", sexual and physical violence against civilians, use of child soldiers, abductions and forced labour, widespread looting and burning of civilian property, and attacks on and abductions of [UN] peacekeepers and humanitarian assistance workers. In short, the prosecution maintains that from an early stage and acting in a private rather than an official capacity he resourced and directed rebel forces, encouraging them in campaigns of terror, torture and mass murder, in order to enrich himself from a share in the diamond mines that were captured by the rebel forces.

...

6. The Applicant argues first that:

a) Citing the judgment of the International Court of Justice ("ICJ") in the case between the *Democratic Republic of Congo v. Belgium* ("*Yerodia* case"), as an incumbent Head of State at the time of his indictment, Charles Taylor enjoyed absolute immunity from criminal prosecution;

b) Exceptions from diplomatic immunities can only derive from other rules of international law such as Security Council resolutions under Chapter VII of the United Nations Charter ("UN Charter");

c) The Special Court does not have Chapter VII powers, therefore judicial orders from the Special Court have the quality of judicial orders from a national court;

...

38. Much issue had been made of the absence of Chapter VII powers in the Special Court. A proper understanding of those powers shows that the absence of

the so-called Chapter VII powers does not by itself define the legal status of the Special Court.... Where the Security Council decides to establish a court as a measure to maintain or restore international peace and security it may or may not, at the same time, contemporaneously, call upon the members of the United Nations to lend their cooperation to such court as a matter of obligation.... It is to be observed that in carrying out its duties under its responsibility for the maintenance of international peace and security, the Security Council acts on behalf of the members of the United Nations. The Agreement between the United Nations and Sierra Leone is thus an agreement between *all* members of the United Nations and Sierra Leone. This fact makes the Agreement an expression of the will of the international community. The Special Court established in such circumstances is truly international.

39. By reaffirming in the preamble to Resolution 1315 'that persons who commit or authorize serious violations of international humanitarian law are individually responsible and accountable for those violations and that the international community will exert every effort to bring those responsible to justice in accordance with international standards of justice, fairness and due process of law', it has been made clear that the Special Court was established to fulfill an international mandate and is part of the machinery of international justice.

...

51. A reason for the distinction, in this regard, between national courts and international courts, though not immediately evident, would appear due to the fact that the principle that one sovereign state does not adjudicate on the conduct of another state; the principle of state immunity derives from the equality of sovereign sates and therefore has no relevance to international criminal tribunals which are not organs of a state but derive their mandate from the international community. Another reason is as put by Professor Orentlicher in her amicus brief that: states have considered the collective judgment of the international community to provide a vital safeguard against the potential destabilizing effect of unilateral judgment in this area.

52. Be that as it may, the principle seems now established that the sovereign equality of states does not prevent a Head of State from being prosecuted before an international criminal tribunal or court. We accept the view expressed by Lord Slynn of Hadley that 'there is... no doubt that states have been moving towards the recognition of some crimes as those which should not be covered by claims of state or Head of State or other official or diplomatic immunity when charges are brought before international tribunals.'

53. In this result the Appeals Chamber finds that Article 6(2) of the Statute is not in conflict with any peremptory norm of general international law and its provisions must be given effect by this court....

59. Before this matter is concluded, it is apt to observe that the Applicant had at the time the Preliminary Motion was heard ceased to be a Head of State. The immunity ratione personae which he claimed had ceased to attach to him. Even if he had succeeded in his application the consequence would have been to compel the Prosecutor to issue a fresh warrant.

QUESTIONS

1. If the UK Government can espouse Al-Adsani's claims directly with the Kuwaiti Government, why can't (or shouldn't) the United Kingdom have Al-Adsani first submit his claims before a national tribunal before taking them up with the foreign government? Would the inclusion of court proceedings not provide a greater degree of independence and impartiality in evaluating private actors' claims?

2. Is the *Al-Adsani* opinion consistent with the *Arrest Warrant* opinion? What are the points of disagreement, if any? Would (and should) the holding in the *Arrest Warrant* decision apply as well to a civil suit against Mr. Yerodia?

3. Should official immunity extend to acts committed by a defendant outside of his country? For example, imagine a Belgian judge proceeding against a Congolese Foreign Minister for allegedly committing an extrajudicial killing in Belgium. Should official immunity extend to acts committed in a third state? For example, consider a Belgian judge proceeding against a Congolese Foreign Minister for acts committed in Rwanda?

4. Do you agree with the reasoning of the Special Court for Sierra Leone? Should the lack of Chapter VII authority have any bearing on whether a defendant enjoys immunity before such a judicial body?

PART F

CURRENT TOPICS

Drawing on the framework created by Parts A–E, the chapters in Part F examine three broad topics of great significance for the human rights movement — three among the larger number of current and vital human rights themes that could as well have been selected. Chapters 14–15 examine consequences of massive human rights tragedies, particularly individual criminal prosecutions and truth commissions; the growing role of nonstate actors, and relationships between globalization and human rights.

14

Massive Human Rights Tragedies: Prosecutions and Truth Commissions

The topics and documents in this chapter grow out of massive human rights tragedies. The illustrations below include the former Yugoslavia, Rwanda, apartheid South Africa and Sierra Leone. Most of these tragedies were stimulated by an oppressor state, but some not. The theme of the chapter can be stated simply: What have been the nature and effects of two types of institutional reactions to such human rights violations — prosecutions before criminal tribunals and truth commissions? How do we understand these institutional responses, how do we assess them, and in what directions do or should they now point?

To approach such questions, the chapter explores a number of related subjects: international crimes and individual culpability, the *ad hoc* international criminal tribunals for the former Yugoslavia and for Rwanda, the permanent International Criminal Court, hybrid tribunals such as the Special Court for Sierra Leone, alternative national approaches such as gacaca courts in Rwanda and truth commissions, particularly in South Africa and Sierra Leone. With some exceptions, the emphasis in the earlier sections is on prosecutions before international tribunals, and in the concluding sections on other tribunals and truth commissions.

Several of the chapter's illustrations of systemic violations grow out of contexts of armed conflict, whether principally international in character or principally internal to a state. Others occurred in periods of severe internal repression that, despite its violence, stopped shy of internal armed conflict. For the first category, the *humanitarian laws of war* become particularly relevant. Hence the chapter builds on the earlier discussions of the law of war in connection with sources and foundations of international law, p. 69, *supra* (Comment on the Humanitarian Law of War), p. 115, *supra* (concerning the Nuremberg Judgment), and in connection with national security and terrorism, p. 395, *supra* (Comment on Relationships between International Human Rights and Humanitarian Law). In cases like Augusto Pinochet's Chile and much (though not all) of the South African experience, the principal source of criticism and judgment has been mainstream *international human rights law* which has developed over the past six decades.

Nonetheless, the trends in both bodies of law over this period have brought them into a closer, intertwined relationship — a relationship vividly illustrated by the statutes of the international criminal tribunals and the judgments of such tribunals. Each field retains a near exclusive interest in a large number of important issues — the laws of war, say, with respect to aspects of *jus in bello* such as military necessity or proportionality in the waging of war; human rights law, say, with respect to free speech, gender equality or political participation. But on numerous issues that are germane to the international crimes and criminal prosecutions described below, the boundary lines are blurring.

The post-Nuremberg growth of the humanitarian laws of war — particularly through the Geneva Conventions and their two Additional Protocols, and the statutes and judicial decisions of international criminal tribunals — as well as the striking success in standard-setting of the human rights movement, have greatly expanded the number of crimes defined by international law that are based on those bodies of law and that impose individual responsibility. Today's international crimes are both conventional and customary in character. Issues of punishment, impunity or immunity, amnesty and pardon of those involved in the most serious violations of human rights have become a feature of today's major conflicts.

A. INTERNATIONAL CRIMINAL TRIBUNALS FOR THE FORMER YUGOSLAVIA AND RWANDA

MARTHA MINOW, BETWEEN VENGEANCE AND FORGIVENESS

(1998), at 25

To respond to mass atrocity with legal prosecutions is to embrace the rule of law. This common phrase combines several elements. First, there is a commitment to redress harms with the application of general, preexisting norms. Second, the rule of law calls for administration by a formal system itself committed to fairness and opportunities for individuals to be heard both in accusation and in defense. Further, a government proceeding under the rule of law aims to treat each individual person in light of particular, demonstrated evidence. In the Western liberal legal tradition, the rule of law also entails the presumption of innocence, litigation under the adversary system, and the ideal of a government by laws, rather than by persons. No one is above or outside the law, and no one should be legally condemned or sanctioned outside legal procedures. . . .

A trial in the aftermath of mass atrocity, then, should mark an effort between vengeance and forgiveness. It transfers the individuals' desires for revenge to the state or official bodies. The transfer cools vengeance into retribution, slows judgment with procedure, and interrupts, with documents, cross-examination, and the presumption of innocence, the vicious cycle of blame and feud. The trial itself steers clear of forgiveness, however. It announces a demand not only for accountability and acknowledgment of harms done, but also for unflinching punishment. At the end of the trial process, after facts are found and convictions are secured, there might be forgiveness of a legal sort: a suspended sentence, or executive pardon, or clemency in light of humanitarian concerns. Even then, the process has exacted time and agony from, and rendered a kind of punishment for defendants, while also accomplishing change in their relationships to prosecutors, witnesses, and viewing public. Reconciliation is not the goal of criminal trials except in the most abstract sense. We reconcile with the murderer by imagining he or she is responsible to the same rules and commands that govern all of us; we agree to sit in the same room and accord the defendant a chance to speak, and a chance to fight for his or her life. But reconstruction of a relationship, seeking to heal the accused, or indeed, healing the rest of the community, are not the goals in any direct sense.... Justice Jackson's own defense of the prosecutorial effort at Nuremberg was more modest than the assertion of deterrence offered by others since. He called for modest aspirations especially because wars are usually started only in the confidence that they can be won. Therefore, he acknowledged, '[p]ersonal punishment, to be suffered only in the event the war is lost, is probably not to be a sufficient deterrent to prevent a war where the war-makers feel the chances of defeat to be negligible'. Does the risk of punishment for human rights violations make the leaders of authoritarian regimes reluctant to surrender power in the first place? Individuals who commit atrocities on the scale of genocide are unlikely to behave as 'rational actors', deterred by the risk of punishment. Even if they were, it is not irrational to ignore the improbable prospect of punishment given the track record of international law thus far. A tribunal can be but one step in a process seeking to ensure peace, to make those in power responsible to law, and to condemn aggression....

MARTTI KOSKENNIEMI, BETWEEN IMPUNITY AND SHOW TRIALS

Max Planck Yearbook of United Nations Law Vol. 6:1 (2002)

...Surely, as many of those involved in the process that led to the signature of the Statute for the International Criminal Court in 1998 seem to have assumed, the value of the new court lies in its deterrent message, the way in which it serves to prevent future atrocities. The force of this argument is, however, doubtful. In the first place, if crimes against humanity really emerge from what Kant labelled "radical evil", an evil that exceeds the bounds of instrumental rationality, that seeks no objective beyond itself, then by definition, calculations about the likelihood of future punishment do not enter the picture. Indeed, there is no calculation in the first place. But even if one remained suspicious about the metaphysics of "radical evil"... the deterrence argument would still fail to convince inasmuch as the atrocities of the 20th century have not emerged from criminal intent but as offshoots from a desire to do good. This is most evident in regard to the crimes of communism, the Gulag, the Ukraine famine, liquidation of the "Kulaks". But even the worst Nazi nightmares were connected to a project to create a better world.... But if the acts do not evidence criminal intent, and instead come about as aspects of ideological programmes that strive for the good life, however far in future, or to save the world from a present danger, then the deterrence argument seems beside the point. In such case, criminal law itself will come to seem a part of the world which must be set aside, an aspect of the "evil" that the ideology seeks to eradicate.

As criminal lawyers know well, fitting crimes against humanity or other massive human rights violations into the deterrence frame requires some rather implausible psychological generalisations. Either the crimes are aspects of political normality — Arendt's "banality of evil" — in which case there is no mens rea, or they take place in exceptional situations of massive destruction and personal danger when there is little liberty of action. This is not to say that in such cases, people act as automatons, losing capacity for independent judgement. Many studies have elucidated the way individuals react to pressure created by either normality or exceptionality, and are sometimes able to resist. But it is implausible to believe that criminal law is able to teach people to become heroes, not least because what "heroism" might mean in particular situations is often at the heart of the confrontation between the political values underlying the criminal justice system (perhaps seen as victor's justice) and the system that is on trial.

...

How to understand the actions of the leaders of the Yugoslav communities — whether they were "criminal" or not — depends on which framework of interpretation one accepts.

...

... Focusing on the individual abstracts the political context, that is to say, describes it in terms of the actions and intentions of particular, well-situated individuals. Indeed, this is precisely what the Prosecutor in the Milosevic trial, Carla del Ponte, said she was doing in The Hague in February 2002. The (Serb) nation was not on trial, only an individual was. But the truth is not necessarily served by an individual focus. On the contrary, the meaning of historical events often exceeds the intentions or actions of particular individuals and can be grasped only by attention to structural causes, such as economic or functional necessities, or a broad institutional logic through which the actions by individuals create social effects. Typically, among historians, the "intentionist" explanations of the destruction of European Jewry are opposed by "functional" explanations that point to the material and structural causes that finally at the Wannsee conference of 1942 — but not until then — turned Nazi policy towards full-scale extermination. When Arendt and others were criticising the Eichmann trial, they pointed to the inability of an individual focus to provide an understanding of the way the Shoah did not come about as a series of actions by deviant individuals with a criminal mind but through Schreibtisch acts by obedient servants of a criminal State.

This is why individualisation is not neutral in its effects. Use of terms such as "Hitlerism" or "Stalinism" leaves the political, moral and organisational structures intact that are the necessary condition of the crime. To focus on individual leaders may even serve as an alibi for the population at large to relieve itself from responsibility....

...

The point here is not to try to settle the epistemological controversy about whether the individual or the contextual (functional, structural) focus provides the better truth but, rather, that neither can a priori override the other and that in some situations it is proper to focus individuals while in other cases — such as Nazi criminality, and perhaps in taking stock of Stasi collaboration in the GDR — the context provides the better frame of interpretation. But if that is so, then there is no guarantee that a criminal process a priori oriented towards individual guilt such as the Milosevic trial necessarily enacts a lesson of historical truth. On the contrary, it may rather obstruct this process by exonerating from responsibility those larger (political, economic, even legal) structures within which the conditions for individual criminality have been created — within which the social normality of a criminal society emerges.

As the German historian Martin Broszat has pointed out, the "one-sided personalisation" and rigid conceptualisation of criminal categories may lead not only to a different kind of truth but also a different way of distributing accountability

. . .

But in the end, individualisation is also impossible. After all, the defences available to the accused refer precisely to the context in which his acts were undertaken. Was there an acceptable motive or an alternative course of action? Did the victim contribute to the action? . . . What was the chain of command that led to the Omarska camp or the Srebrenica massacre? . . . To create that chain will, in the absence of written orders, have to involve broad interpretations and assumptions about the political and administrative culture in the territory, including personal links and expectations between the various protagonists. In this way, even focus on individuals presumes a larger context in which particular individuals rise to key positions and in which their choices and preferences are formulated and come to seem either as "normal" or "deviant". The acts of former Nazis or the Communist Party Politburo — or perhaps more mundanely, Stasi agents or members of apartheid hit-squads — were not anti-social in the way of regular criminality but part of the political "normality" of criminal societies. This is precisely why Milosevic is able to reveal the hypocrisy in the Prosecutor's position: the trial is a trial of the Serbian nation inasmuch as his acts were part of (and not a deviation from) the social normality of Serbia's recent past.

It is at this point that the strategy chosen by Milosevic receives its full significance, and tends to demonstrate the limits of the criminal trial as an instrument of material truth and political reconciliation. . . .

. . .

. . . the West should not be allowed to remain confident that its version of the recent history of the Yugoslavian populations will be automatically vindicated. A trial that "automatically" vindicates the position of the Prosecutor is a show trial in the precise Stalinist sense of that expression. . . . To avoid looking like Vyshinsky, the judges not only must allow Milosevic to speak, but take what he says seriously. They will have to accept being directed by Milosevic into the context within which he will construct his defence in terms of patriotic anti-imperialism. As the political and historical "truth" of the Balkans becomes one aspect of the trial, then the West must accept that some — perhaps quite a bit — of responsibility will be assigned to its weak and contradictory policy. The bombing of Serbia in the spring of 1999 that caused around 500 civilian casualties will become one of the relevant factors. The Tribunal cannot ignore the question of whether that was a reasonable price to pay for flying at high altitudes so as to avert danger to NATO pilots. But who can tell how far in the past the chain of political causality leads, and what will turn up as Milosevic will reveal his interpretation of why the West rejected him as an acceptable interlocutor?

In the course of the trial Milosevic has conducted his defence less in order to save himself than in order to get his version of truth across to the public in Serbia, as well as to "history" by and large. . . .

. . .

Having finally moved away from the Scylla of impunity — however incoherently and in response to external pressure — the West is now heading either towards a lesson in history and politics in which its own guilt will have to be assessed, or to the Charybdis of show trials.

SECURITY COUNCIL RESOLUTIONS ON ESTABLISHMENT OF AN INTERNATIONAL TRIBUNAL FOR THE FORMER YUGOSLAVIA

reprinted in 14 Hum. Rts. L. J. 197 (1993)

Resolution 808, 22 February 1993

. . .

Recalling paragraph 10 of its resolution 764 (1992) of 13 July 1992, in which it reaffirmed that all parties are bound to comply with the obligations under international humanitarian law and in particular the Geneva Conventions of 12 August 1949, and that persons who commit or order the commission of grave breaches of the Conventions are individually responsible in respect of such breaches . . .

Expressing once again its grave alarm at continuing reports of widespread violations of international humanitarian law occurring within the territory of the former Yugoslavia, including reports of mass killings and the continuance of the practice of 'ethnic cleansing',

Determining that this situation constitutes a threat to international peace and security,

Determined to put an end to such crimes and to take effective measures to bring to justice the persons who are responsible for them,

Convinced that in the particular circumstances of the former Yugoslavia the establishment of an international tribunal would enable this aim to be achieved and would contribute to the restoration and maintenance of peace.

. . .

1. *Decides* that an international tribunal shall be established for the prosecution of persons responsible for serious violations of international humanitarian law committed in the territory of the former Yugoslavia since 1991;

2. *Requests* the Secretary-General to submit for consideration by the Council . . . a report on all aspects of this matter, including specific proposals and where appropriate options for the effective and expeditious implementation of the decision contained in paragraph 1 above, taking into account suggestions put forward in this regard by Member States;

. . .

Resolution 827, 25 May 1993

...

Acting under Chapter VII of the Charter of the United Nations,

1. Approves the report of the Secretary-General;

2. Decides hereby to establish an international tribunal for the sole purpose of prosecuting persons responsible for serious violations of international humanitarian law committed in the territory of the former Yugoslavia between 1 January 1991 and a date to be determined by the Security Council upon the restoration of peace and to this end to adopt the Statute of the International Tribunal annexed to the above-mentioned report...

...

4. Decides that all States shall cooperate fully with the International Tribunal and its organs in accordance with the present resolution and the Statute of the International Tribunal and that consequently all States shall take any measures necessary under their domestic law to implement the provisions of the present resolution and the Statute, including the obligation of States to comply with requests for assistance or orders issued by a Trial Chamber under Article 29 of the Statute;...

...

7. Decides also that the work of the International Tribunal shall be carried out without prejudice to the right of the victims to seek, through appropriate means, compensation for damages incurred as a result of violations of international humanitarian law;

...

REPORT OF THE SECRETARY-GENERAL UNDER SECURITY COUNCIL RESOLUTION 808

Doc. S/2504, 3 May 1993, reprinted in 14 Hum. Rts. L. J. 198 (1993)

...

I. The Legal Basis for the Establishment of the International Tribunal

...

18. Security Council resolution 808...[does not] indicate how such an international tribunal is to be established or on what legal basis.

19. The approach which, in the normal course of events, would be followed in establishing an international tribunal would be the conclusion of a treaty by which the States parties would establish a tribunal and approve its statute. This treaty would be drawn up and adopted by an appropriate international body (e.g., the General Assembly or a specially convened conference), following which it would be opened for signature and ratification. Such an approach...would allow the States participating in the negotiation and conclusion of the treaty fully to exercise their sovereign will, in particular whether they wish to become parties to the treaty or not.

20. ...[T]he treaty approach incurs the disadvantage of requiring considerable time to establish an instrument and then to achieve the required number of ratifications for entry into force. Even then, there could be no guarantee that ratifications

will be received from those States which should be parties to the treaty if it is to be truly effective.

21. . . . The involvement of the General Assembly in the drafting or the review of the statute of the International Tribunal would not be reconcilable with the urgency expressed by the Security Council in resolution 808 (1993). The Secretary-General believes that there are other ways of involving the authority and prestige of the General Assembly in the establishment of the International Tribunal.

22. In the light of the disadvantages of the treaty approach in this particular case . . . the Secretary-General believes that the International Tribunal should be established by a decision of the Security Council on the basis of Chapter VII of the Charter of the United Nations. Such a decision would constitute a measure to maintain or restore international peace and security, following the requisite determination of the existence of a threat to the peace, breach of the peace or act of aggression.

23. This approach would have the advantage of being expeditious and of being immediately effective as all States would be under a binding obligation to take whatever action is required to carry out a decision taken as an enforcement measure under Chapter VII. . . .

. . .

28. In this particular case, the Security Council would be establishing, as an enforcement measure under Chapter VII, a subsidiary organ within the terms of Article 29 of the Charter, but one of a judicial nature. This organ would, of course, have to perform its functions independently of political considerations; it would not be subject to the authority or control of the Security Council with regard to the performance of its judicial functions. As an enforcement measure under Chapter VII, however, the life span of the international tribunal would be linked to the restoration and maintenance of international peace and security in the territory of the former Yugoslavia, and Security Council decisions related thereto.

29. It should be pointed out that, in assigning to the International Tribunal the task of prosecuting persons responsible for serious violations of international humanitarian law, the Security Council would not be creating or purporting to 'legislate' that law. Rather, the International Tribunal would have the task of applying existing international humanitarian law.

. . .

II. Competence of the International Tribunal

. . .

33. According to paragraph 1 of resolution 808 (1993), the international tribunal shall prosecute persons responsible for serious violations of international humanitarian law committed in the territory of the former Yugoslavia since 1991. This body of law exists in the form of both conventional law and customary law. While there is international customary law which is not laid down in conventions, some of the major conventional humanitarian law has become part of customary international law.

34. In the view of the Secretary-General, the application of the principle *nullum crimen sine lege* requires that the international tribunal should apply rules of international humanitarian law which are beyond any doubt part of customary law so

that the problem of adherence of some but not all States to specific conventions does not arise. This would appear to be particularly important in the context of an international tribunal prosecuting persons responsible for serious violations of international humanitarian law.

35. The part of conventional international humanitarian law which has beyond doubt become part of international customary law is the law applicable in armed conflict as embodied in: the Geneva Conventions of 12 August 1949 for the Protection of War Victims; the Hague Convention (IV) Respecting the Laws and Customs of War on Land and the Regulations annexed thereto of 18 October 1907; the Convention on the Prevention and Punishment of the Crime of Genocide of 9 December 1948; and the Charter of the International Military Tribunal of 8 August 1945....

STATUTE OF THE INTERNATIONAL TRIBUNAL FOR THE FORMER YUGOSLAVIA

reprinted in 14 Hum. Rts. L. J. 211 (1993)

Article 1 — Competence of the International Tribunal

The International Tribunal shall have the power to prosecute persons responsible for serious violations of international humanitarian law committed in the territory of the former Yugoslavia since 1991 in accordance with the provision of the present Statute.

Article 2 — Grave breaches of the Geneva Conventions of 1949

The International Tribunal shall have the power to prosecute persons committing or ordering to be committed grave breaches of the Geneva Conventions of 12 August 1949, namely the following acts against persons or property protected under the provisions of the relevant Geneva Convention:

(a) wilful killing;
(b) torture or inhuman treatment, including biological experiments;
(c) wilfully causing great suffering or serious injury to body or health;
(d) extensive destruction and appropriation of property, not justified by military necessity and carried out unlawfully and wantonly;
(e) compelling a prisoner of war or a civilian to serve in the forces of a hostile power;
(f) wilfully depriving a prisoner of war or a civilian of the rights of fair and regular trial;
(g) unlawful deportation or transfer or unlawful confinement of a civilian;
(h) taking civilians as hostages.

Article 3 — Violations of the laws or customs of war

The International Tribunal shall have the power to prosecute persons violating the laws or customs of war. Such violations shall include, but not be limited to:

(a) employment of poisonous weapons or other weapons calculated to cause unnecessary suffering;
(b) wanton destruction of cities, towns or villages, or devastation not justified by military necessity;
(c) attack, or bombardment, by whatever means, of undefended towns, villages, dwellings, or buildings;
(d) seizure of, destruction or wilful damage done to institutions dedicated to religion, charity and education, the arts and sciences, historic monuments and works of art and science;
(e) plunder of public or private property.

Article 4 — Genocide

1. The International Tribunal shall have the power to prosecute persons committing genocide as defined in paragraph 2 of this article or of committing any of the other acts enumerated in paragraph 3 of this article.

2. Genocide means any of the following acts committed with intent to destroy, in whole or in part, a national, ethnical, racial or religious group, as such:

(a) killing members of the group;
(b) causing serious bodily or mental harm to members of the group;
(c) deliberately inflicting on the group conditions of life calculated to bring about its physical destruction in whole or in part;
(d) imposing measures intended to prevent births within the group;
(e) forcibly transferring children of the group to another group.

3. The following acts shall be punishable:

(a) genocide;
(b) conspiracy to commit genocide;
(c) direct and public incitement to commit genocide;
(d) attempt to commit genocide;
(e) complicity in genocide.

Article 5 — Crimes against humanity

The International Tribunal shall have the power to prosecute persons responsible for the following crimes when committed in armed conflict, whether international or internal in character, and directed against any civilian population:

(a) murder;
(b) extermination;

(c) enslavement;
(d) deportation;
(e) imprisonment;
(f) torture;
(g) rape;
(h) persecutions on political, racial and religious grounds;
(i) other inhumane acts....

Article 7 — Individual criminal responsibility

1. A person who planned, instigated, ordered, committed or otherwise aided and abetted in the planning, preparation or execution of a crime referred to in articles 2 to 5 of the present Statute, shall be individually responsible for the crime.

2. The official position of any accused person, whether as Head of State or Government or as responsible Government official, shall not relieve such person of criminal responsibility nor mitigate punishment.

3. The fact that any of the acts referred to in articles 2 to 5 of the present Statute was committed by a subordinate does not relieve his superior of criminal responsibility if he knows or had reason to know that the subordinate was about to commit such acts or had done so and the superior failed to take the necessary and reasonable measures to prevent such acts or to punish the perpetrators thereof.

4. The fact that an accused person acted pursuant to an order of a Government or of a superior shall not relieve him of criminal responsibility, but may be considered in mitigation of punishment if the International Tribunal determines that justice so requires....

Article 10 — Non-bis-in-idem

1. No person shall be tried before a national court for acts constituting serious violations of international humanitarian law under the present Statute, for which he or she has already been tried by the International Tribunal.

2. A person who has been tried by a national court for acts constituting serious violations of international humanitarian law may be subsequently tried by the International Tribunal only if:

(a) the act for which he or she was tried was characterized as an ordinary crime; or
(b) the national court proceedings were not impartial or independent, were designed to shield the accused from international criminal responsibility, or the case was not diligently prosecuted....

Article 20 — Commencement and conduct of trial proceedings

1. The Trial Chambers shall ensure that a trial is fair and expeditious and that proceedings are conducted in accordance with the rules of procedure and evidence, with full respect for the rights of the accused and due regard for the protection of victims and witnesses....

4. The hearings shall be public unless the Trial Chamber decides to close the proceedings in accordance with its rules of procedure and evidence.

Article 21 — Rights of the accused

1. All persons shall be equal before the International Tribunal.
2. In the determination of charges against him, the accused shall be entitled to a fair and public hearing. . . .
3. The accused shall be presumed innocent until proved guilty according to the provisions of the present Statute.
4. In the determination of any charge against the accused pursuant to the present Statute, the accused shall be entitled to the following minimum guarantees, in full equality: [provisions for a fair trial omitted]

Article 22 — Protection of victims and witnesses

The International Tribunal shall provide in its rules of procedure and evidence for the protection of victims and witnesses. Such protection measures shall include, but shall not be limited to, the conduct of *in camera* proceedings and the protection of the victim's identity.

. . .

Article 24 — Penalties

1. The penalty imposed by the Trial Chamber shall be limited to imprisonment. In determining the terms of imprisonment, the Trial Chambers shall have recourse to the general practice regarding prison sentences in the courts of the former Yugoslavia.

. . .

Article 29 — Cooperation and judicial assistance

1. States shall cooperate with the International Tribunal in the investigation and prosecution of persons accused of committing serious violations of international humanitarian law.
2. States shall comply without undue delay with any request for assistance or an order issued by a Trial Chamber, including, but not limited to:

   (a) the identification and location of persons;
   (b) the taking of testimony and the production of evidence;
   (c) the service of documents;
   (d) the arrest or detention of persons;
   (e) the surrender or the transfer of the accused to the International Tribunal. . . .

Article 32 — Expenses of the International Tribunal

The expenses of the International Tribunal shall be borne by the regular budget of the United Nations in accordance with Article 17 of the Charter of the United Nations.

. . .

NOTE

The establishment of the International Criminal Tribunal for the former Yugoslavia (ICTY) — the first such tribunal since the International Military Tribunal at Nuremberg, whose membership was indeed limited to the four major victorious powers — was an historic event holding considerable promise and inescapable risk. Consider several aspects of the ICTY and its work.

1. Observers have read different motivations into the Security Council's decision to establish the Tribunal. Some understand the ICTY to be an essential response by the Council to the public outcry after exposure by the media of the outrages in the conflict — a minimum response, an effort to do 'something' that could prove to be significant and that was politically manageable (unlike the failures in efforts at negotiation or in discussions of types of intervention). Others understand the Tribunal as an attempt to salve the conscience of the West, a way of responding to ethnic cleansing and the accompanying brutality without taking effective action.

2. The ICTY is in a radically different situation from a court in a state observing fundamental principles of the rule of law in the sense that the state's executive and legislative branches comply with and execute court judgments. The Security Council has created an independent organ, as must be the case. Nonetheless, the ICTY remains dependent on an uncertain and changing political context; it lacks the relative autonomy of a court in a state with a strong tradition of an independent judiciary. The Tribunal depends for funds on a UN General Assembly whose members hold different views about it and who may judge its work differently. It must receive support from states and from the Security Council with respect to such basic matters as putting pressure on states to comply with its orders. There is no equivalent to a 'national tradition' for the Tribunal to draw on.

3. Beyond its fundamental mission of bringing a sense of justice and reconciliation to the combatants and civilians in the area, the ICTY (and the ICT for Rwanda, *infra*) possess an exceptional opportunity to develop international law in the field of individual criminal responsibility in an authoritative way. The Prosecutor and judges have confronted and will continue to confront numerous vexing issues, some of ancient lineage and some bred by the developments over the last half century in international humanitarian law including the crimes defined at Nuremberg.

QUESTIONS

1. In what respects does the Statute on its face reveal changes in the definitions of war crimes and crimes against humanity from the Nuremberg Charter? What is the direction of those changes?

2. Why do you suppose the Statute lacks a provision for crimes against peace similar to that at Nuremberg?

COMMENT ON BACKGROUND TO THE TADIC LITIGATION BEFORE THE INTERNATIONAL CRIMINAL TRIBUNAL FOR THE FORMER YUGOSLAVIA

The Broad Context:

The 1997 opinion of a Trial Chamber of the ICTY in *Prosecutor v. Tadic, infra,* was the first determination of individual guilt or innocence in connection with serious violations of international humanitarian law by this tribunal. This Comment sketches the context in which this and similar cases arose. For this sketch, it draws on the opinion of the Trial Chamber, which relied on expert witnesses called by the Prosecution and Defence. Where conflict emerged between witnesses, the Trial Chamber sought to resolve it 'by adopting appropriately neutral language.' It did not turn to any other sources. The area stressed by the opinion was northwestern Bosnia and Herzegovina (hereafter Bosnia), particularly Prijedor Opstina (the Prijedor district).

For centuries the population of Bosnia, more than any other republic of the former Yugoslavia, had been mulit-ethnic: Serbs (Eastern Orthodox), Bosnian Muslims and Croats (Roman Catholic); all indeed Slav peoples within a broader conception of ethnicity. In the nineteenth century, a concept of a state of the south Slavs, with a common language and ethnic origin, had developed, together with the growth among Serbs of the concept of a Greater Serbia including within its borders all ethnic Serbs. The collapse of the Ottoman Empire (it withdrew from the former Yugoslavia by 1912) and the Austro-Hungarian Empire after the First World War led to the creation of such a state of the south Slavs: Yugoslavia. The Axis occupation of Yugoslavia during the Second World War left bitter memories: Croatia's status as a puppet state of the Axis powers, the massacres it committed against Serbs and others, the fighting that occurred between the various Serb factions including the partisans under Marshal Tito (as he became later known), the retaliations after the war ended. Much of the fighting and many atrocities against civilians took place in Bosnia.

Nonetheless until about 1991, the different ethnic groups in Bosnia lived 'happily enough together', though particularly in rural areas such as those in the outlying parts of the Prijedor district the three populations tended to live separately. As the opinion stated:

> Many witnesses speak of good inter-communal relations, of friendships across ethnic and coincident religious divides, of intermarriages and of generally harmonious relations. It is only subsequent events that may suggest that beneath that apparent harmony always lay buried bitter discord, which skilful propaganda readily brought to the surface, with terrible results.

Tito and his Communist regime acted sternly to suppress nationalist tendencies. The country consisted of six republics: Serbia (with its autonomous regions, Vojvodina and Kosovo), Slovenia, Croatia, Bosnia, Macedonia and Montenegro. Bosnia alone had no single majority ethnic grouping. During the latter part of Tito's rule from the mid 1960s on, there was a trend toward devolution of power to the republics, a trend which after Tito's death became useful to the overt resurgence of nationalist sentiment.

Economic and political crises developed simultaneously in the late 1980s. Slowly Yugoslavia fell apart as secessionist sentiment grew. A 1990 plebiscite in Slovenia voted overwhelmingly for independence from Yugoslavia, as did one in 1991 in Croatia. Slovenia effectively withdrew from Yugoslavia after brief fighting, but fierce hostilities broke out in Croatia. Both declared their independence, which was ultimately recognized by the European Union. The Bosnian Parliament declared Bosnia sovereign in 1991, and following a 1992 referendum, Bosnia declared itself independent. The United States and European Union states recognized the independence of the three new states in 1992.

With the encouragement and direction of Slobodan Milosevic, the Serbian president, the Serbian media stirred up nationalist feelings. With the break-up of Yugoslavia, the objectives of Serbia, including the Serbian-controlled JNA (Yugoslav People's Army) became the creation of a Serb-dominated western extension of Serbia to include Serb-dominated portions of Croatia and Bosnia, so as to form a new Yugoslavia with a substantially Serb population. But the large Muslim and Croat populations stood in the way. Hence it was deemed necessary to adopt the practice of ethnic cleansing. The media propaganda intensified and began to accuse non-Serbs of plotting genocide against Serbs. Serbs were told that they had to protect themselves against a fundamentalist Muslim threat. The message from the Government of Serbia was, as the tribunal's opinion put it, 'relentless', 'cogent and potent'.

By the end of 1991, Serb autonomous regions in Bosnia had been formed. Serb leadership, the JNA and paramilitary organizations, and special police units began to establish physical and political control over municipalities, sometimes by rigged plebiscites. In March 1992, a Serb Republic of Bosnia (*Republika Srpska*) was formed as a distinct political entity. The JNA, once a multi-ethnic national army although with a disproportionately Serb officer corps, became the instrument of policy of the new rump Federal Republic of Yugoslavia (consisting of Serbia and Montenegro). Gradually only ethnic Serbs were recruited into the armed forces. In late 1991, military units were formed in Serb-populated villages in Bosnia and supplied with weapons. Bosnian Serbs joined such distinct units as well as the JNA. More reliance came to be put on Serb paramilitary forces recruited in Serbia and Montenegro, and used to control non-Serb communities in Bosnia. Such forces acted in conjunction with the JNA.

By mid 1992 there were substantial international demands, including a Security Council resolution, that the JNA quit Bosnia. Serbia responded by ordering all non-Bosnian Serbs in the JNA to serve elsewhere, and by directing to Bosnia all Bosnian Serbs who served in the JNA. The eventual new army of Republika Srpska retained close contacts with and received weapons and funding from the JNA and its successor in the Former Yugoslavia, the VJ (Vojska Jugoslavije, Armed Forces of Yugoslavia).

As the Serb takeover of Serb-dominated areas continued, shelling and round-ups of non-Serbs intensified, leading to many civilian deaths and the flight of non-Serbs, who were forced to meet in stated assembly areas for expulsion from the area. The Prijedor district was important because of its location as part of a land corridor between Serb-dominated areas. Before the fighting and expulsions, Bosnian Muslims were a slight majority in the area. Careful Serbian planning preceded the takeover of the town of Prijedor, and the joining of Prijedor to a Serb region that was part of Republika Srpska. An attack on the nearby town of Kozarac, also in Prijedor municipality and with a concentrated Muslim population, led to great destruction and many deaths. The non-Serb population was effectively expelled. Severe restrictions were imposed on the movement of non-Serbs throughout the region, and forms of economic discrimination were instituted. Massive destruction of Muslim religious and cultural sites began. The population of Bosnian Muslims in the Prijedor district fell from about 50,000 to 6,000.

Thousands of Muslim and Croat civilians were confined to camps in Omarska, a former mining complex near Prijedor, as well as other locations, and were subjected to severe mistreatment. The Trial Chamber heard testimony from about 30 witnesses who survived the brutality, and who reported the frequent killings and torture. Up to 3,000 prisoners were at Omarska at any one time. They were held in very confined space and forced to live in filth and stifling heat. They received one inadequate meal a day, if that. There was rampant sickness. Frequent interrogations included severe beatings and injuries. Prisoners were summoned to be attacked with sticks and iron bars with nails. Bodies were slashed with knives. Many prisoners who were summoned never returned. Women were routinely summoned at night and raped. Dead bodies were a frequent sight. Prisoners heard bursts of machine gun fire in one situation, and were called the next morning to load over 150 bodies on a truck.

Tadic

Doško Tadic was born in 1955 in Kozarac, to a prominent Serb family. He joined the Serb nationalist party in 1990. After the ethnic cleansing of Kozarac was completed, he became a political leader of the town. The military tried several times to enlist him, and he was indeed arrested or threatened with arrest several times by the military police. In June 1993 he was mobilized and posted to the war zone. He managed to escape several times, and ultimately fled to Germany, where he was arrested by German authorities in 1994 on suspicion of having committed offences at the Omarska camp that constituted crimes under German law. The ICTY then issued a formal request to Germany (as contemplated by the Statute and Rules of the ICTY) for deferral of its intended prosecution and surrender of Tadic to the tribunal. Germany enacted the necessary legislation for his surrender (distinct from normal extradition to another state), and Tadic was transferred in 1995 to a UN detention unit in the Hague.

The indictment by the Prosecutor against Tadic and a co-accused charged them with 132 counts involving grave breaches of the Geneva Conventions, violations of the laws or customs of war, and crimes against humanity.

Findings of Fact

The Trial Chamber considered separately each count of the indictment. It discussed the events alleged, the role of Tadic in those events, and the case for the defence. It then made findings of fact, leaving legal issues such as interpretation of the relevant articles of the Tribunal's Statute for the end of the opinion.

Paragraph 7 of the indictment, for example, concerned events in Omarska prison camp. The cruel conduct alleged in some of the many counts in this paragraph included:

> A prisoner was frequently summoned for severe beatings. On one occasion, he was made to go on a hangar floor 'and there for up to half an hour was kicked and beaten by a group of soldiers armed with metal rods and metal cables. Then he was suspended upside down from an overhead gantry for some minutes.' As a result he suffered head fractures, a wasted hand, an injured spine and damage to his kidneys.
>
> A prisoner was struck as he entered the hangar floor. Another prisoner saw him being slashed with a knife and having black liquid poured over him. A third witness saw him being beaten with an iron bar and falling to the floor. This prisoner was never seen again.
>
> Two prisoners were forced to jump into an inspection pit with a third prisoner who was naked and bloody from beatings. One prisoner was ordered 'to suck his penis and then to bite his testicles. Meanwhile a group of men in uniform stood around the inspection pit watching and shouting to bite harder'. One prisoner was made to bite the other's testicles until he bit one testicle off and spat it out. He was then told that he was free to leave.

The opinion reviewed in detail the testimony of each of the witnesses. The defence of the accused to these counts was principally by way of alibi. Tadic said that he never visited the Omarska camp and on the day in question was living in Prijedor and working as a traffic policeman.

In its findings of fact, the tribunal considered all elements of the defence position, and pointed out where prosecution witnesses were vague or seriously inconsistent with each other. Nevertheless, there was 'much evidence from many witnesses' that Tadic was indeed in the Omarska camp on the relevant day. The Trial Chamber was 'satisfied beyond reasonable doubt' that Tadic was among the group beating several of the named prisoners, and that he attacked another prisoner with a knife; and that Tadic was present on the hangar floor on the occasion of the sexual assault on and mutilation of prisoners. The Trial Chamber was 'not satisfied that [Tadic] took any active part' in those assaults and mutilation. However, Tadic's lack of active participation did not preclude the Trial Chamber from finding that he knowingly encouraged or supported the acts and holding that Tadic was liable for having 'intentionally assisted directly and substantially in the common purpose of inflicting physical suffering upon them and thereby aided and abetted in the commission of the crimes'.

Paragraph 4 of the indictment covered events at different locations in the Prijedor district. Several counts alleged that Serb forces including Tadic destroyed and plundered Muslim and Croat residential areas, imprisoned thousands under brutal conditions, and deported or expelled the majority of Muslim and Croat residents of the district. Muslims and Croats inside and outside the camp were subjected to a 'campaign of terror which included killings, torture, sexual assaults, and other physical and psychological abuse'. There was abundant testimony of systematic rape, often repetitive rape of the same victim, attended by great humiliation and cruelty, and sometimes followed by killing.

The Trial Chamber found beyond reasonable doubt that Tadic had participated in many of these events, and that he killed two Muslim policemen in Kozarac. All these events occurred 'within the context of an armed conflict'. Again the legal issues were reserved.

The Trial Chamber described the policy of discrimination instituted against non-Serbs, of which the camps were the most striking illustration. Those remaining were often required to wear white armbands and were continuously subject to beatings and terror tactics. Derogatory, denigrating curse words were common, and non-Serbs were forced to sing Serb nationalist songs. On various counts, the Trial Chamber found beyond a reasonable doubt that Tadic committed acts falling within this pattern of discrimination on religious and political grounds.

Legal Issues Relating to the Offences Charged

The Trial Chamber addressed several legal issues concerning Tadic's acts. Two of the most important issues concerned grave breaches of the Geneva Conventions and the mens rea required for crimes against humanity.

Article 2. The opinion referred to the view of the Appeals Chamber that the Statute restricted prosecution of grave breaches to those committed against 'persons . . . protected under the provisions of the relevant Geneva Conventions'. The Fourth Geneva Convention dealing with civilian populations was directly on point. Under Article 4(1) of the Civilians Convention, protected persons are 'those who, at a given moment and in any manner whatsoever, find themselves, in case of a conflict or occupation, in the hands of a Party to the conflict or Occupying Power of which they are not nationals'. That requirement led the Trial Chamber to inquire whether the armed Serbian groups in Bosnia were under such control from the Federal Republic of Yugoslavia (FRY) that acts of such groups could be imputed to Yugoslavia's government. That the JNA played a role of 'vital importance' in establishing, supplying, maintaining and staffing local Serbian military groups was in itself 'not enough'. It was necessary to show that the FRY government continued to 'exercise effective control' over the operations of such groups.

The Trial Chamber concluded that there was 'no evidence' on which it could state that the armed forces of the *Republika Srpska* 'were anything more than mere allies, albeit highly dependent allies', of the [FRY] Government. Hence the non-Serb civilian population of Bosnia, although it enjoyed the protection of prohibitions contained in Common Article 3 of the Geneva Conventions applicable to all armed conflict, did not benefit from the grave breaches regime of Article 2. It could not be said that the civilian victims 'were at any relevant time in the hands of a party to the conflict of which they were not nationals'. Hence the Trial Chamber found Tadic not guilty with respect to all charges based on grave breaches of the Geneva Conventions.

Article 5. The opinion traced the development of the concept of crimes against humanity from Nuremberg to the present, and underscored such crimes' status as part of customary law. It repeated the statement in an earlier decision of the Appeals Chamber that it was now a 'settled rule of customary international law that crimes against humanity do not require a connection to international armed conflict'. The Trial Chamber stated, 'it is the occurrence of the act within the context of a widespread or systematic attack on a civilian population that makes the act a crime against humanity as opposed to simply a war crime or crime against national penal legislation, thus adding an additional element, and therefore in addition to the intent to commit the underlying offence the perpetrator must know of the broader context in which his act occurs'. The opinion stated that, to constitute a crime against humanity, the perpetrator 'does not commit his act for purely personal motives completely unrelated to the attack on the civilian population'. At another point the opinion stated, 'the act must not be taken for purely personal reasons unrelated to the armed conflict'. However, the Trial Chamber found that Tadic did not act for personal motives, and found him guilty of crimes against humanity beyond a reasonable doubt.

After analyzing other components of the charges, the Trial Chamber found Tadic guilty on numerous counts including Article 5, but not guilty with respect to charges under Article 2 and with respect to several other counts.

The Appeals Chamber in its Judgment of 15 July 1999 reversed several holdings of the Trial Chamber. The opinion of the Appeals Chamber follows.

PROSECUTOR V. TADIC

Appeals Chamber, International Criminal Tribunal for the Former Yugoslavia, Case No. IT-94–1-AR72, 15 July 1999, http://www.un.org/icty/tadic/appeal/judgement/index.htm

[Before reaching legal questions involving the definition of protected persons, the Appeals Chamber held that the armed forces of the *Republika Srpska* constituted a *de facto* organ of the FRY. The Appeals Chamber explained that the Trial Chamber applied an excessively strict test of state responsibility. The Appeals Chamber held that the appropriate test required the FRY to possess only 'overall control' of the Bosnian Serb forces. Under this more lenient standard, the acts of the armed forces of Republika Srpska could be attributed to the FRY.]

IV. [Whether the Victims Were 'Protected Persons' under Article 2 of the Statute]

5. The Status of the Victims

163. Having established that in the circumstances of the case the first of the two requirements set out in Article 2 of the Statute for the grave breaches provisions to be applicable, namely, that the armed conflict be international, was fulfilled, the Appeals Chamber now turns to the second requirement, that is, whether the victims of the alleged offences were "protected persons".

(a) The Relevant Rules

164. Article 4(1) of Geneva Convention IV (protection of civilians), applicable to the case at issue, defines "protected persons" — hence possible victims of grave

breaches — as those "in the hands of a Party to the conflict or Occupying Power of which they are not nationals". In other words, subject to the provisions of Article 4(2),[1] the Convention intends to protect civilians (in enemy territory, occupied territory or the combat zone) who do not have the nationality of the belligerent in whose hands they find themselves, or who are stateless persons. In addition, as is apparent from the preparatory work, the Convention also intends to protect those civilians in occupied territory who, while having the nationality of the Party to the conflict in whose hands they find themselves, are refugees and thus no longer owe allegiance to this Party and no longer enjoy its diplomatic protection (consider, for instance, a situation similar to that of German Jews who had fled to France before 1940, and thereafter found themselves in the hands of German forces occupying French territory).

165. Thus already in 1949 the legal bond of nationality was not regarded as crucial and allowance was made for special cases. In the aforementioned case of refugees, the lack of both allegiance to a State and diplomatic protection by this State was regarded as more important than the formal link of nationality.[2] In the cases provided for in Article 4(2), in addition to nationality, account was taken of the existence or non-existence of diplomatic protection: nationals of a neutral State or a co-belligerent State are not treated as "protected persons" unless they are deprived of or do not enjoy diplomatic protection. In other words, those nationals are not "protected persons" as long as they benefit from the normal diplomatic protection of their State; when they lose it or in any event do not enjoy it, the Convention automatically grants them the status of "protected persons".

166. This legal approach, hinging on substantial relations more than on formal bonds, becomes all the more important in present-day international armed conflicts. While previously wars were primarily between well-established States, in modern inter-ethnic armed conflicts such as that in the former Yugoslavia, new States are often created during the conflict and ethnicity rather than nationality may become the grounds for allegiance. Or, put another way, ethnicity may become determinative of national allegiance. Under these conditions, the requirement of nationality is even less adequate to define protected persons. In such conflicts, not only the text and the drafting history of the Convention but also, and more importantly, the Convention's object and purpose suggest that allegiance to a Party to the conflict and, correspondingly, control by this Party over persons in a given territory, may be regarded as the crucial test.

[1] Article 4(2) of the Civilians Convention provides:

"Nationals of a State which is not bound by the Convention are not protected by it. Nationals of a neutral State who find themselves in the territory of a belligerent State, and nationals of a co-belligerent State, shall not be regarded as protected persons while the State of which they are nationals has normal diplomatic representation in the State in whose hands they are."

[2] In a corresponding footnote, the Appeals Chamber reproduced Articles 44 and 70(2) of the Civilians Convention. Article 44 provides:

"In applying the measures of control mentioned in the present Convention, the Detaining Power shall not treat as enemy aliens exclusively on the basis of their nationality de jure of an enemy State, refugees who do not, in fact, enjoy the protection of any government."

Article 70(2) provides:

"Nationals of the Occupying Power who, before the outbreak of hostilities, have sought refuge in the territory of the occupied State, shall not be arrested, prosecuted, convicted or deported from the occupied territory, except for the offences committed after the outbreak of hostilities, or for offences under common law committed before the outbreak of hostilities which, according to the law of the occupied State, would have justified extradition in time of peace."

(b) Factual Findings

167. In the instant case the Bosnian Serbs, including the Appellant, arguably had the same nationality as the victims, that is, they were nationals of Bosnia and Herzegovina. However, it has been shown above that the Bosnian Serb forces acted as de facto organs of another State, namely, the FRY. Thus the requirements set out in Article 4 of Geneva Convention IV are met: the victims were "protected persons" as they found themselves in the hands of armed forces of a State of which they were not nationals.

168. It might be argued that before 6 October 1992, when a "Citizenship Act" was passed in Bosnia and Herzegovina, the nationals of the FRY had the same nationality as the citizens of Bosnia and Herzegovina, namely the nationality of the Socialist Federal Republic of Yugoslavia. Even assuming that this proposition is correct, the position would not alter from a legal point of view. As the Appeals Chamber has stated above, Article 4 of Geneva Convention IV, if interpreted in the light of its object and purpose, is directed to the protection of civilians to the maximum extent possible. It therefore does not make its applicability dependent on formal bonds and purely legal relations. Its primary purpose is to ensure the safeguards afforded by the Convention to those civilians who do not enjoy the diplomatic protection, and correlatively are not subject to the allegiance and control, of the State in whose hands they may find themselves. In granting its protection, Article 4 intends to look to the substance of relations, not to their legal characterisation as such.

169. Hence, even if in the circumstances of the case the perpetrators and the victims were to be regarded as possessing the same nationality, Article 4 would still be applicable. Indeed, the victims did not owe allegiance to (and did not receive the diplomatic protection of) the State (the FRY) on whose behalf the Bosnian Serb armed forces had been fighting.

C. Conclusion

170. It follows from the above that the Trial Chamber erred in so far as it acquitted the Appellant on the sole ground that the grave breaches regime of the Geneva Conventions of 1949 did not apply.

. . .

VI. [Whether Crimes Against Humanity can be Committed for Purely Personal Motives]

. . .

A. Submissions of the Parties

1. The Prosecution Case

240. The Prosecution submits that there is nothing in Article 5 of the Statute which suggests that it contains a requirement that crimes against humanity cannot be committed for purely personal motives. In the submission of the Prosecution, no such requirement can be inferred from the requirement that the crime must have a nexus to the armed conflict. In fact, to read the armed conflict requirement as requiring that the perpetrator's motives not be purely personal "would [. . .]

transform this merely jurisdictional limitation under Article 5 into a substantive element of the mens rea of crimes against humanity".

...

242. The Prosecution argues that the weight of authority supports the proposition that crimes against humanity can be committed for purely personal reasons and that... [s]ubsequent decisions of the United States military tribunals under Control Council Law No.10 and of national courts are also consistent with the view that a perpetrator of crimes against humanity may act out of purely personal motives.

243. Finally, the Prosecution contends that the object and purpose of the Tribunal's Statute support the interpretation that crimes against humanity may be committed for purely personal reasons, arguing that the objective of the Statute in providing a broad scope for humanitarian law would be defeated by a narrow interpretation of the category of offences falling within the ambit of Article 5. Furthermore, if proof of a non-personal motive was required, many perpetrators of crimes against humanity could evade conviction by the International Tribunal simply by invoking purely personal motives in defence of their conduct.

2. The Defence Case

...

245. The Defence contests the interpretation given to the applicable case law by the Prosecution, arguing that in all the cases cited, the defendants were linked to the system of extermination which formed the underlying predicate of crimes against humanity, and therefore did not commit their crimes for purely personal motives. In other words, the activities of the defendants were linked to the general activities comprising the pogroms against the Jews and thus the Defence submits that the acts of the defendants were not acts committed for purely personal reasons.

246. The Defence also contests the Prosecution's submissions regarding the object and purpose of the Statute of the International Tribunal, arguing, to the contrary, that policy suggests that it would be unjust if a perpetrator of a criminal act guided solely by personal motives was instead to be prosecuted for a crime against humanity.

B. Discussion

247. Neither Party asserts that the Trial Chamber's finding that crimes against humanity cannot be committed for purely personal motives had a bearing on the verdict.... Nevertheless this is a matter of general significance for the Tribunal's jurisprudence. It is therefore appropriate for the Appeals Chamber to set forth its views on this matter.

1. Article 5 of the Statute

248. The Appeals Chamber agrees with the Prosecution that there is nothing in Article 5 to suggest that it contains a requirement that crimes against humanity cannot be committed for purely personal motives. The Appeals Chamber agrees that it may be inferred from the words "directed against any civilian population" in Article 5 of the Statute that the acts of the accused must comprise part of a pattern of widespread or systematic crimes directed against a civilian population and that the accused

must have known that his acts fit into such a pattern. There is nothing in the Statute, however, which mandates the imposition of a further condition that the acts in question must not be committed for purely personal reasons, except to the extent that this condition is a consequence or a re-statement of the other two conditions mentioned.

249. The Appeals Chamber would also agree with the Prosecution that the words "committed in armed conflict" in Article 5 of the Statute require nothing more than the existence of an armed conflict at the relevant time and place. The Prosecution is, moreover, correct in asserting that the armed conflict requirement is a jurisdictional element, not "a substantive element of the mens rea of crimes against humanity" (i.e., not a legal ingredient of the subjective element of the crime).

250. This distinction is important because, as stated above, if the exclusion of "purely personal" behaviour is understood simply as a re-statement of the two-fold requirement that the acts of the accused form part of a context of mass crimes and that the accused be aware of this fact, then there is nothing objectionable about it; indeed it is a correct statement of the law. It is only if this phrase is understood as requiring that the motives of the accused ("personal reasons", in the terminology of the Trial Chamber) not be unrelated to the armed conflict that it is erroneous. Similarly, that phrase is unsound if it is taken to require proof of the accused's motives, as distinct from the intent to commit the crime and the knowledge of the context into which the crime fits.

251. As to what the Trial Chamber understood by the phrase "purely personal motives", it is clear that it conflated two interpretations of the phrase: first, that the act is unrelated to the armed conflict, and, secondly, that the act is unrelated to the attack on the civilian population. In this regard, paragraph 659 of the Judgement held:

> 659. Thus if the perpetrator has knowledge, either actual or constructive, that these acts were occurring on a widespread or systematic basis and does not commit his act for purely personal motives completely unrelated to the attack on the civilian population, that is sufficient to hold him liable for crimes against humanity. Therefore the perpetrator must know that there is an attack on the civilian population, know that his act fits in with the attack and the act must not be taken for purely personal reasons unrelated to the armed conflict. (emphasis added)

Thus the "attack on the civilian population" is here equated to "the armed conflict". The two concepts cannot, however, be identical because then crimes against humanity would, by definition, always take place in armed conflict, whereas under customary international law these crimes may also be committed in times of peace. So the two — the "attack on the civilian population" and "the armed conflict" — must be separate notions, although of course under Article 5 of the Statute the attack on "any civilian population" may be part of an "armed conflict". A nexus with the accused's acts is required, however, only for the attack on "any civilian population". A nexus between the accused's acts and the armed conflict is not required, as is instead suggested by the Judgement. The armed conflict requirement is satisfied by proof that there was an armed conflict; that is all that the Statute requires, and in so doing, it requires more than does customary international law.

. . .

2. The Object and Purpose of the Statute

253. The Prosecution has submitted that "the object and purpose of the Statute support the interpretation that crimes against humanity can be committed for purely personal reasons". The Prosecution cites the Tadic Decision on Jurisdiction, to the effect that "the 'primary purpose' of the establishment of the International Tribunal 'is not to leave unpunished any person guilty of [a] serious violation [of international humanitarian law], whatever the context within which it may have been committed' ". This begs the question, however, whether a crime committed for purely personal reasons is a crime against humanity, and therefore a serious violation of international humanitarian law under Article 5 of the Statute.

254. The Appeals Chamber would also reject the Prosecution's submission concerning the onerous evidentiary burden which would be imposed on it in having to prove that the accused did not act from personal motives, as equally question-begging and inapposite. It is question-begging because if, arguendo, under international criminal law, the fact that the accused did not act from purely personal motives was a requirement of crimes against humanity, then the Prosecution would have to prove that element, whether it was onerous for it to do so or not. The question is simply whether or not there is such a requirement under international criminal law.

3. Case-law as Evidence of Customary International Law

255. Turning to the further submission of the Prosecution, the Appeals Chamber agrees that the weight of authority supports the proposition that crimes against humanity can be committed for purely personal reasons...

256. In this regard, it is necessary to review the case-law... to establish whether this case-law is indicative of the emergence of a norm of customary international law on this matter.

257. The Prosecution is correct in stating that the 1948 case cited by the Trial Chamber supports rather than negates the proposition that crimes against humanity may be committed for purely personal motives, provided that the acts in question were knowingly committed as "part and parcel of all the mass crimes committed during the persecution of the Jews". As the Supreme Court for the British Zone stated, "in cases of crimes against humanity taking the form of political denunciations, only the perpetrator's consciousness and intent to deliver his victim through denunciation to the forces of arbitrariness or terror are required".

...

259. The Prosecution's submission finds further support in other so-called denunciation cases rendered after the Second World War by the Supreme Court for the British Zone and by German national courts, in which private individuals who denounced others, albeit for personal reasons, were nevertheless convicted of crimes against humanity.

260. In *Sch.*, the accused had denounced her landlord solely "out of revenge and for the purpose of rendering him harmless" after tensions in their tenancy had arisen. The denunciation led to investigation proceedings by the Gestapo which ended with the landlord's conviction and execution. The Court of First Instance

convicted Sch. and sentenced her to three years' imprisonment for crimes against humanity. The accused appealed against the decision, arguing that "crimes against humanity were limited to participation in mass crimes and . . . did not include all those cases in which someone took action against a single person for personal reasons". The Supreme Court dismissed the appeal, holding that neither the Nuremberg Judgement nor the statements of the Prosecutor before the International Military Tribunal indicated that Control Council Law No. 10 had to be interpreted in such a restrictive way. The Supreme Court stated:

> [T]he International Military Tribunal and the Supreme Court considered that a crime against humanity as defined in CCL 10 Article II 1 (c) is committed whenever the victim suffers prejudice as a result of the National Socialist rule of violence and tyranny ("Gewalt-oder Willkürherrschaft") to such an extent that mankind itself was affected thereby. Such prejudice can also arise from an attack committed against an individual victim for personal reasons. However, this is only the case if the victim was not only harmed by the perpetrator — this would not be a matter which concerned mankind as such — but if the character, duration or extent of the prejudice were determined by the National Socialist rule of violence and tyranny or if a link between them existed. If the victim was harmed in his or her human dignity, the incident was no longer an event that did not concern mankind as such. If an individual's attack against an individual victim for personal reasons is connected to the National Socialist rule of violence and tyranny and if the attack harms the victim in the aforementioned way, it, too, becomes one link in the chain of the measures which under the National Socialist rule were intended to persecute large groups among the population. There is no apparent reason to exonerate the accused only because he acted against an individual victim for personal reasons.

261. This view was upheld in a later decision of the Supreme Court in the case of *H.* H. denounced his father-in-law, V.F., for listening to a foreign broadcasting station, allegedly because V.F., who was of aristocratic origin, incessantly mocked H. for his low birth and tyrannised the family with his relentlessly scornful behaviour. The family members supposedly considered a denunciation to be the only solution to their family problems. Upon the denunciation, V.F. was sentenced by the Nazi authorities to three years in prison. V.F., who suffered from an intestinal illness, died in prison. Despite the fact that H.'s denunciation was motivated by personal reasons, the Court of First Instance sentenced H. for a crime against humanity, stating that "it can be left open as to whether [. . .] H. was motivated by political, personal or other reasons". Referring to the established jurisprudence of the Supreme Court for the British Zone, the Court of First Instance held that "the motives ("Beweggründe") prompting a denunciation are not decisive (nicht entscheidend)".

. . .

263. Turning to the decisions of the United States military tribunals under Control Council Law No. 10 cited by the Prosecution, it must be noted that they appear to be less pertinent. These cases involve Nazi officials of various ranks whose acts were, therefore, by that token, already readily identifiable with the Nazi regime of terror. The question whether they acted "for personal reasons" would, therefore,

not arise in a direct manner, since their acts were carried out in an official capacity, negating any possible "personal" defence which has as its premise "non-official acts". The question whether an accused acted for purely personal reasons can only arise where the accused can claim to have acted as a private individual in a private or non-official capacity. This is why the issue arises mainly in denunciation cases, where one neighbour or relative denounces another. This paradigm is, however, inapplicable to trials of Nazi ministers, judges or other officials of the State, particularly where they have not raised such a defence by admitting the acts in question whilst claiming that they acted for personal reasons. Any plea that an act was done for "purely personal" motives and that it therefore cannot constitute a crime against humanity is pre-eminently for the defence to raise and one would not expect the court to rule on the issue proprio motu and as obiter dictum.

...

268. ... The Appeals Chamber believes, however, that a further reason why this was not in issue is precisely because motive is generally irrelevant in criminal law, as the Prosecution pointed out in the hearing of 20 April 1999:

> For example, it doesn't matter whether or not an accused steals money in order to buy Christmas presents for his poor children or to support a heroin habit. All we're concerned with is that he stole and he intended to steal, and what we're concerned with...here is the same sort of thing. There's no requirement for non-personal motive beyond knowledge of the context of a widespread or systematic act into which an accused's act fits. The Prosecutor is submitting that, as a general proposition and one which is applicable here, motives are simply irrelevant in criminal law.

269. The Appeals Chamber approves this submission, subject to the caveat that motive becomes relevant at the sentencing stage in mitigation or aggravation of the sentence (for example, the above mentioned thief might be dealt with more leniently if he stole to give presents to his children than if he were stealing to support a heroin habit). Indeed the inscrutability of motives in criminal law is revealed by the following reductio ad absurdum. Imagine a high-ranking SS official who claims that he participated in the genocide of the Jews and Gypsies for the "purely personal" reason that he had a deep-seated hatred of Jews and Gypsies and wished to exterminate them, and for no other reason. Despite this quintessentially genocidal frame of mind, the accused would have to be acquitted of crimes against humanity because he acted for "purely personal" reasons. Similarly, if the same man said that he participated in the genocide only for the "purely personal" reason that he feared losing his job, he would also be entitled to an acquittal. Thus, individuals at both ends of the spectrum would be acquitted. In the final analysis, any accused that played a role in mass murder purely out of self-interest would be acquitted. This shows the meaninglessness of any analysis requiring proof of "non-personal" motives.

...

271. The Trial Chamber correctly recognised that crimes which are unrelated to widespread or systematic attacks on a civilian population should not be prosecuted as crimes against humanity. Crimes against humanity are crimes of a special nature to which a greater degree of moral turpitude attaches than to an ordinary crime.

Thus to convict an accused of crimes against humanity, it must be proved that the crimes were related to the attack on a civilian population (occurring during an armed conflict) and that the accused knew that his crimes were so related.

272. For the above reasons, however, . . . the requirement that an act must not have been carried out for the purely personal motives of the perpetrator does not form part of the prerequisites necessary for conduct to fall within the definition of a crime against humanity under Article 5 of the Tribunal's Statute.

COMMENT ON SIGNIFICANCE OF NATIONALITY

[The nationality test for protected persons received further elaboration in a subsequent decision of the Appeals Chamber, *Prosecutor v. Delalic & Others*, Judgment, Case No. IT-96–21-A (2001) (Celebici camp case). The case involved a prison camp, which held Bosnian Serb detainees near the town of Celebici in central Bosnia and Herzegovina. The defendants included a Bosnian Muslim commander, a deputy commander, and a guard who all served at the camp. The defendants urged the Appeals Chamber to revisit its analysis in *Tadic* on the grounds that they shared the same Bosnian nationality as the alleged victims and that the alleged acts occurred completely within Bosnia and Herzegovina. They contended that the nationality requirement in the Fourth Geneva Convention was specifically intended to preclude application of the grave breaches regime to such internal situations. The Trial Chamber had rejected the defendants' claims, stating, *inter alia*, that a more flexible interpretation of the nationality requirement 'is fully in accordance with the development of the human rights doctrine which has been increasing in force since the middle of this century. It would be incongruous with the whole concept of human rights, which protect individuals from the excesses of their own governments, to rigidly apply the nationality requirement of article 4, that was apparently inserted to prevent interference in a State's relations with its own nationals'. Excerpts of the Appeals Chamber opinion follow.]

. . .

11. The appellants submit that "the traditional rules of treaty interpretation" should be applied to interpret strictly the nationality requirement set out in Article 4 of Geneva Convention IV. The word "national" should therefore be interpreted according to its natural and ordinary meaning. The appellants submit in addition that if the Geneva Conventions are now obsolete and need to be updated to take into consideration a "new reality", a diplomatic conference should be convened to revise them.

12. The Prosecution on the other hand contends that the Vienna Convention on the Law of Treaties of 1969 provides that the ordinary meaning is the meaning to be given to the terms of the treaty in their context and in the light of their object and purpose. It is submitted that the Appeals Chamber in *Tadic* found that the legal bond of nationality was not regarded as crucial in 1949, i.e., that there was no intention at the time to determine that nationality was the sole criteria. In addition,

adopting the appellants' position would result in the removal of protections from the Geneva Conventions contrary to their very object and purpose.

13. The argument of the appellants relates to the interpretative approach to be applied to the concept of nationality in Geneva Convention IV. The appellants and the Prosecution both rely on the Vienna Convention in support of their contentions. The Appeals Chamber agrees with the parties that it is appropriate to refer to the Vienna Convention as the applicable rules of interpretation, and to Article 31 in particular, which sets forth the general rule for the interpretation of treaties . The Appeals Chamber notes that it is generally accepted that these provisions reflect customary rules. The relevant part of Article 31 reads as follows:

> A treaty shall be interpreted in good faith in accordance with the ordinary meaning to be given to the terms of the treaty in their context and in the light of its object and purpose.

14. The Vienna Convention in effect adopted a textual, contextual and a teleological approach of interpretation, allowing for an interpretation of the natural and ordinary meaning of the terms of a treaty in their context, while having regard to the object and purpose of the treaty.

...

24. Relying on the ICRC Commentary to Article 4 of Geneva Convention IV, the appellants further argue that international law cannot interfere in a State's relations with its own nationals, except in cases of genocide and crimes against humanity. In the appellants' view, in the situation of an internationalised armed conflict where the victims and the perpetrators are of the same nationality, the victims are only protected by their national laws.

25. The purpose of Geneva Convention IV in providing for universal jurisdiction only in relation to the grave breaches provisions was to avoid interference by domestic courts of other States in situations which concern only the relationship between a State and its own nationals. The ICRC Commentary (GC IV), referred to by the appellants, thus stated that Geneva Convention IV is "faithful to a recognised principle of international law: it does not interfere in a State's relations with its own nationals". The Commentary did not envisage the situation of an internationalised conflict where a foreign State supports one of the parties to the conflict, and where the victims are detained because of their ethnicity, and because they are regarded by their captors as operating on behalf of the enemy. In these circumstances, the formal national link with Bosnia and Herzegovina cannot be raised before an international tribunal to deny the victims the protection of humanitarian law. It may be added that the government of Bosnia and Herzegovina itself did not oppose the prosecution of Bosnian nationals for acts of violence against other Bosnians based upon the grave breaches regime.

26. It is noteworthy that, although the appellants emphasised that the "nationality" referred to in Geneva Convention IV is to be understood as referring to the legal citizenship under domestic law, they accepted at the hearing that in the former Yugoslavia "nationality", in everyday conversation, refers to ethnicity.

27. The Appeals Chamber agrees with the Prosecution that depriving victims, who arguably are of the same nationality under domestic law as their captors, of the

protection of the Geneva Conventions solely based on that national law would not be consistent with the object and purpose of the Conventions. Their very object could indeed be defeated if undue emphasis were placed on formal legal bonds, which could also be altered by governments to shield their nationals from prosecution based on the grave breaches provisions of the Geneva Conventions. A more purposive and realistic approach is particularly apposite in circumstances of the dissolution of Yugoslavia, and in the emerging State of Bosnia and Herzegovina where various parties were engaged in fighting, and the government was opposed to a partition based on ethnicity, which would have resulted in movements of population, and where, ultimately, the issue at stake was the final shape of the State and of the new emerging entities.

28. In *Tadic*, the Appeals Chamber, relying on a teleological approach, concluded that formal nationality may not be regarded as determinative in this context, whereas ethnicity may reflect more appropriately the reality of the bonds...

29. As found in previous Appeals Chamber jurisprudence, Article 4 of Geneva Convention IV is to be interpreted as intending to protect civilians who find themselves in the midst of an international, or internationalised, conflict to the maximum extent possible. The nationality requirement of Article 4 should therefore be ascertained upon a review of "the substance of relations" and not based on the legal characterisation under domestic legislation. In today's ethnic conflicts, the victims may be "assimilated" to the external State involved in the conflict, even if they formally have the same nationality as their captors, for the purposes of the application of humanitarian law, and of Article 4 of Geneva Convention IV specifically....

30. ...The nationality of the victims for the purpose of the application of Geneva Convention IV should not be determined on the basis of formal national characterisations, but rather upon an analysis of the substantial relations, taking into consideration the different ethnicity of the victims and the perpetrators, and their bonds with the foreign intervening State.

...

43. ...As submitted by the Prosecution, the Trial Chamber correctly sought to establish whether the victims could be regarded as belonging to the opposing side of the conflict.

44. The Appeals Chamber particularly agrees with the Trial Chamber's finding that the Bosnian Serb victims should be regarded as protected persons for the purposes of Geneva Convention IV because they "were arrested and detained mainly on the basis of their Serb identity" and "they were clearly regarded by the Bosnian authorities as belonging to the opposing party in an armed conflict and as posing a threat to the Bosnian State".

...

QUESTIONS

1. 'It is clear that Tadic, a mere foot soldier in these sordid events, was selected for prosecution because the Tribunal did not have custody of a higher ranking, more significant figure. There were hundreds or thousands of people like Tadic, starting with his close

companions in perpetrating the horrors described in the opinion. What is the point of convicting one among them in what seems to be a mere lottery?' Comment.

2. 'It is wrong to imagine the prosecution of Tadic as serving the goal of individualizing guilt, so as to overcome notions of collective guilt and allow peoples like the Serbs to get on with their lives after the war. Tadic is part of a system. His guilt is deeply linked to the guilt of the larger bloody scheme in which he played a role. The opinion indicts an entire leadership and those who executed its plans. These are not the isolated, deviant crimes of murder or torture or rape that occur within all countries and that are sensibly punished as such.' Comment. Also specifically consider this statement in light of the essay by Martti Koskenniemi. Does the prosecution of individuals like Tadic constitute a 'way of distributing accountability' that obscures the systemic causes of atrocities committed during such a conflict?

3. Should individuals who act for purely personal motives be liable for crimes against humanity? Do they deserve the same condemnation, under international criminal law, accorded to perpetrators who are primarily motivated by an interest in advancing the overall attack against the civilian population? Should the definition of elements of the crime be altered if proving the lack of personal motives would impose a highly onerous burden on the prosecution?

4. Is the Appeals Chamber's interpretation of the nationality requirement for 'protected persons' convincing? Is it appropriate for the ICTY to engage in this form of 'flexible' interpretation? What are the perils of this interpretive approach? What are the advantages?

5. Observers have described the aims of the international criminal tribunals in ways that evoke traditional notions of the aims of the criminal law generally, but that also address specific characteristics of this conflict. Consider:

a. *Deterrence.* Whom is the Tribunal attempting to deter: the present leaders in this conflict, or those who might instigate and commit crimes in future conflicts? Should different strategies be at work to achieve one or the other goal? Who indeed can be deterred in an ethnic conflict stirring such deep hatreds and cruel actions — only the leaders, or also the foot soldiers who commit many of the atrocities? Is a court the most effective instrument of deterrence, or does the Tribunal play this role because of failure of other means of addressing the conflict?

b. *Punishment-retribution.* How can the Tribunal best serve this function? Is symbolic justice through the conviction and imprisonment of a small number of people (in relation to the number of people committing the international crimes defined by the Statute) sufficient to create a broad sense of justice among the conflict's victims? What other means (shy of forceful intervention) are available to help build this sense of justice?

c. *Reconciliation*, long-term peace and stability. Can reconciliation and a 'true' lasting peace be achieved partly through the work of the Tribunal? What role are convictions and imprisonment likely to play in this process of reconciliation in comparison with, for example, a Serbian–Bosnian settlement on issues like territorial control and resettlement or an international agreement on compensation of victims that may permit them to get on with their lives?

6. How do you understand the savage cruelty shown by the Serbian captors to their prisoners? (The same question can be put to many parties to ethnic and other conflicts, such as the Rwandan conflict, as well as to members of majority or powerful groups that behave in physically cruel ways to the despised and dehumanized minority or powerless groups.) Is encouragement or condoning of such behaviour by those in charge meant to serve a purpose, like ethnic cleansing? Meant to humiliate? Does the context of weapons and force and killing encourage release of this base side of human nature, in the sense that violence dissolves all bonds and restraints? Is such mass conduct in the context of mass violence deterrable?

NOTE

By Resolution 955 (1994), the Security Council established the International Criminal Tribunal for Rwanda (ICTR) to prosecute persons 'responsible for genocide and other serious violations of international humanitarian law' committed principally in that country in 1994. The new tribunal has the same appeals chamber as the ICTY, but separate trial chambers. The ICTR and ICTY also shared the same chief prosecutor until September 2003, at which point the Security Council appointed separate prosecutors for the two tribunals.

The preamble to Resolution 955 stated that the Council was convinced that prosecution of those responsible for serious violations 'would contribute to the process of national reconciliation and to the restoration and maintenance of peace', and would contribute to 'ensuring that such violations . . . are halted and effectively redressed'.

The Council, 'acting under Chapter VII of the Charter', adopted the annexed Statute of the ICTR, excerpts from which appear below.

STATUTE OF THE INTERNATIONAL TRIBUNAL FOR RWANDA

reprinted in 33 I.L.M. 1590 (1994)

Article 1 — Competence of the International Tribunal for Rwanda

The International Tribunal for Rwanda shall have the power to prosecute persons responsible for serious violations of international humanitarian law committed in the territory of Rwanda and Rwandan citizens responsible for such violations committed in the territory of neighbouring States between 1 January 1994 and 31 December 1994 . . .

Article 2 — Genocide

[The definition of genocide is identical to Article 4 of the ICTY Statute, p. 1252, *supra.*]

Article 3 — Crimes against Humanity

The International Tribunal for Rwanda shall have the power to prosecute persons responsible for the following crimes when committed as part of a widespread or systematic attack against any civilian population on national, political, ethnic, racial or religious grounds:

(a) Murder;

(b) Extermination;

(c) Enslavement;

(d) Deportation;

(e) Imprisonment;

(f) Torture;

(g) Rape;

(h) Persecutions on political, racial and religious grounds;

(i) Other inhumane acts.

Article 4 — Violations of Article 3 common to the Geneva Conventions and of Additional Protocol II

The International Tribunal for Rwanda shall have the power to prosecute persons committing or ordering to be committed serious violations of Article 3 common to the Geneva Conventions of 12 August 1949 for the Protection of War Victims, and of Additional Protocol II thereto of 8 June 1977. These violations shall include, but shall not be limited to:

(a) Violence to life, health and physical or mental well-being of persons, in particular murder as well as cruel treatment such as torture, mutilation or any form of corporal punishment;

(b) Collective punishments;

(c) Taking of hostages;

(d) Acts of terrorism;

(e) Outrages upon personal dignity, in particular humiliating and degrading treatment, rape, enforced prostitution and any form of indecent assault;

(f) Pillage;

(g) The passing of sentences and the carrying out of executions without previous judgment pronounced by a regularly constituted court, affording all the judicial guarantees which are recognized as indispensable by civilized peoples;

(h) Threats to commit any of the foregoing acts.

Article 6: Individual Criminal Responsibility

1. A person who planned, instigated, ordered, committed or otherwise aided and abetted in the planning, preparation or execution of a crime referred to in Articles 2 to 4 of the present Statute, shall be individually responsible for the crime.

...

3. The fact that any of the acts referred to in Articles 2 to 4 of the present Statute was committed by a subordinate does not relieve his or her superior of criminal responsibility if he or she knew or had reason to know that the subordinate was about to commit such acts or had done so and the superior failed to take the necessary and reasonable measures to prevent such acts or to punish the perpetrators thereof.

...

[Many articles in the ICTR Statute are identical to the equivalent articles in the ICTY Statute, p. 1251, *supra*, including articles on personal jurisdiction, individual criminal responsibility, concurrent jurisdiction, *non-bis-in-idem*, investigation and preparation of indictment, review of the indictment, commencement and conduct of trial proceedings, rights of the accused, protection of victims and witnesses, judgment, penalties, appellate proceedings, enforcement of sentences, cooperation and judicial assistance, and expenses of the tribunal.]

NOTE

One of the novel features of the indictments and opinions of the ICTY and ICTR has been the strong attention to sexual crimes, particularly systematic sexual violence against women. Mass rape and other organized forms of sexual violence and humiliation have been frequent, and often used as instruments of fear, shame and ethnic cleansing. Rape itself, long unmentioned in definitions of crimes in the humanitarian law of war, is included in the definition of several crimes in the two statutes. Note the attention to sexual violence against women in the *Akayesu* opinion below.

PROSECUTOR V. AKAYESU

Trial Chamber, International Criminal Tribunal for Rwanda, 1998
Case No. ICTR-96–4-T http://www.ictr.org/ENGLISH/cases/Akayesu/judgement/akay001.htm

[The trial of Jean-Paul Akayesu resulted in the first conviction for genocide by an international court. The indictment charged Akayesu, a Hutu, with genocide, crimes against humanity and violations of Article 3 common to the Geneva Conventions, punishable under Articles 2–4 of the ICTR Statute. All alleged acts took place in Rwanda during 1994. The country is divided into 11 prefectures, which are subdivided into communes placed under the authority of bourgmestres (mayors). From April 1993 to June 1994, Akayesu served as bourgmestre of the Taba commune.

There were 15 counts in the indictment. Some illustrative charges follow: (1) At least 2,000 Tutsis were killed in Taba from April to June 1994. Killings were so open and widespread that the defendant 'must have known about them', but despite his authority and responsibility, he never attempted to prevent the killings. (2) Hundreds of displaced Tutsi civilians sought refuge at the bureau communal. Females among them were regularly taken by the armed local militia and subjected to sexual violence, including multiple rapes. Civilians were frequently murdered on or near the communal premises. Akayesu knew of these events and at times was present during their commission. That presence and his failure to attempt to prevent 'encouraged these activities'. (3) At meetings, Akayesu 'urged the population to eliminate accomplices of the RPF, which was understood by those present to mean Tutsis.... The killing of Tutsis in Taba began shortly after the meeting.' He also 'named at least three prominent Tutsis... who had to be killed because of their alleged relationships with the RPF'. Two of them were soon killed. (4) Akayesu ordered and participated in the kill.ing of three brothers, and took eight detained men from the bureau communal and ordered militia members to kill them. (5) He ordered local people to kill intellectuals and influential people. On his instructions, five secondary school teachers were killed.

The Trial Chamber found it 'necessary to say, however briefly, something about the history of Rwanda, beginning from the pre-colonial period up to 1994'. Prior to and during colonial rule (first under Germany, and from 1917 until independence under Belgium), Rwanda was an advanced monarchy ruled by the monarch's representatives drawn from the Tutsi nobility. The Trial Chamber further explained:

> In those days, the distinction between the Hutu and Tutsi was based on lineage rather than ethnicity. Indeed, the demarcation line was blurred: one could move from one status to another, as one became rich or poor, or even through marriage.
>
> Both German and Belgian colonial authorities, if only at the outset as far as the latter are concerned, relied on an elite essentially composed of people who referred to themselves as Tutsi, a choice which, according to Dr. Alison Desforges, was born of racial or even racist considerations. In the minds of the colonizers, the Tutsi looked more like them, because of their height and colour, and were, therefore, more intelligent and better equipped to govern.
>
> In the early 1930s, Belgian authorities introduced a permanent distinction by dividing the population into three groups which they called ethnic groups, with the Hutu representing about 84% of the population, while the Tutsi (about 15%) and Twa (about 1%) accounted for the rest. In line with this division, it became mandatory for every Rwandan to carry an identity card mentioning his or her ethnicity. The Chamber notes that the reference to ethnic background on identity cards was maintained, even after Rwanda's independence and was, at last, abolished only after the tragic events the country experienced in 1994.

The Chamber explained that the Tutsi were more willing to be converted to Christianity; hence the church too supported their monopoly of power. The Trial Chamber also quoted the following testimony from Dr. Alison Desforges, an expert witness:

> The primary criterion for [defining] an ethnic group is the sense of belonging to that ethnic group. It is a sense which can shift over time.... But, if you fix any given

> moment in time, and you say, how does this population divide itself, then you will see which ethnic groups are in existence in the minds of the participants at that time.... [R]eality is an interplay between the actual conditions and peoples' subjective perception of those conditions. In Rwanda, the reality was shaped by the colonial experience which imposed a categorization which was probably more fixed, and not completely appropriate to the scene.... The categorisation imposed at that time [by the Belgians] is what people of the current generation have grown up with. They have always thought in terms of these categories, even if they did not in their daily lives have to take cognizance of that.... [T]his division into three ethnic groups became an absolute reality.

When the Tutsi led campaigns for independence, the allegiance of the colonizer shifted to the Hutu. In the 1950s, elections were held and political parties were formed. The Hutu held a clear majority in voting power. Violence broke out between Hutu and Tutsi. Independence was attained in 1962. In 1975, a one-party system was instituted under (Hutu) President Habyarimana, whose policies became increasingly anti-Tutsi through discriminatory quota systems and other methods. In 1991, following violence and growing pressures, Habyarimana accepted a multi-party system.

Many Tutsi in exile formed a political organization and a military wing, the Rwandan Patriotic Army (RPA). Their aim was to return to Rwanda. Violence, negotiations and accords led to the participation of the Tutsi political organization (RPF) in the government institutions. Hard-line Hutu formed a radical political party, more extremist than Habyarimana. There were growing extremist calls for elimination of the Tutsi.

The Arusha accords between the Government and the RPF in 1993 brought temporary relief from the threat of war. The climate worsened with assassinations, and the accords were denounced. Habyarimana died in an air crash, of unknown cause, in April 1994. The Rwandan army, Presidential Guard and militia immediately started killing Tutsi, as well as Hutu who were sympathetic to the Arusha accords and to power-sharing between Tutsi and Hutu. Belgian soldiers and a small UN peacekeeping force were withdrawn from the country. RPF troops resumed open war against Rwandan armed forces. The killing campaign against the Tutsi reached its zenith in a matter of weeks, and continued to July. The estimated dead in the conflict at that time, overwhelmingly Tutsi, ranged from 500,000 to 1,000,000.]

❀ ❀ ❀

112. As regards the massacres which took place in Rwanda between April and July 1994, as detailed above in the chapter on the historical background to the Rwandan tragedy, the question before this Chamber is whether they constitute genocide. Indeed, it was felt in some quarters that the tragic events which took place in Rwanda were only part of the war between the Rwandan Armed Forces (the RAF) and the Rwandan Patriotic Front (RPF)....

...

118. In the opinion of the Chamber, there is no doubt that considering their undeniable scale, their systematic nature and their atrociousness, the massacres were aimed at exterminating the group that was targeted.... In this connection,

Alison Desforges, an expert witness, in her testimony before this Chamber... stated as follows: "on the basis of the statements made by certain political leaders, on the basis of songs and slogans popular among the Interahamwe, I believe that these people had the intention of completely wiping out the Tutsi from Rwanda so that-as they said on certain occasions — their children , later on , would not know what a Tutsi looked like, unless they referred to history books"....

119. ... Dr. Zachariah also testified that the Achilles' tendons of many wounded persons were cut to prevent them from fleeing. In the opinion of the Chamber, this demonstrates the resolve of the perpetrators of these massacres not to spare any Tutsi....

120. Dr. Alison Desforges testified that many Tutsi bodies were often systematically thrown into the Nyabarongo river, a tributary of the Nile. Indeed, this has been corroborated by several images shown to the Chamber throughout the trial....

121. ... even newborn babies were not spared. Even pregnant women, including those of Hutu origin, were killed on the grounds that the foetuses in their wombs were fathered by Tutsi men, for in a patrilineal society like Rwanda, the child belongs to the father's group of origin....

122. In light of the foregoing, it is now appropriate for the Chamber to consider the issue of specific intent that is required for genocide (mens rea or dolus specialis). In other words, it should be established that the above-mentioned acts were targeted at a particular group as such. In this respect also, many consistent and reliable testimonies... agree on the fact that it was the Tutsi as members of an ethnic group... who were targeted during the massacres.

123. ... the propaganda campaign conducted before and during the tragedy by the audiovisual media,... or the print media, like the Kangura newspaper.... overtly called for the killing of Tutsi, who were considered as the accomplices of the RPF and accused of plotting to take over the power lost during the revolution of 1959....

...

126. Consequently, the Chamber concludes from all the foregoing that genocide was, indeed, committed in Rwanda in 1994 against the Tutsi as a group....

127. ... as to whether the tragic events that took place in Rwanda in 1994 occurred solely within the context of the conflict between the RAF and the RPF, the Chamber replies in the negative, since it holds that the genocide did indeed take place against the Tutsi group, alongside the conflict. The execution of this genocide was probably facilitated by the conflict, in the sense that the fighting against the RPF forces was used as a pretext for the propaganda inciting genocide against the Tutsi...

128. ... The accused himself stated during his initial appearance before the Chamber, when recounting a conversation he had with one RAF officer and... a leader of the Interahamwe, that the acts perpetrated by the Interahamwe against Tutsi civilians were not considered by the RAF officer to be of a nature to help the government armed forces in the conflict with the RPF.... The Chamber's opinion is that the genocide was organized and planned not only by members of the RAF, but also by the political forces who were behind the "Hutu-power", that it was executed essentially by civilians including the armed militia and even ordinary citizens, and above all, that the majority of the Tutsi victims were non-combatants, including thousands of women and children, even foetuses....

5. *Factual Findings*

[The Chamber noted that in addition to testimony of witnesses, it would take 'judicial notice' of UN reports extensively documenting the massacres of 1994. Its listing included reports of a Commission of Experts established by a Security Council resolution, of a special rapporteur of the Secretary General, and of the High Commissioner for Human Rights. Note that the 'factual findings' *infra* are relevant to determining whether the conditions stated in several articles of the ICTR Statute were met.]

...

178. The Chamber now considers paragraph 12 of the Indictment, which alleges the responsibility of the Accused, his knowledge of the killings which took place in Taba between 7 April and the end of June 1994, and his failure to attempt to prevent these killings or to call for assistance from regional or national authorities.

...

184. There is a substantial amount of evidence establishing that before 18 April 1994 the Accused did attempt to prevent violence from taking place in the commune of Taba. Many witnesses testified to the efforts of the Accused to maintain peace in the commune and that he opposed by force the Interahamwe's attempted incursions into the commune to ensure that the killings which had started in Kigali on 7 April 1994 did not spread to Taba. Witness W testified that on the order of the Accused to the population that they must resist these incursions, members of the Interahamwe were killed. Witness K testified that Taba commune was calm during the period when Akayesu wanted that there be calm. She said he would gather the population in a meeting and tell them that they had to be against the acts of violence in the commune....

185. The Accused testified that he asked for three gendarmes at the meeting with the Prime Minister in Gitarama on 18 April 1994, to help him maintain order and security and to stop the killing of Tutsi.... Given the accused's testimony on this point, and its corroboration in part by the sole prosecution witness who was present at the Murambi meeting, the accused's version of events — that he did call for assistance from the national and regional authorities — must be credited.

186. Moreover, Defence witness DAAX, the former prefect of Gitarama supports the accused's account. Witness DAAX testified that he convened three meetings of bourgmestres between 6 April 1994 and 18 April 1994... At this third meeting, the prefect testified, the accused took the floor and complained of the problems of security in his commune, in common with the Prefect and other bourgmestres. Witness DAAX's testimony agrees with that of the accused that the Prime Minister did not reply directly to the bourgmestre's expressions of concern about security in their Communes, but that he rather read parts of a prepared policy speech and threatened the complaining bourgmestres with dismissal. Witness DAAX further testified that at least one bourgmestre, the bourgmestre of Mugina, was killed shortly after the meeting as a result. Witness DAAX also testified that the accused had to flee his commune due to pressure from the Interahamwe at some point between 6 April 1994 and 18 April 1994.... Witness DAAX said the Accused never officially requested gendarmes from him, unlike the bourgmestre of Mugina....

187. A substantial amount of evidence has been presented indicating that the conduct of the Accused did, however, change significantly after the meeting on 18 April 1994, and many witnesses ... testified to the collaboration of the Accused with the Interahamwe in Taba after this date. Witness A testified that he was surprised to see that the Accused had become a friend of the Interahamwe. The Accused contends that he was overwhelmed. Witness DAX and Witness DBB, both witnesses for the Defence, testified that the Interahamwe threatened to kill the Accused if he did not cooperate with them. The Accused testified that he was coerced by the Interahamwe ...

188. The Chamber recognises the difficulties a bourgmestre encountered in attempting to save lives of Tutsi in the period in question. Prosecution witness R, who was the bourgmestre of another commune, ... He averred that a bourgmestre could do nothing openly to combat the killings after that date or he would risk being killed; what little he could do had to be done clandestinely. The Defence case is that this is precisely what the accused did.

189. Defence witnesses, DAAX, DAX, DCX, DBB and DCC confirm that the accused failed to prevent killings after 18 April 1994 and expressed the opinion that it was not possible for him to do anything with ten communal policemen at his disposal against more than a hundred Interahamwe.

190. The Defence contends that, despite pressure from the Interahamwe, the Accused continued to save lives after 18 April 1994. There is some evidence on this matter ...

191. There is also evidence indicating that after 18 April 1994, there were people that came to the Accused for help, and he turned them away, and there is evidence that the Accused witnessed, participated in, supervised, and even ordered killings in Taba. Witness JJ testified that after her arrival at the bureau communal, where she came to seek refuge, she went to the Accused on behalf of a group of refugees, begging him to kill them with bullets so that they would not be hacked to death with machetes. She said he asked his police officers to chase them away and said that even if there were bullets he would not waste them on the refugees.

192. The Chamber finds that the allegations set forth in paragraph 12 cannot be fully established. The Accused did take action between 7 April and 18 April to protect the citizens of his commune. It appears that he did also request assistance from national authorities at the meeting on 18 April 1994....

193. Nevertheless, the Chamber finds beyond a reasonable doubt that the conduct of the Accused changed after 18 April 1994 and that after this date the Accused did not attempt to prevent the killing of Tutsi in the commune of Taba. In fact, there is evidence that he not only knew of and witnessed killings, but that he participated in and even ordered killings.... The Accused contends that he was subject to coercion, but the Chamber finds this contention greatly inconsistent with a substantial amount of concordant testimony from other witnesses. It is also inconsistent with his own pre-trial written statement. Witness C testified to having heard the accused say to an Interahamwe "I do not think that what we are doing is proper. We are going to have to pay for this blood that is being shed..", a statement which indicates the Accused's knowledge of the wrongfulness of his acts and his awareness of the consequences of his deeds. For these reasons, the Chamber does

not accept the testimony of the Accused regarding his conduct after 18 April, and finds beyond a reasonable doubt that he did not attempt to prevent killings of Tutsi after this date. Whether he had the power to do so is not at issue, as he never even tried and as there is evidence establishing beyond a reasonable doubt that he consciously chose the course of collaboration with violence against Tutsi rather than shielding them from it.

...

[The Chamber continued in its examination of each count of the indictment and, after presenting testimony of witnesses, made findings of fact. Several counts dealt with sexual violence. Some of the Chamber's findings follow.]

449. ...Chamber finds that there is sufficient credible evidence to establish beyond a reasonable doubt that during the events of 1994, Tutsi girls and women were subjected to sexual violence, beaten and killed on or near the bureau communal premises, as well as elsewhere in the commune of Taba.... Hundreds of Tutsi, mostly women and children, sought refuge at the bureau communal during this period and many rapes took place on or near the premises of the bureau communal... Witness JJ was also raped repeatedly on two separate occasions in the cultural center on the premises of the bureau communal, once in a group of fifteen girls and women and once in a group of ten girls and women.... The Chamber notes that much of the sexual violence took place in front of large numbers of people, and that all of it was directed against Tutsi women.

450. ...There is no suggestion in any of the evidence that the Accused or any communal policemen perpetrated rape,...

...

452. On the basis of the evidence set forth herein, the Chamber finds beyond a reasonable doubt that the Accused had reason to know and in fact knew that sexual violence was taking place on or near the premises of the bureau communal, and that women were being taken away from the bureau communal and sexually violated. There is no evidence that the Accused took any measures to prevent acts of sexual violence or to punish the perpetrators of sexual violence. In fact there is evidence that the Accused ordered, instigated and otherwise aided and abetted sexual violence.... On the two occasions Witness JJ was brought to the cultural center of the bureau communal to be raped, she and the group of girls and women with her were taken past the Accused, on the way. On the first occasion he was looking at them, and on the second occasion he was standing at the entrance to the cultural center. On this second occasion, he said, "Never ask me again what a Tutsi woman tastes like." Witness JJ described the Accused in making these statements as "talking as if someone were encouraging a player." More generally she stated that the Accused was the one "supervising" the acts of rape.

...

6. The Law

...

471. The Accused is charged under Article 6(1) of the Statute of the Tribunal with individual criminal responsibility for the crimes alleged in the Indictment.

With regard to Counts . . . on sexual violence, the Accused is charged additionally, or alternatively, under Article 6(3) . . . . Article 6(1) sets forth the basic principles of individual criminal liability, which are undoubtedly common to most national criminal jurisdictions. Article 6(3), by contrast, constitutes something of an exception to the principles articulated in Article 6(1), as it derives from military law, namely the principle of the liability of a commander for the acts of his subordinates or "command responsibility".

. . .

488. There are varying views regarding the mens rea required for command responsibility.

. . .

489. . . . it is certainly proper to ensure that there has been malicious intent, or, at least, ensure that negligence was so serious as to be tantamount to acquiescence or even malicious intent.

490. As to whether the form of individual criminal responsibility referred to Article 6 (3) of the Statute applies to persons in positions of both military and civilian authority, it should be noted that during the Tokyo trials, certain civilian authorities were convicted of war crimes under this principle. Hirota, former Foreign Minister of Japan, was convicted of atrocities — including mass rape — committed in the "rape of Nanking", under a count which charged that he had "recklessly disregarded their legal duty by virtue of their offices to take adequate steps to secure the observance and prevent breaches of the law and customs of war". . . .

It should, however, be noted that Judge Röling strongly dissented . . . and held that Hirota should have been acquitted. Concerning the principle of command responsibility as applied to a civilian leader, Judge Röling stated that:

> "Generally speaking, a Tribunal should be very careful in holding civil government officials responsible for the behaviour of the army in the field. Moreover, the Tribunal is here to apply the general principles of law as they exist with relation to the responsibility for omissions'. Considerations of both law and policy, of both justice and expediency, indicate that this responsibility should only be recognized in a very restricted sense".

491. The Chamber therefore finds that in the case of civilians, the application of the principle of individual criminal responsibility, enshrined in Article 6 (3), to civilians remains contentious. Against this background, the Chamber holds that it is appropriate to assess on a case by case basis the power of authority actually devolved upon the Accused in order to determine whether or not he had the power to take all necessary and reasonable measures to prevent the commission of the alleged crimes or to punish the perpetrators thereof.

Genocide

498. Genocide is distinct from other crimes inasmuch as it embodies a special intent or dolus specialis. Special intent of a crime is the specific intention, required as a constitutive element of the crime, which demands that the perpetrator clearly seeks to produce the act charged. Thus, the special intent in the crime of genocide

lies in "the intent to destroy, in whole or in part, a national, ethnical, racial or religious group, as such".

. . .

523. On the issue of determining the offender's specific intent, the Chamber considers that intent is a mental factor which is difficult, even impossible, to determine. This is the reason why, in the absence of a confession from the accused, his intent can be inferred from a certain number of presumptions of fact. The Chamber considers that it is possible to deduce the genocidal intent inherent in a particular act charged from the general context of the perpetration of other culpable acts systematically directed against that same group, whether these acts were committed by the same offender or by others. Other factors, such as the scale of atrocities committed, their general nature, in a region or a country, or furthermore, the fact of deliberately and systematically targeting victims on account of their membership of a particular group, while excluding the members of other groups, can enable the Chamber to infer the genocidal intent of a particular act.

524. Trial Chamber I of the International Criminal Tribunal for the former Yugoslavia also stated that the specific intent of the crime of genocide

> "may be inferred from a number of facts such as the general political doctrine which gave rise to the acts possibly covered by the definition in Article 4, or the repetition of destructive and discriminatory acts. The intent may also be inferred from the perpetration of acts which violate, or which the perpetrators themselves consider to violate the very foundation of the group — acts which are not in themselves covered by the list in Article 4(2) but which are committed as part of the same pattern of conduct". . . .

Complicity in Genocide

525. Under Article 2(3)(e) of the Statute, the Chamber shall have the power to prosecute persons who have committed complicity in genocide. . . .

527. The Chamber notes that complicity is viewed as a form of criminal participation by all criminal law systems, notably, under the Anglo-Saxon system (or Common Law) and the Roman-Continental system (or Civil Law). Since the accomplice to an offence may be defined as someone who associates himself in an offence committed by another, complicity necessarily implies the existence of a principal offence.

528. According to one school of thought, complicity is borrowed criminality' (criminalité d'emprunt). In other words, the accomplice borrows the criminality of the principal perpetrator. By borrowed criminality, it should be understood that the physical act which constitutes the act of complicity does not have its own inherent criminality, but rather it borrows the criminality of the act committed by the principal perpetrator of the criminal enterprise. Thus, the conduct of the accomplice emerges as a crime when the crime has been consummated by the principal perpetrator. The accomplice has not committed an autonomous crime, but has merely facilitated the criminal enterprise committed by another.

. . .

530. Consequently, the Chamber is of the opinion that in order for an accused to be found guilty of complicity in genocide, it must, first of all, be proven beyond a reasonable doubt that the crime of genocide has, indeed, been committed.

. . .

538. The intent or mental element of complicity implies in general that, at the moment he acted, the accomplice knew of the assistance he was providing in the commission of the principal offence. In other words, the accomplice must have acted knowingly.

539. Moreover, as in all criminal Civil law systems, under Common law, notably English law, generally, the accomplice need not even wish that the principal offence be committed. In the case of *National Coal Board v. Gamble*, Justice Devlin stated

> "an indifference to the result of the crime does not of itself negate abetting. If one man deliberately sells to another a gun to be used for murdering a third, he may be indifferent about whether the third lives or dies and interested only the cash profit to be made out of the sale, but he can still be an aider and abettor."

In 1975, the English House of Lords also upheld this definition of complicity, when it held that willingness to participate in the principal offence did not have to be established. As a result, anyone who knowing of another's criminal purpose, voluntarily aids him or her in it, can be convicted of complicity even though he regretted the outcome of the offence.

. . .

547. Consequently, where a person is accused of aiding and abetting, planning, preparing or executing genocide, it must be proven that such a person acted with specific genocidal intent, i.e. the intent to destroy, in whole or in part, a national, ethnical, racial or religious group as such, whereas, as stated above, there is no such requirement to establish accomplice liability in genocide.

. . .

[Crimes against Humanity — Rape and other inhumane acts]

. . .

691. The Tribunal has found that the Accused had reason to know and in fact knew that acts of sexual violence were occurring on or near the premises of the bureau communal and that he took no measures to prevent these acts or punish the perpetrators of them. The Tribunal notes that it is only in consideration of Counts 13, 14 and 15 that the Accused is charged with individual criminal responsibility under Section 6(3) of its Statute. . . . Although the evidence supports a finding that a superior/subordinate relationship existed between the Accused and the Interahamwe who were at the bureau communal, the Tribunal notes that there is no allegation in the Indictment that the Interahamwe, who are referred to as "armed local militia," were subordinates of the Accused. This relationship is a fundamental element of the criminal offence set forth in Article 6(3). The amendment of the Indictment with additional charges pursuant to Article 6(3) could arguably be interpreted as implying an allegation of the command responsibility required by Article 6(3). In fairness to the Accused, the Tribunal will not make this inference. Therefore, the Tribunal

finds that it cannot consider the criminal responsibility of the Accused under Article 6(3).

...

694. The Tribunal finds, under Article 6(1) of its Statute, that the Accused, having had reason to know that sexual violence was occurring, aided and abetted ... acts of sexual violence, by allowing them to take place on or near the premises of the bureau communal and by facilitating the commission of such sexual violence through his words of encouragement in other acts of sexual violence which, by virtue of his authority, sent a clear signal of official tolerance for sexual violence, without which these acts would not have taken place ...

...

7.8. [Genocide and Complicity in Genocide]

...

704. The Chamber finds that, as pertains to the acts alleged in paragraph 12, it has been established that, throughout the period covered in the Indictment, Akayesu, in his capacity as bourgmestre, was responsible for maintaining law and public order in the commune of Taba and that he had effective authority over the communal police. Moreover, as "leader" of Taba commune, of which he was one of the most prominent figures, the inhabitants respected him and followed his orders. Akayesu himself admitted before the Chamber that he had the power to assemble the population and that they obeyed his instructions. It has also been proven that a very large number of Tutsi were killed in Taba between 7 April and the end of June 1994, while Akayesu was bourgmestre of the Commune. Knowing of such killings, he opposed them and attempted to prevent them only until 18 April 1994, date after which he not only stopped trying to maintain law and order in his commune, but was also present during the acts of violence and killings, and sometimes even gave orders himself for bodily or mental harm to be caused to certain Tutsi, and endorsed and even ordered the killing of several Tutsi.

705. In the opinion of the Chamber, the said acts indeed incur the individual criminal responsibility of Akayesu for having ordered, committed, or otherwise aided and abetted in the preparation or execution of the killing of and causing serious bodily or mental harm to members of the Tutsi group. Indeed, the Chamber holds that the fact that Akayesu, as a local authority, failed to oppose such killings and serious bodily or mental harm constituted a form of tacit encouragement, which was compounded by being present to such criminal acts.

...

728. ... The Chamber is of the opinion that it is possible to infer the genocidal intention that presided over the commission of a particular act, inter alia, from all acts or utterances of the accused, or from the general context in which other culpable acts were perpetrated systematically against the same group, regardless of whether such other acts were committed by the same perpetrator or even by other perpetrators.

729. First of all, regarding Akayesu's acts and utterances during the period relating to the acts alleged in the Indictment, the Chamber is satisfied beyond reasonable doubt, on the basis of all evidence brought to its attention during the trial, that on

several occasions the accused made speeches calling, more or less explicitly, for the commission of genocide.[3] . . .

730. . . . Owing to the very high number of atrocities committed against the Tutsi, their widespread nature not only in the commune of Taba, but also throughout Rwanda, and to the fact that the victims were systematically and deliberately selected because they belonged to the Tutsi group, with persons belonging to other groups being excluded, the Chamber is also able to infer, beyond reasonable doubt, the genocidal intent of the accused in the commission of the above-mentioned crimes.

731. With regard, particularly, to . . . rape and sexual violence, the Chamber wishes to underscore the fact that in its opinion, they constitute genocide in the same way as any other act as long as they were committed with the specific intent to destroy, in whole or in part, a particular group, targeted as such. Indeed, rape and sexual violence certainly constitute infliction of serious bodily and mental harm on the victims and are even, according to the Chamber, one of the worst ways of inflict harm on the victim as he or she suffers both bodily and mental harm. In light of all the evidence before it, the Chamber is satisfied that the acts of rape and sexual violence described above, were committed solely against Tutsi women, many of whom were subjected to the worst public humiliation, mutilated, and raped several times, often in public, in the Bureau Communal premises or in other public places, and often by more than one assailant. These rapes resulted in physical and psychological destruction of Tutsi women, their families and their communities. Sexual violence was an integral part of the process of destruction, specifically targeting Tutsi women and specifically contributing to their destruction and to the destruction of the Tutsi group as a whole.

732. The rape of Tutsi women was systematic and was perpetrated against all Tutsi women and solely against them. A Tutsi woman, married to a Hutu, testified before the Chamber that she was not raped because her ethnic background was unknown. As part of the propaganda campaign geared to mobilizing the Hutu against the Tutsi, the Tutsi women were presented as sexual objects. Indeed, the Chamber was told, for an example, that before being raped and killed, Alexia, who was the wife of the Professor, Ntereye, and her two nieces, were forced by the Interahamwe to undress and ordered to run and do exercises "in order to display the thighs of Tutsi women". The Interahamwe who raped Alexia said, as he threw her on the ground and got on top of her, "let us now see what the vagina of a Tutsi woman takes like". As stated above, Akayesu himself, speaking to the Interahamwe who were committing the rapes, said to them: "don't ever ask again what a Tutsi woman tastes like". This sexualized representation of ethnic identity graphically illustrates that tutsi women were subjected to sexual violence because they were Tutsi. Sexual violence was a step in the process of destruction of the tutsi group — destruction of the spirit, of the will to live, and of life itself.

[3] [Eds. Earlier in the opinion, the Trial Chamber stated that, in a speech delivered on 19 April 1994, Akayesu 'clearly urged the population to unite in order to eliminate what he termed the sole enemy: the accomplices of the Inkotanyi [described by the ICTR as a term for the RPF in its basic meaning and had a number of extended meanings including RPF sympathizer and potentially Tutsi as an ethnic group]' and that 'on the basis of consistent testimonies heard throughout the proceedings and the evidence of . . . [an] expert witness on linguistic matters, the Chamber is satisfied beyond a reasonable doubt that the population understood Akayesu's call as one to kill the Tutsi. Akayesu himself was fully aware of the impact of his speech on the crowd and of the fact that his call to fight against the accomplices of the Inkotanyi would be construed as a call to kill the Tutsi in general.']

733. On the basis of the substantial testimonies brought before it, the Chamber finds that in most cases, the rapes of Tutsi women in Taba, were accompanied with the intent to kill those women. Many rapes were perpetrated near mass graves where the women were taken to be killed. A victim testified that Tutsi women caught could be taken away by peasants and men with the promise that they would be collected later to be executed. Following an act of gang rape, a witness heard Akayesu say "tomorrow they will be killed" and they were actually killed. In this respect, it appears clearly to the Chamber that the acts of rape and sexual violence, as other acts of serious bodily and mental harm committed against the Tutsi, reflected the determination to make Tutsi women suffer and to mutilate them even before killing them, the intent being to destroy the Tutsi group while inflicting acute suffering on its members in the process.

734. In light of the foregoing, the Chamber finds firstly that the acts described supra are indeed acts as enumerated in Article 2 (2) of the Statute, which constitute the factual elements of the crime of genocide, namely the killings of Tutsi or the serious bodily and mental harm inflicted on the Tutsi. The Chamber is further satisfied beyond reasonable doubt that these various acts were committed by Akayesu with the specific intent to destroy the Tutsi group, as such.

[Akayesu appealed the Trial Chamber decision, though primarily on evidentiary and procedural grounds. In a decision issued in 2001, the Appeals Chamber affirmed the guilty verdict on all counts.]

QUESTIONS

1. Consider, as applied to the ICTR and the *Akayesu* decision, question 5 at p. 1272, supra.

2. The Trial Chamber discussed superior responsibility contained in Article 6(3) of the Statute. What are the requirements for establishing such responsibility? Does the tribunal's analysis go too far in suggesting Akayesu could have been found guilty under this rationale? Should a different standard apply to civilian, as opposed to military, leaders? Compare Article 28 of the Rome Statute of the International Criminal Court, p. 1297 *infra.*

3. Does the *Akayesu* opinion (as presented in these excerpts) broaden the crimes defined in the Statute to any considerable degree? How? In particular, how does the ICTR respond to the sexual cruelty to which Tutsi women were subjected? Does the record of systematic rape described in the opinion satisfy the elements of the crime of genocide? If not, should the definition of genocide be changed accordingly?

4. The ICTR concludes 'if the accused knowingly aided and abetted in the commission of... a murder while he knew or had reason to know that the principal was acting with genocidal intent, the accused would be an accomplice to genocide, even though he did not share the murderer's intent to destroy the group.' Does this rule seem appropriate? Does it relax the threshold of liability too far? Would it be more appropriate to require the accused possess specific genocidal intent? Should the individual at least know — not just

have reason to know — that the principle is acting with genocidal intent? Do these questions raise concerns similar to the concerns raised in question 3 following the *Celebici* opinion, p. 1272 *supra*, with respect to acts committed for purely personal motives as part of a crime against humanity?

BARBARA CROSSETTE, INQUIRY SAYS UN INERTIA IN '94 WORSENED GENOCIDE IN RWANDA

New York Times, 17 December 1999, at A1

A strongly worded report issued today by an international panel of experts holds both the United Nations and leading member countries, primarily the United States, responsible for failing to prevent end the genocide in Rwanda in 1994, which cost hundreds of thousands of lives.

The report, commissioned by Secretary General Kofi Annan, who was then head of the peacekeeping department, spares no one, naming those in the highest reaches of the United Nations who were running the operation in Rwanda, including Mr. Annan and his predecessor, Secretary General Boutros Boutros-Ghali.

Mr. Annan and others in his department made weak and equivocal decisions in the face of mounting disaster, the panel found. At the same time the Clinton administration . . . persistently played down the problem, setting the tone for a Security Council generally lacking the political will for a tougher response.

Both the United Nations and the United States sent the wrong message to militias bent on genocide, the report concluded. Today Mr. Annan called the report 'thorough and objective.' 'On behalf of the United Nations, I acknowledge this failure and express my deep remorse,' he said, calling the events in Rwanda 'genocide in its purest and most evil form'. . . .

. . . [T]he leader of the investigation, Ingvar Carlsson, a former Swedish prime minister, said it would 'always be difficult to explain' why the Security Council — managed by the world's major powers and not the United Nations bureaucracy — drastically cut the peacekeeping force in Rwanda, reducing it to a few hundred from 2,500 when the genocide began, and then increasing it to 5,500 when the weeks of massacres were over. The United States, . . . effectively blocked the Security Council in 1993 and 1994 from authorizing significant action in Rwanda. . . .

Today Mr. Carlsson repeated the Clinton administration's explanation that the loss of 18 American Rangers in Somalia in 1993 had scared the United States off peacekeeping, particularly in Africa, for domestic political reasons. . . . On a trip to Rwanda last year, President Clinton apologized for Washington's inaction. . . . The Rwanda report follows by several weeks the release of an internal United Nations inquiry into problems in the Bosnia peacekeeping operation that led to thousands of deaths in Serbian attacks on Bosnian Muslims in Srebrenica and other towns. That report also found fault with both the organization and Security Council members.

The report issued today shows a pattern of ignored warnings and missed signs of the genocide to come in Rwanda.... 'Information received by a United Nations mission that plans are being made to exterminate any group of people requires an immediate and determined response', the panel said.... In the bloody melee that followed [the very first steps in the genocide], groups of United Nations peacekeepers were rounded up by Rwandan Hutu troops and 10 Belgians were executed. The remaining Belgians, the best-qualified soldiers among the peacekeepers, were then abruptly withdrawn.

In the report, Belgium was criticized for this and for abandoning 2,000 civilians hiding in a technical school after telling them they would be protected. They were savagely attacked. The Belgian withdrawal prompted others to pull out, an action supported by the United States, the panel said....

JOSÉ ALVAREZ, CRIMES OF STATES/CRIMES OF HATE: LESSONS FROM RWANDA

24 Yale J. Int. L. 365 (1999), at 400

...[T]he West's complicity in the 1994 killings in Rwanda is a discomforting fact. The scale and seriousness of that complicity take various forms. At one level, certain European powers, namely the colonizers of Rwanda who imported their racist notions of 'superior races' to Rwanda, need to accept their responsibility for creating the 'tribalism without tribes' that helped make genocide possible and continues to characterize Rwanda today. Much greater blame can be attributed to those, like the French, who, in the 1990s and through the 1994 killings themselves, continued to befriend and arm the Habyarimana [Hutu] government. But the circle of blame extends much wider and includes Kofi Annan, who ignored warnings of the impeding genocide; all members of the U.N., and particularly the Security Council, who, in the wake of the fiasco of Somalia, failed to send the 5000 troops that, it is estimated, might have prevented the vast majority of the killings; and the international community as a whole, which, in the wake of the emergence of a new government in Rwanda after the genocide, ignored that new government's pleas for assistance but came to the aid of the Hutu killers in exile while failing to prevent their ongoing incursions into Rwanda to continue the genocide.

For all their attention to the attribution of individual blame for these crimes, international lawyers have not been attentive to these wider circles of guilt. In surreal fashion, international lawyers have argued that judges from some of the very countries that are regarded as partly 'to blame' for these crimes will be readily accepted as neutral arbitrators simply because they do not come from Rwanda. Blind to the colonial-era racism that helped to make the Rwandan genocide possible, and equally blind to the continuing insensitivities of the U.N. and its patrons since the genocide, international lawyers pin their hopes for verdicts that will be accepted as impartial on a U.N.-approved bench, simply because it does not contain a Hutu or a Tutsi. This seems a slim reed on which to rely. To the extent that the U.N., as an organization, was itself derelict in enforcing international humanitarian law, that fact is surely detrimental to the credibility of the ICTR's judgments.

...Knowledge of what led to the Rwandan killings as well as who is to blame in this wider sense strengthens the very premise that individuals must be held responsible. In addition, sensitivity to colonial-era racism and what has occurred in its wake prompts scrutiny of the policies now being touted by the U.N.'s Security Council with respect to Rwanda.... Those who were blind once to the important consequences of acting on the basis of ethnic prejudices could be wrong a second time when they insist that international trials should proceed as if the prejudices they helped to instill can be ignored.

...Knowledge of the West's complicity should make us skeptical of a scheme that would deny to the Rwandan government what each Western state has for centuries enjoyed, namely the right to try its own war criminals.

QUESTIONS

1. Accepting the report of the panel appointed by Kofi Annan and Alvarez's analysis, what follows from them? Do they lessen, or strengthen, the argument for individual punishment of those committing the genocide on the ground? Should they lead to criminal liability under international law of non-Rwandans who are implicated in some other way in the genocide? Against whom, and under what charges?

2. Does this analysis delegitimate the ICTR and its judgments if a panel of the Trial Chamber or the Appeal Chamber consists predominantly of non-African judges, particularly judges from the states that are alleged to bear responsibility? Does it point to resorting to the Rwandan judiciary rather than to an international tribunal — a small judiciary in a country where tens of thousands of prisoners have been long awaiting trial for the genocide? Would analogous problems to those described by Alvarez arise in constituting a judicial bench in state criminal proceedings in countries that have suffered massive tragedies in civil conflict or severe repression? Does the fact that a conflict or political represssion has a strong ethnic dimension in addition to its deep political divisions complicate such issues?

ADDITIONAL READING

Gary Jonathan Bass, *Stay the Hand of Vengeance: the Politics of War Crimes Tribunals* (2000); Theodor Meron, *War Crimes Law Comes of Age* (1998); Stephen Ratner and J. Abrams, *Accountability for Human Rights Atrocities in International Law* (1997); Samantha Power, *A Problem from Hell: America and the Age of Genocide* (2002); Romeo A. Dallaire, *Shake Hands with the Devil: The Failure of Humanity in Rwanda* (2004); Michael Scharf, *Balkan Justice: The Story Behind the First International War Crimes Tribunal since Nuremberg* (1997); Mohamed C. Othman, *Accountability for International Humanitarian Law Violations: The Case of Rwanda and East Timor* (2005); Virginia Morris and M. Scharf, *The International Criminal Tribunal for Rwanda* (1998); Eric Stover, *The Witnesses: War Crimes and the Promise of Justice in The Hague* (2005); Antonio Cassese, 'On the Current Trends towards Criminal Prosecution and Punishment of Breaches of International Humanitarian Law', 9 E.J. Int. L. 2 (1998); José Alvarez,

'Rush to Closure: Lessons of the Tadic Judgment', 96 Mich. L. Rev. 2031 (1998); Steven Ratner, 'New Democracies: Old Atrocities; An Inquiry in International Law', 87 Georgetown L.J. 707 (1999); Cherif Bassiouni, 'Strengthening the Norms of International Humanitarian Law to Combat Impunity', in Burns Weston and S. Marks (eds.), *The Future of International Human Rights* (1999); Symposium, 'Genocide, War Crimes, and Crimes against Humanity', 23 Fordham Int: L. J. 275–488 (1999); Chile Eboe-Osuji, "'Complicity in Genocide'" Versus "'Aiding And Abetting Genocide'" Construing the Difference in the ICTR and ICTY', 3 J. Int. Crim. Just. 56 (2005).

B. THE INTERNATIONAL CRIMINAL COURT

The idea of a permanent international criminal court has been a part of the human rights movement since 1948, when the General Assembly instructed the International Law Commission to study the possibility of establishing one. That initiative was rejuvenated following the end of the Cold War. In 1992, the General Assembly requested the Commission to draft a statute for a permanent criminal court. Those efforts led to a conference held in Rome in 1998, resulting in the adoption of the Statute for the International Criminal Court (ICC). In 2002, the ICC treaty came into force. As of January 2007, 104 states had ratified the treaty, including 26 of the 29 members of NATO (the three exceptions are the Czech Republic, Turkey and the United States). Other state parties include Afghanistan, Australia, Colombia, Central African Republic, Democratic Republic of the Congo, Georgia, Peru and Uganda. States that have not ratified the treaty include Chile, China, India, Indonesia, Iran, Israel, Pakistan, Russia, Rwanda, Sudan, Syria and Zimbabwe.

The first three cases taken up by the Court were the Democratic Republic of Congo (2004), Uganda (2004) and the Central African Republic (2005). The latter two were referred by the governments themselves. The first case, however, was initiated at least informally by the Prosecutor. According to an ICC Press Statement, 'In September 2003 the Chief Prosecutor informed the States Parties that he was ready to request authorization from the Pre-Trial Chamber to use his own powers to start an investigation, but that a referral and active support from the DRC would assist his work. In a letter in November 2003 the government of the DRC welcomed the involvement of the ICC and in March 2004 the DRC referred the situation in the country to the Court'. In March 2005, the Security Council referred the fourth case — the situation in Darfur — to the Court.

As of early 2007, the ICC had only one defendant in custody, a former leader of a militia group in the DRC, who is being tried for allegedly enlisting and conscripting children under the age of 15 years and using them to participate actively in hostilities. In late 2005, the Chief Prosecutor unsealed five warrants of arrest for leaders of the Lords Resistance Army, an armed rebel group fighting in Northern Uganda. In February 2007, the Chief Prosecutor released the first Darfur indictments. The indictments charged two individuals, the incumbent Minister for Humanitarian Affairs (formerly Minister of State for the Interior) and a leader of the Janjaweed militia group, with 51 counts of crimes against humanity and war crimes.

The following excerpts from the Rome Statute include crimes that are within the substantive jurisdiction of the Court, procedural requirements for the exercise of jurisdiction, and standards of liability.

ROME STATUTE OF THE INTERNATIONAL CRIMINAL COURT

37 I.L.M. 999 (1998)

Article 5 — Crimes within the jurisdiction of the Court

1. ... The Court has jurisdiction in accordance with this Statute with respect to the following crimes: (a) The crime of genocide; (b) Crimes against humanity; (c) War crimes; (d) The crime of aggression.

2. The Court shall exercise jurisdiction over the crime of aggression once a provision is adopted in accordance with articles 121 and 123 defining the crime and setting out the conditions under which the Court shall exercise jurisdiction with respect to this crime. Such a provision shall be consistent with the relevant provisions of the Charter of the United Nations.

Article 6 — Genocide

[This section repeats Article 2 of the Genocide Convention, as did the Statutes for the ICTY and ICTR.]

Article 7 — Crimes against humanity

1. For the purpose of this Statute, 'crime against humanity' means any of the following acts when committed as part of a widespread or systematic attack directed against any civilian population, with knowledge of the attack:

(a) Murder;
(b) Extermination;
(c) Enslavement;
(d) Deportation or forcible transfer of population;
(e) Imprisonment or other severe deprivation of physical liberty in violation of fundamental rules of international law;
(f) Torture;
(g) Rape, sexual slavery, enforced prostitution, forced pregnancy, enforced sterilization, or any other form of sexual violence of comparable gravity;
(h) Persecution against any identifiable group or collectivity on political, racial, national, ethnic, cultural, religious, gender as defined in paragraph 3, or other grounds that are universally recognized as impermissible under international law, in connection with any act referred to in this paragraph or any crime within the jurisdiction of the Court;
(i) Enforced disappearance of persons;
(j) The crime of apartheid;

(k) Other inhumane acts of a similar character intentionally causing great suffering, or serious injury to body or to mental or physical health. . . .

2. For the purpose of paragraph 1:

(a) 'Attack directed against any civilian population' means a course of conduct involving the multiple commission of acts referred to in paragraph 1 against any civilian population, pursuant to or in furtherance of a State or organizational policy to commit such attack;

. . .

3. For the purpose of this statute, it is understood that the term 'gender' refers to the two sexes, male and female, within the context of society. The term 'gender' does not indicate any meaning different from the above.

Article 8 — War crimes

1. The Court shall have jurisdiction in respect of war crimes in particular when committed as part of a plan or policy or as part of a large-scale commission of such crimes.
2. For the purpose of this Statute, 'war crimes' means:

(a) Grave breaches of the Geneva Conventions of 12 August 1949 namely, any of the following acts against persons or property protected under the provisions of the relevant Geneva Convention:
   (i) Wilful killing;
   (ii) Torture or inhuman treatment, including biological experiments;
   (iii) Wilfully causing great suffering, or serious injury to body or health;
   (iv) Extensive destruction and appropriation of property, not justified by military necessity and carried out unlawfully and wantonly;
   (v) Compelling a prisoner of war or other protected person to serve in the forces of a hostile Power;
   (vi) Wilfully depriving a prisoner of war or other protected person of the rights of fair and regular trial;
   (vii) Unlawful deportation or transfer or unlawful confinement;
   (viii) Taking of hostages.

(b) Other serious violations of the laws and customs applicable in international armed conflict, within the established framework of international law, namely, any of the following acts: [the designated acts include intentionally directing attacks against a civilian population as such, against civilian objects that are not military objectives, or against a humanitarian assistance or peacekeeping mission in accordance with the UN Charter; killing or wounding combatants who have surrendered; transfer by an Occupying Power of part of its own civilian population into territory it occupies, or deporting the population of the occupied territory outside the territory; employing poisonous gases or weapons that cause superfluous injury or unnecessary suffering; committing rape, sexual slavery, or forced pregnancy.]

[Section (c), concerning armed conflict not of an international character, is omitted.] ...

Article 11 — Jurisdiction ratione temporis

1. The Court has jurisdiction only with respect to crimes committed after the entry into force of this Statute.

2. If a State becomes a Party to this Statute after its entry into force, the Court may exercise its jurisdiction only with respect to crimes committed after the entry into force of this Statute for that State, unless that State has made a declaration under article 12, paragraph 3.

Article 12 — Preconditions to the exercise of jurisdiction

1. A State which becomes a Party to this Statute thereby accepts the jurisdiction of the Court with respect to the crimes referred to in article 5.

2. In the case of article 13, paragraph (a) or (c), the Court may exercise its jurisdiction if one or more of the following States are Parties to this Statute or have accepted the jurisdiction of the Court in accordance with paragraph 3:

(a) The State on the territory of which the conduct in question occurred or, if the crime was committed on board a vessel or aircraft, the State of registration of that vessel or aircraft;

(b) The State of which the person accused of the crime is a national.

3. If the acceptance of a State which is not a Party to this Statute is required under paragraph 2, that State may, by declaration lodged with the Registrar, accept the exercise of jurisdiction by the Court with respect to the crime in question. The accepting State shall cooperate with the Court without any delay or exception in accordance with Part 9.

Article 13 — Exercise of jurisdiction

The Court may exercise its jurisdiction with respect to a crime referred to in article 5 in accordance with the provisions of this Statute if:

(a) A situation in which one or more of such crimes appears to have been committed is referred to the Prosecutor by a State Party;

(b) A situation in which one or more of such crimes appears to have been committed is referred to the Prosecutor by the Security Council acting under Chapter VII of the Charter of the United Nations; or

(c) The Prosecutor has initiated an investigation in respect of such a crime in accordance with article 15.

...

Article 15 — Prosecutor

1. The Prosecutor may initiate investigations proprio motu on the basis of information on crimes within the jurisdiction of the Court.

2. The Prosecutor shall analyse the seriousness of the information received. For this purpose, he or she may seek additional information from States, organs of the United Nations, intergovernmental or non-governmental organizations, or other reliable sources that he or she deems appropriate, and may receive written or oral testimony at the seat of the Court.

3. If the Prosecutor concludes that there is a reasonable basis to proceed with an investigation, he or she shall submit to the Pre-Trial Chamber a request for authorization of an investigation, together with any supporting material collected. Victims may make representations to the Pre-Trial Chamber, in accordance with the Rules of Procedure and Evidence.

4. If the Pre-Trial Chamber, upon examination of the request and the supporting material, considers that there is a reasonable basis to proceed with an investigation, and that the case appears to fall within the jurisdiction of the Court, it shall authorize the commencement of the investigation, without prejudice to subsequent determinations by the Court with regard to the jurisdiction and admissibility of a case.

. . .

Article 16 — Deferral of investigation or prosecution

No investigation or prosecution may be commenced or proceeded with under this Statute for a period of 12 months after the Security Council, in a resolution adopted under Chapter VII of the Charter of the United Nations, has requested the Court to that effect; that request may be renewed by the Council under the same conditions.

Article 17 — Issues of admissibility

1. . . . the Court shall determine that a case is inadmissible where:

(a) The case is being investigated or prosecuted by a State which has jurisdiction over it, unless the State is unwilling or unable genuinely to carry out the investigation or prosecution;
(b) The case has been investigated by a State which has jurisdiction over it and the State has decided not to prosecute the person concerned, unless the decision resulted from the unwillingness or inability of the State genuinely to prosecute;
(c) The person concerned has already been tried for conduct which is the subject of the complaint, and a trial by the Court is not permitted under article 20, paragraph 3;
(d) The case is not of sufficient gravity to justify further action by the Court.

2. In order to determine unwillingness in a particular case, the Court shall consider, having regard to the principles of due process recognized by international law, whether one or more of the following exist, as applicable:

(a) The proceedings were or are being undertaken or the national decision was made for the purpose of shielding the person concerned from criminal responsibility for crimes within the jurisdiction of the Court referred to in article 5;

(b) There has been an unjustified delay in the proceedings which in the circumstances is inconsistent with an intent to bring the person concerned to justice;

(c) The proceedings were not or are not being conducted independently or impartially, and they were or are being conducted in a manner which, in the circumstances, is inconsistent with an intent to bring the person concerned to justice.

3. In order to determine inability in a particular case, the Court shall consider whether, due to a total or substantial collapse or unavailability of its national judicial system, the State is unable to obtain the accused or the necessary evidence and testimony or otherwise unable to carry out its proceedings.

Article 20 — Ne bis in idem

...

3. No person who has been tried by another court for conduct also proscribed under article 6, 7 or 8 shall be tried by the Court with respect to the same conduct unless the proceedings in the other court:

(a) Were for the purpose of shielding the person concerned from criminal responsibility for crimes within the jurisdiction of the Court; or

(b) Otherwise were not conducted independently or impartially in accordance with the norms of due process recognized by international law and were conducted in a manner which, in the circumstances, was inconsistent with an intent to bring the person concerned to justice.

Article 21 — Applicable law

1. The Court shall apply:

(a) In the first place, this Statute, Elements of Crimes and its Rules of Procedure and Evidence;

(b) In the second place, where appropriate, applicable treaties and the principles and rules of international law, including the established principles of the international law of armed conflict;

(c) Failing that, general principles of law derived by the Court from national laws of legal systems of the world including, as appropriate, the national laws of States that would normally exercise jurisdiction over the crime, provided that those principles are not inconsistent with this Statute and with international law and internationally recognized norms and standards.

2. The Court may apply principles and rules of law as interpreted in its previous decisions.

3. The application and interpretation of law pursuant to this article must be consistent with internationally recognized human rights, and be without any adverse distinction founded on grounds such as gender as defined in article 7,

paragraph 3, age, race, colour, language, religion or belief, political or other opinion, national, ethnic or social origin, wealth, birth or other status.

...

Article 28 — Responsibility of commanders and other superiors

In addition to other grounds of criminal responsibility under this Statute for crimes within the jurisdiction of the Court:

(a) A military commander or person effectively acting as a military commander shall be criminally responsible for crimes within the jurisdiction of the Court committed by forces under his or her effective command and control, or effective authority and control as the case may be, as a result of his or her failure to exercise control properly over such forces, where:

(i) That military commander or person either knew or, owing to the circumstances at the time, should have known that the forces were committing or about to commit such crimes; and

(ii) That military commander or person failed to take all necessary and reasonable measures within his or her power to prevent or repress their commission or to submit the matter to the competent authorities for investigation and prosecution.

(b) With respect to superior and subordinate relationships not described in paragraph (a), a superior shall be criminally responsible for crimes within the jurisdiction of the Court committed by subordinates under his or her effective authority and control, as a result of his or her failure to exercise control properly over such subordinates, where:

(i) The superior either knew, or consciously disregarded information which clearly indicated, that the subordinates were committing or about to commit such crimes;

(ii) The crimes concerned activities that were within the effective responsibility and control of the superior; and

(iii) The superior failed to take all necessary and reasonable measures within his or her power to prevent or repress their commission or to submit the matter to the competent authorities for investigation and prosecution.

Article 53 — Initiation of an investigation

1. ... In deciding whether to initiate an investigation, the Prosecutor shall consider whether:

...

(c) Taking into account the gravity of the crime and the interests of victims, there are nonetheless substantial reasons to believe that an investigation would not serve the interests of justice.

. . .

2. If, upon investigation, the Prosecutor concludes that there is not a sufficient basis for a prosecution because:

. . .

(c) A prosecution is not in the interests of justice, taking into account all the circumstances, including the gravity of the crime, the interests of victims and the age or infirmity of the alleged perpetrator, and his or her role in the alleged crime;

the Prosecutor shall inform the Pre-Trial Chamber and the State making a referral under article 14 or the Security Council in a case under article 13, paragraph (b), of his or her conclusion and the reasons for the conclusion.

3. . . . the Pre-Trial Chamber may, on its own initiative, review a decision of the Prosecutor not to proceed if it is based solely on paragraph 1 (c) or 2 (c). In such a case, the decision of the Prosecutor shall be effective only if confirmed by the Pre-Trial Chamber.

. . .

Article 98 — Cooperation with respect to waiver of immunity and consent to surrender

1. The Court may not proceed with a request for surrender or assistance which would require the requested State to act inconsistently with its obligations under international law with respect to the State or diplomatic immunity of a person or property of a third State, unless the Court can first obtain the cooperation of that third State for the waiver of the immunity.

2. The Court may not proceed with a request for surrender which would require the requested State to act inconsistently with its obligations under international agreements pursuant to which the consent of a sending State is required to surrender a person of that State to the Court, unless the Court can first obtain the cooperation of the sending State for the giving of consent for the surrender.

KENNETH ROTH, THE COURT THE US DOESN'T WANT

N.Y. Rev. Books, November 19, 1998, at 45

. . . In favor of the [International Criminal] [C]ourt were most of America's closest allies, including Britain, Canada, and Germany. But the United States was isolated in opposition, along with such dictatorships and enemies of human rights as Iran, Iraq, China, Libya, Algeria, and Sudan. . . .

The Clinton administration's opposition to the ICC stemmed in part from its fear, a plausible one, that hostile states like Cuba, Libya, or Iraq might try to convince the court to launch a frivolous or politically motivated prosecution of US soldiers or commanding officers. The Rome delegates adopted several safeguards against this possibility, most importantly the so-called principle of complementarity. This gives the ICC jurisdiction over a case only if national authorities are 'unwilling or unable' to carry out a genuine investigation and, if appropriate, prosecution. The complementarity principle also reflects the widely shared view that systems of national justice should remain the front-line defense against serious human rights abuse, with the ICC serving only as a backstop. (By contrast, the Yugoslav and Rwandan tribunals are empowered to supersede local prosecutorial authorities at their discretion and have done so repeatedly.)

According to the principle of complementarity, if an American soldier were to commit a serious war crime — say, by deliberately massacring civilians — he could be brought before the ICC only if the US government failed to pursue his case. Indeed, even a national decision not to prosecute must be respected so long as it is not a bad faith effort to shield a criminal from justice. Because of the strength of the US judicial system, an ICC prosecutor would have a hard time dismissing a US investigation or prosecution as a sham. And, under the treaty, any effort to override a nation's decision not to prosecute would be subject to challenge before one panel of international judges and appeal before another.

Much would still depend on the character and professionalism of the ICC prosecutor and judges. The record of the International Criminal Tribunals for Rwanda and the former Yugoslavia suggests that faith in them would be well placed. . . .

There is every reason to believe that the ICC will be run by jurists of comparable stature. . . .

But the Pentagon and its congressional allies were not satisfied with the principle of complementarity as protection against unjustified prosecutions. . . .

Efforts by the US to exempt its nationals from the ICC's jurisdiction contributed to four points in contention during the Rome conference. . . . The resulting concessions [by other states] weakened the court significantly; still the Clinton administration ended up denouncing it.

The first controversy concerned whether and, if so, how the UN Security Council should be permitted to halt an ICC prosecution. The US proposed that before the ICC could even begin an investigation the Security Council would have to expressly authorize it. Because the United States, as a permanent Council member, could single-handedly block Council approval by exercising its veto, this proposal would have allowed Washington to prevent any investigation, including of its own soldiers and those of its allies. The other four permanent Council members — Britain, France, China, and Russia — would necessarily have had the same veto power. As a result, only criminals from a handful of pariah states would have been likely to face prosecution. . . .

Singapore offered a compromise to the veto problem which ultimately prevailed. It granted the Security Council the power to halt an ICC prosecution for a one-year period, which could be renewed. But the Security Council would act in its usual manner — by the vote of nine of its fifteen members and the acquiescence of all five permanent members. Therefore no single permanent Council member could use its veto to prevent a prosecution from being initiated. . . . The third major controversy involved what restrictions should be placed on the ICC's definition of war crimes. . . . Of special concern was the so-called rule of proportionality under international law, which prohibits a military attack causing an incidental loss of civilian life that is 'excessive' compared to the military advantage gained. This less precise rule could implicate activity that US military commanders consider lawful but the

ICC might not. For example, the Gulf War bombing of Iraq's electrical grid was claimed to have killed a disproportionate number of civilians, including the thousands said to have died because of the resulting loss of refrigeration, water purification, and other necessities of modern life. What if the ICC had been in existence and had found such claims well founded?...

To avoid prosecution in such borderline situations, US negotiators successfully redefined the proportionality rule to prohibit attacks that injure civilians only when such injury is 'clearly excessive' in relation to the military advantage....

The United States, joined by France, also proposed that governments be allowed to join the ICC while specifying that their citizens would be exempted from war crimes prosecutions.... [A]s a compromise, the treaty allows governments to exempt their citizens from the court's war crimes jurisdiction for a period of seven years. That would allow a hesitant government to reassure itself about the court's treatment of war crimes without permanently denying the court jurisdiction over its citizens....

The most divisive issue delegates faced was deciding how — once the ICC treaty was ratified by sixty countries — the court would get jurisdiction over a case that was referred by an individual government or initiated by the prosecutor. (This issue does not arise when the Security Council refers a matter for prosecution, since the Council has the power to impose jurisdiction.)... South Korea put forward a more limited proposal which gained broad support. It would have granted the ICC jurisdiction when any one of four governments concerned with a crime had ratified the ICC treaty or accepted the court's jurisdiction over the crime. These were: (1) the government of the suspect's nationality; (2) the government of the victims' nationality; (3) the government on whose territory the crime took place; or (4) the government that gained custody of the suspect. In any given case, some and perhaps all of these governments would be the same, but each separate category increases the possibility that the court could pursue a particular suspect.

Speaking for the Clinton administration, Ambassador Scheffer vehemently insisted that the court should be empowered to act only if the government of the suspect's nationality had accepted its jurisdiction....

Clinton administration officials were not mollified by the fact that, under the doctrine of universal jurisdiction, American soldiers are already vulnerable to prosecution in foreign courts. The US government has many ways of dissuading governments from attempting to try an American — from diplomatic and economic pressure to the use of military force. But the administration fears such dissuasion would be less effective against the ICC. After all, the Pentagon could hardly threaten to bomb The Hague.

...Facing these extraordinary threats [from the United States], the Rome delegates gave in, but only partially. They got rid of two of Korea's proposed conditions for ICC jurisdiction: that the treaty would have to be ratified by the state of the victim's nationality or it would have to be ratified by the state that gained custody of the suspect.

This concession was damaging. Because a state could not give the ICC jurisdiction just by arresting a suspect, a leader who commits atrocities against his own country's citizens, such as a future Pol Pot or Idi Amin, could travel widely without being brought before the ICC — so long as his own government had not ratified the treaty (and assuming the Security Council does not act).... And if the victims' nationality cannot be used as grounds for ICC jurisdiction, then the ICC could not take action against the leader of a nonratifying government that slaughters refugees from a ratifying state who seek shelter on its territory (again, assuming the Security Council fails to act)....

But the Rome delegates did not accept the Clinton administration's demands entirely. They retained two grounds for the ICC's jurisdiction: not only that the government of the suspect's nationality had ratified the treaty (the only ground acceptable to the US) but also that the government on whose territory the crime took place had ratified it. In the case of a tyrant who commits crimes at home, these two governments would be the same.... The United States, however, feared that the territorial hook might catch American troops, or their commanders, for alleged crimes committed while they were abroad. If the country where US troops are present has ratified the treaty, the ICC could pursue a case against them even though the United States had not joined the court.... Can the ICC survive without US participation? The Clinton administration is betting that it cannot. Already Jesse Helms, having declared the ICC treaty 'dead on arrival' in the Senate, has vowed to sponsor legislation forbidding the US government to fund the court or do anything to give it legitimacy. The State Department said publicly it might put pressure on governments not to join the court; and it is considering renegotiating the bilateral treaties that govern the stationing of US forces overseas in order to protect them from the ICC.

The Clinton administration... also contends that, small as the risk is of an American being brought before the court, the ICC will undermine humanitarian goals by making the United States reluctant to deploy troops in times of need.

NOTE

On 31 December 2000, President Clinton signed the Rome Treaty. In signing, he reiterated 'our concerns about significant flaws in the Treaty' and concluded that 'given these concerns, I will not, and do not recommend that my successor submit the Treaty to the Senate for advice and consent until our fundamental concerns are satisfied'. President Clinton also stated, 'Signature will enhance our ability to further protect U.S. officials from unfounded charges and to achieve the human rights and accountability objectives of the ICC. In fact, in negotiations following the Rome Conference, we have worked effectively to develop procedures that limit the likelihood of politicized prosecutions.'

On 6 May 2002, President Bush 'unsigned' the Rome Treaty by informing the UN Secretary-General that 'the United States does not intend to become a party to the treaty. Accordingly, the United States has no legal obligations arising from its signature.... The United States requests that its intention not to become a party, as expressed in this letter, be reflected in the depositary's status lists relating to this treaty.' The US Undersecretary for Political Affairs issued the following statement on the same day. Consider his remarks in comparison with Kenneth Roth's commentary above.

MARC GROSSMAN, UNDERSECRETARY FOR POLITICAL AFFAIRS, AMERICAN FOREIGN POLICY AND THE INTERNATIONAL CRIMINAL COURT

Remarks to the Center for Strategic and International Studies, Washington, DC, 6 May 2002

President Bush has come to the conclusion that the United States can no longer be a party to this process. In order to make our objections clear, both in principle and philosophy, and so as not to create unwarranted expectations of U.S. involvement in the Court, the President believes that he has no choice but to inform the United Nations, as depository of the treaty, of our intention not to become a party . . . These actions are consistent with the Vienna Convention on the Law of Treaties.

The decision to take this rare but not unprecedented act was not arrived at lightly. But after years of working to fix this flawed statute, and having our constructive proposals rebuffed, it is our only alternative.

Historical Perspective

Like many of the nations that gathered in Rome in 1998 for the negotiations to create a permanent International Criminal Court, the United States arrived with the firm belief that those who perpetrate genocide, crimes against humanity, and war crimes must be held accountable — and that horrendous deeds must not go unpunished.

The United States has been a world leader in promoting the rule of law. From our pioneering leadership in the creation of tribunals in Nuremberg, the Far East, and the International Criminal Tribunals for the former Yugoslavia and Rwanda, the United States has been in the forefront of promoting international justice. We believed that a properly created court could be a useful tool in promoting human rights and holding the perpetrators of the worst violations accountable before the world — and perhaps one day such a court will come into being.

A Flawed Outcome

. . .

First, we believe the ICC is an institution of unchecked power. In the United States, our system of government is founded on the principle that, in the words of John Adams, "power must never be trusted without a check." Unchecked power, our founders understood, is open to abuse, even with the good intentions of those who establish it.

But in the rush to create a powerful and independent court in Rome, there was a refusal to constrain the Court's powers in any meaningful way. . . .

Take one example: the role of the UN Security Council. Under the UN Charter, the UN Security Council has primary responsibility for maintaining international peace and security. But the Rome Treaty removes this existing system of checks and balances, and places enormous unchecked power in the hands of the ICC prosecutor and judges. The treaty created a self-initiating prosecutor, answerable to no state or institution other than the Court itself.

In Rome, the United States said that placing this kind of unchecked power in the hands of the prosecutor would lead to controversy, politicized prosecutions, and confusion....

...

Third, the treaty threatens the sovereignty of the United States. The Court, as constituted today, claims the authority to detain and try American citizens, even though our democratically-elected representatives have not agreed to be bound by the treaty. While sovereign nations have the authority to try non-citizens who have committed crimes against their citizens or in their territory, the United States has never recognized the right of an international organization to do so absent consent or a UN Security Council mandate.

Fourth, the current structure of the International Criminal Court undermines the democratic rights of our people and could erode the fundamental elements of the United Nations Charter, specifically the right to self defense.

With the ICC prosecutor and judges presuming to sit in judgment of the security decisions of States without their assent, the ICC could have a chilling effect on the willingness of States to project power in defense of their moral and security interests.

This power must sometimes be projected. The principled projection of force by the world's democracies is critical to protecting human rights — to stopping genocide or changing regimes like the Taliban, which abuse their people and promote terror against the world.

...

The United States has a unique role and responsibility to help preserve international peace and security. At any given time, U.S. forces are located in close to 100 nations around the world conducting peacekeeping and humanitarian operations and fighting inhumanity.

We must ensure that our soldiers and government officials are not exposed to the prospect of politicized prosecutions and investigations. Our President is committed to a robust American engagement in the world to defend freedom and defeat terror; we cannot permit the ICC to disrupt that vital mission.

...

Our Philosophy

While we oppose the ICC we share a common goal with its supporters — the promotion of the rule of law. Our differences are in approach and philosophy. In order for the rule of law to have true meaning, societies must accept their responsibilities and be able to direct their future and come to terms with their past. An unchecked international body should not be able to interfere in this delicate process.

For example: When a society makes the transition from oppression to democracy, their new government must face their collective past. The state should be allowed to choose the method. The government should decide whether to prosecute or seek national reconciliation. This decision should not be made by the ICC.

If the state chooses as a result of a democratic and legal process not to prosecute fully, and instead to grant conditional amnesty, as was done in difficult case of South Africa, this democratic decision should be respected.

Whenever a state accepts the challenges and responsibilities associated with enforcing the rule of law, the rule of law is strengthened and a barrier to impunity is erected. It is this barrier that will create the lasting goals the ICC seeks to attain. This responsibility should not be taken away from states.

International practice should promote domestic accountability and encourage sovereign states to seek reconciliation where feasible.

The existence of credible domestic legal systems is vital to ensuring conditions do not deteriorate to the point that the international community is required to intercede.

In situations where violations are grave and the political will of the sovereign state is weak, we should work, using any influence we have, to strengthen that will. In situations where violations are so grave as to amount to a breach of international peace and security, and the political will to address these violations is non-existent, the international community may, and if necessary should, intercede through the UN Security Council as we did in Bosnia and Rwanda.

. . .

We Will Continue To Lead

. . .

The existence of a functioning ICC will not cause the United States to retreat from its leadership role in the promotion of international justice and the rule of law.

The United States will:

. . .

- Continue our longstanding role as an advocate for the principle that there must be accountability for war crimes and other serious violations of international humanitarian law.

  . . .
- The armed forces of the United States will obey the law of war, while our international policies are and will remain completely consistent with these norms.
- Continue to discipline our own when appropriate.
- We will remain committed to promoting the rule of law and helping to bring violators of humanitarian law to justice, wherever the violations may occur.
- We will support politically, financially, technically, and logistically any post-conflict state that seeks to credibly pursue domestic humanitarian law.
- We will support creative ad-hoc mechanisms such as the hybrid process in Sierra Leone — where there is a division of labor between the sovereign state and the international community — as well as alternative justice mechanisms such as truth and reconciliation commissions.

  . . .
- We will seek to create a pool of experienced judges and prosecutors who would be willing to work on these projects on short-notice.
- We will take steps to ensure that gaps in United States' law do not allow persons wanted or indicted for genocide, war crimes, or crimes against humanity to seek safe haven on our soil in hopes of evading justice.

And when violations occur that are so grave and that they breach international peace and security, the United States will use its position in the UN Security Council to act in support of justice.

We believe that there is common ground, and ask those nations who have decided to join the Rome Treaty to meet us there. Encouraging states to come to face the past while moving into the future is a goal that no one can dispute. Enhancing the capacity of domestic judiciaries is an aim to which we can all agree.... Because, in the end, the best way to prevent genocide, crimes against humanity, and war crimes is through the spread of democracy, transparency and rule of law. Nations with accountable, democratic governments do not abuse their own people or wage wars of conquest and terror. A world of self-governing democracies is our best hope for a world without inhumanity.

QUESTIONS

1. Is the US Government correct that the ICC fails to provide sufficient safeguards against politically motivated prosecutions? Is the US Government's real concern that the Court will apply too much law (i.e., let legal standards determine which situations to investigate and who to prosecute) rather than too much politics? Is it a valid concern that the Court is not subject to sufficient political control?

2. Marc Grossman states that 'the ICC could have a chilling effect on the willingness of States to project power in defense of their moral and security interests.... The principled projection of force by the world's democracies is critical to protecting human rights...' Ken Roth notes the Clinton Administration made a similar claim. Is it likely that powerful states would be deterred by the prospect of a few or more individual prosecutions? Don't decisions to engage in military campaigns routinely involve much greater risks to an intervening state's armed forces? Will the International Criminal Court reduce the likelihood that states engage in humanitarian interventions? If so, is that consequence worth the benefits of having the Court?

3. Article 18 of the Vienna Convention on the Law of Treaties requires states not to defeat the object and purpose of a treaty that they have signed but not yet ratified. Ken Roth refers to bilateral treaties (sometimes called 'immunity agreements' or 'Article 98 agreements') that the United States has crafted to ensure that US nationals and employees are not transferred to the Court. By 2006, the US reportedly finalized 100 agreements and 54 states had publicly refused to enter such agreements.[4] Do these agreements defeat the object and purpose of the Rome Statute or are they consistent with Article 98 of the Statute? Note that a debate exists as to whether the term 'sending state' in Article 98 refers only to specific relationships, such as when US military and civilian personnel are sent to a receiving state under a Status of Forces or Status of Mission agreement. Compare the wording in Article 1 of the Statute of the Special Court for Sierra Leone, p. 1310, *infra*.

[4] See www.iccnow.org/documents/CICCFS_BIAstatusCurrent.pdf.

According to Article 18 of the Vienna Convention, the obligation not to defeat the object and purpose exists 'until [the state] shall have made its intention clear not to become a party to the treaty.' Grossman states that the US administration's 'actions are consistent with the Vienna Convention on the Law of Treaties.' The act of 'un-signing', on this view, constitutes notification of intent under Article 18 and thus the US released itself from any obligations to support the ICC. However, what about the obligations of states that are parties to the ICC and have a bilateral agreement with the United States? Consider Articles 30 and 41 of the Vienna Convention.

SECURITY COUNCIL RESOLUTION ON SITUATION IN SUDAN AND EXPLANATIONS OF VOTE

Res. 1593, 31 March 2005

The Security Council,

Taking note of the report of the International Commission of Inquiry on violations of international humanitarian law and human rights law in Darfur (S/2005/60),

Recalling article 16 of the Rome Statute under which no investigation or prosecution may be commenced or proceeded with by the International Criminal Court for a period of 12 months after a Security Council request to that effect,

Also recalling articles 75 and 79 of the Rome Statute and encouraging States to contribute to the ICC Trust Fund for Victims,

Taking note of the existence of agreements referred to in Article 98–2 of the Rome Statute,

Determining that the situation in Sudan continues to constitute a threat to international peace and security,

Acting under Chapter VII of the Charter of the United Nations,

1. Decides to refer the situation in Darfur since 1 July 2002 to the Prosecutor of the International Criminal Court;

2. Decides that the Government of Sudan and all other parties to the conflict in Darfur shall cooperate fully with and provide any necessary assistance to the Court and the Prosecutor pursuant to this resolution and, while recognizing that States not party to the Rome Statute have no obligation under the Statute, urges all States and concerned regional and other international organizations to cooperate fully; . . .

5. Also emphasizes the need to promote healing and reconciliation and encourages in this respect the creation of institutions, involving all sectors of Sudanese society, such as truth and/or reconciliation commissions, in order to complement judicial processes and thereby reinforce the efforts to restore long-lasting peace, with African Union and international support as necessary;

6. Decides that nationals, current or former officials or personnel from a contributing State outside Sudan which is not a party to the Rome Statute of the International Criminal Court shall be subject to the exclusive jurisdiction of that contributing State for all alleged acts or omissions arising out of or related to operations in Sudan

established or authorized by the Council or the African Union, unless such exclusive jurisdiction has been expressly waived by that contributing State;

7. Recognizes that none of the expenses incurred in connection with the referral, including expenses related to investigations or prosecutions in connection with that referral, shall be borne by the United Nations and that such costs shall be borne by the parties to the Rome Statute and those States that wish to contribute voluntarily;

The draft resolution was adopted by a vote of 11 in favour with 4 abstentions (Algeria, Brazil, China, United States).[5]

Following the vote, ANNE WOODS PATTERSON (United States) said her country strongly supported bringing to justice those responsible for the crimes and atrocities that had occurred in Darfur and ending the climate of impunity there....

While the United States believed that a better mechanism would have been a hybrid tribunal in Africa, it was important that the international community spoke with one voice in order to help promote effective accountability. The United States continued to fundamentally object to the view that the Court should be able to exercise jurisdiction over the nationals, including government officials, of States not party to the Rome Statute. Because it did not agree to a Council referral of the situation in Darfur to the Court, her country had abstained on the vote. She decided not to oppose the resolution because of the need for the international community to work together in order to end the climate of impunity in the Sudan, and because the resolution provided protection from investigation or prosecution for United States nationals and members of the armed forces of non-State parties.

The United States was and would be an important contributor to the peacekeeping and related humanitarian efforts in the Sudan, she said. The language providing protection for the United States and other contributing States was precedent-setting, as it clearly acknowledged the concerns of States not party to the Rome Statute and recognized that persons from those States should not be vulnerable to investigation or prosecution by the Court, absent consent by those States or a referral by the Council. In the future, she believed that, absent consent of the State involved, any investigations or prosecutions of nationals of non-party States should come only pursuant to a decision by the Council.

Although her delegation had abstained on the Council referral to the Court, it had not dropped, and indeed continued to maintain, its long-standing and firm objections and concerns regarding the Court, she continued. The Rome Statute was flawed and did not have sufficient protection from the possibility of politicized prosecutions. Non-parties had no obligations in connection with that treaty, unless otherwise decided by the Council, upon which members of the Organization had conferred primary responsibility for the maintenance of international peace and security.

She was pleased that the resolution recognized that none of the expenses incurred in connection with the referral would be borne by the United Nations, and that instead such costs would be borne by the parties to the Rome Statute and those that contributed voluntarily. That principle was extremely important. Any effort to retrench on that principle by the United Nations or other organizations to which the United States contributed could result in its withholding funding or taking other action in response.

[5] [Eds. The following governmental statements are excerpted from UN Press Release SC/8351.]

The Council included, at her country's request, a provision that exempted persons of non-party States in the Sudan from the ICC prosecution. Persons from countries not party who were supporting the United Nations' or African Union's efforts should not be placed in jeopardy. The resolution provided clear protection for United States persons. No United States person supporting operations in the Sudan would be subject to investigation or prosecution because of this resolution. That did not mean that there would be immunity for American citizens that acted in violation of the law. The United States would continue to discipline its own people when appropriate.

ELLEN MARGRETHE LØJ (Denmark) said that it had been two months since the Council had received the report of the Commission of Inquiry, which had strongly recommended referring the situation in Darfur to the ICC. . . .

Denmark had only been able to support the text after some alterations were made, she said. Regarding the formulation on existing agreements referred to in article 98–2 of the Rome Statute, she noted that that reference was purely factual and referred to the existence of such agreements. Thus, the reference was in no way impinging on the Rome Statute. The result was a valid compromise leading to the first referral of a situation to the ICC. . . .

CÉSAR MAYORAL (Argentina) said he had voted in support of the resolution on the basis of the report to the Council by the High Commissioner for Human Rights, who stated clearly what had been crimes against humanity in Darfur. . . .

He noted that it was the first time the Council had referred to the Court a situation involving crimes over which the Court had jurisdiction. It was a crucial precedent. The letter and spirit of the Rome Statute must be respected, taking into account the legitimate concerns of States. Accordingly, he regretted that the Council had to adopt a text that provided an exemption to the Court, and hoped that that would not become normal practice. The exemption referred to in operative paragraph 6 only applied to those States not party to the Rome Statute.

JEAN-MARC DE LA SABLIERE (France) said the events in Darfur were deeply troubling, and the greatest concern was the plight of the people there. The Secretary-General's reports had provided a detailed picture of those atrocities. The Council had a duty to take action. . . .

ADAMANTIOS TH. VASSILAKIS (Greece) stressed that impunity must not be allowed to go unpunished and that was why his country had turned to the International Criminal Court. It would have preferred a text that did not make exceptions, but it was better than one that allowed violations to go unpunished. The text strengthened the Council's authority, as well as that of the International Criminal Court, which would have the possibility of showing its competence. . . .

Council President RONALDO MOTA SARDENBERG (Brazil), speaking in his national capacity, said his country was in favour of the resolution, but had been unable to join those who had voted in favour. However, Brazil was ready to cooperate fully with the International Criminal Court whenever necessary. The Court provided all the necessary checks and balances to prevent politically motivated prosecutions, and any fears to the contrary were both unwarranted and unhelpful.

However, there were limits to the responsibilities of the Council vis-à-vis international instruments, and Brazil had consistently maintained that position since the negotiations on the Rome Statute. But the Court remained the only suitable institution to deal with the violations in the Sudan. Brazil had been unable to support operative paragraph 6, which recognized exclusive jurisdiction. It would not strengthen the role of the International Criminal Court.

ELFATIH MOHAMED AHMED ERWA (Sudan) said that, once more, the Council had persisted in adopting unwise decisions against his country, which only served to further complicate the situation on the ground. The positions over the ICC were well known. The Darfur question had been exploited in light of those positions. It was a paradox that the language in which the resolution was negotiated was the same language that had buffeted the Council before on another African question. The resolution adopted was full of exemptions. He reminded the Council that the Sudan was also not party to the ICC, making implementation of the resolution fraught with procedural impediments. As long as the Council believed that the scales of justice were based on exceptions and exploitation of crises in developing countries and bargaining among major Powers, it did not settle the question of accountability in Darfur, but exposed the fact that the ICC was intended for developing and weak countries and was a tool to exercise cultural superiority.

The Council, by adopting the resolution, had once again ridden roughshod over the African position, he said. The initiative by Nigeria, as chair of the African Union, had not even been the subject of consideration. Also, the Council had adopted the resolution at a time when the Sudanese judiciary had gone a long way in holding trials, and was capable of ensuring accountability. Some here wanted to activate the ICC and exploit the situation in Darfur. Accountability was a long process that could not be achieved overnight. The Council was continuing to use a policy of double standards, and sending the message that exemptions were only for major Powers....

QUESTIONS

1. Does the US decision not to veto the Resolution represent a significant change in the posture of the United States towards the Court? Does the US acceptance of the competence of the ICC in this case weaken the persuasive appeal of US opposition to the Court?

2. What concessions were made to the US Government in the text of the Resolution? The US representative takes the position, also suggested in Marc Grossman's statement, that nationals of a state not party to the Rome Statute should generally not be vulnerable to investigation or prosecution by the Court without that state's consent. Does the Resolution strengthen the U.S. position or, on the contrary, demonstrate that exemptions from the ICC require affirmative Security Council action?

ADDITIONAL READING

David Scheffer, 'The United States and the International Criminal Court', 93 AM. J. Int. L. 12 (1999); Mahnoush Arsanjani, 'The Rome Statute of the International Criminal Court', 93 AM. J. Int. L. 22 (1999); Darryl Robinson, 'Defining "Crimes against Humanity" at the Rome Conference', 93 AM. J. Int. L. 43 (1999): Antonio Cassese *et al.* (eds.), *The Rome Statute of the*

International Criminal Court: A Commentary (2002); M. Cherif Bassiouni, *The Statute of the International Criminal Court: A Documentary History* (1998); Roy Lee (ed.), *The International Criminal Court: The Making of the Rome Statute* (1999); William Schabas, *An Introduction to the International Criminal Court* (2001); Otto Triffterer (ed.), *Commentary on the Rome Statute of the International Criminal Court* (1999); Jack Goldsmith, 'The Self-Defeating International Criminal Court', 70 U. Chi. L. Rev. 89 (2003).

C. HYBRID TRIBUNALS: THE CASE OF SIERRA LEONE

Since the establishment of the ad hoc tribunals for the former Yugoslavia and Rwanda and the finalization of the Rome Statute, 'hybrid tribunals' — institutions whose structure is part international, part national — have been created to prosecute human rights and humanitarian law violations in Sierra Leone, East Timor, Kosovo, and Cambodia. The first hybrid tribunal was the Special Court for Sierra Leone. That tribunal has been heralded as 'the model' for similar institutions. Its record of successes and failures thus carries special weight.

In the 1990s, Sierra Leone was ravaged by a civil war that claimed over 75,000 lives and displaced a third of the population. In mid 1999, the national government and the Revolutionary United Front (RUF) rebel group negotiated a comprehensive peace agreement at Lomé, Togo. The Lomé Peace Agreement mandated the establishment of a Truth and Reconciliation Commission. However, it did not effectively resolve all outstanding issues of accountability. In June 2000, the President of Sierra Leone asked the UN Secretary-General for assistance in prosecuting individuals who perpetrated atrocities during the civil war. In response, the Security Council authorized the Secretary-General to negotiate an agreement between the UN and the Government of Sierra Leone to establish a criminal tribunal. The subsequent agreement, signed in 2002, created the legal framework for the Special Court for Sierra Leone. The Special Court is seated in the capital Freetown. The Court is composed of international and domestic judges, prosecutors and administrative staff. The jurisdiction of the Court includes international and domestic crimes. These and other features are reflected in the following provisions.

STATUTE OF THE SPECIAL COURT FOR SIERRA LEONE

http://www.sc-sl.org/scsl-statute.html

Article 1: Competence of the Special Court

1. The Special Court shall, except as provided in subparagraph (2), have the power to prosecute persons who bear the greatest responsibility for serious violations of international humanitarian law and Sierra Leonean law...

2. Any transgressions by peacekeepers and related personnel present in Sierra Leone pursuant to the Status of Mission Agreement in force between the United

Nations and the Government of Sierra Leone or agreements between Sierra Leone and other Governments or regional organizations, or, in the absence of such agreement, provided that the peacekeeping operations were undertaken with the consent of the Government of Sierra Leone, shall be within the primary jurisdiction of the sending State....

Article 2: Crimes against humanity...

Article 3: Violations of Article 3 common to the Geneva Conventions and of Additional Protocol II...

Article 4: Other serious violations of international humanitarian law

The Special Court shall have the power to prosecute persons who committed the following serious violations of international humanitarian law:

a. Intentionally directing attacks against the civilian population as such or against individual civilians not taking direct part in hostilities;

...

c. Conscripting or enlisting children under the age of 15 years into armed forces or groups or using them to participate actively in hostilities.

Article 5: Crimes under Sierra Leonean law

The Special Court shall have the power to prosecute persons who have committed the following crimes under Sierra Leonean law:

a. Offences relating to the abuse of girls under the Prevention of Cruelty to Children Act...

b. Offences relating to the wanton destruction of property under the Malicious Damage Act, 1861:

   i. Setting fire to dwelling—houses, any person being therein...;
   ii. Setting fire to public buildings...;
   iii. Setting fire to other buildings....

   ...

Article 12: Composition of the Chambers

1. The Chambers shall be composed of not less than eight (8) or more than eleven (11) independent judges, who shall serve as follows:

a. Three judges shall serve in the Trial Chamber, of whom one shall be a judge appointed by the Government of Sierra Leone, and two judges appointed by the Secretary-General of the United Nations (hereinafter "the Secretary-General").

b. Five judges shall serve in the Appeals Chamber, of whom two shall be judges appointed by the Government of Sierra Leone, and three judges appointed by the Secretary-General....

Article 13: Qualification and appointment of judges

1. The judges shall be persons of high moral character, impartiality and integrity who possess the qualifications required in their respective countries for appointment to the highest judicial offices. They shall be independent in the performance of their functions, and shall not accept or seek instructions from any Government or any other source. . . .

. . .

3. The judges shall be appointed for a three-year period and shall be eligible for reappointment. . . .

Article 15: The Prosecutor

1. . . . The Prosecutor shall act independently as a separate organ of the Special Court. He or she shall not seek or receive instructions from any Government or from any other source.

2. The Office of the Prosecutor shall have the power to question suspects, victims and witnesses, to collect evidence and to conduct on-site investigations. In carrying out these tasks, the Prosecutor shall, as appropriate, be assisted by the Sierra Leonean authorities concerned.

3. The Prosecutor shall be appointed by the Secretary-General for a three-year term and shall be eligible for re-appointment. . . .

4. The Prosecutor shall be assisted by a Sierra Leonean Deputy Prosecutor, and by such other Sierra Leonean and international staff as may be required to perform the functions assigned to him or her effectively and efficiently. Given the nature of the crimes committed and the particular sensitivities of girls, young women and children victims of rape, sexual assault, abduction and slavery of all kinds, due consideration should be given in the appointment of staff to the employment of prosecutors and investigators experienced in gender-related crimes and juvenile justice.

. . .

Article 16: The Registry

1. The Registry shall be responsible for the administration and servicing of the Special Court.

3. The Registrar shall be appointed by the Secretary-General after consultation with the President of the Special Court and shall be a staff member of the United Nations. He or she shall serve for a three-year term and be eligible for re-appointment.

4. The Registrar shall set up a Victims and Witnesses Unit within the Registry. . . .

. . .

Article 20: Appellate proceedings

. . .

3. The judges of the Appeals Chamber of the Special Court shall be guided by the decisions of the Appeals Chamber of the International Tribunals for the former

Yugoslavia and for Rwanda. In the interpretation and application of the laws of Sierra Leone, they shall be guided by the decisions of the Supreme Court of Sierra Leone.

...

Article 22: Enforcement of sentences

1. Imprisonment shall be served in Sierra Leone. If circumstances so require, imprisonment may also be served in any of the States which have concluded with the International Criminal Tribunal for Rwanda or the International Criminal Tribunal for the former Yugoslavia an agreement for the enforcement of sentences, and which have indicated to the Registrar of the Special Court their willingness to accept convicted persons. The Special Court may conclude similar agreements for the enforcement of sentences with other States.

2. Conditions of imprisonment, whether in Sierra Leone or in a third State, shall be governed by the law of the State of enforcement subject to the supervision of the Special Court....

Article 23: Pardon or commutation of sentences

If, pursuant to the applicable law of the State in which the convicted person is imprisoned, he or she is eligible for pardon or commutation of sentence, the State concerned shall notify the Special Court accordingly. There shall only be pardon or commutation of sentence if the President of the Special Court, in consultation with the judges, so decides on the basis of the interests of justice and the general principles of law....

INTERNATIONAL CENTER FOR TRANSITIONAL JUSTICE, THE SPECIAL COURT FOR SIERRA LEONE: THE FIRST EIGHTEEN MONTHS

March 2004

http://www.ictj.org/downloads/SC_SL_Case_Study_designed.pdf

...

The Special Court for Sierra Leone is a tribunal established to try [individuals] for serious violations of international humanitarian law and certain provisions of Sierra Leonean domestic law since November 30, 1996.[6] ... From its outset, the jurisdiction of the Special Court was restricted to "those who bear the greatest responsibility." Clearly, this was intended to prevent the Special Court from expanding in size and expense as a result of an unwieldy prosecutorial policy, as some diplomats had characterized the ICTY and ICTR....

...

Another unique element of prosecutorial strategy in Sierra Leone has been the use of public statements on prosecutorial strategy to reassure the public. For example, the

[6] This limitation on the temporal jurisdiction of the war, based on the date of the failed Abidjan Accord, was intended to keep the budget down in comparison to the other international criminal tribunals.

Prosecutor ... declar[ed] that he did not intend to indict anyone for crimes committed while under the age of 18. He also declared that he would not seek information from the TRC. It is unusual for a Prosecutor to declare his prosecutorial plans or policies in advance, but on both these issues, his announcements have been positively received.

... Especially during the Court's start-up period, most of the key posts in the Office of the Prosecutor were filled by U.S. nationals, which attracted some criticism. By April 2003, 25 percent of the prosecutorial staff comprised Americans, including the Chiefs of Investigations, Prosecutions, and Operations (although two of these posts have been turned over to non-Americans).... As a consequence... some have perceived the Special Court as under undue American influence.

Comparing the Special Court to the Ad Hoc Tribunals

... Both [the ICTY and ICTR] tribunals have been criticized for their slow pace, prosecution strategies, high operational costs, and lack of connection to the societies where crimes were committed. This report mainly uses the ICTR as the reference point against which the Court is assessed.

A. An On-Site Court

The first major difference between the Special Court and the ICTR is geography. The ICTR is located 600 miles from where the crimes were committed. This has contributed to one of the major criticisms against the two ad hoc tribunals: their lack of connection to the people in the countries that suffered the violence.

Ten years after it began to function and seven years after it started trials, the ICTR is criticized as having very little impact on Rwanda's citizens and judiciary. According to some accounts, Rwandans have no sense of ownership of the ICTR and do not necessarily perceive the tribunal to be for them. This is exacerbated by the fact that many ICTR staff members have not even visited Rwanda, with the exception of those who have worked for the Office of the Prosecutor on investigations.

Against this background, there was strong pressure for the Special Court for Sierra Leone to be set up in Freetown, instead of in a neighboring country. In addition, having the Court on site allows for greater analysis of its impact on the Sierra Leonean people and judiciary.

From early on, the Court has demonstrated considerable concern about how it is perceived and understood in Sierra Leone. Between September 2002 and February 2003, the Chief Prosecutor and the Registrar held a series of "town hall meetings" in all 12 districts to explain the Court's work to the population in the provinces and receive feedback. The ad hoc tribunals did not do similar outreach at the outset (although each eventually established such a program).

By April 2003, the Registry had put into place an Outreach Unit that would eventually comprise 17 people, with small offices spread throughout the country in a District Grassroots Network. Through the Network, the Outreach Unit has built the capacity to get information to and from every district in the country within a 36-hour period, despite lack of phone coverage and poor road infrastructure. By September 2003, the Outreach Unit had conducted a number of activities — including targeted outreach among the military and a booklet explaining the Court to schoolchildren — and had developed detailed plans for the future, including the creation of a forum to interface between civil society and the Court (Special Court Interactive Forum). The Special Court has prioritized an outreach policy as part of its regular budget....

Security is the main hazard of housing the Court inside Sierra Leone; the Special Court has faced challenges that the ICTR and ICTY have been spared. Hinga Norman's case [Minister of Internal Affairs and former leader of pro-government militia groups] is the most significant demonstration.... several unprecedented measures were taken following Norman's arrest, such as holding his initial appearance in closed session and seeking to negotiate his detention outside of the country.[7] A balance will have to be struck between security measures and the public nature of the trial (and the Court's ability to have an impact on public debate).

B. A Hybrid Court

A key difference between the Special Court and the ICTR is that the Special Court has both national and international staff members in all organs of the Court, including the Chambers. By April 2003, 23 percent of the Court's professional staff members were Sierra Leoneans, and 56 percent of all employees were nationals. Even though internationals hold most key decision-making positions, the influence of Sierra Leonean staff within the structure is significant. There is a wide consensus that the presence and expertise of Sierra Leoneans has made the process more relevant and efficient....

Incorporating nationals helps the Court to carry out its work in an efficient manner that is sensitive to the country's conditions and to maintain its focus and sense of mandate. Furthermore, a major risk in tipping the balance of a hybrid composition in favor of internationals is that the institution will be seen as detached and will have less legitimacy among Sierra Leoneans. However, Sierra Leonean views on this inevitably vary, and while Freetown residents have often urged more inclusion of Sierra Leoneans at senior levels, many of those outside Freetown distrust the Freetown "elites" and prefer to have internationals in key positions.

Whether most Sierra Leoneans perceive the Special Court as mainly international or domestic is still open to debate....

...Article 5 of the Statute includes Sierra Leonean domestic legal provisions on the abuse of girls and wanton destruction of property. However, to date none of the indictments encompasses charges of domestic crimes....

C. A Lower Budget and Voluntary Contributions

Another critical difference between the ad hoc tribunals and the Special Court lies in the latter's financial structure and management. The Special Court is funded from voluntary contributions, rather than the regular budget of the UN. More than 30 countries have contributed to the Special Court, although four of them (Canada, the Netherlands, the United Kingdom, and the United States) provided two-thirds of the Court's first-year budget. This has two consequences: the budget is tight overall,

[7] Immediately after his arrest, authorities explored the option of flying Hinga Norman to The Hague (or Arusha), where he would be detained until the start of his trial, but it proved difficult to obtain the requisite permission from the various domestic authorities and ICTY/ICTR.

and these few states theoretically have great influence, although the Registrar has said that he has not experienced any interference.... The Special Court might offer a different perspective on what an international tribunal can accomplish with less funding. If the Court succeeds in trying around 15 people in 3 years within these general budgetary provisions, it may be seen as a more efficient model... Because of the voluntary nature of contributions, the Court is often in a precarious financial state. In its second year, the Court has struggled to secure adequate pledges from governments. Allowing the Court to be entirely reliant on donations from a small number of states makes it vulnerable and has potentially negative implications for its independence (a matter that defense counsel has already raised)....

D. State Cooperation

International tribunals depend on state cooperation in matters of enforcement, such as arrest and transfer of suspects, detention, witness protection, and so forth. The ICTY and ICTR have a Chapter VII mandate by virtue of being created pursuant to a UN Security Council Resolution under that Chapter, which makes it mandatory for all UN member states to cooperate. The Special Court for Sierra Leone was not created under a Chapter VII resolution but by an Agreement between Sierra Leone and the UN, and to date it has been at a disadvantage.... As to the arrest of suspects, when the arrests were first announced, the only accused not in Sierra Leone were thought to be in Liberia, a country then at war whose own head of state was indicted by the Special Court. It is worth noting, however, that once the Court failed to attain [Liberian head of state Charles] Taylor's arrest in Ghana, the President wrote to the Secretary-General on June 10, 2003, requesting Chapter VII powers for the Court, but with no result.

...

The other ad hoc tribunals also may have been more inclined to keep Hinga Norman in detention if the Special Court had a similar mandate and powers.

A duty to cooperate would also assist in concluding agreements with states on the enforcement of sentences....

...

NANCY KAYMAR STAFFORD, A MODEL WAR CRIMES COURT: SIERRA LEONE

10 ILSA J. of Int. & Comp. L. 117 (2003)

... Pierre Bourin, Justice of the Court, stated, "[t]he main objective of the court is to reestablish the rule of law in this country and then show to the people of Sierra Leone that justice can be done in this country." The judicial system has been decimated by 10 years of war....

...

... [T]he local population will have greater access to the proceedings of the Special Court if they are local.... The entire population of Sierra Leone is a victim of the war. If the Special Court is not assisting in the healing of the nation, the people of Sierra Leone are present to "judge" the proceedings and ensure the Special Court does not deviate from its mandate or get bogged down in political issues or mismanagement. . . .

. . . The most effective way for the people to reconcile with the past and start building a future is to see justice being done. Having the Special Court located in a third country deprives the local communities — the victims — of being a part of the judicial process. . . . Every war is fought differently. Therefore "cookie cutter" justice is not always the best answer. . . . Just because future atrocities do not fit neatly within the traditional mold of what constitutes a war crime, does not mean that the crimes should not be punished by tribunals. . . . Future hybrid courts would be able to use the relevant aspects of their domestic laws to ensure the prosecutions cover all atrocities that were committed during their particular conflict. . . . Sierra Leone is located in a hot bed of civil unrest. Liberia, Guinea, Burkina Faso and other countries in Western Africa have had tumultuous pasts. Obtaining sustained peace and the return to the rule of law in Sierra Leone would set an exceptional example for both the people and the governments of other West African nations. . . .

There is a certain amount of concern that if the rebel commanders are tried for their crimes, their supporters may be angered and retaliate sending the country back into war. . . . the international community is keeping a close eye on Sierra Leone particularly since this is the first time post World War II, that a war crimes tribunal is being held in the country where the crimes were committed. . . . [T]his is an issue related to prosecution and not the structure of the hybrid court system. Presumably retaliation, if it were to occur, would be planned regardless of where the perpetrators were prosecuted. . . .

The eight judges for the Special Court were sworn in on December 2, 2002. Five, from varying countries outside Sierra Leone, were appointed by the UN Secretary General and three by the Sierra Leone government. Some claim that the inclusion of judges from Sierra Leone renders the proceedings unfair. Issa Sesay, interim Chairperson of the RUF stated, "[i]f the Court is to be neutral then no Sierra Leonean judge should be included because they may have their prejudices."

. . . International judges from Britain, Canada, Austria, Nigeria, Gambia and Cameroon will be impartial and provide the necessary impediment to any prejudices the local judges may have. At the same time, the international judges will be reaffirming the rule of law and helping the local judges to reestablish a working judicial system in the country.

. . . International judges represent the majority in both chambers and therefore will be able to safeguard against any issues of impartiality. Significantly, public judgments subject to external scrutiny, will serve as an additional check on impartiality.

QUESTIONS

1. As the readings above suggest, the location of the Special Court in Freetown is considered a major advance in the development of international criminal tribunals. Yet in mid 2006 the Security Council, acting under Chapter VII, authorized the transfer of

Charles Taylor to The Hague for trial by a 'special chamber' of the Special Court. Some consider this decision a major step backwards. Consider the following remarks by Sierra Leone's former Ambassador (1996–2002) to the United States:

> Mr. Taylor's forthcoming war crimes trial should not be transferred to The Hague, as Liberia's president and the court itself have requested.
>
> Such a transfer would defeat a principal purpose behind the establishment of the special court in Sierra Leone — namely, to teach Africans, firsthand and in their own countries, the fundamentals of justice and to drive home the democratic principle that no one is above the law. The special court has the potential to help raise West Africa's standards for accountability, transparency, fairness and the humane treatment of defendants.
>
> In countries where might makes right, demonstrating the proper administration of justice can be an unbeatable nation-building tool. This is a key part of what the special court was set up to do and has done quite well in Sierra Leone since it commenced operations in late 2002.
>
> ...
>
> True, fears that Mr. Taylor's trial in Freetown could cause instability in Sierra Leone, Liberia and elsewhere in the region have substantial merit....
>
> But the solution is not to rob Africans of the experience of seeing real justice administered to their most powerful tormentor. Potential instability should be addressed not by pandering to thuggish elements but by tightening security in both Sierra Leone and Liberia, under a robust United Nations peacemaking mandate.[8]

Comment.

2. The purported virtues of the Special Court for Sierra Leone include the direct interactions between the Office of the Prosecutor and the public. The ICTJ report refers to such interactions as 'another unique element of prosecutorial strategy in Sierra Leone'. These relationships, for example, are thought to make the Prosecutor more responsive to the people of Sierra Leone. Are these relationships and the expectations placed on the Prosecutor fully desirable? What are the costs and benefits of this arrangement?

3. Is it appropriate for a quasi-international institution to prosecute domestic crimes? Why should the Special Court have jurisdiction over such offences?

4. Nancy Stafford writes about the hybrid tribunal: 'International judges... will be impartial and provide the necessary impediment to any prejudices the local judges may have.' Doesn't the bias of even a single judge taint the entire judicial proceeding? Recall that in *Incal v. Turkey*, p. 437, *supra*, the presence of a single military judge impugned the fairness of that court system. The influence of the nonmilitary judges on their military colleague was not considered material. As another example, consider that the failure of one judge to recuse himself in *Ex Parte Pinochet* required the British House of Lords to rehear that case. Is the hybrid model for criminal tribunals in Sierra Leone distinguishable from these other situations? Do you agree with Stafford's reasoning?

[8] John E. Leigh, Op-Ed, 'Bringing it all Back Home', *New York Times*, 17 April 2006.

D. ALTERNATIVE JUSTICE SYSTEMS: RWANDA'S GACACA COURTS

In addition to the ICTR, the Rwandan Government has undertaken a separate national effort to prosecute crimes related to the 1994 genocide. Several years after the genocide, more than 100,000 Rwandese were awaiting trial in national court, many of them since 1995. These individuals were held in severely overcrowded and abject detention conditions. Between 1996 and 2001, the national court system processed approximately 5,000 individual cases. At that rate, it would have taken several decades to clear the backlog of individuals awaiting trial.

By year 2000, the Rwandan Government formulated a plan to transfer the majority of genocide cases to a new adjudicative system known as 'gacaca' courts. The concept of gacaca courts is borrowed from a traditional practice of community-based dispute resolution. The gacaca courts are intended to provide a participatory form of justice in which the general populace can participate. Local communities elect judges to sit on panels, and the hearings require a quorum of community members to be present. The stated purpose of this system is to achieve truth, accountability and reconciliation. The Government formally launched the gacaca system in 2002 and added some legislative modifications in 2004. In 2005, gacaca courts began delivering their first judgments (hours after some of the trials began). The national legislation envisions establishing 12,103 gacaca courts across the country.

The law classifies offenders into three broad categories. Category One includes planners, organizers, supervisors and leaders of the genocide or crimes against humanity as well as accomplices, and individuals who allegedly committed, or were accomplices in, torture, 'rape or acts of torture against sexual organs', particularly brutal or notorious killings, or 'dehumanizing acts on the dead body'. Category Two includes perpetrators or accomplices of intentional homicides, serious assaults causing death, or serious assaults without intending to cause death. Category Three includes perpetrators of property crimes. Gacaca courts have responsibility, in a pretrial process, for classifying defendants according to these three groups. Category Two and Three defendants are then tried by gacaca courts. Category One defendants are tried by regular national courts.

An official roster lists the names of all currently accused individuals, and the law provides incentives for confessions. It involves a complex scheme allowing individuals who confess to commute their sentences. For example, Category One offences carry a sentence of death or life imprisonment. Individuals who confess to Category One offenses receive a prison sentence of 25 to 30 years. Individuals who confess to Category One offences before being listed on the roster are eligible for partial commutation of sentence apparently to community service. Category Two offences involving intentional homicides or serious assaults causing death carry a prison sentence of 25 to 30 years. Individuals who confess to these offenses after being listed on the roster receive a prison sentence of 12 to 15 years with half of their sentence commuted to community service. Incentives related to other offences are similarly structured.

In practice, the process of making a confession has frequently included the identification of additional suspects. So too has the practice of local community members' naming new suspects during the gacaca process. The first wave of confessions resulted in the incrimination of thousands of additional individuals. In 2005, the Executive Secretary of the National Service of Gacaca Jurisdictions stated, 'Drawing from the experience and figures accruing from the pilot trials, we estimate a figure slightly above 1 million people [an eighth of the population] that are supposed to be tried under the gacaca courts'. Concerns have been raised that these new cases will further overwhelm the system.

A separate criticism of the law is that innocent individuals will be encouraged to confess to crimes they did not commit especially if their time already served in pretrial detention satisfies half of the maximum prison penalty (such that the remaining time would be spent in community service). In addition to these concerns, consider the procedural fairness of the gacaca courts in light of the following material.

ORGANIC LAW NO 16/2004 OF 2004 ESTABLISHING THE ORGANIZATION, COMPETENCE AND FUNCTIONING OF GACACA COURTS CHARGED WITH PROSECUTING AND TRYING THE PERPETRATORS OF THE CRIME OF GENOCIDE AND OTHER CRIMES AGAINST HUMANITY, COMMITTED BETWEEN OCTOBER 1, 1990 AND DECEMBER 31, 1994

Article 29

Every Rwandan citizen has the duty to participate in the Gacaca courts activities.

Any person who omits or refuses to testify on what he or she has seen or on what he or [she] knows, as well as the one who makes a slanderous denunciation, shall be prosecuted by the Gacaca Court which makes the statement of it. He or she incurs a prison sentence from three (3) months to six (6) months. In case of repeat offence, the defendant may incur a prison sentence from six months (6) to one (1) year.

Is considered as refusing to testify on what he or she has seen or knows, any person who apparently knew something on a given matter denounced by others in his or her presence, without expressing his or her own opinion.

Is considered as refusing to testify:

1° Anyone who, once summoned to testify before the Court after knowing that he or she is holder of a testimony, refuses to declare by avoiding to speak or deliberately evading the question put to him or her;

2° Anyone who, once summoned by the Court and does not appear deliberately without reasons, avoiding to be questioned in as much as the summons is clearly notified to him or her.

Is considered as a perjurer, anyone who gives a testimony ascertaining that he or she is telling only the truth and holds evidences for that, takes an oath and signs it; but later on it appears to be false and done on purpose.

The perjury is prosecuted during the very hearing of the matter in which the prosecuted person has given the testimony, if it is discovered that the person did it on purpose.

Article 33

The General Assembly of the Gacaca Court of the Cell exercises the following attributions:

1° electing Seat members of the Gacaca Court of the Cell and their deputies;

2° attending the activities of the Gacaca Court of the Cell for the non-members of the seat and take the floor only upon request;

3° assisting the seat of the Gacaca Court in the establishment of a list of persons

a. who resides in the cell;
b. who resided in the cell before the genocide, locations they kept shifting to and routes they took;
c. killed in their Cell of residence;
d. killed outside their Cell of residence;
e. killed in the cell while they were not residing in it;
f. victimized and their damaged property;
g. alleged authors of the offences referred to in this organic law.

4° presenting evidences or testimonies on all person s suspected of having committed the crime of genocide and on others who took part;

5° examining and adopting activity report established by the Gacaca Court.

All residents of the Cell shall tell the facts of events which took place, especially in their home villages and give evidence, denounce the authors and identify the victims.

Article 34

The Seat for the Gacaca Court of the Cell exercises the following attributions:

1° with the participation of the General Assembly, to make up a list of persons:

a. who reside in the cell;
b. who were residing in the Cell before the genocide, locations where they kept shifting to and routes they took;
c. killed in their Cell of residence;
d. killed outside their Cell of residence;
e. killed in the cell while they were not residing in it;
f. victimized and their damaged property;
g. who took part in the offences referred to in this organic law.

2° to receive confessions, guilt plea, repentance and apologies from the person who participated in genocide;

3° to bring together the files forwarded by the Public Prosecution;

4° to receive evidences and testimonies and other information concerning how genocide was planned and put into execution;

5° to investigate testimonies;

6° to categorize the accused as per the provisions of this organic law;

7° to put on trial and judges cases for the accused whose crimes classify them in the third category;

8° to give a ruling on objection to Seat members for the Gacaca Court of the Cell;

9° to forward to the Gacaca Court of the Sector, the files of the defendants classified in the second category;

10° to forward to the Public Prosecution, the files for the defendants classified in the first category;

11° to elect members of the Coordination Committee.

A victim referred to in point 1°-f is anybody killed, hunted to be killed but survived, suffered acts of torture against his or her sexual parts, suffered rape, injured or victim of any other form of harassment, plundered, and whose house and property were destroyed because of his or her ethnic background or opinion against the genocide ideology.

Article 38

As regards offences relating to rape or acts of torture against sexual parts, the victim chooses among the Seat members for the Gacaca Court of the Cell, on or more to whom she submits her complaint or does it in writing. In case of mistrust in the Seat members, she submits it to the organs of investigations or the Public Prosecution.

. . .

It is prohibited to publicly confess such an offence. No body is permitted to publicly sue another party. All formalities of the proceedings of the that offence shall be conducted in camera.

Article 39

Gacaca Courts have competences similar to those of ordinary courts, to try the accused persons, on the basis of testimonies against or for, and other evidences that may be provided.

They may in particular:

1° summon any person to appear in a trial;

2° order and carry out a search of or to the defendant's. This search must, however, respect the defendant's private property and basic human rights;

3° take temporary protective measures against the property of those accused of genocide crimes;

4° pronounce sentences and order the convicted person to compensate;

5° order the withdrawal of the distrait for the acquitted person's property;

6° prosecute and punish troublemakers in the court;

7° summon, if necessary, the Public Prosecution to give explanatory information on files it has investigated on;

8° issue summons to the alleged authors of offences and order detention or release on parole, if necessary.

Article 53

For the implementation of this organic law, the accomplice is the person who has, by any means, provided assistance to commit offences with persons referred to in article 51 of this organic law.

Article 54

Any person who has committed offences aimed at in article one of this organic law has right to have recourse to the procedure of confessions, guilt plea, repentance and apologies.

Apologies shall be made publicly to the victims in case they are still alive and to the Rwandan Society.

To be accepted as confessions, guilt plea, repentance and apologies, the defendant must:

1° give a detailed description of the confessed offence, how he or she carried it out and where, when he or she committed it, witnesses to the facts, persons victimized and where he or she threw their dead bodies and damage caused;

2° reveal the co-authors, accomplices and any other information useful to the exercise of the public action;

3° apologise for the offences that he or she has committed.

AMNESTY INTERNATIONAL, RWANDA: THE TROUBLED COURSE OF JUSTICE

26 April 2000
http://web.amnesty.org/library/Index/ENGAFR470102000?open&of = ENG-RWA

Amnesty International delegates who visited Rwanda in late 1999 received both positive and negative reactions to the proposals from Rwandese of various backgrounds. Many people expressed a general sense of hope and optimism for the proposals. However, some families of victims of the genocide expressed fears that the gacaca jurisdictions would result in excessively light sentences for those who may have committed terrible crimes. Some of the accused, on the other hand, viewed the proposals as a way of legitimizing popular retribution on those presumed to be guilty for the genocide. Both groups expressed fears that the gacaca jurisdictions would be used as a way of settling personal scores, rather than extracting the truth or delivering justice. . . .

...

Right to legal defence

The draft law on the gacaca jurisdictions does not make any explicit reference to the right of the accused to have access to legal representation. In view of existing safeguards of this right in national and international law, the accused should automatically enjoy this right in the gacaca trials. However, several senior Rwandese government officials, including the Minister of Justice, have stated explicitly and publicly that the accused in the gacaca trials would not be allowed representation by a defence lawyer. This would result in a serious disadvantage for the accused, especially as the majority are likely to have little or no formal education, limited awareness of their rights or knowledge of how to defend themselves in a formal or semi-formal context. The question of the right of defendants to legal assistance in the pre-trial period has not been addressed either.

...

Concerns relating to competence, independence and impartiality

Amnesty International is seriously concerned about the lack of legal training of members of the gacaca jurisdictions. The individuals who would be asked to try the cases which come before the gacaca jurisdictions would be elected into this role by the local population. They would have no prior legal background or training, and yet will be expected to hand down judgments in extremely complex and sensitive cases, with sentences as heavy as life imprisonment.... Even if these individuals are conscientious and striving to act in good faith, it is likely that they will be subjected to considerable pressures both from the accused and the complainants.... Government authorities have indicated that they would receive some "basic" training and have appealed for international assistance for this task, but have stressed that the rules governing the gacaca trials must be kept simple.

...

The search for the truth

One of the main hopes pinned on the gacaca jurisdictions is that they will succeed in revealing the truth — in a manner which the ordinary courts fail to do — by holding hearings at the grassroots level and encouraging people to testify to events they witnessed in their own community. However, it will not be sufficient to instruct people to tell the truth. The search for the truth is extremely important but should not be undertaken at the expense of justice....

International obligations

If the gacaca jurisdictions are set up as outlined in the draft law, the trials would clearly fail to meet basic international standards for fair trial....

A primary guarantee of a fair trial is that decisions will be made by competent, independent and impartial courts. This is reflected in Article 14(1) of ICCPR as well as Article 7 of the African Charter. Principle 2 of the Basic Principles on the Independence of the Judiciary states that "the judiciary shall decide matters before them impartially, on the basis of facts and in accordance with the law, without any restrictions, improper influences, inducements, pressures, threats or interferences, direct or indirect, from any quarter or for any reason". Judges should have legal training and experience (Principle 10 of the Basic Principles states "Persons selected for judicial office shall be individuals of integrity and ability with appropriate training or qualifications in law") and should be impartial: they should not have any interest or stake in a particular case and should not have pre-formed opinions about it.

Among the minimum guarantees for a fair trial, Article 14(3) of the ICCPR includes the right to defend oneself through legal counsel and to be informed of such a right, and the right to examine and call witnesses.

REPUBLIC OF RWANDA, REPLY TO AMNESTY INTERNATIONAL'S REPORT 'RWANDA: THE TROUBLED COURSE OF JUSTICE'

May 2000

http://www.gov.rw/government/06_11_00news_ai.htm#X.%20GACACA

... The observations of the report are critical of the proposed structures. The report, however, does not attempt to offer any alternative to Gacaca. Neither does it offer any practical solutions to the shortcomings that it claims to see in our proposal. The authors of the report are content merely to list a catalogue of things they are unhappy about. We are compelled to reply in detail to the report's comments on Gacaca tribunals.

...

We resolved, in particular, to let the existing court structures handle the genocide cases. The courts in charge of hearing genocide cases have now been in operation for more than three years. . . .. In 1997, they were only able to judge 346 persons. In 1999, the number had risen to 1318. The number for the first quarter of 2000 is almost 600.

In any other country, the successful conduct of 1500 murder trials would be an extraordinary achievement. In Rwanda, this is far from satisfactory in light of the large number of persons awaiting trial. Our court system is overwhelmed. Supporting institutions such as the parquets and police cannot cope. Our prisons are overcrowded. Although the conditions of detention are far from satisfactory for many detainees, the cost of maintaining these prisons takes a disproportionate portion of our budget. Part of this budget could be put to better use financing social programs.

Defendants and complainants alike are equally frustrated by the slow pace of justice. The problem is not the classical system of justice per se. The problem is that the system was never designed or intended to deal with accountability for crimes of such mass violence. . . .

...

The system will encourage confessions by offering incentives to defendants who cooperate. The number of detainees in our overcrowded prisons will be reduced by substituting part of the sentence of every prisoner with a requirement to perform community service. This will reduce government expenditure on prisons and the savings made can help finance desirable social services. Conditions for detainees who will remain in prison will improve dramatically as the number of inmates goes down.... The system will, we strongly believe, produce a climate that will enhance the process for reconciliation.

...

Legal Representation

Rwanda has only around 60 lawyers in private legal practice. On account of various reasons, the majority of these advocates have shown little willingness to defend genocide suspects. We acknowledge the right of genocide suspects to legal defence. However, there should be no question that victims of genocide too are entitled to justice.

A position to the effect that the people who committed genocide in this country should not be tried because we lack lawyers to represent them would be indefensible in light of the crimes that were committed during the genocide. When we were drafting the legislation on the prosecution of genocide suspects in 1996, we chose to adopt the compromise position that legal representation is a right, but the state would not assume responsibility to finance it. We did not have the personnel to provide legal representation for all genocide suspects appearing before ordinary courts. We are unable to provide lawyers to represent genocide suspects whose cases will go to Gacaca tribunals.

Even on the assumption that enough lawyers were available, there would still be problems of financing. Who would bear the cost? And why has such financing not been available for the on-going trials?

...

The task of providing legal representation is already difficult as it is when there are only 12 court chambers specialising in handling genocide cases. There will be something in the range of 10,000 Gacaca tribunals. It is difficult to see how one could conceivably raise enough lawyers to appear in 10,000 jurisdictions across the country....

...

Concerns Relating Competence, Independence and Impartiality

...

There is concern, for example, that judges in Gacaca tribunals will not have any prior legal experience or training. The report misses the whole point about Gacaca tribunals. There would have been no need to turn to Gacaca tribunals in the first place if we had people with the necessary legal background in sufficient numbers to work in our courts.

The report expresses the fear that judges in Gacaca tribunals will be subjected to considerable pressure from both the accused and the complainants, as well as from political authorities. As Amnesty International itself acknowledges in the report, even judges in ordinary courts are themselves not immune to pressure. In any event, we are of the opinion that such pressure is less likely in Gacaca jurisdictions because of the large number of judges involved and the more transparent methods of operation that Gacaca tribunals will use.

The Amnesty International report criticises plans to keep the rules of procedure governing Gacaca simple. One of the reasons why it has become necessary to transfer genocide cases to Gacaca tribunals is because ordinary courts are burdened by cumbersome procedures. There would be absolutely no point in establishing Gacaca tribunals if the intention is to transform them into replicas of ordinary courts which are unable to help us resolve the problem at hand.

...

International Obligations

...

We acknowledge that Gacaca jurisdictions are tribunals to which the international human rights instruments, to which Rwanda is a party, apply. We undertake to honour our obligations under the treaties in question.

... The draft law conforms to the provisions of the requirements of the International Covenant on Civil and Political Rights on all essential issues generally, and the rights to a fair and public hearing and a competent, independent and impartial tribunal in particular.

Whereas there may be certain basic international standards that all parties to human rights treaties must adhere to, international human rights law recognises that circumstances in state parties differ in many respects. That is why many treaties permit states to make their signing of certain treaties subject to some reservations. Opt-out provisions are also common. Indeed, the framers of the International Covenant on Civil and Political Rights recognise that there should be room for exceptions. . . . [The Government quotes Article 4(1)–(2) of the ICCPR.]

No one would doubt that the genocide, which Rwanda experienced in 1994, qualifies as a crisis that threatened the life of the nation.

The matters in respect of which the draft law on Gacaca jurisdictions does not, according to the Amnesty International report, conform to the International Covenant on Civil and Political Rights are matters covered by provisions from which Rwanda as a state party may derogate, and we do not have any doubt that the requisite circumstances that would entitle Rwanda to exercise the right of derogation exist.

...

AMNESTY INTERNATIONAL, RWANDA — GACACA: A QUESTION OF JUSTICE

17 December 2002

http://web.amnesty.org/library/Index/ENGAFR470072002?open&of = ENG-RWA

Despite the promise of gacaca, the legislation establishing the Gacaca Jurisdictions fails to guarantee minimum fair trial standards that are guaranteed in international treaties ratified by the Rwandese government.... If justice is not seen to be done, public confidence in the judiciary will not be restored and the government will have lost an opportunity to show its determination to respect human rights.... The laudable objectives of ending impunity and restoring the social fabric cannot be achieved without respecting human rights.

...

While the contemporary gacaca jurisdictions retain certain characteristics of the customary system — notably their location in the local community and the participation of community members, there are significant differences. Customary gacaca proceedings dealt with interfamily or intercommunity disputes. Offenders voluntarily appeared before *inyangamugayo*. Their appearance before community elders demonstrated their desire to be re-integrated into the community whose mores they had violated....

Contemporary Gacaca Jurisdictions deal, not with local disputes, but with a genocide organized and implemented by state authorities in which hundreds of thousands of individuals lost their lives. The new jurisdictions are state creations. Their operation and sentencing are dictated by national legislation.... If reconciliation is an essentially personal interaction between victim and perpetrator, one can see how gacaca, as previously practiced, would promote it. It is less clear that the state-mandated Gacaca Jurisdictions whose focus remains on retributive justice will achieve the same end.

...

The requirement of equal treatment by the courts in criminal cases demands that equality of arms must be observed throughout the trial process. It is essential that each party is afforded a reasonable opportunity to present its case, under conditions that do not place it at a substantial disadvantage vis-à-vis the opposing party. In criminal trials, where the prosecution has all the machinery of the state behind it, the principle of equality of arms is an essential guarantee of the right to defend oneself. It ensures among others that the defence has a reasonable opportunity to prepare and present its case on a footing equal to that of the prosecution; the right to adequate time and facilities to prepare a defence, including disclosure by the prosecution of material information; the right to legal counsel; the right to call and examine witnesses and the right to be present at the trial.

...

Thus, Article 14(1) of the ICCPR provides that "in the determination of any criminal charge against him, or of his rights and obligations in a suit at law, everyone shall be entitled to a fair and public hearing by a competent, independent and impartial tribunal established by law." The Human Rights Committee has stated that this right "is an absolute right that may suffer no exception". In fact, the right may not be suspended even in states of emergency under the African Charter on Human and Peoples' Rights.

...

Despite government disavowals, the prosecution enjoys a number of other advantages. A majority of cases will be judged on the basis of case-files prepared and passed on to the gacaca benches by the Public Prosecutor's Offices. Lay judges, with virtually no legal training, may be unwilling to challenge the information contained in them. Likewise, it will be difficult for defendants, without counsel, to effectively counter cases prepared by state authorities with infinitely more resources at their disposal....

...

Inyangamugayo were traditionally community elders whose status, experience and historical knowledge of the community gave them the independence, impartiality and competence required to arbitrate local conflicts. Contemporary gacaca judicial arbiters, "*les intègres*" (honest or upright individuals), represent the full spectrum within Rwandese communities. While this is advantageous and commendable, the gacaca judges do not occupy the same community standing as these inyangamugayo, which also calls into question their capacity to insure fair trial proceedings.

...

Cell-level Gacaca Jurisdictions operate at an administrative level small enough to enable community debate to take place. Ministry of Justice officials repeatedly told Amnesty International delegates that truth, if it can or will be told, is known at this level. The same cannot be said for province-level Gacaca Jurisdictions where the conceptualization of gacaca as a community forum breaks down. There is also more room for intervention both from the state and various pressure groups. Since all judges have the same amount of legal training, judges at the province-level would in most cases have neither the legal background nor legal knowledge to compensate for the loss of community discussion.

...

The Rwandese government has to further ensure that its own human rights violations during the genocide and armed conflict are investigated and tried. The Rwandese government can argue, as it does, that its crimes do not equal the magnitude and scale of those committed by the former government. Nonetheless, all human rights violations, regardless of who committed them or whether or not they constitute the crime of genocide have to be investigated and tried in a court of law.

...

IX. Recommendations

...

Amnesty International has already made some of the following recommendations; others are quite new.

...

...Relevant legislation regarding gacaca needs to ensure that:

...

- defendants and their lawyers have access to appropriate information, including documents, information and other evidence necessary to the preparation of their case;
- defendants and their lawyers should be given adequate time and facilities to prepare their defence at all stages of the proceedings. This is essential given the complexity of genocide cases and the fact that defendants will not have access to defence counsel;

...

- defendants have the opportunity to call and examine witnesses on their behalf and to examine witnesses against them;...
- each party in a gacaca hearing is afforded a reasonable opportunity to present its case under conditions that do not place it at a disadvantage;
- gacaca tribunals operate in an independent, impartial and competent manner; ...
- all gacaca sessions and hearings are open to the public, including human rights monitors, and operate in a transparent manner;...

...Amnesty International requests members of the international community to:

use their political influence and financial resources to ensure that the Gacaca Jurisdictions respect international minimum fair trial standards....

QUESTIONS

1. Recall the discussion of derogation rules in Chapter 5, *supra.* Did the Government of Rwanda lawfully derogate from its international obligations? If the Government plausibly satisfied the substantive requirements, does it indicate that those requirements are too weak?

2. In applying international legal standards, should greater deference be accorded to post-conflict societies? Conversely, should governmental decisions in post-conflict societies receive closer scrutiny and less deference given the politically charged atmosphere including the public's thirst for vengeance that often accompanies such situations?

3. Do the gacaca courts satisfy the standards of a fair trial? Should a different standard apply to extremely impoverished countries dealing with such a large number of cases? Do the gacaca courts satisfy the specific requirements for an independent and impartial hearing? How could the Government create an 'impartial' proceeding in such a post-genocidal society?

4. Amnesty International makes a number of consequentialist claims such as '[i]f justice is not seen to be done, public confidence in the judiciary will not be restored' and that 'restoring the social fabric cannot be achieved without respecting human rights'. Are these propositions correct? What empirical assumptions underlie such claims (and is Amnesty International well suited to make such assessments)? Do these types of consequentialist claims help or hurt efforts to promote human rights? What if the public demands trials that fall far short of international standards? For example, what if community leaders explicitly call for summary trials and executions 'to restore the "social fabric" '?

ADDITIONAL READING

John R.W.D. Jones *et al.*, 'The Special Court for Sierra Leone: A Defense Perspective', 2 J. Int. Criminal Justice 211 (2004); Jane Stromseth (ed.), *Accountability for Atrocities: National and*

International Responses (2003); Eric Stover and Harvey M. Weinstein (eds.), *My Neighbor, My Enemy: Justice and Community in the Aftermath of Mass Atrocity* (2004); Laura A. Dickinson, 'The Promise of Hybrid Courts', 97 Am. J. of Int. L. 295 (2003).

E. PEACE VERSUS JUSTICE?

How should institutional efforts to remedy mass human rights violations address concerns that such interventions promote war or social conflict? Efforts to address past wrongdoing, for example, may threaten to unravel a fragile peace agreement or the transition from an authoritarian past. Concerns about such consequences often relate to the prospect of criminal trials. These concerns, however, can also apply to a range of other measures. For instance, a truth commission, under certain circumstances, could be more likely to rupture social relations and foster notions of collective guilt rather than encourage reconciliation. Lustration policies — precluding former perpetrators and their supporters from participating in a successor government — might obstruct social integration and political stability. Civil suits against particular individuals or organizations, such as companies formerly involved in apartheid South Africa, might undermine government efforts to encourage those and other actors to rebuild the country.

The important question may not be whether to adopt particular institutional devices. The most important question may be one of timing. When is it appropriate, or most feasible, to deal with the past through these justice and accountability mechanisms? A central question may also be about who decides. That is, what institution or set of actors should have the authority to decide whether to pursue various strategies? Are local actors best situated to make those decisions, international actors, judicial or political bodies? Does it matter if local actors generally prefer amnesties?[9] What if local actors prefer prosecution, especially for retributive or symbolic reasons, despite a more pragmatic judgment of international exports and institutions? Should the structure of international and domestic legal institutions include a presumption favouring (or disfavouring) certain justice and accountability mechanisms? What factors should overcome that presumption?

Finally, how should decision-makers weigh justice and peace in the instant case versus the precedent set and consequences for dealing with situations of mass violations in the future? For example, trials in the instant case may be important to promoting norms and expectations of punishment in other countries or in the same country's political future. Alternatively, trials might encourage repressive leaders or combatants in the future to conclude that amnesties are not reliable and that conceding political power is not in their best interest.

[9] In general, *amnesties* foreclose prosecutions for stated crimes (often by reference to crimes or conduct that took place before a stated date), whereas *pardons* release convicted human rights offenders from serving their sentences (or the remainders thereof if they are prisoners at the time of pardon). Nonetheless, usage often views these terms as interchangeable, so that persons not yet tried are 'pardoned' and prisoners serving sentences are granted an 'amnesty'.

The following readings emphasize the institutional response that has received the most attention: criminal trials. Efforts to bring individuals to justice through international and domestic prosecutions have bumped up against concerns about endangering peace and stability. As the readings below explain, proponents of prosecution argue that states and international institutions have a legal obligation to punish gross violations of human rights. Recent controversies include the decision of ICTY officials to indict Bosnian Serb leaders during the final stages of peace negotiations in the Balkans, the subsequent decision of the ICTY to indict Slobodan Milosevic while the US Government was encouraging him to leave office, Cambodian Prime Minister Hun Sen's warning that prospective trials of Khmer Rouge leaders could reignite a civil war, Charles Taylor's request to have his indictment by the Special Court for Sierra Leone vacated in exchange for his leaving office, the approval by popular referendum of a broad-based amnesty for serious crimes committed by armed rebel groups in Algeria, the retroactive abolition of amnesties in several Latin American countries, the establishment of the Iraqi Special Tribunal to prosecute former senior officials in Saddam Hussein's Baath Party regime in the midst of an insurgency, indictments of rebel leaders in Uganda by the ICC Prosecutor despite local efforts to achieve peace and reconciliation, Iraqi Prime Minister Nouri al-Maliki's plan to offer amnesty to insurgents in his country. The list is long, and there is no reason to think similar cases will not arise in the future. The following readings begin with a commentary on the indictment of Milosevic in historical perspective. The subsection concludes by examining the particular case of the ICC and its provisions for deferring to national amnesties and local reconciliation processes.

MAX BOOT, COMMENTARY, WHEN 'JUSTICE' AND 'PEACE' DON'T MIX

***Wall Street Journal*, 2 October 2000, at A34**

... Is [Slobodan Milosevic] guilty? Sure. Was the indictment smart? No.

...

There's a better way to deal with dictators who stay past their sell-by date. In fact, we saw an example of this other approach last week too. Vladimiro Montesinos, the much-feared spy chief of Peru, was fired after being taped offering a bribe to a congressman. In order to avert a military coup, the U.S. government pressured Panama to grant him exile.

The Clinton administration's handling of Mr. Montesinos follows in the best Ronald Reagan tradition. In 1986, President Reagan dispatched his friend, Sen. Paul Laxalt, to Manila to inform Ferdinand Marcos, who had just stolen an election, that the jig was up. Sen. Laxalt did not tell Marcos that he would be headed for the slammer if he left Malacanang Palace. Instead, he offered the dictator and his wife the opportunity to move to Hawaii. They wisely accepted the invitation, letting the rightful election winner, Corazon Aquino, take power. The same year, the Reagan administration also helped engineer Jean-Claude "Baby Doc" Duvalier's voyage from Haiti to the French Riviera.

None of these deals was popular with human-rights campaigners, whose favorite slogan is, "No Justice, No Peace." They want to make dictators pay for their crimes. Hence the recent attempted prosecution of Augusto Pinochet. But justice, while a laudable concept, is hard to apply in the lawless realm of international affairs. If a war-crimes indictment keeps a Milosevic in power longer, allowing him to inflict greater suffering on his people and their neighbors, it's hard to see how this is more moral than letting him ride off into the sunset.

There's a place for war-crimes prosecutions — but they need to be smarter and more selective. During World War II, the Allies made no secret of their intention to hold top Germans and Japanese accountable for their atrocities. This helped fire up morale in Allied countries by transforming the war into a moral crusade, and it cost nothing. Since the Allies' stated war aim was unconditional surrender, throwing in war-crimes charges was not likely to make the enemy fight any harder. In 1946, war-crimes tribunals were convened at Nuremberg (19 Nazis were convicted, 12 hanged) and Tokyo (25 convictions, seven hanged). These trials helped Germany and Japan make a break with their nefarious pasts. But the Allies were careful not to go too far, for fear of making the occupied countries ungovernable.

Gen. Douglas MacArthur famously refused to prosecute Emperor Hirohito, even though he was arguably more complicit in war crimes than some subordinates who were hanged. MacArthur figured, probably rightly, that harming their revered emperor would hinder his efforts to transform the Japanese from foe to friend.

In short, the Allies realized after World War II that settling scores can sometimes conflict with the need to create a better world. "Justice" and "peace" aren't always compatible. And when those two imperatives clash[sic], morality dictates that the future win out over the past.

Applying those principles today, it's clear that war-crimes prosecutions make sense in Bosnia. Like post-1945 Germany or Japan, postwar Bosnia is run by an Allied army of occupation. Letting mass murderers like Radovan Karadzic run around loose makes it harder to build a democracy. Just imagine how difficult it would have been to create a free West Germany if Hermann Goring were hanging around Bonn.

It is equally clear that in the case of Slobodan Milosevic — who still holds sway over unconquered Serbia — a war-crimes indictment is counter-productive....
The West has made a mistake in letting the courts take the lead in Balkans policy. Tricky matters like easing dictators out of power should be left to politicians, diplomats and generals, not to lawyers....

JACK SNYDER AND LESLIE VINJAMURI, TRIALS AND ERRORS: PRINCIPLE AND PRAGMATISM IN STRATEGIES OF INTERNATIONAL JUSTICE

28 International Security 5 (2003/04), at 43–44

Advocacy groups such as Human Rights Watch and Amnesty International have made a historic contribution to the cause of international human rights by publicizing the need to prevent mass atrocities such as war crimes, genocide, and widespread political killings and torture. However, a strategy that many such groups favor for achieving this goal — the prosecution of perpetrators of atrocities according to universal standards — risks causing more atrocities than it would prevent…

Amnesties, in contrast, have been highly effective in curbing abuses when implemented in a credible way, even in such hard cases as El Salvador and Mozambique. Truth commissions, another strategy favored by some advocacy groups, have been useful mainly when linked to amnesties, as in South Africa. Simply ignoring the question of punishing perpetrators — in effect, a de facto amnesty — has also succeeded in ending atrocities when combined with astute political strategies to advance political reforms, as in Namibia.

…

Justice does not lead; it follows. We argue that a norm-governed political order must be based on a political bargain among contending groups and on the creation of robust administrative institutions that can predictably enforce the law. Preventing atrocities and enhancing respect for the law will frequently depend on striking politically expedient bargains that create effective political coalitions to contain the power of potential perpetrators of abuses (or so-called spoilers). Amnesty — or simply ignoring past abuses — may be a necessary tool in this bargaining. Once such deals are struck, institutions based on the rule of law become more feasible. Attempting to implement universal standards of criminal justice in the absence of these political and institutional preconditions risks weakening norms of justice by revealing their ineffectiveness and hindering necessary political bargaining.…

…

Trials do little to deter further violence and are not highly correlated with the consolidation of peaceful democracy.… In contrast, the empirical hypotheses underpinning pragmatism… fare better. Amnesties or other minimal efforts to address the problem of past abuses have often been the basis for durable peaceful settlements. The main positive effect of truth commissions has probably been to give political cover to amnesties in transitional countries with strong reform coalitions. The international criminal justice regime should permit the use of amnesties when spoilers are strong and when the new regime can use an amnesty to decisively remove them from power. Deciding what approach to adopt in a particular case requires political judgment. Consequently, decisions to prosecute should be taken by political authorities, such as the UN Security Council or the governments of affected states, not by judges who remain politically unaccountable.

…choices about punishment of past abuses must be made through the application of resolutely forward-looking criteria designed to avert atrocities and secure human rights, not backward-looking strategies based on rigid rule following or on what "feels right."

HELENA COBBAN, THINK AGAIN: INTERNATIONAL COURTS

Foreign Policy (May 2006)

...

"War Crimes Tribunals and Truth Commissions Advance Human Rights"

Not always. War crimes tribunals and truth commissions are well-meaning responses to ghastly atrocities. But the assumption that they advance human rights rests on a deep failure to recognize that nearly all of today's atrocities are committed in the anarchic, violent atmosphere of war zones. Any strategy for limiting atrocities must prioritize the pursuit of providing a stable, sustainable end to armed conflicts.

In some instances, threats of prosecution can actually impede peacemaking, prolong conflict, and multiply the atrocities associated with them. Consider Uganda. In July 2004, the ICC's chief prosecutor-responding to a request from the Ugandan government-launched a judicial investigation into the situation in the north of the country, where the Lord's Resistance Army (LRA) has sustained a barbaric insurgency for some 18 years. In April 2005, two dozen community leaders from northern Uganda went to The Hague to urge the prosecutor to hold off. One delegation member was David Onen Acana II, the chief of the dominant tribe in the war zone. He and his colleagues argued that their communities' traditional approaches would be far more effective than international prosecutions in ending the violence. In October, the Ugandan government, which had escalated its campaign against the LRA, announced that the ICC had issued arrest warrants against five top LRA leaders. LRA fighters responded by stepping up attacks against civilians and aid workers-just as Acana had warned.

Many successful, rights-respecting peace accords-including those in Spain and Mozambique-were built on tacit agreements not to look back. Is modern Spain weaker and less law-abiding because it did not engage in wrenching and divisive prosecutions of those who committed abuses during its decades of civil war and repression? The logic of prosecution-obsessed activists would say yes; common sense says no.

...

"Giving Amnesty to War Criminals Encourages Impunity"

Where's the proof? Post-genocide Rwanda has been dedicated in its pursuit of war crimes prosecutions. But it has borne that country little fruit. At one point when Rwanda was still trying to prosecute all those accused of participating in the 1994 genocide, more than 130,000 of its 8 million citizens were detained. Yet President Paul Kagame has also kept all major elements of society, including the judiciary, the government, and the media, completely under his thumb. That undermines the rule of law in Rwanda, no matter how dedicated the regime is to seeking justice. In 1994, Freedom House gave Rwanda a "Not Free" rating for its political rights and civil liberties-basic components of the rule of law anywhere. In 2004, Rwanda received the same rating.

By contrast, when Mozambique and South Africa ended their internal conflicts in the early 1990s, they enacted widescale amnesties-and in both countries, the rule of law quickly improved. In each of them, political leaders opted to move past the violence and injustices of the past and to focus on the tasks of social and political reconstruction. As part of that reconstruction, each country became a multiparty democracy in which the accountability of leaders and other key norms of the rule of law could finally take root. The restoration of public security, meanwhile, allowed the provision of basic services. And though their criminal-justice systems remained woefully underfunded, both were finally able to start providing citizens basic protections, such as an assurance of "habeas corpus." South Africa's Freedom House score made impressive improvements between 1994 and 2004. In poorer Mozambique, the improvement was smaller but still marked.

"The World Needs the International Criminal Court"

No. We can predict that the ICC will be no more effective than the international courts for the former Yugoslavia and Rwanda in improving the lives of war-zone residents who are its primary stakeholders. That is, not very effective at all.

In a criminal trial, two sets of facts-those of the prosecution and those of the defense-do public battle with each other. Those competing facts are probed and examined in detail and a winner and loser are ultimately decided. When such a trial concerns events that took place in recent memory, in a society that's still highly divided and deeply traumatized, the trial itself too often exacerbates existing political rifts.

That was the case with the ICTY and ICTR, and it risks being true of the ICC, too. The ICC shares with the two ad hoc courts the attribute that-unlike the Nuremberg and Tokyo tribunals-it exercises jurisdiction without being part of any broader administrative body that is responsible under international law for the welfare of the people within its domain....

Meanwhile, these war-shattered communities continue to live under the day-to-day control of their national governments. In the case of the former Yugoslavia, this fact has made it hard (and, in the case of wanted war criminals Radovan Karadzic and Ratko Mladic, impossible) for the ICTY to arrest some of its highest-ranking indictees. In the case of the ICTR, the Rwandan government's control over most of the witnesses and physical evidence involved in the court's cases has given the government a huge bargaining chip. It has used this power to force the ICTR to halt its investigations into well-founded accusations that Kagame's supporters also committed atrocities. In the ICC's work thus far on Uganda, the Ugandan government has similarly been able to deter the prosecutor from pursuing cases against pro-government forces. The idealists who supported the ICC's creation hoped that it would help check the power of governments and improve the well-being of much-abused people. There is little to suggest it will do either.

[The following exchange was published in a subsequent issue of the same journal in which Cobban's article appeared.[10]]

[10] 154 Foreign Policy, (May/June 2006), 4–10.

David Scheffer, Jostling over Justice

Helena Cobban misstates the intentions of international criminal tribunals.... They are convened to pursue justice and, over the long term, influence the attitudes of perpetrators and victims. No one ever assumed that they would have a significant short-term impact on warring parties.

After 1945, most Germans and Japanese despised the Nuremberg and Tokyo trials. But subsequent generations in both countries have absorbed the historical significance of these tribunals and become champions of human rights. Germany's support of the International Criminal Court (ICC) is second to none. When I was the U.S. ambassador at large for war crimes issues, I observed how often German negotiators invoked the memory of Nuremberg in advocating a permanent court. Decades from now, the same will be said of Serbs and Rwandans. Imagine how events would have unfolded if the atrocity lords of the Balkans, Rwanda, and West Africa had not been isolated and brought to credible justice by the international tribunals.

Michael P. Scharf, Jostling over Justice

A major war crimes trial — whether before an international or domestic tribunal — may cost upward of $100 million. But for someone accused of orchestrating the murder of 800,000 Tutsis in Rwanda, 250,000 Muslims in Bosnia, or 500,000 Northern Kurds and Marsh Arabs in Iraq, that is just a few hundred dollars per victim.

The former Yugoslavia is a case study in the benefits of international justice. The indictment of Slobodan Milosevic led to his removal from power and surrender to The Hague, where he no longer posed a threat to the region. During the war crimes trials, the NATO peacekeeping force in Bosnia has been reduced from 60,000 to just 7,000, as peace has taken hold. And though Milosevic's popularity may have climbed in the early days of his trial, it ultimately plummeted. The former Serb leader's nationalist policies were thoroughly discredited when the prosecution presented a graphic video of the genocidal acts committed at Srebrenica-evidence that was subsequently broadcast countless times throughout Serbia and Bosnia.

It is impossible to prove that war crimes prosecutions deter future atrocities. Yet evidence presented at the recent tribunals strongly suggests that the failure to prosecute perpetrators such as Pol Pot, Idi Amin, Saddam Hussein, Augusto Pinochet, and Papa Doc Duvalier convinced the Serbs and Hutus that they could commit genocide with impunity.

Cobban is calling for a return to the days before international accountability, a time when a person stood a better chance of being tried for killing one person than for killing 1 million. There must be no going back.

Helena Cobban, Jostling over Justice

People in conflict-plagued, low-income countries compare the expense of international courts with the development aid they receive. Viewed through this lens, courts look mind-bogglingly dear.

Throughout history, humans have fashioned many different social mechanisms for escaping conflict, and it seems strange that anyone should imagine that Western-style criminal trials can provide the answer around the globe....

... My colleagues in the human rights movement would make a greater contribution to attaining our shared goal of ending atrocities if they emphasized finding sustainable ends to conflicts and to righting the world's glaring economic imbalances.

KATHRYN SIKKINK AND CARRIE BOOTH WALLING, DO HUMAN RIGHTS TRIALS IMPROVE HUMAN RIGHTS?

Paper presented at the Princeton International Relations Faculty Colloquium, March 2006

... The trends in transitional justice follow some distinct patterns. We surveyed data on human rights trials for a 26 year period covering 195 countries and territories. Of the total, 34 countries have used truth commissions, and 51 countries had at least one transitional human rights trial. If we look only at the approximately 85 new and/or transitional countries in the period 1979–2004, we see that well over half of these transitional countries attempted some form of judicial proceeding. If we add to this list the 12 countries that used truth commissions but did not use trials, well over two thirds of transitional countries used either trials or truth commissions as a transitional justice mechanism. Second, of these fifty-one countries, many carried out a series of trials...

In sum, the use of a truth commission and/or human rights trials among transitional countries is not an isolated or marginal practice, but a very widespread social practice occurring in the bulk of transitional countries. Further, amnesties are not an alternative to truth commissions and trials, but more often part of the transitional justice mixture of policies. We believe that processes of international learning and diffusion are part of the explanation for the justice cascade.

...

[The authors turn to analyzing the impact of criminal prosecutions.] ... [W]e try two kinds of empirical comparisons: first, using a quantitative measure, we compare the human rights situation in individual countries before and after trials to see if we can discern the impact of trials on human rights; and second, we compare countries without trials to countries that had trials to gain further insight into the effects of trials. We also compare those countries that had a greater number of trials to those countries that had fewer trials. Note that in the Latin American cases we cannot compare the effectiveness of amnesties to trials because every transitional country in Latin America except Guyana, Grenada and Paraguay had an amnesty. Nor can we compare the efficacy of just using truth commission to the effectiveness of trials, because every country in the region that adopted a truth commission also used trials. There are however, countries that used trials but not truth commissions, so we can compare the effect of using both truth commissions and trials to the effect of using just trials....

...

First, we need to address the argument made by Snyder and Vinjamuri that amnesties "have been highly effective in curbing abuses, when implemented in a credible way, even in such hard cases as El Salvador and Mozambique." At least in Latin America, there is no evidence that amnesties are highly effective because amnesties are almost a constant, and it is difficult to untangle their impact from that of other transitional justice mechanisms. Amnesties were used in various forms in 16 of the 19 transitional countries in Latin America (all except Guyana, Grenada, and Paraguay). Further, many of these countries passed multiple amnesty laws. Of the sixteen countries that passed an amnesty law, only in Brazil did the amnesty appear to have the desired effect of blocking trials. Each of the amnesties in the remaining countries is slightly different, yet each of these countries also had truth commissions and also had human rights trials, and in some cases, frequent human rights trials. So, for example, drawing a case from Snyder and Vinjamuri, El Salvador passed six different amnesty laws (1979, 1980, 1983, 1987, 1992, and 1993), and had a truth commission in 1993, and held human rights trials in 1990, 1991, 1992, and 1998. El Salvador has seen a significant improvement in its human rights record, but it is not clear what explains the improvement: amnesties, the truth commission, trials, redemocratization, or the end of the civil war. There is no evidence that the amnesties in El Salvador or anywhere else in the region were effective by themselves in curbing abuses. At least in the Latin American cases, no generalization can be made at all about the effects of amnesty laws except that they have not been effective in preventing human rights trials.

...

What is the impact of trials on democracy? If we compare regions that have made extensive use of trials to regions that have not made extensive use of trials, we find that Latin America, which has made the most extensive use of human rights trials of any other region, has made the most complete democratic transition of any transitional region. In the 20th century, political instability and military coups were endemic in Latin America. Since 1980, however, the region has experienced the most profound transition to democracy in its history, and there have been very few reversals of democratic regimes. Ninety one percent of the countries in the region are now considered democratic, well above the level for Eastern Europe and the former USSR (67%) or Asia & Pacific (48%) or Africa (40%).

Since 1978 when the first trials were initiated in the region, the only examples of successful coups included President Alberto Fujimori's "self-coup" in Peru in 1992 (which has since experienced a transition to democracy), the coup in Haiti in 2004, and the coup in Ecuador in 2005 (where the military immediately turned power back to civilian leaders). The remaining 14 countries that used trials have not had a successful coup attempt since the use of trials, and in many cases, are increasingly considered consolidated democratic regimes. While we cannot yet attribute causation to the justice cascade, the data from Latin America provides no evidence that human rights trials have contributed to undermining democracy in the region.

...

Another key claim in the security literature is that human rights trials can lead to more conflict. Latin America experienced many internal conflicts between

1979 and 2004 — the years for which we have data on trials. . . . 17 Latin American countries experienced some form of internal or international conflict (from minor to a full fledged war) in the period 1970–2003: Argentina, Chile, Colombia, Ecuador, El Salvador, Grenada, Guatemala, Haiti, Mexico, Nicaragua, Panama, Paraguay, Peru, Suriname, Trinidad and Tobago, Uruguay, and Venezuela. There is clearly some kind of connection between trials and conflict because 16 of these countries also had some form of judicial proceedings for past human rights violations. The only countries that had transnational trials but did not have either type of conflict were Bolivia and Honduras. If we compare the dates of the conflict to the dates of the trials, however, we find that in most cases, judicial proceedings followed rather than preceded conflict . . . . In other cases, there was some overlap between the earliest trials and the armed conflict, but the conflicts did not extend significantly in these cases, and trials continued after conflict had ended. There is not a single transitional trial case in Latin America where it can be reasonably argued that the decision to undertake trials extended or exacerbated conflict.

. . .

Few who work on human rights believe that trials and truth commissions work only by changing the logic of appropriateness. Rather we believe there is an interesting blend of logics of appropriateness and logics of consequences at work for different actors. Actors that propose trials are often motivated by the logic of appropriateness. If we were discussing explanations for the emergence of human rights trials, we would stress the role of such principled action. But if we define effectiveness of such trials in terms of a reduction in human rights violations, the actors that interest us are those capable of carrying out future human rights violations — mainly the security forces. When we ask how trials and truth commissions change the perceptions and motivations of these actors we also need to understand how trials change the strategic context within which they operate. To do so, we first need to distinguish between current members of the security forces, some of whom have already carried out human rights violations, and younger members or future members of the security forces who have not carried out human rights abuses, because they operate in very different contexts. . . .

. . .

More interesting yet is actual deterrence of future human rights violations via the strategic impact of trials on the new generations of military leaders. Young officers who were not involved in the last round of repression may look at their past leaders and draw strategic conclusions about their future choices. They observe their past leaders, perhaps in jail through domestic trials, or in gilded cages of their countries through foreign and international trials, or with tattered international and domestic reputations. If logics of appropriateness are working simultaneously, future military leaders may decide that military coups, torture, or disappearances are not the appropriate standard of behavior for the modern professional military leader. But even if mainly logics of consequences are working, they may decide that trials have made repression and coups too costly for use in the future. . . . The "pragmatists" have only looked at the short term game and have ignored the long term game over the next ten to twenty years.

Second, because of the interconnected nature of international justice, trials in one country may affect the strategic calculations of military leaders in another country. Even trials that do not "succeed" in terms of a conviction can impose other forms of sanctions that are relevant for deterring actors from human rights violations in the future. Individuals are influenced by a range of possible sanctions, including issues that impact their national and international reputation, ability to travel, or to live in desirable international locations during retirement, ability to keep one's assets safe in banks in foreign countries, and the desire to send one's children to study abroad and then to visit them when they do. Foreign trials, even when they do not lead to imprisonment, can lead to indictments and international arrest warrants that affect reputation and make it risky to travel abroad. Civil trials for damages, while they may never result in imprisonment, can permit courts to attack people's assets, and make it difficult to keep funds abroad....

Empirically, we may not yet be able to prove or resolve what exact impact these sanctions have on the likelihood that future regimes will choose to use repression. But the so-called "pragmatic arguments" are not necessarily more realistic than the norm argument.... The passage of time makes a big difference for these scenarios. In the short term, as Snyder and Vinjamuri argue, it may be necessary to offer amnesties to end conflict, but in the long term, these amnesties are not holding in practice. The decision to offer such amnesties is what game theorists call a "time inconsistent commitment"— it is rational to make at the time, but not rational to keep later. Thus, it is more appropriate to think about the interactive nature of the logics of appropriateness and consequences, rather than to conclude that only one logic is at work with regards to transitional justice.

DARRYL ROBINSON, SERVING THE INTERESTS OF JUSTICE: AMNESTIES, TRUTH COMMISSIONS AND THE INTERNATIONAL CRIMINAL COURT

14 European J. of Int. L. 481 (2003)

[Article 53 of the ICC Statute, p. 1297 *supra*, permits the Prosecutor, with the approval of a Pre-Trial Chamber, to forego investigations or prosecutions when doing so is 'in the interest of justice'. This provision is generally understood to permit the ICC to defer to a national amnesty or reconciliation programme. Under Article 16, the Security Council could also potentially preclude prosecutions in such circumstances.]

... Even among international lawyers who argue that prosecution should sometimes give way to alternative means of dealing with the past, many or most would also allow that there are exceptionally serious crimes for which prosecution may be required under international law. The first pertinent question is which crimes are covered by the duty. To summarize very briefly, it is relatively clear that states are under a duty to bring to justice those responsible for genocide, acts of torture, and grave breaches of the Geneva Conventions of 1949. These obligations are derived from treaties, but are now widely considered to be reinforced by equivalent customary international law obligations....

With respect to the other crimes in the ICC Statute (crimes against humanity and serious violations of the laws of armed conflict), the situation is less clear. . . . In fact, it has often been noted that actual state practice has traditionally been distinctively unsupportive of such a duty, and tended in the past to condone the granting of amnesties. Nevertheless, there are convincing reasons to suggest that under current or emerging customary international law, there is a duty to bring to justice perpetrators of genocide, crimes against humanity and war crimes, at least with respect to crimes committed on the state's territory or by its nationals. First, there has been a marked revolution in state practice, decisively shifting from history's tacit endorsement of amnesties to today's consistent rejection of them for serious international crimes. This is illustrated by the disclaimer attached by the UN to the 1999 Lomé peace accord and the subsequent rejection of amnesties, and the exclusion of international crimes from the community reconciliation process in East Timor. Second, this practice is accompanied by numerous declarations affirming a duty to prosecute, in resolutions (such as the Resolution on Impunity adopted by the Commission on Human Rights), declarations (such as the Vienna Declaration and Programme of Action) and even the preamble of the ICC Statute. Without overstating the weight to be given to 'paper practice', these declarations are relevant in combination with the actual practice of states, as it shows that the practice of rejecting amnesties is accompanied by a sense of legal obligation. Third, a growing body of jurisprudence, generated by the Inter-American human rights system, the UN human rights system, and other national and international bodies, affirms that amnesties for serious violations also are incompatible with a state's basic human rights obligations. . . .

The other major question is the extent of that duty. Those critical of the idea of a duty to prosecute have argued that it does not take account of the potentially precarious position of new fragile democracies, that it would be reckless to require fragile democracies to proceed with a course that may lead to their destruction and, in addition, that in situations involving thousands of perpetrators, prosecuting everyone may be logistically impossible, financially ruinous and socially divisive.

In response, many advocates of the duty have recognized two limitations. First, the duty does not necessarily require a transitional government to prosecute all offenders; the duty may be satisfied by prosecuting the ringleaders and persons most responsible. Second, the duty may be subject to an exception of 'necessity' in situations of a 'grave and imminent threat', such that governments would not be required 'to press prosecution to the point of provoking their own collapse'. Such an exception is not to be lightly invoked; the international duty is intended to provide a counterweight to pressure from groups seeking impunity and thereby help embolden fragile democracies to carry out prosecutions rather than seeking an 'easy escape route'. It is proposed . . . that these two suggested limitations provide a useful frame of reference for the ICC in deciding whether to defer to a national programme falling short of full prosecution.

. . .

It is often argued that amnesties are a practical necessity to stop a conflict or to secure and maintain a transition from a military regime to a democratic government. . . .

However, any 'necessity' exception should be very carefully and narrowly construed.

...granting for the sake of argument that a 'necessity' exception is justified on consequentialist grounds, it is appropriate to weigh all of the consequences, including the long-term global consequences of granting impunity to violators. If governments adopt a general approach that 'impunity may be granted whenever expedient', then the consequence of giving into expediency in case after case will be impunity in case after case, thus reinforcing expectations of impunity and encouraging future violators.

Indeed, recent experience has tended to contradict the supposedly 'pragmatic' view that prosecution is destabilizing and that amnesties are necessary for peace, as indeed the very opposite propositions have been recently borne out. For example, in Sierra Leone, blanket amnesties were granted for horrific crimes against humanity in the belief that this was necessary for peace and reconciliation; instead this merely reinforced a culture of impunity in which brutal acts of mutilation and lawlessness continued. After more conflict and more atrocities, the policy was reversed in favour of prosecution and punishment of those bearing the greatest responsibility for international crimes. Likewise, many argued that the indictment of Slobodan Milosevic by the ICTY during the Kosovo conflict would only stiffen his resolve and prolong the conflict, and yet a peace agreement was reached shortly after the indictment, and Mr. Milosevic is now in The Hague facing trial. These and other cases cast considerable doubt on the received wisdom that peace and justice are somehow at odds.

...

This author would suggest that, in deciding whether a 'necessity exception' might apply, one should consider the balance between the extent of the departure from full prosecution, i.e., the quality of the measures taken, and the severity of the factors necessitating a deviation, to decide whether the society has done everything possible to advance accountability-related goals. Different authors have suggested different lists of criteria or factors to consider, but the following seem generally recognized as relevant:

- Was the measure adopted by democratic will?
- Is the departure from the standard of criminal prosecution of all offenders based on necessity, i.e. irresistible social, economic or political realities?
- Is there a full and effective investigation into the facts?
- Does the fact-finding inquiry 'name names'?
- Is the relevant commission or body independent and suitably resourced?
- Is there at least some form of punishment of perpetrators (are they identified, required to come forward, required to do community service, subject to lustration)?
- Is some form of remedy or compensation provided to victims?
- Does the national approach provide a sense of closure or justice to victims?
- Is there a commitment to comply with other human rights obligations?

In the light of the core purpose of the ICC and its prior compact with the state concerned, a programme where even the persons most responsible may apply for amnesties should receive deference 'only in the most compelling of cases'.

QUESTIONS

1. Does the list of factors outlined by Robinson sufficiently resolve problems that might arise in the struggle for both peace and justice? Should some factors weigh more heavily than others? Are there factors that should be added or omitted?

2. What actors or institutions are best equipped to make the determination that amnesty is appropriate in a given case? Does international law, or the ICC structure in particular, place too much weight in favour of prosecutions?

3. Should states in all circumstances have an absolute duty to prosecute the commission of extreme crimes such as genocide and grave breaches of the Geneva Conventions? Or should the extent of the duty to punish, even for these offenses, be qualified? Should any special exceptions be made for situations in which perpetrators and survivors must continue to coexist with one another in the same country?

4. 'Effective deterrence is predicated on strong and reliable incentives directed at rational actors. Some commentators claim it is most unlikely that the prospect of international criminal prosecution will deter future tyrants or genocidaires. Commentators who hold such a position, however, should not also claim that the existing threat of international criminal prosecution deters such individuals from relinquishing power or accepting a peace agreement. The two claims are inconsistent'. Comment.

ADDITIONAL READING

Yasmin Naqvi, 'Amnesty for War Crimes: Defining International Recognition', 85 Int. Review of the Red Cross 583 (2003); David Mendeloff, 'Truth-Seeking, Truth-Telling, and Postconflict Peacebuilding: Curb the Enthusiasm?', 6 Int. Studies Review 355 (2004); Ellen Lutz and Kathryn Sikkink, The Justice Cascade: 'The Evolution and Impact of Foreign Human Rights Trials in Latin America', 2 Chi. J. Int. L. 1 (2001); Robert I. Rotberg and Dennis Thompson (eds.), *Truth v. Justice* (2000).

F. TRUTH COMMISSIONS

Sections A–E examined the role of international, national and hybrid institutions in the prosecution of individuals accused of committing international crimes. The issues to be explored in Section F, like those in earlier sections, arise when systematic and gross human rights violations are committed internally by a controlling state regime (and in some cases by opposition groups as well). At a certain stage, whether because of a strengthening internal opposition, international pressures, economic deterioration, or special international circumstances such as war, negotiations with opposing forces may start to displace the authoritarian regime in power by a popularly elected government committed to human rights. Alternatively, the (often military) regime in power may simply collapse.

The question then arises how the new regime should act towards those suspected of serious human rights violations in the prior period. Should there be trials and punishment of individuals or should other paths be followed? Section F examines one other path, that of truth commissions. It examines the attributes of such institutions on their own terms. It also explores their relationships with criminal tribunals, which are increasingly working alongside truth commissions in response to the same set of violations.

HENRY STEINER, INTRODUCTION TO TRUTH COMMISSIONS

Harvard Law School Human Rights Program and World Peace Foundation, Truth Commissions: A Comparative Assessment (1997), at 7

The cause of the Irish problem, suggested William Gladstone, is that the Irish never forget, while the English never remember. Is there then a golden mean, some 'proper' degree of collective memory appropriate for bearing in mind the cruelties and lessons of a troubled past, while not so consuming as to stifle the possibilities of reconciliation and growth? How might one imprint such a memory on a people's or state's conscience? What kinds of institutions or processes would be appropriate? What purposes might be served by a detailed recording of gross abuses, not only for the collectivity but also for the individuals involved as victims or perpetrators? . . . In a brief fifteen years, 'truth commission' has become a familiar conception and institution for a state emerging from a period of gross human rights abuses and debating how to deal with its recent past. The term serves as the generic designation of a type of governmental organ that is intended to construct a record of this tragic history, and that has borne different titles in the many countries over several continents that have resorted to it. These commissions offer one among many ways of responding to years of barbarism run rampant, of horrific human rights violations that occurred while countries were caught up in racial, ethnic, class, and ideological conflict over justice and power. They may be alternative or complementary to other national responses, including the poles of amnesty and criminal prosecution.

The contemporary surge of truth commissions . . . started in Argentina after the country's defeat in the Falkland Islands war and the military's related retreat from political power. Other prominent examples of commissions that have effectively completed their work include Chile and El Salvador. In some countries such as Uruguay, commissions did not achieve a great deal. In others such as Uganda, hampered by a lack of political will and funds, they have been unable to complete their mission and issue a report. Among the commissions functioning today, the most discussed and — given the degree of reconstruction that will be necessary — potentially the most significant for a country's future operates in South Africa. . . .

The truth commission has been a protean organ, not only in the many institutional forms it has assumed, but also in its varying membership, in the diverse functions that it serves, and in its range of powers, methods, and processes. . . .

Although the general purposes and methods of truth commissions properly figure in a critical discussion of what they have achieved, what rapidly becomes apparent is that concrete examples drawn from different countries must inform abstract description. No architect of these institutions has proceeded by deduction from general principles. The effect of specific historical contexts on the kind of commission created is inconcealable. Consider, for example, one important explanation for the variations among commissions' mandates. When the military continues to hold considerable power as part of a negotiated move toward civilian rule (as in Chile where it retained its commander, the former political leader), severe constraints influence what a truth commission may be empowered to do, or the possibility of prosecution of military personnel. The Argentinian transition following a military disgrace enjoyed greater, though still limited, possibilities.

Commissions are official organs that are generally but not always staffed by citizens. They are organized for a time certain and for the specific purpose of examining through one or another method serious violations of personal integrity. Frequently, victims of gross violations testify before them, and alleged or confessed violators may testify as well. Invariably, the commissions receive or gather evidence of violations committed by state actors, and in some instances also of violations by nonstate actors such as insurgent groups. The investigative capacity given commissions has ranged from extensive staffs armed with legal powers, to reliance principally on voluntary testimony that may or may not be verified. Hearings have been both private and public. The reports of proceedings — including graphic evidence of abuses, sometimes the naming of victims and less frequently of perpetrators, summaries and conclusions, on occasion recommended changes in state institutions or structures — ultimately become public documents. . . .

. . . [T]ruth commissions have addressed state conduct that raises the most politically and morally sensitive issues facing the country as a whole.

Commission's reports have implicated high reaches of state authority in raw and systematic violations of law that claimed victims into the many tens of thousands. This slaughter, rape, torture, imprisonment, and disappearance of victims occurred in the setting of consuming conflicts, sometimes decades long, over a country's basic nature and structure: ethnic hierarchy or equality, military or democratic rule, dictation or participation, repression or expression, mass murder or the rule of law, concentration of wealth and power within a given elite or broader distribution. . . .

. . . [G]overnments have created these commissions principally at the time of a state's transition toward more participatory government expressing ideals of democracy, power bounded by law, formal legal equality, and social justice. Even when the moment of political change has been non-violent — as in Chile where the structural and substantive features of the change were discussed between an opposition and a government, or in South Africa where those features were submitted to the people for its approval — the term 'transition' may understate how radically the successor regime has departed from its predecessor with respect to moral principle and political ideology.

Realization of (or at least the aspiration toward) fundamental change appears to be an almost constant companion to the use of truth commissions. A repressive regime succeeding as repressive a government that it has ousted from power is unlikely to explore prior misdeeds that may be ideally suited to its own malign purposes. The movement toward democratic rule and associated human rights in the years since the Argentinean experiment has become more common in a world informed by the powerful ideals of the international human rights movement. Hence truth commissions have become more likely.

Second, the rules and principles drawn on by commissions in determining what is relevant testimony, in reaching conclusions about criminal conduct, or in making recommendations may be found directly in the international human rights movement. Or they may be found in a state's own internal law, a law that was violated by those holding power in the prior period. Even when the latter is the case, the impact on the national proceedings of such international norms (on murder, torture, disappearances, repression, ethnic discrimination, and so on) seems evident. South Africa offers a striking illustration of the powerful effect on a state of the international system's norms and pressures. Indeed, the term 'human rights' has figured as part of some commissions' titles. . . .

Any assessment of truth commissions must involve comparisons between them and other approaches toward dealing with a tragic period of national history. At one extreme, a state may grant amnesty to those who committed defined crimes — say, crimes with a political objective — during a prior regime. At another, it may criminally prosecute (as did Argentina) a limited number of leading figures who are viewed as ultimately responsible. . . .

Except where barred by amnesty provisions, victims' civil suits for compensatory damages first become possible as the repression lifts. The new government may develop a public program of systematic compensation or restitution. It may make public apology without fresh investigative proceedings — as, for example, the Czech and German governments have done in a recent joint declaration bearing on stated abuses during and after World War II. The so-called process of lustration (purification) may by law dismiss people from or make them ineligible for government or other positions because of their involvement in the criticized conduct of the prior regime.

Truth commissions can stand apart from all these approaches to dealing with the past, or they may be closely linked to one among them, perhaps to amnesty or to prosecution. In South Africa, for example, confession before a commission may lead to a grant of amnesty. . . .

Some possibilities and purposes of truth commissions are distinctive to them; others characterize several of the alternative or complementary processes that have been noted. . . .

[The author then notes some major issues about truth commissions.]

(1) Why should a state deal in some official way with its past? If it selects the path of truth commissions, what assurance can it have that major goals such as reconciliation among groups or catharsis for victims will be realized? For example, will the findings of a truth commission promote reconciliation without companion policies like compensation? Can the goal of deterrence of massive violations of human rights be realized through selective prosecutions of leaders, or through the narratives of truth commissions? (Consider in this respect the title, *Nunca Mas*, used for several reports of commissions.)

(2) What criteria and conditions should lead a state to resort to a truth commission rather than to alternative ways of dealing with the past like prosecution or lustration?

(3) Should commissions restrict themselves to recording facts developed through voluntary testimony or through investigative procedures? Should they also engage in broader causal analysis, as by advancing historical explanations of the sources of a conflict? Should a report include recommendations of structural and substantive changes in government with the purpose of avoiding mass recidivism?

(4) Can such questions be answered in general, or will answers necessarily depend on the particular close context for decision? . . .

JONATHAN D. TEPPERMAN, TRUTH AND CONSEQUENCES

Foreign Affairs, (March/April 2002), at 129–145

. . . [T]rials, the standard mechanism for arranging punishment, are a far from perfect way to establish transitional justice. The upper levels of the outgoing regime often demand immunity from prosecution as part of the transition deal. And even after repressive governments leave office, their civil servants — including judges, prosecutors, and police — usually remain in place. This makes practical sense, since new democracies cannot afford to purge all their experienced technocrats . . . Trials, moreover, with their high standard of proof and extensive evidentiary requirements, are complicated and expensive, and fledgling governments tend to be strapped for cash.

Even in countries eager to confront the past, trials have turned out not to be a good way of doing so. At their best, prosecutions for human rights crimes are limited in number and selective in scope. The Allied-sponsored Nuremberg trials, for example, covered 85,882 individual cases but secured only 7,000 convictions — and this for the Holocaust and all other Nazi atrocities. Moreover, trials focus not on general social or economic forces, but on individuals, and one set of individuals at that: namely, the perpetrators and not their victims.

Truth commissions, in theory, are supposed to address all these shortcomings. By forgoing the right to dispense punishment they make themselves less objectionable to members of the old regime. By avoiding prosecutions, they can delve widely into institutional injustices in the past. And by broadening their focus, commissions allow victims, not just violators, to tell their stories — something thought to have a powerful healing effect on those who have suffered. This, at least, is how truth commissions are supposed to work. . . .

. . .

Eyeing these mixed results in South Africa, Guatemala, or elsewhere, skeptics have raised four types of general objections to the work of truth commissions: that history is so murky and subjective that even well-intentioned investigations cannot establish anything that should actually be called, with a straight face, "truth"; that the panels too often focus on individual violations rather than broad structural problems; that their work does not lead to reconciliation; and that they interfere with, and distract attention from, the prosecution and punishment of past crimes.

A close look at the South African and Guatemalan cases, however, shows that although some of these charges have merit, well-planned commissions can nevertheless make an essential contribution to justice and harmony in fragile societies.

The first question, whether historical truth is a reasonable goal, is crucial. In many cases a commission's actual findings are its sole lasting accomplishment.... And the value of revealing the truth is not abstract.... it is argued, an honest accounting of past injustices is essential before shattered societies can start to rebuild.

Yet truth turns out to be a surprisingly elusive goal. One need not be a postmodernist to recognize that historical narratives are partly constructed rather than merely discovered, and that power and interests affect the process....

Furthermore, commissions have a bad habit of reflecting the prejudices and agendas of their framers. The TRC, for example, placed a disproportionate emphasis on crimes committed against nonblack South Africans. This slant was deliberate: even though blacks had suffered vastly more than other groups, [Chairperson of the TRC Archbishop Desmond] Tutu wanted the TRC to show how apartheid had affected all South Africans. As [Vice Chairperson of the TRC Alex] Boraine explained to me, "[Tutu] said that the major problem in our country is not a black problem, it's a white problem. It's a mixed race, a colored problem. So we mustn't go strictly on proportionality." However noble such a motive, unfortunately, giving nonblack victims more attention than they statistically "deserved" caused many blacks to angrily question the legitimacy of the TRC's findings.

...

Such criticisms, while serious, are best answered by the findings themselves. And there is abundant evidence that even imperfect truth commissions produce a wealth of previously unknown information regarding events that many people care about passionately. Families and friends have learned what happened to loved ones who "disappeared," and victims have had their charges legitimized. This can have a profound impact on sufferers....

Columbia University's Mahmood Mamdani, however, has leveled a somewhat different charge: that the [South African] TRC was not so much unable to locate the truth as it was unwilling to do so. The legislation that founded the commission, he notes, directed it to investigate only "gross violations of human rights." But the commission interpreted this mandate too narrowly, using it as an opportunity to avert its gaze from the broader criminality of the system itself and the racial inequities it perpetuated. Such choices explain why the TRC avoided economic injustice and documented only 21,000 victims — what Mamdani calls a "laughable" figure.

...as Mamdani bitingly explains, "[it] ended up acknowledging as victims only political activists. But apartheid wasn't about political activists; it was about ordinary people. The only reconciliation the TRC can now expect is between two elites."

This hardly means that the TRC report was a total failure. The fact that both de Klerk and Mbeki challenged it in public and in court suggest that it got something right. But Mamdani's critique does highlight the consequences of the choices that commissions make and raises questions about what exactly is meant by all the talk of reconciliation....

...

Reconciliation, then, turns out to involve much more than mere forgiveness; to achieve it seems to require far more than truth telling. In fact, the reconciliation project could better be described as "nation building." Such a process involves addressing fundamental social inequalities. That is a task for politics, however, and not one that truth commissions — however broad their mandate — can hope to accomplish.

If truth commissions tend to achieve somewhat less than their advocates like to think, then the final charge against them — that they overshadow and undermine prosecutions — becomes more important. . . .

. . .

Some governments, moreover, have turned to commissions precisely in order to put off — and eventually escape — formal legal proceedings that could spark confrontation with members or agents of the old regime. . . .

Truth commission advocates such as Priscilla Hayner and Alex Boraine, both of whom are now professional truth-commission consultants at the [International Center for Transitional Justice], deny there is any necessary opposition between commissions and trials. The two processes, they argue, are complementary, not mutually exclusive. Hayner points to the fact that in both Argentina and Chad, evidence uncovered by truth commissions has been used in subsequent prosecutions. "You'll find that truth commissions increase the possibility of prosecutions rather than the other way around," she promises.

So far, at least, there is little evidence to support this claim. . . . Asked whether there is a causal connection between the work of the truth commission and the small number of prosecutions, Paul Seils, a Scottish human rights lawyer working in Guatemala, argues that the effect of the [Guatemalan Commission for Historical Clarification] report was to reduce international pressure on the country. . . .

. . .

. . . Reconciliation turns out to be tremendously difficult to achieve or even understand. Truth too often remains elusive. The most appropriate response to such problems, however, should be not to blame the commissions for what they cannot accomplish, but to appreciate them for what they indisputably can. Although they may not have lived up to the giddy promises of their founders, for example, both the Guatemalan and the South African commissions made invaluable contributions to the health of those countries. Thanks to the TRC and the CEH, basic facts about apartheid in South Africa and the civil war in Guatemala are now part of the general historical record. De Klerk's political career has been ruined and he will never return to office. Even in Guatemala, a country slipping back toward chaos and gangsterism, the genocide of the 1980s is now impossible to deny.

And South Africa, at least, is a different country because of the TRC's collective national therapy. Harmony may not reign, but as Professor Jakes Gerwel, the chancellor of Rhodes University, argues, "notwithstanding the complex divisions and differences of various sorts, levels, and intensities, [it] is decidedly not an unreconciled nation in the sense of being threatened by imminent disintegration and internecine conflict." The fact that there have been no revenge killings in the country since the TRC started its work almost certainly says something about what kind of impact the commission has had.

VIEWS ON FUNCTIONS AND UTILITY OF TRUTH COMMISSIONS

Consider the following excerpts from the roundtable discussion in Truth Commissions: A Comparative Assessment, p. 1345, *supra*.

Bryan Hehir

I think that truth commissions function at three levels. The first entails catharsis.... The second level involves the process of moral reconstruction.... Society must pass judgment on what has been heard. It must establish a moral account of the historical record. The third level verges on the political — what is done with the process of truth telling? A number of options are available. A society may [even] choose to 'forget' or ignore the truth.

Tina Rosenberg

I am struck by how many comments outline the parallels between truth commissions and the therapeutic process of dealing with victims of post-traumatic stress disorder. The similarities are striking. People need to tell their story, but this is not all. Two other levels are important. People need to tell their stories to someone who is listening to them seriously and validating them. This is official acknowledgment. More importantly, victims must be able to reintegrate that narrative into their whole life story.

Lawrence Weschler (Staff Writer, *New Yorker*)

Furthermore, as the victims put their own lives together, they also pull the whole country together.

I detect three overlapping metaphors in our discussion — the realms of law, art and therapy. The most effective truth commissions carry on elements of the theatric, by being broadcast to the public on television for example. Artfulness of presentation makes the commission more effective. The public responds like an audience of a Greek tragedy. People must organize their lives in an artful way that lends them a cathartic life experience at the end.

❁ ❁ ❁

[Use of truth commissions in the context of particular international disputes:]

Yael Tamir

Should Israel and Palestine establish a truth commission?... I can think of three kinds of justifications, which I have ordered from the most to the least convincing.

The first presupposes that we have a moral obligation to know and remember the wrongs that have occurred. If we ignore the injustice that has been done or forget it, we become in some sense accomplice to it. This implies that we have an obligation to know what has happened regardless of the social effects that this knowledge might produce. A truth commission contributes to our ability to reach this goal and is therefore welcome. It signals that no harm will go unnoticed and that those who bear responsibility will not go unpunished.

The second justification is instrumental. It is grounded in the psychological needs of the victims and their relatives: the need to talk about their harsh experiences and to have their suffering publicly acknowledged. . . . I am skeptical about the ability of truth commissions to serve this goal. I also have a deeper doubt about the psychological assumptions — for example, whether victims are better off if they are allowed to recount their experiences.

Truth commissions are also seen as instrumental in promoting reconciliation. I find this claim doubtful. In my experiences in Israeli-Palestinian workshops, I have found that an attempt to expose the facts is not particularly useful. It is often better to assume that injustices have been committed by both sides, and then focus on how to solve the conflict.

The most convincing justifications are then of the first kind, for the arguments for commissions that rest on instrumental justifications are very contingent on detailed contexts. I believe that a truth commission is unlikely to be helpful in the Israeli-Palestinian case. . . . To summarize, if the peace process is to move forward it cannot proceed on the basis of an investigation of the past. Rather, we must disassociate ourselves from the past and build a future based on an abstract acknowledgment of the injustice done by both sides, an injustice grounded in the fact that we share the same small piece of land for which both sides make claims of right. We must therefore reach an agreement regardless of past injustices. Peace cannot be grounded in competition over past suffering.

Fateh Azzam

Basically I agree with Yael Tamir's assessment of the situation and the potential for a truth commission. At the same time, I cannot help but note the urgency of dealing with issues of past injustices.

What should emerge from this strange animal called the peace process? I have some disagreement with Yael. Unless we acknowledge what happened in the past, it will continue to come up. Israelis and Palestinians must redefine their relationship, but not necessarily deny it. We must acknowledge one another in a way that lays a proper foundation for our future. This will take a very long time. The Palestinians need to hear some acknowledgment in order for them to admit that co-existence is possible.

For these reasons, I had thought a truth commission might be a useful exercise. But further reflection has made me realize how much the outcome of the peace process depends on politics and political desires. Our societies need to accept one another, and this has not yet happened. Perhaps it is a question of timing.

QUESTIONS

1. Are you satisfied with Jonathan Tepperman's exposition of the virtues of truth commissions? Do these benefits overcome the potential costs he identifies?

2. Some commentators have argued that a decision to 'name names' in a truth commission's report of those (in armed forces, police) accused of committing serious human rights violations, as was done in the Report on El Salvador, is justified in part by the fact that the state's justice system is incapable of honest investigation and impartial judgment. Do you agree? Are there other reasons pointing towards including names of violators? What form and methods of investigation would you recommend for a truth commission that intended to publish such names?

3. 'Truth commissions are particularly useful where the people involved — violators, victims, those just standing by — will (indeed must) live in close proximity to each other as members of the same state and society. Hence they are less necessary and less effective in many types of international conflicts where the peoples involved, the violators and the victims, will live separately after some accord and end to the conflict.' Do you agree?

PROMOTION OF NATIONAL UNITY AND RECONCILIATION ACT OF SOUTH AFRICA, 1995

Definitions

...

1.

(ix) "gross violation of human rights" means the violation of human rights through —

(a) the killing, abduction, torture or severe ill-treatment of any person; or

(b) any attempt, conspiracy, incitement, instigation, command or procurement to commit an act referred to in paragraph (a), which emanated from conflicts of the past and which was committed during the period 1 March 1960 to the cut-off date within or outside the Republic, and the commission of which was advised, planned, directed, commanded or ordered, by any person acting with a political motive;

Functions of Commission

4. The functions of the Commission shall be to achieve its objectives, and to that end the Commission shall-

(a) facilitate, and where necessary initiate or coordinate, inquiries into —

(i) gross violations of human rights, including violations which were part of a systematic pattern of abuse;

(ii) the nature, causes and extent of gross violations of human rights, including the antecedents, circumstances, factors, context, motives and perspectives which led to such violations;

(iii) the identity of all persons, authorities, institutions and organisations involved in such violations;

(iv) the question whether such violations were the result of deliberate planning on the part of the State or a former state or any of their organs, or of any political organisation, liberation movement or other group or individual; and

(v) accountability, political or otherwise, for any such violation;

(b) facilitate, and initiate or coordinate, the gathering of information and the receiving of evidence from any person, including persons claiming to be victims of such violations or the representatives of such victims, which establish the identity of victims of such violations, their fate or present whereabouts and the nature and extent of the harm suffered by such victims;

(c) facilitate and promote the granting of amnesty in respect of acts associated with political objectives . . . ;

. . .

(f) make recommendations to the President with regard to —

(i) the policy which should be followed or measures which should be taken with regard to the granting of reparation to victims or the taking of other measures aimed at rehabilitating and restoring the human and civil dignity of victims;

(ii) measures which should be taken to grant urgent interim reparation to victims;

. . .

(h) make recommendations to the President with regard to the creation of institutions conducive to a stable and fair society and the institutional, administrative and legislative measures which should be taken or introduced in order to prevent the commission of violations of human rights.

Powers of Commission

5. In order to achieve its objectives and to perform its functions the Commission shall have the power to —

. . .

(d) conduct any investigation or hold any hearing it may deem necessary and establish the investigating unit referred to in section 28;

. . .

(i) in consultation with the Minister [of Justice] and through diplomatic channels, obtain permission from the relevant authority of a foreign country to receive evidence or gather information in that country;

(j) enter into an agreement with any person, including any department of State, in terms of which the Commission will be authorized to make use of any of the facilities, equipment or personnel belonging to or under the control or in the employment of such person or department;

...

(l) hold meetings at any place within or outside the Republic;

(m) on its own initiative or at the request of any interested person inquire or investigate into any matter, including the disappearance of any person or group of persons.

...

[Article 31 provides the power of the Commission to subpoena individuals to testify.]

[Article 34 provides the power of the Commission to authorize entry into premises and the search and seizure of relevant evidence.]

Granting of amnesty and effect thereof

20. (1) If the Committee, after considering an application for amnesty, is satisfied that—

(a) the application complies with the requirements of this Act;
(b) the act, omission or offence to which the application relates is an act associated with a political objective committed in the course of the conflicts of the past in accordance with the provisions of subsections (2) and (3); and
(c) the applicant has made a full disclosure of all relevant facts, it shall grant amnesty in respect of that act, omission or offence.

(2) In this Act, unless the context otherwise indicates, "act associated with a political objective" means any act or omission which constitutes an offence or delict which, according to the criteria in subsection (3), is associated with a political objective, and which was advised, planned, directed, commanded, ordered or committed . . . . by—

(a) any member or supporter of a publicly known political organisation or liberation movement on behalf of or in support of such organisation or movement, bona fide in furtherance of a political struggle waged by such organisation or movement against the State or any former state or another publicly known political organisation or liberation movement;

(b) any employee of the State or any former state or any member of the security forces of the State or any former state in the course and scope of his or her duties and within the scope of his or her express or implied authority directed against a publicly known political organisation or liberation movement engaged in a political struggle against the State or a former state or against any members or supporters of such organisation or movement, and which was committed bona fide with the object of countering or otherwise resisting the said struggle;

(c) any employee of the State or any former state or any member of the security forces of the State or any former state in the course and scope of his or her duties and within the scope of his or her express or implied authority directed—

(i) in the case of the State, against any former state; or

(ii) in the case of a former state, against the State or any other former state, whilst engaged in a political struggle against each other or against any employee of the State or such former state, as the case may be, and which was committed bona fide with the object of countering or otherwise resisting the said struggle;

(d) any employee or member of a publicly known political organisation or liberation movement in the course and scope of his or her duties and within the scope of his or her express or implied authority directed against the State or any former state or any publicly known political organisation or liberation movement engaged in a political struggle against that political organisation or liberation movement or against members of the security forces of the State or any former state or members or supporters of such publicly known political organisation or liberation movement, and which was committed bona fide in furtherance of the said struggle;

(e) any person in the performance of a coup d'etat to take over the government of any former state, or in any attempt thereto;

(f) any person referred to in paragraphs (a), (b), (c) and (d), who on reasonable grounds believed that he or she was acting in the course and scope of his or her duties and within the scope of his or her express or implied authority;

...

(3) Whether a particular act, omission or offence contemplated in subsection (2) is an act associated with a political objective, shall be decided with reference to the following criteria:

(a) The motive of the person who committed the act, omission or offence;

(b) the context in which the act, omission or offence took place, and in particular whether the act, omission or offence was committed in the course of or as part of a political uprising, disturbance or event, or in reaction thereto;

(c) the legal and factual nature of the act, omission or offence, including the gravity of the act, omission or offence;

(d) the object or objective of the act, omission or offence, and in particular whether the act, omission or offence was primarily directed at a political opponent or State property or personnel or against private property or individuals;

(e) whether the act, omission or offence was committed in the execution of an order of, or on behalf of, or with the approval of, the organisation, institution, liberation movement or body of which the person who committed the act was a member, an agent or a supporter; and

(f) the relationship between the act, omission or offence and the political objective pursued, and in particular the directness and proximity of the relationship and the proportionality of the act, omission or offence to the objective pursued, but does not include any act, omission or offence committed by any person referred to in subsection (2) who acted—

(i) for personal gain: Provided that an act, omission or offence by any person who acted and received money or anything of value as an informer of the State or a former state, political organisation or liberation movement, shall not be excluded only on the grounds of that person having received money or anything of value for his or her information; or

(ii) out of personal malice, ill-will or spite, directed against the victim of the acts committed.

...

(7) (a) No person who has been granted amnesty in respect of an act, omission or offence shall be criminally or civilly liable in respect of such act, omission or offence and no body or organisation or the State shall be liable, and no person shall be vicariously liable, for any such act, omission or offence.

...

[Sections 8–10 provide that amnesty shall result in the termination of any criminal prosecution for an act for which amnesty is granted and shall result in the nullification of any conviction and sentence for an offence for which amnesty is granted.]

REPORT OF TRUTH AND RECONCILIATION COMMISSION OF SOUTH AFRICA

5 vols (1998)

[Excerpts from the Report appear below. They are identified by volume, chapter number of the volume, and paragraph number.]

Volume 1

Chapter 4: The Mandate

• *Why the South African Commission is different from other Commissions...*

25. The most important difference between the South African Commission and others was that it was the first to be given the power to grant amnesty to individual

perpetrators. No other state had combined this quasi-judicial power with the investigation tasks of a truth-seeking body. More typically, where amnesty was introduced to protect perpetrators from being prosecuted for the crimes of the past, the provision was broad and unconditional, with no requirement for individual application or confession of particular crimes....

26. Another significant difference can be found in the Commission's powers of *subpoena*, search and seizure, which are much stronger than those of other truth commissions. This has led to more thorough internal investigation and direct questioning of witnesses, including those who were implicated in violations and did not apply for amnesty....

27. The very public process of the South African Commission also distinguishes it from other commissions.... The Latin American truth commissions heard testimony only in private, and information only emerged with the release of the final reports....

29. The South African Commission was the first to create a witness protection programme. This strengthened its investigative powers and allowed witnesses to come forward with information they feared might put them at risk.

30. Finally, the South African Commission was several times larger in terms of staff and budget than any commission before it....

• *Interpreting the mandate*...

34. It was recognised at the outset that the Commission could not carry out all the tasks required of it simultaneously. Thus, it first gave attention to the question of the restoration of the human and civil dignity of (individual) victims of past gross human rights violations. It did so by creating opportunities for victims 'to relate their own accounts' of the violations they had suffered by giving testimony at public hearings across the length and breadth of South Africa between April 1996 and June 1997. These highly publicised hearings were coupled with an extensive statement-taking drive, investigations, research and so-called 'section 29' hearings (where witnesses and alleged perpetrators were *subpoenaed*) in order to 'establish the fate or whereabouts of victims' and the identity of those responsible for human rights violations.

35. During the second half of the Commission's life (from approximately the middle of 1997), the Commission shifted its focus from the stories of individual victims to an attempt to understand the individual and institutional motives and perspectives which gave rise to the gross violations of human rights under examination. It enquired into the contexts and causes of these violations and attempted to establish the political and moral accountability of individuals, organisations and institutions. The goal was to provide the grounds for making recommendations to prevent future human rights violations. Features of this phase were public submissions by, and questioning of, political parties, and a range of institutional, sectoral and special hearings that focused on the health and business sectors, the legal system, the media and faith communities, prisons, women, children and youth, biological and chemical warfare and compulsory national service. It was also during this period that the majority of amnesty hearings took place....

• *Who were victims of gross violations of human rights?...*

51. It is this systemic and all-pervading character of apartheid that provides the background for the present investigation. During the apartheid years, people did many evil things. Some of these are the gross violations of human rights with which this Commission had to deal. But it can never be forgotten that the system itself was evil, inhumane and degrading for the many millions who became its second and third class citizens. Amongst its many crimes, perhaps the greatest was its power to humiliate, to denigrate and to remove the self-confidence, self-esteem and dignity of its millions of victims....

55. ...[T]he Commission resolved that its mandate was to give attention to human rights violations committed as specific acts, resulting in severe physical and/or mental injury, in the course of past political conflict. As such, the focus of its work was not on the effects of laws passed by the apartheid government, nor on general policies of that government or of other organisations, however morally offensive these may have been. This underlines the importance of understanding the Commissions as but one of several instruments responsible for transformation and bridge-building in post-apartheid South Africa....

57. But bodily integrity rights are not the only fundamental rights. When a person has no food to eat, or when someone is dying because of an illness that access to basic health care could have prevented — that is, when subsistence rights are violated — rights to political participation and freedom of speech become meaningless.

58. Thus, a strong argument can be made that the violations of human rights caused by 'separate development' — for example, by migrant labour, forced removals, bantustans, Bantu education and so on — had, and continue to have, the most negative possible impact on the lives of the majority of South Africans. The consequences of these violations cannot be measured only in the human lives lost through deaths, detentions, dirty tricks and disappearances, but in the human lives withered away through enforced poverty and other kinds of deprivation....

• *Just ends, just means and crimes against humanity*

64. In making judgments in respect of the above requirements, the Commission was guided by criteria derived from just war theory..., international human rights principles and the democratic values inherent in the South African Constitution. By using these criteria, the Commission was able to take clear positions on the evils of apartheid, while also evaluating the actions of those who opposed it....

74. The Commission's confirmation of the fact that the apartheid system was a crime against humanity does not mean that all acts carried out in order to destroy apartheid were necessarily legal, moral and acceptable. The Commission concurred with the international consensus that those who were fighting for a just cause were under an obligation to employ just means in the conduct of this fight.

75. As far as justice in war is concerned, the framework within which the Commission made its findings was in accordance with international law and the views and findings of international organisations and judicial bodies. The strict prohibitions against torture and abduction and the grave wrong of killing and injuring defenceless people, civilians and soldiers 'out of combat' required the Commission

to conclude that not all acts in war could be regarded as morally or legally legitimate, even where the cause was just.

76. It is for this reason that the Commission considered the concept of crimes against humanity at both a systemic level and at the level of specific acts. Apartheid as a system was a crime against humanity, but it was also possible for acts carried out by any of the parties to the conflicts of the past to be classified as human rights violations.

77. Thus, the Commission adopted the view that human rights violations could be committed by any group or person inside or outside the state: by persons within the Pan Africanist Congress (PAC), the IFP, the South African Police (SAP), the South African Defence Force (SADF), the ANC or any other organisation.

78. It is important to note, however, that this wider application of human rights principles to non-state entities is a relatively recent international development....

79. The Act establishing the Commission adopted this more modern position. In other words, it did not make a finding of a gross violation of human rights conditional on a finding of state action....

Racism

127. There were cases in which people were victims of racist attack by individuals who were not involved with a publicly known political organisation and where the incident did not form part of a specific political conflict. Although racism was at the heart of the South African political order, and although such cases were clearly a violation of the victim's rights, such violations did not fall within the Commission's mandate.

128. Cases which were interpreted as falling inside the Commission's mandate included instances where racism was used to mobilise people through a political organisation as part of their commitment to a political struggle, or where racism was used by a political organisation to incite others to violence. Examples of these were instances when white 'settlers' or farmers were killed by supporters of the PAC or the ANC, or where black people were killed by supporters of white right-wing organisations....

Naming

152. The Act required the publication of the names of those who received amnesty in the Government Gazette. These individuals had already identified themselves as perpetrators by applying for amnesty. The Commission had therefore, to resolve which of the other perpetrators identified in the course of its work should be named in accordance with its mandate—to enquire into 'the identity of all persons, authorities, institutions and organisations' involved in gross human rights violations, as well as the 'accountability, political or otherwise, for any such violation' (section 4(a)(iii), (V), the Act).

153. In fulfilling this part of its mandate, the Commission was again required to walk a tightrope. This time, it was faced with the tension between the public interest in the exposure of wrongdoing and the need to ensure fair treatment of individuals in what was not a court of law; between the rights of victims of gross violations of human rights to know who was responsible and the fundamentally important question of fairness to those who are accused of crimes or serious wrongdoing.

...

155. Given the investigative nature of the Commission's process and the limited legal impact of naming, the Commission made findings on the identity of those involved in gross violations of human rights based on the balance of probability. This required a lower burden of proof than that required by the conventional criminal justice system. It meant that, when confronted with different versions of events, the Commission had to decide which version was the more probable, reasonable or likely, after taking all the available evidence into account.

Volume 5

Chapter 6: Findings and conclusions...

The Commission's position on responsibility and accountability...

66. In the light of the above and of the evidence received, the Commission is of the view that gross violations of human rights were perpetrated or facilitated by all the major role-players in the conflicts of the mandate era. These include:

a The state and its security, intelligence and law-enforcement agencies, the SAP, the SADF and the NIS.

b Groups and institutions which, to a greater or lesser extent, were affiliated or allied to the state in an official capacity. These include homeland governments and their security forces as well as groups and institutions informally allied to the state....

c White right-wing organizations which, while actively opposing the state, actively and violently took action to preserve the *status quo* in the 1990s....

d Liberation movements and organizations which sought to bring about change through armed struggle and which operated outside South Africa and by covert and underground means inside the country.

e Organizations which sought to bring about change by non-violent means prior to and post-1990, including the United Democratic Front; and

f Non-state paramilitary formations such as the ANC's self-defence units and the IFP's self-protection units (SPUs)....

68. At the same time, the Commission is not of the view that all such parties can be held to be equally culpable for violations committed in the mandate period. Indeed, the evidence accumulated by the Commission and documented in this report shows that this was not the case. The preponderance of responsibility rests with the state and its allies....

71. ... [T]he evidence shows that the perpetration of gross violations of human rights by non-state actors often took place in circumstances where they were acting in opposition to the official state ideology and the policy of apartheid. In this sense, it was the state that generated violent political conflict in the mandate period — either through its own direct action or by eliciting reactions to its policies and strategies.

72. . . . A state has powers, resources, obligations, responsibilities and privileges that are much greater than those of any group within that state. It must therefore be held to a higher standard of moral and political conduct than are voluntary associations. . . .

. . .

74. It would, however, be misleading and wrong to assign blame for the gross violation of human rights only to those who confronted each other on the political and military battlefields, engaged in acts of commission. Others, like the church or faith groups, the media, the legal profession, the judiciary, the magistracy, the medical/health, educational and business sectors, are found by the Commission to have been guilty of acts of omission in that they failed to adhere or live up to the ethics of their profession and to accepted codes of conduct.

75. It is also the view of the Commission that these sectors failed not so much out of fear of the powers and wrath of the state — although those were not insignificant factors — but primarily because they were the beneficiaries of the state system. They prospered from it by staying silent. By doing nothing or not enough, they contributed to the emergence of a culture of impunity within which the gross violations of human rights documented in this report could and did occur.

[The balance of this section on Findings and Conclusions provides detailed findings against each of the state organs, government leaders, internal allies of the state, regional groups, liberation movements and sectors of civil society to which the earlier parts of this section refer.]

DECISIONS OF AMNESTY COMMITTEE, TRUTH AND RECONCILIATION COMMISSION

http://www.truth.org.za/amnesty

Ntamo, VS (4734/97); Peni, NA (5188/97); Nofemela, EM (5282/97); Manqina, MC (0669/96) (Heard in July 1997)

The Applicants were convicted and sentenced to imprisonment for 18 years for the murder of Amy Biehl. . . . The offence was committed on the NY1 Road in the Gugulethu Township, in Cape Town on the 25th August 1993. The applicants are young men whose ages, at the time of the commission of the offence ranged between 18 and 22 years. Except for Ntamo, whose education had not progressed beyond Std 4, the others were high school students.

They have applied for amnesty in terms of section 18 of the Promotion of National Unity and Reconciliation Act No. 34 of 1995.

Amy Biehl their victim was an American Citizen. She was on a Fulbright Scholarship and was affiliated to the Community Law Centre at the University of the Western Cape where she was pursuing her studies for a Ph.D in Political Science. On that fateful afternoon, she was conveying three colleagues in her car. She was on her way to drop some of them off in Gugulethu, when her vehicle came under attack by people who were running towards it and throwing stones at it. The stones smashed the windscreen and windows of the car. One of the stones hit Amy Biehl on her head, causing her to bleed profusely. She could not continue driving. She got out of her car and ran towards a garage across the road. Her attackers did not relent. They pursued her and continued throwing stones at her. Manqina tripped her, causing her to fall. She was surrounded by between 7 and 10 people and while she was being stoned, one of her attackers stabbed her. She died as a result of the injuries they inflicted on her.

According to the evidence of the applicants they were among those who were involved in the attack on Amy Biehl. Peni admitted throwing stones at his victim when he was three to four metres from her. Manqina stabbed her with a knife in addition to throwing stones at her. Nofemela threw stones at her and stabbed at her 3 or 4 times. Ntamo threw many stones at her head when he was only a metre away. They stopped attacking her when the police arrived on the scene.

The attack on the car driven by Amy Biehl was one of many incidents of general lawlessness in NY1 that afternoon. Bands of toyi-toying youths threw stones at delivery vehicles and cars driven by white people. One delivery vehicle was toppled over and set alight and only the arrival of the police prevented more damage....

The applicants explained their behavior by saying that earlier that day they had attended a meeting at the Langa High School where a Pan African Student organization (PASO) unit was relaunched. Peni was elected Chairperson at the meeting. Manqina was Vice Chairperson of the PASO unit at the Gugulethu Comprehensive School and Nofemela was a PASO organizer at the Joe Slovo High School.... The applicants said that speakers dealt with:

- the strike by Teachers in the Western Cape who demanded recognition for the South African Democratic Teachers Union (SADTU);
- the struggles of the Azanian Peoples Liberation Army (APLA) for the return of the land to the African People;
- APLA had declared 1993 as the 'Year of the Great Storm'. Reference was also made to the launching of 'OPERATION BARCELONA' to stop all deliveries into the townships.

The speakers urged the members of PASO to take an active part in the struggle of APLA by assisting APLA operators on the ground by making the country ungovernable.

The speeches were militant and punctuated by shouting the slogan 'ONE SETTLER ONE BULLET'.

Applicants said that they were all inspired by the speakers to such an extent that they left the meeting with many others in a militant mood. They marched through the township toyi-toying and shouting ONE SETTLER ONE BULLET, determined to put into effect what they had been urged to do. This is how they got involved in the activities briefly described above which led to the killing of Amy Biehl.... Although they did not act on the orders or instructions of APLA or PAC [Pan African Congress] on that day, they believed they owed loyalty to the same cause.... As members of PASO, which was a known political organization of students, they were active supporters of the PAC and subscribed to its political philosophy and its policies. By stoning company delivery vehicles and thereby making it difficult for deliveries into the townships, they were taking part in a political disturbance and contributing towards making their area ungovernable. To that extent, their activities were aimed at supporting the liberation struggle against the State. But Amy Biehl was a private citizen, and the question is why was she killed during this disturbance. Part of the answer may be that her attackers were so aroused and incited, that they lost control of themselves and got caught up in a frenzy of violence. One of the applicants said during his evidence that they all submitted to the slogan of ONE SETTLER, ONE BULLET. To them that meant that every white person was an enemy of the Black people. At that moment to them, Amy Biehl, was a representative of the white community. They believed that by killing civilian whites, APLA was sending a serious political message to the government of the day. By intensifying such activity the political pressure on the government would increase to such an extent that it would demoralize them and compel them to hand over political power to the majority of the people of South Africa.

When the conduct of the applicants is viewed in that light, it must be accepted that their crime was related to a political objective.

The PAC regarded the killing of Amy Biehl as a mistake committed by young people who were misguided. They nevertheless supported the application for amnesty.

The parents of Amy Biehl had come from America to attend the hearing. At the conclusion of the evidence Mr Biehl addressed the Amnesty Committee. Part of his speech reads as follows:

> ... We have the highest respect for your Truth and Reconciliation Commission and process. We recognise that if this process had not been a pre-negotiated condition your democratic free elections could not possibly have occurred. Therefore, and believing as Amy did in the absolute importance of those democratic elections occurring we unabashedly support the process which we recognize to be unprecedented in contemporary human history.
>
> At the same time we say to you it's your process, not ours. We cannot, therefore, oppose amnesty if it is granted on the merits. In the truest sense it is for the community of South Africa to forgive its own and this has its basis in traditions of ubuntu and other principles of human dignity. Amnesty is not clearly for Linda and Peter Biehl to grant. . . . . . We, as the Amy Biehl Foundation are willing to do our part as catalysts for social progress. All anyone need do is ask. Are you, the community of South Africa, prepared to do your part?

The applicants have made a full disclosure of all the relevant facts as required by section 20(1) of the Act. On a consideration of all the evidence placed before us, we have come to the conclusion that they be granted amnesty for the murder of Amy Biehl. . . .

Dirk Coetzee (0063/96), David Tshikalange (0065/96), and Butana Almond Nofomela (0064/96) (Heard in November 1996 and January 1997)

... We are dealing now with the applications for amnesty made by the three Applicants in respect of the murder of Griffiths Mxenge. The three Applicants, who were at all relevant times serving members of the South African Police Force, have applied for amnesty in respect of many acts committed by them. [The three applicants had been convicted for one of the offences stated in their application, the murder of Mxenge.] ...

The evidence led before us disclosed that the three Applicants were stationed at a place called Vlakplaas, which was a base established in the country where the police stationed what could perhaps fairly be described as hit squads....

At the relevant time all four groups from Vlakplaas were in Durban for various purposes. The First Applicant who was the commander reported, so he said, daily to Brigadier Van der Hoven, the regional security commander at about 7.30 am and again at 4 pm. On one such occasion, a few days before the 19th of November 1981, Brigadier Van der Hoven called him to make a 'plan' with Mxenge. He understood this to mean that he was to make arrangements to eliminate Mxenge. He was told in very brief terms that Mxenge, who was the victim in this application, was an ex-Robben Island prisoner and was an attorney practising in Durban. He acted on behalf of members of the liberation movement and others who were charged with criminal offences arising out of the struggle against apartheid, and a large amount of money was known to have gone through his account. There was no suggestion in the evidence before us that this money was improperly used in any way....

He was told that the security police had been unable to bring any charges against Mxenge and that he had accordingly become a thorn in their flesh by enabling persons charged with political offences to obtain the protection of the courts.

The First Applicant said that Brigadier Van der Hoven told him that they must not shoot or abduct Mxenge but that they should make it look like a robbery. He was then taken to Captain Taylor who gave him certain information about Mxenge. This information related to where his office was, where his house was, what car he drove and matters of that nature....

The First Applicant took charge of arrangements and set up a squad which was to be responsible for killing Mxenge, consisting of the Second and Third Applicants, [a certain] Mamasela, and a certain Brian Ngulunga, because he was from the Umlazi area and knew the vicinity well. The First Applicant took charge of the general planning of the murder.... He however left the details as to the actual killing to the four members of the squad he had appointed.... They intercepted the car in which Mxenge was travelling and dragged him out of it. While Brian Ngulunga stood by with a pistol in his hand, the others commenced to stab their victim.... The stabbing continued until he was dead. He had been disemboweled; his throat had been cut and his ears had been practically cut off. His body was found to have 45 lacerations and stab wounds.

It is quite clear from his evidence and from the evidence of the other two Applicants, that they considered this to be an act performed as part of their duties as policemen on the instructions of senior officers who would undoubtedly have satisfied themselves as to the necessity for it.

In this regard the First Applicant said the following during the course of his evidence before us:

...

> 'Do you still today believe that those were necessary or lawful orders?'
>
> 'Absolutely not.'
>
> 'Why do you think differently today?'
>
> 'Well, at the time, yes, but with hindsight absurd and absolutely — I mean unjustifiable.'

On the evidence before us we are satisfied that none of the Applicants knew the deceased, Mxenge, or had any reason to wish to bring about his death before they were ordered to do so. We are satisfied that they did what they did because they regarded it as their duty as policemen who were engaged in the struggle against the ANC and other liberation movements. It is, we think clear, that they relied on their superiors to have accurately and fairly considered the question as to whether the assassination was necessary or whether other steps could have been taken. . . .

. . . With regard to the First Applicant, there was no direct evidence to confirm that he acted on the orders of Van der Hoven or Taylor. In fact, it is a matter of public knowledge that Van der Hoven and Taylor denied any involvement; they did so during their recent trial in which they were co-accused with the Applicants on a criminal charge in respect of this very incident. While there may be some doubt about the identity of the person or persons on whose advice, command or order, the First Applicant acted, the fact that he acted on the advice, command or order of one or more senior members of the security branch, admits of no doubt. . . .

. . . We are accordingly of the view that the three Applicants are entitled to amnesty in respect of this offence, that is the murder of Griffiths Mxenge on the 19th of November 1981, and it will accordingly not be necessary for the Trial Court to proceed with the question of sentence.

NOTE

The Report stressed the role of the Truth and Reconciliation Commission (TRC) in communicating to a relevant public the nature of amnesty and the process for submitting applications through visits of its members and staff to institutions such as prisons and through public talks. The amnesty hearings were open to all media, and television coverage became standard.

With respect to the procedure of the hearings, the Amnesty Committee took care to 'avoid overly formalising the process' and to retain flexibility. It took the view of the TRC that 'process should not be equated to that of a court of law and should not be overly regulated.' Nonetheless, the proceedings 'are largely judicial in nature' and included such rights as cross-examination 'within reasonable bounds'. Proceedings were recorded, and the Committee gave 'reasoned decisions' on all issues to be decided. All decisions were published.

Several legal challenges to the legislation underlying the amnesty provisions and the procedure governing the hearings were brought in the courts. The Constitutional Court resolved one such challenge in *Azanian Peoples Organisation (AZAPO) v. President of the Republic of South Africa*, CCT 17/96 (1996). The applicants claimed that certain provisions on amnesty of the Promotion of National Unity and Reconciliation Act 34 of 1995 were unconstitutional, since if amnesty were granted, a perpetrator would not be criminally or civilly liable in respect of the acts subject to the amnesty. The Court upheld the constitutionality of these provisions that limited applicants' right set forth in the Constitution to 'have justiciable disputes settled by a court of law'. The interim Constitution's epilogue on national unity and reconciliation sanctioned this limitation on the applicants' right of access to courts to bring a suit for damages. Absent such provisions, there would be no incentive for offenders to disclose the truth. Moreover, the amnesty provisions were a crucial part of the negotiated settlement leading to the Constitution. Parliament could always act to provide systematic reparations for victims of past abuses, and to provide for individualized reparations taking account of the claims of all victims, rather than preserving civil liability of the state and its officials for provable acts of wrongdoing. The Court also concluded that the amnesty provisions did not violate any international norms.

Upon the release of the TRC's final report, some pressure grew for a general amnesty. The ruling African National Congress, which along with other major political parties had key officials who could face prosecution because of the report, initially expressed willingness to consider another amnesty. In 2003, President Thabo Mbeki announced before Parliament that there would be no blanket amnesty. In 2004, charges brought against former security agents for the notorious 1985 killing of 'the Pebco Three', three black South African anti-apartheid activists, appeared to signal the start of post-TRC prosecutions. All cases dealing with former abuses, however, were suspended in November 2004 while a new prosecutions policy was being developed.

In 2006, the Minister of Justice unveiled a new policy for prosecuting apartheid-era crimes.[11] The policy is highly controversial. Critics argue that it gives the National Prosecutions Authority wider powers than the TRC to grant amnesty and this time to individuals who were refused amnesty by the TRC or who failed to appear before the TRC. The new policy guidelines provide the National Director of Public Prosecutions discretion not to prosecute a person if the individual satisfies the former TRC's amnesty criteria such as providing 'full disclosure' of all relevant facts relating to the past acts and if the individual's commission of an alleged offence was associated with a 'political objective'. The guidelines also stipulate factors such as 'the degree of remorse shown by the alleged offender'; 'the degree of indoctrination to which the alleged offender was subjected', the extent to which prosecution would support or undermine 'nation-building through transformation [and] reconciliation', and '[i]f relevant, the alleged offender's role during the TRC process, namely, in respect of co-operation, full disclosure and assisting the process in general'. Opponents of the new policy include South African civil society organizations, TRC commissioners including the former head of the TRC Archbishop Desmond Tutu, Justice Richard Goldstone, and the International Center for Transitional Justice.

QUESTIONS

1. Assuming that there were no serious political constraints in South Africa on one or another plan, what changes would you have made in the provisions for the TRC, including amnesty? What changes, if any, would you make to the 2006 guidelines for the National Prosecutions Authority?

[11] See Prosecution Policy and Directives Relating to Prosecution of Criminal Matters Arising from Conflicts of the Past, http://www.polity.org.za/pdf/npaProsecutionPolicy.pdf.

2. The TRC required that acts eligible for amnesty be committed for a 'political motive'. Does the 'political motive' element make pragmatic sense? Is it normatively desirable? How does this requirement compare with the issues in *Tadic* concerning acts committed for 'purely personal motives' in association with a crime against humanity? Is the TRC category of eligible crimes too narrow or too broad?

3. Given the conditions for amnesty in the relevant legislation, do you agree with the decisions in the two amnesty cases? Do you agree with the Amnesty Committee's approach to the notion of a 'political motive', as applied in the Amy Biehl case?

4. What is your estimate of the long or short-term consequences of the TRC for South African democracy, growth, political stability and social harmony among the different racial and ethnic groups? Do you view other factors as equally or more important to achieve these goals? How would you assess the significance of the TRC among those other factors?

5. Are the goals of truth and reconciliation necessarily complimentary? Should there be any constraints on seeking the truth if doing so threatens to undermine social harmony? What actors or institutions should make these determinations?

COMMENT ON RELATIONSHIPS BETWEEN TRUTH COMMISSIONS AND CRIMINAL TRIBUNALS

In post-atrocity situations, criminal tribunals and truth commissions are increasingly being called on to operate alongside one another. Such situations are sometimes the result of deliberate planning and other times the coincidence of separate political and institutional developments. Criminal tribunals and truth commissions are often thought to complement one another. Criminal prosecutions, for instance, may focus attention on personal guilt and away from structural or systemic causes, and trials lack opportunities for direct, broad-based public participation. Truth commissions potentially fill those gaps. Truth commissions, however, do not serve other objectives often associated with criminal justice such as deterrence and perhaps retribution. Truth commissions and criminal tribunals might also directly support each other's respective agendas. A truth commission can provide prosecutors and judges with valuable information on the nature of the atrocities and individuals involved. Criminal tribunals can, in turn, assist truth commissions. Indeed, without a credible threat of prosecution, South Africa's conditional amnesty scheme might not have succeeded.

Nevertheless, the two institutions might encounter conflicts, if not fundamental incompatibilities, with one another. Potential suspects may be reluctant to appear before a truth commission for fear that their testimony could be used against them by prosecutors. That is, the specter of a criminal trial can potentially chill participation in a truth commission. In the reverse, witnesses and survivors who have already provided sworn testimony to a truth commission may undermine or complicate their value for prosecutors. Finally and perhaps most fundamentally, problems might arise if two institutions provide conflicting 'authoritative' accounts of the history of events and conclusions about the responsibility of various individuals and organizations. Such competing narratives can undermine the legitimacy of both institutions and the goals they serve.

As the following discussion by Priscilla Hayner explains, the operation of the International Criminal Court is likely to bring many of these issues to the fore. Some of these issues received attention in the context of the ICTY and a proposed truth commission for Bosnia and Herzegovina. Hayner discusses the ICTY experience and lessons for the ICC. Following Hayner's discussion we turn to recent clashes between the truth commission and criminal tribunal operating in Sierra Leone.

PRISCILLA HAYNER, UNSPEAKABLE TRUTHS: CONFRONTING STATE TERROR AND ATROCITY

(2001)

It is... likely that [the ICC's] investigations will focus on those countries where national truth commissions may also be considered, and that the Court's and these commissions' subjects of investigation will overlap. This could raise some delicate legal and political questions, especially around overlapping investigations, access to evidence, and the use of witnesses. Unfortunately... outside of the question of national amnesties, the issues raised by the Court's relationship with future truth commissions were never directly discussed during the several years of intense negotiations around the Court's statute....

Some of the troublesome issues that might arise can be seen in the discussions around a proposed truth commission for Bosnia, and especially in the strong response from the International Criminal Tribunal for the Former Yugoslavia, which opposed the idea of a truth commission that would overlap with its own investigations.... After the Yugoslavia Tribunal was under way for a number of years, in 1997 a truth commission was proposed for Bosnia, intended to serve as a complementary body that would work on the national level to document the massive abuses that took place.

The truth commission idea was rooted in the recognition that three contradictory versions of history were being taught by the three ethnic communities of Bosnia — the Serbs, Muslims, and Croats — and that such radically different understandings of the atrocities of the recent war could well lead to future violence. The efforts of the Tribunal did not seem to be having any impact on these local dynamics, and its proceedings and decisions — undertaken in the Hague, the Netherlands — received little attention from the press or public within the country. Those backing the idea of a truth commission argued that only by taking an assertive step toward reconciling such different conceptions of truth and history would Bosnians be able to find common ground and ease tensions between the three groups. The commission's supporters also insisted that such a body, which would be created by the joint presidency of Bosnia and include both national and international commissioners and staff, would be complementary to the work of the Tribunal... In the process of its investigations, the commission could review, catalog, and summarize thousands of local language documents and press reports and hundreds of videotapes that to date had been out of reach of the Tribunal.

But the leadership of the Tribunal was worried that a Bosnian truth commission could weaken it by creating a parallel structure with overlapping interests... The concerns of the Tribunal's chief prosecutor at the time, Louise Arbour, and its president, Gabrielle Kirk McDonald, were first outlined at a conference in Belgrade, Yugoslavia, in November 1998. They argued that the existence of a truth commission could undermine the Tribunal's work by allowing individuals to cooperate with the commission while continuing to default on their obligations to the Tribunal; that the commission's findings of political responsibility might not be distinguished in the public's eye from those of criminal responsibility, thus leading to unreasonable demands for prosecutions; that there would be a danger that the commission and the Tribunal could arrive at contradictory findings of fact, given the commission's lower standards of evidence; that evidence could be "contaminated" by the commission, especially through repeated interviewing of witnesses; and that the Tribunal already was providing the historical truth, so that a truth commission was not necessary. They also argued that Bosnia was not ready for a truth commission and that the process would likely be manipulated by local political factions. In addition, some observers outside the Tribunal feared that a truth commission, which would depend entirely on international funding, could pull needed funds away from the Tribunal.

While all of these are important concerns, and some would require serious attention before a Bosnian commission were established, many independent legal scholars have concluded that none of these issues should be insurmountable. Whether certain political actors would try to use the truth commission as a means to avoid compliance with the Tribunal is not something the commission could control, except by making public statements to try to deter this ploy. Many countries work under different standards of evidence for different kinds of trials (criminal versus civil), and after mass crimes the public must appreciate that not all of the accused can be tried. The problem of a "contaminated" witness pool is also commonly confronted by prosecutors, and many argue that this should not be a formidable issue for the Tribunal; the commission could further lessen this problem by not taking testimony under oath (to help protect a witness's testimony from being discredited, if a slightly different version were given in court). And finally, it is true that the Tribunal's decisions have included long descriptions of the historical context of each case, thus helping to officially establish the historical record, but unfortunately these decisions are neither easily accessible nor widely read, especially within Bosnia. Whether a truth commission should be established in Bosnia is an open question that ultimately should be decided by Bosnians themselves, not internationals. There may well be important reasons not to have a truth commission at this time — that it would be politically manipulated or not done in good faith could be the strongest arguments against it — but the overlap with the Tribunal is alone not a sufficient reason to drop the commission proposal.

A number of the issues raised by the Yugoslavia Tribunal are likely to be raised in very similar form if the permanent International Criminal Court exists in conjunction with future truth commissions. In addition, there are other questions likely to be pertinent to the International Criminal Court. Perhaps most important, it is not clear how and when information would be shared between a national truth commission and the Court. The Court's statute requires state parties to the treaty to cooperate fully with the Court, and to "comply with requests by the Court to provide... assistance in relation to investigations or prosecutions," including "the provision of records and documents, including official records and documents." The timing and nature of how this information would be shared are not spelled out, however, and could be a critical question both to a commission and to the Court. If a commission discovers evidence or receives testimony that links a person to a crime against humanity, genocide, or a war crime, must the commission immediately report this to the Court? Could a truth commission wait until it has completed its work before handing over evidence, even if that evidence implicates persons already under investigation by the Court, or will the Court's prosecutor be able to request and gain access to such evidence at any time? What about truth commissions that operate independently of a government, such as those created by a peace accord — will they be equally obliged to share all information with the Court?

The answer to these questions could have serious implications for a truth commission. If its records must be made available to the Court, a truth commission's ability to grant confidentiality to its witnesses would be at risk, and therefore its investigating powers constrained. Many past truth commissions have offered a screen of strict confidentiality to entice testimony from key witnesses — a particularly important tool for those truth commissions which have no subpoena power and depend on the voluntary willingness of witnesses to come forward. Some victims and other key witnesses may fear speaking to the commission if they do not trust that their information would remain confidential. And certainly, those perpetrators who otherwise might be willing to quietly cooperate with the commission — often a critical source of information — would surely hesitate if they expected that their testimony might be turned over to the Court for prosecution.

...

Notwithstanding the potential areas of tension suggested above, the overlap between a truth commission and the International Criminal Court could also result in benefits for both bodies. A commission report's outline of the broad pattern of crimes could help focus the Court's investigations, especially if the commission concludes its work before the Court's prosecutor begins investigations in the country. The commission's report, supporting materials, and interviews with thousands of victims could help identify witnesses and evidence for the prosecutor, as took place in Argentina to greatly strengthen domestic prosecutions there. Even if a commission does not name names in its report, its archives would likely identify persons implicated in crimes.... Finally, most truth commission reports comment in some detail on the strength and independence of the judiciary. This analysis could help the Court determine whether the state is "unwilling or unable" to investigate and prosecute a case, which is a key test for the Court to gain jurisdiction over a matter.

...

While some victims may request confidentiality, as suggested above, many who provide testimony to truth commissions are frustrated by the lack of justice and would feel encouraged that their testimony might be used by an international court to prosecute and punish perpetrators. Prospects that its documentation could be used for international prosecutions could add weight to a commission's work, focus its targeted investigations, and help shape or clarify its evidentiary standards.

PROSECUTOR V. NORMAN

(Decision on Appeal of TRC Request for Public Hearing with Chief Norman), Special Court for Sierra Leone, Case No. SCSL-2003–08-PT (2003)

[Sierra Leone provides a useful study of a truth commission operating alongside a criminal tribunal. The Truth and Reconciliation Commission (TRC) of Sierra Leone was a product of the Lomé Peace Agreement between the Government of Sierra Leone and the Revolutionary United Front. It was established as a national body by Parliament in 2000. Some impediments to the TRC involved its formal and informal relationships with the Special Court for Sierra Leone. Potential witnesses were reportedly unwilling to provide statements before the TRC for fear of subsequent prosecution. As one close observer explained:

> The Prosecutor, David Crane... stated publicly that the court has its own investigative procedures and that it will not use evidence presented to the TRC. It has also been suggested that TRC evidence would be inadmissible in court. Unfortunately this message appears not to have reached everyone in Sierra Leone. Some Sierra Leoneans had difficulty distinguishing between the TRC and the court and feared that confessions to the TRC may lead to prosecution.... Arguably, only the Prosecutor's word stood between TRC testimony and court prosecutions, and it was highly likely that defense lawyers would mine TRC testimony, wherever possible, in support of their clients Several of the people I spoke to... mentioned the court as a deterrent to giving statements to the TRC.[12]

Paradoxically, the case that gave rise to a direct dispute between the TRC and Special Court involved the reverse situation: an accused who sought to provide testimony to the TRC.

Chief Sam Hinga Norman was one of the most prominent defendants in the custody of the Special Court. He was arrested in 2003 while serving as Minister of Internal Affairs. Norman was charged for his role as National Coordinator of the Civil Defence Forces, pro-government militias that fought during the civil war. The charges included his responsibility for militias that identified civilian 'collaborators' of rebel forces who were then 'unlawfully killed... often shot, hacked to death, or burnt to death. Other practices included human sacrifices and cannibalism' and

[12] Tim Kelsall, 'Truth, Lies, Ritual: Preliminary Reflections on the Truth and Reconciliation Commission in Sierra Leone', 27 Hum. R. Q. 361 (2005).

'acts of terrorism' in particular regions of the country. Norman's arrest surprised many Sierra Leoneans who viewed him as a national hero.

The TRC approached the Special Court to seek the appearance of Norman before a public hearing. Norman formally notified the Court that he wanted to appear before the Commission. The ensuing confrontation between the TRC and Special Court created what William Schabas described as a 'most unfortunate... quarrel between the [two institutions]... at the close of what had otherwise been a cordial and uneventful relationship.' The Presiding Judge of the Trial Chamber rejected the TRC request. The TRC and Norman appealed to the President of the Special Court, Justice Geoffrey Robertson. Justice Robertson's decision follows.]

2. [This application raises], on any view, a novel and difficult question and one that is likely to recur for other indictees and in other post-war situations where the local or international community considers that the establishment of both a Special Court and a Truth Commission will assist in the restoration of peace and justice.

...

4. ... The Special Court was given, by Article 8 of its Statute, a primacy over the national courts of Sierra Leone (and, by implication, over national bodies like the TRC). It has an overriding duty to prosecute those alleged to bear the greatest responsibility for the war, with which duty the Government bound itself to co-operate. There was nothing in the Court's Agreement or Statute which required the Court to compromise its justice mission by deferring to local courts or national institutions.

...

6. The spirit of co-operation envisaged by the Secretary General had in fact resolved all problems without the need for any formal agreements, until this particular issue concerning whether indictees should give public testimony to the TRC arose late in October 2003. The Office of the Prosecutor, which has substantially more resources than the TRC, has followed a different and independent process of investigation. The Prosecutor even announced that he would not use any evidence collected or heard by the Commission, although this undertaking was made at a time when it was not envisaged that any indictee would testify (and the Prosecutor has made clear that he will not be constrained from using indictee testimony). Even so, this was a very considerable compromise by an organ of the Special Court: if crucial evidence against an author of a crime against humanity were to surface at a TRC hearing, one would expect the Prosecutor to obtain it (if a document) or to subpoena the witness, certainly if the testimony was given in public. Nonetheless, the Prosecutor is entitled to make agreements or announce self-denying ordinances and "no go" areas, and he gave this undertaking precisely to avoid any possible conflict with the TRC process. What he cannot do, of course, is bind defendants: if evidence vital for their defence is given at a TRC hearing, then the Trial Chamber would not be prevented from entertaining a defence application to obtain it.

...

8. ... The TRC, by this application, wishes to go towards the other extreme: it seeks not only to interview indictees, but to do so in public, in a courtroom over several days, in a form that will permit them to broadcast live to the nation, and then face sustained questioning shortly before their trial.

. . .

13. The TRC functions may broadly be divided, in accordance with its title, into those of providing an historical record ("truth") and those of assisting victims to come to terms with their perpetrators ("reconciliation"). The "truth" functions, described in Section 6(2)(a) of its Act, 19 could be interpreted as permitting findings about individual responsibility—the prime function of the Special Court. The "reconciliation" functions, described in Section 6(2)(b) are not so problematic, so long as they invite victims to reconcile with perpetrators who do not bear great responsibility and are not Special Court indictees. It is possible to envisage an indictee pleading guilty and then going before the TRC to beg his victims' forgiveness, and subsequently asking for any such forgiveness to be taken into account by the Court in mitigation of his sentence. But that is not this case and no indictee has yet evinced any intention to plead guilty. . . . .

. . .

15. . . . I was told at the hearing by TRC representatives that the Commissioners are preparing to make some assessments of responsibility, and I have been given no assurance that indictees awaiting or undergoing trial will not be "judged" guilty or innocent by the Commissioners (who are not qualified judges), whether or not they testify to the TRC. . . . its publication may create expectations and anxieties among prospective witnesses and other defendants and prove indirectly damaging to either Prosecution or Defence. For the very reason that it would necessarily be a premature judgement, it might be shaken or reversed after all the evidence is heard and exposed to the test of cross-examination at the trial. Any such result might discredit the TRC report, but the Court must take no account of this: its judges remain committed by oath to reach their verdicts according to the evidence before them.

16. One solution to the problem could be for the TRC to issue a preliminary report in February and then suspend its operations until the trial process has been completed, when it would reconvene to consider the trial evidence and prepare and publish a final report, incorporating the results of the trials. But I am told that no such course can realistically be contemplated.

17. In these circumstances, a competent lawyer would be unlikely to advise an indicted client to run the risk of testifying before the TRC. There are no procedural safe-guards; he might make damaging admissions under questioning from the counsel to the Commission or from the Commissioners themselves and these admissions could be used by the Prosecution, whose self-denying ordinance does not extend to indictee testimony; he might be condemned in the Commission's report in a way which would create an expectation of his conviction by the Special Court and in consequence frighten off potential defence witnesses. When the TRC first approached a number of indictees, earlier in the year, they all declined a chalice that they were doubtless advised was poisoned. There came a point, however, when this applicant changed his mind. . . . Chief Sam Hinga Norman . . . [stated] since, almost 6 months after his arrest, "there is no news about the start of the trial . . . I would prefer to be heard by the people of Sierra Leone and also be recorded for posterity". He refers to the fact that President Kabbah has testified, as have other ministers of the Government.

18. . . . He possesses, even as an indictee remanded in custody, a qualified right to freedom of speech. That right must be capable of assertion, in some meaningful

way, to answer, if he wishes, any allegations that have been made against him in another forum: particular resonance attaches to free speech when it is sought as a "right of reply"....

19. To these claims of the indictee must be added the claim of the TRC itself to be put in a position to decide where the truth lies. The Commission states in paragraph 9 of its Application: The TRC perceives Chief Samuel Hinga Norman JP to have played a central role in the conflict in Sierra Leone. The Commission's report—insofar as it purports to present an impartial historical record—would not be complete without hearing from Chief Hinga Norman....

20. The Special Court was first approached by letter from the Executive Secretary of the TRC... The chief concern of the judges was that indictees should know what they were letting themselves in for if they gave interviews to the TRC, and to ensure that in that event they would be given every reasonable protection against self-incrimination. Thus any prisoner who agreed to participate in the process had to signify his agreement in writing, confirmed by a lawyer who had advised him about it; he had to be provided with a list of written questions and told he was not obliged to answer any particular one; he had to be informed that his answers might be used against him by the Prosecution and that no "finding" by the TRC about him would sway the Court. Any interview had to be supervised by a lawyer appointed by the Registrar and had to be held in the presence of a lawyer for the indictee.

...

21. It must be understood that these were protections laid down not to obstruct the TRC but to provide fundamental protection for men facing charges alleging heinous crimes which if proved could lead to long years of imprisonment. That protection was essential where they were facing impromptu questioning by a skilled counsel for the TRC and by the commissioners themselves. There was not, indeed never has been, any inhibition against an indictee volunteering or communicating information to the TRC in writing, either directly or through his lawyers. The indictee retains freedom of speech to this very considerable extent, that he can write a book, if he wishes... and have it sent to the TRC—by his lawyers, who will sensibly vet it first. It is surprising that the TRC does not appear to have requested information in written form from this indictee. It is also surprising that it has shifted its request from a two day private interview with investigators to a full-scale public hearing broadcast "live" to the nation.

...

22. ... the promulgation of the Practice Direction was followed by TRC objections that it would infringe its powers to take evidence in confidence—powers that it seemed to want to use in respect of Chief Hinga Norman....

26. The Prosecution opposes the joint application, despite admitting that the availability of evidence on oath from the defendant at an open hearing "had a certain appeal" — for reasons that are obvious. Nevertheless, it asserted that such a hearing would undermine the integrity of the Special Court, imperil the security situation in the country and could serve to intimidate witnesses given that the indictee has a large following, even if this was not his intention. The latter claim is always easy for prosecutors to make and often difficult for defendants to refute. It could have

been discounted, but for the TRC's warning that if the Chief did not testify then his supporters might cause unrest and even "unleash powerful emotions" against the Special Court.... the danger of unintended consequences, in a society where factions still have access to arms and where the war ended only last year, must be born in any judicial mind. To allow any accused to testify live-to-air, for several days in an uncontrolled environment, may be asking for unpredictable trouble.

...

30. What is actually proposed by this application may be described in different ways: it might appear as a spectacle. A man in custody awaiting trial on very serious charges is to be paraded, in the very court where that trial will shortly be held, before a Bishop rather than a presiding judge and permitted to broadcast live to the nation for a day or so uninterrupted. Thereafter for the following day or days, he will be examined by a barrister and then questioned from the bench by the Bishop and some five or six fellow Commissioners. In the immediate vicinity will be press, prosecutors and "victims". His counsel will be present and permitted to interject but there are no fixed procedures and no Rules of Evidence. The event will have the appearance of a trial, at least the appearance of a sort of trial familiar from centuries past, although the first day of uninterrupted testimony may resemble more a very long party political broadcast. It is not necessary to speculate on the consequences of this spectacle: there may be none. There may be those the Prosecution fears which could lead to intimidation of witnesses and the rally of dormant forces. There may be those that doubtless informed the original advice of his lawyers against testifying—namely fodder for the Prosecution, an adverse effect on public perceptions of his innocence and a consequent disheartening of potential defence witnesses. There will probably, I fear, be this consequence, namely intense anxiety amongst other indictees, especially from rival factions, and concerns over whether they should testify to the TRC as well, or in rebuttal. The spectacle of the TRC sitting in court may set up a public expectation that it will indeed pass judgement on indictees thus confronted and questioned, whose guilt or innocence it is the special duty of the Special Court to determine.

31. ...If it is the case that local TRCs and international courts are to work together in efforts to produce post-conflict justice in other theatres of war in the future, I do not believe that granting this application for public testimony would be a helpful precedent.

...

33. Let me to return to first principles. Truth Commissions and International Courts are both instruments for effectuating the promise made by states that victims of human rights violations shall have an effective remedy. Criminal courts offer the most effective remedy—a trial, followed by punishment of those found guilty, in this case of those who bear the greatest responsibility. TRC reports can assist society to move forward and beyond the hatreds that fuelled the war. Truth commissions offer two distinct prospects for victims—of truth, i.e. learning how and why they or their loved ones were murdered or maimed or mutilated, and of reconciliation, through understanding and forgiveness of those perpetrators who genuinely confess and regret. It seems to me that these are separate and severable objectives.

34. In what has been termed "transitional justice" periods, truth commissions may be the only option for weak governments. In this context they were common in South America in the 1980s — in Bolivia, Chile, El Salvador, Haiti, Argentina and so forth. They were usually accompanied by blanket amnesties and were not permitted to "name names" of those who might be identified as perpetrators of crimes against humanity, not to avoid prejudice to trials (which were not in prospect), but to avoid political embarrassment. The reports nonetheless shed light on abuses — in some cases, as with "Nunca Mas", very great light. They achieved a degree of truth, but without justice and in many cases without reconciliation — see the recent public demands in these countries to vacate the amnesties and prosecute the perpetrators. The Lomé Accord of 1999 offered both a blanket amnesty and a TRC: only after that agreement was comprehensively violated did the international community deploy its muscle to insist on the prosecution of those bearing the greatest responsibility for the war.

. . .

36. In the case, as here, of Truth Commissions coinciding with court trials of alleged perpetrators, there is a dearth of precedent. In East Timor, a Memorandum of Understanding has been drawn up between the Office of the General Prosecutor (OGP) and the Commission (CAVR) which provides that: The OGP is able to provide information to the CAVR that is relevant to its truth-seeking function only in circumstances where this does not prejudice ongoing investigations or prosecutions or the confidentiality of witnesses or victims and is consistent with the mandate of the OGP. This does not address the specific issue of indictee testimony, although it demonstrates that in balancing the interests of the two processes, the value of fair trial must be overriding.

37. There is some assistance to be drawn from the experience of Peru, where the issue has arisen in relation to testimony by members of Shining Path who were awaiting trial. The TRC chose, I am told, to hear any testimony offered by such indictees in private, so as not to impact on their trial, even though the trial process there was to be inquisitorial rather than adversarial. . . . I note also that the TRC in that case wrestled with the difficulty inherent in public hearings for convicted perpetrators, namely that this can provide a "soapbox" or platform for justification of their crimes. It declined to provide such hearings for persons whose testimony (which it saw in written form in advance) was either self-promoting or at odds with other credible information it had gathered. . . . Despite some well-publicised confessions at the South African TRC, I am informed that it is rare for perpetrators, whether alleged or convicted, to use public hearings to make confessions: these are more likely to be forthcoming in private hearings. . . .

. . .

39. It would clearly not be right that the TRC apply its "reconciliation" processes of public hearing, confrontation with victims, live broadcast and so on to Special Court indictees who have not pleaded guilty. This would, for the reasons given above, be wholly inappropriate. . . . I have to decide how to effectuate the wish to testify of an indictee who, his counsel tell me, intends to plead "not guilty" and to vigorously defend the legality of his actions in putting down an insurrection by use

of what he will contend was reasonable force. His free speech entitlement may only be restricted — like his freedom of movement — to the extent that is consonant with his present status as an indictee.

40. That status does not only restrict his speech in the interests of security. It carries with it a host of considerations about ensuring the fairness of his trial (and "fairness" includes fairness to the Prosecutor and its witnesses) and fairness to other indictees who face trial. . . .

41. In my judgement, Chief Sam Hinga Norman is entitled to testify to the TRC upon condition that he has been fully apprised and advised of the dangers of so doing. I am satisfied that he has been expertly warned. His testimony must, however, be provided in a manner that reduces to an acceptable level any danger that it will influence witnesses (whether favourably or adversely) or affect the integrity of court proceedings or unreasonably affect co-defendants and other indictees. This in my judgement can be achieved by evidence prepared by him in writing (with the benefit of legal advice) and sworn in the form of an affidavit. . . . Should counsel for the TRC have any further questions, these may be put to the indictee in writing and his answers may be sworn and delivered in the same way. There shall be no public hearing of the kind requested or of any other kind prior to the conclusion of the trial. This is without prejudice to his right, if so advised, to make unsworn written statements to the TRC. It is without prejudice to his right to meet with commissioners in the Detention Unit, if they apply for that purpose, or to his right to meet them for a confidential session, if a joint application is made for that purpose.

42. . . . Mr Tim Owen made the point that an affidavit would not be so beneficial as a radio broadcast in getting his message across to his followers, because many of them cannot read. But this begs the question of the legitimate purpose of the TRC hearing, which must be to get information across to the Commissioners for the purpose of their report, rather than to permit indicted political leaders to get messages to their followers. What is important is that followers should know that their leaders have been given an opportunity to put forward their version of events in full detail, and this is achieved by the affidavit method. The indictee will shortly address the Court either to have the seven charges against him dismissed (if his Preliminary Motions fail) or else to refute them by his own defence which he will be given every opportunity to develop under procedures that have been scrupulously laid down to achieve fairness. The time for him to give public testimony will be if and when he exercises his right to give evidence on oath.

44. The work of the Special Court and the TRC is complementary and each must accommodate the existence of the other. The TRC is not in a position to suspend its work once trials begin in order to issue a final report when they are over, taking the evidence and verdicts into account. It would be seemly if the report that the TRC is (I am told) to issue in February refrains from passing concluded judgement on the criminal responsibility of any person who is detained to face trial in this Court. Should comment or conclusion be passed, it will of course have absolutely no effect on the minds of the judges of this Court who sit to provide a fair trial according to international standards. That said, the Special Court respects the TRC's work and will assist it so far as is possible and proper, subject only to our overriding duty to

serve the interests of justice without which there may not be the whole truth and there is unlikely to be lasting reconciliation.

FINAL REPORT OF THE TRUTH AND RECONCILIATION COMMISSION OF SIERRA LEONE: WITNESS TO TRUTH

Vol. 3B (2004)

1. ... In recent times, truth commissions have worked in tandem with national criminal justice processes and in one case a commission has functioned in parallel with a criminal tribunal established under UN regulations. However the Sierra Leonean case has brought into sharp focus the different roles of these institutions and the potential pitfalls in their relationship.......

43. ... While the Special Court has primacy over the national courts of Sierra Leone, the TRC does not fall within this mould. In any event, the relationship between the two bodies should not be discussed on the basis of primacy or lack of it. The ultimate operational goal of the TRC and the Court should be guided by the request of the Security Council and the Secretary-General to 'operate in a complementary and mutually supportive manner fully respectful of their distinct but related functions'.

63. ... For [there to be] any basis for [the] claim that the international Agreement [between Sierra Leone and the United Nations] took precedence over the powers of the TRC, further legislation specifically on that point would have had to enacted. No legislation was ever passed to require "full compliance" of the TRC with the "requests and orders" of the Special Court.

75. ... On 26 August 2003 Chief Samuel Hinga Norman, the former National Co-ordinator of the CDF, wrote a letter requesting his legal counsel to facilitate an appearance before the TRC...

76. Norman's application to testify to the TRC was followed by those of Augustine Bao and Issa Sesay, both members of the RUFP, formerly the RUF.

77. ... There was certainly nothing to prevent them recording their full testimonies in writing and submitting them through their lawyers. What these detainees were seeking, however, was a hearing; an opportunity to present testimony in person to the Commission and to answer questions posed by staff of the TRC. They were asserting their rights to be heard in a manner like that accorded to all other Sierra Leoneans who had so requested and so desired....

79. There is nothing unusual about a prisoner, either awaiting trial or convicted, testifying in proceedings in other cases and even in proceedings between other bodies. Such an occurrence happens regularly in national judicial systems and procedures exist in Sierra Leone and elsewhere to facilitate it. Indeed, the Special Court apparently gave its approval for certain detainees in its custody to give evidence in ongoing proceedings in the Sierra Leonean courts pertaining to charges of treason against other individuals.

80. More specifically, there is considerable precedent to be drawn from other truth and reconciliation commissions. In the South African Commission, both

"awaiting-trial" and convicted prisoners appeared before hearings of the Human Rights Violations Committee in order to supply their versions of events. Prisoners and detainees also appeared before the Amnesty Committee of the South African Commission for purposes of having their amnesty applications heard. Indeed some prisoners and detainees appeared before both Committees. The Sierra Leone TRC was entrusted by the Parliament of Sierra Leone with the responsibility of hearing all relevant evidence and information concerning its mandate. Had Chief Hinga Norman or the other detainees been in prison in Sierra Leone awaiting trial before a national court, there can be no doubt that arrangements would have been made to have enabled them to be heard by the Commission. The TRC succeeded in gaining access to several persons held in Freetown Central Prison in exactly this situation.

83. The Practice Direction was adopted by the Special Court for Sierra Leone on 9 September 2003....

85. In requiring the Commission to make a substantive application to a Special Court Judge for permission to interview a detainee, the Practice Direction was inconsistent with the mandate and powers granted to the Commission under its founding statute. The Commission was granted the power to interview any individual within Sierra Leone at any place in the fulfilment of its mandate. There were no limitations, exceptions or qualifications on this power contained in the Truth and Reconciliation Commission Act 2000.

87. ... The TRC routinely interviews awaiting trial prisoners before the criminal courts of Sierra Leone and there has been absolutely no question of monitoring our interviews or for that matter forwarding information to prosecutors. Indeed to do so would be regarded as an outrage. Our hope is that the Special Court, a body established through international co-operation and which subscribes to international human right standards, will not conduct itself in this way.

122. In an attempt to highlight the profound importance of the issue at hand, the Commission submitted that developments in national and international law created a presumption in favour of permitting Hinga Norman to appear before the Commission. Nationally, the established practice of the Truth and Reconciliation Commission had led to the recognition in national law of a de facto right to testify before the Commission. With regard to international practice, the Commission asserted the following: "In the light of developments in post-conflict societies in the late 20th and early 21st centuries in dealing with past human rights violations, there exists on the part of victims a right to know the truth. Truth Commissions have been created in several countries around the world to meet that recognised obligation. There is considerable weight to the argument that establishing the "truth" is an essential component of the universally recognised "right to an effective remedy." The Special Court is duly bound to consider such a right in respect of the Sierra Leone population in its determination of the parameters of this request "in the interests of justice"."

123. The Commission concluded its representations by suggesting that the historic moment had arrived whereby a decision had to be made as to whether these two institutions were indeed going to work together on a complementary basis or not. The outcome of this proceeding will in large measure determine whether two such institutions can in fact be complementary. The consequences for the people of

Sierra Leone — and indeed for the people in all conflict zones which envisage similar mechanisms of transitional justice — will be far reaching."

140. The Commission submitted that the institutions of the Special Court and the TRC both had important roles to play in reaching the truth and addressing impunity in the context of post-conflict Sierra Leone. The Special Court seeks to prove and establish beyond reasonable doubt the elements of specifically-framed charges against individuals who are alleged to bear the greatest responsibility. It endeavours to reach the truth in relation to the role of those individuals. In so doing it would hopefully provide a deterrent against future abuses.

141. The TRC, on the other hand, endeavours to establish the wider truth in relation to the roles of all key players and factions in the conflict. It was averred on behalf of the Commission that it was only when the full truth (or as close to the full truth as possible) was placed squarely before the public that society is able to examine itself honestly and robustly. It was this exercise that would permit society to take genuine measures to prevent repetition of the horrors of the past.

154. Judge Robertson then wished to know whether the Commission would "make a determination on the guilt or innocence of certain individuals": "Has the Commission addressed the issue of making judgements on people? Would the TRC make judgements?" Mr. Varney explained the nature of findings that truth commissions make and reminded the Judge that "the TRC is not a court". Judge Robertson indicated that it would be preferable if the Commission refrained from making pronouncements on the roles and responsibilities of the indictees held by the Special Court.

156. At this point Mr. Johnson on behalf of the Prosecution said that there were "ongoing efforts to intimidate and scare witnesses right now". He added: "I would hate to see this being used in some effort to promulgate that...."

157. The Judge and the Prosecution then engaged in a discussion on Hinga Norman and the potential volatility of his supporters:

160. The Judge then commented on the wisdom of having two institutions such as the Special Court and the Commission in operation at the same time: "It may be that our hope of working together and at the same time may not be possible." He suggested that the best resolution would be for the Commission to suspend the issuance of its report until all the trials at the Special Court were complete.

161. Mr. Varney pointed out to Judge Robertson that there was no prospect of securing a suspension of the Commission's proceedings. He also advised that it had always been open to the TRC to obtain Chief Norman's testimony by way of a written submission. No approval or intervention by the Special Court was ever required to obtain written testimony.

167. The decision of Judge Robertson was finally issued on 28 November 2003....

172. ...Extracts from the Commission's media statement of 1 December 2003 read as follows: "PRESS RELEASE BY THE TRC Freetown, Sierra Leone, 1 December 2003 SPECIAL COURT DENIES HINGA NORMAN'S RIGHT (AND THAT OF THE OTHER DETAINEES) TO APPEAR PUBLICLY BEFORE THE TRC... The ruling, in the view of the TRC, has dealt a serious blow to the cause of truth and reconciliation in Sierra Leone. As a citizen of Sierra Leone and as a key

role-player in Sierra Leone's recent history, Chief Hinga Norman has a right to appear before the TRC to tell his story. All equivalent role-players have appeared before the TRC, including prisoners awaiting trial at Pademba Road Prison. . . . "

192. The Judge's choice of words to describe the Commission's original approach to the detainees was unfortunate: "When the TRC first approached a number of indictees, earlier in the year, they all declined a chalice that they were doubtless advised was poisoned." The publication of such a theatrical metaphor in a decision under the hand of the President of the Court inferred that there was something poisonous about the agenda of the TRC, supposedly a "complementary" organisation. . . . According to the Judge, the Revised Practice Direction provided "for a confidential process of receiving information." In fact it provided for an official from the Registrar's office to monitor the interview within earshot. In addition, the monitoring officer had authority to intervene should the questions stray off the approved subject areas. In effect it was envisaged that a Court representative would sit at the interview table. The entire interview would be tape recorded and lodged at the Registrar's office. Parties to the proceedings could thereafter apply to the trial judge for the disclosure of the transcript "in the interests of justice". . . .

213. The achievement of "justice" may very well advance the cause of reconciliation. Whether it brings reconciliation in itself is debatable. Whether the kind of justice referred to by the Judge, namely the retributive justice pursued by the Special Court, is capable of producing national reconciliation is equally debatable. Confining the achievement of justice to retributive justice is a narrow interpretation of what justice has come to mean in recent times.

215. If Justice Robertson's proposition is correct then the achievement of reconciliation is presumably dependent on the "successful" outcome of the prosecutions before the Special Court. However, achieving justice and addressing impunity are difficult enough tasks. There are huge uncertainties inherent in criminal trials. Prosecutions fail as often as they succeed. To rest reconciliation on the successful outcome of a legal process is a risky endeavour. This point was made forcefully in a unanimous decision of the South African Constitutional Court in 1996. The applicants in the matter contested the denial of their rights to judicial redress under the amnesty provision of the truth and reconciliation process: "Every decent human being must feel grave discomfort in living with a consequence which might allow the perpetrators of evil acts to walk the streets of this land with impunity, protected in their freedom by an amnesty immune from constitutional attack; but the circumstances in support of this course require carefully to be appreciated. Most of the acts of brutality and torture [that] have taken place have occurred during an era in which neither the laws which permitted the incarceration of persons or the investigation of crimes, nor the methods and the culture which informed such investigations, were easily open to public investigation, verification and correction. Much of what transpired in this shameful period is shrouded in secrecy and not easily capable of objective demonstration and proof. Loved ones have disappeared, sometimes mysteriously and most of them no longer survive to tell their tales. Others have had their freedom invaded, their dignity assaulted or their reputations tarnished by grossly unfair imputations hurled in the fire and the cross-fire of a deep and wounding conflict. The wicked and the innocent have often both been victims. Secrecy and authoritarianism have

concealed the truth in little crevices of obscurity in our history. Records are not easily accessible; witnesses are often unknown, dead, unavailable or unwilling. All that often effectively remains is the truth of wounded memories of loved ones sharing instinctive suspicions, deep and traumatising to the survivors but otherwise incapable of translating themselves into objective and corroborative evidence which could survive the rigours of the law. The Act [that created the Truth and Reconciliation Commission] seeks to address this massive problem. [...] The alternative to the grant of immunity from criminal prosecution of offenders is to keep intact the abstract right to such a prosecution for particular persons without the evidence to sustain the prosecution successfully, to continue to keep the dependants of such victims in many cases substantially ignorant about what precisely happened to their loved ones; to leave their yearning for the truth effectively unassuaged; to perpetuate their legitimate sense of resentment and grief..."

217. Judge Robertson's assertion of the power of the Court does not exclude other means of pursuing reconciliation, but his notion does not leave room for a lasting reconciliation to be built without resorting to criminal trials. Based on the practice of other countries, it does not appear to be accurate to say that criminal trials are a prerequisite for reconciliation. Mozambique, which experienced one of the bloodiest civil wars in the second half of the twentieth century, enjoys a measure of reconciliation even though there were no criminal trials, or for that matter a truth and reconciliation commission. South Africa, which deprived many victims of judicial redress, through its "truth for amnesty" formula, also enjoys a measure of reconciliation notwithstanding its bitter and divided past.

227. Ultimately where there is no harmonisation of objectives a criminal justice body will have largely punitive and retributive aims, whereas a truth and reconciliation body will have largely restorative and healing objectives. Where the two bodies operate simultaneously in an ad-hoc fashion, conflict between such objectives is likely. Confusion in the minds of the public is inevitable.

228. Harmonisation of objectives means that neither body can operate in a manner that is oblivious of the other. It is highly incongruous for one body to engage in intensive truth seeking and reconciliation exercises involving former participants in the conflict, while another body is independently pursing punitive actions against the same individuals....

230. It is likely that in the future there will be more truth commissions that work alongside international judicial bodies. This will particularly be the case as the International Criminal Court commences operations in different post-conflict countries....

233. In the light of developments in post-conflict societies in the late twentieth and early twenty-first centuries in dealing with past human rights violations, there exists on the part of victims a right to know the truth. Truth Commissions have been established in several countries around the world to meet this recognised obligation. The Commission finds that there is considerable weight to the argument that establishing the "truth" is an essential component of the universally recognised "right to an effective remedy".

234. The Commission also recognises that victims have a right to justice and to pursue this right through legal means.

QUESTIONS

1. What changes in structural design and legal rules could resolve the potential conflicts between truth commissions and criminal tribunals? Do the different goals of the two institutions make such conflicts likely, if not inevitable? Do Hayner's suggestions overcome the types of concerns raised by ICTY officials? Are the concerns of the ICTY officials reasonable?

2. Truth commissions and criminal tribunals can also potentially benefit one another. What formal rules or procedures can improve upon the positive relationships between these institutions?

3. It is both explicit and implicit in Justice Robertson's reasoning that trials should have primacy over alternative remedial strategies in dealing with mass human rights violations. Does international law support his assessment? The TRC Final Report suggests that normative questions about whether such primacy is warranted might boil down to an empirical debate about the potential effectiveness of trials in different situations. Do you agree? What potential is there for trials ever to succeed in the aftermath of a collapsed state or where 'secrecy and authoritarianism have concealed the truth' for decades?

4. Is the Special Court the appropriate institution for addressing issues such as a defendant's rights before another body and the relative value of the TRC's work? Does the fact that the Special Court constitutes a quasi-international institution affect your evaluation?

5. Could permitting defendants to testify in public hearings before a truth commission be advantageous to criminal tribunals? For example, such an arrangement could provide an incentive for key suspects to offer important information about the history of events and their particular actions. Similarly, are there conditions under which a truth commission's exerting pressure on a tribunal to pursue convictions would be advantageous? What if the commission can be trusted to produce a fair and objective set of conclusions? What if a criminal tribunal would, in the absence of a commission's report, surrender to outside political pressure to acquit perpetrators?

ADDITIONAL READING

N. Kritz (ed.), *Transnational Justice: How Emerging Democracies Reckon with Former Regimes* (3 Vols. 1995); N. Roht-Arriaza (ed.), *Impunity and Human Rights in International Law and Practice* (1995); M. Minow, *Between Vengeance and Forgiveness* (1998); Deborah Posel and Graeme Simpson (eds.), *Commissioning the Past: Understanding South Africa's Truth and Reconciliation Commission* (2003); Priscilla B. Hayner, *Unspeakable Truths: Confronting State Terror and Atrocity* (2001); Naomi Roht-Arriaza and Javier Mariezcurrena (eds.), *Transitional Justice in the Twenty-First Century: Beyond Truth versus Justice* (2006); Ruti G. Teitel, *Transitional Justice* (2001); Dugard, 'Possible Conflicts of Jurisdiction with Truth Commissions', in A. Cassese *et al.* (eds.), *The Rome Statute of the International Criminal Court: A Commentary* (2002).

15

Non-State Actors and Human Rights

One of the most dramatic developments within international human rights law over the past decade or more has been the growing importance of a range of non-state actors. The centrality of the state is one of the defining features of international law and the human rights system builds upon this by seeking to bind states through a network of treaty obligations to which, in the vast majority of cases, only states can become parties. Non-state actors are thus, by definition, placed at the margins of the resulting legal regime. The problem is that actors such as transnational corporations, civil society groups, international organizations and armed opposition groups, to name just the most prominent among a wide range of potentially important non-state actors, have all assumed major roles in relation to the enjoyment of human rights, especially in recent years.

Various factors have contributed to this development. They include: (i) the privatization of functions previously performed by governments, including in relation to social welfare services, prisons, asylum processing, schools, adoptions, health care provision for the poor, and the supply of water, gas and electricity; (ii) the ever-increasing mobility of capital and the increased importance of foreign investment flows, facilitated by market deregulation and trade liberalization; (iii) the expanding responsibilities of multilateral organizations, some of which are now called upon to exercise a wide range of governmental functions in areas ranging from Kosovo and East Timor to Afghanistan and Iraq; (iv) the enormous growth in the role played by transnational civil society organizations, many of which now have multimillion dollar budgets, employ very large staffs, and perform public-type functions in a large number of countries; (v) the changing nature of conflicts which has seen a growth in the number and proportion of internal conflicts and a subsequent rise in the importance of organized armed groups controlling territory and population and aspiring to gain international legitimacy; and (vi) the growth of international terrorist networks such as Al Qaeda, and international criminal networks, such as drug cartels, which are not confined to any one state and some of whose activities have become global in scope.

These developments have increased the risk that a human rights regime which addresses itself effectively only to states will become increasingly marginalized in the years ahead. The ILO recognized this as long ago as 1994 when it launched a new initiative based upon a Declaration on Fundamental Principles and Rights at Work which was said to be applicable to all actors. The new approach was said to be designed to move beyond 'the "state-centred" nature of ILO standards' and 'the fact that the obligations arising from Conventions apply directly only to States'.[1] More recently, the importance of devising means by which to ensure the applicability of human rights standards to non-state actors has been highlighted by the dilemmas flowing from 'outsourcing' of military and military-support functions in many contexts. This development is the opposite of concerns which were prevalent in the 1980s which led to widespread condemnation of the role of mercenaries in a range of different conflicts. In contrast, the twenty-first century has witnessed a broad and potentially almost unlimited role being accorded to private contractors in conflict situations. In relation to Iraq, for example, a class action lawsuit was brought in the US Federal Court against two corporations (Titan International and CACI International) accused of having conspired with US officials to 'humiliate, torture and abuse persons detained' in Iraq. The contractors provided a range of services to the US Government, including carrying out prisoner interrogations, a role they had also played in Guantánamo.[2]

This chapter looks at the role of non-state actors in three specific situations. The first concerns the attempts, primarily within the United Nations setting, to articulate and implement human rights obligations for corporations, particularly those that operate transnationally. The second looks at the extent to which the existing framework of human rights law is capable of addressing the role of armed opposition groups and the third considers the dilemmas created for freedom of speech by the privatization of traditionally public spaces.

Before engaging with these specific contexts it is useful to set the scene with an excerpt from a General Comment adopted by the ICCPR Human Rights Committee in 2004 which addresses, albeit somewhat obliquely, the position of non-state actors:

> The article 2, paragraph 1, obligations ['to respect and to ensure to all individuals within its territory and subject to its jurisdiction the rights recognized...'] are binding on States Parties and do not, as such, have direct horizontal effect as a matter of international law. The Covenant cannot be viewed as a substitute for domestic criminal or civil law. However the positive obligations on States Parties to ensure Covenant rights will only be fully discharged if individuals are protected by the State, not just against violations of Covenant rights by its agents, but also against acts committed by private persons or entities that would impair the enjoyment of Covenant rights in so far as they are amenable to application between private persons or entities. There may be circumstances in which a failure to ensure Covenant rights as required by article 2 would give rise to violations by States Parties of those rights, as a result of States Parties' permitting or failing to take appropriate measures or to exercise due diligence to prevent, punish, investigate or redress the harm caused by such acts by private persons or entities. States are reminded of the interrelationship between the positive obligations imposed under article 2 and the need to provide effective remedies in the event of breach under article 2, paragraph 3. The Covenant itself envisages in some articles certain areas where there are positive obligations on States Parties to address the activities of private persons or entities. For example, the privacy-related guarantees of article 17 must be protected by law.

[1] *Defending Values, Promoting Change: Social Justice in a Global Economy: An ILO Agenda* (1994), at 56.

[2] The text of the class action lawsuit is available at http://www.ccr-ny.org/v2/legal/september_11th/docs/Al_Rawi_v_Titan_Complaint.pdf.

It is also implicit in article 7 that States Parties have to take positive measures to ensure that private persons or entities do not inflict torture or cruel, inhuman or degrading treatment or punishment on others within their power. In fields affecting basic aspects of ordinary life such as work or housing, individuals are to be protected from discrimination within the meaning of article 26.[3]

QUESTION

Does it follow from the Human Rights Committee's interpretation of Article 2(1) that states' positive obligations to address non-state actors are limited to matters concerning privacy, torture or discrimination? Would this be a tenable reading of the Covenant? If not, what criteria might apply to determine the extent of such obligations?

A. TRANSNATIONAL CORPORATIONS AND HUMAN RIGHTS

Globalization has contributed to, and in part been driven by, the increasingly central role of transnational corporations (TNCs) in the international and domestic economic orders. Since the 1970s there has been an immense expansion in the wealth and power of TNCs, and this trend has accelerated in recent years. As Macklem has noted:

> Processes of economic globalization are dramatically enhancing technological, commercial and financial integration of national economies. Traditional geographical and political barriers are becoming increasingly irrelevant to the production, placement and sale of goods and services. States are gradually dismantling tariff barriers and actively seeking new forms of direct foreign investment. Multinational corporations, participating in spatially concentrated clusters often referred to as transnational production chains, are cutting across national economic and juridical boundaries, exploiting efficiency gains associated with economic globalization and technological innovation, and wielding unprecedented power and influence in local and global markets and domestic and international affairs.[4]

Along with greater power comes an enhanced potential to promote or undermine respect for human rights:

> The corporate world touches the lives of people more closely than any other constituency, giving it immense potential for good or harm.... [In addition to its great benefits] has come collateral damage — to individuals, to the environment,

[3] Human Rights Committee, General Comment No. 31 (2004) on (Article 2) The Nature of the General Legal Obligation Imposed on States Parties to the Covenant, para. 8.

[4] Patrick Macklem, 'Corporate Accountability under International Law: The Misguided Quest for Universal Jurisdiction', 7 *International Law Forum* 281 (2005).

> to communities. Whether directly or indirectly, companies encounter problems which we would now classify under the generic heading of human rights. In their supply chains they can meet exploitative child labour, discrimination, risks to health and life, forced labour. The extractive industries can be involved in the spoliation of the environment and the destruction of communities. In contexts of conflict and human rights violations they confront a need for security which is too often provided by ill-disciplined state security forces.
>
> Simply through their presence companies provide economic support and moral sanction to oppressive governments. If they lack appropriate policies and principles, companies risk the legitimate charge of complicity with oppression in pursuit of profit.[5]

The scale of corporate power is illustrated by the case of the world's biggest company, Wal-Mart. Its 2003 sales of $256 billion made it larger than the economies of all but the world's 30 richest nations.[6] Its sales on a single day alone were greater than the annual Gross Domestic Product (GDP) of 36 countries in the world.[7] In Mexico it is the largest private employer, accounts for 2% of the country's GDP, and is credited with single-handedly reducing the national inflation rate.[8]

For human rights proponents the growth of corporate power raises the question of how to ensure that the activities of transnational corporations in particular are consistent with human rights standards and of how to promote accountability when violations of those standards occur. In principle, the answer is straightforward. The human rights obligations assumed by each government require it to use all appropriate means to ensure that actors operating within its territory or otherwise subject to its jurisdiction comply with national legislation designed to give effect to human rights.

In practice, however, various problems arise: (1) governments are often loathe to take the measures necessary to ensure compliance by TNCs, especially, but not only, in relation to labour matters; (2) such measures are costly and perceived to be beyond the resource capabilities of governments in developing countries; (3) in the context of increasing global mobility of capital, competition among potential host countries discourages initiatives that may push up labour costs and make one country less attractive than others with lower regulatory standards (the so-called 'race to the bottom'); (4) the transnational complexity of manufacturing and related arrangements in an era of globalization makes it increasingly difficult to identify who is responsible for what activities and where; and (5) especially in the labour area, difficult issues arise about the different levels of minimum acceptable standards from one country to another.

The past decade or so has seen extensive activity aimed at developing corporate human rights accountability. Such responsibilities were barely recognized in the early 1990s but the situation today is very different. According to one prominent participant in the debate the change of attitude 'has come about not because of corporate initiative, but as the result of reputational disaster. It was the damaging

[5] G. Chandler, 'Corporate Liability: Human Rights and the Modern Business', Conference organized by JUSTICE and Sweet & Maxwell, 12 June 2006.

[6] Tim Weiner, 'Wal-Mart Invades, and Mexico Gladly Surrenders', *New York Times*, 5 December 2003, A1 at A9.

[7] Jerry Useem, 'One Nation Under Wal-Mart', *Fortune Magazine*, 3 March 2003, at http://www.ufcw135.org/z_news/n_onenation_under_wmt.htm.

[8] Weiner, n. 6 above.

experience of Shell and BP in Nigeria and Colombia respectively which proved the catalyst for a change of attitudes and provided a lesson about corporate responsibility which was reinforced by the experience of Nike and other major international brands with reputations to protect.'[9] An additional element which has emerged only recently is the extent to which Chinese-owned TNCs have emerged in many countries, and especially in Africa, and are generally seen to be resistant to the notion of human rights responsibilities. One result is that the debate is no longer only about Northern corporations and their activities in the global South.

The following materials provide illustrations of some of the principal contexts in which major human rights issues have arisen concerning TNCs. The notion of 'complicity' is prominent and the excerpt from a Human Rights Watch report on Internet regulation in China demonstrates the dilemmas for TNCs when confronted by national laws and policies that are incompatible with human rights. Leisinger analyses the issues from a business perspective and seeks to differentiate the levels of responsibility which corporations might be considered to have in different situations.[10] The materials then consider the role played by voluntary codes and standards in this area.

IRENE KHAN, UNDERSTANDING CORPORATE COMPLICITY: EXTENDING THE NOTION BEYOND EXISTING LAWS

London, 8 December 2005, Amnesty International Index: POL 34/001/2006[11]

...

On 4 February 2005, soldiers from the Nigerian Joint Task Force fired on protesters from Ugborodo, a small community of the Itsekiri ethnic group, who had entered Chevron Nigeria's Escravos oil terminal on the Delta State coast. One demonstrator was shot and later died from his injuries, and at least 30 others were injured, some of them seriously, by blows from rifle butts and other weapons. Chevron Nigeria, which operates the terminal, said that 11 employees and security officers received minor injuries....

The protest was over a Memorandum of Understanding signed by Ugborodo community representatives and Chevron Nigeria in 2002. The protesters said that Chevron Nigeria had not provided the jobs and development projects they were promised. The company denied charges and said that the responsibility for protecting its facilities rests with the state security forces, and it could not control the actions of the security forces in any way. Chevron, like other oil companies operating in Nigeria, does provide the state security forces with allowances in line with industry practice, as well as interacts regularly with the JTF.

[9] Chandler, n. 5, above.

[10] An important legal analysis of the same issues is provided by Ratner who identifies four 'clusters of issues' which determine the nature of a TNC's obligations in a specific context: the closeness of the relationship between the TNC and host government; the TNC's nexus to affected populations; the specific human right concerned; and the place within the corporate structure of the individuals violating human rights. S. Ratner, 'Corporations and Human Rights: A Theory of Legal Responsibility', 111 Yale L.J. 443 (2001), at 496.

[11] The author is Secretary-General of Amnesty International.

Human rights law is clear that the state has primary responsibility for respecting and promoting human rights. Human Rights law is also clear that non-state actors such as companies have a responsibility to uphold human rights — as an organ of society, in the words of the Universal Declaration of Human Rights — within their area of control and sphere of influence — whether in the context of their operations or in the communities in which they operate.

But what happens when the company itself does not commit an abuse but benefits from an abuse committed by a government or armed group? Or funds those who commit abuses? Or remain[s] silent in the face of abuse? Or complies with national laws and policies which are clearly in violation of international human rights?

The Second Principle of the Global Compact calls upon companies not to be complicit in human rights abuses.

...

A legal or moral case?

Corporate complicity is an emerging area of law — it is also an area where moral questions are as important as legal ones — at least until there is more legal clarity — of what is good practice, what is right and wrong, fair and unfair. It extends from a situation where a company has knowingly funded, supported or benefited from human rights abuse to a situation where it has been a silent witness of abuse committed by others. Where do the boundaries of complicity begin and end? On one side there is law which tells us what can and cannot be done. But we must not stop where the law rests; in protecting human rights sometimes we have to go beyond the law, where there are values and principles which are worth fighting for. . . .

In some cases, criminal or civil liability may be clear. . . .

But there are many other cases where the parameters of complicity are only emerging . . . . [L]et me start by laying out some examples of real cases where companies can risk complicity.

Armed Conflict

Companies may provide money, resources, infrastructure, products or services that facilitated human rights violations in the context of armed conflict.

An apparently innocuous trade in rough diamonds was used to fund weapons with which gross human rights abuses were then committed. No court case had to be fought to make the diamond industry realize that the risk to their reputation of complicity in crimes against humanity. That led to the Kimberly Process certification scheme.

So, what is the corporate liability if an oil company provides aviation fuel to the Sudanese air force to bomb villages? This is a case where the company concerned withdrew from its contract with the Sudanese government. Naming and shaming — or reputational damage on moral grounds — can be as strong an incentive as legal action . . .

Slavery and Forced Labour

. . . UNOCAL was sued in the United States under the ATCA for participating in a joint venture with the government of Myanmar in which the Myanmar army had used forced labour to build a pipeline. UNOCAL settled the case of out[sic] court.

Companies that use migrant labour directly or through their suppliers may need to be particularly careful, given the increase in human trafficking and abuse of migrant workers. When a gang master hires undocumented foreigners to work under inhumane conditions in certain industries, the companies that benefit from the products they make could run the risk of being complicit, even though they themselves do not own the factories.

Child Labour

... If a company in the developed world turns a blind eye to [inherently exploitative, dangerous and unacceptable forms of] child labour and continues to contract work to offending subcontractors, it could run the risk of being complicit in the abuse of children's rights.

Trade Union Rights

A company provides residential addresses of its employees who are active trade union members to a government which is hostile to trade unions. Or calls in the police which brutally disperses trade unions officials. Or remains silent when its trade unions officials are systematically killed by the authorities or "disappear".

Technology

There have also been instances where companies have provided technology to governments to commit human rights abuses, for instance, surveillance technology to authoritarian governments which then used that technology to track down and punish dissidents, and, the international tribunal at Nuremberg after World War II sentenced senior executives of German firms that provided the Zyklon B gas to the Nazis. Other executives, who facilitated the abuses in concentration camps, were also sentenced.

...

Discrimination

At the heart of human rights law is the principle of non-discrimination. Many companies operating in South Africa during the apartheid era not only followed the discriminatory laws of that time, some of them also aided and abetted the South African government's policies — by providing technology, infrastructure, and other means to implement its policies. The Truth and Reconciliation Commission established three levels of moral responsibility for business[es] in the context of apartheid:

First order involvement — companies that actively helped to design and implement apartheid policies e.g. the mining industry that worked with the government to shape the migrant labour system from which it benefited.

Second order involvement— when companies knew their products would be used for repression. For instance arms producers who knew that their weapons would be used by the security forces in the townships or banks that provided covert credit cards to repressive security operations.

Third order involvement— companies that benefited indirectly by virtue of operating within a racially segregated environment.

...

Non discrimination may be particularly relevant also for companies that run hospitals, food distribution systems or school. Acquiescing with discriminatory policies of states may expose a company to the risk of complicity in a wide range of human rights, including economic, social and cultural rights.

Many companies seek to hide behind national laws, but what may be legal at the national level could be wholly unacceptable at the international level. Standards for human rights are set internationally.... Some of the toughest campaigns against corporate behaviour were not fought in the court of law but in the court of public opinion.

...

HUMAN RIGHTS WATCH, 'RACE TO THE BOTTOM': CORPORATE COMPLICITY IN CHINESE INTERNET CENSORSHIP

August 10, 2006, HRW Index No. C1808

...[China] now attracts more foreign investment than any other country in the world [but the] rule of law continues to seriously lag behind economic expansion. The judiciary, a pillar of a rights-respecting society, remains poorly trained and under the political control of the Chinese Communist Party. Access to justice remains severely limited for citizens with grievances, particularly the poor. The Party retains its monopoly on political power and shows no signs of allowing political pluralism or challenges to its authority. Torture continues to be rampant.... As a result, there is enormous social unrest, as evidenced by tens of thousands of street protests annually.

Since President Hu Jintao came to power in 2003, the trend towards greater freedom of expression — a core right upon which the attainment of many other rights depends — has been reversed. Many critical (and popular) media outlets that have exposed corruption or criticized government policies have been closed. Large numbers of journalists have been jailed.

One of the most distressing trends has been a steady crackdown on the Internet. While in the past decade the Internet has ushered in an era of unprecedented access to information and open discussion, debate, and dissent, since President Hu took office the authorities have taken a series of harsh steps to control and suppress political and religious speech on the Internet, including the jailing of Internet critics and bloggers for peaceful political expression.

In fact, China's system of Internet censorship and surveillance is the most advanced in the world. While tens of thousands of people are employed by the Chinese government and security organs to implement a system of political censorship, this system is also aided by extensive corporate and private sector cooperation — including by some of the world's major international technology and Internet companies. In China, the active role of censor has been extended from government offices into private companies. Some companies not only respond to instructions and pressures from Chinese authorities to censor their materials, they actively engage in self-censorship by using their technology to predict and then censor the material they believe the Chinese government wants them to censor.

...

In this report, we have documented the different ways in which companies such as Yahoo!, Microsoft, Google, and Skype are assisting and reinforcing the Chinese government's system of arbitrary, opaque and unaccountable political censorship. This report documents the way in which these companies actively, openly, and deliberately (by their own admission) collaborate with the Chinese government's system of Internet censorship:

Yahoo!: Yahoo! has handed over user information on four Chinese government critics to the Chinese authorities, resulting in their trial and conviction. Yahoo!'s Chinese search engine is heavily censored....

Microsoft: In June 2005 ... Microsoft came under criticism from the press and bloggers around the world for censoring words such as "democracy" and "freedom" in the titles of its Chinese blogs, at the request of the Chinese government. Microsoft has made efforts in recent months to revise its practices and minimize censorship of Chinese bloggers....

Google: In January 2006 Google rolled out its censored search engine, Google.cn. Google.cn does provide notice to users when search results have been censored but provides no further details....

Skype: ... Skype executives have publicly acknowledged that [its Chinese] software censors sensitive words in text chats, and have justified this as in keeping with local "best practices" and Chinese law. However Skype does not inform Chinese users of the specific details of its censorship policies, and does not inform them that their software contains censorship capabilities.

Yahoo!, Microsoft and Google have not publicized the list of sites or keywords being censored, and have not clarified which Chinese laws are being violated by the terms and web addresses censored by their Chinese search engines or services (and also blog-hosting services in the case of Microsoft). Thus it is impossible to evaluate the veracity of the claim each company makes that it is simply following Chinese law....

The above companies are complicit in the Chinese government's censorship of political and religious information and/or the monitoring of peaceful speech....

In response to criticism, these companies all insist that despite the constraints under which they operate they are still helping to increase the Chinese people's access to the Internet, access to more information, and greater means for self-expression.... But we believe that companies are only [contributing to freedom of expression in China] if they are improving or maintaining high ethical standards that, at the very least, are consistent with international law and norms. The burden of proof as to whether they are making a positive impact in comparison to their domestic competitors should be on the companies themselves, rather than leaving the public to guess or discover the companies' ethical standards on their own — in some cases by going to jail.

These companies also argue that they have no choice but to comply with Chinese law and regulations in order to access the Chinese market. Human Rights Watch does not believe that the choice for companies is to either continue current practices or to leave China. Rather, we believe companies can and should make ethical choices about what specific products and services they will provide to the Chinese people — and the manner in which they are provided — without playing a pro-active role in censorship or collaborating in repression. While some companies have said that they have adopted more rigorous processes and procedures to determine when to censor or abide by government demands, none of the companies discussed in this report have said they will refuse such demands, or appear to have actively resisted them. . . .

KLAUS M. LEISINGER, ON CORPORATE RESPONSIBILITY FOR HUMAN RIGHTS

Basel, April 2006[12]

1. Accepting a Conceptual Challenge

. . . The fact is that 8 out of 10 people in an opinion poll conducted among 21,000 respondents in 20 industrial countries and emerging markets assign to large companies at least part of the duty to reduce the number of human rights abuses in the world. While this public opinion — at least in the short run — will not have legal consequences for companies, it is a strong indicator of the perceived legitimacy of corporate activities . . . .

. . .

. . . Some [human rights] groups go so far as to present companies that operate on the international stage as "major violators of human rights" . . . . In doing so, they usually point to the worst-case examples from the extractive sector, which — regardless of the specifics of the individual cases — present unique human rights issues that do not always apply to other sectors (such as textiles, leather processing, the construction and electricity generating sector, or pharmaceuticals).

. . . The challenge — both intellectually and politically — lies in working out a meaningful and broadly accepted package of corporate human rights responsibilities . . . .

. . .

2. Corporate Human Rights Commitment as Values Management

. . .

. . . [O]n the one hand, there are those who regard companies (especially multinationals) as the "source of all evil"; on the other hand, there are those who have a touching faith in the ability of companies, economic growth, and the laws of the market to solve all human rights problems. Yet reality is more complex and indeterminate than these extreme views: the expectations directed at companies remain unclear.

[12] The author is Special Advisor to the UN Secretary-General on the Global Compact and President and CEO of the Novartis Foundation for Sustainable Development.

... [Corporate management needs to engage] in an informed discussion of critical questions such as:

- What are the human rights-related risks of our business operations? If there are any, in what priority should we approach them? Are there human rights-related opportunities?
- Is there, to the best of our knowledge and belief, any reason to change our business practices in the context of the human rights principles laid down in the UN Global Compact?
- In what areas of activity do those things we consider morally imperative and reasonable differ from what influential human rights groups demand of companies?
- Where and on the basis of what special circumstances (such as market failures or failing states) do we recognize particular demands for the fulfilment of economic or social human rights (such as the offer of life-saving medicines at special conditions), and what concrete deliverables result from this?
- In what areas of activity and in which countries does a corporate policy aimed only at meeting basic legal requirements create vulnerabilities, such as not meeting the expectations of civil society?
- Are there priority arrangements in place for overcoming such conflicts?
- Which actors of civil society (NGOs, media, churches, etc.) do we want to include in our internal analysis of the problem to ensure that the information (fact-based and value-based knowledge) on which we base our decision is appropriate to the complexity and the many-layered context of the issue under debate?
- Where do we draw the limits of our responsibility for the respect, support, and fulfilment of human rights — in other words, how do we define our sphere of influence?
- What do we understand by "complicity"?

... The distinction between "must", "ought to", and "can" norms helps to distinguish what is essentially *good management practice* and what constitutes *corporate responsibility excellence*, partly having a "nice to have" character.

All responsibilities in the context of [civil and political] human rights are an integral part of the "must" dimension and hence an essential ingredient of good management practices.... [A] company must do all in its power to ensure that there are no violations within its own sphere of influence and that it also does not benefit from human rights abuses by other parties. This implies the obligation to strive for all relevant knowledge in this respect as far as is reasonably possible.

As far as [economic, social and cultural] rights are concerned, the normal business operations of a company form the main corporate contribution to the preservation of these rights....

All activities subject to the criterion of "legality" are part of the "must" dimension. Activities that go beyond what is legally required fall under the "ought to" dimension. Most of them are moral obligations but nevertheless constitute good management practice. This includes, for example, ... a "living wage" ..., affirmative efforts for greater gender justice, ... corporate pension funds, and more.

... [Companies might also for example, offer discounted or free medicines in certain circumstances], finance philanthropic foundations, do pro bono research, make donations, and, on a case-by-case basis, contribute to the fulfilment of economic, social, and cultural rights in other ways.

...

NOTE

Codes of conduct have been adopted by thousands of TNCs and they vary hugely in their content, participation, arrangements for monitoring, follow-up, etc. For a compilation of corporate codes on human rights see www.business-humanrights.org/Documents/Policies. In 1999, then UN Secretary-General Kofi Annan launched the Global Compact designed to encourage corporations to commit to following a list of principles in their activities. In addition to principles governing the environment the Compact includes:

Human Rights

Principle 1: support and respect the protection of international human rights within their sphere of influence;

Principle 2: make sure their own corporations are not complicit in human rights abuses.

Labour Standards

Principle 3: freedom of association and the effective recognition of the right to collective bargaining;

Principle 4: the elimination of all forms of forced and compulsory labour;

Principle 5: the effective abolition of child labour;

Principle 6: the elimination of discrimination in respect of employment and occupation.

The Global Compact (www.unglobalcompact.org) has attracted significant corporate support but has generally elicited scepticism from human rights proponents because of their vagueness and their apparent failure to generate significant pressure upon corporations to improve their performance.

One of the most important international initiatives is the Voluntary Principles on Security and Human Rights ('VPs') which were adopted in 2000 at the initiative of the US and UK Governments working with key TNCs and NGOs.[13] They aim 'to guide extractives companies in maintaining the safety and security of their operations within an operating framework that ensures respect for human rights'. They focus particularly on risk assessment, and interactions between companies and public and private security. In relation to effective risk assessment, for example, they

[13] See www.voluntaryprinciples.org.

call upon corporations to: (i) identify security risks; (ii) estimate the potential for violence in a given area; (iii) take account of the human rights records of public security forces, paramilitaries, local and national law enforcement, and the reputation of private security; (iv) take account of the local prosecuting authority and judiciary's capacity to hold actors accountable for human rights abuses; (v) identify the root causes and nature of local conflicts; and (vi) consider the risks of transferring equipment to public or private security and the feasibility of measures to mitigate foreseeable negative consequences.

In addition to the US and the UK, the Netherlands and Norway have joined the initiative along with TNCs such as Amerada Hess, Anglo American, BHP Billiton, BP, Chevron, ExxonMobil, Freeport, Norsk Hydro, Occidental Petroleum, Rio Tinto, Shell and Statoil. Key NGO participants include Amnesty International, Human Rights First, Human Rights Watch, and International Alert, and there are three observer organizations: the International Committee of the Red Cross, the International Council on Mining & Metals, and the International Petroleum Industry Environmental Conservation Association.

Major NGOs have been critical of the extent to which TNCs, especially in the extractive industries, have failed to take the VPs seriously in their operations in countries such as Nigeria.[14] While they continue to support the initiative, they have warned that their continuing participation was dependent upon progress in implementation and reporting (AI Index: IOR 40/003/2006). John Ruggie, Special Representative of the UN Secretary-General on the issue of human rights and transnational corporations and other business enterprises, has called upon the VP system to transform its potential into reality by: (i) adopting 'internal and external reporting criteria, including specific performance measures'; (ii) establishing 'a coherent and effective in-country presence' involving intensive interaction among all stakeholders; (iii) systematic sharing of information and best practices; (iv) supporting capacity-building in host countries; and (v) providing an adequately staffed Secretariat.[15]

In May 2007 the annual meeting of VPs participants adopted new criteria including: minimum requirements for participation; a dispute resolution process to raise concerns about the performance of a participant; clear accountability mechanisms; more transparent procedures for accepting new members; and a commitment by participants to report publicly on their implementation of the VPs.

One publicly available case study of the application of the principles by BP (British Petroleum) concerns an agreement with the Papuan Police in the context of a major oil and gas project in Indonesia.[16] In terms of practical impact, John Ruggie has cited the example of the Colombian Government which, although not yet a formal VPs participant, 'has established a National Committee for the VPs. The government and companies have incorporated VPs language into their legal agreements

[14] E.g. Amnesty International, Nigeria: Ten Years On: Injustice and Violence Haunt the Oil Delta (2005).

[15] J. Ruggie, 'Voluntary Principles on Security and Human Rights', Remarks at Annual Voluntary Principles on Security and Human Rights Plenary (2007).

[16] See 'Field Guidelines for Joint Security Measures Within the Work Area of the Tangguh Lng Project, at http://www.bp.com/liveassets/bp_internet/globalbp/STAGING/global_assets/downloads/T/Tangguh_Field_Guidelines_BP_Papaun_Police.pdf.

regulating public security forces that protect company operations. And company-supported human rights training programs for the armed forces are up and running. Both parties have established complaints procedures for alleged abuses, and the army has established human rights offices all the way down to the brigade level.'

The strategy reflected in the VPs and in some other voluntary code contexts is to gradually ratchet up the levels of commitment and accountability. Some observers, such as the International Commission of Jurists, however, are not content with the incrementalism reflected in such approaches and have insisted upon the need for binding legal rules. This is the thrust of the excerpt below by Howen. A first step in this direction was thought to have been the adoption of a set of Norms on the Responsibilities of Transnational Corporations and Other Business Enterprises with Regard to Human Rights (the so-called 'UN Norms'). The Norms were drafted by a working group of the UN Sub-Commission on the Promotion and Protection of Human Rights, chaired by David Weissbrodt.

NORMS ON THE RESPONSIBILITIES OF TRANSNATIONAL CORPORATIONS AND OTHER BUSINESS ENTERPRISES WITH REGARD TO HUMAN RIGHTS,

U.N. Doc. E/CN.4/Sub.2/2003/12/Rev.2 (2003)

Preamble

Bearing in mind the [UN Charter] . . . ,

Recalling [the UDHR] . . . ,

Recognizing that even though States have the primary responsibility to promote, secure the fulfilment of, respect, ensure respect of and protect human rights, transnational corporations and other business enterprises, as organs of society, are also responsible for promoting and securing the human rights set forth in the Universal Declaration of Human Rights,

Realizing that transnational corporations and other business enterprises, their officers and persons working for them are also obligated to respect generally recognized responsibilities and norms contained in United Nations treaties and other international instruments such as the [Conventions on Genocide, Torture, Slavery, Racial Discrimination, Discrimination against Women, the Rights of the Child, and Migrant Workers; the two International Covenants; the four Geneva Conventions of 1949 and two Additional Protocols thereto; the Declaration on human rights defenders; the Rome Statute of the International Criminal Court; the UN Convention against Transnational Organized Crime; the Convention on Biological Diversity; the International Convention on Civil Liability for Oil Pollution Damage; the Declaration on the Right to Development; the Rio Declaration on Environment and Development; the UN Millennium Declaration; the WHO's Ethical Criteria for Medical Drug Promotion; conventions and recommendations of the International Labour Organization; the Refugee Convention and Protocol; the African Charter on

Human and Peoples' Rights; the American Convention on Human Rights; the European Convention on Human Rights; the Charter of Fundamental Rights of the European Union; and other instruments],

...

Conscious also of the Commentary on [these UN Norms[17]], and finding it a useful interpretation and elaboration of the standards contained in the Norms,

...

Solemnly proclaims these Norms ... and urges that every effort be made so that they become generally known and respected.

A. General obligations

1. States have the primary responsibility to promote, secure the fulfilment of, respect, ensure respect of and protect human rights recognized in international as well as national law, including ensuring that transnational corporations and other business enterprises respect human rights. Within their respective spheres of activity and influence, transnational corporations and other business enterprises have the obligation to promote, secure the fulfilment of, respect, ensure respect of and protect human rights recognized in international as well as national law, including the rights and interests of indigenous peoples and other vulnerable groups.

[Eds. The Commentary to the Norms elaborates on this provision by stating:

> (b) Transnational corporations and other business enterprises shall have the responsibility to use due diligence in ensuring that their activities do not contribute directly or indirectly to human abuses, and that they do not directly or indirectly benefit from abuses of which they were aware or ought to have been aware. Transnational corporations and other business enterprises shall further refrain from activities that would undermine the rule of law as well as governmental and other efforts to promote and ensure respect for human rights, and shall use their influence in order to help promote and ensure respect for human rights. Transnational corporations and other business enterprises shall inform themselves of the human rights impact of their principal activities and major proposed activities so that they can further avoid complicity in human rights abuses. The Norms may not be used by States as an excuse for failing to take action to protect human rights, for example, through the enforcement of existing laws.]

B. Right to equal opportunity and non-discriminatory treatment

2. Transnational corporations and other business enterprises shall ensure equality of opportunity and treatment, as provided in the relevant international instruments and national legislation as well as international human rights law, for the purpose of eliminating discrimination based on race, colour, sex, language, religion, political opinion, national or social origin, social status, indigenous status, disability, age — except for children, who may be given greater protection — or other status of the individual unrelated to the inherent requirements to perform the job, or of complying with special measures designed to overcome past discrimination against certain groups.

[17] UN Doc. E/CN.4/Sub.2/2003/38/Rev.2 (2003).

C. Right to security of persons

3. Transnational corporations and other business enterprises shall not engage in nor benefit from war crimes, crimes against humanity, genocide, torture, forced disappearance, forced or compulsory labour, hostage-taking, extrajudicial, summary or arbitrary executions, other violations of humanitarian law and other international crimes against the human person as defined by international law, in particular human rights and humanitarian law.

4. Security arrangements for transnational corporations and other business enterprises shall observe international human rights norms as well as the laws and professional standards of the country or countries in which they operate.

D. Rights of workers

5. Transnational corporations and other business enterprises shall not use forced or compulsory labour. . . .

6. Transnational corporations and other business enterprises shall respect the rights of children to be protected from economic exploitation. . . .

7. Transnational corporations and other business enterprises shall provide a safe and healthy working environment. . . .

8. Transnational corporations and other business enterprises shall provide workers with remuneration that ensures an adequate standard of living for them and their families. Such remuneration shall take due account of their needs for adequate living conditions with a view towards progressive improvement.

9. Transnational corporations and other business enterprises shall ensure freedom of association and effective recognition of the right to collective bargaining. . . as provided in national legislation and the relevant conventions of the International Labour Organization.

E. Respect for national sovereignty and human rights

10. Transnational corporations and other business enterprises shall recognize and respect applicable norms of international law, national laws and regulations, as well as administrative practices, the rule of law, the public interest, development objectives, social, economic and cultural policies including transparency, accountability and prohibition of corruption, and authority of the countries in which the enterprises operate.

11. Transnational corporations and other business enterprises shall not offer, promise, give, accept, condone, knowingly benefit from, or demand a bribe or other improper advantage, nor shall they be solicited or expected to give a bribe or other improper advantage to any Government, public official, candidate for elective post, any member of the armed forces or security forces, or any other individual or organization. Transnational corporations and other business enterprises shall refrain from any activity which supports, solicits, or encourages States or any other entities to abuse human rights. They shall further seek to ensure that the goods and services they provide will not be used to abuse human rights.

12. Transnational corporations and other business enterprises shall respect economic, social and cultural rights as well as civil and political rights and contribute to their realization, in particular the rights to development, adequate food and drinking

water, the highest attainable standard of physical and mental health, adequate housing, privacy, education, freedom of thought, conscience, and religion and freedom of opinion and expression, and shall refrain from actions which obstruct or impede the realization of those rights.

F. Obligations with regard to consumer protection

13. Transnational corporations and other business enterprises shall act in accordance with fair business, marketing and advertising practices and shall take all necessary steps to ensure the safety and quality of the goods and services they provide, including observance of the precautionary principle. Nor shall they produce, distribute, market, or advertise harmful or potentially harmful products for use by consumers.

G. Obligations with regard to environmental protection

14. Transnational corporations and other business enterprises shall carry out their activities in accordance with national laws, regulations, administrative practices and policies relating to the preservation of the environment of the countries in which they operate, as well as in accordance with relevant international agreements, principles, objectives, responsibilities and standards with regard to the environment as well as human rights, public health and safety, bioethics and the precautionary principle, and shall generally conduct their activities in a manner contributing to the wider goal of sustainable development.

H. General provisions of implementation

15. As an initial step towards implementing these Norms, each transnational corporation or other business enterprise shall adopt, disseminate and implement internal rules of operation in compliance with the Norms. Further, they shall periodically report on and take other measures fully to implement the Norms and to provide at least for the prompt implementation of the protections set forth in the Norms. Each transnational corporation or other business enterprise shall apply and incorporate these Norms in their contracts or other arrangements and dealings with contractors, subcontractors, suppliers, licensees, distributors, or natural or other legal persons that enter into any agreement with the transnational corporation or business enterprise in order to ensure respect for and implementation of the Norms.

16. Transnational corporations and other businesses enterprises shall be subject to periodic monitoring and verification by United Nations, other international and national mechanisms already in existence or yet to be created, regarding application of the Norms. This monitoring shall be transparent and independent and take into account input from stakeholders (including non governmental organizations) and as a result of complaints of violations of these Norms. Further, transnational corporations and other businesses enterprises shall conduct periodic evaluations concerning the impact of their own activities on human rights under these Norms.

17. States should establish and reinforce the necessary legal and administrative framework for ensuring that the Norms and other relevant national and international laws are implemented by transnational corporations and other business enterprises.

. . .

I. Definitions

20. The term "transnational corporation" refers to an economic entity operating in more than one country or a cluster of economic entities operating in two or more countries — whatever their legal form, whether in their home country or country of activity, and whether taken individually or collectively.

21. The phrase "other business enterprise" includes any business entity, regardless of the international or domestic nature of its activities, including a transnational corporation, contractor, subcontractor, supplier, licensee or distributor; the corporate, partnership, or other legal form used to establish the business entity; and the nature of the ownership of the entity. These Norms shall be presumed to apply, as a matter of practice, if the business enterprise has any relation with a transnational corporation, the impact of its activities is not entirely local, or the activities involve violations of the right to security as indicated in paragraphs 3 and 4.

22. The term "stakeholder" includes stockholders, other owners, workers and their representatives, as well as any other individual or group that is affected by the activities of transnational corporations or other business enterprises. . . .

NICHOLAS HOWEN, BUSINESS, HUMAN RIGHTS AND ACCOUNTABILITY

Copenhagen, 21 September 2005, at
http://www.icj.org/IMG/pdf/NICK_Speech_DK_2.pdf[18]

. . . I see at least seven reasons why there is need to develop clear, common and binding global rules on corporate accountability and human rights.

1. Documented abuses and complicity

. . . When we talk about accountability we must answer how to ensure the worst [corporations], and not only the best, respect the rules. . . .

2. Market forces are not enough

Some have argued that we should leave it to the marketplace — economic forces — to regulate the behaviour of companies. This argument overlooks, however, that respecting human rights are not, unfortunately, always good for business. It is clear that companies can thrive in countries with abusive regimes, such as in South Africa under the *apartheid* regime, in Burma now, in Nigeria under military rule. . . .

3. Need for binding, common benchmarks

We must go beyond voluntarism. Voluntary codes of conduct and initiatives have been important steps on the road to accountability but they're not enough. We need a mix of voluntary initiatives *and* legally binding rules.

Voluntary codes can be useful: individual company or industrywide codes, ethical programmes. They can build a consensus around some rights, such as not using

[18] Secretary-General, International Commission of Jurists.

child labour. They can build a culture of compliance, to a certain extent. Some codes even go beyond the minimum human rights standards, which are set out in documents like the Universal Declaration of Human Rights. Voluntary codes are, however, only respected by those who want to respect them. Too often they fall by the wayside when there is a clash against hard commercial interests. They can be easily rejected when faced with the harsh competitiveness of the commercial world. Studies of voluntary codes have shown how most codes leave out the most difficult rights for business, such as the freedom of association and collective bargaining. There is a proliferation of voluntary standards that has brought confusion. . . .

4. Victims' rights to remedy and reparation

Victims of human rights violations need rights and remedies, not merely charity or philanthropy.

We need to move from the good intentions of voluntary codes to the idea that if victims suffer and their rights are violated, they do have a right to compensation and restitution. . . .

Providing remedies for victims is not about engaging in costly and drawn out court cases, but it is about building legal rights that encourage a culture of compliance . . . .

5. Inability or failure of host states to hold business accountable

We need global rules because most large corporations have outgrown the ability of many individual states to regulate them effectively.

We find that the balance has often tilted in favour of transnational corporations. Often the government of a host country is worried that tough regulation will scare away foreign direct investment. . . . Governments in countries where multinationals have their headquarters have little interest in holding companies accountable for behaviour far away from home.

International law is not a substitute for effective national laws and policies. But international standards do help to provide common guidance to states, to harmonize rules at times of weak national regulation. . .

6. Why human rights standards?

. . . Aspects of consumer law, criminal law, environmental law or corporate law can all help companies decide what they should do and not do. But only human rights standards provide the comprehensive normative guide about how human beings should be treated.

7. Power needs to be constrained by law

A role of law is to balance power and obligations and to limit the arbitrary exercise of power. Large corporations are beginning to challenge the traditional economic and political dominance of governments.

Some states are dwarfed by the power of transnational corporations. Governments are losing authority up to supranational organisation bodies and internally as state functions are privatized.

. . .

To sum up, . . . [t]he controversy is on the table now. We have a set of [UN] Norms . . . drafted . . . after wide consultation with business, governance and civil society. They have brought everyone out into the open, those who have fiercely opposed the norms such as the International Chamber of Commerce and those that see these Norms as one important, imperfect step . . . .

The Norms do not change international law; they do not create new law. They bring together what already exists and point the direction towards a common, universal set of benchmarks. They are not the devil incarnate as they have been portrayed by some. They are a starting point.

NOTE

Responses to the UN Norms varied dramatically. The most involved NGO groups — notably Amnesty International, Human Rights Watch, and the International Commission of Jurists — all endorsed them as an appropriate basis upon which to move forward to develop corporate accountability. Some scholars were supportive. Kinley and Chambers, for example, argued that the Norms ought to be supported as a viable first step in the establishment of an international legal framework through which companies can be held accountable for any human rights abuses they inflict, or in which they are complicit.[19] Others were critical. Baxi highlighted the Norms' 'dense intertextuality' reflected in the fact that they are built upon the foundations of at least 56 sets of norms of varying types. As a result, the Norms suffer from 'immense orders of self-referentiality', in a process of 'self-generating normative cannibalism'. Baxi[20] also noted that each of the main actors to whom the Norms are addressed would have good reason to oppose them:

> Strategic transnational business interests cannot but contest a network conception of corporate governance that makes these liable for each infraction of human rights by all and sundry associates and affiliates. Local, small and medium-sized business (no matter how defined) may, with equal vigour, similarly contend that such massive exposure to wide-ranging human rights standards not merely spells the ruin of their micro-entrepreneurial activity but also the precious opportunities they may otherwise offer for millions of impoverished to cheat their way into survival. State actors may also, particularly but not exclusively in the South, voice similar concerns because strict enforcement of labour-related human rights obligations for business enterprises may swell, beyond actually existing governmental coping capabilities, the already harrowing numbers of the impoverished un-/under-employed. [As a recent UN study notes]:
>
> > Imposing inappropriate standards, which constrain the value creation role of business lead to job losses, under-investment, lack of services, and ever-widening gap between developed, and developing countries.

[19] D. Kinley and R. Chambers, 'The UN Human Rights Norms for Corporations: The Private Implications of Public International Law', 6 Hum. Rts. L. Rev. 447 (2006).

[20] U. Baxi, 'Market Fundamentalisms: Business Ethics at the Altar of Human Rights', 5 Hum. Rts. L. Rev. 1 (2005).

Governmental reaction was largely negative. Most developing countries were not keen on intrusive regulation and most developed countries felt that the Norms were either unnecessary or over-reaching. The USA, for example, criticized the 'anti-business agenda pursued by many' in the UN, the effect of which had been to hold back 'the economic and social advancement of developing countries'. The response of industry representatives was mixed but most were hostile. In 2004 the UN Commission on Human Rights noted that the Norms contained 'useful elements and ideas', but that the draft had no legal standing. The following year, after intensive lobbying, the Commission opted (CHR Res. 2005/69) not to act on the Norms but instead to appoint an independent expert as Special Representative of the Secretary-General with a mandate to '(a) To identify and clarify standards of corporate responsibility and accountability . . . ; (b) To elaborate on the role of States in effectively regulating [corporations] . . . , including through international cooperation; (c) To research and clarify the implications . . . of concepts such as "complicity" and "sphere of influence"; (d) To develop materials and methodologies for undertaking human rights impact assessments of [corporate activities]; and (e) To compile a compendium of best practices of States and [corporations].'

John Ruggie was appointed as Special Representative on the issue of human rights and transnational corporations and other business enterprises. In his initial report (UN Doc. E/CN.4/2006/97), he was strongly critical of the Norms, characterizing it as an exercise that had 'became engulfed by its own doctrinal excesses'. He noted its 'highly contentious though largely symbolic proposal to monitor firms', but singled out 'its exaggerated legal claims and conceptual ambiguities'. In his view, the Norms had taken 'existing State-based human rights instruments and simply [asserted] that many of their provisions now are binding on corporations as well', an assertion which in his view had 'little authoritative basis in international law — hard, soft, or otherwise'.

Another problem was the Norms' 'imprecision in allocating human rights responsibilities to States and corporations . . . . By their very nature . . . corporations do not have a general role in relation to human rights as do States; they have a specialized one. The Norms . . . articulate no actual principle for differentiating human rights responsibilities based on the respective social roles performed by States and corporations. Indeed in several instances, and with no justification, the Norms end up imposing higher obligations on corporations than on States . . . '. As a result, he suggested that the 'concept of "spheres of influence" is left to carry the burden'. But it could not do so because of the elusive nature of its legal meaning.

A further criticism was that because 'corporations are not democratic public interest institutions, attempts to make them co-equal duty bearers for the broad spectrum of human rights . . . may undermine efforts to build indigenous social capacity and to make Governments more responsible to their own citizenry.' He concluded that the Norms' flaws made them 'a distraction' rather than a basis for moving forward. In 2007, Ruggie provided his own assessment of the existing legal and other landscape.

REPORT OF THE SPECIAL REPRESENTATIVE OF THE SECRETARY-GENERAL ON THE ISSUE OF HUMAN RIGHTS AND TRANSNATIONAL CORPORATIONS AND OTHER BUSINESS ENTERPRISES, JOHN RUGGIE

Business and human rights: mapping international standards of responsibility and accountability for corporate acts, UN Doc. A/HRC/4/35 (2007)

Introduction

1. There is no magic in the marketplace. Markets function efficiently and sustainably only when certain institutional parameters are in place. The preconditions for success are generally assumed to include the protection of property rights; the enforceability of contracts; competition; and the smooth flow of information. But a key requisite is often overlooked: curtailing individual and social harms imposed by markets. History demonstrates that without adequate institutional underpinnings, markets will fail to deliver their full benefits and may even become socially unsustainable.

2. In recent decades, especially the 1990s, global markets expanded significantly as a result of trade agreements, bilateral investment treaties, and domestic liberalization and privatization. The rights of transnational corporations became more securely anchored in national laws and increasingly defended through compulsory arbitration before international tribunals. Globalization has contributed to impressive poverty reduction in major emerging market countries and overall welfare in the industrialized world. But it also imposes costs on people and communities — including corporate-related human rights abuses, for reasons detailed in the interim report of the Special Representative of the Secretary-General.

3. These are challenges posed not only by transnational corporations and private enterprises. Evidence suggests that firms operating in only one country and State-owned companies are often worse offenders than their highly visible private sector transnational counterparts. Clearly, a more fundamental institutional misalignment is present: between the scope and impact of economic forces and actors, on the one hand, and the capacity of societies to manage their adverse consequences, on the other. This misalignment creates the permissive environment within which blameworthy acts by corporations may occur without adequate sanctioning or reparation. For the sake of the victims of abuse, and to sustain globalization as a positive force, this must be fixed.

4. Realigning the relationships among social institutions is a long-term process. While Governments representing the public interest must play a key role, they need to be joined by other social actors and to utilize other social institutions to achieve this goal, including market mechanisms themselves. . . .

. . .

6. The report is organized into five clusters of standards and practices governing corporate "responsibility" (the legal, social, or moral obligations imposed on companies) and "accountability" (the mechanisms holding them to these obligations).

For ease of presentation, the five are laid out along a continuum, starting with the most deeply rooted international legal obligations, and ending with voluntary business standards....

I. State Duty To Protect

10. Many claims about business and human rights are deeply contested. But international law firmly establishes that States have a duty to protect against non-State human rights abuses within their jurisdiction, and that this duty extends to protection against abuses by business entities....

...

14. The human rights treaty bodies express concern about State failure to protect against business abuse most frequently in relation to the right to non-discrimination, indigenous peoples' rights, and labour and health-related rights. But the duty to protect applies to all substantive rights....

15. Current guidance from the Committees suggests that the treaties do not require States to exercise extraterritorial jurisdiction over business abuse. But nor are they prohibited from doing so. International law permits a State to exercise such jurisdiction provided there is a recognized basis: where the actor or victim is a national, where the acts have substantial adverse effects on the State, or where specific international crimes are involved.

...

II. Corporate Responsibility and Accountability for International Crimes

19. ... Individuals have long been subject to direct responsibility for the international crimes of piracy and slavery, although in the absence of international accountability mechanisms they could be held liable only by national legal systems. [The report then refers to the Nuremburg and Tokyo Tribunals and the ICC Statute.]

20. Long-standing doctrinal arguments over whether corporations could be "subjects" of international law, which impeded conceptual thinking on this issue and the attribution of direct legal responsibility to corporations, are yielding to new realities. Corporations are increasingly recognized as "participants" at the international level, with the capacity to bear some rights and duties under international law. As noted, they have certain rights under bilateral investment treaties; they are also subject to duties under several civil liability conventions dealing with environmental pollution. Although this has no direct bearing on corporate responsibility for international crimes, it makes it more difficult to maintain that corporations should be entirely exempt from responsibility in other areas of international law.

21. The ICC preparatory committee and the Rome conference on the establishment of the ICC debated a proposal that would have given the ICC jurisdiction over legal persons (other than States), but differences in national approaches prevented its adoption. Nevertheless, just as the absence of an international accountability mechanism did not preclude individual responsibility for international crimes in the past, it does not preclude the emergence of corporate responsibility today.

22. Indeed, corporate responsibility is being shaped through the interplay of two developments: one is the expansion and refinement of individual responsibility by

the international ad hoc criminal tribunals and the ICC Statute; the other is the extension of responsibility for international crimes to corporations under domestic law. The complex interaction between the two is creating an expanding web of potential corporate liability for international crimes, imposed through national courts.

23. Individual responsibility under international law may arise by directly committing or instigating a crime, or for crimes committed by subordinates that a superior had reason to know would be committed, but failed to prevent. The international tribunals have also imposed liability for "aiding and abetting" a crime, or for engaging in a "common purpose" or "joint criminal enterprise". No one-to-one mapping can be assumed between standards for natural and legal persons. But national courts interpreting corporate liability for international crimes have drawn on principles of individual responsibility, as the United States Court of Appeals for the Ninth Circuit did in its *Unocal* ruling.[21]

24. At the same time, the number of jurisdictions in which charges for international crimes can be brought against corporations is increasing, as countries ratify the ICC Statute and incorporate its definitions into domestic law....

...

27. In this fluid setting, simple laws of probability alone suggest that corporations will be subject to increased liability for international crimes in the future. They may face either criminal or civil liability depending on whether international standards are incorporated into a State's criminal code or as a civil cause of action (as under the United States Alien Torts Claims Act, or ATCA). Furthermore, companies cannot be certain where claims will be brought against them or what precise standards they may be held to, because no two national jurisdictions have identical evidentiary and other procedural rules. Finally, civil proceedings may be brought for related wrongs under domestic law, such as assault or false imprisonment. In short, the risk environment for companies is expanding slowly but steadily, as are remedial options for victims.

...

30. Few legitimate firms may ever directly commit acts that amount to international crimes. But there is greater risk of their facing allegations of "complicity" in such crimes. For example, of the more than 40 ATCA cases brought against companies in the United States (now the largest body of domestic jurisprudence regarding corporate responsibility for international crimes), most have concerned alleged complicity where the actual perpetrators were public or private security forces, other government agents, or armed factions in civil conflicts.

31. Corporate complicity is an umbrella term for a range of ways in which companies may be liable for their participation in criminal or civil wrongs....

32. ... Mere presence in a country and paying taxes are unlikely to create liability. But deriving indirect economic benefit from the wrongful conduct of others may do so, depending on such facts as the closeness of the company's association with those actors. Greater clarity currently does not exist. However, it is established that even where a corporation does not intend for the crime to occur, and regrets its commission, it will not be absolved of liability if it knew, or should have known, that it

[21] *Doe v. Unocal*, 395 F.3d 932 (9th Cir, 2002). The case settled and the decision was vacated.

was providing assistance, and that the assistance would contribute to the commission of a crime.

III. Corporate Responsibility for other Human Rights Violations under International Law

...

34. At national levels, there is enormous diversity in the scope and content of corporate legal responsibilities regarding human rights....

...

37. [The UDHR is addressed to "every individual and every organ of society...".... But that does not equate to legally binding effect.

...

41. In short, the treaties do not address direct corporate legal responsibilities explicitly, while the commentaries of the treaty bodies on the subject are ambiguous. However, the increased attention the Committees are devoting to the need to prevent corporate abuse acknowledges that businesses are capable of both breaching human rights and contributing to their protection.

42. On purely logical grounds, a stronger argument could be made for direct corporate responsibilities under the ILO core conventions.... But logic alone does not make law, and the legal responsibilities of corporations under the ILO conventions remain indirect.

...

IV. Soft Law Mechanisms

...

47. A prominent example of the normative role of soft law is the ILO Tripartite Declaration of Principles Concerning Multinational Enterprises and Social Policy, endorsed not only by States but also by global employers' and workers' organizations. It proclaims that all parties, including multinational enterprises, "should respect the Universal Declaration of Human Rights and the corresponding international Covenants".

48. The OECD Guidelines [for Multinational Enterprises, revised in 2000] acknowledge that the capacity and willingness of States to implement their international human rights obligations vary. Accordingly, they recommend that firms "respect the human rights of those affected by their activities consistent with the host Government's obligations and commitments"....

49. Both instruments are widely referenced by Governments and businesses and may, in due course, crystallize into harder forms....

...

51. For its part, the International Finance Corporation [the private sector arm of the World Bank Group] now has performance standards that companies are required to meet in return for IFC investment funds. They include several human rights elements....

52. Beyond the intergovernmental system, a new multi-stakeholder form of soft law initiatives is emerging. Most prominent among them are the Voluntary Principles

on Security and Human Rights (Voluntary Principles), promoting corporate human rights risk assessments and training of security providers in the extractive sector; the Kimberley Process Certification Scheme (Kimberley) to stem the flow of conflict diamonds; and the Extractive Industries Transparency Initiative (EITI), establishing a degree of revenue transparency in the taxes, royalties and fees companies pay to host Governments.

53. Driven by social pressure, these initiatives seek to close regulatory gaps that contribute to human rights abuses. But they do so in specific operational contexts, not in any overarching manner....

...

55. In these collaborative ventures, there is no external legislative body that sets standards and no separate adjudicative body to assess compliance. Both functions are internalized within the operational entity itself. But without such mechanisms, how can they be judged?

...

[The report then identifies factors such as credibility of governance structures — reflected in participation, transparency, and status reviews — and effectiveness in terms of operational impact and demonstration effect.]

...

61. ...As they strengthen their accountability mechanisms, they also begin to blur the lines between the strictly voluntary and mandatory spheres for participants. Once in, exiting can be costly....

...

V. Self-regulation

63. In addition to legal standards, hard or soft, the mandate of the Special Representative includes evolving social expectations regarding responsible corporate citizenship, including human rights. One key indicator consists of the policies and practices that business itself adopts voluntarily, triggered by its assessment of human rights-related risks and opportunities, often under pressure from civil society and local communities. This section maps such standards of self-regulation.

64. However, mapping the entire universe of business enterprises is impossible. More than 77,000 transnational corporations currently span the globe, with roughly 770,000 subsidiaries and millions of suppliers. Those numbers are dwarfed by local firms, and an even bigger informal sector in developing countries.

...

74. [Based on a survey of the practice of leading companies, the report concludes that] leading business players recognize human rights and adopt means to ensure basic accountability. Yet even among the leaders, certain weaknesses of voluntarism are evident. Companies do not necessarily recognize those rights on which they may have the greatest impact. And while the rights they do recognize typically draw on international instruments, the language is rarely identical. Some interpretations are so elastic that the standards lose meaning, making it

difficult for the company itself, let alone the public, to assess performance against commitments.

75. There are also variations in the rights companies emphasize that seem unrelated to expected sectoral differences, but which appear instead to reflect the political culture of company home countries. For example, European-based firms are most likely to adopt a comprehensive rights agenda, including social and economic rights, with American firms tending to recognize a narrower spectrum of rights and rights holders.

76. Where self-regulation remains most challenged, however, is in its accountability provisions. The number, diversity, and uptake of instruments have grown significantly. But they also pose serious issues about the meaning of accountability and how it is established. Only three can be touched on here: human rights impact assessments (HRIAs); materiality; and assurance.

77. For businesses with large physical or societal footprints, accountability should begin with assessments of what their human rights impact will be. This would permit companies and affected communities to find ways of avoiding negative impacts from the start. Several SRI [socially responsible investment] funds strongly promote HRIAs, coupled with community engagement and dialogue. However, relatively few firms conduct these assessments routinely and only a handful seem ever to have done a fully-fledged HRIA, in contrast to including selected human rights criteria in broader social/environmental assessments. And apparently only one company, BP, has ever made public even a summary of an HRIA. No single measure would yield more immediate results in the human rights performance of firms than conducting such assessments where appropriate.

78. The concept of materiality refers to the content of company reporting — whether it conveys information that really matters. The number of firms reporting... has risen exponentially. But quality has not matched quantity....

79. Assurance helps people to know whether companies actually do what they say. A growing proportion of sustainability reports (circa 40 per cent) include some form of audit statement, typically provided by large accounting firms or smaller consultancies....

...

81. For several reasons, the initiatives described in this section have not reached all types of companies. First, because many of the tools were developed for large national and transnational firms, they are not directly suitable for small- and medium-sized enterprises. Existing tools need to be adapted or new ones developed. Second, as noted, large developing country firms are just beginning to be drawn into this arena. Third, a more serious omission may be major state-owned enterprises based in some emerging economies: with few exceptions, they have not yet voluntarily associated themselves with such initiatives, nor is it well understood when the rules of State attribution apply to their human rights performance. Finally, as is true of all voluntary — and many statutory initiatives — determined laggards find ways to avoid scrutiny. This problem is not unique to human rights, nor is it unprecedented in history. But once a tipping point is reached, societies somehow manage to mitigate if not eliminate the problem. The trick is getting to the tipping point — a goal to which this mandate is dedicated.

...

NOTE

Following the presentation of his 2007 report, above, Ruggie identified four key dilemmas for which he did 'not yet have good answers'.[22] (1) Few if any voluntary efforts have reached a scale where they can move markets. 'Uptake is significant but has slowed down and in some areas, like non-financial reporting, appears to have levelled off. There still are lots of laggards in industrialized countries. And firms from emerging market countries are vastly underrepresented.' (2) Relatively few companies conduct 'human rights impact assessments in contexts where significant uncertainty prevails or adverse effects could be expected'. (3) There are 'few if any widely accepted process standards... that firmly establish the effectiveness and credibility of voluntary accountability mechanisms. There has been a proliferation of codes, social auditing, reporting systems, indices, and so on....' This has created mounting frustration all around. (4) There is a 'dearth of viable grievance and alternative dispute resolution mechanisms for business and human rights'. This lack 'virtually invites campaigning and excessive litigation by other social actors'.

QUESTIONS

1. What do you consider to be the responsibility of corporate lawyers in relation to human rights. Do you agree with Chandler who has argued that it is extraordinary that Amnesty International 'should have had to tell some of the biggest and most sophisticated multinational companies in the world about the [UDHR and other standards]. Where were the company lawyers who should have been aware of the relevance, if not applicability, of these instruments to the companies they served before disaster struck?... They should surely be guardians of principle, not just protectors of narrow commercial interest.'

2. How do you view the conclusion that, 'in the absence of effective means of reporting non-compliance, provisions for monitoring and training, and incentives for managerial compliance, a corporate code is "at best a form of public relations for powerful multinationals and at worst a misleading seal of approval affixed by those with no legitimate claim to judge these matters"'?[23]

3. After reviewing the saga of the Norms, a key Amnesty International adviser, and former business leader, concluded that they 'were not a failure. I personally fought for them publicly until it was obvious they were no longer politically viable and that we needed to direct our energies to keeping the process of discussion alive'. How do you assess the Norms? Would you have advised your NGO, your corporation, or your government to endorse them as an appropriate basis for moving forward?

4. After reviewing Ruggie's 2007 'mapping' exercise, do you consider that binding treaty obligations governing corporate human rights conduct are appropriate, feasible and necessary?

[22] 'Remarks at International Chamber of Commerce Commission on Business in Society', Paris, 27 April 2007, at http://www.reports-and-materials.org/Ruggie-speech-to-ICC-27-Apr-2007.pdf.

[23] See Macklem, n. 4 above.

NOTE

In addition to the various proposals outlined above, two other approaches warrant mention. The first relies upon the concept of universal jurisdiction and is inspired by the use of the Alien Tort Statute as a form of US civil litigation for foreign torts. See Chapter 13, *supra*. But Macklem argues that this is not the way to go: [24]

> What would universal jurisdiction add to [the law of state responsibility and state treaty obligations]? Universal jurisdiction would entitle a state — say, Belgium — to bring criminal proceedings against a multinational corporation that has no legal presence in Belgium for a small class of human rights violations it commits outside of Belgium....
>
> But by establishing independent multinational corporate liability in international law, the principle of universal jurisdiction would contribute to a conception in the field of multinational corporations as international legal actors with obligations owed to individuals and states. And with international corporate obligations comes international corporate rights. Such rights would emerge incrementally as corporations seek to defend themselves from criminal prosecution by states exercising universal jurisdiction. Prosecutions inevitably would require distinguishing between criminal and lawful activity, thereby producing over time a zone of freedom derived from international law itself — a realm of international corporate liberty — that would protect from state sanction a set of corporate actions that raise human rights concerns but which do not constitute criminal acts. This realm of international corporate liberty would combine easily with the emerging set of economic rights that multinational corporations enjoy under international economic law. Multinational corporations would possess even greater international economic freedom to exploit the opportunities afforded by globalization in ways that evade state efforts to promote human rights compliance.

Nowak, on the other hand, advocates the adoption of a Statute for a World Court of Human Rights, to which non-state actors could also possibly become parties. This would include inter-governmental organizations, such as the UN, the international financial institutions, the EU, the WTO and NATO. In addition, transnational corporations:

> might be invited and encouraged to accept the binding jurisdiction of the World Court in relation to selected human rights in the sphere of their respective influence, such as the prohibition of forced or child labour; the right to form and join trade unions; the right to collective bargaining; and the prohibition of discrimination. The World Court would not only be in a position to decide in a binding judgment whether or not a business corporation subject to its jurisdiction has violated any human right of an employee, a client or any other person affected, but it might also provide proper reparation to the victim concerned. In principle, any non-State actor might be interested, for various reasons including upholding ethical

[24] Ibid.

standards, marketing, corporate identity or a genuine interest in strengthening human rights, to recognise the jurisdiction of the World Court of Human Rights.[25]

QUESTION

What do you see as the pros and cons of the proposals relating to universal jurisdiction over corporate acts and the creation of a World Court of Human Rights which could issue judgments binding upon corporations?

ADDITIONAL READING

The most comprehensive and up-to-date source for information on corporations is www.business-humanrights.org. See also Steven Ratner, 'Corporations and Human Rights: A Theory of Legal Responsibility', 111 Yale L.J. 443 (2001); International Council on Human Rights Policy, *Beyond Voluntarism: Human Rights and the Developing International Legal Obligations of Companies* (2002); John Ruggie, Business Recognition of Human Rights: Global Patterns, Regional and Sectoral Variations, UN Doc. A/HRC/4/35/Add.4 (2007); Philip Alston (ed.), *Non-State Actors and Human Rights* (2005); Paul Redmond, 'Transnational Enterprise and Human Rights: Options for Standard Setting and Compliance', 37 Int. L. 69 (2003); and Marius Emberland, *The Human Rights of Companies: Exploring the Structure of ECHR Protection* (2006).

B. ARMED OPPOSITION GROUPS

At one level, armed opposition groups are simply outlaws. They have rejected or resisted the authority of the state and opted to act outside the applicable legal framework. But at another level, such groups are often involved in a quest for legitimacy, designed to convince the relevant population and the world at large of the illegitimacy of the existing form of state power, and perhaps invoking by way of justification the state's violations of the rights of the group concerned. Two questions arise. First, should we seek to encourage such groups to accept human rights commitments? Second, what would the legal basis of any such obligations be?

One clear example of practical engagement is reflected in the work of the Special Representative of the UN Secretary-General for Children and Armed Conflict. Invoking the Convention on the Rights of the Child, as well as the Geneva Conventions, the Special Representative has in recent years sought and obtained commitments from groups as diverse as the Sudan People's Liberation Movement, the Revolutionary United Front in Sierra Leone, the Liberation Tigers of Tamil Eelam in Sri Lanka, and the Revolutionary Armed Forces of Colombia.[26]

[25] Manfred Nowak, 'The Need for a World Court of Human Rights', 7 Hum. Rts. L. Rev. 251 (2007), at 256.

[26] http://www.un.org/special-rep/children-armed-conflict/English/Commitments.html.

International humanitarian law has long accepted that armed opposition groups engaged in an internal armed conflict are bound by IHL, even though they are not parties to the relevant treaties. Even though the structure and assumptions of human rights law are different there have been examples of governments and opposition groups combining both human rights and IHL commitments in a single agreement. Thus, in the context of peace negotiations, the Government of the Philippines on one side and the Communist Party of the Philippines and New Peoples' Army on the other jointly signed the Comprehensive Agreement on the Respect for Human Rights and International Humanitarian Law (CARHRIHL) in 1998.

In the readings that follow Sivakumaran outlines the theoretical bases upon which the application of IHL to armed opposition groups might be grounded. Cockayne then makes the case for a radically different approach to the structure of IHL, in response to what he describes as the global reorganization of legitimate violence. Some of his arguments raise questions that might also apply to human rights law. Finally Clapham considers how the UN human rights regime has dealt with the issue.

SANDESH SIVAKUMARAN, BINDING ARMED OPPOSITION GROUPS

55 ICLQ 369 (2006)

The vast majority of conflicts being fought today are internal in character. Internal armed conflicts are fought between a state and an armed opposition group, or between two armed opposition groups, within the boundaries of a single state. Armed opposition groups are becoming increasingly sophisticated and are responsible for some of the most egregious atrocities committed in conflicts. Given the proliferation of internal armed conflicts, the number of armed opposition groups that take part in them, and the atrocities that are committed by such groups, it is essential that international humanitarian law regulates such conflicts and governs the behaviour of such groups.

There exist, however, only a minimum of international humanitarian law rules that pertain to armed conflict of an internal character. [They include, in particular, Common Article 3 of the four Geneva Conventions, and Additional Protocol II.] ...

A treaty binds parties to it, thus these instruments bind states parties fighting in an internal armed conflict. The language of these instruments also purports to bind armed opposition groups fighting in such a conflict. This raises the question of how armed opposition groups are bound by the law governing internal armed conflict when they are not party to the relevant treaties....

...

Four reasons that are commonly put forward to explain the binding nature of the rules governing internal armed conflict on armed opposition groups — customary international law; general principles; the rules governing the effect of treaties on third parties; and the principle of succession — are not in fact capable of binding all types of armed opposition groups by all the rules of internal armed conflict. This is so even when all four reasons are used in conjunction with one another.

The legislative jurisdiction explanation — the principle whereby the state binds all individuals within its territory upon ratification of a treaty — is the only one that is capable of binding all types of armed opposition groups by all the rules that govern internal armed conflict.

There is a more fundamental theoretical difference between the four limited explanations on the one hand and the legislative jurisdiction explanation on the other hand. The four limited explanations apply the rules that are applied to states to armed opposition groups. In this way, they are treated like states. The legislative jurisdiction approach treats armed opposition groups as entities subordinate to states. The default positions of the two also differ. The four limited explanations start off from the position that armed opposition groups are not bound by the rules governing internal armed conflict while the legislative jurisdiction explanation begins from the view that armed opposition groups are so bound. Consequently, the four limited explanations are more attractive to armed opposition groups while the legislative jurisdiction approach is more appealing to states. As a result, a question that has to be asked is whether using the legislative jurisdiction approach will lead to a decrease in compliance with the rules on the part of the armed opposition group.

Compliance in this regard is likely affected more by the degree of legitimacy the armed opposition group sees in the rules than the precise manner in which they are bound. One of the threads underlying this article has been the degree of legitimacy of the rules from the perspective of the armed opposition group. In order to increase the degree of legitimacy of and foster a sense of respect for the laws governing internal armed conflict, participation of armed opposition groups in the formation of the rules is vital. Participation may range from the formal — for example involvement of armed opposition groups in the conclusion of new international humanitarian law treaties using their practice for the purposes of customary international law, concluding Common Article 3 agreements and encouraging unilateral declarations of acceptance — to the less formal — such as creating linkages with armed opposition groups that do respect international humanitarian law and pointing to the positive practice of other armed opposition groups.

That armed opposition groups are bound by the rules governing internal armed conflict is beyond doubt; quite how to increase their compliance with these rules is the next big question.

JAMES COCKAYNE, THE GLOBAL REORGANIZATION OF LEGITIMATE VIOLENCE: MILITARY ENTREPRENEURS AND THE PRIVATE FACE OF INTERNATIONAL HUMANITARIAN LAW

863 Int. Rev Red Cross 459 (2006), at 486

[The author begins by noting fundamental changes in the global organization of legitimate violence. He observes that 'private actors operating through global networks — whether pursuing profit or power — now rival states in their ability globally to mobilize and project violence. In some cases, these actors may attract aspects of legitimacy allowing their privately organized violence to rival or even resemble law.']

What unifies contemporary debates over private military companies, terrorism, organized crime and even the Responsibility to Protect is a profound reconsideration [of]... the extent to which violence ought be organized and regulated by public — and in the global context, universal — standards of legitimacy and organizational systems. It is a debate over the scope and content of the social responsibilities of a variety of organizational forms, whether states, business, religious institutions or civil society organizations, in particular the extent to which they ought be responsible for providing physical and social protection to human beings — particularly those outside their groups or exchange relationships — and over the question of to whom they ought be accountable for the provision of that protection. This is, in other words, in part a quest to find a new constitutional settlement at the global level between the public and the private in the organization and regulation of legitimate violence....

...

What would a system of globally organized legitimate violence be like, and where would international humanitarian law figure in it?...

First, we must consider whether humanitarian action in such a deterritorialized setting can continue to rely on state consent alone as the basis for its legitimacy. What sources of legitimacy are required to underpin humanitarian action worldwide in a setting populated by military entrepreneurs ranging from private military companies to global terrorist networks and local warlords, all fuelled by access to global markets?

Interstate reciprocity alone seems insufficient as a basis for a humanitarian law that enmeshes all these actors. Confronted by adversaries who are unwilling or unable to offer state personnel the same protections that international humanitarian law requires states to offer each other and to offer to non-state actors, many states will continue to be tempted to corral or to avoid altogether the application of international humanitarian law. Many of those non-state actors will, themselves, justify their actions not by reference to state sanction but by reference to "global" norms such as humanitarianism, shareholder value and divine authority.

Given these vulnerabilities, humanitarian law will need to find additional sources of legitimacy, for example by drawing in global business, civil society and even trans-national armed groups....

We shall need to think about ways of treating non-state actors not only as objects of governance, but as sources of normativity and legitimacy. This will require a highly creative approach to global governance, going well beyond state-centric international legal approaches, emphasizing non-territorial and non-hierarchical aspects of global "public" citizenship. Mechanisms for promoting such public citizenship could include voluntary arrangements such as the Deed of Commitment promoted by Geneva Call or the US–UK Voluntary Principles on Security and Human Rights; national regulatory strategies and mechanisms incentivizing or mandating private actors' compliance with certain standards...; and public advocacy engaging individual consumers, voters and worshippers.

ANDREW CLAPHAM, HUMAN RIGHTS OBLIGATIONS OF NON-STATE ACTORS IN CONFLICT SITUATIONS

863 Int. Rev Red Cross 491 (2006), at 503

... For Dieter Fleck it is simply "logical" that if ... insurgents can have obligations under humanitarian law they should also be able to bear human rights obligations. From here it is a small step to suggest that such international human rights obligations apply at all times to all armed opposition groups (even before the appeals of the Security Council [which has frequently called upon such groups to respect IHL and sometimes human rights]). The resolution adopted by the distinguished expert body the Institute of International Law, at its Berlin session in 1999, stated that "All parties to armed conflicts in which non-State entities are parties, irrespective of their legal status ... have the obligation to respect international humanitarian law as well as fundamental human rights." With regard to disturbances short of armed conflict the resolution includes an Article X to similar effect concerning fundamental human rights: "To the extent that certain aspects of internal disturbances and tensions may not be covered by international humanitarian law, individuals remain under the protection of international law guaranteeing fundamental human rights. All parties are bound to respect fundamental rights under the scrutiny of the international community."

To those who would still prefer to rely simply on humanitarian law I would respond as follows: first, humanitarian law does not usually apply in the absence of protracted armed conflict; second, even when there is a reasonable claim that there is a protracted armed conflict, governments have often denied the existence of a conflict, making dialogue with the parties about the application of humanitarian law rather problematic; and, third, the human rights framework allows for a wider range of accountability mechanisms, including monitoring by the Special Rapporteurs of the UN Commission of Human Rights and the field offices of the High Commissioner for Human Rights.

Most recently, the UN's Special Rapporteur on Extrajudicial, Summary or Arbitrary Executions, Philip Alston, grappled with the question in the context of his report on Sri Lanka [UN Doc. E/CN.4/2006/53/Add.5]. Alston concluded in the following terms:

> 25. Human rights law affirms that both the Government and the LTTE [Liberation Tigers of Tamil Eelam] must respect the rights of every person in Sri Lanka. Human rights norms operate on three levels — as the rights of individuals, as obligations assumed by States, and as legitimate expectations of the international community. The Government has assumed the binding legal obligation to respect and ensure the rights recognized in the International Covenant on Civil and Political Rights (ICCPR). As a non-state actor, the LTTE does not have legal obligations under ICCPR, but it remains subject to the demand of the international community, first expressed in the Universal Declaration of Human Rights, that every organ of society respect and promote human rights.
>
> 26. I have previously noted that it is especially appropriate and feasible to call for an armed group to respect human rights norms when it 'exercises significant control over territory and population and has an identifiable political structure'. This visit clarified both the complexity and the necessity of applying human rights

> norms to armed groups. The LTTE plays a dual role. On the one hand, it is an organization with effective control over a significant stretch of territory, engaged in civil planning and administration, maintaining its own form of police force and judiciary. On the other hand, it is an armed group that has been subject to proscription, travel bans, and financial sanctions in various Member States. The tension between these two roles is at the root of the international community's hesitation to address the LTTE and other armed groups in the terms of human rights law. The international community does have human rights expectations to which it will hold the LTTE, but it has long been reluctant to press these demands directly if doing so would be to treat it like a State'.
>
> 27. It is increasingly understood, however, that the human rights expectations of the international community operate to protect people, while not thereby affecting the legitimacy of the actors to whom they are addressed. The Security Council has long called upon various groups that Member States do not recognize as having the capacity to formally assume international obligations to respect human rights. The LTTE and other armed groups must accept that insofar as they aspire to represent a people before the world, the international community will evaluate their conduct according to the Universal Declaration's "common standard of achievement".

Alston goes on to include specific human rights recommendations addressed to the non-state actor:

> The LTTE should refrain from violating human rights, including those of non-LTTE-affiliated Tamil civilians. This includes in particular respect for the rights to freedom of expression, peaceful assembly, freedom of association with others, family life, and democratic participation, including the right to vote. The LTTE should specifically affirm that it will abide by the North-East Secretariat on Human Rights charter.

This approach is applied in the joint report on Lebanon and Israel by a group of four special rapporteurs [UN Doc. A/HRC/2/7 (2006)] [in dealing with the situation of Hezbollah, to the extent that it is a non-state actor].

...

The Office of the UN High Commissioner for Human Rights (OHCHR) has a human rights field operation in Nepal. The Office reports on the human rights situation. Reports include a special section on incidents involving the Communist Party of Nepal (Maoist) (CPN-M). Often these cannot be expressed in terms of violations of international humanitarian law since they took place during the cease-fire outside the context of an armed conflict. At one level there is apparently a commitment to human rights by the CPN-M, but this does not really seem dispositive to the UN's reporting. Another section in the report covered killings by an "illegal armed groups" known as Pratikar Samiti (retaliation groups) later renamed "Peace and Development Committees" as well as killings by a group known as the Special Tiger Force. The UN report does not allege that these groups were supported by the state. Their killings are simply detailed as part of the human rights situation. One recent press release by the OHCHR Nepal Office illustrates the approach:

> OHCHR has continued to emphasize in its meetings with CPN-M leaders that abductions of civilians for any reason are in violation of CPN-M's commitment to

> international human rights standards. These abductions and related investigations and punishment fail to provide even minimum guarantees of due process and fair trial. As a consequence, victims of abductions are vulnerable to other violations of their human rights, particularly their right to life and physical integrity, as in the noted cases. OHCHR concerns in this regard also apply to CPN-M cadres accused of crimes.

To conclude this section, the assumption of many humanitarian law experts that human rights law applies only to governments, and not to unrecognized insurgents, is no longer a universally shared assumption.

QUESTIONS

1. In 2004, both the USA and the EU voted against a resolution in the Commission on Human Rights because it referred to 'gross violations of human rights perpetrated by terrorist groups'. They did so on the grounds that such a formulation equated states with terrorists, when the latter were in fact simply criminals. In response India argued that 'non-state actors were armed groups that could be criminal, but in condemning them and asking them to follow international law, they were not being equated with States'. In light of such perceptions, how persuasive are the arguments recounted by Clapham in favour of attributing human rights obligations to certain non-state actors? What are the alternatives to such an approach?

2. 'Arguments based upon the approach of IHL to armed opposition groups have no relevance to human rights law. The latter's assumptions are fundamentally different and the label of human rights respecter is one that, by definition, can and should only be conferred on a legitimate state actor.' Discuss.

ADDITIONAL READING

M. Schmitt, 'Humanitarian Law and Direct Participation in Hostilities by Private Contractors or Civilian Employees', 5 Chi. J. Int. L. 511 (2005); D. PoKempner, 'The "New" Non-State Actors in International Humanitarian Law', 38 Geo. Wash. Int. L. Rev. 551 (2006); J. Hessbruegge, 'Human Rights Violations Arising from the Conduct of Non-State Actors', 11 Buff. Hum. Rts. L. Rev. 21 (2005); L. Zegveld, *Accountability of Armed Opposition Groups in International Law* (2002); and International Council on Human Rights Policy, *Ends and Means: Human Rights Approaches to Armed Groups* (2000).

C. INTERNATIONAL NON-GOVERNMENTAL ORGANIZATIONS

The non-state actors which have featured most prominently throughout this book are human rights nongovernmental organizations (NGOs), both domestic and international (INGOs). They were at the outset, and continue to be today, an indispensable component in the functioning of the international human rights regime. Their contributions are especially important in relation to fact-finding, reporting, standard-setting, and the overall promotion, implementation and enforcement of human rights norms. They provoke and energize. They spread the message of human rights and mobilize people to realize that message. Decentralized and diverse, they proceed with a speed, decisiveness and range of concerns impossible to imagine in relation to most of the work of bureaucratic and politically constrained intergovernmental organizations.

NGOs operate on the basis of differing mandates, each responding to its own priorities and methods of action, bringing a range of viewpoints to the human rights movement. It is inconceivable that the state of human rights in the world, whatever its shortcomings, could have progressed as much since the Second World War without the spur and inventiveness of NGOs.

At the international level, and particularly in the United Nations context, the frequent reluctance of governmental actors to criticize their counterparts from other countries and the limited supply of independent sources of information have contributed to making NGOs the lynchpins of the system as a whole. In situations in which NGO information is not available or where the NGOs are either unable or unwilling to generate political pressures upon the governments concerned, the chances of a weak response by the international community, or of none at all, are radically increased. A high proportion of the most significant initiatives to draft new international instruments, to establish new procedures and machinery, and to identify specific governments as violators have come as a result of concerted NGO campaigns designed to mobilize public opinion and lobby governmental support.

Human rights NGOs have experienced a quantum leap in their professionalism from the days of the 'amiable amateurs' importuning delegates for a brief chat to the high level of professionalism of many groups today. By comparison with the situation even as recently as 20 years ago, the output of the major international NGOs is more visible and better marketed, their strategies are more clearly mapped out, their level of technical expertise is greater, and their funding more adequate to the task. The communications revolution has assisted them in gathering timely and compelling information, in disseminating it, in running well coordinated campaigns, and in enlisting public opinion.

Moreover, their impact is often more obvious and tangible than it was in an earlier era. The 1997 Ottawa Conference to draft a Landmines Treaty, the 1998 Rome Conference to draft the Statute of an International Criminal Court, and the drafting of the 2006 Convention on the Rights of Persons with Disabilities represent a high water mark in terms of NGO involvement and influence. Perhaps most significant is the blurring of the distinction between the insiders and the outsiders as NGO representatives have become part of governmental delegations. They have also increasingly become key partners in the delivery of humanitarian and other forms of development assistance, partners with government in performing a variety of functions such as human rights education, the monitoring of voluntary codes of conduct and even the delivery of basic social services, as well as partners with businesses and labour unions in various areas.

But along with this growing influence has come strong criticism, much of which is now expressed in terms of the debate over accountability and transparency. The question 'who elected the NGOs?' has become a rallying cry for those who feel that NGOs wield too much power and cannot be constrained by governmental actors. Many within the human rights field also consider that greater accountability and transparency will make the groups more effective and more strongly supported.

Attacks on the leading human rights NGOs are often led by officials and supporters of particular states whose policies have been criticized. In May 2005, for example, Amnesty International released a report citing the US prison camp in Guantanamo Bay as 'the gulag of our time'. President Bush called the report 'absurd'. 'The United States is a country that promotes freedom around the world.' And he noted that the US Government had 'investigated every single complaint against (sic) the detainees'. The Amnesty allegations, he said, had come from 'people who were held in detention, people who hate America, people who had been trained in some instances to disassemble (sic) — that means not tell the truth.' Vice President Cheney opined that '[f]or Amnesty International to suggest that somehow the United States is a violator of human rights, I frankly just don't take them seriously. . . . I was offended by it.' The Chairman of the Joint Chiefs of Staff Chairman called the report 'absolutely irresponsible' and characterized Guantanamo as a 'model facility'. And the Wall Street Journal saw the report as 'one more sign of the moral degradation of Amnesty International'.

In August 2006 a Human Rights Watch report, 'Fatal Strikes: Israel's Indiscriminate Attacks Against Civilians in Lebanon', led Martin Peretz of *The New Republic* to conclude that the NGO had 'utterly destroyed its credibility' while Professor Alan Dershowitz wrote in *The Jerusalem Post*, 'When it comes to Israel and its enemies, Human Rights Watch cooks the books about facts, cheats on interviews, and puts out predetermined conclusions that are driven more by their ideology than by evidence.'[27]

Such attacks are of course evidence of the impact of the reports themselves, and the contested facts and interpretations can be fought out in the public domain in light of constantly emerging new evidence. More problematic, from the perspective of NGOs in general, have been the generic critiques of the very legitimacy of such organizations. After the Seattle riots against the WTO in 1999 *The Economist* asked whether NGOs were 'the first steps towards an "international civil society" (whatever that might be)', or whether they instead represented 'a dangerous shift of power to unelected and unaccountable special-interest groups?'[28] A year later, the same magazine asked:

> who elected Oxfam . . . ? Bodies such as these are, to varying degrees, extorting admissions of fault from law-abiding companies and changes in policy from democratically elected governments. They may claim to be acting in the interests of the people — but then so do the objects of their criticism, governments and the despised international institutions. In the West, governments and their agencies are, in the end, accountable to voters. Who holds the activists accountable?[29]

[27] For a detailed defence of HRW's reporting, see Aryeh Neier, 'The Attack on Human Rights Watch', *New York Review of Books*, 2 November 2006.

[28] 'The Non-Governmental Order', *The Economist*, 18 December 1999, at 23.

[29] 'Angry and Effective, *The Economist*, 23 September 2000.

The call was taken up with relish by conservative groups. In 2003 the American Enterprise Institute and the Federalist Society established NGO Watch, the stated rationale of which is:

> NGO officials are widely cited in the media and relied upon in congressional testimony; corporations regularly consult with NGOs prior to major investments. NGOs also use their growing influence inside international organizations to push for the establishment of globalized standards and international legal norms. Yet this growing local and global role has in large part been unchecked and unregulated. Coupled with sparse (or reluctant) practices of public disclosure and a spate of high-profile NGO scandals in the last decade, calls for greater transparency in NGO operations have been resounding. Who funds NGOs? How effective are their programs? How do they influence governments and international organizations? What are their agendas? And to whom are they accountable?[30]

Even Judge Guillaume, subsequently President of the International Court of Justice, criticized NGOs in an Advisory Opinion rendered by the Court. He suggested that the Court could have declined to answer two requests submitted respectively by the UN General Assembly and the World Health Assembly for advisory opinions on the legality of nuclear weapons on the grounds that they had resulted from advocacy by an NGO coalition, led by the International Association of Lawyers Against Nuclear Arms:

> These associations worked very intensively to secure the adoption of the resolutions referring the question to the Court and to induce States hostile to nuclear weapons to appear before the Court. Indeed, the Court and the judges received thousands of letters inspired by these groups, appealing both to the Members' conscience and to the public conscience.
>
> ... I wondered whether, in such circumstances, the requests for opinions could still be regarded as coming from the Assemblies which had adopted them or whether, piercing the veil, the Court should not have dismissed them as inadmissible. However, I dare to hope that Governments and intergovernmental institutions still retain sufficient independence of decision to resist the powerful pressure groups which besiege them today with the support of the mass media.[31]

The dilemma is straightforward. On the one hand, as Kingsbury has observed, '[i]nternational civil society in its widest sense is bound to be a largely unregulated free-for-all, with markets in prestige, influence, membership, fundraising capability, and other markers of organizational success.'[32] Efforts to regulate or control NGOs are in some respects contrary to their nature and ethos. They are inevitably suspect when coming from those who have been obliged to change their policies and practices as a result of NGO campaigning. On the other hand, the NGOs unyielding demands for accountability on the part of governments, corporations, and IGOs

[30] www.ngowatch.org.

[31] The Legality of the Threat or Use of Nuclear Weapons, Advisory Opinion [1996] ICJ Rep. 226 at 287.

[32] Benedict Kingsbury, 'First Amendment Liberalism as Global Legal Architecture: Ascriptive Groups and the Problems of the Liberal NGO Model of International Civil Society', 3 Chicago J. Int. L. 183 (2002), at 193.

like the World Bank and the World Trade Organization necessarily serve to focus attention on shortcomings in terms of their own accountability. In decades past such demands have been shrugged off by most NGOs. Some have argued that they could not be held to the same standards of accountability as those who hold 'real' power. As one recent study put it, '[i]n the grand scheme of societal relations, NGOs ultimately have very little power. They do not have coercive power, financial power, or even the authority and power that derives from representation.'[33] Others note that they are in any event answerable to their supporters and funders, and that their impact and effectiveness is largely dependent upon their perceived legitimacy and credibility. Such responses have not satisfied the critics and as the impact of NGOs has become greater so too have the calls for enhanced accountability become stronger and more concerted.

The reluctance of many, although not all, human rights NGOs to come to grips with this issue is illustrated by the fate of a project launched in 2002 by the International Council on Human Rights Policy focusing on the Accountability of NGOs. It was designed to consider: (i) what are the essential elements of 'legitimacy' and 'accountability' for human rights NGOs; and (ii) what benefits will human rights NGOs obtain by demonstrating clearly that they are accountable and legitimate — and what risks might they face? By 2007 the report had still not emerged. The group's website noted only that responses by NGOs and others to a first draft in 2003 had 'demonstrated both the sensitivity of this issue and the need to address it well'. In other words, the achievement of some sort of consensus position had proved elusive.

In the readings that follow Kenneth Anderson argues that INGOs are essentially elitist groups which lack democratic legitimacy. Isobelle Jacques explores the sources of NGO legitimacy and Kumi Naidoo reviews the type of accountability mechanisms being used by NGOs. The readings then conclude with excerpts from the International Non-governmental Organisations' Accountability Charter (2005) and an evaluation of Amnesty International's accountability performance by the One World Trust.

KENNETH ANDERSON, THE OTTAWA CONVENTION BANNING LANDMINES, THE ROLE OF INTERNATIONAL NON-GOVERNMENTAL ORGANIZATIONS AND THE IDEA OF INTERNATIONAL CIVIL SOCIETY

11 Eur. J. Int. L. 92 (2000)

. . . The Ottawa Convention [on the Prohibition of the Use, Stockpiling, Production and Transfer of Anti-Personnel Mines and on their Destruction] represents the first time in over a century in which a major, traditional weapon system has been banned outright and not simply regulated in its use . . . .

. . .

[33] Lisa Jordan, Mechanisms for NGO Accountability, Global Public Policy Institute, Research Paper Series No. 3 (2005) 13.

3. The Romance Between NGOs and International Organizations

A. Seven lessons from the Landmines Ban Campaign

[The author recalls the origin of the international campaign to ban landmines in the form of efforts by the ICRC. These were subsequently overtaken by a coalition of INGOs with diverse standpoints and coming together to form the International Campaign to Ban Landmines (ICBL). The groups that came together in 1992 included HRW, Handicap International (France), Medico International (Germany), Mines Awareness Group (UK), Physicians for Human Rights (US), and Vietnam Veterans of America Foundation (US). The campaign eventually numbered more than 1,200 NGOs in 60 countries. For mandate reasons, the ICRC was not a formal part of the coalition but actively supported the process leading to the Ottawa Convention.]

Second, governments were initially entirely uninterested; it was regarded by governments everywhere as pie-in-the-sky, even if they were not actively hostile to the idea....

Third, the ban campaign had a simple, easily understood message — a complete and comprehensive ban, nothing more, nothing less....

Fourth, although... the world's militaries [felt threatened, the campaign] did not represent an overwhelming economic threat to arms makers.... As a consequence, no industrial and private sector groups had a strong incentive within the NATO countries to contribute money to a counter-campaign.

...

Fifth,... largely in response to [INGO] pressures [consensus was not the rule for negotiations. Instead] sympathetic governments adopted a new principle of negotiating a treaty among 'like-minded' states...

Sixth, governments eventually began to come on board the landmines ban cause for three principal reasons. NGO pressure, first, brought them to an awareness of the genuine extent of the problem and put it on their policy agendas....

Seventh,... the ban campaign [came to be seen as] a genuine partnership between NGOs, international organizations and sympathetic states....

B. The partnership between 'international civil society', sympathetic states, and international organizations

...

The central assumption underlying the idea that the landmines campaign is a new and better way of doing international lawmaking is that international NGOs are somehow 'international civil society'....

... [INGOs] are therefore a force for democratizing international relations and international institutions and, moreover, the authoritative bearers of 'world opinion'. They are therefore the legitimate representatives in the international sphere of 'people' in the world, in a way in which their states, even democratic states, and their state representatives, are not.... As [Canadian] Foreign Minister Axworthy put it in an address to NGOs in the midst of the Ottawa process:

> One can no longer relegate NGOs to simple advisory or advocacy roles in this process. They are now part of the way decisions have to be made. They have been

the voice saying that government belongs to the people, and must respond to the people's hopes, demands and ideals.

...

C. But who elected the International NGOs?

...

... [The international bureaucracy] has adopted this theory of politics, of the legitimacy of the independent international NGO sector ... [because] public international organizations *themselves* are in desperate need of legitimacy.... [I]nternational organizations have volunteered and been volunteered for a variety of tasks that, in a word, require forms of legitimacy that international organizations have never had.

By 'legitimacy' in this context I mean merely that institutions act and be understood to act with authority that is accepted as proper and moral and just.... [W]e call this apperception 'democracy' and the consent of the governed.

... [I]nternational lawyers ... fundamentally believe that international organizations, and their underlying concept of 'world government' — what is today taken as the vision of Grotius — *are* legitimate, and deserve to be understood as the world's constitutionally supreme sources of authority and the exercise of power....

... [They] tend to form a church of those converted to belief in supranationalism....

...

... [But] the brutal fact remains that international organizations as they exist today do not have the perception of legitimacy to carry out the functions that international elites would assign to them ....

...

... Yet now it is urgently needed, and where to get it?

... International organizations claim to have overcome the democratic deficit as an impediment to their legitimacy by having as their partners, and having the moral and political approval of, international NGOs, the voice of 'world opinion', and the loud and incessant invocation of 'international civil society'....

...

... International NGOs, for their part, are happy to accept the accolade of 'international civil society', the voice of the people, and so on, for the obvious reason that it increases their power and authority within international organizations, international elites, and beyond....

...

[The author suggests that some legitimacy might inhere in INGOs if they could claim to be] authentic intermediaries of the 'people'.... But this is implausible, for at least two reasons.

First, [INGOs] are not very often connected, in any direct way, to masses of 'people'. International NGOs, in virtue of their role to operate globally rather than locally, are fundamentally elite organizations. There are exceptions, to be sure, but they are prototypically large religious affiliations.... There are certain large secular exceptions, as well; Amnesty International is perhaps one, in that at least it has a large base membership. But that membership comes mostly from wealthy countries, and its membership even in those countries tends to be educated and at least middle class... [T]he far more typical 'international' NGO of the kind whose approval and favour international organizations seek is much closer to the model of Human Rights Watch — a relatively small, highly professional, entirely elite organization funded by foundations and wealthy individuals in the Western democracies, and having no discernible base outside international elites. This is not to denigrate Human Rights Watch or the vital work it does, but it would be the first to declare that its legitimacy is not based on democratic roots among the masses but on its fidelity to its own conception of the meaning of international human rights....

International NGOs collectively are not conduits from the 'people' or the 'masses' or the 'world citizenry' from the 'bottom up'. They are, rather, a vehicle for international elites to talk to other international elites about the things — frequently of undeniably critical importance — that international elites care about. The conversation is not vertical, it is horizontal. It has a worthwhile, essential function in making the world — sometimes at least, a better place — but it does not reduce the democratic deficit.

Second, if the idea of 'international civil society' is drawn by an analogy to civil society in domestic society, then it bears noting that at least in the United States, with its vigorous and diverse civil society, civil society is *not* conceived of as being a substitute for democratic processes, let alone conveying democratic legitimacy. On the contrary, the glory of civil society is precisely that it is something different from democracy and democratic processes...

Put bluntly, the glory of organizations of civil society is not democratic legitimacy, but the ability to be a pressure group...

ISOBELLE JAQUES, STRENGTHENING DEMOCRATIC GOVERNANCE: THE ROLE OF CIVIL SOCIETY

Report on Wilton Park Conference S06/10 (2006), at http://www.wiltonpark.org.uk/documents/conferences/WPS06-10/pdfs/WPS06-10.pdf

...

The non-profit sector is coming under closer scrutiny, both from its proponents and those wishing to curtail its activities. Issue arising include: concern among donors wishing to engage with civil society organisations that transaction costs are too high; the relationship between northern and southern NGOs, and between international and national entities, with criticism that larger and northern-based organisations are not able fully to represent concerns of the South and, in some situations, adopt lifestyles inappropriate to local context; and the extent to which organisations can be professional yet able to represent, or facilitate the expression of, grassroots views. Undemocratic governments or emerging democracies are often uncomfortable with or, in some cases, hostile to the activity of civil society organisations.

There is overwhelming agreement that if the voluntary sector is to hold governments and business accountable, it needs to ensure its own legitimacy, openness and transparency. Legitimacy stems from several sources: firstly, from a strong moral conviction, through acting on the basis of universally-recognised rights and freedoms of speech, assembly and association to articulate public concerns inadequately addressed by government; secondly, a political legitimacy or credibility, through approval of the community or constituency represented by the voluntary association, asserting people's sovereignty and community control; thirdly, competence or performance legitimacy, by delivering results through being closer to local reality than governmental institutions, helping to bridge a government-community gap and promote social cohesion; fourthly, legal recognition, although in some countries, in the Middle East region for example, laws may prevent truly independent NGOs from functioning, or formal registration may undermine rather than enhance their reputation; and, most importantly, legitimacy comes from accountability and transparency.

NGOs should be accountable to a wide range of stakeholders: peoples whose rights they seek to protect and advance; their own members, supporters and staff; to those who contribute finance, goods or services; to partner institutions, both governmental and non-governmental; to regulatory bodies; to those whose policies, programmes or behaviour they wish to influence; and, more broadly, to the media and general public. They should be able to demonstrate a democratic structure, participative decision-making and non-partisan approach if they claim legitimacy on political grounds. They should focus on whatever is their primary agenda and not be diverted from this by demands of donors or obstacles in their operational environment. Some express concern that, in recent years, some civil society organisations, for example in the Philippines, have veered away from contentious issues like political reform and redistributive justice, with preference for 'doable' programmes such as delivery of social services. While there are urgent basic service needs which civil society organisations are equipped to fill, the need to address structural issues such as ineffectual government, distribution of resources and rampant corruption remains. Civil society organisations should pursue both. They should follow through on projects they undertake, conducting long-term programmes with sustainable results.

Fiscal accountability is, of course, vital, with effective reporting and monitoring systems, and sources of funding fully divulged. Some argue against accepting government support and foreign funding if civil society organisations are involved in promoting political and democratic reform; others, acknowledging the potential sensitivity of this, believe assuring a diversity of funding from public and private sources will overcome accusations of undue influence of donors.

The evolution towards national and international codes of conduct for voluntary self-regulation is regarded as a healthy development, although given the tremendous difference in size and scope of civil society organisations all cannot be brought under one approach. It will, however, introduce common principles which all can use in their work....

...

INTERNATIONAL NON-GOVERNMENTAL ORGANIZATIONS' ACCOUNTABILITY CHARTER (2005)

at www.ingoaccountabilitycharter.org

[The initial signatories include Amnesty International, Greenpeace, Oxfam International, International Save the Children Alliance, Terre des Hommes International, and Transparency International.]

We, international non-government organisations (INGOs) signatory to this Charter, are independent non-profit organisations that work globally to advance human rights, sustainable development, environmental protection, humanitarian response and other public goods.

...

Our right to act is based on universally-recognised freedoms of speech, assembly and association, on our contribution to democratic processes, and on the values we seek to promote.

Our legitimacy is also derived from the quality of our work, and the recognition and support of the people with and for whom we work and our members, our donors, the wider public, and governmental and other organisations around the world.

We seek to uphold our legitimacy by responding to inter-generational considerations, public and scientific concerns, and through accountability for our work and achievements.

By signing this Charter we seek to promote further the values of transparency and accountability that we stand for, and commit our INGO to respecting its provisions.

...

INGOs can complement but not replace the over-arching role and primary responsibility of governments....

We also seek to promote the role and responsibilities of the private sector....

We can often address problems and issues that governments and others are unable or unwilling to address on their own....

...

Wherever we operate, we seek to ensure that the high standards which we demand of others are also respected in our own organisations.

...

Our first responsibility is to achieve our stated mission effectively and transparently, consistent with our values. In this, we are accountable to our stakeholders.

Our stakeholders include:

- Peoples, including future generations, whose rights we seek to protect and advance;
- Ecosystems, which cannot speak for or defend themselves;
- Our members and supporters;
- Our staff and volunteers;

- Organisations and individuals that contribute finance, goods or services;
- Partner organisations, both governmental and non-governmental, with whom we work;
- Regulatory bodies whose agreement is required for our establishment and operations;
- Those whose policies, programmes or behaviour we wish to influence;
- The media; and
- The general public.

...

INGOs are founded on the rights to freedom of speech, assembly and association in the Universal Declaration of Human Rights. We seek to advance international and national laws that promote human rights, ecosystem protection, sustainable development and other public goods.

Where such laws do not exist, are not fully implemented, or abused, we will highlight these issues for public debate and advocate appropriate remedial action.

...

We aim to be both politically and financially independent. Our governance, programmes and policies will be non-partisan, independent of specific governments, political parties and the business sector.

...

We will ensure that our advocacy is consistent with our mission, grounded in our work and advances defined public interests.

...

We are committed to openness, transparency and honesty about our structures, mission, policies and activities. We will communicate actively to stakeholders about ourselves, and make information publicly available.

...

We seek to comply with relevant governance, financial accounting and reporting requirements in the countries where we are based and operate.

...

We should be held responsible for our actions and achievements. We will do this by: having a clear mission, organisational structure and decision-making processes; by acting in accordance with stated values and agreed procedures; by ensuring that our programmes achieve outcomes that are consistent with our mission; and by reporting on these outcomes in an open and accurate manner.

The governance structure of each organisation will conform to relevant laws and be transparent. We seek to follow principles of best practice in governance. . .

...

We seek continuously to improve our effectiveness. We will have defined evaluation procedures for our boards, staff, programmes and projects on the basis of mutual accountability.

...

We will be responsible in our public criticisms of individuals and organisations, ensuring such criticism amounts to fair public comment.

...

'AMNESTY INTERNATIONAL', IN ONE WORLD TRUST, 2006 GLOBAL ACCOUNTABILITY INDEX

at http://www.oneworldtrust.org/?display=amnesty

[The One World Trust is itself an NGO. It publishes an annual accountability index which rates some of the most prominent IGOs, INGOs and TNCs in terms of their accountability to both internal and external stakeholders. The excerpt that follows focuses on Amnesty International. Other INGOs surveyed included: ActionAid International, the International Chamber of Commerce, the International Confederation of Free Trade Unions, Oxfam International, World Vision International and WWF International.]

Amnesty International

...

Amnesty International does not seek or accept funds from governments; instead the organisation relies primarily on funding from national sections and local volunteer groups. Their income for 2006 was £29.4 million (US$58 million).

The Amnesty International secretariat is based in London, UK and employs approximately 450 people. They have more than two million supporters in over 140 countries.

...

Conclusion

Amnesty International's accountability capabilities are strongest in relation to participation. They have well developed policies and systems from engaging external stakeholders, specifically human rights organisations, in decision-making and fostering equitable member control.

Amnesty International's capabilities for handling and responding to complaints are the least developed dimension of their accountability and one of the areas where they need to focus their efforts. They need to develop mechanisms to handle and responds to complaints from both internal and external stakeholders and in doing so, they need to provide protections that are based on good practice principles.

Amnesty International's transparency capabilities also need strengthening. For much of its existence, Amnesty has faced government pressure in countries where it has exposed state sponsored human rights abuses. Historically, therefore Amnesty International has not disclosed information as a mean of both protecting itself and more importantly, its informants. The context in which AI works however, has changed and INGOs are now faced with growing calls to be more open about what they do. This changing context necessitates that Amnesty International develop the capabilities to ensure a consistent flow of information, not only to its membership, but also to the general public on its activities. In light of this, Amnesty International should consider developing an organisation-wide information disclosure policy that clearly states what, when and how information will be made publicly available.

QUESTIONS

1. Does the INGOs' Accountability Charter respond adequately to the criticisms that have been made of the major human rights INGOs?

2. Is it reasonable to expect Amnesty International to deal with complaints, and to become transparent in all of its operations, when most of the governments and corporations which are subject to its criticism have not adopted comparable measures?

3. The role played by NGOs at the Rome Conference on the International Criminal Court, in 1998, has been much criticized. Serge Sur notes that they were active partners in the negotiations, either indirectly by putting pressure on delegations or directly by being members of governmental delegations and being allowed to speak on their behalf. What are the appropriate limits to NGO involvement in such contexts and what criteria would you suggest for determining whether such involvement had gone too far?

ADDITIONAL READING

For a list of the websites of international and national human rights NGOs see http://docs.lib.duke.edu/igo/guides/ngo/db/rights.asp. See also Hugo Slim, *By What Authority? The Legitimacy and Accountability of Non-governmental Organizations* (2002); Jem Bendell, Debating NGO Accountability, UN Doc. UNCTAD/NGLS/ 2006/1 (2006); Stephen Hopgood, *Keepers of the Flame: Understanding Amnesty International* (2006); Robert Blitt, 'Who will Watch the Watchdogs? Human Rights Non-Governmental Organizations and the Case for Regulation', 10 Buffalo Hum. Rts. L. Rev. 261 (2004); M. Keck and K. Sikkink, *Activists Beyond Borders: Advocacy Networks in International Politics* (1998) S. Charnowitz, 'Two Centuries of Participation: NGOs and International Governance', 18 Michigan J. Int. L. 183 (1997); P. Chiang, *Non-Governmental Organizations at the United Nations* (1981); C. Welch Jr. (ed.), *NGOs and Human Rights: Promise and Performance* (2000); Menno Kamminga, 'The Evolving Status of NGOs under International Law: A Threat to the Inter-State System?', in P. Alston (ed.), *Non-State Actors and Human Rights* (2005), R. Lagoni, 'Article 71', in B. Simma *et al.* (eds.), *The Charter of the United Nations: A Commentary* 902–15 (2nd edn. 2000), at 902.

16

Human Rights, Development and Climate Change

One of the most important developments over the past decade or so has been the attempt to apply human rights standards and obligations to activities in specific sectoral areas such as development, environment, trade, debt, migration, labour and conflict prevention. Each of these different areas is complex and the challenge of making the relevant arrangements more human rights sensitive or compliant requires an understanding of the substantive issue areas and of the normative and institutional arrangements that govern. Rather than provide an inevitably superficial treatment of issues such as the relevance of human rights in the global trading regime, the nature of rights in relation to protection of the environment, the role of human rights in relation to labour rights, or the human rights responsibilities of key international economic actors such as the World Trade Organization, the World Bank or the International Monetary Fund, this chapter focuses primarily on the central issue of development. This requires looking at both its relationship to human rights in general, and the notion of the right to development. In addition, consideration is given to the challenge of considering whether there are specific human rights implications that flow from the rapidly developing global crisis of climate change.

A. HUMAN RIGHTS AND DEVELOPMENT

Less than two decades ago, human rights considerations were rarely addressed in the context of development policy. The reasons were diverse. Some economists considered human rights to be political in contrast to the more technical challenges of promoting economic development, some felt that many or even most human rights concerns were not able to be quantified effectively and thus could not be factored into the development equation, others were sympathetic to the idea that respect for civil and political rights was an issue that first required a significant degree of development to be attained, and some rejected the notion of economic and social rights as running counter to the functioning of free markets. It was not until the early 1990s that a more sophisticated debate began to take place. It was fuelled partly by the failure of old development models, and partly by the realization that notions of good governance, participation, accountability and transparency inevitably had human rights dimensions and could not be promoted adequately without addressing those dimensions. One of the most influential contributors to the debate has been Amartya Sen (whose related writings appear at pp. 180 and 371, *supra*). In the following excerpt, Sen argues that freedom should be seen as both the ends and the means of development. The need to relate human rights more closely to development is then taken up by the Human Development Report of 2000.

The materials then consider one of the main strategies that have been promoted over the past decade or so in order to promote the relevance of human rights in relation to development policies and practices. This is the so-called 'human rights based approach' ('HRBA') to development which argues that human rights norms and methodologies should be of central importance at all stages of the development process — in deciding who is to participate in decision-making, in determining the objectives to be sought, in shaping the relevant policies and in evaluating progress. This process is often referred to as one of seeking to 'mainstream' human rights policies into the activities of other actors. The relevant materials below include an excerpt from a key UN policy in relation to HRBA and a critique of some of the assumptions and techniques used in promoting such mainstreaming efforts.

AMARTYA SEN, DEVELOPMENT AS FREEDOM

(1999), at 35

Chapter 2: The Ends and the Means of Development

Let me start off with a distinction between two general attitudes to the process of development that can be found both in professional economic analysis and in public discussions and debates. One view sees development as a 'fierce' process, with much 'blood, sweat and tears' — a world in which wisdom demands toughness. In particular, it demands calculated neglect of various concerns that are seen as 'soft-headed' ... [T]he temptations to be resisted can include having social safety nets that protect the very poor, providing social services for the population at large, departing from rugged institutional guidelines in response to identified hardship, and favoring — 'much too early' — political and civil rights and the 'luxury' of democracy. These things, it is argued in this austere attitudinal mode, could be supported later on, when the development process has borne enough fruit: what is needed here and now is 'toughness and discipline'. The different theories [diverge] in pointing to distinct areas of softness that are particularly to be avoided, varying from financial softness to political relaxation, from plentiful social expenditures to complaisant poverty relief.

This hard-knocks attitude contrasts with an alternative outlook that sees development as essentially a 'friendly' process. Depending on the particular version of this attitude, the congeniality of the process is seen as exemplified by such things as mutually beneficial exchanges (of which Adam Smith spoke eloquently), or by the working of social safety nets, or of political liberties, or of social development — or some combination or other of these supportive activities.

The approach of this book is much more compatible with the latter approach than with the former. It is mainly an attempt to see development as a process of expanding the real freedoms that people enjoy. In this approach, expansion of freedom is viewed as both (1) the *primary end* and (2) the *principal means* of development. They can be called respectively the 'constitutive role' and the 'instrumental role' of freedom in development. The constitutive role of freedom relates to the importance of substantive freedom in enriching human life. The substantive freedoms include elementary capabilities like being able to avoid such deprivations as starvation, undernourishment, escapable morbidity and premature mortality, as well as the freedoms that are associated with being literate and numerate, enjoying political participation and uncensored speech and so on. In this constitutive perspective, development involves expansion of these and other basic freedoms. Development, in this view, is the process of expanding human freedoms, and the assessment of development has to be informed by this consideration.

Let me refer here to an example.... Within the narrower views of development (in terms of say, [Gross Domestic Product] growth or industrialization) it is often asked whether the freedom of political participation and dissent is or is not 'conducive to development'. In the light of the foundational view of development as freedom, this question would seem to be defectively formulated, since it misses the crucial understanding that political participation and dissent are *constitutive* parts of development itself.... Development seen as enhancement of freedom cannot but address [deprivations of freedom]. The relevance of the deprivation of basic political freedoms or civil rights, for an adequate understanding of development, does not have to be established through their indirect contribution to *other* features of development (such as growth of GDP or the promotion of industrialization). These freedoms are part and parcel of enriching the process of development.

This fundamental development point is distinct from the 'instrumental' argument that these freedoms and rights may *also* be very effective in contributing to economic progress.... [T]he significance of the instrumental role of political freedom as *means* to development does not in any way reduce the evaluative importance of freedom as an *end* of development.

...The instrumental role of freedom concerns the way different kinds of rights, opportunities, and entitlements contribute to the expansion of human freedom in general, and thus to promoting development.... The effectiveness of freedom as an instrument lies in the fact that different kinds of freedom interrelate with one another, and freedom of one type may greatly help in advancing freedom of other types. The two roles are thus linked by empirical connections, as relating freedom of one kind to freedom of other kinds.

...

...I shall consider the following types of instrumental freedoms: (1) *political freedoms*, (2) *economic facilities*, (3) *social opportunities*, (4) *transparency guarantees*, and (5) *protective security*. These instrumental freedoms tend to contribute to the general capability of a person to live more freely, but they also serve to complement one another. While development analysis must, on the one hand, be concerned with the objectives and aims that make these instrumental freedoms consequentially important, it must also take note of the empirical linkages that tie the distinct types of freedom *together*, strengthening their joint importance. Indeed, these connections are central to a fuller understanding of the instrumental role of freedom. The claim that freedom is not only the primary object of development but also its principal means relates particularly to these linkages.

Let me comment a little on each of these instrumental freedoms. [Discussion of political freedoms omitted.]

Economic facilities refer to the opportunities that individuals respectively enjoy to utilize economic resources for the purpose of consumption, or production, or exchange. The economic entitlements that a person has will depend on the resources owned or available for use as well as on conditions of exchange, such as relative prices and the working of the markets. Insofar as the process of economic development increases the income and wealth of a country, they are reflected in corresponding enhancement of economic entitlements. It should be obvious that in the relation between national income and wealth, on the one hand, and the economic entitlements of individuals (or families), on the other, distributional considerations are important, in addition to aggregative ones. How the additional incomes generated are distributed will clearly make a difference.

...

Social opportunities refer to the arrangements that society makes for education, health care and so on, which influence the individual's substantive freedom to live better. These facilities are important not only for the conduct of private lives (such as living a healthy life and avoiding preventable morbidity and premature mortality), but also for more effective participation in economic and political activities. For example illiteracy can be a major barrier to participation in economic activities that require production according to specification or demand strict quality control (as globalized trade increasingly does). Similarly, political participation may be hindered by the inability to read newspapers or to communicate in writing with others involved in political activities.

...

Finally, no matter how well an economic system operates, some people can be typically on the verge of vulnerability and can actually succumb to great deprivation as a result of material changes that adversely affect their lives. *Protective security* is needed to provide a social safety net for preventing the affected population from being reduced to abject misery, and in some cases even starvation and death. The domain of protective security includes fixed institutional arrangements such as unemployment benefits and statutory income supplements to the indigent as well as ad hoc arrangements to generate income for destitutes.

These instrumental freedoms directly enhance the capabilities of people, but they also supplement one another, and can furthermore reinforce one another. These interlinkages are particularly important to seize in considering development policies.

...

Similarly the creation of social opportunities, through such services as public education, health care, and the development of a free and energetic press, can contribute both to economic development and to significant reductions in mortality rates. Reduction of mortality rates, in turn, can help to reduce birth rates, reinforcing the influence of basic education — especially female literary and schooling — on fertility behavior.

...

This approach goes against — and to a great extent undermines — the belief that has been so dominant in many policy circles that 'human development' (as the process of expanding education, health care and other conditions of human life is often called) is really a kind of luxury that only richer countries can afford. Perhaps the most important impact of the type of success that the East Asian economies, beginning with Japan, have had is the total undermining of that implicit prejudice. These economies went comparatively early for massive expansion of education, and later also of health care, and this they did, in many cases, *before* they broke the restraints of general poverty. And they have reaped as they have sown....

...

UNDP, HUMAN RIGHTS AND DEVELOPMENT

Human Development Report 2000, at 85

...

History shows that even without the full set of civil and political rights, rapid progress is possible in economic, social and cultural rights. But withholding civil and political rights in no way helps achieve these rapid advances. Quite the reverse, for civil and political rights empower poor people to claim their economic and social rights — to food, to housing, to education, to health care, to decent work and to social security. These rights empower them to demand accountability — for good public services, for pro-poor public policies, for a transparent participatory process open to hearing their views. This propels dynamic public policy for equitable development and accelerated human development.

Moreover, neglect of economic and social rights can undermine civil and political liberties, reversing recent progress. Economic stagnation, high unemployment, scant economic opportunities for urban youth, growing gaps between rich and poor, inflows of the international Mafia — all are sources of enormous strain on fragile transition democracies, in many parts of Africa, Latin America, Eastern Europe and the former Soviet Union. Consider the fear and insecurity in the streets, felt across the globe from Bogotá to Nairobi, from Moscow to Manila. Economic and social policies that increase inequalities, particularly in the context of economic stagnation and unemployment, often lead to crime and put pressure on the judicial system. The ensuing failures in the administration of justice lead to quasilegal investigative methods, violations of constitutional guarantees and the use of coercive powers by the police. Communities end up facing a false dichotomy — a supposed choice between respecting human rights and fighting crime. That sets in motion a downward spiral pitting communities, especially poor communities, against the police and judiciary.

In sum: progress towards a democratic society that respects human rights will be consolidated if laws and institutions to protect civil and political rights are accompanied by investments in accelerating human development and poverty eradication. Economic revival and an equitable distribution of the economic gains are a vital companion to constitutional advance.

Four challenges that public policy must recognize:

- Equitable economic and social policies have direct connections to sustaining civil and political liberties. One policy priority all countries can consider deserves priority attention — meeting the 20:20 compact target of increasing expenditures for human priorities, including primary health and education, by restructuring national and aid budgets or protecting them in balancing budgets.
- Civil and political liberties empower poor people — advancing social and economic progress, reducing economic and social poverty and inequality. Promoting the work of civil society organizations — including NGOs, workers organizations and the free media — will help vibrant societies secure human rights. Lifting archaic regulations that restrict activities of NGOs and censor the media is a priority.
- The human rights obligations of public institutions — and other important actors — are to implement pro-poor policies and policymaking processes that guarantee the right to participation by the poor.
- The human rights obligations of global actors — state and non-state — are to put in place global institutional and legal arrangements that promote the eradication of poverty.

...

THE HUMAN RIGHTS-BASED APPROACH TO DEVELOPMENT COOPERATION: TOWARDS A COMMON UNDERSTANDING AMONG UN AGENCIES

in Report of the Second Interagency Workshop on Implementing a Human Rights-Based Approach in the Context of UN Reform (Stamford, USA, 5–7 May 2003)

[In 2003 the Office of the High Commissioner for Human Rights, the UN Development Programme and a range of other UN agencies, funds and programmes, met to adopt an agreed position on human rights-based approaches to development cooperation ('HRBA'). The outcome is the following 'Common Understanding'.]

...

1. All programmes of development co-operation, policies and technical assistance should further the realisation of human rights as laid down in the Universal Declaration of Human Rights and other international human rights instruments.

...

2. Human rights standards contained in, and principles derived from, the Universal Declaration of Human Rights and other international human rights

instruments guide all development cooperation and programming in all sectors and in all phases of the programming process.

...

Among these human rights principles are: universality and inalienability; indivisibility; interdependence and inter-relatedness; non-discrimination and equality; participation and inclusion; accountability and the rule of law.

...

3. Programmes of development cooperation contribute to the development of the capacities of duty-bearers to meet their obligations and of 'rights-holders' to claim their rights.

...

Experience has shown that the use of a human rights-based approach requires the use of good programming practices. However, the application of "good programming practices" does not by itself constitute a human rights-based approach, and requires additional elements.

The following elements are necessary, specific, and unique to a human rights-based approach:

a) Assessment and analysis in order to identify the human rights claims of rights-holders and the corresponding human rights obligations of duty-bearers as well as the immediate, underlying, and structural causes of the non-realization of rights.
b) Programmes assess the capacity of rights-holders to claim their rights, and of duty bearers to fulfill their obligations. They then develop strategies to build these capacities.
c) Programmes monitor and evaluate both outcomes and processes guided by human rights standards and principles.
d) Programming is informed by the recommendations of international human rights bodies and mechanisms.

Other elements of good programming practices that are also essential under a HRBA, include:

1. People are recognized as key actors in their own development, rather than passive recipients of commodities and services.
2. Participation is both a means and a goal.
3. Strategies are empowering, not disempowering.
4. Both outcomes and processes are monitored and evaluated.
5. Analysis includes all stakeholders.
6. Programmes focus on marginalized, disadvantaged, and excluded groups.
7. The development process is locally owned.
8. Programmes aim to reduce disparity.
9. Both top-down and bottom-up approaches are used in synergy.
10. Situation analysis is used to identity immediate, underlying, and basic causes of development problems.

11. Measurable goals and targets are important in programming.
12. Strategic partnerships are developed and sustained.
13. Programmes support accountability to all stakeholders.

PHILIP ALSTON, SHIPS PASSING IN THE NIGHT

27 Hum. Rts. Q. (2005)755, at 802

. . . [S]everal general observations are prompted by the sort of criteria that are commonly put forward as defining a human rights based approach. The first is that such criteria are often expressed at a level of abstraction and generality that is not uncharacteristic of some human rights discourse but that is likely to seem abstract, untargeted, and untested to the community of development economists. . . .

The second observation is that some of the formulations do little more than restate the fundamental dilemma and do not actually offer a lot of guidance as to how to resolve it. For example, identifying "the corresponding human rights obligations of duty-bearers," as one of the above-listed elements suggested, may be extremely difficult to do . . . .

Similarly, the Statement of Common Understanding calls for identification of "the immediate, underlying, and structural causes of the non-realization of rights." This will usually be even more fraught with difficulty because most human rights problems are subject to diverse and heavily contested causal explanations. . . .

A third general observation . . . is that there is a good deal of optimism implicit in the suggestion that decisions on complicated matters of development programming should be "informed by the recommendations of international human rights bodies and mechanisms." At the current relatively embryonic and certainly underfunded stage of development of such bodies and mechanisms, a great many of the recommendations emerging from them are not at all operational, and some of them are not especially well grounded. . . .

A fourth observation concerns the disparate items contained in the second list of the Statement of Common Understanding, all of which are said to be essential for a human rights based approach. In many cases, the advice proffered does not seem to follow inexorably from human rights principles per se, but rather to be a reflection of what the authors consider to be sound policy on the basis of their own experise . . . .

In other cases, the criteria seem somewhat platitudinous, offer little real practical guidance, or fail to exhibit any clear human rights based origins. For example, the suggestion that "both top-down and bottom-up approaches [should be] used in synergy" tells us very little. . . . Finally, some of the criteria, while unquestionably correct, seem to do little more than implicate further questions. To insist that strategies be "empowering, not disempowering" leaves open the question of what strategies are actually empowering, particularly when so few of those pursued in the name of empowerment seem to succeed in any marked way. Moreover, how does one resolve the dilemma created by situations in which the result of empowering local communities is the rejection of broader priorities identified in order to ensure compatibility with human rights standards....

A related issue concerns the emphasis on the "marginalized, disadvantaged, and excluded." One of the potentially misleading claims contained in much of the literature about rights based approaches is that they reflect a preference for the poor and disadvantaged or that their purpose is to "set out the rights and entitlements within which the poor and their representatives can make claims."[1] At one level such a claim is certainly correct in the sense that if the poor enjoyed all of the rights recognized in human rights declarations they would be infinitely better off than they are at present. But at another level, it is almost naive not to acknowledge that human rights systems have historically benefited the well-off even more than the downtrodden, and that the consequences of highlighting rights will depend very significantly on the power relations that exist within the society or the group....

...

Strengthening the Human Rights-Based Approach

...

One clearly emerging policy prescription is the need to be more selective and to set priorities. If every possible human rights element is deemed to be essential or necessary, then nothing will be treated as though it is truly important. A list of requirements that is too demanding or ignores trade-offs and dilemmas is unlikely to be taken seriously by practitioners who are operating under major resource and time constraints and are faced with competing priorities and the need to make difficult choices. Two caveats are in order at this point. First, the call for prioritizing is not to suggest that any obvious violation of rights can be ignored, let alone that human rights shortcuts can be acceptable in the development process. Second contextually identified priorities must be distinguished from fixed hierarchies. While the latter are unacceptable in human rights law in so far as they purport to authorize one set of rights to trump another, the former are also somewhat alien to the analytical frameworks of many human rights specialists who are carefully trained to avoid any form of selectivity in the name of the indivisibility and interdependence of all rights. It is, however, a misunderstanding of the consequences of this principle to suggest that setting priorities is unacceptable.

Another policy prescription is that human rights proponents need to be more realistic about the obstacles that impede those working in the area of development from adopting human rights methodologies....

...Two elements will be important in charting the way forward. The first is that the onus will largely be on the human rights community to demonstrate the feasibility of the advocated approaches, to demonstrate their adaptability to different circumstances, and to show a greater engagement with the alternative methodologies employed within the development community. The second is that incremental change is far more likely to succeed than is an approach assuming that a paradigm shift can be achieved almost overnight....

[1] Department for International Development, *supra* note 163, at 2.

QUESTIONS

1. Can Sen's approach be characterized as a human rights-centred one? Does it matter if he does not specifically embrace the discourse of international human rights law in his analysis?

2. What, in your view, are the strengths and weaknesses of the human rights-based approach to development?

B. THE RIGHT TO DEVELOPMENT

Article 56 of the UN Charter commits all member states to take 'joint and separate action in co-operation' with the UN for the achievement of the purposes identified in Article 55, which includes human rights, 'higher standards of living...and conditions of economic and social progress and development' and 'solutions of international economic, social, health and related problems'. Similarly, Article 28 of the UDHR provides that '[e]veryone is entitled to a social and international order in which the rights and freedoms set forth in this Declaration can be fully realized'. These provisions, although expressed at a level of great generality, have often been invoked by those who posit the existence of a broad international 'duty to cooperate' or a 'right to solidarity'. In a world of deep-rooted and growing inequalities among nations, the question inevitably arises whether the international community bears some responsibility for assisting states whose resources are inadequate to ensure the human rights of their own citizens, or for providing direct assistance to those individuals in dire need.

Since 1977 much of this debate has been pursued within the field of human rights under the rubric of the 'right to development'. The debate touches upon a number of themes raised in earlier chapters: the basis for recognition of new rights, the priority to be accorded to the different sets of rights, the links between human rights and democratic governance, and the relationship between individual and collective rights (including peoples' rights).

The list of internationally recognized human rights is by no means immutable. Just as the British sociologist T. H. Marshall characterized the 18th century as the century of civil rights, the 19th as that of political rights and the 20th as that of social rights, so too have some commentators over the past three decades put forward claims for the recognition of the new rights, in particular a category known as the 'third generation of solidarity rights'. By analogy with the slogan of the French Revolution these rights have been said to correspond to the theme of *fraternité*, while first generation civil and political rights correspond with *liberté* and second generation economic and social rights with *egalité*. Karel Vasak's list of solidarity rights included 'the right to development, the right to peace, the right to environment, the right to the ownership of the common heritage of mankind, and the right to communication'.[2]

Far more significant has been the impact of the right to development. First recognized by the UN Commission on Human Rights in 1977 (CHR Res. 4 (XXXIII)), it was enshrined in the following very carefully negotiated Declaration:

DECLARATION ON THE RIGHT TO DEVELOPMENT

General Assembly Res. 41/28 (1986)

The General Assembly,

...

Proclaims the following Declaration on the Right to Development:

Article 1

1. The right to development is an inalienable human right by virtue of which every human person and all peoples are entitled to participate in, contribute to, and enjoy economic, social, cultural and political development, in which all human rights and fundamental freedoms can be fully realized.

2. The human right to development also implies the full realization of the right of peoples to self-determination, which includes, subject to the relevant provisions of both International Covenants on Human Rights, the exercise of their inalienable right to full sovereignty over all their natural wealth and resources.

Article 2

1. The human person is the central subject of development and should be the active participant and beneficiary of the right to development.

2. All human beings have a responsibility for development, individually and collectively, taking into account the need for full respect for their human rights and fundamental freedoms as well as their duties to the community, which alone can ensure the free and complete fulfilment of the human being, and they should therefore promote and protect an appropriate political, social and economic order for development.

3. States have the right and the duty to formulate appropriate national development policies that aim at the constant improvement of the well-being of the entire population and of all individuals, on the basis of their active, free and meaningful participation in development and in the fair distribution of the benefits resulting therefrom.

Article 3

1. States have the primary responsibility for the creation of national and international conditions favourable to the realization of the right to development.

[2] K. Vasak, 'For the Third Generation of Human Rights: The Rights of Solidarity', International Institute of Human Rights, July 1979, at 3.

2. The realization of the right to development requires full respect for the principles of international law concerning friendly relations and cooperation among States in accordance with the Charter of the United Nations.

3. States have the duty to co-operate with each other in ensuring development and eliminating obstacles to development. States should realize their rights and fulfil their duties in such a manner as to promote a new international economic order based on sovereign equality, interdependence, mutual interest and co-operation among all States, as well as to encourage the observance and realization of human rights.

Article 4

1. States have the duty to take steps, individually and collectively, to formulate international development policies with a view to facilitating the full realization of the right to development.

2. Sustained action is required to promote more rapid development of developing countries. As a complement to the efforts of developing countries, effective international co-operation is essential in providing these countries with appropriate means and facilities to foster their comprehensive development.

. . .

Article 6

. . .

2. All human rights and fundamental freedoms are indivisible and interdependent; equal attention and urgent consideration should be given to the implementation, promotion and protection of civil, political, economic, social and cultural rights.

. . .

Article 8

1. States should undertake, at the national level, all necessary measures for the realization of the right to development and shall ensure, inter alia, equality of opportunity for all in their access to basic resources, education, health services, food, housing, employment and the fair distribution of income. Effective measures should be undertaken to ensure that women have an active role in the development process. Appropriate economic and social reforms should be carried out with a view to eradicating all social injustices.

2. States should encourage popular participation in all spheres as an important factor in development and in the full realization of all human rights.

. . .

Article 10

Steps should be taken to ensure the full exercise and progressive enhancement of the right to development, including the formulation, adoption and implementation of policy, legislative and other measures at the national and international levels.

NOTE

The right to development has never ceased to be controversial among governments as well as among scholars and commentators. While the right is generally grounded in claims relating to the material conditions required to ensure realization of the full range of existing human rights, it is also sometimes grounded in claims of appropriate reparations for colonialism and other forms of exploitation of the South by the North, or on arguments that the existing international economic order is loaded against developing countries and that compensation should follow.[3]

The international community has underlined its importance on many occasions, including a statement endorsed by the 1993 Vienna World Conference on Human Rights to the effect that it is 'a universal and inalienable right and an integral part of fundamental human rights'. Despite such ringing endorsements, prolonged efforts to clarify its content and, more importantly, its implications, have yielded little agreement on concrete issues. Since the adoption of the Declaration, the UN Commission and its successor, the Human Rights Council, have employed various mechanisms designed to shed light on these issues. They include four different 'working groups', two composed of 'experts' and two of governmental representatives, as well as an independent expert. While a great many reports have been produced, they have yet to lead to any consensus about the practical consequences of the recognition of the right.

In the readings below Abi-Saab and Bedjaoui present the case for the existence in international law of a right to development, while Donnelly argues that the right is not only without foundation but is dangerous as well. Their analyses are followed by an excerpt from the 2007 report to the Human Rights Council by the Working Group on the Right to Development. The report reflects the current state of the debate at the international level.

GEORGES ABI-SAAB, THE LEGAL FORMULATION OF A RIGHT TO DEVELOPMENT

in Hague Academy of International Law, The Right to Development at the International Level (1980), at 163

[Abi-Saab begins by noting that, for the right to development to be considered a legal right, it must be possible to identify the active and passive subjects of the right and its content. But those elements depend on the legal basis of the right, which in turn depends on whether the right is an individual or collective one.]

It is possible to think of different legal bases of the right to development as a collective right. The first possibility... is to consider the right to development as the aggregate of the social, economic and cultural rights not of each individual, but of

[3] These arguments were examined in detail in the first major UN report on the right to development. See UN Doc. E/CN.4/1334 (1978).

all the individuals constituting a collectivity. In other words, it is the sum total of a double aggregation of the rights and of the individuals. This version…has the merit of shedding light on the link between the rights of the individual and the right of the collectivity; a link which is crucial….

Another way…is to approach it directly from a collective perspective…by considering it either as the economic dimension of the right of self-determination, or alternatively as a parallel right to self-determination, partaking of the same nature and belonging to the same category of collective rights.

…

As far as the beneficiaries or active subjects are concerned, the first answer that comes to mind is that they are those societies possessing certain characteristics which lead the international community to consider them wanting in terms of development and to classify them as 'developing' or 'less developed' countries (LDC)….

…

…Up to now, we have used societies, communities, countries and States as interchangeable, which they are not. In fact, here as with self-determination, the common denominator of these different ways of describing the beneficiary collectivity is the 'people' they designate, which constitutes the socially relevant entity or group in this context…. Suffice it to say here that the distinction between 'people' and 'State', though in theory it is as important in relation to the right to development as to the right of self-determination, in practice it is not….

…

…[T]he passive subject of the right to development can only be the international community as such. But as the international community does not have at its disposal the means (organs, resources) of directly fulfilling its obligations under the right to development, it can only discharge them through a category of its members, that of the 'developed' States….

…

…[S]atisfaction of the collective right is a necessary condition, a condition-precedent or a prerequisite for the materialization of the individual rights. Thus without self-determination it is impossible to imagine a total realization of the civil and political rights of the individuals constituting the collectivity in question. Such rights can be granted and exercised at lower levels, such as villages and municipalities, but they cannot reach their full scope and logical conclusion if the community is subject to colonial or alien rule.

…

The same with the right to development, which is a necessary precondition for the satisfaction of the social and economic rights of the individuals. And here, even more than in the case of self-determination, the causal link between the two levels is particularly strong; for without a tolerable degree of development, the society will not be materially in a position to grant and guarantee these rights to its members, i.e., of providing the positive services and securing the minimum economic standards which are required by these rights.

…

MOHAMMED BEDJAOUI, THE RIGHT TO DEVELOPMENT

in M. Bedjaoui (ed.), International Law: Achievements and Prospects (1991), at 1182

...

14. The right to development is a fundamental right, the precondition of liberty, progress, justice and creativity. It is the alpha and omega of human rights, the first and last human right, the beginning and the end, the means and the goal of human rights, in short it is the *core right* from which all the others stem....

...

15. ...In reality the international dimension of the right to development is nothing other than *the right to an equitable share in the economic and social well-being of the world.* It reflects an essential demand of our time since four fifths of the world's population no longer accept that the remaining fifth should continue to build its wealth on their poverty.

...

IV. Basis of the Right to Development

19. The most essential human rights have, in a sense, a meta-juridical foundation. For example, the right to life is independent both of international law and of the municipal laws of States. It pre-exists law. In this sense it is a 'primary' or 'first' law, that is to say a law commanding all the others.... Thus the right to development imposes itself with the force of a self-evident principle and its natural foundation is as a corollary of the right to life....

...

22. The 'right to development' flows from this right to self-determination and has the *same nature.* There is little sense in recognizing self-determination as a superior and inviolable principle if one does not recognize *at the same time* a 'right to development' for the peoples that have achieved self-determination. This right to development can only be an 'inherent' and 'built-in' right forming an inseparable part of the right to self-determination.

23. ... [This makes the right to development] much more a right of the State or of the people, than a right of the individual, and it seems to me that it is better that way.

...

26. The present writer considers that international solidarity means taking into account the interdependence of nations. One may identify three stages in this search for the foundation of the right to development based on international solidarity:

(i) interdependence, the result of the global nature of the world economy;
(ii) the universal duty of every State to develop the world economy, which makes development an international problem *par excellence*;
(iii) preservation of the human species as the basis of the right to development.

...

V. Content of the Right to Development

34. … [This right] has several aspects, the most important and comprehensive of which is the right of each people freely to choose its economic and social system without outside interference or constraint of any kind, and to determine, with equal freedom, its own model of development.…

…

48. … [T]he State seeking its own development is entitled to demand that all the other States, the international community and international economic agents collectively *do not take away from it what belongs to it, or do not deprive it of what is or 'must be' its due in international trade.* In the name of this right to development, the State being considered may claim a '*fair price*' for its raw materials and for whatever it offers in its trade with the more developed countries.

…

49. This second meaning of the right to development which is due from the international community seems much more complex. It implies that the State is *entitled if not to the satisfaction of its needs at least to receive a fair share of what belongs to all, and therefore to that State also.*

…

50. … [T]he satisfaction of the needs of a people should be perceived as a right and not as an act of charity. It is a right which should be made effective by *norms and institutions.* The relation between the donor and the recipient States is seen in terms of responsibility and reciprocal rights over goods that are considered as belonging to all. There is no place in such an analysis for charity, the 'act of mercy', considered as being a factor of inequality from which the donor expects tokens of submissiveness or political flexibility on the part of the receiving State. The concept of charity thus gives place to that of justice. *The need,* taken as a criterion of equity, gives greater precision to the concept of '*equitable distribution*' which would otherwise be too vague.

…

VI. Degree of Normativity of the Right to Development

53. Learned opinion is divided in its view of the legal validity of the right to development. Many writers consider that while it is undoubtedly an inalienable and imperative right, this is only in the moral, rather than in the legal, sphere. The present writer has, on the contrary, maintained that the right to development is, by its nature, so incontrovertible that it *should* be regarded as belonging to *jus cogens.*

…

55. It is clear, however, that a right which is not opposable by the possessor of the right against the person from whom the right is due is not a right in the full legal sense. This constitutes *the challenge which the right to development throws down to contemporary international law* and the whole of the challenge which the underdevelopment of four fifths of the globe places, in political terms, before the rulers of the world.…

…

JACK DONNELLY, IN SEARCH OF THE UNICORN: THE JURISPRUDENCE AND POLITICS OF THE RIGHT TO DEVELOPMENT

15 Calif. Western Int. L. J. 473 (1985), at 482

III. Legal Sources of the Right to Development

. . .

. . . If the right to development means the right of peoples freely to pursue their development, then it can be plausibly argued to be implied by the Covenants' right to self-determination. However, such a right to development is without interest; it is already firmly established as the right to self-determination.

A substantially broader right to development, however, cannot be extracted from this right to self-determination. The right to self-determination recognized in the Covenants does not imply a right to live in a developing society; it is explicitly only a right to *pursue* development. Neither does it imply an *individual* right to development; self-determination, again explicitly, is a right of peoples only. In no sense does it imply a right to be developed. Thus the claim that the right to development is simply the realization of the right to self-determination is not based on the Covenants' understanding of self-determination.

It might also be argued that because development is necessary for self-determination, development is itself a human right. Such an argument, however, is fallacious. Since we will come across this form of argument again, let us look briefly at this 'instrumental fallacy'. Suppose that A holds mineral rights in certain oil-bearing properties. Suppose further that in order to enjoy these rights fully, she requires $500,000 to begin pumping the oil. Clearly A does not have a right to $500,000 just because she needs it to enjoy her rights. . . . The same reasoning applies to the link between development and the right to self-determination. Even assuming that development is necessary for, rather than a consequence of, full enjoyment of the right to self-determination, it simply does not follow that peoples have a right to development.

Allowing such an argument to prevail would result in a proliferation of bizarre or misguided rights. . . .

. . .

The second promising implicit source of a right to development is Article 28 of the [UDHR] . . .

. . .

[O]ne might question whether 'development' falls under the notion of a social and international order referred to in Article 28. 'Development' suggests a process or result; the process of development or the condition of being developed. 'Order', by contrast, implies a set of principles, rules, practices or institutions; neither a process nor a result but a structure. Article 28, therefore, is most plausibly interpreted as prohibiting *structures* that deny opportunities or resources for the realization of civil, political, economic, social or cultural human rights. . . .

. . .

Suppose, though, that Article 28 *were* to be taken to imply a human right to development. What would that right look like? It would be an *individual* right, and only an individual right; a right of persons, not peoples, and certainly not States. It would be a right to the enjoyment of traditional human rights, not a substantively new right. It would be as much a civil and political as an economic and social right — Article 28 refers to *all* human rights — and would be held equally against one's national government and the international community . . .

. . .

[V. Subjects of the Right to Development]

. . .

If human rights derive from the inherent dignity of the human person, collective human rights are logically possible only if we see social membership as an inherent part of human personality, and if we argue that as part of a nation or people, persons hold human rights substantively different from, and in no way reducible to, individual human rights. This last proposition is extremely controversial. . . .

The very concept of human rights, as it has heretofore been understood, rests on a view of the individual person as separate from, and endowed with inalienable rights held primarily in relation to, society, and especially the state. Furthermore, within the area defined by these rights, the individual is superior to society in the sense that ordinarily, in cases of conflict between individual human rights and social goals or interests, individual rights must prevail. The idea of collective *human* rights represents a major, and at best confusing, conceptual deviation.

I do not want to challenge the idea of collective rights *per se* or even the notion of peoples' rights; groups, including nations, can and do hold a variety of rights. But these are not *human* rights as that term is ordinarily understood. . . .

. . .

A further problem with collective human rights is determining who is to exercise the right; the right-holder is not a physical person, and thus an institutional 'person' must exercise it. In the case of a right held by a people, or by society as a whole, the most plausible 'person' to exercise the right is, unfortunately, the state. Again this represents a radical reconceptualization of human rights — and an especially dangerous one.

. . .

UN HUMAN RIGHTS COUNCIL, REPORT OF THE WORKING GROUP ON THE RIGHT TO DEVELOPMENT ON ITS EIGHTH SESSION

(Geneva, 26 February–2 March 2007) UN Doc. A/HRC/4/47

. . .

18. Algeria . . . on behalf of the Group of African States . . . underscored the centrality of the right to development in the framework of promoting and protecting

human rights and its importance in relation to the mandate of the Human Rights Council. The Group of African States reaffirmed that only a non-fragmented approach, including equitable international trade rules and responses to energy, raw material and debt burden issues, could reduce the growing gap between developing and developed countries. In a framework of fighting poverty, the Group of African States called for international cooperation exclusive of conditionality. In relation to the future work of the task force, the African Group recommended examining questions contributing to the elaboration of a convention on the right to development.

19. Cuba, on behalf of the Non-Aligned Movement (NAM), reasserted the importance and centrality of the right to development... and stressed that, since the adoption of the Declaration on the Right to Development, 20 years ago, very little had been shown in terms of implementation of this right by the international community.... NAM underscored inter alia the lack of autonomy of developing countries as regards decision-making to formulate development policies suitable to their realities; unfair trade rules and practices that restrict market access and allow for export subsidies; a decrease in and failure to comply with commitments to official development assistance and transfer of technology and heavy debt burdens, as a factor of permanent decapitalization of developing countries. Referring to the Declaration on the Right to Development, NAM reaffirmed the duty of States to cooperate for the creation of conditions conducive to realizing the right to development. In this context, it called for international cooperation that is not subject to conditionality, nor be treated as a matter of charity.... NAM called for... the elaboration of a convention on the right to development....

20. In a general statement on behalf of the European Union (EU)... Germany reaffirmed the firm commitment of the EU to the realization of the right to development. The EU underscored the primary responsibility of States for the promotion and protection of all human rights, including the right to development; responsibility to create internal conditions favourable to their development, and to cooperate at an international level in eliminating obstacles to development. The EU reiterated its support to the work of the task force, and welcomed the development of innovative instruments and indicators, as reflected in the consideration of the African Peer Review Mechanism [designed to facilitate self-assessment of governance and other performance by African States, in a process subject to peer review by representatives of other states].... The EU noted elements of clarification of responsibilities between developing countries and development partners and important linkages to a human rights-based approach to development, such as non-discrimination, inclusion of vulnerable groups and principles of transparency and accountability.... By focusing on identified rights, such as rights of the child and gender aspects, the EU expressed the view that the Working Group could contribute to conceptualizing implementation strategies for particular human rights in the field of development cooperation.

...

A. Conclusions

...

52. ...The experience gained from further work of the task force in applying, refining and developing the criteria would be conducive to the elaboration

and implementation of a comprehensive and coherent set of standards. These standards could take various forms, including guidelines on the implementation of the right to development, and evolve into a basis for consideration of an international legal standard of a binding nature, through a collaborative process of engagement.

...

Annex III

Comments submitted by groups and member states

Explanation of position by the Non-Aligned Movement

60. The Non-Aligned Movement interprets the phrase "international legal standard of a binding nature", contained in paragraph 52 of the conclusions and recommendations, to mean "internationally legally binding convention."

...

Explanation of position by the European Union

63. ... [T]he EU joins consensus on [paragraph 52] on the understanding that it does not imply a process leading to an international legal standard of a binding nature. Rather, the EU considers that paragraph 52 describes an open-ended process of developing criteria promoting the operational implementation of the right to development.

...

QUESTIONS

1. Compare the different conceptions of the right to development put forward by Abi-Saab, Bedjaoui, and Donnelly with the text of the 1986 General Assembly Declaration. Key concerns voiced by some of the governmental and other opponents of the right to development include objections to collective human rights and especially to any idea that a human right can be vested in a state, resistance to the idea that resource transfers from the North to the South are obligatory, and fears that a right to development gives priority to development over human rights. To what extent does the Declaration provide a foundation for each of these concerns?

2. In 1986, at the same time as it adopted the Declaration, the General Assembly (Res. 41/120) also adopted guidelines that states were to 'bear in mind' in developing new human rights instruments. New rights should (a) be consistent with the existing body of international human rights law; (b) be of fundamental character and derive from the inherent dignity and worth of the human person; (c) be sufficiently precise to give rise to identifiable and practicable rights and obligations; (d) provide, where appropriate, realistic and effective implementation machinery, including reporting systems; and (e) attract broad international support. Does the right to development meet these criteria?

3. What conclusions can be drawn from the 2007 report of the Working Group on the Right to Development. Which groups of states are the principal protagonists and what are the major stumbling blocks? What might be the content of a potentially binding Convention on the Right to Development and what are the arguments for and against the proposal?

C. ENVIRONMENT, DEVELOPMENT AND HUMAN RIGHTS

The most contentious issue which emerges from the debates on the right to development is whether there is some sort of transnational obligation on the part of wealthy states to provide assistance to developing states to enable them to achieve the right to development. An instrumentalist case in favour of that proposition, already considered in Chapter 4, *supra* (see p. 265), concluded in the following terms:

> The world's richest 500 individuals have a combined income greater than that of the poorest 416 million. Beyond these extremes, the 2.5 billion people living on less than $2 a day — 40% of the world's population — account for 5% of global income. The richest 10%, almost all of whom live in high-income countries, account for 54%. An obvious corollary of extreme global inequality is that even modest shifts in distribution from top to bottom could have dramatic effects on poverty. Using a global income distribution database, we estimate a cost of $300 billion for lifting 1 billion people living on less than $1 a day above the extreme poverty line threshold. That amount represents 1.6% of the income of the richest 10% of the world's population.[4]

Note that such analyses are usually based upon the notion that there is, or should be, a moral or ethical responsibility upon the rich to assist the poor. But many of the claims made in the name of the right to development go much further and posit a legal obligation requiring the provision of such assistance. Such an obligation could possibly be grounded in the framework of the (usually unspecified) obligation of 'international cooperation' which is reflected in the UN Charter and a range of human rights treaties, or in a provision such as Article 28 of the UDHR which provides that '[e]veryone is entitled to a social and international order in which the rights and freedoms set forth in this Declaration can be fully realized'.

Other variations on this theme of international responsibility also warrant consideration. Two in particular will be dealt with here. The first is the argument that people in rich countries have an obligation to seek to improve the conditions of the workers in developing countries who produce the goods which the rich consume. The 'anti-sweatshop' movement has been especially prominent in recent years in asserting that the often exploitative working conditions in the factories of the global South that produce goods such as footwear, clothing and textiles for export to the North give rise

[4] International Cooperation at a Crossroads: Aid, Trade And Security in an Unequal World, UNDP, Human Development Report 2005 (New York, 2005), p.1

to obligations upon Northern consumers. The principal objection to such claims is that the latter group have not themselves caused the relevant exploitation and thus could have no personal responsibility for improving the relevant conditions. The excerpt below from Iris Marion Young seeks to provide a philosophical justification for imposing a particular type of responsibility in such situations.

The second variation on the theme concerns claims upon the rich to compensate or assist those developing countries which are likely to be the worst affected by global climate change. These claims may be based either upon the specific attribution of responsibility to the countries of the North for the carbon emissions which are responsible for global warming, or upon a human rights-based claim that the wealthy must assist those who are at risk of large-scale rights deprivation and are effectively unable to help themselves. In each case the question arises as to the moral and/or legal foundation of such a claim. Some consideration was given to the question of international responsibility for poverty alleviation in Chapter 4, at p. 308 above. In the materials that follow consideration is given to the challenges stemming from climate change and to an analysis in which Iris Marion Young seeks to develop a philosophical argument that rejects a fault or liability based model as being inadequate and instead develops a political responsibility model which would have far-reaching implications in relation to all of the issues canvassed above.

INTERGOVERNMENTAL PANEL ON CLIMATE CHANGE, CLIMATE CHANGE 2007: IMPACTS, ADAPTATION AND VULNERABILITY

Working Group II Contribution to the Intergovernmental Panel on Climate Change, Fourth Assessment Report, Summary for Policymakers, April 2007

...

Africa

By 2020, between 75 and 250 million people are projected to be exposed to an increase of water stress due to climate change. If coupled with increased demand, this will adversely affect livelihoods and exacerbate water-related problems.

Agricultural production, including access to food, in many African countries and regions is projected to be severely compromised by climate variability and change. The area suitable for agriculture, the length of growing seasons and yield potential, particularly along the margins of semi-arid and arid areas, are expected to decrease. This would further adversely affect food security and exacerbate malnutrition in the continent. In some countries, yields from rain-fed agriculture could be reduced by up to 50% by 2020.

Local food supplies are projected to be negatively affected by decreasing fisheries resources in large lakes due to rising water temperatures, which may be exacerbated by continued over-fishing.

Towards the end of the 21st century, projected sea-level rise will affect low-lying coastal areas with large populations. The cost of adaptation could amount to at least

5–10% of Gross Domestic Product (GDP). Mangroves and coral reefs are projected to be further degraded, with additional consequences for fisheries and tourism.

New studies confirm that Africa is one of the most vulnerable continents to climate variability and change because of multiple stresses and low adaptive capacity. Some adaptation to current climate variability is taking place, however, this may be insufficient for future changes in climate.

Asia

Glacier melt in the Himalayas is projected to increase flooding, and rock avalanches from destabilised slopes, and to affect water resources within the next two to three decades. This will be followed by decreased river flows as the glaciers recede.

Freshwater availability in Central, South, East and Southeast Asia, particularly in large river basins, is projected to decrease due to climate change which, along with population growth and increasing demand arising from higher standards of living, could adversely affect more than a billion people by the 2050s.

Coastal areas, especially heavily-populated mega-delta regions in South, East and Southeast Asia, will be at greatest risk due to increased flooding from the sea and, in some mega-deltas, flooding from the rivers.

. . .

It is projected that crop yields could increase up to 20% in East and Southeast Asia while they could decrease up to 30% in Central and South Asia by the mid-21st century. Taken together and considering the influence of rapid population growth and urbanisation, the risk of hunger is projected to remain very high in several developing countries.

Endemic morbidity and mortality due to diarrhoeal disease primarily associated with floods and droughts are expected to rise . . .

. . .

Small islands

Small islands, whether located in the tropics or higher latitudes, have characteristics which make them especially vulnerable to the effects of climate change, sea level rise and extreme events.

Deterioration in coastal conditions, for example through erosion of beaches and coral bleaching, is expected to affect local resources, e.g., fisheries, and reduce the value of these destinations for tourism.

Sea-level rise is expected to exacerbate inundation, storm surge, erosion and other coastal hazards, thus threatening vital infrastructure, settlements and facilities that support the livelihood of island communities.

Climate change is projected by the mid-century to reduce water resources in many small islands, e.g., in the Caribbean and Pacific, to the point where they become insufficient to meet demand during low rainfall periods.

With higher temperatures, increased invasion by non-native species is expected to occur, particularly on middle and high-latitude islands.

. . .

. . . At present we do not have a clear picture of the limits to adaptation, or the cost, partly because effective adaptation measures are highly dependent on specific, geographical and climate risk factors as well as institutional, political and financial constraints.

The array of potential adaptive responses available to human societies is very large, ranging from purely technological (e.g., sea defences), through behavioural (e.g., altered food and recreational choices), to managerial (e.g., altered farm practices) and to policy (e.g., planning regulations). . . . For developing countries, availability of resources and building adaptive capacity are particularly important. . . .

. . .

MARGARETT BECKETT, CLIMATE CHANGE: 'THE GATHERING STORM'

Annual Winston Churchill Memorial Lecture, New York, 16 April 2007

[Ms Beckett was, at the time, the United Kingdom Foreign Secretary, a position equivalent to that of Minister for Foreign Affairs in other countries.]

. . .

. . . [T]he potential effects on our biodiversity from climate change range, under differing scenarios, from serious to catastrophic. And the image of polar bears on melting glaciers is a simple one that has had a role in raising awareness and drumming up public support.

But the, perhaps rather sad, truth is that the international community will not move with the necessary urgency or the necessary resolve if climate change is seen as primarily something that effects insects, animals and plants: although they may in turn hold the key to our own survival. To steal a slogan from Amnesty International, we need to show that tackling climate change is about saving the human [sic].

So let's look at the effect on humans if we do nothing.

[The IPCC report excerpted *supra*, p. 1454] paints a stark picture. Let me give just one example from it: by 2020 crop yields in some African countries, for example, could have halved.

So science is giving us a clear picture of the scale and severity of the physical impacts that will happen if we don't do anything about climate change. It is simply inconceivable that there will not be a profound and possibly devastating effect on our collective and individual security.

There are some consequences of climate change that we can identify with some confidence and that should give us very specific reason to be worried. So, for example, rising sea-levels could displace millions in Bangladesh alone and add a dangerous new dynamic to an already tense region. Or, another example, the Middle East (a classic security challenge, if you like) — where five per cent of the world's population share one per cent of the world's water — will have even less of that water to go round with the Nile flow being particularly badly affected. Increased incidence of drought in Sudan has been said to be one of the factors that brought pastoralists and nomads into conflict in Darfur. . . .

…

If you are looking for a simple, linear connection between climate change and a particular flash-point, you are only picking up a glimpse of a much wider picture. The implications of climate change for our security are more fundamental and comprehensive than any single conflict.

For a start, there is that potential devastating effect on the global economy. If there is one resounding thing we have learnt in the past 150 years it is that there is a deadly and complex link between the global economy, economic nationalism and increased global tensions. . . .

…

The former Chief Economist at the World Bank, Nick Stern, . . . estimated that the dangers of unabated climate change — based on the science available in 2001 and on a narrow range of effects — would be at least five per cent of global GDP. Taking on board more recent scientific evidence and the economic effects on human life and the environment, he estimates that the global economy could take a hit equivalent to 20 per cent of GDP or more.

…

Add to that mixture the sense in certain parts of the world that climate change is a developed world problem for which the developing world will pay the price and you can see how easily it could serve to exacerbate an existing sense of grievance. President Museveni of Uganda was the first African leader to describe climate change as an act of aggression by the rich against the poor: he won't be the last.

But there's more to it even than that.

I argue that there are some fairly basic needs that underpin our collective security — as much within communities and societies as between states. Take them away, fail to prepare adequately and you raise the chances of conflict and instability. If people don't have enough food to eat it can lead to instability. If — perhaps even more so — they can't get the water they need for themselves and their families: again, the risk of heightened tension. Make it more difficult for them to secure the energy they need to power their homes and their businesses — in any or all of these instances they might decide to go out and take what they need for themselves.

…

CHRISTIAN AID, HUMAN TIDE: THE REAL MIGRATION CRISIS

(2007)

Climate change

Scientific forecasts about the effects of climate change are frightening. They suggest a world in which people in already poor countries will have an even harder struggle to survive. Although there are no up-to-date statistics to show how many people are being displaced by climate change, it is clear that the numbers are potentially in the hundreds of millions. This, in turn, is likely to fuel conflicts that will push still more people to flee. It is poor people who will suffer most as a result of climate change, but rich people who are most to blame for it. In sub-Saharan Africa, people emit less than one tonne of CO2 per year while in the US it is 24 tonnes.

The latest scientific studies suggest that the climate is changing more quickly than was previously predicted. In addition, because of international prevarication over reducing CO2 emissions, the scale and speed of action needed now is greater than previously imagined. A massive, international effort is needed to reduce CO2 emissions and keep global average temperature increases below 2°C. Even then, climate change will cause serious disruption, especially in poor communities.

- A new international, science-based and equitable agreement is needed along the lines of a 'global carbon budget'. This must be consistent with the 2°C-limit and recognise the right of developing and less-developed countries to increase the size of their economies and reduce poverty in a way that does not lead to further growth in global CO2 emissions.
- The agreement should have at its heart development-friendly mechanisms with which rich countries will fund adaptation and clean-development activities in poor countries.
- As part of the agreement, rich countries that have emitted most pollution must establish a US$100 (£50) billion a year global fund to help poor, vulnerable counties to adapt to sealevel rises, increasing drought and more extreme weather. Funding could be based on CO2 taxation or trading, or both.
- This money should not be taken from existing aid budgets — it is partial compensation for the damage done by climate change. It should be paid in proportion to countries' CO2 emissions since 1990 (when negotiations on the UN Framework Convention on Climate Change began), and national wealth.

...

CENTER FOR INTERNATIONAL ENVIRONMENTAL LAW, INUIT CASE

at www.ciel.org/Climate/Climate_Inuit.html

[This note outlines the content of a petition presented to the Inter-American Commission on Human Rights in March 2007.]

[According to the IPCC, if] global warming continues unchecked it threatens to destroy [the Arctic peoples'] culture, render their land uninhabitable, and rob them of their means of subsistence. The harm caused to their way of life, largely by the United States, as biggest global contributor of carbon dioxide emissions, is already serious enough so as to violate [human rights] recognised in the American Declaration of the Rights and Duties of Man, [including]: the right to life (Art. I), the right to residence and movement (Art.VIII), the right to inviolability of the home (IX), the right to preservation of health and to well-being (Art. XI), the rights to benefits of culture (Art. XIII), and the right to work and to fair renumeration (Art. XIV).

... The effects of global warming have already begun to impact the homes and communities of many individuals and groups in the Arctic. Subsidence due to permafrost melting is destroying homes, roads and other vital structures in the Arctic. Effects such as these violate the rights of each individual to protection of "private and family life", "the inviolability of his home" and, in some situations, "not to leave [the territory of the state of which he is a national] except by his own will." International tribunals have recognized that harm to the environment that affects one's home can violate these rights. For example, in Lopez Ostra v. Spain, the European Court of Human Rights held that Spain's failure to prevent a waste treatment plant from polluting nearby homes violated the petitioner's "right to respect for her home and her private and family life", and held the state liable for damages.

CIEL and Earth Justice (EJ) are petitioning the Inter-American Commission of Human Rights on behalf of the Inuits. The Commission has in the past recognized the relationship between human rights and the environmental effects of development activities, and its interpretation of this relationship suggests that it would recognize the human rights implications of the effects of global warming. The United States has not ratified the Convention and as such is not subject to the jurisdiction of the court. However, a report by the Commission examining the connection between global warming and human rights could have a powerful impact on worldwide efforts to address global warming. It would demonstrate that the issue is not merely an abstract problem for the future, but is instead a problem of immediate concern to all people everywhere. Recognition by the Commission of a link between global warming and human rights may establish a legal basis for holding responsible countries that have profited from inadequate greenhouse gas regulation and could provide a strong incentive to all countries to participate in effective international response efforts.

NOTE

Two questions that the preceding materials raise are: (1) whether climate change is appropriately addressed as a human rights issue? and (2) what is the basis upon which the rich world might be required to assume particular financial and other responsibility for the resulting plight of the poorer countries? In relation to the first of these, consider the following comments by former UN High Commissioner for Human Rights, Mary Robinson:

> ... We now recognise that respect for human rights is at the core of sustainable development.... [Climate change raises an issue of justice]: it is poor communities who are suffering most from the effects of climate change, and it is rich countries that are contributing most to the problem. The human rights approach, emphasising the equality of all people, is a direct challenge to the power imbalances that allow the perpetrators of climate change to continue unchecked. And the human rights framework gives us the legal and normative grounds for empowering the poor to seek redress.

> … [W]e can no longer think about climate change as an issue where the rich give charity to the poor to help them to cope with its adverse impacts. Rather, this has now become an issue of global injustice that will need a radically different framing to bring about global justice.
>
> …
>
> There are strict limits to adaptation — the poor cannot buy their way out of trouble…. These [resulting] changes, in sum, will have a profound impact on the fulfilment of human rights: on people's right to food, right to water, right to health, and even to life itself….
>
> …
>
> [Existing international] legal frameworks — on climate change and on human rights — are not only mutually compatible — they powerfully reinforce each other.
>
> At the global level it is obviously ethical, rational and feasible to take action now. The technology exists — what we lack is the political commitment to act….
>
> …
>
> It is clear that human rights advocates need to do more thinking about climate change as a rights issue. Part of the reason for the lack of innovative ideas may stem from the inherent emphasis to date on 'humans' in the context of human rights, without sufficient concern for the environmental stewardship that underpins so many social and economic rights. But within the human rights framework lies the possibility of embracing environmental concerns more explicitly.[5]

In contrast, an editorial in *The Economist* magazine was pessimistic that anything much would come in response to the claim made by President Museveni, and cited by Margaret Beckett above, in which he characterized climate change as an act of aggression by the rich world against the poor and demanded compensation. After noting that African governments had themselves done far less than they could have in response to the climate change crisis, the magazine concluded that Africa 'should not expect much new [foreign aid] money to protect the environment. In the short run, Africa's own politicians need to take a lead, even if the people most culpable for the damage done by climate change live elsewhere.'[6]

And there are many philosophers who hold that arguments in favour of transnational justice are misplaced. For example, according to 'Michael Walzer, there is no room for transnational distributive justice in international law because states ought to determine their own internal distributive arrangements. According to Walzer, each distinct society is engaged in an on-going process of developing and revising shared social meanings that ground distinctive principles of distributive justice, and the identity and well-being of individuals depends upon their participation in this cultural project. The benefits that individuals derive from the process depend upon its integrity, and this in turn requires that their shared meanings be worked out among themselves without standards being imposed from outside. Thus, the whole enterprise of transnational distributive justice is illegitimate,

[5] Mary Robinson, 'Climate Change and Justice', Barbara Ward Lecture, London, 11 December 2006.

[6] Global Warming in Africa: Drying Up and Flooding Out, *The Economist*, 12 May 2007, p. 43.

because it is an attempt to impose an external conception of distributive justice, with the result that the integrity of the indigenous process will be undermined.'[7]

Others have argued that fault or liability based arguments are unhelpful in resolving such issues and that a broader conception of political responsibility is necessary instead. Thus for example, in addressing the question of how agents should think about responsibility in relation to structural social injustice Iris Marion Young distinguishes the liability and responsibility models in five respects: '(1) Unlike responsibility as liability, political responsibility does not isolate some responsibility parties in order to absolve others. (2) Whereas blame or liability seeks remedy for a deviation from an acceptable norm, usually by an event that has reached a terminus, with political responsibility we are concerned with structural causes of injustice that are normal and ongoing. (3) Political responsibility is more forward-looking than backward-looking. (4) What it means to take up or assign political responsibility is more open and discretionary than what it means to hold an agent blameworthy or liable. (5) An agent shares political responsibility with others whose actions contribute to the structural processes that produce injustice.' In Young's view, the political responsibility model she proposes is applicable to any issue of structural social injustice. She argues that only collective action can succeed in rectifying injustices that result from the product of the mediated actions of many. Her argument draws heavily upon Hannah Arendt's concept of political responsibility which envisaged:

> a kind of collective responsibility, and one where the responsibility borne collectively is not dissolvable to the self-conscious collaborative acts of individuals. Whereas responsibility as liability assigns responsibility according to what particular agents have done, on the model of political responsibility individuals are responsible precisely for things they themselves have *not* done. The reason to assume political responsibility involves not individual fault, but derives from "my membership in a group (a collective) which no voluntary act of mine can dissolve, that is, a membership which is utterly unlike a business partnership which I can dissolve at will." Arendt clearly takes the political community of a nation-state as her paradigm of such a collective.[8]

QUESTIONS

1. In what respects, if any, would you consider that the climate change crisis raises problems that are properly, or helpfully, classified as human rights issues? Does it necessarily reflect badly on the human rights regime if it has nothing much to add in relation to one of the most pressing problems of the twenty-first century?

[7] A. Buchanan and D. Golove, 'The Philosophy of International Law' in J. Coleman and S. Shapiro (eds.), *Oxford Handbook on the Philosophy of Law* (2002) 808 at 900. In relation to Walzer, see his book *Spheres of Justice: A Defense of Pluralism and Equality* (1983).

[8] Iris Marion Young, 'Responsibility and Global Labor Justice', 12 J. Polit. Phil. 365 (2004), at 388. Young's reference is to Hannah Arendt, 'Collective Responsibility,' in J. Bernauer (ed.), *Amor Mundi: Explorations in the Faith and Thought of Hannah Arendt* (1987), p. 45.

2. Does Young's notion of collective action based on a concept of shared responsibility help in articulating a human rights-based theory for allocating international responsibilities for issues such as climate change?

3. Thomas Pogge has argued, primarily on the basis of Article 28 of the UDHR, that the global institutional order 'must afford the persons on whom it is imposed secure access to the objects of their human rights' and that there is 'a negative duty not to cooperate in the imposition of this global order if feasible reforms of it would significantly improve the realization of human rights'.[9] What are the reasonable limits of such an obligation? Do national boundaries make a major difference in terms of such obligations? Is it sufficient for the international community to establish institutions devoted to the promotion of different aspects of development? Does it matter if some of these institutions, such as the WTO, explicitly exclude human rights from their fields of activity?

4. The United States Government did not respond to the complaint filed on behalf of the Inuits before the Inter-American Commission. If you were a member of the Commission, how would you deal with the case? Note that the Inuits are from Canada, and not the US.

ADDITIONAL READING

Frequently Asked Questions on a Human Rights-Based Approach to Development Cooperation, UN Doc. HR/PUB/06/8 (2006); OECD, *The Development Dimension: Integrating Human Rights into Development: Donor Approaches, Experiences and Challenges* (2006); M. Foresti et al., *Aid Effectiveness and Human Rights: Strengthening the Implementation of the Paris Declaration* (ODI, 2006); B.A. Andreassen and S.P. Marks (eds.), *Development as a Human Right* (2006), Patricia Smith, *Liberalism and Affirmative Obligation* (1998); Thomas Nagel, 'The Problem of Global Justice', 33 Philosophy and Public Affairs (2005), p. 113; T. Pogge, *World Poverty and Human Rights* (2002); Polly Vizard, *Poverty and Human Rights* (2006); Arjun Sengupta *et al.* (eds.), *Reflections on the Right to Development* (2006); Peter Uvin, *Human Rights and Development* (2004).

[9] Pogge, 'The International Significance of Human Rights', in 4 J. of Ethics 45 (2000).

DOCUMENTS SUPPLEMENT

An accompanying website, www.oxfordtextbooks.co.uk/orc/ihr3e/, contains a documentary supplement for this coursebook. Part I of the supplement sets forth documents that are essential to an understanding of materials in different parts of the coursebook. Since they have been edited to delete provisions that are unnecessary for an understanding of those materials, you should not rely on any of them as full and official versions. Part II of the web-based supplement sets forth an extended set of documents. It contains additional conventions and protocols, including recently adopted instruments that have not yet entered into force. The list below comprises those documents found on the website.

In the list below, after the official title of a document, there appear within parentheses the acronym or abbreviated name(s) by which the text or the readings are sometimes referred.

CONTENTS

I. Texts required for coursebook purposes

Geneva Convention (III) relative to the Treatment of Prisoners of War (POWs Convention)

Geneva Convention (IV) relative to the Protection of Civilian Persons in Time of War (Civilians Convention)

Protocol Additional to the Geneva Conventions of 12 August 1949, and relating to the Protection of Victims of International Armed Conflicts (Protocol I)

Protocol Additional to the Geneva Conventions of 12 August 1949, and relating to the Protection of Victims of Non-International Armed Conflicts (Protocol II)

Vienna Convention on the Law of Treaties

Constitution of the United States

II. Other important texts

Convention on the Elimination of All Forms of Racial Discrimination (CERD)

Convention on the Rights of the Child (CRC)

Convention for the Protection of All Persons from Enforced Disappearance (not yet in force)

Convention on the Rights of Persons with Disabilities (not yet in force)

Optional Protocol to the Convention on the Rights of Persons with Disabilities (not yet in force)

Optional Protocol to the Convention against Torture and Other Cruel, Inhuman or Degrading Treatment or Punishment

Annex on CITATIONS TO HUMAN RIGHTS INSTRUMENTS

Unless otherwise indicated, details of the number of parties to a treaty are current as of 1 July 2007. The principal abbreviations used are as follows: ILM for *International Legal Materials*, UNTS for *United Nations Treaty Series* and ETS for *European Treaty Series.*

Human Rights Document Collections

I. Brownlie and G. Goodwin-Gill (ed.), *Basic Documents on Human Rights* (5th. edn., Oxford University Press, 2006).

M. Evans and R. Murray (eds.), *Compendium of Key Human Rights Documents of the African Union* (Compendium of Key Human Rights Instruments of the African Union (Pretoria University Law Press, 3rd edn., 2007); African Union treaties webpage, at www.africa-union.org/root/au/Documents/Treaties/treaties.htm University of Minnesota Human Rights Library at www1.umn.edu/humanrts/instree/afrinst.htm

Human Rights: A Compilation of International Instruments, 2 vols. (Geneva: United Nations, 2002).

Human Rights in International Law: Basic Texts (Strasbourg: Council of Europe Press, 2nd edn. 2001).

International Labour Conventions and Recommendations 1919–1995, 3 vols. (Geneva: International Labour Office, 1996). Comprehensive listing available at http://www.ilo.org/ilolex/english/index.htm

Religion and Human Rights: Basic Documents (New York: Columbia University, Center for the Study of Human Rights, 1998). Up-dated version available at http://www.religlaw.org/interdocs/rhrbdtoc.htm

Roberts, A. and R. Guelff, *Documents on the Laws of War* (3rd edn., Oxford: Oxford University Press, 2000).

United Nations Treaties

Note: most of the human rights treaties and other instruments adopted by the UN are available at www.ohchr.org/english/law/index.htm

Charter of the United Nations, adopted 26 June 1945, entered into force 24 Oct. 1945, as amended by G.A. Res. 1991 (XVIII) 17 Dec. 1963, entered into force 31 Aug. 1965 (557 UNTS 143); 2101 of 20 Dec. 1965, entered into force 12 June 1968 (638 UNTS 308); and 2847 (XXVI) of 20 Dec. 1971, entered into force 24

Sept. 1973 (892 UNTS 119), *available at* http://www.un.org/aboutun/charter/. 192 Member States.

Convention Against Torture and Other Cruel, Inhuman or Degrading Treatment or Punishment, adopted 10 Dec. 1984, entered into force 26 June 1987, 1465 UNTS 85, reprinted in 23 ILM 1027 (1984), minor changes reprinted in 24 ILM 535 (1985), *available at* http://www.ohchr.org/english/law/cat.htm. 144 states parties.

Optional Protocol to the Convention against Torture and Other Cruel, Inhuman or Degrading Treatment or Punishment, adopted 18 Dec. 2002, entered into force 22 June 2006, reprinted in 42 ILM 26 (2003), *available at* http://www.ohchr.org/english/law/cat-one.htm. 34 states parties.

Convention for the Protection of All Persons from Enforced Disappearance, adopted 20 Dec. 2006, G.A. Res. 61/177, 61 UN GAOR, Supp. (No. 49), UN Doc. A/61/488, at 408 (2006), *available at* http://www.ohchr.org/english/law/disappearance-convention.htm. Not yet in force.

Convention on the Elimination of All Forms of Discrimination against Women, adopted 18 Dec. 1979, entered into force 3 Sept. 1981, 1249 UNTS 13, reprinted in 19 ILM 33 (1980), *available at* http://www.un.org/womenwatch/daw/cedaw/text/econvention.htm. 185 states parties.

Optional Protocol to the Convention on the Elimination of All Forms of Discrimination against Women, adopted 6 Oct. 1999, entered into force 10 Dec. 1999, 2131 UNTS 83, reprinted in 39 ILM 281 (2000), *available at* http://www.ohchr.org/english/law/cedaw-one.htm. 88 states parties.

Convention on the Prevention and Punishment of the Crime of Genocide, adopted 9 Dec. 1948, entered into force 12 Jan. 1951, 78 UNTS 277, *available at* http://www.ohchr.org/english/law/genocide.htm. 140 states parties.

Convention on the Rights of Persons with Disabilities, adopted 13 Dec. 2006, G.A. Res. 61/106, 61 UN GAOR, Supp. (No. 49), UN Doc. A/RES/61/106/AnnexI, at 65 (2006), *available at* http://www.ohchr.org/english/law/disabilities-convention.htm. 2 states parties.

Optional Protocol to the Convention on the Rights of Persons with Disabilities, adopted 13 Dec. 2006, G.A. Res. 61/106, 61 UN GAOR, Supp. (No. 49), UN Doc. A/RES/61/106/AnnexII, at 65 (2006), *available at* http://www.ohchr.org/english/law/disabilities-op.htm. 1 state party.

Convention on the Rights of the Child, adopted 20 Nov. 1989, entered into force 2 Sept. 1990, 1577 UNTS 3, reprinted in 28 ILM 1448 (1989), *available at* http://www.ohchr.org/english/law/crc.htm. 193 states parties.

Convention Relating to the Status of Refugees, adopted 28 July 1951, entered into force 22 April 1954, 189 UNTS 137, *available at* http://www.ohchr.org/english/law/refugees.htm. 140 states parties.

Protocol Relating to the Status of Refugees, opened for signature 31 Jan. 1967, entered into force 4 Oct. 1967, 606 UNTS 267, reprinted in 6 ILM 78 (1967), *available at* http://www.ohchr.org/english/law/protocolrefugees.htm. 138 states parties.

International Convention for the Elimination of All Forms of Racial Discrimination, adopted 21 Dec. 1965, entered into force 4 Jan. 1969, 660 UNTS 195, reprinted in 5 ILM 352 (1966), *available at* http://www.ohchr.org/english/law/cerd.htm. 173 states parties.

International Convention on the Protection of the Rights of All Migrant Workers and Members of Their Families, adopted 18 Dec. 1990, entered into force 1 July 2003, reprinted in 30 ILM 1517 (1991), *available at* http://www.ohchr.org/english/law/cmw.htm. 37 states parties.

International Covenant on Civil and Political Rights, adopted 16 Dec. 1966, entered into force 23 March 1976, 999 UNTS 171, reprinted in 6 ILM 368 (1967), *available at* http://www.ohchr.org/english/law/ccpr.htm. 160 states parties.

Optional Protocol to the International Covenant on Civil and Political Rights, adopted 16 Dec. 1966, entered into force 23 March 1976, 999 UNTS 171, reprinted in 6 ILM 383 (1967), *available at* http://www.ohchr.org/english/law/ccpr-one.htm. 109 states parties.

Second Optional Protocol to the International Covenant on Civil and Political Rights, adopted 15 Dec. 1989, entered into force 11 July 1991, 1642 UNTS 414, reprinted in 29 ILM 1464 (1990), *available at* http://www.ohchr.org/english/law/ccpr-death.htm. 60 states parties.

International Covenant on Economic, Social and Cultural Rights, adopted 16 Dec. 1966, entered into force 3 Jan. 1976, 993 UNTS 3, reprinted in 6 ILM 360 (1967), *available at* http://www.ohchr.org/english/law/cescr.htm. 156 states parties.

Supplementary Convention on the Abolition of Slavery, the Slave Trade, and Institutions and Practices Similar to Slavery, adopted 7 Sept. 1956, entered into force 30 April 1957, 226 UNTS 3, *available at* http://www.ohchr.org/english/law/slavetrade.htm. 121 states parties.

Other Universal Treaties

Geneva Convention for the Amelioration of the Condition of the Wounded and Sick in Armed Forces in the Field, adopted 12 Aug. 1949, entered into force 21 Oct. 1950, 75 UNTS 31, *available at* http://www.icrc.org/ihl.nsf/FULL/365?OpenDocument. 194 states parties.

Geneva Convention for the Amelioration of the Condition of Wounded, Sick and Shipwrecked Members of Armed Forces at Sea, adopted 12 Aug. 1949, entered into force 21 Oct. 1950, 75 UNTS 85, *available at* http://www.icrc.org/ihl.nsf/FULL/370?OpenDocument. 194 states parties.

Geneva Convention Relative to the Treatment of Prisoners of War, adopted 12 Aug. 1949, entered into force 21 Oct. 1950, 75 UNTS 135, *available at* http://www.ohchr.org/english/law/prisonerwar.htm. 194 states parties.

Geneva Convention Relative to the Protection of Civilian Persons in Time of War, adopted 12 Aug. 1948, entered into force 21 Oct. 1950, 75 UNTS 287, *available at* http://www.ohchr.org/english/law/civilianpersons.htm. 194 states parties.

Protocol I Additional to the Geneva Conventions of August 12, 1949, and relating to the Protection of Victims of International Armed Conflicts, adopted 8 June 1977, entered into force 7 Dec. 1978, 1125 UNTS 3, reprinted in 16 ILM 1391 (1977), *available at* http://www.ohchr.org/english/law/protocol1.htm. 167 states parties.

Protocol II Additional to the Geneva Conventions of August 12, 1949, and relating to the Protection of Victims of Non-International Armed Conflicts, adopted 8 June 1977, entered into force 7 Dec. 1978, 1125 UNTS 609, reprinted in 16 ILM

1442 (1977), *available at* http://www.ohchr.org/english/law/protocol2.htm. 163 states parties.

Vienna Convention on the Law of Treaties, adopted 23 May 1969, entered into force 27 Jan. 1980, 1155 UNTS 331, reprinted in 8 ILM 679 (1969), *available at* http://untreaty.un.org/ilc/texts/instruments/english/conventions/1_1_1969.pdf. 108 states parties.

Other United Nations Instruments

Declaration on the Elimination of All Forms of Intolerance and of Discrimination Based on Religion or Belief, adopted 25 Nov. 1981, G.A. Res. 36/55, 36 UN GAOR, Supp. (No. 51), UN Doc. A/36/51, at 171 (1981), reprinted in 21 ILM 205 (1982), *available at* http://www.un.org/Depts/dhl/res/resa36.htm.

Declaration on the Elimination of Violence Against Women, adopted 20 Dec. 1993, G.A. Res. 48/104, 48 UN GAOR, Supp. (No. 49), UN Doc. A/48/29, at 217, reprinted in 33 ILM 1049 (1994), *available at* http://www.un.org/Depts/dhl/res/resa48.htm.

Declaration on the Granting of Independence to Colonial Countries and Peoples, adopted 14 Dec. 1960, G.A. Res. 1514 (XV), 15 UN GAOR, Supp. (No. 16), UN Doc. A/4684, at 66 (1960), *available at* http://www.un.org/documents/ga/res/15/ares15.htm.

Declaration on Principles of International Law concerning Friendly Relations and Co-operation among States in accordance with the Charter of the United Nations, adopted 24 Oct. 1970, G.A. Res. 2625 (XXV), 25 UN GAOR, Supp. (No. 28), UN Doc. A/8028, at 121 (1970), reprinted in 9 ILM 1292 (1970), *available at* http://www.un.org/documents/ga/res/25/ares25.htm.

Declaration on the Protection of All Persons from Being Subjected to Torture and Other Cruel, Inhuman or Degrading Treatment or Punishment, adopted 9 Dec. 1975, G.A. Res. 3452 (XXX), 30 UN GAOR, Supp. (No. 34), UN Doc. A/10034, at 91 (1976), *available at* http://www.un.org/documents/ga/res/30/ares30.htm.

Declaration on the Protection of All Persons from Enforced Disappearance, adopted 18 Dec. 1992, G.A. Res. 47/133, 47 UN GAOR, Supp. (No. 49), UN Doc. A/RES/47/133, at 207 (1992), reprinted in 32 ILM 903 (1993), *available at* http://www.un.org/Depts/dhl/res/resa47.htm.

Declaration on the Right and Responsibility of Individuals, Groups and Organs of Society to Promote and Protect Universally Recognized Human Rights and Fundamental Freedoms, adopted 9 Dec. 1998, G.A. Res. 53/144, 53 UN GAOR, Supp. (No. 49), UN Doc. A/RES/53/144/Annex, at 261(1998), *available at* http://www.un.org/Depts/dhl/resguide/r53.htm.

Declaration on the Right to Development, adopted 4 Dec. 1986, G.A. Res. 41/128, 41 UN GAOR, Supp. (No. 53), UN Doc. A/RES/41/128, at 186 (1986), *available at* http://www.un.org/Depts/dhl/res/resa41.htm.

Declaration on the Rights of Disabled Persons, adopted 9 Dec. 1975, G.A. Res. 3447 (XXX), 30 UN GAOR, Supp. (No. 34), UN Doc. A/10034, at 88 (1975), *available at* http://www.un.org/documents/ga/res/30/ares30.htm.

Declaration on the Rights of Persons Belonging to National or Ethnic, Religious or Linguistic Minorities, adopted 15 Dec. 1992, G.A. Res. 47/135, 47 UN GAOR,

Supp. (No. 49), UN Doc. A/RES/47/135, at 210 (1992), reprinted in 32 ILM 911 (1993), *available at* http://www.un.org/Depts/dhl/res/resa47.htm.

Declaration on the Rights of the Child, adopted 20 Nov. 1959, G.A. Res. 1386 (XIV), 14 UN GAOR, Supp. (No. 16), UN Doc. A/4354, at 19 (1959), *available at* http://www.un.org/documents/ga/res/14/ares14.htm.

Standard Minimum Rules for the Treatment of Prisoners, adopted 31 July 1957, E.S.C. Res. 663C (XXIV), 24 UN ESCOR, Supp. (No. 1) at 11 (1957), extended 13 May 1977, E.S.C. Res. 2076 (LXIII), 62 UN ESCOR, Supp. (No. 1) at 35 (1977), *available at* http://www.ohchr.org/english/law/treatmentprisoners.htm.

Universal Declaration of Human Rights, adopted 10 Dec. 1948, G.A. Res. 217A (III), 3 UN GAOR, UN Doc. A/810, at 71 (1948), *available at* http://www.un.org/documents/ga/res/3/ares3.htm.

United Nations World Conference on Human Rights, Vienna Declaration and Programme of Action, adopted 25 June 1993, UN Doc. A/CONF.157/24 (Part I), at 20 (1993), reprinted in 32 ILM 1661 (1993), *available at* http://www.ohchr.org/english/law/vienna.htm.

Instruments adopted by United Nations Agencies

Convention Concerning Forced or Compulsory Labour (I.L.O. No. 29), adopted 28 June 1930, entered into force 1 May 1932, 39 UNTS 55, *available at* http://www.ilo.org/ilolex/cgi-lex/convde.pl?C029. 172 states parties.

Convention Concerning Indigenous and Tribal Peoples in Independent Countries (I.L.O. No. 169), adopted 27 June 1989, entered into force 5 Sept. 1991, reprinted in 28 ILM 1382 (1989), *available at* http://www.ilo.org/ilolex/cgi-lex/convde.pl?C169. 18 states parties.

Convention Concerning the Abolition of Forced Labour (I.L.O. No. 105), adopted 25 June 1957, entered into force 17 Jan. 1959, 320 UNTS 291, *available at* http://www.ilo.org/ilolex/cgi-lex/convde.pl?C105. 167 states parties.

Convention Concerning the Protection and Integration of Indigenous and Other Tribal and Semi-Tribal Populations in Independent Countries (I.L.O. No. 107), adopted 26 June 1957, entered into force 2 June 1959, 328 UNTS 247, *available at* http://www.ilo.org/ilolex/cgi-lex/convde.pl?C107. 18 states parties.

Convention Concerning the Worst Forms of Child Labour (I.L.O. No. 182), adopted 17 June 1999, entered into force 19 Nov. 2000, 2133 UNTS 161, reprinted in 38 ILM 1207 (1999), *available at* http://www.ilo.org/ilolex/cgi-lex/convde.pl?C182. 164 states parties.

UNESCO Convention against Discrimination in Education, adopted 14 Dec. 1960, entered into force 22 May 1962, 429 UNTS 93, *available at* www.unesco.org/education/pdf/DISCRI_E.PDF. 91 states parties.

Regional Instruments

(a) The Council of Europe

European Convention for the Prevention of Torture and Inhuman or Degrading Treatment or Punishment, signed 26 Nov. 1987, entered into force 1 Feb. 1989,

2206 UNTS 230, Doc. No. H(87)4 1987, ETS 126, reprinted in 27 ILM 1152 (1988), *available at* http://conventions.coe.int/Treaty/en/Treaties/Html/126.htm. 47 states parties.

European Convention for the Protection of Human Rights and Fundamental Freedoms, signed 4 Nov. 1950, entered into force 3 Sept. 1953, 213 UNTS 221, ETS 5, *available at* http://conventions.coe.int/Treaty/en/Treaties/Html/005.htm. 47 states parties.

Protocol No. 1 to the European Convention for the Protection of Human Rights and Fundamental Freedoms, adopted 20 March 1952, entered into force 18 May 1954, 213 UNTS 262, ETS 9, *available at* http://conventions.coe.int/Treaty/en/Treaties/Html/009.htm. 44 states parties.

Protocol No. 4 to the European Convention for the Protection of Human Rights and Fundamental Freedoms, adopted 16 Sept. 1963, entered into force 2 May 1968, 1496 UNTS 263, ETS 46, *available at* http://conventions.coe.int/Treaty/en/Treaties/Html/046.htm. 41 states parties.

Protocol No. 6 to the European Convention for the Protection of Human Rights and Fundamental Freedoms, adopted 28 April 1983, entered into force 1 March 1985, 1496 UNTS 281, ETS 114, reprinted in 22 ILM 539 (1983), *available at* http://conventions.coe.int/Treaty/en/Treaties/Html/114.htm. 46 states parties.

Protocol No. 7 to the European Convention for the Protection of Human Rights and Fundamental Freedoms, adopted 22 Nov. 1984, entered into force 1 Nov. 1988, 1525 UNTS 195, ETS 117, reprinted in 24 ILM 435 (1985), *available at* http://conventions.coe.int/Treaty/en/Treaties/Html/117.htm. 40 states parties.

Protocol No. 9 to the European Convention for the Protection of Human Rights and Fundamental Freedoms, adopted 6 Nov. 1990, entered into force 1 Oct. 1994, 1934 UNTS 295, ETS 140, reprinted in 30 ILM 693 (1991), *available at* http://conventions.coe.int/Treaty/en/Treaties/Html/140.htm. 24 states parties.

Protocol No. 11 to the European Convention for the Protection of Human Rights and Fundamental Freedoms, adopted 11 May 1994, entered into force 1 Nov. 1998, 2061 UNTS 7, ETS 155, reprinted in 33 ILM 960 (1994), *available at* http://conventions.coe.int/Treaty/en/Treaties/Html/155.htm. 47 states parties.

European Social Charter, signed 18 Oct. 1961, entered into force 26 Feb. 1965, 529 UNTS 89, ETS 35, *available at* http://conventions.coe.int/Treaty/en/Treaties/Html/035.htm. 27 states parties.

Additional Protocol to the European Social Charter, adopted 5 May 1988, entered into force 4 Sept. 1992, 1704 UNTS 313, ETS 128, *available at* http://conventions.coe.int/Treaty/en/Treaties/Html/142.htm. 13 states parties.

Protocol Amending the European Social Charter, adopted 21 Oct. 1991, ETS 142, reprinted in 31 ILM 155 (1992), *available at* http://conventions.coe.int/Treaty/en/Treaties/Html/142.htm. Not yet in force. 22 states parties.

European Social Charter (Revised), adopted 3 May 1996, entered into force 1 July 1999, 2151 UNTS 277, ETS 163, reprinted in 36 ILM 31 (1997), *available at* http://conventions.coe.int/Treaty/en/Treaties/Html/163.htm. 23 states parties.

Framework Convention for the Protection of National Minorities, adopted 10 Nov. 1994, opened for signature 1 Feb. 1995, entered into force 1 Feb. 1998, 2151 UNTS 243, ETS 157, reprinted in 34 ILM 351 (1995), *available at* http://conventions.coe.int/Treaty/en/Treaties/Html/157.htm. 39 states parties.

Statute of the Council of Europe, adopted 5 May 1949, entered into force 3 Aug. 1949, 87 UNTS 103, ETS 1, *available at* http://conventions.coe.int/Treaty/en/Treaties/Html/001.htm. 47 states parties.

(b) The Organization of American States

American Convention on Human Rights (Pact of San José), signed 22 Nov. 1969, entered into force 18 July 1978, 1144 UNTS 123, OASTS 36, O.A.S. Off. Rec. OEA/Ser.L/V/11.23, doc.21, rev.6 (1979), reprinted in 9 ILM 673 (1970), *available at* http://www.oas.org/juridico/english/treaties/b-32.html. 24 states parties.

Additional Protocol to the American Convention on Human Rights in the Area of Economic, Social and Cultural Rights (Protocol of San Salvador), adopted 17 Nov. 1988, entered into force 16 Nov. 1999, OASTS 69, reprinted in 28 ILM 156 (1989), corrections at 28 ILM 573 and 1341 (1989), *available at* http://www.oas.org/juridico/english/treaties/a-52.html. 14 states parties.

Protocol to the American Convention on Human Rights to Abolish the Death Penalty, adopted 8 June 1990, entered into force 28 Aug. 1991, OASTS 73, reprinted in 29 ILM 1447 (1990), *available at* http://www.oas.org/juridico/english/treaties/a-53.html. 8 states parties.

American Declaration of the Rights and Duties of Man, signed 2 May 1948, OEA/Ser.L./V/11.71, at 17 (1988), *available at* http://www.cidh.oas.org/Basicos/English/Basic2.American%20Declaration.htm.

Charter of the Organization of American States, signed 1948, entered into force 13 Dec. 1951, amended 1967, 1985, 14 Dec. 1992, 10 June 1993. Integrated text of the Charter as amended by the Protocols of Buenos Aires and Cartagena de Indias, the Protocol of Amendment of Washington; and the Protocol of Amendment of Managua, reprinted in 33 ILM 981 (1994), *available at* http://www.oas.org/juridico/English/charter.html. 35 member states.

Inter-American Convention on the Forced Disappearance of Persons, signed 9 June 1994, entered into force 28 Mar. 1996, reprinted in 33 ILM 1529 (1994), *available at* http://www.oas.org/juridico/english/treaties/a-60.html. 13 states parties.

Inter-American Convention on the Prevention, Punishment and Eradication of Violence Against Women, signed 9 June 1994, entered into force 3 March 1995, reprinted in 33 ILM 1534 (1994), *available at* http://www.oas.org/juridico/english/treaties/a-61.html. 32 states parties.

Inter-American Convention to Prevent and Punish Torture, signed 9 Dec. 1985, entered into force 28 Feb. 1987, OASTS 67, GA Doc. OEA/Ser.P, AG/doc.2023/85 rev. I (1986) pp. 46–54, reprinted in 25 ILM 519 (1986), *available at* http://www.oas.org/juridico/english/treaties/a-51.html. 17 states parties.

(c) The Organization of African Unity

Charter on Human and Peoples' Rights, adopted 27 June 1981, entered into force 21 Oct. 1986, O.A.U. Doc. CAB/LEG/67/3 Rev. 5, reprinted in 21 ILM 58 (1982). 53 states parties.

Protocol to the African Charter on Human and Peoples' Rights on the Establishment of an African Court on Human and Peoples' Rights, adopted 10 June 1998, O.A.U. Doc. CAB/LEG/66/5. Not yet in force. 3 states parties.

African Charter on the Rights and Welfare of the Child, adopted July 1990, entered into force 29 Oct. 1999, O.A.U. Doc. CAB/LEG/TSG/Rev. 1.15 states parties.

Charter of the Organization of African Unity, adopted 25 May 1963, 47 UNTS 39, reprinted in 2 ILM 766 (1963). 53 states parties.

Convention Governing the Specific Aspects of the Refugee Problems in Africa, adopted 10 Sept. 1969, entered into force 20 June 1974, 1001 UNTS 45, reprinted in 8 11-M 1288 (1969). 44 states parties.

(d) The Organization for Security and Co-operation in Europe

Document of the Copenhagen Meeting of the Conference on the Human Dimension of the Conference of Security and Co-operation in Europe, adopted 29 June 1990, reprinted in 29 ILM 1305 (1990); 11 HR LJ 232 (1990), *available at* http://www.osce.org/documents/odihr/1990/06/13992_en.pdf.

Document of the Moscow Meeting of the Conference on the Human Dimension of the Conference on Security and Co-operation in Europe, adopted 3 Oct. 1991, reprinted in 30 ILM 1670 (1991), *available at* http://www.osce.org/item/13995.html.

Final Act of the Conference on Security and Co-operation in Europe, adopted 1 Aug. 1975, reprinted in 14 ILM 1292 (1975), *available at* http://www.osce.org/documents/html/pdftohtml/4044_en.pdf.html.

Index of Topics

Index of Names

Note: This is not only an index of authors, but rather of all individuals cited in the book, except for: (a) those mentioned in the Additional Reading sections; (b) those referred to only in footnotes or questions; (c) editors or translators; (d) the authors of judgments; and (e) newspaper reporters.